DATE DUE

GROVES DICTIONARY OF
MUSIC AND MUSICIANS
SONG-Z
MacMillan

DATE DUE	BORROWER'S NAME	

GROVES DICTIONARY OF MUSIC AND
MUSICIANS
SONG-Z
MacMillan

A DICTIONARY

OF

MUSIC AND MUSICIANS

THE MACMILLAN COMPANY
NEW YORK · BOSTON · CHICAGO · DALLAS
ATLANTA · SAN FRANCISCO

MACMILLAN AND CO., Limited
LONDON · BOMBAY · CALCUTTA · MADRAS
MELBOURNE

THE MACMILLAN COMPANY
OF CANADA, Limited
TORONTO

ENGLISH ROTA "Sumer is icumen in" (c. 1225)

British Museum (Harley 978)

GROVE'S

DICTIONARY OF MUSIC

AND MUSICIANS

THIRD EDITION

EDITED BY

H. C. COLLES, M.A. (OxON.)

IN FIVE VOLUMES

VOL. V

NEW YORK
THE MACMILLAN COMPANY
1947

SET UP AND ELECTROTYPED BY J. S. CUSHING CO.
PRINTED IN THE UNITED STATES OF AMERICA
BY BERWICK & SMITH CO.

CONTRIBUTORS

W. B. Chase, Esq., New York . . . . . W. B. C.
Alexis Chitty, Esq. . . . . . . A. C.
Mons. Gustave Chouquet . . . . . G. C.
Mons. Ernest Closson, Professor at Brussels Conservatoire . . E. C^N.
W. W. Cobbett, Esq. . . . . . . W. W. C.
A. D. Coleridge, Esq. . . . . . . A. D. C.
Frederick Corder, Esq. . . . . . . F. C.
George Arthur Crawford, Major . . . . G. A. C.
Walter R. Creighton, Esq. . . . . . W. R. C.
W. H. Cummings, Esq., Mus.D., F.S.A. . . . . W. H. C.
Sir William George Cusins . . . . . W. G. C.

William H. Daly, Esq., Edinburgh . . . . W. H. D.
H. G. Daniels, Esq., Berlin . . . . . H. G. D.
Edward Dannreuther, Esq. . . . . . E. D.
Paul David, Esq. . . . . P. D.
J. H. Davie, Esq. . . . . J. H. D.
Sir H. Walford Davies, Mus.D., Gresham Professor of Music, etc. . H. W. D.
J. W. Davison, Esq. . . . . . . J. W. D.
H. C. Deacon, Esq. . . . . H. C. D.
Edward J. Dent, Esq., Professor of Music in Cambridge University . E. J. D.
L. M'C. L. Dix, Esq. . . . . . . L. M'C. L. D.
Miss Janet Dodge . . . . J. D.
Herr Alfred Dörffel . . . . . . A. D.
Edward H. Donkin, Esq. . . . . . . E. H. D.
George Dyson, Esq., Mus.D., Director of Music in Winchester College G. D.

Clarence Eddy, Esq. . . . . . . C. E.
F. G. Edwards, Esq. . . . . . . F. G. E.
H. Sutherland Edwards, Esq. . . . . . H. S. E.
Dr. Alfred Einstein, Editor of Riemann's Lexikon, 1922 . . A. E.
Thomas Elliston, Esq. . . . . . . T. E.
Carl Engel, Esq., Librarian of Music, Library of Congress, Washington C. E^L.
Edwin Evans, Esq. . . . . . . E. E.

The Rev. E. H. Fellowes, Mus.D. . . . . E. H. F.
Gustave Ferrari, Esq. . . . . . . G. F.
Shelley Fisher, Esq. . . . . . . S. F.
Chevalier Wm. Hy. Grattan Flood, Hon. Mus.D., N.U.I., K.S.G. . W. H. G. F.
Walter Ford, Esq. . . . . . . W. F.
The Rt. Rev. Walter H. Frere, D.D., C.R., Lord Bishop of Truro . W. H. F.
Arthur M. Friedlander, Esq. . . . . . A. M. F.
Dr. Max Friedländer . . . . . . M. F.
H. Frederick Frost, Esq. . . . . . H. F. F.
John T. Fyfe, Esq. . . . . . . J. T. F.
Charles Alan Fyffe, Esq. . . . . . C. A. F.

The Rev. Canon F. W. Galpin . . . . F. W. G.
Signor Guido M. Gatti . . . . . . G. M. G.
Nicholas Comyn Gatty, Esq., Mus.B. . . . N. C. G.
Dr. Franz Gehring, Vienna . . . . . F. G.
Scott Goddard, Esq. . . . . . . S. G.
M. van Someren Godfery, Major . . . . M. v. S. G.
Harvey Grace, Esq. . . . . . . H. G.
Charles L. Graves, Esq. . . . . . C. L. G.

J. C. GRIFFITH, Esq.   .   .   .   .   .   .   J. C. G.
Sir GEORGE GROVE, C.B., D.C.L., Editor of the First Edition   .   .   G.

Sir W. HENRY HADOW, Mus.D., Vice-Chancellor of Sheffield University   W. H. H^w.
H. V. HAMILTON, Esq.   .   .   .   .   .   .   H. V. H.
Mrs. ROBERT HARRISON   .   .   .   .   .   .   B. H.
Herr KARL HASSE   .   .   .   .   K. H^x.
L. W. HAWARD, Esq., Curator of the Manchester Art Gallery   .   .   L. W. H.
The Rev. T. HELMORE   .   .   .   .   .   .   T. H.
WILLIAM HENDERSON, Esq.   .   .   .   .   .   .   W. H.
W. J. HENDERSON, Esq., New York   .   .   .   .   .   W. J. H.
GEORGE HERBERT, Esq.   .   .   .   .   .   .   G. H.
ARTHUR F. HILL, Esq.   .   .   .   .   .   .   A. F. H.
Dr. FERDINAND HILLER   .   .   .   .   .   .   F. H^x.
A. J. HIPKINS, Esq., F.S.A.   .   .   .   .   .   .   A. J. H.
Miss EDITH J. HIPKINS   .   .   .   .   .   .   E. J. H^s.
CLAUDE HOBDAY, Esq.   .   .   .   .   .   .   C. H.
EDWARD JOHN HOPKINS, Esq., Mus.D.   .   .   .   .   .   E. J. H.
The Rev. Canon T. PERCY HUDSON (Canon Pemberton)   .   .   .   T. P. H.
FRANCIS HUEFFER, Esq.   .   .   .   .   .   .   F. H.
The Rev. Dom ANSELM HUGHES, O.S.B.   .   .   .   .   .   A. H.
A. HUGHES-HUGHES, Esq.   .   .   .   .   .   .   A. H.-H.
A. EAGLEFIELD HULL, Esq., Mus.D.   .   .   .   .   .   A. E. H.
JOHN HULLAH, Esq. .   .   .   .   J. H.
DUNCAN HUME, Esq.   .   .   .   .   .   .   D. H.
W. HUME, Esq.   .   .   .   .   .   .   W. H^x.
HUBERT W. HUNT, Esq., Mus.D.   .   .   .   .   .   .   H. W. H.
Miss KATHLEEN D. HURST   .   .   .   .   .   .   K. D. H.
WILLIAM H. HUSK, Esq.   .   .   .   .   .   .   W. H. H.

IVOR JAMES, Esq.   .   .   .   .   I. J.
F. H. JENKS, Esq. .   .   .   .   F. H. J.
Mons. ADOLPHE JULLIEN   .   .   .   .   .   .   A. J.

H. J. KALCSIK, Esq.   .   .   .   .   .   .   H. J. K.
A. KALISCH, Esq.   .   .   .   .   A. K.
J. A. KAPPEY, Esq. .   .   .   .   J. A. K.
CUTHBERT KELLY, Esq.   .   .   .   .   .   .   C. K.
FRANK KIDSON, Esq.   .   .   .   .   .   .   F. K.
HERMAN KLEIN, Esq.   .   .   .   .   .   .   H. K.
The Rev. Dr. ALOIS KOLIČEK   .   .   .   .   .   .   A. K^x.
E. KRALL, Esq.   .   .   .   .   E. K.
H. E. KREHBIEL, Esq.   .   .   .   .   .   .   H. E. K.
Mons. MAURICE KUFFERATH, Brussels   .   .   .   .   .   M. K.

Herr ROBERT LACHMANN   .   .   .   .   .   .   R. L.
MORTON LATHAM, Esq.   .   .   .   .   .   .   M. L.
JAMES LECKY, Esq. .   .   .   .   J. L.
ROBIN H. LEGGE, Esq.   .   .   .   .   .   .   R. H. L.
J. MEWBURN LEVIEN, Esq.   .   .   .   .   .   .   J. M. L.
CECIL LEWIS, Esq. .   .   .   .   C. L.
H. J. LINCOLN, Esq.   .   .   .   .   .   .   H. J. L.
R. B. LITCHFIELD, Esq.   .   .   .   .   .   .   R. B. L.
R. E. LONSDALE, Esq.   .   .   .   .   .   .   R. E. L.
STANLEY LUCAS, Esq.   .   .   .   .   .   .   S. L.

R. F. M'Ewen, Esq. . . . . R. F. M'E.
Sir G. A. Macfarren, Mus.D. . . . . . G. A. M.
The Rev. Charles Mackeson, F.R.S. . . . . C. M.
Charles Maclean, Esq., Mus.D. . . . . . C. M².
H. S. Macran, Esq. . . . . H. S. M.
Herr A. Maczewsky . . . . A. M.
J. A. Fuller Maitland, Esq., F.S.A., Editor of the Second Edition . M.
Jeffery Mark, Esq. . . . . J. M^X.
Mrs. Julian Marshall . . . . F. A. M.
Julian Marshall, Esq. . . . . . . J. M.
Russell Martineau, Esq. . . . . . . R. M.
H. J. L. J. Massé, Esq. . . . . . . H. J. L. M.
Signor Giannandrea Mazzucato . . . . G. M.
The Rev. J. H. Mee . . . . J. H. M.
Senhor Carlos de Mello . . . . . . C. de M.
Herr Rudolf Mengelberg . . . . . . R. M^G.
Miss Louisa Middleton . . . . . . L. M. M.
The Rev. J. R. Milne . . . . . . J. R. M.
R. O. Morris, Esq. . . . . R. O. M.
D. L. Murray, Esq. . . . . D. L. M.

V. E. Negus, Esq., F.R.C.S. . . . . . V. E. N.
Mrs. Rosa Newmarch . . . . R. N.

E. M. Oakeley, Esq. . . . . E. M. O.
Sir Herbert S. Oakeley, Mus.D. . . . . H. S. O.
C. B. Oldman, Esq., British Museum . . . . C. B. O.
The Rev. Sir F. A. Gore Ouseley, Bt., Mus.D. . . . F. A. G. O.

Sidney H. Pardon, Esq. . . . . . . S. H. P.
Henry Parr, Esq. . . . . H. P.
Sir Walter Parratt, Mus.D., M.V.O. . . . W. P^A.
Sir C. Hubert H. Parry, Bt., C.V.O., Mus.D. . . C. H. H. P.
Mons. K. Paucitis, Riga . . . . . . K. P.
Edward John Payne, Esq. . . . . . . E. J. P.
The Rev. Hugh Pearson . . . . . . H. P^N.
Edward H. Pember, Esq., K.C. . . . . . E. H. P.
The Rev. Canon T. P. Pemberton (formerly Hudson) . T. P. P.
Mlle. Marie Louise Pereyra . . . . . M. L. P.
Miss Phillimore . . . . C. M. P.
F. Piggott, Esq. . . . . F. P.
Mons. Marc Pincherle . . . . . . M. P.
Herr C. Ferdinand Pohl . . . . . . C. F. P.
William Pole, Esq., F.R.S., Mus.D. . . . . W. P.
E. Polonaski, Esq. . . . . E. P^I.
Victor de Pontigny, Esq. . . . . . . V. de P.
Reginald Lane Poole, Esq. . . . . . R. L. P.
Mons. J. G. Prod'homme . . . . . . J. G. P.
Ebenezer Prout, Esq., Mus.D. . . . . . E. P.
The Rev. W. Pulling . . . . . . W. P^G.
Charles H. Purday, Esq. . . . . . . C. H. P.

Miss Olga Racster . . . . O. R.
Mons. Félix Raugel, Paris . . . . . . F. R^L.

WILLIAM HENRY REED, Esq. . . . . . W. H. R.
LUIGI RICCI, Esq. . . . . . L. R.
EDWARD F. RIMBAULT, Esq., LL.D. . . . . E. F. R.
Signor F. RIZZELLI . . . . . F. R^Z.
W. S. ROCKSTRO, Esq. . . . . . W. S. R.
Dr. KURT ROGER, Vienna . . . . . K. R.
DESMOND LUMLEY RYAN, Esq. . . . . D. L. R.

Mons. GUSTAVE SAMAZEUILH, Paris . . . . G. S.
H. A. SCOTT, Esq. . . . . . H. A. S.
J. S. SHEDLOCK, Esq. . . . . . J. S. S.
A. J. SHELDON, Esq. . . . . . A. J. S.
CARL SIEWERS, Esq. . . . . . C. S^B.
The Hon. Mrs. SINCLAIR . . . . . G. A. S.
WARREN STOREY SMITH, Esq., Boston . . . . W. S. S.
Miss BARBARA SMYTHE . . . . . B. S.
O. G. SONNECK, Esq., New York . . . . O. G. S.
Dr. Ing. OTTOKAR SOUREK, Prague . . . . O. S.
T. L. SOUTHGATE, Esq. . . . . . T. L. S.
WALTER R. SPALDING, Esq., Professor of Music in Harvard University, Cambridge, Mass. . . . . . W. R. S.
Dr. PHILIPP SPITTA . . . . . P. S.
S. J. SPURLING, Esq. . . . . . S. J. S.
WILLIAM BARCLAY SQUIRE, Esq., M.V.O. . . . W. B. S.
Miss C. STAINER . . . . . C. S.
Sir JOHN STAINER, Mus.D. . . . . . J. S.
J. F. R. STAINER, Esq. . . . . . J. F. R. S.
W. W. STARMER, Esq. . . . . . W. W. S.
E. IRENAEUS PRIME STEVENSON, Esq. . . . . E. I. P. S.
Sir ROBERT P. STEWART, Mus.D. . . . . R. P. S.
T. L. STILLIE, Esq. . . . . . T. L. S^E.
WILLIAM H. STONE. Esq., M.D. . . . . W. H. S.
E. VAN DER STRAETEN, Esq. . . . . . E. v. d. s.
A. H. FOX-STRANGWAYS, Esq. . . . . . A. H. F.-S.
R. A. STREATFEILD, Esq. . . . . . R. A. S.
The Rt. Rev. THOMAS B. STRONG, D.D., Lord Bishop of Oxford . T. B. S.
J. STUTTERFORD, Esq. . . . . . J. S^D.
Sir ARTHUR SEYMOUR SULLIVAN, Mus.D. . . . A. S. S.

FRANKLIN TAYLOR, Esq. . . . . . F. T.
CHARLES SANFORD TERRY, Esq., Litt.D. (Cantab.), Hon. Mus.D. (Edin.), Hon. LL.D. (Glasgow) . . . . . C. S. T.
Mons. ANDRÉ TESSIER, Paris . . . . . A. T.
ALEXANDER W. THAYER, Esq. . . . . . A. W. T.
Miss BERTHA THOMAS . . . . . B. T.
HERBERT THOMPSON, Esq., D.Litt., Leeds . . . . H. T.
G. H. THRING, Esq., Incorporated Society of Authors, Playwrights and Composers . . . . . G. H. T.
H. JULIUS W. TILLYARD, Esq., Professor in Birmingham University . H. J. W. T.
FRANCIS TOYE, Esq. . . . . . F. T^YE.
J. B. TREND, Esq. . . . . . J. B. T.

Mons. RICHARD VEŠELÝ, Prague . . . . . R. V.
Dr. BOLESLAV VOMAČKA . . . . . B. V.

ERNEST WALKER, Esq., Mus.D., Fellow of Balliol College, Oxford   .   E. W.
WILLIAM WALLACE, Esq.   .   .   .   .   .   W. W.
S. H. WALROND, Esq.   .   .   .   .   .   S. H. W.
Miss SYLVIA TOWNSEND WARNER   .   .   .   .   .   S. T. W.
EDWARD WATSON, Esq., National Institute for the Blind   .   .   E. Wᴺ.
P. G. L. WEBB, Esq.   .   .   .   .   .   P. G. L. W
C. WELCH, Esq.   .   .   .   .   .   C. W.
FREDERICK WESTLAKE, Esq. .   .   .   .   .   F. W.
H. A. WHITEHEAD, Esq.   .   .   .   .   .   H. A. W.
W. E. WHITEHOUSE, Esq.   .   .   .   .   .   W. E. W.
C. F. ABDY WILLIAMS, Esq.   .   .   .   .   C. F. A. W.
R. VAUGHAN WILLIAMS, Esq., Mus.D.   .   .   .   .   R. V. W.
C. W. WILSON, Esq., Dublin   .   .   .   .   C. W. W.
Mrs. EDMOND WODEHOUSE   .   .   .   .   .   A. H. W.
J. MUIR WOOD, Esq.   .   .   .   .   .   J. M. W.
H. E. WOOLDRIDGE, Esq.   .   .   .   .   .   H. E. W.
H. SAXE-WYNDHAM, Esq., Secretary of the Guildhall School of Music   .   H. S.-W.

THE EDITOR   .   .   .   .   .   .   C.

CONTRIBUTORS

LIST II. ARRANGED IN ALPHABETICAL ORDER OF THE INITIALS BY WHICH ARTICLES
ARE SIGNED

The names of deceased writers are printed in italics

A. C.	ALEXIS CHITTY, Esq.
A. C. B.	ADRIAN C. BOULT, Esq., Mus.D.
A. D.	*Herr ALFRED DÖRFFEL.*
A. D. C.	*A. D. COLERIDGE, Esq.*
A. E.	Dr. ALFRED EINSTEIN.
A. E. H.	A. EAGLEFIELD HULL, Esq., Mus.D.
A. F. H.	ARTHUR F. HILL, Esq.
A. H.	Rev. Dom ANSELM HUGHES, O.S.B.
A. H. F.-S.	A. H. FOX-STRANGWAYS, Esq.
A. H.-H.	A. HUGHES-HUGHES, Esq.
A. H. W.	*Mrs. EDMOND WODEHOUSE.*
A. J.	*Mons. ADOLPHE JULLIEN.*
A. J. H.	*A. J. HIPKINS, Esq., F.S.A.*
A. J. S.	A. J. SHELDON, Esq.
A. K.	A. KALISCH, Esq.
A. Kᴋ.	Rev. Dr. ALOIS KOLIČEK.
A. M.	*Herr A. MACZEWSKY.*
A. M. F.	ARTHUR M. FRIEDLANDER, Esq.
A. S. S.	*Sir ARTHUR S. SULLIVAN, Mus.D.*
A. T.	Mons. ANDRÉ TESSIER.
A. W. T.	*ALEXANDER W. THAYER, Esq.*
B. H.	Mrs. ROBERT HARRISON.
B. S.	Miss BARBARA SMYTHE.
B. T.	Miss BERTHA THOMAS.
B. V.	Dr. BOLESLAV VOMAČKA.
C.	THE EDITOR.
C. A.	*CARL ARMBRUSTER, Esq.*
C. A. F.	*CHARLES ALAN FYFFE, Esq.*
C. B.	Mons. CHARLES BOUVET.
C. B. O.	C. B. OLDMAN, Esq.
C. E.	Clarence EDDY, Esq.
C. Eᴸ.	CARL ENGEL, Esq.
C. F. A. W.	*C. F. ABDY WILLIAMS, Esq.*
C. F. P.	*Herr C. FERDINAND POHL.*

C. H.	.	.	.	.	. Claude Hobday, Esq.
C. H. P.	.	.	.	.	. *Charles H. Purday, Esq.*
C. H. H. P.	.	.	.	.	*Sir C. Hubert H. Parry, Mus.D., C.V.O.*
C. K.	.	.	.	.	. Cuthbert Kelly, Esq.
C. L.	.	.	.	.	. Cecil Lewis, Esq.
C. L. G.	.	.	.	.	. Charles L. Graves, Esq.
C. M.	.	.	.	.	. *Rev. Charles Mackeson, F.R.S.*
C. M^N.	.	.	.	.	. *Charles Maclean, Esq., Mus.D.*
C. de M.	.	.	.	.	. Senhor Carlos de Mello.
C. M. P.	.	.	.	.	. Miss Phillimore.
C. S.	.	.	.	.	. Miss C. Stainer.
C. S^a.	.	.	.	.	. Carl Siewers, Esq.
C. S. T.	.	.	.	.	. Charles Sanford Terry, Esq., Mus.D.
C. W.	.	.	.	.	. *C. Welch, Esq.*
C. W. W.	.	.	.	.	. C. W. Wilson, Esq.
D. B.	.	.	.	.	. *David Baptie, Esq.*
D. H.	.	.	.	.	. *Duncan Hume, Esq.*
D. J. B.	.	.	.	.	. D. J. Blaikley, Esq.
D. L. M.	.	.	.	.	. D. L. Murray, Esq.
D. L. R.	.	.	.	.	. *Desmond Lumley Ryan, Esq.*
E. B.	.	.	.	.	. Eric Blom, Esq.
E. B^L.	.	.	.	.	. Mons. E. Borrel.
E. C.	.	.	.	.	. *E. C. Chadfield, Esq.*
E. C^N.	.	.	.	.	. Mons. Ernest Closson.
E. D.	.	.	.	.	. *Edward Dannreuther, Esq.*
E. E.	.	.	.	.	. Edwin Evans, Esq.
E. F. R.	.	.	.	.	. *Edward F. Rimbault, Esq., LL.D.*
E. H.-A.	.	.	.	.	. E. Heron-Allen, Esq.
E. H. D.	.	.	.	.	. Edward H. Donkin, Esq.
E. H. F.	.	.	.	.	. Rev. E. H. Fellowes, Mus.D.
E. H. P.	.	.	.	.	. *Edward H. Pember, Esq., K.C.*
E. I. P. S.	.	.	.	.	. E. Irenaeus Prime Stevenson, Esq.
E. J. D.	.	.	.	.	. Edward J. Dent, Esq.
E. J. H.	.	.	.	.	. *Edward John Hopkins, Esq., Mus.D.*
E. J. H^s.	.	.	.	.	. Miss Edith J. Hipkins.
E. J. P.	.	.	.	.	. *Edward John Payne, Esq.*
E. K.	.	.	.	.	. E. Krall, Esq.
E. M. O.	.	.	.	.	. E. M. Oakeley, Esq.
E. O. B.	.	.	.	.	. Mrs. Edith Oldham Best (Miss Oldham).
E. P.	.	.	.	.	. *Ebenezer Prout, Esq., Mus.D.*
E. P^I.	.	.	.	.	. E. Polonaski, Esq.
E. v. d. S.	.	.	.	.	. E. van der Straeten, Esq.
E. W.	.	.	.	.	. Ernest Walker, Esq., Mus.D.
E. W^N.	.	.	.	.	. Edward Watson, Esq.
F. A. G. O.	.	.	.	.	. *Rev. Sir F. A. Gore Ouseley, Bt., Mus.D.*
F. A. M.	.	.	.	.	. *Mrs. Julian Marshall.*
F. B.	.	.	.	.	. F. Bonavia, Esq.
F. C.	.	.	.	.	. Frederick Corder, Esq.
F. G.	.	.	.	.	. *Dr. Franz Gehring.*
F. G. E.	.	.	.	.	. *F. G. Edwards, Esq.*
F. H.	.	.	.	.	. *Francis Hueffer, Esq.*
F. H^R.	.	.	.	.	. *Dr. Ferdinand Hiller.*

F. H. J.	. . . . .	F. H. Jenks, Esq.
F. K.	. . . .	Frank Kidson, Esq.
F. P.	. . . .	F. Piggott, Esq.
F. R^z.	. . . .	Signor F. Rizzelli.
F. R^L.	. . . .	Mons. Félix Raugel.
F. T.	. . . .	Franklin Taylor, Esq.
F. T. A.	. . . .	F. T. Arnold, Esq.
F. T^{YE}.	. . . .	Francis Toye, Esq.
F. W.	. . . .	Frederick Westlake, Esq.
F. W. G.	. . . .	Rev. Canon F. W. Galpin.
G.	. . . .	Sir George Grove, C.B., D.C.L.
G. A. C.	. . . .	Major George Arthur Crawford.
G. A. M.	. . . .	Sir G. A. Macfarren, Mus.D.
G. A. S.	. . . .	The Hon. Mrs. Sinclair.
G. C.	. . . .	Mons. Gustave Chouquet.
G. D.	. . . .	George Dyson, Esq., Mus.D.
G. E. P. A.	. . . .	G. E. P. Arkwright, Esq.
G. F.	. . . .	Gustave Ferrari, Esq.
G. H.	. . . .	George Herbert, Esq.
G. H. T.	. . . .	G. H. Thring, Esq.
G. M.	. . . .	Signor Giannandrea Mazzucato.
G. M. G.	. . . .	Signor Guido M. Gatti.
G. S.	. . . .	Mons. Gustave Samazeuilh.
G. S. K.-B.	. . . .	G. S. Kaye-Butterworth, Esq.
H. A.	. . . .	Herbert Antcliffe, Esq.
H. A. S.	. . . .	H. A. Scott, Esq.
H. A. W.	. . . .	H. A. Whitehead, Esq.
H. B.	. . . .	Hugh Butler, Esq.
H. B^Y.	. . . .	Dr. Hermann Budy.
H. C. D.	. . . .	H. C. Deacon, Esq.
H. E. A.	. . . .	Lieut. H. E. Adkins.
H. E. K.	. . . .	H. E. Krehbiel, Esq.
H. E. W.	. . . .	H. E. Wooldridge, Esq.
H. F. B.	. . . .	Horatio Robt. Forbes Brown, Esq.
H. F. F.	. . . .	H. Frederick Frost, Esq.
H. G.	. . . .	Harvey Grace, Esq.
H. G. D.	. . . .	H. G. Daniels, Esq.
H. J. K.	. . . .	H. J. Kalcsik, Esq.
H. J. L.	. . . .	H. J. Lincoln, Esq.
H. J. L. M.	. . . .	H. J. L. J. Massé, Esq.
H. J. W. T.	. . . .	Professor H. Julius W. Tillyard.
H. K.	. . . .	Hermann Klein, Esq.
H. P.	. . . .	Henry Parr, Esq.
H. P^N.	. . . .	Rev. Hugh Pearson.
H. S. E.	. . . .	H. Sutherland Edwards, Esq.
H. S. M.	. . . .	H. S. Macran, Esq.
H. S. O.	. . . .	Sir Herbert S. Oakeley, Mus.D.
H. S.-W.	. . . .	H. Saxe-Wyndham, Esq.
H. T.	. . . .	Herbert Thompson, Esq., D.Litt.
H. V. H.	. . . .	H. V. Hamilton, Esq.
H. W. D.	. . . .	Sir H. Walford Davies, Mus.D.
H. W. H.	. . . .	Hubert W. Hunt, Esq., Mus.D.

I. J.	.	. IVOR JAMES, Esq.
J. A. K.	.	. *J. A. KAPPEY, Esq.*
J. B.	.	. Dr. JOSEF BARTOŠ.
J. B. T.	.	. J. B. TREND, Esq.
J. C. B.	.	. J. C. BRIDGE, Esq., Mus.D.
J. C. G.	.	. J. C. GRIFFITH, Esq.
J. D.	.	. Miss JANET DODGE.
J. F. R. S.	.	. J. F. R. STAINER, Esq.
J. G. P.	.	. Mons. J. G. PROD'HOMME.
J. H.	.	. *JOHN HULLAH, Esq.*
J. H. D.	.	. J. H. DAVIE, Esq.
J. H. M.	.	. *Rev. J. H. MEE.*
J. L.	.	. JAMES LECKY, Esq.
J M.	.	. *JULIAN MARSHALL, Esq.*
J. M^K.	.	. JEFFERY MARK, Esq.
J. M. L.	.	. JOHN MEWBURN LEVIEN, Esq.
J. M. W.	.	. *J. MUIR WOOD, Esq.*
J. R. M.	.	. Rev. J. R. MILNE.
J. R. S.-B.	.	. J. R. STERNDALE-BENNETT, Esq.
J. S.	.	. *Sir JOHN STAINER. Mus.D.*
J. S^D.	.	. J. STUTTERFORD, Esq.
J. S. S.	.	. J. S. SHEDLOCK, Esq.
J. T. F.	.	. JOHN T. FYFE, Esq.
J. W. C.	.	. J. W. CAPSTICK, Esq.
J. W. D.	.	. *J. W. DAVISON, Esq.*
K. D. H.	.	. Miss KATHLEEN D. HURST.
K. H^E.	.	. Herr KARL HASSE.
K. P.	.	. Mons. K. PAUCITIS.
K. R.	.	. Dr. KURT ROGER.
L. B.	.	. *LEONARD BORWICK, Esq.*
L. M^CL. L. D.	.	. L. M'C. L. DIX, Esq.
L. M. M.	.	. Miss LOUISA MIDDLETON.
L. R.	.	. *LUIGI RICCI, Esq.*
L. W. H.	.	. L. W. HAWARD, Esq.
M.	.	. J. A. FULLER MAITLAND, Esq.
M. B.	.	. *The Hon. Mrs. M. BURRELL.*
M. C. C.	.	. Mrs. WALTER CARR.
M. D. C.	.	. M. D. CALVOCORESSI, Esq.
M. F.	.	. Dr. MAX FRIEDLÄNDER.
M. K.	.	. *Mons. MAURICE KUFFERATH.*
M. L.	.	. *MORTON LATHAM, Esq.*
M. L. P.	.	. Mlle. M. L. PEREYRA.
M. P.	.	. Mons. MARC PINCHERLE.
M. V. S. G.	.	. Major M. VAN SOMEREN GODFERY.
N. C. G.	.	. NICHOLAS C. GATTY, Esq.
O. G. S.	.	. O. G. SONNECK, Esq.
O. R.	.	. Miss OLGA RACSTER.
O. S.	.	. Dr. Ing. OTTOKAR ŠOUREK

P. C. B.	.	.	PERCY C. BUCK, Esq., Mus.D.
P. D.	.	.	*PAUL DAVID, Esq.*
P. G. L. W.	.	.	P. G. L. WEBB, Esq.
P. S.	.	.	*Dr. PHILIPP SPITTA.*
R. A.	.	.	RICHARD ALDRICH, Esq.
R. A. S.	.	.	*R. A. STREATFEILD, Esq.*
R. B. L.	.	.	*R. B. LITCHFIELD, Esq.*
R. E. L.	.	.	R. E. LONSDALE, Esq.
R. F. M'E.	.	.	*R. F. M'EWEN, Esq.*
R. H. L.	.	.	ROBIN H. LEGGE, Esq.
R. H. M. B.	.	.	*R. H. M. BOSANQUET, Esq.*
R. L.	.	.	Herr ROBERT LACHMANN.
R. L. P.	.	.	REGINALD LANE POOLE, Esq.
R. M.	.	.	*RUSSELL MARTINEAU, Esq.*
R. M^G.	.	.	Herr RUDOLF MENGELBERG.
R. N.	.	.	Mrs. ROSA NEWMARCH.
R. O. M.	.	.	R. O. MORRIS, Esq.
R. P. S.	.	.	*Sir ROBERT P. STEWART, Mus.D.*
R. V.	.	.	M. RICHARD VEŠELÝ.
R. V. W.	.	.	R. VAUGHAN WILLIAMS, Esq., Mus.D.
S. F.	.	.	SHELLEY FISHER, Esq.
S. G.	.	.	SCOTT GODDARD, Esq.
S. H. P.	.	.	*SIDNEY H. PARDON, Esq.*
S. H. W.	.	.	S. H. WALROND, Esq.
S. J. S.	.	.	S. J. SPURLING, Esq.
S. L.	.	.	*STANLEY LUCAS, Esq.*
S. T. W.	.	.	Miss SYLVIA TOWNSEND WARNER.
T. B. S.	.	.	The Rt. Rev. THOMAS B. STRONG, D.D., Lord Bishop of Oxford.
T. E.	.	.	THOMAS ELLISTON, Esq.
T. H.	.	.	*Rev. THOMAS HELMORE.*
T. L. S.	.	.	*T. L. SOUTHGATE, Esq.*
T. L. S^E.	.	.	*T. L. STILLIE, Esq.*
T. P. H.	.	.	*Rev. Canon T. PERCY HUDSON (Canon Pemberton).*
T. P. P.	.	.	*Rev. Canon T. P. PEMBERTON (formerly Hudson).*
V. E. N.	.	.	V. E. NEGUS, Esq., F.R.C.S.
v. de P.	.	.	*VICTOR DE PONTIGNY, Esq.*
W. A. A.	.	.	W. A. AIKIN, Esq., M.D.
W. B. C.	.	.	W. B. CHASE, Esq.
W. B. S.	.	.	*WILLIAM BARCLAY SQUIRE, Esq.*
W. C.	.	.	*WILLIAM CHAPPELL, Esq., F.S.A.*
W. E. W.	.	.	W. E. WHITEHOUSE, Esq.
W. F.	.	.	WALTER FORD, Esq.
W. G. C.	.	.	*Sir WILLIAM GEORGE CUSINS.*
W. H.	.	.	*WILLIAM HENDERSON, Esq.*
W. H^E.	.	.	W. HUME, Esq.
W. H. C.	.	.	*W. H. CUMMINGS, Esq., Mus.D.*
W. H. D.	.	.	WILLIAM H. DALY, Esq.
W. H. F.	.	.	The Rt. Rev. W. H. FRERE, D.D., C.R., Lord Bishop of Truro.
W. H. G. F.	.	.	W. H. GRATTAN FLOOD, Esq., Mus.D.

W. H. H.	.	.	.	.	. WILLIAM H. HUSK, Esq.
W. H. H^w.	.	.	.	.	. Sir W. HENRY HADOW, Mus.D.
W. H. R.	.	.	.	.	. WILLIAM HENRY REED, Esq.
W. H. S.	.	.	.	.	. WILLIAM H. STONE, Esq., M.D.
W. J. H.	.	.	.	.	. W. J. HENDERSON, Esq.
W. P. .	.	.	.	.	. WILLIAM POLE, Esq., F.R.S., Mus.D.
W. P^A.	.	.	.	.	. Sir WALTER PARRATT, Mus.D., M.V.O.
W. P^G.	.	.	.	.	. Rev. W. PULLING.
W. R. C.	.	.	.	.	. WALTER R. CREIGHTON, Esq.
W. R. S.	.	.	.	.	. WALTER R. SPALDING, Esq.
W. S. R.	.	.	.	.	. W. S. ROCKSTRO, Esq.
W. S. S.	.	.	.	.	. WARREN STOREY SMITH, Esq.
W. W.	.	.	.	.	. WILLIAM WALLACE, Esq.
W. W. C.	.	.	.	.	. W. W. COBBETT, Esq.
W. W. S.	.	.	.	.	. W. W. STARMER, Esq.

LIST OF PLATES

VOLUME I

xvii

VOLUME II

VOLUME IV

VOLUME V

ABBREVIATIONS

PERIODICALS AND WORKS OF REFERENCE, Etc.

Allgemeine Musikalische Zeitung	A.M.Z.
American Supplement of Grove's Dictionary	Amer. Supp.
Bach-Gesellschaft (complete critical edition of J. S. Bach's works)	B.-G.
Bach Jahrbuch	B. J.-B.
Baker's Biographical Dictionary	Baker.
British Musical Biography	Brit. Mus. Biog.
British Musical Society's Annual, 1920	B.M.S. Ann., 1920.
Davey's *History of English Music*	Hist. Eng. Mus.
Denkmäler deutsche Tonkunst	D.D.T.
Denkmäler der deutsche Tonkunst in Österreich	D.T.Ö.
Dictionary of National Biography	D.N.B.
Eitner's *Quellen-Lexikon*	Q.-L.
Fétis's *Biographie universelle* (with Supplement)	Fétis.
Imperial Dictionary of Universal Biography	Imp. Dict. Univ. Bio.
Mendel's Lexicon	Mendel.
Monatshefte für Musikgeschichte, Leipzig	M.f.M.
Musical Antiquary	Mus. Ant.
Musical Association's Proceedings	Mus. Ass. Proc.
Musical Times	Mus. T.
Music and Letters	M. and L.
Oxford History of Music	Oxf. Hist. Mus.
Quarterly Musical Review	Q. Mus. Rev.
Revista de Filogia española, Madrid	R.F.E.
Revista musical Catalona, Barcelona	R.M.C.
Revista musical de Bilbao	R.M.B.
Revista musicale italiana, Turin	R.M.I.
Revue musicale, Paris	R.M.
Riemann's Musik Lexikon, 1922	Riemann.
Sammelbände der Internationalen Musikgesellschaft, Leipzig	S.I.M., also I.M.G.
Studien zu Musikwissenschaft	S.z.M.W.
Walker's *History of Music in England*	Hist. Mus. Eng.
Zeitschrift für Musikwissenschaft, Leipzig	Z.M.W.

ENGLISH LIBRARIES AND COLLECTIONS

Batten Organ Book at St. Michael's College, Tenbury	Tenb. O.B.
Bodleian Library, Oxford	Bodl. Lib.
British Museum	B.M.
Buckingham Palace Library (now in the British Museum)	Roy. Lib. B.M.
Caius College, Cambridge	Caius.
Christ Church, Oxford	Ch. Ch.
Commonplace Book of John Baldwin	Baldwin.
Durham Cathedral	Durh.
Ely Cathedral	Ely.
First Book of Selected Church Music, edited by John Barnard, 1641	Barnard.
Fitzwilliam Library, Cambridge	Fitzw.

Harleian MSS., British Museum . . . . Harl.
Lambeth Palace . . . . Lambeth.
Organ Book at Christ Church . . . . Ch. Ch. O.B.
Organ Book at Durham Cathedral . . . . Durham O.B.
Oxford Music School Collection (now in the Bodleian Library) . . Bodl. Mus. Sch.
Peterhouse, Cambridge . . . . PH.
Royal Collection Appendix MSS., British Museum . . . . Roy. MSS.
Royal College of Music . . . . R.C.M.
Sadler Partbooks (now in the Bodleian Library) . . . . Sadler.
St. George's Chapel, Windsor . . . . St. G. Ch.
St. Michael's College, Tenbury . . . . Tenb.
Wimborne Minster . . . . Wimb.
Worcester Cathedral . . . . Worc.
York Minster . . . . Yk.

CHURCH MUSIC

Benedicite . . . (Bcte.)	Litany . . . (L.)
Benedictus . . (B.)	Magnificat . . (M.)
Creed . . . (C.)	Nunc Dimittis . . (N.D.)
Gloria . . . (G.)	Sanctus . . . (S.)
Jubilate . . . (J.)	Te Deum . . (T.D.)
Kyrie . . . (K.)	Venite . . . (V.)

INSTITUTIONS, Etc.

Bibliothèque National, Paris . . . . Bibl. Nat. Paris.
Breitkopf & Härtel . . . . B. &. H.
Guildhall School of Music, London . . . . . . G.S.M.
Incorporated Society of Musicians . . . . . . I.S.M.
International Musik Gesellschaft . . . . Int. Mus. Ges.
Musical Antiquarian Society . . . . Mus. Ant. Soc.
Musical Association . . . . Mus. Ass.
Real Conservatorio di Musica, Naples . . . . . R.C.M. Naples.
Royal Academy of Music, London . . . . . . R.A.M.
Royal College of Music, London . . . . R.C.M.
Royal College of Organists, London . . . . . . R.C.O.

DICTIONARY

OF

MUSIC AND MUSICIANS

VOL. V

SONG—Z

SONG. In relation to the study of music, a song may be defined as a short metrical composition, whose meaning is conveyed by the combined force of words and melody. The song, therefore, belongs equally to poetry and music.

The history of song in this article is treated in regard to country and not to period; it is confined to European [1] nations which have developed special characteristics of style, and is concerned rather with such characteristics than with the achievements of individual masters, whose work is discussed under their own names. It may safely be asserted that certain successions of sounds or intervals, varying with different nationalities, have in all ages possessed some particular significance and conveyed some message of meaning from man to man. So that the song of each nation has qualities and idioms of its own as distinct and definite as those of its language.

Vocal music is probably the oldest branch of the art; but from the fact that dance-songs preponderate in the music of nations whose musical culture remains in a primitive stage it is reasonable to conclude that vocal music may have been at first a mere accessory of the dance. (See DANCE-RHYTHM.) Choral singing at religious and other festivals was also a practice of very remote antiquity. Recitations by bards, commemorative of the exploits of heroes, were a further and distinct development of vocal music. Hence the work done by the minstrels, TROUBADOURS and TROUVÈRES, MINNESINGER and MEISTERSINGER (*q.v.*), will call for notice in their different countries.

FRANCE

France may legitimately occupy the first place in this scheme, as the European country which possesses one of the oldest songs in a written notation. This is a *Complainte* on the death of Charlemagne, 813. It may be found in a MS. in *fonds-latin* dated 1154, in the Bibliothèque Nationale in Paris,[2] and has been attri-

buted to S. Columbanus. The music has been reduced to modern notation by both Cousse-

1. FACSIMILE OF 'PLANCTUS KAROLI' [3]

[1] Originally this article contained a short section on song in the United States of America, now withdrawn since the subject could not be treated on historical lines parallel with those adopted for the song of European nations. The following books, however, offer material for the study of the several folk-songs implanted in America. See also the article NEGRO MUSIC.

H. E. Krehbiel, *Afro-American Folk-Songs*. A study in racial and national music. Pp. 176. New York, 1914.

Eleanor Hague, *Spanish-American Folk-Songs*. Collected by E. Hague. Pp. 113. Lancaster, Pa., and New York, 1917. (*Memoirs of the American Folk-Lore Society*, vol. 10.)

Frances Densmore, *Teton Sioux Music*. Pp. xxviii, 561. Washington, 1918. (Smithsonian Institution. Bureau of American Ethnology. Bulletin 61.)

Olive Dame Campbell and C. J. Sharp, *English Folk-Songs from the Southern Appalachians*. Pp. 341. New York and London, 1917.

Songs from the Hills of Vermont. . . . Texts collected and edited by Edith B. Sturgis. Tunes collected and piano accompaniments arranged, with historical notes, by Robert Hughes. Pp. 57. New York, 1919.

Twenty Kentucky Mountain Songs. The words collected by Loraine Wyman, the melodies collected and the pianoforte accompaniment by Howard Brockway. Pp. 115. Boston, 1920. (Cf. *Lonesome Tunes: Folk-Songs from the Kentucky Mountains*, by the same collectors. Vol. 1, pp. 102. New York, 1916.)

Several types of Oriental song are described under their own headings in the Dictionary.

[2] Another song in the same MS. on the battle of Fontanet, 841, is said to be by one Angelbert, a Frankish warrior, who was present. Fétis, *Histoire générale de la musique*, iv. 473 *et seq.*

[3] Fétis, *Histoire générale de la musique* iv. 474.

maker and Fétis, but their versions vary. It must be remembered that there is less certainty on the subject of early music than on early language, for music was handed down solely by oral tradition. And even when about the year 1000 the necessity was felt for some method of musical NOTATION (*q.v.*), the plans adopted were so numerous and confused that the question of time or rhythm or actual notes of a mediæval MS. is constantly interpreted differently by musical historians. We therefore give in facsimile a fragment of the MS. and a few bars of both versions for comparison :

2.   COUSSEMAKER'S VERSION [1]

A so-lis or-tu us-que ad oc-ci-du--a Lit-to-ra ma-ris

3.   FÉTIS'S VERSION

A so-lis or-tu us-que ad oc-ci-du-a lit-to-ra ma-ris

The melody has only four notes ; indeed, up to the last phrase only three, showing that the peculiar French fondness for a small compass has survived for 1000 years. Since the 10th century the practice existed of using well-known tunes (which later would be called *timbres*) to different Latin words.[2] And most of the Crusaders' songs which have come down to us from the 11th century are in Latin.[3] But an important exception amongst them is a song beginning 'O Marie, Deu maire,' dated 1096, which is in the vernacular, and this date marks the epoch when the Latin language began to be superseded by the French.

It is necessary to emphasise the close connexion which has ever existed—and perhaps in France more than in any other country—between the folk-song and the Church. There is reason to believe that some melodies, or fragments of melodies, of Celtic origin have been preserved from the ages before Christianity was introduced into France. The old heathen popular songs were in the early centuries of the Christian era a subject of much trouble to the Church, and Christian people were forbidden to frequent places where they were sung. Even Charlemagne, who ordered a collection of epic songs to be made, condemned the vulgar, reprehensible type of songs which

were sung round about the churches. In speaking of the music of the Church it must be remembered that it had two distinct groups ; first, the liturgical portion, or plain-song, without regular rhythm ; and second, the music to the hymns (prose or sequence, *sequentia*), which was both melodious and rhythmical, and represented the popular part of the service. By degrees, the secular spirit crept into these *proses* [4] and from the 11th century onwards popular songs [5] are to be found in the vulgar tongue side by side with the Latin canticles. These were called *proses farcies* or *épîtres farcies* [6] Laudable attempts also were made by the Church to adapt secular festivals and customs to Christian purposes. Thus the Christian festival of Easter corresponded with the heathen celebration of the spring. Many of the old Celtic May-day songs [7] still exist, and a great similarity of melody can be traced between them and the Easter music of the Church. The origin of the well-known Easter hymn ' O filii et filiae ' is unknown, but it is certainly as old as the 12th century, and has usually been attributed to French sources. It is unlike Gregorian music in character, but its affinity with some of the following examples of old May-day songs, called *Chansons de quête*, still sung in different parts of France, is incontestable.[8]

4.

O fi-li-i et fi-li-ae,

Rex coe-les-tis, rex glo-ri-ae

5.

En re-ve-nant de-dans les champs, En re-ve-nant de-dans les champs.

6.

Mois de mai qu'est ar-ri-vé, c'est au-jour-d'hui qu'il faut chanter.

Another example of the resemblance between the church and folk-songs is afforded by the Tonus Peregrinus, the chant sung to the Psalm

---

1 Weckerlin, ' Chansons populaires du pays de France,' i. 86.
2 Fétis speaks of two Latin poems sung to tunes called *Modus libidinis* (l'air de l'amour), and *Modus florum* (l'air des fleurs). *Ibid.* iv. 430.
3 Such as the beautiful ' Jerusalem Mirabilis,' which is a solemn piece, like a Gregorian hymn, and probably sung by the people in the open air. *Ibid.* iv. 482

4 Lavoix, *La Musique française*, p. 20.
5 Usually *Complaintes*, recognisable by their rhythm.
6 For example see Fétis, v. 103.
7 These contain strange relics of old Celtic words such as *Trimoussette*. See Tiersot, *Histoire*, p. 192.
8 Tiersot, *Histoire de la chanson populaire en France*, p. 361. Other pagan or Celtic festivals, such as midwinter (called *la fête de l'Aguilaneuf* or *l'Aguilaneuf*) or midsummer, answering respectively to the Church festivals of Christmas (see CAROL), the Epiphany, or St. John the Baptist, gave rise to masses of songs still sung in France, and common to both kinds of music. Space debars further mention of this subject, but full and interesting information will be found in M. Tiersot's above-quoted volume, p. 186 *et seq.* (In this same chapter the famous ' Maumariée ' *Chansons* are alluded to.)

'When Israel came out of Egypt.' Again the origin is obscure, but already in the 9th century it was held to be very old. Like 'O filii et filiae' it differs in many ways from Gregorian music, but several old French songs could be given where the melody is almost note for note that of the Tonus Peregrinus. For instance, the 'Chant des livrées,' a very old song still sung at country weddings; or the beautiful 16th-century 'Rossignolet des bois.'[1]

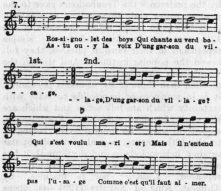

7.

Ros-si-gno-let des boys Qui chante au verd bo-
As-tu ou-y la voix D'ung gar-son du vil-

1st.   2nd.

--ca-ge,   --la-ge,D'ung gar-son du vil-la-ge?

Qui s'est voulu ma-ri-er; Mais il n'entend

pas l'u-sa-ge Comme c'est qu'il faut ai-mer.

Modal melodies have existed for hundreds of years, and still exist all over France, but the commonest scales for the French folk-songs are the modern major and minor scales.[2] Among the most beautiful modal tunes are those found in Brittany, such as 'Le Clerc du Trémélo,' which is in the ecclesiastical Dorian or first mode; a singularly pathetic religious song sung in a time of famine, 'Disons le chapelet' in the Phrygian or third mode; and the well-known 'Ma douce Annette,' or the beautiful 'Le Paradis' (given below) in the Aeolian or ninth mode.[3]

8.

Je crois au pa-ra-dis   J'es-père al-ler un
Jé-sus nous la pro-mis.

1st.   2nd.

jour au glo-ri-eux sé-jour.

The narrative form of song is very popular in France, and the generic term for this class

of song is the *Complainte*. The old Celtic epics and the later collection of epics made by Charlemagne, the *chansons de geste*, the early *romances*, the *légendes* of the Passion and of the Christian saints, and the old pathetic *ballades* of the peasants would all come under that name. The wonderful *légende* called the 'Ballade de Jésus Christ' is still sung in Picardy.[4] The simplicity of the language and the modal melody point to its being of popular origin. The 'Chanson de la Perronelle,' which has lived in the mouths of the people for centuries,[5] resembles the oldest *complaintes* in its poetic form, consisting of couplets of two lines without a refrain.[6]

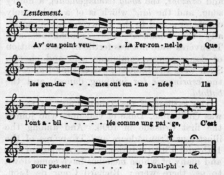

9.

Lentement.

Av' ous point veu-... La Per-ron-nel-le Que

les gen-dar-...mes ont em-me-née? Ils

l'ont a-bil-...lée comme ung pai-ge,   C'est

pour pas-ser......le Daul-phi-né.

Tiersot calls attention to the strange fact, that although these *chansons narratives* were known to exist, they were far less often included in the collections made from the 13th to the 17th centuries than the *chansons satiriques*, *chansons d'amour*, *pastourelles*, etc. Of recent years their extreme beauty has claimed more attention, and many modern collections of them have been published.

Some strong impulse was evidently given to the human mind in Europe towards the close of the 11th century, and the songs of the Troubadours, like the numerous schools of philosophy which illuminated the 12th century, were fruits of an awakened ardour for intellectual pursuits. With the TROUBADOURS (*q.v.*) a new type of music was introduced, which may be described as songs written with conscious art. The Troubadours and Trouvères belonged respectively to the south and north of France, and wrote in the Langue d'Oc and Langue d'Oïl. At first the Troubadours and Trouvères sang their own verses, but the functions of the poet and singer soon became distinct. Hence a class of professional musicians arose, who sang the songs of their own lords and other composers. These wandering singers from Provence and Picardy, known as *Jongleurs*

---

[1] Tiersot, 'Mélodies,' p. 73.
[2] *Ibid.*, *Histoire*, p. 322.
[3] The above are included in M. Bourgault-Ducoudray's 'Trente mélodies populaires de la Basse-Bretagne'; and here it would be convenient to state briefly M. Bourgault-Ducoudray's theory. He denies that these modal songs have their origin in the Church. His argument is that the modes found in these and other popular melodies, not only of France, but of Ireland, Scotland, Greece, etc., are actually the survival of music common to the early Indo-European race. He maintains that the Greeks alone cultivated music as an art; that the Church, taking its scales from Greece and afterwards carrying them to other countries, brought to Brittany, for instance, a kind of music which was already familiar to the Bretons in their popular songs; that the so-called modes may be as old and as common to many nationalities as many of the familiar words common to the different languages of the Indo-European family. On the strength of this, Ducoudray's nomenclature of the modes is the Greek and not the ecclesiastical, and this has been adopted by other Continental writers (see MODES). Throughout this article, however, the Church names and Gregorian numbers of the modes are retained, except in the section relating to song in Greece.

[4] This legend is widely spread in France. I. is found in connexion with several saints in the *Legenda Aurea* of Jacobus de Voragine. See Champfleury and Weckerlin's 'Chansons populaires des provinces de France.'
[5] The earliest record of the words and music of this song is to be found in a MS. in the Bibliothèque Nationale called 'Chansons du 15ème siècle,' published by Gaston Paris and Gevaert.
[6] Tiersot, *Histoire*, p. 12.

or *Chanteors* in the south, and *Ménétriers* or minstrels in the north,[1] went from court to court, country to country, and joining the Crusaders they returned from the Holy Land filled with enthusiasm and singing songs of love and war. The war-songs or *chansons de geste* were musically uninteresting ; they were merely long chanted tales where the melody only occurs in the short refrain. But the love-songs were poems of exquisite grace, perfect rhythm and highly expressive. Their very names reveal their origin, such as the *pastourelle*, *alba* and *serena*, *tensons* and *sirvente*.[2] To the Troubadours likewise may be ascribed the *canzo* and *canzone*, the *soula* (soulagement), a merry song, and the *lai*,[3] which is of a melancholy character ; and to the Trouvères more especially the *romance*.[4] The Troubadours and Trouvères were not less fertile in the invention of dance songs, combining solo and chorus. Such were the famous *carol* or *rondet de carol*, the *espringerie* (or jumping dance), and the *ballata*.

The earliest of the Troubadours on record was Guillaume, Duke of Guienne, who joined the first Crusade in 1096. And among the illustrious Troubadours and Trouvères of the 12th and 13th centuries, whose names survive and many of whose melodies have come down to us, there were : Richard Cœur de Lion, Bertran de Born, Pierre Rogier, Bernart de Ventadour, the Châtelain de Coucy, Guirant de Borneil, Blondel de Nesle, Gracé Brulé, Hugues de Lusignan, Thibaut de Champagne (King of Navarre), Jehan Erars, Giraut de Calenson, Perrin d'Angecourt, Adam de la Bassée, Adenet le Roi and Adam de la Hale. The prime of the Troubadours was past when in the year 1320 the Troubadour Academy of Toulouse was founded for the cultivation and preservation of their art.[5]

The Troubadours and Trouvères owe great debts to the Church and to the folk-song. Their music was a compound of the folk-song for its melody and form ; and of the Gregorian chant for its declamation and ornament. But inasmuch as the art of literature was then highly developed, and music was still in its infancy, it was impossible to combine the elaborate and highly finished forms of poetry with the music then existing, and a new kind of song, more artistic and more developed, was the result. The Troubadours were eager to invent new, ingenious and graceful phrases, metres and rhythms,[6] and their work was of real value in handing down the rhyming stanza as the most perfect vehicle for lyrical expression. Also, by the preference the Troubadours gave to the modern major scale they helped to establish it in European music before the close of the 13th century. In this, and in the simple repetitions of their musical phrases, they followed the popular instinct. And though the Troubadour melodies are more developed and finished than those of the *chansons populaires*, it is in many cases impossible to state with certainty which are folk-songs and which are the work of trained musicians. For instance, a pastoral song, ' La reine d'Avril,' belonging to the 12th century, is said to be of popular origin ; it is melodious and rhythmical, it has a refrain, and the first little phrase is four times repeated. ' L'autrier par la matinée,' by Thibaut, King of Navarre (1201–54), opens with a phrase exactly similar, which is also

10.   *Quant le Rossignol.*

CHÂTELAIN DE COUCY.

Quant li lou - sei - - gnolz jo - lis chante
sur la flor . . . . . d'es - té, que naist la
ro - se et le lys et la ro - - - -
- - sée et vert pré plains de bon - ne vo - len
- - té chan-te-rai . . confins a - mis, mais di tant
suis es-ba - his . . que . . . j'ai si très haut
pen - - sé qu'a pai - nes iert ac-com-plis . . li
ser - - virs . dont jai - - 6 grè.

[1] The *Ménétrier* seems to have attained a higher standard of culture and taste than the *Jongleur*, who soon added other modes of popular diversion (such as juggling and acrobatic feats) to his musical accomplishments. It must, however, be remembered that the lower classes in France were untouched by the Troubadour movement, which covered the time from the 11th to the 14th centuries. They had nothing more in common with the *lais*, *sirventes*, etc. than they had with the old *chansons de geste*. The *Jongleurs* were the sole connecting link between the people and the courts.

[2] In the *pastourelle* the poet feigned to meet and woo a shepherdess ; the *alba* and *serena* were aubades and serenades. The *tensons* were metrical dialogues of lively repartee on some disputed point of gallantry, and the *sirvente* was an address of a devoted lover to his mistress. To this latter form of composition, which was also much employed in satire, a special celebrity belongs, because its metre—the *terza rima*—was adopted by Dante and Petrarch.

[3] See F. Wolf, *Über die Lais*.

[4] The *romance* is the lyrical outcome of the narrative *complaintes* and *chansons de geste* in Northern France. ' Belle Yolans ' of the 12th century is an example. See Tiersot, *Histoire*, p. 414.

[5] There were schools in other parts of France where the Gay Science was taught, and whither the Troubadours repaired in Lent (when not allowed to appear in public) to learn new songs and melodies. The minstrels also had rights granted to them to form corporations or guilds in several towns. The earliest charter dates 1338, signed by Robert de Caveran, and lasted until the 18th century.

[6] See P. Aubry, *Le Rhythmique musicale des Troubadours, etc.*, Paris, 1907.

repeated.[1] There is the same charm of sincerity and pretty sentiment about an older song, the Châtelain de Coucy's (1192) ' Quant le rossignol,' [2] though the form is less concise. It is composed in phrases of seven bars each, like many other mediæval songs.[3] Both are good illustrations of Troubadour songs.[4]

Very few *sirventes*, but many *pastourelles*, have been preserved from the 12th century. This period was specially rich in sacred and secular dramatic representations; and, as before stated, proses and canticles in plain-chant melody are found side by side with light, rhythmical popular tunes. It is thus in ' Daniel Ludus ' by one Hilaire, played in 1250. The ' Jeu de S. Nicolas ' and ' Le Juif ' were of the same type, at once sacred and comic. The character of the mysteries remained faithful to tradition ; these were only a continuation of the liturgical dramas of the 11th century.[5] But by the end of the 13th century the Trouvères had broken loose from the Church, and resorted to little village histories or love-stories for their material. ' Aucassin et Nico-lette,' the well-known *chant-fable*, belongs to this time. Musically more important was Adam de la HALE's celebrated pastorale ' Le jeu de Robin et de Marion,' which was played at the court of Charles of Anjou at Naples in 1285. Tiersot has now shown that A. de la Hale probably wrote the play, and then strung together a number of popular tunes (many of them of far older date) to suit his words.[6] Thus this pastoral comedy forms probably the oldest collection of French folk-tunes in existence. Adam de la Hale, together with Guillaume de MACHAUT, should more properly be classed among the *Chansonniers*, or the early musicians, who in the 13th century paved the way for the contrapuntal school, which for two centuries was to be the predominating influence in European music. To Adam de la Hale and G. de Machaut French music owes much ; not only can the form of the future *vaudeville* be detected in the *pastorale* ' Robin et Marion,' but its chansons are strictly similar in structure and character to chansons of modern date. In the old and new alike we find a strongly marked rhythm, easy intervals, and a paucity of notes, repetition of one short melodic phrase, the major mode, the favourite 6–8 time, and an extreme simplicity of general plan.[7] Though hundreds of years have passed since ' Robin

et Marion ' was written, the song ' Robin m'aime ' (Ex. 11) is still sung in Hennegau.[8]

11.

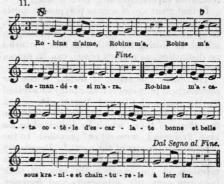

Ro - bins m'aime, Robins m'a, Robins m'a

Fine.

de - man - dé - e si m'a - ra. Ro - bins m'a - ca-

- - ta co - tè - le d'es - car - la - te bonne et belle

Dal Segno al Fine.

sous kra - ni - e et chain - tu - re - le à leur ira.

It should be noted that in the songs of this early period the melody is never protracted and drawn out to the detriment of the words, but closely follows the quick succession of syllables without visible effort. And these old melodies often have the Iambic rhythm, for instance [9] :

12.
ADAM DE LA HALE.

Il n'est si bon - ne vi - an-de que ma - tons.

Contemporary with, or a little junior to Machaut, was Jehannot Lescurel, who wrote *romances* which are still extant in MS. One of these, ' A vous douce débonnaire,' which has been translated into modern notation by Fétis,[10] exhibits a more developed melody and a more modern tendency than other productions of the same date.

If it be true that during the 14th and 15th centuries the Church exercised an exclusive dominion over music, she was nevertheless a friend to secular songs. By taking popular tunes for the themes of their masses and motets, such as ' L'omme armé,' ' Tant je me déduis,' ' Se la face ay pale ' (used by Dufay) ; or ' Baisez-moi ' (by Roselli), ' Malheur me bat ' (by Josquin des Prés), etc.,[11] the musicians of the Church preserved many a melody which would otherwise have perished. ' L'omme armé ' is undoubtedly the most famous song of the Middle Ages, and it owes its notoriety not so much to its beauty as to the fact that contrapuntal composers, from Dufay, at the end of the 14th century, to CARISSIMI (*q.v.*) in the 17th, used it more than any other folk-song. (See L'HOMME ARMÉ, Vol. III. p. 151.) From want of such adoption by the Church, some of the airs have been lost to which the curious old Noëls, printed in black letter at the end of

1 Ambros, *Geschichte der Musik*, ii. 227, and Tiersot, *Hist.* p. 371.
2 Ambros, *ibid.* ii. 223. Burney and Perne put these into modern notation, and, where they differ, Burney's are the lower notes.
3 Another of Thibaut's songs, ' Je me quidoie partir d'amour,' given by Ambros, ii. 228, has an alternating rhythm of two and three bars, but it preserves a perfect symmetry of form.
4 Further examples of Troubadour songs will be found in Wolf's *Über die Lais*, Kiesewetter's *Schicksale und Beschaffenheit des weltlichen Gesanges* ; J. Stafford Smith's ' Musica antiqua,' and in the histories of music by Ambros, Fétis, Burney and others. Also for modernised versions see Weckerlin's ' Échos du temps passé,' vol. i.
5 See Lavoix, *La Musique française*, p. 41.
6 Tiersot's interesting and conclusive arguments are given in different places in his *Histoire de la chanson populaire*. See especially p. 422 *et seq.*, and the article HALE, Adam de la, Vol. II. p. 495.
7 Tiersot, *Histoire*, p. 373.

8 This example is taken from M. Lussy and E. David's *Histoire de la notation musicale*, p. 105.
9 Ambros, *Ges. der Musik*, ii. 295.
10 This song is to be found in the *Revue musicale*, vol. xii. No. 34.
11 Ambros, *Ges. der Musik*, iii. 15 *et seq.*

the 15th century, were sung, though the names of the airs (such as 'Faulce trahison,' etc.) remain as superscriptions. (See Noël.[1])

In that great age of serious polyphonic music a high place was held by the French school, or, to speak more correctly, by the Gallo-Belgian school, for during the 14th and 15th centuries no distinction, as regards music, can be drawn between northern France and Flanders.[2]

The direct use made of secular music for ecclesiastical purposes is remarkably illustrated by the works of Clément Marot. He was a translator of a portion of the Psalms ; and the first thirty of them, which he dedicated to his king, François I., were set or ' parodied ' to the favourite dance-airs of the court.[3] Popularity was thus at once secured for the Psalms, which members of the court could sing to their favourite *courantes, sarabandes* and *bourrées*. After Marot's death Béza continued his work at Calvin's instance.[4] Much doubt existed for a long while as to whom belonged the credit of having set the Psalms to music. Some ascribed it wholly to Marot, others to Goudimel ; but M. Douen has now made it clear that these men, together with Jambe de Fer, Franc, Claudin and others, adapted the Psalms to old secular songs.[5] In the ' Psautier flamand primitif ' (1540) all the psalms are for one voice, and with only two exceptions they can all be traced back to their sources in popular French and Flemish songs.[6] (See PSALTER.)

While secular music was thus made to minister to the Church, it had a separate though less conspicuous sphere of its own. This is attested by the *vaux-de-vire* (or drinking-songs),[7] *voix-de-ville* (better known by their

modern name of *vaudevilles*) and *airs de cour*, collected and published in the 16th century. Much grace, indeed, and gaiety were evinced in the poetry and music of the songs and *romances* of this period, and it would be wrong to disparage such writers as Guillaume le Heurteur, Noë Faignient, Pierré Vermont, and François I., whose song, ' O triste départir,' with music by A. Muret, is full of feeling. But more important work was undoubtedly being done by their polyphonic contemporaries.[8]

The effects of the great change which came over vocal music at the end of the 16th century were perhaps more marked in France and in the Netherlands than elsewhere. When once the monodic system had gained universal recognition polyphonic music began to decline, even where it had flourished most. Henceforward original melodies of their own invention were expected of musicians, and the old practice of choosing themes for their compositions in folk-songs or popular dance-songs died out, though its disappearance was gradual.[9] Songs for one voice, such as the ' Airs de cour ' of the early 17th century, accompanied by lute or harpsichord, began to find favour and to drive airs for several voices from the ground they had occupied for more than 150 years And that most characteristic type of French song, the *romance*, was soon to begin, or rather resume, a reign of popularity which is not yet ended.

Scudo[10] defines the *romance* as a song divided into several ' couplets,' the air always simple, naïve and tender, the words to treat of sentiment and love. Unlike the *chanson* it is never political or satirical. It was one of the very earliest fruits of French grace, sensibility and gallantry ; and though its attributes may have varied from time to time, it remained unchanged in its essence from the era of the Troubadours until the 19th century. There was, it is true, a period after the disappearance of the Troubadours, when the *romance* was threatened with extinction by its formidable rival the polyphonic *chanson*, but the 17th century saw it again in possession of all its

[1] A list of collections of Noëls is given by Tiersot, *Hist.* p. 242.

[2] The importance of the French chanson as a factor in the transformation of the whole of European music in the second half of the 15th century can scarcely be overrated. Its extraordinary vogue is attested not only by the numerous publications of French music-printers, but by publications issued in foreign countries such as those of Venice, Louvain, Antwerp, Nuremberg. Moreover, as early as the second half of the 15th century, the chanson becomes an important element in instrumental music, through its transcriptions for the keyboard instruments, and later on for the lute. An important general bibliography forms the sequel of three articles by A. Jeanroy, J. Tiersot and E. Muret, in the *Grande Encyclopédie*.
M. L. P.

[3] Weckerlin says in his 'Échos du temps passé,' iii. 136, that when any dance-air became popular, rhymers immediately ' parodied ' it, *i.e.* put words to it, so that it could be sung. The term ' parody ' thus had no sense of burlesque, but it simply meant adaptation. The Ballards issued a quantity of these songs. 'L'Abeille,' a well-known example, is really a minuet.

[4] Calvin, who detested the arts, recommended music, nevertheless, from the purely utilitarian point of view, ' la parole chantée qui porte beaucoup plus fort.'

[5] See *Clément Marot et le psautier huguenot*, i. 606. One of the most noted is the magnificent Huguenot Battle Hymn, ' Que Dieu se montre seulement ' (Psalm 68), sometimes called ' La Marseillaise huguenote.' It is a secular tune of Alsatian origin, and it appeared first in the first edition of the Strassburg Psalter.

[6] For *cantiques*, moreover, as well as masses and psalms, secular airs were openly utilised. And according to Douen (pp. 688 and 703) the Roman Catholics have never ceased to adapt secular airs to ecclesiastical uses from the 16th century down to the present time. He supports this statement by reference to ' La pieuse alouette avec son tire-lire ; chansons spirituelles, le plupart sur les airs mondains, par Ant. de la Cauchie, 1619 ' ; ' Imitations de Jésus-Christ en cantiques sur des airs d'opéras et de vaudevilles, par Abbé Pelegrin, 1727 ' (Paris) ; and ' Concerts spirituels,' a collection published at Avignon in 1835, of masses, hymns, Requiems, prayers, etc., on operatic melodies by Gluck, Piccinni, Mozart, Cimarosa, Rossini, Méhul and others.

[7] Basselin and Jean le Houx, who lived in the little valleys (*vaux*) around Vire in Normandy, in the second half of the 15th century, wrote many favourite drinking-songs, and hence drinking-songs came to be called *vaux-de-vire*. Some writers have confused this term with the *voix-de-ville*, which applied to chansons sung in the streets, and later to any songs with gay airs and light words. Jehan

Chardavoine's famous collection of monodic songs of the 16th century is described as containing *vaux-de-ville* and *voix-de-ville*, chansons de ville, pièces littéraires avec leur musique originale, telle que ' Mignonne, allons voir si la rose,' by Ronsard, etc. See Tiersot, *Histoire*, pp. 228 and 433 for other similar collections.

[8] A celebrated collection, with a dedication to Charles IX., by Ronsard, was published in 1572, under the title of ' Meslanges de chansons,' and it contained songs for four, six and sometimes eight voices by all the best-known Gallo-Belgian composers, such as Josquin, Mouton, Claudin, etc. These songs, like others of the same date, have strong melodies, and are full of canonic devices. Pierre Ronsard's sonnets were set to music by Philippe de Monte, in five, six and seven parts, and his songs in four parts, by Bertrand and Reynard. Mention should also be made of Crespel, Raif, and Clement Jannequin, whose descriptive songs (such as the *Cris de Paris*) formed a new feature in music, also Gombert and Certon. But with the true polyphonic song this article is not concerned.

[9] When public opinion first ceased to approve this practice composers did not at once abandon it, but they no longer produced vocal pieces which were avowedly parodies or adaptations ; it now became their habit to attach their names to all their melodies, whether they were original or borrowed. As a typical case ' Charmante Gabrielle ' may be quoted : neither the words of which were by Henri IV. nor the music by his maître de chapelle, Du Caurroy. The air is really an old Noël of unknown authorship, and probably some court poet, Desportes, perhaps, wrote the words. See also J. B. Weckerlin, ' Chansons populaires du pays de France,' ii. 217.

[10] Scudo, *Critique et littérature musicales*, vol. ii.

old supremacy. Louis XIII. wrote several; and his music-master, Pierre Guédron, was perhaps the foremost composer of *romances* of that time. One of the best examples of his work, ' Aux plaisirs, aux délices, bergères,' [1] contains modulations which are remarkable for that date. Guédron's son-in-law, Boesset, was the author of a very famous *romance*, 'Cachez beaux yeux.' And the names of Beaulieu, Deschamps, Colasse, Bernier, Lefêvre, Lambert and Pierre Ballard may be recorded as composers of this age. The last (whose ' Belle, vous m'avez blessé,' was a favourite) was a member of the famous Ballard family of music-printers and also composers. As printers they preserved a large quantity of *brunettes* (see BRUNETTE), *musettes* [2] and other dance - songs and drinking - songs. Several *brunettes* were included in the great collection of the old French popular songs which A. Philidor copied out with his own hand and dedicated to Louis XIV. Many were undoubtedly written on old Noël airs, especially those in parts.[3] After the 17th century they became scarcely distinguishable from romances.

For excellent and typical specimens of the romances of the 18th century we may quote J. J. Rousseau's ' Le Rosier ' and ' Au fond d'une sombre vallée,' both of which are found in his collection entitled ' Les Consolations des misères de la vie.' The musicians of this period seem to have been inspired by the grace and delicacy of contemporary poetry to create tender and simple melodies. Insipid as these songs must seem to us now, they are thoroughly representative of the age which produced them. It was the time of that singular phase of thought and feeling which will be for ever associated with the name of J. J. Rousseau; a time of yearnings to return to some imagined state of native innocence, to an ideal pastoral life in some visionary and often artificial Arcadia. All this was faithfully reflected in the works of its poets and musicians. Monsigny instinctively returned to the style of the folk-song, even to the *pastourelle* and *complainte*. His frequent use of the minor seventh of the scale gives a touch of mediævalism to his songs [4]:

13.

Son pe-tit cœur sou - - hai - te.

[1] Published in Weckerlin's ' Échos du temps passé,' vol. iii. p. 10. It is taken from a very rare collection entitled ' Airs de cour de différents auteurs, 5 livres, publiés de 1615 à 1628. Paris, chez Pierre Ballard.' (Guédron's melody is in the first book.)
[2] Here on we may mention the drone-bass which occurs so frequently in musettes and other dance-songs. Numerous examples may be found in Weckerlin's ' Échos du temps passé.'
[3] In Weckerlin's second vol. of his ' Échos du temps passé' he states that this collection especially characterises the 17th and 18th centuries, and ' though written earlier the songs were only published when their popularity was great enough to justify it.' Weckerlin gives a valuable list of the collections drawn upon for this volume with full descriptions and dates. The favourite ' Menuet d'Exaudet ' (Exaudet was a famous dancing-master), with words by Favart, is included among the *chansons à danser.* All these dance-songs, except the minuet, are in common or 2-4 time, and in regular periods.
[4] Tiersot, *Histoire*, p. 525.

Grétry, on the other hand, who was a far more advanced musician, consciously set himself the task of reproducing the old melodic form of the folk-song. He confesses to have written the *romance* of Richard Cœur de Lion, ' Une fièvre brûlante,' *dans le vieux style.*[5] And certainly when the little art-songs or *romances* of this period are closely examined, they show externally but little difference from the folk-songs, though in their essence they are wide apart, being artificial rather than natural and spontaneous. As examples it will suffice to mention a few favourites such as : Monsigny's ' O ma tendre musette ' (words by La Harpe) ; ' Il pleut, bergère,' by Simon ; ' Les petits oiseaux,' by Rigel ; ' L'amour fait passer le temps,' by Solié ; ' Le point de jour,' by Dalayrac ; ' Annette et Lubin,' by Favart and ' Que j'aime à voir les hirondelles,' by Devienne.

Although romances were so much in vogue and reached so high a degree of popularity there were songs of other kinds written by the composers of the 18th century of equal importance. Amongst these, political songs are prominent, and in no country have they been more so than in France. The Mazarinade of the 17th century was a vast collection of more than 4000 satirical effusions against Mazarin, adopted to popular airs. Early in the 18th century was heard the famous song, ' Malbrouk s'en va-t-en guerre,' [6] and later on, in the first throes of the Revolution, the Royalists were singing ' Pauvre Jacques ' (words by the Marquise de Travenet), and the air resounded with ' Ça ira,' from the throats of the insurgent rabble of Paris. ' O Richard, ô mon roi ' and ' Où peut-on être mieux ' have become historical by their use at the same terrible period. As might have been expected of so profound a movement, the Revolution gave birth to many remarkable songs. To the stormy years at the close of the 18th and the opening of the 19th centuries are due the finest *chants* or patriotic songs of France. Supreme among these stands the MARSEILLAISE (*q.v.*), which has won immortality for its author and composer, Rouget de Lisle. Next in fame come three songs of Méhul's, the ' Chant du départ ' (words by Chénier), the ' Chant de retour,' and the ' Chant de victoire.' And by the side of these may be set the fine ' Réveil du peuple ' by Gaveaux, and the ' Père de l'univers ' by Gossec. Contemporary with these songs, but on a lower level of political importance and musical value, were ' Cadet Rousselle,' the ' Chanson de Dagobert,' ' Fanfan la tulipe,' [7] ' Te souviens-tu,' the ' Récit du caporal,' and many others it would be tedious to enumerate. Of a different kind was the official national anthem of the Restoration — the beautiful

[5] Grétry, *Essais sur la musique*, i. 368.
[6] For the tunes see J. B. Weckerlin's Chansons populaires du pays de France.'
[7] An old song of irregular metre by Souriquère de St. Marc, set to an old tune, and extremely popular between 1792 and 1802.

old song 'Vive Henri IV,'[1] which was much in vogue in 1814 after the Allies entered Paris.

After the accession of Napoleon and the accompanying revival of monarchical traditions, the demand for *romances* was more eager than ever, and there was no lack of composers ready to supply it.[2] The most successful were Plantade, Garat, Pradher and Lambert. Another popular contemporary, possessing more musical erudition, was Dalvimare, whose 'Chant héroïque du Cid' is a fine song. Choron was founder of a school whence issued Duprez, Scudo and others, who were both singers and song composers. The names of several women should also be included among *romance* writers : Mme. Gail, Queen Hortense, Mme. Duchambge and Loïsa Puget. The first named was the best musician. About Queen Hortense there was more of the amateur composer, and she would trust to Drouet, Carbonnel, or Plantade to put her airs into musical shape. Her best songs were 'Partant pour la Syrie' and 'Reposez-vous, bon chevalier.' Mme Duchambge owed her reputation to the skill with which Nourrit sang her songs, and Loïsa Puget was a favourite in schools and convents. Of others who wrote about the same time and in the same manner, it will suffice to mention A. de Beauplan, Panseron, Jadin, Bruguière, Mengal, Dolive, Berton, Lis and Pollet. As a general reflection on these songs, it may be said that their most common fault is the endeavour to express inflated sentiment with inadequate means. A discrepancy is constantly felt between the commonplace simplicity of the accompaniments and modulations, and the intense sentimentality or turgid pomposity of the words. The disparity could only be concealed by highly dramatic or expressive singing.

Out of the revolutionary era of 1830 there came in France a splendid outburst of lyric poetry. This was the era of Victor Hugo, Lamartine, Delavigne, Alfred de Musset and Béranger. And it was natural that the song should be responsive to the poetic movement of the time. In 1828 Monpou's setting of Béranger's 'Si j'étais petit oiseau' attracted the notice of the poets of the Romantic School. Many of de Musset's and Victor Hugo's ballades and romances were also composed by him. But MONPOU (*q.v.*) was not a highly trained musician ; though striking and original, his music was faulty. He was a slave to the influence of the Romantic School, and his songs well illustrate the extreme exaggeration to which it was prone. Similar qualities were likewise displayed by an incomparably greater musician, Hector BERLIOZ (*q.v.*). In him there was a

depth of poetic insight and a subtle sense of beauty to which Monpou could make no pretension. Another musician allied to the Romantic School was Félicien David, who, without being a song-writer, indirectly influenced later composers' songs by introducing the element of orientalism into French music. This, with its strange Eastern rhythms and tonalities, has attracted many subsequent composers.

The 19th-century opera-composers, such as A. Thomas, Gounod, Saint-Saëns, Delibes, Bizet, Reyer, Joncières and Massenet, wrote some truly lyric songs. Gounod had a distinct lyric talent, and strongly influenced his generation. Among his best may be named 'Le Vallon,' 'Le Soir,' 'The fountain and the river,' 'Ring out, wild bells,' 'Le Printemps,' 'Medjé,' and the collection of twenty songs entitled 'Biondina,' which are full of the Southern spirit. Massenet possessed much the same sensuous vein of melody, but the form of his songs is more concise, and his accompaniments more brilliant. In the songs of Saint - Saëns, Lalo, Bizet and A. Chabrier there is individuality ; but they, as well as Widor, Joncières, Guiraud, Dubois, Paladilhe, Pierné, Boisdeffre, Lefebvre, Augusta Holmès, Thomé, Chaminade and other lesser composers are greatly indebted to Gounod, and generally speaking may be said to belong to the old school. Delibes and Godard should also be included, but their music has a distinct character of its own. Amongst his other works, Léo Delibes wrote many graceful, refined and typically French songs, full of colour ; whilst Benjamin Godard chiefly distinguished himself in this lyric form by the peculiar charm and melancholy sentiment of his songs.[3]

A totally different school of song from that above described now exists in France. At the present day the old rules of form, cadence and harmony are discarded ; a studied simplification of melody, restless modulation, vague tonalities and a preference for prose rhythms[4] prevail and indicate a radical change of method. The causes, direct and indirect, are varied. M. Bruneau attributes the new seriousness of French composers to the results of the disastrous war of 1870, and the misery and gloom which overshadowed France. Wagner's influence again penetrated through opera to song, realising the importance of the sound of words as well as their meaning, and equalising the importance of the instrumental part and the voice parts. Another incitement to change is based on the revival of the folk-song now used by modern song-writers, not only as a medium of national or local colour but as a source of

---

[1] Henri IV., 1553–1610. The melody is certainly older than his date, as it first appears as the *timbre* of a Noël in a collection published in 1581.
[2] Specimens of these little songs are to be found in Weckerlin's 'Chansons populaires du pays de France.'

[3] Godard has been aptly described as a musician of the autumn or of the twilight (see *French Music in the 19th Century*, by Arthur Hervey).
[4] A. Bruneau, in *La Musique française*, at p, 233, speaks of his efforts to combine prose with music, and adds that Saint-Saëns and he himself agree in thinking that in time prose will supplant poetry in drama and song.

inspiration.[1] Musicians, no less than painters, have their *plein - air* school. The love of nature and its elements, of the earth and of the growths of the soil has asserted its empire in the kingdom of art.[2] But while the influence of the folk-song conduced to simplicity, another influence stamped French song with a new impress. César Franck (a Belgian by birth but a naturalised Frenchman), a profound scholar, an idealist by character and aims alike, raised the level of contemporary art to a greater seriousness, and gave it a more complete emancipation. The special quality assimilated by the younger school of French song-writers is the element of mysticism. In César Franck's song, ' La Procession,' a noble simplicity and fervid mysticism are displayed, which exemplifies what has been said above. In adopting Franck's mysticism, it is stated that some of his followers have forfeited their race qualities of clearness of design and straightforwardness of expression. But their gains are manifest if we study the songs of Gabriel Fauré, Vincent d'Indy and Alfred Bruneau, and compare them with the romances and songs of the older school. In this generation song-writing was raised to a far higher plane. Gabriel FAURÉ (*q.v.*) was a song-writer *par excellence*. After these comes DEBUSSY (*q.v.*), with his conspicuous originality and aloofness of thought, the passing impressions of his dreams and ideals, and the atmosphere of the poem he sets.

To the above names may be added as typical of recent developments in French song : G. Charpentier, Reynaldo Hahn, E. Chausson, L. Wurmser, C. Blanc, E. Moret, P. de Bréville, H. Duparc, H. de Gorsse, E. Trémisot, L. Moreau, P. Vidal, G. Marty, S. Rousseau, Hillemacher frères, G. Ropartz, A. Chapuis, A. Gédalge, De Castillon, G. Hüe, M. Ravel.

It is necessary to add that modern French poets have had a great influence on these composers, and there exists a close sympathy between them. Obscurity of form, eccentricity, a feverish egoism which tends to over-subjectiveness, a subtlety which to an exaggerated degree substitutes suggestion for expression may be defects ; but an aptitude for intensity in the presentment of emotional themes, and an acute perception of the artistic values of personal emotion, a keen appreciation of evasive effects, of the fugitive and illusive beauty of sounds, implied or felt rather than heard—these are amongst the gifts they have utilised to the full.

[1] M. Tiersot truly remarks that ' the element of the folk-song vivifies and refreshes art, for it comes direct from the deepest source of inspiration in a nation.' But it is not only the spirit of the peasant's lyric and dramatic songs that modern composers have assimilated ; they also make use of the old forms, such as the *chansons à danser*, *ballades* and *légendes*. These are frequently found in Bruneau's and his contemporaries' works ; and Charpentier, in his opera ' Louise,' has used the old *cris de Paris* as Clément Jannequin did centuries ago. Many composers also have thought it worth their while to collect and arrange the folk-songs ; see for instance Vincent d'Indy's ' Chansons populaires recueillies dans le Vivarais,' and Bourgault-Ducoudray's beautiful volume of ' Trente mélodies populaires de la Basse-Bretagne.'
[2] Bruneau's ' Lieds de France,' and ' Chansons à danser ' form a striking example of the above qualities.

BIBLIOGRAPHY [3]

BURNEY, DR. *History of Music* (especially vol. ii.). 1776–89.
DELABORDE, J. B., and ROUSSIER, P. J. *Essai sur la musique.* Paris, 1780.
GRÉTRY, A. E. M. *Mémoires ou essais sur la musique.* Paris, 1796.
TOULMON, BOTTÉE DE. *De la chanson mus. en France.* Paris, 1836.
WOLF, F. *Über die Lais.* Heidelberg, 1841.
SCUDO, J. P. *Critique et littérature musicales.* Paris, 1850, 1859.
CHOUQUET, G. *Les Chants nationaux de la France* (*L'Art musical,* Oct. 1867).
AMBROS, A. W. *Geschichte der Musik* (especially vols. ii. and iii.). 1869.
FÉTIS, F. J. *Histoire générale de la musique* (especially vol. iv.). 1869.
BARTSCH, C. *Romances et pastourelles.* Leipzig, 1870.
HUEFFER, F. *The Troubadours.* 1878.
DOUEN, E. O. *Clément Marot et le psautier huguenot.* 1878.
DAVID, E., ET LUSSY, M. *Histoire de la notation musicale.* Paris 1882.
JULLIEN, A. *Musiciens d'aujourd'hui.* Paris, 1882.
TIERSOT, J. *Histoire de la chanson populaire en France.* Paris, 1889.
LAVOIX, H. *La Musique française.* 1891.
IMBERT, H. *Profils de musiciens.* Paris, 1888. *Portraits et études.* Paris, 1894.
BRUNEAU, A. *La Musique française.* 1901.
HERVEY, A. *Masters of French Music,* 1894 ; *French Music in the XIXth Cent.* 1904.
DIETZ, F. *Leben und Werke der Troubadours.* Breslau, 1862–82.
JEANROY, A. *Bibliographie sommaire des chansonniers français du moyen âge, manuscrits et éditions.* pp. viii, 78. Paris, 1918.

COLLECTIONS [4]

CAPELLE, P. ' La Clé du caveau,' 2nd ed. 1816.
RIVAREZ, FRÉDÉRIC ' Chansons et airs populaires du Béarn.' Pau, 1844.
BOUILLET, J. B. ' Album auvergnat.' Moulins, 1848.
WECKERLIN, J. B. ' Échos du temps passé.' Paris, 1855.
KASTNER, GEORGES. ' Les Voix de Pris.' Paris, 1857.
DUMERSAN, and COLET, H. ' Chants et chansons populaires de la France.' Paris, 1860.
CHAMPFLEURY, ET WECKERLIN, J. B. ' Chansons populaires des provinces de France.' Paris, 1860.
ARBAUD, DAMAS. ' Chants populaires de la Provence.' Aix, 1862–1864.
GAGNON, E. ' Chansons populaires du Canada.' Quebec, 1864, 1880, 1894 and 1900.
PUYMAIGRE, B. DE. ' Chants populaires recueillis dans le pays Messin.' Paris and Metz, 1865.
NISARD, M. E. C. ' Des chansons populaires.' Paris, 1867.
VILLEMARQUÉ, HERSAT DE LA. ' Barzas Breiz, chants populaires de la Bretagne.' Paris, 1867.
PARIS, GASTON, ET GEVAERT, A. ' Chansons du XVe siècle.' Paris, 1875.
MONTEL ET LAMBERT. ' Chants populaires de Languedoc.' Paris, 1880.
ROLLAND, E. ' Recueil de chansons populaires.' Paris, 1885.
BOURGAULT-DUCOUDRAY, L. A. ' Trente mélodies populaires de la Basse-Bretagne.' 1885.
TIERSOT, JULIEN. ' Mélodies populaires des provinces de France.' 3 vols. Paris, 1887 1890–91.
' Chants de la vieille France.'
' Chansons populaires françaises.'
' Noëls français.'
' Chansons populaires des Alpes françaises. Grenoble, 1903.
D'INDY, V., ET TIERSOT, J. ' Chansons recueillies dans le Vivarais et le Vercors.' Paris, 1892.
BUGEAUD, J. ' Chants et chansons populaires de l'Ouest.' 1895.
WECKERLIN, J. B. ' Chansons populaires du pays de France.' 2 vols. Paris, 1903.
GUILLERM, H. ' Recueil de chants populaires bretons du pays de Cornouailles.' Rennes, 1905.
BRANCHET, L., ET PLANTADES, J. ' Chansons populaires du Limousin.' Paris, 1905.
WECKERLIN, J. B. ' Chansons populaires de l'Alsace.'
DONCIEUX, G. ' Le Romancero populaire de la France.'
GEROLD, TH. ' Chansons populaires du XVe et XVIe siècles avec leurs mélodies.
' Le Manuscrit de Bayeux.' Strassburg, 1921.
' L'Art du chant en France au XVIIe siècle.' 1913.
DROZ, E., and THIBAULT, G. ' Poètes et musiciens du XVe siècle.'
SEVRETTE, G. ' Les Vieilles Chansons des pays de France.' Paris, 1922.
Volumes of chansons of special provinces have been published by Bourgault-Ducoudray (Brittany), Moullé (Normandy), C. de Malaret (Auvergne), M. Emmanuel (Burgundy), V. d'Indy (Vivarais).
Numerous old collections of French polyphonic songs are mentioned in Tiersot's *Histoire de la chanson populaire en France.* Paris, 1889.
A. H. W. rev. with addns. M. L. P.

SPAIN AND THE BASQUE COUNTRY

In Spain song has a long and varied history. Art-song developed early, in the works of the Spanish lutenists, or *vihuelistas* (*v.* VIHUELA) ; and the first book of tablature, ' El Maestro ' of Luis MILAN (1535), contains a number of songs and settings of ballads, which are not necessarily folk-songs, and have accompaniments written in a real instrumental style.

[3] The writer is also indebted to Mr. Walter Ford for permission to quote from his Lectures on French Song, 1905.
[4] Most of the collections contain valuable information about the songs given.

1.   L. MILAN. (1535.)

Y por siem - pre

Vihuela.
(effect: 8ve lower.)

vos a ma - ré

It is curious, however, that the later lute-songs tend more and more to become transcriptions of madrigals or madrigalesque compositions founded on folk-songs. The Italian chamber-cantata with figured bass did not find many imitators in Spain. To judge from existing MSS., Spanish singers of the 17th century preferred genuine Italian works (especially Alessandro Scarlatti) to native imitations. There are a few MS. songs by Hidalgo and other 17th-century composers, to figured bass, and the surviving works of MARÍN (q.v.) for bass or guitar (on which, in Spain, the continuo was often rendered) show a considerable and original talent. In the 18th century the art-song appeared chiefly as a part of the TONADILLA (q.v.); in the 19th it degenerated into drawing-room ballads mainly intended for exportation, and it was only in the 20th century that the Spanish art-song, in the hands of Falla, Granados, Pahissa, Turina, Vives and others, regained the position it had held 400 years earlier in the time of Luis Milan.

Poverty in art-songs is, however, amply rewarded by the wealth and variety of Spanish folk-songs. There is an initial difficulty in determining whether many of them are more properly songs or dances, for song is now (and apparently has always been) an accompaniment to dancing. But the basic form is the VILLAN-CICO (q.v.), which goes back to the time of the Muslim occupation of Southern Spain, and seems to be connected with two forms of vulgar Arabic verse (muwashshah and zajal), which had their origin in the Spanish Peninsula. It is found in the early songs of all the different regions of Spain (except the Basque Provinces). These may be divided as follows: (1) Galicia; (2) Catalonia and the Balearic Isles; (3) Castille, including Estremadura, León, Asturias, the 'Montaña' of Santander and also Aragon and Navarre; (4) Andalucía and Murcia; (5) the 'Levante' (S.E. coastal provinces); and (6) the Basque Provinces.

(1) GALICIA.—To the N.W. corner of Spain belong the earliest Peninsular songs which have

been preserved: the so-called 'Siete Canciones de Amor' of Martin CODAX (q.v.), which are in parallelistic verse-form and free musical rhythm, e.g.:

2.   MARTIN CODAX. (13th cent.)

On - das do . . mar de Vi - go,

se vis - tes . . meu a - mi - go,

e, ay De-us, se ve-rra . . ce - do.

and the 'Cantigas' of ALFONSO X. (q.v.), which are in Villancico-form and based on rhythmic principles analogous to those of the songs of the Troubadours, e.g.:

3.   ALFONSO X. (13th cent.)

A - le - gri - a, a - le - gri - a,
[Fin.]

Fa - ça - mos iá to - da - vi - a.
[D.C. al fin.]

Mui grand' a - le - gri - a fa - cer
de - ve - mos; ca Deus quis mo - rrer.

These are of mixed origin; some have been referred to French types.[1] Others have been compared (somewhat unconvincingly, perhaps) with modern songs and dances heard in Andalucía.[2] The melodies of Martin Codax, however, are admitted to be genuinely Galician in feeling. Their tonality, melodic formulæ and cadences are like those of the Alalás (v. infra), still sung by country people in remote parts of Galicia; the example quoted shows this clearly in the opening phrase. There is no real difference between the ancient Galician melodies in free rhythm and similar melodies which appear later in rhythms of 6-8 or 3-4 The essential feature is the melodic line, together with certain set turns of phrase, typical cadences and a tonality which is strongly diatonic. These qualities are largely due to the influence of the native instrument, which is not the guitar, but the bagpipes (gaita gallega), a diatonic instrument, with a compass extending from the b below the middle c^1 up to d^2 and including b^1 flat as well as natural. Another traditional instrument is the hurdy-gurdy (zanfonia), also diatonic, tuned in G and producing this scale (with F♮ as well as F♯) for two octaves The modes found in Galician popular song include Dorian, Phrygian, Mixolydian and Æolian

[1] Collet and Villalba, Bulletin Hispanique. Bordeaux, 1911. P. 270 ff.
[2] Ribera, La Música de las cantigas. Madrid, 1923.

(D, E, G and A modes) in their authentic and plagal forms. Among twenty or more *Alalás* in the collection of the Archæological Society of Pontevedra, 5 are Hypodorian, 5 Mixolydian, 4 Hypophrygian, 4 Lydian, 1 Phrygian and 1 Hypomixolydian. Another characteristic of Galician tunes is the resemblance of some of them to Gregorian melodies, not only in the mode, but also in melodic formula and cadence. The difference is rhythmical, not melodic.

The *Alalá* is a short melody sung to 4 8-syllable lines of verse. It is always repeated in the course of the stanza, and the singer is apparently allowed to add as many grace notes and flourishes as he pleases. Related to the *Alalá* are many types of popular song : cradle-songs, ploughing-songs, songs for ' braking ' the flax, *arrieros* (the songs of muleteers) and *canteros*, formerly sung in quarries, before the introduction of modern machinery, for the ' Altogether . . . Up ! ' (*In arriando . . . alto !*) The ancient songs of pilgrims to the shrine of St. James of Compostela also bear a certain likeness to the modern *alalás*.

Instrumental forms include the ALBORADA (*q.v.*) ; while dance music is represented by the *Muiñeira*, a form in 6–8 time, which has given rise (from the rhythm of the words which can be fitted to it) to an anapæstic measure known as the ' rhythm of the Galician bagpipes ' (*ritmo de gaita gallega*). Various sword-dances are known ; there is one to be seen on the day of Corpus Christi at Redondela, a town famous in folk-song for the beauty of its women and the fatness of its priests. The dialect of this region, and the language of its folk-songs, has more affinity with Portuguese than with Castilian Spanish.[1]

(2) CATALONIA (including Valencia and the Balearic Isles). On the E. coast of Spain it is still possible to hear music actually performed in a traditional manner, which dates at latest from the 14th cent. This is the *Song of the Sibyl*, heard every year at Christmas in the cathedral at Palma de Mallorca (also reported from Manacor and Marratxi, Mallorca, and from the Catalan-speaking district of Alghero, in Sardinia), and the *Virgin's Plaint* sung in the MYSTERY OF ELCHE (*q.v.*).

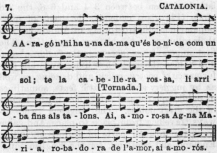

The 14th cent. MS. known as the ' Llibre Vermell ' (Montserrat) contains a number of songs (sometimes in 2 or 3 parts) sung by pilgrims to the shrine. One of these, *Polorum*

[1] *Music and Letters* (1924), v. i, 15 ff.

Regina, is a fine 6–4 tune which was heard and recorded 200 years later in the neighbourhood of Salamanca by SALINAS (*q.v.*).

In Catalonia, Valencia and the Balearic Isles the language is not Castilian Spanish, but *Catalan* (related to Provençal), and the songs have often a French rather than a Spanish character. The subjects, too, are sometimes identical, as for instance ' La bona viuda ' and the French ' Jean Renaud,' though the tunes vary.[2]

Many Catalan songs possess a *tornada* or refrain (equivalent to the *vuelta* or *estribillo* of a *villancico*), which may occur at the beginning, middle, or end of the song. It may be heard in ' La Dama d'Aragó,' one of the best and most popular songs in Catalonia.

Numbers of old ballads exist (*e.g.* the legend of Count Arnold, ' El Comte Arnau ') together with epic, lyric and dance songs ; while the religious or legendary songs are especially numerous, and the melodies often beautiful. Both melodies and words seem to have reached

[2] The many varying versions of this famous song, known in Italy as ' Comte Angiolino ' and in Brittany and Scandinavia as ' Sire nan,' and ' Sire Olaf,' are familiar to all students of folk-lore. A Branchet and Gaston Paris have published articles on this song in the *Revue critique d'histoire et de littérature*. It is remarkable how many Catalan songs have their counterparts among Scandinavian songs, especially as regards the words. A. H. W.

their present forms at the end of the 17th cent. or the beginning of the 18th.

The national dance of Catalonia is the *Sardana*, which has seen a great revival in recent years. It is danced in a large ring to the accompaniment of the *fluviol* (or *flaviol*) a small flute played with one hand, while the other beats a drum.

(3) CASTILLE. The songs of central Spain, including Old and New Castille, Estremadura (S.W.), León (N.W.), the Asturias and the Montaña of Santander (N.) have often been dismissed as less interesting than those of other regions, just as English folk-songs were neglected in favour of those from the Celtic parts of the British Isles. Recent research, however, tends to show that Castilian songs have great variety and individuality, though they have not that curious property of Andalucian song, of forcing its way into other provinces and contaminating the melodies found there with ' Andalucisms.'

Castilian folk-songs were first noted by Francisco SALINAS (*q.v.*), professor of music at Salamanca at the end of the 16th century, though the melodies he printed in his ' De musica libri septem ' (1577) were used to illustrate a discussion of rhythm and prosody. They did not escape the notice of Dr. Burney,[1] who quoted several of them in his ' General History of Music.' Subsequent authors have sometimes been less accurate in their transcriptions, making arbitrary alterations in the rhythm as well as the words.[2] Considered merely as tunes, the *villancicos* of this period are generally more interesting than the ballads (*romances*); but the latter, besides their literary and historical interest, are of great importance in the history of Spanish music. They are remarkable for their rhythms, *e.g.* the constant and characteristic hesitation between 3–4 and 6–8, the 3rd mode (Phrygian) cadence, the basis of most popular music heard to-day in Andalucía, and their influence on the history of variation. The first singers of *romances* were the *juglares*,[3] men and women who made their living by public performance of poetry, music and dancing, as well as by jugglery and acrobatic feats, sometimes in public squares and sometimes in the houses of the great nobles. The ' jugglers ' were always travelling from place to place, and came to Spain from all parts of Europe including England and Scotland, for the English ' jugglers ' of the 14th cent. were famous for their playing on the harp. While the Galicians were singing parallelistic love-songs like those of Martin Codax (see above), and the Catalans and Provençaux were displaying their carefully turned rhymes, the Castilians preferred the recital of heroic deeds and fragments of epic

chansons de gestes (see French section above), which were eagerly listened to by the official chroniclers and afterwards included in their histories as a true account of what had taken place. These wandering musicians were the inventors of Castilian poetry. They were the first singers of the old ballads, which are now known to be the remains of long *chansons de gestes*, detached episodes which struck the imagination of audiences and were more easily remembered than entire epics. They were sung to tunes resembling a litany or psalmody, simple melodic or rhythmic formulæ which would be repeated again and again. The type of *tonada* to which ballads were originally sung is illustrated by the tune of ' Conde Claros ' which, from its popularity or simplicity, or the fact that so many ballads could be sung to it, became a favourite subject for variation with the Spanish *vihuelistas* (lutenists) in the 16th century ; indeed, variation - form arose, in Spain, through the necessity for relieving the monotony of the lute accompaniment during the recitation of a long *romance*. The *vihuelista* ENRIQUEZ (*q.v.*) wrote no less than 120 variations on this tune. An example of those by MUDARRA (*q.v.*) is the following :

The *romances*, however, were by no means always sung to the same tune, as Salinas shows. The most curious fragment of early Castilian folk-song preserved by Salinas is a dance-tune which, besides Spanish words, has words which are recognisably Arabic, and was still sung to them when Salinas wrote in 1577.

It was evidently a well-known tune, for there are references to it in Spanish and Portuguese literature from the 14th century to the 17th.

[1] *Hist.* iii. 306 ff.
[2] See, however, *The Music of Spanish History*, Oxford, 1926, Examples 34-42 ; and *Z.M.W.*, 1921, iv. ii, 65 ff.
[3] R. Menéndez Pidal, *Poesia juglaresca y juglares* Madrid, 1924 ; H. Anglès, *Report Mus. Hist. Congress*, Basel, 1924, 55-66.

The 'Cancionero Musical' (MS., Royal Palace, Madrid) and the 16th-century Spanish lute-books have preserved many other tunes of old ballads and *villancicos*. Descendants of ballads belonging to the Carolingian and Arthurian cycles (with their tunes), have been collected in modern times in Castille and Asturias.

10.   LEDESMA. (1907.)

A ca - za va el ca - za - dor, etc.

a ca - za co - mo so - lí - a .

A 16th-century folk-song was used as a canto fermo by MORALES, for one of his masses,

11.   MORALES. (c. 1540)

Tris - te - zas me ma - tan, tris - te de mi;

Hol - gan - do y ri - en - do tris - te de mi.

La que yo mas quie - ro,
con o - tro la ve - o.

while another Spanish tune, 'Nunca fué pena mayor' was employed in the same way by Pierre de la Rue. A song made on the occasion of the expulsion of the Jews (1492) was used as a canto fermo by ANCHIETA (*q.v.*); but the mass based on it has not been preserved. The tune is printed by Burney.

The different types of Castilian folk-songs which have been collected in modern times will be found in the works of Calleja, Ledesma, Olmeda and Torner, mentioned at the end of this article. The melodies in 5–8 time from the neighbourhood of Burgos are especially noteworthy, as it is in Castille (and probably not, as is usually stated, in the Basque provinces) that a genuine 5-beat melody has been developed.

Aragon and Navarre are memorable for the characteristic JOTA (*q.v.*). A good account of the music of this region (which has little connexion with Castille) is given by Laparra, 'La Musique et les danses populaires en Espagne,' *Encl. de la musique*, 1920.

(4) ANDALUCIA.—Folk-songs from Andalucía were used in madrigalesque compositions by Juan VASQUEZ (*q.v.*), of Seville, who published two sets of partbooks, in 1551 and 1560. The folk-song is treated on the same principle as the ' first singing part ' in the ' Psalms, Sonnets and Songs ' of Byrd (1588).

These melodies, however, have nothing specifically Andaluz about them, and it was not until the end of the 18th century that *Polos* and other characteristic forms began to be

written down, and sung in the TONADILLAS, performed at Madrid. There is a *polo* in the comic opera ' El Criado fingido ' (1804) of

12.   VASQUEZ. (1560.)

1. De los á - la - mos ven - go,
2. De los á - la - mos de Se -

ma - - - dre,   de ver
- vi - - - lla,   de ver

co - mo los me - ne - a el ai - - - re.
a mi lin - da a - mi - - ga.

Manuel GARCIA (*q.v.*); and the famous song of the same composer, ' El Contrabandista ' is also a *polo*. Mitjana[1] points out that though the *polo* from ' El Criado fingido ' is not really popular in the sense of being traditional, yet it was treated as a folk-song by Bizet, and used in the prelude to the fourth act of ' Carmen.' The same authority points out undoubted Spanish popular effects in Rossini's 'Barbiere.' Since the end of the 18th century Andaluz types of melody and rhythm have made their way into all the Spanish provinces, mainly through the *zarzuelas* (comic operas) into which they were introduced. So much has this been the case that the only type of music which people of other nations can immediately recognise as ' Spanish ' is the type which belongs to Andalucía.

Much has been written on the Moorish origin of this kind of music (*v.* CANTE HONDO). It is probable, however, that the Moorish influence is to be found in the manner of performance, rather than in the music itself ; it is a primitive way of singing (permitting ' hockets ' and other mediæval devices) which has been exaggerated by gipsy singers. A performance of Andaluz song begins with a long prelude on the guitar. This is an improvisation, but follows certain rules which are well-defined although unwritten, while the rhythmic figure varies according to the nature of the song to follow. A good player on the guitar will give his prelude a sense of form recalling that of Domenico Scarlatti ; and it is interesting, in this connexion, to find (from numerous instances in Scarlatti's sonatas) how often he had in mind turns of rhythm and phrase and effects of harmony which could only have been suggested by hearing a good guitar-player from Andalucía.

The different forms of Andaluz song can hardly be defined, though they can be recognised by one who is accustomed to them, partly from the guitar prelude, partly from the melody itself and partly from the form of verse. Thus the *Soleá* (plur. *Soleares*) has a verse of three 8-syllable lines, the *Seguidilla*, seven lines, the

[1] *Encl. de la musique* : ' Espagne.' Paris : Delagrave, p. 2256.

Siguiriya gitana (Gipsy Seguidilla) also known as the *Playera*, three 6-syllable lines and one of eleven syllables, with a break (and a characteristic musical effect) in the middle of the long line. Most forms, however, have four lines of eight syllables; and these include forms such as *Granadinas, Rondeñas, Malagueñas, Murcianas*, descended directly or indirectly from the FANDANGO (*q.v.*). The *Fandanguillo* seems (to a foreigner) like a mixture of Andaluz and northern tunes. *Saetas* and *Carceleras* are sung unaccompanied, the former during the halt of a procession; the latter (derived from the Saeta) is literally the song of a prisoner in gaol. Other forms such as *Peteneras* and the 18th-century *Tiranas*, take their names from celebrated singers The most ancient form still existing is (according to Falla) the *Siguiriya gitana*, mentioned above; and it is the gipsy singers, and singers influenced by gipsy ways of singing (*v.* CANTE HONDO) who have given Andaluz song its most characteristic qualities. Others also may be mentioned : the long wail (*Ay !* or *Leli, leli !*) with which the voice-part sometimes begins, the cross-rhythms of guitar, castanets and hand-clapping ; and the interjections of the audience, *Olé, Olé !* (said, on somewhat doubtful authority, to be derived from an invocation to Allah). These three qualities are found also in music heard in Morocco and other Muslim countries. The actual modes of Muslim music, however, are of rarer occurrence in Spanish music than is usually believed. The characteristic cadence of Southern Spanish song is the Phrygian (third mode) cadence A-G♮-F♮-E ; while among Muslim peoples this mode (though sometimes used) is generally replaced by another, with the cadence A-G♯-F♮-E, which gives it an entirely different effect. This cadence, however, is not unknown in Spanish folk-song (see above, Ex. 10). The effects of the *Flamenco* style on Southern Spanish song, and the intensification of its 'oriental' qualities have been defined under CANTE HONDO (*q.v.*). What is sometimes called the 'Spanish idiom' in music depends on the use of certain effects borrowed from the folk-music of Andalucía. It is noteworthy that this is folk-music still in process of formation. While the words are anonymous or unacknowledged (Spanish poets holding it an honour that their lines should be sung as if they were traditional), the melodies were and are the composition of the singers themselves, or at any rate the modification of something they have heard yesterday or may hear to-morrow.

(5) THE 'LEVANTE.'—The S.E. coastal districts of Spain, including a great part of the old province of Valencia, have forms of popular music which are little known outside the Peninsula. The scale systems they exhibit have been used as a basis for cultivated symphonic music by Oscar ESPLÁ (*q.v.*). Examples of folk-songs from this district are given by Pedrell (see below).

(6) THE BASQUE PROVINCES.—Doubts have recently been cast on the originality of many Basque melodies ; and the exclusiveness with which the Basques have kept themselves a distinct and separate race has made it difficult to trace their music to a primeval source. It has a curious suggestion of 19th-century music, which may be due to the constant use of the leading note and the rapid changes of key. Basque melodies are not founded on any particular scale. The rhythm is irregular and a dance exists in 5–8 time, the *Zortziko*, e.g.

18.

O id o gui-puz-coa nos   en-sen ei-lla-can-cion . . . .
                                                              etc.

It has been conjectured, however, that such tunes now in 5–8 were originally in 6–8, the change having taken place during the 19th century.[1] In any case, the sense of rhythm is not very strongly developed in Basque singers. The placidity of the Basque temperament is reflected in folk-song ; almost all are andante, while those which move a little faster are usually of instrumental origin. However, many fine tunes exist in the Basque provinces. The modes chiefly used are Dorian and Mixolydian, though the modern major and minor are most usual. The melodies are diatonic, and they are syllabic ; there is nothing like the endlessly decorated ploughing songs (*Aradas*) of Castille or the S.E. The words have no refrain, like the *villancicos* of Castille ; indeed, the use of a refrain is said to be unknown in Basque popular literature. There is also an absence of epic and legendary words. Gasqué concluded that the majority of Basque melodies were imported by sailors from Brittany, Wales, or the Isle of Man, but not from the neighbouring parts of Spain. One tune bears a striking resemblance to 'There was a Jolly Miller,' which is said to have been introduced by Wellington's troops, since it appeared in San Sebastian not long after. On the whole the Basque songs are much closer to the types found normally in Europe, in France, England, or Germany, than they are to those of Castille or Andalucía.

The Basques have a fine communal dance, the *Aurresku*, usually in four figures, of which the third is a *Zortziko* in 5–8.[2] The Basque *Fandango* has no relation to that of Andalucía, and is more related to the JOTA. The melody, however, is that of the fandango in Gluck's ballet 'Don Juan,' which was afterwards used by Mozart in 'Figaro.'

[1] See the review *Euskalerrian Alde*, San Sebastian, 1915–16, where the theory is upheld by Gasqué and disputed by other writers.
[2] See Gasqué, F., *L'Aurresku, danse basque*, Paris, *S.I.M.*, Sept.-Oct. 1912, with photographs and musical illustrations.

COLLECTIONS

(Those marked * contain introduction and notes.)

GENERAL

FALLA, M. DE. '7 canciones populares españoles.' Paris, Eschig,
    1920.
*INZENGA, J. 'Cantos y bailes populares de España.' Madrid,
    Romero, 1888.
*LAPARRA, R. 'La Musique et la danse populaires en Espagne.'
    Paris, Delagrave (*Encl. de la musique* : Espagne), 1920.
*MÖLLER, H. 'Spanische katalanische, portugiesische u. baskische
    Volkslieder.' Schott, 1924.
NIN, J. ' 20 Chants populaires espagnols.' Paris, Eschig, 1924.
*OCÓN, E. 'Cantos Españoles con notas esplicativas y biográficas.'
    (Span. and Ger. text.) Málaga, 1874, 1906.
*PEDRELL, F. 'Cancionero musical popular español.' Valls, E.
    Castells, 1918–19.
SCHINDLER, K. 'Spanish Sacred and Secular Songs.' Boston,
    Oliver Ditson Co., 1918, etc.
TORNER, E. M. ' 40 Canciones españolas' (for male vv.). Madrid,
    Residencia de Estudiantes, 1924.

1. GALICIA

ADALID, M. DE C. 'Cantares viejos y nuevos de Galicia.' La
    Coruña, Canuto Berea. (See also Inzenga, Laparra and
    Pedrell.)

2. CATALONIA AND THE BALEARIC ISLES

ALIÓ, F. 'Cançons populars catalanes.' Barcelona, Union Mus.
    Española, 1917.
ARS CHORUM. ' 1a Serie : Cançons populars catalanes (male and
    mixed vv.). Barcelona, Iberia Musical.
BELTRAN Y BROS, P. 'Cançons i follies populars.' Barcelona, 1885.
*CAPMAÑY, A. 'Cançoner popular' 3 Series. Barcelona.
CARRERA, A. 'Cançons populars catalanes.' 4 Series. Barcelona,
    Bibl. populaires de 'L'Avenç,' 1910–16.
*MILLET, LL. 'De la cançó popular catalana.' Barcelona, Bloud &
    Gay, 1917.
  * ' El cant popular religiós.' Barcelona, 1912.
MORERA, E. 'Cançons catalanes' (mixed and male vv.). Barcelona,
    Union Mus. Española.
*NOGUERA, A. 'Memoria sobre los cantos, bailes y tocatas populares
    de la Isla de Majorca.' Palma, 1893.
*PELAY BRIZ. 'Cançons de la terra.' Barcelona, 1866–74.
POL, A. 'Colección de canciones populares mallorquinas.' Barce-
    lona, Iberia, Musical, 1925.
SERRA Y VILARÓ, J. 'El cançoner de Calic.' Barcelona, 1913.

3. CASTILLE, LEÓN, ASTURIAS, ETC.

*CALLEJA, R. 'Colección de canciones populares de la Provincia de
    Santander.' Madrid, R. Rodriguez, 1901.
FERNÁNDEZ NUÑEZ, 'Canciones leonesas.' Madrid, Fernando Fé,
    1909.
LAVANDERA, F. R. 'Alma asturiana : Selección de cantos.' Gijon,
    Casa David.
*LEDESMA, D. 'Cancionero salmantino.' Madrid, Imprenta
    Alemana, 1907.
*OLMEDA, F. 'Cancionero popular de Burgos.' Seville, 1903.
*OTAÑO, N. 'El canto popular montañés.' Santander, 1915.
  'Canciones montañesas.' Valencia, M. Villar, 1918.
*TORNER, E. M. 'Cancionero musical de la lirica popular asturiana.'
    Madrid, Nieto y Cia, 1920.

4. BASQUE PROVINCES

*ANTONIO DE DONOSTIA, J. 'La Música popular vasca.' Bilbao,
    Union Musical Española, 1918.
  'Euskel Eres-Sorta (Cancionero vasco).' Bilbao, Union Musical
    Española, 1922.
AZKUE, R. M. DE. 'Cancionero popular vasco.' Bilbao, 1922– .
BORDES, C. 'Cent Chansons populaires basques.' Paris, 1894.
  '12 Noëls basques anciens.' Paris, 1897.
  '12 Chansons amoureuses du pays basque français.' Paris,
    Rouart Lerole, 1910.
*GASCUE, F. 'Origen de la música popular vascongada.' Bilbao,
    Rev. internat. de Estud. vascos, 1913.
  'L'Aurresku, danse basque.' Paris, *S.I.M.*, Sept.-Oct. 1912.
GURIDI, J. 'Cantos populares vascos harmonizados' (male and
    mixed vv.). Bilbao, Mar y Compa, 1913.
*SALABERRY, J. D. J. 'Chants populaires du pays basques.'
    Bayonne, 1870.
SANTESTEBAN, J. A. 'Colección de aires vascongadas.' San
    Sebastian, 1860.
  'Chansons basques.' Bayonne, 1870.

ANDALUCÍA

(See under 'General,' and especially in the collectons of Falla,
Ocón and Pedrell.)
                                        J. B. T.

PORTUGAL

The folk-music of Portugal bears a certain
affinity to that of Spain, especially in dance-
songs. But there are certain clearly-marked
differences. The Portuguese is more pensive
and tranquil than the quicker, dramatic
Spaniard ; and as all national music is more
or less a reflection of racial characteristics,
there is a repose and subdued melancholy, and
an absence of exaggeration in Portuguese music,
qualities seldom found in the more vivacious
and stirring music of Spain. From the same
cause, and perhaps because the Moorish ascendancy was of briefer duration in Portugal than in
Spain, there is less ornament in what music
remains to us of an undoubtedly oriental character. The poetry of the two countries has also
much in common. Many of the Portuguese
ballads are of Spanish origin, and even at the
present day the Spanish and Portuguese ballad
forms are almost identical.

In the lyrics of both races the rhyme
follows the assonance principle, and is a more
important element than the metre. Moreover, Gil Vicente and other poets of Portugal
used the Castilian language as much as their
own, especially for poetry intended to be
sung.

Portugal shares with her neighbour in collections of early music, for the songs of Martin
Codax and Alfonso X. (in Galician-Portuguese
dialect) belong as much to Portugal as to
SPAIN (*q.v.*). Unfortunately a mass of valuable manuscript and printed music which
existed in the splendid library founded by
King D. João IV. (1604–56), perished in the
Lisbon earthquake in 1755. Much was also
destroyed during the demolition of the monasteries and convents which followed the revolution of 1834.

The earliest and most important musical
records preserved in Portugal belong to the
Troubadour period. D. Diniz, sixth King of
Portugal (1261–1325), who founded a university with a chair for music at Coimbra, was a
grandson of Alfonso X., and well versed in the
art of the Troubadours.[1] The *Jogral* (*jongleur*)
also played an important part in Troubadour
life in Portugal ; and the last was Gil Vicente
(*c.* 1465–1536 ?), at once poet, actor, musician
and composer. His works, which give interesting information about the various customs and
forms of song of his time,[2] are written partly
in Portuguese and partly in Castilian. Interspersed in his pieces are *vilhancetes, cançonetas,
cantigas, romances, canções pastoris, cantigas de
berço, cantigas maritimas,* etc. ; and in his
enselladas songs with Latin and French words
also occur, such as the *chanson,* ' Ay de la nobl*
ville de Paris.*'

The *vilhancetes* or *vilhancicos, autos* and *loas*
were similar to the Spanish in character ; semi-
sacred, popular, and yet a form which learned
musicians adopted and elaborated, such as Fr.
Francisco de Santiago, Gabriel Diaz, and many
contrapuntists from Duarte Lobo's celebrated
school, as, for instance, Felipe de Magalhães.

---

[1] For the various *Cancioneiros* (song-books) of his time, and that
of his bastard son, D. Pedro, Count of Barcellos, see A. F. G. Bell,
Portuguese Literature, Oxford, 1922.
[2] It is said that Erasmus learnt Portuguese simply to be able to
read Gil Vicente's works. See A. F. G. Bell, *Lyrics of Gil Vicente*
(with translations), Oxford, Blackwell 1921 ; and the *Oxford Book*
of Portuguese Verse, 1925.

The earliest *vilhancicos* we hear of were those by Juan del ENZINA (*q.v.*) and Gil Vicente[1] in the late 15th century, and the last by the Abbot Luiz Calisto da Costa e Feria in 1723.[2]

The old Pagan festivals and the mediæval Christian festivals blended in Portugal as elsewhere, and heritages from those times are the *Maias* and *Janeiras* songs. These festival songs are still sung on certain days of the year; the principal ones are ' O São João,' sung on St. John the Baptist's Day (Midsummer) ; ' As Janeiras,' sung at the New Year; and ' Os Reis,' sung at the Epiphany.[3]

Various forms of songs are given in the works of the poets of the Renaissance, Ribeiro, Gil Vicente, Sà de Miranda and Camoëns, and these were clearly intended to be sung, as the accompanying instruments and the manner of singing them are frequently recorded.[4] Many are identical with the Troubadour forms, for example the *serranilha* and *solão*, which answer to the *pastoralla* and *soula*. We read also of the *endeixas* or funeral songs; the *celeumas* sung in chorus by sailors or workmen[5]; the *descantes* which are always 8-syllabled and have *estribilhos* (refrains) and the *sonetos*. And among the dance-songs the *xacara* (a gipsy song) and the *chula* which is similar to it, the *captiva* or *mourisca* and the *judenga*. The two latter naturally disappeared with the expulsion of the Moors and Jews.[6]

It is difficult to trace the music of the above-mentioned songs. Still no one can deny the antiquity of many of the *cantigas* and *canções* still sung among the peasants in the country districts of Portugal ; and here, unlike Spain, the dance-songs are not more prevalent than other kinds. In some the oriental element is still evident; there is a careless ease, tinged with melancholy, about them, which is the secret of their charm. They are generally sung by one voice without any accompaniment; and to the ears of foreigners have the sound of recitatives, as the rhythm is often wholly obscured by the singer.[7] The following

little song, which the women sing whilst reaping, always inventing new verses, is a fair example :

Foi me acci-fa ao Por-to San-to As ce-a-ras ama-re-las.

And on the plains the shepherds and labourers may be heard any evening chanting in a minor key, with a pointless, halting measure and vague rhythm *cantigas* which are purely Moorish in character.[8] In the province of Minho it is quite common to hear one peasant in his harsh, guttural Eastern voice challenge another to sing one or more verses against him. The curious custom for the men and women to sing in fourths and fifths still exists in the southern province of Alemtejo. This example, wholly Moorish in character, was heard on a popular feast-day in the little town of S. Thiago do Cacem in 1897[9] :

2.   *Ribandeira.*

Although the words *cantiga* and *cançao* are used indiscriminately for all kinds of songs, the so-called *Cantiges das ruas* are a special form, and chiefly sung in the towns by blind beggars. Many of the tunes are very old, but the words are constantly changed.[10] The *fado* is the most purely national type of dance-song which exists in Portugal, and it has always maintained its integrity.[11] It is seldom heard outside towns, and properly belongs to the lowest classes of the population, though during the last century it acquired popularity among the higher classes.[12] The guitar (which is much less used than in Spain) is always employed for the *fados*, and has a strongly rhythmical and uniform accompaniment :

[1] Gil Vicente was among the first to write *autos*, ' religious pieces resembling in their nature the miracle-plays common all over Europe at the time. . . . Most of these are Christmas pieces, and the dramatists often took advantage of the story of the shepherds to introduce the elements of what may be called pastoral comedy.' *History of Portugal*, by Morse Stephens.

[2] Vasconcellos, ii. 191.

[3] 'As Janeiras ' and ' Os Reis ' are especially sung on the respective eves of the New Year and of the Epiphany. The minstrels go from door to door in the evening, singing the praises of the inmates of the house, and accompanying their songs with metal triangles, bells, etc. They are generally rewarded by the master of the house with money, sausages or dried figs. But if they get nothing they sing :

  ' Esta casa cheira a bren
  Aqui mora algum Juden.'
(This house smells of tar ; some Jew lives here) ; or else:
  ' Esta casa cheira a unto
  Aqui mora algum defunto.'
(This house smells of ointment ; there is a dead body in it.)

[4] Gil Vicente speaks of ' the pleasing way the *sonetos* were sung with guitar accompaniment.' See Th. Braga's *Historia da litteratura portugueza*, vol. viii. p. 228.

[5] See Camoëns, *Lusiads*, ii. 15.

[6] See *Portugiesische Musik*, Mendel's *Mus. Con. Lex.* p. 499 *et seq.* (Platon von Waxel).

[7] Nos. 3, 7 and 11 of J. A. Ribas's collection give some idea of this kind of song, but they are spoilt by their accompaniment.

[8] It is curious that in the mountainous parts of Portugal no Arab music is heard. The voices also are sweeter.

[9] Sent by D. Augustò Machado (Director of the Lisbon Conservatoire) to A. Hammerich. *Studien übe.· isländische Musik, Sammelbände*, I.M.G. 1899, p. 341.

[10] Numerous examples are given in Das Neves' and other collections.

[11] Platon von Waxel derives this dance-form from the *xacara* of the Portuguese gipsies, and the word from *fatiste* or verse-maker. See also M. Roeder's Essay *Dal Taccuino*, p. 145.

[12] A celebrated modern singer of *fados* was José Dias (1824–69), who improvised with wonderful skill. He was a great favourite at the Court, and in the salons at home and abroad. Pinto de Carvalho and Alberto Pimentel have written on the Fados.

There are many varieties of *fados* and *fadinhos* in the different towns, but they are all binary in form and have the same rhythm

Except during the period when the Netherlanders exercised their influence upon the ecclesiastical music of Portugal (that is, during the 16th and 17th centuries) this country can claim no great composers nor school of its own. For when not avowedly borrowing various forms from other countries, Portugal fell unconsciously under their influence. The *trovas* (Troubadour songs) were merely adopted Provençal forms, the *vilhancicos, autos* and *loas* were borrowed from Spain and France; the polyphonic 17th century *tonos* were in reality Italian madrigals written to Spanish words, with *estribilhos* added to them. And late in the 18th century all attempts to form a national opera failed, owing to the invasion of the Italian opera, which has exercised complete hold over Portuguese music for the last two centuries.

It is only in two small and unimportant forms of vocal music, the *fado* and the *modinha*, that Portugal can claim to have created and established a distinct genre of her own. Of the *fados* we have already spoken. The *modinha*, which is the only kind of art-song that Portugal has as yet produced, is, moreover, the direct offspring of the Italian opera. Though written by trained musicians and sung by educated people, neither as regards form nor character can the *modinhas* be assigned high rank as artistic music. Still they have retained their popularity from early in the 18th century down to the present day, and are written as a matter of course by every Portuguese composer.

These *modinhas*, or Portuguese romances, are of a literary as well as a musical form.[1] The first mention of them occurred in the so-called 'Jewish operas,'[2] which rapidly became popular. In the burgher classes *modinhas* remained simple sentimental melodies; but at the court and among the more educated classes they developed into highly elaborate brilliant arias, and celebrated composers and poets did not disdain to use this form. In Das Neves' *Cancioneiro de musicas populares* there are twelve songs (*modinhas*) from Gonzaga's *Marilia de Dirceu*, which, according to good evidence,[3] were set to music by Marcos Antonio, better known as Portogallo. In 1793 F. D. Milcent published a monthly *Jornal de modinhas* at

Lisbon, from which the following example is taken, to show the brilliant type of *modinha*:

Moda a Solo del S. Ant. da S. Leite M. de Capela no Porte.

Since the 16th century, when Portugal colonised Brazil, there has been continual intercourse between these countries; and during the first quarter of the 19th century, whilst the Portuguese court was domiciled in Brazil, the *modinhas* were as fashionable there as in Portugal. But they differed in character; the *modinhas brazileiras* were always very primitive in form, devoid of workmanship, somewhat vulgar, but expressive and gay. In short, a mixture between the French *romance* of the 18th century and *couplets* from the vaudevilles. And this description applies to the type of Portuguese *modinhas* of the present day, which are written for one or two voices, strophic in form, with easy guitar or pianoforte accompaniments.

A complete list of greater and lesser composers who have tried their hand at this form of song is too long to give, but the following are amongst the most celebrated. In the 18th century Portogallo and also Cordeiro da Silva and João de Sousa Carvalho; a little later, Rego, Bomtempo, Soares, Pereira da Costa, Coelho, Cabral, and João de Mesquita. In Coimbra,[4] José Manricio; in Oporto, Silva Leite, Nunes, Pires, João Leal and Edolo[5]; and nearer our own time, Domingos Schiopetta, the two monks J. M. da Silva and José Marquis de Santa Rita, Frondoni (an Italian, long resident in Lisbon), R. Varella and Vasconcellos de Sà. But the most popular *modinhas*, such as 'A Serandinha,' 'O Salvia,' 'As Peneiras,' 'Mariquinhas meu Amor,'[6] and 'Tem minha amada'[7] are anonymous. An exception is Vasconcellos de Sà's canção, 'Margarida vae à fonte,' which is the favourite *modinha* of the moment.[8]

There are many patriotic and political songs in every collection. The pianist Innocencio wrote a whole series; Portogallo's 'Hymno da

---

[1] The derivation of the word is doubtful. Some say it came from *mote* or *moda*, and that it had its origin in Brazil. We certainly read in a folio dated 1729 (*Annals of the Bibl. of Rio de Janeiro*, ii. 129) that on a wedding-feast of the Viceroy ' *um alegre divertimento musico de cantigas e modas da terra, de que ha abundancia n'este paiz.*' Also many travellers of that time describe with admiration the *modinhas brazileiras*. For further information see Th. Braga's *Historia da litteratura portugueza* (*Filinto Elysio e os dissidentes da Arcadia*), vol. xx. p. 603 *et seq.*

[2] Thus named from Antonio José da Silva, born in 1705, a baptized Jew from Brazil, who wrote Portuguese comedies with these interspersed.

[3] Braga, *Historia da litteratura portugueza*, vol. xv. p. 604, note.

[4] The *modinhas* vary somewhat in the different districts.

[5] Between 1820 and 1840 José Edolo, a violinist at the opera, was the favourite contributor to the *Jornal de modinhas*.

[6] These last two are included in Ribas's Collection.

[7] In Berggreen's Collection.

[8] The difference between the *canções* and *modinhas* is slight, and the names are constantly interchanged.

Patria ' was the customary national anthem until King Pedro IV.[1] composed his ' Hymno da Carta ' in 1826 ; and Frondoni was the author of the popular hymn of the revolution of Maria da Fonte in 1848.

Of late, serious attention has been directed to the national poetry and music of Portugal. One of the first to do so was the poet Almeido Garrett in his *Romanceiro*. He was followed by Vasconcellos and Th. Braga, who in his numerous volumes on the history of Portuguese literature often touches on the musical form.[2] Leading musicians, such as B. Moreira de Sà, A. Machado (Director of the Conservatoire), and J. Vianna da Motta and others have shown their practical interest in the subject.

BIBLIOGRAPHY

MACHADO, D. B. *Bibliotheca lusitana.* Lisbon, 1741–59.
WOLF, F. *Proben portugiesischer und catalanischer Volkslieder und Romanzen.* Vienna, 1856.
BELLERMANN, C. F. *Portugiesische Volkslieder und Romanzen.* Leipzig, 1864.
MENDEL'S *Mus. Cons. Lex.* ; *Portugiesische Musik* (PLATON VON WAXEL).
Gazeta da Madeira, 1866–69. *A Musica em Portugal* (PLATON VON WAXEL).
MARQUES, JOAQUIM J. *Estudios sobre a historia da musica em Portugal.*
BRAGA, TH. *Historia da litteratura portugueza. Hist. da poesia pop. portugueza.* Oporto, 1867.
VASCONCELLOS, JOAQUIM DE. *Os musicos portuguezes.* Oporto, 1870.
ROEDER, MARTIN. *La musica en Portogallo ; Dal Taccuino,* etc. Milan, 1877.
LEITE DE VASCONCELLOS, J. *Romances populares portuguezas.* 1880 ; *Tradigoes populares.* Oporto, 1882 ; *As Mais* (May day songs).
COMTE DE PUYMAIGRE. *Romanceiro ; Choix de vieux chants portugais, traduits et annotés.* Paris, 1881.
SOUBIES, A. *Histoire de la musique en Portugal* 1898.
LAMBERTINI, M. A. *Encl. de la musique : Portugal.* Paris, 1920.
(The writer is also indebted to Senhor Bernardo Moreira de Sà for much information kindly supplied to her by letter.)

COLLECTIONS

MILCENT, F. D. ' Jornal de modinhas, com acompanhamento de Cravo, pelos milhores autores.' Lisbon, 1793.
JOSÉ DO REGO, A. ' Jornal de modinhas.' 1812.
EDOLO, JOSÉ. ' Jornal de modinhas.' 1823.
FERREIRA, ANTONIO J. ' Collecçao de modinhas portuguezas e brazilleras.' 1826.
KESTNER, H. ' Auswahl spanischer und portugiesischer Lieder.' Hanover, 1859.
GARCIA, JOSÉ M., and MACHADO, R. COELHO. Two large collections of Brazilian Modinhas. 1851.
BERGGREEN, A. P. ' Portugisiske Folke-sange og Melodier.' 1866.
RIBAS, J. A. ' Album de musicas nacionaes portuguezas.'
NEVES, A. DAS E MELLO-FILHO. ' Musicas e canções populares.'
PIRES. ' Canções populares do Alemtejo.'
COLAÇO, A. R. ' Collecção de fados.'
THOMAZ, F. PEDRO. ' Canções populares da Beira ' (with introduction by Leite de Vasconcellos).
SALVINI, G. R. ' Cancioneiro mus. portuguez.' Lisbon, 1884.
CLASING, J. H. ' Zwölf brasilianische Volkslieder.' Hamburg.
NEVES, CÉSAR DAS, and CAMPOS, GUALDINO DE. ' Cancionero de musicas populares.' 3 vols. Porto, 1893–98. (These volumes contain valuable prefaces by Th. Braga, Viterbo and Ramas, and consist of : *canções, serenatas, chulas, danças, descantes, cantigas dos campos e das ruas, fados, romances, hymnos nacionaes, cantos patrioticos, cantigas religiosas de origem popular, canticos liturgicos popularisados, cantilenas, canções do berço,* etc.)

A. H. W. ; rev. J. B. T.

ITALY

Italy was more slowly caught by the poetic flame which the Provençal troubadours had kindled, than other southern countries. For not until the middle of the 13th century, when Raymond Berenger, Count of Provence, visited the Emperor Frederick II. at Milan, bringing Troubadours and Jongleurs in his train, do we hear of them in this country. A similar patronage was extended to them by Raymond's son-in-law, Charles of Anjou, king of Naples and

Sicily. Through which of these two gates the Provençal language entered Italy has ever been a disputed point. But taught by these singers, whom the common people called *uomini di corti*,[3] Italy soon produced her own *trovatori* and *giocolini*. At first they deemed their native dialect unsuitable to poetry, and used the Provençal language. But it is certain that already, by the time of Dante, the *volgar poesia*, which sprang from it, had reached a stage when it was capable of receiving rules and of being taught in the schools founded for the purpose. After Dante, no Italian could longer doubt the capacities of his own tongue for all forms of poetry. It must not be forgotten that the *terza rima,* used by the Provençal troubadours for the *sirvente,* was adopted by Dante for the ' Divina Commedia ' and by Petrarch in his ' Trionfi.' But soon the verse of the troubadours began to pale before the splendours of the great poet ; and towards the middle of the 14th century the *trovatori* declined in numbers and popularity, and after 1450 were heard of no more.[4]

Notwithstanding the subordination of lyric song to other branches of poetry and music in Italy, her long and careful study of *la melica poesia*—poetry wedded to music—has not been surpassed elsewhere. Dante's sonnets and Petrarch's ' Trionfi ' were among the earliest poems set to music. Dante's own contemporary and friend Casella[5] (b. 1300), who set his sonnet ' Amor che nella mente ' to music, is believed to have also composed the music for a *ballata* by Lemmo da Pistoja, still extant in the Vatican.[6] The *ballate* and *intuonate* were perhaps the oldest forms of songs written in the vernacular ; both were love-songs sung to a dance.[7] After them the *maggiolate* or May-day songs had their popularity. These also were love-songs, sung in the spring-time by bands of young men. The hunting-songs or *cacci*[8] equally deserve mention. The most celebrated were written by Soldaniere and Sacchetti, and the words are far better than their music by Nicolaus da Perugia, Laurentius and Ghirardellus. Some are realistic, imitating the sounds of the hunt[9] ; others are canonic in form, and others again interesting from the historic side, as they bring in the street-cries of the time.[10]

---

[1] Dom Pedro IV., the first constitutional king of Portugal, was a pupil of Sigismund Neukomm, and wrote several choral and operatic works.
[2] Braga also collected the folk-songs of the Azores.

[3] So called because these singers appeared as retainers from princely courts. Also *ciarlatani,* because the exploits of Charlemagne were a constant theme of their songs.
[4] For further information about the *Trovatori* see H. von der Hagen's work on the *Minnesinger,* vol. iv.
[5] See the fourth Canto of the *Purgatorio* and the second Canzone in the *Convito,* where Casella's name occurs several times.
[6] Burney tells us that the Vatican MS. No. 3214 is a poem on the margin of which is written : ' Lemmo da Pistoja, e Casella diede il suono.'
[7] Arteaga gives the words of a *ballata* of the 13th century by Frederick II., and of another by Dante. See *Le rivoluzioni del teatro musicale italiano.* i. pp. 187, 190.
[8] They may have been written specially for hunting, but Gaspari, in his history of Italian Literature, proves that any quick movement at that time would be called a *Caccia.*
[9] In this they resemble the FROTTOLE.
[10] They are counterparts of the *Cris de Paris,* which Jannequin brought into his motet ' Voulez'ouyr les cris de Paris,' the ' Cries of London,' and ' Court Cries ' used by Richard Deering. See J. Wolf's article *Florenz in der Musikgeschichte des 14ten Jahrhunderts, Sammelbände.* I.M.G., 1901–02. iii.

When later the *canti carnascialeschi* came into vogue they at first were Carnival songs, but under the skilful hand of Lorenzo di Medici a kind of consecutive drama grew out of them.[1]

During the 14th century there existed a class of dilettante musicians called *cantori a liuto,* whose business it was to set other poets' verses to music and sing them. They differed from the *trovatori,* who were poets, and who sang their own verses to their own music or to that of others, and equally from the *Cantori a libro,* who were the learned professional musicians.[2] Casella (see above) and Minuccio d' Arezzo, mentioned by Boccaccio,[3] would belong to the *cantori a liuto.* It was the habit of these musicians to improvise,[4] for until the 16th century musical notation remained so difficult that only learned musicians were able to avail themselves of it. This is the reason why the melodies of the strophic songs, which contemporary writers[5] show to have been so popular and universal during the 14th and 15th centuries, have not survived.

The compositions of the Netherlands school of music, with their severe contrapuntal style, found their way into Italy in the 15th century, and in time began to exercise a strong influence there. But the prevailing type of Italian secular songs continued to be of a very light order during this and the following century. Petrucci, who issued in 1502 the motets and masses of the Netherland composers, had nothing better to offer of native productions than *frottole* and *villanelle,* tuneful but light partsongs. In form the *villanelle* adhered to the contrapuntal style, though in spirit they were essentially popular. Gradually the term *frottola* disappeared; the more serious *frottole* passed into the madrigal, while the gayer, merrier type was merged in the *villanelle.*[6] But although the *frottole* were despised by contrapuntists they showed a sense of form in repeating the first part again, and attention was paid to the words by having different music for each verse, whereas the *villanelle* were strophical—that is, the same melody was repeated for each stanza.[7] Other songs, light in character, were the rustic songs, *canzone*

villanesche, or *villotte,* which peasants and soldiers used as drinking-songs. More refined and yet more trifling were the *villotte alla Napoletana.*[8] The so-called *fa-la-la* was a composition of a somewhat later date and more merit. Those which Gastoldi wrote (about 1590) were good, and so too his *balletti.* (See MADRIGAL.)

The vocal music to which our attention has been thus far directed, consisted either of songs in parts, or unisonous chorus with little or no accompaniment. Sometimes the principal or upper voice had a sort of *cantilena.* but solo-singing was yet unknown. An early recorded instance of solo singing with independent instrumental accompaniment is the oft-quoted one of Sileno, who in 1539 sang in an Intermezzo[9] the upper part of a madrigal by Corteccia, accompanying himself on the violone, while the lower parts which represented the satyrs were taken by wind instruments. But the piece itself shows it was far from being a song for one voice with accompaniment; the under parts are as much independent voices as the upper one. (See Ex. 1.)

Fragment of a Madrigal. Sonato da Sileno con violone, sonando tutte le parti, e cantando il soprano.

---

[1] Many of these were written by special invitation by Heinrich Isaak (b. 1445). Naumann's *Hist. of Mus.* i. 438.
[2] The important part played in Italian music by such a one as Francesco Landini (1325–90) is well described by Fétis, v. 310 *et seq.*
[3] *Decam.* Giorn. X. No. 7. See Ambros, *Ges. der Mus.* ii. 497.
[4] The *improvisatore* has been for centuries a well-known figure in Italian life.
[5] We read in Sacchetti's novels that Dante's *ballate* were everywhere known and sung, and how Dante overheard a blacksmith singing his song and scolded him for having altered it. And Trucchi quotes, in proof of Dante having made the music for his own poems, an anonymous writer of the 13th century, who says Dante was 'dilettossi nel canto e in ogni suono' (*Poesie italiane inedite,* ii. 140). See also Ambros, *Ges. der Mus.* ii. 489, for further account of the songs in the *Decameron.*
[6] A *frottola,* printed in Junta's Roman collection of 1526, evidently became, ere long, a *villanella,* for it is still sung in Venice with the same words and melody, 'Le son tre fantinelle, tutti tre da maridar.' Originally, however, it was a partsong with the tune in the tenor. Ambros, iii. 495.
[7] See FROTTOLA, also Ambros, iv. 150 *et seq.*; *Florenz in der Musikgeschichte d. 14ten Jahrhunderts,* J. Wolf; *Sammelbände,* I.M.G., 1901–02, iii.; *Die Frottole im 15ten Jahrhunde.* t, R. Schwartz, *Vierteljahrsschrift f. Musikwissenschaft* 1886.
[8] These were gallant addresses from singing-masters to their feminine pupils. They were as popular in northern Italy as in Naples. For examples, see in Kiesewetter's *Schicksale und Beschaffenheit des weltlichen Gesanges,* app. Nos. 12, and 13 by Cambio (1547) and Donati (1555). Several collections of these songs still exist in the various libraries, and a specially important one at Naples.
[9] The Intermezzi were usually madrigals interspersed in the earlier Italian plays.

During the last decades of the 16th century a sweeping change came over music in Italy. The spirit of the Renaissance, which had affected the other arts of poetry, painting and sculpture many years earlier, gradually asserted an influence over music. Each individual now desired to think and speak for himself, and was no longer content to be merged in the mass. Thus ecclesiastical music was gradually driven from the field by secular music, and choral or collective song by pure solo-song, which was the medium best fitted for the expression of the thoughts, emotions and actions of individuals. Poetry, which had hitherto been smothered in the web of contrapuntal music (where many voices were simultaneously singing different words) once again asserted herself, and claimed attention to her meaning and form.[1] Further, the art of singing, which by the close of the 16th century had reached a highly advanced stage [2] demanded the prominence of the solo-singer. In short, a different kind of music was now required, and the monodic style supplied the want. Historians have clearly shown that the latent germs must have been present wherever folk-music existed.[3] The predilection for a marked rhythm, the disuse of the old church scales, the feeling for the dominant, the use of the leading-note [4]—all these elements were instinctively present in folk-music before being formulated and taught in schools.

According to the historian G. B. Doni,[5] V. Galilei was the first composer who wrote actual melodies for one voice.[6] He further tells us that Galilei set to music the passage of the *Inferno* which narrates the tragic fate of Count Ugolino, and that he performed it himself 'very pleasingly,' with viola accompaniment. But be that as it may, an epoch in musical history was undoubtedly marked by Giulio CACCINI (*q.v.*) when he published in 1601, under the title of ' Le nuove musiche,' a collection of *madrigali*, *canzoni* and *arie* for one voice. These compositions have a figured bass, and some are embellished with *fioriture*. In the preface [7] to his collection, Caccini gives minute directions as to the proper mode of singing his pieces, and his airs are well supplied with marks of expression, as the following example will show [8] (see ORNAMENTS, Vocal, and THOROUGH-BASS):

2.
(*Scemar di voce. Esclamazione spiritosa.*)   CACCINI.

Deh! Deh! do-ve son fug-gi-ti, deh! do-ve

(*Escl. più viva.*)   (*Escl.*)

son spa-ri-ti gl'oc-chi de quali er-ra-i Io son

(*Trillo.*) (*Senza misura quasi favellando,*

ce-ne-re o-ma-i Au-re au-re di-vi-ne ch'er-

in armonia con la suddetta sprezzatura.)   (*Trillo.*)

ra-te pe-re-gri-ne in ques-ta par-te e quel-

(*Escl.*)

-la, Deh re-ca-te no-vel-la dell'al-ma lu-ce

(*Escl. con misura più larga.*)

1st.   (*Trillo.*)

lo-ro, au-re ch'io me-ne mo-ro deh re-

2nd.   (*Escl. rinf.*)   (*Trillo una mezza battuta.*)

au-re ch'io me-ne mo-ro.

Jacopo Peri succeeded Caccini with a work entitled ' Le varie musiche del Sig. J. Peri a una, due, tre voci per cantare nel clavicembalo o chitarrone ' (Florence, 1609). They are simpler than those by Caccini, and less declamatory.[9] Caccini had numerous followers in the path he had opened, and thus the ' expressive monodia,' *i.e.* the attempt to render certain thoughts and feelings in music, and to adapt music to the meaning of the words, was virtually established.

---

1 Ambros, iv. 178 *et seq.*

2 This advanced technique in solo singing was the outcome of generations of cultivation in the Church, whose polyphonic music by no means excluded the use of the solo voice. See Henderson, *Early History of Singing*, chap. v. and vi.

3 See Parry's *Art of Music.*

4 Zarlino writes in 1558 that the peasants who sing without any art all proceed by the interval of the semitone in forming their closes.

5 *Op. omn.* Florence, 1763, tom. ii.

6 This statement may be doubted, as we hear of Caccini, Viadana, Peri and Cavalieri all exhibiting the same double talent as Corteccia and Galilei at the same period, *i.e.* in the last decades of the 16th century.

7 Translated into German in Kiesewetter's *Schicksale und Beschaffenheit*, etc.

8 For other examples see the beautiful aria ' Fere selvagge,' reprinted in Gevaert's ' Les Gloires de l'Italie.' and ' Amarilli mia bella ' in Parisotti's ' Arie antiche.'

9 See ' Bellissima Regina ' in Parisotti's ' Piccolo album.'

But these early pioneers of solo-song were amateurs, and it remained for trained musicians to carry on their work systematically. With MONTEVERDI (1562 – 1654) a turning-point in music was reached. To him we owe the development of the recitative which led to the beginning of the OPERA (*q.v.*)—the most important moment in the whole history of music. We also owe to him a debt in the history of song for having established the so-called ternary form which was soon to become stereotyped for the ARIA (*q.v.*) and song. This consisted of an air in three parts ; the last part being a mere repetition of the first, while the middle part contained a passage of contrast. This form was already familiar in the folk-songs of the Middle Ages ; Monteverdi's application of it is well seen in the 'Lamento' from 'Ariadne' (1610).[1] Monteverdi's successors, Cesti and Cavalli, both showed aptitude for pleasant melodious solo-music of this form, although Cavalli sometimes wrote arias with only two contrasting portions.

Other composers of the transition period which witnessed the growth of the opera and cantata were Radesca da Foggia, who published five books of 'Monodie' in 1616 ; A. Brunelli, who published in the same year and in 1618 two books of 'Scherzi, Arie, Canzonette, and Madrigali '[2]; G. F. Capello, whose most remarkable work was a set of 'Madrigali a voce sola ' ; G. Fornacci, celebrated for his 'Amorosi respiri musicali,' which appeared in 1617 ; Sigismondo d' India, Pietro della Valle, Luigi Rossi[3] and finally Salvator Rosa.[4] A great quantity of these vocal compositions are treated in the strophic form, and the words of all are love-poems of a stilted, artificial character.[5]

If Corteccia's madrigal be compared with the following example from Capello, it will be seen how great an advance had been made in solo-singing in less than a century. And a striking resemblance may be observed between Capello and his successor STRADELLA (*q.v.*).

3.

Madrigale a voce sola. G. F. CAPELLO.

During the 17th century the influence of Carissimi was great. He had a strong sense for modern tonality and for secular rhythm, and hence his style grew different from that of the older school. The cantata, which was to become the chief form of chamber-music, reached a high stage of maturity under CARISSIMI, LEGRENZI, CALDARA, STRADELLA and finally A. SCARLATTI. Legrenzi's 'Cantate e canzonette a voce sola ' (published 1676) show his position in the development of the art of his time. (See CANTATA.) With A. Scarlatti's name the *da capo* form of the *aria* is associated, and for the many other debts the classical *aria* owes him, both in the opera and the cantata, see SCARLATTI.

No sooner were the 'expressive monodia' and the recitative started than the opera became firmly established. And in the same way the madrigal and the cantata,[6] which were both important, at least as regards vocal chamber-music during the 16th and 17th centuries, were doomed to insignificance by the use of this great and overshadowing rival. For an account of the origin and marvellous popularity of the OPERA, the reader must turn to that article. It need only be said here that all other kinds of secular vocal music had and still have to yield precedence in Italy to the opera and its off-shoots, the *scena, cavatina* and *aria.*

If we closely examine the vocal works of the great composers of the 17th and 18th centuries, we see how little the *arie, ariette, canzonette,* etc., published separately in collections [7] differ either in form or spirit from the arias extracted from their cantatas and operas. In the latter class some of the most beautiful examples of pure lyrics may be found, like Salvator Rosa's 'Star vicino ' ; Cesti's 'Intorno all' idol mio ' ; Stradella's 'Ragion sempre addita '; Leo's 'Ahi, che le pena mia'; A. Scarlatti's 'Voi fuggiste.'

[1] This was afterwards arranged as a madrigal in five parts. See Parry, *Music of the Seventeenth Century (Oxford History of Music)*, p. 47. Parry further clearly shows how this simple form later dominated one branch of music completely, and indeed 'became the bane of one period of Italian art.'
[2] Brunelli's collection included several pieces by other composers of the Florentine group.
[3] For the numerous existing collections of Rossi's 'Monodie' see ROSSI.
[4] Salvator Rosa certainly was Carissimi's contemporary, but the example Burney gives shows that he wrote much like the aforementioned composers.
[5] Ambros, iv. 330.

[6] Cantatas, which are really vocal sonatas, became by degrees a mixture of the formal aria and recitative. There was practically no difference in structure and style between the arias from these 'slices out of the opera ' and the opera itself. Parry, *Music of the Seventeenth Century (Oxford History of Music).*
[7] See such collections as—' Arie antiche,' 'Piccolo album di musica antica,' Parisotti ; 'Echi d' Italia,' Viardot ; 'Gloires de l'Italie,' Gevaert; 'Tesori antichi,' M. Roeder; 'Gemme d' antichità,' published by Ashdown; 'Alt-italienische Canzonetten und Arien,' Lindner.

'Le violette,' and 'Cara tomba'; and Caldara's 'Come raggio di sol.' Many of the operas and cantatas from which such lovely airs are taken are dead and forgotten, or their names only remain in history as the shells which contained such treasures.

Turning to another branch of the subject, namely the folk-song, it is clear that in Italy it never held the same place as among other nations. That Italian composers ranked the folk-songs of other countries higher is proved by their choosing French or Gallo-Belgian folk-songs for their masses and motets in preference to their own.[1] In Petrucci's 'Canti cento cinquanta,' published in 1503, the best songs belong to France, Germany and the Netherlands; and the partsongs called *Canzoni alla francese* [2] were among the most popular songs in Italy in the early 16th century. Traces no doubt exist of *canti popolari* of the 15th, 16th and 17th centuries, but very few have come down to us in their complete or native form. It was in the gay, busy town of Venice that the folk-song first became recognised and found free development. It was there that Petrucci printed the many *frottole, ballate, barcajuoli*, etc., which contained folk-songs like 'Le son tre fantinelli' (mentioned above), or the popular 'La Bernardina' used by Josquin des Prés, or 'Lirum bilirum' and 'Quando andarete al monte' used respectively by Rossini di Mantua and J. B. Zesso. It was here, too, that G. Scotto printed the Venetian master A. Willaert's collection which has preserved to us the celebrated 'Canzon di Ruzante.' [3] But though many of the songs used for the polyphonic works bear Italian titles, there is nothing to prove their Italian origin. Only in a few instances have the words been preserved in their integrity, and the melodies have no distinguishing characteristics. They are somewhat dull and formless.[4] Much more akin to the typical *canti popolari* in liveliness and simplicity of style were the hymn-tunes, known as 'Laudi spirituali.' These, in the Middle Ages, were introduced in the oratorios in order to popularise such performances; and the connexion between these Laudi with popular dance-songs is obvious. (See LAUDI SPIRITUALI.)

But although we find within recent years that the study of the folk-lore of Italy has received serious attention, materials for a satisfactory treatment of the *canti popolari* are in-complete. Much has been written about the words of traditional songs, and innumerable collections of popular poetry have been published,[5] but no attempt has been made towards a scientific and systematic work on the melodies, tracing their origin and development and various forms. In the many volumes of the *Archivio per lo studio delle tradizioni popolari*, edited by Giuseppe Pitrè and S. Salomone-Marino, and in G. Pitrè's excellent work, *Bibliografia delle tradizioni popolari d' Italia* (Clausen, Turin, 1894), mention is made of the various collections of *canti popolari*; and in the former volumes there are occasional short articles which refer to the tunes, and give a few musical examples. During the latter half of the 19th century Ricordi and other publishers issued large quantities of modern *canti popolari* in volumes entitled 'Canzonette veneziane,' 'Stornelli toscani,' 'Canti lombardi,' 'Napolitani,' 'Siciliani,' etc., purporting to be local songs belonging to the several provinces of Italy, not all authenticated.[6] The melodies of the 'Canti lombardi,' at least are genuine; also the 'Canti siciliani,' edited by Frontini, and the 'Canti abruzzesi,' collected by P. Tosti and G. Finamore. The last named, in an interesting article [7] on the harvest-songs of this district, draws attention to the solemn, religious character of the melodies, in contrast to the words, which are merry love-songs. This peculiarity Finamore attributes to the great antiquity of the melodies,[8] which have remained unchanged for centuries, though the words have altered. The following *Canti della meititura* (harvest) are amongst the commonest; the tonality of both is curious, the first being pure Lydian and the second of more or less Phrygian character.[9]

Largo.   Given by G. FINAMORE.

Ji' mè - ta mè - ta e la faggij - ja mè-te ca la pa-

- - - tron - a m'a da - dà la fij - je.

---

1 'L'Homme armé' is a well-known example. It must not be forgotten, though, that Italy was for many centuries the meeting-place for musicians from all countries — hence the cosmopolitan character of the themes chosen for the great contrapuntal works.

2 'Canzoni francesi a due voci, buone da cantare e suonare,' published by Gardano, Venice, 1539. The words are love-songs, and the music chiefly by Sermisy, Peletier, Herteur and Gardano himself. Gardano had published in the previous year 'Venticinque canzoni francesi,' consisting chiefly of four-part songs by Jannequin.

3 This collection is called 'Canzon Villanesche alla Napolitana di Messer Adriano; a quattro voci cor 'a canzon di Ruzante. Libro i. Venezia, Girolamo Scotto, 1548.'

4 For an example see 'La Bernardina in Kiesewetter's *Schicksale*, etc. App. p. 13.

5 See, for instance, G. Pitrè's *Studii di poesia popolare* (Palermo, 1872); Rubieri's *Storia della poesia popolare italiana* (Florence, 1877); A. D' Ancona's *La poesia popolare italiana* (Leghorn, 1878). See also Carducci's *Cantilene e ballate, strambotti e madrigali nei sec. XIII e XIV* (Pisa, 1871); and an interesting but unfinished work entitled *Canzoni antiche del popolo italiano, riprodotte secondo le vecchie stampe a cura di Mario Menghini*, Rome.

6 Speaking of Tuscan songs, Miss Busk shows how in these days of cheap printing and half-educated editing 'the literary songs (i.e. art-songs) have got mixed up with the folk-songs.' As instances, she quotes 'Stella confidente,' 'Non mi amara,' 'Ritorna! che t' amo' which were sung in London drawing-rooms as much as on the waysides and in the slums of Italy. Such songs also as Tosti's 'Vorrei morire' are constantly heard in the streets. *The Folk-songs of Italy*, p. 261 *et seq.*

7 *Melodie popolari abruzzesi; i canti della mietitura*, G. Finamore; see vol. 13 of the *Archivio per lo studio delle tradizioni popolari*, 1894.

8 'Chaque acte de la vie de l'agriculture était accompagné de sacrifice, et on exécutait les travaux en récitant des hymnes sacrés.' De Coulanges, *La Cité antique*, p. 184.

9 From the Vasto district, noted by L. Anelli. It should be accompanied by the cornemuse.

Aria della notte.[1]

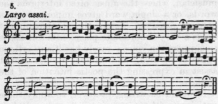

Some of the songs from the Abruzzi collected by Tosti are of extreme beauty in form, melody and words. Many of the Sicilian and Neapolitan songs begin with a long-drawn high note ; they are sung very fast and strongly accented.

The wealth of *canti popolari* is prodigious, and although (as mentioned above) they vary greatly in the different districts, their general characteristics are the same   The harmonic and formal structure is simple. The accompaniment, which is usually intended for the guitar, consists merely of the tonic and dominant chords, and rarely modulates into anything except the nearest related keys.[2] Few modal *canti popolari* are extant, although the flattened supertonic which is characteristic of the Sicilian and Neapolitan folk - songs recalls the Phrygian mode.[3] The time is more frequently triple than duple, and this especially applies to the dance-songs. The largest proportion of folk-songs consists of eight-lined verses of eleven syllables, and are variously called *strambotti, rispetti,*[4] *dispetti, siciliani,* or *ottavi.* The three-lined verses are called *ritornelli, stornelli, fiori* or *fiorette.* But it should be added that the terms *canti, canzoni, canzonette, stornelli* are very loosely and indiscriminately employed.[5] But speaking generally, *stornelli* are lively songs of love, *canzoni* and *canzonette* narrative songs, and *canto* is a generic term applicable to almost any form. Modern composers generally use the word *melodia* for a lyric song (*Lied*).

A strong claim to the title of *canti popolari* may be advanced in favour of the popular melodies taken from operas. Ambros tells us that during the 17th and 18th centuries, favourite ' couplets ' from operas, which at first had nothing in common with the folk-song beyond being melodious and simple, acquired by degrees a place similar to that held by the *Volkslied* in Germany.[6] And the immense popularity of operatic tunes in Italy during the last century cannot surprise us when we remember the theatre is a ubiquitous institution there, and that the quick ear of the Italian instantly catches melodies with a distinct rhythm and an easy progression of intervals.[7] Having regard, therefore, to the wide diffusion of the opera and its influence on all classes during nearly three centuries, it is reasonable to conclude that it may have checked the normal development of independent songs, and perhaps helped to obliterate the traces of old traditional tunes. It will be seen later that the exactly contrary process took place in some countries, where in order to make their operas popular, composers introduced favourite folk-songs or dances, or indeed whole operas were based on national melodies.

The so-called *canti nazionali* belong to a period beginning about the year 1821. They have all been inspired by the political movement of the 19th century for the regeneration of Italy. Their tone is naturally warlike, but the melodies are ultra-simple and rather weak. The most celebrated of them are : ' Addio, mia bella '[8] ; ' O dolce piacer, goder libertà ' ; ' Daghela avanti un passo '[9] ; 'Inno di Mameli' ; ' Fratelli d' Italia ' ; ' La bandiera tricolore ' ; ' Inno di Garibaldi,' and ' All' armi ' by Pieri. The years in which Italy has been most deeply stirred by struggles for independence were 1821, 1848 and 1859, and all the songs whose names have just been cited can be traced to one or other of those revolutionary periods.

For many important forms of both vocal and instrumental music we are primarily and especially indebted to the Italians, but as regards the art-song proper we owe them little. From the latter part of the 17th to the early part of the 19th century, the *canzoni* and *canzonette da camera* exhibited neither merit nor improvement. Several collections were published at intervals, yet apparently they attracted little attention. Many were of a religious tendency ; not hymns but *canzoni spirituali e morali,* as they were called. Even when the *canzoni madrigaleschi* were reduced to two voices (as, for instance, those by Benedetto Marcello, published at Bologna in 1717) they continued to be essentially polyphonic, one voice imitating the other.

[1] From the Guardiagrelle district, noted by M. Bruni. Finamore adds that they are sung in turn by one voice at a time, accompanied by the *chitarra battente,* a sort of *colascione.* The verses are of interminable length.

[2] A weak and very modern colouring is imparted to the harmony of the published folk-songs by an excessive use of the chord of the seventh.

[3] It has been remarked that the flat supertonic may be found in the canzonette from the comic operas by Vinci and Leo ; and that an air from A. Scarlatti's cantata ' Andate o miei sospiri,' marked *alla Siciliana,* has the same characteristic, showing that Scarlatti realised it as essential to the native quality of the melody. (See E. J. Dent's *A. Scarlatti, His Life and Works,* 1905.)

[4] *Rispetti* are always sung, and, as eight lines is the normal number, the popular mode of speaking either of inventing or singing them is, *dar l' ottava.* R. Busk, *The Folk-songs of Italy,* p. 20.

[5] *Canzune* is the Sicilian equivalent of *rispetto,* and *ciuri* of *stornello.* The children's songs in Italy are very numerous, and are usually called *Ninne-Nanne* or *Nane* in Venice. Busk, *op. cit.* p. 47.

[6] Orloff recounts how an aria from an opera by P. Cafaro (b. 1706), ' Belle luci,' was for half a century the best-known and most widely sung song all over Italy ; the melody was even painted on china and embroidered on robes (*Essai sur l'histoire de la musique en Italie,* i. 293). See also the account of the popularity of Piccinni's opera ' La Cecchina ' in the *Oxford History of Music,* vol. v., *The Viennese Period,* p. 97, W. H. Hadow.

[7] The chorus of an opera is frequently chosen from amongst the workmen and labourers of the place where it is performed ; and thus even difficult choruses may be heard in the streets and suburbs of towns which possess a theatre.

[8] This is an adaptation of Italian words to ' Partant pour la Syrie ' and was probably made during the war of 1820, in which France assisted Italy to liberate herself from the yoke of Austria.

[9] A ballet-song written by P. Giorza in 1858.

During the 18th century the lyric poet Metastasio exercised a certain effect on vocal music,
and many of his *ariette* were set by contemporary musicians ; but his influence was not lasting. A little later, a few inferior composers,
such as Asioli, Barni, Federici, Blangini and
Romagnesi [1] (all born in the second half of the
18th century) turned their attention to song-
writing, and published quantities of *ariette,
canzonette, rondi, notturni* and *romanze,* but
they were too weak to stand the test of time,
and such popularity as they may once have
known has been brief and fleeting. In fact,
few Italian composers of merit ever deemed it
worth while to bestow pains on this kind of
work ; to write an opera was their natural
ambition, and on this they concentrated their
powers. ' With all the best talent devoted to
the service of the Church or the theatre there
was little room left for the more solitary and
self-contained expression of lyric feeling.' [2] Nor
was there any demand for lyric songs. Just as
the ' couplets ' and favourite tunes from the
operas supplied the people with many *canti
popolari,* the *aria* and *cavatina* provided the
vocal pieces which the educated classes preferred. If we look through the work of Paisiello, Cimarosa, Mercadante, Bellini, Donizetti, Verdi and other celebrated composers
of opera, very numerous examples of the above-
mentioned miscellaneous kinds of songs may
be found, but none evince any serious thought.
They were obviously thrown off in leisure
moments, and now they are never heard of.
An exception, however, must be made in favour
of Rossini, some of whose songs have fine
melodies and interesting accompaniments.[3]
Among song-writers who lived nearer our own
time Gordigiani, Mariani and Giordani are undoubtedly the best for simple melodious songs.[4]
They wrote in the true Italian style, with the
utmost fluency and sentimentality.

With few exceptions Italian songs are marked
in a greater or less degree by the same qualities.
The voice-part is ever paramount in them, and
all else is made to yield to it. The beautiful
quality and the wide compass of Italian voices,[5]
and the facility with which they execute difficult vocal phrases, tempt the composer to
write brilliant and effective passages where a
simple melody would be far more appropriate
to the words. The words may indeed give the
form to the song, and the music may substantially agree with them, but we miss that delicate

subtle understanding between the poet and the
musician, where the music often interprets the
words, or a single word gives importance to a
note or passage. Again, the accompaniment
holds a very subordinate place. Its sole use is
to support the voice ; rarely has it any artistic
value of its own,[6] and seldom, if ever, does it
assist in expressing the poetic intention of the
work.

It would be wrong, however, to apply these
criticisms without reserve to all modern Italian
composers. P. Tosti, for instance, possessed a
genuine lyric talent, and some of his melodies
are charming. Clever accompaniments also
are met with in the compositions of Marco Sala,
Faccio, Bozzano, Coronaro and Smareglio.
The last two have paid especial attention to
the words of their songs. A cycle of songs,
entitled ' La Simona,' by Benedetto Junck,
would have a high rank assigned to them in
any country ; and the same can be said of
Sgambati's beautiful songs, with their highly
developed accompaniments. E. de Leva's,
Enrico Bossi's, P. Tirindelli's and Rotoli's
songs have merit ; and Leone Sinigaglia, writes
with grace and originality, and the increased
scientific interest in the folk-song characteristic
in all countries of the early years of the 20th
century is producing its effect in the work of
such composers as PIZZETTI, RESPIGHI and
CASTELNUOVO-TEDESCO.

BIBLIOGRAPHY [7]

ARTEAGA, S.   *La rivoluzione del teatro mus. ital.*   Venice, 1785.
ORLOFF, G.   *Essai sur l'histoire de la mus. en Italie.*   Paris, 1822.
LICHTENTHAL, P.   *Dizionario e bibliog. della musica.*   Milan, 1826.
VON DER HAGEN, F.   *Die Minnesinger.*   Leipzig, 1838.
DIETZ, F.   *Leben und Werke des Troubadours.*
WOLF, F.   *Über die Lais.*   Heidelberg, 1841.
KIESEWETTER, R. G.   *Schicksale und Beschaffenheit des weltl. Ge-
    sanges.*   Leipzig, 1841.   *Geschichte der europ.-abendländ.
    Musik.*   Leipzig, 1834.
AMBROS, W.   *Geschichte der Musik.*   Breslau, Leipzig, 1862–82.
FLORIMO, F.   *Cenno storico sulla scuola mus. di Napoli.*   Naples,
    1869–71.
NAUMANN, E.   *Italienische Tondichter.*   Berlin, 1876.
PFLEIDERER, R.   *Das ital. Volk im Spiegel seiner Volkslieder.*   Leipzig,
    1879.
PITRÈ, G., E SALOMONE-MARINO, S.   *Archivio per lo studio delle tradi-
    zioni popolari.*   Palermo, 1882, etc.
BUSK, RACHEL.   *The Folk-songs of Italy.*   London, 1887.
CHILESOTTI, O.   *Sulla melodia popolare del Cinquecento.*   Milan, 1889.
PARRY, C. H. H.   *Music of the Seventeenth Century (Oxford History
    of Music,* vol. iii.).   Oxford, 1902.

COLLECTIONS

FLORIMO, F.   ' Eco di Napoli.'   Napoli, 1840–60.
TOMMASEO, N.   ' Canti popolari toscani.'   Venice, 1841–42.
ALVERÀ, ANDREA.   ' Canti popolari tradizionali.'   Vicenza, 1844.
GORDIGIANI, L.   ' Collezione dei canti popolari toscani ' ; ' Stornelli
    d' Arezzo ' ;   ' Eco dell' Arno,' etc.   Milan, 1850.
FEA, L. A.   ' Chants populaires de la Corse.'   Paris, 1850.
RICORDI, G.   ' Canti popolari lombardi.'   1857–1900.
GIAMBONI, A.   ' I veri canti popolari di Firenze.'   Milano, 1862.
COMPARETTI, D.   ' Saggi dei dialetti greci dell' Italia merid.'   Pisa,
    1866.
SALOMONE-MARINO, S.   ' Canti popolari siciliani.'   Palermo, 1867.
FERRARO, G.   ' Canti popolari monferrini.'   Turin, 1870.
CASETTI, A.   ' Canti popolari delle provincie merid.'   Rome, 1871–72.
BORTOLINI, G.   ' Canzoni naz. della Laguna.'   Milan, 1873.
MARCHETTI, F.   ' Canti popolari romaneschi.'   Milan, 1874.
IVE, A.   ' Canti popolari istriani.'   Rome, 1877.
D' ANCONA, A.   ' Canti popolari italiani.'   Rome, 1877.
GIALDINI, G., E RICORDI, G.   ' Eco della Lombardia.'   Milan,
    1881–84.
DE MIGLIO, V.   ' 50 canzoni popolari napolitani.'   Milan, 1882.
FINAMORE, G.   ' Canti popolari abruzzesi.'   Milan, 1882–94.
TOSTI, F. P.   ' Canti popolari abruzzesi.'   Milan, 1882.

---

[1] These last two composers were better known in Paris than in
their own country.
[2] W. H. Hadow, *Oxford Hist. of Music,* v. 325.
[3] See for example ' La regata veneziana,' No. 2, where the
rhythmical figure in the left-hand represents the regular movement
of the oars, whilst the right hand has continuous *legato* passages
in double notes.
[4] Rossini once aptly summed up the Italian ideal of a song ; ' Il
diletto dev' essere la basa e lo scopo di quest' arte—Melodia semplice
—Ritmo chiaro.'
[5] It is curious to note how limited is the compass of voice for
which modern Italian composers write songs intended for circulation in foreign countries, while the songs they write for the home-
market often exceed the compass of two octaves.

[6] A point to be taken into consideration as greatly impoverishing
and limiting the accompaniments is that, on account of the climate
and the outdoor life the Italians lead, the guitar and mandoline
are as much used as the pianoforte.
[7] The writer also owes her thanks to Signor Domenico Comparetti
for information on the folk-songs of Italy.

FRONTINI, F. 'Eco della Sicilia.' Milan, 1883.
SINIGAGLIA, O. 'Stornelli d' Amore.' Palermo, 1884.
JULIA, A. 'Baci,' 'Ninne-Nanne.' Naples, 1884.
ORTOLI, J. F. B. 'Les voceri de l'île de Corse.' Paris, 1887.
NIGRA, CONST. 'Canti popolari del Piemonte.' Turin, 1888.
PARISOTTI, A. 'Le melodie popolari romane.' Rome.
TESCHNER, G. W. 'Sammlung italienischer Volkslieder.'
PARGOLESI, C. 'Eco del Friuli.' Trieste.
PITRÈ, G. 'Canti popolari siciliani.' Palermo, 1891; 'Bibliografia
   delle tradiz. popolari d' Italia,' Parte ii. 'Canti e melodie.'
   Torino, Palermo, 1894.
GIANNINI, G. 'Canti popolari Lucchesi.' Lucca, 1890–92.
SAVIOTTI, A. 'Canti e Ninne-Nanne arpinati.' Palermo, 1891.

SWITZERLAND

Although this country is bound together by a strong national feeling, it contains great diversities of idiom. More than half the population speak German; the rest either French or Italian, and a small fraction Romansch or Ladin. Hence there is little specifically national music, as it generally resembles that of the country to which it lies nearest. For instance, the folk-songs on the southern side are essentially Italian in character, while the French-Swiss and German-Swiss folk-songs are included in the collections of France and Germany. A purely indigenous feature in Swiss music is the cow-call, or *Kuhreihen*, which has been already treated. (See RANZ DES VACHES.) The old watchman-songs should also be mentioned. These date back for centuries, but are probably of German origin; as in the canton of Tessin, where Italian is the common language spoken, the night watch-call is still sung in Old German. Nearly all the true Alpine songs can be played on the Alphorn, to which in fact they owe their birth. The Swiss peasants have always possessed a remarkable harmonic aptitude. The herdsmen can skilfully improvise songs in many parts, and vary them with *Jodels* as ritornels or refrains. In many of the dance-songs the rhythm, too, is highly developed, necessitating constant changes of time-signature. Otherwise the melodies, like the poetry, are of the simplest character in form and metre.

Looking back on the past history of music in Switzerland, we find that the composers of any note in this country have generally identified themselves with other nationalities. Thus in the 16th century the great contrapuntist Ludwig Senfl's [1] name appears among German composers; in the 18th, J. J. Rousseau is claimed by France, just as Nägeli, Raff and Schnyder von Wartensee, nearer our own time, are by Germany. But Switzerland has never been without her own musicians, who have striven in all ages to keep up the national feeling, although their names are now scarcely remembered.

The Reformation exerted a great influence in French Switzerland. The Psalms of G. Franc, the two Bourgeois and Davantes are still heard around Geneva. Some of the *coraules* of the Fribourgeois have beautiful

refrains, recalling the ecclesiastical sequences; and in many of the old songs used in the peasants' *Festspiele* are traces of Goudimel's fine hymns adapted to secular words. These festival-plays, in which the peasants represent some national legend or historic event by word, dance and song, are held in different districts, and form a powerful factor in the musical life of Switzerland. They have incited such Swiss musicians as Baud-Bovy, G. Doret and F. Niggli to take down the songs sung on these occasions by the peasants and to write simple popular melodies in the same spirit. Whilst the Church cultivated the taste for hymns and Chorals,[2] the frequent wars gave rise to innumerable songs of satire, strife and politics. Some of the earliest French collections of these songs were printed by P. de Vingle at Neuchâtel in the 16th century.[3] He also printed many books of carols (Noëls Nouveaultx, 1533), usually with very irreverent words set to favourite sacred and secular tunes.

In the 17th and 18th centuries music-schools were formed in the various towns of Zürich, Basle, Berne and Coire, and their libraries have preserved numerous collections of songs by Dillhern, Simler, Krüger, Briegel, Musculi, the Molitors, Dietbold, Menzingen, and especially L. Steiner (b. 1688)—the first Swiss composer to cultivate a love for his country's music. J. Schmidli, who set Lavater's 'Chansons suisses' to music, and Egli, who published several 'Chansons suisses avec mélodies,' followed in his steps. After Egli's death in 1810, his pupil Walder carried on his work, together with Ott, Albertin, Bachofen (a special favourite) Greuter, Felix Huber, Kuhn and Zwinger, some of whom were national poets as well as musicians and collectors. J. G. Nägeli (as much a German as a Swiss song-composer) did much to promote musical education in the country of his birth. He was joined in this movement by Kunlin, Wachter, Krausskopf, the brothers Fröhlich, and Ferdinand Huber. As song-writers Karl Attenhofer, F. Grast and Ignaz Heim should be especially mentioned, the latter being perhaps the most popular. Zwyssig composed the 'Cantique suisse' (the national hymn) and Baumgartner the fine *chant* 'O ma Patrie.' The names of Methfessel, C. and F. Munziger, G. Weber, A. Meyer and F. Hegar (who is principally famous for his choral songs) may complete the list of that period.

During the latter part of the 19th century a new impetus was given to Swiss music by a group of young and enthusiastic musicians, who felt the necessity of preserving the tradi-

---

[1] Senfl contributed largely to the various collections of the 16th century; and in one of these called *Bicinia Gallica*, dated 1545, there occurs the oldest known version of a *ranz des vaches.*

[2] Towards the end of the 15th century L. Moser of Basle contributed largely to the popularisation of the church songs. His book, *Ein vast nothdürftige Materi*, etc. contains a large number of German songs adapted to familiar church melodies. See Becker, *Hist. de la musique suisse.*

[3] The collection of 1509 contains the celebrated *complainte* on the heretics burnt at Berne: 'Die war History von den vier Ketzer Prediger ordens zu Bern in den Eydgenossenschaft verbrannt.'

tional treasures of their country and developing them with all the resources of modern art. They endeavoured to prove the essential unity of feeling in the nation. Though composed of such various races, the same patriotism, love of liberty and independence have animated this little republic in all times of its history. The leaders of this movement are Hans HUBER and E. JAQUES-DALCROZE (*q.v.*). The latter's numerous volumes of 'Chansons romandes,' 'Chansons populaires et enfantines,' 'Chansons des Alpes,' 'Chansons patriotiques,' etc. contain graceful little pictures of national life, in which Jaques-Dalcroze cleverly introduces the types of melody, harmony, and rhythm characteristic of the various cantons.[1]

In the year 1900 the 'Union of Swiss Musicians' was formed, which holds yearly festivals for the performance of new works of all kinds by these composers. Especial interest is attached to those of the younger generation, all of whom have included song as an important branch of their art. The principal names are as follows: E. Jaques-Dalcroze, V. Andrae, Otto Barblan, E. Bloch, E. Combe, A. Dénéréaz, G. Doret, F. Klose, H. Kling, E. Reymond, Fritz Niggli, J. Ehrhart, R. Ganz, F. Karmin, J. Lauber, W. Pahnke, P. Maurice, W. Rehberg, G. Pantillon, L. Kempter, etc.

BIBLIOGRAPHY

TOBLER. *Appenzellischer Sprachschatz.* Zürich, 1837.
SCHUBIGER, A. *Die Sängerschule St. Gallens vom 8ten bis 12ten Jahrhundert.* Einsiedeln, New York, 1858.
BECKER, G. *La Musique en Suisse depuis les temps les plus reculés jusqu'à la fin du 18me siècle,* etc. Geneva, 1874.
BECKER, G. *Kulturhistorische Skizzen aus der romanischen Schweiz.* 1878.
SOUBIES, A. *Suisse (Histoire de la musique).* Paris, 1899.
JAQUES-DALCROZE, E. *Die Musik in der Schweiz (Die Musik,* July, 1905.)

COLLECTIONS

HUMBRECHTIKON, GREUTER DE. 'Bundtner Lieder.' Coire, 1785.
EGLI, J. H. 'Schweizer Lieder.' Zürich, 1798.
WALDER, J. J. 'Lieder zum gesellschaftlichen Vergnügen.' Zürich, 1804.
WAGNER, S. VON. 'Acht schweizer Kuhreihen.' Berne, 1805.
KUHN, G. 'Sammlung von schweizer Kuhreihen und alten Volksliedern.' Berne, 1812–18.
TARENNE, G. 'Recherches sur les ranz des vaches ou sur les chansons pastorales des bergers de la Suisse avec musique.' Paris, 1813.
WYSZ, J. and HUBER, F., edited the 4th edition of Kuhn's work in 1826.
HUBER, FELIX. 'Schweizerliederbuch' (532 Lieder). Aarau, 1824.
'Recueil de ranz de vaches.' 1830.
ROCHHOLZ, E. 'Eidgenössische Lieder-Chronik.' Berne, 1835–42.
HUBER, FELIX. 'Chants pour la guerre de la confédération.' Berne, 1840.
OTTO, F. 'Schweizer-Sagen in Balladen, Romanzen und Legenden.' Basle, 1842.
SHUDI. 4 vols. of old Swiss songs.
'Chants valanginois accompagnés de textes historiques.' Neuchâtel, 1848.
FORBES, DR. JOHN. 'A Physician's Holiday, or a month in Switzerland.' (This contains some interesting specimens of the hymns and chants used by the night-watchmen in Switzerland.) London, 1849.
ROCHHOLZ, E. 'Alemannisches Kinderlied und Kinderspiel aus der Schweiz' (no music). Leipzig, 1857.
KURZ, H. 'Schlacht- und Volkslieder der Schweizer.' Zürich, 1860.
BUHLER, J. A. 'Canzuns en lungatz rhäto-roman ch.' Coire, 1865.
KOELLA. 'Chansonnier suisse.' Zürich, 1882.
WYSZ, J., and HUBER, F. 'Der Schweizer-Sänger.' Lucerne, 1883.
'Chansons et coraules fribourgeoises.' Fribourg, 1894.
'Chants et coraules de la Gruyère.' Leipzig, 1894.
'Chansonnier des Zofingiens de la Suisse romande.' Lausanne, 1894.
DIETERICH, G. A. 'XXII Alpenlieder.' Stuttgart.

ROUMANIA

Roumania is a Romance country, and embraces both Moldavia and Wallachia. The

character of its national music is, therefore, very mixed. Among the educated classes a preference is shown for French and Italian music, and thus the Latin origin is betrayed. The real folk-music has also much in common with its Slavonic neighbours, and the gipsy element is strongly represented by the *Laoutari*.[2] Without these gipsy lutenists, no christening, wedding,[3] or funeral is held to be complete among the peasants, though at funerals in Roumania, as in Russia, it is the village women who are the professional 'wailers.' Their song of wailing is a monotonous recitative chanted on a few notes, interspersed by a succession of sharp little cries, whilst the words enumerate all the qualities of the deceased.

The most beautiful of the Roumanian folk-songs are enshrined in their *doinas*.[4] This is a generic term, as it includes songs of various origins. In times past, both pastoral and war-songs were alike called *doinas*, but at the present time they resemble the French *complaintes*, as indeed their name—*doina* = lament—indicates. They are usually in the minor key; the melody is full of turns, trills and other embellishments, yet throughout they are of a melancholy cast.

Though the folk-songs may be less original and striking than the national dances, they are extremely melodious and full of sentiment. The poetry is rhymed and often in five-lined stanzas. The metre is irregular, and refrains frequently occur either at the end of the line or the stanza, as the following well-known folk-song (*cantec popular*) shows:

Pentru tine Jana

[1] E. Jaques-Dalcroze, *Die Musik in der Schweiz.*
[2] Both Verdi and Liszt have testified their approval of the *Laoutari* in enthusiastic language. See J. Schorr, *Musik in Roumänien,* in *Die Musik,* 1903, No. 22.
[3] A Roumanian proverb says: 'Mariage sans *Laoutari* c'est-à-dire chose impossible.'
[4] The name *doina,* according to Hăsdeů, is of Dacian origin, and may also be found in Sanscrit, as *d'haina.*

The oldest and most celebrated dance is the *hora*, a slow choral dance written in rondo form usually in this rhythm:

Another dance, equally written in rondo form, but usually in a major key, is the *sarba* (or *sirba*). Though the prevailing tendency of this country's national music is melancholy, some of the dance-tunes are, nevertheless, gay and light. The occurrence of the augmented second between unusual intervals is frequent, and doubtless due to gipsy influence. Melodies of more recent date consist usually of the first phrase in the major and the second and concluding phrases in the relative minor, as in so many Slavonic tunes. The melody is also often played by the chief singer on the *cobza*, a sort of flute.

The renaissance of music in this country did not begin until the middle of the 19th century, and its principal promoters were Professor Wachmann (who especially called attention to the national music), Flechtenmacher and Caudella. The latter was the creator of the Roumanian national opera, and together with Ventura, Scheletti and Cavadi, composed numerous and favourite songs. These closely resemble the typical French and Italian *romances*, and have little in common with the German or Russian art-song. Mention should also be made of Eduard Hübsch, the composer of the national hymn. Musicescu and Kiriac have reproduced in their compositions the old Roumanian church and folk-songs. Margaritesco, Stephănescu, Spirescu, Ciran, Ercole and Dumitresco have written numerous songs and ballads, besides other works; and among a younger generation, Enescu, better known in western Europe as ENESCO (*q.v.*), and Lcarlatescu, who have won for themselves European reputations in more than one branch of music, perhaps stand the highest.

The cultivation of the national poetry and songs is due to the poet Vasili Alexandri,[1] to Asaki, Carmen Sylva, H. Vacaresco, Wachmann, Adamescu, Kogolniceanu and others. There are Conservatoires at Bucarest and Jassy, where young musicians can obtain a scientific training in their own country.

There is also a considerable Roumanian colony of Balkan origin in Hungary, who first established themselves here in 1230. They lead a more or less wandering life among the mountains, pasturing flocks. Their language, of a Latin stem, is much intermixed with Albanian, Slavonic and Hungarian words, but

[1] Vasili Alexandri was the first to collect the folk-ballads. His collection was published in 1852. See Otto Wagner's article *Das rumänische Volkslied, Sammelbände,* I.M.G. No. 1, 1902, where the treatment of the literary side of the folk-song is far superior to the musical.

their folk-songs and dances are quite distinct, and essentially their own. Among the dances we find the true Roumanian *hora, sirba, tarina* and *ardeleana*; and their innumerable songs and ballads are of Balkan rather than Hungarian origin. The oldest are theological or mystical in subject, but in the historical ones the heroes fight against the Turks. Among the *kolindas*, the religious kind are the commonest, treating of the life of our Lord, of the Virgin and saints, and the melodies are in plain-song.[2]

BIBLIOGRAPHY

SULZER, F. J. *Geschichte des transalpinischen Daciens.* Vienna. 1781–82.
Zustand der Musik in der Moldau, Allg. Musik. Zeitung, xxiii. Leipzig, 1821.
GRENVILLE MURRAY, E. C. *Doine, or the National Songs and Legends of Roumania.* London, 1854.
WAGNER, O. *Das rumänische Volkslied, Sammelbände,* I.M.G., 1902, i.
SCHORR, J. *Musik in Rumänien, Die Musik,* 1903, No. 22.
(The principal material for the above sketch was kindly supplied to the writer by M. Margaritesco, Bucarest.)

COLLECTIONS

PANN, A. 'Cântece de stea' (Cantiques de Noël). Bucarest, 1830–1848.
MUSICESCU, G. '12 Melodii nationale armonizate.' Jassy, 1889.
GEBAUER, C., and FÉDER, M. 'Volkslieder und Volkstänze.' Bucarest.
WACHMANN, J. A. 'Mélodies valaques pour le piano.' Müller, Vienna. 'Rumänische Volksmelodien.' Vienna, 1865.
MIKULI, C. 'Airs nationaux roumains.' Léopol.
IONESCU, M. 'Col. de cântece nationale.' Bucarest.
VACARESCO, H. 'Airs populaires roumains.' Bucarest, 1900.
PAUMANN, S. 'Album national, colecţiune de arii romanesci.' Bucarest, 1902.
'Chitaristui român' (Colecţiune de arii si romanţi naţionale). Bucarest, 1903.
KIRIAC, D. G. 'Coruri populare romanesti.' Bucarest, 1904–05.

MODERN GREECE

It is difficult if not impossible to avoid the mention of oriental songs, when treating those of Greece, because in the islands and on the mainland the songs are intermingled. Bourgault-Ducoudray says that in Greece the oriental chromatic scale is often found:

And again in Smyrna and other parts of Asia Minor the Aeolian scale [3] is in constant use. The melodies sung along the coast and in the Ionian islands are very Italian in character, and are easily distinguished from the genuine Greek melodies by being in the European minor scale. But inland, and away from the coast of Asia Minor, the pure Greek songs predominate.[4]

Until within a recent period there existed a number of minstrels or bards who combined the profession of musicians with that of chroniclers, and whose function it was to hand down by word of mouth, and thus keep alive, the great traditions of their country's history. These

[2] These Roumanians belong to the Greek Church. See G. Moldarau's article *Die Rumäner,* in *Die österreichisch-ungarische Monarchie,* vol. vi.

[3] The Greek names of the modes are here retained in preference to the ecclesiastical, and those readers not conversant with the interchange of nomenclature are referred to the article on MODES, ECCLESIASTICAL.

[4] M. Bourgault-Ducoudray says in the preface to his 'Trente mélodies populaires de Grèce et d'Orient' (using the Greek names) that the Greek Hypodorian, which only differs from the European A minor scale by the absence of the leading-note, is of frequent occurrence among the popular melodies of Greece. The Greek Dorian, Phrygian, Hypophrygian and Mixolydian modes are also fairly often met with; and the Hypolydian with the fourth lowered (which may easily be confused with the western major scale of F) is at the present time the commonest of all.

men were held in high esteem in their time ; but, as in other countries, education and the introduction of printing have brought about their rapid disappearance. Yet we are told that only a few years ago an old and blind minstrel, by name Barba Sterios,[1] sat, surrounded by a crowd, on the roadside by the gate of Kalamaria in Thessalonica. He played and sang in a melancholy and monotonous tone to his λύρα,[2] without raising his voice to a high pitch, and in pathetic parts drew deep emotion from his audience. In epic recitations of this kind the lyre is only used as an accompaniment in succession to the chanted words, and not with them. For instance, the old man to whom reference has just been made would start by touching a prelude on his lyre, and then begin intoning a couple of verses, after which the instrument came in again, and so on to the end, alternately playing and singing.[3]

The τραγούδια τοῦ χοροῦ, or choral songs, are ballads in the original sense of the word, for they are sung as an accompaniment to a complicated set of steps and mimic evolutions. At weddings, Christmas, on May-Day and similar festivals, men and women may be seen dancing together in a ring, hand in hand, outside their country inns. The leader of the dance, as he sweeps on, waves a handkerchief and sings a verse, accompanying it with appropriate gestures, while the rest of the dancers sing alternate verses in chorus. There are also other dance-songs, which are sung antiphonally by distinct sets of voices. This music is of a light and gay kind, consisting of short phrases which often end on the high octave :

with little or no variety in melody or rhythm. The words of the many Greek cradle-songs are of great beauty, but the melodies are monotonous and limited in compass.[4] Greater interest is imparted to the lyric folk-songs belonging to the eastern parts of Greece and the adjacent islands (where the melodies are naturally of an oriental character), by the irregular rhythms and constant change of time, such as alternate 2–4 and 3–4 time.

The Greeks have a gift for improvising or reciting in verse, and the preponderance of open vowels and the facility of rhyming in the Romaic language [5] render their task easy. Also they are keenly sensitive to emotions roused by striking events and incidents, both of past and present history. Many of their songs have reference to the customary periods of absence from home, when the villagers, who follow the professions of merchants or pedlars, descend from their hills to ply their trades in foreign lands.[6] Thus a youth who quits his home for the first time is accompanied a certain distance on the road by his family and friends. Before taking final leave of her son the mother laments his departure in a song either improvised or traditional, and in response the youth bewails the hard fate which drives him from his home.[7] There is proof that among the mass of folk-poetry still extant much of it dates back to old classical times. For example, the famous swallow-songs, when boys go about the streets greeting in song the reappearance of the swallows, embody a very ancient custom.[8] Serenades and aubades are most in vogue in the large towns, and each province has its own special songs ; but there are some ancient songs of great celebrity, such as ' The Fall of Constantinople,' which are the common heritage of all the provinces.

The Fall of Constantinople.[9]

3.

Τά - πά-νω βῆ - - μα 'πάρ - - δη-κεν, τό

κά - τω 'πο-κοι - μᾶ - ται, τό με - σα-κὸ . . . ἐ

στράγ - γι-σε, παι - διά, 'πάρ - δη ἡ Πόλι.

In the Greek folk-songs, as among other nations, the last words or lines are often repeated, or the words are broken up into meaningless syllables, recurring three or four times before the word is completed. Or it may be that the words are interrupted by interjections or refrains. It should be noted also that the accents of the words and music do not always agree, which clearly proves that different words were set to already extant melodies. It is difficult to represent these Eastern songs in our present notation, but the following example, of which a few bars are given, is a love-story from the Island of Samos,[10] and shows many of the above-mentioned features, including the peculiar tonality, limited compass, changing time and deep melancholy inherent to them. Stringed instruments are used to accompany

---

[1] Barba = uncle, is used as a term of endearment, like dyadya = uncle in Russian.

[2] A rough sort of stringed instrument, recalling the classic λύρα with five sheep-guts ; the bow consisting of a stick bent at one end and a bunch of horse-hair strung along it.

[3] G. F. Abbott's Songs of Modern Greece.

[4] The lullabies are called Βαυκαλήματα, Ννυρισματα, Ναναρισμα from ναναρίζω, to lull to sleep.

[5] The words of the folk-songs are all in modern Greek, i.e. Romaic, though they vary in dialect. The vernacular language is never taught, but many of the best modern poets have adopted it, and the effort made at the time of the War of Independence for the restoration of the classical language has had but a poor success. The Romaic language is more easily translated into Italian than any other tongue. Hence the reason that song-collectors such as Bourgault-Ducoudray, Bürchner and others, make use of it.

[6] Like the Vlachs in the Valley of Zagari who go to Spain.

[7] See Garnett's Greek Folk-Poesy, and Passow's song 'The Exile.'

[8] For the words of the Swallow and May-time songs see Kind and Passow. Many have been translated into English by Miss Lucy Garnett in Greek Folk-Poesy and Greek Folk-Songs.

[9] This song was taken down by Bürchner from an old woman of eighty, who again had heard it from her infancy, sung by old people.

[10] Bürchner, 'Griechische Volksweisen,' p. 406.

these songs, and nowadays principally guitars
and mandolines.

etc.

The literary revival which followed the War
of Independence, and the abundance of poetry
written in the present day, have, however,
produced no effect on the music of the country.
The Greek song-writers worthy of mention are
lamentably few; the generality of their published songs are with few exceptions either
trivial or sentimental. Among the Greek composers who have won European fame, Spiro
SAMARA (q.v.) may be noted as the best. At an
early period of his career he achieved success in
Paris by his graceful little songs. Other song-
composers are: Zacharopoulos, Sidere, Be-
loudion, Lampalete, Karrĕrĕ, Rodios and
Leonardos.

The few and best exceptions to the general
average of songs are those in which either the
composer has taken the folk-song as his model,
or the actual folk-songs themselves, such as are
to be found in L. A. Bourgault-Ducoudray's
'Trente mélodies populaires de Grèce et
d'Orient'; and more recently in the collection
of M. Pakhtikos, Director of the School of Music
in Constantinople, who personally noted them
down in remote districts of Thrace, Macedonia,
Crete, the Aegean Islands, etc.

BIBLIOGRAPHY AND COLLECTIONS

SULZER, F. J. Geschichte des transalpinischen Daciens. Vienna,
  1781–82, 3 vols. (Contains Greek, Wallachian and Turkish tunes.)
FAURIEL, C. Chants populaires de la Grèce moderne (no music).
  Paris, 1824.
KIESEWETTER, R. Über die Musik der neueren Griechen. Leipzig,
  1838.
SANDERS, D. Das Volksleben der Neugriechen. Mannheim, 1844.
KIND, TH. 'Neugriechische Volkslieder.' Leipzig, 1849.
PASSOW, A. Liebes- und Klagelieder des neugriechischen Volkes
  (no music). Magdeburg, 1861; 'Romaic Songs' (Τραγούδια
  'Ρωμαίικα). 1860.
TANTALIDES, E. 'Collection of songs, including nursery rhymes
  and school-songs with music.' Athens, 1876.
BOURGAULT-DUCOUDRAY. 'Trente mélodies populaires de Grèce
  et d'Orient.' Paris, 1876.
RANGABÉ, A. R. Histoire littéraire de la Grèce moderne. Paris, 1877.
SIGALA, A. 'Recueil de chants nationaux.' Athens, 1880.
MATZA, PERICLES. '80 mélodies grecques.' Constantinople, 1883.
GARNETT, L., and STUART-GLENNIE, J. Greek Folk-Songs (nothing
  about music). London, 1888.
GARNETT, L., and STUART-GLENNIE, J. Greek Folk-Poesy. London,
  1896.
ABBOTT, G. F. Songs of Modern Greece (no music). Cambridge, 1900.
BÜRCHNER, L. 'Griechische Volksweisen.' (Sammelbände of the
  I.M.G. iii. 403.)
PERNOT, H., and LE FLEM, P. 'Mél. pop. de Chio en pays turc.'
  Appendix. Paris, 1903.
PAKHTIKOS, G. D. ' 260 Greek songs (Asia Minor, Macedonia, Cyprus,
  Albania, etc.).' Athens, 1905.

RUSSIA

No country is richer in national music than
Russia, and nowhere has it been more carefully
preserved from neglect or oblivion. For many
years the folk-songs and dances of the most
remote districts were collected by order of the
Imperial Government: musicians and savants
of the highest rank [1] joined in folk-song research and assisted in the task of compilation.
Moreover, the modern school of Russian music,
which holds so important a place in art, owes,
in part, its strength and magnetic attraction to
the ingrain colour derived from race temperament. Though it was only in the 19th century
that Russian music achieved European renown,
it has always been loved and cultivated in its
own country. Hence from birth onwards the
peculiar harmonies and rhythms of his native
land have so possessed the ear of every Russian
musician that consciously or unconsciously he
has re-echoed them in his works.

The oldest form of national poetry would
seem to be the builini, of which there is evidence
that they existed 1000 years ago. They are
national epics akin to the historical romances;
of great length and in unrhymed metre.[2] The
music, which is a kind of monotonous chant,
accompanies one line, or at most two lines of the
song, repeating to the end.

As it befell in the capital Kieff.[3]

1.

etc.

The horovodi or choral songs belong solely to
the Slav races. They celebrate the change of
seasons and the successive festivals of the
ecclesiastical or agricultural calendar, while
some are especially appropriate to various
peasant occupations.[4] These horovodi are sung
in a curious manner: the first voice sings a
melody, the other voices in succession sing
variants of the same melody, and as the voices
fall in with one another a kind of counterpoint
is established, whilst each voice retains its
independence.

2.

1st Voice.

2nd Voice.

etc.

[1] Such as Balakirev, Rimsky-Korsakov, Serov, Melgounov.
[2] One of the most interesting small collections of builini was
made by R. James, an English clergyman, who spent the winter of
1619 in the far north of Russia. His MSS. are now in the Bodleian
Library.
[3] Rimsky-Korsakov, 'Chants nationaux russes,' No. 1. (Communicated by Moussorgsky.)
[4] The singers of the christening, wedding, funeral, or even con-
scription songs are always elderly women, and no ceremony is
considered properly conducted without them. They are to some
extent 'improvisatrici'—reflecting in their song, past and present,
individual and general conditions. See preface to Dioutsh, Liapounov and Istomin's 'Songs of the Russian People.'

MELGOUNOV (*q.v.*) contended that from the earliest time it was essentially polyphonic in structure, and he refuted the general idea that folk-songs were sung in unison.[1] In taking down the songs from the peasants he carefully recorded each voice separately, and attributed great importance to the preservation of the popular counterpoint. His examples show that the secondary parts (*podgoloski*) constitute really a free imitation of the main melody:

The *piessni* or solo songs are very often sung to the accompaniment of the *balalaïka*, a guitar-like instrument. These are mainly lyrical in character, and reflect the emotions and episodes of peasant life. Some of the love-songs are beautiful, and the wailing songs—*zaplachki*—most pathetic. The melancholy and monotonous cradle-songs have a strange charm of their own ; and the so-called 'laudatory' songs (glorifying some individual indiscriminately, before or after death), which are the peculiar property of the Slav, rank high in importance among the songs of the peasants.[1]

The rhythm of Russian folk-songs is often characterised by extreme irregularity. The tunes usually begin on the first beat of the bar, but the phrases are of unequal length ; they are frequently in 7–4 or 5–4 time, or 2–4 and 3–4 time alternating ; but it must be remembered on the authority of Sokalski and others that the division of the melodies into bars is arbitrary.[2] The original tunes, handed down by oral tradition, owed their rhythm to no symmetrical repetition of accents, but to the cadences suggested by the flow of the verse itself. Again it frequently happens that the accent of the verse varies, which renders it difficult to arrange under the regular metrical accentuation of the time system. The accent moves from one syllable or one word to another, for instance, *gòry* or *gorỳ* (hills)—as if to avoid monotony ; and the inequality of the number of syllables in each half verse, each of which has one main accent, appears to be one of the characteristics of Russian folk-songs.[3] Naturally the dance-songs have more regular accents and rhythms, especially those of gipsy origin, when the dancers mark the time with their feet.

[1] See preface to J. Melgounov's ' Russian Songs.'
[2] The numerous other kinds of songs which the above classifications do not include cannot here be dealt with. They will be found under their different headings in any standard collection. See also Ralston's *Songs of the Russian People*, pp. 34, 39 *et seq.*
[3] Sokalski's *Russian Folk-Songs.*

Peasants do not like singing solos : they prefer to sing in *artels* or companies in which each member is a performer and composer, owing to the above-mentioned structure of the songs.

Glinka and many other theorists have made the peculiar tonality and harmonisation of Russian songs their life-long study. Melgounov says that they are based on the so-called natural (untempered) scale, which is impossible to represent in our present notation ; and that the foundation of the major and minor scales is contained in this simple formula : $11\frac{1}{2}111\frac{1}{2}$. That is, if the relative minor of the scale of C is taken descending from dominant to its octave the result is :

$$e_1 \; d_1 \; c_{\sharp} \; b_1 \; a_1 \; g_1 \; f_{\sharp} \; e.$$

This when reversed will be found to be identical with the ecclesiastical Phrygian mode.[4] Certainly there is an indisputable connexion between the musical theory of the ancient Greeks and the oldest and actually existing Slavonic melodies founded on these scales, more especially those of the western part of Russia. To modern ears the tonality, therefore, is of an uncertain character, and many melodies start in the major and bear distinctly the stamp of the major key until towards the end, where they modulate into the minor key in which they conclude. Further they more often begin and end on the supertonic, or indeed on any degree of the scale rather than the tonic. Another peculiarity we find in the folk and art-songs alike are the florid passages on one syllable. This and many other features in Russian song could be traced to Asiatic influence, for in Russia the eastern and western temperaments meet and intermingle.[5]

Early in the 19th century national representation was lacking in the music of Russian born composers. It awaited emancipation from the foreign influences under which it had so long lain. It was GLINKA who first began to effect its liberation, and the importance of his work cannot be exaggerated. Though his national opera, ' A Life for the Tsar ' (except for a few bars in the opening chorus) incorporates no single folk-song, Glinka so identified himself with the feeling and spirit of the national music that his melodies became at once familiar to his countrymen. Glinka has truly been named the father of the Russian art-song. Previous to him, other song-composers, such as Alabiev, Varlamov, Kozlovsky, Verstov-

[4] See preface to Lineiev's ' Peasant Songs of Great Russia.'
[5] Tchaikovsky's remarks on the character of the folk-songs are worth quoting. In writing to Tolstoi to acknowledge some songs he had sent him, Tchaikovsky says, ' I must frankly say the songs have not been skilfully treated, and thereby all their original beauty has been lost. The chief fault is, that they have been forced into a regular, formal rhythm. The *buïlinï* have nothing in common with the dances. Besides this, the greater part of these songs is written in the cheerful D major scale, and this does not agree in the least with the tonality of the true Russian Volkslied, which is always of an uncertain tonality, so that one can really only compare them with the old church modes.'
[6] C. Cui remarks that the ' Tartar influence is so strong that there is hardly one Russian folk-song not affected by it,' but that is an overstatement.

sky[1] and Lvov, wrote songs of the simple, popular type, imitating so faithfully the external qualities of the real folk-song, that some, such as Alabiev's ' Nightingale ' and Varlamov's ' Red Sarafan,' have been accepted as national melodies. Lvov was the composer of the Russian national hymn,[2] the tune of which, though fine and suitable to the words, is not Russian in character.[3] Again, others like Gurilev, Vassilev and Dübüque arranged a number of national airs, and some gipsy tunes, to modern words in rhyme and four-line stanzas, with a simple pianoforte accompaniment. Glinka's songs stand on a higher level, though they vary in merit ; some of the earlier ones betray the Italian influence, and have elementary accompaniments ; some are in dance-rhythm pervaded by a local colouring ; others are pure lyrics and very expressive, but his finest effort is the powerful ballad ' The Midnight Review.' DARGOMIJSKY was nearly Glinka's contemporary, and shared the same enthusiasm for his country's music. His songs show more dramatic power ; many consist of short declamatory phrases akin to recitative, and all evince a high regard for the meaning and metre of the words. Dargomijsky has, moreover, caught the intense but languorous spirit of the East. His ballads take high rank, especially one called ' Knight Errant.'[4] RUBINSTEIN is a strange paradox.[5] More cosmopolitan and western in feeling than any other Russian composer, it is his eastern songs which are the best. Many of his songs belong to the German *Lied*, the accompaniments being clearly based on Schumann as a model, as for instance, ' Nun die Schatten dunkeln ' (Geibel), and ' Nacht ' (Eichendorff). But his settings of Mirza Schaffy's words are by far the most beautiful and original of all his songs, and all are essentially vocal.

The five composers, BORODIN, BALAKIREV, CUI, MOUSSORGSKY and RIMSKY - KORSAKOV, formulated certain principles of their art, one of which directly concerns song, ' that vocal music should be in perfect accordance with the meaning of the text.' And though each composer with his individual tendencies reached this end by his own route, they were unanimous on this point, as may be seen on closer examination of their songs. TCHAIKOVSKY stands alone. He was more cosmopolitan than the afore-mentioned composers, and more individual than

national in his music. The emotional value and the beautiful melodies of his songs compensate for the inadequacy of ill-chosen words and for the defects of a certain diffuseness of treatment. But notwithstanding these artistic demerits, as an expression of passion, tragic or triumphant, his songs make a direct appeal and elicit a direct response. To this quality may be attributed his wide popularity in non-Slavonic countries.

Sacred and spiritual songs are greatly sung in Russia, and in connexion with them the names of Lvov, Bortniansky, Bachmetiev and Dmitriev are well known.

In conclusion it remains to give the names of some later song-writers whose work is discussed under their own names : ARENSKY, ARTCIBOUCHEV, S. and F. BLUMENFELD, DAVIDOV, GLAZOUNOV, GRETCHANINOV, KOPYLOV, LIADOV, LIAPOUNOV, RACHMANINOV, REBIKOV, SCRIABIN, SOKOLOV, STCHERBATCHEV, WIHTOL.

BIBLIOGRAPHY

The general histories of Russian music by Youri von Arnold, Famintsine (on old Slavonic music), Sacchetti, Beresovsky, Sokalski (Folk-Song), etc.
RASOUMOVSKY. *Le Chant de l'Église en Russie.* Moscow, 1867–69.
RALSTON, W. R. S. *Songs of the Russian People.* London, 1872.
CUI, C. *La Musique en Russie.* Paris, 1880.
PEREPELITZINE. *History and Dictionary of Russian Music.* 1884.
HABETS, A. *Borodin and Liszt.* London, 1895.
SOUBIES, A. *Histoire de la musique en Russie.* Paris, 1898.
MIKHNIEVITCH. *L'Aperçu de l'histoire de la musique en Russie.*
Lectures and articles by Mrs. NEWMARCH.
See also the Russian edition of Riemann's *Lexikon* with supplement by J. ENGEL. Jurgenson, Moscow, 1905.
Extensive work has also been done by the St. Petersburg Song Commission of the Imperial Geographical Society, and the Moscow Musico Ethnographic Committee.

COLLECTIONS

TROUTOVSKY, V. F. ' Russian Songs.' (The first collection.) 1782.
PRACH, IVAN. ' Russian Popular Songs.' St. Petersburg, 1806 and 1815. (Introduction by N. A. Lvov.) 1790.
DOFFELMAIR, G. VON. ' Russische Volkslieder.' Leipzig, 1809.
GOETZE, P. O. v. ' Stimmen des russ. Volks in Liedern.' Stuttgart, 1828.
STANOVITCH, M. ' Recueil de chants populaires russes.' 1834.
SAKAROV, I. P. ' Songs of the Russian People.' St. Petersburg, 1838–39.
KIRIYEVSKY, P. V. ' Russian Folk-songs.' Moscow, 1860.
KASTALSKY, A. D. ' The Peasant's Harmonization of Russian Folk songs.'
RUIBNIKOV, P. N. ' Songs of the Russian People.' St. Petersburg, 1861–67.
KUBA, L. ' Slovantsvo ve soych zperech ' (' The Slavs in their Songs.' Russian section). Prague.
KASHIN, D. ' 115 Russian National Songs.' Moscow, 1833, 1841, 1868.
BERNARD, M. ' Chants populaires russes.' St. Petersburg, 1868.
EDLICHKA. ' Chants nationaux de la Petite-Russie.' St. Petersburg, 1868.
PHILIPPOV and RIMSKY-KORSAKOV. ' Chants nationaux russes.' 1870.
HILPERING, A. ' Collection of Builini (Bylinas).' 1873.
PROKOUNIN, K., and TCHAIKOVSKY, P. ' Chants populaires russes.' Moscow, 1873.
MELGOUNOV, J. ' Russian Folk-songs.' Moscow, 1879.
SOKALSKI, P. P. ' Russian Folk-songs.' Kharkov, 1888.
DIOUTSH, LIAPOUNOV, and ISTOMIN. ' Songs of the Russian People.' St. Petersburg, 1894.
PALTCHINOV, N. ' Peasants' Songs.' Moscow, 1896.
BALAKIREV, M. ' Recueil de chants populaires russes.' Leipzig, 1898.
ISTOMINE and NEKRASOV. ' 50 Chants du peuple russe.' St. Petersburg, 1901.
LINEIEV, EUGÉNIE. ' Peasant Songs of Great Russia ' (transcribed from phonograms). St. Petersburg and London, 1905.

YUGO-SLAVIA AND OTHER SLAVONIC NATIONS

Much that has been said about the national music of Russia would apply also to other branches of the Slavonic people.[6] There are,

---

[1] Verstovsky, who was hailed for a time as the true Messiah of Russian music, owed his fleeting popularity to his operas more than to his songs.
[2] Composed to order in 1833, the words by Zhukovsky.
[3] It has been said that Lvov was not the true composer of this hymn, but merely took the melody of the trio of a *Geschwindmarsch*, composed by F. Bogdanovitch Haas, bandmaster of the St. Petersburg regiment of the Guards, and published in a March Collection in 1822. The notes are identical, the only change being made in the time.
[4] C. Cui says of this ballad : ' It is impossible to put into adequate words all the laconic strength, the picturesque qualities and vivid realism conveyed by this song. It breathes the spirit of the past and appeals to the mind as vividly as a picture.'
[5] The paradox, however, is explained by Rubinstein's Semitic race and his career as a virtuoso.

[6] Since the war of 1914–18, the political distribution of the Slav peoples is as follows : Great Russia, White Russia, Ukraine and the Transcaucasian Federation are included in the Union of Soviet Socialist Republics ; the Czechs (Bohemians), Moravians, Slovaks, Silesians and Ruthenians (of sub-Carpathian Russia) constitute a republic ; the Serbs, Croats, Slovenes and Dalmatians form the

nevertheless, important variations in the traits they appear to have in common, and certain characteristics peculiar to each nation which claim notice. The remarks will, however, refer chiefly to the folk-music, as in many of the countries music remains still in its primitive state, or can hardly be said to have developed beyond the stage of national airs ; no musical schools have been formed, and the composers would merely be classed under the generic term Slavonic.[1] But of the beauty and enormous wealth of the folk-songs in these countries proof has been afforded by the many and valuable collections which already exist and yearly increase.

Indigenous to the Ukraine[2] is a kind of epic song of irregular rhythm recited to a slow chant. These *doumas* were originally improvised by the *Bandurists*, but these wandering minstrels are now nearly extinct, and their function has devolved upon the village women, who invent both the poetry and melodies of the songs which they sing　Among the peculiarities of these interesting songs, one is that if the song ends on the dominant or lower octave, the last note of the closing verse is sung very softly, and then without a break the new verse begins loud and accented, the only division between the two being such a shake as described by the German phrase *Bocktriller*. This feature is common also to Cossack songs,[3] and to the songs of that Wendic branch of the Slavonic race which is found in a part of Saxony.

1. *Wendic Folk-song.*

The Wendic songs, except when dance-tunes, are generally sung *tremolando* and very slowly. And the exclamation 'Ha' or 'Hale,' with which they almost invariably begin, may be compared with the 'Hoj,' or 'Ha' of the Ruthenians and the 'Ach' of Great Russia. One of the most popular Ruthenian songs is 'The Cossack Ride,' better known under the name of 'Pretty Minka.'[4] The superior charm of the songs of Little Russia is due, for the most part, to a prevailing cast of melancholy.

Inhabited by a people who vie with the Poles in susceptibility to poetic sentiment, Little Russia is naturally rich in songs. The greater part are in the minor, or based on the Church scales, of a slow tempo, and frequently with a halt or drag in the rhythm produced by shortening the first syllable and prolonging the second, thus :

Croatian peasants, men or women, never use songs already composed ; they improvise the words as well as the melodies themselves. Hence only those songs which sprang from the people are sung by them.[5] This does not apply to the ritual songs which have been handed down by oral tradition for centuries, and in which the Croatians are very rich. The following song is sung at Midsummer as the men and women leap and dance round the fires lighted on the hill-tops and call to the heathen goddess ' Lado.'[6]

2.

La-do! La-do! Bog pomana tomu stanu liepa J' La-do!

The chief dance-song of the Croatians and Serbs is the *kolo*, of which there are many kinds　To the *oro kolo* the peasants sing religious songs ; to the *junačko kolo* heroic ballads ; to the *zensko kolo* love-songs ; and to the *salgivo kolo* humorous songs. There is a marked difference between the town and village songs. The latter exhibit the truest Croatian feeling ; the town songs are more cosmopolitan, and are much influenced by the wandering *Tanburists*, who, like the Hungarian gipsies, sing and play the *tanbura* (the national instrument) in taverns.

Since the Illyrian movement of 1835, a national school of music has arisen in Croatia, and been fostered by educated musicians of the country. Previous to this, a Conservatoire of music had been founded at Agram, but it was not until 1846, when Vatroslav Lisinski's popular opera ' Ljubovi zlova ' was given, that Croatian art-music gained notice.[7] Lisinski. Ferdo Livadić, Ferdo Rusan, Ivan Zajc and his pupil G. Eisenhuth, the historian V. Klaić, and Vilko Novak have contributed to the lyric music of Croatia.[8] F. Z. Kuhač's large collec-

kingdom of Yugo-Slavia ; Poland and Lithuania are independent republics ; Bulgaria remains as before, but with curtailed territory ; the Banat, Bessarabia, Bukovina, Crisana, Maramuresh and Transylvania are incorporated in the kingdom of Roumania.

[1] As for instance Borodin, a Georgian composer, who is mentioned under Russia.

[2] 'Le dialecte de l'Oukraine en est tout différent du russe. Ce n'est pas un patois, c'est un dialecte constitué, qui possède une brillante littérature. C'est surtout la noblesse de Kiev, de la Volhynie, Podolie qui a subi l'influence polonaise ; le *moujik* de l'Oukraine est resté en dehors de son action par la nature de sa vie, et surtout par la différence de religion, car il pratique toujours le rite grec.' Dr. A. Bonmariage, *Notes pour la Russie d'Europe*, p. 430 *et seq.*

[3] The Don Cossacks are Great Russians, and the Zaparogues Cossacks are Little Russians. Dr. A. Bonmariage, *Notes pour la Russie d'Europe*, p. 417.

[4] The music and original words are given in Prach's collection, and the German version in Fink's *Hausschats*, No. 157

[5] F. Kuhač in a letter to W. Barclay Squire from Agram in 1893.

[6] From F. Z. Kuhač's article in the *Österreichisch-ungarische Monarchie*, vol. vii. p. 110 *et seq.*

[7] *Musik in Croatien*, by Ferdo Miler, p. 174 *et seq.* in *Öst.-ung. Mon.*

[8] Although Haydn was a Croatian by birth and freely used his native folk-songs in his instrumental works, he is rightly classed among German composers. But the remarkable resemblance between his greatest German song, ' Gott erhalte,' the Austrian national hymn, and a folk-song from the Bistritz district of Croatia cannot be passed over in silence. It has given rise to much discussion ; see for instance, H. Reimann and F. Kuhač in the *Allgemeine deutsche Musikzeitung*, 1893 (Nos. 40-42) ; also Hugo Conrat's article in *Die Musik*, Jan. 1, 1905 ; and *Josip Haydn*, by Dr. Kuhač. The tune is as follows :

Stal ve jesem.

O. Fleischer, whilst admitting the resemblance of Haydn's melody to the folk-song, prefers to trace its origin back to the Church

tion of South Slavonic folk-songs is of great value. The composer of the Croatian national anthem, 'Liepa naša domovina,' was an officer named Josip Runjanin.

All the Serb songs are of remarkable beauty and expressiveness, and although they resemble the Russian songs as regards their scale and tonality and the same elastic metre prevails, yet the melodies are more rhapsodical. And among these south-eastern nations the affinity with the music of the Arabs and other nations of Western Asia is more often indicated. The Serbian drinking-songs are noticeable; grave, solemn and devotional, they are quite unlike those of any other country; but as among the Serbs the hymns and secular songs are so frequently intermingled, this may be accounted for. Most of the Serbian and many of the Bulgarian songs end on the supertonic, as in the Serbian national hymn:

3.

The Bulgarian songs show Turkish influence; they are also quite irregular in metre, and far more fragmentary than the Serbian:

4.
Lento.

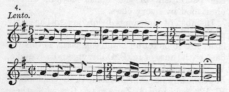

The Bulgarians have a great love for the folklore of their country, and the volumes of the Sbornik, which the State publishes yearly, contain legends, ballads and songs with music.

COLLECTIONS

LIPINSKI, C. 'Chants du peuple de Gallicie.' Lemberg, 1833.
KOLLAR, J. 'Národnie Zpiewanky.' Buda Pest, 1834.
ACHAZEL and KORYTHO. 'Carniolian Songs.' 1839.
PAULI, I. Z. 'Pieśne ludu Ruskiego w Galicyi.' Lemberg, 1839–40.
HAUPT und SCHMALER. 'Volkslieder der Wenden.' Grimma, 1841.
KRASINSKI, H. 'The Cossacks of the Ukraine.' London, 1848.

and quotes many examples of hymns which open with the same phrase as 'Gott erhalte,' thus:

Di - es i - rae   Di - es   il - la

from the Franciscan Requiem; and

Stand die   Mut - ter   qua - len - tra - gend

An dem   Kreu - ze   und er - kla - gend.

a Stabat Mater from Cantarium S. Galli, 1845 (see *Zur vergleichenden Liedforschung*; *Sammelbände* of the I.M.G. iii. 2). See also Hadow. *A Croatian Composer.*

KOCIPINKIM, A. 'Chansons populaires russes en Podolie, l'Oukraine, etc.' 1862.
ROUBETZ, A. 'Chansons populaires de l'Oukraine.' Moscow, 1872; 'Chansons populaires petit-russiens.' St. Petersburg, 1875.
KUHAĆ, F. Z. 'Chansons nationales des Slaves du Sud.' Agram, 1878–81. (This contains Serbian, Dalmatian, Bosnian, Croatian, etc., songs.)
CHODŹKO, A. B. 'Les Chants historiques de l'Ukraine.' Paris, 1879.
DE VOLLAU. 'Rutheno-Galician Folk-songs.' 1885. (Publ. by Russian Geog. Soc.)
STOIANOV and RATSCHOW. '24 Chansons notées (bulgares).' 1887.
KALANZ, A. 'Serbische Volksmelodien.' Vienna, 1890.
VASILEV, G. P. '225 Chansons populaires bulgares.' Tirnovo, 1891.
The publications in the *Sbornik* vols. for 1894 and 1897.
BOSILJEVA, S. 'Album des chansons nationales de la Bosnie.' Agram, 1895.
GEORGEWITCH, V. R. 'Mélodies nationales serbes.' Belgrade, 1896.
GEMTCHOUNOV, A. and VL. 'Les Chants des Cosaques de l'Oural.' St. Petersburg, 1899.
HADOW, W. H. 'A Croatian Composer, Joseph Haydn' (contains many specimens of Croatian songs).
STÖHR, A. 'Album croatien.'
Das musikalische Österreich contains Croatian, Carniolian, Dalmatian and Bosnian songs. Vienna.
PARLOVIC. 'Serbian Songs.' Agram.
KOCORA. '15 Chants nationaux des Serbes lusaciens.' Prague.
MANTEUFFEL, GUSTAV. FREIHERR VON. 'Deutsche altlivländische Volkslieder.' 1906.

POLAND

The songs of the Poles are mainly presented to us in the form of hymns, or in the form of their national dance-rhythms. One of the earliest and most celebrated examples of the former, dating from the 10th century, is St. Adalbert's hymn to the Virgin ('Boga Rodziça'), which is engraved in plain-chant on his tomb in the cathedral of Gnesen.[1] Here and at Dombrova on the Warka, it is still sung every Sunday. The hymn is, however, well known throughout Poland, as it is used on all solemn occasions, for triumphant or sad ceremonials and on the battlefield [2]:

1.

Bo - ga   Ro - dzi - ça   Dzie - wi - ça

Bogiem W Slawio - na   Ma - ry - - a

Another familiar hymn is the 'Hajnaly,' which is heard every morning from the towers of Cracow to awaken the sleeping town. In the old sacred song-books called *Kancyonaly* or *Cancionales*[3] preserved in cathedrals, convents, and in the libraries of the great nobles, many old secular folk-songs are to be found incorporated in masses and motets[4]; likewise many *kolendas* which are peculiar to the Polish people. These *kolendas* (noëls) are old folk-songs, some dating from the 13th century, and are still sung in every house and street at Christmas time, and it is in one of these *kolendas* that we meet with the rhythm of the polonaise:

[1] St. Adalbert was born in 936. A member of the Polish hierarchy, St. Adalbert was by birth, however, a Bohemian, and, at one time, Bishop of Prague.
[2] For the hymn (translated into modern notation by F. Lessel) see Sowinski, *Les Musiciens polonais*, p. 64.
[3] The Bohemian Brothers first printed the *Cancionales* at Prague and at Cracow, in 1558.
[4] This is not the place to speak of the interesting polyphonic school of music which flourished in Poland during the late 15th and 16th centuries, and of the work done by the so-called College of Roratists at Cracow. This school was represented by such composers as Felzstyn, Leopolita, Szamotulski, Szadek, etc., all of whom were clearly under Flemish influence.

W Zlobie lezy.

1. W zlobie lezy Ktoz po biezy Ko-len-do wac ma le mu.

2. Je-su so-wi Chrys-tu so-wi Dzis nam na-rod-zo rem-u.

Ras-tusz ko-wie   przy-by - waj - cie,   Je mu welzie cznie

przy-gry-waj-cie   Ja - ko Pa - nu   na - sze - mu.

The Poles have ever loved their simple, dignified hymns, and are so familiar with them that they may be truly called their national music.[1]

Unlike the Russian and other Slavonic races the Poles are singularly exempt from Asiatic influences. At an early date they accepted the Roman Catholic faith ; and while adhering to the Slav language, they adopted the characters of the Latin alphabet. The Poles are excitable and more finely susceptible to romance than the Russians, and their music is full of fire and passion. Their songs are somewhat wanting in melodic invention, though this deficiency is hidden by the wonderful skill with which they are varied and embellished ; and they are marked by a poetic melancholy which makes them attractive. In colouring they are instrumental rather than vocal, as revealed in their difficult intervals :

3.

etc.

Ej ej sla - zy   dow-ka   ej ej   wedie

It is rather to their characteristic and striking rhythms, free, varied and elastic and yet contained in dance forms, such as the *polonez*, *krakowiak*, and especially the *mazur* or *mazurek*, that they owe their rare beauty and brilliance. The *mazurek* (see MAZURKA) is usually a melancholy yet quick and strongly accented dance-song in 3–4 time ; the *tempo* is irregular and closely follows the words. These may treat of peasant occupations—hay-making, harvest, vintage, or of love, sorrow, parting, or meeting. Some of the oldest *mazurs*, *polonezes* (see POLONAISE), and more especially the hymns, take their name from a battle or historic event recounted in the text. The *krakowiak* (see CRACOVIENNE) is described by C. Miaskowski in a book of poems published in 1632, proving that this lively dance-song in duple time has long been popular in the country. And to the same date and genre belong the *gregorianki*— songs which the market-women of Cracow sing on the festival of their patron-saint.

In scientific and ecclesiastical composers

Poland excelled for many centuries, but in the 17th century these gave place to Italian musicians, who reigned supreme at court. The first efforts to counteract the Italian influence were made by KAMINSKY, J. STEFANI and J. ELSNER in the second half of the 18th century. These founders of Polish national opera, by incorporating a large number of their country's songs into their works, won immense popularity. Elsner also wrote many volumes of songs, besides two treatises on the rhythm and prosody of the Polish language and its suitableness for singing.

Rather earlier in the same century the charming poems of François Karpinski were set to music—either to original or adapted tunes, and, sung by rich and poor alike, belonged in their turn to the national song-group, such for instance, as ' Yuz miesionç zeszell ' (' Déjà la lune se lève '), which is still heard. In 1816 the poet Niemcewicz published his great work, *Spiewy historyczne z muzyka i rycinami* (Historical Songs with Music), and invited the best-known musicians (men and women) of the day to compose or arrange melodies for it. This work, which included some of the oldest hymns (amongst them the celebrated ' Boga Rodziça '), war-songs and legends, stimulated the patriotism of the Polish nation, and is cherished by every class.

In most of the songs belonging to the early part of the last century the national characteristics are to be found ; and especially is this the case with those of Ig. F. Dobrzynski, E. Jenicke, W. Kazynski, Ig. Komorowski, M. Madeyski, J. Nowakowski, A. Sowinski, C. J. Wielhorski, K. Wysoçki and A. Zarzycki. But while these composers are hardly known beyond their native country, CHOPIN and MONIUSZKO attained a world-wide reputation. Though neither were wholly Poles by birth, they closely identified themselves with the Polish national spirit. Both drew from the beautiful Lithuanian[2] folk-music, and especially from the *dainos*,[3] which, monotonous as they are, yet possess a peculiar charm.[4] Moniuszko borrowed many traditional tunes from other Slavonic provinces, but all his songs are deservedly loved and sung throughout Poland, Galicia and Lithuania. Chopin's seventeen songs, op. 74, were written at different periods of his life, and vary widely in character. The words of most are by his friend S. Witwicki, others are by A. Mickiewicz, Zaleski and Krasinski. Some of the songs may be traced to traditional sources, so far as the melody goes,[5] but Chopin's exquisitely refined harmony raises them to a high artistic

---

[1] Two hymns to the Virgin and a Resurrection hymn are especially celebrated, and these were printed by the Abbé Mioduzewsky in his collections of sacred songs at Cracow in 1838. For further information on these historic hymns, see E. Oloff, *Polnische Liedergeschichte*, '744.

[2] The Lithuanians are said to be of Sanscrit origin, and their language differs widely from that of other Slavonic nations.

[3] A term for secular songs in contradistinction to *ge'sme*, sacred songs.

[4] L. D. Rhesa collected a large quantity of old Lithuanian songs and published them at Berlin in 1826, with remarks on their metre and rhythm.

[5] Karasowski states that many songs sung by the people in Poland are attributed to Chopin, and chief among them one called ' The third of May,' Fr. *Chopin*, p. 162.

value. Three of the most beautiful are the 'Lithuanian Song' (written in 1831), the tender and sad 'Melodya' (1847), and the strange 'Dwojaki koniec' (Two corpses), with the simple Choral-like air. But those in the mazurka form, such as 'Zyczenie' ('Maiden's Desire'), 1829; 'Moja Pieszezotka' ('My Joys'), and 'Pierścień' ('The Ring'), 1844, are more widely known and sung.

Ig. PADEREWSKI resembles Chopin in one respect; he is national without being a slave to it, and yet on hearing his songs one feels that no one but a Pole could have written them. In some an undercurrent of sadness prevails, veiled by a proud reserve, as for instance in op. 7. Others are brilliant and effective, and the accompaniments always developed and interesting. Other modern song-writers of Poland are SZYMANOWSKI, SZOPSKI, FITELBERG and RÓŻYCKI (q.v.).

BIBLIOGRAPHY

OLOFF, E. *Polnische Liedergeschichte.* Danzig, 1744. (Chiefly on Sacred songs.)
POTOCKI, TG. *La Littérature mus polonaise.* 1818.
SIKORSKI, J. *Ruch Musyjozny.* 1857–62.
SOWINSKI, A. *Les Musiciens polonais.* Paris, 1857.
CHODZKO, J. L. *Histoire populaire de la Pologne.* Paris, 1864.
GLOGER, Z. *Singt noch das polnische Volk.*
JARZEMSKI, A. *Histoire de la musique en Pologne.*

COLLECTIONS

FONTANA, J. 'Polish National Melodies.' Chappell, London, 1830.
SOWINSKI, J. 'Chants polonais nationaux.' Paris, 1832.
KONOPKA, J. 'Pieśni ludu Krakowskiego.' Cracow, 1840.
RHESA, R. S. 'Dainos, oder Litthaunische Volksl.' Berlin, 1843.
MIODUSZEWSKI (ABBÉ). 'Pastoralki i Kolendy z Melodyami.' Cracow, 1845.
NESSELMANN. '410 Dainos, mit deutscher Übersetz. und Mus.' Berlin, 1843.
KOLBERG, H. O. Pieśni ludu polskiego.' Warsaw, 1857–90.
ROGER, J. ' Pieśne ludu Polskiego w Gornym Szlasku.' Breslau, 1863.
BERGGREEN. 'Folke-Sange og Melodier.' Copenhagen, 1866.
KOLBERG, H. O. ' Pieśni ludu litewskiego.' Cracow, 1879.
GLOGER, Z. 'Rutheniche und lithauische Volkweisen.'
BARTSCH, C. ' Dainu Balsai. Melodien lithauischer Volkslieder.' Heidelberg, 1886–89.
KOLBERG, H. O. ' La Mazowsze.' Cracow, 1885–90.
GLOGER, Z., and NOSZKOWSKI, Z. ' Pieśni ludu.' Cracow, 1892.
NAST, L. ' Die Volkslieder der Lithauer.' Tilsit, 1893.
JUSZKIEWICZ, A. ' Litauische Volksweisen ' (new edition). Cracow, 1900.

CZECHOSLOVAKIA (BOHEMIA)

When Christianity was first introduced into Bohemia, the influence of the Church was strenuously exerted to suppress the songs of the people; but the effort was made in vain, and the nation continued to sing its popular songs. The *Koledy* (Christmas songs), which are still in use, are generally acknowledged to be of pagan origin. As in other countries, the early Christian Church allowed the congregation to join in the Kyrie Eleison, and the oldest Bohemian hymn is merely a translation and development of this ' Krleš.' Tradition ascribes it to St. Adalbert[1]; it was really a prayer for peace and mercy, and was sung both in churches and on the battlefield as the national song. Another celebrated hymn, which holds the same place, was dedicated in the 13th century to St. Wencelas, the patron saint of Bohemia.[2] These national hymns and the so-called

Rorate,[3] are a compound of liturgical melodies and secular folk-songs. They are peculiar to Bohemia, and were allowed to be sung in the vernacular, and thus belonged to the people not less than the Church. Then later, during the Hussite movement, a like popular spirit reasserted itself in the Church. The Hussites and the Bohemian Brothers chose many secular melodies for their hymns, and thus again the hymns passed into genuine folk-songs.[4] One of the earliest and most famous of examples belonging to the first half of the 15th century is the Hussite Battle-Song, of which the first line runs thus:

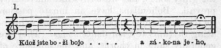

1.

Kdož jste bo - ži bojo . . . . a zá - ko-na je - ho,

As samples of the secular music of the 15th and 16th centuries the folk-songs preserved in the *Cancionales* are of great value. The Hussite songs are for the most part of a grave and stern character; while those of the Bohemian or Moravian Brothers have a more tender and sensuous cast. It should be observed that the Bohemians have long been called Czechs, and that name has been adopted for the national language and music. But in their origin the Czechs were only one of the many Slavonic tribes which constitute the nationality of Bohemia and Moravia. There are some differences between the Bohemian and Moravian songs. In the former there is a predominance of songs in the major scale, while those which seem to be in the minor scale more properly belong to the ecclesiastical modes. In Moravia the balance is equal; the tunes are of a bold decisive character, with a strongly marked rhythm. In this country also the songs of each district are distinct,[5] and hence flows a greater wealth and variety of song. In Bohemia, on the other hand, which is homogeneous, all parts being alike, a fuller unity exists in the songs. They are more tuneful and tender, their rhythm is simpler and the form is more regular and developed owing to the influence which German music has exercised in Bohemia.[6] Common to both and characteristic of all Bohemian songs is a vein of natural, unaffected humour, and a close connexion between the verbal and musical accents. The tunes rarely begin on the weak beat of the bar, just as in the speaking language the accent is always on

---

[1] It is given in facsimile in Hostinsky's article on Bohemian Music in *Die öst.-ung. Monarchie.*
[2] This hymn was composed by Arnest, Archbishop of Prague, and is given in Hostinsky's article referred to above.

[3] The *Rorate* are joyful Advent hymns, and some have been preserved in a beautiful *Cancionale* of the 14th century at Prague.
[4] To John Hus (Huss) only one sacred song can with authority be attributed. ' Stala matka zalostiva,' which contains three strophes of equal length, and a melisma of three notes to a syllable, and is nearly diatonic.
[5] The Slovaks and Slavonic Czechs are the principal inhabitants of Moravia.
[6] It is interesting to note the difference between the two Slavonic countries. The song may belong to both of them, but with distinct variants, though more perhaps in the words than in the music. The love of nature is a strongly marked characteristic in the Bohemian folk-songs. For instance most of their songs refer to a flower, or a tree, or a bird, or a stream, or a lake, whether it be employed in a literal or metaphorical sense.

the first syllable. The form is sometimes in three-bar phrases, which in the longer songs develops into four bars in the middle, returning again to the three-bar phrase for the close :

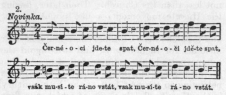

2.
Novinka.

Čer-né - o - ci jde-te spat, Čer-né - o - či jdě-te spat,

vsák mu-sí-te rá-no vstát, vsak mu-sí-te rá-no vstát.

The harmony is always simple, and except in the gipsy songs, the western scales universally prevail. Bohemians have an innate passion for dancing, which imparts marked and exhilarating rhythms to their dance songs. They are generally sung in chorus, and the influence of their national instrument, the ' Dudy,' or bagpipe, is often apparent.

Their many and varied dances (such as the *beseda, dudík, furiant, hulan, kozak, polka, sedlák, trinožka,* etc.) take their names from the occasions on which they have been danced, or even more frequently from the songs with which they are accompanied. There is a close association between the folk-songs and the folk-dances of Bohemia. The greater part of the songs met with in modern collections are of no older date than the 18th century, but there are several exceptions, such as the Hussite Battle-Song, or the tune of ' Proč Kalino,' which was constantly sung in the 15th and 16th centuries, and ' Sedlák z Prahy,' which was composed in 1609.

In the 17th century there was a widespread cultivation of music in Bohemia ; both part-singing and instrumental music were salient features of domestic life. Wenzel Karl Holan (Rovensky) published a large song-book called ' Kaple Kralovská zpèvní.' The harmony is bold and varied, and the accompaniments for lute and violin, organ or wind-instruments, are skilfully composed.

In the 18th century foreign influences were more marked. German, French and Italian musicians crowded the principal towns of Bohemia, while the native musicians, such as BENDA, DUSSEK, REICHA, GYROWETZ (*q.v.*), etc., on the other hand, sought a living abroad, where their compositions were more likely to attract notice and interest. Meanwhile, the true national music of the country was being kept alive chiefly by the village schoolmasters, who acted as organists, choir and bandmasters. Each parish had its own choir, chorus and band; and every child was taught the study of music with as much precision as reading, writing and arithmetic. Naturally, therefore, village music attained to a high level under such conditions.[1]

Early in the 19th century attempts were

made by certain Czech composers to restore the lost prestige of their country's music and language. One of the first composers of real Bohemian songs was Ryba, who was followed by Kanka, Doležalek and Kniže.[2] But a more important factor in music was the national opera. The first opera was written by F. Škroup and the poet Chmelensky. Škroup's name is, however, best preserved by his song ' Kde domov muj ? '[3] (' There, where my home is '), now adopted as the national hymn of the Czechs. Between 1823 and 1830 Chmelensky and F. Škroup, together with TOMASCHEK and Th. Krov̌ published many songs. Among other song-writers there may be cited the names of Zvonař, Procházka, Malat, Shukerský, Vojaček and Smetana's precursor, KŘIŽKOVSKY (*q.v.*). The general characteristics of their songs may be described as a flowing and clear *cantilena*, recalling to mind the traits of Italian song. Their harmony and rhythm are very simple ; and their sentiment and humour have the grace of spontaneity.

F. SMETANA reproduced in his own works the true Bohemian spirit, and mostly so in his national operas and symphonic poems. In the latter he has used occasional folk-songs, and one called ' Tabor ' is really a splendid polyphonic fantasia on the Hussite battle-song (see SMETANA). Nor are the national songs forgotten in DVOŘÁK's music. In the overture called ' Husitska ' he introduces the St. Wencelas and the Hussite hymns. Dvořák, W. Blodek, Rozkošný, Šebor and Karel Bendl have tried to carry the merry humorous spirit of the Bohemian peasant into their music.

The extraordinary development of Bohemian music during the later half of the 19th century is mainly owing to the enthusiasm of modern Czech composers for their country's melodious folk-songs and merry dances. The reason for this enthusiasm was partly political. The patriotic songs kept alive the aspirations of a misgoverned people. Music played its part in the renaissance of the 19th century. Smetana gave the art the earnestness of a national cult ; Dvořák's music is penetrated by fervent racial sentiment. These two composers created a school of Czech music and left disciples to carry on their work. The neighbourhood of Slovakia with its grand scenery and characteristic customs exercised an influence upon Czech artists and musicians comparable with that of Scotland upon our romanticists. Of the many musicians who experienced the lure of Slovakia Vítezlav NOVÁK (*q.v.*) is the best known outside Czechoslovakia.

With the establishment of the republic in 1918, a fresh stimulus was given to social and

---

[1] See Burney's *Present State of Music in Germany,* ii. 12, 14, 41.

[2] Kniže's popular ballad ' Bretislava Jitka ' is to be found in most collections. For other well-known songs, such as Krov̌'s ' Husitská,' Škroup's ' Kde domov muj,' Rosenkranz's ' Chaloupka,' Dietrich's ' Moravo,' see Fr. Zahorsky's ' Českých národních písní.'

[3] This is the blind fiddler's song which Škroup wrote for J. Tyl's musical play *Fidlovačka,* in 1831.

artistic life. Modern tendencies and new impulses made themselves felt in the country. The folk-songs are sung as much as ever. The schools and the Sokols (gymnastic clubs) will not let them be forgotten. Every year brings a crop of new collections and arrangements. But they are no longer regarded as essential creative material. The folk-song school is dying out, and while the veneration of Smetana as seer and patriot has lost nothing of its old fervour, he is no longer, musically, the ideal model of the younger generation of composers. JANÁČEK (q.v.) is the chief representative of the folk idea in music, but in technique and conception he stands at the opposite pole to Smetana. He is, however, an enthusiastic connoisseur and collector, and to him we are indebted for the list of collections here given.

COLLECTIONS

BLAHOSLAV, JAN. 'Musica.' 1569.
ČELAKOVSKY. 'Slovanské národní písně' (Slavonic Folk-songs). 1822.
'Pisně národ' (Folk-songs). 1824.
SUŠIL, F. 'Morav. nár písně (Moravian Folk-songs), 1832; a second collection, 1859.
ERBEN, K. J. 'Pisně České' (Czech songs). 1862.
KOŽELUH, FR. Kytice znárodní písně' (A bouquet of National Songs). 1873.
'Radhost.' 1874.
'Slavia.' 1877–80.
'Slovenské spěvy' (Slovak Songs). 1880.
PECK, E. 'Národní pisně (Folk-songs). 1884.
'Staré zpěby národ. ve Vel. Ořechově' (Old Folk-songs of Great Ořechov). 1888.
BARTOŠ, F. 'Pisně moravské' (Moravian Songs). 1889.
'Morav. Svatba ',(Moravian Wedding Songs). 1892.
BARTOŠ and JANÁČEK. 'Nár. písně Moravské' (Folk-songs of Moravia). 1901.
BAKEŠOVA, L. 'Královnicky' (Festival Dancing Songs). 1891.
ZÍBRT, DR. C. 'Bibliografický přehled Čes. národ. pisně' (Bibliographical Survey of Czech National Songs). 1895.
KOCMAN, MET. 'Pisně lida z Tronbska' (Folk-songs from Tronbsko). 1895.
CERNÍK, J. 'Zpěvy morav. Kopaničářů' (Songs of the Moravian Cotters). 1908.
LISA, V, 'Slovensky lidové pisně' (Songs of the Slovak People). 1912.
'Pisničky modlosluzcbníki' (Songs of the Idolators). 1917.

To Janáček's list may be added a few more popular and accessible collections:

MALÁT, J. 'Česky národni Poklad' (A Treasury of Czech (also Moravian and Slovak) Folk-songs). Prague, 1886–95.
KUBA (q.v.) 'Slovanstvo ve svych zpěvech' (The Slavs in their Songs). Hudební Matice, Prague.
ERBEN. 'Chansons tchèques populaires.' Prague, 1886.
NOVÁK, VÍT. Slovak Songs for voice and piano, also for male voice choir (several collections). Hudební Matice.
See also FIGUŠ-BYSTRI, FRANCISI, LICHARD and SCHNEIDER-TRNAVSKY.

BIBLIOGRAPHY

Articles in Bohemian newspapers Dalibor, and Literárni přiloha, 1860–65. L. ZVONAŘ.
MELIŠ, E. Böhmische Musik.
Articles in Die österreich.-ungarische Monarchie: Böhmen; (a) Volkslied und Tanz der Slaven; (b) Musik in Böhmen, by O. HOSTINSKY, 1894–96.
MAURICE, E. Bohemia from the Earliest Times, etc. London, 1896.
SOUBIES, A. Histoire de la musique. Bohème. Paris, 1898.
Geschichte des vorhussitischen Gesanges in Böhmen (pub. by the Kgl. böhmische Gesellschaft). Prague, 1904.
BATKA, R. Geschichte der Musik in Böhmen (still appearing), 1st vol. Prague, 1906.

A. H. W.; rev. R. N.

HUNGARY

The songs of Hungary comprise both those of the Slavs and the Magyars, but the music of the Slovaks, who now form a part of the Czechoslovak Republic, is of Slavonic origin and has been noticed under Czechoslovakia. The music of the Magyars,[1] which is generally accepted as the national music, is of Oriental origin. It should be observed that the Hungarian language has nothing in common with the Indo-Germanic. Together with the Finnish and Turkish (and possibly Basque) languages, it stands isolated in Europe, and belongs to the Turanian or Ural-Altaic family.

Gipsy music also plays an important part in Hungary (see MAGYAR MUSIC). Although the same melodic intervals and rhythmic peculiarities occur in Tsigane music all over the world, it was in Hungary, where an affinity of scale existed, that gipsy music reached its highest point. Among the Magyar gipsies—i.e. those gipsies who live among the Magyars and can speak their language—the songs may have gipsy words, but the actual tune and rhythm are Magyar. Moreover, the gipsies rarely sing and nearly always play the songs of other nations, imparting their own fire, impetuosity and embellishments to the music of their adoption.[2] It is often difficult, when the gipsies play the csárdás, verbunkos, hallgatós, or palatos and other dances, to recognise the original folk-song on which they are based.

As in other countries, so in Magyar-land, the introduction of Christianity was followed by a burst of hymn-poetry. But so strong was the national feeling that the hymns were sung even in the churches in the vernacular instead of Latin; also it seems that the ecclesiastical tonal system never took the same hold of the sacred music as it did elsewhere. A few of these venerable hymns are still sung. Such, for instance, is one sung to the Virgin, by Andreas Vásárheli (printed at Nuremberg, 1484) and another to King Stephen, the patron saint of Hungary. Again, the influence of the Reformation was deeply felt both in music and poetry; and there arose among the Protestants a literature of hymn-music, such as had already been stirred among the Hungarian Roman Catholics. In 1560 the Roman Catholic Church forbade, under severe penalties, the use in church of any popular Magyar songs, but the old collections of both churches offer proof that the tunes of the secular songs were always freely used, set either to Latin or Hungarian sacred words.

Further evidence of the cultivation of music in the 16th century is supplied by the Hoffgraff collection[3] and by the songs of Sebastian Tinódi, both published by G. Matray in 1859. Tinódi, commonly called Sebastian the Lutenist, died about 1559, and was the last survivor of Hungary's wandering minstrels. His 'Cronica,' dedicated to King Ferdinand, contains songs of battles lost and won, of the joys and sorrows of the Magyar people and the vicissitudes of their

---

[1] The origin of their language can hardly be traced with certainty. Hungarian philologists are divided; the 'Orientalists' assert its affinity with the Turco-Tartaric languages, while the 'Finnists' contend that it belongs to the Ugric branch of the Finnish group. That some likeness exists between the Magyar and Finnish language and music has long been recognised.

[2] The true gipsy songs are never sung by the 'professional' gipsy in public. Those songs are reserved exclusively for themselves in their tented wanderings, and there they are never played but always sung. See Archduke Joseph's article in vol. vi. (Ungarn) of Die österreich.-ungarische Monarchie, 1902.
[3] The collection contains nineteen songs, chiefly Biblical narrative songs, by K. Bajnaj, M. Szártary, M. Tarjai, A. Farkas and others.

destiny. Such songs being truly national in their spirit soon passed into folk-songs, and are sung at this day.[1] It should also be noticed that dramatic representations interspersed with songs were introduced by these wandering minstrels, harpists and lutenists, and secured a great popularity.

Neither in the 17th nor 18th century did the development of music keep pace with that of poetry, except in sacred lyrics. The difference between the melodies of the Roman Catholic churches on the one hand and of the Protestants on the other is curious and worthy of note. The Roman Catholic melodies were of a florid and ornamented character, with passing notes and chromatic intervals, which may have been due to the instrumental music used in their churches. But the Protestants adhered to severely simple melodies in the style of Goudimel, for a time at least. As the hymns became folk-songs, the strong national rhythm prevailed, and changed their character. Thus:

1.

The most remarkable feature, both of the poetry and the music of the Hungarians, is the rhythm. At an early date their lyric poetry shaped itself into sharp and bold strophical sections, and their melodies underwent a corresponding division into distinct phrases and periods. Great diversity of accents, and the unequal length of the lines, impart richness and variety to the musical rhythm. In the music of some nations there is a rhythmical and metrical sameness, but in Hungarian it is far more varied. The prevailing metrical feet are the choriambus: $|-\cup\cup-|$ and the antispastus: $|\cup--\cup|$. Most tetrapodics are like this: $|$ ♪ ♪ ♪ ♪ $|$ ♩ ♩ $|$ ♪ ♪ ♩ $|$ ♩ ♪ ♪ $|$, but constantly three or even five and seven-bar rhythms are met with. The correct accentuation and phrasing of Hungarian music is closely interwoven with the language. Every first syllable has an emphasis of its own, whether short, as in Ex. 2, or long, as in Ex. 3, and

2.
Lento.

3.

Far & high the cranes give cry & spread their wings.

[1] For Tinódi's life see Áron Szilády's *Régi Magyar Költök Tára*, a recent work on old Maygar poets.

hence the reason why no song begins with the up-beat.[2] The constant recurrence of syncopation and the augmented intervals have already been alluded to under MAGYAR MUSIC. The scales in which the songs fall are very varied; numerous instances of the Dorian and Phrygian modes occur, nor are the augmented seconds in the minor scale so prevalent as is generally believed. The following example begins with the peculiar ' call ' found in many Hungarian songs[3]:

4.　　　　　　　　　　Long pause.

All Hungarian music has a strongly individual character. Its abrupt transition from deep melancholy to wild merriment, its variations of tempo, its richly applied cæsuras, constant ⌢ on different beats of the bar, its unexpected modulations, and its many peculiarities, both melodic and rhythmic, give to it the charm of distinctive originality. A few bars of this beautiful folk-song[4] will suffice to indicate the characteristics here named.

5.
Slow.

The time of Hungarian national airs, whether songs or dances, is mostly 2–4. Triple and compound time are rare, excepting 5–4 or 5–8, or 7–4 and 7–8, of which many examples may be found in any collection. The Hungarians are rich in their historic ballads relating to national events. For instance, during the Rakoczy period the celebrated and sturdy Kurutzen songs, or old Crusaders' songs, were revived and widely sung[5] (see RAKOCZY MARCH). The ballads from the Szekler district are very old; they are mostly sad and simple, as may be seen in the example on next page.[6]

Many districts have kept strictly to their own special songs; and have jealously excluded any outside influence or innovation. Such are the above-named Szekler ballads, the oldest and the most beautiful of the national Hungarian songs; or the Puszten songs, in which

[2] F. Korbay, *Nationality in Music.* The English words given in Ex. 3 are those of Korbay's setting.
[3] Given by Béla Bartók. An examination of any good collection of these folk-songs would prove the truth of the above remarks.
[4] Called ' Autumn ' in J. Kappey's ' Songs of Eastern Europe.'
[5] Julius Káldy published in 1892 about thirty ' Liedweisen aus der Thököly- und Rakoczi-zeit,' under the title of ' Kurutzenlieder.'
[6] This was taken down from the lips of the peasants by Béla Bartók.

the true Magyar peasant life is reflected, and the Betyar songs. The different classes of

songs fall into clearly distinct sets, such as love and wedding songs, drinking, soldiers', peasants', funeral and satirical songs, all of which Jokai has described in an interesting manner.[1]

The first national opera ('Béla's Flight') was written in 1823 by Ruzsicska, and though a slight work it contained some songs which immediately became popular. Heinisch and Bartay followed, but the first unmistakably successful opera was Franz Erkel's 'Maria Bathori,' given in 1840, with words by the famous Benjamin Egressy; and Erkel may with justice be designated as the creator of the Hungarian national opera. Erkel was also a prolific composer of songs, some of which were embodied in his operas; and he was the author of the Hungarian national hymn. Other successful writers of opera were F. and K. Doppler, Reyer. K. Huber, Szerdahelyi, A. Erkel, G. Császár, and most of these composers freely used their country's folk-songs. Moreover, there is a specifically Hungarian form of drama called the folk-play (Volkschauspiel), the matter for which is taken from the domestic life of the people, and its music consists entirely of folk-songs and folk-dances. E. Szigligetti was the originator of this form, and J. Szerdahelyi, Ig. Bognár, Jul. Káldy, Jul. Erkel, A. Nikolits and others contributed to establish it. These folk-plays have at least served to rescue many beautiful melodies from oblivion.

Among the song-writers of the 19th century who adhered to the national school, the best-known names are Michael Mosonyi[2] and his pupils, the two Erkels and E. Mihalovich. The Magyar songs of this last-mentioned composer are more especially beautiful and poetical. Béla M. Végvölgyi is also worthy of notice on account of the originality and popularity of his songs entitled 'Szerelmi dalok'; and not less worthy of notice is his valuable collection of national airs under the title of 'Népdalgyöngyök.' Other names may be cited, such as E. Székely, Cornel, L. Zimay, K. Huber, Abrányi senior (his ballads are essentially Hungarian), E. Bartay, E. Moór, S. Bartalus and V. Langer, whose song-cycle 'Ögyek's songs' is especially noteworthy. Benjamin Egressy likewise main-

tained a great popularity among the peasants and burghers during the first half of the 19th century. His songs may be found in every national collection, together with those of E. Szentirmay, Limbay, Simonffy, Erkel, Horváth, Füredy, Janko, Bolla, Zagonyi, etc.

F. Korbay's songs, either original or arranged, are well known in England. In the two volumes entitled 'Hungarian Songs,' and the volume of 'Twelve Magyar Songs,' Korbay has taken some of the most beautiful songs of his country.[3]

The greatest song-writer of Hungarian birth is Franz Liszt (q.v.); although considering the fact that the larger number of his songs have German texts they would be more accurately classed as belonging to the German school. Moreover, the national elements—the Magyar rhythms and melodies, and the gipsy ornaments which abound in his instrumental music—are, with two exceptions—'Farewell' and the 'Three Gipsies'—absent from his vocal music.[4]

Among Hungarian song-writers of the present day, Emil Abrányi, Pista Dankó, Béla Bartók and Ernö Lanyi stand on a high level. Many, such as Erdélyi, Bartalus, Káldy, Bognár, Bartók, Kodály and others, have devoted their time to exploring, collecting, arranging and publishing the old and modern folk-music of their country, greatly assisted by the Kisfaludy Society, which was formed for the express purpose. The Raaber collection, which is still appearing, must also be named.

BIBLIOGRAPHY:

Liszt, F. Die Zigeuner und ihre Musik in Ungarn. Presburg, 1861. Die österreichisch-ungarische Monarchie: vol. i. (Ungarn) contains Die magyarische Volksdichtung, by M. Jokai; Die ungarische Palastmusik und die Volkslieder, by S. Bartalus. 1888. Vol. iii. Die kirchliche Musik, by S. Bartalus, and Die weltliche Musik, by Julius Káldy. 1893. (Detailed accounts of numerous collections of songs are given in the above articles.)
Soubies, A. Hongrie. (Hist. de la musique), Paris, 1898.
Korbay, F. Nationality in Music.
Dr. Pressel's account of Hungarian music in vol. xxxvi. of the Neue Zeitschrift für Musik, and the article on Magyar music in this Dictionary.

COLLECTIONS

Matray, G. 'Magyar népdalok, etc.' Budapest, 1852–59.
Füredi, M. '100 Magyar Népdal.' Budapest, 1853.
Bartalus, S. 'The Hungarian Orpheus.' 1869. (A collection of 18th and 19th century music, containing many old folk-songs from the Adam Paloczi-Horvath MS.)
Bartalus, S. 'Magyar népdalok.' (7 vols.)
Györffy, J. 50 Magyar népdal, etc.' Budapest, 1871.
László, Arany. 'Magyar népköltési gyujtemény.' Budapest, 1872–82.
Földes, J., and Demeter, R. 'Emlék.' Budapest, 1876.
Kalmany, L. 'Szeged népe.' Aradon, 1881–82, 1882.
Goll, J. 'Enektan polgári iskolák. Budapest, 1884–88.
Bornemiszza, Y. '150 Bordal, etc.' Budapest, 1888.
Berger-Henderson, Mme. 'Album of 16 Hungarian Songs.' London, 1889.
Deák, G. 'Daloskönyv Két és harom szólamu, etc.' Budapest, 1892.
Káldy, G. 'Schätze der alten ungarischen Musik' (1672–1838). Budapest, 1892.
Végvölgyi, B. M. 'Népdalgyöngyök.'
Elemér, Limbay, Bolla G. and Nemesovits, E. 'Magyar dal Album.' Budapest.
Korbay, F. 'Hungarian Songs' and '12 Magyar Songs.'
László, Kún. '1000 Népdalok.' (Still appearing), 1905. 'A Magyar Dal.' Budapest, 3 vols. 1906–7.
Palotasy, G. '101 Legszebb Magyar Nepdal.' Budapest.

---

[1] Die österreich.-ungarische Monarchie (Ungarn), vol. i. p. 347.
[2] His real name was Michael Brandt.

[3] Amongst them several by Elemér Szentirmay, Benjamin Egressy, Füredy, Kalman de Simonffy, etc.
[4] For detailed descriptions see Liszt; also Vogel's essay published by Kahnt, Leipzig, 1887, and Finck's Songs and Song-Writers.
[5] The writer also owes her warmest thanks to Béla Bartók for information, and for examples from his MS. collection of folk-songs.

FINLAND

Finland (Finnish *Suomi*) is 'the land of a thousand lakes,' vast stretches of moors, deep silent woods and long dark winters. These elements and scenery are reflected in the gloomy, mystical, fantastic yet monotonous poetry and music of the in-dwellers. No country is more poetic than Finland, as the *Kalevala* proves. This glorious national epic of nearly 23,000 verses has been transmitted from generation to generation from long past ages. The Finns also possess a very large quantity of lyric songs and ballads ; and to Elias Lönnrot (*d.* 1884) the credit is due for having given the nation these two treasures in a collected form : the national epics which form the *Kalevala* and the collection of lyrics which are entitled the *Kanteletar*.

The Finnish language, a branch of the Finnish-Ugric stem, is peculiarly melodious and full of open vowels. The verse metre is simple, and consists mostly of trochees, four times repeated—the last foot being lengthened in order to mark the close of the line :

hŭwă | kĕllŏ | kăŭwăs | kŭŭlŭŭ

This is the usual explanation of the five-beat rhythm in the music, which is the commonest in the old Finnish songs or *runos*,[1]

1.

Kĕwy kasky tai-wa has-ta, Kĕwy kasky tai-wa has-ta,

Kaiken luondon Hal-di al-da, Kaiken luondon Haldi al-da. [2]

2.   RUNO.

Jos mun tut-tu-ni tulisi ja-tu li--si,

Ar-ma-ha-ni as-te-lei-si, as-te-lei-si

and it is clear that in aiming to make these melodies agree with their poetry the irregular and unsymmetrical 5- or 7-time did not appear to the Finns either forced or unnatural.

As in all other national music, the musical instruments are closely connected with the melodies of the country. In Finland the oldest and most popular instrument is the *kantele*, a kind of lyre or harp with five copper strings tuned *g, a, b♭, c, d*, on which five notes a large mass of the old *runo* melodies are formed (see above example). These melancholy and monotonous *runolaulua*, characterised by con-

[1] *Runo* or *runolaulua* means 'air' or 'ballad,' and has nothing to do with the Anglo-Saxon *runes* or runic writing-stones.
[2] Ilmari Krohn, in an article entitled *De la mesure à cinq temps dans la musique populaire finnoise*, *Sammelbände* of the Int. Mus. Ges. ii. 1. 1900, considers that the above example (which is a type of the *Kalevala* melodies) is wrongly noted, and suggests two alternative metrical schemes.

stant repetition, are usually accompanied by the *kantele*. Mention is made in the *Kalevala* of this instrument being used to accompany the songs ; also of the 'sighing verses ' which in the *runo* songs are a refrain of actual realistic sobbing sighs. Dance tunes also adhere to the *kantele* intervals, and at the same time to the song-rhythms, as :

3.

Some writers,[3] however, deny that this instrument had so great an influence on the old Finnish tunes, and contend that, as vocal music is older than instrumental, it is more probable that the melodies were based on the pentatonic scale. A further proof of this theory is that the Finnish-Ugric race is of Asiatic origin.

The *Kanteletar* is a large collection of lyrics and ballads. These songs reflect the restrained melancholy of the national character ; they are full of deep feeling and tenderness, and absolutely natural and spontaneous. A few of these lyric songs are to be found in 5-time, though this time is chiefly confined to the old sacred folk-songs, and more especially to the ancient *runo* melodies. In common with other folk-songs of Western Europe, some of the Finnish melodies have their basis in the ecclesiastical modes ; but there are traces of an older and as yet unfathomed and unexplained tonal influence which gives a peculiar interest to the music of this country. Those which come from the southern part of Finland, where nature is less severe, possess a certain idyllic cheerfulness, and many which are sung along the coast are undoubtedly of Scandinavian origin. These melodies range over a wider compass, the rhythm is more varied, and they are usually in common or triple time and more often than not in our modern tonality[4] :

4.

Tuuti las-ta Tuonelahan, Alla nurmen nukkuma-han

Tuonen lasten lau-la-tel-la manan nei-to-jen pi-del-lä.

The herdsmen's songs (*Paimen loilottamus*), as in Scandinavia, are numerous. They are closely akin to the notes of the herdsman's pipe, and of no definite form in tune or words.

Between the 12th and 14th centuries Sweden took possession of and christianised Finland, but it was only in towns and at court that the Swedish language was used. Finland has always been an apple of discord between Sweden and Russia, and the perpetual wars

[3] See Engel, *Introduction to the Study of National Music*, p. 59 *et seq.*
[4] For some of the most beautiful, see G. Hägg's collection, 'Soreimmat Soinnut Suomesta.'

hindered this country's artistic development. Finally, from 1809 onwards, when it was conquered by Russia, strenuous efforts towards its complete Russification never ceased. Russia never succeeded, however, in taking away from Finland her own peculiar character and culture.

The modern history of music in Finland begins early in the 19th century, when F. Pacius and B. Crusell, both Germans by birth, settled there. By using Finnish folk-songs in their works, and taking the words of Finnish poets, such as Runeberg, Qvanten, Topelius, etc., for their national songs and hymns, they awoke the spirit of patriotism in Finland, and hence have been justly called the fathers of Finnish music. PACIUS (q.v.), who died at a great age in 1891, wrote many fresh and effective songs, but his name will live for having given Finland her national hymns : ' Our Country ' (' Värt Land ') and ' Finland's Song ' (' Suomen laulu '), which every Finn knows and sings from his childhood. (See Ex. 5.)

His son-in-law, Karl Kollan, wrote also patriotic songs in the peculiar march-like rhythm which is popular in Finland. Crusell was a prolific and favourite composer, but his melodies are commonplace. K. Greve, L. Bergström, M. Wegelius, Ph. von Schantz, G. Wasenius, F. Ehrstrom, K. Flodin, S. Linsén, H. Borenius, R. Faltin and a younger generation which includes O. Merikanto,

5.

F. PACIUS.

Hear, the glorious song is ring-ing Thro' the ancient halls of Wai - - no: It is Suomi's song! It is Suo-mi's song!

etc.

O. Katilainen, P. Hannikainen and S. Palmgren all belong, more or less, to the same school of song-writers. Whilst introducing many of the old Finnish folk-songs into their works and choosing the words of Finnish poets for their songs, the music practically belongs to the German Mendelssohn-Spohr period, and cannot in any sense be called racial.

The true national period of Finnish music begins with R. Kajanus. Imbued with the classic-romantic traditions, yet heart and soul a Finn, Kajanus drew his inspirations from the *Kalevala*, and did much to originate and stimulate interest in his country's music. But the actual representative of Finnish music is Jean SIBELIUS (q.v.) His songs, whilst original, dramatic and powerful, are the true counterpart of the Finnish folk-song. Essentially

modern in feeling, yet Sibelius uses frequently the old, simple scale, limited harmony and the curious uneven rhythm of the folk-songs. One of his most beautiful songs, with a modal melody, is ' Men min Fogel märks dock icke ' ; ' Svarta Rosar ' (' Black Roses ') is effective ; and ' Atinares Säng,' perhaps the best known, is a fine war-song in march-rhythm. If Sibelius be the lyric and dramatic representative of Finnish music, A. JÄRNEFELT (q.v.) may be called the epic. He has written many songs, but it is the peculiarly national ballad-like feeling in his orchestral works which arrests attention. Mention must also be made of Ilmari Krohn and E. Melartin (b. 1875), whose songs are of distinct merit.

BIBLIOGRAPHY

Über die finnische Musik (*Neue Zeitschrift f. Musik*), vol. xxxiv. p. 205. Leipzig, 1851.
FLODIN, K. *Die Entwickelung der Musik in Finnland* (*Die Musik*, Jahrgang ii.).
KROHN, ILMARI. *De la mesure à cinq temps dans la musique populaire finnoise, Sammelbände, I.M.G. i. 1900.
MENDEL. *Mus. Lexikon.*
WILLIBRAND, M. VON. *Finlande en XIXme siècle.* Paris, 1900.
PUDOR, H. *Zur Geschichte der Musik in Finnland, Sammelbände, I.M.G., II. i. 1900.
(The writer is also indebted to Dr. Ilmari Krohn for his kind help.)

COLLECTIONS

SCHRÖTER. ' Finnische Runen.' Stuttgart, 1834.
KOLLAN, K., and REINHOLM, A. ' Suomen Kansan Lautaatoja, Helsingfors, 1849 ; and ' Valituita Suomalaisia Kansan-Lauluja, Helsingfors, 1854.
ILBERG, F. V. ' Suomalaisia Kansan-Lauluja ja Soetelmia.' Helsingfors, 1867.
BORENIUS, A., and LINSÉN, G. ' Suomalaisia Kansan-Lauluja.' Helsingfors, 1880.
KROHN, ILMARI. ' Uusia Suomalaisia Kansanlauluja.' Helsingfors, 1886.
LAGUS, E. ' Nyländska Folkvisor ' (2 parts). Helsingfors, 1887–1900.
KAJANUS, R. ' Suomen Kansan Sävelmiä.' Helsingfors, 1888–92.
' Suomen Kansan Sävelmia ' (Melodies of the Finnish People), three series, published by the Finnish Literary Society [1] at Helsingfors ; 1st series, ' Hengellisiä Sävelmiä ' (Sacred Melodies), 1898 ; 2nd series, ' Kansanlauluja ' (Popular Songs), 1888 ; 3rd series, ' Kansantansseja ' (Popular Dances), 1893 (complete with German Introduction). The whole work is edited by I. Krohn.
HÄGG, G. ' Soreimmat Soinnut Suomesta.' Stockholm (5th edition), 1904.

SCANDINAVIA

To this group belong Sweden, Norway, Denmark, parts of Finland, Iceland and the adjacent islands. There is a great affinity between the Scandinavian languages. At the present time Danish is the language of the educated class in Norway, although it has a harder pronunciation.[2] And in an article written early in the last century, entitled *Alte Volksmelodien des Nordens*,[3] it was pointed out that the Swedish songs only differed from the Danish in dialect and not in language. Danish is also as much spoken as Norwegian in the Faroë Islands,[4] where also many Icelandic and Danish songs are heard.

The poetry of Scandinavia is peculiarly rich in ballads, legends and tales of ancient and mediæval warriors on sea or land—the heroic-epic element being abundant, while the lyric element plays little part except in the refrains

[1] *Suomalaisen Kirjallisuuden Seura.* Dr. Ilmari Krohn says that this publication, which is still in progress, will, when completed, be the fullest and most systematic collection.
[2] Chambers's *Encyclopædia*, 1891 edition.
[3] *Allg. mus. Zeitung*, No. 35, Aug. 18, 1816.
[4] 'Tanz, Dichtung und Gesang auf den Färöern,' *Sammelbände* of the I.M.G., III. pt. ii. 1902, H. Thuren.

to the ballads. The Scandinavians have always been a music-loving nation, but not until comparatively recent times have systematic collections of their folk-music been made.[1] Collectors have found great difficulty in taking down the music of the *Kämpavisor*,[2] owing to the free declamatory way in which they were sung. The formal melody occurs only in the refrains, or *Omkväde*, of the *Kämpavisor*. The *Omkväd*[3] (Danish *Omkvæd*), which is undoubtedly of very ancient origin, forms an important part of northern songs.[4] It may be a line at the end of each verse, used to strengthen the meaning of the poem, or a line interpolated in the middle of the verse corresponding with its contents ; or it may contain satirical or contemptuous remarks sung by a chorus ; or it may only concern the reciter, applauding and encouraging him.[5] Musically the *Omkväd* was the most important part of the song and remained always intact and unvaried, whereas the actual song was often improvised or changed according to the solo-singer's desire. In the Faroë Islands, for instance, the old ballads are still sung to the mediæval dances, and collectors often find variants in the songs themselves, whilst the refrains are identical in every part of the islands. The *Omkväd* naturally influences both the form and harmony of the songs. It necessitates the extension or repetition of a musical phrase, and sometimes a change of time and accent, which imparts a great freedom of form to the Scandinavian songs. Again, if the song be in the minor, the *Omkväd* would be in the major, or *vice versa* ; also if the song be sung as a solo, or in unison, the *Omkväd* is most frequently sung in parts.

1.   *Och Jungfrun.*

Och, jungfrun hon skul-le sig åt   ot-te sån-gen gå:
Oh ! the maiden she hurries   to   evensong;

OMKVÄD.

Tiden görs mig lång. Så gick hon den   vägen åt
Time   is   long. So   she went the   way by

höga   berget låg; Men jag vet att sor-gen är tung.
the   high hill; But I wot that sorrow is heavy.

These refrains are universal in Scandinavian songs, and occur as often in other forms as in the *Kämpavisor*.

It is a well-known fact (and has been briefly alluded to in several sections of this article) that some of the most famous folk-songs of different countries are founded on the same subject, whether it be a legendary or historical event, or an incident of ordinary life. The accessories of course vary and impart a local colouring to each version of the song, but the central theme is in all the same. In like manner the same tunes are the property of different countries.[6] Their identity may not, perhaps, be detected at first, beneath the disguises in which it is enveloped by national varieties of scale and rhythm and harmony ; but it is certain that closer examination would establish many relationships hitherto unsuspected. An especially strong affinity exists between the English, Scottish, Welsh, German and Scandinavian folk-poetry. This interesting subject, which is well worth separate study, can only be dwelt on shortly, and a few examples given. Geijer in his ' Svenska Folk-visor ' quotes three lines of a Norwegian folk-song, also heard in Wermland and Småland—

> Månan skinar (the moon shines),
> Dödman rider (dead men ride),
> Är du inte rädder än, Bolla ?
>   (Are you not afraid thereof, Bolla ?)

which correspond to the German Lenore ballad [7]

> Der Mond scheint so helle,
> Die Todten reiten schnelle,
> Feins Liebchen ! graut Dir nicht ?

Geijer also gives the Swedish version of the legend of the Swimmer,[8] the classical story of Hero and Leander, which has a local habitation in Holland, Germany (' Ach Elslein '), Russia, etc. ' The Jolly Beggar ' of Scotland is identical with the ' Bettlerlied ' still sung in many parts of Germany and Sweden.[9] The ' Edward ' ballad as given in Percy's *Reliques* is the well-known Swedish ' Sven i Rosengård,' the Danish ' Svend i Rosengaard,' and the Finnish ' Welisurmaäja.' [10]

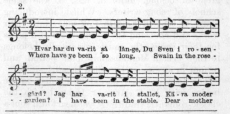

2.

Hvar har du va-rit så   lån-ge, Du Sven i ro-sen-
Where have ye been   so   long,   Swain in the rose-

- - gård? Jag har   va-rit i   stallet, Kä-ra moder
- - garden? I have been in the stable. Dear mother

1 T. Norlind, in his *History of Swedish Music*, speaks of certain isolated collections, such as ' Petri Piae Cantiones,' dated 1582, which contains folk-songs written in parts to sacred words. He calls attention especially to the melodious ' School and Spring Songs.'

2 That is, the heroic epic folk-poetry or ballads of the Middle Ages. The wandering players called *Leikarar* (or in modern Danish *Legere*) were the professional preservers or ' spreaders ' of Scandinavian music at that period, and are mentioned in the old chronicles as honoured guests of the northern kings and nobles.

3 *Om* (German *um*)=round, about ; *Kvæd*=song, singing, ' quoth.'

4 Jamieson, in his *Popular Ballads and Songs*, Edinburgh, 1806, remarks : ' In our ancient songs equally remarkable and incomprehensible *Omqvads* occur.'

5 Geijer contends in his *Svenska Folk-visor*, p. 226, that the *Omkväde* had no other significance than that the extemporiser of the song or the listener should use them to gain time—the one to produce his own thoughts and the other to remember what he had just heard.

6 See F. Böhme's ' Altdeutsches Liederbuch,' and Oscar Fleischer's " Zur vergleichenden Liedforschung," *Sammelbände*, I.M.G. III. ii. 1902.

7 See also ' Fair Margaret and Sweet William,' and ' Margaret's Ghost ' in Percy's *Reliques*.

8 See ' Svenska Folk-visor,' vol. i. p. 106, and vol. ii. p. 210.

9 See Crosby's *Caledonian Musical Repository*, 1811, p. 58.

10 The Swedish and Danish songs are given in Berggreen's collections ; the Finnish in Schröter's ' Finnische Runen ' and in ' Suomalaisen Kirjallisuuden Seuran Toimituksia '; Helsingfors, 1849.

BURDEN.

vår! I vänten mig sent, men jag kommer ald - rig.
of ours! A - wait me late, but I come never.

3.

Og hvor har du vaeret saa laenge, Svend i Rosens -
O where have ye been so long, Swain in the Rose-

- - gaard? Og jeg har vaeret i Lun - den, Kjaer Moder
- - garden? I have been in the grove, Dear Mother

BURDEN.

vor! I ven - te mig seent eller ald - rig.
of ours! A - wait me late or never.

4. *Welisurmaäja.*

Mis-täs tu-let Kus-tas tu-let, Poi-kan-i i - lo - nen?

Meren ran-nal-ta, meren rannalta äi-ti-ni Kul-ta-nen!

The tunes of the three last-named countries appear to have a common origin, but the tune of the ' Edward ' ballad cannot with certainty be traced. Still, as Engel points out, many of our old English tunes bear a strong resemblance to the Scandinavian, both in character and construction ; and the remarkable affinity, especially between the Welsh and Danish songs, has been noticed by Dr. Crotch and others.[1]

But although the Scandinavian nations may have many songs in common, it is evident, on comparing as a whole the collections of the different countries, that there is a great difference in their general character.[2] The Swedish folk-songs are the most beautiful and poetical, and though tinged with melancholy they are not gloomy and tragic like the Norwegian, nor monotonous and regular like the Danish. The latter, however, possess a peculiarly idyllic and pastoral beauty of their own ; they recall the upland meadows, fertile plains and wooded valleys of the country. The 4- or 8-bar rhythm is usually clearly defined, independently of the refrain [3] :

[1] Engel says, ' One of the most popular of the Welsh tunes, " Ar hyd y nôs," is also current in Denmark, especially among the peasantry in Jutland. It may be worth noticing that Jutland is generally believed to have been inhabited in ancient times by the same Celtic race which we find in Wales. But whether the tune originated in Denmark or in Wales is a question which will probably never be solved ' (*Introduction to the Study of National Music*, p. 360). In the introduction to his *Ballad Book*, Allingham calls attention to the similarity between many Scotch ballads, such as the ' Douglas Tragedy,' ' Mary Colvin,' ' Clerk Saunders,' and others, and those contained in the Swedish Folk-song collection by Afzelius and Arvidsson. See also Motherwell's *Minstrelsy, Ancient and Modern*, Glasgow, 1827.

[2] Berggreen, the great Danish collector of folk-songs, draws attention to the close connexion between the word-accent and the melodic outline of the three nations' songs.

[3] This is from the old song-cycle, ' King Dietrich Bern,' and is one of the few early northern songs preserved in writing. As here given it was noted down in 1675 by J. Lorentz, an organist at Copenhagen.

5.

De va - re syv og syv-sind sty-ve der de drog

ud fra Hald, og der de komme ti Brat-tings-

OMKVÄD.

- - borg, der sloge de der-es tjald. Det don-ner under

ros. de don - ske hofmond der de ud - ri - de.

The northern melodies usually begin with the up-beat, and by preference with the step of the fourth (as ' Och Jungfrun '). They are very frequently in common or 2–4 time and adhere to the simplest modulations. The phrases are not repeated on different steps of the scale as in so many other countries, and this gives the melodies great variety. The ' Vermelandsvisa,' one of the most beautiful folk-songs in the world, exemplifies the above qualities ; it begins thus :

6. *Vermelandsvisa.*

O Ver-me-land du skö-na du herr - li-ga land, Du

Krona bland Sve - a - ri - kes län - der.

It may be safely asserted that nine out of every twelve Scandinavian songs are in the minor, or partly so, for many begin in the minor, and end in the major or *vice versâ*. Some of the older melodies recall the Church scales, and especially the Mixolydian and Phrygian modes, but these occur most frequently among the Norwegian and Danish songs.[4] The epic songs which have been collected in Telemarken (in the S.W. of Norway) are evidently of great antiquity, as for instance, the following relating

7.

Slow.

Eg va - no meg saa li - ten ein gut, eg sjatta

fe un-de li - e, saa Kom den frie Flan-ar-

OMKVÄD.

- - ormin han monne i grase skrie. För - di lig-ger

ormin i Y - se-land u - ti flo - i.

[4] There are many examples of modal tunes in Kristensen' ' Gydske Folkeviser.'

to Sigurd's fight with the dragon, with its curious rhythm and melancholy original melody.[1] Important sections of the people's songs are those of the foresters and wood-cutters and the herdsmen. The words of these songs are often mere exclamations and contain no formal verses. The herdsman or girl calls the cattle home from the mountain-side, either with the cowhorn or *Lur*, or by singing a melody with the echo formed on that instrument. Another class of songs are those of the sailors and fishermen. Many old ballads relating to the brave deeds of the sea-fighting heroes are to be found in the Swedish and Norwegian collections, and many typically nautical songs in the more modern.[2]

The national dances have greatly influenced the melodies, though the *Syvspring, Slängdansar. Halling* and many others are not usually accompanied by singing.[3] The famous ring or chain-dances, and children's game-songs and certain festival-songs (such as the old May-Day and Epiphany songs) are relics from mediæval times. In the province of Dalecarlia the 3–4 time dance-songs are especially cultivated ; one called ' Necken's Polska '[4] is widely known. The Norwegian *Springer* is its equivalent. Both dances are sung, whilst the drone fifths in the bass show the old national instrument used. The *Hardangerfele* (*fele*=fiddle) belonging to the Norwegian highlands is the most perfect of their instruments, but it is only used for marches and dances. The peasant marks the time by double tapping of the toe and heel uninterruptedly, playing all the while brilliantly. The richest districts in national songs are Telemarken in the S.W. of Norway, the centre of Jutland[5] and the southern part of the Faroë Islands. These islands were ever in close connexion with Iceland, and many songs show their Icelandic origin. Doubtless the Icelandic sagas incited many Scandinavian songs, and the poetry and language of this island have much in common with the rest of Scandinavia ; but the music is of such a totally different character that a few words must be devoted to its most salient points.

Iceland has ever been a land of history. With true love and devotion its inhabitants have preserved their old tales, traditions and customs. Their language, which the Nor-

wegians brought with them when they settled there at the close of the 9th century, remains unchanged, as also their strangely mediæval music.

The chief source for studying Icelandic music is the Arnamagnäan MS. in the University Library at Copenhagen. And if we compare this collection with those of a far later, or even quite recent date, we find the same forms now as then. There has been no development of music in Iceland ; it has been stationary. Iceland, indeed, adopted the form prevailing in the Middle Ages, and has clung to it up to the beginning of the 20th century. The music of her secular songs[6] is of an ecclesiastical character ; instrumental music hardly exists ; the old scales or modes are retained,[7] for the wave of modern tonality which swept over Europe in the 17th century never reached Iceland. An even stronger evidence of mediævalism than the modal tonality is afforded by the peculiar form of part-singing in Iceland, called *Tvisöngur*, which closely resembles Hucbald's *Organum.* Examples are to be found in the Arnamagnäan MS. of the 15th century ; and although earlier traces of it are extant in other countries, Iceland alone has retained it for her secular music down to the present day. This is proved by the following example taken from the ' Icelandic Student's Söngbók,' of 1894[8] :

8.

NATIONAL SONG—*Island.*

Lento.   Given by PASTOR THORSTEINSSON.

Island! far-sæl-da frón, og hagsæl-da hrimhvita móðir!

Tenor (Melody).

Hvar er þin forn-al-dar frægð frels-ið og mann - dáð-in bezt?

Until the last generation the *Tvisöngur* held its own all over Iceland ; but now in the 20th century it only exists in certain isolated localities. The increasing development of communication with other countries, coupled with the knowledge of musical notation, the spread of choral societies and the publication of numerous collections of songs and hymns, have all combined to induce the Icelanders to adopt at last the more sophisticated methods of music. ' The *Tvisöngur* is, therefore, fast dying out,

---

[1] Thus given by Lindemann. In Telemarken the refrain is often called *Stev*, but the *Stev* consists really of improvised verses of love or satire, sung on certain festive occasions and gatherings, to traditional tunes. See Landstad and Dr. von Ravn in Mendel's *Lexikon.*

[3] See L. A. Smith's *Music of the Waters*, p. 218.

[2] This does not apply to the Faroë Islands, where musical instruments are practically unknown. Here the inhabitants are passionately fond of dancing, and, as mentioned above, accompany their dances with singing the old epics and ballads.

[4] Lindgren in his *Ur Svenska Musikens Häfder*, p. 137, tells us that the Polska is not of national origin, but was introduced from Poland in the 17th century in the Lute-books under the name of *Polonessa* (polonaise).

[5] This district was called the ' knitting-district,' because until quite recently the peasants used to meet during the winter evenings in different houses knitting woollen goods, and relating or singing tales, songs, ballads and legends. Their wealth of songs was so great that in many places the same song was not allowed to be sung more than once a year.

[6] See especially Olafur Davidsson's ' Islenzkar Skemtanir.'

[7] The Icelanders have an especial love for the Lydian mode with its tritone.

[8] The parallel fifths do not sound so harsh if the melody is taken by loud full voices, and the second (upper) part by a few singers, very subdued, and the whole song sung very slowly and emphatically.

and with it the last remains of an interesting episode in musical history.'[1]

The so-called Scandinavian school of music is of very recent birth; for until the close of the 18th century it was greatly under foreign influence. Thus, during the 16th century, the court-music of Denmark was chiefly in the hands of Flemish musicians, whilst in the 17th, Dowland and many other Englishmen, besides French, German, Polish and Italian composers, visited and settled in Copenhagen and Stockholm. The latter part of the 17th and the first part of the 18th were monopolised by the ballet, and French melodies (especially in Sweden) predominated over all others. A fresh impetus was given to northern music by the operas and Singspiele of German composers, such as B. Keiser, J. A. P. Schulz and Kunzen. And in the imitations of these by Weyse, Kuhlau and Hartmann,[2] Scandinavian folk-songs were first introduced on the stage. The compositions in which the vernacular was first used were the sacred and secular cantatas, oratorios and hymns, both by Danish and German composers, such as Iversen, A. Scheibe and J. E. Hartmann in Denmark, and in Sweden, J. Roman, Per Frigel and J. B. Struve. But the chief impulse towards a national school of music was given by the literature of the country. Towards the end of the 18th century the didactic school of poetry began to give way to a more natural lyrical style; and by the beginning of the 19th (influenced by the romanticism of Germany) a strong intellectual national movement arose in Northern poetry. It was greatly promoted in Denmark by the poet Oehlenschläger, in Norway and Sweden by the patriotic 'Norwegian Society,' and by the founding of the so-called 'Götiska förbundet' (Gothic union). About this time the first collections of national songs appeared. Poets and musicians became interested in the old epics and ballads, with their beautiful melodies and their wealth of new materials both in ideas and form, and hastened to avail themselves of the treasure. Thus within the last hundred years or so a new school of music has arisen, containing in its ranks the distinguished names of LINDBLAD, GADE, KJERULF, GRIEG, SJÖGREN, SINDING, etc.

DENMARK.—In Denmark, the homely, humorous, or idyllic Singspiele especially took root, and it would be legitimate to say that the Kunstlied originated in the theatre-songs. Some of these melodies by the elder Hartmann, Schulz, Kunzen and Zinck—singing of social pleasures, friendship and wine, or those of a more romantic and sentimental type—are still popular in Denmark, in the Faroë Islands

and far into the north of Norway. It is worthy of notice that the three founders of the Danish school of music, C. E. F. Weyse, F. Kuhlau and J. Hartmann, were Germans by birth, and that a strong tinge of the German element has prevailed through the works of Danish musicians to the present day. J. Hartmann, the founder of the Hartmann family of composers, is the author of one of Denmark's most national songs, 'King Christian stood by the mast.' Weyse is considered the creator of the Danish romance. Full of romantic feeling, and possessing a fluent gift of melody, the songs from his Singspiele, his child-like, pious 'Morning and Evening Songs,' and more especially his 'Nine Danish Songs' to words by the national lyrists Oehlenschläger, Ewald, Grundtvig, Heiberg and Winther, are justly popular. Later in life Weyse (d. 1842) devoted himself to collecting and harmonising two volumes of 'Gamle Kæmpewise-Melodier' (Old Hero-songs). His contemporary, F. Kuhlau, also loved the simple, noble melodies of the Kämpeviser, which he had noted down in his youth. These he used later with success in the romance form, and it is difficult to distinguish them from the genuine folk-songs of this kind. Still Kuhlau never cared for Danish poetry and always preferred to use German words. Contemporary native musicians were less celebrated, and Sörenson, Claus Schall and Niels Schiorring are names now scarcely remembered. But the improvement in literature due to the poets Oehlenschläger, Heiberg, Hertz, Hans C. Andersen and the publications at Copenhagen of the numerous collections of Scandinavian folk-songs, naturally influenced and stimulated the musical feeling and inventive powers of the song-writers. The consequent development of Danish song we owe to J. P. E. Hartmann, Niels Gade and P. Heise. The songs of the latter vary very much in merit, but his fine song-cycles, 'Gudrun's Sorg' and 'Dyvekes Sange' (words by Drachmann), have never received their due appreciation. J. P. E. Hartmann's songs are gloomy and northern in colouring, and in form less perfect than Heise's and Gade's. Among the best are the six to Winther's poem 'Hjortens Flugt,' and the nine entitled 'Salomon and Sulamith,' op. 52. At first Gade, who was steeped in the atmosphere of Schumann and Mendelssohn, wrote only German songs. But by degrees— influenced, doubtless, by his old master, Berggreen (the great folk-song collector)—he became more national in feeling, and joined the ranks of the northern romanticists, writing music to Oehlenschläger's and Heiberg's romances. His influence has been great over all subsequent Scandinavian composers. Gade's lyrics are always expressed in the simplest language, and suffer from a certain poverty of rhythm. He shares with other Danes the preference for the

---

[1] Studien über isländische Musik, by A. Hammerich (Sammelbände of the I.M.G. I. iii. 1900), to whom the writer is indebted for the above information.
[2] Kuhlau's romantic 'Der Erlenhügel' (1828), and later J. P. Hartmann's 'Liden Kirsten' (1846), (the latter consisting almost wholly of folk-songs) are still popular in Denmark.

monotonous, swaying 6–8 time, and he rarely modulates beyond the nearest keys. A group of composers who have treated the song in the same simple and popular way are : H. Rung, Barnekow, A. Winding, J. O. Hornemann, S. Salomon ; and Gade's pupils, K. Attrup and L. Schytte. More individual and more developed in the accompaniment are those by Emil C. Hartmann, C. F. Hornemann, A. Hamerik, O. Malling, A. Enna and notably R. Hansen and P. E. Langemüller, whose 'Sulamith' cycle is interesting, and as well known abroad as in Denmark. A new note in Danish music was touched by Carl Nielsen (b. 1865). He wrote only a few, but remarkable songs, evincing in his rhythm and modulation a strong originality.

NORWAY.—Although Norway was for a time joined to Sweden and in the past shared the destinies of Denmark, whose language it still retains, it ever remained the most independent branch of the Scandinavian kingdom. The people are intelligent and well educated, and intensely jealous of their national rights. Foreign music and literature never had the same influence in Norway as in Sweden and Denmark, and the *Singspiel* and the opera were never popular. The modern period in poetry and music began with the awakening of national life which received its first impulses in 1772 from the 'Norwegian Society'[1]; from the national poets, Wergeland, (called the Schiller of Norway) Welhaven, Münch, Moë and Jensen ; from the folk-tale collector Faye, the hymn-writer Landstad and most of all from the folk-song collectors Bagge and L. M. Lindemann. The latter did valuable work in familiarising the national melodies of his country. He published them as psalms, hymns, songs and dances, and his work was carried on by C. Elling. The first real song-writer of Norway was Halfdan KJERULF (q.v.), whose lyrics long suffered from unaccountable neglect. His two books of 'Sänger och Visor' contain songs of real beauty, as for instance, 'Lokkende Toner,' 'Kärlekspredikan,' 'Saknaden,' 'Eremiten,' 'Mit Hjerte og min Lyre' ('My Heart and Lute'), and 'Natten pas Fjorden.' The voice-part and accompaniments are well written and interesting,[2] and there is no straining for effect or originality. Among the song-writers born between the years 1837 and 1847 we find the same inclination to represent the national spirit in their art. But neither Winter-Hjelm, J. Selmer, C. Cappelen, nor even J. S. Svendsen, who wrote two books of highly expressive songs, touched the true note. This was reserved for R. NORDRAAK and Eduard GRIEG (q.v.). An intimate friend of Grieg, a celebrated

pianist, Agathe BACKER-GRÖNDAHL (q.v.), has written simple and expressive songs, which are very popular in Norway. Other song-writers, born in the second half of the last century, are : J. Holter, Ole Olsen, C. Sinding, Per Winge and his cousin Per Lasson, C. Elling, J. Halvorsen, Andersen, Alnaes and Sigurd Lie.

SWEDEN.—In the 16th century musical art in Sweden reached a high level. Gustav Vasa was a connoisseur in music, and encouraged composers of the Netherland and Italian Schools to his court. The Thirty Years' War brought Sweden into contact with other European nations, and many Germans flocked thither. Under Charles XII., French music reigned supreme and long held its sway over all native composers. The Düben family (Germans by origin), who settled in Sweden early in the 17th century, and have been called the 'founders of Swedish music,' hardly deserve this name, for though they did much to further and develop music in Sweden they were entirely under foreign influence. Gustav Düben (d. 1690) wrote songs of the type of Heinrich Albert in Germany, whilst his brother Anders Düben, who inclined more to French music, wrote only little arias for the court of the French chanson kind. In the 18th century the music of German and Italian composers, such as Fux, Graun and Handel, Scarlatti and Lotti, predominated, but simultaneously the Swedish composers J. H. Roman, Agrell and Zellbell were pursuing the right road towards founding a national school by using the vernacular in their vocal works. The opera, which has always played an important part in Stockholm, remained chiefly French under Dalayrac and Monsigny, though German dramatic influence was exerted by Gluck, Naumann, Haeffner, etc. The only dramatic composer of Swedish descent was the popular K. Stenborg, who used his native folk-songs in his operas, and led the way through Dupuy and Randel to Hallström, the real creator of the national opera.

The song of the Gustavian period (i.e. the close of the 18th century) answers exactly to that of J. A. Hiller, Schulz, Reichardt and Zelter of Germany, and bore the same homely, popular character, without, however, being in any sense national. The forerunner of the true Swedish song was Olof Åhlström, who published at the beginning of the 19th century a collection of eighteen volumes called 'Skaldestycken Satte i Musik,' containing songs by himself, by Haeffner, Stenborg, Palm and others. Many songs in this collection, as well as those by Dupuy, Nordblom, Crusell,[3] etc., still show the same tendency towards the Berlin School, but the words of Swedish poets

[1] A band of patriotic Norwegians living in Copenhagen, who combined to found a native university in Christiania in 1811, and to recover their native independence in 1814.
[2] To a certain degree Kjerulf resembles the German song-writer Robert Franz. Both pay the same strict regard to the words and accent, and in both the accompaniments are often treated polyphonically. (See for example Kjerulf's op. 23, No. 2.)

[3] Crusell would really be considered a Finnish composer, but the interests and destinies of Finland and Sweden have been closely interwoven. This indeed applies to most of the literature and music of the Scandinavian countries, and it is often hard to define to which country the several poets and composers belong.

were used, and attention was thus called at last to Swedish composers. A yet greater service Åhlström did was to edit the songs of that strange original genius C. M. Bellmann, under the title of 'Fredmans Epistlar och Sanger' (1790–95). These are in reality splendidly humorous pictures of Stockholm life skilfully adapted to favourite foreign (chiefly French) and native airs; very few tunes are original, but they remain household words in Sweden to the present day.

Literature and music kept pace during the early 19th century, and both drank from the same national source. It is difficult to say whether poetry or music owes most to the so-called Gothic revival, of which Geijer, Afzelius, Tegner, Arvidsson and Atterbom were the leaders. The first impetus towards the new lyric was given by Afzelius and Geijer in their publication of old Swedish folk-songs in 1814–1816.[1] The melodies in these volumes were revised and harmonised by Haeffner and Groenland. A little later Erik Drake published another series, in which Afzelius joined. Arvidsson (a Dane by birth) devoted himself to the same subject, and published, between 1833 and 1837, three volumes of old war, hunting and love songs; Bergström, Hoijer, R. Dybeck and K. Södling following suit.

The earliest composers who breathed the romantic national atmosphere and sang the characteristic melodies of Sweden were Geijer, A. Lindblad, J. A. Josephson, Wennerberg, Berwald, Hallström, Rubenson, L. Norman and A. Södermann. The classic time of the Romanze belongs to the three first named. Geijer's songs are impregnated with the true folk-song spirit, and are powerful and expressive, but Lindblad's won wider fame. These also bear the national stamp; they are pure, natural, unaffected and withal really poetic and graceful compositions. Among the most interesting are those to Atterbom's words, especially 'Trohet.'[2] And others worthy of mention are 'Saknad,' 'O kom, nij droj,' 'Am Aaren See,' 'Strykningsvisa,' and the nine Heine songs which have more developed and original accompaniments. Lindblad's songs owe their fame and popularity in a great measure to having been sung by Jenny Lind. Josephson surpasses the others in the real lyric; and the melancholy tenderness which pervades his songs is a racial characteristic. Wennerberg's collection of duets, 'Gluntarne' (Scenes of student-life in Upsala), were once famous, but though his thoughts show independence, his musical treatment is somewhat amateurish. Norman was a truly idyllic composer, and amongst his songs the beautiful 'Skogs Sånger' and 'Månestrålar' should be better known. With the great ballad composer, A. Södermann, Swedish romanti-

cism reached its highest point. Among his solo-ballads and songs, such as 'Tannhäuser,' 'Kvarnruinen,' and the 'Black Knight,' we find a great development in the accompaniment. Södermann filled the old forms with new dramatic life, and is therefore considered the great reformer of Swedish song. Less well-known names are those of J. A. Hägg, A. Körling (whose songs 'Weisse Rosen' and 'Abendstimmung,' of the Mendelssohn type, are favourites), A. Myrberg, V. Svedbom, F. Arlberg (also a fine singer), Henneberg, Kjelander, Byström, Nordquist, A. Bergenson, etc. Emil SJÖGREN holds an important place. Grieg's influence may be traced in his harmonies and Schumann's in his rhythms, but withal he is an independent and interesting composer.

Towards the end of the 19th century a change came over Swedish music. The genius of Berlioz, Liszt and Wagner dominated the talents of the living representatives of Swedish romanticism. Of the later school of songwriters, Vilhelm STENHAMMAR (b. 1871) stands pre-eminent. His father, P. W. Stenhammar, was a prolific composer of ultra-simple religious, old-fashioned songs. V. Stenhammar is equally successful in any form of song he touches, whether it be the ballad, such as his fine setting of 'Florez and Blanchiflur,' or a little folk-song like 'Irmelin Rose,' or the true lyric, such as the splendid song 'Fylgia.' In W. Peterson-Berger's Swedish songs, 'Svensk Lyrik' and the cycle entitled 'Ut Fridolin's Lustgård,' the tender, melancholy national tone is reflected; whereas in his German songs, such as the 'Gesänge nach Nietzsche,' he is more directly under Wagner's spell. Hugo Alfvén, Tor Aulin and E. Åkerberg belong also, with others, to this group.

SCANDINAVIAN BIBLIOGRAPHY

RAVN, DR. VON. *Skandinavische Musik* (Mendel).
HÜLPHER, A. *Histor. Afhandling om Musik och Instrumenter* Westerås, 1773.
'Alte Volksmelodien des Nordens.' (*Allg. musikal. Zeitung*). Aug. 1816.
LINDGREN, A. *Ur Svenska Musikens Häfder.*
CRISTAL, M. *L'Art scandinave.* Paris, 1874.
GRÖNVOLD, AIMAR. *Norske Musikere.* Christiania, 1883.
VALENTIN, CARL. *Studien über die schwedischen Volksmelodien.* Leipzig, 1885.
SCHWEITZER. *Geschichte d. skandinavischen Literatur.* Leipzig, 1886–89.
SPITTA, P. *Niels Gade, Zur Musik.* Berlin, 1892.
NORLIND, TOBIAS. *Schwedische Musikgeschichte.* Lund, 1901. *Zur Geschichte der schwedischen Musik (Die Musik).* Aug. 1904. *Die Musikgeschichte Schwedens in den Jahren 1630–1730.* (*Sammelbände,* I.M.G., I. ii. 1900.)
THUREN, HJALMAR. *Tanz, Dichtung und Gesang auf den Färöern.* (*Sammelbände,* I.M.G., III. ii. 1902.)
SOUBIES, A. *États scandinaves.* (*Histoire de la musique.*) Paris, 1901–3.
NIEMANN, W. *Die schwedische Tonkunst.* (*Sammelbände,* I.M.G., V. i. 1903.)
NIEMANN, W. *Die Musik Skandinaviens.* Leipzig, 1906.
See the publications of Catharinus Elling: *Vore folkemelodier,* 1909; *Vore kjæmpeviser,* 1914, etc.
SANDVIK, OLE MØRK. *Folke-Musik i Gudbrandsdalen,* pp. vi, 72 and 128 pp. of musical examples. Christiania, 1919.

COLLECTIONS

ABRAHAMSON, NYERUP and RAHBEK. 'Udvalgte danske Viser fra Middelalderen.' Copenhagen, 1812–14.
ÅHLSTRÖM and AFZELIUS. 'Traditioner af Svenska Folkviser,' 1814.
GEIJER and AFZELIUS. 'Svenska Folk-visor från Forntiden.' Stockholm, 1814–16.
RASMUSSEN und NYERUP. 'Udvalg af Danske Viser.' Copenhagen, 1821.
LYNGBYE, H. C. 'Foerøske Qvoeder.' Randers, 1822 (no music).
ARVIDSSON, A. 'Svenska Fornsänger.' Stockholm, 1834–42.

---

[1] These volumes contain valuable prefaces and notes.
[2] Written on the death of the poet's wife.

LINDEMANN, L. 'Aeldre og nyere Norske Fjeldmelodier.' Christiania, 1840.
DYBECK, R. 'Svenska Vallviser och Hornlåtar.' Stockholm, 1846; 'Schwedische Weisen,' 1847–48 ; 'Svenske Viser,' 1853–56.
LANDSTAD, M. B. 'Norske Folkeviser.' Christiania, 1853.
BERGGREEN, A. P. 'Danske, Norske og Svenske Folkesange og melodier.' Copenhagen, 1861–63.
LUNDQUIST. '100 Svenska Folkviser.' Stockholm, 1866.
KRISTENSEN, E. 'Jydske Folkeviser,' 1871–76–91.
BOHLIN, K. T. P. 'Folktöner från Jämtland.' Stockholm, 1883.
HANSEN, W. 'Danske Melodier.' (Melodier fra alle Lande, vol. i.) Copenhagen, 1885.
HAMMERSHAIMB, V. 'Foerøsk Anthologi.' Copenhagen, 1891. (Chiefly dances and dance-songs.)
CARLHEIM - GYLLENSKIÖLD, V. 'Viser och Melodier.' Stockholm, 1892.
LAUB, T. 'Danske Folkeviser med gamle Melodier.' Copenhagen, 1899.
GARBORG, H. 'Norske Folkevisor.' 1903. No. 8 of the 'Norske Folkeskriften.')
'August Bondeson's Visbok.' Stockholm, 1903.
HANSEN, W. 'Svenske og Norske Melodier.' (Melodier fra alle Lande, vol. ii.) Copenhagen.
ROCKE, L. 'Nordische Volkslieder.'
ÅHLSTRÖM, J. '300 Svenska Folkeviser.' Stockholm. 'Nordiska Folkeviser.' Stockholm.
BOGGE, J. '73 Polkskor från Gottland.' Stockholm.
WEYSE, C. E. F. '50 gamle Kampevise melodier.'
BLUMENTHAL, I. G. 'Delsbostintens Visor.'

ICELANDIC.—BIBLIOGRAPHY AND COLLECTIONS

DE LA BORDE, J. B. Essai sur la musique ancienne et moderne. (Several Icelandic songs in vol. ii. p. 397 et seq.) Paris, 1780.
BERGGREEN, A. P. 'Folke-Sange og Melodier' (vol. i.). Copenhagen, 1869.
DAVIDSSON, OLAFUR. 'Islenzkar Skemtanir.' Copenhagen, 1888–1892. 'Söngbók hins islenzka Studentafjelags.' Reykjavik, 1894.
PILET, RAYMOND. Nouvelles Archives des missions scientifiques et littéraires (vol. vii. pp. 243-71). Paris, 1897.
PANUM and BEHREND. Illustreret Musikhistorie (vol. i. p. 44, has a reference to the Tvisöngur). Copenhagen, 1897–1905.
HAMMERICH, ANGUL. 'Studien über isländische Musik.' (Sammelbände, I.M.G., I. iii. 1900.)
THUREN, HJALMAR. 'Tanz, Dichtung und Gesang auf den Färöern.' (This contains many Icelandic songs.) Sammelbände, I.M.G., III. ii. 1902.

THE NETHERLANDS

Under this comprehensive term are included the countries which extend from the North Sea to the Somme in France, comprising Holland, Flanders, Belgium, the Walloon country and the chief part of the old province of Artois. The population is partly Teutonic, represented by the Flemings ; partly of Romance origin, represented by the Walloons. Two languages are spoken—Dutch and French, for Flemish is nearly akin to Dutch and the Romance dialect spoken by the Walloons is closely allied to French, which is the official language of Belgium. Still, until the 19th century when Holland and Belgium were formed into independent kingdoms, the Netherlands was practically one country. In dealing with the folk-songs, however, a distinction must be made, as each division of the country possessed its own songs. Yet even so the subject is confusing, for while the official designation of 'Netherlands' is retained by what we now call Holland, the 'Spanish Netherlands,' which in the 16th and early 17th centuries played so important a part in history and gave birth to the finest songs, comprised rather the districts of Flanders and Belgium. Again, the songs of the North of France and Flanders and the Low German and Dutch songs, have so much in common that to write the history of one is to write the history of the other.

The Trouvères of the 11th and 12th centuries, with their langue d'oïl, belonged equally to Northern France and to Belgium, and as they

have already been mentioned under the section FRANCE it is unnecessary to refer to them again here. Further, the Old French and Flemish schools of music were practically identical, and the Gallo-Belgian School, whose most successful period lies between 1360 and 1460, was considered by other nations as French, and the composers indiscriminately called Galli (see ante, p. 6). But with the Netherland School proper we are treading on different ground. This school penetrated into every cultured country in Western Europe, formed schools of its own, identified itself with other nationalities and was held in universal esteem until, in the latter part of the 16th century, the Italians became the leading musical nation in Europe. This great school, however, was essentially polyphonic, and with it and its chief representatives (such as Okeghem, Obrecht, Josquin des Prés, Gombert, Orlandus Lassus and others) this article is only indirectly concerned. These prefatory remarks will explain to some extent the complex character of the history of song in the Netherlands.

Among the earliest traces of the langue d'oïl is the 'Cantique de Ste Eulalie' (without music), preserved in the Valenciennes Library, and belonging to the 9th or early 10th century.[2] This language of the Trouvères was spoken in Northern France and Belgium for some centuries and during the 11th, 12th and 13th numerous songs were composed which, with their melodies, still exist. With regard to the Flemish songs, Fétis says it is more difficult[3] to decide with certainty whether they are as old as they are reputed to be. Of these, one famous song, to judge by the character of the poetry, reaches back to the Norman traditions of the 10th century.[4] It is known by the name of 'Heer Halewijn,' and Willems, who published the song in 1836 with the original text, says it is still heard in Brabant and Flanders.[5] The many versions of the melody make it impossible to date it with accuracy, but the following (in the Hypomixolydian mode) is considered the oldest and purest :

1.

Heer Halewijn.

Heer Halewijn zong een lie-de-kijn, al die dat hoor-de
wou bi hem zijn, al die dat hoor-de wou bi hem zijn.

[1] See Coussemaker's Chants des Flamands de France ; and Böhme's 'Altdeutsches Liederbuch.'

[2] Fétis, Histoire gén. de la mus. iv. 485.   [3] Ibid. v. 55 et seq.
[4] Oscar Fleischer, in Ein Kapitel vergleichender Musikwissenschaft (Sammelbände I.M.G., I. i. 1899), shows the resemblance between the Halewijn melody and a Brittany ballad, 'Die drei Monniken' (see Villemarqué, p. 185), and the melody of a hymn, 'Sidus solare,' from a Neapolitan MS. of the 11th and 12th centuries and discusses which is the older.
[5] F. van Duyse corroborates this by saying that Pol de Mont (poet and folk-lorist) heard the 'Halewijnslied' in 1896 in the environs of Leuwen. (See Het oude Nederlandsche Lied, i. 13.) In this standard work Duyse practically includes all the songs found in the Netherlands, with the words and tune of each and their variants. The valuable preface explains the verse metre, rhythm, scales and general form, and is indispensable to the student.

Although it is true that the aim of the representative Netherland School (1425–1625) was polyphonic, it is a mistake to suppose that the work of these learned contrapuntists was the only form of music prevailing in the country at this time. National songs existed contemporaneously with it; and the tunes these great masters used as themes for their masses, motets and polyphonic chansons were practically their own folk-songs. That such historic French and Flemish tunes as ' L'Homme armé,' ' Cents mille écus,' ' Forseulement,' ' Je me demande,' ' Myn Hert,'[1] ' Het daghet,'[2] were not merely worthy of local recognition is proved by their constant use throughout Europe. The Netherland masters, however, rarely gave the whole melody even to the leading part, and seldom more than one *couplet* of the words, and hence the fragmentary character of the songs they bequeathed to us. But gradually the spirit of the folk-song began to influence their highest forms of composition, and they realised that in their *chansons*, *villanelles* and *canzonettes*, written in four, five, six, seven, or eight parts, ' mechanical invention must be subservient to idea, and euphony and expression should equally be the objects of the composer.'[3] Amongst the works of Dufay, Binchois, Faugues, Busnois, and in Petrucci's ' Canti cento cinquanta,' there are songs which, in regularity of form and simplicity of character, rival the folk-songs. Nor are examples wanting in the minor works of Okeghem, Pierre de la Rue, Josquin des Prés, Gombert, Willaert,[4] Goudimel, Clemens non Papa, Jannequin,[5] Arcadelt and Orlandus Lassus, of secular melodies conceived in a strain of freshness, naïveté, humour and brightness, or marked by a power of lyric expression belonging to a much later time.

The picture of an age and its culture is always vividly reflected in its folk-songs; it was therefore the natural result of the intensity of the impulse given to religious life by the ' mystics ' that so great a number of sacred songs was created during the 14th century.[6] The ground had already been prepared by the celebrated ascetics Greert Groote and Johann Ruysbrock, and the numerous sacred *Minne-songs*[7] were the especial outcome of the mystic movement. About the middle of the 15th century the early *Rederykers*[8] (who correspond with the German *Meistersinger*)

substituted for the harshly realistic secular songs of the day their own carefully prepared sacred songs.[9] For these they either altered the words of the secular songs to give them a sacred meaning, or they adapted totally new religious words, retaining the secular tune unchanged.[10] And this practice prevailed in the Netherlands throughout the 16th and 17th centuries. In 1561 Tylman Susato published his ' Souterliedekens,' consisting of portions of the Psalms according to the rhymed Flemish version, set unaltered to the popular song-tunes of the day. This publication was succeeded by Fruytier's ' Ecclesiasticus ' (1565) and the various Catholic song-books, such as ' Theodotus,' ' Het Paradijs ' (Antwerp, 1621), which similarly contained a mass of secular melodies. Whilst the Church scales were still in use the greater part of the earlier melodies were in the Dorian mode, though the Phrygian and Lydian were also represented.[11]

Very different in character from the sacred songs of the mystics, of the *rederykers*, of the Catholics, or those which the Reformation produced, were the songs of liberty and patriotism sung a generation later during the Spanish oppression. Amongst other collections the famous song-book of the Gueux[12] (' Geusen-Liedenboecxkens,' 1588) and Adrianus Valerius' ' Gedenck-Clanck ' (1621–26)[13] (see VALERIUS), contain the classics of Dutch musical literature, and are historically of inestimable value. They give us the ballads of ' Egmont and Horn,' the ' Storm of Leyden '; the splendid political songs of satire on the Spanish generals, such as the ' Spotlied op de Bossu,' ' Spotlied op de Alva,' or the patriotic songs such as ' Ein Liedje op den Briel,' or ' De Geuzen bij Antwerpen,' and ' Wilhelmus van Nassouwe '— the Dutch national anthem. (See WILHELMUS VAN NASSOUWE.) These grand old Netherland songs breathe a spirit of protest against tyranny and of warlike determination tempered with resignation under disaster, which sets them on a distinct plane of their own. In many of the collections only the name of the tune (*stem*) is mentioned to which the song was sung. Such is the case with those in the ' Geusen Liedenboecxkens,' but Valerius has given the actual melodies as well. Many tunes are derived from

1 Used by Pierre de la Rue in a 4-part chanson. See Ambros, iii. 241.
2 Used by Clemens non Papa in a 3-part chanson. See Duyse, i. 124.
3 Naumann's *Hist. of Mus.* i. 368.
4 In Willaert we clearly see the modern spirit, not only in what he did for harmony but also for his recognition of the value of the solo-voice. In 1536 he arranged some of Verdelot's madrigals for solo-song with accompaniment of lute.
5 Wooldridge gives a lovely little song, ' Ce moys de Mai,' by Jannequin, showing the transition between the two styles, where the harmony is in plain chords, but ' the polyphonic element is still present in the melodious flow and independent interest of the separate parts.' *Oxford Hist. of Music*, ii. 277.
6 See W. Bäumker, *Niederländische geistliche Lieder, Vierteljahrsschrift*, 1888.
7 All these songs deal with Christ as the Bridegroom for Whom the loving soul yearns.
8 For information on the guilds of poets and musicians in the Netherlands, see Motley's *Rise of the Dutch Republic*, i. 75 et seq.

9 For examples from the later *rederyker*, M. van Castelyn's songs (*Diversche Liederkens*), see Duyse, ii. 1530 et seq. One of Castelyn's songs, ' Ghepeys, Ghepeys, vol van euvijen,' is included in most collections.
10 In this manner many secular songs have been preserved intact, instead of only in a fragmentary or mutilated form, such as we have seen the polyphonic writers reduced them to.
11 Bäumker has given examples of these interchangeable sacred and secular songs from two old MS. collections : one is in the K. K. Fideikommissbibliothek in Vienna, and the other in the Staats Bibliothek in Berlin. The tunes are nearly all to be found in Böhme's ' Altdeutsches Liederbuch,' and frequently occur again in Dutch collections. See also ' Geistliche und weltliche Compositionen des XV. Jahrhunderts,' bearbeitet von Guido Adler und Oswald Koller.
12 Or ' Gentlemen beggars.' For the origin of the word see Motley's *Rise of the Dutch Republic*, i. 432 et seq.
13 Dr. A. Loman has harmonised a selection from the ' Geusenliedenboecxkens ' and the ' Gedenck-Clanck.' Both, with his interesting prefaces and notes, were published by the Maatschappij tot bevordering der Toonkunst for 1871 and 1872. (See VEREENIGING.)

foreign sources, and especial interest is attached to those of English origin, of which the following collections contain the most: 'Friesche Lusthof' (1621) [1]; 'Gedenck-Clanck' (1621–26) [2]; 'Den singende Zwaen' (1664); 'Stichtelycke Rymen' (1624) [3]; 'Bellerophon' (1633) [4]; and Thysius's and Vallet's lute-books. At the time of Queen Elizabeth, when the cultivation of music in England was at its height, intercourse between this country and the Netherlands was most frequent. English traders arrived in Dutch harbours, English students studied at Leyden, English actors played in Amsterdam, [5] and English soldiers fought side by side with the Dutch against the Spaniards. And it is clear that Dutch musicians were well acquainted with English ballads, for certain songs, such as 'Fortune,' 'What if a day' (which may be compared with ' Bergen op Zoom '), 'Barafostus' Dream,' and the 'Cobbler's Jig,' [6] were evidently favourites, as they occur so frequently. The last-named tune is used in the 'Gedenck-Clanck' for the song ' Wie dat sich selfs verheft,' and

2.   *Wie dat.*

Wie dat sich selfs ver-heft te-met, wert wel een ar-me duc d'Alf u beeld, tot spijt ge-set, waer af-ge-bro-ken

sle-ter, u boose daed, die ghij begaet bij al-len toch on-be-ter,

lij - dig is en strij-dig is met on-ser Landen staet.

Valerius calls the *stem* ' Engelslapperken.' On comparing this Dutch song of satire on Alva's standard with the English version, it will be seen that not a note has been altered.

One of the most beautiful songs in this collection, ' Waer datmen sich al keerd of wend ' (a fine patriotic poem by Valerius), set to the *stem* ' Pots hondert duijsent [7] slapperment ' (named also by Valerius 'Allermande Pekelharing'), bears a strong resemblance to ' Walking in a country town.' [8]

3.   *Waer datmen.* [9]

Waer dat-men sich al keerd of wend, End' waer-men
Waer dat-men reijst of rotst, of rend, End' waer-men

loopt of staet,
he - nen gaet,   Daer vint-men, 'tsij oock op wat ree d'Hol-

lan-der end de   Zeeuw: Sij loopen door de

woe-ste   Zee, Als   door het bosch de Leeuw.

Valerius has also included nineteen purely Dutch folk-tunes in the ' Gedenck-Clanck,' and one cannot fail to be struck by the bold sweeping melodic lines, massive structure and stately dignity of these songs. The Dutch and North Flemish folk-songs have, in fact, much in common with the German Volkslied, which is explicable when we consider the consanguinity of the races, the resemblance of temperament and the similarity of language and poetical forms. [10] Many of the tunes are modal and yet have a feeling for harmony which is unusual in such tunes. The melodies most frequently

4.   *Het daghet.* [11]

Het daghet in den Oosten, het lich-tet o - ver-

- al . . . . .;   hoe luttel weet mijn lief

- - ken, och   waer Ick he-nen   sal!

---

[1] J. Starter.
[2] See J. P. Land's article on Valerius's ' Gedenck-Clanck ' in vol. i. of the *Tijdschrift der Vereeniging voor Noord-Nederlands Muzickgeschiedenes.* (Land's references are to the 1st edition of Chappell's *Pop. Music.*)   [3] Camphuysen.   [4] D. P. Pers.
[5] *Die Singspiele der englischen Komödianten*, Dr. J. Bolte, 1893.
[6] See Chappell's *Old English Pop. Music* (new edition), i. 75, 100, 148, 279.
[7] *Tausent* in some versions. See Starter's, from whom Valerius possibly took the tune.   [8] Chappell, i. 117.
[9] Thus arranged by Loman. (The opening phrase recalls the Swedish song ' O Wermeland.'

[10] It may be safely asserted that two-thirds of the songs given in Duyse's famous collection occur also in F. Böhme's ' Altdeutsches Liederbuch ' and other German collections, with only slight differences in the words and melodies. As one example, take ' Daer staet een clooster in Oostenrije ' (Duyse, i. 472) and ' Es liegt ein Schloss im Österreich (Böhme, 154). Böhme drew attention to this point in his preface, saying : ' The German and old Netherland folk-songs are indistinguishable, for from the last half of the 15th to the end of the 16th century they had a fund of folk-poetry in common. And amongst the songs contained in the Netherland collections (see especially those in the Antwerp Song-book of 1544) many were written both in High and Low German ; and in the German collections (see for instance, Rhau's ' Bicinia ') songs occur with Netherland text and sometimes with the mark *Brabantica* annexed. This interchange need cause no surprise when the close intercourse promoted by the Hanseatic League is taken into account.'
[11] This 15th-century song is set to Psalm iv. in the ' Souterliedekens ' (1540), and was used by Clemens non Papa in a chanson for three voices, and published in Antwerp in 1556. It occurs also in a different form in the Gueux song-book (1575), set to ' Och God will doch vertroosten,' also in Camphuysen's and many other collections. See Duyse, i. 124.

begin on the up-beat, and as the musical rhythm follows the words very closely[1] frequent changes of time are necessitated, although the actual rhythmical figures present little variety.

The songs are by no means always in regular periods; constantly the first part consists of eight and the second part of five or six bars, or of five and seven bars each as in the 'Spotlied.' (See Example 5.) Sometimes only one bar is

5.   *Spotlied op de Bossu.*[2]

Ma-xi-mi-lia-nus de Bos-su ben ick een Graef Ge-hee - - - ten, ick heb ge-weest sijn ad - mi-rael, de Geu-sen te doo-den prin - ci-pael, dit had ick mij ver-me-ten.

added, as if to give emphasis to the last words. Melodic *melismas* are of frequent occurrence, even in strophical songs, and are probably due to the influence of the Church. And yet, paradoxical as it may seem, the songs never lose their classical character of regularity of form.

Belgium being a bilingual country the folk-songs are divided into two classes, Flemish and Walloon.[3] The Flemish are more numerous and widespread; indeed they extend north into Holland, where they intermingle with the Dutch. The Walloon songs are more local, though they include all those sung in French or in the Walloon dialect.[4] Just as the Flemish people show affinity with the German, the Walloons resemble the French. The grace and liveliness of the French chanson, the love the French have for satirical words and strongly marked dance-rhythms,[5] are qualities exhibited by the Walloons. In the district round Liège a particular genre of satirical song exists, called *la pasqueye*, and amongst the numerous Belgian dance-songs, the 'Crâmignons' of the same district should be especially noticed. Example 6 is a favourite.

The traditional ballads of the old French provinces, Lorraine, Picardy, Auvergne and Provence, survive in the Ardennes. In the Walloon songs the refrains follow much the same lines as other countries; rhyme is by no means universal and is often replaced by mere assonance; the dialogue form is very common, and consists of innumerable strophes.[6] Modal

6.   *Crâmignon.*[7]

Pauv' mohe! quu n'tu sâ-vér' tu? Wiss' don? po dri les ca - bus.   Vo - chal vi-now' l'a-règne, Po v'ni ma-gni l'mohe.   1st. l'mohe, l'a-règne li 2nd. *Solo.* mohe, l'a-regne li mohe.   *Tutti.*   Pauv' mohe! quu n'tu sâvér' tu? Wiss' don?   po dri les ca - bus.

melodies are frequently found amongst the Noëls and other religious songs. The profound sincerity and naïveté of the Noëls must appeal to all, and if a vein of realistic familiarity, attractive to the peasantry, is repellent to the more cultivated taste, none will deny that they possess a touching charm of their own, difficult to convey in words.

It is inevitable that songs handed down century after century should undergo changes, but this is less so in the Netherlands than in most other countries. Conscious of their value, Flemish and Dutch musicians have at all times been assiduous in forming collections of their songs and thus preserving them in their original condition.[8] This has not been the case with the French and Walloon-speaking inhabitants of the country. They have depended on oral tradition, and hence their songs have suffered considerable deterioration in the course of time. Indifference to the folk-song steadily gained ground among this people, and their preference for debased tunes from the *vaudeville* and *opéra-comique* was fostered by inferior composers, who wrote in accordance with the prevailing taste. Fortunately this evil is now being counteracted by earnest musicians,[9] who are devoting themselves to the task of rescuing the folk-songs from neglect and issuing exhaustive collections from the various districts. The wealth of songs and their beauty have fully justified their labours.

---

1 Following the verse-metre closely is peculiarly characteristic of Dutch folk-songs.
2 This song does not appear in the first editions of the Gueux song-book, but the melody is given in Luther's hymn-book of 1524 to words by Speratus, ' Es ist das Heil '; afterwards it was used by the Bohemian Brothers, and by the Lutherans in Antwerp in 1573. Winterfeld says in his *Evang. Kirchengesang*, i. 41, that in its original form it was undoubtedly a secular folk-song.
3 'Chansons pop. des provinces belges ' (preface), Ernest Closson.
4 This dialect was dying out, but within the last twenty years efforts have been made by the Liège poet Nicolas Defrecheux and by folk-lorists to preserve it.
5 3–4 and 6–8 time are very common among the Walloon songs.

6 The (Flemish) lace-makers for instance have their own especial songs with apparently meaningless words, but which represent to them a given number or kind of stitch. Each worker takes up one of these endless verses in turn. See Lootens and Fey's ' Chants pop. flamands.'
7 Terry and Chaumont's collection, from which the above is taken, includes over 200.
8 The efforts of the members of the Maatschappij tot bevordering der Toonkunst and their interesting publications have greatly contributed to this end. H. Rogge, J. P. Land, A. D. Loman, J. Röntgen, F. van Duyse, D F. Scheuleer, and Enschedé also deserve special recognition in this connexion.
9 Among these the names of L. Terry and Chaumont, Lootens and Feys, L. Jouret, E. Closson, O. Colson (the director of the Liège review *Wallonia*, which contains much information about the Walloon folk-songs) and the curé J. Bols hold an honoured place.

After the 16th century the glory of the Flemish school [1] waned. As representative songs of the 18th century we may mention those by the Flemish composer G. de Fesch, who came over to England about 1730 and published there a volume entitled ' Canzonette ed arie a voce sola.' They are sentimental like the French songs of the period, regular in form, with fairly agreeable harmony. Of greater interest are the songs interspersed in the short allegorical, mythological and pastoral plays then much in vogue. Van der Straeten [2] gives as a characteristic example a pretty little ' Bergère flamande,' from Lambrecht's ' Vlaemsche Vrede-Vreucht '; but whether it was original or an adopted folk-song is an open question. 'Le Voegge de Chofontaine,' an opéra-bouffe by the Liège composer G. Noël Hamal, contained the favourite couplets and dances in the district in which it was written.[3] By degrees, however, these unimportant local operas died out,[4] and composers sought their laurels in Paris. Both Belgium and France lay claim to Gossec and Grétry as national composers; and similarly Grisar, César Franck and many others, who, although Belgians by birth, are practically regarded as French composers, having identified themselves with the French school.

BELGIUM.—The year 1834 witnessed the constitution of Belgium as a separate kingdom, and the formation of a Belgian nationality. Up to that date there are no songs worthy of mention, with the possible exception of LA BRABANÇONNE, the national song of Belgium, composed by Van Campenhout in 1830. The generality of composers had hitherto continued to use indiscriminately French and Flemish words for their songs, until towards the end of the 19th century a group of musicians arose who avowedly are endeavouring to give Flemish art once more a national character. This has been designated the *mouvement flamingant*, and the foremost personalities belonging to it were P. BENOIT, whose songs set to Flemish words are full of life and colour, and Edgar TINEL. The latter is an interesting composer with a strong individuality, but his songs are few. Many other excellent musicians, who have all written ballads and songs, joined this movement, such as Lenaerts, Wambach and Jan Blockx, the most brilliant of them all. Mention must also be made of Blockx's pupil, Vleeshower, and of Van den Eeden, who succeeded Huberti as director of the Mons Conservatoire. Less exclusively Flemish song-writers are Eyken and Tilman, who chiefly confined themselves to sacred songs; Miry, C. Meerens

and A. Goovaerts, who wrote for the most part nursery or school songs; and Van Gheluwe, J. Radoux, A. Samuel, J. Meertens, G. Huberti and E. Mathieu, who are the best-known names. Meertens and Huberti have written songs both graceful and melodious, and of a simple character; whilst those of Jan Blockx, G. Lekeu and Paul Gilson, if somewhat eclectic, manifest originality, novelty and boldness of invention. The curious phase of thought and the peculiar qualities shown in the literature of Belgium by the writings of Maeterlinck, Rodenbach and Verhaeren, cannot fail to leave their mark also on the music of the period.

HOLLAND.—After the numerous song-books which appeared in Holland between 1600 and 1700, Dutch composers devoted themselves principally to instrumental music. Even on the title-pages of vocal pieces we find *om te singen of te spelen*; and Sweelinck's skilful organ and clavier variations on the songs were greater favourites than the songs themselves. As lutenists, organists, carillonneurs or theoreticians, Dutch musicians held a high place in Europe [5]; and although among the works of various members of musical families (and music in Holland was an essentially hereditary gift) we find incidental mention of songs or song-collections, it is evident that this form of art was on the wane. Hooft's anonymous publication, ' Emblemata amatoria,' is the last collection of any value in the 17th century, though Jacques Vredeman (a member of the Vredeman family of lutenists) is known to have written some *canzoni* and *villanelle* to words in the Frisian dialect.

To the 18th century belong De Koninck and Snep, who were the authors of some ' Nederlandsche Liederen met een en twe Stemmen,' with figured bass, but these are of no musical value. The same may be said of the vocal works of the following composers who lived in the early part of the 19th century: A. Ten Cate, J. G. Wilms, G. Hutschenruijter, G. W. Smits, J. Boers and D. H. Dijkhuijzen. Their names still appear in all popular collections of school and patriotic songs, together with those by composers of a later date and higher rank, such as J. Viotta, J. Antheunis, Van Eyken, Richard Hol, S. de Lange (the elder), Prudens van Duyse and J. van Riemsdijk. The songs of the last-named composers are best described under the German term *volkstümlich*, though some of them have shown more interesting and original work, as, for example, Riemsdijk in his ' Tranenkruikje ' and ' Sant Jans Gheleide,' from the *Loverkens*.[6]

The most typical Dutch composers of the last century, the words of whose songs are in

---

[1] Technically, the term Flemish has no longer the same significance as it had earlier; that is to say, it is now more identified with Belgian than with Dutch art.
[2] *La Musique aux Pays-Bas*, E. van der Straeten, iii. 22.
[3] The opera was revived in Paris, edited by L. Terry.
[4] In 1810 Van der Ghiste wrote an opera with Flemish words; and later Miry, Van den Acker and Meertens attempted Flemish vaudevilles, achieving, however, only local success.

[5] D. F. Scheurleer gives an interesting picture of musical life in Holland, *Amsterdam in de 17de eeuwe, Het Muziek leven*, The Hague, 1904.
[6] Hoffmann von Fallersleben's *Loverkens* were favourite words with Dutch composers.

the vernacular, were undoubtedly Richard HOL, J. VERHULST and W. F. G. Nicolai. The first named is better known for his patriotic songs and choruses. Nicolai, who was a prolific writer and a great favourite, wrote melodious and expressive songs, somewhat resembling Mendelssohn. Verhulst was one of the most gifted Dutch musicians, a friend of Schumann and also well known abroad. He set a number of the Flemish poet Heije's words to music, amongst others a volume of children's songs, 'Kinderleeven, 29 Liederen voor eem Stem,' which are of great charm. Another very favourite writer of children's songs in Holland is Catarina van RENNES.

Modern Dutch song-writers approach more closely to the German school than to the French; and, although at this moment a strong national feeling is asserting itself amidst some of the Dutch composers, the general tendency towards Germany cannot be denied. Space forbids more than the mere enumeration of the following names, many of whom have written songs possessing high qualities: J. BRANDTS-BUYS, J. WAGENAAR, Hendrika van Tussenbroek, J. Smulders, S. de Lange, DIEPENBROCK, Gottfried Mann, Julius RÖNTGEN, B. ZWEERS, K. Kuiler, A. Spoel, J. H. Loots, H. Viotta, van Brucken-Fock and Cornelie van Oosterzee.

BIBLIOGRAPHY[1]

LEJEUNE, J. C. W. Letterkundig Oversigt en Proevein van de Nederlandsche Volkszangen sedert de 15d eeuw. Gravesande, 1828.
COUSSEMAKER, C. E. H. DE. Histoire de l'harmonic au moyen âge. Paris, 1852.
GRÉGOIR, E. G. Essai historique sur la musique et les musiciens dans les Pays-Bas. Brussels, 1861.
DINAUX, A. Les Trouvères de la Flandre ; Trouvères, jongleurs et ménestrels du nord de la France et du midi de la Belgique. Paris, 1863.
STRAETEN, E. VAN DER. La Musique aux Pays-Bas avant le XIXme siècle. Brussels, 1867, etc.
KALFF, DR. G. Het Lied in de Middeleeuwen. Leyden, 1884.
SOUBIES, A. Belgique, le XIXme siècle ; Hollande, le XIXme siècle. Paris, 1901.
DUYSE, F. VAN. Het eenstemmig, Fransch en Nederlandsche wereldlijk Lied. Brussels, 1896. De Melodie van het Nederlandsche Lied en hare rhythmische vormen. The Hague, 1902.
Various articles in the Tijdschrift der Vereeniging voor Noord-Nederlands Muziekgeschiedenes, and general histories by Fétis, Naumann, Ambros, etc.

COLLECTIONS. (a) OLD

(This list contains only the most famous of the old collections.)
SUSATO, TYLMAN. 'Souterliedekens.' Antwerp, 1561.
FRUYTIERS, JAN. 'Ecclesiasticus.' Antwerp, 1565.
'Geusen-Lieden Boeckxens' 1588, etc.
VALLET, NICOLAS. 'Le Secret des Muses.' Amsterdam, 1618-19.
VAERIUS, A. 'Nederlandsche Gedenck-Clanck.' Haarlem, 1626.
STARTER, J. 'Friesche Lusthof.' Amsterdam, 1621.
CAMPHUYSEN, D. R. 'Nieuwen Jeuchtspiegel' (no music). 1620. 'Stichtelycke Rymen.' 1624.
THEODOTUS, S. 'Het Paradijs.' 1646.
SWAEN, G. DE. 'Den Singende Zwaen.' Antwerp, 1664.
'Het Liutboek van Thysius.'
'Cupido's Lusthof' (no music). 1613.
PERS, D. F. 'Bellerophon.' 1633.

COLLECTIONS. (b) MODERN AND GENERAL

FALLERSLEBEN, HOFFMANN VON. 'Holländische Volkslieder,' Breslau, 1833 ; 'Horae Belgicae.' (This contains the 'Antwerpsh Liedebock van 1544.')
CARTON, C. 'Oud vlaemsche Liederen en andere Gedichten der 14e en 15e eeuwen.' (Vlaem. Biblioph.), 1847.
WILLEMS, J. F. 'Oude Vlaemsche Liederen.' (This contains a valuable list of printed and MS. collections.) Ghent, 1848.
GEVAERT, F. A. 'Verzameling van acht oude Vlaemsche Liederen.' Ghent, 1854.
COUSSEMAKER, C. E. H. DE. 'Chants populaires des Flamands de France.' Ghent, 1856.
SNELLAERT, F. A. 'Oude en nieuwe Liedjes.' Ghent, 1864.
WYTSMAN, KLEMENS. 'Anciens airs et ch. populaires de Termonde.' 1868.
BRANDTS-BUYS, M. A. 'Liedjes van en voor Nêderlands Volk.' Leyden, 1875.

LUMMEL, H. J. VAN. Nieuw Geuzenliedboek.' Utrecht, 1874 and 1892.
LOOTENS, A., and FEYS, J. 'Chants populaires flamands recueillis à Bruges.' Bruges, 1879.
SCHELTEMA, J. H. 'Nederl. Liederen uit vroegeren tijd.' Leyden, 1885.
WILDER, V. 'Chansons populaires flamandes des 15me, 16me et 17me siècles.' Paris.
TERRY, L., et CHAUMONT, L. 'Recueil d'airs de crâmignons et d'airs populaires à Liège. Liège, 1889.
BRAEKMAN. 'Oude Nederlandsche Liederen.' (Melodiee uit de Souterliedekens.) Ghent, 1889.
BAMPS, C. 'Recherches sur le Mey-Liedje' (hymne populaires). Hasselt, 1889.
RIEMSDIJK, J. C. VAN. 'Vier en twintig Liederen uit de 15de en 16de eeuw met geestelijken en wereldlijken Tekst.' Amsterdam, 1890.
VLOTEN, J. VAN, and BRANDTS-BUYS, M. 'Nederlandsche Baker-en kinderrijmen.' Leyden, 1894.
JOURET, L. 'Chansons du pays d'Ath.' Brussels, 1894.
GILSON, P. 'Chansons populaires du pays Borain.' 1894.
FREDERIC ., P. 'Onze hist. Volksl. van vóór de godsdienstige Beroerten der 16de eeuw.' Ghent, 1894.
'Nederlandsche Liederboek' (pub. by the Willemsfond). Ghent, 1896.
LANGE, D. DE, RIEMSDIJK, C. VAN, and KALFF, G. 'Nederlandsch Volksliederenboek.' Amsterdam, 1896.
LOON, J. VAN, and BOER, M. DE. 'Frysk Lieteboek.' Leeuwaaden, 1899.
BLYAU, A., and TASSEEL, M. 'Iepersch (Ypres) oud Liedboek.' Ghent, 1900.
COCK, A. DE, and TEIRLINCK, I. 'Kinderspel i Kinderlust en Zuid-Nederland.' Ghent, 1902.
COERS, F. R. 'Liederboek van Groot-Nederland.' Amsterdam, 1898-1902.
RÖNTGEN, JULIUS. 'Altniederländische Kriegs- und Siegeslieder nach A. Valerius' (1626) ; '14 Altniederländische Volkslieder nach A. Valerius.' Leipzig, 1903.
CLOSSON, E. 'Chansons populaires des provinces belges.' Brussels, 1905.
DUYSE, F. VAN. 'Het oude Nederlandsche Lied.' The Hague, 1903-5.
TROELSTRA, P. J., and GROOT, P. DE. (New edition by Halbertsma.) 'Nij Frysk Lieteboek.' Leeuwaaden, 1905.
See also the publications of the Maatschappij tot bevordering der Toonkunst, and of the Maatschappij der Vlaemsche Bibliophilen.

ENGLAND [2]

English song has as long and as honourable a genealogy as that of any country in Europe. Moreover the recent research into ENGLISH FOLK-SONG (q.v.) has brought to light the popular sources of its melody and discovered a wealth of song of which for many generations sophisticated musicians had been lamentably ignorant. If John Dunstable who lived early in the 15th century cannot claim to have invented polyphony, at least he was one of the first to bring scientific and artistic order into the chaos of harmony and raise vocal music to the rank of a structural art. But about the year 1240 [3]— two centuries before the time of Dunstable—the song 'SUMER IS ICUMEN IN' (q.v.) was written by John of Fornsete, a monk of Reading Abbey. Whether this beautiful canon is the sole survivor of many such compositions, or was a solitary inspiration, is hidden from us, but it certainly implied a long previous course of study and practice.

As France gave birth to the troubadours and Germany to the Minnesinger, so did England in a remote age produce her own bards and afterwards her scalds and minstrels, her gleemen and harpers, all of whom were held in high repute by their countrymen. And there is a record of a company or brotherhood, called 'Le Pui,' formed by some merchants in London, at the end of the 13th century, for the encouragement of musical and poetical compositions. With this purpose they assembled

---

[1] The writer owes her warm thanks to Professor Julius Röntgen of Amsterdam for his kind help.

[2] See the articles on IRISH, SCOTTISH and WELSH MUSIC, with bibliographies for accounts of the characteristics of song in those countries.
[3] Or 1226, according to Dr. Wilibald Nagel's Geschichte der Musik in England, i. 76, et seq., where an interesting discussion of that song will be found. (See SUMER IS ICUMEN IN.)

periodically, and competitions were held, though the reluctance of the brotherhood to admit any but members to those meetings prevented their influence being widespread. The name denotes a French origin, which is easily possible considering the close intercourse between France and England after the Norman Conquest and during the time of the Crusades.[1] Of the abundance of popular tunes in the 14th century evidence is supplied by the number of hymns written to them. For instance, 'Sweetest of all, sing,' 'Good-day, my leman dear,' and many others were secular stage-songs, to which the Bishop of Ossory, who lived about 1350, wrote Latin hymns. While the minstrels flourished, notation was difficult and uncertain, and they naturally trusted to memory or improvisation for the tunes to which their tales should be sung. (See MINSTREL.) But with the end of the 15th century the minstrels disappeared, their extinction accelerated by the invention of printing. When the pedlar had begun to traverse the country with his penny books and his songs on broadsheets the minstrel's day was past.[2] To the time of the minstrels belongs, however, the famous 'Battle of Agincourt' song,[3] with the date 1415.

To the reigns of Henry VI. and Edward IV. belong also many carols, and amongst them the

1.

The Song of Agincourt.

De - o gra - ci - as an - - - gli - a, red-

- - de pro vic - to - - ri - a. Owre kynge went forth to

Nor-man-dy, With grace and myght of chy-val - ry:

Ther God for him wrought mar-velus-ly, Wher-fore Eng-

- londe may call and cry De - - - - - o gra - - ci-

Chorus.

- as, De - o gra - ci - as an - - gli - -

- a, red - de pro vic-to - - - - ri - - a.

celebrated 'Nowell, Nowell' and the 'Boar's Head' Carol, sung even now every Christmas at Queen's College, Oxford.[4] Some of these carols may have been composed by John Dunstable or his contemporaries. Although in England there is little left of this earliest English school of composers[5] on the Continent recent discoveries have been important. 'O rosa bella,' a three-part love-song, by Dunstable, was found at Rome, and afterwards in a different version at Dijon,[6] and it is evidently counterpoint on a popular song. A number of other MSS. of English composers' works of this period exist at Modena and Trent, and the latter library contains another secular song 'Puisque m'amour' by Dunstable.[7] (See DUNSTABLE.)

In the period between 1485 and 1547,[8] which covers the reigns of Henry VII. and Henry VIII., social and political ballads multiplied fast; and among the best-known productions of these reigns are the following: 'Pastyme with good companye,' composed by Henry VIII. himself; 'The three ravens,' 'John Dory,' 'The hunt is up,'[9] 'We be three poor Mariners,' 'Robin, lend me thy bow,' 'My little pretty one,' 'Sellenger's Round,' 'Westron Wynde,'[10] etc. It should be noticed here that many variations in the copies of old tunes indicate uncertainty in oral traditions. Formerly the general opinion was that the old secular music of European countries was based upon the same scale or mode as the modern major scale, *i.e.* the Ionian mode. But it is now generally acknowledged that the ecclesiastical modes were fully used in England in the composition of all kinds of secular music until early in the 17th century, and many of the popular songs were written throughout this period in the Dorian, Mixolydian and other modes.[11] Thus, amongst

[1] See H. I. Riley's *Liber Custumarum*, p. 589. The languages of Latin, French and English were for a time intermingled, but by the middle of the 14th century French had become a foreign language, Latin was reserved for ecclesiastics and scholars, and every Englishman, high or low, spoke his own tongue. *Ges. d. Musik in England*, Dr. W. Nagel, ii. 8 *et seq.*

[2] For further information about the minstrels see *Old English Popular Mus.*, Chappell, i. 1 *et seq.*; and *Ges. d. Musik in England*, Nagel, i. 96 *et seq.*

[3] *Old English Popular Music*, i. 25. Chappell further says that when Henry V. entered the city of London in triumph after the battle of Agincourt . . . boys with pleasing voices were placed in artificial turrets singing verses in his praise. But Henry ordered this part of the pageantry to cease, and commanded that for the

future no ditties should be made and sung by minstrels or others in praise of the recent victories 'for that he would whollie have the praise and thanks altogether given to God.' Nevertheless among many others, a minstrel piece soon appeared on the *Seyge of Harflet* (Harfleur), and the *Battayle of Agynkourt*, evidently, says Warton, adapted to the harp, and of which he has printed some portions (*History of English Poetry*, ii. 257). The above song, which was printed in the 18th century by Percy, Burney and J. Stafford Smith, from a MS. in the Pepysian collection in the Library of Magdalene College, Cambridge, has been shown by J. A. Fuller Maitland to be an incomplete transcript from one in Trinity College, Cambridge, in which the melody stands as above. (See 'English Carols of the 15th Century.')

[4] The words to this carol were printed by Wynkyn de Worde in 1521, but the music appears to be of an earlier date.

[5] See, however, Wooldridge's discussion, MSS. *Oxf. Hist. Mus.* ii. 127.

[6] See Ambros, *Geschichte der Musik*, Musik Beilage, p. 22, where the Roman version is reprinted.

[7] These were discovered in 1892 by W. Barclay Squire, and copies are now in the British Museum.

[8] Here the chapter on 'The English School' in Prof. H. Wooldridge's second vol. of the *Oxford Hist. of Mus.* may be studied with advantage.

[9] Any song intended to arouse in the morning, even a love-song, was formerly called a *hunt's up* (Shakespeare so employs it in *Romeo and Juliet*, Act iii. Scene 5). There are many different versions of the tune.

[10] This song is famous for being the only secular song which our church composers employed; it was the subject of three Masses by Taverner, Tye and Shepherde in the 16th century. See Chappell, *op. cit.* i. 38, for the melody.

[11] At the time the previous editions of Chappell's work were published this fact had not been freely accepted, and a certain number of the tunes had had sharps and flats added to them, which transformed an ecclesiastical mode into a major or minor key. In the 1893 edition, these signs have been removed. Moreover, in this edition it is stated that there are 44 Dorian, 19 Mixolydian and 12 Aeolian tunes out of 118. The other 43 are mostly in the major. The Phrygian and Lydian modes occur less often, however, in English music than in that of other countries. See Wooldridge's preface to Chappell's *Old Eng. Pop. Music.*

the early songs, The King's Ballad,' ' Westron Wynde,' and others agree in some of their many versions with the Dorian mode. And, as will be later shown, modal influences exist to the present day in our simplest folk-songs. But in the 16th century the easy Ionian mode was the favourite of strolling singers and ballad-mongers; and in spite of prohibition and censure by the Church and the disdain with which skilled musicians treated what they contemptuously termed *il modo lascivo*, this popular scale triumphantly survived and has formed the basis of our modern system of scales and keys.

Of secular songs antecedent to the middle of the 16th century few have come down to us in writing. The aurally transmitted folk-song cannot be dated with any accuracy. The principal relics are the songs in the Fayrfax MS.[1] This manuscript, which once belonged to and was probably written down by Dr. Robert FAYRFAX (*q.v.*), consists of forty-nine songs by the best musicians of that time.[2] They are all written in 2, 3 and 4 parts in the contrapuntal style; some in the mixed measure—four-time in the one part and three-time in another—which was common at the end of the 15th century. During the latter half of the 16th century musicians of the first rank seldom composed airs of the short rhythmical kind appropriate to ballads, and poets rarely wrote in this metre, for ballad-writing had become a separate employment. It should also be noted that 'English church composers rarely took popular or folk-songs for the subjects of their masses[3] and motets as was the custom in foreign countries, though they were freely used as themes for variations or *canti fermi* for polyphonic works by instrumental composers.

In Queen Elizabeth's reign music was generally cultivated and song was universal: 'tinkers sang catches; milkmaids sang ballads; carters whistled; each trade, even the beggars, had their special songs.'[4] The best-known songs of this period from 1558–1603 were ' The Carman's Whistle,' ' All in a Garden Green,' ' Dulcina,' ' The British Grenadiers,' ' Death and the Lady,'[5] ' Near Woodstock Town,' ' Light o' Love,' ' Children in the Wood,'[6] ' The Bailiff's Daughter of Islington,' ' Willow Song,'[7] ' Greensleeves,' ' The Friar of Orders Gray,' ' O Death, rock me asleep,'[8] and ' Frog

Galliard.' This last song by John Dowland is almost the only instance to be found in the Elizabethan period of a favourite folk - tune known to have come from the hand of a celebrated composer. Dowland originally wrote it to the words, ' Now, O now, I needs must part,' and it appeared in his First Book of Airs (see ENGLISH SCHOOL OF LUTENIST SONG-WRITERS, Vol. II.) in the double form of a song to the lute and a four-part song. William Byrd's adoption of the ' Carman's Whistle ' in the Fitzwilliam Virginal Book is well known; it is a dance-tune, and so also is ' Greensleeves,' and many others. In fact, nearly all the dance-tunes contained in these and somewhat later collections of lute and virginal music are the most valuable sources we possess for accurate and trustworthy versions of the music of the folk-songs (see VIRGINAL MUSIC). They are trustworthy because they were written down at the time by skilled musicians and therefore escaped the risks of transmission by ear alone. The names or words of many ballads are handed down to posterity in the works of Shakespeare[9] and other Elizabethan dramatists.[10]

A few words may be introduced here on the form of popular English ballads, or folk-songs.[11] In dance, or march, or ballad music which has grown from the recitation of words to a chant, or to a short rhythmical tune, the musical design is found to reside chiefly in the rhythm. The ordinary rhythm of ballads was the even fashion of four-bar phrases, as, for instance, in ' The hunt is up ':

2.   *The Hunt is up.*

1st Phrase. 1   2   3   4

The hunt is up, the hunt is up, and it is well nigh day;

2nd Phrase. 1   2   3   4

And Harry our King is gone hunting to bring his deer to bay.

The three-bar phrase rhythm is generally met with in the jig and hornpipe tunes of England, such as ' Bartholomew Fair,' but it sometimes occurs in songs of other kinds. Of the rhythm in ' My little pretty one ' (Ex. 3), which has three phrases of two bars each, and a fourth of three bars, there are several other examples; and, indeed, there are abundant varieties of irregular rhythm. But it may be held as a general conclusion that the musical rhythm follows the rhythm and metre of the words and varies with

---

[1] Mention must also be made of three MSS. in the British Museum. Add. MSS. 5665 contains some ballads. This MS. was discovered by Ritson, and a few pieces were printed in J. S. Smith's ' Musica antiqua.' Add. MSS. 31,922 is a volume containing no less than thirty-three songs by King Henry VIII. (amongst them ' Green grow the holly,' which is a fine song), the rest by Cornyshe, Farding, John Fluyd, Pygott and others. Royal MSS. appendix 58 contains tenor-parts of twenty secular songs, perhaps written before 1500. This collection contains many dance-tunes, such as ' My Lady Carew's Dompe,' also printed in ' Musica antiqua,' with several of the older songs. Davey, *History of English Music*, p. 94 et seq.   [2] Burney, ii. 539.
[3] The ' Westron Wynde ' masses of Tye, Shepherd and Taverner are noteworthy instances of the practice adopted from the Netherlands. See *Oxf. Hist. Mus.* ii. 325.   [4] Chappell, i. 59.
[5] A series of ballads from ' The Dance of Death.'
[6] ' Chevy Chace ' was sung to this tune.
[7] ' A poor soul sat sighing.'
[8] This was the first ballad known to have an independent accompaniment; it was for the lute. Chappell, i. 111.

[9] The following are some of the ballads Shakespeare refers to: ' The hunt is up,' ' Heartsease,' ' Willow, Willow,' ' It was a lover and his lass,' ' Greensleeves,' ' Under the greenwood tree,' ' Bonny Sweet Robin,' etc.
[10] Ben Jonson's poem, ' Drink to me only,' is for ever associated with the equally beautiful 18th-century tune ascribed to Col. Mellish, about 1760.
[11] The word 'ballad' was applied in a loose sense to every kind of song. The ballad of this period and, indeed, up to the 18th century usually means ' pieces of narrative verse in stanzas,' the music of the first stanza being repeated for every successive one. It was also used in England for that which in other countries is designated a ' folk-song,' and this term has of recent years been also accepted in England for any form of song which essentially belongs to the people.

them. Compound time is very common in English ballads, especially during and after the

3.   *My Little Pretty One.*

My ly-tell pre-ty one, my pretie bo-ni one,

She is a joy-lie one, and gentle as can be;

With a beck she comes anon, with a wincke she wil be gon,

No doubt she is alone of all that ev-er I see.

reign of Charles II., and may be accounted for by the influence of the French dance-music, which Charles II. brought into England. In modulations they exhibit but little variety. The most frequent arrangement is the half-close on the dominant, and the leading note preceding the tonic at the end of the melody, as in ' The hunt is up.' In another arrangement the half-close is on the sub-dominant and the penultimate note is on the supertonic. In minor-key ballads the relative major-key often takes the place which is held by the dominant in major-key ballads. Another peculiarity of many old ballads are ' burdens.' Sometimes the burden was sung by the bass or basses underneath the melody to support it, as in ' Sumer is icumen in ' ; or it took the shape of ' ditties,' the end of old ballads, introduced to eke out the words of the story to the length of the musical phrase, as in the ' Willow Song.' In this case the burden was sung continuously by the same voice, but in other instances it was taken up by the chorus at the end of a solo song, or solo and chorus combined, as for instance in the burden of ' Sir Eglamore.' The burdens often consist

4.   *Sir Eglamore.*[1]

Sir Eg-la-more, that va-liant knight, Fa la

lanky down dilly. And as he rode o'er hill and dale, All

arm'd upon his shirt of mail, Fa la

la fa la la, Fa la lanky down dilly.

[1] J. Stafford Smith's ' Mus. Ant.' i. 66, taken from the ' Merry Drollery Compleat.'

of meaningless syllables, as in ' It was a lover and his lass,' or the last example quoted.[2] The same feature is characteristic of the SHANTY (*q.v.*).

With the end of the 16th century comes in England the first great period of the art-song ushered in by the publication of John Dowland's ' First Booke of Songs or Ayres of foure parts with tablature for the Lute ' (1597). The historical importance of this publication is that while the songs may be sung in parts in accordance with prevalent fashion, Dowland has evidently conceived them for his own solo performance to his instrumental accompaniment. From this date to 1612 some thirty sets of songs to the lute were published, four by DOWLAND, the acknowledged master of the school, five each by Thomas CAMPIAN and Robert JONES (*q.v.*) ; others by MORLEY, ROSSETER, FORD, CORKINE and PILKINGTON (see ENGLISH SCHOOL OF LUTENIST SONG-WRITERS). Nearly all the above-mentioned composers were among the contributors to the collection published by Sir W. Leighton in 1614. This collection was entitled ' Teares or Lamentacions of a sorrowfull soule,' but its contents were mostly songs in four parts.[3]

The popularity of masques at court offered opportunities to composers for the introduction of lyric songs and dance-tunes. Some scientific musicians may have disdained this kind of work, which only required simple little ditties akin to the folk-songs. Nevertheless Campian, Johnson, and later on Henry LAWES, won great favour in this branch. Lawes published several books of Ayres and Dialogues for one, two and three voices, with the assistance of his brother, William Lawes, whose fame chiefly rests on his music to Herrick's words ' Gather ye rosebuds.' The high reputation won by Henry Lawes in his own day, the enthusiastic praise of the poets, Milton and Herrick, whose verses he set and the disparagement of his work by musical historians of a later age, together call for a word of comment. Milton accorded him the undeserved credit of being the first English musician to set words ' with just note and accent,' and Burney[4] criticised his most famous song, ' Sweet Echo,' one of the five which have survived of his music to Milton's ' Comus,' for its defects in the very matter for which the poet praised him. The changed attitude towards rhythm which was invading music in the 17th century accounts both for the success and failure of Lawes. The BAR (*q.v.*) was gaining in influence, and regular barring of music according to accentual principles was becoming the fashion.

Dowland could write such a phrase as the following without the least hint of undue accent

[2] For the above remarks on form, see Miss O. Prescott's article entitled *Form or Design in Vocal Music* (*Musical World*, 1881).
[3] Want of space precludes mention in detail of Playford's, Ravenscroft's, D'Urfey's, Leighton's and the various interesting collections of others, and the reader is referred to the articles under their several names in this Dictionary.   [4] *History*, iii. 382.

on ' the ' and ' of '; the bar line was for him still a matter of convenience dictating no accent.

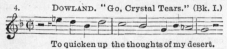

4. DOWLAND. "Go, Crystal Tears." (Bk. I.)

To quicken up the thoughts of my desert.

Lawes on the other hand had to guard the first beat of the bar, generally to accept and sometimes to disguise, but always to respect its implied accent. In the passage from ' Sweet Echo ' which Burney criticises so trenchantly he deals with this bar line accent in several ways and certainly with more success than Burney allows him.

5. LAWES. " Sweet Echo."

And in the vi - o - let embroider'd vale,

Where the love-lorn Night-in-gale nightly to

thee her sad . . song mourn-eth well,

Canst thou not tell me of a gen-tle pair that

lik - est thy Nar-cis-sus are

In bars 1 and 3 of the above he begins the vocal phrase after the accent; in bar 2 he diminishes its prominence by the length which he has given to the first syllable of the word ' violet '; in bar 4 he uses the bar accents to enforce the play on the words ' Nightingale nightly.' Lawes here and elsewhere tackled a problem which his predecessors had not had to face, and in doing so he did a certain amount of pioneer work in the technique of the new style which dance-rhythms and the Italian recitative were combining to impose on musical interpretation. He had not the musical genius for supreme success, but he prepared the way for PURCELL (q.v.), whose declamation of the English language ultimately combined elasticity

of musical rhythm with the regular bar structures of duple, triple and quadruple times.

It was a custom with poets in the 16th and 17th centuries to write new words to favourite old tunes, and this practice has made it almost impossible to assign precise dates to many songs and ballads. Thus in Sir Philip Sidney's poems the heading ' to the air of ' etc. —often a French or Italian tune—constantly recurs ; and many of the folk-tunes were sung to three or four sets of words bearing different dates and having little or no relation to each other. Among songs to be found in the principal collections of the first half of the 17th century was the tune of ' Cheerily and Merrily,' afterwards sung to George Herbert's ' Sweet day,' and better known by its later name. ' Stingo, or oil of barley,' ' The country lass,' and ' Cold and raw ' were all sung to the same tune, and many another example might be adduced.

During the Commonwealth secular music flourished in England, and, notwithstanding the abolition by the Puritans of cathedral choirs and theatre music, domestic music was much cultivated. A few of the favourite ballads of that time, both Puritan and Loyalist, were, ' Hey then, up we go,' ' Love lies bleeding,' ' I live not where I love,' ' When love was young,' ' When the king enjoys his own again,'[1] and ' I would I were in my own country.' At the end of the Commonwealth the secularisation of music was complete, and with the Restoration of the Stuarts in 1660 a lighter and more melodious kind of music was introduced. In his exile Charles II. had grown fond of French dance music. Ballads, too, came into popular favour again, as the king was partial to lively tunes with strongly marked rhythms. Of the abundant songs of that period, amongst the most celebrated were : ' Here's a health unto his Majesty,' ' Come, lasses and lads,' ' Troy Town,' ' Barbara Allen,' ' Under the greenwood tree,' ' Dulce Domum,' ' LILLIBURLERO ' (q.v.), and ' May Fair,' now better known as ' Golden Slumbers.'[2]

As already mentioned, educated musicians of England were about this time very much under the influence of the Italian and French schools. The style of Pelham Humfrey, whom Charles II. sent to France to study under Lully, was entirely founded on that of his teacher. His song, 'I pass all my hours in a shady old grove,'[3] has hardly yet ceased to be sung, and it is a good example of his work, ' which shows a continually varying adaptation of music to changing sentiment of words, and the most

1 Ritson calls this the most famous and popular air ever heard in this country. See Chappell, i. 214.
2 During the 17th century many of our ballad-tunes had found their way into the Netherlands and were there printed with Dutch words (only preserving the English titles) in most of the miscellaneous collections of songs. For instance ' The hunt is up ' and ' Fortune my foe ' appear severally in the Leyden Lute-Book and the ' Nederlandtsche Gedenck-Clanck,' 1626. Chappell, Old English Popular Music, i. xv. 76, 84. (See The Netherlands section of this article.)
3 The words are attributed to Charles II.

fastidious observance of their emphasis and quantity.'[1] Many songs of his may be found in the various collections of the time.[2] A fellow-student in the Chapel Royal, to whom Humphrey taught much, was John Blow. In 1700 Blow published a volume of his own songs under the title of 'Amphion Anglicus,' and his setting of Waller's 'Self-Banished' is evidence that he could sometimes compose with tenderness and grace. Then Matthew Locke, the famous masque-composer who wrote 'The delights of the bottle,' a most popular song in its day, is worthy of notice, and he had the honour paid to him of an elegy by Purcell at his death in 1677.

Had Henry Purcell never written anything but songs, he would still have established his claim to be the greatest of English musicians. After his death, his songs were collected under the title of 'Orpheus Britannicus'; and 'Full fathom five,' 'Come unto these yellow sands,' 'From rosy bowers,' 'I attempt from love's sickness to fly,' amongst others, have been sung down to our own times. He was a contributor also to Playford's publication 'Choice Ayres and Dialogues,' but his finest songs will be found in the operas and plays for which he composed the incidental music. The qualities of his style and particularly his masterly use of the ground bass as a principle of design in song-writing have received some analysis above. (See PURCELL.) Between 1683 and 1690 Purcell devoted himself to the study of the great Italian masters, and their teachings are manifest in his music. He did not indeed lose any of his individuality, but the melody of his songs became henceforth smoother and more flowing, and the accompaniments more varied. A common fault of the music of Purcell's time was a too servile adherence to the meaning of the text, and the changing sense of the words was too often blindly followed to the sacrifice of musical construction.[3] Purcell avoided these faults; with his fine instinct for melody and harmony and his thorough scientific education, no extravagances of any school could lay a strong or permanent hold upon his genius.

From 1700–1800 England's previous repute as a land of music sank to a low ebb. Purcell had no successor as a great creative and original musician.[4] There were, however, a number of tunes produced in the 18th century which are still familiar to us. John Eccles and Richard Leveridge published large selections of songs; and to the latter we owe the famous songs, 'Black-eyed Susan' and 'The Roast Beef of Old England.' A beautiful song called 'Felton's Gavotte,' or 'Farewell, Manchester,' said to have been played by the troops of Charles Stuart in quitting Manchester in December 1745, was originally part of a concerto composed by the Rev. W. Felton. Other popular songs of this period were 'Old King Cole,' 'Down among the dead men,' 'Cease your funning,' 'The Vicar of Bray,' and 'Pretty Polly Oliver.' A marked stimulus was given to song-culture in George II.'s reign by the ballad-operas, of which the 'Beggar's Opera' (1727) was the first; and it was these operas which brought about the first reaction of the popular taste against Italian music (see BALLAD OPERA). They were spoken dramas with songs interspersed, the songs being set to old ballad tunes, or imitations of them. Thenceforth most of the popular songs were composed by educated musicians, but the great and enduring popularity of some would entitle them to be classed as national songs. In regard to musical structure they are generally strophical, with an easy accompaniment, a marked rhythm and a pleasing melody very simply harmonised.

Very popular in his day was Henry Carey, to whom our splendid national anthem was for a time attributed (see GOD SAVE THE KING). William Boyce also claims recognition for the spirited 'Come, cheer up, my lads' ('Heart of Oak'), which he wrote to Garrick's words in 1759. A greater composer was Thomas Arne, who has been pronounced to be our most national song-writer. 'Rule, Britannia' was written by Arne in 1740 as a finale for the masque of 'Alfred'; and as the song passed from mouth to mouth it soon grew pre-eminent among national airs. It was said by Wagner that the first eight notes of 'Rule, Britannia' express the whole character of the British people. In that same year Arne produced his beautiful songs in *As You Like It*, which he followed with songs in other plays of Shakespeare. In later years Arne's style deteriorated. An imitator of Handel without his genius, Arne overloaded his airs with florid passages, as may be seen in the songs of his opera, 'Artaxerxes.' The obligations of the English people to opera-writers, and of the latter to them, have been reciprocal. While some of the best national airs were due to the opera-writers, they in turn won applause by the free introduction of current popular songs into their operas.[5]

Passing on to another generation, we meet with William Jackson of Exeter, who was thirty years younger than Arne. About Jackson's songs there clings a sense of tameness and in-

[1] Hullah's *Transition Period of Musical History*, p. 203.
[2] J. Stafford Smith prints five songs in 'Mus. Ant.' ii. 170 *et seq.*, and also one of John Blow's.
[3] In fact Lawes's meritorious efforts in this direction were soon exaggerated and overdone by his followers.
[4] Handel's contribution to English song, apart from his arias in oratorio and cantata, was slight. Reference is made under Germany in this article to his songs published with English words, p. 68.

[5] Most indeed of the best songs of a period extending from Purcell's time down to the early part of the 19th century were once embedded in dramatic pieces; but these pieces have faded into oblivion, while the songs have survived through successive generations. As dramatic forms of song, these compositions lie outside the scope of this article, but as national and popular songs, they come within it. A list of forty operas entirely set to current popular airs is given under ENGLISH OPERA.

sipidity, but in his day no collection was held to be complete without his ' Time has not thinned my flowing hair,' or ' When first this humble roof I knew.' Among his contemporaries, but a little junior to him, were Thomas Carter, Samuel Arnold, Samuel Webbe and Charles Dibdin, who was a patriotic ballad-writer rather than a musician. The pathos of ' Tom Bowling ' has rescued it from neglect, but only by sailors are his other songs remembered now. To Dibdin's generation also belonged John Percy, the composer of ' Wapping Old Stairs,' and James Hook, best known for ' The Lass of Richmond Hill,' and ' 'Twas within a mile of Edinboro' Town,' a pseudo-Scotch song, like Carter's ' O, Nanny, wilt thou gang with me ? ' Two better musicians than the foregoing appeared a little later, namely, William Shield and Stephen Storace, both of whom were distinguished by a gift of melody. But their songs are seldom heard now, excepting perhaps ' The death of Tom Moody ' by Shield, and Storace's ' With lonely suit.' A well-known song of that period was ' The Bay of Biscay ' by John Davy of Exeter.

The special merit of English songs of the late 18th century is their melody, which seems to have then been a common gift ; but the strongest feeling of the nation was patriotism, and the compositions that survive are almost all short songs expressive of patriotic sentiment, or connected with it by their nautical subjects,[1] John Braham, Charles Horn, and Henry Bishop were all born in the 18th century, but so near its close that their works must be ascribed to the 19th century. Braham himself was a celebrated singer, and his sea-song ' The Death of Nelson ' [2] merits the fame which it has won. To Horn we owe ' Cherry Ripe,' and ' The deep, deep sea.' Sir Henry Bishop stood foremost among all his contemporaries and immediate predecessors, alike in science, taste and facility, and possibly also in invention. His accompaniments are varied and skilful, and though his melodies contain rapid divisions requiring vocal skill, they are graceful and effective. With such care also did he study correctness of accent that in his songs the metre of the poetry is seldom disturbed by the rhythm of the music. ' Bid me discourse,' ' Should he upbraid,' and ' Home, Sweet Home ' are well-established favourites, which need no eulogy. As other illustrations of the songs of the first part of the 19th century may be mentioned, ' I'd be a butterfly,' by Haynes Bayly ; ' She wore a wreath of roses,' by Knight ; ' The blue bell of Scotland,' by Mrs. Jordan, and others by Rooke, Rodwell, Thomas Cooke, Lee and Lover. But speaking generally of these songs and of many others like them, their sole and

only merit consisted in the voice-part being pleasant and melodious, and the accompaniments very easy.

It can be easily understood that although this type of song was popular it had nothing in common with the genuine folk-song. There is indeed an impression that by the end of the 18th century traditional song had died out in England,[3] but this is by no means the case. The many valuable books of traditional songs collected and published during the 19th and present centuries afford proof that the popularity of song has never been lost in England. Each part of England preserves its special songs as much as its own customs for certain days and seasons. And collectors of songs can bear witness that the habit of inventing songs is not yet extinct among the country people. This circumstance may account for the existence of many quite distinct airs for a set of favourite words.[4] Recent collections also show that the modal influence (already spoken of in this article) is still evident in many of the English folk-songs. Many of the more recently collected folk-songs are mere variants of older versions, and it is often very difficult to trace them back to their original form. The districts where music is largely cultivated among the poorer classes are not those where the old tunes are most carefully preserved and handed down. The reason of this is that the popular song of the day is ever the enemy of folk-music ; and, although the neighbourhood of a town may afford opportunities of musical instruction and cultivation, it likewise offers facilities for acquiring familiarity with this commoner and less desirable class of song. As a general rule the English folk-songs are diatonic in melody and regular in form, and lack any striking characteristics as regards either rhythm or harmony. They hold, however, a high place among the folk-songs of other nations, and they owe it to symmetry of form, simplicity and directness of melody and the absence of sentimentality.[5]

It would be difficult at this date to write a just appreciation of English songs of the 19th century. Although there have been many composers of real merit, the standard of the general public taste was low, and the demand for high or serious work was limited. A numerous section of song-writers clung to the ever-popular ballad-form, and, as they considered the voice-part to be their paramount consideration, they attempted nothing more than the simplest harmonies and accompaniments and disregarded alike the accent and meaning of the poem for the sake of repeating the same commonplace

---

[1] Davey's *History of English Music*, p. 425 *et seq.*
[2] On the curious similarity of musical idea between this and Méhul's ' Chant du départ ' (amounting almost to identity), see Davey, *op. cit.* p. 477.

[3] Chappell's ' Old English Popular Music ' ends with the close of the 18th century.
[4] See preface to ' English County Songs,' by Lucy Broadwood and J. A. Fuller Maitland.
[5] Sir Hubert Parry said in his inaugural address to the Folk-song Society : ' The folk-songs are characteristic of our race ; of the quiet reticence of our country folk, courageous and content to meet what chance shall bring with a brave heart. All the things that mark the folk-music of the race also betoken the qualities of the race, and as a faithful reflection of ourselves we needs must cherish it.'

tune again and again. Yet within these narrow limits there are songs of various degrees of merit ; some composers have raised their songs by force of natural gifts and instinctive taste to a high level.

For a considerable period it seemed as if England knew not how to speak her own language in music. It is an open question whether the effects produced by the Italian opera in Handel's time, and succeeded later by the strong influence of Mendelssohn, were baneful or beneficial to English music. But it is certain that during the first two-thirds of the 19th century very few genuine English songs—that is, purely English in idiom and turn of expression, as well as in thought and feeling—could be met with. Of these few exceptions we may name J. L. Hatton's ' To Anthea ' and ' Simon the Cellarer,' J. Hullah's ' Three Fishers,' F. Clay's ' The Sands of Dee,' A. S. Sullivan's ' Orpheus ' and his other songs from Shakespeare and Tennyson. In excellence of workmanship many of the above songs cannot compete with those of a perfectly distinct class of writers, among whom W. Sterndale Bennett stands pre-eminent. Of the refinement, delicacy and perfect symmetry of his songs, such as ' May Dew ' and ' Dawn, gentle flower ' there could be no question ; and had he not shared in common with Mendelssohn a tiresome mannerism of frequent repetition of the same phrase, his songs would have been more fully recognised and appreciated. To much the same period belong the songs of E. J. Loder, whose graceful ' Booklet ' is one of the best of English songs, W. Davison, G. A. Macfarren, Henry Hugo Pierson and Edward Bache. The last died very young, but not before he had given promise of high merit in the clearness of his ideas. Pierson's songs displayed strength and originality and broke through the established traditions of form. The true English ring of Arthur Sullivan's songs has already been noticed, but there was some other undefined quality which contributed to secure his great successes. It was not his brilliant humour, for that quality hardly appears in his songs. Possibly the charm lay in some veiled touch of emotion. He wrote various kinds of songs : some descended to the sentimental type known as the ' drawing-room ballad,' while others rose to a far higher level, such as his Shakespeare songs and the setting of Tennyson's ' The Window, or the Loves of the Wrens.' [1] In this last beautiful little cycle there are a tenderness and grace combined with fine workmanship which are enduring qualities.

During the last third of the 19th century song in England along with other forms of music showed signs of revival. The group of com-

posers to whom this was due includes the names of Parry, Stanford, Mackenzie, Goring Thomas, Cowen and a little later Elgar. Parry indeed took up the subtle problems of the declamation of the English language where Purcell had left them, and his 12 books of ' English lyrics ' (two published posthumously) will stand beside ' Orpheus Britannicus.' Stanford, profiting by his heritage of Irish melody and a peculiar deftness of handling in which he surpassed all his contemporaries, was the most instinctive song-writer of his generation. To name the successful song-writers who have followed these leaders in revival would be merely to recount most of the names of living English composers who are included in this Dictionary. It is worth while, however, to note the names of several women who have done distinctive work in this direction ; particularly Maude Valerie White, Liza Lehmann and Ethel Smyth.

With the end of the 19th century came that revival of the English folk-song which has already been mentioned (see FOLK - SONG SOCIETY; SHARP, Cecil J.; and ENGLISH FOLK-SONG), and the best of the younger composers have profited by it to recover the traditional idiom of native song in their own compositions.

BIBLIOGRAPHY

BURNEY, DR. CHARLES. *History of Music.* London, 1776–89.
HAWKINS, SIR JOHN. *History of Music.* Edition of 1853.
HULLAH, JOHN. *The Third or Transition Period of Musical History.* London, 2nd edition, 1876.
ROCKSTRO, W. S. *History of Music.* London, 1886.
NAUMANN, EMIL. *History of Music* (edited and added to by Sir F. Gore Ouseley). London, 1882–86.
PARRY, SIR C. H. H. *The Evolution of the Art of Music.* London, 1894.
NAGEL, DR. WILIBALD. *Geschichte der Musik in England.* Strassburg 1894–97.
DAVEY, H. *History of English Music.* London, 1895 (rev. edn. 1921).
PARRY, SIR C. H. H. *Music of the Seventeenth Century.* (*Oxford Hist. of Music,* vol. iii.). Oxford, 1902.
FULLER MAITLAND, J. A. *The Age of Bach and Handel* (*Oxford Hist. of Music,* vol. iv.). Oxford, 1902.
WOOLDRIDGE, H. *The Polyphonic Period.* (*Oxford Hist. of Music,* vol. ii.). Oxford, 1905.
SHARP, CECIL J. *English Folk-Song, some Conclusions.* 1907.
WALKER, ERNEST. *A History of Music in England.* 1907 (rev. edn. 1924).

COLLECTIONS

SMITH, J. STAFFORD. ' Musica antiqua.' London, 1812.
SANDYS, W. ' Christmas Carols, Ancient and Modern.' London, 1833.
CHAPPELL, W. ' Popular Music of the Olden Time.' London, 1855–59.
WOOLDRIDGE, H. A new edition of above, called ' Old English Popular Music.' London, 1893.
HULLAH, JOHN. ' 58 English Songs of the 17th and 18th Century.' London, 1871.
SMITH, LAURA. ' The Music of the Waters.' London, 1888.
BARRETT, W. A. ' English Folk-Songs.' London, 1891.
GOULD, S. BARING, and SHEPPARD, H. ' Songs of the West.' London, 1891.
KIDSON, F. ' Traditional Tunes.' Oxford, 1891.
SOMERVELL, A. ' Songs of the Four Nations.' London, 1892.
BROADWOOD, L. E., and FULLER MAITLAND, J. A. ' English County Songs.' 1893.
GOULD, S. BARING, and SHEPPARD, H. J. ' A Garland of Country Song.' London, 1895–97.
STOKOE, J., and REAY, S. ' Songs and Ballads of Northern England.' Newcastle and London, 1899.
SHARP, CECIL. (See bibliography under SHARP, CECIL J.)
MOFFAT, ALFRED, and KIDSON, FRANK. ' The Minstrelsy of England.' 1902.
HADOW, W. H. ' Songs of the British Islands.' London, 1903.
O'NEILL, NORMAN. ' A Golden Treasury of Song.' London, 1903.
NICHOLSON, SYDNEY. ' British Songs for British Boys.' 1903.
SHARP, C. J., and MARSON, C. L. ' Folk-Songs from Somerset.' 1905–7.
DUNCAN, EDMONSTOUNE. ' The Minstrelsy of England.' London, 1905.
STANFORD, SIR C. V. ' The National Song-Book.' London and New York, 1906.
GOULD, S. BARING, and SHARP, C. ' English Folk-Songs for Schools.' London, 1906.
KIDSON, FRANK, and MOFFAT, ALFRED. ' English Songs of the Georgian Period.' London, 1907.
KIDSON, F., and SNOW, MARTIN. *Songs of Britain.*
BUCK, PERCY C. *The Oxford Song Book,* 1916.
See also the Journal of the Folk-Song Society, 1899, etc., and bibliographies under ENGLISH FOLK-SONG and SHANTY.

---

[1] These words were written by Tennyson expressly for Sullivan at Sir George Grove's request. The latter had proposed in Oct. 1866 to Tennyson, to write a ' Liederkreis ' for Millais to illustrate, and Sullivan to set to music. *Life and Letters of Sir George Grove,* by C. L. Graves, p. 133.

GERMANY

The history of German song has been so thoroughly explored by German writers that its course may be followed from very remote ages, when song was scarcely distinguishable from speech, and *singen* and *sagen* were convertible terms.[1] But until the time of the Minnesinger the song had not acquired form either in metre or melody, and this therefore must be our starting-point.

The Minnesinger were the German counterparts of the Troubadours, but they were of rather later date, and the tone of their compositions was somewhat different. While the Troubadours sang generally of love and gallantry, the Minnesinger constantly introduced into their songs praises of the varied beauties of nature. The Minnesinger always sang and accompanied their own compositions and took no remuneration for the entertainment they gave. They were more numerous in Southern than in Northern Germany; Austria was especially prolific in them. (See MINNESINGER.)

The most representative names in the first period, 1150–1190, were Dietmar von Aiste, Meinloh von Sevelingen, Der von Kürenberc and Spervogel. The second and best period, which was the stage of maturity, was covered by the last years of the 12th century and at least half of the 13th century. To this period belonged Heinrich von Veldecke, Friedrich von Hausen, Heinrich von Morungen, Reinmar der Alte (the master of Walther von der Vogelwiede), Hartmann von der Aue (the author of the celebrated poem 'Der arme Heinrich') and Walther von der Vogelwiede himself, whose fine lyrics won for him a place among national poets. Early in the 13th century the Sängerkreig, or Minstrel-contest, was held on the Wartburg by the Landgrave Hermann of Thuringia, and among the champions who took part in it were Heinrich von Ofterdingen, Tannhäuser and Wolfram von Eschenbach. Wolfram's Minnelieder had some success, but higher renown was gained for him by his Wächterlieder and his 'Parsifal.' The third period was a time for decline and of transition to the Meistersinger. The art of the Minnesinger then descended to trivial and unpoetic themes, and a growing carelessness as to the forms of poetry plainly revealed its deterioration. Nithart von Reuenthal (whose poems were chiefly descriptive of peasant life), Ulrich von Lichtenstein, Reinmar von Zweter, der Marner and Konrad von Würzburg were the principal Minnesinger of this period.

Mediæval MSS. contain a great number of the poems of the Minnesinger and the large Jena and Colmar MSS. the melodies also. These remains attest the special pains bestowed on the poetic words, the finish of their verses as regards metre and rhythm and in short the superiority of their poetry to their music. But this perfection was only reached by degrees. Beginning with alliterative words they advanced to regular rhymes, and then rules of composition were laid down prescribing the number of lines of which different kinds of song should consist. The structure of the verses was closely followed by the Minnesinger melodies, and as there was necessarily a pause wherever the rhyme fell, a certain form was thus imparted to them. Their mode of notation was similar to that then used in the Church and their melodies were founded on the ecclesiastical modes. These compositions were of three principal kinds : the *Lied* (song), the *Leich* (lay) and the *Spruch* (proverb). The *Lied* was usually divided into three parts ; the first and second were called *Stollen* (props) and were of the same metre. These constituted the *Aufgesang*. The third or concluding section, the length of which was not prescribed, was called the *Abgesang*. This, after beginning with a contrasting metre and melody, usually (but not invariably) repeated the *Stollen*. A good example is the 'Rügelied' from the Jena MS., arranged by R. von Kralik thus [2]:

The *Leich*, according to its character, was formed either from the Church *sequences* or from the old dance tunes (*Reigen*). If the latter was the case the *Leich* was composed of differently constructed strophes and each of these had a different melody. If taken from the *sequentia* it exhibited the same monotony and absence of rhythm as the ecclesiastical melodies of that time [3]:

[1] Fragments exist of the Hildebrandlied of the 8th century (see list of MSS. and printed collections at end of this section), of which the well-known Volkslied of the 13th century 'Ich will zu Land ausreiten' is an offshoot (Böhme, 'Altdeutsches Liederbuch,' p. 3). Also of the Ludwigslied which was sung in honour of Ludwig III. when he gained the victory over the Normans in 882 at Sancourt. These are the earliest songs in the German language.

[2] 'Poesie und Musik der Minnesinger,' R. v. Kralik. (*Die Musik*, Apr. 1, 1904.)
[3] From the Jena MSS. Fr. Heinrich von der Hagen gives this example in its original notation (iv. 843, No. xxix.). His work on the Minnesinger is the best authority to consult. In the fourth volume a very instructive essay on the music of the Minnesinger will be found, together with many examples of their melodies, some of which are transcribed in facsimile, whilst others are given in modern notation. See also the new editions of the Colmar MSS. by Paul Runge and Hugo Riemann (1896) ; and of the Jena MSS. by G. Holz, E. Bernoulli and Fr. Saran (1902).

Heynrich von Ofterdingen In des e-deln vur - sten dhon.

The *Spruch* was composed of one entire strophe,
or, if other strophes were added they could be
all sung to the same tune. Walther von der
Vogelwiede's solitary surviving song (which is
in the Colmar MSS., folio 734) is a *Spruch*[1];
it is clearly meant to be sung and differs from
the ordinary didactic *Sprüche*. It must be
remembered that in speaking of the 'tone' of
a song, the Minnesinger referred exclusively to
the metrical structure of the strophe, and the
word did not therefore indicate the use of any
special melody or mode.

The 'fahrenden Sänger' (wandering minstrels),
also called merely *die Fahrenden* or *Gaukler*,
formed a link between nobles and people. Belonging clearly to the 'Jongleur' class, discouraged by the priests and patronised by courts,
they were at once acrobats, ballad-mongers
and performers on various instruments. Their
ranks comprised unfrocked monks, disbanded
crusaders, soldiers, serving-men. Essentially
musical, they made known the people's songs
at courts, and transmitted the songs of Church
and Minnesinger to the people. The music was
a fusion of secular and ecclesiastical elements,
their language a mixture of German and Latin.[2]
But they especially loved the Volkslied, and it
is to them that we owe the preservation of these
priceless songs which found their way into the
numerous collections published in the first half
of the 16th century.[3]

In the 14th century feudalism had passed its
prime. With the extinction of the art-loving
Hohenstaufen dynasty, the taste for poetry
and music declined at court and with it the
patronage extended to the Minnesinger. Power
was slipping from the grasp of princes, prelates
and nobles into the hands of burghers and
artisans. Out of these middle classes came the
Meistersinger,[4] who supplanted the more patri-
cian Minnesinger. The name of Heinrich von
Meissen (1260–1318), commonly called Frauenlob, forms the connecting-link, for by some
he is considered the last of the Minnesinger

and by others the founder of the Meistersinger.
In 1311 he came to Mainz and instituted
a guild or company of singers, who bound
themselves to observe certain rules. Though
somewhat stiff and pedantic, Frauenlob's poems
evince intelligence and thought[5]; and the
example set by him was widely imitated. Guilds
of singers soon sprang up in other large towns
in Germany; and it became the habit of the
burghers, especially in the long winter evenings,
to meet together and read or sing narrative or
other poems, either borrowed from the Minnesinger and adapted to the rules of their own
guild, or original compositions. By the end of
the 14th century there were regular schools of
music at Colmar, Frankfort, Mainz, Prague and
Strassburg, and a little later they were found
also in Nuremberg, Augsburg, Breslau, Regensburg and Ulm. In short, during the 15th and
16th centuries, there was scarcely a town of any
magnitude or importance throughout Germany
which had not its own Meistersinger. The
17th century was a period of decline, both in
numbers and repute. The last of these schools
of music lingered at Ulm until 1839 and then
ceased to exist; and the last survivor of the
Meistersinger is said to have died in 1876.

Famous among Meistersinger were Hans
Rosenblüt, Till Eulenspiegel, Muscatblüt, Heinrich von Müglin, Puschman, Fischart and
Seb. Brandt; but the greatest of all by far
was Hans Sachs, the cobbler of Nuremberg,
who lived from 1494–1576. His extant
works are 6048 in number, and fill 34 folio
volumes. 4275 of them are Meisterlieder or
Bar, as they were called.[6] To Sachs's pupil,
Adam Puschman, we are indebted for accounts
of the Meistergesang.[7] The works of the
Meistersinger had generally a sacred subject,
and their tone was religious. Hymns were
their lyrics and narrative poems founded on
Scripture were their epics. Sometimes, however, they wrote didactic or epigrammatic
poems. But their productions were all alike
wanting in grace and sensibility; and by a too
rigid observance of their own minute and complicated rules of composition or *Tablatur* (as
they were termed) they constantly displayed
a ridiculous pedantry. The Meistersinger
clearly adopted (especially in lyric-song) the
forms of the Minnesinger, such as the two
Stollen and the *Auf-* and *Abgesang*, but without
the instrumental preludes, interludes or postludes.[8] Churches were their ordinary place

---

[1] R. von Kralik gives this song in his above-mentioned work. It
is too long to quote, and the words are certainly of later date.

[2] Schneider, *Das musikalische Lied*, i. 193.

[3] The 'fahrenden Sänger' were also counted as Meistersinger, but
belonged to a different circle. In the 15th century, the greatest
was Michael Beheim (or Behaim), who was a favourite in the courts
of the princes on the Rhine and Danube and at Copenhagen. Reimann in his collection gives an example of his songs, and the
Dresden MSS. of the 15th century contain some mystical hymns
to the Virgin by Behaim. (R. v. Liliencron, *Deutsches Leben im
Volkslied um 1530*.)

[4] The origin of the term Meistersinger is uncertain. Ambros
says that it was applied to every Minnesinger who was not a noble,
and thus became the distinguishing appellation of the burgher
minstrels. Reismann, however, maintains that the title 'Meister'
indicated excellence in any act or trade; and that having been at
first conferred only on the best singers, it was afterwards extended
to all members of the guild.

[5] A complete collection of Frauenlob's poems were published in
1843 by Ettmüller, Quedlinburg.

[6] The celebrated Choral 'Warum betrübst du dich, mein Herz,'
was long believed to be the work of Hans Sachs; but it has been
conclusively shown by Böhme ('Altdeutsches Liederbuch,' p. 748)
that the words were written by G. A. Oemler, and then set to the
old secular tune, 'Dein gsund mein Freud.'

[7] They bear the titles of *Gründlicher Bericht des deutschen
Meistergesangs* (Görlitz, 1571); and *Gründlicher Bericht der deutschen Reimen oder Rithmen* (Frankfort a. O., 1596). Both are
partially reprinted in the *Sammlung für altdeutsche Literatur*,
edited by F. H. v. der Hagen, J. G. Büsching, and others. Breslau,
1812. See also *Das Singebuch des A. Puschman nebst den Original-
melodien des M. Behaim und H. Sachs*, by G. Münzer (Leipzig, 1906).

[8] *Von den Meistersingern und ihrer Musik*. Curt Mey, 1903.

of practice. At Nuremberg, for instance, their singing-school was held in St. Katherine's church and their public contests took place there. The proceedings began with the *Frei-singen*, in which any one, whether a member of the school or not, might sing whatever he chose, but no judgments were passed on these preliminary performances. Then followed the contest, in which Meistersinger alone might compete. They were limited to Scriptural subjects, and their relative merits were ad-judged by four *Merker* or markers who sat hidden by a curtain at a table near the altar. It was the duty of one of the four to heed that the song faithfully adhered to Holy Writ ; of another to pay special attention to its prosody ; of a third to its rhyme, and of the fourth to its melody. Should the singer fail in any of the rules of the *Tablatur*, the *Merker* declared him *versungen* and *verthan*, and the competitor who had the fewest faults obtained the prize, a chain with coins.   One of the coins, bearing the image of King David, had been the gift of Hans Sachs, and hence the whole *Gesänge* were called the 'David' and the prizeman the 'Davidwinner.' Every Davidwinner might have his apprentices, but no charge was made for teaching. The term ' Meister ' (strictly speaking) applied only to those who invented a new metre or melody ; the rest were simply ' Sänger.'

The Meistersinger possessed a store of melodies for their own use ; and these melodies were labelled with distinctive but apparently meaningless names, such as the blue-tone,[1] the red-tone, the ape-tune, the rosemary-tune, the yellow-lily-tune, etc. A Meistersinger might set his poems to any of these melodies. The four principal were called the *gekronten Töne*, and their respective authors were Müglin, Frauenlob, Murner and Regenbogen. So far were the Meistersinger carried by their grotesque pedantry that in setting the words of the twenty-ninth chapter of Genesis to Müglin's *lange Ton*,[2] the very name of the book and the number of the chapter were also included. Thus :

1 With the Meistersinger the word *Ton* referred to the music only, and not to the poetry, as with the Minnesinger.
2 Wagner has made us familiar with Müglin's *lange Ton*, in his Meistersinger fanfare :

and it is evident that Wagner studied and fully understood the Meistersinger melodies and adopted many genuine ones.

To all external appearance the melodies of the Meistersinger (like those of the Minnesinger) had a strong affinity with church music and kept to the ecclesiastical modes. But on closer scrutiny many melodies may be found which would sound just like our major and minor scales, were it not for their modal cadences and the many liturgical fragments introduced. Still their songs are for the most part poor and simple and too devoid of rhythm ever to be really popular, and very few of them found sufficient favour to become *Volkslieder* in the 15th and 16th centuries.[3] On the other hand, the Meistersinger themselves sometimes appro-priated Volkslieder. Thus Hans Sachs has reproduced the beautiful old Mailied (May-song) in his *Fastnachtsspiel*, ' Der Neydhart mit dem Feyhel,' written Feb. 7, 1562.[4] He calls it a *Reigen* or roundelay, and its original date was evidently anterior to the 14th century. In its 16th-century form it is as follows :

In fine, the Meistersinger cannot be said to have reached a high level of excellence either in poetry or in music, but they undoubtedly exercised an important influence on the forma-tion of the song by the attention they paid to rhyme and by their numerous inventions of new metrical arrangements. And they rendered a still greater service to music when they carried it into every German home and made it a grace and pastime of domestic life.

While more regular and formal varieties of the song were thus being studied and practised, it had never ceased to issue in its own spon-taneous form of Volkslied from the untutored hearts of a music-loving people. From that source it came in native vigour, unforced and untrammelled. And far more was done for melody and harmony by the obscure authors of the Volkslieder than was ever done by Minne-singer or Meistersinger. Ambros[5] claims that the importance of the part played by the Volks-lied in the history of the music of Western Europe was second only to that of the Gregorian modes. Further, the moral struggle against the anti-humanism of the mediæval Church found victorious expression in the assertive

3 According to Böhme, in the preface to his 'Altd. Liederbuch,' p. xxiii, the writers of the Volkslieder never signed their names, whilst the Meistersinger generally introduced his own name, and very often the date of his composition, into the last rhyme of the poem. A Meistersinger's song can thus be distinguished from a true Volkslied.   4 See Böhme's ' Altd. Liederbuch,' p. 366.
5 Ambros, *Gesch. der Mus.* ii. 276.

humanism of the folk-song—anathematised by spiritual authority. A partial reconciliation of the contending forces followed when the great polyphonic masters adopted Volkslied melodies as theme or foundation of their greatest sacred and secular works. Later, a yet closer union was effected in the CHORAL (*q.v.*) of the reformation period. Whoever were the authors of the Volkslieder, it was not their habit to write them down; the songs lived on the lips and in the hearts of the people. But happily, even in remote times, there were collectors who made it their business to transcribe these popular songs; and of collections thus made none are more important than the 'Limburger Chronik' and the 'Locheimer Liederbuch.' The former work consists of Volkslieder which would seem to have been in vogue from 1347–80 [1]; while songs of a little later date are found in the other collection.[2] This book contains forty-four songs, some of great melodic beauty and showing considerably developed rhythm and structure as well as a delicate sense of poetic feeling. The *Lehrcompendium* of H. de Zeelandia also contains some very fine Volkslieder of the 14th and 15th centuries.[3] Finally, among the many Minnesinger and other MS. collections named after the various towns (such as the Nuremberg, Prague, Dresden MSS.), numbers of genuine Volkslieder are to be found.[4]

The subjects of the earliest Volkslieder were historical [5]; they were indeed epic poems of many stanzas set to a short melody. But by the time that the Volkslied had attained to its meridian splendour, about the beginning of the 16th century, almost every sentiment of the human heart and every occupation of life had its own songs. Students, soldiers, huntsmen, pedlars, apprentices and other classes had their own distinctive songs. The best are undoubtedly the love-songs—those, in fact, where feeling is the strongest. Amongst them the songs of parting (Abschiedslieder) are the most numerous and beautiful, especially the Wächterlieder [6] or Tagelieder, in which the watchman announces the dawn.[7] As a rule, the music of the Volkslied was better than the words. So loose was the structure of the verse that syllables without any sense were inserted to fill up the length of the musical phrase, as :

'Dort oben auf dem Berge
Dölpel, dölpel, dölpel
Da steht ein hohes Haus.'

[1] In the 'Limburger Chronik' we are told of a leper monk living by the Rhine, *c.* 1370. Despite his leprosy, the beauty of his compositions drew men to his cell from all quarters.
[2] Ambros, *Gesch. der Mus.* iii. 375.
[3] From the Prague MS. Ambros (ii. 277) gives one, 'Herr Conrad ging,' both in its original and in modern notation.
[4] For the history of the Meistersinger see J. C. Wagenseil's *Buch von der Meistersinger holdseligen Kunst.* 1697.
[5] For the best authority consult R. von Liliencron's *Die historischen Volkslieder,* etc.
[6] A Wächterlied still sung, 'Der Wächter auf dem Türmlein sass,' is given in Erk's 'Deutsche Liederhort,' No. 135.
[7] These Abschiedslieder are full of the sounds of nature—described with poetic charm. They were the special property of the Minnesinger (Wolfram von Eschenbach's were the most famous), but equally loved by the people.

or a sentence was broken off in the middle, or meaningless *unds* and *abers* were lavishly interspersed. But notwithstanding these laxities of composition there was a close connexion between the words and the melody.

The Volkslied was always strophical in form, and therein differed from the *Sequences* and *Proses* of the Church and the *Leichen* of the Minnesinger. Another marked feature was its rhyme. When the final rhyme had been substituted for mere alliteration and assonance, a definite form was imparted to the verse, and its outline was rendered clearer by the melody of the Volkslied which emphasised the final rhyme, and by covering two lines of the poetry with one phrase of the melody constructed a symmetrical arrangement.

5. *Meine liebe Frau Mutter.*

Meine lie-be Frau Mut-ter, mit mir ist's 'aus; jetzt bald
wer-dens mich bald füh-ren beim Schand-thor hin-aus.

It will be noted in the above example that the half-close is on the dominant harmony and the full-close on the tonic, and this principle, which was originally a peculiar attribute of the Volkslied, was gradually introduced into all other kinds of music, to become one of the most important factors of form. (See FORM.) Many of the Volkslieder were composed in different ecclesiastical modes, but by degrees the Ionian mode, in which alone the dominant principle can have full weight, obtained pre-eminence. The form of the Volkslied is generally very concise as in the above example, and this perhaps is the secret of its great charm. But looser forms are sometimes met with, and were probably

6. *Abschied.*

Ent-laubet ist der Wal-de gegn die-sem Win---
Be-raubt werd' ich, so bal-de mein Feinslieb macht . .
ter kalt. Das ich die schönst' muss
mich alt.
mei------den, die mir ge-fal----len
thut, bringt mir das heymlich lei-den und
macht mir schwe o------ren Mut.

due to the influence of the Church. To the same influence may be ascribed the melodic *melismata* or vocal flourishes which occur even in strophical songs. These melodic *melismata* also allow the voice great scope in the so-called *Kehrrein* or refrain. Another noticeable peculiarity of rhythm in the Volkslied is the variety of ways in which the metre is treated. In many cases the time changes with every bar, and the above example illustrates a different representation of the metre in every line of the stanza.[1] Few of the Volkslieder begin on the first beat of the bar; and therefore the usual metre is Iambic, thus:

Ich will zu Land aus - rei - ten.

and a preference has always been shown by the Germans for equal or common time; it is a quieter and more formal time than the triple, which is essentially dance-rhythm.[2] Other common, though not invariable attributes of the Volkslied are a diatonic intervallic progression, the reiteration of one note, a limited compass, the key or mode steadily adhered to, and unlike the songs of many other countries, the melody of the Volkslied always maintained a complete independence of the accompanying instrument. In character the old Volkslieder are marked by a certain earnestness and dignified self-restraint. They are cheerful and even gay, but without impetuosity or excitability. There is no attempt at word-painting; the same tune must serve for the numerous verses. Hence the necessity for concise melodies.

The Volkslied would seem to have fixed, as it were, instinctively our modern major tonal system; and, moreover, songs even of the 15th century are extant, which correspond to our minor keys. The following example clearly belongs to the old system, but the beginning and close and the intervals on which the principal rhymes fall, make it evident that the key of A minor was intended.[3]

7.   *Ach Elslein.*

Ach Els - lein,lie-bes Els-lein mein, wie gern wär' ich bei dir!

So sind zwei tief-e Was - - - ser wol zwischen dir und mir!

In Hans Judenkünig's (1523) and Hans Neusiedler's (1536) Lute-books this melody is always in A minor with the G♯ marked. In the song-books the sharp was never marked, but undoubtedly always used.

Consideration has thus far been given to the very important contributions of the Volkslied to the determination of permanent form in music; but its influence on contemporary music also requires notice.

It has already been shown that the composers of other countries in the 14th, 15th and 16th centuries, took secular tunes as themes for their masses, motets and other sacred works. The German composers did the same to a certain extent, but they more commonly employed the secular tunes in their secular polyphonic works. Nevertheless, as regards church music the Volkslied occupied a higher place in Germany than elsewhere; for it is not too much to say that more than half the melodies of the choral-books were originally folk-songs, and these melodies were among the simplest and most beautiful ever created. (See CHORAL.) Heinrich von Lauffenberg (or Loufenberg) in the 15th century systematically set his sacred words to secular tunes,[4] especially using the favourite *Tage* and *Wächterlieder*; but the reformation made the practice very much more common. The reformers wished the congregation to join as much as possible in the singing of hymns, and with that object they naturally preferred words in the vernacular and melodies which were familiar with the people.[5] A well-known example of the combination of sacred words and secular melody is the song 'Isbruck, ich muss dich lassen,' set by Heinrich Isaak in four parts in 1475,[6] with the melody in the upper part—a rare arrangement at that time. After the reformation this tune was adapted by Dr. Hesse to the sacred words 'O Welt, ich muss dich lassen'; and in 1633 Paul Gerhardt wrote to it the evening hymn 'Nun ruhen alle Wälder,' in which form it still remains a favourite in all Lutheran churches.[7] After many transformations the old love-song 'Mein Gmüt ist mir verwirrt'[8] now lives in one of the most beautiful and solemn Chorals of both the Lutheran and Catholic churches, namely 'O Haupt voll Blut und Wunden,' which Bach has introduced so often in his Passion music. Again 'Könt ich von Hertzen singen' (one of the most famous of the many *Wächterlieder* and *Tageweisen* melodies

---

[1] See Böhme, p. 335, No. 257. The melody and words of this song are taken from the *Gassenhawerlin*, 1535, No. 1. There are many versions of this fine melody; and in collections subsequent to 1540 it is often to be found set to the morning hymn ' Ich dank Dir, lieber Herre,' and with this setting it appears in all choral books down to the present day.

[2] Böhme, however, maintains that until the 14th century no trace of any time except *Tempus perfectum* (which means triple time) can be found. ' Altd. Liederbuch,' Preface, p. 54.

[3] Another good example is ' Es warb ein schöner Jüngling ' (Georg Forster, *Ein Aufzug guter alter und newer Teutscher Liedlein*, etc., 1539–56, i. 49). This and ' Ach Elslein, liebes Elslein,' are some of the numerous versions of the legend of the Swimmer. ' Ach Elslein ' is found in all the old collections of the 16th century. for instance, in Joh. Ott, 1534, No. 37; Schmeltzel, Quodlibet x. 544; Rhau, Bicinia, ii, 1545, No. 19, etc.

[4] Ambros, iii. 375.

[5] Naumann (*Hist. of Mus.* p. 454 *et seq.*) points out that Luther being both a practical and theoretical musician saw clearly how powerful a factor the Volkslied had become in tonal practice, and in using it he insisted on the importance of the appropriateness of the melody to the sacred words, and on correctness of accent.

[6] Georg Forster, i. No. 36. The words are supposed to be by the Emperor Maximilian I., in whose court Isaak was living.

[7] See ISAAK. Also Böhme, 'Altd. Liederbuch,' p. 332, where the song is given in its original form with a *melisma*. Böhme also gives an interesting remark on the admiration Bach and Mozart evinced for this song.

[8] This song is to be found in Hans Leo Hassler's *Lustgarten neuer teutscher Gesänge*, etc., Nuremberg, 1601. The melody was also used for a death-song ' Herzlich thut mich verlangen,' and later it was set to the universally sung ' Befiel du deine Wege ' (Handel employed it in 1709, previous to Bach).

the Church borrowed) was adapted to the Choral ' Hilf Gott, das mir gelinge ' ; ' Ich hört ein Frewlein klagen ' to ' Hilf Gott, wem soll ich klagen ' ; ' O lieber Hans, versorg dein Gans ' to ' O lieber Gott, das dein Gebot' ; and ' Venus du und dein Kind ' to ' Auf meinen lieben Gott.' Many dance-songs, especially the so-called *Ringel* and *Reigentänze*, were likewise set to sacred words.[1]

It is clear that the Choral gained rather than lost by the adoption of secular melodies ; they emancipated it from stiffness and formality ; they gave it heart and living warmth. So far removed from irreverence were the secular melodies, and so appropriate to the sacred text, that the music is generally more expressive of the words in the Choral than in the Volkslied. But perhaps the true explanation of this is, that in the case of the Choral the words were either written expressly for a chosen melody, or the melody was selected for its appropriateness to particular words.[2] The melody of that just mentioned, ' O Haupt voll Blut und Wunden,' is obviously secular, but what melody could better express a deep and poignant religious sorrow ? In the Catholic Church the use of the Volkslied was chiefly confined to the hymns to the Blessed Virgin (*Marienlieder*) and to the saints, and to the Christmas Carols, especially the sacred cradle-songs, such as the lovely ' Josef, lieber Josef mein.' But upon the whole, the Catholic hymns are all conceived in the ' traditional fixed cadence of the Gregorian song.'

The progress of polyphonic music in Germany had been checked by the discontinuance of the Mass after the reformation, but a new impetus was given to it by the contrapuntal treatment of the Volkslied by great composers. As examples of such treatment may be mentioned Allein dein G'stalt,' ' Ach herzig's Herz,' by H. Finck ; ' Mir ist ein rot Goldfingerlein,' by L. Senfl ; ' Der Gutzgauch auf dem Zaune sass,' by L. Lemlin. This brings us to the Kunstlied, which in its primary sense signified only the contrapuntal treatment of the song by learned musicians.[3] With the polyphonic Kunstlied we have here no concern, beyond what just suffices to point out the changes through which it successively passed, and the important part the Volkslied held in it. The composers who used the Volkslied thus were masters of every form of counterpoint ; sometimes they worked one melody with another, as Arnold von Bruck, who combined the song ' Es taget vor dem Walde ' with ' Kein Adler in der Welt '[4] ; or if they did not treat the

melody as a canon, as Eckel treated ' Ach Jungfrau, ihr seid wolgemuth,'[5] they broke it up into fragments for imitation. They were careful always to choose familiar and favourite tunes, so that they might stand out and be easily recognised amidst the web of other parts surrounding them. When composing their own melodies, they always adhered to the ecclesiastical modes, using the new system only when they adopted a Volkslied.[6] The contrapuntal treatment had, however, one great disadvantage—it constantly necessitated the severance of the melody into fragments, and thus the clear, concise form of the song, which the Volkslied had done so much to establish, was in danger of disappearing. But happily at this juncture (about 1600) Hans Leo Hassler came to its rescue. Having studied in Italy, he breathed into his songs the light secular spirit of the Italian *villanella* and *fa-la-la*, and gave more prominence to the melody than to the other voice-parts. His dance-songs also, with their short rhythmical phrases, did much to restore the concise form. Similar characteristics are noticeable in Melchior Franck's, Regnart's and other contemporary collections of songs.[7]

In the beginning of the 17th century solo songs were first heard in Germany. There, as everywhere else, the introduction of the monodic system was due to the influence of Italy. The revolution begun by that country would seem to have first affected the church music rather than the secular music of Germany. Innovations of Italian origin are plainly discernible in the sacred works of Praetorius and Heinrich Schütz ; but neither of these composers improved the secular monodic song. German poetry had now fallen to a debased condition. It produced nothing better than songs of a vapid and artificial sentiment addressed to a conventional Phyllis or Amaryllis. And the language it employed was a nondescript mixture of French, Latin and stilted German. Since Luther's death the simple vernacular had ceased to be in repute. But on August 24, 1617, a meeting of German patriots was held, who set themselves to restore

---

[1] See Böhme, 'Altd. Liederbuch,' p. 368 *et seq.* Böhme gives a list at p. 810 of secular melodies with sacred words.
[2] The sacred Volkslieder (*geistliche Volkslieder*) differ from the Choral in that the former were printed on broadsheets and sung by the people of every class, whereas the Chorals were written for and sung by the cultivated only.
[3] The very much wider signification which the term *Kunstlied* afterwards acquired has been referred to at the outset of this article.   [4] Reismann, *Gesch. d. deutschen Liedes*, p. 69.

[5] *Ibid.* p. 72.
[6] Georg Forster's collections contain a large quantity of songs thus treated. See FORSTER.
[7] See, for example, ' Tricinia nova lieblicher amorosischer Gesänge mit schönen poetischen Texten gezieret und etlicher Massen nach italienischer Art mit Fleiss componirt durch Melchior Francken,' Nuremberg, 1611 ; and ' Kurzweilige teutsche Lieder zu dreien Stimmen nach Art der neapolitanen oder welschen Villanellen durch Jacobus Regnart in Druck verfertigt,' Nuremberg, 1578. The so-called *Gesellschaftslieder* of the 16th and 17th centuries belong to this category of song. They arose when song was cultivated among the burgher and middle classes to a high extent, and ceased with the efforts of the Silesian poets in 1617. At first they resembled the Volkslied in form and spirit, but later they approached more closely to the Kunstlied. Most contemporary musicians took part in this popular development of music, and collected and arranged the favourite songs of the time in parts, either retaining or altering the words. The editors and publishers encouraged the introduction of Italian melodies with translated or imitated words. Between 1540 and 1624, the following musicians (amongst many others) issued collections of such songs : Georg Forster, Orlandus Lassus, Ivo de Vento, Jacob Regnart, Joh. Eccard, C. Demantius, H. L. Hassler, M. Praetorius, M. Franck, E. Widmann, H. Schein and several Italians. For further information see Hoffmann von Fallersleben, *Die deutschen Gesellschaftslieder*, etc., and R. v. Liliencron, *Deutsches Leben im Volkslied*, etc.

their native tongue to honour, and with that view to study the introduction of method and rule into its grammar and poetry. Other patriotic groups were soon formed with a like purpose, and by the year 1680 these associations numbered 890 members. Their labours quickly bore good fruit. The success of a group of Königsberg poets was specially remarkable, and was doubtless due in a great measure to the skill with which one of the best of them—Heinrich Albert—set his own and his associates' songs to music. His compositions consequently won great popularity, and he has been named ' the father of the volkstümliches Lied.' Schein and Hammerschmidt had preceded Albert in the right path, but their taste and talent had been frustrated by the worthlessness of the words they set to music. The poetry on which Albert worked was not by any means of a high order, although it had sufficient merit to demand a certain measure of attention. And from his uncle, Heinrich Schütz, Albert had learnt the new Italian methods of singing with correct expression and brilliant execution, introducing vocal embellishments.[1] Several of his songs are for one voice with clavicembalo accompaniment, but their harmony is poor. The movement begun by Albert was carried on by J. R. and J. G. Ahle and Adam and Joh. Krieger. Johann's songs are good, and exhibit a marked improvement in grace and rhythm. The first bars of his song, ' Komm', wir wollen wandeln,' have all the clearness of the best Volkslieder :

8.

Komm', wir wol - len uns spa - zie - ren

weil die Zeit so gün - stig ist etc.

Meanwhile the Kunstlied or polyphonic song had ceased to advance. Other branches, especially instrumental and dramatic music, had absorbed composers, songs began to be called ' odes ' and ' arias,' and French and Italian influence was strongly felt, both in music and literature. Writing in 1698, Keiser tells us that cantatas had driven away the old German songs, and that their place was being taken by songs consisting of mixed recitatives and arias.[2]

Among the writers of the 18th century who almost invariably called their songs ' odes ' and ' arias' were Graun, Agricola, Sperontes, Telemann, Quantz, Doles, Kirnberger, C. P. E. Bach, Marpurg, Nichelmann, J. G. Krebs, Neefe and many others. Also large quantities of collections of ' Arien und Oden ' were published at this time, either separately or in numbers, of which the most famous was Sperontes' ' Singende Muse an der Pleisse ' (Leipzig, 1742–45).[3] J. P. Kirnberger has been called (perhaps not with perfect accuracy) the inventor of the ' durchkomponirtes Lied,' that is, a song with different music for every stanza. C. P. E. Bach used the same form, and his best-known vocal work is his setting of Gellert's ' Geistliche Oden '[4] (1758); but he was a musician of a higher and more genial type than the afore-mentioned. Still, this group of composers rendered some services to the song. They set a good example of attention to the words, both as regards metre and expression[5]; they varied the accompaniments by arpeggios and open chords and displayed a thorough command of the different forms they employed. But notwithstanding these merits their songs (with few exceptions) must be pronounced to be dry, inanimate and either deficient in melody, or the melody is overburdened with florid passages and tasteless ornaments and rarely, if ever, spontaneous.[6]

It might strike the reader as strange if the great names of J. S. Bach and Handel were passed by in silence ; but neither Bach nor Handel ever devoted real study to the song. Such influence as they exercised upon it was indirect. Bach, it is true, wrote a few secular songs, and a little love-song, ' Bist Du bei mir,' is simple and sincere.[7] His two comic cantatas also contain several of great spirit and show his use of the Volkslied.[8] And amongst his ' Geistliche Arien ' we have the beautiful ' Gieb dich zufrieden ' and ' Schlummert ein, ihr matten Augen.' But these are isolated instances, and it was through his choral works that he most powerfully affected the song.

[1] In the preface to the fourth part of his Arien Albert says he has borrowed some melodies from other composers, 'Aus Liebe und Wohlgefallen zu denselben Weisen.' He rarely names the composers, but merely calls the songs ' Aria gallica,' ' Aria polonica,' etc. He only used one Italian air, which is the more curious, as in the preface to the sixth part of his Arien he says, ' Was für herrliche und geistreiche Compositionen aus Italien . . . sehe ich oftmals mit höchster Verwunderung an.' See L. H. Fischer, Fremde Melodien in H. Albert's Arien, Vierteljahrsschrift, 1886.

[2] See the preface to his cantata collection. See also Lindner, Gesch. d. deutschen Liedes, p. 53.

[3] Schneider, Das mus. Lied, ii. 206 and B. Seyfert, Das mus. volksthümliche Lied. Although this collection was popular, it was of a very mixed nature, containing solemn odes, vulgar drinking-songs, parodies, or arrangements of French instrumental pieces, and Italian arias.

[4] In his life of C. P. E. Bach, C. Bitter says : ' Mit diesem schönen, edlen Werke ist C. Bach der Begründer und Schöpfer des deutschen Liedes in seiner jetzigen Bedeutung geworden,' i. 143.

[5] Generally speaking, expression and tempo marks were sparingly used until the end of the 18th century. But it is curious to see how the composers of this period indicated the tempo by such words as fröhlich, munter, ängstlich, traurig, showing, thereby, their wish to express, above all, the mood or character of the song.

[6] Full information and abundant examples of these songs will be found in Lindner's and Schneider's histories of the song.

[7] Another in praise of tobacco, of a different character, is ir. the same book.

[8] P. Spitta, J. S. Bach, ii. 561 et seq. The English folk-song, ' When Adam was first created ' (see Kidson's Traditional Tunes, p. 153), was used by Bach in one of these cantatas.

Handel's name is frequently assigned to songs in 18th-century English song-books, or single sheets, or in collections, but it is difficult to say which are original and which are adaptations of Italian songs or minuets set to English words. ' Stand round, my brave boys,'[1] ' From scourging rebellion,'[2] ' The unhappy lovers,'[3] and ' 'Twas when the seas were roaring '[4] were some of the best-known examples. The Händel-Gesellschaft has published a whole volume of ' German, Italian and English Songs and Airs,' but Handel's real influence upon the song was through his operas and oratorios, and there it was immense.[5] Equally indirect, as will be seen presently, were the effects produced on it by the genius of Gluck, Haydn and even of Mozart.

At the period we have now reached, namely, the end of the 18th century, a group of poets, called the ' Göttinger Dichterbund,' or ' Hainbund,' were actively engaged in providing simple lyrics for the people.[6] Simultaneously in music, a new and popular form of the Kunstlied appeared which was the ' volkstümliches Lied.' This term defies exact translation ; but, speaking broadly, it means a simple and popular form of the art-song The decline of the Volkslied during the 17th century has been sometimes attributed to the distracted state of Germany ; and certainly the gloomy atmosphere of the Thirty Years' War and the desolation of the Palatinate, cannot have been favourable to it. But no political or social troubles could affect its existence so deeply as an invasion upon its own ground by the Kunstlied. So long as the Kunstlied dwelt apart among learned musicians the Volkslied had little to fear. But when once it had become simple and melodious enough to be caught by the people the Volkslied was supplanted. In churches and schools, at theatres and concerts the public grew habituated to the Kunstlied, and where civilisation existed the old Volkslieder faded from memory.[7] The ' volkstümliches Lied ' is, in short, a combination of the Volkslied and the Kuntslied, and its area of capacity is a very wide one. It may rise to a high level of poetic beauty, and may descend to low depths of stupidity or triviality without ceasing to be ' volkstümlich.' Songs there were, undoubtedly, before the time of J. A. Hiller, to which this epithet could be properly applied, but he was the first to secure for them

[1] A song made for the Gentlemen Volunteers of the city of London, and printed in the *London Magazine*, Nov. 1745.
[2] *London Magazine*, July 1746.
[3] *Merry Musician*, iv. p. 33, c. 1733.
[4] From a *Select Collection of English Songs with their original Airs*, by J. Ritson, London, 1813.
[5] See Schneider, *Das mus. Lied*, ii. p. 190.
[6] This group consisted of the poets Boie, Hölty, Overbeck, Bürger, Claudius, Voss and the Stolbergs. They revered Klopstock and opposed the French tendency.
[7] It is, however, well to remember that this new departure of German song which we have been describing may—paradoxical as it sounds—be traced to the zeal displayed by Herder, Goethe and others in collecting and arousing the enthusiasm for the folk-poetry of Germany and other kindred nations. It was the same desire to return to simple, natural forms, though it led in poetry as in music in different directions.

a thorough recognition.[8] He belonged to the second half of the 18th century, and was really an operatic composer. It was indeed the songs in his Singspiele which took so strong a hold of the public, and a favourite tune of his, ' Die Jagd,' will serve as a specimen of his work :

9.   Die Jagd.
                                      J. A. HILLER.
Commodetto.

Als ich auf meine
Da kam aus dem Ge-

Blei - che ein Stück-chen garn be - goss Das
sträu - che ein Mädchen a- them - los.

sprach, ach habt er-bar-men, steht meinem Va - ter bei ! Dort

schlag ein Fall dem Armen das linke Bein ent-zwei !

Another, ' Ohne Lieb und ohne Weib,' taken from his Singspiel ' Der Teufel ist los,' and still sung in Germany with much zest, was one of the first Kunstlieder to be received into the ranks of the Volkslieder. J. André, the author of the ' Rheinweinlied,' and J. A. P. Schulz, were contemporaries of Hiller, and did much for the volkstümliches Lied. Schulz was careful above others of his time to select poetic words for his music, and so long as he kept to the simpler forms, he was always successful ; many of his songs are still the delight of German children. Composers were now provided with a store of fresh and natural poems of a popular type by the poets of the Göttingen school, to whom later the names of Körner, Brentano, Arnim and Uhland[9] may be added ; and the love of poetry and song steadily increased in the German nation.

Starting from Hiller and Schulz, the volkstümliches Lied pursued two different roads. Its composers in the Hiller school, such as F. Kauer, Wenzel Müller and Himmel were

[8] It would have seemed more methodical to trace the rise and decline of particular kinds of songs in separate and clearly defined sections of time, but this is altogether impossible, because their respective periods are interlaced with one another. Thus the volkstümliches Lied had come into existence while the Ode and the Aria were at their zenith ; and again composers were using the aria form even after the introduction of the lyric song.
[9] Körner's patriotic poems and the publication of ' Des Knaben Wunderhorn ' acted as powerful incentives to song.

shallow and imperfectly cultivated musicians, whose sentimental melodies had for a time a certain superficial and undeserved repute, such as Himmel's 'An Alexis send' ich dich,' or 'Vater, ich rufe dich.' The dramatic composers Winter and Weigl may be reckoned among this school, in so far as they were songwriters; and its tendencies reappeared nearer our own day in Reissiger and Abt. On the other hand, Schulz's followers were real musicians; and if they became too stiff and formal it was the outcome of a strict regard to form and symmetry and of a praiseworthy contempt for false sentiment. Whenever they chose the volkstümliches Lied they proved their mastery of it; but most of them could write at will in more than one style, and their names must therefore be mentioned in more than one class of song. The first and best of Schulz's school was Mendelssohn's favourite J. F. Reichardt, but his most valuable services to the song were given on other ground, as will appear later. Next to him came Kunzen, A. Weber and Nägeli. Zelter, Klein, L. Berger and F. Schneider are entitled by their songs for male chorus to be counted among the followers of Schulz. The operatic songs of C. Kreutzer and H. Marschner, and the simple melodious songs by C. Krebs, F. Kücken, Silcher, Gersbach and Gustav Reichardt have proved themselves to be truly *volkstümlich* by their firm hold on the hearts of the people.

In the many collections of so-called Volkslieder, beginning with the South German 'Blumenlese' (1782) and the North German 'Mildheimisches Liederbuch' (1799), down to those which are continually issuing from the musical press of to-day, there will be found numerous volkstümliche Lieder converted into Volkslieder. Some of these are by celebrated authors whose fame was won in other fields,[1] and some

by men who wrote nothing but volkstümliche Lieder. Of many songs the authorship is wholly unknown, and of others it is disputed.[2] Worthy to be mentioned as representative songs of this class are: 'Es ist bestimmt in Gottes Rat'; 'Ach, wie ist's möglich dann'; 'Prinz Eugenius'; 'Zu Mantua in Banden'; 'Wir hatten gebaut ein stattliches Haus'; 'Es zogen drei Burschen'; 'Morgen muss ich fort von hier'; 'Ännchen von Tharau'; 'Bekränzt mit Laub'; 'Gaudeamus'; 'Es geht bei gedämpftem Trommelklang'; 'Was blasen die Trompeten'; 'Morgenrot'; 'Ich weiss nicht, was soll es bedeuten'; 'In einem kühlen Grunde'; 'Mädele ruck, ruck, ruck'; 'So viel Stern am Himmel stehen'; 'Es kann ja nicht immer so bleiben'; 'Der Mai ist gekommen'; 'O Tannenbaum'; 'Ich hatt' einen Kameraden'; 'Was ist des Deutschen Vaterland'; 'Die Wacht am Rhein,' etc.[3] They are familiar in all classes, young and old; and the heartiness with which they are everywhere sung attests their vitality. Singing in unison is comparatively rare among Germans; their universal love and knowledge of music naturally predispose them to singing in parts. A regiment on the march, a party of students on a tour, or even labourers returning from work, all alike sing their favourite songs in parts, with remarkable accuracy and precision. And the natural aptitude of the nation for this practice is perpetually fostered by the *Singvereine* which exist in the most secluded corners of Germany.

The mere enumeration of the qualities by which the volkstümliches Lied can be recognised explains its popularity. It is strophical in form and is easy to sing; it has an agreeable, usually diatonic melody, a simple and pure harmony, an unpretentious accompaniment, a regular rhythm, and words inspired by natural sentiment. But it lacked the poetic and thoughtful treatment, both of words and music, which subsequently raised the lyric song to the level of true art.

It is now time to inquire in what manner the song was treated by some of the greatest composers of the 18th and 19th centuries— by Gluck, Haydn, Mozart, Beethoven, Spohr and Weber. Gluck was the contemporary of Graun, Agricola and Kirnberger; and like them he called most of his songs odes. But the standpoint from which he regarded the song was very different from theirs. Applying his theories about the opera to the song, he steadfastly aimed at a correct accentuation of the words in the music and the extinction of the

---

[1] The *Blumenlese*, edited by H. P. Bossler, contains Beethoven's earliest song, 'Schilderung eines Mädchens,' composed when he was eleven. A very good and typical example of the *volkstümliches Lied* may here be added. It is taken from his Sketch-book of 1815 and 1816 (cited by Nottebohm in the *Mus. Wochenblatt*, Nov. 1878).

Die Zufriedenheit.

BEETHOVEN.

Was frag' ich viel nach Geld und Gut, wenn ich zufrie-den bin? Giebt Gott mir nur ge-sun-des Blut, so bin ich fro-her Sinn, und sing aus dankbar-em Gemüth, mein Morgen- und mein Abendlied.

The words of the song are by J. Müller. It has been set also by Mozart and Neefe.

[2] Böhme, in his work entitled *Volkstümliche Lieder der Deutschen im 18. und 19. Jahrhundert*, has done much to rectify current errors as regards the authorship of these songs, such as attributing 'Herz, mein Herz, warum so traurig' to Beethoven instead of to F. Glück, and 'Willst du dein Herz mir schenken' to J. S. Bach instead of to Giovannini, etc.

[3] In the various collections mentioned at the end of this article, the reader will find a multitude of other similar songs, including *Studenten-, Soldaten-, Trink-, Fest-, Tanz-, National-, Begräbniss-, Geistliche-, Kinderlieder.* etc.

Italian form of the melody, which required the complete subordination, if not the entire sacrifice to itself, of every other element of composition. ' The union,' wrote Gluck to La Harpe in 1777, ' between the air and the words should be so close that the poem should seem made for the music no less than the music for the poem,' and he conscientiously strove to be true to this ideal in all his work. But though he revolutionised the opera, he left no deep mark on the song, for indeed he never devoted to it the best of his genius. His few songs, chiefly Klopstock's odes, have no freshness about them, they are dry and pedantic ; and with all Gluck's superiority to his contemporaries in aims and principles of composition, his odes are scarcely better than theirs.[1]

With J. Haydn the influence of the Volkslied is once more apparent. Hence the vitality of his melodies where this element is strongest. His finest song, the Austrian National Anthem, ' Gott erhalte Franz den Kaiser,' closely resembles a Croatian folk-song[2] (see EMPEROR'S HYMN), and in his instrumental works numerous instances of his use of his native songs could be adduced. Yet, taking the bulk of Haydn's songs it cannot be denied that they are lacking in the freshness displayed in his instrumental works. The melodies are carefully and elaborately written, and the accompaniments often interesting and developed (see for instance ' O süsser Ton,' ' Rückerinnerung,' or ' Der erste Kuss ') ; but his want of interest in the words he chose and his disregard both for their meaning and proper accentuation, rob them of the first conditions necessary for the true lyric. His songs are conceived too exclusively from the instrumental point of view. As Schneider truly says, Haydn ' treats the vocal melody exactly as a pianoforte or violin motif, under which he places some words which only superficially agree in rhythm with the melody.'[3] Freest from these defects and amongst his best and most popular songs are the twelve canzonets, containing such graceful and melodious numbers as ' My mother bids me,' ' Recollection,' and ' The Mermaid.' These and such simple little German songs as ' Jede meint das holde Kind ' and the pretty serenade ' Liebes Mädchen, hör' mir zu ' will never lose their charm.

The versatility of Mozart's powers is visible in his songs. Some of them might be described as arias and others as volkstümliche Lieder ; some are lyrical and others dramatic, and yet Mozart cannot be said to have impressed his own great individuality upon the song except in a few instances. It was in the opera that he put forth his whole strength, and his operatic songs often derive from their simple joyous melodies a truly popular character. It is evident that he treated song, pure and simple, as mere recreation, and bestowed little pains thereon. Many faults of accentuation could be pointed out in his songs, but his exquisite melodies and skilful accompaniments almost obliterate such defects. Mozart wrote many volkstümliche Lieder ; some humorous, like ' Die Alte ' (with its amusing expression-mark, ' Ein wenig durch die Nase zu singen ') ; some fresh and joyous as ' Komm', lieber Mai,' and the favourite ' Ich möchte wohl der Kaiser sein.'[4] But it is in the form of the aria and *durchkomponirtes Lied* that we find his most perfect song - writing. ' Abendempfindung,' with the most beautiful opening phrases expressive of the calm moonlight evening, and his masterpiece, ' Das Veilchen,' which he wrote to words by Goethe, are on a level with his best work in other branches.

Some of Beethoven's earlier songs, such as ' An einen Säugling,' ' Das Kriegslied,' ' Molly's Abschied,' and ' Der freie Mann,' are volkstümlich ; the form is small and the accompaniment nothing more than the melody simply harmonised. The structure is similar in Gellert's sacred songs, op. 48, except in the ' Busslied,' where there is a fuller development, both of voice and accompaniment. ' Adelaide ' is also an early work, but it is written in a larger form and shows signs of the dramatic treatment which for a while influenced Beethoven's vocal writing. Many other songs cast in the scena and aria form could be instanced, but of far higher interest are those written in the lyrical vein. He set six poems of Goethe's as op. 75, and three as op. 83, and although there is much in these songs which might have tempted Beethoven to use the scena or the cantata form, he resisted it. He adhered to the strophical divisions, and left it to the instrumental part to satisfy their dramatic requirements. In Mignon's song, ' Kennst du das Land,' each stanza has the same beautiful melody, and the accompaniment alone varies and intensifies. In Jeitteles' Liederkreis, ' An die ferne Geliebte,' op. 98, the unity which makes the cycle is wholly the work of the composer and not of the poet. It is Beethoven who binds the songs together by short instrumental interludes modulating into the key of the next song, and by weaving the exquisite melody with which the cycle begins into the last song. Most of the songs of this immortal cycle are strophical, but with great variety of accompaniment ; and the just balance of the vocal and instrumental parts, and the warmth and fervour of the expression, equally contribute to the faithful representation of lyric thought and feeling. Enough stress cannot be laid on the importance of Beethoven's work in song-writing, for having effectively shown the power of harmony and

---

[1] For a good example see ' Willkommen, o silberne Mond,' given by Schneider, ii. 267.
[2] See the Yugo-Slavonic section of this article, p. 32, note 8.
[3] Schneider, *Das mus. Lied*, ii. 269.

[4] The little cradle-song, ' Schlafe, mein Prinzchen,' long attributed to Mozart, has recently been proved by Dr. Max Friedländer to have been written by Bernhard Flies.

modulation as means of expression; also for having enlarged the part sustained by the pianoforte. He taught his instrument, as it were, to give conscious and intelligent utterance to the poetic intention of the words. Furthermore, we must recognise that although Beethoven's genius rose to its loftiest heights in other branches of music, it was he who first raised song from the entirely subordinate position it had hitherto held to an honourable place in the ranks of musical art.

Spohr also wrote lyric songs, and was fitted for the work by his romantic and contemplative nature. But his songs are marred by excessive elaboration of minutiæ, and in the profusion of details clearness of outline is lost. Again, his modulations, or rather chromatic transitions, are so frequent as to be wearisome. Of all his songs, ' Der Bleicherin Nachtlied ' and ' Der Rosenstrauch ' are freest from these faults, and they are his best.

A greater influence was exercised upon the song by Carl Maria von Weber.[1] He published two books of Volkslieder, op. 54 and op. 64, perfect in their simplicity and of real distinction. Of his other seventy-eight songs the most celebrated are those from Körner's ' Leyer und Schwert'; the cradle-song, 'Schlaf Herzenssöhnchen,' ' Die gefangenen Sänger,' and the finest of all, ' Das Mädchen an das erste Schneeglöckchen.' These songs deserve their celebrity, and there are indeed many others which are not so well known, nor as often heard as they deserve to be. Weber's fame as a song-writer has perhaps suffered somewhat from the circumstance that many of his best songs are in his operas, and it has been partially eclipsed by the supreme excellence of one or two composers who were immediately subsequent to him.

Incidental reference has already been made more than once to Goethe, to whom the obligations of the song are great. The fine outburst of lyric song which enriched the music of Germany in his lifetime was very largely due to him. The strong but polished rhythm and the full melody of his verse were an incentive and inspiration to composers. J. Fr. Reichardt was the first to make it a systematic study to set Goethe's lyrics to music, and between 1780 and 1810 he issued several collections.[2] So long as Reichardt merely declaimed the words in melody, or otherwise made the music subordinate to the verse, he was successful. Goethe's words were, in short, a sure guide for a talent like his. Reichardt was not a great master, but he may claim the honour of having struck the true keynote of lyrical songs, and greater artists

than himself immediately followed in his footsteps. Nothing he ever wrote is better than his setting of Tieck's ' Lied der Nacht,' and in this song he clearly shows himself to be the forerunner of Schubert and Schumann. A younger contemporary, Zelter, also made his reputation by setting Goethe's words to music. Zelter was himself a friend of Goethe, and so great an admirer was the poet of Zelter's settings that he preferred them to Reichardt's and, through some strange obliquity of taste or judgment, to those of Beethoven and Schubert. Zelter's early songs were strophical, but in later years he adopted more freely the *durchkomponirte* form. Others of this group of writers were Ludwig Berger and Bernard Klein, albeit they differed somewhat in their treatment, both of the voice and instrumental parts.

If the general results of the period through which we have just passed be now regarded as a whole, it will be seen that the various conditions requisite for the perfection of the song had matured. The foundations and all the main structure had been built; it required only to crown the edifice. Starting from the *volkstümliches Lied*, the Berlin composers had demonstrated the necessity of full attention to the words. Mozart and Weber had given it a home in the opera. Mozart and Beethoven had developed its instrumental and dramatic elements; and had further shown that the interest of the song is attenuated by extension into the larger scena-form. Nothing, therefore, of precept or example was wanting, by which genius might be taught how to make the compact form of the song a perfect vehicle of lyrical expression. The hour was ripe for the man; and the hour and the man met when Schubert arose.

This wonderful man, the greatest of songwriters, has been so fully and appreciatively treated in other pages of this Dictionary,[3] that it would be superfluous to do more here than examine the development of the song under him. So fertile was Schubert's genius that we have more than 600 of his songs, and their variety is as remarkable as their number. He was master of the song in every stage—whether it were the Volkslied, or the Ode, or the volkstümliches Lied, or the pure lyric song, or the Ballade and Romanze. And the secret of his greatness was largely due to his complete recognition of the principle that the balance between the melodic form and emotional meaning should be perfectly adjusted. The essence of true song, as Schubert clearly saw, is deep, concentrated emotion, enthralling words and music alike. Full of poetry himself, he could enter into the very heart and mind of the poet; and so wide was his range of sympathetic intuition that he took songs from all the great German

---

[1] It is worth while to note that Weber himself says in his literary works, that ' strict truth in declamation is the first and foremost requisite of vocal music. . . . Any vocal music that alters or effaces the poet's meaning and intention is a failure.'

[2] Some of Goethe's words appeared among Reichardt's miscellaneous songs as early as 1780 ; but in 1793 he published a separate collection, entitled ' Goethes lyrische Gedichte,' containing thirty poems. And in 1809 he issued a more complete collection under the title of ' Goethes Lieder, Oden, Balladen, und Romanzen mit Musik, von J. Fr. Reichardt.'

[3] The reader should also consult Reissmann's *Das deutsche Lied in seiner historischen Entwickelung* and his *Geschichte des deutschen Liedes.* Also Hadow's vol. v. of the *Oxford History of Music.*

poets, and as their styles varied, so did his treatment. His best compositions are lyrical, and it is scarcely possible to conceive higher excellence than is displayed in these masterpieces. Beauty and finish are bestowed with so even a hand, both on the voice-part and on the accompaniment, that it would be difficult to say that either takes precedence of the other. In the music which he wrote to the more dramatic, legendary, or ballad-like forms, such as Schiller's ' Der Taucher,' and ' Gruppe aus dem Tartarus,' Collins's ' Der Zwerg,' Mayrhofer's ' Memnon,' or Goethe's 'Ganymed' and 'Schwager Kronos,' the accompaniment is more important than the voice-part. Schubert's treatment of the song-cycle differed from that of Beethoven, inasmuch as Schubert did not weld together the music of the set, but bound them to one another by community of spirit. They can all be sung separately, but the ' Müllerlieder ' and ' Winterreise,' which tell a continuous tale, lose much of their dramatic power if they be executed otherwise than as a whole. Some of Schubert's finest songs are strophical in form, and others have a change of melody or accompaniment, or both, for every stanza. But whatever treatment the words might call for, that Schubert gave them with unerring instinct.

Mendelssohn, although he comes after Schubert, belongs to an earlier school of song-writers. His songs exhibit all the best characteristics of the Berlin school ; they are perfect in form, melodious and easy of comprehension. But they lack the marvellous variety we find in Schubert's songs. This is partly owing to the fact that Mendelssohn could not surrender himself completely to the poet whose words he was setting [1]; the words to him were only an aid or incentive to the composition of a song already preconceived in his own mind. He also adhered to certain clearly pronounced types of melody and harmony; so that his songs all bear a strong resemblance to each other. He preferred the strophic form ; and ranked the independence of the melody higher than the variations of expression the words demanded. Hence the slight influence Mendelssohn has exercised upon the song in Germany. Yet granted these limitations, the joyousness of his spring-tide songs, the tranquil beauty of such compositions as ' Scheidend ' and the ' Nachtlied,' and the true Volkslied tone of ' Es ist bestimmt,' have rendered his songs popular in the best sense of the word. (See MENDELSSOHN.)

Meyerbeer's songs in general are but little known ; but amongst the ' 40 Mélodies ' published in 1840 by Brandus, Paris, many are

remarkable and well worth reviving ; as, for instance, ' Le Moine,' ' Le Poëte mourant,' ' Sur le balcon,' ' Du schönes Fischermädchen.' Still, they are open to Mendelssohn's criticism, that they are too pretentious and exaggerated, and are wanting in naïveté and spontaneity. Methods were adopted by Meyerbeer more suitable to the exigencies of opera than to the simple song.

With Robert SCHUMANN (q.v.) we approach a new departure in song-writing; and no composer since Schubert has exerted so wide and deep an influence upon the subsequent development of this art, both in Germany and in other countries. Schumann was at once poet and musician. His songs are the very soul of romantic poetry. With scrupulous art he reproduces all that runs in the poet's mind, be it ever so subtle and delicate, but he also permeates it with a deeper shade of meaning. This may be seen especially in his settings of the poets Heine, Reinick, Kerner, Geibel, Chamisso,[2] Rückert [3] and Eichendorff, the last five of whom were essentially romantic poets. It is to Heine that Schumann's nature most deeply responded. Whether the poet be in a mood of subtle irony or bitter mockery, of strong passion or delicate tenderness, of joy or sorrow, with equal fidelity is he portrayed in the composer's music. What Schubert was to Goethe, Schumann was to Heine ; but the requirements of the two poets were not the same. Goethe's thought is ever expressed in clear and chiselled phrase ; while it is a habit of Heine to veil his meaning and leave whatever may be wanting to be supplied by the reader's imagination. The composer who would adequately interpret him must, therefore, have poetic fancy no less than a mastery of his own art. This Schumann had, and none of his songs rank higher than the splendid cycle ' Dichterliebe ' from Heine's Buch der Lieder. Their melodic treatment is declamatory ; not in recitative, but in perfectly clear-cut strophes, with great attention bestowed on the accentuation of emphatic words. As a general rule the instrumental part of Schumann's songs is too important, too independent to be called an accompaniment ; it is an integral factor in the interpretation of the poem. While the voice-part often seems only to suggest, the pianoforte part unfolds the sentiment of the song and evolves from the poem a fuller significance than it could ever have owed to the poet's own unaided art.

We will here allude to another branch of modern German song, which comprises the Ballade, the Romanze and the Rhapsodie. In the ordinary English sense, the ballad is

---

[1] It is a strange paradox that Mendelssohn, with all his finished culture and literary tastes, never realised his responsibilities towards the poet, and did not hesitate to change the words if it suited his music better. To give one instance out of many : in Heine's ' Ich wollt' meine Schmerzen ergössen sich,' Mendelssohn substitutes ' Liebe ' for ' Schmerzen ' thereby wholly altering the sense. Another strange contradiction is the fact that although Mendelssohn was steeped in Bach and possessed great contrapuntal skill, his accompaniments are never polyphonic.

[2] Chamisso's cycle ' Frauenliebe und Leben ' is described fully under SCHUMANN.
[3] Rückert's verse did not perhaps evoke in Schumann so full a measure of spontaneous melody as Eichendorff and Kerner. The most melodious, and perhaps the best known of the Rückert collection, are Nos. 2, 4 and 11, and these are by Frau Clara Schumann.

primarily a poem descriptive of an event or chain of incidents, leaving the reader to gather sentiment and reflection from bare narration. But the Ballade, as a German form of song, has some other properties. Goethe says it ought always to have a tone of awe-inspiring mystery, which fills the reader's mind with the presence of supernatural powers, and contain strong dramatic elements. The Romanze is of the same class as the Ballade, but is generally of more concise form, and by more direct references to the feelings which its story evokes approaches nearer to the lyric song. As distinguished from the Ballade and Romanze, the Rhapsodie is deficient in form, and its general structure is loose and irregular. The first poet who wrote poems of the true Ballade type was Bürger; his example was followed by Goethe, Schiller, Uhland and others, and then the attention of composers was soon caught. Inspired by Schiller, Zumsteeg composed in this vein, and his work is interesting as being the first of its kind. But Zumsteeg had too little imagination to handle this form successfully, and his best songs belong more correctly to the Romanze. We miss in his Balladen the bold, melodic, principal theme (which should stand out in relief from all secondary themes and ideas, and be repeated wherever the story needs it),[1] although in some of them the details are very well and truthfully painted—for instance, the fine gloomy opening phrase of the 'Pfarrers Tochter.' Neither Reichardt nor Zelter succeeded any better with the Ballade. They treated the 'Erlkönig' as a Romanze, and Schiller's Balladen, 'Ritter Toggenburg,' and 'Der Handschuh,' as rhapsodies. And even Schubert in his longer pieces was inclined to compose in a rhapsodical form. In some, such as 'Der Taucher,' 'Die Bürgschaft,' 'Der Sänger,' where he is faithful to the Ballade form, and where there are exquisite bits of melody appositely introduced and the accompaniments are thoroughly dramatic, the general effect of the piece is overlaid and marred by multiplicity of elaborate details and drawn out to too great length. To the Romanze Schubert gave the pure strophical form, as, for instance, in Goethe's 'Heidenröslein.'

The founder of the true Ballade in music was J. C. G. Loewe, who caught, as it were instinctively, the exact tone and form it required. His method was to compose a very short, distinct, though fully-rounded melody for one or two lines of a stanza and then repeat it throughout with only such alterations as were demanded by the narrative. This secures unity for the Ballade, but it necessitates a richly-developed accompaniment to contribute to the dramatic colouring of the incidents. The simpler the metrical form of the Ballade, the better will this treatment suit it. Take,

for example, Uhland's 'Der Wirthin Töchterlein.' All Loewe's music to it is developed from the melody of the first line; though other resources are brought into play as the tragic close draws near, the original idea is never lost to view, and the character with which the accompaniment began is preserved intact to the end. Still more importance is given by Loewe to the pianoforte part in the gloomy Northern Balladen ' Herr Olaf ' and ' Der Mutter Geist,' and to his wonderful setting of ' Edward,' ' Archibald Douglas,' and the ' Erlkönig.' But his popular Balladen are ' Heinrich der Vogler,' ' Die Glocken zu Speier,' and ' Goldschmieds Töchterlein.' These have fresh and genial melodies, accompaniments full of characteristic expression and, stroke upon stroke, they effect a vivid presentment of animated scenes.

Mendelssohn never touched the Ballade form for the solo voice; and Schumann greatly preferred the Romanze. To his subjective lyric cast of mind the underlying thought was of more concern than external facts. In his beautiful music to Kerner's ' Stirb, Lieb' und Freud'' he treats the melody as a Romanze and puts the Ballade form into the accompaniment. On the same plan are his ' Entflieh' mit mir,' ' Loreley,' and ' Der arme Peter,' from Heine. More developed is the powerful ' Löwenbraut,' and the most complete as regards unity in variety and impressiveness is ' Die beiden Grenadiere.' When Schumann essayed to treat the Ballade melodramatically he failed. Singing, in his opinion, was a veil to the words; whenever, therefore, he wished them to have emphatic prominence he left them to be spoken or ' declaimed,' and attempted to illustrate the narrative of the song by the musical accompaniment. Still the Ballade form was too small and contracted for this kind of treatment, which is better suited to larger and more dramatic works aided by the orchestra. Subsequent composers have used the Ballade and Romanze form in various ways,[2] but with the exception of Martin Plüddemann none can be said to have devoted themselves exclusively to it. Plüddemann was at first under Wagner's influence: in his musical phrases he attempted to introduce the peculiarly pathetic declamatory utterances, and the Leitmotiv (see, for instance, ' Volkers Nachtgesang ' or ' Jung Siegfried '). But, later, he recognised Loewe to be the only true exponent of this form, and on Loewe's methods Plüddemann achieved his greatest success. It is a vexed question whether the repetition of the melody for every verse or its variation throughout is the better structure for the Ballade; but the former arrangement would seem to be the best adapted for short and simple pieces, and the latter for lengthier ones. If the melody be repeated for every verse in long Balladen, and unless the varied instrumental

---

[1] Loewe's ballads strikingly illustrate the value of this characteristic.

[2] See Brahms's ' Balladen und Romanzen.'

part be of paramount importance, an impression of monotony is apt to be created, and the necessarily varying aspects of the poem are imperfectly represented in the music.[1]

The lyric song continued to hold in Germany the high place to which it was raised by Schubert and Schumann, and their traditions were worthily sustained by their successors, Robert Franz and Johannes Brahms. FRANZ (q.v. for a special study of his songs) devoted himself almost exclusively to the song, which was the form of music best suited to his lyrical temperament. His favourite poets are writers of quiet, pensive verse like Osterwald, Lenau, Geibel and Eichendorff.

All the best tendencies of the 19th century were summed up in the songs of Johannes Brahms The perfection of formal structure, the high distinction of melody, the beauty and fitness of the accompaniments, the depth of thought and throughout the ring of truth and sincerity place his songs among the immortal works of the great classical masters. At all times Brahms gave earnest attention to the Volkslied.[2] The simple sentiment and originality of conception in the poetry of the folk-songs of his own and other countries were a strong incitement to him, and were reflected in his music with unsurpassable truth. Even where he uses Hungarian or other idioms, his language is always his own.[3] His use of the old modes and of complex rhythms which had long fallen into disuse,[4] show he had drunk deeply of the past in music, but he ever amalgamated it with his own living musical utterance. Brahms's full, rich accompaniments have also a character of their own. It is clear that he attached the highest importance to the fundamental bass, and there are many songs in which the bass alone is sufficient to support the voice. Again, whilst his consummate skill in the contrapuntal line is shown by the melodic life he has given the inner parts, his complete mastery over every technical resource of his art is visible in the multifarious rhythms and exquisite harmonies he employs.[5] His accompaniments sometimes lead, sometimes follow the voice, or they pursue their own independent course. Many instances of these occur in the magnificent song-cycle from Tieck's *Magelone*. The poetical and intellectual qualities of Brahms's songs, as well as their more serious and spiritual properties, have been fully described elsewhere. (See BRAHMS.)

Turning to a side-group of composers who

have worked more on the lines laid down by Mendelssohn, we find the names of Curschmann, Taubert, F. Lachner, F. Ries, Eckert, Rietz, Reinecke, Raff and Fanny Hensel. Their best work is unpretending and simple, but they lack the higher qualities of song-writing. Far more interesting and very different names are those of Cornelius, Jensen, Brückler, Herzogenberg and Lassen. Jensen was richly responsive to the vein of tender sentiment brought into prominence by the romantic school. The exquisite ' Dolorosa ' cycle, the brilliant ' Spanisches Liederbuch ' and gay student songs have won success for him. Both he and Hugo Brückler, whose posthumous songs Jensen edited, possessed the true lyric feeling for melody, and both wrote elaborate and interesting accompaniments. But in each of these song-writers we find a want of self-restraint and self-criticism and an over-feverish imagination. Heinrich von Herzogenberg did not err in this respect ; his refined and thoughtful songs, if lacking in spontaneity, are carefully worked out, and appeal to those who care for the intellectual side of song-writing. The number of E. Lassen's songs is great, and they vary much in merit. He had a sensitive feeling for the æsthetic side of art ; and the slightness of means and material wherewith he obtains his effects is admirable.[6] But his over-sentimentality and desire for popularity place Lassen on a far lower level than the above-mentioned composers. P. Cornelius stands on a wholly different plane, being as much a poet as a musician, and having too strong an individuality in thought and mode of expression to belong to any school. In Cornelius's personality there is a strange combination of subtle mysticism and transparent simplicity, which imparts a rare charm to his songs. The beautiful ' Weihnachtslieder ' cycle, with their childlike sincerity and the exquisitely poetical ' Brautlieder ' cycle represent his best work, but all his songs need to be intimately studied before they can make their full impression.

The history of German song during the last century bears witness to a continuous attempt towards heightening, by means of melody, harmony and rhythm, the effect of the words. The musical idea, nevertheless, did not subserve the literary, nor were the essentials of pure musical art forgotten. The latest development of German song has carried to the extreme the tendency of giving a place of primary importance to the words, and musical form is sacrificed to literary construction. The composer selects poems with regard to their literary value ; the exigencies of verbal accent are enforced ; repetition or alteration of words and other verbal licences countenanced in past days are prohibited. Musically regarded, the importance and independence of the instrumental part

---

[1] See Vischer's *Ästhetik*, pt. iii. p. 996 ; Albert Bach's *The Art Ballad* ; Reissmann's *Das deutsche Lied*, p. 236 ; and M. Runze's *Schiller und die Balladenmusik* (*Die Musik*, 4. Jahr. Heft 15).

[2] P. Spitta, *Zur Musik*.

[3] To show the power Brahms had to limit this form to its own compact structure, and without change evolve fresh meaning for every verse, see the pathetic Volkslied ' Schwesterlein.' And that he could equally raise it to the highest development of the art-song is exemplified by his treatment of the Wendic folk-song ' Von ewiger Liebe.'

[4] Compare his use of the *hemiolia* with those which occur in Handel's ' Duetti da Camera.' Spitta, *Zur Musik*.

[5] See, for example, ' Frühlingstrost ' and ' O wüsst' ich doch,' from op. 63.

[6] See P. Bachmann's essay on Lassen in *Die Musik*, Feb. 1904.

has reached its climax ; declamatory passages have replaced melodic phrases ; all the resources of modern music in modulation, in harmonic and rhythmical combinations have been expended on the song-form with a lavish and often undiscriminating hand.[1] Sounds, musically chaotic, are tolerated by the æsthetic principle which recognises no obligation save the obligation to emphasise the mood or meaning of the verse. Expression, not beauty, is now the composer's ideal. This song-formula was adopted by Hugo Wolf and Richard Strauss and carried to its apogee by Max Reger and others belonging to the same school of thought —each engrafting thereon his individual qualities and idiosyncrasies. No one can deny the sincerity of these composers' methods of writing. They have realised the æsthetic value of complexity and ugliness, and it needs no defence in their minds. And yet all have shown that if they wished to write anything simple and beautiful they could do so—every resource in musical art being at their command.[2] Strauss and Reger will probably not rank among musicians primarily as song-writers, but with Hugo Wolf his songs are his master-work, and as such he justly holds the highest place. His earliest works show an unerring penetration into the very heart of the poet. His art demanded lyrical objectivity, and he deliberately avoided the subjective poets. This objectivity of theme requires a more vivid imaginative grasp and a wider sympathy than is necessary to a composer who makes the songs only represent his own emotion. There is no diffuseness in Wolf's writing ; the finest thought is compressed into the smallest possible space. He seems to have triumphantly solved the problem of imparting a feeling of unity into the most declamatory and fragmentary phrases of his songs. He produces the effect on the one hand by concentration of imaginative conception and on the other hand by the more mechanical method of retaining one figure or *motif* throughout the whole song, which adapts itself with wonderful elasticity to each change in the situation. Wolf's accompaniments are usually polyphonic, or consist of kaleidoscopic and unconventional successions of chords and discords, the latter extended also to the voice-part. Songs of extreme beauty are to be found both in the 'Italienisches' and 'Spanisches Liederbuch,' and the 'Geistliche Lieder' of the latter cycle testify to the depth of his nature. In short, what music Wolf wrote was in all sincerity what Wolf felt. Fantastic, realistic and original he may be, but never wilfully affected or extravagant. Many interesting and beautiful songs have,

moreover, been written by Weingartner, Henschel, Hans Schmidt, Hans Sommer, E. d'Albert, Max Schillings, Th. Streicher and others.[3] It may also be said that every German composer of modern times, with every diversity of talent, has cultivated the song as a serious branch of his art.

BIBLIOGRAPHY AND COLLECTIONS

A. *MSS. from the 8th to the 17th Century*

1. Fragments of the 'Hildebrandlied' (8th century) in the Landesbibliothek, Cassel. (Facsimile published by W. Grimm in 1830. See O. Schade's *Altdeutsches Lesebuch*, 1862–66.)
2. The Wolfenbüttel MSS. (10th century), in the Ducal Library, Wolfenbüttel. (Contains some of the oldest secular songs in Germany.)
3. MSS. of the 'Ludwigslied' (10th century) in the Valenciennes Library. (See Schade's *Altdeutsches Lesebuch*.)
4. The St. Gall Cod. Lat. No. 393 (11th century).
5. 'Nithart's Song-book '—MSS. (13th century). In the possession of Professor v. der Hagen. (Printed in his work on the Minnesinger.)
6. The Limburg Chronicle (1347–80), in the Limburg Library. (This MS., reprinted in 1617, 1826 and 1860, contains chiefly knights' and monks' songs.)
7. The 'Jena Minnesinger Codex' (14th century) in the University Library. (Contains fine specimens of Minnesinger melodies, and amongst them Vogelweide's 'Reiselied.' Reprint, 1902.)
8. The Colmar Minnesinger MSS. (14th century), at Munich. (Reprint, 1896.)
9. H. von Loufenberg's Song-book (1415–43), at Strassburg. (Destroyed by fire, 1870, but copied previously by Wackernagel.)
10. Spörl's Song-book (end of 14th and beginning of 15th century), in the Imperial Library, Vienna.
11. The Prague MS. (early 15th century), in the University Library, entitled *Ein musikalischer Lehrcompendium d. H. de Zeelandia*.)
12. The Locheim Song-book (1452–60), in the Ducal Library, Wernigerode. (Edited in 19th century by Arnold and Bellermann.)
13. The Dresden Minnesinger MS. (15th century), in the Public Library. (Contains M. Behaim's hymns.)
14. The Vienna Song-book (1533), in the Imperial Library. (Consists of sacred and secular partbooks, words and music.)
15. Hager's Meisterliederbuch (1600). (Contains portrait of Hans Sachs and many Meisterlieder melodies from the Nuremberg School.)
16. Werlin's Song-book (1646), in the State Library, Munich. (Contains many thousand songs ; some are genuine Volkslieder of the 15th and 16th century and others later and more artificial.)

B. *Modern Collections of Volkslieder, Volkstümliche Lieder and Chorals, and Works relating to the History of German Song, chronologically arranged.*[4]

BECKER, R. Z. 'Mildheimisches Liederbuch.' Gotha, 1799.
ACHIM V. ARNIM,[5] L. and C. BRENTANO. 'Des Knaben Wunderhorn.' Berlin, 1806–46.
HERDER.[6] 'Stimmen der Völker.' Tübingen, 1807.
BÜSCHING, J. G. G., and F. H. V. D. HAGEN. 'Sammlung deutscher Volkslieder.' Berlin, 1807.
GRIMM, J. *Über den altdeutschen Meistergesang*. Göttingen, 1811.
GÖRRES, J. VON. Altdeutsche Volks- und Meisterlieder (from MSS. in the Heidelberg Library). Frankfort-on-M., 1817.
ERLACH, F. K. VON. *Die Volkslieder der Deutschen*. Mannheim, 1834–37.
SILCHER, F. 'Deutsche Volkslieder,' etc. Tübingen, 1837–40.
ZUCCALMAGLIO and KRETZSCHMAR, A. 'Deutsche Volkslieder.' 1838–44.
ERK, L., and IRMER, W. 'Die deutschen Volkslieder.' Berlin. 1838–45.
HAGEN, F. H. V. D. *Die Minnesinger*. Leipzig, 1838.
BECKER, C. F. 'Die Hausmusik in Deutschland in dem 16., 17. und 18. Jahrhunderte,' etc. Leipzig, 1840.
WOLF, F. *Über die Lais, Sequenzen und Leiche*. Heidelberg, 1841.
FALLERSLEBEN, HOFFMANN VON, and RICHTER, E. 'Schlesische Volkslieder,' etc. Leipzig, 1842.
BECKER, C. F. 'Lieder und Weisen vergangener Jahrhunderte.' Leipzig, 1843–53.
LYRA, J., and LÖWENSTEIN, R. 'Deutsche Lieder. Leipzig, 1843–1858.
FINK, G. W. 'Mus. Hausschatz der Deutschen.' Leipzig, 1843–1878.
SCHOTTKY, J., and ZISKA, F. 'Österreichische Volkslieder.' Pest, 1844.
FALLERSLEBEN, HOFFMANN v. *Die Deutschen Gesellschafts Lieder des 16. und 17. Jahrhunderts*. Leipzig, 1844–60.
UHLAND, L.[7] *Alte hoch- und niederdeutsche Volkslieder*. Stuttgart, 1844–46.
SPAUN, A. v. 'Die österreichischen Volksweisen.' Vienna, 1845.
WINTERFELD, CARL v. *Der evangelische Kirchengesang*, etc. Leipzig, 1843–47.
FALLERSLEBEN, HOFFMANN v. 'Deutsches Volksgesangbuch.' Leipzig, 1848.
MEISTER, C. S. *Das katholische deutsche Kirchenlied*, etc. Freiburg, 1852. (Later edition with Bäumker, 1862–91.)

---

[1] The application of Wagner's methods to the song cannot here be discussed, as he practically stood apart from this form, although his indirect influence upon song has been undeniable, and the few examples he left are of great beauty.
[2] Wolf's 'Verborgenheit,' Strauss's 'Traum durch die Dämmerung ' and 'Heimliche Aufforderung,' and Reger's 'Mit Rosen bestreut ' may be mentioned as isolated examples.

[3] See Dr. Kretzschmar's article, 'Das deutsche Lied seit dem Tode R. Wagners,' in the *Jahrbuch der Musikbibliothek Peters*, 1898.
[4] It was considered advisable to combine the bibliography and collections together in this section, as the one work frequently embraces both. Take, for instance, Böhme's 'Altdeutsches Liederbuch,' which is at once the best history of the Volkslied and the best collection.
[5] This work contains practically no music, but is necessary to the student of the German Volkslied.
[6] *Ditto.* [7] *Ditto.*

STADE, W., and LILIENCRON, R. v. *Lieder und Sprüche aus der letzten Zeit des Minnesanges.* Weimar, 1854.
BECKER, C.F. *Die Tonwerke d. 16. und 17. Jahrhunderts.* Leipzig, 1854.
SILCHER, F., and ERK, F. A. 'Allgemeines deutsches Commersbuch.' 1858–88.
REISSMANN, A. *Das deutsche Lied in seiner historischen Entwickelung.* Cassel, 1861.
AMBROS, A. W. *Geschichte der Musik.* Breslau and Leipzig, 1862 1882.
SCHNEIDER, C. E. *Das musikalische Lied in geschichtlicher Entwickelung.* Leipzig, 1863–65.
WACKERNAGEL, C. E. P. *Das deutsche Kirchenlied,* etc. Leipzig, 1862–77.
LILIENCRON, R. v. *Die historischen Volkslieder der Deutschen,* etc. Leipzig, 1865–69.
HÄRTEL, A. 'Deutsches Lieder-Lexicon.' Leipzig, 1867.
VILMAR, A. 'Handbüchlein für Freunde d. deutschen Volksliedes.' Marburg, 1867.
FALLERSLEBEN, HOFFMANN V. *Unsere volksthümlichen Lieder.* Leipzig, 1869.
LINDNER, E. O. *Geschichte d. deutschen Liedes im XVIII. Jahrhundert.* Leipzig, 1871.
VON CAROSFELD, SCHNORR. *Zur Geschichte d. deutschen Meistergesanges.* Berlin, 1872.
SARAN, A. *Robert Franz und d. deutsche Volkslied.* Leipzig, 1872.
REISSMANN, A. *Geschichte d. deutschen Liedes.* Berlin, 1874.
SCHURÉ, E. *Histoire du Lied.* Paris, 1876.
EITNER, R. *Das deutsche Lied d. 15. und 16. Jahrhunderts.* Berlin, 1876–80.
BÖHME, F. M. *Altdeutsches Liederbuch aus dem 12. bis zum 17. Jahrhundert,* etc. Leipzig, 1877.
LILIENCRON, R. v. *Deutsches Leben im Volkslied um 1530.* Leipzig, 1884.
BÖHME, F. M. *Geschichte des Tanzes in Deutschland.* Leipzig, 1886.
NECKHEIM, H. 'Kärnthner Lieder.' 1891–1902.
FRIEDLÄNDER, M. 'Commersbuch.' Leipzig, 1892.
REIMANN, H. 'Das deutsche Lied.' Berlin, 1892–93.
WOLFRAM, E. H. 'Nassauische Volkslieder.' Berlin, 1894.
ERK, L., and BÖHME, F. M. 'Deutsche Liederhort.' Leipzig, 1894.
BÖHME, F. M. *Volkstümliche Lieder der Deutschen im 18. und 19. Jahrhundert.* Leipzig, 1895.
KUFFERATH, M. *Les Maîtres-Chanteurs de R. Wagner.* Paris, 1898.
MEY, KURT. *Der Meistergesang in Geschichte und Kunst.* Leipzig, 1901.
FRIEDLÄNDER, M. *Das deutsche Lied im 18. Jahrhundert.* Berlin, 1902.
RIEMANN, H. *Geschichte des neueren deutschen Liedes.* Leipzig, 1904.
MÜLLER VON DER WERRA, F.C. 'Allgemeine Reichs-Kommersbuch für deutsche Studenten' (edited by Felix Dehn and C. Reinecke). Leipzig, 1904.
RIEMANN, H. *Geschichte der Musik des 19. Jahrhunderts.* Leipzig, 1905.
BISCHOFF, H. *Das deutsche Lied.* Leipzig, 1906.
LILIENCRON, R. v. 'Neue deutsche Volkslieder-Sammlung.' Leipzig, 1906.
Articles in the *Vierteljahrsschrift für Musikwissenschaft, Monatshefte für Musikgeschichte,* and *Sammelbände* of the I.M.G.
JOLIZZA, W. K. VON. *Das Lied und seine Geschichte . . . mit 122 Notenbeispielen und Liedern der früheren Epochen bis zum Ende des 18. Jahrhunderts.* Vienna and Leipzig, 1910.
KRETZSCHMAR, HERMANN. *Geschichte des neuen deutschen Liedes.* 1 Teil: von Albert bis Zelter. Leipzig, 1911. 8vo.
(In spite of the word 'neu' this history starts with the 17th century.)
HAZAY, OE. VON. *Entwickelung und Poesie des Gesanges und die wertvollen Lieder der Gesamt-Musikliteratur.* 2nd ed. 2 Bd. Leipzig, 1915.
MAUTNER, KONRAD. *Alte Lieder und Weisen aus dem steiermärkischen Salzkammergute.* Pp. xxi, 412. Vienna (1919).
MOSER, HANS JOACHIM. 'Zur Rhythmik der altdeutschen Volksweisen.' *Z.M.W.,* Jan. 1919, pp. 225-52.
RADANOWICZ, EDITHA. *Das Wiener Lied, 1789–1815.* Vienna Dissertation, 1921.
MERSMANN, HANS. 'Grundlagen einer musikalischen Volksliedforschung.' *A.M.,* Apr. 1922, pp. 141-54; July 1922, pp. 289-321; Apr. 1923, pp. 83-135.
URSPRUNG, OTTO. 'Vier Studien zur Geschichte des deutschen Liedes.' *A.M.,* Oct. 1922, pp. 413-19; Jan. 1922, pp. 11-30.
KRABBE, WILHELM. 'Das Liederbuch des Johann Heck.' *A.M.,* Oct. 1922, pp. 420-38.
WALLNER, FRANZ. *Das musikalisch Volkstümliche im Lied des 17. Jahrhunderts.* Erlangen Dissertation, 1923.
R'ETSCH, HEINRICH. 'Einige Leitsätze für das ältere deutsche einstimmiges Lied.' *Z.f.M.W.,* Oct. 1923, pp. 1-15.

For further additions to this list refer to F. M. Böhme's 'Altdeutsches Liederbuch' and 'Volkstümliche Lieder der Deutschen,' where ample catalogues at end, with annotations, will be found.

A. H. W.; rev. with addns.: M. L. P. (France); J. B. T. (Spain and Portugal); R. N. (Slavonic countries); c. (England, etc.).

SONG-CYCLE, see LIEDERKREIS.

SONGE D'UNE NUIT D'ÉTÉ, LE (A Midsummer Night's Dream), opéra-comique in 3 acts, an absurd caricature of scenes in the life of Queen Elizabeth and Shakespeare, with no relation to his play; words by Rosier and De Leuven, music by Ambroise Thomas; produced Opéra - Comique, Paris, Apr. 20, 1850.   G.

SONG-SCHOOL. A considerable part in the development of the art of music has been played by Song-Schools. It was the establishment of the *Schola cantorum* at Rome (see SISTINE CHOIR) that led to the development of Gregorian plain-song in the 5th and 6th centuries, and it was the establishment of other such schools at St. Gall, Reichenau, Metz, etc., which disseminated widely the knowledge of the Roman music. In England such musical centres were set up in the earliest days of the Roman mission, and in the 6th and 7th centuries there was great enthusiasm and much good work done under a succession of teachers who came from the Roman *Schola.* After the Danes had devastated monastic life, and with it the bulk of Saxon culture, musical and other, a Benedictine revival under St. Ethelwold took place which recovered music among other things, and English music long preserved some special features which it had learnt in French Benedictine music-schools, particularly at Fleury-sur-Loire.

In the later period before the Reformation two forces were at work in giving practical musical training. In connexion with the monasteries a song-school was almost a necessity. In such song-schools not only foreigners, like Guido d'Arezzo or Regino of Prüm, learnt their music, but English musicians too, such as Odington, Tunsted, Hothby, Fayrfax and, finally, Tallis. At Durham, for example, there was in the monastic days a song-school in which six children were taught and kept under a master, who was also bound to play the organ at the chief services. After the dissolution the building was pulled down, but the school continued under its old master in a different position; and still the song-school flourishes in connexion with the present cathedral. Like the monasteries the secular cathedrals had also a song-school, and others were maintained not only by the King for the Chapel Royal, but also by great ecclesiastics and nobles. Secondly, the foundation of chantries tended to multiply song-schools; for the work stipulated for from the chantry priest after he had said his Mass daily was usually schoolmaster's work, and in many cases either a song-school or a grammar school was annexed to the foundation. Hundreds of these smaller schools were mostly destroyed when Edward VI. confiscated the chantries, and English music has never recovered from the loss. The prevalence of song-schools made it possible for England to be a nation of musicians in the 15th and 16th centuries; but few survived the Reformation, except in connexion with great collegiate or cathedral churches, and England lost its skill. (Cf. MAÎTRISE.)   W. H. F.

In Scotland 'Sang Schools' flourished from the 13th century onwards. A 'scule' for teaching singing existed in almost every one of the cathedral cities in Scotland, and in many of the smaller towns, such as Ayr, Dumbarton, Lanark, Cupar and Irvine. Even in the far north, in 1544, Bishop Reid founded and endowed a 'Sang School' in Orkney. Before the Reformation the teaching in these schools was principally confided to 'musick, meaners and vertu,' but at a later date it extended to the proverbial 'three R's.' Music, however, seems to have been the chief course of instruction, and the original idea of confining its study to the cathedral singers was so far enlarged, that laymen were admitted to the schools, in which the Gregorian chant had naturally an early and important place. The master of the school was held in high esteem, and was occasionally selected from the clergy, the appointment at times leading to important preferment—thus William Hay, master of the Old Aberdeen School in 1658, was made Bishop of Moray; and John Leslie, Bishop of Ross, was once a teacher in the Aberdeen School.

Great attention seems to have been paid by the Parliament of the day to the study of music, for a statute was passed in 1574

'instructing the provest, baillies, and counsale, to sett up ane sang scuill, for instruction of the youth in the art of musick and singing, quhilk is almaist decayit and sall schortly decay without tymous remeid be providit.'

Comparatively little interest seems to have attended either the Edinburgh or Glasgow schools, and from a minute of the Town Council of the latter we gather that the institution collapsed in 1588, 'the scuile sumtyme callit the sang scuile' being sold to defray the expenses incidental to the heavy visitation of a plague. The Aberdeen school appears to have been the one of chief celebrity, attracting teachers of even Continental fame, and the Burgh records contain references of a curious and amusing description. The school existed so early as the year 1370, its class of pupils being the same as those attending the grammar school. Both vocal and instrumental music were taught, as we learn from the title of Forbes's scarce work, 'Cantus, Songs and Fancies both apt for Voices and Viols as is taught in the Music School of Aberdeen' (1662). About this period, Mace, in his *Musick's Monument*, directed the attention of his countrymen to the sang school of Scotland as an institution well worthy of imitation south of the Tweed. A few excerpts from the Burgh records of Aberdeen and other places may not be uninteresting, and we give the following as a fair example of the attention paid by the civic authorities of the day to the subject of music. On Oct. 7, 1496, a contract was entered into between the Town Council of Aberdeen and Robert Huchosone, sangster, 'who obliges himself by the faith of his body all the days of his life to remain with the community of the burgh, upholding matins, psalms,

hymns,' etc., the Council also giving him the appointment of master of the Sang School. The four following extracts are also from the Aberdeen Burgh records, as faithfully transcribed by the editors of the Spalding Club publications :

4th October, 1577.

The said day the counsell grantit the soume of four poundis to the support of James Symsonne, doctour of thair Sang Scuill, to help to buy him cloythis.

23 Novr., 1597.

The maister of the sang schoole sall serve bayth the Kirkis in uptacking of the psalmes theirin.

1594.

Item to the Maister of the sang schoile xiiij.

1609.

'The bairnis and scoleris of the sang schoolis' are ordered to find caution for their good behaviour.

From Dundee Records, 1602.

Item to the master of the sang scule lxxx lbs.

From Air Records, 1627.

Item to the M^r of musick scule for teaching of the musick scule and tacking up the psalmes in the kirk x bolls victuall and xiiij of silver.

From Irving Records, 1633.

Our doctour and musicianer jcii.

On Nov. 27, 1579, Andrew Buchan was appointed master of the Edinburgh Sang School and 'for uptaking the Psalms in the Kirk of said borough.'

The stipend of the master of the Edinburgh Sang School appears to have been the modest allowance of ten pounds in sterling money.

J. T. F.

SONG WITHOUT WORDS, see LIED OHNE WORTE.

SONNAMBULA, LA, an opera in 2 acts; libretto by Romani, music by Bellini. Produced Teatro Carcano, Milan, Mar. 6, 1831; King's Theatre, July 28, and Paris, Oct. 28 of the same year; Drury Lane in English, May 1, 1833; New York, Park Theatre, Nov. 13, 1835.   G.

SONNECK, OSCAR GEORGE (b. Jersey City, New Jersey, Oct. 6, 1873), American writer on music, editor and librarian.

Educated in Germany at the Frankfort Gymnasium and the universities of Heidelberg and Munich, he studied music also in Germany. In 1902–17 he was in charge of the Music Division of the Library of Congress in Washington, which under his direction became one of the great and well-ordered music libraries of the world (see LIBRARIES). In 1911 he represented the United States government at the international music congresses at Rome and London. Since 1915 he has been editor of *The Musical Quarterly*, published by Schirmer (see PERIODICALS), and since 1921 he has been vice-president of that house.

As composer Sonneck is chiefly known through numerous songs. As historian and critic his work has been notable, particularly in the field of early American music. Aside from two volumes of poems his more important books are :

Classification of Music and Literature of Music. (1904; revised 1917.)
Francis Hopkinson and James Lyon. (1905.)
Bibliography of Early Secular American Music. (1905.)
Early Concert-Life in America. (1907.)
Historical Report on 'The Star-Spangled Banner,' 'America,' 'Hail Columbia' and 'Yankee Doodle.' (1909.)
Critical History of the 'Star-Spangled Banner.' (1914.)
Catalogue of Opera Librettos printed before 1800. (2 vols., 1914.)
Early Opera in America. (1915.)
Catalogue of First Editions of Edward MacDowell. (1917.)
Catalogue of First Editions of Stephen C. Foster. (1917.)
A book of Essays, Suum Cuique. (1916.)
Miscellaneous Studies in the History of Music. (1921.)

W. S. S.

SONNLEITHNER, a noted Viennese family of musical amateurs. (1) CHRISTOPH (b. Szegedin, May 28, 1734 ; d. Dec. 25, 1786) came to Vienna at 2 years old and learned music from his uncle Leopold Sonnleithner, choirmaster of a church in the suburbs. He also studied law, became an advocate of some eminence, was employed by Prince Esterhazy, and thus came into contact with Haydn. He composed several symphonies, which his friend Von Kees (often mentioned in Haydn's life) frequently played with his orchestra ; and also thirty-six quartets, mostly for the Emperor Joseph, who used to call him his favourite composer. His church compositions, remarkable for purity of form and warmth of feeling, have survived in the great ecclesiastical institutions of Austria, and are still performed at High Mass. His daughter Anna was the mother of Grillparzer the poet.

His son (2) IGNAZ (d. 1831), Doctor of Laws and professor of commercial science (ennobled 1828), was an energetic member of the Gesellschaft der Musikfreunde, and took part in their concerts as principal bass-singer. At the musical evenings held at his house (the so-called ' Gundelhof ') in 1815–24, in which his son Leopold took part as chorus-singer, Schubert's ' Prometheus,' though only with piano accompaniment, was first heard (July 24, 1816), as were also partsongs, ' Das Dörfchen ' (1819), ' Gesang der Geister über den Wassern ' (1821), and the 23rd Psalm for female voices (1822).

A second son, (3) JOSEPH (b. 1766 ; d. Dec. 26, 1835), devoted himself with success to literature and the fine arts, and in 1799 was sent abroad by the Emperor Franz to collect portraits and biographies of savants and artists for his private library. During this tour he made the acquaintance of Gerber and Zelter. In 1804 he succeeded Kotzebue as secretary of the court theatres, and as such had the entire management of both houses till 1814, and also of that ' an der Wien ' till 1807. He directed his endeavours principally to German opera, and himself wrote or translated several libretti, including Beethoven's ' Leonore ' from the French of du Bouilly (the title of which was changed against the composer's wish to ' Fidelio ')[1] ; ' Agnes Sorel ' and others for Gyrowetz ; ' Kaiser Hadrian,' and ' Die Weihe

der Zukunft '—a pièce d'occasion for the visit of the Allies — for Weigl ; ' Faniska ' for Cherubini ; an oratorio, ' Die vier letzten Dinge,' for Eybler, and numerous plays from various languages. He edited the Viennese Theater-Almanach for 1794, 1795 and 1796, which contains valuable biographies, and articles on the then condition of music in Vienna. For his services as founder (1811) and honorary secretary of the ' Gesellschaft adeliger Frauen zur Beförderung der Guten und Nützlichen ' he was made a counsellor. With indefatigable energy he next applied himself to founding (1813) the Gesellschaft der Musikfreunde, and continued to act as its honorary secretary till his death, devoting himself unremittingly to the welfare of the society. Another institution in which he took equal interest was the Conservatorium, founded in 1817.[2] The formation of the archives, and especially of the library, was almost entirely his work, through his acquisition of Gerber's literary remains in 1819, and his legacy of 41 MS. volumes in his own hand, full of valuable materials for the history of music. His discovery of the S. Gall Antiphoner in 1827 was an important event in the history of old liturgical music. The curious incident of the unique copy of Forkel's collection of 16th century church music, undertaken at Sonnleithner's instance, has been narrated under FORKEL. He lived in close friendship with Schubert and Grillparzer up to his death. He received the Danebrog Order and honorary diplomas from several musical societies.

His nephew, (4) LEOPOLD EDLER VON SONNLEITHNER (b. Nov. 15, 1797 ; d. Mar. 3, 1873), son of Ignaz, advocate and eminent amateur, was a great friend of the sisters Fröhlich, Schubert, Schwind the painter, and Grillparzer. He took great care to preserve Schubert's songs, and to introduce the composer to the musical world, by publishing, with the help of other friends, his ' Erlkönig ' and other early songs, for the first time. The ' Erlkönig ' was sung by Gymnich[3] at a soirée of the Gesellschaft der Musikfreunde, Jan. 25, 1821, and for the first time in public on Mar. 7 following, at the old Kärnthnerthor theatre, by Vogl, with immense success. As member of the Gesellschaft der Musikfreunde (from 1860 an honorary one), Sonnleithner took an unwearied interest in the concerns of the society, to whose archives he left, among other papers, his highly valuable notes on the operas produced, on concerts, and other musical events in Vienna. His numerous articles on music are scattered through various periodicals. He was an intimate friend of Otto Jahn, and furnished him with much valuable material for the life of Mozart, as Jahn acknow-

---

[1] Revised by Treitschke for the revival of the opera in 1814.

[2] The first scheme of instruction was drawn up by Hofrath von Mosel.
[3] August von Gymnich, an imperial official, and a much esteemed tenor, d. Oct. 6, 1821, aged 36.

ledges in his preface. Leopold von Sonnleithner was Ritter of the Order of the Iron Crown, an honorary member of the Gesellschaft der Musikfreunde, and of the Musikvereine of Salzburg, Innsbruck, etc. With his death disappeared a most persevering investigator and collector of facts connected with the history, of music in Vienna, a class which daily becomes rarer, though its labours were never of more value than in the present age of new appearances and general progress.   C. F. P.

SONS OF THE CLERGY, THE CORPORATION OF THE. This venerable institution, which was founded in 1655 by sons of clergymen, has for its objects the assisting necessitous clergymen, pensioning and assisting their widows and aged single daughters, and educating, apprenticing and providing outfits for their children. To aid in procuring funds for these purposes it holds an annual festival (at no fixed date), consisting of a choral service with a sermon, followed by a dinner. The first sermon was preached in the year of foundation at St. Paul's Cathedral by the Rev. George Hall, D.D., of St. Botolph's, Aldersgate Street. That similar meetings took place in following years is most probable, but there are no means of proving it, owing to the unfortunate destruction of the early records of the institution by fire, in 1838. We find, however, that in 1674 and 1675 sermons were preached at St. Michael's, Cornhill; that from 1676–96 they were delivered at Bow Church, Cheapside; and that from 1697 down to the present year (1926) they have been invariably given at St. Paul's Cathedral. The association was incorporated by charter of Charles II. in 1678. It was in 1698, according to the records, that ' music ' (i.e. orchestral accompaniment to the service and anthems) was first introduced at the festivals. The compositions then performed were Purcell's Te Deum and Jubilate in D, composed for the celebration on St. Cecilia's Day, 1694, and these were annually repeated until 1713, when Handel's Te Deum and Jubilate, composed on the Peace of Utrecht, were given, from which time the two compositions were alternately performed until 1743, when both were laid aside in favour of the Te Deum composed by Handel to celebrate the victory at Dettingen, which continued to be annually performed (with the exception of one or two years when Purcell's Te Deum was revived) until 1843, after which its performance was discontinued in consequence of the services of the instrumental band being dispensed with in deference to the wishes of the Bishop of London (Blomfield). Handel's overture to the oratorio ' Esther ' was almost invariably played as a prelude to the service from near the time of its production in 1720 until 1843. Dr. W. Hayes was at one time conductor of the festivals, and added instrumental parts to the Old Hundredth

Psalm tune for their use. Dr. Boyce also was for many years their conductor, and composed for them his two anthems, ' Lord, Thou hast been our refuge,' and ' Blessed is he that considereth the poor and needy,' besides adding accompaniments to Purcell's Te Deum and Jubilate, and expanding several movements in them. After 1843 the services were for some thirty years accompanied by the organ only, the choir being, as before, very largely augmented. Since 1873 orchestral accompaniment has again been called into requisition; Evensong has taken the place of Matins; and modern compositions by various living composers, often written expressly for the festival, have been introduced. A history of the corporation, by Rev. E. H. Pearce, was published in 1904.   W. H. H.

SONTAG, HENRIETTE, COUNTESS ROSSI (b. Coblenz, Jan. 3, 1806; d. June 17, 1854). Her father was a good comedian, her mother an actress of no ordinary merit, to whom the daughter, when at the height of fame, continued to turn for instruction. At 6, Henriette made her first public appearance, at the Darmstadt theatre, as Salome, in Kauer's 'Donauweibchen.' Three years later her mother, then a widow, settled at Prague, where Weber was conductor at the theatre. Here Henriette acted in juvenile parts, and in 1815 was admitted, though under the prescribed age, as a pupil at the Conservatorium of the city. She studied singing under Bayer and Frau Czegka, and when only 15 was suddenly called upon to replace the prima donna at the opera in the part of the Princess in Boieldieu's ' Jean de Paris.' Her precocity, appearance and vocal gifts at once created a great impression, but shortly afterwards her mother removed with her to Vienna, where the next few years were spent, Henriette Sontag singing both in Italian and German opera, and deriving, according to her own statement, incalculable benefit from the counsels and example of Mme. Fodor-Mainvielle. Here Weber, in 1823, after hearing her in the ' Donna del Lago,' went next day to offer her the title-rôle in his ' Euryanthe,' whose production, Oct. 25, was a triumph for Mlle. Sontag. Beethoven could not hear her, but ' How did little Sontag sing ? ' was his first question to those who had been at the performance. When, in 1824, his ninth symphony and Mass in D were produced, it was she who sustained the difficult and ungrateful soprano part. She was next engaged at Leipzig, and then for Berlin, making her first appearance at the Königstadt theatre, Aug. 3, 1825, as Isabella in the ' Italiana in Algieri.'

Henceforward her career was one unbroken triumph. She made her début in Paris in June 1826, as Rosina in the ' Barbiere,' and became a favourite at once. Her introduction of Rode's air and variations created a furore. She sang also in the ' Donna del Lago' and ' Italiana in Algieri,' and returned to Germany in July with heightened prestige. Everywhere her beauty, charming voice, and exquisite vocalisation combined to excite an admiration amounting to frenzy. At Göttingen her post - chaise was thrown into the river by the ardent crowd, no mortal being counted worthy to make use of it after her. Even Ludwig Börne, after commenting humorously on the extravagance of the public, confesses to have yielded in his turn to the prevailing infatuation. Her figure was slender and *mignonne*, her hair between auburn and blonde, her eyes large, and her features delicate. Her voice, a soprano of clear and pleasing quality, was specially good in the upper register, reaching the E in alt with facility, and in execution she seems to have been unsurpassed by any singer of her time. But she was deficient in dramatic power, and only appeared to the highest advantage in works of a light and placid style. On her return to Paris, in Jan. 1828, she essayed parts of a different order, such as Donna Anna and Semiramide, with success, but in passion and emotion never rose to the distinction she attained as a songstress.

In England she appeared first on Apr. 19, 1828, at the King's Theatre, as Rosina, and met with a most flattering reception, sharing with Malibran the honours of that and the succeeding season.

At Berlin, Mlle. Sontag had formed the acquaintance of Count Rossi, then in the diplomatic service of Sardinia. An attachment sprang up between them, and was followed by a secret marriage. It was feared that the young diplomat's future might be compromised were he to acknowledge an artist of low birth as his wife. But after a time Count Rossi's efforts to procure court sanction to his union were successful—the King of Prussia bestowed a patent of nobility on the lady, who henceforth appeared in documents as *née de Launstein*, and she definitely bade farewell to artistic life. As Countess Rossi she accompanied her husband to the Hague, where he was representative of the Sardinian court. Occasionally she would sing for public charities, in concerts or oratorio —a style in which she is said to have been unrivalled ; still, for nearly half her lifetime she remained lost to the musical public, following the career of her husband at the courts of Holland, Germany and Russia. As to her domestic felicity and the character of her husband, we quote the positive testimony of her brother, Carl Sontag : ' Rossi made my sister happy, in the truest sense of the word. Up to the day of her death they loved each other as on their wedding-day ! ' But the disorders of 1847–48 had impaired their fortunes, and she was tempted to return to the opera. It was notified to Rossi that he might retain his

ambassador's post if he would formally separate from his wife—on the tacit understanding that so soon as her operatic career was concluded she should be allowed to return to him. This he, however, at once refused, and resigned his post, though remaining on a friendly footing with the court. Lumley, then manager of Her Majesty's Theatre, having offered the Countess Rossi £6000 for six months, it was accepted, and in July 1849 her reappearance in London as ' Linda ' was announced. The curiosity excited was extreme. Her voice and charms were unimpaired, and the unanimous opinion seems to have been that, in the words of Adolphe Adam, she now united to youth and freshness the qualities of a finished artist. As Amina, though Jenny Lind was fresh in the public memory, she was rapturously received, as also in Desdemona, and Susanna in the ' Nozze,' one of her favourite parts, and pronounced by a German critic the most perfect thing he had seen on any stage. Her extraordinary preservation of her powers was partly due, no doubt, to long exemption from the wear and tear of incessant public singing ; but Sontag was always extremely careful of her voice, discarding any rôle that did not lie well within her register. Thus, in an early contract at Berlin, she expressly stipulates that she shall not be bound to sing in the operas of Spontini !

After a tour in the English provinces in the winter of 1849, she went to Paris, where a successful series of concerts, also under Lumley's management, preceded in the spring of 1850 her reappearance at Her Majesty's to win fresh laurels as Norina in ' Don Pasquale,' Elvira in the ' Puritani,' and Miranda in Halévy's new opera ' La Tempesta.' As Zerlina and the ' Figlia del reggimento,' she appeared for the first time, and with pre-eminent success. In the autumn of 1850 she sang in Italian opera at Paris, Lumley again being director of the company. During this season Alary's ' Tre nozze ' was produced, and the polka-duet between Sontag and Lablache never failed to send the public into ecstasies. It was brought out in London in 1851, with similar results. During this season, Mme. Sontag's last in London, she sang in a round of her favourite parts, and in the production of ' L'Enfant prodigue.'

In Germany, wherever she went she carried all before her. At a concert at Munich she was expressly requested to stay to hear the last piece. It proved to be a ' Huldigungs Chor '— verses composed expressly in her honour by the Crown Prince, and set to music by Lachner.

In 1852, Mme. Sontag received offers from the United States, which tempted her thither with her husband in the autumn. The results were brilliant. Her voice was strengthened by the climate, and at this time she could sing in ' Lucrezia Borgia ' and the ' Figlia del reggimento ' on a single evening without over-

fatigue ! Her last appearance was made in
'Lucrezia' at Mexico in 1854. She was attacked by cholera, and a brief illness cut short
a life of unchequered prosperity.   B. T.

BIBL.—THÉOPHILE GAUTIER, Portraits contemporains (1847,
3rd ed.).

SOPRANO, the name given to the highest
of the three classes into which the voices of
women are generally divided. (See CONTRALTO
and MEZZO-SOPRANO.) The term is etymologically synonymous with 'Sovrano,' the
head, chief or highest. But apart from the
height to which the compass of the voice can
climb, the true soprano is further distinguished
by the unmistakable brightness and ring of
its tone-quality. It may be classified as the
dramatic, the lyrical and the *coloratur*. A
compass which extends to f''' is necessary for a
voice in the last-named category (see AGUJARI).
B flat is about the effective limit downwards.

The voices of boys usually cover about two
octaves—*a* to *a″* of the soprano range, with
something approximating to the soprano
quality. For artificial soprano see CASTRATO.

SORCERER, THE, comic opera in 2 acts ;
libretto by W. S. Gilbert ; music by Sullivan.
Produced Opéra-Comique Theatre, Nov. 17,
1877.

SORDINO, see MUTE.

SORGE, GEORG ANDREAS (*b*. Mellenbach,
Schwarzburg, Mar. 21, 1703 ; *d*. Lobenstein,
Apr. 4, 1778). After a period of but indifferent
tuition he was appointed court and town
organist at Lobenstein, which post he held to
the time of his death. He was a prolific composer, not without merit, but he is best known
by his theoretical work, being one of the dis-
coverers of the 'combination tones,' which he
discusses in his *Vorgemach der mus. Komposi-
tion*, published before Tartini made his discoveries known to the world. Sorge was unfortunately a very conceited man, who thought
that he alone possessed true knowledge, which
led to bitter controversies, especially with
Marpurg and Quantz. Sorge introduced the
system of building up chords by the super-
imposition of thirds which is still used in the
teaching of harmony. A list of his theoretical
works and his compositions is given in *Riemann*
and *Q.-L.*

SORIANO (SURIANO, SURIANUS, SURIANI),
FRANCESCO (*b*. Rome, 1549 ; *d*. there, Jan.[1]
1620), entered the choir at St. John Lateran
at the age of 15. After the breaking of his
voice he became a pupil of Montanari, then of
G. M. Nanini, and lastly of Palestrina. After
this his fame went on always increasing. In
1581 we find him maestro di cappella at
St. Ludovico dei Francesi ; in 1583 he was at
the court of Mantua ; in 1587 at Sta. Maria
Maggiore ; in 1599 at St. John Lateran. He
returned, however, to Sta. Maria Maggiore, and

[1] *Riemann.*

in 1603 made his final step to the head of the
choir of St. Peter's. He was buried at Sta. Maria
Maggiore.

Soriano published his first work in 1581, a
book of madrigals, *a* 5. This was followed by
a second in 1592 ; by a book of motets, *a* 8,
1597 ; by a second book of madrigals, *a* 4, 1601,
1602 ; by a book of masses for 4, 5 and 6 voices,
1609 ; by a collection of 110 canons on Ave
Maris Stella, 1610, and by a second book of
psalms and motets, *a* 8, 12 and 16, 1616. His
last work was a Magnificat and Passione, *a* 4,
Rome, 1619, containing his portrait. A complete list of his works is given in *Q.-L.* He
arranged Palestrina's Missa Papae Marcelli for
8 voices. The Passion already mentioned, a
Magnificat and five Antiphons are included in
Proske's 'Musica Divina,' vols. iii. and iv., and
two masses in the 'Selectus novus.'   G.

SORIANO FUERTES, MARIANO (*b*. Murcia,
Mar. 28, 1817 ; *d*. Madrid, Mar. 26, 1880),
Spanish musical historian. In spite of musical
upbringing, he was forced into a cavalry regiment ; but soon retired and devoted himself
to music. He founded two musical journals
(1841 and 1860), and was for some time teacher
at the Madrid Conservatoire (1843) and director
of a musical institution at Córdoba. He held
various posts as conductor of opera at Seville,
Cadiz and Barcelona. He completed a *History of Spanish music from the times of the
Phœnicians down to 1850* (Madrid, 1855–59).
It is confused and inaccurate, and is now
superseded by the works of Riaño, Pedrell and
Mitjana. He also wrote a treatise (of doubtful
value), *Musica Arabe-Española* (1853).   J. B. T.

SORS (SOR), FERNANDO (*b*. Barcelona,
Feb. 17, 1780 ; *d*. Paris, July 8, 1839), Spanish
guitarist. Like SOLER he was a pupil of the
Escolanía at Montserrat ; at 17 he composed
an opera, 'Telemaco,' which was produced at
Barcelona. In Paris he made the acquaintance
of Méhul and Cherubini, and during the
Napoleonic invasion, in 1809, fled to London,
where he had much to do with stimulating
interest in the guitar. He became a fashionable teacher, and was the only guitar-player
who ever appeared at one of the Philharmonic
Society's concerts. His studies are still in
the repertory of every serious player of the
guitar.   J. B. T.

SORTE, BARTOLOMEO, lived at Padua, his
native town, between 1570–90. He was singer
at the cathedral, and composed masses (1596),
Psalms, etc., and two books of madrigals (*Q.-L.*).

SOSTENUTO, 'sustained' ; a direction
which has of late come to be used with a
considerable degree of ambiguity. It originally
signified that the notes were to be held for their
full value, and was thus equivalent to *tenuto* ;
but in music of the 'romantic' school it very
often has the same meaning as *meno mosso*, or
something between that and *ritenuto*—*i.e.* the

passage so marked is to be played at an uniform rate of decreased speed until the words *a tempo* occur. No precise rule can be given for its interpretation, as its use varies with different masters, and even in different works by the same master.   M.

SOSTINENTE PIANOFORTE. A term used in connexion with several attempts, none of them permanently successful, to make a pianoforte capable of producing a sustained sound, such as that of the organ or violin. The lyrichord, melopiano, claviol and piano-violin, names adopted by inventors for certain of these attempts, are discussed below.

THE HURDY-GURDY (*q.v.*) is the germ of *sostinente* keyed instruments; allied to the harpsichord we meet with it in the Gamben-werk[1] of Hans Haydn of Nuremberg, dating about 1610. An instrument of Spanish origin, dated 1625, is in the Museum of the Conserva-toire of Music at Brussels (see Mahillon, Cat. IV. p. 282 ff.). Pepys records in 1664 the ex-hibition of an ARCHED VIOL (*q.v.*), an instru-ment similar in principle. The lyrichord, patented by Roger Plenius[2] in London in 1741, demands notice as being a harpsichord strung with wire and catgut, made on the sostinente principle, and actuated by moving wheels in-stead of the usual quills, so that the bow of the violin and the tone of the organ were imitated. There is no specification to the patent, but a magazine article of 1755[3] gives a drawing and complete description of the instrument, which was otherwise remarkable for sustaining power by screws, springs and balanced tension weights for tuning; for silver covering to the bass strings, like the largest bass-violins; for the use of *iron* to counteract the greater pull of the octave strings (in the drawing there are apparently four iron bars connecting the wrest-plank and sound-board, thus anticipating the later intro-duction of steel arches in grand pianofortes for similar service); and lastly for the Swell ob-tained by dividing the lid or cover into two parts, one of which is movable up and down by means of a pedal governed by the foot of the player. Another patent of Plenius, in 1745, added the 'Welch harp,' or buff stop (in his patent by a pedal), to the instrument. Another 'sostinente' harpsichord was the CELESTINA of Adam Walker, patented in London in 1772.

The melopiano was a grand piano with a *sostinente* attachment, the invention of Caldera, applied in England by Kirkman, who secured the sole right to use it here and made several instruments with it. The principle was original, the apparently sustained sounds being pro-duced by reiterated blows of small hammers placed nearer the wrest-plank bridge than the striking place of the ordinary hammers, and

suspended by a bar above and crossing the strings.[4]

An important 'sostinente' instrument was the claviol[5] or finger-keyed viol, the in-vention of Dr. John Isaac Hawkins[6] of Border-town, New Jersey, U.S.A., an Englishman by birth, who invented the real upright pianoforte. This upright piano (called 'portable grand') and the claviol, which was in form like a cabinet piano, with ringbow mechanism for the sostinente, were introduced to the public in a concert at Philadelphia, by the inventor, June 21, 1802. Hawkins was in England in 1813 and 1814, exhibiting his claviol, and in the latter year complained of his idea being appro-priated by others through the expiration of his patent. Isaac Mott's 'Sostinente Piano Forte,' patented by him in 1817, was a further de-velopment of the idea, and is fully described in the patent, No. 4098. Mott claimed the power to increase or diminish the tone at will; and by rollers acting on silken threads, set in action by a pedal, the 'sostinente' was brought into action or stopped. Mott's instrument had some success, he being at the time a fashionable pianoforte-maker. Another instrument of this period was Kaufmann's HARMONICHORD (*q.v.*).

In 1865 Hubert Cyrille Baudet introduced an instrument in Paris named 'Piano Quatuor,' patenting it in England as piano violin. The strings were of wire as in the PF., but of greater thickness, there being only one to each note. The strings were vertical, and attached to a nodal, or nearly nodal, point of each was a piece of stiff catgut, projecting in front more than an inch. A roller, covered with fine linen and slightly rosined, was made to turn by means of treadles with great rapidity. Motion was communicated through the ties to the wires and their musical vibration excited. The impression on the ear was that of the tone of a violin.   A. J. H., with addns.

SOTO DE LANGA, FRANCISCO (*b.* Langa, near Osma, 1539; *d.* Rome, Sept. 25, 1619), Spanish priest and adapter of *Laude Spirituali*. He came to Rome at an early age and entered the Papal Choir as a soprano in 1562. Shortly afterwards he became one of the followers of St. Philip Neri, and eventually joined the congregation of the Oratory. He still re-mained a member of the Papal Choir, of which he was dean for many years, but he sang at the Chiesa Nuova up to the end of his life, and preserved his voice to the age of 80.

Examples from Soto's collections of Laude are given by D. Alaleona, *Storia dell' oratorio musicale in Italia* (Turin, 1908), and E. J. Dent, *Proc. Mus. Ass.* xliii. (1916–17), 80 ff. He includes a great many folk-songs, as being

---

[1] Figured in Praetorius's *Theatrum instrumentorum*, 1620.
[2] Plenius is said to have been the first to attempt to make a pianoforte in England.
[3] Formerly in the possession of A. J. H.

[4] The mechanism was more fully described under MELOPIANO in earlier editions of this Dictionary. See also Hipkins, *History of the Pianoforte*.
[5] For descriptions see *Rees's Cyclopædia*, 1819; *Mechanic's Magazine*, 1845, No. 1150, p. 136.
[6] See *Scribner's Magazine*, 1888.

well known and suitable for congregational singing, and has no objection to consecutive fifths ; though he also uses tunes of a more sophisticated type. Again, the words of many of his hymns are nothing more than parodies *a lo divino* of secular poems ; in the example quoted by Mitjana (*Encl. de la musique, Espagne*, p. 1987), 'Esclarecida Madre' is a sacred version of a Spanish villancico, ' Esclarecida Juana' (Bibl. Medinaceli, MS. 13,230). The originals of many of the Italian folk-songs used by him have also been identified. Soto was responsible for the musical part of the five books of ' Laude filippine ' :

Il primo libro delle laudi spirituali, a 3 v. Rome, 1583. (Rome, Vallicelliana ; Berlin ; B.M.)
Il secondo libro delle laudi spirituali, a 3 et a 4 v. Rome, 1583. (Rome, Vallicell. ; Florence, Riccardiana ; Berlin ; B.M.)
Il terzo libro delle laudi spirituali, a 3 e 4 v. Rome, 1588. (Rome: Vallicell., Casanatense ; Berlin ; B.M.)
Libro delle laudi spirituali dove in uno sono compressi i 3 libri già stampati. (Florence, Instituto musicale ; Bologna, Liceo : B.M.)
Il quarto libro delle laudi a 3 et 4 v. Rome, 1591. (Rome, Vallicell., Casanat. ; Bologna, Liceo ; Berlin ; Brussels, Conservatoire ; B.M.)
Il quinto libro delle laudi spirituali a 3 et 4 v. del Reverendo P. Francesco Soto. Ferrara, 1598. (Rome, Vallicell. ; B.M.)

Other compositions or arrangements by Soto are to be found in Ancina's ' Tempio armonico ' (Rome, 1599) and Arascione's ' Nùovi laudi ariose ' (Rome, 1600). The statement that many of the Laude were composed by Palestrina is an invention of Baini.   J. B. T.

SOTTO VOCE, ' under the voice,' in an undertone ; a direction of frequent occurrence in instrumental as well as vocal music.   M.

SOUBIES, ALBERT (*b.* Paris, May 10, 1846 ; *d.* there, Mar. 19, 1918), was educated at the Lycée Louis-le-Grand, but, after studying for the legal profession, he entered the Conservatoire, where he studied under Savard, Bazin and Guilmant. His first essay as a writer on music, a career in which he had remarkable success, was in the continuation of the *Almanach Duchesne* under the title of *Almanach des spectacles* (1874 onwards). His principal work was a history of music in a series of small volumes arranged under different countries : *Allemagne et Russie* occupy two volumes ; *L'Espagne*, three more ; *Le Portugal, La Hongrie et la Bohême*, three ; *Suisse and Hollande*, one each ; *Belgique*, two ; *États scandinaves*, three ; and *Îles britanniques*, two. *Les Grands Théâtres Parisiens* deals with the Comédie Française, the Opéra (for sixty-seven years), the Opéra-Comique (for sixty-nine years), the Théâtre Lyrique, 1851–70, and the Théâtre Italien. *Une Première par jour* was crowned, with other of Soubies's works, by the Opéra, and other non-musical books are in his list. His last work was *Les Membres de l'Académie des Beaux Arts depuis la fondation de l'Institut* (Paris, 1917). He collaborated with Ch. Malherbe in the *Histoire de l'Opéra-Comique* (*1840–87*), *Mélanges sur Richard Wagner*, *L'Œuvre dramatique de Richard Wagner* ; with H. de Curzon in *Documents inédits sur le Faust de Gounod* (1912) ; and in a

Précis de l'histoire de l'Opéra-Comique, the last under the name of B. de Lomagne. He wrote for the *Soir* from 1876, and for the *Revue de l'Art dramatique* from 1885, and was a frequent contributor to the *Guide musical*; the *Ménestrel*; *Encyclopédie de la musique et Dictionnaire du Conservatoire*.   G. F.

SOUND-BOARD (SOUNDING-BOARD). (1) In the organ the sound-board is the upper portion of the wind-chest, upon which the pipes stand.

(2) In the pianoforte the sound-board is usually called the BELLY (*q.v.*).

SOUND-HOLES (*ff* HOLES) (Fr. *ouïe* ; Ger. *Schalloch* ; Ital. *occhi*). The two apertures in the form of italic *f*'s which face one another in the tables of violins—and the instruments of that family—on either side of the bridge.

These exercise a powerful influence upon the tone, regulating as they do the entire system of vibrations of the various parts of the instruments, by governing the amount of air which is contained within the body. Scientific investigation has proved that the best tonal results are arrived at when the contained mass of air in the body of a violin answers to 512 vibrations (*i.e.* corresponding to c''; see PITCH), and for this reason that standard of vibration has been generally adopted by all good violin-makers since the days of Stradivarius, whose violins are perfect examples of this system. The principle, however, cannot be applied by way of extension to the viola, or violoncello, a fact which was proved by those large violoncellos made by 17th century *luthiers* in accordance with violin measurements by mere augmentation, all of which have had to be reduced in size. According to Savart[1] the pitch of the viola being a fifth below that of the violin, and an octave above the violoncello, the instrument should contain a mass of air answering to 341·33 vibrations (*f'*: a system, however, not generally followed) ; and the violoncello, being pitched a fifth plus an octave below the violin, should give 170·66 vibrations (*f*)—neither of which, again, can be said to be arbitrary laws.

Savart at first questioned the necessity of curved sound-holes, but his later experiments proved that any deviation from the *f* form, where the belly was arched, had a disastrous effect upon the tone of the instrument. He also tested the effect of dispensing with one sound-hole by covering it with paper, with the result that the tone was immediately diminished, and the note given by the contained mass of air was flattened. A similar effect is produced when the holes are too small ; but when they are too large the vibratory note of the air rises. Practically the proportions of the *ff* holes must depend upon the dimensions, thickness, height, etc., of the instrument, and they must be cut in strict relation to these conditions.

[1] *Mémoire sur la construction des instruments à cordes et à archet.*

Although an established form and position of the sound-holes did not exist until the latter half of the 16th century, still there are evidences that sound-holes were employed in very early times. The monochord attributed to Ptolemy (*circa* A.D. 139) was apparently provided with a circular sound-hole, like some of the guitars depicted in ancient Egyptian frescoes, which show small sound-holes pierced in the upper table, on either side of the strings. To-day those presumptive descendants of the original inhabitants of Egypt—the Berbers—monopolise a musical instrument called the 'kissar,' considered to be of very ancient origin, which has a circular sound-hole placed in the now generally adopted position. In the 9th century we find a figure from the MS. found by Gerber in the Monastery of St. Blasius in the Black Forest, and copied by him, which shows (Fig. 1) C-shaped sound-holes well placed, but from that time to the 16th century pictorial and sculptural representations afford evidence that the various small predecessors of the viol properly so called depended entirely upon the whim of their makers for the shape of their sound-holes. Some of the viol's forerunners had as many as six sound-holes pierced in their diminutive bodies, others had four, and others two, but none among them approached the *f* form finally adopted by the violin-makers proper. At the beginning of the 16th century, makers began to show

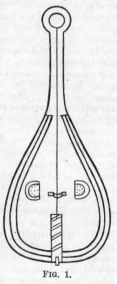

FIG. 1.

more dexterity in cutting the sound-holes, and even in the previous century some Italian makers had already come very near to realising their correct position. A glance at Fig. 2, reproduced from an early woodcut representation of a seven-stringed viol which ornaments the front page of the 'First Book of Songs' by 'Aurelius Augurellus Ariminensis' (Verona, 1491), a copy of which is in the library of the British Museum, will corroborate this statement. During the first half of the 16th century the woodcut illustrations of bow instruments which appeared in the works of Sebastian Virdung (*Musica getutscht*, 1511), of Martin Agricola (*Musica instrumentalis*, 1528), and of Hans Gerle (*Musica teusch*, 1532), show rebecs with the C-shaped sound-holes on either side of the strings—sometimes turned

inward and sometimes outward; also viols with a 'rose' in the centre and the C-shaped sound-holes set high up in the upper bouts. Far in advance of the German work was that of the contemporary Italians as revealed by Ganassi del Fontego (Venice, 1542), in his *Regola Rubertina,* wherein graceful viols with large *f*-shaped sound-holes appear, and later in the century the still more elegant curves portrayed in Domenichino's bass, in his picture of St. Cecilia (Fig. 3). Another form of sound-hole prevalent among viol-makers and extensively employed by them for the viola da gamba is that shown in Fig. 4,

FIG. 2.

known as the 'flaming sword.' Generally speaking, the true era of the *f*-shaped sound-hole began with Andreas Amati (Cremona, about 1520–80) and Gasparo da Salò (Brescia, 1542–1609), and was the outcome of the ceaseless pursuit of perfection which marked the period of the Renaissance. The C-shaped (Fig. 2) sound-holes, it

FIG. 3.

was observed, lacked grace, so makers began to twist them about until they assumed the greater elegance of form. An example of this progression is shown in Fig. 5, which is taken from a tenor viol on one of the carved screens of Cremona Cathedral, dating from the first part of the 16th century. This was a distinct step in the right direction ; but neither Gasparo da Salò nor Andreas Amati could quite throw aside the C-shape, and the first employed that form for some of his grand tenors. Gasparo da Salò's *ff* holes are very long and pointed, stiff

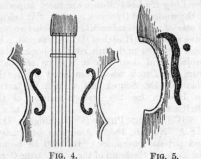

FIG. 4.   FIG. 5.

in appearance and parallel in position, while Andreas Amati's lack symmetry by reason of their being cut too wide. Gasparo's pupil Paolo Maggini (Brescia, 1590–1640), according to Savart's experiments, committed the same error, the muffled tone of his instruments being due to this cause, the contained volume of air within the body of his violins answering to the vibrations of middle D. The brothers Amati and Jerome's son Nicolas—who added a touch of boldness to his father's *ff*—put grace of design into their sound-holes, but robbed their violins of power by placing them too far apart on the table. The fallacies inherent to these first attempts were discovered and rectified by Antonius Stradivarius (Cremona, 1644–1737), whose graceful, converging *ff* holes are acknowledged to be perfect in form, position, proportion, and intent. Although Stradivari had an ingenious method for ascertaining the correct place for his *ff* holes on the belly of the violin, and fixed upon the main features of these, yet on no two of his instruments can the *ff* holes be called identical. The spontaneous feeling and charm which characterised the work of his predecessors, who knew neither template nor pattern, or at least did not employ them, were by him preserved with an added touch of necessary exactitude. He realised the efficacy of flatter surfaces and the influence exercised by the contained mass of air, and made his *ff* holes to suit these ruling factors with a resulting balance of parts impossible to surpass. Deviations from the form or position established by Stradivari have never proved satisfactory. What Joseph Guarnerius gained in power by his more heroic form of sound-hole—magnificent as it is in many cases—was at the sacrifice of the tone of the G string. The E A D of his violins are sonorous and brilliant, but the fourth string suffers from combined effects due to the excessive thickness of the plates and the size of the sound-holes. In these days the form and position of the sound-holes have reached a point of almost mechanical perfec-

tion. With the exception of the attempted innovations made by Savart and Chanot, the present *f* shape has retained its position unchallenged for quite 300 years.

BIBL.—SAVART, *Mémoire sur la construction des instruments à cordes et à archet*; GALLAY, (1) *Les Luthiers italiens*; (2) *Les Ancêtres du violon*; VIDAL, *Les Instruments à archet*; YUSSOPOFF, *Luthomonographie*; MORDRET, *Lutherie artistique*; MAUGIN ET MAIGNE, *Nouveau Manuel complet du luthier*; P. DAVIDSON, *The Violin*; HART, *The Violin*; HILL, *Antonio Stradivari*; HERON-ALLEN, *Violin-making*; *Violin Monthly Magazine*, No. 5 (edited by J. M. Fleming); GERBER, *Musical Lexikon*; VON LUTGENDORFF, *Die Geigen- und Lautenmacher*; BACHMANN, *Le Violon*.   E. H.-A.

SOUND-POST (Fr. *âme*; Ger. *Stimmstock*; Ital. *anima*), a small pillar of pine wood which stands vertically within the body of the violin and the other instruments of that family. Originally it was a mere structural precaution, brought about by the introduction of the higher pitch, and consequent greater pressure upon the table of the instrument; but it is in reality the centre round which the vibrations of the body of the instrument focus, and from which they proceed. This important tone-producing factor is made either of fine-grained Swiss pine or spruce wood, and it is placed so that the fibres of its wood run at right angles to those of the table. Closely fitting against the arching of the back and table of the instrument, it retains its position under, and slightly behind, the right foot of the bridge, and is kept in position solely by the pressure of the strings upon the table. Its length depends upon the depth between the back and table of the instrument for which it is intended, and its diameter is subject to slight alteration, according to the modelling. If the sound-post is too slight, the tone of the instrument in which it is placed will be relatively thin, and the opposite effect is produced where it is too thick. The correct position to be assigned to the sound-post is an important matter, as the smallest variation of position materially alters the tone. The extreme range over which it may be moved is comprised within an area of about a quarter of an inch. As a general rule, when the vibrations of the back of an instrument are sluggish and require to be accelerated before the highest quality of tone of which it is capable can be produced, the sound-post should be brought nearer the bridge; in a contrary condition of things it should be moved farther away; and high-built instruments require the sound-post nearer the bridge than do those of flatter model.

The interesting series of experiments made in connexion with the sound-post by Savart, and later by Huggins, have proved the following axioms:

(1) That the sound-post conveys the combined vibrations of the table and sides to the back of the instrument, controlling the action of these parts, and bringing them into unison and equilibrium with the contained mass of air in the body of the instrument.

(2) That the material of which the sound-post is made influences the tone of the

instrument, as was evidenced by Huggins's introduction of lead, and of sealing-wax, into the centre of the post, whereby the volume of tone was diminished greatly. A sheet. of india-rubber firmly wedged in at the upper and lower end of the sound-post, when in position, influenced the tone in a still more disastrous manner.

(3) That the sound - post placed directly under the right foot of the bridge diminished the intensity of tone, rendering it as meagre in quality as it is when the sound-post is dispensed with ; placed under the left foot of the bridge, on the same side as the bass-bar, similarly unsatisfactory results were produced.

The object of the sound-post, therefore, is not so much to convey the vibrations of any of the sections of the violin one to another, as to render the vibrations regular and consonant, and experiment has proved that these results are best obtained by placing the 'sound-post slightly behind the right foot of the bridge. This conclusion has been borne out by the fact that trial has shown the fallacy and inefficacy of all innovations such (to name but a few) as Petizeau's hollow glass sound-post (brought before the Academy of Sciences in Paris a few years ago) ; Haussel's broad, flat, thin sound-post (described in the *A.M.Z.*, 1881, p. 75) ; and P. Davidson's sound-post with drilled holes, together with such patents as David Herring's sound-post made elastic, so as to double the amplitude of the vibrations (No. 18,028) ; Simoutre's round - legged or oval sound-post (No. 11,936), and others to be found in the *Abridgements of Specifications relating to Music and Musical Instruments*, published by the Commissioners of Patents.   E. H.-A.

BIBL.—SIR W. HUGGINS, LL.D., F.R.S., *On the Function of the Sound-post* (1883) ; FELIX SAVART, *Mémoire sur la construction des instruments à archet* ; OTTO MIGGE, *The Secret of the Celebrated Italian Violin-makers* ; J. GALLAY, *Les Luthiers italiens* ; J. C. MAUGIN, *Manuel de luthier* ; P. DAVIDSON, *The Violin* ; HERON - ALLEN, *Violin-making*.

SOUPIR (a sigh), the French name for a crotchet rest. A quaver rest is called *un demi-soupir* ; a semiquaver ditto, *un quart de soupir*, and so on.   G.

SOURDINE, (1) an obsolete instrument of wood, with a small cylindrical bore, played with a double reed. The larger instruments of this family had two parallel tubes arranged much in the same way as those of the bassoon, and were furnished with several keys, as well as six finger-holes. The CURTAL (*q.v.*) was a very similar if not an identical instrument.   D. J. B.

(2) See MUTE.

ŠOUREK, OTAKAR (*b.* Prague, 1883), musical critic of *Lidové Noviny* and *Venkov* (1919). An engineer by training, Šourek has devoted his literary energies chiefly to Dvořák and his work. His thematic catalogue of the works of Dvořák (Simrock) has been very useful in setting right the chronological errors which have accumulated round this musician's

compositions on account of the publishers having given them fictitious opus numbers. His numerous articles in the *Hudebni Revue* and the *Listy Hudebni Matice* are most important to the student of Dvořák's music. *The Life and Works of Antonín Dvořák*, of which two vols. have appeared (Hudebni Matice, Prague), is the most detailed and authoritative book on the subject, and doubtless it will be translated from the Czech when completed by a third volume. Dr. Šourek has written the article on Dvořák for the present edition of this Dictionary.   R. N.

SOUSA, JOHN PHILIP (*b.* Washington, D.C., U.S.A., Nov. 6, 1856), American bandmaster and popular composer. In 1880 he became the leader of the band of the U.S. Marine Corps. In 1892 his band was formed. Sousa's compositions include numerous comic operas, but it is by his marches that he is best known.
                                        W. S. S.

SOUTH PLACE SUNDAY CONCERTS. A series of weekly concerts which for 6 or 7 months each winter enables music-lovers in London (especially the poorer ones) to hear the masterpieces of chamber music adequately performed by first-rate artists, the funds being provided by collections among the audience. Originally the Finsbury branch of the PEOPLE'S CONCERT SOCIETY (*q.v.*), the South Place Institute, was asked to take over the work in 1887. This was done with remarkable success, thanks to an energetic committee, and to the indefatigable exertions of A. J. Clements, the secretary, who has kept in touch with the most competent instrumentalists in or visiting London. About 1000 [1] Sunday concerts have been given, and there is every prospect of a continuance of the work for an indefinite period, though not necessarily at South Place.

The chamber music of all periods and all schools has been placed before the public with remarkable completeness. On rare occasions the South Place Orchestral Society, an amateur organisation conducted by R. H. Walthew, has given performances ; but chamber music has been the staple fare, with the addition of songs and instrumental solos. A salient feature has been the devotion of special evenings to the music of one composer, chiefly on the occasion of an anniversary or centenary celebration. In this way the following composers have been honoured : Haydn, Mozart, Beethoven, Bach, Schubert, Brahms, Schumann, Dvořák, Richard Strauss, Robert Fuchs, Parry, Stanford, Walford Davies, R. H. Walthew and Elgar. Modern British music has been represented, the programmes including the phantasies associated with the Cobbett Competitions (see COBBETT and FANCY), attention being also given on special evenings to modern French, Scandi-

1 The 1000th concert was given on the 40th anniversary of the first concert, Feb. 20, 1927.

navian and Slavonic music. The name of the artists performing is legion, and all have given their services for a merely nominal fee. Exceptional mention should be made of the late John SAUNDERS, a violinist and quartet leader, who is the subject of a special notice. w. w. c.

SOWERBY, LEO (b. Grand Rapids, Michigan, May 1, 1895), American pianist and composer. Educated at the American Conservatory of Music in Chicago, he subsequently became a teacher in that institution. During the Great War he served as bandmaster with the American forces in England and in France. In 1922 he was awarded the American Prix de Rome. In the United States he has been soloist with various orchestras ; he has also given recitals in London and in Italy, and in 1923 he took part in the Salzburg (contemporary music) Festival. His compositions include :

Pianoforte concerto; ballad for two pianos and orchestra; an orchestral suite, 'From the Northland,' and other orchestral pieces; chamber music; pieces for organ and pianoforte; and choral compositions. He has also written a 'Sinconata' for jazz orchestra.

w. s. s.

SPAGNOLETTI, P. (b. Cremona, 1768[1]; d. London, Sept. 23, 1834), violinist, who held the post of leader of the King's Theatre orchestra for nearly thirty years. According to some MS. notes sent by the late George Bently—who was acquainted with some of Spagnoletti's relatives—to Dr. T. Lamb Phipson in 1877, this artist's real name was Paolo Diana. At the age of twelve he was introduced to the director of the Naples Conservatorio as a very promising pupil, whereupon the director placed an elaborate composition before the young aspirant, who, it is said, astonished his auditors by glancing at the printed sheet for a few moments, and then playing the piece through with the music turned upside down before him. About 1802 he was brought to London by the celebrated tenor Vagnoni, who heard him play at Milan, and shortly after, he was engaged as second violin in the King's Theatre orchestra. In 1812 he was leading the orchestra at the Pantheon, where Italian Opera was being played, under the patronage of many of the nobility who had become disgusted with the management of the King's Theatre. The following year with the establishment of the Philharmonic, Spagnoletti became one of the first thirty-eight Associates of that Society, and led a septuor with Vaccari, Lindley, Hill, Petuder, Cramer and Holmes, at one of the first of the season's concerts on Apr. 19, 1813. In 1817 he was leader of the King's Theatre orchestra, and his services were requisitioned by nearly every important orchestral society in London. At the Lenten Oratorios at the King's Theatre, at the Ancient Concerts, at the Philharmonic, at the R.A.M. concerts in the Hanover Square Rooms, at numberless benefit concerts during the season, Spagnoletti in-

[1] Not, as Q.-L. says, in 1761.

variably led the orchestra, besides which he frequently led quartets at the Philharmonic, and gave a benefit concert in the Argyll Rooms each year. Frequent notices of his performances, ' which were characterised by an excellent and spirited attack,' appear in the Harmonicon between the years 1823 and 1833. When Paganini came to London in 1831, the management proposed to engage another leader for his concerts ; but when Paganini heard of this, he immediately demanded that Spagnoletti should be engaged for all his performances, accompanying his request with a well-merited compliment on his abilities. This occasioned some unpleasant feeling between the leader and Laporte, especially when the latter underpaid Spagnoletti for his services at thirteen Paganini concerts. A law-suit ensued, and a letter from Spagnoletti on the subject appeared in the Harmonicon of that year. Spagnoletti was of a modest, retiring disposition, and so ardently devoted to his art that he invariably put it before all private interests, the result of which was his acknowledged pre-eminence as an orchestral leader rather than as a virtuoso.

One of his last appearances—if not his last—was at Alsager's Queen's Square Select Society on Mar. 28, 1834, some months before his death, when he led the first performance of Cherubini's Requiem in England. For several years he had been in a delicate state of health, owing to two severe strokes of paralysis, and it was a third seizure which deprived him of speech and the use of one side of his body, and to which he eventually succumbed. He was buried beside Madame Spagnoletti in Brompton Cemetery, but all trace of the grave-stone which marked the place where he rested has disappeared. Spagnoletti's favourite violin was a Joseph Guarnerius of excellent tone but poor preservation. It eventually became the property of the late Sir Howard Elphinstone, V.C., at one time comptroller to the household of H.R.H. the Duke of Edinburgh. An engraving of Spagnoletti and Lindley was published by Sharp, after a picture by Mrs. Wigley of Shrewsbury, in 1836. He composed various rather unimportant violin pieces and some songs.

BIBL.—PARKE, Musical Memoirs; MASON CLARKE, Biog. Dict. Fiddlers, Musical World, vol. ii.; JAMES T. BROWN, Biog. Dict. Mus. Q.-L., The Harmonicon (1823-41), Musical World (1836); W. GARDINER, Music and Friends, Musical Recollections of the last Half Century, chap. iv. vol. i.; T. LAMB PHIPSON, Celebrated Violinists, The Times, and Morning Post, Sept. 26, 1834.   E. H.-A.

SPALDING, ALBERT (b. Chicago, Aug. 15, 1888), American violinist and composer. After study of the violin at the Bologna Conservatorio and in Paris under Lefòrt, he made his début in Paris in 1905. Following numerous European appearances, his New York début was made with the New York Symphony Society in 1908, and in 1920 he was soloist in that orchestra's first European tour. In 1917–19 he served with the American Expeditionary Forces as artillery observation-officer in France and Italy. Since then he has toured in Europe and America, playing with the leading orchestras of both continents.

Spalding was the first American violinist to play at the regular concerts of the Société des Concerts du Conservatoire in Paris (1922), and the first American to be a member of the jury awarding the prize in the graduating violin class of the Conservatoire (June, 1923).

Besides 2 violin concertos, an orchestral suite and a violin sonata that are unpublished, Spalding's compositions include :

String Quartet, E minor, op. 10.
' Etchings,' Theme and Improvisation for violin and pianoforte.
Suite, C major, violin and pianoforte.
Pianoforte pieces, songs, many violin pieces and transcriptions.

w. s. s.

SPANGENBERG, (1) JOHANNES (b. Hardegsen, Hanover, Mar. 30, 1484 ; d. Eisleben, June 13, 1550) ; first Protestant pastor of Hardegsen, 1521 ; preacher at Nordhausen, 1524 ; from 1546 superintendent at Eisleben. He published Lutheran church songs ; also a little book on musical theory for use at the school of Nordhausen ; (2) CYRIAK, son of the former (b. Nordhausen, Jan. 17, 1528 ; d. Strassburg, Feb. 10, 1604), wrote an important work on the Meistersinger, *Von der edlen hochberühmten Kunst der Musica*, etc., republished by Ad. v. Keller, 1861 ; also the ' Eislebener Gesangbüchlein,' 1568 (7 melodies republished by Zahn) ; a Psalter (1582) ; and school-dramas (Q.-L. ; *Riemann*).

SPANO, DONAT ANTONIO, of Naples, early 17th century, a pupil of Giov. de Macque, under whose supervision he composed, Madrigaletti ariosi, e vilanelli 4 v. (1607) ; 1 lib. de Madrigali 5 v. (1608).

SPARK, (1) WILLIAM, Mus.D. (b. Exeter, Oct. 28, 1823 ; d. Leeds, June 16, 1897), son of a lay-vicar of Exeter Cathedral, became a chorister there, and in 1840 was articled for five years to Dr. S. Sebastian Wesley. On Wesley's leaving Exeter for the Parish Church, Leeds, his pupil went with him, and soon became deputy-organist of the parish church, and organist of the churches of Chapeltown and St. Paul's successively. He was next chosen organist to Tiverton, Devon, and Daventry, Northampton ; and on Wesley's removal to Winchester, in 1850, was appointed to St. George's Church, Leeds. His activity in Leeds, outside his own parish, was remarkable. Within a year of his appointment he founded the Leeds Madrigal and Motet Society, and the People's Concerts, held in the Town Hall, just then built. Municipal business had long required a new Town Hall, the central portion of which has ever since served the city for its chief concert-room. The organ was built by Gray & Davison, from the designs of Henry Smart and Spark. The hall was opened Apr. 1, 1859, and after a severe competition Spark was elected

the Borough organist, a post he held until his death. He took his degree of D.Mus. at Dublin in 1861. In 1869 he started the *Organists' Quarterly Journal* (Novello). It was followed by the *Practical Choir-master* (Metzler), and in 1881 by a biography of Henry Smart (Reeves, 8vo). *Musical Memoirs* (1888), and *Musical Reminiscences* (1892), contain an amusing picture of his time, and he did good work in many Yorkshire towns as a lecturer on music. He also published three cantatas, various anthems, services, glees, and other compositions.

His brother, (2) FREDERICK ROBERT (b. Feb. 26, 1831 ; d. Nov. 14, 1919), became editor and publisher of the *Leeds Express* in the fifties. He was officially connected with the Leeds Festival from its beginning in 1858, being honorary secretary from 1877. After the festival of 1907 he retired from active service, and was presented with a portrait of himself painted by Sir George Reid. He was joint author, with Joseph Bennett, of *A History of the Leeds Musical Festivals 1858–89* (1892).

G. ; addns. F. K.

SPATARO (SPADARO SPADARIUS), GIOVANNI (b. Bologna, c. 1458 ; d. there, 1540), maestro di cappella of S. Petronio, which post he held from 1512 till his death. He was a learned musical theorician, a pupil of Ramis de Pareira, whom he supported in his controversies with Gafurius and Burtius. Apart from controversial writings he published a treatise on the fifth (1531). Of his compositions only one Mass is still in existence (Q.-L. ; *Riemann*).

SPAZIER, JOHANN GOTTLIEB KARL (b. Berlin, Apr. 20, 1761 ; d. Leipzig, Jan. 19, 1805), much esteemed in his time as the composer of 4-part and solo songs. He was founder and editor of the *Berlinische musikalische Zeitung* (1793) ; contributor to the *Leipziger allgemeine Musikzeitung* and author of a number of pamphlets on musical subjects (*Riemann*).

SPEAKER-KEYS. On wind instruments of the reed family, certain keys are fitted to facilitate the production of harmonics. These are known as ' speaker-keys.' Two are usually supplied on the oboe, and one on the clarinet, giving octaves on the one instrument and twelfths on the other. These keys open small holes by which the continuity of the air-column is broken, and the setting up of a ' loop,' or point of least variation of pressure, is made easy.

D. J. B.

SPEAKING-LENGTH. The pitch of the ordinary open flue-pipe on the organ is chiefly determined or controlled by the length of the portion above the mouth of the pipe, which is called the ' speaking-length.' Instances, however, occur in which the speaking-length differs from the true open flue length. See STOPPED PIPE ; HARMONIC STOPS ; DIAPASONS. T. E.

SPECIFICATION. The working specification of an organ consists of a detailed description of the stops, materials, pipes, action movements, etc., and the method of procedure requiring to be followed in building the instrument.　　　　　　　　　　　　　　T. E.

SPEE, FRIEDRICH (of the noble house VON LANGENFELD) (b. Kaiserswerth-on-the-Rhine, Feb. 25, 1591; d. Trier, Aug. 7, 1635), a Jesuit; was a poet and probably also composer of the famous book of songs, 'Trutznachtigall oder geistlich-poetisches Lustwäldlein,' which since 1649 has appeared in a great many editions, the text also in Reclam's *Universal Bibliothek*; he also wrote 'Güldenes Tugendbuch' (1645, 1656), 28 songs.　　　　　　　E. V. D. S.

SPEER, (1) CHARLTON T. (b. Cheltenham, Nov. 21, 1859). In 1873 he entered the R.A.M., winning the Sterndale Bennett Scholarship in the following year ; for some time he studied composition under Sir George Macfarren, the piano under Walter Macfarren, and the organ under Dr. Steggall ; in 1885 he became professor of piano-playing at the R.A.M. He has held several posts as organist, and since 1899 has been honorary organist and director of music at the parish church, Sutton. His compositions include two operas, 'Odysseus' and 'Zara,' and several works for chorus and orchestra, of which 'The Battle of Lake Regillus' is perhaps the best known. He has also written a symphonic poem ('King Arthur') and an overture in C, a ballade 'Guinevere,' a suite 'Cinderella,' and other works for orchestra, besides songs, piano pieces and church music.

(2) WILLIAM HENRY (b. London, Nov. 9, 1863), cousin of the above, studied under Dr. C. H. Lloyd when the latter was organist of Gloucester Cathedral, and subsequently entered the R.C.M., where he studied the organ under Sir Walter Parratt and composition under Sir Charles Stanford. At the age of 18 he went to Trinity College, Cambridge, took the M.A. and Mus.B. degrees in 1890, and the Mus.D. in 1906. He held more than one organist's post before 1903, when he was appointed to that at the parish church, Bexhill. Of his compositions the best known is 'The Jackdaw of Rheims,' a ballad for chorus and small orchestra, which has been performed by many choral societies in this country, and also in British Columbia. His cantata 'The Lay of St. Cuthbert' was produced in London (Queen's Hall) by the Edward Mason Choir in 1912. His orchestral works include a rhapsody in E♭, a festival overture, and a symphony in E♭, all of which were produced at the Bournemouth Symphony Concerts. He has also written a number of songs, and a string quartet in B♭ was first heard at the British Chamber Music Concerts in 1894 (see *B.M.S. Ann.*, 1920).　　　　G. S. K. B., with addns.

SPEER, DANIEL (b. Breslau between 1620–1625), town-musician at Breslau; in 1680

cantor at Göppingen; in 1688–89 imprisoned for political publications; in 1692 cantor at Waiblingen. He composed a number of sacred partsongs, with organ, and some also with instruments. (See list in *Q.-L.*)

SPENCER DYKE STRING QUARTET, THE. This Quartet (composed of the following artists, all of British nationality: Spencer Dyke (b. 1880), leader ; Edwin Quaife (b. 1889), 2nd violin; Ernest Tomlinson (b. 1879), viola; and B. Patterson Parker (b. 1871), violoncello) made its first appearance on Jan. 26, 1920, three of the party having played together in other quartets since 1900. A perfect *ensemble* results from this constant association, an annual series of recitals of quartet music forming a very attractive feature of London musical life.

First performances have been given of works by Herbert Howells, York Bowen, J. B. M'Ewen, Jaques-Dalcroze, L. Durey and others.　　　　　　　　　　　　　W. W. C.

SPENDIAROV, ALEXANDER (b. Kharkov, 1871), composer, at present (1926) living in the Crimea, was a pupil of Rimsky-Korsakov, and was accounted one of his close disciples. His compositions include: a concert-overture, op. 4; Crimean Sketches, op. 9; a memorial cantata to the art critic Vladimir Stassov; and many songs. His best-known work, the symphonic picture 'The Three Palm Trees' (op. 10), based upon a poem by Lermontov, was introduced to this country by Sir Henry J. Wood, at a Promenade Concert, Sept. 4, 1917.　　　　　　　　　　　　　R. N.

SPERGER, JOHANN MATHIAS (d. Ludwigslust, May 13, 1812), a contrabass player, who served in the chapels of Cardinal Batthyanyi, in 1780, of Prince Esterhazy (under Haydn), and from 1787 of the Duke of Mecklenburg at Ludwigslust. He composed motets, cantatas, symphonies, concertos, divertimenti, quartets, trios, sonatas, etc., mostly in MS. (*Q.-L.*; *Riemann*).

SPEYER, WILHELM (b. Frankfort-on-the-Main, June 21, 1790; d. there, Apr. 5, 1878), composer. He received his musical education at Offenbach under Thieriot (the friend of Weber) and André. He was already a prominent violinist when he went to Paris in 1812, to become a pupil of Baillot, from whose instruction and from the acquaintance of such men as Cherubini, Boieldieu, Méhul, etc., he derived much benefit. Returning to Germany afterwards, he settled down at Frankfort and exchanged the musical profession for that of a merchant, but continued to compose—at first chiefly chamber music. He published string quartets and quintets, and also violin duets, which last became widely popular. He afterwards devoted himself chiefly to vocal music. Amongst his Lieder—of which he published several hundred—many, such as 'The Trumpeter,' ' Rheinsehnsucht,' ' Die drei Liebchen,' etc., acquired great popularity.　He also wrote vocal quartets and some choral works　G.

SPIANATO (Ital.) = ' level,' 'even.'　A word used by Chopin in the Andante which precedes the Polonaise in E♭, op. 22, to denote a smooth and equal style of performance, with but little variety.　　　　　　　　　　　　　　　　　F. T.

SPICCATO (Ital.) = ' separate,' ' distinct.' The term is applied to a type of staccato bowing on instruments of the violin family, chiefly used for the execution of quick passages formed of notes of equal duration, e.g.

HAYDN.　Quartet, Op. 64, No. 5.

The middle of the bow is used and a spring is obtained by a loose movement of the wrist.

SPIES, HERMINE (b. Löhnberger foundry, near Weilburg, Nassau, Feb. 25, 1857 ; d. Wiesbaden, Feb. 26, 1893), daughter of the resident manager.　She was taught singing by Frau Fichtenberg at the Conservatorium of Wiesbaden, by Sieber at Berlin, and by Stockhausen at Frankfort.　In July 1880, while still a student, she sang at the Mannheim Festival, and in 1882 she made her début at a concert at Wiesbaden ; in 1883 she sang in concerts at Leipzig, Berlin, etc., speedily establishing her reputation as an excellent mezzo-soprano or contralto singer.　She also sang in Austria, Hungary, Holland, Denmark and Russia.　On June 3, 1889, she made her début in England at St. James's Hall at a Richter Concert, when she sang ' Che farò ' and Lieder of Schubert, Schumann and Brahms.　She attracted immediate attention on account of her fine voice and her excellent phrasing, expression and general intelligence.　She confirmed her success at her two recitals in a selection of Schumann's ' Dichterliebe,' etc., also at the Philharmonic, where she sang in English Handel's ' Return, O God of hosts,' etc.　In 1892 she married Dr. W. A. F. Hardtmuth, of Wiesbaden, a doctor of jurisprudence, and died the following year. She was unrivalled in her singing of the contralto part in Brahms's Rhapsody, op. 53, and in the Lieder of the same composer.　A memoir by her sister, Minna Spies, appeared in 1894.　　　　　　　　　　　　　　　　　A. C.

SPIESS, MEINRAD (b. Housolgen, Suabia, Aug. 24, 1683 ; d. monastery of Yrsee, Bavarian Suabia, July 12, 1761), prior of the monastery at Yrsee at the time of his death. He studied music under Gius. Ant. Bernabei at Munich ; from 1712–49 was musical director at Yrsee ; and from 1743 member of Mizler's ' Society of Musical Sciences.'　He composed masses, Requiems and other church music ; 12 trio sonatas for violins, violoncello and organ, and a theoretical treatise (Riemann ; Q.-L.).

SPINA, CARL ANTON, the successor of the

Diabellis in that famous publishing house at Vienna, which for so long stood in the Graben, No. 1133, at the corner of the Bräunerstrasse. He succeeded them in 1852, and was himself succeeded by F. Schreiber in July 1872 (see DIABELLI).　During that period Spina's activity showed itself especially in the publication of Schubert's works, a mass of whose MSS. he acquired from Diabelli.　Chief among these were the octet, quintet in C, quartets in D minor, G, and B♭ ; the overture in the Italian style, those to ' Alfonso und Estrella,' ' Fierrabras,' ' Rosamunde,' with entr'actes in B minor and B♭ ; the B minor symphony, sonata for PF. and arpeggione, etc., all in score.　Spina's enthusiasm for Schubert was not that of a mere publisher, as the writer from personal experience of his kindness can testify.　It was he who allowed the Crystal Palace Company to have copies of several of the orchestral works for playing, long before there was sufficient public demand to allow of their being published.　　　　　　　　　　　　　　　　　G.

SPINACCINO, FRANCESCO, a 15th - 16th century lutenist of Fossombrone ; author of 4 books in lute tablature containing arrangements of songs, ricercari and dances by himself and other masters ; only a few of the latter are named, among whom Josquin appears once or twice.　Books 1 and 2 were published by Petrucci in 1507 ; Book 4 in 1508 ; Book 3 is unknown.　There is a bassa-dance in a 16th-century MS. lute-book, Vienna Hofburg lib. (Q.-L.).

SPINDLER, FRITZ (b. Wurzbach, Lobenstein, Nov. 24, 1817 ; d. Niederlössnitz, near Dresden, Dec. 26, 1905), pianoforte-player and composer for that instrument, was a pupil of F. Schneider of Dessau, and was for many years resident in Dresden.　His published works are more than 330 in number, the greater part brilliant drawing-room pieces, but amongst them much teaching-music, and some works of a graver character—trios, sonatinas, two symphonies, concerto for PF. and orchestra, etc. Favourite pieces in their day were—' Wellenspiel ' (op. 6) ; ' Schneeglöcklein ' (op. 19) ; ' Silberquell ' (op. 74) ; ' Husarenritt '; six dance themes; transcriptions of ' Tannhäuser ' and ' Lohengrin.'　　　　　　　　　　　　　　G.

SPINET (Fr. épinette, clavicorde ; Ital. spinetta, clavicordo ; Span. clavicordio ; Eng. spinet, virginal).　A keyed instrument, with plectra or jacks, used in the 16th, 17th and 18th centuries ; according to Burney [1] ' a small harpsichord or virginal with one string to each note.'

DERIVATIONS.—The following definitions are from Florio's New World of Words, 1611 : ' Spinetta, a kind of little spina . . . also a paire of Virginalles ' ; ' Spinettegiare, to play upon Virginalles ' ; ' Spinetto, a thicket of

[1] Rees's Cycl. 1819, Harpsichord.

brambles or briars.'[1] We first meet with the
derivation of spinet from *spina*, a 'thorn,' in
Scaliger's *Poetices* (1484–1550; lib. i. cap.
lxiii.). Referring to the plectra or jacks of
keyed instruments, he says that, in his recollection, points of crowquill had been added to
them, so that what was named, when he was a
boy, 'clavicymbal' and 'harpichord' (*sic*), was
now, from these little points, named 'spinet.'
(See JACK.) He does not say what substance
crowquill superseded, but we know that the old
cithers and other wire-strung instruments were
twanged with ivory, tortoiseshell, or hard wood.
(See HARPSICHORD, Vol. II. p. 544.) Another
origin for the name has been discovered, to
which we believe that Signor Ponsicchi [2] was the
first to call attention. In a very rare book,
*Conclusioni nel suono dell' organo, di D. Adriano
Banchieri Bolognese* (Bologna, 1608), is this
passage :

'Spinetta riceve tal nome dall' inventore di tal
forma longa quadrata, il quale fù un maestro Giovanni
Spinetti, Venetiano, ed uno di tali stromenti hò veduto
io alle mani di Francesco Stivori, organista della
magnifica comunità di Montagnana, dentrovi questa
inscrizione : JOANNES SPINETUS VENETUS FECIT.
A.D. 1503.'

According to this, the spinet received its name
from Spinetti, a Venetian, the inventor of the
oblong form, and Banchieri had himself seen
one in the possession of Stivori, bearing the
above inscription. Becker of Geneva [3] regards
this statement as totally invalidating the passage from Scaliger ; but this is not necessarily
so, since the year 1503 is synchronous with the
youth of Scaliger. The invention of the crowquill points is not claimed for Spinetti, but the
form of the case—the oblong or table shape of
the square piano and older clavichord, to which
Spinetti adapted the plectrum instrument ; it
having previously been in a trapeze-shaped
case, like the psaltery, from which, by the addition of a keyboard, the instrument was derived.
(See VIRGINAL ; and also for the different construction and origin of the oblong clavichord.)
Putting both statements together, we find the
oblong form of the Italian spinet, and the
crowquill plectra, in simultaneous use about
the year 1500. Before that date no record has
been found. The oldest German writers, Virdung and Arnold Schlick, whose essays appeared in 1511, do not mention the spinet, but
Virdung describes and gives a woodcut of the
virginal, which in Italy would have been called
at that time 'spinetta,' because it was an instrument with plectra in an oblong case. Spinetti's adaptation of the case had therefore
travelled to Germany, and, as we shall presently
see, to Flanders and Brabant, very early in the
16th century ; whence Becker conjectures that
1503 represents a late date for Spinetti, and
that we should put his invention back to the

second half of the 15th century, on account of
the time required for it to travel, and be accepted as a normal form in cities so remote
from Venice.

EARLY SPECIMENS.—Considerable light has
been thrown upon the hitherto profoundly
obscure invention of the keyboard instrument
subsequently known as the spinet, by Edmond
van der Straeten. He quotes [4] from a testa-
mentary inventory of musical instruments
which had belonged to Queen Isabella, at the
Alcazar of Segovia, dated 1503 ? 'Dos Clavicin-
banos viejos ' that is to say, two old clavecins
(spinets). One of her chamberlains, Sancho de
Paredes (p. 248), owned in 1500 'Dos Clabior-
ganos '—two claviorgans or organised clavecins.
In a previous inventory, dated 1480 (and
earlier), the same chamberlain appears to have
possessed a manicorde or clavichord with tan-
gents. But van der Straeten is enabled to
give a positive date, 1387 (p. 40, *et seq.*), when
John the First, King of Aragon, had heard and
desired to possess an instrument called 'ex
aquir,' which was certainly a keyboard stringed-
instrument. He describes it later on as resembling an organ but sounding with strings.
The name 'exaquir' may be identified with
'l'eschuaqueil d'Angleterre,' which occurs in a
poem entitled 'La Prise d'Alexandrie,' written
by Guillaume de Machaut in the 14th century.
Van der Straeten inquires if this appellation
can be resolved by 'échiquier' (chequers) from
the black and white arrangement of the keys.
The name échiquier occurs in the romance
'Chevalier du cygne ' and in the 'Chanson sur
la journée de Guinegate,' a 15th-century poem,
in which the poet asks to be sounded—

'Orgius, harpes, naquaires, challemelles,
Bons echiquiers, guisternes, doucemelles.'

The inquirer is referred to the continuance of
van der Straeten's notes on this interesting
question, in the work above mentioned. It is
here sufficient to be enabled to prove that a
kind of organ sounding with strings was existing
in 1387—and that clavecins were catalogued
in 1503, that could be regarded as old ; also
that these dates synchronise with Ambros's
earliest mention of the clavicymbalum, in a
MS. of 1404.

Van der Straeten [5] has discovered the following references to the spinet in the household
accounts of Margaret of Austria :

'A ung organiste de la Ville d'Anvers, la somme de
vi livres auquel madicte dame en a fait don en faveur
de ce que le xve jour d'Octobre xv. xxii [1522] il a
amené deux jeunes enffans, filz et fille, qu'ils ont
jouhé sur une espinette et chanté à son diner.
'A l'organiste de Monsieur de Fiennes, sept livres
dont Madame lui a fait don en faveur de ce que le
second jour de Décembre xv. xxvi [1526] il est venu
jouher d'un instrument dit espinette devant elle à
son diner.'

The inventory of the Château de Pont d'Ain,

1 See Rimbault's *History of the Pianoforte*, 1860.
2 *Il pianoforte*, Florence, 1876.
3 *Revue et Gazette musicale*, in the *Musical World*, June 15, 1878.

4 *La Musique aux Pays-Bas*, vol. vii. p. 246 (*Les Musiciens
néerlandais en Espagne*, 1re partie), Brussels, 1885.
5 *La Musique aux Pays-Bas*, vol. i.

1531, mentions ‘una espinetta cum suo etuy,’ a spinet with its case ; meaning a case from which the instrument could be withdrawn, as was customary at that time. Becker transcribes also a contemporary reference from the Munich Library :

‘ Quartorze Gaillardes, neuf Pavannes, sept Bransles et deux Basses-Dances, le tout reduict de musique en la tablature du ieu [jeu] Dorgues, Espinettes, Manicordions et telz semblables instruments musicaux, imprimées à Paris par Pierre Attaignant MDXXIX.’

The manichord was a clavichord. Clement Marot (Lyons, 1551) dedicated his version of the Psalms to his countrywomen :

‘ Et vos doigts sur les Espinettes,
Pour dire Saintes Chansonettes.’

With this written testimony we have fortunately the testimony of the instruments themselves, Italian oblong spinets (*spinetta a tavola*), or those graceful pentangular instruments, without covers attached, which are so much prized for their external beauty. Miss Marie Decca owned [1] a Rosso spinet dated 1550, and there is another by the same maker (signed Annibalis Mediolanesis) dated 1569, recently in the possession of H. Kohl, Hamburg, who obtained it from the palace of the San Severino family, at Crema, in Lombardy. These spinets are usually made entirely of one wood, the soundboard as well as the case. The wood appears to be a kind of cedar, from its odour when planed or cut, at least in some instances that have come under the writer’s notice. The next oldest bearing a date is in the Conservatoire at Paris, by Francesco di Portalupis, Verona, 1523. The next by Antoni Patavini, 1550, is at Brussels. In the Bologna Exhibition, 1888, Historical Section, was shown a spinet bearing the inscription ‘ Alessandro Pasi Modenese,’ and a date, 1490. It was exhibited by Count L. Manzoni. It is a true Italian spinet in a bad state of repair. The date, which has been verified, does not invalidate the evidence adduced from Scaliger and Banchieri concerning the introduction of the spinet, but it places it farther back and before Scaliger (*b.* 1484) could have observed it. There are at S. Kensington two by Annibal Rosso of Milan, 1555 and 1577, and one by Marcus Jadra (Marco dai Cembali ; or dalle Spinette), 1568.[2] Of the date 1568 is also a virginal, or *spinetta tavola*, from the collection of Terme of Liège and now (1927) in the Victoria and Albert Museum. It had belonged originally to the family of Anne of Cleves ; its compass is A–*f'''*. It has boxwood keys, but the arrangement of the short octave is uncertain, as the lowest note may be G, F, or A. Kraus had, at Florence, two 16th-century spinets, one of which is signed and dated, Benedictus Florianus, 1571 (see *PLATE CX*.

[1] Ownership ascertained on publication of the 2nd edition of this Dictionary.
[2] A spinet in the Dublin Museum of Science and Art, which A. J. Hipkins described in his *History of the Pianoforte*, p. 60, as dated 1590, and the work of Domenico da Pesaro, has since been discovered to be by Francesco da Brescia and to bear the much earlier date 1564. W. H. G. F.

No. 3) ; and at the Hôtel Cluny, Paris, there is one by the Venetian Baffo, date 1570, whose harpsichord (clavicembalo) at S. Kensington is dated 1574.

For the pentangular or heptangular model with the recessed keyboard, it is probable that we are indebted to Annibal Rosso, whose instrument of 1555 was engraved here in preceding editions Carl Engel reprinted in the S. Kensington Catalogue (1874, p. 273) a passage from *La nobilita di Milano* (1595), which he thus renders :

‘ Hannibal Rosso was worthy of praise, since he was the first to modernise clavichords into the shape in which we now see them,’ etc.

The context clearly shows that by ‘ clavichord ’ spinet was meant, *clavicordo* being used in a general sense equivalent to the German *Clavier*. If the modernising was not the adoption of the beautiful forms shown in the splendid examples at South Kensington— that by Rosso, of 1577, having been bought at the Paris Exhibition of 1867 for £1200 on account of the 1928 precious stones set into the case—it may possibly have been the wing-form, with the wrestpins above the keys in front, which must have come into fashion about that time, and was known in Italy as the *spinetta traversa* ; in England as the Stuart, Jacobean or Queen Anne spinet, or couched harp. There is a very fine *spinetta traversa*, emblazoned with the arms of the Medici and Compagni families, in the Kraus Museum (1878, No. 193). Praetorius illustrates the Italian spinet by this special form, speaks [3] of larger and smaller spinets, and states that in the Netherlands and England the larger was known as the virginal. The smaller ones he describes as ‘ the small triangular spinets which were placed for performance upon the larger instruments, and were tuned an octave higher.’ Of this small instrument there are specimens in nearly all museums ; the Italian name for it being ‘ ottavina ’ (also ‘ spinetta di serenata ’). We find them fixed in the bent sides of the long harpsichords, in two remarkable specimens ; one of which, by Hans RUCKERS (*q.v.* Vol. IV. p. 474), is preserved in the Schloss Museum, Berlin (there is a painting of a similar double instrument inside the lid) ; the other is in the Maison Plantin, Antwerp, and was made as late as 1734–35, by Joannes Josephus Coenen at Ruremonde in Holland. In rectangular instruments the octave one was removable, as it was in those double instruments mentioned under RUCKERS, so that it could be played in another part of the room.

COMPASS AND SHORT OCTAVES.—According to Mersenne,[4] who treats of the spinet as the principal keyed instrument, there were three sizes : one of 2½ feet, tuned to the octave of the

[3] *Organographia*, Wolfenbüttel, 1619.
[4] *Harmonie*, 1636, liv. 3, p. 101, etc.

'ton de chapelle' (which was about a tone higher than our old 'Philharmonic' or high concert pitch); one of 3½ feet, tuned to a fifth above the same pitch; and the large 5-feet ones, tuned in unison to it. We shall refer to his octave spinet in another paragraph.

The compass of the 'ottavine' was usually from E to c''', three octaves and a sixth (a); of the larger 16th-century Italian spinette, four octaves and a semitone, from E to f''' (b). The French épinettes of the 17th century were usually deeper, having four octaves and a semitone from B to c''' (c).

The reason for this semitonal beginning of the keyboard is obscure unless the lowest keys were used for 'short octave' measure, an idea which suggested itself simultaneously to the writer and to Professor A. Kraus, whose conviction is very strong as to the extended practice of the short octave arrangement. The Flemish picture of St. Cecilia, in Holyrood Palace, shows unmistakably a short octave organ keyboard as early as 1484.[1]

Fortunately, we are not left to such suggestion for the spinet short octave. Mersenne,[2] describing his own spinet, which, according to him, was one of the smallest in use, says :

'The longest string has little more than a foot length between the two bridges. It has only thirty-one steps in the keyboard, and as many strings over the sound-board, so that there are five keys hid on account of the perspective [referring to the drawing] —to wit, three principals and two chromatics ("feintes"), of which the first is cut in two; but these chromatics serve to go down to the third and fourth below the first step, or C *sol*, in notation

in order to arrive at the third octave, for the eighteen principal steps only make an eighteenth; that is to say, a fourth over two octaves.'

Here is the clearest confirmation of short-octave measure in the spinet, the same as in the organ, both keyboards, according to Mersenne, being conformable. But owing to the fact that the woodcut represents a different spinet from that described (apparently descending to B), the description is not clear. To reach the third octave would require an F, for which one-half the cut chromatic in the spinet described may be reserved. But the B of the drawing would, by known analogy with organ

[1] Hubert, or Jan Van Eyck's St. Cecilia, in the famous 'Mystic Lamb,' may be referred to here although appertaining to the organ and not the spinet, as a valuable note by the way. The original painting, now at Berlin, was probably painted before 1426 and certainly before 1432. The painter's minute accuracy is unquestionable. It contains a chromatic keyboard like the oldest Italian, with boxwood naturals and black sharps. The compass begins in the bass at the half-tone E. There is no indication of a 'short-octave,' but there is one key by itself, convenient to the player's left hand; above this key there is a latchet acting as a catch, which may be intended to hold it down as a pedal. D is the probable note, and we have in Van Eyck's organ, it seems to us, the same compass, but an octave lower, as is the German Positif of the next century at South Kensington—viz. D, E, then three chromatic octaves from F, and finally F♯, G, A. There is no bottom-rail to the keyboard, nor is there in the painting at Holyrood.

[2] *Harmonie*, liv. 3, p. 107.

practice, sound G, and A would be found on the C♯, the B also on the D♯ key, though this is generally found retained as E♭ on account of the tuning.[3] It is inferred that F was reached by dividing the lowest natural key; these diagrams therefore represent what we will call the C short measure, as that note gave the pitch.

Mersenne's express mention of C as the longest string shows that the still deeper G and A were made so, in his spinet, by weight: an important fact, as we have not seen a spinet in which it could have been otherwise, since in large instruments the bridge is always unbroken in its graceful curve, as it is also in the angles—always preserved—of the bridge of an octave one. The intimate connexion of the spinet and organ keyboards must palliate a trespass upon ground that has been covered in ORGAN (Vol. III. p. 748). It is this connexion that incites inquiry into the origin of the short octaves, of which there are two measures, the French, German or English C one, which we have described, and the Italian F one, which we will now consider. We propose to call this F, from the pitch note, as before. We have reason to believe these pitch notes originally sounded the same, from which arose the original divergence of high and low church-pitch; the C instrument being thus thrown a fourth higher. The Italian short measure having been misapprehended the question of its construction was submitted to Professor Kraus, and of W. T. Best, who made a careful examination of the organs in Italy. Both are in perfect agreement. Kraus describes the Italian short octave as a progression of three dominants and tonics, with the addition of B *molle* (♭) and B *quadro* (♮) for the ecclesiastical tones. The principle, he writes, was also applied to the pedal keyboards, which are called 'Pedaliera in Sesta,' or 'Pedaliera a ottava ripiegata.'[4] Kraus maintains the nearly general use of the short octave in Italian spinets, harpsichords, clavichords, and organs, and to some harpsichords he adds even another dominant.

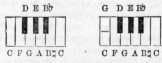

[3] It may have been on account of the tuning that A and D were left unfretted in the old 'gebunden' or fretted clavichords; but the double Irish harp which Galilei (*Dissertation on Ancient and Modern Music*, A.D. 1581) says had been adopted in Italy, had those notes always doubled in the two rows of strings, an importance our tuning hypothesis fails to explain.

[4] But not 'Ottava Rubata,' which some inaccurately apply to the lowest octave of the short octave manual. This is a contrivance in small organs with pedals to disguise the want of the lowest diapason octave on the manual, by coupling on to it the contrabasso of the pedals with the register of the octave above.

According to this, the oldest harpsichord known to exist, the Roman one of 1521, at S. Kensington, is a short-octave F instrument. When, in the 18th century, the C short octaves were made long, it was by carrying down the G and A, and giving back the semitonal value to the B and C♯ (sometimes also the D♯) ; but G♯ was not introduced, since it was never required as a drone. The drones had sometimes given way to semitones as early as the 14th and 15th centuries.

A THEORY of ' SHORT MEASURE.'—What was, then, the original intention of ' short measure '? We find it indicated in Mersenne's psaltery (G C D E F G A B♭ C d e f g) and in many delineations of portatives or regals in pictures of the old masters, whose sincerity, seeing the accurate manner in which they have painted lutes, cannot be questioned. We will confine our references to Orcagna's ' Coronation of the Virgin ' (1350), in the National Gallery, London, and Master Stephen's ' Virgin of the Rosary ' (1450), at Cologne, with the Holyrood picture of 1484, already referred to as an illustration of a Positive organ with short measure. May not Hopkins's quotation (see ORGAN, Vol. III. p. 745) of two long pipes in an organ of 1418 count as evidence for short measure as much as for pedals ? We think so. In fine, we regard short measure as having been intended to supply, in deeper-toned instruments, drones for cadences, and in the shriller regals (which were no more than boxes of pitch-pipes, one, two, or three to a key) to prompt the intonation of the plain-song. The contraction of the keyboard, whether diatonic or chromatic, to suit the size of the hand, was probably due to these small instruments—

> ' Orgues avait bien maniables,
> A une seulle main portables,
> Ou il mesmes souffle et touche.'
> *Roman de la rose.*

The contraction to the short-octave measure might have been intended to get rid of the weight of the heavier pipes not needed for dominants or intonation, and, at the same time, to keep the keyboard narrow. Both contractions—the keyboard and the short measure— were thus ready-made for the spinet, harpsichord and clavichord, when they came into use.

The short-octave group was finally partially doubled, so as to combine with the dominant fourths the ordinary chromatic scheme, by dividing the lowest sharps or chromatics, of which there is an example in a spinet by Pleyer or Player, made between 1710 and 1720, exhibited by Kirkman at S. Kensington in 1872. This instrument, with black naturals, and apparently 4¼ octaves from B to D, has the lowest C♯ and D♯ divided, called in the quotation in the Catalogue (p. 12) ' quarter tones.' But it is difficult to imagine enharmonic intervals provided for the deepest notes. We believe it to

have been intended for a ' short octave,' and to be thus explained :

			$\dfrac{D♭}{C♯}$	$\dfrac{E♭}{D♯}$	
Apparent notes	B	C		D	E
			$\dfrac{C♯}{A}$	$\dfrac{E♭}{B}$	
Real notes		G	C	D	E,

			$\dfrac{C♯}{D♭}$	$\dfrac{D♯}{E♭}$	
or Apparent notes	B	C		D	E
			$\dfrac{A}{C♯}$	$\dfrac{B}{E♭}$	
Real notes		G	C	D	E

A detailed examination of instruments contributed to the Historic Loan Collection (1885) proves that the natural keys of the Patavini Spinet mentioned on p. 92 are marked with their names. The lowest E key is clearly inscribed Do—C ; on the next, the F, is written F. This writing is not so early as 1550, because Do was not then used for Ut. The probable date is about one hundred years later, when the solmisation was finally giving way before the simple alphabetic notation. There are other instances. As to the cut sharps [1] : the small Maidstone clavichord, said to have been Handel's, has the two nearer or front divisions intended for fourths below the next higher naturals, the two further or back divisions being the usual semitones.

Two spinets by Keene, dated 1685, in private hands,[2] have the same apparently enharmonic arrangement. One by Player (*sic*), sent to South Kensington about 1882, is to be included with Kirkman's and the Keenes, and also a Player which belongs to Dr. A. H. Mann of Cambridge ; but a Keene of Sir George Grove's, undated, has not the cut sharps, which we are disposed to regard as for mixed dominants and chromatics, because the independent keynote value of the chromatics was, about A.D. 1700, beginning to be recognised, and the fretted clavichords were soon to give way to those without frets. It was Bach who set all notes free as tonics. We see in Keene's and Player's spinets the blending of old and new—that which was passing away, and our modern practice.

THE TRANSVERSE SPINET.—Returning to the *spinetta traversa*, we find this model preferred in England in the Stuart epoch, and indeed in fashion for 150 years. The favourite makers during the reigns of Charles I. and II. were Thomas and John Hitchcock and Charles Haward ; but there is an unaccountable differ-

[1] The oldest spinet with cut sharps in the Historic Loan Collection was, according to the Facies, by Edward Blount ; but on the first key, and less legibly on the jacks, is written ' Thomas Hitchcock his make in 1664.' A similar autographic inscription of this maker, but dated 1703, was brought forward by Taphouse of Oxford. We are thus enabled to find Thomas Hitchcock's working time. We think John Hitchcock came after him, and was probably his son.
[2] Formerly H. J. Dale of Cheltenham and E. R. Hughes of Chelsea.

LXXVI

1

2

1. ENGLISH SPINET (C. Haward, *c.* 1660).
2. ENGLISH SPINET (T. Hitchcock, *c.* 1700).

1. Dale Collection.   2. Messrs. Broadwood & Sons, Ltd.

ence between John Hitchcock's and Charles Haward's spinets [1] in the fine specimens known to the writer, the latter of much older character, though probably made after the former.

Thomas Hitchcock's spinets are better known than John's. The one on *PLATE LXXVI.* No. 2 belongs to Broadwood, and is numbered 1379.[2] (The highest number we have met with of Thomas Hitchcock, is 1547.) Broadwood's differs from the John Hitchcock of 1630 in having a curved instead of an angular bent side, and from the naturals being of ivory instead of ebony. The compass of these instruments—five octaves, from G, to g'''—is so startling as to be incredible, were it not for the facts that several instruments are extant with this compass, that the keyboard did not admit of alteration, and that the Sainsbury Correspondence (see RUCKERS) mentions that a greater compass existed in England in the time of Charles I. than was expected or required on the Continent. The absence also of the sound-hole, regarded as essential in all stringed instruments of that time, where the sound-board covered the whole internal space, shows how eminently progressive the Hitchcocks must have been. Not so Haward, in the instrument represented on *PLATE LXXVI.* No. 1. Charles Haward appears to have been contemporary with the Hitchcocks, and yet he is as conservative to old Italian or French practice as if John Hitchcock had never made an instrument in England.

A John Hitchcock spinet exists numbered 1676. Thomas and John were probably father and son. The Charles Haward spinet is small, with short keys and limited compass, being only of 4 octaves and a semitone, B,–c'''. The naturals are of snakewood, nearly black ; the sharps of ivory. There are wires on each bridge over which the strings pass, and along the hitchpin block, precisely the same as in a dulcimer. The decoration of the sound-board, surrounding an Italian rose, is signed ' I H,' with ' Carolus Haward Fecit ' above the keys ; and the name of each key is distinctly written, which we shall again have occasion to refer to. Pepys patronised Haward (or Hayward, as he sometimes writes the name). We read in his Diary :

' April 4, 1668. To White Hall. Took Aldgate Street in my way and there called upon one Hayward that makes Virginalls, and there did like of a little espinette, and will have him finish it for me : for I had a mind to a small harpsichon, but this takes up less room.
' July 10, 1668. To Hayward's to look upon an Espinette, and I did come near to buying one, but broke off. I have a mind to have one.
' July 13, 1668. I to buy my espinette, which I did now agree for, and did at Haward's meet with Mr. Thacker, and heard him play on the harpsichon, so as I never heard man before, I think.
' July 15, 1668. At noon is brought home the espinette I bought the other day of Haward ; costs me 5l.'

---

[1] Formerly in the possession of William Dale of London.
[2] This is the instrument in Millais's picture of ' The Minuet,' 862. Thomas dated his spinets ; John numbered them.

Another reference concerns the purchase of triangles for the spinet—a three-legged stand, as in our illustration. A curious reference to Charles Haward occurs in *A Vindication of an Essay to the Advancement of Musick*, by Thomas SALMON, M.A., London, 1672. This writer is advocating a new mode of notation, in which the ordinary clefs were replaced by B. (bass), M. (mean), and T. (treble) at the signatures :

' Here, Sir, I must acquaint you in favour of the aforesaid B. M. T. that t'other day I met with a curious pair of Phanatical Harpsechords made by that Arch Heretick Charles Haward, which were ready cut out into octaves (as I am told he abusively contrives all his) in so much that by the least hint of B. M. T. all the notes were easily found as lying in the same posture in every one or their octaves. And that, Sir, with this advantage, that so soon as the scholar had learned one hand he understood them, because the position of the notes were for both the same.'

The lettering over the keys in W. Dale's Haward spinet is here shown to be original. I. is very curious, however, to observe Haward's simple alphabetical lettering, and to contrast it with the hexachord names then passing away. There is a virginal (oblong spinet) in York Museum, made in 1651 by Thomas White, on the keys of which are monograms of Gamaut (bass G) and the three clef keys, F *fa ut,* C *sol fa ut,* and G *sol re ut* !

Mace, in *Musick's Monument* (London, 1676), refers to *John* Hayward as a ' harpsichon ' maker, and credits him with the invention of the pedal for changing the stops. There was a spinet by one of the Haywards or Hawards left by Queen Anne to the Chapel Royal boys. It was used as a practising instrument until the chorister days of the late Sir John Goss, perhaps even later.[3]   A. J. H.

SPIRIDIO (SPER' IN DIO), BERTHOLD, a late 17th-century Carmelite monk ; first at the court of Savoy ; in 1668 preacher in the diocese of Würzburg ; finally (from 1670) in the monastery St. Theodor near Bamberg. He composed masses and other church music, and wrote an important work *Neue bis dato unbekannte Unterweisung,* etc., giving instructions in the art of composition, as well as in organ-, spinet-, monochord-playing, etc. (1670). Of this part 2-4 appeared separately as *Nova instructio pro pulsandis organis spinettis, manuchordis,* etc. (1671–79), and part 5 as *Musikalische Erzgruben,* etc. (1683). A selection therefrom as *Musica Romana* containing vocal compositions with 2 violins *ad lib.* by various composers included himself (1665) (*Q.-L.* ; *Riemann*).

SPIRITOSO, *i.e.* ' spiritedly,' is, like CON SPIRITO, a designation of style rather than of pace. The variant ' spirituoso ' occurs in some of Beethoven's arrangements of national airs.

SPITTA, JULIUS AUGUST PHILIPP (*b.* Wechold, Hanover, Dec. 27, 1841 ; *d.* Berlin,

---

[3] Details of the private ownership of further specimens known to the writer have been withheld from this edition as verification was impossible.—ED.

Apr. 13, 1894), a well-known musical *littérateur*, son of the author of the 'Psalter und Harfe'; studied at Göttingen, and afterwards taught at Reval, Sondershausen and Leipzig, where he took part in the founding of the Bachverein in 1874. So great was his progress during this time, that in 1875 he was made professor of musical history in the Berlin University, and Perpetual Secretary to the Academy of Arts there. At Easter of the same year he became teacher of musical history in the Hochschule für Musik; in 1876 entered the direction, and at midsummer 1882 became a permanent director of that establishment. His principal literary work—*J. S. Bach*, in two vols. (B. & H.; vol. i. 1873, vol. ii. 1880), an authoritative treatise of all relating to the subject, but sadly wanting a better index—has remained the foundation of all modern Bach research and criticism. A translation by Clara Bell and J. A. Fuller Maitland was published in three volumes by Novello & Co. in 1884-85. He published a smaller biography of the same master, forming No. 1 of B. & H.'s *Musikalische Vorträge*, and another of Schumann, which, though issued as Nos. 37, 38 of the same series, was written for this Dictionary. (See Vol. IV. pp. 648-686.) His article on SPONTINI, written for the first edition of this Dictionary, was the first adequate treatment of that singular individual. An article on Homilius will be found in the *Allg. deutsche Biographie*, and many other productions of his pen in the *Leipzig A.M.Z.* for 1875-78, 1880-82, and in the earlier numbers of Eitner's *M.f.M.* He was co-editor with Chrysander and Adler of the *Vierteljahrsschrift für Musikwissenschaft*, from 1885 to his death. His critical edition of the organ works of Buxtehude, in two volumes (B. & H., 1875, 1876), is an admirable specimen of editing, and, in addition to the music, contains much valuable information. He also edited the complete edition of Heinrich Schütz, and was a prominent member of the directorate of the *D.D.T.* A monument by Hildebrandt, the eminent sculptor, was erected to his memory in Berlin.

G. REV.

SPITZFLÖTE, SPITZFLUTE; *i.e.* pointed flute. An organ stop, so-called because its pipes are slightly conical, that is, taper gradually from the mouth upwards. The diameter of the top is generally one-third of that of the pipe at its mouth. The tone is thin and reedy, but pure and effective. The Spitzflöte may be of 8 ft., 4 ft., or 2 ft. pitch; in this country, stops of this kind are most commonly of 4 ft. pitch.

J. S.

SPOFFORTH, (1) REGINALD (*b.* Southwell, Nottingham, 1770; *d.* Brompton, Sept. 8, 1827), glee composer. His uncle, Thomas Spofforth, was organist of the Minster at Southwell. From him and from Dr. Benjamin Cooke he probably derived all his instruction in music.

About 1787 or 1788 he wrote a glee—probably his first—for three male voices, 'Lightly o'er the village green,' and in 1793 obtained two prizes from the 'Glee Club,' for his glees 'See! smiling from the rosy East,' and 'Where are those hours,' which brought him prominently forward. In 1796 he ventured into the theatre with his music to the farce 'The Witch of the Wood,' produced at Covent Garden.[1] About 1799 he published a 'Set of Six Glees,' one of which, 'Hail, smiling morn,' at once caught the public ear, and has ever since retained its popularity. Another, 'Fill high the grape's exulting stream,' gained a prize in 1810. Spofforth's masterpieces, however, are not among his prize glees, and 'Come, bounteous May,' 'Mark'd you her eye,' 'Health to my dear,' and 'How calm the evening'—all for male voices—are among the finest specimens of his genius. For several years before his death his health was bad. He was buried at Kensington, where a monument was erected to his memory in St. Mary Abbotts Church. After his death W. Hawes published a number of his MS. glees, but some of these pieces are crude and imperfect, and probably not intended for publication.

Reginald's younger brother, (2) SAMUEL (*b.* 1780; *d.* London, June 6, 1864), was appointed organist of Peterborough Cathedral when only 18, and in 1807 was made organist of Lichfield Cathedral.

D. B.

SPOHR, LOUIS[2] (*b.* Brunswick, Apr. 5, 1784; *d.* Cassel, Oct. 22, 1859), great violinist and composer. He was born in the house of his grandfather, a clergyman. Two years after, his father, a young physician, took up his residence at Seesen, and it was there that young Spohr spent his early childhood. Both parents were musical: the father played the flute; the mother was pianist and singer. The boy showed his musical talent very early, and sang duets with his mother when only 4 years of age. At 5 he began to play the violin, and when hardly 6 was able to take the violin-part in Kalkbrenner's trios. His first teachers were Riemenschneider and Dufour, both amateurs. The latter, a French émigré, was so much impressed with his pupil's exceptional talent that he persuaded the father to send him for further instruction to Brunswick. Along with his first studies on the violin went his earliest attempts at composition, which consisted chiefly of violin duets.

EDUCATION AND TRAVEL.—At Brunswick he attended the grammar-school and continued his musical studies. His teachers were Kunisch, a member of the Duke's band, for the violin, and Hartung, an old organist, for counterpoint. This was the only instruction in the theory of music he ever received. According to his own

1 Information from W. B. S.
2 So, and not Ludwig, he calls himself in his Autobiography.

statement, it was principally through an eager study of the scores of the great masters, especially Mozart, that he acquired mastery over the technicalities of composition. His first public appearance was at a school-concert, when he played a concerto of his own with so much success that he was asked to repeat it at one of the concerts given by the Duke's band. Kunisch then insisted on his taking lessons from Maucourt, the leader of the band, and the best violinist at Brunswick. Spohr was only 14 when he undertook his first artistic tour. With a few letters of introduction in his pocket he set out for Hamburg. But there he failed even to get a hearing, and after some weeks had to return to Brunswick on foot, greatly disappointed, his slender means thoroughly exhausted. In his despair he conceived the idea of presenting to the Duke a petition asking for means to continue his studies. The Duke was pleased with the lad's open bearing, heard him, was struck with his talent, at once gave him an appointment in his band, and after a short time expressed his willingness to defray the expenses of his further musical education under one of the great recognised masters of the violin. Viotti and Ferdinand Eck both declined to receive a pupil, but the latter recommended his brother, Franz Eck, who was just then travelling in Germany. He was invited to Brunswick, and as the Duke was greatly pleased with his performances, an agreement was made that young Spohr should accompany him on his journeys and receive his instruction, the Duke paying one-half of the travelling expenses and a salary besides. In the spring of 1802 they started, master and pupil, for Russia. They made, however, prolonged stays at Hamburg and Strelitz, and it was on these occasions that Spohr profited most from his master's tuition. Latterly this became very irregular. Spohr, however, derived much benefit from constantly hearing Eck, who certainly was a very excellent violinist, though but an indifferent musician. At this period Spohr, who had an herculean frame and very strong constitution, often practised for ten hours a day. At the same time he composed industriously, and among other things wrote the first of his published violin concertos (op. 1) which is entirely in the manner of Rode, and also the violin duets op. 3. In St. Petersburg he met Clementi and Field, of whom he tells some curious traits; and after having passed the winter there without playing in public, returned to Brunswick in the summer of 1803. There he found Rode, and heard him for the first time. The playing of this great master filled him with the deepest admiration, and for some time it was his chief aim to imitate his style and manner as closely as possible. After having given in a public concert highly satisfactory proof of the progress made during his

absence, he again entered on his duties in the Duke's band. An intended journey to Paris in 1804 was cruelly cut short by the loss of his precious Guarnerius violin, the present of a Russian enthusiast. Just before entering the gates of Göttingen the portmanteau containing the violin was stolen from the coach, and all endeavours to recover it proved fruitless. He returned to Brunswick, and after having acquired, with the help of his generous patron, the Duke, another, though not equally good violin, he started on a tour to Berlin, Leipzig, Dresden and other German towns. His success was everywhere great, and his reputation spread rapidly. At his Berlin concert he was assisted by Meyerbeer, then only a boy of 13, but already a brilliant pianist.

In 1805 Spohr accepted the post of leader in the band of the Duke of Gotha. It was there he met and married his first wife, Dorette Scheidler, an excellent harp-player, who for many years appeared with him in all his concerts, and for whom he wrote a number of sonatas for violin and harp, as well as some solo-pieces. Having at his disposal a very fair band, Spohr now began to write orchestral works and vocal compositions of larger dimensions. His first opera, ' Die Prüfung,' which belongs to this period, was performed at a concert. In 1807 he made a very successful tour with his wife through Germany, visiting Leipzig, Dresden, Prague, Munich, Stuttgart (where he met Weber), Heidelberg and Frankfort. In 1808 he wrote his second opera, ' Alruna '; but this, again, never reached the stage, although accepted for representation at Weimar and apparently gaining the approval of Goethe, at that time manager of the Weimar theatre, who was present at a trial-rehearsal of the work. In the course of this year Napoleon held the famous Congress of Princes at Erfurt. Spohr, naturally anxious to see the assembled princes, went to Erfurt, where a French troupe, comprising Talma and Mars, performed every evening to a pit of monarchs. But on arrival he heard, to his great disappointment, that it was impossible for any but the privileged few to gain admittance to the theatre. In this dilemma he hit on a happy expedient. He persuaded the second horn-player of the band to allow him to take his place; but as he had never before touched a horn, he had to practise for the whole day in order to produce the natural notes of the instrument. When the evening came, though his lips were black and swollen, he was able to get through the very easy overture and entr'actes. Napoleon and his guests occupied the first row of stalls; but the musicians had strict orders to turn their backs to the audience, and not to look round. To evade this fatal regulation Spohr took with him a pocket looking-glass, and by placing it on his desk got a good view of the famous personages assembled.

In 1809 he made another tour through the north of Germany, and at Hamburg received a commission for an opera, ' Der Zweikampf mit der Geliebten '—or ' The Lovers' Duel '—which was produced with great success the year after. At this time he had already written six of his violin-concertos, and as a player had hardly a rival in Germany. The year 1809 is memorable for the First Music Festival in Germany, which was celebrated under Spohr's direction at Frankenhausen, a small town in Thuringia. It was followed by another, in 1811, for which Spohr composed his first symphony, in E♭. In 1812 he wrote his first oratorio, ' Das jüngste Gericht ' (not to be confounded with ' Die letzten Dinge,' or ' The Last Judgment'), on the invitation of the French Governor of Erfurt, for the ' Fête Napoléon ' on Aug. 15. He naïvely relates [1] that in the composition of this work he soon felt his want of practice in counterpoint and fugue-writing ; he therefore obtained Marpurg's treatise on the subject, studied it assiduously, wrote half-a-dozen fugues after the models given therein, and then appears to have been quite satisfied with his proficiency !

VIENNA.—The oratorio was fairly successful, but after two more performances of it at Vienna in the following year, the composer became dissatisfied, and laid it aside for ever. In autumn 1812 he made his first appearance at Vienna, and achieved as performer a brilliant, as composer an honourable, success. The post of leader of the band at the newly established Theatre ' an der Wien ' being offered to him under brilliant conditions, he gave up his appointment at Gotha and settled at Vienna. During the next summer he composed his opera ' Faust,' one of his best works, and soon afterwards, in celebration of the battle of Leipzig, a great patriotic cantata. But neither of these works was performed until after he had left Vienna. During his stay there Spohr naturally came into contact with Beethoven ; but in spite of his admiration for the master's earlier compositions, especially for the quartets, op. 18, which he was one of the first to perform at a time when they were hardly known outside Vienna (indeed, he was the very first to play them at Leipzig and Berlin)—yet he was quite unable to understand and appreciate the great composer's character and works, as they appeared even in his second period. His criticism of the C minor and Choral Symphonies has gained for Sophr, as a critic, an unenviable reputation.[2]

Although his stay at Vienna was on the whole very successful, and did much to raise his reputation, he left it in 1815, after having quitted his appointment on account of disagreements with the manager of the theatre. He passed the summer at the country-seat of Prince Carolath in Bohemia, and then went to

conduct another festival at Frankenhausen, where he brought out his cantata ' Das befreite Deutschland,' after which he set out on a tour through the west and south of Germany, Alsace, Switzerland and Italy. On his road, with the special view of pleasing the Italian public, he wrote the eighth concerto — the well-known ' Scena cantante.' He visited all the principal towns of the Peninsula, played the concerto in Rome and Milan, and made acquaintance with Rossini and his music — without approving much of the latter, as will be readily believed.

Returned to Germany, in 1817 he visited Holland, and then accepted the post of conductor of the opera at Frankfort-on-the-Main. Here, in 1818, his opera ' Faust ' was first produced. It was quickly succeeded by ' Zemire und Azor,' which, though hardly equal to ' Faust,' gained at the time even greater popularity. Owing again to differences with the manager he left Frankfort, after a stay of scarcely two years.

LONDON AND PARIS.—In 1820 he accepted an invitation from the Philharmonic Society in London, and paid his first visit to England. He appeared at the opening concert of the season (Mar. 6),[3] and played with great success his concerto No. 8, ' Nello stilo drammatico.' At the second Philharmonic concert he led his solo quartet in E. At the next he would naturally have been at the head of the violins to lead the band, while Ries, according to the then prevailing fashion, presided at the piano. But, after having overcome the opposition of some of the directors, Spohr succeeded in introducing the conductor's stick for the first time into a Philharmonic concert. It was on this occasion (Apr. 10) that he conducted his MS. symphony in D minor, a fine work, composed during his stay in London. At the last concert of the season another symphony of his was played for the first time in England, as well as his nonetto for strings and wind (op. 31). Spohr was delighted with the excellent performance of the Philharmonic orchestra, especially the stringed instruments. Altogether his sojourn in London was both artistically and financially a great success. At his farewell concert his wife made her last appearance as a harp-player, and was warmly applauded. Soon after she was obliged, on account of ill-health, to give up the harp for the piano, on which she would occasionally play in concerts with her husband, who wrote a number of pianoforte and violin duets especially for her.

On his journey home Spohr visited Paris for the first time. Here he made the personal acquaintance of Kreutzer, Viotti, Habeneck, Cherubini and other eminent musicians, and was received by them with great cordiality and esteem. His success at a concert which he gave

---

[1] *Selbstbiogr.* i. 169.   [2] *Ibid.* i. 202, etc.

[3] At a miscellaneous concert on Mar. 22 Spohr was described on the programme as making his first appearance in England.

at the Opéra was complete, although his quiet unpretentious style was not, and could not be, as much to the taste of the French as it was to that of the German and English public. Cherubini appears to have felt a special interest in Spohr's compositions, and the latter takes special pride in relating how the great Italian made him play a quartet of his three times over. Returned to Germany, Spohr settled at Dresden, where Weber was just then engaged in bringing out his 'Freischütz.' Spohr was no more able to appreciate the genius of Weber than that of Beethoven. It is curious that, without knowing of Weber's opera, he had had the intention of setting a libretto on the same story; but when he heard that Weber had treated the subject, he gave it up. During Spohr's stay at Dresden, Weber received an offer of the post of Hofkapell-meister to the Elector of Hesse-Cassel; but being unwilling to leave Dresden, he declined, at the same time strongly recommending Spohr, who soon after was offered the appointment for life under the most favourable conditions.

APPOINTMENT AT CASSEL.—On New Year's Day, 1822, he entered on his duties at Cassel, where he remained for the rest of his life. He had no difficulty in gaining at once the respect and obedience of bands and singers, and soon succeeded in procuring a more than local reputation for their performances. Meanwhile he had finished his 'Jessonda,' which soon made the round of all the opera-houses in Germany, with great and well-deserved success. It must be regarded as the culminating point of Spohr's activity as a composer. At Leipzig and Berlin, where he himself conducted the first perform-ances, it was received with an enthusiasm little inferior to that roused a few years before by the 'Freischütz.' In the winter of 1824 he passed some time in Berlin, and renewed and cemented the friendship with Felix Mendelssohn and the members of his family, which had been begun when they visited him at Cassel in 1822. In 1826 he conducted the Rhenish Festival at Düsseldorf, when his oratorio 'The Last Judg-ment' (Die letzten Dinge), previously given at Cassel (see Vol. III. p. 111), was performed. It pleased so much that it was repeated a few days later in aid of the Greek insurgents. His next large work was the opera 'Pietro von Abano,' which, however, like his next operas, 'Der Berggeist' and 'Der Alchymist,' had but a temporary success. In 1831 he finished his great *Violin School*, which has ever since its publication maintained the place of a standard work, and which contains, both in text and exercises, a vast amount of extremely interesting and useful material. At the same time, it cannot be denied that it reflects some-what exclusively Spohr's peculiar style of playing and is therefore of especial value for the study of his own violin-compositions. It is also true that its elementary part is of less

practical value from the fact that the author himself had never taught beginners, and so had no personal experience in that respect.

The political disturbances of 1832 caused a prolonged interruption of the opera perform-ances at Cassel. Spohr, incensed by the petty despotism of the Elector, proved himself at this time, and still more during the revolu-tionary period of 1848 and 1849, a strong Radical, incurring thereby his employer's dis-pleasure, and causing him innumerable annoy-ances. However, he made good use of the interruption to his official duties by writing his symphony 'Die Weihe der Töne' (The Consecration of Sound, No. 4, op. 86), which was produced at Cassel in 1832. During the next year he composed the oratorio 'Des Heilands letzte Stunden' (Calvary), on a libretto which Rochlitz had offered to Mendels-sohn, but which the latter, being then engaged on 'St. Paul,' had declined. Spohr's oratorio was first performed at Cassel on Good Friday, 1835. His first wife had died in 1834; in 1836 he married Marianne Pfeiffer, a pianist, who survived him, dying at Cassel, Jan. 4, 1892.

ORATORIOS FOR ENGLAND.—In 1839 he paid his second visit to England, where meanwhile his music had attained great popularity. He had received an invitation to produce his 'Calvary'[1] at the Norwich Festival, and in spite of the opposition offered to the work by some of the clergy on account of its libretto, his reception appears to have surpassed in enthusiasm anything he had before experienced. It was a real success, and Spohr for the rest of his life refers to it as the greatest of his triumphs. Soon after his return to Cassel he received from Professor Edward Taylor the libretto of another oratorio, 'The Fall of Babylon,' with a request that he would compose it for the Norwich Festival[2] of 1842.

In 1840 he conducted the Festival at Aix-la-Chapelle. Two years later he brought out at Cassel Wagner's 'Der fliegende Holländer.' That Spohr, who, in the case of Beethoven and Weber, exhibited such inability to appreciate novelty—and who at bottom was a conservative of conservatives in music—should have been the very first musician of eminence to interest himself in Wagner's talent is a curious fact not easily explained. To some extent his pre-dilection for experiments in music—such as he showed in his 'Weihe der Töne,' his symphony for two orchestras, the 'Historic Symphony,' the 'Quartet-Concertante' and some other things—may account for it; while his long familiarity with the stage had doubtless sharpened his perception for dramatic effect, and thus enabled him to recognise Wagner's eminently

[1] Previously given with an English translation by Edward Taylor at Hanover Square Rooms, London, by the VOCAL SOCIETY, under Taylor, Mar. 27, 1837.
[2] For the circumstance of the Norwich Festival performances, see *Annals of the Norfolk and Norwich Musical Festivals*, by R. H. Legge and W. E. Hansell, 1896.

dramatic genius. But there was in Spohr, both as man and as artist, a curious mixture of the ultra-conservative, nay almost philistine element, and of the radical spirit.

To the great disappointment of himself and his English friends, he was unable to conduct the 'Fall of Babylon' at Norwich, since the Elector refused the necessary leave of absence. Even a monster petition from his English admirers and a special request from Lord Aberdeen, then at the head of the Government, to the Elector, had not the desired result. The oratorio, however, was performed with the greatest success, and Spohr had to be satisfied with the reports of his triumph, which poured in from many quarters. On the first day of his summer vacation he started for England, and soon after his arrival in London conducted a performance of the new oratorio at the Hanover Square Rooms. On this and other occasions his reception here was of the most enthusiastic kind. The oratorio was repeated on a large scale by the Sacred Harmonic Society in Exeter Hall. The last Philharmonic concert of the season (July 3) was almost entirely devoted to Spohr, having in its programme a symphony, an overture, a violin-concerto and a vocal duet of his. By special request of the Queen and Prince Albert an extra concert with his co-operation was given on July 10, in which also he was well represented. A most enjoyable tour through the South and West of England, and Wales, brought this visit of Spohr to a happy end.

The year 1844 was marked by the composition of his last opera, 'Die Kreuzfahrer' (The Crusaders), for which he had himself arranged the libretto from a play of Kotzebue. It was performed at Cassel and Berlin, but had no lasting success. During his vacation he made a journey to Paris, and witnessed at the Odéon the 32nd performance of the 'Antigone' with Mendelssohn's music. The members of the Conservatoire orchestra arranged in his honour a special performance of his 'Consecration of Sound.' In the same year he conducted the 'Missa Solennis' and the Choral Symphony at the great Beethoven Festival at Bonn. The year 1847 saw him again in London, where the Sacred Harmonic Society announced a series of three concerts for the production of his principal sacred compositions : 'The Fall of Babylon,' 'Calvary,' 'The Last Judgment,' 'The Lord's Prayer' and Milton's 84th Psalm. However, on grounds similar to those which had roused so much opposition at Norwich, 'Calvary' was omitted from the scheme, and 'The Fall of Babylon' repeated in its place.

LAST YEARS.—On his return to Cassel, Spohr seems to have been quite absorbed by the great political events then going on in Germany. In the summer of 1848 he spent his vacation at Frankfort, where the newly created German Parliament was sitting, and he was never tired of listening to the debates of that short-lived political assembly. In 1849 he composed a fresh symphony, 'The Seasons' —his ninth. With 1850 a long chain of annoyances began. When his usual summer vacation time arrived, the Elector, probably intending to show displeasure at his political opinions, refused to sign the leave of absence—a mere formality, as his right to claim the vacation was fixed by contract. After several fruitless attempts to obtain the signature, Spohr, having made all his arrangements for a long journey, left Cassel without leave. This step involved him in a law-suit with the administration of the theatre, which lasted for four years, and which he finally lost on technical grounds.

For the London season of 1852 Spohr had received an invitation from the new Opera at Covent Garden to adapt his 'Faust' to the Italian stage. He accordingly composed recitatives, in place of the spoken dialogue, and made some further additions and alterations. It was produced with great success under his own direction on July 15, the principal parts being sustained by Castellan, Ronconi, Formes and Tamberlik. In 1853, after many fruitless attempts which were regularly frustrated by the Elector, he at last succeeded in bringing out Wagner's 'Tannhäuser' at Cassel. In reference to it he says in his Autobiography, ' This opera contains a great deal that is new and beautiful, but also some things which are ugly and excruciating to the ear,' and speaking of the 2nd finale he says : ' In this finale now and then a truly frightful music is produced.' That he considered Wagner by far the greatest of all living dramatic composers he declared as soon as he became acquainted with 'The Flying Dutchman.' From 'Tannhäuser' he would have proceeded to 'Lohengrin,' but owing to the usual opposition of the court, all his endeavours to bring it out were frustrated. In the same year he came for the sixth and last time to England, to fulfil an engagement at the New Philharmonic concerts. At three of these he conducted not only many of his own works—especially the symphony for two orchestras—but also the Choral Symphony. At the same time 'Jessonda' was in preparation at Covent Garden. But as it could not be produced before the close of his vacation, Spohr was unable to conduct it himself.

From this time his powers began to decline. He still went on composing, but declared himself dissatisfied with the results. In 1857 he was pensioned off, very much against his wish, and in the winter of the same year had the misfortune to break his arm, which compelled him to give up violin-playing. Once more, in 1858, at the celebration of the fiftieth anniversary of the Prague Conservatorium, he con-

LXXVII

SPOHR

Photographische Gesellschaft

From a painting in the possession of Countess Rosalie von Sauerma

SPONTINI

From a lithograph by Maurin

ducted his ' Jessonda ' with wonderful energy. It was his last public appearance. He died quietly on Oct. 22, 1859, at Cassel,[1] and thus closed the long life of a man and an artist who had to the full developed the great talents and powers given to him ; who throughout a long career had lived up to the ideal he had conceived in youth ; in whom private character and artistic activity corresponded to a rare degree, even in their foibles and deficiences. That these last were not small cannot be denied.

QUALITIES OF THE MUSICIAN.—His utter want of critical power in reference both to himself and to others is fully exposed in his interesting Autobiography,[2] which, however, bears the strongest possible testimony to his rare manly straightforwardness and sincerity in word and deed, and to the childlike purity of mind which he preserved from early youth to latest age. Difficult as it is to understand his famous criticisms on Beethoven and his interest for Wagner, their sincerity cannot be doubted for a moment. According to his lights he ever stood up for the dignity of his art, with the same unflinching independence of character with which he claimed, not without personal risk, the rights of a free citizen. It is true that he called himself a disciple of Mozart. But the universality of Mozart's talent was the very reverse of Spohr's exclusive individualism; and except in their great regard for form, and in a certain similarity of melodic structure, the two masters have hardly anything in common. Spohr certainly was a born musician, second only to the very greatest masters in true musical instinct; in power of concentration and of work hardly inferior to any. But the range of his talent was not wide ; he never seems to have been able to step out of a given circle of ideas and sentiments. He never left the circle of his own individuality, but drew everything within it.

He was fond of experiments in composition— such as new combinations of instruments (to wit the double quartets, the symphony for two orchestras, the quartet-concerto and others), or adoption of programmes (' Consecration of Sound ' ; concertino, ' Past and Present,' etc.), and thus showed his eagerness to strike out new paths. (See SYMPHONY, pp. 221-3.) But after all, what do we find under these new dresses and fresh-invented titles but the same dear old Spohr, incapable of putting on a really new face, even for a few bars ? ' Napoleon,' says Robert Schumann[3] (àpropos of Spohr's Historical Symphony),

' once went to a masked ball, but before he had been in the room a few minutes folded his arms in his well-known attitude. " The Emperor ! the Emperor ! " at once ran through the place. Just so, through disguises of the Symphony, one kept hearing " Spohr, Spohr " in every corner of the room.'

---

[1] A Spohr Museum was founded at Cassel in 1921.
[2] *Louis Spohr's Selbstbiographie* ; Cassel und Göttingen, G. H. Wigand, 1860. Two volumes, with portrait and seventeen facsimiles.
[3] *Gesammelte Schriften*, iv. 89.

Hence there is considerable sameness—nay, monotony—in his works. Be it oratorio or concerto, opera or string-quartet—he treats them all very much in the same manner, and it is not so much the distinctive styles peculiar to these several forms of music that we find, as Spohr's peculiar individuality impressed upon all of them. He certainly was not devoid of originality—in fact his style and manner are so entirely his own that no composer is perhaps so absolutely unmistakable as he is. That an originality so strong and so inalienable, unless supported by creative power of the very first order and controlled by self-criticism, would easily lead to mannerism is obvious ; and a mannerist he must be called. Certain melodious phrases and cadences, chromatic progressions and enharmonic modulations, in themselves beautiful enough, and most effective, occur over and over again, until they appear to partake more of the nature of mechanical contrivances than to be the natural emanations of a living musical organism.

To his violin-concertos—and among them especially to the 7th, 8th and 9th—must be assigned the first place among his works. They are distinguished as much by noble and elevated ideas as by masterly thematic treatment ; while the supreme fitness of every note in the solo-part to the nature of the violin need hardly be mentioned. His duets and concertantes for two violins, and for violin and viola, are of their kind unsurpassed. By the frequent employment of double stops great sonority is produced, and, if well played, the effect is charming. The mass of his chamber music, a great number of quartets, quintets, double quartets, trios, etc., is nowadays not often heard in public. Spohr as a composer of quartets was rarely able to shake off the great violin-virtuoso. Some of the quartets—the so-called ' Quatuors brillants ' or solo quartets —are avowedly violin-concertos accompanied by violin, viola and violoncello, and appear to have been written to supply a momentary want. And even those which claim to be quartets in the proper sense of the term, almost invariably give to the first violin an undue prominence, incompatible with the true quartet-style. Allowing all this, it must be maintained that many of the slow movements are of great beauty; and together, in spite of undeniable drawbacks, his quartets contain so much fine and noble music as certainly not to deserve the utter neglect they have fallen into.

His oratorios, still enjoying a certain popularity in England, are but rarely heard in other countries. They contain, no doubt, much beautiful music, and occasionally rise even to grandeur and sublimity. Yet one cannot help feeling a certain incongruity between the character of the words and the musical treatment—between the stern solemnity of such subjects as 'Calvary' or ' The Last Judgment ' and the quiet charm and sweetness of Spohr's music, which even in its most powerful and passionate moments lacks the all-conquering force here demanded.

Of his many songs a few only have attained great popularity, such as ' The Bird and the Maiden.'

SPOHR AS VIOLINIST. — As an executant Spohr counts amongst the greatest of all times. Through Franz Eck he received the solid principles of the Mannheim School, and Rode's example appears afterwards to have had some influence on his style. He was, however, too original to remain fettered by any school, still less under the influence of a definite model. He very soon formed a style of his own, which again—like his style as a composer—was a complete reflex of his peculiar individuality. It has often been remarked that he treated the violin pre-eminently as a singing instrument, and we can readily believe that the composer of the Scena Cantante and of the slow movements in the 9th and other concertos, played with a breadth and beauty of tone and a delicacy and refinement of expression almost unequalled. A hand of exceptional size and strength enabled him to execute with great facility the most difficult double-stops and stretches. His manner of bowing did not materially differ from that of the old French School (Viotti, Rode). Even in quick passages he preserved a broad full tone. His staccato was most brilliant and effective, moderately quick, every note firmly marked by a movement of the wrist. The lighter and freer style of bowing, that came in with Paganini, and has been adopted more or less by all modern players, was not to his taste. He appears to have had a special dislike to the use of the 'springing bow,' and it is a characteristic fact that, when he first brought out Mendelssohn's ' Midsummer Night's Dream' overture at Cassel, he insisted on the violins playing the quick passage at the opening with firm strokes.

If Spohr's compositions for the violin do not present abnormal difficulties to the virtuoso of the present day, such was not the case at the time when they were written. They were then considered the *ne plus ultra* of difficulty. We must also remember that he was too great an artist and musician to care for display of executive skill for its own sake, and that in consequence the difficulties contained in his works do not by any means represent the limit of his powers as an executant. He had a large number of pupils, the best known of whom were St. Lubin, Pott, Ferdinand David, Kömpel, Blagrove, Bott, Bargheer. Spohr was considered one of the best conductors of his time. An unerring ear, imperturbable rhythmical feeling, energy and fire, were combined with an imposing personal appearance and great dignity of bearing.

As a man he was universally respected, although, owing to a certain reserve in his character and a decided aversion to talking, he was not rarely reproached with coldness and brusqueness of manner. At the same time he gained and kept through a long life certain intimate friendships—with Hauptmann [1] and others—and in many instances showed great kindness, and extended not a little courtesy, to brother artists. That this was not incompatible with an extraordinary sense of his own value and importance is evident in every page of his Selbstbiographie, a most amusing work, deserving a better translation than it has yet found.[2]

His works, of which a catalogue is given below, comprise 9 great symphonies ; a large number of overtures ; 17 violin-concertos and concertinos ; many other concert pieces (Potpourris, Variations, etc.) for the violin, for violin and harp ; 15 violin-duets ; duets for violin and PF. ; 4 concertos and other pieces for clarinet ; 33 string quartets ; 8 quintets ; 4 double quartets ; 5 PF. trios ; 2 sextets ; an octet ; and a nonet ; 4 great oratorios ; a Mass ; several psalms and cantatas ; 10 operas ; a great many songs, partsongs and other vocal pieces—over 200 works in all.

LIST [3] OF WORKS

Op.		Op.	
1.	Concerto for violin (No. 1, A min.).	23.	Potpourri on themes of Mozart (No. 3, G) for vln. with acc. of Quartet, flute, oboe, clarinet, 2 bassoons and 2 horns.
2.	Concerto for vln. (No. 2, D min.).		
3.	3 Duos Concertants for 2 vln.	24.	Potpourri on themes of Mozart (No. 4, B) for vln. with acc. of 2nd vln., viola and bass.
4.	2 String Quartets (C, G min.).		
5.	First Potpourri on Air of Dalayrac for vln. with acc. of 2nd vln., viola and bass.	25.	6 German Songs.
		26.	Concerto for clarinet (No. 1, C min.).
6.	Variations (No. 1, D) for vln. solo, 2nd vln., viola and bass.	27.	Quartet for 2 vln., viola and violone (No. 6, G min.).
7.	Concerto for vln. (No. 3, C min.).	28.	Concerto for vln. (No. 6, G min.).
8.	Variations (No. 2, A min.) for vln. solo, 2nd vln., viola and bass.	29.	3 String Quartets (Nos. 7, 8, 9 ; E♭, C min., F min.).
9.	2 Duos Concertants for 2 vln. (Nos. 4, 5).	30.	String Quartet (No. 10, A).
		31.	Grand Nonetto (F. maj.) for vln., viola, v'cl., bass, flute, oboe, clarinet, bassoon and horn.
10.	Concerto for vln. (No. 4, B min.).		
11.	Quatuor Brillant for 2 vln., viola and v'cl. (No. 3, D min.).	32.	Octet (E maj.) for vln., 2 violas, v'cl., clarinet, 2 horns, and bass.
12.	Overture (No. 1, C min.).		
13.	Grand Duo for vln. and viola (No. 6).	33.	2 Quintets for 2 vln., 2 violas and v'cl. (No. 1, E♭ ; No. 2, G).
14. *			
15.	2 String Quartets (Nos. 4, 5 ; C, A).	34.	Notturno (in C) for wind instruments and Turkish band.
15a.	Overture (No. 2, D), ' Die Prüfung.'		
16.	Grande Sonate for PF. (or harp) and vln. (B.).	35.	Fantasia for harp (A♭).
		36.	Variations for harp (F).
17.	Concerto for vln. (No. 5, E♭).	37.	6 German Songs (2nd book of Songs).
18. *			
19. *		38.	Concerto for vln. (No. 7, E min.).
20.	First Symphony (E♭). Peters.		
		39.	3 Duets for vln. (Nos. 7, 8, 9 ; D min., E♭, E).
21.	Overture (No. 3, E♭), ' Alruna.'	40.	Grande Polonaise (A min.) for vln. with orch.
22.	Potpourri on themes of Mozart (No. 2, B♭) for vln. with acc. of 2nd vln., viola and bass.	41.	6 German Songs (3rd book of Songs).
		42.	Potpourri. Arrangement for vln. and PF. of op. 24.

[1] Hauptmann's letters to Spohr have been published by Schoene and Hiller. See also *Letters of a Leipzig Cantor*, translated and edited by A. D. Coleridge (1892).
[2] *Louis Spohr's Autobiography*, Longmans, 1865.
[3] Founded on the catalogue edited by H. M. Schletterer, B. & H., 1881. An earlier catalogue, imperfect but very useful in its time, was that of Jantzen—*Verzeichniss*, etc., Cassel, Lückhardt.
* Unknown and not to be found in Schletterer's Catalogue Probably represented by works left in manuscript.

Op.
43. Quatuor Brillant for stringed instr. (No. 11, E).
44. 6 4-part Songs for male voices.
45. 3 String Quartets (Nos. 12, 13, 14 ; C, E min., F min.).
46. Introduction and Rondo (E) for PF. and vln.
47. Concerto for vln. No. 8, A min. 'In modo d' una scena cantante' (' Gesangsscene ').
48. First Concertante for 2 vln. and orch. (A min.).
49. Second Symphony (D min.) Ded. to Philharmonic Society.
50. Potpourri (F♯ min.) for vln. and PF. on Airs from ' Die Zauberflöte.' Peters.
51. Grand Rondo for vln. and PF. concertants.
52. Quintet for PF., flute, clarinet, horn and bassoon (C min.).
53. Arrangement of op. 52 for PF. and stringed instr.
54. Mass for 5 solo voices and 2 5-part choirs.
55. Concerto for vln. (No. 9, D min.).
56. Potpourri for vln.and PF. on Airs from ' Das unterbrochene Opferfest.'
57. Concerto for clarinet (No. 2, E♭).
58. 3 String Quartets (Nos. 16, 17, 18 ; E♭, A min., G).
59. Potpourri (A min.) on Irish Airs for vln. and orch.
60. ' Faust,' Opera.
61. QuatuorBrillant for stringed instr. (No. 15, B min.).
62. Concerto for vln. (No. 10, A min.).
63. ' Jessonda,' Opera.
64. Potpourri (A♭) on Airs from ' Jessonda,' for vln. and v'cl. with orch.
65. Double String Quartet (No. 1, D min.).
66. Potpourri (A min.) on Airs from ' Jessonda,' for vln. and orch.
67. 3 Duos Concertants for 2 vln. (Nos. 10, 11, 12 ; A min., D, G min.).
68. Quatuor Brillant (No.19, A).
69. Quintet for stringed instr. (No. 3, B min.).
70. Concerto for vln. (No.11, G).
71. Scena and Aria for soprano.
72. 6 German Songs (Book 4 of Songs).
73. ' Der Berggeist,' Opera.
74. 3 String Quartets (Nos. 20, 21, 22 ; A min. B♭, D min.).
75. Overture, ' Macbeth ' (B min.).
76. ' Pietro von Abano,' Opera.
77. Double Quartet for stringed instr. (No. 2, E♭).
78. Third Symphony (C min.).
79. Concerto for vln. (A min.).
80. Potpourri for clarinet (F).
81. Fantasia and Variations for clarinet (B♭).
82. 3 String Quartets (Nos. 23, 24, 25 ; E, G, A min.).
83. Quatuor Brillant for stringed instr. (No. 26, E♭).
84. 3 String Quartets (Nos. 27, 28, 29 ; D min., A♭, B min.).
85. 3 Psalms for double choir and solo voices.
86. Fourth Symphony, 'The Consecration of Sound.'
87. Double Quartet for stringed instr. (No. 3, E min.).
88. Second Concertante for 2 vln. with orch.
89. ' Erinnerung an Marienbad,' valses for orch. (A min.).
90. 6 4-part Songs for male voices.
91. Quintet for stringed instr. (No. 4, G min.).
92. Concertino for vln. (No. 2, E (maj.).
93. Quatuor Brillant for stringed instr. (No. 30, A min.).
94. 6 Songs for contralto or baritone (Book 5 of Songs).
95. Duo Concertant for PF. and vln. (G min.).

Op.
96. Duo Concertant for PF. and vln. (F).
97. Hymn, ' St. Caecilia,' chorus, soprano solo.
97a. Psalm 24, for chorus, solo voices and PF.
98. Hymne, ' Gott, du bist gross' (God, thou art great), for chorus, solo voices, and orch.
99. Fantasia on Raupach's ' Die Tochter der Luft ' in form of a concert-overture for orch. (See op. 102.)
100. *
101. 6 German Songs (Book 6 of Songs).
102. Fifth Symphony (C min.). Fantasia op. 99 used as first movement.
103. 6 German Songs with acct. of PF. and clarinet (Book 7 of Songs).
104. ' Vater unser ' (words by Klopstock).
105. 6 Songs (Book 8 of Songs).
106. Quintet for stringed instr. (No. 5, G min.).
107. 3 Duets for soprano and tenor with PF.
108. 3 Duets for 2 sopranos.
109. *
110. Concertino for vln., ' Sonst und Jetzt ' (No. 3, A min.).
111. Rondo alla Spagnuola (C) for PF. and vln.
112. Duo Concertant for PF. and vln. (No. 3, E).
113. Sonate Concertante for harp and vln. (E♭).
114. Do. (E♭).
115. Do. (A♭).
116. Historical Symphony (No. 6, G). Dedicated to the Philharmonic Soc., London.
117. Fantasia for PF. and vln. on Airs from 'Der Alchymist.'
118. Fantasia for PF. (or harp) and vln. on Airs of Handel and Abt Vogler.
119. Trio Concertant (E min.) for PF., vln., and v'cl.
120. 6 4-part Songs for mixed voices.
121. Double Symphony, ' Irdisches und Göttliches im Menschenleben,' for double orch.
122. Psalm 128. Chorus and solo voices with organ or PF.
123. Trio Concertant for PF., vln. and v'cl. (No. 2, F maj.).
124. Trio Concertant for PF., vln. and v'cl. (No. 3, A min.).
125. Sonata (A♭) for PF. Dedicated to Mendelssohn.
126. Concert-Overture, ' Im ernsten Styl ' (D).
127. ' Elegisch u. humoristisch,' 6 Duettinos for PF. and vln.
128. Concerto for vln. (No. 15, E min.).
129. Quintet for stringed instr. (No. 5, E min.).
130. Quintet for PF., 2 vln., viola and v'cl.
131. Quartet Concerto for 2 vln., viola and v'cl., with orch.
132 String Quartet (No. 31, A).
133. Trio for PF., vln., and v'cl. (No 4, B♭).
134. Psalm 84 (Milton). Chorus and solo voices with orch.
135. Sechs Salonstücke for vln. and PF.
136. Double Quartet (No. 4, B♭).
137. Symphony (No. 8, G min.). Dedicated to the Philharmonic Soc. of London.
138. Sonatina for PF. and voice, ' An Sie am Clavier.'
139. 5 Songs (Book 9). Lückhardt.
140. Sextet for 2 vln., 2 violas and 2 v'cl. (C maj.).
141. Quartet (No. 32, C).
142. Trio for PF. vln. and v'cl. (No. 5, G min.).
143. Symphony ' The Seasons' (No. 9).
144. Quintet for stringed instr. (No. 7, G min.).
145. Sechs Salonstücke for vln. and PF.
146. String Quartet (No. 33, G).
147. Septet for PF., flute, clarinet, horn, bassoon, vln. and v'cl.

Op.
148. 3 Duets for 2 vln. (No. 1, F) —dedicated to the brothers Holmes. (See opp. 150, 153.)
149. Rondoletto for PF. (G).
150. 3 Duets for 2 vln. (No. 2, D). (See opp. 148,153.) Peters.
151. 6 4-part Songs for mixed voices.
152. String Quartet, No. 34 (E♭).
153. 3 Duets for 2 vln. (No. 3, C).
154. 6 Songs for a baritone voice with acc. of vln. and PF.

WORKS WITHOUT OPUS-NUMBER

' Der Zweikampf mit der Geliebten.' Opera.
Overture and Bass Air from the Cantata, ' Das befreite Deutschland.'

' Zemire und Azor.' Opera.
' Die letzen Dinge ' (The Last Judgment). Oratorio.
' Vater unser ' (words by Mahlman).
' Der Alchymist.' Opera. Violinschule.
' Des Heilands letzte Stunden ' (Calvary). Oratorio. Overture and Song for the play ' Der Matrose.'
' Der Fall Babylons.' Oratorio.
' Die Kreuzfahrer ' (The Crusaders). Opera.
36 Violin Studies by Fiorillo, with a 2nd vln.part added,fingered and bowed.
A number of Songs, written for and published in various Albums and Collections.
A considerable number of works remain in manuscript.

P. D.

SPONDEE (Lat. *spondæus*). A metrical foot, consisting of two long syllables (– –). (See METRE.)

SPONTINI, GASPARO LUIGI PACIFICO (*b.* Majolati, near Jesi, Nov. 14, 1774 ; *d.* there, Jan. 14, 1851), opera composer, the son of simple peasants. With a view to the priesthood, an uncle gave him elementary instruction and showed at first no sympathy with the boy's love of music, resorting indeed to harsh measures to drive it out of him. The result was that Spontini ran away to Monte San Vito, where he had another uncle of a milder disposition, who procured him music lessons from a certain Quintiliani. In the course of a year the uncle at Jesi relented, took back his nephew, and had him well grounded by the local musicians.

In 1791 his parents took him to Naples, where he was admitted into the Conservatorio de' Turchini, studying counterpoint and composition under Sala and Tritto and singing under Tarantino.[1] In the Neapolitan Conservatorios a certain number of the more advanced pupils were set to teach the more backward ones. These ' monitors,' as we should say, were called *maestrini* or *maestricelli*.[2] In 1795 Spontini became a candidate for the post of fourth *maestrino*, but the examiners gave the preference to another pupil. This seems to have roused the lad to special industry, and in a short time he was appointed first *maestrino*. His exercise for the competition of 1795 has been preserved, and is now in the archives of the Real Collegio di Musica at Naples. It must be the earliest of his compositions now in existence.[3]

Having already composed some cantatas and church music performed in Naples and the neighbourhood, in 1796 Spontini had an opportunity of attempting opera. The invitation came from one of the directors of the Teatro Argentina in Rome, who had been pleased with some of Spontini's music which he had heard at Naples. The professors seem to have refused him leave to go, so he left the Conservatorio by stealth, and, reaching Rome, quickly composed ' I puntigli delle donne ' with brilliant success.

---

* Unknown and not to be found in Schletterer's Catalogue. Probably represented by works left in manuscript.

[1] Florimo's *Cenno storico sulla scuola musicale di Napoli* (Naples, 1869), vol. i. p. 50. On p. 673 Florimo speaks of Salieri and not Tarantino as Spontini's master.
[2] Lichtenthal, *Dizionario e bibliografia della musica* (Milan, 1826), vol. ii. p. 20.
[3] Florimo, pp. 595, 609, and elsewhere.

He was readmitted into the Turchini at the intercession of Piccinni, who had lived at Naples since his return in 1791, and gave Spontini valuable advice with regard to composition, particularly for his next opera, 'L' eroismo ridicolo.'[1] This also was produced in Rome (1797), as well as a third, ' Il finto pittore ' (1798). Next followed three operas for Florence, all in 1798. Meantime Naples had begun to fix its attention on Spontini. ' L' eroismo ridicolo ' (one act) was given at the Teatro Nuovo during the Carnival of 1798, and reproduced in two acts as ' La finta filosofa ' at the same house in the summer of 1799. In the Carnival of 1800 the same theatre brought out a new work, ' La fuga in maschera.'[2] At the close of 1798 the court, alarmed at the advance of the French troops, had taken flight to Palermo, and Cimarosa, who as maestro di cappella should have gone too, refusing to stir, Spontini was put in his place and during 1800 composed for the court in Palermo no less than three operas, in the facile and rapid style of a true disciple of the Neapolitan School. This is specially worth noting, as he afterwards completely changed in this respect, and elaborated most slowly and carefully the very works on which his European fame rests. In Palermo he also began to teach singing, but towards the end of 1800 was forced to leave, as the climate was affecting his health. After supplying more operas for Rome and Venice, he paid a visit to Jesi, and then took ship at Naples for Marseilles. His objective was Paris, and there he arrived in 1803.

From Lully downwards all Italian composers seem to have been impelled to try their fortunes in the French capital, and invariably have had to encounter the onslaughts of the national jealousy. The Bouffonists, Gluck, Cherubini, all went through the same experience ; it was now Spontini's turn. The work by which he introduced himself at the Théâtre Italien, ' La finta filosofa,' was, it is true, well received ; but when he entered on the special domain of the French opéra-comique he was roughly disillusioned. His first work of the kind, ' Julie, ou le pot de fleurs ' (Mar. 1804), failed, and though remodelled by the composer and revived in 1805, could not even then keep the boards.[3] The second, ' La Petite Maison ' (June 23, 1804), was hissed off. This fate was not wholly undeserved. Spontini had fancied that the light, pleasing, volatile style, which suited his own countrymen, would equally please the Parisians ; the melodies, though very attractive, are often trivial. Stronger work than this was needed to compete with Méhul, and Boieldieu, who had

already written the ' Calife de Bagdad.' During this period Spontini was making a livelihood by giving singing-lessons.

His next opera, ' Milton ' (Nov. 27, 1804), a little work in one act, is of an entirely different character, the melodies more expressive, the harmony and orchestration richer, the whole more carefully worked out, and the sentiment altogether more earnest. But the most interesting point in the score is the evidence it affords of Mozart's influence. One is driven to the conclusion that Spontini had now for the first time made a solid acquaintance with the works of the German masters. Even in old age he used to speak of Don Giovanni as ' that immortal chef-d'œuvre,' and it was one of the very few works besides his own which he conducted when director-general at Berlin.

' Milton ' took at once with the French, and made its way into Germany, being produced in Berlin (translated by Treitschke) Mar. 24, 1806,[4] Weimar, Dresden and Vienna.

The writer of the libretto, Étienne Jouy, played a considerable part in Spontini's life. He saw in him a man of great dramatic talent, and offered him the libretto of ' La Vestale.'[5] It was originally intended for Cherubini, but he could not make up his mind to compose it, and after a long delay returned it.[6] To Spontini it afforded the means of ranking himself at once with the first operatic composers of the day. The score was finished in 1805, and the first performance took place Dec. 15, 1807.

Spontini was now fortunately in favour with the Empress Josephine—to whom he dedicated the score of ' Milton '—and was appointed her ' Compositeur particulier.' A cantata, ' L' eccelsa gara,' performed Feb. 8, 1806, at the fêtes given in honour of Austerlitz, helped to increase this goodwill, which proved of vital importance to Spontini in maintaining his ground against the opposition of the Conservatoire. To such a length was this opposition carried that at one of the Concerts Spirituels in Holy Week, 1807, an oratorio of his was yelled off the stage by the students. Meantime, however, through the Empress's patronage, ' La Vestale ' was in rehearsal at the Opéra. But so prejudiced were the artists against the work that the rehearsals went on amid ridicule and opposition, both inside and outside the theatre. Some foundation for this no doubt did exist.[7]

---

[1] I can find no quite satisfactory ground for the statement so often made in print that it was Cimarosa and not Piccinni who gave Spontini instruction in composition.

[2] Fétis speaks of yet another opera, 'L' Amore segreto' (Naples, 1799), but there is no mention of it in Florimo's 4th volume.

[3] At least so says Fétis, who was living in Paris from the middle of 1804-11, and who not only took great interest in Spontini's works but was personally acquainted with him. Ledebur, in his Berliner Tonkünstler-Lexicon (Berlin, 1861), p. 501, gives a wholly opposite account, but Fétis seems the more credible witness.

[4] Teichmann's Literary Remains, edited by Dingelstedt (Stuttgart, Cotta, 1863), p. 415.

[5] See Jouy's own account, Notes anecdotiques sur l'opéra de la Vestale, in the Théâtre d'Étienne Jouy (Paris, 1824), vol. ii. p. 149 et seq.

[6] So says Fétis. Others have stated that besides Cherubini it had been offered to Méhul, Boieldieu, Paër and others, and that the then unknown Spontini was a last resource. That the latter part of the statement is positively untrue we know from Jouy himself, and the rest will not bear examination. The mistakes as to the details of Spontini's life are very numerous. Jouy even did not know the correct date of his birth, for he speaks of him in 1804 as ' à peine âgé de vingt-cinq ans.' For a long time he was universally supposed to have been born in 1778.

[7] The ' Vestale ' was a marvel of noise for its day, and a good story was current about it in Paris at the time. A well-known physician had advised a friend to go and hear it as a remedy for his deafness, and accompanied him to the theatre. After one of the loudest

Spontini's thoughts were throughout fresh and significant, but, not having before attempted lyric tragedy, he did not in all cases succeed in giving them a satisfactory form. Then began an interminable altering and remodelling on his part; the most trying experiences at rehearsals did not discourage him from again and again re-casting passage after passage, until he had hit on the best possible form. This indefatigable polishing and experimenting became henceforth one of his characteristics, and instead of diminishing, as he acquired command of his means, as might have been expected, each new work seemed to strengthen the habit.

The success of 'Vestale' was the most brilliant imaginable, and it long remained a favourite with the Parisians, having been performed 200 times as early as the year 1824. The cast on the first night was as follows:

Licinius, Nourrit; Cinna, Laïs; the High-Priest, Dérivis; the Chief-Augur, Bonel; A Consul, Martin; Julia, Mme. Branchu; the Chief Vestal, Mme. Armand.'

It soon became known beyond France. The first performances at San Carlo in Naples (to an Italian translation by Giovanni Schmidt) took place Sept. 8, 1811.[1] In Berlin it was given on Jan. 18, 1811, to a translation by Herklots, at Munich on Jan. 14, and Würzburg, Jan. 10, 1812.

Jouy drew the material of his poem, the action of which takes place in the year of Rome 269, from Winckelmann's *Monumenti antichi inediti.* As for the music it is so entirely new, and so utterly unlike the Neapolitan style, that it is not to be wondered at if the malicious story that Spontini was not the composer of it has occasionally been believed. Of the influence of Mozart we have already spoken, but that of Gluck, with whose works he became acquainted in Paris, was more important still. With Gluck he shares that touch of grandeur, the refined melancholy of which is often so peculiarly attractive, though as a rule the depth of Gluck's sentiment is beyond the reach of the Italian master. As with Gluck too the dramatic gift preponderates in Spontini over the purely musical.

Between the 'Vestale,' which we take to have been finished in 1805, and Spontini's next opera four years elapsed. To this period apparently belongs a collection of six songs, with accompaniment for PF. or harp, entitled

'Sensations douces, mélancoliques et douloureuses, exprimées en vers par M. de G.—L., et en musique avec accompagnement de piano ou harpe par Gaspare Spontini, Maître de Chapelle du Conservatoire de Naples.'

His next opera was 'Fernand Cortez,' the first performance of which took place Nov. 28, 1809. The libretto was again by Jouy, and not

by Esménard,[2] who merely made some alterations and additions. Napoleon took an interest in the production of 'Cortez,' from an idea that it might influence public opinion in favour of his plans for the Spanish war, then in progress.[3] Its success was very great, equalling if not exceeding that of the 'Vestale.' On the whole we should not be wrong in pronouncing 'Cortez' the more finished work of the two. The harmony is stronger, the tendency (latterly so exaggerated) to pile up means in order to produce imposing effects is still kept within due bounds. Remarkable skill is shown in the treatment of the masses, and the construction of the larger dramatic forms. Throughout we are brought in contact with an individual artist, who has created for himself his own means of expression.[4] The certainty of touch, too, in the different characters is worthy of all praise. Here Spontini is seen to be a worthy successor of Gluck, who was the first to attempt this kind of problem in his 'Paris et Hélène.'

The form in which we know 'Cortez' is not that in which it first appeared. After a long interval it was revived May 26, 1817, in an entirely new shape. Esménard was dead, and for the alterations in the poem Jouy was entirely responsible. The third act became the first, the first act the second, and a part of the second the third; some passages were suppressed and others added, and the part of Montezuma was entirely new.

In 1810 Spontini became conductor of the Italian opera, which was united with the Comédie Française under the title of 'Théâtre de l'Impératrice,' and located at the Odéon. He formed a distinguished company of singers, improved the orchestra, and threw more variety into the repertory. One signal service was his production, for the first time in Paris, of 'Don Juan' in its original form. He also instituted Concerts Spirituels, at which he successfully introduced such works as Mozart's Requiem, Haydn's Symphonies, and extracts from the 'Creation.' But he did not keep the conductorship long. Differences arose between himself and Alexandre Duval, the director of the theatre, and in 1812 Spontini was dismissed from his post by de Rémusat, surintendant of the imperial theatres.

On the restoration of the Bourbons in 1814 Spontini was reinstated, but soon gave up the post to Catalani for a money consideration. His conduct as conductor of the opera does not give a favourable idea of his character. When Count Brühl was in Paris, Spontini was described to him by the managers of the Opéra as 'grasping

bursts, 'Doctor,' cried the friend in ecstasy, 'Doctor, I can hear!' but alas, the doctor made no response, the same noise which had cured his friend had deafened him.
[1] See Florimo, *Scuola musicale di Napoli*, iv. 268. In his earlier work, *Cenno storico sulla Scuola musicale di Napoli* (Naples, 1869), p. 631, he says the first performance took place in 1809.

[2] Riehl (*Musikalische Charakterköpfe*, 5th ed., Stuttgart, Cotta, 1876, vol. i. p. 192); following Raoul Rochette, *Notice historique sur la vie et les ouvrages de M. Spontini* (Paris, Firmin Didot, 1852).
[3] *Théâtre d'Étienne Jouy*, vol. ii. p. 199 et seq.
[4] In face of this self-evident fact but little importance will be attached to the discovery made in Paris that the trio 'Créateur de ce nouveau monde,' was an imitation of an 'O Salutaris Hostia' of Gossec. See *Journal des Débats* for June 1, 1817.

and indolent ; ill-natured, treacherous, and
spiteful.' [1] Catalani, too, always averred that
he had treated her badly. Some, however,
took a more favourable view, and maintained
that he had been both zealous and successful
in his efforts for the furtherance of art. Fétis
believed that it was not Spontini but Duval
who should have been dismissed in 1812. It is
curious thus to find the same difference of
opinion in Paris with regard to Spontini's
character which was afterwards so noticeable
in Berlin.

On May 30, 1814, Louis XVIII. became king
of France, and in commemoration of the event
Jouy and Spontini wrote a festival-opera in
two acts called 'Pélage, ou le Roi de la paix.'
The first performance took place Aug. 23, 1814.
The work is of no value and must have been
very quickly composed.

He next took part with Persuis, Berton and
Kreutzer in an opéra-ballet, 'Les Dieux rivaux,'
produced June 21, 1816, in honour of the
marriage of the Duc de Berri. Spontini's share
was confined to two or three dances, and a song,
'Voici le Roi, Français fidèles,' of little value.
Other ballet - music, however, composed for
Salieri's 'Danaïdes,' rises to the level of
'Cortez' and the 'Vestale.' The opera, revived with this addition Oct. 22, 1817, was
enthusiastically received.

But these *pièces d'occasion* sink into insignificance before the grand opera 'Olympie,'
'imitated' by Briffaut and Dieulafoy from Voltaire's tragedy. Spontini took a most unusual
length of time for the composition. He was at
work upon the last act in Dec. 1815, and yet
the opera was not finished by Jan. 1819.[2] After
so much trouble and pains he not unnaturally
considered it his best work. At the first performance (Paris, Dec. 15, 1819) a bitter disappointment awaited him, for the opera failed
in spite of his numerous supporters, and of the
generally favourable disposition of the Parisians
towards him. Spontini, however, was not the
man to throw up his cause for a first failure.
The libretto was chiefly to blame. The writers
had adhered too closely to Voltaire, without
remembering the requirements of the music, or
the established forms of 'Grand' opera. The
tragical conclusion especially was objected to
as an innovation. This was remedied first of
all, and a happy ending substituted. By Feb.
1820, Spontini was at work on the revision,
which he completed in less than a year, and
the opera was produced in its new form, May
14, 1821, at Berlin. In 1822 it was again
revised, the changes this time being in the airs
for Olympie and Cassandre, the duet for the
same in the first act, and a new scene with
terzetto in the third. As this last is not in-

cluded in the printed edition it looks as if the
final form of the opera had not even yet been
attained. Schlesinger of Berlin published a
complete pianoforte score in 1826.[3] The opera
was again put on the stage in Paris, Feb. 28,
1826, and by Mar. 15 it had already been
played six times.[4] Each time it pleased more,
and at last Spontini was able to count it among
his great triumphs. It was, however, only in
Berlin, where he settled in 1820, that it kept a
place in the repertory, though it has now completely disappeared from musical life.

'Olympie' stood alone at this period for
grandeur of conception. True, in isolated
scenes of the 'Huguenots' and the 'Prophète,'
Meyerbeer approached his predecessor, but
he never succeeded in creating so well-proportioned a whole. The unity of design is remarkable, each act seems to be cast in one mould ;
and this from the fact that musically the
several scenes of each act run into each other
in a much more marked manner than in
'Cortez' or the 'Vestale.' The principal
characters are well defined, and the tone
assigned to each at the start is skilfully maintained. But these qualities are accompanied
by defects, the lack of charm in the details
and of variety in the accompaniments; nor
is there plasticity of melody nor the power of
assigning the instrumental music its due share
in the dramatic development. In all these
respects he was far surpassed by Cherubini and
Weber, each in his own line.

Whilst Spontini was busy in Paris composing
'Olympie,' the way was being prepared for
the most important event in the second half
of his life—his summons to Berlin.[5] King
Frederick William III., during a visit of two
months to Paris (Mar. 31 to the beginning of
June 1814), heard Spontini's operas several
times, and was deeply impressed by them.
Not only was 'Cortez' at once put in rehearsal
at Berlin and produced Oct. 15, 1814, but the
King, on the return of peace, occupied himself
with various plans for improving the state of
music in Prussia, one of which was to give
fresh impulse to the court Opera by engaging
a conductor of acknowledged ability. For
this last post Spontini was the man fixed upon.
So far back as the autumn of 1814 proposals
had been made to him at Vienna, offering him
the then immense salary of 5000 thalers (£750)
on condition of his furnishing two operas a
year for Berlin. Spontini was inclined to
accept, but the plan did not meet with the
approval of the Intendant of the royal theatre
—Count Brühl, who had succeeded Iffland in
Feb. 1815. Brühl's opinion was entitled to
the more weight as there had scarcely ever

1 Letter of Brühl to Frederick William III., Oct. 8, 1819.
2 Letters from Spontini to Count Brühl, dated Dec. 22, 1815, and
Jan. 14, 1819.

3 A full score, in 3 vols., was published by Erard at Paris.
4 Marx's *Berliner A.M.Z.* for 1826, p. 104.
5 Papers belonging to the royal theatres of Berlin and the
Prussian Royal Family were consulted for the facts here related.
The details were discussed more fully by the writer in former
editions of the Dictionary.

been a theatrical manager in Germany who knew his business so well, and he was doubtful of Spontini's capabilities as a conductor. (See BERLIN, section OPERATIC HISTORY.)

It was not until 1819 that the contract was drawn up, signed by the King on Sept. 1, giving Spontini the titles of chief Kapellmeister, and general director of music, with an additional one of 'Superintendent-General of the Royal Music' to be borne abroad.

Although nominally subordinate to Brühl, Spontini was by this contract virtually made his colleague. Brühl's experienced eye, however, soon detected certain passages in the document admitting of two interpretations, and exposing the management to all the dangers of a divided authority. He could not help feeling mortified at the way he had been superseded in the business ; this would naturally make him mistrust Spontini, and thus the two came together under unfavourable auspices. The Opera was at this time, thanks to Brühl's exertions, in a high state of efficiency. The company was unusually good, and the band had been well trained by Bernhard Weber. Brühl took immense pains to secure finish in the performances, had added to the repertory all the great masterpieces, and had introduced 'Fidelio' and 'Armida,' besides establishing permanently in Berlin other operas of Gluck. He had also mounted the 'Vestale' and 'Cortez' with the utmost care and intelligence, and was entitled to boast that he had made the Berlin opera the first in Germany, as indeed every one allowed. Spontini found neither blemishes to remove nor reforms to introduce.

He started with the best intentions. Brühl was informed of various plans for increasing the orchestra, establishing a training-school for the chorus, and introducing new methods into the existing singing-school. He was considering the best means of educating the singers in the dramatic part of their art, and drew up a new set of rules for the band. Little, however, came of all this, partly because several of Spontini's proposals were already in existence in other forms, and partly because of his own want of purpose and temper. In fact, it soon came to a trial of strength between him and Brühl, leading to ill-concealed irritation on both sides.

During the preparations for the performance of 'Olympia,' Spontini had an opportunity of appearing before the court and public with a new composition. In the beginning of 1821 the Grand Duke Nicholas, heir-presumptive to the throne of Russia, and his consort, paid a visit to Berlin, and court festivities on a grand scale were instituted in their honour. Moore's *Lalla Rookh* was then much talked of, and Brühl conceived the idea of representing the principal scenes in a series of *tableaux vivants*. Schinkel undertook the scenery and arrangement of the groups, and Spontini composed the songs, introductory march, and dance-music.[1] The performance took place Jan. 27, 1821, at the Royal Palace, and was pronounced to be the most brilliant and quaintly beautiful thing of the kind ever seen.

The first performance of 'Olympia' was eagerly anticipated. Mar. 5, 1821, was first fixed, but it was postponed till May 14, a delay for which Spontini was to blame. The translator, E. A. Hoffmann, only got the last act from him bit by bit, the chorus-master had not seen a note of it by Feb. 18, nor had the ballet-master been consulted. Spontini insisted on at least three months' rehearsals. The expenditure on the *mise-en-scène* was so lavish that even the king remonstrated. The chorus and orchestra were materially strengthened, the scenery was by Schinkel and Gropius, and there were forty-two rehearsals. The result was one of the most brilliant and perfect performances ever seen, and an enormous success. Even Brühl was carried away, and Spontini's triumph was complete. Even his opponents acknowledged that 'Olympia' had no rival among modern operas.

Spontini's supremacy in the musical world lasted exactly five weeks, for on June 18, 1821, 'Der Freischütz' was produced at the newly erected theatre in Berlin. Its immediate success may not have more than equalled that of 'Olympia,' but it soon became evident that the chief effect of the latter was astonishment, while the former set the pulse of the German people beating. 'Olympia' remained almost restricted to the stage of Berlin, while 'Der Freischütz' spread with astonishing rapidity throughout Germany and the whole world. Spontini could not conceal that he had, on the morrow of a great triumph, been completely vanquished by an obscure opponent, and that, too, after consciously doing his very utmost. Even this might not have discouraged him, but that in 'Der Freischütz' he was brought face to face with a phase of the German character totally beyond his comprehension. He had no weapons wherewith to encounter this opponent. A man of weaker will would have contented himself with such success as might still be secured in Germany ; but Spontini could brook no rival, and finding that he could not outdo Weber's music, tried to suppress him by means wholly outside the circle of art. The success of 'Der Freischütz' did not improve his relations with Brühl, a personal friend of Weber, and a great admirer of his music.

From the first night of 'Der Freischütz' the public was divided into two parties. The national party, far the strongest in intellect and cultivation, rallied round Weber. The King and the court persistently supported Spontini, though even their help could not

[1] 'Lalla Rukh. A festival play with songs and dances, performed at the Royal Palace of Berlin, Jan. 27, 1821. Edited by Count Brühl and S. H. Spiker. Berlin, L. W. Wittich, 1822.'

make him master of the situation. The Censorship interfered to check the expression of public opinion against him, and his complaints of supposed slights were always attended to.[1] But his artistic star, which had shone with such lustre after the first night of ' Olympia,' was now slowly setting.

Whether Spontini had a specific talent for conducting cannot be determined, for as a rule he conducted only two operas besides his own —' Armida ' and ' Don Giovanni,' and these he knew thoroughly.[2] But if he never completely mastered the technicalities of the art, his manner of conducting recitatives especially being clumsy and undecided,[3] and was thus very slow in rehearsing a work, the same laborious accuracy which he showed in composing was carried into every detail of the performance. He never rested till each part was reproduced exactly as it existed in his own imagination, which itself had to be cleared by repeated experiments. His rehearsals not unfrequently lasted from 8 A.M. till 4 P.M., or from 5 P.M. till 11 at night. He only treated others, however, in the same way that he treated himself, for no trouble was too great for him to take in revising his work down to the smallest particulars. When the first night arrived, every member of the orchestra knew his work by heart, and Spontini might beat as he liked, all went like clockwork.[4] He insisted on the complete fusion of the vocal and instrumental, the dramatic and the musical elements, and demanded from the chorus, as well as the solo-singers, an entire absorption in their parts, and an intelligent rendering of each situation. His love for the grandiose and the awe-inspiring led him to employ all the resources of decoration, and what then seemed enormous masses of musicians, singers and dancers ; and also to employ the strongest accents and most startling contrasts. ' His *forte*,' says Dorn, ' was a hurricane, his *piano* a breath, his *crescendo* made every one open their eyes, his *diminuendo* induced a feeling of delicious languor, his *sforzando* was enough to wake the dead.'[5] His appearance at the head of his musicians was almost that of a general leading an army to victory. When he glided rapidly through the orchestra to his desk every member of the band was in position, and on the alert to begin. At such moments he looked an aristocrat to the backbone ; but also an autocrat who would insist on subjugating all other wills to his own. The pedantic side of his character also came out in many little traits—he could only conduct from a MS. score, and his desk must be of a certain peculiar construction. His baton was a

thick stick of ebony with a solid ivory ball at each end ; this he grasped in the middle with his whole fist, using it like a marshal's staff.[6]

By May 14, 1821, the ' Vestalin,' ' Cortez ' and ' Olympia ' had all been produced according to the composer's own ideas at the Berlin opera, where they long remained stock-pieces. But their frequent repetition was more to gratify the king than the public, and indeed the theatre had soon to be filled by a large issue of free admissions. A new opera of his was, however, still an exciting event, partly because of his own personality and position, partly because the public was sure of a splendid spectacle. He was bound to furnish two grand operas every three years ; ' Olympia ' counted as one, and by the end of 1821 he was thinking of the second, and chose the ' Feast of Roses,' from Moore's *Lalla Rookh*, influenced, no doubt, by the success of his earlier Festspiel, and the prospect, welcome to a slow worker, of using portions of his old material ; but the subject did not seem very congenial. The libretto was written by Herklots, librettist to the Opera. The first performance of ' Nurmahal ' took place May 27, 1822, in honour of the marriage of the Princess Alexandrina of Prussia, to whom the Emperor dedicated the PF. score (Schlesinger). This is not, as has often been said, merely a revised version of ' Lalla Rookh,' comparatively little of that music having been used in it.

The merits of the libretti of the ' Vestale,' ' Cortez ' and ' Olympia ' outweigh their defects. Not so, however, that of ' Nurmahal ' ; its plot and characters are alike insipid, and it is in fact a mere *pièce d'occasion*. The Oriental colouring, which must have been its attraction for Spontini, still forms its sole interest. But, inferior as it is to ' Oberon,' it gives a high idea of its author's dramatic instinct, when we consider the inability French and Italian composers as a rule showed in dealing with the fantastic and mythical.

On June 9, 1821, Spontini started for a seven months' leave. He went first to Dresden, and there met Weber. Weber was cordial and obliging, while Spontini, though polite in manner, took pains to make his rival feel the newness of his reputation as a composer.[7] By June 29 he was in Vienna trying to arrange a performance of ' Olympia ' for the following season ; but this did not take place. Thence he went to Italy, revisiting his birthplace ; and by September was in Paris at work on the revision of ' Olympie.' He also made some experiments on ' Milton,' telling Brühl (Jan. 12, 1823) that he would put it before him in three different forms. By the end of January he was back in Berlin, apparently anxious to keep on good terms with Brühl, though such good

1 Gubitz, *Erlebnisse*, vol. iii. p. 241. Berlin, 1869.
2 He conducted the 99th performance of ' Der Freischütz ' (Nov. 6, 1826), for the benefit of Weber's widow and children, which was much to his credit, considering his dislike to the piece.
3 Dorn, *Aus meinem Leben*, Part III. p. 3.
4 Blume on *Alcidor*, in the Theatre archives.
5 *Aus meinem Leben*, first collection, p. 127.

6 Richard Wagner, *Erinnerung an Spontini*; *Gesammelte Schriften*, vol. v. p. 116 (Leipzig, Fritzsche, 1872).
7 *C. M. von Weber*, by Max von Weber, ii. 433.

resolutions seldom lasted long. One of their many differences was on the subject of star-singers (*Gastspieler*). These Brühl wished to encourage, as a means of testing the artists, and their chance of popularity ; but Spontini disliked the system.

He had now been in office four years, and the stipulated two grand operas every three years, or smaller one each year, were only represented by a *scena* or two for ' Olympia,' and a couple of pieces for ' Nurmahal.' It was plain that he had undertaken a task wholly beyond his strength, owing to his pedantic manner of working. He thought (Aug. 2, 1823) of turning ' Milton ' into a grand opera with recitatives, choruses and ballets, but soon relinquished the idea, and by Oct. 17 was 'busy, night and day, with "Alcidor ".' The libretto was by Théauleon, who had formerly altered ' Cortez.' The first performance was on May 23, 1825, and the reception from Spontini's adherents was unmistakably hearty, many outsiders being dazzled by its new effects of scenery and music ; the national party, however, were louder than ever in their disapprobation.[1]

Another grand opera was due for the summer of 1826, and a week after the production of ' Alcidor ' Spontini asked Count Brühl whether a revised and lengthened version of ' Milton ' would do for the purpose. The Count thought the material too scanty, but the King (June 29) agreed to the proposal. Spontini, having obtained eleven months' leave, started for Paris, where he was present at a revival of ' Olympie ' on Feb. 28, 1826, returning immediately afterwards to Berlin. Nothing more was heard of ' Milton,' and during this year he furnished no work for the King's theatre. Ernst Raupach was now librettist to the Opera, and Spontini agreed with him on a subject from German mediæval history, which eventually became the opera ' Agnes von Hohenstaufen.' He set to work with the seriousness which was his main characteristic as an artist : read, studied, and did everything to imbue himself with the spirit of the epoch, one wholly foreign to anything he had before attempted.[2] The first act—long enough for a complete opera—was ready by 1827, and performed May 28. The whole three acts were finished in 1829, and produced June 12 for the marriage of Prince Wilhelm (afterwards the Emperor William I.). Spontini, dissatisfied with his work, had the libretto altered by Baron von Lichtenstein and other friends, and made more vital changes in the music than in almost any other of his grand operas. In this form it was revived Dec. 6, 1837.

It was the last opera which Spontini completed. Various new plans and schemes continued to occupy him, and some progress was made with a poem by his old friend Jouy, ' Les Athéniennes,' first offered him in 1819, and accepted in a revised form in 1822. In a review of the poem [3] written in 1830, Goethe implies that the music was complete, but at Spontini's death nothing was found but unimportant fragments.[4] An opera founded on English history occupied him longer. We have already mentioned the revision of his ' Milton.' His studies for this deepened his interest in the English history of the 17th century. In 1830 Raupach wrote a libretto for a grand opera, ' Milton,' which was bought by the committee of management for 30 Friedrichs d'or, and placed at Spontini's disposal.[5] The only portion of the smaller opera retained was the fine Hymn to the Sun. After completing the revision of 'Agnes von Hohenstaufen,' Spontini wrote to the Intendant (May 9, 1837) that he hoped in the winter of 1838 to produce ' Miltons Tod und Busse für Königsmord ' (Milton's death, and repentance for the King's execution). He spent the summer of 1838 in England, studying historical, national and local colouring for this ' historico-romantic ' opera. Raupach's poem, extended and revised by Dr. Sobernheim, had now assumed a political and religious tendency, so distasteful to the King as to make him prohibit the opera. Further alterations ensued, and it became ' Das verlorene Paradies ' (Paradise Lost). By May 1840 the score of part of the 1st, and two-thirds of the 2nd act was complete. Up to Mar. 1841 he certainly intended finishing it, but not a note of it has ever been heard.

Spontini's other compositions during his residence in Berlin are unimportant. A hymn for the coronation of the Emperor Nicholas of Russia, to words by Raupach, was performed at Berlin, Dec. 18, 1826, and May 9, 1827.[6] A cantata to Herklots' words, ' Gott segne den König,' had a great success at the Halle Musical Festival in Sept. 1829, which Spontini conducted so much to the general satisfaction as to procure him an honorary Doctor's degree from the University, and a gold medal inscribed *Liricae Tragoediae Principi Germania meritorum cultrix*. A ' Domine salvum fac regem,' *a* 12, with accompaniment of organs, trumpets, violoncelli and basses, was written on Oct. 15, 1840, for presentation to the King. Besides these he published a number of French, German and Italian vocal pieces, with PF. accompaniment, the best of which is ' Die Cimbern,' a war-song for three men's voices.[7]

Considering his great position, Spontini did

1 *Briefwechsel von Goethe und Zelter*, iv. 39, 40.
2 *Spontini in Deutschland*, p. 102 (Leipzig, Steinacker und Hartknoch, 1830)

3 Goethe's *Works*, Goedecke's edition, vol. xiii. p. 632, Cotta. Also *Spontini in Deutschland*, p. 22. Leipzig, 1830.
4 Robert's *Spontini*, p. 34. Berlin, 1883.
5 In *Spontini in Deutschland* this libretto is said to be by Jouy. I have not been able to ascertain whether it was Jouy's work revised by Raupach, or an original production.
6 Raupach had intended to have *tableaux vivants* to each five stanzas ; but this was not carried out.
7 Ledebur gives a tolerably complete catalogue of Spontini's smaller works ; see p. 570. Also Marx, in the *Berliner allg. mus. Zeitung* for 1826, p. 306.

not accomplish much for music in Berlin. His efforts as a rule were concentrated on the operas which he himself conducted; the pieces directed by his vice-conductors went badly, partly because Spontini exhausted the singers, and partly because he took little interest in the general repertory. He had, too, no power of organisation or administration. As long as the excellent material lasted which Brühl transferred to him in 1820 this defect was not glaring, but when his solo-singers began to wear out and had to be replaced, it was found that he had not the judgment, the penetration, nor the impartiality necessary for such business. The art of divining the taste of the public, of at once meeting it, elevating and moulding it— the art, in fact, of keeping the exchequer full without sacrificing artistic position—this was wholly out of his reach. At the King's theatre, the audiences steadily fell off, especially after the opening of the Königstadt theatre in 1823. In time even the admirers of his music felt that his personal influence was bad, and that the opera would never prosper as long as he remained at its head.

Spontini was to have the receipts of the first nights of his own operas for his annual benefit, or in default of such representations a sum of 4000 francs. In the latter case he might give a concert, and in fact he gave a considerable number, both vocal and instrumental. 'My concerts,' in his own words, 'are dedicated to the great masters, whose memory I strive to keep alive with the public, while testifying my own respect by performing their works in the most brilliant and complete manner possible.'[1] His programmes consisted principally of German music, Handel, Haydn, Mozart and Beethoven. The first performance in Berlin of Beethoven's symphony in A was at a concert of Spontini's on May 12, 1824, and on Apr. 30, 1828, he gave Beethoven's C minor symphony, the Kyrie and Gloria from his Mass in D, the overture to 'Coriolan,' and the Credo from Bach's B minor Mass. As Bach's Mass had only just been published by Nägeli of Zürich, Spontini was the first to introduce a portion of it to the public of Berlin, as he had been to acquaint them with Beethoven's masses.[2]

As we have already mentioned, Spontini's late operas had no success outside Berlin. Except a couple of stray performances of 'Olympia' at Dresden and Darmstadt, they did not even gain a hearing. Occasionally he conducted one of his own works, as for instance the 'Vestale' at Munich[3] (Oct. 7 and 11, 1827), and Hamburg[4] (Sept. 18, 1834). But such personal contact does not seem to have led to sympathetic relations. Speaking generally, the 'Vestale' and 'Cortez' were the only operas of his appreciated in Germany.

In Berlin itself, each year added to the number of his opponents. He was morbidly sensitive to public opinion, and, against the advice of judicious friends, he replied in person to anonymous attacks, suffered flatterers to use unpractised pens in his behalf, and even called in the Censorship. Such steps could but damage his cause.[5] His ten years' contract finished in 1830; it was renewed, on terms more favourable to the Intendant-General— Brühl had resigned in 1828, being succeeded by Count Redern—and this, with the fact of his ceasing to compose, gave an opportunity to his enemies.

On June 7, 1840, King Frederick William III. died, and Spontini's one mainstay was gone. Though obliged occasionally to express displeasure at his perpetual squabbles with the Intendant, the King had been steadfast in his attachment to Spontini and his music. The new King made no change in his position, but his sympathies were in a different direction, and no place was destined for Spontini in the grand designs he was elaborating. This soon became known. If Spontini could have kept himself quiet the change might have been delayed, but he was injudicious enough to lay before the King a paper complaining of the Management and of Count Redern. The King questioned the Intendant, and was satisfied with his explanations, but to obviate all appearance of partisanship he appointed a commission to inquire into Spontini's grievances. In the meantime the press had taken up the matter. A definite attack was made, to which Spontini was unwise enough to reply (Leipzig *Allgemeine Zeitung* of Jan. 20, 1841) in such a manner as to give Count Redern ground for an indictment for *lèse-majesté*, and (on Feb. 5) to a direct reprimand from the King.

But this treatment of the royal house by a foreigner who had enjoyed for years almost unexampled court favour immensely increased the public feeling against Spontini, and for two months he remained in private. On Apr. 2, however, in spite of repeated warnings, he took his seat to conduct 'Don Juan.' His appearance was the signal for a tremendous uproar, and cries of 'hinaus! hinaus!'—'off! off!' He stood firm, began the overture, and would have proceeded with the opera, but a rush was made to get at him on the stage, and he was forced to retire from the theatre. He never entered it again as conductor.

The trial kept Spontini in Berlin all the

1 Gubitz's *Erlebnisse*, iii. 242.
2 Marx, *Berliner allg. mus. Zeitung*, 1828, pp. 146 and 152.
3 Grandaur, *Chronik des königl. Theaters in München*, p. 106. Munich, 1878.
4 Schmidt's *Denkwürdigkeiten*. Edited by Uhde. Part ii. p. 314. Stuttgart, Cotta, 1878.

5 See Marx's *Musikzeitung*, Nos. 23-29, 1827; Dorn's *Über mein Verhältniss als Kritiker zu Herrn Spontini* (Leipzig, Whistling, 1827); *Spontini in Germany, an impartial consideration of his productions during his ten years' residence in that country* (Leipzig, 1830); under RELLSTAB, H. F. L., and *The Lament of Herr Ritter Gasparo Spontini . . . over the decline of dramatic music. Translated from the French, with explanatory remarks by a body of friends and admirers of the great master*. Leipzig, Michelsen, 1837.

summer, but he obtained leave from Aug. 31-
Dec. 10, and went to Paris. His connexion
with the opera was severed by the King on Aug.
25, on terms of royal generosity. He was to
retain his title and full salary, and live where he
pleased, ' in the hope that in repose he might
produce new works, which the King would hail
with pleasure if he chose to conduct them in
person at Berlin.' To these munificent arrangements no conditions whatever were attached.
Spontini was convicted of *lèse-majesté*, and
condemned to nine months' imprisonment, a
sentence confirmed by the higher court to which
he appealed, but remitted by the King. In
the face of all this he had the effrontery to
demand a further sum of 46,850 thalers, on
the ground that the Management had not supplied him with a sufficient number of libretti,
whereby he had lost the sum guaranteed him
for first nights, besides profits from other performances and from publishers—reckoned at
3000 thalers for each opera ! The King referred
him to the Law Courts, but Spontini's better
nature seems at length to have prevailed, and
he withdrew his application Dec. 23, 1841.
When he finally left Berlin in the summer of
1842, the King granted him a further sum of
6000 thalers. His friends gave him a farewell
concert on July 13, 1842, for which he wrote
both words and music of an ' Adieu à mes amis
de Berlin.' [1]

He left few friends behind him. He was, however, long and gratefully remembered by the
members of the King's band. The orchestra
were proud of their majestic conductor, who
so often led them to triumph, and who,
moreover, had a tender care for their personal
interests. The poorer members found his purse
ready of access, and in 1826 he established a
fund for them, called by special permission the
' Spontini-Fonds,' to which he devoted the
whole proceeds of his annual benefit concerts.
The fund speedily attained to considerable proportions, and still exists, though the name has
been changed.

Of his last years there is little to relate. On
leaving Berlin he went to Italy, and in Jan.
1843 was in Majolati. In that year he left
Italy and settled at Paris, where he had many
pleasant connexions through his wife, an Erard,
whom he had married soon after the production
of ' Cortez.' He had been a member of the
Institut since 1838. In 1844 the Pope made
him Count of S. Andrea, and other distinctions
followed. But the hope expressed by King
Frederick William IV. that he would produce
other works was not realised ; Berlin had
broken him down physically and mentally.
He revisited Germany two or three times. In
1844 he was in Dresden, where Richard Wagner
had prepared for him a performance of the
' Vestale,' which he conducted with all his old

[1] Robert, p. 52, etc.

energy.[2] He was invited to the Cologne Musical
Festival of May 1847 to conduct some excerpts
from ' Olympia,' and had a warm reception,
but was too infirm to conduct, and his place
was taken by Dorn, then Kapellmeister at
Cologne.[3] In August he visited Berlin, and
was most graciously received by the King, who
gave him an invitation to conduct some of his
own operas at Berlin during the ensuing winter.
He was much delighted, and thought a great
deal about the performances after his return
to Paris, and also of the best manner in which
he could express his gratitude and devotion to
the King ; but the project was never realised,
as he was ill all the winter. In 1848 he became
deaf, and his habitual gravity deepened into
depression. He went back to Italy, and settled
at Jesi, where he occupied himself in founding
schools and other works of public utility. In
1850 he removed to Majolati. Having no
children he left all his property to the poor of
Jesi and Majolati.   P. S., abridged.

SPONTONE (SPONTONI), BARTOLOMMEO, a
madrigal composer, a pupil of Nicola Mantovano, and maestro di cappella in the cathedral
of Verona. He published a first book of Masses,
a 5, 6 and 8, in 1588 ; a book of four-part
madrigals in 1558 ; and three sets of madrigals
for five voices at Venice in 1561 (2nd ed. 1583),
1567 and 1583. Others are contained in the collections of Waelrant (1594) and others. Cipriano
de Rore prints a Dialogo, *a* 7, by him in 1568.
A Mass, *a* 6, is in vol. ii. of Torchi's ' L' arte
musicale in Italia.'   G.

SPRING GARDEN, see VAUXHALL GAR-
DENS.

SQUARCIALUPI, ANTONIO (*d.* Florence,
c. 1475) (also called Antonio degl' organi), a
famous Florentine organist who lived in the
15th century, and who was living in Siena in
1450, and at the Florentine court in 1467, as
organist of Santa Maria. None of his compositions are extant, and he is only known as
an esteemed contemporary of Dufay. A letter
written by him to Dufay, dated 1467, is given by
Otto Kade in the *Monatshefte* for 1885, No. 2.
See also Haberl's ' Dufay ' in the *Vierteljahrsschrift*, i. 436. A volume of music by various
early composers, which was in Squarcialupi's
possession, is in the Bibl. Laurenziana in Florence, and is described in J. Wolf's *Geschichte
der Mensural-Notation*, pp. 228 ff. There is a
monument to his memory in the Duomo at
Florence. (*Q.-L.* ; *Riemann*.)   M.

SQUIRE, WILLIAM BARCLAY (*b.* London,
Oct. 16, 1855 ; *d.* there, Jan. 13, 1927), one of the
most distinguished musical scholars of his day,
was educated privately, at Frankfort, and at
Pembroke College, Cambridge, where he took
the B.A. degree in 1879, taking honours in the
History Tripos. He proceeded to the M.A.

[2] For a clever and amusing account of it see Wagner's *Gesammelte Schriften*, v. 114.
[3] Dorn's *Aus meinem Leben*, vol. iii. p. 21.

degree in 1902. While still an undergraduate he was asked by Sir George Grove to contribute to the first edition of this Dictionary an account of the music in the Fitzwilliam Museum. He was also a prominent member of the Cambridge University Musical Society. He became a solicitor in 1883, and practised until 1885, when he was appointed an assistant in the library of the British Museum, his special knowledge of music and of modern languages fitting him for the superintendence of the printed music. In this capacity he earned the gratitude of students by the unfailing generosity with which he placed his great knowledge at the disposal of those who genuinely desired to make researches among the treasures of the museum. After his retirement (1917) his connexion with the British Museum was maintained since he undertook the charge of the valuable Buckingham Palace collection of music placed there by King George V. and known as the Royal Music Library. Squire was engaged in arranging and cataloguing this collection up to the time of his death, and his catalogue of the Handel MSS. was then in the press.

For some years he acted as musical critic, writing in 1890–94 for the *Saturday Review*, in 1893 for the *Westminster Gazette*, for the *Globe* in 1894–1901, and for the *Pilot* in 1900–04. He also wrote the libretti of Stanford's 'Veiled Prophet' and Bridge's 'Callirhoë.' He was honorary secretary of the Purcell Society, and for several years was joint honorary secretary to the International Musik-Gesellschaft. For the three editions of this Dictionary, for the *Encyclopædia Britannica*, for the *Dictionary of National Biography*, and for *Archæologia* and other periodical publications, English and foreign, he wrote much that is of permanent value, as his sound knowledge of the art went hand in hand with minute historical accuracy. He was elected a fellow of the Society of Antiquaries in 1888. His *Catalogue of Accessions to the old Printed Music in the British Museum since 1886* appeared in 1899, a list of music in the Chapter Library of Westminster Abbey was printed as a Supplement to the *Monatshefte* for 1903, and a *Catalogue of the Printed Music in the Library of the Royal College of Music appeared in* 1909. (This library was arranged by him and was under his supervision.) He edited Purcell's harpsichord music for the Purcell Society, and prepared new editions of Byrd's masses and Palestrina's Stabat Mater; and he issued a valuable series of madrigals (see AUSGEWÄHLTE MADRIGALE) and several motets, etc. Squire collaborated with J. A. FULLER MAITLAND (*q.v.*) in the issue of the 'Fitzwilliam Virginal Book' and other publications. Apart from music, he edited a reprint of Robert Jones's *Muses Gardin for Delights* (words only, 1901), and worked with Helena, Countess of Radnor, in preparing the sumptuous *Catalogue of the Pictures in the Collection of the Earl of Radnor* (1909). During the war Squire did valuable work for the Foreign Office, and his handbook on Tunis, prepared there, was officially adopted by the French Government after the Versailles Conference.   C. L. G., addns.

SQUIRE, (1) WILLIAM HENRY (*b.* Ross, Aug. 8, 1871). His father was a clever amateur violinist, and the boy's first teacher. He gained a violoncello scholarship at the R.C.M. in 1883, which was extended for a further period of three years. He studied under Edward Howell, and made his début at a concert of Albeniz at St. James's Hall, Feb. 12, 1891. At the Crystal Palace he first appeared on Apr. 20, 1895, in Saint-Saëns's concerto in A. In the same year he held the place of principal violoncello at the Royal Opera, Covent Garden. He was elected an associate of the R.C.M. in 1889. He has written a concerto for his instrument, very numerous and successful works in a popular style, many songs, two operettas (unpublished), and has had a useful and prosperous career as a concert-player and in orchestras; he was a prominent member of the original Queen's Hall Orchestra, and for some time belonged to the London Symphony Orchestra.

His sister, (2) Mme. EMILY SQUIRE, a pupil of the R.C.M. and the R.A.M., became a successful soprano singer. She first appeared at Bath in 1888, and at the Crystal Palace in 1891.   M.

SRB-DEBRNOV, JOSEF (*b.* Prague, 1836; *d.* there, 1904). A Czech musical writer who was an intimate friend of SMETANA and Karel BENDL (*q.v.*) and played an active part in the musical life of Prague. He adopted the name of Debrnov as a pseudonym. For many years he undertook the business management of the choral society Hlahol (1864–65 and 1874–91). He wrote (in Czech): *The Science of Instrumentation* (1883); *A Short History of the Prague Conservatoire* (1877); *A History of Music in Bohemia and Moravia.*   Ř. N.

STAATSOPER, see BERLIN.

STABAT MATER. This mediæval poem, which has had a greater popularity than any similar composition, is of uncertain authorship. It is generally ascribed to Jacopone. It was not liturgical, and had originally no music of its own; but it came into popular use as a devotion in the 13th century; indulgences were granted to those who used it, and finally it crept into liturgical books and was provided with musical settings. It did not obtain its place in the Roman Missal as a Sequence till 1727, nor did a cento from it obtain a place as a hymn in the Breviary till even later. The musical history of the poem, therefore, is concerned with the polyphonic and later writers.   M.

The classical polyphonic settings are those of

JOSQUIN DES PRÉS (Vol. II. p. 792), PALESTRINA (Vol. IV. p. 28). Famous later examples are by ASTORGA, CLARI, STEFFANI, PERGOLESE, HAYDN. Outstanding examples of the 19th century and after are by ROSSINI, VERDI, DVOŘÁK, STANFORD (1907).   C.

STABILE, ANNIBALE (b. Padua), pupil of Palestrina, maestro di cappella at the Lateran, Rome, 1575 ; from 1576–90 at the German college ; in 1592 at S. Maria Maggiore, Rome ; and in 1604 Kapellmeister at the Polish court at Cracow. He composed 3 books of motets, 5-8 v., 3 books 5-part madrigals, and 4-part litanies, and single numbers in various collective volumes (Q.-L. ; Riemann).

STABILINI, GIROLAMO (HIERONYMO) (b. Rome, c. 1762 ; d. Edinburgh, July 13, 1815), violinist. Having attained some distinction in Italy he was invited to Edinburgh, to replace Giuseppe Puppo, as leader of the St. Cecilia Hall concerts.

Stabilini arrived at Edinburgh in 1783, and died of dropsy there, being buried in the graveyard of St. Cuthbert's or the 'West Kirk.' His tombstone is still to be seen built into an old boundary wall. Stabilini, though he does not appear to have been of very extraordinary talent, was eminently popular in Scotland, a popularity heightened by his performance and arrangement of Scots airs ; 'I'll gang na mair to yon toon' being especially associated with him.

There is a head of him in Kay's Edinburgh Portraits.   F. K.

STACCATO (Ital.) (Fr. détaché) = 'detached,' a word used in all languages to mean the shortening of notes in a phrase so as to separate each from each.

The staccato style is indicated either by pointed dashes (׳׳) or round dots (· ·). The distinction between them, not very strictly preserved in practice, is discussed under DASH (q.v.). The staccato, unlike its opposite the legato, is susceptible of degree, and its effect varies very much according to the amount of accent with which it is allied. Pianists therefore recognise different types of staccato according to the technical method by which the effect is obtained, e.g. from the fingers, the wrist or the forearm. The staccato varies even more widely on bowed strings according as it is obtained from the point, the middle or close to the nut of the bow, or by means of a springing bow (see SPICCATO and SAUTILLÉ). Notation gives no accurate indication of these different types, but it recognises the mezzo staccato (half-detached) in the use of dots combined with a slur, indicating that while the notes are to be separated their relation to one another as parts of the same phrase is to be carefully observed. In the mezzo staccato the separation must be no more than a slight check in the tone.

The term staccato is occasionally used as a general direction at the beginning of a movement or passage.   C.

STADEN, (1) JOHANN (b. Nuremberg, 1581[1]; d. there, Nov. 15, 1634). From 1603 to about 1616 he was in the service of the Margrave Christian Ernst of Kulmbach and Bayreuth as court organist. In 1616 he returned to Nuremberg, where he received the appointment of organist, first to the St. Lorenz - Kirche, and shortly afterwards to the more important St. Sebald-Kirche, in which latter post he remained till his death.

Staden occupies a place of some importance in the transition period of musical history at the beginning of the 17th century, when German musicianship was endeavouring to combine with the older style of pure vocal music the advantages of the newer style of instrumental accompaniment with its greater freedom of harmonic modulation. Staden, however, was on the whole more conservative and less enthusiastically progressive than his contemporaries Michael Praetorius and J. H. Schein, not to mention Heinrich Schütz. His publications were fairly numerous, though all are not preserved complete. There are six of church works proper, partly with Latin, partly with German texts, entitled respectively, 'Harmoniae sacrae pro festis praecipuis' 4-8 voc., 1616 ; 'Harmoniarum sacrarum continuatio' 1-12 voc., 1621 ; 'Kirchenmusik,' 1 Theil mit 2-14 St., 1625 ; 'Kirchenmusik,' 2 Theil zu 1-7 St. mit Violen und anderen Inst., 1626 ; 'Harmoniae novae' 3-12 voc., 1628 ; 'Harmoniae variatae,' 1-12 voc., 1623. In these works three styles of church music are represented : the pure vocal motet, in which basso continuo is not required ; the motet with only basso continuo ; and the sacred concerto with obbligato accompaniment and instrumental preludes and interludes denominated respectively symphonies and ritornelli.

Another series of Staden's publications consists of sacred music on German texts intended more for private or domestic performance, a kind of music which would seem to have been much in vogue among the Nuremberg citizens of those days. His chief publication of the sort is expressly entitled 'Hausmusik,' which originally appeared in four separate parts in 1623–28, and afterwards in a complete edition in 1646. This work contains 118 mostly short and comparatively simple pieces a 3-4 for voices, or instruments ad libitum, in a few cases instruments obbligati. Another work of the same kind, a little more elaborate, is entitled 'Musicalischer Freuden- u. Andachtswecker oder geistliche Gesänglein' zu 4-6 St., 1630. Other works belonging to the same class entitled 'Hertzentrosts-Musica,' 1630, and 'Geistlicher Music-Klang,' 1633, contain mostly Lieder for one voice only with continuo accompaniment for organ, lute, or theorbo. Several of Staden's Lieder found their way into later Choral-books. Another department of Staden's activity as a composer consists of secular songs and instrumental dances. Three collections of secular songs *a* 4-5 with an appendix of instrumental dances appeared 1606, 1609 and 1610. Two other collections of dances alone, Pavanes, Galliardas, Courantes, etc., appeared 1618 and 1625. A comprehensive collection of instrumental works by Staden was published posthumously in 1643, containing not only dances, but pieces described as sonatas, symphonies and canzonas. Staden would appear to have been incited to the composition of these instrumental works by his official connexion for a time with the Stadtpfeifer or town musicians of Nuremberg. It only remains to add, *D.D.T.* (second series), VII. i. and VIII. i., contains a selection of Staden's vocal works, including ten Latin motets *a* 4-8 and twenty-five German pieces *a* 3-8, with a full biographical and critical introduction.

(2) SIGMUND GOTTLIEB (or THEOPHIL) (*b.* 1607; *d.* Nuremberg, July 30, 1655), son of Johann. At the age of 13 he was sent by the town authorities of Nuremberg, at the request of his father, to receive further musical instruction from Jacob Baumann, organist and Stadtpfeifer' or town musician of Augsburg. This might seem strange, considering that Johann Staden was himself a more distinguished musician than Baumann, but Baumann appears to have had during his lifetime a greater reputation as an instrumentalist. Later on, in 1626, Sigmund was again sent at the expense of the Nuremberg authorities to Berlin to receive instruction in the playing of the viola bastarda, a form of the gamba, from one Walter Rowe or Roy, an English instrumentalist in the service of the Elector of Brandenburg. In 1627 Staden received an appointment as one of the 'Stadtpfeifer' or town musicians of Nuremberg. On the death of his father, he became organist to the St. Lorenz-Kirche in succession to Valentin Dretzel, who took the elder Staden's place as organist to the St. Sebald-Kirche. Whether Staden received any further promotion is unknown. He is now chiefly known as the composer of the first German operatic work that was ever published, an allegorical SING-SPIEL (*q.v.*), the full title of which is :

' Das geistliche Waldgedicht oder Freudenspiel genannt Seelewig. Gesangweis auf italianische Art gesetzet, 1644.'

The work is an interesting example of the early monodic style for solo voices with accompaniment of figured bass, but having also short instrumental preludes and interludes, sometimes for viols or violins only, sometimes for three flutes, at other times for two or three ' schalmeien ' or oboes. It has been republished by Eitner in modern form with the harmonies of the figured bass written out. The text is by G. P. Harsdörffer, one of the founders of the Pegnitzschäferei Gesellschaft in Nuremberg, who brought from Italy to Nuremberg the peculiar taste for artificial pastoralism in poetry, and for the Florentine monodic style of music in association with allegorical and spiritual dramas. Other poetical texts by Harsdörffer were set by Staden as simple Lieder for one voice with figured bass. He did not, however, forsake altogether the older style of choral music. In 1637 he put forth a new edition of Hans Leo Hassler's ' Kirchengesänge mit vier stimmen simpliciter gesetzt ' (1608), in which he included eleven new Choral-tunes and settings by his father, and five by himself. He also followed in the wake of his father in the encouragement of domestic sacred music, by publishing, in 1644, two collections entitled ' Seelenmusik,' with settings of hymns *a* 4 with basso continuo, and furnishing new melodies to the various Gesangbücher of the time. *Q.-L.* mentions an Instruction-Book for singing by him, 1648.

J. R. M.

STADLER, MAXIMILIAN, ABBOT (*b.* Melk, Lower Austria, Aug. 4,[1] 1748; *d.* Vienna, Nov. 8, 1833), a sound and solid composer. At 10 he became a chorister in the monastery of Lilienfeld, where he learnt music, completing his education in the Jesuit College at Vienna. In 1766 he joined the Benedictines at Melk, and after taking priest's orders worked as a parish priest and professor till 1786, when the Emperor Joseph, who had noticed his organ-playing, made him abbot first of Lilienfeld, and three years later of Kremsmünster. Here his prudence averted the suppression of that then famous astronomical observatory. After this he lived at various country-houses, then privately at Linz, and finally settled in Vienna. Between 1803 and 1816 he was parish priest at Alt-Lerchenfeld and afterwards in Bohemia. Haydn and Mozart had been old friends of his, and at the request of the widow he put Mozart's musical remains in order, and copied from the autograph score of the Requiem, the Requiem and Kyrie, and the Dies irae, both copy and original being now in the Hofbibliothek at Vienna. (See Vol. III. p. 566.) He also came forward in defence of the Requiem against Gottfried Weber, in two pamphlets—*Vertheidigung der Echtheit des Mozart'schen Requiem* (Vienna, 1825–26), and *Nachtrag zur Vertheidigung*, etc. (*ib.* 1827). Stadler was an excellent contrapuntist, and an authority in musical literature and history. His printed compositions include sonatas and fugues for PF. and organ ; partsongs ; two Requiems ; several masses ; a Te Deum ; ' Die Frühlingsfeier,' cantata, with orchestra, to Klopstock's words ; psalms, Misereres, responses, offertoriums, etc.; also a response to Haydn's farewell-card for two

[1] *Riemann* gives Aug. 7.

voices and PF. (See Vol. II. p. 579.) Among his numerous MSS. are fine choruses for Collin's tragedy, 'Polyxena.' Stadler's greatest work, 'Die Befreiung von Jerusalem,' an oratorio in two parts, words by Heinrich and Matthäus von Collin, was given with great success in 1816 at the annual extra concert of the Gesellschaft der Musikfreunde, for the benefit of the proposed Conservatorium, and in 1829 at Zürich. (For list of works see *Q.-L.*) C. F. P.

STADLMAYR, JOHANN (*b.* Freising, Bavaria; *d.* Innsbruck, July 12, 1648). Fétis dates his birth 1560,[1] but in the absence of precise documentary evidence Eitner, in *Q.-L.*, considers this far too early, as the works published by the composer himself only begin in 1603 and continue to 1645. On the basis of the indications furnished by the title-pages and dedications of his works, Eitner gives the appointments which he held, as stated below. In 1603 Stadlmayr subscribes himself as a musician in the service of the Archbishop of Salzburg. In 1610 he was Kapellmeister to the Archduke Maximilian of Austria probably at Innsbruck. In 1625 he acts in the same capacity to the Archduke Leopold at Innsbruck, and from 1636 he subscribes himself as music-director to the Archduchess Claudia at Innsbruck. He is described, at the time of his death, as having been hof-Kapellmeister. Stadlmayr's works are all for the services of the Roman Church, but show the gradual supersession of the earlier pure vocal style of church music by the modern style of instrumental accompaniment. There is, first, the regular employment of basso continuo, followed by the substitution *ad libitum* of an instrumental choir, *a* 4 or 8 as the case may be, for one or other of the vocal choirs, and the culminating point is reached in the definite specification of instruments which are now written for in a definitely instrumental style. The dates and titles, somewhat abbreviated, of Stadlmayr's chief publications as given below, will serve to confirm what we have said :

1603. Magnificat *a* 5-8, 10 n. (No mention of basso continuo in the title of this or the work following.)
1608. Magnificat *a* 4-8, 13 n.
1610. Missae 8 voc., cum duplici basso ad organum. 5 n.
1614. Magnificat. Symphoniae variae secundum varios modos musicos, aliae octonis, una 12 voc., cum Bc.
1616. Missae 12 voc., cum triplici Bc.
1618. Cantici Mariani septies variati cum 12 voc. c. triplici bass. org.
1625. Musica super cantum gregorianum. Pars 1. Missarum dominicalium introitus . . . 52 n. Pars 11 Festorum introitus. 50 n. 5 voc. c. Bc. *ad libitum.*
1628. Hymni totius anni . . *a* 4, quibus et alii pro festis solemnioribus cum symphoniis *a* 4-8, accesserunt in quibus pro ratione variari possunt instrumenta musica cum basso continuo.
1631. Missae concertatae *a* 6 adjuncto choro secundo sive ripieni.
1638. Odae sacrae . . . *a* 5 v., et totidem instr.
1640. Salmi *a* 2 et 3 v. c. 2 v. o cornetti.
1641. Psalmi integri *a* 4 voc. concertantibus, quatuor aliis accessoriis ad lib. accinendis cum 2 cornet, sive violin.
1642. Missae concertatae *a* 10-12 et instrum., cum 4 partibus pro secundo choro.
1643. Missae ix voc. primo choro concert. *a* 5 voc. Secundo pleno cum symphoniis.
1646. Apparatus musicus sacrarum cantorium 6-24 vocib. et instr.

Of all these works, the only one which has as yet appeared in a modern reprint is the Hymni *a* 4, 1628, edited by J. E. Haberl for the *D.T.Ö.*,

III. i. But Haberl has only given the simple Hymns *a* 4, without accompaniment. It might have been more interesting, historically, if he had also given the Hymns with instrumental accompaniment and ritornelli. J. R. M.

STÄNDCHEN (Ger.), 'Serenade.'

STAFF, see STAVE.

STAFFORD, WILLIAM COOKE (*b.* York, 1793; *d.* Norwich, Dec. 23, 1876 [2]), published at Edinburgh in 1830 a 12mo volume entitled *A History of Music*, a work chiefly noted for its inaccuracy, but which notwithstanding was translated into French (12mo, Paris, 1832) and German (8vo, Weimar, 1835). W. H. H.

STAGGINS, NICHOLAS (*d.* 1705), was taught music by his father, a musician of little standing. Although of slender ability he won the favour of Charles II., who, in 1674,[3] appointed him Master of the King's Band of Musick ; and in the same year the University of Cambridge, upon the King's request, conferred upon him the degree of Mus.D. The performance of the customary exercise being dispensed with, great dissatisfaction was occasioned, to allay which Staggins, in July 1684, performed an exercise, whereupon he was appointed professor of music in the University, being the first who held that office. Staggins composed the Odes for William III.'s birthday in 1693 and 1694, and for Queen Anne's birthday, 1705. In 1693 he was allowed £200 per annum as Master of the Musick (Calendar of Treasury Papers). In 1697 he gave a concert of his own music in York-buildings, London ; in the following year Eccles succeeded him as Master of the King's Musick. Songs by him are contained in 'Choice Ayres, Songs and Dialogues,' 1675, and other collections of the time ; and a dialogue, 'How unhappy a lover am I,' composed for Dryden's 'Conquest of Granada,' Part II., is included in J. S. Smith's 'Musica Antiqua.'

W. H. H. ; addns. W. H. G. F. and *Q.-L.*

STAHLSPIEL (Ger. *Stahl*, 'steel,' and *Spiel* 'play'). (1) An instrument consisting of a series of accurately-tuned steel bars loosely fastened to a frame and generally played by means of two small hammers—one in each hand of the performer—but sometimes constructed so as to be played from a keyboard. It is used in military music and known by the name Lyra, the steel bars being arranged on a lyre-shaped frame. For orchestral use the bars are arranged in two rows, in the exact relative positions of the white and black keys of the pianoforte. The compass is from two to two and a half octaves, and the tone is incisive and penetrating ; but although the instrument is susceptible of very charming effects it should be sparingly used. It is very frequently written for under the names GLOCKEN-SPIEL and CARILLON, so much so that in modern use the three names are alternatives for one and

[1] *Riemann* accepts 1560.
[2] *Brit. Mus. Biog.*
[3] Date given by W. H. G. F., who adds that he was appointed musician for the violin, Dec. 21, 1671.

the same thing. Originally the two latter were applied to an instrument consisting of a series of small *bells*; but steel bars have been found to be more convenient, more easily manipulated, better in tone—being free from the dissonant overtones so particularly prominent in *small* bells—and capable of the most accurate tuning. Excellent examples of the effective treatment of the instrument will be found in the works of Wagner ('Walküre' and 'Meistersinger '), Tchaikovsky, Strauss, Elgar, Parry, Mackenzie, Cowen, etc.

(2) An organ stop consisting of a series of steel bars played from the manuals and generally extending from middle C upwards, but rarely exceeding three octaves in compass.   w. w. s.

STAINER, (1) JACOB (*b.* Absam, near Hall, Austria, July 14, 1621 ; *d.* 1683), a celebrated German violin-maker. According to one story, the boy had a love of music, which induced the parish priest to send him to an organ-builder at Innsbruck. This trade, however, he found too laborious. He therefore took to making stringed instruments, serving his apprenticeship to an Innsbruck 'Lautenmacher '; after which he proceeded to travel, working, according to tradition, at Cremona, under Antonio or Nicolo Amati, and visiting other places in Italy, including Venice, where he wrought in the shop of Vimercati. Of all this, however, there is not a particle of evidence. It may be said that violins are in existence, signed by Stainer and dated from Cremona ; but these are now believed to be spurious. He began at a very early age, if we may trust an apparently genuine label dated 1641. He married in 1645 Margaret Holzhammer, by whom he had eight daughters, and one son who died in infancy. Henceforward, to his death in 1683, the life of Stainer shows little variety. He made a great number of stringed instruments of all sorts, which he chiefly sold at the markets and fairs of the neighbouring town of Hall. The forests of ' Haselfichte ' (see KLOTZ), which clothe the slopes of the Lafatsch and the Gleirsch, supplied him with the finest material in the world for his purpose. In 1648 the Archduke Ferdinand Charles became his patron. Ten years later he received by diploma the title of Hofgeigenmacher to the Archduke. In 1669, having fallen under a suspicion of Lutheranism, he was imprisoned and forced to recant. He was still at work in 1677, in which year he made two fine instruments for the monastery of St. Georgenburg. Soon after this date he ceased from his labours. In his latter years Stainer became of unsound mind, in which condition he died in 1683.

Stainer's place in the history of German fiddle-making is strongly marked. He was the first to introduce into Germany those Italian principles of construction which are the secret of sonority, but his originality cannot be

precisely determined. Some trace his model to the early Tyrolese viol-makers, others say the peculiarities of the Stainer violins are strictly original. As a mere workman Stainer is entitled to the highest rank. He made an immense number of instruments, some more, and others less, finely finished, but all substantially of the same model : the main design of which bears a rough resemblance to that of the Amati. Stainer's best instruments have written labels : some of the common ones have in very small Roman letterpress in the middle of a large slip of paper, ' Jacobus Stainer in Absom prope Oenipontum Anno (1678).' It is not impossible that some of these may have been made by other hands under his direction.

E. J. P., abridged.

BIBL.—RÜF, *Der Geigenmacher Jacobus Stainer von Absam in Tirol*, Innsbruck, 1872 ; F. OKA, *J. Stainer der erste deutsche Meister in Geigenbau* published in the *Neue Berliner Musikzeitung*, Nos. 22, 23, 31, May 7, June 1854 ; OTTO, *A Treatise on the Structure and Preservation of the Violin* (first edition, German, 1817 ; three English editions translated by John Bishop) ; STOEVING, *Von der Violine* ; WASIELEWSKI, *Die Violine* ; VON LUTGENDORFF, *Die Geigen- und Lautenmacher* ; HAWKINS, *History of Music* ; VIDAL, *Les Instruments à archet* ; GRILLET, *Les Ancêtres du violon* ; PEARCE, *Violins and Violin-Making* ; READE, *A Lost Art Revived* ; RACSTER, *Chats on Violins* (containing an English translation of Von Gilm's poem) ; HILL, *Violins and their Makers* (two pictures of Stainer's house) ; HERON-ALLEN, *A Pilgrimage to the House of Jacob Stainer* (*Mus. T.* Aug. 1900).   E. H.-A.

(2) MARCUS, brother of Jacob, from whom he learned his trade, set up for himself at the village of Laufen. The famous Florentine player Veracini had two violins by this maker, christened ' St. Peter ' and ' St. Paul,' and he reckoned them superior to all Italian violins. In sailing from London to Leghorn in 1746 Veracini was shipwrecked and the fiddles were lost. The instruments of this maker are extremely rare. They are made of unusually fine material, of somewhat large size, covered with dark varnish, and are sweet though decidedly feeble in tone. Like those of Jacob Stainer, they usually contain written labels. One of these runs thus : ' Marcus Stainer, Bürger und Geigenmacher in Küfstein, anno 1659.' Occasionally Marcus Stainer yielded to an obvious temptation, and sold his violins under the name of his more famous brother.

E. J. P.

STAINER, SIR JOHN, Mus.D. (*b.* London, June 6, 1840 ; *d.* Verona, Mar. 31, 1901), son of a schoolmaster, entered the choir of St. Paul's Cathedral in 1847—by which time he was already a remarkable player and an excellent sight-singer—and remained there till 1856, very often taking the organ on occasion. In 1854 he was appointed organist and choirmaster of St. Benedict and St. Peter, Paul's Wharf, of which the Rev. J. H. Coward, classical master to the choristers, was rector. At the same time he learnt harmony from Bayley, master of the St. Paul's boys, and counterpoint from Dr. Steggall, for whom he sang the soprano part in his Mus.D. exercise at Cambridge in 1852. Through the liberality of Miss Hackett (see CHORISTER) he received a course of lessons on the organ from George Cooper at St. Sepulchre's. In 1856 he was selected by Sir F. Ouseley as organist of his then newly founded College at Tenbury, where he remained for some time. In 1859 he matriculated at Christ Church, Oxford, and took the degree of Mus.B. Shortly after, he left Tenbury for Magdalen College, Oxford, where, after six months' trial, he was appointed organist and *informator choristarum*. He then entered St. Edmund Hall as a resident undergraduate, and while discharging his duties at Magdalen, worked for his B.A. degree in Arts, which he took in Trinity Term 1863. Meantime, on the death of Stephen Elvey, he had been appointed organist of the University of Oxford, and was conductor of a flourishing College Musical Society and of another association at Exeter College. At Magdalen he raised the choir to a very high state of efficiency. In 1865 he proceeded to his Mus.D. degree, and 1866 to his M.A., and became one of the examiners for musical degrees. In 1872 he left Oxford and succeeded Goss as organist of St. Paul's Cathedral. The services were at that time by no means what they should have been ; but Stainer possessed the confidence of the Dean and Chapter, and his hard work, knowledge and tact at last brought them to a worthier pitch of excellence.

Stainer did not confine his activity to his own University. He was a member of the Board of Musical Studies at Cambridge, and for two years was also examiner for the degree of Mus.D. there. He was examiner for musical degrees in the University of London ; an Hon. Member of the R.A.M. and Hon. Fellow of the Tonic Sol-fa College ; President of the College of Organists and of the Musical Association, of which he was virtually the founder. He was a juror at the Paris Exhibition of 1880, and at its close was decorated with the Legion of Honour. He was attached to the NATIONAL TRAINING SCHOOL FOR MUSIC (*q.v.*) as a professor of organ and harmony, from its foundation, and at Easter 1881 succeeded Sullivan as principal. In 1882 he succeeded Hullah as inspector of music in the elementary schools of England for the Privy Council. He was also a member of Council of the R.C.M. In 1888 he was obliged to resign his post at St. Paul's owing to his failing sight. In the same year he received the honour of knighthood. He was appointed professor of music in the University of Oxford in 1889, and was master of the Company of Musicians in 1900. He was buried at Holywell Cemetery, Oxford, Apr. 6, 1901.[1]

His compositions embrace an oratorio, 'Gideon' ; a cantata, 'The Daughter of Jairus,' composed by request for the Worcester Festival of September 1878 ; a cantata, ' St. Mary Magdalen ' (Gloucester Festival, 1883) ; and an oratorio, ' The Crucifixion '—his most

[1] See *Mus. T.*, 1901, p 297, etc.

popular work—1887. He also wrote many services and anthems, and among his most successful pieces of church music must be named the well-known ' Sevenfold Amen.' He was the author of the two very useful manuals of *Harmony* and *The Organ* in Novello's series, and of a work on Bible music, and was part editor with W. A. Barrett, of a *Dictionary of Musical Terms* (see DICTIONARIES OF MUSIC). He also edited the interesting *Dufay and his Contemporaries*, 1898. His son, J. F. R. Stainer, and daughter, Miss Cecilia Stainer, collaborated with him in that production. Both, like their father, have done valuable research work and have been contributors to this Dictionary.

Sir J. Stainer was beloved and esteemed by all who knew him, and was an admirable and efficient musician in all branches ; but his great excellence was in his organ-playing, and especially his accompaniments, which were unsurpassed. He was a shining example of the excellent foundation of sound musical knowledge which may be got out of the various duties and shifts of the life of a clever chorister in one of our cathedrals. G., addnc.

STAMATY, CAMILLE MARIE (*b.* Rome, Mar. 23, 1811; *d.* Paris, Apr. 19, 1870), son of a Greek father and a very musical French mother. After the death of his father in 1818 his mother returned to France, remained some time at Dijon, and finally went to Paris. There, after long coquetting between music and business as a profession, Stamaty, in 1828, took an employee's post in the Prefecture of the Seine. But music retained its influence on him, and under Fessy and Kalkbrenner he became a remarkable player. An attack of rheumatism forced him from playing to the study of composition. In Mar. 1835 he made his first public appearance in a concert, the programme of which contained a concerto and other pieces of his composition. This led to his being much sought after as a teacher. But he was not satisfied, and in Sept. 1836 went to Leipzig, attracted, doubtless, by the fame of Mendelssohn and Schumann, then both resident there. After a short course of instruction from Mendelssohn, he returned to Paris early in 1837, and introduced much more classical music—Bach Mozart, Beethoven, etc.—into his programmes. In 1846 he lost his mother, in 1848 he married, and in 1862 was made Chevalier of the Legion of Honour. From a crowd of pupils it is sufficient to name Gottschalk and Saint-Saëns. His most permanent works are educational— ' Le Rhythme des doigts,' much praised ; ' Études progressives ' (opp. 37-39) ; ' Études concertantes ' (opp. 46, 47) ; ' Esquisse ' (op. 19) ; ' Études pittoresques ' (op. 21) ; ' Six études caractéristiques sur Obéron,' and 12 transcriptions entitled ' Souvenir du Conservatoire.'

Besides these, his solo sonatas in F minor and

C minor ; a PF. trio, op. 12 ; a concerto in A minor, op. 2 ; sonatas, opp. 8 and 14 ; and other works, were much esteemed at the time. The concerto and some brilliant variations on an original theme (op. 3) were reviewed very favourably by Schumann (*Ges. Schriften*, ii. 155, 181).   G.

STAMITZ (STEINMETZ), a Bohemian musical family of much renown in the 18th century. (1) JOHANN WENZL ANTON [1] (*b.* June 19, 1717 ; *d.* Mannheim, Mar. 30,[2] 1757), son of the schoolmaster at Deutschbrod ; a man evidently of great originality and force. In 1742 he took part as a solo violinist in the festivities at the coronation of the Emperor Carl VII., and shortly afterwards was taken to Mannheim by the Elector, who in 1745 appointed him his leading violin and director of chamber-music ; he remained there till his death. He wrote much music for the violin, which shows him to have been a great and brilliant player. Six concertos, 3 sets of 6 sonatas, and some solo exercises, giving the effect of duets, were published at Paris, and 21 concertos and 9 soli are still in MS. He also wrote symphonies, of which several sets of 6 were published, as well as concertos and sonatas for the harpsichord. The thematic catalogue of 45 symphonies and 10 orchestral trios is given in *D.D.T.* (second series) III. i., which contains four of the symphonies and a trio. The introduction by Hugo Riemann is the most detailed account of the family that has yet appeared. Other works of Johann Stamitz are to be found in VII. i., XV. and XVI. of that publication, and recent criticism has assigned a place of first-rate importance to him as a pioneer of symphonic design (see SYMPHONY). The music shows a great advance in effect and expression on anything that preceded it.

(2) His brother, ANTON THADDÆUS (*b.* 1721 ; *d.* Allbunzlau, Aug. 23, 1768), was a violoncello-player ; according to Gerber, he was also in the Mannheim band. He became a priest, and rose to many dignities. Another brother, Joseph, was distinguished as a painter. Cannabich was one of Johann's pupils ; but a still more memorable one was his eldest son, (3) CARL (*b.* Mannheim, May 7, 1746 ; *d.* Jena, 1801) ; like his father, a remarkable violinist and composer. He was a second violin in the Mannheim band in 1762–70. In 1770 he went to Paris, and was known there as a player of the viola and viola d' amore. He played in London in 1778. His opera, ' Der verliebte Vormund,' was given at Frankfort. In 1785 he returned to Germany, and in 1787 we find him at Prague and Nuremberg, in 1790 at

Cassel, and then at St. Petersburg, where he remained for some years, and where he brought out a grand opera, ' Dardanus.'

His works include 70 symphonies, many published in opp. 1, 2, 3, 4, 6, 9, 13, 15, 16, 18, 19 and 24 ; others are in MS. They are mostly for a larger orchestra than that employed by his father ; some have two ' concertante ' violin parts ; there are also many concertos, quartets, trios, etc. (see the summary in Riemann's preface to *D.D.T.* III. i.). Another son of Johann was (4) ANTON (*b.* Mannheim, Nov.[3] 1754 ; *d. circa* 1820). He went to Paris with Carl, and published 13 symphonies, 3 piano concertos, a violin concerto, a violoncello concerto, and many quartets, trios, and duets. The family had a great influence on the development of the symphonic form ; the father raised the band to a pitch of superlative excellence, and Carl's experiments in orchestration pointed the way for later men.   G., addns.

BIBL.—Riemann's Preface to *D.D.T.* (second series) III. i. R. SONDHEIMER, *Die formale Entwicklung der vorklassichen Sinfonie* (*A.M.* Jan. 1922) ; *Riemann* and *Q.-L.*

STANDISH, (1) FREDERIC, a 16th- or 17th-century composer. A MS. anthem of his is in Ely Cathedral. The following were all organists at Peterborough Cathedral : (2) DAVID (1661–76) ; (3) WILLIAM (1677–90) ; (4) ROGER (1690–1713) (*Q.-L.*).

STANFORD, SIR CHARLES VILLIERS, Mus.D., D.C.L., LL.D. (*b.* Dublin, Sept. 30, 1852 ; *d.* London, Mar. 29, 1924), was distinguished both as composer and conductor, and was eminent as a teacher of composition.

His father, an enthusiastic amateur vocalist, was Examiner in the Court of Chancery in Dublin.[4] His first teachers were Arthur O'Leary and Sir Robert Stewart, and various efforts in songs, piano pieces, etc., were published while he was yet a child. His first composition is stated to have been a march composed in 1860, and played in the pantomime ' Puss in Boots,' at the Theatre Royal, Dublin, 1863–64.[5] He matriculated at Queens' College, Cambridge, in 1870, as choral scholar. On his appointment in 1873 to the important post of organist to Trinity College, in succession to Dr. J. L. Hopkins, Stanford ' migrated ' as an undergraduate to that college, from which he graduated in 1874 in Classical Honours. He had filled the post of conductor of the Cambridge Amateur Vocal Guild for a year or two before this, and had brought Sir R. Stewart's cantata, ' The Eve of St. John,' to a hearing in 1872. This Society was soon joined to the Cambridge University Musical Society (the choir of which had hitherto consisted of male voices only), and Stanford raised the position of the Society to a remarkably high level, incidentally making Cambridge an important musical centre (see

---

[1] The confusion between Johann and Carl, his son, is made worse by the habit of calling the father ' Johann Carl ' as many authorities have done. Eitner says that his son Carl sometimes used the name Johann.
[2] Riemann discovered the exact date ; it is given in the Registry of Deaths in the Catholic parsonage at Mannheim.

[3] Baptized Nov. 25.
[4] The house where Stanford was born, 2 Herbert Street, Dublin, is now marked with a limestone tablet commemorating the fact.
[5] See *Mus. T.*, 1898, p. 785.

CAMBRIDGE). He was appointed conductor of the Society in 1873, and his activity was not long in bearing good fruit, in the first performances in England of Schumann's 'Faust' (pt. iii.) and many other things, such as Brahms's 'Alto Rhapsodie.' In each year, from 1874–76, he was given leave of absence in order to prosecute his studies, first with Reinecke at Leipzig, and then with Kiel at Berlin. In the spring of 1876, on the production of Tennyson's 'Queen Mary' at the Lyceum Theatre, the incidental music was provided by Stanford, having been composed at the poet's suggestion. This work, and a symphony which gained the second prize in a competition held at the Alexandra Palace, in the same year, brought the young composer's name into prominence, and from that time onwards he was more or less regularly before the public as composer and conductor. In 1877, when he proceeded M.A., he organised and directed a concert at which works by Brahms and Joachim were performed for the first time in England, on the occasion when the Honorary Mus.D. degree was offered to both composers, and accepted by the latter. This was the first of many concerts at which the recipients of honorary musical degrees were similarly honoured. In 1877, too, a Festival Overture by Stanford was played at the Gloucester Festival, and subsequently given at the Crystal Palace. A setting of Psalm xlvi. was produced at Cambridge, and afterwards at a Richter concert.

The symphony just mentioned, in B flat, was played at the Crystal Palace in Mar. 1879, but like a second 'Elegiac' symphony in D minor, played at Cambridge in 1882, concertos for PF. and for violoncello, etc., is not included in the list of opus-numbers. Stanford's first opera, 'The Veiled Prophet of Khorassan,' to a libretto by W. Barclay Squire, produced at the Court Theatre, Hanover, Feb. 6, 1881, was only given once in England, at Covent Garden, July 26, 1893 ; an orchestral serenade (op. 17) was produced at the Birmingham Festival of 1882. In 1883 he received the hon. degree of Mus.D. at Oxford, and the same degree at Cambridge in 1888. In 1885 he succeeded Otto Goldschmidt as conductor of the Bach Choir, and held that position until 1902 when he resigned it; in 1887 he was elected professor of music in the University of Cambridge, on the death of Sir G. A. Macfarren, and this appointment he retained till his death in 1924. He devoted his energies to improving the standard of general education required for the musical degrees at Cambridge, and in this and many other ways his influence on the music of the University, and the country at large, has been of great importance. On the opening of the R.C.M. he became professor of composition, conductor of the orchestra and of the operatic class. In the annual performances of opera he maintained a high standard of excellence, and brought many neglected works, old and new, to a hearing. In 1892 he resigned the post of organist to Trinity College, and henceforth lived in London. In 1901 he was appointed conductor of the Leeds Festival in succession to Sullivan, and directed four triennial festivals there (1901–10). He received the honour of knighthood in 1901 and in 1904 he was elected a member of the Royal Academy of Arts at Berlin. Through all his later years Stanford's most important work, apart from his composition, was done at the R.C.M. In the course of forty years of composition teaching a very large proportion of the English composers who have since gained distinction passed through his hands and benefited by his influence.[1]

Stanford's Irish descent gives his music a strong individuality, which is not only evident in his arrangements of Irish songs and in his work as a collector (see IRISH MUSIC), but stands revealed in his 'Irish Symphony' (op. 28), in the opera, 'Shamus O'Brien' (op. 61), the orchestral 'Irish Rhapsodies,' the 'Irish Fantasies' for violin, and in many other definitely Irish compositions. The easy flow of melody, and the feeling for the poetical and romantic things in legendary lore (illustrated in the early song, 'La Belle Dame sans Merci,' the 'Voyage of Maeldune,' and in other works), are peculiarly Irish traits ; but his rare mastery of the resources of orchestra or voices, the thoroughness of his workmanship, and his remarkable skill as a teacher of composition, are qualities not generally associated even with the more brilliant natives of Ireland. His wonderful versatility allowed him to adopt, successfully, styles far removed from one another ; that of the Latin settings of Te Deum, Requiem, Stabat Mater, and of the Mass in G, has an affinity with the Italian composers of the 18th century. Part of his oratorio 'Eden' is strictly modal in utterance, a large number of his instrumental compositions are in the classical idioms of Germany, and all these contrast with his use of the fantastic or rhapsodical style of Ireland already referred to.

In yet another style he won what is perhaps the greatest success he achieved : the early song, 'In praise of Neptune,' from op. 19, may have been a kind of essay in the nautical style, which reached its full fruition in the splendid 'Revenge' (Tennyson) (Leeds Festival, 1886), the choral ballad, which is known and loved wherever the best choral music is practised. The five 'Songs of the Sea' (op. 91), for baritone solo, male chorus, and orchestra, and the 'Songs of the Fleet' (op. 117) for baritone solo, mixed choir and orchestra (the poems of both sets by Henry Newbolt), have

[1] A stone tablet has been placed by his pupils in the wall of the room in which Stanford taught at the R.C.M. His own collection of photographs of his pupils also decorates the walls.

had hardly a less success, and in all these there is a breezy and unmistakably English atmosphere that endears them to all hearers. His use of orchestral colour is full of interest, and his scores are models of effective yet not exaggerated writing; but in one and all the colouring is properly subordinated to the design, and in the thematic development of his subjects will be found the central interest of these compositions.

Although his 'Shamus O'Brien' was a great success, running for many weeks, his more serious operas have not as yet been heard by enough English people to be properly assessed on their real merits. The first, already mentioned, was only given for one extra night after the close of one of Harris's seasons; his second, 'Savonarola,' brought out at Hamburg Apr. 18, 1884, was only performed for a single night under Richter at Covent Garden, July 9, 1884, owing to difficulties connected with its publication; the third, 'The Canterbury Pilgrims,' had four performances at Drury Lane Theatre by the Carl Rosa Company, in 1884; 'Much Ado about Nothing' (words by Julian Sturgis) was produced with great care and effect at Covent Garden, May 30, 1901, but in spite of the success of its two performances it also disappeared quickly from the repertory. Of course it is necessary to remember the singular methods of operatic management in England before assuming that these works have failed to attract the English public. Neither 'Savonarola' nor 'The Canterbury Pilgrims' has a really good libretto; the former, which begins with a passionately emotional prologue, loses its dramatic interest before the end is reached, and the frequent allusions to the lovely 'Angelus ad virginem,' though beautiful musically, are of small value on the stage. In the same way, 'Sumer is icumen in' is used as a kind of motto to 'The Canterbury Pilgrims,' and with all the brightness of its first act, and the romantic charm of the second, the impression left by the trial in the third act is not very strong. 'Much Ado about Nothing,' alone of these works, has a remarkably effective close, and the dirge to Hero strikes a note of welcome pathos. 'Shamus O'Brien' was furnished with regular recitatives in place of the original spoken dialogue, for the performance in Germany (Breslau, 1907); in its original form, and interpreted by capable actors, it is deliciously bright and characteristic, with a touch of wild and fantastic beauty in the 'caoine' of the banshee.

It is always difficult to prophesy within a few years of a composer's death what place his works will ultimately gain; and the task is especially hard in the case of Stanford, for before we can predict what place he will hold in the history of the art, we must know what is to be the fate of that 'modern' music with which he had so very little sympathy. If, as is not improbable, we shall see a return to something like the normal conditions, and the re-establishment of the old ideals, then we may be sure that the best works of Stanford will gain in the general estimation of musicians as time goes on. But if the artistic revolution of our own day should be a repetition of that great revolution when the rich polyphony of the 16th century gave way before the halting utterances of the early monodists, then it is to be feared that Stanford's name will be known by only a few compositions.

All through his career a similar fate befell nearly all his works, as if some malevolent fairy had been unpropitiated at his birth. Each piece of music as it was brought out was received with favour and often with enthusiasm by the public and the press; and after a single performance it would be neglected or eventually forgotten. Of course there are brilliant exceptions, like 'The Revenge,' 'The Voyage of Maeldune,' the Irish rhapsodies, many of his partsongs, and the opera 'Shamus O'Brien.' But the greater number of his operas, all his oratorios, many of his choral and orchestral works in the larger form, have undergone the same fate. The conditions of musical production in England at the end of the 19th century were partly responsible, for it had not then been realised that anything mattered except a first performance of a new work. Nowadays we are wiser and our concert-managers know the importance of repetition in winning the favour of the public. There may also have been personal reasons for the neglect.

As a teacher of composition he was without a rival in Europe. Some artistic creators have found the work of creation so easy that they are unable to help less gifted people through difficulties unfelt by themselves; but Stanford had so thoroughly fought out his own problems that he could sympathise with those that lay before his pupils, and he had a natural gift of imparting his great knowledge. He knew the resources of orchestra and voices as very few have known them; and there is none of his works that may not be profitably studied for the perfection of its presentment. His melodic ideas, too, were of the highest quality, and full of suggestion for the development to which they were subjected. So rich was his endowment in the invention of these that he poured them out lavishly, seldom caring to make sure that they were indeed his own. The curiously numerous instances in which themes of his have been discovered in older works would have laid a lesser man open to a charge of plagiarism; but with him the fitness of some phrase for some particular word or idea often led him to use it without realising that some one else had used it before. Perhaps the most instructive instance is the Dogberry theme in 'Much Ado about Nothing,' where 'write me down an ass' receives the most vivid musical illustration in a theme well known to all admirers of Corelli.

As he wrote with such consummate skill and ease, it was inevitable that much of his work, especially in his later years, should deserve the oblivion which for the time has befallen so many of the compositions in which his best qualities were exhibited. And unless the whole *corpus* of classical music should be swept away or become merely food for the antiquary, there is little doubt that Stanford's operas, with their knowledge of musical stage effect, his symphonies with their adroit manipulation of themes, the many songs in which the natural accentuation of the word seems always to have suggested the musical idea, and his beautiful works in chamber-music, will regain a firm place in the affections of musicians.   M.

LIST OF WORKS

(Unpublished works are indicated by an asterisk.)

Op.
1. Eight songs from George Eliot's 'Spanish Gypsy.'
2. Suite for pf.
3. Toccata for pf.
4. Six songs by Heine.
5. 'Die Auferstehung,' Resurrection Hymn by Klopstock, for choir and orchestra.
6. Incidental music for Tennyson's 'Queen Mary.' (Lyceum Theatre, 1876.)
7. Six songs by Heine.
8. Ps. xlvi. for soli, choir and orchestra.
9. Sonata, pf. and v'cl., in A.
10. Morning, Communion, and Evening Service in B flat.
11. Sonata for pf. and vln. in D.
12. Evening Service in A (Festival of the Sons of the Clergy, 1880), for choir, orchestra and organ.
13. Three Intermezzi, pf. and clarinet.
14. Six songs ('Requiescat,' 'Ode to the Skylark,' 'Sweeter than the violet,' 'There be none of Beauty's daughters,' 'Tragödie,' and 'Le bien vient en dormant ').
15. Quartet, pf. and strings in F.
16. 'Awake, my heart,' Hymn by Klopstock.
17. Serenade for full orchestra in G.
18. Three Cavalier Songs (Browning), for baritone and male choir.
19. Six songs ('A Hymn in praise of Neptune,' 'Lullaby,' 'To the Rose,' 'Come to me when the earth is fair,' 'Boat Song,' 'The Rhine Wine ').
20. Pf. Sonata in D flat.*
21. Elegiac Ode (Walt Whitman), for soli and chorus and orch. (Norwich Festival, 1884.)
22. Oratorio, 'The Three Holy Children.' (Birmingham Festival, 188b.)
23. Incidental Music to the 'Eumenides.' (Cambridge, 1885.)
24. 'The Revenge' (Tennyson), choral ballad. (Leeds Festival, 1886.)
25. Quintet for pf. and strings, in D minor.
26. Carmen Saeculare (Tennyson), for soprano solo and chorus. Composed for Queen Victoria's Jubilee, 1887.
27. Psalm cl. for soprano and chorus. (Opening of Manchester Exhibition, 1887.)
28. 'Irish Symphony ' in F minor. (Richter, 1887.)
29. Incidental music to the 'Oedipus Tyrannus.' (Cambridge, 1887.)
30. A Child's Garland of Songs (Stevenson).
31. Symphony in F. (Berlin, Jan. 14, and Crystal Palace, Feb. 23, 1889.)
32. Suite for vln. and orchestra. (Berlin, Jan., and Philharmonic, Mar. 28, 1889.)
33. Overture, 'Queen of the Seas.' (Armada Tercentenary.)
34. 'The Voyage of Maeldune' (Tennyson), soli, choir and orchestra. (Leeds Festival, 1889.)
35. Trio in E flat for pf. and strings.
36. Morning, Communion, and Evening Service in F.
37. Two Anthems.
38. Anthem, 'The Lord is my Shepherd.'
39. Second Sonata for pf. and v'cl. in D minor.
40. Oratorio, 'Eden' (Robert Bridges). (Birmingham Festival, 1891.)
41. Choral Ballad, 'The Battle of the Baltic.' (Hereford Festival, 1891.)
42. Six pf. pieces.*
43. Six Songs, to poems by R. Bridges.
44. String Quartet in G.
45. String Quartet in A minor.
46. Mass in G, for soli, choir and orchestra.
47. Four partsongs.
48. Incidental Music to Tennyson's 'Becket.' (Lyceum Theatre, 1893.)*
49. Six Elizabethan Pastorals for unaccompanied choir, 1st set.
50. Ode, 'The Bard ' (Gray), for baritone, chorus and orchestra.
51. Three Motets for unaccompanied chorus.
52. Ode 'East to West' (Swinburne), for chorus and orchestra.
53. Six Elizabethan Pastorals, 2nd set.
54. Six Irish Fantasies for vln. and pf.

Op.
55. Opera, 'Lorenza.' *
56. Symphony in D, 'L' Allegro ed il Pensieroso.' *
57. Fantasia and Toccata for organ.
58. Ten Dances for pf. (five of them also scored for orchestra as a Suite of Ancient Dances).
59. Concerto, pf. and orchestra, in G.*
60. Moore's Irish Melodies, restored, edited and arranged.
61. Opera, 'Shamus O'Brien.' (Opera-Comique, London, Mar. 2, 1896.)
62. Choral Ballad, 'Phaudrig Crohoore ' (J. S. Le Fanu), for choir and orchestra. (Norwich Festival, 1896.)
63. Requiem for soli, choir and orchestra in memory of Lord Leighton. (Birmingham Festival, 1897.)
64. String Quartet in D minor.
65. The Clown's Songs from 'Twelfth Night.'
66. Te Deum, for soli, choir and orchestra. (Leeds Festival, 1898.)
67. Six Elizabethan Pastorals 3rd set.
68. Cycle of Quartets from Tennyson's 'Princess ' with pf. accompaniment.
69. Opera.*
70. Sonata for pf. and vln. in G.*
71. Variations on an English Theme ('Down among the dead men '), for pf. and orchestra.
72. Ballad, 'Die Wallfahrt nach Kevlaar ' (Heine), voice and pf.
73. Trio, No. 2, for pf. and strings in G minor.
74. Concerto for vln. and orchestra in D. (Leeds Festival, 1904.)
75. 'The Last Post ' (Henley), for choir and orchestra. (Hereford Festival, 1900.)
76. 'Songs of Erin,' a collection of 50 Irish folk-songs.
76a. Opera, 'Much Ado about Nothing.' (Covent Garden, May 30, 1901; Leipzig, 1902.)
77. An Irish Idyll (Moira O'Neill), for voice and pf.
78. Irish Rhapsody, No. 1 in D minor.
79. Four Irish Dances for Orchestra.
80. Concerto for clarinet and orchestra.*
81. Morning, Communion, and Evening Service in G.
82. Five sonnets from 'The Triumph of Love ' (E. Holmes), for voice and pf
83. Motet, 'The Lord of Might,' for chorus and orchestra. (Festival of the Sons of the Clergy, 1903.)
84. Irish Rhapsody, No. 2, for orchestra.*
85. Quintet for strings, No. 1, in F.*
86. Quintet for strings, No. 2, in C minor.*
87.
88. Six Preludes for Organ.
89. Four Irish Dances for orchestra.
90. Overture in the style of a Tragedy.*
91. Songs of the Sea, for baritone, male choir and orchestra. (Leeds Festival, 1904.)
92. Three Rhapsodies from Dante, for pf. solo.
93. Five Characteristic Pieces for vln. and pf. (also for v'cl. and pf.).
94. Symphony in E flat.* (In memoriam G. F. Watts.)
95. Serenade-Nonet in F for strings and wind.*
96. Stabat Mater, Symphonic Cantata for soli, choir and orchestra. (Leeds Festival, 1907.)
97. Six 'Songs of Faith ' (Tennyson and Walt Whitman).
98. Evening Service on Gregorian Tones.
99. String Quartet in G minor.*
100. Wellington (Tennyson) for soli, chorus and orchestra. (Bristol Festival, 1908.)
101. Six Short Preludes and Postludes for Organ, 1st set.
102. Overture and Incidental Music to 'Attila ' (Binyon). (His Majesty's Theatre, 1907.) *
103. Fantasia and Fugue for organ.
104. String Quartet in B flat. (In memoriam Joseph Joachim.)
105. Six Short Preludes and Postludes for organ, 2nd set.
106. Four Partsongs for male voices.
107. A Welcome Song for the opening of the Franco-British Exhibition, 1908 (to words by the Duke of Argyll), for chorus and orchestra.
108. Installation March for the Chancellor of the University of Cambridge, for wind band, published in an arrangement for organ.
109. Three Military Marches.
110. Four Partsongs for mixed choir.
111. Three Partsongs for mixed choir.
112. Four Songs.
113. Four Bible Songs, for voice and organ.
114. Ave atque Vale, overture with choral portions, written for the Haydn Centenary. (Bach Choir. London, 1909.)
115. Morning, Evening, and Communion Service in C.
116. Two organ pieces, 'Te Deum Laudamus ' and ' Canzona.'
117. Five 'Songs of the Fleet,' for baritone solo and chorus. (Leeds Festival, 1910.)
118. Cushendall an Irish song cycle.
119. Eight Partsongs (S.A.T.B.).
120. Anthem for Harvest, and 2 Choral Hymns.
121. Idyll and Fantasia, for organ.
122. Quartet for strings, in A minor.
123. Anthem, 'Ye choirs of New Jerusalem.'
124. Seventh Symphony, in D minor, for orchestra. (Philharmonic Society, 1912.)
125. Four Songs : 'John Kelly,' 'The Song of Asia,' 'Phoebe,' 'The Song of the Spirit of the Hour.'
126. Second Concerto, in C minor, for pf. and orchestra. (Norfolk Va., Musical Festival, June 3, 1915.)
127. Eight Partsongs (S.A.T.B.).
128. Festal Communion Service, in B flat (including Coronation Service, 'Gloria in Excelsis '), for voices and orchestra.
129. Sonata, for clarinet (or viola) and pf.
130. Incidental music to 'Drake ' (Louis N. Parker).*
131. Three Idylls, 'Fairy Day,' for women's choir and small orchestra.
132. Six characteristic pieces, for pf.
133. Quartet, for pf. and strings.*
134. Anthem, 'Blessed City, heavenly Salem.'
135. Three Motets : 'Ye Holy Angels,' 'Eternal Father,' 'Powerful God.'
136. Five Capricci, for pf.
137. Irish Rhapsody, No. 3, for v'cl. and orchestra.*

Op.
138. Six Two-part Songs (two soprani).*
139. Cycle of Seven Songs, 'A Fire of Turf,' for voice and pf. ; 'A
      Fire of Turf,' 'The Chapel on the Hill,' 'Cowslip Time,'
      'Scared,' 'Blackberry Time,' 'The Fair,' 'The West Wind.'
140. 'A Sheaf of Songs from Leinster,' for voice and pf. ; 'Grandeur,'
      'Thief of the World,' 'A Soft Day,' 'Little Peter Morrissey,'
      'The Bold Unbiddable Child,' 'Irish Skies.'
141. Irish Rhapsody, No. 4, in A minor, for orchestra.
142. An Eight-part Ode, 'Time.'
143. Choral Work, 'Thanksgiving Hymn.'
144. Opera, 'The Critic' (Sheridan). (Shaftesbury Theatre, Jan.
      1916.)
145. Anthem, 'Lo I raise up.'*
146. Opera, 'The Travelling Companion' (Newbolt, after Hans
      Andersen). (Published Carnegie Trust.) (Theatre Royal,
      Bristol, Oct. 25, 1926.)
147. Irish Rhapsody, No. 5, for orchestra.*
148. 'Night Thoughts,' six pieces for pf.
149. First Sonata, in F, for organ.
150. Scènes de Ballet, for pf.
151. Second Sonata, 'Eroica,' for organ (including 'Verdun,' 1916).
152. Third Sonata, 'Britannica,' for organ.
153. Fourth Sonata, 'Celtica,' for organ.
154. Six Pieces, for vln.
155. Six Easy Pieces, for vln.
156. Ten Partsongs.*
157. Eight Songs.
158. Third Trio, in A, for pf., vln. and v'cl.
159. Fifth Sonata, in A, 'Quasi una Fantasia,' for organ.
160. 'Ballata and Ballabile,' for v'cl. and orchestra.
161. Irish Concertino, for vln., v'cl. and orchestra.*
162. Second Concerto, in G minor, for vln. and orchestra.*
163. Twenty-four Preludes (in all the keys), for pf.
164. Magnificat, for unaccompanied choir.
165. Two Sonatas, for vln. solo, with pf. accompaniment.*
166. Quartet in C, for strings.*
167. Quartet in C minor, for strings.*
168. 'A Song of Agincourt,' for orchestra.*
169. Mass in D minor (a cappella).*
170. Ballade, in G minor, for pf.
171. Third Concerto, for pf. and orchestra.*
172. 'Merlin and the Gleam' (Tennyson), for baritone solo, chorus
      and orchestra.
173. Mass, 'Via Victrix.'
174. Six Songs, from 'The Glens of Antrim' (Moira O'Neill).
175. Six Songs.
176. Mass (a cappella).*
177. 'At the Abbey Gate' (Judge Darling), for baritone solo,
      chorus and orchestra.

WITHOUT OPUS-NUMBERS

Festival Overture. (Gloucester Festival, 1877.)
Symphony in B flat. (Alexandra Palace, 1876.)
Elegiac Symphony, in D minor. (Cambridge, 1882.)
Scherzo in B minor for pf.*
Songs—'Irish Eyes,' 'A Valentine,' 'Three Ditties of the olden
      Time,' 'La Belle Dame sans Merci,' 'Prospice' (Browning),
      'The Tomb,' contr. to an album published by Teague and
      King (Winchester), 'I liken my love' (contr. to album of
      Twelve New Songs by British Composers, 1891).
Arrangements of Irish Songs—'Songs of Old Ireland,' 1882 ; 'Irish
      Songs and Ballads,' 1893.
The 'Petrie Collection of Irish Music' was edited by Stanford for the
      Irish Literary Society in 1902–05.
The operas, 'The Veiled Prophet,' 'Savonarola' and the 'Canterbury
      Pilgrims,' which have no opus-numbers, are referred to above.
Mention should also be made of an Installation Ode for the Chancellor
      of the University (the Duke of Devonshire), in 1892, which
      is a 'quodlibet' on well-known tunes (cf. op. 108).

LITERARY WORKS

Studies and Memories. (1908.)
A collection of articles on various musical subjects which had
      appeared previously in periodicals.
History of Music, with Cecil Forsyth.
Musical Composition (1911). A short treatise for students.
Pages from an Unwritten Diary. (1914.)
Further occasional papers.

STANLEY, CHARLES JOHN, Mus.B. (b. London, Jan. 17, 1713 ; d. May 19, 1786), at 2 years old became blind by accident, at 7 began to learn music from John Reading, organist of Hackney, and a few months later was placed with Maurice Greene, under whom he made such rapid progress that in 1724 he was appointed organist of All Hallows, Bread Street, and in 1726 organist of St. Andrew's, Holborn. On July 16, 1729, he graduated as Mus.B. at Oxford. In 1734 he was appointed one of the organists of the Temple Church. In 1742 he published 'Six Cantatas, for a Voice and Instruments,' the words by Hawkins, the future historian of music, which proved so successful that a few months later he published a similar set to words by the same author. In 1757 he produced his 'Jephthah,' and in 1760 joined

J. C. Smith in carrying on the oratorio performances formerly conducted by Handel, for which he composed 'Zimri,' 1760, and 'The Fall of Egypt,' 1774. In 1761 he set to music Robert Lloyd's dramatic pastoral, 'Arcadia, or The Shepherd's Wedding,' written in honour of the marriage of George III. and Queen Charlotte. Eight soli for a German flute, violin or harpsichord appeared as op. 1, and six concertos in seven parts, for strings, as op. 2 ; another set of flute soli was made from these latter. He published also 'Three Cantatas and Three Songs for a Voice and Instruments,' and three sets, of ten each, of organ voluntaries. In 1774, on the retirement of Smith, he associated Thomas Linley with himself in the conduct of the oratorios. In 1779 he succeeded Boyce as Master of the King's Band of Music. Burney says he was 'a neat, pleasing, and accurate performer, a natural and agreeable composer, and an intelligent instructor.' His portrait by Gainsborough was finely engraved by Mary Ann Rigg (afterwards Scott), and another portrait, at the organ, was engraved by MacArdell. (See *D.N.B.*)   W. H. H., addns.

STANSBURY, GEORGE FREDERICK (b. Bristol, 1800 ; d. June 3, 1845), son of Joseph Stansbury, a player upon the flute, bassoon and viola, residing in Bristol. When only 12 years old he was proficient on the pianoforte, violin and flute, and at 19 was engaged by Mme. Catalani as accompanist during a concert tour through England. He was, in 1820–23, musical director at the Theatre Royal, Dublin. In 1828 he appeared at the Haymarket Theatre as Capt. Macheath in 'The Beggar's Opera,' and on Jan. 15, 1829, at Covent Garden in A. Lee's 'Nymph of the Grotto.' He sang there and at Drury Lane for several years. He was re-engaged at Dublin from 1833–35 ; his music for 'Life in Dublin' was given there in 1834.

He was engaged as musical director and conductor at the St. James's, the Surrey, and other theatres. He composed music for 'Waverley' (with A. Lee) and 'Puss in Boots,' 1832 ; 'The Elfin Sprite' and 'Neuha's Cave,' 1833, and other pieces, besides many songs, etc. His voice was of poor quality, but he was an excellent musician and a ready composer. He died of dropsy.   W. H. H. ; addn. by W. H. G. F.

STANSFIELD, ELY, a Yorkshire musician, settled at or near Halifax in the early part of the 18th century. He issued

'Psalmody Epitomiz'd, being a brief collection of plain and
useful Psalm Tunes, both old and new, in four parts, London,
second ed., 1731, 8vo.'

The book is of considerable interest as a volume of Yorkshire psalmody, many of the tunes being by Stansfield himself, and named after Lancashire and Yorkshire towns.   F. K.

STARCK (VON BRONSART), INGEBORG (b. St. Petersburg, 12/24 Aug. 1840 ; d. Munich, June 17, 1913), pianist and composer, of Swedish parentage. Henselt was one of her first masters. When 18 she studied for some time under Liszt at Weimar, and then made a long concert tour through the principal towns of Germany, playing at the Gewandhaus Concerts in 1858 and 1859, at Paris and St. Petersburg. In 1862 she married Hans von Bronsart. After staying some time in Leipzig, Dresden and Berlin, Bronsart and his wife settled in Hanover, where he was intendant of the theatre. Here she devoted herself entirely to composition. An opera by her, ' Die Göttin von Sais,' had been unsuccessful in Berlin ; but her next dramatic work, a setting of Goethe's ' Jery und Bätely,' was played with great success in Weimar, Cassel, and many other places. In 1870 she wrote a ' Kaiser Wilhelm March,' which was played at Berlin at a state performance, to celebrate the return of the troops. In 1891 her four-act opera, ' König Hiarne,' was produced, the libretto by Hans von Bronsart and Friedrich von Bodenstedt. ' Manfred,' a dramatic tone-poem in five pictures, was given at Weimar in 1901, and another opera, ' Die Sühne,' appeared at Dessau, 1909. After settling in Hanover, Frau von Bronsart, who was a pianist of rare excellence, was seldom heard in public. Her compositions further include a concerto and other PF. pieces, many songs, and some music for strings.   w. b. s.

STARK, LUDWIG (b. Munich, June 19, 1831 ; d. Stuttgart, Mar. 22, 1884), was educated at the University there, and learned music in the school of the Lachners. In 1856 he went to Paris, and after a short residence there removed to Stuttgart, and in conjunction with Faisst, Lebert, Brachmann and Laiblin, founded the Stuttgart Music School. Stark's energies were since that time continually concentrated on the school, which flourished accordingly, and in July 1865 was allowed to assume the title of Conservatorium.

A large number of works have been prepared for the use of the students, among which the ' Grosse Klavierschule ' of Lebert and Stark, in 4 vols., is conspicuous. Also by the same— ' Instruktive Klavierstücke ' in four grades ; ' Jugendbibliothek' and ' Jugendalbum,' each in twelve parts ; 'Instruktive klassicher Ausgabe,' of various writers, in 21 vols., by Lebert, Faisst, I. Lachner, Liszt, and Bülow; and many more. The famous Cotta edition of Beethoven's PF. sonatas is the best-known of these publications.

Stark was made Royal Professor in 1868, and Hon. Dr. Ph. 1873, and had many other distinctions.

STARKE, FRIEDRICH (b. Elsterwerda, Saxony, 1774 ; d. Hamburg, early in 1836).[1] As town musician he learned to play all the usual instruments, and studied theory and composition. In later years he continued these under Albrechtsberger in Vienna, after

[1] Schilling says Dec. 18, 1835.

a roving life as Kapellmeister of a circus, theatres, and an Austrian military band. After settling at Vienna, Beethoven entrusted him with the musical education of his nephew. He composed masses and other church music, a cantata and chamber music, and published the *Journal für Militärmusik,* the *Journal für Trompeterchöre,* etc. (*Q.-L.* ; *Riemann*).

STAR-SPANGLED BANNER, THE, long accounted an American national song, by regulation the official anthem of the Army and Navy of the United States and of late years generally accepted as the national anthem, it has never been officially so adopted.

The words were written by Francis Scott Key (1779–1843) in Sept. 1814, inspired by his witnessing of the defence of Fort M'Henry, near Baltimore, Md., against the British bombardment, Sept. 13-14 of that year. Concerning the melody to which it is sung, English in origin and known as ' To Anacreon in Heaven,' there has, however, been much discussion and disagreement. Long attributed to Dr. Samuel Arnold, it is now generally conceded to have been composed by John Stafford SMITH (1750–1836), to words of Ralph Tomlinson.

In an exhaustive and authoritative *Historical Report* in 1909, further elaborated in 1914, O. G. Sonneck establishes Smith's claim to the composition of the ' Anacreontick Song,' as it was popularly called. This was a song so widely familiar that the peculiar form and metre of its text unquestionably served as model for Key's poem. It is undetermined whether he himself consciously fitted it to that melody or whether, as some hold, it was Judge Joseph Hopper Nicholson who was responsible for the actual wedding of words and music that now live, with some slight modifications and variations, as 'The Star-Spangled Banner.'
w. s. s.

BIBL.—O. G. SONNECK, *Report on ' The Star - Spangled Banner,' 'Hail Columbia,' 'America,' 'Yankee Doodle,'* p. 255 (Washington, 1909), Library of Congress publications. ' *The Star - Spangled Banner* ' (revised and enlarged from the Report on the above and other airs, issued in 1909), p. 115, with 25 plates (1914).

STASSOV, VLADIMIR VASSILIEVICH (b. St. Petersburg, Jan 14, 1824 ; d. there, Oct. 23, 1906), a celebrated art critic and the literary champion of the ' new Russian school of music ' (see BALAKIREV). He was the son of an architect of great talent, and was educated, like Serov and Tchaikovsky, at the School of Jurisprudence, which he left in 1843. From 1851–54 he resided abroad, chiefly in Rome and Florence, as private secretary to Prince Demidov. In the former city he wrote his first important contribution to musical literature, *L'Abbé Santini et sa collection musicale à Rome.* On his return to St. Petersburg he began by being private assistant to the director of the Imperial Public Library, Baron Korf, and in 1872 was himself appointed director of the department of Fine Arts, a position which he held until his death.

Stassov wrote indefatigably on a great number of subjects, artistic and literary, and was much preoccupied with the theory—which he shared with Glinka—that the national epics of Russia were mainly of Eastern origin. His earlier musical articles had chiefly an erudite and archæological interest, but with the birth and struggles of the young Russian school they assumed a new and far more vigorous character, and henceforth he stood as the representative champion of nationality in art. His views are clearly and trenchantly defined in such remarkable essays as *Twenty-five Years of Russian Art, The Tracks of Russian Art, Art in the XIXth Century*, etc. His style is intensely individual, his sincerity unquestionable; while his views invariably inclined to the progressive and liberal side. The value of his criticisms was increased by his extensive and accurate learning, which enabled him to use comparative methods most effectually. Apart from polemics, Stassov collected and published the most valuable materials for the biographies of the chief Russian composers. His monographs upon Glinka, Moussorgsky, Borodin, Cui and Rimsky-Korsakov are indispensable to those who desire to study the development of Russian national music. His influence on contemporary Russian art was immense, and can best be realised in the number of works undertaken at his suggestion, and dedicated to him. His collected works from 1847–86 were published by his admirers in a jubilee edition (3 vols., St. Petersburg, 1894), and a fourth volume, dedicated to Count Tolstoi, was added in 1905.   R. N.

STATE SYMPHONY ORCHESTRA, see New York.

STATUE, LA; opéra-comique in 3 acts, text by Carré and Barbier; music by Ernest Reyer. Produced Opéra-Comique, Paris, Apr. 11, 1861; revived at the Opéra, 1903.

STAUDIGL, (1) Joseph (b. Wöllersdorf, Lower Austria, Apr. 14, 1807; d. Mar. 28, 1861), one of the most distinguished and accomplished singers of his time. His father destined him for his own calling, that of Imperial huntsman (*Revierjäger*), but for this he was not sufficiently strong, and in 1816 he entered the Gymnasium of Wiener Neustadt, where his beautiful soprano voice soon attracted attention in the church. In 1823 he attended the philosophical college at Krems, and was persuaded, in 1825, to enter upon his noviciate in the Benedictine Monastery at Melk. Here his voice, which had developed into a fine sonorous bass, was invaluable for the church services. A vague impulse drove him in Sept. 1827 to Vienna to study surgery, but money ran short, and he was glad to accept a place in the chorus at the Kärnthnerthor Theater. Here he took occasional secondary parts, until the sudden illness of one of the solo singers brought him forward as Pietro in the 'Stumme von Portici' ('Mas-

aniello '), after which all the principal parts fell into his hands. High as was his position on the stage, he was still greater as a singer of oratorio and church music. In 1831 he was admitted to the court chapel, and in 1837 sang for the first time at the great musical festival of the Gesellschaft der Musikfreunde in the 'Creation.' In 1833 he sang in the 'Seasons' for the Tonkünstler Societät, a society to which he rendered the greatest services. Though not even a member, he sang at no less than eighty of its concerts, and absolutely declined to accept any fee. Differences with the management of the court theatre led him to the theatre 'an der Wien' on its reopening in 1845. There he acted as chief manager, and, with Pischek and Jenny Lind, entered on a series of fresh triumphs. He returned to the court theatre in 1848, but only to expose himself to fresh annoyance up to Feb. 1854, when an abrupt dismissal embittered the rest of his life. His last appearance in public was in 'St. Paul,' at the Tonkünstler Societät, on Palm Sunday, 1856. A few days after, insanity developed itself, and he was taken to an asylum, which he never quitted alive. His repeated tours abroad spread his fame far and wide, and he had many admirers in England, which he often visited, and where he sang in English. He created the part of 'Elijah' at the Birmingham Festival of 1846, singing the music at sight at the grand rehearsal. As a singer of Schubert's Lieder he was without a rival.

His youngest son, (2) Joseph (b. Mar. 18, 1850; d. Apr. 1916), possessed a flexible sonorous baritone, which he cultivated with success under Rokitansky at the Vienna Conservatorium till 1874, when he left. He made his mark as an oratorio singer in the principal towns of Germany and Switzerland. In 1875–1883 he was frequently engaged at the court theatre of Carlsruhe, and was chamber-singer to the Grand Duke. In 1885 he married Gisele Koppmayer, an Austrian, pupil of Mme. Marchesi, who was a favourite contralto singer in opera at Hamburg, Berlin, Bayreuth, etc. They sang together in a concert tour in America (*Musik. Wochenblatt*, 1888, p. 349).

c. f. p. ; addn. a. c.

STAVE (Eng. *stave, staff*; Fr. *portée*; Ger. *Liniensystem, System*; Ital. *sistema*; Lat. *systema*). A series of horizontal lines, so arranged that the signs used for the representation of musical notes may be written upon or between them.

Their number is now invariably five. For the history of the stave's development see Notation, Vol. III. p. 659.

STAVELESS NOTATION. The staveless designation of notes, according to the system long used in Germany, has been adopted in England for the names of the notes in various octaves, but in past times in England the nomenclature was very vague. Organists and writers on the organ have been in agreement for many years, and 'great C,' 'double C,' and 'tenor C' have been long recognised as denominating the notes sounded by pipes of 16, 8, and 4 feet respectively. 'High C' and 'low C' are terms which can only be understood in relation to different voices or instruments, and even then are sufficiently vague. The terms 'in alt' and 'in altiss' are rather loosely used, and, though as a general rule it may be taken that the octave called 'in alt' begins on the G above the treble stave, yet many persons call the F above it the 'F in altiss' instead of the 'F in alt.' It is greatly to be wished that the reasonable plan of designation shown above the notes in the following example should be generally understood by scientists and musicians. The main difficulty in regard to its universal adoption is that the note C of

the 'Great Octave' (German system) is identical with CC of the organ-nomenclature.   M.

STAVENHAGEN, BERNHARD (*b.* Greiz, Reuss, Nov. 25, 1862; *d.* Geneva, Dec. 26, 1914), studied with Kiel and Rudorff, and became one of the most beloved of Liszt's own pupils. He received the Mendelssohn prize for pianoforte-playing in 1880, and lived till 1885 in Berlin, when he settled in Weimar, where in 1890 he became court pianist to the Grand Duke and in 1895 Kapellmeister. In 1898 he went to Munich in the latter capacity, and was elected director of the Royal Academy of Music there in 1901, but gave up the post in 1904 and returned to Weimar, where he was teacher, pianist and conductor until 1907, when he removed to Geneva to conduct the subscription concerts there. He composed two piano concertos, some piano pieces, of which a minuet is well known. In 1890 Stavenhagen married the singer Agnes Denis.   H. V. H.

STCHERBATCHEV, (1) NICHOLAS VLADIMIROVICH (*b.* Aug. 24, 1853), pianist and composer, spent part of his youth in Rome, but on his return to Russia became closely associated with the young Russian School. His compositions, mostly published by Belaiev in Leipzig, are as follows :

A. *Orchestral.*—' Serenade,' op. 33 ; two Idylls.
B. *Pianoforte.*—' Féeries et pantomimes,' op 8 (two books) ; ' Mosaics,' op. 15 ; ' Scherzo-Caprice,' op. 17 ; ' Echoes,' op. 18 ; ' Allegro appassionato,' op. 22 ; three Idylls, op. 23 ; two pieces, op. 28 ; ' Expromptu,' op. 29 ; ' Melancholia,' op. 31 ; ' The First Snow,' op. 32 ; ' Barcarolle,' op. 35 ; ' two Expromptus,' op. 36 ; ' Impromptu Vilanelle,' op. 38 ; ' Valses,' op. 21 (3), op. 27 (2), op. 34 (Valse entr'acte) ; Mazurkas, opp. 16, 40, 42 ; Preludes and Interludes, opp. 20, 35, 37 ; Études, opp. 19, 26, 30.
C. *Vocal.*—Six songs to words by Count A. Tolstoi, op. 24 ; six songs to words by Heine.

(2) ANDREW VLADIMIROVICH (*b.* Government of Poltava, Jan. 29, 1869), entered the St. Petersburg Conservatoire in 1887, where he studied under F. Blumenfeld, Liadov and Rimsky-Korsakov, composer of a march for orchestra, op. 5, a pianoforte sonata, op. 6, and a considerable number of songs and piano pieces.

(3) VLADIMIR VLADIMIROVICH (*b.* Jan. 24, 1889), was educated at the St. Petersburg Conservatoire and has composed symphonies, PF. sonatas and chamber music.   R. N.

STEDMAN'S PRINCIPLE, see CHANGE-RINGING.

STEFANINI (STEFFANINI), GIOVANNI BATTISTA, of Modena, maestro di cappella in 1608 of S. Maria della Scala, Milan ; between 1608 and beginning of 1614 of Turin Cathedral ; in 1614 of Madonna della consolatione, Rome ; in 1618 and in 1626 of Modena Cathedral. He composed 4 books of motets, 1 book of 'Concerti ecclesiastici,' also a masque, together with ' Capilupi,' performed at Modena, Jan. 26, 1600 (*Q.-L.*).

STEFFANI, AGOSTINO (*b.* Castelfranco, July 25, 1654 ; *d.* Frankfort, Feb. 12, 1748), composer and diplomatist, was one of the most remarkable men of his age. He appears to have entered one of the Conservatori early and become a singing-boy at St. Mark's in Venice,[1] where, in 1667, he was heard by a Count von Tattenbach, probably an emissary of the court of Bavaria. The Count was so delighted with his voice and intelligence that he carried him off to Munich. He was educated at the expense of the Elector Ferdinand Maria and apprenticed to Johann Kaspar Kerl to learn to play the organ. At the beginning of Oct. 1673 he travelled to Rome in order to perfect himself in his art. Here he began to compose assiduously.

In 1674 Bernabei succeeded Kerl as Kapellmeister at Munich. After his return Steffani again took up his position as Kammermusikus, and almost immediately published his first work :

' Psalmodia vespertina volans 8 plenis vocibus concinenda ab Augost. Steffana in lucem edita aetatis suae anno 19,[2] Monachii, 1674.'

This work was a brilliant success for the young composer, and a portion of it was thought worthy of being included by Padre Martini in his *Saggio di contrappunto*, published just a hundred years later. On Mar. 1, 1675, he was appointed court organist.

MUNICH.—But music was not the only study which had occupied his mind ; he had studied mathematics, philosophy and theology, and in 1680 he was ordained a priest with the title of Abbate of Lepsing. Such was the favour shown to him by the new Elector, his old

[1] *Riemann* says he was brought up at Padua.
[2] On this erroneous statement of age see *Q.-L.* It is from the same dedications that we know him to have learnt from Bernabei.

friend Ferdinand Maria having died the year before, that a decree of Nov. 3, 1680, accords to the ' Honourable priest, Court and Chamber musician, and Organist Steffani,' a present of 1200 florins for ' certain reasons and favours ' (gewissen Ursachen und Gnaden). Hitherto he had confined himself to the composition of motets and other church music, but now appeared his first work for the stage. The title, taken from the contemporary MS., evidently the conducting score, in the Royal Music Library B.M. (formerly at Buckingham Palace), in an Italian hand, probably that of his secretary and copyist Gregorio Piva, runs thus:

' Marco Aurelio, Dramma posto in Musica da D. Agostino Steffani. Direttor della Musica di Camera di S. A. S. etc. di Baviera, l' anno 1681.'

It will be seen that a further step had been gained—he was now director of chamber-music. In 1683 appeared some Sonate da Camera for two violins, alto and bass, and in 1685 a collection of motets entitled ' Sacer Janus Quadrifrons 3 voc. Monachii,' but no trace of these works is to be found. For the Carnival of 1685 he composed the opera ' Solone,' which appears to have been an opera buffa in three acts ; the score, however, like all the Munich operas by Steffani with the exception of ' Marco Aurelio,' is lost. He also composed in this year a musical introduction for a tournament, with the title : ' Audacia e rispetto.' The new Elector Maximilian Emanuel was married at the end of 1685 to the Archduchess Maria Antonia, daughter of Leopold I., and the wedding festivities in Munich in the first days of January 1683 began with the opera ' Servio Tullio,' again by Steffani, with ballets arranged by Rodier, and music to them by Dardespin, the Munich Konzertmeister, danced by twelve ladies and gentlemen of the court, with costumes from Paris. On Jan. 18, 1687, the birthday of the young Electress, we have an opera—the text of which was by the new Italian secretary Luigi Orlandi, whose wife sang on the stage—called ' Alarico il Balto, cioè l' audace, rè dei Gothi,' with ballets composed, arranged and danced as before. For this opera fresh Italian singers were brought from Italy. In 1688 he composed the opera ' Niobe, regina di Tebe,' probably for the Carnival, the text again by Orlandi. This was his last work for the court of Munich.

Various reasons have been put forward to account for his leaving a court where he had been so well treated, and where the art of music was held in such esteem, for Munich had not only at this time good singers, a good orchestra and experienced and intelligent audiences, but had likewise a splendid musical history. The Elector had granted him 750 florins on account of his two operas and for a ' Badekur ' in Italy in June 1686. In May 1688 gracious permission was given to him to go again to Italy, in consideration of his twenty-one years' service ; his salary was not only paid to the end of June, but from the beginning of July he was given three years' salary as a reward ! Not only so, but his debts were paid by the court treasurer out of this, and the balance was sent to him in Venice, where he had gone. The main reason for his deserting Munich was no doubt that on the death of the elder Bernabei at the end of the year 1687 his son, who had come from Italy in 1677 to fill the post of vice-Kapellmeister, was in the early part of 1688 made Kapellmeister, thus debarring Steffani from further promotion. Added to this, the Duke of Brunswick, Ernst August, who had been present at the festivities when ' Servio Tullio ' was performed, was so delighted with Steffani's music and singing that he had already made him an offer to go to Hanover, and Steffani appears actually to have made use of the leave granted for the Badekur in Italy in 1686 to spend his time in Hanover instead of there. The appointment then of the younger Bernabei to the Munich Kapell-meistership must have decided him at once to leave Munich, and from Venice at the end of 1688 or early in 1689 he made his way to Hanover, there to remain and become Kapell-meister, and a good deal besides.

HANOVER.—The court of Hanover was renowned for its magnificence and courtesy, which were, however, combined with a friendly simplicity held to be the best in Germany.[1] One of its principal ornaments was the great philosopher Leibniz, who had resided there since 1676, and who, with the Duchess Sophia, had raised the tone of the court to a very high intellectual standard. Up to this time the operas at Hanover (chiefly imported from Venice) were given in the small French theatre, but that being deemed too small a new opera-house was built, which was pronounced to be the most beautiful in all Germany. It created the reputation of its architect, Thomas Giusti, and caused him to be called to Berlin and other towns for similar purposes. The new house was opened in 1689 with ' Henrico Leone,' by Mauro and Steffani. The score[2] gives a list of the scenes, machinery, etc., which might astonish even a 20th-century reader. It had a very great success, was given in German in 1696 at Hamburg and in 1697 at Brunswick, and acquired great celebrity. The opera shows marked advance on ' Marco Aurelio.'

' Henrico Leone ' was followed in the summer of this year by ' La lotta d' Alcide con Achelaò,' a divertimento drammatico in one act, a charming work, written probably also by Mauro. It seems to have been performed at the Summer Theatre at Herrenhausen. The next opera was ' La superbia d' Alessandro,' in 1690 (the conducting score gives 1691 as the date), the words by Mauro ; a fine work. ' Orlando generoso '

[1] See Chrysander's *Händel*.   [2] Roy. Lib., B.M.

came out in 1691—another fine work written in conjunction with Mauro. ' Le rivali concordi' appeared in 1692 (1693, *Riemann*), written again by Mauro, and afterwards performed at Hamburg. We now come to ' La libertà contenta' (Mauro) in 1693, in which evidence is given of great further progress, for nothing of such importance had hitherto come from his pen.

It was in the next year that Steffani issued his celebrated pamphlet entitled

' Quanta certezza habbia da suoi Principii la Musica, ed in qual pregio fosse perciò presso gli Antichi. Amsterdam, 1695. Risposta di D. A. Steffani Abbate di Lepsing Protonotario della San Sede Apostolica. Ad una lettera del Sⁿ. March^e. A. G. In difesa d' una Proposizione sostenuta da lui in una Assemblea. Hannovera Sett, 1694.'

Steffani ably discusses the question whether music exists only in the imagination, or is grounded on nature and science. In 1695 we have the opera ' I trionfi del Fato, o le glorie d' Enea.' It found its way to Hamburg in 1699. An opera in one act, ' Baccanali,' was also composed this year for the small theatre in Hanover. For the Carnival of 1696 the grand opera of ' Briseide ' was composed, the words by Count Palmieri. No composer's name is mentioned, and Chrysander thinks it is not by Steffani; but the two scores and collections of Steffani's songs in the Roy. Mus. Lib., B.M., leave little doubt on examination that it is his work, and in his usual manner.

DIPLOMATIC CAREER.—A change was now about to take place in Steffani's circumstances. He was no longer to be the active composer of operas, and Kapellmeister, but from this time forth was destined to devote his time chiefly to diplomacy, though he never forsook the art of which he was so great an ornament. Ernst August had sent 5000 men to assist the Emperor against the Turks, and some 8000 against the French; his two eldest sons, George (afterwards King of England) and Frederick Augustus, had served in the field, and three others had been killed in the wars.' The Emperor as a reward determined, in 1692, to create a ninth Elector, and raise the younger branch of the house of Brunswick-Lüneburg to the Electorate. This was generally deemed just, but many difficulties stood in the way, and during four years the position of Ernst August as Elector became more and more difficult, so that, in 1696, it was determined to send an Envoy Extraordinary round to the various German courts to smooth matters over, and Ernst August and Leibniz could find no one among the court *personnel* in Hanover so well fitted for the post as Abbate Steffani. So admirably did he succeed that at the end of the mission he was not only granted a considerably larger salary than he had hitherto had at court, but Innocent XI. was induced to raise him in 1706 to the dignity of Bishop (*in partibus infidelium*) of Spiga in Anatolia, Asia

Minor—the ancient Cyzicus. In the early part of 1698 he was sent to Brussels as ambassador, and there had his first audience on Mar. 1. In this year the Elector Ernst August died, and Steffani afterwards transferred his services to the Elector Palatine at Düsseldorf, where he became a Privy Councillor and, in 1709, the Pope's Protonotarius for North Germany, though at what time this occurred is not known. In 1707 the opera ' Arminio ' was composed. In 1709 we find Steffani again with two new operas. Both are stated in the scores of the Roy. Mus. Lib., B.M., to be by Gregorio Piva —his secretary, whose name he adopted for his compositions after he became a statesman. The opera given at Hanover is called ' Enea, or Amor vien dal destino,' in the large copy, but in the conducting score ' Il Turno '—in three acts. The Düsseldorf opera, ' Tassilon: Tragedia in 5 Atti,' is only represented in the Roy. Mus. Lib., B.M., by a vocal score; the overture and all instrumental effects are wanting, only the bass being given to the different pieces; but the singers' names, all Italian, are mentioned.

VOCAL DUETS.—Though, however, his operas were his greatest works, they could not attain the same universal popularity as his well-known duets for various voices, with a bass accompaniment. These are mostly in three long movements, some with recitatives and soli, in the cantata form, following Carissimi and Stradella. Of these celebrated duets there are more than a hundred in the British Museum, and in the splendid copy in 3 vols. in the Roy. Mus. Lib. The words were mostly by Ortensio Mauro, Averara, Abbate Conti, Conte Francesco Palmieri, etc. The testimony to the great excellence of these compositions is abundant. Burney says in speaking of these duets, ' Those of the admirable Abbate Steffani were dispersed in MS. throughout Europe.' Mattheson again, ' In these duets Steffani is incomparable to all I know, and deserves to be a model, for such things do not easily become old.' Chrysander also writes, ' These duets are the greatest of their kind.' The most renowned singers, Senesino, Strada and others, delighted in them, and used them constantly for practice in both expressive and florid singing.[1] No copies of these duets are dated, but they were probably all composed after he went to Hanover; and some of them are known to have been written for the Princess Sophia Dorothea.

Steffani was in Italy on a diplomatic mission to the Papal Court from Oct. 1708 to June 1709.[2] It was then that he met HANDEL (see Vol. II. p. 506), whom he induced to visit Hanover. Handel testifies to Steffani's great kindness to him while at Hanover. He was

[1] Several movements from these duets are included in ' Duetti da camera,' edited by J. A. Fuller Maitland.
[2] Woker, *Aus den Papieren des kurpfälzischen Ministers Agostino Steffani.* (*Vereinsschrift der Görresges.* 1885) See also Streatfeild's *Händel,* p. 44.

anxious, too, that Handel should become Kapellmeister at this court.

The Duke of Brunswick, Anton Ulrich, was converted to Catholicism in 1710, and we find Steffani going from Düsseldorf to Brunswick to accept in the name of the Pope a piece of ground as a site for a church. About the year 1712 the new church in Brunswick was so far ready that the Pope sent Bishop Steffani to consecrate the building and perform the opening service. Two years later the Elector of Hanover became King of England, but Steffani did not accompany him to London ; indeed, we do not meet with his name again till 1724, when the ACADEMY OF ANCIENT MUSIC (q.v.) in London unanimously elected him its Hon. President for life. Steffani appears to have sent over the following four works for performance—the fine and well-known madrigal ' Qui diligit Mariam,' for S.S.A.T.B. ; another madrigal, called ' La Spagnuola,' ' Al rigor d' un bel sembiante,' for two altos and tenor, not so remarkable ; and the beautiful madrigal ' Gettano i Rè dal soglio.' These are generally found in the MS. collections of the time. The fourth piece was the great Stabat Mater, composed for S.S.A.T.T.B., accompanied by strings and organo, and undoubtedly one of the finest works of any composer of the period immediately preceding that of the giants Bach and Handel. His great contemporaries Alessandro Scarlatti and Purcell produced nothing finer. No exact dates can be assigned to these four works, but they all belong to his later manner. In Steffani is to be found the perfection of counterpoint without stiffness, and with that real sign of genius, exhaustless variety. As in Bach, there is marvellous freedom in the movement of the parts, and no hesitation at a good clashing dissonance produced by this freedom. He was an adept too at writing the charming minuets and gavottes which were then so fashionable, and in which his operas abound. At the British Museum there is likewise a ' Confitebor ' for three voices with violins and bass in E minor, said to be of the year 1709, with a splendid bass solo ('Sanctum et terribile')—a species of accompanied recitative ; the whole work being full of exquisite beauties. In the R.C.M. there is a book of ' XII Motteta per celeberrimum Abbatem Stephanum ' for three voices with soli and recitatives, but it is only a vocal score, without the symphonies and accompaniments which all undoubtedly had. In another book in the same library, however, we find two of them complete. Early in 1727 Steffani was once more and for the last time in Italy. At the palace of Cardinal Ottoboni, who still kept up his Monday performances of music, Steffani, now 74 years old, occasionally sang.[1] Hawkins reports

on the authority of ' those who heard him that

' He was just loud enough to be heard, but that this defect in his voice was amply recompensed by his manner, in the chasteness and elegance of which he had few equals.'

From Hawkins we also learn that

' As to his person he was less than the ordinary size of men, of a tender constitution of body, which he had not a little impaired by intense study and application. His deportment is said to have been grave, but tempered with a sweetness and affability that rendered his conversation very engaging ; he was perfectly skilled in all the external forms of polite behaviour, and, which is somewhat unusual, continued to observe and practise them at the age of fourscore.'

He was back in Hanover in a short time, and the next year, going to Frankfort on some public business, died and was buried there after a short illness.

The last word has not yet been said about this remarkable musician, and it is to be hoped that some of his duets, and perhaps his glorious Stabat Mater and Confitebor, may still be heard in the concert-room. His career was certainly one of the most extraordinary in musical history. Born of obscure parents he raised himself by his talents and industry from the position of a poor choir-boy, not only to be one of the foremost musicians of his age, but likewise the trusted confidant of princes and the friend of such a man as Liebniz. The only other instance of an artist having become an ambassador is to be found in the painter Rubens. The materials for this notice have been chiefly gathered from Rudhardt, Hawkins and Chrysander, the latter having supplied some important information hitherto unpublished. Besides these authorities the following may be consulted : A. Neisser's *Dissertation* on ' Servio Tullio,' 1902 ; F. W. Woker's article in the *Vereinschriften* of the *Görresgesellschaft* (see p. 127, n. 2). (For list of extant works, see Q.-L.)

w. g. c. ; rev. s. g. and c.

STEFFKINS, (1) THEODORE (THEODORUS), a foreign professor of the lute and viol, who lived in London in the latter half of the 17th century. He is commended in Thomas Salmon's *Essay to the Advancement of Music*, 1672. His brother, (2) DIETRICHT, was one of the band of Charles I. in 1641, and his two sons, (3) FREDERICK and (4) CHRISTIAN, were famous performers on the viol. They were members of the King's band in 1694, and Christian was living in 1711.   w. h. h.

STEGGALL, (1) CHARLES, Mus.D. (b. London, June 3, 1826 ; d. there, June 7, 1905), was educated at the R.A.M., from June 1847, principally by Sterndale Bennett. In 1848 he became organist of Christ Church Chapel, Maida Hill ; in 1851 a professor at the R.A.M., and in the same year accumulated the degrees of Mus.B. and Mus.D. at Cambridge. In 1855 he was appointed organist of Christ Church, Lancaster Gate, and in 1864 organist of Lin-

[1] The statement formerly accepted that Handel met Steffani on this occasion and heard him sing is unfounded. Handel was in London in the spring of 1727.

coln's Inn Chapel. In 1884 he was elected on the Board of Directors of the Academy, and in 1887 was one of those who carried on the duties of head of the institution between the death of Macfarren and the appointment of Mackenzie. In 1903 he resigned his professorship. He was one of the founders of the R.C.O. in 1864, and was examiner for the Mus.D. degree at Cambridge in 1882 and 1883. He was hon. secretary to the Bach Society, founded by Bennett, from 1849 to its dissolution in 1870. He composed anthems and other church music, and lectured upon music in the metropolis and elsewhere.

w. h. h., addns.

His youngest son, (2) Reginald (b. London, Apr. 17, 1867), was educated at the R.A.M., where he gained the Balfe Scholarship in 1887, afterwards becoming an Associate, in due course a Fellow, and, in 1895, organ professor. In 1886 he was appointed to the post of organist of St. Anne's Church, Soho, and some years afterwards became his father's assistant at Lincoln's Inn Chapel, being appointed to succeed him in 1905.

He first came prominently before the public as a composer at a concert organised by Granville Bantock in 1896 at the Queen's Hall, when a scena, 'Elaine,' was performed; an Ave Maria was given at another concert of the same kind, and his scena 'Alcestis' was given at the Crystal Palace earlier in the year. His 'Variations on an Original Theme' for orchestra were played at Bournemouth in Feb. 1903,[1] and later orchestral works include a Fantasy Overture, produced there in Mar. 1914. A symphony, and a Mass, together with many anthems, a Festival Evening Service, and organ pieces, are included among his compositions.

m., addns.

STEGMANN, Karl David (b. Dresden, c. 1751; d. Bonn, May 27, 1826), a pupil of the Kreuzschule, afterwards of Weisse and Homilius. He appeared at Breslau successfully in 1772 as operatic tenor, and after engagements in that capacity at Königsberg, Danzig, Gotha and Hamburg, became Kapellmeister at the Hamburg Theatre in 1798, retaining that position until 1811, when he retired to Bonn. For a list of his numerous compositions (operas, singspiele, concertos, etc.), see Gerber, i. and ii. (Q.-L.; Riemann).

STEIBELT, Daniel (b. Berlin, 1765; d. Sept. 20, 1823), was so celebrated in his day as a pianoforte-player and composer that many regarded him as the rival of Beethoven.

He was the son of a Berlin harpsichord and pianoforte maker, and coming under the patronage of the Crown Prince, afterwards Frederick William II., was sent to Kirnberger for instruction in the harpsichord and composition. His musical education was interrupted by his joining the army for a while,[2] and was finally

brought to an end, as far as Berlin was concerned, by his departure from that city, probably in 1784.

His career as a composer and virtuoso began in Paris at some date between 1787 and 1790. Besides winning success as a pianist and writer of pianoforte music, Steibelt also essayed opera, his 'Romeo and Juliet,' a setting of a libretto written by the Vicomte de Ségur, one of his patrons, being produced at the Théâtre Feydeau on Sept. 10, 1793, meeting with considerable approval.

This completely confirmed Steibelt's position in Paris. His pianoforte music, though considered difficult, was extremely popular, and as a teacher he counted amongst his pupils the most eminent amateurs of the time; but he presently injured his reputation by selling as new some pieces in a slightly altered form which had already been published elsewhere, and in consequence he felt it desirable to leave Paris, at any rate for a time. England attracted his attention, and, journeying by way of Holland, he reached London about the close of 1796.[3] His first public performance seems to have been at Salomon's Benefit Concert on May 1, 1797, and a fortnight later (May 15) he played a pianoforte concerto of his own at an opera concert. Not long after this he wrote the pianoforte concerto in E (No. 3), containing the 'Storm Rondo,' a work of enormous popularity, in all probability first performed in public at Salomon's concert on Mar. 19, 1798. At the close of the same year (Dec. 11) its author again came forward as an opera composer, 'a new grand Heroic Romance, in three acts, called Albert and Adelaide; or the Victim of Constancy,' being produced at Covent Garden; a medley this, both words and music, the latter being only in part original, eked out by the insertion of a quintet from 'Lodöiska' and the like expedients. Even the 'original' music was not all written by Steibelt, as Attwood contributed some of it.[4] As teacher and performer Steibelt appears to have been as fully employed during his stay of three years or so in London as he had been previously in Paris. Two circumstances of interest connected with his visit to England may be mentioned. The first of these is the fact that he conceived a decided predilection for English pianofortes, always using them in preference to any others; the second is his marriage with a young Englishwoman, described as possessed of considerable personal attractions and as a good player on the pianoforte and tambourine. The last-named accomplishment led her husband to add a tambourine accompaniment to many of his subsequent pieces.

[3] According to Fétis, Steibelt did not leave Paris till 1798; but Broadwood & Sons have records in their possession which prove that he was established in London by Jan. 2, 1797.   a. j. h.
[4] This information is derived from an advertisement of Longman, Clementi & Co. in The Morning Chronicle of Jan. 22, 1799. These pasticcios were common enough then, and until the end of the first quarter of the 19th century.

[1] See Dan Godfrey's Memories and Music, p. 304.   [2] A.M.Z. ii. 622.

Steibelt now resolved on visiting his native country, reaching Hamburg in Sept. or Oct. 1799, and going on to Dresden, where he gave a concert on Feb. 4, 1800, Prague, Berlin [1] and *Vienna. For the account of his meeting and contest with Beethoven, see BEETHOVEN. His discomfiture on this occasion naturally affected his success at Vienna, and a concert that he gave at the Augarten-Saal was rather thinly attended. His German tour as a whole was only partially successful, and Steibelt determined to return to the more congenial atmosphere of Paris. He arrived there in Aug. 1800, carrying with him the score of Haydn's ' Creation,' giving a performance of the work, with a translation by de Ségur and with some alterations and additions of his own to the music, at the Opéra on Christmas Eve, 1800.[2] The adaptation of the words seems to have been fairly performed ; at the alterations made in the score competent judges were, naturally enough, extremely indignant. Moreover, the circumstances of his departure some four or five years before had not been forgotten, and thus, in spite of the success of the performance of the ' Creation ' and of that of his ballet ' Le Retour de Zéphyr,' given at the Opéra on Mar. 3, 1802, Steibelt did not feel very comfortable in Paris. On the 22nd of the same month he returned to London.

The next six years of his life were about equally divided between London and Paris. His popularity in London was as great as ever. For the King's Theatre in the Haymarket he wrote two ballets, ' Le Jugement du berger Pâris ' [3] in 3 acts (produced May 24, 1804), and ' La Belle Laitière ' [4] (produced Jan. 26, 1805). Returning to Paris, Steibelt produced an intermezzo, ' La Fête de Mars,' composed in celebration of the Austerlitz campaign, at the Opéra on Mar. 4, 1806, while ' La Princesse de Babylone,' an opera in three acts, was accepted by the Opéra, and was in active preparation when the importunity of his creditors compelled the composer to leave Paris suddenly in the autumn of 1808. But his energies were by no means confined to writing for the stage. Much of his chief pianoforte music dates from these years; the two concertos in E♭ (Nos. 4 and 5), the Méthode published in French, German and Spanish, in which he claims to have invented the signs for the use of the pedals adopted by Clementi, Dussek and Cramer (see MUTE), and his Étude—a collection of fifty studies in two books.

Having received the offer of a very advantageous appointment from the Emperor Alexander, Steibelt left Paris for St. Petersburg in

Oct. 1808. He stopped at Frankfort to give a concert on Nov. 2,[5] and at Leipzig made a stay of some weeks and repeated the programme of the Frankfort concert.

It is not very clear when he was appointed director of the Opéra Français at St. Petersburg, but when Boieldieu left, at the close of 1810, Steibelt received the title of maître de chapelle to the Emperor in his place. In managing and writing for the opera, and in teaching and composing for the pianoforte, the remaining years of Steibelt's life were spent. His early years in the city were marked by production of the ballets ' La Fête de l'Empereur ' in 1809, and ' Der blöde Ritter ' (before the end of 1812) ; he also wrote two operas, each in three acts, ' Cendrillon ' [6] and ' Sargines ' ; a third, ' Le Jugement de Midas,' he did not live to finish. He also spent some time in revising ' Roméo et Juliette.' In the midst of these avocations he was seized with a painful disease, of which, after lingering some time, he died. A number of his friends combined to honour him with a quasi-public funeral, and the military governor of St. Petersburg, Count Milarodowitsch, organised a subscription concert for the benefit of his family, who were left in very straitened circumstances.

A comprehensive list of Steibelt's compositions appeared in the former editions of this Dictionary.   J. H. M., abridged.

STEIGLEDER, HANS ULRICH (*b. circa* 1580 ; *d.* 1635) came of an organist family settled at Stuttgart. After serving as organist at Lindau on the Bodensee, he was appointed in 1617 Stifts-Organist at Stuttgart, in which capacity he had also to serve as musician generally to the court of Würtemberg. For the organ he published two works, the first of which is so far remarkable as being the first specimen in Germany of copper-plate engraving for organ or clavier music. As the title informs us, the engraving was by his own hands,

Ricercar Tabulatura. Organis et Organoedis unice inserviens et maxime conducens adornata a J.U.S. . . . . ejusdemque Autoris sumptibus et manibus propriis Aeri Cupreo insculpta et excusa. Anno 1624.'

Although mentioned by Gerber, this work was unknown to modern musicians, until a copy sent from the Royal (now State) Library at Stuttgart was shown at the Vienna Musical Exhibition of 1892. The engraving is said to be rather coarsely done. Some account of the music is given in Seiffert, *Geschichte der Klaviermusik*, Bd. I. p. 105. It consists of ricercari of the earlier Italian fugal type. The other published work of Steigleder is entitled,

' Tabulatur-Buch darinnen dass Vater Unser auf 2, 3 und ÷ Stimmen componirt und vierzig mal variirt würdt . . . auf Orgeln und allen andern Instrumenten ordentlich zu appliciren . . . 1627.

This work consists of forty ' Bearbeitungen ' or Variations on the melody of the ' Vater Unser

---

[1] All authorities seem to place the visit to Berlin between his concert at Prague and his arrival at Vienna. Otherwise, it would be natural to conjecture from the dates that he went to Berlin before going to Dresden.

[2] See PLEYEL for the original plan regarding this production at the Opéra.

[3] See *Morning Chronicle*, May 25, 1804.

[4] *Ibid.* Jan. 28, 1805.

[5] The correspondent of the *A.M.Z.* (xi. 170) oddly describes him as ' Steibelt of London.'

[6] It is worth noting that some authorities declare this was written for Paris. This opera has been considered his greatest work.

im Himmelreich,' which show the influence of the newer technique of the English-Dutch Variation School of Sweelinck, as well as of the South German toccata style of George Muffat. Two specimens are given in Ritter, *Geschichte des Orgelspiels*, Nos. 87 and 88.   J. R. M.

STEIN, a family of pianoforte makers and players.

(1) JOHANN ANDREAS (*b.* Heidesheim, Palatinate, 1728 ; *d.* Feb. 29, 1792), the founder of German pianoforte - making.   He appears to have been in Paris in 1758, and to have remained there for some years.   We may conclude that he was engaged in organ-building and harpsichord-making, since he was not only a good musician, but a proficient in both handicrafts, before he turned to pianoforte-making. After Paris we find him at Augsburg, organist of the Barfüsserkirche, the famous organ of which he built, as well as that of the Kreuzkirche.   Several examples of Stein's pianoforte, exhibited at Vienna in 1892, are now in the collection of Mr. Steinert of New Haven, Conn., U.S.A.   A grand piano, which was secured by Victor Mahillon for the Museum of the Conservatoire, Brussels, is inscribed

'Jean André Stein
  Facteur d'orgues et des Clavecins
  Organiste à l'Eglise des Minorites
      Augsbourg, 1780.' [1]

The action of this bichord grand piano is the same as that illustrated in Fig. 10 of the article PIANOFORTE, which was copied from a scarce pamphlet preserved in the Library of the Gesellschaft der Musikfreunde at Vienna.   The wedge damper is Cristofori's ; the escapement and other parts of the action differ entirely from that maker's and from Gottfried Silbermann's as preserved in three instruments at Potsdam, in which the Florentine maker Cristofori is closely followed.   This instrument has also the *genouillière* or knee-pedal for raising the dampers, which preceded the foot-pedal. (See MUTE.) The genouillière and Stein's escapement are described by Mozart with great gusto in a letter addressed to his mother, in Oct. 1777, only a very few years before Mahillon's piano was made.   What action was used by Spaeth of Ratisbon, also referred to by Mozart, we do not know, but Mahillon's discovery at Brussels of a square piano, with the rudiments of Stein's action—that is, the same centred percussion without the hopper escapement—leads directly to the conclusion that this simple action, clumsy as Mozart found it without the escapement, was in common use before Stein brought his inventive genius to bear upon its improvement.[2]

[1] The last figure is indistinct, and Mahillon thought that it might be 5 or 6 instead of 0.
[2] The small Viennese piano now at the R.C.M. has these attributes of Stein, action and knee-pedals, and of so clever a mechanism that it was said by an expert to be fifty years in advance of its time. It was found in Italy by Heron-Allen—who gave it to Mrs. Rudolph Lehmann—and she bequeathed it to A. J. Hipkins ; but it came too late for him to gratify his curiosity as to its maker. E. J. Hⁿ.

Welcker von Gontershausen (*Der Clavierbau*, Frankfort, 1870, p. 173) gives a drawing of this action without hopper escapement, attributing it to Silbermann ; but, as far as we can see, without proof.   Many of the early German pianos have neither date nor inscription, which makes the attribution to a maker difficult. We are disposed to think that Silbermann would not have abandoned the good action of Cristofori, which he knew how to finish well, for a crude tentative mechanism ; we therefore conclude that the Seven Years' War having entirely stamped out Saxon pianoforte-making, a new era began with the restoration of peace, and that the merit of founding that German pianoforte-making which was so long identified with the school of Vienna, belongs to Stein, whose inventive talent and artistic devotion were displayed in the good instruments he made, which by 1790 at latest, were adopted as models both in North and South Germany, as the two grand pianos formerly belonging to Queen Louise, made by Huhn, '*Organ - builder*,' of Berlin,[3] and preserved in memory of her at Potsdam, unmistakably show.

Gerber, in his *Lexicon*, has preserved a list of numerous inventions by Stein (of one, the 'Melodica,' the inventor published an account in 1772) of which none are now of value save the escapement and the keyboard shifting by means of a pedal.   He introduced the latter in his 'Saitenharmonica' in 1789, carrying the hammers from three strings to one, which he spaced rather away from the other two unisons. This 'una corda' he named 'Spinettchen.' A. W. Thayer[4] unearthed a record of Pastor Junker, showing that Beethoven in 1791, when residing at Bonn, always used an instrument of Stein's.

Stein died, leaving two sons, MATTHÄUS ANDREAS and FRIEDRICH, and a daughter, Maria Anna, known as NANNETTE, who married STREICHER (*q.v.*), and was really the most prominent of the group.

Though Streicher ultimately succeeded to the business, which had been removed from Augsburg to Vienna, his name does not appear for several years in connexion with it.   (See PIANOFORTE, Vol. IV. p. 158, note 5.)   The firm as late as 1801 was 'Geschwister Stein'; subsequently 'Nannette Stein' only, which appears as the maker's name on a grand pianoforte with six pedals, existing (1882) in Windsor Castle.   A. J. H.

(2) MARIA ANNA (NANNETTE) (*b.* Augsburg, Jan. 2, 1769 ; *d.* Jan. 10, 1838).   When barely 8 she played to Mozart on his visit to Augsburg in 1777, and, in spite of the bad habits she had contracted, he said of her ' She

[3] One of these instruments, and apparently the older one, bears no name outside, but internal examination shows that the maker was the same who made the 1790 one ; both closely resemble Mozart's piano by Walther, at Salzburg, and the original model by Stein of 1780.   [4] *Beethoven*, ii. 209-15.

may do yet, for she has genius ' (Jahn, i. 368). Her talent and capacity were so obvious that her father early initiated her into the details of his business, and on his death she carried it on, in conjunction with her brother, Matthäus Andreas, with a decision and energy almost masculine. In 1793 she married Johann Andreas STREICHER, an excellent pianist and teacher from Stuttgart, and then she, her husband and mother, moved to Vienna. The new firm of ' Nannette and Andreas Stein ' (constituted by Imperial decree, Jan 17, 1794) established itself in the ' Red Rose,' No. 301 in the Landstrasse suburb. In 1812 the factory was removed to premises of their own, which had been rebuilt and enlarged some years before, No. 27 in the Ungargasse. In 1802 the brother and sister dissolved partnership, each setting up for themselves, as ' Matthäus Andreas Stein,' and ' Nannette Streicher, geborene Stein.' Streicher, who had hitherto managed only the commercial part of the business, now took his full share of the work. Both firms endeavoured to perfect their instruments in every possible way,[1] while still adhering to the traditions of their father, and Stein of Vienna became as celebrated as Stein of Augsburg had been. In 1823 the Streichers took into partnership their son Johann Baptist (b. Vienna, 1796). Nannette Streicher was at once an energetic and capable woman of business, a pianist of remarkable excellence, a person of great general cultivation, and a model wife and mother. Her name is closely connected with that of Beethoven. It is well known that she did much to help him in his domestic arrangements, lightened the burden of his housekeeping, and even looked after his bodily health. Thayer, in his Beethoven (iii. 239), gives us a striking picture of their relationship. (See also BEETHOVEN, Vol. I. p. 290.) Her husband died in the same year as his wife, on May 25. The business was carried on successfully by their son, J. B. Streicher, and his son, Emil. Her brother,

(3) MATTHÄUS ANDREAS (b. Augsburg, Dec. 12, 1776 ; d. May 6, 1842), accompanied his sister to Vienna, set up for himself in 1802, marrying on Nov. 12, 1796. His son,

(4) KARL ANDREAS (b. Vienna, Sept. 4, 1797 ; d. Aug. 28, 1863), also a pianoforte-maker and composer, early showed talent for music, and became an excellent pianist and teacher. He was a pupil of Förster in harmony and composition, and published a considerable number of works principally for his instrument. He also left in MS., among others, two PF. concertos with orchestra, two orchestral overtures, and a comic opera, ' Die goldene Gans,' words by Langbein. He appeared several times in

public, but latterly devoted himself entirely to the factory, in the working of which his father had early initiated him. In 1829 a patent was granted to him. Karl Andreas travelled much, and his pianos were appreciated abroad, as well as by the first artists of his own country. In 1844 he was appointed court pianoforte-maker. His book ' on the playing, tuning, and preservation of Stein pianofortes,'[2] contains valuable matter.

C. F. P.

(5) FRIEDRICH (b. Augsburg, May 26, 1784), younger son of Johann Andreas (1), at the age of 10 went to Vienna, and studied counterpoint and composition with Albrechtsberger. He became one of the first pianoforte-players of the capital, and was considered to be a very promising composer. He appeared rather frequently in the Augarten and Burgtheater concerts as a player of concertos, especially those of Mozart. Reichardt (Apr. 1, 1809) calls him :

' A performer of great power and genius. . . . A rare power, combined with the deepest feeling, characterised his performance. He played some of Beethoven's most difficult pieces, and variations of his own composition, full of invention and deep sentiment, and of monstrous difficulty. Since then I have heard him at home on his magnificent Streicher pianoforte, and am confirmed in my opinion of his assiduous study and great talents.'

These eulogies are borne out by other contemporary notices.

Friedrich Stein is the subject of Ries's anecdote (Notizen, p. 115). Beethoven had played his concerto in G at his own concert, Dec. 22, 1808 (Vol. I. p. 286), with astonishing spirit and speed, and immediately after called upon Ries to play it in public, with only five days for its study. Ries naturally shirked such a task, preferring to play the C minor one instead. At this his master was offended, and turned to Stein, who accepted the task, but was unable to accomplish it, and played the C minor instead, not satisfactorily.

Stein was an industrious composer, but few of his vocal compositions reached the stage. He left three operettas and a ballet, of which only one—' Die Fée radiante '—came to public performance. Also a set of songs, a violin concerto, a grand sonata for the PF., and a PF. trio. He also arranged Beethoven's fourth and sixth symphonies for two PFs.

A. W. T.

STEINBACH, (1) EMIL (b. Lengenrieden, Baden, Nov. 14, 1849 ; d. Mainz, Dec. 6, 1919), studied at the Leipzig Conservatorium 1867–1869, in 1877 became conductor of the town band, and in 1898 director of the town theatre of Mainz. He was especially known as a conductor of Wagner, in which capacity he appeared at Covent Garden in 1893. He composed much chamber and orchestral music and many songs.

---

[1] From this period dates the so-called ' Viennese mechanism,' the principle of which was really the same as that of the Augsburg pianos.

[2] Kurze Bemerkungen ü. d. Spielen, Stimmen, u. Erhalten d. F.P., etc., Wien, 1801.

(2) FRITZ (b. Grünsfeld, Baden, June 17, 1855; d. Munich, Aug. 13, 1916), brother of the above, whose pupil he was till he went to the Leipzig Conservatorium in 1873. In 1880 he became second Kapellmeister at Mainz till 1886, when he was summoned by the Grand Duke of Meiningen to the post of conductor of his celebrated orchestra, and later on became his general music-director. In 1902 he visited England with the whole of the Meiningen orchestra, and made one of the greatest sensations that has been caused by any musical performances within recent years in this country, his renderings of Bach and Brahms being specially appreciated. All the four symphonies of Brahms were included in his programmes. He was also a frequent visitor to England in later years, when he conducted concerts of the LONDON SYMPHONY ORCHESTRA (q.v.). In 1902 he succeeded Wüllner as town Kapellmeister and director of the Conservatorium at Cologne. He was also well known as a composer, chiefly through his septet (op. 7) and a violoncello sonata.   H. V. H.

STEINWAY & SONS, a firm of pianoforte-makers in New York, the merit of whose instruments early gave them equal rank with those of famous European make.

The founder of the Steinway house, Henry Engelhard Steinway (originally Steinweg), a piano-maker, with three of his four sons emigrated to New York from the Duchy of Brunswick in 1849, and in that city in 1853 established the firm of Steinway & Sons (incorporated in 1876). In 1855 they exhibited a square piano in which the principle of a single casting was combined with a cross or overstrung scale, the foundation of the so-called Steinway system.

From that year onward the Steinway piano was awarded honours and prizes at exhibitions and expositions in England, Europe and America. The first Steinway grand piano was built in 1856; the first upright in 1862. In 1865 Theodore, the eldest son of Henry Steinway, joined the firm in New York, and to him were due many of the inventions which gave the Steinway its signal merit and made it a model for the German makers of that day.

In 1866 Steinway & Sons opened a concert-hall in New York. This was sold in 1925 when the firm moved to West 57th Street. In 1875 a branch was opened in London, also with a concert-room attached (see STEINWAY HALL and GROTRIAN STEINWEG); and in 1880 a Hamburg branch was added. In 1925 the London house was moved to 1-2 George Street, Conduit Street, W.   W. S. S.

STEINWAY HALL. This small concert-hall attached to the original premises of Steinway & Sons in Lower Seymour Street, now renamed Wigmore Street, was formerly known as the Quebec Institute, where various literary

societies held their meetings. In 1878 it was used for music, Hans von Bülow giving the inaugural concert. For many years it was the principal small concert-hall in London and many well-known musicians appeared there. In later years it was greatly used for first appearances of young performers and singers. When the lease of the premises expired and the firm moved to Conduit Street the hall was closed, the last concert being given there in December 1924. The seating capacity was 400. It was reopened in 1925 as Grotrian Hall (see GROTRIAN STEINWEG).

STEINWEG, see GROTRIAN STEINWEG.

STENHAMMAR, VILHELM EUGEN (b. Stockholm, Feb. 7, 1871), one of the foremost Swedish pianists and leaders of music since the beginning of this century, has also earned a reputation, at home and abroad, as a composer. His father was Per Ulrik Stenhammar, who wrote several church choruses and solo pieces which became very popular. He studied the piano, first under Rich. Andersson (1888), and later in Berlin (1892–93) under Barth, and was taught composition by E. Sjögren and others. He qualified as an organist at the Conservatoire in 1890. His first noted work, 'The Princess and the Page,' for solo, chorus and orchestra, was produced in Stockholm by the Philharmonic Society in 1892. For the inauguration of the new Opera-House, Stenhammar wrote the musical drama 'Tirfing,' which was produced at the Royal Theatre in 1898. He had already written 'Gildet på Solhaug,' first performed in Stuttgart in 1899 and afterwards at the Royal Theatre, Stockholm, in 1902. He held a prominent position as conductor of the Royal Orchestra in Stockholm and later extended his musical leadership to Gothenburg, where he has gained great popularity.

Stenhammar is a noted song-composer and has also written chamber music, orchestral works and opera. In 1900 he became a member of the Academy of Music.

Among his works are :

'Ett folk' ('A People'); Ithaka (both for barytone and orchestra); 'Midvinter'; the second piano-concerto in D minor; 'Two sentimental romances,' for violin; 'Folket i Nifelhem,' op. 30 and 'Intermezzo.'

There is a striking portrait of Stenhammar at the piano, by Robert Thegerström (b. 1857), in the National Museum, Stockholm.

See articles in *Swedish Musical Journal*, 1895, 1897, 1902, 1906, 1909; German biogr. by T. Norlind in 'Die Musik,' Berlin, 1904.

                                        G. A. S.

STENHOUSE, WILLIAM (b. Roxburghshire, Scotland, 1773; d. Nov. 10, 1827), a writer on Scottish music. He was an accountant in Edinburgh, and before 1817 conceived the idea of annotating Johnson's *Scots Musical Museum*, with historical references regarding both words and music. He contributed specimens of these notes to *Blackwood's Magazine* for July 1817. For a republication of the *Scots Musical Museum* Stenhouse's notes were printed in 1820, but laid aside for a considerable period, being ultimately published in 1839 and again in 1853. Stenhouse's work has been a bone of contention among musical antiquaries since its publication.

There is undoubtedly a vast mass of interesting and trustworthy information in the notes, together with many careless and slipshod references which have caused the whole work to be condemned. (See SCOTTISH NATIONAL MUSIC, section LATER COLLECTIONS.)

Stenhouse edited the musical portion of James Hogg's *Jacobite Relics*, 1819–21. F. K.

ŠTĔPÁN, VÁCLAV (*b.* Pečky, 1889), Czech composer, pianist and musical critic. Ph.D. of the University of Prague. He studied the piano with J. Čermák and composition with Vít. Novák, professor of æsthetics in the Prague Conservatoire. He has appeared as a pianist in many European centres (England, 1919), and done much to make modern Czech music known to the world. His ' Musical Symbolism in Programme Music ' (1914) first came out as a series of articles in the defunct *Hudební Revue*, to which he was a frequent contributor. His published works include the poem ' Pohoda Života ' (Life's Halcyon Days), for violoncello and piano (Hudební Matice, Prague).

R. N.

STEPHENS, (1) CATHERINE (*b.* London, Sept. 18, 1794 ; *d.* 9 Belgrave Square, London, Feb. 22, 1882), the daughter of Edward Stephens, a carver and gilder in Park Street. Having given early indications of aptitude for music, she was in 1807 placed under the instruction of Gesualdo Lanza, whose pupil she remained for five years. Early in 1812 she appeared in subordinate parts at the Pantheon as a member of an Italian Opera Company. Soon afterwards her father, dissatisfied with the apparently small progress she made under Lanza, placed her under the tuition of Thomas Welsh. On Sept. 23, 1813, she appeared anonymously at Covent Garden as Mandane in ' Artaxerxes ' with decided success. She repeated the part on Sept. 28, as ' Miss Stevens,' and on Sept. 30 under her proper name. On Oct. 22 she sang Polly in ' The Beggar's Opera,' Rosetta in ' Love in a Village,' and afterwards Clara in ' The Duenna,' in each gaining ground in public favour. In Mar. 1814 she was engaged at the Concert of Ancient Music, and later in the year she sang at the festivals at Norwich and Birmingham. She sang in Edinburgh in 1814, and at Dublin in 1816, 1821 and 1825. She continued at Covent Garden from 1813–22, when she broke with the managers on a question of terms and transferred her services to Drury Lane. She occupied the principal position on the English operatic stage, at the first concerts, and the festivals, until 1835, when she retired into private life. Her voice was a pure soprano, rich, full, and powerful, and of extensive compass, and her execution neat,

although not very remarkable 'or brilliancy. She somewhat lacked dramatic instinct and power, and her enunciation was very bad, but she excelled in the expression of quiet devotional feeling and simple pathos. In such songs as Handel's ' Angels, ever bright and fair,' and ' If guiltless blood,' and in ballads like ' Auld Robin Gray,' and ' Savourneen Deelish,' she captivated every hearer. On Apr. 19, 1838, she was married to the widowed octogenarian Earl of Essex in his house No. 9 Belgrave Square,[1] and on Apr. 23, 1839, became his widow. She survived him for nearly forty-three years. A portrait by John Jackson is in the National Portrait Gallery. W. H. H., addns.

(2) CHARLES EDWARD (*b.* Edgware Road, London, Mar. 18, 1821 ; *d.* London, July 13, 1892), nephew of the preceding. Displaying early tokens of musical organisation, he was placed under Cipriani Potter for pianoforte, J. A. Hamilton for harmony, counterpoint and composition, and Henry Blagrove for the violin. In 1843 he was elected organist of St. Mark's, Myddelton Square, and subsequently held the same office at Holy Trinity, Paddington, 1846 ; St. John's, Hampstead, 1856 ; St. Mark's, St. John's Wood, 1862–63 ; St. Clement Danes, 1864–69, and St. Saviour's, Paddington, 1872–1875. In 1850 he was elected an associate, and in 1857 a member of the Philharmonic Society, of which he was repeatedly chosen a director. In 1865 he was elected a Fellow of the R.C.O., in 1870 an honorary member of the R.A.M., and in 1877 a licentiate, *honoris causa*, of Trinity College, London. His trio for pianoforte, violin and violoncello was produced at the Society of British Musicians, himself performing the pianoforte part ; his works also include several concert overtures of merit, No. 4 of which, ' A Dream of Happiness,' was played at the Crystal Palace, Nov. 13, 1875. His partsong, ' Come, fill ye right merrily,' gained the prize given by Henry Leslie's Choir in 1858, and in Apr. 1879 he was awarded both the first and second prizes given by Trinity College, London, for the best string quartet. His symphony in G minor was performed at the Philharmonic Concert in Mar. 1891.

W. H. H., addns.

STEPHENS, JOHN, Mus.D. (*d.* Dec. 15, 1780), was educated as a chorister in Gloucester Cathedral, and in 1746 succeeded Edward Thomson as organist of Salisbury Cathedral. He graduated as Mus.D. at Cambridge in 1763, and conducted the Gloucester Festival in 1766.

[1] In the Parish Register of St. George's, Hanover Square, the marriage was originally entered as having been celebrated in ' the Parish Church.' These last three words were, however, subsequently *erased* (in two places) *with a sharp instrument*, and ' 9 Belgrave Square ' written upon the erasures, but without any note, or authentication of the alteration being made in the Register. The original entry is proved by the words ' the Parish Church ' remaining unaltered in the certified copy of the Register at Somerset House, until Mar. 1882, when the discrepancy was pointed out by the present writer, and measures taken for its correction. It is to be hoped that this is a solitary instance of so flagrant a violation of the directions of the Act of Parliament as to the mode in which erroneous entries in Registers are to be rectified.

A volume of ' Cathedral Music ' by him, edited by Highmore Skeats, was published in 1805.

W. H. H.

STERKEL, JOHANN FRANZ XAVER (Abbé Sterkel) (b. Würzburg, Dec. 3, 1750; d. there, Oct. 21, 1817), was a distinguished amateur. He went through his college course at Würzburg University, took orders and became vicar and organist of Neumünster. In 1778 he was called to the court of the Elector of Mainz at Aschaffenburg as chaplain and pianist. Next year the Elector sent him on a journey through Italy; success attended him everywhere, and at Naples he brought out an opera, ' Farnace,' in 1780, with éclat. In 1781 he returned to Mainz and was promoted to a canonry. He wrote about this date some German songs which were great favourites, and he formed some excellent pupils—among composers Hofmann and Zulehner, among singers Grünbaum and Kirschbaum. In Sept. 1791 occurred the great musical event of Sterkel's life, though he probably did not know its significance—his meeting with Beethoven, then a youth of 20. Beethoven came to Aschaffenburg with the band of the Elector of Bonn, and was taken by Ries and Simrock to call on the great player, whose reputation was something like that of Liszt in after years. Sterkel was the first great executant that Beethoven had heard, and the extreme refinement and finish of his style evidently struck him much. He watched him with the closest attention, and not unnaturally declined to play in his turn, till Sterkel induced him to do so by speaking of his twenty-four variations on Righini's 'Venni Amore.' They had been published only a few months previously, and Sterkel declared that they were so hard that he did not believe even the composer could play them. Beethoven played what he could recollect, and improvised others fully equalling the originals in difficulty—but the curious thing was that he adopted Sterkel's delicate style all through. They do not appear to have met again. In 1793 Sterkel succeeded Righini as Kapellmeister to the Elector, and this threw him still more into serious composition; but the French war forced the Elector to leave Mainz, and his Kapellmeister returned to Würzburg. In 1805 he became Kapellmeister at Ratisbon, where all his old energy revived, and he taught and composed with the greatest vigour and success. The war of 1813 at length drove him back from Ratisbon to Würzburg.

The list of Sterkel's published compositions is immense. (See Q.-L.) It embraces:

10 symphonies; 2 overtures; a string quintet; a quartet for PF. and strings; 6 string trios; 6 do. duos; 6 PF. concertos; a very large number of sonatas for PF. both for two and four hands; variations, and minor pieces; 10 collections of songs for voice and PF.; Italian canzonets, duets, etc.

The number of editions which some of these went through shows how widely popular

Sterkel was in his day. A Mass and a Te Deum are in MS.

G.

STERLING, ANTOINETTE (b. Sterlingville, State of New York, Jan. 23, 1850 ?; d. Hampstead, Jan. 9, 1904), singer. She possessed, even in childhood, a voice of extraordinary range, which afterwards settled into a contralto of great richness and volume, with a compass from e♭ to f″. Her first serious study of singing began in 1867 in New York under Abella, better known as the husband of Mme. d'Angri. She came to England in 1868 and remained a few months, singing chiefly in the provinces, en route for Germany. There she was first a pupil of Mme. Marchesi at Cologne, then of Pauline Viardot at Baden-Baden, and lastly of Manuel Garcia in London. She returned to America in 1871, and soon took a high position as a concert singer. On May 13, 1873, she took leave of her native country in a concert at the Irving Hall, Boston, arrived in England, and made her first appearance on Nov. 5 at the Covent Garden Promenade Concert, under the conductorship of Sir Julius Benedict. At the Crystal Palace she first sang on Dec. 6, and shortly after appeared at the Saturday Popular, Feb. 21, 1874, Sacred Harmonic, Philharmonic, Albert Hall and London Ballad Concerts. At Gloucester, in the following September, she sang at the Festival. She was married on Easter Sunday 1875, at the Savoy Chapel, to John MacKinlay; and from that time, excepting a few months in the same year, when she sang in America in a series of forty concerts under Theodore Thomas, resided in London, and was one of the most popular singers there. She was not unknown in classical music. On her first arrival here she sang the Cradle Song from Bach's Christmas Oratorio with much effect, and her repertory contained songs of Mendelssohn and Schumann. But she was essentially a ballad singer. Her voice was one of great beauty and attractiveness; but it was her earnestness and intention, the force which she threw into the story—especially if it was weird or grim, such as 'The Three Fishers,' 'The Sands of Dee,' or 'The Three Ravens'— and the distinctness with which she declaimed the words, that formed the real secret of her success. Her son, Sterling MacKinlay, a baritone singer, published a memoir in 1906.

G.

STERN, JULIUS (b. Breslau, Aug. 8, 1820; d. Berlin, Feb. 27, 1883), removed at an early age to Berlin, where he learned music under Maurer, Ganz and Rungenhagen, at the Singakademie and the Royal Academy of Arts and soon began to compose. ' Please enquire about Mr. Julius Stern of Berlin,' says Mendelssohn,[1] ' who has sent me a book of songs with a kind note. From the first glance I think they show talent, but I have not seen or heard anything else about him.' In 1843 he received a

[1] Mendelssohn Family, ii. 57.

travelling scholarship from the King, which led him first to Dresden, for the special study of singing, and then to Paris, where he soon became known as conductor of the German 'Gesangverein.' Here he performed the 'Antigone,' first in the studio of Henry Lehmann the painter,[1] and then at the Odéon Theatre, which drew from Mendelssohn a very characteristic letter (May 27, 1844). In 1846 he returned to Berlin, and in 1847 founded the Society which bore his name (Stern'scher Gesangverein). The first performance of ' Elijah ' in Oct. 1847 gave a specimen of the powers of the new Association, and the level was fully maintained subsequently by performances of a very wide range of works both ancient and modern. In 1874 ill-health obliged Stern to retire from the conductorship, and he was succeeded by STOCKHAUSEN.

Meantime, in 1850, with Kullak and Marx, he had founded his Conservatorium, which, notwithstanding the defection of his two colleagues, flourished and educated many good musicians. From 1869–71 he conducted the Berlin ' Sinfonie-Kapelle,' and at Christmas 1873 undertook the Reichshall concerts, which, however, only lasted for two seasons. He then confined himself to his Conservatorium till his death. Stern published many vocal pieces and arrangements, but his most enduring work will probably be his edition of Exercises by Vaccaj (Bote & Bock), Crescentini (Peters), etc. He was made a ' Königliche Musikdirector ' in 1849 and ' Königliche Professor ' in 1860.   G.

STERN, LEOPOLD LAWRENCE (b. Brighton, Apr. 5, 1862; d. London, Sept. 10, 1904), violoncellist. He belonged to a musical family, his father being a German violinist and his mother (née Annie Lawrence) an English pianist. From his early youth he showed strong musical leanings, and as a boy played the drum in the ' Brighton Symphony Society,' of which his father was the conductor. In 1877 he became a student at the South Kensington School of Chemistry, keeping up his music meanwhile, and eventually began the violoncello under Hugo Daubert. In 1880 he accepted a business appointment at Thornliebank, near Glasgow; but three years later he finally abandoned chemistry in favour of music and, returning to London, entered the R.A.M., studying the violoncello first under Pezze and then under Piatti, and subsequently visiting Leipzig in order to take lessons from Julius Klengel and Davidov. Returning to England in 1886, he played both in London and the provinces, accompanied Patti on one of her tours, and later on played in concerts with Sauret and Paderewski. In Paris he played with Godard and Massenet. In 1895 he visited Prague, where, being favourably impressed by his playing,

[1] Mendelssohn Family, ii. 295.

Dvořák selected him to bring out his violoncello concerto, and came himself to London to conduct in person the first public performance of the same, which took place at the Philharmonic Concert in Mar. 1896, when Stern achieved his greatest success. He subsequently played it at Prague, the Leipzig Gewandhaus, and the Berlin Philharmonic.

In 1897 and 1898 Stern toured through the United States and Canada, and henceforth appeared but rarely before an English audience.

Stern was twice married : firstly, in 1891, to Nettie Carpenter, a violinist of some distinction; and secondly, in 1898, to Suzanne Adams, the accomplished operatic singer.

In his early years Leo Stern played upon a violoncello by Guidantus, later on the ' General Kyde ' Stradivari (an instrument of large proportions), and finally on the ' Baudiot ' Stradivari.   W. W. C.

STERNDALE BENNETT, see BENNETT.

STERNHOLD, see PSALTER.

STEURLEIN (STEURLIN), JOHANN (b. Schmalkalden, July 5, 1546; d. Meiningen, May 5, 1613), was town clerk of Wasungen in 1575; government clerk at Weimar, 1588; imperial notary and poet-laureate, 1604. He was a very successful and gifted amateur composer of several books of sacred and secular songs, motets, psalms and occasional songs (Q.-L.).

STEVENS, RICHARD JOHN SAMUEL (b. London, Mar. 27, 1757; d. Sept. 23, 1837), was educated in St. Paul's Cathedral choir under William Savage. He distinguished himself as a glee composer, and obtained prizes from the Catch Club for his glees ' See, what horrid tempests rise,' 1782, and ' It was a lover and his lass,' 1786. He was appointed organist of the Temple Church, 1786, organist of the Charter House, 1796 (retaining his appointment at the Temple), and on Mar. 17, 1801, was elected to the GRESHAM MUSICAL PROFESSORSHIP (q.v.). He published three sets of glees, three harpsichord sonatas (op. 1) and songs. Nine glees and a catch by him are included in Warren's collections. Among his best glees may be mentioned ' Ye spotted snakes,' ' Blow, blow, thou winter wind,' ' Crabbed age and youth,' ' Sigh no more, ladies,' ' The cloud-capt towers,' ' From Oberon in fairy land,' all of which still retain their popularity with lovers of that class of composition. He edited ' Sacred Music for one, two, three and four voices, from the works of the most esteemed composers, Italian and English,' an excellent collection in 3 vols. fol. He left a valuable collection of music to the R.A.M.   W. H. H.

STEVENSON, SIR JOHN ANDREW, Knight, Mus.D. (b. Dublin, Nov. 1761; d. Headfort House, Sept. 14, 1833), son of John Stevenson, a violinist in the State Band in Dublin, was admitted a chorister of Christ Church Cathedral, Dublin, in 1771, and in 1775–80 was in the choir of St. Patrick's Cathedral. He became a vicar-choral of St. Patrick's in 1783 and of Christ Church in 1800. He composed new music to O'Keeffe's farces, 'The Son-in-Law' (1781), 'The Dead Alive' (1781) and 'The Agreeable Surprise' (1782), to enable them to be performed in Dublin, and also composed for the Irish stage some of the music of 'The Contract,' 1782 ; 'Love in a blaze,' 1799 ; 'The Patriot,' 1810 ; 'The Burning of Moscow' and 'Bedouins,' 1801. He obtained his honorary Mus.D. degree at Dublin in 1791, and his knighthood from the Lord-Lieutenant (Lord Hardwicke) in 1803. In 1814 he was appointed the first organist and musical director at the Castle Chapel. He composed some services and anthems (a collection of which he published, with his portrait prefixed, in 1825), 'Thanksgiving' (Dublin Musical Festival, Sept. 1831), an oratorio, and numerous glees, duets, canzonets, songs, etc. But he is best known by his symphonies and accompaniments to the collection of Irish Melodies, the words for which were written by Thomas Moore. He died at Headfort House, while on a visit to his daughter, the Marchioness of Headfort. A monument was erected to his memory in St. Patrick's Cathedral. A biographical sketch, by John Bumpus, appeared in 1893.

w. h. h. ; addns. and corr. w. h. g. f.

STEVENSON, Robert, Mus.D. Oxon. (2nd half of 16th cent.), English composer of church music. He had supplicated for his Mus.B. degree in 1583, but did not obtain it until 1587, when he had been for thirty-three years a student of music. He proceeded Mus.D. in 1596 (C. F. Abdy Williams, *Degrees in Music*). He was organist of Chester Cathedral from 1570–99 (West's *Cath. Org.*). A whole Service by him (including V. ; T.D. ; B. ; K. ; C. ; M. and N.D.) is in Durham Cathedral Library (Durh. C 8 and 13 ; Durh. O.B. A 3/23); an anthem, 'When yᵉ Lord turned,' is at Peterhouse, Cambridge (tenor cantoris part in B.M. Add. MSS. 30,478-9); and 4 parts of a 6-part medley beginning 'Miserere' (with a plain-song in the tenor) by 'Dr. Stevenson' are also in the British Museum (Add. MSS. 18,936-9).

J. Mᴷ.

STEWART, Neil, one of the early Edinburgh music-publishers. In 1759 he was at the sign of the 'Violin and German Flute' in the Exchange, but before 1761 he had removed to a shop, 'opposite the Head of Blackfriar's Wynd,' which had probably been Bremner's place of business. He again removed to the Exchange, and then to Miln's Square (now demolished), facing the Tron Church. Afterwards the business was in Parliament Square, and finally in South Bridge Street. The stock-in-trade and plates were sold off by auction in 1805. Originally founded by the elder Neil

Stewart, the business afterwards developed into a partnership as 'Neil Stewart & Company,' and finally belonged to Neil and Malcolm Stewart, the two sons.

The Stewart publications comprise a great bulk of important works of Scottish music, and include republications of M'Gibbon ; collections of reels and country dances ; marches and minuets ; M'Glashan's works ; Scots Songs ; and great quantities of interesting music sheets.

F. K.

STEWART, Sir Robert Prescott, Knight, Mus.D. (*b.* Dublin, Dec. 16, 1825 ; *d.* there, Mar. 24, 1894), son of Charles Frederick Stewart, librarian of the King's Inns, Dublin, was educated as a chorister of Christ Church Cathedral, Dublin, of which he was appointed organist in 1844, in which year he was also appointed organist of Trinity College, Dublin. In 1846 he became conductor of the University of Dublin Choral Society, the members of which defrayed the expenses of the performance of his music for degrees of Mus.B. and Mus.D. which took place in 1851, besides presenting him with his graduate's robes and a jewelled baton. In 1852 he became a vicar-choral of St. Patrick's Cathedral, and in 1861 was appointed professor of music in the University of Dublin. For the great Peace Festival held in America at Boston, in 1872, he composed a fantasia on Irish airs for orchestra, organ and chorus, but declined the invitation to represent Ireland there. On this occasion he received knighthood from the Lord-Lieutenant (Earl Spencer) and became professor of theory in the Royal Irish Academy of Music. In 1873 he was appointed conductor of the Dublin Philharmonic.

Amongst Stewart's many compositions, his glees deserve particular mention. In this branch of his art he won numerous prizes and well-merited renown. His more important works include an ode for the opening of the Cork Exhibition of 1852 ; 'Ode on Shakespeare,' produced at the Birmingham Festival, 1870 ; and two cantatas, 'A Winter Night's Wake' and 'The Eve of S. John,' given by Stanford at Cambridge in 1872. He edited the Irish 'Church Hymnal' (1876).

Sir Robert Stewart enjoyed a high reputation as an organist and extemporiser ; his playing at the Great Exhibition of 1851 and at that of Manchester in 1857 excited general admiration. His musical memory was remarkable. As occupant of the Dublin Chair of Music, his excellent lectures and writings on music bore evidence to his wide culture and literary skill, as well as to his high musical attainments. He was the first to require candidates for the musical degrees to pass a literary test, and the good example was afterwards followed at Cambridge. A portrait by Sir T. A. Jones is in the Royal Irish Academy of Music, and his statue is on

Leinster Lawn, Dublin. A biography by Olinthus John Vignoles appeared in 1898, and Dr. Culwick's *The Works of Sir R. P. Stewart*, with a catalogue of his compositions (Dublin, 1902), may be consulted. w. h. h., addns.

STIASTNÝ, (1) BERNARD WENZEL (*b.* Prague, 1770; *d.* there, 1835), violoncellist, was a member of the Prague orchestra. He studied with Seegr and was probably professor at the Conservatorium, to which he dedicated his work on the violoncello. It is remarkable for what may be almost called a treatise on the accompaniment of recitative as it was then practised.

(2) JOHANN (*b.* Prague, 1764; *d. circa* 1820), brother of the above, was in the orchestra at Prague in 1800–20. He seems to have studied harmony and the violoncello at Prague, under his brother, but he must have soon left that city, as he is described on the title of his op. 3 as 'Violoncelle de S. A. R. le Grand Duc de Frankfort.' According to Fétis he was musical director at Nuremberg in 1820, and from thence went to Mannheim. He is known to have been in London, and he dedicated two of his finest compositions to Lindley and Crosdill, as well as his three duets, op. 8, to Sir W. Curtis. His last and perhaps finest work was published and probably written in London. He was also in Paris, where he arranged his op. 11 for violoncello and piano, and he dedicated his op. 3 to the pupils of the Conservatoire. There exists a beautiful French edition of his six grand duets, op. 1, and also of his two sonatas, op. 2, the latter in score. Though the list of his works only amounts to thirteen in number, the originality and purity of them all entitle him to rank among the very first writers for the instrument. A list of his works follows:

Op.
1. Six grand duets for two v'cls., dedicated to his brother.
2. Two sonatas for v'cl. solo with accompaniment for a second v'cl.
3. Divertissement for v'cl. solo with accompaniments for tenor and second v'cl.
4. Twelve ' Petites pièces pour violoncelle et basse à l'usage de commençants.'
5. Six pièces faciles for v'cl. and bass.
6. Three grand duets for two v'cls.
7. Concertino for v'cl. with accompaniments for flute, two tenors, v'cl. and contrabass, dedicated to Lindley.
8. Three duets for two v'cls.
9. Six pièces faciles for v'cl. and bass.
10. Andante with variations for v'cl. solo with accompaniments for flute, two violins, tenor and v'cl., dedicated to Crosdill.
11. Six solos for v'cl. and bass.
12. Theme with variations and rondo with quartet accompaniment.
13. Grand trio for v'cl. solo with accompaniment for tenor and second v'cl., published in London by Welsh & Hawes, but unknown on the Continent.
G. H.

STICCADO-PASTROLE, an early name for a kind of wooden dulcimer formed of a graduated series of rods which being struck give forth musical sounds. (See XYLOPHONE.) A trade card, in date about 1770, advertises that ' G. Smart, Sticcado - Pastrole maker, from Mr. Bremner's music shop . . . continues to make the above instruments with improvements.' The above G. Smart was afterwards a music-publisher, and was the father of Sir George SMART (*q.v.*). F. K.

STICH, JOHANN WENZEL, known as PUNTO (*b.* Bohemia, *c.* 1755; *d.* Feb. 16, 1803), eminent horn - player; was taught music and the French horn by Matiegka and Hampel of Dresden, at the expense of Count Thun. On his return to the Count's household he considered himself ill-treated, and ran away with some of his comrades. To avoid recognition he Italianised his name to Punto, and travelled in Germany and France, settling for a time in Würzburg, Treves, Coblenz, Paris, etc., and attracting considerable attention. In Paris he made the acquaintance of Mozart, who composed for him a Sinfonie Concertante for flute, oboe, horn and bassoon, never played and now unfortunately lost. ' Punto plays magnificently' (*bläst magnifique*), writes Mozart to his father. In 1788 he was engaged by Mara (with Graff, Fischer and Florio) for her concerts at the Pantheon, London. In Vienna, Beethoven composed his sonata for PF. and horn (op. 17) for him, and they played it together without rehearsal, at Punto's concert, Apr. 18, 1800. It was received enthusiastically, and at once encored. After this Punto made another tour with Dussek, returned to Prague and gave a concert at the theatre there in 1801. He died after a long illness. His epitaph runs:

'Omne tulit punctum Punto, cui Musa Bohema
 Ut plausit vivo, sic morienti gemit.'

His compositions were published in Paris by Sieber, Nadermann, Cochet, Imbault, Le Duc and Pleyel. C. F. P.

STICKER, a light wooden rod used in organ action for conveying motion by a pushing movement. (See TRACKER.) T. E.

STIEHL, HEINRICH (*b.* Lübeck, Aug. 5, 1829; *d.* Reval, May 1, 1886), second son of J. D. Stiehl (1800–73), an esteemed organist there. He studied at Lübeck and Weimar, and at Leipzig under Moscheles, Gade and Hauptmann. In 1853 he settled in St. Petersburg as organist to the St. Peter's Church, and director of the Singakademie. In 1867 he moved to Vienna, and after staying there two years went on to Italy. In 1872 and 1873 he was in London, and from Oct. 1874–77 resided in Belfast as conductor of the Philharmonic Society and founder of the Cecilia Society there. He then returned to England, settling as a teacher at Hastings, and in 1880 was called to Reval in Russia, where he held a leading position as professor of music, organist and conductor of the Musical Society of the town. He gave an excellent performance of Bach's ' Matthew-Passion ' (the first in Russia) on Mar. 17, 1883, and repeated it at St. Petersburg, Apr. 6.

Stiehl's compositions are numerous. They include two operas, ' Der Schatzgräber ' and ' Jery und Bätely.' A little orchestral piece called ' The Vision ' was produced at the

Crystal Palace, Apr. 12, 1873, and was much applauded for its delicate fanciful character. A ' Hexentanz,' ' Ungarisch,' Waltzes, and a gavotte are also well known in Germany. He published three PF. trios, a sonata for PF. and v'cl., sonata quasi fantasia for PF. solo, and many other works, the latest being a string quartet, op. 172.   G.

STIMME (Ger.), is used both for the human voice and for the individual parts in polyphonic composition or concerted music, whether vocal or instrumental.

STIMMFÜHRUNG (Ger.), see PART-WRIT-ING.

STIMPSON, JAMES (b. Lincoln, Feb. 29, 1820 ; d. Birmingham, Oct. 4, 1886), son of a lay-vicar of Lincoln Cathedral, who removed to Durham in 1822, where James became a chorister in 1827. In Feb. 1834 he was articled to Ingham, organist of Carlisle Cathedral ; in June 1836 was appointed organist of St. Andrew's, Newcastle ; and in June 1841, on Ingham's death, was made organist of Carlisle. In Feb. 1842 James Stimpson was unani-mously chosen organist at the Town Hall and St. Paul's, Birmingham, out of many com-petitors, and in the following year justified the choice by founding the Festival Choral Society and its Benevolent Fund, in connexion with the Triennial Festivals. (See BIRMINGHAM.) He continued organist and chorus-master to the Society until 1855. In 1844 he was instru-mental in starting the weekly Monday Evening Concerts, of which, in 1859, he took the entire responsibility, to relinquish them only after heavy losses in 1867.

In 1845 Stimpson had the satisfaction of having the pedals of the Town Hall organ increased from 2 to 2½ octaves, so that he was able to perform the works of J. S. Bach un-mutilated. From his weekly recitals in the Town Hall, given throughout the year to audiences varying from 600 to 1000, many a young amateur has derived his first taste for classical music. He was permanent organist of the Birmingham festivals, and Mendelssohn's last visit there was to conduct ' Elijah ' for Stimpson's benefit, Apr. 25, 1847. He intro-duced Sims Reeves and Charles Hallé to Birmingham, and laboured from 1849–68, in many ways, in the service of good music, gain-ing thereby the gratitude and respect of his fellow-townsmen. He was for many years professor of music at the Blind Institution.

D'Almaine published in 1850 ' The Organists' Standard Library,' edited by Stimpson, consist-ing principally of pieces hitherto unpublished in this country. His other publications consist mostly of arrangements and a manual of theory published by Rudall, Carte & Co. G.

STIRLING, ELIZABETH (b. Greenwich, Feb. 26, 1819 ; d. London, Mar. 25, 1895), an eminent English organist and composer,

learned the organ and piano from W. B. Wilson and Edward Holmes, and harmony from J. A. Hamilton and G. A. Macfarren. She attained a remarkable degree of execution on the organ pedals, as may be inferred from her first public performance, given at St. Katherine's Church, Regent's Park, when, out of fourteen numbers, the programme contained five pedal fugues and preludes, three pedal trios, and other pieces, by J. S. Bach. In Nov. 1839 she was elected organist of All Saints', Poplar, which she retained till Sept. 1858, when she gained the same post at St. Andrew's Undershaft, by com-petition. This she resigned in 1880. In 1856 she submitted an exercise (Ps. cxxx. for five voices and orchestra) for the degree of Mus.B. Oxon. ; but though accepted it was not per-formed, since at that time women were not eligible for degrees. She published some original pedal fugues and slow movements, and other pieces for her instrument, as well as arrangements from the works of Handel, Bach and Mozart. Also songs and duets, and many partsongs for four voices, of which a well-established favourite is ' All among the barley.' In 1863 she married F. A. Bridge.   G.

STIVORI, FRANCESCO, a 16th-17th century organist and church composer, pupil of Claudio Merulo. From 1579–1601 or 1602 he was town organist at Montagnana, afterwards in the service of the Archduke Ferdinand of Austria, until 1605. He composed 6 books of sacred songs (' Sacrae cantiones '), 5-8 v. (1579–1601) ; 6 books of madrigals (1583–1605), also masses, Magnificat, etc., and 3 books of ricercari, etc. for instruments (. . . , 1594, 1599) (Q.-L. ; Riemann).

STOBAEUS, JOHANN (b. Graudenz, West Prussia, July 6, 1580 ; d. Königsberg, Sept. 11, 1646). In 1595 he was sent, for his further education, to Königsberg, where also from 1600 he attended the University. In 1599 he became the pupil in music of Johann Eccard, then ducal Kapellmeister at Königsberg. In 1601 Stobaeus was bass singer in the ducal chapel, and in 1602 was appointed cantor at the Dom-kirche and the school in connexion therewith. In 1626 he received the appointment of Kapell-meister to the Elector of Brandenburg at Königsberg, which he retained till his death.

Stobaeus followed Eccard in the contrapuntal setting of the Choral-tunes for voices alone, in a style midway between that of the motet proper, and that of mere note-for-note har-mony. In 1634 he published :

' Geistliche Lieder auf gewöhnliche Preussische Kirchen-Melodeyen durchaus gerichtet und mit fünff Stimmen componirt.'

This work contains 102 settings a 5 of the Choral-tunes, half of them by Eccard, the remainder by Stobaeus. In 1642 and 1644 appeared two parts of ' Preussische Fest-Lieder mit 5, 6, 8 Stimmen,' 27 by Eccard, 21 by Stobaeus. In this work the tunes, as well as the settings, are by the composers. It has been reproduced in modern score by Teschner. An earlier publication of Stobaeus is his ' Cantiones sacrae 5, 6, 7, 8 et 10 vocibus item aliquot Magnificat 5 et 6 vocibus adornatae,' Frankfort, 1624. The Königsberg Library also contains a large number of occasional compositions by Stobaeus, sacred and secular.

J. R. M.

STOCK, FREDERICK AUGUST (b. Jülich, Germany, Nov. 11, 1872), German-American conductor and composer : Mus.D., Northwestern University, 1915. The son of a bandmaster in the German army, Stock began his musical studies with his father, and at 14 entered the Cologne Conservatorium. Graduating as a violinist, he then studied theory and composition under Humperdinck, Gustav Jensen and Franz Wüllner.

After five years as violinist in the Cologne Orchestra, in 1895 Stock went to the United States to become a violinist in the Chicago Symphony Orchestra (see CHICAGO). Made assistant to Theodore THOMAS (q.v.), then conductor, in 1899, from 1903 he conducted the orchestra's out-of-town concerts, and in January 1905, upon Thomas's death, he succeeded to the conductorship. In that post, which he still holds (1926), he has proved himself an able conductor, unusually catholic in his tastes.

As composer Stock is less widely known, although certain of his works have been played repeatedly at Chicago, and others were brought forward by KNEISEL (q.v.) The more important include :

Symphony, C minor.
Symphony, E flat.
' Variations,' orchestra.
' Life,' symphonic poem.
3 Overtures.
Symphonic Sketches.
Concerto, violin.
' Psalmodic Rhapsody,' solo, chorus and orchestra.
Chamber music, songs, violin and pianoforte pieces.

W. S. S.

STOCK EXCHANGE ORCHESTRAL AND CHORAL SOCIETY, THE, was founded in Nov. 1883, and gave its first concert on Mar. 5, 1885. On Dec. 18, 1885, the first subscription concert was given in the Prince's Hall ; and continuously from that date the Society has given a series of concerts in each season at St. James's and Queen's Hall. The Male Voice Choir was established in Oct. 1886, and gave its first concert in Feb. 1887. The choir made its first appearance with the orchestra in May 1888. In Oct. 1899 the orchestra and choir amalgamated under the present title. One of the objects of the Society is the production of new works by native composers. George Kitchin, an amateur, was honorary conductor of both orchestra and choir from their foundation until his retirement in 1897. Arthur W. Payne conducted the orchestra from Oct. 1897, and Munro Davison the choir from Oct. 1898. In 1925 the Society was conducted

by Cecil Engleheart with Francis H. Harper as deputy conductor. The hon. secretary is C. F. Hipwell, Stock Exchange, E.C.2.

S. J. S., addns.

STOCKFLÖTE, see CZAKAN.

STOCKHAUSEN, (1) née MARGARETE SCHMUCK (b. Gebweiler, 1803; d. Oct. 6, 1877), was trained in Paris as a concert-singer by Cartruffo. She became the wife of the harpist and composer Franz Stockhausen (1792–1868), and the mother of the singer Julius Stockhausen (2). Husband and wife travelled, giving not very remunerative concerts in Switzerland (1825). Paris was visited later, but Mme. Stockhausen's greatest successes attended her in England, where she was induced to return almost every year from 1828–40, singing at some of the concerts of the Philharmonic and Vocal Societies, and also taking part in the principal private and benefit concerts. She had little or no dramatic feeling, but as she gained in power she grew in public favour, and came to be recognised as a true musician and an accomplished singer. She was frequently engaged at provincial festivals, and her delivery of the music of Mary in Spohr's ' Calvary ' evoked special praise among her oratorio parts.

A few years after her farewell appearance in London, a home was made in Colmar, whither the Stockhausens retired to devote themselves to the education of their six children. Up to 1849 Mme. Stockhausen was heard with her son at local concerts ; she left Alsace only occasionally to appear in public, and in her last visit to Paris (1849) her singing showed a great falling off.

L. M. M.

(2) JULIUS (b. Paris, July 22, 1826 ; d. Sept. 22, 1906), son of the foregoing, one of the most remarkable singers of his time. His gifts showed themselves early, and his mother was accustomed to say that he could sing before he could speak. He and his younger brother Edward (who died early) accompanied their parents on a concert tour to England, and learnt there to sing Bishop's duet ' Where are you going, sweet sister Fay ? ' In 1833 Julius was placed at a school at Gebweiler in Alsace, where he remained till 1840, with a view to taking orders. But such intentions were dispelled by the violent turn for music which asserted itself after a concert at Basle in 1842, in which Mme. Stockhausen took part. He took a prominent part in the concerts at Gebweiler as singer, accompanist, violin-player and even drummer. In 1844 he moved to the seminary of Strassburg, and there his performances on the violoncello and organ sealed his fate as a priest. In 1845 and 1846 he visited Paris with his father, took lessons in the piano from Charles Hallé and Stamaty, and in singing from Manuel Garcia, and entered thoroughly into the abundant musical life of the French capital, to the great advantage of his musical

education. His devotion to the profession of music was, however, not absolutely decided till 1848, when, at the invitation of Ernst Reiter, the conductor, he suddenly took the part of Elijah in a performance of that oratorio at Basle. His success decided his future course, and he at once threw himself energetically into the art, and for the next few years travelled in all directions, singing at innumerable concerts Schubert's 'Schöne Müllerin' and other songs. In 1849 he came to England, renewed his lessons with Garcia and sang at various concerts. In 1851 he returned, and sang three times at the Philharmonic, Apr. 7, in the Choral Symphony, Apr. 28, in two trios, and June 9 in a scena from Boieldieu's 'Chaperon rouge.' Taste in England was not then sufficiently advanced to call for the Lieder just mentioned. To these, at the instance of Schröder-Devrient, he shortly added Schumann's 'Dichterliebe' and others. His first appearance on the stage seems to have been at Mannheim in 1852–53, and he joined the Opéra - Comique at Paris in 1857–59, taking such parts as the Seneschal in 'Jean de Paris.' At this time he became intimate with Ary Scheffer; and with Mme. Viardot, Berlioz, Duprez, Saint - Saëns and others, formed one of the circle by whom much German music was performed in the studio of the great painter.

The years 1859–62 were occupied in more concert tours, and it was during this time at Leipzig and Cologne that he first attempted Schumann's 'Faust' music. In 1862 he came to an anchor at Hamburg as director of the Philharmonic Concerts and of the Singakademie, a position which he retained till 1869, when he was made Kammersänger to the King of Würtemberg at Stuttgart with a salary of 2000 gulden, residing at Canstatt. During all this time he made many concert tours, especially with Mme. Schumann, Joachim and Brahms. In the latter part of 1870 he brought over his pupil Sophie Löwe to England, sang at the Popular Concerts, and remained till late in 1871. He once more sang at the Philharmonic, and appeared at the Crystal Palace, and the Monday Populars, where he introduced several fine unknown Lieder of Schubert. He and Frl. Löwe reappeared here the next winter, and remained till the end of the summer season of 1872.

In 1874 he moved from Stuttgart to Berlin, and took the direction of the Sternscher Gesangverein, founded by STERN (q.v.), which under his genial and able direction rose to the highest point of excellence. In the four years that he conducted it there were no less than twenty-eight performances of great works, including Beethoven's Mass in D, Mozart's Requiem, Bach's Matthew-Passion, Schumann's 'Faust' music (complete), and 'Paradise and the Peri,' Brahms's Requiem, etc. In 1878 he again

changed his residence, this time to Frankfort, to take the department of singing in the Conservatorium founded by Dr. Hoch, and presided over by Raff. This post, however, he soon gave up, and retired to his house at Frankfort, teaching the many private pupils who resorted to him there. After the death of Raff in 1882 he returned to the Conservatorium. In 1886–1887 he published his *Method of Singing* (translated by Mme. Sophie Löwe, new edition, 1907).

Stockhausen's singing in his best days must have been wonderful. Even to those who, like the writer, only heard him after he had passed his zenith, it is a thing never to be forgotten. Perhaps the maturity of the taste and expression made up for a little falling off in the voice. His delivery of opera and oratorio music—his favourite pieces from 'Euryanthe,' 'Jean de Paris,' 'Le Chaperon rouge,' and 'Le Philtre'; or the part of Elijah, or certain special airs of Bach—was superb in taste, feeling and execution; but it was the Lieder of Schubert and Schumann that most peculiarly suited him, and these he delivered in a truly remarkable way. The rich beauty of the voice, the nobility of the style, the perfect phrasing, the intimate sympathy, and, not least, the intelligible way in which the words were given—in itself one of his greatest claims to distinction—all combined to make his singing of songs a wonderful event. Those who have heard him sing Schubert's 'Nachtstück,' 'The Wanderer,' 'Memnon,' or the Harper's songs; or Schumann's 'Frühlingsnacht,' or 'Fluthenreicher Ebro,' or the 'Löwenbraut,' will corroborate all that has just been said. But perhaps his highest achievement was the part of Dr. Marianus in the third part of Schumann's 'Faust,' in which his delivery of the scene beginning 'Hier ist die Aussicht frei,' with just as much of acting as the concert-room will admit—and no more —was one of the most touching and remarkable things ever witnessed. G.

STOCKHORN, a rude musical instrument mentioned by early writers as being in use among the Scottish peasantry. It appears to have been identical with or similar to the PIBGORN (q.v.). The instrument is figured in a vignette in Ritson's 'Scotish Songs,' 1794, also on the frontispiece to the editions of Ramsay's 'Gentle Shepherd,' illustrated by David Allan, 1788 and 1808. It was then almost obsolete, for Robert Burns, the poet, had much difficulty in obtaining one. It appears to have been made in divers forms, with either a wooden or a bone stock, the horn being that of a cow. Burns, in a letter to George Thomson, Nov. 19, 1794, thus describes it:

'Tell my friend Allan . . . that I much suspect he has in his plates mistaken the figure of the stock and horn. I have at last gotten one; but it is a very rude instrument. It is composed of three parts, the stock, which is the hinder thigh bone of a sheep . . . the horn which is a common Highland cow's horn cut off at the smaller end until the aperture be large enough to admit the stock to be pushed up through the horn, until it be held by the thicker end of the thigh bone ; and lastly, an oaten reed exactly cut and notched like that which you see every shepherd-boy have, when the corn stems are green and full grown. The reed is not made fast in the bone, but is held by the lips, and plays loose on the smaller end of the stock ; while the stock with the horn hanging on its larger end, is held by the hand in playing. The stock has six or seven ventages on the upper side, and one back ventage, like the common flute. This of mine was made by a man from the braes of Athole, and is exactly what the shepherds are wont to use in that country. However, either it is not quite properly bored in the holes, or else we have not the art of blowing it rightly, for we can make little of it.'

An example of the Stockhorn is preserved in the Library of the R.C.M. and was once the property of Charles Keene. It consists of a cylindrical tube pierced through the stock or body of the instrument, having seven holes for the fingers in front and one at the back. The lower end terminates in a short bell of natural horn. The reed is covered by a pierced wooden cap like that of the practice chanter of the bagpipe, within which the reed vibrates under the breath of the performer. Unfortunately, a double-reed has been substituted for the single-beating reed which is characteristic of the instrument (*PLATE LIV*. No. 5). Another and probably unique example is in the Museum of Scottish Antiquities, Edinburgh ; it has fourteen finger-holes, and two thumb-holes at the back, arranged in pairs, so that each finger closes or opens two holes at once. The total length of this instrument is about twenty-two inches, with a bell - mouth expanding to $2\frac{1}{8}$ inches, and its scale is from f' to g''. The object of the double bore appears to have been the production of a strong beating tone from mistuned consonances, as is commonly found in the Egyptian Zummarah or double reed-pipe of the present day, which also has single-beating reeds. (See PIBGORN).   F. K. and F. W. G.

STOCKMARR, JOHANNA (b. Copenhagen, Apr. 21, 1869), pianist, studied in Copenhagen and later in Paris, and established her reputation as an artist of first-rate ability. In England she was associated with Lady Hallé at the Monday Popular Concerts, and from 1900 onwards she was frequently to be heard with the orchestra under Richter and Wood.   c.

STODART. A family of eminent pianoforte-makers, whose business was founded in Wardour Street, Soho, about the year 1776, by (1) ROBERT STODART. It is said he had been in the Royal Horse Guards, to be a private in which corps involved at that time the payment of £100, an amount that must now be estimated by the then higher value of money. Having little duty and much leisure, Stodart became a pupil of John Broadwood to learn pianoforte-making, and in the books of Broadwood's firm appears, during the year 1775, to have taken his share in tuning for customers. It was while he was under Broadwood that he had the privilege, enjoyed by them as friends, of assist-

ing Americus Backers in the invention of the new movement for the grand pianoforte since generally known as the ' English ' action. After Backers's death, Stodart, now upon his own account, entered upon grand pianoforte making with energy and ability, and soon made a considerable reputation. The pianoforte was at that time hardly emancipated from the harpsichord, and there were frequent endeavours to combine both principles in one instrument. An endeavour of this nature was patented by Stodart in 1777, which is otherwise remarkable by the first mention of the word ' grand ' in connexion with a pianoforte. In it he worked his crow-quill registers, and also a swell, by means of pedals.

We find the business in 1795 removed to Golden Square, (2) WILLIAM STODART in that year taking out, from that address, a patent for an 'Upright Grand.' This was the horizontal grand turned up vertically in the same way the upright harpsichord had been. The giraffe-like upright grand was then coming into fashion, and the speciality of Stodart's patent was to introduce one in the form of a bookcase. Of the highest importance was the patent of James Thom and William Allen, who were in Stodart's employ, a compensating framing of metal tubes and plates at once secured by Stodart's firm. This meritorious invention, which was really Allen's, was brought out in 1820, and paved the way to the general introduction of iron in pianofortes as a resisting power. (See PIANOFORTE and the writer's *Pianoforte Primer*, p. 16.) When (3) MALCOLM STODART, who had shown great promise, died, the interest of the survivors ceased, and the business, which had been declining, came, in 1861, to an end.   A. J. H.

STOELZEL (STÖLTZEL) GOTTFRIED HEINRICH (b. Grünstädel, Saxony, Jan. 13, 1690 ; d. Gotha, Nov. 27, 1749), a pupil of Umlauf at Schneeberg and of Musikdirektor Hofmann at Leipzig, where he also studied at the University and joined Telemann's Musical Society. From 1710–12 he was teacher of music at Breslau, where he produced his first opera ' Narcissus ' in 1711, which was followed by several operas for Naumburg. In 1713 he went to Italy and on his return he remained at Prague for three years where he produced several operas and oratorios ; thence he went to Bayreuth. In 1718 he was in the service of the Count of Gera and from 1719 was Kapellmeister to the Duke of Gotha. Stoelzel was a prolific composer (22 operas, 14 oratorios, masses, trio-sonatas, concertos, etc., mostly MS.) who possessed melodic invention, and imbued his orchestral parts with individuality ; but he lacked true genius and never rose beyond fluency of melody. He wrote also some theoretical essays. A violin concerto of his was republished by Prof. A. Schering in *D.D.T.*   E. v. d. S.

STOJOWSKI, Sigismond Denis Antoine (*b.* Strzelce, Poland, Apr. 8,[1] 1870), Polish pianist and composer. In his early youth he studied with Zenlenski at Cracow : later at the Paris Conservatoire under Diémer, Dubois, Delibes and Massenet, and finally with Gorski and Paderewski. After numerous European tours, in 1905–11 he was head of the pianoforte department of the Institute of Musical Art (New York). He has taught extensively in that city. As soloist he has played with most of the leading orchestras of America.

The list of Stojowski's compositions is a long one and includes :

Symphony, D minor, op. 21.
Concerto, piano, F-sharp minor, op. 3.
Romanza, violin and orchestra, op. 20.
Concerto, violin, G minor, op. 22.
Symphonic Rhapsody, pianoforte and orchestra, op. 23.
Concerto, violoncello, D, op. 31.
Concerto, pianoforte, op. 32.
'A Prayer for Poland,' chorus, organ and orchestra, op. 40.
A cantata ; numerous sonatas and other chamber music ; many
     pianoforte pieces and songs.   w. s. s.

STOKES, Charles (*b.* 1784 ; *d.* London, Apr. 14, 1839), an excellent musician who received his first instructions as a chorister in St. Paul's Cathedral. He was afterwards a pupil of Webbe, the glee composer, who was his godfather—and of other masters ; but he was most indebted for his musical knowledge to Samuel Wesley, with whom he was long and intimately acquainted. He officiated for several years as assistant-organist to Callcott, at St. Paul's, Covent Garden and Bartleman at Croydon ; but he latterly preferred the quiet pursuit of his own studies, in domestic retirement, to the exertion and fatigue of public engagements. Yet his musical acquirements were of the highest order. Vincent Novello speaks of him as a most able teacher, an excellent organist, a delightful pianoforte-player, a refined and tasteful composer, and one of the most profound musical theorists then living. His name was little known, and his published music was almost confined to the pieces printed in Novello's ' Select Organ Pieces ' (from which this notice is derived). That collection contains ten pieces by Stokes, full of quiet feeling, and real, though somewhat antiquated, musicianship. Novello also published an Anthem of his, ' I will lay me down in peace.'   G.

STOKOWSKI, Leopold (*b.* London, Apr. 18, 1882), orchestral conductor. Of Polish parentage, his early education was obtained in England, France and Germany, and included instruction in violin, piano and organ. At the R.C.M. his teachers included Stevenson Hoyte (organ), Walford Davies and Stanford. From 1900 he was organist of St. James's, Piccadilly. Going to America in 1905 he was for three years organist of St. Bartholomew's Church in New York ; then, after a year's conducting in Europe, he became, in 1909, the conductor of the Cincinnati Symphony Orchestra.

Since 1912 Stokowski has been conductor of the Philadelphia Symphony Orchestra, where his rise to fame and popularity has been notable. He has brought that orchestra to a high place among the orchestras of the world, and he has been hospitable to the music of American composers and to the newer works of Europeans. In 1911 he married the pianist, Olga Samaroff (*q.v.*) ; they were divorced twelve years later.   w. s. s.

STOLTZ, Rosine (*b.* Paris, Feb. 13, 1815 ; *d.* there, July 28,[2] 1903), celebrated French singer, whose chequered life has afforded materials for more than one romance. Her real name was Victoire Noël, but she entered Ramier's class in Choron's school in 1826 as Rosine Niva. She became a chorus singer at one of the theatres after the Revolution of 1830, and in 1832 made a very modest début at Brussels. She first adopted her mother's maiden name of Stoll, which she converted into Stoltz. In 1833 she sang at Lille under the name of Heloïse Stoltz. Her knowledge of music was deficient and she never became a perfect singer, but nevertheless made a considerable mark in lyric tragedy. The first time she displayed her powers was when acting with A. Nourrit as Rachel in ' La Juive ' at Brussels in 1836. There she married the following year A. Lescuyer, manager at the Théâtre de la Monnaie.

She reappeared in the part of Rachel at the Opéra in Paris, Aug. 25, 1837. Though inferior to Mlle. Falcon, who had created the rôle, the public was interested by a talent so original and full of fire, though so unequal, and Mme. Stoltz became a favourite from the day she appeared in parts written expressly for her. Indeed throughout Léon Pillet's management (1841–1847) she reigned without a rival. She created the following mezzo-soprano parts : Lazarillo in Marliani's ' Xacarilla ' (1839) ; Léonore in ' La Favorite ' (1840) ; Agathe in ' Der Freischütz ' (1841) ; Catarina in ' La Reine de Chypre ' (1841) ; Odette in ' Charles VI' (1843) ; Zayda in Donizetti's ' Dom Sébastien ' (1843) ; Beppo in Halévy's 'Lazzarone,' Desdemona in Rossini's ' Otello,' Marie Stuart in Niedermeyer's opera of that name (1844) ; Estrelle in Balfe's ' Étoile de Séville ' (1845) ; David in Mermet's opera of that name and Marie in Rossini's pasticcio ' Robert Bruce ' (1846). The last three were failures, and in 1849 she left Paris, but appeared for some time longer in the provinces and abroad. She appeared at the Opéra in Sept. 1854 and in 1855 as Fidés (' Prophète '). In 1857 she sang at Montpellier, and in 1860 at Lyons—the end of her dramatic career. Then no more was heard of her excepting the fact of her several marriages, by which she became successively a Baroness, Countess of Kestschendorf, and

Princess of Bassano. Schoen and Laval published in her name six melodies for voice and PF. in 1870.

Among the works based on the life of Rosine Stoltz may be mentioned :

SCUDO, *Histoire d'une cantatrice de l'Opéra* ; LAMER, *Mme. Rosine Stoltz* (Paris, 1847, 16mo) ; CANTINJOU, *Les Adieux de Mme. Stoltz* (Paris, 1847, 18mo); and Mlle. EUGÉNIE PÉRIGNON, *Rosine Stoltz* (Paris, 1847, 8vo) ; GUSTAVE BORD, *Rosine Stoltz de l'Académie Royale de Musique* (1815–1903) (Paris, 1909).

G. C.

STOLTZER, THOMAS (*b.* Schweidnitz, Silesia, early 16th cent.), became Kapellmeister at Ofen or Buda to King Louis, who reigned over both Hungary and Bohemia from 1517–26. Fétis gives the date of Stoltzer's death as Aug. 29, 1526, but although the fact has not been noticed by musical historians, it is somewhat significant that this is merely the date of the Battle of Mohacs, at which King Louis with the flower of the Hungarian nobility fell in fighting against the Turks. But there is no evidence that Stoltzer was with King Louis on this occasion, or that his life came to an end with the taking of Buda shortly afterwards by the Turks. It is very probable that he was still alive between 1536 and 1544, when the greater part of his works appeared in the Collections of the time. A letter of his, addressed to Duke Albert of Prussia, dated Feb. 23, 1526, is extant, which seems to refer to some offer made to him from the Duke to become his Kapellmeister at Königsberg. He sent to the Duke an elaborate composition of the 37th Psalm in Luther's German Prose version in seven divisions (' motettisch gesetzt ') for three to seven voices. There are four other psalms of the same kind which, with the one above mentioned, Otto Kade considers to represent the high-water mark of Stoltzer's abilities as a composer. The MSS. of these are now in the State Library at Dresden, for which Kade negotiated their purchase in 1858, and one of them, Psalm xii., ' Hilf, Herr, die Heiligen sind abgenommen,' he has since published in score in the *Beilagen* to Ambros's *Geschichte*. Ambrose gives considerable praise to the Latin psalms and motets of Stoltzer, which appeared in the various collections 1538 to 1545 and 1569. This praise he largely qualifies in the case of the thirty-nine settings *a* 4-5 of Latin Church Hymns, which constitute Stoltzer's contribution to Rhau's ' Hymni sacri ' of 1542. These latter he considers somewhat heavy, though showing solid workmanship. Other German works of Stoltzer are seven settings of Geistliche Gesänge and ten of Weltliche Lieder in the collections of Schöffer, 1536, Forster, 1539, and Ott, 1544. One of the secular songs, ' Entlaubet ist der Walde,' deserves mention, because the tune in Stoltzer's tenor was afterwards adopted as the Choral - tune for the hymn ' Ich dank dir, lieber Herre.' The tune itself is said to have been known about 1452, and it also appears in Hans Gerle's Lautenbuch

of 1532. Harmonised by Bach, it forms the conclusion of his cantata, ' Wer da glaubet und getauft wird.' It is given with Stoltzer's own harmony in Schöberlein's *Schatz*, Bd. iii. n. 443. One of the Geistliche Gesänge also deserves mention, ' König, ein Herr ob alle Reich,' because the first words of the three verses form the acrostic ' König Ludwig ' (King Louis of Hungary), and the hymn itself first appears in company with the better-known ' Mag ich Unglück nicht widerstehn,' which also forms the acrostic ' Maria,' for Queen Maria, the wife of Louis, and daughter of the Emperor Charles V. A large number of Latin motets by Stoltzer exist in MS. in the Library at Zwickau.

J. R. M.

STOLZ, TERESA (*b.* Elbe Kosteletz, 1836 ; *d.* Milan, 1902), dramatic soprano, lives in musical history from her connexion with two of Verdi's most famous works. She was the first Aïda in Italy—at La Scala in 1872—and the soprano of the great quartet that, with Verdi conducting, sang in the Requiem Mass at the Albert Hall in 1875. She was the Aïda, under Verdi, at Vienna in 1875 and at Paris in 1876. Her various engagements at La Scala extended from 1865–77. Like Madame Waldmann, who sang with her in ' Aïda ' and the Requiem Mass, Madame Stolz was a pupil of Lamperti. A woodcut portrait of Madame Stolz, together with those of Madame Waldmann, Masini and Medini, the bass, appeared in the *Graphic* in 1875.

S. H. P.

STONARD (STONNARD, STONERD), WILLIAM, Mus.B. Oxon. (*d.* 1630), English composer of church music. In 1608, when he took his degree (not Mus.D. as Hawkins says) he was required to compose an 8-part choral hymn (C. F. Abdy Williams, *Degrees in Music*). In this year he became organist of Christ Church, Oxford, and held this post until his death. A 4 - part catch by him, ' Ding dong bell,' is in four different MSS. (B.M. Add. MSS. 29,386, 31,463, 31,811, 31,809). The 5-part Evening Service in C included in the Tudway Collection (Harl. 7337-42) is noted as being ' composed by Mr. Stonard . . . . in 1558.' Unless this date is a mistake, this is obviously the work of a Stonard of an earlier generation. The words of some of his anthems are given in Clifford's collection (1663).

SERVICES

Evening Service in C, *a* 5.   (M. ; N.D.)   Harl. 7337-42.
Evening Service in D.   (M. ; N.D.)   Ch. Ch. 1227.   Organ score.

ANTHEMS

Be merciful unto me, O God.   Tenb. O.B./277.
Behold how good, *a* 5.   B.M. Add. MSS. 17,797.
Harken, all yee people, *a* 5.   B.M. Add. MSS. 17,797.
Hear, O my people.   PH.
My God, my God (verse anthem).   Durh. C11/159 ; Durh. O.B. A6/36b.   B.M. Add. MSS. 30,478-9.   Tenor cantoris part only.
Sing unto God (' for a Bass ').   PH. ; R.C.M. 1048-51 (Barnard's MS. Collection).
When the sorrows of Hell.   PH.

J. MK.

STONE (STONES), ROBERT (*b.* Alphington, Devon,[1] 1516 ; *d.* July 2, 1613), English com-

[1] Q.-L.

poser of church music. He was early connected with Exeter Cathedral,[1] but entered the Chapel Royal about 1543, and remained there until his death. His name appears in the Establishment Book for 1552 in a list of ' The Master of the Children and forty Gentleman of the Chapel ' (B.M. Stowe 571), and in 1603 among the gentlemen who received an allowance of mourning livery for the funeral of Queen Elizabeth.[2] He is important as the harmoniser of Cranmer's Litany, and composed a setting of the Lord's Prayer for the first Morning Service in Day's ' Certaine Notes ' (1560).   J. M^K.

STONINGS (?) (STONINGES, STENINGS) (16th cent.), English composer. B.M. Add. MSS. 31,390 is a collection of In Nomines, fancies and anthems, madrigals and motets by 16th century (chiefly English) composers arranged for 5 viols, and contains an In Nomine, a Miserere and a ' Browninge, my dere,' by Stonings. A 4-part Latin Magnificat by him is bound up in a late 16th century MS. (B.M. Add. MSS. 17,802-5), with four other settings by W. Mundy, Tallis, Shepherd and Taverner.   J. M^K.

STOPPED PIPE, an organ pipe, the upper end of which is closed by a wooden plug, or cap of metal. The pitch of a stopped pipe is one octave lower (roughly speaking) than that of an open pipe of the same length ; it is usual, therefore, in a specification, to state the pitch of a stopped pipe instead of its length ; thus, ' Open Diapason 16 ft.,' ' Bourdon 16 ft.-tone,' etc. By the former it is understood that the longest pipe is 16 ft. long ; by the latter that the longest pipe (though only 8 ft. in length) gives the same note as an open pipe of 16 ft.   J. S.

STOPPING is the term used for the action of the fingers of the left hand in playing instruments with strings stretched over a finger-board, in order to produce sounds higher in pitch than those produced by the ' open ' strings. To obtain such notes the vibrating part of the string must be shortened by stopping the vibration at a certain point between nut and bridge, i.e. by using one of the fingers of the left hand as an artificial nut or stopping-point. The nearer this point is to the bridge, the shorter the vibrating part of the strings, and the higher in pitch therefore the sound produced. A correct intonation or playing in perfect tune obviously depends entirely on exactness of stopping. See FINGERING (VIOLIN), DOUBLE STOPPING and HARMONICS.   P. D.

For stopping as applied to brass instruments, see HORN.

STOPS (HARPSICHORD). Like the organ, the harpsichord had stops, by which, with double keyboard, contrasts as well as changes could be made. The principle, borrowed from the organ, was the simple movement of each

rack of jacks forming a register, so that the quills of the jacks might or might not touch the strings. The earliest notice of stops to a keyed stringed instrument appears in the Privy Purse Expenses of Henry VIII., Apr. 1530, published by Sir N. Harris Nicholas in 1827 (Rimbault, History of the Pianoforte, 1860, p. 33). The item mentions ' ii payer of Virginalls in one coffer with iiii stoppes.' The term ' virginals ' in England under the Tudors and up to the Commonwealth, had, like ' Clavier ' in German, the general signification of any keyed stringed instrument. (See VIRGINAL.) We therefore interpret this quotation as a double harpsichord, in one case, with four stops. If this be so, we must perforce limit Hans Ruckers's invention to the ' ottava,' the octave string (see RUCKERS), withdrawing from him the double keyboard and stops. In all unaltered Ruckers' harpsichords, we find the registers made as in the old Positive organs,[3] by the prolongation of the racks as rails or slides, so as to pass through and project beyond the right-hand or treble side of the case. Each rail-end has a short loop of cord to pull it by. The late Miss Twining's Andries Ruckers of 1640, and the Countess of Dudley's Hans Ruckers the younger of 1642 have only this simple arrangement. But subsequently, to be nearer the hands, the registers were shifted by iron crank levers, and manipulated by brass knobs divided into two groups on either side of the nameboard, and immediately above the keys. The older instruments were often altered and modernised by the addition of this contrivance. The two unison stops were placed to the player's right hand, and as the reversed position of the quills when acting upon the strings required, could be brought into play by squeezing the two brass knobs together, or made silent by pushing them apart. The ottava was placed to the player's left hand, with the Lute and Harp stops, which were of later introduction, and require separate description.

The Lute, a timbre or colour stop, doubtless arose from observation of the power which lute-players, like viol- and guitar-players, had of changing the quality of the tone by touching the strings closer to the bridge. Perhaps the earliest reference to an attempt to imitate these instruments on the harpsichord has been found by Count L. F. Valdrighi, of Modena, in a letter in the Este records dated Mar. 3, 1595, by Giacomo Alsise, horn-maker of Padua, who says :

' I have let Messer Alessandro see and hear one of my quill instruments (da penna), of new invention, that with two unisons (due mani di corde) forms three changes of sound.'

The passage is obscure, but if, as is probable, two jacks touched one string in Alsise's

---

[1] Q.-L.   [2] See H. C. de Lafontaine, The King's Musick.

[3] See the organ depicted in ' Music,' attributed to Melozzo Forli (1438–94), in the National Gallery, London.

instrument, one must touch nearer the bridge than the other, and produce a different quality of sound. This might seem far-fetched were not Lady Dudley's Antwerp harpsichord of 1642 actually so made. Here are four certainly original changes, with three strings, two unisons and an octave, and the different quality is sought for upon the octave string. A few years later, and in England, Thomas Mace (*Musick's Monument*, 1676) speaks of the 'Theorboe' stop, which may have been only another name for the Lute stop. Certainly in England in the next century the use of the Lute stop, with its fascinating oboe quality, was universal,[1] and it was frequently added to old harpsichords.

The second fancy stop, the 'Harp,' was contrived to push small pieces of firm leather against the second unison.[2] We have unquestionable authority for this in a double harpsichord of Shudi's, of 1771, that has never been disturbed. From the material being leather, this is often called the 'buff' stop, and a single harpsichord, now at Torquay, inscribed 'Longman & Broderip,' but bearing inside the real maker's name, 'Culliford,' and date 1775, which has all the stops named, has this one marked 'Silent.' The earliest mention of the Harp stop (as 'Welch harp') is in a patent taken out by Roger Plenius in 1745. The combination of the Lute stop by the first unison on the upper keyboard, and the second unison, which could be muted by the Harp stop on the lower, was effected by a pedal for the left foot. But to allow this pedal to be used, a stop placed inside the case, at the bass end of the keyboards, away from the other stops, had to be pushed back. Culliford's harpsichord gives the name for this pedal stop, the 'Machine,' derived from the ironwork of the pedal movement placed outside the case, and usually concealed by a box covering. The alternation of Lute and Harp with the normal registers of the upper and lower keyboards, is the most pleasing colour effect of the harpsichord. In Kirkman's harpsichord we find the Lute muted, without knowing for certain if this was the original plan. This muting has the high authority of the late Carl Engel, who transferred Kirkman's description of the stops from the *Catalogue of the Special Exhibition at South Kensington*, 1872, to his admirable *General Catalogue of Musical Instruments in the Museum*, 1874, p. 352.

The right-foot pedal is for the SWELL (*q.v.*). Mace attributes the inventions of the harpsichord pedal to John Hayward, a 'harpsichon' maker. Kirkman and Shudi did not place

their fancy stops alike. Kirkman's arrangement (and Culliford's), proceeding from the bass, was Harp, Lute, Octave; Shudi's was Lute, Octave, Harp. In all, the Lute, Octave and first Unison move to the right; the Harp and second Unison to the left. Shudi marked this on Frederick the Great's harpsichords, still preserved at Potsdam, with arrows and the English words 'ring' and 'dumb'; the Machine stop, 'open,' 'shut.' The Germans do not appear at that time to have cared for the varieties in the harpsichord given by stops. C. P. E. Bach makes no remarks in his *Versuch* about them. He merely says (1753, p. 131) that on a Flügel with more than one keyboard, the player has the forte and piano; that is to say, the lower and upper keyboards make those changes.[3] (See *Pianoforte Primer*, p. 86.)

A. J. H.

STOPS (ORGAN). This word is used in two senses—for the handles or draw-stops which are placed near the organ-player, and by which he can shut off or draw on the various registers; and for the registers themselves. Thus we speak of a 'stop' being half-out, meaning the actual handle communicating with the sliders, and at the same time we speak of 'an organ having twenty stops,' meaning twenty registers. The latter use of the word has caused the appearance of a new expression, namely, 'sounding stops' or stops acting on pipes, as opposed to couplers and other accessory movements governed also by a stop-handle. When the pipes governed by a stop do not go through the whole compass, it is said to be a 'short-stop,' 'incomplete stop,' or 'half-stop.' When a complete row of pipes is acted upon by means of two stops, treble and bass, it is called a 'divided stop.' (See ORGAN: VOCABULARY OF STOPS; REGISTER; REGISTRATION.)

J. S.

STORACE, (1) ANN (ANNA) SELINA (*b.* London, 1766; *d.* Dulwich, Aug. 24, 1817), daughter of Stefano Storace (originally Sorace), an eminent Italian contrabassist who had settled in England, and who lived and taught in Dublin in 1750–56. She was first instructed in music by her father, and when only 8 years old appeared as a singer at the Haymarket Theatre in a concert given by Evans, the harper, Apr. 15, 1774. She was afterwards a pupil of Rauzzini, and in 1777 sang in the oratorios at Covent Garden and at Hereford Festival. On Apr. 27, 1778, she had a benefit concert at the Tottenham Street Rooms 'to enable her to pursue her studies, as she intends to go to Italy in the course of the ensuing summer.' She accordingly repaired to Venice, where she became a pupil of the Conservatorio dell' Ospedaletto, under Sacchini. In 1780 she appeared at La Pergola, Florence, with

---

[1] Queen Charlotte's Shudi harpsichord at Windsor Castle has an original Lute stop, and the date is 1740. This instrument, long at Kew Palace, was probably made for Frederick, Prince of Wales, George the Third's father.

[2] Shudi put a spring on the second unison slide, so that it could not be pushed off without moving a rail outside the case, next the 'Machine.'

[3] In the posthumous second edition, 1797, he recommends Hohlfeld's pedal, which appears to have been a sostenente, for a dynamic change.

great success.[1] In 1781 she sang at Parma, and in 1782 at La Scala, Milan. In 1784 she was engaged at the Imperial Theatre, Vienna, at a salary equal to £500 sterling for the season, a then unprecedented sum. During her stay in the Austrian capital two important events in her career happened, (1) her appearance on May 1, 1786, as the original Susanna in Mozart's 'Nozze di Figaro,' and (2) her ill-starred marriage with Fisher the violinist. (See FISHER, John Abraham.) She returned to England in Mar. 1787, and appeared at the King's Theatre, Mar. 24, as Gelinda, in Paisiello's 'Gli schiavi per amore,' and afterwards in other comic operas, but she soon abandoned the Italian for the English stage, on which she made her first appearance at Drury Lane, Nov. 24, 1789, in her brother's opera, 'The Haunted Tower,' and for several years afterwards sustained, with the greatest success, a variety of characters in comic opera. In 1791 she sang at the Handel Festival in Westminster Abbey, and in 1792 at Hereford Festival. She formed an intimacy with BRAHAM (q.v.) and toured with him on the Continent. In 1801 she was engaged at Covent Garden, where she continued to perform till May 30, 1808, when she took her leave of the public in the opera of 'The Cabinet.' She lived at Dulwich until her death, and was buried at St. Mary's, Lambeth. She accumulated a considerable fortune, and by her will, dated Aug. 10, 1797 (twenty years before her death), bequeathed upwards of £11,000 in pecuniary legacies alone, including two munificent gifts of £1000 each to the old Musical Fund (Royal Society of Musicians) and New Musical Fund. This will was proved Oct. 11, 1817, the personalty being sworn under £50,000. It was said in 1820 that after payment of all the legacies, there remained but little short of £40,000 for her cousin, Miss Trusler, the residuary legatee. Her studious concealment, after her return to England, of her marriage, is evidenced by her having made her will in her maiden name and avoided any description in it of her quality or condition, and also by the fact that her executor, in proving the will, describes her as a spinster. A miniature of her is in the Soane Museum.

W. H. H.

(2) STEPHEN (b. London, Jan. 4, 1763; d. there, Mar. 19,[2] 1796), opera composer, brother of the preceding. His early taste for music was cultivated by his father, so that when 10 years old he was able to perform the most difficult violin music of Tartini and Giardini with correctness and steadiness. When 12 years old he was placed in the Conservatorio of St. Onofrio at Naples, where he studied the harpsichord, violin and composition. On his sister's arrival in Italy, a few

years later, he joined her and visited with her the principal cities of that country, and eventually went to Vienna, where he produced his two operas, 'Gli sposi malcontenti' (June 1, 1785) and 'Gli equivoci,' the subject taken from Shakespeare's 'Comedy of Errors,' Dec. 27, 1786. He gained great advantage whilst there from his association with Mozart. He wrote, no doubt, during his Viennese period, two quintets and a sextet. Many amusing stories of Storace and his sister are told in Michael Kelly's *Reminiscences.* In Mar. 1787 he returned to England and was engaged to superintend the production of the opera in which his sister appeared at the King's Theatre, but soon became disgusted with the prevalent petty jealousies and intrigues, and retired for a time to Bath, where he devoted his attention to drawing, for which he had considerable talent. He returned to his musical pursuits in the ensuing year, and on Oct. 25, 1788, produced at Drury Lane the musical farce of 'The Doctor and the Apothecary,' adapting some of the well-known 'Doctor und der Apotheker' of Dittersdorf. On Nov. 24, 1789, he brought out his three-act opera 'The Haunted Tower,' the success of which was unbounded; it was performed fifty nights in the first season and kept its place upon the stage for nearly half a century. On Apr. 16, 1790, he produced his charming little opera 'No Song no Supper,' in which he introduced some of the music of 'Gli equivoci.' In the same year he wrote music for 'La cameriera astuta.' Jan 1, 1791, witnessed the production of the opera 'The Siege of Belgrade,' in which he introduced much of the music of Martini's 'La cosa rara.' This also long continued an established favourite. On May 3, in the same year, he produced the 'Cave of Trophonius,' an adaptation of Salieri's 'La grotta di Trofonio,' with some additional music by himself, but with no success. He fared better when, on Nov. 20, 1792, he brought out 'The Pirates,' in which he incorporated several pieces from 'Gli equivoci.' The finale to the first act is regarded as his masterpiece. In the same year he produced his opera 'Dido, Queen of Carthage,' which met with but small success, notwithstanding that the heroine was undertaken by Mara. 'The Prize,' musical entertainment, first performed on his sister's benefit night, Mar. 11, 1793; 'My Grandmother,' musical farce, produced Dec. 16, 1793; 'Lodoiska,' musical romance, the music partly adapted from Cherubini and Kreutzer, and partly composed by himself, performed June 9, 1794; 'The Glorious First of June,' occasional piece, produced July 2, 1794; the ballet of 'Venus and Adonis' (1794), and the 'Cherokee,' comic opera, Dec. 20, 1794, were all well received, as was also 'The Three and the Deuce,' musical drama, performed Sept. 2, 1795. On

---

[1] See Michael Kelly's *Reminiscences* and the *D.N.B.*
[2] The day of his death is given on his monument as the 16th.

Mar. 12, 1796, Colman's 'Iron Chest,' with Storace's music, was performed for the first time. He was then recovering from a severe attack of gout and fever; yet he determined to attend the first rehearsal. The consequence was fatal; he took cold, the gout attacked his stomach, and on March 19 he died.

At the time of his death he had an opera, 'Mahmoud, or The Prince of Persia,' in preparation for Braham's début in London. This work was left incomplete, but by the assistance of Kelly and the selection of some music by the composer's sister, Ann Storace, it was fitted for performance and produced for the benefit of his widow (a daughter of John Hall the engraver) and his children, Apr. 30, 1796, was well received, and performed many times. Storace's melodies are thoroughly English in character, whilst in his instrumentation the influence of Mozart and the Italian composers is evident. He was almost the first English composer who introduced into his works the type of finale, in which the business of the scene is carried on by concerted music.[1] Some fine examples occur in his works.

w. h. h.

STORIONE, Lorenzo (*b.* Cremona, 1751), one of the last famous Cremonese violin-makers, who worked on the model of Stradivari from 1776–95. His violoncellos are particularly admired for their full tone.

STORNELLO. 'A short poem, in lines of eleven syllables each: it is peculiar to, and liked by the people in Tuscany, who extemporise it with elegant simplicity.' This is the definition of Stornello we find in Tommaseo's Dictionary. The *Vocabolario degli Accademici della Crusca*, the stronghold of the purity of the Italian language, does not contain the word; this fact added to the other, not less significant, that neither Crescimbeni, nor Quadrio, nor Tiraboschi, mention the word in their elaborate works, inclines us to believe that the word *stornello* has not the definite meaning that, for instance, *sonnetto* has, but is merely a name given in some parts of Italy to very short poems, more with regard to their purport than their form. Tommaseo again, somewhere else, speaking of Tonio and Beatrice, two peasants who sang and recited popular songs and popular poems to him, says: 'Tonio makes a difference between *rispetti* and *ramanzetti*: the latter are composed of only three lines, the former of eight or ten. And those that Tonio called *ramanzetti* Beatrice called *strambotti*, as Matteo Spinello and King Manfredi did; and in the territory of Pistoja and in Florence they are distinguished by the name of *stornelli*.' The two stornelli we subjoin may be taken as fair examples of this kind of poem.[2]

(1) 'Tutta la notte in sogna mi venite;
    Ditemi, bella mia, perchè lo fate?
    E chi viene da voi quando dormite?'

(2) 'Fiori di pepe.
    So giro intorno a voi come fa l' ape
    Che gira intorno al fiore della siepe.'

The first line may contain either five or eleven syllables; the other two are of eleven syllables each. The first line rhymes with the third, *i.e.* the two have the last syllable, and the vowel of the last syllable but one, alike; the intermediate line, while corresponding in its last syllable with the last syllable of the other two lines, changes the vowel of the accented one. In the second form given above, the verse begins with the name of a flower. A stornello is embodied in Browning's 'Fra Lippo Lippi,' and Lola, in 'Cavalleria rusticana,' sings one.

The etymology of 'stornello' is very uncertain; Tommaseo, however, has some ground for asserting that it is a corruption of 'ritornello,' or 'refrain.'   G. M., addns.

STOUGHTON MUSICAL FESTIVAL, see Boston, sub-section Handel and Haydn Society.

STRADA DEL PÒ, Anna. An Italian soprano, brought from Italy by Handel in 1729, with Bernacchi, Merighi, Fabri, and others, for the opera in the Haymarket. She appeared there in 'Lotario,' Dec. 2, 1729; in 'Partenope,' Feb. 24, 1730; 'Poro,' Feb. 2, 1731; 'Ezio,' Jan. 15, 1732; 'Sosarme,' Feb. 19, 1732; in 'Acis and Galatea,' June 10, 1732; and in 'Orlando,' Jan. 23, 1733. She was the only one of Handel's company who did not desert him for the rival new opera in Lincoln's Inn in the end of 1733, and she remained faithful to him till her departure from this country in June 1738, when a quarrel with Heidegger, the manager, put an end to her connexion with England. In the interval between 1733 and the last-named date she took part in Handel's 'Ariodante,' 'Alcina,' 'Atalanta,' 'Arminio,' 'Giustino,' 'Berenice'; also in 'Athaliah' and 'Alexander's Feast.'

Even on her arrival, though according to Handel,[3] 'a coarse singer with a fine voice,' Strada must have had some brilliant execution, for the first air which she sang on those boards contains no less than thirty opportunities to display her shake. Coming after Cuzzoni and Faustina, and having so little to recommend her to the eye that she was nicknamed the 'pig,' it took her some time to get into favour. But Handel took pains with her, wrote for her, and advised her, and at length rendered her equal to the first singers of the Continent.   G.

STRADELLA. (1) Lyric drama, music by Flotow. Produced Palais Royal Theatre, Paris, Feb. 1837. Then recomposed, as a Grand Opera, and produced at Hamburg, Dec. 30, 1844, as 'Alessandro Stradella.' In English

---

[1] Dibdin had foreshadowed it in his 'Quaker.'
[2] From Tigri's 'Canto populare Toscani' (Florence, 1869).

[3] Burney's *History*, iv. 342. The above information is compiled from the same volume, pp. 339-427.

(altered by Bunn) as ' Stradella,' Drury Lane, June 6, 1846 ; in German, Drury Lane, May 21, 1849 ; in Italian, Covent Garden, 1864. (2) Opera in 5 acts, by Niedermeyer; produced Opéra, Mar. 3, 1837.   G.

STRADELLA, ALESSANDRO (*b. circa* 1645 ; *d.* 1682), Italian composer. The place of birth is uncertain ; Genoa (Arteaga) and Venice (Carrier) are unlikely. Naples (Burney and, following him, Fétis and Riemann) is more generally accepted. Hess makes out a very fair case for the province of Modena, probably Vignola or Montefestino. Stradella's father, Marcantonio, was governor of Vignola for Prince Boncompagni in 1642, and at the siege of the town by the Papal troops in 1643 is said to have retreated to Montefestino. Rumour has it that Marcantonio Stradella evacuated Vignola after an insufficient defence, and when help was practically in sight. This point is worth mentioning, if only as a faint sign of a possibly weakening hereditary influence. Of Stradella's mother nothing is known. The date of Alessandro's death (1682) is obtained from a document in the archives at Modena quoted by Hess, who thus corrects the early authorities. (Bourdelot has 1670 and Burney 1678, both palpably in error, seeing that the score of ' Il barcheggio' is dated 1681, that work having been commanded for a wedding ceremony on July 6 of that year.) Hess's Modena document also corrects the date 1681 which had been accepted by Adler, Riemann, Combarieu and others.

The true facts of Stradella's life are in part unknown and for the rest so overlaid with legend and conjecture as to be equally problematical. The truth, were it discoverable, would probably be stranger than any of the fictions which at present abound with regard to this musician's life. The earliest authority is Bourdelot,[1] and from him there starts the fictive account of the happenings that befell Stradella. The tale which until recently has obtained credence is that Stradella went to Venice, where he taught and composed. Here he fell in love with the mistress of a Venetian nobleman and eloped with her to Rome (*via* Naples, according to Burney, whose statement lacks further verification). In Rome he first encountered the assassins who had been set on his path by the enraged Venetian nobleman. These ruffians are said not only to have desisted from their monstrous intent, after having their hearts melted by the exquisite strains of Stradella's oratorio ' S. Giovanni Battista ' in the church of S. Giovanni Lateran, but to have warned the two young people of the danger threatening them. At this point, with evident art, the tale breaks off. Little more is told. We hear that Stradella and his lady fled there and then to Turin, where, ' about 1670,' the musician was

finally run to earth and murdered by a fresh band of hirelings. Thus far Bourdelot. Burney follows him except for the one point mentioned above and for the fact of Stradella's death being placed in 1678, a statement which Burney was able to uphold by the possession of the score of an opera, ' La forza d' amore ' (since lost), dated Genoa, 1678, and which Burney takes to be Stradella's last composition. Fétis follows Burney in the main details. Since then the dated score of ' Il barcheggio ' lengthens Stradella's life up to 1681, and, as has been noted, the latest research puts his death early in 1682.

Heinz Hess, in his *Die Opern Alessandro Stradellas*, has gathered together the conflicting versions of the musician's life and sifted the evidence. His is the most complete and reliable account, and from his book the following is taken. Stradella's position in Venice (it is not known in what year he went there) was that of a teacher of singing, not, as Bourdelot says, composer of operas commissioned by the Republic. Burney (*General History*) says that Stradella ' was not only an excellent composer but a great performer on the violin and, besides these qualifications, was possessed of a fine voice and an exquisite manner of singing.' The lady with whom Stradella eloped, generally called Ortensia, was not[2] the mistress of the Venetian nobleman Pignaver, but ' una giovane patrizia destinata sposa ' of the Venetian senator Alvise Contarini.[3] The flight to Rome is not vouched for by any contemporary document. It is possible that Stradella visited Rome from Venice and returned thither to embark on his love affair. (The couple may, in that case, have fled straight to Turin, where, according to contemporary documents, an abortive attempt at the assassination of Stradella was carried out.[4]) This assumption still leaves room for a second visit to Rome, this time with his lady, where the first attempt at assassination may have taken place. It seems that Stradella entered into service as a court musician under the Regent Marie de Nemours, Duchess of Savoy, in Turin. It is not related definitely whether he married Ortensia. From a document in the archives of Modena,[5] his death in 1682 at Genoa is placed beyond doubt. Another document from the same source mentions a son.

Of Stradella's musical education nothing is known. The dates of his compositions are equally undiscoverable. Larousse[6] mentions, without giving sources, the performances of operas in Venice between 1665 and 1668. Cesti's ' Dori ' is dated 1672, and to this work Stradella wrote a Prologue. The score of ' S. Giovanni Battista ' bears the date 1676. Burney says that his copy of ' La forza d'amore '

<hr />

[1] *Histoire de la musique et de ses effets.*

[2] According to Bourdelot.

[3] Carutti, *Storia della diplomazia della corte di Savoia.* (Rome, 1875.)

[4] Hess, p. 6.   [5] *Ibid.* p. 9.   [6] *Dictionnaire des opéras.*

was dated 1678. It is known that 'Il bar-cheggio' was written for performance in 1681.

Stradella's compositions, comprising operas, serenades, religious and secular cantatas, oratorios, motets, madrigals and string concertos, are nearly all in MS. Hess gives a full account of the operas and discusses them from the point of view of their novelty of structure and treatment. Burney traces the influence of Stradella on Purcell, founding this hypothesis on the latter's use of the ground-bass, which, he says, was fostered 'by viewing the works of an author who, according to tradition, was his greatest favourite.' Parry [1] mentions Stradella at some length in regard to his use of ground-bass and his position as a composer of cantatas and oratorios. The oratorio 'S. Giovanni Battista' is probably Stradella's greatest work and is undoubtedly of interest, showing, as it does, an important step in the evolution of that form from Carissimi to later oratorio writers like Handel. Parry says of it, 'The genuine musicianship and breadth of treatment in this work are indeed remarkable for the time when it appeared. . . .' In this respect it is of interest to notice the two sides of Stradella's character. On the one hand there is the free-living, amorous gallant; on the other, the composer of moving and apparently deeply felt religious music.

The serenata which Handel laid under contribution for 'Israel in Egypt' is 'Qual prodigio ch'io miri,' and is to be found in the supplement of the German Handel Society's edition.

An exhaustive catalogue of the Stradella MSS. will be found in Hess. The following list shows the principal printed works:

Scelta di canzonette italiane di diversi autori. Printed at London by Godbid and Playford. (1679.)
SILVANI MARINO : Scielta delle suonate con il B. C. per organo. (Bologna, 1680.)
CHRYSANDER : Supplemente, enthaltend Quellen zu Händels Werken, iii.
CROSTI : Les Airs célèbres. (Paris, 1896)
EITNER : Acht Gesänge.
GEVAERT : Les Gloires d'Italie, i. and ii.
HALÉVY : Canti a voce sola dell' insigne A. Str. (Paris, 1861.)
NOVELLO : Fitzwilliam Music. (1825.)
PARISOTTI : Libro secondo di arie antiche. (Milan, 1890.)
RUNG : Musica scelta di antichi . . . musici italiani. . (Copenhagen.)

BIBLIOGRAPHY

Apart from the usual Dictionaries and Histories the following should be consulted :
ADEMOLLO : I teatri di Roma nel secolo XVII. (Rome, 1888.)
BOURDELOT : Histoire de la musique et de ses effets. (Paris, 1715.)
BURNEY : General History of Music. (London, 1789.)
DENT : Alessandro Scarlatti. (London, 1905.)
GALVANI : I teatri musicali di Venezia nel secolo XVII. (Milan, 1878.)
HESS : Die Opern Alessandro Stradellas. (Leipzig, 1906.)
MAZZUCATO : Article in this Dictionary, 2nd edition.
RICHARD : Stradella et les Contarini, Le Ménestrel. (Paris, 1865–66.)
Delle opere di' A. Stradella esistenti dell' Archivio mus. della R. Bibl. Palatina di Modena. (Modena, 1865.)
                                                S. G.

STRADIVARI (STRADIVARIUS), (1) ANTONIO (b. ? 1644 ; d. Cremona, Dec. 18, 1737), 'brought the violin to perfection and left to Cremona an imperishable name as master of his craft'; thus the inscription now affixed by the municipality of Cremona to the house in the Piazza Roma where the great violin-maker passed the

most successful years of his life [2] and where he died.

Regarding the etymology of the name, E. J. Payne, in the first edition of this Dictionary, pronounced it to be derived from 'the plural form of 'Stradivare,' a Lombard variety of 'Stradiere,' a tollman or douanier, a feudal official who was posted on the Strada (or high road) for the purpose of exacting dues from passengers'; while Mandelli, quoting from the catalogue of ancient rolls of the community of Cremona, compiled by the Piedmontese professor, Astegiano, to the year 1300, and printed at Turin in 1899, states that :

'The form of the name "de Stradaverta" as used in 1298 is derived from "Strada Averta" of the Cremonese dialect ; in Italian, "Strada Aperta."'

A further outcome of Mandelli's researches is the remarkable genealogy of the Stradivari family which he traced down to 1883. Beginning with Giulio Cesare Stradivari of the parish of S. Michele Vecchio, who married Doralice Milani, a widow of the cathedral parish, on Apr. 10, 1600, we find Antonio Stradivari's father recorded in the register entry of the son born to them two years later and christened Alessandro, Jan. 15, in the same church. Later we find this same Alessandro, son of Giulio Cesare Stradivari, entering into the bonds of matrimony with Anna, daughter of Leonardo Moroni, on Aug. 30, 1622, which fact is duly recorded in the marriage register of the parish of S. Prospero. Three children are recorded to have been born of this union : Giuseppe Giulio Cesare, (b. Mar. 1623) ; Carlo Felice (b. Sept. 1626) ; Giovanni Battista (b. Oct. 1628). After the birth of the last-mentioned child documentary evidence concerning the family ceases entirely, and no effort has yet dissipated the obscurity which enshrouds the birth of Antonio Stradivari. Every record relating to the subject has, it would seem, been destroyed, or lost, and the only available explanation of this singular deficiency has been furnished by the wars and famine which visited Cremona in 1628, the year Giovanni Battista was born, and again in 1629. Again in 1630 the inhabitants were further harassed by the ravages of a plague which caused innumerable deaths, and compelled all those who could do so to leave the city. It is further recorded that Hieronymus Amati, his wife and his daughters, succumbed to the disease ; but there is no indication that Alessandro Stradivari and his family were still at Cremona at the time, and Mandelli has perhaps rightly interpreted the complete lack of documentary evidence regarding the date and place of Antonio Stradivari's birth, to signify that

---

[1] Oxf. Hist. Mus vol. iii. pp. 181 et seq.

[2] It should be stated at once that the whole of the facts available as the reward of untiring effort and research concerning the family of the great 'Stradivarius,' as well as his own personality and work, have been amassed in the monumental study which has been, it may be said, the life-work of the sons of William Ebsworth Hill—Antonio Stradivari, his Life and Work (1644–1737), by W. Henry Hill, Arthur F. Hill, F.S.A., and Alfred Hill (London, 1902). To this work the writer acknowledges his great indebtedness.

his parents had fled to some haven of refuge where in the fullness of time Antonio first saw the light. The names of the three children above mentioned are the only entries to be found in the birth registers relating to children born in wedlock to Alessandro Stradivari, and the only direct allusion to the relationship existing between Antonio and Alessandro Stradivari is furnished by the contract for the purchase of his house wherein he signs himself 'Antonio Stradivari, son of the late Alessandro.'

The earliest authentic evidence of Antonio Stradivari's residence in Cremona has been supplied by a violin—dated 1666—recorded by Alfred Hill, in whose hands it has been. The original label in this instrument runs as follows:

'Antonius Stradiuarius Cremonensis Alumnus Nicolai Amati, Faciebat Anno 1666,'

followed by the familiar Maltese cross and the initials A. S. enclosed within a double circle. He was then—as will be gathered later—22 years of age and, it may be assumed, had probably served an apprenticeship to Nicolo Amati (see AMATI, 4) for the seven or eight preceding years. It is quite possible that he began to insert his own labels some years before 1666, but this date may be said to have marked the later limit of his pupilage; in any case it proved his competence to claim the authorship of his own instruments, and the labels found in his violins of the following year bear no allusion to Nicolo Amati, nor is there any further reference to his master on the labels of any of his later instruments. Following the same lines of deduction, the year in which Antonio Stradivari was born has been generally accepted as 1644, by reason of his custom of adding his age to his labels during the latter part of his life. In 1732 he states himself to be '89,' in 1736, '92,' and in 1737, '93.' Another noticeable feature of these labels is the alteration in the spelling of his name. About the year 1730 he seems to have discarded the first orthography, i.e. 'Antonius Stradiuarius,' and replaced the u with a roman v. The origin of this change may have been a chance misprint which commended itself to him; but it was certainly not due to any orthographical views on the part of the Stradivari family, for his son, Omobono, still continued to employ the earlier, while Francesco adopted the later spelling.

Accepting the year of Antonio Stradivarius's birth as 1644, we find that he was twenty-three years of age when he married Francesca Feraboschi in 1667. This lady was the widow of Giovanni Giacomo Capra, who had committed suicide in the Piazza S. Agata, Cremona, three years previously, and was Stradivari's senior by a few years. After the union Stradivari and his wife settled in a house known as the Casa del Pescatore, which was situated in his wife's

parish of S. Matteo; and a year after the marriage the Cremona census reports record that a daughter, christened Giulia Maria, had been born to them. Until 1680 Stradivari continued to live at the Casa del Pescatore, where his family was increased by the birth of a second daughter, Catterina (b. Mar. 25, 1674; d. June 17, 1748), and four sons: Francesco (b. Feb. 6, 1670), who only lived a week; Francesco (2); Alessandro (b. May 25, 1677; d. June 26, 1732); Omobono (3). In 1680 Stradivari and his family removed to the house he had purchased in the Piazza San Domenico of a Cremonese family named Picenardi. According to the deed of sale, first brought to light by Lombardini,[1] and now preserved in the National Archives of Cremona, Stradivari paid 7000 imperial lires (about £840) for his new home. 2000 lire of this amount he paid in cash, 4990 he agreed to pay within four years, and the balance of ten lire was foregone by the vendors provided he paid the Canons of the Cathedral the yearly tithe of six imperial sols. Until his death Stradivari resided in this house, known in his day as No. 2 Piazza San Domenico, but since 1870 as No. 1 Piazza Roma, and for nine years after his demise the remaining members of his family lived there. In 1746 it was let to Stradivari's pupil, Carlo Bergonzi, who occupied the house until 1758. In the following year it was tenanted by Giacomo Caraffe, and until 1777 by Giuseppe Paleari and others; but in that year Stradivari's grandson, named Antonio after him, sold the house to Signor Giovanni Ancina. During these years the building escaped alteration, but in 1888 the proprietor of the adjoining caffè purchased it and carried out such extensive alterations that little of the original form of the structure remained.

Eighteen years of domestic tranquillity followed the establishment of the Stradivari family—which included Susanna Capra, his wife's only daughter by her first husband—in their new abode, until May 25, 1698, when a break was caused in the home circle by the death of the violin-maker's wife, Francesca Feraboschi. She was buried with conspicuous honours in a tomb situated in the choir of the church of St. Domenico, and fifteen months after her death Stradivari consoled himself, becoming united in Aug. 1699 to Antonia Maria Zambelli, daughter of Antonia Zambelli, of the parish of S. Donato. This second marriage was blessed with five children: one daughter—named after the first wife—Francesca Maria (b. Sept. 19, 1700; d. Feb. 11, 1720); Giovanni Battista Giuseppe (b. Nov. 6, 1701; d. July 8, 1702); Giovanni Battista Martino (b. Nov. 11, 1703; d. Nov. 1, 1727); Giuseppe (b. Oct. 27, 1704; d. Dec. 2, 1781), who became a priest; Paolo Bartolomeo (b. Jan. 26, 1708; d. Oct. 14,

[1] Antonio Stradivari e la celebre scuola cremonese. 1872.

1776), a cloth-merchant. The last named, together with Stradivari's first child, Giulia Maria (by his first wife), were apparently the only members of his family who married.

TOMB AND RELICS. — It was in 1729 that Stradivari is recorded to have purchased, from the heirs of Francesco Villani, the burial-place and tombstone belonging to that noble family. The exact locality of this vault has been entirely lost since the total destruction (1869) of the church of S. Domenico and its chapel—named after the Blessed Virgin of the Rosary—which contained the Villani, afterwards the Stradivari tomb. A commemorative inscription on one of the decorative vases in the grounds (now a public garden) perpetuates the memory of the church of S. Domenico, but the fact that it was the last resting-place of the illustrious violin-maker is not alluded to. The Villani tombstone, however, from which the coat of arms and family inscriptions were so imperfectly effaced that they are still visible under Stradivari's name, is now preserved in the Municipal Museum, and the Parish Register of S. Matteo records that Stradivari's second wife was interred in the Villani vault on Mar. 4, 1737. She was the first member of the family to be buried there, and nine months later she was followed by her husband, who was laid to rest on Dec. 19, 1737. The following members of his family were also interred in the same vault :

Omobono Stradivari, June 9, 1742 ; Francesco Stradivari, May 13, 1743 ; Paola Bartolomeo Stradivari, Oct. 15, 1776 ; Giuseppe Antonio Stradivari, Dec. 3, 1781 ; Catarini Stradivari (spinster) June 18, 1784.

After the departure from the house in the Piazza San Domenico of Stradivari's son Paolo Bartolomeo, with his wife Elena Tempiari and their four children, in 1746, the new tenant, Bergonzi, presumably became the owner of Stradivari's tools and violin-making appurtenances ; but during the thirty-nine years or so which elapsed between Stradivari's death and the sale of his designs, moulds, etc., by his descendants to Count Cozio di Salabue, many of these interesting relics necessarily became scattered abroad and passed into different hands. With the exception of his callipers, the great violin-maker's tools were not included in the Count's collection, which subsequently passed to the Marchese Dalla Valle in Turin. There are sixteen moulds for violins, and three for violas, in this collection, besides various drawings and designs for the minutest details of his art, which are of great interest. Vuillaume, it is said, also preserved some of Stradivari's moulds, and these were presented by him to the Musée of the Paris Conservatoire, whilst the French luthier, Chanot-Chardon, owned a set of small planes said to have belonged to Stradivari.

As no genuine portrait of Stradivari exists, we still have to rely on the verbal description of him handed down to us by Polledro from his master Pugnani, for an idea of his personal appearance. According to Fétis (Biog. des Mus.), on whose authority we have the account, Polledro (d. 1882), formerly first violin at the court of Turin, records that his master, Pugnani, knew Stradivari during the latter part of his life, and delighted in talking about him. He described him as tall and thin. As a rule his head was covered with a white woollen cap in the winter, and a white cotton cap in the summer ; over his clothes he wore an apron of white leather, and, as he rarely ceased from work, his costume varied seldom. Fétis also recounts that Stradivari's untiring industry and his frugal habits brought him to an old age of such easy circumstances that his affluence became a standard of comparison to the people of Cremona, who adopted the phrase Ricco come Stradivari.

METHOD AND WORKMANSHIP.—In the opinion of Messrs. Hill, Stradivari was undoubtedly an apprentice in Nicolo Amati's workshop, but they unhesitatingly repudiate the idea that Stradivari assisted Amati in the construction of his later instruments, and this on the grounds that there is no indication of any such help to be found in the latter's work. The explanation of this is possibly to be found in the fact that Stradivari's superior gifts placed him in a high position of trust, freed him from many of the duties exacted from his comrades, and gave him the privilege of making his own instruments and using his own labels. The question must still be somewhat a matter of surmise, but the above conclusion is certainly strengthened by the excellent violins which issued from Stradivari's hands whilst apparently he still worked in the studio of the great Amati. Again, the termination of Stradivari's apprenticeship can only be approximately stated to have taken place a couple of years before he purchased his house in the Piazza Roma in 1680. Already in 1666—and possibly as early as 1660—Stradivari was making violins in which he affixed his own labels. These early violins are particularly noticeable for their poor material, thick yellow varnish, solid build, and their proportions, which follow those of Amati's smaller pattern, i.e. about $13\frac{7}{8}$ long ; $7\frac{15}{16}$ width of lower bouts ; $6\frac{3}{8}$ width of upper bouts ; $1\frac{3}{16}$ lower ribs ; $1\frac{1}{8}$ upper ribs. With one or two exceptions, notably the ornamented violin known as the 'Hellier' Strad (1679), which tends towards the grand Amati in measurement, and is remarkably heavy in style of work, Stradivari adhered to the small model until 1684, after which date he definitely turned his attention to larger-built instruments. There is little doubt that by this time he had gained some prestige as a maker, and this, combined with the loss of his master's living influence, gave freedom to and further awakened his inventive faculties. Until 1684 he merely proved himself to be an uncommonly skilled craftsman, but the years which intervened between 1684 and 1700 marked the progress of those experiments which were to culminate in the uttermost perfection of form and balance. It must be observed, however, that notwithstanding the changes which took place in Stradivari's work during this period—generally alluded to as the ' Amatisé period '—the perfect poise and equilibrium, so characteristic of his later work, is to some extent lacking. That Nicolo Amati's precepts still strongly influenced him is proved by his first innovation, which consisted in adopting a standard of length, varying from 14 inches to $14\frac{1}{16}$ inches, and proportions similar to those of the ' grand ' Amati. In some instances he flattened the model, in others arched it almost to a central point, more generally he adhered entirely to the Amati model, though the solidity of his edges always remained the same. The scrolls also, during these years, evidence the master's indecision by the deviating vigour and occasional feebleness.

A marked alteration in the detail of his work took place in 1688, when Stradivari first outlined the curves of the scroll in black, and also similarly accentuated the centre-line or back rib of the scroll. This original idea was one which evidently commended itself to him and to his patrons as, with but few exceptions, he continued to place it on his scrolls until the end of his life. Briefly to summarise this early period, we may say that, between 1684 and 1690, Stradivari principally strove to avoid the defects of others, while seeking new paths for himself ; but in the meantime the beauty, accuracy, and finish of his work was gaining steadily every year. The cutting of his ff holes, the carving of his scrolls, the exquisite precision of the purfling, all prove the complete dexterity with which he handled his knife. Then, as a crowning point to this perfect craftsmanship a new set of proportions suddenly suggested themselves to his maturing brain, and we find him in 1690 creating the ' Long Strad.' The abrupt appearance of this complete innovation is not easy to account for, but the growing demand for strongly toned instruments for use in the churches doubtless influenced Stradivari in the first place, and as the authors of *Gio. Paolo Maggini, his Life and Work* (Hill & Sons), state, the form and proportions were suggested by a Maggini violin which came under his notice. This search for power in Stradivari's work is observable from the moment that he threw off the yoke of the ' small ' Amati pattern. He gradually increased his breadths year by year, and even contemporaneously with the ' Long Strad,' he made violins in 1691 and 1692 of still larger proportions, by combining extreme breadth with the utmost length of the long pattern. The dimensions of a typical

' Long Strad ' of 1690 will be found recorded in Messrs. Hill's Appendix to their work already mentioned.

During the years following 1684 the varnish upon Stradivari's violins became gradually deeper in colour, and, as on the ' Long Strads,' it is of a rich hue of amber and light red. Until 1698 Stradivari adopted the ' long pattern ' almost entirely, then came a return to the proportions which preceded the year 1690, and we get violins of about 14 inches in length, with widths similar to those of the ' Long Strad,' but with outlines more curved, corners longer, body fuller, and a whole of more harmonious appearance. It is interesting to note before leaving this period that the backs of the ' Long Strads ' are nearly always cut in one piece ; that the model is rather flat, but sloping gracefully from the centre to the purfling ; that the ff holes, to fall in with the general design, are set rather upright, nearer together, and more open ; the pine is fine grained, the mitres square, and the exquisitely carved scrolls are proportionately long.

With the year 1700 dawned the finest decade of his greatest period. Slowly but surely he discarded the Amati tradition which had again asserted itself in 1698 and continued to a certain extent until about 1702. We find him still adhering to the 14-inch length, but broadening, developing, and arching the model, until it assumes an unsurpassable grandeur and symmetry. His years of experiment have resulted in a neatly compacted instrument, with light edges, accurate corners, round arching, broadly treated but exquisitely graceful sound-holes and scroll, and a varnish soft in texture, which shades deliciously from orange to red. From 1703 until about 1709, the year of those famous violins ' La Pucelle ' and the ' Viotti,' Stradivari seems to have settled upon certain points of construction, from which he rarely departed afterwards. A slight variation of curve is observable, but the main features and general dimensions agree with one another. Then followed years of indecision, in which no consistency of plan is to be traced, and until the end of his career, some minute changes of thickness, width, or length, characterise his work. Yet, in spite of these diversities, the years following 1710 undoubtedly mark the production of some of his finest instruments. In 1711 he made the fine violin known as the ' Parke ' ; in 1713, the ' Boissier,' which belonged to Sarasate; in 1714 the ' Dolphin ' ; in 1715 the ' Gillot ' and ' Alard,' which experts look upon as the master's finest creation ; and in 1716 came the ' Messiah ' (see Tarisio). These years also mark the production of some of his grandest violoncellos, such as the ' Duport,' 1711 ; the ' Batta,' 1714 ; and—the most superb of all— the ' Piatti ' in 1720. All of these are instruments of smaller proportions (about $29\frac{1}{2}$ inches long) than those he made anterior to the years following 1700, which kept to the dimensions of his contemporaries. That Stradivari did not occupy himself with the proportions of the violoncello, as he did with those of the violin, is hardly to be wondered at, seeing that the capacities of the violoncello were hardly understood in his day. It was not until the latter years of his life that such artists as FRANCIS-CELLO employed it as a solo instrument, and Stradivari—with his usual quick responsiveness to the demands of artistic appreciation—gradually modified the proportions of his instruments from about 31½ inches to about 29½ inches in length, as the progressing technique of the contemporary virtuosi exacted a diminution in size.

His violas bear a more distinctive stamp of his creative genius than do his violoncellos. The changes so apparent in his violins are quite as evident in these larger instruments, and the models marked ' TV ' and ' CV ' preserved in the Dalla Valle collection evidence that he made these in two sizes, i.e. ' Tenor Viola ' and ' Contralto Viola.' Before 1690 the influence of the Brescian school, and of the Amatis, still ruled the proportions of his violas, but after that year he adopted a smaller model—about 16₁⁵₆ in length—and to this he mainly adhered. These three members of the string quartet seem to have occupied Stradivari's attention almost exclusively. No authentic double basses or any designs for the same have as yet come to light, and with the exceptions of the remains of a viola da gamba, a kit—now in the Musée of the Paris Conservatoire—two handsome guitars, dating from the early years of his career, and the head of a third, it may be said with truth that Stradivari's fame rests entirely upon his violins, violas and violoncellos.

Stradivari's methods have been preserved from century to century, until they have become the fundamental basis of the art of violin-making. No detail of his work was too unimportant for the master's vigilant observation. That he personally designed the pegs, finger-boards, tail-pieces, inlaid patterns, bridges, and even the minutest details of his violin cases, is attested to by the numerous drawings of these in the Dalla Valle collection, while the several sketches for bow-tips and nuts reveal the interesting fact that he also made bows. His material, as already stated, was not always of the finest, owing to the restriction of limited funds during the early part of his career. However, it may be said that in the classification of the relative importance of the various factors required to make a perfect violin, material and dimensions are subservient to varnish, and it was in the application of this that Stradivari surpassed his contemporaries, rather than in the discovery of any new compound for the same.

Generally speaking, the so-called ' Lost Cremona Varnish ' was, in the writer's opinion, no secret in Stradivari's lifetime, but the common property of the luthiers of the day, who compounded it from the materials used by the great painters of the epoch. Space will not admit of our discussing the many theories put forth regarding the component parts which constituted this varnish. Suffice it to state here that, in the opinion of the writer—an opinion which, it must be said, is controverted with some skill by Messrs. Hill—the late Charles Reade's hypothesis of an oil varnish over a spirit varnish is the most fundamentally correct solution of Stradivari's varnishing (vide *Readiana* and the *Pall Mall Gazette*, Letters, 1872). The exigencies of time-limits which have brought a demand for quick-drying varnishes in modern times sounded the death-knell of the brilliant, tender, transparent varnish of the Cremona School, so that the world has been forced to acknowledge that it is now a mere memory. Stradivari's own recipe was inscribed on the fly-leaf of a family Bible, but his descendant Giacomo Stradivari destroyed this, though it is said that he kept a copy of it which he carefully preserved for any future members of the family who might adopt the profession of their illustrious ancestor.

SYNOPSIS OF THE MOST NOTICEABLE VIOLINS, ETC., MADE BY ANTONIO STRADIVARI.—According to Messrs. Hill's careful calculations Stradivari made 1116 instruments between the years 1666 and 1737 ; of these, 540 violins, twelve violas, and fifty violoncellos are actually known to them to-day, whilst they have traces (unconfirmed) of over one hundred more. The earliest dated instruments seen by them are of the years 1666, 1667 and 1669. Count Cozio di Salabue states, however, that Stradivari was working and inserting his own labels in 1659. The following are the names of some of Stradivari's most noticeable violins : The ' Hellier,' 1679 ; the ' Sellière,' made between 1666 and 1680 ; the ' Tuscan,' 1690 (see MOSEL) ; the ' Betts,' 1704 ; the ' Ernst,' 1709 (presented to Lady Hallé by Earl Dudley and others) ; ' La Pucelle,' 1709 ; the ' Viotti,' 1709 ; the ' Vieuxtemps,' 1710 ; the ' Parke,' 1711 ; the ' Boissier,' 1713 ; the ' Dolphin,' 1714 (so named from its iridescent varnish) ; the ' Gillot,' 1715 ; the ' Alard,' 1715 ; the ' Cessol,' 1716 ; the ' Messie,' 1716 (preserved in Count Cozio di Salabue's collection for fifty years without being played on ; hidden by Luigi Tarisio for thirty years in an isolated farm near the village of Fontenato, Italy ; purchased by Vuillaume when Tarisio died in 1854 ; preserved by him in a glass case in his shop ; sold to E. Crawford, an enthusiastic musical amateur, for £2000, and now the property of Messrs. William Hill). The ' Sasserno,' 1717 ; the ' Maurin,' 1718 ; the ' Lauterbach,' 1719 ; the ' Blunt,' 1721 ;

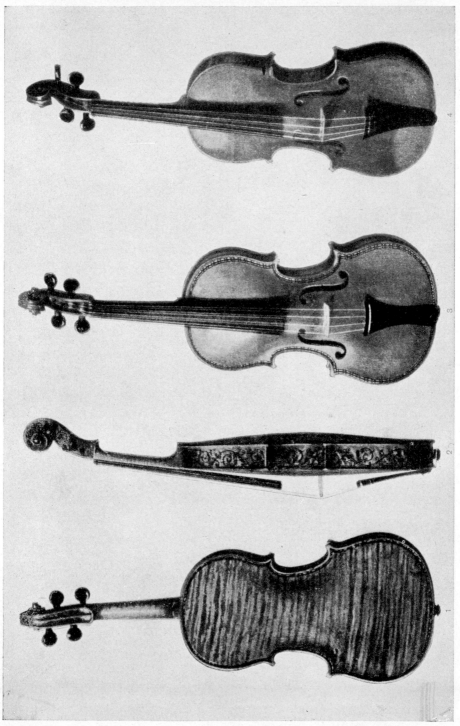

LXXVIII

1, 2, 3. The 'Hellier' Stradivari Violin, 1679.   4. The 'King' Guarneri del Gesù Violin, 1735.
From Hipkins & Gibbs's *Musical Instruments*.   By permission of The Encyclopædia Britannica Co., Ltd.

the 'Sarasate,' 1724 ; the 'Rode,' 1722 ; the 'Deurbroucq,' 1727 ; the 'Kiesewetter,' 1731 ; the 'Habeneck,' 1736; the 'Muntz,' 1736 (both of these show the shaky hand of the veteran master).

Violas : The 'Tuscan,' 1690, preserved in the Municipal Institute, Florence—it bears Stradivari's monogram stamped on the mortice of the neck, the original finger-board, tail-piece, tail-nut, and bridge ; two violas, 1696, belonging to the quintet of inlaid instruments for some years owned by King Philip IV. of Spain; the 'Archinto,' 1696 (named after Count Archinto who owned a Quartet of Strads) ; the 'Macdonald,' 1701 ; Paganini's viola, 1731, which inspired Berlioz to write his symphony 'Harold in Italy.'

Violoncellos : The 'Archinto,' 1689 ; the 'Tuscan,' 1690 ; the 'Aylesford,' 1696 ; the 'Cristiani,' 1700 ; the 'Servais,' 1701 ; the 'Gore - Booth,' 1710 ; the 'Duport,' 1711 ; the 'Adam,' 1713 ; the 'Batta,' 1714 ; the 'Piatti,' 1720 ; the 'Baudiot ' and ' Gallay,' 1725, comprise some of the finest instruments made by Stradivari (see also QUARTETS OF INSTRUMENTS).

BIBL.—ALFONSO MANDELLI, *Nuove indagini su Antonio Stradivari* ; W., A F. & A. HILL, *Antonio Stradivari* ; VINCENZO LANCETTI, *Biografica cremonese* ; CARL SCHULZE, *Stradivaris Geheimnis* ; HORACE PETHERICK, *Antonio Stradivari* ; FEDERICO SACCHI, *Gli istrumenti di Stradivari (Estratto della Gazzetta Musicale)*, Milano, anno 1892 ; EDOUARD ROCHE, *Stradivarius* ; JULIET VON LEPEL GUITZ (*née* Buchanan Austin), *Ein Stradivarius* ; ANONYMOUS (*Enrico Stradivari*), *Cenni sulla celebre scuola cremonese*, Cremona, 1872 ; F. J. FÉTIS, *Antonio Stradivari luthier célèbre*, Paris, 1856 (English translation by John Bishop, London, 1864) ; H. R. HAWEIS, *My Musical Life*, pp. 314-28, *Stradivarius of Cremona, his House* ; C. READE, *Cremona Violins* (vide *Readiana*) : ANON., *A Short Account of a Violin by Stradivari dated 1690* ; W. E. HILL & SONS, *The Tuscan Strad* ; E. J. PAYNE, *The Violins of Stradivari*, pp. 202-4 ; *Musical Standard*, vol. xxxiv., London, 1888 ; GIOVANNI DI PICCOLELLIS, *Liutai antichi e moderni* ; JULES GALLAY, (1) *Les Luthiers italiens aux XVIIe et XVIIIe siècles*, Paris, 1869 (only 500 copies printed) ; (2) *Les Instruments des écoles italiennes* ; RICHARD G. WHITE, *Antonius Stradivarius (The Atlantic Monthly)*, Boston, vol. xlv. p. 253, 1880 ; *The Stradivarius case at the Violin Loan Exhibition (Musical Star)*, Edinburgh (secular), No. 167, July 1885 ; J. M. FLEMING, *The Stradivarius Violin, the Emperor*, London, 1891 ; JOSEPH PEARCE (jun.), *Violins and Violin-makers* ; A. VIDAL, *Les Instruments à archet* ; G. HART, *The Violin* ; *The Salabue Strad* (the Messie), W. E. Hill & Sons, London, 1891 ; LOUIS PERRARD, *Le Violon, son histoire* ; VON LUTGENDORFF, *Die Geigen- und Lautenmacher* ; GEORGE ELIOT, *Stradivari* (poem) ; LONGFELLOW, *Tales of a Wayside Inn* ; ROBERT FISSORE, *Les Maîtres luthiers*.

E. H.-A.

(2) FRANCESCO (*b.* Cremona, Feb. 1, 1671 ; *d.* May 11, 1743), son of the above by his first wife, *née* Francesca Feraboschi.

(3) OMOBONO (*b.* Cremona, Nov. 14, 1679 ; *d.* June 8, 1742), also a son by the first wife. Both were interred in the Villani vault. They were the only members of Stradivari's family who embraced their father's profession, and although their work is not without merit, their brilliant and long-lived father entirely eclipsed them. During the latter years of Stradivari's life there is little doubt that they assisted him, probably in conjunction with Carlo Bergonzi, in constructing his violins. This would account for those specimens of the great master's work that frequently gave rise to controversy. But for the hand of the vandal these 'doubtful' instruments would bear the label 'sotto la disciplina d'Antonio Stradivari,' by which inscription he distinguished the instruments made in co-operation

with his sons. These tickets have, however, in almost every case, been removed, and fresh ones, bearing Antonio Stradivari's name alone, inserted. Of the two brothers, Francesco was the better *luthier*. His work is not without originality, the outline of his *ff* holes in particular differing greatly from that of his father. A picture of one of his violas is included in George Hart's *The Violin*. E. H.-A.

STRAETEN, EDMOND VAN DER (*b.* Oudenarde, Flanders, Dec. 3, 1826 ; *d.* there, Nov. 25, 1895), distinguished Belgian musician and writer on music, was educated for the law, first at Alost, and afterwards in the University of Ghent.

On his return to Oudenarde he continued the cultivation of his taste for music, in combination with numismatics and archæology, the last-named pursuit powerfully influencing the determination of his career. While in his native town he organised and directed performances of excerpts from operatic works, and in 1849 himself set to music a three-act drama, entitled ' Le Proscrit.' At this early age he began that research in the rich musical archives of his native country which he later gave to the public in his literary works. Van der Straeten next became secretary to Fétis, who was then director of the Brussels Conservatoire, at the same time continuing his studies in harmony and counterpoint, the latter under Fétis, with whom he entered into active collaboration, in cataloguing the historical section of the Royal Library and contributing numerous articles to Fétis's biographical dictionary. He thus spent fourteen years in preparation for his own historical productions. During this time he acted as musical critic to *Le Nord*, *L'Écho du Parlement* and *L'Étoile belge*, and wrote, as well, in various reviews. His early books are *Coup d'œil sur la musique actuelle à Oudenarde* (1851) ; *Charles Félix de Hollandre* (1854) ; *Les Carillons d'Oudenarde* (1855) ; *Recherches sur la musique à Oudenarde avant le XIXe siècle* (1856); *Examens des chants populaires des Flamands de France* (1858) ; *Jacques de Goüy* (1863) ; and *J. F. J. Janssens* (1866).

The first volume of his great work, *La Musique aux Pays-Bas*, appeared in 1867, and the eighth in 1888 ; it marks the period of his entire devotion to the publication of his archæological discoveries. He had formed an important library of materials for the musical history of the Low Countries, and had also collected musical instruments bearing upon his studies, including his beautiful Jean Ruckers clavecin of 1627, figured in his third volume.

The Belgian Government now charged van der Straeten with artistic and scientific missions which involved his visiting Germany, Italy, France and Spain. He visited Weimar in 1870, for the model representations of Wagner's operas, and his reports are alike distinguished by æsthetic sentiment and clearness of analytical vision. He was appointed by his government, in concert with the Académie Royale, on the committee for the publication of ancient Belgian compositions. The most important of his later books are : Le Théâtre villageois en Flandre, 2 vols. (1874 and 1880) ; Les Musiciens néerlandais en Italie (1882); Les Musiciens néerlandais en Espagne (first part, 1885); Charles V musicien (1894), and Les Willems luthiers gantois du XVII⁰ siècle (with C. Snoeck, 1896). A complete bibliography of his works to 1877 is appended to an interesting biographical notice, written by Charles Meerens, and published at Rome. (See also RIEMANN.)

A. J. H.

STRAETEN, EDMUND SEBASTIAN JOSEPH VAN DER (b. Düsseldorf, Apr. 29, 1855), violoncellist, writer and composer ; living in London since 1881. For over thirty years he has identified himself with the revival of the viols and ancient chamber music as player of the viola da gamba and lecturer on the viols and musical history. He instituted chamber concerts at the North-East London (now Hackney) Institute under the auspices of Ebenezer Prout, and in the West End between 1890–1910; played as soloist in London and the provinces in the last concert of Mme. Trebelli's farewell tour ; played the gamba at the Handel Festival at Halle in 1922; and founded the Tonal Art Club at St. John's Wood in 1900. He has been an extensive contributor to the 3rd edition of this Dictionary. His publications include The History of the Violoncello, The Romance of the Fiddle, The Technics of Violoncello Playing, Handbook of Musical Form, The Revival of the Viols (in The Strad), a series of books on How to play Violin Solos and Violoncello Solos. Compositions : two albums, a suite, ' Romance ' and other solos for violoncello and violin, Méthode de Violoncello, 3 books. His unpublished include ' The Lily of Kashmir,' 3-act opera, and a Christmas cantata, Elegy and other pieces for orchestra.

STRAIGHT & SKILLERN, a firm of London music-publishers. Thomas Straight and Thomas Skillern were established in Great Russell Street, Covent Garden, and issued a set of Country Dances for 1768. On the death of James Oswald about 1769, they appear to have taken over his business at 17 St. Martin's Lane, and to have reissued some of the Oswald publications, in some instances in conjunction with William Randall. About 1777 or 1778, Thomas Straight either died or gave up business, and Skillern was left alone at 17 St. Martin's Lane, where he remained until about 1799 or 1800, at which time his death occurred, his plates and stock-in-trade being bought by Preston. Skillern's son (presumably) now went into partnership with Challoner (evidently Neville Butler Challoner, the harpist) at 25 Greek Street ; they afterwards, c. 1815, were near the corner of Regent Street and Oxford Street.

Thomas Straight, jun., after his father's death, set up a music business at 138 St. Martin's Lane, removing about 1796, and apparently devoting himself to music engraving solely, at 7 Lambeth Walk. Another address of the same or another Straight is 4 Green Street, Leicester Square.   F. K.

STRAKOSCH, (1) MAURICE (b. Lemberg, Moravia, 1825 [1]; d. Paris, Oct. 9, 1887), well known in the United States as an entrepreneur of operatic and concert ventures, the elder of two brothers, studied at the Vienna Conservatorium, and from 1845–60 lived in the United States, first as a teacher and then as an impresario. After Rossini's death he gave performances of the ' Messe solennelle ' at the Salle Ventadour, Paris, where he organised a successful opera season in 1873–74. He was European agent for his sister-in-law, Mme. Patti, from her début in 1859 until her marriage, and also for many other distinguished singers. In 1857 he managed his first season of Italian opera in New York and in 1859 took his company to Chicago. Two operas of his composition, ' Sardanapalus ' and ' Giovanna di Napoli,' were given in New York. He joined his brother in management of the Apollo Theatre in Rome in 1884–85. In 1887 he published a volume of memoirs, Souvenirs d'un impresario, and died suddenly in the same year.

His younger brother, (2) MAX (b. 1834 ; d. New York, Mar. 17, 1892), remained in America when Maurice went to Europe, and managed in his stead. He directed many successful enterprises of Italian opera, and managed the Apollo Theatre in Rome with his brother in 1884–85.

A. C.; addns. Amer. Supp.

STRALOCH MS., a famous MS. collection of airs written in lute tablature, for Robert Gordon of Straloch, and dated 1627 and 1629. The MS. was in small oblong octavo of ninety-two leaves, and was entitled,

' An playing Booke for the Lute. Where in ar contained many cvrrents and other mvsical things. . . . At Aberdein. Notted and Collected by Robert Gordon [Sir Robert Gordon of Straloch.] In the year of our Lord 1627. In Februarie.'

On the back of the title was a sketch of a person playing on the lute.

It was given, in 1781, by Dr. George Skene of Aberdeen, to Dr. Burney, who does not appear to have mentioned it or to have made any use of it. It afterwards came into the possession of James Chalmers of London, at the sale of whose effects it disappeared. In 1839 it was lent to George Farquhar Graham, who made some extracts from it. Graham's original transcript was in the library of the late T. W. Taphouse of Oxford, and was sold in 1905. A fair copy was made by Graham, and deposited in the

[1] Musical World gave 1823.

Advocates' Library, Edinburgh ; other copies, too, have been made from the original transcript, one by the present writer. Though the Straloch appears to be the earliest MS. containing Scottish airs, yet the list of contents (see *Gentleman's Magazine*, Feb. 1823) shows how small a proportion they bear to the English and foreign airs.   F. K.

STRANIERA, LA (The Stranger), opera in 2 acts ; libretto by Romani, music by Bellini. Produced La Scala, Milan, Feb. 14, 1829 ; King's Theatre, June 23, 1832.   G.

STRANSKY, JOSEF (*b.* Hupoleč, Bohemia, Sept. 9, 1874), orchestral conductor, who after studying medicine at Prague, Vienna and Leipzig, studied music under such famous masters as Fibich and Dvořák in Prague, Fuchs and Bruckner in Vienna.

His career as conductor began at the German theatre in Prague and was continued at the Hamburg Opera (1900–09). He followed Mahler as conductor of the New York Philharmonic Society (1911–22), and since then has been in charge of other orchestral and operatic organisations in America. His compositions include an opera, ' Der General,' given at Hamburg.
Amer. Supp.

STRATHSPEY, a Scottish dance, closely allied to the REEL (*q.v.*), derives its name from the strath or valley of the Spey, in the North of Scotland, where it appears to have first been danced. The word does not appear in connexion with music till late in the 18th century, but much earlier than that tunes are found suited for the style. Though slower in time than the Reel, the Strathspey calls for more exertion. The former is a gliding dance, while the Strathspey abounds in those jerky motions which call every muscle into play. Thus the music of the Reel is composed of a series of passages of equal quavers, while the Strathspey consists of dotted notes and semiquavers. The latter frequently precede the long note, and this peculiarity has received the name of the SCOTCH SNAP (*q.v.*). That the two words were formerly almost synonymous, is shown by a volume which is still of the highest authority and of which the title-page runs thus :

' A Collection of Strathspeys or Old Highland Reells, with a Bass for the Violincello [*sic*], Harpsichord, or Pianoforte. By Angus Cumming, at Granton. Strathspey. 1780.'

The word Strathspey is here printed in very large letters, while ' Old Highland Reells ' are in the smallest. Moreover, throughout the volume the word Strathspey is not once used, but always *Reell So-and-so*. No. 5, for example, though clearly a Strathspey, is entitled ' Acharnae Reell.' (See REEL and SCOTTISH MUSIC.) The Strathspey differs from the Reel in *tempo* ; the Strathspey ♩=94, the Reel ♩=126 is an approximate indication. Another difference is the smoothness of the notes in the Reel as compared with the broken notes of the Strathspey.

REEL. *Clydeside Lasses.*

STRATHSPEY. *Tullochgorum.*

With the Reels and Strathspeys of Scotland the name of Neil Gow (*q.v.*) is indissolubly associated.   T. L. S.

STRAUBE, KARL (*b.* Berlin, Jan. 6, 1873), organist and conductor, is the son of a German father and an English mother. He studied the organ under Heinrich Reimann, and from 1894–1897 gave organ recitals all over Germany and elsewhere, arousing wide admiration for both the virtuosity and the musical quality of his playing. In 1897 he was appointed organist of the Willibrode Dom at Wesel. In 1902 he went to Leipzig as organist of the Thomaskirche, a post he retained until 1918. In 1903 he became conductor of the Leipzig Bach Society, and in 1904 conducted the second German Bach Festival. In 1908 he conducted the Leipzig Bach Festival on the occasion of the unveiling of Seffner's Bach monument, and further Bach Festivals at Leipzig in 1911, 1914, 1920 and 1923—this last one being held to commemorate the bicentenary of Bach's appointment as cantor.

Meanwhile, in 1907, he had been appointed organ-teacher at the Leipzig Conservatorium, and was granted the title of ' Royal Professor ' in 1908. In 1918 he succeeded Gustav Schreck as cantor of the Thomasschule, and in 1919 effected the merging of the Bach Society in the Gewandhauschor, of which he is conductor. In 1925 he was the chief organiser of an important Handel Festival at Leipzig and conducted the greater part of it. Since his appointment as cantor in 1918, his duties have been so exacting and multifarious that he has almost given up playing the organ in public, but the general German opinion is that he is the finest organist that Germany has produced in recent generations. His repertory includes all the best organ music, new and old, and his powers of improvisation are unrivalled. Max Reger met him in early years, and it is owing to his admiration for Straube's playing that he produced most of his finest organ works. At one time, indeed, there was a kind of friendly warfare between them. Reger was determined that he would write works which would defeat even Straube's virtuosity, but after each onslaught Straube was left with the victory. As a conductor, whether of the Thomanerchor or the Gewandhauschor, he has done an immense amount of admirable work, introducing music hitherto unknown in Germany—early Netherland, Italian and English church music, as well as modern choral works of different nationalities, including Vaughan Williams's unaccompanied Mass in G minor ; while his interpretation of accepted masterpieces such as Bach's Passion Music and the B minor Mass or Handel's oratorios is always masterly. His profound knowledge of music of all periods, coupled with his exceptionally wide general culture and his ever - fresh curiosity about anything that touches human affairs, makes him one of the leading figures in the artistic and intellectual life of present-day Germany.

H. B.

STRAUS, LUDWIG (b. Pressburg, Mar. 28, 1835; d. Cambridge, Oct. 23,[1] 1899), an excellent violin-player ; entered the Vienna Conservatorium in 1843, and remained there till the revolution in 1848 ; was pupil of Böhm for the violin, and Preyer and Nottebohm for counterpoint ; made his first appearance (at the same time with Fräulein Csillag) in a concert at the hall of the Musikverein, Vienna, in June 1850. During the next few years he made various public appearances, besides playing in the private concerts of several patrons of music, especially Ober-Finanzrath Baron von Heintl, at whose réunions he played second fiddle to Mayseder for three years. At the Mozart Centenary Festival in 1856 he met Liszt, and, like many other young artists, benefited by his kindness. Straus's first concert tour was made in 1855, and extended as far as Venice and Florence. In 1857 he made the acquaintance of Piatti, with whom he took a second tour through Germany and Sweden. In 1860 he was appointed Konzertmeister of the theatre (till 1862) and of the Museum-concerts in Frankfort (till 1864), giving also quartet concerts, and leading the subscription concerts in the neighbouring towns. In 1860 he first visited England, played at the Musical Union, June 5, etc., and at the Monday Popular Concert of June 18. In 1861 he returned, and appeared twice at the Philharmonic, Apr. 29 and June 24.

In 1864 he took up his residence in England, settling after a time in Manchester, where he was leader of Hallé's orchestra. But he often visited London, to take either first fiddle or viola in the Popular Concerts, or to play soli at the Crystal Palace or the Philharmonic ; during his residence in England he played at Dresden, Vienna, etc. Straus was a member of the Queen's private band, and 'solo violinist' to Queen Victoria. In 1888 he resigned the leadership of the Hallé orchestra, and settled altogether in London. In 1893 he gave up all active work, being crippled with arthritis ; he went to live at Cambridge, where,

[1] Not 15th, as Riemann states.

a short time after his retirement, his many friends and admirers presented him with a fine Stradivarius violin.   G., addns.

STRAUSS, (1) JOHANN (b. Vienna, Mar. 14, 1804 ; d. there, Sept. 25, 1849), composer of dance music of world-wide celebrity.

As a child he showed talent for music, and a love for the violin, but his parents, small inn-keepers, apprenticed him to a bookbinder, from whom he ran away. A friend met him, took him back, and persuaded the parents to entrust him with the boy's education as a musician. With the son of this benefactor he learnt the violin from Polyschansky, afterwards studying harmony and instrumentation with Seyfried. He soon played the viola in string quartets at private houses, and at fifteen entered Pamer's orchestra at the 'Sperl,' a favourite place of amusement in the Leopoldstadt. At that time the excellent playing of LANNER (q.v.) and the brothers Drahanek was exciting attention ; Strauss offered himself, and was accepted as fourth in the little band. Soon, however, their numbers had to be increased to meet their numerous engagements, and Strauss acted as deputy-conductor till 1825, when he and Lanner parted.

In the Carnival of 1826 Strauss and his little orchestra of fourteen performers appeared in the hall of the 'Swan' in the Rossau suburb, and took the hearts of the people by storm. His op. 1, the 'Täuberl-Walzer' (Haslinger), was speedily followed by others, the most successful being the 'Kattenbrücken-Walzer,' called after the Hall of that name. Strauss was next invited to return with his now enlarged orchestra to the 'Sperl,' and with such success as to induce the proprietor, Scherzer, to engage him for six years, which virtually founded the reputation of the 'Sperl' and its orchestral conductor. Meantime Strauss was appointed Kapellmeister of the first Bürger-regiment, and entrusted with the music at the court fêtes and balls. As his band was daily in request at several places at once, he increased the number to over 200, from which he formed a select body for playing at concerts, in music of the highest class. He now began to make tours in the provinces and abroad, visiting Pest in 1833 ; Berlin, Leipzig and Dresden in 1834 ; West Germany in 1835 ; and North Germany, Holland, Belgium and the Rhine in 1836.

His next tour began in Oct. 1837, and embraced Strassburg, Paris, Rouen, Havre, Belgium, London, and the larger towns of Great Britain ; he then returned to Belgium, and back to England and Scotland. His success in Paris was unprecedented, notwithstanding the formidable rivalry of Musard and Dufresne, with the former of whom he wisely joined for a series of thirty - concerts. A disagreeable intrigue nearly made him throw up the journey to England, but it was only there that his profits at all remunerated him for his enormous expenses. In London he played at seventy-two concerts, and at innumerable balls and fêtes given in honour of Queen Victoria's coronation (June 28, 1838). On his second visit he had great difficulty in keeping his band from dispersing, so weary were they of continual travelling. He managed, however, to go again to Birmingham, Liverpool and Dublin, besides visiting Reading, Cheltenham, Worcester, Leicester, Derby, Nottingham and Sheffield. At Sheffield his receipts were small, and at Halifax still less, but when the amateurs of both places discovered the kind of musician they had been neglecting, a deputation was sent with post-horses to Leeds to bring him back again. He was taken ill at Derby, and only reached Vienna with great difficulty in Dec. 1838.

His first reappearance at the ' Sperl ' was quite a popular fête. On May 5, 1840, he conducted for the first time in the imperial Volksgarten, which was crowded whenever his band performed. Strauss now introduced the quadrille, which he had studied in Paris, in place of the galop. His first work of the kind was the ' Wiener Carneval-Quadrille ' (op. 124). Henceforward, except waltzes—among which the ' Donaulieder ' (op. 127) are still played—he composed only quadrilles, polkas, and marches, including the favourite ' Radetzky-March.' On Apr. 16, 1843, he and the band of his old Bürger-regiment accompanied the body of his old colleague Lanner to the grave. An excursion to Olmütz, Troppau, etc., in the autumn of 1844, was succeeded in the next autumn by one to Dresden, Magdeburg and Berlin, where he was immensely fêted. The King appeared in person at Kroll's Garden, and invited Strauss to play at the palace. The Prince of Prussia, afterwards the Emperor William I., ordered a performance at Kroll's by more than 200 bandsmen, conducted by the Kapellmeister General Wipprecht, before Strauss and his orchestra, when the royal princes, the generals, and the pick of the nobility attended. On his departure a grand torchlight procession and serenade were given in his honour. On his return to Vienna he was made conductor of the court balls. In the autumn of 1846 he went to Silesia, and the year following again to Berlin and Hamburg, where he revenged himself for some slights caused by professional jealousy by giving a concert for the poor. He returned to Vienna by Hanover, Magdeburg and Berlin. During the stormy days of Mar. 1848 he did homage to the spirit of the times in the titles of his pieces, but Strauss was at heart a Viennese of the olden time, a fact which caused him much unpleasantness on his next tour, in 1849, by Munich, Stuttgart, Frankfort, the Rhine, and Brussels to England.

He stayed in London and the provinces from Apr. to July. After a brilliant farewell concert he was accompanied down the Thames by a fleet of boats, one of which contained a band playing the popular air, ' So leb' denn wohl du stilles Haus,' from Raimund's ' Verschwender.' In the midst of this gay scene poor Strauss was oppressed with a presentiment that he should never revisit London. Shortly after his return to Vienna he was taken ill with scarlet fever, to which he succumbed on the fourth day. With him departed a feature of Viennese life, and that the people themselves felt this was shown by the vast concourse at his funeral. A Requiem was performed in his honour on Oct. 11 by his own band, and the Männergesangverein of Vienna, the soli being sung by Mesdames Hasselt and Ernst, Aloys Ander and Staudigl, all from the court opera. Strauss married, in 1824, Anna Streim, daughter of an innkeeper, who bore him five children, Johann (2), Joseph (3), Eduard (4), Anna and Therese. They separated after eighteen years, on the ground of incompatibility of temper.

There are numerous portraits from which an idea can be gathered of Strauss's personal appearance. Though small he was well made and distinguished-looking, with a singularly formed head. His dress was always neat and well chosen. Though lively in company he was naturally rather silent. From the moment he took his violin in his hand he became another man, his whole being seeming to expand with the sounds he drew from it.

As an artist he furnished many pleasant hours to thousands, and high and low combined to do him honour, while great masters like Mendelssohn, Meyerbeer and Cherubini acknowledged his talent. He raised dance music to a higher level than it had ever reached before, and invested his copious melodies with all the charm of brilliant instrumentation. Full of fire, life, and boisterous merriment, they contrasted well with Lanner's softer and more sentimental airs, and must be judged by a totally different standard from that of mere dance music. As a conductor it was his constant endeavour to mingle classical names in his programmes, and thus to exercise an elevating influence on the masses. His works, published almost entirely by Haslinger, number 251, and comprise 152 waltzes, 24 galops, 6 cotillons and contredanses, 32 quadrilles, 13 polkas, and 18 marches, including some without opus numbers. The bulk of these have made, so to speak, the tour of the world ; each new waltz was in its way an event, not only in Vienna, but wherever the first printed copies penetrated. Innumerable pens, including those of poets, celebrated his works, and the stage itself took part in the general homage, ' Strauss and Lanner ' being the title of a one-act comedy by Töpfer, and a three-act piece by Anton Langer. His complete works were published in 1889 by B. & H., in seven volumes.

Of his three sons, the eldest, (2) JOHANN

(*b.* Vienna, Oct. 25, 1825 ; *d.* there, June 3, 1899), was scarcely less gifted than his father. In accordance with the father's wish that none of his sons should adopt his own line of life, Johann, after finishing his education at the Gymnasium and Polytechnic Institute, became a clerk in the savings bank, although he had, with his mother's help, long taken lessons in secret on the violin, and even studied composition with Drechsler. When only six he composed, at Salmannsdorf near Vienna, where the family used to spend the summer, his first waltz, which was performed on his fiftieth birthday as ' Erster Gedanke.' The constraint put upon him became at length unbearable, and on Oct. 15, 1844, he first appeared as a conductor at Dommayer's, at Hietzing, playing compositions of his own, and his father's 'Loreley Walzer.' His success on that occasion decided his future career. After his father's death he incorporated the two bands, and made a tour to the country towns of Austria, Warsaw and the more important towns of Germany. He also undertook for ten years the direction of the summer concerts in the Petropaulovski Park at St. Petersburg. On Aug. 28, 1862, he married the popular singer Henriette (' Jetty ') Treffz, and in 1863 became conductor of the court balls. This post he resigned after his brilliant success on the stage, but he had in the meantime composed nearly 400 waltzes, of as high a type as those of his father.

His music is penetrated with Viennese gaiety and spirit, and has made its way into all countries. The waltz, 'An der schönen blauen Donau ' (' The Blue Danube ') (op. 314), became a kind of musical watchword in Vienna, and was played on all festive occasions. 'Tausend und eine Nacht,' ' Man lebt nur einmal,' ' Weiner Blut,' and ' Künstlerleben ' are among the most famous. Besides Russia, Strauss visited Paris (during the Exhibition of 1867), London, New York, Boston, and the larger towns of Italy. The Theatre 'an der Wien' was the scene of his triumphs as a composer of operettas, which rapidly spread to all the theatres, large and small. ' Indigo und die vierzig Räuber' (his first, 1871), 'Der Karneval in Rom ' (1873), ' Die Fledermaus ' (1874), ' Cagliostro ' (1875), 'Prinz Methusalem' (1877), ' Blindekuh ' (1878), ' Das Spitzentuch der Königin ' (1880), ' Der lustige Krieg ' (1881), ' Eine Nacht in Venedig ' (1883), ' Der Zigeunerbaron' (1885), 'Simplicius' (1887), 'Ritter Pasman ' (1892), ' Fürstin Ninetta ' (1893), ' Jabuka ' (1894), ' Waldmeister ' (1895), and ' Die Göttin der Vernunft ' (1897), all published by Spina, were soon known all over the world, and were sung everywhere. Posthumously produced were a ballet, 'Aschenbrödel,' and an orchestral piece, ' Traumbilder.' A biography by R. von Prochâzka is in Riemann's series of *Berühmte Musiker.* (See *Riemann.*) After the

death of his wife on Apr. 8, 1878, he married another dramatic singer, Angelica Dittrich.

His next brother, (3) JOSEPH (*b.* Vienna, Aug. 22, 1827 ; *d.* there, July 22, 1870), was also obliged to accommodate himself to his father's wishes, and became an architect. He had, however, studied music in secret, and during an illness of his brother's in 1853 he conducted for him with a baton, as he did not learn the violin till later. He next collected a band, began to compose, and published in rapid succession 283 works (Haslinger and Spina) not less popular than those of his brother. He had always been delicate, and the excitement incidental to his calling increased the mischief year by year. A visit to Warsaw in 1870, against the wish of his friends, was very disastrous. Some Russian officers, having sent for him in the middle of the night to play for them, so shamefully ill-treated him for his refusal that he had to take to his bed. Under the devoted nursing of his wife (married in 1857) he rallied sufficiently to return to Vienna, but sank a few days afterwards.

The youngest of his brothers, (4) EDUARD (*b.* Vienna, Feb. 14, 1835 ; *d.* there, Dec. 28, 1916), was educated at the Schotten and Akademien Gymnasiums. His father having died before he grew up he devoted himself entirely to music, learnt the harp, and studied composition with Preyer. In 1862 he made his first appearance as a conductor in the Dianasaal, and was well received for his father's sake. In 1865 he took his brother Johann's place at the concerts in St. Petersburg, and in 1870 became conductor of the court balls. He and his band made repeated tours to Dresden, Leipzig, Breslau, Berlin, Hamburg, Frankfort, etc. He appeared regularly in Vienna on fixed days at the Volksgarten, and in the winter in the large hall of the Musikverein, when his programmes were always attractive. He composed over 200 pieces of dance music, published by Haslinger, and latterly, with few exceptions, by Spina (Schreiber). Eduard Strauss married in 1863. In 1885 his orchestra was engaged at the Inventions Exhibition in London, when the daily concerts created a furore. He came also a few days later and played at the Imperial Institute.   C. F. P.

BIBL.—FRITZ LANGE, *Josef Lanner und Johann Strauss* (Vienna, 1904 ; 2nd ed. Leipzig, 1919) ; ERNST DECSEY, *Johann Strauss* (Stuttgart, Berlin, 1922) ; ED. STRAUSS, *Erinnerungen,* 1906.

STRAUSS, RICHARD (*b.* Munich, June 11, 1864), eminent alike as composer and conductor, was without a doubt the greatest figure in music of the last decade of the 19th century.

His father, Franz Strauss, was well known in Munich as the leading horn-player in the Munich Opera Orchestra. He was credited with having, at Wagner's own request, reduced the famous horn-call in ' Siegfried,' which in its original form was almost unplayable, to its final shape. The composer's mother was one of the famous brewing family of Pschorr. The boy Richard early showed musical talent, and his father, who was a conservative of the straitest sect, took care that he should be brought up in the strictest classical traditions. His earliest teacher was F. W. Meyer. At the age of 6 he composed a ' Schneiderpolka ' and a Christmas song. He pursued the ordinary education of a German boy at an elementary school from 1870–74, after which he entered the Gymnasium, whence he proceeded to the University of Munich in 1882. In 1871 he had already published a Festival March for orchestra and written a Serenade for wood-wind instruments, published as opus 7. In view of later happenings the fact that he composed the chorus from the *Elektra* of Sophocles, which was performed at a school concert, has a certain historical interest. The first record of a public performance of any of his works is of the singing of three of his songs by Frau Meysenheim. His quartet, opus 2, was played in Mar. 1881, by a quartet led by his violin master, Benno Walter. A still greater distinction was the performance of a symphony in D minor (at present unpublished) by Hermann Levi. All this time his musical and general education were proceeding side by side. He left the University in 1883 with the intention of devoting himself to music. Until that time even Schumann and Brahms had been too advanced for him, and although there are a few prophetic hints, certain turns of phrase, which are still characteristic of him, his earliest works remain strictly classical.

In the winter of 1883–84 Strauss was in Berlin, and this proved a turning-point in his career, for some of his works attracted the attention of von Bülow, who had his Serenade played at one of the concerts of the Meiningen Orchestra. Bülow also helped him to start his career as a conductor. In Oct. 1885 Bülow secured for him an appointment as Assistant Music Director at Meiningen. During this period he played solos and concertos and conducted his own symphony in F minor, opus 12, which had already been performed in 1884 at New York under Theodore Thomas. The two last works and the choral work ' Wanderers Sturmlied,' though not lacking in individuality, clearly show the very strong influence of Brahms.

At this period comes the real beginning of Strauss's career as a composer. He himself attributes his change of view to Alexander RITTER (*q.v.*), who had been at school with Bülow, and was a convinced adherent of Wagner and Liszt. The question has often been discussed at length and will never be answered fully how far Strauss's conversion is due to ideas that germinated in his own brain and how far to the external influence of Ritter. The probabilities are that both answers are true, or at any rate the question may now be considered as a purely academic one. For most people

Strauss's own account of his relationship to Ritter is sufficient :

' His influence was in the nature of the stormwind. He urged me on to the development of the poetic, the expressive in music, as exemplified in the works of Liszt, Wagner and Berlioz. My symphonic fantasia, " Aus Italien," is the connecting link between the old and the new methods.'

It was not long before this change in Strauss's outlook, which may be briefly described as a conversion to the new German school which had as its motto ' Music as Expression ' ('Musik als Ausdruck '), became evident. Strauss was appointed successor to Bülow at Meiningen in 1885 and spent a good deal of the spring of 1886 in Italy, and brought back with him the fantasia ' Aus Italien,' which was first performed in Munich in the spring of 1887. In the meantime, in Aug. 1886, he was appointed subconductor at the Munich Opera, a position which he held till July 1889, and in the following August he became assistant to Lassen at Weimar.

In 1886 was published the first group of songs, op. 17, of which the one now best remembered is ' Seitdem dein Aug' in meines schaute.' In this the new ideal of music expressionism is first fully realised. The violin sonata, op. 18, in which there are many turns of phrase suggestive of the later Strauss, appeared in 1887, and in 1888 ' Don Juan,' op. 20, was first performed in Berlin ; ' Tod und Verklärung ' was first performed in 1889. Although it is numbered op. 23, ' Macbeth ' had been written earlier than either of these. They show that the conversion to the new ideals was complete.

At this time Strauss's works were generally becoming known, and the controversies which their audacity aroused, controversies which to-day seem to belong to an age long past, began. The chief events of Strauss's stay at Weimar, which extended to June 1894, were a severe illness in 1892 which made necessary a voyage to Egypt and Sicily in 1892, and the composition during this time of the opera ' Guntram,' first performed at Weimar in 1894. The part of the heroine Freihild was played by Pauline de Ahna, who shortly afterwards became the composer's wife. In the following winter Strauss was appointed conductor of the Philharmonic concerts in Berlin in succession to Bülow, and shortly before that he had conducted the first performance of ' Tannhäuser ' at Bayreuth.

During this period Strauss became one of the most prominent German travelling conductors. He visited London in 1897 for the first time and all the other important European towns. At this time came the composition of ' Till Eulenspiegels lustige Streiche,' which was first performed at Frankfort in Sept. 1895. Here may be interpolated mention of the fact that on Mar. 21, 1896, Manns played 'Till Eulenspiegel' at the Crystal Palace, this being the first time that Strauss's name appeared in an English orchestral programme. Manns thought the work so hard to understand that he had it played twice. ' Don Quixote,' op. 35, written in 1897 (first performance at Cologne, Mar. 8, 1898), and ' Ein Heldenleben,' op. 40, written in 1898, followed quickly. On Nov. 1, 1898, he was appointed conductor of the Royal Opera House at Berlin. Next came his second opera ' Feuersnot,' op. 50, first produced in Dresden on Nov. 21, 1901. In June 1903, came the series of concerts, known as the Strauss Festival, in London in the old St. James's Hall, given in conjunction with the Amsterdam orchestra, which he and Mengelberg conducted alternately, and at which several of his works were introduced to England.

The controversies about Strauss had all this time continued to rage fiercely in all the musical centres of Europe and America. They reached their height after the production, in Dresden, on Sept. 9, 1905, of his opera ' Salomé ' to Oscar Wilde's text. The greater part of the year 1904 was devoted to the composition of the ' Symphonia Domestica,' which was first performed in New York in April of that year under the composer's direction, for the first time in Europe on June 1, at the Tonkünstler-Verein Festival at Frankfort, and on Nov. 6 in London.

The chief event of 1905 was the first performance at Dresden of ' Salomé,' under von Schuch with Frau Wittich and MM. Burrian and Perron in the chief parts. This period of 1906–09 may be passed over rapidly. It was filled simply with many successes as conductor, culminating in the appointment as conductor of the Berlin Opera Orchestra, a post which Weingartner had retained when he relinquished the conductorship of the opera.

The first performance of ' Elektra ' (text by von Hofmannsthal) was at Dresden on Jan. 25, 1909, and Strauss conducted the opera the first time in London in Mar. 1910. During this time ' Der Rosenkavalier ' was being composed and was completed on Sept. 26, 1909, at his country house in Garmisch. Its first performance took place at Dresden on Jan. 26, 1911. In November 1910 Strauss resigned from the conductorship of the Berlin Opera. Since that date there have been few external events in his life, and the history of Strauss is chiefly that of his compositions.

After the composition of ' Der Rosenkavalier,' which to a certain extent showed that a modification of Strauss's style was inevitable and impending, came ' Ariadne auf Naxos,' which in its first version is an integral part of Molière's Le Bourgeois gentilhomme. It was first produced in Stuttgart, Oct. 25, 1912,[1] and in 1913 in London at His Majesty's

[1] Given in the small house of the newly opened Hoftheater as the chief event in a festival of Strauss's works to celebrate the opening of the new theatre on Oct. 14.

Theatre under BEECHAM (q.v.). This showed a further tendency towards simplification, of which, however, there were few, if any, signs in the ' Legend of Joseph,' op. 63, first produced by Diaghilev's Russian Ballet in Paris shortly before the war (1914), and a few weeks later given in London under the conductorship of the composer at Drury Lane Theatre (in June 1914). It was due to the war that it was not heard in Germany till 1921. The most important works of the war period were the opera ' Die Frau ohne Schatten,' text by Hugo von Hofmannsthal, which was first produced at Vienna on Oct. 1, 1919, and, for the present, the last of the orchestral compositions, the ' Alpine Symphony,' 1915, which was first heard in England under Sir Thomas Beecham at Queen's Hall in 1923. He also composed ' Parergon to the Domestic Symphony,' in other words, a free fantasia on themes from that work, for the one-armed pianist Paul von Wittgenstein, who had been wounded in the war. This is for the piano (left hand alone) and orchestra. It was played privately by von Wittgenstein in arrangement for two pianos in London.

The two other works of this last period are the ballet-pantomime ' Schlagobers ' (Whipped Cream), Vienna, 1924, and the comic play opera ' Intermezzo,' for which Strauss wrote his own text (a thing he had not done since the days of ' Guntram '), produced in 1925 in Vienna.

He is engaged (1926) in the composition of another opera, text by von Hofmannsthal, on the subject of Helen of Egypt. Among his other works the only ones calling for mention here are editions of Gluck's ' Iphigenia in Tauris,' and editions of his father's post-humous works, chiefly studies for horn.

Since the war Strauss has paid three visits to London, one in the beginning of 1923 as conductor of his works, and two in 1926. On the first of these (April) he conducted the film version of ' Der Rosenkavalier,' for which he had adapted the music of his opera ; on Nov. 9 he conducted the ' Alpine Symphony ' and other works at a concert of the B.B.C.

QUALITIES OF STRAUSS'S ART

The history of the appreciation of Strauss's music in England is peculiar. It has probably never before happened to a composer of his rank that, just when the popularity of his works seemed to be steadily growing and controversy was dying down and the good was being separated from the bad, his works have suddenly been for about 10 years made inaccessible to the public. The 10 years in question are just the period in which musical as well as other history moved faster than at any time since the world began, while, for reasons totally independent of music itself, we were not able to hear it or write an opinion about it. Russian and French music held our world, and native music, both old and new, had a vogue such as it had never had before.

When Strauss's music was heard again in England, it came into a world totally different from that in which we had last known it, and revaluation became indispensable. It was quickly realised that much which had been most eagerly fought about in the pre-war years had passed beyond the realm of controversy. The later developments of Russian music made much which had seemed strange and cacophonous before 1914 now seem harmless and ordinary. Ears which had not flinched at the ' Sacre du printemps ' found the Battle Scene of ' Ein Heldenleben ' quite innocent. On the other hand, lasting qualities of much of Strauss's work which controversialists had not allowed us to enjoy in peace were shown in a clearer light. Pre - war controversy as to the justification of programme music and ' hearing vertically ' began to have no more than antiquarian interest at the time when Strauss's music was heard again. But it is as well not to forget that at the time the problems had been acute.

THE SYMPHONIC POEMS.—At the time when Strauss first came under the influence of Alexander Ritter and professed himself a ' musician of expression ' (' Ausdrucks Musiker ') the world had hardly begun to understand the true functions and scope of programme music, and many wild experiments were made. The first of Strauss's really modern works was, as has already been said, ' Macbeth,' in which, however, he did not carry the development of the symphonic poem beyond the point where Liszt had stopped (see SYMPHONIC POEM). He had realised the truth of what Wagner said in writing of Liszt's works, that, under the guise of describing the individual, they really helped to interpret the universal. Each successive symphonic poem of Strauss carried the effort to enlarge the descriptive scope of music beyond the depicting of the elementary emotions. It was not enough for him to associate with ' Don Juan ' one or two themes expressive of violence and restlessness. He attempted to delineate the various phases of his mental development.

It would almost appear that at this period, perhaps subconsciously, a feeling grew on him that the Symphonic Poem, which in its beginnings in the hands of Liszt had been a protest against the formalism into which symphony was degenerating, or at any rate running a risk of degenerating, was in its turn creating a rigid dogma of its own. A very large percentage of symphonic poems, whether they attempted merely to tell stories in music—an error which Strauss never committed—or not began to conform to an unvarying pattern, of which the chief characteristic was that the composition must end with a coda based on a ' glorification ' of the themes of the chief character. Strauss tried to shake himself free of such fetters, until, in ' Till Eulenspiegel,' the highest splendour of the themes of ' Till ' is the central, not the final, feature of the work, and at the end there is a return to the simplicity with which the composition began, that is the æsthetic justification of its rondo form.

The variation form of ' Don Quixote ' is, for analogous reasons, equally appropriate to the subject, for the main object of the whole work is to show the modifications which the knight's mind and temperament undergo till he returns to sanity and rises to a higher spirituality. ' Ein Heldenleben ' has really two main subjects, the hero and his mate, and the real text of the work is the development of the two chief characters.[1]

Inevitably, in his efforts to enlarge the expressive scope of his music, Strauss wandered into fields hitherto deemed inaccessible to music, or at least inappropriate to music of high aims. But to say this without qualification is to leave out of account the element of humour and satire. There is real humour in all these works, except ' Macbeth,' although there is, and probably will be for a long time to come, much controversy as to the quality of the humour. Whatever may be our ultimate judgment on passages like those associated with the attack on the windmills, the wind machine and the herd of bleating sheep in ' Don Quixote ' or the music of the ' Adversaries ' in ' Ein Heldenleben,' one thing about them should be borne in mind; although they have perhaps been talked about more than the whole of the rest of the works put together, in actual performance they only occupy one or two minutes out of forty or forty-five. If such a thing as musical humour is at all possible, that quality can no more be denied to the music associated with Sancho Panza in ' Don Quixote ' or to the passage associated with the Wandering Friars in ' Till Eulenspiegel ' or the Penitents in ' Don Quixote,' than to Beethoven in his more irresponsible moments or the subtler comedy of Mozart. ' Till ' is in a different category, for there the humour is inherent in the themes themselves.

Strauss has never given to the world a long reasoned exposition of his views of the function of music, but it is possible to gather the principal features of what may be called his musical system from his scattered utterances, and of course from his works themselves. The

[1] Perhaps one might call ' the Adversaries ' the third topic ; but they are important more because they influence the Hero, and the way in which finally the themes coalesce is a subtle piece of psychology.

fundamental principle on which he has worked, ever since the days when he came under the influence of Ritter, may be summed up briefly thus: he refuses to recognise the distinction between abstract music and programme music; the only two categories he recognises are good music and bad music, and he defines good music as that which expresses most. How far this belief can be reconciled with the very marked preference which he has always shown for the music of Mozart over that of Beethoven is an interesting but hardly practical speculation. This taste, however, finds its expression in certain passages of his later music of which more will be said presently. Music he contends can do more than merely describe outward occurrences; it can express inner states of the mind and more than that, can arouse in the hearer the same emotions as the thing described. The answer given by himself and his adherents to the argument that it is impossible to set to music a system of philosophy and the accusation that he attempts to do so in 'Also sprach Zarathustra' is that he aims only at putting the hearer into a frame of mind analogous to that which would result from the study of philosophy. (See PROGRAMME MUSIC.)

This is perhaps the best place in which to deal with the charge of formlessness and the want of logic which was so often brought against his music in the past. It is not without interest to note that others have accused him with equal vehemence of cold-blooded calculation which takes the place of artistic impulse. It may be said with a good deal of force that in his earlier works, as for instance 'Aus Italien' and 'Macbeth,' he was preoccupied rather with the question how much can be expressed within the limits of a given form of music, whereas in later symphonic poems his chief anxiety was to find the musical form which would best express what he had to say. The difference in shape between 'Till Eulenspiegel,' who returns to a new life in legend, and 'Don Quixote' is accounted for by this modification of his æsthetic theory, which also explains the peculiarity of the structure of 'Ein Heldenleben,' especially at its eloquent close.

Later events have made it almost superfluous to discuss at any length his theories of 'vertical hearing' which at the time caused so much heart-burning. The problems which he set the musical world in this direction now seem almost elementary, and the resulting tonal effects which at first seemed irredeemably cacophonous to contemporary opinion are now accepted as completely innocuous.

Both their original strangeness and their subsequent familiarity have been quoted over and over again as proof of his artistic worthlessness on the one hand, and as proof of commanding ability on the other. It may be noted in passing that in the nature of things a good deal depends on the way in which the outstanding passages in the various works are presented by different conductors. To take two extreme instances: Strauss himself rather emphasises their asperities and freakishness in performance whereas Arthur Nikisch used rather to tone them down, and when Strauss was once told by a friend that Nikisch made his music sound more amiable his reply was, 'I don't want it to be always beautiful.'

That Strauss is an almost unapproached master of orchestral effect and tone colour is a point that need not be laboured. (See ORCHESTRATION.) The two most characteristic passages in which he has set out to paint the beauties of nature are the movements 'At Sorrento' in 'Aus Italien' and at the opposite end of his career the passage depicting the sun shining on the Alpine waterfall in the 'Alpine Symphony.' For sensuous charm there are not many passages in modern music to be quoted which equal the love music in 'Ein Heldenleben' and the 'Domestic Symphony' and, above all, the variation chiefly concerned with Dulcinea in 'Don Quixote.'[1] The rich colour of these is in strong contrast to the more incisive tones of much of 'Till Eulenspiegel,' 'Don Quixote' and, above all, 'Don Juan' with its reckless gaiety. The closes of 'Don Quixote' and 'Ein Heldenleben,' which are closely akin in mood, could hardly be surpassed as expressions of serenity and resignation. It would be possible to quote endless passages descriptive of every variety of mood from tragedy to force. One peculiarity of Strauss remains to be mentioned; he is reputed to have said once that every theme in his symphonic poems occurs to him as connected with a certain instrument. He hears it first on the violin, the horn, the oboe, as the case may be, but, he added, it does not follow that it is on that instrument that it makes its appearance in the work itself.

It will be well to consider next Strauss's way of making a certain instrument of the orchestra personify a certain character in his symphonic poems. The salient instances which will occur to every one are the solo violin which represents the Mate and the bassoons which typify the Adversaries in 'Ein Heldenleben,' and the oboe d' amore which stands for the Child in the 'Symphonia domestica,' and in 'Don Quixote' again the viola which is Sancho Panza's mouthpiece, so to speak. Strauss had to a certain extent been anticipated by Berlioz in the 'Symphonie Fantastique' and 'Harold in Italy,' but he extended the scope of this use of the individual instruments, making them more an integral part of the orchestra, and his choice has an unfailing felicity. This brings

[1] It is not without interest as bearing on Strauss's sensibility to the emotional values of keys to remark in passing that one is in G♭ and the other in F♯ major.

as again to another aspect of Strauss's works, the use of humour. It cannot be denied that often with him humour is synonymous with unlovely realistic sounds, but there are occasions when humour is combined with fine music. The viola passages in 'Don Quixote' connected with Sancho Panza, referred to above, are good instances of this, while the music which illustrates the death of Till Eulenspiegel may be quoted as being on the border-line. Thus in many cases with Strauss's music it is difficult to make a sharp distinction between descriptive realism, in the strict sense, as, for instance, the bleating of sheep in 'Don Quixote,' and the wind machine, and merely suggestive passages without raising the vexed question of humour in music, which is also illustrated by the parodied ecclesiastical music in 'Don Quixote' and 'Till Eulenspiegel.'

THE SONGS.—Coming now to Strauss as a writer for the voice, we find among the songs a great variety of music on various levels of excellence. His most rabid opponents cannot deny the beauty of songs like 'Traum durch die Dämmerung' (op. 29), 'Morgen,' 'Heimliche Aufforderung,' 'Ruhe meine Seele,' and 'Cäcilie' (op. 27), 'Ich schwebe' (op. 48) and 'Allerseelen' (op. 10), which are remarkable both for lyrical charm of melody and extraordinary insight into the meaning of the text and picturesque accompaniment. He has, however, another vein which is almost equally well developed, the musical value of which is perhaps doubtful, such as 'Steinklopfers Lied' (op. 49), and many others, in which the composer has the excuse that the text which he has chosen does not deal with the beautiful things of this life but with the ugly side of the world, and violent subversive feelings. He has also a group of songs which are full of delightful *naïveté*, of which 'Muttertändelei' (op. 43) is a good specimen; in them are found genial themes of Mozartian simplicity.

In a letter to Franz von Hausegger, dated 1903, he wrote an extremely interesting confession as to his methods of composing songs, which it will be best to transcribe in full:

'For some time,' he says, 'I will have no impulse to compose at all. Then one evening I will be turning the leaves of a volume of poetry; a poem will strike my eye. I read it through; it agrees with the mood I am in; and at once the appropriate music is instinctively fitted to it. I am in a musical frame of mind, and all I want is the right poetic vessel into which to pour my ideas. If good luck throws this in my way, a satisfactory song results.'

But often, he says, the poem that presents itself is not the right one; then he has to bend his musical mood to fit it the best way he can; he finds then that he works laboriously and without the right kind of enthusiasm at it.

His texts are mostly taken from modern German poets, of whom he is in particular sympathy, and his choice is happy, but sometimes his literary judgment fails him. He has

also, it cannot be denied, written a good many songs which bear traces of being composed without an inner impulse. A word should be spared for the beautiful 'Enoch Arden' (op. 38), a recitation for voice and piano, which is as nearly a song as such a hybrid can be. He has written, too, some fine songs for voice and orchestra, as distinct from those the piano accompaniment of which was later transcribed for orchestra, of which 'Hymnus' and 'Gesang der Apollopriesterin' (op. 33) are the most characteristic of Straussian rapture.

THE OPERAS.—It remains now to speak of Strauss as an operatic composer. His first work for the stage, 'Guntram' (op. 25), dates from 1892. He wrote his own libretto on a subject obviously inspired by Wagner's idea of what Nietzsche called the 'inevitable redeeming female' (*das obligat erlösende Frauenzimmer*). Its defect was the lack of action, which was not redeemed by the merits of the music, amongst which a long confession of faith by the hero and a duet between the hero and heroine are the best numbers. Next, in 1900, came 'Feuersnot' (op. 50), the libretto of which was by von Wolzogen. Here Strauss is more himself. The story of 'legendary time' (*fabelhafte Unzeit*) gave him full scope for brilliantly effective treatment of the folk-song elements of music, for musical sarcasm and for voluptuous love music. The finale remains one of the most gorgeously coloured of his tone pictures, and the choruses are remarkable for almost unsuspected powers of solid choral architecture, which is also observable in the choral ballad 'Taillefer' (op. 52), composed three years later.

After an interval of six years, during which he composed the 'Symphonia domestica' and 'Taillefer,' came 'Salomé,' which, with the exception of 'Elektra,' is the most hectic opera, or music-drama, ever written. These two works make the end not only of a period of Strauss's development, but of the development of music-drama in general. The force of passionate excitement could go no further.

'Salomé'—apart from the religious objections to the subject—was critised when it first appeared on the ground that it misrepresented the archaism of Wilde's style with its cold glitter, but the real opposition is between Wilde and the subject. In 'Salomé' Strauss's short sharp themes are found in their fullest development. The use of the *Leitmotiv* is carried to the utmost extent, and the excitement is worked up to the highest pitch by the almost physical violence of the unusually large orchestra. Its great defect is the almost inhuman demand which Strauss makes on the voice, and the brutality of the *dénouement*, which, however, is brought about with lightning rapidity. The reasons of its undoubted success (for it is still played in Germany after twenty years) are the gorgeous colour of the instrumentation, the vivid contrast between the music of Salomé, Herodias and Herod and that of Jochanaan, which comes as a relief after the hysterical excitement which precedes his entries. The Dance of the Seven Veils and Salomé's address to the head of Jochanaan are still to be heard on the concert platform in this country and each has a beauty of its own. ' Salome ' was first played in Dresden on Dec. 9, 1905, and in New York in Jan. 1907. The censor's objections to its production in England were overcome by altering the names of the principal characters and some few modifications in the text.

With Strauss's next music-drama, ' Elektra,' his partnership with Hugo von Hofmannsthal, which still (1926) lasts, began. ' Elektra ' was first performed at Dresden on Jan. 25, 1909. The poet took as his subject the drama of Sophocles, while the psychology is to some extent that of Euripides. It affords the composer ample scope for his gifts of musical characterisation, both with regard to the themes and their orchestral treatment. It has been said that it is more brutal and sordid than ' Salomé,' but it must not be forgotten that, whereas in ' Salome ' the viciousness is unredeemed, the brutality of Elektra has its foundations in her noble desire to avenge her father. The musical characterisation in ' Elektra ' has great power. The contrast between Elektra and Chrysothemis is incisively illustrated, and the musical picture of the neurotic over-wrought Clytemnestra, who is the female counterpart of Herod in ' Salomé,' is drawn with a firm hand. The first solo of Elektra, the duet of Elektra and Chrysothemis and the scene of the recognition of Orestes by Elektra contain magnificent vocal passages which stand out from the somewhat unvocal main body of the work. The recognition scene is in itself a refutation of the common accusation that Strauss is merely a cerebral musician without keen emotion.

When he had finished ' Elektra ' Strauss no doubt felt that he had gone as far as was possible in the way of stirring the emotions of his hearers by violence, orchestral and otherwise, and his next opera ' Der Rosenkavalier '—of which the text was also by Hugo von Hofmannsthal—shows a complete change of style. It has been rightly called his ' Meistersinger.' Three elements are to be discerned in the music, and the skill with which they are combined in a homogeneous whole is masterly. The first element is the dramatic Strauss, who is represented in the overture, with which he had dispensed in ' Salomé ' and ' Elektra '; the second element is that of Viennese folk-song and dance, and the third is naïve Mozart-like melody. It must suffice to mention a few of the salient passages in the opera, such as the

valses, the brilliant scene of the entry of the Rosenkavalier in Act II., the trio of three female voices, and the soliloquy of the Princess at the end of Act I., wherein she deplores her lost youth. Nothing in German opera, except the quintet of the ' Meistersinger,' can stand by the side of the trio for beauty and skill of workmanship. Here, too, Strauss's great gifts of characterisation show themselves, and nowhere more successfully than in the delineation of the character of the licentious Baron Ochs von Lerchenau.

His next work for the stage was ' Ariadne auf Naxos ' which has had a strange history. In its first version, produced in Stuttgart on Oct. 25, 1912, the ' Ariadne ' drama was incorporated with Molière's Le Bourgeois gentilhomme and the comedy of ' Zerbinetta and her Companions.' In a second version the two are separated and more prominence is given to the ballet scenes of Molière. In the third Le Bourgeois gentilhomme and all connected with it was scrapped and von Hofmannsthal wrote an entirely new prologue, and the rest is left practically unchanged.[1] Here Strauss went a step further in the direction of simplicity; the orchestra is small and the musical texture less complicated. Strauss has caught the spirit of the Italian commedia d' arte in the ' Zerbinetta ' episodes completely, and in the drama of ' Ariadne ' he has aimed at the creation of a new musical idiom, which, however, retains the hall-mark of his personality. The most remarkable part of the score is the long coloratura aria of Zerbinetta. This was considerably shortened and partly transposed in the new version.[2] It has been said that this is not in keeping with the Italian ideal, but it may be assumed that Strauss is not aiming so much at reproducing as at further developing it.

The ballet of the ' Legend of Joseph,' which he composed for Diaghilev's Russian Ballet, also contains a certain amount of music of greater simplicity, but it cannot be considered as a great success. Except in the ' Alpine Symphony,' this movement towards simplicity has been uninterrupted, and it is to be noticed also in his ballet, ' Schlagobers,' and in his ' Intermezzo.' Whether it is to be discerned also in the ' Egyptian Helen,' which is to be produced in 1927, remains to be seen. In ' Die Frau ohne Schatten '—libretto also by Hugo von Hofmannsthal—produced in Vienna on Oct. 10, 1919, he was rather hampered by a mystical and unintelligible libretto, and in it he seems to have returned to his older style.

[1] The chief reason for the changes made by Strauss : first, that the interest was not concentrated enough ; and secondly, the practical financial difficulties of employing a dramatic and an operatic ensemble on one and the same evening. Such difficulties did not, however, weigh much with Strauss in the cases of ' Salomé ' and ' Elektra,' both of which are too short for a whole evening and too long to go with any other work.
[2] The first English performance of ' Ariadne ' in the new version took place at Covent Garden in 1924.

CONDUCTING AND PERSONALIA.—Strauss's activities as a conductor have been manifold, and he would have earned fame in that capacity alone if he had not composed. He is a complete master of all his orchestral forces, and his interpretations are always distinguished by youthful fire [1] and impulse, and a keen sense of musical beauty : these qualities have made him pre-eminent as a conductor of Mozart. When he conducts his own work, however, he often over-accentuates the bizarre and realistic points, but latterly he has not, as far as one can judge from his recent appearance in London, conducted his own work with the same zeal that he used to show.

In person Strauss is tall and thin. His appearance is rather that of a successful business man than of a musician. In the society of his friends he is extremely genial, but he has great power of sarcasm. The chief article of his musical creed, as far as can be gathered from his conversation is adoration of Mozart, of which indeed his music bears ample traces, especially in his later works. His great relaxation is playing cards, especially ' skat,' at which he is a past-master and which he has illustrated musically in ' Intermezzo.' He has done admirable work in the ' Deutsche Tonkünstler-Verein,' and elsewhere, in safe-guarding the practical interests of his fellow-musicians. One feature of his character which cannot remain unnoticed is his keen business sense, which indeed is sometimes carried to excess. When during his first visit to America, he conducted concerts in a large drapery store, he was severely attacked for his inartistic behaviour in so doing, but he replied to his detractors that the conditions under which he gave his concerts were perhaps even more artistic than those in ordinary concert halls, and it was better to earn money honestly than to complain to those who do. But he cannot be absolved from all blame in some later incidents, as when he rearranged the score of the ' Rosenkavalier ' to fit a film and himself conducted the performances with inferior orchestras in cinemas.

TO SUM UP.—With the example of Verdi before us, there is no reason to suppose that his creative career is at an end, but it is probably safe to draw certain conclusions. He passed through the phase of severe classicism to that of modernity and is now partly retracing his steps. His chief services, which have made him the most prominent figure in the music of the day, may be said to be that he has settled the boundaries of descriptive music, at least till the old but ever-new conflict between programme music and absolute music revives once more. When it does revive it will be on a different field of battle, so to speak ; and it

[1] Thus, of his reading of ' Die Meistersinger ' it used to be said that while Richter approached it from the point of view of Hans Sachs, Strauss looked at it through the eyes of Walter.

is chiefly to his work that this is due. One thing must not be forgotten. It is a necessary result, for good or for evil, of present-day criticism that more stress is always laid in a new work on the startling features, which may be mere externals, than on the essentials. What chiefly distinguishes him from the ultra-moderns who have come after him (and later movements have left him untouched) is that he claims (and his claim can be fully established) to have built on the foundation well and truly laid by his great predecessors ; whereas some later composers assert that they have laid new foundations altogether. Time alone can decide between them. Though his work is not all on the highest level (whose is ?), he has written enough music to insure him, by reason of its true beauty, its sincerity and above all its vast technical skill, a lasting place among the great ones of music.

LIST OF COMPOSITIONS

(With dates of first performances in England.)

Op.
1. Festival March for orch.
2. String Quartet in A.
3. Five pieces for PF. solo.
4. PF. Sonata in B min.
5. Sonata for PF. and v'cl.
6. Serenade for Wind Instruments.
7. Violin Concerto.
8. Eight Songs.
9. Stimmungsbilder, five pieces for PF.
10. Eight Songs.
11. Concerto for French Horn.
12. Symphony in F min. Nov. 28, 1896.
13. Quartet for PF. and Strings.
14. ' Wanderers Sturmlied ' for 6-part choir with orch.
15. Five Songs.
16. ' Aus Italien '—Symphonic Fantasia.
17. Six Songs.
18. Sonata, violin and PF. in E flat.
19. Six Songs (' Lotosblätter ').
20. ' Don Juan,' tone poem for orch. May 24, 1897.
21. Five Songs (' Schlichte Weisen ').
22. Four Songs (' Mädchenblumen ').
23. ' Macbeth,' tone-poem for orch. June 5, 1903.
24. ' Death and Transfiguration,' tone-poem for orch. Dec. ?, 1897.
25. ' Guntram,' opera in 3 Acts.
26. Two Songs.
27. Four Songs.
28. ' Till Eulenspiegel's Merry Pranks,' tone-poem for orch. Aug. 21, 1896.
29. Three Songs.
30. ' Also sprach Zarathustra,' tone-poem for orch. Mar. 6, 1896.
31. Four Songs.
32. Five Songs.
33. Four Songs, with orchestral accompaniment.
34. Two Anthems for 16-part chorus.
35. ' Don Quixote,' Fantastic Variations for v'cl. and orch. June 4, 1903.
36. Four Songs.
37. Six Songs.
38. ' Enoch Arden,' melodrama (music for recitation).
39. Five Songs.
40. ' Ein Heldenleben,' tone-poem for orch. Dec. 6, 1902.
41. Five Songs.
42. Two Male Choruses.
43. Three Songs.
44. Two ' Grössere Gesänge ' for low voice with orch.
45. Three Choruses for Male Voices.
46. Five Songs.
47. Five Songs.
48. Five Songs.
49. Eight Songs.
50. ' Feuersnot,' opera in 1 Act. July 9, 1910.
51. ' Das Thal,' for bass Voice and Orch.
52. ' Taillefer,' Choral Ballad with soli and orch. 1905.
53. ' Symphonia domestica ' for orch. Feb. 25, 1905.
54. Opera, ' Salomé,' in 1 Act. Dec. 8, 1910.
55. Bardengesang,' 1906.
56. Six Songs. 1906.
57. Two Military Marches. 1906.
58. ' Elektra,' opera in 1 Act. Feb. 19, 1910.
59. ' Der Rosenkavalier ' opera in 3 Acts. Jan. 29, 1913.
60. ' Ariadne on Naxos,' opera. 1st version, May 27, 1913 ; new version, May 27, 1924.
' Le Bourgeois gentilhomme,' comedy with dance.
61. ' Festliches Präludium.' Nov. 4, 1913.
62. German Motet.
63. Alpine Symphony. Nov. 16, 1923.
65. ' Die Frau ohne Schatten,' opera.
66. ' Krämerspiegel,' twelve songs for voice and PF.
67. Six Songs.
68. Six Songs.

Op.
69. Five Small Songs.
70. ' Schlagobers,' ballet.
71. ' Drei Hymnen,' for voice and orch.
72. ' Intermezzo,' opera.
    Suite for orch. from the music of ' Le Bourgeois gentilhomme.'
    Dance suite from piano pieces of François Couperin for orch.

A. K.

BIBLIOGRAPHY

R. SPECHT : *R. Strauss und sein Werk.* 1920.
    Catalogue (*Verzeichnis*). 1911.
MAX STEINITZER : *R. Strauss.* 1911.
    R. Strauss und seine Zeit. 1914.
O. BIE : *Die moderne Musik und R. Strauss.* 1906–16.
E. SCHMITZ : *R. Strauss als Musikdramatiker.* 1907.
W. H. VON WALTERSHAUSEN : *R. Strauss.* 1921.

In addition there are a number of comparatively early German biographies, analyses of works, etc. English readers should consult
E. NEWMAN : *Richard Strauss.* 1908.
    Musical Studies. 1905.

STRAVINSKY, IGOR (*b.* Oranienbaum, near St. Petersburg, June 5 (18), 1882), composer, was the son of an operatic singer who took care to develop his son's precocious and astonishing musical gifts. There was no question, however, of making a professional musician of him, and he was induced to prepare himself for a legal career. A classical education was followed by a few years' study at the University of St. Petersburg. But Stravinsky did not neglect music, and by the time he was 22 years of age, his talent had so far matured that Rimsky-Korsakov, whom he met at this time, strongly advised him to drop the law and devote himself entirely to musical studies. It was under Rimsky-Korsakov, accordingly, that he received his first systematic training.

The first work of importance figuring in the list of Stravinsky's published compositions, is a symphony, begun in 1905 and finished in 1907. A song-cycle with orchestra, ' Faun and Shepherdess,' followed soon afterwards and was in its turn succeeded by two orchestral pieces, ' Fireworks ' and ' Scherzo fantastique.' At a performance of the latter, Serge Diaghilev, whose ' Russian Ballet ' came into vogue at that time, was so struck by the young composer's uncommon gifts that he invited him to write the music for one of his forthcoming productions. This was ' The Firebird,' a brilliant score which, next to its unmistakable indebtedness to Rimsky-Korsakov, reveals more than the germs of a remarkable individuality. It appeared in 1910, and only a year later followed a new ballet, ' Petroushka,' which completely unfolded the composer's striking personality. As regards brilliancy and originality of scoring, and aptness of characterisation, this work still remains Stravinsky's undisputed masterpiece.

Although many critics deny that Stravinsky ever surpassed ' Petroushka,' all are agreed that he went on developing with disconcerting rapidity. In 1913 appeared his third ballet, ' Le Sacre du printemps,' which created a sensation at its production in Paris by its deliberate primitiveness and uncouthness of rhythm and orchestral colour. Even those who disliked the elemental brutality of the work were compelled to own that it was

expressed to perfection and in a manner that had never been attempted in music before.

Next came an opera, ' The Nightingale,' based on a tale by Hans Andersen. This was not finished until 1914, but included a good deal of music of much earlier date. The result was a certain incongruity of style, which the composer cleared away in 1917 by converting the second and third acts alone into a symphonic poem, ' The Song of the Nightingale.' It has been staged as a ballet with a scenario based on the original libretto.

Between 1915 and 1920 Stravinsky wrote and published a number of small works, including the three pieces for string quartet, the ' Pribaoutki ' (Pleasant Songs) for voice and eight instruments, the easy pieces for piano duet, the ' Berceuses du chat ' for voice and three clarinets, the three pieces for solo clarinet, the ' Ragtime ' for small orchestra or piano, the ' Piano Rag-Music,' and some songs. But along with these minor works, all of which, though of a somewhat tentative character, are too highly finished to be dismissed as mere sketches, several new compositions for the stage gradually took shape, and consolidated the composer's newly acquired views and principles. Among these are ' Renard ' (1918 ; produced in Paris, May 1922), ' Les Noces ' (produced in Paris, June 1923), ' Pulcinella,' a ballet on music by Pergolesi in a modernised setting (1919 ; produced in Paris, May 1920), and ' L'Histoire du soldat ' (published 1920).

Of later date still are the ' Concertino ' for string quartet, the symphony for wind instruments, dedicated to the memory of Debussy, and the opera in one act, ' Mavra,' based on a tale by Pushkin, where the composer reverts to the traditions, if not to the actual forms, of the *bel canto*. It is in the latter work and in ' Pulcinella ' that Stravinsky's recent affectation of facing two ways at once first manifests itself clearly. In ' Mavra ' he claims spiritual kinship with Glinka and Tchaikovsky, in ' Pulcinella ' he makes actual use of music by Pergolesi, while his own personality remains uppermost in either work. ' Mavra ' was a failure, but the revival of an 18th-century Italian scenario with music of the same period, presented in a modern version that sparkles with humour and technical adroitness, is brilliantly successful in spite of the fact that the old and the new elements fail to blend. Less satisfactory is the first piano concerto, where the composer professes to write in the style of Bach. If the pretence of taking that master for its model is left out of account, the work is dreary and hollow ; compared with Bach it is too completely lacking in the latter's spirituality to be taken seriously and too devoid of wit to be amusing as a parody.

Thanks to the extensive tours undertaken by

the 'Russian Ballet,' Stravinsky made his first successes outside Russia, more particularly in France and England. He left his native country at an early age, and has since lived in Paris and at various places round the Lake of Geneva.

The dominating principle that governs the art of Stravinsky from 'Petroushka' onward, is his belief that music should make a purely physical appeal to the hearer, and should be free from any literary and pictorial associations which address themselves to the intellect. It may appear curious that his chief output should fall into the domain of the ballet, a form of art in which music is apt to assume a subordinate function; but it is precisely in his mature works of this type that we may observe how his music is raised from the subsidiary form of a mere accompaniment to the dignity of an independent organism by being made to appeal exclusively to the senses, while the scenario occupies the mind. The composer's intention is that these two entities should make their impression simultaneously on two distinctly separate human faculties, and that they should thus assist each other without servility on either side. We find that a ballet like 'Le Sacre du printemps' can be staged at will in a realistic or a fantastic manner, without regard for the music, and that in works like 'Renard' and 'L'Histoire du soldat' a series of musical pieces are used whose form is in no way determined by the stage action. In 'Les Noces' the running accompaniment of solo song and chorus is to all appearance entirely irrelevant to the subject of the dances, but nevertheless produces a similar mental and emotional reaction.

The composer sees no reason why an impression that is already conveyed by one art should be merely duplicated by another. A fine poem, to him, gains nothing by being set to music, and this explains how, in his later songs, he came to choose words which in themselves possess no beauty and very little sense. The 'Pribaoutki,' the 'Berceuses du chat,' the '4 Chants russes' and the '3 Histoires pour enfants' are all written to childish or simple popular texts of no literary significance. The early 'Pastorale' for voice and piano has no words at all.

Stravinsky's art in its later stages obeys no rules but those of its own making, and these again are subject to no definite system. His music is far from shapeless, but questions of form are invariably determined by the nature of the work itself, and not by any rigid patterns deliberately chosen beforehand. Nor is Stravinsky's harmony subject to any laws of progression or combination. He shuns no dissonance and avoids no orthodox chord if it happens to serve his purpose. No mode of expression is considered illegitimate by him, so long as a desired effect can be gained by it, but it must always remain a means to an end, for Stravinsky never sets out to startle his hearers at any price, as he has been unjustly accused of doing. On the other hand, he is frequently experimental, and has allowed the publication of some smaller works which will probably be regarded by future generations as little more than unimportant essays in the new media subsequently exploited by him in more significant compositions. This is not to say, however, that any of the published works are lacking in finish from the technical point of view: Stravinsky handles his material with remarkable virtuosity even where he fails to reach his ultimate aim with complete success.

Everything that Stravinsky writes is admirably suited to the medium for which it is intended. He is obviously incapable of inventing a musical phrase without simultaneously realising the particular instrument it calls for. His orchestral scores are not only full of colour and brilliance, but they have a thematic variety that is the direct outcome of his feeling for the peculiarities of each instrument. In the later works he frequently uses very small orchestral combinations, which are capable of bringing to light instrumental characteristics with still greater lucidity. These transparent scores ('Japanese Lyrics,' 'Pribaoutki,' 'L'Histoire du soldat,' 'Pulcinella,' 'Ragtime,' etc.) have in their turn led to new discoveries in the way of harmonic and thematic combination. The composer found, for instance, that a chord played by a number of instruments of vastly different timbres has a far greater plasticity than one given to a group of closely related ones, the ear being enabled in the former case to hear each sound separately and to follow the melodic thread of each part more easily. Thus even in passages that proceed in harmonic blocks, the feeling of a sort of colour-counterpoint is gained, and the musical fabric acquires immense point and clarity.

A final estimate of Ivor Stravinsky's work can scarcely be arrived at while it still continues to advance towards the ultimate solution of the problems that constantly arise out of its development; but there can be no doubt that a composer who provokes such bitter controversy must be a personality of exceptional strength, whose firm belief in his principles, be they right or wrong, is indisputable. Adverse criticism has, indeed, seldom denied his genius: arguments about his art are generally confined to the question whether his exceptional gifts are being properly employed.

The following is a complete list of Stravinsky's works up to 1925, each section being arranged as strictly as possible in chronological order:

ORCHESTRA

Symphony in E flat maj.
Faun and Shepherdess, 3 Songs for voice and orch.
Lament on the Death of Rimsky-Korsakov.
Scherzo fantastique.
Fireworks.
Suite from ' L'Oiseau de feu.'
Song of the Haulers on the Volga, for wind instr.
The Song of the Nightingale, symphonic poem.
Suite from ' L'Histoire du soldat,' for small orch.
Ragtime, for small orch.
March, Valse, Polka and Galop, for small orch. (arr. from the pieces for PF. duet).
Symphony for wind instr.

DRAMATIC WORKS

The Firebird, ballet.
Petroushka, ballet.
Le Sacre du printemps, ballet.
The Nightingale, opera.
Renard, burlesque.
Les Noces, ballet with songs and chor.
The Song of the Nightingale, ballet.
L'Histoire du soldat, a story, told, acted and danced.
Pulcinella, ballet with songs, after Pergolesi.
Mavra, comic opera in 1 act.

CHAMBER MUSIC

3 Japanese Lyrics, for voice and instr.
Pribaoutki (Chansons plaisantes), for voice and 8 instr.
Berceuses du chat, for voice and 3 clarinets.
3 Pieces for str. quartet
3 Pieces for clarinet solo.
Suite from ' L'Histoire du soldat,' for clarinet, vln. and PF.
Concertino for str. quartet.
Octet for wind instr.

PIANOFORTE MUSIC

4 Études
3 Easy Pieces for PF. duet.
5 Easy Pieces for PF. duet.
Ragtime.
Piano Rag-Music.
Les Cinq Doigts, very easy pieces on 5 notes.
Étude for pianola.
2 Concertos for PF. and orch.
Sonata (1925).

VOCAL WORKS

Faun and Shepherdess, 3 songs.
2 Songs : Spring (The Cloister)—A Song of the Dew.
2 Songs on Poems by Paul Verlaine.
Pastorale, wordless song.
3 Japanese Lyrics.
3 Russian Songs.
2 Songs on Poems by K. Balmont.
Cantata, ' Le Roi des étoiles,' for male voices and orch.
3 Histoires pour enfants.
4 Chants russes.
Pribaoutki (chansons plaisantes).
Berceuses du chat

(See also under Dramatic Works.) **E. B.**

STREET, JOSIAH, a Yorkshire musician, who issued ' A Book containing great variety of Anthems in two, three, and four parts.' London, second edition, 1746. This was published by Joseph Lord of Wakefield. A previous edition is stated to be *circa* 1729, but this is probably too early. A later one is dated 1785. F. K.

STREICHER, (1) JOHANN ANDREAS (*b.* Stuttgart, Dec. 13, 1761; *d.* May 25, 1833), a professor of music in Vienna, and, by marriage with Nannette STEIN (see STEIN, (2) MARIA ANNA) the founder of the pianoforte-making firm in that city, derived from Stein of Augsburg, that was to become in course of time the famous house of Streicher und Sohn.

Streicher was a man of education and great intelligence, and was, moreover, distinguished by his friendship with Schiller. He brought up his son (2) JOHANN BAPTIST (*b.* Jan. 3, 1796; *d.* Mar. 28, 1871) to the business, and long before his death, resigned it to the son's complete control. Johann Baptist maintained the excellent traditions of his worthy predecessors; and when he died left his son (3) EMIL the proprietor of this historical business, the services of which in the improvement of pianoforte construction are duly recognised in the articles PIANOFORTE and STEIN. Ernst

PAUER (*q.v.*) was a grandson of J. A. Streicher and Nannette Stein, and a great-grandson of the object of Mozart's admiration, J. A. Stein of Augsburg. A. J. H.

STRETTO (Ital.), literally ' close ' or ' narrow ' (Ger. *Engführung*), a term used in two ways. (1) In fugue it designates the following of response to subject at a *closer* interval of time than at first. (See FUGUE, subsection STRETTO.)

(2) The second use of the word occurs more especially in Italian opera, when towards the end of a piece the time is quickened, bringing the accents closer together.

STRIGGIO, ALESSANDRO (*b.* Mantua, *c.* 1535; *d.* there, after Sept. 22, 1587). In the judgment of his contemporaries he was a cultivated musician, an organist of renown, a fine lutenist and viola-player. Bartoli[1] writes that Striggio was most excellent in playing of the viola

' e far sentir in essa quatro parti a un tratto con tanta leggiadria e con tanta musica, che fa stupire gli ascoltanti,'

adding that his compositions were as musical and as good as any to be heard at that time ; and Garzoni[2] mentions among famous players of various instruments ' il Striggio passato nel lauto.' From about 1560 Striggio was at Florence, attached to the court of Cosmo de Medici, who died 1574 ; on the title-pages of Striggio's works published in 1560, 1565–66 and 1569, he is described as

' gentilhuomo mantovano. Servitore dell' illustrissimo et eccellentissimo Cosmo de Medici, Duca di Firenze e di Siena,'

but from 1570–85 he is merely ' gentilhuomo mantovano '· and probably was living in Mantua at this later period. He was certainly there in 1574, the bearer of a letter dated Sept. 1, 1574, in which the Emperor Maximilian II. recommends Striggio, ' a man eminent in the art of music,' to the good offices of the Duke Guglielmo of Mantua, with the result that Striggio was released from a dragging lawsuit in which he had been involved.

Striggio was one of the first to compose music for the Intermedii in representations at court festivities. An interesting example and one of the earliest is *La Cofanaria, commedia di Francesco d' Ambra, con gl' intermedii di G. B. Cini*, Firenze, 1566, written on the occasion of the marriage of Francesco de Medici with Johanna of Austria. Striggio set the first, second and fifth intermedio[3] to music. A copy of this work is in the British Museum ; on p. 16 a description of the music is given with a list of the instruments required, including :

4 Gravicembali doppi.
4 Viole d' arco.
2 Tromboni.
2 Tenori di flauti.
1 Cornetto mute.
1 Traversa.
2 Leuti, a dolzaina, a stortina, and a ribechino.

---

[1] *Ragionamenti accademici*, 1567, p. 37b.
[2] *La piazza universale*, Venetia, 1585, p. 450.
[3] For description of Striggio's intermedi see *Mus. Ant.* iii. 40.

In the *Dialoghi di Massimo Troiano* (Venetia, 1569), recounting the principal events in the festivities celebrated at the wedding of Wilhelm VI. of Bavaria and Renata di Loreno, mention is made (*Lib.* 3, p. 147) of a motet in 40 parts composed by Striggio, 'il quale fu degno d' ogni honore e laude'; it was written for 8 tromboni, 8 viole da arco, 8 flauti grossi, uno instrumento da penna, and un liuto grosso, the rest of the parts being supplied by voices, and was twice performed before large audiences.

In a little book published at Florence in 1579, *Feste nelle nozze del sereniss. Dom Francesco Medici, e della sereniss. Sig. Bianca Cappello, da Raffaello Gualterotti*, p. 20, there is an allusion to the 'diverse musiche, con molte voci ed infiniti strumenti' composed by Striggio, that most excellent musician. He was also responsible for music to the first, second and fifth intermediô in the Commedia written for the wedding of Cesare d' Este and Virginia de Medici at Florence (Bastiano de' Rossi, *Descrizione.* Firenze, 1585).

Striggio also composed a great many madrigals; Morley in his *Plaine and easie Introduction*, 1597, p. 35, gives illustrations of various proportions in 'measured' music from Striggio's madrigal 'All' acqua sagra' for six voices, and also includes Striggio's name in the list of 'practitioners the moste parte of whose works we haue diligently perused, for finding the true use of the moods.' Burney scored several of the madrigals : one, 'Invidioso amor' for five voices, from the 'Secondo libro de la muse,' 1559, is in the British Museum, Add. MSS. 11,583 ; and another, 'Gravi pene' from 'Madrigali a 4 voci di Cipriano e Annibale,' 1575, is in the Add. MSS. 11,588. Another of his madrigals, 'Chi fara fed' al cielo' for four voices, afterwards used by Peter Philips as a theme for a fantasia (in the 'Fitzwilliam Virginal Book,' i. 312), is to be found rather unexpectedly in a rare book published at Frankfort in 1615, called *Les raisons des forces mouvantes avec diverses machines*, etc., par Salomon De Caus ; in the account of 'La roue musicale (un orgue mécanique)' it is the 'pièce de musique qui est posée sur ladite roue,' and the music, the four parts scored, is reproduced on the back of plate 38.

The following works by Striggio were published, some during his lifetime, others after his death by his son Alessandro :

Di Alessandro Striggio, gentil'huomo mantovano, servitore del-l' illustriss. et eccellentiss. Cosmo de Medici, Duca di Firenze e di Siena. Il primo libro de madrigali a sei voci.
(The earliest edition of this book is not known; it was reprinted in Venice by Antonio Gardano in 1560, 1565, 1569, and later editions were published there by Francesco Rampazetto in 1566, by Girolamo Scotto and his successors in 1566, 1578 and 1585, and by Angelo Gardano in 1579 and 1592.)
Il secondo libro de madrigali a sei voci.
(This was also reprinted in Venice, by Girolamo Scotto and his successors in 1571, 1573, 1579 and 1582, and by Angelo Gardano in 1592 : the earliest edition is unknown.)
Di Alessandro Striggio, gentil'huomo mantovano, servitore, etc. Il primo libro de madrigali a cinque voci.
(Of this work again only reprints are known, by Antonio Gardano in 1560 and in 1569, by Scotto in 1560, 1566 and 1585, and by Fr. Rampazetto, *circa* 1566.)

Il secondo libro de madrigali a cinque voci di M. Alessandro Striggio, gentil'huomo mantovano, nouamente posti in luce. In Vinegia appresso Girolamo Scotto, 1570.
(It was reissued by Scotto in 1571, 1573, 1579 and 1583.)
Il terzo libro de madrigali a cinque voci del Sig. Alessandro Striggio, etc. Venetia, Angelo Gardano, 1596.
(Dedicated to the Duke of Mantua by Striggio's son Alessandro, who in alluding to his father, writes of this work 'd' uno che nacque suo suddito e visse alcun tempo servitore della felice memoria del sereniss. Sig. suo Padre, che sia in gloria, e mori finalmente servendo l' A.V.')
Il quarto libro de madrigali a cinque voci, etc. Venetia, Angelo Gardano, 1596.
Il quinto libro de madrigali a 5 voci, etc. Venetia, Angelo Gardano, 1597.
(Both books edited by Striggio's son.)
Il cicalamento delle donne al bucato et la caccia di Alessandro Striggio, con un lamento di Didone ad Enea per la sua partenza di Cipriano Rore, a 4, 5, 6 e 7 voci. Di nouo posto in luce per Giulio Bonagionta da San Genesi, musico della illus. Signoria di Venezia in S. Marco, Vinegia. Girolamo Scotto, 1567.
(Reprinted in 1569, and again in 1584, with a slightly different title) :
Il cicalamento delle donne al bucato e la caccia di Alessandro Striggio a 4, 5, 6 e 7 voci, con il gioco di primiera a cinque voci del medesimo, novamente agionto.
(There is a manuscript copy in five partbooks in Ch. Ch. Library, Oxford.)
Other MSS. are to be found in the libraries at
Berlin.—MS. Z, 28, date 1599, a score of 'Faciem tuam' (' nasco la pena ') for six voices ; the same composition in MS. Z, 32, a 16th-century lute-book. (Eitner.)
Bologna.—A 1613 MS. contains four madrigals for six voices in score. (Gasperini's Cat.)
Brieg.—Imperfect copies of 'Nasce la pena.' (Kuhn's Cat.)
Brussels.—Madrigals in MS. 2289. (Fétis, *Bibl. royale.*)
Liegnitz.—Eight madrigals for six voices. (Pfudel's Cat.)
Milan.—Conservatoire.—A Mass for four voices and a Mass for five voices. (Canal.)
Modena.—Bibl. palatina. A canzone with lute accompaniment.
Munich.—MS. 218, dated 1628, 'Ad nitida' (' Chi fara ') for five, 'Nascitur cum dolore' (' Nasce la pena mia ') for six, 'Quae mulier' (' All' apparir ') for eight voices. (Maier's Cat.)
Proske Library.—In MS. 774 and 75, thirteen madrigals. (Eitner.)
R.C.M, *London.*—In MS. 1881, four partbooks of 17th century, 'Love hath proclaimed' for six voices. A lute piece in MS. 1964.
Upsala.—MS. J. mus. 108, a piece in organ tablature.
Zwickau.—MS. 732, dated 1587, 'Ecce beatum lucem' a 40 vocibus in 4 chori, Bassone canato dalle parti più basse del 40 persone. Chorus I. eight voices ; Chorus II. ten voices ; Chorus III. sixteen voices ; Chorus IV. six voices (Vollhardt's Cat.)
About 41 of Striggio's compositions were also published at Venice in collected works, ranging from the year 1559 to 1626. Five of his madrigals are in Torchi, *L' arte musicale in Italia*, vol. i.

C. S.

(2) ALESSANDRO, son of the above, was a violin and lyre player at the court of Mantua, and is memorable in musical history as the author of the book of Monteverdi's 'Orfeo' (1607). He published certain of his father's madrigals (see list above).

STRIKING REED, a beating reed. One in which the vibrator or tongue strikes the face of the reed. (See REED and REED-STOP.) T. E.

STRINASACCHI, REGINA (*b.* Ostiglia, near Mantua, 1764 ; *d.* Gotha, *c.* 1823), was a distinguished violin and guitar player, educated at the Conservatorio della Pietà in Venice, and in Paris. From 1780-83 she travelled through Italy, and won great admiration by her playing, her good looks, and her attractive manners. She next went to Vienna, and gave two concerts at the National Court Theatre in the Burg on Mar. 29 and Apr. 24, 1784. For the second of these Mozart composed a sonata in B♭ (Köchel 454), of which he wrote out the violin-part complete, but played the accompaniment himself from a few memoranda which he had dashed down on the PF. staves.[1] The Emperor Joseph, noticing from his box above the blank look of the paper on the desk, sent for Mozart and obliged

---

[1] This interesting MS. came into the possession of F. G. Kurtz of Liverpool. Mozart filled in the complete accompaniment afterwards in an ink of slightly different colour from that which he first employed, so that the state of the MS. at the first performance can be readily seen. See Zahn, *W. A. Mozart*, 2nd ed. II. 25.

him to confess the true state of the case. 'Strinasacchi plays with much taste and feeling,' writes Mozart to his father, who quite agreed with him after hearing her at Salzburg. 'Even in *symphonies*,' Leopold writes to his daughter, 'she always plays with expression, and nobody could play an adagio more touchingly or with more feeling than she; her whole heart and soul is in the melody she is executing, and her tone is both delicate and powerful.' In Vienna she learnt to appreciate the gaiety of Haydn's music, so congenial to her own character. She played his quartets before the court at Ludwigslust, and also at Frau von Ranzow's, with peculiar naïveté and humour, and was much applauded for her delicate and expressive rendering of a solo in one of them. She is also said to have been an excellent guitar-player. She married Johann Conrad SCHLICK (*q.v.*), a distinguished violoncellist in the ducal chapel at Gotha. The two travelled together, playing duets for violin and violoncello, and appeared at Leipzig between 1793 and 1800. The last concert spoken of in the *Leipziger Zeitung* was at Rome in 1809. Schlick died at Gotha in 1825, two years after the death of his wife.

C. F. P., with addns.

STRING (Fr. *corde*; Ger. *Saite*; Ital. *corda*), a slender length of gut, silk, or wire, stretched over raised supports called bridges, between which it is free to vibrate. When weighted to resist the drawing power or tension, the rapidity of its transverse vibrations depends upon the tension, the length, and the specific gravity of the material; and in exact ratio with this rapidity the ear is sensible of the difference of musical pitch. From the 6th century B.C. the MONOCHORD (*q.v.*) or single string, stretched over a sound-board and measured by movable bridges, has been the canon of musical intervals, the relative scale pitch. The string by itself would give but a faint tone in the surrounding air, and a sound-board is necessary to reinforce the tone, and make it sufficiently audible.

Of the materials employed for strings, silk has been much used in the East, but in European instruments gut and wire have had the constant preference. Gut ($\chi o\rho\delta\dot{\eta}$; in Greek, whence the familiar 'chord') was the musical string of the Egyptians, Greeks and Romans; wire was practically unknown to them, since wire-drawing was invented only about A.D. 1350, synchronising with the probable invention of keyed instruments with strings, such as the clavichord, harpsichord, or virginal. From that epoch gut and wire have held divided rule, as they do in our own day in the violin and the piano. The general name for gut strings is catgut,[1] but it is really made from the intestines of sheep and goats, chiefly the former; the best and strongest being of lamb's gut when the lamb is of a certain age and development, whence it

comes that September is the month for fiddle-string making; particularly for first (or E) fiddle-strings, which are the smallest though they have to bear the greatest strain of the four. For the deeper-toned strings the gut is overlapped with silver, copper, or mixed metal. According to J. Rousseau (*Traité de la viole*, 1687) this loading of the string was introduced in France by Sainte Colombe about A.D. 1675. The tension of the four strings of a violin was stated by Tartini, in 1734, to be 63 lb.

Wire strings were originally of latten or brass, with which psalteries and dulcimers were strung. As late as the first half of the 18th century, clavichords were generally strung with brass wire only; pianofortes retained a batch of brass strings until about 1830. Steel wire, as the special iron music-wire was called, was, however, very early introduced, for Virdung (*Musica getutscht und ausgezogen*, A.D. 1511) expressly states that the trebles of clavichords were then strung with steel. Early in the 19th century Nuremberg steel was in great request, but about 1820 the Berlin wire gained the preference. The iron of both came from the Harz Mountains. About 1834 Webster of Birmingham brought out cast steel for music wire, and gave piano strings a breaking weight of about one-third more than the German. But in 1850 Miller of Vienna was able to contend for the first place, and in the following year actually gained it at the Great Exhibition, for cast steel wire-drawing. After that, Pöhlmann of Nuremberg came forward and was considered by some experts to have surpassed Miller.[2] Webster's firm was not idle during a competition to the results of which the present power of the pianoforte to stand in tune owes so much. A trial made under direction of the writer gives for average breaking weight of 24 inches, of No. 17½ wire, Pöhlmann's 297 lb., Miller's 275 lb., Webster and Horsfall 257 lb., all nearly doubling the tension required for use. It is not, therefore, with surprise that we accept the eminent authority of Dr. William Pole, who regarded cast steel music-wire as the strongest elastic material that exists. The earliest covered piano strings, about a hundred years ago, spun in long interstices of brass over steel, have in time become close spun in single, double, and even treble overlayings of copper, or mixed metal composed of spelter and copper, gaining in the largest strings a diameter of 0·21 of an inch, and considerable power of strain. The greatest tension of a string recorded by Messrs. Broadwood in the technical part of their Exhibition book of 1862 is 315 lb. — for the *highest* single string of a concert grand. They give the whole tension at that time for Philharmonic pitch (viz. A 454, C 540 double vibrations per second) of two of their

---

[1] The origin of the term catgut has not yet been traced.　　G.

[2] Unpublished correspondence of Theobald Böhm, the flautist, shows that Pöhlmann was indebted to him for improving his manufacture.

concert grands, as well as the tension of each separate note. The first of the two is 34,670 lb. (15 tons 9 cwt., etc.) ; the other, a longer scale, 37,160 lb. (16 tons 11 cwt., etc.). In later years tension was much increased, but not sufficiently so to account for the much higher totals or for the breaking - weights of wire recorded in Mendel's *Lexikon*. (See A. J. Hipkins's *History of the Pianoforte*, pp. 39, 83, 86.)   A. J. H.

STRINGENDO (Ital.), 'forcing, compelling' ; pressing or hastening the time. This word conveys, besides the idea of simple acceleration of pace, that of growing excitement, working up to some climax.   M.

STRING-PLATE (Fr. *sommier en fer* ; Ger. *Anhängeplatte, metallner Saitenhalter* ; Ital. *cordiera*). The iron plate on the hitch - pin block of pianofortes to which the farther ends of the strings are attached. Formerly it formed with the tension bars the metal framing of the instrument. The frame made in a single casting has superseded the separate stringplate. See under PIANOFORTE, the section on the modern frame.

STRINGS. A term used colloquially to mean the bowed stringed instruments used in the orchestra : violins, violas, violoncelli and double basses. (See VIOLIN FAMILY.)

It is similarly used in combination with other words, *e.g.* string quartet (Fr. *quatuor à cordes* ; Ger. *Streichquartett*) means a body of four bowed stringed instruments (normally 2 violins, viola and violoncello).

STROGERS (STROWGER), E. (early 16th cent.), English composer. An organ score of a Miserere by him is in the British Museum (Add. MSS. 29,996/6b). This MS. is in the hand of John Redford (*d. circa* 1545). Two 5-part madrigals by him, in Italian tablature, ' If the, my dere ' and ' By croked ways,' are also in the British Museum (Add. MSS. 31,992/51b, 52b). Add. MSS. 31,390 contains a collection of In Nomines, fancies and arrangements of anthems, madrigals, motets, etc., for 5 viols by 16th cent. (chiefly English) composers and includes 2 In Nomines by Strogers. The treble viol parts of two others for 5 viols and two more for 6 are in B.M. Add. MSS. 32,377/18b, 19b (c. 1584). Some of the compositions attributed to Nicholas STROGERS (*q.v.*) are possibly by E. Strogers.

J. Mᴷ.

STROGERS, NICHOLAS (late 16th and early 17th cent.), English organist and composer. Two In Nomines and a piece ' upon ut re my fa soul la ' for organ are at Oxford (Ch. Ch. 371), as well as a soprano solo, ' O doleful deadly pang,' with accompaniment for 5 instruments (Ch. Ch. 984-8). He contributed a fantasia to the ' Fitzwilliam Virginal Book,' and a galliard to Jane Pickering's Lute Book, *c.* 1616 (B.M. Egerton MSS. 2046/17). His Morning and Evening Service in D is one of the ' six services

for the Kings Royall Chappell ' included in Benjamin Cosyn's Virginal Book. The cantoᵣ alto and tenor parts of a pavan for 5 viols by him are in the British Museum (Add. MSS. 30,826-8). A 6-part In Nomine arranged in Italian tablature (B.M. Add. MSS. 29,426/55b —after 1611) is probably his also, but with regard to two pieces ' Poore downe ' and ' The world is a world ' in the Batten Organ Book, as well as some Latin church music, it is not certain whether they are his or the work of E. STROGERS (*q.v.*). (See *Mus. Ant.* iv. 113.)

SERVICES, ETC.

First Whole Service. (V. ; T.D. ; B. ; K. ; C. ; M. ; N.D.) B.M. Add. MSS. 29,289/46. Altus part only.
Whole Service in D. (T.D. ; B. ; K. ; C. ; M. ; N.D.) B.M. Add. MSS. 17,784/105. Bass part only.
Whole Service (of 4 parts in D min.). (T.D. ; B. ; K. ; C. ; M. ; N.D. and Deus Misereatur.) B.M. Add. MSS. 30,085/41. Score.
Short Service, *a* 4. (V. ; T.D. ; B. ; C. ; K. ; M. ; N.D.) Barnard.
Benedictus. B.M. Add. MSS. 17,853/12. Tenor part only.
Magnificat. fragments (Esurientes, *a* 3, Sicut locutus, *a* 2). Ch. Ch. 45/33, 40.

ANTHEMS

God be merciful. Durh. O.B. A3/356 ; B.M. Add. MSS. 29,289. Altus part only.
Mistrust not truth. Tenb. O.B. 389/96.
O God be merciful. Durh. ; PH.

MOTETS

A solis ortus. Tenb. O.B. 389/77.
Domine non est exaltatum. PH.
In Nomines, 3 *a* 5. Ch. Ch. 984-8.
In Nomine. Tenb. O.B. 389/13.
Non me vincat, *a* 5. Ch. Ch. 984-8.

J. Mᴷ.

STROHMEYER, CARL (*b.* Stollberg district, 1780 ; *d.* Weimar, Nov. 11, 1845), a bass singer, a Kammersänger at Weimar, who sang in a festival at Frankenhausen in June 1810, and is mentioned by Spohr for the extraordinary compass of his voice from D to *g'* (see Spohr's *Selbstbiographie*, i. 142). He was employed successively at Gotha and at Weimar.   G.

STROLLERS, THE, see DUBLIN.

STROLLING PLAYERS' AMATEUR ORCHESTRAL SOCIETY, THE, was founded in 1882 by Norfolk Megone, who gave up his position as conductor of the School of Mines Orchestra to fulfil the duties of honorary conductor. He remained at the head of the Society's operations for 20 years, being succeeded in 1902 by William Shakespeare, who conducted till 1905, when Joseph Ivimey was appointed. The first concert was given Dec. 13, 1882, at the School of Dramatic Art, Argyll Street, London. Soon afterwards St. James's Hall was used for the ' Ladies' Concerts,' the smoking concerts being held in St. Andrew's Hall, Newman Street. Subsequently the concerts of both kinds have been given in the Queen's Hall. The president is H.R.H. the Duke of Connaught, and the hon. secretary is Miss W. M. Elder. During the war 1914-18 many concerts were given for war charities and for the entertainment of soldiers and sailors.   M.

STRONG, GEORGE TEMPLETON (*b.* New York City, May 26, 1856), an American composer whose career has been made chiefly in Europe. Both of his parents were musical. His mother was a good pianist and sang agreeably, and his father, G. T. Strong, a lawyer associated with the corporation of Trinity Church and a trustee of Columbia College, was an amateur organist, and for four years was president of the Philharmonic Society of NEW YORK (q.v.). In 1879 he went to Leipzig, where he entered the Conservatorium, abandoned the oboe in favour of the viola, studied harmony with Richard Hofmann, counterpoint and fugue with Jadassohn, and horn with Gumbert of the Gewandhaus orchestra. In Leipzig he belonged to the coterie of Liszt champions of which men like Siloti, Friedheim, Dayas and Krause were members, and frequently visited that master in Weimar. From 1886–89 he lived in Wiesbaden, associating much with his friend and fellow-countryman MacDowell, and falling under the influence of Raff. He then settled at Vevey, Switzerland, having spent one year (1891–92) in the United States as teacher at the New England Conservatory of Music in Boston. In Vevey he turned his thoughts for a time to water-colour painting, and founded the *Société Vaudoise des Aquarellistes*, having become discouraged by the failure of American composers to find recognition in their native land. Of Strong's published pieces the most important are two for soli, male chorus, and orchestra : 'Wie ein fahrender Hornist sich ein Land erblies,' op. 26, and ' Die verlassene Mühle,' op. 30, and a symphony entitled 'Sintram,' based on de la Motte Fouqué's romance of that name and Dürer's famous print ' Ritter, Tod und Teufel.' A symphonic poem 'Undine' and a symphony 'In den Bergen' have been successfully played at home and abroad. A considerable number of chamber music pieces, two ' American Sketches ' for violin solo and orchestra, a short dramatic cantata, arrangements for four hands pianoforte of some of Bach's organ works, songs, instrumental soli, etc., remain in manuscript. Later works include a third symphony, ' An der See,' a symphonic idyll, ' An der Nixenquelle ' (2 PF.s), ' Knights and Dryads ' (soli, choir and orch.) and various pieces for piano. A humorous trio (2 vlns. and vla.) called ' A Village Music-Director ' was played by the Flonzaley Quartet in America in 1917. H. E. K. ; addns. *Amer. Supp.*

STROUD, CHARLES (*b. circa* 1705 ; *d.* Apr. 26, 1726), was educated as a chorister of the Chapel Royal under Dr. Croft. After quitting the choir he officiated as deputy organist for his instructor and became organist of Whitehall Chapel. He was buried in the west cloister of Westminster Abbey. He is known as a composer by his beautiful anthem, ' Hear my prayer, O God,' included in Page's ' Harmonia sacra,' and long a favourite in English Cathedrals.

w. h. h.

STROZZI, BARBERA, a 17th-century Venetian lady, the adopted daughter of the poet Giulio Strozzi. Nicolo Fontei, who composed his ' Bizzarrie poetiche ' for her in 1636, calls her a ' virtuosissima cantatrice.' She was her-

self a talented composer, who wrote 5 books of cantatas, ariettas and duets, 1 book of madrigals, 2-5 v., 1 book of sacred songs for one voice basso continuo, published between 1644 and 1664, also single numbers in collective volumes (*Q.-L.*).

STRUNGK, (1) DELPHIN (*b.* 1601 ; *d.* Brunswick, 1694), was a capable organist, and held posts successively at the Wolfenbüttel Hauptkirche, 1630–32 ; at Celle, and at the church of St. Martin, Brunswick. In a complimentary dedication to the Burgomaster of Brunswick of his work on music published in 1652, Conrad Matthaei alludes to ' der sehr berühmte Organist, Herr Delphin Strungk.' [1]

Strungk composed music for the organ—an example is printed in Ritter's *Geschichte des Orgelspiels*, 1884, ii. 207, a Choralvorspiel in 4-part writing ' Lass mich dein sein ' ; Max Seiffert published two more. In a Lüneburg MS. there are six of these organ arrangements [2]; other compositions for voices with instruments, as well as a Choralvorspiel, are in MS. in Berlin. In the Wolfenbüttel Library is an autograph MS. of music for five voice and eight instrumental parts, composed in June 1671,

' Musikalischer Glückwunschender Zuruff (Kommt und sehet die Wercke des Herrn) als . . . Rudolphus Augustus, Herzog zu Braunschweig und Lüneburg in der Erbhuldigungsstadt Braunschweig den Gottesdienst in der Kirchen zum Brüdern erstesmahls beigewohnt.'

His son,

(2) NICOLAS ADAM STRUNGK (or STRUNCK) (*b.* Celle, Nov. 1640 ; *d.* Dresden, Sept. 23, 1700) studied music with his father and at the age of 12 was acting as organist at the Magnuskirche, Brunswick. Later he entered Helmstadt University, and worked there for some years, taking violin lessons in the vacations from Schnittelbach of Lübeck. In 1660 he was appointed first violin in the Wolfenbüttel Hofkapelle, but changed subsequently to a similar post at Celle, with a yearly salary of 200 thalers. In 1665 he joined the Hofkapelle of the Elector Johann Friedrich of Hanover.

About this time he paid his first visit to Vienna, and played the violin before the Emperor Leopold I. In 1678 he was appointed director of music in Hamburg, where a great effort was being made to foster German musical talent, long overshadowed by Italian influences. There he wrote and produced many operas : ' Der glückselig-steigende Sejanus,' and 'Der unglücklich-fallende Sejanus ' in 1678, the German libretto by Christoph Richter being adapted from the Italian of Nicola Minato ; 'Esther,' ' Die drei Töchter Cecrops,' ' Doris ' and ' Alceste ' in 1680 ; 'Theseus,' ' Semiramis ' and ' Floretto ' in 1683.

Friedrich Wilhelm of Brandenburg, when visiting Hamburg, tried to secure Strungk's services as Kapellmeister, but this was not allowed,

1 Vogel, *Handschr. zu Wolfenbüttel*, 1890. p. 182.
2 Prof. Junghans, *Bach als Schüler*, 1870.

Hanover having a prior claim. The Elector Ernst August appointed Strungk chamber organist, and presented him to a canonry at Einbeck, and eventually Strungk accompanied him to Italy and remained there some time. It was at Rome that the meeting between Strungk and Corelli took place, so graphically described by Hawkins (ed. 1875, vol. ii. p. 676). Strungk again visited Vienna, this time playing on the clavier before the Emperor with much success. From 1682–86 he remained a member of the Hanover Hofkapelle, but on Jan. 26, 1688, Johann Georg II. of Saxony appointed him Kammerorganist and vice-Kapellmeister to the Dresden Hofkapelle, with a salary of 500 thaler. He was the successor of Carlo Pallavicini, who died on Jan. 29, leaving an unfinished opera which Strungk was asked to complete. The libretto was by Pallavicini's son, Stefano. Strungk apparently contributed the music to the third act, and the opera, 'L'Antiope,' was performed four times in Feb. 1689, at Dresden. Strungk seems to have suffered at Dresden from the usual friction between the Italian and German musicians, although the Germans were gradually gaining the upper hand, for on Mar. 30, 1688, Elector Johann Georg III. was appealed to because the Italians refused to join in any performance of Strungk's compositions, and would only acknowledge his authority when Bernhard the Kapellmeister was absent through illness. This resulted in the dismissal of the ringleader Fedeli in the following September. Bernhard died on Nov. 14, 1692, and was succeeded by Strungk, who composed some music in his memory.

On June 13, 1692, Strungk obtained permission from Johann Georg IV. of Saxony to found an opera-house in Leipzig. With the aid of two associates, Glaser and Sartorio, an architect, the work was put in hand in Mar. 1693, and a theatre of wood was erected in the Brühl, at a cost of 10,000 thaler. It was opened on May 8, 1693, with Strungk's opera 'Alceste'; the German libretto by Paul Thiemich was adapted from the original Italian of Aurelio Aureli. A contemporary chronicle [1] narrates that pictured announcements were suspended in the streets of Leipzig, giving a description of the opera, and the time of its performance. Johann Georg IV. came from Dresden to be present at the opening performance. In 1693 Strungk's opera 'Nero' was also given, and his 'Agrippina' in 1699. Strungk was financially much embarrassed by his Leipzig undertaking, although he retained his Dresden post and salary until 1697, when he retired with a pension. His daughters Philippine and Elisabeth were two of the principal singers in the Leipzig theatre from 1705–09.

Very little of Strungk's music is known at the present day, and it nearly all remains in MS.

[1] *Leipzigisches Geschicht-Buch*, 1714, p. 883.

He composed a 'Ricercar auf den Tod seiner Mutter, verfertiget zu Venedig am 20. Dec. 1685,' also 'Die Auferstehung Jesu,' first performed on Apr. 21, 1688 ; and he published at Dresden in 1691—

'Musikalische Übung auf der Violin oder Viola da gamba, so wohl zur Ehre Gottes als menschlicher Ergötzlichkeit bestehend, in etlichen Sonaten über die Festgesänge, dann auch etliche Ciaconen mit zwei Violinen.'

A selection of his opera airs was published in Hamburg, 1684—

'Ein hundert auserlesene Arien zweyer Hamburgischen Operen, Semiramis und Esther. Mit beigefügten Ritornellen.'

A MS. copy is in the Königsberg Library as well as some MS. Choralvorspiele also attributed to Strungk, although they may be the work of his father, Delphin Strungk (see Müller's Cat.). MS. copies of a sonata for two violins and viola da gamba, and a sonata for six strings, are in the Upsala Library. Various MSS. are also in the Berlin and Dresden Libraries, and in the Wolfenbüttel Library, MS. 253 'Les Aires avec les Flauts douces pour son Altesse Seren^me monseigneur le Prince Ludwig Rudolf, Duc de Bruns. et Lüneberg,' containing ten numbers, chiefly dances.   C. S.

BIBL.—MAX SEIFFERT, *Zur Biographie Delphin Struncks.* A.M. Jan. 1920 ; FRITZ BEREND, *Nicolaus Adam Strungk, 1640–1700, Sein Leben und seine Werke, mit Beiträgen zur Geschichte der Musik und des Theaters in Celle, Hannover, Leipzig.* Freiburg i. B., 1915.

STRUTIUS (STHRUCIUS), THOMAS (*b.* Rathenow, Brandenburg ; *d.* Danzig, 1678), organist at Stargard in 1603, of Holy Trinity, Danzig, in 1656, and of S. Mary's, Danzig, in 1668. In all his works he gives prominence to the Choral which he strives to present in its most artistic form. Winterfeld counts him among the best composers of his time. He composed psalms, sacred songs, etc., also a sonata for eight instruments (1658) (*Q.-L.*).

STUBBS, SIMON (late 16th and early 17th cent.), English composer of church music. He contributed several settings to Ravenscroft's 'Whole Book of Psalms' (1621), as well as the first two anthems in the list of his music below to Thomas Myriell's collection 'Tristitiae remedium' (1616).

Evening Service.   Tenb. O.B./296.

ANTHEMS

Father of love.   B.M. Add. MSS. 29,372-7 ; Ch. Ch. 56-60. Bass part wanting.
Have mercy.   B.M. Add. MSS. 29,372-7.
The Lord is my Shepherd.   Tenb. O.B./280.   J. Mᴷ.

STUCK, JOHANN BAPTIST, see BATISTIN, Jean.

STUCKEN, FRANK VAN DER (*b.* Fredericksburg, Texas, Oct. 15, 1858), American conductor and composer, of German and Belgian parentage. Educated in Europe, he numbered among his teachers Benoît, Reinecke and Grieg. In 1884–95 he was conductor of the Arion Society (male chorus) of New York, and in 1892 he took that organisation on a tour of Germany. He was also active as an orchestral conductor during those years and was the first to present 'all-American' orchestral programmes. In 1895–1903 he was director of the Cincinnati College of Music, and (1895–1907) conductor of the Cincinnati Symphony Orchestra. In 1906–12 (and also in 1923) he was conductor of the Cincinnati Music Festival, succeeding Theodore Thomas, and he has conducted numerous other festivals both in Europe and America. Since 1908 he has spent much of his time in Europe.

In addition to an opera, 'Vlasda' (Weimar, 1883), his compositions include :

Incidental music to 'The Tempest.'
Prologue to Heine's 'William Ratcliff,' orchestra, op. 10.
'Pax Triumphans,' symphonic prologue, op. 26.
'Louisiana,' festival march, orchestra, op. 32.
Other orchestral pieces, choral music and many songs.

W. S. S.

STUDIES, see ÉTUDES.

STURGEON, NICHOLAS (*d. circa* 1454), English ecclesiastic and composer of church music. He was prebendary of Reculverand in 1440, and two years later became a canon of Windsor. In July of this year he also became precentor of St. Paul's, but still held office at Windsor, as he became steward there in 1443, and was in residence in 1444 and more or less continuously from 1446–52, when he obtained the prebend of Kentish Town in St. Paul's.[1] He is important in that he either possessed or wrote out the 15th century MS. preserved at the College of St. Edmund's, Old Hall, near Ware, Herts, which contains music by members of the English Dunstable group of composers. The MS. was probably connected with St. George's Chapel, Windsor, and Sturgeon's compositions, which each bear his name, are :

'Et in terra pax '—3 settings *a* 3 v.
'Patrem omnipotentem '—2 settings *a* 3 v.
'Sanctus '—*a* 3 v.
'Et in Nomine Domini '—*a* 3 v.

J. Mᴷ.

STURGES, EDWARD, see TURGES.

STURTON (TURTON), EDMUND (late 15th and early 16th cent.), English composer of church music. He is probably the 'Turton' who was clerk and instructor of the choristers at Magdalen College, Oxford, in 1509–10, when he received 3s. 4d. and 4s. 10d. ' pro notacione diversorum cantorum.'[2] An Ave Maria by him is at Lambeth, and he is the composer of a 6-part 'Gaude Virgo Mater,' one of the 43 hymns to the Virgin, preserved in an early 16th century MS. in the library of Eton College. He is referred to by Morley in his *Plaine and Easie Introduction* (1597).

J. Mᴷ.

SUB. The Latin preposition 'under' is used in connexion with the organ, and denotes the octave below, as ' Sub Bass,' ' Sub Octave couples,' etc. (See COUPLER.)

SUBDIAPENTE. A polyglot word, part Latin, part Greek, to signify a fifth below, just as ' Epidiapente ' signified a fifth above. A ' Canon in Subdiapente ' was a canon in which the answer was a fifth below the lead. Similarly ' Subdiatessaron ' is a fourth below, and ' Epidiatessaron ' a fourth above.

G.

[1] W. Barclay Squire. *Sammelb.* Int. Mus. Ges. vol. ii.
[2] *Ibid. Archæologia*, vol. lvi.

SUBDOMINANT, the fourth note of the scale upwards. The note below the dominant, as F in the key of C. The radical bass of the penultimate chord in the Plagal CADENCE (*q.v.*). When groups of movements are balanced together in threes the central one is most frequently in the key of the subdominant, as in sonatas of three movements, the minuet and trio form, marches, valses, etc. In the actual body of a large movement in forms of the sonata order, the key of the subdominant is not antithetically acceptable, and examples of its occurrence in modern music as the key of the second section or second subject are extremely rare, and evidently not well advised. But in dependence on the tonic key it is one of the most important of harmonic centres, and digressions in that direction are very common in modern music (cf. FORM ; SONATA).

C. H. H. P.

SUBJECT (Fr. *sujet* ; Ital., *tema, soggetto* ; Ger. *Thema, Subjekt*) is used generally to mean a phrase of melody, with or without harmony, of sufficient distinction to be regarded as a musical thought.

Every species of musical FORM (*q.v.*) is dependent for consistency on the use of subjects of one kind or another, and the history of musical form is largely concerned with the increasing clearness in articulating the subjects, from the rhythmless adoption of *canti fermi* by mediæval composers to the incisive rhythmic figures of the classical era (see CANTO FERMO and FIGURE). The whole of the fugal style of writing is generated by the recognition of one or more prevalent subjects as a starting-point. The immanence of the subject is as important to the free use of IMITATION (*q.v.*) in the modern style as it was to the strict writers of FUGUE (*q.v.*). Each form (see SONATA ; SYMPHONY ; SUITE) has had its own kinds of subjects suitable to its special method of development.

C.

SUBMEDIANT, the sixth note of the scale rising upwards. The note next above the dominant, as A in the key of C. The submediant of any major scale is chiefly brought into prominence as the tonic of its relative minor.

C. H. H. P.

SUCCENTOR, *i.e.* sub-cantor, a cathedral officer, deputy to the precentor. His duty is to supply his principal's place during absence, in the regulation of the service, and other duties of the precentor.

G.

SUCH, (1) HENRY (*b.* London, Mar. 31, 1872), violinist, son of Edwin C. Such, Mus.B. He began studying at the age of 6, and made his first public appearance when 8 years old. Following the advice of Joachim he entered the Hochschule at Berlin in 1885, remaining there till 1892, in which year his first public appearance in Berlin was successfully made. After touring in Germany he studied during 1895–96 with Wilhelmj, and again travelled in Holland and Scandinavia. He then visited Vienna, meeting and playing with Brahms, and in 1896 made two public appearances with Richter conducting. Settled in London in 1898, and was appointed professor at the Guildhall School of Music. He has a large repertory and an excellent technique. His violin is one of the Stradivari instruments formerly possessed by Paganini.

(2) PERCY FREDERICK (b. London, June 27, 1878), brother of the above, went to Berlin in 1887 and studied the violoncello under Otto Ludemann, pupil of Robert Hausmann, who accepted him as private pupil in 1889, and continued to give him lessons when he joined the Hochschule in 1892. In the latter institution he remained until 1898, having the advantage of lessons in ensemble-playing from Joachim. His first public appearance in Berlin was with the Philharmonic Orchestra in 1898. Besides playing as soloist, he assisted the Joachim Quartet as second violoncello at many concerts in Germany and Holland, including the Beethoven Festival at Bonn in 1899. He appeared in London first at St. James's Hall with the Joachim Quartet in 1901, and followed with a series of recitals. Held the post of principal violoncello during the two final seasons of the Popular Concerts. His training and purity of style fit him especially for the performance of chamber music. He plays upon an exceptionally fine Gagliano violoncello.   W. W. C.

SUCHER, JOSEF (b. Döbör, Eisenburg, Hungary, Nov. 23, 1844 ; d. Berlin, Apr. 4, 1908), was brought up in the Löwenburg Konvict at Vienna, as a chorister in the Hofkapelle, which he joined on the same day with Hans Richter, the conductor. On completing his course at the Konvict he began to study law, but soon threw it aside, worked at counterpoint with Sechter, and adopted music as his profession. Beginning as sub-conductor of a Singing Society in Vienna, he advanced to be 'Repetitor' of the solo singers at the imperial court Opera, and conductor at the Comic Opera, and in 1876 went to Leipzig as conductor of the City Theatre. In the following year he married ROSA HASSELBECK (b. Velburg, Feb. 23, 1849; d. Berlin, 1027), the then prima donna of the same house. Her first engagement was at Trèves. Thence she went to Königsberg and thence to Berlin and Danzig, where she was engaged by her future husband for Leipzig. From Leipzig in 1879 husband and wife went to Hamburg, where they settled as conductor and prima donna, and where the latter attracted immediate attention by her performance of Chryssa in Rubinstein's 'Nero.' They visited England in 1882, and Mme. Sucher proved her eminent qualities both as a singer and an actress by the extraordinary range of parts in which she appeared at the German opera at

Drury Lane. She made her début as Elsa on May 18, and besides singing as Elizabeth and Senta, she sang Eva on May 30, and Isolde on June 20, on the respective productions in England of 'Die Meistersinger' and 'Tristan,' and as Euryanthe on the revival of that opera. Her husband produced a 'scene' or cantata entitled 'Waldfräulein' ('The Wood Maiden') for soli, chorus and orchestra, at the Richter Concert of June 5. Sucher's early compositions had included songs, masses, cantatas and overtures, one of which, to an opera called 'Ilse,' was brought forward at a concert in Vienna in 1873. One of his best-known published works is a Liedercyclus entitled 'Ruheort.' Frau Sucher gained great renown by her singing of Isolde at Bayreuth in 1886. From 1888–99 Sucher was conductor at the Hofoper at Berlin.

Frau Sucher, after successful performances of Kundry and Eva at Bayreuth in 1888, became a prima donna at Berlin, where she remained until 1898, as a noted Wagner singer. On leave of absence, she sang at Bayreuth and other cities of Germany, and in 1892 sang both at Covent Garden and Drury Lane as Brünnhilde in 'Siegfried,' and once as Isolde, and was warmly received. She would have played Isolde again but for a peremptory recall to Berlin, where her services were urgently required. On Nov. 3, 1903, she took a final farewell of the stage at Berlin as Sieglinde. She wrote a book of reminiscences, *Aus meinem Leben*, in 1914.   A. C.

SÜSSMAYER,[1] FRANZ XAVER (b. Steyer, Upper Austria, 1766 ; d. Sept. 16, 1803), composer and Kapellmeister, educated at the monastery of Kremsmünster, where he attempted composition in several branches. Some MS. operas still existing at Kremsmünster are mentioned in Q.-L.

At Vienna he had instruction from Salieri and Mozart. With the latter he formed the closest attachment, becoming, to use Seyfried's expression, 'the inseparable companion of the immortal Amphion.' Jahn details the work he did for the 'Clemenza di Tito' on its production at Prague, whither he accompanied Mozart. Süssmayer was at the composer's bedside the evening before Mozart's death, while the latter tried to give him the necessary instructions for completing his Requiem, a task for which he was peculiarly fitted by his knack of imitating Mozart's handwriting. Jahn has stated in detail (ii. 172) how much of that work is in all probability Süssmayer's. (See MOZART, Vol. III. p. 566.)

As a composer Süssmayer's name (as 'pupil of Salieri and Mozart') first appears at Schikaneder's Theatre, where his opera 'Moses' was brought out May 4, 1792, revived in 1796, and again in concert form in 1800. This was

---

[1] He signs himself on a symphony SIESSMAYR.

followed by ' L' incanto superato,' a ' musico-romantic fable ' (Burgtheater, 1793), and by ' Der Spiegel von Arkadien ' (Schikaneder's Theatre, 1794), libretto by Schikaneder, which became a favourite, and was eulogised by the *Wiener Zeitung.* He became in 1794 composer, and in 1795 Kapellmeister, to the Kärnthnerthor Court Theatre, where he produced successively ' Die edle Rache ' (1795), ' Die Freiwilligen ' (1796), ' Der Wildfang ' (1797), ' Der Marktschreier ' and ' Soliman der Zweite' (1799), 'Gulnare '(1800), and ' Phasma' (1801). His patriotic cantata, ' Der Retter in Gefahr,' was performed at an entertainment to the Vienna volunteers in the large Redoutensaal at a time of threatened war (1796), and several times repeated in the same building, and by the Tonkünstler - Societät. Süssmayer also composed two operas for Prague. Several of the above works were printed, some only in part, while others—masses, and smaller church - works, instrumental pieces, etc. — exist only in MS. Though wanting in depth and originality his works are melodious, and have a certain popular character peculiar to himself. Prince Esterhazy bought his entire MSS. from his widow.   C. F. P.

SUEVUS (SUEVIS ; real name ' Schwab '), FELICIANUS (*b.* Altdorf Weingarten, Würtemberg, 1639), a Franciscan monk in the monastery of Weingarten. In 1656 he was made priest and Musikdirektor at the monastery at Constance, and afterwards guardian at his own monastery. He composed 3 books of masses, and a large amount of other church music of all kinds between 1634–56 (*Q.-L.*).

SUGGIA, GUILHERMINA (*b.* Oporto, June 27, 1888), violoncellist. Having played in the Oporto City Orchestra from an early age (leading violoncellist at 12 years old), she studied with Paul Klengel at Leipzig (1904) and made her appearance as a soloist at one of the Gewandhaus concerts conducted by Nikisch. After a tour in Europe she worked for a time with Casals, and made another extensive tour in 1912. Since the war Madame Suggia has lived in London ; her beauty of style and perfection of phrasing and intonation have never been surpassed. Her portrait has been painted by Augustus John.   J. B. T.

SUITE. (1) THE CLASSICAL TYPE.—In the period between the latter part of the 16th and the beginning of the 18th century the most conspicuous feature of universal instrumental music is the profusion of dance tunes. All the most civilised nations of that time took equal pleasure in them ; and partly owing to the itinerant musicians who traversed divers countries, and partly to the wars which brought representatives of different nationalities into frequent contact, both friendly and hostile, the various characteristic types were spread from one land to another, were adopted uni-

versally by composers, irrespective of nationality, and were so acclimatised as to become in many cases as characteristic of and as popular in the countries of their adoption as in that of their origin.

ENGLISH AND GERMAN PROTOTYPES.—This is sufficiently illustrated in Morley's *Plaine and easie Introduction,* 1597. For when he comes to treat of dance-music, the first things he takes notice of are pavans and galliards, almanes and branles ; of which the first two are of Italian origin, the third probably Suabian, and the last French. The first two were not only in common use for dancing purposes in Queen Elizabeth's time, but were adopted by the great composers of the day and a little later as a favourite basis for instrumental pieces, which were intended as much for private enjoyment as music as for accompaniments to dances ; and they are found plentifully scattered in such collections as the ' Fitzwilliam Virginal Book ' and ' Parthenia,' among sets of variations, preludes and fantasias. (See VIRGINAL MUSIC.) A large proportion of such dances were naturally taken singly, but composers early perceived the advantage of contrasting one with another. Thus Morley, in the same part of the work just mentioned, speaks of the desirableness of alternating pavans and galliards ; since the first was ' a kind of staid musick ordained for grave dancing,' and the latter ' a lighter and more stirring kind of dancing'; and he further describes more obscurely the contrast arising from the 4-time and 3 - time which subsists between them. Spitta[1] mentions the same contrast as popular in Germany a little later, and refers to the publication of thirty paduans and gaillards by Johann Ghro of Dresden in 1604. In such a manner originated the idea of joining different dance tunes together to make an artistic balance and contrast, and in this lies the germ of the suite ; in which, by selecting dances of various nationalities, and disposing them in the order which displayed their relative bearings on one another to the best advantage, composers established the first secular instrumental cyclic art-form.

It is not possible, for want of materials, to trace fully the process of selection. The pavans and galliards dropped out of fashion very early, and allemandes and courantes came in, and soon became a sort of established nucleus, to which was sometimes appended a sarabande, or even several other dance movements, and a prelude. Indeed, when the principle of grouping movements together was once accepted, the speculations of composers in that line seem to have been only limited by their knowledge of dance-forms. It was in fact by experimenting with various methods of grouping that the most satisfactory succession was arrived at ;

[1] *Life of Bach* (i. 681, Engl. trans. ii. 73).

and thus many of the earlier suites contain a greater profusion and variety than is found in those of the maturer period. In Purcell's suites, for instance, which date from the last ten or twenty years of the 17th century, besides the allemande and courante, which occupy just the very position in which they are found in the suites of Bach and Handel, in one case the group also comprises a sarabande, cebell, minuet, riggadoon, intrade and march ; while another contains a trumpet tune and a chacone, and another a hornpipe. One of the most curious features in them is the absence of the jig, which in the mature suite-form was the only one admitted of English origin. The opening with a prelude is almost invariable ; and this is not astonishing, since this kind of movement (which can hardly be described as a ' form ') was as familiar as the dances, from having been so often attempted by the early instrumental composers, such as Byrd, Orlando Gibbons, Bull and Blow among Englishmen. The order of four movements which served as the nucleus in the large proportion of suites of the mature period is also occasionally, by accident, found very early ; as for instance in one of the suites of Froberger, which Nottebohm says was written in 1649 ; and another by Lully, which was probably written early in the second half of the same century.

GROUPING AND TITLES.—These groups had, however, as yet no uniform distinctive title. In England, in common with other combinations of divisions or movements, they were generally called lessons, or suites of lessons, and continued to be so called till after Handel's time. In Italy similar groups were called sonate da camera ; in Germany they were called Parties or Partitas, as in the Clavierübung of Kuhnau published in 1689, and the set of six by Johann Krieger [1] published in 1697 ; and in France they were as yet commonly known as ordres. Thus the fact evidently existed universally for some time before the name by which it is now known came into general use.

The composers of different countries illustrated in different degrees the tendency towards consolidation which is inevitable in an art-form. The steps taken by the Italians appear to be particularly important as illustrating the distinct tendencies of the suite and the sonata. Corelli's earlier sonate da camera are scarcely distinguishable from the suite type, as they consist of a string of dance tunes preceded by a prelude. The later sonatas or solos of his Opera Quinta, however, represent different types. Some still consist of dance tunes, but many also show a fair proportion of movements of more abstract nature ; and in several the dance element is, in name at least, quite absent. These are indeed a sort of combination of the

church and chamber sonata into a secular form, adding a canzona or free fugal movement in the place of the allemande, and transmuting the other dance types into movements with general qualities analogous to the earlier sonatas. Where this abstract character prevailed, the type approached more distinctly to that of the modern sonata ; and where the uniformity of a dance rhythm prevailed throughout, it approached more nearly to the suite type. In these cases the arrangement had already ceased to be a mere crude experiment in antithesis, such as the early balance of galliard and pavan, and attained to the dignity of a complete art-form. With the Italians the remarkable distinction of their violin school led to the greater cultivation of the violin SONATA (*q.v.*), which, though retaining a few danceforms, differed markedly in their distribution, and even in the structure of the movements.

THE FRENCH STYLE.—In both France and Germany more attention seems to have been paid to the clavier, and with it to the suite form. The former country very early showed many proofs of appreciation of its principles ; as an instance, the suite by Lully in E minor, mentioned above, has the complete series of allemande, sarabande, courante, minuet and gigue. But a little later, theatrical influences seem to have come into play, and Rameau and Couperin, though in many cases adopting the same nucleus to start with, added to it a profusion of rondeaux and other short movements called by various eccentric names. In one of Couperin's ordres the number of little pieces amounts to no less than twenty-three ; and in such a case it is clear that a sense of form or complete balance in the whole can hardly have been even aimed at. The movements are strung together in the same key, according to the recognised rule, as a series of agreeable ballet pieces, and the titles point to their belonging to quite a different order of art from that illustrated by the suite in its maturity. In fact their kinship must be attributed mainly to the order of programme music. Thus in the tenth ordre of Couperin, the first number is called ' La Triomphante ' and also ' Bruit de guerre.' In the eleventh ordre a series of pieces represents ' Les Fastos do la grande et ancienne Mxnxstrxndxsx,' in five acts, the fourth of which is ' Les Invalides,' etc., in which the right hand is made to represent ' Les Disloqués ' and the left ' Les Boiteux,' and the last is ' Désordre et déroute de toute la troupe : causés par les Yvrognes, les Singes, et les Ours.'

In Germany, composers kept their faces more steadfastly set in the direction of purer art-form, and the prevalence of uniformity in their distribution of movements soon became remarkable. Kuhnau's examples have been already referred to, and an example given in Pauer's 'Alte Clavier-Musik ' illustrates the usual order absolutely. Spitta mentions that the famous organist Buxtehude made a complete suite out of variations on the Choral 'Auf meinem lieben Gott' in the form of sarabande, courante and gigue. Twelve sets of 'Pièces de clavecin' by Mattheson, which were published in London as early as 1714, two years before Couperin's first set, are remarkably regular. The first, in D minor, has a prelude, allemande and double, courante and double, sarabande, and gigue. The second begins with a toccatina, the fifth with a fantasia, the ninth with a 'boutade,' and the tenth with a 'symphonie,' but in other respects most of them follow the same outlines of general distribution. The 'Six Suits of Lessons' of the Dutchman Johann Loeillet, published a little earlier still, are equally precise. From these facts it is quite clear that by the beginning of the 18th century certain definite principles of grouping the movements were generally known and accepted; and that a nucleus, consisting of allemande, courante, sarabande and gigue, had become the accepted type of the art-form.

CONTRAST WITH SONATA.—The differences between the structure of suite movements and sonata movements have already been traced in the article SONATA. It remains here only to summarise, with more special reference to the suite. While sonata movements constantly increased in complexity, suite movements remained almost stationary. They were based upon the persistence of the uniform type of a dance rhythm, throughout the whole of each several movement. Hence the ground principles of subject in sonata and suite are altogether different. In the former the subjects are concrete, and stand out in a marked manner both in contrast to one another and to their immediate context; and it is a vital point in the form that they shall be fully and clearly recapitulated. In the suite, on the other hand, the subject does not stand out at all prominently from its context, but is only a well-marked presentation of the type of motion and rhythm which is to prevail throughout the movement. To this there is no contrasting subject or episode, and definite recapitulation is no part of the scheme at all. In a few cases—which must be regarded as accidents in relation to the logical principles of the form—the opening bars happen to be sufficiently marked to have something of the character of a sonata subject; and in such cases it may also happen that they are repeated with sufficient simplicity to have the effect of recapitulation. But nevertheless it must be maintained that this is not part of the principle of construction. And with reference to this point it is well to remember that composers did not attain the ultimate distinct outlines of sonata and suite with a definite purpose and plan before them; but that in working with particular materials

they were led almost unconsciously to differentiate the two forms. The plan is found to exist when the work is done; but it is not theoretically propounded and then worked up to. It is not therefore a matter for surprise that in early times some points in the development of abstract form of the sonata kind were worked out in dance movements of the suite type, and applied and extended afterwards in works which had more distinctly the sonata character. Nevertheless the sonata is not an outgrowth from the suite; but, inasmuch as both were descended from a kindred stock, before the distinctions had become well defined, it is natural that many works should have continued to exhibit suggestions and traits of both sides promiscuously. On the whole, however, it is remarkable how soon the distinct types came to be generally maintained; and from the number of instances which conform, the system can be fairly deduced.

PRINCIPLES OF THE CLASSICAL FORM.—The most marked external point is the uniformity of key. In Corelli's earlier sonate da camera, which in general are decided suites, the one exception which marks a sonata tendency is that the slow dance is often in a different key from the rest of the movements. In later suites of all sorts the uniformity of key throughout is almost universal. In the whole of Bach's the only exceptions are the second minuet of the fourth English suite, and the second gavotte in that known as the 'Overture in French Style.'[1] Hence the contrast is purely one of character between the several movements; and this is emphasised by the absence of any marked contrast of key or subject in the movements themselves. They are almost invariably constructed upon the simple principle of balanced halves, each representing the same material in different phases, and each strengthened by repetition. The first half sets out from the tonic key, and without any marked pause or division modulates so as to settle into the key of the dominant or relative major, and closes in that key. The second half begins afresh from that point, and proceeding in most cases by way of the key of the subdominant, settles well back again into the original key and concludes. The only break therefore is in the middle; and the two halves are made purposely to balance one another, as far as may be, without definite recapitulation. In a few movements, such especially as sarabandes and intermezzi, the second half is somewhat extended to admit of a little development and free modulation, but the general principles in the average number of cases are the same, namely, to diffuse the character of the principal figures and features throughout, rather than to concentrate the interest of the subject in definite parts of the

[1] 'Ouverture à la manière française.'

movement. In order, however, to strengthen the effect of balance between the two halves, certain devices are common and characteristic, especially with regard to the beginnings and endings of each half. Thus though composers do not seem to have aimed at recapitulation, there is frequently a clear relation between the opening bars of each half. This often amounts to no more than a subtle equivalence in the distribution of the group of rhythms in the bar, or a very loose transcript of its melodic features. But in some cases, most especially in Bach, the opening bars of the latter half present a free inversion of the beginning of the first half, or a sort of free shuffling of the parts approximating to double counterpoint. The first mode is clearly illustrated by the courante of the third partita in A minor as follows :

The Allemande of the fourth 'Suite anglaise' supplies a remarkable example of free inversion of figures and parts at the same time :

The other point, of even more common occurrence, is the correspondence of the ends of each half, which prevails particularly in allemandes, courantes and gigues. A very fine and full example is supplied by the allemande of Bach's first 'Suite anglaise'; the courante of his second 'Suite française' supplies another of some length; and among works of other composers the allemande of Lully's suite in E minor, the courante of Mattheson's suite No. 5 in C minor, the courante of Handel's fourth suite, the gigue of his eighth suite, and most of his allemandes, are instances to the point. In the particular manner of the suite movements both these devices are exceedingly effective as emphasising the balance of halves, and in the finest movements the balance of material and modulation is carefully distributed for the same end. Thus much of form applies more or less to all the movements which are based on dance rhythms, or developed on that principle.

ORDER AND CHARACTER OF MOVEMENTS.— Each of the movements has also severally distinct characteristics, upon which the form of the suite as a whole is mainly based. For the better understanding of this it will be best to take the group which forms the average nucleus or so-called canon of the suite. In the severest simplicity of the form the ALLEMANDE comes first, as in all Bach's French suites, in some of Couperin's, and many by earlier composers. The origin of the movement is obscure, and it is maintained that it is not based upon any dance, since the allemande of Suabian origin, said to be the only dance-form of that name known, is quite distinct from it. However that may be, its constitution, which is most important, consists mainly of moderately slow 4-time, with regular smooth motion—most frequently of semiquavers—distributed in a figurate manner between the various parts, and its character has been generally regarded as appropriately quiet and sober ; which Mattheson described as the ' Ruhe des Anfangs.' To this the COURANTE, which almost invariably follows it in the mature suite, is supposed and intended to supply a contrast, but it cannot be maintained that it always does so successfully. The character of this movement varies considerably, owing chiefly to the fact that there are two decidedly distinct forms derived from different sources. The one of Italian origin which is found most frequently in Corelli's sonatas, in most of Handel's, in some but not all of Purcell's suites, and in Bach's fifth and sixth French suites, and fifth partita, is in 3–4 time, of quick, light and direct movement, full of rapid passages of simple character, with simple rhythm, and free from complication. This in general supplies in an obvious sense a fair contrast to the allemande. The other courante, of French origin, is nominally in 3–2 time, but its characteristic is a peculiar intermixture of 3–2 and 6–4, which is supposed to produce a stronger antithesis to the smooth motion of the allemande. In the original dance it is said that this characteristic was chiefly confined to the last bars of each half, but in mature suite movements it was elaborately worked into the body of the movement with very curious effect. The quality is shown as early as Kuhnau, but more frequently in Couperin's suites, from whom it is said Bach adopted it. The following example from Couperin's third suite is characteristic :

It is possible that Bach adopted this form as affording opportunities for rhythmic experiments ; he certainly carried it to great lengths, such as giving the right hand a passage in 3–2 and the left in 6–4 :

but the result is not on the whole very successful. In most cases the French courantes are the least interesting movement of his suites, and as contrasts to the allemande do not compare favourably with the Italian courante. As an element of contrast the crossing of the time is rather theoretical than real, and the necessity of keeping the time moderate in order to make it intelligible brings the strong beats and the average quickness of the shortest notes, as well as the full spread of the bar, too near to those of the allemande ; and in the general effect of the suite these externals tell more strongly than the abstract restlessness of crossing rhythms. It is possible, however, that the French courante has one advantage over the Italian : that inasmuch as the latter has more stability in itself, it calls less for a succeeding movement, and presents less perfectly the aspect of a link in the chain than of a movement which might as well stand alone. There is a slight touch of uneasiness about the French courante which, as a step towards the SARABANDE, is very appropriate. In this latter movement, which is of Spanish or possibly Moorish origin, rhythmic principle is very pronounced, and at the same time simple. Its external aspect is chiefly the strong emphasis on the second beat of a bar of three in slow time, as is clearly illustrated in Handel's sarabande in the G minor suite, in his ' Lascia ch' io pianga,' and in the sarabande of Bach's F major ' Suite anglaise.' This is an obvious source of contrast with both the preceding members of the suite, since in both allemande and courante there is no pronounced and persistent rhythm, and the pace, though not necessarily quick, scarcely ever comes within the range of motion or style characteristic of definitely slow movements. There is also a further and equally important element of contrast. The first two numbers are characterised in a considerable proportion of instances by a similar free motion of parts. The process of carrying on the figures is sometimes knit by a kind of free imitation, but, however desirable it may be theoretically to regard them so, they cannot fairly be described as movements of imitation. The process is rather that of free figuration of two or three parts, giving in general a contrapuntal effect to the whole. In the sarabande the peculiar rhythmic character puts both systematic imitation and regular contrapuntal motion equally out of the question. Consequently as a rule a more decidedly harmonic style obtains ; the chords are fuller, and move more simultaneously as blocks of harmony. The character of the finest examples is necessarily very pliable, and varies between free melody with simple accompanying harmony, such as those in Bach's 'Suites anglaises' in F and D minor, Handel's suites in G minor and E minor ; examples in which the prominent melodic features are distributed successively without regularity between the parts, as in those in the ' Suites anglaises ' in G minor and A minor, the ' Suite française ' in B minor, the partita in B♭. and several of Couperin's ; and a few examples in which a figure or characteristic mode of motion is made to prevail almost throughout, as in the ' Suite française ' in E♭. The general effect of the sarabandes is noble and serious, and the music is more concentrated than in any other member of the group of movements. It is thus in various respects the central point of the suite : in position ; in musical interest and unique quality ; and in the fact, as observed and curiously commented on by Nottebohm, that the preceding movements generally tend to the solidity and the succeeding movements to lightness and gaiety. The order is in this respect somewhat similar to that of average sonatas, and seems to be the art-exposition of the same ideas of form from the point of view of the musical sense, though differently carried out as far as the actual manner and material of the movements are concerned.

In the most concise examples of the suite the sarabande is followed by the final gigue ; but it is so common with all the most notable writers of suites to interpolate other movements, that it may be well to notice them first. These appear to have been called by the older writers galanterien, and more lately intermezzi ; and seem to have been regarded as a sort of concession to popular taste. But in any way they answer the purposes of form exceedingly well. A very great variety of dances is introduced at his point. The most familiar are the GAVOTTES, BOURRÉES, MINUETS and PASSEPIEDS. But besides these the most distinguished writers introduced LOURES, POLONAISES, movements called arias and other less familiar forms. Their character on the average is especially light and simple, and in the dance numbers it is remarkable that they always preserve their dance character more decidedly and obviously than any other member of the group. It is not possible to describe them all in detail, as they are too numerous, but their aspect in the group is for the most part similar, and is analogous to that of the scherzo or minuet and trio in the modern sonata. They evidently strengthen the balance on either side of the sarabande both in quality and amount. In many cases there is a considerable group of them, and in these cases it is that the ARIA is sometimes introduced. This movement has little connexion with the modern piece of the same name, as it is generally a short movement in the same balanced form as the other movements, but free from the dance basis and rule of time. It is generally moderately slow, and sometimes consistently melodious, as in Mattheson's suite in A; but often it is little more than a string of figures, without even melody of much importance. The group of intermezzi is generally contrasted with the sarabande and the gigue either by a square time or by the interchange of moderate movement, such as that of the minuet; and the conciseness and distinctness of the type is always sufficient to make the relations on both sides perfectly clear.

The GIGUE which concludes the series is theoretically, and in most cases actually, of light and rapid style. It is usually based on some rhythmic combination of 3 feet, but even this is not invariable. The balance is in favour of 12–8 time; but 6–8 is also common, and 12–16 and 3–8 not unfrequent; while a few are in some form of common time, as the slow gigue in the first French suite of Bach, and the remarkable example in his last partita in E minor. The old fancy for concluding a work with a fugue is illustrated by the common occurrence of fugal treatment in this member alone of the regular group of the true suite series. The treatment is met with in all directions; in Kuhnau, Mattheson, Handel, Couperin, as well as Bach. The method of application is commonly to begin and carry out a free sort of fugue in the first half, concluding like the other movements in the dominant key; and to take up the same subject freely 'al rovescio' or by contrary motion in the second half, with regular answer as in a fresh fughetta, and carry it out on that basis with the usual direction of modulation, concluding in the original key. Thus the fugal treatment is an accessory to the usual form of

the suite movement, which is here as regularly and invariably maintained as in the other members of the group.

The most important accessory which is commonly added to this nucleus is the PRELUDE. It appears in a variety of forms, and under a great variety of names. (It is worth noticing that all six introductory movements of Bach's partitas have different titles.) The chief point which is most obvious in relation to the other movements is that their characteristic form of nearly equal halves is systematically avoided; in fact any other form seems to have been taken in preference. In many important examples it is the longest and most elaborate movement of all. In some it is a sort of rhapsody or irregular group of arpeggios and other figures based on simple series of chords. Bach commonly developed it on the same broad outlines as some of his largest sonata movements, and the first and last of the Italian concerto—that is, the distinct balancing section of clear musical character and full close at the beginning and end of the movement, and the long passage of development and modulation in the middle, sometimes embracing new figures. This is illustrated by the preludes to the 'Suites anglaises' in A minor, G minor, F and E minor. In other examples the treatment is fugal, or contains a complete fugue along with other matter of more rhapsodical cast, as in the toccata of the partita in E minor; or yet again it is in the form of a fantasia, or of the overture as then understood. The effect is certainly to add breadth and stability to the group in no mean degree, and the contrast with the rest of the movements is in every respect unmistakable. This completes the general outline of the suite in its finest and most consistently complete form, as illustrated in Bach's 'Suites anglaises,' which must be regarded as the culminating point of the suite as an art-form.

EXCEPTIONAL TYPES.—In the matter of actual distribution of movements there are plenty of examples of experiments, even in the time when the usual nucleus had come to be generally recognised; in fact, there is hardly any large collection of suites which does not present some exceptions to the rules. Bach's departures from the usual outline are chiefly in the earliest examples, such as the partitas, in one of which he concludes with a rondo and a caprice. The 'Ouverture à la manière française,' for clavier, is in appearance a suite, but it is clear that Bach had not only the clavier suite type in his mind in laying out its plan, but also the freer distribution of numbers in the so-called French overture said to date from Lully. In this there is no allemande; the sarabande has intermezzi on both sides of it, and it concludes with an 'Echo' after the gigue. The works of his which are now commonly known as orchestral suites must be put in the same category. For the inference suggested by Dehn's trustworthy observations on the MSS. is that Bach regarded them as overtures, and that the name suite was added by some one else afterwards. They depart from the average order of the clavier suite even more conspicuously than the above-mentioned work. In his later compositions for clavier, as has been already remarked, he was very strict. Handel's suites, on the other hand, are conspicuous departures from the usual order. They are, in fact, for the most part hybrids, and very few have the genuine suite character as a whole. The introduction of airs with variations, and of fugues, in the body of the work, takes them out of the category of strict interdependent art - forms and makes them appear rather as casual strings of movements, which are often as fit to be taken alone or in different groups as in the group into which he has thrown them. Moreover they illustrate somewhat, as Nottebohm has also observed, the peculiar position which Handel occupied in art, as not pure German only, but also as representative of some of the finest traits of the Italian branch of the art. The tendency of the Italians after Corelli was towards the violin sonata, a distinct branch from the original stem, and to this order some of Handel's suites tend to approximate. It was chiefly by thorough Germans that the suite-form was developed in its austerest simplicity ; and in that condition and in relation to their keyed instruments it seems that the usual group is the most satisfactory that has been devised.

It is obvious that the suite as an art-form is far more elementary and inexpensive than the sonata. In fact it attained its maturity long before the complete development of the latter form ; and not a little of the interest which attaches to it is derived from that and collateral facts. It was the first instrumental form in which several movements were combined into a complete whole. It was the first in which the ecclesiastical influences which had been so powerful in all high-class music were completely supplanted by a secular type of equally high artistic value. Lastly, it was the highest representative instrumental form of the contrapuntal period, as the sonata is the highest of the harmonic period. It was brought to perfection when the modern sonata was still in its infancy, and before those ideas of key and of the relations of harmonies which lie at the root of sonata-form had become tangible realities to men's minds. In some respects the complete plan has the aspect of formalism and rigidity. The uniformity of key is sometimes taken exception to, and the sameness of structural principle in each movement is also undoubtedly somewhat of a drawback ; but it must be remembered that the form is a representative product of a peculiar artistic period,

and devised for a particular keyed instrument, and for minds as yet unaccustomed to the varied elaboration of the sonata. The results are remarkable and valuable in a high degree ; and though this may be chiefly owing to the exceptional powers of the composers who made use of the form, it is possible that as a pattern for the combination of small pieces it may still be worthy of regard. In fact the combination of short lyrical movements such as are characteristic of modern times has strong points of analogy with it. Moreover, since it is obviously possible to introduce modifications of some of the details which were too rigid in the early scheme without destroying the general principles of the form, it seems that genuine and valuable musical results may still be obtained by grafting characteristics of modern treatment and expression upon the old stock.   C. H. H. P.

BIBL.—C. H. H. PARRY, The Seventeenth Century (Oxf. Hist. Mus. vol. iii.) ; J. A. FULLER MAITLAND, The Age of Bach and Handel (Oxf. Hist. Mus. vol. iv.) ; S. CONDAMIN, La Suite instrumentale (1905) ; KARL NEF, Geschichte der Sinfonie und Suite (Leipzig, 1921) ; ELISABETH NOACK, Ein Beitrag zur Geschichte der älteren deutschen Suite (A.-M., Apr. 1920) ; LUDWIG BRAV, Die Entwicklung der Tanzfolgen für Orchester bis zur Mitte des 30 jähr. Krieges (Berlin Dissertation, 1921).

(2) MODERN VARIETIES.—The classical type of suite, so completely rounded off in the first half of the 18th century, received a certain measure of revival in the latter part of the 19th century by composers who found an attraction in experimenting with old forms. The suites of Lachner and Bargiel among the minor composers of Germany set a new fashion followed with conspicuous success by Grieg, in his 'Aus Holberg's Zeit,' and many others. Among English composers none contributed to that revival more decisively than Parry, whose 'Lady Radnor Suite' for strings and 'English Suite in G' (published posthumously) are perfect examples of that grafting on the old stock to which his last sentence above refers.

But the widespread modern use of the name has generally nothing to do with the old form. The works of Tchaikovsky may be pointed to as giving salient examples of two types quite distinct from the old dance forms. On the one hand, the orchestral suites (opp. 43, 53, 55) trace descent from the DIVERTIMENTI, CASSATIONS (q.v.) and similar groups of pieces of the late 18th century ; on the other, the popular 'Casse - noisette' suite is typical of the very prevalent practice of compiling suites for independent performance from ballet music.

The most common uses of the term in current practice approximate to one or other of these types. The composer groups his numbers together on any principle, either of purely musical affinity or contrast or in accordance with some descriptive programme, which appeals to him. He accepts the term 'suite' as one which allows him a freer hand than symphony and one which indicates more definiteness of design than symphonic poem. Rimsky-Korsakov's 'Scheherazade' suite and Holst's 'The

Planets ' are outstanding instances. The other use is commonly adopted by the composer of ballet music and of incidental music to plays who wishes subsequently to throw his work into a form suitable to concert performance. From Grieg's ' Peer Gynt ' to Stravinsky's ' Firebird ' their number is legion. A third distinct use of the term is that of the arranger and orchestrator of old music for modern use. Among English composers none has been more drawn on for this purpose than Henry Purcell. The many charming suites of his theatre tunes and dances heard in concert-rooms to-day must not be confused with his own harpsichord suites referred to in the foregoing article.   c.

SUK, JOSEF, (b Křečovice, S. Bohemia, Jan. 4, 1874), a leading Czech composer, and member of the BOHEMIAN (CZECH) STRING QUARTET (q.v.). His father was school- and choir-master of Křečovice. Suk, therefore, springs from that old pedagogic stock which has made the musical culture of Bohemia famous.[1] His father, his first teacher, laid the solid foundations of his musical education. In 1885 he entered the Prague Conservatoire where, under the guidance of the Director, Ant. Benne-witz, he became an excellent violinist. At the same time he studied piano (Jiránek) and theory (Foerster, Stecker and Knittl). After passing his final examinations, in 1891, he remained another year at the Conservatoire to work at chamber music under Wihan and composition under Dvořák. He was the favourite pupil of Dvořák, with whom he after-wards entered into close relationship by marriage with his daughter Otilie. In Wihan's class Suk met his colleagues, K. Hoffmann, O. Nedbal, and O. Berger (a violoncellist who died young), and in 1892 they founded the well-known Bohemian Quartet. Suk, nevertheless, found time to work hard at composition. At the beginning of this century, he was already regarded as joint leader with NOVÁK (q.v.) of the modern Czech school. Since 1922 he has been professor of composition in the ' master school ' of the Prague Conservatoire. In the years 1924–26 he was elected director of this institution.

Suk's first essays in composition date from very early in his career, and the first to be known outside his own country (the pianoforte quartet in A minor, op. 1, and the serenade for string orchestra, op. 6) belong to his student days at the Conservatoire. They are remark-able for an assured mastery of the art of com-position ; the Viennese classicists, Schubert, Brahms, and more especially his teacher, Dvořák, are his models ; classical sonata-form is the keystone of his work. But already his individuality is clearly apparent. He is far more tender, intimate and melancholy than Dvořák ; his rhythm is not so racially ele-

[1] See Burney, *The Present State of Music in Germany.*

mentary, therefore richer ; his breadth of melody is not greatly concerned with period-icity; polyphony stands well in the foreground; the harmony is very original. In his ' Dramatic overture,' op. 4, he already shows great tragic pathos and profound passion ; the serenade and early piano works stamp him as a delicate lyrical composer. The great wealth of inven-tion shown in his first group of chamber music (the piano quartet; piano quintet, op. 80; string quartet in B, op. 11) and in his first symphony (E flat) assured him an outstanding position among Czech composers.

During the time of his love for Dvořák's daughter, and in the early years of their short married life, the lyrical quality of Suk's art became most prominent ; his subjective side increased in power, and, from this point, his works gradually became autobiographical con-fessions. In connexion with this tendency came a remarkable growth of individuality in his technique, especially as regards harmony. The first work he composed at this time, the text of which reflected his mood, was the music to a dramatic fairy tale, ' Radúz and Mahulena,' by the Czech poet Julius Zeyer. Suk set to music chiefly those parts of the work which stirred his lyrical instincts : the entr'actes and melo-dramatic scenes. Only in the description of the curse of the wicked queen Runa he shows once more the passionate side of his art. The poet was so enthusiastic about Suk's work that he begged him also to compose incidental music for his dramatic legend ' Pod jabloní ' (Under the Apple-trees). This is an idyll pervaded by an atmosphere of Catholic mysticism. Suk, however, was most interested in depicting the happiness of the young married couple—the principal characters in the legend—just as in the preceding work the love of Radúz and Mahulena became the central point of his music. Moreover, in these two works Suk succeeded in catching the atmosphere of the old Slavonic legendary world, thus introducing something new into Czech music. Here, too, is shown that fantastic element which became so marked in his later works. The scherzo of the first sym-phony and the bacchanal from the legend are forerunners of similar movements, such as the fantasy for violin and orchestra, op. 24 ; the fantastic scherzo, op. 25 ; and the scherzo movements in the later symphonic works

The presentiment of an unhappy destiny, which pursued him as the result of much pon-dering upon the instability of human joy and drove him to feverish imaginative activity, is reflected in the fantasy. The same dreamy, fanciful mood prevails in the scherzo, op. 25. Upon this followed the symphonic poem ' Prague,' the apotheosis of the noble past, and the hopeful future, of the capital city of his fatherland.

With Prague,' however, this period of Suk's

creative activity ended, for now came the dreaded catastrophe which so deeply influenced the composer's life and achievement. In 1905 his wife died, a year after her father. After a nervous breakdown Suk returned to the composition of his second symphony, begun in 1904. He called it 'Asrael' and dedicated it to the memory of the two beloved persons whom he had lost. The work is the starting-point of what, so far, is the latest phase of Suk's art; a period which has meant for him a slow victory over the blows of fate, and a gradual working towards life's affirmation. Besides the important orchestral works in which he has embodied this mental and emotional process— 'Asrael,' 'Midsummer Tale,' 'Maturity' and 'Epilogue'—Suk has written smaller works belonging, however, to the same spiritual impulse. These consist of piano pieces and a string quartet. The pianoforte cycle 'About Mother' was written for his little son; it contains a series of intimate reminiscences. The symphonic poem in five movements, 'A Summer Tale,' gives us pictures from Nature, in which the composer sought, and believed he had found, consolation. The later cycle of piano pieces, 'Things lived and dreamed,' is rich in many new methods of expression, and, together with the string quartet, op. 31, gives us a further picture of the soul's conflict. Here we find much inward sorrow and also much bitter irony. The victory over all the shadows cast by fate is expressed in the symphonic poem 'Maturity' (based on a poem by Ant. Sova). It is the most modern of Suk's compositions up to the present time. Subtlety of harmony, richness yet clearness of polyphony, rhythm and periodicity liberated from all fetters, breadth of melody, brilliance of orchestration and freedom of form and tonality—all these qualities reach their highest level here. The latest of Suk's works—unfinished at the time of writing—is called 'Epilogue,' and is intended to complete the cycle of symphonic works mentioned above. All these works are fundamentally subjective, while aiming at something wider. They speak for all; expressing in music what humanity has experienced from the beginning of time. During the war (1914–18) Suk wrote two works intended for his own country. The 'Meditation on the Chorale St. Wenceslaus' originated in the nation's greatest hour of need; the 'Legend of dead victors' is the apotheosis of the heroes who died for their convictions on the battlefield (the Czechoslovak legionaries who fought with the Allies).

Suk's early works (in manuscript), without opus numbers, include :

Str. quartet, D min. ; fantasy for str. orch. ; funeral march for strings ; Mass in B flat maj. ; ballade for str. quartet ; fugue for PF. and str. quartet ; ballade for vln. and PF. ; cradle song with PF. accompaniment.

WORKS WITH OPUS NUMBER

ORCHESTRAL.—Dramatic overture, op. 4, orch. (PF., 4 hands, M. Urbánek, Prague) ; Serenade, op. 6, strings (score parts and PF., 4 hands, Simrock) ; overture to Shakespeare's 'A Winter's Tale,'

op. 9 (MS.) ; incidental music to Zeyer's 'ramatic fairy tale, 'Radúz and Mahulena' (PF. score, Hudební Matice, Prague) ; prologue for vln. and PF., 4 hands, (M. Urbánek) ; symphony in E maj., op. 14 (score parts and arrangement for 4 hands, N. Simrock) ; 'Pohádka' (A Tale), op. 16 ; a suite from the music to 'Radúz and Mahulena, op. 13 (Simrock) ; 'Pod jabloni' (Under the Apple-trees), op. 20 ; music to a dramatic legend by Zeyer (five numbers for mixed chorus, alto solo, PF. (4 hands) and harmonium, German and Czech words, N. Simrock) ; fantasia for vln. and orch., op. 24 (N. Simrock) ; fantastic scherzo for large orch., op. 25 (Breitkopf & Härtel) ; 'Prague,' symphonic poem, op. 26 (MS. arrangement for PF., 4 hands, M. Urbánek) ; symphony, 'Asrael,' op. 27 (score and parts, Breitkopf & Härtel ; arrangement for PF., 4 hands, Hudební Matice, Prague) ; 'Pohádka léta' (A Summer Tale), op. 29, symphonic poem in five movements (Universal Edition, Vienna) ; 'Zrani' ('Maturity,' sometimes translated 'Ripening,' though 'Harvest-tide' best represents its meaning), a symphonic poem for large modern orch., op. 34 (Hudební Matice, Prague ; J. & W. Chester, London) ; 'Epilogue,' for full orch., baritone solo and women's choir, op. 37 (unfinished as yet).

CHORAL.—Ten songs for women's voices, op. 15, with accompaniment for PF., 4 hands ; Slavonic folk - poems (Simrock) ; four songs for male-voice chorus, op. 18, from Serbian folk-poetry (M. Urbánek) ; three songs for mixed chorus with accompaniment for PF. ad lib. (M. Urbánek) ; male-voice choruses with folk-texts, op. 32 (Hudební Matice).

PIANOFORTE.—Polish fantasia, op. 5 (F. A. Urbánek, Prague) ; PF. pieces, op. 7 (F. A. Urbánek) ; 'Nálady' (Moods), op. 10 (Simrock) ; PF. pieces, op. 12 (Simrock) ; PF. suite, op. 21 (M. Urbánek) ; 'Jaro' (Spring) and 'Letní dojmy' (Summer Impressions), two cycles of pieces, op. 22 (M. Urbánek) ; 'O matince' (About Mother), op. 28 (J. Otto, Prague) ; 'Zivotem a snem' (Things lived and dreamed), ten pieces, op. 30 (Breitkopf & Härtel) ; 'Ukolébavky' (Slumber Songs), op. 33 (Simrock) ; 'Opřátelstve' (Friendship), op. 36 (Hudební Matice and J & W. Chester, London).

CHAMBER MUSIC, ETC.—PF. quartet, op. 1, A min. ; PF. trio, op. 2, C min. (both by F. A. Urbánek, Prague) ; str. quartet No. 1, in B flat, op. 11 (Simrock) ; str. quartet No. 2, op. 31 (Simrock) ; str. quartet, 'Meditation on the Chorale St. Wenceslaus,' op. 35a (also for str. orch. and arrangement for organ, F. A. Urbánek) ; ballade and serenade for v'cl., PF. accompaniment, op. 3 (M. Urbánek) ; elegy for vln. and v'cl. with accompaniment for str. quartet, harmonium and harp, suggested by Zeyer's epic 'Vyšehrad,' op. 23 (M. Urbánek).

Also a few small works recently printed, without opus : Humoreske for PF. (Neldner, Riga) ; a male-voice chorus, words by J. Kollár (F. A. Urbánek) ; 'Vesnická Serenáda' (Village Serenade) for PF. (J. Otto, Prague) ; 'Episody,' for PF. (Hudební Matice and J. & W. Chester) ; Bagatelle, 'S Kytice v luce' (With nosegay in hand), for flute, vln. and PF. (Hudební Matice and J. & W. Chester).

R. V. (translated R. N.)

SULLIVAN, SIR ARTHUR SEYMOUR (b. 8 Bolwell Terrace, Lambeth, May 13, 1842; d. Westminster, Nov. 22, 1900), was the son of an Irish soldier who became Sergeant of the Band at the Royal Military College, Sandhurst, and eventually professor of the clarinet at Kneller Hall (see ROYAL MILITARY SCHOOL OF MUSIC), upon that Institution being opened in 1857. The opportunity for a thoroughly practical parental grounding in orchestral instruction was thus provided for the boy, whose general education was also not neglected, for he attended a private school at Bayswater, kept by a Mr. W. G. Plees. On Apr. 12, 1854, he had the good fortune to enter the Chapel Royal as a chorister upon the recommendation of Sir George Smart. There he received invaluable and systematic instruction in music from the Rev. Thomas Helmore, master of the children, and there, we cannot doubt, since it rests upon his own written word, he received the

' care and attention bestowed upon every branch of my education and the constant and kindly interest taken in my progress [that] have been in no small manner influential in making me what I am, viz. an earnest labourer in the cause of true Art.'

His first published composition, an anthem, ' O Israel,' was accepted by Novello in 1855 while he was yet a chorister.

In July 1856 he became, in open competition, the first holder of the recently established MENDELSSOHN SCHOLARSHIP (q.v.) at the R.A.M., where he became a pupil of Sterndale Bennett, Sir John Goss and O'Leary. He

LXXIX

SULLIVAN

SANTLEY

Photo, W. & D. Downey, Ltd.

Photo, Ellis & Walery

retained his choristership until 1858, although we may suspect that, as a boy of 16, his voice had become uncertain. But under the terms of the Scholarship he was enabled to go to Leipzig to further his education, and he arrived there in the autumn of 1858. Here he entered upon a yet more intensive period of study at the Conservatorium under teachers of European renown. Moritz Hauptmann for counterpoint and fugue, Rietz for composition, David for orchestral conducting, Moscheles and Plaidy for the pianoforte. There he had as contemporaries John Francis BARNETT, Walter BACHE, Franklin TAYLOR and Carl ROSA, and there he remained till 1861 steeping himself in German taste and tradition, full of reverence for German thoroughness and method, yet still maintaining sturdily his own remarkable artistic individuality. He then returned to London, having won golden opinions of his teachers, and for the last months of his stay, above and beyond the period of his Scholarship, having been partly maintained by the self-denying exertions of his devoted father.

On Apr. 12, 1862, his music to Shakespeare's 'Tempest,' composed at Leipzig, was produced at a Crystal Palace Saturday concert by August Manns. The following week—an unprecedented occurrence—it was repeated, and Sullivan awoke to find himself famous in the world of music. A few months later it was again heard, this time at a Hallé concert in Manchester, and so the two leading orchestras of the day set the seal of their approval upon the young composer's début In the preceding autumn he had become organist at St. Michael's, Chester Square, a position he occupied for several years, during which period his time was occupied partly by teaching (a profession he detested) and partly, and largely, by composition.

In 1864 he composed the music for a ballet, 'L'Île enchantée,' which was produced at Covent Garden, and was, we may conjecture, the means of procuring him the post of organist at the theatre, then under the sway of Sir Michael Costa. This was his first practical experience of the theatre from the professional side of the curtain, and it had the further advantage of bringing him into touch with Costa, probably the most influential musician in England of his time. Through Costa's good offices Sullivan was invited to write a cantata for the Birmingham Festival of 1864, of which the former had been conductor for many years. The result was 'Kenilworth,' written in collaboration with his friend Henry F. CHORLEY. In this year he also wrote some music to an opera libretto by Chorley, entitled 'The Sapphire Necklace,' which was never produced, and the music for which Sullivan thriftily used in later works.

At this time he also came under the influence of Sir George Grove, of whom he became a devoted friend and disciple, a friendship only terminated by their deaths within a few months of each other. The year 1864 was full of importance to Sullivan, for he composed the Irish symphony during a visit to the land of his fathers. It also was produced at the Crystal Palace. In 1866 he was appointed a professor of composition at his alma mater, the R.A.M., and in September of that year he suffered a severe bereavement by the death of his father, which was the *motif* expressed by his 'In Memoriam' overture produced at the Norwich Festival on Oct. 30 of that year.

A concerto for violoncello and orchestra was played by Piatti at the Crystal Palace on Nov. 24. The following year he was commissioned by the Philharmonic Society to write an overture, 'Marmion,' and the composition was duly performed on June 3, 1867. This year was, however, even more memorable to Sullivan for the journey he took with Grove to Vienna in search of the lost Schubert MS. scores of 'Rosamünde,' the triumphal result of which is related elsewhere (see SCHUBERT). At the same time his 'In Memoriam' overture was produced at the Gewandhaus at Leipzig, the scene of his boyish experiences and successes.

In 1867 the first of those works which have brought such enduring and world-wide fame to Sullivan was heard. It was an adaptation by F. C. Burnand (sometime editor of *Punch*) of Maddison Morton's famous farce, *Box and Cox*. The title was reversed and the libretto 'Cox and Box' handed to Sullivan. The performance was to take place a fortnight later at Moray Lodge, Campden Hill, the residence of Mr. Arthur Lewis, a wealthy and cultured amateur of the day. With incredible labour and rapidity this was accomplished, and on Apr. 27, 1867, the little masterpiece was born. Later in the year it was added to the repertory of Mr. and Mrs. German Reed, with whom it had a long run.[1]

In December of the same year, 1867, 'Contrabandista,' a 2-act libretto by Burnand, was set to music by Sullivan, and produced at St. George's Hall by the German Reeds, not meeting, however, with the success of its predecessor. In 1869 his first oratorio, the 'Prodigal Son,' was performed on Sept. 8 at the Worcester Festival, Mmes. Tietjens and Trebelli, with Sims Reeves and Charles Santley, taking the solo parts.

In 1870 the overture 'Di ballo' (in E♭) was heard at the Birmingham Festival, a work which, while couched throughout in dance-rhythm, is constructed in regular classical form. To continue the list of his commissioned works, in 1871, in company with Gounod, Hiller and Pinsuti, he wrote a piece for the opening, on May 1, of the Annual International Exhibition

---

[1] It was revived in London by the D'Oyly Carte Opera Company (Prince's Theatre, Monday, Nov. 28 1921), until then exclusively occupied with the works in which Sullivan had collaborated with Gilbert.

at the Albert Hall. This was a cantata, to words by Tom Taylor, ' On Shore and Sea,' for solo, chorus and orchestra.

In the same year at the Prince's Theatre, Manchester, his music to a revival of the ' Merchant of Venice ' was heard, and at the close of the year another attempt at comic opera was made, not wholly successfully, with ' Thespis, or The gods grown old ' (Gaiety, Dec. 26, 1871). The importance of this lies in its being the occasion of his first association with W. S. Gilbert, the famous humorist, whose name is for ever associated with that of the composer.

At this time Sullivan was also closely engaged in editing the collection of ' Church Hymns with Tunes ' for the S.P.C.K. and the Hymnary for Novello, for both of which he wrote a large number of original tunes, among them his famous setting of ' Onward! Christian Soldiers ' (1872). Another popular work was, perhaps, his best-known partsong, ' Oh hush thee, my babie' (Novello), first sung at St. James's Hall, May 23, 1867.

In 1872, at the call of the Crystal Palace Company, he composed a Festival Te Deum, for soprano solo, orchestra and chorus for the rejoicings to honour the recovery of the Prince of Wales from typhoid fever.

By this time Sullivan's life had become so strenuous that he found it expedient to resign the two organistships he held, at St. Michael's, Chester Square, and St. Peter's, Cranley Gardens. He had undertaken the conductorship of the Royal Aquarium, Westminster, and of the Promenade Concerts at Covent Garden Theatre, and was besides in continuous request for social and musical functions in many quarters.

In 1873 he made a third appearance at Birmingham, this time with the leading feature of the Festival, an oratorio entitled the ' Light of the World,' the words, like those of the ' Prodigal Son,' selected from the Bible by himself. Shortly afterwards he was honoured by the bestowal of the degree of Doctor of Music by Cambridge University. He had also become in a special degree the intimate friend of the Royal Family in particular of the Duke of Edinburgh, an enthusiastic amateur violinist (see ROYAL AMATEUR ORCHESTRAL SOCIETY). In 1874 he wrote music for ' The Merry Wives of Windsor,' produced at the Gaiety Theatre, Jan. 2, 1875, by John Hollingshead.

In 1875 Richard D'Oyly CARTE (q.v.) procured Sullivan's collaboration with Gilbert for the production, entitled a Dramatic Cantata, of ' Trial by Jury ' at the Royalty Theatre, Soho, then under the temporary direction of Mme. Selina Dolaro, for a season of Offenbach opera with Carte as manager. It was produced on Mar. 25, 1875, with instantaneous success, owing in part to the very humorous conception of the character of the Judge by Sullivan's brother Frederick. It was the only Gilbert and Sullivan opera set to music entirely without spoken dialogue.

In June of that year, 1875, Sullivan also collaborated with B. C. Stevenson in a comic operetta entitled ' The Zoo,' produced at the St. James's Theatre. About the same busy period he began a connexion with the Choral and Orchestral Union of Glasgow. The following year D'Oyly Carte took a lease of the Opéra-Comique Theatre and formed a syndicate for the express purpose of producing operas by Gilbert and Sullivan. The first result was the production, on Nov. 17, 1877, of ' The Sorcerer,' which ran uninterruptedly for 175 nights, and was responsible for the introduction to the London public of George Grossmith, Rutland Barrington and Richard Temple, who created leading parts in the subsequent series of these operas.

In May 1876 the National Training School (see ROYAL COLLEGE OF MUSIC) was opened by the Duke of Edinburgh, and after strenuous persuasion Sullivan was induced to become its first director. This was a colossal addition to an already overburdened man's work, but he undertook it and retained it for three years, resigning definitely in 1881. In 1878 he wrote incidental music for Charles Calvert's revival of Shakespeare's ' Henry VIII.,' produced at Manchester. In January of this year he suffered the loss of his elder brother Frederick, to which was directly due the composition of his most popular song, ' The Lost Chord.'

The ' Sorcerer ' was followed at the Opéra-Comique by ' H.M.S. Pinafore' on May 25, 1878. This not only ran in London for 700 consecutive nights (besides an unauthorised series of performances at another theatre), but had an extraordinary vogue in the provinces, and was adopted and pirated in the United States to a degree exceeding all previous records. At one time it was stated

' the spectacle was presented at every theatre and every Concert Company of importance in the big Cities, producing the same piece without the author and composer receiving a farthing for their work.'

To attempt to protect their interests Gilbert and Sullivan visited New York in 1879 to produce the authorised version at the Fifth Avenue Theatre.

An attempt to bring out the piece in Berlin as ' Amor am Bord ' failed owing to the difficulty of anything like stage political caricature in Germany. But it was published by Litolff in 1882.

The next and fifth of the joint productions, ' The Pirates of Penzance ' (produced Apr. 3, 1880) was given a copyright performance at Paignton on Tuesday, Dec. 30, 1879, almost simultaneously with the New York premiere at the Fifth Avenue Theatre, in which Jessie Bond, Rosina Brandram and Alice Barnett all appeared.

For the Leeds Festival of 1880 Sullivan succeeded Costa as conductor and wrote for it 'The Martyr of Antioch,' to words selected by W. S. Gilbert from Dean Milman's poem. Following a run of nearly 400 nights by the 'Pirates,' 'Patience,' the sixth opera, was produced on Apr. 25, 1881. It was a satire upon the ridiculous 'æsthetic' craze of the day, led by the pose of the brilliant but erratic writer, Oscar Wilde. During the run of the opera it was transferred (Oct. 10) from the Opéra-Comique to D'Oyly Carte's new theatre at the Savoy, where, in conjunction with its previous performances, it enjoyed a run of 408 performances.

On Saturday, Nov. 25, 1882, three nights after the last night of 'Patience,' 'Iolanthe' (seventh of the series) was produced, and six months later the popular musician received the honour of knighthood. 'Iolanthe' ran for more than a year, and was followed on Jan. 5, 1884, by the eighth opera, and possibly the least successful, 'Princess Ida.' When this was withdrawn in October, as if to compensate the public for any disappointment, its successor, ninth of the series, 'The Mikado' (produced Mar. 14, 1885), proved the Savoy composer, librettist and manager to be literally at the top of their form. It is impossible to relate the history of this amazing production here, and it must suffice to say that it ran for 672 nights continuously from its first night, and is still probably the prime favourite of an enormous public.

The authors and D'Oyly Carte had to take the closest precautions against American piracy, in which they happily succeeded. In the same year, 1885, Sullivan added to his many activities the conductorship of the Philharmonic Society, which he only retained, however, until 1887. In 1880 he had written the 'Martyr of Antioch' for the Leeds Festival Committee, but had not followed this up by a contribution in 1883.

In 1886, however, he wrote the 'Golden Legend,' to a libretto by his friend Joseph Bennett from Longfellow's poem. It was produced on Oct. 16, 1886, and achieved, with press and public alike, an immense and overwhelming success, greatly to the surprise of those who could not reconcile it with such compositions as 'The Pirates of Penzance' and 'Pinafore.'

'Ruddigore, or the Witch's Curse,' the tenth opera, succeeded 'The Mikado,' after its prodigious run, on Jan. 22, 1887, and ran for eight months, including the hottest weather of the Jubilee Year, no slight drawback. Between the date of its termination and the next production Sullivan found time to compose his incidental music for Irving's revival of 'Macbeth' at the Lyceum. On Oct. 3, 1888, eleventh in the succession, 'The Yeomen of the Guard' was produced, which is understood to have been regarded by its composer

and author as the best and most meritorious of the great series. The libretto and plot were entirely set free from the peculiar—and popular—form of humour known as Gilbertian, and the musical setting followed the spirit of this lead. But the twelfth and next opera, 'The Gondoliers,' produced Dec. 7, 1889, reverted to the earlier type of success and easily secured a similar measure of popularity. Among its many claims to distinction it secured the signal honour of a 'command performance' at Windsor Castle before Queen Victoria. During its run, there was an unhappy rupture between the famous partners, and while the differences were still unsettled, Carte relied on revivals of the repertory that had been formed. Sullivan himself, however, collaborated with Sidney Grundy in the production of 'Haddon Hall' on Sept. 24, 1892. The reconciliation which followed was a matter of national rejoicing, and on Oct. 7, 1893, the thirteenth Gilbert and Sullivan opera was produced, called 'Utopia Limited.' This enjoyed a run of 245 nights. In 1894 Sullivan wrote incidental music for Irving's production of Comyns Carr's version of 'King Arthur' at the Lyceum, and it is known that the subject of the play was one which the composer had in his mind to use as the libretto for a serious opera.

There were five more light operas written, viz.: 'The Chieftain' (Dec. 12, 1895)—a modernised and elaborated version of the old 'Contrabandista,' written as far back as 1867—'The Grand Duke' (Mar. 7, 1896), in which for the last time he and Gilbert worked together; 'The Beauty Stone' (May 28, 1898), to a libretto by Pinero and Comyns Carr; and 'The Emerald Isle,' to a book by Basil Hood, upon which he was at work in 1900 when seized by his fatal illness. None of the first three can, however, be credited as successful, but 'The Rose of Persia' (produced Nov. 29, 1899), to a libretto by Basil Hood, received such warm welcome from the public that a new period of success seemed to have been begun. 'The Emerald Isle' was completed by Edward German and produced on Apr. 27, 1901.

We have related the story of this unique series of productions as far as possible without interruption. We must now revert to the years 1889–90, during which Sullivan—probably urged to some extent by public sentiment,[1] and partly influenced by his own consciousness that the attempt was due—determined to write a 'grand' opera. Gilbert, whom he asked for a libretto, declined the task, feeling that it was not the kind of work the public would take from him, and himself suggested the name of Julian Sturgis, to whom eventually the composer turned, and in collaboration with whom his

[1] In the 1st Edition of this Dictionary, Sir George Grove expressed the hope that Sullivan would apply his gifts to the production of a serious opera on some 'subject of abiding human or national interest.'

first and last 'grand' opera, 'Ivanhoe,' was produced on Saturday, Jan. 31, 1891. This is not the place to relate the story of the building in which the long-anticipated production was achieved. D'Oyly Carte had, after infinite labour, at enormous expense, borne upon his own shoulders the titanic task of constructing a new English Opera House in Cambridge Circus, a district at that time quite outside the London theatre-goer's range. A fine list of singers was engaged, and in order to secure a long run and save the voices of the principals, alternate casts were provided, but in spite of the success of this manœuvre, a run extending to 160 nights, and the friendly reception at the outset, other circumstances intervened, notably the colossal expenses involved, and the difficulty of providing an English repertory, and so the courageous scheme collapsed. Messager's charming 'La Basoche' was put on to follow 'Ivanhoe,' and after a few weeks Carte decided to sell the theatre to a music hall syndicate.

The Diamond Jubilee of Queen Victoria was celebrated by Sullivan in two compositions: the ballet 'Victoria and Merrie England' (Alhambra, May 25, 1897), in which a danced fugue was the best and most interesting number, and a 'Festival Te Deum,' given at the Chester Festival, 1897.

Sullivan had, we may here remark, for many years been looked to on occasions of national rejoicing for some musical expression of public feeling. As far back as 1872 this was evident on the recovery of the Prince of Wales, and almost the last effort of his failing powers was his attempt to assist the sale of a popular song by Rudyard Kipling, 'The Absent-Minded Beggar,' during the Boer War in 1899. Sullivan's songs were in their day as well known as his comic operas, but the most prolific period of his success as a song-writer ended in the year 1877 with the writing of the 'Lost Chord' and the production of the 'Sorcerer.' For very many years now we may safely say few ballads have approached the vogue that was enjoyed by such compositions as 'The Arabian Love Song' and 'If Doughty Deeds' (1866). The Shakespeare songs and the Tennyson cycle of 'The Window' (1871), 'O fair Dove' (1868), 'The Sailor's Grave' (1872), 'Sleep, my love, Sleep' (1874), 'The Distant Shore,' 'Let me dream again,' 'Thou'rt passing hence,' 'Sweethearts,' 'My dearest Heart' and 'The Lost Chord'

The same tunefulness and appropriateness that have made his songs such favourites also distinguish his numerous hymns and anthems. Public taste has, in fact, altered less in this latter respect than in the former.

The easy flow of the voices, the display of excellent and learned counterpoint, and the frequent examples throughout of that melodious style and markedly independent treatment

in which they bring to mind certain periods of the older English Schools, are still recognised by the frequency with which his name occurs in Church of England Services. The whole of his hymn tunes, fifty-six in number, were republished in one volume in 1902 (Novello).

His musical gifts were so amazingly varied that although we have enumerated many claims to fame we have hardly yet done justice to his orchestral music. The output in this was relatively small, but his music to 'The Tempest,' 'The Merchant of Venice,' 'Macbeth,' his oratorios, the 'In Memoriam' overture, the symphony in E—unfortunately his only work in this department—show what remarkable gifts he had for the orchestra. Form and symmetry he seemed to possess by instinct, rhythm and melody clothe everything he touched; the music shows not only sympathetic genius, but sense, judgment, proportion and a complete absence of pedantry; while the orchestration is distinguished by a happy and original beauty hardly surpassed by the greatest masters.

He had received the Cambridge degree of Doctor of Music in 1876, and Oxford followed suit in 1879. In 1878 he acted as British Commissioner for Music at the International Exhibition at Paris, and was decorated with the Légion d'honneur. He also bore the Order of Saxe-Coburg and Gotha, and on May 22, 1883, was knighted by Queen Victoria, on the recommendation of Gladstone.

At the 1898 Leeds Festival performances, of which he had been conductor for fifteen years, it was evident that he was in failing health, but he accomplished the difficult task of conducting although suffering much pain. A terribly painful malady from which he had been a lifelong sufferer had undermined his constitution. It is a harrowing thought that a very great number of his most sparkling and delicious melodies were written during the intervals between spasms of the illness. It was little short of heroism that enabled him to conceal this from the public, and, indeed, to all save his most intimate friends, his spirits ever appeared buoyant, cheery and even jocular. His old friend, Sir George Grove, predeceased him by only a few months, though at a greater age, and the cultured manager who associated his name for ever with those of Gilbert and Sullivan, Richard D'Oyly Carte, passed away soon afterwards.

Sullivan was taken ill by a chill in Nov. 1900, and on the morning of the 22nd at his residence, 58 Victoria Street, Westminster, he died at the age of 58. A vast concourse of people lined the streets on Nov. 27 to see the last honours paid to the composer, whose remains were laid to rest in St. Paul's Cathedral.

It is not to be denied that his more serious works, including his oratorios, cantatas and his one 'grand' opera, have declined in popularity within the last quarter of a century. It is quite obvious, however, that in this respect they have but shared the fate that has largely overtaken many oratorio performances on the grand scale. In the North of England this is not so noticeable as in London and the Home Counties in the South. He would be a bold man, however, who argued from this that they are permanently extinct. It is quite probable that the pendulum will swing back some day and a new period of popularity begin. Meanwhile in ever-increasing circles the fountain of joy which he created sparkles and gushes out to the inexpressible pleasure of the third generation of playgoers whose purest pleasures are found in the delights of ' Savoy ' Opera.

H. S. W.

A chronological list of Sullivan's stage works, with date of production, is given below, to facilitate reference :

' The Tempest.' Incidental music. Crystal Palace, Apr. 12, 1862.
' L'Ile enchantée.' Ballet. Covent Garden, 1864.
' The Sapphire Necklace.' Libretto by Chorley, 1864 (never produced).
' Cox and Box.' Adaptation by F. C. Burnand from Maddison Morton. Moray Lodge, Campden Hill, Apr. 27, 1867.
' Contrabandista.' Libretto by F. C Burnand. St. George's Hall, 1867
' Merchant of Venice.' Incidental music. Prince's Theatre, Manchester, 1871.
' Thespis, or the gods grown old.' With Gilbert. Gaiety, Dec. 26, 1871.
' Merry Wives of Windsor.' Incidental music. Gaiety, Jan. 2, 1875.
' Trial by Jury.' With Gilbert. Royalty Theatre, Soho, Mar. 25 1875.
' The Zoo.' With B. C. Stevenson. St. James's Theatre, June 1875.
' The Sorcerer.' With Gilbert. Opéra-Comique, Nov. 17, 1877.
' Henry VIII.' Incidental music Manchester, 1878.
' H.M.S. Pinafore.' With Gilbert. Opéra-Comique, May 25, 1878.
' The Pirates of Penzance.' With Gilbert. Opéra-Comique, Apr. 3, 1880.
' Patience.' With Gilbert. Opéra-Comique, Apr. 25, 1881.
' Iolanthe.'   „   Savoy, Nov. 25, 1882.
' Princess Ida.'   „   „   Jan. 5, 1884.
' The Mikado.'   „   „   Mar. 14, 1885.
' Ruddigore.'   „   „   Jan. 22, 1887.
' Macbeth.' Incidental music. Lyceum, 1888.
' The Yeomen of the Guard.' With Gilbert. Savoy, Oct. 3, 1888.
' The Gondoliers.' With Gilbert. Savoy, Dec. 7, 1889.
' Ivanhoe.' With Julian Sturgis. Jan. 31, 1891.
' Haddon Hall.' With Sidney Grundy. Sept. 24, 1892.
' The Foresters' (Tennyson). Incidental music. Daly's Theatre, 1892.
' Utopia Limited.' With Gilbert. Savoy, Oct. 7, 1893.
' King Arthur.' Comyns Carr's version. Incidental music. Lyceum, 1894.
' The Chieftain.' With Burnand. Savoy, Dec. 12, 1895.
' The Grand Duke.' With Gilbert. Savoy, Mar. 7, 1896.
' The Beauty Stone.' With Pinero and Comyns Carr. Savoy, May 28, 1898.
' The Rose of Persia.' With Basil Hood. Savoy, Nov. 29, 1899.
' The Emerald Isle.' With Basil Hood. Completed by Edward German. Savoy, Apr. 27, 1901.

A complete and tabulated list of Sullivan's compositions will be found in the memoir *Arthur Seymour Sullivan* by H. SAXE-WYNDHAM (London, 1926).

SUL PONTICELLO, see PONTICELLO.

SULZER, (1) SALOMON (*b.* Hohenems, Vorarlberg, Mar. 30, 1804 ; *d.* Vienna, Jan. 18, 1890), precentor of the Jews' synagogue in Vienna, and reformer of their musical service. The name was derived from Sulz in Würtemberg, the ancient residence of the family. When only 13 he was made cantor of the synagogue at his native village by the Emperor Franz I., and in 1825 was called to Vienna to conduct the music at the newly built synagogue there. There he took lessons in composition from Seyfried, and set himself earnestly to reform the service by reducing the old melodies to rhythm and harmonising them. His collection of Jewish hymns, under the name of 'Schir

Zion' (the Harp of Zion), was used all over Germany, Italy and even America ; but it was not till 1838 that he could succeed in publishing it. It contains a setting of the 92nd Psalm (in Moses Mendelssohn's version) by Schubert, for baritone solo and four men's voices, made in July 1828, the autograph of which is in possession of the synagogue (Nottebohm's *Catalogue*, p. 229). In 1842 a second edition appeared, and in 1865 a second volume. A collection of home and school songs, entitled ' Dudaim ' (Mandrakes), appears to be still in MS. In 1866 a fête was held in his honour and a silver laurel presented to him with the inscription ' The Artists of Vienna to the Artist Sulzer.' From 1844–47 he was professor of singing at the Vienna Conservatorium. He was a Knight of the Order of Franz Joseph (1868), and carried the medals of various societies. His voice, a baritone, is said to have been magnificent.

G.

(2) JOSEPH (*b.* 1850–51; *d*, Vienna, Jan. 14, 1926), son of Salomon, was a violoncellist in the opera orchestra of Vienna, and composer of several works for his instrument. He brought out a revised edition of his father's work ' Schir Zion.'

SUMER IS ICUMEN IN. No English or foreign history of music is without its account of this 13th-century composition, which is *facile princeps* among specimens of mediæval music. In six directions is it pre-eminent, for (i.) it is the oldest known canon ; (ii.) it is the oldest known harmonised music which is frequently performed and enjoyed by singers and listeners to-day ; (iii.) it is the oldest known 6-part composition ; (iv.) it is one of the oldest known specimens of the use of what is now the major mode ; (v.) it is the oldest known specimen of ground-bass ; (vi.) it is the oldest known manuscript in which both secular and sacred words are written to the music. The last point gives us some idea of the estimation in which it was held in its own day. In addition to the numerous references of the histories, it has been made the subject of a 56-page monograph by J. B. Hurry (Novello, 1914), which is chiefly valuable for its collection of 32 verdicts from the writings of English and foreign experts. From among these we select for quotation that of Dr. Ernest Walker[1] :

' It combines beauty of sound and ingenuity of workmanship in a way that has no parallel in early music. Artistically we may say that nothing written for two hundred years afterwards can touch it.'

The date is generally accepted now as 1240 ; it may possibly be as early as 1227 (*vide* Hughes-Hughes, Catalogue of MS. Music in the British Museum), but is probably not earlier than 1239 ; the question seems to turn on whether the MS. (British Museum, Harl. 978)

[1] *History of Music in England*, p. 9.

was written all at one time, or at separate dates. The scribe is supposed to have been one John of Fornsete (? Forncett in Norfolk). But the MS. is from Reading Abbey, and the English words are certainly in Wessex dialect.

The form of the composition is an infinite canon at the unison for four voices, accompanied by two ground-basses singing in canon with one another. The directions shown in the facsimile may be translated thus :

' Four companions can sing this rota. But it ought not to be rendered by fewer than three, or two at the least, in addition to those who sing the bass. Now it is sung thus : the others keeping silent, one begins, with those who sing the bass, and when he shall have arrived at the first note after the cross, another begins : and so on with the rest. And each one shall pause at the written rests, and not elsewhere, for the space of one long.
' *Bass.* (i.) One performer repeats this as often as there is need, counting a rest at the end.
' (ii.) The second sings this, with a rest in the middle, but not at the end, where he repeats the beginning at once.'

Certain alterations, some made at the time of writing, some shortly afterwards, are of interest but not of vital importance. If rightly discerned, they show that the music in its original form was still a canon susceptible of a satisfactory performance ; also that the original system of notation was partly independent of the Franconian scheme, each note deriving its value from the corresponding value (after a trochaic scheme) of the syllable which was sung to it.

The Latin text ' Perspice Christicola ' was presumably added to make this musical gem available for performance within the Abbey Church of Reading.

Musical historians of a speculative turn of mind have often thought that the relatively marvellous height of perfection reached by the Rota made it certain that other music of a like character once existed, and have held that this one specimen is sufficient to prove the existence of an early English school of composition. Evidence in support of this claim was, however, entirely lacking until a German scholar, Fr. Ludwig, pointed out that the same MS. contained a catalogue of organa and motets (the actual music having disappeared) coinciding in part with the famous contemporary collections from Notre Dame at Paris (now at Florence, Wolfenbüttel, Madrid, Turin, etc.), but ascribed here to ' W. de Winc ' (=? Wulfstan of Winchester). One such motet, *Ave gloriosa mater*, survives in this MS., Harl. 978. (See also PES.)

The many facsimile reprints, and translations into modern notation, reliable and otherwise, are too numerous to list here. Nearly all those published in the present century are substantially accurate, though all require some very slight adaptation of the text to produce a satisfactory final close. *Mus. T.* No. 95 (Novello) is a typical handy performing edition,

while *Oxf. Hist. Mus.* vol. i. p. 333 is the most complete. The facsimile shown on the Frontispiece to this volume has been made for this edition of the Dictionary by photography of the original.   A. H.

SUMMATIONAL TONES, see RESULTANT TONES.

SUMMER'S NIGHT, A, opera in one act; text and music by G. H. Clutsam, based on a story from the *Heptameron*. Produced His Majesty's Theatre, July 23, 1910.

SUNDAY CONCERT SOCIETY, see QUEEN'S HALL.

SUNDAY MUSICAL UNION, see QUEEN'S HALL.

SUNDERLAND, MRS. (*b.* Brighouse, Yorkshire, Apr. 30, 1819; *d.* there, May 6, 1905), singer, the daughter of a gardener. Her maiden name was Susan Sykes.

Her voice first attracted the attention of Luke Settle, a blacksmith at a village near Brighouse, who, hearing her singing in her father's garden, offered to teach her. She afterwards joined the Halifax Choral Society, under the leadership of Dan Sugden, who gave her her first fee, of five shillings, for singing a solo at the quarterly concert of the Society. Her next important appearance as a solo singer was on Feb. 19, 1838, at a concert given in the Exchange Rooms, Bradford. She then had five months' training in London, and soon became a local celebrity, was styled the 'Yorkshire Queen of Song,' and for more than a quarter of a century was the leading vocalist in the North of England. She was physically robust, and her voice was a high soprano of great force and volume, which she managed with much expression. Her repertory was chiefly composed of the principal songs in the ' Messiah,' ' Judas ' and the ' Creation '; but she had also some secular songs, mostly of a popular kind. Her first appearance in London was in the ' Messiah ' at Exeter Hall, Nov. 2, 1849, and she continued to sing first soprano for the Sacred Harmonic Society and other bodies in the ' Messiah,' ' Creation,' ' Elijah,' etc., until 1856. The directors of the Ancient Concerts esteemed her voice and expression so much that they offered to send her abroad for further tuition. Indeed, had her early training equalled the quality of her voice and her natural feeling, there can be little doubt that she would have risen to very great general eminence. She frequently sang at Leeds concerts, notably at the opening of the Town Hall by Queen Victoria in 1858, and at the first of the Leeds Festivals in the same year. Her last appearance in public was in the ' Messiah,' at Huddersfield, June 3, 1864. Mrs. Sunderland married at the age of 19, her husband being a butcher. Their golden wedding was celebrated by a concert on June 7, 1888, the proceeds of which helped to found the Sunderland Vocal

Prize for natives of the West Riding of York-shire.   G. ; addns. F. K.

SUOR ANGELICA, opera in one act ; text by Gioachimo Forzano ; music by Puccini. Produced Metropolitan Opera House, New York, Dec. 14, 1918 ; Costanzi Theatre, Rome, Jan. 11, 1919 ; Covent Garden, June 18, 1920.

SUPER. (1) The Latin preposition, ' above,' is used in organ terminology to denote the octave above, and is sometimes, but erroneously, used for ' octave ' (see COUPLER). (2) The supernumeraries in a theatre, who appear in crowded scenes, but do not speak, sing or dance, are colloquially called ' Supers.'

SUPERTONIC, the second note of the scale upwards, as D in the key of C. It is brought into much prominence as the dominant note of the dominant key. The strong tendency to find the chief balance and antithesis in that key, and to introduce the second subject of a movement in it, as well as the tendency to make for that point even in the progress of a period, necessarily throws much stress upon the root-note of the harmony which leads most directly to its tonic harmony, and this is the dominant of the new key or supertonic of the original one. It has consequently become so familiar that its major chord and the chord of the minor seventh built upon it, although chromatic, are freely used as part of the original key, quite irrespective of the inference of modulation which they originally carried.

                                        C. H. H. P.

SUPPÉ, VON (b. Spalato, Apr. 18, 1820 ; d. Vienna, May 21, 1895), light operatic composer, known as FRANZ VON SUPPÉ, was of Belgian descent, though his family for two generations had lived at Cremona ; he was born at Spalato, or on board ship near it, and his full baptismal name was FRANCESCO EZECHIELE ERMENEGILDO CAVALIERE SUPPÉ DEMELLI.

His taste for music developed early. At 11 he learned the flute, at 13 harmony, and at 15 produced a Mass at the Franciscan church at Zara. A piece called ' Der Apfel ' was produced privately at Zara in 1834. His father, however, had other views for him, and sent him to the University of Padua. But music asserted itself ; he learned from Cigala and Ferrari, and wrote incessantly. At this moment his father died, the mother settled in Vienna, where Francesco joined her ; and after a little hesitation between teaching Italian, practising medicine and following music, he decided on the last, got lessons from Seyfried, and obtained a gratuitous post as conductor at the Josephstadt theatre. This was followed by better engagements at Pressburg and Baden, and then (about 1862) at the theatres ' an der Wien,' Quai and Leopoldstadt in Vienna, with the last-named of which he was connected from 1865 until his death. His work at these houses,

though for long mere patching and adding, was excellent practice, and he gradually rose to more independent things. In 1844 a ' Sommernachtstraum,' founded on Shakespeare, and composed by him, is mentioned in the A.M.Z. ' Der Krämer und sein Commis ' followed. In 1847 he was at the theatre ' an der Wien ' and (Aug. 7) brought out a piece, ' Das Mädchen vom Lande ' (The Country Girl), which met with wild success. Ten years later (Jan. 8, 1858) a Singspiel, ' Paragraph 3,' spread his fame into North Germany, and from that time a stream of pieces flowed from his pen. His works are said by the careful Wurzbach[1] to reach the astonishing number of 2 grand operas, 165 farces, comediettas and vaudevilles, etc., as well as a Mass (' Missa dalmatica,' Spina, 1877), a Requiem produced at Zara in 1860 under the title of ' L' estremo Giudizio,' etc. etc. A list of 49 of his operatic pieces is given by Wurzbach, but a few only are dated. Another list of 21 is given by Batka in Pougin's supplement to Fétis, but the titles are French, and it is hard to make the dates agree. Some of the pieces are mere parodies, as ' Tannenhäuser,' ' Dinorah, oder die Turnerfahrt nach Hütteldorf.' One, ' Franz Schubert,' is founded on the life of Schubert, and contains five of his songs. In Riemann the number of his operettas is given as 31, and 180 ' possen ' and slighter pieces are mentioned. The only pieces of Suppé's known out of Germany are ' Fatinitza,' produced at Vienna, Jan. 5, 1876 ; at the Alhambra, London, June 20, 1878 ; and at the Nouveautés, Paris, Mar. 1879 ; and ' Boccaccio ' (originally produced in 1879, and brought out in London, at the Comedy Theatre, Apr. 22, 1882). The overture to ' Dichter und Bauer,' known in England as ' Poet and Peasant,' must be his most popular work abroad, since it has been arranged for no less than 59 different combinations of instruments, all published by Aibl of Munich. The overture to ' Light Cavalry ' (1886) has also had a long-maintained popularity.   G.

SURETTE, THOMAS WHITNEY (b. Concord, Mass., Sept. 7, 1862) ; American teacher, composer and writer on music. Graduating from Harvard in 1891, where he studied piano with Foote and theory with Paine, he was for some years an organist in Concord and later in Baltimore. Since 1895 he has been a lecturer on music, and his activities in this field have been extensive both in England and America. In 1921 he was made director of music at Bryn Mawr College, Pennsylvania. His books include : The Appreciation of Music (with Daniel Gregory Mason, 1907) ; The Development of Symphonic Music (1915) ; and Music and Life (1917). His compositions include an opera, ' Cascabel ' (Pittsburgh, 1899) ; ' Priscilla,' an operetta frequently performed ;

[1] Biog. Lexikon des Österreich. Part 40 ; 1880.

'The Eve of St. Agnes,' dramatic ballet for soli, chorus and orchestra; anthems and instrumental pieces.   w. s. s.

SURIANO, see SORIANO.

SUSANNA, oratorio in 3 parts by Handel; the author of the words is not known; begun July 11, and finished Aug. 24, 1748. It was produced during the season of 1749.   G.

SUSATO, TYLMAN (b. at or near Cologne, end of 15th cent.; d. before 1564 [1]), printer and composer of music His name is regularly written by himself in the full form given above, although the spelling of the first part of it is extremely irregular.[2] A document referred to by Fétis[3] describes Susato as ' son of Tylman.' It is therefore only through an inexplicable forgetfulness of diplomatic usage that Fétis and others[4] have taken Tylman for a surname.[5] These writers have also accepted a conjecture of Dehn[6] that 'Susato' indicated the place of the composer's birth, namely, the town of Soest (Susatum); in one of his books, however, he expressly describes himself as 'Agrippinensis,'[7] which can only refer to Cologne.[8] Consequently we have to consider ' Susato ' (or ' de Susato '—as it once occurs, in a document of 1543[9]) as a family name, ' van (or ' von ') Soest,' doubtless originally derived from the Westphalian town. By the year 1529 Tylman is found settled at Antwerp, where he maintained himself by transcribing music for the chapel of the Virgin in the cathedral; in 1531 he is mentioned as taking part, as trumpeter, in the performance of certain masses there. He was also one of the five musicians supported by the city (' Stadsspeellieden '), and as such possessed, according to a list of 1532, two trumpets, a ' velt-trompet ' and a 'teneur-pipe.' Losing his post on the arrival of Philip II. in 1549 he appears, for some unexplained reason, never to have been again employed by the city. Before this date however, in 1543, he had found another occupation as a printer of music. For a short time[10] he worked in company with some friends; but from 1543 onwards he published on his own account, bringing out between that year and 1561 more than fifty volumes of music, nearly every one of which contains some compositions of his own.

1 Goovaerts, p. 31.
2 In works with Latin titles Susato writes himself in a great majority of cases Tilemannus; Tielmannus, Tilmannus, Tylenannus and Tylmannus occurring but rarely. In Flemish his favourite form seems to have been Tielman. In French Tylman, the spelling adopted by Fétis and Mendel, is found most frequently; Thielman, which is preferred by Goovaerts, is less usual; while Tilman, the spelling which is adopted by Van der Straeten and is now practically the accepted one in the Netherlands, is met with only twice.
3 Biogr. univ. des Musiciens viii. 276; 2nd ed.
4 Thus Mendel and Reissmann, Musikal. Convers.-Lex. x. 355; Berlin, 1881.
5 Cp. Alphonse Goovaerts, Histoire et bibliographie de la typographie musicale dans les Pays-bas, pp. 26, 27; Antwerp, 1880.
6 See his letter in Fétis, l.c.
7 Goovaerts, p. 191.
8 At the same time Goovaerts notes (pp. 26, 27) we are not to confound Susato, as Fétis and Mendel have done, with a contemporary Thielman van Ceulen, who was a brewer, and whose father's name was Adolf.
9 Edmond van der Straeten, La Musique aux Pays-bas avant le sixme siècle, v. 258; Brussels, 1880.
10 Goovaerts, pp. 18-26.

Susato's first publication is a first book of four-part ' Chansons ' (1543), and his next is entitled ' Premier Livre de chansons à trois parties, auquel sont contenues trente et une novvelles chansons conuenables tant à la voix comme aux instrumentz ' (1544). Eight of these pieces are by himself. The rest of his publications,[11] so far as they are now extant, include

(1) In French, sixteen books of ' Chansons ' in 3-8 parts.
(2) ' Madrigali e canzoni francesi a 5 voci ' (1558).
(3) In Latin, three books of ' Carmina,' three of masses, one of ' Evangelia Dominicarum,' fifteen of ' Ecclesiastical Cantiones ' or motets (1553-60), ' Motecta quinis vocibus, auctore Clemente non Papa ' (1546), and five books of ' Cantiones sacrae quae vulgo Moteta vocant ' [sic] (1546).
(4) In Dutch there are his three books of songs, etc. (1551), entitled ' Musyck boexken,' and one book (1561), apparently the second of a series of ' Souter-Liedekens ' (Psalter-ditties), which are of peculiar interest.

The third of the Musyck boexken contains some dances by Susato himself, which are described[12] as ' full of character ' and excellently written. The souterliedekens, which Ambros further[13] states to be found in four more Musyckboexken, are pieces from the Psalms according to the rhymed Flemish version, set without change to the popular song-tunes of the day (' gemeyne bekende liedekens '[14]). The charm, however, of these compositions lies less in the airs adapted in them than in the independence and originality of the part-writing, an art in which Susato was so proficient that some of his three-part songs are composed in such a manner as to be suitable, he states, equally for three and for two voices with omission of the bass. Susato appears also to have co-operated with Clemens non Papa in some of his work, and not to have been merely his publisher. Still, it is as a publisher[15] that Susato has hitherto been almost exclusively known, the masters whose works he printed being very numerous and including such names as Créquillon, Gombert, Goudimel, O. de Lassus, P. de Manchicourt, J. Mouton, C. de Rore, A. Willaert, etc.   R. L. P.

BIBL.—P. BERGMANS, Un Imprimeur musicien, Tilman Susato. Bulletin de la Société de Bibliophiles anversois (Antwerp, 1923).

SUSPENSION is the process of arresting the conjunct motion of one or more parts for a time, while the rest of the components of the chord proceed one step onwards, and thereby come to represent a different root. The part which is stayed in this manner commonly produces dissonance, which is relieved by its then passing on to the position it would have naturally occupied sooner had the motion of the parts been simultaneous. (See HARMONY, Vol. II. p. 530.)

SUTOR, WILHELM (b. Edelstetten, Bavaria, c. 1774; d. Linden, near Hanover, Sept. 7, 1829), studied singing under Valesi, and under

11 Further details of compositions are given in Q.-L.
12 Van der Straeten, v. 261, who says that these dances have been reprinted by Eitner in the M. f. M., Jahrg. vii. No. 6.
13 Geschichte der Musik, iii. 313 (Breslau, 1868). These, however, are not mentioned by Goovaerts, whose general accuracy may lead one to suspect a mistake on Ambros's part.
14 Ambros, iii. 313.
15 His publications are rarely found in England, the B.M. only possessing one volume of masses.

other masters, also composition, violin and pianoforte. He entered the court chapel of the Prince-Bishop of Eichstaett as tenor singer. In 1800 he was chorus-master at the Stuttgart opera, and in 1801 Konzertmeister. From 1818 he was court Kapellmeister at Hanover. He composed 5 operas for Stuttgart, an oratorio, 2 cantatas, a melodrama, incidental music to *Macbeth*, partsongs for male voices, canzonets and songs with PF. (*Q.-L.* ; *Riemann*).

SVENDSEN, JOHAN SEVERIN (*b.* Christiania, Sept. 30, 1840 ; *d.* Copenhagen, June 14, 1911), composer.

His father was a military bandmaster at Christiania. At the age of 11 he wrote his first composition for the violin. When 15 he enlisted in the army, and soon became band-master. Even at that age he played, with considerable skill, flute, clarinet and violin. He soon left the army, and worked during the next few years in the orchestra of the Christiania theatre, and at a dancing academy, for which he arranged some études by Paganini and Kreutzer for dancing. A strong desire to travel drove him, at 21, on a roving tour over a great part of Sweden and north Germany. Two years after, being in Lübeck in extremely reduced circumstances, he fortunately met with the Swedish-Norwegian Consul Herr Leche, whose interest he gained, and who shortly after obtained a stipend for him from Charles XV. to enable him to perfect himself as a violinist ; but being soon afterwards attacked with paralysis in the hand, he was compelled to give up the bow for composition. He went to Leipzig in 1863, and his works being already known there, he was placed in the finishing class of the Conservatorium, receiving, however, instruction in elementary theory of music, which he had never been taught. His instructors were Hauptmann, David, Richter and Reinecke. He wrote a quartet in A, an octet and a quintet, all for strings ; quartets for male voices ; and a symphony in D.

On leaving Leipzig in 1867 he received the great honorary medal of the Academy. After travelling in Denmark, Scotland and Norway, Svendsen went in 1868 to Paris. The Second Empire was then at its zenith, and his sojourn in the capital of France influenced the composer to a very great extent. Whilst there he played in Musard's orchestra, and at the Odéon, and became intimately acquainted with Wilhelmine Szarvady, De Bériot, Vieuxtemps and Léonard. He arranged the incidental music to Coppée's ' Le Passant,' in which both Sarah Bernhardt and Agar performed, but on the whole his Paris productions were few—a concerto for violin in A, and orchestral arrangements of studies by Liszt and Schubert ; he also began ' Sigurd Slembe,' the overture to a Norwegian drama of that name. He left Paris at the beginning of the war in 1870 for Leipzig,

where he had been offered the conductorship of the Euterpe Concerts, which, however, were discontinued owing to the war. At a great musical festival at Weimar in the same year, he first met Liszt and Tausig, and his octet was played by a party containing David, Hellmesberger, Grützmacher and Hechmann, with great approbation. Early in the following year his symphony in D was performed at the Gewandhaus, and his fame as a composer established. He composed in that year his concerto for violoncello in D. In the autumn he went to America to be married to an American lady, whom he had met in Paris, and returned the same year to Leipzig, where, after the end of the war, he undertook the leadership of the Euterpe Concerts for one year. There he finished the overture to ' Sigurd Slembe,' which was played at the Euterpe then, and in the following year at the musical festival at Çassel, both times with great success. In this year he met Wagner at Bayreuth, and soon became his intimate associate. For the next five years (1872–77) he was conductor of the Christiania Musical Association and teacher of composition, and composed comparatively few works, which may be explained by the unfortunate want of pecuniary independence. The pieces of this period are numbered opp. 10-22 in his list.

In 1874 his labours found some appreciation from his countrymen in the shape of an annuity granted by the Storthing, and several decorations conferred on him by the king. After five years of hard work, he was enabled once more to proceed abroad. In 1877 he revisited Leipzig, and conducted a new work at the Gewandhaus ; went thence to Munich, and eventually to Rome, where he spent the winter. In 1878 he visited London for the first time, and there met Sarasate, who assisted him in the performance of his quartet, quintet and octet. From London he went to Paris, where he stayed until 1880, during which time his works were several times performed—as also at Angers, where the post of conductor was offered him by the Musical Association. But Svendsen refused this lucrative appointment, and in the autumn of that year we again find him in his old post as conductor of the Musical Association in Christiania. In 1883 he became court conductor at Copenhagen : in 1888 he visited England again, conducting his symphony in D at the Philharmonic Concert of May 31. In later years he produced only some minor compositions, besides arranging for orchestra several studies by foreign composers.

Svendsen's music is all of high character, remarkable for strong individuality and conciseness, as well as for an elaborate finish strictly in harmony with the traditions of the great masters.

His printed works are as follows :

Op.		Op.	
1.	String quartet in A minor.	15.	Symphony No. 2 in B♭.
2.	Songs for men's voices.	16.	Carnava' des artistes nor-
3.	Octet for strings in A minor.		végiens
4.	Symphony in D.	17.	Rhapsodie norvégienne No. 1,
5.	String quintet in C.		for orch.
6.	Concerto for violin and orch.	18.	Overture to Romeo and
	in A		Juliet.
7.	Do. for violoncello and orch.	19.	Rhapsodie norvégienne No. 2.
	in D minor.	20.	Scandinavian airs arranged
8.	Overture in C to Björnson's		for string quartet.
	drama of ' Sigurd Slembe.'	21, 22.	Rhapsodies norvégiennes
9.	Carnaval à Paris, for orch.		Nos. 3, 4.
10.	Funeral march for Charles	23.	Five songs, French and Ger-
	XV.		man, for voice and PF.
11.	Zorahayde, legend for orch.	24.	Four songs, French and Nor-
12.	Polonaise for orch.		wegian, for voice and PF.
13.	Coronation march for Oscar	25.	Romance by Popper, arranged
	II.		for violoncello and PF.
14.	Marriage Cantata, for chor.	26.	Romance for violin and orch.
	and orch.		in G.

C. S.

SVENDSEN, Oluf (*b.* Christiania, Apr. 19,
1832 ; *d.* London, May 15, 1888), a distinguished
flute - player. He learnt the rudiments of
playing from his father, a musician ; when 12
years old played the flute in small orchestras ;
and at 14 was engaged as first flute in the
Christiania theatre. In 1851 he went to
Copenhagen, and took lessons from Nils
Petersen, then a flute-player there. In 1853
he entered the Conservatoire at Brussels, where
he studied for two years, after which he was
engaged by Jullien for his concerts in London.
In Sept. 1856 he joined the band of the
Crystal Palace, Sydenham, where he remained
till the end of 1858. In 1861 Svendsen was
appointed first flute in the Queen's private
band, and the same year joined the Philharmonic Orchestra. He was ten years in the
orchestra at Her Majesty's Theatre ; and from
1867 was professor of his instrument at the
R.A.M.   G.

SWAEN, Guillaume de, a 16th - century
Netherlander, author of ' Den Singende
Zwaan,' a collection of Catholic sacred songs
published in 1654, which appeared in various
editions, the latest (?) being of the year
1759 (*Q.-L.*).

SWAIN, Freda (*b.* Portsmouth, Oct. 31,
1902), composer and pianist, studied piano
playing under Dora Matthay (1913–19) and
Arthur Alexander (1920–21), to whom she was
married in December 1921 ; composition under
Stanford at the R.C.M., where she also received
some instruction in violin-playing from Achille
Rivarde. Her student works include a sonata
in C minor and a ' Mauresque ' for violin and
piano, 3 preludes for piano and a sonata-
poem, ' The Sea,' for the same instrument.

Having appeared several times on the concert platform with her husband, interpreting
works for two pianos, Freda Swain for the first
time introduced an extensive composition of
her own to the public when ' The Harp of
Ængus,' a work for violin and orchestra on a
poem by W. B. Yeats, was played by Achille
Rivarde at Queen's Hall in Jan. 1925. The
same artist produced the sonata in B minor,
' The River,' at two recitals in May 1925, with
the composer at the piano.

Other important works by Freda Swain are
a sonata in C minor in one movement for
violoncello and piano, a piano sonata in F
minor and a string quartet (' Norfolk ') in E
minor. An operatic setting of ' The Shadowy
Waters ' by Yeats has so far remained unfinished.

The work of Freda Swain at its best shows
intellectual vigour and an uncompromising
earnestness which at times verges on austerity.
The workmanship is at once solid and imaginative, and in the later works there is always a
remarkable agreement between the thought
expressed and the medium through which it is
conveyed. The unaccompanied duets for two
violins and the ' Danse barbare ' for violin and
violoncello, for instance, make the most of
the limited possibilities of unsupported string
instruments ; the ' Barbaric Scherzo ' for 3
pianos exploits the qualities of keyboard instruments very effectively ; the songs are
admirably vocal ; and the numerous works
for violin and piano show a fine sense of how
to combine two essentially antagonistic
values.

Among the smaller works are a ' Poem-
nocturne ' and a ' Lament ' for violin and
piano ; an arrangement for the same instruments of the Irish air, ' The Valley lay smiling before me ' ; a number of piano pieces
(some of which are published) ; and several
sets of songs to words by Bridges, Burns,
Housman, Stephens and translations of
Chinese and Japanese poems.   E. B.

SWEELINCK (Swelinck),[1] (1) Jan Pie-
terszoon (*b.* 1562 ; *d.* Amsterdam, Oct. 16,
1621), the greatest of Dutch organists, was born
of a Deventer family.

His father, ' Mr. Pieter,' was organist of the
Old Church at Amsterdam, which place disputes with Deventer the honour of having
given the son birth.[2] He was taught by Jacob
Buyck (Buchius), the pastor of the Old Church.
There is a tradition that he was sent to Venice
to study music under Zarlino and Gabrieli ; but
with this is connected a mistake of old standing, which places his birth in 1540, twenty-two
years too early.[3] Now, as we know that he
was in Holland from 1577, at latest, onwards,
it becomes barely credible that the lad of 15
could have followed the instruction of the

---

[1] Of the seven or more ways in which the name is spelled, these
two have the warrant of the musician's own signature. The
Germans of the time seem to have naturalised him as Schweling ;
in Amsterdam he was known as plain Jan Pietersz.
[2] Deventer is consistently mentioned by Sweelinck's later biographers ; but the Amsterdam claim has the support of the official
entry of his marriage there in 1590, in which his birthplace is not
stated. The omission was the rule when the person was a native
of the city. Else documentary evidence is equally wanting on
both sides.
[3] The correction of this and the rest of the mistakes which confuse
every single date in Sweelinck's life is due to the essay of F. H. J.
Tiedeman, *J. P. Sweelinck, een bio-bibliografische Schets,* published
by the Vereeniging voor Nederlandsche Muziekgeschiedenis (Amsterdam, 1876), which supersedes a shorter sketch published by the same
writer as an introduction to the ' Regina Coeli,' in 1869. Both are
based upon a biography (which remains in MS. in the possession of
the Vereeniging) by Robert Eitner, who did good service by
rescuing the works of Sweelinck from the obscurity of the Graue
Kloster at Berlin.

Venetian masters to any important extent; and it is likely that the whole story is based upon the close study which his works prove him to have devoted to those of ' the apostle of musical science,' [1] whose ' Istitutioni harmoniche' he translated.[2] Some time between 1577 and 1581 Sweelinck was appointed to the organistship previously held by his father (who died in 1573); and this post he filled until his death. For a generation he was the glory of Amsterdam. When he played the organ there, says a contemporary, ' there was a wonderful concourse every day; every one was proud to have known, seen, heard the man.' [3] And when he died it was the greatest of Dutch poets, Vondel, who wrote his epitaph, and surnamed him ' Phoenix of Music.' He must also have been a distinguished figure in the society of Amsterdam, then in its greatest brilliancy, not only for his unmatched powers as an organist, but also for his skill, fancy and charming versatility on the clavicymbel.[4] The town bought him for public service a new ' clavecimpbel' from Antwerp at a cost of 200 gulden; and the instrument seems to have travelled with him all over the country.[5]

What was published, however, by Sweelinck in his lifetime was entirely vocal music, and includes, besides occasional canons, marriage-songs, etc.—his ' Chansons françaises' (three parts, Antwerp, 1592–94), ' Rimes françoises et italiennes' (Leyden, 1612), and the great collections of sacred music on which, with his organ works, his fame chiefly rests. These are the ' Pseaumes mis en musique' for 4–8 voices (published in several editions at Leyden, Amsterdam and Berlin), and the ' Cantiones sacrae' (Antwerp, 1619). A ' Regina Coeli' from the latter, three chansons and eight psalms in six parts were reprinted, in organ-score, by the Association for the History of Dutch Music (pts. i., v., vi. and vii.; Utrecht and Amsterdam, 1869–77); which has also published for the first time seven of Sweelinck's organ works [6] (pt. iii.) (see VEREENIGING). In 1894–1901 B. & H. published Sweelinck's complete works in twelve volumes, edited by Max Seiffert, who added prefaces, etc., see below. The chanson, ' Tu as tout seul' is in vol. i. of ' Arion,' and two of the Italian madrigals are in ' Ausge-

wählte Madrigale.' The beautiful ' Hodie Christus natus est' is in the Bach Choir Magazine, etc.

The psalms make an interesting link between the tranquillity of the old polyphonists and the rhythm of modern music. Formally they stand nearest to the earlier style, but the strictness of their counterpoint, the abundance of imitation and fugue in them, does not hinder a general freedom of effect, very pure and full of melody, to a greater degree than is common in works of the time. The organ pieces are also historically of signal importance. Though they may not justify the claim made for Sweelinck as ' the founder of instrumental music,' [7] they at all events present the first known example of an independent use of the pedal (entrusting it with a real part in a fugue), if not with the first example of a completely developed organ-fugue.

It is as an organist and the founder of a school of organists that Sweelinck had most influence, an influence which made itself felt through the whole length of northern Germany.[8] In the next generation nearly all the leading organists there had been his scholars; his learning and method were carried by them from Hamburg to Danzig. His pupil Scheidemann handed down the tradition to the great Reincke [9]—himself a Dutchman—from whom, if we accept a statement supported alike by unanimous testimony and by exhaustive analysis of their works, it turned to find its consummation in Sebastian Bach.[10]

The contents of the complete edition are as follows:

Two portraits are reproduced, and the prefaces by Dr. Seiffert are given in Dutch and German.   R. L. P.

(2) DIRK JANSSON (bapt. Amsterdam, May 26, 1591; d. there, Sept. 1652 [11]), followed his father, Jan Pieter, as organist of the Oude Kerk at Amsterdam. He published an edition of the ' Livre septième des chansons vulgaires,' with the addition of some of his own songs (Q.-L.).

SWELL (HARPSICHORD). The desire for a power of increase and decrease on keyboard instruments like the harpsichord and organ, so as to emulate the bow instruments, and even the human voice, in that flow and ebb which are at the foundation of form no less than of expression, has led to the contrivance of

[1] So Zarlino is entitled by his biographer, F. Caffi, Della vita e delle opere del prete G. Zarlino (Venice, 1836). Neither here nor in the chapters on Zarlino and Andrea Gabrieli contained in his Storia della musica sacra, vol. i. p. 129, etc. (Venice, 1854) does Caffi take any notice of the Dutch scholar. Nor have I been able to discover any trace of his residence at Venice in the MS. collections of S. Marco.
[2] MS. at Hamburg, formerly belonging to the great organist Reincke.
[3] Sweertius, in Tiedeman, p. 16. Sweelinck's portrait at Darmstadt gives his strong irregular features a kindly expression, with a touch of sadness in them. It is reproduced in photograph by F. H. J. Tiedeman.
[4] On this he was the master of Christina van Erp, the famous lutenist, and wife of the more famous poet, Pieter Corneliszoon Hooft. See the Bouwsteenen of the Vereeniging, vol. i. pp. 13 f.
[5] See an anecdote in Baudartius, Memoryen, xiii. p. 163; cited by Tiedeman, p. 16.
[6] The bibliography of Sweelinck is given at length by Tiedeman, pp. 43–75. To this should be added some supplementary particulars communicated by Dr. J. P. Heije in the Bouwsteenen, vol. i. pp. 39–46.

[7] See Eitner's preface to the edition, and Tiedeman, pp. 54 ff.
[8] The wide distribution of his works is shown by early transcripts existing in the British Museum, and by copies of the extremely rare printed works preserved in the Bibliotheque Nationale. Curiously enough not a single MS. of Sweelinck remains in Holland.
[9] Or Reincken.
[10] Spitta, J. S Bach, i. 96. 192-213.
[11] Buried Sept. 20.

mechanical swells as the only possible approach to it. A swell was first attempted on the organ; the harpsichord swell was introduced by Robert Plenius in a sostinente (see SOSTINENTE PIANOFORTE) variety of the instrument, named by him Lyrichord, and is described (in 1755) as the raising of a portion of the lid or cover of the instrument by means of a pedal. Kirkman adopted this very simple swell, and we find it also in many small square pianos of the 18th century. About 1765 Shudi introduced the Venetian swell, and patented it in 1769. This beautiful piece of joinery is a framing of louvres which open or close gradually by means of the right pedal and thus cause a swell, which may be as gradual as the performer pleases. Shudi bequeathed this patent to John Broadwood, who inherited it on the death of Shudi in 1773. When the patent expired, Kirkman and others adopted it, and it was fitted to many old harpsichords, and even to pianos, but was soon proved unnecessary in an instrument where power of *nuance* was the very first principle.

The English organ-builders perceived the great advantage of Shudi's Venetian swell over the rude contrivance they had been using (see ORGAN, Vol. III. p. 753), and it became generally adopted for organs, and has since been constantly retained in them as an important means of effect. A. J. H.

SWELL-ORGAN. The clavier or manual of an organ which acts upon pipes enclosed in a box, such box having shutters, by the opening of which, by means of a pedal, a crescendo is produced. The shutters are made to fold over each other like the woodwork of a Venetian blind, hence the expressions ' Venetian Swell ' and ' Venetian Shutters ' sometimes found in specifications. To the swell-organ a larger number of reed-stops is assigned than to other manuals.

The first attempt at a ' swelling-organ ' was made by Jordan in 1712. The crescendo was obtained by raising one large sliding shutter which formed the front of the box. The early swell-organs were of very limited compass, sometimes only from middle C upwards, but more generally taken a fourth lower, namely, to ' fiddle G.' For many years the compass did not extend below tenor C. (See ORGAN, Vol. III. p. 753) J. S.

SWELL-PEDAL, the pedal in the organ and harpsichord by which the shutters of the swell are opened and closed. (See PEDAL.) T. E.

SWERT, JULES DE (b. Louvain, Aug. 16, 1843 ; d. Ostend, Feb. 24, 1891), a representative violoncellist of the Belgian school. When only 8 years of age he began playing in public, though his studies were not completed until 1858, in which year he took first prize in the class of Servais at the Brussels Conservatoire. His subsequent career was that of a travelling virtuoso until 1865, when he became Konzertmeister at Düsseldorf. Between 1869 and 1873 he resided at Berlin, where his functions were those of royal Konzertmeister and professor at the Hochschule. He also held appointments at Weimar, Wiesbaden, Leipzig and finally at Ostend. At the last-named town he was appointed in 1888 director of the local music school, acting as professor at the neighbouring Conservatoires of Bruges and Ghent, until his death. As a soloist he visited London first in 1875, and was esteemed as a warm, temperamental player, producing a tone of exceptional volume. Three concertos, one of which was produced with great success at the Berlin Philharmonic in 1886 ; a symphony, ' Nordseefahrt ' ; and two operas, ' Die Albigenser ' (Wiesbaden, 1878) and ' Graf Hammerstein,' represent his more serious work as a composer. W. W. C.

SWIETEN, GOTTFRIED, BARON VAN (b. Vienna, 1734 ; d. there, Mar. 29, 1803), a musical amateur of great importance, who resided at Vienna at the end of the 18th century and beginning of the 19th. The family was Flemish, and Gottfried's father, Gerhard,[1] returned from Leyden to Vienna in 1745, and became Maria Theresa's favourite physician. Gottfried was brought up to diplomacy, but his studies were much disturbed by his love of music, and in 1769 he committed himself so far as to compose several of the songs in Favart's ' Rosière de Salency ' for its public production at Paris. In 1771 he was made ambassador to the court of Prussia, where the music was entirely under the influence of Frederick the Great, conservative and classical. This suited Van Swieten. Handel, the Bachs and Haydn were his favourite masters ; in 1774 he commissioned C. P. E. Bach to write six symphonies for orchestra. He returned to Vienna in 1778 ; succeeded his father as prefect of the Public Library, and in 1781 was appointed president of the Education Commission. He became a kind of musical autocrat in Vienna, and in some respects his influence was very good. He encouraged the music which he approved ; had regular Sunday-morning meetings for classical music, as well as performances of the great choral works of Bach, Handel and Hasse, etc. ; employed Mozart to add accompaniments to Handel's ' Acis,' ' Messiah,' ' St. Cecilia ' and ' Alexander's Feast,' and Starzer to do the same for ' Judas ' ; translated the words of the ' Creation ' and the ' Seasons ' into German for Haydn [2] ; and himself arranged Handel's ' Athaliah ' and ' Choice of Hercules.' He supplied Haydn now and then

[1] Evidently not a very wise person. See Carlyle's *Frederick*, Bk. xxi. ch. 5.
[2] Max Friedlaender, *Van Swieten und das Textbuch zu Haydns Jahreszeiten*, shows from an examination of the MS. libretto that Van Swieten made many suggestions that actually guided Haydn in his musical setting (*J.M.P.* 1909).

with a few ducats, and gave him a travelling-carriage for his second journey to England.[1] In his relation to these great artists he seems never to have forgotten the superiority of his rank to theirs ; but this was the manner of the time. Van Swieten patronised Beethoven also (see BEETHOVEN, Vol. I. p. 274); but such condescension would not be at all to Beethoven's taste, and it is not surprising that we hear very little of it. His first symphony is, however, dedicated to Van Swieten. He was the founder of the 'Musikalische Gesellschaft,' or Musical Society, consisting of twenty-five members of the highest aristocracy, with the avowed object of creating a taste for good music—a forerunner of the 'Gesellschaft der Musikfreunde,' founded in 1808. G.

SWINEY (MACSWINEY), OWEN (b. near Enniscorthy, Ireland, 1680 ; d. Oct. 2, 1754), was the son of the rector of Enniscorthy. In a letter,[2] dated Oct. 5, 1706, and addressed to Colley Cibber, whom he calls in turn 'puppy,' 'his Angel' (twice), 'his Dear' and finally 'Unbeliever'—this singular person describes how Rich had sent for him from his 'Quarters in the North,' and how 'he was at a great charge in coming to town, and it cost him a great deal of money last winter,' and 'he served him night and day, nay, all night and all day, for nine months.' He had 'quitted his post in the army' on the faith of promises that, in return for managing 'the playhouse in the Haymarket' under Rich, he was to have '100 Guineas per annum Salary, a place at Court, and the Devil and all.' Having come up to London, as described, in 1705, he soon found that Rich intended nothing seriously for his advantage ; and he announces (in the same letter) that, in consequence of the general discontent of the actors with Rich, and although Rich might have had the house for £3 or £3 : 10s. a day, he (Swiney) had taken a lease for seven years at £5 a day, and meant to begin in a few days.

In 1707 we find him in partnership with Wilks, Dogget and Cibber in the King's Theatre, having taken the lease from Vanbrugh, and very soon quarrelling with them and petitioning the Lord Chamberlain's interference in his favour. He was mixed up in most of the quarrels and intrigues of the time.

In May 1709 Swiney engaged the famous Nicolini for three years, produced Handel's 'Pastor Fido' (Nov. 1712) and 'Teseo' (Jan. 1713) and became bankrupt (Mar. 1713).

After this he lived for some years in Italy ; but on his return to England (1718) a place in the Custom-house was found for him, and he was appointed Keeper of the King's Mews. While in Italy with Lord Boyne and Walpole, he wrote to Colman (July 12, 1730) from

1 Griesinger, Biog. Not. p. 66.
2 Formerly in the writer's possession.

Bologna, on the subject of engaging singers for the Opera, then in the hands of Handel. He was given a benefit at Drury Lane, Feb. 26, 1735. Swiney died, leaving his fortune to Mrs. Woffington. He was the author of several dramatic pieces, viz. 'The Quacks, or Love's the Physician' (1705) ; 'Camilla' (1706) ; 'Pyrrhus and Demetrius' (1709) ; and an altered version of the first piece.

Two years before his death a fine portrait of Swiney, after Van Loo, was scraped in mezzotint by J. Faber, junr. It represents him, in black velvet, holding in his hand a book, of which the title seems to be *Don Quixote*.

     J. M. ; addns. W. H. G. F.

SYKES, SUSAN, see SUNDERLAND, Mrs.

SYLPHIDE, LA, ballet in 2 acts ; libretto by A. Nourrit ; music by Schneitzhöffer. Produced Opéra, Paris, Mar. 12, 1832 ; Covent Garden, July 26, 1832. G.

SYLVANA, see SILVANA.

SYLVIA, OU LA NYMPHE DE DIANE, 'ballet-pantomime' in 2 acts and 3 tableaux ; libretto by Barbier ; music by Léo Delibes. Produced Opéra, Paris, June 14, 1876. G.

SYMPATHETIC TONE, RESONANCE, or VIBRATION is the term used to describe one of the commonest and most beautiful of acoustical phenomena. Any sound-producing body, such as a stretched string, or any cavity, has one particular note to which it will respond if the same note be sounded in its neighbourhood. The easiest illustration of the fact is given by raising the dampers from the strings of a piano by pressing the right pedal, and then singing a note over the strings ; these will be found to give forth the same notes uttered by the voice, in faint 'sympathy.' The fact has been turned to account in various ways in practical music. The viola d' amore was provided with 'sympathetic' strings below the finger-board, which were usually tuned to the chord of D major, and resounded when notes of that chord were played. The charm of the pianoforte pedal is not so much in prolonging the tone of the notes that are actually struck, as in allowing the sympathetic resonance to be heard from the strings corresponding to the upper partial tones of the lower notes. This power, again, is easy to analyse by placing the fingers successively or simultaneously upon the notes of the chord of C major from middle C upwards (without sounding them), and then striking the bass C firmly ; on releasing this latter key, the upper notes, or overtones, of the chord will be distinctly heard, sounded by sympathetic vibration from the upper strings. The effect of all sympathetic vibration is to enrich the quality of the tone produced ; and the fact that the harp, with its obvious poverty of tone as a solo instrument, is one of the most effective members of the full orchestra, is no doubt partly due to the sympathetic vibration reacting on the large surface of strings that are capable of resonance. M.

SYMPHONIA was apparently a keyboard [1] instrument, and although named by Schlick [2] and Praetorius [3] neither writer describes what is meant by this name, a fact which shows it to have been popular. Cocleus,[4] in Latin text, speaks of the ' clavichordium ' with brass or iron wires touched by keys and says ' if the instrument is softer it is called " symphonia " ; if louder, " clavicymbalum," ' indicating gradations in power ; but how achieved is not explained.

Praetorius gives a complete list of musical instruments that includes ' symphonies.' Again, it is mentioned by Chaucer in his ' Tale of Sir Thopas.'

' Heer is the queen of fayerie
With harp, and lute and symphonye.'

The name occurs once in the Bible in Daniel (iii., 5, 10, 15) as ' Symphoniah ' but wrongly translated as ' dulcimer.' By comparing the name with almost identical form in Greek and Italian, it would seem to have been a kind of bagpipe, the use of which was known from remote antiquity in Persia, Egypt and Phœnicia.

It would have been better translated ' sackbut ' ; and the passage read thus ' Harp (sebeka) ; dulcimer (psanterin) ; bagpipe (symphonia).' [5]   E. J. H.

SYMPHONIC POEM (Fr. poème symphonique ; Ger. sinfonische Dichtung). The phrase was the happy invention of Liszt as the general title for a series of orchestral works the production of which occupied the decade 1850–60 (see LISZT, LIST OF WORKS). It has become a generic term used to describe orchestral works generally of large design but not according with any of the accepted categories of musical form, and having some reference to a programme (see PROGRAMME MUSIC ; also SYMPHONY, subsection SPOHR'S PROGRAMME SYMPHONIES) more or less governing the style and course of the music.

Liszt's connotation of the term was more definite than this. Eight of the series refer to actual poems ; ' Ce qu'on entend sur la montagne ' after a poem of Victor Hugo, ' Tasso ' after Byron's Lament of Tasso, ' Les Préludes ' after one of Lamartine's Méditations poétiques, are typical. His intention was to produce a musical paraphrase of the thought, feeling and colour of the poem, to say in the language of music what the poet says in that of words. How far he succeeded or could succeed is immaterial here. The point is that to him the symphonic poem meant a certain tone of mind

[1] History of the Pianoforte. (Novello, 1897.) A. J. Hipkins, pp. 43-6.
[2] Schlick, Spiegel des Orgelmacher. (1511.) p. 101.
[3] Praetorius, Reprint, pp. 72-3.
[4] Cocleus, Krebs, Tetrachordum Musices. (Nuremberg, 1512.) Cap. 9.
[5] The Bible, Helps to the Study of, n.d. Musical Instruments, p. 111.

in the composer. He laid no claim to the origination of a new ' Form.' His emphasis laid on certain characteristics of style, such as the use of representative themes and rhythmical transformations of themes, was merely the adaptation to his own needs of methods which Berlioz had used in the programme symphony and Wagner was even then developing in the music drama. His position was not that form was unimportant but that the poetic impulse of the composer could be trusted to produce a satisfactory form according to the needs of each individual case ; in fact, that form should be conditioned by content not by a prearranged pattern.

The example of Liszt had the most immediate effect on his contemporaries. His own contributions to the type were still incomplete when Smetana, the champion of Czech nationalism, produced his series of six symphonic poems, ' Mà Vlast ' (My Country). The nationalistic movement, characteristic of the second half of the 19th century, and pursued with peculiar eagerness among the Slavonic races of Europe, favoured the extension of the ideas set on foot by Liszt. Works descriptive of the life and scenery, the folklore, dance and song, of the several countries flowed from innumerable pens and were given the title (not necessarily by the composers themselves) of ' Symphonic Poem.' They ranged geographically from Borodin's ' Steppes of Central Asia ' to Saint-Saens's ' Africa ' (PF. and orch.), and in later times from Delius's ' Appalacchia,' to Sibelius's ' Finlandia,' and embraced every type and style of orchestral fantasia or rhapsody which attempted the record in music of impressions from without.

Two composers of the generation after Liszt stand out for their treatment of the symphonic poem apart from national sentiment or scenic representation. Tchaikovsky in Russia and César Franck in Paris have little in common in temperament or musical style, but they were alike in this, that each contributed something essential to the renaissance of the symphony proper, and each also worked on the lines of the symphonic poem. Tchaikovsky in ' Hamlet,' ' Romeo and Juliet,' and ' Francesca da Rimini ' seized on the central features of dramatic situations and characterised them in strong theatrical colouring. Franck in ' Les Éolides,' ' Le Chasseur maudit ' and ' Les Djinns ' (PF. and orch.), with less concern for the external effects and indeed much less power of visualising them objectively, allowed his symphonic style to be dominated by the mood of the poem chosen. The symphonic poems of Tchaikovsky are propelled forward by the human personality and the clash of incident ; in Franck the influence of the poetic idea is felt more generally in texture and colouring. The application by Franck of the term ' poème symphonique' to certain choral works with words, notably 'Rédemption' and 'Psyché,' must here be noted.

The composer most acclaimed as the direct successor of Liszt is Richard Strauss, whose period of symphonic poems, usually called by him *Tondichtung* (tone-poem, a term practically synonymous), ranges from 'Don Juan' (1889) to 'Ein Heldenleben' (1899). The first of these, 'after Lenau,' begins by preserving something of the literary flavour of Liszt's attitude, but it is noticeable that Strauss's tone-poems become increasingly objective in the point of view—till at last poetry gives way to prose in the details of the 'Sinfonia domestica' (1904), which, as its title suggests, belongs more to the category of the programme symphony than to that of the symphonic poem. Strauss brought to his task a full equipment; the power to amalgamate both the subjective and the objective views of his literary matter in his musical presentation; he used a richer orchestral palette than any of his predecessors and evolved a technical style for his purpose which was very much more supple than anything known to his predecessors. 'Don Juan,' 'Tod und Verklärung,' 'Also sprach Zarathustra' probe deeply into the psychological situations propounded by these subjects. In two of the series, 'Till Eulenspiegel' and 'Don Quixote' (violoncello and orch.), it is noteworthy that he declares allegiance to two of the classical forms, the rondo and variations, respectively. The general structure of 'Ein Heldenleben' in a series of movements contrasted in mood and rhythm, unified by identity of theme, shows him tending more towards the plan of the programme symphony. It also shows him creating his own images, as Berlioz had done in the 'Symphonie fantastique,' no longer projecting himself into the mind of poet or of dramatist, which process seems to be the true *raison d'être* of the symphonic poem.

Among the innumerable symphonic poems produced by English composers of the post-Victorian generation [1] it will suffice to name two examples, Bantock's 'Fifine at the Fair' (produced 1912) and Elgar's 'Falstaff' (produced 1913). Neither bears the words 'symphonic poem' or 'tone-poem' on its title-page; the one is described as 'an orchestral drama with a prologue,' the other as 'symphonic study, with two interludes.' Both, however, accord precisely with that tone of mind which Liszt indicated in his adoption of the term. The one takes a poem of Robert Browning, the other the character of 'Falstaff' as represented by Shakespeare in *Henry IV.*, and both are concerned rather with the psychology of their several subjects than with the portrayal of incident.

[1] The first to use the term was William WALLACE (*q.v.*).

The dates from Liszt to Elgar seem to outline an historical period of the prevalence of the symphonic poem. While many later specimens appear there has been a distinct reaction in modern music from the tone of mind which generated works of the type, and the tendency to reassert the independence of purely instrumental music from association with literary ideas is one of the marked characteristics of the present day (1926).

BIBL.—E. NEWMAN, *Musical Studies* (Programme Music, 1905); ZADOR-ZUCKER, *Über Wesen und Form der sinfonischen Dichtung. Beiträge zu ihrer Entwicklungsgeschichte von Liszt bis Strauss* (Münster Dissertation, 1922).   C.

SYMPHONY (Lat. *sinfonia*; Ger. *Sinfonie*; Fr. *symphonie*). The terms used in connexion with any branch of art are commonly very vague and indefinite in the early stages of its history, and are applied without much discrimination to different things. In course of time men consequently find themselves in difficulties, and try, as far as their opportunities go, to limit the definition of the terms, and to confine them at least to things which are not obviously antagonistic. In the end, however, the process of sifting is rather guided by chance and external circumstances than determined by the meaning which theorists see to be the proper one; and the result is that the final meaning adopted by the world in general is frequently not only distinct from that which the original employers of the word intended, but also in doubtful conformity with its derivation.

In the case of the word 'symphony,' as with 'sonata,' the meaning now accepted happens to be in very good accordance with its derivation, but it is considerably removed from the meaning which was originally attached to the word. It seems to have been used at first in a very general and comprehensive way, to express any portions of music or passages whatever which were thrown into relief as purely instrumental in works in which the chief interest was centred upon the voice or voices. Thus, in the operas, cantatas and masses of the early part of the 17th century, the voices had the most important part of the work to do, and the instruments' chief business was to supply simple forms of harmony as accompaniment. If there were any little portions which the instruments played without the voices, these were indiscriminately called symphonies; and under the same head were included such more particular forms as overtures and ritornelli. The first experimentalists in harmonic music generally dispensed with such independent instrumental passages altogether. For instance, most if not all of the cantatas of Cesti and Rossi [2] are devoid of either instrumental introduction or ritornel; and the same appears to have been the case with many of the operas of that time. There were, however, a few independent little instrumental movements even

[2] MSS. in the Christ Church Library, Oxford.

in the earliest operas. Peri's 'Euridice,' which stands almost at the head of the list (having been performed at Florence in 1600, as part of the festival in connexion with the marriage of Henri IV of France and Marie de' Medici), contains a 'Sinfonia' for three flutes, which has a definite form of its own and is very characteristic of the time. The use of short instrumental passages, such as dances and introductions and ritornels, when once fairly begun, increased rapidly. Monteverdi, who followed close upon Peri, made some use of them, and as the century grew older they became a more and more important element in dramatic works, especially operas. The indiscriminate use of the word 'symphony' to denote the passages of introduction to airs and recitatives, etc., lasted for a very long while, and got so far stereotyped in common usage that it was even applied to the instrumental portions of airs, etc., when played by a single performer. As an example may be quoted the following passage from a letter of Mozart's— 'Sie [meaning STRINASACCHI, q.v.] spielt keine Note ohne Empfindung; sogar bei den Sinfonien spielte sie alles mit Expression,' etc.[1]

With regard to this use of the term, it is not necessary to do more than point out the natural course by which the meaning began to be restricted. Lully, Alessandro Scarlatti and other great composers of operas in the 17th century, extended the appendages of airs to proportions relatively considerable, but there was a limit beyond which such dependent passages could not go. The independent instrumental portions, on the other hand, such as overtures or toccatas, or groups of ballet tunes, were in different circumstances, and could be expanded to a very much greater extent; and as they grew in importance the name 'symphony' came by degrees to have a more special significance. The small instrumental appendages to the various airs and so forth were still symphonies in a general sense, but the symphony *par excellence* was the introductory movement; and the more it grew in importance the more distinctive was this application of the term.

GENESIS FROM THE OPERATIC OVERTURE.— The earliest steps in the development of this portion of the opera are chiefly important as attempts to establish some broad principle of form; which for some time amounted to little more than the balance of short divisions, of slow and quick movement alternately. Lully is credited with the invention of one form, which came ultimately to be known as the 'Ouverture à la manière française.' The principles of this form, as generally understood, amounted to no more than the succession of

a slow solid movement to begin with, followed by a quicker movement in a lighter style, and another slow movement, not so grave in character as the first, to conclude with. Lully himself was not rigidly consistent in the adoption of this form. In some cases, as in 'Persée,' 'Thésée' and 'Bellérophon,' there are two divisions only—the characteristic grave opening movement and a short free fugal quick movement. 'Proserpine,' 'Phaéton,' 'Alceste' and the Ballet piece, 'Le Triomphe de l'amour,' are characteristic examples of the complete model. These have a grave opening, which is repeated, and then the livelier central movement, which is followed by a division marked *lentement*; and the last two divisions are repeated in full together. A few examples are occasionally to be met with by less famous composers than Lully, which show how far the adoption of this form of overture or symphony became general in a short time. An opera called 'Venus and Adonis,' by Desmarets, of which there is a copy in the Library of the R.C.M., has the overture in this form. 'Amadis de Grèce,' by Des Touches, has the same, as far as can be judged from the character of the divisions; 'Albion and Albanius,' by Grabu, which was licensed for publication in England by Roger Lestrange in 1687, has clearly the same, and looks like an imitation direct from Lully; and the 'Venus and Adonis' by Dr. John Blow, yet again the same. So the model must have been extensively appreciated. The most important composer, however, who followed Lully in this matter, was Alessandro Scarlatti, who certainly varied and improved on the model both as regards the style and the form. In his opera of 'Flavio Cuniberto,'[2] for instance, the 'Sinfonia avanti l' opera' begins with a division marked *grave*, which is mainly based on simple canonical imitations, but has also broad expanses of contrasting keys. The style, for the time, is noble and rich, and very superior to Lully's. The second division is a lively allegro, and the last a moderately quick minuet in 6–8 time. The 'Sinfonia' to his serenata 'Venere, Adone, Amore,' similarly has a Largo to begin with, a Presto in the middle, and a movement, not defined by a *tempo*, but clearly of moderate quickness, to end with. This form of 'Sinfonia' survived for a long while, and was expanded at times by a succession of dance movements, for which also Lully supplied examples, and Handel at a later time more familiar types; but for the history of the modern symphony, a form which was distinguished from the other as the 'Italian Overture,' ultimately became of much greater importance.

This form appears in principle to be the exact opposite of the French overture; it was similarly divided into three movements, but

1 'She does not play a note without feeling, and even in the symphonies played all with expression.' The same use of the name for the ritornelli between the verses of a song was common in England down to the middle of the 19th century.

2 MS. in Christ Church Library.

the first and last were quick and the central one slow. Who the originator of this form was it seems now impossible to decide; it certainly came into vogue very soon after the French overture, and quickly supplanted it to a great extent. Certain details in its structure were better defined than in the earlier form, and the balance and distribution of characteristic features were alike freer and more comprehensive. The first allegro was generally in a square time and of solid character; the central movement aimed at expressiveness, and the last was a quick movement of relatively light character, generally in some combination of three feet. The history of its early development seems to be wrapped in obscurity, but from the moment of its appearance it has the traits of the modern orchestral symphony, and composers very soon obtained a remarkable degree of mastery over the form. It must have first come into definite acceptance about the end of the 17th or the beginning of the 18th century; and by the middle of the latter it had become almost a matter of course. Operas, and similar works, by the most conspicuous composers of this time, in very great numbers, have the same form of overture. For instance, the two distinct versions of 'La clemenza di Tito' by Hasse, 'Catone in Utica' by Leonardo Vinci (1728), the 'Hypermnestra,' 'Artaserse' and others of Perez, Piccinni's 'Didone,' Jommelli's 'Betulia liberata,' Sacchini's 'Œdipus,' Galuppi's 'Il mondo alla reversa'—produced the year before Haydn wrote his first symphony—and Adam Hiller's 'Lisuart und Dariolette,' 'Die Liebe auf dem Lande,' 'Der Krieg,' etc. And if a more conclusive proof of the general acceptance of the form were required, it would be found in the fact that Mozart adopted it in his boyish operas, 'La finta semplice' and 'Lucio Silla.'

With the general adoption of the form came also a careful development of the internal structure of each separate movement, and also a gradual improvement both in the combination and treatment of the instruments employed. Lully and Alessandro Scarlatti were for the most part satisfied with strings, which the former used crudely enough, but the latter with a good deal of perception of tone and appropriateness of style; sometimes with the addition of wind instruments. Early in the 18th century several wind instruments, such as oboes, bassoons, horns, trumpets and flutes, were added, though not often all together; and they served, for the most part, chiefly to strengthen the strings and give contrasting degrees of full sound rather than contrasts of colour and tone. (See ORCHESTRATION.) Equally important was the rapid improvement which took place simultaneously in internal structure; and in this case the development followed that of certain other departments of

musical form. In fact the progress of the 'Sinfonia avanti l' opera' in this respect was chiefly parallel to the development of the clavier sonata, which at this time was beginning to attain to clearness of outline and a certain maturity of style.

It will not be necessary here to repeat what has elsewhere been discussed from different points of view in the articles on FORM, SONATA and SUITE; but it is important to realise that in point of time the form of this 'Sinfonia avanti l' opera' did not lag behind in definition of outline and mastery of treatment; and it might be difficult to decide in which form (whether orchestral or clavier) the important detail first presents itself of defining the first and second principal sections by subjects decisively distinct. A marked improvement in various respects appears about the time when the symphony first began to be generally played apart from the opera; and the reasons for this are obvious. In the first place, as long as it was merely the appendage to a drama, less stress was laid upon it; and, what is more to the point, it is recorded that audiences were not by any means particularly attentive to the instrumental portion of the work. The description given of the behaviour of the public at some of the most important theatres in Europe in the middle of the 18th century seems to correspond to the descriptions which are given of the audience at the Italian Operas in England in the latter half of the 19th. Burney, in the account of his tour, refers to this more than once. In the first volume he says:

'The music at the theatres in Italy seems but an excuse for people to assemble together, their attention being chiefly placed on play and conversation, even during the performance of a serious opera.'

In another place he describes the card-tables, and the way in which the 'people of quality' reserved their attention for a favourite air or two, or the performance of a favourite singer. The rest, including the overture, they did not regard as of much consequence, and hence the composers had but little inducement to put out the best of their powers. It may have been partly on this account that they took very little pains to connect these overtures or symphonies with the opera, either by character or feature. They allowed it to become almost a settled principle that they should be independent in matter; and consequently there was very little difficulty in accepting them as independent instrumental pieces. It naturally followed as it did later with another form of overture. The 'Symphonies' which had more attractive qualities were played apart from the operas, in concerts; and the precedent being thereby established, the step to writing independent works on similar lines was but short; and it was natural that, as undivided attention would now be given to them, and they were no more in a secondary position in connexion with the opera, composers should take more pains both in the structure and in the choice of their musical material. The symphony had, however, reached a considerable pitch of development before the emancipation took place ; and this development was connected with the progress of certain other musical forms besides the sonata, already referred to.

INFLUENCE OF OTHER FORMS.—It will accordingly be convenient, before proceeding farther with the direct history of the symphony, to consider some of the more important of these early branches of musical art. In the early harmonic times the relationships of nearly all the different branches of composition were close. The symphony was related even to the early madrigals, through the 'Sonate da Chiesa,' which adopted the canzona or instrumental version of the madrigal as a second movement. It was also closely related to the early fantasias, as the earliest experiments in instrumental music, in which some of the technical necessities of that department were grappled with. It was directly connected with the vocal portions of the early operas, such as airs and recitatives, and derived from them many of the mechanical forms of cadence and harmony which for a long time were a necessary part of its form. The solo clavier suite had also something to do with it, but not so much as might be expected. As has been pointed out elsewhere, the suite-form, being very simple in its principle, attained to definition very early, while the sonata-form, which characterised the richest period of harmonic music, was still struggling in elementary stages. The ultimate basis of the suite-form is a contrast of dance-tunes ; but in the typical early symphony the dance-tunes are almost invariably avoided. When the symphony was expanded by the addition of the minuet and trio, a bond of connexion seemed to be established; but still this bond was not at all a vital one, for the minuet is one of the least characteristic elements of the suite-form proper, being clearly of less ancient lineage and type than the allemande, courante, sarabande or gigue, or even the gavotte and bourrée, which were classed with it, as ' Intermezzi ' or ' Galanterien.' The form of the clavier suite movements was in fact too inelastic to admit of such expansion and development as was required in the orchestral works, and the type did not supply the characteristic technical qualities which would be of service in their development. The position of Bach's orchestral suites was somewhat different ; and it appears that he himself called them overtures. Dehn, in his preface to the first edition printed, says that the separate MS. parts in the Bach archives at Hamburg, from which he took that in C, have the distinctive characteristics of the handwriting of John Sebastian, and have

for title ' Ouverture pour 2 violons,' etc. ; and that another MS., probably copied from these, has the title ' Suite pour orchestre.' This throws a certain light upon Bach's position. It is obvious that in several departments of instrumental music he took the French for his models rather than the Italians. In the suite he followed Couperin, and in the overture he also followed French models. These therefore appear as attempts to develop an independent orchestral work analogous to the symphony, upon the basis of a form which had the same reason for existence and the same general purpose as the Italian overture, but a distinctly different general outline. Their chief connexion with the actual development of the modern symphony lies in the treatment of the instruments ; for all experiments, even on different lines, if they have a common quality or principle, must react upon one another in those respects.

Another branch of art which had close connexion with the early symphonies was the concerto. Works under this name were not by any means invariably meant to be show pieces for solo instruments, as modern concertos are ; and sometimes the name was used as almost synonymous with symphony (see CONCERTO GROSSO). The earliest concertos seem to have been works in which groups of ' solo ' and ' ripieno ' instruments were used, chiefly to obtain contrasts of fullness of tone. For instance, a set of six concertos by Alessandro Scarlatti, for two violins and violoncello, ' soli,' and two violins, tenor and bass, ' ripieni,' present no distinction of style between one group and the other. The accompanying instruments for the most part merely double the solo parts, and leave off either to lessen the sound here and there, or because the passages happen to go a little higher than usual, or to be a little difficult for the average violin-players of that time. When the intention is to vary the quality of sound as well, the element of what is called instrumentation is introduced, and this is one of the earliest phases of that element which can be traced in music. The order of movements and the style of them are generally after the manner of the ' Sonate da Chiesa,' and therefore do not present any close analogy with the subject of this article. But very soon after the time of Corelli and Alessandro Scarlatti the form of the Italian overture was adopted for concertos, and about the same time they began to show traces of becoming show-pieces for great performers. Allusions to the performance of concertos by great violin-players in the churches form a familiar feature in the musical literature of the 18th century, and the three-movement form (to all intents exactly like that of the symphonies) seems to have been adopted early. This evidently points to the fact that this form appealed to the instincts of composers generally, as the most promising for free expression of their musical thoughts. It may seem curious that J. S. Bach, who followed French models in some important departments of instrumental music, should exclusively have followed Italian models in this. But in reality it appears to have been a matter of chance with him; he always followed the best models which came to his hand. In this department the Italians excelled; and Bach therefore followed them, and left the most important early specimens of this kind remaining—almost all in the three-movement form, which was becoming the set order for symphonies. Setting aside those specially imitated from Vivaldi, there are at least twenty concertos by him for all sorts of solo instruments and combinations of solo instruments in this same form. It cannot therefore be doubted that some of the development of the symphony-form took place in this department. But Bach never to any noticeable extent yielded to the tendency to break the movements up into sections with corresponding tunes; and this distinguishes his work in a very marked manner from that of the generation of composers who followed him. His art belongs in reality to a different stratum from that which produced the greater forms of abstract instrumental music.

It is probable that his form of art could not, without some modification, have produced the great orchestral symphonies. In order to get to these, composers had to go to a different, and for some time a decidedly lower, level. It was much the same process as had been gone through before. After Palestrina a backward move was necessary to make it possible to arrive at the art of Bach and Handel. After Bach men had to take up a lower line in order to get to Beethoven. In the latter case it was necessary to go through the elementary stages of defining the various contrasting sections of a movement, and finding that form of harmonic treatment which admitted the great effects of colour or varieties of tone in the mass, as well as in the separate lines of the counterpoint. Bach's position was so immensely high that several generations had to pass before men were able to follow on his lines and adopt his principles in harmonic music. The generation that followed him showed scarcely any trace of his influence. Even before he had passed away the new tendencies of music were strongly apparent, and much of the elementary work of the modern sonata-form of art had been done on different lines from his own.

THE 18TH-CENTURY TYPE.—The 'Sinfonia avanti l' opera' was clearly by this time sufficiently independent and complete to be appreciated without the opera, and without either name or programme to explain its meaning; and within a very short period the demand for these sinfonias became very great. Burney's tours in search of materials for his History, in France, Italy, Holland and Germany, were made in 1770 and 1772, before Haydn had written any of his greater symphonies, and while Mozart was still a boy. His allusions to independent 'symphonies' are very frequent. Among those whose works he mentions with most favour are Stamitz, Emanuel Bach, Christian Bach and Abel. Works of the kind by these composers and many others of note are to be seen in great numbers in sets of partbooks in the British Museum.[1] These furnish most excellent materials for judging of the status of the symphony in the early stages of its independent existence. The two most important points which they illustrate are the development of instrumentation and the definition of form. They appear to have been generally written in eight parts. Most of them are scored for two violins, viola and bass; two hautboys, or two flutes, and two 'cors de chasse.' This is the case in the six symphonies of op. 3 of John Christian Bach; the six of Abel's op. 10, the six of Stamitz's op. 9, op. 13 and op. 16; also in a set of 'Overtures in 8 parts' by Arne, which must have been early in the field, as the licence from George II., printed in full at the beginning of the first violin part, is dated January 1740/41. The same orchestration is found in many symphonies by Galuppi, Ditters, Schwindl and others. Wagenseil, who must have been the oldest of this group of composers (having been born in the 17th century, within six years after Handel, Scarlatti and Bach), wrote several quite in the characteristic harmonic style, 'à 4 parties obligées avec cors de chasse ad libitum.' The treatment of the instruments in these early examples is rather crude and stiff. The violins are almost always playing, and the hautboys or flutes are only used to reinforce them at times as the 'ripieni' instruments did in the early concertos, while the horns serve to hold on the harmonies. The first stages of improvement are noticeable in such details as the independent treatment of the strings. In the 'symphonies before the opera' the violas were cared for so little that in many cases [2] not more than half-a-dozen bars are written in, all the rest being merely 'col basso.' As examples of this in works of more or less illustrious writers may be mentioned the 'Sinfonias' to Jommelli's 'Passione' and 'Betulia liberata,' Sacchini's 'Œdipus,' and Sarti's 'Giulio Sabino.' One of the many honours attributed to Stamitz by his admiring contemporaries was that he made the violas independent of the basses. This may seem a trivial detail, but it is only by such details, and the way in which

1 See also D.D.T. (second series) for examples by Stamitz and other members of the Mannheim School.
2 It is notorious that Mozart gave fuller parts to the second violin because of the incompetence of the viola-players.

they struck contemporary writers, that the character of the gradual progress in instrumental composition can now be understood.

The general outlines of the form were extremely regular. The three movements as above described were almost invariable, the first being a vigorous broad allegro, the second the sentimental slow movement and the third the lively vivace. The progress of internal structure is at first chiefly noticeable in the first movement. In the early examples this is always condensed as much as possible, the balance of subject is not very clearly realisable, and there is hardly ever a double bar or repeat of the first half of the movement. The divisions of key, the short 'working-out' portion and the recapitulation are generally present, but not pointedly defined. Examples of this condition of things are supplied by some MS. symphonies by Paradisi in the Fitzwilliam Museum at Cambridge, which in other respects possess excellent and characteristically modern traits. The first thing attained seems to have been the relative definition and balance of the two subjects. In Stamitz, Abel, J. C. Bach and Wagenseil, this is already commonly met with. The following examples from the first movement of the fifth symphony of Stamitz's op. 9 illustrate both the style and the degree of contrast between the two principal subjects.

1st subject.

2nd subject.

etc.

The style is a little heavy, and the motion constrained, but the general character is solid and dignified. The last movements of this period are curiously suggestive of some familiar examples of a maturer time; very gay and

obvious, and very definite in outline. The following is very characteristic of Abel:

etc.

It is a noticeable fact in connexion with the genealogy of these works, that they are almost as frequently entitled 'overture' as 'symphony'; sometimes the same work is called by the one name outside and the other in; and this is the case also with some of the earlier and slighter symphonies of Haydn, which must have made their appearance about this period. One further point which it is of importance to note is that in some of Stamitz's symphonies the complete form of the mature period is found. One in D is most complete in every respect. The first movement is allegro with double bars and repeats in regular binary form; the second is an andante in G, the third a minuet and trio, and the fourth a presto. Another in E♭ (which is called No. 7 in the partbooks) and another in F (not definable) have also the minuet and trio. A few others by Schwindl and Ditters have the same, but it is impossible to get even approximately to the date of their production, and therefore little inference can be framed upon the circumstance, beyond the fact that composers were beginning to recognise the fourth movement as a desirable ingredient.

THE STYLE OF C. P. E. BACH.—Another composer who precedes Haydn in time as well as in style is Emanuel Bach. He was his senior in years, and began writing symphonies in 1741, when Haydn was only nine years old. His most important symphonies were produced in 1776; while Haydn's most important examples were not produced till after 1790. In style Emanuel Bach stands singularly alone, at least in his finest examples. It looks almost as if he purposely avoided the form which by 1776 must have been familiar to the musical world. It has been shown that the binary form was employed by some of his contemporaries in their orchestral works, but he seems determinedly to avoid it in the first movements of the works of that year. His object seems to have been to produce striking and clearly outlined passages, and to balance and contrast them one with another according to his fancy, and with little regard to any systematic distribution of the successions of key. The boldest and most striking subject is the first of the symphony in D:

The opening passages of that in E♭ are hardly less emphatic. They have little connexion with the tendencies of his contemporaries, but seem in every respect an experiment on independent lines, in which the interest depends upon the vigour of the thoughts and the unexpected turns of the modulations; and the result is certainly rather fragmentary and disconnected. The slow movement is commonly connected with the first and last either by a special transitional passage, or by a turn of modulation and a half-close. It is short and dependent in its character, but graceful and melodious. The last is much more systematic in structure than the first; sometimes in definite binary form, as was the case with the early violin sonatas. In orchestration and general style of expression these works seem immensely superior to the other early symphonies which have been described. They are scored for horns, flutes, oboi, fagotto, strings, with a figured bass for 'cembalo,' which in the symphonies previously noticed does not always appear. There is an abundance of unison and octave passages for the strings, but there is also good free writing, and contrasts between wind and strings; the wind being occasionally left quite alone. All the instruments come in occasionally for special employment, and considering the proportions of the orchestras of the time Bach's effects must have been generally clear and good. The following is a good specimen of his scoring of an ordinary full passage:

CHARACTERISTICS OF HAYDN AND MOZART.

—It has sometimes been said that Haydn was chiefly influenced by Emanuel Bach, and Mozart by John Christian Bach. At the present time, and in relation to symphonies, it is easier to understand the latter case than the former. In both cases the influence is more likely to be traced in clavier works than in those for orchestra. For Haydn's style and treatment of form bear far more resemblance to most of the other composers whose works have been referred to, than to Emanuel Bach. There are certain kinds of forcible expression and ingenious turns of modulation which Haydn may have learnt from him; but their best orchestral works seem to belong to quite distinct families. Haydn's first symphony was written in 1759 for Count Morzin. It is said by Pohl [1] to be ' a small work in three movements for two violins, viola, bass, two oboes and two horns' [2] from which particulars it would appear to correspond exactly in externals to the examples above described of Abel and J. C. Bach, etc. In the course of the next few years he added many more ; most of which appear to have been slight and of no great historical importance, while the few which present peculiarities are so far isolated in those respects that they do not throw much light upon the course of his development, or upon his share in building up the art-form of the symphony. Of such a kind is the movement (dramatic in character, and including long passages of recitative) in the symphony in C, which he wrote as early as 1761.[3] (No. 2.) For, though this kind of movement is found in instrumental works of an earlier period, its appearance in such a manner in a symphony is too rare to have any special historical bearings. The course of his development was gradual and regular. He seems to have been content with steadily improving the edifice of his predecessors and with few exceptions to have followed their lines. A great deal is frequently attributed to his connexion with the complete musical establishment which Prince Esterhazy set up at his great palace at Esterház ; where Haydn certainly had opportunities which have been the lot of scarcely any other composer who ever lived. He is described as making experiments in orchestration and ringing the bell for the band to come and try them ; and, though this may not be absolutely true in fact, there can scarcely be a doubt that the very great improvements which he effected in every department of orchestration may to a great extent be attributed to the facilities for testing his works which he enjoyed. At the same time, the really important portion of his compositions were not produced till his patron, Prince Nicolaus Esterhazy, was dead and the musical establishment broken up ; nor, it must be remembered, till after that strange and important episode in Haydn's life, the rapid flitting of Mozart across the scene. When Haydn wrote his first symphony, Mozart was only three years old ; and Mozart died in the very year in which the famous Salomon concerts in London, for which Haydn wrote nearly all his finest symphonies, began. Mozart's work, therefore, comes between Haydn's lighter period and his greatest achievements ; and his symphonies are in some respects prior to Haydn's, and certainly had an effect upon his later works of all kinds.

Mozart's authentic symphonies are numbered at 39.[4] The first, in E♭ (K 16), was written in London in 1764, when he was 8 years old, and only five years after Haydn wrote his first. It was on the same pattern as those which have been fully described above, being in three movements and scored for the usual set of instruments, viz. two violins, viola, bass, two oboes and two horns. Three more followed in close succession, in one of which clarinets are introduced instead of oboes, and a bassoon is added to the usual group of eight instruments. In these works striking originality of purpose or style is hardly to be looked for, and it was not for some time that Mozart's powers in instrumental music reached a pitch of development which is historically important ; but it is nevertheless astonishing to see how early he developed a free and even rich style in managing his orchestral resources. With regard to the character of these and all but a few of the rest it is necessary to keep in mind that a symphony at that time was a very much less important matter than it became fifty years later. The manner in which symphonies were poured out, in sets of six and otherwise, by numerous composers during the latter half of the 18th century, puts utterly out of the question the loftiness of aim and purpose which has become a necessity since the early years of the 19th century. They were all rather slight works on familiar lines, with which for the time being composers and public were alike quite content ; and neither Haydn nor Mozart in their early specimens seem to have specially exerted themselves.

The general survey of Mozart's symphonies presents a certain number of facts which are worth noting for their bearing upon the history of this form of art. The second symphony he wrote (K. 17) had a minuet and trio ; but it is hardly possible that he can have regarded this as an important point, since he afterwards wrote seventeen others without them ; and these spread over the whole period of his activity, for even in that which he wrote at Prague in 1786 (K. 504), and which is last but three in the whole series, the minuet and trio are absent. Besides this fact, which at once connects them with the examples by other composers previously discussed, there is the yet more noticeable one that more than twenty of the series are written for the same peculiar little group of instruments, viz. the four strings, a pair of oboes or flutes, and a pair of horns. His use of clarinets in the symphony only begins [5] with the Paris Symphony in D (K. 297) and subsequently is exceedingly sparing, Mozart having added clarinet parts to the score of that in G minor (K. 550). Even bassoons are not common ; the most frequent addition to the little nucleus of oboes or flutes and horns being trumpets and drums. The

1 *Joseph Haydn*, vol. i. p. 284 (1875).
2 Not in Mandyczewski's list. See HAYDN, Vol. II. p. 585.
3 Pohl's *Haydn* pp. 287, 397.

4 See MOZART, List of Works, Series 8.
5 The early symphony in E♭ (K. 18) with clarinets is not now regarded as authentic.

two which are most fully scored are the Parisian, in D, just alluded to, which was written in 1778, and that in E♭, which was written in Vienna in 1788, and stands first in the famous triad. These facts explain to a certain extent how it was possible to write such an extraordinary number in so short a space of time. Mozart's most continuously prolific period in this branch of art seems to have been when he had returned to Salzburg in 1771 ; for between July in that year and the beginning of 1773 it appears to be proved that he produced no fewer than fourteen. But this feat is fairly surpassed in another sense by the production of the last three in three successive months, June, July and Aug. 1788 ; since the musical calibre of these is so immensely superior to that of the earlier ones.

One detail of comparison between Mozart's ways and Haydn's is curious. Haydn began to use introductory adagios very early, and used them so often that they became quite a characteristic feature in his plan. Mozart, on the other hand, did not use one until his symphony in C (K. 425), written in 1783. What was the origin of Haydn's employment of them is uncertain. The causes that have been suggested are not altogether satisfactory. In the orthodox form of symphony, as written by the numerous composers of his early days, the opening adagio is not found. He may possibly have observed that it was a useful factor in a certain class of overtures, and then have used it as an experiment in symphonies, and finding it answer, may have adopted the expedient generally in succeeding works of the kind. It seems likely that Mozart adopted it from Haydn, as its first appearance (in the symphony which is believed to have been composed at Linz for Count Thun) coincides with the period in which he is considered to have been first strongly influenced by Haydn.

The influence of these two great composers upon one another is extremely interesting and curious, more especially as it did not take effect till comparatively late in their artistic careers. They both began working in the general direction of their time, under the influences which have been already referred to. In the department of symphony each was considerably influenced after a time by a special circumstance of his life ; Haydn by the appointment to Esterház before alluded to, and the opportunities it afforded him of orchestral experiment ; and Mozart by his stay at Mannheim in 1777. For it appears most likely that the superior abilities of the Mannheim orchestra for dealing with purely instrumental music, and the traditions of Stamitz, who had there effected his share in the history of the symphony, opened Mozart's eyes to the possibilities of orchestral performance, and encouraged him to a freer style of composition

and more elaborate treatment of the orchestra than he had up to that time attempted. The Mannheim band had in fact been long considered the finest in Europe ; and in certain things, such as attention to *nuances* (which in early orchestral works had been looked upon as either unnecessary or out of place), they and their conductors had been important pioneers ; and thus Mozart must certainly have had his ideas on such heads a good deal expanded. The qualities of the symphony produced in Paris (K. 297) early in the next year were probably the first-fruits of these circumstances ; and it happens that while this symphony is the first of his which has maintained a definite position among the important landmarks of art, it is also the first in which he uses orchestral forces approaching to those commonly employed for symphonies since the latter part of the 18th century.

Both Haydn and Mozart, in the course of their respective careers, made decided progress in managing the orchestra, both as regards the treatment of individual instruments, and the distribution of the details of musical interest among them. It has been already pointed out that one of the earliest expedients by which contrast of effect was attempted by writers for combinations of instruments was the careful distribution of portions for 'solo' and 'ripieno' instruments, as illustrated by Scarlatti's and later concertos. In J. S. Bach's treatment of the orchestra the same characteristic is familiar. The long duets for oboes, flutes or bassoons, and the solos for horn or violin, or viola da gamba, which continue throughout whole recitatives or arias, all have this same principle at bottom. Composers had still to learn the free and yet well-balanced management of their string forces, and to attain the mean between the use of wind instruments merely to strengthen the strings and their use as solo instruments in long independent passages. In Haydn's early symphonies the old traditions are most apparent. The balance between the different forces of the orchestra is as yet both crude and obvious. In the symphony called 'Le Matin' (No. 6), for instance, which appears to have been among the earliest, the second violins play with the first, and the violas with the basses to a very marked extent—in the first movement almost throughout. This first movement, again, begins with a solo for flute. The slow movement, which is divided into adagio and andante, has no wind instruments at all, but there is a violin solo throughout the middle portion. In the minuet a contrast is attained by a long passage for wind band alone (as in J. S. Bach's second Bourrée to the 'Ouverture' in C major) ; and the trio consists of a long and elaborate solo for bassoon. Haydn early began experiments in various uses of his orchestra, and his ways of grouping his solo instruments for effect are often curious and original. C. F. Pohl, in his life of him, prints from the MS. parts a charming slow movement from a symphony in B♭ which was probably written in 1766 or 1767. It illustrates in a singular way how Haydn at first endeavoured to obtain a special effect without ceasing to conform to familiar methods of treating his strings. The movement is scored for first and second violins, violas, *solo violoncello* and bass, all ' con sordini.' The first and second violins play in unison throughout, and the violoncello plays the tune with them an octave lower, while the violas play in octaves with the bass all but two or three bars of cadence ; so that in reality there are scarcely ever more than two parts playing at a time. The following example will show the style :

Towards a really free treatment of his forces he seems, however, to have been led on insensibly and by very slow degrees. For over twenty years of symphony-writing the same limited treatment of strings and the same kind of solo passages are commonly to be met with. But there is a growing tendency to make the wind and the lower and inner strings more and more independent, and to individualise the style of each within proportionate bounds. A fine symphony in E minor (No. 44), which appears to date from before 1772, is a good specimen of Haydn's intermediate stage. The strings play almost incessantly throughout, and the wind either doubles the string parts to enrich and reinforce them, or else has long holding notes while the strings play characteristic figures. The passage from the last movement, given in the next column, will serve to illustrate pretty clearly the stage of orchestral expression to which Haydn had at that time arrived.

In the course of the following ten years the progress was slow but steady. Many other composers [1] were writing symphonies besides Haydn and Mozart, and were, like them, improving that branch of art. Unfortunately the difficulty of fixing the dates of their productions is almost insuperable ; and so their greater representatives come to be regarded, not only

[1] The work of Michael Haydn is important. Several of his symphonies were accepted as Mozart's at the time of Köchel's Catalogue.

as giving an epitome of the history of the epoch, but as comprising it in themselves.

Mozart's first specially notable symphony (K. 297) falls in 1778. This was the one which he wrote for Paris after his experiences at Mannheim ; and some of his Mannheim friends who happened to be in Paris with him assisted at the performance. It is in almost every respect a very great advance upon Haydn's E minor symphony, just quoted. The treatment of the instruments is very much freer, and more individually characteristic. It marks an important step in the transition from the kind of symphony in which the music appears to have been conceived almost entirely for violins, with wind subordinate, except in special solo passages, to the kind in which the original conception in respect of subjects, episodes and development, embraced all the forces, including the wind instruments. The first eight bars of Mozart's symphony are sufficient to illustrate the nature of the artistic tendency. In the firm and dignified beginning of the principal subject, the strings, with flutes and bassoons, are all in unison for three bars, and a good body of wind instruments gives the full chord. Then the upper strings are left alone for a couple of bars in octaves, and are accompanied in their short closing phrase by an independent full chord of wind instruments, *piano*. This chord is repeated in the same form of rhythm as that which marks the first bars of the principal subject, and has therefore at once musical sense and relevance, besides supplying the necessary full harmony. In the subsidiary subject by which the first section is carried on, the quick lively passages of the strings are accompanied by short figures for flute and horns, with their own independent musical significance. In the second subject proper, which is derived from this subsidiary, an excellent balance of colour is obtained by pairs of wind instruments in octaves, answering with an independent and very characteristic phrase of their own the group of strings which give out the first part of the subject. The same well-balanced method is observed throughout. In the working out of this movement almost all the instruments have something special and relevant of their own to do, so that it is made to seem as if the conception were exactly apportioned to the forces which were meant to utter it. The same criticisms apply to all the rest of the symphony. The slow movement has beautiful independent figures and phrases for the wind instruments, so interwoven with the body of the movement that they supply necessary elements of colour and fullness of harmony, without appearing either as definite solos or as meaningless holding notes. The fresh and merry last movement has much the same characteristics as the first in the matter of instrumental utterance, and in its working-out section all the forces have, if anything, even more independent work of their own to do, while still supplying their appropriate ingredients to the sum total of sound.

The succeeding ten years saw all the rest of the work Mozart was destined to do in the department of symphony; much of it showing in turn an advance on the Paris symphony, inasmuch as the principles there shown were worked out to greater fulness and perfection, while the musical spirit attained a more definite richness, and escaped farther from the formalism which characterises the previous generation. Among these symphonies the most important are the following: the 'Haffner' (K. 385), which was a modification of a serenade, and had originally more than the usual group of movements; the 'Linz' symphony in C (K. 425); and the last four, the crown of the whole series. The first of these (in D major) was written for Prague in 1786 (K. 504), and was received there with immense favour in Jan. 1787. It appears to be far in advance of all its predecessors in freedom and clearness of instrumentation, in the breadth and musical significance of the subjects, and in richness and balance of form. It is one of the few of Mozart's which open with an adagio, and that, too, of unusual proportions; but it has no minuet and trio. This symphony was in its turn eclipsed by the three great ones in E♭, G minor and C (K. 543, 550, 551), which were composed at Vienna in June, July and Aug. 1788.

These symphonies are almost the first in which certain qualities of musical expression and a certain method in their treatment stand prominent in the manner which was destined to become characteristic of the great works of the early part of the 19th century. Mozart, having mastered the principle upon which the mature art-form of symphony was to be attacked, had greater freedom for the expression of his intrinsically musical ideas, and could emphasise more freely and consistently the typical characteristics which his inspiration led

him to adopt in developing his ideas. It must not, however, be supposed that this principle is to be found for the first time in these works. They find their counterparts in works of Haydn's of a much earlier date; only, inasmuch as the art-form was then less mature, the element of formalism is too strong to admit of the musical or poetical intention being so clearly realised. It is of course impossible to put into words with certainty the inherent characteristics of these or any other later works on the same lines; but that they are felt to have such characteristics is indisputable, and their perfection as works of art, which is so commonly insisted on, could not exist if it were not so. Among the many writers who have tried in some way to describe them, probably the best and most responsible is Otto Jahn. Of the first of the group (K. 543), he says, 'We find the expression of perfect happiness in the charm of euphony' which is one of the marked external characteristics of the whole work.

'The feeling of pride in the consciousness of power shines through the magnificent introduction, while the Allegro expresses the purest pleasure, now in frolicsome joy, now in active excitement, and now in noble and dignified composure. Some shadows appear, it is true, in the Andante, but they only serve to throw into stronger relief the mild serenity of a mind communing with itself and rejoicing in the peace which fills it. This is the true source of the cheerful transport which rules the last movement, rejoicing in its own strength and in the joy of being.'

Whether this is all perfectly true or not is of less consequence than the fact that a consistent and uniform style and object can be discerned through the whole work, and that it admits of an approximate description in words, without either straining or violating familiar impressions.

The second of the great symphonic trilogy— that in G minor (K. 550)—has a still clearer meaning. The contrast with the E♭ is strong, for in no symphony of Mozart's is there so much sadness and regretfulness. This element also accounts for the fact that it is the most modern of his symphonies, and shows most human nature. E. T. A. Hoffmann (writing in a spirit very different from that of Jahn) says of it,

'Love and melancholy breathe forth in purest spirit tones; we feel ourselves drawn with inexpressible longing towards the forms which beckon us to join them in their flight through the clouds to another sphere.'

Jahn agrees in attributing to it a character of sorrow and complaining; and there can hardly be a doubt that the tonality as well as the style, and such characteristic features as occur incidentally, would all favour the idea that Mozart's inspiration took a sad cast, and maintained it so far throughout; so that, notwithstanding the formal passages which occasionally make their appearance at the closes, the whole work may without violation of probability receive a consistent psychological explanation. Even the orchestration seems appropriate from this point of view, since the prevailing effect is far less soft and smooth than that of the previous symphony. A detail of historical interest in connexion with this work is the fact that Mozart originally wrote it without clarinets, and added them afterwards for a performance at which it may be presumed they happened to be specially available. He did this by taking a separate piece of paper and rearranging the oboe parts, sometimes combining the instruments and sometimes distributing the parts between the two, with due regard to their characteristic styles of utterance.

The last of Mozart's symphonies (K. 551) has so obvious and distinctive a character throughout that popular estimation has accepted the definite name 'Jupiter' as conveying the prevalent feeling about it. In this there is far less human sentiment than in the G minor. In fact, Mozart appears to have aimed at something lofty and self-contained, and therefore precluding the shade of sadness which is an element almost indispensable to strong human sympathy. When he descends from this distant height he assumes a cheerful and sometimes playful vein, as in the second principal subject of the first movement, and in the subsidiary or cadence subject that follows it. This may not be altogether in accordance with what is popularly meant by the name 'Jupiter,' though that deity appears to have been capable of a good deal of levity in his time ; but it has the virtue of supplying admirable contrast to the main subjects of the section ; and it is so far in consonance with them that there is no actual reversal of feeling in passing from one to the other. The slow movement has an appropriate dignity which keeps it in character, and reaches, in parts, a considerable degree of passion, which brings it nearer to human sympathy than the other movements. The minuet and the trio again show cheerful serenity, and the last movement, with its elaborate fugal treatment, has a vigorous austerity, which is an excellent balance to the character of the first movement. The scoring, especially in the first and last movements, is fuller than is usual with Mozart, and produces effects of strong and clear sound ; and it is also admirably in character with the spirit of dignity and loftiness which seems to be aimed at in the greater portion of the musical subjects and figures.

In these later symphonies Mozart certainly reached a far higher pitch of art in the department of instrumental music than any hitherto arrived at. The characteristics of his attainments may be described as a freedom of style in the ideas, freedom in the treatment of the various parts of the score, and independence and appropriateness of expression in the management of the various groups of instruments employed. In comparison with the works of his predecessors, and with his own and Haydn's earlier compositions, there is through-

out a most remarkable advance in vitality. The distribution of certain cadences and passages of *tutti* still appear to modern ears formal ; but compared with the immature formalism of expression, even in principal ideas, which was prevalent twenty or even ten years earlier, the improvement is immense. In such structural elements as the development of the ideas, the concise and energetic flow of the music, the distribution and contrast of instrumental tone, and the balance and proportion of sound, these works are generally held to reach a pitch almost unsurpassable from the point of view of technical criticism. Mozart's intelligence and taste, dealing with thoughts as yet undisturbed by strong or passionate emotion, attained a perfection in the sense of pure and directly intelligible art which later times can scarcely hope to see approached.

Haydn's symphonies up to this time cannot be said to equal Mozart's in any respect ; though they show a considerable improvement on the style of treatment and expression in the 'Trauer' or the 'Farewell' Symphonies (Nos. 44, 45). Of those which are better known of about this date are 'La Poule' and 'Letter V' (Nos. 83, 88), which were written (both for Paris) in or about 1786. 'Letter Q,' or the 'Oxford' Symphony (No. 92), which was performed when Haydn received the degree of Doctor of Music from that university, dates from 1788, the same year as Mozart's great triad. 'Letter V' and 'Letter Q' are in his mature style, and thoroughly characteristic in every respect. The orchestration is clear and fresh, though not so sympathetic nor so elastic in its variety as Mozart's ; and the ideas, with all their geniality and directness, are not up to his own highest standard. It is the last twelve, which were written for Salomon after 1790, which have really fixed Haydn's high position as a composer of symphonies ; these became so popular as practically to supersede the numerous works of all his predecessors and contemporaries except Mozart, to the extent of causing them to be almost completely forgotten. This is owing partly to the high pitch of technical skill which he attained, partly to the freshness and geniality of his ideas, and partly to the vigour and daring of harmonic progression which he manifested. He and Mozart together enriched this branch of art to an extraordinary degree, and towards the end of their lives began to introduce far deeper feeling and earnestness into the style than had been customary in early works of the class. The average orchestra had increased in size, and at the same time had gained a better balance of its component elements. Instead of the customary little group of strings and four wind instruments, it had come to comprise, besides the strings, two flutes, two oboes, two bassoons, two horns, two trumpets and drums. To these were occasionally added two clarinets, as in Haydn's last three (the two in D minor and one in E♭ (Nos. 101, 104, 103)), and in one movement of the 'Military' symphony (No. 100). Neither Mozart nor Haydn ever used trombones in symphonies; but uncommon instruments were sometimes employed, as in the 'Military,' in which Haydn used a big drum, a triangle and cymbals.

In his latest symphonies Haydn's treatment of his orchestra agrees in general with the description already given of Mozart's. The bass has attained a free motion of its own; the violas rarely cling in a dependent manner to it, but have their own individual work to do, and the same applies to the second violins, which no longer so often appear merely 'col 1mo.' The wind instruments fill up and sustain the harmonies as completely as in former days; but they cease merely to hold long notes without characteristic features, or slavishly to follow the string parts whenever something livelier is required. They may still play a great deal that is mere doubling, but there is generally method in it; and the musical ideas they express are in a great measure proportioned to their char-

acters and style of utterance. Haydn was rather fond of long passages for wind alone, as in the slow movement of the 'Oxford' symphony, the opening passage of the first allegro of the 'Military' symphony, and the 'working out' of the symphony in C, No. 1 of the Salomon set (No. 97). Solos in a tune-form for wind instruments are also rather more common than in Mozart's works, and in many respects the various elements which go to make up the whole are less assimilated than they are by Mozart. The tunes are generally more definite in their outlines, and stand in less close relation with their context. It appears as if Haydn always retained to the last a strong sympathy with simple people's-tunes; the character of his minuets and trios, and especially of his finales, is sometimes strongly defined in this respect; but his way of expressing them within the limits he chose is extraordinarily finished and acute. It is possible that, as before suggested, he got his taste for surprises in harmonic progression from C. P. E. Bach. His instinct for such things, considering the age he lived in, was very remarkable. The passage below, from his symphony in C, just referred

etc.

to, illustrates several of the above points at once.

The period of Haydn and Mozart is in every respect the principal crisis in the history of the symphony. When they came upon the scene, it was not regarded as a very important form of art. In the good musical centres of those times—and there were many—there was a great demand for symphonies; but the bands for which they were written were small, and appear from the most natural inferences not to have been very efficient or well organised. The standard of performance was evidently rough, and composers could neither expect much attention to *pianos* and *fortes*, nor any ability to grapple with technical difficulties among the players of bass instruments or violas. The audiences were critical in the one sense of requiring good healthy workmanship in the writing of the pieces—in fact much better than they would demand in the present day; but with regard to deep meaning, refinement, poetical intention, or originality, they appear to have cared very little. They wanted to be healthily pleased and entertained, not stirred with deep emotion; and the purposes of composers in those days were consequently not exalted to any high pitch, but were limited to a simple and unpretentious supply, in accordance with demand and opportunity. Haydn was influenced by these considerations till the last. There is always more fun and gaiety in his music than pensiveness or serious reflection. But in developing the technical part of expression, in proportioning the means to the end, and in organising the forces of the orchestra, what he did was of the utmost importance. It is, however, impossible to apportion the value of the work of the two masters. Haydn did a great deal of important and substantial work before Mozart came into prominence in the same field. But after the first great mark had been made by the ' Paris ' symphony, Mozart seemed to rush to his culmination; and in the last four of his works reached a style which appears richer, more sympathetic and more complete than anything Haydn could attain to. Then, again, when he had passed away, Haydn produced his greatest works. Each composer had his distinctive characteristics, and each is delightful in his own way; but Haydn would probably not have reached his highest development without the influence of his more richly gifted contemporary; and Mozart for his part was undoubtedly very much under the influence of Haydn at an important part of his career. The best that can be said by way of distinguishing their respective shares in the result is that Mozart's last symphonies introduced an intrinsically musical element which had before been wanting, and showed a supreme perfection of actual art in their structure; while Haydn in the long series of his works cultivated and refined his own powers to such an extent that when his last symphonies had made their appearance, the status of the symphony was raised beyond the possibility of a return to the old level. In fact he gave this branch of art a stability and breadth which served as the basis upon which the art of succeeding generations appears to rest; and the simplicity and clearness of his style and structural principles supplied an intelligible model for his successors to follow.

GOSSEC AND OTHERS.—One of the most important of the contemporaries of Haydn and Mozart in this department of art was F. J. Gossec. He was born in 1733, one year after Haydn, and lived like him to a good old age. His chief claim to remembrance is the good work which he did in improving the standard of taste for instrumental music in France. According to Fétis such things as instrumental symphonies were absolutely unknown in Paris before 1754, in which year Gossec published his first, five years before Haydn's first attempt. Gossec's work was carried on most effectually by his founding, in 1770, the Concert des Amateurs for whom he wrote his most important works. He also took the management of the famous Concert Spirituel, with Gaviniés and Leduc, in 1773, and furthered the cause of good instrumental music there as well. The few symphonies of his to be found in this country are of the same calibre, and for the same groups of instruments, as those of J. C. Bach, Abel, etc., already described; but Fétis attributes importance to him chiefly because of the way in which he extended the dimensions and resources of the orchestra. His symphony in D, No. 21, written soon after the founding of the Concert des Amateurs, was for a full set of strings, flutes, oboes, clarinets, bassoons, horns, trumpets and drums; and this was doubtless an astonishing force to the Parisians, accustomed as they had been to regard the compositions of Lully and Rameau as the best specimens of instrumental music. But it is clear from other indications that Gossec had considerable ideas about the ways in which instrumental music might be improved, analogous on a much smaller scale to the aspirations and attempts of Berlioz at a later date. Not only are his works carefully marked with *pianos* and *fortes*, but in some (as the symphonies of op. 12) there are elaborate directions as to how the movements are to be played. Some of these are curious. For instance, over the first violin part of the slow movement of the second symphony is printed the following:

' La différence du Fort au Doux dans ce morceau doit être excessive, et le mouvement modéré, à l'aise, qu'il semble se jouer avec la plus grande facilité.'

Nearly all the separate movements of this set have some such directions, either longer or shorter; the inference from which is that Gossec had a strong idea of expression and style in performance, and did not find his bands very easily led in these respects. The movements themselves are on the same small scale as those of J. C. Bach, Abel and Stamitz; and very rarely have the double bar and repeat in the first movements, though these often make their appearance in the finales. The style is to a certain extent individual; not so robust or so full as that of Bach or Stamitz, but not without attractiveness. The following quotation from the last movement of a symphony in Bb will serve to give some idea of his style and manner of scoring:

Another composer of symphonies, who is often heard of in juxtaposition with Haydn and Mozart, and sometimes as being preferred to them by the audiences of the time, is Gyrowetz. His symphonies appear to be on a larger scale than those of the prior generation of composers of second rank like himself. A few of them are occasionally to be met with in collections of 'Periodical overtures,' 'symphonies,' etc., published in separate orchestral parts. One in C, scored for small orchestra, has an introductory adagio, an allegro of about the dimensions of Haydn's earlier first movements, with double

bar in the middle; then an andante *con sordini* (the latter a favourite device in central slow movements); then a minuet and trio, and, to end with, a rondo in 2-4 time, allegro non troppo. Others, in Eb and Bb, have much the same distribution of movements, but without the introductory adagio. The style of them is rather mild and complacent, and not approaching in any way the interest or breadth of the works of his great contemporaries; but the subjects are clear and vivacious, and the movements seem fairly developed. Other symphony writers, who had vogue and even celebrity about this time and a little later, such as Krommer (beloved by Schubert), the Rombergs and Eberl (at one time preferred to Beethoven), require no more than passing mention. They certainly furthered the branch of art very little, and were so completely extinguished by the exceptionally great writers who came close upon one another at that time that it is even difficult to find traces of them.

BEETHOVEN.—The greatest of all masters of the symphony followed so close upon Haydn that there is less of a gap between the last of Haydn's symphonies and his first than there was later between some of his own. Haydn's last was probably written in 1795. When Beethoven wrote his first cannot be ascertained; sketches for the finale are found as early as the year last mentioned; but it was not actually produced in public till Apr. 2, 1800. Like Schumann and Brahms in later days, he did not turn his attention to this branch of composition till comparatively late. The opus-number of his first symphony is 21. It is preceded by eleven pianoforte sonatas, several works for pianoforte combined with other instruments, the well-known septet in Eb and several chamber compositions for strings. So that by the time he came to attacking symphony he had had considerable practice in dealing with structural matters. The only works in which he had tried his strength with the orchestra were the two piano concertos—the Bb, op. 19, which was written in or about 1795, and the C major, op. 15, which was written about 1796. He showed himself at once a master of the orchestra; but it is evident that at first he stepped cautiously in expressing himself with such resources.

The first symphony is less free and rich in expression, and has more elements of formality, than several works on a smaller scale which preceded it. This is explicable on the general ground that the orchestra, especially in those days, was not a fit exponent of the same kind of things which could be expressed by solo violins or the pianoforte. The scale must necessarily be larger and broader; the intricate development and delicate or subtle sentiment which is quite appropriate and intelligible in the intimacy of a domestic circle is out of place in the more public conditions of orchestral performance,

This Beethoven must have instinctively felt, and he appears not to have found the style for full expression of his personality in either of the first symphonies. The second is even more curious in that respect than the first, as it comes after one of the richest and most interesting, and another of the most perfectly charming and original of the works of his early period, namely, the sonatas in D minor and Eb of op. 31. However, even in these two symphonies there is a massiveness and breadth and seriousness of purpose which mark them as products of a different and more powerfully constituted nature than anything of the kind produced before. At the time when the first symphony appeared, the opening with the chord of the minor 7th of C, when the key of the piece was C major, was looked upon as extremely daring; and the narrow-minded pedants of the day felt their sensitive delicacy so outraged that some of them are said never to have forgiven it. The case is very similar to the famous introduction to Mozart's C major string quartet, about which the pedants were little less than insulting. Beethoven had to fight for his right to express what he felt to be true; and he did it without flinching; sometimes with an apparent relish. But at the same time, in these early orchestral works he seems to have experimented with caution, and was content to follow his predecessors in a great deal that he put down. There are characteristic things in both symphonies; for instance, in the first the transitional passage which begins at the 65th bar of the allegro, passing from G to G minor and then to Bb and back again, and the corresponding passage in the second half of the movement. The working out of the andante cantabile and the persistent drum rhythm are also striking points. In the second symphony the dimensions of the introduction are unusual, and the character of all the latter part and the freedom of the transitions in it are decisive marks of his tendencies. The slow movement has also a warmth and sense of genuine sympathy which is new; the scherzo, though as yet short, has a totally new character about it, and the abrupt sforzandos and short striking figures, and still more the coda, of the finale are quite his own. In the orchestra it is worth noting that he adopted clarinets from the first, apparently as a matter of course; in the first two symphonies he continued to use only the one pair of horns, as his predecessors had done; in the third he expanded the group to three. In the fourth he went back to two, and did not use four till the ninth. The disposition of his forces even in the first two is more independent and varied than his predecessors.' The treatment of the several groups of instruments tends to be more distinct and appropriate, and at the same time more perfectly assimilated in the total effect of the music.

'EROICA' AND THE NEW ERA.—The step to the third symphony is, however, immense, and at last shows this branch of composition on a level with his other works of the same period. It is surrounded on both sides by some of his noblest achievements. Op. 47 was the sonata in A for violin and pianoforte, known as the 'Kreutzer.' Op. 53 is the sonata in C major, dedicated to Count Waldstein. Op. 54 is the admirable little sonata in F major. Op. 55 is the symphony, and op. 57 the sonata known as the 'Appassionata.' It appears that Beethoven had the idea of writing this symphony as early as 1798, but the actual work was probably done in the summer and autumn of 1803. There seems to be no doubt that it was written under the influence of his admiration for Napoleon. His own title-page had on it 'Sinfonia grande. Napoleon Bonaparte,' and, as is well known, the name 'Eroica' was not added till Napoleon became Emperor; after which event Beethoven's feelings about him naturally underwent a change. To call a great work by the name of a great man was quite a different thing from calling it by the name of a crowned ruler. However, the point remains the same, that the work was written with a definite purpose and under the inspiration of a special subject, and one upon which Beethoven himself assuredly had a very decided opinion. The result was the richest and noblest and by far the biggest symphony that had ever yet appeared in the world. It is very possible that Beethoven meant it to be so; but the fact does not make the step from the previous symphonies any the less remarkable. The scoring throughout is most freely distributed. In the first movement especially there is hardly any one of the numerous subjects and characteristic figures which has not properties demanding different departments of the orchestra to express them. They are obviously conceived with reference to the whole forces at command, not to a predominant central force and appendages. The strings must necessarily have the greater part of the work to do, but the symphony is not written for them with wind as a species of afterthought. But it is still to be noticed that the balance is obtained chiefly by definite propositions and answers between one group and another, and though the effect is delightful, the principle is rendered a little obvious from the regularity of its occurrence. The second movement is specially noticeable as reaching the strongest pitch of sentiment as yet shown in an orchestral slow movement. In the earliest symphonies these movements were nearly always remarkably short, and scored for fewer instruments than the first and last. Frequently they were little better than 'intermezzi,' attached on both sides to the more important allegros. Even Mozart's and Haydn's latest examples had more grace and sweetness than deep feeling, and frequently showed a tendency to formalism in the expression of the ideas and in the ways in which the ornamental *fioriture* were introduced. In the Eroica the name ' Marcia funebre ' at once defines the object ; and though the form of a march is to a certain extent maintained, it is obvious that it is of secondary importance, since the attention is more drawn to the rich and noble expression of the finest feelings of humanity over the poetically imagined death of one of the world's heroes than to the traditional march form. The music seems in fact to take almost the definiteness of speech of the highest order ; or rather, to express the emotions which belong to the imagined situation with more fulness and comprehensiveness, but with scarcely less definiteness, than speech could achieve. In the third movement appears the first of Beethoven's large orchestral scherzos. Any connexion between it and the typical minuet and trio it is hard to see. The time is quicker and more bustling ; and the character utterly distinct from the suave grace and somewhat measured paces of most of the previous third movements. The main points of connexion with them are firstly the general outlines of form (that is, the principal portion of the scherzo corresponding to the minuet comes first and last, and the trio in the middle) and secondly the humorous element. In this latter particular there is very great difference between the *naïf* and spontaneous fun of Haydn and the grim humour of Beethoven, sometimes verging upon irony, and sometimes, with evident purpose, upon the grotesque. The scherzo of the Eroica is not alloyed with so much grimness as some later ones, but it has traits of melancholy and seriousness here and there. The effect in its place is chiefly that of portraying the fickle crowd who soon forget their hero, and chatter and bustle cheerfully about their business or pleasure as before ; which has its humorous or at least laughter-making ironical side to any one large-minded enough to avoid thinking of all such traits of humanity with reprobation and disgust. The last movement is on a scale more than equal to that of all the others, and, like them, strikes an almost entirely new note in symphonic finales. The light and simple character of Haydn's final rondos is familiar to every one ; and he was consistent in aiming at gaiety for conclusion. Mozart in most cases did the same ; but in the G minor symphony there is a touch of rather vehement regretfulness, and in the C major of strength and seriousness. But the finale of the Eroica first introduces qualities of massiveness and broad earnest dignity to that position in the symphony. The object is evidently to crown the work in a totally different sense from the light cheerful endings of most previous symphonies, and to appeal to fine feelings in the audience instead of aiming at

putting them in a cheerful humour. It is all the difference between an audience before the revolutionary epoch and after. The starting-point of the movement is the same theme from the Prometheus music as that of the pianoforte variations in E♭ (op. 35). The basis of the whole movement is mainly the variation-form, interspersed with fugal episodes ; and a remarkable feature is the long andante variation immediately before the finale presto—a somewhat unusual feature in such a position, though Haydn introduced a long passage of adagio in the middle of the last movement of a symphony in F written about 1777, but of course in a very different spirit. The finale of the Eroica as a whole is so unusual in form that it is not wonderful that opinions have varied much concerning it. As a piece of art it is neither so perfect nor so convincing as the other movements ; but it has very noble and wonderful traits, and, as a grand experiment in an almost totally new direction, has a decided historical importance.

THE MIDDLE PERIOD.—It is not necessary to go through the whole series of Beethoven's symphonies in detail, for one reason because they are so generally familiar to musicians, and for another because they have been so fully discussed from different points of view in this Dictionary. Some short simple particulars about each may, however, be useful and interesting. The order of composition of the works which succeeded the Eroica symphony is almost impossible to unravel. By opus-number the fourth symphony in B♭ comes very soon, being op. 60 ; but the sketches for the last movement are in the same sketch-book as parts of 'Fidelio,' which is op. 72, and the concerto in G, which is op. 58, was begun after 'Fidelio' was finished. It can only be seen clearly that his works were crowded close together in this part of his life, and interest attaches to the fact that they represent the warmest and most popular group of all. Close to the B♭ symphony come the overture to 'Coriolan,' the three string quartets, op. 59, the violin concerto, the PF. concerto in G major, the symphony in C minor and the 'Sinfonia Pastorale.' The B♭ is on a smaller scale than its predecessor, and of lighter and gayer cast. The opening bars of the introduction are almost the only part which has a trace of sadness in it ; and this is probably meant to throw the brightness of the rest of the work into stronger relief. Even the slow movement contains more serenity than deep emotion. The scherzo is peculiar for having the trio repeated—altogether a new point in symphony-writing, and one which was not left unrepeated or unimitated. What the symphony was meant to express cannot be known, but it certainly is as complete and consistent as any.

The C minor which followed has been said to

be the first in which Beethoven expressed himself freely and absolutely, and threw away all traces of formalism in expression or development to give vent to the perfect utterance of his musical feeling. It certainly is so far the most forcible, and most remote from conventionalism of every kind. It was probably written very nearly about the same time as the B♭. Nottebohm says the first two movements were written in 1805 ; and, if this is the fact, his work on the B♭ and on the C minor must have overlapped. Nothing, however, could be much stronger than the contrast between the two. The C minor is, in the first and most striking movement, rugged, terrible in force ; a sort of struggle with fate, one of the most thoroughly characteristic of Beethoven's productions. The second is a contrast : peaceful, though strong and earnest. The scherzo again is one of his most original movements ; in its musical spirit as utterly unlike anything that had been produced before as possible. Full of fancy, fun and humour, and, notwithstanding the pauses and changes of time, wonderful in swing ; and containing some devices of orchestration quite magical in their clearness and their fitness to the ideas. The last movement, which follows without break after the scherzo, is triumphant ; seeming to express the mastery in the wrestling and striving of the first movement. It is historically interesting as the first appearance of trombones and contrafagotto in modern symphony ; and the most powerful in sound up to that time. The next symphony, which is also the next opus-number, is the 'Pastoral,' probably written in 1808, the second of Beethoven's which has a definitely stated idea as the basis of its inspiration, and the first in which a programme is suggested for each individual movement ; though Beethoven is careful to explain that it is 'mehr Empfindung als Malerei.' Any account of this happy inspiration is clearly superfluous (see PASTORAL SYMPHONY). The situations and scenes which it brings to the mind are familiar, and not likely to be less beloved as the world grows older. The style is again in great contrast to that of the C minor, being characterised rather by serenity and contentment ; which, as Beethoven had not heard of all the troubles of the land question, might naturally be his feelings about country life. He used two trombones in the last two movements, but otherwise contented himself with the same group of instruments as in his earliest symphonies.

After this there was a pause for some years, during which time appeared many noble and delightful works on other lines, including the pianoforte trios in D and E♭, the Mass in C minor, op. 86, the music to 'Egmont,' op. 84, and several sonatas. Then in one year, 1812, two symphonies appeared. The first of the two, in A major, numbered op. 92, is looked upon by many as the most romantic of all of them ; and certainly has qualities which increase in attractiveness the better it is known and understood. Among specially noticeable points are the unusual proportions and great interest of the introduction (*poco sostenuto*) ; the singular and fascinating wilfulness of the first movement, which is enhanced by some very characteristic orchestration ; the noble calm of the slow movement ; the merry humour of the scherzo, which has again the same peculiarity as the fourth symphony, that the trio is repeated (for which the world has every reason to be thankful, as it is one of the most completely enjoyable things in all symphonic literature) ; and finally the wild headlong abandonment of the last movement, which might be an idealised national or rather barbaric dance-movement, and which sets the crown fitly upon one of the most characteristic of Beethoven's works. The symphony in F, which follows immediately as op. 93, is again of a totally different character. It is of specially small proportions, and has rather the character of a return to the old conditions of the symphony, with all the advantages of Beethoven's mature powers both in the development and choice of ideas, and in the treatment of the orchestra. Beethoven himself, in a letter to Salomon, described it as 'eine kleine Symphonie in F,' as distinguished from the previous one, which he called 'Grosse Symphonie in A, eine meiner vorzüglichsten.' It has more fun and light-heartedness in it than any of the others, but no other specially distinctive external characteristics, except the substitution of the graceful and humorous 'Allegretto scherzando' in the place of the slow movement, and a return to the 'Tempo di menuetto' for the scherzo.

THE NINTH SYMPHONY.—After this came again a long pause, as the greatest of all symphonies did not make its appearance till 1824. During that time, however, it is probable that symphonic work was not out of his mind, for it is certain that the preparations for putting this symphony down on paper spread over several years. Of the introduction of voices into this form of composition, which is its strongest external characteristic, Beethoven had made a previous experiment in the 'Choral Fantasia' ; and he himself spoke of the symphony as 'in the style of the Choral Fantasia, but on a far larger scale.' The scale is indeed immensely larger, not only in length but in style, and the increase in this respect applies to it equally in comparison with all the symphonies that went before.

The first movement is throughout the most concentrated example of the qualities which distinguish Beethoven, and the new phase upon which music entered with him, from all the composers of the previous half-century. The other movements are not less characteristic of him in their particular ways. The second is the largest example of the typical scherzo which first made its appearance for the orchestra in the Eroica ; and the supreme slow movement (the theme with variations) is the finest orchestral example of that special type of slow movement ; though in other departments of art he had previously illustrated it in a manner little less noble and deeply expressive in the slow movements of the B♭ trio and the B♭ sonata (op. 106). These movements all have reference, more or less intelligible according to the organisation and sympathies of the hearer, to the finale of the symphony, which consists of a setting of Schiller's ode ' An die Freude.' Its development into such enormous proportions is of a piece with the tendency shown in Beethoven's previous symphonies, and in some of his sonatas also, to supplant the conventional type of gay last movement by something which shall be a logical or poetical outcome of the preceding movements, and shall in some way clench them, or crown them with its weight and power. The introduction of words, moreover, gives a new force to the definite interpretation of the whole as a single organism, developed as a poem might be in relation to definite and coherent ideas.

The dramatic and human elements, which Beethoven introduced into his instrumental music to a degree before undreamed of, find here their fullest expression ; and most of the forms of music are called in to convey his ideas. The first movement of the symphony is in binary form ; the second in scherzo, or idealised minuet and trio form ; the third in the form of theme and variations. Then follows the curious passage of instrumental recitative, of which so many people guessed the meaning even before it was defined by the publication of the extracts from the MS. sketch-books in the Berlin Library ; then the entry of the noble tune, the theme of the entire finale, introduced contrapuntally in a manner which has a clear analogy to fugal treatment ; and followed by the choral part, which treats the theme in the form of variations apportioned to the several verses of the poem, and carries the sentiment to the extremest pitch of exultation expressible by the human voice. The instrumental forces employed are the fullest ; including, with the usual complement, four horns, three trombones in the scherzo and finale, and contrafagotto, triangle, cymbals, and big drum in the finale. The choral forces include four solo voices and full chorus, and the sentiment expressed is proportionate to the forces employed.

In Beethoven's hands the symphony has again undergone a change of status. Haydn and Mozart, as above pointed out, ennobled and enriched the form in the structural sense. They took up the work when there was little more expected of the orchestra than would have been expected of a harpsichord, and when the object of the piece was slight and almost momentary entertainment. They left it one of the most important branches of instrumental music, though still to a great extent dependent on formal perfection and somewhat obvious artistic management for its interest. Their office was in fact to perfect the form, and Beethoven's to use it. But the very use of it brought about a new ratio between its various elements. In his work first clearly appears a proportion between the forces employed and the nobility and depth and general importance of the musical ideas. In his hands the greatest and most pliable means available for the composer could be no longer fit for lightness and triviality, but only for ideal emotions of an adequate standard. It is true that earlier composers saw the advantage of adopting a breadth of style and largeness of sentiment when writing for the orchestra ; but this mostly resulted in positive dulness. It seems as if it could only be when the circumstances of history had undergone a violent change that human sentiment could reach that pitch of comprehensiveness which in Beethoven's work raised the symphony to the highest pitch of earnest poetic feeling : and the history of his development is chiefly the co-ordination of all the component elements ; the proportioning of the expression and style to the means ; the expansion of the form to the requirements of the expression ; the making of the orchestration perfectly free, but perfectly just in every detail of expression, and perfectly balanced in itself ; and the eradication of all traces of conventionalism both in the details and in the principal outlines, and also to a great extent in the treatment of the instruments. It is chiefly through Beethoven's work that the symphony now stands at the head of all musical forms whatever ; and though other composers may hereafter misuse and degrade it as they have degraded the opera, the cantata, the oratorio, the mass, and such other forms as have equal possibilities with the symphony, his works of this kind stand at such an elevation of human sympathy and emotion, and at such a pitch of individuality and power in expression and technical mastery, that it is scarcely likely that any branch of musical art will ever show anything to surpass them.

THE POST-BEETHOVEN SCHOOL.—It might seem almost superfluous to trace the history of symphony further after Beethoven.[1] Nothing since his time has shown, nor in the changing conditions of the history of the race is it likely anything should show, any approach to

[1] This was written some fifty years ago, when only the first two of Brahms's symphonies had made an appearance, and others of the later 19th-century symphonists were unknown. The fulness of Parry's appreciation of Brahms's first two symphonies is sufficiently shown in the latter part of this article. It is doubtful whether he would have modified this sentence in 1926. Readers may decide for themselves in the light of what is added under LATER DEVELOPMENTS.　s.

the vitality and depth of his work. But it is just these changing conditions that leave a little opening for composers to tread the same path with him. In the millions of the human species there are endless varieties of mental and emotional qualities grouped in different individuals and different bands or sets of men; and the many-sided qualities of artistic work, even far below the highest standard, find their excuse and explanation in the various groups and types of mind whose artistic desires they satisfy. Those who are most highly organised in such respects find their most perfect and most sustained gratification in Beethoven's works; but others who feel less deeply, or are less wide in their sympathies, or have fewer or different opportunities of cultivating their tastes in such a musical direction, need musical food more in accordance with their mental and emotional organisation. Moreover, there is always room to treat an accepted form in the mode characteristic of the period. Beethoven's period was much more like ours than that of Haydn and Mozart, but yet it is not so like that a work expressed entirely in his manner would not be an anachronism. Each successive generation takes some colour from the combination of work and changes in all previous generations; in unequal quantities proportioned to its amount of sympathy with particular periods.

By the side of Beethoven there were other composers, working either on parallel lines or in a different manner on the same lines. The succeeding generations were influenced by them as well as by him; and they have introduced some elements into symphony which are at least not prominent in his. One of the contemporary composers who had most influence on the later generation was Weber; but his influence is derived from other departments, and in that of symphony his contribution is next to nothing—two only, so slight and unimportant as probably to have had no influence at all.

Another composer's symphonies did not have much immediate influence, chiefly because they were not performed. In delightfulness, Schubert's two best works in this department stand almost alone; and their qualities are unique. In his earlier works of the kind there is an analogy to Beethoven's early works. Writing for the orchestra seemed to paralyse his particular individuality; and for some time after he had written some of his finest and most original songs, he continued to write symphonies which were chiefly a mild reflex of Haydn and Mozart, or at most of the early style of Beethoven. His first attempt was made in 1813, the last page being dated Oct. 28 of that year, when he was yet only 16 years old —one year after Beethoven's symphonies in A and F, and more than ten years before the great

D minor. In the five following years he wrote five more, the best of which is No. 4, the 'Tragic,' in C minor; the andante especially being very fine and interesting, and containing many characteristic traits of the master. But none of the early works approach in interest or original beauty to the unfinished one in B minor, and the very long and vigorous one in C major; the first composed in 1822, before Beethoven's No. 9, and the second in 1828, after it. In these two he seems to have struck out a real independent symphony-style for himself, thoroughly individual in every respect, both of idea, form and orchestration. They show singularly little of the influence of Beethoven, or Mozart, or Haydn, or any of the composers he must have been familiar with in his early days at the Konvict; but the same spirit as is met with in his songs and pianoforte pieces, and the best specimens of his chamber music. The first movement of the B minor is entirely unlike any other symphonic first movement that ever was composed before. It seems to come direct from the heart, and to have the personality of the composer in it to a most unusual degree. The orchestral forces used are the usual ones,[1] but in the management of them there are numbers of effects which are perfectly new in this department of art, indicating the tendency of the time towards direct consideration of what is called 'colour' in orchestral combinations, and its employment with the view of enhancing the degree of actual sensuous enjoyment of a refined kind, to some extent independent of the subjects and figures. Schubert's mature orchestral works are, however, too few to give any strong indication of this in his own person; and what is commonly felt is the supreme attractiveness of the ideas and general style. As classical models of form none of Schubert's instrumental works take the highest rank; and it follows that no compositions by any writer which have taken such hold upon the musicians of the present time [2] depend so much upon their intrinsic musical qualities as his do. They are therefore in a sense the extremest examples that can be given of the degree in which the status of such music altered in about thirty years. In the epoch of Mozart and Haydn, the formal elements absolutely predominated in importance. This was the case in 1795. The balance was so completely altered in the course of Beethoven's lifetime, that by 1824 the phenomenon is presented of works in the highest line of musical composition depending on the predominating element of the actual musical sentiment. It must be confessed that Schubert's position in art is unique; but at the same time no man of mark can be quite unrepresentative of his time, and Schubert in this way represents the

---

[1] Excepting only that he uses three trombones, an unusual thing in first movements at the date.　　[2] I.e. about 1880.

extraordinary degree in which the attention of musical people and the intention of composers in the early years of the 19th century were directed to the actual material of music in its expressive sense as distinguished from the external or structural aspect.

The relation of the dates at which more or less well-known symphonies made their appearance about this time is curious and not uninstructive. Mendelssohn's 'Reformation' symphony was produced only two years after Schubert's great symphony in C, namely in 1830. His Italian symphony followed in the next year; and Sterndale Bennett's, in G minor, in 1834.

SPOHR'S PROGRAMME SYMPHONIES.—The dates and history of Spohr's productions are even more striking, as he was actually a contemporary of Beethoven's and senior to Schubert, while in all respects in which his style is characteristic it represents quite a later generation. His first symphony (in Eb) was composed in 1811, before Beethoven's 7th, 8th and 9th, and when he himself was 27 years old. This was followed by several others, which are not without merit, though not of sufficient historical importance to require special consideration. The symphony of his which is best remembered at the present day is that called the 'Weihe der Töne,' which at one time enjoyed great celebrity. The history of this work is as follows. He intended first to set a poem of the same name by his friend Pfeiffer. He began the setting in 1832, but finding it unsatisfactory he abandoned the idea of using the words except as a programme; in which form they are appended to the score. The full description and purpose of the work as expressed on the title is ' Characteristisches Tongemälde in Form einer Sinfonie, nach einem Gedicht von Carl Pfeiffer '; and a printed notice from the composer is appended to the score directing that the poem is to be either printed or recited aloud whenever the symphony is to be performed. Each movement also has its title, like the Pastoral of Beethoven; but it differs from that work not only in its less substantial interest, but also in a much more marked departure from the ordinary principles of form, and the style of the successive movements.

The earlier part of the work corresponds fairly well with the usual principles of structure. It opens with a short largo of vague character, passing into the allegro, which is a continuous movement of the usual description, in a sweet but rather tame style. The next movement might be taken to stand for the usual slow movement, as it begins andantino; but the development is original, as it is broken up by several changes of tempo and time-signatures, and is evidently based upon a programme, for which its title supplies an explanation. The next movement again might be taken as an

alternative to the minuet and trio, being marked 'Tempo di Marcia,' which would suggest the same general outline of form. But the development is again independent, and must be supposed to follow its title. From this point all connexion with the usual outlines ceases. There is an andante maestoso, based upon the plain-song of the Te Deum, a larghetto containing a second hymn-tune, and a short allegretto in simple primary form to conclude with. From this description it will be obvious that the work is an example of thoroughgoing ' programme music.' It is clearly based rather on the musical portrayal of a succession of ideas in themselves independent of music, than upon the treatment of principles of abstract form and ideas intrinsically musical. It derives from this fact a historical importance which its musical qualities taken alone would not warrant, as it is one of the very first German examples of its kind possessing any high artistic excellences of treatment, expression and orchestration. It contains a plentiful supply of Spohr's characteristic faults, and is for the most part superficial, and deficient in warmth of feeling and nobility of thought; but it has also a fair share of his good traits—delicacy and clearness of orchestration, and a certain amount of poetical sentiment. Its success was considerable, and this, rather than any abstract theorising upon the tendencies of modern music, led him to several further experiments in the same line. The symphony (in C minor) which followed the ' Weihe der Töne ' was on the old lines, and does not require much notice. It contains experiments in unifying the work by unusual references to subjects, as in the first movement, where conspicuous reference is made in the middle part of the allegro to the characteristic feature of the slow introduction; and in the last, where the same subject is somewhat transformed, and reappears in a different time as a prominent feature of the second section. In the next symphony, and in the seventh and ninth, Spohr again tried experiments in programme.

Two of these are such curiosities as to deserve description. The sixth, op. 116, in G is called ' Historische Symphonie,' and the four movements are supposed to be illustrations of four distinct musical periods. The first is called the Period of Handel and Bach, and dated 1720; the second, the Period of Haydn and Mozart, and dated 1780 (i.e. before any of the greatest instrumental works of either Haydn or Mozart were produced); the third is the Period of Beethoven, and dated 1810; and the fourth, ' Allerneueste Periode,' and dated 1840. This last title seems to imply that Spohr regarded himself as belonging to a different generation from Beethoven. The first period is represented by an introductory largo in contrapuntal style, and an allegro movement, part after the manner of the old canzonas, and part a pastorale, intro-

duced for contrast. The style has scarcely the
least affinity to Bach, but the Handelian character is extremely easy to imitate, and hence in
some respects it justifies its title fairly well.
The slow movement which follows has good
qualities and graceful points. It has more the
flavour of Mozart than Haydn, and this is
enhanced by the Mozartian turns and figures
which are introduced. One which is very conspicuous is the short figure--

which is found in several places in Mozart's
works. The second subject, moreover, is only
an ingenious alteration of the second subject
in the slow movement of Mozart's Prague
symphony in D:

Nevertheless, the whole effect of the movement is not what its title implies. The scoring
is fuller, and the inner parts richer and freer in
their motion than in the prototypes, and the
harmonisation is more chromatic, after Spohr's
manner. The Scherzo professes to be in Beethoven's style, and some of his characteristic
devices of harmony and rhythm and treatment
of instruments are fairly well imitated (e.g. the
drums in G, D, and E♭), though in a manner
which shows they were but half understood.

The last movement, representing the then
'latest period,' has of course no names appended. Spohr probably did not intend to
imitate any one, but was satisfied to write in
his own manner, of which the movement is not
a highly satisfactory example. It is perhaps
rather to the composer's credit that his own
characteristics should peep out at all corners
in all the movements, but the result can hardly
be called an artistic success. However, the
experiment deserves to be recorded and described, as unique among works by composers
of such standing and ability as Spohr; and the
more so as it is not likely to be often heard in
future.

His next symphony (No. 7, in C major,
op. 121) is in many respects as great a curiosity
of a totally different description. It is called
'Irdisches und Göttliches im Menschenleben,'
and is a double symphony in three movements
for two orchestras. The first movement is called
'Kinderwelt,' the second 'Zeit der Leidenschaften,' and the last (Presto) 'Endlicher Sieg
des Göttlichen.' In the first two the second
orchestra, which is the fuller of the two, is

little more than an accompaniment to the first.
In the last it has a good deal of work to do,
uttering chiefly vehement and bustling passages
in contrast with quiet and sober passages by
the first orchestra; until near the end, when it
appears to be subdued into consonance with the
first orchestra. The idea seems to be to depict
the divine and the worldly qualities more or
less by the two orchestras: the divine being
given to the smaller orchestra of solo instruments, and the worldly to the fuller orchestra.
The treatment of the instrumental forces is on
the whole very simple; and no very extraordinary effects seem to be aimed at.

Spohr wrote yet another programme symphony after this (No. 9, in B, op. 143) called
'Die Jahreszeiten,' in which Winter and
Spring are joined to make Part I., and Summer
and Autumn to make Part II. The work
approaches more nearly to the ordinary outlines of the symphony than his previous
experiments in programme, and does not seem
to demand so much detailed description. In
fact, but for his having been so early in the
field as a writer of thoroughgoing programme-
music, Spohr's position in the history of the
symphony would not be an important one;
and it is worthy of remark that his being so at
all appears to have been an accident. The
'Weihe der Töne' would not have been a
programme symphony but for the fact that
Pfeiffer's poem did not turn out to be very
suitable for a musical setting. It is not likely
that the work would have attained such popularity as it did but for its programme; but
after so good a result in relation to the public,
it was natural that Spohr should try further
experiments on the same lines; and hence he
became one of the earliest representatives of
artistic speculation in a direction which has
become one of the most conspicuous subjects of
discussion among modern musical philosophers.
As far as intrinsic qualities are concerned it is
remarkable how very little influence he has had
upon the subsequent history of the symphony,
considering the reputation he enjoyed in his
lifetime. His greatest excellence was his treatment of his orchestra, which was delicate,
refined and extremely clear; but it must be
confessed that he erred on the side natural to
the virtuoso violinist, and was too fond of
bringing his first violins into prominence. His
ideas and style generally were not robust or
noble enough to stand the test of time. His
melodies are not broad or strong; his harmonisation, though very chromatic to look at,
is not radically free and vigorous; and his
rhythm, though sometimes complicated and
ingenious, is neither forcible nor rich in variety.
None of his works, however, can be said to be
without their good points, and the singularity
of his attempts at programme-music gives them
an interest which the unlikelihood of many

performances in the future does not by any means diminish.

An interesting fact in connexion with Spohr and the history of the symphony is that he was the first to conduct an orchestra in England with a baton ; the practice having previously been to conduct ' at the pianoforte.' The occasion was one of the Philharmonic Concerts in 1820 (see BATON ; CONDUCTING ; SPOHR). The habit of conducting at the pianoforte was evidently a tradition continued from the days when the symphony was an appendage of the opera, when the principal authority, often the composer in person, sat at the principal clavier in the middle of the orchestra giving the time at his instrument, and filling in the harmonies under the guidance of a figured bass. Almost all the earlier independent symphonies, including those of Philip Emanuel Bach of 1776, and some of Haydn's earlier ones, have such a figured bass for the clavier-player, and an extra bass part is commonly found in the sets of parts which may be reasonably surmised to be for his use.[1] The practice was at last abrogated in England by Spohr, possibly because he was not a clavier but a violin player. In Germany it was evidently discontinued some time earlier.

MENDELSSOHN'S POSITION.—The most distinguished composers of symphonies who wrote at the same time as Spohr, were entirely independent of him. The first of these is Mendelssohn, whose earliest symphonies even overlap Beethoven, and whose better-known works of the kind, as before mentioned, begin about the same time as Spohr's best examples, and extend over nearly the same period as his later ones. The earliest which survives in print is that in C minor dedicated to the London Philharmonic Society. This work was really his thirteenth symphony, and was finished on Mar. 31, 1824, when he was only 15 years old, in the very year that Beethoven's ninth symphony was first performed. The work is more historically than musically interesting. It shows, as might be expected, how much stronger the mechanical side of Mendelssohn's artistic nature was, even as a boy, than his poetical side. Technically the work is extraordinarily mature. It evinces not only a perfect and complete facility in laying the outline and carrying out the details of form, but also the acutest sense of the balance and proportion of tone of the orchestra. The limits of the attempt are not extensive, and the absence of strong feeling or aspiration in the boy facilitated the execution. The predominant influence is clearly that of Mozart. Not only the treatment of the lower and subordinate parts of the harmony, but the distribution and management of the different

[1] Mendelssohn's early Symphonies are marked ' Klavier mit dem Basse.' (See Vol. III. p. 378, note 1.)

sections and even the ideas, are like. There is scarcely a trace of the influence of Beethoven, and not much of the features afterwards characteristic of the composer himself. The most individual movements are the slow movement and the trio. The former is tolerably free from the influence of the artificial and mannered slow movements of the Haydn and Mozart style, and at the same time does not derive its inspiration from Beethoven ; it contains some very free experiments in modulation, enharmonic and otherwise, a few characteristic figures similar to some which he made use of later in his career, and passages of melody clearly predicting the composer of the 'Lieder ohne Worte' and the short slow movements of the organ sonatas. The trio is long and very original in intention, the chief feature being ingenious treatment of arpeggios for the strings in many parts. The other movements are for the most part formal. The minuet is extraordinarily like that of Mozart's G minor symphony, not only in accent and style, but in the manner in which the strings and the wind are grouped and balanced, especially in the short passage for wind alone which occurs towards the end of each half of the movement. It was possibly owing to this circumstance that Mendelssohn substituted for it the orchestral arrangement of the scherzo of his octet when the work was performed later in his life. In the last movement the most characteristic passage is the second subject, with the short chords of pizzicato strings, and the tune for the clarinet which comes after the completion of the first period by strings alone. He used the same device more than once later, and managed it more satisfactorily. But it is just such suggestions of the working of the musical spirit in the man which make an early work interesting.

His next symphony happened to illustrate the supposed tendency of the age towards programme. It was intended for the tercentenary festival of the Augsburg Protestant Confession in 1830, though owing to political circumstances its performance was deferred till later. He evidently had not made up his mind what to call it till some time after it was finished, as he wrote to his sister and suggested ' Confession Symphony,' or ' Symphony for a Church Festival,' as alternative names. But it is quite evident, nevertheless, that he must have had some sort of programme in his mind, and a purpose to illustrate the conflict between the old and new forms of the faith, and the circumstances and attributes which belonged to them. The actual form of the work is as nearly as possible what is called perfectly orthodox. The slow introduction, the regular legitimate allegro, the simple pretty scherzo and trio, the short but completely balanced slow movement, and the regular last movement preceded by a second slow introduction, present very little that is out of the way in point of structure ; and hence the work is less dependent upon its programme than some of the examples by Spohr above described. But nevertheless the programme can be clearly seen to have suggested much of the detail of treatment and development in a perfectly consistent and natural manner. The external traits which obviously strike attention are two : first, the now well-known passage which is used in the Catholic church at Dresden for the Amen, and which Wagner has since adopted as one of the most conspicuous religious motives of ' Parsifal ' ; and secondly, the use of Luther's famous hymn, ' Ein' feste Burg,' in the latter part of the work. The Amen makes its appearance in the latter part of the opening andante, and is clearly meant to typify the old church ; and its recurrence at the end of the working out in the first movement, before the recapitulation, is possibly meant to imply that the old church still holds its own ; while in the latter portion of the work the typical hymn-tune, introduced softly by the flute and by degrees taking possession of the whole orchestra, may be taken to represent the successful spread of the Protestant ideas, just as its final utterance fortissimo at the end of all does the establishment of men's right to work out their own salvation in their own way. There are various other details which clearly have purpose in relation to the programme, and show clearly that the composer was keeping the possible succession of events and circumstances in his mind throughout. The actual treatment is a very considerable advance upon the symphony in C minor. The whole work is thoroughly Mendelssohnian. There is no obvious trace, either in the ideas themselves or in the manner of expression, of the Mozartian influence which is so noticeable in the symphony of six years earlier. And considering that the composer was still but 21, the maturity of style and judgment is relatively quite as remarkable as the facility and mastery shown in the work of his 15th year. The orchestration is quite characteristic and free ; and in some cases, as in part of the second movement, singularly happy.

The principle of programme here assumed seems to have been maintained by him thenceforward ; for his other symphonies, though it is not so stated in the published scores, are known to have been recognised by him as the results of his impressions of Italy and Scotland. The first of them followed very soon after the ' Reformation ' symphony. In the next year after the completion of that work he mentioned the new symphony in a letter to his sister as far advanced ; and said it was ' the gayest thing he had ever done.' He was in Rome at the time, and it appears most probable that the first and last movements were written

there. Of the slow movement he wrote that he had not found anything exactly right, ' and would put it off till he went to Naples, hoping to find something to inspire him there.' But in the result it is difficult to imagine that Naples can have had much share. Of the third movement there is a tradition that it was imported from an earlier work ; and it certainly has a considerable flavour of Mozart, though coupled with traits characteristic of Mendelssohn in perfect maturity, and is at least well worthy of its position ; and even if parts of it, as is possible, appeared in an earlier work, the excellences of the trio, and the admirable effect of the final coda which is based on it, point to considerable rewriting and reconstruction at a mature period. The actual structure of the movements is based upon familiar principles, though not without certain idiosyncrasies ; as, for instance, the appearance of a new prominent feature in the working-out portion, and the freedom of the recapitulation in the first movement. In the last movement, called ' Saltarello,' he seems to have given a more free rein to his fancy in portraying some scene of unconstrained Italian gaiety of which he was a witness ; and though there is an underlying consistency in the usual distribution of keys, the external balance of subjects is not so obvious. The last movement is hence the only one which seems to depend to any extent upon the programme idea ; in all other respects the symphony belongs to the ' classical ' order.

Indeed such a programme as the purpose to reproduce impressions of particular countries is far too vague to lend itself to exact and definite musical portrayal of external ideas, such as might take the place of the usual outlines of structure. In fact it could lead to little more than consistency of style, which would be equally helpful to the composer and the audience ; and it may well have served as an excuse for a certain laxity and profusion in the succession of the ideas, instead of that difficult process of concentrating and making relevant the whole of each movement upon the basis of a few definite and typical subjects The characteristics of the work are for the most part fresh and genial spontaneity. The scoring is of course admirable and clear, without presenting any very marked features ; and it is at the same time independent and well proportioned in distribution of the various qualities of sound, and in fitness to the subject-matter.

In orchestral effects the later symphony—the ' Scotch,' in A minor—is more remarkable. The impressions which Mendelssohn received in Scotland may naturally have suggested more striking points of local colour ; and the manner in which it is distributed from first page to last serves to very good purpose in unifying the impression of the whole. The effects are almost invariably obtained either by using close harmonies low in the scale of the respective instruments, or by extensively doubling tunes and figures in a similar manner, and in a sombre part of the scale of the instruments ; giving an effect of heaviness and darkness which were possibly Mendelssohn's principal feelings about the grandeur and uncertain climate of Scotland. Thus in the opening phrase for wind instruments they are crowded in the harmonies almost as thick as they will endure. In the statement of the first principal subject again the clarinet in its darkest region doubles the tune of the violins an octave lower. The use of the whole mass of the strings in three octaves, with the wind filling the harmonies in rhythmic chords, which has so fine and striking an effect at the beginning of the ' working out ' and in the coda, has the same basis ; and the same effect is obtained by similar means here and there in the scherzo ; as, for instance, where the slightly transformed version of the principal subject is introduced by the wind in the coda. The same qualities are frequently noticeable in the slow movement and again in the coda of the last movement. As in the previous symphony, the structure is quite in accordance with familiar principles. If anything, the work errs rather on the side of squareness and obviousness in the outlines both of ideas and structure ; as may be readily perceived by comparing the construction of the opening tune of the introduction with any of Beethoven's introductions (either that of the D or B♭ or A symphonies, or his overtures) : or even the introduction to Mozart's Prague symphony. And the impression is not lessened by the obviousness of the manner in which the succeeding recitative passages for violins are introduced ; nor by the squareness and tune-like qualities of the first subject of the first movement, nor by the way in which the square tune pattern of the scherzo is reiterated. In the manipulation of the familiar distribution of periods and phrases, however, he used a certain amount of consideration. For example, the persistence of the rhythmic figure of the first subject of the first allegro, in the inner parts of the second section of that movement, serves very good purpose ; and the concluding of the movement with the melancholy tune of the introduction helps both the sentiment and the structural effect. The scherzo is far the best and most characteristic movement of the whole. In no department of his work was Mendelssohn so thoroughly at home ; and the obviousness of the formal outlines is less objectionable in a movement where levity and abandonment to gaiety are quite the order of the day. The present scherzo has also certain very definite individualities of its own. It is a departure from the ' Minuet and Trio ' form, as it has no

break or strong contrasting portion in the middle, and is continuous bustle and gaiety from beginning to end. In technical details it is also exceptionally admirable. The orchestral means are perfectly suited to the end, and the utterances are as neat and effective as they could well be ; while the perfect way in which the movement finishes off is delightful to almost every one who has any sense for art. The slow movement takes up the sentimental side of the matter, and is in its way a good example of his orchestral style in that respect. The last movement, allegro vivacissimo, is restless and impetuous, and the tempo-mark given for it in the preface to the work, 'Allegro guerriero,' affords a clue to its meaning. But it evidently does not vitally depend upon any ideal programme in the least ; neither does it directly suggest much, except in the curious independent passage with which it concludes, which has more of the savour of programme about it than any other portion of the work, and is scarcely explicable on any other ground. It is to be noticed that directions are given at the beginning of the work to have the movements played as quickly as possible after one another, so that it may have more or less the effect of being one piece.

Mendelssohn's only other symphonic work was the ' Lobgesang,' a sort of ecclesiastical counterpart of Beethoven's ninth symphony. In this the programme element is important, and is illustrated by the calls of the brass instruments and their reiteration with much effect in the choral part of the work. The external form, as in Beethoven's ninth symphony, is that of the three usual earlier movements—(1) introduction and allegro, (2) scherzo, or minuet and trio, and (3) slow movement (which in the present case have purposely a pietistic flavour), with the finale or last movement supplanted by the long vocal part.

The consideration of these works shows that though Mendelssohn often adopted the appearance of programme, and gained some advantages by it, he never, in order to express his external ideas with more poetical consistency, relaxed any of the familiar principles of structure which are regarded as orthodox. He was in fact a thoroughgoing classicist. He accepted formulas with perfect equanimity, and aimed at resting the value of his works upon the vivacity of his ideas and the great mastery which he had attained in technical expression, and clearness and certainty of orchestration. It was not in his disposition to strike out a new path for himself. The perfection of his art in many respects necessarily appeals to all who have an appreciation for first-rate craftsmanship ; but the standard of his ideas is rather fitted for average musical intelligences, and it seems natural enough that these two circumstances should have combined successfully to obtain for him an extraordinary popularity. He may fairly be said to present that which appeals to high and pure sentiments in men, and calls upon the average of them to feel at their best. But he leads them neither into the depths nor the heights which are beyond them ; and is hence more fitted in the end to please than to elevate. His work in the department of symphony is historically slight. In comparison with his great predecessors he established positively nothing new ; and if he had been the only succcesor to Beethoven and Schubert it would certainly have to be confessed that the department of art represented by the symphony was at a standstill. The excellence of his orchestration, the clearness of his form, and the accuracy and cleverness with which he balanced and disposed his subjects and his modulations, are all certain and unmistakable ; but all these things had been attained by great masters before him, and he himself attained them only by the sacrifice of the genuine vital force and power of harmonic motion and freedom of form in the ideas themselves, of which his predecessors had made a richer manifestation. It is of course obvious that different orders of minds require different kinds of artistic food, and the world would not be well served without many grades and standards of work. Mendelssohn did good service in supplying a form of symphony of such a degree of freshness and lightness as to appeal at once to a class of people for whom the sternness and power of Beethoven in the same branch of art would often be too severe a test. He spoke also in the spirit of his time, and in harmony with it ; and as illustrations of the work of the period in one aspect his symphonies will be among the safest to refer to.

Among his contemporaries the one most natural to bracket with him is Sterndale Bennett, whose views of art were extraordinarily similar, and who was actuated in many respects by similar impulses. His published contribution to the department we are considering is extremely slight. The symphony which he produced in 1834 was practically withdrawn by him, and the only other work of the kind which he allowed to be published was the one which was written for the Philharmonic Society, and first played in 1864. The work is slight, and it is recorded that he did not at first put it forward as a symphony. It had originally but three movements, one of which, the charming minuet and trio, was imported from the Cambridge Installation Ode of 1862. A slow movement called 'Romanze' was added afterwards. Sterndale Bennett was a severe classicist in his views about form in music, and the present symphony does not show anything sufficiently marked to call for record in that respect. It is singularly quiet and unpretentious, and characteristic of the composer, showing his taste and delicacy of sentiment together with his admirable sense of

symmetry and his feeling for tone and refined orchestral effect.

SCHUMANN'S EVOLUTION.—The contemporary of Mendelssohn and Sterndale Bennett who shows in most marked contrast with them is Robert Schumann. He seems to represent the opposite pole of music ; for as they depended upon art and made clear technical workmanship their highest aim, Schumann was in many respects positively dependent upon his emotion. Not only was his natural disposition utterly different from theirs, but so was his education. Mendelssohn and Sterndale Bennett went through severe technical drilling in their early days. Schumann seems to have developed his technique by the force of his feelings, and was always more dependent upon them in the making of his works than upon general principles and external stock rules, such as his two contemporaries were satisfied with. The case affords an excellent musical parallel to the common circumstances of life : Mendelssohn and Sterndale Bennett were satisfied to accept certain rules because they knew that they were generally accepted ; whereas Schumann was of the nature that had to prove all things, and find for himself that which was good. The result was, as often happens, that Schumann affords examples of technical deficiencies, and not a few things which his contemporaries had reason to compare unfavourably with the works of Mendelssohn and Sterndale Bennett ; but in the end his best work is far more interesting, far more deeply felt, and far more really earnest through and through than theirs. It is worth observing also that his feelings towards them were disinterested admiration and enthusiasm, while they thought very slightly of him. They were also the successful composers of their time, and at the head of their profession, while he was looked upon as a sort of half amateur, part mystic and part incompetent. Such circumstances as these have no little effect upon a man's artistic development, and drive him in upon his own resources. Up to a certain point the result for the world in this instance was advantageous. Schumann developed altogether his own method of education. He began with songs and more or less small pianoforte pieces. By working hard in these departments he developed his own emotional language, and in course of time, but relatively late in life as compared with most other composers, he seemed to arrive at the point when experiment on the scale of the symphony was possible.

In a letter to a friend he expressed his feeling that the pianoforte was becoming too narrow for his thoughts, and that he must try orchestral composition. The fruit of this resolve was the symphony in B♭ (op. 38), which was produced at Leipzig in 1841, and was probably his first important orchestral work. It is quite extraordinary how successfully he grappled with the difficulties of the greatest style of composition at the first attempt. The manner is thoroughly symphonic, impressive and broad, and the ideas are more genuinely instrumental both in form and expression than Mendelssohn's, and far more incisive in detail, which in instrumental music is a most vital matter. Mendelssohn had great readiness for making a tune, and it is as clear as possible that when he went about to make a large instrumental work his first thought was to find a good tune to begin upon. Schumann seems to have aimed rather at a definite and strongly marked idea, and to have allowed it to govern the form of period or phrase in which it was presented. In this he was radically in accord with both Mozart and Beethoven. The former in his instrumental works very commonly made what is called the principal subject out of two distinct items, which seem contrasted externally in certain characteristics and yet are inevitable to one another. Beethoven frequently satisfied himself with one principal one, as in the first movements of the Eroica and the C minor; and even where there are two more or less distinct figures, they are joined very closely into one phrase, as in the Pastoral, the eighth and the first movement of the ninth. The first movement of Schumann's B♭ symphony shows the same characteristic. The movement seems almost to depend upon the simple but very definite first figure quoted in Vol. IV. p. 677, which is given out in slow time in the introduction, and worked up as by a mind pondering over its possibilities, finally breaking away with vigorous freshness and confidence in the 'Allegro molto Vivace.' The whole first section depends upon the development of this figure; and even the horns, which have the last utterances before the second subject appears, continue to repeat its rhythm with diminishing force. The second subject necessarily presents a different aspect altogether, and is in marked contrast to the first, but it similarly depends upon the clear character of the short figures of which it is composed, and its gradual work up from the quiet beginning to the loud climax, ends in the reappearance of the rhythmic form belonging to the principal figure of the movement. The whole of the working-out portion depends upon the same figure, which is presented in various aspects and with the addition of new features and ends in a climax which introduces the same figure in a slow form, very emphatically, corresponding to the statement in the introduction. To this climax the recapitulation is duly welded on. The coda again makes the most of the same figure, in yet fresh aspects. The latter part is to all intents independent, apparently a sort of reflection on what has gone before, and is so far in definite contrast as to explain itself. The whole movement is direct and simple in style, and, for Schumann, singularly bright and cheerful.

The principles upon which he constructed and used his principal subjects in this movement are followed in the first movements of the other symphonies; most of all in the D minor; clearly in the C major; and least in the E♭, which belongs to the later period of his life. But even in this last he aims at gaining the same result, though by different means; and the subject is as free as any from the tune-qualities which destroy the complete individuality of an instrumental subject in its most perfect and positive sense. In the first movement of the D minor he even went so far as to make some important departures from the usual outlines of form, which are rendered possible chiefly by the manner in which he used the characteristic figure of his principal subject. It is first introduced softly in the latter part of the introduction, and gains force quickly, so that in a few bars it breaks away in the vigorous and passionate allegro in the following form—

which varies in the course of the movement to

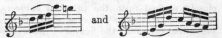

In one or other of these forms it continues almost ceaselessly throughout the whole movement, either as actual subject or accompaniment; in the second section it serves in the latter capacity. In the latter part of the working-out section a fresh subject of gentler character is introduced, seeming to stem and mitigate the vehemence expressed by the principal figures of the first subject; from the time this new subject makes its appearance there continues a sort of conflict between the two; the vehement subject constantly breaking in with apparently undiminished fire, and seeming at times to have the upper hand, till just at the end the major of the original key (D minor) is taken, and the more genial subject appears in a firm and more determined form, as if asserting its rights over the wild first subject; and thereupon, when the latter reappears, it is in a much more genial character, and its reiteration at the end of the movement gives the impression of the triumph of hope and trust in good, over the seeds of passion and despair. The result of the method upon which the movement is developed is to give the impression of both external and spiritual form. The requirements of key, modulation, and subject are fulfilled, though, from the point of view of classical orthodoxy, with unusual freedom. The spiritual form—the expression in musical terms of a type of mental conflict, so depicted that thinking beings can perceive the sequence to be true of themselves

—is also very prominent, and is the most important element in the work, as is the case in all Schumann's best works; moreover in this movement everything is strongly individual, and warm with real musical life in his own style; which was not altogether the case with the first movement of the B♭.

In the C major symphony (op. 61) the first allegro is ushered in by a slow introduction of important and striking character, containing, like those of the two just mentioned, anticipations of its principal figures. In the allegro the two principal subjects are extremely strong in character, and the consistent way in which the whole movement is developed upon the basis of their constituent figures, with allusions to those of the introduction, is most remarkable. Here again there is a sort of conflict between the principal ideas. The first subject is just stated twice (the second time with certain appropriate changes), and then a start is instantly made in the dominant key, with new figures characteristic of the second section; transition is made to flat keys and back, and an allusion to the first subject ends the first half; but all is closely consistent, vigorous and concise. The development portion is also most closely worked upon the principal subjects, which are treated, as it seems, exhaustively, presenting especially the figures of the second subject in all sorts of lights, and with freshness and warmth of imagination, and variety of tone and character. The recapitulation is preceded by allusions to the characteristic features of the introduction, considerably transformed, but still sufficiently recognisable to tell their tale. The coda is made by fresh treatment of the figures of the principal subjects in vigorous and brilliant development.

The symphony in E♭ has no introduction, and Schumann seems to have aimed at getting his strong effects of subject in this case by means other than the vigorous and clear rhythmic forms which characterise the first movements of the earlier symphonies. The effect is obtained by syncopations and cross rhythms, which alternately obscure and strengthen the principal beats of the bar, and produce an effect of wild and passionate effort, which is certainly striking, though not so immediately intelligible as the·rhythmic forms of the previous symphonies. The second subject is in strong contrast, having a more gentle and appealing character; but it is almost overwhelmed by the recurrence of the syncopations of the principal subject, which make their appearance with persistency in the second as in the first section, having in that respect a very clear poetical or spiritual meaning. The whole development of the movement is again consistent and impressive, though not so fresh as in the other symphonies. As a point characteristic of Schumann, the extreme

conciseness of the first section of the first movement in the B♭, D minor and C major symphonies is to be noticed, as it bears strongly upon the cultivated judgment and intelligence which mark his treatment of this great instrumental form. The first half is treated almost as pure exposition; the working-out having logically the greater part of interesting development of the ideas. The recapitulation is generally free, and in the D minor symphony is practically supplanted by novel methods of balancing the structure of the movement. The coda either presents new features, or takes fresh aspects of the principal ones, enhanced by new turns of modulation, and ending with the insistence on the primary harmonies of the principal key, which is necessary to the stability of the movement.

In all these respects Schumann is a most worthy successor to Beethoven. He represents his intellectual side in the consistency with which he develops the whole movement from a few principal features, and the freshness and individuality with which he treats the form; and he shows plenty of the emotional and spiritual side in the passionate or tender qualities of his subjects, and the way in which they are distributed relatively to one another. Schumann's symphonic slow movements have also a distinctive character of their own. Though extremely concise, they are all at the same time rich and full of feeling. They are somewhat in the fashion of a 'Romanze,' that in the D minor symphony being definitely so called; and their development depends rather upon an emotional than an intellectual basis; as it seems most just that a slow movement should. His object appears to have been to find some noble and aspiring strain of melody, and to contrast it with episodes of similar character, which carry on and bear upon the principal idea without diverting the chain of thought into a different channel. Hence the basis of the movements is radically lyrical; and this affords an important element of contrast to the first movement, in which there is always an antithetical element in the contrast of the two principal subjects. The 'Romanze' of the D minor is constructed on a different principle; the sections and musical material being strongly contrasted; this may be partly owing to the closeness of its connexion with other parts of the symphony, as will be noticed farther on.

MODIFICATIONS OF SCHERZO FORM.—The scherzos, including that in the 'Overture, Scherzo and Finale' (op. 52), have a family likeness to one another, though their outlines are different; they all illustrate a phase of musical and poetical development in their earnest character and the vein of sadness which pervades them. The light and graceful gaiety of most of the minuets of Haydn and

Mozart is scarcely to be traced in them ; but its place is taken by a certain wild rush of animal spirits, mixed up in a strange and picturesque way with expressions of tenderness and regret. These scherzos are in a sense unique ; for though following in the same direction as Beethoven's in some respects, they have but little of his sense of fun and grotesque, while the vein of genuine melancholy which pervades them certainly finds no counterpart either in Spohr or Mendelssohn ; and, if it may be traced in Schubert, it is still in comparison far less prominent. In fact Schumann's scherzos are specially curious and interesting, even apart from the ordinary standpoint of a musician, as illustrating a phase of the intellectual progress of the race. Schumann belonged to the order of men with large and at the same time delicate sympathies, whose disposition becomes so deeply impressed with the misfortunes and unsolvable difficulties which beset his own lot and that of his fellow-men, that pure unmixed lightheartedness becomes almost impossible. The poetical and thoughtful side of his disposition, which supplied most vital ingredients to his music, was deeply tinged with sadness ; and from this he was hardly ever entirely free. He could wear an aspect of cheerfulness, but the sadness was sure to peep out, and in this, among thoughtful and poetically disposed beings, he cannot be looked upon as singular. Hence the position of the scherzo in modern instrumental music presents certain inevitable difficulties. The lively, almost childish, merriment of early examples cannot be attained without jarring upon the feelings of earnest men ; at least in works on such a scale as the symphony, where the dignity and importance of the form inevitably produce a certain sense of responsibility to loftiness of purpose in the carrying out of the ideas. A movement corresponding to the old scherzo in its relation to the other movements had to be formed upon far more complicated conditions. The essential point in which Schumann followed his predecessors was the definition of the balancing and contrasting sections. The outlines of certain groups of bars are nearly always very strongly marked, and the movement as a whole is based rather upon effects attainable by the juxtaposition of such contrasting sections than upon the continuous logical or emotional development which is found in the other movements. The structural outline of the old dance-forms is still recognisable in this respect, but the style and rhythm bear little trace of the dance origin ; or at least the dance quality has been so far idealised as to apply rather to thought and feeling than to expressive rhythmic play of limbs. In Schumann's first symphony the scherzo has some qualities of style which connect it with the minuets of earlier times,

even of Mozart ; but with these there are genuine characteristic traits of expression. In the later scherzos the poetical meaning seems more apparent. In fact the scherzo and the slow movement are linked together as the two sections of the work most closely representative of human emotion and circumstance ; the first and last movements having more evident dependence upon what are called abstract qualities of form.

In its structural outlines Schumann's scherzo presents certain features. In the symphonies in B♭ and C he adopts the device of two trios. Beethoven had repeated the trio in two symphonies (4th and 7th), and Schumann advanced in the same direction by writing a second trio instead of repeating the first, and by making the two trios contrast not only with the scherzo, but also with each other ; and as a further result the trios stand centrally in relation to the first and last statement of the scherzo, while it in its turn stands centrally between them, and thus the whole structure of the movement gains in interest. It is worthy of note that the codas to all Schumann's scherzos are specially interesting and full ; and some of them are singular in the fact that they form an independent little section conveying its own ideas apart from those of the principal subjects. His finales are less remarkable on general grounds, and on the whole less interesting than his other movements. The difficulty of conforming to the old type of light movements was even more severe for him than it was for Beethoven, and hence he was the more constrained to follow the example set by Beethoven of concluding with something weighty and forcible, which should make a fitting crown to the work in those respects, rather than on the principle of sending the audience away in a good humour. In the B♭ symphony only does the last movement aim at gaiety and lightness ; in the other three symphonies and the ' Overture, Scherzo and Finale ' the finales are all of the same type, with broad and simple subjects and strongly emphasised rhythms. The rondo form is only obscurely hinted at in one ; in the others the development is very free, but based on binary form ; and the style of expression and development is purposely devoid of elaboration.

INTERLACING OF MOVEMENTS.—Besides the points which have been already mentioned in the development of the individual movements, Schumann's work is conspicuous for his attempts to bind the whole together in various ways. Not only did he make the movements run into each other, but in several places he connects them by reproducing the ideas of one movement in others, and even by using the same important features in different guises as the essential basis of different movements. In the symphony in C there are some interesting examples of this ; but the symphony in D minor is a still more remarkable experiment, and may be taken as a fit type of the highest order.

In the first place all the movements run into each other except the first and second ; and even there the first movement is purposely so ended as to give a sense of incompleteness unless the next movement is proceeded with at once. The first subject of the first movement and the first of the last are connected by a strong characteristic figure, which is common to both of them. The persistent way in which this figure is used in the first movement has already been described. It is not maintained to the same extent in the last movement ; but it makes a strong impression in its place there, partly by its appearing conspicuously in the accompaniment, and partly by the way it is led up to in the sort of intermezzo which connects the scherzo and the last movement, where it seems to be introduced at first as a sort of reminder of the beginning of the work, and as if suggesting the clue to its meaning and purpose ; and is made to increase in force with each repetition till the start is made with the finale. In the same manner the introduction is connected with the slow movement or romanze, by the use of its musical material for the second division of that movement ; and the figure which is most conspicuous in the middle of the romanze runs all through the trio of the succeeding movement. So that the series of movements are as it were interlaced by their subject-matter ; and the result is that the whole gives the impression of a single and consistent musical poem. The way in which the subjects recur may suggest different explanations to different people, and hence it is dangerous to try and fix one in definite terms describing particular circumstances. But the important fact is that the work can be felt to represent in its entirety the history of a series of mental or emotional conditions such as may be grouped round one centre ; in other words, the group of impressions which go to make the innermost core of a given story seems to be faithfully expressed in musical terms and in accordance with the laws which are indispensable to a work of art. The conflict of impulses and desires, the different phases of thought and emotion, and the triumph or failure of the different forces which seem to be represented, all give the impression of belonging to one personality, and of being perfectly consistent in their relation to one another ; and by this means a very high example of all that most rightly belongs to programme music is presented. Schumann, however, wisely gave no definite clue to fix the story in terms. The original autograph has the title ' Symphonische Fantaisie für grosses Orchester, skizzirt im Jahre 1841 ; neu instrumentirt 1851.' In the published score it is called ' Symphony,' and

numbered as the fourth, though it really came second.

Schumann left several similar examples in other departments of instrumental music, but none so fully and carefully carried out. In the department of symphony he never again made so elaborate an experiment. In his last, however, that in E♭, he avowedly worked on impressions which supplied him with something of a poetical basis, though he does not make use of characteristic figures and subjects to connect the movements with one another. The impressive fourth movement is one of the most singular in the range of symphonic music, and is meant to express the feelings produced in him by the ceremonial at the enthronement of a Cardinal in Cologne Cathedral. The last movement has been said to embody ' the bustle and flow of Rhenish holiday life, on coming out into the town after the conclusion of the ceremony in the Cathedral.' [1] Of the intention of the scherzo nothing special is recorded, but the principal subject has much of the ' local colour ' of the German national dances.

As a whole, Schumann's contributions to the department of symphony are by far the most important [2] since Beethoven. As a master of orchestration he is less certain than his fellows of equal standing. There are passages which rise to the highest points of beauty and effectiveness, as in the slow movement of the C major symphony ; and his aim to balance his end and his means was of the highest, and the way in which he works it out is original ; but both the bent of his mind and his education inclined him to be occasionally less pellucid than his predecessors, and to give his instruments things to do which are not perfectly adapted to their idiosyncrasies. On the other hand, in vigour, richness, poetry and earnestness, as well as in the balance which he was able to maintain between originality and justness of art, his works stand at the highest point among the moderns whose work is done ; and have had great and lasting effect upon his successors.

DIVERGENT VIEWS OF THE 19TH CENTURY.— The advanced point to which the history of the symphony has arrived is shown by the way in which composers have become divided into two camps, whose characteristics are most easily understood in their extremest representatives. The growing tendency to attach positive meaning to music, as music, has in course of time brought about a new position of affairs in the instrumental branch of art. We have already pointed out how the strict outlines of form in instrumental works came to be modified by the growing individuality of the subject. As long as subjects were produced upon very simple lines, which in most cases resembled one another in all but very trifling external particu-

[1] For Schumann's intention see Wasielewski, 3rd ed., pp. 269 272.
[2] This is from the point of view of 1880. c.

lars, there was no reason why the structure of the whole movement should grow either complex or individual. But as the subject (which stands in many cases as a sort of text) came to expand its harmonic outlines and to gain force and meaning, it reacted more and more upon the form of the whole movement; and at the same time the musical spirit of the whole, as distinguished from the technical aspects of structure, was concentrated and unified, and became more prominent as an important constituent of the artistic ensemble. In many cases, such as small movements of a lyrical character for single instruments, the so-called classical principals of form were almost lost sight of, and the movement was left to depend altogether upon the consistency of the musical expression throughout. Sometimes these movements had names suggesting more or less of a programme; but this was not by any means invariable or necessary. For in such cases as Chopin's Preludes, and some of Schumann's little movements, there is no programme given, and none required by the listener. The movement depends successfully upon the meaning which the music has sufficient character of its own to convey. In such cases the art form is still thoroughly pure, and depends upon the development of music as music. But in process of time a new position beyond this has been assumed. Supposing the subjects and figures of music to be capable of expressing something which is definite enough to be put into words, it is argued that the classical principles of structure may be altogether abandoned, even in their broadest outlines, and a new starting-point for instrumental music attained, on the principle of following the circumstances of a story, or the succession of emotions connected with a given idea, or the flow of thought suggested by the memory of a place or person or event of history, or some such means; and that this would serve as a basis of consistency and a means of unifying the whole, without the common resources of tonal or harmonic distribution. The story or event must be supposed to have impressed the composer deeply, and the reaction to be an outflow of music expressing the poetical imaginings of the author better than words would do. In some senses this may still be pure art; where the musical idea has really sufficient vigour and vitality in itself to be appreciated without the help of the external excitement of the imagination which is attained by giving it a local habitation and a name. For then the musical idea may still have its full share in the development of the work, and may pervade it intrinsically as music, and not solely as representing a story or series of emotions which are, primarily, external to the music. But when the element of realism creeps in, or the ideas depend for their interest upon their connection with a given programme,

the case is different. The test seems to lie in the attitude of mind of the composer. If the story or programme of any sort is merely a secondary matter which exerts a general influence upon the music, while the attention is concentrated upon the musical material itself and its legitimate artistic development, the advantages gained can hardly be questioned. The principle not only conforms to what is known of the practice of the greatest masters, but is on abstract grounds perfectly unassailable; on the other hand, if the programme is the primary element, upon which the mind of the composer is principally fixed, and by means of which the work attains a specious excuse for abnormal development, independent of the actual musical sequence of ideas, then the principle is open to question, and may lead to most unsatisfactory results. The greatest of modern programme composers came to a certain extent into this position.

BERLIOZ AND THE 'PROGRAMME.'—The development of pure abstract instrumental music seems to have been almost the monopoly of the German race; French and Italians have had a readier disposition for theatrical and at best dramatic music. Berlioz had an extraordinary perception of the possibilities of instrumental music, and appreciated the greatest works of the kind by other composers as fully as the best of his contemporaries; but it was not his own natural way of expressing himself. His natural bent was always towards the dramatic elements of effect and dramatic principles of treatment. It seems to have been necessary to him to find some moving circumstance to guide and intensify his inspiration. When his mind was excited in such a manner he produced the most extraordinary and original effects; and the fluency and clearness with which he expressed himself was of the highest order. His genius for orchestration, his vigorous rhythms, and the enormous volumes of sound of which he was as much master as of the most delicate subleties of small combinations of instruments, have the most powerful effect upon the hearer; while his vivid dramatic perception goes very far to supply the place of the intrinsically musical development which characterises the works of the greatest masters of abstract music. But on the other hand, as is inevitable from the position he adopted, he was forced at times to assume a theatrical manner, and a style which savours rather of the stage than of the true dramatic essence of the situations he deals with. In the 'Symphonie fantastique,' for instance, which he also called 'Episode de la vie d'un artiste,' his management of the programme principle is thorough and well-devised. The notion of the ideal object of the artist's affections being represented by a definite musical figure, called the 'idée fixe,' unifying the work throughout by its constant reappearance in various aspects and surroundings, is very happy; and the way in which he treats it in several parts of the first movement has some of the characteristic qualities of the best kind of development of ideas and figures, in the purely musical sense; while at the same time he has obtained most successfully the expression of the implied sequence of emotions, and the absorption consequent upon the contemplation of the beloved object. In the general laying out of the work he maintains certain vague resemblances to the usual symphonic type. The slow introduction, and the succeeding allegro agitato—representing his passion, and therefore based to a very great extent on the ' idée fixe '—are equivalent to the familiar opening movements of the classical symphonies; and moreover there is even a vague resemblance in the inner structure of the allegro to the binary form. The second movement, called ' Un bal,' corresponds in position to the time-honoured minuet and trio; and though the broad outlines are very free there is a certain suggestion of the old inner form in the relative disposition of the valse section and that devoted to the ' idée fixe.' In the same way the ' Scène aux champs ' corresponds to the usual slow movement. In the remaining movements the programme element is more conspicuous. A ' Marche au supplice ' and a ' Songe d'une nuit de Sabbat ' are both of them as fit as possible to excite the composer's love of picturesque and terrible effects, and to lead him to attempt realistic presentation, or even a sort of musical scene-painting, in which some of the characteristics of instrumental music are present, though they are submerged in the general impression by characteristics of the opera. The effect produced is of much the same nature as of that of passages selected from operas played without action in the concert-room. In fact, in his little preface, Berlioz seems to imply that this would be a just way to consider the work, and the condensed statement of his view of programme music there given is worth quoting :'

' Le compositeur a eu pour but de développer, dans ce qu'elles ont de musical, différentes situations de la vie d'un artiste. Le plan du drame instrumental, privé du secours de la parole, a besoin d'être exposé d'avance. Le programme (qui est indispensable à l'intelligence complète du plan dramatique de l'ouvrage) doit donc être considéré comme le texte parlé d'un Opéra, servant à amener des morceaux de musique, dont il motive le caractère et l'expression.' [1]

This is a very important and clear statement of the position, and marks sufficiently the essential difference between the principles of the most advanced writers of programme music and those adopted by Beethoven. The results are in fact different forms of art. An instrumental

drama is a fascinating idea, and might be carried out perfectly within the limits used even by Mozart and Haydn; but if the programme is indispensable to its comprehension those limits have been passed. This does not necessarily make the form of art an illegitimate one; but it is most important to realise that it is on quite a different basis from the type of the instrumental symphony; and this will be better understood by comparing Berlioz's statement with those symphonies of Beethoven and Mendelssohn, or even of Raff and Rubinstein, where the adoption of a general and vague title gives the semblance of a similar use of programme. Beethoven liked to have a picture or scene or circumstance in his mind [2]; but it makes all the difference to the form of art whether the picture or story is the guiding principle in the development of the piece, or whether the development follows the natural implication of the positively musical idea. The mere occurrence, in one of these forms, of a feature which is characteristic of the other, is not sufficient to bridge over the distance between them; and hence the ' instrumental drama ' or poem, of which Berlioz has given the world its finest example, must be regarded as distinct from the regular type of the pure instrumental symphony. It might perhaps be fairly regarded as the Celtic counterpart of the essentially Teutonic form of art, and as an expression of the Italo-Gallic ideas of instrumental music on lines parallel to the German symphony; but in reality it is scarcely even an offshoot of the old symphonic stem; and it will be far better for the understanding of the subject if the two forms of art are kept as distinct in name as they are in principle.

The earliest and most eminent follower of Berlioz, working on similar lines to his in modern times, is Liszt; and his adoption of the name SYMPHONIC POEM (q.v.) for such compositions sufficiently defines their nature without bringing them exactly under the head of symphonies. Of these there are many, constructed on absolutely independent lines, so as to appear as musical poems or counterparts of actual existing poems. A work [3] which, in name at least, trenches upon the old lines is the ' Faust Symphony,' in which the connection with the programme-principle of Berlioz is emphasised by the dedication of the piece to him. In this work the connection with the old form of symphony is perhaps even less than in the examples of Berlioz. Subjects and figures are used not for the purposes of defining the artistic form, but to describe individuals, ideas, or circumstances. The main divisions of the work are ostensibly three, which are called ' character-

---

[1] ' The composer has aimed at developing various situations in the life of an artist, so far as seemed musically possible. The plan of an instrumental drama, being without words, requires to be explained beforehand. The programme (which is indispensable to the perfect comprehension of the dramatic plan of the work) ought therefore to be considered in the light of the spoken text of an Opera, serving to lead up to the pieces of music, and indicate the character and expression.'

[2] This important admission was made by Beethoven to Neate : ' I have always a picture in my thoughts when I am composing, and work to it.' (Thayer, iii. 343.)
[3] Liszt's ' Dante ' symphony, which does not seem to have come under the notice of Sir Hubert Parry at the time this article was written, is a further illustration of the same method.

pictures of Faust, Margaret and Mephistopheles severally ; and the whole concludes with a setting of the ' Chorus mysticus.' Figures are used after the manner of Wagner's ' Leitmotive' to portray graphically such things as bewildered inquiry, anxious agitation, love, and mockery, besides the special figure or melody given for each individual as a whole. These are so interwoven and developed by modifications and transformations suited to express the circumstances, as to present the speculations of the composer on the character and the philosophy of the poem in various interesting lights ; and his great mastery of orchestral expression and fluency of style contribute to its artistic importance on its own basis ; while in general the treatment of the subject is more psychological and less pictorially realistic than the prominent portions of Berlioz's work, and therefore slightly nearer in spirit to the classical models. But with all its striking characteristics and successful points the music does not approach Berlioz in vitality or breadth of musical idea.

MINOR COMPOSERS.—Mention must be made of a few composers of symphonies in the mid-19th century who belonged essentially to the German school, even when adopting the general advantage of a vague title. Prominent among these are Raff and Rubinstein, whose methods of dealing with instrumental music were at bottom closely related. Raff almost invariably adopted a title for his instrumental works ; but those which he selected admit of the same kind of general interpretation as those of Mendelssohn, and serve rather as a means of unifying the general tone and style of the work than of pointing out the lines of actual development. The several Seasons, for instance, serve as the general idea for a symphony each. Another is called ' Im Walde.' In another several conditions in the progress of the life of a man serve as a vague basis for giving a certain consistency of character to the style of expression, in a way quite consonant with the pure type. In one case Raff comes nearer to the Berlioz ideal, namely in the 'Lenore' symphony, in some parts of which he clearly attempts to depict a succession of events. But even when this is most pronounced, as in the latter part of the work, there is very little that is not perfectly intelligible and appreciable as music without reference to the poem. As a matter of fact Raff is always rather free and relaxed in his form ; but that is not owing to his adoption of programme, since the same characteristic is observable in works that have no name as in those that have. The ease and speed with which he wrote, and the readiness with which he could call up a certain kind of genial, and often very attractive idea, both interfered with the concentration necessary for developing a closely-knit and compact work of art. His ideas are clearly defined and very

intelligible, and have much poetical sentiment ; and these facts, together with a very notable mastery of orchestral resource and feeling for colour, ensured his works great success on their production ; but there is too little self-restraint and concentration both in the general outline and in the statement of details, and too little self-criticism in the choice of subject-matter, to give permanence. In the broadest outlines he generally conformed to the principles of the earlier masters, distributing his allegros, slow movements, scherzos and finales according to precedent.

Rubinstein's works are conspicuous examples of the same class ; but the absence of concentration, self-criticism in the choice of subjects, and care in statement of details, is even more conspicuous in him than in Raff. His most important symphonic work is called ' The Ocean '—the general title serving, as in Raff's symphonies, to give unity to the sentiment and tone of the whole, rather than as a definite programme to work to. In this, as in Raff, there is much spontaneity in the invention of subjects, and in some cases a higher point of real beauty and force is reached than in that composer's works ; and there is also a good deal of striking interest in the details. The most noticeable external feature is the fact that the symphony is in seven movements. There was originally the familiar group of four, and to these were added, some years later, an additional slow movement, which stands second, and a further genuine scherzo, which stands fifth, both movements being devised in contrast to the previously written adagio and scherzo. The third added movement is a ' storm.' Another symphony of Rubinstein's, showing much vigour and originality, and some careful and intelligent treatment of subject, is the ' Dramatic.' This is in the usual four movements, with well-devised introductions to the first and last. The work as a whole is hampered by excessive and unnecessary length, which is not the result of the possibilities of the subjects or the necessities of their development ; and might be reduced with nothing but absolute advantage.

CONTEMPORARY ESTIMATE OF BRAHMS.—The greatest representative of the highest art in the department of symphony is Johannes Brahms.[1] His first two[2] examples have that mark of intensity, loftiness of purpose, and artistic mastery which sets them above all other contemporary work of the kind. Like Beethoven and Schumann he did not produce a symphony till a late period of his career, when his judgment was matured by much practice in other kindred forms of instrumental composition, such as pianoforte quartets, string sextets and quartets, sonatas, and such forms of orchestral

[1] This estimate would seem inconsistent with what was said above of Schumann were it not that the writer is evidently thinking of Brahms as a contemporary and not comparing him with predecessors. C.
[2] Only the symphonies in C minor and D major had appeared when this article was written. C.

composition as variations and two serenades. He seems to have set himself to prove that the old principles of form are still capable of serving as the basis of works which should be thoroughly original both in general character and in detail and development, without either falling back on the device of programme, or abrogating or making any positive change in the principles, or abandoning the loftiness of style which befits the highest form of art ; but by legitimate expansion, and application of careful thought and musical contrivance to the development. In all these respects he is a thorough descendant of Beethoven, and illustrates the highest and best way in which the tendencies of the age in instrumental music may yet be expressed. He differs most markedly from the class of composers represented by Raff, in the fact that his treatment of form is an essential and important element in the artistic effect. The care with which he develops it is not more remarkable than the insight shown in all the possible ways of enriching it without weakening its consistency. In appearance it is extremely free, and at available points all possible use is made of novel effects of transition and ingenious harmonic subtleties ; but these are used in such a way as not to disturb the balance of the whole, or to lead either to discursiveness or tautology.

In the laying out of the principal sections as much freedom is used as is consistent with the possibility of being readily followed and understood. Thus in the recapitulatory portion of a movement the subjects which characterise the sections are not only subjected to considerable and interesting variation, but are often much condensed and transformed. In the first movement of the second symphony, for instance, the recapitulation of the first part of the movement is so welded on to the working-out portion that the hearer is only happily conscious that this point has been arrived at without the usual insistence to call his attention to it. Again, the subjects are so ingeniously varied and transformed in restatement that they seem almost new, though the broad melodic outlines give sufficient assurance of their representing the recapitulation.

The same effect is obtained in parts of the allegrettos which occupy the place of scherzos in both symphonies. The old type of minuet and trio form is felt to underlie the well-woven texture of the whole, but the way in which the joints and seams are made often escapes observation. Thus in the final return to the principal section in the allegretto of the second symphony, which is in G major, the subject seems to make its appearance in F♯ major, which serves as dominant to B minor, and going that way round the subject glides into the principal key almost insensibly.[1] In

the allegretto of the symphony in C minor the outline of a characteristic feature is all that is retained in the final return of the principal subject near the end, and new effect is gained by giving a fresh turn to the harmony. Similar closeness of texture is found in the slow movement of the same symphony, at the point where the principal subject returns, and the richness of the variation to which it is subjected enhances the musical impression. The effect of these devices is to give additional unity and consistency to the movements. Enough is given to enable the intelligent hearer to understand the form without its appearing in aspects with which he is already too familiar.

Similar thoroughness is to be found on the other sides of the matter. In the development of the sections, for instance, all signs of 'padding' are done away with as much as possible, and the interest is sustained by developing at once such figures of the principal subjects as will serve most suitably. Even such points as necessary equivalents to cadences, or pauses on the dominant, are by this means infused with positive musical interest in just proportion to their subordinate relations to the actual subjects. Similarly, in the treatment of the orchestra, such a thing as filling up is avoided to the utmost possible; and in order to escape the over-complexity of detail so unsuitable to the symphonic form of art, the forces of the orchestra are grouped in masses in the principal characteristic figures, in such a way that the whole texture is endowed with vitality. The impression so conveyed to some is that the orchestration is not at such a high level as the other elements of art ; and certainly the composer does not aim at subtle combinations of tone and captivating effects of a sensual kind so much as many other great composers of modern times ; and if too much attention is concentrated upon the special element of his orchestration it may doubtless seem at times rough and coarse. But this element must only be considered in its relation to all the others, since the composer may reasonably dispense with some orchestral fascinations in order to get broad masses of harmony and strong outlines ; and if he seeks to express his musical ideas by means of sound, rather than to disguise the absence of them by seductive misuse of it, the world is a gainer. In the putting forward and management of actual subjects, he is guided by what appears to be inherent fitness to the occasion. In the first movement of the symphony in C minor, attention is mainly concentrated upon one strong subject figure, which appears in both the principal sections and acts as a centre upon which the rest of the musical materials are grouped; and the result is to unify the impression of the whole movement, and to give it a special sentiment in an unusual degree. In the first movement of the symphony in D there are even several subjects in each section,

---

[1] For a counterpart to this see the first movement of Beethoven's pianoforte Sonata in F, op. 10, No. 2.

but they are so interwoven with one another, and seem so to fit and illustrate one another, that for the most part there appears to be but little loss of direct continuity. In several cases we meet with the devices of transforming and transfiguring an idea. The most obvious instance is in the allegretto of the symphony in D, in which the first trio in 2–4 time (*a*) is radically the same subject as that of the principal section in 3–4 time (*b*), but very differently stated. Then a very important item in the second trio is a version in 3–8 time (*c*) of a figure of the first trio in 2–4 time (*d*).

Of similar nature, in the symphony in C minor, are the suggestions of important features of subjects and figures of the first allegro in the opening introduction, and the connexion of the last movement with its own introduction by the same means.

In all these respects Brahms illustrates the highest manifestations of actual art as art; attaining his end by extraordinary mastery of both development and expression. And it is most notable that the great impression which his larger works produce is gained more by the effect of the entire movements than by the attractiveness of the subjects. He does not seem to aim at making his subjects the test of success. They are hardly seen to have their full meaning till they are developed and expatiated upon in the course of the movement, and the musical impression does not depend upon them to anything like the proportionate degree that it did in the works of the earlier masters. This is in conformity with the principles of progress which have been indicated above. The various elements of which the art-form consists seem to have been brought more and more to a fair balance of functions, and this has necessitated a certain amount of 'give and take' between them. If too much stress is laid upon one element at the expense of others, the perfection of the art-form as a whole is diminished thereby. If the effects of orchestration are emphasised at the expense of the ideas and vitality of the figures, the work may gain in immediate attractiveness, but must

lose in substantial worth. The same may be said of over-predominance of subject-matter. The subjects need to be noble and well marked, but if the movement is to be complete, and to express something in its entirety and not as a string of tunes, it will be a drawback if the mere faculty for inventing a striking figure or passage of melody preponderates excessively over the power of development; and the proportion in which they are both carried upwards together to the highest limit of musical effect is a great test of the artistic perfection of the work. In these respects Brahms's symphonies are extraordinarily successful. They represent the austerest and noblest form of art in the strongest and healthiest way.

C. H. H. P.

LATER DEVELOPMENTS

Brahms's third symphony, which appeared in 1884, has been called the finest and certainly the clearest of all his orchestral compositions. To Hans Richter it was Brahms's 'Eroica' symphony; yet only the first and last movements are of heroic character; and that character is without warlike implication. Its fundamental note is of proud strength that rejoices in deeds; so Hanslick wrote. Brahms made interesting and highly effective use in it of a 'motto' phrase, suggestive of the 'community of theme' that he and others had found valuable in the sonata form. The phrase is the three introductory chords of the first movement, whose upper voice, F, A flat, F, present a short theme, which recurs significantly throughout the movement. It is heard immediately as the bass of the first real theme of the movement, and is repeated in the inner voices, mounting in a peculiarly exultant manner to the higher octave. The 'cross relation' thereby produced has an incisive and penetrating effect that gives the movement a savour of its own. In this movement Brahms has so far modified the usage of earlier masters as to condense the working-out section within unusually narrow limits, making up for it with a very full elaboration of the recapitulation. In the second movement there are hints of the 'motto' theme of the opening measures, and such hints reappear more clearly and indeed unmistakably in the coda of the last movement, bringing the work to an end with a grave, sweet reminiscence of the fiery outburst of the beginning.

The fourth symphony, coming two years later, in 1886, the last work of Brahms in this form, is in strong contrast with its predecessor. It seems at first, and in its opening, barer, lacking in the rich warmth of that. The first theme of the first movement, taken by itself, gives a thin and cold effect, as do certain themes of Beethoven so taken. It is raised to a higher power and significance by the treatment ; and is, indeed, one of the most notable examples of the power of a great master in the development, from apparently insignificant germs, of broad, noble and stirring utterance. There is a curious effect in the tonality of the andante, as of hesitation between the key of E, in which it really stands, and of C, into which it seems to slip. It is of an unusually developed form for a slow movement, with a well-marked second subject appearing first in the dominant and then in the tonic, as in the sonata-form. The last movement presents an unexpected novelty from the hands of one who so consistently stood for the preservation of the classical tradition in the symphony. It is a PASSACAGLIA (*q.v.*) (a form that had never before been used as a constituent part of a symphony) based on a theme of eight measures, eight notes in all, over a grim and austere ' ground.' From this simple germ Brahms develops innumerable variations, also of eight measures each, with an amazing fertility of resource, lavishness of invention and variety of expression. ' Sometimes it appears as a melody, sometimes as a bass, while more often it is suggested by a melody of wider range. It is often rather implied than expressed, but never really absent, and its influence is always felt beneath the wealth of melody and contrapuntal device applied to it.' [1]

At one time Brahms's orchestration was spoken of by some as dark, muddy, rough, coarse. It no longer seems so, as presented by the finest orchestras under the hands of discriminating and sympathetic conductors—in other words, as Brahms intended it to sound. It has not the glowing brilliancy of Wagner nor the scintillation of Strauss ; but for the expression of Brahms's ideas it seems most perfectly fitted. It has warmth, depth, drastic power— as those qualities are required. The scoring is economical, even restrained, refraining from excess. Brahms, as has been remarked, avoids in general mixture of colours ; and is apt to treat the instruments by themselves. He uses doublings, as a rule, only when he sets entire groups in strong opposition to each other. Then they have a powerful effect, rounded rich and glowingly shadowed, gaining a fullness of tone not really to be gained by the accumulation of mass. It is the business of conductors, as Weingartner truly says, to dispense with ' impressionism ' in conducting Brahms's orchestral works and to study the proper balancing and contrasting of his instrumentation in such a way as to show it in its true light.

In his four symphonies Brahms made the greatest contribution to the literature of the form since Beethoven, and showed conclusively the unsoundness of the contention that with Beethoven the possibilities of the symphonic

form were exhausted. He attempted, and apparently thought of, no radical change or development or innovation in the form. He used it in the main as it was handed down to him by his great predecessors, and found within its outlines ample opportunity for the expression of a great range of ideas of a symphonic sort. His ideas were, in fact, of the symphonic sort, sufficient unto themselves and for symphonic purposes, dependent upon no sister art for their existence and needing no sister art for their explanation or justification. Some of his commentators have tried to read into these symphonies implications of a programmatic kind. But Brahms, perhaps more than any other composer, turned his face in the other direction and undertook to find in music, and in music alone, a great world of ideas that are in themselves music and music alone. He justified supremely the independence of symphonic art in a period when so many composers were turning to the programme and the anecdote as crutches to support the interest and validate the very existence of their musical production.

It cannot be said that Brahms in his symphonic works has formed a school or has deeply influenced the course of music since his day. The great influence that has so long prevailed has been that of Wagner and then of Strauss ; and in France, of Franck ; others are now taking their place. The great symphonic works of Brahms and Franck stand alone, and the course of modern music has strayed past them into ways that cannot be traced back to any of the great creative forces of the 19th century. Brahms may seem at this time a figure of lonely eminence, the last of his race, the summation of a great series of symphonists. It is given to no man to foretell the future of the art. To many it will seem that the tendencies that now have so much prevalence therein are self-destructive and lead nowhere. Whether there will be a return, in some way, or in some approximation, to the principles and ideals that governed the great symphonists and found their final exemplification in Brahms, it seems certain that his works will remain among the great and inspiring landmarks, looming larger the farther we recede from the composer's lifetime, which coming generations of music lovers will not willingly lose from view.

THE GERMAN SCHOOL.—A contemporary of Brahms, who for a time, owing to the zealous activities of their respective partisans, was considered his rival, was Anton Bruckner.[2] He wrote nine symphonies. He was an ardent admirer of Wagner and paid him, sometimes to a considerable extent, the tribute of imitation. Bruckner was unfortunate in that he was regarded, justly or unjustly, as a musician pitted

---

[1] H. C. Colles : *Brahms* (' Music of the Masters '), p. 84.

[2] For a modern German estimate of Bruckner, see the article under his name by A. Einstein.

against Brahms the symphonist by the extreme Wagnerites, who were said to have no symphonist among them and were thought to be disturbed by the prominence of Brahms in the realm of ' absolute ' music. It was even declared by some, however absurdly, that Bruckner was following in the symphony the same ideals as Wagner followed in the music drama. This is, of course, based not on the underlying significance of those ideals but only on such minor considerations as the physiognomy of his themes, sometimes resembling almost to the point of plagiarism certain themes of Wagner ; the quality of his harmony ; his use of dissonance ; his manner of combining certain figurations in the several orchestral choirs ; in a kind of free modern polyphony characteristic of Wagner ; and finally in the abundance and richness of his orchestration, especially in the resonance of his brasses and the use, probably for the first time in the symphony, of the ' Bayreuth tubas.' Though Bruckner's first symphonies were written in the late 'sixties and early 'seventies, it was not till Nikisch and Levi played them in 1884 and 1885 that their composer attracted much attention. These symphonies are marked by a singular unevenness of texture and value. Grandiose and imposing, even noble and elevated, pages are alternated with trivial ones, with laborious prolixity, dry pedantry and fruitless over-elaboration. Bruckner was a professor of counterpoint, and was inordinately fond of certain contrapuntal technicalities, such as the inversion of themes ; but in a larger view the technical structure of many of his movements discloses a singular ineptitude and clumsiness of writing, and his treatment of the symphonic form is often illogical, fragmentary and episodic. His peasant naïveté, his lack of well-considered artistic principles, are evident in his music. Of his symphonies, the fourth is entitled the ' Romantic ' ; the third is dedicated to Wagner. There is in none of them any hint or suggestion of a ' programme ' nor of any extra-musical allusion ; and Bruckner is said to have been roused to fury by writers who professed to discover such. Though Bruckner's symphonies are much played in Germany and Austria, and are much admired there, they have never found much favour in England, the United States or France.

Gustav Mahler's career as a conductor had the effect that such a career may be supposed to have upon a composer. The results of a constant flow of other men's ideas through his brain is shown in the ' eclectic ' character of his symphonic writing. He produced nine symphonies, several of them being of colossal dimensions, and all representing, in greater or less degree, the programmatic tendency. Nevertheless he was violently opposed to the disclosure of his intentions in that direction

through the medium of explanatory notes. The composer, he contended, should force on his hearers the sensations which streamed through his own mind ; then he reaches his goal. There are, however, frequently explanatory or allusive titles upon his symphonies and upon individual movements of them. Mahler also declared that in conceiving a great musical picture he always arrived at the point where he must employ the ' word ' ; and in several of his symphonies he introduced vocal parts into one or more movements. This is the case with the second (C minor), in which there is a text to be sung in the third and fourth movements ; in the third (D minor) where the ' second part,' in five movements, demands an alto voice, a choir of children and a women's chorus ; in the fourth, which has a soprano solo in the fourth movement ; in the eighth, in which an enormous apparatus is used—two mixed choruses, a chorus of boys and seven solo singers. In these respects and in other, perhaps more important, details of form Mahler's symphonies depart widely from accepted canons, often in the pursuit of the programmatic purpose which he kept to himself or indicated only by general suggestions or through the words of the texts of the vocal numbers. The value of his musical inspiration in these symphonies varies widely. He had a predilection for very long themes ; also for a certain sort of tunes of the naïve character of folk-song, with which, however, he could not get far without submitting them to all sorts of incongruous sophistications. His predilection for the naïve is also suggested by his frequent resort to the texts of ' Des Knaben Wunderhorn,' a collection of old German songs.

On the whole, Mahler lacked in his symphonies a truly individual inspiration, a potent inventive power. He attempted to make up for this lack by great elaboration and involution of his material, by the use of very large orchestral resources and of rich and lavish colouring. He not infrequently produced pages of beauty and real splendour, but they are buried in long stretches of dullness. He is another case of one whose invention panted in vain after his hurrying ambition. Much played in Germany and Austria, and by Mengelberg at Amsterdam, his symphonies have never taken deep root in other lands.

In his youthful days Richard Strauss wrote a symphony in F that quite soberly complies with all the symphonic rules, creditably for one of his age—it was in 1884 and he was 20 years old—but it is a wholly derived work and shows strongly the influences to which he was then subjected. His ' Symphonia domestica ' came in 1904, after his long series of symphonic poems, and is scarcely a symphony in more than name. It is really a symphonic poem in four movements, and the highly realistic programmatic intention is as clearly marked as in any of the symphonic poems. The 'Alpine Symphony' (1915), even more elaborately realistic and descriptive in its purpose, is perhaps still less of a symphony in the older acceptance of the term.

INFLUENCE OF NATIONALISM.—A tendency that made great headway in the 19th century was the making of the symphony an expression of nationalism in music, through the use of national colour, usually as suggested in folk-song elements ; not always of folk-songs themselves, but through an assimilation of their spirit, of their characteristic melodic turns, of the harmony expressed or implicit in them. It was not new in the 19th century. Sir W. H. Hadow has shown in his examination of Haydn's works [1] the strong inclination of that composer to use Croatian tunes in his music. Mendelssohn made an attempt on foreign soil to suggest national colour in his ' Scotch ' and ' Italian ' symphonies. Niels W. Gade pursued the suggestion by putting a Scandinavian colour and an allusion to the quality of Scandinavian folk-tunes into his eight symphonies : though, as Schumann says, he would have been the last to deny his debt to German masters.

In modern times the tendency has been exhibited in symphonic music by the Russians. Tchaikovsky, though he was not recognised as one of them by the most thorough-going Russian nationalist composers, the ones who claimed that title exclusively, discloses a fondness for the use of Russian folk-tunes or themes conceived in the most obvious imitation of them. It was objected by those composers, or their spokesmen, that Tchaikovsky's frequent use of folk-tunes is in a manner associated with Western traditions ; that he is rarely successful in imparting to their treatment the special complexion requisite to preserve their character as an indigenous product. This is all a little difficult ; and perhaps it needs a Slavic inheritance properly to be appreciated. Of Tchaikovsky's six symphonies, only the last three have gained much foothold outside of Russia, the fifth and sixth having been extravagantly popular in England and the United States. The fourth and fifth show most decisively the composer's inclination toward the use of a distinctively Russian idiom. In the fourth a true folk-tune is introduced into the finale as the second theme. The first theme of the first allegro of the fifth symphony is said to be derived from a Polish folk-song. There is an obvious Russian spirit in the last movement of this symphony, with its characteristic *ostinato* effects. In his first symphony Tchaikovsky gives some indication of a programmatic intention of the more general sort which he did not carry out in his succeeding ones. He entitled it ' Winter Day Dreams ' ; the first two movements are inscribed ' Dreams on the

High Road in Winter ' and ' Dreary Land : Land of Mists ' respectively. The last two have no titles. In the second symphony there is no attempt at a programme, but the composer was, it is said, persuaded to use a Little Russian folk-tune as the subject for his last movement, and there is the Russian imprint on several themes occurring earlier. The slow prelude to the third is marked ' Tempo di marcia funebre' ; the third ' Andante Elegiaco,' which in themselves contain some hint of programme not pursued in the other three movements—there are five.

Tchaikovsky also made use of the device of ' community of theme,' foreshadowed in the works of some of his predecessors and destined to take a still more important place a little later. A sort of seal is set upon the fourth symphony by the fanfare that introduces it and that reappears at the close of the last movement. The device is carried much further in the fifth symphony. There is a unifying force in the strongly rhythmed phrase of fateful import that appears in the introduction, reappears imposingly near the end of the second movement, is suggested as in a whisper at the end of the slow movement, is proclaimed imposingly in the introduction to the last movement, and recurs emphatically in the working out of the second theme of that movement.

Tchaikovsky's preoccupation was not with the exploitation of the national spirit, nor did he, as some have suggested, seek programmatic effects by the use of an affiliated theme. He had a very decided personality of his own that gave his music a larger flight and a greater power than the somewhat parochial efforts of the avowedly national party, the members of which affected to treat him condescendingly, though they themselves had, after all, hardly emerged from the state of amateurs. Tchaikovsky, especially in his last three symphonies, shows a rich and individual expression. He is addicted to a haunting melancholy or a wild and unrestrained passion, to startling contrasts of moods. His luxuriant melodic invention has sometimes a luscious and overripe quality, sometimes a feverishness and lack of poise, that are characteristic of the man ; but it is always free and liberally spontaneous. These things are most forcibly set forth in the sixth symphony, where there are the most drastic contrasts, the greatest intensity of mood, that to many will be morbid. His workmanship is skilful, though he does not always follow the accepted canons of symphonic form—departing most widely from them in his last symphony. In structural power, in harmonic originality and richness, in command of all the resources of the orchestra, he takes a high place among modern symphonists. Yet there are not seldom lapses into triviality in his style ; the use of *ad captandum* effects, especially of these *ostinato*

[1] A Croatian Composer : Notes on Josef Haydn.

passages that seem particularly dear to the Russian heart, and frequent mannerisms of expression, such as persistently repeated scale passages and unimportant figurations with no special freight of meaning.

The 'Invincible Five,' as they liked to call themselves — Rimsky - Korsakov, Balakirev, Borodin, Moussorgsky and Cui—embarked deliberately upon a nationalistic campaign, in writing music that should be ˙unmistakably Russian, rooted in the soil and racy with the native musical idiom. Most of the works that decisively embody this intention are in the form of symphonic poems and so do not come within the scope of this article. But there are several symphonies in which the composers have tried to give a deep and prevailing tinge of nationalism. Of the 'Five,' Balakirev and Borodin produced symphonies (leaving out of account a couple of unimportant early attempts by Rimsky-Korsakov)—the former two, the latter three. In Balakirev's C major symphony the last movement begins with a Russian tune, so called in the ʹscore ; the third theme of this rondo-like movement is also distinctively Russian in character. Borodin's first symphony contains no definitely labelled Russian theme, but there are one or two that betray their nationality. Borodin is said to have told a friend that in the adagio of his second symphony he intended to recall the songs of the old Slavonic 'boyars' (troubadours) ; in the first movement the assemblage of the Russian princes, in the finale the banquet of heroes to the tones of the 'guzla' and the bamboo flute. Above and beyond the use of these specifically nationalistic elements there is a strenuous attempt to attain a distinctive Russian spirit in the music of these composers ; an attempt that must in many cases be considered successful. The value of it all, apart from this special quality, has been diverse. Borodin's symphonies still survive in the concert-rooms ; and it may be said that the 'Five' made on the whole a considerable contribution to the sum of modern symphonic music.

Although the nationalistic movement in Russia is declared to have reached its height in Rimsky-Korsakov (whose mark was not made as a symphonic composer), and to have begun to decline with his death in 1908, there are some traces of the aggressive Russian influence in the symphonies of some of his younger contemporaries. Glazounov has written no fewer than eight symphonies and is still apparently writing them—with far too much facility and lack of concentration to produce results of lasting value. The use he makes of characteristically Russian themes has steadily diminished in his later works. At the same time—not necessarily because of this—there has been a steady diminution in the pregnancy and individuality of his musical ideas.

The nationalistic movement has pretty well come to an end in Russia, and had done so before the great revolution. Of the more recent representatives of the school, Rachmaninov has been the most prominent. He has been most strongly influenced by Tchaikovsky. His three symphonies show little trace of a distinctively national physiognomy. As for Scriabin, who wrote but two symphonies, of a character and structure doubtfully entitling them to the name, the influences to which he has chiefly submitted have been those of Wagner and Liszt and, as is said by his expounders, the ideas of theosophy, whatever they may mean in music.

The nationalist movement had a strong repercussion in that other Slavic nation, the Czechs. Their earliest distinguished composer, Smetana, devoted his orchestral talents to the symphonic poem ; but Antonín Dvořák, who came later, wrote five symphonies, besides some discarded earlier ones. He resorted largely to the national colour and rhythms. In none of his symphonies has he avowedly made use of folk-tunes or dances, such as appear often in his instrumental music in the smaller forms. Yet the 'dumka' and 'furiant' can be traced in spirit, at least, in several. A notable attempt in assimilating a foreign idiom after the same fashion is his fifth symphony, 'From the New World,' op. 95, written during his sojourn in the United States (1892–95), wherein, as also in his string quartet and string quintet (opp. 96 and 97), he avowedly submitted himself to the influence of the negro folk-songs of North America, as ho heard them around him and found them noted by American collectors. His success in so doing was for a time the subject of debate among American critics, some of whom found marked traces, in rhythm and melodic quality, of the negro tunes. He used no existing tunes (though he came near to one or two), but tried to mould his ideas on their salient characteristics, and publicly declared that he did so. Others found in this symphony (as in the chamber works) only the utterance of a 'homesick Bohemian' vainly trying to escape from his musical heritage. However this may be, the 'New World' symphony immediately found and has hitherto maintained a remarkable popularity in America, where the negro idiom is most familiar, and in England. The other symphonies of Dvořák have in recent years steadily sunk below the musical horizon and are less and less frequently heard. In all of them the composer shows himself a fertile melodist, a master of brilliant orchestration and what has been called 'the lesser gift of writing brilliant dialogue for his instruments, of making each stand out salient and expressive against a background of lower tone.' He is 'even more successful in those combinations of timbre which harmonize the separate voices and give the full chord its peculiar richness and euphony.'[1] In the matter of form Dvořák was a conservative and held in general to the classical models, though he often enough departed from them in details, nor did he hesitate in certain places to experiment with modifications of them, as in the finales of the G major and F major symphonies.

THE FRENCH SCHOOL.—For a long time it was supposed that the French genius was incapable of symphonic music ; that its nature impelled it exclusively to opera. The fate that first befel the attempts of Berlioz was taken as a confirmation of this belief. These attempts remained the only ones in French symphonic composition for a generation or more. It is remarkable, as d'Indy points out in his life of Franck, that in the years between 1884 and 1889 there was a serious return in France to pure symphonic music ; a renewed effort to escape from the circumscription of opera and dramatic music. Camille Saint-Saëns had written his first symphony in 1853 as a boy of 16, and had followed it six years later with another ; but very little was heard of the first and not much of the second, which was not published till 1878. In 1836 he published his third, in C minor, one of his most important compositions. In this symphony Saint-Saëns attempted a modification of the traditional symphonic form, by dividing it into two parts, which include, however, at least in outline, the four canonical movements, with two brief slow introductions. The composer's purpose is said to have been to eliminate some of the repetitions that belong to the accepted form. He also embodied in his work an elaborate system of thematic transformation and community of theme : a device by no means new. The work is based largely on the first theme and on its transformations in various guises in the several movements. The orchestral forces include the organ and the pianoforte, the latter played by two and then by four hands. The work is remarkable for skill, ingenuity and technical adeptness. It was the flight of creative faculty that Saint-Saëns lacked. Mastery of technique, a certain hard-surfaced finish and a paucity of deeply felt inspiration characterise this symphony ; which, nevertheless, because of the skill and resourcefulness shown in the transformation of its themes and its outward effectiveness, is a landmark in modern French art and has retained a certain place in the modern orchestral repertory.

Another French symphony appeared in the same year as Saint-Saëns's—that in G minor by Edouard Lalo, already a distinguished musician, a work to be remembered more by what it foreshadowed in French art than by its intrinsic musical value, for it has hardly kept its place in

the orchestral repertory. Its most important foreshadowing was of the symphony in D minor by César Franck, produced in 1889.

Much has been said about this symphony as one of the starting-points of the younger French school of instrumental music, and, in common with other works of Franck in the sonata form, as marking the 'creation and consecration' of the cyclical method, called by d'Indy 'the basis of modern symphonic art.' It is music greatly superior to its predecessors in the field of French symphony, in poetical warmth, eloquence and a certain high mysticism that characterises so much of the master's limited output. It was, as were all the other chief works of Franck, a new utterance, in a new and wholly original and individual style. The symphony is constructed out of two primary themes, developed now singly, with or without a counter-subject, now combined in a clear and melodious counterpoint. Here is to be found something more than transformation of themes, such as takes so prominent a part in the works of some of Franck's predecessors and is in them effected with an ingenuity that sometimes borders on the mechanical. There is transformation, but there is also development in a more largely structural way. With Franck such transformation was not merely a technical procedure ; it was a means of heightening the beauty and value of a number of melodies enhanced by combining them contrapuntally with each other and making of them something richer and finer than their sum. There is a strongly original quality in Franck's themes, an unmistakable personal note in them ; but there is a still greater originality in the poignant beauty of his harmony. This is of a richness and unexpectedness entirely individual with him. This harmony is largely based on an elaborate and, in the final analysis, deeply learned and skilful chromatic movement of the parts ; but its learning and skill are concealed in the intensity of beauty and the emotional significance of the result. It is hard to believe that Franck was not in this respect to a certain extent influenced by Wagner, whose 'Tristan' can now and again be heard in his harmonies. But it is undoubtedly true that he took no part in the Wagnerian movement that for a time so strongly influenced the French composers of the period, and it would be an entire misjudgment to consider Franck's music 'Wagnerian' in its substance or in its tendencies. He was one of the greater original forces of modern symphonic art ; and his single symphony seems destined long to keep its place as one of its finest exemplifications.

César Franck was the centre and inspiration of a group of young French composers, his pupils, who have made contributions of diverse value to modern French symphonic music.

[1] W. H. Hadow, Studies in Modern Music.

Ernest Chausson produced a symphony in 1891, largely influenced by Wagner in its style and orchestration, that has many attractive qualities in thematic invention and expression of mood. More individual and independent, especially in his later work, is Vincent d'Indy, who himself was submitted for a time to the spell of Wagner that fascinated the younger French composers at the close of the last century ; but who later emerged into a path of his own, with a strong individuality and with a method that may be characterised as austere and has frequently been called ' cerebral.' He produced three symphonies, in which he has shown in varying degrees the influence of his master, Franck, in the matter of structure and thematic development. He passes beyond him, indeed, in the logic and resource with which he has applied Franck's principles ; though he is far from showing a similar warmth and emotional quality in his music. His first symphony (1886) is based on a folk-tune of the Cévennes, a ' mountaineer's air.' In it the pianoforte plays an important part which, though elaborate and requiring the skill of a virtuoso, is treated generally as a constituent of the orchestra and not as a solo instrument. The folk-tune, of a pastoral character, is stated at the very beginning. It is consorted with other themes and occupies a prominent, though by no means a preponderating, place throughout the work : assuming new forms in the second movement and variants in the third, portions of it being used in combinations with other themes ; all in a manner that testifies to the composer's ingenuity in devising new sources of beauty by his skill of treatment. Even more elaborate is the method pursued in the second symphony in B flat (1904). By this time the composer had outgrown the most obvious influences that Franck and Wagner had had upon him. His style had become more severe and carries out with a sterner and more unflinching logic the principles of thematic development that he had learned from Franck. The themes appear first in the state of simple ' cells,' as the composer himself was pleased to call these brief phrases afterwards united to larger issues. Two themes dominate the whole symphony, though others are used frequently. These undergo numberless changes, rhythmic and melodic transformations, the particular physiognomy of the themes being sometimes radically changed, sometimes more strictly retained. These persist through the four movements of the work. The last movement is an ' Introduction, fugue and finale,' in which all the chief thematic elements of the preceding movements are employed with a remarkable and unfailing readiness of resource and constructive skill. As may be imagined from the account of this method, the symphony gives a certain excuse for the use of the term ' cerebral ' in describing it. It is severe, and it is obvious

that the composer took little thought of affording facile pleasure to his listeners.

In 1918 d'Indy produced a symphony, entitled ' De Bello Gallico,' inspired or suggested by the Great War, in which the contending French and German armies are typified, with a final apotheosis of victory. It is of less value than his other symphonies, however, and is open to the charge of being a ' pièce d'occasion,' with all that implies, in which patriotism has taken the place of purely musical promptings.

ENGLISH COMPOSERS.—The writing of symphonies in England hardly reached a point entitling it to serious consideration till the last quarter of the 19th century. The ' renaissance ' that had gained a good headway by that time brought several men of high attainment to the front, men who have established an English symphonic school that now, in its latest manifestations, occupies as high a place as any in the modern musical world.

Frederic Cowen is the composer of six symphonies. His ' Scandinavian ' symphony, No. 3, in C minor (1880) had great popularity for a time within and without the borders of England, on account of its melodiousness and its pleasing use of Scandinavian colour. Parry produced five ; that in C, entitled the ' English ' (1889), lays emphasis on certain English characteristics. His symphonies have occupied a less important place in the sum of his work than his choral compositions and other instrumental pieces. In the long tale of Stanford's compositions there are seven symphonies, of which the ' Irish ' (1887) has been the most popular, embodying as it does some of the composer's heritage as an Irish musician. Elgar has produced two symphonies, in A flat (1908) and in E flat (1911), which have been recognised as among the most serious and important of his compositions. They are thoroughly characteristic of his musical inspiration as it had been made known in his preceding great choral works, showing the same closely woven texture and logical treatment of thematic material, in itself often of apparent slight significance, till it is transfigured by the highly intellectual power with which it is developed, and by the composer's brilliant mastery of the orchestra.

The most significant of recent symphonies by a modern Englishman have been Ralph Vaughan Williams's three—' A Sea Symphony ' with chorus, the ' London Symphony ' (1914) and the ' Pastoral Symphony ' (1922). They are all of a very general programmatic tendency, the last being ' Malerei '—tone painting— even less than Beethoven's symphony of the same title and purpose. A profoundly serious tone prevails in them. The ' London ' symphony, undertaking to suggest various aspects of the great capital, sombre in spirit, is a remarkable achievement in the embodiment of the moods with which it deals ; and no less so is the ' Pastoral,' deeply poetical in its contents and less definite in its outward suggestion. Vaughan Williams is an ardent devotee of the English folk-song. While he has not used actual folk-songs in his symphonies, his musical thought has been much cast in their mould and coloured by them, especially by the modal character that inheres in many of those tunes.

Looking elsewhere, we must notice the seven symphonies of Jean Sibelius. Some of them display singular originality and power. Though he studied in Berlin and Vienna, he brought back to his native Finland much less of their influence than many other northern composers have done. He stands alone, as do few symphonists of less than the highest rank, in the independence and individuality of his work. He has not drawn on the rich stores of Finnish folk-song, so far as appears, for his symphonic material, nor has he undertaken to illustrate programmes; yet there is a strong national colour in much of his music. He avows that he loves the mysterious sounds of fields, forests, water and mountains and wishes to be considered a poet of Nature. His style has a certain innate gloom and severity; qualities that are intensified in his later symphonies. In these he has cast loose from many of the prescriptions of form and shows a radical departure from his previous manner, in his use of dissonances, of the whole-tone scale and sundry other modern effects, as well as in a certain boisterousness, abruptness and fantasticality. It is difficult to trace Sibelius's artistic lineage, as it is to class him among contemporary symphonists, with none of whom he has any marked affinity. His work is not completed; and whither the most recent divagations of his style may lead him is not to be foretold.

Though in Italy in recent years there has been a great growth of interest in purely instrumental music, it has not resulted in important contributions to symphonic literature. Almost the only notable contributions in this direction have been Sgambati's two symphonies in D and E flat, the former of which gained for a time considerable notice outside of Italy, and Martucci's two in D minor and F, strongly influenced by Wagner and Liszt.

AMERICAN COMPOSERS have not produced lasting works, apparently, in the form of the symphony. John Knowles Paine's ' Spring ' symphony was for a time popular, leaning heavily on Schumann and filled with a ' romantic ' spirit. George Whitfield Chadwick, one of the most independent and muscular of American musicians, has written three symphonies and a ' sinfonietta ' that disclose vigour of invention and skill in technique; also a certain quality that might be held to come from the American soil, though not through the use or imitation of any of the various ' folk-songs ' that exist on that soil. Edgar Stillman Kelley

has written two symphonies both more or less suggestive of a programme; one entitled ' Gulliver,' the other ' New England.' Henry Hadley, somewhat handicapped in high endeavour by an excess of fluency and facility, has written four symphonies, three of them also bearing suggestive titles. Of these the second, ' The Four Seasons,' won the Paderewski prize in 1902; the fourth, ' North, South, East, West,' was produced at the Norfolk (Connecticut) Festival in 1911.   R. A.

SYMPHONY, see HURDY GURDY.

SYMPSON, CHRISTOPHER, see SIMPSON.

SYNCOPATION. (1) An alteration of the normal time accents of the bar (see ACCENT, METRE, TIME) by the setting up of contrary accents. This may be done either by indications of emphasis or of phrasing in passages of notes of equal value; e.g.

where bar 1 is thus syncopated, or by making the longer notes of the passage begin on the weak parts of the bar; e.g.

The latter is the commoner. In either case the practical effect of syncopation depends on the conflict created between the syncopated accents and the normal time accents either already set up in the hearer's mind and maintained by him imaginatively or simultaneously heard in another part.

In Example 3 there is a double effect of syncopation, (a) the imaginative one as a result of displacing the accents of the original tune (which in the jargon of American music has been called ' ragging the time '), and (b) the actual syncopation of the accent on the second beat of the bar in the flute tune conflicting with the regular time-beat of the bassoon.

Such a passage as Schumann's opening to the Manfred overture

is only a syncopation on paper, because neither ear nor imagination has any experience which can suggest a contrary accent.

(2) Syncopation has become a general term for all that class of 20th-century dance music which has sprung from the American adoption of rag-time. Dance bands are frequently spoken of as 'Syncopated Orchestras' less because their music employs syncopation than because their constitution with saxophones, percussive instruments, etc., is designed to emphasise the effects essential to dance music of the American type.   C.

SYNTAGMA MUSICUM, see PRAETORIUS.

SYREN, see SIREN.

SYRINX, see PANDEAN PIPE.

SYSTEM. The collection of staves necessary for the complete score of a piece—in a string quartet, or an ordinary vocal score, four; a PF. trio, four; a PF. quartet, five; and so on. Two or more of these will go on a page, and then we speak of the upper or lower system, etc.   G.

SZARVADY, MME., see CLAUSS - SZARVADY.

SZOPSKI, FELICJAN (b. Galicia, June 5, 1865) studied music with Zelenski and also in Berlin with Urban. He became a teacher at the Cracow Conservatoire (1894) and in 1908 removed to Warsaw, where he attained a prominent position as a teacher of theory and a newspaper critic. In 1918 he became musical adviser to the Ministry of Education. He has done important work as an editor of folk-songs and is himself a song-writer. His opera ('The Lilies') was produced at Warsaw in 1916.   C.

SZYMANOWSKA, MARIE (b. circa 1790; d. St. Petersburg, Aug. 1831), a distinguished pianist of her day, who would, however, hardly have been remembered but for Goethe's infatuation for her. She was born of Polish parents named Wolowski, and was a pupil of John Field at Moscow. She travelled much in Germany, France and England. She died of cholerà. One of her daughters married the famous Polish poet Mickiewicz, whom she had introduced to Goethe in July 1829. Goethe knew her as early as 1821, and even then overpraised her, setting her above Hummel; 'but those who do so,' says Mendelssohn, who was then at Weimar,[1] 'think more of her pretty face than her not pretty playing.' Goethe, who renewed the acquaintance in Aug. 1823, at Eger, where she and Anna Milder were both staying, calls her 'an incredible player,' and expresses his excitement at hearing music after an interval of over two years in a remarkable letter to Zelter of Aug. 24, 1823, again comparing her with Hummel, to the latter's disadvantage. Mme. Szymanowska appears to have helped to inspire the 'Trilogie der Leidenschaft,' and the third of its three poems, called 'Aussöhnung,' is a direct allusion to her. In 1824 she was in Berlin. 'She is furiously in

love (rasend verliebt) with you,' says Zelter to the poet, 'and has given me a hundred kisses on my mouth for you.'

Her compositions were chiefly for the PF., with a few songs.   G.

SZYMANOWSKI, KAROL (b. Timoshovka, govt. of Kieff, Ukraine, 1883), studied under Sigismund Noskowski at Warsaw. The latter being a pupil of Moniuszko, he is in the direct line of the Polish tradition, and is now regarded as the leader of a Polish musical renascence.

The national element is, however, not obtrusive in his music, and it rarely, if ever, assumes a form attributable to folklore. As one of his countrymen has pointed out, it is necessary to bear in mind that, if the Poles are Slavs, their ancient culture is Latin and not Byzantine, which constitutes an important difference. Yet Szymanowski's first works show side by side with piety toward Chopin and occasional tributes to Scriabin, a marked and almost inevitable effect of the Teutonic preponderance. There is an occasional touch of Brahms in the earlier songs and some of the piano pieces, and until recent years there was also a tendency to over-elaboration and a confusing plethora of notes which recall, in romantic moments, the exuberance of Richard Strauss, and at other times, the polyphony of Reger. In short, Pole that he was, Szymanowski had to achieve his own emancipation from the influences which prevailed in his studentship. In spite of these, however, his personality was quick to detach itself from the inherited background, and even in the 'Nine Preludes' (op. 1) one is conscious of a pronounced individuality. The Four Studies (op. 4) were soon made familiar to recital audiences, among others, by Myra Hess. In those early days he was fortunate in his friends, notably Arthur Rubinstein and Paul Kochanski, who not only championed his works, but whose enthusiasm for all that is good in modern music was a valuable stimulant. The piano accounts for a large proportion of his works. Besides those mentioned there are variations (opp. 3 and 10), sonatas (I. C minor, op. 8; II. A major, op. 21; III. D minor, op. 36), a fantasy (op. 14). Three poems ('The Isle of the Sirens,' 'Calypso,' 'Nausicaa.' op. 29), a later set of twelve études (op. 33), three masks (Scheherazade, 'Tantris the Fool,' and a 'Don Juan Serenade,' op. 34), and a recent set of mazurkas introduced by Rubinstein at his recitals. Songs are also numerous, the most important being opp. 2, 7, 11, 13, 17 (twelve), 22, 24 ('Hafiz'), and of more recent date, the "Songs of the Infatuated Muezzin' and some settings of Tagore. One of his best-known works consists of three pieces for violin and piano entitled 'Myths' ('The Fountain of Arethusa,' 'Narcissus,' 'Dryads and Pan,' op. 30) bearing some relationship to the Poems for piano   Other violin works are the sonata in D minor (op. 9), Romance (op. 23), Notturno and Tarantella (op. 28) and the concerto (op. 35) played in 1924 at the Prague Festival of the International Society for Contemporary Music. His orchestral works comprise a symphonic poem, ' Penthesilea,' Overture Concertante (op. 12), three symphonies, of which the third (op. 27) requires a solo tenor and chorus, a ' Song of the Night ' completed in 1916, and ' Mandragore,' being incidental music to a comedy of Molière. The two last-named have been performed by the London Symphony Orchestra. He has also composed an opera, ' Hagith ' (op. 25), and two large choral works : ' Demeter ' for contralto, female chorus and orchestra, and ' Agave ' for soprano, chorus and orchestra. His opus-list is rich in works which, whatever their appeal to individual taste, possess the valuable attribute of character and are the utterances of a composer who has something personal to say.

The string quartet in C (op. 37) which was performed in 1925 at the Venice Festival of the International Society for Contemporary Music seems to indicate a new orientation, the thematic material being simpler, and its treatment more direct. In this respect it approaches more nearly than most of his works to the prevalent conception of Slavonic tendencies as indicated by the Russian composers. In some of his larger works, sonatas and symphonies, Szymanowski has adopted a form consisting of a sonata-allegro, theme with variations, and final fugue on previous subjects, which is peculiarly suited to a certain stage of his development, notably in the second piano sonata and second symphony. The third sonata denotes a further development in form and is of remarkable interest. As regards texture, Szymanowski is no avowed disciple either of atonality or of polytonality, which, however, does not debar him from having recourse to either method as occasion dictates. Despite the generally elaborate character of his style his instinct for design preserves him from excesses which would impair the tonal plan. In conclusion, it has been remarked that apart from all stages of development his work exhibits a kind of duality, certain groups of compositions exhaling charm and poetic grace, whilst others have a profounder, more intellectual purport and are more robustly conceived. E. E.

T

TABARRO, IL, opera in one act; text by Giuseppe Adami (from Didier Gold's *La Houppelande*); music by Puccini. Produced Metropolitan Opera House; New York, Dec. 14, 1918; Costanzi Theatre, Rome, Jan. 11, 1919; Covent Garden, June 18, 1920.

TABLATURE (Lat. *tabulatura*, from *tabula*, a table or flat surface, prepared for writing; Ital. *intavolatura* or *intabolatura*; Fr. *tablature*; Ger. *Tabulatur*). (*a*) The word applied to their list of rules by the Meistersinger from the 'tables' upon which they were recorded. (*b*) A system of indicating musical sounds (in general use between the 15th and 18th centuries for the music of certain instruments) which, not following normal notation, made use of letters, numbers or other signs. The chief difference of principle between notation and tablature is that in the former pitch and time values are combined in one sign; in the latter two are necessary. (It will be seen that some guitar tablature is an exception to this.) Of this system there are two different classes: (1) That in which the signs employed directly indicated the musical note. To this class belong most organ and clavier tablature; rarely that for string and wind instruments; and, in the rare cases in which notation is not used, that for vocal works. (2) That in which the signs employed indicated the musical notes only through the medium of frets, stops or keys—that is, where the sign indicated the fret

few exceptions, employing notation for keyboard music, and tablature of the second class for that of other instruments. The word was, however, often and wrongly used for organ and clavier music which was printed in ordinary notation: *tablature des orgues, espinettes,* etc., *intabolatura d' organo.* German organ tablature is probably the oldest of any of the systems which were in use during the 16th and 17th centuries, and the most ancient examples are of a mixed notation and tablature, the former for right hand, the latter for left hand. This particular variety was in use in south-west Germany only between 1440 and 1530, and is not to be confused with the mixed notation and tablature used for songs with accompaniments. The ordinary or normal kind was a simple and fairly elastic method of indicating the notes by means of letters without the assistance of the stave. The various octaves were differentiated by different styles of letters, and were called great, little, one-line, two-line, etc., octaves, according to those letters. Sharps were indicated by means of a little tail attached to the letter, and the confusion of such a system is exhibited in the fact that, for the greater part of the time when keyboard tablature was in use, the scale possessed but one flat—*bb*. There were considerable variations in the manner of writing the different octaves, and the following three different explanations of the keyboard will be of use in transcribing the signs:

1.—VIRDUNG: *Musica getutscht,* 1511.

2.—AGRICOLA: *Musica instrumentalis deudsch,* 1528.

3.—AMERBACH: *Orgel oder Instrument Tabulatur,* 1571.

on the string, the hole of the pipe or the number of the key on the keyboard where the finger should rest in order to produce the required note (see LYRA VIOL). To this class belongs tablature for all the different varieties of lute (theorbo, arch-lute, chitarrone, etc.), for mandora, cittern, angelica, calichon, orpharion, vihuela da mano, guitar, viols, violin, etc., also for wind instruments and (rarely) keyboard.

(1) It was chiefly in Germany that tablature of the first class was used, other countries, with

The compass in the first two examples is from

to , in the third from

to ; and in the latter the short compass in the bass may be seen by the two lowest tones occupying the black keys otherwise sounding *f♯* and *g♯*.

Although Praetorius (*Syntagma musicum,* 1615) recommended a better differentiation of intervals (the tail pointing up for a flat, down for a sharp), the signs given above continued in general use as long as tablature was employed for keyed instruments.

Time-values had separate signs attached to them, and the following were usual :

A dotted note was indicated the same way as in notation, *i.e.* |. for ⌒ · etc. Rests were indicated as follows : ▪ or ⁻ for ⊞ the others having the same signs as the notes themselves, ▪ or ⊥ for ⌒ only being attached to no letters there was no confusion. When notes of identical value followed each other their tails were generally connected : ⊓ ⊓⊓ ⊞ etc. These signs were placed above every part in the music, *i.e.* in a polyphonic composition of four parts each one had its sign attached, so that there should be no misunderstanding in playing them together. This method, as will be seen, was a much more thorough-going one than that employed by lutenists in setting their polyphonic arrangements. An illustration follows, taken from Amerbach's book referred to above, together with a transcription of the same, and it will be noticed that *d♯* is written for *e♭* repeatedly.

AMERBACH, *Orgel oder Instrument Tabulatur*, 1571.

(2) With regard to tablature of the second class, it is acknowledged by Virdung that its first appeal was to those who ' had not learned singing,' *i.e.* who could not read notation and therefore knew the required musical note only when it was found by means of the fret or stop.

' Den andern dye das nitt singen künden, den ist eyn modus erdacht, der tabulaturen, sye zu underweisen, uff den instrumenten zu lernen.'

The practice, however, of employing tablature for the music of many instruments on which notes had to be ' made ' by the performer, was a very general one among trained musicians as well as amateurs, and whether the system was musical or not it remained more or less unquestioned so long as the instruments were patronised. Under this class of tablature there are two special divisions, *i.e.* (*a*) that without lines ; and (*b*) that with lines.

(*a*) This is the least important division, as it includes only German lute tablature of the 15th and 16th centuries. The inventor of this uncouth system was Conrad PAUMANN (*q.v.*; *d.* 1473). He was celebrated as an organist as well as lutenist, and was blind besides. There were critics of the system from the beginning, and Agricola makes merry over it, saying that only a blind man could have been capable of inventing it. Its unusual ways were probably the reason that the fame of early German composers for the lute never went very far away from home, for not until they discarded it for the French method do we find them taking their proper place. That there was some national pride and jealousy concerned in keeping it up as long as possible seems probable, for Melchior Newsidler tried to introduce Italian tablature into his country in the middle of the 16th century, only to meet with great opposition and some reproaches. It finally died a natural death at the end of the 16th century, 1592 being the date of the last published collection. French tablature was thereafter employed in Germany exclusively.

The system being invented in the days of lutes of five strings, its alphabet (which indicated the frets) fitted the five strings and no more. When a sixth became common, as it did early in the 16th century, other signs had to be invented. The ordinary alphabet therefore began on the tenor or *Mittelbrummer*, the string next to the lowest in the usual six-string lute. The letters read *across* the finger-board, not down the strings as in Italian and French systems ; open strings were indicated by large numerals. We give a diagram of the finger-board, with the indications of all frets in the five strings, as well as the various ways that different lutenists had of indicating the lowest bass string, or *Grossbrummer*. The Gothic letters of the German alphabet have been replaced by the ordinary ones.

A seventh string, which was used by many Germans in the 16th century (although it was common to lower the *Grossbrummer* a whole tone when demanded by the compass of a piece, a practice known as playing *im Abzug*), further added to the confusion by being sometimes indicated in capital letters, the same as Judenkünig employs for the *Grossbrummer* ; but as this seventh string was not stopped very often it did not so much matter.

Time-values were indicated by signs above the letters, one sign doing work for all parts played together, and holding good until replaced by another sign. Most German tablature, however, especially up to the middle of the 16th century, repeats its signs over every retter. They are the same as those in organ tablature, given on p. 246.

The music thus written was barred not altogether according to modern ideas, but on the whole fairly systematically. Time - signatures were common, but not by any means invariable, some printers always ignoring them. The tablature was further complicated by signs for left-hand fingering (sometimes right hand), generally one, two, three or four points (· : ⁚) or (· ·· ··· ····), and another sign, sometimes an asterisk (✳), sometimes a single or double cross (+ ✕) which indicated that the fret which it referred to must be held down as long as possible by the left-hand finger stopping it. This was the only means lutenists had of arriving at contrapuntal effects.

The tuning in use in Germany throughout the 16th century was what was universally called the ' normal ' tuning :

that is, from lowest to highest, but this often varied according to the size of the lute. Praetorius mentions seven different sizes (see LUTE) ; and in any case the pitch was by no

means definite, for the top string was only tuned as high as it could bear and the other strings accordingly. All instruction-books in all countries make a particular point of this (to quote only one, Thomas Robinson's *Schoole of Musick*, 1603, ' First set up the treble so high as you dare venter for breaking,' etc.), so that the actual key in which transcriptions of lute music are made reproduces the original with no exactitude of pitch. The intervals are the only important consideration. An example of German lute tablature is given below, together with a literal transcription.

(b) The tablature which made use of lines includes all that except the German kind which we have been considering. The lines, when tabulating music for plucked-string or bowed instruments, indicated the strings; when for the pipe they indicated the holes; when for the keyboard they referred to the four parts of the music, cantus, altus, tenor, bass. As the examples of the latter kind of tablature are comparatively few, being confined to some Spanish organists, they may be here dismissed with the explanation that the forty-two keys of the keyboard, from ⋯ to ⋯ , were numbered and the numbers were placed upon the four lines representing the different voice parts. An example of this may be seen at p. 30 of Tappert's *Sang und Klang*; also (p. 44) of another kind of keyboard tablature in which the four lines represent the note *f*, while the octaves are differentiated by dots or lines attached to the letters.

HANS GERLE, *Tabulatur*, 1533.

FRENCH AND ITALIAN LUTE TABLATURES.—
These are by far the most important of all, and
it extends over three centuries—from the early
16th to the early 19th. The principle made
use of by both kinds was the same, although
details varied considerably. It may be roughly
said that Italian tablature was confined to its
own country and to Spain (with here and there
exceptions to be met with in England and
Germany); French tablature was adopted in
France, the Netherlands, England and Germany
in the 17th and 18th centuries. The French
kind is undoubtedly the earliest in origin, but
the earliest known examples of lute tablature
are Italian. This latter system made use of
six lines (some time before the six-string lute
was common in the rest of Europe) upon each
of which were placed numbers to indicate frets.
(The numbers were sometimes upon, sometimes
above the line.) The lowest line represented
the highest string and the numbers began at
the first fret, repeating themselves down each
string, the open string being indicated by the
figure nought (0). Above the ninth fret Italian
tablature progressed in either Arabic or Roman
numerals with points above them, i.e. 10 or x,
11 or ẋ, 12 or ẍ. The chromatic scale would
therefore appear as follows :

from 𝄢 ≡ to 𝄞 ≡ .

When diapasons, or extra bass strings became
general, they were indicated by numerals
above the top line, which varied with different
printers, some using Arabic, some Roman. As
a rule the following are met with : θ 8 9 X
11 12 13, indicating the 7th to the 13th string,
or the 1st to the 7th string (octave) below the
bass. As no lute before the beginning of the
17th century had so many diapasons these signs
are of course lacking in 16th-century tablature
—until about 1590, when they begin.

Time-values were indicated by the same
means described above under organ tablature,
although the signs employed by different
printers naturally varied in small details. As
a rule, except in the earliest books where the
signs are repeated for every note, they did duty
for as long as the value remained unchanged.
Later on, towards the end of the 16th century,
and generally throughout the 17th, ordinary
notes were used, rather than the signs above
described, i.e. 𝅝 𝅗𝅥 𝅘𝅥 𝅘𝅥𝅮 etc. There were further
signs for fingering (mostly right hand, indicated
by one point under the letter, ọ for the thumb,
and two points ọ̤ for other fingers); signs for
holding the fingers down on the frets, indicated

by × or ⚹; slurs and bows for legato playing;
signs for arpeggi, ≡; for shakes, twc points
above a letter (2̈), or a capital T under a letter.
(²/T). The following example, with transcription
according to the normal tuning (see above),
which prevailed until the middle of the 17th
century, will illustrate what has been said :

ANT. ROTTA's *Intavolatura*, 1546.

By the French method the tablature lines
(of which for the better part of the 16th century
there were but five, after that six) were reversed, the top line representing the highest
string, the bottom the lowest. Moreover,
letters of the alphabet were employed instead
of numerals, the open string being indicated by
a, the first fret on each string by b, the second
by c, and so on. The ascending chromatic
scale, from 𝄢 ≡ to 𝄞 ≡, was therefore
written thus :

≡

(In five-line tablature frets on the sixth string
were indicated by letters underneath the fifth
line.) Diapasons, which were not in use until
after 5-line tablature had become superseded
by that of six, were indicated by letters underneath the bottom line, and varied a good deal
according to the tuning. When there was but
one diapason (during the early years of the 17th
century) it was generally, at least in England,
tuned a fourth below the bass or sixth string
and stopped like the other strings. When
there were two diapasons, the second was tuned
a whole tone below the first. In this case they
were indicated as follows :

Where diapasons increased to four, five or (in
theorboes) six, they were tuned in descending
diatonic intervals, and appeared as follows,
according to the key of the piece :

i.e.

These, being often coupled with octaves, like some of the 'fingered' strings, we sometimes find (in the 18th century) a direction for the pair to be played as two separate tones ; in which case it was indicated by a capital and a small letter, *i.e.* ///A ///a which, translated, would sound 𝄞⸺ .

Time-values were written in the same way as in Italian or German lute tablature, except that the tails were scarcely ever run together, and in the 17th century notes, together with a very free version of them, became general, *i.e.* ♩♪♪𝅘𝅥𝅮 etc. What has been said of bar lines in German lute tablature holds good for Italian and French ; also the use of time signatures. Fingering signs (much the same as Italian, except for the use of a *p* or the number 1 for the right hand thumb— 𝑎/𝑝 or 𝑎/1); *tenues* or signs for holding the finger on the fret (expressed by a stroke or bow under the letters); *estouffements* or signs for suddenly deadening the sound of a string (*i.e.* e× or e//; called the Tut by Mace, and indicated so— ÷α); arpeggi, ; and numerous signs for ornaments of which the following are most commonly found in French and German collections of the 17th and 18th centuries ; shakes and mordents (the signs generally at the right or left of the letter, sometimes below) (×, ⸴, ∧, ⸚, 𝑧. ⸱ ⋔ ✳ 7 ♮ //); appoggiature (⸱, ⸰⸱, / ∧ ⌢⸱); the vibrato (× ⁂ ,. 𝓂); besides these Mace has the following, whose explanation is lengthy and best found by referring to his *Musick's Monument*, 1676—the Elevation (÷ ⸱), single relish (∴), and double relish (∷). It will be seen that the same sign employed by different lutenists meant sometimes two quite different ornaments, and this confusion makes any study of lute ornamentation extremely complicated (cf. ORNAMENTS).

The normal tuning mentioned above gave place generally, in the middle of the 17th century to what was known as the normal French tuning, *i.e.* 𝄞 (although others besides were frequently em-

ployed, notably by Mace), and with this key we may transcribe the following illustration :

LE SAGE DE RICHÉE, *Cabinet der Lauten*, 1695.

Tablature of all other stringed instruments, with one exception (the shorthand kind employed for guitar music), is founded on one of those systems for the lute already explained, and it is only necessary to know the tuning of the instrument in order to be able to transcribe. The French method was by far the most general, and the only variations consisted in the number of lines employed. These followed the number of strings upon the instrument up to six (very exceptionally eight) beyond which the strings were indicated in some such way as lute diapasons were. 16th-century Germans used their own tablature for the viols and violin, while the French and Italian methods were employed in other countries for instruments of those families. Much gamba music in England was written in tablature (called lyra or leero way), and a great many collections of this have been mistaken for lute music. The test is to observe whether there are any gaps in the letters of the chords ; where there are none throughout a collection it may be safely considered viol music, as of course chords played by a bow could not leave out any string, and lutenists rarely made their chords so close as not to do that fairly often.   J. D.

ENGLISH LUTE TABLATURE. — It remains to say something briefly as to the form of tablature used for the lute in England at the close of the 16th century. The Italian method is occasionally found in the MSS. of this period, more especially in transcriptions of polyphonic vocal music. By this method, as already stated, the highest string was represented by the lowest of the six lines in the tablature, and numerals were more commonly employed than letters to indicate the fingering of the frets. But with the rarest exceptions the English lutenists, whether in the printed books of Ayres, or in the MSS. of their compositions for the lute as a solo instrument, adopted in the main the French system of tablature. Six lines were used to represent the six strings, the extra diapasons, when more than one came to be employed early in the 17th century, being denoted, as already described, by the signs / /! /// before the letter beneath the sixth line. The normal tuning of the mean lute was

and when two lutes were employed for accompanying duets the second lute was ordinarily tuned to a fourth lower as in Dowland's 'Come when I call.' Occasionally, as in Jones's *Second Book of Ayres*,[1] the second or bass lute was tuned

. Letters were employed to show which frets were to be stopped, and the signs for the note-values have already been described. Rests were left blank on the lines, but the same signs were placed above to show their value.

The following is the opening phrase of the accompaniment of Dowland's song 'Flow, my tears,' with a translation into ordinary notation:

E. H. F.

THE GUITAR.—As there were a number of

'Nova inventione d' intavolatura per sonare li balletti sopra la chitarra spagniuola senza numeri e note,'

which was adopted with modifications and additions by all countries, although not to the exclusion of the earlier method. It was a kind of shorthand, a series of letters and signs to indicate whole chords; and it differed from all other tablature by the fact that in each sign employed both pitch and time values were combined. The following is the table of signs with their translation and a transcription. Montesardo's tuning of the guitar was the normal one, and resembled that of the lute without the chanterelle, *i.e.*

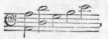

although the pitch varied as it did in lute tuning, depending upon the amount of stretching the highest string could bear. The three highest tones were coupled with unisons, the two lowest generally with octaves, although this was not invariable. (In the transcription the octaves are given, but not the unisons.)

Time-values were indicated by capital and small letters, the former having twice the value of the latter; dotted notes were represented by letters with dots, *i.e.* (A ♩), (a ♪), (a. ♩.). There were no bar divisions, and as the above were the

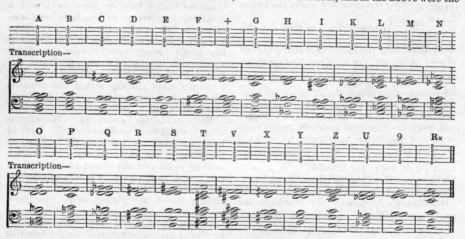

ways of writing guitar music, the confusion of these is sometimes considerable. During the 16th century it was written in ordinary French or Italian lute tablature (numbers or letters on four or five lines according to the number of strings); but in 1606 Montesardo brought out a method—

only signs employed, there was some confusion in differentiation, for example, *a. a a* standing for ♩ ♪ ♩. The manner of striking these chords (either from the lowest upwards, *da giù in sù*, or from the highest downwards, *da sù in giù*) was further indicated by a line which divided the letters from each other, letters below the line being struck upwards, above the line downwards, *i.e.*

1 See *The English School of Lutenist Song-writers.* Robert Jones in the Preface of his *Second Book of Ayres* (1601) claims to have been the first to use ordinary notes in the place of the usual signs for the note-values.

translated thus:

Other methods, in either capital or small letters only, made use of bar lines, with strokes above or below the horizontal line to indicate upward or downward striking of the chords. The time-values were sometimes indicated by notes, sometimes left vaguely to the imagination, *i.e.*

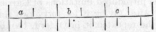

translated thus:

translated thus:

Mersenne's *Harmonie universelle*, 1636, gives the Italian and Spanish methods translated as follows into French tablature, using the alphabet only as far as P. (The open strings are implied.)

Different masters of the instrument somewhat varied the chords of the alphabet according to their own fancy, and later ones added many new, which were generally explained in a table prefixed to the music. Another tuning was also in use later in the 17th century, *i.e.* Some guitarists who employed ordinary lute tablature with its time-values, indicated by the tails of the latter the striking upwards or downwards of their chords, thus: Others of a later date, of whom Francesco Corbetta is the best known, employed a combination of ordinary lute tablature with the shorthand alphabet, and this of course was much better suited to solo music. It will be seen from the illustration that Corbetta makes use of the ordinary time-values, while for playing the chords he uses strokes above or below the line.

CORBETTA: *Varii Capricii*, **1643.**

He also advises that the fourth string should be coupled with an octave instead of unison, which looks as if unisons were general in the lower strings. His reason is that the 'harmony' is thereby improved ('les deux unisones ne composent point d'harmonie'), and indeed the chief defect of this kind of tablature is the anomalous 'harmony' it sometimes produces, chords frequently lacking their fundamental

In the Spanish signs it will be seen that the dot beside the number indicates the minor of the chord represented by a number without the dot. This kind of shorthand was of great convenience in indicating the accompaniments to songs, for the economy of space resulting from the lack of stave was considerable, *i.e.*

Pieta - - te occhi

notes, even at the beginning or end of pieces, a defect which not even Corbetta could remedy.

Signs for fingering, *tenues*, ornaments, legato, etc., were also freely used in guitar tablature, being in some cases identical with those used by lutenists. After the fashion of lute playing began to make way for that of the guitar, tablature for the latter instrument took on many of the characteristics of the other, especially in regard to solo music, and we find the same tables of signs which are met with in 17th- and 18th-

century lute collections. (See GUITAR and
VIHUELA.)

TABLATURE FOR WIND INSTRUMENTS (German flute, hautboy, flageolet, etc.) also employed lines (six, seven or eight) which represented the holes, and dots placed upon them indicated the particular hole to be stopped, This method, founded on the same principle as lute tablature, lasted into the 18th century, but did not survive the better-known system. A clear exposition of pipe tablature is to be found in Thomas Greeting's *Pleasant Companion . . . for the Flageolet*, 1682. The music is indicated by dots or small strokes on six lines, and when all the holes are open by ○ ; a cross through the stroke refers to the 'pinching notes' or octave higher than the ordinary dots. Time signatures are indicated the same way as in lute tablature. Ornaments (beats and shakes), slurs, etc., are also freely used. The method may be studied in the following illustration :

GREETING : *The Pleasant Companion*, 1682.

Printed tablature books are legion, and range from the earliest Italian publication (Petrucci, 1507) to as late as 1760 (in MS. to the early 19th century), lute tablature beginning as well as ending the list. The name Tablature was, probably even later than this, used for figured bass (in the 17th and 18th centuries this was often called theorbo tablature, because of the strictly accompanying qualities of that instrument), and we might even apply it to our own Tonic Sol-fa system. The student who has not the opportunity to consult the original collections may find examples and facsimiles of many different kinds of tablature not illustrated here, in Tappert's *Sang und Klang aus alter Zeit* referred to above, and in Chilesotti's various publications on the subject ; explanations of different methods may also be found scattered through the volumes of the *M.f.M.* and the International Musical Society.   J. D.

BIBL.—ED. BERNOUILLI, *Chansons und Tänze. Pariser Tabulaturdrucke für Tasteninstrumente aus dem Jahre 1530, von Pierre Attaingnant. Nach dem einzigen bekannten Exemplar in der k. Hof- und Staatsbibliothek zu München*, 5 vols. 1914 (Facsimiles : vol. 5 contains some notes) ; MELANIE GRAFCZYNSKA, *Die Orgeltabulatur des Martin Leopolita* (16. Jhdt.), Vienna Dissertation, 1919 ; MAX SEIFFERT, *Das Mylauer Tabulaturbuch von 1750* (*A.M.* 14, 1919); W. MERIAN, *Drei Handschriften aus der Frühzeit des Klavierspiels*, 25 pp. (*A.M.* Jan. 1920).

TABLE ENTERTAINMENT, a species of performance consisting generally of a mixture of narration and singing delivered by a single individual seated behind a table facing the audience. When or by whom it was originated seems doubtful. George Alexander Steevens gave entertainments in which he was the sole

performer at Marlborough Gardens, Dublin, in Aug. 1752. In May 1775, R. Baddeley the comedian (the original Moses in *The School for Scandal*) gave an entertainment at Marylebone Gardens, described as ' an attempt at a sketch of the times in a variety of caricatures, accompanied with a whimsical and satirical dissertation on each character ' ; and in the June following George Saville Carey gave at the same place ' A Lecture on Mimicry,' in which he introduced imitations of the principal theatrical performers and vocalists of the period. John Collins, an actor, in 1775 gave in London a table entertainment, written by himself, called ' The Elements of Modern Oratory,' in which he introduced imitations of Garrick and Foote. After giving it for forty-two times in London he repeated it in Oxford, Cambridge, Belfast, Dublin and Birmingham. He subsequently gave, with great success, an entertainment, also written by himself, called ' The Evening Brush,' containing several songs which became very popular.

Charles DIBDIN (*q.v.*) began in 1789 a series of table entertainments in which song was the prominent feature, and which he continued with great success until 1801. Dibdin's position as a table entertainer was unique. He united in himself the functions of author, composer, narrator, singer and accompanist. On Apr. 3, 1816, the elder Charles Mathews gave, at the Lyceum Theatre, his ' Mail Coach Adventures,' the first of a series of table entertainments which he continued to give for many years, and with which he achieved an unprecedented success. Into these his wonderful power of personation enabled him to introduce a new feature. After stooping behind his table he quickly reappeared with his head and shoulders in costume, representing to the life some singular character. His success led to similar performances by others. Foremost among these were the comedians John Reeve and Frederick Yates, whose *forte* was imitation of the principal actors of the day. W. S. Woodin gave for several seasons, with very great success, table entertainments at the Lowther Rooms, King William Street, Strand. Henry Phillips, the bass singer, and John Wilson, the Scotch tenor, gave similar entertainments, of a more closely musical kind ; and Edney, the Frasers and others have followed in their wake. (See PHILLIPS, Henry ; WILSON, John.)   W. H. H.

TABOR. See DRUM (5). (*PLATE XXV.* No. 2.)

TABOUROT, see ARBEAU.

TACCHINARDI, NICCOLÒ (*b.* Leghorn, Sept. 3, 1772 ; *d.* Florence, Mar. 14, 1859), a distinguished tenor singer. He was intended for an ecclesiastical career, but his artistic bias was so strong that he abandoned the study of literature for that of painting and modelling.

From the age of 11 he also received instruction in vocal and instrumental music. When 17 he joined the orchestra at the Florence theatre as violin-player, but after five years of this work, his voice having meanwhile developed into a beautiful tenor, he began to sing in public. In 1804 he appeared on the operatic stages of Leghorn and Pisa; afterwards on those of Venice, Florence and Milan, where he took a distinguished part in the gala performances at Napoleon's coronation as king of Italy.

At Rome, where his success was as permanent as it was brilliant, his old passion for sculpture was revived by the acquaintance which he made with Canova, in whose studio he worked for a time. Canova executed his bust in marble, thus paying homage to him in his worst aspect, for he was one of the ugliest of men, and almost a hunchback. When he appeared at Paris in 1811, his looks created a mingled sensation of horror and amusement; but such was the beauty of his voice and the consummate mastery of his style, that he had only to begin to sing for these personal drawbacks to be all forgotten. He is said to have taken Babini for his model, but it is doubtful if he had any rival in execution and artistic resource. The fact of so ugly a man sustaining the part of Don Giovanni (transposed for tenor) with success shows what a spell he could cast over his audience.

After three successful years in Paris, Tacchinardi returned in 1814 to Italy, where he was appointed chief singer to the Grand Duke of Tuscany, with liberty to travel. He accordingly sang at Vienna, and afterwards in Spain, distinguishing himself especially at Barcelona, although then 50 years old. After 1831 he left the stage, and lived at his country house near Florence. He retained his appointment from the Grand Duke, but devoted himself chiefly to teaching, for which he became celebrated. He built a little private theatre in which to exercise his pupils, of whom the most notable were Mme. Frezzolini, and his daughter Fanny, Mme. Persiani, perhaps the most striking instance on record of what extreme training and hard work may effect, in the absence of any superlative natural gifts. His other daughter, Elisa, was an eminent pianist. Tacchinardi was the author of a number of solfeggi and vocal exercises, and of a little work called *Dell' opera in musica sul teatro italiano, e de' suoi difetti.*   F. A. M.

TACET, *i.e.* ' is silent.' An indication often found in old part-books, meaning that the instrument to which it refers is to leave off playing. An equivalent direction ' contano ' means that the players ' count ' their bars till they come in again.   G.

TADOLINI, GIOVANNI (*b.* Bologna, *c.* 1785; *d.* there, Nov. 29, 1872), learned composition from Mattei, and singing from Babini, and in

1811 was appointed by Spontini accompanist and chorus-master at the Théâtre des Italiens, Paris. He kept this post till the fall of Paris in 1814, when he returned to Italy. There he remained, writing operas and occupied in music till 1830, when he went back to the Théâtre des Italiens, with his wife, Eugenia Savorini (*b.* Forlì, 1809), whom he had married shortly before, and resumed his old functions till 1839, when he once more returned to Italy. His operas are

' La Fata Alcina ' (Venice, 1814), ' La Principessa di Navarra' (Bologna, 1816), ' Il credulo deluso ' (Rome, 1817), ' Tamerlano' (Bologna, 1818), ' Il Fato Molinaro ' (Rome, 1820), ' Moctard (Bologna, 1824), ' Mitridate ' (Venice, 1826), ' Almanzor ' (Trieste, 1827).

One of his canzonets, ' Eco di Scozia,' with horn obbligato, was much sung by Rubini. Tadolini was at one time credited with having written the concluding fugue in Rossini's Stabat (see Berlioz, *Soirées de l'orchestre*, 2ème Épilogue). (Fétis.)   G.

TÄGLICHSBECK, THOMAS (*b.* Ansbach, Bavaria, Dec. 31, 1799; *d.* Baden-Baden, Oct. 5, 1867), of a musical family, studied at Munich under Rovelli and Gratz, and by degrees became known. Lindpaintner in 1820 gave him his first opportunity by appointing him his deputy in the direction of the Munich theatre, and about this time he produced his first opera, ' Weber's Bild.' After this he forsook Munich and wandered over Germany, Holland and Denmark, as a violinist, in which he acquired great reputation. He then settled in Paris, and on Jan. 24, 1836, a symphony of his (op. 10) was admitted to the unwonted honour of performance at the Conservatoire. A second symphony was given there on Apr. 2, 1837.

In 1827 he was appointed Kapellmeister of the Prince of Hohenzollern-Hechingen, a post which he retained till its abolition in 1848. The rest of his life was passed between Löwenberg in Silesia, Dresden and Baden-Baden. His works extend to op. 33, and include 4 symphonies, a Mass, op. 25; a psalm, op. 30; a trio for PF. and strings; a great quantity of concertos, variations and other pieces for the violin; partsongs, etc.   G.

TAFFANEL, CLAUDE PAUL (*b.* Bordeaux, Sept. 16, 1844; *d.* Paris, Nov. 22, 1908), famous flautist and conductor in Paris. He was educated at the Paris Conservatoire, where he gained the first flute prize in 1865. The year before he had become solo flautist at the Opéra (1864–90). He held the same position with the Société des Concerts du Conservatoire from 1867 onwards. He was conductor of these orchestras from 1890–1903, and became professor of the flute at the Conservatoire in 1893. Among his pupils there were Fleury, Blancard and Gaubert. His name is associated with the last in the *Méthode complète de flûte en 8 parties* (Paris, 1823). He was the founder of the Société des Instruments à Vent (1879).

      G. F.

TAG, CHRISTIAN GOTTHILF (b. Bayerfeld, Saxony, 1735; d. Niederzwönitz, near Zwickau, July 19, 1811), studied at the Kreuzschule, Dresden, under Homilius, and became cantor at Hohenstein, Saxony, in 1755. He was a prolific composer who, living in modest circumstances, wrote only for art's sake, without troubling about publicity, as Rochlitz tells us, who knew him well. He composed 72 cantatas, 11 masses, motets, secular vocal compositions, symphonies for organ and orchestra, and other organ pieces (Q.-L.; Riemann).

TAGLIA, PIETRO (mid-16th century), composed madrigals : lib. i. a 4 v. (Milan, 1555); lib. i. a 5 v. (Milan, 1557), lib. ii. (Venice, 1564); also canzons and other songs in collective volumes (1569–1600) (Q.-L.).

TAGLIAFICO, JOSEPH DIEUDONNÉ (b. Toulon, Jan. 1, 1821; d. Nice, 1900), of Italian parents, was educated at the Collège Henri IV, Paris. He received instruction in singing from Piermarini, in acting from Lablache, and made his début in 1844 at the Italiens, Paris. He first appeared in England, Apr. 6, 1847, at Covent Garden Theatre, as Oroe in 'Semiramide,' on the occasion of the opening of the Royal Italian Opera. From that year until 1876 he appeared at Covent Garden season by season, almost opera by opera. His parts were small, but they were thoroughly studied and given, and invariably showed the intelligent and conscientious artist. In the intervals of the London seasons he had engagements in St. Petersburg, Moscow, Dublin, Paris and America ; was stage manager at the Théâtre des Italiens, Monte Carlo, etc., and for many years was correspondent of the Ménestrel under the signature of ' De Retz.' In 1877, on the death of Desplaces, he was appointed stage manager of the Italian Opera in London, which post he resigned in 1882 on account of ill-health. Mme. Tagliafico, formerly Cotti, was for many years a valuable ' comprimaria ' both at Covent Garden and Her Majesty's. A. C.

TAGLIATO (Ital. ' cut '), an obsolete term for the signs ₵ and ₵. (See ALLA BREVE; BREVE; NOTATION; TIME.)

TAGLIETTI, GIULIO (b. Brescia, c. 1660), maestro at the Jesuit college of St. Antonio, Brescia. He composed 13 or more volumes of instrumental compositions, chiefly for 2 vlns. and bass, with and without organ or harpsichord, and violin sonatas with basso continuo, mostly published between 1695–1715 (Q.-L.; Fétis).

TAGLIONI, (1) MARIE SOPHIE (b. Stockholm, Apr. 23, 1804 [1] or 1809 [2]; d. Marseilles, c. Apr. 24, 1884) [3] the daughter of Filippo Taglioni (1777–1871), an Italian dancer and balletmaster (début, Paris Opéra, 1806), by his marriage with Marie, the daughter of a Swedish actor named Karsten. She was taught dancing by her father, himself the son of a dancer, SALVATORE TAGLIONI, [4] and on June 10, 1822, made her début at Vienna in a ballet of the former, ' La Réception d'une jeune nymphe à la cour de Terpsichore.' In 1824–25, according to her own account to A. D. Vandam, [5] she danced at St. Petersburg, and on her journey thence to Germany she had to dance before a highwayman (à la Claude Duval), with the ultimate loss to her of nothing more than the rugs on which she had danced. In 1825 she was engaged at Stuttgart, then at Munich, and on July 23, 1827, she made her début at the Opéra, Paris, in ' Le Sicilien,' with extraordinary success, confirmed on Aug. 1 when she danced in the ' Vestale ' and with her brother in Schneitzhöffer's ballet ' Mars et Vénus.' From 1828–37 she was engaged there (dancing in London and Berlin, etc., on leave of absence), and reigned supreme as the greatest dancer of the day, albeit inferior to Fanny Elssler as a pantomimist and in versatility. She danced there on the production of Rossini's ' Guillaume Tell,' as Zoloe in Auber's ' Dieu et la bayadère,' as Hélène in ' Robert,' and in new ballets, Hérold's ' La Fille mal gardée ' and ' La Belle au bois dormant,' Halévy's ' Manon Lescaut,' Carafa's ' Nathalie,' Schneitzhöffer's ' La Sylphide ' (scenario by Nourrit), founded on Nodier's ' Trilby ' ; as Zulma in Labarre's ' Révolte au sérail,' and in 1836 as Fleur des Champs in Adam's ' La Fille du Danube.' The dances in most of these ballets were arranged by her father, then choreographist at the Opéra. She danced in London, both in 1830 and 1831, at the King's Theatre in Venua's ballet ' Flore et Zéphyre,' wherein she made her début June 3, 1830, also in mutilated versions of ' Guillaume Tell ' with her ' Tyrolienne,' and the ' Bayadère ' with her noted ' Shawl Dance,' etc. (nearly all the vocal music of the opera being left out). In 1832 she was at Covent Garden, and on July 26 for her benefit appeared for the first time here as the Sylphide, described by Thackeray (Pendennis) as

' That prettiest of all ballets now faded into the past with that most beautiful and gracious of all dancers. Will the young folks ever see anything so charming, anything so classic, anything like Taglioni ? '

In 1833 and for several seasons she danced again at the Opera, in the Haymarket. In 1839 she danced in the ' Gitana ' on the night of Mario's début in ' Lucrezia.' In 1840 she danced in ' L'Ombre,' both that and the ' Gitana ' being originally produced at St. Petersburg where she was engaged after Paris. In 1840 she danced in Paris for a few nights, and again made a farewell visit, four years

---

[1] According to Regli. [2] According to Fétis.
[3] This is the date given in D.N.B. and the Era, the Annual Register gives the day of death as Apr. 22, and Brockhaus, Larousse, etc., as the 23rd.

[4] Salvatore (b. Palermo, 1790; d. Naples, Oct. 5, 1868), made his début at the Paris Opéra in 1799 with his sister Luigia. He married the dancer, Mlle. Perrot, and in 1812 founded at Naples the Royal School of Dancing, and was ballet-master of the San Carlo Theatre. [5] An Englishman in Paris.

later, between which she danced at Milan. In 1845 she danced at Her Majesty's in the celebrated *pas de quatre* with Carlotta Grisi, Cerrito, and Lucile Grahn (*d.* 1907), in 1846 with Cerito and Grahn in ' Le Jugement de Paris,' and for the last time in 1847, soon after which she retired, and the supremacy of the ballet ceased to exist. With no pretensions to beauty, even hump-backed according to de Boigne, wherever she danced she was acclaimed as the greatest dancer of her time, being remarkable for the aerial grace of her movements, the embodiment of poetry in motion. She was noted for the decency of her poses and gestures, points whereon her father always laid particular stress. Besides Thackeray and Chorley other writers such as Balzac, Feydeau, Arsène Houssaye, FitzGerald in his *Letters to Fanny Kemble*, etc., have all in some shape or other recorded the charm of her movements. Alfred Chalon executed sketches of her in five of her parts, bound up with verses by F. W. R. Bayley (London, 1831, fol.). In the print-room at the British Museum are also engravings of her after Bouvier and others (*D.N.B.*).

In 1832 she married Count Gilbert de Voisins, Vice-Consul of France (*d.* Figueira, Spain, June 1863), by whom she had a son Gilbert, and a daughter Marie, who married Prince Troubetzkoi. The marriage was unfortunate and they soon separated. On her retirement, she lived for some time in Italy. In 1860 she was the choreographist of Offenbach's ballet ' Le Papillon ' on its production at the Paris Opéra, being interested in the début of her protégée Emma Livry, a dancer of great promise, soon after burned to death during a performance of ' La Muette.' In 1871, after the death of her father, owing to the loss of her fortune, she settled in London as a teacher of dancing and deportment. In 1874, to her great delight, she was a guest at the Mansion House at a Banquet given to Representatives of Literature and Art. Later she lived with her son at Marseilles. Her brother PAUL (*b.* Vienna, 1808 ; *d.* Berlin, 1884) was also a noted dancer. The date of his début at the Paris Opéra was 1827. He and his wife danced with Taglioni on the production in England of the ' Sylphide.' He was dancing-master at the San Carlo Theatre, Naples, and was for many years ballet-master at Berlin. By his wife Amalie, *née* Galster, he had a daughter Marie (1833–1891), who danced at Her Majesty's in 1847, and was a favourite dancer on the Continent until her retirement on her marriage in 1866 with Prince Joseph Windisch-Grätz.

BIBL.—REGLI ; LAROUSSE, *Dictionnaire universel* ; CHORLEY ; CASTIL-BLAZE, *Les Adieux à Mlle. Taglioni suivis d'une notice biographique sur cette célèbre danseuse* (Paris, 1837) ; DE BOIGNE, *Les Petits Mémoires de l'Opéra* (Paris, 1857) ; DR. VÉRON, *Mémoires d'un bourgeois de Paris* (Paris, 1854) ; VANDAM ; *Nouvelle Biographie générale* (Firmin-Didot) ; *D.N.B.*, etc.). TIETZ, *Marie Taglioni* (Berlin, 1866). A. C. ; addns. M. L. P.

TAILER (TALER, TAYLOR), DANIEL (*d.* Apr. 1643 [1]), English composer of church music. He was a singing man at Westminster Abbey, and his name appears in lists in this capacity in 1625 (see H. C. de Lafontaine, *The King's Musick*). An anthem, ' Singe we merrily,' by him is in some partbooks at Durham Cathedral (tenor cantoris book of this set in B.M. Add. MSS. 30478-9 ; bass part in Ch. Ch. 1219). A motet by Tailer, ' Christus resurgens,' is in Ch. Ch. 984-8. The alto part of a ' song ' or madrigal by him, ' Appollo [*sic*] did in Musick's art,' is also in Ch. Ch. 1219.

J. Mᴷ.

TAILLE. Originally the French name for the tenor voice, basse-taille being applied to the baritone ; but most frequently employed to designate the tenor viol and violin (viola). It properly denominates the large tenor, as distinguished from the smaller contralto or haute-contre : but is often applied to both instruments. The tenor violoncello clef was originally appropriated to the Taille. (See VIOL.)

E. J. P.

TAILLEFERE, GERMAINE (*b.* Pau St. Maur, near Paris, Apr. 19, 1892), has made a name for herself as a composer, and first became prominent as one of the Parisian group who called themselves ' les six.' Her ' Pastorale ' for small orchestra, and ' Songs ' heard in Paris in 1920, made at once a distinctive impression. A quartet, a violin sonata, produced 1922 by Thibaud and Cortot, and other chamber works followed. Her piano concerto in D was first played in London by Cortot at a concert of the Women's Symphony Orchestra in 1924, and has since been repeated at Queen's Hall under Wood.

C.

TAILOUR, ROBERT, ' one of Prince his Highnes Musicians ' in 1618. Author of

' Sacred Hymns, consisting of Fifti select Psalms of David and others, Paraphrastically turned into English Verse [by Sir Edwin Sandys] and by Robert Tailour set to be sung in 5 parts, as also to the Viol and Lute or Orpharion. Published for the use of such as delight in the exercise of music in hir original honour, London, 1615.'

W. H. C.

TALES OF HOFFMANN, see CONTES D'HOFFMANN.

TALEXY, ADRIEN (*b. circa* 1820 ; *d.* Paris, Feb. 1881), a pianist and voluminous composer ; produced between 1872 and 1878 six one-act operettas at the Bouffes-Parisiens and other Paris theatres, none of which met with any special favour. He was the author of a *Méthode de piano* ; twenty ' Études expressives,' op. 80 (with Colombier) ; and of a large number of salon and dance pieces for piano solo, some of which enjoyed great popularity in their day. In 1860 Talexy conducted a series of French operas at the St. James's Theatre, London, for F. B. Chatterton, beginning with ' La Tentation,' May 28, which did not prove successful.

G.

TALICH, VÁCLAV (*b.* Kroměříž, Moravia, May 28, 1883), chief conductor of the Prague Philharmonic Orchestra since 1918. His father, a music teacher, settled at Klatov, where the son received his early education at the gymnasium. He distinguished himself as a pupil of Ševčík at the Prague Conservatoire (1897–1903). In 1905 he was leader in the orchestra of the Opera at Odessa, where he made his first essay in conducting, the branch of his art which most attracted him. From 1906–07 he was professor of violin in Tiflis. On his return to Prague he found opportunities of deepening his experience as choirmaster and conductor of the Orchestral Association. The newly founded Philharmonic Society of Lubanja (Laibach), Jugoslavia, engaged him as conductor (1908–12), after which he fulfilled his wish to study for a time in Leipzig. There he worked under Reger (piano, composition and counterpoint), and Nikisch (conducting). In 1911 he went to Milan, where he worked with the conductor Arturo Vigno. He returned to Bohemia in 1912, as conductor at Plzen (Pilsen), where he remained three years. At Plzen he showed his mastery of the art of conducting, combining the grace and tenderness of Kovařovic with the rhythmic sensibility and fire which are, in part, his Slavonic heritage, and, in part, acquisitions from his studies with Nikisch. Under his permanent direction the Prague Philharmonic Orchestra has become a high y disciplined and responsive organisation, equal to the great variety of music it is called upon to interpret in the course of the season, for Talich's programmes have the widest possible basis. He toured with this orchestra in Italy (1921), and has visited Vienna Liverpool, Glasgow and Edinburgh as a guest conductor. In 1926 he undertook the direction of the Scottish Orchestra's season.   R. N.

TALISMANO, IL, opera in 3 acts; text, after Scott's *Talisman*, by A. Mattheson (Italian translation by Zaffira), music by Balfe. Produced Her Majesty's Theatre, June 11, 1874; in English, Carl Rosa Co., Liverpool, Jan. 15, 1891. The work, left unfinished by Balfe, was completed by G. A. Macfarren.   G.

TALLIS, THOMAS (*b. circa* 1505; *d.* Greenwich, Nov. 23, 1585). Composer and organist. The date of Tallis's birth is not known, but it is a matter of some consequence to attempt to discover it approximately because it also determines relatively the date at which he began to compose. And at a period of rapid musical development this becomes a considerable factor in comparing his style with that of his contemporaries throughout a long life. In this connexion it is well to remember that Tallis was very probably writing some of his most important music while holding the responsible position of organist of the Abbey of the Holy Cross at Waltham : and if we are

right in putting his birth as early as about 1505, for reasons which will be stated presently, the earliest work of Tallis would have been contemporary with that of Taverner, whose death took place five years after the dissolution of Waltham Abbey, and Tallis may have been at Waltham before Taverner left Christ Church.

Davey in the *D.N.B.* conjectures that Tallis was born about 1510. It is likely that his birth was four or five years earlier. For in 1577, when Tallis and Byrd petitioned Queen Elizabeth for the grant of a lease, Tallis described himself as ' verie aged,' an expression implying that he was at least 70 at that time : and it is not unreasonable to assume from this that he would have been about 80 at the time of his death in 1585. Born in the opening years of the sixteenth century he thus bridges the gap between Fayrfax and the late Elizabethans, a period of tremendous musical change. The name of Tallis, Tallys or Talles is uncommon. Robert Talles, or Tallys, died in 1571, and was buried at Islington parish church.[1] He had relatives living at Leicester, and Clement Tallis, who matriculated at Christ Church, Oxford, in 1581 [2] as ' of co. Leic.' seems to have been the son of his brother Clement. The name is found at Burton Overy in 1669, when Henry Tallis left a legacy to the poor of that parish.[3] No connexion between these families and that of the composer can be proved on the known facts, yet they suggest that Thomas Tallis may have been a native of Leicestershire.

There is no evidence to support the conjectures that Tallis was one of the ' children ' of the Chapel Royal or that he was under Thomas Mulliner at St. Paul's Cathedral. The earliest known fact about him is that he held an official position, presumably musical, at the Abbey of the Holy Cross at Waltham in Essex. His name is not included in the list of those who received pensions on the dissolution of Waltham Abbey in 1540, but it appears in a long list of some 70 persons who received small sums in reward for services when they were deprived of their offices. This list is appended to an inventory of the goods belonging to the abbey dated March 24, 31 Hen. VIII.[4] Tallis received a larger sum than any one else in the list, namely 20s. for wages and 20s. ' in reward,' or as a gratuity. Another item of interest in the same list shows that five ' children ' in the church, evidently choristers, jointly received 20s. for wages and 20s. in reward. The names in this long list also, no doubt, include the singing men. From these details it may fairly be assumed that Tallis was master of the choristers or organist. The inventory shows that there was ' a lytell payre of organes ' valued at xxs in the Lady Chapel, and that

1 P.C.C. 11 Daper.   2 Foster's *Alumni Oxon.*
3 Nichols's *History of Leicestershire*, vol. i. p. 20.
4 P.R.O. Exchequer K.R. Church goods ⁸⁄₄.

in the choir was ' a great larg payre of organs '
and also 'a lesser payr.' No organ is mentioned
in the inventory as being ' in the church.'

A very interesting manuscript belonging to
Waltham Abbey seems to have passed into
the possession of Tallis at the time of the dissolution. It is now in the British Museum.[1]
It was written in the hand of John Wylde,
formerly precentor of Waltham Abbey and
contains a number of treatises on musical
subjects. Its chief interest to-day lies in the
fact that Tallis wrote his name upon the last
page and this autograph is here reproduced.[2]

The name was written again on the same
page in large block letters, and this may also
be in the composer's hand, but it is more
than doubtful whether the succeeding notes,
referring to certain books—possibly choir
books—were written by Tallis.

Tallis may have become known to Henry
VIII. before the dissolution of the abbey, for
the King was a frequent visitor there. His
appointment as one of the gentlemen of the
Chapel Royal must have been made about the
year 1540 or even earlier, for in a petition,
made jointly with Byrd in 1577, he stated that
he had served ' these fortie yeres ' [3] referring,
without doubt, to his position in the Chapel
Royal. His name appears in several lists of
the ' gentlemen of the chapel.' In one list,[4]
for example, given in connexion with the
accounts of the King's household, his name
stands sixteenth out of thirty-two; this list
is undated, but was about the year 1545; the
rate of stipend was £1 per diem between the
thirty-two men. Tallis does not appear to
have been organist of the chapel at this time;
Richard Bowyer was master of the children.
At the funeral of Henry VIII. and the coronation of Edward VI. Tallis's name stands
sixteenth out of twenty of those who received
liveries on those occasions.[5] In 1557 Tallis
and Bowyer jointly were granted by Queen
Mary a lease for 21 years of the Manor of
Minster in the isle of Thanet.[6] In the first
year of Queen Elizabeth's reign the Royal
Household Accounts show that Tallis received
a sum of £40, presumably as a gratuity.[7]

On Jan. 22, 1574–75 Tallis and Byrd were
granted a licence[8] by letters patent which gave
them the sole right for printing music and
music paper in England.[9] This was intended as
a royal boon which should have been lucrative,
and such it proved to be at a later date; but
in the first two years it resulted in loss, and the
two composers presented a petition to the
Queen asking her to compensate them by
granting them a lease for twenty-one years of
the annual value of £30. They pleaded that
Tallis ' is now verie aged and hath served
yᵒ maᵗⁱᵉ and yᵒ Royall ancestors these fortie
yeres and hadd as yet never anie manner of
preferment except onely one lease . . . which
being now the best pᵗᵉ of his lyvinge is wᵗʰ in
one yere of expiration.' They further stated
that the printing licence had brought a loss of
200 marks. Byrd pleaded that his daily
attendance in the royal service had interfered
with his teaching and that his income had
diminished since he left Lincoln Cathedral.
The lease was granted.

Tallis and Byrd were acting as joint organists
of the Chapel Royal at this time, and were so
described on the title page of the set of their
motets which they published in 1575. This
was entitled :

' Cantiones quae ab argumento sacrae vocuntur, quinque et sex
partibus autoribus Thoma Tallisio & Gulielmo Birdo Anglis
Serenissimae Reginae Maiestati a priuato Sacello generosis &
Organistis.'

It was dedicated to the Queen, and contained
16 numbers by Tallis and 18 by Byrd. In a
rather unusually large amount of prefatory
matter two poems were included in praise of
the two composers written in Latin elegiacs,
one by Richard Mulcaster and the other by
Ferdinand Richardson. In this latter poem
is the much quoted line ' Tallisius magno
dignus honore senex.'

The only other works of Tallis published in
his lifetime were five anthems set to English
words included by John Day in his ' Certaine
notes ' (1560–65).

The closing years of Tallis's life seem to have
been spent at Greenwich where he owned a
house. He was married in 1552, the date
being calculated from his epitaph; he had no
children. The surname of his wife is not
known, but her Christian name was Joan. She
survived him. Tallis died at Greenwich on
Nov. 23, 1585 and was buried in the parish
church of St. Alphege, just inside the chancel
rails, and near the grave of his colleague
Richard Bowyer. A brass plate was placed
on his tombstone; the inscription on this plate
was fortunately recorded by Strype in his
Continuation of Stowe's Survey of London,
for shortly after this the church was pulled
down and rebuilt and the tombstone of Tallis

1 B.M. Lansdowne MS. 763.
2 It has been photographed afresh from the original for the
present edition of this Dictionary   3 Hatfield MSS.
4 B.M. Stow MSS. 571 fo. 36ᵇ.
5 *The King's Musicke,* by H. C. de Lafontaine, pp. 6-7.
6 B.M. Harl. MSS. 239 fo. 75ᵇ.
7 B.M. Lansd. MSS. 3 fo. 200.

8 P.R.O. Rot. Pat. 17 Eliz. para 7. m. 2.
9 Printed in full in *William Byrd ; a Short Account of his Life and
Work,* by E. H. Fellowes.

disappeared. The inscription may be seen in vol. vi. of the Carnegie Edition of 'Tudor Church Music'; it was also printed by Hawkins, Burney and Boyce, but Strype's spelling has not been accurately reproduced by them. Hawkins [1] says that Dean Aldrich repaired Tallis's gravestone.

The will of Tallis (P.C.C. 52 Brudenell) was dated Aug. 20, 1583, and proved on Nov. 29 of the same year. Joan, his wife, was sole executrix; William Byrd and Richard Cranwell, also of the Chapel Royal and the intimate friends of Tallis, were his 'overseers.' Byrd was one of the witnesses. The will provides no clue to his family history except that he had a cousin in Thanet named John Sayer. He left his share of the printing licence to his godson Thomas Byrd, the composer's son.

Mrs. Tallis died in 1589 and was buried in her husband's grave. Her will (P.C.C. 54 Leicester) is chiefly interesting as containing a very full list of the furniture and other personal property belonging to Tallis and his wife.[2]

It may be assumed that in the early part of his career while at Waltham Abbey Tallis confined himself exclusively to the composition of music for the Latin rites of the Church. There is no means of dating any of his music with any degree of certainty, but it seems likely that the motet 'Gaude gloriosa' belongs to the Waltham period; it includes prolonged phrases, sometimes split up by rests, set to single syllables of the words; a good illustration of this style of writing is to be found at the word ' glorificat ' at the end of the ' Gaude Virgo ' section of this motet. ' Ave Rosa ' and ' Ave Dei Patris ' contain similar passages, and for other reasons also these may be assigned to the earlier period of Tallis's work. The five-part Mass and the Lamentations are far more concise in treatment, but the four-part Magnificat is another work that may be early. The four-part Mass looks like a very early work; only one source of text is known and this seems to be faulty, but judged by this text the counterpoint in some places seems feeble and unsatisfactory if it really represents the composer's work. The motets of Tallis published in the 'Cantiones sacrae' of 1575 show a marked advance in style compared with the work of the pre-Elizabethan composers. In this collection Tallis exhibited those qualities which have made his name so famous; and some of these same motets, for instance, the ' Miserere nostri,' are constructed with that marvellous contrapuntal skill in which both he and Byrd were supreme.

In contrast to these elaborate pieces are such beautiful and simple works as ' O nata lux ' and ' Procul recedant ' which were printed in the same set. These are little more than hymn tunes, quite regular in melodic outline

and for the most part homophonic in treatment. There are several further examples of this character by Tallis surviving in MS., notably in the Mulliner MS.[3]

The motet ' Spem in alium ' is written for 8 choirs, each of 5 voices. Tudway [4] mentions 'the original MS.' as being extant in his time. The earliest text known is now (1927) owned by M. Brook of Southport, and formerly was at Gresham College. This MS. dates before 1612; the text is English, and the 40 voice parts are complete. Hawkins [5] wrongly states that the English version was made in the time of Charles I. or II.

Tallis has been called ' the Father of English Cathedral music,' but this title has been assigned to him in comparatively recent times when the work of most Tudor musicians, including most of that of Tallis himself, had passed into neglect. It was Byrd who in his own day was styled ' a Father in Musicke,' and Byrd did more than Tallis to establish what may be called the tradition of English Cathedral music. Again, if it were a matter of who was first in the field, it is commonly thought that Tye's setting of the evening canticles is even earlier than Tallis's ' short ' service, and some others in the Bodleian MS. Mus. Sch. e. 420-2 are also probably earlier. (See SERVICE.) Nevertheless Tallis undoubtedly was among the first composers who wrote music to English words for use with the English rites of the Church. It must have been very soon after the publication of The Booke of Common Praier noted, in which Merbecke had provided a fixed version of the plain-song for the English Preces, Responses and Litany, that Tallis, as Hawkins describes it, ' added three parts,' to the plain-song, making a version in four-part harmony, and Hawkins was probably referring here to Tallis's four-part setting of the Preces and Responses which differs entirely from his five-part setting. Other composers of this period also left more than one independent setting of the Preces and Responses. The two versions of the Litany ascribed to Tallis, one in four parts and one in five, have given rise to much discussion. The five-part setting was printed by Barnard, and is also found in Barnard's MSS. (R.C.M. 1045-51). On internal evidence, in spite of some ' forbidden ' progressions as printed by Barnard which may be due to faulty transcription, this five-part setting is unquestionably the work of Tallis. The four-part setting of the Litany, found in the Peterhouse MSS. and also in one of the Durham organ books, and ascribed there to Tallis, is almost certainly an adaptation of the five-part setting. In the Durham book it is called ' the New Litany ' which lends support to this theory. It was also printed by Lowe

[1] Vol. iii. p. 266.
[2] These two wills are printed in full in vol. vi. of the Carnegie edition of ' Tudor Church Music.'

[3] B.M. Add. MSS. 30513.   [4] B.M. Harl. MS. 3782 fo. 95.
[5] Hawkin's Hist. vol. iii. p. 262.

in his *Short Directions*, 1661. When Boyce in 1760 reprinted Tallis's five-part Litany he emended Barnard's text in a manner consistent with the orthodoxy of his own time, and quite probably in accordance with the original version of Tallis ; it is unlikely that he had access to any independent text at that date.

The 'short' service of Tallis, known as 'Tallis in D minor ' or 'in the Dorian mode ' includes, besides the ordinary morning and evening canticles, a full setting of the Venite (for which Boyce in his 'Cathedral Music' substituted a chant), Kyrie, Creed, Sanctus and Gloria in excelsis. It was probably composed at least as early as 1550, for scarcely any settings of the English 'Gloria in excelsis' are of later date although there are several in the Bodl. MS. Mus. Sch. e. 420-2. And another detail points to this early date ; early texts of the Tallis Te Deum give the phrase 'the Holy Ghost also being the Comforter ' which is found only in the King's Primer and the First Prayer Book. A. H. D. Prendergast pointed out in the *Zeitschrift* of the Int. Mus. Ges. ix. p. 65 how Tallis in the Creed of this service deliberately departed from the universal tradition of the musical setting of the Mass by making no break before the words 'And was incarnate.' This entire service was written in conformity with the principle of securing verbal clearness by means of homophony as opposed to polyphony, yet it is marked by a good deal of rhythmic freedom and flexibility as well as some melodic interest ; it has been better understood in Cathedral circles since the freely-barred edition of Dr. Kitson has been published. Tallis's five-part service has unfortunately perished with the exception of the bass part alone, and the known text of another English Te Deum is far from complete. A four-part English Benedictus is in the Lumley MSS. in the B.M. ; these MSS. were almost certainly in Cranmer's library and date from about 1547.

The Anglican chants commonly attributed to Tallis are of more than doubtful origin ; but the ninth of his 'tunes' written for Archbishop Parker's Psalter (1567) is in general use as a modern hymn tune under the name of 'Tallis,' and the so-called 'canon' is an adaptation from the eighth tune.

Tallis's work as an English anthem-writer has been much misunderstood. Hawkins and Burney wrote as if all his English anthems were adaptations of Latin motets ; and they attributed much of the work of adaptation to Aldrich. Hawkins said it was Aldrich who adapted Tallis's 'O sacrum convivium ' to the English words 'I call and cry.' In more recent times it has been freely but incorrectly stated that John Barnard was responsible for the earliest of these adaptations, and there were some who went so far as to aver that all the English anthems of the Tudor composers were originally written as Latin motets.

In the case of Tallis four out of the five of his English anthems printed by Barnard in 1641 were adaptations of motets, but the adaptations were made many years earlier ; indeed many of these and other adaptations are found in the 16th century MSS. and it is more than probable that they are the work of the composer himself or at least had his sanction.

But apart from adaptations there are a fair number of original English anthems by Tallis, and some of these date from the time when the English language was first being used in the church services. For example, 'Hear the voice and prayer ' and 'If ye love me ' are both to be found in the Bodl. MS. Mus. Sch. e. 420-2, the date of which is *circa* 1546–49; and 'Remember not ' is in the Lumley MS., already quoted, dating *circa* 1547.

Such secular and instrumental work by Tallis as has survived is of small importance.

The church music of Tallis has been collected and scored with as much completeness as was possible by the editors of the Carnegie edition of 'Tudor Church Music.' The Latin music is the subject of vol. vi. of the series, and the English church music is intended to be printed in a later volume. The following is a list of known compositions by Tallis :

A. CHURCH MUSIC

I. LATIN

Missa, *a* 4. B.M. Add. MSS. 17802-5, 18936.
Missa, ' Salve intemerata,' *a* 5. B.M. Add. MSS. 29246 ; Pet. MSS. 31, 32, 40, 41.
Magnificat, *a* 4. B.M. Add. MSS. 17802-5.
Magnificat and Nunc Dimittis, *a* 6. Ch. Ch. MSS. 979-83.
Lamentations, *a* 5. B.M. Add. MSS. 5059, 17792-6, 32377, 34070, 34726 ; Pet. MSS. 35, 37, 44 ; Bodl. MS. Mus. Sch. e. 1-5 ; Ch. Ch. MSS. 979-83 ; Tenb. MSS. 341-4.

MOTETS, ETC.

Absterge Domine, *a* 5. Can. Sac. (1575), No. 2 ; B.M. Add MSS. 5059, 29247 ; Bodl. MS. Mus. Sch. e. 1-5.
Adesto nunc propitius, *a* 5. Ch. Ch. MSS. 979-83 ; Pet. MSS. 35, 37, 44, 45 ; Tenb. MSS. 341-4.
Alleluia, *a* 4. B.M. Add. MSS. 17802-5.
Audivi media nocte, *a* 4. B.M. Add. MSS. 17802-5.
Ave Dei Patris, *a* 5. B.M. Add. MSS. 29246 ; R.C.M. MSS. 2035 ; Tenb. MSS. 342, 354-8.
Ave Rosa sine spinis, *a* 5. B.M. Add. MSS. 34049 ; Pet. MSS. 31, 32, 40, 41 ; R.C.M. MSS. 2035.
Benedictus qui venit, *a* 5 Tenb. MSS. 341-4.
[Candidi] facti sunt Nazarei, *a* 5. Can. Sac. (1575), No. 22 ; B.M. Add. MSS. 30480-4 ; Ch. Ch. MSS. 984-8.
Claro paschali, *a* 5. Can. Sac. (1575), No. 16 (2).
Derelinquit impius, *a* 5. Can. Sac. (1575), No. 13 ; Tenb. MSS. 341-4.
Domine quis habitabit, *a* 5. B.M. Add. MSS. 5059, 29247 ; Bodl. MS. Mus. Sch. e. 1-5 ; Ch. Ch. MSS. 979-83 ; Tenb. MSS. 341-4.
Ecce tempus. B.M. Add. MSS. 30513.
Euge coeli porta, *a* 5. Tenb. MSS. 354-8.
Gaude gloriosa, *a* 6. B.M. Add. MSS. 29246 ; Roy. Lib., Baldwin's MS. ; Bodl. MS. Mus. Sch. e. 423 ; Ch. Ch. MSS 45, 979-83 ; Tenb. MSS. 354-8, 807-11.
Gloria in excelsis, *a* 4. B.M. Add. MSS. 17802-5.
Gloria tibi, *a* 5. Can. Sac. (1575), No. 16 (4).
Haec Deum coeli, *a* 5. Ch. Ch. MSS. 979-83 ; Tenb. MSS. 341-4.
Hic nempe mundi gloria, *a* 5. Tenb. MSS. 341-4.
Hodie—gloria in excelsis, *a* 4. B.M. Add. MSS. 17802-5
Iam lucis. B.M. Add. MSS. 30513.
Illae dum pergunt, *a* 5. Can. Sac. (1575), No. 16 (1).
In ieiunio et fletu, *a* 5. Can. Sac. (1575), No. 26.
In manus tuas, *a* 5. Can. Sac. (1575), No. 3.
In pace si dedero, *a* 4. B.M. Add. MSS. 17802-5.
Iste confessor. B.M. Add. MSS. 30513.
Laudate Dominum, *a* 5. Ch. Ch. MSS. 979-83 ; Tenb. MSS. 341-4.
Mihi autem nimis, *a* 5. Can. Sac. (1575), No. 7 ; B.M. Add. MSS 29247.
Miraculum videte, *a* 5. Ch. Ch. MSS. 979-83.
Misere nostri, *a* 7. Can. Sac. (1575), No. 34 ; B.M. Add. MSS. 5054, 14398.
Natus est nobis. B.M. Add. MSS. 30513.
O nata lux de lumine, *a* 5. Can. Sac. (1575), No. 8.
O sacrum convivium, *a* 5. Can. Sac. (1575), No. 9 ; B.M. Add MSS. 29247 ; Bodl. MS. Mus. Sch. e. 1-5 ; Ch. Ch. MSS. 984-8.

O salutaris hostia, *a* 5. B.M. Add. MSS. 22597, 29247, 30480-4
34049 ; Ch. Ch. MSS. 984-8 ; Tenb. MSS. 341-4, 389.
Pange lingua. B.M. Add. MSS. 30513.
Per haec nos. B.M. Add. MSS. 30513.
Procul recedant somnia, *a* 5. Can. Sac. (1575), No. 20. ; B.M. Add.
MSS. 31822 (without words).
Quidem fecit coenam, *a* 6. Ch. Ch. MSS. 979-83.
Rex Christi, *a* 5. Can. Sac. (1575), No. 16 (3).
Rex sanctorum, *a* 4. B.M. Add. MSS. 19836-9.
[Sabbatum] dum transisset, *a* 5. Can. Sac. (1575), No. 14 ; B.M.
Add. MSS. 29247 ; Bodl. MS. Mus. Sch. e. 1-5 Ch. Ch. MSS.
979-83 ; Tenb. MSS. 341-4.
Salvator mundi (I.), *a* 5. Can. Sac. (1575), No. 1 ; B.M. Add.
MSS. 5059, 22597, 29247 ; Bodl. MS. Mus. Sch. e. 1-5 ; Ch. Ch
MSS. 984-8.
Salvator mundi (II.), *a* 5. Can. Sac. (1575), No. 21 ; Ch. Ch. MSS.
984-8.
Salve intemerata, *a* 5. B.M. Add. MSS. 4900, 18936-7-9, 24049,
29246, 30513 ; Harl. 1709 ; Roy. Lib., Baldwin's MS. ; Bodl.
MS. Mus. Sch. e. 1-5, 423 ; Pet. MSS. 31, 32, 40, 41 ; Ch. Ch.
MSS. 979-83 ; Tenb. 341-4, 354-8, 807-11 ; R.C.M. MSS. 2035.
Sancte Deus, *a* 4. B.M. Add. MSS. 17802-5.
Solemnis urgebat dies, *a* 5. Ch. Ch. MSS.
Spem in alium, *a* 40. B.M. Add. MSS. 29968 ; Roy. Lib., Baldwin's
MS. ; Tenb. MSS. 1270, M. Brook of Southport.
Suscipe quaeso Domine, *a* 7. Can. Sac. (1575), Nos. 27-28 ; B.M.
Add. MSS. 29247 ; Tenb. MSS. 341-4.
Tu fabricator omnium, *a* 5. Ch. Ch.MSS. 979-83 ; Tenb. MSS. 341-4.
Variis linguis, *a* 7. B.M. Roy. Lib., Baldwin's MS. ; Ch. Ch. MSS.
979-83.
Veni Redemptor. B.M. Add. MSS. 30513.
Virtus honor et potestas, *a* 5. Can. Sac. (1575), No. 15.

Note.—In the above list fragmentary sections of the motets are
not given separately, as in some instances in former editions of the
Dictionary, but the text referred to under the principal titles in
many cases only covers small sections.

II. ENGLISH

SERVICES, ETC.

Preces, *a* 5. Barnard (1641) ; R.C.M. MSS. 1045-51.
Preces, *a* 4. Pet. MSS. 35, 36, 42, 44 ; St. John's Oxf. MSS. 180.
Responses, *a* 5. Barnard (1641) ; R.C.M. 1045-51 ; Durh. MSS.
C. 1.
Responses, *a* 4. Pet. MSS. 33, 34, 38, 39.
Litany, *a* 5 Barnard (1641).
Litany, *a* 4. Pet. MSS. 35, 37, 42, 44 ; Durh. MSS. A. 5.
Psalms (First Set)—
Blessed are those. St. John's Oxf. MSS. 180.
Wherewithal. Barnard (1641) ; St. John's Oxf. MSS. 180.
O do well. Barnard (1641) ; St. John's Oxf. MSS. 180.
My soul cleaveth. Barnard (1641) ; St. John's Oxf. MSS. 180.
Psalms (Second Set)—
The Lord said unto my Lord. St. John's Oxf. MSS. 180 ; Ch. Ch.
in MS. at end of Barnard (formerly at Hereford).
Lord remember David. St. John's Oxf. MSS. 180.
Psalms (Third Set)—
I call with my whole heart. St. John's Oxf. MSS. 180.
O consider mine adversity. St. John's Oxf. MSS. 180.
Princes have persecuted me. St. John's Oxf. MSS. 180.
Let my complaint. St. John's Oxf. MSS. 180.
' Short ' Service, *a* 4 [V., T.D., B., K., Cr., S., Glo., M., N.D.]
Barnard (1641) ; B.M. Add. MSS. 17784, 29289 ; Roy. Lib.
Cosyn's MS. ; Pet. MSS. 35-37, 42-45 ; Ch. Ch. MSS. 1001 ;
R.C.M. MSS. 1045-51 ; Durh. MSS. A. 6, C. 1, 8, 13 ; York
MSS., Windsor MSS., Wimborne MSS.
Service, *a* 5 [V., T.D., B., K., Cr., Gl., M., N.D.]. St. John's Oxf.
MSS. 180-1.
Te Deum, *a* 5. R.C.M. MSS. 1046-7, 1049-51 ; Ch. Ch. MSS. 1001.
Benedictus, *a* 4. B.M. Roy. App. MSS. 74-76.
Psalm Tunes printed in Archbp. Parker's Psalter (1567) :
1. Man blest no doubt.
2. Let God arise.
3. Why fumeth in fight.
4. O come in one.
5. Even like the hunted hind.
6. Expend, O Lord.
7. Why brag'st in malice high.
8. God grant with grace.
9. Come Holy Ghost eternal God.

ANTHEMS

(a) Original Settings

A new commandment. B.M. Add. MSS. 15166, 29289.
Blessed are those that be undefiled. B.M. Add. MSS. 22597,
29401-5 ; Bodl. MS. Mus. Sch. e. 423 ; Tenb. MSS. 354-8, 389.
Hear the voice and prayer. Day (1560-65) ; B.M. Add. MSS.
15166, 29289 ; Bodl. MS. Mus. Sch. e. 420-2 ; Pet. MSS. 33.
38 ; Durh. MSS. A. 3, C. 11, 17.
I give you a new commandment. Day (1560-65) ; B.M. Add. MSS.
30513.
If thast a giver's sighs. Tenb. MSS.
If ye love me. Day (1560-65) ; B.M. Add. MSS. 15166, 29289,
Bodl. MS. Mus Sch. e. 420-2 ; Durh. MSS. A. 3, C. 11, 17.
O give thanks. Tenb. MSS. 791.
O God be merciful. Pet. MSS. 35, 37, 42, 44.
O Lord give Thy Holy Spirit. Barnard (1641) ; B.M. Add. MSS.
15166, 29289, 30478, 31443 ; York MSS.
O Lord God of hosts. B.M. Add. MSS. 29289.
O Lord in Thee is all my trust. Day (1560-65).
O sing unto the Lord. Bodl. MS. Mus. Sch. e. 423.
Purge me, O Lord. B.M. Add. MSS. 30480-4.
Remember not, O Lord. Day (1560-65) ; B.M. Roy. App. MSS.
74-76, Add. MSS. 29289.
Teach me Thy way, O Lord, and I will walk. B.M. Add. MSS.
15166 ; Ch. Ch. MSS. 1001.
This is My commandment. B.M. Add. MSS. 30478 ; Pet. MSS.
35-37, 42, 43 ; Durh. MSS. A. 1, 3, C. 11, 17.
Verily, verily, I say unto you. B.M. Add. MSS. 15166 ; Pet. MSS.
34, 38, 39 ; Ely MSS.
When shall my sorrowful sighing. B.M. Roy. App. MSS. 74-76,
Add. MSS. 33933.

Note.—Anthems quoted in former editions of the Dictionary from
' St. Paul's List ' are not included here. They are not found in any
early MSS., and are probably late adaptations.

(b) Early Adaptations of Latin Motets to English Words

Arise, O Lord (Salvator mundi, No. 1). B.M. Add. MSS. 30478-9
Durh. MSS. C. 1, 2, 3, 7, 11, 14, 16.
Blessed be Thy name (Mihi autem nimis). Barnard (1641) ; B.M.
Add. MSS. 17792-6, 29289, 30478-9 ; Ch. Ch. MSS. 1001 ;
R.C.M. MSS. 1045-51 ; Durh. MSS. A. 3, C. 4-6, 10-12, 15, 16 ;
York MSS.
Discomfit them (Absterge Domine). Pet. MSS. 42, 44, 45 ; Ch. Ch.
MSS. 1001.
I call and cry (O sacrum convivium). Barnard (1641) ; B.M. Add,
MSS. 15117, 17784, 22597, 29427, 30478-9 ; R.C.M. MSS.
1046-51 ; Ch. Ch. MSS. 1001 ; Durh. MSS. A. 1, C. 4, 11, 12.
16 ; York MSS., Windsor MSS., Wimborne MSS.
O holy and sacred banquet (O sacrum convivium). B.M. Add. MSS.
29372-7.
O praise the Lord (O salutaris hostia). R.C.M. MSS. 1051 ; Wim-
borne MSS.
When Jesus went into Simon the Pharisee's house (Salvator mundi,
No. 2) ; B.M. Add. MSS. 30480-4, 31226.
Wipe away my sins (Absterge Domine). Barnard (1641). B.M.
Add. MSS. 17792-6, 30478, 30480-4 ; R.C.M. MSS. 1045-7-9 ;
Tenb. MSS. 1176-82.
With all our hearts (Salvator mundi, No. 1). Barnard (1641) ;
B.M. Add. MSS. 17784, 17792-6, 29289, 29372-7, 30478, 30480-4;
R.C.M. MSS. 1045-7-9 ; York MSS., Tenb. MSS. 1180.

(c) Uncertain and Erroneous Ascriptions

All people that on earth. Not found earlier than Ch. Ch. MSS.
1220-4. Adapted by Aldrich as ' from Tallis.' Printed by
Arnold (1842) as by Tallis.
Come Holy Ghost. Printed anonymously by Lowe (1661). Not
found in MS. earlier than Ch. Ch. MSS. 1220-4, where it is
ascribed to Tallis.
How long shall mine enemies ? Ascribed to Tallis in B.M. Add.
MSS. 29247 (lute tablature), is certainly by Byrd.
I give you a new commandment. Ascribed to Tallis in B.M. Add.
MSS. 30513, but by Day (1560-65) to Shepherd. The Tallis
ascription is probably correct.
O thou God Almighty. Ascribed to Tallis in Ch. Ch. MSS. 1001, is
certainly by Hooper.
Out from the deep. Ascribed to Tallis in Ch. Ch. MSS. 6, may be an
adaptation.
Praise the Lord, ye servants. Stated in a former edition of the
Dictionary to have been in a MS. in possession of Joseph
Warren, cannot be traced.
Teach me, O Lord. Adapted from Salvator mundi, No. 1, mentioned
in the list in a former edition of the Dictionary, cannot be
traced at Ch. Ch. or elsewhere.
This is my commandment. Is ascribed to Tallis in the Durham
MSS. One of the Pet. MSS. (37) ascribes it to John Mundy,
and the other MS. quoted above gives no ascription. There
is little doubt that it is by Tallis. In B.M. Add. MSS. 30478 it
comes between ' If ye love me ' and ' Hear the voice and
prayer.'

B. SECULAR MUSIC

VOCAL

As Cæsar wept. Ascribed to Tallis in B.M. Add. MSS. 18936-9, is
ascribed to Byrd in other MSS., and is possibly by Byrd.
Fond youth is a bubble. B.M. Add. MSS. 30513.
Like as the doleful dove. B.M. Add. MSS. 30513.
O ye tender babes. B.M. Add. MSS. 30513.
Note.—These last two have all the appearance of being hymn
tunes.

INSTRUMENTAL

Two In nomines in Bodl. MSS.
In nomine. Tenb. MSS.
In nomine. B.M. Add. MSS. (in lute tablature).
Note.—These have not been collated and possibly the last two
are the same as these in Bodl.

Felix namque. Fitz Virg. Book, No. 109, dated 1562.
Felix namque. Another setting. Fitz Virg. Book, No. 110, dated
1564.
Felix namque. Another setting The Lady Nevill Book. B.M.
Add. MSS. 30485 (extracts from the Lady Nevill Book), and
Add. MSS. 31403.
Poyncte for the Virginals. B.M. Add. MSS. 30513.
Two Pieces for the organ : (i.) Gloria tibi Trinitas ; (ii.) ' parts on
a round tyme ' ; and an unnamed piece. Ch. Ch. MSS. 371.
An unnamed piece. Ch. Ch. MSS. 1034. E. H. F.

TAMAGNO, FRANCESCO (*b.* Turin, 1851 ;
d. Varese,[1] Aug. 31, 1905), tenor singer, was
educated at the Conservatorio of Turin, and
entered the chorus of the opera, but only remained there a short time, being compelled to
join the army. At the close of his military
service he made his début at the Teatro Bellini,
Palermo, in ' Un Ballo in maschera,' in 1873.
A more important event was his appearance in
' Ernani ' at La Scala, in 1880. Verdi saw in
him the ideal impersonator of Otello, and on
his creation of this part at La Scala, in 1887,
he leapt at once into the front rank of operatic
tenors. His first actual [2] visit to London was

[1] Buried at Turin.
[2] His name had appeared in the prospectuses of Covent Garden
and Her Majesty's about 1877

in the production of this work in 1889 at the Lyceum Theatre, after which he made a rare success in America, receiving terms that were then unparalleled for any male performer. M.

TAMBERLIK, ENRICO (b. Rome, Mar. 16, 1820; d. Paris, Mar. 13, 1889), tenor singer, received instruction in singing from Borgna and Guglielmi, and made his début in 1841 at the Teatro Fondo, Naples, in Bellini's ' I Capuletti.' He sang with success for several years at the San Carlo, also at Lisbon, Madrid and Barcelona. He first appeared in England Apr. 4, 1850, at the Royal Italian Opera, as Masaniello, and obtained immediate popularity in that and other parts. He remained a member of the company until 1864 inclusive, excepting the season of 1857, singing in the winters at Paris, St. Petersburg, Madrid, North and South America, etc. His other parts included Aug. 9, 1851, Phaon (' Saffo'); Aug. 17, 1852, ' Pietro il Grande'; June 25, 1853, ' Benvenuto Cellini'; May 10, 1855, Manrico (' Trovatore ')—on production of those operas in England ; also, May 27, 1851, Florestan (' Fidelio ') ; July 15, 1852, Ugo (Spohr's 'Faust'); Aug. 5, 1858, 'Zampa'; July 2, 1863, Gounod's ' Faust '—on the revival or production of the operas at Covent Garden. He reappeared at the same theatre in 1870 as Don Ottavio, the Duke (' Rigoletto '), and John of Leyden ; and in 1877, at Her Majesty's, as Ottavio, Otello and Manrico, and was well received, though his powers were on the wane. In the autumn of that year he sang at the Salle Ventadour, Paris, and retired soon after. He lived at Madrid, and carried on a manufactory of arms, occasionally singing in public. A. C.

TAMBOURA, see PANDORA.

TAMBOURIN, an old Provençal dance, in its original form accompanied by a flute and Tambour de Basque, whence the name was derived. The drum accompaniment remained a characteristic feature when the dance was

adopted on the stage, the bass of the tune generally consisting of single notes in the tonic or dominant. The Tambourin was in 2-4 time, of a lively character, and generally followed by a second Tambourin in the minor, after which the first was repeated. A well-known example occurs in Rameau's ' Pièces de clavecin,' and has often been reprinted. It was introduced

in Scene 7, Entrée III, of the same composer's ' Fêtes d'Hébé,' where it is entitled ' Tambourin en rondeau,' in allusion to its form, which is that of an 8-barred Rondeau followed by several ' reprises.' The same opera contains (in Entrée I, Scenes 5 and 9) two other Tambourins, each consisting of two parts (major and minor). Above we give the first part of one of them as an example. Mlle. Camargo is said to have excelled in this dance. W. B. S.

TAMBOURIN. A long narrow drum used in Provence. See DRUM (5).

TAMBOURINE (O.E. timbrel). A shallow ring of wood covered on one side with skin and struck with the fingers or the hand. The old English name timbrel is a diminutive derived from tymbyr, a little tabor or drum. In the late 18th century, upon the revival of the timbrel as an adjunct to the Janissary music of military bands, it became known as the tambourine (tamburino), of which an illustration is given on PLATE XXIV. No. 5.

The ancestry of this simple instrument is most remote, as the timbrel is found in use amongst the most ancient nations of the world, such as those of Assyria and Egypt : its distribution, too, seems to be world-wide, the hoop-drums of China, the rectangular Daff of India, the Chilchiles of the Peruvian Incas and the Aelyau of Greenland being but varied forms of the timbrel. Its introduction into Britain is certainly prehistoric, for not only did the Gauls use it, but the advent of the Romans to our shores must have increased its popularity, as, with little bells or metal discs, called ' jingles,' attached, it marked the rhythm of the dance or roused to frenzy the devotees of Bacchic rites. Under the Hebrew name Tof (see HEBREW MUSIC) it was presumably the instrument used by Miriam and her maidens to celebrate Israel's triumph over the Egyptian foe ; hence it is frequently depicted in ecclesiastical carving and placed by artists in the hands of angels. In mediæval times a cord of catgut was stretched across the parchment head in order to produce a sharp rattling sound when struck (see SNARES). Its introduction into orchestral works was occasioned by the need for special effects of the Spanish or Gipsy character, as for instance in Weber's overture to ' Preciosa.' It is now a recognised member of the percussion group. F. W. G.

TAMBURA (TANBUR), an instrument of the lute family, having wire strings played with a plectrum, found in Arabia, Persia and elsewhere under slightly differing names. The Indian tambura, (tamburi), a four-stringed instrument, is described in Day's Music and Musical Instruments of Southern India (see INDIAN MUSIC). The tampur, another variety of this instrument found in the Caucasus, has three strings, and is played with a bow.

TAMBURINI, ANTONIO (b. Faenza, Mar. 28,

1800; d. Nice, Nov. 9, 1876), baritone singer, eminent among the great lyric artists of the 19th century. His father was director of military music at Fossombrone, Ancona. A player himself on horn, trumpet and clarinet, he instructed his son, at a very early age, in horn - playing. At 9 the boy played in the orchestra, but seems soon to have been passed on to Aldobrando Rossi for vocal instruction. At 12 he returned to Faenza, singing in the opera chorus, which was employed not only at the theatre but for Mass. At 18, and in possession of a fine voice, he was engaged for the opera of Bologna. The piece in which, at the little town of Cento, he first appeared was ' La contessa di colle erboso,' of Generali. His favourable reception there at Mirandola, Correggio and Bologna, attracted the notice of several managers, one of whom secured him for the Carnival at Piacenza, where his success in Rossini's ' Italiana in Algeri ' procured for him an engagement that same year at the Teatro Nuovo at Naples. The political troubles of 1820, however, closed the theatres, and Tamburini sang next at Florence, where, owing to indisposition, he did himself no justice. The memory of this was speedily wiped out by a series of triumphs at Leghorn, Turin and Milan. At Milan he married the singer Marietta Gioja, for whom, together with him, Mercadante wrote ' Il posto abbandonato.'

Proceeding to Trieste, he passed through Venice, where an unexpected toll was demanded of him. Special performances were being given in honour of the Emperors of Austria and Russia, then at Venice, and Tamburini was not allowed to escape scot-free. He was arrested ' by authority,' and only after a few days, during which he achieved an immense success, was he allowed to proceed. From Trieste he went to Rome, where he remained for two years; thence, after singing in ' Mosè ' at Venice, with Davide and Mme. Meric-Lalande, he removed to Palermo, where he spent another two years. He now received an engagement from Barbaja for four years, during which he sang in Naples, Milan and Vienna. At Vienna he and Rubini were decorated with the Order of the Saviour, an honour previously accorded to no foreigner but Wellington.

Tamburini first sang in London in 1832, and soon became an established favourite. His success was equally great at Paris, where he appeared in October of the same year as Dandini in ' Cenerentola.' For ten years he belonged to London and Paris, a conspicuous star in the brilliant constellation formed by Grisi, Persiani, Viardot, Rubini, Lablache and himself, and was long remembered as the baritone in the famous ' Puritani quartet.' His non-engagement by Laporte in the season of 1840 was the cause of the series of riots which began in Apr. 29, and resulted in victory for Tamburini's

admirers. His voice, a baritone, of over two octaves extent, was full, round, sonorous and perfectly equal throughout. His execution was unsurpassed and unsurpassable; of a kind which at the present day is well-nigh obsolete, and is associated in the public mind with soprano and tenor voices only. The Parisians, referring to this florid facility, called him ' Le Rubini des basse - tailles.' Although chiefly celebrated as a singer of Rossini's music, one of his principal parts was Don Giovanni. His readiness, versatility and cleverness are well illustrated by the anecdote [1] of his exploit at Palermo, during his engagement there, when he not only sang his own part in Mercadante's ' Elisa e Claudio ' but adopted the costume and the voice—a soprano sfogato—of Mme. Lipparini, the prima donna, who was frightened off the stage, went through the whole opera, duets and all, and finished by dancing a pas de quatre with the Taglionis and Mlle. Rinaldini.

In 1841 Tamburini returned to Italy and sang at several theatres there. Although his powers were declining, he proceeded to Russia, where he found it worth his while to remain for ten years. When, in 1852, he returned to London, his voice had all but disappeared, in spite of which he sang again after that in Holland and in Paris. His last attempt was in London, in 1859. From that time he lived in retirement at Nice.   F. A. M.

TAMBURO (Ital.) ' drum,' generally used in the phrase ' gran tamburo,' for the big drum, the word ' timpani ' being reserved for the orchestral drums. (See Drum.)

TAMERLANO, opera in 3 acts; libretto by Piovene; music by Handel. Composed between July 3 and 23, 1724, and produced at the King's Theatre, London, Oct. 31, 1724. g.

TAMING OF THE SHREW, see Widerspänstigen Zähmung.

TAMPON, a two-headed drumstick (tampon or mailloche double), used for the bass drum when a roll is required on that instrument, as in the overture to 'Zampa' and elsewhere, when the direction is ' Grosse caisse en tonnerre.' It is held in the middle, where it is $1\frac{3}{16}$ inch in diameter, so that the roll is easily made by an alternate motion of the wrist. The stick, ending in a round knob at each end, is turned out of a piece of ash ; the knobs are thickly covered with tow and a cap of chamois leather, and are both of the same size. When finished the heads are about $2\frac{3}{4}$ inches in diameter, and the same in length. The length of the whole stick is $12\frac{1}{2}$ inches.   v. de P.

TAM-TAM. See Gong.

TANBUR, see Tambura.

TANCREDI, opera in 2 acts ; libretto by Rossi, after Voltaire, music by Rossini. Produced Teatro Fenice, Venice, Feb. 6, 1813 ; in

1 See Sutherland Edwards, History of the Opera, ii. 272.

Italian, Théâtre des Italicns, Paris ; in French (Castil Blaze) Odéon ; in Italian, King's Theatre, London, May 4, 1820.   G.

TANEIEV, ALEXANDER SERGEIEVICH (b. St. Petersburg, Jan. 5/17, 1850 ; d. there, June 20, 1915). On leaving the university he entered the service of the State and rose to the post of chief chancellor. He studied music with Reichel at Dresden, and, after a lapse of some years, with Rimsky-Korsakov and Petrov in St. Petersburg. He was also influenced by Balakirev. The list of his works includes : An opera in one act, ' Cupid's Revenge ' ; 3 symphonies No. 2 in B minor (op. 21) published ; 2 orchestral suites (op. 14) ; 2 quartets ; pianoforte pieces ; ' Rêverie ' for violin (op. 23) ; choruses and partsongs, and a symphonic poem 'Alesha Popovich.'   R. N.

TANEIEV, SERGIUS IVANOVICH (b. Government of Vladimir, Nov. 13/25, 1856 ; d. Moscow, June 1915), pianist and composer, was the son of a government official.

He attended the Moscow Conservatoire at the early age of 10, taking pianoforte lessons from Langer. In 1869 Taneiev's parents purposed removing him from the Conservatoire in order to send him to a public school, but were persuaded by the director, Nicholas Rubinstein, not to break off his musical education. During the years which followed he studied the pianoforte with Nicholas Rubinstein, form and fugue with Hubert, and composition with Tchaikovsky. He left the Conservatoire in 1875, having gained the first gold medal ever awarded in that institution, and soon afterwards started on a concert tour through Russia in company with the famous violinist Auer. During 1877–78 he visited Paris, and gave concerts in various towns of the Baltic Provinces, after which he returned to Moscow to succeed Tchaikovsky as professor of instrumentation at the Conservatoire. He also became the chief professor of pianoforte after the retirement of Klindworth and the death of N. Rubinstein. In 1885 he succeeded Hubert as director of the Conservatoire, being replaced by Safonov in 1889. During his directorate, Taneiev completed the organisation of the students' orchestra.

He made his début as a pianist in 1875, at one of the concerts of the Imperial Russian Musical Society at Moscow. On this occasion he played Brahms's pianoforte concerto, and Tchaikovsky wrote of him that he had more than fulfilled the hopes of his teachers, and added :

' Besides purity and strength of touch, grace and ease of execution, Taneiev astonished every one by his maturity of intellect, his self-control and the calm objective style of his interpretation. He has his own artistic individuality which has won him a place among virtuosi from the very outset of his career.'

In December of the same year Taneiev played Tchaikovsky's pianoforte concerto in B♭ minor

for the first time in Moscow. Henceforth he became one of the chief exponents of this master's pianoforte works. Master and pupil were united by bonds of close friendship, and corresponded frequently. Taneiev sometimes criticised Tchaikovsky's music with an unsparing freedom of expression characteristic of youth. But this in no way interfered with the cordiality of their relations, for Tchaikovsky had every confidence in his pupil's opinion. ' I beg you not to be afraid of over-severity,' he wrote to him in 1878. ' I want just those stinging criticisms from you. So long as you give me the truth, what does it matter whether it is favourable or not ? '

In later years Taneiev rarely appeared in public as pianist. As a teacher he always laid stress on the necessity for a thorough theoretical education and the study of the older classical masters. His own compositions are more remarkable for sound workmanship and a cultured taste than for charm or warmth of inspiration. The list of his principal works is as follows :

ORCHESTRAL.

Symphony No. 1, in C minor, op. 12 (1902) (published). Three other symphonies. Suite de Concert (op. 28) for vln. and orch. Overture in C on Russian themes.

CHAMBER MUSIC

Six string quartets : B minor (op. 4), C major (op. 5), D minor (op. 7), A minor (op. 11), A major (op. 13), B flat (op. 19) ; PF. quartet in E (op. 20) ; two string trios (op. 21 in D, op. 31 in E flat) ; PF. trio in D (op. 22) ; Prelude and Fugue G sharp minor for 2 PF.'s (op. 29).

OPERATIC AND CHORAL

' Orestes,' a trilogy in eight scenes, libretto from Æschylus by A. Benkstern ; performed at the Maryinsky Theatre, St. Petersburg, 1895. Cantata ' John of Damascus ' for soli, chorus and orchestra (1884). Three choruses for male voices to words by Fet ; two choruses for male voices in Albrecht's collection ; ' Sunrise ' for mixed voices. Other choral pieces and about 40 songs.

Taneiev has also written an important work on counterpoint, and done useful service in arranging for pianoforte orchestral works by Tchaikovsky, Glazounov, Arensky and others.
                                                       R. N.

TANGENT, in a clavichord, is a thick pin of brass wire an inch or more high, flattened out towards the top into a head one-eighth of an inch or so in diameter. It is inserted in the back end of the key, and being pushed up so as to strike the pair of strings above it, forms at once a hammer for them and a temporary bridge, from which they vibrate up to the sound-board bridge. (See CLAVICHORD.)
                                                       A. J. H.

TANGO, a dance of Mexican origin, in which the movements of the negroes were imitated. The music is rhythmically similar in style to the HABANERA, but played half as fast again, and worked up faster and faster till it ends abruptly like the conventional dances of the modern ballet. The frequent habit of writing five notes, sometimes of equal value, sometimes a dotted semiquaver, a demi-semiquaver and a triplet of semiquavers, in the melody against four notes in the accompaniment, and vice versa, and many other varieties of rhythm of a similar nature, added to the peculiar colour of Spanish harmonic progressions which are the stamp of so-called Musica flamenca, give it a weird

fascination. The movements of the dance are
less presentable to a polite audience than those
of the Habanera, and as now performed in the
cafés chantants of Madrid and other cities of
Spain the Tango has become nothing but an
incitation to desire. As such it never fails to
draw forth vociferous applause. A modified
form of the dance is often introduced into a
ZARZUELA at better - class theatres. Tangos
have been written by modern composers for
solo instruments, and one, by Arbós, for violin
with orchestral accompaniment (also with
pianoforte) is extremely graceful, refined and
characteristic.　　　　　　　　　　H. V. H.

TANNHÄUSER UND DER SÄNGER-
KRIEG AUF WARTBURG, opera in 3 acts ;
words and music by Wagner. Produced Dres-
den, Oct. 19, 1845 ; New York, Staadt Theatre,
Apr. 4, 1859 ; Opéra, Paris [1] (French transla-
tion by Ch. Nuitter), Mar. 13, 1861 ; Covent
Garden, in Italian, May 6, 1876 ; in English,
Her Majesty's Theatre, Feb. 14, 1882, Carl
Rosa Co. ; in German, Drury Lane, under
Richter, May 23, 1882 ; in French, Covent
Garden, May 27, 1896. The overture was first
performed in England by the Philharmonic
Society (Wagner conducting), May 14, 1855.
　　　　　　　　　　　　　　　　G.

TANS'UR, WILLIAM (b. Dunchurch, Warwickshire, 1706 ; d. St. Neot's, Oct. 7, 1783), a
composer chiefly of psalm tunes, though some
secular pieces are also by him. In the preface
to one of the many works he issued, The Elements of Musick display'd, 1772, he informs us
that he was born at Dunchurch, Warwickshire,
in 1700. He further confirms this by append-
ing to his engraved portrait the words 'Aetatis
suae 70 Christi 1770.' It is likely that he has
made a mistake regarding the date of his birth,
for the parish register [2] of Dunchurch states
that William Tanzer, the son of Edward Tanzer
and Joan Tanzer, was baptized Nov. 6, 1706.
This year may be taken as the year of his birth,
for John, a previous son of Edward and Joan
Tanzer, was baptized on May 14, 1704, and it is
unlikely that William would remain unbaptized
six years after his birth.

The original name 'Tanzer' implies a German origin, and we learn from the register that
Edward Tanzer, the father, was a labourer, and
that he died, aged about 60, on Jan. 21, 1712,
while Joan, his wife, followed on Feb. 16 of the
same year, aged 51. Why Tans'ur changed his
name does not appear. The chief details of
Tans'ur's biography occur in the prefaces and
imprints of his books. It appears that he was
a teacher of psalmody from early youth, and

[1] For the extraordinary uproar which it created see Prosper
Mérimée's Lettres à une inconnue, ii. 151-3. One of the jokes was
'qu'on s'ennuie aux récitatifs, et qu'on se tanne aux airs.' Even
a man of sense like Mérimée says that he 'could write something
as good after hearing his cat walk up and down over the keys of the
piano.' Berlioz writes about it in a style which is equally discredit-
able to his taste and his penetration (Correspondance inédite, Nos.
iii. to cvi.). See also the Bayreuther Taschen-Kalender, for 1891.
[2] The entries in the Parish Register were kindly contributed by
the Rev. C. T. B. McNulty. Vicar of Dunchurch

he seems to have settled at many different
places in this pursuit, notably at Ewell near
Epsom and Barnes in Surrey, and Stamford in
Lincolnshire, at which places he was organist.
He had a son who was chorister at Trinity College, Cambridge. Tans'ur's books and editions
are numerous. They consist chiefly of collections of psalm tunes prefaced by the usual instructions for singing. A great number of the
tunes are either composed or arranged in parts
by himself, and he is also author of much of the
verse. His earliest publication appears to have
been 'The Royal Melody Compleat or the new
Harmony of Sion ' in three books, oblong 4to,
1735. Of this work there appeared many editions. Others were, ' Heaven on Earth or the
Beauty of Holiness,' 1738 ; ' Sacred Mirth or
the Pious Soul's daily Delight,' 1739 ; 'The
Psalm Singer's Jewel,' 1760, etc., etc. He was
also the author of an excellent work, A New
Musical Grammar, 1746-56, etc., which developed into The Elements of Musick Display'd,
1772. It is, for its time, an excellent treatise,
and at the present day contains much of antiquarian interest. An edition of it was published so late as 1829, and one about ten years
before this was issued at Stokesley.　　F. K.

TANTO (Ital.), ' as much,' or ' so much ' ;
it is used correctly in many musical directions,
and by Beethoven with the same force as
' troppo,' as if it was the equivalent of ' too
much.'

TANTUM ERGO. The first words of the
last two stanzas of the hymn ' Pange lingua '
written by S. Thomas Aquinas for the office
of Corpus Christi. This excerpt has acquired
a separate status through being sung at
Benediction and other services of the Roman
Catholic Church in connexion with the Eucharist. It has therefore received some special
attention from musicians.　　　　　　W. S. R.

TAPHOUSE, THOMAS WILLIAM (b. Oxford,
Feb. 11, 1838 ; d. there, Jan. 8, 1905), worked
as a cabinet-maker after leaving school at the
age of 14. In 1857 he started with his father
in business as a music-seller in Broad Street,
Oxford, and the business is still a flourishing
one, though it has been moved to a short
distance from the original house. Taphouse
was a skilful pianoforte-tuner, and held various
organ appointments in the city ; but his chief
claim to permanent notice is based on his zeal
and knowledge as a collector of old music and
musical instruments. His library (dispersed at
his death) was of very great value, including,
among many other treasures, the autograph
of Purcell's sonata for violin ; he had collected
materials for a history of music in Oxford ; and
his scholarship was rewarded by the University in an honorary M.A. degree, conferred on
him in 1904. He was elected a member of
the Oxford City Council in 1888, was sheriff
in 1892-93, and curator of the municipal

buildings from 1897 when they were opened. In Nov. 1904 he was elected Mayor of Oxford.

M.

TAPISSIER, JOHANNES, one of the three early 15th-century composers named by Martin le Franc (see CARMEN, Johannes). There is a Credo of his in three parts in Cod. Mus. 37 of the Liceo Musicale at Bologna, an early 15th-century MS. written in the old black-and-red notation. Immediately preceding it in the same MS. is a three-part Gloria by Tomas Fabri, who is described as ' scolaris Tapisier,' in evident allusion to the master's reputation ; this is probably the Tomas Fabri who was succentor at the church of St. Donatus at Bruges in 1412. A four-part motet by Tapissier, printed in Stainer's *Dufay and his Contemporaries* from the Bodleian MS. Canonici. Misc. 213, seems to have been written at Rome. It shows many signs of immaturity, and enables us to realise how great was the advance in musical art made by Dufay and Binchois.

J. F. R. S.

A Sanctus by him has been published in the ' Collection choisie des maîtres polyphonistes des XIIe, XIIIe, XIVe and XVe siècles ' (Gastoué) (Paris, Bureau d'édition de la Schola Cantorum).

BIBL.—A. GASTOUÉ, *Les Primitifs de la musique française* (Paris, 1922). M. L. P.

TAPPERT, WILHELM (*b.* Ober - Thomas - waldau, Silesia, Feb. 19, 1830 ; *d.* Berlin, Oct. 27, 1907), German critic and writer on music. He began life as a schoolmaster, but in 1856 adopted music, under Dehn for theory and Kullak for practice. From that time he resided in Berlin, where he was well known as a teacher and musical writer, and an able and enthusiastic partisan of Wagner. He was a teacher in Tausig's school for higher PF. playing. His *Wagner Lexikon* (1877) contains a collection of the abuse lavished on that composer and his friends. Much more important are his researches into ancient Tablatures, on which much may be learnt from his *Katalog der Spezialausstellung*, *Die Entwicklung der Musiknotenschrift*, etc. From 1876–80 he edited the *Allgemeine deutsche Musikzeitung.* He was a contributor to the *Musikalisches Wochenblatt* and published several pamphlets. His valuable library was purchased by the Berlin State Library (*Riemann*). G.

TARANTELLA, a South Italian dance, which derives its name from Taranto, in the old province of Apulia. The music is in 6–8 time, played at continually increasing speed, with irregular alternations of minor and major. It is generally danced by a man and a woman, but sometimes by two women alone, who often play castanets and a tambourine. It was formerly sung, but this is seldom the case now. The Tarantella has obtained a fictitious interest from the idea that by means of dancing it a strange kind of insanity, attributed to the effects of the bite of the Lycosa Tarantula, the largest of European spiders, could alone be cured. It is certain that a disease known as Tarantism prevailed in South Italy to an extraordinary extent, during the 15th, 16th and 17th centuries, if not later, and that this disease—which seems to have been a kind of hysteria, like the St. Vitus dance epidemic in Germany at an earlier date—was apparently only curable by means of the continued exercise of dancing the Tarantella ; but that the real cause of the affection was the bite of the spider is very improbable, later experiments having shown that it is no more poisonous than the sting of a wasp. The first extant notice of Tarantism is in Niccolo Perotto's *Cornucopia linguae Latinae* (p. 20 *a*, ed. 1489). During the 16th century the epidemic was at its height, and bands of musicians traversed the country to play the music which was the only healing medicine. The forms which the madness took were very various ; some were seized with a violent craving for water, so that they were with difficulty prevented from throwing themselves into the sea, others were strangely affected by different colours, and all exhibited the most extravagant and outrageous contortions. The different forms which the disease assumed were cured by means of different airs, to which the Tarantists—the name by which the patients were known—were made to dance until they often dropped down with exhaustion. The epidemic seems only to have raged in the summer months, and it is said that those who had been once attacked by it were always liable to a return of the disease.

Most of the songs, both words and music, which were used to cure Tarantism no longer exist, but the Jesuit Kircher, in his *Magnes* (Rome, 1641), Book III., cap. viii., has preserved a few specimens. He says that the Tarantellas of his day were mostly rustic extemporisations, but the airs he gives (which are printed in Mendel's *Lexicon*, *sub voce* Tarantella) are written in the Ecclesiastical Modes, and with one exception in common time. They bear no resemblance to the tripping melodies of the modern dance.[1] Kircher's work contains an engraving of the Tarantula in two positions, with a map of the region where it is found, and the following air, entitled ' Antidotum tarantulae,' which is also to be found in Jones's ' Maltese Melodies ' (London, 1805) and in vol. ii. of Stafford Smith's ' Musica antiqua ' (1812), where it is said to be derived from Zimmermann's ' Florilegium ' : [2]

---

[1] It has been suggested that these fragments of melodies—for they are little more—are ancient Greek tunes handed down traditionally in Taranto.

[2] In Mazella's ' Balli, Correnti,' etc. (Rome, 1689), is a Tarantella in common time in the form of a short air with ' partite,' or variations. Mattheson (*Vollkommener Kapellmeister*, 1739) says there is one in the *Quintessence des Nouvelles* for 1727.

For further information on this curious subject we must refer the reader to the following works :

N. Perotto, *Cornucopia* (Venice, 1480) ; A. Kircher, *Magnes* (Rome, 1641) ; *Musurgia* (Rome, 1650) ; Hermann Grube, *De ictu tarantulae* (Frankfort, 1679) ; J. Müller, *De tarentula et vi musicae in ejus curatione* (Hafniae, 1679) ; G. Baglivi, *De praxi medica* (Rome, 1696) ; Dr. Peter Shaw, *New Practice of Physic*, vol. i. (London, 1726) ; Fr. Serao, *Della tarantola* (Rome, 1742) ; Dr. R. Mead, *Mechanical Account of Poisons* (3rd ed., London, 1745) ; J. D. Tietz, *Von den Wirkungen der Töne auf den menschlichen Körper* (in Justi's *Neuen Wahrheiten*, (Leipzig, 1745) ; P. J. Buc'hoz, *L'Art de connaître et de designer le pouls par les notes de la musique* (Paris, 1806) ; J. F. E. Hecker, *Die Tanzwuth* (Berlin, 1832) ; A. Vergari, *Tarantismo* (Naples, 1839) ; De Renzi, in *Raccoglitore medico* for 1842 ; C. Engel, *Musical Myths*, vol. ii. (London, 1876).

The Tarantella has been used by many modern composers. Auber has introduced it in 'La Muette de Portici,' Weber in his E minor sonata, Thalberg wrote one for piano, Heller two. More famous in piano music are those of Chopin and Liszt, and Rossini wrote a vocal Tarantella, 'La Danza' (said to have been composed for Lablache). The ballet 'La Tarantule' in which Fanny Elssler danced in Paris and London is notable.

One of the finest examples is in the finale to Mendelssohn's Italian symphony, where it is mixed up with a Saltarello in the most effective and clever manner. Good descriptions of the dance will be found in Mme. de Staël's *Corinne* (Book VI. ch. i.), Mercier Dupaty's *Lettres sur l'Italie* (1797), and Goethe's *Fragmente über Italien*, see J. Case's *Praise of Musick*, 1586, p. 85. It was danced on the stage with great success by Cotellini (1783–85) at the Teatro dei Fiorentini at Naples, and later by Charles Mathews.

         W. B. S.

To the above it may be added that a curious account of the cure of a person bitten by the tarantula spider is given, in a letter signed Stephen Storace (the father of the better-known musician), in *The Gentleman's Magazine*, for Sept. 1753. Storace says that he was called upon to play the particular tune associated with the cure ; but this he did not know, and tried sundry jigs without effect, until, learning the proper tune from the lips of an old woman, he played it with a satisfactory result. He

gives the following as the traditionary melody, and states that the scene of the occurrence was a village ten miles from Naples.   F. K.

The Tarantula Tune.

etc.

TARARE, opera, in prologue and 5 acts (afterwards 3) ; words by Beaumarchais ; music by Salieri. Produced Opéra, Paris, June 8, 1787 ; in Italian (with many changes of text and music) as 'Axur, Rè d' Ormus,' Vienna, Jan. 8, 1788 ; in English as 'Tarrare, the Tartar Chief,' London, Aug. 15, 1825.

         G.

TARCHI, ANGELO (*b.* Naples, 1760 ; *d.* Paris, Aug. 19, 1814), a pupil of Tarantino and Sala at the Turchini conservatoire, Naples. In his time he was a very popular composer, whose operas, numbering about 46, were performed all over Europe. In 1786 he was in London where, according to Burney, he contributed to a pasticcio some songs for Rubinelli (*Q.-L.* ; *Fetis*).

TARDITI, ORAZIO (*b.* Rome, towards end of 16th cent. ; *d.* Faënza, *c.* 1670 ?), organist at various Italian towns from 1622 ; Calmaldulian monk and abbate at Ravenna, 1647 ; maestro di cappella of Faënza Cathedral, 1648. He was an important church composer (masses, motets, etc.), and wrote also several books of secular madrigals, canzonets and other songs (*Q.-L.* ; *Fétis*).

TARISIO, LUIGI (*d.* Milan, 1854), an able and perhaps the first judge of old violins, who created and supplied a demand for old Italian instruments both in England and in France at a time when the work of Stainer and his school practically monopolised the market. Originally an obscure Italian carpenter who plied a house-to-house trade, he gradually became cognisant of the valuable violins which were scattered among the Italian peasantry at the beginning of the 19th century, and the carpenter became merged in the collector, dealer and connoisseur. Tarisio's talent for detecting the characteristics of the great Italian luthiers amounted to genius, but, in addition to this, he possessed a shrewd knowledge of human nature, and he drove excellent bargains. His *modus operandi* was principally based on the system of a so-called exchange, whereby he himself invariably benefited. His humble profession admitted him not only into the homes of the cottagers, but into many sacristies and convents also, whence he more than frequently emerged with a fine Italian instrument, obtained in exchange for a shining new fiddle from his own pack. In 1827 Tarisio made his way to Paris, introduced himself and his sack of fine instruments first to M. Aldric, a dealer of dilettante tastes, who, after some doubts occasioned by the pedlar's shabby appearance, was eventually compelled to recognise him as one of the greatest violin connoisseurs of the day. For over twenty years after his first visit to Paris, Tarisio's advent there was welcomed by all the foremost dealers, and through his importation numbers of the finest Italian violins came into France, and, after his appearance in London in 1851, into England also. Despite his nomadic life, Tarisio considered Italy his home always. He owned a small farm in the province of Novara, and shortly before his death he settled in Milan, where he established himself in an attic over a restaurant in the Via Legnano, Porta Tenaglia. Here, amid comfortless surroundings, he was found dead one morning in 1854, with over 200 violins, violoncellos and altos in his small domicile. To his family he left a fortune of 300,000 francs, a sum which represented his profits in violin-dealing during twenty years; and in addition to this his relatives received the purchase-money paid by J. B. Vuillaume after Tarisio's death for the instruments found in the Milanese attic, and for the five magnificent violins which had been hidden away at his farm. Among the latter number was the 'Messie' Stradivarius, which had been preserved for over sixty years in the collection of Count Cozio di Salabue. Tarisio purchased it on the death of the latter in 1824, and concealed its whereabouts until his death, with a view, no doubt, to enhancing its value from a sensational point of view. During his visits to the various dealers he frequently referred to the treasure he would reveal to them one day, i.e. a Stradivarius violin in superb condition that had never known the touch of a bow, and it was its promised advent that gained for it the title of the 'Messiah' in professional circles.

BIBL.—HILL, *Antonio Stradivari*; HAWEIS, *Old Violins*; VIDAL, *Les Instruments à archet*; READE, *Readiana*; RACSTER, *Chats on Violins*.   E. H.-A.

TARTAGLIONE, IPPOLITO (b. Modena, c. 1539; d. Naples, c. 1580), maestro di cappella at S. Maria Maggiore, Rome, 1575, and at Naples Cathedral, 1577. He is spoken of as one of the foremost composers of his time and one of the first who wrote masses and motets for 3 and 4 choruses (*Fétis*: Q.-L.).

TARTINI, GIUSEPPE (b. Pirano, Istria, Apr. 8, 1692; d. Padua, Feb. 26, 1770), famous violinist and composer, founder of an important school of violin-playing at Padua, and originator of certain improvements in the construction and technique of the bow.

Fanzago,[1] his contemporary, records that Tartini's father was a member of a good Florentine family; a man whose philanthropic nature led him to give largely to the Church, which charitable practices gained him a title. From documents belonging to another contemporary, the Bishop of Capo d' Istria, Paolo Naldini, now preserved in the Episcopal Archives at Trieste, it would appear that Tartini's father became a member of the staff of the Public Salt Works in Pirano on Sept. 16, 1692; but he doubtless settled there some years before this, for the marriage-registers for the year 1685—preserved among the Archives of the Collegiata di Pirano—announce that Giovanni Antonio Tartini espoused Catarina, daughter of Pietro Zangando (not *Giando* as stated by Fanzago, and others), on Mar. 5, in that year at Pirano. Here also is recorded the baptism of 'Iseppo,' son of the above, ' by me Pre Giov Maria Vanturini, Canon : Godfather, Signor Simon Testa ; Godmother, Signora Bartolemea, wife of Signor Girolamo Apollonio.' Tartini's father, besides being ennobled, would appear to have been wealthy, being the owner of the beautiful villa Struegnano, and much property in its neighbourhood. It was here that Giuseppe, his brothers Domenico, Antonio, Pietro, and a sister—who died in infancy— were born. One of the priests belonging to the order of St. Filippo Neri of Pirano superintended Giuseppe's earliest education, and as soon as his capacities permitted he was admitted into the Collegio dei Padri delle Scuole Pie, at Capo d' Istria. According to Fanzago, he learnt the rudiments of music and the violin here. He remained at Capo d' Istria until 1709, in which year his father obtained permission from the Bishop (Paolo Naldini) for him to pursue his studies at the University of Padua. The Bishop's consent was dated Feb. 22, 1709, and it caused a good deal of variance between the father and son as to his destined avocation. The father's wish was to see his son one of the brotherhood of the Minori Conventuali, and to this end he even went as far as to promise a handsome contribution to the 'Convento' of Pirano should his desire be attained. But the prospect of studying theology held no attractions for the youthful Tartini, who was of an ardent and vivacious nature, and, in spite of the fact that his father's counsels were endorsed by the Bishop, he gained his point, and entered the Padua University as a law student.

He was just 17, passionately fond of art, and above all devoted to fencing, in which he became so excellent that few could stand against him. In addition to this he was devoted to music, and at one time seriously contemplated opening a fencing-school at Naples which should form his means of subsistence whilst he followed his inclination as a violinist.

[1] *Lodi di G. Tartini*, Padua, 1770.

Instead, however, he remained at the University until his 20th year (1713) when his love for one of his pupils—by name Elisabetta Premazone—changed the tenor of his life. This lady has frequently been alluded to as the niece of Cardinal Giorgio Cornaro. More recently it has been thought that she was no connexion of the Cardinal, but a daughter of one of his dependants. In any case, the Cardinal occupied himself with her welfare, and in the matter of her runaway marriage with Tartini his interest took the form of wrathful disapproval, which he demonstrated by ordering Tartini's arrest. To this were added the strong objections of his family, who deprived him of all support, and in this predicament the young man found himself compelled to fly from the city disguised as a monk, leaving his wife at Padua. The story goes that he wended his way towards Rome in the first instance, then wandered wearily over the country, living from hand to mouth, until he fortunately met a relative who occupied a position as custodian in the Monastery of Assisi, where he found a haven of refuge. Little is known of Tartini's residence at Assisi, except that it was a time of serious study and contemplation for him. Here, according to his great friend Gian Rinaldo Carli, professor of Navigation and Astronomy at the University of Padua, he discovered what is generally known as the 'third sound,' a problem in acoustics beyond his scientific knowledge to explain, but since lucidly expounded by HELMHOLTZ (see also RESULTANT TONES). He also inaugurated the use of violin-strings thicker than those that had hitherto served violinists, and in addition he had his bow made of lighter wood, corrected the outward bulge of the stick, diminished the size of the head, and fluted the wood at the heel of the bow so as to obtain a surer grip. It was here also that he wrote his famous 'Trillo del Diavolo' which, according to the account of its composition which he gave to Lalande the great astronomer, came to him in a dream. The story is recounted by Lalande in his *Voyage d'un François en Italie* (1765–66, vol. viii. p. 292) in the following manner :

'One night I dreamt that I had made a bargain with the devil for my soul. Everything went at my command ; my novel servant anticipated every one of my wishes. Then the idea suggested itself to hand him my violin to see what he would do with it. Great was my astonishment when I heard him play, with consummate skill, a sonata of such exquisite beauty as surpassed the boldest flights of my imagination. I felt enraptured, transported, enchanted ; my breath failed me, and—I awoke. Seizing my violin I tried to reproduce the sounds I had heard. But in vain. The piece I then composed, The Devil's Sonata, although the best I ever wrote, how far was it below the one I had heard in my dream !'

Tartini remained at Assisi nearly two years studying composition with the 'padre Boemo' (see ČERNOHORSKY), and attracting people to the Monastery Chapel by the fame of his violin-

playing. No member of the congregation knew who the wonderful artist was, as he always remained shrouded from view behind a heavy curtain. But the moment of his discovery and release came at last.

It was on Aug. 1, 1715, when the greatest number of Italians made a customary pilgrimage to the tomb of St Francis to implore his grace, that the deacon in presenting incense to the Fathers inadvertently pulled aside the curtains concealing the entry to the choir, and revealed the figure of Tartini, who was instantly recognised by some Paduans present. The news quickly spread to Padua, where his wife languished for him ; the Cardinal's heart became softened, and he removed all obstacles to the reunion of the couple. Thus Tartini was now free to return to his home in Padua. Here he mixed with the most cultured and aristocratic people of his day, devoting himself entirely to music. His fame as a violinist began to spread, so that when Veracini visited Venice in 1716, Tartini was invited to compete with the eminent Florentine at the Palace of His Excellency Pisano-Mocenigo to honour the visit of the Elector of Saxony. But to his chagrin, Tartini discovered, on hearing Veracini at Cremona before the contest, that that artist excelled him in many ways, especially in his management of the bow. Humiliated and mortified by the disclosure, he again left his wife—this time in the care of his brother Domenico at Pirano—and returned to Ancona, where he applied himself assiduously until he had obtained the perfection he desired. Whether he had any master at Ancona the authorities fail to state, but it may have been that he profited by the teaching of a certain obscure musician named Giulio Terni, whom Tartini stated to have been his first master, adding that he had studied very little until after he was 30 years of age. However this may be, it was before that age that he received an invitation to accept the post of first violin at the famous Cappella del Santo at Padua. The document which called him to the appointment is dated Apr. 3, 1721, and states that the bearer is asked to conduct 'Signor Giuseppe Tartini, an extraordinary violinist, thither,' and that he shall have an annual stipend of 150 florins, also that any proof of his excellence in his profession shall be dispensed with. The latter was an exceptional favour, as the choir and players of the Chapel, numbering sixteen singers and twenty-four instrumentalists, was considered one of the finest in Italy, and the musicians were subjected to strict annual examinations. A further benefit was extended to Tartini by the granting to him of permission to play at other places besides the Chapel, but he availed himself of this privilege very rarely until 1723, when he accepted the invitation of a passionate musical devotee, the Chancellor of Bohemia

—Count Kinsky—to come to Prague. With
him went Antonio Vandini, the principal violoncellist of the Cappella del Santo, and they both
assisted at the Festival held in honour of the
Coronation of the Emperor, Charles VI , at
Vienna. In Prague Tartini created a veritable
furore, remaining there from 1723–25 as conductor of Count Kinsky's band. But success
could not lighten the life of a man who was
harassed by family worries, and uncongenial
surroundings. His letters addressed to his
brothers from Prague [1] reveal that his troubles
were many. His family—and more especially
his brother Domenico—seemed to be threatened
with some terrible financial crisis, and Tartini
was constantly called upon for aid, and, writing
to Domenico on Aug. 10, 1725, the devout
maestro feels he can do but little to alleviate
his brother's miseries, and turns to God
Almighty for help, praying

'that he may assist you and me . . . and teach me,
and help me to remain in a place where the air, the
food, and the people are equally distasteful to me.
I see clearly I cannot live here without being reduced
very shortly by so many ills, that I shall have to go
constantly about with a physick bottle in my hands.'

He tells his brother that he is firmly resolved
to return to his own country, ' for the skin is
nearer than the purse.' At last in 1726 he left
Prague for his beloved Padua, delaying his
return only by a visit to one of his great admirers at Venice, his Excellency Michele Morosini di San Stefano. This dignitary interested
himself in the misfortunes of Tartini's family,
and advised him to apply to the Fisc of the
Public Salt Works on behalf of his brother, all
of which Tartini immediately posted on to
Domenico, advising that in sending the application to the Fisc, ' it would be wise to present
him with a barrel of that good black Moscato.'

FOUNDATION OF THE ' SCHOOL.'—The year
1728 saw the installation of Tartini's school
of violin-playing at Padua, an establishment
whose excellence gained for it the title of 'School
of the Nations,' while its prime instigator himself was known as the ' Master of Nations.' In
a letter written by Tartini from Padua on Sept.
18, 1739, to the Padre Martini of Bologna, who
was interesting himself on behalf of a youth, a
protégé of Count Cornelio Pepoli, we can form
an idea of students' fe s for tuition at this school.
' The expenses,' he writes,

'for his board (not in my house, as I do not care to
take scholars in my home, but) in the house of my
assistant, would be fifty paoli a month, because
living is dearer in Padua than in Venice. As for my
own honorarium it will be two zecchini a month for solo
violin alone ; if he wishes counterpoint also, my fee
will be three zecchini. Some of my pupils pay me
more, but I am accustomed to two zecchini for the
violin alone. If the youth is gifted, in one year,
if God wills, his studies will be completed, as scholars
with small talents have completed their studies in
two years. . . .'

From the time that Tartini returned to Padua
after his residence at Prague not even the most

1 See Hortis, *Lettere di Giuseppe Tartini.*

tempting offers could induce him to leave
his native country again. For this, his wife—
for whom the biographies have no praise—
was mainly responsible. She was apparently a
nervous, suffering, exacting creature, who yet
commanded her husband's patient devotion to
the end of his life. On her account he was content to forgo conquests farther afield, and thus
refused the proposal of Sir Edward Walpole—
who heard him while passing through Padua in
1730—to come to London. His wife ' agreed
with him ' that it was best for them to be satisfied with their state. ' Although not rich, I
have sufficient and do not need for more,' is the
manner in which he is reported to have declined
the offer. The invitation of Louis Henri,
Prince of Condé, to come to Paris met with a
similar reply in the same year. Then came the
renewal of the offer by the Duc de Noailles ; in
1734 this again was declined, as was also the
tempting offer of Lord Middlesex, who thought
that 3000 lire would surely lure the great violinist from his native land to London. However,
although gifted with an apparently modest
ambition, Tartini occasionally toured in his own
country.

A little before 1740 he journeyed to Rome at
the request of Cardinal Olivieri, at whose Palace
he met all the *noblesse* of the city, and even
Pope Clement XII. himself. It was at the
request of this Pontiff that Tartini wrote his
Miserere, which was performed on Ash Wednesday in the Sistine Chapel. This was said to be
Tartini's only vocal composition until Tebaldini pointed out that among the Archives of
the Santo at Padua is preserved a MS. entitled
' Salve Regina : a quattro voci ripieni,' which
is the ' Ultima compositione del celeb. maes.
Giuseppe Tartini.' In the same place there are
also some *canzone* of Tartini for two and three
voices. On his way to Cardinal Olivieri's Tartini visited Venice, Milan, Florence, Livorno,
Bologna, Naples and Palermo, receiving enthusiastic ovations wherever he went. The
admiration of the Neapolitans reached such a
climax that it is said they tried to carry the
astonished violinist round the town. At the
conclusion of his visit to Rome Tartini returned
to Padua, never to leave it until his death,
although he was pressed by the Prince of Clermont to visit Paris and London in 1755.

Stancovitch [2] says that the rumour of Tartini's coming to Paris spread all over that city
in 1755, and was ventilated at a public meeting,
but Tartini, firm in his principles, soon put an
end to their hopes, and finally disappointed the
Parisians. During all this time Tartini employed his days in indefatigable musical studies,
in playing, composing and teaching, and his
hours of repose were passed in the society of
most of the great men of the day. Even when

2 *Biografia degli uomini distinti dell' Istria* (Capodistria, n.d.
p. 278).

declining years prevented him from playing, he continued composing. (Some of these works are preserved in the Cappella del Santo at Padua.) In 1768 his health began to fail him. He wrote to his friend Riccati in that year, telling him that he had suffered from an attack of convulsive paralysis, and it had confined him to the house for nearly six months. This was the beginning of the end. A month later he was moved from his bed to a sofa, and became more hopeful of recovery, but instead of this he grew worse. A cancerous growth formed in his foot, and caused him terrible suffering until his death. Tartini's last moments were soothed by the presence of his affectionate pupil Nardini, who came expressly from Leghorn to be with his master, and followed his remains to the grave. The great violinist was buried in the church of St. Catherine of Padua. A Requiem composed by his friend Vallotti was sung in the church of the Santo, and the Abbé Fanzago delivered a laudatory oration which was published at Padua in the same year.

CHARACTER OF TARTINI. — Tartini practically divided his personal property, which consisted of certain investments, amongst his family during his lifetime, so that, as he states in a letter to his people dated 1769,

'there is nothing to leave you at my death except my furniture and my money. That may pass to my legitimate heirs at Pirano. In the absence of such (I mean males) the inheritance may pass to the Tartinis of Florence.'

Some of his manuscripts and other articles he left to his pupil Giulio Meneghini of Padua, and some to the Postmaster-General, Count Thurn and Taxis. To his friend Professor Colombo he entrusted his literary work *Delle ragioni e delle proporzioni* (six books), that he might superintend its publication. Colombo unfortunately died shortly after, and the manuscripts were apparently all lost except those portions of the materials which served for the work now preserved in the Archives of Pirano.

As a man Tartini was universally beloved and respected by his fellows. He was of a pious nature, and frequently told his friends that his happiness consisted in his submission to the will of the Almighty, and not to his own. He devoted his life to the highest forms of art and science, although his practical knowledge was not always sufficiently sound to place the result of his researches upon a solid basis. An instance of this is found in his *Trattato di musica secondo la vera scienza dell' armonia*, and in his *De' principii dell' armonia musicale*, wherein he attempted to fathom some difficult acoustical problems, and raised some literary controversy on the subject, but entirely failed to come to a clear conclusion. Briefly, his observations led to the discovery of the generating sound which proceeds from two notes vibrated together, and this he employed

as an excellent guide to perfect intonation in double-stopping. 'If you do not hear the bass,' he told his pupils, 'your thirds and sixths are not in tune'; but neither he nor his pupils could explain the phenomenon of this 'third sound,' since explained by Helmholtz under the title of 'differential tones.' His humble nature imbued him with a serene content, which was perhaps detrimental to his fame as a solo-player, for there is no doubt that he was the greatest scientific as well as practical violinist of his day. In spite of Quantz's oft-quoted but improbable statement that Tartini resorted to tricks, we have ample proof in his music, and in his *Arte del arco*, that he was a magnificent cantabile player. Indeed, so sensible were the Italians of this exquisite quality in the great violinist that Mainwaring [1] tells us that his contemporaries often said of him : 'Non suona, ma canta sul violino.' Yet it was his success as a teacher, rather than as a player, that made him world-famous. Such pupils as Nardini, Pasqualino, Bini, Alberghi, Manfredi, Ferrari, Graun, Carminato, Maddalena Lombardini (Madame Sirmen), to whom he addressed the oft-quoted Letter of Instruction, Pagin, Lahoussaye and others were living proofs of his ability as a teacher, which attracted all the talent of the day to the 'School of Nations' in Padua. As a composer he combined the serenity and dignity of Corelli with an added grace and passion all his own, and his writing for the violin was technically more advanced and complicated than that of his predecessors. He contrived to infuse a variety of expression into his music lacking in the works of Corelli, and this is stated to have been due to his custom of selecting some phrase from Petrarch before he began to compose, and keeping the sense mirrored on his mind while at work. He not only thought of the chosen lines, but inscribed them in a cipher known only to himself and a chosen few, at the top of his MSS. A certain Melchior Babbi of Padua possessed the key to this cipher, and according to his account Tartini inscribed on one sonata the words 'Ombra sacra' (' Sacred shade '). On another 'Volge il riso in pianto o miei pupille' (' Turn laughter into tears, oh my eyes '). Tebaldini confirms this statement and says that many of the MSS. preserved in the Cappella del Santo at Padua bear such inscriptions. There is a story that when Lipinski visited Trieste in 1818 he met one of Tartini's oldest pupils in the person of the lawyer Constantino Massarana, who placed one of his master's MSS. before the violinist. Lipinski failed to play it to the satisfaction of his listener, who said, ' Read the inscription, and that will inspire you to play it with the right spirit,' which it is said he did.

SUMMARY OF WORKS. — A complete and com-

[1] *Memoirs of the Life of Handel*, 1760.

prehensive list of Tartini MSS. is given in
Q.-L., and according to this authority they are
to be found in the public and State Libraries
of Dresden, Konigsberg, Mecklenburg-Schwerin,
at Padua, and in the British Museum. The
Journal encyclopédique de Venise for 1775
contains a paragraph stating that Captain
P. Tartini, a nephew of Giuseppe Tartini, had
deposited the following MS. compositions of
his uncle with Antonio Zazzini (an excellent
violinist): 42 sonatas, 6 sonatas and trios, 114
concertos, 13 concertos, etc., which were offered
for sale by Carminer at Venice.

The number of his published compositions is
very extensive. His first book of sonatas, ' a
5 e 6 istrumenti,' op. 1, was published in
Amsterdam, 1734. The second book appeared
in Rome in 1745, and a large number of concertos for violin solo with orchestral accompaniment, as well as a trio for two violins and a bass,
were published at various times at Amsterdam,
Paris and London. A considerable number
has been arranged and edited in recent years
by Emilio Pente.

His contributions to the literature of music
were almost as numerous. The Municipio di
Pirano possesses twenty-five of his MS. writings
on matters dealing with various theoretical
problems. His published works comprise:
Trattato di musica, etc., Padua, 1754 (Giov.
Manfre), 2nd edition, Paris, 1767 (Leduc).
French translation, *Traité des agréments*, etc.
. . . *traduit par Sig. Denis*, Paris, 1782. *Riposta
di G. T. alla critica del di lui trattato di
musica di Monsieur Serre di Ginevra*, Venice,
1767. *De' principi dell' armonia musicale*,
Padua, 1767. English translation by Stilling-
fleet, London, 1771 (S. Baker and G. Leigh).
*Lettera del defonto Sig. G. T. alla signora
Maddalena Lombardini*, Venice, 1770. Italian
with English translations by Doctor Burney,
London, 1771, 2nd edition, 1779. German
translation of the same by H. H. Rohrmann,
Hanover, 1786.

PORTRAITS, ETC.—A committee of Paduan
admirers erected a life-size statue of Tartini in
1807 in the Prato della Valle, Padua. On the
second centenary of Tartini's birth in 1892, the
President of the Arca del Santo had a stone
slab with a memorial inscription upon it placed
in the first cloister of the Basilica. There is
a portrait of him in the Gallery of the Filarmonico, Bologna. The engraver, Antoine
Bonaventura Sberti, engraved a portrait of
Tartini and placed the following distich upon
it, written by Antonio Piombolo, professor of
medicine at the University of Padua :

'Hic fidibus scriptus claris, hic magnus alumnus
Cui par nemo fuit, forte nec ullus erit.'

The Abbate Vincenzo Rota of Padua prefaced his poem, ' L' incendio di tempio di
S. Antonio,' published in Padua (by Conzatti
in 1753), in which every stanza celebrates

Tartini's genius, with a portrait of Tartini
taken from life, and placed the following lines
beneath it :

'Tartini haud potuit veracius exprimi imago.
Sive lyram tangat seu meditetur, is est.'

This engraving also serves as a frontispiece
to Fanzago's *Orazione* published in 1754. The
Bibliotheca of Pirano possesses a portrait in
oils of Tartini, and there is a memorial bust
of him executed by Rosa in the Concert-hall of
the Casino of Pirano. George Hart of Wardour
Street possessed the original painting of Tartini's dream by Charles Joseph Hullmandel,
who seems to have brought it out as an engraving. A drawing formerly in the possession of
the late Julian Marshall was reproduced in
earlier editions of this Dictionary. An engraving
by C. Calcinoto is shown on *PLATE LVI.*

BIBL.—FANZAGO, *Orazione del Signor Abate Fanzago*, Padua, 1770 ;
FANZAGO, *Elogi di Giuseppe Tartini* ; FAYOLLE, *Notice sur Corelli,
Tartini, etc.*, Paris, 1810 (Swed·sh translation, Stockholm, 1811 ;
Burgh) ; *Anecdotes of Music*, London, 1814, German translation
(Leipzig, 1820) ; HILLER, *Lebensbeschreibungen*, Leipzig, 1784, pp.
267-85; RUBBI, *Elogi italiani*, Venice, 1782 (12 vols.), vol. viii. ;
UGONI, *Della letteratura italiana*, Brescia, 1820 ; ORTLEPP, *Ein
musikalische Anthologie*, Stuttgart, 1841, vol. ix. pp. 1-33 ; DR.
HORTIS, *Archeografo triestino*, Nuova seria, vol. x. pp. 209-229 ;
HORTIS, *Lettere di G. T.* (also printed separately) ; STANCOVITCH,
Biografia degli uomini distinti dell' Istria ; SERRE, *Analyse critique
de l'ouvrage de M. Tartini*, 1763 ; THURN AND TAXIS (Count of),
Risposta di un anonimo al celebre Sig. Rousseau, Venice, 1769 ;
LALANDE, *Voyage d'Italie*, Paris, 1749, vol. viii. p. 292, etc. ; HUET,
École de violon, Châlons-sur-Marne, 1880 ; BURNEY, *The Present
State of Music in France* ; HOGARTH, *History of Music* ; VIDAL, *Les
Instruments à archet* ; HART, *The Violin and its Music* ; *Inaugura-
zione del monumento di G. T.*, Trieste, 1898 ; TEBALDINI, *L' archivio
musicale della cappella Antoniana a Padova*, 1895 ; VERNON LEE,
The European Review, vol. xx. f. 11. iv. ; *Good Words*, vol. xxxiv.
p. 18 ; TAGLIAPIETRA, *G. Tartini* (poem), Milan, 1865 ; PARISINI,
Carteggio del P. G. B. Martini, Bologna, 1888 ; DUBOURG, *The
Violin*; PHIPSON, *Sketches and Anecdotes* ; BELL, *Ole Bull*; ANONY-
MOUS (Michel Lambert), *The Chorister Boy*, pp. 33-63 ; *The Little
Pilgrim, or Giuseppe Tartini* ; MONTROND, *Musiciens les plus célèbres*,
Lille, 1853 ; *Strad*, vol. ix. 1898, Aug. ; *Strad*, vol. xvi. June, July,
1905 ; CHARLES BOUVET, *Une Leçon de Giuseppe Tartini et une femme
violiniste au XVIIIe siècle*, 1915.
E. H.-A.

TASKIN, (1) PASCAL (*b.* Theux, province of
Liège, 1723; *d.* Paris, Feb. 9, 1793[1]), celebrated
instrument - maker, and head of a family of
musicians, migrated early to Paris, and was
apprenticed to Etienne Blanchet, the best
French clavecin - maker of the period. Succeeding eventually to the business, he improved
the tone of his spinets and harpsichords by
substituting slips of leather for the crowquills
then in use in the jacks (1768). This ' peau de
buffle ' appliance was claimed as Taskin's invention, but was in use in the 16th and 17th
centuries. (See JACK.) In 1772 Louis XV.
offered him the post of Keeper of the Musical
Instruments and the Chapel Royal, vacant by
the death of Chiquelier, but the life at Versailles
would not have suited the inventor, who wished
to be at liberty to continue his experiments,
and he contrived to get his nephew and pupil,
Pascal Joseph (2), appointed in his stead.
Having thus succeeded in preserving his independence without forfeiting the royal favour,
he was shortly after elected an acting member
of the corporation of musical instrument-
makers (1775).

He was brought more before the public by a
piano in the shape of our present ' grands,'
made for the Princess Victoire, the first of the

1 See Ernest Closson's article *Taskin*, S.I.M. xii. 237-38.

kind made in France. Other inventions were his use of a single string doubled round the pin in his two-stringed pianos, working the pedal by the foot instead of by the knee, and the 'Armandine'[1] (1789). This fine instrument, now in the museum of the Paris Conservatoire, is like a grand piano without a keyboard, and with gut strings, and is therefore a cross between the harp and the psaltery. Other specimens of his manufacture are the harpsichord with two keyboards made for Marie Antoinette and still to be seen in the Petit Trianon, the pretty instrument in the possession of the distinguished pianist Mlle. Joséphine Martin, and those in the Conservatoire and the Musée des Arts Décoratifs in Paris. He repaired and enlarged the Ruckers harpsichord now in the possession of Sir Edgar Speyer. (See RUCKERS.) His nephew,

(2) PASCAL JOSEPH[2] (b. Theux, Nov. 20, 1750; d. Paris, Feb. 5, 1829), Keeper of the King's Instruments and the Chapel Royal from 1772 to the Revolution, was his uncle's best pupil and assistant. He married a daughter of Blanchet, and was thus brought into close connexion with the Couperin family. (See COUPERIN, Armand Louis, 6.) Of his two sons and two daughters, all musicians, the only one calling for separate mention here is the second son,

(3) HENRI JOSEPH (b. Versailles, Aug. 24, 1779; d. Paris, May 4, 1852). He learned music as a child from his mother, and so charmed the court by his singing and playing that Louis XVI. made him a page of the Chapel Royal. Later he studied music and composition with his aunt, Mme. Couperin, a talented organist, and early made his mark as a teacher, virtuoso and composer. Three operas were neither performed nor engraved, but other of his compositions were published, viz., trios for PF., violin and violoncello; a caprice for PF. and violin; a concerto for PF. and orchestra; solo pieces for PF.; and songs. A quantity of Masonic songs remained in MS. Like his father he had four sons; none of them became musicians.   G. C.

(4) ÉMILE ALEXANDRE (b. Paris, Mar. 18, 1853; d. there, Oct. 5, 1897), descendant of the same family, studied at the Conservatoire, gaining, in 1874, accessits in harmony and opéra-comique. On Jan. 10, 1875, he sang the music of Joseph and Herod in the revival of Berlioz's 'L'Enfance du Christ' at the Colonne concerts, and made his stage début the same year at Amiens as Roland in Halévy's 'Mousquetaires de la Reine.' In 1878 he made successful débuts at the Théâtre Ventadour, Paris, in Pessard's 'Capitaine Fracasse,' and in D'Ivry's 'Amants de Vérone.' In 1879 he was

[1] Called after Mlle. Armand, a pupil of his niece, who became an excellent singer at the Opéra and the Opéra-Comique.
[2] Fétis confuses the uncle and nephew. The writer of this article, having had access to family papers, has been able to correct the errors of previous biographers.

still more successful at the Opéra-Comique as Malipieri in 'Haydée,' Michel in 'Le Caïd' and Peter the Great in 'L'Étoile du nord,' and remained there during his stage career as one of the best artists of the company, being excellent alike in singing and acting and an accomplished musician. He sang the baritone parts in several new operas. On May 25, 1887, he was singing the part of Lotario in 'Mignon' on the night of the burning of the theatre, on which occasion he showed great coolness and presence of mind. On May 13, 1894, he sang Lotario on the 1000th night of 'Mignon,' soon after which he retired and devoted himself to teaching at the Conservatoire.   A. C.

BIBL.—H. DE CURZON, Croquis d'artistes (Paris, 1898); CONSTANT PIERRE, Les Facteurs d'instruments de musique, les luthiers et la facteur instrumentale (Paris, 1893); CHARLES BOUVET, Une Dynastie de musiciens français; les Couperins, organistes de l'église Saint Gervais (Paris, 1919); E. CLOSSON, Pascal Taskin (Liège, 1913).

TASSO, GIOVANNI MARIA, a 16th-century composer who, together with Lupacchino, wrote 'Il i. libro a note negre a 2 voci,' published by Scotto, 1559, and appearing in many editions until 1701. Fifteen of the 2-part solfeggi without words, which it contains, are by Tasso (Q.-L.).

TASTO SOLO. Tasto (Fr. touche) means the part in an instrument which is touched to produce the note; in a keyed instrument, therefore, the key. 'Tasto solo,' 'the key alone,' is in old music written over those portions of the bass or continuo part in which the mere notes were to be played by the accompanist, without the chords or harmonies founded on them. (See THOROUGH-BASS.)
                                          G.

TATTOO[3] (rappel; Zapfenstreich), the signal in the British army by which soldiers are brought to their quarters at night. The infantry signal begins at twenty minutes before the hour appointed for the men to be in barracks, by the bugles in the barrack-yard sounding the 'First Post' or 'Setting of the Watch.' This is a long passage of twenty-nine bars, beginning as follows:

and ending with this impressive phrase:

[3] The word is derived by Johnson from the French tapotez tous; and its original form seems to have been 'tap-to' (see Count Mansfield's Directions of Warre, 1624), as if it were the signal for the tap-rooms or bars of the canteen to put-to or close. Curiously enough, however, 'tap' seems to be an acknowledged term for the drum—'tap of drum.' Tapoter is probably allied to the German zapfen, the tap of a cask, and zapfenstreich, the German term for tattoo; this also may mean the striking or driving home of the taps of the beer barrels. The proverbial expression 'the devil's tattoo'—meaning the noise made by a person absorbed in thought drumming with foot or fingers—seems to show that the drum and not the trumpet was the original instrument for sounding the tattoo.

This is succeeded by the 'Rolls,' [1] consisting of three strokes by the big drum, each stroke followed by a roll on the side-drums :

The drums and fifes then march up and down the barrack-yard playing a succession of quick marches at choice, till the hour is reached. Then 'God save the King' is played, and the tattoo concludes with the 'Second Post,' or 'Last Post,' which begins as follows :

and ends like the 'First Post.' [2]

Since the time of Wallenstein the Zapfenstreich in Germany has had a wider meaning, and is a sort of short, spirited march played not only by drums and fifes or trumpets but by the whole band of the regiment. It is in this sense that Beethoven uses the word in a letter to Peters (1823 ?) :

'There left here last Saturday three airs, six bagatelles, and a tattoo, instead of a march . . . and to-day I send the two tattoos that were still wanting . . . . the latter will do for marches.'   G.

TAUBERT, KARL GOTTFRIED WILHELM (b. Berlin, Mar. 23, 1811; d. there, Jan. 7, 1891), composer, was the son of an official in the Berlin Ministry of War. Though not actually brought up with Mendelssohn, he trod to a certain extent in the same steps, learned the piano from Ludwig Berger, and composition from Klein, and went through his course at the Berlin University 1827–30. He first appeared as a PF.-player; in 1831 was made accompanist to the court concerts, and from that time his rise was steady. In 1834 he was elected member of the Academy of Arts, in 1841 became music-director of the Royal Opera, and in 1845 court Kapellmeister—a position which he held till his retirement from the Opera in 1869 with the title of Oberkapellmeister. From that time he conducted the royal orchestra at the court concerts and soirées. In 1875 he was chosen member of council of the musical section of the Academy. Among his first compositions were various small instrumental pieces, and especially sets of songs. The songs attracted the notice of Mendelssohn, and not only drew from him very warm praise and anticipation of

future success (see the letter to Devrient, July 15, 1831), but led to a correspondence, including Mendelssohn's long letter of Aug. 27, 1831. In these letters Mendelssohn seems to have put his finger on the want of strength and spirit which, with all his real musician-like qualities, his refined taste and immense industry, prevented Taubert from writing anything that will be remembered.

The list of his published works is an enormous one :

3 Psalms and a Vater unser; 6 operas, 'Die Kirmess' (1832), 'Der Zigeuner' (1834), 'Marquis und Dieb' (1842), 'Joggeli' (1853), 'Macbeth' (1857) and 'Cesario' (1874). Incidental music to 8 dramas, including 'Medea' and 'The Tempest' (Nov. 28, 1855); 4 cantatas; 294 solo-songs, in 52 Nos., besides duets and partsongs; 3 symphonies and a festival-overture for full orchestra; 2 trios for PF. and strings; 3 string quartets; 6 sonatas for PF. and violin; 6 sonatas for PF. solo; and a host of smaller pieces. The most successful of all are the charming 'Kinderlieder.' For complete catalogue see Ledebur's *Tonkünstler-Lexikon Berlins.*

                            G.

TAUDOU, ANTOINE ANTONIN BARTHÉLEMY (b. Perpignan, Aug. 24, 1846 ; d. Paris, July 6, 1925), composer and violinist. He early evinced such aptitude for music that he was sent to Paris and entered at the Conservatoire, where he carried off successively the first prizes for solfège, violin (1866), harmony (1867), fugue (1868) and, finally, after two years' study of composition with Reber, the Grand Prix de Rome (1869). The subject of the cantata was 'Francesca da Rimini,' and the prize score was distinguished for purity and elegance.

His works include a trio for flute, viola and violoncello, another for PF., violin and violoncello; a violin-concerto played at the Société des Concerts du Conservatoire; string quartet in B minor, often heard in Paris; and for orchestra a 'Marche - Ballet,' a 'Chant d'automne' and a 'Marche - Nocturne.' He published songs and pieces for PF., and a cantata written for the inauguration of a statue to Arago (1879), at Perpignan, is still in MS. In Jan. 1883 he was chosen professor of harmony and accompaniment at the Conservatoire. G. C.

TAUSCH, JULIUS (b. Dessau, Apr. 15, 1827 ; d. Bonn, Nov. 11, 1895), composer and conductor, a pupil of F. Schneider at Dessau. In 1844 he entered the Conservatorium of Leipzig, then in the second year of its existence, and on leaving that in 1846 settled at Düsseldorf. Here he gradually advanced ; on Julius Reitz's departure in 1847 taking the direction of the artists' Liedertafel, and succeeding Schumann as conductor of the Musical Society, temporarily in 1853, and permanently in 1855. He was associated in the direction of the Lower Rhine Festivals of 1863, 1866 (with O. Goldschmidt), 1869, 1872 and 1875. In the winter of 1878 he conducted the orchestral concerts at the Glasgow Festival. He retired in 1888, and lived at Bonn.

Tausch published a Fest-overture, music to 'Twelfth Night,' various pieces for voices and orchestra, songs and pianoforte pieces, solo and accompanied. G.

TAUSIG, CARL (*b.* Warsaw, Nov. 4, 1841; *d.* Leipzig, July 17, 1871), ' the infallible, with his fingers of steel,' as Liszt described him, was, after Liszt, the most remarkable pianist of his time.

He was first taught by his father, Aloys Tausig, a professional pianist of good repute, who outlived his more famous son, dying Mar. 24, 1885. When Carl was 14, his father took him to Liszt, who was then at Weimar, surrounded by a very remarkable set of young musicians. It will suffice to mention the names of Bülow, Bronsart, Klindworth, Pruckner, Cornelius, Joseph Joachim (Konzertmeister), Joachim Raff (Liszt's amanuensis) to give an idea of the state of musical things in the little Thuringian town. During the interval from 1850–58 Weimar was the centre of the ' music of the future.' Liszt, as Kapellmeister in chief, with a small staff of singers and a tolerable orchestra, had brought out ' Tannhäuser ' and ' Lohengrin,' Berlioz's ' Benvenuto Cellini,' Schubert's ' Alfonso und Estrella,' etc. He was composing his ' Poèmes symphoniques,' revising his pianoforte works, writing essays and articles for musical papers. Once a week or oftener the pianists met at the Alte Burg, Liszt's residence, and there was an afternoon's ' lesson ' (gratis of course). Whoever had anything ready to play, played it, and Liszt found fault or encouraged as the case might be, and finally played himself. Peter Cornelius used to relate how Liszt and his friends were taken aback when young Tausig first sat down to play. ' A very devil of a fellow,' said Cornelius, ' he dashed into Chopin's A♭ Polonaise, and knocked us clean over with the octaves.' From that day Tausig was Liszt's favourite. He worked hard, not only at pianoforte-playing, but at counterpoint, composition and instrumentation. In 1858 he made his début in public at an orchestral concert conducted by Bülow at Berlin. Opinions were divided. It was admitted on all hands that his technical feats were extraordinary, but sober-minded people talked of noise and rant, and even those of more impulsive temperament, who might have been ready to sympathise with his ' Lisztian eccentricities,' thought he would play better when his period of ' storm and stress ' was over. In 1859 and 1860 he gave concerts in various German towns, making Dresden his headquarters. In 1862 he went to reside at Vienna, when, in imitation of Bülow's exertions in Berlin, he gave orchestral concerts with very ' advanced ' programmes. These concerts were but partially successful in an artistic sense, whilst pecuniarily they were failures. After this, for some years, little was heard of Tausig. He changed his abode frequently, but on the whole led the quiet life of a student. The ' storm and stress ' was fairly at an end when he married and settled in Berlin, 1865. Opinions were now unanimous. Tausig was hailed as a master of the first order. He had attained self-possession, breadth and dignity of style, whilst his technique was as ' infallible ' as ever. At Berlin he opened a ' Schule des höheren Clavierspiels,' and at intervals gave pianoforte recitals, of which his ' Chopin recitals ' were the most successful. He played at the principal German concert-institutions, and made the round of the Russian towns. He died of typhoid fever.

His manner of playing at its best was grand, impulsive and impassioned, yet without a trace of eccentricity. His tone was superb, his touch exquisite and his manipulative dexterity and powers of endurance such as to astonish even experts. He made a point of executing his *tours de force* with perfect composure, and took pains to hide every trace of physical effort. His repertory was varied and extensive, and he was ready to play by heart any representative piece by any composer of importance from Scarlatti to Liszt. A virtuoso *par excellence*, he was also an accomplished musician, familiar with scores old and new, a master of instrumentation, a clever composer and arranger.

Shortly before his death Tausig published an op. 1—' Deux Études de Concert.' With this he meant to cancel various compositions of previous date, some of which he was sorry to see in the market. Amongst these latter are a pianoforte arrangement of ' Das Geisterschiff, symphonische Ballade nach einem Gedicht von Strachwitz, op. 1,' originally written for orchestra; and ' Réminiscences de Halka, Fantaisie de concert.' A pianoforte concerto, which contains a Polonaise, and which, according to Felix Draeseke, was originally called a Phantasie, several ' Poèmes symphoniques,' etc., remain in manuscript. Tausig's arrangements, transcriptions and fingered editions of standard works are as follows :

Wagner : Die Meistersinger von Nürnberg, PF. score ; ' Walkürenritt,' transcription.
Bach : Organ Toccata and Fugue in D minor, Choral-Vorspiele: Praeludium, Fugue and Allegro ; ' Das wohltemperirte Clavier,' a selection of the Preludes and Fugues, carefully phrased and fingered.
Berlioz : ' Danse des gnomes ' and ' Danse des sylphes ' from the ' Damnation de Faust.'
Schumann : El contrabandista.
Schubert : Andantino and Variations, Rondo, Marche militaire, Polonaise mélancolique.
Weber : Invitation à la valse.
Scarlatti : three Sonatas, Pastorale, and Capriccio.
Chopin : Concerto in E minor ; score and PF. part.
Beethoven : six Transcriptions from the string quartets, opp. 59, 130, 131 and 135.
' Nouvelles Soirées de Vienne—Valses caprices d'après Strauss.' 1-5. (These are pendants to Liszt's ' Soirées de Vienne ' after Schubert.)
' Ungarische Zigeunerweisen ' (fit to rank with the best of Liszt's ' Rhapsodies hongroises ').
Clementi : Gradus ad Parnassum, a selection of the most useful Studies, with additional fingering and variants.

Tausig's ' Tägliche Studien ' is a posthumous publication, consisting of ingeniously contrived finger exercises, edited by H. Ehrlich ; among the many ' Indispensables du pianiste,' it is one of the few really indispensable. E. D.

TAVERNER JOHN (*b. circa* 1495 ; *d.* Oct. 25, 1545), organist and composer. Taverner was commonly described by Foxe and other early writers as ' of Boston ' in Lincolnshire, and without doubt he died and was buried there ; but that he was a native of Boston is not certainly known. The name was not uncommon in this district. In 1335 Walter le Taverner ' of St. Botolph ' (Boston) was one of the first members of the Guild of Corpus Christi in Boston. It is quite likely that the composer was a native of Tattershall, where there were Taverners living at the close of the 15th century, for the first facts that can be cited in his personal history associate him with Tattershall. These facts are contained in a letter from the Bishop of Lincoln to Cardinal Wolsey in 1526, recommending Taverner, a singing man, for the post of ' Informator ' of the children of Wolsey's newly founded College at Oxford. At the time he was evidently a lay clerk in the establishment at Tattershall, and he took up his appointment at Cardinals' College, Oxford, in Nov. 1526. His duties as Master of the Choristers at St. Frideswide's, as the College Chapel was called until it became the Cathedral Church of Christ in 1546, included the playing of the organ. Anthony Delaber describes how he ' heard Master Taverner play and others of the chappell there sing.' For his duties he received a salary of £10, with further liberal allowances for livery and commons. Some confusion has arisen, as in Fuller's *Church History*, because a Richard Taverner, of the family of Elmham in Norfolk, was at this time one of the junior canons in Wolsey's College. There is no reason to suppose that the two were even nearly related.

Taverner was at Oxford no more than three years and a half ; for, on May 20, 1530, John Benbow of Manchester was appointed Master of Choristers in his place. It must have been during this period, and while he was at Tattershall, that he wrote all his fine church music, because after this date his religious views, and indeed his whole career, underwent a complete change. The College was at that time a hotbed of Lutheranism, and Taverner became deeply involved in the religious controversies of the day. In 1528 he, with others, was accused of heresy and imprisoned, the charge being that he had hidden some heretical books ' under the bordes in his schoole,' yet ' the Cardinal for his musick excused him, saying that he was but a musitian, and so he escaped.' It seems to be true, as Foxe says, that ' this Taverner repented him very muche that he had made Songes to Popish Ditties in the time of his blindnes.' His subsequent career was spent in fanatical persecution, as the paid agent of Thomas Cromwell, in the destruction of the monastic establishments ; musicians of all shades of religious opinion may be grateful for the fact that this great composer was not, at an earlier age, exposed to those influences which terminated his musical career.

It was at Boston that the remaining years of his life were spent. Three autograph letters of his, surviving in the Public Record Office, refer to the scenes with which he was connected, including the burning of the Rood at Boston, and even greater horrors in the market-place. The musician's sensitive temperament in a man of such strong character, as the portrait sketches in Bodl. MS. Mus. Sch. e 376-81 indicate, reacted in fierce fanaticism when he felt compelled to abandon music under pressure of religious conviction.

In 1537 he was elected a member of the Guild of Corpus Christi in Boston ; in 1541 he was one of the stewards of this Guild and still held office in 1543 when the Register ends abruptly. He left no will that has yet been discovered, but the Inquisition post-mortem dealing with his property gives the date of his death on Oct. 25, 1545. John Baldwin, the famous Windsor musical scribe, in a footnote in Ch. Ch. MS. 983, fo. 46, stated that ' Master John Tavernar of Cardinall Wolsayes chappell died at bostone and there lieth.' We gather from his widow's will that he was buried under the bell-tower, familiarly known as ' Boston stump,' but no trace of his grave can now be found. He married Rose Parrowe and left two daughters : Isobel, married to Richard Hodge, and Emma, married to Stephen Salmon. He owned landed property in and around Boston at the time of his death.

Taverner's position in the history of English church music is one of the highest importance. The merits of his music were recognised, before the close of the 16th century, by such writers as Thomas Morley, John Case and Meres, and without question he was pre-eminent among the English composers of his own day, working as he did just a generation before Tye and Tallis. His work, in fact, represents the climax of the development of the early Tudor School, following, as it did, upon that of Fayrfax, Hugh Aston and Nicholas Ludford. In this connexion we may quote from the preface of ' Tudor Church Music,' vol. i. p. xxiv :

' The greatest exponent of the style developed in the post - Fayrfax period was John Taverner. . . . No account of English polyphony could be complete that did not insist upon his eminence, not only relatively but absolutely. Relatively, he sums up all the qualities of his precursors and contemporaries, and expresses all their ideals. . . . Absolutely, his mastery of a most intricate idiom and his amazing vitality and virility "secure for him a high place among the composers of church music of all periods."'

It is a noteworthy fact that two of Taverner's Masses, ' Sine Nomine ' and ' Small Devotion,' were at a very early date, possibly in Taverner's lifetime, adapted for use in English. These adaptations are found in the Bodl. MSS. Mus. Sch. e 420-22 (see SERVICE.) Some similarity in the script of this MS. to that of Taverner's autograph letters has given rise to the conjecture that the Bodleian MS. is in his hand. On internal evidence this is improbable, because the adaptations are a poor piece of workmanship, very unlikely to have been approved by a composer of Taverner's rank, while it is scarcely credible that the adaptations as they stand should have been his work. Moreover, the MS. would seem to be at least as late at 1545, which was the year of Taverner's death.

Taverner's church music has been collected and edited in the Carnegie edition of ' Tudor Church Music,' vols. i. and iii., with full biographical details and a critical notice of his work. Besides his church music, he wrote three small secular pieces for Wynkyn de Worde's Song-book in 1530 : ' My harte, my minde," ' Love wyll I ' and ' The bella ' ; and a two-part song ' For women no season is rest or patience ' (Roy. Lib. B.M.).

Appended is a list of Taverner's church music, which comprises eight Masses, three settings of Christe Eleison and the Kyrie called ' Kyrie Leroy ' ; a Sanctus, Benedictus and Agnus Dei ; three Magnificats and a Te Deum, besides 28 Motets. Day's ' Certaine Notes,' etc. (1560), includes an adaptation of words beginning ' In trouble and adversity ' to one of his ' In nomines,' and a later adaptation of the same composition is found in B.M. Add. MSS. 30480-3 to words beginning ' O give thanks unto the Lord.'

In the opinion of the editors of ' Tudor Church Music ' the ' Osanno in excelsis,' ascribed to Taverner in BM. Add. MSS. 18936-9, is not authentic.

I. MASSES

(B.M.=British Museum; Bodl.=Bodleian Library; R.C.M.= Royal College of Music; Ch. Ch.=Christ Church, Oxford; Tenb.= St. Michael's College, Tenbury; Pet.=Peterhouse, Cambridge; C.U.Lib.=Cambridge University Library; St. John's=St. John's College, Cambridge.)

Gloria tibi Trinitas, *a* 6. B.M. Add. 29246 ; B.M. Roy. Lib.; Bodl. Mus. Sch. e 376-81 ; R.C.M. 2035 ; Ch. Ch. 979-83; Tenb. 354-8 and 342.
Corona spinea, *a* 6. B.M. Add. 29246 ; Bodl. Mus. Sch. e 376-81; R.C.M. 2035 ; Tenb. 342.
O Michaell, *a* 6. B.M. Add. 11586 (Burney's MS. score) ; Bodl. Mus. Sch. e 376-81.
Sine nomine, *a* 5. B.M. Add. 29246 ; R.C.M. 2035 ; Tenb. 354-8; Pet. 31, 32, 35, 37, 40, 41, 43, 44.
English adaptation. Bodl. Mus. Sch. e 420-2.
Small Devotion, *a* 5. Tenb. 342 ; Pet. 31, 32, 40, 41.
English adaptation. Bodl. Mus. Sch. e 420-2.
Mater Christi, *a* 5. Pet. 31, 32, 40, 41.
The Western Wynde, *a* 4. B.M. Add. 17802-5 ; Bodl. Mus. Sch. e 1-5.
Playn Song Mass, *a* 4. B.M. Add. 17802-5.

II. LATIN SERVICES

Kyrie (Le Roy), *a* 4. B.M. Add. 17802-5.
Christe Eleison, *a* 3 (three settings). B.M. Add. 18936-7-9.
Sanctus, *a* 3. B.M. Add. 18936-7-9.
Benedictus, *a* 3. B.M. Add. 18936-7-9.
Agnus Dei, *a* 3. R.C.M. 2035.
Magnificat I., *a* 4. B.M. Add. 17802-5.
Magnificat II., *a* 5. Pet. 31, 32, 40, 41.
Magnificat III., *a* 6. B.M. Add. 18936-9 ; Bodl. Mus. Sch. e 423 ; Ch. Ch. 45 ; Tenb. 354-8, 807-11.
Te Deum, *a* 5. Ch. Ch. 979-83.

III. MOTETS

Alleluya I., *a* 4. B.M. Add. 17802-5.
Alleluya II., *a* 4. B.M. Add. 17802-5.
Audivi media nocte, *a* 4. B.M. Add. 17802-5. (In MS. 17804 the Pars ad placitum is stated to be by Whitbroke.)
Ave Dei Patris Filia, *a* 5. Bodl. Mus. Sch. e 1-5, e 423 ; Ch. Ch. 979-83 ; R.C.M. 2035 ; Pet. 31, 32, 41 ; St. John's K 31 ; C.U.Lib. Dd 13, 27.
Ave Maria. Pet. 31, 32, 41.
Christi Jesu, *a* 5. Ch. Ch. 979-83 ; Pet. 31, 32, 40, 41.
Dum transiset Sabbatum I., *a* 5. Ch. Ch. 979-83, 984-8.
Alternative version, *a* 4. B.M. Add. 17802-5.
Dum transisset Sabbatum II., *a* 5. B.M. Add. 31390 ; Ch. Ch. 979-83.
Ecce Mater. Ch. Ch. 982.
Esto nobis. R.C.M. 2035.
Fac nobis, *a* 5. Pet. 31, 32, 41.

Gaude plurimum, *a* 5. B.M. Add. 34049, 34191, 18936-9 ; Harl. 1709 ; Roy. Mus. Lib. ; Bodl. Mus. Sch. e 1-5, e 423 ; Ch. Ch. 979-83 ; C.U.Lib. Dd 13, 27 ; Pet. 31, 32, 40, 41 ; St. John's K 31 ; R.C.M. 2035 ; Tenb. 354-8, 342.
Gloria in excelsis (Respond, Christmas Day), *a* 4. B.M. Add. 17802-5.
Jesu spes penitentibus, *a* 3. B.M. Roy. Lib.
In pace, *a* 4. B.M. Add. 17802-5.
Mater Christi, *a* 5. B.M. Add. 34049 ; Bodl. Mus. Sch. e 1-5; Ch. Ch. 979-83 ; Pet. 31, 32, 40, 41 ; Tenb. 341-4, 354-8.
O splendor gloriae, *a* 5. B.M. Roy. Lib. ; Bodl. Mus. Sch. e 1-5; Ch. Ch. 979-83.
Prudens Virgo, *a* 3. B.M. Roy. Lib.
Quemadmodum, *a* 6. B.M. Add. 31390 ; Ch. Ch. 979-83.
Rex anabilis, *a* 3. B.M. Roy. Lib.
Sancte Deus, *a* 5. Pet. 31, 32, 41.
Sospitati dedit, *a* 5. B.M. Add. 34049 ; R.C.M. 2035 ; Tenb. 341-4, 354-8.
Sub tuum presidium, *a* 5. Pet. 31, 32, 41.
Tam peccatum, *a* 3. B.M. Roy. Lib.
Traditur militibus, *a* 3. B.M. Roy. Lib.
Tu angelorum Domina, *a* 3. B.M. Roy. Lib.
Tu ad liberandum, *a* 3. B.M. Roy. Lib.
Virgo pura, *a* 3. B.M. Roy. Lib.

E. H. F.

TAYBER (TEYBER), (1) ANTON (*b.* Vienna, Sept. 8, 1756 ; *d.* there, Nov. 18, 1822), court composer to the Imperial Chapel from Mar. 1, 1793 ; later also teacher of the archdukes. He composed an oratorio, a Passion, masses and other sacred music, symphonies, and chamber music for various instruments. Several theoretical works in MS. are in the library of the Musikfreunde, Vienna. (2) FRANZ (*b.* Vienna, Nov. 15, 1756 ; *d.* there, Oct. 22, 1810), brother of the above, conductor of Schikaneder's opera company. Shortly before his death he became court organist at Vienna. He composed an oratorio, various church music, operas, singspiele and songs (*Riemann* ; *Q.-L.*).

TAYLOR, bell-founders. For generations this bell-foundry has been carried on at Loughborough, and so successfully that at the present time it is the largest and most important one in the world. The buildings cover an area of 7000 square yards, and every department is equipped with the most modern machinery electrically driven. Messrs. Taylor have succeeded in reducing the designing and tuning of bells to an exact science, and have proved themselves pre-eminent founders and tuners of bells. Most of the great bell projects in England and elsewhere during the past fifteen years have been carried out by this firm. Their business connexions date back directly to Johannes de Stafford of York in the reign of Edward III. He removed to Leicester about the middle of the 14th century, where, by his good repute and successful business capabilities, he became mayor in 1366 and 1370. Under various ownerships (including the eight Newcombes, 1516–1612) the foundry passed to Edward Arnold, who had also a foundry at St. Neot's at which Robert Taylor was apprenticed and eventually succeeded Arnold in 1780. In 1820 Robert Taylor removed to Oxford and died there in 1832. His son John removed to Loughborough in 1840 and died there in 1858. His son, John William Taylor, succeeded, and, under his energetic command, the foundry was very greatly extended. He died in 1906, after which the business continued with even greater success under the management of his sons John and Denison. John died in 1919, since which time the foundry has increased its work under the most capable direction of E. Denison Taylor, and its importance now is greater than it has ever been before.

The following is a list of the most famous peals made by Taylor :

	No. of Bells.	Weight of Tenor. cwts.
Beverley Minster . . .	10	41
„ St. Mary's .	10	35
Bristol : St. Mary Redcliffe .	12	51
Dublin : St. Patrick's Cathedral	13	45
Edinburgh : St. Mary's Cathedral	10	42
Exeter Cathedral . .	12	72½
London : St. Paul's Cathedral	12	62
Manchester Town Hall . .	10	52
Newcastle Cathedral . .	10	37
Shrewsbury : St. Chad's . .	12	40
Truro Cathedral . . .	10	34
Worcester Cathedral . . .	12	50

The great bells and carillons made by this firm are to be found enumerated under BELL.

W. W. S.

TAYLOR, EDWARD (b. Norwich, Jan. 22, 1784 ; d. Brentwood, Mar. 12, 1863), as a boy attracted the attention at Norwich of Dr. Beckwith, who gave him instruction. Arrived at manhood he embarked in business as an ironmonger in his native city, but continued the practice of music as an amateur. He possessed a fine, rich, full-toned bass voice, and became not only solo vocalist, but an active manager of the principal amateur society in Norwich. He was sheriff of Norwich in 1819. He took a leading part in the establishment in 1824 of the existing triennial Norwich Musical Festival, training the chorus, engaging the band and singers, and making out the entire programmes. In 1825 he removed to London, and, in connexion with some relatives, entered upon the profession of civil engineer, but not meeting with success he, in 1826, adopted music as a profession, and immediately attained a good position as a bass singer. He sang at the Norwich Festival of 1827. In 1830 he translated and adapted Spohr's ' Last Judgment.' This led to an intimacy with Spohr, at whose request he subsequently translated and adapted the oratorios, ' Crucifixion ' (or ' Calvary '), 1836, and ' Fall of Babylon,' 1842. On Oct. 24, 1837, he was appointed professor of music in Gresham College in succession to R. J. S. Stevens. He entered upon his duties in Jan. 1838, by the delivery of three lectures, which he subsequently published. His lectures were admirably adapted to the understanding of a general audience ; they were historical and critical, excellently written, eloquently read, and illustrated by well-chosen extracts from the works described, efficiently performed. His lecture on madrigals, delivered at Bristol in 1837, resulted in the formation of the BRISTOL MADRIGAL SOCIETY (q.v.). In 1839 he published, under the title of ' The Vocal School of Italy in the 16th century,' a selection of twenty-eight

madrigals by the best Italian masters adapted to English words. He conducted the Norwich Festivals of 1839 and 1842. He wrote and composed an ode for the opening of the present Gresham College, Nov. 2, 1843. In 1844 he joined James Turle in editing ' The People's Music Book.' In the same year he contributed to The British and Foreign Review two anonymous articles entitled The English Cathedral Service, its Glory, its Decline, and its designed Extinction, a production evoked by some then pending legislation connected with the cathedral institutions, which attracted great attention and in 1845 was reprinted in a separate form. He was one of the originators of the VOCAL SOCIETY (of which he was the secretary), of the MUSICAL ANTIQUARIAN SOCIETY (for which he edited Purcell's ' King Arthur '), and of the PURCELL CLUB (q.v.). Besides the before named works he wrote and adapted English words to Mozart's Requiem, Graun's ' Tod Jesu,' Schneider's ' Sündfluth,' Spohr's ' Vater unser,' Haydn's ' Jahreszeiten,' and a very large number of compositions introduced in his lectures. He was in 1829–43 musical critic to The Spectator. He was buried in the old dissenting burial-ground in King's Road, Brentwood. His valuable library was dispersed by auction in the following December.

W. H. H. ; addns. D.N.B.

TAYLOR, FRANKLIN (b. Birmingham, Feb. 5, 1843 ; d. Mar. 19, 1919), a well-known pianoforte-player and teacher in London, began music at a very early age ; learned the pianoforte under Chas. Flavell, and the organ under T. Bedsmore, organist of Lichfield Cathedral, where at the age of 13 he was able to take the service. Returning to Birmingham soon afterwards, he appeared as a pianist and composer, and was appointed organist of the Old Meeting-house. In 1859 he went to Leipzig and studied in the Conservatorium together with Sullivan, J. F. Barnett, etc., under Plaidy and Moscheles for pianoforte, and Hauptmann, Richter and Papperitz for theory. He left in 1861, and made some stay in Paris, where he had lessons from Mme. Schumann, and was in close intercourse with Heller, Schulhoff, Mme. Viardot, etc. In 1862 he returned to England, settled permanently in London, and began teaching, and playing at the Crystal Palace (Feb. 18, 1865, etc.), the Monday Popular Concerts (Jan. 15, 1866, etc.), as well as at the Liverpool Philharmonic, Birmingham Chamber Concerts and elsewhere. At the same time he was organist successively of St. Peter's, Charlotte Street, Buckingham Gate, Twickenham Parish Church and St. Michael's, Chester Square. In 1876 he joined the National Training School as teacher, and in 1882 the R.C.M. as professor of the pianoforte, a position which he retained till his death. He was president of the Academy for the higher development of pianoforte-playing from its foundation by Oscar Beringer in 1873 until its dissolution in 1897.

His *Primer of the Pianoforte* (1879)—emphatically a 'little book on a great subject,' and a most useful and practical book too—was translated into German. He also compiled a PF. Tutor, and a valuable series of Progressive Studies in 56 books. He contributed extensively to the first edition of this Dictionary. He translated Richter's treatises on Harmony, Counterpoint and Canon and Fugue; and arranged Sullivan's 'Tempest' music for four hands on its production. His attention to his pupils was unremitting, and his power of imparting tone, touch and execution to them remarkable. Gifted with a fine musical organisation himself, he invoked the intelligence of his pupils, and succeeded in making them musicians as well as fine technical performers.

G.: addns. from *Mus. T.*, 1899, p. 798, *et seq.*

TAYLOR, SAMUEL COLERIDGE, see COLE-RIDGE-TAYLOR.

TAYLOR, CAPTAIN SILAS (SILAS DOMVILL, *alias* TAYLOR) (*b.* Harley, Shropshire, *c.* 1624; *d.* Harwich, *c.* 1678). He studied at Oxford, became a puritan, and joined Cromwell's army, where he rose to the rank of captain. He devoted himself to antiquarian studies, and, together with his brother, took an active part in the music performances at Oxford. After the Restoration he became a customs officer at Dunkerque, and later at Harwich. He contributed to Hilton's 'Catch that Catch can' and Playford's 'Court Ayres,' and composed also anthems and other sacred music. Autograph MSS. of theoretical essays are in the British Museum. The autograph of two canons by Mathew Locke were inscribed by the composer in 1669 to Silas Domvill, *alias* Taylor. He wrote also some historical works, on the title-pages of which he calls himself Silas Taylor, *alias* Domvill (*Q.-L.*).

E. v. d. s.

TCHAIKOVSKY, PETER ILICH (*b.* Kamsko-Votinsk, Government of Viatka, May 7, 1840 (N.S.); *d.* St. Petersburg, Nov. 6/Oct. 25 1893), one of the most famous composers of the Russian school.

His father was inspector of the Government mines. The boy's musical gift does not appear to have been hereditary. On the contrary, his family was unusually deficient in musical feeling, and could not discern that his capacity in this respect was greatly above the average. At 5 years old he was a winning and precociously intelligent child, devoted to his French governess, who exercised a wholesome influence upon his excitable and morbidly sensitive disposition. Mlle. Fanny Dürbach, not being in the least musical, was inclined to curtail the boy's time at the piano, and on the other hand to encourage his early attempts at literature. When he

was about 7 years old, a music-mistress gave him his first regular instruction on the pianoforte. The Tchaikovsky family took up their abode in St. Petersburg in 1850, and Peter Ilich was then placed under a good teacher, Philipov, with whom he made rapid, but not phenomenal progress. No thought of devoting their child to music ever crossed the minds of his parents, and at 10 years of age he was sent to the preparatory classes for the School of Jurisprudence, from which, nine years later (1859), he passed into the Ministry of Justice as a first-class clerk.

At the School of Jurisprudence Tchaikovsky joined the choral class directed by the famous chorus-master Lomakin, and continued his pianoforte lessons under Kündinger; but neither of these musicians seems to have suspected a budding genius. The whole of this period of his life was distinctly inimical to his artistic development; for he appears to have simply acquiesced in the commonplace ideas of the majority; and on leaving the School he entered upon a somewhat frivolous and worldly life. Music was the highest of his pleasures, but his dealings with it were not very lofty; at 20 he improvised pleasantly, and composed valses and polkas which he did not venture to put on paper. After a time, however, he saw with disgust the emptiness of his daily existence. With this moral awakening came also the first suspicion that he had chosen the wrong career. In the autumn of 1861 he began to study theory under Zaremba at the newly-opened classes of the Russian Musical Society. They increased his misgivings, but he cautiously resolved to hold on to his place in the Ministry of Justice until he felt confident that he was 'no longer a clerk but a musician.' Two years later these classes had developed into the Conservatoire, and Tchaikovsky's musical studies had become so much more serious and absorbing that he felt the need for some decisive action. Consequently, early in 1863, he relinquished his official work and began to face a life of poverty for the sake of his art. His mother, to whom he had been devotedly attached, had died of cholera in 1855; while his father had experienced such sharp reverses of fortune that he could now offer Peter Ilich nothing but bare board and lodging, until he should be able to maintain himself in the profession of his choice. To supply his further needs Tchaikovsky took some private teaching offered to him by Anton Rubinstein, but his earnings at this time did not exceed £5 a month. The composer's most intimate friend, the critic Hermann Laroche, gives an interesting account of their student days. The leading spirits of the Conservatoire in its infancy were Zaremba and Anton Rubinstein. With the former Tchaikovsky studied harmony, strict counterpoint and the Church

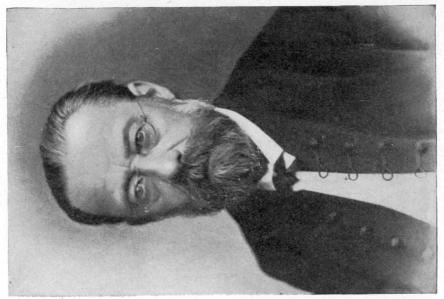

LXXX

SMETANA

Photo, Deutsche Anstalt, Berlin

TCHAIKOVSKY

Modes; with the latter composition and instrumentation. For Rubinstein his attitude was almost that of adoration; a sentiment which survived much harsh criticism and apparent unkindness. Tchaikovsky himself always attributed Rubinstein's coolness to him as a composer to the radical difference in their musical temperaments; but in reading the life of Tchaikovsky it is difficult to accept this as the sole reason for Rubinstein's persistent rejection in St. Petersburg of works which were received with considerable enthusiasm in Moscow. Both Zaremba and Rubinstein seem to have had power to stimulate their pupil's innate indolence, so that he soon threw off the last traces of his old dilettantism, and kept a single aim perpetually before him—'to be a good musician and earn my daily bread.' Tchaikovsky completed his course at the Conservatoire in 1865. For his diploma-work (a setting of Schiller's 'Ode to Joy') he received a silver medal and a good deal of unflattering criticism.

Early in 1866 Nicholas Rubinstein organised the Conservatoire in Moscow, and offered Tchaikovsky the post of professor of harmony. The pay was poor, but it was an honourable position, and the change to the artistic life of Moscow proved in many ways beneficial to him. Here he enjoyed the companionship of such talented musicians as Kashkin, Albrecht and Klindworth, men who were older, or at least more experienced, than himself. Here, too, he met the enterprising young publisher Jurgenson, who afterwards played such an important part in his life. During the first years of his career in Moscow Tchaikovsky lived with Nicholas Rubinstein, a man of somewhat irritable and overbearing temper, but a loyal and devoted friend. Whether Rubinstein's masterful guidance did not check the free development of Tchaikovsky's character and talent is an open question.

On the other hand, it was an inestimable advantage to have such an influential friend; for, year by year, Nicholas Rubinstein brought out Tchaikovsky's compositions—even the earliest ones—at the concerts of the Russian Musical Society, of which he was the conductor. In spite, however, of the favourable auspices under which his works were produced, a note of dissatisfaction is apparent in Tchaikovsky's letters at this time. The appreciation of Moscow meant far less to him than that of St. Petersburg, and he was always more keenly sensitive to any slight, real or imaginary, which emanated from the northern capital. During the first two years of his life in Moscow Tchaikovsky completed three works of importance in their different styles. A Festival Overture on the Danish national hymn, his first symphony in G minor ('Winter Daydreams'), and an opera on a libretto by Ostrovsky, 'The Voyevode.' To accomplish so much besides his teaching he had to work very hard, and suffered greatly from disordered nerves and insomnia. From this time dates that 'hankering after a quiet country life' which pursued him through life. Until he was able to gratify this desire he found his chief consolation in the long visits he paid every summer to his married sister, Alexandra Davidov, whose husband was manager of a large family estate at Kamenka, near Kiev. This sister was the chief confidante of Tchaikovsky's early troubles and difficulties; he was bound to her and to her children by lifelong ties of sympathy and affection.

About Easter 1868, while on a visit to St. Petersburg, Tchaikovsky first came in contact with that group of young musicians who were working for the cause of nationality in art. There is no doubt that he was stirred by the enthusiasm of Balakirev, Stassov and Rimsky-Korsakov, and that they exercised a temporary influence upon his choice of musical subjects. His second symphony, based upon Little Russian folk-songs, and the two 'programme' works 'Romeo and Juliet' (dedicated to Balakirev) and 'The Tempest' (dedicated to Stassov) bear witness to the effect of his intercourse with the men who were then regarded as the musical radicals of Russia. He was never unreservedly in sympathy with the 'Invincible Band.' On the contrary, as time went on, he grew more and more alienated from these contemporaries, until ten years later, we find him—in his letters to Nadejda von Mack—betrayed into criticisms as superficial as they are ungenerous. The year 1868 was marked by another event of a more intimate nature. In the course of the winter season an opera company visited St. Petersburg under the direction of Merelli, who brought as a star the singer Désirée Artôt (*q.v.*), then at the zenith of her fame and power. Artôt, who was several years older than Tchaikovsky, took a friendly interest in his work, and invited him to visit her. At first the young composer responded shyly to her friendly advances, but soon fell under the spell of her rare charm, with the result, as he subsequently informed his father, 'that we began to feel a mutual glow of tenderness, and an understanding followed immediately.' Tchaikovsky's feelings for Artôt were not so ardent as to blind him to the possible disadvantages of a marriage with her. We find him, even in the first flush of happiness, speculating as to what might become of his own career if he were expected to run about the world at the beck and call of a successful *prima donna* in the pitiable rôle of 'the husband of my wife.' Artôt herself put a term to his uncertainties. A few weeks after their first parting, in Jan. 1869, Tchaikovsky received the totally unexpected news of her marriage to the baritone Padilla, in Warsaw. Owing to the fact that he was completely absorbed in superintending the preparations for his first opera, 'The Voyevode,' the blow affected him far less than his friends expected. In years to come he resumed his friendly relations with the artist, whom he still admired, perhaps far more than he had ever loved the woman.

The five years which followed this episode was a period of great activity. His first symphonic poem, 'Fatum'; an opera, 'Undine,' the score of which he destroyed in 1873; the quartet, op. 11; an historical opera 'The Oprichnik'; a setting of 'The Snow Maiden'; the pianoforte concerto in B flat minor; the third symphony, and the humorous opera 'Vakoula the Smith'—are some of the more important works which followed each other in quick succession between 1869 and 1875. In 1872 he was appointed musical critic of the *Russky Viedomosti*, and continued to write for this paper at intervals until 1876. Add to all this work the strain of daily teaching—always most uncongenial to him—and it is not surprising that during the winter of 1875 he suffered from depression and was threatened with a nervous collapse. The longing to be relieved of all hindrances to his creative work now possessed him increasingly. In the summer of 1876 he went to Vichy for a cure and afterwards to the Bayreuth festival, as special correspondent to the *Russky Viedomosti*. Mentally and physically exhausted, pondering incessantly on the future, and firmly persuaded that 'things could not go on much longer,' Tchaikovsky returned to Russia early in the autumn. A long visit to his sister somewhat restored his health and spirits, and at the end of October he travelled to St. Petersburg to be present at the first performance of his humorous opera 'Vakoula the Smith' (afterwards known as 'Oxana's Caprice'). He had counted greatly upon the success of this work, which had been most carefully mounted and rehearsed. Nevertheless it proved, in Tchaikovsky's own words, 'a brilliant failure.' Other disappointments were in store for him. His 'Romeo and Juliet,' hissed in Vienna, met with a chilling reception at the Pasdeloup Concerts in Paris. Yet, contrary to expectation, he rose to meet these troubles with energy and self-reliance. Writing of him at this time, his brother Modeste says:

' Just before committing the rash act which was to cut him off for ever from Moscow, and change all his habits and social relations, he gave us the impression of a man whose mind was at rest, who had no ungratified desires, and displayed more purpose and cheerfulness than formerly.'

The 'rash act' referred to was Tchaikovsky's marriage, which took place in the summer of 1877. The engagement was ill-considered, and the marriage turned out miserably. From a

letter to his friend Nadejda von Meck, dated July 3 (15), 1877, those who are curious in the matter may gather a fairly clear idea of how Tchaikovsky drifted into matrimony with 'a woman with whom I am not the least in love.' In his correspondence with his family the composer completely exonerates his wife from all responsibility for the separation which followed about nine weeks after the wedding. In that short period he seems to have suffered acutely for the weakness, or illusion, which led him to marry in haste at the age of 37. Broken in health and spirits, he fled from Moscow to St. Petersburg, where he arrived in a state of collapse. For several days he lay on the verge of brain fever, and as soon as the dangerous crisis was over the doctors ordered him abroad, in the care of his brother Anatole.

Almost at the same time that Tchaikovsky met his wife he made the acquaintance of another woman who, for the next thirteen years, was destined to play the part of an invisible fairy godmother in his life. The circumstances of this friendship were unusual, for during the whole period of their intimacy the friends never came into personal contact. Their correspondence, however, was frequent and intimate. Nadejda Filaretovna von Meck was Tchaikovsky's senior by nearly ten years. She had married, early in life, a railway engineer who had amassed a large fortune and left her a widow, with eleven children, in 1876. A great lover of nature, a woman of strong and sane intellect, with an excellent head for business, Nadejda von Meck cared nothing for society and lived an extremely secluded existence. She was, however, passionately fond of music, and engaged the services of a young violinist named Kotek as a kind of domestic musician. From him she learnt many particulars about the private life of Tchaikovsky, whom she greatly admired as a composer. She heard of his poverty, of his yearning to be delivered from the drudgery of teaching, and of his phases of nervousness and depression. At first she restricted her philanthropy to the offer of one or two small commissions, for which, however, she paid the composer on such a liberal scale that he could not fail to suspect a charity in disguise. Finally, with tact and delicacy, she persuaded him to accept a yearly allowance which permitted him to devote his time entirely to composition. One of the first-fruits of this friendship was the fourth symphony, dedicated to 'My Best Friend.'

On leaving Russia after his disastrous marriage, Tchaikovsky settled for a time at Clarens, on the Lake of Geneva, and afterwards moved on to Italy, where he remained until Mar. 1878. A year's rest was considered necessary for his complete restoration to health, and thanks to the kindness of Nicholas Rubinstein and Nadejda von Meck he was now master of his own time. It is a curious psychological fact that during these dark days of his life, when he wrote of himself as 'un homme fini,' he produced some of the most delightful and least stressful of his music. The completion of the fourth symphony and the 'Lyrical Scenes' from Poushkin's 'Eugen Oniegin' occupied him chiefly during his travels abroad. In the summer he enjoyed some weeks of solitude on Madame von Meck's estate of Brailov, near Kiev. Here he composed the Kinderalbum and the twelve pieces for pianoforte, op. 40, and completed the pianoforte sonata in G major, dedicated to Klindworth. In September he returned to Moscow to take up his work again, in accordance with his promise to Nicholas Rubinstein. But the atmosphere of the Conservatoire was now more distasteful than ever, and he very soon resigned his professorship. After a short visit to St. Petersburg, where he witnessed the second failure of his opera 'Vakoula the Smith,' Tchaikovsky left for Florence, a town which had a strong fascination for him.

At this time he was full of a project for a new opera on the subject of Joan of Arc. He therefore returned to the quiet of Clarens and threw himself into the task, with his usual ardour for a new work. This time he determined to write his own libretto, which gave him far more trouble than the music. However, as early as Mar. 1879, he wrote to his brother from Paris that he had 'unexpectedly finished the opera.' Shortly afterwards he was recalled to Moscow to be present at the first performance of 'Eugen Oniegin,' given by the students of the Moscow Conservatoire in the theatre of that institution. Modeste Tchaikovsky attributes the cool reception of this work—afterwards the most popular of all the composer's operas—to the poor interpretation it then received at the hands of such inexperienced singers. The composer himself seems to have been elated by the moderate success which awaited him on this occasion. He left for the country in the best of spirits and spent the four summer months between Kamenka, Brailov and Simaki, a smaller country house belonging to Nadejda von Meck to which he retired when she herself came to occupy Brailov. At Simaki he finished the orchestration of his latest opera, 'The Maid of Orleans,' and corrected the proofs of his first suite for orchestra, op. 43. In November he left Russia, travelling by Berlin and Paris to Rome, where he remained until Mar. 1880.

The year 1880 marks a distinct increase in Tchaikovsky's popularity as a composer. He had now reached his fortieth year, and, thanks to Nicholas Rubinstein, all his principal orchestral works had received the best possible interpretations at the concerts of the Musical Society in Moscow; while his operas had all

been given in both capitals. His reputation was therefore well established in Russia; but, so far, his successes abroad had been very dubious. In Vienna he was still the object of Hanslick's almost venomous hostility; in Berlin the Press had unanimously condemned 'Francesca da Rimini'; in Paris 'Romeo and Juliet' and 'The Tempest' had proved failures, and, as recently as Jan. 1880, his fourth symphony had been received with 'icy coldness' at the Colonne concerts. This was a discouraging record, even if we bear in mind that in England and America his music had met with a far more cordial reception. Now, however, came news of the success of his quartet No. 3, op. 30, and the serenade for violin and piano at the Société de Sainte-Cécile in Paris; of the excellent reception of the first suite in America and the triumph of the pianoforte concerto in B♭ minor, which had been played by Bülow and Friedenthal in Berlin, by Breitner in Buda-Pest and Rummel in New York. Tchaikovsky now stood on the brink of universal fame and recognition.

From Nov. 1880 until Sept. 1881 he composed nothing. There are several reasons which may account for this gap in his creative activity. In the spring of 1881 he was deeply affected by the death of Nicholas Rubinstein. He was now confronted with the question: Could he consent to fill his friend's place as director of the Moscow Conservatoire? He decided in favour of freedom and his creative work; yet wise as the decision was, it cost him some twinges of conscience, and so disturbed his peace of mind that he felt no inclination to embark upon an important composition. Another reason for his being unable to work with his usual zest was the illness of his sister Alexandra Davidov. Kamenka, thus overshadowed, was never again to be the ideal place of refuge in the summer months. In December, while staying in Rome, he took up his pen once more, and began to compose the beautiful pianoforte trio, op. 50, 'dedicated to the memory of a great artist'(Nicholas Rubinstein). The work was completed by the end of Jan. 1882.

The chief work of 1882–83 was the opera 'Mazeppa,' based upon Poushkin's poem 'Poltava.' In the course of its completion his enthusiasm flagged considerably. Writing to Nadejda von Meck in Sept. 1882 he says:

'Never has any important work given me such trouble as this opera. Perhaps it is the decadence of my powers—or have I become more severe in self-judgment?'

The Opera Direction showed extraordinary zeal in the staging of the work. It was decided to give it simultaneously in Moscow and St. Petersburg, a course so unusual that the composer was justified in thinking the Emperor must have interested himself personally in the matter. In spite of these favourable auspices the work was not very cordially received, the public applause being obviously intended for the man rather than the music. Exhausted by nervous anxiety as to the fate of his opera, Tchaikovsky went to Paris to avoid the first performance in St. Petersburg (Feb. 15, 1883). He had hardly arrived in the French capital before he was summoned to appear before their Imperial Majesties in order to be invested with the order of St. Vladimir. From St. Petersburg he went to Kamenka, where he set to work upon his third suite. During the autumn 'Eugen Oniegin' was given in St. Petersburg under the direction of Napravnik. This proved the turning-point in its favour. The critics still remained cold, but the crowded houses signified the first popular success of a native opera since Glinka's 'A Life for the Tsar,' and henceforward it remained almost an unrivalled favourite with the Russian public.

The year 1884 closes the second, or 'Kamenka' period in Tchaikovsky's life, so called to distinguish it from the 'Moscow' period, which is inseparably connected with his teaching at the Conservatoire. From the time of his serious illness in 1877, Kamenka, with its peaceful family atmosphere, entirely satisfied his requirements. But with a gradual change to a happier and more independent state of mind, its circle became too narrow for him. His desire for complete liberty, coupled with social intercourse, may be regarded as a sign of his complete recovery.

'The Tchaikovsky of 1885,' says his brother, 'seemed a new man compared with the nervous and misanthropical Tchaikovsky of 1878.' Recognition seemed to endow him with strength and energy for a public career. He was no longer satisfied to stand aloof and leave to others the propaganda of his works. Conquering his former dislike to publicity, he now accepted invitations to conduct his own compositions in person. These new conditions of life are reflected in the ever-widening circle of his acquaintances, which included such interesting personalities as Liadov, Altani, Grieg, Sophie Menter, Emil Sauer, Louis Diémer, Colonne and Carl Halir. Besides these, he knew and corresponded more or less intimately with the famous singer Emilie Pavlovskaya, the Grand Duke Constantine Constantinovich, the pianists Sapellnikov and Siloti, Glazounov, Désirée Artôt, Brodsky and many others. In these new friendships he found the affection and appreciation so indispensable to his temperament, but few of them were so deep and lasting as the ties of earlier days. The dearest of all his later affections was for his nephew Vladimir Davidov, for whom Tchaikovsky felt the same protecting affection he had lavished upon his brothers the twins Anatole and Modeste, in their youth. The difference of age was no hindrance to their companionship. Tchai-

kovsky confided his inmost thoughts to his nephew, dedicated to him his last great work, the 'Pathetic Symphony,' and made him his heir and executor, confiding to his care all those whom he still wished to help, even after his death.

For many years Tchaikovsky had desired to possess a small country house of his own. When, in the early spring of 1885, the moment came to decide upon his usual trip abroad, he was suddenly seized by a nervous terror of the journey and sent his faithful servant Alexis to take a furnished house in the country. The manor-house of Maidanovo, near Klin, once the abode of an aristocratic family, had gradually fallen into decay. Nevertheless it was not an unpleasant temporary residence, and had the advantage of being on the direct line between Moscow and St. Petersburg. The view from the windows, the quiet and sense of being at home, delighted Tchaikovsky. 'I am contented, cheerful, and quiet,' he wrote to his brother, soon after his arrival at Maidanovo.

'I read a great deal, and am getting on with English, which I enjoy. I walk, eat, and sleep when—and as much as—I please—in fact, I live.'

He was occupied at this time in the revision of 'Vakoula the Smith,' which was to be brought out again under the title of 'Oxana's Caprice,' and also upon a new opera, founded upon Shpajinsky's play 'The Enchantress.' He was also greatly absorbed in the affairs of the Moscow Conservatoire, being set upon securing the directorship for his favourite pupil Taneiev. In June he began to fulfil a promise, made to Balakirev three years earlier, to compose a symphonic work on the subject of 'Manfred.' The programme was alluring, moreover it was not out of harmony with contemporary feeling; for, as Balakirev puts it,

'all the troubles of modern man arise from the fact that he does not know how to preserve his ideals. Hence all the suffering of our times.'

The work cost Tchaikovsky an immense effort. Writing of it to Nadejda von Meck he says: 'It is so highly tragic—so complicated and difficult—that at times I myself become a Manfred.' It was finished in Dec. 1885.

After spending nearly six months in the manor-house at Maidanovo Tchaikovsky moved into a smaller house in the same neighbourhood. From this time dates that quiet country existence which earned for him the sobriquet of 'the Hermit of Klin.' The routine of his life at this time was as follows:—He rose between 7 and 8 A.M. Part of his morning was devoted to reading, the remainder to proof-correcting, or composition. At one o'clock he dined, and, wet or fine, always went for a walk after dinner. He had read somewhere that in order to keep in health, a man ought to walk for two hours a day, and observed this rule so conscientiously that it distressed him to return five minutes too soon. Most of the time during these solitary rambles was spent in composition. He thought out the leading ideas, pondered over the construction of the work, and jotted down the chief themes. The next morning he looked over these notes and worked them out at the piano, so that he should not trust entirely to his indifferent memory. He wrote out everything very exactly, and indicated the instrumentation here and there. In these sketches the greater part of a work was generally quite finished. When it came to the orchestration, he only copied it out clearly, without essentially altering the first drafts. While speaking of his methods of composing, it may be added that his close reserve as to his compositions also dates from this time. In earlier days Tchaikovsky had been very communicative about his work; even before his compositions were finished, he was ready to discuss them, and ask the advice of his friends. Gradually the circle to whom he communicated the fruits of his inspiration became smaller, until after 1885 he ceased to show his works to any one. The first person to see them was the engraver in Jurgenson's publishing house. Tchaikovsky never worked at night after his alarming breakdown in 1866. His lonely evenings were spent at the piano, or in reading—mostly historical books— and playing 'patience.' When his intimate friends, Kashkin or Laroche, visited him, they would read aloud, or play cards till 11 P.M., when Tchaikovsky retired to bed.

In Apr. 1886 Tchaikovsky left the seclusion of Maidanovo to visit his youngest brother Hippolyte in the Caucasus. At Tiflis, where he had an excellent friend and interpreter in Ippolitov-Ivanov, he met with a triumphant reception. A concert was organised consisting entirely of his works, followed by a supper, and the presentation of a silver wreath. It was the first great public honour accorded to the composer, and revealed to him what he had hitherto hardly begun to realise—the extent of his popularity and his real relation to the Russian public. From the Caucasus he travelled to Paris, where by this time his reputation had considerably increased; but it cannot be said that his popularity has been maintained there in the same degree as in England. Late in June he returned to the little home which he had left deep in snow, and now found embowered in foliage and flowers. He was still busy with his 'Enchantress,' and believed, as he always did of his latest operatic work, that it was the finest thing he had ever conceived. At the beginning of the autumn he paid a visit to St. Petersburg to be present at the first performance of Napravnik's 'Harold,' and was very much gratified at his reception there. The composers, headed by Rimsky-Korsakov, welcomed him in a most friendly spirit, while at the same time he received,

through the medium of Stassov, an anonymous gift of 500 roubles, usually bestowed on the composer of the best musical novelty of the season, judged, in this instance, to be 'Manfred.'

The first performance of 'Oxana's Caprice' took place in Moscow on Jan. 31, 1887, and had a far-reaching influence on Tchaikovsky's future, because he then made his first successful attempt as a conductor. The work had a brilliant success, perhaps due to the composer's presence on the occasion; for it only remained in the repertory for two seasons. He was not long in following up his first success in the conductor's rôle. On Mar. 17 he appeared in this capacity at one of the Philharmonic Society's concerts in St. Petersburg, and this was the beginning of a whole series of similar concerts which made his name known throughout Russia, western Europe and America. Tchaikovsky's diary contains the following laconic reference to this occasion : ' My concert. Complete success. Great enjoyment—but still, why always this drop of gall in my honey-pot?' 'In this question,' says his brother Modeste, 'lie the germs of all the weariness and suffering which sprang up in Tchaikovsky's soul simultaneously with his pursuit of fame, and reached their greatest intensity at the moment of his greatest triumphs.'

Tchaikovsky spent most of the spring at Maidanovo, devoting himself to the orchestration of 'The Enchantress.' This work was a step in the direction of purely dramatic and national opera. The composer declared that he was attracted to the subject by a long-cherished desire to illustrate in music Goethe's famous words, 'Das Ewig-Weibliche zieht uns hinan,' and to demonstrate the irresistible witchery of woman's beauty. The opera was produced at the Maryinsky Theatre, St. Petersburg, on Nov. 1/Oct. 20, 1887, and was conducted by the composer. Tchaikovsky did not at first realise that in spite of a personal ovation the opera was actually a failure. He was bitterly disappointed when, on the fifth night, the work was sung to a half-empty house, and almost immediately withdrawn. Nor did it meet with a better fate when given in Moscow in the following February.

With the year 1888 Tchaikovsky began his new mode of life with a lengthy concert tour which included Leipzig, Berlin, Prague, Hamburg, Paris and London. It was not without inward misgivings that he set out on the chase for fame, and in a few weeks the sense of disillusionment had already crept over him. 'My reputation will probably increase,' he wrote to Nadejda von Meck,

'but would it not be better to stay at home and work? God knows! . . . I regret the time when I was left in peace in the solitude of the country.'

In Berlin his success was not sufficiently marked to console him for the exertion and loss of time involved by his visit; Leipzig received him with far greater cordiality; in Prague and Paris he met with brilliant receptions, but the results in both instances have proved transient. It was in London that the seeds of his popularity struck the deepest and most abiding roots. Generally speaking, the London papers were favourable to Tchaikovsky, although some regret was expressed that he had not made his début at the Philharmonic Society with some more solid works than the Serenade for strings and the Variations from the third suite.

By the end of April 1888 he was back in Russia, and settled in a new country house at Frolovskoe near Klin, less pretentious than Maidanovo, but more picturesque and secluded. Here he was free from the inroads of summer excursionists—and could enjoy the little garden on the edge of the forest and the wide outlook beyond, which opened .upon the homely landscape of Central Russia, dearer to Tchaikovsky than all the beauties of Italy or the grandeurs of the Caucasus. He became greatly attached to the place and only left it on account of the wholesale destruction of the surrounding forests. The summer went by peacefully. 'I cannot tell you,' he writes to Nadejda von Meck, early in August,

'what a pleasure it has been to watch my flowers grow, and see daily—even hourly—new blossoms coming out. When I am quite old and past composing I shall devote myself to growing flowers. Meanwhile, I have been working with good results, for half the symphony (the Fifth) is now orchestrated.'

He was also engaged in completing the Fantasia-Overture 'Hamlet.' But these happy summer months were followed by an unusually arduous and depressing winter season. Early in autumn he lost his niece Vera Rimsky-Korsakov, née Davidov, and his old comrade Hubert. The fifth symphony and 'Hamlet' were well received in St. Petersburg, but the criticisms of the former were very discouraging. In December he conducted a successful performance of 'Eugen Oniegin' at Prague, and during the course of the winter season retired to the country for six weeks to compose a ballet ('The Sleeping Beauty') commissioned by the directors of the Opera.

Towards the close of Jan. 1889 Tchaikovsky started on his second tour abroad. Hardly had he crossed the German frontier than he experienced 'the usual feelings of home-sickness' and looked forward to his return. On Feb. 13 he made his first appearance as composer and conductor at a Gürzenich concert in Cologne, and afterwards wrote to Glazounov in high praise of the orchestra: 'They read the scherzo of the third suite, which is particularly difficult, as though they were playing it for the tenth time.' From Cologne he went to Frankfort, Dresden, Berlin, Leipzig and Geneva, after which he travelled north to Hamburg. Here he found himself in the same hotel as Brahms,

and was gratified to hear that the German composer was prolonging his visit on purpose to attend the rehearsal of the fifth symphony. Afterwards, at luncheon, Brahms confided his opinion of the work to its composer 'very frankly and simply': it pleased him on the whole, with the exception of the finale. This meeting increased Tchaikovsky's respect and personal liking for Brahms, but their musical temperaments differed too radically to find any common meeting-ground. Tchaikovsky took no part in the conflict between the partisans of Brahms and Wagner which divided all musical Germany. The personality of the former, his purity and loftiness of aim, and earnestness of purpose won Tchaikovsky's sympathy. Wagner's personality and views were, on the contrary, antipathetic to him; but his music awoke his enthusiasm, while the works of Brahms left him unmoved to the end of his life. Between the Hamburg concert and his arrival in London Tchaikovsky spent a few weeks in Paris, but made no public appearance.

On Apr. 11, 1889 Tchaikovsky appeared for the second time at the London Philharmonic Concerts, conducting his first suite and the pianoforte concerto in B flat minor (Sapellnikov). From London he returned to Russia by the Mediterranean and the Caucasus. He spent a few days in Moscow, where a coup d'état had taken place in the Conservatoire, Taneiev having resigned the directorship, in which he was succeeded by Safonov. The summer was spent as usual in the country, and the time was occupied by the completion and orchestration of 'The Sleeping Beauty' ballet. He was delighted with the results, and pronounced it to be 'one of my best works.' Consequently he experienced a severe disappointment when on the occasion of the gala rehearsal in St. Petersburg, Jan. 13, 1890, at which the Imperial court was present, 'very nice' constituted the sole expression of approval which passed the Emperor's lips. The public showed itself equally cool; but, as in the case of 'Eugen Oniegin,' the ballet grew in favour until it became in time one of the most popular of the composer's works.

During the greater part of the winter 1889–90 Tchaikovsky was obliged to remain in Moscow, to superintend the rehearsals for 'Eugen Oniegin.' At this time he looked forward with apprehension to the Jubilee Festival of Anton Rubinstein, which was to take place in St. Petersburg in November, for which he had undertaken to compose a chorus and a pianoforte piece. This part of his task was easily fulfilled, but the conductorship of the concerts was another matter; for although he had been conducting his own compositions for two seasons, he had but little experience with the works of others. 'There were moments,' he wrote, 'when I experienced such a complete loss of strength that I feared for my life . . . from the 1st to the 19th of November I endured martyrdom, and I am still marvelling how I lived through it.'

Tired out with four months' arduous work, Tchaikovsky went to Florence about the middle of February. Italy did not interest him at the moment; his one thought was to get away from the turmoil of life in the capitals and to work at his new opera 'Pique-Dame' (The Queen of Spades), the libretto for which had been prepared from Poushkin's novel of the same name, by the composer's brother Modeste. Tchaikovsky attacked the work with intense enthusiasm, wept copiously over the hero's sad end, and was persuaded—as with each new opera—that he had at last found the ideal subject. 'Either I am mistaken, or "Pique-Dame" is a masterpiece,' he wrote to his brother on the completion of the work. In this instance he was not disappointed. On the first representation of the opera in St. Petersburg, Dec. 19, 1890, its success, though clearly evident, was not extraordinary. The Press almost unanimously condemned the libretto, and spoke slightingly of the music, and there was little to predict that the work would hold its own and continue to bring the composer a substantial revenue. Of all Tchaikovsky's operas it is the one most accessible to foreigners, and best calculated to win success abroad.

The summer was spent happily enough in the seclusion of Frolovskoe, but an exceedingly bitter experience was awaiting Tchaikovsky in the near future. In Dec. 1890 he received a letter from Nadejda von Meck, informing him that she was on the brink of ruin, and therefore unable to continue his allowance. In the course of their correspondence, which had lasted thirteen years, Nadejda von Meck had more than once hinted at pecuniary embarrassments, but had always hastened to assure her friend that his allowance of 6000 roubles a year could not affect her position one way or the other. Her letter on this occasion has not been made public, but it is evident from the tone of Tchaikovsky's reply that it was so worded as to wound his feelings. After sympathising with her troubles, and begging her not to be anxious on his account, he says:

'The last words of your letter [1] have hurt me, but I do not think you meant them seriously. Do you really think me incapable of remembering you when I no longer receive your money? . . . I am glad . . . that I may show my unbounded and passionate gratitude which passes all words. Perhaps you hardly suspect how immeasurable has been your generosity. If you did, you would never have said that now you are poor I am "to think of you *sometimes*." I can truly say that I have never forgotten you and never shall, for when I think of myself my thoughts turn immediately to you.'

Shortly afterwards he heard that her financial difficulties were satisfactorily arranged, and with the sense of relief which followed on this

[1] 'Do not forget, and think of me sometimes.'

news a very human feeling of resentment crept into his heart. He could not banish the idea that his friend's letter had been merely 'an excuse to get rid of him on the first opportunity.' After a short time, however, his sincere affection overcame his mortification and wounded pride. But all advances on his part were met with absolute silence and indifference on hers. The old, ideal friendship now appeared to him as the mere caprice of a wealthy woman —the commonplace ending to a fairy-tale; while her last letter rankled in his heart to the end of his days. According to his brother:

'Neither the triumph of "The Queen of Spades," nor the profound sorrow caused by the death of his beloved sister, in Apr. 1891, nor even his American triumphs, served to soften the blow she had inflicted.'

Let it be said in extenuation of her apparent heartlessness that Nadejda von Meck was already the victim of a terrible nervous disorder 'which changed her relations not only to him, but to others.' The news of the composer's end reached her on her own death-bed, and two months later she followed him to the grave, Jan. 25, 1894.

With the opening of the new year 1891, a note of weariness and vacillation becomes evident in Tchaikovsky's correspondence. Writing to his brother shortly after the splendid success of 'The Queen of Spades' in Kiev, he says:

'It was indescribable, but I am very tired, and in reality I suffer a great deal. My uncertainty as to the immediate future weighs upon me. Shall I give up the idea of wandering abroad or not? Is it wise to accept the offer of the Opera Direction (to compose an opera in one act and a ballet, for the season 1891–92)? My brain is empty; I have not the least pleasure in work. "Hamlot" [2] oppresses me terribly.'

About the middle of January he retired to Frolovskoe, and cancelled his engagements in Mainz, Buda-Pest and Frankfort. It was not only the composition of 'Hamlet' which caused him to give up these concerts; at this time he was suffering from an affection of the right hand, and conducting was a matter of difficulty. But when a pressing invitation to visit America reached him in his solitude, Tchaikovsky replied accepting the offer. He had already promised the Direction of the Imperial Opera an opera on the subject of Herz's play, 'King René's Daughter,' and a ballet, 'Casse-Noisette' ('The Nut-cracker'). Neither of these subjects stirred him to enthusiasm like 'Pique-Dame' and 'The Sleeping Beauty,' and he was filled with misgivings as to the possibility of composing so much in the time at his disposal.

Early in March he left Frolovskoe for Paris, where he was to conduct one of the Colonne Concerts on Apr. 5. He was wretchedly homesick, and his brother Modeste, who joined him in Paris on Mar. 22, was unfavourably impressed by his mental and physical condition

[2] Incidental music to the tragedy for Guitry's benefit.

'A chilling and gloomy look, his cheeks flushed with excitement, a bitter smile on his lips—this is how I shall always remember Peter Ilich during that visit to Paris.'

The success of the concert, which consisted entirely of his own works, did not soothe his acute nostalgia, or console him for his over-fatigue. Worse troubles were in store for him. On Apr. 9 Modeste Tchaikovsky received a telegram announcing the death of their sister Alexandra Davidov. Through all the early troubled years of the composer's life she had been his chief moral support and comfort; her affection, and that of Nadejda von Meck, had sustained him in times of dejection and physical suffering. Modeste Tchaikovsky hastened to Rouen, where his brother was taking a few days' rest before embarking at Havre for New York. Knowing that the news of his sister's death would be a crushing blow to Peter Ilich, and that it was too late to put off his journey to America, Modeste resolved to let him go in ignorance of the sad event. Unfortunately Tchaikovsky was no sooner left alone in Rouen than he resolved to return to Paris for a day or two, to distract his anxiety as to the approaching journey. There, in a reading-room, he picked up the *Novoe Vremya* and learnt the melancholy truth. 'For God's sake, send all details to New York,' he wrote in his last letter of farewell. 'To-day, even more than yesterday, I feel the absolute impossibility of depicting in music the "Sugar-plum Fairy."'

Tchaikovsky sailed from Havre on Apr. 18, 1891, and landed in New York on the 27th. On the voyage, and during the whole of his American visit, he kept a bright and entertaining journal of his experiences. He conducted six concerts in America: four in New York, one in Baltimore and one in Philadelphia. The works performed were: (1) The Coronation March, (2) the third suite, (3) two sacred choruses—The Lord's Prayer and The Legend, (4) the pianoforte concerto No. 1 and (5) the serenade for strings. Everywhere he met with 'unprecedented success,' and the Press notices were mostly written 'in a tone of unqualified praise.' By the end of May he was back in St. Petersburg.

As Frolovskoe was becoming rapidly denuded of its forests, Tchaikovsky returned for the summer to Maidanovo. Here he completed the 'Casse-Noisette' ballet and the opera 'King René's Daughter'(afterwards called'Iolanthe'); the remodelling of his sextet and the instrumentation of a symphonic poem, 'The Voyevode,' also engaged him during these months. At this time his health was good, and he enjoyed the society of his old friend Hermann Laroche, who paid him a long visit during the autumn. His correspondence with concert agents, publishers and all kinds of applicants had become a burden to him; and although his earnings were considerable, his generosity more than

kept pace with his income, so that he was often short of funds. Undoubtedly he had aged prematurely, and looked at this time far more than his years. All these things probably conduced to the mood of melancholy and discontent reflected in his correspondence. Late in October he went to Moscow to be present at the first performance of 'The Queen of Spades,' and to conduct 'The Voyevode' at Siloti's concert. The work made little impression on the audience, and this fact, added to some rather hasty critical remarks by Taneiev, so annoyed Tchaikovsky that he is said to have torn up the score. The fragments, however, were carefully preserved by Siloti, and after the composer's death the symphonic poem was reconstructed, and had considerable success under Nikisch and other conductors.

On Dec. 29 Tchaikovsky left Moscow on a concert tour, visiting Kiev and Warsaw before going to Germany. At Warsaw, where he arrived about the middle of January, he was overcome by that despairing home-sickness which towards the close of life attacked him whenever he left Russia. From Warsaw he went *via* Berlin to Hamburg to be present at the first performance of 'Eugen Oniegin,' conducted by Gustav Mahler. In consequence, however, of his increasing depression, he abandoned the concerts for which he was engaged in Holland, and returned to Maidanovo after a short visit to Paris. On Mar. 19 he travelled to St. Petersburg to conduct his 'Romeo and Juliet' overture and the first performance of the 'Casse-Noisette' suite. The latter was received with immense enthusiasm, five out of the six movements having to be repeated.

At this time Tchaikovsky moved into another new home, destined, however, to be his last. The house stood on the outskirts of the little town of Klin, and was surrounded by fields and woods. It was simple and far from picturesque, but it suited the composer's modest tastes. After Tchaikovsky's death it was bought by his servant Alexis Safronov and repurchased in 1897 by Modeste Tchaikovsky and his nephew Vladimir Davidov. All relics and documents connected with the composer were preserved there.

In the summer of 1892, after a short cure at Vichy, he returned directly to Klin to work upon a new symphony—the sixth—which he was anxious to complete by the end of August. At the same time he began also to busy himself with the correction of his compositions and the revision of the pianoforte arrangements of them. The vast accumulation of proof-correcting weighed heavily upon him. 'Even in dreams,' he wrote to his nephew, Vladimir Davidov, 'I see corrections, and flats and sharps that refuse to do what they are ordered.' His psychological condition was at this time rather peculiar. Since he first took up the baton in 1887 the number and importance of his touring engagements steadily increased. Every journey cost him agonies of home-sickness, and he vowed it should be the last. Yet no sooner was he home again than he began to plan for the next tour. 'It seemed as though he had become the victim of some blind force which drove him hither and thither at will,' says Modeste Tchaikovsky. . . .

'This mysterious force had its origin in an inexplicable, restless, despondent condition of mind, which sought appeasement in any kind of distraction. I cannot explain it as a premonition of his approaching death; there are no grounds whatever for such a supposition. . . . I will only call attention to the fact that he passed through a similar phase before every decisive change in his life. As at the beginning of the sixties, when he chose a musical career, and in 1885 when he resolved "to show himself in the eyes of the world," so also at this juncture we are conscious of a feeling *that things could not have gone on much longer;* we feel ourselves on the brink of a change, as though something had come to an end and was about to give place to a new and unknown presence. His death, which came to solve the problem, seemed fortuitous—yet I cannot shake off the impression that the years 1892 and 1893 were the dark harbingers of a new and serener epoch.'

In the summer of this year (1892) he was invited to conduct a concert at the Vienna Exhibition, and gladly availed himself of the chance of overcoming the unfriendly attitude of the Viennese, due chiefly to Hanslick's influence. On his arrival he found that the concert was to be given in what was practically a restaurant, amid the rattling of knives and plates, and the fumes of beer and tobacco. Thereupon the composer refused to fulfil his contract until the tables had been moved and the room converted into something more resembling a concert-hall. From Vienna he went to be the guest of Madame Sophie Menter at the Castle of Itter, in Tyrol, and afterwards to Salzburg and Prague to be present at the first performance of 'The Queen of Spades' in the Bohemian capital. Early in November he had to be in St. Petersburg·to superintend the rehearsals for the new opera 'Iolanthe.' Two honours were now conferred upon him: he was elected a Corresponding Member of the French Academy, and the University of Cambridge invited him to accept the degree of Doctor of Music, *honoris causa.*

On Dec. 17 'Iolanthe' and the 'Casse-Noisette' ballet were performed at the Opera-house in the presence of the Emperor and the court. The opera was conducted by Napravnik, but in spite of an admirable interpretation it met with a mere complimentary success. Nor has it, like some of Tchaikovsky's works, grown in popularity. The ballet, too, was a momentary disappointment; its unconventional treatment and the delicate charm of the musical ideas did not appeal to the public on a first hearing.

Early in January 1893 Tchaikovsky visited Brussels and Paris, and travelled homewards by way of Odessa, where for a whole fortnight he was the object of such ovations as eclipsed all previous receptions at home and abroad. The year opened with a period of cheerfulness and serenity for which the sixth, so-called 'Pathetic,' symphony seems partly accountable. Modeste Tchaikovsky speaks of this work as 'an act of exorcism,' whereby his brother cast out all the dark spirits which had possessed him in the preceding years. The first mention of the symphony occurs in a letter to the composer's brother Anatole, dated Feb. 22, 1893. The following day he wrote a more detailed account to his nephew Vladimir Davidov, to whom eventually the work was dedicated:

'I must tell you how happy I am about my work. As you know, I destroyed a symphony which I had partly composed and orchestrated in the autumn. I did wisely, for it contained little that was really fine—an empty pattern of sounds without any inspiration. Just as I was starting on my journey (the visit to Paris in Dec. 1892), the idea came to me for a new symphony. This time with a programme; but a programme of a kind which remains an enigma to all—let them guess it who can. The work will be entitled "A Programme Symphony" (No. 6). This programme is penetrated by subjective sentiment. During my journey, while composing it in my mind, I frequently shed tears. Now I am home again I have settled down to sketch out the work, and it goes with such ardour that in less than four days I have completed the first movement, while the rest of the Symphony is clearly outlined in my head. There will be much that is novel as regards form in this work. For instance, the finale will not be a great Allegro, but an Adagio of considerable dimensions. You cannot imagine what joy I feel at the conviction that my day is not yet over, and that I may still accomplish much. Perhaps I may be mistaken, but it does not seem likely. Do not speak of this to any one but Modeste.'

The happier mood of this year was not proof against the old malady of nostalgia and restlessness. On May 29 Tchaikovsky arrived in London in a phase of the darkest depression and misanthropy, which does not seem to have been suspected by those who saw him at the time. In a letter to Vladimir Davidov he says:

'I suffer, not only from torments that cannot be put into words (there is one place in the sixth symphony where they seem to me to be adequately expressed), but of a hatred to strangers, and an indefinable terror—though of what, the devil only knows.'

This season the London Philharmonic Society gave two concerts at which the foreign composers, recipients of the honorary degree at Cambridge, were invited to conduct compositions of their own. At the first of these, on June 1, Tchaikovsky was represented by his fourth symphony, which appears to have been a brilliant success. The festivities at Cambridge —in honour of the Jubilee of the University Musical Society—began on June 12, with a concert, the programme of which contained a work by each of the five doctors of music *honoris causa:* Boïto, Saint-Saëns, Max Bruch, Tchaikovsky and Grieg (the last of whom was unable to be present on account of illness). For this concert Tchaikovsky chose his symphonic poem 'Francesca da Rimini.' The day after the ceremony he left for Paris, whence he wrote in a characteristic mood to his old friend Konradi:

'Now that all is over it is pleasant to look back on my visit to England, and to remember the extraordinary cordiality shown to me everywhere, although, in consequence of my peculiar temperament, while there, I tormented and worried myself to fiddle-strings.'

No sooner was he back in Klin than he returned to work upon the sixth symphony, completing it by the end of August, after which he started, in excellent spirits, for a flying visit to Hamburg. That he had the highest opinion of his new symphony is evident from his correspondence at this time, especially from a letter to the Grand Duke Constantine Constantinovich, in which he says: 'Without exaggeration I have put my whole soul into this work.' Tchaikovsky left Klin on Oct. 19 for the last time. As the train passed the village of Frolovskoe he pointed to the churchyard, remarking to his fellow-travellers: 'I shall be buried there, and people will point out my grave as they go by.' The following day he attended the memorial service for his friend Zvierev in Moscow, and spoke to Taneiev of his wish to be buried at Frolovskoe. These two references to death were probably prompted by the melancholy occasion, for otherwise he showed no signs of depression or foreboding.

Tchaikovsky arrived in St. Petersburg on Oct. 22, and was met by his brother Modeste and his favourite nephew Vladimir Davidov. The rehearsals of the sixth symphony discouraged him, because it made so little impression on the band, and he was afraid lest their coldness would mar the interpretation of the work. But his opinion that 'it was the best thing he ever had composed, or ever should compose,' was not shaken by the indifferent attitude of the musicians. He did not, however, succeed in impressing this view on the public or the performers. At the concert on Oct. 28 the work fell rather flat. A few weeks later, under Napravnik's conductorship, it made a profound sensation, since repeated in many other cities. The following day, before sending the score to his publisher, P. Jurgenson, he decided to give the symphony some distinctive title. Various names were suggested by his brother, from which he selected the qualification 'pathetic.' Afterwards he changed his mind, and desired Jurgenson, if it were not too late, merely to put this inscription on the title-page:

To Vladimir Lvovich
Davidov
(No. 6.)
Composed by P. Tchaikovsky.

During the last days of his life his mood was fairly equable. There was nothing which gave the least hint of his approaching end. On the evening of Oct. 31 he went to bed well and serene. The following day he complained of his digestion being upset and of a sleepless night, but refused to see a doctor. He joined his nephew and Modeste Tchaikovsky at lunch and, although he declined to eat anything, he drank a copious draught of water which had not been boiled. The others were dismayed by his imprudence, but he assured them he had no dread of cholera. All day his indisposition increased, until at night his brother, in alarm, sent for the eminent physician Bertenson. Tchaikovsky was rapidly growing weaker, and remarked more than once: 'I believe this is death.' Bertenson sent for his equally famous brother, and after a consultation they pronounced it to be a case of cholera. The next day his condition seemed more hopeful, but on Saturday, Nov. 4, his mental depression returned, and he begged those around him to waste no more time on useless remedies. Gradually he passed into a state of collapse. Sometimes he wandered in his mind, and repeated the name of Nadejda von Meck in accents of indignation or reproach. By the time his old servant had arrived from Klin Tchaikovsky was unable to recognise him. At 3 A.M. on the morning of Nov. 6 (Oct. 25), 1893, he passed away in the presence of his brothers Nicholas and Modeste, his nephews Litke, Buxhövden and Davidov, the two Bertensons, the district doctor and Alexis Safronov. Several sensational accounts of the composer's end have been widely circulated, and received credence, but in view of the medical opinions clearly expressed, and the numerous trustworthy witnesses of his last days, the foregoing account may be accepted as authentic.

Qualities of the Composer

In reviewing Tchaikovsky's career as a whole we are struck by the absence of salient landmarks and clearly defined points of fresh departure. The customary and convenient division of a master's work into distinct 'periods' is impossible in his case. His progress was seldom in a straight line. In his brother's words, 'he moved in spiral convolutions.' His constant fluctuations between old and new forms of expression seems to argue a lack of strong intellectual conviction. In his orchestral music he alternated from first to last between traditional symphony and the freer forms of programme music; while in opera he sometimes left the purely lyrical forms which suited him best to experiment with declamatory drama, as in 'The Enchantress.' As regards symphonic music, his predilection seems to have been for classic form, for while engaged on 'Manfred'—which dates, however, as late as 1885—he wrote to Taneiev that he much preferred to compose without any definite literary basis. 'When I write a programme symphony,' he says, 'I always feel I am not paying in sterling coin, but in worthless paper money.' Yet 'Manfred' had two successors in the sphere of programme music,—the overture-fantasia 'Hamlet' and the symphonic ballad 'The Voyevode.' The fact that Tchaikovsky's progress was based upon impulse rather than upon intellectual conviction is, I think, the clue to the understanding of all his charm and his weakness. It lends the fascination of the *imprévu* to the study of his works. He never forced his thoughts and feelings into a mould merely from compliance with the demands of traditional form; and although—having tarried too long in dilettante circles—he ended by preaching that a 'professional' musician should not shrink from the conscientious fulfilment of any commission imposed upon him, as a matter of fact, thanks to his enthusiastic and not too critical temperament, he wrote very little which had not actually the sanction of his inner feelings. He had, to a great extent, the powers of adaptation and assimilation peculiar to Russians; and if he lost in concentration thereby, he certainly gained in range and variety of accomplishment. It is this sincere response to emotional impulse, and the freedom with which he ranges almost every field of musical creation, which make Tchaikovsky as great as he is. At the same time, when we come to estimate his place in the history of music, we cannot forget that a more logical continuity of development, closer concentration, more searching self-criticism, more ruthless elimination of all that is merely facile and sentimental, have always been the characteristics of supreme genius. If this judgment appears somewhat paradoxical, it results from the fact that Tchaikovsky himself is one of the most striking of musical paradoxes.

An artist's earliest musical impressions are rarely obliterated in his after-career. Much has been written as to Tchaikovsky's right to be termed a national composer. In the more exclusive sense of the word he was not one of the Levites of national music. This is obvious from the beginning. While Glinka, Rimsky-Korsakov, Balakirev and Moussorgsky started life saturated with the folk-music, Tchaikovsky tells us that his unchanging affection for Mozart and the Italian school dated from his 6th year. There is no mention of his having imbibed the music of the people in his cradle, but undoubtedly he came to know it and employ it in later years—as an acquirement, not as an integral part of his nature. He was 23, and his musical tastes in many ways quite formed, before he came into contact with the music of Bach and Beethoven. On the other hand, he had frequented the Italian opera at a much earlier age. Therefore it is not surprising that he never ceased to blend with the melody of his own race an echo of the sensuous beauty of the south. Perhaps, indeed, it would be truer to say that in much of his music it is the racial element which is the echo, and the cosmo-

politan element which forms the actual basis of his inspiration. This may be said without reproach to Tchaikovsky's patriotism. To read his letters is to understand that he had no home but Russia. The ideals of the world save themselves from extermination by assuming strange disguises, and we have every reason to be grateful that at a moment when Wagner and Brahms were the paramount influences in music, a belated Russian youth, knowing nothing of either, caught up all that was most gracious and ideally beautiful not only in the Italian school, but, above all, in the music of Mozart. The tenderness and radiance of the latter shine through the darkness of Tchaikovsky's innate pessimism; while as regards the Italian influence it is one of the secrets of the quick and popular appeal of his music. Lest it should be thought that I exaggerate the importance of the Italian element, I refer those who only know his later works to his early operas, 'The Voyevode' and 'The Oprichnik.' The latter, based upon a historical and national subject, suffered greatly from this incongruous and crude combination of Russian and Italian elements. They had not as yet had time to fuse into that wonderfully penetrating, glowing and moving language of the emotions which speaks from the later symphonies and symphonic poems. We often hear it said: 'None but a Russian could have written the Pathetic Symphony.' This may be easily conceded. But only a Russian, penetrated like Tchaikovsky by a strong strain of Italian sensationalism and sensuousness, could have arrayed its funereal gloom in such ample folds of purple, and perfumed its odour of mortality with such subtle blends of incense. What underlies a great part of the symphony is the almost intolerable realisation of death and the futility of human achievements; what draws the crowd to hear it time after time is its attractive luxury of woe.

THE OPERAS.—In his opera 'Oxana's Caprice,' founded upon Gogol's tale 'Christmas Eve Revels,' Tchaikovsky found a subject which might have led him entirely away from the form and spirit of conventional Italian opera. This work dates from the early 'seventies, a time at which he came under the influence of Balakirev and Stassov, and passed through a mild phase of ultra-nationalism and what was then ultra-modernism. The second symphony and the symphonic poems 'Romeo and Juliet,' 'The Tempest' and 'Francesca da Rimini' were more or less the direct outcome of these new influences. The opera 'Oxana's Caprice' belongs also to this period. But this work must be reckoned one of the least successful of his operas. The more modern and realistic style which he here strove to assume hangs upon him too obviously like a borrowed garment, and his limited fund of subdued and whimsical humour, so charmingly displayed in the 'Casse-Noisette' suite, could hardly keep pace with Gogol's robust and racy wit. The comparative failure of this work was only a momentary check to his operatic ambition. It is evident that his friend Nadejda von Meck, who had no faith in the future of the opera in general, more than once hinted that his gifts might be more profitably applied to purely instrumental music. To this he replied that opera increased the circle of a composer's hearers in a degree impossible to symphonic art. He writes:

'To refrain from writing operas is the act of a hero, and we have only one such hero in our time— Brahms. Such heroism is not for me. The stage, with all its glitter, attracts me irresistibly.'

So, within two years of the failure of 'Oxana's Caprice,' we find him absorbed in the composition of 'Eugen Oniegin.' As with so many of his operatic subjects, he was so completely enamoured of Poushkin's poem as to be blind to all its practical difficulties. But this time his instinct served him well. The delicate, poetic realism, the elegiac sentiment, and, above all, the intensely subjective character of this novel in verse, were so completely in harmony with his temperament that he was able to triumph over all minor drawbacks. The result was his first really popular work for the stage. Tchaikovsky himself was careful not to call this unique creation an opera. 'Lyric scenes' describes more accurately a work of art which in many ways defies criticism as completely as it eludes classification. It answers to no particular standard of dramatic truth; its weaknesses are many, and its absurdities not a few. Yet to all emotional natures it makes an irresistible appeal, for the music is as much a part of the touching, old-world story as the perfume is a part of the flower which exhales it. It was not surprising that in Russia, where Poushkin's poem holds a permanent place in the hearts of the cultivated classes, Tchaikovsky's opera soon rivalled Glinka's 'A Life for the Tsar' in the popular favour. We must not judge this work as the composer's greatest and most strenuous effort, but as the outcome of a passionate, single-hearted impulse. Consequently the sense of joy in creation, of perfect reconciliation with his subject, is conveyed in every bar of the music. 'Eugen Oniegin' is the child of Tchaikovsky's fancy; born of his passing love for the image of Tatiana and tinged throughout with those moods of romantic melancholy and tender sentiment which the composer and his heroine share in common.

Twelve months after the completion of 'Eugen Oniegin' we find Tchaikovsky writing:

'The idea of "The Maid of Orleans" has taken furious possession of me. I want to finish the whole work in an hour, as sometimes happens in a dream.'

Looking through the score with eyes more coolly critical than the composer's, we now see that, in spite of effective moments, the music of this opera displays in abundance all those weaknesses which were the result of Tchaikovsky's unsettled convictions as regards style. The transition from a subject so Russian in colour and so lyrical in sentiment as 'Eugen Oniegin' to one so universal and so epic in character as 'The Maid of Orleans' presented difficulties which only time and reflexion could have successfully overcome. But Tchaikovsky threw off two-thirds of this opera in a little over a fortnight, and the natural result of this blind haste is that much of the music has the patchiness and lack of coherence of an improvisation. Just as the national significance of 'The Oprichnik' suffers from moments of purely Italian influence, so 'Joan of Arc' moves at times in an incongruously Russian atmosphere. Tchaikovsky started upon his sixth opera, 'Mazeppa,' without any of the fervent enthusiasm which carried him through his two preceding works. Although 'Mazeppa' failed to win immediate success, it has shown greater staying power than many of Tchaikovsky's earlier operas, and still holds a place in the repertory of the capitals and provincial cities of Russia. It contains some of the composer's most inspired and forcible pages. 'The Enchantress,' which followed in 1887, only serves to show that the further Tchaikovsky strayed from lyric forms in opera, the less satisfactory were the results. We may presume he realised this at last, for in 'Pique-Dame' and his last opera, 'Iolanthe,' he returns in a great measure to purely lyrical methods. 'Pique-Dame,' which now vies in popularity with 'Eugen Oniegin,' is perhaps the most successful of all his works for the stage, and the one most interesting to a foreign audience. We may sum up Tchaikovsky's operatic development as follows: Beginning with conventional Italian forms, he passed on in 'Oxana's Caprice' to more modern methods, to the use of melodic recitative and arioso; while 'Eugen Oniegin' shows a combination of both these styles. This first period is purely *lyrical*. Afterwards, in 'The Maid of Orleans,' 'Mazeppa' and 'The Enchantress,' he passed through a second period of *dramatic* and *declamatory* tendency. With 'Pique-Dame' he reaches the climax of his operatic progress; but this work is the solitary example of a period which may be characterised as *lyrico-dramatic*. In 'Iolanthe' he returns to simple lyric forms.

Of Tchaikovsky's eight operas, two only have so far achieved popular success—'Eugen Oniegin' and 'The Queen of Spades.' The others have enjoyed in varying degrees the negative triumphs of a *succès d'estime*. The choice of libretti may have had something to do with this; for the books of 'The Oprichnik' and 'Mazeppa,' though dramatic, are exceedingly lugubrious. But Polonsky's charming text to 'Cherevichek' ('Oxana's Caprice') should at least have pleased a Russian audience.

We must find another reason for the comparative failure of so many of Tchaikovsky's operas. It was not so much that the subjects he chose were poor in themselves, as that they did not always suit the particular temperament of the composer; and he rarely took this important fact sufficiently into consideration. Tchaikovsky's outlook was essentially subjective, individual, particular. He himself knew very well what was requisite for the creation of a great and effective opera: 'breadth, simplicity and an eye to decorative effect,' as he says in a letter to a friend. But it was exactly in these qualities, which would have enabled him to treat such subjects as 'The Oprichnik,' 'The Maid of Orleans' and 'Mazeppa' with greater power and freedom, that the composer was lacking. Tchaikovsky had great difficulty in escaping from his intensely emotional personality, and in viewing life through any eyes but his own. Now opera, above all, cannot be 'a one-man piece.' For its successful realisation it demands breadth of conception, variety of sentiment and sympathy, powers of subtle adaptability to all kinds of situations and emotions other than our own. In short, opera is the one form of musical art in which the objective outlook is indispensable. Of Tchaikovsky's operas, the two which seem destined to live longest are those into which he was able, by the nature of their literary contents, to infuse most of his own temperament and lyrical inspiration; but they are not masterpieces of lyric opera.

SYMPHONIC WORKS.—Although it is remarkable that Tchaikovsky constantly alternated between the symphonic poem and the symphony, his progress in the latter form was fairly logical and continuous. Omitting the first ('Winter Day–dreams') as standing essentially apart from the rest, each of his symphonies shows a steady advance on its predecessor. A few critics have ranked the fifth above the sixth, but this opinion is probably the reaction which follows upon satiety, and is hardly likely to be the verdict of posterity. Individually each symphony has its own definite character and colour-scheme, and reflects the prevailing influence under which it was written. The second ('Little-Russian') shows the composer strongly dominated by national tendencies. The third is clearly a reaction from exclusive nationalism, and is tinctured throughout by his increasing eclecticism, and particularly by his newly awakened enthusiasm for Schumann. The fourth, which was almost contemporary with 'Eugen Oniegin,' is remarkable for its brighter qualities and gleams of unwonted humour. Written during a time of profound

mental depression, it is something of a psychological paradox, and, like Beethoven's second symphony, might be described as 'a heroic falsehood.' The fifth has touches of religious sentiment—in the Choral-like introduction to the second movement and the *Andante maestoso* which precedes the finale—that are lacking in all the others. In the sixth, Tchaikovsky has concentrated the brooding melancholy which is the most characteristic and recurrent of all his emotional phases. Tchaikovsky never carried out his intention of writing down the programme of this symphony, but he tells us that 'it is penetrated by subjective sentiment.' The overwhelming energy of the third movement and the abysmal sorrow of the finale seem, however, to express something more than personal apprehension and despair. The last movement is calamitous rather than 'pathetic,' and truly Elizabethan in the intensity of its tragic significance. It voices 'une lamentation large et souffrance inconnue.' This latest inspiration of Tchaikovsky's will always remain the most profoundly moving of all his works, because it ponders one of the great preoccupations of all ages,—the impenetrable mystery of death and futility of all human speculation.

Of the works avowedly composed upon a literary basis, three stand out as worthy to rank with the fifth and sixth symphonies: the vigorous and picturesque orchestral fantasia 'The Tempest'; the overture 'Romeo and Juliet,' suggested by Balakirev and carried out with such ardent conviction that the work seems to glow and throb with youthful passion and tenderness; and the orchestral fantasia 'Francesca da Rimini,' one of those fateful and poignant subjects so perfectly adapted to Tchaikovsky's temperament that he has made of it the most poetical and beautiful of all his examples of programme music.

Tchaikovsky's orchestral suites count among his most popular works. They show off his masterly orchestration more completely perhaps than any of his compositions. The third, in G major, which ends with the well-known air and variations, although not more richly scored than the second (op. 53), is far the better of the two as regards thematic material. The fourth is constructed upon certain themes borrowed from his favourite composer, Mozart, and is appropriately scored for a small orchestra, without trombones. The 'Casse-Noisette' suite (op. 71a) is, however, his *chef-d'œuvre* as regards charm and novelty of instrumentation. It has conveyed a lesson which is both useful and dangerous; that musical ideas which have no pretensions to sublimity may be made exceedingly fascinating by means of brilliant orchestration and piquant accessories. In this work Tchaikovsky employed the celesta for the first time, and we must give him credit for an innovation which now threatens to become as great a commonplace of orchestration as the xylophone. While speaking of Tchaikovsky's instrumentation, mention must be made of the Italian Capriccio, a work of unshadowed gaiety and abounding in striking effects.

The greater part of Tchaikovsky's compositions for piano were written to order, and show very little inspiration or even ingenuity. Unlike most Russian composers he had no special mastery of pianoforte technique, such as makes the works of Balakirev, Liadov and Stcherbatchev acceptable to virtuosi. His single pianoforte sonata is heavy in material and in treatment, and cannot be reckoned a fine example of its kind. A few of his fugitive pieces are agreeable, and the variations in F show that at the time of their composition he must have been interested in thematic development, but the world would not be much the poorer for the loss of all that he has written for piano solo. In combination with other instruments, however, he rises to a much higher level in his handling of the pianoforte. His first pianoforte concerto, composed in 1874, was very severely handled by Nicholas Rubinstein. Von Bülow, on the other hand, pronounced it 'perfect and mature in form, and full of style —in the sense that the intentions and craftsmanship are everywhere concealed.' In after years Tchaikovsky must have concurred with Rubinstein's opinion that the solo part was capable of considerable improvement, and the brilliant 'duel between piano and orchestra,' now so popular with pianists, is the completely revised version of 1889. The second concerto, in G major, is a sound piece of workmanship, more conventional in form than its predecessor, but not to be compared with it as regards the interest of its thematic material, or those qualities of warmth and pulsing vitality which carry us away in the B flat minor concerto.

CHAMBER MUSIC.—Kashkin, in his reminiscences of Tchaikovsky, tells us that the latter knew very little chamber music in his early years, and that the timbre of the string quartet was absolutely distasteful to him. He soon modified this opinion, however, and wrote his first string quartet, in D major, in 1871. It is a clear, perfectly accessible work, which shows the composer in one of his sanest and tenderest moods. The lovely folk-song on which the slow movement is built has largely contributed to the popularity of this quartet. Tchaikovsky followed it up by two others, belonging respectively to the years 1873 and 1876. The second quartet, in F, betrays the orchestral composer in its solidity of structure and straining after too weighty effects. The finale, in rondo form, is an interesting and vigorous movement. The third quartet, in E flat minor, dedicated to the memory of the violinist Laub, is undoubtedly the finest work of the three, both as regards mastery of form and the quality of the musical

ideas. In its emotional mood it is distinctly akin to the sixth symphony and the pianoforte trio. It leaves us with the conviction that had he cared to persevere with the string quartet as persistently as with the symphony, he might have achieved increasingly fine results. For a long time Tchaikovsky resisted the entreaties of Nadejda von Meck to compose a pianoforte trio, assuring her that it was torture to him to have to listen to the combination of the piano with violin and violoncello. But the day came when—as with the string quartet—he relinquished this prejudice and wrote his pianoforte trio (op. 50) 'in memory of a great artist'— Nicholas Rubinstein. In the second movement of this work appear the twelve variations which embody Tchaikovsky's memories of Rubinstein and his musical characteristics at various periods of his life. In spite of its great length, the trio never wearies us in the hands of artists who know how to bring out its depth of feeling and endless variety of effects. Tchaikovsky is always profoundly touching in his elegiac vein, and this trio is worthy to rank among the loveliest of musical laments. Another work belonging to the category of chamber music, but totally different in character, is the sextet for strings, op. 70. It was completely revised before its publication in 1892, and it is a pity that it is so seldom heard, for, like the Italian Capriccio, it is written in one of the composer's rare veins of happiness and serenity.

SONGS.—Tchaikovsky was a prolific songwriter, and left in all about 107 songs. Of these, a comparatively small portion are really of fine quality. The chief defect of his instrumental writing—the repetition and development *ad nauseam* of an idea which is too thin to bear such over-elaboration—is even more obvious in his songs. Another, and even more radical defect, springs from an indiscriminate choice of words. This want of respect for the relationship between music and fine verse leads to an irritating trick of interrupting his phrases by frequent and unnecessary pauses. Tchaikovsky was a gifted melodist, and some of his cantilenas are remarkable for their beauty and touching qualities. His songs, moreover, are eminently vocal, and usually end in a showy climax that endears them to the singer's heart. As regards harmony, they are generally interesting, but not so strikingly original in this respect as those of Borodin and Rimsky-Korsakov. Another fault—though some consider it an added fascination—is the monotonous vein of sentimental melancholy which runs through about two-thirds of Tchaikovsky's songs. But notwithstanding these deprecatory remarks, which apply more particularly to his earlier songs, it is not difficult to pick out a good number which show the master hand. There are also many potentially fine songs in spite of their imperfections of form, and a whole group of songs that we love in spite of their faults, because when we hear them they take our emotions by storm. In the first category I should place the 'Modern Greek Song,' founded on a mediæval *Dies Irae* and treated with consummate skill. As specimens of intensity of emotion few of his songs equal ' The Dread Moment ' (op. 28) and ' Day reigns ' (' Only for thee ') ; in the first we have the utterance of despairing passion, in the second the exultation and fervour of love crying aloud for recognition and fulfilment. In complete emotional contrast to these are the ' Slumber Song ' (op. 16)—the words of which are a Russian version by Maikov of a Greek folk-poem—which is remarkable for tender and restrained sentiment, and ' Don Juan's Serenade ' (op. 38), a dashing song, with a characteristic ritornelle. Tchaikovsky has been very happily inspired by the verses of Count Alexis Tolstoi, who wrote the text for his popular song ' A Ballroom Meeting,' in which the music, with its languid valse rhythm, reflects so subtly the paradoxical musings of the lover, vaguely captivated by a vision of radiant beauty that may signify ' woe or delight.' In op. 54, Sixteen Songs for Children, the ' tearful minor ' is less conspicuous and the majority of the songs has an echo of national melody. It is impossible to deny the charm, the penetrating sweetness and sadness and the vocal excellence of many of Tchaikovsky's songs. At the same time, if we compare him with Schubert or Schumann, with Brahms or Hugo Wolf—or even with his own countrymen Dargomijsky and Balakirev—it is equally impossible to place him in the front rank of song-writers.

The time of prejudice against Tchaikovsky's music on the ground of its national peculiarities has long since gone by ; at least in this country, where his reception has always been more enthusiastic than critical. As regards its powers of endurance, the prophetic spirit is hardly needed in order to foresee the waning popularity of a few of his works which have run a course of sensational success. The world is growing weary of the overture ' 1812,' and perhaps also of the evanescent charms of ' The Chinese Dance ' and the ' Sugar-plum Fairy.' But it would be a rash critic who would venture to set a term for the total extinction of such of Tchaikovsky's symphonic and operatic music as bears the full impress of his individuality. There is enough fire, human and divine, in such works as the four later symphonies, the overture 'Romeo and Juliet,' ' Francesca da Rimini,' the pianoforte concerto in B flat minor, the third string quartet, and the operas ' Eugen Oniegin ' and ' Pique-Dame ' to ensure them a long lease of life. If Tchaikovsky does not bear a supreme message to the world, he has many things to say which are of the greatest interest to humanity, and he says them with such warmth and intimate feeling that they seem less a revela-

tion than an unexpected effluence from our own innermost being. His music, with its strange combination of the sublime and the platitudinous, will always touch the average hearer, to whom music is—and ever will be—more a matter of feeling than of thought. Therefore, if we must pose the inevitable question—How long will Tchaikovsky's music survive ?—we can but make the obvious reply : As long as the world holds temperaments akin to his own : as long as pessimism and torturing doubt overshadow mortal hearts who find their cry re-echoed in the intensely subjective, deeply human music of this poet who weeps as he sings, and embodies so much of the spirit of his age ; its weariness, its disenchantment, its vibrant sympathy and morbid regretfulness.

LIST OF TCHAIKOVSKY'S WORKS

Op.
1. Two Pianoforte Pieces (Russian Scherzo, and Impromptu).
2. Three Pianoforte Pieces (Souvenir de Hapsal).
3. Fragments of Opera, ' The Voyevode.'
4. Valse Caprice in D for pianoforte.
5. Romance in F minor for pianoforte.
6. Six Songs.
7. Valse Scherzo (A major) for pianoforte.
8. Capriccio (G flat) for pianoforte.
9. Three Pianoforte Pieces (Rêverie, Polka, Mazurka).
10. Two Pianoforte Pieces (Nocturne and Humoreske).
11. Quartet No. 1 (D major) for strings.
12. Music to Ostrovsky's ' Sniegourochka ' (The Snow-Maiden).
13. Symphony No. 1 in G minor (' Winter Day-Dreams ').
14. ' Vakoula the Smith ' (also known as ' Cherevichek and ' Le Caprice d'Oxane '), opera in three acts.
15. Overture on the Danish National Hymn.
16. Six Songs.
17. Symphony No. 2 in C minor (' Little Russian ').
18. Symphonie Fantasia ' The Tempest,' for full orchestra.
19. Six Pianoforte Pieces.
20. ' The Swan Lake ' (Ballet).
21. Six Pianoforte Pieces.
22. Quartet No. 2 (in F major) for strings.
23. Pianoforte Concerto No. 1 in B♭ minor.
24. ' Eugen Oniegin,' opera in three acts.
25. Six Songs.
26. Sérénade mélancolique in B flat minor for violin.
27. Six Songs.
28. Six Songs.
29. Symphony No. 3 (in D major), 'The Polish.'
30. Quartet No. 3 (in E flat minor) for strings.
31. Slavonic March for full orchestra.
32. Symphonic fantasia, ' Francesca da Rimini,' for full orchestra.
33. Variations on a Rococo Theme for violoncello and orchestra.
34. Valse scherzo for violin and orchestra.
35. Concerto for violin and orchestra.
36. Symphony No. 4 (in F minor).
37. Pianoforte Sonata in G major.
37a. ' The Months.' Twelve pieces for the pianoforte.
38. Six Songs.
39. Twenty-four easy Pianoforte Pieces (Kinderalbum).
40. Twelve pieces for pianoforte.
41. Liturgy of St. John Chrysostom for four-part mixed choir.
42. ' Souvenir d'un lieu cher,' three pieces for violin with pianoforte accompaniment.
43. First Suite in D major for full orchestra.
44. Pianoforte Concerto No. 2 in G major.
45. Caprice Italien for full orchestra.
46. Six vocal duets.
47. Seven Songs.
48. Serenade in C major for stringed orchestra.
49. ' The Year 1812,' festival overture for full orchestra.
50. Pianoforte trio in A minor.
51. Six Pianoforte Pieces.
52. Russian service, ' First Vespers,' for four-part choir.
53. Second Suite in C major for full orchestra.
54. Sixteen children's songs with pianoforte accompaniment.
55. Third Suite in G major for full orchestra.
56. Fantasia for Pianoforte and orchestra.
57. Six Songs.
58. ' Manfred,' Symphonic Poem for full orchestra.
59. ' Dumka,' Russian village scene, for pianoforte.
60. Twelve Songs.
61. Fourth Suite, ' Mozartiana,' for full orchestra.
62. ' Pezzo capriccioso ' for violoncello with orchestral accompaniment.
63. Six Songs.
64. Symphony No. 5 in E minor.
65. Six Songs to French words.
66. ' Sleeping Beauty ' (Ballet in three acts and prologue).
67. ' Hamlet,' Overture fantasia for full orchestra.
67a. Incidental music to ' Hamlet.'
68. ' Queen of Spades ' (' Pique-Dame '), opera in three acts, and seven scenes.
69. ' Iolanthe,' lyrical opera in one act.
70. ' Souvenir de Florence,' sextet in D minor for strings.
71. ' Casse-Noisette,' Fairy Ballet in two acts and three scenes.
71a. ' Casse-Noisette ' suite, arranged for orchestra from the above.
72. Eighteen Pianoforte Pieces.

Op.
73. Six Songs.
74. Symphony No. 6 in B minor, ' The Pathetic,' for full orchestra.
75. Pianoforte Concerto No. 3, in E flat.
76. Overture to Ostrovsky's ' The Storm.'
77. ' Fatum,' Symphonic Poem.
78. ' The Voyevode,' Symphonic ballad for full orchestra.
79. Andante and Finale, for pianoforte and orchestra.

WORKS WITHOUT OPUS NUMBERS

Operas : ' Undine,' ' Mazeppa,' ' The Oprichnik,' ' Joan of Arc,'
    ' The Enchantress.'
Orchestral Works : ' Romeo and Juliet,' Symphonic Poem ; ' Corona-
    tion March ' ; ' Marche solennelle ' ; ' Elegy ' for stringed
    orchestra.
Vocal Music : Choruses, ' Moscow.' Cantata, ' Nature and Love.'
    Hymn in honour of SS. Cyril and Methodius. Nine Church
    choruses. ' The Nightingale.' ' Hommage à A. Rubinstein.'
    Male Voice Chorus.
Solo : Five Songs.
Duet : ' Romeo and Juliet.'
Quartet : ' Night.'
Pianoforte Music : Three Impromptus.
Pianoforte Music : Valse scherzo. Perpetuum mobile (Weber) for
    left hand.
Theoretical : Guide to the Study of Harmony. Various literary
    and critical Essays.

BIBLIOGRAPHY

The Life and Letters of Peter Ilich Tchaikovsky, by his brother
MODESTE TCHAIKOVSKY. Russian edition. 3 vols., P. Jurgenson,
Moscow, 1900–02. German edition, 2 vols., P. Jurgenson, Leipzig
and Moscow, 1900–02. English edition, translated and edited with
a preface by Rosa Newmarch, 1 vol., demy 8vo, John Lane, London
and New York, 1906. *Tchaikovsky, His Life and Works*, by ROSA
NEWMARCH (embodying most of Kashkin's *Reminiscences*, extracts
from the composer's critical writings and the Diary of his Tour
Abroad in 1888), Grant Richards, London, 1900. The same book
reissued, without the author's co-operation, with additional matter
by EDWIN EVANS, William Reeves, 1907. *Tchaikovsky* by E.
MARKHAM LEE, M.A., Mus.D. Vol. ii. of the *Music of the Masters*
series, John Lane, London. These are the chief sources of information in the English language.   R. N.

TCHEREPNIN, (1) NICOLAI NICOLAIEVITCH
(*b.* St. Petersburg, May 15, 1873), pianist, conductor and composer, abandoned a legal career
to devote himself to music. He entered the
Conservatoire of his native city in 1895, his
principal studies being pianoforte and composition, the latter under Rimsky-Korsakov, whose
influence is obvious in his earlier works. Before
leaving the Conservatoire in 1898, he already
appeared as pianist and conductor in the
Russian capital and provinces. In 1901 he
became conductor of the Belaiev Symphony
Concerts, and an appointment in a similar
capacity at the Marinsky Theatre followed soon
afterwards. Tcherepnin was also for a time
in charge of the orchestral class at the Conservatoire. In 1908 he went to Paris to conduct
Russian opera for the company directed by
Sergei Diaghilev, to which he remained attached
until 1914, visiting various European capitals.
He was in Petrograd 1914–18, at the end of
which term he was appointed principal of the
Conservatoire at Tiflis. In 1921 he left Russia
and settled permanently in Paris.

Tcherepnin's music seems curiously influenced by the outward circumstances of his
career. In his early works, where the influence
of his master, Rimsky-Korsakov, is uppermost,
he scarcely distinguishes himself by any
strongly personal characteristics from the
numerous eclectic composers of his generation
who emerged in considerable numbers from the
Conservatoires of St. Petersburg and Moscow.
Up to and including the ballet, ' Le Pavillon
d'Armide,' his music, though not wanting in
technical finish and a certain smooth attractiveness, lacks individuality and a Lefinite æsthetic
direction. Such personal features as began to

emerge about this time—the piano concerto in
C sharp minor is typical of this period—show a
tendency to harden into mannerisms, due to
a certain uniformity of inventive resource,
especially as regards formal construction. The
visit to Paris brought Tcherepnin under French
influence, which is particularly apparent in the
ballet of ' Narcissus,' a refined and delightful
work performed with much success by the
Diaghilev company. The composer's return
to his native country seems to have awakened,
perhaps by way of reaction, his national consciousness, which, it is true, manifests itself to
some extent even in the earlier works, such
as the charming piano pieces on the Russian
alphabet, based on a children's picture-book,
which also show his happy gift of pictorial
suggestion. But the Russian national note is
sounded more strongly in works of the last
period, of which the ballet, ' A Russian Fairy
Tale,' produced by Anna Pavlova, may serve
as a typical example. This work also shows
indebtedness to Stravinsky. The latest Ballet
(1925), entitled ' The Romance of a Mummy,'
is comparatively poor.

Among the works not mentioned above are :

Ballets, ' The Masque of the Red Death ' (after Poe), ' The Tale
of the Princess Oulyba,' and ' Dionysius ' ; an early Symphony ;
a Sinfonietta ; symphonic poems, ' Narcissus and Echo ' and ' The
Enchanted Kingdom ' ; the Witches' Scene from ' Macbeth ' for
orchestra ; an orchestral suite, ' The Enchanted Garden ' ; Overture to Rostand's ' La Princesse lointaine ' ; Lyric Poem for
violin and orchestra ; String Quartet in A minor ; 2 Masses ; and
a long series of songs and piano pieces.

His son (2) ALEXANDER NICOLAIEVITCH
(*b.* St. Petersburg, Jan. 8 (O.S.), 1899), pianist
and composer, studied theory and composition
under his father, Liadov, Sokolov and Thomas
Alexandrovitch Hartmann, and the piano
under Anna Essipov. Precociously gifted, he
showed great facility at the piano and composed tentatively from early childhood. His
first three works for piano were published by
Belaiev when he was still in Russia, but in
1921 he accompanied his father to Paris.
There he continued his studies at the Conservatoire, Gédalge being his professor of composition
and Philipp giving the final polish to his already
brilliant piano-playing. He appears frequently
as pianist in Paris and in the French provinces,
and has also given recitals in London, Berlin,
Vienna and other European centres.

As a composer Alexander Tcherepnin has
already proved extraordinarily prolific. At the
age of 25 he had between thirty and forty
published works to his credit. His music is
not free from influences, those of his father
and of Prokofiev predominating. His work,
however, never falls into the somewhat sentimental lyricism that occasionally mars the
former's music, or into the dry angularity that
is so characteristic of the latter. It shows an
exuberant gift of fantastic invention, tempered
by a certain sense of humour and proportion
which generally keeps the composer from

inflating small ideas to fill large forms. His most successful works are therefore those on a small scale, especially many of the sets of fanciful and attractive pieces for his own instrument. The larger works, such as the sonatas and the piano concertos, although well made, show less individuality.

Apart from the numerous shorter pieces for piano, Tcherepnin has written:

Two concertos, a sonata and a number of studies for PF. ; a sonata for violin and PF. ; two for violoncello and PF. ; a 'Rapsodie géorgienne ' for violoncello and orchestra ; a trio for violin, violoncello and PF. in D minor ; a ' concerto da camera ' for flute, violin and small orchestra ; a string quartet ; 3 pieces for chamber orchestra ; ' Ol-Ol,' an opera in 3 acts ; and the ballet, ' The Frescoes of Ajanta,' produced by Anna Pavlova in 1923 ; unpublished incidental music to Oscar Wilde's *Salome*, Hugo von Hofmannsthal's *Elektra*, Romain Rolland's *L'Esprit triomphant* and Gerhard Hauptmann's *Hannele*.

E. B.

TECHNICON. In the last quarter of the 19th century an American invention obtained some considerable success under this name (Brotherhood's Patent). Besides the keys, made on the pattern of the DIGITORIUM (*q.v.*) there are various appliances for strengthening the *lifting* power of the fingers, and thus helping in the acquirement of muscular control ; all the springs can be regulated so as to offer different degrees of resistance. See the *Proceedings of the Mus. Association*, 1888–89, p. 1.

M.

TECHNIPHONE, See VIRGIL PRACTICE CLAVIER.

TEDESCA, ALLA (Italian), ' in the German style.' ' Tedesca ' and ' Deutsch ' are both derived from an ancient term which appears in mediæval Latin as *Theotisca*. Beethoven employs it twice in his published works—in the first movement of op. 79, the sonatina in G and in the fifth movement of the B♭ quartet (op. 130).

In one of the sketches for this movement (in B♭) it is inscribed ' Allemande Allegro.'

In a Bagatelle, No. 3 of op. 119, he uses the term in French—' A l'allemande,' but in this case the piece has more affinity to the presto of the sonatina than to the slower movement of the dance. All three are in G. The term ' tedesca,' says Bülow, has reference to waltz rhythm, and invites changes of time. (See TEUTSCHE.)

G.

TE DEUM LAUDAMUS. It is now generally agreed that this great canticle owes its origin to Nicetas, Bishop of Remesiana in Dacia (*fl.* A.D. 400). It soon found an abiding-place in Latin services as the climax of the service of Nocturns or Matins on festivals, and it has been continually utilised separately as an act of thanksgiving on special occasions.

The traditional melody described below is coeval with the words, and indeed in some respects it is older than they in their present form, and reveals the history of the development of the canticle. It consists of three sections (*a*) recounting the praise of the Trinity from ' We praise Thee ' to ' the Comforter ';

(*b*) the praise of Christ, from ' Thou art the King,' onward, ending with two verses of prayer,' ' We therefore pray Thee, etc.,' and ' Make them to be numbered, etc.' ; (*c*) a series of versicles and responses like the sets in use elsewhere in services both Latin and English, ' O Lord, save Thy people, etc.,' to the end. These sections are treated separately so far as music goes. The first section (*a*) is freely set partly to a plastic chant-form but partly to independent music, thus :

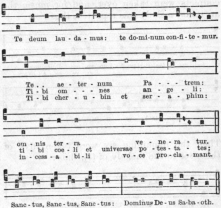

The second strain is then resumed, being modified as the words require, *e.g.* :

With section (*b*) the melody changes to one which may be thus represented in its full and its compressed forms :

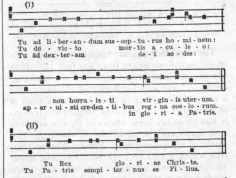

This tune is of the nature of a psalm tone of the 4th mode ; it is natural, therefore, to find the last verse of the section set independently as an antiphon, thus :

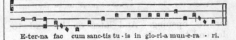

E-ter-na fac cum sanc-tis tu - is in glo-ri-a mun-e-ra ri.

This is probably the original close of the canticle. But when it was inserted into the Nocturn service (taking the place of the old morning hymn, the *Gloria in Excelsis*, which was promoted to form part of the Eucharist), it found itself closely associated with a set of versicles and responses which had hitherto followed the *Gloria in Excelsis*. It incorporated them, therefore, and extended its music to them. Apparently the incorporation took place in two stages (1) the first two couplets were taken over, and for music the antiphon melody was repeated, thus :

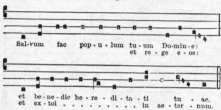

Sal-vum fac pop-u-lum tu-um Do-min-e:
                          et re-ge e-os:

et be-ne-dic he-re-di-ta-ti   tu-ae.
et ex-tol . . . . in ae-ter-num.

Then the remaining six were taken, five of them set to the melody of (*b*), thus :

Per sing-u- . . . . . los di-es:
Et lau-da-mus nomen   tu-um in sae-cu-lum':
Dig-na-re domine   di- is-to:

be-ne-di-ci-mus   te:'
et in sae-cu-lum sae- - cu-li.
si-ne pec-ca-to   nos cus-to-di- - re:

Then for the sixth and last the antiphon melody is again used, as follows :

In te do-mi-ne spe-ra-vi: non con-fun-dar in ae-ter-num.

The simplicity and magnificence of this treatment, even apart from the fact that it is the original and proper music of the canticle, ought to have won for it greater attention and a more lasting place in church services than is at present its lot. So far as English services go it has probably been obscured by the adaptation made and published by Merbecke in the *Booke of Common Praier Noted*. The restriction which seems to have been imposed upon Merbecke of setting only one note to a syllable made a satisfactory adaptation impossible. He was reduced, *e.g.* to

We prayse the o lorde: we know-lege the to be the lorde:

for his opening. And later on he had to descend to—

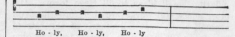

Ho-ly,   Ho-ly,   Ho-ly

instead of the rolling phrase of the original. Happily now a proper adaptation to the English text is to be found among the publications of the Plain-song Society or in Novello's *Manual of Plain-song*.

The canticle has sometimes profited by, and sometimes suffered from, many later settings.[1] (See SERVICE.)   W. H. F.

The beauty of the old melody has led to its frequent adoption as a canto fermo for polyphonic masses ; as in the case of the fifth and sixth masses—'In Te, Domine, speravi,' for five voices, and 'Te Deum laudamus,' for six—in Palestrina's ninth book. But the number of polyphonic settings is less than that of many other hymns of far inferior interest. The reason of this must be sought for in the immense popularity of the plain-song melody in Italy, and especially in the Roman States. Every peasant knows it by heart ; and from time immemorial it has been sung in the crowded Roman churches at every solemn thanksgiving service by the people of the city and the wild inhabitants of the Campagna, with a fervour which would have set polyphony at defiance. There are, however, some very beautiful examples ; especially one by Felice Anerio, printed by Proske in vol. iv. of 'Musica divina,' from a MS. in the Codex Altaemps. Othobon., based on the ancient melody, and treating the alternate verses only of the text. The 'Tertius tomus musici operis ' of Jakob Händl contains another very fine example, in which all the verses are set for two choirs, which, however, only sing alternately. Another important setting of the 16th century is that for 8 voices by Jacobus VAET (*q.v.*). For the treatment of the English text as part of the office of Matins see SERVICE.

It remains to notice another method of treatment by which the text of the Te Deum has been illustrated with extraordinary success. The custom of singing the hymn on occasions of national thanksgiving naturally led to the composition of great works, with orchestral accompaniment and extended movements, both for solo voices and chorus. Among these must be classed the compositions for many choirs, with organ and orchestral accompaniment, by Benevoli and other Italian masters of the 17th century, which were composed for special festivals, and never afterwards permitted to see the light. Sarti wrote a Te Deum to Russian text, by command of the Empress Catherine II., in celebration of Prince Potemkin's victory at Otchakous, in which he introduced fireworks and cannon. Notwithstanding

---

[1] The attention of composers may well be drawn to the Bishop of Salisbury's exposition of the principles which should govern settings in his little brochure, *The Te Deum* (S.P.C.K., 1902).

this extreme measure the work is a fine one; but far inferior to that composed by Graun in 1756 by command of Frederick the Great, in commemoration of the Battle of Prague, and first performed at Charlottenburg in 1762 at the close of the Seven Years' War.

The earliest English setting of this type was that written by Purcell for St. Cecilia's Day, 1694; a work which must at least rank as one of the greatest triumphs of the school of the restoration. For many years it was known only in the curiously garbled version of Boyce, but the true text was restored by Sir J. F. BRIDGE (*q.v.*). In 1695 Blow wrote a Te Deum, with accompaniments for two violins, two trumpets and bass—the exact orchestra employed by Purcell; and not long afterwards Croft produced another work of the same kind, and for the same instruments.

The first sacred music which Handel composed to English words was the 'Utrecht Te Deum,' the MS. of which is dated Jan. 14, 1712.[1] Up to this time Purcell's Te Deum had been annually performed at St. Paul's, for the festival of the SONS OF THE CLERGY (*q.v.*). In 1713 Handel's 'Utrecht Te Deum' found a place in that festival, where also subsequently the 'Dettingen Te Deum' received frequent performance. In contrapuntal resources the 'Utrecht Te Deum' is even richer than that with which Handel celebrated the Battle of Dettingen, fought June 27, 1743.

w s. r., rev. with addns.

Among 19th-century settings of the Te Deum on the festival scale that of Berlioz for three choirs, orchestra and organ (written for the Paris Exhibition of 1855) is pre-eminent. Other notable examples are by Bruckner (Vienna, 1885), Dvořák (op. 103) (1896) and Verdi for double choir and orchestra (Paris, 1898). Outstanding English works of the type are those of Sullivan (written for the Diamond Jubilee of Queen Victoria, 1897), Stanford (Leeds Festival, 1898) and Parry. Sullivan's was written to the English text, Stanford's to the Latin. Parry's Latin Te Deum (Hereford Festival, 1900) was revised, amplified and adapted to the English words for the Gloucester Festival of 1913. Another Te Deum was written by Parry to English words for the Coronation of King George V. (1911). Stanford also wrote a Te Deum intended for the peace celebrations of 1918 but not then performed.   c.

TELEMANN, (1) GEORG PHILIPP (*b.* Magdeburg, Mar. 14, 1681; *d.* Hamburg, June 25, 1767), German composer, son of a clergyman, was educated at Magdeburg and at Hildesheim. He received no regular musical training, but by diligently studying the scores of the great masters—he mentions in particular Lully and Campra—made himself master of the science

[1] *I.e.* 1712-13.

of music. In 1700 he went to the university of Leipzig, and while carrying on his studies in languages and science, became in 1704 organist of the Neukirche, and founded a society among the students, called 'Collegium musicum.' He wrote various operas for the Leipzig Theatre before his church appointment. In 1704 he became Kapellmeister to a Prince Promnitz at Sorau, in 1708 Konzertmeister, and then Kapellmeister, at Eisenach, and, still retaining this post, became Musikdirector of the church of St. Catherine, had an official post in connexion with a society called 'Frauenstein' at Frankfort in 1712, and was also Kapellmeister to the Prince of Bayreuth, as well as at the Barfüsserkirche. In 1721 he was appointed cantor of the Johanneum, and Musikdirector of the principal church at Hamburg, posts which he retained till his death. A few details concerning his duties at the Johanneum were found, and published by Max Schneider in the *Sammelbände* of the Int. Mus. Ges. vii. 414 (1906). He made good musical use of repeated tours to Berlin, and other places of musical repute, and his style was permanently affected by a visit of some length to Paris in 1737, when he became strongly imbued with French ideas and taste.

Telemann, like his contemporaries Mattheson and Keiser, is a prominent representative of the Hamburg school in its prime during the first half of the 18th century. In his own day he was placed with Hasse and Graun as a composer of the first rank, but the verdict of posterity has been less favourable. With all his undoubted ability he originated nothing, but was content to follow the tracks laid down by the old contrapuntal school of organists, whose ideas and forms he adopted without change. His fertility was so marvellous that he could not even reckon up his own compositions; indeed it is doubtful whether he was ever equalled in this respect. He was a highly skilled contrapuntist, and had, as might be expected from his great productiveness, a technical mastery of all the received forms of composition. Handel, who knew him well, said that he could write a motet in eight parts as easily as any one else could write a letter, and Schumann quotes an expression of his to the effect that 'a proper composer should be able to set a placard to music'[2]; but these advantages were neutralised by his lack of any earnest ideal, and by a fatal facility naturally inclined to superficiality. He was over-addicted, even for his own day, to realism; this, though occasionally effective, especially in recitatives, concentrates the attention on mere externals, and is opposed to all depth of expression, and consequently to true art. His shortcomings are most patent in his church works, which are of greater historical importance than his operas

[2] *Gesammelte Schriften,* ii. 235. Compare Rameau's 'Qu'on me donne la Gazette de Hollande.'

and other music. The shallowness of the church music of the latter half of the 18th century is distinctly traceable to Telemann's influence, although that was the very branch of composition in which he seemed to have everything in his favour—position, authority and industry. But the mixture of conventional counterpoint with Italian opera air, which constituted his style, was not calculated to conceal the absence of any true and dignified ideal of church music. And yet he composed twelve complete sets of services for the year, forty-four Passions, many oratorios, innumerable cantatas and psalms, thirty-two services for the installation of Hamburg clergy, thirty-three pieces called 'Capitäns-musik,' twenty ordination and anniversary services, twelve funeral and fourteen wedding services—all consisting of many numbers each. Of his oratorios several were widely known and performed, even after his death, especially a 'Passion' to the well-known words of Brockes of Hamburg (1716) (see PASSION MUSIC); another, in three parts and nine scenes, to words selected by himself from the Gospels (his best-known work); 'Der Tag des Gerichts'; 'Die Tageszeiten' (from Zechariah); and the 'Tod Jesu' and the 'Auferstehung Christi,' both by Ramler (1730 and 1757). To these must be added forty operas for Hamburg, Eisenach and Bayreuth, and an enormous mass of vocal and instrumental music of all kinds, including no less than 600 overtures in the French style. Many of his compositions were published, and he even found time to engrave several himself; Gerber (*Lexicon*, ii. 631) gives a catalogue. He also wrote an autobiography, printed in Mattheson's *Ehrenpforte* and *Generalbassschule* (1731, p. 168). 'Der Tag des Gerichts' and 'Ino' are published together in *D.D.T.* xxviii. A fine chorus for two choirs is given in Rochlitz's 'Sammlung' and Hullah's Vocal Scores. Others will be found in Winterfeld, and in a collection—'Beitrag zur Kirchenmusik'—published by Breitkopf. Organ fugues have been printed in Körner's 'Orgel Virtuos.' Very valuable examinations of his church cantatas, and comparisons between them and those of Bach, will be found in Spitta's *Bach* (Transl. i. 490, etc.). Besides the autobiography referred to above, the following contain information about the composer:

CARL ISRAEL, *Frankfurter Konzertchronik im 1730–80* (1876); JOS. SITTARD, *Geschichte des Musik- und Konzertwesens in Hamburg*, 1890; CURT OTTZENN, *Telemann als Opernkomponist* (1902); ROMAIN ROLLAND, *Voyage musical aux pays du passé* (Paris, 1919), Eng. trans. by BERNARD MIALL, 1922; *Singe-, Spiel- und Generalbass-Übungen* (Hamburg, 1733–34), ed. by MAX SEIFFERT (Berlin, 1921); MAX W. FREY, *G. Ph. Telemanns Singe-, Spiel- und Generalbass-Übungen, ein Beitrag zur Geschichte des begleiteten Kunstliedes* (Zürich Dissertation, 1922); *Riemann*.
A. M., addns.

(2) GEORG MICHAEL (*b.* Plöu, Holstein, Apr. 20, 1748; *d.* Riga, Mar. 4, 1831), grandson of Georg Philipp, was accompanist at the Hamburg church choir. He studied theology (1773) and music (1775), becoming cantor and director

of music at Riga, *c.* 1775. He wrote theoretical and didactic works, 2 hymn-books, and composed choral works, a book of trio-sonatas, 6 violin sonatas, and 6 organ preludes. (*Q.-L.*)

TELFORD & TELFORD. WILLIAM TELFORD (*d.* 1885) established an organ factory at 45 Bride Street, Dublin, in 1830. In 1838 he built an organ with pedals for the chapel of Trinity College, replacing that erected by Green. At this date he had just removed into larger premises in Stephen's Green. He added German pedals to the organ of Christ Church Cathedral, and did the same for St. Patrick's. His largest organ was that built for St. Peter's, Radley, which instrument was exhibited at the Great Exhibition in Dublin, in 1853. On his death the business was continued by his two sons, and the firm have built fine organs for the cathedrals of Limerick, Lismore, Thurles, Monaghan, Letterkenny, Enniscorthy and Queenstown, as also for numerous parish churches. The elder brother, W. H. Telford, Mus.B., died Oct. 2, 1905, but the business was carried on by the younger brother, Edward, in Stephen's Green. In 1913 it was turned into a Limited Company and the factory removed to Charlemont Street. W. H. G. F.

TELLEFSEN, THOMAS DYKE ACLAND (*b.* Dronthjem, Nov. 26, 1823; *d.* Paris, Oct. 7, 1874), a Norwegian musician, probably named after an Englishman, well known in his day as M.P. for North Devon, who was much in the habit of travelling in Norway.

Tellefsen was a pupil of Chopin, and first came to England with his master in 1848. He was in the habit of returning to this country, had many pupils, and used to give concerts, at one of which he was assisted by Madame Lind-Goldschmidt. Besides publishing several compositions of small value he edited a collection of Chopin's PF. works (Paris, Richault), valuable as embodying the master's personal traditions, and was interesting chiefly from his intimate connexion with that remarkable composer and player. G.

TELL-TALE. A simple mechanical contrivance for giving information to an organblower (and sometimes also to an organist) as to the amount of wind contained in the bellows. A piece of string is fixed by one end to the top board of the bellows and carried over a pulley; a small metal weight is attached to the other end of the string. As the bellows rise the weight descends, as they sink the weight ascends; and the words 'Full' and 'Empty' mark the limits of the journey down and up.
J. S.

TEMPERAMENT (Fr. *tempérament*; Ger. *Temperatur*; cf. Ital. *temperare*, to tune) is the name given to various methods of TUNING, in which certain of the consonant intervals, chiefly the fifth and major third, are intentionally made more or less false or imperfect;

that is to say, either sharper or flatter than exact consonance would require. If, on the contrary, all the consonant intervals are made perfectly smooth and pure, so as to give no BEATS, the tuning is then called JUST INTONATION (*q.v.*).

We shall omit from the present article all reference to the arithmetical treatment of temperament (see INTERVAL), and simply deal with its physical and audible effects. We shall describe the means by which any student may obtain for himself a practical knowledge of the subject, and point out some of the conclusions to which such knowledge will probably lead him.[1] The first and most important thing is to learn by experience the effect of temperament on the quality of musical chords. To carry out this study properly it is necessary to have an instrument which is capable of producing all the combinations of notes used in harmony, of sustaining the sound as long as may be desired, and of distinguishing clearly between just and tempered intonation. These conditions are not fulfilled by the pianoforte ; for, owing to the soft quality of its tones, and the quickness with which they die away, it does not make the effects of temperament acutely felt. The organ is more useful for the purpose, since its full and sustained tones, especially in the reed stops, enable the ear to perceive differences of tuning with greater facility. The harmonium is superior even to the organ for illustrating errors of intonation, being less troublesome to tune and less liable to alter in pitch from variation of temperature or lapse of time.

By playing a few chords on an ordinary harmonium and listening carefully to the effect, the student will perceive that in the usual mode of tuning, called equal temperament, only one consonant interval has a smooth and continuous sound, namely, the octave. All the others are interrupted by *beats*, that is to say, by regularly recurring throbs or pulsations, which mark the deviation from exact consonance. For example, the fifth and fourth, as at (*x*), are each made to give about *one* beat per second. This error is so slight as to be hardly worth notice, but in the thirds and sixths the case is very different. The major third, as at (*y*), gives nearly *twelve* beats per

second : these are rather strong and distinct, and become still harsher if the interval is extended to a tenth or a seventeenth. The major sixth, as at (*z*), gives about *ten* beats

[1] Those who wish to study the subject more in detail may consult — (1) Bosanquet, *Elementary Treatise on Musical Intervals and Temperament* (Macmillan) ; (2) Helmholtz, *Sensations of Tone*, chapters xiv. to xvii., and Ellis's Appendix xix. sections A to G, tables i. to vi. ; (3) Perronet Thompson, *On the Principles and Practice of Just Intonation* ; (4) Woolhouse, *Essay on Musical Intervals*.

per second, which are so violent that this interval in its tempered form barely escapes being reckoned as a dissonance.

The Difference - Tones resulting from these tempered chords are also' thrown very much out of tune, and, even when too far apart to beat, still produce a disagreeable effect, especially on the organ and the harmonium (RESULTANT TONES). The degree of harshness arising from this source varies with the distribution of the notes ; the worst results being produced by chords of the following types :

By playing these examples, the student will obtain some idea of the alteration which chords undergo in equal temperament. To understand it thoroughly, he should try the following simple experiment :

Take an ordinary harmonium and tune two chords perfect on it. One is scarcely enough for comparison. To tune the triad of C major, first raise the G a very little, by scraping the end of the reed, till the fifth, C–G, is dead in tune. Then flatten the third E, by scraping the shank, till the triad C–E–G is dead in tune. Then flatten F till F–C is perfect, and A till F–A–C is perfect. The notes used are easily restored by tuning to their octaves. The pure chords obtained by the above process offer a remarkable contrast to any other chords on the instrument.' [2]

It is only by making one's self practically familiar with these facts, that the nature of temperament can be clearly understood, and its effects in the orchestra, or in accompanied singing, properly appreciated.

EQUAL TEMPERAMENT TUNING.—Against its defects, equal temperament has one great advantage which specially adapts it to instruments with fixed tones, namely, its extreme simplicity from a mechanical point of view. It is the only system of tuning which is complete with *twelve* notes to the octave. This result is obtained in the following manner. If we start from any note on the keyboard (say G♭), and proceed along a series of twelve (tempered) fifths upwards and seven octaves downwards thus—

we come to a note (F♯) identical with our original one (G♭). But this identity is only arrived at by each fifth being tuned somewhat too flat for exact consonance. If, on the contrary, the fifths were tuned perfect, the last note of the series (F♯) would be sharper than

[2] Bosanquet, *Temperament*, p. 6.

the first note (G♭) by a small interval called
the 'Comma of Pythagoras' (see COMMA),
which is about one-quarter of a semitone.
Hence in equal temperament, each fifth ought
to be made flat by one-twelfth of this Comma;
but it is extremely difficult to accomplish this
practically, and the error is always found to be
greater in some fifths than in others. If the
theoretic conditions, which the name 'equal
temperament' implies, could be realised in the
tuning of instruments, the octave would be
equally divided into twelve semitones, six tones,
or three major thirds. Perfect accuracy, indeed, is impossible even with the best-trained
ears, but the following rule, given by Ellis, is
much less variable in its results than the
ordinary process of guesswork. It is this:

> Make all the fifths which lie entirely within the
> octave middle *c'* to treble *c''* beat *once* per second;
> and make those which have their upper notes above
> treble *c''* beat *three* times in *two* seconds. Keeping
> the fifth treble *f'* and treble *c''* to the last, it should
> beat *once* in between *one* and *two* seconds.[1]

In ordinary practice, however, much rougher
approximations are found sufficient.

The present system of tuning by equal temperament was introduced into England at a
comparatively recent date (see TUNING). In
1854 organs built and tuned by this method
were sent out for the first time by Gray &
Davison, Walker and Willis. That year is therefore the date of its definite adoption as the
trade usage in England. There was no equally
tempered organ of English make in the Great
Exhibition of 1851; and before that time the
present system appears to have been only
used in a few isolated cases, as in the organ of
St. Nicholas, Newcastle-upon-Tyne, which was
returned in 1842. For the pianoforte equal
temperament came into use somewhat earlier
than for the organ. It was introduced into
the works of Broadwood about 1846. In
France the change had already taken place,
for Aristide Cavaillé-Coll stated that from 1835
he consistently laboured to carry out the equal
principle in the tuning of his organs.[2] What
little is known of the history of temperament
in Germany seems to show that the new tuning
was employed there at a still earlier date, but
there are reasons for believing that equally
tuned organs had not become general even as
late as the time of Mozart. Emanuel Bach
seems to have been the first musician who
advocated in a prominent manner the adoption
of equal temperament, whence we may infer
that it was unusual in his day.[3] His father is
also said to have employed this system on his
own clavichord and harpsichord; but even
his authority was not sufficient to recommend
it to his contemporary Silbermann, the famous
organ-builder (1683-1753). Still he must have

1 Bosanquet, *Temperament*, p. 5.
2 Ellis, in *Nature* for Aug. 8, 1878, p. 383. For Mersenne's
advocacy of equal temperament as early as 1636 see TUNING.
3 C. P. E. Bach, *Versuch über die wahre Art das Clavier zu spielen*,
Einleitung. sect. 14; published 1753.

obtained some practical system of temperament, since the 'Wohltemperirtes Clavier'
would not have been tolerable to the ear
without some modification of just intonation,
however rough. An earlier builder, Schnitger,
is said to have used something approaching it
in the organ built by him about 1688-93, in the
S. Jacobi church at Hamburg. Before that
time the system appears to have had hardly
more than a theoretic existence in Europe.

THE MEANTONE SYSTEM.—The mode of
tuning which prevailed before the introduction
of equal temperament is called the Meantone
System.[4] Till late in the 18th century this
tuning, or a closely allied variety, was almost
universally employed, both in England and
on the Continent. It was invented by the
Spanish musician Salinas, who was born at
Burgos in 1513, lived for many years in Italy,
and died at Salamanca in 1590.[5] On account
of its historical interest, as well as its intrinsic
merits, the meantone system requires a short
explanation. It will be convenient to take
equal temperament as the standard of comparison, and to measure the meantone intervals
by the number of equal semitones they contain.
The relations of the two systems may therefore
be described as follows.

If we start from say D on the keyboard, and
proceed along a series of four equal temperament fifths upwards and two octaves downwards, thus—

we arrive at a note (F♯) which we employ as
the major third of our original note (D). This
tempered interval (D–F♯) is too sharp for exact
consonance by nearly one-seventh of a semitone; but if we make these fifths flatter than
they would be in equal temperament, then the
interval D–F♯ will approach the perfect major
third. We may thus obtain a number of
systems of tuning according to the precise
amount of flattening we choose to assign to the
fifth. Of this class the most important is the
Meantone System, which is tuned according
to the following rule. First, make the major
third (say D–F♯) perfect; then make all the
intermediate fifths (D–A–E–B–F♯) equally flat
by trial. After a little practice this can be
done by mere estimation of the ear; but if
very accurate results are desired, the following
method may be used. A set of tuning-forks
should be made (say at French pitch) giving
$c' = 260.2$, $g' = 389.1$, $d' = 290.9$, $a' = 435$ vibra-

4 Otherwise Mesotonic; so called because in this tuning the tone
is a *mean* between the major and the minor tones of Just Intonation:
or half a major third. It lingered in England in the tuning of a few
organs in country churches, and according to Yñiguez, organist of
Seville Cathedral, was generally maintained on Spanish organs
until late in the 19th century. See Ellis, *Hist. of Musical Pitch*, in
Journal of Soc. of Arts, Mar. 5, and Apr. 2, 1880, and Jan. 7, 1881.
5 The invention of this temperament has also been attributed to
Zarlino and to Guido d'Arezzo.

tions per second. The notes c', g', d', a' of the instrument should be tuned in unison with the forks, and all other notes can be obtained by perfect major thirds and perfect octaves above or below these (see Tuning).

There is one difficulty connected with the use of the Meantone System, namely, that it requires more than twelve notes to the octave, in order to enable the player to modulate into any given key. This arises from the nature of the system ; for as twelve meantone fifths fall short of seven octaves, the same sound cannot serve both for G♭ and for F♯. Hence if we tune the following series of meantone fifths

E♭–B♭–F–C–G–D–A–E–B–F♯–C♯–G♯

on the piano, or on any other instrument with twelve notes to the octave, we shall have only six major scales (B♭, F, C, G, D, A), and three minor scales (G, D, A). When the remoter keys are required, the player has to strike G♯ instead of A♭, or E♭ instead of D♯, producing an intolerable effect. For in the Meantone System the interval G♯–E♭ is sharper than the perfect fifth by nearly one-third of a semitone, and the four intervals B–E♭, F♯–B♭, C♯–F, G♯–C, are each sharper than the perfect major third by more than three-fifths of a semitone. The extreme roughness of these chords caused them to be compared to the howling of wolves. (See Wolf.)

To get rid of the ' wolves ' many plans were tried. For instance, the G♯ was sometimes raised till it stood half-way between G and A ; but the result was unsatisfactory, for the error thus avoided in one place had to be distributed elsewhere. This was called the method of Unequal Temperament, in which the notes played by the white keys were left in the meantone system, while the error was accumulated on those played by the black keys. The more usual scales were thus kept tolerably in tune while the remote ones were all more or less false. Such a make-shift as this could not be expected to succeed, and the only purpose it served was to prepare the way for the adoption of Equal Temperament.

The Meantone System is sometimes described as an Unequal Temperament, but wrongly, since in it the so-called ' good keys ' are all equally good ; the ' bad keys ' are simply those for which the necessary notes do not exist when the system is limited to twelve notes per octave. The defect therefore lies not in the system itself, but in its application, and the only legitimate remedy is to increase the number of notes, and so provide a more extended series of fifths. This was well understood from the first, for we find that as early as the 16th century many organs were constructed with extra notes.[1] Salinas

tells us that he had himself played on one in the Dominican Monastery of Santa Maria Novella at Florence. Similar improvements were attempted in England. (See Organ, Vol. III. p. 751.)   J. L.

In former editions of this Dictionary the writer of the above here developed at length an argument for the partial restoration of meantone temperament. This argument was based largely on the researches of Bosanquet,[2] and included a description of the modified keyboard invented by Bosanquet, and now preserved in the Victoria and Albert Museum, South Kensington. The writer further discussed with musicians the experiments made by Helmholtz[3] and by two French savants, Cornu and Mercadier,[4] and pointed to possible modifications in the practice of musicians to which these considerations might lead. Fifty years of experience since the article was written, however, show that music has not taken the directions indicated. On the contrary composers and players of instruments capable of Just Intonation have increasingly tended to think in terms of Equal Temperament, witness the whole-tone scale and other developments of Harmony (q.v.) as well as the proposals of individuals (Busoni, Haba, etc.) to further subdivide the intervals of the scale on arithmetical principles.   c.

TEMPEST, THE. There have been many musical settings of the whole or part of Shakespeare's play, although we have no definite information as to the music used at its earliest representation.

(1) Robert Johnson's settings of ' Full fathom five ' and ' Where the bee sucks ' were first published in Wilson's ' Cheerful Ayres ' in 1600, and are held to be the original settings.

(2) In 1667 Pepys saw the version by Davenant and Dryden which was published in 1670. The version provided considerable scope for music, a ' dialogue sung in parts ' by two devils leading to a dance, one song ' Dry those Eyes ' additional to those of Shakespeare, and further dances. The music used in this production has not been certainly identified.

(3) In 1673, according to Downes,[5] but more probably early in 1674, Shadwell's version, ' made into an Opera,' was produced at the Dorset Gardens Theatre. It is probable that the music by Matthew Locke, the instrumental numbers from which were published, together with his ' Psyche,' in 1675, was composed for Shadwell's version, and that there were ' Entries and Dances ' by another hand (conjectured to be Draghi) omitted from the same publication. It seems equally probable that to this production may be assigned ' the Vocal Musick in the

---

[1] The extra notes were sometimes called ' quartertones,' not a very suitable name, since a quartertone is not a sound, but an interval, and the semitone is not divided equally in the Meantone System.

[2] See Mus. Ass. Proc., May 1, 1875.
[3] Sensations of Tone (Ellis).
[4] Ellis's Appendix to Sensations of Tone, p. 640.
[5] Roscius Anglicanus. W. J. Lawrence, examining the MS. prologue and epilogue written by Shadwell for this production, has shown that the date must have been early in 1674 (The Elizabethan Playhouse, 1912).

Tempest by Mr. Pelh. Humfrey,' since its contents, 'The song of the 3 Divells,' the Masque, the song 'Arise ye subterranean winds' supply the lacunae in Locke's publication.[1] About the same time appeared a collection called 'The Ariel's Songs in the Tempest,' containing four vocal compositions by Banister, including 'Come unto these yellow sands' and 'Full fathom five,' and Pelham Humfrey's 'Where the bee sucks.' In 1676 and 1690 Davenant and Dryden's version was reprinted, and both reprints contain the song, 'Arise, ye subterranean winds,' a setting of which by Pietro Reggio was published in his collection of songs in 1680. There are in the same reprints opportunities for music, such as the masque in Act V. for which no contemporary composition seems to be forthcoming.

(4) The song 'Dear pretty youth' (published in 'Deliciae musicae' in 1695–96) is the only part of Henry Purcell's music to the play that was printed in his lifetime, and there is a remarkable absence of early MSS. of the music he wrote, which was published in 1790 by Goodison. A MS., probably an old theatre copy, of about 1700–10, was bought at Julian Marshall's sale in 1905 by the British Museum; it presents the same compositions as are in Goodison's edition, and in a MS. formerly in Dr. Cummings's possession, which probably dates from the third decade of the 18th century.[2] Purcell's music is held by Barclay Squire to represent a third alteration of Dryden and Davenant's version of the play, and these garbled versions held the stage down to 1745–46, when a return was made to the original form of the play, with Arne's famous music. In 1747 Dryden's version was again revived, but without composer's name for the music performed.[3]

(5) A new transformation of the play into an 'Opera' was brought out by Garrick at Drury Lane in 1756, with music composed or arranged by John Christopher Smith. In 1777 Sheridan brought out the play with music by Thomas Linley.

(6) In 1861 Arthur Sullivan, when a student at the Leipzig Conservatorium, composed incidental music to the play, apparently for no special revival, as its first performance took place at the Crystal Palace, Apr. 5, 1862. It is among the composer's most charming works, although it bears the opus number 1.[4]

M.; with addns. c.

(7) Arthur Bliss composed an overture (chiefly drums, with trumpet, trombone, voices, etc.) and some incidental music for Viola

[1] See W. Barclay Squire in *Musical Quarterly*, vol. 7. p. 571. The discovery of this MS. was made by Mlle. Pereyra in the library of the Paris Conservatoire, and it was first described by her in the *Bulletin de la Société Française de Musicologie*, Oct. 1920, No. 7. See also *Revue Musicale*, 1921, No. 3.
[2] See Preface to the Purcell Society's edition, vol. xix., by Edward J. Dent.
[3] See, on the whole question of these early versions, and in particular of Purcell's music, Barclay Squire's article in the *Sammelbände* of the Int. Mus. Ges. vol. v. pp. 551-55.
[4] *Sammelbände* of the Int. Mus. Ges. vol. v. pp. 551, etc.: information from F. K.

Tree's production of *The Tempest*, Aldwych Theatre, London, 1921.

The following are operas on this subject: (1) text by Scribe, music by Halévy, produced Covent Garden, June 8, 1850 ; Paris, Théâtre Italien, Feb. 25, 1851 ; (2) by Fibich, Prague, 1895 ; (3) in 3 acts, text arranged by Reginald Gatty, music by Nicholas Gatty, Surrey Theatre, Apr. 17, 1920.   c.

TEMPLER UND DIE JÜDIN, DER, opera in 3 acts, text by W. A. Wohlbrück (founded on *Ivanhoe*) ; music by Marschner. Produced Leipzig, Dec. 1829. See also IVANHOE.

TEMPLETON, JOHN (*b*. Riccarton, Kilmarnock, July 30, 1802 ; *d*. New Hampton, July 2, 1886), tenor singer. At the age of 14 he made his first appearance in Edinburgh, and continued to sing in public until his 16th year, when his voice broke. Appointed precentor in Dr. Brown's church, Edinburgh, at the age of 20, he began to attract attention, until Scotland became too limited for his ambition, and he started for London, where he received instruction from Blewitt in thorough-bass, and from Welsh, De Pinna and Tom Cooke in singing. His first theatrical appearance was made at Worthing, as Dermot in 'The Poor Soldier,' in July 1828. This brought about engagements at the Theatre Royal, Brighton, Southampton and Portsmouth, and Drury Lane. He made his first appearance in London, Oct. 13, 1831, as Belville in 'Rosina.' Two days later he appeared as Young Meadows in 'Love in a Village,' Wood taking the part of Hawthorn, with Mrs. Wood (Miss Paton) as Rosetta. After performing for a few months in stock pieces, he created the part of Raimbaut in Meyerbeer's 'Robert le Diable' on its first performance in England, Feb. 20, 1832. He appeared as Lopez in Spohr's 'Der Alchymist' when first produced (Mar. 20, 1832), Bishop's 'Tyrolese Peasant' (May 8, 1832) and John Barnett's 'Win her and wear her' (Dec. 18, 1832) ; but the first production of 'Don Juan' at Drury Lane, Feb. 5, 1833, afforded Templeton a great opportunity. Begrez, after studying the part of Don Ottavio for eight weeks, threw it up a week before the date announced for production. Templeton undertook the character, and a brilliant success followed.

Madame Malibran, in 1833, chose him as her tenor, and 'Malibran's tenor' he remained throughout her brief but brilliant career. On the production of 'La sonnambula,' at Drury Lane, May 1, 1833, Templeton's Elvino was no less successful than Malibran's Amina. After the performance Bellini embraced him, and, with many compliments, promised to write a part that would immortalise him. 'The Devil's Bridge,' 'The Students of Jena' (first time June 4, 1833), 'The Marriage of Figaro,' 'John of Paris,' etc., gave fresh opportunities for Templeton to appear with Malibran, and with marked success. In Auber's 'Gustavus the Third,' produced at Covent Garden, Nov. 13, 1833, he made another great success as Colonel Lillienhorn. During the season the opera was repeated one hundred times. Alfred Bunn, then manager of both theatres, so arranged that Templeton, after playing in 'La Sonnambula' or 'Gustavus the Third' at Covent Garden, had to make his way to Drury Lane to fill the rôle of Masaniello—meeting with equal success at both houses.

On the return of Malibran to England in 1835, the production of 'Fidelio' and of Balfe's 'Maid of Artois' (May 27, 1836) brought her and Templeton again together. Templeton took the leading tenor parts in Auber's 'Bronze Horse' (1836), in Hérold's 'Corsair' (1836), Rossini's 'Siege of Corinth' (1836), in Balfe's 'Joan of Arc' (1837) and 'Diadeste' (1838), in Mozart's 'Magic Flute' (1838), Benedict's 'Gipsy's Warning' (1838), H. Phillips's 'Harvest Queen' (1838), in Donizetti's 'Love Spell' (1839) and in 'La favorita' (1843) on their first performance or introduction as English operas; altogether playing not less than eighty different leading tenor characters.

In 1836–37 Templeton made his first professional tour in Scotland and Ireland with great success. Returning to London, he retained his position for several years. In 1842 he visited Paris with Balfe, and received marked attention from Auber and other musical celebrities. The last twelve years of his professional career were chiefly devoted to the concert-room. In 1846 he starred the principal cities of America with his 'Templeton Entertainments,' in which were given songs illustrative of England, Scotland and Ireland, and as a Scottish vocalist he sang himself into the hearts of his countrymen. He gave his entertainment in Dublin in 1849, with Blewitt as accompanist. Templeton retired in 1852.

With splendid voice, graceful execution and exquisite taste, he excelled alike in the pathetic, the humorous and the heroic; his rendering of 'My Nannie O,' 'Had I a cave,' 'Gloomy winter,' 'Jessie, the Flower o' Dunblane,' 'Corn Rigs,' 'The Jolly Beggar' and 'A man's a man for a' that,' etc., left an impression not easily effaced.   w. h.

TEMPO (PACE). Theoretically, it is an easy matter to fix the pace of a piece of music. The first movement of a symphony consisting of 250 bars of common time takes, let us say, ten minutes to play through, and we mark it accordingly $\downarrow=100$; or we play a piece, naturally and flexibly, for fifteen seconds by the watch and find we have played twenty-five crotchets, multiply these by 4 and write down $\downarrow=100$. Pace is also easy to check. The normal watch ticks 300 to the minute; we put it to our ear and three ticks give us the time of the crotchet as the conductor is taking it,

viz. $\downarrow=100$. All of these may be accurate, but for a single performance only, that is, in one set of conditions.

PACE IS RELATIVE.—But the conditions may vary much. What is right under one conductor, with one orchestra, in one building, is wrong with another. Mozart said that nothing seemed to him so important as the right choice of *tempo*, and he could hardly have said that if it were merely a question of adjusting a tape or a *Taktmesser* (see CONDUCTING, METRONOME). Beethoven's metronome marks, which puzzle us occasionally, dismayed him so much that he thought there must be something wrong with his metronome. The truth is that time is relative to the things that take place in it: an hour is long or short according as we spend it upon half a dozen little jobs or on an exciting book; and to a musician pace is not the number of minutes it takes to play the pages which contain the notation, but the amount of experience he can cram into the music.

PACE AND CHARACTER.—To describe that experience we use words, and these start life meaning degrees of speed—*Lento, Adagio, Andante, Allegro, Presto,* and so forth. But as they go on we find them describing not so much speed as character. Nobody is quite sure, for instance, whether *Andantino* is faster or slower than *Andante,* because composers have used it both ways; but every one agrees that it is livelier than *Poco Andante* and less playful than *Allegretto.* The slow movement of a symphony was (rather than is) frequently called 'the' ADAGIO (*q.v.*), although it is quite commonly marked *Largo* or *Andante.*

ITALIAN TERMS.—If these expressions of *tempo* indicated pace only, there would be a strong argument apart from sentiment for continuing to use the Italian forms of them, which have become technical terms. But since what we chiefly want to know is the composer's own conception of his work, there is much to be said for his expressing it in a language he knows intimately (provided it is one that we may hope to understand) rather than in one which he probably has to learn, perhaps for the occasion and out of a dictionary. There is very little to be said for the Englishman who gives his indications in German or French, as has been done; since these are neither technical nor in a *lingua franca,* which, for music at least, Italian is.

TEXTURE OF MUSIC.—Armed with a knowledge of the composer's style and mood it is not difficult to arrive at the true pace from the texture of the music itself. Full and, especially, spaced harmonies, elaborate counterpoint, variety in the time-units of the melody, the limitations of brass as against wood, or wind against strings, even the comparative somnolence of an afternoon as against an evening performance or the unresponsive acoustics of a large hall, are all factors which, as far as they count, make for slower pace. A capable musician will be alive to these, and his decision should be worth more than the pronouncement of an unthinking machine.   A. H. F. S.

TEMPO ORDINARIO (Ital.), common time, four crotchets in a bar. The time-signature is an unbarred semicircle C, or in modern form C, in contradistinction to the barred semicircle $\mathcal{C}$ or $\mathcal{C}$, which denotes a diminished value of the notes, i.e., a double rate of movement. In consequence of the notes in *tempo ordinario* being of full value (absolutely as well as relatively), the term is understood to indicate a moderate degree of speed. It is in this sense that Handel employs it as an indication for the choruses ' Lift up your heads,' ' Their sound is gone out,' etc.   F. T.

TEMPO RUBATO, see RUBATO.

TEMPUS PERFECTUM ; TEMPUS IMPERFECTUM, see NOTATION, subsection TIME SIGNATURES ; TIME.

TENAGLIA, ANTONIO FRANCESCO, was a Florentine by birth, but it was in Rome that he came under the strong influence of the musicians of the 17th century, who had developed the operatic song or aria into a thing of beauty in which music and words responded to each other. Tenaglia was an apt pupil. In an able appreciation of his musical gifts, Torchi (' Canzoni ed arie italiane ad una voce nel secolo XVII,' 1894) writes that his power of dramatic colouring places him on the level of Carissimi ; the aria ' Non è mai senza duol ' (from a MS. in the Bologna Library), that he picks out for especial praise, contains musical phrases of much pathos, representing closely the feeling of the words.

Little of Tenaglia's music is known, two of his madrigals, ' Madonna udite ' and ' E così pur languendo,' are in the ' Florido concento di madrigali in musica a tre voci. Parte seconda,' published in Rome in 1653.

The Cecilia Society's publications of old Italian music (' Musica scelta ' : published by P. W. Olsen at Copenhagen, about 1855) included a duet, ' Ma se non moto,' for two soprani and the aria ' Begl' occhi mercè ! ' with a pianoforte accompaniment arranged by Enrico Rung.

This aria was again printed with an English translation, ' Take pity, sweet eyes,' by Mary A. Robinson, in Vol. I. of ' Cecilia,' edited by Prof. Schimon and others (published by J. André, Offenbach o.M., 1881–82), and an arrangement for violin or violoncello was made by Franz Ries (' Album-Blätter,' Leipzig,1884).

There is record of an opera composed by Tenaglia ; it is described in Allacci's *Drammaturgia* as

' Cleano. Favola musicale. In Roma per Giacomo Dragondelli. 1661. Poesia di Lodovico Cortesi. Musica di Anton Francesco Tenaglia.'

Nothing more seems to be known of it.

MSS. containing various compositions are in :

British Museum. The Harleian MS. 1265, p. 237, and 1863, p. 201. Copies of ' Son disperato, abbandonato ' for three voices, by Sig. Gio. Franco. Tenaglia.
Bologna Liceo Musicale. In vol. iv. of secular music by composers in Rome, ' Se fosse così conforme voi dite ' and ' Misero chi si fida ' for soprano with basso continuo, by Gio. Fr. Tenaglia. (Gaspari's Catalogue, iii. 258.)
Vienna Hofbibliothek. In MS. 17,763, ' Il nocchier, che torna,' and ' O che bizzarro humor,' arie by Antonio Francesco Tenaglia. (Mantuani's Catalogue.)
Florence R. Istituto Musicale. MS. includes three arie for solo voice with figured bass by Tenaglia. Eitner mentions compositions in the Bibliothek Wagener and in the Modena Library.
                                            C. S.

TENDUCCI, GIUSTO FERDINANDO (b. Siena, c. 1736 ; d. Italy, early 19th century), a celebrated sopranist, very popular in England. Like a still greater singer, he was sometimes called Senesino from his birthplace. His earliest stage appearances in Italy were made at about 20 years of age, and in 1758 he came to London, where he first sang in a pasticcio called ' Attalo.' But it was in the ' Ciro riconosciuto ' of Cocchi that he first attracted special notice. Although he had only a subordinate part, he quite eclipsed, by his voice and style, the principal singer, Portenza, and from that time was established as the successor of Guadagni. He appeared in Dublin, at the Smock Alley Theatre, in Arne's ' Artaxerxes,' on Feb. 18, 1765. O'Keeffe says that his singing of ' Water parted from the sea ' created a furore ; in July he appeared in ' Amintas ' (his own alteration of Rolt's ' Royal Shepherd '), and on Dec. 12, in his own adaptation of ' Pharnaces,' called ' The Revenge of Athridates.' He remained in Ireland till 1768, when he went to Edinburgh. He married [1] a pupil, Miss Dora Maunsell of Limerick, in Aug. 1766. A romantic account of their elopement was published by the lady in 1768, as *A True and Genuine Narrative of Mr. and Mrs. Tenducci*. He published six sonatas for harpsichord in Dublin in 1768, and ' A Collection of Lessons ' in Edinburgh, where he stayed during 1768–69. His vanity and extravagance were so unbounded that in 1776 he was forced to leave England for debt. In a year, however, he found means to return, and remained in London many years longer, singing with success as long as his voice lasted, and even when it had almost disappeared. In 1783 he sang again in Dublin with Mrs. Billington in ' Orpheus and Eurydice,' an adaptation from Gluck, and in 1785 he appeared in the same work in London ; he appeared at Drury Lane Theatre as late as 1790. He also sang at the Handel Commemoration Festivals at Westminster Abbey, in 1784 and 1791. Ultimately he returned to Italy.

[1] On July 16, 1766, Tenducci eloped with Miss Dorothy Maunsell (daughter of Councillor Thomas Maunsell), a pretty girl not quite 16 years old, of a good Limerick family, and in August he got married by a Roman Catholic priest in Cork. The Limerick correspondent of the *Dublin Journal* (Aug. 28, 1766) reports the fact of the elopement as ' a most extraordinary matter of amazement.' On July 4, 1767, this marriage was legalised in the parish church of Shaurahan, Co. Tipperary. Councillor Maunsell ultimately procured its annulment in a decree signed Jan. 1775.
                                            W. H. G. F.

Tenducci was on friendly terms with the Mozart family during their visit to London in 1764. In 1778, at Paris, he again met Mozart, who, remembering their former intercourse, wrote a song for him, which has been lost. He was the author of a treatise on singing and the composer of an overture for full band (Preston, London), and of 'Ranelagh Songs,' which he sang at concerts. He also composed music for Captain Jephson's comic opera, 'The Campaign,' about 1784. A sketch of him by Cosway is in Lord Tweedmouth's possession, and an exquisite medallion portrait, etched, is on the title-page of the *Instructions of Mr. Tenducci to his Scholars*, published by Longman & Broderip about 1785.

F. A. M.: addns. W. H. G. F., F. K.; information from R. Hitchcock's Irish Stage, Faulkner's Journals, etc.

TENEBRAE, a somewhat fanciful name given to the MATINS (*q.v.*) and LAUDS (*q.v.*) service of the last three days of Holy Week, owing to the ceremonial extinction of the lights, which goes on increasingly through the service till it ends in the dark. (See LAMENTATIONS; MISERERE.)

TENERAMENTE (CON TENEREZZA), 'tenderly'; a term slightly stronger and used more emphatically than *dolce*, but having very much the same meaning and use in music. A good instance of the distinction between the terms is found in the second movement of Beethoven's sonata in E minor, op. 90, where the subject, at its first entry labelled *dolce*, is subsequently directed to be played *teneramente*, it being evidently intended that the music should become slightly more impassioned as it goes on.

TENOR, the term used to denote the highest natural voice of men. It is derived from the Latin *teneo*, 'I hold,' the voice being that which in early times held, took or kept the plain-song (see DESCANT; MOTET). The compass is usually of about two octaves from *cc*, the first two or three notes being more or less ineffective. A notable exception was the compass of Caruso, who could sing with ease and effect down to G. Tenor voices may be roughly classified as being 'robust' or 'lyrical.' N. C. G.

TENOR, the largest bell of a 'ring' or 'peal,' sounding the lowest note—the keynote of the ring. W. W. S.

TENOR COR, a brass valve instrument of tenor pitch and circular or French horn form, designed and introduced by Henry Distin about 1860. The difficulty of training French horn-players for military bands, and the inadequacy of the tenor saxhorn as a substitute for the French horn, suggested the new instrument as a compromise. In tone quality the tenor cor is intermediate between the tenor saxhorn and the French horn, and is much used in

cases where the latter instrument is not available. It is usually made in F, with an extra slide for E♭. D. J. B.

TENOR DRUM, see DRUM (4).

TENOR HORN, a name used indiscriminately for two brass valve instruments of the saxhorn type.[1]

1. In E flat, with a compass of two octaves from the second harmonic sounding a major sixth lower (the valves give a complete chromatic compass from); it is also known as the althorn in E flat.

2. In B flat; sounding a ninth lower it is the German equivalent of the BARITONE (*q.v.*). (See also SAXHORN.)

In the U.S.A. the E♭ tenor is known as the E♭ alto, and the B♭ baritone of small bore as the B♭ tenor. The name B♭ tenor is not used in this country. The tenor instrument is frequently made in F, and the baritone in C. D. J. B.

TENOROON, see BASSOON (3).

TENOR TUBA, the equivalent to the euphonium. (See TUBA, where also are discussed the so-called tubas designed by Wagner for the 'Ring.')

TENOR VIOL, see VIOL (2).

TENOR VIOLIN, see VIOLIN FAMILY, subsection (2) VIOLA.

TENUTO, 'held'; a direction (or its contraction *ten.*) used to draw attention to the fact that particular notes or chords are intended to be sustained for their full value, in passages where staccato phrases are of such frequency that the players might omit to observe that some notes are to be played smoothly in contrast. Its effect is almost exactly the same as that of *legato*, save that this last refers rather to the junction of one note with another, and *tenuto* to the note regarded by itself. M.

TERCE (Lat. *officium (vel oratio) ad horam tertiam. Ad tertiam*); the second division of the lesser Hours in the Roman Breviary. W. S. R.

TERNINA, MILKA (*b.* Begizse, Croatia, Dec. 19, 1863), singer, one of the most eminent exponents of the soprano parts of Wagner.

Having lost her father when a child, she was adopted by her uncle, the Imperial State Councillor, J. Jurkovic of Agram, who gave her there an excellent education in music and foreign languages. When 12 years old she studied singing there with Frau Ida Winterberg. From about 1880–82 she studied singing with Gänsbacher at Vienna, both privately and at the Conservatorium. While still a student she made her débuts on the stage at Agram, as a guest, as Amelia ('Ballo in Maschera'),

---

[1] This is correct if applied to Europe generally and to the U.S.A. particularly, but not to this country.

Gretchen, Aida and Selika. In 1883–84 she sang light operatic parts at Leipzig. From 1884–86 she sang at Graz in the whole repertory. From 1886–90 she sang at Bremen, as successor to Klafsky, and from 1890–99 at Munich, where she was a great favourite, both in Wagner's operas and the general repertory. She also sang as Chimène in the revival of Cornelius's ' Cid,' and as the heroines in Schilling's ' Ingwelde ' and Chabrier's ' Gwendoline,' in the presence of their respective composers, and on May 7, 1899, as the heroine in Heinrich Vogl's ' Der Fremdling.' Soon after her engagement she was appointed court chamber singer to the Regent of Bavaria. On leave of absence, she sang in the principal cities of Germany, the Rhenish Festival (Aix-la-Chapelle, 1894), etc. On Apr. 25, 1895, she made her début in England at an orchestral concert at Queen's Hall under Hermann Levi, and by her singing of Elizabeth's Greeting and the scena from ' Fidelio ' made a highly favourable impression, ' by reason of her noble voice and powerful dramatic style.' In 1896 she sang at the German ambassador's concert at Moscow on the occasion of the Czar's coronation, and visited America for the first time. On June 3, 1898, she made her début at Covent Garden as Isolde with very great success, both as a singer and actress, confirmed later as Brünnhilde and Leonora (' Fidelio ').

In 1899 she sang for the first time at Bayreuth as Kundry, and later in the year went to America, where she sang several winter seasons with her usual success, not disdaining to sing the small part of the 1st Lady in ' Die Zauberflöte ' in a cast including Eames, Sembrich, De Lussan and Schumann-Heink. In Dec. 1904 she sang Kundry at the Metropolitan Opera-House. From 1900–06 she sang frequently at Covent Garden, principally in the Wagner operas, her only other part being, July 12, 1900, the heroine in Puccini's 'Tosca,' which she sang both to the satisfaction of the composer and the public. In Germany she was a favourite singer of the Lieder of Brahms and others. Her last appearance in London took place on May 28, 1906, in the part of Elizabeth. Soon after she retired from the profession. The combination of a perfect vocal method with dramatic force and sympathetic personality gave to each of her impersonations a rare and individual beauty.

A. C.

TERPODION, a musical friction-instrument, invented by Buschmann of Berlin in 1816, and improved by his sons in 1832. The principle appears to have been the same as that of Chladni's clavicylinder, except that instead of glass, wood was employed for the cylinder (see CHLADNI). In form it resembled a square piano, and its compass was six octaves. Warm tributes to its merits by Spohr, Weber, Rink and Hummel are quoted (*A.M.Z.* xxxiv. 857, 858, see also 634, 645 ; and l. 451 note), but notwithstanding these, the instrument is no longer known.

G.

TERRADELLAS (TERRADEGLIAS), DO-MENICO (Domingo Miguel Bernabé) (*b.* probably Barcelona, Feb. 1711 ; *d.* Rome, 1751), a Spanish musician, baptized in the cathedral at Barcelona, Feb. 13, 1711.[1] He began his musical studies at a monastery in Catalonia, but desiring greatly to go to Italy, he secured the aid of a merchant, a friend of his father's, who shipped the boy to Naples on one of his own vessels, and there, through the influence of the Spanish ambassador, Terradellas was entered as a pupil at the Conservatorio di San Onofrio under Durante.

His earlier efforts at dramatic composition quickly gained popular favour, and throughout his life it was to that branch of music that he principally devoted his talents, as the following long list of operas shows :

' Artaserse,' ' dramma per musica,' in three acts, the text by Pietro Metastasio, was performed at the San Carlo Theatre, Naples, in 1736, and in 1744 was played in Venice at the Teatro S. Gio. Grisostomo.

' Astarte,' text by Apostolo Zeno, was first performed at the Teatro alle Dame, in Rome, in 1736, and at Naples in 1739.

' Gl' intrighi delle cantarine,' a comic opera, was given at the Teatro del Fiorentini at Naples in 1740.

' Artemisia,' opera in three acts, was performed in Rome about 1740 ; in the same year part of Latilla's ' Romolo ' was composed by Terradellas.

' Issifile,' text by Metastasio, performed in Florence, 1742, is said to have been a failure.

' Merope,' ' dramma per musica ' in three acts, first performed in the Teatro alle Dame, Rome, in 1743, was, however, a great success. A MS. score is in the Fitzwilliam Museum, and MS. scores of this work and of Terradellas's opera ' Epitide,' text by Apostolo Zeno, are in the library of the Bologna Liceo Musicale. (Gaspari's *Catalogue*, III, 342.)

' Giuseppe riconosciuto,' text by Metastasio, performed at Naples about 1745.

' Mitridate,' London, 1746.

' Bellerophon,' London, 1747.

' Imeneo in Atene,' in three acts, text by Silvio Stampiglia, was performed at Venice at the Teatro S. Samuele in 1750.

' Sesostri,' text by Zeno, was given at Rome in 1751.

It is said that he composed a Mass for four voices, and also some motets, but only one sacred composition of his seems to be known ; it is included in the catalogue [2] of church music acquired by J. F. Libau, a priest of S. Gudule, Brussels, 1765, a *Nocturna procella* for solo voice.

In 1746 Terradellas was in London ; his opera ' Mitridate,' the text by Zeno, was first performed at the ' great theatre in the Haymarket,' on Dec. 2, 1746, and ran for ten nights ; on Mar. 24 following, his opera ' Bellerophon,' in three acts, was produced, and was performed ten times also. The interest aroused in Terradellas's music resulted in a good deal of it being printed by J. Walsh, of Catherine Street in the Strand. In the British Museum are copies of two collections of the ' Favourite songs in the opera call'd Mitridate by Sigr. Terradellas,' with instrumental accompaniment—Burney [3] writes that those sung by Reginelli, an old but great singer, are admirable, the others very agreeable ; also copies of ' The favourite Songs in the opera call'd Bellerofonte by Sigr. Terradellas,' with instrumental accompaniment ; and of ' The favourite

1 Saldoni's *Efemérides de musicos españoles*, Madrid, 1860.
2 Printed by Van der Straeten, *Pays-Bas*, l. 89.
3 *Hist. of Music*, iv. 455.

Songs in the opera call'd Annibale in Capua, by Sigr. Hasse and others.' This last work includes an aria for soprano, ' L' augellin che in lacci stretto,' by Signore Terradeglias, with accompaniment of flutes, viols and violins ; a MS. copy of ' L' augellin ' is·in the Fitzwilliam Museum Library, headed ' alle Dame 1743,' and it is probably part of either ' Epitide ' or ' Merope,' operas of that date.

Finally a work published by Walsh, which contained music from Terradellas's earlier operas :

'Dodici arie e due duetti. All' eccellenza di Melusina Baronessa di Schulemburg, Contessa di Walsingham, Contessa di Chesterfield, Queste composizioni di musica delle alme grandi nobile sollievo qual tributo di rispetto e d' ammirazione dedica e consacra l' umilissimo e devotissimo servo, Domenico Terradellas.'

Terradellas returned to Rome in 1747, passing through Paris, where he is said to have visited the grand opera and was much astonished at the amount of noise made on the stage, the singers shouting their loudest.

He was appointed maestro di cappella at S. Giacomo, on his return to Rome.

Two reports found currency as to the manner of his death ; one has it that he died from grief at the failure of his opera ' Sesostri,' the other that owing to the great success of ' Sesostri,' Jommelli, his musical rival in Rome, caused him to be assassinated ; the latter account seems to be discredited by the fact that Jommelli continued to reside in Rome quite peacefully until 1754.

LIST OF COMPOSITIONS IN MS.

Berlin State Library.—An aria, duetto, and terzetto for voices with instrumental accompaniments in MS. L. 268. An aria for soprano, ' Se perde l' usignolo,' in MS. 139. (Published in *Bellerofonte,* 1747.)

British Museum.—In Add. MSS. 31,598 : ' Terradellas. In Roma,' ' Fra l' ombre del timore,' for soprano with figured bass. In Add. MSS. 31,624 : ' In Venezia 1744, del Sigre. Domco. Terradellas,'four arie for soprano with instrumental accompaniment and figured bass : ' L' onda dal mar divisa ' ; ' Deh respirar lasciatemi ' (a MS. copy also in Fitzwilliam Museum) ; ' Conservati fedele,' and ' Se d' un amor tiranno ' ; the last two were published in Terradellas's ' Dodici arie,' 1747. All four airs are probably part of the opera 'Artaserse,' performed at the theatre S. Gio. Grisostomo, Venice, in 1744. In Add. MS. 14,219, p. 117 : 'Alle Dame, 1751, Scena del Signor Domenico Terradellas,' for soprano with instrumental accompaniment ; ' Solitudini amene, ombre gradite.' (Possibly from the opera ' Sesostri ' performed at the Teatro alle Dame, Rome, in 1751.)

Brussels Conservatoire Library.—(See Wotquenne's *Catalogue,* vol. 2.) No. 4903, aria ' Dove si vide mai ' (a MS. copy also in Naples), and ' Figlio ascolta ' from ' Merope,' Rome, Teatro alle Dame, 1743. No. 8154, the separate MS. parts of an overture by Terradellas.

Darmstadt Library.—Aria ' Oh Dei quel mi sorprende,' for soprano, with instrumental accompaniment (a MS. copy also in Fitzwilliam Museum, dated 1743). It was published in ' Dodici arie,' 1747, the phrase ' l' amato figlio Epitide,' which comes in it, points to it being from the opera ' Epitide ' (1743).

Dresden Library.—(Eitner's *Catalogue.*) Twenty-seven Arien with instrumental accompaniment.

Fitzwilliam Museum, Cambridge.—(Fuller Maitland and Mann's *Catalogue,* 1893.) In MS. 142, score of overture and songs in ' Merope ' (' alle Dame, 1743'). In MS. 145 three arie, ' alle Dame, 1743,' ' O Dei ' (see Darmstadt Library) ; ' L' augellin (published in ' Anibale in Capua ') ; ' Un bel gentil ' (see Naples Library) ; and a song, ' Deh respirar ' (another MS. copy in British Museum, dated 1744).

Milan Conservatorio Library.—(Eitner.) Seven arie with instrumental accompaniment.

Naples Real Collegio Library. — (Florimo's *La scuola musicale in Napoli,* 1880.) Solfeggio with pianoforte accompaniment ; six arie with instrumental accompaniments, including ' Non sperar che cangi affetto ' published in ' Dodici arie,' 1747 ; and a cantata with violins, viola and bass, ' Un bel gentile sembiante ' (a MS. copy also in the Fitzwilliam Museum dated 1743. The music is probably from ' Merope ' or ' Epitide ' of that date).

Schwerin Library.—(Kade's *Catalogue,* 1893.) Aria for soprano with accompaniment of two violins, viola and cembalo.

Vienna Hofbibliothek. — (Mantuani's *Catalogue.*) In MS. 17,033 an aria, ' Io son quel pellegrino,' by D. M. B. Terradellas.

Wolfenbüttel herzogliche Bibliothek.—(Vogel's *Catalogue,* p. 66.) MS. 302, an aria, ' Dono d' amica sorte,' in score.

BIBL.—J. M. CARRERAS, *D. Terradellas* (1908) ; H. VOLKMANN, *Journal of Int. Mus. Ges.* xiii. 306.   C. S.

TERRY, CHARLES SANFORD (*b.* Newport Pagnell, Bucks, 1864), professor of history in the University of Aberdeen since 1903, has, in addition to many researches embodied in publications which lie outside the field of this Dictionary, specially devoted himself to the study of J. S. Bach and his epoch. The product of his study in this direction is contained in articles in the present edition of this Dictionary (see BACH, CHORAL, PASSION MUSIC, etc.). His publications in this field include *Bach Chorales* (3 vols.), 1915–21 ; *J. S. Bach's Original Hymn-tunes for Congregational Use,* 1922 ; a *Bach Hymn-book of 16th-Century Melodies,* 1923 ; *J. S. Bach, Cantata Texts, Sacred and Secular,* 1925. The last-named includes English translations of all Bach's cantatas, together with a reconstruction of the Leipzig Liturgy of Bach's day, founded on hitherto unexamined documents. *Bach's Four-Part Chorals,* 1926, is a complete Bach hymn-book. In 1920 Terry published an English translation of Forkel's *Johann Sebastian* ; he has also arranged and published a stage version of Bach's 'Coffee Cantata,' which has been performed by the B.N.O.C. under the title ' Coffee and Cupid.' An exhaustive biography of Bach is in preparation. Terry is the holder of many academic distinctions, including honorary D.Mus. of Edinburgh, and hon. D.Litt. Durham.   C.

TERRY, SIR RICHARD RUNCIMAN, Mus.D. (*b.* Ellington, Northumberland, 1865), became organist and music-master at Elstow School in 1890, organist and choirmaster of St. John's Cathedral, Antigua, West Indies, in 1892. In 1896 he was appointed to a similar position at Downside Abbey, Somerset, where he began the admirable work of reviving the music written for the Latin ritual by early English composers ; he was the first to perform liturgically the three- and five-part Masses of Byrd, Tye's ' Euge bone,' Tallis's four-part Mass and his ' Lamentations,' Mundy's Mass ' Upon the square,' and motets by Morley, Parsons, White and others.

A larger sphere of work was opened to him when Westminster Cathedral was built and he was appointed organist and director of music in 1901, a post which he held with great distinction until 1924, when he resigned. Here, from the first, he set a high standard of performance as well as influencing the choice of music and demonstrating the great wealth of English liturgical music of the finest period. He revived the whole of Peter Philips's ' Cantiones sacrae,' Byrd's ' Gradualia ' and ' Cantiones sacrae,' the ' Cantiones ' of Tallis and Byrd, White's ' Lamentations,' and motets by Deering, Fayrfax, Shepherd, Tye and others. Among continental compositions of special interest, it may be mentioned that the contents of the fourth volume of Jacob Hándl's ' Opus musicum' were brought to a hearing at the cathedral. It is worth noticing that this great work was set on foot two years before the issue of the papal decree which directed Roman Catholic church musicians to give due regard to the polyphonic music of the past.   M.

Terry was able to establish at Westminster Cathedral a complete tradition of musical treatment for the whole of the Roman liturgy in England based on principles laid down in the *Motu Proprio*, so that the Use of Westminster has offered an example to Roman Catholic church musicians unequalled anywhere else outside of Rome itself. Moreover, the great wealth of his repertory of English polyphonic music did much to arouse general interest in this music as a national, apart from an ecclesiastical, possession. This latter aspect of Terry's work was emphasised in the speech [1] with which Sir Henry Hadow presented him for the degree of Mus.D. conferred *honoris causa* by Durham University in 1911. Soon after this date when the Carnegie Trust entertained proposals for the publication of 'Tudor church music,' Terry was appointed chairman of the Trust's editorial committee. Unfortunately the pressure of other affairs made it impossible for him to carry through this scheme to its conclusion. Terry's publications include editions of various works of old English church music, five Masses, a Requiem Mass and motets of his own composition and the *Westminster Hymnal* (1912), which is the official hymnal for Roman Catholic use in England. They all bear the stamp of his musicianship, though the official acceptance of the hymnal necessitated the inclusion of a number of tunes which his own fine taste would naturally have rejected. A book, *Catholic Church Music* (1907), was designed as a handbook for the guidance of choirmasters both in the choice of music and the manner of its performance. A controversial chapter put forward some propositions as to the effect of the Reformation on English church music which the author has since admitted were historically untenable. Apart from this, however, the book is valuable. Terry's minor activities have included much lecturing, musical journalism (after his retirement from the cathedral he edited *Musical News* for a time) and folk-song collection. His *Shanty Book* (2 parts, see SHANTY) is the fruit of a long experience. He is among the most able of judges at the musical competition festivals. He was knighted in 1922.   C.

TERTIS, LIONEL (*b.* West Hartlepool, Dec. 29, 1876), studied the violin at Leipzig and afterwards at the R.A.M., where he was encouraged by Sir Alexander Mackenzie to take up the viola for the sake of quartet-playing. He became an exceptionally fine player of that instrument, arranged a number of violin

[1] See *Mus. T.*, Aug. 1911, p. 525.

concertos for it, and has toured widely in Europe and America as a virtuoso. The lack of solo music written for the viola was at first an obstacle to his success, but this, like all other prejudices against the viola as a solo instrument, has been largely overcome by his talent. Many of his contemporaries among English composers have written important works for him. These include concertos with orchestra by J. B. McEwen, A. Carse, Arnold Bax, B. J. Dale and York Bowen ; sonatas, etc., with PF. by the last-named three with others, Ernest Walker, W. H. Bell, Cyril Scott, Frank Bridge and H. Farjeon (see *Mus. T.*, Mar. 1922). Tertis's performance has shown that while all the resources of violin technique are at command of the viola-player, its characteristic tone gives it a personality which is quite distinct from that of the violin.   C.

TERZETTO (Ital.), generally a composition for three voices. Beyond one instance in Bach, and a few modern examples consisting of pieces not in sonata-form, the term has never been applied to instrumental music. It is now becoming obsolete, being superseded by trio, which is the name given to music written for three instruments, and now includes vocal music as well.

A terzetto may be for any combination of three voices, whether for three trebles—as the unaccompanied Angels' Trio in 'Elijah' those of the three women and three boys in 'Die Zauberflöte,' the famous trio in 'Il matrimonio segreto,' and that for three florid sopranos in Spohr's 'Zemire und Azor'—or for three male voices, like the canonic trio in the last-named opera. More frequent, naturally, are terzetti for mixed voices, the combinations being formed according to the exigencies of the situation.   F. C.

TERZI, GIOVANNI ANTONIO, a 16th-17th century lutenist, wrote lib. 1 and lib. 2 of 'Intavolatura di liuto' containing motets, canzones, etc., by various Italian and French authors, published at Venice respectively in 1593 and 1599. Chilesotti republished 15 of Terzi's own lute pieces (*Q.-L.*).

TESCHNER, GUSTAV WILHELM (*b.* Magdeburg, Dec. 26, 1800 ; *d.* Dresden, May 7, 1883), studied singing and composition under Zelter and Klein at Berlin, and afterwards went to Italy, where his acquaintance with the Abbé Santini was the means of inducing him to take a greater interest in the older church music, both Latin and German. Returning to Germany, he settled in Berlin as a teacher of singing on Italian principles, and published various collections of Italian solfeggi, as well as some of his own. But his name is even better known by his republication, in score, of such works as H. L. Hassler's 'Psalmengesänge' of 1608, Eccard's 'Geistliche Lieder' of 1597, Eccard and Stobaeus's 'Preussische Festlieder' of

1642–44, and by his editorship of other collections of sacred and secular music of the 16th and 17th centuries.   J. R. M.

TESCHNER, MELCHIOR, Lutheran cantor at Fraustadt, in Silesia, at the beginning of the 17th century. His name chiefly appears in connexion with the Choral-tune to an acrostic hymn, 'Valet will ich dir geben,' written by Valerius Herberger, Lutheran pastor at Fraustadt, and a famous preacher of the time. The hymn, written in 1613, during a time of pestilence in Silesia, appeared in a publication of Herberger's in 1614, accompanied by two simple musical settings, a 5, by Teschner. Both melodies are given in Zahn's Collection, but only one has survived in modern use. Hymn and tune were received into the Gotha Cantionale Sacrum of 1648, and have thence passed into most modern Choral-books. Teschner's original setting, a 5, appears in Schöberlein's 'Schatz' to Paul Gerhardt's hymn, 'Wie soll ich dich empfangen,' with which the tune is also now associated. With some alteration the tune has been adopted into English hymn-books to the Palm Sunday hymn, 'All glory, laud, and honour.' Two other works of Teschner are mentioned in Q.-L.   J. R. M.

TESI-TRAMONTINI, VITTORIA (b. Florence, Feb. 13, 1700 [1]; d. Vienna, May 9, 1775 [2]), a celebrated singer. Her first instructor was Francesco Redi, and at a later date she studied under Campeggi, at Bologna, but it is evident that she sang on the public stage long before her years of study were over. She was singing in Italy in 1716, when she appeared with Cuzzoni, in a pastoral called 'Dafni'; in 1718 she was at Venice, and went in 1719 to Dresden, just at the time when Handel arrived there in quest of singers for the newly established Royal Academy of Music in London. The story of her singing in Handel's 'Rodrigo,' in 1707, and of her falling in love with the master, is due to a mistake of Chrysander.[3] Her voice was of brilliant quality and unusual compass. Quantz, who heard her at Dresden, defines it as 'a contralto of masculine strength,' but adds that she could sing high or low with equally little effort. Fire, force and dramatic expression were her strong points, and she succeeded best in men's parts; in florid execution she did not greatly excel. Her fame and success were at their zenith in 1719, but it does not appear that Handel made any effort to secure her for England. At some time or other, possibly at this period, she visited Poland with her father, where she attracted the admiration of the king. From 1721–47 there are traces of her singing each year in Italy. She married a barber

named Tramontini and appeared as 'Tesi-Tramontini, virtuosa di Camera della Granduchessa di Toscana,' from 1743. In the autumn of 1739 she was at Madrid. In 1747 or 1748 she went to Vienna, and opened a school for vocal instruction. In 1749 she played in Jommelli's 'Didone.' The book was by Metastasio, who wrote of this occasion, 'The Tesi has grown younger by twenty years.' She was then 49. Burney met her at Vienna in 1772, and speaks of her as more than 80. This mistake, and various statements by other historians, are settled by the discovery of the baptismal register.

Her nature was vivacious and emporté to a degree, and many tales were told of her freaks and escapades. Perhaps most wonderful of all is the story of her marriage, as told by Burney in his Present State (Germany), i. 318 ; in which, to avoid marrying a certain nobleman, she went into the street, and addressing herself to a poor labouring man, said she would give him fifty ducats if he would marry her, not with a view to their living together, but to serve a purpose. The poor man readily consented to become her nominal husband, and they were formally married ; and when the Count renewed his solicitations, she told him that she was already the wife of another. This may be a version of her marriage with Tramontini, for as he was living in 1753, there would be no reason for her to make a marriage of convenience before that date, and after it, it is unlikely that such a marriage would be required. Among the pupils of La Tesi were the 'Teuberinn,' and Signora de Amicis, who took a friendly interest in the boy Mozart, and sang in his earliest operatic efforts in Italy.
       F. A. M., with addns.

TESS, opera in 4 acts, founded on Hardy's novel by Luigi Illica ; music by F. D'Erlanger. Produced San Carlo Theatre, Naples, Apr. 10, 1906 ; Covent Garden, July 14, 1909.

TESSARINI, CARLO (b. Rimini, 1690), an eminent violinist, probably a pupil of Corelli. He was violinist at St. Mark's, Venice, 1729 ; afterwards at SS. Giovanni e Paolo, and finally in the service of the Cardinal Wolfgang Hannibal at Brünn. GERBER (1) relates that in 1762 he appeared, still a vigorous old man, as a soloist at Amsterdam. Tessarini, who left a considerable number of violin sonatas and concerti grossi, played an important part in the evolution of the sonata and the instrumental concerto. (See A. Schering, Geschichte des Instrumentalkonzerts, p. 107 ; Q.-L. ; Riemann.)

TESSIER, CHARLES (or CARLES), composer and lutenist, was born, according to Fétis, at Pézénas (Dep. Hérault) about 1550. He visited England some time before 1597, for in that year his Le Premier Livre de chansons et airs de court, tant en françois qu'en italien et en gascon à 4 et 5 parties was printed in London by

1 The baptismal register, of Feb. 15, is copied in A. Ademollo's articles on the singer, in the Nuova antologia, xxii. 308, and the Gazzetta musicale, 1889, p. 283, etc.
2 Riemann.
3 The documents referred to in note 1 correct Chrysander's error. See also Streatfeild, Handel, p. 30 et seq.

Thomas Este, and from a dedicatory preface, written in Italian and addressed to Lady Penelope Riche (the ' Stella ' of Sir Philip Sidney's Sonnets), we learn that these songs were composed in England and published at the request of friends. On the title-page Tessier is described as ' Musitien de la Chambre du Roy ' (*sc.* Henri IV. of France). His only other published song-book was entitled *Airs et vilanelles françois, italiens, espagnols, suices et turcqs, mis en musique à 3, 4 et 5 parties*, and was printed in Paris in 1604. A setting by ' Tesseir ' [sic] of the eighth song from Sidney's *Astrophel and Stella* was published in Robert Dowland's *A Musicall Banquet* (1610). Eitner suggests that the presence of certain manuscript compositions of Tessier, dedicated to Maurice, Landgrave of Hessen, in Kassel, indicates that he spent some time in that town. P. H.

TESSITURA (Ital.), literally texture, from *tessere*, to weave. A term used to indicate how the music of a piece ' lies ' ; that is to say, what is the prevailing or average position of its notes in relation to the compass of the voice or instrument for which it is written, whether high, low or medium. ' Range ' does not at all give the idea, as the range may be extended, and the general *tessitura* limited ; while the range may be high and the *tessitura* low or medium. In place of a corresponding word we say that a part ' lies high or low.' For diagrammatic examples of tessitura see SINGING, Vol. IV. p. 764. H. C. D.

TESTORE, a family of violin-makers at Milan in the first half of the 18th century, consisting of a father, CARLO GIUSEPPE (1690–1715), and two sons, CARLO ANTONIO and PAOLO ANTONIO (1715–45). Carlo Giuseppe was the best of the three. His instruments have often passed for the work of his master, Giovanni GRANCINO (*q.v.*). In 1884 the violoncello called the ' Lindley Grancino ' being under repair, the removal of its spurious label revealed the fact that it is the work of the old Testore, the original label, which was found well preserved, running thus :

' Carlo Giuseppe Testore allievo di Gio. Granzino in Contrada Larga di Milano, 1690.' [1]

Bottesini's famous double-bass is another specimen of the old Testore's work. His instruments are strongly made, and often irregular in design. The model is generally of medium height, and the finish varies considerably, many being left very rough, and extremely plain in appearance. The tone, however, is usually good, and in exceptional cases very powerful and telling.

The instruments of the sons are less esteemed ; they are lighter in colour, and a tendency to imitate Joseph GUARNERIUS (*q.v.*) is observable. The Testores worked at the sign of the Eagle

[1] Communicated by W E. Hill and Sons.

in the same narrow street where the Grancinos worked at the sign of the Crown. Alberti, Landolfi, Tanegia, Mantegazza, Giuseppe Guadagnini, Mezzadri, Lavazza and others complete the group of Milanese makers who followed the Testores in general plainness of style, aiming at producing instruments rather useful and lasting than ornamental. E. J. P.

TETRACHORD (Gr. τετράχορδον), a system of four sounds, comprised within the limits of a perfect fourth (see GREEK MUSIC ; MONOCHORD ; Guido D' AREZZO ; HEXACHORD).

TETRAZZINI, LUISA (Signora Bazelli) (*b.* Florence, June 29, 1871), received her musical instruction there from Ceccherini at the Liceo Musicale, and from her sister Eva, the wife of Cleofonte CAMPANINI (*q.v.*), the conductor. In 1895 she made her début at the Teatro Pagliano (now Teatro Verdi) as Inez in ' L'Africaine.' She next sang at Rome, and later toured with great success in the other cities of Italy, having in the meantime acquired a great reputation in Spain, Portugal, Russia, Mexico, South America, etc. On Nov. 2, 1907, she made her début at Covent Garden as Violetta (' La traviata ') and made a success both as singer and actress, confirmed the same season in her next parts of Lucia and Gilda. She next sang in the United States (Manhattan, Jan. 15, 1908), where she again made a great reputation. Since 1908 her principal operatic engagements have been either in North America or at Covent Garden, where she has sung for the first time there as Rosina, Marguerite de Valois (' Huguenots '), Leila in ' Les Pêcheurs de perles,' and Amina in ' La sonnambula.' She sang with the Chicago Opera Company 1913–14, and has since toured in concerts as an International Celebrity. In 1921 she published reminiscences called *My Life of Song*. A. C., addns.

TEUFELS LUSTSCHLOSS, DES (The Devil's Country-house), comic opera in 3 acts, by Kotzebue ; music by Schubert ; composed between Jan. 11 and May 15, 1814, and rewritten in the autumn, but not performed. The overture was played by the London Musical Society, June 17, 1880. It contains a singular anticipation of the muted violin passage in the overture to ' Euryanthe.' G.

TEUTSCHE. Mozart's way of spelling Deutsche, *i.e.* Deutsche Tänze—little German waltzes in 3-8 or 3-4, of which he, Beethoven, and Schubert, wrote many. For Schubert's ' Atzenbrucker Deutsche, July 1821,' see Vol. IV. p. 598. The famous ' Trauer - Waltzer,' sometimes called ' Le Désir ' (op. 9, No. 2), for long attributed to Beethoven, is a Teutsch. (See ALLEMANDE, 2.) G.

THACKRAY, THOMAS, an 18th - century composer of minuets, country-dance tunes, etc. He resided in York, and was probably a native of that city. About 1770 he issued ' A Collection of Forty-four Airs, properly adapted for one, or two Guittars,' London, John Johnston, folio ; also 'Six Lessons for the Guittar,' printed at York by Thomas Haxby for the author. Other 'Lessons' by him are extant.

F. K.

THAÏS, opera in 3 acts ; text by Louis Gallet (after Anatole France) ; music by Massenet. Produced Opéra, Paris, Mar. 16, 1894 ; Covent Garden, July 18, 1911.

THALBERG, SIGISMOND (b. Geneva, 1812 [1] ; d. Posilipo, Apr. 27, 1871), was one of the outstanding pianists of the 19th century.

He was the natural son of Prince Moritz Dietrichstein and Baroness von Wetzlar. At the age of 10 his father sent for him to Vienna, intending him for the diplomatic career ; he attended the Polytechnic School, and had for a fellow-student the Duc de Reichstadt, who fired him with so much military ardour that he nearly became a soldier. He received his early musical education from Mittag, the first bassoonist at the opera. Later he learnt theory from Sechter, and developed his pianoforte technique under Hummel. He played at private parties in Vienna from the age of 13, and made a public appearance in 1826 at the house of Prince Metternich.[2] In 1830 he went on his first concert tour in different parts of Germany, three of his early compositions having already been published. In 1834 he was appointed Kammervirtuoso to the Emperor of Austria. In 1835 he had a great success in Paris, where he studied again under Pixis and Kalkbrenner ; and in the following year appeared in London at the Philharmonic Concert of May 9, 1836, in his fantasia, opus 1, in which the special peculiarity of his technique was commented on in the Musical World. This consisted of so dividing a melody between the two hands that a bass could be played with the left and an accompaniment with the right, giving the effect of three independent hands. This seems to have been adopted by Mendelssohn in his E minor prelude after hearing Thalberg play ; at all events the priority of publication is with Thalberg, in whose fantasia on 'Moïse' it appears. From this time forth he was an idolised figure all the world over, and endless were the comparisons made by musicians and others between him and Liszt. For some years the controversy raged, Fétis taking the side of Thalberg and Berlioz that of Liszt.[3] In the following year he again visited London, in 1839 he went to Belgium, Holland and Russia, in 1845 to Spain, and in 1846 he played at the Wednesday Concerts in Exeter Hall. In 1855

he visited Brazil, and in 1857 he went to the United States with Vieuxtemps (during which time he essayed operatic management with Ullman and Strakosch). In 1843 he married, in Paris, Mme. Boucher, widow of the painter and daughter of Lablache. In 1851 his opera 'Florinda' was brought out in London without success, and his second attempt at dramatic writing, 'Cristina di Suezia,' brought out at Vienna in 1855, was no more successful. In 1858 he bought a villa at Posilipo near Naples ; but he reappeared in England in 1862 and 1863, and after that year, in which he went again to Brazil, he settled down as a wine-grower at Posilipo, where he died.

Thalberg's demeanour at the piano was always quiet, and his prodigies in manual achievement depended, not on force, but gradation of tone, and on the incomparable art of singing on the keyboard. Schumann refers to Thalberg very often, and gives a very trustworthy account of his qualities.[4]

Apart from his gift of melodic invention, he was a piano composer pure and simple. He was only really at home on the keyboard ; but there he was, in his style, a king. His remarkable and well-developed power of singing on the piano (legato sostenuto), which he possibly gained from Clementi through Kalkbrenner and Moscheles, enabled him to produce melodic effects which had not hitherto been heard ; and his clever use of the sustaining pedal made it possible to render the melody smoothly, while both hands were free to give the rushing scales, brilliant arpeggi and other sparkling passages with which he loved to surround his melodies.

With an intense feeling for melody, a wide span, and a peculiar shape of finger-tip, Thalberg was able to produce many and fine melodic and harmonic effects in legato playing, as well as in extended chords and arpeggi. His strongest points seem to have been 'pearly passage playing' (a light, rapid, silvery percussion), his knack of uniting the tones in long skips by means of the pedal, together with a singularly deft wrist-action. It is stated that he played Bach's fugues in incomparably beautiful style. In his directions to students he writes that he recommends, above all things, 'the slow, conscientious practice of fugues'; again, 'The performance of one fugue in three parts, in moderate time, without errors, and in good style, demands and proves more talent than the most rapid and complicated morceau'; and once more, 'Generally pupils work too much with their hands and too little with their minds.'

The following is a list of his published compositions, in the order of their opus numbers

1 The date Jan. 7 is given by Fétis, followed by Riemann ; Mendel gives May 5, and a half-brother of Thalberg informed the writer of the article in the first edition of this Dictionary that the true date was Feb. 7. A search of the archives at Geneva reveals the fact that the birth was never registered.

2 A pamphlet in the British Museum, entitled Thalberg and Vieuxtemps Grand Concert Book, supports Fétis's statement that Thalberg made his first appearance in London in 1830, and states that his tour in Germany was in consequence of his success in England.

3 See correspondence in Gazette musicale, 1837.

4 See Gesammelte Schriften, third edition, i. 290, ii. 67, 160, 212, 221, 310. For other appreciations see Rubinstein, Kunst und ihre Meister and Ernst Pauer, A Contemporary Appreciation of Thalberg Performances 1863).

from the *Biographical Lexicon of the Austrian Empire*, of Dr. von Wurzbach (1882) :

Op.
1. Fantaisie et variations (' Euryanthe ').
2. Do. do. (' Thème écossais ').
3. Impromptu (' Siège de Corinthe ').
4. Souvenirs de Vienne.
5. Gran Concerto (F minor).
5 bis. Hommage à Rossini (' Guil. Tell ').
6. Fantaisie ('Robert le Diable').
7. Grand Divertissement (F minor).
8. Sechs deutsche Lieder (1-6).
9. Fantaisie (' La straniera ').
10. Gr. Fantaisie et variations (' I Montecchi ').
11. Sechs deutsche Lieder (7-12).
12. Gr. Fantaisie et variations (' Norma ').
13. Sechs deutsche Lieder (13-18).
14. Gr. Fantaisie et variations (' Don Juan ').
15. Caprice (E minor).
16. 2 Nocturnes (F♯, B).
17. 2 Airs russes variés (G).
18. Divertissement (' Soirées musicales ') on motifs of Rossini.
19. Second Caprice (E♭).
20. Fantaisie (' Huguenots ').
21. 3 Nocturnes.
22. Grand Fantaisie.
23. Sechs deutsche Lieder (19-24).
24. Do. do. (25-30).
25. Do. do. (31-36).
26. 12 Études.
27. Gr. Fantaisie ('God save the Queen ' and ' Ruie Britannia '), A♭.
28. Nocturne (E).
29. Sechs deutsche Lieder(37-42).
30. Do. do. (43-48).
31. Scherzo (A).
32. Andante in D♭.
33. Fantaisie (' Moïse ').
34. Divertissement (' Gipsy's Warning ').
35. Grand Nocturne (F♯).
35 bis. Étrennes aux jeunes pianistes. Nocturne.
36. (1) La Cadence. Impromptu (A minor). (2) Nouv. Étude de perfection. (3) Mi manca la voce (A♭). (4)La Romanesca. (5) Canzonette italienne. (6) Romance sans paroles.
37. Fantaisie (' Oberon ').
38. Romance et Étude (A).
39. Souvenir de Beethoven. Fantaisie (A minor).
40. Fantaisie ('Donna del Lago').
41. 2 Romances sans paroles.
42. Gr. Fantaisie (Sérénade et Menuet, ' Don Juan ').
43. Gr. Fantaisie No. 2 (' Huguenots ').
44. Andante final de ' Lucia,' variée.

Op.
45. Thème orig. et Étude (A minor).
46. Gr. Caprice (' Sonnambula ').
47. Gr. Valses brillantes.
48. Gr. Caprice (' Charles VI ').
49. German Songs.
50 Fantaisie (' Lucrezia ')
51. Gr. Fantais e (' Sémiramide').
51 bis. 3rd Nocturne.
52. Fantaisie (' La Muette ').
53. Gr. Fantaisie (' Zampa ').
54. Thalberg et de Bériot. Gr. Duo concertante (' Sémiramide ').
55. Le Départ, varié en forme d'Étude.
56. Grand Sonate (C minor).
57. 10 Morceaux, servant d'école préparatoire (also called ' Irish Fantasia' and 'Decameron musical ').
58. Gr. Caprice (Marche de Berlioz).
59. Marche funèbre variée.
60. Barcarole.
61. Mélodies styriennes, Gr. Fant. arr. par Wolff.
62. Valse mélodique.
63. Gr. Fantaisie (' Barbier ').
64. Les Capricieuses, Valses.
65. Tarantelle.
65 bis. Souvenir de Pesth
66. Introd. et var. sur la Barcarole de L'Élisire.
67. Gr. Fantaisie (' Don Pasquale ').
68. Fantaisie (' Fille du régiment ').
69. Trio, pf. and strings.
70. L'Art du chant appliqué au piano. 4 Series containing 22 transcriptions.
70a. Ballade de ' Prec osa '; transcription.
70b. Grand duo de ' Freischütz.'
71. F.orinda, opera. 6 transcriptions.
72. Home, sweet home ! . . . Variée.
73. The last rose of summer. . . . Variée.
74. Lily Dale. . . . Variée.
75. Les Soirées de Pausilippe, 24 Pensées musicales in 6 books.
76. Célèbre Ballade.
77. Gr. Fantaisie de Concert (' Il Trovatore ').
78. Do. do. (' Traviata ').
79a. 3 Mélodies de F. Schubert transcrites.
79b. Romance dramatique.
80. La Napolitaine. Danse.
81. Souvenir du ' Ballo in maschera.'
82. Ditto de ' Rigoletto.'
83. Air d'Amazily ('Fernand Cortez ').

Unnumbered Pieces.—Auf Fiügeln (Mendelssohn) transcr.—2 Morceaux sur Lucrezia.—Arietta, ' Non so fremar.'—Zwei Gedichte.—Thalberg and Fanoika, Grand Duo.—Duo on ' Trovatore ' with Gottschalk.—Graciosa, Rom. sans paroles.—Nocturno in D♭.—Romance variée in E♭.—Viola Mélodie.—Thalberg Galoppe.—La Berceuse.—' Le Fils du Corse.'—Pauline, Valse.—Larmes d'une jeune fille.—' Tre giorni.'—Pianoforte School.

D. H.

THALBERG, ZARÉ (*b.* Derbyshire, Apr. 16, 1858 ; *d.* Finchley, Middlesex, 1915), operatic soprano. Not, as was generally supposed, the daughter of Sigismond Thalberg, but a pupil who took his name, and, after vocal study in Paris and Milan, made her début on the stage at Covent Garden, under Gye's management in 1874, as Zerlina in ' Fra Diavolo.' In that part she was thought to rival even Pauline Lucca, thanks to the unusual charm of her personality, the sweetness and purity of her voice (a very flexible *soprano leggiero*) and the grace and intelligence of her singing and acting. She also pleased in the Mozart operas, as well as those of Donizetti and Rossini, and quickly became a favourite. Then, after six successful seasons in London and on the Continent, she lost her voice, owing to an affection of the vocal cords, and had to retire from the operatic stage. The fact of her English parentage appears to have remained unknown during this important part of her career ; nor was her identity with the ' Zaré Thalberg ' of opera disclosed when she subsequently resumed her maiden name of Ethel Western and took to the drama as an exponent of Shakespearian parts.[1] She was engaged by Edwin Booth and toured with him for some time in America, winning a notable success as Lady Anne in ' Richard III.' Her career as an actress ended in the early 'nineties, when, on her return to England, she married John Oliver, a well-known Queen's Messenger (' Master of the Silver Greyhounds '), whom she accompanied on many of his journeys. Through him she became acquainted with some of the leading statesmen of her time, including Lord Beaconsfield. On her husband's death in 1908 she went to live at Finchley, and was married again, this time to one Belcher, whom she also survived.   H. K.

THAYER, ALEXANDER WHEELOCK (*b.* South Natick, Mass., U.S.A., Oct. 22, 1817 ; *d.* Trieste, July 15, 1897), the biographer of Beethoven.

In 1843 he graduated at Harvard University, took the degree of Bachelor of Laws there, and was for a few years employed in the College library. In 1849 he left America for Europe, and remained for more than two years in Bonn, Berlin, Prague and Vienna, studying German, corresponding with newspapers at home, and collecting materials for a life of Beethoven, the idea of which had presented itself to him while at Harvard, and which was his one serious pursuit for the rest of his life. In 1852 he tried journalism on the staff of the *New York Tribune*, but only to the detriment of his health. *Dwight's Journal of Music* was started at Boston in Apr. 1852, and Thayer soon became a prominent and favourite writer therein. In 1854 he returned to Germany, and worked hard at the rich Beethoven materials in the Royal (now State) Library at Berlin for nearly a year. Ill-health and want of means drove him back to Boston in 1856, and amongst other work he there catalogued the musical library of Lowell Mason. In the summer of 1858, by Mason's help, he was enabled to cross once more to Europe, remained for some months in Berlin and Frankfort-on-the-Oder, and in 1859 arrived at Vienna more inspired than ever for his mission. A severe and able review of Marx's Beethoven in the *Atlantic Monthly*, republished in German by Otto Jahn, had made him known in Germany, and henceforth the Biography became his vocation. The next year was passed in Berlin, Vienna, Graz, Linz, Salzburg, Frankfort, Bonn,

[1] The personal details newly set forth in this article have been communicated by the artist's intimate friend, Mr. David Smart, her neighbour at Finchley during the later years of her life.

LXXXI

THALBERG

From a bust by E. H. Baily, R.A., at the Royal College of Music

Photo, Fritz Luckhardt

RUBINSTEIN

etc., in intercourse with Hüttenbrenner, Wegeler, Schindler and other friends of Beethoven, in minute investigation of documents, and in a fruitless visit to Paris, for the sake of papers elucidating the history of Bonn. His next visit was to London, where he secured the reminiscences of Neate, Potter and Hogarth, and received much substantial kindness [1] from Chorley. From England he returned to Vienna, and in 1862 accepted a small post in the U.S. Legation there, afterwards exchanged for that of U.S. Consul at Trieste, where he died.

His book is entitled *Ludwig van Beethovens Leben.* It was written in English, translated into German by Dr. H. Deiters of Bonn and published by Weber of Berlin—vol. 1 (1770–96) in 1866 ; vol. 2 (1792–1806) in 1872 ; vol. 3 (1807–16) in 1879. Vol. 4 was unfinished at Thayer's death, and Deiters undertook to revise and complete the work, but died before accomplishing more than the revision of the first volume, which came out in 1901. Riemann completed the fourth volume in 1907, the fifth and last in 1908, and brought out the revisions of volumes 2 and 3 in 1910–11. Krehbiel's edition in English (3 volumes, New York, 1921) is the product of the whole of the above material. (See KREHBIEL.)

The quantity of new letters and facts, and of rectifications of dates, contained in the book is very great. For the first time Beethoven's life is placed on a solid basis of fact. At the same time Thayer was no slavish biographer. He viewed his hero from a perfectly independent point of view, and often criticised his caprice or harshness (as in the cases of Mälzel and Johann Beethoven) very sharply.

Thayer wrote countless articles in American newspapers ; he was the author of *Signor Masoni* (Berlin, Schneider, 1862) ; of *Ein kritischer Beitrag zur Beethoven-Literatur* (Berlin, Weber, 1877) ; and of *The Hebrews and the Red Sea* (Andover, Mass., Draper).

G., with addns.

THEILE, JOHANN (*b.* Naumburg, Saxony, July 29, 1646 ; *d.* June 1724 [2]), received his earlier instruction, musical and otherwise, at Magdeburg and Halle. He afterwards attended the University at Leipzig, where he also took part in various musical performances, partly as singer, partly as player on the viola da gamba. For further instruction in composition he betook himself to Heinrich Schütz, who was then for a time at Weissenfels. He found employment as teacher of music first at Stettin, then at Lübeck ; at which latter place he is said to have had Dietrich Buxtehude as one of his pupils. Some doubt, however, attaches to this statement, as according to all accounts Buxtehude (*b.* 1637) was nine years Theile's senior,

and was already in 1668 organist at the Marienkirche of Lübeck. It is just possible that Theile, being a gambist, may have given instruction on the viola da gamba to Buxtehude, who afterwards wrote sonatas for that instrument. In 1673 Theile accepted the invitation of Duke Christian Albert of Holstein to be his Hof-Kapellmeister at Gottorp, but in 1675, when the duchy was invaded and occupied by the troops of the King of Denmark, Theile and the Duke himself were obliged to take refuge in Hamburg. It was while Theile was in Hamburg that in 1678 an opera-house was built, and operatic performances became an established institution there. The first opera at Hamburg was one upon a Scriptural subject, the music of which was composed by Theile. It was entitled ' Adam und Eva, oder Der erschaffene, gefallene, und wieder aufgerichtete Mensch.' The text of this has been preserved, but not the music. It is remarkable that most of these early Hamburg operas are on sacred subjects, among them another by Theile performed in 1681 entitled ' Die Geburt Christi.' Mention is also made of a secular opera by him entitled ' Orontes.' In 1676 Theile had been an unsuccessful candidate for the St. Thomas cantorship at Leipzig, but in 1685 succeeded Rosenmüller as Kapellmeister at Wolfenbüttel, and in 1689 held a similar post at Merseburg. The latter years of his life he spent at his birthplace, Naumburg, where his son was organist.

Theile had a great reputation as a master of counterpoint, and several MS. treatises remain, partly written by himself, partly compiled by some of his pupils, in which all the artificialities of canon and fugue are elaborately set forth with examples. The most important is one which bears the title

' Musicalisches Kunstbuch worinnen 1¢ gantz sonderbare Kunststücke und Geheimnisse welche aus den doppelten Contrapuncten entspringen, anzutreffen sind.'

In 1708 Theile had printed a catalogue of his church compositions, in which are specified twenty-three whole masses, eight Magnificats, twelve psalms *a* 4-11 with and without instruments. The only works which were ever published are ' Missarum juxta veterem contrapuncti stylum Pars I.' and ' Passio Domini nostri Jesu Christi sec. Matthaeum.' This latter work was published at Lübeck, 1673, and dedicated to Duke Christian Albert of Schleswig-Holstein. It is provided with an instrumental accompaniment *a* 5, consisting of two viole da braccia and two viole da gamba with basso continuo. The words of the Evangelist are accompanied by the gambas in a somewhat florid fashion, while the words of our Lord are accompanied by the other violas in a simpler and more subdued style ; the other single parts have only basso continuo. The dramatic choruses *a* 5 are accompanied in unison by all the instruments. There are four solo arias of a pathetic devotional cast with basso continuo, but followed by full instrumental *ritornelli*. Theile permits the work to be performed also without instruments; in this case the place of the solo arias is to be taken by familiar Chorals, and the recitatives must be simplified into a form of plain-song. But the instrumental form of the work with its devotional arias is the more interesting as preparing the way for the fuller combination of voices and instruments, and the grander devotional style in the Passion Music of Sebastian Bach. (See PASSION MUSIC.) The work has now been republished in the *D.D.T.*, vol. xvii. Other works of Theile in MS. are church cantatas with German texts for various combinations of voices and instruments. (See *Q.-L.*; also a monograph on Theile by Dr. Friedrich Zelle.)

J. R. M.

THEINRED, a 14th-century Benedictine and singer at the monastery of Dover, wrote a treatise, *De legitimis ordinibus pentachordum et tetrachordum*, dedicated to Alueredo Cantuariensi, 1371. The examples are in letter notation (MS. Bodl., No. 842).

THEME (Fr. *thème, air*; Ger. (from Lat.) *thema*, (from Ital.) *motiv*; Ital. *tema, soggetto, motivo*) is used as an alternative to SUBJECT (*q.v.*), but more particularly in the phrase 'Theme with Variations' (*Tema con variazioni*) of the kind of subject developed into a self-contained form which is susceptible of further treatment in the form of VARIATIONS (*q.v.*).

THEORBO (Fr. *théorbe, tuorbe*; Ital. *tiorba* or *tuorba*, also *arciliuto*), the large double-necked lute with two sets of tuning-pegs, the lower set holding the strings which lie over the fretted finger-board, while the upper set are attached to the bass strings, or so-called diapasons, which are used as open notes.

According to Baron's *Untersuchung des Instruments d. Lauten* (Nuremberg, 1727, p. 131) the Paduan theorbo was the true one. The English archlute of that time, so frequently named as an alternative to the harpsichord or organ for the basso continuo or 'Through Base' accompaniment, was such a theorbo. Baron gives

—eight notes on the finger-board and nine off. This is the old lute-tuning of Thomas Mace,[1] who says that the theorbo is no other than the old English lute. But early in the 17th century many large lutes had been altered to theorbos by substituting double necks for the original single ones. These altered lutes, called, according to Mersenne, 'luth téorbé' or 'liuto attior-

bato,' retained the double strings in the bass. The theorbo engraved in Mersenne's *Harmonie universelle* (Paris, 1636) is really a theorboed lute. He gives it the following accordance :

The Chanterelle is single. For the 'Tuorbe' as practised at Rome the same authority gives (p. 88)—

In the musical correspondence of Huygens, (*Musique et Musiciens*) edited by Jonckbloet and Land, and published (1882) at Leyden, is to be found a letter of Huygens, wherein he wishes to acquire a large lute, to elevate it to the quality of a theorbo, for which he considered it from its size more fit. (See LUTE.)

Praetorius (*Organographia*, Wolfenbüttel, 1619, p. 50), with whom Mersenne agrees, states that the difference between lute and theorbo is that the lute has double and the theorbo single basses. The Paduan theorbo is about 4 ft. 7 ins. high. Praetorius, in the work referred to (p. 52), seems to prefer the Roman theorbo or CHITARRONE, which, although according to his measurement about 6 ft. 1 in. in height, is not so broad in the body or so awkward to hold and grasp as the Paduan. Baron praises especially the Roman theorbos of Buchenberg or Buckenberg, a German lute-maker, who was living at Rome about A.D. 1606. His instruments had ' oval-round ' bodies of symmetrical form and a delicate and penetrating metallic timbre—a criterion of good tone in a stringed instrument.

Mace regards the lute as a solo instrument, and the theorbo as a concert or accompanying instrument : the name theorbo, however it originated, certainly became fixed to the double-necked lute, which first appeared with the introduction of opera and oratorio, when real part-playing was exchanged for the chords of the figured bass. Mersenne [2] calls it ' Cithara bijuga.' One account credits the invention of the double neck to a Signor Tiorba about 1600. Athanasius Kircher [3] attributes the introduction of the theorbo to a Neapolitan market follower, who gave it the name in a joke. His idea, says the same authority, was brought to perfection by a noble German, Hieronymus Capsberger. Victor Mahillon, in his catalogue of the Brussels Museum (1880, p. 249), names as the inventor a Roman called BARDELLA (properly Antonio Naldi) who was in the service of the Medicis, and was much praised by Caccini in the preface to ' Nuove musiche ' (A.D. 1601). Dr. Plume (MS. Pocket Book, 1657) writes : ' Inigo Jones

1 *Musick's Monument*, London, 1676, p. 207.

2 *Harmonicorum lib. xii.*, Paris, 1636.
3 *Musurgia*, Rome, 1650, cap. ii. p. 476.

first brought the theorbo into England presently
after the Popish conspiracy, 1605. At Dover
it was thought some engine brought from
Popish countries to destroy the king, and he
and it were sent up to the Council Table '
(of the Star Chamber). These attributions all
centre in the same epoch, that of the rise
of accompaniment. The theorbo was last
written for by Handel, as late as 1732, in the
oratorio of 'Esther,' in combination with a
harp, to accompany the song 'Breathe soft, ye
winds,' a fact which would seem to support
Mace's view of its being an orchestral instrument. The arciliuto also appears in 'Athaliah,'
1733, in 'Gentle Airs.' It remained in occasional
use until the end of the 18th century. (See
PLATE XLV. No. 4.)   A. J. H.

THÉRÈSE, opera in 2 acts by Massenet.
Produced Monte Carlo, 1907 ; Covent Garden,
May 22, 1919.

THESIS, see ARSIS AND THESIS ; METRE.

THESPIS, OR THE GODS GROWN OLD,
comic opera in 2 acts ; words by W. S. Gilbert,
music by A. Sullivan. Produced Gaiety
Theatre, Dec. 26, 1871.

THIBAUD, JACQUES (*b.* Bordeaux, Sept.
27, 1880), violinist. His father was his first
teacher till the age of 13, when he was sent
to Paris to the Conservatoire, studying under
Marsick, and gaining in 1896 a *premier prix.*
To supplement his modest means he played
for some years in the Café Rouge, and was
heard there by Edouard Colonne, who was
struck with his talent, and engaged him for
his orchestra.

On one occasion, the leader being unable to
play the incidental solo in an orchestral work,
Thibaud was asked to take his place, and did so
with such conspicuous success that he became a
regular soloist at the Colonne Concerts, appearing no less than fifty-four times during the
winter of 1898, and completely establishing his
fame in Paris. Since then he has travelled as
a soloist in America (1903) and in every European musical centre. He has visited England
frequently, playing chamber music at the Popular Concerts and soli on most of our concert
platforms. In his own country he has played
a good deal in concerted music with his two
brothers, one a pianist and the other a violoncellist of ability. He is in the foremost rank of
living violinists, a representative player of the
French classic school, producing not a large,
but an exceptionally pure and lovely tone, bowing with elegance, and in rapid passages he is as
accurate as Sarasate. In the playing of cantabile passages he has a caressing style peculiar
to himself, and is yet by no means wanting
in virility. After the French composers he is
heard at his best in the concertos and sonatas of
Mozart, of which he gives an exquisite account.
He played for some time on a violin by Carlo
Bergonzi, but is now the possessor of the fine

Stradivari which was once the property of
Baillot.   W. W. C.

THIBAUT, ANTON FRIEDRICH JUSTUS
(*b.* Hameln on the Weser, Jan. 4, 1772 ; *d.* Heidelberg, Mar. 25, 1840), studied law at Göttingen,
became tutor at Königsberg, and law-professor
at the University of Kiel, then at Jena, and in
1805 at Heidelberg, where he remained till his
death. The Archduke of Baden made him
Geheimrath. He was an ardent admirer of
the old Italian church-composers, especially of
Palestrina, and founded a society for the
practice of such music at his own house.

MENDELSSOHN (*q.v.* Vol. III. p. 383) writes
with the greatest enthusiasm about Thibaut,
' There is but one Thibaut,' he says, ' but he is
as good as half a dozen. He is a man.' [1]

One of Thibaut's greatest services to the
cause of art was his collection of music, which
included a very valuable series of Volkslieder of
all nations. The catalogue was published in
1847 (Heidelberg) and Thibaut's widow endeavoured to sell it to one of the public libraries
of Germany, but was unable to do so till 1850,
when it was acquired for the court library of
Munich. Of still greater value is his book
Ueber Reinheit der Tonkunst (Heidelberg, 1825,
with portrait of Palestrina ; 2nd edition, 1826).
The title does not indicate (as his friend Bähr
observes in the preface to the 3rd edition, 1853)
purity either of construction or execution, but
purity of the art itself. The treatise may
justly claim to have exercised a moral influence.
Thibaut maintains that as there is music which
acts as a powerful agent in purifying and cultivating the mind, so there is music which has
as depraving an influence as that exercised by
immoral literature. From this point of view he
urges the necessity of purity in music, and sets
himself firmly against all that is shallow, common, unhealthy or frivolous. His idea of im-
purity may be gathered from the fact that in
the essay on instrumentation he unhesitatingly
condemns the flutes, clarinets and bassoons
added by Mozart to ' The people that walked
in darkness,' urging that they entirely change
the character of the piece. He also strongly
censures the frequent changes of tempo and
expression by which Mozart gives colour to his
splendid motet ' Misericordias Domine.' It is
not too much to say that this book, dealing
as it does in a spirit of great earnestness
with questions which must ever attract the
musical world, will always be of interest. The
last German edition came out in 1861. The
English version (*Purity in Musical Art*, John
Murray, 1877) is by W. H. Gladstone.   F. G.

THIBAUT IV. (*b.* Troyes, 1201 ; *d.* Pam-
pelune, July 8, 1253), King of Navarre and
Count of Champagne, famous TROUVÈRE (*q.v.*).
Bishop La Ravallie republished 63 of his songs

[1] See also *The Mendelssohn Family*, vol. i. p. 138, for an extract,
from Mendelssohn's letter to his mother, dated, from Heidelberg
Sept. 20, 1827, and printed here in previous editions.

in 1742, unfortunately with imperfect rendering of the melodies, of which some have since been often republished and become very popular.   E. v. d. s.

THIEME, CLEMENS (b. Gross-Dietmansdorf, near Dresden, Sept. 7, 1631 ; d. Zeitz, Mar. 27, 1668). He went to Copenhagen in 1642 as choir-boy in the court chapel, and returned in 1646 to Dresden, where he was appointed instrumental player in the court chapel. In 1663 he went to the court at Zeitz on the recommendation of Schütz, and became successively Konzertmeister and director of the chapel. In addition to masses and other church music, he composed sonatas for 2 violins, as well as for 5-8 instruments (Q.-L.).

THIERRY, the name of a celebrated family of Paris organ-builders. (1) PIERRE (b. 1605 ; d. Sept. 16, 1665), built the organ at the Hôtel-Dieu, Pontoise, now in the church of Notre Dame in that town, and carried out important work on the organs in the church of St. Gervais, Paris, during 1636. (2) CHARLES (b. Paris, 1641), son of the preceding, directed and enlarged the workshops started by his father. (3) ALEXANDRE, carried on the reputation of the firm. His masterpiece is the organ in the church of St. Louis des Invalides (1679). He restored the organs of St. Gervais, 1684–85, built that of the chapel of the Château at St. Germain-en-Laye, 1684, and of Saint-Cyr, 1688. (4) FRANÇOIS, the most celebrated of the family, built the great organ of the church of the Innocents, 1723–25, now in St. Nicholas du Chardonnet, and the great organ of Notre Dame, Paris, 1730–33, an instrument of 45 stops which was received by Calvière, Du Mage, Daquin and Clérambault, in the second fortnight of June 1733.   F. Rᴸ.

THILLON, SOPHIE ANNE (ANNA), (b. London, c. 1816 ; d. Torquay, May 5, 1903), singer. Her father's name was Hunt. At the age of 14 she left England for France with her mother and sister, and received instruction from Bordogni, Tadolini and Claude Thomas Thillon, conductor of the Havre Philharmonic Society, whom she afterwards married. She appeared at Havre, Clermont and Nantes, with such success as to obtain an engagement at the Théâtre de la Renaissance, Paris (Salle Ventadour), where she made her début, Nov. 15, 1838, as the heroine, on the production of Grisar's 'Lady Melvil.' She also sang as Argentine in his 'L'Eau merveilleuse,' and in Monpou's 'La Chaste Suzanne,' etc. Her voice was a 'soprano sfogato' of marvellous timbre, from B♭ below the stave to E♭ in alt., and, combined with her personal charms, it obtained for her the favour of the public in a remarkable degree. On Aug. 11, 1840, she first appeared at the Opéra-Comique as Mathilde in 'La Neige.' She next played Elizabeth in 'Lestocq,' and became a great favourite with Auber, who gave her

instruction, and at whose request she sang the part of Catarina in 'Les Diamants de la couronne' (produced Mar. 6, 1841).

On May 2, 1844, she first appeared in public in England at the Princess's in the 'Crown Diamonds,' and met with extraordinary success, and the opera, then first produced in England, ran to the end of the season. She was also well received at the Philharmonic and other concerts. She afterwards appeared in England in 1845 and 1846 at Drury Lane, playing Stella in the 'Enchantress,' on its production May 14, 1845, a part composed expressly for her by Balfe ; in 1846 at the Haymarket in 'Le Domino noir' and 'L'Eau merveilleuse' ; and in 1848 at the Princess's in 'La Fille du régiment.' She also played at Brussels and in the French and English provinces, and from 1851–1854 in America, first introducing opera at San Francisco. She reappeared in 1854 at Jullien's concerts, after which she was only heard at intervals, on account of a severe throat attack. Her last appearances in opera were in 1855 at the Lyceum as Catarina. She was last heard in public at the Brighton Festival of 1867.

                                                A. C.

THIRD. One of the most important intervals in harmonic music, since by one or other of its principal forms it supplies the means of definition in all the most characteristic chords. Three forms are generally met with—major, minor and diminished. The first of these occurs most characteristically in the major scale between the tonic and the mediant—as between C and E in the key of C (a). It is also an important factor in the Dominant chord, whether in the major or minor mode—as between G and B in the Dominant of the key

of C (b). The minor third occurs most characteristically in the minor scale as the converse to the principal major third in the major scale ; that is, between tonic and mediant ; as C and E♭ in C minor (c). It also makes its appearance characteristically in the chord of the subdominant—as F–A♭ in C minor (d) ; but both this minor third and the major third of the dominant chord are sometimes supplanted by major and minor thirds respectively for the convenience of melodic progression in the minor mode.

The ratio of the sounds of the major third is 4 : 5, and that of the minor third 5 : 6. Thirds were not accepted by the ancients as consonances, and when they began to come into use in the early Middle Ages as so-called imperfect consonances the major third used was that commonly known as the Pythagorean third, which is arrived at by taking four fifths from the lower note. The ratio of this interval is 64 : 81, and it is therefore considerably sharper than the just or natural third; while the major third of equal temperament generally used in modern music lies between the two, but a little nearer to the Pythagorean third. (See TEMPERAMENT.)

The resultant tones of thirds are strong. That of the major third is two octaves lower than the lower of the two notes, and that of the minor third two octaves and a major third.

Diminished thirds are rough dissonances; they occur in modern music as the inversions of augmented sixths, as F♯–A♭ (e); and their ratio is 225 : 256. (See INTERVAL; HARMONY.)

C. H. H. P.

THIRLWALL, (1) JOHN WADE (b. Shilbottle, Northumbria, Jan. 11, 1809; d. June 15, 1875), was the son of an engineer who had been the playmate of George Stephenson. He appeared in public before he was 8 years old, at the Newcastle Theatre, afterwards became music-director at the Durham Theatre, and was engaged by the Duke of Northumberland to collect Northumbrian airs. He subsequently came to London, was employed in the Opera band, and was music-director at Drury Lane, the Haymarket, Olympic and Adelphi Theatres successively. After the death of Nadaud in 1864 he was appointed conductor of the ballet music at the Royal Italian Opera. In 1843 he composed the music for 'A Book of Ballads,' one of which, 'The Sunny Days of Childhood,' was very popular; also many songs, violin solos, and instrumental trios. He was for some time music critic to the Pictorial Times, Literary Gazette and Court Circular. Besides music he cultivated poetry and painting, and in 1872 published a volume of poems.

His daughter and pupil (2) ANNIE, a soprano singer, first appeared at the National Concerts, Exeter Hall, in 1855. On Feb. 4, 1856, she first performed on the stage at the Strand Theatre, whence she removed to the Olympic, Oct. 12, 1856. In Oct. 1859 she joined the Pyne and Harrison company at Covent Garden. A few years afterwards she became the leading member of an English Opera company which performed in the provinces. She retired in 1876.

W. H. H.

THIRTEENTH, CHORD OF THE, see HARMONY (2), CLASSIFICATION OF CHORDS.

THOINAN, ERNEST, the nom de plume of ANTOINE ERNEST ROQUET (b. Nantes, Jan. 23, 1827; d. Paris, between May 27 and June 3, 1894), a distinguished amateur and collector of works on music. From collecting he advanced to writing, first as a contributor to La France musicale, L'Art musical and others. His essays in these periodicals he afterwards published: La Musique à Paris en 1862 (Paris, 1863); L'Opéra des Troyens au Père Lachaise (1864); Les Origines de la Chapelle musique des souverains de France (1864); Les Déplorations de Guillaume Crestin

(1864), Maugars (1865), Antoine de Cousu (1866); Curiosités musicales (1866); Un Bisaïeul de Molière : recherches sur les Mazuel (1878); Louis Constantin, roi des violons (1878); Notes bibliographiques sur la guerre des Gluckistes et des Piccinnistes (1878). These pamphlets contain much curious information, and many corrections of Fétis's mistakes. He also republished the very scarce Entretien des musiciens, by Annibal Gantez (1878), with notes and explanations. Les Hotteterre et les Chédeville (1894) is the last of his works.

G. C.

THOMAS, ARTHUR GORING (b. Ratton Park, Sussex, Nov. 20, 1850; d. Mar. 20, 1892), opera composer, was educated for the Civil Service, and did not begin to study music seriously until after he came of age. In 1873 he went to Paris, and studied for two years under Émile Durand. In 1877 he entered the R.A.M., studied there for three years under Sullivan and Prout, and twice gained the Lucas medal for composition. He studied orchestration later with Max Bruch. An opera in three acts (MS.), libretto by Clifford Harrison, on Moore's 'The Light of the Harem,' performed in part at the R.A.M. on Nov. 7, 1879, procured him a commission from Carl Rosa which he fulfilled in 'Esmeralda.' Of his four concert-scenas, two were performed in London and one at the Crystal Palace; an anthem for soprano solo, chorus and orchestra, 'Out of the deep,' was performed at St. James's Hall in 1878; and a cantata, 'The Sun-worshippers,' was given with success at the Norwich Festival of 1881.

Ever since the composition of an early unfinished opera, 'Don Braggadocio,' to a libretto by his brother, Thomas had shown strong leanings towards dramatic writing, and it was no wonder that the work commissioned by Carl Rosa was at once recognised as a very remarkable production. The book of 'Esmeralda' was written by T. Marzials and A. Randegger, and the opera was produced at Drury Lane with great success, Mar. 26, 1883. It was afterwards given in a German version at Cologne and Hamburg, and was revived in a French version at Covent Garden in 1890. The original English version was again revived by the Royal Carl Rosa Company at Covent Garden in Jan. 1908; and the opera must be regarded as a classic of English art in its own way. Its characteristic and appropriate music, its originality of idea and skill of treatment as well as the mere beauty of the musical themes and the grace of many of the songs, entitle it to a very high place.

Two years afterwards, on Apr. 16, 1885, the Carl Rosa Company followed up this success with 'Nadeshda,' a romantic opera in four acts, to a libretto by Julian Sturgis. This, too, was given in a German version, at Breslau in 1890. The subject is more serious and less brilliant than that of 'Esmeralda,' and the popularity of the work has not been as great, although the contralto song, ' O my heart is weary ' (written for the German version), is one of the composer's best-known compositions. In June 1887, the Cambridge University Musical Society produced his orchestral ' Suite de Ballet.' A delightful comic opera, ' The Golden Web,' to a libretto by F. Corder and B. C. Stephenson, was not produced until after the composer's death ; it was given at Liverpool, Feb. 15, 1893, and at the Lyric Theatre, London, Mar. 11 of the same year. Another important posthumous work was the cantata, ' The Swan and the Skylark,' to words by Mrs. Hemans, found in pianoforte score after his death ; it was orchestrated by Stanford, and produced at the Birmingham Festival of 1894. In 1891 symptoms of mental disease began to appear, and on Mar. 20, 1892, his career ended tragically. He was buried in Finchley Cemetery. A great number of songs, duets, etc. were published in his lifetime, and some after his death ; a practically complete list of his works was in the programme of the memorial concert given in St. James's Hall, July 13, 1892, with the object of founding a scholarship in his memory ; this was duly established at the R.A.M. Some of his MSS. are now in the British Museum, and others in the R.C.M.   w. b. s.

THOMAS, CHARLES LOUIS AMBROISE (b. Metz, Aug. 5, 1811 ; d. Paris, Feb. 12, 1896), eminent French composer. The son of a musician, he learnt his notes with his alphabet, and while still a child played the piano and violin. Having entered the Paris Conservatoire in 1828, he carried off the first prize for piano in 1829, for harmony in 1830, and the Grand Prix de Rome in 1832. He also studied the piano with Kalkbrenner, harmony with Barbereau, and composition with the venerable Lesueur, who used to call him his ' note sensible ' (leading-note), because he was extremely sensitive, and the seventh of his pupils who had gained the Prix de Rome. His cantata ' Hermann et Ketty ' was engraved, as were also the works composed during his stay in Italy, immediately after his return. The latter comprise a string-quartet and quintet ; a trio for PF., violin and violoncello ; a fantasia for PF. and orchestra ; PF. pieces for two and four hands ; six Italian songs ; three motets with organ ; and a ' Messe de Requiem ' with orchestra.

Early works of this calibre gave promise of a musician who would work hard, produce much, and by no means rest content with academical honours. He soon gained access to the Opéra-Comique, and produced there with success ' La Double Échelle,' one act (Aug. 23, 1837) ; ' Le Perruquier de la Régence,' three acts (Mar. 30, 1838) ; and ' Le Panier fleuri,' one act (May 6, 1839). Ambition, however, prompted him to attempt the Opéra, and there he produced ' La Gipsy ' (Jan. 28, 1839), a ballet in three

acts, of which the second only was his, the rest being by Benoist ; ' Le Comte de Carmagnola ' (Apr. 19, 1841) ; ' Le Guerilléro ' (June 2, 1842), both in two acts ; and ' Betty ' (July 10, 1846), ballet in two acts ; but it was hard for so young a composer to hold his own with Auber, Halévy, Meyerbeer and Donizetti, so Thomas returned to the Opéra - Comique. There he composed successively

' Carline,' 3 acts (Feb. 24, 1840).
' Angélique et Médor,' 1 act (May 10, 1843).
' Mina,' 3 acts (Oct. 10, 1843).
' Le Caïd,' 2 acts (Jan. 3, 1849).
' Le Songe d'une nuit d'été,' 3 acts (Apr. 20, 1850).
' Raymond,' 3 acts (June 5, 1851).
' La Tonelli,' 2 acts (Mar. 30, 1853).
' La Cour de Célimène,' 2 acts (Apr. 11, 1855).
' Psyche,' 3 acts (Jan. 26, 1857, revived with additions May 21, 1878).
' Le Carnaval de Venise,' 3 acts (Dec. 9, 1857).
' Le Roman d'Elvire,' 3 acts (Feb. 3, 1860).
' Mignon,' 3 acts (Nov. 17, 1866).
' Gille et Gillotin,' 1 act, composed in 1861, but not produced till Apr. 22, 1874.

To these must be added two cantatas composed for the inauguration of a statue to Lesueur at Abbeville (Aug. 10, 1852), and for the Boieldieu centenary at Rouen (June 13, 1875) : a ' Messe solennelle ' (Nov. 22, 1857), a ' Marche religieuse ' (Nov. 22, 1865) composed for the Association des Artistes Musiciens ; and a quantity of partsongs and choral scenas, such as ' France,' ' Le Tyrol,' ' L'Atlantique,' ' Le Carnaval de Rome,' ' Les Traîneaux,' ' La Nuit du Sabbat,' etc. The life and dramatic movement of his unaccompanied partsongs for men's voices showed the essentially dramatic nature of Thomas's genius, which, after enlarging the limits of opéra - comique, found a congenial though formidable subject in ' Hamlet,' five acts (Mar. 9, 1868). The Prince of Denmark was originally cast for a tenor, but there being at that time no tenor at the Opéra capable of creating such a part, Thomas altered the music to suit a baritone, and entrusted it to Faure. The success of this great work following immediately on that secured by ' Mignon,' pointed out its composer as the right man to succeed Auber as director of the Conservatoire [1] (July 6, 1871). (See CONSERVATOIRE.) A post of this nature leaves scant leisure for other employment, and from the date of his appointment Thomas composed nothing beyond the solfèges and exercises for the examinations, except one opera ' Françoise de Rimini ' (Apr. 14, 1882), the prologue and fourth act of which are entitled to rank with his ' Hamlet.'

He was made a knight of the Legion of Honour in 1845, an officer in 1858, and received the Grand Cross in 1894, on the occasion of the thousandth performance of 'Mignon.'

There is a fine oil-painting of him by Hippolyte Flandrin, a terra-cotta bust by Doublemard, and a marble bust and medallion, the last a striking likeness, by Oudiné. Berlioz wrote an interesting article on the witty satire, ' Le Caïd,' collected in Les Musiciens, p. 241.   G. C.

[1] He had been professor of composition since 1852, and a member of the Institut from 1851.

THOMAS, (1) JOHN (b. Bridgend, Glamorganshire, Mar. 1, 1826 ; d. Mar. 19, 1913), known in Wales as 'Pencerdd Gwalia,' i.e. chief of the Welsh minstrels, a title conferred on him at the Aberdare Eisteddfod of 1861, was a very distinguished harpist, born on St. David's Day. He played the piccolo when only 4, and when 11 won a harp at an Eisteddfod. In 1840 he was placed by Ada, Countess of Lovelace (Byron's daughter), at the R.A.M., where he studied under J. B. Chatterton (harp), C. J. Read (piano) and Lucas and Cipriani Potter (composition). He remained there for about eight years, during which time he composed a harp concerto, a symphony, several overtures, quartets, two operas, etc. On leaving the R.A.M. he was made in succession Associate, Honorary Member and professor of the harp. In 1851 he played in the orchestra of Her Majesty's Opera, and in the same year went a concert tour on the continent, a practice he continued during the winter months of the next ten years, playing successively in France, Germany, Russia, Austria and Italy. He played a harp concerto of his own at a Philharmonic Concert in 1852. In 1862 Thomas published a valuable collection of Welsh melodies, and in the same year gave with great success the first concert of Welsh music in London. In 1871 he was appointed conductor of a Welsh Choral Union, which for six years gave six concerts annually. In 1872, on the death of J. B. Chatterton, he was appointed harpist to Queen Victoria ; he also taught the harp at the R.C.M.

Thomas always took a deep interest in the music of his native country. There was scarcely an Eisteddfod of importance at which he did not appear as judge or performer, and he collected a large sum with which in 1883 he endowed a permanent scholarship for Wales at the R.A.M. In 1866, at the Chester Eisteddfod, he was presented with a purse of 500 guineas in recognition of his services to Welsh music. Thomas was a member of the Academies of St. Cecilia and the Philharmonic of Rome, the Florentine Philharmonic, and the R.A.M., Royal Philharmonic, and Royal Society of Musicians, of London. His compositions include a large amount of harp music, amongst which are two concertos ; 'Llewelyn,' a cantata for the Swansea Eisteddfod (1863) ; and 'The Bride of Neath Valley,' for the Chester Eisteddfod (1866). 'Llewelyn' was revived at the Chicago Exhibition of 1893, where he acted as judge at an Eisteddfod.   W. B. S.

(2) THOMAS (AP THOMAS) (b. Bridgend, 1829 ; d. Ottawa, Canada, May 1913), younger brother of the above, was also a distinguished harpist. He gave many successful concerts in Europe (1851-67), appeared at the Gewandhaus, Leipzig (Jan. 18, 1872) and went to America in 1895. His compositions include a cantata,

'The Pilgrim's Progress,' and he wrote a history of the harp. (See Mus. T., June 1913, p. 388.)

THOMAS, KURT (b. Tönning, Schleswig-Holstein, May 25, 1904), composer. After passing his school years at Lennep in Rhineland and receiving some musical instruction from Hermann Inderan at Barmen, he entered the Leipzig Conservatorium in 1922, where he studied the piano with Robert Teichmüller, theory with Max Ludwig and composition with Hermann Grabner. He also had lessons in composition from Arnold Mendelssohn and, though he was never a direct pupil, owes much to Karl Straube for constant help and advice. In 1925 he was appointed a teacher of theory at the Leipzig Conservatorium. He is a composer of quite exceptional promise and has already written several notable works. His a cappella Mass in A minor for solo voices and two choirs, composed when he was 19, is a work of singular beauty and of remarkable maturity and sureness of touch. While intensely modern and individual in technique and idiom, it is by no means extravagant or revolutionary. It has been performed twice at the Leipzig Thomaskirche and in other towns, and has always produced a profound impression, notably at the 55th Festival of the Allgemeiner Deutscher Musikverein held in 1925 at Kiel, when the critics from all over Germany showed a rare unanimity in declaring it to be the outstanding feature of the Festival. His pianoforte trio, performed in 1925 at a concert of the International Society for Contemporary Music, is also a fine and admirably written work, sometimes a little ruthless in its dissonances but full of real substance and vigorous life. Published works (Breitkopf & Härtel) :

Mass in A min. for soli and 2 choirs, op. 1 ; sonata in E min. for PF. and vln., op. 2 ; PF. trio in D min. op. 3 ; Psalm 137, 'An den Wassern zu Babel,' for 2 a cappella choirs, op. 4.   H. B.

THOMAS, LEWIS WILLIAM (b. Bath, Apr. 1826 ; d. London, June 13, 1896), of Welsh parentage, learnt singing under Bianchi Taylor, and in 1850, when 24, was appointed lay-clerk in Worcester Cathedral. In 1852 he was made master of the choristers, and during the next few years sang frequently at Birmingham, Gloucester, Hereford and Worcester. In 1854 he made his first appearance in London, at St. Martin's Hall ; in 1855 he sang at the Sacred Harmonic, and in 1856 settled in London, with an appointment at St. Paul's. In the following year Thomas left St. Paul's for the choir of the Temple Church, and in the same year was appointed a gentleman of Her Majesty's Chapel Royal. In 1857 he had lessons of Randegger, and appeared under his direction on the operatic stage, which however he soon abandoned for the concert-room, where he was chiefly known as a bass singer of oratorio music. For a time he contributed musical criticisms to the *Daily Telegraph*.   w. b. s.

THOMAS, ROBERT HAROLD (*b.* Cheltenham, July 8, 1834; *d.* London, July 29, 1885), a favourite pupil of Sterndale Bennett, under whom he was placed at the R.A.M. at a very early age. His other masters were Cipriani Potter (theory), and Henry Blagrove (violin). He made his first appearance as a pianist at a R.A.M. Concert, May 25, 1850, and after this appeared frequently at the same concerts, both as pianist and composer. In 1858 Thomas played before the Queen and Prince Consort at Windsor, and in 1864 played Bennett's first concerto at the Philharmonic. A few years later, he retired from public life and devoted himself to teaching, becoming professor of the piano at the R.A.M., and the G.S.M. His compositions include many original piano pieces, some songs, many arrangements, etc., and three overtures for orchestra : Overture to ' As You Like It,' produced by the Musical Society of London in 1864 ; and ' Mountain, Lake and Moorland,' produced at the Philharmonic in 1880.   w. b. s.

THOMAS, THEODORE (*b.* Esens, Hanover, Oct. 11, 1835; *d.* Chicago, Jan. 4, 1905), conductor, was eminent as one of the pioneers of music, especially orchestral music, in the United States. (See NEW YORK ; CHICAGO.)

He received his first musical instruction from his father, a violinist, and at the age of 6 made a successful public appearance. The family emigrated to the United States in 1845, and for two years Theodore made frequent appearances as a solo violinist in concerts at New York. In 1851 he made a trip through the Southern States. Returning to New York he was engaged as one of the first violins in concerts and operatic performances during the engagements of Jenny Lind, Sontag, Grisi, Mario, etc. He occupied the position of leading violin under Arditi, and subsequently, the same position in German and Italian troupes, a part of the time officiating as conductor, until 1861, when he withdrew from the theatre. In 1855 he began a series of chamber-concerts at New York, with W. Mason, J. Mosenthal, Carl Bergmann, G. Matzka and F. Bergner, which were continued every season until 1869.

In 1864 Thomas began his first series of symphony concerts at Irving Hall, New York, which were continued for five seasons, with varying success. In 1872 the symphony concerts were resumed and carried on until he left New York in 1878. Steinway Hall was used for these concerts, and the orchestra numbered eighty performers. In the summer of 1866, in order to secure that efficiency which can only come from constant practice together, he began the experiment of giving nightly concerts at the Terrace Garden, New York, removing, in 1868, to larger quarters at the Central Park Garden.

In 1869 he made his first concert tour through the Eastern and Western States. The orchestra, at first numbering forty players, was, in subsequent seasons, increased to sixty. The programmes presented during these trips, as well as at New York, were noticeable for their catholic nature, and for the great number of novelties brought out. But it was also noticeable that the evenings devoted to the severer class of music, old or new, in the Garden concerts at New York were often the most fully attended. Thomas's tendencies, it was plainly seen, were toward the new school of music ; but he was none the less attentive to the old, and he introduced to American amateurs a large number of compositions by the older masters. The repertory of the orchestra was very large, and included compositions in every school.   F. H. J.

Thomas, who had been a member of the Philharmonic Society of New York since 1853, was elected conductor of the organisation in 1877, but after a single season's activities was called to Cincinnati, Ohio, to become director of the College of Music, an institution which had grown up as one of the fruits of the enthusiasm created by the Music Festivals instituted by him in 1873. In Cincinnati he organised an orchestra to give concerts in connexion with the College, but after a year accepted re-election to the New York post, journeying to the metropolis once a month in order to prepare and direct the concerts. In Feb. 1880 differences of opinion between him and the other officials of the College led to his resignation and return to New York, where, besides conducting the concerts of the Philharmonic Society, he called his own orchestra back into existence. With it he gave high - class symphony concerts, popular concerts, and concerts for young people until the end of the season 1887–88, when, discouraged for want of popular support, he abandoned all activities except those which devolved on him as conductor of the Philharmonic Societies of New York and Brooklyn.

In 1891 the Chicago Orchestra (later known as the Theodore Thomas Orchestra, and now since 1912 as the Chicago Symphony Orchestra) was organised for him by wealthy music-lovers in the metropolis of the North-West, and he transferred his labours to that city. The twelve years of his connexion with the Philharmonic Society as its conductor were for the society a period of uninterrupted prosperity, towards which he contributed greatly, not only by his artistic zeal and skill, but also by voluntarily relinquishing, year after year, a portion of the sum which under his contract he was entitled to collect. The story of his labours in Chicago belongs to the history of the orchestra which bore his name. In 1886 and 1887 he was concerned in a disastrous effort to put opera in the vernacular on a high plane in America. He died having been privileged to conduct only three concerts in the new home of the orchestra over whose artistic fortunes he had presided for fourteen years.   H. E. K.

THOMAS AND SALLY, a short opera which kept the stage, as a secondary piece, for a great number of years. The music was by Dr. Arne, and it was first produced at Covent Garden on Nov. 28, 1760.[1] It was published by the composer himself, in folio, with the engraved date 1761 ; afterwards the plates were acquired by Walsh, who erased date, name of engraver and author's imprint. Walsh also issued a copy in oblong folio. The libretto was written by Isaac Bickerstaff, and the piece has the sub-title, ' The Sailor's Return.' The opera formed a model for a great number of plays up to the middle of the 19th century. Beard and Mattocks, with Miss Brent and Mrs. Vernon, were the original performers.   F. K.

THOMAS DE WALSYNGHAM, prior of Wymondham in 1396, and monk and singer at the abbey of St. Albans, c. 1440. He wrote a treatise, *Regulae Magistri Thomae Walsingham de figuris compositis* . . ., which is contained in the Waltham Holy Cross MS. in the British Museum (*Q.-L.*).

THOMASSCHULE, see LEIPZIG.

THOMÉ, FRANCIS LUCIEN JOSEPH (FRANÇOIS LUC JOSEPH) (*b.* Port Louis, Mauritius, Oct. 18, 1850 ; *d.* Nov. 16, 1909), composer, was brought as a child to Paris, where he entered the Conservatoire. He studied with Marmontel and Duprato, obtaining the second prize for piano and harmony (1869), and first prize for counterpoint and fugue (1870). On the completion of his studies he soon made a name for himself as a composer of works of small calibre, such as songs, piano pieces, etc., and was in great request as a teacher. His opera, ' Martin et Frontin,' was produced at Eaux-Bonnes in 1877, and his ballet, ' Djemmah,' at the Eden-Theatre, Paris, in 1886. Another ballet, ' La Folie parisienne,' was given at the same theatre ; an operetta, ' Barbe-Bleuette,' was brought out in 1889, and ' Endymion et Phœbé ' was given at the Opéra-Comique. One of his most important works was the music to the beautiful ' Mystère,' ' L'Enfant Jésus,' first heard in 1891. In 1892 his opera, ' Le Caprice de la reine,' was brought out at Cannes, and in 1898 another ballet, ' La Bulle d'amour,' was produced. Other works for the Paris stage were ' Le Papillon,' ' Le Trottin,' ' Mademoiselle Pygmalion ' ; and Thomé wrote also incidental music for many plays. A choral ' Hymne à la nuit ' had a great success ; but Thomé's name is best known to the English public by his popular ' Simple Aveu,' originally for piano.   M.

[1] An earlier date for the production of the opera is undoubtedly wrong.

THOMPSON, a family of London music-publishers, of great note, in the second half of the 18th century. The firm started with PETER THOMPSON, who was established at the sign ' The Violin and Hautboy ' (or, as sometimes given, ' The Violin, Hautboy and German Flute ') at the west end of St. Paul's Church-yard. This address was afterwards named 75 St. Paul's Churchyard. Peter Thompson was publishing small musical works, as Country Dances, Instructions for the Flute, etc., in 1751. The sets of yearly Country Dances began with those for this year, and were continued throughout the whole period of the Thompson firm's existence and that of their successors. About 1758–59 Peter took his son Charles into partnership, and in 1762 his other son, Samuel, also. In 1764 Peter had either died or retired from the business.

The various changes in the firm and the dates for them are best shown in tabular form. They will serve to give accurate date to the published music and the instruments made or sold by the Thompson family :

Peter Thompson, 1751–58.
Charles and Ann, c. 1758.
Thompson & Son, 1758–59 to 1760–61.
Thompson & Sons, 1761–62 to 1763–64.
Charles and Samuel, 1764 to 1776–78.
• Samuel and Ann, 1778.
Samuel, Ann and Peter, 1779–80 to c. 1794.
Samuel, Ann, Peter and Henry, 1792.
Samuel, Ann and Henry, 1795–96.
Ann and Henry, 1796–97 (or later).
Henry, 1798–99 to 1802–03.

In addition to this it may be mentioned that after 1790 the imprints frequently merely give ' Messrs. Thompson ' or ' Thompsons' ware-house.'

About 1804 Henry Thompson gave up the business, and it was taken over by Purday & Button, which, in 1807, is transposed into ' Button & Purday.' S. J. Button, the senior partner, on the retirement of Purday in 1808, took into partnership John Whitaker the musician. As BUTTON & WHITAKER (*q.v.*) the firm built up a large business, which in 1820 became ' Whitaker & Co.'

In the early years of its existence the Thompson firm published many minor musical works, now of considerable interest. At a later date their trade was of a very extensive character, and they became among the most important of London music firms. Many violins bear their labels, but it must be remembered that these have been made by fiddle-makers in their employ. Dictionaries of violin-makers promulgate a great many errors of dates and facts relating to the Thompson firm.

ROBERT THOMPSON, probably a brother of Peter Thompson, had a shop also in or near St. Paul's Churchyard. His sign and address was at the Bass Violin at number 1 Paul's Alley. A violin label of his (not very trust-worthy evidence) would certify him at this address in 1749. He was certainly there in 1755, and publishing a small quantity of half-sheet music. He remained in Paul's Alley until 1771, when he removed to 8 Lombard Street, remaining there for about ten years. He was perhaps more of an instrument-maker than a music-publisher.   F. K.

THOMPSON, HERBERT (b. Hunslet, Leeds, Aug. 11, 1856), has been critic both of music and of pictures to the *Yorkshire Post* since 1886.

Thompson was educated privately in Germany (Wiesbaden) and at St. John's College, Cambridge. He entered the Inner Temple and was called to the Bar in 1879. At Cambridge he was strongly influenced by Stanford, who was then stirring up new musical life in the University ; and it was largely through Stanford that music became the primary interest of Thompson's career. During the forty years of his association with the *Yorkshire Post* Thompson has steadily devoted himself to the improvement of musical cultivation in the North of England, and he holds there a position of exceptional authority. In 1925 the University of Leeds conferred on him the honorary degree of D.Litt. Outside journalism his influence has been exercised through the many musical institutions whose activities he has assisted as a member of committee ; and also through his ably written analytical notes to concerts, and especially the Leeds Festival. He has been a valued contributor to this Dictionary, in both its second and third editions.   C.

THOMSON, CÉSAR (b. Liège, Belgium, Mar. 18, 1857), violinist, began to study the violin in childhood under his father, who sent him, at the age of 7, to the Liège Conservatoire of Music. There he joined the class of Jacques Dupuis, a very exacting task-master, with whom he studied to such purpose that before reaching the age of 14 he had acquired executive powers far exceeding those of any other of the many talented pupils, some of them since famous, of the Conservatoire ; and two years later was recognised as possessing a technique unrivalled by any violinist then living. Later he went for some finishing lessons to Léonard, with whom he studied interpretation, but his career has been mainly noteworthy for achievements in the domain of pure technique. In 1875 he travelled in Italy, and became a member of the private orchestra of Baron de Derwies. In 1879 he joined Bilse's orchestra in Berlin as Konzertmeister, and in 1882, after a very successful appearance at the annual musical festival at Brussels, he was appointed violin professor at the Liège Conservatoire. This post he held until 1897, when he left Liège, and the following year succeeded Ysaÿe as principal professor of the violin at the Brussels Conservatoire. He has travelled much as a soloist in the principal cities of the Old and New Worlds, and

has scored many successes, notably at the Gewandhaus concert in Leipzig in 1891, and at Brussels in 1898, but in England and America he never succeeded in completely capturing the sympathies of his audiences. Practising emotional reticence to the verge of austerity he was considered greatest as an exponent of Paganini, whose works he revived at a time when they were fast becoming a dead letter. He also devoted himself to the editing, arranging and performing of works of the early Italian school.   W. W. C.

THOMSON, GEORGE (b. Limekilns, Dunfermline, Mar. 4, 1757 ; d. Leith, Feb. 18, 1851[1]), was for fifty years Secretary to the Board of Trustees for the Encouragement of Arts and Manufactures in Scotland. His place in musical history is that of the most enthusiastic, persevering and successful collector of the melodies of Scotland, Wales and Ireland, a work begun in his youth and continued for forty years or more.

I. (1) *Scotland.* He proposed to rescue from oblivion, so far as it could possibly be accomplished, every existing Scots melody, in all its forms and varieties. Being in correspondence with and knowing personally gentlemen in every part of Scotland, no man had greater facilities for the work. He proposed, further, to publish ' all the fine airs both of the plaintive and lively kind, unmixed with trifling and inferior ones.' The first ' set ' of 25 was published in Edinburgh in June 1793.

(2) *Ireland.* At first he included twenty favourite Irish airs in his ' sets,' denoting them in the index by an asterisk. Burns persuaded him to undertake a separate publication of Irish melodies, and offered to write the new texts. This was the origin of the two volumes under that title, 1814 and 1816 respectively, for the collection of which Thomson was indebted especially to Dr. J. Latham of Cork, and other friends in various parts of Ireland, who are responsible for whatever faults of omission and commission they exhibit. (See IRISH MUSIC.)

(3) *Wales.* Meantime he undertook to collect the melodies played by Welsh harpers and adapt them to the voice. The project found favour in Wales, and friends in all parts of it sent them to him as played by the harpers ; ' but the anxiety he felt to have a complete and authentic collection induced him to traverse Wales himself, in order to hear the airs played by the best harpers, to collate and correct the manuscripts he had received, and to glean such airs as his correspondents had omitted to gather.' There was of course no deciding as to the original form of an air on which no two harpers agreed, and Thomson could only adopt that which seemed to him the most simple and

----

[1] Dates verified by registers and gravestone in Kensal Green Cemetery.

perfect. Very few if any had Welsh texts, or were at all vocal. To make them so, he in some cases omitted monotonous repetitions; in some repeated a strain ; in most discarded the ornaments and divisions of the harpers; but no changes were made in the tunes except such as were absolutely necessary to ' make songs of them.' [1]

II. In regard to their texts, these three collections of melodies consisted of four classes : (1) without words ; (2) with none in English ; (3) with English texts, silly, vapid, or indecent; (4) a few with unimpeachable words, even in which cases he mostly thought it well to add a new song. In fact, in the first twenty-four Scottish airs, sixteen have two songs each, most if not all written expressly for the work. A large number of eminent authors, including Peter Pindar, Mrs. Grant, Sir Alexander Boswell, Joanna Baillie and Sir Walter Scott, were employed by Thomson for this purpose.

When the melody was known to the poet, there was no difficulty in writing an appropriate song ; when not, Thomson sent a copy of it with its character indicated by the common Italian terms, Allegro, etc., which were a sufficient guide. Burns was the principal writer. Allan Cunningham, in his *Life and Works* of the poet, leaves the impression that Thomson was niggardly and parsimonious towards him. Thomson disdained to take any public notice of Cunningham's charges ; but in a copy of the work in possession of his son-in-law, George Hogarth (1860), there are a few autograph notes to the point. Thus in July 1793, Burns writes:

'I assure you, my dear sir, that you truly hurt me with your pecuniary parcel. It degrades me in my own eyes. However, to return it would savour of affectation ; but as to any more traffic of this debtor and creditor kind, I swear by that HONOUR which crowns the upright statue of ROBERT BURNS'S INTEGRITY—on the least motion of it I will indignantly spurn the by-past transaction, and from that moment commence entire stranger to you ! ' [2]

Thomson writes, Sept. 1, to Burns :

'While the muse seems so propitious, I think it right to inclose a list of all the favours I have to ask of her—no fewer than twenty and three ! . . . most of the remaining airs . . . are of that peculiar measure and rhythm that they must be familiar to him who writes for them.'

III. As to the instrumental accompaniments, Thomson's plan was as new and original as it was bold. Besides the pianoforte accompaniment each song was to have a prelude and coda, and parts *ad libitum* throughout for violin, or flute, and violoncello, the composition to be entrusted to none but the first composers. In the years 1791–93, Pleyel stood next to Haydn and Mozart ; they in Vienna, he at that time much in London. Thomson engaged Pleyel for the work, but he soon ceased to write, and Thomson was compelled to seek another composer. Mozart was dead : Haydn seemed

to occupy too lofty a position ; and Kozeluh of Vienna was engaged. But the appearance of Napier's Collection of Scots Songs with pianoforte accompaniments, written by Haydn during his first visit to London, showed Thomson that the greatest living composer did not disdain this kind of work. Thomson applied to him ; and Haydn worked for him until about 1806. In 1806–07 Haydn arranged the Scots songs published in Wm. Whyte's collection. The star of Beethoven had now risen, and he did not disdain to continue the work. But he, too, died before Thomson's work was completed, and Bishop and George Hogarth made up the sixth volume of Scots songs (1841).

The following, based on a list supplied by Thomson to G. F. Graham, exhibits each composer's share in the work :

SCOTS SONGS

Vol. I. originally all by Pleyel. 1st set, June 1793 ; 2nd Aug. 1798.
Vol. II. originally all by Kozeluh (?). July 1799.
   In the second edition of these (1803) Thomson substituted arrangements by Haydn for several which were ' less happily executed than the rest,' and in various re-issues other changes were made.
Vol. III., IV. all by Haydn. July 1802 and June 1805 respectively.

Vol. V. (Pref. dated June 1, 1818)	Haydn . .	4
	Beethoven .	26
		30
Vol. VI. (dated Sept. 1841)	Haydn . .	12
	Beethoven .	13
	Kozeluh .	1
	Hogarth .	21
	Bishop . .	5
		52

Hummel also supplied some arrangements for a new edition issued in folio sheets. Besides these there was issued an edition in royal 8vo, which, in 1822, reached five volumes, with a sixth added in 1825.

WELSH MELODIES

The Preface is dated May 1809.

Vol. I.	Kozeluh	10
	Haydn	20
		30
Vol. II.	1811 Kozeluh . . .	15
	Haydn	17
	Kozeluh and Haydn .	1
		33
Vol. III.	1814 Haydn . . .	4
	Beethoven	26
		30

As a means of extending the knowledge of the Scottish melodies, Thomson, at the beginning of his intercourse with Pleyel and Kozeluh, ordered sonatas based upon such airs. Both composed works of this kind ; but how many does not appear. It is evident from a letter of Beethoven to Thomson (Nov. 1, 1806) that, besides arrangements of melodies,[3] the latter had requested trios, quintets and sonatas on Scottish themes from him also. Beethoven's price for compositions, which could only sell in Great Britain and Ireland, was such as could not be acceded to, and none were written. About 1818–20 he wrote variations on a dozen Scots melodies, which Thomson published, but which never paid the cost of printing either in Great Britain or Germany. At the lowest estimate Beethoven received for his share in Thomson's publications not less than £550. It is stated that Haydn was paid £291 : 18s. for arranging 230 airs. In 1825 Thomson paid £19 to Weber for arranging ten Scots songs. George Hogarth,

---

[1] This of course detracts largely from the value of his labour. G.
[2] This protest evidently refers to all songs written or to be written, and thus disposes of Cunningham's arguments.

[3] All Beethoven's Scots and Irish songs are contained in Breitkopf's complete edition of his works, Series 24, Nos. 257-260.

who married Thomson's daughter, told the writer that the Scots songs only paid their cost.

In the winter of 1860–61 there appeared in Germany a selection of these songs from Beethoven's MSS., edited by Franz Espagne, in the preface to which he writes : ' The songs printed in Thomson's collection are, both as to text and music, not only incorrectly printed, but wilfully altered and abridged.' These groundless charges were made honestly, but with a most plentiful lack of knowledge. They need not be discussed here, as they were amply met and completely refuted in the Vienna *Deutsche Musikzeitung* of Nov. 23 and Dec. 28, 1861.

There are at least two portraits of Thomson in existence, one, a small water-colour in the National Collection, Edinburgh, and the other, almost a caricature, in Crombie's *Men of Modern Athens*. Both have been frequently reproduced. *George Thomson, the Friend of Burns ; his Life and Correspondence*, by J. Cuthbert Haddon, was published in 1898.

A. W. T. ; addns. F. K.

THOMSON, JOHN (*b.* Ednam, Kelso, Oct. 28, 1805 ; *d.* May 6, 1841), first professor of music at Edinburgh University, was the son of an eminent clergyman. His father afterwards became minister of St. George's Church, Edinburgh. He made the acquaintance of Mendelssohn during the visit of the latter to Edinburgh in the summer of 1829, and showed him much attention, which Mendelssohn requited by a warm letter of introduction to his family in Berlin, in which he says of Thomson [1] ' he is very fond of music ; I know a pretty trio of his composition and some local pieces which please me very well ' (*ganz gut gefallen*). During his visit to Germany he studied at Leipzig, kept up his friendship with Mendelssohn, and made the intimate acquaintance of Schumann, Moscheles and other musicians, and of Schnyder von Wartensee, whose pupil he became. In Oct. 1839 he was elected the first Reid Professor at EDINBURGH (*q.v.*). He gave the first Reid Concert on Feb. 12, 1841, and the book of words contains analytical remarks by him on the principal pieces—probably the first instance of such a thing. Thomson died deeply lamented. He wrote three operas or dramatic pieces, ' Hermann, or the Broken Spear,' ' The House of Aspen ' and ' The Shadow on the Wall.' The last two were brought out at the Royal English Opera (Lyceum) on Oct. 27, 1834, and Apr. 21, 1835, respectively, and had each a long run. Two of his songs, ' Harold Harfager ' and ' The Pirates' Serenade,' are mentioned as spirited and original. G.

THOMSON, WILLIAM, the editor of the first printed collection of Scottish songs united to their melodies. This is a folio named ' Orpheus Caledonius [*q.v.*], a collection of the best Scotch songs set to Musick,' entered at Stationers' Hall, Jan. 5, 1725. He is said to have been the son of Daniel Thomson, one of the king's trumpeters for Scotland. As a boy-singer he sang at a concert—' The Feast of St. Cecilia ' —in 1695. Before 1722 he had settled in London, and according to Burney had a benefit concert in that year. He appears to have become a fashionable singer and teacher, for his volume, dedicated to the Princess of Wales, contains a lengthy list of notable personages as subscribers. The book consists of fifty songs with their airs, having a slight accompaniment fitted to them. A second edition, in two volumes octavo, has another fifty added. The two editions have value and interest, although Hawkins speaks of him as ' a tradesman,' and says that the collection is injudicious and incorrect. The words of the songs were mainly taken from Allan Ramsay's *Tea-Table Miscellany*, published in 1724. Thomson was living in 1753. F. K.

THOMYRIS, QUEEN OF SCYTHIA, an opera acted at Drury Lane, Apr. 1, 1707. The libretto was by Peter Motteux, and adapted to airs by Scarlatti and Bononcini. These were arranged, and recitatives composed by Pepusch. After a few performances at its original place of production it was revived in the following year, 1708, at the Haymarket, the singers being Valentini, Hughes, Laurence, Leveridge with Margarita de l'Épine, Mrs. Tofts and Mrs. Lindsey. The songs from the opera were published in folio by Walsh. F. K.

THORN, THE. An English song by William Shield which has attained a considerable popularity. It seems to have been first sung in public about 1802 or 1803 by Charles Incledon in a monologue entertainment called ' Variety,' with which he travelled the country. It was issued on music-sheets about this date with the statement that the words were by Robert Burns. They do not appear in the usual editions, but research has shown that they formed one of several epigrams which Burns sent to William Creech the Edinburgh bookseller, May 30, 1789. After the death of Burns they were published in the *Edinburgh Advertiser* for Aug. 8, 1800. The second verse of ' The Thorn ' has been added by an inferior writer, and the name ' Chloris,' which Burns used, changed into ' Chloe.' F. K.

THORNE, EDWARD H., Mus.D.[2] (*b.* Cranbourne, Dorsetshire, May 9, 1834 ; *d.* Dec. 26, 1916), received his musical education at St. George's Chapel, Windsor, where he was articled to Sir George Elvey. In 1853 he was appointed to the Parish Church, Henley, and in 1863 to Chichester Cathedral, which appointment he resigned in 1870 in order to devote himself more closely to the more congenial work of teaching the pianoforte. Thorne re-

---

[1] He spells the name Thompson, but it must surely be the same man. See *Die Familie Mendelssohn*, i. 243.

[2] Degree conferred by the Archbishop of Canterbury in 1913

moved to London, and was successively organist at St. Patrick's, Brighton ; St. Peter's, Cranley Gardens ; St. Michael's, Cornhill ; and St. Anne's, Soho, where from 1891 to the end of his career he maintained the fine traditions of the church in regard to Bach's music, directing the regular performances of the Christmas Oratorio and St. John Passion, as well as other cantatas, and giving organ recitals entirely composed of the master's works. His published works comprise several services, including a Magnificat and Nunc Dimittis for chorus, soli and orchestra, written for the Festival of the Sons of the Clergy ; the 125th Psalm ; a festival march, toccata and fugue, funeral march, overture and six books of voluntaries for the organ ; some pianoforte pieces ; several songs and partsongs ; the 47th Psalm (for female voices), etc. An overture to ' Peveril of the Peak ' won a prize at the Promenade Concerts in 1885. His unpublished works include trios for piano, violin and violoncello ; sonatas for the violoncello and the clarinet ; the 57th Psalm for tenor solo, chorus and orchestra ; and many other compositions. 　　　　　　　　　　　w. b. s.

THORNE, JOHN (*d.* Dec. 7, 1573), English composer of church music. He is mentioned among the ' practicioners ' of music in Morley's ' Plaine and Easie Introduction ' (1597). He is referred to as ' of York ' in the Commonplace Book of John BALDWIN (*q.v.*), which contains the following motets by Thorne :

' Stella coeli ' ; ' Ipsa stella ' (printed by Hawkins) ; ' Gloriosa Stella maris ' ; ' Pro quibus virgo.'

West (*Cath. Org.*) conjectures that he was organist of York Minster from 1550–73. B.M. Add. MSS. 29,996/37b contains the organ score of another motet by ' Thorne of York ' —' Exultabunt sancti.' Drake, in his *Eboracum* (1736), says that Thorne lies ' buried in the middle aisle from the west door ' of the Minster, and gives his epitaph as below :

' Here lyeth Thorne, musician most perfect in his art,
In Logick's Lore who did excell : all vice who set apart :
Whose Lief and conversation did all men's Love allure,
And now doth reign above the Skies in joys most firm and pure
　　　　　Who dyed Decemb. 7, 1573.' 　j. mᴷ.

THOROUGH-BASS, or, as it used to be called, ' Through-Bass,' is obviously a translation of the Latin *bassus continuus* (Italian *basso continuo*), so called because, as originally employed, it continued without a break from the beginning of a piece to the end. Thorough-bass is often regarded as synonymous with figured bass (Ital. *basso numerato*; Fr. *basse chiffrée*; Ger. *bezifferter Bass*), but though the terms are, for most practical purposes, interchangeable, they are not, actually, identical in meaning. If one were to figure the bass of a composition for several voices or instruments, in which bass *rests* occurred, we

should have, it is true, a *figured* bass, but not, in the strict sense of the term, a *thorough*-bass. If, on the other hand, wherever rests occurred in the bass, we incorporated in it whichever happened at the moment to be the lowest sounding part, tenor, alto, or even (as might easily happen in a fugal entry) treble, we should have, whether figured or unfigured, a true *continuo* or thorough-bass.

Because, for some two hundred years, a practical acquaintance with harmony was first gained through the medium of the thorough-bass, the latter word has come to be used to denote the science of harmony, just as has been the case with the word *General-Bass*, the German equivalent of the Latin *bassus generalis*.

The origin of the latter term is not quite so obvious as that of *bassus continuus*, but the *bassus generalis* was probably so called because, instead of being individual, it is concerned in a general way with all the other parts, both because any one of them is liable to be incorporated in it (as explained above), and also because they combine to constitute the harmony which the accompanist deduces *ex tempore* from the *general bass* before him. Such, at least, seems to be the opinion of Niedt, who, in the first chapter (' On the Etymology of the *bassus generalis* and why it is so called ') of his celebrated little work,[1] tells us that it is because ' all, or nearly all the other parts are comprised *generaliter*, that is to say in common (*insgemein*), in this single part.' He adds :

' It is also called *bassus continuus*, or, with the Italian termination, *b sso continuo*, because it plays on continuously, whereas the other parts occasionally pause the while. But nowadays this Bass, too, frequently pauses, espe ially in Operas and cleverly (*künstlich*) compose 1 secular pieces ; moreover, any *Violone*- Bass [2] might be styled *bassus continuus*, therefore the name *General*-*Bass* seems more convenient here.'

THE BEGINNINGS OF THE BASSUS CONTINUUS. —It may very well be (though in the absence of fresh and unexpected evidence any such theory is incapable of proof) that the thorough-bass has a dual origin. It will be shown presently that the *bassus continuus*, which in 1602 became widely known through its employment by Lodovico Grossi (better known to us by the name of his birthplace, VIADANA, *q.v.*), had been in existence some years previously, though not under that name, in the form of ' Organ Basses ' (presently to be described), which were used for the accompaniment of polyphonic compositions. The figured basses of Cavalieri, Peri and Caccini, which appeared in 1600, and which formed the basis of the accompaniment of their recitative, may possibly have had a similar origin, but it seems not improbable that they

[1] *Musicalische Handleitung*, etc. (Musical Guide, etc), by Friderich Erhard Niedt. Part I. Hamburg, Spieringk, 1700.
[2] Any such part, played by a bass instrument to support the organ or harpsichord would, if manuscript, be unfigured, but, if printed, would usually be a duplicate of the part figured for the use of the accompanist. As Niedt says, the term *continuo* is as applicable to the one as to the other, and indeed, was regularly used by J. S. Bach in this double sense.

were intended to replace the written-out harp-sichord accompaniments of vocal solos which are known to have existed some years pre-viously.[1]

The substitution of figures for a written-out accompaniment would, in the instance of the composers named above, have possessed a dis-tinct advantage over and above the obvious one of saving trouble, for, besides the harpsichord,

instruments of the lute tribe co-operated in the accompaniment.[2]

Unless, therefore, a separate accompaniment were written out for each instrument in accord-ance with the requirements of its particular technique, a plain bass, with figures as a guide to the harmony, would obviously be a more convenient basis for an accompaniment extem-porised on different instruments than written-out harmony adapted to the requirements of the harpsichord (or any one instrument) alone.

Let us briefly examine the facts attending the first appearance of the *bassus continuus* or Thorough-bass :

(1) In the year 1600 there appeared works by the three composers already mentioned, all three with figured basses.[3] Cavalieri was first

[1] Otto Kinkeldey describes a set of Madrigals for one, two and three soprano voices, with accompaniment for the harpsichord, by Luzzasco Luzzaschi (*Orgel und Klavier in der Musik des 16. Jahr-hunderts*, Leipzig, B. & H., 1910, p. 157 *sq.*). The title is as follows : '*Madrigali di Luzzasco Luzzaschi per cantare e sonare a uno, e doi, e tre soprani, fatti per la musica del già Serma Duca Alfonso d' Este. Stampata in Roma appresso Simone Verovio, 1601.*' The Harpsi-chord is not actually specified as the instrument to be used, but the nature of the accompaniment plainly shows (as Kinkeldey points out) that no other can have been intended. Although the date of publication is 16 1, a passage in the dedication proves definitely that the music was written before the death of Duke Alfonso in 1597. In an appendix Kinkeldey prints *in extenso* two of the madrigals, one for a single voice, and another for two, in modern notation (*o.c.* pp. 286 *sqq.*). The opening bars of the first of the two are given below, and will suffice to show the character of the accompaniment. The latter is in four parts nearly throughout (and this, as Kinkeldey tells us, is also the case in the madrigals for more than one voice, when only a single voice is singing, as in fugal entries), and the upper part of the accompaniment is identical with the voice part, except where the latter indulges in 'diminutions,' a. in bars 13, 14, of the following extract :

[2] In the preface, *A Lettori*, to his 'Euridice' (1600) Peri enumerates the *gravicembelo* (harpsichord), the *chitarrone* (theorbo), the *lira grande* (*violone*) and the *liuto grosso* (tenor lute)—Caccini, in the preface to the *Nuove musiche* (1602, 2nd ed. 1607), speaks of the *chitarrone* as best fitted to accompany the voice, 'particularly the tenor voice.' Guidotti, who edited Cavalieri's 'Rappresentatione di anima e di corpo' (1600), tells us that ' a *lira doppia*, a *clavicembalo*, a *chitarrone*, or so-called theorbo, together produce an excellent effect, as also a soft-toned Organ with a *chitarrone*.' And he adds : ' And Signor Emilio [Cavalieri] would approve of the instruments being changed in accordance with the effect of [*i.e.* to be produced by] the reciter.' A further most interesting detail was disclosed by the discovery, on the part of Signor Domenico Alaleone, of an original copy of the 'Rappresentatione ' in addition to the two pre-viously known. It was found (catalogued under the name of Guidotti) in the library of the Vallicella, where it had been used in the performances which took place there. The word *Tiorba* entered on the first page shows that it was appropriated to that instrument, and the word *tace*, prefixed to all the solo numbers shows that it was in operation only when more voices than one were singing. Cavalieri did not, therefore, agree with Caccini in regarding the *chitarrone* as specially fitted to accompany the voice, 'particularly the tenor voice.'

[3] The figuring of all three had one important point in common : they all used double figures (10, 11, etc.) as a means of distinguishing the compound intervals. This practice, which survived only a very short time, enabled the accompanist to know with certainty in

in the field with his allegorical oratorio, the 'Rappresentatione di anima e di corpo,' which

what octave the composer desired the interval in question to be taken, and, when the composition was in several parts, it was thus possible to make the accompaniment an almost exact reproduction of the vocal or instrumental score. Neither Peri nor Caccini, whose figured basses were used only to accompany a *single voice*, went beyond the figure 14 (Peri not beyond 11), but Cavalieri, who employed a figured bass to accompany three, four, and even five vocal or instrumental parts, went as far as 18 = a double octave plus a fourth). The final *Ritornello* of the 'Rappresentatione' will serve as an example, and it will be seen that if the figuring is carefully followed, as in the set out accompaniment supplied below in small notes, it is practically impossible to arrive at a version which differs in any important particular from the instrumental score. It must be mentioned that, in accordance with one of the few rules given by Guidotti in his preface, a ✕ over a bass note, when un-accompanied by the figure 3 (as on the last crotchet of bars 3 and 8), is to be taken as equivalent to ✕10, *not* ✕3.

It will be observed that Cavalieri's figuring necessitates the occasional use of extended harmony; compare, for instance, the different treatment of the same harmony on the last crotchet of the third and seventh bars.

In one important particular Cavalieri is far in advance of his Florentine colleagues: he occasionally uses two (and, in

was performed in February, and Peri and Caccini followed late in the year, each with a primitive opera, 'Euridice.' Peri had written an opera, 'Dafne,' as early as 1594, but it is unfortunately lost, and we have no means of knowing what form of accompaniment was provided and, in particular, whether figures were used. We must, therefore, accept 1600 as the date of their first known appearance.

(2) In the year 1602 Viadana published the first instalment of his famous work, entitled :

'Cento concerti ecclesiastici, a una, a due, a tre, & a quattro voci. Con il basso continuo per sonar nell' organo Nova inventione commoda per ogni sorte de cantori, & per gli Organisti di Lodovico Viadana. Opera duodecima In Venetia, appresso Giacomo Vincenti MDCII.'

The wording of this title, 'A New invention, suitable for all kinds of Singers, and for Organists,' alone makes it clear that the novelty of the invention resided, not in the continued bass only, but in the character of the vocal compositions as well. With regard to the former, indeed, it is noteworthy that two years earlier Guidotti, in his preface to Cavalieri's work, speaks of the *basso continuato*. On the other hand, Viadana mentions in his preface that he had composed the concertos (first published in 1602) five or six years ago in Rome, and he adds the significant statement that they ' found such favour with many singers and musicians that they were not only found worthy to be sung again and again in many leading places [of worship], but that some persons actually took occasion to imitate them very cleverly and to print some of these imitations.' This means that the year in which Viadana's work became known to the world was not 1602 but 1596 or 1597. It is improbable that either Cavalieri or the Florentines were the imitators to whom Viadana refers, as their works were of so widely different a character, but that they must have known of, and perhaps derived ideas from, Viadana's work is pretty certain.

Viadana's basses differ from theirs in one important particular : they are not figured, the nearest approach to figures being ※ and ♭ placed a third above, and slightly to the left of, the bass note, to indicate an accidentally sharpened or flattened third. A ※, intended to be placed a sixth above the bass (but always misplaced by the printer), was also used in a few instances to indicate an accidental major sixth. It is, however, very probable (indeed almost certain) that Viadana, though only very occasionally, used the figure 6, which the printers, not being familiar with figures over a

one instance, three) figures one above the other, chiefly to indicate a $\frac{6}{4}$ chord, which appears oftenest as $1\frac{7}{6}$ or $1\frac{3}{2}$. In the basses of Peri and Caccini, on the other hand, if a $\frac{6}{4}$ chord seems appropriate, it must be supplied at the discretion of the accompanist. Cavalieri's single example of the use of triple figures is $\frac{10}{X4}$, denoting the second inversion of a seventh on an accidentally sharpened lead'ng note, which at a later period was figured $\#\frac{6}{3}$ or $\frac{6}{4}$, omitting the 6.

bass, mistook for a ♭ (which in those days was often rounded at the bottom, ♭) and printed as such.[1]

(3) We know, mainly through the researches of Kinkeldey published in the work already mentioned (cf. p. 326, note 1), that basses for the organ, similar in character to the *basso continuo* in Viadana's concertos for several voices, were in existence some years before the close of the 16th century. When the composition was for two, or even three choirs, the organist either had the two (or three) vocal basses, written one above the other, before him and selected from them whichever note was lowest, or else he had a single bass part, prepared on the same principle, and was thus saved a considerable amount of trouble. In some cases the highest of the voice parts was printed over the organ-bass, thus enabling the player the better to divine the harmony.

The earliest example recorded by Kinkeldey is printed by Vincenti of Venice and dated 1594.[2] It is an organ part to some 8-part motets for double choir by Giovanni Croce and is marked 'Spartidura.'[3]

The two vocal basses are printed one above the other, and ✕ and ♭ above the bass are used, as by Viadana (and as throughout the figured bass age), to denote accidentally sharpened or flattened thirds.

A similar bass, to Adriano Banchieri's 'Concerti ecclesiastici a 8 voci,' was printed by Vincenti in 1595. Here, however, only the bass of the first choir is given and the cantus part is printed on the upper stave. The accidentals ✕ and ♭ are used as in Croce's 'Spartidura,' but are sometimes placed over the cantus instead of the bass. Though only one bass is printed, the organist is told how to remedy the

---

[1] The evidence on which this statement is based is embodied in two articles by the present writer in the correspondence columns of the *Musical Times* of July and Sept. 1922. There it was also conclusively proved that Viadana used the *signum cancellatum* ✕ placed a sixth above the bass note (as stated in the text), to indicate an accidentally sharpened major sixth. Adriano Banchieri, in his *L'organo suonarino*, 1605, and Galeazzo Sabbatini, in his *Regola facile*, etc., 1628, allude to the similar practice of placing the ✕ a *third be'ow* the bass to denote a sharpened sixth (or inverted third) : the latter speaks of it as 'virtually obsolete.' The following example from the Concerto 'Peccavi super numerum' shows both the meaningless flats which have replaced Viadana's sixes and also the ✕ (here restored to its right position, but misplaced in the German reprint of 1613 from which the example was taken) indicating the sharpened sixth :

3.

Cantus vel Tenor.

B.c.

N.B.—The strokes through the first ♭ and the ✕ are leger lines. It will be noticed that the ♭ over the crotchet *g* is the only one of the three which has any justification, *as* a flat, namely, as marking the modulation to D minor. But it is more likely that here, too, Viadana wrote a 6, leaving the accidental flattening of the third to the musical instinct of the accompanist.

[2] Kinkeldey thinks that the date may possibly be a misprint on the ground that no edition of the voice parts of 1594 is known to exist, though he points out that the extant edition of 1599 is shown by the words *Novamente ristampati* in the title to be a reprint, which consideration seems to invalidate his doubt.

[3] So called because the organ basses, unlike the voice parts, were generally barred. *Partire* or *spartire* originally denoted the division of the music by bar-lines.

---

omission, namely, by selecting the highest and lowest notes of the second choir and incorporating them in the printed *cantus* and bass parts respectively.

Kinkeldey mentions and describes other interesting examples. Apart from all these there can be little doubt that he is right in his assumption that organists had been in the habit of preparing manuscript organ parts, on the principles described above, long before any were printed. The thorough-bass, therefore, dates much farther back than was formerly supposed.

VIADANA

As it has been seen that Viadana did not invent the *bassus continuus*, as he was for so long believed to have done, it may well be asked what he did to deserve the reputation for invention which he undoubtedly enjoyed in his own day, both in Italy and abroad. This question is best answered by Viadana himself. He tells us in the preface to his 'Cento concerti' that, when one, two or even three singers wished to sing with the organ, they 'were sometimes forced by the lack of compositions suitable to their purpose to take one, two or three parts from motets in five, six, seven or even eight parts '; after describing the effect of these mutilated performances he continues :

'Accordingly, having repeatedly given no little thought to these difficulties, I have tried very hard to find a way of remedying so notable a deficiency, and I believe, thank God, that I have at length found it, having to this end composed some of these concertos of mine for a single voice (for sopranos, altos, tenors, basses) and some others for the same parts in a variety of combinations. . . .'

Thus we see that it was a new application of the continued bass, and not the thing itself, that Viadana claimed, and was acknowledged, to have invented.[4]

His actual basses, however, in the 'Concerti a voci pari' (S.A.T.B.) mark an advance upon the old organ basses, for, whereas the latter were entirely derived from the vocal parts, Viadana's are occasionally independent of the vocal bass. Whether the application of the continued bass, on his part and that of the monodists, Peri, Caccini and Cavalieri, to compositions in which the complete harmony was not supplied by the voices (particularly to compositions for a single voice) was an idea derived entirely from the old organ basses, or whether it was partly suggested by written-out harpsichord accompaniments, such as those of Luzzaschi (cf. p. 326, note 1), as suggested above, it is at present impossible to determine.

---

[4] In speaking of the 'Bassus generalis seu continuus,' Praetorius teils us (*Syntagma*, 1619, vol. iii. ch. 6) that it 'has now in particular been brought to light and put into print by that excellent musician Lodov. Viadana, *nove inventionis primario*, when he invented the fashion of singing with one, two, three, or four voices to the accompaniment of an organ, regal, or any other similar instrument of foundation. . . .'

The Bassus continuus in the 17th Century

(*a*) It seems strange that the advantages of using figures to indicate the harmonies should not have been at once and unanimously recognised ; such, however, was the case, and there were musicians who were definitely opposed to the practice, which nevertheless soon gained ground, at all events in the case of compositions in which no vocal part (or parts) appeared above the bass to give a clue to the harmony.[1]

(*b*) The whole system, too, of accompanying from a bass was opposed by some, partly on the ground that those who practised it were inclined to be satisfied with that accomplishment and were thus diverted from the practice of improvisation, playing from score, etc., and partly on the ground that it was impossible to play as perfect an accompaniment (even though figured) as from a detailed score.[2]

(*c*) This idea, that the accompaniment should exactly reproduce the harmonic texture of the principal parts, and in particular that the upper parts of each should coincide, was, however, gradually abandoned,[3] and by the end of the 17th century such identity had come to be regarded as a positive blemish.[4]

(*d*) While some musicians were not enthusiastic about the *bassus continuus*, there were, on the other hand, others who were so enamoured of it that they must needs add it to the works of composers of an older generation. As early as 1610 there appeared (according to

Eitner) an edition of Masses for 4 and 5 voices by Palestrina (first published 1582) with a figured bass part for the organ with the soprano printed above it. Perhaps the most notable example of this barbarous procedure on a large scale was the *Promptuarium musicum* of Abraham Schadaeus—a collection of 5-8-part motets by various composers, the first instalment of which appeared at Strassburg in 1611, to which a *Basis* [sic] *vulgo generalis dicta* and *ad organa musicaque instrumenta accommodata* was added by Caspar Vincentius (Gaspard Vincent, a Frenchman by birth), organist in the same city.

(*e*) It is difficult to say exactly when the *bassus continuus* first became known in England. In all probability it was imported direct from Italy. The earliest instance, known to the writer, of a figured *continuo* by an Englishman is in the 'Cantiones sacrae' of Richard Dering, published by Phalèse at Antwerp, where Dering was organist at the time, in 1617. There is, however, direct internal evidence [5] that the Cantiones were composed, some years before publication, at Rome, where Dering must have become familiar with the continued bass, both figured and unfigured.

That the thorough-bass was on its way to being well established in Germany before the end of the second decade of the 17th century [6] is abundantly clear from the chapter (chap. vi.) of the third volume of the *Syntagma musicum* which Praetorius devotes to the subject ; on the other hand, we know that its acceptance in that country, as far as the music of the Church was concerned, was considerably retarded by the obstinate adherence of many organists to the old German organ-tablature.[7]

Praetorius gives an example of a bass from one of his own works,[8] and also the *Resolutio*, or

---

[1] No vocal part is printed over any of the basses in Viadana's 'Cento concerti' but in one of the celebrated twelve *avertimenti* in his preface he recommends the organist to prepare an *intavolatura* for himself. The latter would, therefore (if he followed this advice), make a manuscript 'short score' of the pieces in several parts and would, no doubt, make a copy, with the voice part above the bass, of the pieces for a single voice, except, perhaps, of those for a bass voice, in which (except for the rests) the voice part was often identical with the continued bass.

[2] Viadana's recommendation to the organist to make an *intavolatura* (cf. note 1 above) shows that he, like Cavalieri (cf. p. 326, note 3) desired the accompaniment to be an exact reproduction of the vocal score. His harmony was more archaic than that of Cavalieri, and in the successions of triads, which are of frequent occurrence, consecutives are avoided by the crossing of parts, a device which on a keyed instrument has no reality ; he therefore gives a rule to the effect that consecutive 5ths and 8ves may be disregarded in the accompaniment, though not in the voices, for, without this liberty, the reproduction of his vocal score on the organ would have been impossible.

[3] As early as 1607 Agostino Agazzari, maestro di cappella at the Collegium Germanicum at S. Apollinare in Rome, and a great admirer of Viadana, as is proved by the number of the latter's works which he acquired for the church in question, tells us that, when only a few voices are singing, the accompanist should avoid the territory of the upper voices, and should avoid, as far as he can, playing the same note as the soprano is singing. Agazzari's little treatise *Del suonare sopra il basso*, etc., Siena, 1607, is reprinted by Kinkeldey in an appendix. Among the *avertimenti*, or rules, which form the concluding (21st) chapter of *Li alberi musicali* by Lorenzo Penna (1st edn. 1672), the 10th, 11th and 12th are as follows :

'In playing with a soprano or contralto one must not play above the voice part, or make divisions (*diminuire*).'

'With a tenor one can go above, and also remain above, but not play in the octave the notes which he is singing, or make divisions.'

'With a bass one can introduce a certain amount of movement (*si puo far qualche poco di movimento*), but, if the bass is singing passages (*passeggia*), it is not good to move at the same time.'

In the case of a soprano or contralto, Penna tells us in a previous chapter (ch. 14), the accompanist is to play the same notes, or, when the voices move rapidly, to adhere to the general outline, selecting the Consonances, and playing 'at least the first and the last of the down-beat (*battere di mano*) and of the up-beat (*levar di mano*), each being (ordinarily) equivalent to a minim.

[4] Werckmeister tells us that the accompanist must ' be careful to avoid continually moving in octaves [the term is here loosely used to include the *unison*] with the vocalists and instrumentalists ' (*Die nothwendigsten Anmerckungen*, etc., 1698 ; cf. § 69 of the somewhat enlarged reprint of 1715).

[5] The Latin dedication contains the following passage (as translated by Sir F. Bridge) : 'For long my Music has desired to come forward. She is not unpolished (for she was born in the first City of the World), but she is modest.' (cf. Bridge, *Twelve good Musicians*, 1920, pp. 56-60).

[6] A complete edition of Viadana's 'Cento concerti' was issued in Germany by Nikolaus Stein of Frankfort, in 1613, under the title *Opera omnia sacrarum concentuum 1, 2, 3, 4 vocum*, etc., with the addition of a Latin and German translation of Viadana's preface.

[7] Niedt, writing in 1700, tells us, through the mouth of an imaginary character in the delightfully quaint little romance which forms the preface of the work already alluded to, that ' 60 years ago, or a little more, one hardly ever saw a German organist who played from a thorough-bass or from notes ' [i.e. as opposed to the letter-tablature].

[8] 'Wir glauben,' from the *Polyhymnia Caduceatrice seu Pacis nuncia*. The writer has unfortunately been unable to give the vocal parts, which would have added greatly to the interest of the example, as the parts in question are missing from the copy of this extremely rare work in the British Museum (G. 131).

4.   *Bassus Generalis.*

the same bass with the harmony set out as he would, no doubt, have played it himself. Such examples are so extremely rare that it is worth recording here.[1] It will be noticed that in the *Resolutio* (from the fifth bar onwards) Praetorius has altered the irregular barring of the *Bassus generalis* :

1. *Resolutio.*

[N.B.—The figures in the *Bassus generalis*, and the notes in the *Resolutio*, omitted in the original by obvious inadvertence, have here been added in square brackets.]

By comparing the *Bassus generalis* with the *Resolutio* it will be seen that the 6 on the last crotchet (*C*) of the fourth bar of the former is used (whether carelessly or intentionally) to indicate a $\frac{6}{4}$ chord on the passing bass note. One would have expected Praetorius to figure it ⨯4 or ⨯$\frac{4}{2}$.

The only points of the *Resolutio* to which serious exception could have been taken by the best authorities of the 18th century are: (1) the wide interval between the upper part and the close chords in the lower region of the keyboard in the first half of the fifth bar, (2) the consecutive 8ves $\frac{b\,c}{b\,c}$ between treble and tenor in the third and fourth crotchets of the same bar (to which, in a four-part accompaniment, all but the laxest would certainly have objected), and (3) the consecutive 8ves $\frac{c\,d}{c\,d}$ between alto and bass in the penultimate bar. The augmented fourth *f-b* in the alto, at the

[1] It has already been recorded by A. Dolmetsch in his invaluable work, *The Interpretation of the Music of the XVIIth and XVIIIth Centuries.*

end of the second bar, is also contrary to strict rule.

THE GENERAL CHARACTER OF A FIGURED BASS ACCOMPANIMENT IN THE 18TH CENTURY

(*a*) The instruments most commonly used were the organ and the harpsichord. Philip Emanuel Bach ('Versuch' etc., part ii., 1762, Introd.) mentions the pianoforte and the clavichord as well. He writes (*l.c.* § 6):

'The pianoforte and clavichord give the best support to a performance in which the greatest refinements of taste occur. Only certain singers like to be accompanied on the clavichord or harpsichord rather than on the instrument first named.'

Both the pianoforte and clavichord possess the advantage of enabling the player easily to regulate the loudness of the sound by the strength of his touch, though the tone of the latter instrument is too delicate to provide an adequate accompaniment to any but the very softest voice. On the harpsichord, on the other hand, the strength of the touch makes very little difference, and gradation of tone can be secured only (1) by passing from the louder to the softer manual, and *vice versâ*; and (2) by the use of registers, calling fresh sets of strings (of 4-foot and 16-foot tone) into play, and operated by knobs or pedals; or (3) by playing in more or fewer parts. On the smaller instruments of the harpsichord tribe, with only one manual and no 'stops,' this last method is the only one available.

The use of the organ was not necessarily restricted to sacred, nor that of the harpsichord to secular music : in Bach's 'St. Matthew Passion' an harpsichord is employed (allocated to the second choir) as well as the two organs; and in Corelli's op. 1 and 3, 'Suonate da Chiesa' for two violins and bass, the bass parts are headed *Basso per organo*, whereas in his op. 2 and 4 ('Suonate da camera' for the same instruments) they are headed *Violone ò cembalo*.

Too much stress must not be laid on the use of the word *ò* ('or') instead of *e* ('and'). Sometimes, no doubt, only a stringed instrument (violone or violoncello) was used to accompany a solo, but there can also be no doubt that such an accompaniment was regarded as more or less of a *pis aller*; moreover, it is not uncommon to find 'Organo *ò* violoncello' on a title-page and 'Organo *e* violoncello' on the parts themselves. That the co-operation of both instruments was intended is often shown by the provision of a bass part in duplicate.

Ph. Em. Bach expresses himself exceedingly strongly on the necessity for using a keyed instrument for the accompaniment, quite irrespective of any considerations which might seem to militate against the need for its employment. After explaining the purposes to which the organ and harpsichord, etc., are respectively appropriate, he continues (*l.c.* § 7) :

'No piece, therefore, can be performed satisfactorily without the accompaniment of a keyed instrument (*Clavierinstrument*). Even in the case of music on the largest scale (*bey den stärksten Musiken*), in operas, even in the open air, when one would feel confident of not hearing the harpsichord in the very least, one misses it if it is left out. If one listens from a height, one can distinctly hear every note. I am speaking from experience, and anybody can try it.'

'The most complete accompaniment to a solo, to which nobody can take any exception,' he tells us (*l.c.* § 9), ' is a keyed instrument in conjunction with the violoncello.'

Sometimes the violoncello (or gamba) was given a part, not really independent of the figured bass, but a more or less ornate variant of it. Examples of this may be found (in the 17th cent.) in the canzonas of Purcell's sonatas for two violins and bass (1683 and 1697),[1] and, in the 18th century, in the first book of Leclair's sonatas for violin solo and bass.[2] This treatment of the violoncello (or viol di gamba) is strongly reminiscent of the ' instruments of ornamentation ' which we know to have been employed early in the 17th century.[3]

(*b*) The most usual form of accompaniment, when four- (or three-) part harmony was adhered to, consisted of the bass, played by the left hand, and doubled in the lower, or sometimes (especially if the hands had got somewhat far apart) the upper octave, at the discretion of the player,[4] and of chords played by the right hand in close harmony.

Sometimes, again, either as a matter of taste or to obtain a better progression, extended harmony, equally divided between the two hands, was used. Ph. Em. Bach is very fond of recommending this form of accompaniment. A third form of four-part harmony, namely, with the chords in the left hand and a single part in the right, was sometimes employed. It was, obviously, possible only when the bass moved slowly and without leaps, and not advisable except when it was desired to execute a more or less elaborate figure in the right hand.[5]

---

[1] *E.g.* 'Sonatas of four parts,' 1697, No. iii., Canzona.
[2] *E.g.* Sonata viii., *Tempo gavotta* and *Altro* (= Gavotte II.). In the latter the violoncello part is practically independent of the harpsichord bass. Instead of executing mere divisions, as in the example from Purcell (see note above), it has a rhythmical figure, based on the harmony played by the harpsichord.
[3] Agostino Agazzari, in the short treatise already mentioned (cf. p. 329, note 3), divides the instruments on which the accompaniment is to be extemporised into ' instruments of foundation,' ' such as the organ, *gravicembalo*, etc., and similarly, in the case of few or single voices, the lute, theorbo, harp, etc.,' and ' instruments of *ornamentation*.' ' As ornamentation,' he writes, ' there are those which disport themselves (*scherzando*) and play counterpoints *contrapontegiando*) and make the harmony more agreeable and sonorous : such are the lute, theorbo, harp, lirone, cither, spinet, chitarrina, violin, pandora and the like.' It will be noticed that the theorbo is included in both categories. Later on Agazzari speaks of the treatment of the violone and viol di gamba as instruments of ornamentation. A bass instrument could therefore be employed in either capacity.
[4] It is, naturally, chiefly in loud passages, and when the bass is fairly slow, that it is suitable to play it in octaves. This, however, may never be done when a C clef (tenor or alto) is employed in the bass part. These C clefs (or *Bassetti* as they were called) are really a relic of the old practice of incorporating one of the higher parts into the *Basso continuo* during a pause in the vocal bass.
[5] This would occur only during a prolonged rest (or sustained notes) in the principal part or parts, for it was the cardinal principle of good accompaniment, throughout the whole of the figured bass age that the accompanist must never seek to shine at the expense of the soloist.

Mattheson gives the following example [6] :

[Note the use of the ' French ' violin clef on the *lowest* line of the upper stave. In the original the third quaver ✳ in the upper part of the left hand is misprinted ♭♭.]

(*c*) Besides the forms of accompaniment just described there was one, much used on the harpsichord (but not on the organ), in which the number of notes struck simultaneously was limited only by the capacity of the two hands. This was known in German treatises as a *vollstimmiges Accompagnement*, or filled-in accompaniment. It is described in great detail by Heinichen (*General-Bass*, etc., 1728). The main points to be observed, he tells us, are these : (1) The extreme parts (upper part and bass) *must* be absolutely correct in their relation to each other, as consecutives arising between them could not, on a keyed instrument, be excused by the assumption of a crossing of parts (*i.e.* between the upper and a middle part) ; (2) in the middle parts, on the other hand, or between an extreme and a middle part, consecutives may be entirely disregarded, as they can then be ' excused by the usual crossing of the parts.' There is, however, one important condition attached, namely, that the hands should be kept close together, in order that consecutive octaves may not be apparent to the ear, either between the upper parts of the respective hands, or between the thumbs of the two hands, or between the extreme parts of the right hand. The great importance of this condition becomes apparent when we learn that Heinichen permitted the duplication in the left hand, not only of the consonances played by the right hand, but of the dissonances as well. These were resolved in the right hand according to rule (generally, therefore, a degree downwards), and in the left hand in three ways : either (1) a degree downwards, in octaves with the right hand ; or (2) a degree upwards ; or (3) they might leap to another interval of the chord.

Heinichen went even further, in allowing the resolution of certain suspended discords to be anticipated in the left hand, as :

---

[6] *Organisten-Probe* (Organists' Test), 1719 ; *Mittel-Classe* (Middle Grade) ; *Prob-Stück* (Test Piece) 11 ; *Erläuterung* (Explanation),

Example [1] 4 will give an idea of his treatment of this form of accompaniment :

It will be seen that the tied 3 on the second note of bar 1, the 7 on the last note of bar 2, the diminished 5 on the last note of bar 6, and the 7 on the last note of bar 10, all resolve in octaves between the right and left hands, while the 7 on the third crotchet of bar 8 leaps a fourth downwards in the left hand, and that the resolution of the 7 on the first note of bar 8 is anticipated in the left hand.

[1] *O.c.* part i. ch. iii. § 88, p. 244 *sq.*

It may be mentioned that, in the fullest accompaniment, Heinichen never, so far as the present writer has observed, doubles an accidentally sharpened leading note.

The question now arises how far Heinichen's rules were in accordance with the practice of his time and of the later part of the century. No other writer goes into the matter in anything like the same detail, and those who make a brief mention of it (as Ph. Em. Bach) for the most part speak of the left hand doubling the *consonances* (but not the dissonances) played by the right ; and of the anticipation of a resolution in the left hand no mention is made. It seems more than likely that Heinichen's precepts reflect the Italian practice, with which (as may be seen from references in the course of his work) he must have become intimately acquainted during his travels in Italy, the home of that harsh, but most effective ornament, the *acciaccatura.*

That J. S. Bach made abundant use of the filled-in accompaniment (whether he doubled the dissonances or not) is clear from a much-quoted passage in a work of his pupil Johann Christian Kittel.[2]

Kittel describes how Bach would become impatient with the inadequate accompaniment of a pupil (presumably at rehearsals), and how ' one had to be prepared to find Bach's hands and fingers mingling with the hands and fingers of the player, and, without further troubling the latter, adorning the accompaniment with masses of harmony, which were even more impressive than the unexpected proximity of the strict teacher.'

(*d*) Apart from the filling-in of the accompaniment described above it is often necessary, when playing in four-part harmony, to take in a fifth part temporarily, either (1) when the hands have got too close together, in order to gain a higher position for the right hand (in which case the extra part, which must always be a consonance, is added at the top of the chord and its lower octave subsequently dropped, so that the process is very closely akin to the crossing of parts)[3] ; or (2) in order to get out of a position in which consecutive fifths

[2] *Der angehende praktische Organist.* Erfurt, 1808, part iii. p. 33.
[3] The two processes are illustrated by the following example :

The same object (that of preventing the hands from getting too close together) can also be attained, as both Heinichen and Ph Em. Bach tell us, by the repercussion of an entire chord, *which must be a consonant one,* in a higher position   In the following example we see both this process and also the one above mentioned : at * a consonant chord is repeated, while at † † a consonant fifth part is added at the top, and its lower 8ve subsequently dropped, as indicated by the crotchet rest after it.   Finally, at ‡ a fifth part is added below the upper part of the last chord, which, owing to the

would result; or (3) in order to prepare a subsequent discord; or (4) to give fulness to a particular chord (*e.g.* one which, owing to the downward resolution of a previous discord, would otherwise lack a consonant interval); or for other reasons.

(*e*) A very important question arises as to how far the accompaniment was expected to possess independent interest and, in particular, whether contrapuntal devices, such as imitation, were regularly employed. It was quite accepted, as has already been mentioned, that any display on the part of the accompanist should be limited to occasions when the solo part or parts were either silent (as in *Ritornelli* and during long pauses) or were executing something of comparatively little interest. It is, then, of such cases that we are now speaking.

With regard to imitation, surprisingly little is said about it in any of the text-books. Mich. de Saint Lambert tells us (*Nouveau Traité*, etc., 1707, ch. ix. 12) that in accompanying a single voice, if the music lends itself to such treatment, imitation may be used; ' but,' he adds, ' this demands consummate science, and, to be a success, must be of the first order.' Heinichen expresses the very definite opinion (*o.c.* part i., ch. vi. § 40, p. 578) that, in pieces in which the composer has used all his opportunities in the written parts, there will very rarely indeed be occasion for *ex tempore* imitation on the part of the accompanist. He admits, however, that such cases may arise, especially in [solo] cantatas and arias without the accompaniment of instruments, and gives an example accordingly. Ph. Em. Bach gives some examples, of which the following is one, in which a rhythmical

8 7 progression over the preceding bass note, would otherwise lack the 5:

Apart from this repetition of an entire consonant chord, it may perhaps be mentioned here that, in the case of the chord of the
seventh (which in four-part harmony may be taken either as ⁷ or ⁷)
circumstances may arise which make it necessary to change from one form of the chord to the other, over the same bass note, leaving the dissonant interval (the 7) unchanged. In the following example from Ph. Em. Bach (*o.c.* Ch. 36 § 14 *d*), given on a single stave and an 8ve lower than here, we see that the previous harmony makes
it necessary to take the 7 on E as ⁷₅ and that it must be changed
to ⁸₇ (or else taken in five parts) to prepare the following 7 on ♯F:

figure in the solo is imitated in the accompaniment (*o.c.* ch. xxxiii. § 7):

[*N.B.*—The part here given in small notes is omitted by Bach, who gives the example (according to his custom) on a single stave, an octave lower than here.]

The following example of imitation is given by Bach (*o.c.* ch. xxxii. § 9) to illustrate cases in which ' certain skips with the harmony in the right hand ' are admissible:

The account which Johann Friedrich Daube [1] gives of the performance of J. S. Bach leaves no room for doubt but that the latter would, upon occasion, draw upon his marvellous contrapuntal resources for the embellishment of the accompaniment; but it is rather suggested that he did so chiefly when accompanying music by other composers with very little inherent interest of its own.

Daube writes:

' Through him [Bach] the principal part was bound to shine. He gave it life by his perfect accompaniment when it had none. He knew how to imitate it so skilfully with the right or left hand, or unexpectedly to bring in a countersubject, that his audience could swear it had been so composed with all care. At the same time the regular accompaniment [*i e.* the harmonies prescribed by the figures] was very little curtailed. . . .'

A similar enthusiastic account in Lorenz Mizler's *Musikalische Bibliothek* (Part 4, 1738, p. 48) makes no mention of contrapuntal feats, but speaks of Bach playing

' any Thorough-Bass to a Solo in such a way that one imagines that it is a Concerto and that the melody which he plays with his right hand has been composed like that beforehand.'

(*f*) Apart from contrapuntal device there were many ways in which the accompaniment was embellished. These are well described by Heinichen in a long chapter devoted to the subject (*o.c.* Part I. ch. vi. pp. 521-83). Apart from the practice of following the bass in

1 *General-Bass in drey Accorden*, 1756, ch. xi., footnote.

thirds,[1] to which he makes frequent allusion in his pages, he divides these embellishments into two classes.

In the first class he includes those embellishments ' which always remain immutable, as one learns them from one's teacher,' and, in the second, those which depend on the invention of the player. The former comprise (1) the shake, (2) the *Transitus in tertiam*,[2] (3) the appoggiatura, (4) the slide, (5) the mordent and (6) ' the so-called acciaccatura '[3]; the latter include (1) melody,[4] (2) passage-work, (3) arpeggios, etc., and (4) imitation.

[1] As in the following:

[2] This consists in filling up the interval of a third between two consecutive notes with a passing note (with or without a shake), and may, Heinichen tells us, be employed in the bass itself. Heinichen's example begins as follows : (a) shows the plain accompaniment, and (b) the same embellished as described—

[3] Heinichen, as he himself tells us, learnt this ornament from *L'armonico pratico al cembalo* (Venice, 1708) of Francesco Gasparini. The latter made a curious distinction : when the ornament in question was a *semitone* below the harmony note, he called it a *mordente*, and when it was a whole tone below (or above), an *acciaccatura*. Either ornament is to be struck together with the harmony notes and immediately released, the whole chord being played with a slight *arpeggio*. Heinichen gives numerous examples, of which the following (*l.c.* § 18, p. 536) is one :

The *acciaccatura* may also be double, as in the next example *ib.* § 19, p. 537) :

Heinichen adds directions for the introduction of the *acciaccatura* or *mordente* (according to Gasparini's definition of the latter) by the accompanist (*ib.* § 24, p. 540 *sq.*) :
The latter is to note where there is an interval of a third between the harmony notes in either hand and, at the same time, a finger unemployed. The intervening note is to be struck with the others, and immediately released, as described above. Three cautions are added : (1) The ornament must not be used too often, but only by way of variety ; (2) it is not good for more than 3 or 4 contiguous notes to be struck together ; (3) the chord must be slightly spread (*mit einem gelinden Arpeggio*).

[4] Heinichen gives two excellent examples showing how a melody may be founded on the simple bass :

In the first example the harmony is divided equally between the hands ; in the second the right hand has the melody alone, and the left hand chords.

(g) There were definite rules for the compass of the accompaniment. Most text-books of the 18th century give e'' or f'' as the limit of the upward compass,[5] and some mention g or f as the lowest notes permissible in the right hand. The only occasions when the upward compass might be extended was when a C clef was used in the bass, or when the latter was exceptionally high.

With regard to the pitch of the accompaniment in relation to the principal part or parts, the main rules were (1) that the upper part of the accompaniment should not be continuously in unison with the upper principal part, and (2) that it should be rather below than above it.[6]

(h) A considerable change took place during the first half of the 18th century (if we may judge by the examples given in text-books) in the attitude of musicians towards consecutives in a figured bass accompaniment. In the works of Mattheson [7] and Heinichen [8] we find con-

[5] Heinichen makes the amusing comment on this rule (*o.c.* p. 548, footnote) that ' when trying to play a melody, passages, arpeggios and all kinds of variations in the right hand alone,' a person may ' go up to X in alt (*das dreigestrichene X*), if he thinks that there is any good to be got there.'
[6] Considerable difference of opinion existed as to the pitch at which bass instruments or voices should be accompanied. Quantz (*Versuch*, etc., 1752, *Hauptstück* (Section) xvii., *Abschnitt* (Subsection) vi. § 21) states explicitly that the violoncello should not be accompanied at the same pitch as the violin, and Ph. Em. Bach (*Versuch*, etc., Part II., 1762, ch. xxix. § 23) shares this point of view. Türk (*Kurze Anweisung*, etc., 1791, § 198), on the other hand, expresses the opinion that ' one may, in various cases, accompany a bass or tenor voice, as also the bassoon, violoncello, etc., a whole octave higher, because, namely, middle C (c'), for instance, sung by a bass, is in so far accepted on keyed instruments, etc. as the C above (c'').'
[7] In the *Organisten-Probe*, 1719 (*Mittel-Classe*, Prob. Stück 22, *Erläuterung*, § 4) we find the following :

Of this he says (*l.c.* § 8) that ' Should some critical creature perhaps think to detect octaves in the second bar, he must allow himself to be informed of what is meant by crossing of the parts.' He would probably have excused the following progressions from the *Kleine General-Bass-Schule*, 1735 (*Aufsteigender Classe*, 4te Aufgabe § 7, bars 7-8 ; *Höherer Classe*, 2te Aufgabe, § 9, 6th bar from end ; *Höherer, Classe*, 4te Aufgabe, § 4, bars 9 and 10), in the same way :

[*N.B.*—In the original the chords are not given, but every interval of them is figured above the bass, and in the order (as Mattheson explains) in which they are to be taken.]
[8] It must be admitted that octaves like those in the following example (*o.c.* Part I. ch. vi. § 7, pp. 525, 526) are rare in Heinichen's work, in *four-part* harmony :

[*N.B.*—Heinichen here uses the *custos W* to indicate a (long) *appoggiatura*.]
On the other hand, he uses octaves arising between passing notes

secutives in four-part harmony (quite apart from those arising in a filled-in accompaniment) which neither Marpurg, nor Ph. Em. Bach, nor Kirnberger, nor Türk would have tolerated for an instant.

It was generally admitted by even the stricter authorities, about the middle of the 18th century and later, that somewhat more latitude might be allowed (in the matter of correctness of progression) in accompanying from a figured bass than in composition, but Ph. Em. Bach apparently did not share this view. The following progression, in which consecutive 5ths cannot be avoided except in the position in which the 9 is in the tenor, is a case in point:

etc.

Of this Marpurg writes as follows in his *Handbuch bey dem Generalbasse* (1755, 2nd ed. 1762):

' There are certain sequences of harmonic progressions in which consecutive fifths *between the inner parts* are fairly tolerable. See Fig. 24 [= Ex. 7 and another example not given here]. The dissonance here stifles the annoyance to the ear which would otherwise arise from the succession of fifths.'

In the *first* edition of the *Handbuch* there follows a passage which concludes:

' At least they [the 5ths] can be used without fear in accompanying.'

In the second edition this passage is cancelled and the following substituted:

' However, it is better to arrange (*setzen*) the three upper parts differently and to transform the fifths into fourths.'

Ph. Em. Bach in commenting on the same progression (*Versuch*, etc., Part II., 1762, ch. xvii. I. § 8) prescribes the position in which the 9 is in the tenor, and adds:

in the bass and an upper part quite freely, as in the following example (o.c. Part I. ch. iv. § 16, p. 274, bar 2):

Ph. Em. Bach (as he explains in similar cases) would have corrected the progression as follows:

' The fifths which arise in the other two positions, however much they may be defended, are, and remain, disgusting to the ear.'

Of the same progression, again, Christoph Gottlieb Schröter (no mean authority) writes (*Deutliche Anweisung*, etc., 1772, § 234, p. 123): ' Mock fifths (*Scheinquinten*) are not real fifths.'

(*i*) The device of a nominal crossing of parts, as a means either of evading consecutives or of maintaining a higher position of the right hand than the necessary preparation and resolution of discords would otherwise admit, is not much discussed in the old text-books. Heinichen, as we saw above, absolutely refused to recognise it as an excuse for consecutives between extreme parts, but admitted it in the case of those arising between middle (or middle and extreme) parts in a filled-in accompaniment. Ph. Em. Bach's sole reference to the device is purely negative. He speaks (*o.c.* ch. xxv. § 5) of

' . . . a crossing of parts in the thorough-bass-which is not allowed, as otherwise many mistakes might be justified without the ear after all being satisfied.'

Marpurg, however, as we have already been led to expect, allows more latitude. He forbids the evasion of consecutives by an assumed crossing of the parts only when (1) the harmony is not full enough (*i.e.* in less than four parts), (2) when both chords are consonant, (3) when the consecutives are between extreme parts, and (4) when most of the parts progress by similar motion.

He therefore sanctions the following progressions:

Handbuch, etc. 1755, Tab. VII (2nd Ed. 1762, Tab. V) Fig 5.   *Ibid.* Tab. VIII (2nd Ed. Tab. VI) Fig. 12.

Kirnberger gives the following example in which the crossing of parts is used in order to maintain the position of the right hand[1]:

etc.

(*j*) A principle, fully recognised in the 18th century, but often disregarded to-day, was that a discord should be played more loudly than its resolution. Very few definite instructions, however, are given in the text-books. Ph. Em.

[1] Cf. *Grundsätze des Generalbasses*, 1781, § 172; Volume of examples, Part III. Fig. xxvi.

Bach makes the following brief allusion to the matter [1] :

'It may, however, be noted that dissonances are generally played more loudly and consonances more softly, because the former stimulate and accentuate the emotions (*die Leidenschaften mit Nachdruck erheben*) while the latter calm them.'

Quantz, however, in his famous essay on the flute,[2] goes into great detail. He divides the discords into three classes according to the amount of emphasis which they require : (1) *mezzoforte*, (2) *forte*, (3) *fortissimo*. These degrees of loudness, he explains, are not absolute but relative, and his classification is based on the assumption that the normal level of the accompaniment, in an adagio, is *mezzo piano*. He tells us, moreover, that when discords of various kinds follow one upon another, and discords resolve on discords, the intensity of expression must be kept on the increase by strengthening the tone and increasing the number of parts. Among the discords to be played *m.f.* is the ' second with [perfect] fourth ' $\frac{6}{4}$, among those to be played *f.*, the ' second with augmented fourth ' $\frac{6}{4}$, and among those to be played *ff.*, the diminished seventh with its three inversions. Quantz gives an example to illustrate his rules in the shape of an entire movement (*Affettuoso di molto*) for solo (presumably flute) and figured bass. There can be no doubt that he carries the didactic principle too far, but what he says is nevertheless well worth careful (if critical) study.

It remains, in conclusion, to say a few words concerning the disregard of the composers' intentions, often shown in present - day performances of the masterpieces of the past, by omitting the figured bass accompaniment whenever the harmony is supplied in a more or less (often less) complete form by the vocal and instrumental parts. For this omission there is absolutely no justification. If the organist is unable to play from the figures, the accompaniment should be set out from them, and on no account arranged, as sometimes happens, from the vocal or instrumental parts, which very often lack an interval prescribed by the figures, quite apart from the fact that, in quickly moving parts, the harmony note is often present in a very transient form. The opinion, which the writer has heard expressed, that the figured bass accompaniment was intended to be used (or not) at the discretion of the organist, in order to support a weak performance, is entirely without foundation in fact and is as pernicious a fallacy as can well be. Let Ph. Em. Bach's words be remembered : ' No piece . . . can be performed satisfactorily without the accompaniment of a keyed instrument.' If any impartial musician had the opportunity of listening to a

[1] *Versuch*, etc., Part I. 2nd ed. 1757 (1st ed. 1753), *Hauptstück* (Section) 3, § 29
[2] *Versuch*, etc., 1752, *Hauptstück* (Section) xvii., *Abschnitt* Subsection) vi., §§ 12-17.

performance of one of J. S. Bach's violin concertos, or of the concerto in D minor for two violins, with the accompaniment of strings and of the harpsichord (or, failing that, of the pianoforte), and then to a performance of the same work *without* the figured bass accompaniment, he would inevitably be driven to the conclusion that the former was as much more satisfying to the ear as is a chalk drawing on toned paper to the eye, when compared with a similar drawing upon a dead white.

BIBLIOGRAPHY

Among the sources of information relating to accompaniment from a Thorough-Bass, as practised during the 17th and 18th centuries, the following are, in their different ways, of special interest :

LODOVICO VIADANA : Twelve rules (*avertimenti*) contained in the Preface to the *Cento concerti ecclesiastici*. Venice (Vincenti), 1602.
AGOSTINO AGAZZARI : *Del suonare sopra il basso con tutti stromenti ed uso loro nel conserto*. Siena, 1607. (Reprinted by O. Kinkeldey, *Orgel und Klavier in der Musik des 16. Jahrh.* (Leipzig, 1910, Appendix).
MICHAEL PRAETORIUS : *Syntagma musicum*, Tom. III. 1619 ch. vi. ' De Basso generali seu continuo.'
LORENZO PENNA : *Li primi albori musicali*, etc. Bologna (Monti), 1672. The Third Book of the above contains ' Li fondamenti per suonare l' organo sopra la parte.'
   A work of extraordinary interest.
MATTHEW LOCKE : *Melothesia, or Certain General Rules for playing a Continued-Bass*, etc. London (J. Carr), 1673.
FRIDRICH ERHARD NIEDT : *Musicalische Handleitung*, etc. ' Erster Theil handelt vom General-Bass,' etc. Hamburg (Spieringk) 1700.
MICHAEL DE SAINT - LAMBERT : *Traité de l'accompagnement du clavecin, de l'orgue et de quelques autres instruments*. Paris, (Ballard), 1680.
   The writer has been unable to trace this edition except in a manuscript Italian translation of chapters v.-ix. preserved in the library of the Liceo Musicale at Bologna. A second edition appeared under the title *Nouveau traité*, etc., Paris (Ballard), 1707, reprinted by Estienne Roger, Amsterdam. A most interesting and well written work.
FRANCESCO GASPARINI : *L' armonico pratico al cembalo*, etc. Venice (Bortoli), 1708, last reprint 1802.
JOHANN MATTHESON : *Exemplarische Organisten-Probe*, etc. Hamburg, 1719. 2nd ed. entitled *Grosse General-Bass-Schule*, 1731.
JOHANN DAVID HEINICHEN : *Der General-Bass in der Composition*, etc. Dresden, 1728.
JOHANN JOACHIM QUANTZ : *Versuch einer Anweisung die Flöte traversiere zu spielen*, etc. Berlin, 1752, Hauptstück (Section) xvii. ' Von den Pflichten derer, welche accompagniren.' etc., Abschnitt (Subsection) vi. ' Von dem Clavieristen insbesondere.'
FRANCESCO GEMINIANI : *The Art of Accompaniament* [sic], etc. Op. 11. London, undated (1755 ?).
   A most original and instructive work, far too little known.
FRIEDRICH WILHELM MARPURG : *Handbuch bey dem General-Basse*, etc. Berlin, 1755, 2nd ed. 1762.
   This is mainly theoretical, but contains instructive allusions to the practice of accompaniment.
CARL PHILIPP EMANUEL BACH : *Versuch über die wahre Art das Clavier zu spielen. Zweyter Theil, in welchem die Lehre von dem Accompagnement und der freyen Fantasie abgehandelt wird*. Berlin (Winter), 1762.
   Some later editions.
CHRISTOPH GOTTLIEB SCHRÖTER : *Deutliche Anweisung zum General-Bass*, etc. Halberstadt (Gross), 1772.
DANIEL GOTTLOB TÜRK : *Kurze Anweisung zum Generalbassspielen*, etc., Leipsic (Schwickert), 1791.
   Later editions 1800-41.

Among the works enumerated above, Ph. Em. Bach's *Versuch* is quite indispensable to the student, and Heinichen's *General-Bass* almost equally so.

F. T. A.

THOROWGOOD, HENRY, a London music-publisher at the sign of the ' Violin and Guittar,' at Number 6, under the North Piazza of the Royal Exchange. He flourished about 1760 to 1770, and published many interesting works, some of which were reprints from earlier publications. These include such operas as ' Thomas and Sally,' ' Maid of the Mill,' ' Artaxerxes,' etc., while Galleotti's sonatas, Zannetti's soli, Spadino's minuets and other similar collections bear his imprint. It is difficult to determine exactly whether he preceded or succeeded Maurice Whitaker, who was at the same address ; probably the latter.

At one time (about 1760) there was a partnership, Thorowgood & Horn, music-sellers in Cheapside, and this, no doubt, was the prior firm.   F. K.

THREE CHOIRS FESTIVAL, the popular name for the MEETING OF THE THREE CHOIRS OF GLOUCESTER, WORCESTER AND HEREFORD held annually in the week beginning on the first Sunday in September in the cathedrals of these three cities by rotation. This is the oldest of the English provincial musical festivals, and in its modern form it provides each city with a triennial festival, consisting of an Opening Service with choir and orchestra on the Sunday and four days of musical performances (Tuesday to Friday), for the most part in the Cathedral, but with one or two secular concerts (Wednesday and Friday evenings) in the Shire Hall.

HISTORY.—Definite records of the ' Music Meeting ' date from 1724, in which year Dr. Thomas Bisse, Chancellor of Hereford and brother of Dr. Philip Bisse, Bishop of that diocese, first proposed to associate the meeting with a charity for the education and maintenance of orphans of the poorer clergy of the three dioceses. The idea was suggested by the festival of the SONS OF THE CLERGY (q.v.), for which Dr. Bisse had preached in St. Paul's Cathedral, London. For some years previously the members of the three cathedral choirs had met in one or other of the cathedrals for the combined singing of service music, but the collection for the clerical charity at Gloucester in 1724 and the appointment of six stewards (a clergyman and a layman from each diocese) to administer the fund gave the meeting a definite status, and the sermon in aid of the charity and in praise of the art preached by Dr. Bisse at Hereford in 1726 [1] sealed the association of the two objects. The sermon (now preached at the Sunday service) has remained a constant feature ever since.

The advertisements and reports in the Gloucester Journal (1724) show that the meetings already included secular evening concerts then held in the ' Boothall ' (at Worcester and Hereford in the College halls), and organised by the musical clubs of the cities. The music in the cathedrals included the singing in alternate years of Purcell's Te Deum and Handel's Te Deum for the Peace of Utrecht, the latter being presently superseded by Handel's Dettingen Te Deum. The performance of these works with instruments was the starting-point from which the oratorio performances were later to proceed. The following list of events are landmarks in the development of the festival-scheme.

1737. Dr. Boyce was appointed conductor of the

---

1 Rimbault declared that the meetings date probably from 1716 or 1717. He possessed a printed sermon entitled ' A Rationale on Cathedral Worship or Choir Service ' preached by Bisse at Hereford, Sept. 7, 1720. See Annals, p. 3, note.

music meeting and held that position for several years.

1739. Handel's ' Alexander's Feast ' performed.

1743. Boyce composed an anthem for the festival, apparently given as part of a ' Grand Concert of Musick ' in which members of London choirs brought by Dr. Greene co-operated.

1745. A dramatic pastoral, ' Love's Revenge ' (music by Greene), and Handel's ' Acis ' performed in the Boothall, Gloucester.

1748. Handel's Dettingen Te Deum and Jubilate on the first day, Purcell's Te Deum and Handel's ' Coronation Anthem ' on the second day, in the Cathedral.

1752. Worcester. Handel's ' Samson ' at the evening concert.

1753. Hereford. The programme extended to three evening concerts. At the third ' The Shepherd's Lottery ' (music by Boyce) was given.

1754. Gloucester. Handel's ' Judas Maccabæus ' given at a concert.

1755. Worcester. For the first time we get full accounts of the performers engaged. The solo singers include a Miss Turner, Beard the famous tenor, Wass of the Chapel Royal ; Abraham Brown led the orchestra.

1757. Gloucester. Handel's ' Messiah ' first given in the Boothall.

1759. Hereford. Handel's ' Messiah ' first given in the Cathedral. This was the beginning of oratorio performances in the Cathedral. It was conducted by Clack, organist of Hereford.

For some time ' Messiah ' was the only oratorio admitted in the cathedrals (and it was often given at the secular concerts), and the programmes retained generally the form of Te Deum, Jubilate and anthem performances in the Cathedral with an increasing number of Handel's oratorios elsewhere for many years.

1784. Gloucester. The first day's music of the HANDEL COMMEMORATION (q.v.) held in Westminster Abbey was given in a morning performance in the Cathedral, substituted for the usual church service. A charge was made for admission to the Cathedral for the first time.

1786. Hereford. Owing to the dangerous condition of the Cathedral, the Handel Commemoration selection and ' Messiah ' were sung in St. Peter's Church.

1787. Gloucester. Handel's ' Israel in Egypt ' first given in the Cathedral.

1788. Worcester. The meeting was held in the first week in August for the convenience of King George III. and members of the Royal family who attended.

The meetings had become by this time virtually Handel Festivals, and a touch of unconscious humour is provided in the information that at Gloucester, 1790, Mme. Mara introduced the air ' Pious orgies ' in the course of the morning service on the first day. The famous singers of the day all appeared in turn, and the original performers (the choirs of the three cathedrals) became merely the ripieno. The original purpose of improving the service music by combined singing is more or less lost sight of, though the services are still maintained. We find portions of Haydn's ' Creation ' taking their place in the early years of the 19th century, and at Gloucester (1832), a year of disaster owing to the outbreak of cholera in the town, the following enterprising selection was given in the Cathedral : portions of Spohr's ' Last Judgment,' Neukomm's ' Mount Sinai,' Mozart's ' Requiem ' and Handel's ' Israel.' These works, with a considerable portion of Crotch's

Z

'Palestine,' at Worcester (1833) show the festival to be gradually outgrowing the Handel fever.

The appointment of S. S. Wesley to Hereford is a landmark of importance. His first programme shows the music, given for the first time in the nave of the Cathedral, assuming a more varied form.

1834. Hereford. First day, Spohr's overture to 'The Last Judgment,' Handel's Dettingen Te Deum, Attwood's coronation anthem 'I was glad,' Boyce's anthem 'Lord Thou hast been our refuge.' Second day, Spohr's 'Last Judgment,' Haydn's 'Creation,' Pt. I., 'Antiphona' by S. Wesley, 'Sanctus' by S. S. Wesley. Third day, Mozart's 'Requiem' and selections from Handel's 'Messiah.'

The whole thing is now on the larger scale befitting performances in the nave. At Gloucester (1835) the following is the schedule of performers :

10 principal singers (including Mmes. Caradori Allan and Clara Novello, Mr. and Mrs. Knyvett, Signori Rubini, Lablache).
71 instrumentalists.
119 choralists.

At Worcester (1836) a fourth day was added to the festival. With these enlargements began an era of financial difficulty resulting from the system maintained to the present time (1926) by which the charity takes all the profits [1] and the stewards bear all the loss. No money is carried over from a successful year to meet possible reverses or defray increased costs, consequently the conveners of the meetings have to make a bid for popularity in framing their programmes.

Throughout the 19th century the principal additions to the programmes were naturally the works of the composers who had for the time being the ear of the large public. The appearance of Mendelssohn's 'Hymn of Praise' (Lobgesang) at Gloucester (1841) marks the beginning of the Mendelssohn period crowned with the introduction of 'Elijah' at Gloucester (1847), and his works, with the oratorios of Spohr, Rossini's 'Stabat Mater' and, more occasionally, Beethoven's 'Mount of Olivet,' were, with Handel's oratorios, the chief ingredients of the festival programmes throughout the middle years of the century.

At Gloucester (1868) a short instrumental work 'Intermezzo Religioso' by Hubert Parry, then known only as the son of the squire of Highnam, was played in the cathedral. The critics who treated it slightingly were unaware that its appearance was the beginning of a new era in the life of the festival. They could not be expected to foresee the future eminence of the composer; what they might have welcomed was the fact that the festival was now opening its doors to the works of young and native talent. In the following year (Worcester, 1869) Sullivan conducted his oratorio 'The Prodigal Son,' and from about this time ora-

torios by native composers, mostly ephemeral, become frequent. The progress of English music and the discovery of the great choral work of J. S. Bach are the things which stand out in the history of the Three Choirs of the next twenty years. The principal events of the period may be summarised thus :

1871. Gloucester. J. S. Bach's 'St. Matthew Passion,' first given under S. S. Wesley's direction.
1872. Worcester. Bach's 'St. Matthew Passion' repeated.
1875. Worcester. The most virulent of the periodical attacks on the plan and methods of the festival resulted in an experimental return to something like the original design. A series of choral services with anthems by such favourite composers as Handel, Mendelssohn, Spohr, S. S. Wesley, took the place of the oratorio performances.
1880. Gloucester. The first of Parry's mature works, 'Scenes from Prometheus Unbound,' was produced at the Shire Hall. Of this event Sir Henry Hadow says : 'No one seems to have had any idea that on that evening in the Shire Hall English music had, after many years, come again to its own, and that it had come with a masterpiece in its hand.' [2]
1883. Gloucester. Stanford's 'Elegiac' symphony was performed in the Cathedral.
1884. Worcester. Bach's 'God so loved the world,' and Dvorak's 'Stabat Mater' given.
1885. Hereford. Bach's 'A stronghold sure.'
1889. Gloucester. Parry's 'Judith' (produced at Birmingham) first given here.
1890. Worcester. Elgar's 'Froissart' overture produced in the Shire Hall.
1891. Hereford. Parry's 'De profundis' for three choirs, written expressly for this festival.
1892. Gloucester. Parry's 'Job' produced and repeated in the two following years at Worcester and Hereford, the first time that such an event had occurred with the work of a native living composer.

As Gloucester brought Parry, so Worcester brought Elgar to renew the vitality of the Three Choirs Festival. The 'Froissart' overture named above is the latter's first appearance in a festival programme, and the several productions of his lesser choral works are discussed elsewhere (see ELGAR). The Worcester festival of 1902 brought forward 'The Dream of Gerontius' after its comparative failure at Birmingham and its conspicuous continental success at Düsseldorf. It with Elgar's later works, both choral and orchestral, became the mainstays of the festival as far as native composition was concerned, though many other composers, notably Bantock, Walford Davies, Vaughan Williams, produced important works which have lived in the years between 1902 and 1913.

For six years of war, 1914–19, the Three Choirs festival was suspended. It was revived at Worcester in 1920, and has been carried on with renewed vigour and success since. To Ivor Atkins fell the privilege of negotiating the revival. The organists of Gloucester and Hereford, Brewer and Hull, the one a veteran, the other a newcomer to the work, threw themselves with equal enthusiasm into the cause. Arrangements were made to increase greatly the number of stewards and so ease the burden of individual financial responsi-

[1] That is, the collections taken at the doors intact, and any profit which may be made by the sale of tickets.

[2] Address on 'Sir Hubert Parry,' read before the Musical Association, June 17, 1919. See *Mus. Assoc. Proc.*, 1918–19, p. 137.

bility, but the old financial defect which creates no reserve fund for the future was unfortunately allowed to remain. New works have been shorter and generally less important than they were in the pre-war festivals, but the programmes up to and including 1926 have contained some interesting revivals and notable performances of Bach with other favourite classics. The festival of 1925 (Gloucester) was designed to be as far as possible representative of English music from Orlando Gibbons, whose tercentenary it celebrated, to modern times. The programme included, besides works by composers already mentioned, part of Ethel Smyth's Mass, and a new motet by G. Holst.

BIBL.—*Origin and Progress of the Meeting of the Three Choirs of Gloucester, Worcester and Hereford, and the Charity connected with it,* REV. DANIEL LYSONS (to 1812), JOHN ARNOTT (to 1864), C. LEE WILLIAMS and H. GODWIN CHANCE (to 1894), 1 vol. ; *Annals of the Three Choirs from 1895–1922,* by C. LEE WILLIAMS and H. GODWIN CHANCE.

                                                                     C.

THREE MUSKETEERS, THE, opera in 4 acts; libretto, founded on Dumas, by H. Cain and L. Payen (English translation by A. Kalisch); music by Isidore de Lara. Produced (in French), Cannes, 1921; in English (Carl Rosa Co.), Newcastle, May 2, 1924.

THREE-QUARTER FIDDLE, see VIOLINO PICCOLO.

THUILLE, LUDWIG (*b.* Bozen, Nov. 30, 1861; *d.* Munich, Feb. 5, 1907). His father, Johann Thuille, was a timber merchant, and an enthusiastic amateur musician. From him the boy had his first lessons, and soon he developed a quite remarkable talent for music; in fact, he was a prodigy. On the death of his father the boy was sent as a chorister to the Benedictine Abbey at Kremsmünster in Upper Austria; where, in addition to receiving a thorough instruction in church music, he attended the High School and gained an excellent elementary education. In 1876, when he was 15 years old, Thuille returned to his home and became a pupil of Joseph Pembaur, principal of the Innsbruck School of Music, and a good sound musician. Here the boy was well grounded in piano-playing as well as in theory, and also entered the gymnasium. Having completed his course there in three years, he in 1879 removed to Munich and joined the School of Music. This, on account of his extreme poverty, would have been impossible except for the kindness of the widow of Matthäus Naziller, the late principal of the Innsbruck School of Music, who generously paid the boy's expenses. Thuille remained at the Munich School of Music until July 1881, in all three years; during this period his chief teachers were Karl Bärmen (a pupil of Liszt) for piano, and Rheinberger for organ, counterpoint and composition. On leaving Munich Thuille obtained a scholarship on the Frankfort Mozart foundation, and in the following year, 1882, he

made the friendship with Alexander RITTER which was destined to affect his career very materially.

In 1883 Thuille was appointed to a professorship at the Munich School of Music, and to Munich came also Alexander Ritter when in 1885 Richard Strauss was appointed successor to von Bülow at Meiningen. Strauss was an old friend and fellow-student of Thuille, and he produced at Meiningen a piano trio and a symphony by the latter which enhanced the reputation of the now rising composer. Under Ritter's good influence Thuille turned his attention to opera. For his first essay in this direction Ritter himself prepared the libretto, which was founded on Herman Schmid's comedy, 'Theuerdank.' The music was completed in 1894, but the opera was not heard until Mar. 12, 1897, when it was very favourably received, but did not keep the stage, owing to defects in the libretto. The only published number was the Prelude to Act I., which appeared under the title of 'Romantic Overture.' The second opera, 'Lobetanz,' poem by O. J. Bierbaum, was written in 1896, and was even spoken of as superior to Humperdinck's 'Hänsel und Gretel,' and in the same style. The third opera, ' Gugeline,' poem also by O. J. Bierbaum, was finished in 1900, and was considered (especially in the third act) superior to the two already mentioned.

Thuille, whilst giving his attention to opera, did not neglect other branches of music. Following on his original brilliant success in chamber music—a sextet for piano and wind instruments, composed in 1887 and performed at the National German Music Union at Wiesbaden in 1889— he produced, just after ' Lobetanz,' the quintet for piano and strings, and, after ' Gugeline,' the violoncello sonata which has been considered as one of the most important works for the violoncello since the time of Beethoven. As conductor of the ' Liederhort,' an important malevoice choir in Munich, Thuille was naturally led to compose music for men's voices, in which field his ' Weihnacht im Walde ' stands out as a very high-class composition. Also by way of contrast he wrote the beautiful choruses for female voices, ' Dreamy Summer night,' with harp and violin soli, and ' Rosenlied,' with only piano accompaniments, besides a number of songs.

His best-known works are as follows :

Op.
3. Drei Klavierstücke.
4. Fünf Lieder.
5. Drei Frauenchöre. Poems by Karl Stiehler.
6. Sextet for Piano and Wind.
7. Von Lieb und Leid. Poem by Karl Stiehler.
14. Männerchor, ' Weihnacht im Walde.'
20. Quintet, Piano and Strings.
22. Sonata, Violoncello and Piano.
25. Frauenchor, ' Traum Sommernacht.'
29. Frauenchor, ' Rosenlied.'

OPERAS

Theuerdank. Lib. by Ritter, 1894, produced Munich, Mar. 12, 1897
Lobetanz. Poem by Bierbaum, produced Mannheim, 1898.
Gugeline. Poem by Bierbaum, produced Bremen, 1901.
Prelude to Theuerdank (' Romantic Overture ').   D. H.

BIBL.—FRIEDRICH MUNTER, *Ludwig Thuille* (Munich, 1923).

THUMOTH,[1] Burk, was editor of an early printed collection of Irish melodies.

This was issued in two octavo books, the first containing twelve Scotch and twelve Irish airs, and the second twelve English and twelve Irish airs. Both are ' with Variations, set for the German Flute, Violin or Harpsichord,' and are printed for John Simpson at the Bass Viol and Flute in Sweeting's Alley, opposite the east door of the Royal Exchange. Bunting asserted that they were published in 1720 ; but Simpson did not begin printing till long after that date, and the two collections of Curious Scots Tunes by James Oswald which are advertised on the title-page of the first book were certainly not issued before 1742. The two books were reprinted from Simpson's plates about 1765 'for Henry Thorowgood at the Violin and Guitar under the North Piazza of the Royal Exchange,' and about twenty years later they were re-engraved and published in one volume by A. S. and P. Thompson of 75 St. Paul's Churchyard, under the titl eof ' Forty-eight English, Irish, and Scotch Airs.' The only other known publication of Thumoth is

' Six Solos for a German Flute, Violin or Harpsichord, the First Three compos'd by Mr. Burk Thumoth, the Three Last by Sigr. Canaby.'

This is a thin folio volume, undated, which seems to have been issued about the same time as the Irish Airs, between 1740 and 1745.

J. F. R. S.

THURSBY, Emma (b. Brooklyn, New York, Feb. 21, 1857), singer, came of English ancestors on her father's side and a Dutch family on her mother's. Her great-grandparents were American. She received instruction in singing first from Julius Meyer and Achille Errani, then in 1873 at Milan from Lamperti and San Giovanni, and finally completed her studies in America under Madame Rudersdorff and Maurice Strakosch. In 1875 she undertook a tour through the United States and Canada. She made her début in England, May 22, 1878, at the Philharmonic, with such success that she was engaged at a subsequent concert of the Society in the same season. She remained in England until the end of 1879, singing with acceptance at the Crystal Palace, the Popular Concerts, Leslie's Choir, etc., and in the summer of the same year sang in Paris and the French provinces. In 1880–81 she made an extended concert-tour through Germany, Austria, Holland, Belgium, Spain, Norway, Denmark, etc., and returned to America at the end of 1882. In 1883 she was singing in the States and Canada. Later she abandoned her public career and became a teacher in New York, where among her pupils in 1897 and 1898 was Geraldine Farrar. She made a tour of China and Japan in 1903.

A. C. : addns. H. E. K.

[1] Real name Burke of Thomond.   W. H. G. F.

THYL UYLENSPIEGEL, see Till Eulen-spiegel.

TICHATSCHEK, Joseph Aloys (b. Ober Weckelsdorf, Bohemia, July 11, 1807 ; d. Blase-witz, near Dresden, Jan. 18, 1886), German operatic tenor, began by studying medicine, but abandoned it for music, and received in-struction in singing from Ciccimara, a favourite Italian singing-master. In 1830 he became a chorus singer at the Kärnthnerthor theatre, was next appointed chorus inspector, played small parts, and afterwards those of more im-portance, viz. Idreno (' Semiramide '), Alphonse (' Stumme '), and Raimbaud (' Robert '). He sang for two years at Graz, and again at Vienna, as principal tenor. On Aug. 11, 1837, he made his début at Dresden as Gustavus III. (Auber), with such success as to obtain an engagement for the following year. At this period he at-tracted the attention of Schroeder-Devrient, who gave him the benefit of her advice and experience, with the result of a long and inti-mate friendship, which terminated only with her death. Until his retirement in 1870 he remained permanently in Dresden, where, on Jan. 16, as Idomeneo, he celebrated the 40th anniversary of his professional career, having previously, on Jan. 17, 1863, celebrated his 25th anniversary at Dresden, as Fernando Cortes (Spontini). On Oct. 20, 1842, and Oct. 19, 1845, respectively, he was the original Rienzi and Tannhäuser. In 1841 he sang for a few nights in German at Drury Lane Theatre as Adolar, Tamino, Robert, etc. ; also at Liver-pool and Manchester.   A. C.

TIE, a curved line uniting two notes of the same pitch, whereby they form a single note which is sustained for the value of both. The tie is also called the Bind (q.v.), and by some writers the Ligature, although this term properly refers to certain slurred groups of notes which occur in ancient music. (See Notation.)

In pianoforte music ties are occasionally met with where the note, though tied, is actually repeated. To effect this repetition properly some skill and care are required ; the finger which strikes the first of the two tied notes is drawn inwards, and the following finger falls over it as closely and rapidly as possible, so as to take its place before the key has had time to rise to its full distance, and therefore before the damper has quite fallen.[2] Thus there is no actual silence between the two sounds ; the repetition takes place before the first sound has ceased, and an effect is produced which re-sembles the old effect of Bebung (q.v.) as nearly as the modern pianoforte can imitate it. The particular occasions on which this effect is required are not indicated by any specific sign, since an experienced performer can always

[2] The effect, however, is generally most readily obtained by the aid of the sustaining pedal.

judge from the nature of the passage. As a rule, it may be said that whenever two tied notes are written for which a single longer note might have been substituted, repetition is indicated—for the use of the tie proper is to express a note-value which *cannot* be represented by a single note, *e.g.* five quavers. Thus Ex. 1, which is an instance in point, might, if no repetition had been required, have been written in quavers, as in Ex. 2.

BEETHOVEN, Sonata, Op. 106, Adagio.

Another instance of the employment of this close repetition sometimes occurs when an unaccented note is tied to an accented one, as in Ex. 3. Here the rhythm would be entirely lost if the tied notes were sustained instead of repeated.

CHOPIN, Valse, Op. 34, No. 1.

In the same sense it seems quite possible that the subject of the scherzo of Beethoven's Sonata for piano and violoncello, op. 69, and other similar phrases, may have been intended to be played with repetition ; and in support of this view it may be mentioned that an edition exists of the Sonata Pastorale, op. 28, by Cipriani Potter, who had opportunities of hearing Beethoven and becoming acquainted with his intentions, in which the analogous passage in the first movement is printed with what is evidently meant for a sign of separation between the tied notes, thus :

Ex. 4.

F. T.

TIEFFENBRUCKER, see DUIFFOPRUGCAR.

TIEFLAND, opera in a prelude and 2 acts ; text after A. Guimera, by Rudolph Lothar ; music by Eugen d'Albert. Produced Prague, 1903 ; Covent Garden (in English), Oct. 5, 1910.

TIERCE, *i.e. Tiers*, third. (1) A name given to the interval of the third, whether major or minor.

(2) The fourth of the series of natural harmonics, being the major third in the third

octave above the ground-tone or prime ; its vibrations are five times as numerous as those of its prime.

(3) An open metal organ stop of the same pitch as the similarly named harmonic, *i.e.* if the note CC is held down and the Tierce-stop drawn, the E above middle C will be heard. That such a stop can only be used in combination with certain other harmonics, and then but sparingly, will be evident when it is remembered that if C, E and G be held down there will be heard at the same time G sharp and B. Hence the Tierce when found in a modern organ is generally incorporated as a rank of the Sesquialtera or Mixture, in which case it is of course combined with other harmonics, its near relat ons. Most organ-builders, however, altogether exclude it. A serious difficulty is now met with, if a Tierce be introduced; it is this—modern organs are tuned to ' equal temperament,' whereas the Tierce (whether a separate stop or a rank) certainly ought to be tuned to its prime in ' just intonation,' in which case tempered and natural thirds would be heard simultaneously when the Tierce is used. (See TEMPERAMENT.)   J. S.

TIERCE DE PICARDIE. The practice of ending polyphonic compositions with a major third in the final chord, even though the third degree of the mode formed a minor interval with the final, came to be known by this name. The reason for the name is not known.   C.

The reason for the practice is the presence of the major 17th as the fourth harmonic of the bass-note (see TIERCE). This must jar, in sensitive ears, with the minor third (or 17th) if sounded at the same time.   L. M'C. L. D.

TIERSCH, OTTO (*b.* Kalberieth, Thuringia, Sept. 1, 1838 ; *d.* Berlin, Nov. 1, 1892), received instruction from Toepfer of Weimar, Bellermann, Marx and Erk ; was then teacher in Stern's Conservatorium, and subsequently teacher of singing to the city of Berlin. His writings are practical, and concern themselves much with an endeavour to make the modern discoveries of Helmholtz and others, in acoustics, available in teaching singing. The principal are as follows : *System und Methode der Harmonielehre* (1868) ; *Elementarbuch der musikalischen Harmonie und Modulationslehre* (1874) ; *Kurze praktische Generalbass - Harmonielehre* (1876) ; the same for counterpoint and imitation (1879) ; *Allgemeine Musiklehre*, with Erk (1885) ; *Die Unzulänglichkeit der heutigen Musikstudien an den Konservatorien* (1883) ; and *Rhythmik, Dynamik und Phrasierungslehre* (1886). The article on ' Harmonielehre ' in Mendel's *Lexikon* is by him.   G.

TIERSOT, JEAN BAPTISTE ELISÉE JULLIEN (*b.* Bourg-en-Bresse, July 5, 1857), studied at first under the direction of his father, an excellent amateur. From 1871 he lived in Paris, and, after studying medicine for a time, entered the Conservatoire in 1877, where he worked under Savard, Massenet and César Franck. In 1883 he was appointed sub-librarian of the institution, then librarian, a post which he filled with distinction until 1920. His writings on music are highly valued, and his researches into folk-lore of different countries have borne good fruit. His *Histoire de la chanson populaire en France*, which obtained the Prix Bordin in 1885, was published in 1889 ; another prize was won by his *Rouget de Lisle, son œuvre, sa vie*, which appeared in 1892. His 'Chansons populaires recueillies dans le Vivarais et le Vercors' were compiled with Vincent d'Indy, and appeared in 1892 ; 'Chants populaires pour les écoles' (1893–96) ; *Les types mélodiques dans la chanson populaire française*, 1894 ; other collections are 'Mélodies populaires des provinces de France' (8 series), 'Noëls français,' 'Chants de la vieille France' ; 'Chansons populaires recueillies dans les Alpes françaises' came out in 1903 ; his *Berlioz et la société de son temps* was awarded a prize by the Académie Française in 1905 ; *Notes d'ethnographie musicale* (1905, 1910, 2 series) ; *Étude sur les maîtres chanteurs* ; *Musiques pittoresques* (1889) ; *Les Années romantiques* ; the first volume of the *Correspondance générale d'Hector Berlioz ;* *Les Fêtes et les chants de la Révolution française* (1908) ; *Gluck* (1910), *J.-J. Rousseau* (1912), *Un Demi-siècle de musique française* (1870–1917), all three in the series *Maîtres de la musique* (Alcan) ; *Histoire de la Marseillaise* (1915). His most recent works are *La Musique dans la comédie de Molière* (1922), *Lettres de musiciens écrites en français du XVe au XXe siècle* (1924), and works on Couperin and Smetana. Numerous articles in *Le Ménestrel*, the *Revue des traditions populaires*, the *Revue Internationale de musique*, the *Sammelbände* of the Int. Mus. Ges., the *Temps*, the *Revue bleue*, the *Revue encyclopédique*, etc., testify to his industry and skill. He has edited a series of French folk-songs for America (Ditson, Schirmer), and he collaborated with Saint-Saëns in the preparation of the Pelletan edition of Gluck's works. His own compositions include a rhapsody on popular songs of La Bresse, for orchestra ; 'Hellas,' for chorus and orchestra, after Shelley ; incidental music to Corneille's *Andromeda*, performed 1897 ; 'Chansons populaires françaises,' for choir and orchestra ; 'Sire Halewyn,' a symphonic legend, performed at Nancy in 1897 ; and an orchestral suite of 'Danses populaires françaises' (1900). Tiersot was for a time professor at the École des Hautes Études Sociales de Paris. He has been president of the 'Société française de musicologie' and a contributor to its publications, and has given series of lectures on folk-lore in the United States of America, Canada, Belgium, Holland and Sweden. G. F. ; addns. M. L. P.

TIETJENS (Titiens), THERESE CATHLINE JOHANNA (*b.* Hamburg, July 17, 1831 ; *d.* Oct. 3, 1877), opera singer, came of Hungarian parentage.

Her voice, even in childhood, gave so much promise of future excellence that she was educated for the lyric stage. She appeared for the first time at the Hamburg Opera, in 1849, as Lucrezia Borgia, and achieved an immediate success. She proceeded to Frankfort, and thence, in 1856, to Vienna, where her performance of Valentine raised her at once to the highest rank.

Madame Jullien heard her at this time, and it was largely due to her glowing accounts that Mlle. Tietjens was quickly engaged by Lumley for his last season at Her Majesty's Theatre in London ; and when, on Apr. 13, 1858, she appeared in 'The Huguenots,' her impersonation of Valentine achieved a success which increased with every repetition of the opera. England from that time became her home, and with the exception of a visit to Paris in 1863 and to America in 1876, she never henceforth appeared elsewhere. She remained at Her Majesty's Theatre during the successive managements of E. T. Smith and Mapleson, and after the burning of the theatre in 1867 followed the fortunes of the company to Drury Lane. She sang at Covent Garden during the two years' coalition of the rival houses in 1869 and 1870, returning to Drury Lane in 1871, and finally, just before her death, to the new house in the Haymarket.

Her voice had none of a soprano's shrillness or of that peculiar clearness called 'silvery' ; when it declined, as it eventually did, in power, it never became wiry. It had a mezzo-soprano quality extending to the highest register, perfectly even throughout, and softer than velvet. Her acting in no way detracted from her singing ; she was earnest, animated, forcible, in all she did conscientious and hearty, but not electric. Her style of singing was noble and pure. When she first came to England her rapid execution left much to be desired ; it was heavy and imperfect. Fluency and flexibility were not hers by nature, but by dint of hard work she overcame all difficulties, so as to sing with success in the florid music of Rossini and Bellini. Indeed she attempted almost everything, and is perhaps the only singer, not even excepting Malibran, who has sung in such completely opposite rôles as those of Semiramide and Fidès. But her performance of light or comic parts was a mere *tour de force* ; her true field was grand opera. As Lucrezia, Semiramide, Countess Almaviva, she was great ; as Donna Anna and Valentine she was greater ; best of all as Fidelio, and as Medea in Cherubini's opera, revived for her and not likely to be forgotten by any who heard it.

In the 'Freischütz,' as in 'Fidelio,' her appearance was unsuited to her part, but she

sang the music as no one else could sing it.
In her later years she set a good example by
undertaking the rôle of Ortrud in ' Lohengrin.'
The music, however, did not show her voice to
advantage, and this was still more the case
with the music of Fidès, although her acting
in both parts was very fine.   Her repertory also
included Leonora (' Trovatore '), the Favorita,
Alice, Lucia, Amalia (' Un ballo in maschera '),
Norma, Pamina, Margherita, Marta, Elvira
(' Ernani '), Reiza (' Oberon ') and Iphigenia
(in Tauris).

Her voice was as well suited to sacred as to
dramatic music, and she applied herself assiduously to the study of oratorio, for which
her services were in perpetual request.

The first symptoms of the internal disorder
which proved fatal to her appeared in 1875,
but yielded to treatment. They recurred
during a visit to America in the next year, but
were again warded off for the time, and throughout a subsequent provincial tour in England she
sang ' as well as she had ever done in her life.'
In 1876 she had her last benefit concert at the
Albert Hall, but she sang at a benefit concert
in Dublin on Jan. 8, 1877. In Apr. 1877 her
illness increased to an alarming extent, and
her last stage appearance was on May 19, as
Lucrezia. She fainted twice during the performance, in her dressing-room ; but she would
appear, though she had to undergo a painful
operation on the following Tuesday. ' If I am
to die,' she said to a friend, ' I will play Lucrezia
once more.' Those who then heard her will
always recall her rendering of the despairing
cry after Gennaro's death. She died Oct. 3,
1877, and was buried in Kensal Green Cemetery.

F. A. M.

TIGRINI, ORAZIO (b. Arezzo), was canon at
Arezzo in 1588, and maestro di cappella of the
cathedral in 1591. He composed 1 book of
madrigals a 4 v. (1573), 2 books a 6 v. (1582,
1591), and wrote Il compendio della musica,
a work on counterpoint in 4 books (1588, 2nd
ed. 1602). (Q.-L.)

TILL EULENSPIEGEL. (1) Symphonic
poem, ' Till Eulenspiegels lustige Streiche,'
by Richard Strauss, op. 28 (1894).

(2) Opera, ' Thyl Uylenspiegel,' in 3 acts,
text by Henri Cain and Lucien Solvarg, music
by Jan Blockx. Produced Théâtre de la
Monnaie, Brussels, early in 1900.

TILMANT, (1) THÉOPHILE ALEXANDRE
(b. Valenciennes, July 9, 1799 ; d. Asnières,
May 8, 1878), French conductor, was educated at
the Paris Conservatoire, where he took the first
violin prize in R. Kreutzer's class in 1819. He
played with great fire and brilliance, and had a
wonderful instinct for harmony, though without
much scientific knowledge. On the formation
of the Société des Concerts in 1828 he was
appointed vice-conductor, and also played solo
in a concerto by Mayseder. In 1834 he

became vice- and in 1838 chief-conductor at
the Théâtre Italien, where he remained till
1849. In 1838, with his brother (2) ALEX-
ANDRE (b. Valenciennes, Oct. 2, 1808 ; d. Paris,
June 13, 1880), a distinguished violoncellist, he
founded a quartet-society, which maintained
its popularity for some ten years or so.

In 1849 Théophile succeeded Labarre as conductor of the Opéra-Comique, an enviable and
responsible post, which he held for nearly twenty
years (1849–68). The composers whose operas
he mounted found him earnest and conscientious, and he conducted with a fire and a dash
perfectly irresistible, both there and at the
Concerts du Conservatoire, which he directed
from 1860–63. In 1868 he left the Opéra-
Comique, and retired to Asnières, where he
died. He received the Legion of Honour in
1861.   G. C.

TIMBALES is the French word for Kettle-
drums. (See DRUM, 2.)

TIMBRE (Fr.) ; (Ger. Klangfarbe) has been
adopted in English with more recently ' tone
colour ' as equivalent to the German [1] as an
expression for quality. (See ACOUSTICS, subsection QUALITY.)

TIMBREL, see TAMBOURINE.

TIME. Under this general heading it will
be well to define the sense in which certain
technical terms which concern time rather than
tune are used in this book. Those in capitals
are the subjects of separate articles. [2]

ACCENT is an importance given to one note
over another. This may be done by deliberate
stress, i.e. greater volume of sound ; but there
are five other ways, which may, or may not, be
accompanied by stress. When accent recurs
regularly it becomes the strong BEAT or pulse,
a moment of action as against one of reaction,
which marks the beginning of a group, bar or
period. Music is written within bars as a
design may be drawn on squared paper ; the
squares are rubbed out and the bar-lines are
not heard. The BAR is an arbitrary division
providing orderly accents round which phrases
may cluster. This orderliness is called TIME.
There are many orders of time ; time-
signatures establish the rule, and various
corrective or contradictory time-signs the
exceptions which prove it. The PERIOD differs
from the bar in being larger (as the group is
smaller) and in not being marked off by bar-
lines ; whereas in poetry the (larger) verse is
marked off and the (smaller) foot is not.
Irrespective of its divisions large or small,
music goes at a certain pace (TEMPO) ; in a
sense, pace is absolute, capable of exact
definition, but in a truer sense it is relative, like
everything else in music.

Those are the formal elements of time ; they

---

[1] Tyndall adopted ' Clang-tint ' as a translation of the German term.
[2] They form a group, all by the same writer.   C.

stand over against the substance of music which is expressed in METRE. Metre is concerned with durations as such, their combinations and contrasts, and their suitable notation, and it thus builds the musical sentence.

Behind form and substance, and combining them, is RHYTHM. Rhythm, *lit.* 'flow,' is a reading of, a judgment as to the meaning of, music. Into this judgment accent, time, period, pace and metre all enter in their degree; but in any concrete instance rhythm is personal to the musician in a sense in which the others are not. If these others are the vital forces of music, rhythm is the life itself.

TIME PROPER.—We need not try, as the ancients did, to measure absolutely the time-unit (see BEAT). We may be content to notice that *tempo giusto*, the pace which is neither fast nor slow to us, corresponds to the healthy pulse of the blood, and when we think of that pulse as fast to contrast it with a slower, and conversely. So long as the words of poetry rule the melody, music has no need to establish a numerical relation between the short and the long; it merely arranges them in patterns like the feet of verse,[1] and the solution of the problems offered by the treatises of the 12th and 13th centuries is to be found in the verse structure of the period. (See RHYTHMIC MODES.) The precedence there given to triple time, *tempus perfectum* (normal), is probably to be explained, not by any fancied ascription to the Trinity but by the fact that the trochee (‒ ◡, ◯ ̄) and iamb (◡ ‒, ̄ ◯), both involving triple time, were the normal metrical feet of poetry, whereas the dactyl (‒ ◡ ◡, ̄ ◯ ◯) and anapæst (◡ ◡ ‒, ◯ ◯ ̄) involving duple time, were abnormal (*imperfectum*).

But with the concurrent growth of instrumental music and its emergence as an art independent of poetry, measurement of note-lengths became necessary.

Neither pitch nor duration can be accurately measured before instruments have made considerable progress, for though these are only what man chooses to make them, and he chooses only what his songs have taught him to want, yet arguments from what singers have said of scale and time are apt to lack the precision which an instrument with its ancillary notation supplies.

TIME-SIGNATURES.—(Cf. NOTATION.) About the time of a piece of music we want to know two things—where do the bar divisions and where do the group divisions come? The first is answered by the bar-lines, and the second is sometimes to be seen in the numerator of the time-signature and sometimes to be inferred from it. The information given by the denominator is otiose, because a glance at the music supplies it. As one of our questions is better answered elsewhere and the other only half answered, it is not surprising that musicians usually ignore the time-signature. The fact is that we have superinduced the bar-line upon the Elizabethan time-signatures and have not noticed that it renders them largely nugatory. Erik Satie, quite logically, writes time-signatures and omits the bar-lines. D'Indy, equally logically, has sometimes written bar-lines and omitted the denominator of the time-signature.

THE EXISTING SYSTEM.—The time is given in the signature, which is a fraction of the semibreve. Of this fraction the denominator is always a power of 2 (2, 4, 8, 16, etc.) and states the component time-units (minim down to semiquaver, etc.). The numerator tells us how many of these compose a bar, and though this may be any number whatever, it is usually one of the following:

2, 4, 8 ; 3, 6, 9 ; 12, 24 ; 5, 7.

Time is duple or triple, and simple or compound. Duple used to be called common, a name now usually restricted to $\frac{4}{4}$.

	Duple				Triple				Quintuple		Septuple	
Simple	2/2	2/4	2/8		3/2	3/4	3/8	3/16	5/4	5/8	7/4	7/8
Common	4/2	4/4	4/8	4/16					10/4	10/8	14/4	14/8
			8/8	8/16								
Compound	6/2	6/4	6/8	6/16	9/2	9/4	9/8	9/16	15/4	15/8		
	12/4	12/8	12/16	12/32			18/8	18/16		27/32		
			24/16					36/64				

SIMPLE TIME has a prime number for the numerator, viz. 2 (duple), 3 (triple), 5 (quintuple), 7 (septuple). The ear embraces immediately 2 and 3 as unities; it only gradually recognises 5 and perhaps 7 as a unity; a chorus in 'Sadko' (Rimsky-Korsakov) is written with 11 as a unity. Simple time has one strong beat in the bar, *e.g.* $\frac{2}{4}$ |♩ or $\frac{3}{4}$ |♩.|, which may break up into groups,

$\frac{2}{4}$ ♩ ♩ | ♫ ♫ | ♬ ♬ ♬ | , etc.,

each with a beat of its own, but *the signature is not changed* in consequence.

---

[1] See *Oxf. Hist. Mus.* i. 102-56 and Riemann's *Geschichte der Notenschrift*, pp. 189-224.

COMPOUND TIME.—In Germany simple times are divided into 'equal' (duple) and 'unequal' (triple), and all combinations of both of these are called compound. In England the practice has been to reserve the name 'compound' to those times whose numerator is a multiple of 3 (viz. 6, 9, 12, 15, etc.), and to call those which are multiples of 2, *but not of* 3, 'common' (viz. 4, 8, 10, 14, etc.). The above diagram will make this clear. Observe that there is no common triple time, because its signature would have been indistinguishable from that of the corresponding compound duple ; the simple triple is used subdivided.

GROUPS.—A bar is defined by the number of its groups, not of its time-units, as may be shown by taking 12 quavers and varying the groups. The following are from the ' Wohltemperirtes Clavier ' :

1.

$\frac{3}{8}$ Prel. II, 10, E mi.

$\frac{6}{8}$ Fug. II, 18, G♯ mi.

$\frac{12}{8}$ Prel. I, 11, F ma.

$\frac{6}{16}$ Fug. II, 11, F ma.

$\frac{12}{16}$ Prel. I, 13, F♯ ma.

$\frac{24}{16}$ Prel. I, 15, G ma.

$\frac{2}{4}$ Fug. II, 12, F mi.

$\frac{3}{2}$ Prel. II, 11, F ma.

$\frac{3}{4}$ Fug. I, 6, D mi.

$\frac{6}{4}$ Prel. I, 4, C♯ mi.

In no two of these ten ways is both bar and group exactly the same, and we see it to be likely that there is no distinction of any practical value which notation cannot express. If it is desired to alter the size of the time-unit (see under METRE, subsection CHOICE OF TIME-UNIT) the denominator is multiplied or divided by 2, and the beat remains the same. The larger the number of time-units within the bar, the smoother the flow of the time. Prelude and Fugue II. 11, for instance, make an effective contrast.

ADDED TIMES.—Until lately $\frac{5}{4}$ and $\frac{7}{4}$ have been taken as ' added ' times, and as such they are outside the European system, which multiplies. $\frac{5}{4}$ has been taken more commonly as $2+3$ than as $3+2$, and $\frac{7}{4}$ as $3+4$ rather than $4+3$. The same applies to five-bar periods ; seven-bar periods are too uncommon as yet to dogmatise about. We are beginning to reach the conception of $\frac{5}{4}$ and $\frac{7}{4}$ as simple times, *i.e.* as taken in one sweep : common times $\frac{10}{4}$ and $\frac{14}{4}$ are possible, but rare.

REMARKS.—It is worth while to examine closely the Arietta of Beethoven, op. 111. It begins by expressing $\frac{3}{8}$ as $\frac{9}{16}$, which obviates the necessity of writing the semiquavers as triplets. The first variation is marked *L' istesso tempo*, which must mean that the ♪. of $\frac{9}{16}$ now reverts to the ♪ of $\frac{3}{8}$ (♫). That is incorrectly described as $\frac{6}{16}$ (which would be ♫). In the second variation, with $\frac{12}{32}$, the ♬'s are tripleted ; but, thinking these triplets away, we get the motion , which again is $\frac{3}{8}$ (for $\frac{12}{32}$ would be). $\frac{3}{8}$ is the only possible signature ; for $\frac{36}{64}$, suggested in the *Ency. Brit.* (to avoid triplets), would be (four times over), which is $\frac{12}{32}$ again.

In Ravel's ' D'Anne qui me jecta ' $\frac{6}{4}$ (meaning $\frac{3}{2}$) occurs after $\frac{5}{4}$ to save trouble. In a similar interchange of $\frac{6}{4}$ (correctly used) and $\frac{5}{4}$ D'Indy in op. 45 draws a dotted line to make the division clear. Five-time being either $2+3$ (Tchaikovsky, 6th symphony, and many folksongs) or $3+2$ (Holst, ' Mars '), it is possible either to follow D'Indy or to place, with Brahms (C minor trio, andante), $\frac{3}{4}\frac{2}{4}$ and $\frac{9}{8}\frac{6}{8}$ for the signatures ; in this case Brahms obtains by his barring a mixture of $3+4$, $6+8$, and $3+2$ (see under BEAT, subsection NUMBER OF BEATS).

INTERNAL TIME-SIGNS.—Notation must always lag behind the swift grace of performance, and motions which are intended to be perfectly flexible to the ear must often be set down rigidly for the fingers. When duplets are set against six-eight or triplets against two-four, it is not intended that one note shall be two-thirds or three-halves of the other, but that each melody shall be felt as an independent whole. When duplets and triplets occur in the same melody, as in Schumann's ' Eusebius,' in much of Chopin, or at Brahms's climaxes, they are to be taken less at their face value than as written out rubatos. And the same when two different times are set against one another, as in Brahms's G major violin sonata.

Here the piano keeps on with its $\frac{6}{4}$ time but breaks a sextolet into two triplets, beginning this in the right hand a little before the left. The violin thinks in the larger sweep of $\frac{9}{4}$ tripleted. The piano also gives a hint of $\frac{9}{4}$ by the slight accents in the right hand, after slipping, by the figuration from $\frac{6}{4}$ into $\frac{3}{2}$. The general effect of this *ritardando*-without-retarding is greatly to broaden the passage.

ALTERNATIVE TIME-INDICATIONS.—Of alternations within the bar that of 3 and 2 is commonest. Either the group is equal to the group, as in $\frac{2}{4}$ | ♪♪ ♪♪♪ | and $\frac{6}{8}$ | ♪♪♪ ♪♪ |, or the bar to the bar, as when two dotted crotchets $\frac{6}{8}$ | ♪♪♪ ♪ | appear as three crotchets $\frac{3}{4}$ | ♪♪♪♪♪♪ | (the quaver being the common unit) but it is not worth while to alter the signature $\frac{6}{8}$, because such a simple equation is within every one's understanding. But the time-unit can be maintained only by changing the signature, as in $\frac{2}{4}$ | ♩ ♩ $\frac{6}{8}$ | ♪♪♪ ♪ |. There are also ways of temporarily contradicting the bar-accent which are exemplified under SYNCOPATION.

A. H. F. S.

TIMPAN (Lat. *tympanum*; Irish, *tiompan*; English, *timpe*). A form of psaltery with wire strings plucked by the fingers or a quill plectrum, and in later times struck with a rod or short stick. It was formerly in use in Ireland, Scotland and England. Dunstan, Archbishop of Canterbury, excelled not only on the harp but 'in timphano,' and Giraldus (12th cent.) records that amongst the Irish and the Scots the *Tympanum*, as well as the *Cithara*, was popular. It was sometimes called *Benn Crot* or the 'pointed' Cruit (see CRWTH), and in a 13th-century English version of the French *Romance de Brut* the word *Timpe* is given as a translation of ROTTE (*q.v.*), in the same way as in the 10th century the word *Rotte* is used as a translation of *Tympanum*. The French still call the dulcimer *Tympanon*. (See PSALTERY and DULCIMER.)

F. W. G.

TIMPANI is the Italian word for kettledrums. Printers and copyists often substitute *y* for *i* in this word, a mistake, since the letter *y* does not exist in the Italian language. (See DRUM, 2.)

V. de P.

TINCTORIS, JOANNES DE (*b.* Poperinghe, Belgium, *c.* 1446; *d.* Nivelles, Brabant, before Oct. 12, 1511),[1] known in Italy as Giovanni del Tintore, and in England as John Tinctor. The peculiar form of his name has led to the supposition that he was the son of a dyer; but the custom of using the genitive case, when translating proper names into Latin, was so common in Flanders during the middle ages, that it cannot, in this instance, be accepted as a proof of the fact. All we really know of his social status is, that his profound learning and varied attainments were rewarded with honourable appointments, both in his own country and in Italy. In early youth he studied the law; took the degree of Doctor, first in Jurisprudence, and afterwards in Theology; was admitted to the priesthood, and eventually obtained a Canonry in his native town. In 1476 he was in the service of Ferdinand of Aragon, King of Naples, who appointed him his chaplain and cantor, and treated him with marked consideration and respect. Between 1484 and 1500 he was a member of the Papal Chapel.[2] At Naples he founded a public music-school, composed much music, and wrote the greater number of his theoretical works. Franchinus Gafurius makes honourable mention of him in several places. Few of his compositions have been printed, but several exist in MS. among the Archives of the Pontifical Chapel, at Dijon, etc. Petrucci's 'Odhecaton' (1501) and his 'Lamentationes' (1506) contain examples of Tinctor's work. A Mass, 'Virgo Dei trono,' *a* 4, is in an incomplete copy at St. Gall. One of these, a 'Missa l'homme armé,' *a* 5, is remarkable for the number of extraneous sentences interpolated

[1] Q.-L.   [2] Haberl, *Vierteljahrsschrift*, iii. 254.

into the text. In the Sanctus the tenor is made to sing ' Cherubim ac Seraphim, caeterique spiritus angelici Deo in altissimis incessabili voce proclamant ' ; in the first Osanna, the altus sings ' Pueri Hebraeorum sternentes vestimenta ramos palmarum Iesu filio David, clamabant ' ; and in the Benedictus, the tenor interpolates ' Benedictus semper sit filius Altissimi, qui de coelis huc venit ' ; while, in each case, the other voices sing the usual words of the Mass.

The theoretical works of J. de Tinctoris are more numerous and important, by far, than his compositions. Their titles are *Expositio manus*; *Liber de natura et proprietate tonorum* (1476); *De notis ac pausis*; *De regulari valore notarum*; *Liber imperfectionum notarum*; *Tractatus alterationum*; *Super punctis musicalibus*; *Liber de arte contrapuncti*; *Proportionale musices*; *Complexus effectuum musices*; *Terminorum musicae diffinitorium* (undoubtedly the first musical dictionary that ever was printed); and *De inventione et usu musicae*, recently recovered and described by Weinmann (see Bibliography below). The *Terminorum musicae diffinitorium* is of such extreme rarity that, until Forkel discovered a copy in the library of the Duke of Gotha, in the latter half of the 18th century, it was altogether unknown. About the same time Dr. Burney discovered another copy in the library of King George III., now in the British Museum.[1] A third copy is in the Library of the Ges. der Musikfreunde at Vienna. The work is undated, and the place of publication is not mentioned ; but there is reason for believing that it was printed at Naples about the year 1474. It contains 291 definitions of musical terms, arranged in alphabetical order, exactly in the form of an ordinary dictionary. The language is terse and vigorous, and, in most cases, very much to the purpose. Indeed it would be difficult to overestimate the value of the light thrown, by some of the definitions, upon the musical terminology of the middle ages. Some of the explanations, however, involve rather curious anomalies, as for instance, ' MELODIA idem est quod armonia.'

Forkel reprinted the entire work in his *Literatur der Musik*, p. 204, etc. ; and his reprint was republished, in the original Latin, under the editorship of John Bishop, of Cheltenham, by Cocks & Co.[2] It appears with the other treatises in Coussemaker's *Scriptores* ; it was translated by H. Bellermann in Chrysander's *Jahrbuch*, i. 1863. MS. copies existing in various libraries are noted in *Q.-L.*

　　　　　　　　　　　　　　　w. s. r., with addns.

BIBL.—G. PANNAIN, *La teoria mus. di G. Tintoris* (Naples, 1913); KARL WEINMANN, *Johannes Tinctoris (1445-1511) und sein unbekannter Traktat ' De inventione et usu musicae '* (Regensburg, 1917). (See review in *Z.M.W.*, June 1919, p. 546.)

1 King's Lib. 66. e. 121.
2 At the end of Hamilton's *Dictionary of 2000 Musical Terms*.

TINEL, EDGAR (*b.* Sinay, Belgium, Mar. 27, 1854 ; *d.* Brussels, Oct. 28, 1912), composer and teacher, for four years director of the Brussels Conservatoire, was educated at the Brussels Conservatoire under Brassin, Gevaert and Kufferath, obtaining the Prix de Rome with a cantata, ' Klokke Roeland,' in 1877 ; the work afterwards appeared as op. 17.

In 1882 he was appointed to succeed Lemmens as director of the institute for church music at Malines ; in 1889 he became inspector of musical studies in the state schools, and in 1896 succeeded Kufferath as the professor of counterpoint in the Brussels Conservatoire. His op. 1 was a set of four ' nocturnes ' for voice and piano, and various works obtained success before the production of his oratorio, ' Franciscus,' op. 36, one of his most important choral works. The sound workmanship, and the contrapuntal and orchestral skill shown throughout, won it success in various countries ; its first important English performance was at the Cardiff Festival of 1895. Effective as it is, there are moments when reminiscences of other composers cannot be disguised, and a sense of incongruity, due perhaps to the libretto, is felt in the portions of the work which set the worldly and spiritual elements in contrast. A Te Deum, op. 26, and a later setting of the same hymn, op. 46 (1907), show the composer in a more serious light ; as do also his beautiful ' Geistliche Gesänge ' for mixed choir, op. 33, the ' Marienlieder,' an Alleluia for equal voices and organ, the Mass in honour of the Holy Virgin of Lourdes (op. 41), etc. For the stage he wrote music to Corneille's ' Polyeucte,' from which an orchestral suite was arranged and brought out in 1906 ; two religious music dramas, ' Godoleva ' (produced 1897) and ' Katharina ' (Brussels, 1909). Two works for tenor and baritone solo respectively, with chorus and orchestra, are ' Kollebloemen ' and ' De drie Ridders.' A valuable treatise on *Le Chant gregorien, théorie sommaire de son exécution*, appeared in 1895, and was translated into Italian in 1901.　　　　　M., with addns.

BIBL.—VAN DER ELST, *Edgar Tinel* (Ghent, 1901); PAUL TINEL, *Edgar Tinel: Le récit de sa vie et l'exégèse de ses œuvres de 1854 à 1886* (Bruxelles, 1923).

TIORBA (Ital.), see THEORBO.

TIRABOSCHI, GIROLAMO (*b.* Bergamo, Dec. 28, 1731 ; *d.* Modena, June 3, 1784), writer on Italian literature, was educated by the Jesuits, to which order he at one time belonged. He was librarian of the Brera in Milan for some years, and in 1770 removed to a similar post at Modena. His *Storia della letteratura italiana* (13 vols. quarto, 1772 to 1782) includes the history of Italian music. He published besides *Biblioteca modenese* (6 vols., 1781 to 1786), the last volume of which, ' Notizie de' pittori, scultori, incisori, ed architetti, nati degli Stati del Sig. Duca di Modena,' has an appendix of musicians.　　　　　　　　　F. G.

TIRANA, an Andalusian dance of a very graceful description, danced to an extremely rhythmical air in 6–8 time. The words which accompany the music are written in 'coplas' or stanzas of four lines, without any 'estrevillo.' (See SEGUIDILLA.) There are several of them in Preciso's 'Colleccion de Coplas,' etc. (Madrid, 1799), and in Paz's 'Collection d'airs espagnols,' c. 1816.

Tiranas are generally danced and sung to a guitar accompaniment. The music of one ('Si la mar fuera de tinta') will be found in 'Arias y Canciones Nacionales Españoles' (London, Lonsdale, 1871). See SONG, subsection SPAIN (4).

                            W. B. S.

TIRARSI, DA, see TROMBA DA TIRARSI.

TIRÉ, the French designation for a downstroke of the bow in violin, viola and violoncello music.

TITELOUZE, JEAN, canon and organist of Rouen Cathedral, 1563–1633, was often summoned to Paris as an expert at the time of the reception of the great organs (the Abbey of Saint Denis, 1604; Notre - Dame, 1610). In 1623 he published his 'Hymnes de l'Église pour toucher sur l'orgue, avec les fugues et recherches sur leur plain - chant.' He also published some verses of the Magnificat. This founder of French organ music wrote in a serious and lofty style, with very skilful counterpoint. His works have been republished by Guilmant and Pirro ('Archives des maîtres de l'orgue'), vol. 1.   F. R.

TITIENS, see TIETJENS.

TITOV, a family of amateurs of music who made important contribution to the early development of the national music of Russia.

(1) ALEXIS NICHOLAIVITCH (b. 1769; d. St. Petersburg, Nov. 2, 1827), an officer in the cavalry guards, was a well-known dilettante, and the composer of several operas on Russian subjects, the music being more or less imitated from Mozart.

(2) SERGIUS NICHOLAIVITCH (b. 1770), brother of Alexis (1), was also a composer of operas. He is supposed to have supplied music to 'The Forced Marriage' (text by Plestchiev). It is probable that he had a hand in the long list of works attributed to his brother.

(3) NICHOLAS ALEXEIVITCH (b. St. Petersburg, May 10, 1800; d. Dec. 22, 1875), the son of Alexis (1), followed his father's profession and rose to the rank of lieutenant-general. Although obviously gifted for music he declined to study seriously in his boyhood, and was content with such knowledge as he could pick up from his father. In spite of their technical weakness, Titov's songs soon began to be exceedingly popular in his own country, and, being the first in the field, he acquired the title of 'the father of Russian song.' Later in life he became acquainted with Glinka and Dargomijsky, and profited by their advice and more

thorough theoretical training. Titov wrote about sixty songs, besides a good deal of light pianoforte music and several popular marches. He had a command of fluent melody of an old-fashioned kind, and many of his songs are agreeably tinged with local colour. His warmth of feeling often degenerates into sentimentality, but a few examples of his ballads— or 'romances' as the Russians call them—have enjoyed a long popularity. Of these the best known are 'Prayer,' 'The Branch' and 'The Postillion's Song.'   R. N.

TO ANACREON IN HEAVEN, see STAR-SPANGLED BANNER.

TOCCATA (Ital.), from *toccare*, to touch, is the name of a kind of instrumental composition originating in the beginning of the 17th century. As the term sonata is derived from the verb *suonare*, to sound, and may thus be described as a sound-piece, or *Tonstück*, so the similarly-formed term toccata represents a touch-piece, or a composition intended to exhibit the touch and execution of the performer. In this respect it is almost synonymous with the prelude and fantasia; but it has its special characteristics, which are so varied as to make them difficult to define clearly. The most obvious are a very flowing movement in notes of equal length and of a homophonous character, there being often indeed in the earlier examples but one part throughout, though occasionally full chords were employed. There is no decided subject which is made such by repetition, and the whole has the air of a showy improvisation. Giovanni Gabrieli (1557–1613) and Claudio Merulo (1533–1604) were the first writers of any importance who wrote in this style, the toccatas of the latter being scarcely as brilliant as those of the former, though more elaborate. Frescobaldi, Luigi Rossi and Scherer developed the idea and sometimes altered the character of the movement, using chords freely and even contrapuntal passages. It was Bach, however, who raised the toccata far beyond all previous and later writers. His toccatas for harpsichord are in many cases a chain of short movements of markedly different tempi and styles. (See B.-G. vol. iii. pp. 311 and 322, vol. xxxvi. pp. 26, 36, 47, 54, 63.[1]) Bach's organ toccatas are very grand, one of the finest being that in F (B.-G. vol. xv. p. 154), the semiquaver figure of which is treated at great length alternately by the two hands in thirds and sixths over a pedal bass, and then by the pedals alone. Another in C (B.-G. vol. xv. p. 253) is equally brilliant. Bach sometimes begins and ends with rapid cadenza-like passages in very short notes divided between the two hands, as in the well-known toccata in D minor, with its fugue (B.-G. vol. xv. p. 276).

---

[1] The toccata in A, printed in the same edition, vol. xiii. p. 250, is now known to be by Purcell. It is contained in vol. vi. of the Purcell Society's edition, p. 42. See also *The Toccatas of Bach* by J. A. Fuller Maitland, *Mus. Ass. Proc.*, 1912–13.

Probably from the fact of its faint individuality the toccata has in later times had but a flickering vitality, though composers of organ music have made considerable use of the name and general style. A collection of six toccatas for piano published by E. Pauer has resuscitated as prominent specimens one by F. Pollini (not the famous one of his 32) in G, and others by Czerny, Onslow, Clementi, etc. That by Pollini is of the form and character of a bourrée, and the others would be better named études in double notes, having all definite subjects and construction. The same may be said of Schumann's toccata in C (op. 7), which is a capital study for practice, and is in sonata form. Contemporary musicians have given us two or three specimens of real toccatas worth mention, prominent among them being that in G minor by Rheinberger, which is a free fugue of great boldness and power. The same composer has used the diminutive term Toccatina for one of a set of short pieces ; and another instance of the use of this term is the toccatina in E♭ by Henselt, a short but very showy and difficult piece. Dupont has published a little PF. piece entitled Toccatella. Toccatas by Stanford and Walter Macfarren provide English examples. In these later examples the unchanging movement of rapid notes, in the manner of the *moto perpetuo*, has become almost an essential characteristic of the form. (See Touch ; Tucket.)

          F. C., with addns.

TODI, Luiza Rosa d' Aguiar (*b.* Setubal, Jan. 9, 1753 ; *d.* Lisbon, Oct. 1, 1833), known as Madame Todi (from her husband, Francesco Severio Todi), was a famous mezzo-soprano singer.

After appearing on the Lisbon stage in comedy in 1768, she received her musical education from David Perez, at Lisbon. She made her début in London in 1777, in Paisiello's ' Due contesse,' but was not successful.[1] At Madrid, in the same year, her performance of Paisiello's ' Olimpiade ' won warm admiration, but her European fame dates from 1778, when her singing at Paris and Versailles created a lasting sensation. She returned for one year to Lisbon, but in 1781 was at Paris again. In 1782 she engaged herself for several years to the Berlin Opera, at a yearly salary of 2000 thalers. But the Prussian public thought her affected and over-French in manner, and at the end of a year she gave up her engagement and returned to Paris, where she always found an enthusiastic welcome. Madame Mara was also in Paris, and the two queens of song appeared together at the Concert Spirituel. The public was divided into ' Maratistes ' and ' Todistes ' and party spirit

ran high. The contest was not conducted without wit : ' Laquelle étoit la meilleure ? C'est Mara. C'est bien Todi (bientôt dit).' [2]

Todi returned to Berlin in 1783, where she sang the part of Cleofide in ' Lucio Papirio.' The King wished her to remain, but she had already signed an engagement for St. Petersburg. There her performance of Sarti's ' Armida ' was an immense success. She was overwhelmed with presents and favours by the Empress Catherine, between whom and the *prima donna* there sprang up a strange intimacy. Todi acquired over Catherine an almost unbounded influence, which she abused by her injustice to Sarti, master of the Imperial Chapel, whom she disliked. Seeing that she was undermining his position at court, Sarti revenged himself by bringing Marchesi to St. Petersburg, whose wonderful vocal powers diverted some part of the public admiration from Todi. Todi retorted by procuring Sarti's dismissal.

Meanwhile the King of Prussia was tempting her back to Berlin, and she, in 1786, accepted his offers and was far more warmly received than upon her first visit. With the exception of six months in Russia, she remained at Berlin till 1789, achieving her greatest triumphs in Reichardt's ' Andromeda ' and Neumann's ' Medea.' In Mar. 1789 she reappeared in Paris, and among other things sang a scena composed for her by Cherubini, ' Sarete alfin contenti,' eliciting much enthusiasm. After a year's visit to Hanover she proceeded to Italy, and sang with great success. In 1793 she returned to Lisbon. Her farewell performance, however, took place at Naples in 1796.

At the time of the French occupation she was in Oporto, and was caught in the crowd which tried to escape across the river, losing the greater part of her possessions and being nearly drowned in her flight. The French general, however, knew her name and helped her. The rest of her life was spent at Lisbon.

There is a pretty and scarce portrait of her in character, singing, called ' L' Euterpe del secolo XVIII ' (1791). She was twice married, and left to her husband and her eight children, who survived her, a sum of 400,000 francs, besides jewels and trinkets worth a fortune. (See Vasconcellos, and a separate biography of Todi by him, published in 1873.)

     F. A. M., addns. J. B. T.

TOD JESU, DER, *i.e.* the Death of Jesus, a ' Passions-Cantate,' words by Ramler, music by K. H. Graun. It was first performed in the Cathedral of Berlin, on Wednesday before Easter, Mar. 26, 1755, and took such hold as to become an essential part of the Passion week

---

[1] Lord Mount-Edgcumbe speaks of her as having 'failed to please here,' and Burney, later in her career, writes of her, 'She must have improved very much since she was in England, or we treated her very unworthily, for; though her voice was thought to be feeble and seldom in tune while she was here, she has since been extremely admired in France, Spain, Russia and Germany as a most touching and exquisite performer' (*Hist.* iv. p. 509).

[2] Their rivalry gave rise to the following stanza :
' Todi, par sa voix touchante,
De doux pleurs mouille mes yeux ;
Mara, plus vive, plus brillante
M'étonne, me transporte aux cieux
L'une ravit et l'autre enchante,
Mais celle qui plaît le mieux
Est toujours celle qui chante.'

at Berlin. It was first given in England at St. Gabriel's, Pimlico, in Lent 1877, and at the R.A.M., Apr. 1 of the same year. There are three editions of the full score—1760, 1766, 1810 ; and PF. arrangements without number, beginning with one by J. Adam Hiller, 1783, and ending with one in Novello's 8vo series.   G.

TOEPFER, JOHANN GOTTLOB (b. Niederrossla, Thuringia, Dec. 4, 1791 ; d. Weimar, June 8, 1870), was at first taught by the cantor of the place, and afterwards sent to Weimar to study under Destouches, Riemann and A. E. Müller. In 1830 he was appointed town organist of Weimar, a post which he held until his death. He wrote many works on the organ : Die Orgelbaukunst (1833) ; Die Scheiblersche Stimmmethode (1842) ; Die Orgel, Zweck und Beschaffenheit ihrer Teile (1843) ; Organistensehule (1845) ; Lehrbuch der Orgelbaukunst (1856), with two appendices by Max Allihn (1888). Toepfer was also a composer of organ pieces, a cantata, 'Die Orgelweihe,' a sonata for flute and piano, a trio for piano and strings ; he edited an ' Allgemeines Choralbuch ' (Riemann).   M.

TOËSCHI (TOËSCA DELLA CASTELLA-MONTE), CARLO GIUSEPPE (b. Italy, 1722 or 1724 ; d. Munich, Apr. 12, 1788), became violinist in the Mannheim Orchestra, 1752, and Konzertmeister in 1759. He was a pupil of Joh. Stamitz, and a prolific composer in all branches of orchestral and chamber music (Q.-L. ; Riemann).

TOFTS, MRS. CATHERINE (d. Venice, 1756), ' little inferior, either for her voice or her manner, to the best Italian women,' [1] was the first of English birth who sang Italian Opera in England. A subscription concert was instituted in Nov. 1703 at the Theatre in Lincoln's Inn Fields, where Mrs. Tofts sang several songs, both Italian and English.[2] In the following year she continued to sing at the ' Subscription Music.' On Jan. 29, Margherita de l'Épine sang for the first time, at Drury Lane. On the second appearance of this, Tofts's future rival, a disturbance occurred at the theatre, while she was singing, which ' was suspected [3] to have been created by her emissaries,' a suggestion which she denied in the Daily Courant, Feb. 8, 1704. In the same year she sang and played the part of Pallas in Weldon's ' Judgment of Paris.'

In 1705 came the first attempt to plant Italian, or pseudo-Italian, Opera in England ; and to the success of this endeavour Mrs. Tofts and her rival were the chief contributors, the former playing successively the chief parts in ' Arsinoe,' ' Camilla,' ' Rosamond,' ' Thomyris,' and ' Love's Triumph.'

' Mrs. Tofts, who took her first grounds of musick here in her own country, before the Italian taste had so highly prevailed, was then not an adept in it ; yet

[1] Hawkins.   [2] Burney.   [3] Ibid.

whatever defect the fashionably skilful might find in her manner, she had, in the general sense of her spectators, charms that few of the most learned singers ever arrive at. The beauty of her fine proportioned figure, and the exquisitely sweet, silver tone of her voice, with that peculiar rapid swiftness of her throat, were perfections not to be imitated by art or labour.'[4]

At a very early stage of her short but brilliant career, she drew a salary of £500,[5] higher than that which was paid to any other member of the company—a sure test of the estimation in which she was held by the management and the public ; at the same time, Valentini and de l'Épine only drew £400 apiece, and the Baroness £200. At another time, this salary was commuted[6] into a share in the profits of the theatre. Again, we find her[7] offering to sing for 20 guineas a night, or ' in consideration the year is so far advanced ' for 400 guineas till the 1st of July, provided she was allowed to sing in another play, to be produced elsewhere, if not on an opera night. These were high terms in 1708. She sang also at the concerts at court. Meanwhile, she was no stranger to the quarrels and disputes which seem to have prevailed at the Opera then as in later times. There was a warm correspondence[8] about a bill of 80 guineas for Camilla's dress, which Rich declined to pay ; but Camilla refused to appear in ' Thomyris ' till it was paid ; and Rich then compromised the matter. She further demanded[9] an allowance for ' locks for hair, jewells, ribbons, muslin for vails, gloves, shoes, washing of vails, etc.,' for which she modestly affirmed that ' £100 was not sufficient for the season.'

Were it not that similar complaints and demands were common from other singers, there would seem to be here some foundation for the charge brought against Mrs. Tofts in the epigram, attributed to Pope :

' So bright is thy beauty, so charming thy song,
    As had drawn both the beasts and their Orpheus along;
But such is thy avarice, and such is thy pride,
    That the beasts must have starved, and the poet
        have died ! '

She must, however, have had a great passion for money, and a great disregard of the means of raising it, if Lady Wentworth's contemporary account may be trusted. ' Mrs. Taufs,' says that delightful writer and most eccentric speller,

' was on Sunday last at the Duke of Somerset's, where there were about thirty gentlemen, and every kiss was one guinea ; some took three, others four, others five at that rate, but none less than one.' [10]

This unfortunate singer lost her reason early in 1709. In a most ungenerous vein Steele alludes to her affliction,[11] and attributes it to the habit she had acquired of regarding herself as really a queen, as she appeared on the stage, a habit from which she could not free herself.

[4] Cibber's Apology.
[5] Coke Papers, formerly in the writer's possession.
[6] Ibid.   [7] Ibid.   [8] Ibid.   [9] Ibid.
[10] Letter, Mar. 17, 1709, in Wentworth Papers, p. 66.
[11] Tatler, No. 20, May 26, 1709.

Burney supposes that this was an exaggeration, by means of which the writer intended only to

'throw a ridicule on opera quarrels in general, and on her particular disputes at that time with the Margarita or other female singers.'

Hawkins says that she was cured, temporarily at least, and

'in the meridian of her beauty, and possessed of a large sum of money, which she had acquired by singing, quitted the stage (1709), and was married to Mr. Joseph Smith, afterwards English consul at Venice. Here she lived in great state and magnificence, with her husband, for a time ; but her disorder returning' [which, if true, upsets Burney's theory], 'she dwelt sequestered from the world in a remote part of the house, and had a large garden to range in, in which she would frequently walk, singing and galops way to that innocent frenzy which had seized her in the earlier part of her life.'

She died at Venice, and is buried in the old cemetery in the fort of San Nicolo, Lido.

Her voice did not exceed in compass [1] that of an ordinary soprano, and her execution, as shown by the *printed* airs which she sang, 'chiefly consisted in such passages as are comprised in the shake, as indeed did that of most other singers at this time.' It may be observed, however, that all singers ' at this time ' added a good deal to that which was ' set down for them ' to execute ; and probably she did so too.

It is somewhat strange that, of a singer so much admired as Mrs. Tofts undoubtedly was, no portrait should be known to exist, either painted or engraved.   J. M.

TOLBECQUE, a family of Belgian musicians, who settled in France after the Restoration. The original members were four brothers : (1) ISIDORE JOSEPH (b. Hanzinne, Apr. 17, 1794 ; d. Vichy, May 10, 1871), was a good conductor of dance music. (2) JEAN BAPTISTE JOSEPH (b. Hanzinne, 1797 ; d. Paris, Oct. 23, 1869), violinist, composer and excellent conductor, directed the music of the court balls during Louis Philippe's reign, and also those at Tivoli, when those public gardens were the height of the fashion. He composed a quantity of dance music—quadrilles, valses and galops —above the average in merit ; an opéra-comique in one act, ' Charles V et Duguesclin ' (Odéon, 1827), with Gilbert and Guiraud ; and with Deldevez, ' Vert-Vert ' (Opéra, 1851), a three-act ballet, his most important work. He was a member of the Société des Concerts du Conservatoire from its foundation in 1859. (3) AUGUSTE JOSEPH (b. Hanzinne, Feb. 28, 1801 ; d. Paris, May 27, 1869), was a pupil of Rudolph Kreutzer: he took the first violin prize at the Conservatoire in 1821, made some mark as a virtuoso, was an original member of the Société des Concerts, and one of the best violinists at the Opéra, and for several seasons was well known in London, where he played first violin at Her Majesty's Theatre. (4) CHARLES

JOSEPH (b. Paris, May 27, 1806 ; d. there, Dec. 29, 1835), was also a pupil of R. Kreutzer, and an original member of the Société des Concerts. He took a prize at the Conservatoire in 1824, and became conductor at the Variétés in 1830. In this capacity he composed songs and pieces for interpolation in the plays, several of which attained some amount of popularity.

Later members of the family were (5) AUGUSTE (b. Paris, Mar. 30, 1830; d. Niort, Mar. 8, 1919), son of Auguste Joseph (3), a distinguished violoncellist, took the first violoncello prize at the Conservatoire in 1849, and published some fifteen works of various kinds for his instrument, including ' La Gymnastique du violoncelle ' (op. 14), an excellent collection of exercises and mechanical studies. He was also a clever restorer of old instruments, and formed a collection, which he sold to the Brussels Conservatoire in 1879. He was professor of the violoncello at the Marseilles Conservatoire from 1865–79, after which he went to Paris, where he became a member of th Société de Concerts du Conservatoire. In 1890 his interesting contribution to the literature of the violin, entitled *Quelques considérations sur la lutherie*, was published by Gand and Bernadel in Paris, and on Dec. 22, 1894, his opéra-comique in one act, ' Après la valse,' was produced at Niort. His *Souvenirs d'un musicien en Provence* was published at Niort, in 1896.

                                   E. H.-A.

In 1903, at Niort, he published his great work, *L'Art du luthier*. He was decorated with the Légion d'Honneur in 1909. He had made a fresh collection of instruments, also of old instrumental music, which was dispersed in 1922. A catalogue, without the name of the publisher, was printed by F. Aubéry, Valréas.   M. P.

His son (6) JEAN (b. Niort, Oct. 7, 1857 ; d. 1890), took the first violoncello prize at the Paris Conservatoire in 1873, and studied the organ with César Franck.   G. C.

TOLLET, THOMAS, one of the Dublin city musicians in 1668–88. He went to London in 1689 and set a song in D'Urfey's *Marriage-Hater Matched* in 1692. In 1692, in conjunction with John Lenton, he published ' A Consort of Musick in three parts,' and was author of *Directions to play on the French Flageolet*. He was also a composer of act tunes for the theatre. ' Tollet's Ground,' printed in the Appendix to Hawkins's *History*, is by one George Tollet.

w. h. h. ; addns. w. h. g. f. and w. b. s.

TOLLING. Sounding a bell a number of times in slow succession, sometimes with an interval between every two or three blows of the clapper (' tellers ') to announce a death or a funeral.   w. w. s.

TOLLIUS, JAN (b. Amersfort, Holland, c. 1550 ; d. circa 1603), was maestro di cappella at Assisi in 1587, went to Rome in that year, and lived at Padua in 1591 under the patronage of the bishop. Thence he went to Denmark, where he was engaged as singer in the court chapel from Oct. 10, 1601, to Jan. 18, 1603, in which year he probably died. He composed several books of motets and madrigals (*Q.-L.*; *Riemann*).

TOMASCHEK, Václ. Jar. (Johann Wenzel), *b.* Skutsch, Bohemia, Apr. 17, 1774; *d.* Apr. 3, 1850), distinguished organist, composer and teacher, was the youngest of a large family.

His father, a well-to-do linen-weaver, having been suddenly reduced to poverty, two of his brothers, a priest and a public official, had him educated. He early showed talent for music, and was placed at Chrudim with Wolf, a well-known teacher, who taught him singing and the violin. He next wished to learn the piano and organ, and his brother the priest sent him a spinet, on which he practised day and night. The Minorite fathers of Iglau offered him a choristership, with instruction in theory. On the breaking of his voice in 1790 he went to Prague to study philosophy and law, supporting himself the while by giving lessons. All his spare time, even the hours of rest, was spent in studying the works of Marpurg, Kirnberger, Mattheson, Türk and Vogler, and he thus laid a solid foundation of scientific knowledge. Neither did he neglect practical music, but made himself familiar with the works of Mozart and Pleyel, and became acquainted with Winter, Kozeluh and, above all, Beethoven, who exercised a lifelong influence over him. In his autobiography, published in a periodical called *Libussa* (1845, etc.), Tomaschek writes:

'It was in 1798, when I was studying law, that Beethoven, that giant among players, came to Prague. At a crowded concert in the Convict-hall he played his concerto in C (op. 15), the Adagio and Rondo grazioso from the sonata in A (op. 2), and extemporised on a theme from Mozart's "Clemenza di Tito," "Ah tu fosti il primo oggetto." His grand style of playing, and especially his bold improvisation, had an extraordinary effect upon me. I felt so shaken that for several days I could not bring myself to touch the piano; indeed it was only my inextinguishable love for the art, that, after much reasoning with myself, drove me back to the instrument with even increased industry.'

Before long, however, the critical faculty returned. After hearing Beethoven twice more he says:

'This time I was able to listen with greater calmness of mind, and though I admired as much as ever the power and brilliancy of his playing, I could not help noticing the frequent jumps from subject to subject which destroyed the continuity and gradual development of his ideas. Defects of this kind often marred those most magnificent creations of his superabundant fancy.'

Three years later Tomaschek declared Beethoven to have still further perfected his playing. He himself about this time published some 'Ungarische Tänze' (without ever

having heard a Hungarian air) and Hölty's 'Elegie auf eine Rose,' an early specimen of programme music. Twelve waltzes had a great success at the Prague Carnival of 1797: but these he burnt. He was known as a pianist, and esteemed as a teacher by the principal nobility, but hesitated between the profession of music and an official career. Meantime Count Bucquoi von Longueval offered him the post of composer in his household, with such a salary as to place him at ease in money matters; and this he accepted. Prague continued to be his home, but he made occasional journeys, especially to Vienna. In Nov. 1814 he paid Beethoven a visit, of which he has left an account (*Libussa*, 1846) in the form of a conversation.

Tomaschek's house became the centre of musical life in Prague, and the list of his pupils includes Dreyschock, Kittl, Kuhe, Schull off, Bocklet, Dessauer, Worzischek and Würffel. In 1823 he married Wilhelmine Ebert, remaining in Count Bucquoi's service, though with a house of his own, where he was much visited by strangers, especially by English. He was hospitable and pleasant except on the subject of music, on which he was given to laying down the law. In person he was tall, and of a military carriage. The superficial was his abhorrence. Even in his smaller works there was a technical completeness, which procured him the title of the 'Schiller of music.' His church music includes three masses (two published) and two Requiems (still in MS.), but his predilection was for dramatic music, to which he was led by its connexion with the Ballad and the Lied. He set several of Goethe's and Schiller's poems, and also old Czech songs from the Königinhof MS.[1]

Tomaschek played his setting of Goethe's poems before the poet himself at Eger, and was very kindly received. His opera 'Seraphine' (1811) was well received at the National Theatre in Prague, in spite of a poor libretto; but notwithstanding this success he declined to permit the appearance of two other operas, 'Alvara' and 'Sakuntala.' He left *scenas* from Goethe's 'Faust,' and from 'Wallenstein,' 'Maria Stuart,' and the 'Braut von Messina,' as well as other vocal compositions, which were presented with his other remains to the Bohemian National Museum in Prague, by his nephew Freiherr von Tomaschek.

Besides a symphony, a piano concerto, string quartets, a trio, some piano sonatas, opp. 11, 14, 15, 21 and 48, and a quantity of smaller works, chiefly Lieder, Tomaschek published 110 with opus numbers, including the interesting 'Eklogues' (opp. 35, 39, 47, 51, 53, 66 and 83) and two sets of 'Ditirambi,' opp. 52 and 65, which would still repay the attention of pianists.

---

[1] The authenticity of which has been disproved by Sembora, the great authority on Czech literature.

His works exercised a material influence on such an artist as Robert Schumann.

Tomaschek was buried in the churchyard of Koschir, near Prague.   F. G.

TOMASI, BIASIO (b. Comachio, near Rome), was organist of Comachio in 1611 and 1615. In 1635 he calls himself arch-presbyter and vicar at Massa Fiscaglia (Ferrara). He composed 2 books of ' Sacri fiori,' 1-8 v., 1 book of motets and 2 books of madrigals (Q.-L.).

TOMASINI, (1) LUIGI (ALOYSIUS) (b. Pesaro, 1741 ; d. Apr. 25, 1808), eminent violinist and distinguished member of Prince Esterhazy's band under Haydn. In 1757 he became a member of Prince Paul Anton's household at his palace of Eisenstadt in Hungary, and on Haydn becoming second Kapellmeister in 1761 was at once promoted by him to be first violin. He was afterwards leader and director of the chamber music, with a largely increased salary. Prince Nicholas (successor to Paul Anton) left him a pension in 1790, but Tomasini remained in the service till his death. He was on the most intimate terms with Haydn, who wrote all his quartets with a view to Tomasini's playing, and remarked to him, ' Nobody plays my quartets so much to my satisfaction as you do.' He only once appeared in public in Vienna, at a concert of the Tonkünstler-Societät (1775), of which he had been a member from its foundation in 1771. In all probability Haydn gave him instruction in composition. He published violin-concertos, quartets, duos, concertants (dedicated to Haydn), etc. For the Prince he wrote ' 24 Divertimenti per il paridon (barytone), violino, e violoncello,' now in the archives of the Gesellschaft der Musikfreunde in Vienna. A few of Haydn's violin-concertos were written expressly for Tomasini (' fatto per il Luigi '). Besides two daughters, who sang in the church and opera at Eisenstadt, Tomasini had two talented sons.

(1) LUIGI (b. Esterház, 1779), an excellent violinist, was received into the chapel in 1796, dismissed several times for incorrigible levity, but as often readmitted at Haydn's request. The latter speaks of his ' rare genius,' and so did Hummel. He played in Vienna in 1796 and 1801 at the Tonkünstler-Societät, and in 1806 at the Augarten Concerts. In 1808 he had to fly, for having married, without the Prince's leave, Sophie Groll, a singer in the chapel, but he secured an appointment as Konzertmeister to the Duke of Mecklenburg-Strelitz. In 1812 he and his wife gave a concert in Berlin, when Luigi played Beethoven's concerto, and his wife, a pupil of Righini, was much applauded. In 1814 he gave a concert in the court theatre in Vienna, after which he wholly disappears.

(2) ANTON (b. Eisenstadt, 1775 ; d. there, June 12, 1824), played in the chapel as an amateur from 1791–96, when he became a regular member. His instrument was the viola. He married the daughter of a Polish General in 1803, in which year he also became a member of the Tonkünstler-Societät. He resembled his brother both in talent and disposition, and, like him, was several times dismissed, and taken on again with increased salary. In 1820 he became leader of the band.   C. F. P.

TOMKINS. The name of a family of musicians living in the 16th and 17th centuries.

(1) JOHN (fl. circa 1590), mentioned in Noake's Monastery, p. 476, as organist of Worcester Cathedral in 1590. Atkins (The Early Occupants of the office of Organist . . . of the Cathedral of . . . Worcester) failed to trace him. He does not seem to have been nearly related to the family discussed below.

(2) THOMAS (b. circa 1545 ; d. circa 1626–1627), organist and precentor. His chief claim to notice rests on the fact that he was the father of a notable family of musicians. As the pedigrees recorded at the College of Arms show, he was descended from a family seated for several generations at Lostwithiel, in Cornwall. He left Cornwall for St. David's, and became ' Master of the Choristers and Organ-player ' at the cathedral. He married twice. By his first wife, Margaret Poher or Pore, he had, besides one who died in infancy, two sons ; both of these, not an unusual circumstance at that period, received the name of Thomas (3) and (4) (see below). By his second wife, Ann Hargest, daughter or sister of Richard Hargest, of Penarthur Farm, near St. David's, he had five more sons : John (5), Nicholas (7), Giles (8), Robert (9), Peregrine (10). Later he took holy orders and became Minor Canon of Gloucester and vicar of St. Mary de Lode in the same town. In 1625 he succeeded Richard Marwood as precentor of the cathedral and died shortly after that date. There is no evidence that he had special musical gifts ; and there can be no doubt that the madrigal ' The Fauns and Satyrs,' contributed in 1601 to ' The Triumphes of Oriana,' was the work of his famous son (4), who for some years before that date had been organist of Worcester Cathedral.

(3) THOMAS (b. circa 1570 ; d. 1596), lay-clerk. Eldest son of Thomas (2). While still a boy he was appointed to ' enjoy all the profits and commodities of a Vicar's stall ' on the recommendation of the Archbishop's Commissioners ' to the end that his poor Father, at whose finding he is, may thereby the rather be relieved.' He was subsequently expelled for misbehaviour, went to sea, and lost his life in Grenville's famous action in the Revenge in 1596.

(4) THOMAS (b. St. David's, 1573 ; d. Martin Hussingtree, June 1656), composer and organist. The second son of Thomas Tomkins (2)

and Margaret, his first wife. He was born at St. David's, a fact that tallies with his statement in the dedication of his book of 'Songs' in 1622 to Lord Pembroke, that he was born in the 'country' from which his patron took the title of his earldom. He was a pupil of Byrd, as we learn from the dedication of No. 14 of his 'Songs.' He became organist of Worcester Cathedral about the year 1596. He married Alice, daughter of — Hassard and widow of Nathaniel PATTRICK (q.v.). In 1607 he took the B.Mus. degree at Oxford. In 1621 he was appointed one of the organists of the Chapel Royal, and he received 40s. for music composed for Charles I.'s coronation in 1625. In 1628 he was appointed to succeed Alphonso FERRABOSCO (q.v.) as composer in ordinary to Charles I., but the appointment was revoked by the King, it having been promised to Ferrabosco's son. Tomkins retained his position as organist of Worcester until 1646, when the services in the cathedral were suspended after the second siege of Worcester.

Tomkins's latter days were spent in all probability at the Manor House, Martin Hussingtree, owned by the wife of his son Nathaniel. He continued to compose to the end of his life, for one of his virginal pieces is dated 1654. He was buried at Martin Hussingtree ; the entry in the register reads :

'Mr. Thomas Tomkins, organist of yᵉ King's Chappell and of the Cathedrall church of Worcester, was buried yᵉ ixth day of June 1656.'

Although Tomkins lived till the middle of the 17th century, he adhered for the most part to the polyphonic style, and he must be regarded as belonging to the great group of English composers who flourished at the close of the 16th century ; and it is a fact that much of his work was written before the close of the first two decades of the 17th century. He was some ten years older than Orlando Gibbons, and much the same age as Weelkes and Wilbye. The greater part of his work was printed, his secular music in his 'Songs of 3. 4. 5. and 6. parts' (1622), and the sacred music in Musica Deo sacra (1668). The former of these publications has been reprinted together with a full account of the Tomkins family in Engl. Madr. Sch. vol. xviii. Musica Deo sacra has been completely scored by Rev. A. Ramsbotham ; for the services see Tudor Church Music, vol. vii.

Though he used the term 'Songs,' the compositions in the 1622 publication are mostly madrigals and ballets, and some are set to Scripture words. As a madrigal writer Tomkins ranks very high. He had a fine technique and showed remarkable power of expression. This is well exemplified in 'When David heard that Absalom was slain.' And he also rises to great heights in 'Weep no more, thou sorry

boy,' 'When I observe,' with its lovely ending, 'Oft did I marle,' and 'Music divine.' In this last are some splendid sequences of quavers, of rather unusual character, at the word 'harmony.' The ballets in the set are worthy to be classed with those of Morley and Weelkes, though they are of a somewhat different character; among the best are 'See the shepherds' queen' and 'Fusca, in thy starry eyes.' Musica Deo sacra was not published until several years after the composer's death. It contains five services. Tomkins, like Weelkes, did something to develop the form of the SERVICE (q.v.), and was not content with the conventional 'short' service, note against note. Besides a 'short' service and a 'great' service, he wrote 'verse' services, and used the organ independently of the voices. There are 95 anthems in Musica Deo sacra ; many of the later works among them are of the nature of verse anthems. A notable anthem is the twelve-part 'O praise the Lord, all ye heathen.'

Tomkins records two interesting details in some notes in the 'Pars organnica' of Musica Deo sacra. He states that the sound produced by a 36-inch pipe represents F to him. In modern days it is nearer to G sharp. He also states that the beat of a 24-inch pendulum, or the beat of the human heart, is the normal speed of a minim beat (4 minims in a bar). These two important notes have survived only in the Tenbury copy of Musica Deo sacra. Tomkins wrote a good deal of instrumental music both for the virginal and for viols. One virginal-book in the library of the Conservatoire de Musique in Paris is in Tomkins's hand ; besides a large number of his own works, it contains pieces by Byrd, Bull and Gibbons.

The following church music by Thomas Tomkins was not printed in Musica Deo sacra, but survives in MS.

SERVICES

(1) M., N.D. (verse) ; Tenb. 791 fo. 208v ; Durh. A2 fo. 214
   A5 fo. 171v ; Cl fo. 167 ; C13 fo. 73, 74vv ; C18 fo. 21.
(2) M., N.D. ; Tenb. 791 fo. 211.

ANTHEMS

Dear Lord of life. Ch. Ch. 61-66.
From deepest horror. B.M. Add. MSS. 29,372-7.
Jesus came when the doors were shut. Tenb. 791 fo. 203 ; B.M.
   Add. MSS. 30,478-9 ; Durh. A1, A3, C1, C2, C3, C11, C16 ;
   Pet. 35, 36, 39, 42, 44, 45, and org. book.
Know you not. Ch. Ch. 61.
Sweet Saviour. Tenb. 791 fo. 188.

(5) JOHN (b. circa 1586, d. London, Sept. 27, 1638), eldest son of Thomas Tomkins (2) by his second marriage. He was a scholar of King's College, Cambridge, and in 1606 was appointed organist of the College. He took the B.Mus. degree in 1608. In 1619 he left King's and became organist of St. Paul's Cathedral. In 1625 he was appointed a gentleman extraordinary of the Chapel Royal 'for the next place of an organist there.' He married Margaret, daughter of Dr. Sylvanus Griffiths, Dean of Hereford. Two of his three sons were choristers and king's scholars at Worcester Cathedral

The youngest, Thomas, became Fellow of All Souls', Chancellor and Prebendary of Exeter. He was buried in St. Paul's Cathedral, but his epitaph was destroyed in the fire of London. Some anthems by him are in the R.C.M. MSS. 1043–51 and Tenb. 791; and a set of variations on ' John come kiss me now ' is in B.M. Add. MSS. 29,996. He wrote a short dedicatory poem which is printed in his brother's ' Songs of 3. 4. 5. and 6. parts,' and No. 26 of these songs was inscribed to him. John had a son (6) ROBERT, who was one of the king's musicians in 1641 and in 1662.

(7) NICHOLAS, 5th son of Thomas (2), did not follow music as a profession, though he is said by Anthony Wood to have been musical. He was one of the gentlemen of the Privy Chamber to Charles I. in 1634. His brother Thomas (4) inscribed the 4th of his ' Songs ' to him.

(8) GILES (d. Salisbury 1668), 6th son of Thomas (2), like his brother John (5), became organist of King's College, Cambridge, where he succeeded Matthew Barton in 1624. On the death of John HOLMES (q.v.), organist of Salisbury Cathedral, in 1629, he was put forward in rivalry to Holmes's son as a claimant to a prebend in the cathedral and was supported by the King. After a long dispute the claim seems to have been settled in favour of Holmes; but Tomkins became master of the choristers and organist. In 1630 he received the additional appointment of ' Musician for the Virginalls ' to Charles I. in succession to Richard DERING (q.v.). He was buried at Salisbury on April 4, 1668. Little of his church music has survived. No. 12 of his brother's ' Songs ' was inscribed to him.

(9) ROBERT, 7th son of Thomas (2), was one of the musicians in the household of Charles I. in 1633 and held office till 1641 or later. Anthems by him are in Tenb. MS. 791 and in the B.M. His brother inscribed No. 11 of his ' Songs ' to him.

(10) PEREGRINE, 8th and youngest son of Thomas (2), was described as ' of London and Dronfield, co. Derby.' He married Jane, daughter of Sir Henry Hastings, and had three sons. He took up arms for the King against Parliament. He was mentioned in his mother's will in 1627; and in 1623 he was a witness to the will of John Patten, father-in-law of Orlando Gibbons. No. 10 of his brother's ' Songs ' was inscribed to him.

(11) NATHANIEL (b. Worcester 1599, d. Martin Hussingtree, Oct. 20, 1681), only son of Thomas (4), organist of Worcester Cathedral. He took the degree of B.D. at Balliol in 1629, and in the same year became a Canon of Worcester. His wife inherited the Manor of Martin Hussingtree, and the latter part of his life was spent there.

(12) GILES (b. Salisbury 1633, d. Martin Hussingtree, July 24, 1725), son of Giles Tom-

kins, organist of Salisbury Cathedral. He was appointed organist of Worcester Cathedral in 1661, when the services were resumed after the Restoration. Very shortly afterwards he was dismissed by the Dean for contumaciously absenting himself. He subsequently took holy orders and was rector of Martin Hussingtree for over 50 years. He had six children.

BIBL.—SIR IVOR ATKINS, *The Early Occupants of the Office of Organist and Master of the Choristers of the Cathedral Church of Christ and the Blessed Virgin Mary, Worcester.* Printed for the Worcester Historical Society, 1918. E. H. FELLOWES. Preface of vol. xviii. of *Engl. Mad. Sch.* Both these books contain many further details concerning the Tomkins family.   E. H. F.

TOMMASINI, VINCENZO (b. Rome, Sept. 17, 1880), composer, studied the violin under Ettore Pinelli and composition under Stanislao Falchi at the Liceo di Santa Cecilia, the Accademia di Santa Cecilia admitting him as an associate later on. His early works, which are conventional and no longer representative, include an overture to Calderon's ' Life is a Dream,' dating from 1904, and the opera, ' Medea,' produced at Trieste in 1906.

Several years' travel made Tommasini conversant with modern methods which his early academic training had withheld from him, and he altered his style radically. The first work to reveal his new outlook was a string quartet in F (1910). This was succeeded by the ' Erotic Poem ' for orchestra, and by the comic opera in one act, ' Uguale Fortuna,' both composed in 1911. The new opera was awarded the first prize at a national competition instituted by the city of Rome, and it was staged for the first time in 1913 at the Teatro Costanzi.

In 1912 took place the first performance of an orchestral prelude to Baudelaire's ' Hymne à la beauté,' and in 1914 that of a suite for orchestra in four movements; but Tommasini's most successful orchestral work so far is the ' Chiari di Luna,' consisting of two movements entitled ' Chiese e rovine ' and ' Serenate.' It was presented for the first time by Toscanini in 1916. The same year saw the composition of a sonata for violin and piano.

It was in 1917 that Vincenzo Tommasini finished the work which has made his name known all over the world. This was the ballet, ' The Good - humoured Ladies,' based on a comedy of Goldoni, and accompanied by a series of sonatas by Domenico Scarlatti, orchestrated with impeccable taste by Tommasini, if somewhat grievously cut and unsatisfactorily strung together. The ballet was produced in Rome in Apr. 1917, and it remains one of the most delightful entertainments in the repertory of Serge Diaghilev's Russian Ballet Company.

In 1918 Tommasini issued four choral settings of poems by Dante, Petrarch and Matteo Frescobaldi, in which he attempted, with no very happy result, an imitation of the Italian madrigal of the 16th century. The next two works of large dimensions are both orchestral, ' Il Beato Regno ' (1921) draws its material from liturgical music, while the other, 'Paesaggi toscani' (1923), is based on Tuscan folksongs.   E. B.

TONADA, see SONG, subsection SPAIN (3).

TONADILLA, see MISSON, Luis.

TONAL FUGUE, see FUGUE.

TONALITY is that element of key-feeling which was gradually evolved out of the increasingly harmonic organisation of modal polyphony. In the end it completely supplanted the less universal values which had depended on the particular character of a particular mode. Throughout the whole development of classical forms key-definition has occupied a paramount place, and without it neither the harmonies nor the architecture of the music of the last three centuries can be made intelligible. Tonality in general rests mainly on a balance of tonic harmonies rendered stable and convincing by the use of a context of such related or leading chords as appear to find their ultimate solution in the desired key. Of these leading chords those of the dominant of the key in question are the most important, and a satisfying definition is almost impossible without harmonic inferences which are ultimately derived from the relation between the chosen key and its dominant. Subdominant harmonies also have harmonic inferences which can be used to consolidate a tonality, though these are not so powerful as those of the dominant. The simplest definitions of a tonality are to be found in the various cadences which were organised to this end. Examples will be found in the articles on CADENCE and HARMONY.

Those extended forms of the sonata order on which classical instrumental music has been mainly built, have acknowledged an unqualified allegiance to rigid tonalities. And this is almost equally true of every musical form which has an intrinsic architectural coherence. Keys and their relations are in this sense the postulates on which melodic, harmonic and formal arguments were alike founded, and it was by an unfailing sensitiveness to these values that composers were able to display a wealth of imaginative fancy and yet preserve a formal balance and coherence that made an extended movement an artistically proportioned whole (see FORM; SONATA).

It must be admitted, however, that three centuries of development have not left these fundamental conceptions of tonality altogether unqualified. Dramatic music in particular has always claimed a certain freedom to obey ideas external to music proper, and has therefore subjected many formal considerations to demands of an alien kind. Moreover, increasing familiarity with idioms thus externally suggested has made it possible to transfer even to the most absolute music a noticeable licence in the treatment of keys and their definitions.

Opera and programme music alike have shown this power of indirect infection. It must further be remembered that the more sensitive the mind of the composer may be to the inferences of tonality, the more novel and subtle are likely to be the relations which he will comprehend within it. There can be no doubt that many of the idioms which the 19th century has accepted as having a clear basis in tonality would have appeared to the musicians of an earlier day too vague and fantastic to be intelligible on any traditional principles. And to this must be added the fact that the very strength of the tonal organisation which three centuries of masterpieces has inculcated, has served to give a certain attraction to devices of expression not so rigidly proportioned.

There has recently been a decided renaissance of such values as belonged to more modal systems, and whether these are practised as a form of conscious archaism, or are less directly culled from the half-forgotten idioms of folk-music, they are equally subversive of key-definition in the stricter classical sense. Nor have contemporary composers scrupled to derive novel idioms from various arbitrarily chosen formulæ, many of which are deliberate negations of the traditional associations of tonality. Some of the consequences of these phenomena have been outlined in the article on HARMONY.

The word *atonality* has recently been coined to describe these non-tonal idioms. It is not of much use for purposes of exact description, because it logically includes modal, neo-modal, and all kinds of arbitrary melodic or harmonic dialects, even to the degree of complete chromaticism. These various features have been dealt with under their respective headings, and in the article on HARMONY.

Polytonality is a synonym for *Multiple Tonality*, and refers to certain features of contemporary experiment in which more than one tonality is involved in a single harmonic structure. This also is discussed in the article on HARMONY.   G. D.

TONE. In scientific treatises this term is used to denote a musical note which is free from harmonics. A musical note in general consists of a fundamental and a series of harmonic overtones. Each of these constituents is a Tone.

The word tone is also commonly used with the same meaning as quality. (See ACOUSTICS, subsection QUALITY.)   J. W. C.

TONELLI, ANTONIO (b. Carpi, Italy, Aug. 19, 1686; d. there, Dec. 25, 1765), one of the most active pioneers of the violoncello as a solo instrument. His father, Giuseppe Michele Santo de Pietri, called (*detto*) Tonelli, was a lieutenant in the Carpigenian cavalry, and an amateur musician of repute. Tonelli's mother, *née* Caterina Pisa, or Pisi, excelled in music, and was his first instructor. She was succeeded by D. Nicolo Pace, choirmaster of the cathedral of Carpi. In due course Tonelli proceeded to Bologna, where he learnt to play the organ, the viola d' amore, the violoncello, and, as a recreation, devoted himself to the art of fencing. Later Tonelli went to the Collegio de' Nobili in Parma, where his musical attainments gained him much honour, and attracted the attention of Antonio Francesco, Duke of Parma, who became his patron. Tonelli's biographers differ widely in their accounts of the length of his stay in Parma, and his supposed three years' sojourn in Denmark. One authority denies that Tonelli ever visited the latter country at all, while another declares that he made a resolve to roam the world without money or provisions. ' Money,' he told his friends, ' is the greatest enemy of man, and in a city where there is an organ Tonelli will not want bread.' Dressed entirely in black—as was ever his wont—and carrying a small cane in his hand, Cabassi tells us that Tonelli left Parma suddenly, and started on his pilgrimage to Denmark, where he received an appointment at the royal court. He remained there exactly three years, after which he returned in precisely the same condition as he left. On one occasion he appeared in Genoa without any means of subsistence, whereupon he sat down in a corner of the *piazza grande*, and began to play on his violoncello so divinely that he soon attracted a crowd around him, who supplied him with more than a sufficiency for his return journey to Carpi. The year 1724 saw him in Carpi busily engaged in composition, and in that year he wrote an oratorio in honour of the birth of a son and heir to the house of Este. In 1726 Benedict XII. canonised Louis Gonzago at Guitalla, and Tonelli was invited to play the violoncello at the solemn after-festival ordered by the ducal court to celebrate the occasion. Tonelli willingly assented to the request, and during a performance in the principal church is said to have distinguished himself in an artistic rivalry with the eminent violinist d'Ambreville. The latter tried to excel Tonelli in a difficult passage, whereat Tonelli repeated the phrase in a more elaborate and beautiful form, after which the contest for supremacy between violin and violoncello grew in ardour until the whole assemblage burst into involuntary applause. On Mar. 27, 1730, Tonelli was appointed maestro di cappella to the cathedral of Carpi on the resignation of D. Gio. Batt. Zarani. Here he composed some of the interludes of his musical drama, ' Lucio Vero,' which was produced at Alassio during the Carnival of 1741. But the ties of a settled occupation were repellent to the dictates of Tonelli's restless spirit, and he soon ceded his post to his stepbrother Giuseppe, of whom he

was very fond, and disappeared, no one knew where, with his violoncello under his arm. He wandered about Italy for some time, and at length accepted a post in the Cappella di Alassio, near Albenga. There he remained until 1745, when he again returned to Carpi and opened a free school of singing for poor children, on a special method of teaching, entirely his own. One of his pupils, Rosa Parteggotti, a child barely 6 years of age, created a great sensation, by appearing in public in 1753, singing and accompanying herself on the spinet with extraordinary dexterity. In the same year that she appeared Tonelli closed his academy, left Carpi, and returned to Alassio, where he remained for three years. It is possible that his gifted little pupil may have accompanied him, as he seems to have conceived a great affection for her. When she reached the age of 15, Rosa accepted the direction of the choir of the nuns of the Convent of St. Clare at Carpi, and at the same time resolved to join the sisterhood. Tonelli grew distracted with grief. He was then 76, but entreated Rosa to marry him, and when he found it impossible to shake her resolution he threatened to commit suicide. He lived long enough, however, to write a clever *canzoniere* against nuns, and died from the effects of a chill at the age of 78.

As a composer Tonelli was thorough; he shone on the concert platform as a violoncellist and in church as an organist, besides which he was a gifted poet. Published compositions : ' Il trionfo dell' umiltà di S. Filippo Neri,' ' Oratorio a tre voci ' (Paolo Ferrari, Carpi, 1724 ?); ' Cantate per musica ' (Paolo Ferrari, Carpi, 1724) ; ' Intermezzi musicali di Canoppo e Lisetta ' (Paolo Ferrari), ' Lucio Vero ' ; on the fourth page there is the following : *La Musica è del Sig: Antonio Tonelli, virtuoso delle altezze serenissime Duca e Duchessa di Modena. Vari sonetti stampati ed intermezzi tra quali le Quattro Stagioni, ed un sonetto in fine dell' oratorio intitolato : Il Trionfo dell' Umiltà* (Paolo Ferrari). A number of his MSS. are preserved in the cathedral at Carpi, and his *Tratto di musica* with some other MS. belonged (according to Count Valdrighi) to Tonelli's biographer Cabassi in 1880.

Bibl.—Valdrighi, *Il violoncellista Tonelli (Musurgiana,* No. 4), reprinted from the *Atti e memorie delle R. R. Deputazione di Storia Patria per la Provincia dell' Emilia.* Nuova Seria, vol. 5, part 11, Modena.

E. H.-A.

TONES, THE GREGORIAN. See Gregorian Tones and Psalmody. Under the latter heading the tones with their several endings are given in full.

TONIC, the name given in harmonic music to the Keynote, *i.e.* the note from which the key is named. The functions of the tonic are in all respects identical with those of the final of the ancient modes. The tonic harmony is the common chord or triad, major or minor as the case may be, which is built upon the keynote as its bass. (See TONALITY.)

TONIC SOL-FA is the name of a method of teaching sight singing from a special form of notation which has had the most far-reaching effect in promoting popular choral singing throughout the British Isles. (See CURWEN, John; COMPETITION FESTIVALS; TONIC SOL-FA COLLEGE.)

Its leading principle is that of 'key relationship' (expressed in the word 'Tonic'), and it enforces this by the use of the ancient soundnames *do, re, mi,* etc., as visible, as well as oral, symbols. These names are first put before a class of beginners in the form of a printed picture of the scale, called a 'Modulator.' For simplicity's sake they are spelt English-wise, and *si* is called *te* to avoid having two names with the same initial letter. In the first lessons the teacher practises the class in the singing of the sounds as he points to the name of each, first taking the *do, me, soh,* of the common chord, making his pupils feel the special character of each sound, its distinguishing melodic effect, and afterwards training them to recognise the intermediate sounds in the same way. It is on this 'feeling' of the different character of each sound, the difference due to its place in the scale, that the greatest stress is laid. When the pupil has caught the perception of these differences, and has learnt to associate the difference of the feeling with the difference of the name, he has grasped, in its essential principle, the secret of singing at sight.—The central column only of the modulator is used at first. The lateral columns are for teaching and explaining change of key. The *fe, se,* etc., represent the occasionally used 'chromatic' sounds, *i.e.* 'flats' and 'sharps' not involving modulation into a new key. The names of the sounds are so placed on the modulator as to show, accurately, the true positions of the sounds in the natural (untempered) scale. When the class can, with some readiness, sing the sounds as the teacher points to them on the modulator, they are introduced to exercises printed in a notation formed out of the initials of the scalenames; **d** standing for *doh,* **r** for *ray,* etc. The duration of each sound is indicated by the linear space it occupies, each line of print being spaced out into divisions by bars and dots. A 'rest' is shown by a blank space, the prolongation of a sound by a line (—) occupying the space. Sounds in upper and lower octaves are distinguished by small figures; thus, d^1, r^1, etc. signify an upper octave; d_1, r_1, etc., a lower. An example of a vocal score is given on the following page.

The method is, it will be seen, identical in principle with the old system known by the name of the 'Movable Do,' and the notation is only so far new in that symbols are written down which have been used, orally, for some eight centuries. The syllables attributed to Guido (see HEXACHORD; SOLMISATION), were a notation, not of absolute pitch, but of tonic relation; his *ut, re, mi,* etc., meaning sometimes

, and so on, according as the tonic changed its pitch; and this ancient use of the syllables to represent, not fixed sounds, but the sounds of the scale, has been always of the greatest service in helping the singer, by association of name with melodic effect, to imagine the sound. The modern innovation of a 'fixed Do' is one of the many symptoms (and effects) of the domination of instruments over voices in the world of modern music.[1]

The Tonic Sol-fa method is really a reversion to a principle many centuries old. Its novelty of aspect, when Curwen[2] first promulgated it, resulted from its making this principle more prominent, by giving it visual, as well as oral, expression; that is, by using the old soundnames as written symbols. Those who follow the old Italian and old English practice of the 'Movable Do' are, in effect, Tonic Sol-fa-ists. The question of notation is a distinct one, and turns on considerations of practical convenience. The argument for adhering to the old tonic use of the syllables rests broadly on the ground that the same thing should be called by the same name; that, for example, if

is to be called *do, do, re | si, do, re,* it is not reasonable that

the essential effect of which on the ear is the

---

[1] Sir John Herschel said in 1868 (*Quarterly Journal of Science,* art. 'Musical Scales'): 'I adhere throughout to the good old system of representing by Do, Re, Mi, Fa, etc., the scale of natural notes *in any key whatever,* taking *Do* for the keynote, whatever that may be, in opposition to the practice lately introduced (and soon, I hope, to be exploded), of taking *Do* to represent one fixed tone C,—the greatest retrograde step, in my opinion, ever taken in teaching music, or any other branch of knowledge.' The 'fixed Do' is the system preferred in France and Belgium, but has been definitely rejected in England.

[2] Curwen's system grew out of his adoption of a plan of Sol-fa-ing from a modulator with a letter notation, which was being used with success for teaching children some years before by a benevolent lady living at Norwich. He always spoke of this lady, Miss Elizabeth Glover (d. 1867), as the originator of the method.

Key D. M. 60.   THOMAS FORD.

same—for the tune is the same, and the tune is all that the ear feels and remembers—should be called by another set of names, *si, si, do | la, si, do.* And, conversely, it is not reasonable that if, for example, in the passage

the last two sounds are called *do, la,*—the same sounds should be also called *do, la,* in the passage

where they sound wholly different; the identity of pitch being as nothing compared with the change of melodic effect—a change, in this case, from the plaintive to the joyous. It is on this perception of the ' mental effect ' of the sounds of the scale that the Tonic Sol-fa teacher relies as the means of making the learner remember and reproduce the sounds. And it is this that constituted the novelty of the system as an instrument of teaching. To make the beginner feel these effects for himself is the teacher's first object. As a help to such perception a set of descriptive names is used in the earliest lessons. The pupil is told he may think of the *do* as the 'strong' tone, of the *me* as the 'steady' or ' calm ' tone, of the *lah* as the ' sad ' tone, and so on; these epithets giving, in a rough way of course, some indication of the ' mental effect.' When in this way the pupil has learnt to associate the names with the several sounds, he refers the letters on the printed page to a mental picture of the modulator, and though the music does not ' move up and down,' as in the Staff notation, the syllable-initials suggest to him the names; he sees these names, mentally, in their places on the scale, and with the remembrance of the name comes the remembrance of the sound.

This constant insistence on the scale and nothing but the scale carries the singer with ease over the critical difficulties of modulation. He has been taught to follow with his voice the teacher's pointer as it moves up and down the modulator. When it touches *soh* he sings *soh.* It moves to the *doh* on the same level to the right, and he sings the same sound to this new name. As he follows the pointer up and down the new scale he is soon taught to understand that a new sound is wanted to be the *te* of the new *doh*, and thus learns, by the ' feeling ' of the sounds, not by any mere machinery of symbols, what modulation is. When he has been made familiar with the change from scale to scale on the modulator, he finds in the printed music a sign to indicate every change of key. Thus the changes between tonic and dominant in the following chant are shown as follows (taking the soprano part only) :

ROBINSON

the ᵐl meaning that the singer is to sing the sound which is the *me* of the scale in which he began, but to call it *lah* while singing it, and sing onwards accordingly. When the key changes again to the original tonic he is informed of it by the ᵈs, which means that he is to sing again the sound he has just sung as *doh*, but to think of it and sing it as *soh*. These indications of change of key give the singer direct notice of what, in the Staff notation, he is left to find out inferentially from the occurrence of a sharp or flat in one of the parts, or by comparing his own part with the others. To make these inferences with any certainty requires a considerable knowledge of music, and if they are not made with certainty the ' reading ' must be mere guess-work. Remembering that in music of ordinary difficulty—say in Handel's choruses—the key changes on an average every eight or ten bars, one can easily see what an advantage the Tonic Sol-fa-ist has in thus being at every moment sure of the key he is singing in. The method thus sweeps out of the beginner's way various complications which puzzle him in the Staff notation—'signatures,' ' sharps and flats,' varieties of clef. To transpose, for instance, the above chant into the key of F, all that is needed is to write ' Key F ' in place of ' Key E♭.' Thus the singer finds all keys equally easy. 'Accidentals' are wholly unknown to him, except in the comparatively rare case of the accidental properly so called, that is a ' chromatic ' sound, one not signifying change of key.[1]

These advantages can, it is true, be in part secured by a discreet use of the ' tonic ' principle—a ' movable *do* '—with the Staff notation. But the advocates of the letter notation urge that the old notation hampers both teacher and learner with difficulties which keep the

principle out of view : that the notes of the staff give only a fictitious view of interval. To the eye, for instance, a major third (*a*) looks the same as a minor third (*b*) ; which of the two is

meant can only be determined by a process of reasoning on the ' signature.' A like process is needed before the reader can settle which sound *of the scale* any note represents. In the above

Key E♭.   Key B♭.

| s͡ | d' : l | s :— ‖ ᵐl͡ | t : d' | d' : t | d' :— ‖

f. Key E♭.

ᵈs͡ | f : m | l :— ‖ s͡ | r : m | r : r | d :— ‖

chant, for example, before the singer can sing the opening phrase he must know that the first sound is the *soh* of the key. The staff notation shows him a mark on a particular line, but it is only after he has made certain inferences from the three ' flats ' on the left that he can tell where the sound is in the scale. How much better, the Sol-fa-ists say, to let him know this at once, by simply printing the sound as *soh*. Why impede the singer by troubling him with a set of signs which add nothing to his knowledge of the facts of music, and which are only wanted when it is desired to indicate absolute pitch, a thing which the sight-reader is not directly concerned with ?

An exposition of the details of the method would be here out of place, but one or two points of special interest may be noticed.[2] One is the treatment of the minor scale—a crux of all Sol-fa systems, if not of musical theory generally. Tonic Sol-fa-ists are taught to regard a minor scale as a variant of the *relative* major, not of the tonic major, and to sol-fa the sounds accordingly. The learner is made to feel that the special ' minor ' character results from the dominance of the *lah*, which he already knows as the plaintive sound of the scale. The 'sharpened sixth ' (reckoning from the *lah*), when it occurs is called *ba* (the only wholly new soundname used (see the modulator, above), and the ' leading ' tone is called *se* by analogy with *te* (Italian *si*) of the major mode. Thus the air is written and sung as shown on the opposite page.

Experience appears to show that, for sight-reading purposes, this is the simplest way of treating the minor mode. Some musicians object to it on the ground that, as in a minor scale the lowest (and highest) sound is essentially a tonic, in the sense that it plays a part analogous to that of the *do* in a major scale,

---

[1] In the soprano part, for instance, of the ' Messiah ' choruses there are but three real ' accidentals.' Nevertheless, a great quantity of modern and highly chromatic music has now (1927) been published in Tonic Sol-fa Notation and is read with extraordinary assurance by its singers.

[2] The best summary account of this system for the musician is given in ' Tonic Sol-Fa,' one of the *Music Primers* edited by Sir John Stainer (Novello).

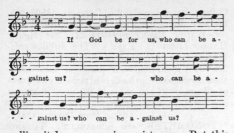

Key Bb. Lah is G.

l₁	d : t₁ : l₁	m : m : l	s :-.1: f
If	God be	for us, who	can be a-

m :1₁:		: :	: :1₁	m :-.r :d
gainst us?			who	can be a-

t₁ :1₁ :d	s :-.f : m	r :d
gainst us? who	can be a -	gainst us?

calling it *la* seems an inconsistency. But this seems a shadowy objection. The only important question is, what sign, for oral and ocular use, will best help the singer to recognise, by association with mental effect, one sound as distinguished from another? Experience shows that the Tonic Sol-fa plan does this effectually. The method is also theoretically sound. It proceeds on the principle that similarity of name should accord with similarity of musical effect. Now as a fact the scale of A minor is far more closely allied to the scale of C major than it is to the scale of A major. The identity of 'signature' itself shows that the substantial identity of the two first-named scales has always been recognised. But a proof more effective than any inference from signs and names is that given by the practice of composers in the matter of modulation. The scales most nearly related must evidently be those between which modulation is most frequent; and changes between tonic major and *relative* minor (type, C major to and from A minor) are many times more frequent than the changes between tonic major and *tonic* minor (type, C major to and from C minor). If therefore the Tonic Sol-fa-ist, in passing from C major to A minor, changed his *doh*, he would be adopting a new set of names for what is, as near as may be, the same set of sounds.

The examples above given show the notation as applied to simple passages; the following will show how peculiar or difficult modulations may be rendered in it:

They stand be-fore God's throne, and serve him day and night. And the Lamb shall lead them to fountains of living waters.

Af-fright-ed fled hell's spi-rits black in throngs.

Down they sink in the deep a-byss to end-less night.

In the teaching of harmony the Tonic Sol-fa method puts forward no new theory, but it uses a chord-nomenclature which makes the expres-

sion of the facts of harmony very simple. Each chord is represented by the initial letter, printed in capitals, of the sol-fa name of its essential root, thus—

D   S   R

the various positions of the same chord being distinguished by small letters appended to the capital, thus—

Da or D   Db   Dc   S   7S   7Sb   7Sc

Harmony being wholly a matter of relative, not absolute pitch, a notation based on key-relationship has obvious advantages as a means of indicating chord-movements. The learner has from the first been used to think and speak of every sound by its place in a scale, and the familiar symbols **m, f,** etc., convey to him at once all that is expressed by the generalising terms 'mediant,' 'subdominant,' etc. Another point in the method, as applied to harmony teaching, is the prominence given to training the ear, as well as the eye, to recognise chords. Pupils are taught, in class, to observe for themselves how the various consonances and dis-

Key Gb.

{m	f :-.r	s :-.t₁	d :	:d
r	:-.r	f :-t₁	d:	:d .r

G : Seven removes.

| ᵐar., l₁ : d .t₁, t₁ | m .r, r: t₁ ₌ s₁ | r. d ‖

Key Eb. Lah is C.

{m	l :—	: :d'	m' :d'	l :m
d :-.t₁	l₁ :—	: :	l :—	— :l
l	:—	s : s	f :—	m :—
r :—	d :—	t₁ :—	l₁ :1₁	m :— ‖

sonances sound; and they are practised at naming chords when sung to them.

Writing down a tune sung by a teacher has

now become a familiar school exercise for English children, a thing once thought only possible to advanced musicians ; and it has become common to see a choir two or three thousand strong singing in public, at first sight, an anthem or partsong fresh from the printer's hands. In the great spread of musical knowledge among the people this method has played a foremost part, and the teaching of the elements is far from being all that is done. Some of the best choral singing now to be heard in England is that of Tonic Sol-fa choirs. The music so printed amounts to a vast library of choral masterpieces.

Of the ' Galin - Chevé ' method of teaching sight-reading, which is based, broadly speaking, on the same principle as the Tonic Sol-fa method, a notice is given under CHEVÉ.   R. B. L.

TONIC SOL-FA COLLEGE, THE, was founded by John CURWEN (q.v.), in 1863, in order to give stability and permanence to the Tonic Sol-fa system of teaching, and was definitely established in its present form in 1875 by incorporation. The College is chiefly an examining body, but it also carries on the teaching of music (mainly directed to the training of teachers) by means of lectures and correspondence classes. The buildings, lecture-rooms, etc., are at Forest Gate, E.

The examinations are based on a system of graded certificates and diplomas, arranged so as to test the progress of pupils from the earliest stage. From the elementary certificate upwards, the power to sing at sight and to name or write down notes by ear is demanded. The diplomas of associateship, licentiateship and fellowship are granted upon a paper examination combined with vocal and ear tests, on the rendering of which the local examiners have to report to the College. On the occasion of the Jubilee of incorporation (1925) it was announced that the total number of certificates issued was 1,051,625, of which number 979,694 were for Tonic Sol-fa, 45,058 for staff notation and 26,873 for both notations. Correspondence classes are also held in the following subjects : harmony, counterpoint, musical composition, orchestration, musical form, musical and verbal expression, acoustics, theory of teaching, staff notation, and also in English grammar and composition. The College further organises a summer term of study, lasting for four weeks in vacation time, which is attended by teachers and students from Great Britain, the Colonies, etc. The tuition fees and travelling expenses of the majority of these are defrayed by means of scholarships, some of which are endowed. A great point is made of the art of presenting facts to the learner, and of cultivating the intelligence as well as the ear and voice. The students give model lessons, which their teachers criticise. Since 1876 the College has held annually a summer holiday course. The presidents of the

College have been John CURWEN (1863–80), his son John Spencer CURWEN (1880–1911), Sir Walter PARRATT (1911–24), Sir Henry HADOW (1924–   ) (q.v.). The Jubilee celebration held in the hall of the R.C.M. on June 27, 1925, included, with practical demonstrations, evidence from leaders in musical education of all grades of the value of the work achieved (see The School Music Review, July 15, 1925).

R. B. L. ; addns. from the Secretary.

TONOMETER, see SCHEIBLER ; TUNING FORK.

TONSOR, MICHAEL (b. Dünkelsbühl, near Jugolstadt), cantor at the church of Our Lady, at Dünkelsbühl, in 1566, and from c. 1570–90 organist at St. George's, Öttingen. Duke William V. of Bavaria supported him in the publication of his works, consisting of a large number of motets, a Missa Solennis and other church compositions. Some have appeared in modern editions (Q.-L. ; Riemann).

TORELLI, GIUSEPPE (b. Verona, c. mid-17th cent. ; d. Anspach, c. 1708), violinist and composer, lived in Bologna from 1686 as leader of a church orchestra, but in 1701 accepted the post of leader of the band of the Markgraf of Brandenburg-Anspach at Anspach in Germany, where he died.

To him has been ascribed the invention of the ' concerto ' but that is not tenable. His most important work, however, the Concerti Grossi, op. 8, was published at Bologna, 1709, three years earlier than Corelli's Concerti Grossi. They are written for two obbligato violins and stringed orchestra, and clearly present the main features of the concerto-form, as used by Corelli, Handel and others. According to Eitner, eight works of his were published—all in concerted style, for 2, 3, or 4 stringed instruments, and Q.-L. refers to many in MS.   P. D.

TORNADA, see SONG, subsection SPAIN (2).

TORQUATO TASSO, lyric drama in 4 acts ; libretto by Ferretti ; music by Donizetti. Produced Teatro Valle, Rome, autumn of 1833 ; at Her Majesty's Theatre, Mar. 3, 1840.   G.

TORRANCE, REV. GEORGE WILLIAM, M.A., Mus.D. Dublin (b. Rathmines, Dublin, 1835 ; d. Aug. 20, 1907). Educated as a chorister in Christ Church Cathedral, he afterwards became successively organist of Blackrock, Dublin, and of the city churches of St. Andrew and St. Anne. Among his earlier compositions was a Te Deum and Jubilate, sung in Christ Church Cathedral. At 19 he composed his first oratorio, ' Abraham,' which was performed in 1855 at the Ancient Concert Rooms, Dublin, by all the leading musicians of the city, Sir Robert Stewart presiding at the organ and the composer conducting. ' Abraham ' was performed four times in two years. It was rightly deemed a wonderful work for a mere lad to produce ; the airs were written after the manner of Beethoven, the choruses followed that of

Handel : of plagiarism there was none, and if the work was lacking in experience, it was yet a bold and successful effort for a boy in his teens. In 1856 Torrance visited Leipzig, and during his studies in that city became acquainted with Moscheles and other eminent musicians. Upon his return he produced an opera, ' William of Normandy,' and several minor works, some of which have since been published. In 1859 Torrance entered the University of Dublin, with a view to studying for the ministry of the Church of Ireland ; here he graduated in Arts in 1864, and produced the same year a second oratorio, ' The Captivity,' to Goldsmith's words. He took the degree of M.A. at the University in 1867, was ordained deacon in 1865, and priest in 1866. In 1867 he returned to Dublin, being appointed curate of St. Bride's.

In 1869 he emigrated to Melbourne, Victoria, where he held the curacy of Christ Church, S. Yarra, Melbourne. Subsequently he held the incumbencies of All Saints, Geelong ; Holy Trinity, Balaclava ; and St. John's, Melbourne. In 1879 he obtained the degrees of Mus.B. and Mus.D. from Dublin University, on the recommendation of Sir Robert Stewart, professor of music in the University, the ' Acts ' publicly performed for the degree being; for Mus.B. a Te Deum and Jubilate (composed 1878), for Mus.D. a selection from his oratorio ' The Captivity.' He received an honorary degree of Mus.D. *ad eundem* from the Melbourne University, the first degree conferred in Music by that University.

In 1882 Dr. Torrance produced a third oratorio, ' The Revelation ' ; this was performed with great success in Melbourne, the composer conducting. It was published by Novello. He was elected president of the Fine Arts section of the ' Social Science Congress ' held in Melbourne in 1880, when he delivered the opening address on Music, since published. In 1883 he was appointed by the Governor of Victoria to be one of the Examiners for the ' Clarke Scholarship ' in the Royal College of Music.

He returned to Ireland in 1897, and after being appointed Chaplain to the Bishop of Ossory, he was raised to the dignity of Prebendary of Killamery, and Canon of St. Canice's Cathedral, Kilkenny, in 1900—being also made Registrar of the united dioceses of Ossory, Ferns and Leighlin, and Librarian of St. Canice's Library. In his last years Canon Torrance composed much sacred and secular music, and his madrigal ' Dry be that tear ' obtained the Molyneux Prize and the Society's medal, offered by the Madrigal Society of London in 1903. Many of his hymn tunes obtained wide popularity ; and a Chant Book for the Church of Ireland was completed before his death, which took place two days after that of his wife.   R. P. S. ; addns. W. H. G. F.

TORRI, Pietro (*b.* Peschiera, Lago d' Iseo, *c.* 1655 ; *d.* Munich, July 6, 1737), a pupil of Ag. Steffani, was chamber-organist at Munich, 1689 ; Kapellmeister at Hanover, Carneval, 1696; director of chamber music at Munich, 1703 ; Kapellmeister or Hof-Kapell-director, 1715. With Abaco he followed the elector Max Emanuel, exiled to Brussels, and was appointed first Kapellmeister in 1732. He wrote a number of operas, in which he made characteristic use of obbligato solo instruments. His chamber duets are greatly praised. He also wrote an oratorio and a concerto per camera (*Q.-L.* ; *Riemann*).   E. v. d. S.

TORRIAN, Jehan, of Venice, lived at the end of the 15th century, and built in 1504 the organ of Notre Dame des Tables, Montpellier. A copy of the curious contract may be seen in Roret's *Manuel des facteurs d'orgues* (Paris, 1849).   v. de P.

TOSCA, ' Melodramma ' in 3 acts, text by L. Illica and G. Giacosa (founded on Sardou's play) ; music by G. Puccini. Produced Costanzi Theatre, Rome, Jan. 14, 1900 ; Covent Garden, July 12, 1900 ; Buenos Aires, June 16, 1900 ; New York, Metropolitan Opera House, Feb. 4, 1901 ; in English, Moody-Manners Co., Court Theatre, Liverpool, Oct. 29, 1909.

TOSCANINI, Arturo (*b.* Parma, Mar. 25, 1867), the most celebrated Italian conductor of his time. Toscanini began his musical studies at the Conservatoire of his native city, with the violoncello as his principal subject. Apparently his extraordinary gifts were not noted by his instructors. But no sooner had he begun his career as an orchestral player than his exceptional memory marked him out as a musician of unusual calibre, for he could play his part by heart after a few rehearsals, and he often did it. A conductor once noticing the closed copy on his desk challenged him to play without music. Toscanini accepted the challenge and soon convinced the conductor that a single reading was all he needed to know the score by heart. This great gift stood him in good stead when he was suddenly called upon to conduct the orchestra for the first time in very odd circumstances. South America is one of the countries where theatres often rely on Italians for their orchestras, and Toscanini was playing as a violoncellist in the spring season of 1886 at Rio Janeiro when the audience, owing to a series of incidents and misunderstandings, rose *en masse* against the conductor, and a noisy demonstration made it impossible for the performance to begin. The impresario, who happened to be also a keen musician, attempted to take his place, but again a storm of hisses broke out and it looked as if the performance would have to be suspended when Toscanini's colleagues, knowing his qualities, forced the shy, youthful violoncellist on to the conductor's desk. The appearance of so young a man in so responsible a position quieted the demonstration. The performance was allowed to proceed and ended in unbounded enthusiasm. The inexperienced conductor knew the score of the opera ('Aïda') by heart; he carried in his mind a clear conception of what the rendering should be; he possessed, moreover, the personal magnetism which bound to his will at once players and singers. The verdict of that first audience has since been confirmed by the public wherever Toscanini has appeared. In 1898 as chief conductor of the Metropolitan Opera House in New York he began a series of conspicuously fine performances there which lasted till his resignation of the post in 1915.

In the long and successful career which thus opened for him he has performed many remarkable feats, and his influence has been of great benefit also to Italian theatres and music. When Franchetti's 'Cristoforo Colombo' was being rehearsed for the first production at Genoa, the conductor, Mancinelli, fell ill at the last moment. Toscanini was sent for and conducted with great success after studying the new score for only twenty-four hours. He was the first to make known to his countrymen Wagner's 'Götterdammerung,' Verdi's Te Deum and Stabat Mater, and numberless Italian operas including Puccini's 'Bohème' and 'Turandot' and Boïto's 'Nerone,' the score of which, left unfinished at the composer's death, was revised by Toscanini. His advice was followed in the radical alterations made at La Scala, and when the famous Milanese theatre was reopened in 1922 he was appointed its director.

It may be said of Toscanini that his tastes know no limitations. His interpretations of German music are as finished and distinguished as his readings of Verdi or Debussy. He is said to be something of a martinet, and he certainly does not suffer compromise in anything connected with artistic matters or even in minor questions of details. Having made up his mind that encores were an intolerable nuisance he never again gave way, in spite of the hostility his refusal evoked from the public that had been taught by long tradition to expect them as a matter of course. He demands implicit obedience from singers and players, and thus, quite apart from extraordinary beauty and mastery of the orchestral playing, performances under his direction possess an authority and character impossible where unity of control is lacking.　　F. B.

TOSI, GIUSEPPE FELICE (b. Bologna, c. 1630), organist of S. Petronio, Bologna, 1683; afterwards maestro di cappella at S. Giovanni, Monte, and member of the Accademia dei Filarmonici, of which he was president in 1679. He was maestro di cappella at the cathedral in Morte di Ferrara. He composed a number of

operas, salmi concertati and cantate da camera (Q.-L.).

TOSI, PIER FRANCESCO (b. circa 1650; d. after 1730), the son of a musician of Bologna, must have been born about 1650, since we learn from the translator of his book that he died soon after the beginning of George II.'s reign above 80 years old.[1] In the early part of his life he travelled a great deal, but in 1693 we find him in London, giving regular concerts,[2] and from that time forward he resided there almost entirely till his death, in great consideration as a singing-master and a composer. A volume in the Harleian Collection of the British Museum (No. 1272) contains seven songs or cantatas for voice and harpsichord, with his name to them. Galliard praises his music for its exquisite taste, and especially mentions the pathos and expression of the recitatives. When more than 70 Tosi published the work by which his name is still known, under the modest title of *Opinioni de' cantori antichi e moderni, o sieno osservazioni sopra il canto figurato* . . . (Bologna, 1723), which was translated after his death into English by GALLIARD—*Observations on the Florid Song, or Sentiments of the Ancient and Modern Singers*, London, 1742—second edition, 1743; and into German by AGRICOLA—*Anleitung zur Singkunst*, Berlin, 1747. It is a practical treatise on singing, in which the aged teacher embodies his own experience and that of his contemporaries, at a time when the art was probably more thoroughly taught than it has ever been since.　　G. M.

TOSTI, FRANCESCO PAOLO (b. Ortona sul mare, Abruzzi, Ap. 9, 1846; d. Rome, Dec. 2, 1916), an Italian composer.

In 1858 his parents sent him to the Royal College of St. Pietro a Majella at Naples, where he studied the violin under Pinto, and composition under Conti and the venerable Mercadante. The young pupil made wonderful progress, and was by Mercadante appointed *maestrino* or pupil teacher, with the not too liberal salary of 60 francs a month. He remained in Naples until the end of 1869, when, feeling that his health had been much impaired by overwork, he went back to Ortona with the hope of regaining strength. However, as soon as he got home he was taken seriously ill with bronchitis, and only after seven months recovered sufficiently to go to Rome and resume work. During his illness he wrote 'Non m' ama più' and 'Lamento d' amore'; but it was with difficulty that the young composer could induce a publisher to print these songs, which subsequently became popular, and it was not till a considerable time after they sold well that he disposed of the copyright for the insignificant sum of £20 each. Sgambati, the leader of the new musical school in Rome,

1 Galliard's Prefatory Discourse, p. viii.
2 Hawkins, *History*, v. 5.

was among the first to recognise Tosti's talent, and in order to give his friend a fair start in the fashionable and artistic world, he assisted him to give a concert at the Sala Dante, where he achieved a great success, singing several of his own compositions, and a ballad purposely written for him by Sgambati, ' Eravi un vecchio.' The Queen of Italy, then Princess Margherita of Savoy, was present and showed her appreciation by immediately appointing him as her teacher of singing. Shortly afterwards he was entrusted with the care of the Musical Archives of the Italian court.

It was in 1875 that Tosti first visited London, where he was well received in the best circles, both as an artist and as a man. He paid yearly visits to the English capital, and in 1880 was called in as teacher of singing to the Royal Family of England. About that time he settled in London ; he received the honour of knighthood in 1908.

He wrote Italian, French and English songs. He had an elegant, simple and facile inspiration, a style of his own, a genuine Italian flow of melody, and great skill in finding the most appropriate and never-failing effects for drawing-room songs.

His songs reflect the advance in public taste as well as the progress of his own artistic development. They are very numerous, and his Vocal Albums, and fifteen duets, ' Canti popolari abruzzesi,' enjoyed a great success for many years. Among his early favourites in London were ' Forever,' ' Good-bye,' ' Mother,' ' At Vespers,' ' Amore,' ' Aprile,' ' Vorrei morire,' and ' That Day ' ; but none are up to the artistic level of his later lyrics, such as ' Mattinata,' ' Serenata ' and many others.

G. M.

TOUCH (Ger. *Anschlag*), term used of keyboard instruments and also of their performers.

(1) Of the instruments it denotes the weight required to bring the key into effective action, and also the distance traversed by the key in depression. This applies equally to the pianoforte and the organ. An instrument is spoken of as possessing a light or a heavy, a deep or shallow touch. Neither weight nor measurement has been precisely standardised. (See the description of actions under PIANOFORTE ; and ORGAN-PLAYING, subsection TECHNIQUE.)

(2) As regards performers it is applicable primarily to pianists, since the manner of pressing or striking the keys of their instrument directly affects the tone, which is not the case with organists. The production of pianoforte tone by means of touch is one of the most subtle problems of the pianist and the teacher (see PIANOFORTE - PLAYING). The control of duration (the holding or releasing of a note) gives a secondary meaning to the term applicable alike to both pianists and organists. (See LEGATO, STACCATO and PHRASING.)

TOUCH. By old writers the word is used as equivalent to sound, in which sense it occurs in Massinger's ' Guardian ' (Act ii. Sc. 4), where Severino says ' I'll *touch* my horn '—(blows his horn). An earlier example will be found in the Romance of Sir Gawayne and the Green Knight (*c.* 1320), line 120, p. 4 of the edition of 1864. The word appears also to have been used in English music during two centuries for a toccata. ' A touche by Mr. Byrd ' is found in the MS. of a virginal piece in the British Museum ; and ' Mr. Kelway's touches,' as a heading to several passages of a florid character, appears in a MS., probably in the handwriting of Dr. B. Cooke, in the R.C.M.   W. B. S.

TOUCH, see CHANGE-RINGING.

TOUCHEMOULIN (TOUCHMOLIN), JOSEPH (*b.* Châlons, *c.* 1727 ; *d.* Ratisbon, Oct. 25, 1801), an excellent violinist at the courts of Bonn and Cologne, played with success at the Concert Spirituel, Paris, in 1754. He made further studies under Tartini, and was appointed at the court of Ratisbon after 1761. He composed church music as well as operas, symphonies and sonatas (*Q.-L.*).

TOUR DE GOSIER, an *agrément* of the French school which resembles a very rapid *grupetto*. (See ORNAMENTS, VOCAL.)   E. B^L.

TOURDION (TORDION), ' a turning or winding about ; also a tricke or pranke ; also, the daunce tearmed a Round.' (Cotgrave.) The early French dances were divided into two classes, ' Danses basses ' or ' Danses nobles,' and ' Dances par haut.' The former of these included all regular dances, the latter were mere improvised romps or ' baladinages.' The regular Basse Dance consisted of two parts, the first was twice repeated, and the last, or ' Tourdion,' was probably something like our modern round dances. The Tourdion was therefore the French equivalent for the German Nachtanz, Proportio or Hoppeltanz, and the Italian SALTARELLO (*q.v.*). Tabourot says that the Tourdion was nearly the same as the GALLIARD (*q.v.*), but the former was more rapid and smooth than the latter. Hence he defines it as a ' Gaillarde par terre,' *i.e.* a galliard deprived of its characteristic jumps and springs. Both dances were in 3-time. The following is the tune of the Tourdion given in the *Orchésographie*:

Further particulars as to these dances may be found in the *Provinciales* of Antonio de Arena (1537). (See TRIHORIS.)   W. B. S.

TOURJEE, EBEN, Mus.D. (*b.* Warwick, Rhode Island, June 1, 1834 ; *d.* Boston, Apr. 12,

1891), father of the Conservatory or class system of musical instruction in America. His family being in humble circumstances it became necessary to put him to work at the early age of 8; but his thirst for knowledge was so great, that he soon became a laborious student at the East Greenwich seminary. At the age of 15 he became clerk in a music store in Providence, and thus had opportunities for study which he did not fail to improve. At the age of 17 he opened a music store in Fall River, where he also taught music in the public schools and formed classes in piano, voice and organ. This was in 1851, and was really the beginning of the class system, which has since been so largely developed. He afterwards removed to Newport, and continued his work as organist and choirmaster of Old Trinity Church there, and as director of the local choral society. In 1859 he founded a Musical Institute at East Greenwich, where he had an opportunity of carrying out his ideas regarding class-teaching under more favourable auspices than before.

In 1863 he visited Europe, in order to gain information regarding the methods employed in France, Germany and Italy in conservatory teaching. He took this opportunity of studying with many eminent masters, amongst others August Haupt, of Berlin. On his return to America he removed to Providence, and established the ' Providence Conservatory of Music,' which had great success. In 1867 he extended his work by founding ' The New England Conservatory of Music,' in BOSTON (*q.v.*) and continued for a time to keep both schools in operation. He drew round him the most eminent teachers in Boston, and placed a good musical education within the reach of the poorest students. In 1869 his executive and organising abilities were made use of by the projectors of the great ' Peace Jubilee,' and there is no doubt that the success of that enterprise was largely due to his efforts. During the same year the degree of Doctor of Music was conferred upon him by Wesleyan University. From the foundation of Boston University he was Dean of the College of Music attached thereto. But his greatest work was the establishment of the great Conservatory just mentioned, from which have graduated thousands of pupils, filling honourable positions as teachers, pianists, organists and vocalists, and proving themselves able musicians.   G.

TOURNEMIRE, CHARLES ARNOULD (*b.* Bordeaux, Jan. 22, 1870), studied at the Paris Conservatoire, where he gained first organ prize in 1891; he afterwards studied with Vincent d'Indy. He succeeded César Franck as organist of Sainte-Clotilde (1898) soon after completing his education. He is professor of a chamber-music class at the Conservatoire. He has written chamber music, a symphony, songs and pieces for piano and organ. ' Le Sang de

la Sirène,' for chorus, soli and orchestra, gained the Prix de la Ville de Paris, and was performed at the Théâtre Municipal de la Gaîté on Nov. 17, 1904. The work was also given at Toulouse, Leyden and The Hague. A lyric tragedy in seven scenes, ' Nittetis,' has not yet been performed. Tournemire has given many organ recitals—in Berlin, Amsterdam, The Hague, Marseilles, Turin, Liège, etc. His principal works are :

Organ.—Opp. 2, 3, 10, 16, 19, interlude, scherzetto, adagio, toccata; op. 24, 'Itε Missa est'; ' Pièces symphoniques,' various pieces, versets, Noëls, entrées, offertoires, etc.; triple Choral (op. 41).
Songs.—A collection containing ' Sept Mélodies,' ' Solitude ' (1923).
Chamber Music.—PF. quartet, PF. trio, etc.; ' Sagesse,' vln. and PF., etc.
Dramatic Works.—' Les Dieux sont morts ' (Paris, 1923), lyric drama in 2 acts; words by E. Berteaux; first performed, Opéra, Mar. 19, 1924.   G. F.; addns. M. L. P.

TOURS, BERTHOLD (*b.* Rotterdam, Dec. 17, 1838; *d.* London, Mar. 11, 1897). His early instruction was derived from his father, Barthélemy Tours (1797–1864), who was organist of the St. Laurence church, and from Verhulst. He afterwards studied at the Conservatoires of Brussels and Leipzig and then accompanied Prince George Galitzin to Russia, and remained there for two years. From 1861 he resided in London, writing, teaching and playing the violin in the band of the Royal Italian Opera, and other good orchestras. He was appointed organist of the Swiss Church, Holborn, 1862, and in 1878 he became musical adviser and editor to Novello, and in that capacity arranged several important works from the orchestral scores, such as Beethoven's Mass in C, four of Schubert's Masses, ' Elijah,' Gounod's ' Redemption,' etc. etc., besides writing the 'Primer of the Violin ' in the series of that firm. His compositions are numerous. He wrote for the piano and other instruments, and a large number of songs, some of which were very popular. But his best work is to be found in his hymn tunes, anthems and services for the Anglican Church.   G.

TOURTE, FRANÇOIS (*b.* Paris, 1747; *d.* there, Apr. 1835), the most famous of violin bowmakers. His father and elder brother were bow-makers also; and the reputation which attaches to the family name is not due to François alone. To François Tourte's father is generally attributed the substitution of the screw for the crémaillière. Xavier Tourte, the elder brother, known in France as ' Tourte l'aîné,' was also an excellent workman : tradition says that the brothers started business in partnership, François making the sticks, and Xavier the nuts and fittings. They quarrelled and dissolved partnership, and each then set up for himself, Xavier reproducing as well as he could the improvements in the stick which had been introduced by François. The latter has been called the Stradivari of the bow : and there is some truth in this ; for as Stradivari finally settled the model and fittings of the violin, so Tourte finally settled the model and fittings of the bow. But he had more to do for the bow than Stradivari for the fiddle. The Cremona makers before Stradivari had nearly perfected the model of the violin : it only remained for him to give it certain finishing touches. But Tourte, properly speaking, had no predecessors. He found bow-making in a state of chaos, and he reduced it to a science ; and he may be said to have invented the modern bow. Perhaps the best idea of the bows which were in use in Tourte's youth may be gained from the illustrations given under Bow. Before his time all the modern forms of staccato must have been impossible, and the nuances of piano and forte extremely limited ; a rawness, especially on the treble strings, and a monotony which to our ears would be intolerable, must have deformed the performances of the best of violinists. The violin, under Tourte's bow, became a different instrument : and subsequent bow-makers have exclusively copied him, the value of their productions depending on the success with which they have applied his principles.

An examination of Tourte's bows proves that his first care was to select wood of fine but strong texture, and perfectly straight grain, and his second to give it a permanent and regular bend. This was effected by subjecting it in a state of flexion to a moderate heat for a considerable time. Tourte's first experiments are said to have been made on the staves of old sugar hogsheads from Brazil : probably the bent slabs of Brazil wood employed for this purpose had acquired a certain additional elasticity from the combined effect of exposure to tropical heat and the absorption of the saccharine juices : and in connexion with the latter it has been suggested that the dark colour of the Tourte sticks is not wholly attributable to age, but partly to some preparation applied to them in the process of heating. The writer cannot agree with this suggestion, especially as some of Tourte's finest bows are extremely pale in colour. Be this as it may, it is certain that the greater elasticity which he secured in the stick by the choice and preparation of the wood enabled him to carry out to the fullest extent the method of bending the stick of the bow the reverse way, that is, inwards, and thus to realise what had long been the desideratum of violinists, a bow which should be strong and elastic without being heavy. By thus increasing and economising the resistance of the stick he liberated the player's thumb and fingers from much useless weight. On the subject of the wood employed by Tourte, Fétis in his chapter on bows at the end of his *Antonio Stradivari* (English translation by John Bishop, 1864) says that Tourte's indefatigable investigations led him to experiment in all kinds of wood which seemed likely to bring about the realisa-

tion of his ideal. He soon discovered that Pernambuco wood alone combined the requisite lightness and stiffness. Unfortunately the maritime wars between France and England were a serious obstacle to the importation of Pernambuco wood during the period—from 1775–80—during which Tourte's most important discoveries were made. The price of this wood, used mostly for dyeing purposes, rose to nearly five shillings a pound, and in addition to this pecuniary consideration, there was great difficulty in finding a straight billet, for the wood is of a knotty and crooked growth. Sometimes in eight or ten tons of Pernambuco wood scarcely one piece of wood suitable for making bow-sticks can be found. By a series, no doubt, of patient experiments, he determined the right curvature for the stick, and the rule for tapering it gradually towards the point [1] so as to have the centre of gravity in the right place, or in other words to ' balance ' properly over the string in the hand of the player. He determined the true length of the stick, and the height of the point and the nut, in all which particulars the bow-makers of his time seem to have erred on the side of excess. Previously to the year 1775, nothing had been determined regarding the length, weight and condition of equilibrium of the bow. Tourte's penetration, aided by the actual experience of the virtuosi of his day, enabled him to decide the most perfect proportions of the bow to be between 29·134 and 29·528 inches in length including the button. He decreased the diameter up to the head, giving a difference of ·13 inches between the extremities, and also determined the distance of the hair from the stick by the heights of the head and rest. Lastly, he invented the method of spreading the hairs and fixing them on the face of the nut by means of a movable band of metal fitting on a slide of mother-of-pearl. The bow, as we have it, is therefore the creation of the genius of Tourte.

Tourte's improvements in the bow were effected after 1775. Tradition says that he was materially assisted in his work by the advice of Viotti, who arrived in Paris in 1782. Nothing is more likely ; for only an accomplished violinist could have formulated the demands which the Tourte bow was constructed to satisfy. Viotti no doubt contributed to bring the Tourte bow into general use, and it is certain that it quickly drove the old barbarous bows completely from the field, and that in Paris there at once arose a school of bow-makers which has never been excelled.

Tourte never stamped his bows. Genuine ones are sometimes found stamped with the name, but this is the work of some other hand. His original nuts are usually of tortoise shell,

---

1 Mathematically investigated, Tourte's bow, when unstrung, is found to form a logarithmic curve, the ordinates of which increase in arithmetical proportion, and the abscissas in geometrical proportion.

finely mounted in gold, but wanting the metallic slide on the stick, which was introduced by Lupot.

Tourte continued to work to within a very few years of his death, at an advanced age. His atelier was on the fourth floor of No. 10, Quai de l'École : after making bows all day he would descend in the evening, and recreate himself by angling for gudgeon in the Seine. (See Bow.)　　　　　　E. J. P. ; addns. E. H.-A.

TOVEY, DONALD FRANCIS (*b.* Eton, July 17, 1875), pianist and composer, has been Reid Professor of Music in Edinburgh University since 1914.

The son of an Eton master, the Rev. Duncan Crooks Tovey, his education, both musical and general, was up to the age of 19 in the hands of Miss Sophie Weisse, who trained him for the career of a pianist. (In after years he had advice and help from Deppe, but was never his pupil.) His encyclopædic knowledge of the music of Bach was already manifested in his teens, when he played the thirty variations from memory. His playing of the six-part 'Ricercar' from the 'Musikalisches Opfer' is perhaps his greatest achievement as a pianist. As early as the age of 8 years he began to compose works in sonata form, and soon was allowed to learn counterpoint, Walter Parratt being his teacher. He subsequently studied with James Higgs, and when he was 13 had a few lessons from Hubert Parry. In June 1894 he was elected Lewis Nettleship scholar at Balliol College, Oxford, and graduated in classical honours in 1898. In 1894 he had given a concert at Windsor, at which he was assisted by Joachim, who took the keenest interest in his artistic development, often bearing testimony to the remarkable nature of Tovey's gifts.

He definitely entered the musical profession in 1900, when he gave a series of four concerts in St. James's Hall, at which several of his own compositions were given. Two more sets of concerts were given in 1901, and in 1901–02 he gave concerts in Berlin and Vienna. A more important concert, with orchestra, in Nov. 1903 showed his powers of orchestration in his own pianoforte concerto which produced a strong impression ; it was conducted by Henry J. Wood and played by the composer, and was repeated under Richter in 1906.

In the following years Tovey played much in London and elsewhere, particularly in chamber music, with such artists as Robert Hausmann and Lady Hallé. He organised several series of such concerts at the Chelsea Town Hall, took part in those of the CLASSICAL CONCERT SOCIETY (*q.v.*), and brought forward some of his own compositions as well as giving distinguished performances of the classics.

His appointment in July 1914 as Reid Professor of Music (see REID: EDINBURGH), gave a

more definite direction to his activities and called into play his depth of scholastic knowledge of music. Early in his residence at Edinburgh he created the Reid Orchestral Concerts, conducted the orchestra, and thus co-ordinated practice and theory. His lectures show the high quality of his mind, and his writings, mostly in the form of pamphlets on works to be performed at the concerts and also analytical notes to the concerts, are of a kind far above the level of first steps to knowledge usually expected from such work. His unswerving devotion to the highest manifestations of art has made him a great teacher.

The list of Tovey's major compositions below shows that his output has been considerable. His mind steeped in the classics and superior to popular demand has produced works which musicians respect, but the public is apt to ignore to its own loss. Most of the chamber music has been published by Schott.

Trio in B minor for pf. and strings.
Sonata in F for pf. and v'cl.
Quintet in C for pf. and strings.
Sonata in F for pf. and vln.
Twelve songs for a low voice.
Three anthems for unaccompanied male voices.
Trio in C minor, for pf., clarinet and horn, with a free arrangement of the wind parts for vln. and v'cl.
Divertimento in B flat for oboe and pf., embodying three 'duets' brought forward before the completion of the work.
Offertorium ' in festo sanctorum Innocentium ' for unaccompanied vocal quartet.
Quartet in E minor for pf. and strings.
Aria and Variations in B flat for string quartet.
Trio in D minor for pf. and cor anglais.
Concerto in A for pf. and orch.
Sonata in B flat for pf. and clarinet.
Several short pf. pieces.
Twenty-five Rounds for equal voices.
Prelude and entr'actes for Maeterlinck's ' Aglavaine et Sélysette for string orch.
Balliol Dances for pf. duet.
Suite for wind band, written for the Oxford Pageant of 1907.
String quartets in G and D (Chelsea Concert, 1909).
National March composed for the Sultan of Zanzibar, for military band.
Variations for pf. and v'cl. ' In Memoriam Robert Hausmann,' 1909.
Symphony in D (op. 32). (Aix-la-Chapelle, 1913.)
Sonata ' Eroica ' in C. Vln. alone.
Sonata in D. V'cl. alone.
Sonata in G. 2 v'cl.
Trio in D. Pf., vln. and v'cl.
Variations on a theme by Gluck. Flute and string quartet.
Opera. ' The Bride of Dionysus.' 3 acts. Text by R. C. Trevelyan.
　　　See *B.M.S. Ann.* 1920.　　　　　M. ; addns. C.

TOWER, a group of organ pipes arranged in the form of a turret or tower.　　　T. E.

TOWER DRUMS, THE. Handel frequently borrowed a pair of kettledrums from the Master-General of the Ordnance for his own performances of his oratorios ; and as they were kept in the Tower of London, they were usually called ' the Tower Drums.' They were in frequent request after his death, including the Commemoration Festival in Westminster Abbey in 1784. Dr. Burney, in his account of this Festival, says they were taken by Marlborough at the battle of Malplaquet in 1709.

A much larger pair, 39 and 35 inches in diameter, were made expressly for that Festival from the design of Asbridge, of Drury Lane orchestra, and have since obtained the name of ' Tower Drums,' from a notion that the head of one of them was made from the skin of a lion in the Tower menagerie. These drums came into the possession of T. P. Chipp.

the well-known kettledrummer, and on the sale of his instruments at his death were bought by H. Potter & Co., military musical instrument makers. They added a brass T-shaped key to each tuning-screw, and presented them (1884) to the Crystal Palace Company, who placed them in their large orchestra.

Larger drums were made for the Sacred Harmonic Society (47 and 43 inches in diameter), but no tone can be got from such overgrown instruments.   v. de P.

TOWER OF THE VOÏVOD, THE, opera, text after a novel of H. H. Ewers, music by Dohnányi; produced Budapest, Mar. 18, 1922.

TOYE, (1) JOHN FRANCIS (b. Winchester, Jan. 27, 1883), writer on music in several journals and a contributor to this Dictionary, became musical critic to the *Morning Post* in 1925. In 1913 he published a musical novel, *Diana and Two Symphonies*, and some songs by him have also been published. In 1925 appeared *The Well-tempered Musician*, epitomising his outlook on the art. His brother, (2) GEOFFREY (b. Feb. 17, 1889), was educated in music at the R.C.M. (exhibitioner and scholar), and gained experience as a conductor at several London theatres. He conducted the first performance of Vaughan Williams's ' London Symphony ' (see VAUGHAN WILLIAMS) in 1914. He attained the rank of major in the R.F.C. during the War, commanding the photographic section. Returning to music he conducted performances of the Beecham Opera Company and concerts of the Royal Philharmonic Society (1918–19). He conducted two London seasons of the D'Oyly Carte Opera Company in the Gilbert and Sullivan repertory. He is a member of Lloyds, and has founded and conducted the Lloyds Choir.   c.

TOY SYMPHONY (Fr. *La Foire des Enfants*, or *symphonie burlesque*; Ger. *Kindersinfonie*), the English name by which a certain work of Haydn's is known. A tradition which there is no reasonable cause for doubting says that the composer got seven toy instruments at a fair at Berchtesgaden, and taking them to Esterház, summoned some of his orchestra to an important rehearsal. When they found that they were expected to play a new symphony upon these toys (the only real instruments in the score are two violins and a double bass) the most experienced musicians in the band failed to keep their time for laughing. The original parts are entitled ' Sinfonia Berchtolsgadensis '; the toy instruments employed are a ' cuckoo ' playing E and G, a trumpet and drum in G, a whistle, a triangle and a ' quail ' in F. There are three movements, the last of which is played three times over, faster and faster each time. The symphony is in C major, and was written in 1788 (see Pohl's *Haydn*, vol. ii. p. 226, etc.).

Andreas Romberg wrote a symphony for much the same instruments, with the addition of a pianoforte duet, a rattle and a bell. He attempts more elaborate modulations than Haydn ventures to use, but his symphony lacks the fun and freshness of the older master's work, although his slow movement, an Adagio lamentabile, is very humorous. Mendelssohn wrote two—the first for Christmas 1827, for the same orchestra as Haydn's, the second for Christmas 1828. Both seem to have vanished. (See MENDELSSOHN, Vol. III. pp. 383-4.) Franklin Taylor wrote one for piano and toys which was frequently played, and later examples have had a more or less ephemeral popularity.   M.

TRABACI, GIOVANNI MARIA, a Neapolitan by birth, appears in 1603 as organist to the Royal Chapel at Naples, and somewhat later as magister capellae. His publications consist of several books of masses, psalms, motets and madrigals, hardly any of which, however, seem to be preserved complete; but they also include two books of organ pieces, one described in the title as containing Ricercate, Canzone francesi, Capricci, Canti fermi, Gagliarde, Partite diverse, Toccate di durezze e ligature, Consonanze Stravaganti, opere tutte da Sonare a 4 v., Lib. 1, 1603; the other, Ricercate ed altri varii Capricci con 100 versi sopra li otti finali ecclesiastici, Napoli, 1615. From the first of these organ books L. Torchi in ' L' arte musicale in Italia,' vol. iii. has reprinted some short pieces, two of which serve to illustrate the somewhat crude attempts of the time in the employment of dissonances and chromatic harmony. The first piece, ' Terzo tono con tre fughe,' which is diatonic enough, hardly appears to be transcribed or at least printed correctly. The answers and the theme do not correspond.

     J. R. M.

TRACKER, a thin flat strip of wood used in the mechanism of an organ for the purpose of conveying motion from one portion of the instrument to another. (See ORGAN, Vol. III. p. 756.)

TRACKER PNEUMATIC ACTION, see ORGAN.

TRACTULUS, the *Guidon* or sign used at the end of a stave to indicate the note with which the next stave begins. In English it is called a DIRECT (*q.v.*).   W. S. R.

TRACTUS. The position of the tract in the Latin service has already been indicated (see GREGORIAN MUSIC). In character it differs from the other classes of plain-song of the Mass and is probably a survival of old ways which has been retained for penitential occasions though superseded elsewhere. A tract consists of a psalm or excerpt from a psalm sung between the Epistle and Gospel in chorus with no solo or alternation. In practice nearly all tracts belong to one or other of two classes, the first of which utilises a plastic melody of the

2nd mode and the second a similar melody of the 8th mode. Specimens of the latter are given here showing a comparison of the opening parts of three of the tracts of Easter Even.

1. Can - - te - - mus   Do - - min - - o
2. Vi - - ne - - riam   fac - - ta est   (domin-)
3. At - - ten - - de   cae - - lum   (et loqu-)

(b)

glo - ri - o - se e - - - nim
                                  o
                             ar

(c)

hono-ri - fi-ca-tus est, e-quum et ascen-sor - em
in cor - nu in   loco   u - be - ri
et au - di - at   terra . . ore me - o.

The first then repeats the last two divisions, (b) and (c), to the remaining words left over from verse one. Verse two then proceeds thus :

1.   Hic Deus e - - - - - um: Deus   )
2. Et ma-ce - riam ... fo - - - - - dit: et plantavit }
3. Ex-pec - ten-tur .... me - - - - um: et descendant)

{etc. as (b) above {et ex - al - ta - bo   } as (c)
                   {et ae-di - - fi - ca - vit } above.
                   . . . . verba mea

It will be seen that the treatment is quite methodical, and each verse is set to a melody in three divisions, each of which consists of (a) an intonation, (b) a recitation and (c) a cadence. (See INFLEXION.)   W. H. F.

TRAETTA, TOMMASO MICHELE FRANCESCO SAVERIO (b. Bitonto, Terra di Bari, Mar. 30, 1727 ; d. Venice, Apr. 6, 1779), an Italian composer of the 18th century. Formerly it was believed that his name was Trajetta, and the date of his birth May 19, 1727 ; but the certificate of birth published by the *Gazzetta musicale di Milano* of 1879, No. 30, settles beyond question that he was the legitimate son of Filippo Traetta and Anna Teresta Piasanti, and that his date of birth was that given above.

At 11 years of age he became pupil of Durante at the ' Conservatorio di Santa Maria di Loreto ' at Naples, to which institution he belonged until the autumn of 1748, when we find him teaching singing, and occasionally writing some sacred music for several churches of Naples. Two years afterwards his first opera, ' Farnace,' produced at the San Carlo at Naples, Nov. 4, 1751, met with such success that he was forthwith commissioned to compose six more operas for the same house. Of these nothing is known, except the title of one, ' I pastori felici,' 1753 ; yet they were probably not less successful than ' Farnace,' since his

name spread rapidly, and he received engagements at Florence, Venice, Rome, Turin, Verona, Parma, etc. Goldoni and Metastasio did not disdain to write libretti for him ; Goldoni a comic opera ' Buovo d' Antona ' (Florence, 1756) ; and Metastasio ' L' Olimpiade ' (Verona, 1758). Towards the end of 1759 Traetta accepted the appointment of maestro di cappella and teacher of singing to the Princesses, offered to him by Don Filippo, Infanta of Spain, and Duke of Parma. The first opera he composed for the ducal theatre of Parma was ' Solimano ' (Carnival, 1759), followed in the spring by ' Ippolito ed Aricia.' This appears to have been a masterpiece, as both the Duke and the audience were exceedingly pleased with it, and on its reproduction six years later for the wedding of the Princess Maria Luisa with Charles III., King of Spain, a life pension was granted to the composer. In 1759 and 1760 Traetta went twice to Vienna to witness the performance of two operas purposely written for the Austrian capital, ' Ifigenia in Aulide ' (1759) and ' Armida ' (1760).

In 1765, after the death of the Duke, Traetta left Parma and settled in Venice, as principal of the ' Conservatorio dell' Ospedaletto.' He held the appointment for nearly three years, and resigned it on the invitation of Catherine II. of Russia, to succeed Galuppi as ' Maestro di Corte.' The severe climate of Russia, however, did not agree with the Italian maestro ; in 1775 he gave up his position, and accepted an engagement in London, where, however, he was not very successful, owing chiefly to the firm hold which Sacchini had taken of the English public. He accordingly returned to Naples, but the climate of Russia and the anxieties of London had impaired both his health and his genius, and the few operas he wrote before his death show that the spring of his imagination was dried up. He died in Venice and was buried in the church of Santa Maria Assunta, where the following epitaph is engraved on his tomb :

THOMAE TRAJETTA
BITUNTI NATO
SUBLIMIORIS MUSICES PERITISSIMO
HUJUS CHORI
AD AMPLITUDINEM ARTIS SUAE
INSTAURATORI MODERATORI
OPTIME MERITO
ANNO SALUTIS MDCCLXXIX
AETATIS SUAE LII
VITA FUNCTO
MONUMENTUM POSITUM.

Though Traetta was gifted with great intelligence, and his music is full of vigour and not wanting in a certain dramatic power, yet his works are now entirely forgotten.[1] Burney, Galvani, Grossi, Florimo and Clément all praise him, and Florimo even finds in him a tendency towards the same dramatic expression and dignity in the musical treatment of the libretto

---

[1] His name does not occur once in the programmes of the Philharmonic Society, and only once in all the three indexes of the *A.M.Z.*

that a few years afterwards made the name of Gluck immortal. However this may be, nobody can deny that Traetta had, as a man, a very peculiar character, an extraordinary estimation of his own talent, and an unusual readiness in making it clear to everybody : 'Traetta,' says Florimo,

'at the first performance of the operas, when presiding at the *clavicembalo*, as was customary at that time, convinced of the worth of his works, and persuaded of the special importance of some pieces—was in the habit of turning towards the audience and saying: "*Ladies and gentlemen, look sharp, and pay attention to this piece.*"'

LIST OF WORKS

OPERAS	
Farnace. Napoli, 1751.	with the Infanta Doña Isabella di Borbone, at Parma, Sept. 1761.
I pastori felici. Do. 1753.	
Ezio. Rome, 1754.	Il tributo campestre, 'componimento pastorale,' on the occasion of Maria Carolina of Austria, wife to Ferdinand IV. King of Sicily, passing through Mantua in 1768.
Le nozze contrastate. Do. 1754.	
L' incredulo. Napoli, 1755.	
La fante furba. Do. 1756.	
Buovo d' Antona. Firenza, 1756.	
Nitteti. Reggio, 1757.	In the same year he wrote an Oratorio, 'Salomone,' for the Conservatorio dell' Ospedaletto in Venice ; and about 1770 he wrote a 'divertimento for four orchestras' with the title 'Le quattro stagioni e i dodici mesi dellanno' (the four seasons and the twelve months of the year).[1]
Didone abbandonata. Venezia, 1757.	
Ifigenia in Tauride. 1758.	
Olimpiade. Verona, 1758.	
Solimano. Parma, 1759.	
Ippolito ed Aricia. Do. 1759.	
Ifigenia in Aulide. Vienna, 1759.	
Armida. Do. 1760.	
Sofonisba. Parma, 1760.	
Enea nel Lazio. Torino, 1760.	
I Tindaridi. Parma, 1760.	A Stabat Mater of his for four voices and accompaniment of several instruments is known, and was republished at Naples in 1878 ; and the Archives of the 'Real Collegio di Napoli' contain the following :
Enea e Lavinia. Do. 1761.	
Antigono. Padova, 1764.	
La francese a Malghera. Venezia, 1764.	
La buona figliuola maritata. Parma, 1765.	
La pace di Mercurio. 1765.	Lezione terza for soprano.
Semiramide. Venezia, 1765.	39 Arie (some with accompaniment of violin and basso, and some with accompaniment of several instruments).
Le serve rivali. Do. 1766.	
Amor in trappola. Do. 1768.	
L'isola disabitata. Bologna, 1768.	
Germondo. London, 1776.	7 Duetti.
Merope. Milano, 1776.	Aria, 'Terrore m' inspirava,' with pianoforte accompaniment.
Il cavaliere errante. Napoli, 1777.	
La disfatta di Dario. Venezia, 1778.	Aria, 'Ah ! consola il tuo dolore,' arranged for two violins, viola and basso.
Artenice. Do. 1778.	
Siroe, Lucio Vero, Il ritornale da Londra, and Astarto are undated. (See *Quellen-Lexikon*.)	A Canon, 'Sogno, ma te non miro,' for two soprani and basso.
	A Solfeggio, with pianoforte accompaniment.
Gli eroi dei Campi Elisi. Venezia, 1779. Written on the composer's death-bed, and finished by Gennaro Astaritta.	A cantata for soprano and instruments, 'Dei, qual mi sorprende,' is in the State Library at Berlin, and a 'Hymn to the Creator' (published) is in the British Museum.
Le feste d' Imeneo, a prologue and trilogy, viz. Il trionfo d' Amore, Triole, Saffo, and Egle, for the wedding of the Archduke Joseph of Austria	

G. M.

TRAÎNÉE, name of an *agrément* of the French School, also called Chute (see ORNAMENTS).   E. B^L.

TRAINING SCHOOL FOR MUSIC, THE NATIONAL, see NATIONAL TRAINING SCHOOL FOR MUSIC ; ROYAL COLLEGE OF MUSIC.

TRAIT, an ornament of the French School. It differs from the COULADE (*q.v.*) in that all the notes are articulated in the trait, in contrast with the slur in the coulade. The trait comprises, moreover, all kinds of *diminutions* (see DIMINUTION, 3) improvised by the executant. (See ORNAMENTS.)   E. B^L.

TRAMIDAMENTE. This strange direction, with *ängstlich* below it as its German equivalent, is found at the recitative with the trumpets in the 'Agnus' of Beethoven's Mass in D, in

[1] This composition is mentioned in a letter dated Dec. 21-3, 1770, written by Catherine II. of Russia to Voltaire.

the old score (Schott). In Breitkopf & Härtel's edition it appears as 'timidamente,' which is good Italian, and is the translation of 'ängstlich '—with distress.   G.

TRANQUILLO, an Italian term, meaning 'calmly,' 'quietly.'   G.

TRANSCRIPTION, see ARRANGEMENT.

TRANSFORMATION OF THEMES, see METAMORPHOSIS.

TRANSITION is a musical term which has several different senses. It is most commonly used in a vague way as synonymous with modulation. Some writers, wishing to limit it more strictly, use it for the actual moment of passage from one key to another ; and again it is sometimes used to distinguish those short subordinate flights out of one key into another, which are so often met with in modern music, from the more prominent and deliberate changes of key which form an important feature in the structure of a movement. The following example from Beethoven's sonata in B♭, op. 106, is an illustration of the process defined by this latter meaning of the term ; the transition being from F♯ minor to G major and back :

etc.

See MODULATION.   C. H. H. P.

TRANSPOSING INSTRUMENTS. This is a name often given to those wind instruments for which, for the sake of the player's convenience in reading, the parts are written in one key while the instrument sounds in another. Players of the clarinet, cor anglais, horn and trumpet, among the ordinary orchestral instruments, are required to play from parts which indicate the physical production of certain notes, not their accurate sound.   M.

TRANSPOSING KEYBOARDS. The difficulties of transposition at the keyboard seem early to have prompted the alternative of a shifting keyboard, applied in the first instance to the diatonic arrangement of the keys, which in the 16th century was still to be met with in old organs : in other words, whatever the key might be, to play apparently in C. The oldest authority on the organ extant is the blind organist of Heidelberg, Arnold Schlick, who in 1511 published the *Spiegel der Orgelmacher und Organisten*, of which only one copy is now

known to exist.[1] Schlick is quoted by Sebastian
Virdung, who also published his book in 1511,
and (2nd cap. p. 19, Berlin reprint, p. 87) has
an interesting passage on transposing organs,
which we will freely translate.

' When an organ in itself tuned to the right pitch can
be shifted a tone higher or lower, it is a great advantage to both organist and singers. I have heard
years ago of a Positive so made, but I only know of
one complete organ, and that one I use daily, which
together with its positive, two back manuals, pedals,
and all its many and rare registers, may be shifted
higher and back again as often as necessity requires.
For chapels and singers ad Cantum Mensurabilem
such a contrivance is specially useful. Two masses
or Magnificats may be in the same tone, and set in the
same notation of line and space, and yet it may be
desirable to sing the one a note higher than the other.
Say both masses are in the Sixth Tone with Clef C ;
the counter bass going an octave lower [2]—in the other
the counter bass goes a note or more lower, to B or
A,[3] which are too low for bass singers, and their
voices heard against others would be too weak, if
it were not possible to sing the part a note higher.
Now in the first mass the counter bass in C can be
played on an organ as set, but the other demands
transposition to D, with the semitones F♯ and C♯,
which to those who have not practised it is hard and
impossible. So therefore, with an organ, as described,
the organist may go on playing in C (C-sol fa-ut)
on the keyboard, although the pipes are in D
(D-la-sol-re).'[4]

We may assume that in course of time the
increasing skill of organists rendered mechanical transpositions unnecessary, since for the
organ we hear no more about them ; but for
the harpsichord they were to be met with in
the 16th and following centuries. Praetorius
(A.D. 1619) speaks of transposing clavicymbals
(harpsichords) which by shifting the keyboard
could be set two notes higher or lower, and
describes a ' Universal-Clavicymbal ' capable
of gradual transposition by semitones to the
extent of a fifth. Burney in his musical tour
met with two transposing harpsichords ; one
a German one, made under the direction of
Frederick the Great, at Venice ; the other (a
Spanish one, also with movable keys) at
Bologna, belonging to Farinelli.[5]

The transposing harpsichord mentioned by
Burney as belonging to Count Torre Taxis of
Venice, had also a pianoforte stop, a combination in vogue at the time it was made, 1760.
A German pianoforte with movable keyboard
was made for the Prince of Prussia in 1786,
and about the same period Sébastien Erard constructed an ' organised ' pianoforte, another
favoured combination of the latter half of the
18th century, which transposed a semitone,
whole tone, or minor third each way, to suit
the limited voice of Marie Antoinette. Roller
of Paris is also said to have made transposing
pianos.

[1] Reprinted in the M. f. M. Berlin, 1869 ; edited with explanatory
notes by Robert Eitner.
[2] To the C, second space of the bass clef, but evidently, as will be
obvious, sounding the F lower.
[3] In our pitch the double E and D.
[4] This very difficult passage in the quaint original has been
rendered from an elucidatory footnote by the editor, Eitner.
[5] See A. J. Hipkins, History of the Pianoforte, pp. 87, 88, for a
description of the late Sir Bernard Samuelson's interesting Ruckers
harpsichord. Also p. 83, for Van Blankenburg's account of such
transpositions.

The most prominent instances of transposing
pianofortes made in England in the 19th century are the following : (1) The square piano of
Edward Ryley, patented in 1801, and acting
by a false keyboard, which was placed above
the true one, and could be shifted to any semitone in the octave. Ryley's idea as stated in
his specification went back to the original one
of playing everything in the so-called natural
scale of C. The patent for this complete trans-
poser was bought by John and James Broadwood, and an instrument so made is in the
possession of the present firm. (2) The Royal
Albert Transposing piano, brought out by
Addison & Co. soon after the marriage of Queen
Victoria, a piccolo or cottage instrument, is
described by Rimbault in his History of the
Pianoforte as having the keys divided at half
their length, the front and back ends being
capable of moving independently of each other.
(3) Broadwood's transposing Boudoir Cottage
pianos, made about 1845, displayed the novel
feature of the instrument itself moving while
the keyboard and action were stationary. In
some of their pianos made in this way, the instrument was suspended between two pivoted
metal supporters which allowed the gradual
movement, semitone by semitone, effected by
turning a pin at the side with an ordinary
tuning hammer. Subsequently the instrument
was moved in a groove at the top and on two
wheels at the bottom of the outer fixed case,
but neither contrivance was patented, nor
was long continued to be made. (4) Another
attempt at transposing by the keyboard was
brought forward in 1884 by Hermann Wagner
of Stuttgart. He names his invention ' Trans-
ponir-Pianino.'[6] (5) The last transposing contrivance to be mentioned is the ' Transpositeur '
of Pleyel, Wolff et Cie of Paris, invented by
Auguste Wolff in 1873. The Transpositeur
being an independent false keyboard, could be
applied to any pianoforte by any maker. It
was patented and sold by the Pleyel firm in
Paris and London at a moderate price.

A. J. H.

TRANSPOSITION, change of key, the notation or performance of a musical composition in a different key from that in which it is
written.

In order to transpose a phrase, each note
must be written, sung or played a certain fixed
distance higher or lower, that it may occupy the
same position in the new scale that it held at
first in the original one. Thus Exs. 2 and 3 are
transpositions of Ex. 1, one being a major second
higher, and the other a major second lower ;
and the notes of the original phrase being
numbered, to show their position as degrees of
the scale, it will be seen that this position
remains unchanged in the transpositions.

[6] Zeitschrift für Instrumentenbau, Band 4, No. 12 (Leipzig
Jan. 12 1884).

1.   Original Key C.

2.   Transposed into D.

3.   Transposed into B♭.

It is, however, not necessary that a transposition should be fully written out, as above. By sufficient knowledge and practice a performer is enabled to transpose a piece of music into any required key, while still reading from the original notation. To the singer such a proceeding offers no particular difficulty, since the relation of the various notes to the key-note being understood, the absolute pitch of the latter, which is all that has to be kept in mind, does not matter. But to the instrumental performer the task is by no means an easy one, since the transposition frequently requires a totally different position of the fingers. This arises from the fact that in transposition it often happens that a natural has to be represented by a sharp or flat, and *vice versa*, as may be seen in the above examples, where the B♮ of Ex. 1, bar 2, being the 7th degree of the scale becomes C♯ which is the 7th degree of the scale of D, in Ex. 2 ; and again in bar 3, where F♯, the 4th degree, becomes E♭ in Ex. 3. The change of a flat to a sharp, though possible, is scarcely practical. It could only occur in an extreme key, and even then could always be avoided by making an enharmonic change, so that the transposed key should be more nearly related to the original ; for example :

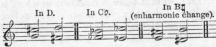

In D.   In C♭.   In B♮ (enharmonic change).

Hence it will not suffice to read each note of a phrase so many degrees higher or lower on the stave ; in addition to this, the relation which every note bears to the scale must be thoroughly understood, and reproduced in the transposition by means of the necessary sharps, flats or naturals ; while the pianist or organist, who has to deal with many sounds at once, must be able also instantly to recognise the various harmonies and modulations, and to construct the same in the new key.

The faculty of transposition is extremely valuable to the practical musician. To the conductor, or to any one desiring to play from orchestral score, it is essential, as the parts for the so-called 'transposing instruments'—horns, trumpets, clarinets—being written in a different key from that in which they are to sound, have to be transposed back into the key of the piece, so as to agree with the strings and other non-transposing instruments. (See SCORE.) Orchestral players and accompanists are frequently called upon to transpose, in order to accommodate the singer, for whose voice the written pitch of the song may be too high or too low, but it is probably extremely seldom that transposition takes place on so grand a scale as when Beethoven, having to play his concerto in C major, and finding the piano half a tone too flat, transposed the whole into C♯ major ; or the scarcely less remarkable feat of Brahms, who, as a young man, playing with the violinist Remenyi, and finding the piano at Celle at too low a pitch to suit the violinist, transposed Beethoven's C minor sonata into C♯ minor.

Transposed editions of songs are frequently published, that the same compositions may be made available for voices of different compass, but transpositions of instrumental music more rarely.   F. T.

TRANSPOSITION OF THE ECCLESIASTICAL MODES. By means of the B♭ which was available for use in the ancient scale derived from the Greeks (see GREEK MUSIC ; MODES ; MONOCHORD), a melody could be written in a transposed position either a fourth above or a fifth below. This liberty was employed particularly in the case of melodies of the second mode that ranged low. It was also employed in order to get chromatic effects. For example, fourth mode melodies were set a fourth higher, and could use both B♭ and B♮ as the note above their final. See, for example, the antiphon analysed at the end of the article ANTIPHON. To a limited extent other transposition was utilised. A melody could be transposed a fifth higher without change so long as the note fourth above its final did not occur. In some cases even with such a note occurring the transposition was made, and thus the effect was obtained of an F♯.

But all such statements as the above must be made and taken with great caution because of the uncertainty that prevails as to the theory that originally governed the composition of early plain-song and as to possible changes which the melodies may have undergone in transmission. In a case like that last mentioned, for example, the F♯ effect may be regarded as a primitive feature which it has happily been possible to retain, in spite of the restricted possibilities of the plain-song scale, by the expedient of transposition : or it may be regarded as a curious perversion which has come about as the melody has been handed down from mouth to mouth : or it may be regarded as a bold venture of a composer who saw his way to secure an effect which pleased him though it did not fall in with the strict theory of his art.   W. H. F.

Composers of the polyphonic period made use

of the legitimate liberty of transposing which the B♭ afforded. During the transitional period—but very rarely earlier than that—a double transposition was effected, in a few exceptional cases, by means of two flats; B♭ raising the pitch a fourth, and E♭ lowering it, from thence, by a fifth—thus really depressing the original pitch by a tone. A beautiful example will be found in Wilbye's 'Flora gave me fairest flowers,' composed in 1598; yet Morley, writing in 1597, severely condemns the practice.

W. S. R.

TRASUNTINO, VITO, a Venetian harpsichord-maker, who made an enharmonic (quarter-tone) archicembalo or large harpsichord for Camillo Gonzaga, Conte di Novellara, in 1606, now preserved in the Museum of the Liceo Communale at Bologna. It was made after the invention of Don Nicola Vicentino, an enthusiast who tried to restore Greek music according to its three genera, the diatonic, chromatic and enharmonic, and published the results of his attempt at Rome in 1555, under the title of *L' antica musica ridotta alla moderna prattica.* From engravings in this work illustrating a keyboard invented to include the three systems, Trasuntino contrived his instrument. A photograph of it is in the South Kensington Museum. It had one keyboard of four octaves C–C, with white naturals; the upper or usual sharps and flats being divided into four alternately black and white, each division being an independent key. There are short upper keys also between the natural semitones, once divided, which makes thirty-two keys in the octave; 125 in all. Trasuntino made a Tetracorda, also preserved at Bologna, with intervals marked off to tune the archicembalo by—an old pitch-measurer or quadruple monochord. When Fétis[1] noticed Trasuntino, the archicembalo was in the possession of Baini. It was not the first keyboard instrument with enharmonic intervals; Vicentino had an organ built, about 1561, by Vicenzo Colombo of Venice. There is a broadsheet describing it quoted by Fétis as obtained by him from Signor Gaspari of Bologna.

<small>'Descrizione dell' arciorgano, nel quale si possono eseguire i tri generi della musica, diatonica, cromatica, ed enarmonica,' in Venetia, appresso Niccolo Bevil'acqua, 1561, a di 25 ottobrio.</small>

A harpsichord dated 1559, made by a Trasuntini, is cited by Giordano Riccati ('Delle corde ovvero fibre elastiche'), and was probably by Vito's father, perhaps the Giulio Trasuntino referred to by Thomas Garzoni ('Piazza universale di tutte le professioni del mondo,' Discorso 136) as excellent in all 'istrumenti da penna'—quilled instruments, such as harpsichords, manichords, clavicembalos and cithers. A harpsichord[2] by Alexander Trasuntino, dated 1531, is in the Donaldson Museum,

<small>[1] *Biographie universelle,* 1865, p. 250.
[2] The instrument is engraved in A. J. Hipkins's *History of the Pianoforte,* p. 76.</small>

R.C.M. This maker may have been the grandfather of Vito Trasuntino. Of Vito, Fioravanti[3] says:

'Guido [or Vito] Trasuntino was a man of much and learned experience in the art of making harpsichords, clavicembalos, organs and regals, so that his instruments were admired by every one before all others, and other instruments he improved, as might be seen in many places in Venice.'

These citations are rendered from Fétis. 'Manicordo,' as in the original, is the clavichord. It is doubtful whether 'arpicordi' and 'clavicembali' here distinguish upright and horizontal harpsichords, or harpsichords and spinets.

A. J. H.

TRAUER-WALZER, *i.e.* Mourning-waltz, a composition of Schubert's (op. 9, No. 2), dating from the year 1816,

which would not be noticed here but for the fact that it is often attributed to Beethoven, under whose name a 'Sehnsuchts-walzer,' best known as 'Le Désir' (first of a set of ten all with romantic titles), compounded from Schubert's waltz and Himmel's 'Favoritwalzer,' was published by Schott in 1826. Schubert's op. 9 was issued by Cappi and Diabelli, Nov. 29, 1821, so that there is no doubt to whom it belongs. The waltz was much played before publication, and got its title independently of Schubert. In fact, on one occasion, hearing it so spoken of, he said, 'Who could be such an ass to write a *mourning-waltz*?' (Spaun's *Memoir,* MS.) Schubert's Waltz is a perfect type of a German 'Deutsch.' (See TEUTSCH.)

G.

TRAUTMANN, MARIE, see JAELL, Alfred.

TRAVERS, JOHN (*b. circa* 1703; *d.* June 1758) began his musical education as a chorister of St. George's Chapel, Windsor, where he attracted the attention of Dr. Godolphin, Dean of St. Paul's Cathedral and Provost of Eton College, by whom he was placed with Maurice Greene as an articled pupil. He soon afterwards made the acquaintance of Dr. Pepusch, who assisted him in his studies to his great advantage. About 1725 he was appointed organist of St. Paul's, Covent Garden, and subsequently organist of Fulham Church. On May 10, 1737, he was sworn in organist of the

<small>[3] *Specchio di scientia universale,* fol. 273.</small>

Chapel Royal in the room of Jonathan Martin, deceased, upon which he relinquished his place at Fulham. He composed much church music : his well-known Service in F, a Te Deum in D, and two anthems were printed by Arnold, and another anthem by Page ; others are in MS. in the books of the Chapel Royal. He published about 1750 ' The Whole Book of Psalms for one, two, three, four and five voices, with a thorough bass for the harpsichord,' 2 vols. fol. But the work by which he is best known is his ' Eighteen Canzonets for two and three voices, the words chiefly by Matthew Prior,' which enjoyed a long career of popularity, and two of which—' Haste, my Nanette,' and ' I, my dear, was born to-day '—are still occasionally heard. The canzonet ' I, like a bee ' enjoyed an even longer popularity. A set of ' XII voluntaries for the organ or harpsichord ' was published after his death. An autograph MS. by him, containing four melodies in some of the ancient Greek modes, for four voices with instrumental accompaniments, the fruit, doubtless, of his association with Pepusch, is amongst Dr. Cooke's MS. collections now in the R.C.M. Upon the death of Dr. Pepusch he became the possessor, by bequest, of one-half of the Doctor's valuable library.   W. H. H.

TRAVERSO, see FLUTE.

TRAVIATA, LA, opera in 4 acts ; libretto by Piave (founded on ' La Dame aux camélias '), music by Verdi. Produced Teatro Fenice, Venice, Mar. 6, 1853 ; New York, Academy of Music, Dec. 3, 1856 ; Théâtre Italien, Paris, Dec. 6, 1856 ; Her Majesty's Theatre, May 24, 1856 ; in English, Surrey Theatre, June 8, 1857.   G.

TREBELLI (GILBERT [1]), ZELIA (b. Paris, 1838 ; d. Étretat, Aug. 18, 1892), an operatic singer who took the public by storm, and stepped early into the high position which she maintained until her death.

She was taught the piano at the age of 6. Guided by her German teacher, she learnt to reverence and enjoy the works of Bach and Beethoven. After ten years her wish for instruction in singing was encouraged by her parents, who only thought thereby to add one other graceful accomplishment to those which were to render their daughter useful and acceptable in society. The services of Wartel were secured, and so delighted was he with his clever pupil that he never rested until he had persuaded her parents to allow of his training her for the lyric stage. Five years of close study prepared for her début, which was made at Madrid as Mlle. Trebelli, under the most favourable circumstances and with complete success, Mario playing Almaviva to her Rosina, in ' Il barbiere.'

Trebelli's appearances in the opera-houses of Germany in 1860–61 were a series of brilliant

1 ' Trebelli ' is obviously intended as the reverse of Gillebert.

triumphs. Public and critics were alike carried away by enthusiasm when they heard her rendering of the parts of Rosina, Arsaee, Orsini, Urbano, Azucena and others. No member of Merelli's Italian troupe was gifted with so brilliant a voice and so much executive power. Nor could the audiences fail to be impressed by the actress's varied powers so rarely at the command of one individual, Trebelli expressing at one time the fire of an almost manly vigour, and at another the charm of womanly tenderness and delicacy. The German criticisms which declared the voice a contralto, comparing it with Alboni's in quality and with Schechner's in power, were not supported by English opinions. As a mezzo-soprano, its brilliancy, power and flexibility were appreciatively noticed ; the artist's control over voice and action enthusiastically praised. Trebelli appeared first in London at Her Majesty's Theatre, May 6, 1862, as Orsini in ' Lucrezia.' ' A more encouraging reception has seldom been awarded to a débutante.' From that time she was a recognised favourite with our opera and concert audiences. Those who were familiar with her appearances in frequent co-operation with Mlle. Tietjens in the chief Italian operas, will not easily forget the performances of Oberon, where Trebelli's impersonation of the captive, Fatima, was invested with peculiar charm. More recent and more widely known was her intelligent and refined impersonation of Carmen, though it lacked the vivid animalism now preferred.

In 1884 Madame Trebelli made a tour through the United States with Mr. Abbey's troupe. Her marriage to Bettini, about 1863, was, in a few years, followed by a separation. Her last appearance in England was at Mapleson's benefit concert in the Albert Hall in June 1889, when she was already ill. Her daughter, Antoinette Trebelli, had a considerable success at first under her own name, from about 1889, and subsequently, as Antonia Dolores, won a place among the most artistic singers of the day.   L. M. M.

TREBLE (BELL). The bells of a ' ring ' or ' peal ' are numbered, beginning with 1 for the smallest, which is called the ' treble,' and continuing 2, 3, 4, etc., to the largest, called the ' tenor.' The smaller bells are sometimes described as ' trebles.' Other than the treble and tenor the bells are known by their numerical places in the peal.   W. W. S.

TREBLE CLEF, the sign for the treble clef, 𝄞, is a modification of the letter G. For the earlier forms of this sign see CLEF. The double G clef, 𝄞𝄞, indicates that the music is to be sung an octave lower than written. (See TENOR.)

TREBLE (Ital. *canto*; Ger. *Diskant*; Fr. *dessus*), a general term applied to the highest voices in a chorus or other concerted vocal piece, and to the upper parts in concerted instrumental music; also to soprano voices generally. The treble clef is the G clef on the second line of the upper (our treble) stave; the eighth line of the great stave of eleven lines (*chiave di sol, chiave di violino*; *clef de sol*) (see CLEF).

Its etymology does not refer it to any special class of voice. It is generally held to be a corruption of triplum, a third part superadded to the altus and bassus (high and low) (see MOTET). At what time 'treble' may have found its way into English it is difficult to say. 'Childish treble,' as the voice of old age, appears in Shakespeare, and 'faint treble' used to be applied to what is commonly known as falsetto.　　　　　　　　　　　H. C. D.

TREBLE OR DESCANT VIOL, see VIOL (3).

TREE, ANN MARIA (b. London, Aug. 1801 or 1802; d. there, Queen's Gate Terrace, Feb. 17, 1862), was taught singing by Lanza and Tom Cooke. After singing in the chorus at Drury Lane, where her elder sister (afterwards Mrs. Quin) was a popular dancer, she was engaged at Bath, where she appeared as Polly in 'The Beggar's Opera,' Nov. 13, 1818. She made her début at Covent Garden as Rosina in 'The Barber of Seville,' Sept. 10, 1819; she made a great success as Luciana, in Reynold's and Bishop's operatic adaptation of 'The Comedy of Errors,' Dec. 11, 1819. She became a popular performer in other Shakespearean parts (original or adapted)—Viola, Nov. 8, 1820; Julia, Nov. 29, 1821; Imogen, June 19, 1822; Rosalind, Dec. 10, 1824. Her principal new parts were Louison in 'Henri Quatre,' Apr. 22, 1820; Zaide in the younger Colman's 'Law of Java,' May 11, 1822; Lady Matilda in Bishop's 'Maid Marian,' adapted by Planché from Peacock's novel, Dec. 3, 1822; Clari the Maid of Milan, in Payne's operatic play, wherein she originally sang 'Home, sweet Home,' May 8, 1823 (see BISHOP, Sir Henry). On May 21 of the same year she played Viola to the Olivia of her younger sister Ellen, afterwards Mrs. Charles Kean, and on the same evening sang Susanna in a mutilated version of 'The Marriage of Figaro,' to the Cherubino of another sister, afterwards the wife of John Philip Chapman. On Nov. 26, 1824, she sang as Matilda in 'The Frozen Lake,' an adaptation of Auber's 'Neige,' produced two months previously. On June 15, 1825, she took a farewell benefit as Clari, and as Mary Copp in Payne and Bishop's 'Charles II.' originally played by her the year before. She married James Bradshaw, afterwards member for Canterbury, Aug. 15, 1825. Chorley described her as a singer with a cordial, expressive mezzo-soprano voice, and much real feeling.　　A. C.

TREGIAN, FRANCIS, see VIRGINAL MUSIC, p. 546.

TRE GIORNI SON CHE NINA. See CIAMPI.

TREIBENREIF, see TRITONIUS, PETRUS.

TREMBLEMENT, the name of an ornament of the French school (see ORNAMENTS and SHAKE).　　　　　　　　　　　　E. BL.

TREMOLO (Ital.). The term is properly applied to the rapid reiteration of a single note or chord without regard to measured time values.

(1) INSTRUMENTAL.—(a) It is an important effect on all stringed instruments played with the bow which by rapid up and down movement achieves the true tremolo most readily.

In string music it is noted thus [♪] with the word *tremolo, tremolando* (*trem*) added to distinguish between it and the reiteration according to time values.[1]

(b) The wind instruments cannot produce the *tremolo*, but the drum roll (see DRUM) is actually a *tremolo*.

(c) The effect is obtained on keyboard instruments, more especially the pianoforte, by a shake in octaves or on two or more notes of a chord, with the use of the sustaining pedal. A similar device is used where string *tremoli* are transferred to wind instruments, especially clarinets in arrangements of orchestral music for military band.

(2) VOCAL.—The production of the true tremolo (rapid reiteration of a note without variation of pitch) is one of the most difficult technical feats of the singer. But here terminology has become confused, and this, as it appears in such ornaments as Caccini's *trillo* (see ORNAMENTS, VOCAL, also the quotation from Playford under SHAKE), is generally known as VIBRATO (*q.v.*). On the other hand, the term tremolo is commonly applied to a wavering of pitch in sustaining a single note which corresponds to the string player's vibrato. Both have been used as legitimate means of expression, but the second, since it often appears as the result of technical incompetence, is peculiarly liable to abuse.　　　　　　　　　　　　　　　C.

TREMULANT, a contrivance in the organ producing the same effect as *tremolando* in singing.

The air before reaching the pipes is admitted into a box containing a pallet to the end of which is attached a thin arm of metal with a weight on the end of it; when the air on its admission raises the pallet the metal arm begins to swing up and down, thus producing alternately an increase and diminution of wind-

---

[1] The shake on two notes of a chord thus [♪] is spoken of as the fingered tremolo.

pressure. Its use is generally limited to such stops as the vox humana and a few other stops chiefly of the reed family. The tremulant is happily much less in vogue in this country than on the Continent, where its abuse is simply offensive. It is difficult to conceive how good taste can tolerate these rhythmical pulsations of a purely mechanical pathos.   J. S.

TRENCHMORE, an old English country dance frequently mentioned by writers of the 16th and 17th century. According to Chappell (*Popular Music*) the earliest mention of it is in a Morality by William Bulleyn, published in 1564. The character of the dance may be gathered from the following amusing quotation from Selden's *Table Talk* (1689) [1] :

'The Court of *England* is much altered. At a solemn Dancing, first you had the grave Measures, then the Corrantoes and the Galliards, and this is kept up with Ceremony ; at length to *Trenchmore*, and the Cushion-Dance, and then all the Company dance, Lord and Groom, Lady and Kitchen-Maid, no distinction. So in our Court, in Queen *Elizabeth's* time, Gravity and State were kept up. In King *James's* time things were pretty well. But in King *Charles's* time there has been nothing but *Trenchmore*, and the Cushion-Dance, *omnium gatherum* tolly-polly, hoite come toite.'

Trenchmore appears first in the *Dancing Master* in the fifth edition (1675), where it is directed to be danced ' longways for as many as will.' The tune there given (which we reprint) occurs in *Deuteromelia* (1609), where it is called ' To-morrow the fox will come to town.'

W. B. S.

TRENTO, VITTORIO (*b.* Venice, 1761 or 1765), composer, pupil of Bertoni, and composer of ballets. His first, ' Mastino della Scala ' (1785), was successful enough to procure him commissions from various towns. A drama in two acts, ' La finta ammalata,' was given at Florence in 1793. He was induced by Dragonetti to come to London, and there he composed the immensely popular ' Triumph of Love ' (Drury Lane, 1797). His first opera-buffa, ' Teresa Vedova,' succeeded, and was followed by many others. In 1804 he composed ' Ifigenia in Aulide.' In 1806 he became impresario in Amsterdam, and there produced with great success an oratorio, ' The Deluge ' (1808). Soon afterwards he went to Lisbon, also as impresario. His ' Climene,' the MS. score of which is in the British Museum, was given in 1811 for Catalani's benefit (*Q.-L.*). In 1824 he returned to Venice, and after that his name disappears. He composed about ten ballets, twenty operas, and a few oratorios,

[1] Written in the reign of Charles I., some fifty years before publication.

one being the ' Maccabees.' His scores are in the collection of Ricordi of Milan.   F. G.

TRÉSOR DES PIANISTES, LE. A remarkable collection of ancient and modern pianoforte music, made and edited by Madame FARRENC (*q.v.*), and published part by part by Leduc of Paris, from June 1861–72. Farrenc contributed some of the biographical notices to the work, but his death in 1865 prevented his having any large share in it ; the rest of the biographies were written by Fétis, jun. The collection has been since superseded by separate publications and more thorough editing.   G.

TRÉSOR MUSICAL, a collection of music edited by Robert van MALDEGHEM (*q.v.*), whose researches in the monasteries and libraries of the Continent, including the Vatican, were made with the encouragement of the Belgian Government, and rescued from obscurity many works of the old Flemish and Belgian composers. Every year since 1865 saw the publication, in a magnificent edition, by Musquardt, Brussels, of two books (' Musique religieuse, Musique profane ') of the series, which was completed in 1893, in which year an index-volume was advertised. In the following index the more usual forms of certain composers' names are preferred to those given in Maldeghem's list.[2]

ANONYMOUS OR DOUBTFUL		
Sacred		
a 4 :		
Ave Regina Coelorum	1880	29
Pange lingua	,,	32
O Dulcis	,,	44
Laus Deo	,,	35
Beata Immaculata	1881	35
Felix Anna (2 parts)	1884	10
a 6 :		
Ave Maris stella	1880	36
Secular		
Song, La Buissonnette	1883	9
Duet (for 2 basses)	1882	21
a 3. Partsongs :		
Toutes les nuits	1877	38
On ne peut	,,	39
Pour ung jamais	1887	7
Tous nobles cueurs	,,	11
A vous mon aultre	,,	13
Va-t-en, regret	,,	15
Se je souspère	,,	19
Ce povre mendiant	,,	21
O dévots	,,	23
L'heure est venue	,,	25
Despitant fortune	,,	27
Je ne scay plus	,,	29
J'ay mis mon cueur	1888	5
Triste suis	,,	8
Ne vous chaille	,,	14
L'hirondelle	1877	40
Ghequetst ben ic	1878	10
a 4 :		
Mijn hertken	1875	41
Il me sufit	1878	14
Bon homme vieil	1879	23
Mais qui est celui	,,	24
Dans son château	,,	25
Le mois de Mai	,,	28
De la nuit le doux flambeau	,,	30
Que serviront grands-thrésors	,,	38
Soupirs ardents	,,	40
Par le moyen	1880	12
Les forts	,,	14
Femme de sens	,,	15
O mère des flatteurs	,,	16
Aussi n'est rien	,,	16
L'âme est le feu	,,	18
La médiocrité	,,	19

Qui vers le ciel	1880	20
Par les sentiers	,,	21
Chacun court	,,	28
Page du roi	,,	30
Ce grand Dieu	,,	32
Or tout plaisir	,,	34
La vertu précieuse	,,	35
La volupté	,,	37
Aux uns il fait	,,	39
Or, quand la mort	,,	40
Tout sceptre	,,	41
Aussi n'est il blason	,,	42
Le corps malsein	,,	43
Au fond des bois	,,	45
Où planterai-je	,,	46
Celui ne s'aime en rien	,,	48
Infame	,,	50
Quand plus un homme	1881	4
Nos jours	,,	5
De peut de bien	,,	6
Biens successifs	,,	10
Car à la vertu	,,	12
O bien heureux	,,	13
Entre mille vertus	,,	14
L'honneur	,,	15
Bien heureux	,,	16
Le corps malsein	,,	18
Si je me plains	,,	20
Heil aen den Mensch	1882	3
O qu'à bon droit	,,	8
O bien heureux	,,	10
Ib. (transposed)	,,	11
Celui est fol	,,	12
L'âme n'endure	,,	13
Tout ce qui est	,,	16
Soit que le ciel	,,	18
Il est donc vrai	1883	3
O trop Ingrat !	,,	4
O doux printemps	,,	7
De sin verblijd	,,	11
Sainte Barbe	,,	14
Un visage	,,	16
Mon cœur couvert	,,	18
Réjouissez-vous	,,	20
Vous marchez	1884	3
Ah mon Dieu	,,	6
Vignons, vignettes	,,	13
Amor che deggio	,,	14
Entrée suis	1886	8
Changier ne veulx	,,	21
Plaine de deuil	1887	3
Hélas seray-je	1888	11
a 6 :		
Je ne dis mot	,,	1

[2] The volumes are numbered merely by the date of publication, as in the following list, where the last column of figures indicates the page of the volume. The division into Sacred and Secular is not strictly observed : the words in this list are used for convenience of reference simply.

AGRICOLA, ALEXANDER

Sacred

a 4 :
Nobis sancte Spiritus . 1867 19
Sancte Philippe . . „ 21
Salve Regina . . 1893 1

a 5 :
Haec dies . . . 1867 25

Secular

a 3 :
Sur tous regrets . 1875 46

a 4 :
Si vous m'aimez . „ 43
Misérable . . . „ 47
Il est bien . . . 1885 15
Belle, pour l'amour . 1888 18

ARCADELT, JACOB

Sacred

a 4 :
Ave Maria . . . 1866 23

a 5 :
O sacrum . . . 1884 3

Secular

a 3 :
Quand je compasse . 1874 46
Sincérité . . . „ 47
Si j'ai deux serviteurs „ 48
Si l'on pouvait . . „ 49
Tout le désir . . „ 50
Soupirs ardans . . „ 51

a 4 :
Il bianco e dolce cigno 1889 9
Voi ce n'endare al cielo „ 12
Quanta bella . . „ 16
Ahi se la donna mia . „ 19
Io dico che . . 1890 1
Ancidete mi . . „ 4
Dunque credete . . „ 7
Chi potrà dir . . „ 10
Deh dimmi amor . . „ 13
Non ch' io non voglio „ 16
Quant' è Madonna . „ 19
Felice me . . . „ 21
Giovinetta real . . „ 24
Amor tu sai . . „ 27
Lodar voi donne . 1891 1
Deh come pur' al fin . „ 4
Os' io potessi . . „ 7
Che più foco al mio . „ 10
Se vi place Signora . „ 13
Il ciel che rado virtu „ 16
Bella Fioretta . . „ 19
S' il tuo partir . . „ 22
Non v' accorgete . „ 25
Quanti travagli . . „ 28
Se per colpa . . 1892 2
Sapete amanti . . „ 4
Ahi me . . . „ 6
Vero infern' è il mio
petto. . . . „ 9
Quand' io penso . „ 12

BASTON, JOSQUIN

Secular

a 6 :
Déploration de Lupus 1876 3

BARRA. [See HOTIN]

BENEDICTUS. [See HERTOGHS]

BERCHEM, JACOB VAN

Sacred

a 4 :
O Jesu Christe . . 1865 12
Noë (2 parts) . . 1881 36
Ecclesiam tuam . „ 40
Sabbato Sancto . „ 42
Veni Sancte Spiritus . „ 47

Secular

a 5 :
Dat ick mocht . . 1875 25
Gy nachtegael . . „ 29

a 4 :
L'aultre jour . . 1888 20

BERGHE, VAN DEN. [See MONTE]

BISSCHOP. [See EPISCOPIUS]

BRUMEL, ANTON

Sacred

a 4 :
O Domine Jesu Christe 1866 43
Laudate Dominum . 1875 4
Mass (Kyrie, Gloria,
Credo, Sanctus) . 1874 35
Agnus Dei of the same 1875 3

Secular

a 4 :
Ach gheldeloos . . 1874 45

BULTEL, JACOBUS

Sacred

a 5 :
O lux et Deus . . 1892 14

CABILLIAU

Secular

a 4 :
L'an et le mois . . 1882 14

CLAUDE. [See LE JEUNE]

CLEMENS, NON PAPA

Sacred

a 5 :
Ave Verum . . . 1884 6

Secular

a 4 :
Doux Rossignol . 1865 14
Je prends en gré . 1878 30
Ib. (transposed) . „ 32

CLEVE, JOANNES DE

Sacred

a 5 :
Mass, Tribulatio . 1879 3

a 6 :
Mass, Dum transisset
Sabbatum . . 1878 15

a 4 :
Doctor bonus (2 parts) 1877 8
Ego sum via „ „ 12
Filiae Jerusalem „ „ 16
In nomine Jesu . 1878 3
Miserere mei . . „ 46
Adjuva nos . . „ 50
Convertimini . . 1879 29
Gregem tuum . . „ 32
Impia. . . . „ 35
Deus quis similia (2
parts) . . . „ 38

a 5 :
Regina coeli . . 1877 3
Tribulatio . . . „ 21
Gaudeamus . . „ 25
Doctor bonus (2 parts) „ 29
Domine Jesu . . „ 35
Domino clamavi „ . „ 39
Inter natos mulierum
(2 parts) . . 1879 47
Timete (2 parts) . 1880 3
Inclina . . . „ 8

a 6 :
Alma (2 parts) . . 1876 47
Dum transisset (2 parts) 1878 8
Mirabile . . . 1865 38
Spes mea . . . 1880 15
Respexit Elias . . „ 20

Secular

a 4 :
Caesaris haec animo
(2 parts) . . 1873 16
In Deo spem . . 1876 34

a 6 :
Forti qui celebres . 1865 23
Carole, sceptrigeri pa-
tris . . . „ 28
Si data conveniunt . 1873 7
Principis Ausoniae fili
(2 parts) . . „ 10
Caesaris haec animo (2
parts) . . . „ 20

COMPERE, LOYSET

Secular

a 3 :
Venez, ami . . 1877 30
Va-t-en, regret . „ 32
Recueillez-vous . „ 34
Sourdes Regretz . 1837 17

CORNETS, PIERRE DES

Secular

a 4 :
Reveille-toi . . 1881 8

CRECQUILLON, THOMAS

Sacred

a 4 :
Super montem (2 parts) 1876 32

a 5
Ave virgo (2 parts) . „ 27
Dum aurore . . „ 23
Nigra sum (2 parts) . „ 37

Secular

a 4 :
C'est un grand tort . 1865 17
Je suis contraint . 1872 42
En espérant . . 1878 15
Qui la dira . . „ 16
Si j'ay l'amour . 1888 26

a 5 :
Caroli magnus erat . 1876 15
Quis te victorem dicat „ 21

DESPRÉS. [See PRÉS]

DUCIS. [See HERTOGHS]

**EPISCOPIUS (or EPISCOPUS),
LUDOVICUS**

a 4 :
Antiphon, Salve Regina 1875 9

FAIGNIENT, NÖE

Secular

a 4 :
Basciami . . . 1877 15
Questi ch' inditio . „ 16
Le seul espoir . . 1892 17
Le tien espoir . . „ 19

FEYS, ARNOLDUS

Sacred

a 5 :
Responsorium, Emen-
demus in meiius . 1892 1

FOSSA, JOANNES DE

Sacred

a 4 :
Litaniae de B. Mariâ . 1866 8

GHEERKIN

Secular

a 4 :
Mon pauvre cœur . 1879 42
Si je l'aimais . . „ 43
Ton amitié . . „ 45
Le mois de Mai . . „ 47
Nature a pris . . „ 49
Het was mij . . „ 51
Het was mij wel be-
voren gezeit . . 1889 5

GOMBERT, NICOLAS

Sacred

a 4 :
Salve Regina . . 1866 3
Ave Sanctissima . 1884 15

a 5 :
Pater noster . . 1876 15
Ave Maria . . . 1884 15

a 6 :
Ave Maria . . . 1880 49

Secular

a 4 :
Genuckelycke dingen 1875 23
Si je me plains . . 1878 19
Force sera . . „ 21
En espoir . . . „ 23
Page du Roi . . „ 25
Je n'en puis plus . „ 27
Hors, envieux . . 1881 3
Qui me donnerait . 1875 16

a 6 :
Sous l'ombre . . „ 20

GOSSE. [See JUNCKERS]

GOUDIMEL, CLAUDE

Sacred

a 4 :
Domine quid multipli-
cati . . . 1867 15
A la voix . . . „ 18
3 choirs, Salve Regina „ 3

Secular

a 3 :
Il faut aimer . . 1875 3
Où planterai-je . „ 4
Si c'est un grand tour-
ment . . . „ 5

HELLINCK. [See LUPUS]

HERTOGHS, BENEDICTUS

Secular

a 4 :
Musae, Jovis (2 parts) 1878 34
Mijn hertken . . „ 38

Quand de Noël . . 1878 40
Au fond des bois . „ 42
De la nature . . „ 43
Considérant . . „ 44
Ib. (transposed) . „ 46
N'allez-vous pas, trou-
badour . . „ 48
Ib. (transposed) . „ 49
On dit bien vrai . 1879 8
A bien dire . . „ 11
D'être paien . . „ 12
Mon cher troupeau . „ 14
Heil hem . . . „ 17
En espérant . . „ 18
Grootmachtig God ! . „ 20
Petite fleur . . „ 22
Il n'y a qu'un seul Dieu 1882 5

a 4 :
Danse, Pavane, La Rote 1879 3
„ „ La Fasane „ 4
„ „ „ „ 5
„ „ „ „ 6
„ „ „ „ 7
Basse danse . . „ 7
„ „ „ „ 8

HOLLANDE, JOANNES DE

Secular

a 4 :
Le rossignol . . 1880 22
Du vrai fumeur . „ 23
O malheureux . . „ 25
Qui veut nombrer . „ 27

HONDT. [See GHEERKIN]

HOTIN, or HUTIN

Sacred

a 4 :
Peccantem me . . 1884 13

JOSQUIN. [See PRÉS]

JUNCKERS, GOSSEN

Sacred

a 4 :
Misit me . . . 1885 25

KERLE, JACOB DE

Sacred

a 4 :
Mass, Pro defunctis . 1886 3
„ Regina Coeli . 1887 3
„ Ut, re, mi, fa,
sol, la . . 1888 1
Missa de Beata Virgine 1889 1
Missa Lauda Sion sal-
vatorem . . 1890 1
Missa Resurrexit pas-
tor bonus, Kyrie,
Gloria, Credo . 1891 1
Missa Resurrexit pas-
tor bonus (con-
tinued), (Sanctus),
(Agnus Dei, 8 voices) 1892 32
Te Deum . . . 1865 1
Domine quid multipli-
cati (3 parts) . „ 7
Venite ad me (3 parts) 1881 3
Egressus Jesus . „ 7
Similitudo (2 parts) . „ 12
Cum autem esset (2
parts) . . . „ 16
Super omnia ligna . „ 20

LAMBERTO. [See MONTE]

LAPPERDEY, PHILIPS

Secular

a 4 :
Tant plus un bien . 1882 19

LARUE. [See RUE]

LASSO, ORLANDO DI

Sacred

a 4 :
Ave Jesu . . . 1867 3
Tribulationem (2 parts) „ 36
Cognovi, Domine . „ 40
Ave Regina Coelorum 1876 45
Laudent Deum . . 1880 52
Regina Coeli . . 1888 27

Secular

a 4 :
Lorsque je chante . 1865 1
Vous qui brillez . „ 3
Alma Nemes . . 1867 3
Fertur in conviviis . „ 5
A ce matin ce serait
bonne . . . 1873 25
Soyons joyeux . . „ 27
Si près de moi . . „ 29
Maître Robin . . „ 31
Quand mon mari
revient . . . „ 33
Ardant amour . . „ 35

ROGIER, PHILIPPE

Sacred

a 4:

Mass, Inclyta stirps
Jesse . . . 1885   3

RORE, CIPRIANO DE

Sacred

a 5:

Agimus Tibi . . 1865   18
Da pacem . . 1876   19

Secular

a 3:

Tout ce qu'on peut . 1875   7

a 4:

Tu veux quitter . 1872   44

a 5:

Vergine bella . . 1875   8
Ib. . . . „   12
Hesperie . . 1876   29

ROY, BARTHÉLEMY VAN

Secular

a 6:

Verdi piaggie . . 1866   34

RUE, PIERRE DE LA

Sacred

a 3:

Cum coelum . . 1883   12
In pace (3 parts) . „   15

a 4:

Salve, Regina . . 1882   3
Gaude Virgo (2 parts) „   7
Vexilla Regis . . „   17
Dulces exuviae . . „   18
Anima mea . . „   20
Fama malum . . 1883   3
Sancta Maria . . „   5
Doleo super te . . „   10
Salve, Regina . . „   23
Salve, Regina . . 1893   17

a 5:

Maria, mater . . 1883   7

a 6:

Et exultavit . . 1893   23
Ave Sanctissima . 1882   13
Proh dolor ! . . 1883   20

Secular

a 3:

Il me fait mal . . 1886   27

a 4:

Vous tous regrets . 1884   16
De l'œil . . „   18
Ce n'est pas jeu . „   21
Regrets . . „   23
Deuil et ennui . 1885   3
Bien plus secret . „   5
Ce m'est tout un . „   7
Quand il survient . „   9
Autant en emporte . „   11
Pourquoy non . . „   13
Pour ce que je suis . „   17
Je n'ay deuil . . „   19
Mijn hert . . „   21
Je n'ay deuil . . „   23
Du tout plougiet . „   27
Car Dieu voulut . „   29
Soubs ce tombel . 1886   3
C'est ma fortune . „   12
Hélas . . . „   13
Aprez regrets . . „   23
Me fauldra il . . „   25

a 5:

Quant il advient . „   10
Cueurs désolez . . „   15

SALE (or SOLE), FRANCISCUS

Sacred

a 5:

Mass, Exultandi . 1868   3
Antiphona, Asperges
me . . . 1865   14

Offices (Int. Grad. Comm.)
for the following feasts :

B. Andreae Ap. . 1868   36
S. Nicolai Ep. . . „   43
S. Thomae Ap. . 1869   3
Nativitatis (in prima
Missa) . . „   6

a 6:

Nativitatis (in summa
Missa) . . . 1869   11

a 5:

S. Stephani M. . . „   20
S. Joannis Ev. . . „   30

a 6:

Circumcisionis . . „   39
Epiphaniae . . „   41

a 5:

Conversionis S. Pauli . „   48
Ib. (continued) . 1870   3
Purificationis . . „   8
S. Matthiae . . „   14
Anuntiationis . . „   17
De Communi S.Mariæ „   24

SCHUERE, D'OUDE

Secular

a 4:

Mon cher troupeau . 1883   9

SERMISY. [See LE JEUNE]

VAET, JACOB

Secular

a 6:

Hymn (In laudem Fi-
liorum Maxim. II).
Currite felices (3
parts) . . . 1877   20

VERDELOT, PHILIPPE

Sacred

a 4:

Sancta Maria . . 1866   35
Tanto tempore . . 1887   26

a 5:

Motetto. Si bona sus-
cipimus . . 1892   8

Secular

a 6:

Ick wil de valsche
wereldt . . . 1875   37

VERDONCK, CORNELIUS

Sacred

a 4:

Ave gratia . . . 1865   13

a 5:

Magnificat . . . 1866   41

Secular

a 4:

Dame belle . . „   38
A che più strali amor „   40
Le Feu couvert . . 1892   15

a 6:

Pro me novas . . 1876   27

WAELRANT, HUBERT

Secular

a 4:

Adieu mon frère . 1865   8

WILLAERT, ADRIAN

Sacred

a 4:

Simulacra gentium . 1865   19
Pater noster . . 1866   25
Quia devotis . . „   30
O gemma . . „   32
Da pacem . . 1880   42

Secular

a 4:

Sasso ch' io ardo . 1877   42
Mon pauvre cœur . 1878   3
Ib. . . . „   4
„ (transposed) . „   5
„ „ . . „   6

WOLF. [See LUPUS]

YVER, A

Secular

a 4:

Ung pauvre sot . . 1889   1

L. M. M.

TRESTI, FLAMINIO (*b.* Lodi, *c.* mid-16th cent.), organist of S. Pietro di Bergolio, Alessandria, 1613, composed masses, motets, 4 books of madrigals, canzonette and vesper-

songs, published in Milan, Venice and Frankfort-on-Main between 1585 and 1610 (*Q.-L.*).

TREU, DANIEL GOTTLIEB (called FEDELE in Italy (*b.* Stuttgart, 1695 ; *d.* Breslau, Aug. 7, 1749), violinist and composer, pupil of J. S. Kusser. He went to Venice in 1716 for further study under Vivaldi, and after producing a number of operas in Italy he went to Breslau, 1725, became Kapellmeister at Prague, 1727, and, finally, was in the service of Count Schaffgotsch at Hirschberg, 1740. He composed operas, cantatas and orchestral works (Matthe-son ; *Riemann* ; *Q.-L.*).

TRIAD is a chord of three notes standing in the relation to one another of bottom note, third and fifth. It is of no consequence what the quality of the combination is, whether consonant or dissonant, major or minor. The following are specimens of major, minor, diminished and augmented triads respectively :

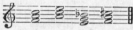

C. H. H. P.

TRIAL, (1) JEAN CLAUDE (*b.* Avignon, Dec. 13, 1732 ; *d.* June 23, 1771), French composer, was educated at the *maîtrise*, and early studied the violin, for which his first compositions were intended, under Garnier at Montpellier. Settling in Paris he became intimate with Rameau. He became conductor at the Opéra and was taken up by the Prince de Conti, who made him conductor of his own music, and procured him the joint-directorship with Berton of the Opéra (1767). He composed ' Ésope à Cythère ' (1766) and ' La Fête de Flore ' (1771), each in one act, and with Berton ' Sylvie,' three acts (1765), and ' Théonis,' one act (1767) ; also short overtures, orchestral divertissements, cantatas, ariettes and the music for ' La Chercheuse d'esprit.' He died of apoplexy.

(2) ANTOINE (*b.* Avignon, 1736 ; *d.* Feb. 5, 1795), his brother and junior by four years, was educated at the *maîtrise*, but forsook ecclesiastical plain-song for stage ariettas. Having appeared with success as a comedy-tenor in several provincial towns, he went to Paris in 1764, and made his début at the Théâtre Italien, July 4, 1764 in Philidor's ' Le Sorcier.' For thirty years composers eagerly vied with each other in writing parts for him, and he left permanent traces at the Opéra-Comique, where the comedy-tenor part is still called by his name. Like Dugazon, Antoine Trial embraced with fervour the doctrines of the Revolution, and on the fall of Robespierre was constrained by the mob to atone for his previous exploits by singing the ' Réveil du Peuple ' on his knees. Forced to give up his post in the municipality, and subjected to many cruel humiliations, his mind gave way, and he poisoned himself. His wife, Marie Jeanne

Milon (b. Paris, Aug. 1, 1746; d. Feb. 13, 1818) made her début at the Théâtre Italien, Jan. 15, 1766, singing under the name of Mme. Mandeville. She had a voice of remarkable compass and flexibility, and brought into fashion airs full of roulades and vocalises.

(3) ARMAND EMMANUEL (b. Paris, Mar. 1, 1771; d. Paris, Sept. 9, 1803), their son, began early to compose, and produced at the Comédie Italienne 'Julien et Colette' (1788); 'Adelaïde et Mirval' (1791); 'Les Deux Petits Aveugles' (1792); 'Le Siège de Lille' (1793); 'La Cause et les effets, ou le Réveil du peuple en 1789' (1793), besides taking part in the celebrated revolutionary piece 'Le Congrès des rois.' A first-rate accompanist, Armand Trial might have made both name and money, but though he married Jeanne Méon, a charming artist at the Théâtre Favart, he plunged into dissipation, and died from its effects.

G. C.; with addns. M. L. P.

TRIAL BY JURY, a very extravagant extravaganza; words by W. S. Gilbert; music by Sullivan. Produced Royalty Theatre, London, Mar. 25, 1875.   G.

TRIANGLE, an instrument of PERCUSSION (q.v.), much used in the modern orchestra, consisting of a steel rod bent in a triangular form, but open at one angle. The beater is of the same metal, and should be somewhat of a spindle shape, so as to give a heavier or lighter stroke at the performer's discretion. The triangle is hung by a string at the upper angle, held in the performer's hand, or more frequently attached to his desk or to one of his drums, as it is seldom that a man has nothing else to play besides this little instrument, except in military bands. It suits all keys, as besides the fundamental tone there are many subordinate ones, *not* harmonics. The woodcut is from an instrument of the pattern used at the Opéra in Paris. It is an isosceles triangle, the longest side 7½ inches, and the short side or base 7 inches. Thickness $\frac{7}{16}$ of an inch.   v. de P.

TRIBUT DE ZAMORA, LE, opera in 4 acts; words by d'Ennery and Brésil; music by Gounod. Produced Opéra, Paris, Apr. 1, 1881.   G.

TRICINIUM, see BICINIUM.

TRICKLIR, JEAN BALTHASAR (b. Dijon, c. 1745; d. Dresden, Nov. 29, 1813), violoncellist, formed a string quartet with Schick, Benda and Hofmann, touring in Germany c. 1782. He was appointed at the Dresden court in 1783. He composed concertos and sonatas for violoncello, and wrote two theoretical treatises (E. v. d. Straeten, *Hist. of Violoncello*).

TRIÉBERT, (1) CHARLES LOUIS (b. Paris, Oct. 30, 1810; d. Gravelle-St. Maurice, July 18, 1867), French oboist, son of a wind-instrument

maker, was educated at the Conservatoire, and took the first oboe prize in Vogt's class in 1829. He had an excellent tone, great execution and good style, and was long remembered at the Théâtre des Italiens and the Société des Concerts. Although much occupied with instrument-making, he carried on his artistic cultivation with earnestness, and composed much for the oboe—original pieces, arrangement of operatic airs, and (in conjunction with Jancourt) fantaisies-concertantes for oboe and bassoon. At the Paris Exhibition of 1855 Triébert obtained a medal for his adaptation of Boehm's contrivances to the oboe, and for improved bassoons. This skilled manufacturer and eminent artist succeeded Verroust as professor of the oboe at the Conservatoire in Apr. 1863, and retained the post till his death.

His brother, (2) FRÉDÉRIC (b. circa 1813; d. Paris, Mar. 1878), was his partner, and showed considerable inventive genius. He constructed bassoons after Boehm's system, a specimen of which may be seen in the Museum of the Conservatoire. He left a son, (3) FRÉDÉRIC, one of the best oboists of the French school.   G. C.

TRIEMER, JOHANN SEWALD (b. Weimar, c. 1700; d. Amsterdam, 1761). He studied the violoncello under Eylenstein and composition under Ehrhardt, and from 1727 under Boismortier in Paris. He went to Alkmar in 1729 and afterwards settled in Amsterdam. In 1739 he published a work on the rudiments of music, and composed sonatas for violoncello, and psalms (E. v. d. Straeten, *Hist. of Violoncello* : Q.-L.).

TRIHORIS, TRIORI, TRIHORY, TRIORY, an old Breton dance, long obsolete. Cotgrave describes it as 'a kind of British and peasantly daunce, consisting of three steps, and performed, by three hobling youths, commonly in a round.' It is mentioned by Rabelais (*Pantagruel*, bk. iv. chap. xxxviii.) and by his imitator, Noël du Fail, Seigneur de la Herrisaye, in chap. xix. of his *Contes et Discours d'Eutrapel* (1585). From this passage it would seem that it was a 'Basse Danse,' and was followed by a 'Carole'—a Low Breton name for a dance in a round, or according to Cotgrave 'a kind of daunce wherein many daunce together.'[1] (See TOURDION.) Du Fail says the dance was 'trois fois plus magistrale et gaillarde que nulle autre.' It was the special dance of Basse Bretagne, as the PASSEPIED was of Haute Bretagne. Jehan Tabourot, in his *Orchésographie* (see ARBEAU), says the Trihoris was a kind of Branle, and that he learnt it at Poitiers from one of his scholars. He gives the following as the air to which it was danced:

---

[1] Compare the Italian 'Carola,' described in Symonds' *Renaissance in Italy*, vol. iv. p. 261, note.

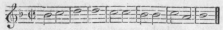

According to Littré, the name is allied to the Burgundian 'Trigori,' a joyful tumult. w. b. s.

TRILL, see SHAKE.

TRILLO DEL DIAVOLO, IL, a famous sonata for violin solo with bass by TARTINI (q.v.).

TRINITY COLLEGE, see DUBLIN.

TRINITY COLLEGE OF MUSIC, LONDON. This institution is the development of a Musical Society founded in 1872. In 1875 it was incorporated under the title of Trinity College, London, which was altered in 1904 to Trinity College of Music, London. Its constitution is that of an unlimited company without shares and without division of profits.

The teaching of the College began in 1872 with vocal music; harmony, counterpoint, etc., being added in 1875, and in 1876 the teaching was extended to include all musical subjects.

The original scheme of higher examinations was instituted in 1874, the local examinations in musical knowledge (theory) in 1877, and the local examinations in instrumental and vocal music in 1879. These examinations are held in London, and at some 400 local centres in the British Isles, India, the Dominions, South America, etc.

As at present (1926) constituted the College is under the direction of a Council (the Corporation, W. W. Cobbett, Chairman) and a Board (of management, Professor J. C. Bridge, M.A., Mus.D., F.S.A., Chairman). Professor J. C. Bridge and Dr. E. F. Horner hold the respective offices of Director of Studies and Director of Examinations. The first Warden of the College was the Rev. H. G. Bonavia Hunt, Mus.D., but the office is now in abeyance.

The College has maintained during recent years a terminal average number of students of about 680. Between forty and fifty scholarships entitling to complete musical instruction at the College, and in some cases to grants toward maintenance, are offered for open competition terminally, and in connexion with the local examinations there are sixty-two exhibitions tenable at local centres and of the value of £9 : 9s. to £3 : 3s. each.

The College is situated in Mandeville Place, Manchester Square, where all information respecting courses of studies and examinations can be obtained from the Secretary.

TRIO, (1) TERZET. A composition for three instruments or three voices was formerly called trio in the one case and terzet (Fr. terzette; Ger. Terzett; Ital. terzetto) in the other. Trio is now more usual for both.

The leading instrumental trio is that for pianoforte, violin and violoncello, and has grown out of the early sonata a tre in the contrapuntal style such as that of Bach for two violins and figured bass. The sonata style was adopted for trios as it was for quartets. (See QUARTET.) In Haydn's 'Sonatas for pianoforte with accompaniment of violin and violoncello' the strings do little if anything of a really independent character, but a rightly proportioned interest and balance of tonal effect was achieved by Beethoven, a balance which, possibly owing to the increased tonal resources of the pianoforte, has not always by any means been preserved by later writers. The combination has been largely used. Beethoven left six, Schubert two, Schumann three, Mendelssohn two, Brahms three, Dvořák four, and the trios of Bax, Bridge, Chausson, Ireland, Novák, Parry, Reger, Saint-Saëns, Scott, Stanford, Tchaikovsky and Tovey must also be mentioned.

The string trio, violin, viola and violoncello, has been taken up much less by comparison (in spite of the obvious advantage of pure intonation), owing to the fact that the texture is apt to become monotonous unless a part is dropped out occasionally, and it is difficult to do that successfully when only two are left without a resulting tenuity of harmony and tone. Beethoven left five string trios and Mozart a divertimento. There is one by Reger.

There are various other combinations employed. Beethoven wrote for flute, violin and viola and two oboes and cor anglais, subsequently rewriting the latter for two violins and viola, and for pianoforte, clarinet and violoncello. There are two trios for two flutes and violoncello of Haydn, for flute, violoncello and pianoforte of Weber, and for pianoforte, clarinet and viola of Mozart, Schumann's 'Märchenerzählungen' being for the same combination. Beethoven's op. 11 is for pianoforte, clarinet and violoncello. Brahms's trios for pianoforte, violin and horn and pianoforte, clarinet (or viola) and violoncello should also be mentioned. Later examples are by Bax, flute, viola and harp; Holbrooke, pianoforte, violin and horn; Reger, flute, violin and viola; and Tovey, pianoforte and wind. Still more unusual are the trios for three violoncellos, of Reicha, for three flutes, of Kuhlau and Quantz, and for oboe, clarinet and bassoon, of Flegier. (See CHAMBER MUSIC.)

The combination of three solo voices with or without accompaniment has a character of its own, of which composers have always been aware. The parts stand out clearly, as there are just enough and no more than are required to suggest the harmonic basis of the music. Songs or canzonets of three voices take an important place in the output of the English madrigalists (see ENGLISH MADRIGAL SCHOOL). In opera the vocal trio of course has been freely used, especially to realise the particularly beautiful effects to be obtained from combining three women's voices.

(2) For 'trio,' in the sense of the central or contrasting section of a symphonic movement, see MINUET; SCHERZO; and MARCH.

TRIONFO DI DORI, IL. The title of a famous collection of madrigals, first published in Venice by Gardano in 1592. There are twenty-nine madrigals by as many Italian composers, and all are in six parts. All end with the refrain, 'Viva la bella Dori,' and the names of the writers of the words are given as well as those of the composers of the music. The contents are as follows:—

Hippolito Baccusi.   Un giorno a Pale sacro.
Hippolito Sabino.   Dove sorge piacevole.
Horatio Vecchi.   Hor ch' ogni vento tace.
Giovanni Gabrieli.   Se cantano gl' augelli.
Alfonso Preti.   Ninfe a danzar venite.
Luca Marenzio.   Leggiadre Ninfe e pastorelli amanti.
Giovanni de Macque.   Vaghe Ninfe selvagge.
Horatio Colombano.   All' apparir di Dori.
Giovanni Cavaccio.   Giunta qui Dori.
Annibale Stabile.   Nel tempo che ritorna Zefiro.
Paolo Bozzi.   All' ombra d' un bel faggio.
Tiburtio Massaino.   Su le fiorite sponde.
Giovanni Matteo Asola.   In una verde piaggia.
Giulio Eremita.   Smeraldi eran le rive.
Filippo de Monte.   Lungo le chiare linfe.
Giovanni Croce.   Ove tra l' herbe e i fiori.
Pietr' Andrea Bonini.   Quando lieta e vezzosa.
Alessandro Striggio.   Eran Ninfe e Pastori.
Giovanni Florio.   Piu trasparente velo.
Leon Leoni.   Di pastorali accenti.
Felice Anerio.   Sotto l' ombroso speco.
Gasparo Zerto.   L' inargentato lido.
Ruggiero Giovanelli.   Quando apparisti.
Gasparo Costa.   Mentr' a quest' ombra intorno.
Lelio Bertani.   Dori, a quest' ombre e l' aura.
Ludovico Balbi.   Mentre Pastori e Ninfe.
Giacomo Gastoldi.   Al mormorar de' liquidi cristalli.
Costanzo Porta.   Da lo spuntar de' matutini albori.
Giovanni Palestrina.   Quando dal terzo cielo.

Two complete copies (sets of partbooks) are known, at Cassel and Bologna. In 1596 Phalèse of Antwerp brought out a new edition, retaining Gardano's dedicatory letter to Leonardo Sanudo. Incomplete parts are at Ghent. At Augsburg and Vienna there are complete sets of Gardano's reissue of 1599, and incomplete parts of Phalèse's edition of 1601 are at Ghent and in the R.C.M. In 1612 Johann Littich prepared for the press (dying before it could be brought out), a selection of sixteen of the madrigals, which were published at Nuremberg with the title 'Musicalische Streitkräntzlein,' and translations of the words into Latin and German. In the following year, Salomon Engelhart, Littich's successor at the Gymnasium of Count Mansfeld, brought out the remainder, which Littich had also prepared, reprinting the contributions of Croce and Luca Marenzio, and adding one German madrigal by Johann Leo Hasler. There are complete copies of the first set, and incomplete copies of the second, at Berlin and Grimma. Another Antwerp edition appeared in 1614, and in 1619 a new German translation of the words by Martinus Rinckhardt was printed together with the music at Leipzig (complete parts at Grimma). The work derives its chief interest from the fact that the more famous English publication, 'The TRIUMPHES OF ORIANA' (q.v.), was suggested, as to scheme and the recurring refrain, by the Italian series of madrigals.

BIBL.—DR. EMIL VOGEL, *Bibliothek der gedruckten weltlichen 'ocalmusik Italiens.*   **M.**

TRIPLE TIME (Fr. *mesure à trois temps*; Ger. *Tripeltakt*), see TIME.

TRIPLET (Fr. *triolet*; Ger. *Triole*; Ital. *terzina*). In modern notation each note is equal to two of the next lower denomination, and the division of a note into three is not provided for, although in the ancient 'measured music' it was an important part of time (see NOTATION; TIME). On this account notes worth one-third of the next longer kind have to be written as halves, and are then grouped in threes by means of curved lines, with the figure 3 usually placed over the middle note as an additional distinction. Such a group is called a triplet, and is executed at a slightly increased speed, so that the three triplet-notes are equal to two ordinary notes of the same species: for example—

BEETHOVEN, Sonata, Op. 2, No. 1.

Triplets may be formed of notes of any kind, and also of rests, or of notes and rests together.

BEETHOVEN, Sonata, Op. 22.

So also a group of two notes, one twice the length of the other, is read as the equivalent of a triplet, provided it is marked with the distinctive figure 3.

SCHUMANN, Trio, Op. 63.

In instrumental music, when the fingering is marked, there is some risk of the figure 3 of a triplet being confounded with the indication for the third finger. To obviate this, the two figures are always printed in different type, or, better still, the triplet figure is enclosed in brackets, thus (3). This plan appears to have been first introduced by Moscheles, in his edition of Beethoven, published by Cramer & Co.

Groups of a similar nature to triplets, but consisting of an arbitrary number of notes, are also frequently met with in instrumental music. These groups, which are sometimes called *quintolets*, *sextolets*, etc., according to the number of notes they contain, always have their number written above them, as an indication that they are played at a rate different from ordinary notes of the same form (usually quicker). Their proper speed is found by referring them to ordinary groups of the same kind of notes ; thus, if the general rhythm of the bar indicates four semiquavers to a beat, as in common time, a group of five, six or seven semiquavers would be made equal to four semiquavers, while a group of eight notes of the value of one beat would of course be written as demisemiquavers ; if, however, the natural grouping of the bar were in threes, as in 9–16 time, a group of four or five (or sometimes two) semiquavers would be equal to three, while a group of six would require to be written as demisemiquavers. On the performance of triplets in certain passages in 18th-century music, see DOT.   F. T.

TRISTAN UND ISOLDE, music-drama (' eine Handlung ') in 3 acts, words and music by Wagner ; produced Munich, June 10, 1865 ; Drury Lane (Franke & Pollini's German Opera), June 20, 1882 ; New York, Metropolitan Opera House, Dec. 1, 1886 ; in English, Carl Rosa Co., Liverpool, Apr. 15, 1898 ; in French, Théâtre Nouveau, Paris, under Lamoureux, Oct. 28, 1899.   G.

TRITONE, the interval of the augmented fourth, consisting of three whole tones, whence the name is derived. In pure ecclesiastical music the use of the *Tritonus* or augmented fourth is strictly forbidden ; as is also that of its inversion, the *Quinta falsa* or diminished fifth. It is scarcely necessary to say that the presence of these intervals is felt, whenever F and B are brought either into direct or indirect correspondence with each other, whatever may be the Mode in which the contact takes place. In the hexachordal system of Guido d' Arezzo, B, the third sound of the *Hexachordon durum*, was called MI ; and F, the fourth sound of the *Hexachordon naturale*, was called FA. Mediæval writers, therefore, expressed their abhorrence of the false relation existing between these two sounds, in the proverb—

Mi contra fa est diabolus in musica.

W. S. R.

TRITONIUS, PETRUS (b. ? Bozen or Sterzing, before end of 15th cent.) (PETER TREIBENREIF or TRAYBENRAIFF),[1] belonged to a family of some consequence long settled in the Etschthal of Austrian Tyrol. He was born some time before the end of the 15th century, and the name being found about that time in the two Tyrolese towns of Bozen and Sterzing gives some colour to the conjecture that one or the other was his birthplace. He studied at the University of Padua, where he took the degree of Master of Arts ; and then, following the custom of the humanist scholars of the time, adopted the Latin name of Tritonius. Return-

ing home, he was appointed teacher of Latin, possibly also of Music, to the Cathedral School of Brixen. In Italy Tritonius had made the acquaintance of the classical humanist scholar Conrad Celtes, who was afterwards appointed University Professor at Vienna, and under the patronage of the Emperor Maximilian had founded a learned Society (Literaria Sodalitas Danubiana) for the furtherance of literature and art on the new classical humanist principles. Tritonius became a member of this Society, and was invited by Celtes to settle in Vienna to be the instructor to the Society in song and instrumental music. At the instigation of Celtes Tritonius set a considerable number of the Odes of Horace to music in simple note for note counterpoint and strict observance of classical metre and quantities. Celtes had these sung by his pupils at the end of his own prelections on Horace. These and similar compositions of other Latin poems and church hymns by other members of the Society were printed and published in 1507 by Erhart Oeglin of Augsburg under the title :

' Melopoeae sive Harmoniae tetracenticae super xxii genera carminum heroicorum elegiacorum, lyricorum et ecclesiasticorum hymnorum per Petrum Tritonium et alios doctos sodalitatis literariae nostrae musicos secundum naturas et tempora syllabarum et pedum compositae et regulatae ductu Chunradi Celtis Feliciter impressae.'

At the foot of the title the following direction is appended :

' Optime musiphile, strophos id est repetitiones carminum collisiones syllabarum, conjugationes et connubia pedum pro affectu animi, motu, et gestu corporis diligenter observa.'

The whole title is printed in the form of a cup with the words added ' Krater Bachi.' Later in the same year Oeglin published a second impression of the settings by Tritonius alone, nineteen in number, with the shorter title, ' Harmoniae Petri Tritonii super odis Horatii Flacci.' These two publications appear to be the earliest specimens of German music-printing with movable types, the first in folio with wooden types, the other in 4to with metal. The settings by Tritonius must have met with much favour at the time. In 1532 and again in 1551 they were republished by Egenolph of Frankfort. The style found many imitators and a greater musician like Ludwig Senfl did not disdain to take the tenor of the settings by Tritonius and provide them with other harmonies. Freiherr von Liliencron described in Chrysander and Spitta's *Vierteljahrsschrift* for 1887 and afterwards separately published with a preliminary dissertation the settings of these Horatian Odes by Tritonius, Senfl and Hofheimer, and also a ' Schulausgabe ' with transcription in modern score. The main importance of these works consists in the fact that they gave the first suggestion to the setting of German Chorals and afterwards of psalm

---

[1] See Dr. F. Walder, Eitner's *Monatshefte*, xxvii. 13, 14.

tunes generally, in simple four-part note for note counterpoint.

After the death of Celtes in 1508, the literary society which he had founded was dissolved, and Tritonius returned to the Tyrol and undertook the direction of the Latin School at Bozen. In 1521 he was settled at Schwatz on the Inn, not far from Innsbruck, where he was chiefly engaged in literary work.   J. R. M.

TRITTO (TURITTO ?), (1) GIACOMO (*b.* Altamura, near Bari, Apr. 2, 1733 ; *d.* Naples, Sept. 26 ?, 1824), studied under Cafaro and N. Saia at the Conservatorio della pietà de' Turchini, where he became a teacher in 1780, co-director with Paisiello in 1798, and Sala's successor as professor of counterpoint and composition in 1800. Between 1764 and 1815 he composed 50 operas, and wrote also a considerable amount of church music, including a number of important works, which all remained in MS. La Fage credits him with the introduction of the *Finale* in opera, which was hitherto attributed to Piccinni. He wrote also several theoretical works. (See *Q.-L.*) His son (2) DOMENICO (*b.* Naples, June 1, 1776 ; *d.* Loreto, Dec. 1851), was also a composer of operas, church music and a symphony (*Q.-L.* ; *Riemann*).

TRIUMPHES OF ORIANA, THE, a collection of madrigals written in honour of Queen Elizabeth and edited by Thomas Morley. The title-page of the original edition bears the date 1601, but the entry of the book in the Stationers' registers shows that it was not actually published until 1603, after the queen was dead. There is no reason to doubt that the collection was modelled on the TRIONFO DI DORI (*q.v.*), and the refrain, ' Long live fair Oriana,' corresponds with ' Viva la bella Dori ' so closely that one of the Dori set, that by Giovanni Croce, was adapted to English words, and reprinted from the second book of MUSICA TRANSALPINA (*q.v.*). The contents of the collection are as follows :

Michael Este.   Hence stars, *a* 5 (printed at the back of the dedication, with a note explaining that it was sent in too late for inclusion in the proper place).
Daniel Norcome.   With angel's face, *a* 5.
John Mundy.   Lightly she tripped, *a* 5.
Ellis Gibbons.   Long live fair Oriana, *a* 5.
John Benet.   All creatures now are merry-minded, *a* 5.
John Hilton.   Fair Oriana, beauty's Queen, *a* 5.
George Marson.   The Nymphs and Shepherds danced Lavolto's, *a* 5.
Richard Carlton.   Calm was the air, *a* 5.
John Holmes.   Thus Bonny-boots, *a* 5.
Richard Nicolson.   Sing Shepherds all, *a* 5.
Thomas Tomkins.   The Fauns and Satyrs tripping, *a* 5.
Michael Cavendish.   Come gentle swains, *a* 5.
William Cobbold.   With wreaths of rose and laurel, *a* 5.
Thomas Morley.   Arise awake, *a* 5.
John Farmer.   Fair Nymphs, *a* 6.
John Wilbye.   The Lady Oriana, *a* 6.
Thomas Hunt.   Hark, did ye ever hear so sweet a singing ? *a* 6.
Thomas Weelkes.   As Vesta was from Latmos hill descending, *a* 6.
John Milton.   Fair Orian, *a* 6.
Ellis Gibbons.   Round about her chariot, *a* 6.
G. Kirbye.   Bright Phoebus, *a* 6.   (With angel's face.)
Robert Jones.   Fair Oriana, *a* 6.
John Lisley.   Fair Cytherea, *a* 6.
Thomas Morley.   Hard by a crystal fountain, *a* 6.
Edward Johnson.   Come blessed bird, *a* 6.
Giovanni Croce.   Hard by a crystal fountain, *a* 6.

Thomas Bateson.   When Oriana walked to take the air,[1] *a* 6.
Francis Pilkington.   When Oriana walked to take the air[2] *a* 5.
Thomas Bateson.   Hark, hear you not ? (Oriana's Farewell)[1] *a* 5.

---

[1] First printed in Bateson's first set, in 1604.
[2] First printed in Pilkington's first set, 1613.

Michael East's contribution came too late for insertion in the proper place, and was printed at the back of the dedication to Charles Howard, Earl of Nottingham, Lord High Admiral. The original number was twenty-six, for Bateson's two and Pilkington's one were not in the original edition ; adding these three pieces, the last two of which change the refrain to ' In Heaven lives Oriana,' we get the number twenty-nine, the same as that of the Trionfo di Dori. There were two issues of the first edition ; Kirbye's madrigal in one has the words ' With angel's face,' the same words that Daniel Norcome used, and in the other the same music is set to ' Bright Phoebus.' [3]

There have been several reprints of the ' Triumphes ' beginning with that of William Hawes (1814) and including an edition by Lionel Benson (Novello) and ENGLISH MADRIGAL SCHOOL, vol. xxxii.   M., with addns.

TROCHEE (Lat. *trochaeus chorius*). A metrical foot, consisting of a long syllable followed by a short one. See METRE.

TROILO, ANTONIO, a 16th-17th century town musician of Vicenza, wrote 4-5-part instrumental canzons (1606) ; ' Sinfonie, scherzi . . . a 2 voci,' to sing and play on any instruments (1608) ; also 10 psalms *a* 5 v. and a Magnificat in G. B. Biondi's ' Salmi intieri ' (1607) (*Riemann* ; *Q.-L.*).

TROJANO, MASSIMO (*b.* Corduba da Napoli, 1st half of 16th cent.), poet, comedian and musician, a male alto in the chapel of Jacob Fugger, *c.* 1568. In the same year he was appointed to the electoral chapel at Munich. In Apr. 1570 a warrant was issued against him as being connected with the murder of the violinist Battista Romano, and he fled the country. He wrote 4 books of ' Canzoni alla Napolitana,' a valuable collection of compositions by composers attached to the Bavarian court (Venice, 1569), and an account of the nuptials of William V., Duke of Bavaria in 1568, which appeared in a German translation by F. Wirthmann (1872) (*Q.-L.*).

TROMBA. The Italian word for TRUMPET (*q.v.*).

TROMBA DA TIRARSI, a form of trumpet used by Bach in his church cantatas which was fitted with a slide to ' draw out ' (*tirarsi*), thereby enabling the player to obtain some of the missing notes of the scale in the ordinary harmonic series. It is generally supposed to have been identical with the little soprano trombone (*PLATE LXXXIII.* No. 7) used in Germany during the 18th century ; but Altenburg (*Trompeter- und Pauker-Kunst*, 1795) compares it with the alto trombone. In the museum of the Berlin Hochschule für Musik there is a specimen of an ordinary D trumpet, by Hans

---

[3] The writer concluded that ' Bright Phoebus ' belonged to the second issue, but Fellowes (*English Madrigal Composers*, p. 248) supports the opposite view with careful evidence.   c.

2 c

Veit of Nuremburg, 1651, in which the smaller end is fitted with a single sliding tube (cf. Catalogue, No. 639: Illustration Plate 24). This may be a primitive tromba da tirarsi, anticipating Hyde's invention by 150 years (see TRUMPET); or it may be merely an early attempt to supersede the use of crooks for putting the instrument in a lower key as noted by Praetorius (*Organographia*, 1618). A similar tuning slide is to be found in some of the early cornopeans or cornets of the 19th century. Bach also employs a 'corno da tirarsi'; but no details of a true 'slide horn' of his period are at present forthcoming, though such an addition to the horn was made by Dikhuth of Mannheim in 1812. (See TRUMPET.)   F. W. G.

TROMBA MARINA (TRUMMSCHEIDT, BRUMMSCHEIDT, TYMPANISCHIZA, NONNEN- GEIGE, MARINE TRUMPET). A portable mono- chord played with the bow, probably the oldest bowed instrument known, and the archetype of all others. The country of its origin is uncer- tain, but is probably Germany. Once exten- sively employed in Germany and France as a popular instrument, and even used in the ser- vice of the church, it was almost disused early in the 18th century : but it figured in the 'Musique des Escuries' of the French mon- archs, down to the year 1767 : and L. Mozart, in his *Violinschule* (1756), describes it as then in use. It was in use later still in German nunneries.[1]

The name Trummscheit or Trumbscheit is certainly derived from the word Trumba or Tromba—a Trumpet (compare the old German Trummete for Trompete and Krumhorn for Krumbhorn): the second syllable 'scheit' signifies 'a piece of wood.' The name Tym- panischiza is very curious and has created some misunderstanding. It is used by Glareanus in his Dodecachordon Lib. 1 (1547) as an attempt to latinise the word Trummscheit : the writer evidently imagined that the first syllable of the popular name was connected with an old Ger- man form of the word Trommel—a drum, while 'schiza' is the nearest he could attain to 'scheit.' There is no reason to believe that the word existed outside his treatise, which Praetorius in his Syntagum (1618) carefully copies in this respect, although, as he says, the instrument itself was commonly used in Germany, France and the Netherlands. Such a barbaric name is unknown to the earlier writers Virdung, Agricola or Luscinius, though the last mentioned treatise is also written in Latin.

Most existing specimens date from the latter half of the 17th century. In its latest form the instrument has a fiddle head fitted with an iron screw. Some heads have rack-wheels to facilitate tuning ; others have iron screw button

tops, a double iron ring working on the screw, into the outer ring of which the string is knotted. It has a round neck or handle about the size of a broomstick, dove-tailed into a top block or shoulder which forms the end of the body. The latter is a resonant box broadening towards the bottom, where it rests on the ground, and having a thin pine table, quite flat. The back or shell of the box is polygonal, being built up of very thin straight staves of maple. The num- ber of staves in the shell is usually either five or seven : the joints are fortified internally, and sometimes externally also, with slips of cart- ridge paper or vellum.[2] Three pine bars are glued transversely across the table before it is glued to the outer edges of the shell. The table is sometimes pierced with a rose. In some specimens the box is constructed in two separ- ate portions. In others, of later date, the bottom of the box spreads out at the edges like the bell of a trumpet. The total length is usually somewhat less than 6 feet ; some speci- mens are a few inches over that length. (See *PLATE LXXXVII*. No. 2.)

The string is a very thick violoncello D string, or a double bass G string, stretched over a peculiar bridge. This is of hard and close- grained wood, and rests firmly on the table with the right foot only, upon which side the string bears with its whole weight. Properly, the bridge should be shaped something like a shoe, the heel being the right foot, the toe the left. The left foot touches the table lightly : and when the string is put in vibration this foot rattles rapidly on the table, like an organ reed. To increase the tone, a thin metallic plate is sometimes attached to the foot, and some bridges have a mechanical apparatus for adjusting its tension.

The marine trumpet is played with a heavy violoncello bow, plentifully rosined. (See *PLATE LXXXII*.) The open string is ordin- arily tuned to CC : and when sounded with the bow, it yields a powerful note, of harsh and nasal character, something like an 8-feet *wooden* organ reed-pipe. Played by stopping in the ordinary way, the marine trumpet produces tones far less melodious than the bray of an ass. But this is not its legitimate use. It is properly played wholly in natural harmonics[3] (see ACOUSTICS, subsection HARMONIC SERIES); hence the following scale arises :

Rühlmann omits the three last notes from the scale : but the writer has seen them marked on several specimens. The facility with which the

---

[1] Rühlmann, *Geschichte der Bogeninstrumente*, pp. 29, 31.

[2] In Mersenne's time, and doubtless in the original instrument, the box was a shallow triangular shape tapering like a sword- sheath, and open at the lower end.

[3] The bow must be drawn across the string a short distance below the upper nut, as described by Mersenne, and not between the thumb (or fingers) and the bridge as often wrongly depicted.   F. W. G.

LXXXII

P 123,

LXIV *Tromba Marina*

A TRUMPET MARINE PLAYER

Bonnani's Gabinetto Armonico-Edition, 1776

marine trumpet yields the natural harmonics is due to its single string and its lopsided bridge. Paganini's extraordinary effects in harmonics on a single string were in fact produced by temporarily converting his violin into a small marine trumpet. As is well known, that clever player placed his single fourth string on the treble side of the bridge, screwing it up to a very high pitch, and leaving the bass foot of the bridge comparatively loose. He thus produced a powerful reedy tone, and obtained unlimited command over the harmonics.[1] According to information procured by Rühlmann from Marienthal, the Trummscheidt will bear lowering to B♭ and raising to E♭, but no more. According to him, it can also be made to yield the notes D and F in the lower octave, though less distinctly. The nuns use the instrument in their choral singing. On the festivals of the Church, and sometimes as a special compliment to a new-comer on her matriculation, they jubilate upon four marine trumpets accompanied by drums ; one takes a principal part, the others are secondary.[2]

An inspection of the scale will explain how the marine trumpet became *par excellence* the Nonnen-geige : its scale corresponds with the female voice, with which its tone, resembling that of a clarinet, but more piercing and nasal, has something in common. Added to this it is extremely easy to play : the neck being rested on the breast or shoulder, and the string lightly touched with the thumb where the letters are marked on the neck, it yields its few notes with absolute accuracy. It was anciently used as a street instrument by mendicant musicians : and those who have heard it will agree with an ancient author that it sounds best at a distance. M. Jourdain, in a well-known passage in the *Bourgeois Gentilhomme* (1670), expresses a preference for it, thereby proclaiming his uncultivated taste.[3] About the end of the 17th century the acoustical peculiarities of the Trummscheidt were the object of much investigation by the learned societies of England and France : the reader who desires to pursue the subject will find the necessary clues in Vidal and Hawkins. The name ' marine trumpet ' (tromba marina) was probably given to the Trummscheidt on its introduction into Italy, on account of its external resemblance to the large speaking-trumpet used on board Italian

vessels, which is of the same length and tapering shape. A more recent theory is that, as the curious trembling bridge, which gives the instrument its trumpet-like tone, was added in the latter half of the 15th century, it was either due to the celebrated French trumpeter of the period, Marin or Maurin, or else the instrument with this improvement was named in his honour.

Specimens are not uncommon : several will be found in the museums of Bologna, Munich, Salzburg, Nuremberg, etc., and there are two good ones in the collection of the Conservatoire in Paris, one of which has sympathetic strings attached to the table internally. The Victoria and Albert Museum possesses a handsome but rather undersized French specimen (oddly described in the Catalogue as ' probably Dutch ' also having sympathetic strings inside.

The Trummscheidt, in the Middle Ages, was sometimes fitted with two, three, and even four strings, one or more of which were Bourdons or drones. Illustrations of the 14th and 15th centuries show it as held and played at the shoulder, the open end pointing outwards like a trumpet.   E. J. P. ; addns. F. W. G.

It is quite evident that the instrument was made in a variety of forms, and probably few specimens existed precisely alike. Grassineau, in his *Musical Dictionary*, 1740, describes it as having ' three tables which form its triangular body ' ; also that the neck was very long, and the single string very thick, and not stopped by pressure, but merely gently touched with the thumb. He says its sound was scarcely distinguishable from that of a trumpet, and that it had the trumpet's defect of some notes being either too flat or too sharp. One of its peculiar qualities of tone was by reason of the bridge being firm on one side and tremulous on the other.

In Michael Praetorius's *Syntagma musicum* it is engraved on Plate XXI. under the title the ' Trumscheit.' This is apparently about 7 feet long and, as Grassineau describes it, formed by three tapering boards placed triangularly, and open at the bottom. There are four circular sound-holes, one covered by an ornamental ' rose,' but it differs from the usual ones described by having four strings of varying length tuned by pegs inserted in a peg-box similar to that of an ordinary violin.   F. K.

In the year 1667 Pepys records in his diary that he heard ' one Monsieur Priu play on the trump-marine, which he do beyond belief.' The Frenchman's instrument was fitted with sympathetic strings inside which caused Pepys to hear ' a whole concert of chords together at the end of a pause,' but he would not let the inquisitive diarist into the secret. In 1699 a book of ' Trumpet tunes, ayres, marches and minuets ' was published in London for the

---

[1] The interesting experiments of Sir Wm. Huggins, printed in the *Transactions of the Royal Society*, tend to show that the principle of the violin bridge is radically identical with that of the marine trumpet bridge, one foot serving as a *point d'appui*, the other as the conductor of vibration.

[2] The quartet of marine trumpets appears to be of ancient date. Hawkins (ch. 158) quotes from the *London Gazette*, Feb. 4, 1674, an advertisement of ' A rare Concert of four Trumpets Marine, never heard of before in England,' to be heard daily at the Fleece Tavern near St. James's.

[3] The music-master recommends the citizen to have a concert at his house every Wednesday or Thursday, and thus describes the requirements : ' Il vous faudra trois voix, un dessus, une hautecontre, et une basse, qui seront accompagnées d'une basse de viole, d'un théorbe, et d'un clavecin pour les basses continues, avec deux dessus de violon pour jouer les ritornelles.' M. Jourdain : ' Il y faudra mettre aussi une trompette marine. La trompette marine est un instrument qui me plaît, et qui est harmonieux.'

'molk-trumpet.' The following extracts from a 17th century MS. entitled 'Sonata per la trompa marina' by Don Lorenzo de Castro will show the sort of music played upon this interesting instrument :

F. W. G.

TROMBA SPEZZATA, an instrument of the trumpet kind, formerly popular among the Italian peasantry. It was generally made of two slides, and was, probably, originally identical with the old English Sackbut.　　F. K.

TROMBETTI, Ascanio, a Bolognese musician of the last quarter of the 16th century. On the title-page of his chief work published at Venice, 1589, he is described as Musico della illustrissima Signoria di Bologna. The work itself consists of motetti accomodati per cantare e far Concerti a 5, 6, 7, 8, 10 e 12, and shows the influence of the Venetian style of Andrea and Giovanni Gabrieli. From this work L. Torchi, in 'L' arte musicale in Italia,' vol. i., has reprinted 'Paratum est cor meum' a 5, and 'Misericordiae tuae' a 12, divided into three choirs. Several of these motets were also taken over into the German collections of Lindner in 1590 and Caspar Hasler 1600 and 1613. Other publications of Trombetti are Napolitane a 3, Venice, 1573, and two books of Madrigals a 4 and 5, Venice, 1583, 1586.

J. R. M.

TROMBONCINO, Bartholomaeus, a fertile composer of Frottole—the popular songs of that day—belonged to Verona, and was probably born in the latter half of the 15th century, since his works are contained in Petrucci's nine books of Frottole dating from 1504. He was in Mantua in 1487–95, being in the service of the Duke in 1494 and going to Venice in the follow-

ing year. In 1499 he was at the courts of Vicenza and Casale, and in 1501 again at Mantua, living there until 1513, when he went to Ferrara (Q.-L). The lists given in Eitner's Bibliographie, pp. 879-82, contain 107 of his compositions to secular and 2 to sacred words, all for 4 voices, as well as 9 Lamentations and 1 Benedictus for 3 voices. One of the Lamentations is reprinted in vol. i. of Torchi's 'L' arte musicale in Italia.'　　G., addns.

TROMBONE, formerly styled Sackbut (Fr. and Ital. trombone; Ger. Posaune), a brass instrument characterised by its ' slide ' which affecting the length of the tube instantaneously alters the pitch.

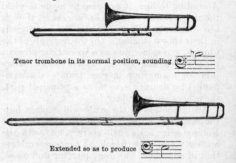

Tenor trombone in its normal position, sounding

Extended so as to produce

The Italian term trombone signifies a big trumpet, and another Italian name is Tromba Spezzata, i.e. ' broken trumpet.' For the etymology and use of the name 'sackbut' see under that heading.

It should be noted that the name trombone is specially applicable to an instrument the shifting slide of which is sufficiently long to lower the pitch three and a half tones, whereas the older instruments or sackbuts were more limited in this respect.

The two chief groups of brass instruments are the trumpets and horn classes, the greater length of tubing being in the one class cylindrical and in the other conical, with corresponding difference of tone quality. Differentiating in more detail, trombones are distinguished from trumpets by having a greater fullness of tone in the middle and lower registers, the ' tessitura ' of trumpets lying higher than that of trombones of the same length and fundamental pitch. For instance, the trumpet in E♭ differs in calibration but very slightly from the E♭ alto trombone, but the difference in character is that between a soprano and an alto voice. This difference is chiefly due to the larger mouthpieces used on trombones, by means of which the lower notes are more easily produced, with a certain dignity and solemnity of tone which stands contrasted with the brilliancy of the trumpet. This difference, however, is merely one of degree, and is not obtrusive, therefore the trombone, when instruments are grouped in families, is properly regarded as the natural bass of the trumpet.

DESCRIPTION. — The trombone is a very simple instrument, consisting essentially for about two-thirds of its length of cylindrical tubing, the remaining third being occupied by the gradual expansion of the bell. It might be regarded as perfect were it not that the great advantage obtained by the slide is to some extent interfered with by the fact that the outer or moving slide is necessarily rather larger than the inner one over which it works. In consequence of this difference of diameter certain notes are rather apt to 'break' and require humouring. The mouthpiece is usually cup-shaped, but sometimes more conical, and is held steadily to the player's lips by the left hand, which, chiefly, bears the weight of the instrument, the right hand controlling the movement of the slide and aiding in the balance. For the shorter shifts the movement should be almost entirely from the wrist, but the longer ones require more or less extension of the arm. For the bass trombone the full reach of the arm is insufficient, however, and is increased by means of a jointed handle.

To obviate the great extension required for the extreme shifts, the whole slide has been sometimes doubled, and by this means the shifts are reduced to half-length. This arrangement is necessary on the contrabass trombone in C or B♭, and has been used on the bass instrument in F or E♭. Its application, however, to the tenor trombone and to the bass in G, although not unknown, serves no useful purpose, and cannot be considered an improvement.

By the introduction of the slide, it is obvious that the trombone, alone of all the wind-family, has the accuracy and modulative power of stringed instruments. Its notes are not fixed, but made by ear and judgment. It is competent to produce at will a major or minor tone, or any one of the three different semitones.

POSITIONS AND COMPASS. — There are seven 'positions' for the movable slide, successive elongations of the tube, each of which produces its own harmonic series. The seven positions may be said in a general way to be each a semi-tone lower than the last. The first is with the slide entirely undrawn. But in the hands of a good player, the length of slide used for each successive position is not the same. But a judicious player, with a sensitive ear, has the remedy in his own power; and the mechanism as well as the mental sensation of trombone-playing, more nearly approaches that of voice production than that of any other instrument.

The trombone has been made in every register from soprano to contra-bass and in every key; those now generally used are the tenor trombone in B♭, the bass trombone in G or F and, more rarely, E♭, and the contra-

bass trombone. The alto trombone in E♭ (sometimes styled *trombonino* in Italian; Ger. *Altposaune*) is to all intents and purposes now obsolete, as are such other varieties as the 17th-century discant trombone, an octave above the tenor, used by Purcell in the canzona for the funeral of Queen Mary.

The following table gives the slide position for tenor and bass trombones:

TABLE OF TROMBONE POSITIONS

	Tenor.	G Bass.	F Bass.
First position . .	B♭	G	F
Second position .	A	F♯	E
Third position . .	A♭	F	E♭
Fourth position .	G	E	D
Fifth position . .	F♯	E♭	D♭
Sixth position . .	F	D	C
Seventh position .	E	C♯	B

It is here seen that the player has in use the equivalent of seven different instruments, any one of which can be converted into any other by a single movement of the right arm; though some sequences involve more change, and are consequently of greater difficulty than others.

The harmonic series is the same as that of the horn and other cupped instruments. The lowest tones or fundamentals are somewhat difficult to produce, and are usually termed pedal notes. The available scale therefore begins with the second harmonic, runs without break to the sixth, omits the dissonant seventh harmonic, and may be considered to end with the eighth, though some higher notes are possible, especially in the longer positions.

The complete chromatic compass of the tenor trombone is from ... to ... , two or three semitones higher being also possible, while the three available pedal notes are

The contrabass trombone as introduced by Wagner was in B♭, an octave lower than the tenor trombone. It has been made in England in C, a tone higher, unfortunately placing the low E ... required in the 'Ring' out of reach. But the serious difficulty about this instrument is the strain on lungs and lip in the production of such deep tones. They are undoubtedly more easily sounded on the larger bore instruments of the saxhorn type.

THE VALVE TROMBONE. — The efficiency of the slide as applied to the trombone leaves nothing to be desired, and therefore the application of the valve action to this instrument as a substitute for the slide cannot be regarded as an improvement. The long study and practice required for the mastery of the slide trombone left the way open for an instrument more easily learnt, hence the adaptation of the valve to the trombone family, and the instrument so furnished is largely used in military and other wind bands. It is true that the valve trombone has not quite the brilliancy of the slide, but it is a mistake to class it with the tenor and baritone saxhorns, as is sometimes done.

The usual number of valves is three, as on saxhorns, but the six-valve system, introduced by Adolphe Sax in 1850, has been applied to the trombone as well as to other instruments. A seventh valve, lowering the pitch from B♭ to F, has been added to an instrument made for Sir Henry Wood.[1] (See VALVE.)

Parts for the trombone are written as sounded, the tenor trombone needing the tenor clef for the higher register; for the alto trombone the alto clef was used. It is usual to find three trombones, two tenor and a bass (or in France, three tenor, the third being preferably of larger calibre than the first and second), in the ordinary orchestra; the addition of a bass-tuba for four-part harmony is normal, although by no means completely satisfactory from the point of view of pure tone-colour. In such cases the tenor trombones will have a stave to themselves, the bass trombone and tuba taking another.

HISTORY.—Although the story respecting the finding of two Roman sackbuts in 1738 has been completely disproved, there is reason to credit the use of the slide as a means of slightly altering the pitch of an instrument, or even (when freely moving) of introducing tones foreign to those obtainable from its normal length, with some antiquity. Some such use can be traced among Eastern nations and in ancient times, but the evidence of gradual development cannot be introduced in a brief article. It must suffice to say that by the end of the 14th century the doubled slide was in use, and that in Virdung's *Musica getutscht* (published in 1511) there is a drawing of a Busaun (posaune or trombone) very similar in its general proportions to the present-day instrument, having the slide sufficiently long to give a 'shift' of three and a half tones, and therefore a complete chromatic scale. Towards the end of the 15th century there was a famous player and maker, Hans Neuschel of Nuremberg, whose work was continued by his sons, Hans and Jorg. (See *PLATE LXVIII.* No. 4.)[2]

It is noticeable that whereas the trumpet was regarded in the Middle Ages as an instrument reserved for the service of royalty and the nobility, the trombone was from the first more freely employed by the various town-bands in festivals and pageants. Its use in churches, orchestras and town-bands was universal in Germany, Krüger publishing in 1585 'Psalmodia sacra,' which contains four-part chorals with organ accompaniment and from four to six trombone parts.

There is an excellent representation of an angel playing a slide trombone in a ceiling-picture given in the appendix to Lacroix (*Arts de la Renaissance*), and in one replica of Paolo Veronese's great 'Marriage of Cana' (not that in the Salon Carré in the Louvre) a negro is performing on the same instrument. Michael Praetorius, in the *Theatrum seu Sciagraphia instrumentorum*, dated 1620, gives excellent figures of the Octav-Posaun, the Quart-Posaun, the Rechtgemeine Posaun, and the Alt-Posaun.

In this country, during the Tudor and Stuart reigns, the English school of playing was in high repute. Henry VIII. had ten players, and Mary and Elizabeth each maintained four. Towards the end of the 18th century, however, the interest taken in the instrument, or perhaps merely the number of players, appears to have fallen low, for Burney (*Commemoration of Handel*, 1784) relates the difficulty experienced in obtaining players on the sackbut or double trumpet, the only performers to be found in England being the six German musicians of the royal band. Handel and Bach used the trombone. For a time it appears to have been neglected, possibly owing to the improved French horn. Gluck and Mozart, however, wrote for it in opera, and Beethoven introduced it into the symphonic orchestra first in the finale of his symphony in C minor.

N. C. G.; incorporating material from
W. H. S. and D. J. B.

TROMLITZ, JOHANN GEORG (*b.* Gera, 1726; *d.* Leipzig, Feb. 1805), flautist, composer and flute manufacturer, composed concertos, sonatas and solos for the flute, songs and some instructive work (Tutor for Flute) (*Riemann*; *Q.-L.*).

TROMMEL, see DRUM.

TROPE. There arose in the 8th or 9th century, probably under Byzantine influence, a custom of making interpolations into the church chant, which in course of time spread through almost the whole range of liturgical song. Such interpolations had the generic name of trope. They speedily affected all the music of the Ordinary of the Mass; till then only one or two melodies of the simplest sort had been utilised for the congregational elements, viz. the Kyrie, Gloria, Credo, Sanctus and Agnus: now new melodies of an elaborate character grew up, and even the new melodies were further elaborated by tropes. Similarly

---

[1] For some years valve trombones were used in the Queen's Hall Orchestra, but now (1926), the slide instruments have been restored.

[2] This instrument, in the Rev. Canon F. W. Galpin's collection, dated MDLVII. by these makers, agrees very closely with the illustration in Virdung's work. Canon Galpin states that, as far as can be ascertained, this is the oldest specimen of the instrument in existence. (See *Proceedings of the Musical Association*, 1906–07, p. 1.)

long melodies were added in other parts of the Mass, particularly at the end of the Alleluia ; and the ornamentation extended also on great occasions to special parts of the Hour services.

Soon a need arose for words to be fitted to these elaborate intercalated *vocalizzi*, and then the habit came in of intercalating words as well as music. The words were either adapted to the already existing music, or both words and music arose together. Thus the sequence developed as a trope, and acquired an independent position of its own (see SEQUENCE). Words were also fitted to Kyrie, Gloria in excelsis, Sanctus and Agnus in the form of tropes ; but never to the Credo. Similarly, Epistles were ' farced ' but not Gospels. In the Hour services the tropes invaded especially the closing respond of Matins, thus making a final peroration to that service ; but as the development went on there was little left that had not suffered from these parasites. Even the short closing versicle and response ' Benedicamus domino , Deo gratias ' was troped, and here as elsewhere the trope grew into an elaborate and almost independent composition. Then came a revulsion ; as the 16th century drew on the tropes began to disappear, and finally, in the Tridentine revision of the Latin service-books all trace of tropes was banished, unless the one or two surviving sequences may be counted as such. But some tropes had sufficient merit to preserve their existence in a separate form ; *e.g.* the popular melody set to ' Of the Father's love begotten ' [1] is in origin a trope to the Sanctus, while the popular poem *O filii et filiae* [2] is a trope to Benedicamus.   W. H. F.

TROPPO, *i.e.* ' too much ' ; ' Allegro ma non troppo '—' Allegro ; but not too much so.'

TROUBADOUR, THE, opera in 4 acts ; words by Francis Hueffer ; music by Mackenzie. Produced (Carl Rosa Co.) Drury Lane, June 8, 1886.   M.

TROUBADOUR (Old Provençal nominative *trobaire*, accusative *trobador*), ' inventor (of a melody),' the name given to the poet-musicians of Southern France whose art flourished from the end of the 11th till the end of the 13th century. The names of 460 troubadours have been recorded, and poems by the great majority of these are extant. Although the troubadours always set their lyrics to music, the melodies have in many cases been lost. Only 259 melodies have been preserved, whereas we have the words of over 2500 songs. The principal MSS. containing troubadour music are :

Milan, Biblioteca Ambrosiana, R 71 superiore (81 melodies).
Paris, Bibliothèque Nationale, fonds français 22,543 (160 melodies).
   ,,   ,,   ,,   ,,   844 (51 melodies).
   ,,   ,,   ,,   ,,   20,050 (24 melodies).

A few songs have been preserved in other MSS. For a complete list of the MSS. and of their contents, see J. B. Beck, *Die Melodien der Troubadours*, Strassburg, 1908.

Troubadour songs fall into two main categories, the ' poésie courtoise ' and the ' chanson à personnages.' The latter genre was, however, little cultivated by the troubadours. It was far more popular with their Northern French contemporaries, the TROUVÈRES (*q.v.*).

' Courtly Poetry ' consists chiefly of purely lyrical songs, *vers* and *canso*, the characteristic love-poetry of the troubadours. It comprises also the *sirventes*, a political or moral satire, the *tenso*, a dispute between two or more troubadours, the *partimen*, a debate on a given subject, and other minor genres.

The troubadours wrote their poems in stanzas and each stanza of a song was sung to the same melody (the only exception is the *descort* ; see below). The music is therefore given at the beginning of each song in the MSS., the words of the first stanza being written underneath the notes. The remaining stanzas follow without music. The music is purely melodic, and there is no indication in the MSS. as to how the songs were accompanied. The melodies are written on staves, usually of four lines, in plain-song notation (MS. 20050 uses Messenian neumes). This shows the pitch of the notes quite clearly, but gives no clue as to the rhythmic principle on which the melodies are composed. Many different views have been put forth as to the way in which they should be interpreted as regards their rhythm. H. Riemann [3] proposed a system which reduces all the melodies to phrases of four measures, each measure having four beats. P. Aubry [4] and J. B. Beck,[5] arguing from slightly different premises, both arrived at the same conclusion—namely that the melodies are written in the RHYTHMIC MODES (*q.v.*). Their arguments, though ingenious and supported by the evidence of a few songs that are actually written in proportional notation, were not found convincing by J. Combarieu,[6] or by A. Gastoué,[7] neither of whom considers that the music of the troubadours belongs to the *musica praecise mensurata* of the Middle Ages.

As regards tonality, some of the melodies have a distinctly modal character, others approximate to the modern major mode.

The metrical form of the songs is very varied (it was a rule that no two songs should exactly correspond in form), but in the majority, the stanza falls into two main divisions, and the first half—often also the second half—contains two equal subdivisions, *e.g.* a b a b c c d, or a b a b c d c d. The musical form does not always correspond exactly with the metrical form, indeed it is rare to find a repeated musical phrase in the second half of the stanza. In many songs the melody flows on without

[1] *Hymns Ancient and Modern*, No. 56.   [2] *Ibid.* No. 130.

[3] *Handbuch der Musikgeschichte*, 1905.
[4] *La Rythmique musicale des troubadours et des trouvères*, 1907.
[5] *Die Melodien der Troubadours*, 1908.
[6] *Histoire de la musique*, vol. i. chapter xxi. 1923.
[7] *Les Primitifs de la musique française*. 1922.

repetition through the stanza. A repeated melodic phrase in the first half is, however, often found. A closer approximation of musical to metrical form is found in the songs of the trouvères.

Guilhem Molinier, author of ' Las leys d'amors,' a 14th-century *Ars poetica* written for the ' most gay company ' of Toulouse (see below), gives the following definitions of the principal genres, and of the style of music suitable to them :

' *Vers* is a poem in Romance (*i.e.* in the vernacular, not in Latin) which has from five to ten *coblas* (stanzas) with one or two *tornadas* (envoys). And it should treat of *sens* (intelligence, sense).' He adds that since the word is derived from *verto*, 'which means turn or change,' a *vers* may also treat of other matters, ' for it is ever changing, for it treats of love or praise or blame.' ' A *vers* should have a slow quiet new melody, with fair and melodious rises and falls and with fair modulations and pleasing rests.'

' *Canso* is a poem which has from five to seven *coblas*. And it should treat principally of love or of praise. . . . A *canso* should have a slow melody, like a *vers*.'

' *Sirventes* is a poem which is served by *vers* and *canso* principally in two things, the one as regards the compass of its stanzas, the other as regards its melody.' That is to say, a *sirventes* copied the metrical form of some well-known song and was sung to its melody. ' And it should treat of blame or of general invective to reprove the foolish and the wicked, or it may treat, if desired, of the affairs of some war.'

' *Descort* is a very strange poem, and it may have as many *coblas* as the *vers*, that is from five to ten, and they must be singular, variable and not corresponding in rime, in melody and in language.' There is a *descort* by Raimbaut de Vaqueiras, of which the first five stanzas are written respectively in Provençal, Italian, French, Gascon and Portuguese, the last stanza, of ten lines, having two lines in each of these languages. Unluckily the music has not been preserved.

Melodies by 41 troubadours have been preserved, in addition to 27 anonymous songs. Many of the composers are represented by only one song.

The first of the troubadours—at all events the first whose works are extant—was Guilhem IX., Duke of Aquitaine (*d.* 1127). Only one of his melodies has survived.

Among the more famous troubadours may be mentioned :

Bernart of Ventadorn (*d.* 1195), the finest poet of them all. Forty-five of his poems and 19 of his melodies have survived. Some of the latter are extremely beautiful.

Bertran de Born (*d. circa* 1215), best known as a sower of discord between Henry II. of England and his sons. The majority of his 46 extant poems are *sirventes*, written to melodies by other troubadours. One original melody by him has survived.

Folquet of Marseilles (*d.* 1231), who wrote between 1180 and 1195, then renounced the world and died as Bishop of Toulouse. We have 27 poems and 13 melodies by him.

Peire Vidal (*d. circa* 1215), an eccentric character, but a fine poet and melodist. Fifty of his poems and 12 of his melodies have survived.

Guiraut de Bornelh (*d. circa* 1220), called in his own day ' Master of the Troubadours.' We have over 80 poems by him, but only 4 melodies. Two of these were used by Bertran de Born for *sirventes*.

Raimon de Miraval (22 melodies) and Peirol (17 melodies) (both *d. circa* 1220), though not among the greatest troubadour poets, were unusually fortunate as regards the number of their melodies that have survived.

Guiraut Riquier, the last of the troubadours (*d.* 1292), was also one of the most important. The music of 48 of his 89 songs has been preserved.

At the end of the 13th century the art of the troubadours died out. In the following century an attempt to revive it was made by certain citizens of Toulouse, who founded a kind of academy, ' la sobregaya companhia,' and offered prizes for the best *cansos*, dance-songs and *sirventes*. The academy is still in existence, but its members cannot be regarded as having been at any period successors of the troubadours.

(For Bibliography, see under TROUVÈRE.)

B. S.

TROUPENAS, EUGÈNE (*b.* Paris, 1799 ; *d.* there, Apr. 11, 1850), French music-publisher. As a child he showed decided taste for music, but his family intended him for an engineer, and put him to study mathematics with Wronsky, a Polish professor, who, however, dissuaded him from entering the École Polytechnique and indoctrinated him with his own misty transcendentalism. The results of this early training came out when, left in easy circumstances by the death of his parents, he became a music-publisher, for to the last it was the metaphysical side of the art which interested him. He never gave his ideas in full to the world, but a couple of letters which originally came out in the *Revue musicale* were published in pamphlet form with the title

' Essai sur la théorie de la musique, déduite du principe métaphysique sur lequel se fonde la réalité de cette science ' (1832).

Troupenas took up the brothers Escudier when they came to seek their fortune in Paris, and it was with his assistance that they founded their journal *La France musicale*. A man of the world, a good musician, and a fascinating talker, his friendship was sought by many artists of eminence. Rossini, Auber and de Bériot were sincerely attached to him, and found him always devoted to their interests. He also published Halévy's operas, Donizetti's 'La Favorita,' and all Henri Herz's pianoforte pieces at the time of his greatest popularity; indeed it is not too much to say that from 1825–50 his stock was one of the largest and best selected of all the publishing-houses in Paris. At his death it was purchased by the music publishers, Brandus (see SCHLESINGER), and the larger part still remains in their hands.   G. C.

TROUTBECK, the REV. JOHN (b. Blencowe, Cumberland, Nov. 12, 1832; d. Westminster, Oct. 11, 1899), a well-known translator of libretti into English, was educated at Rugby and Oxford, where he graduated B.A. 1856, and M.A. 1858. He took orders in 1855, and rose through various dignities to be precentor of Manchester, 1865–69, and minor canon of Westminster, 1869. He was buried in the East Walk of the Cloisters.[1] He translated the following for Novello & Co.'s 8vo series:

Bach. St. Matthew and St. John Passions; Christmas Oratorio; Magnificat. etc.	**Graun.** Der Tod Jesu.
Beethoven. Mount of Olives.	**Hiller.** Song of Victory.
Brahms. Song of Destiny.	**Jensen.** Feast of Adonis.
David. Le Désert.	**Liszt.** 13th Psalm.
Dvořák. Mass; St. Ludmilla; Spectre's Bride.	**Mozart.** Il seraglio.
Gade. Crusaders; Comala; Psyche; Zion.	**Reinecke.** Little Snowdrop.
Gluck. Iphigenia in Aulis; Iphigenia in Tauris; Orpheus.	**Romberg.** Lay of the Bell.
Goetz. Taming of the Shrew; By the Waters of Babylon; Naenia.	**Saint-Saëns.** Ps. xix.
	Schumann. Advent Hymn; the King's Son. Mignon's Requiem; New Year's Song.
Gounod. Redemption; Mors et Vita.	**Tchaikovsky.** Nature and Love.
	Wagner. Flying Dutchman.
	Weber. Jubilee Cantata; Preciosa.

besides many minor works. He also published The Manchester Psalter (1868), and Hymn-Book (1871), A Music Primer for Schools, and A Primer for Church Choir Training (1870), and compiled the hymn-book in use at Westminster Abbey in 1883. The Cathedral Paragraph Psalter followed in 1894, and he joined Sir J. F. Bridge in preparing the 'Westminster Abbey Chant Book.'   G.

TROUVÈRE (old French nominative trovere, accusative troveor). The name given to the lyric poets of Northern France is etymologically identical with that of their Provençal predecessors and contemporaries, whose art they imitated (Hypothetical Latin tropator, tropatorem). (Cf. TROUBADOUR.)

The popularising in Northern France of the art and ideas of the Southern poets was largely the work of Eleanor of Aquitaine, granddaughter of the first of the troubadours. Her marriage with the French King Louis VII. in 1137 brought about important developments in the history of French literature. A patroness of the troubadours (to her Bernart of Ventadorn addressed many of his finest songs), she and her daughters after her encouraged the poets of the North to practise a similar form of art. From the middle of the 12th century a

school of poetry similar to that of the troubadours flourished in Northern France, dying out with the decay of chivalry at the end of the 13th century.

About two hundred trouvères are known to us by name, and melodies by nearly all of them have survived. Altogether about two thousand Northern French songs, including many anonymous works, have been preserved. The principal MSS. are:

Arras, Bibliothèque, 657.
London, British Museum, Egerton 274.
Paris, Bibliothèque de l'Arsenal, 5198.
Paris, Bibliothèque Nationale, fonds français 844.

,,	,,	,,	,,	,,	845.
,,	,,	,,	,,	,,	846.
,,	,,	,,	,,	,,	847.
,,	,,	,,	,,	,,	1,591.
,,	,,	,,	,,	,,	12,615.
,,	,,	,,	,,	,,	20,050.
,,	,,	,,	,,	,,	24,406.
,,	,,	,,	,,	,,	25,566.
,,	,,	,,	,,	nouvelles acquisitions fr. 1050.

Rome, Biblioteca Vaticana, Christina 1490.
Siena, Biblioteca, H. X. 36.

The most important of all these manuscripts is that of the Bibliothèque de l'Arsenal. It contains words as well as melodies of 482 songs. Pierre Aubry undertook the publication of this MS. in photographic facsimile with a transcription of the melodies into modern notation. His great work was nearing completion at the time of his death in 1910.

The 'courtly poetry' of the trouvères is written in the same style as that of the troubadours, and the music is of the same type. The form, both musical and metrical, used by the trouvères, is generally that of two Stollen and an Abgesang; that is to say, the first half of the stanza falls into two equal parts sung to a repeated melodic phrase, and the second half is sung to one melodic phrase. A repetition in the second half is, however, not unknown. The lai was similar to the Provençal descort in changing melody and metre for each stanza, but it was written in French throughout.

The chanson à personnages was more popular with the French than with the Provençal poets. The fact that many of the extant songs of this type are anonymous was formerly held to be a proof that they were of popular origin, or at least imitated from popular models. This view has now been given up, and it is generally admitted that even the anonymous songs are the work of skilled trouvères in their less serious moments. A good account of the different types of chanson à personnages is given in Pierre Aubry's Trouvères et troubadours, pp. 37-94. The most numerous are pastourelles, and the dancing-songs written to accompany various kinds of dances. The latter, which always have a refrain, have a special importance in the history both of literature and of music, since it was from them that the fixed forms of song, such as the ballade and the rondeau, were developed.

The pastourelle, which usually takes the form of a dialogue between the poet and a shepherdess, was cultivated by the troubadours, but was much more popular in Northern France. Over 100 French pastourelles are extant.

Among the principal trouvères of the 12th century are:

Gace Brulé, to whom 90 songs are attributed in the MSS., though his editor, G. Huet, thinks that only 34 are certainly his work.

Conon de Béthune (10 songs, 9 of which have music).

The Châtelain of Coucy (15 songs with music).

Blondel de Nesle (22 songs), whose name is probably best known in connexion with the charming but apocryphal story of his search for his imprisoned master, Richard Cœur de Lion (himself a trouvère).

In the 13th century, the best-known name, with the exception of Adam de la Hale, is that of Thibaut, Count of Champagne, afterwards King of Navarre. The extant songs attributed to him number over 70, and the melodies of all but 2 of these have survived. He wrote pastourelles, religious songs and jeux-partis (the French equivalent of the Provençal partimen), but the majority of his lyrics are love-songs in the Provençal style. As a writer of these he is unequalled among the trouvères and has few rivals even among the troubadours.

Colin Muset, a jongleur (15 songs, 8 with music), deserves mention for the charm and good humour of his songs.

Many literary academies were founded during the 13th century in Northern France. They were known as puys, from the town of Puy Notre Dame, where the earliest society of the kind had been founded in the 12th century by the troubadours. The most celebrated of the Northern French puys was that of Arras, and this town produced many trouvères in the 13th century. The name of Adam de la HALE (q.v.), eclipses that of all his fellow-citizens.

BIBLIOGRAPHY

The following are indispensable :
J. B. BECK : *Die Melodien der Troubadours* (Strasbourg, 1908).
P. AUBRY : *La Rythmique musicale des troubadours et des trouvères.* (Paris, 1907.)
Le Chansonnier de l'Arsenal. This contains by far the largest published collection of trouvère melodies in modern notation.
Le Chansonnier de Saint-Germain des Prés, published by the 'Société des anciens textes français,' is a photographic facsimile of MS. ff. 20050 in the Bibliothèque Nationale.
C. APPEL : *Bernart von Ventadorn.* (1915.) (Contains photographic facsimiles of 15 of this troubadour's melodies, namely those preserved in Milan Ambrosiana, R 71, sup., and in Paris Bibl. Nat. ff. 22543.)
J. BÉDIER : *Les Chansons de Colin Muset.* (1912.) (With transcription of the melodies by J. B. Beck.)
P. AUBRY : *Trouvères et troubadours.* (1909.)
J. B. BECK : *La Musique des troubadours.* (1910.)
A full bibliography of all works on the subject published up till 1908 is given in each of the two last-named works. See also the bibliography in Combarieu, *Histoire de la musique,* vol. i. p. 349.

B. S.

TROVATORE, IL, opera in 4 acts ; libretto by Cammarano, music by Verdi. Produced Teatro Apollo, Rome, Jan. 19, 1853 ; Théâtre des Italiens, Paris, Dec. 23, 1854 ; in French, Opéra, Jan. 12, 1857 ; New York, Apr. 30, 1855 ; Covent Garden, May 17, 1855 ; in English, Drury Lane, Mar. 24, 1856.

TROYENS, LES, 'lyric poem,' words and music by Berlioz ; originally forming one long

opera, but afterwards divided into two— (1) ' La Prise de Troie ' ; (2) ' Les Troyens à Carthage.' No. 1 was performed at the Paris Opéra, Nov. 15, 1899, after the composer's death.[1] No. 2 was produced at the Théâtre Lyrique, Nov. 4, 1863, revised at the Opéra-Comique, June 9, 1892, Opéra, June 10, 1921, and published in PF. score by Choudens. (See Berlioz's *Mémoires.*) The first performance of the work as a whole took place on Dec. 6 and 7, 1890,[2] at Carlsruhe, under Mottl.   G., rev.

TRUELOVE (TROULUFFE), JOHN, a 15th-16th century English composer, wrote a sacred duet and some carols *a* 2 v. in conjunction with Richard SMERT (q.v.) of Plymtree, co. Devon (B.M. Add. MSS. 5665), MS. *c.* 1510.

TRUHN, FRIEDRICH HIERONYMUS (b. Elbing, Oct. 14, 1811 ; d. Berlin, Apr. 30, 1886), became scholar of Klein and Dehn, and also had a few lessons from Mendelssohn. He lived chiefly in Berlin and Dantzig, but with many intervals of travelling. One of his tours was made with Bülow. His operetta, ' Der vierjährige Posten,' was produced at Berlin, 1833, and his opera, ' Trilby,' 1835 ; but he is chiefly known by his partsongs—amongst them ' The Three Chafers.' He also contributed to the *Neue Zeitschrift für Musik* and the *Neue Berliner Musikzeitung.* He founded the Neue Liedertafel in Berlin.   G.

TRUINET, see NUITTER.

TRUMPET (natural trumpet, Fr. *trompette ;* Ger. *Trompete, Trummet, Tarantara ;* Ital. *tromba,* tr. *doppia, clarino ;* valve trumpet, Fr. *trompette à pistons ;* Ger. *Ventiltrompete ;* Ital. *tromba ventile*). An instrument, usually of brass consisting of a tube mainly cylindrical in bore doubled back on itself and played with a mouthpiece of the hemispherical variety (see MOUTHPIECE).

It will be well at the outset to define clearly the term trumpet as distinguished from horn, both to remove ambiguity and to afford a ready means for a broad classification of all lip-blown instruments. By trumpets, then, with which trombones must be included, we understand instruments of a peculiarly incisive and brilliant tone-quality, due partly to the tubing being cylindrical for a great portion of its length, and partly to the hemispherical form of the mouthpiece cup. Horns, whether short, as the natural horns of animals, or long, as the modern orchestral horns and tubas, are mainly conical in form, and are played with mouthpieces deeper in the cup than those suitable for trumpets. There are great varieties of tone-quality among horns, but, speaking generally, their tone is less brilliant, but broader, and more vocal, than that of the trumpet. The ordinary infantry bugle may be regarded as typical of the horn class, and the modern cornet as a somewhat

[1] See Jullien's *Berlioz.*
[2] Date from playbills in the possession of Ernest Newman.

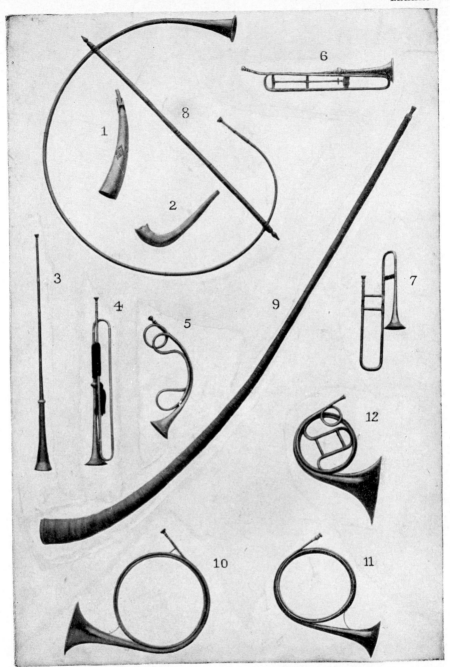

LXXXIII

Galpin Collection

1. AFRICAN WAR HORN.   2. JEWISH SHOFAR.   3. BUZINE (S. Hainlein, 1460).   4. CLARINO
or CLARION (J. Haas, *c.* 1650).   5. HAND TRUMPET (Lintner, 1786).   6. ENGLISH SLIDE
TRUMPET (*c.* 1820).   7. TREBLE TROMBONE or TROMBA DA TIRARSI (J. Schmied, 1781).
8. ROMAN BUCCINA (*c.* 100 B.C.)—a copy.   9. ALPHORN (19th cent.).   10. GERMAN
HUNTING HORN (F. Ehe, *c.* 1650).   11. ENGLISH HUNTING HORN (W. Bull, 1690).
12. HAND HORN (18th cent.).

hybrid instrument, intermediate in character between the trumpet and horn.

The true trumpet character requires considerable length of tube. The Roman lituus, judging by one discovered in 1827, was pitched in G, or a major third higher than the modern cavalry trumpet, which is in E♭, and although small valve trumpets in B♭ are now in use, the characteristic quality of the instrument is to be found at its best in the natural trumpets in D, with a total length of about eighty-eight inches.

NATURAL TRUMPET.—This is an instrument without side-holes, slide, valves, or in short, any means of altering its length. (See *PLATE LXXXIII.* Nos. 3, 4, 5.) Such an instrument is limited to the harmonic scale, and although the prime of the harmonic series can easily be obtained on wide-bore conical instruments, the proportions of the trumpet make it practically impossible to give this note; so that in actual practice the scale begins with the octave of the prime, and even this note is difficult on trumpets of small bore. To complete the diatonic scale, we find an early introduction of side-holes on small conical-bore instruments, such as the zinckes or cornetts, on which the prime and its octave are easily produced, and this was followed later on the larger conical instruments such as serpents and ophicleides, by side-holes closed or opened by keys. The side-hole method of altering fundamental pitch, although it has been attempted on the trumpet, is utterly unsuited to it, and therefore the natural trumpet long held the field, and this is the instrument which must now be more particularly described.

Instruments such as the Greek salpinx and the Roman tuba, corresponding approximately to the modern coach-horn, being straight tubes with bell-mouths, cannot be conveniently handled if more than about 4 feet in length, and on such short tubes no harmonic higher than the eighth is practicable. An increase of length makes it possible to produce notes up to the tenth, twelfth and even the sixteenth notes of the harmonic series, covering many notes in the diatonic scale.

That the necessary increase of length might be practicably adopted, the tube was doubled upon itself in various ways; but by the time of Virdung (1511) and Praetorius (1618) the natural trumpet had settled down to the form in which we still use it. Such an instrument is cylindrical in bore for about three-fourths of its length, the diameter being from $\frac{40}{100}$ to $\frac{46}{100}$ of an inch, the remaining fourth being the 'bell' with an increasing conical expansion terminating in a 'flange' of from four to five inches diameter. The mouthpiece has a somewhat shallow or hemispherical cup, and a rim with an internal diameter varying from that of a threepenny to a sixpenny piece.

The natural notes begin with 8-foot C, which is not used, and follow the harmonic series, up

to the C above the soprano clef. The actual sounds from the trumpet in D are a tone higher. Pedal notes seem to be unknown.[1]

The trumpet is adapted for other keys than that in which it is built by the use of CROOKS (*q.v.*). Praetorius mentions the use of a crook by which the trumpet could be put from D into C, and this means of altering the pitch-note and key was extended downwards to B♭ and A♮, and by an inversion of the process the higher pitches of F and G were introduced, and in anticipation it may here be stated that the raising of the pitch has been extended to the B♭ soprano, or cornet pitch, although the really characteristic trumpet tone diminishes after F as a fundamental is reached.

The limitations imposed by the harmonic scale of the 'natural' trumpet led to various attempts to introduce means of making its scale completely diatonic and even chromatic. There are four possible means of achieving this result, and all have been tried. These are (1) the use of side-holes covered by keys, (2) the stopping or muting of the bell by means of the hand as on the French horn, (3) the alteration of fundamental length by means of a slide, and (4) a similar but more extended alteration by means of valves.[2] The first of these systems was introduced by Kölbel of St. Petersburg in 1770, and in 1795 Weidinger of Vienna produced a trumpet which had five keys covering side-holes. The general principle of side-holes, although within certain limits, as noted above, fairly satisfactory on conical instruments such as the bugle and the ophicleide, is not really applicable to instruments of cylindrical bore such as the trumpet, and in consequence, the keyed trumpet soon died out. The second method, that of muting and changing the pitch by placing the hand in the bell, was introduced by Michael Wöggel in 1780. His instrument, although called the 'Invention horn,' was really a hand-stopped trumpet, and to make the hand-stopping practicable, the general form of the instrument was bent to a curve; but as hand-stopped notes are utterly foreign to the true trumpet tone, the instrument had no value.

THE SLIDE TRUMPET.—The third plan, the change of length by means of a slide, has more merit than either of the foregoing. It was introduced by John Hyde

[1] Eichborn names 'Das kontra Register' or 'Posaunen Register,' but says 'es spricht sehr schwer an.'

[2] In the *Monatshefte für Musik-Gesch.* for 1881, No. III. is a long and interesting article by Eitner, investigating the facts as to the inventor of the 'Ventil trompete,' which is said to date from 1802 or 1803. The writer seems, however, to confuse entirely the key-system or 'Klappen Trompete' with the ventil or valve. Eitner's error is exposed in the preface to Eichborn's *Die Trompete.*

about the end of the 18th century, and although it never obtained general acceptance throughout Europe, and is now disused owing to the improvement of the piston-valve instrument, its good points gave it a strong position in England for the rendering of classical trumpet music (see *PLATE LXXXIII*. No. 6). The slide trumpet as used by Harper may be thus described.[1]

It consists of a tube sixty-six inches and three-quarters in length, and three-eighths of an inch in diameter. It is twice turned or curved, thus forming three lengths ; the first and third lying close together, and the second about two inches apart. The last fifteen inches form a bell. The slide is connected with the second curve. It is a double tube five inches in length on each side, by which the length of the whole instrument can be extended. It is worked from the centre by the second and third fingers of the right hand, and after being pulled back is drawn forward to its original position by a spring fixed in a small tube occupying the centre of the instrument. There are five crooks, a tuning bit, and the mouthpiece.

In the slide trumpet the slide is so placed and used as to be limited to an extension giving one tone only, but there appears to be no sufficient reason against the adoption of a long slide on the trombone principle. Trumpets are the natural treble to the trombones, and in this way the family could be made complete.

Slide trumpets have also been made with a double slide, having four limbs in all and affording twice the extension obtainable from the more ordinary model.

An attempt to amplify the scale of the slide trumpet by the addition of a single valve tuned to lower the pitch a minor tone was brought under the notice of the Musical Association in 1876, but the system did not come into general use.

THE VALVE TRUMPET.—The modern valve-trumpet in F has three valves, and crooks are but little used. (For the details of the valve-action, see VALVE.) This instrument is the only really effective substitute for the old natural trumpet, and it is to be regretted that it has gone so much out of favour, especially where the performance of classical music is concerned. Owing to its length and large bore it has a weight and nobility of tone which cannot be produced by the shorter, more popular high-pitched valve-trumpet in C, or B flat, the more usual key (see *PLATE LXXXIV*. No. 2).

The effective compass of the F trumpet is chromatically from ♯𝄞 to 𝄞 , sounding a fourth higher, the part being written as though in the key of C.

[1] Harper, *School for the Trumpet*. Rudall, Carte & Co.

It is practically superseded now by the high-pitched instrument having a chromatic compass from 𝄞 to 𝄞 .

If built in B flat, or played with a B flat crook, the part is written a tone higher. The use of an A crook necessitates the part being written a minor third higher. It is usual nowadays to give the part the correct key-signature, thus avoiding accidentals, and at the same time giving the player a better idea of the tonality of the music.

If this instrument has lost some of the nobility of tone which is characteristic of the natural trumpet and the valve trumpet in F, it has gained greatly in flexibility. Without it the latter-day effects demanded by composers would be impossible.

The trumpet is muted by the insertion into the bell of a pear-shaped stopper, and the part marked ' con sordino.'

The bass trumpet is a valve trumpet in C-*basso*, *i.e.*, an instrument sounding an octave lower than the trumpet in C, the pitch of which is given above. Bass trumpets in B♭ and E♭ are also built for military bands.

HISTORY.—The mediæval use of the trumpet is well given in Eichborn's book *Die Trompete in alter und neuer Zeit*, published by Breitkopf & Härtel in 1881. Eichborn states that Henry VIII. of England had fourteen trumpeters, one ' Dudelsack ' (or bagpipe), and ten trombones in his band, and Elizabeth, in 1587, ten trumpets and six trombones. Indeed, it is in the 16th century, according to him, that the ' building up of the art of sound ' made a great advance. He divides the band of that day into seven groups, of which group 3, Zinken or Cornetts, Quart-Zinken, Krumm-horns, Quint-Zinken, Bass-Zinken and Serpents of the Bugle type ; group 6, Trumpets, ' Klarinen,' and ' Principal or Field-Trumpets,' with group 7, the Trombones, from soprano to bass, most concern us.

Claudio Monteverdi names among the instruments for his ' Orfeo ' (1607), one clarino, three trombe, and four tromboni ; and Benevoli, in a Mass at Salzburg Cathedral in 1628, has ' Klarinen, Trompeten, Posaunen ' ; Praetorius in 1620 waxes enthusiastic, and says :

' Trummet ist ein herrlich Instrument, wenn ein gute Meister, der es wohl und künstlich zwingen kann, darüber kömmt.'

It is to be noticed that trumpets at the time of Praetorius, although used in ' choirs ' or sets, were not made of different pitches or keys like other wind instruments similarly used, but were all pitched in D, and the difference in register or mean compass between the higher and lower parts was obtained by difference in bore, and in the proportions of the mouthpiece.

The higher trumpets or ' clarini ' were of small bore, and were played with very shallow mouth-pieces. The ' tromba,' or third part in the choir, was slightly larger in bore and mouth-piece, and the ' principale,' or lowest part, required a still wider tubing and larger mouth-piece. The range of the different parts is here indicated :

THE ' BACH ' TRUMPET.—It was the merit of Kosleck of Berlin to introduce a high trumpet specially to perform Bach's trumpet parts in their integrity in the B minor Mass, which was produced under Joachim's direction at Eise-nach on the occasion of the unveiling of the statue of J. S. Bach in Sept. 1884. A perform-ance of the same work, in which Kosleck again

Compass of the Trumpet.

In the above scale it is to be noted that the note [music] and its octave are slightly flat as major tones below C, being the seventh and fourteenth notes of the harmonic scale. The eleventh of this scale is represented by [music] and its true pitch lies between the two. These notes as written could only be obtained by a modification of lip-action, and this remark applies also to the A above the stave, which does not exist in the true harmonic series. However, whether the trumpeters from the 15th to the 18th centuries played only the natural harmonics, or modified them to suit the growing needs of harmony, it is certain that they attained to an excellence which in the 19th century passed away.

The trumpet parts in the works of Bach and Handel are written very high and floridly ; so high that they cannot be performed on the modern valve trumpet. Praetorius (1618) gives for the trumpet in D the higher range that should be produced (a), that is to say from the seventeenth to the twenty - first proper tones of the instru-ment. All these notes (a) [music] are beyond the highest limits of the modern instrument.

The distinction into clarini and principale is found in Handel's scores, notably in the Dettingen Te Deum. To the clarino I. and II. of the score were allotted florid, but less fundamental passages, chiefly in the octave above those of the principale. A like arrange-ment for three trumpets occurs in J. S. Bach's cantata ' Lobe den Herrn,' though the princi-pale is not definitely named. The mode of scoring is an exact parallel to that for the three trombones. A good example of it also occurs in Haydn's Imperial Mass, where, besides the 1st and 2nd trumpets, there is a completely in-dependent 3rd part of principale character.

took part, was given by the London Bach Choir in the Albert Hall, London, March 21, 1885. This trumpet is not bent back but straight, and is fitted with two pistons. It is an A trumpet with posthorn bore and bell. Kosleck's trumpet was improved by Walter Morrow, the well-known English trumpeter, who altered the bore and bell to that of the real trumpet. Morrow's trumpet, like Kosleck's, is straight and has two pistons, measuring in length $58\frac{1}{2}$ inches. It is also an A trumpet. With it the twentieth, and at French pitch the twenty-first proper tone of the 8-foot or normal trumpet can be reached. An instrument of this straight type is sometimes made in D, an octave higher than the old natural trumpet, or a tone higher than the modern valve trumpet in C, but owing to its limited length the proper tone-quality is somewhat lost (see ORCHESTRATION).

Bearing in mind the distinction already referred to between the trumpet and horn it will be clear that the ancestry of the trumpet is to be traced to the LITUUS (q.v.), rather than to the tuba (see TUBA, Roman). From the latter, which still keeps its name, are derived bugles, serpents, horns, euphoniums and bombardons and the like. It was early seen that two distinct varieties of tone-quality could be obtained, the large core and bell of the tuba favouring the production of the fundamental note and the lower partial tones, the long contracted pipe of the lituus breaking easily into harmonics and speaking freely in its upper octave.

N. C. G. ; incorporating material from W. H. S. and D. J. B.

TRUMPETER, SERGEANT-, an officer of the royal household, who presides over sixteen trumpeters in ordinary. The first mention of the office occurs in the reign of Edward VI., when it was held by Benedict Browne (who had been one of the sixteen trumpeters to Henry VIII. at a salary of 16d. a day), at an annual salary of £24 : 6 : 8. The office does not appear to have been regularly kept up for a very long period. It is not again mentioned in any list of royal musicians until 1641. No further notice of it occurs until 1685, when Gervase Price held it, and appointments to it have since been continuously made. Price was succeeded by Matthias SHORE (*q.v.*), one of the trumpeters in ordinary, who was followed in 1700 by his son William, who in his turn was replaced, a few years later, by his brother John, the most celebrated trumpeter of his time. On John Shore's death in 1752 Valentine SNOW (*q.v.*), for whom Handel wrote the difficult obbligato trumpet parts in his oratorios, .etc., obtained the appointment. Snow died in 1770, and for a long time the majority of his successors were not even musicians. One of them, however, John Charles Crowle, who held the office in 1812, deserves mention for having bequeathed to the British Museum the splendidly illustrated copy of Pennant's *London*, so dear to lovers of London topography. About 1858 it was decided that the office should again be given to a musician, although not to a trumpeter, and Joseph Williams, clarinettist, a member of the Queen's band of music, received the appointment, and upon his death in Apr. 1875, J. G. Waetzig, bassoon-player, also a member of the Queen's band, was appointed his successor. The salary of the office has long been £100 per annum. The Sergeant-Trumpeter formerly claimed, under letters patent, a fee of 12d. a day from every person sounding a trumpet, beating a drum, or playing a fife in any play or show without his licence (for which licence 20s. a year was demanded), and Matthias and William Shore successively issued advertisements in the newspapers authorising all magistrates to receive such fees for them and apply them to the relief of the poor. Such privileges were, however, long since abrogated.

W. H. H.

TRUMPET MARINE, see TROMBA MARINA.

TRYDELL, REV. JOHN, an Irish writer on music who issued by subscription a work on the art : *Two Essays on the Theory and Practice of Music*, Dublin, printed for the editor . . . 1766, 8vo. In the preface he says ' there is no such thing as Irish music since the trade hath been opened with Italy ' ; and refers to the ' little remains or reliques preserved in the few Irish airs which have miraculously survived the changes of time.'

F. K.

TSCHUDI, BURKHARDT, founder of the house of Broadwood. (See SHUDI.)

TUA, MARIA FELICITA, known as TERESINA (*b.* Turin, May 22, 1867), completed her musical education at the Paris Conservatoire, where she received instruction on the violin from Massart, and obtained in 1880 a ' premium ' or first prize. She afterwards played with brilliant success in concert tours over the greater part of the continent. On May 5, 1883, she made her first appearance in England at the Crystal Palace, and played with so much success that she was re-engaged for the concert of the following week. She played at the Philharmonic on May 9 and 30 ; at the Floral Hall Concerts, June 9 ; at W. G. Cusins's concert, with whom she was heard in Beethoven's ' Kreutzer ' sonata ; and at other concerts. She returned to the continent, and did not reappear for the season of 1884 as was expected. She next made tours on the continent, and in 1887 visited America. In 1891,[1] she married Giuseppe Ippolito Franchi-Verney, Conte della Valetta, a musical critic. She retired for a time, but later she made tours in Italy and elsewhere. She contributed an appreciation of Joachim to the literature called forth by his death. In 1914 she married Count Emilio Quadrio de Maria Pontaschielli.[2]

A. C.

TUBA, (1) this name, originally signifying a short, straight horn or trumpet, corresponding to our modern coach-horn, is now used as a generic name, vaguely perhaps, but conveniently given to the deeper-toned valve brass instruments, the euphonium (or tenor-tuba), and the bombardon in its two forms—basstuba and contrabass tuba.

Wagner's five tubas as employed in ' The Ring ' were, with one exception, not tubas but modified horns with a funnel mouthpiece which, it was originally intended, were to be played by four of the eight horn-players required at other times in the score. They consisted of two ' tenor ' tubas in B flat compass [music notation] to [music notation], and two ' bass ' tubas in F compass [music notation] to [music notation]. The fifth instrument was a contrabass tuba. In practice these tubas were eventually redesigned on the plan of the SAXHORN (*q.v.*), but still possessing the funnel, and not cupshaped, mouthpiece, to which is due the softer and quieter tone-quality. (See *PLATE LXXXIV*. No. 4.)

Complete sets of these instruments have been used in England for performances of 'The Ring.' Abroad, the two highest parts have been played on the E flat FLÜGELHORN (*q.v.*), sometimes known as althorn. True tubas have a cup mouthpiece and are the modern substitutes for the old bass-horns and ophicleides, and are distinct from the bugle or higher-pitched type of brass instrument in that they are able to play all the notes lying between the fundamental note and the second harmonic. The bombardon is made in two forms, upright like the euphonium, and as used in military bands, circular (when it is called helicon), being so built to pass over the player's shoulder for convenience in marching.

The compass of these instruments is as follows : euphonium, corresponding to what

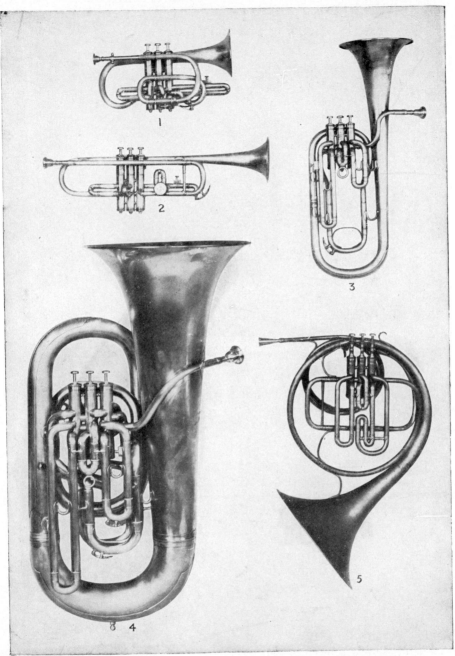

1. CORNET. 2. VALVE TRUMPET. 3. SAXHORN.

4. TUBA. 5. ORCHESTRAL HORN.

the Germans call baryton; the term tenor-tuba in B is also used (in B flat, 4 valves) chromatically from to . This is the equivalent to the bass saxhorn in B flat.

Bombardon (bass tuba, helicon) (E flat, 4 valves) chromatically from to . This instrument, however, for the concert orchestra is generally built in F one whole tone higher.

Bombardon (contrabass tuba) (B flat, 3 valves) chromatically from to , the fundamental is possible. A fourth valve is sometimes added. This instrument, built in c′, was the lowest of the Wagner group.

Tubas are made both with three and four valves, but for the full use of the pedal octave between the fundamental note and the second harmonic the four valves are necessary. A fifth valve has occasionally been introduced to correct the sharpening effect of valves used in combination, but the true remedy for this is a system of compensating lengths automatically brought into operation by the fourth VALVE (q.v.). The lowest note shown above for the B♭ contrabass is produced with the three valves in combination: for the other instruments the lowest note shown is the fundamental without valves, but several lower notes can be obtained with the valves. The upper limit given is the eighth harmonic, but the ninth and even the tenth can be used. As in all brass instruments the upper limit of compass is indefinite, and depends upon the skill of the player.

The notation of tuba parts has been variable. Wagner wrote for his first four 'tubas' as though they were horns in B flat alto and in F, and alternatively as horns in E flat and B flat basso. In brass bands the tubas are sometimes written for as transposing instruments, in which case the second harmonic, the octave above the fundamental, is always placed on the 'middle' C. In the concert orchestra and in military bands in England the usual and most satisfactory plan is to write the actual sounds required.

The tone-quality of the tubas is broad and round and they are a valuable part of the constitution of the military and brass band, the euphonium, with its extensive compass, vocal

tone, and great flexibility, being particularly well suited for solo work. In the concert and opera orchestra the tuba forms a solid bass to trombone harmony, although the tone is apt to become obtrusive unless used with great care or for special effect, e.g. those of Strauss's 'Don Quixote.'

For further details as to the general mechanism of the instrument, see SAXHORN, to which it is closely allied.

N. C. G. incorporating material from D. J. B.

TUBA, (2) (TUBA MIRABILIS; TUBA MAJOR; TROMBA; OPHICLEIDE), a high-pressure reed-stop of 8 ft. pitch on an organ. (See ORGAN: VOCABULARY OF STOPS.)

TUBA, ROMAN, a straight conical metal horn with cup mouthpiece, somewhat similar to the modern coach-horn, and about 3½ or 4 feet in length. It is frequently referred to as the Roman trumpet, but as the characteristic of the trumpet is the great proportion of cylindrical tubing in its length, the tuba should be regarded rather as belonging to the horn family. The origin of such an instrument is doubtless to be found in the natural ox-horn or elephant's tusk, and must be regarded as prehistoric, as there are many evidences of great antiquity illustrating the use of metal horns and trumpets. The tuba was one of the four military instruments used by the Romans, the other three being the LITUUS, the CORNU and the BUCCINA (q.v.). D. J. B.

TUBUPHONE, a variety of GLOCKEN-SPIEL (q.v.) which differs from it in that the steel bars are replaced by small tubes of metal arranged like the keyboard of a piano and struck with a hammer. The compass is chromatic, from to , and the part is written two octaves below the actual pitch.

TUCK, see TUCKET.

TUCKER, EDMUND (late 16th and early 17th century), English composer of church music, and possibly the father of the Rev. William TUCKER (q.v.). An Edward Tucker was organist of Salisbury Cathedral from c. 1626–33 (West's Cath. Org.). An anthem by Edmund Tucker, 'Christ Rising' is in R.C.M. 1045–51 (Barnard's MS. collection), and another, 'He blessed is,' in Tenb. O.B/356. Some of the anthems in the list of compositions by the Rev. William Tucker, described simply as by 'Tucker,' may be the work of Edmund. Barnard's 'Selected Church Music' (1641) was definitely prepared as a collection of compositions by composers then deceased, and the 'Benedicite' bound up with the Barnard part-books (R.C.M. (I. A1) may also be by Edmund Tucker. J. Mᴷ.

TUCKER (TUCKERE, TUCKERS), REV. WILLIAM (d. Feb. 28, 1679), English composer of church music. He was admitted a gentleman of the Chapel Royal, where he appears also to have been a copyist. In 1660 he was a minor canon and precentor of Westminster Abbey. His anthem ' O Give thanks unto yᵉ Lord,' is described in Harl. MSS. 7339, Tudway collection, as by ' Will. Tucker, gentleman of yᵉ Chappell to King Charles yᵉ 2d and Praecentor of yᵉ Abby Church in Westminster.' His name occurs many times in the lists and accounts of payments to the royal musicians.[1] He was buried in the Abbey Cloisters, Mar. 1, 1679. Besides the compositions given below, there are a service and six anthems at Ely Cathedral ; and the following is included in a catalogue of ' severall Services and Anthems that have been transcribed into the books of his Majesty's Chappell Royal since anno 1670 to Midsummer 1676.'[2]

' Benedicite Service '; ' O clap your Hands '; 'I was glad '; ' Praise the Lord, ye Servants '; ' Unto Thee, O Lord.'

SERVICES, Etc.

Whole Service in F (B. ; J. ; K. ; C. ; M. ; N.D.). B.M. Add. MSS. 30,478-9. Tenor cantoris part only.
Evening Service in F (M. ; N.D.). B.M. Add. MSS. 34,203/19. Organ score.
Benedicite.[3] R.C.M. I A 1. 4 single parts bound up with the part books of Barnard's ' Selected Church Music,' 1641.

ANTHEMS

Comfort ye, my People. B.M. Add. MSS. 30,932/68. Score. B.M. Add. MSS. 30,478-9. Tenor cantoris part only.
I will magnifie Thee (verse anthem). B.M. Add. MSS. 31,203/83b. Organ score ; B.M. Add. MSS. 30,478-9. Tenor cantoris part only ; B.M. Add. MSS. 31,404/85b. Organ score.
Lord, how longe wilt Thou. B.M. Add. MSS. 30,478-9. Tenor cantoris part only.
My Heart is fixed. B.M. Add. MSS. 30,478-9. Tenor cantoris part only.
O give thanks. Harl. MSS. 7339/45b. Score. B.M. Add. MSS. 31,404/95b. Organ score. These 2 references are to a ' full ' anthem a 4 and 5, but there is also a ' solo ' anthem setting of these words. Other copies of either the full or solo setting are as follows : B.M. Add. MSS. 17,820/61 ; Ch. Ch. 525. Score without words ; B.M. Add. MSS. 30,478-9. Tenor cantoris part only ; Ch. Ch. 1 ·20-4. Alto, tenor, and bass parts only.
This is the Day. Verse anthem. B.M. Add. MSS. 17,784/63. Bass part only. B.M. Add. MSS. 30,478-9. Tenor cantoris part only.
There were Shepherds B.M. Add. MSS. 30,478-9. Tenor cantoris part only.
Wherewithal shall a younge Man. B.M. Add. MSS. 30,478-9. Tenor cantoris part only. B.M. Add. MSS. 17,820/59. Score.

J. Mᴷ.

TUCKERMAN, SAMUEL PARKMAN, MUS.D. (b. Boston, Mass., U.S.A., Feb. 11, 1819 ; d. Newport, Rhode Island, June 30, 1890). At an early age he received instruction in church music and organ-playing from Charles Zeuner. From 1840, and for some years after, he was organist and director of the choir in St. Paul's Church, Boston, and during that time published two collections of hymn tunes and anthems, ' The Episcopal Harp ' (chiefly original compositions) and ' The National Lyre,' the latter with S. A. Bancroft, and Henry K. Oliver. In 1849 he went to England, to make himself thoroughly acquainted with the English cathedral school of church music, both ancient and modern. In 1851 he took the Lambeth degree of Doctor of Music, and then returned to the United States and resumed his connexion with

[1] See H. C. de Lafontaine, The King's Musick.
[2] See The King's Musick, 1st Aug. 1766.
[3] See Edmund TUCKER.

St. Paul's Church in his native city. He lectured upon Church Music in the Old World and the New, and gave several public performances of cathedral and church music from the 4th to the 19th century. In 1856 he returned to England, and remained eight years, forming a fine musical library. In 1864 he returned to the United States and succeeded Dr. Edward Hodges as organist of Trinity Church, New York. Many of Tuckerman's compositions were published by Novello. In 1852 he received a diploma from the Academy of St. Cecilia, Rome.   G.

TUCKET, TUCK, the name of a trumpet sound,[4] of frequent occurrence in the works of the Elizabethan dramatists. Shakespeare (Henry V., Act. iv. Sc. 2) has, ' Then let the trumpets sound The tucket-sonance, and the note to mount ' ; and in The Devil's Law Case (1623) is a stage direction, ' Two tuckets by several trumpets.' The word is clearly derived from the Italian toccato, which Florio (A Worlde of Wordes, 1598) translates ' a touch, a touching.'

Like most early musical signals, the tucket came to England from Italy, and though it is always mentioned by English writers as a trumpet sound, the derivation of the word shows that in all probability it was originally applied to a drum signal. (See MILITARY SOUNDS AND SIGNALS.) Francis Markham (Five Decades of Epistles of Warre, 1622) says that a ' Tucquet ' was a signal for marching used by cavalry troops. The word still survives in the French ' Doquet ' or ' Toquet,' which Larousse explains as ' nom que l'on donne à la quatrième partie de trompette d'une fanfare de cavallerie.' There are no musical examples extant of the notes which were played.

Closely allied with the word tucket is the Scotch term ' tuck ' or ' touk,' usually applied to the beating of a drum, but by early writers used as the equivalent of a stroke or blow. Thus Gawin Douglas's Virgil has (line 249) ' Hercules it smytis with ane mychty touk.' The word is also occasionally used as a verb, both active and neuter. In Spalding's History of the Troubles in Scotland (vol. ii. p. 166) is the following : ' Aberdeen caused tuck drums through the town,' and in Battle Harlaw, Evergreen (i. 85), the word is used thus : ' The dandring drums alloud did touk.' ' Tuck of drum ' is of frequent occurrence in Scottish writers of the 19th century (see Scott's Rokeby, canto iii. stanza 17; Carlyle's Life of Schiller ; Stevenson's Inland Voyage, etc. ; also Jamieson's Dictionary of the Scottish Language, s.v. ' Tuck ' and ' Touk '). (See TUSCH.)   W. B. S.

TUCZEK, a Bohemian family of artists—the same name as Duschek or Dussek. The compilers of dictionaries have fallen into much confusion between the different members.

[4] Johnson says ' a musical instrument,' but this is inaccurate.

(1) FRANZ (d. circa 1780) was choirmaster of S. Peter's at Prague (1771). His son and pupil,

(2) FRANZ (b. circa 1755; d. Pest, 1820) was a singer in Count Sweert's theatre, became accompanist to the theatre at Prague in 1796, Kapellmeister at Sagan to the Duke of Courland in 1797, conductor of the theatre at Breslau in 1799, and of the Leopoldstadt theatre in Vienna in 1801. He was a versatile composer, writing masses, cantatas (one was performed at Sagan in 1798, on the recovery of the King of Prussia), oratorios (' Moses in Egypt,' and ' Samson,' 1803), operettas (' Le Charme du baiser,' Vienna, 1803, etc.), and music for a tragedy, ' Lanassa,' his best work, given at Pest in 1813. His chief printed work is the PF. score of ' Dämona,' a fairy opera in three acts, performed at Vienna, 1802. Pieces for piano and for guitar were also printed.

(3) FRANZ (b. Königgratz, Jan. 29, 1782 ; d. Charlottenburg near Berlin, Aug. 4, 1850), another son, a musician first in Vienna, and afterwards in Berlin, had two daughters, of whom one married Rott the actor. The other,

(4) LEOPOLDINE TUCZEK - HERRENBURG (b. Vienna, Nov. 11, 1821 ; d. Baden, near Vienna, Sept. 1883), was a pupil of Josephine Fröhlich's at the Vienna Conservatorium in 1829–34, played little parts at the court theatre with Unger, Garcia and Moriani, from the time she was 13, and thus formed herself as an actress. She was also thoroughly trained as a singer by Mozatti, Gentiluomo and Curzi, and made her first appearance in Weigl's ' Nachtigall und Rabi.' In 1841, on the recommendation of Franz Wild, Count Redern offered her a star-engagement in Berlin, as successor to Sophie Löwe in ingénue parts. Her Susanna, Zerlina, Sonnambula, Madeleine, etc., pleased so much as to lead to an offer of engagement on liberal terms, which she accepted on her release from the court theatre at Vienna. She sang at the unveiling of the Beethoven memorial in Bonn (1845). She made her farewell appearance in Berlin, Dec. 6, 1861, when the king himself threw her a laurel-wreath, and sent her a miniature laurel-tree in silver, bearing sixty-five leaves, on which were written the names of her parts, including Mrs. Ford in ' The Merry Wives of Windsor.' Her voice had a compass of $2\frac{1}{2}$ octaves, and her refined and piquant acting made her a model soubrette.   F. G.

TUDOR CHURCH MUSIC. A critical edition of the English masters of the 16th and 17th centuries, published by the Oxford University Press for the CARNEGIE TRUST (q.v.). The editorial committee consists of Prof. P. C. Buck, Dr. E. H. Fellowes, Miss S. Townsend Warner, Rev. A. Ramsbotham. The ten vols. (some still, 1927, in the press) consist of :

1. Taverner (Masses).
2. Byrd (English Services, etc.).
3. Taverner (Motets).
4. Gibbons (Services and Anthems).
5. Robert Whyte.
6. Tallis (Latin).
7. Byrd (Gradualia).
8. Tomkins (Services, etc.).
9. Byrd (Masses and Misc.).
10. Merbecke, Aston and Parsley.

TUDWAY, THOMAS, Mus.D. (d. Nov. 23, 1726),[1] was admitted a chorister of the Chapel Royal in or soon after 1660. On Apr. 22, 1664, he was elected a lay vicar (tenor) of St. George's Chapel, Windsor. About Michaelmas, 1670, he became organist of King's College, Cambridge, in succession to Henry Loosemore (whose name disappears from the College accounts after Midsummer, 1670), and received the quarter's pay at Christmas, and an allowance for seven weeks' commons. He obtained the post of instructor of the choristers at King's College at Christmas, 1679, and retained it until Midsummer, 1680. He was also organist at Pembroke College. In 1681 he graduated as Mus.B. at Cambridge, his exercises being Ps. xx. in English, and Ps. ii. in Latin, both with orchestral accompaniment.[2] On Jan. 30, 1704–05, he was chosen as professor of music in the University in succession to Dr. Staggins. Shortly afterwards he proceeded Mus.D., his exercise for which—an anthem, ' Thou, O Lord, hast heard our desire ' —was performed in King's College Chapel on Apr. 16, in the presence of Queen Anne, who bestowed upon the composer the honorary title of Composer and Organist-extraordinary to her. On July 28, 1706, he was suspended from his offices for ' speaking words highly reflecting upon Her Majesty and her administration.'[3] On another occasion his inveterate habit of punning got him into trouble.[4] His suspension continued until Mar. 10, 1706–07, when he recanted, and was formally absolved and reinstated in his offices.[5] In 1714–20 he was engaged in the work by which his name is preserved. It was undertaken at the desire of Edward, Lord Harley, afterwards Earl of Oxford, and forms an important collection[6] of cathedral music, in six thick 4to vols., now in the B.M. (Harl. MSS. 7337-7342), an Evening Service, eighteen anthems, and a Latin motet by Tudway himself being included in it. Another Service by him is in a MS. at Ely Cathedral, and some songs and catches were printed in the collections of the period. He wrote anthems and a Te Deum with orchestral accompaniment, for the consecration of Lord Oxford's private chapel at Wimpole, in 1720. His portrait, formerly in the Music School at Oxford, is now in the Bodleian.   W. H. H.

[1] D.N.B.   [2] Ibid.
[3] Records of Pembroke College, Cambridge.
[4] Burney, Hist. of Music, iii. 459 n., relates the following anecdote, which may possibly include the obnoxious pun. In the time of the Duke of Somerset's Chancellorship at Cambridge, during the discontents of several members of the University at the rigours of his government and paucity of his patronage, Tudway, himself a malcontent, and joining in the clamour, said, '' The Chancellor rides us all, without a bit in our mouths.''
[5] Register of Emmanuel College in Hist. MSS. Comm., 4th Report, p. 419.
[6] For an alphabetical list, under composers, see Oliphant's Catalogue of MS. Music in the Brit. Mus. (1842). p. 31, etc.

The contents of the collection are as follows :

VOL. I.

Tallis. Whole Service, D minor with B♮ (Benedictus).
Anthem, I call and cry. a 5.
Do. Wipe away my sins. a 5
Do. With all our hearts. a 5.
Do. O Lord give Thy Holy. a 4.
Bird. Whole Service, D minor with B♮ (Benedictus).
Anthem, Sing joyfully. a 6.
Do. O Lord, turn Thy wrath. a 5.
Do. Bow thine ear. a 5.
Do. O Lord, make. a 5.
Do. Save me, O God. a 5.
Do. Prevent us, O Lord. a 4.
Tallis. Anthem, Discomfit them. a 5.
Tye. Even. Serv., G minor, 1545. a 5.
Bull. Anthem, 2 trebles. Almighty God 1592. (Organ pt.)
Morley. Even. Serv., D min. a 5.
Barcroft. Morning Service, G minor, 1532 (Benedictus).
Stonard. Evening Service in C. a 5. 1558.
Amner. Whole Service, D min. a 4 (Benedictus).
Anthem, Christ rising again.
Mundy. Do. O Lord I bow. a 5.
O. Gibbons. Service, 1635 (Benedictus).
Anthem, O Lord, increase. a 4.
Do. Why art thou so heavy. a 4.

O. Gibbons. Anthem, Behold Thou hast made. a 5.
H. Molle. Even. Serv. D min. with B♮.
Portman. Whole Service, G (Benedictus).
H. Molle. Evening Service, F.
Patrick. Whole Service, G minor (Benedictus).
Farrant. Whole Service, called 'Farrant's High,' A minor (Benedictus).
Morley. Funeral Anthem, I am the resurrection.
Do. Man that is born.
Do. I heard a voice.
Giles. Anthem, O give thanks. a 5.
Tomkins. Do. Almighty God. a 5.
Hooper. Do. Behold this is Christ. a 5.
Batten. Do. Hear my prayer. a 4.
Loosemore. Put me not to rebuke. a 4.
Lawes [W.]. Anthem, The Lord is my light. a 4.
Canon, Non nobis, Morley (Byrd).
Do. I am so weary. a 3 (Ford).
Do. O that men would. a 3.
Do. Haste thee, O Lord. a 3 (Ramsey).
Do. Music Divine. a 3.
Do. She weepeth sore. a 4. (Lawes).
Do. Miserere. a 3.

VOL. II.

Child. Whole Service, D. a 4 (Jubilate).
Anthem, Sing we merrily. a 8.
Do. O Lord God. a 5.
Do. O praise the Lord. a 6.
Whole Service, F. (Jubilate and Cantate).
Evening Service, A.
Do. C minor (given in D).
Humphrey. Even. Serv., E min. Verse.
Anthem, Thou art my king. a 4.
Do. Haste Thee, O God a 4.
Do. O Lord my God. a 4.
Do. Like as the hart. a 3.
Do. By the waters. a 3.
Do. O give thanks. a 4.
Do. Have mercy. a 3.
Farrant. Kyrie and Credo from High Service.
Child. Whole Service, E minor. Verse (Jubilate).
Anthem. Praise the Lord. a 4.
Do. O Lord, grant the King. a 6.
Evening Service in G. a 4.
Humphrey. Anthem, O praise the Lord. a 3.
Funeral Anthem, Lord, teach us. a 3.
Do. O be joyful. a 3. Orch.
Do The King shall rejoice. a 4. Orch.
Do. Hear, O heavens. a 3.
Rogers. Whole Service, in D (Jubilate).
Loosemore. Whole Service, in D minor. a 4, 5, 6.
Wise. Whole Service, D minor (Jubilate).
Anthem, Awake, put on. a 3.
Do. The ways of Zion. a 2.
Holder. Evening Service, C.
Anthem, Thou O God.
Creyghton. Whole Service, C (Jubilate).
Anthem, I will arise.
Aldrich. Anthem (from Latin). We have heard. a 4.

Aldrich. Anthem (from Latin), Why art thou so. a 4.
Do. (do.) My heart is fixed. a 4.
Do. (do.) The eye of the Lord. a 4.
Do. (do.) O God the King. a 4.
Do. (do.) Hold not Thy tongue. a 4.
Do. (do.) Give ear, O Lord. a 4.
Do. (do.) Behold now praise. a 5.
Do. (do.) Hide not Thou. a 4.
Do. (do.) I looked for the Lord. a 5.
Do. (do.) O Lord, rebuke me not. a 5. (? M. White.)
Do. (do.) O how amiable. a 2.
Do. (do.) Haste Thee, O Lord. a 2.
Do. (do.) For Sion's sake. a 2 and 3.
Do. (do.) O pray for the peace.
Do. (do.) I am well pleased.
Bryan. Whole Service, in G. a 4. Morning Service.
Ferabosco. Evening Service.
Jackson. Anthem, The Lord said. a 4.
Blow. Evening Service in E. Verse.
Anthem, O Lord, I have sinned. a 4.
Do. I said in the cutting off. a 3. (Orch.)
Do. The Lord is my Shepherd. a 4. (Orch.)
Purcell. Anthem, My beloved spake. a 4. (Orch.)
Do. They that go down. a 2. (Orch.)
Do. My song shall be alway. (Orch.)
Tudway. Anthem, The Lord hear thee. (Orch.)
Do. Quare fremuerunt. (Orch.)

VOL. III.

Henry VIII.[1] Anthem, O Lord the Maker.
Bevin. Whole Service, Dorian.
Tomkins. Anthem, O praise the Lord. a 12.
Do. Glory be to God. a 10.
Do. O God, the proud. a 8.
Do. Turn Thou us. a 8.
Matth. White. Anthem, O praise God. a 8.

Matth. White. Anthem, The Lord bless us. a 5.
Parsons. Anthem, Deliver me. a 6.
Weelkes. Do. O Lord, grant the king. a 6.
Loosemore. Anthem, Glory be to God. a 4.
Holden. Do. O praise our God. a 4.
Lowe. Do. O give thanks. a 4.

---

1 This anthem is more probably by William Mundy, although the Durham partbooks assign it to John Shepherd.

Tucker. Anthem, O give thanks. a 4.
Do. I will magnify. a 4.
Jewett. Do. I heard a voice. a 4.
Creyghton. Whole Service in E♭.
Anthem, Praise the Lord. a 3.
Aldrich. Whole Service in G.
Anthem, Out of the deep.
Do. O praise the Lord. a 4.
Do. Sing unto the Lord. a 4.
Amner. Whole Service in G ('Caesar'). a 5.
Wise. Evening Service in E♭.
Anthem, How are the mighty.
Do. I will sing a new song. a 4.
Do. O praise God. a 3.
Do. Behold how good. a 3.
Turner. Whole Service, in A.
Anthem, O praise the Lord.
Do. The King shall rejoice.
O. Gibbons. Do. Hosanna. a 6.
Aldrich. Do. O Lord, grant the King. a 5.

Giles. Anthem, I will magnify. a 5.
Lugg. Do. Behold how good. a 5.
Blow. Whole Service, in G.
Anthem, Save me, O God.
Do. O Lord God. a 8.
Do. O God, my heart. a 4.
Do. And I heard a great voice. a 4.
Do. The kings of Tharsis. a 4.
Do. Praise the Lord. a 5.
Aldrich. Even. Serv. in F. Verse.
Purcell. Whole Service, in B♭.
Do. Rejoice in the Lord.
Do. Praise the Lord. a 2.
Do. I was glad.
Do. O God, Thou art.
Do. Lord, how long a 5.
Do. O God, Thou hast cast. a 6.
Do. Save me, O God. a 5.
Humphrey, Blow, Turner. Anthem, I will alway give thanks.

VOL. IV.

Amner. Whole Service, in D minor. ('Caesar's ').
Anthem, O sing unto the Lord.
Do. Lord, I am not.
Do. Remember not.
Tye. Do. O God, be merciful.
Barcroft. Anthem, O Almighty God.
O. Gibbons. Do. Lift up your heads. a 6.
Farrant. Do. O Lord God Almighty. a 4.
Wilkinson. Do. I am the resurrection. a 6.
Laud. Do. Praise the Lord.
Shepherd. Anthem. Haste Thee, O God. a 4.
Fox. Do. Teach me Thy way. a 4.
Gibbs. Do. Have mercy upon me. a 4.
Hilton. Do. Lord for Thy tender. a 4.
Mudd. Do. O God, that hast prepared. a 4.
Wilkinson. Do. O Lord God. a 4.
Lugg. Whole Service, in D.
Hooper. Antaem, Almighty God. a 5.
Tye. Do. O Lord, deliver me. a 5.
Amner. Anthem, Sing, O heavens. a 7.
Hutchinson. Do. Behold how good. a 4.
Ramsey. Whole Service, in F.
Locke. Anthem, When the Son of man.
Do. Sing unto the Lord.
Chr. Gibbons. Anthem, How long wilt thou ?
Blow. Whole Service, in A.
Anthem, I beheld and lo a great.
Do. O sing unto God.

Blow. Anthem, Why do the heathen.
Do. We will rejoice.
Do. O Lord Thou hast searched.
Do. Thy righteousness, O Lord.
Do. God is our hope. a 8.
Do. O God, wherefore. a 5.
Purcell. Whole Service, in B♭.
Anthem, O give thanks.
Do. Behold I bring you.
Do. Be merciful.
Aldrich. Whole Service in A.
Anthem, I will love Thee.
Do. The Lord is King.
Do. Give the king thy judgment.
Do. If the Lord Himself.
Do. O Lord, I have heard.
Locke. Anthem, Lord, let me know mine end.
Do. Not unto us.
E. Gibbons. Anthem, How hath the city sat desolate.
Hall. Whole Service, in E♭.
Anthem, Let God arise. a 2.
Do. O clap your hands. a 3.
Do. By the waters. a 3.
Norris. Morning Service, in G minor.
Anthem, Blessed are those.
Do. I will give thanks.
Wildbore. Anthem, Almighty and everlasting.
Clark. Anthem. The earth is the Lord's. a 3.
Do. I will love Thee.
Do. Praise the Lord. Full.
Do. Bow down Thine ear. a 3.
Tudway. Anthem, The Lord hath declared.
Purcell. Do. Blessed is the man.
Do. Thou knowest, Lord.

VOL. V.

Purcell. Te Deum, in D. Jubilate, in D.
Tudway. Anthem, Is it true ?
Do. Sing we merrily.
Do. My God, my God.
Do. Man that is born.
Do. I am the resurrection.
Do. I heard a voice.
Do. I will lift up.
Do. I cry, O heavens.
Do. I will sing (Blenheim).
Do. Thou, O God.
Evening Service, in B♭.
Turner. Whole Service, in E.
Anthem, The Queen shall rejoice.
Do. Behold now, praise.
Do. Lord, Thou hast been.
Do. The Lord is righteous.
Hawkins. Whole Service, in A.
Anthem, O Lord, grant the Queen.
Do. My God, my God.
Do. Lord, Thou art become.
Do. Lord, who shall dwell.
Do. Bow down Thine ear.
Holmes. Anthem, Arise, shine !
Cooper. Do. I waited patiently.
Wanless. Do. Awake up my glory.
Richardson. Do. O Lord God of my salvation.
Bishop. Morning Service, in D.
Anthem, O Lord our Governor.
Wilson. Evening Service, in G.
Hart. Anthem, I will give thanks.

Hart. Anthem, Praise the Lord.
Lamb. Evening Service, in E minor.
Anthem, Unto Thee have I cried.
Do. O worship the Lord.
Goldwin. Whole Service in F.
Anthem, O Lord God of hosts.
Do. Hear me, O God.
Croft. Anthem, We will rejoice.
Do. I will sing.
King. Whole Service, in F.
Anthem. Hear, O Lord.
Do. Hear my crying.
Do. Sing unto God.
Holmes. Anthem, I will love Thee, O Lord.
Williams. Evening Service, in A minor.
Woolcot. Morning Service in G.
Anthem, O Lord, Thou hast cast.
Bowman. Anthem, Shew yourselves joyful.
Croft. Anthem, Praise the Lord, O my soul.
Do. I will always give thanks.
Church. Whole Service, in F.
Anthem, O Lord, grant the Queen.
Do. Righteous art Thou.
Do. Praise the Lord.
Do. Lord, Thou art become.
Weldon. Anthem, Hear my crying.

TÜRK, DANIEL GOTTLOB (b. Clausswitz, near Chemnitz, Saxony, Aug. 10, 1756 ; d. Halle, Aug. 26, 1813), writer on theory, son of a musician in the service of Count Schönburg, learned first from his father, and afterwards from Homilius at the Kreuzschule in Dresden. In 1772 he went to the University of Leipzig, where he became the pupil and friend of J. A. Hiller, who procured his admittance as a violinist to the opera and the Grosses Concert. About this period he produced two symphonies and a cantata. In 1776, owing to Hiller's influence, he became cantor of S. Ulrich at Halle, and in 1779 Musikdirector of the University. In 1787 he was made organist of the Liebfrauenkirche. Türk was the author of several books on the theory of music which have become recognised text-books : *Von dem wichtigsten Pflichten eines Organisten* (1787) ; *Clavierschule* (1789),[1] and a Method for beginners compiled from it (1792) ; and *Kurze Anweisung zum Generalbassspielen* (1791) ; all of which passed through several editions. In 1806 he prepared and in 1808 published an *Anleitung zu Temperaturberechnung* . . . with special reference to Kirnberger's *Kunst des reinen Satzes*. In 1808 he was made doctor and professor of musical theory by the University. He died after a long illness. His compositions—PF. sonatas and pieces, and a cantata ' The Shepherds of Bethlehem ' (1782) —once popular, have wholly disappeared.

F. G.

TULOU, JEAN LOUIS (b. Paris, Sept. 12, 1786 ; d. Nantes, July 24, 1865), eminent French flute-player and composer. He was the son of a good bassoon-player named Jean Pierre Tulou (b. Paris, 1749 ; d. 1799), and entered the Conservatoire very young, studied the flute with Wunderlich, and took the first prize in 1801. He first made his mark at the Théâtre Italien, and in 1813 succeeded his master at the Opéra. In 1816 the production

of ' Le Rossignol,' an insignificant opera by Lebrun, gave him an opportunity of showing his powers in a series of passages *à deux* with the singer, Mme. Albert, and proving himself the first flute-player in the world. Drouet himself acknowledged the superiority of a rival whose style was so pure, whose intonation was so perfect, and who drew so excellent a tone from his 4-keyed wooden flute. His droll comments on the *régime* of the Restoration were resented by the Ministry in a practical form, for he was passed over in the appointment of flute-player to the Chapelle du Roi, and also in the professorship at the Conservatoire on Wunderlich's death. In consequence of this slight he left the Opéra in 1822, but returned in 1826 with the title of first flute solo. On Jan. 1, 1829, he became professor at the Conservatoire, where his class was well attended. Among his pupils may be mentioned V. Coche, Rémusat, Forestier, Donjon, Brunot, Altès and Demersseman. Tulou frequently played at the Société des Concerts, and wrote much for his instrument, especially during the time he was teaching. His works include innumerable airs with variations, fantasias on operatic airs, concertos, and grand soli with orchestra, a few duets for two flutes, a grand trio for three flutes, soli for the Conservatoire examinations, etc. In 1856 Tulou retired from the Conservatoire and the flute-making business. His trade-mark was a nightingale, doubtless in allusion to the opera in which he made his first success. Both as performer and manufacturer he opposed Boehm's system. Nevertheless he took medals at the Exhibitions of 1834, 1839, 1844 and 1849, was honourably mentioned at that of 1851 in London, and gained a medal of the first class at the Paris Exhibition of 1855. After his retirement he lived at Nantes.   G. C.

TUMA, FRANZ (b. Kosteletz, Bohemia, Oct. 2, 1704 ; d. Convent of the Barmherzigen Brüder, Vienna, Feb. 4, 1774), a distinguished church-composer, and player on the viola da gamba. He was a pupil of Černohorsky (Regens cho at Prague, with whom he also fulfilled an engagement as tenor-singer), and of J. J. Fux in Vienna. In 1741 he became Kapellmeister to the Dowager Empress Elisabeth, on whose death in 1750 he devoted himself entirely to his muse. In 1768 he retired to the Premonstratensian monastery of Gera, but after some years returned to Vienna. Tuma was greatly respected by connoisseurs of music amongst the court and nobility, and received many proofs of esteem from Maria Theresa. His numerous church-compositions (see *Q.-L.* for list) are distinguished by a complete mastery of construction, and a singular appropriateness between the harmony and the words, besides striking the hearer as the emanations of a sincerely devout mind. Especially celebrated are his Masses in D minor and E minor, which are masterpieces in the line of Bach. As a chorister in the cathedral of Vienna, Haydn had the opportunity of becoming practically acquainted with the works of this solid master. C. F. P.

TUNDER, FRANZ (b. Lübeck, 1614; d. there, Nov. 5, 1667), organist and church composer.

While still a pupil of Frescobaldi at Rome, he was recalled to Lübeck in 1641 to take the important position of organist to the Marienkirche. His abilities found speedy recognition at the hands of his fellow-citizens, who granted him successive increases of salary and other advantages. His efforts, too, for the artistic development of church music with the aid of instrumental accompaniment were heartily seconded. Taking advantage of the fact that a violist and lutenist were usually engaged to perform in church, on the occasion of the official attendance of the magistrates, he gradually increased the number of instrumentalists for service on festival occasions, and surrounded himself with a phalanx of efficient violin, viola and trombone players. Out of these small beginnings originated the afterwards famous ' Abendmusiken ' of Lübeck, which took place more especially in the season of Advent. One of his instrumentalists, who is also said to have been his pupil in composition, was Thomas Baltzar, who afterwards acquired celebrity in England as the most astonishing violin-player of his day. Tunder was succeeded on his death by Dietrich BUXTEHUDE (q.v.), who, it would appear, married the daughter of his predecessor in order to succeed to the position, a condition which was afterwards insisted upon in the case of Buxtehude's own successor.

Of Tunder's compositions nothing was ever printed during his lifetime, and nothing was known until a happy accident led to the discovery in the Royal Library at Upsala in Sweden of a large number of church compositions by Buxtehude, Tunder, and other North German masters, which a former Swedish Royal Kapellmeister at Stockholm, Gustav Düben by name, had made it his business to collect and copy. Seventeen of Tunder's church works have thus been rescued from oblivion, and are now accessible in D.D.T. (first series), vol. iii., edited by Seiffert. They include pieces for solo voices with accompaniment for one or more strings and organ, as well as choral works designed on a larger scale. Some are Choralcantatas with the Choral-melody sometimes as vocal solo with full accompaniment of strings, and also arranged and varied with other combinations of voices and instruments. One expressive little piece, ' Ach Herr, lass deine lieben Engelein,' for soprano solo with accompaniment of strings and organ, has frequently been performed in Germany. It may be observed that the texts are mostly suitable for the season of Advent. Besides these vocal

works of Tunder seven Choral-variations for organ by him exist in MS. in the Library at Lüneburg. Of these, two have been published in modern times, one, ' Komm Heiliger Geist,' is lithographed in Eitner's *Monatshefte* for 1886; the other, ' Jesus Christus unser Heiland,' has appeared in a collection of ' Choral-Vorspiele älterer Meister,' edited by Karl Straube.

BIBL.—WILHELM STAHL, *Franz Tunder und Dietrich Buxtehude*, Leipzig, 1926; CARL STIEHL, *Die Organisten an der St. Marien Kirche*, etc., Bd. 5, heft 2 of the *Zeitschrift des Vereins für Lübeckische Geschichte und Altertumskunde*. J. R. M.

TUNE appears to be really the same word as tone, but in course of a long period of familiar usage it has come to have a conventional meaning which is quite different.

The meaning of both forms was at first no more than ' sound,' but tune has come to mean not only a series of sounds, but a series which appears to have a definite form of some kind, either through the balance of phrases or periods or the regular distribution of groups of bars or cadences. It may be fairly defined as formalised melody : for whereas melody is a general term which is applicable to any fragment of music consisting of single notes which has a contour—whether it is found in inner parts or outer, in a motet of Palestrina or a fugue of Bach—tune is more specially restricted to a strongly outlined part which predominates over its accompaniment or other parts sounding with it, and has a certain completeness of its own. Tune is most familiarly illustrated in settings of short and simple verses of poetry, or in dances, where the outlines of structure are always exceptionally obvious. (See MELODY.)

C. H. H. P.

TUNING (to tune; Fr. *accorder*; Ger. *Stimmen*; Ital. *accordare*); the adjustment to a recognised scale of any musical instrument capable of alteration in the pitch of the notes composing it.

The violin family, the harp, piano, organ and harmonium, are examples of instruments capable of being tuned. The accordance of the violin, viola and violoncello, as is well known, is in fifths which are tuned by the player.[1] The harpist also tunes his harp. But the tuning of the piano, organ and harmonium is affected by tuners who acquire their art, in the piano especially, by long practice, and adopt tuning as an independent calling, having little to do with the mechanical processes of making the instrument. At Antwerp, as early as the first half of the 17th century, there were harpsichord-tuners who were employed in that vocation only ; for instance, in *De Liggeren der Antwerpsche Sint Lucasgilde*, p. 24, edited by Rombouts and Van Lerius (the Hague), we find named as a master Michiel Colyns, *Claversingelstelder Wynmeester*, i.e.

[1] The accordances of the guitar, lute, theorbo and similar instruments tuned by fifths, fourths and thirds will be found in the descriptions of the instruments.

harpsichord-tuner and son of a master (in modern Flemish *Clavecimbel-steller*).

In all keyboard instruments the chief difficulty has been found in what is known as 'laying the scale, bearings, or groundwork,' of the tuning; an adjustment of a portion of the compass, at most equal in extent to the stave with the alto clef [music], from which the remainder can be tuned by means of simple octaves and unisons. We have records of these groundworks by which we are enabled to trace the progress of tuning for nearly four hundred years. The earliest are by Schlick (1511), Ammerbach (1571), and Mersenne (1636). It is not, however, by the first of these in order of time that we discover the earliest method of laying the scale or groundwork, but the second. Ammerbach published at Leipzig in 1571 an *Orgel oder Instrument Tabulatur*, in which he gives the following directions for the groundwork. We will render this and the examples which follow into modern notation, each pair of notes being tuned together.

For the Naturals—(*das gelbe Clavier*).

[music]

For the Sharps (*Obertasten*).

[music] must be Major Thirds (*müssen grosse Terzen sein*).

[music] are Minor Thirds (*tiefer erklingen*).

There is not a word about temperament!

By the stave for the naturals we may restore the tuning of the Guido scale of the earliest organs and clavichords, which had only the B♭ as an upper key in two octaves. These would be provided for either by tuning up from the G (a minor third) or down from the F (a fifth), all the intervals employed being approximately just. We may also suppose that from the introduction of the full chromatic scale in organs before 1426, to the date of Schlick's publication 1511, and indeed afterwards, such a groundwork as Ammerbach's may have sufficed. There was a difference in clavichords arising from the fretting, to which we will refer later. Now, in 1511, Arnolt Schlick, a blind organist alluded to by Virdung, in his *Spiegel der Orgelmacher* (Mirror of Organbuilders)— republished in Berlin in 1869,—came out as a reformer of tuning. He had combated the utter subordination of the sharps or upper keys to the natural notes, and by the invention of a system of tuning of fifths and octaves had introduced a groundwork which afforded a kind of rough-and-ready unequal temperament and gave the sharps a *quasi* independence. This

is his scale which he gives out for organs, clavicymbals, clavichords, lutes, harps, intending it for wherever it could be applied.

He gives directions that ascending fifths should be made flat to accommodate the major thirds, particularly F–A, G–B♮, and C–E,—excepting G♯, which should be so tuned to E♭ as to get a tolerable cadence or dominant chord, the common chord of E to A. The G♯ to the E♭, he calls the 'wolf,' and says it is not used as a dominant chord to cadence C♯. Indeed, from the dissonance attending the use of C♯ and A♭, they being also out of tune with each other, he recommends the player to avoid using them as keynotes, by the artifice of transposition.

The fact of Ammerbach's publication of the older groundwork 60 years later proves that Schlick's was slow to commend itself to practice. However, we find Schlick's principle adopted and published by Mersenne (*Harmonie universelle*, Paris, 1636), and it was doubtless by that time established to the exclusion of the earlier system. With this groundwork Mersenne adopted, at least in theory, equal temperament (see TEMPERAMENT), of which in Liv. 2, Prop. xi. p. 132, of the before-named work, he gives the correct figures, and in the next volume, Prop. xii., goes on to say that equal temperament is the most used and the most convenient, and that all practical musicians allow that the division of the octave into twelve half-tones is the easiest for performance. Ellis, in his exhaustive Lecture on the History of Musical Pitch (*Journal of the Society of Arts*, Appendix of Apr. 2, 1880), considers corroboration of this statement necessary. We certainly do not find it in Mersenne's notation of the tuning scale, which we here transpose from the baritone clef. For the tuner's guidance

Les Feintes. The Sharps and Flats.

the ascending fifths are marked as flat, the descending as sharp, but the last fifth, G♯–E♭, is excepted as being the 'defect of the accord.' With this recognition of the 'wolf' it is clear that Mersenne was not thinking of equal temperament. But Schlick's principle of fifths and octaves had become paramount.

We will now go back to the interesting 'gebunden' or fretted CLAVICHORD (*q.v.*). The octave open scale of this instrument is F G A B♭ C D E♭ F, or C D E♭ F G A B♭ C, according to the note which may be accepted as the starting-point. Both of these are analogous to church modes, but may be taken as favourite popular scales, before harmony had fixed the present major and minor and the feeling had arisen for the leading note. We derive the fretted clavichord tuning from Ammerbach thus :

Later on, no doubt, four fifths up, F C G D A' and two fifths down, F B♭ E♭, would be used with octaves inserted to keep the tuning for the groundwork, in the best part of the keyboard for hearing. We have found the fretted or stopped semitones, which included the natural B and E, adjusted by a kind of rough temperament, intended to give equal semi mean-tones and resembling the lute and guitar semitones.

When J. Sebastian Bach had under his hands the 'bundfrei' or fret-free clavichord, each key having its own strings, he could adopt the tuning by which he might compose in all the twenty-four keys, from which we have the 48 Preludes and Fugues.[1]

Emanuel Bach (*Versuch*, etc., Berlin, 1753) gives, p. 10, very clear testimony as to his own preference for equal temperament tuning. He says we can go farther with this new kind of tuning although the old kind had chords better than could be found in musical instruments generally. He does not allude to his father, but brings in a hitherto unused interval in keyboard instrument tuning—the fourth. Not, it is true, in place of the fifth ; but as one of the trials to test the accuracy of the tuning. At the present time beginners in tuning find the fourth a difficult interval when struck simultaneously with the note to which it makes the interval : there is a feeling of dissonance not at all perceptible in the fifth. It is therefore not strange that for centuries we do not find it used for instruments capable of more or less sustained harmony. The introduction of a short groundwork for the piano, confined to the simple chromatic scale between

is traditionally attributed to Robert Wornum, early in the 19th century. In this now universally adopted system for the piano, the

[1] He did not get this tuning on the organ, it would appear, although his preference for it is shown in Ellis's *History of Musical Pitch* already referred to. (See the *Journal of the Society of Arts*, Mar. 5, 1800.)

fourth is regarded and treated as the inversion of the fifth ; and for the intentional 'Meantone' system (see TEMPERAMENT) employed almost universally up to about 1840–50, the following groundwork came into use :

—the wolf being, as of old, at the meeting of G♯ and E♭. The advantages of the short system were in the greater resemblance of vibration between notes so near, and the facilities offered for using common chords as trials. It will be observed that the pitch-note has changed from F to the treble C ; possibly from the introduction of the TUNING-FORK in 1711. In Great Britain and Italy a C-fork has been nearly always adhered to since that date for keyboard instruments ; but for the violins, A (on account of the violin open string), which in France and Germany has been also adopted as the keyboard tuning-note. But the pitch-pipe may have also had to do with the change of pitch-note.

The long tuning scale did not at once go out of use ; it was adhered to for organs, and for pianos by tuners of the old school. It went out in Broadwood's establishment with the last tuner who used it, about the year 1869. The change to intentional equal temperament in pianos in 1846, in England, which preceded by some years the change in the organ, was ushered in by an inclination to sharper major thirds : examples differing as different tuners were inclined to more or less 'sweet' common chords of C, G and F. The wolf ceasing to howl so loudly, another short groundwork, which went through the chain of fourths and fifths without break, became by degrees more general with the piano until it prevailed entirely. It is as follows :

and is also the groundwork for tuning the harmonium.

The old way of tuning pianos by the tuning hammer (or a tuning lever) remains in vogue, notwithstanding the ever-recurring attempts to introduce mechanical contrivances of screws, etc., which profess to make tuning easy and to bring it more or less within the immediate control of the player. Feasible as such an improvement appears to be, it has not yet come into the domain of the practical. The co-ordination of hand and ear, possessed by a skilled tuner, still prevails, and the difficulty of getting the wire to pass over the bridge continuously and equally, without the governed strain of the tuner's hand, is still to be overcome before a mechanical system can rival a tuner's dexterity.

In considering practical tuning we must at once dismiss the idea that the ear of a musician is capable of distinguishing small fractions of a complete vibration in a second. Professor Preyer of Jena limited the power of perception of the difference of pitch of two notes heard in succession by the best ears to about one-third of a double vibration in a second in any part of the scale. By the phenomena of beats between two notes heard at the same time we can make much finer distinctions, which are of great use in tuning the organ and harmonium; but with the piano we may not entirely depend upon them, and a good musical ear for melodic succession has the advantage. In fact the rapid beats of the upper partial tones frequently prevent the recognition of the slower beats of the fundamental tones of the notes themselves until they become too faint to count by. The tuner also finds difficulty in tuning the treble of a piano by beats only.

Still, to tune the groundwork of a piano to a carefully measured set of chromatic tuning-forks, such as Scheibler formerly provided, would ensure a nearer approach to a perfect equal temperament than the existing system of fourths and fifths, with the slight flattening upwards of fifths and downwards of fourths, to bring all within the perfect octave. But to achieve this, a normal pitch admitting of no variation is a necessity, because no tuner could give the time to work by a set of forks making beats with the pitch wanted. A. J. H.

THE ORGAN TUNER'S PRACTICE.—The organ no longer remains with the groundwork of fifths and octaves only; modern tuners use fifths and fourths in the treble C–C, of the Principal of 4-ft. pitch; the organ being tuned entirely by the rapidity of the beats arising from the slight deviation from perfection of these intervals. (See ORGAN, Vol. III. p. 762.)

In equal or even temperament each fifth is tuned slightly narrower than a perfect fifth, (see TEMPERAMENT), and each fourth slightly wider than a perfect fourth; the fourth being rather more imperfect intervals—pitch for pitch—than the fifths.

The pulsations or beats in tuning necessarily follow the law of vibrations and double their rate in the octave above; and the number of beats or pulsations of these intervals in this octave has been computed to *average* 75 per minute in 8-ft. pitch (Diapason), for the pitch C = 264 to C = 528, which is somewhat sharper than the Diapason Normal, now (1926) in general use (see PITCH). These figures must be doubled for use with the Principal of 4-ft. pitch, viz. 150 beats per minute. Music being a science of ratios no two intervals of the same degree should beat at the same rate, but *evenly* quicken, as the pitch rises, to double the rate at the octave above, as before mentioned. Below is given the order of the intervals used in tuning the bearings on the Principal 4 ft.

 * A♯ = B♭.   Organ-builders call all black notes sharps.

When the tuning of this series is completed the D♯ and G♯ above should prove to be an evenly wide fourth with the others. Before proceeding farther it is well to test these bearings in such major thirds, minor sixths, and triads as lie within the compass of this septave, after which the octaves above and below must be carefully tuned, and tested with their own fifths and fourths (below or above) already tuned.

When the full compass of the Principal 4 ft. has been tuned and tested in fifths, fourths, major thirds, major tenths and common chords in chromatic order, the remainder of the stops may be tuned to the Principal 4 ft., in the order in which they stand on the sound-board, each stop being tested independently afterwards.

Mutation stops are tuned as pure intervals to the ground or prime tone; and in the VOIX CÉLESTES (*q.v.*) one rank of pipes is tuned to beat with the other (see VOIX CÉLESTES).

The means by which the various pipes are tuned are given in the article ORGAN.

Harmoniums and American organs are tuned by scraping the metal tongue of the reed near the free end to sharpen it, and near the attached end to flatten it.

Of equal or even temperament tuning it must be said that it can only be tolerated by means of fine tuning, any deviation from which offends and ultimately vitiates the ear; such tuning can only be quickly achieved by years of study and practice.

Space will not permit of entering into the minuter details, or of dealing with the side issues connected with this subject, but the reader may be referred to the Bibliography of organ-literature to be found in vol. iii., and to such works as: *An Essay on the Theory and Practice of Tuning in General, and on Scheibler's Invention of tuning Pianofortes and Organs by the Metronome in Particular* (Robt. Cocks & Co., 1853); *The Tuner's Guide* (Musical Bouquet Office); *The History of the Piano-*

forte, by Edgar Brinsmead (Cassell, Petter & Galpin); *Construction, Tuning and Care of the Pianoforte*, by Dr. Henry Fisher (J. Curwen & Sons); *Pianos* ('Work' Handbook, Cassell & Co.).   T. E.

TUNING-FORK (Fr. *diapason*; Ger. *Stimmgabel*; Ital. *corista*). This familiar and valuable pitch-carrier was invented in 1711 by John Shore, Handel's famous trumpeter. From a musical instrument it has become a philosophical one, chiefly from its great permanence in retaining a pitch; since it is flattened by heat and sharpened by cold to an amount which is determinable for any particular observations. A fork is tuned by filing the ends of the prongs to sharpen, and between them at the base, to flatten; and after this it should stand for some weeks and be tested again, owing to the fact that filing disturbs the molecular structure. Rust affects a fork but very little, the effect being to flatten it slightly. Tuning-forks have been used to construct a keyboard instrument, but the paucity of harmonic upper partial tones causes a monotonous quality of tone. An account of the combination of tuning-forks into a tonometer for the accurate measurement of pitch will be found under SCHEIBLER, the inventor.   A. J. H.

The valuable collection of tuning-forks made by Dr. A. J. Ellis is now in the Royal Institution, together with those of the writer, A. J. HIPKINS.

BIBL.—ERNST A. KIELHAUSER, *Die Stimmgabel, ihre Schwingungsgesetze und Anwendungen in der Physik.* (Leipzig, 1907.)

TUNING-SLIDE (organ), an adjustable metal clip or cylinder, attached to the upper end of open metal flue-pipes, for convenience in tuning.   T. E.

TUNSTED, SIMON (*b.* Norwich, 14th century), the reputed author of the treatise *De quatuor principalibus musice*, though himself born at Norwich, derived his surname from Tunstead in Norfolk, of which place his father was a native.

He became one of the Fratres Minores of the Order of St. Francis at Oxford, and it was there that he is said to have taken the degree of Doctor of Theology. He appears to have been well versed in all the seven liberal arts, but, like Walter Odington, especially in music and astronomy. The only literary works attributed to Tunsted, besides that above referred to, are a commentary on the *Meteora* of Aristotle and additions to Richard Wallingford's *Albion*; but the work by which his name has been, rightly or wrongly, handed down to posterity is the musical one. Of this there are two MSS. in the Bodleian Library, numbered Bodley 515 and Digby 90. Owing to the former MS. being described in the old catalogue of 1697 as 'De musica continua et discreta cum diagrammatibus,' many musical historians have believed that there are two distinct works by

this author; but the only real difference is that the Digby MS. contains the prologue beginning 'Quemadmodum inter triticum et zizania,' which the Bodley MS. omits. The work itself contains warrant for both titles. From the colophon to each MS. we learn that the treatise was written in 1351, when Simon Tunsted was Regent of the Minorites at Oxford. He is said to have afterwards become Head of the English branch of his Order,[1] and to have died in the nunnery of St. Clara, at Bruisyard, in Suffolk, in 1369.

The *De quatuor principalibus* treats of music in almost every form then known, from definitions of musical terms in the *Primum principale* down to an account of 'Musica mensurabilis' in the *Quartum principale*. This latter part is perhaps the most important of the whole work. Tunsted quotes Philip de Vitry 'qui fuit flos totius mundi musicorum.' The whole treatise has been printed by de Coussemaker. The British Museum contains a third copy of *De quatuor principalibus* (Add. MSS. 8866), and in another MS. (Add. MSS. 10,336) there is an epitome of several chapters of the *Secundum principale*, written by a Fellow of New College, Oxford, early in the 16th century.   A. H. H.

TUOTILO (TUTILO), monk of St. Gall, *c.* 900, pupil of Marcellus and Iso, a master in all arts and sciences, who could play all the musical instruments of his time, and instructed the sons of the nobility in their use. He composed a Christmas tropos, 'Hodie cantandus est nobis puer,' which is looked upon as the origin of the Christmas (Miracle) plays (Ambros, vol. 2; *Riemann*, under both names).

TURANDOT, a 5-act play of Schiller (after Carlo Gozzi), founded on a Chinese subject, orchestral music to which was composed by Weber in 1809. His music consists of an overture and six numbers, three of them marches, all more or less founded on a Chinese melody, which Weber took from Rousseau's Dictionary of Music (vol. ii. plate N), and which opens the overture exactly as Rousseau gives it.

The overture was originally composed as an 'Overtura Chinesa' in 1806, and afterwards revised. The first performance of the overture in its present shape was at Strassburg, Dec. 31, 1814. The play has been 'freely

---

[1] Twenty-ninth Provincial of the English Friars Minor in 1360.

W. H. G. F.

translated' into English by Sabilla Novello (1872).   G.

For other works (operas, etc.) on this subject see REISSIGER, VESQUE VON PUTTLINGEN (J. Hoven), BUSONI, PUCCINI.

TURBAN, CHARLES PAUL (b. Strassburg, Oct. 3, 1845 ; d. Paris, May 11, 1905), was educated at the Paris Conscrvatoire, where he obtained a second and first accessit for clarinet in 1862 and 1863 respectively, a second prize in 1864 and a first in 1865. He was a member of the orchestras of the Gymnase, the Théâtre Italien, and the Opéra successively. He held the position of solo clarinet at the Opéra and at the Conservatoire concerts. He was associated with Taffanel in the foundation of the Société des Instruments à vent (see PARIS) in 1879, and made many journeys with the other members of the society, winning a European reputation. He became professor of the clarinet in the Paris Conservatoire in 1900, and shortly afterwards retired from the Opéra.   M.

TURCA, ALLA, i.e. in Turkish style ; the accepted meaning of which is a spirited simple melody, with a lively accentuated accompaniment. The two best examples of this are the finale to Mozart's PF. Sonata in A (Köchel, 331), which is inscribed by the composer ' Alla Turca ' (and which has served on occasion as ballet-music for the ' Seraglio ') and the theme of Beethoven's variations in D (op. 76), which he afterwards took for the ' Marcia alla Turca,' which follows the Dervish chorus in the ' Ruins of Athens.'   G.

TURCO IN ITALIA, IL, opera by Rossini. Produced La Scala, Milan, Aug. 14, 1814 ; His Majesty's, May 19, 1821.   G.

TURE-LURE (soft u), or TOURE-LOURE, a very ancient lyrical burden or refrain, probably of Provençal origin. The old English form is ' tirra-lirra ' (Shakespeare, ' The lark that tirra-lirra chants.' Compare the French ' Turlut,' a titlark ; ' Turlutaine,' a bird-organ). In old French music it is also found as ' Tur-lu-tu-tu,' ' Tur-lu-ru ' (in a popular air ' Io canto tur-lu-ru '), ' tur-lur-ibo,' etc. The form ' turelure ' was also employed for ' chanson.' It often occurs in the old French burlesques. The following specimens, taken from Les Parodies du Nouveau Théâtre Italien, 1731, will illustrate its use.

1. ' Ho ! Ho ! toure-louribo.'

Al-lons tôt, que ma ri - vale ex - pi - re, oh !

oh ! tou-re lou-ri - bo ! Quoi con - tre moi tout con -

spir-e, oh ! oh ! tou-re lou-ri - bo ! Quand j'a-vance, on

me re - ti - re, oh ! oh ! oh ! tou-re lou - ri - bo.

2. Vaudeville in ' Les Cahos.'

On ne peut, quoi-que l'on faa - se, s'em-pê-cher d'ai-mer

à son tour ; Les pois-sons tom-bent dans la nas - se,

Les cœurs se tou-re lou-re lou-re lou-re lou-re lou-re

lour. Les cœurs se ren - dent à l'a - mour.

The term still survives in English popular music in the forms " tooral-looral-looral,' and ' tol-de-rol.'   E. J. P.

TURGES (STURGES), EDMUND (late 15th and early 16th cent.), English composer. Barclay Squire (Archaeologia, vol. lvi.) refers to two Turges, William and Edmund (both of Petworth), who came to King's College, Cambridge, the former in 1513, the latter in 1522. An ' Inventarye of the Pryke Songys longynge to the Kyngys College in Cambryge (in 1529) ' —printed in The Ecclesiologist for 1863—refers to ' 6 bokys off parchmente conteyninge Turges massys and antems '; but as many of Turges's compositions date back to the first years of the century, he cannot be identified with either of the Petworth Turges mentioned above. He is more likely to have been, as Barclay Squire suggests, the son of a John Turges of an earlier generation, who was harper to Queen Margaret. One of Turges's part-songs beginning :

' From stormy wyndis and grevous whethir
Good Lord preserve the estrige fethir,'

celebrates the marriage of Prince Arthur and Catherine of Aragon, and must therefore have been written between Nov. 14, 1501 (the date of the marriage), and Apr. 2, 1502 (that of the Prince's death). The Kyrie and Gloria. from a 3-part Mass by Turges are in B.M. Add. MSS. 5665/109b, which also contains compositions by Mower, Cornyshe and Sir Thomas Packe, and was written before 1510, as copies of documents bearing this date are bound up in it. A Magnificat by Turges is at Caius College, Cambridge, and a 4-part ' Gaude flore virginale ' is in the Eton College MS.—written between 1490 and 1504 (see Davey, Hist. Eng. Mus.). This MS. originally contained 97 pieces, of which only 43 remain, and the index shows that another Hymn to the Virgin by Turges is among the missing compositions.

Alas, it is I, a 3. B.M. Add. MSS. 5465/17b ; B.M. Add. MSS 11,583/7b. Score.

Enforce yourselfe, *a* 3
(2nd part) Soverayn Lord, *a* 3 ⎫
(3rd part) God hath gyfť you. *a* 3 ⎬ B.M. Add. MSS. 5465/115b.
From stormy wyndis, *a* 3 ⎭
(2nd part) O blessid lord of hevyn, *a* 3 ⎫ B.M. Add. MSS. 5465/104b.
(3rd part) Wherfor, good Lord, *a* 3 ⎬ R.C.M 810/100b.
(4th part) Now good Lady, *a* 3 ⎭
I am he that you dayly served. B.M. Add. MSS. 5465/19b. Treble
　and portion of bass part only.

J. M^K.

TURIN. If in some ways the musical organisations of Turin cannot boast the great traditions of other Italian cities, the catholic tastes and the enterprise of its musicians and music-lovers have given to the Piedmontese capital the primacy in other respects. The Conservatorio does not equal in importance the schools of Milan and Bologna, yet the orchestral concerts of Turin have long had the reputation of being second to none. In its devotion to the classics Turin perhaps stands first amongst the Italian centres. Established by Pedrotti in 1872 the popular concerts have served their purpose to make the public familiar with symphonic music, and the great German composers have ever found a ready welcome. At the same time the orchestra grew steadily in number and in excellence, and its visit to the Paris exhibition of 1878 was a triumph for the players and their conductors, Pedrotti and Mancinelli. Pedrotti retired in 1882 and the popular concerts ceased, but during the Exhibition of 1884 the local orchestra conducted by Franco Faccio gave a remarkable series of concerts with programmes in which the most popular name was that of Wagner. A number of symphonic works by Italians were also performed, and although it would be idle to pretend that the symphonies of such men as Foroni and Bolzoni compare favourably at any point with their classical models, it should not be forgotten that they, with Sgambati and Martucci, devoted themselves to symphonic music at a time when, for most Italians, music and opera were synonymous. In 1895 another concert society was formed under the chairmanship of Count E. de Villanova, and during the exhibition of 1898 a very successful series of forty-eight concerts was given, mainly conducted by Arturo Toscanini.

The Teatro Regio plays an important part in the musical life of the city. Giovanni Bolzoni, who did much to create a tradition and establish a high standard of critical appreciation in the public, was appointed conductor in 1884 (on Verdi's recommendation); five years later he became director of the Liceo Musicale, a position he held for twenty-nine years. It was at the Teatro Regio that Wagner's 'Lohengrin' triumphed (in 1877) for the first time in Italy, and the Turinese since have been supposed to nourish a warmer admiration for Wagner than any other Italian audience. The theatre was considerably altered and renovated in comparatively recent years and reopened in 1906. Two operas of Puccini were produced at the Teatro Regio for the first time : 'Manon Lescaut' (1893) and 'Bohème' (1896). F. B.

TURINA, JOAQUIN (*b.* Seville, Dec. 9, 1882), Spanish composer, pianist and teacher. After preliminary studies in his native town and Madrid, he worked from 1905–14 with Vincent d'Indy at the Schola Cantorum in Paris, and has written a small Spanish *Enciclopedia abreviada de la música* (Madrid, 1917), which embodies the teaching of his master. His musical outlook is different from that of FALLA ; his style is distinctive. Yet they are alike in their Spanish seriousness of purpose and their attitude to music as being an art, and not a diversion ' for the frivolity of women and the dissipation of men.' Turina's chief interest is chamber music ; but his 'Procesión del Rocío' is a brilliant orchestral study, which never fails to make its effect. His stage works include a lyric comedy, 'Margot,' music for the old morality play, *La Adúltera penitente* (by Moreto, arranged by Martínez-Sierra) and ' Jardín de oriente' (1923). His chamber music includes a PF. quintet, string quartet, 'Escena Andaluza,' viola, PF. and string quartet ; 'Poema de una Sanluquena,' violin and PF. ; and numerous songs of great merit. J. B. T.

TURINI, FRANCESCO (*b.* Prague, *c.* 1595 ; *d.* Brescia, 1656), learned contrapuntist, son of Gregorio Turini, cornet-player to the Emperor Rudolph II., and author of 'Teutsche Lieder' *a* 4, in imitation of the Italian Villanelle (Frankfort, 1610). His father dying early, the Emperor took up the young Francesco, had him trained in Venice and Rome, and made him his chamber-organist. Later he became organist of the cathedral at Brescia. He published 'Messe a 4 e 5 voci a Capella,' op. 1 (Gardano, 1643) ; 'Mottetti a voce sola,' for all four kinds of voices (1629 and 1640) ; 'Madrigali a 1, 2, e 3, con sonate a 2 e 3 ' (1621, 1624, etc.) ; and 'Motetti commodi.' A canon of his is quoted by Burney, the theme of which—

Chris-te　e · le · · · · · · · · i- son.

was a favourite with Handel, who employs it in his organ fugue in B♭, and in his oboe concerto, No. 2, in the same key. The phrase had been previously used by Thomas Morley, who begins his canzonet, ' Cruel, you pull away too soon your dainty lips,' with the same theme. It is also the initial phrase of Palestrina's 'Tu es Petrus,' and was employed by Bach in his well-known pedal fugue in E♭, and by Dr. Croft in his psalm-tune, ' St. Anne's.' F. G.

TURKEY, see MUHAMMEDAN.

TURKISH CRESCENT, see GLCCKENSPIEL.

TURKISH MUSIC (*Türkische,* or *Janitscharen Musik* ; Ital. *banda turca*), a term which was at one time used to denote the percussion instruments in the orchestra, bass-drum, cymbals and triangle. The band of the Janissaries abolished in 1825, is said to have comprised a piccolo and oboes in addition to the percussion instruments named. The modern use of percussive effects is too individual to make the collective term appropriate.   G.

TURLE, (1) JAMES (*b.* Taunton, Somerset, Mar. 5, 1802 ; *d.* London, June 28, 1882), was a chorister at Wells Cathedral, under Dodd Perkins, from July 1810 to Dec. 1813. He was organist of Christ Church, Southwark, from 1819–29, and from the latter date to 1831 organist of St. James's, Bermondsey.

From 1819–31 he was assistant to Thomas Greatorex as organist and master of the choristers of Westminster Abbey, and upon Greatorex's death in 1831 was appointed his successor. In 1840–43 he was part conductor of the Ancient Concerts. In 1875 he was released from active duty by the appointment of J. F. BRIDGE (*q.v.*) as his assistant. From 1829–56 he was music master at the School for the Indigent Blind. He composed and edited many services, anthems, and chants, and edited, with E. Taylor, *The Art of Singing at Sight* (1846) and ' The People's Music Book.' He also composed many glees (MS.). His remarkable skill and ability as a teacher were strikingly manifested by the number of those who received their early training from him, and rose to eminence in their profession. He was buried in Norwood Cemetery.

(2) ROBERT (*b.* Taunton, Mar. 19, 1804 ; *d.* Salisbury, Mar. 26, 1877), his brother, was a chorister at Westminster Abbey from 1814 to Aug. 1821 ; and organist of Armagh Cathedral from 1823–72.

(3) WILLIAM (*b.* Taunton, 1795), first cousin of the preceding two, was a chorister of Wells Cathedral from 1804–10. After quitting the choir he paid a short visit to America, and on his return to England in 1812 became organist of St. James's, Taunton, which he quitted upon being appointed organist of St. Mary Magdalen's n the same town.   W. H. H.

TURN (Fr. *brisée* ; Ger. *Doppelschlag* ; Ital. *grupetto*), an ornament much used in both ancient and modern music, instrumental as well as vocal. Its sign is a curve ∽ placed above or below the note, and it is rendered by four notes—namely, the note next above the written note, the written note itself, the note below, and the written note again (Ex. 1). It is thus identical with a figure frequently employed in composition, and known as the *half-circle* (*Halbzirkel, circolo mezzo*). The written note is called the principal note of the turn, and the others are termed respectively the upper and lower auxiliary notes.

1.   *Written.*   *Played.*

On account of its gracefulness, and also no

doubt in consequence of its presenting little difficulty of execution, the turn has always been a very favourite ornament, so much so that C. P. E. Bach says of it :

' This beautiful grace is as it were too complaisant, it suits well everywhere, and on this account is often abused, for many players imagine that the whole grace and beauty of pianoforte-playing consist in making a turn every moment.'

Properly introduced, however, it is of the greatest value, both in slow movements, in which it serves to connect and fill up long notes in a melody, and also in rapid tempo and on short notes, where it lends brightness and accent to the phrase.

When the sign stands directly above a note, the four notes of the turn are played rapidly, and, if the written note is a long one, the last of the four is sustained until its duration is completed (Ex. 2) ; if, however, the written note is too short to admit of this difference, the four notes are made equal (Ex. 3).

2. MOZART, Violin Sonata in G major.

Played.

3.   MOZART, Rondo in A minor.

Played.

When the sign is placed a little to the right of the note, the written note is played first, and the four notes of the turn follow it, all four being of equal length. The exact moment for the beginning of the turn is not fixed ; it may be soon after the written note, the four turn-notes being then rather slow (Ex. 4), or later, in which case the turn will be more rapid (Ex. 5). The former rendering is best suited to a slow movement, the latter to one of a livelier character.

4. BEETHOVEN, Sonata, Op. 10, No. 1.

Played.

5. BEETHOVEN, Sonata, Op. 2, No. 1.

Both the turn upon the written note and that which follows it may be expressed in small grace-notes, instead of by the sign. For this purpose the turn upon the note will require three small notes, which are placed before the principal note though played within its value, and the turn *after* the note will require four (Ex. 6). This method of writing the turn is usually employed in modern music in preference to the sign.

6. MOZART, Sonata in F.   Turn on the note.

MOZART, Tema con Variazioni.

The upper auxiliary note of a turn is always the next degree of the scale above the principal note, and is therefore either a tone or a semitone distant from it, according to the position in the scale held by the written note. Thus, in a turn on the first degree, the upper note is a tone above (Ex. 7), while a turn on the third degree is made with the semitone (Ex. 8). The lower auxiliary note may likewise follow the scale, and may therefore be also either a tone or a semitone from its principal note ; but the effect of the smaller distance is as a rule the more agreeable, and it is therefore customary to raise the lower note chromatically in those cases in which it would naturally be a tone distant from its principal note (Ex. 9).

This alteration of the lower note is in accordance with a rule which governs the use of auxiliary notes in general, but in the construction of both the ordinary turn and the turn of the SHAKE (*q.v.*), the rule is not invariably followed. The case in which it is most strictly observed is when the principal note of the turn is the fifth degree of the scale, yet even here, when it is accompanied by the tonic harmony, an exception is occasionally met with. That Bach did not object to the use of a lower auxiliary note a tone below the principal note is proved by the four semiquavers in the subject of the C♯ major fugue in the Well-tempered Clavier, and by other similar instances. Another and more frequent exception occurs when the *upper* note is only a semitone above the principal note, in which case the lower note is generally made a tone below (Ex. 10). In the case of a turn on the fifth degree of the *minor* scale the rule is always observed, and both notes are

a semitone distant (Ex. 11). A turn of this kind is termed a chromatic turn, because its notes form part of a chromatic scale.

10. MOZART, Violin Sonata in G.

11. MOZART, Clarinet Trio in E♭.

All chromatic alterations in a turn can be indicated by means of accidentals placed above or below the sign, although they frequently have to be made without any such indication. An accidental above the sign refers to the upper auxiliary note, and one underneath it to the lower, as in the following example from Haydn :

12.   Sonata in E♭.

When the note which bears a turn is dotted, and is followed by a note of half its own length, the last note of the turn falls in the place of the dot, the other three notes being either quick or slow, according to the character of the movement (Ex. 13). When, however, the dotted note is followed by two short notes (Ex. 14), or when it represents a full bar of 3–4, or a half-bar of 6–8 or 6–4 time (Ex. 15), the rule does not apply, and the note is treated simply as a long note.

13   MOZART, Sonata in D.

14.   BEETHOVEN, Sonata, Op. 13, Adagio.

15.   BEETHOVEN, Sonata, Op. 10, No. 1.

A turn on a note followed by two dots is

played so that the last note falls in the place of the first dot (Ex. 16).

16.   MOZART, Sonata in C minor.

Played.

The turn on the dotted note was frequently written by Mozart in a somewhat ambiguous fashion, by means of four small notes (Ex. 17), the fourth of which has in performance to be made longer than the other three, although written of the same length, in order that it may represent the dot, according to rule.

17.   MOZART, Sonata in F, Adagio.

Played.

An apparent exception to the rule that a turn is played during some portion of the value of its written note occurs when the sign is placed over the second of two notes of the same name, whether connected by a tie or not (Ex. 18).

18.   HAYDN, Trio in G.

Played.

In this case the turn is played *before* the note over which the sign stands, so that the written note forms the *last* note of the turn. This apparently exceptional rendering may be explained by the assumption that the second of the two notes stands in the place of a dot to the first, and this is supported by the fact that any such example might be written without the second note, but with a dot in its stead, as in Ex. 19, when the rendering would be precisely the same. If, however, the first of two notes of the same name is already dotted, the second cannot be said to bear to it the relation of a dot, and accordingly a turn in such a case would be treated simply as a turn over the note (Ex. 20).

19.

20.   HAYDN, Sonata in G minor.

Played.

INVERTED TURNS.—When the order of the notes of a turn is reversed, so as to begin with the lower note instead of the upper, the turn is said to be inverted, and its sign is either placed on end thus, *{*, or drawn in the contrary direction to the ordinary sign, thus ∿ (Ex. 21). The inverted turn is however more frequently written in small notes than indicated by a sign (Ex. 22).

21.   C. P. E. BACH, Sonata in B♭, Largo.

Played.

22.   MOZART, Rondo in A minor.

In certain cases, particularly at the beginning of a phrase, the effect of the ordinary turn starting with the upper note is unsatisfactory and deficient in accent. The perception of this fact led to the invention of a particular form of turn (called by C. P. E. Bach the *Geschnellte Doppelschlag*), in which the four notes of the ordinary turn were preceded by a short principal note, written as a small grace-note (Ex. 23).

23.   *Written.*   C. P. E. BACH, Sonata.

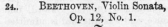

Played.

A similar turn of five notes (instead of four), also frequently met with, is indicated by the compound sign ∿, and called in German the *Prallende Doppelschlag*. The difference of name

24.   BEETHOVEN, Violin Sonata, Op. 12, No. 1.

Played.

is unimportant, since it merely means the same ornament introduced under different circumstances ; but the sign has remained longer in use than the older mode of writing shown in Ex. 23, and is still occasionally met with (Ex. 24).

When a note bearing a turn of either four or five notes is preceded by an appoggiatura (Ex. 25), or by a slurred note one degree higher than itself, the entrance of the turn is slightly delayed, the preceding note being prolonged, precisely as the beginning of the 'bound trill' is delayed. (See SHAKE.)

25.   W. F. BACH, Sonata in D.

Played.

Like the shake, the turn can occur in two parts at once, and Hummel indicates this by a double sign, $\approx$; this is, however, rarely if ever met with in the works of other composers, the usual method being to write out the ornament. in full, in ordinary notes.   F. T.

TURNER, AUSTIN T. (b. Bristol, 1823 ; d. Sydney, New South Wales, Apr. 13, 1901), was a chorister at the Cathedral at Bristol, and at the age of 20 was appointed vicar choral at Lincoln. He went to Australia in 1854, and was selected as singing-master to the Government School at Ballarat. He was the pioneer of music in that place, being the first conductor of the Philharmonic Society, which among other oratorios performed Mendelssohn's 'St. Paul' and Spohr's 'Last Judgment,' and, for the first time in Australia, Sullivan's 'Prodigal Son.' His sacred cantata 'Adoration,' for soli, chorus and full orchestra, was produced by the Melbourne Philharmonic Society on Nov. 24, 1874. He was also the author of a choral song ; two masses, sung with full orchestral accompaniments at St. Francis' Church, Melbourne ; several glees, madrigals and minor works. He was organist of Christ Church, Ballarat, for many years.   G.

TURNER, WILLIAM, Mus.D. (b. 1651 ; d. Duke Street, Westminster, Jan. 13, 1739/40), son of Charles Turner, cook at Pembroke College, Oxford, began his musical education as a chorister of Christ Church, Oxford, under Edward Lowe, and was afterwards admitted a chorister of the Chapel Royal under Captain Henry Cooke. Whilst in the latter capacity he joined his fellow-choristers, John Blow and Pelham Humfrey, in the composition of the 'Club Anthem,' his contribution being a bass solo in the middle. After quitting the choir his voice settled into a fine counter-tenor, and

he became a member of the choir of Lincoln Cathedral. On Oct. 11, 1669, he was sworn in as a gentleman of the Chapel Royal, and soon afterwards became a vicar choral of St. Paul's, and a lay vicar of Westminster Abbey. He set an ode by Nahum Tate, for St. Cecilia's Day, 1685. He graduated as Mus.D. at Cambridge in 1696. A birthday ode for the Princess Anne was composed in 1698. He composed much church music ; two services and six anthems (including 'The King shall rejoice,' composed for St. Cecilia's Day, 1697, and 'The Queen shall rejoice,' for the coronation of Queen Anne) are contained in the Tudway collection (Harl. MSS. 7339 and 7341). Eight more anthems are at Ely Cathedral, and others in the choir books of the Chapel Royal and Westminster Abbey. Boyce printed the anthem 'Lord, Thou hast been our refuge' in his Cathedral Music. Many of Turner's songs were printed in the collections of the period. He contributed songs to D'Urfey's[1] 'Fond Husband' (1676) and 'Madam Fickle' (1677), and wrote the music for a masque 'Presumptuous Love' given at Lincoln's Inn Fields in 1716. A large collection of his songs and catches is in the Fitzwilliam Museum, Cambridge. Playford's 'Harmonia Sacra,' 1688, contains a solo hymn, 'Thus mortals must submit to fate.' He died at his house in Duke Street, Westminster, having survived his wife (with whom he had lived nearly seventy years) only four days, she dying on Jan. 9, aged 85. They were buried, Jan. 16, in one grave in the west cloister of Westminster Abbey. Their youngest daughter, Anne, was the wife of John ROBINSON (q.v.), organist of Westminster Abbey.

      W. H. H. ; addns. from D.N.B., etc.

TURNER, WILLIAM, published in 1724 a treatise on the grammar of music entitled

'Sound Anatomiz'd, in a Philosophical Essay on Musick. To which is added A Discourse concerning the Abuse of Musick.'

He tells us incidentally that violins on some occasions go ten degrees higher than E la, i.e. up to g''', and that some organs are made to go a whole octave lower than Gamma Ut. A third edition was published by Walsh in Sept. 1739. Turner also edited Ravenscroft's Psalms, 8vo, 1728, and 4to, 1746. Some sonatas, published about the same date, were probably by him, as well as songs for several plays.

      J. F. R. S.

TURNHOUT (1) GERARD DE (GHEERT JACQUES, called DE TURNHOUT) (b. Turnhout, Belgium, c. 1520 ; d. Madrid, Sept. 15, 1580), singer, 1545, master in the Confrérie de la Vierge, 1562, and Kapellmeister, 1563, of Antwerp Cathedral. In 1572 Philip II. summoned him to Spain. He composed masses, motets, chansons, etc., some in collective volumes of Phalèse and of Tylman Susato. (2) JEAN

[1] See D'Urfey's New Collection of Songs and Poems, 1683.

DE (JEAN JACQUES), son of Gerard, maître de chapelle of Philip II., and the governor of the Netherlands at Brussels. In 1611 he is mentioned as second master, and in 1618 as first master (Kapellmeister) of the royal chapel there. He composed one book each of 6-part madrigals, 1589, 5-part madrigals, 1595, and 5-8-part motets, 1594 (*Riemann*; *Q.-L.*).

TURPIN, EDMUND HART (*b.* Nottingham, May 4, 1835; *d.* London, Oct. 25, 1907), organist, was local organist at the age of 13; he also studied composition and piano, and became practically acquainted with the instruments of the orchestra and military band. He gave an organ recital at the Great Exhibition of 1851, and in 1857 came to live in London; in 1869 he was appointed to the organ at St. George's, Bloomsbury, and in 1886 to that of St. Bride's, Fleet Street. In 1875 he became Hon. Secretary of the R.C.O., to which institution he devoted much attention, especially in developing the examinations. He received the degree of Mus.D. from the Archbishop of Canterbury in 1889, and in 1892 was appointed warden of Trinity College of Music, London. Dr. Turpin was for long connected with the musical press of London, and from 1880 edited the *Musical Standard*, as well as other musical papers such as the *Musical World*, of which, as of *Musical News*, he was joint-editor. In 1883 he was conductor of the London orchestra at the Cardiff Eisteddfod. His works embrace two masses, a Stabat Mater, the oratorios 'St. John the Baptist' and 'Hezekiah,' 'A Song of Faith,' produced in London, 1867; 'Jerusalem,' a cantata; anthems; services; a symphony-overture for orchestra and military band; chamber music and pianoforte pieces; songs, hymn-tunes and much organ music. He also edited the 'Student's Edition' of classical pianoforte music (Weekes & Co.), with marginal analyses and directions. He succeeded W. T. Best as editor of a complete edition of Bach's organ works. He was buried on Oct. 30, 1907, at Highgate Cemetery, a memorial service being held at St. Bride's.   G.

TURTON, see STURTON.

TUSCH, probably a form of *Touche*, that is, *toccata*, and that again related to TUCK, TUCKET (*q.v.*).

TUTTI (Ital.), all; a term used to designate those parts of a vocal or instrumental composition which are performed by the whole of the forces at once. In the scores, and more frequently in the chorus parts of masses, cantatas, etc., the parts for the solo quartet (where such is employed) are often written on the same set of staves as the chorus parts, in which case the words solo and tutti are used to distinguish the one from the other. The same thing is done in the solo part of a pianoforte concerto, and also in the band parts of concertos generally, so that the orchestra may know where to avoid

overpowering the solo instrument. The term ripieno was formerly applied to those violins which only played in the tuttis. For this end in some scores the string parts are marked S and T or S and R where requisite.

The term tutti has also been applied to those portions of a concerto in which the orchestra—not necessarily the whole orchestra—plays while the solo instrument is silent. See CONCERTO.

In pure orchestral music, especially up to Beethoven's time, we speak of the forte passages as 'the tuttis,' from the fact of their being the places where the full orchestra is used in a mass.   F. C.

TYE, CHRISTOPHER (*b. circa* 1500; *d.* before Mar. 15, 1572/3), composer, was for the chief part of his life closely connected with Cambridge and Ely, and may have been a native of the eastern counties, where the surname was not uncommon. The statement that he was born at Westminster is a mistake arising from a misunderstanding of Fuller, who places him among the Worthies of Westminster. Wood's conjecture that he 'seems to be a Western man born' has nothing to support it. If he is to be identified with a boy named Tye who was in the choir of King's College, Cambridge (fifth in the list of choristers in 1511, and second in the list in 1512), his birth may be placed between 1497 and 1500; but it is not certain, though it is extremely likely, that Christopher is identical with either this chorister, or a singing-man named Tye, who was in the choir in 1527; for there was a Richard Tye who was lay-clerk from 1535–45, to whom these entries may refer.

The full name, Christopher Tye, first appears in the extant Chapel documents of King's College in 1537 as that of one of the lay clerks. He had taken his degree of Mus.B. at Cambridge in 1536; the Grace for his degree speaks of his ten years' study in the art of music, with much practice in composition and teaching boys. He was required to compose a Mass to be sung 'vel paulo post comitia vel eo ipso die quo serenissimi principis observabitur adventus.' Tye was appointed Magister Choristarum, with a yearly salary of £10, at Ely Cathedral in 1541 or 1542, soon after the establishment of the Ely Bishopric, and in 1545 he proceeded Mus.D. at Cambridge, when again he was directed to compose a Mass for his exercise. Three years later, in 1548, he was incorporated in the University of Oxford. It is possible that Tye owed a good deal to the influence of Dr. Richard Cox, who was made Archdeacon of Ely in 1541, and was elected Chancellor of the University of Oxford in 1547. He had been at King's College in 1519, where he may have become acquainted with Tye: afterwards when he was Bishop of Ely, he was certainly Tye's friend. That Cox was schoolmaster to Edward VI. from 1544 to 1550, lends some support to the belief that Tye was the Prince's music-master. This has been questioned, chiefly on the ground that the sole authority for the statement is Samuel Rowley's play *When You see Me, You Know Me*, 1605, in which Edward addresses Tye as ' our music's lecturer.' The Preface to the ' Actes of the Apostles,' however, certainly points to some friendly relation between the two, such as might exist between master and pupil, and there seems to be no need to reject the tradition. In Rowley's play the Prince repeats what we may believe to be a genuine saying of Henry VIII. with regard to Tye :

> 'I oft have heard my Father merrily speake
> In your hye praise, and thus his Highnesse sayth,
> England, one God, one truth, one Doctor hath
> For Musicks Art, and that is Doctor *Tye*.'[1]

It has also been suggested that Tye was music-master to the Princesses Mary and Elizabeth, but there is no evidence on the subject.

The short reign of Edward VI. was marked by great activity among the writers of music for the English Service, in which it has been presumed that Tye took a leading part (see List of Works). The one work, however, which he published, and by which his name is remembered, was not written for church use. This was

> ' The Actes of the Apostles, translated into Englyshe Metre, and dedicated to the kynges most excellent Maiestye, by Christofer Tye, Doctor in Musyke, and one of the Gentylmen of hys graces moste honourable Chappell, wyth notes to eche Chapter, to synge and also to play vpon the Lute, very necessarye for studentes after theyr studye, to fyle theyr wyttes, and also for all Christians that cannot synge, to reade the good and Godlye storyes of the lyues of Christ hys Apostles. 1553.'

A rimed Preface addressed to Edward, of which a considerable part is given by Hawkins, sets forth the object of the publication, which was to spread the knowledge of Bible stories, by treating them much as Sternhold had treated the Psalms :

> 'That such good thinges your grace might moue
> Your lute when ye assaye :
> In stede of songes of wanton loue
> These stories then to playe.'

As a matter of fact the Chapters of the ' Actes ' (of which no more than fourteen are printed) are arranged for four voices, and the parts are so disposed on the page that a lute-player could make nothing of them as they stand. In some copies of the book the colophon runs ' Imprynted at London by Wyllyam Seres dwellynge at the signe of the Hedghogge ' ; in others, ' Imprynted at London by Nycolas Hyll, for Wyllyam Seres.'[2] Two of the settings are Canons, and in each of the others a little point of imitation is introduced to give interest to the music, but what Tye aims at is simplicity and tunefulness ; as he says :

---

[1] The chief part of the scenes in which Tye is introduced will be found in Hawkins's *History*, 1875, p. 452.
[2] Steele, *Earliest English Music Printing*, 1903.

> 'And thoughe they be not curious
> But for the letter mete :
> Ye shall them fynde harmonious
> And eke pleasaunt and swete.'

It is an interesting testimony to the success with which he adopted a popular style that two of the best-known Psalm tunes (WINDSOR OR ETON (*q.v.*) ; and Winchester Old), have been traced to their sources in the ' Actes of the Apostles.' The music indeed is excellent, but when Burney writes of Tye that he was ' perhaps as good a poet as Sternhold,' he was doing an injustice to Sternhold.

Tye describes himself here as gentleman of the King's Chapel, an appointment which is not recorded elsewhere. His name is not in the list of Edward VI.'s Chapel, printed by both Burney and Hawkins ; nor is it to be found in the *Old Cheque-Book of the Chapel Royal* (ed. Rimbault, 1872), which, however, does not begin till 1561. Fuller adds that ' he was probably the organist,' which Wood amplifies into the statement that ' he was chief organist of Edward 6 and first organist of Elizabeth,' but this seems to be mere conjecture. There is no reason to doubt that Tye continued to hold his place of magister choristarum at Ely, from his first appointment up to 1561 ; for though the Treasurer's Rolls are lost excepting that for 1547 (which shows a payment to Tye), there is a special ' Donatio ' made to him on behalf of the Dean and Chapter, dated May 23, 1559, ' pro diligenti servitio . . . hactenus impenso.' By this document, in which he is described as organist as well as magister choristarum, he is granted the power of distraining on the Manor of Sutton, to ensure the payment of his annuity of £10.

In the early part of 1561 Tye resigned his places at Ely, being succeeded as magister choristarum by the composer, Robert White, who may have been his son-in-law. Tye had already been ordained deacon by Bishop Cox in July 1560, and priest in Nov. of the same year. Before Sept. 1560 he was presented to the living of Doddington-cum-Marche in the Isle of Ely, and was established there with his family before Mar. 1561, when we learn that he, as rector of Doddington, ' est Sacerdos residet ibidem et est Doctor Musice non tamen habilis ad predicandum ' (not, however, skilful at preaching) ' nec ad id specialiter licenciatus et alit ibidem familiam ' (*Certificatorium Dioc. Eliensis*, a return to Archbishop Parker in answer to questions about the Ely clergy). In 1564 Tye was in possession of two other livings. On May 13, 1564, he paid first-fruits for the rectory of Newton-cum-capella, near Doddington ; the other was Wilberham (or Wilbraham) Parva, near Cambridge, to which he was presented, probably in 1561. This living was sequestrated in June 1564, as Tye had neglected to pay first-fruits, but the amount due was paid on the following Oct. 19. In June 1570 the living of Doddington was also sequestrated, in consequence of some payments not having been made to the Bishop. Viewed in connexion with an unusual bond taken from Dr. Tye at his wife's request, with regard to the living of Doddington, ' that he should not let any part of his Benefice ' without the Bishop's consent, ' but from year to year,' this second sequestration seems to point to some habitual carelessness or incapacity in business matters on Tye's part. He resigned the living of Newton in 1570 ; he had already resigned Wilberham in 1567.

Tye continued to write verses till the last years of his life ; in 1571 John Lesley, Bishop of Ross, who was then a prisoner in the custody of Bishop Cox, notes in his Diary, Sunday, Aug. 26 : ' I maid certanes versis upon the hunting the day precedent, and gave them to Doctour Ty, doctour in music, for ane argument, to mak the same in Inglis ' (*Bannatyne Miscellany*, 1855, vol. iii. p. 144). Whether Tye was the author of a poem called ' A Notable Historye of Nastagio and Trauersari,' a translation in verse of a tale from Boccaccio, by C. T., 1569, is not certain ; there is nothing in it which he could not have written.

There is one more notice of Tye as rector of Doddington on Aug. 27, 1571, when he signed some Articles of Doctrine, with the other Ely clergy, in a volume now at Ely. He died before Mar. 15, 1572/73, when his successor was appointed.

Of his family, his son Peter was rector of Trinity Church, Ely, and also held livings in Norfolk. Bishop Cox says of him that

'he is a common Dicer, a common Bowler, and a common Hunter, and is indicted for killing of Deer. . . . His Father Dr. Ty hath told me and others, not without Grief, that he wrote a Letter, counterfeiting his Father's hand, and carried it to my Lord of Canterbury ; and by that Means was made Minister.' [1]

Peter Tye was married at Trinity Church, where seven of his children were baptized. It is therefore very likely that Mary Tye, who married Robert Rowley at the same church in 1560, was Dr. Tye's daughter. If so, we may conjecture that Ellen Tye, who married the composer Robert White, was also his daughter ; for by her Will, dated Nov. 21, 1574, Ellen White left legacies to her mother, Katherine Tye, and a sister Mary Rowley, besides a sister Susan Fulke and a brother-in-law Thomas Hawkes. It is conjectured that a Richard Tye who married Alice Smyth at Trinity Church, 1568, and possibly an Agnes Tye who married John Horner at Wilberham Parva in 1575, may have been Dr. Tye's children.

Anthony Wood's story of Dr. Tye and Queen Elizabeth is given here for what it is worth.

' Dr. Tye was a peevish and humoursome man, especially in his latter dayes, and sometimes playing on ye Organ in yᵉ chap. of qu. Elizab. wh. contained much musick, but little delight to the ear, she would send yᵉ verger to tell him yt he play'd out of Tune : whereupon he sent word yt her eares were out of Tune.' [2]

Tye occupies an important place in the history of English church music. ' Music,' says Fuller, ' which received a grievous wound in England at the dissolution of abbeys, was much beholding to him for her recovery ; such his excellent skill and piety, that he kept it up in credit at court and in all cathedrals during his life.' This is a traditional account, but it is probably correct. He has been called ' the Father of the Anthem,' and it is most likely that he helped to set the model which was accepted by Edwardian and early Elizabethan church composers (see ANTHEM). In writing for the English Service, his ' direct, homely, almost popular ' manner of writing is strongly marked ; [3] that he adopted it deliberately may be seen by comparing it with the greater elaboration of his Latin works, which in many cases must have been written side by side with the English. For it must not be assumed that his settings of Latin words are necessarily earlier than those of English words. Some of course are, and may belong to his pre-Reformation days (among them perhaps we may place the contents of B.M. Add. MSS. 17,802-5), but the only dated composition by him which we possess is the ' In quo corriget ' (MS. Mus. Sch. E, 423), which bears the date 1568, near the end of his life. We have seen that two of his masses (possibly the Peterhouse Mass and the ' Euge Bone ') were written as exercises for his degrees, and it is quite likely that many of his settings of Latin words, and those of other writers were similarly composed without any view to their performance in the Latin Service.

Tye's settings of the ' Actes of the Apostles ' have often been reprinted, singly or all together, fitted with a great variety of new words. The only other work of his which was printed in his lifetime was a prayer, ' O Lord of Hosts,' in Day's Psalter, 1563, where no composer's name is given but the initial ' S,' by which Shepherd is probably meant. This has been edited for the Church Music Society. It is a curious fact that no other work by Tye is to be found in Day's publications. Barnard printed (1641) ' I will exalt Thee ' and ' Sing unto the Lord ' (reproduced in Boyce's ' Cathedral Music ') ; ' O God be merciful ' ; and ' I lift my heart ' ; also ' Haste Thee, O God ' under the name of Shepherd, with which it has been reprinted by the Motet Society, and as one of Novello's Octavo Anthems. Shepherd's setting of these words is quite different. Rimbault's ' Cathedral Music ' contains the Ely Evening Service ;

---

[1] Strype, *Annals*, vol. ii. App. I., No. 51.

[2] MS. Notes on Musicians in Bodleian.
[3] *Oxford History of Music*, ii. 342.

and Page, in 'Harmonia sacra,' 1800, printed part of 'From the depths.' 'Give almes' and part of 'Praise ye the Lord, ye children' are in the 2nd vol. of the *Oxf. Hist. Mus.*

Of Tye's Latin works, the 'Euge Bone' Mass has been printed in No. X. of the OLD ENGLISH EDITION (*q.v.*); part of the Gloria from it was given in Burney's *History*, whence it was reproduced in Hullah's 'Vocal Scores.' Specimens of the 'Western Wynd' Mass will be found in vol. ii. of the *Oxford History*; and of Miserere and 'Omnes Gentes' in Dr. Walker's *History of Music in England.*

MASSES, ETC.

Missa, 'Euge Bone' (' Et in terra pax '). B.M. Add. MSS. 11,587/7*b*. Score.
Missa (sine nomine). PH.
Do.   do.   B.M. Add. MSS. 17,802-5.
M. (quia fecit). Ch. Ch. 45/17.

SERVICES, ETC.

Evening Service. PH.; Harl. 7337/72*b*. Score.
N.D. B.M. Add. MSS. 30,480-3.
K. and Alleluia. B.M. Add. MSS. 17,802-5.

MOTETS

Ad te clamamus exules. Ch Ch. 984-8.
Amavit, *a* 5. Baldwin/45*b*.
Ave caput. Ch. Ch. 45/26.
Cantate Domino. Ch. Ch. 979-83.
Deus misereatur. B.M Add MSS. 30,480-4.
Da illi pectus. Baldwin/151*b*.
Domine Deus celesti Pater. Baldwin/151*b*.
Et cum pro notis. Ch. Ch. 979-83.
Gloria laus et honor. B.M. Add. MSS. 17,802-5.
In Nomine. Ch. Ch. 984-8.
In pace si dedero. B.M Add. MSS. 17,802-5.
In quo corrigit, *a* 3. Baldwin/152*b*.
Jesus Nazarenum. B.M. Add. MSS. 30,480-4.
Laudate Nomen Dei. B.M. Add. MSS. 31,415.
Miserere mei Deus. Ch. Ch. 979-83 ; B.M. Add. MSS. 5059/38. Score.
Omnes gentes plaudite } Ch. Ch. 984-8.
(2nd part) Psallite Deo }
Quaesumus omnipotens. Ch. Ch. 979-83.
Sub tuam protectionem. B.M. Add. MSS. 17,802-5.
Tellus flumina. Ch. Ch. 45/28.
Unde nostri. Ch. Ch. 45/20.

ANTHEMS

Christ rising } Ch. Ch. 56-60. Bass part wanting.
(2nd part) Christ is risen }
Deliver us, good Lord. B.M. Add. MSS. 30,480 4.
From the depth I called. B.M. Add. MSS. 30,480-4.
I have loved. B.M. Add. MSS. 30,480-4.
I lift up my heart, *a* 5. Barnard.
I will exalt Thee }
(2nd part) Sing unto the Lord } Barnard.
My trust, O Lord, in Thee is grounded. B.M. Add. MSS. 30,480-4.
O God be merciful }
(2nd part) That we may know } Barnard.
(3rd part) O let the people }
O Lord, deliver me. Harl. 7340/56*b*. Score.
O Lord of Hosts. B.M. Add. MSS. 15,166/37*b*. Treble part only.
   B.M. Add. MSS. 29289/94. Altus part only.
Praise ye the Lord, ye children. PH.; B.M. Add. MSS. 30,480-4.
Save me, O God. B.M. Add. MSS. 30,480-4.
Sit fast, *a* 3. Baldwin/113*b*.
To Father, Son, and Holy Ghost. Ch. Ch. 56-60. Bass part wanting.

Besides his church music, Tye left a large number of In Nomines and other pieces without words, which seem to have been used either as solfa-ing songs or as instrumental pieces. They deserve more attention than they have received. Many of these will be found in B.M. Add. MSS. 31,390; others are in B.M. Add. MSS. 32,377 (treble only); and in MS. Bodl. Mus. Sch. D, 212-16. At Ch. Ch., besides an In Nomine which is also found elsewhere, are 'Ascendo' *a* 5 (which in B.M. Add. MSS. 31,390 is attributed to 'Mr. Maillart Italyon'); 'Madonna' *a* 5 (which appears in Add. MSS. 31,390 without composer's name, as 'Madona sû mia corto'), and 'Rubum quem' *a* 5. A 3-part 'Sit fast' is in Roy. Lib. B.M.

It may be added that some of the compositions of the 16th century which have come down to us without their authors' names, have been claimed for Dr. Tye; such as 'Lord, for Thy tender mercy's sake' (*Sammelbände*, of the Int. Mus. Ges., 1906); and 'In going to my naked bed' (*Oxf. Hist. Mus.* vol. ii. p. 366).

G. E. P. A.; list of works rev. by J. M^K

TYMBAL (TYMPANUM) (cf. TIMBALES; TIMPANI), an early name for the kettle-drum. (See DRUM, 2.)

TYNDALL, JOHN, LL.D., F.R.S. (*b*. Leighlin Bridge, Co. Carlow, Ireland, Aug. 2, 1820; *d*. Dec. 4, 1893), the eminent natural philosopher and lecturer, added to a very varied education and experience in his native country and in England a course of study under Bunsen at Marburg and Magnus at Berlin; he succeeded Faraday as Superintendent of the Royal Institution, London, and was President of the British Association at Belfast in 1874. His investigations into subjects connected with music are contained in a book entitled *Sound*, published in 1867, and frequently reprinted. (See *Times*, Oct. 23, 1884, p. 10 *c*.)   G.

TYPOPHONE, the French name for the DULCITONE (*q.v.*).

TYROLIENNE, a modified form of LÄNDLER (*q.v.*). 'The Tyrolienne' never had any distinctive existence as a dance; the name was first applied to ballet music, supposed more or less accurately to represent the naïve dances of the Austrian or Bavarian peasants. In a similar manner it was adopted by the compilers of trivial school-room pieces, with whom it was as much a rule to print their title-pages in French as their marks of time and expression in Italian. The fashion for Tyrolean music in England was first set by the visit of the Rainer family, in May 1827; several similar performances followed. Most of these companies of peasant musicians came from the Ziller Thal, where the peculiar forms of Tyrolean music may still be heard better than anywhere else. The best-known example of an artificial 'Tyrolienne' is the well-known 'Chœur Tyrolien' in Act iii. of Rossini's 'Guillaume Tell.' For examples of the genuine Ländler we must refer the reader to Ritter v. Spaun's 'Österreichische Volksweisen' (Vienna, 1845), M. V. Süss's 'Salzburger Volkslieder' (Salzburg, 1865), or Von Kobell's 'Schnadahüpfeln' (Munich, 1845).

A characteristic feature of the original form of Ländler as sung in Austrian and Bavarian Tyrol is the *Jodel*. This term is applied to the abrupt but not inharmonious changes from the chest voice to the falsetto, which are a well-known feature in the performances of Tyrolese singers. The practice is not easy to acquire, unless the voice has been accustomed to it from early youth: it also requires a powerful organ and considerable compass. Jodels form an impromptu adornment to the simple country melodies sung by the peasants ; they are also used as ritornels or refrains at the end of each verse of the song. They are not sung to words, but merely vocalised, although passages resembling them in form are of frequent occurrence in Tyrolean melodies. The following example

I bin á junga Bür-scherl, Und

han á frisch's Bluát, Und so wie's beim Tanz

geig-nen, So dräht si mein Huát.

will be found in a dance song from von Spaun's collection. Moscheles ('Tyrolese Melodies,' 1827) tried to note down some of the Jodels sung by the Rainer family, but the result was neither accurate nor successful.   w. b. s.

The Tyrolean songs of the Rainer family were published in two folio volumes, by Willis, in 1827 and 1828. How far the melodies may claim to be the genuine folk-tunes of the district is to some extent questionable. A footnote informs us that two, out of the twelve which comprise the first volumes, are by one of the family, and two others considerably altered from the originals by him. Some of the verses are also claimed as his, and one song is headed ' composed by M. I. Seidel.' Moscheles noted and arranged the tunes in four parts, and the English words are by William Ball. ' The [Merry] Swiss Boy,' the first song in the book, is the sole survivor of the series. This song had an immense run of popular favour, and its simple melody figured largely in the old pianoforte Tutors.   f. k.

U

UBER, (1) CHRISTIAN BENJAMIN (b. Breslau, Sept. 20, 1746; d. there, 1812), studied law at Halle and became a barrister at Breslau in 1774, holding eventually some high offices at the law courts. At Halle he continued his early musical studies under Türk. Uber's house at Breslau became the rendezvous of distinguished musicians, artists and literary men, and every Wednesday and Saturday public performances took place there, ranging from chamber music to opera; sometimes also a play would be given, owing to the presence of some famous actor. Uber was a talented composer, and wrote a comic opera in 3 acts, ' Clarisse,' an ode from the history of 'Miss Fanny Welkes' (Weelkes ?) (1772); a divertimento for harpsichord, 2 violins, 2 flutes, 2 horns, viola and bass (1777); 6 divertimentos for harpsichord, flute, violin, 2 horns and bass (1783); 6 trios for harpsichord, violin and violoncello, and a number of harpsichord sonatas with and without accompaniment of other instruments.

(2) CHRISTIAN FRIEDRICH HERMANN (b. Breslau, Apr. 22, 1781; d. Dresden, Mar. 2, 1822), son of Christian Benjamin, studied law at Halle University, and music under Türk, for whom he deputised as conductor of the subscription concerts, where he played a violin concerto in D, of his own composition, and also brought out a cantata, ' Das Grab,' both being well received. Soon after he devoted himself entirely to music, became chamber musician to Prince Louis Ferdinand of Prussia, after whose death in 1806 he was first violinist at Brunswick; and in 1808 he became Kapellmeister at the Opera, Cassels, where he wrote several French operas (' Les Marins '), an Intermezzo ' Der falsche Werber,' music to Schiller's ' Der Taucher,' Klingemann's ' Moses,' etc. In 1814 he was Kapellmeister at Mayence theatre (opera, ' Der frohe Tag ') and in 1816 musical director of Seconda's theatrical troupe at Dresden. Having long been in delicate health he retired into private life at Leipzig, but in 1818 accepted the position of cantor and musical director of the ' Kreuzkirche,' Dresden. There he wrote, among other works, an Easter cantata and a Passion (' Die letzten Worte des Erlösers '), which proved his swan song, as he was buried on Good Friday 1822, the day of its first performance.

(3) ALEXANDER (b. Breslau, 1783; d. there, 1824), another son of Christian Benjamin, started his musical career as violinist but soon exchanged the violin for the violoncello, which he studied under Jäger. He was an intimate friend of C. M. v. Weber, Berner and Klingohr. In 1804 he toured with great success as a violoncellist in South Germany. In 1820 he settled at Basle, where he married a singer, returning to Breslau in 1821, and becoming Kapellmeister to Prince Schönaich-Carolath in 1823, which post he held till his death. He composed several concertos, variations, etc., for violoncello, several overtures, vocal music, etc. (Schilling; Mendel; E. van der Straeten, *Hist. of the Violoncello*). E. V. D. S.

UBERTI, ANTONIO (b. Verona, 1697; d. Berlin, Jan. 20, 1783), of German parents named Hubert, was a pupil of Porpora, and was usually called Porporino from that circumstance. He was an eminent singer in the Italian opera in Germany, and was appointed chamber singer to Frederick the Great at Berlin. His most distinguished pupil was Mme. MARA. (*Riemann.*) M.

UBERTI, GIULIO (b. Milan, 1805; d. 1876), poet, patriot and teacher of declamation. Together with his friends, Modena and Mazzini, by the power of the pen he succeeded in raising the youth of Italy to action against the tyranny of a foreign domination, and to the establishment of the national independence. His poems are noticed at length by Cesare Cantù in his *History of Italian Literature*. He lived at Milan the greater portion of his life, engaged as a teacher of declamation. He numbered Malibran and Grisi amongst his pupils, and was the last of the masters of declamation who still preserved the old traditions of classical tragic acting. He died by his own hand in 1876, a patriot but a republican to the end.

J. C. G.

U.C., see UNA CORDA.

UCCELLINI, DON MARCO, of Modena, master of the instrumental music of the Duke of Modena, 1645; also maestro di cappella at Modena Cathedral, 1654. In 1669 he appears again under the former title only. Fétis's statement that he was maestro di cappella at the court of Parma appears to lack confirmation. He wrote psalms for 3-5 concerted parts with instruments, and litanies of the Holy Virgin, 5 v., with instruments, op. 6 (Venice, 1654); Canto dell' ozio regio, opera di musica (1660); 3 books of ' sonate,' arie, correnti, etc., published between 1639 and 1645; sonatas or canzonas for violin solo and bass, op. 5 (Ven., 1649); ' Compositioni armoniche ' for violin and other instruments, in 4 and 5 parts, lib. 7 (Antwerp, 1668); Sinfonie boscarecie for solo violin and bass with addition of 2 other violins, op. 8 (Antwerp, 1669; other ed., 1677). His violin compositions prove him a virtuoso who was probably unequalled in his time, as he already made use of the 6th position. Schering[1] mentions Sinfonici concerti, brievi e facili (1667), in which, so he says, the violin soli show here and there a distinct *concerto* character,

1 *Geschichte des Instrumentalkonzerts*, p. 26.

420

and some cadenzas in his sonatas remind one, almost of de Bériot. E. v. d. s.

UGALDE, DELPHINE, *née* BEAUCÉ (*b.* Paris, Dec. 3, 1829 ; *d.* there, July 19, 1910). She was taught music by her mother, an excellent musician and teacher of singing, and a good comedian ; and singing by Moreau - Sainti and, according to Soubies and Malherbe, by Cinti - Damoreau. She married a Spanish musician, Ugalde (*d.* 1858). In July 1848 she made her début at the Opéra - Comique as Angèle (' Domino noir '), became a great favourite, being a brilliant singer and actress, and remained there until 1858, except for a short season at the Variétés in a revival of Favart's ' Trois sultanes.' At the former theatre she sang in the many successful new operas of the period, viz. in ' Le Caïd,' ' Songe d'une nuit d'été,' and as Eros in ' Psyché ' (A. Thomas), ' Les Monténégrins ' (Limnander), ' Le Toréador ' (Adam), ' La Fée aux Roses ' and ' Dame de Pique ' (Halévy), ' Galathée ' (Massé), etc. In 1851, on leave of absence, she sang at Her Majesty's as Nefte in ' L'Enfant prodigue ' and Corilla in Gnecco's ' Prova,' with moderate success. She sang here again in 1857 in concerts, with better effect. On Aug. 28, 1858, she sang as Leonora (' Trovatore ') at the Opéra, for Roger's benefit. She was then engaged at the Lyrique, where she made a great success as Susanne, Blonde, Reiza, as the heroine in Massé's ' Fée Carabosse ' and the hero in Semet's ' Gil Blas.' Later she sang there again as Papagena and Taven (' Mireille '), having in the meantime sung at the Opéra-Comique, and in 1863 at the Bouffes as Roland in ' Les Bavards ' (Offenbach). She sang there again, under the management of Varcollier, her second husband, as Eurydice in ' Orphée aux Enfers,' and in 1867 in an operetta of her own composition, ' La Halte au moulin,' favourably reviewed at the time. In 1870 she sang at the Opéra-Comique for the last time, as Juana in ' Déa ' (Jules Cohen), and in 1871 at the Athénée in ' Javotte ' (Jonas). Among her pupils were Marie Sass of the Opéra (a successful Elizabeth in ' Tannhäuser ' and Sélika in ' L'Africaine ') and her own daughter (by her second husband) known as Marguerite Ugalde who, after successful débuts at the Opéra-Comique in the ' Fille du régiment ' and as Niklausse on the production of ' Contes d'Hoffmann,' became identified with opéra-bouffe, in which she made a reputation.

A. C. ; rev. M. L. P.

UGOLINI, VINCENZO (*b.* Perugia), a 16th-17th century church composer of the Roman school. He was a pupil of Bernardino Nassini, and teacher of Benevoli. Appointed maestro di cappella of Santa Maria Maggiore, Rome, in 1603 [1] he was attacked in 1604 by a severe illness which left him in delicate health for the

rest of his life. Although he had to interrupt his work, he was left in the possession of his place on account of his exceptional merit. In 1609 he went to Benevento as maestro di cappella of the cathedral, but in 1614 he was in the service of Cardinal Arigoni at Rome, and from 1616–20 he was at the French church of St. Louis at Rome. In the latter year he succeeded Soriano at the Cappella Giulia of St. Peter's, Rome, where he remained until 1626, when he resigned, but remained active until 1630 or after, as the dedication of his 12-part psalms is signed in the latter year. He was one of the most learned church musicians and a profound and dignified representative of Palestrina's school. He composed 2 books of 5-part madrigals (1615) ; 4 books of 1-4-part motets with *continuo* (1616–19) ; 2 books of 8-part psalms (1620) ; 2 books of 8 and 12-part masses and motets (1622) ; 1 book of 8-part psalms and Vespers with bass for the organ (1628) ; 1 book of 12-part Vesper-psalms and motets, one with a bass for the organ (1630) ; various sacred songs, etc., in collective volumes.

E. v. d. s.

UHLIG, THEODOR (*b.* Wurzen, near Leipzig, Feb. 15, 1822 ; *d.* Dresden, Jan. 3, 1853), learnt the violin from Schneider at Dessau, in 1837–1840, and entered the royal band at Dresden in 1841. His compositions, though very numerous, and ranging over a wide variety of forms, are not as important as his theoretical works, *Die Wahl der Taktarten, Die gesunde Vernunft und das Verbot der Fortschreitung in Quinten,* and *Druckfehler in der Symphonie-Partituren Beethovens* ; nor is he as famous for these as for the fact that Wagner corresponded with him during an interesting period of the great composer's career. The letters were published in 1888. (*Riemann.*) M.

UILLEANN PIPES. This is the correct name of the Irish domestic pipes, a name which, by a strange Anglicised corruption, was for a century written ' Union.' (See *PLATE IV.* No. 7.) The Uilleann pipes are to be identified with the ' woollen ' bagpipes of Shakespeare (*Merchant of Venice*), but the etymology is from the Irish *uilleann* = the elbow, inasmuch as the wind is supplied by a bellows acted on by the elbow, whereas the Irish Piob Mor (or warpipe) is blown by the mouth. For long, the name was supposed to be derived from the period of the Union between England and Ireland (1800), but there are numerous references to players on the ' Union pipes ' between the years 1750 and 1780. At the close of the 16th century they came into vogue, but the instrument was much improved in the 18th century, and Burney praises it highly in 1780. Uilleann pipes are made in Dublin, Belfast and Cork, and there are Pipers' Clubs in each of those cities. (See BAGPIPE ; IRISH MUSIC.)

W. H. G. F.

[1] Riemann says 1592–1603.

UKELELE, a small guitar very common in Hawaii, but only introduced into the Sandwich Islands about the year 1877 by the Portuguese. It resembles in outline the Machête. (See GUITAR.) Other names given to it are taropatch fiddle ' and ' the flea ' (the smallest size). The ordinary tuning of the 4 strings is b', $f\sharp'$, d', a''.   F. W. G.

ULBRICH, MAXIMILIAN (b. Vienna, c. 1752 : d. there, Sept. 14, 1814), son of a bass singer in the Imperial Chapel. He studied music under Wagenseil and Reuter, and held a remunerative office in the civil service which enabled him to follow his art without the fear of material want. His oratorio, ' The Israelites in the Desert,' was performed at Vienna in 1779 and 1783. He wrote a four-part litany and other church music ; also two operas, symphonies and a harpsichord concerto with orchestra.   E. V. D. S.

ULIBISCHEW, the German mode of spelling the Russian name more generally transliterated as OULIBICHEFF ($q.v.$).   G.

ULRICH, HUGO (b. Oppeln, Silesia, Nov. 26, 1827 ; d. Mar. 23, 1872), a composer of great ability, whose life was wasted owing to adverse circumstances, and probably also to want of strength of character. His father was schoolmaster at Oppeln. By 12 he had lost both his parents, and was thrown helpless on the world. He then got into the Gymnasium or Convict at Breslau ; subsequently went to Glogau, and in 1846 to Berlin. From Mosewius, the excellent director of the University of Breslau, he had an introduction to A. B. Marx ; but Ulrich had no money to pay the fees. With Meyerbeer's help, however, he became a pupil of Dehn for two years, and then produced his op. 1, a PF. trio, followed by two symphonies, all of which excited much attention. The B minor symphony (1852) went the round of Germany, and the ' Symphonie triomphale ' obtained the prize of 1500 francs from the Royal Academy of Brussels in 1853, and was very much performed and applauded. In 1855 he went to Italy and lived for long in the various great towns, but was driven back by want of means to Berlin. He brought with him an unfinished opera, ' Bertrand de Born ' (still in MS.). He taught for a short time in the Conservatorium, but teaching was distasteful to him ; he had not the strength to struggle against fate, and after attempting a third symphony (in G) he appears to have broken down, or at least to have relinquished his old high standard, and to have betaken himself to pot-boilers of various kinds. Amongst these his arrangements of symphonies and other orchestral works are prominent, and of first-rate merit. He left a quartet, two overtures, a violoncello sonata, and various PF. works.   G.

UMBREIT, KARL GOTTLIEB (b. Rehstedt, near Gotha, Jan. 9, 1763 ; d. there, Apr. 28,

1829), a pupil of Kittel, was organist at Sonneborn in Coburg. He enjoyed a great reputation as organist, organ-composer and teacher. He wrote several books of Chorals, one of these being edited in French by A. Choron (1824), and a number of preludes and fugues for the organ. Three books of easy Choral-preludes were republished by Simrock at Bonn, and a book of posthumous preludes and fantasias, edited by his son, Dr. Fr. Wm. C. Umbreit, at Gotha (Lampert), 1833–34.   E. V. D. S.

UMLAUF,(1) IGNAZ(b. Vienna, 1756 ; d. there, June 8, 1796), popular dramatic composer in his day. In 1772 he entered the orchestra of the court theatre as violin-player, in 1778 became Kapellmeister of the German Singspiel, in 1789 deputy Kapellmeister (with Salieri as chief) at the court theatre, and later was associated with Weigl in a similar manner at the Opera. His first opera, ' I rovinati,' was composed to Italian words by Boccherini (court theatre, 1772). When the Emperor Joseph instituted the national Singspiel (for which Mozart composed the ' Entführung ') he chose Umlauf to start it, and his ' Bergknappen ' (edited by Haas, $D.T.\ddot{O}$. vol. xviii.) was the first German Singspiel produced at the Burgtheater (Feb. 17, 1778). This was succeeded by ' Die Apotheke ' ; ' Die pucefarbenen Schuhe,' or ' Die schöne Schusterin ' (long a favourite with the charming singer Mme. Weiss in the principal part) (1779) ; ' Das Irrlicht,' comic opera in three acts, with Mme. Lange ; and ' Der Oberamtmann und die Soldaten ' (after Calderon), a five-act play with airs and serenade (1782) ; ' Die glücklichen Jäger,' and ' Der Ring der Liebe,' both Singspiele (1786).

These operas are all distinguished by a pleasing style, a fine flow of melody, and plenty of striking tunes. Umlauf never left Vienna but once, and that was in 1790, when he went with Salieri and a part of the court band to the Coronation of the Emperor Leopold II. at Frankfort.[1] A set of variations on the favourite air from ' Das Irrlicht,' ' Zu Steffan sprach in Traume,' composed for the celebrated basssinger Fischer, was long attributed to Mozart, but they were really written by Eberl (see Köchel's $Verzeichniss$, Appendix V. No. 288). Pianoforte scores appeared of ' Die schöne Schusterin ' and ' Das Irrlicht,' while several of the airs from the other Singspiele were published singly or in arrangements. Umlauf's son

(2) MICHAEL (b. Vienna, Aug. 9, 1781 ; d. Baden, near Vienna, June 20, 1842), was violinist at the Opera, in 1804 began to compose ballets, was Kapellmeister of the two court theatres from 1810–25, and was engaged again in 1840. He is said to have been a clever musician, published PF. sonatas, etc., and

---

[1] Mozart was there too, but in a private capacity, and at his own expense ; he gave a concert, at which he played himself.

composed a Singspiel, 'Der Grenadier' (Kärnth-nerthor Theatre, 1812), an opera 'Das Wirths-haus in Granada,' and some church composi-tions.

His chief interest, however, is the important part he took in the performance of Beethoven's works. On these occasions they both acted as conductors, Umlauf standing by the side of, or behind, Beethoven; but it was his beat only which the orchestra followed, as Beethoven was either carried away by his impetuosity and went too fast, as at the performance of 'Fidelio' in 1814, or, owing to his deafness, lost the time altogether, as at concerts in 1814, 1819 and 1824. At the first two performances of the ninth symphony in May 1824, Beethoven merely gave the tempo at the beginning of each movement, an arrangement which the pro-gramme announced in the following diplomatic terms: 'Herr Schuppanzigh will lead the orchestra, and Herr Kapellmeister Umlauf con-ducts the whole performance. Herr L. v. Beethoven will take part in conducting the whole performance.'   C. F. P.

UNA CORDA (Ital. 'one string'; Fr. petite pédale; Ger. mit Verschiebung). An indication of the use of the left pedal of the pianoforte, by means of which the action is shifted a little to the right, and the hammers made to strike a single string (in modern instruments generally two strings) instead of the three which are ordinarily struck. The direction is sometimes abbreviated into U.C. The return to the use of three strings is indicated by the letters t.c., tre corde, tutte le corde, or sometimes tutto il cembalo. (See PEDAL; MUTE.)

The shifting pedal produces a beautiful and delicate quality of tone, arising from the sym-pathetic vibrations of the unused strings, which is by no means the same thing as the ordinary pianissimo, but is of the greatest service in pro-ducing certain special effects. Beethoven uses it frequently, in the later sonatas (from op. 101), and in the Andante of the G major concerto, op. 58, the whole of which movement is to be played a una corda, except the long shake in the middle, in which Beethoven requires the gradual addition of the other strings, and after-wards the gradual return from three strings to one. His directions are 'due, e poi tre corde,' and afterwards 'due, poi una corda,' but it is not possible to carry them out strictly on the modern pianoforte, as the shifting action now only reduces to two strings instead of one.

In music for string instruments, the direction a una corda is occasionally given, to denote that the passage is to be played upon a single string, instead of passing from one string to the next, in order to avoid any break in the quality of tone produced.   F. T.

UNDA MARIS (the sea-wave), a name for the undulating organ-stop, more generally known as VOIX CÉLESTES.   G.

UNEQUAL TEMPERAMENT, an uneven distribution of the 'beats' in tuning, resulting in some keys being better in tune than others. See TEMPERAMENT and TUNING.   T. E.

UNEQUAL VOICES, a term generally used in music for mixed choirs of male and female singers. (See EQUAL VOICES.)

UNGER, CAROLINE (b. Stuhlweissenburg, near Pest, Oct. 28, 1805; d. at her villa, 'La Concezione,' near Florence, Mar. 23, 1877), a great singer.

Her father was master of the household (Wirthschaftsrath) to Baron Hakelberg at Stuhlweissenburg. Unger was one of Schu-bert's friends, and recommended him to Count Johann Esterhazy in 1818, so that his daughter must have been brought up in the midst of music. She was trained by no meaner singers than Aloysia Lange, Mozart's sister-in-law, and Vogl, Schubert's friend and best interpreter,[1] and is said to have made her début at Vienna, Feb. 24, 1821, in 'Così fan tutte.' Early in 1824 Sontag and she came into contact with Beethoven in studying the soprano and con-tralto parts of his Mass in D and Choral Sym-phony. No efforts or representations could induce the master to alter the extreme range of their parts. 'I remember once saying to him,' writes Unger, 'that he did not know how to write for voices, since my part in the sym-phony had one note too high for my voice.' His answer was, 'Learn away, and the note will soon come.' On the day of performance, May 7, the note did come; the excitement of the audience was enormous, and it was then, at the close of the symphony, that the happy idea occurred to Unger of turning the deaf Beethoven round to the room, in order that he might see the applause which he could not hear, and of which he was therefore unaware. After this she took an engagement from Barbaja in Italy, and sang there many years (spelling her name UNGHER), during which Donizetti wrote for her 'Parisina,' 'Belisario' and 'Maria di Rudenz'; Bellini, 'La straniera'; Merca-dante, 'Le due illustre rivali'; Pacini, 'Niobe,' etc. etc. In Oct. 1833 she sang in Paris at the Théâtre-Italien for one season only. It was perhaps on this occasion that Rossini is said to have spoken of her as possessing 'the ardour of the South, the energy of the North, brazen lungs, a silver voice, and a golden talent.' She then returned to Italy, but in 1840 married Sabatier, a Florentine gentleman, and retired from the stage. In 1869 she was in London, and at one of the Saturday Concerts at the Crystal Palace confirmed to the writer of this article the anecdote above related of her turn-ing Beethoven round. Her dramatic ability and intelligence, says Fétis, were great; she was large, good-looking and attractive; the lower and middle parts of her voice were broad

[1] Her own statement, in Nohl's Beethoven, vol. iii. p. 486.

and fine, but in her upper notes there was much harshness, especially when they were at all forced. Mme. Regan Schimon was one of her principal pupils.   G.

UNGER, GEORG (b. Leipzig, Mar. 6, 1837 ; d. there, Feb. 2, 1887), was at first a student of theology, but made his début on the operatic stage of his native town in 1867 with such success that he soon fulfilled engagements in different German towns ; in 1876 he was chosen by Wagner to create the part of Siegfried at Bayreuth. In the following year he came to London for the famous series of Wagner concerts in the Albert Hall, but his frequent inability to appear caused the composer to take a dislike to him, and he returned to Leipzig in the same year, singing in the opera there until 1881. He was the earliest of a class of ' Heldentenor ' that has since been numerous in Germany.   M.

UNGER, HERMANN (b. Kamenz, Saxony, Oct. 26. 1886), first studied classical philology at Freiburg and Leipzig, then went to Munich, where he took a musical training under Edgar Istel and Joseph Haas, proceeding later to Meiningen, where he stayed for some considerable period of time with Reger. Fine counterpoint with the structural methods of chambermusic mark even his works for solo pianoforte. Without any revolutionary tendencies, his works are imbued by a fresh naturalness and reveal the characteristics of the folk-songs which are their source. Unger may justly be termed the founder of musical miniatures.

WORKS.—PF., opp. 1, 2, 3, 7, 16, 18, 28, 29 ; songs, opp. 14, 15, 19. 20, 21, 22, 23 ; Anthem of Life, op. 25 ; orch. symphony, op. 31 ; an *a cappella* choir, op. 12 ; old German songs for chorus and orch., op. 30 ; ' Night,' a suite, op. 8 ; German Dances, op. 16 ; Pictures from the Orient, op. 18 ; Rondo, op. 22 ; Rustic Scenes, op. 24 ; symphonic suite, op. 26 ; symphony in D min., op. 27 ; in MS., ' Narrenlieder,' for baritone ; trio for PF., clar. and vla. ; string trio ; sonata for vcl. ; divertimento for string quartet ; variations for 2 PF's. ; numerous songs and choral compositions.
          K. D. H.

UNGER, JOHANN FRIEDRICH (b. Brunswick, 1716 ; d. there, 1781), a councillor of justice at Brunswick. It is claimed in the *Dictionary of Musicians* (1827) that he was an inventor of a machine to be attached to a harpsichord which recorded the notes played. A description of it was published in 1774 under the title *Entwurf einer Maschine.*   F. K.

UNION OF GRADUATES IN MUSIC (INCORPORATED). The formation of this Union was suggested by Sir John Stainer, who took the chair at a meeting held at the R.C.O., Jan. 4, 1893, at which the Union was formally constituted, Sir John being the first president, and Thomas Lea Southgate the hon. sec. Those only are eligible for membership

' upon whom Degrees in Music have been conferred by one of the Universities of the United Kingdom of Great Britain and Ireland, or by any authority in the said United Kingdom which confers degrees by virtue of a Royal Charter or by the sanction of the Crown or of Parliament.'

The Union was incorporated in 1897. A ' Roll

and Kalendar ' is issued annually since 1893, and latterly an annual conference of members has been held at one or other of the Universities. Many distinguished musicians have held the office of president. (See DEGREES.)

UNION PIPES, see UILLEANN PIPES.

UNISON, simultaneous occurrence of two sounds of the same pitch. Passages in octaves are sometimes marked *Unis.*, but this is not strictly correct.   C. H. H. P.

UNIVERSAL EDITION, a music publishing combine which began in 1901 by the purchase of a number of the individually owned businesses of Vienna, and issued editions of the classics in large quantities. By the purchase of the Munich business of Joseph Aibl (1904) it acquired the majority of the works of Richard Strauss, which together with the works of Bruckner, Mahler, Delius and other prominent composers gave it a representative catalogue of modern music. The Universal Edition has also specialised in the works of the younger generation, and from 1920 has produced the *D.T.Ö.* Emil Hertzka is managing director. (*Riemann.*)

UNIVERSITY CHORAL SOCIETIES, see CAMBRIDGE ; DUBLIN ; EDINBURGH ; OXFORD.

UPBEAT and OFFBEAT. The Greeks had a word ' anakrousis ' which they used as we talk of ' striking up ' a piece of music. Of this the French made ' *anacrouse*,' while the Germans use ' *Auftakt* ' to express what we call ' offbeat.' The cry of nearly all animals, including man, proceeds from an unaccented note (generally low) to an accented (high), and it is therefore in the nature of things that much music should begin on the offbeat, a doctrine associated with the names of Westphal and Riemann.

The offbeat in this sense is not necessarily limited to the last note of the bar. It would include, for instance, the three preliminary notes of the ' Marseillaise,' but eventually it includes all phrases that do not begin with the first of the bar. Westphal calls all such phrases ' auftaktig,' as we might say, ' offbeaten.' It is convenient to confine ' upbeat ' to the last of the bar, leaving ' offbeat ' for any other note than the first.   A. H. F. S.

UP BOW, see BOWING.

UPPER PARTIALS. The higher or more acute partial tones. (See ACOUSTICS, subsection HARMONIC SERIES.)

UPRIGHT PIANOFORTE, see PIANOFORTE.

URBANI, PIETRO (b. Milan, 1749 ; d. South Cumberland Street, Dublin, Dec. 1816[1]), appears to have been an excellent theoretical musician, and his singing was considered good and tasteful.

He came to London, but about 1780 made his way into Scotland. In Glasgow he resided three years, singing Scottish songs, and in 1784 he was in Edinburgh, being engaged at the St. Cecilia Hall Concerts. He was eminent as a teacher, and his arrangements of the vocal melodies of Scotland were much admired. Between 1792 and 1804 he issued six folio books of his arrangements of Scottish songs, and these are remarkable for being the first to have opening and concluding symphonies, and elaborate accompaniments which employ two violins, viola and pianoforte.

The books were dedicated to different Scottish ladies of title, and some of the poetry was by Burns, who knew and esteemed the musician. About 1795–96 Urbani entered into a music-selling and publishing business, and the firm of Urbani and Liston was at 10 Princes Street, Edinburgh, until about 1808–9. It was then broken up, and Urbani's books of Scottish song were reissued by other firms. He attempted to introduce Handel's oratorios to the Glasgow and Edinburgh public, but this entailed heavy losses, and with the failure of his music business Urbani retired, broken in health and fortune, to Dublin. He died there in poverty, leaving his widow destitute. Two of his operas were performed in Dublin, viz. 'Il Farnace' and 'Il trionfo di Clelia.'   F. K.

URBANI VALENTINO, see VALENTINI (3).

URFEY, THOMAS D' (b. Exeter, 1653; d. Feb. 26, 1723), the grandson of a French Huguenot, who fled from La Rochelle before the siege in 1628 and settled at Exeter, his mother being of the family of the Marmions of Huntingdonshire. Thomas D'Urfey was educated for the law, but abandoned that profession for poetry and the drama.

Between 1676 (when his 'Siege of Memphis' was given at the King's Theatre) and his death, he produced upwards of thirty plays, which were at first very popular, but were in the course of a few years afterwards banished from the stage on account of their licentiousness and indecency. The songs in a few of them still survive, being preserved through having had the good fortune to be allied to the music of Henry Purcell. These are in *A Fool's Preferment*, 1688; *Bussy d'Amboise*, 1691; *The Richmond Heiress*, 1693; and the three parts of *Don Quixote*, 1694–95. His comic opera, 'Wonders in the Sun,' 1706, was set by Giovanni Baptista Draghi. Much of his fame was owing to his songs and to the lively manner in which he himself sang them, which procured him the favour of Charles II., William III. and Queen Anne. In this he resembled Tom Moore, and like him he was particularly apt at adapting his verses to existing music. He published, between 1683 and 1685, three collections of songs written by himself, and set to music by the best composers of the period. His connexion with the early edition of the celebrated collection of songs called 'Wit and Mirth; or,

Pills to purge Melancholy,' is uncertain. Editions of this range from 1682 to 1720; that with the airs first appeared in two volumes in 1698–1699, and the number of volumes increases with almost every edition. The dates of these later ones are 1707–1712, 1714 and 1719, when it had reached five volumes 12mo. In 1720 a sixth was added. These six volumes were recently reprinted. In the musical part he appears to have had the assistance of John Lenton. The collection is disfigured with the grossest obscenity, but it is valuable for its important bearing on vocal music of the period, and for the many early airs that it contains. D'Urfey wrote several of the birthday and New Year's odes which were set to music by Purcell and Blow, and supplied the former with the words for his fine ode known as 'The Yorkshire Feast Song.' In the latter part of his life he was reduced to great distress, from which he was relieved by the profits of a performance of his own comedy 'The Fond Husband; or, The Plotting Sisters,' which the managers of the theatre generously gave for his benefit on June 15, 1713. D'Urfey was buried at St. James's, Piccadilly, where, against the outer south wall of the tower of the church, may be seen a tablet with the simple inscription, 'Tom D'Urfey, Dyed Feb^ry ye 26, 1723.'

        W. H. H.; addns. F. K.

URHAN, CHRÉTIEN (b. Montjoie, near Aix-la-Chapelle, Feb. 16, 1790; d. Belleville, Paris, Nov. 2, 1845), was the son of a violinist. He early showed great taste for music, and while still untaught began to compose for his two favourite instruments, the violin and piano. The Empress Josephine, happening to hear him at Aix-la-Chapelle, was so struck with his precocious talent that she brought him to Paris, and specially recommended him to Lesueur, whose influence was of much service to Urhan.

The latter entered the orchestra of the Opéra in 1816, was promoted first to a place among the first violins, and finally, on Baillot's retirement (1831), to that of first violin-solo. As a concert-player he made his mark as one of the foremost violinists of the day with Mayseder's brilliant compositions, which he was the first to introduce in Paris. He was frequently heard at the 'Concerts du Conservatoire,' of which he was one of the originators, and where his performances on the viola and the viole d'amour excited great attention. He also contributed to the success of the memorable evenings for chamber-music founded by Baillot, and of Fétis's 'Concerts historiques.'

He left two string quintets; two quintets for three violas, violoncello, double-bass and drums *ad lib.*; PF. pieces for two and four hands; and melodies for one and two voices, including a romance on two notes only, all published by Richault, and now almost unprocurable. Urhan styled all his music

' romantic.' He was godfather to Julius Stockhausen the singer.   G. C.

URHEEN, the Chinese fiddle, consists of a small circular block of wood hollowed out and covered at one end with the skin of a serpent, forming the table or sounding-board. The two strings (usually of silk) are tuned in the interval of a fifth from each other. (See *PLATE LII.* No. 4.) The hairs of the bow pass under the strings, and as the strings are close together the chief difficulty of the novice is to learn to press the bow squarely on one string without touching the other. Tradescant Lay [1] says that :

' Out of this wretched thing performers contrive sometimes to draw sounds of great brilliancy, so that I have heartily wished them a better tool for their pains.'

There is no mention of the Urheen or of any kind of fiddle in the Chinese sacred books which record the teaching and doings of Confucius. The instrument probably came into China from India with the Buddhist religion during the first century of our era.   E. H.-A.

URIO, FRANCESCO ANTONIO, Milanese composer of the 17th and 18th centuries. The title of his first published work, of which there are copies in the library of the Liceo Musicale of Bologna, in the State Library of Berlin, the British Museum, etc., is as follows :

' Motetti di concerto a due, tre e quattro voci, con violini, e senza. Opera prima. Composti e Dedicati all' Eminentissimo e Reverendissimo Prencipe Il signor Cardinale Pietro Ottoboni . . . da Francesc° Antonio Urio de Milano Minore Conventuale, Maestro di Cappella nell' Insigne Basilica de' Santi Dodici Apostoli di Roma. In Roma MDCXC. nella Stamperia di Gio. Giacomo Komarek, Boemo, etc.'

Between this date and that of his second work —also contained in the Bologna Library—he had migrated from Rome to Venice, and was maestro di cappella of the church of the Frari.

' Salmi concertati a trè voci con Violini à beneplacito del Padre Francesco Antonio Urio Maestro di Cappella nella Chiesa dei Frari di Venetia. Opera Seconda dedicata all' Eccellenza del signor Don Filippo Antonio Spinola Colonna, Duca del Testo, Gentilhuomo della Camera di S. M. Cattolica, suo Generale della Cavalleria nello Stato di Milano, e Castellano del Castel Nuovo di Napoli, etc. In Bologna per Martino Silvani, 1697, etc.'

Arthur Pougin, in his Supplement to Fétis' *Biographie,* states that Urio wrote a Cantata di camera (1696), and two oratorios, ' Sansone accecato da' Filistri ' (1701), and ' Maddalena covertita ' (1706), for Ferdinand de' Medici, Prince of Tuscany, but neither the authority for the statement nor the place where the works are to be found can now be ascertained. A Tantum Ergo for soprano solo and figured bass is in the R.C.M., and a nameless oratorio is at Modena. The most important known work ascribed to Urio, however, is a Te Deum for voices and orchestra, which owes its interest, not only to its merits, which are considerable, but to the fact that Handel used it largely, taking, as his custom was, themes and passages from it, principally for his Dettingen Te Deum (10 numbers), and also for ' Saul ' (6 numbers), ' Israel in Egypt ' (1 ditto) and ' L' Allegro ' (1 ditto).

1 *The Chinese as They Are,* London, 1841.

Of this work three MSS. are known to be in existence: (1) In the R.C.M., which is inscribed ' John Stafford Smith,' A.D. 1780. Te Deum by Urio—a Jesuit of Bologna. Apud 1682.' Over the score : ' Te Deum Urio. Con due Trombe, due Oboe, Violini & due Viole obligati & Fagotto a 5 Voci.' (2) In the B.M. Add. MSS. 31,478, ' Te Deum Laudamus con due Trombe, due Oboe et Violini, et due [2] Viole obligati. Del Padre Franco Uria [*sic*] Bolognese.' This title is followed by a note in ink, apparently in the handwriting of Dr. Thomas Bever, Fellow of All Souls, Oxford, and a collector of 18th-century music :

' This curious score was transcribed from an Italian Copy in the Collection of Dr. Samuel Howard, Mus. D., organist of St. Bride's, and St. Clement's Danes. It formerly belonged to Mr. Handel, who borrowed from hence several Verses in the Dettingen Te Deum, as well as some other passages in the Oratorio of Saul. T. B.

' This copy was written by John Anderson, a Chorister of St. Paul's 1781. Pri. 1*l.* 8*s.* 0*d.*'

Above this in pencil, in another hand :

' In the copy purchased by J. W. Callcott at the sale of Warren Horne, the date is put as 1661.'

(3) The copy just mentioned as having been sold at Warren Horne's sale came into the possession of Schoelcher (as stated in a note of Joseph Warren on the fly-leaf of No. 2), and is now in the library of the Conservatoire at Paris. It is an oblong quarto, with no title-page, but bearing above the top line of the score on p. 1, ' Te Deum, Urio, 1660.' [3]

The ' Italian copy,' which was first Handel's and then Dr. Howard's, if not that in the R.C.M. (which is certainly in an Italian hand), has vanished for the present. [4]

The whole subject of this Te Deum is reviewed in close detail by Percy Robinson in *Handel and his Orbit* (London, 1908). Robinson's researches have led to the discovery that URIO and ERBA (*q.v.*) are places in the neighbourhood of Milan (Urio is north of Como on the shores of the lake), and on this he founds the theory that the MSS. which bear these names are Handel's own composition and date from the Italian period.

The Te Deum was published by Chrysander (from what original the writer does not know) as No. 5 of his ' Denkmäler ' of Handel (Bergedorf, 1871). It has been examined chiefly in its connexion with the Dettingen Te Deum by Prout, in the *Monthly Musical Record* for Nov. 1871, and we recommend the student to read the very interesting analysis there given, as well as Robinson's book. See also Sedley Taylor, *The Indebtedness of Handel* (Cambridge, 1906).   G. ; rev.

2 In the score itself these are given as ' Violetta ' (in alto clef) and ' Violetto tenore ' (in tenor clef).
3 Notes by J. W. Callcott and Vincent Novello having reference to Handel's ' borrowings ' are appended to this copy and are reproduced in former editions of this Dictionary.
4 A manuscript of the work bearing the words ' Te Deum Uria ' [*sic*] was purchased at a sale in London in 1925 by W. Barclay Squire. It was fully described by P. Robinson in the *Bulletin de la Société Union Musicologique* (6me année, 1re fascicule).

URLUS, JACQUES (b. Amsterdam, Feb. 1868), operatic tenor. Educated at Utrecht, he studied singing at the Conservatoire, Amsterdam, and first sang in public at a concert in Utrecht in 1887. After that he went through a careful preparation for the operatic stage and made his début in the same city in 1894 as Canio in 'Pagliacci.' One by one he mastered the leading Wagnerian parts, for which his robust voice and declamatory gifts obviously fitted him, and ere long was engaged for Bayreuth, where he sang for several seasons with invariable success. During the Beecham spring season of 1910 he made his début at Covent Garden as Tristan, making a favourable impression, and returned in the following winter to sing Tannhäuser. He also appeared at Covent Garden in 1914 as Parsifal and Siegmund, under Bodanzky; and again in 1924 as Siegmund and Tristan under Bruno Walter. On the Continent he was engaged for considerable periods at the Paris Opéra and at Leipzig, while from 1912–17 he sang regularly at the Metropolitan Opera House, New York. He has many decorations, including one from the Queen of Holland.

BIBL.—*International Who's Who in Music*; NORTHCOTT, *Covent Garden and the Royal Opera.*   H. K.

URQUHART, THOMAS, an early London violin - maker, who worked in the reign of Charles II. The dates on his violins are chiefly in the 'seventies and 'eighties. The model superficially resembles Gasparo da Salo; it is high, straight and flat in the middle of the belly, and has a rigid and antique appearance. The corners have but little prominence. The sound-holes are 'set straight,' and terminate boldly in circles, the inner members being so far carried on and introverted that the straight cut in each is parallel to the axis of the fiddle. This is Urquhart's distinctive characteristic. The purfling is narrow, coarse and placed very near the edge. The violins are found of two sizes; those of the larger size would be very useful chamber instruments but for the height of the model, which renders them somewhat unmanageable. The varnish, of excellent quality ('equal to that on many Italian instruments,' says Hart), is sometimes yellowish brown, sometimes red. Urquhart is considered to have been a Scotsman; he made flutes as well as violins, and one of his flutes was formerly in the possession of the late John Glen of Edinburgh. Edward Pamphilon, a London violinmaker on London Bridge, about 1680–90, is said to have been his pupil.   E. J. P.; addn. F. K.

USANDIZAGA, JOSÉ MARÍA (b. San Sebastian, Mar. 31, 1887; d. Oct. 1915), Spanish (Basque) composer, who, had he lived, might have done much for modern Spanish opera. His 'Mendy-Mendiyan' was produced at Bilbao (1910), and 'Las Golondrinas' at Madrid (1914). A posthumous work, not yet performed, is 'La Llama,' and there are works for chorus and orchestra and a string quartet. Usandizaga was a student at the Schola Cantorum, Paris.

J. B. T.

USE, the name given to any special group of rites or ceremonies belonging to a particular Church. Fundamentally all the Western Latin Services are the same; but local differences, both in rite and ceremony, naturally arose, and in the 13th century these crystallised into orderly Uses. Thus in England many dioceses other than that of Salisbury adopted the ways of that Cathedral, or in other words followed Sarum Use. Similarly in the North, York Use was popular, and in the West the Use of Hereford. Abroad a similar state of things prevailed; Rome had its Use, but it was in the main a local or at most an Italian Use, while elsewhere in France, Germany, etc., diocesan Uses preserved their local distinctions. At the Reformation a desire for uniformity in all quarters alike altered this. In England the local Uses were superseded by 'The Book of Common Prayer . . . according to the Use of the Church of England': while abroad after the Council of Trent the reformed Roman Use was widely adopted to the exclusion of the local Uses. The Old Religious Orders had Uses of their own; the Franciscans were instrumental in forming and disseminating the Roman Use, and even after the Tridentine reform the Old Religious Orders kept their own Uses. In the 17th and 18th centuries, France rebelled against the uniformity, and a new set of French diocesan Uses grew up which were only with difficulty suppressed when the pendulum again swung back in the direction of uniformity in the middle of the 19th century.

At the present time the Roman Use prevails almost through the whole of the West where the Latin Services are in use; and revisions both of the text and of the music which are in progress under the guidance of the Vatican will no doubt tend to make this uniformity of Use all the more general and the more satisfactory; though the ancient Orders (which have been foremost in the work of revision) will no doubt retain their own Uses: and still more the Uniat Churches of the East, Armenians, Syrians, Greeks, etc., who, while in communion with Rome, use a language and a rite other than Latin. The English Prayer-Book has similarly disseminated 'the Use of the Church of England' throughout the world. This Use, though very definite as far as rite and ceremonial go, is not specific on the side of music pure and simple, for no official music is specified in conjunction with it as the old plain-song is specified in the case of the Latin Uses. At the beginning of the present century [1] the Vatican insisted more strongly than ever on the claim of this plain-song to be the official ritual music of the Church, though not to the exclusion of

[1] *Motu Proprio* of Pope Pius X., Nov. 22, 1903.

more modern or of harmonised music : and the result should be the banishing, not only of much unworthy modern music, but also of the debased or frankly modern plain-song that obtained currency in many of the French Uses, and has been too much adopted from them for English Services.   W. H. F.

USPER, FRANCESCO SPONGIA (SPONZA), DETTO, also called simply Franc. Sponga, a 15th-16th century Venetian priest and organ virtuoso, pupil of Monteverdi. About 1614 he was organist at San Salvatore, Venice. When Grills, the organist at St. Mark's, fell ill in 1621, Usper became his deputy, but when Grills died in 1623 Carlo Fillago was appointed as his successor. In 1627 he was principal of the great school of St. John the Evangelist at Venice. In a catalogue at Bologna it is surmised that he was born at Parenzo. He composed : ' Ricercari et arie francesi,' 4 v. (1595) ; 1 book madrigals, 5 v. (1604) ; ' Messa e Salmi,' 5 v., with organ and various instruments, together with symphonies and motets, 1-6 v. (1614) ; 1 book motets, symphonies, sonatas, canzons and capriccios, 1-8 parts, with basso continuo ; also ' La Battaglia,' a 8, to sing and play . . ., op. 3 (1619) ; Vesper-psalms for the whole year, partly for 2 choirs . . ., a 4, 5 and 8 v., with basso continuo, op. 5 (1627) (Q.-L.).

UT, the first note of the major scale in the nomenclature of France and Italy : =C. In naming the note C, Ut has been generally supplanted by Do ; but for the key of C, Ut is retained. See HEXACHORD ; SOLMISATION.

UTTENDAL (UTENTHAL), ALEXANDER (d. Innsbruck, May 8, 1581), a Netherlander by birth, is first heard of as a boy-chorister in the chapel of the Archduke Ferdinand at Prague. In 1568 he appears as singer in the chapel of the same Archduke at Innsbruck. In 1573, in return for various compositions dedicated to the Archduke, he received the title of court composer (Hofkomponist), and in 1579 or earlier was appointed second Kapellmeister with certain special duties for the care and instruction of the choir-boys. He enjoyed special favour with the Archduke, who generously assisted him in the publication of his works. In 1580 he was offered, but declined, the post of Kapellmeister to the Saxon court at Dresden, vacant by the death of Antonio Scandelli.

His works were all published at Nuremberg, and are as follows :

1. Septem Psalmi Poenitentiales, adjunctis ex Prophetarum scriptis Orationibus ejusdem Argumenti Quinque, ad Dodecachordi

modos duodecim aptissima tam vivae voci quam diversis musicorum instrumentorum generibus harmonia accommodati . . . 1570.

2. Sacrarum Cantionum quas vulgo motetas vocant, antea nunquam in lucem editarum sed nunc recens admodum tam Instrumentis musicis quam vivae melodiae quinque vocibus attemperatarum Liber Primus. 1571.

3. Sacrae Cantiones . . . Sex et plurium vocum . . . Liber Secundus, 1573.

4 Tres Missae, quinque et Sex Vocum . . Item Magnificat per octo Tonos quatuor vocibus . . . 1573.

5. Fröliche neue Teutsche und Frantzösische Lieder, lieblich zu Singen, auch auf allerley Instrumenten zu gebrauchen nach sonderer Art der Music componirt, mit vier, fünff und mehr Stimmen . . . 1574. This work contains 26 secular songs, 13 German a 4-8 and 13 French a 4-6.

6. Lib. 3 Sacrarum Cantionum . . . 5 et 6 voc. 1577.

A special distinction of this master is said to be that he is particularly careful in the notation of all accidentals in his works, so that the principles deduced from his works afford a good clue to the right application of these in other works of the period. He is also one of the earliest to use the natural ♮ instead of ♯ to cancel the flat ♭. Only a few of his works have appeared in modern editions. In the fourth volume of Proske's ' Musica divina,' there is a musicianly and deeply expressive setting of the Psalm Miserere, composed throughout in motet style, a 5, in six divisions. In Commer's collection ' Geistliche und weltliche Lieder aus den xvi.-xvii. Jahrhundert ' there are three German secular songs a 4, very melodious, and W. Barclay Squire has published one of the French songs, a 4, ' Petite nymphe folastre.'

J. R. M.

BIBL.—JOSEF LECHTHALER, Die kirchenmusikalischen Werke von Uttendal. (Vienna Dissertation, 1919.)

UTTINI, FRANCESCO ANTONIO BARTOLOMEO (b. Bologna, 1723 ; d. Stockholm, Oct. 25, 1795), pupil of Sandoni and Perti, member of the Accademia dei Filarmonici in 1743, and ' Prince ' of that society in 1751. In 1753 he was at Copenhagen, and on Oct. 30, 1754, he gave a concert at Hamburg, when he appeared also as a singer. Thence he went to Stockholm as court Kapellmeister, where he wrote, and produced, between 1754 and 1765 8 Italian and 5 French operas. In 1768 he visited London, where Henry Fougt published his ' Six sonatas for 2 violins and a bass . . ., one sonata for the violoncello and another for the harpsichord, op. 1.' He was the first composer of operas in the Swedish language, viz., ' Thetis och Peleus ' (1773) and ' Aline ' (1776). Apart from the above-named works he wrote 3 symphonies for 4, 6 and 8 instruments, 12 sonatas and 9 trios for 2 violins and bass. Apparently he did not excel as a conductor, for when Naumann was called to Stockholm in 1776 for the reorganisation of the orchestra he found it in a deplorable condition (Riemann ; Q.-L.).

V

VACCAJ (VACCAI), NICOLA (b. Tolentino, Italy, Mar. 15, 1790; d. Pesaro, Aug. 5, 1848), a prolific composer of Italian operas. He passed the first ten or twelve years of his life at Pesaro, a few more at Rome with a view to the law, and it was not till his seventeenth or eighteenth year that he threw off this, and took lessons of Jannaconi in counterpoint. In 1811 he went to Naples and put himself under Paisiello for dramatic composition, and there wrote a couple of cantatas and some church music. In 1815 he brought out his first opera, 'I solitari di Scozia,' at Naples. The next seven years were passed at Venice, each one with its opera. None, however, was sufficiently successful, and he therefore took up the teaching of singing, and practised it in Trieste and in Vienna. In 1824 he resumed opera composition, and in 1825 wrote amongst several others his most favourite work, 'Giulietta e Romeo,' for Naples. In 1829 he visited Paris, and stayed there two years as a singing-master in great popularity. He then passed a short time in London, and in 1831 we again find him writing operas in Italy, amongst others 'Marco Visconti' and 'Giovanna Grey'—the latter for Malibran, for whose death in 1837 he wrote an elegiac cantata. In 1833 and 1834 he was again in London, singing occasionally at Lady Morgan's and elsewhere. In 1838 he succeeded Basili as head and principal professor of composition of the Conservatorio of Milan. In 1844 he left his active duties, returned to Pesaro, and wrote a fresh opera, 'Virginia,' for the Argentina Theatre, Rome (1845): it was his last work. His works contain fifteen operas besides those mentioned above, twelve Ariette per Camera (Cramer, London), and a Method (Ricordi). 'Giulietta e Romeo' was performed at the King's Theatre, Haymarket, London, Apr. 10, 1832, and its final scene, with the beautiful song, 'Ah, se tu dormi,' was often substituted for the last act of Bellini's 'Capuletti ed i Montecchi.'   G.; addn. w. H. G. F.

BIBL.—G. VACCAI (son), Vita di N. Vaccai. (1882.)

VACCARI, FRANÇOIS (b. Modena, 1775; d. Portugal, after 1823), an excellent violinist, who at the age of 10 studied under Nardini at Florence; three years later he was giving concerts at Mentone, and here it was that Pichl induced him to astonish his auditors with a concerto played at first sight. Following upon this, he achieved successes at Parma, Piacenza, Verona, Padua and Venice, after which he spent some years at Milan. In 1804 he was appointed a member of the court band of Spain, but the troubles of 1808 brought about his resignation. He toured in Spain until the following year, when he visited Paris, and travelled in Germany. In 1815 he came to England. He also went to Lisbon in the same year, and subsequently returned to Madrid, where he was appointed leader of the royal music. He was again in Paris in 1823, and also in London, where he was heard at the Philharmonic Concerts. He composed several potpourris of popular airs, for violin and piano; also some popular variations for the same instruments, on 'God save the King.' An 'Aria' by him for soprano was published in London in 1814.

BIBL.—GERBER, Neues historisch-biographisches Lexikon; CHORON ET FAYOLLE, Dict. de Mus.; DUBOURG, The Violin; MASON CLARKE, Dict. of Fiddlers; FÉTIS, Biog. des Mus.   E. H.-A.

VACCHELLI, GIOVANNI BATTISTA, of Rubiera, Modena, a 17th-century Minorite friar, organist in 1646 of the town of Rubiera. In 1664 he was a member of the Accademia della morte del final da Modona l' Accademia Naufragante, and in 1667 was also maestro di cappella di Pesaro. He wrote motetti concertati, 2-4 v., with a bass for the organ, op. 1 (1646); motetti a voce sola, book 1, op. 2 (1664); sacri concerti, 1-4 v., with and without violins, op. 3 (1667) (Q.-L.).

VACH, FERDINAND (b Jažlovice, near Řičan, 1860), Moravian conductor and choirmaster. He received his musical education at the Organ School, Prague, and then conducted for a time at the Brno Theatre. He made his reputation as a choral conductor with the choir 'Moravan' at Kroměříž (1886). Appointed singing master at the training school for teachers, he founded a male voice choir among his pupils (1903), which became the now famous Choral Society of Moravian Teachers (Pěvecké sdružení moravskych učitelů). Vach has since transferred his activities to Brno, where he is professor at the Teachers' School, the Organ School and the State Conservatoire. He has composed orchestral works, cantatas, choruses and church music, and made many admirable arrangements of folk music for his choir. Over twenty years' work under the same conductor gave a wonderful unanimity of feeling and technical perfection to this body of singers. The P.S.M.U. with their director have toured Czechoslovakia, Germany, Austria and Russia. In 1919 they were heard in London, at Queen's Hall. A choir of women teachers was founded in 1914.   R. N.

VACHER (LEVACHER), PIERRE JEAN (b. Paris, Aug. 2, 1772; d. there, 1819), violinist and composer. At 8 years of age he began his violin studies, first with Alfred Monin, and then with Viotti. When the French Revolution broke out, Vacher—then 19 years of age—went to Bordeaux and became leader of the orchestra at the principal theatre there. His stay in Bordeaux was brief, however, and he returned to Paris, where he

fulfilled similar duties at the Théâtre du Vaudeville, and made several of his tasteful romances
popular through introducing them into the
theatrical programme. From the Vaudeville
he went to the Théâtre-Feydeau, and from
thence to the Opéra orchestra. A number of
Vacher's trios and airs were published in Paris
by Nadermann, Gaveaux, Janet, Frey and
Omont.

BIBL.—CHORON ET FAYOLLE, *Dict. des Mus.*; FÉTIS, *Dict. des
Mus.*; MASON CLARKE, *Dict. of Fiddlers.*
　　　　　　　　　　　　　　　　　　　E. H.-A.

VACHON, PIERRE (*b.* Arles, 1731 ; *d.* Berlin,
1802), violinist and composer. The foundation
of his education as a violinist was laid in his
native town. At the age of 20 he went to Paris
and became the pupil of Chabran. In 1758
he was heard at the Concert Spirituel in Paris,
in a concerto of his own. According to the
contemporary account of the concert in the
Mercure de France, Vachon achieved a brilliant
success. In 1761 he was appointed leader of
the Prince de Conti's band. In 1772 he was
in London. In 1784 he toured in Germany,
where the Emperor appointed him director of
the court music. He remained in this post
until superannuated in 1798, when he retired
on a pension. La Borde [1] states that Vachon
excelled in chamber music. He wrote several
operas, a number of instrumental pieces, quartets, trios and concertos for violin and orchestra.
Most of these were published by Chevardière
in Paris, but six sonatas for violin and bass
were published in London in 1770.

BIBL.—LA BORDE, *Essai sur la musique* ; GERBER, *Neues historisch-
biographisches Lexikon*; CHORON ET FAYOLLE, *Dict. de Mus.* ; MASON
CLARKE, *D'ct of Fiddlers.*
　　　　　　　　　　　　　　　　　　　E. H.-A.

VACQUERAS, BELTRAME (BERTRANDUS,
BERNARDUS, *alias* de Crassia), a Spaniard, and
singer in the Papal Chapel, 1483–1507 ; probably identical with Bertrandus the bass (*contra-
bassista*, singer, who appears in the lists of
singers at St. Peter's, Rome, 1481–82. Petrucci
published a chanson and a motet in 1501 and
1503. The song, ' Ve ci la danse barbare,' is
remarkable for the interwoven dance tune.
Glarean, who valued him highly as a composer,
included his psalm, ' Domine non secundum
peccata,' in his Dodecachordon. The Sistine
Chapel at Rome possesses in MS. a Mass ' Obon
du cœur,' 4 v., a Mass ' Lomme arme,' 4 v.,
and a number of minor vocal compositions,
2-6 v. (*Q.-L.* ; Ambros ; *Riemann*).

VAET, JACOBUS (*d.* Jan. 8, 1567), church
composer, was a native of Flanders.

He was in the service of Maximilian, King of
Bohemia, to whom he acted as ' chori musici
praefectus,' in 1562, the year that his work,

' Modulationes quinque vocum (vulgo motecta) nuncupate, serenissimi Bohemiae Regis, musicarum modulationum, rectoris celeberrimi,' Venetiis apud Antonium Gardanum,

was published in two volumes. He was appointed chief Kapellmeister at Vienna, Dec. 1,
1564, four months after Maximilian II. had
succeeded Ferdinand as Emperor. He retained

this post, in which he had been preceded by
Jachet Buus (see JACHET) until his death. A
motet in his memory, ' In obitum Jacobi Vaet,'
by Jacob Regnart, ' Defunctum charites vaetem
merore requirunt,' set for seven voices, was
published in 1568, in the fifth and last volume
of Pierre Joannellus's ' Novus Thesaurus,' a
work containing many of Vaet's own compositions, notably the great Te Deum set for
eight voices, considered his finest production.
Both this work and the earlier ' Thesaurus
musicus ' published in 1564, show Vaet as pre-
eminently a court musician, for among the large
number of his motets included in these volumes
are compositions in honour of Emperor Ferdinand I. ; of Maximilian II. ; of Maximilian's
two sons, Rudolf and Ernst ; of Albert Duke of
Bavaria ; and of Queen Katherine of Poland ;
many of these with other motets and the Te
Deum have been reprinted by Franz Commer
(Coll. op. mus. bat., vols. 2, 4, 5 and 9).

Some of Vaet's sacred compositions were included in the great collection ' Evangelia
domin. et fest. dierum,' in six volumes, published at Nuremberg, 1554–56, and in the four
volumes of ' Eccles. cant. quatuor vocum,'
published by Tylman Susato at Antwerp,
1553 ; four are in ' Novum et insigne op. mus.,'
Noribergae, 1558 ; three motets are in Dietrich
Gerlach's ' Tricinia sacra,' 1567 ; others are in
' Lib. II suav. et jucund. harm.,' 1568, and in
' Select. sac. cant.' three books, published in
1569. The usual transcriptions of these vocal
compositions into tablature for organ or lute
took place ; specimens are to be seen in Joh.
Rühling's ' Tabulaturbuch,' 1583, and in
Emanuel Adriansen's ' Pratum musicum,'
1584.

Only two secular compositions can be found
to balance this mass of sacred music, ' Sans
vous ne puis ' in ' Premier livre des chansons a
quatre parties,' Louvain 1554 and 1558, and
' Amour leal ' in the first book of the ' Jardin
musical,' Antwerp, 1556.

Allusions to Vaet's methods of composition
are sometimes to be found in early theoretical
works. Zacconi [2] refers to the introduction of
' proportione imperfetta ' or duple time into
the ' Hymni ' of ' Jacobo Vaed, musico antico
e celebrato.' A century later Angelo Berardi [3]
bases his conclusion that there is little difference
to be found between the ' cantilene ecclesia-
stiche e le volgari ' on his examination of 16th-
century compositions by various musicians,
among them Jac. Vaet.

A stray little bit of information garnered by
Van der Straeten [4] may possibly be connected
with Vaet. He extracts it from ' Les comptes
de la châtellerie d'Ypres,' 1499. It runs :

' Meester Jean Vaet ende Joos Gheeraerd, pen-
sionaris van Ypre, was ghepresenteert twee kannen
wyns, van XXXII stuuvers.'

---

[1] *Essai sur la musique*, vol. iii.

[2] *Prattica*, 1592, p. 49.　　　[3] *Misc. musicale*, 1689, p. 40.
　　　　　　[4] *Pays-Bas*, i. p. 120.

Van der Straeten also states that in the *Poemata* of François Haemus published at Antwerp, 1578, is an elegy on the death of Jacques Vasius, first Kapellmeister to the Emperor Maximilian, doubtless identical with Jacques Vaet; this tends to confirm Vaet's supposed Flemish nationality, for Haemus devotes many of his poems to dwellers in Courtrai and other towns close by. Moreover, Guicciardini [1] definitely states that among native musicians

'di presente vivono Giaches de Waet, Giachetto di Berckem, etc., e molti altri tutti maestri di musica celeberrimi, & sparsi con honore & gradi per il mondo.'

Manuscript copies of a Magnificat, of motets and masses composed by Vaet are in the following libraries:

Augsburg.— Missa sex vocum super carmen 'Tityre tu patulae,' Jacobus Vaet, 1595.
Berlin.—Missa sex vocum super 'Ego flos campi'; a motet for five, and one for four voices.
Breslau.—MS. 203, dated 1583, Magnificats, I.-VIII. toni, for four voices. MS. 97, Missa super 'Vitam quae faciunt,' dated May 17 1593, and Missa super 'Tityre tu patulae,' both for six voices. Eighteen motets for 4, 5, 6, and 8 voices, are in MSS. 1, 2 (dated 1573), 3, 5, 6 (dated 1567), 7 and 11 (dated 1583). (See Bohn's Catalogue.)
Brieg.—One motet for five, and one for six voices. (See Kuhn's Catalogue.)
Dresden.—MS. 276. The Te Deum in three movements, for eight voices, scored by Wilhelm Fischer. (See Kade's Catalogue.) Another MS. score made by J. G. Bastiaans is in the library of the Maatschappij tot Bevordering der Toonkunst.
Liegnitz.—Motet for five voices. (See Pfudel's Catalogue.)
London—British Museum. Add. MS. 31,992, in lute tablature; 'Salve Regina,' 'Aspice Domine,' 'In tenebris' and 'Huc me sideris.'
Lübeck.—In a cantional 'Reges terrae' for five voices; 'Beata es' for four voices.
Munich.—MS. 45. An unpublished Mass 'Dissimulare' for six voices. Mus. MS. 82, 'Magnificat VIII. tonorum, autore Jacobo Paet (!) Caesar. maj. Capellae magister. Anno Domini, 1565,' for four voices, unpublished. Mus. MS. 41, Hymn, 'O gloriosa domina,' for eight voices, in two movements. Mus. MS. 1536. An incomplete set of partbooks, dated 1583, with sixteen motets and hymns, for six and eight voices. Mus. MS. 1501. Motet for four voices. (See J. J. Maier's Catalogue.)
Nuremberg.—Lorenzkirche Bibliothek, MS. Sign. 227, S. Egyd, dated Sept. 3, 1573; Missa Quodlibetica cum quinque vocibus a Jacobo Vaet excellentissimo musico composita. Missa sex vocum facta ad imitationem cantilenae 'Si me tenes,' auctore Jacobo Vaet. (See H. Botstiber's Catalogue.)
Proske Library.—Missa super 'Tityre tu patulae' for six voices. Magnificat VIII. tonorum for four voices, and six motets.
Stuttgart.—Landes-Bibl. MS. 5. 'Dum steteritis' for five voices.
Vienna.—MS. 15,950. Three masses for six voices; 'Ego flos campi,' 'Dissimulare' and 'Tityre tu patulae.' A Mass, 'J'ay mis, mon cœur,' for eight voices. MS. 19,280. Canon, sex vocum, dedicated to 'Maximiliano Bohemorum Regi, Archiduci Austriae,' and with the text 'Qui operatus est Petro,' etc. A minute description of this work, printed at Vienna by Raphael Hofhalter, in 1560, is to be found in Schmid's *Ottaviano dei Petrucci*, 1845, p. 215. MSS. 15,613, 18,828 and 19,189, contain motets. (See Mantuani's Catalogue.)
Zwickau.—MS. 742, date about 1560, an incomplete copy of the Mass super 'Si me tenes' (See Vollhardt's Catalogue.)

C. S.

VAGANS, *i.e.* wandering, uncertain—an old name for the Quinta Pars in a mass or motet, so called because it was not necessarily of any particular compass, but might be a second soprano, or alto, or tenor; though usually a tenor.

G.

VAISSEAU-FANTÔME, LE, opera in 2 acts; words translated or imitated from the FLIEGENDE HOLLÄNDER (*q.v.*), of Wagner (from whom the scenario was purchased), music by Dietsch. Produced Opéra, Paris, Nov. 9, 1842.

G.

VAL, FRANÇOIS DU, see DUVAL.

VALDERRÁBANO, ENRIQUEZ DE, see ENRIQUEZ.

VALDRIGHI, COUNT LUIGI FRANCESCO (*b.* Modena, 1837; *d.* there, Apr. 20, 1899),

musical historian to whose untiring zeal we owe a number of new facts as well as corrections, especially with regard to Modenese musicians. They are contained in a collection of small pamphlets, called *Musurgiana*, comprising biographies, descriptions of famous instruments for the compilation of which his position of honorary librarian or curator of the Este Museum afforded him special facilities. His most important work is perhaps his *Nomocheliurgographia*, the most extensive record of musical instrument makers, ancient and modern, in existence. He wrote also a continuation of Gandini's *Chronicle of Modenese Theatres*, and other minor works. He was an amateur violoncellist, and possessed a very valuable collection of ancient instruments which he left to the Este Museum. The Academy of Sciences and Arts of Modena and the Academy of S. Cecilia at Rome both elected him an honorary member.

E. v. d. s.

VALENTINE, JOHN (*d.* ? Leicester, 1791), a composer, mainly of instrumental pieces, settled at Leicester in the latter half of the 18th century. His works include some songs, an 'Ode on the Birthday of the Marquis of Granby,' a set of 'Thirty Psalm Tunes,' and several books of marches and minuets, among which are, 'Twenty-four Marches, Minuets, and Airs in Seven parts,' 'Eight easy Symphonies for two Violins and two Hautboys,' 'Sixteen Marches and Minuets,' etc. etc.

F. K.

VALENTINE, ROBERT, a violinist and composer of the early 18th century. He may be identical with a flautist who lived at Rome in 1714, and appeared in London in 1731, and who was known in Italy as Roberto Valentino or Valentini. Long before the date of his appearance in London (if the two men are identical) he had published with Walsh numerous works as follows:

Op.
1. Twelve sonatas for two violins and bass.
2. Twelve sonatas or soli for a flute.
3. Twelve sonatas for a flute (1701).
4. Six sonatas for two violins, two oboes or German flutes, with bass.
5. Twelve sonatas for flute.
6. Twelve sonatas for two flutes (or Six sonatas for two violins).
7. Six sonatas for two flutes. or two violins.
9 and 10. Setts of Aires, for two flutes and bass.
11 and 13. Flute sonatas, and six Setts of Aires and a Chacoon for two flutes (*c.* 1720).

Sonatas for flute, adaptable for violin, mandola or oboe, appeared in Rome about 1730, and MS. compositions are at Upsala, Rostock and Wolfenbüttel. In Alfred Moffat's 'Meisterschule' two are reprinted (*Q.-L.*, etc.). M.

VALENTINI, GIOVANNI, was from 1614 court organist to the Archduke Ferdinand at Grazi; after the latter's enthronement as the Emperor Ferdinand II., Valentini was his Imperial court organist in Vienna. [2]

Books of masses were published in 1617, 1621

(2), some motets, and in 1618, madrigals with accompaniment in 1619, 1621 and 1625, and 'Musiche a 2 voci' in 1622. A four-part setting of the 'Vesperae integrae' and other sacred compositions are in MS. The four sonatas 'a 5 e 4' for strings, at Cassel, one of which was published as 'Enharmonische sonate' in Riemann's 'Alte Kammermusik,' are probably, as Eitner surmises, the work of Giuseppe VALENTINI.   M.

VALENTINI, GIUSEPPE (GIUSEFFO) (*b.* Florence *c.* 1680), was in the service of the Grand Duke of Tuscany. His concerted chamber music was published at Rome, Amsterdam (op. 1 appeared at both in 1701), London and Bologna, and MS. compositions are in many libraries.

Op.
1. Twelve sinfonie *a* 3.
2. 'Bizzarerie' for three stringed instruments with bass.
3. Twelve Fantasie for the same.
4. 'Idee per camera' for the same.
5. Twelve 'Suonate' for the same.
6 and 7. Concerti grossi.
8. 'Sonata da camera,' or 'Alletamenti,' for violin and violoncello with bass.

The Roman edition of op. 8 is dated 1714. For a sonata reprinted by Riemann see under the name of Giovanni VALENTINI.   M.

VALENTINI, PIETRO FRANCESCO (*d.* Rome, 1654), a great contrapuntist, scholar of G. M. Nanini. Various books of canons, madrigals, 'favole' (possibly for the stage), appeared in 1629, 1631 and 1645, and canzonets, etc., by him were published before and after his death (lists in *Q.-L.* and *Riemann*). His canons were his greatest achievement, and two of them are famous. The first, on a line from the Salve Regina, was published in Rome in 1629, 'con le sue Resolutioni in piu di Duemilia Modi'; it is given by Kircher (*Musurgia*, vol. i. p. 402), and was selected by Marpurg, more than a century later (1763), as the theme of seven of his Critical Letters on Music, occupying fifty quarto pages (vol. ii. p. 89). He speaks of the subject of the canon with enthusiasm, as one of the most remarkable he had ever known, for containing in itself all the possible modifications necessary for its almost infinite treatment —for the same qualities in fact which distinguish the subject of Bach's 'Art of Fugue' and the 'Et vitam venturi' of Cherubini's great 'Credo.'

The first subject is :

Il - los tu - os mi - se - ri - cor - des

o - cu - los ad nos con - ver - te.

which gives direct rise to three others ; viz.—

Second subject, the first in retrograde motion.

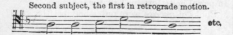
etc.

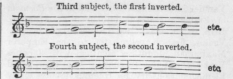

Third subject, the first inverted.

etc.

Fourth subject, the second inverted.

etc.

Each of these fits to each or all of the others in plain counterpoint, and each may be treated in imitation in every interval above and below, and at all distances, and may be augmented or diminished, and this for 2, 3, 4, 5 or 6 voices. Kircher computes that it may be sung more than 3000 different ways.

The second canon—'Nel nodo di Salomo (like a Solomon's knot) a 96 voci' —published in 1631, consists of the common chord of G, and may be varied almost *ad infinitum,* with insufferable monotony it must be allowed. (See also Burney, *Hist.* vol. iii. p. 522.)   G.

Valentini's productions further include :

Two Favole (stage works with intermezzi) : 'La Mitra' and 'La transformazione di Dafne.'
Two books of Madrigals. 5 v. with basso continuo *ad lib.*
Two books 'Motetti ad una voce con istromenti.'
Two books of Motets. 2 to 4 v.
Two books 'Canzonetti spirituali a voce sola.'
Two books similarly called for 2 and 3 v. and two for 2 to 4 v.
Canoni musicali.
Two books, 'Musiche spirituali per la Natività N.S. Gesu Cristo.'
Two books, 'Canzoni, sonetti ed arie a voce sola.'
Four books, similarly called for 1 and 2 v.
Two books, Litanies and Motets.
A theoretical work, MS. in Barbarine library at Rome.   (*Riemann.*)

VALENTINI (VALENTINO URBANI), a celebrated *evirato,* who came to London, Dec. 6, 1707.

He seems to have arrived here possessed of a contralto voice of small power, which fell afterwards to a high tenor, and with an opera, 'Il trionfo d' Amore,' in his pocket. The translation of this piece he entrusted to Motteux ; and he subsequently sold to Vanbrugh,[1] for a considerable sum, the right of representation. The 'Baroness,' Margherita de l'Épine, Mrs. Tofts, and Leveridge sang with him in this opera ('Love's Triumph '), and, if the printed score may be trusted, they all, including Valentini, sang English words. The piece was produced at the end of Feb. 1708, and he took a benefit in it on Mar. 17. Meanwhile, he had already sung (Dec. 1707) as Orontes, a 'contratenor,' in 'Thomyris,' Hughes understudying the part. Valentini's dress [2] in this piece cost £25 : 17 : 3, a very large sum in those days ; his *turban and feathers* cost £3 : 10s., and his 'buskins' 12s. We find him [3] (Dec. 31, 1707) joining with the 'Seigniora Margaritta' (de l'Épine), Mrs. Tofts, Heidegger, and the chief members of the orchestra in a complaint against the dishonesty and tyranny of Rich. They claimed various amounts due for salaries, 'cloaths,' etc. Valentini's pay was fixed at £7 : 10s. a night, as large a sum as any singer then received ; but he seems to have had

1 The Coke papers formerly in the possession of Julian Marshall.
2 *Ibid.*   3 Busby.

difficulty in extracting payment of it from Vanbrugh.

There is extant a curious letter, in which de l'Épine appeals to the Vice-Chamberlain (Coke) for '*juste reuange*' for the '*impertinance*' of which '*cette créature*' (Valentini) had been guilty, in preventing her from singing one of her songs a few days before ; and declares that she would never suffer '*ce monster, ennemi des homes des fames et de Dieu*' to sing one of her songs without her singing one of his ! The letter is simply endorsed by the Vice-Chamberlain, 'Mrs. Margarita about Mr. Valentini.'

Valentini sang, with Nicolini, in 'Pyrrhus and Demetrius,' a part which he resumed in 1709. Nicolini and he sang their music to the Italian words, while the rest of the company sang in English, as was not unusual in the *gallimaufries*[1] of the time. Valentini reappeared (1710) in 'Almahide,' and (1711) in the original cast of 'Rinaldo,' as Eustazio, a tenor. In 1712 he sang another tenor part, that of Silvio in 'Pastor Fido'; and in the following year another, Egeo in 'Teseo,' as well as that of Ricimer in 'Ernelinda.' In the season (1713) he again joined in a petition, with Pepusch and his wife, la Galeratti, and other artists, for the better regulation of their benefits. Valentini sang again in 'Creso,' 1714, and had a benefit concert at Hickford's Great Room on Mar. 31, 1715, when he was assisted by Anastasia Robinson.

Galliard says of him that, 'though less powerful in voice and action than Nicolini, he was more chaste in his singing.'

J. M. ; addn. W. H. G. F.

VALENTINO, Henri Justin Armand Joseph (*b.* Lille, Oct. 14, 1787 ; *d.* Versailles, Jan. 28, 1865), eminent French conductor. His father, of Italian origin, was an army-chemist, and intended him for a soldier, but at 12 he was playing the violin at the theatre, at 14 was suddenly called upon to supply the place of the conductor, and henceforth made conducting his special business.

In 1813 he married a niece of Persuis, the composer, on whose recommendation he became in 1818 deputy-conductor of the Opéra under R. Kreutzer, and in 1820 was rewarded with the reversion of the title of first conductor conjointly with Habeneck. The decree did not take effect till Kreutzer's resignation in 1824, when the two deputies had long been exercising the function of conductor in turn. Amongst the works produced under Valentino's direction between 1827 and 1830 may be mentioned 'Moïse,' 'La Muette de Portici,' 'Guillaume Tell' and 'Le Dieu et la Bayadère.' He also held from Apr. 10, 1824, the reversion after Plantade of the post of maître de chapelle honoraire to the King, but this he lost by the Revolution of 1830, which also brought about

[1] The Coke papers.

changes at the Opéra. Dr. Véron, the new director, inaugurated his reign by cutting down salaries, and Valentino, determined not to sacrifice the musicians who served under him to his own interests, resigned. He soon after succeeded Crémont as chief conductor of the Opéra-Comique, an enviable post which he occupied from Apr. 1831 to Apr. 1836. Here he produced 'Zampa,' 'Le Pré aux Clercs,' 'Le Prison d'Édimbourg,' 'Le Châlet,' 'Robin des Bois' ('Der Freischütz'), 'Le Cheval de bronze,' 'Actéon' and 'L'Éclair.' On the direction of all these popular works he bestowed a care, zeal and attention to *nuances* beyond all praise.

On resigning the Opéra-Comique, Valentino settled at Chantilly, but was soon offered the direction of the popular Concerts of classical music. Fascinated by the idea of rivalling the Concerts du Conservatoire and spreading the taste for high-class instrumental music, he courageously put himself at the head of the enterprise. The spot selected was the hall at 251 Rue St. Honoré, where Musard had given masked balls and concerts of dance-music, and which was now destined to hear the classical masterpieces interpreted by a first-rate orchestra of eighty-five players—and all for 2 francs ! But the public was not ripe for classical music, and preferred the 1 franc nights and dance-music, under a less eminent conductor. The 'Concerts Valentino,' started in Oct. 1837, came to an end in Apr. 1841. He came to London in 1839, and gave concerts at the Crown and Anchor Tavern (see Promenade Concerts).

Valentino retired to Versailles in 1841 and lived in obscurity for twenty-four years. He was indeed asked in 1846 to return to the Opéra, but declined.   G. C.

VALENZUELA (Valenzola), Pedro (16th cent.), Spanish madrigalist, resident in Italy, and described as cantor in St. Mark's, Venice, and maestro de l' Accademia Filarmonica, Verona. His madrigals, which are all to Italian words, were published under the title :

Madrigali *a* 5 v., con uno a 6 et un Dialogo a 8.   Venice, Gardano, 1578.   5 partbooks (B.M.).

One of these, 'La Verginella,' has been included by Barclay Squire in 'Ausgewählte Madrigale.'   J. B. T.

VALERIANO (Cavaliere Valeriano Pellegrini), a very distinguished *musico*, attached to the court of the Elector Palatine, about 1712. In that year he visited London, replacing Nicolini, who left in June. Valeriano, who had a counter-tenor voice of great beauty, 'created' the principal parts in 'Pastor Fido,' produced Nov. 21, and in 'Teseo,' first performed Jan. 10, 1713. He sang also the chief rôle in 'Ernelinda,' and drew the highest salary of the season (about £650). His engagement terminated, Valeriano left England, and did not return here again.   J. M.

VALERIUS, ADRIANUS (b. Middelburg; d. Veere, Jan. 27, 1625), was the author of a famous collection of Netherland Songs, published at Haarlem in 1621 and 1626, under the title of 'Nederlandtsche Gedenck-clanck.' He spent much of his life at Veere, where from 1606 until his death he held various legal offices.

Although many of the splendid national songs of the Netherlands are included in other contemporary collections, a special value is attached to the 'Gedenck-clanck,' because Valerius gave the tunes in musical notation exactly as they were sung, while other collectors only indicated by name the tune (stem) to which the verses were set. Valerius also prefixed short histories of the patriotic events which had inspired the songs. It is probable that many of the songs, both words and music, were written by himself; and he did not hesitate to use many English, German, French and Italian tunes in his collections (see SONG, p. 49). There are about seventy-six songs altogether, varying in merit. Some are written in parts, and all have lute or cithern accompaniment.[1]   A. H. W.

VALESI, FULGENTIO, of Parma. In 1611 he calls himself 'Monache San Ambrosiana.' He wrote one book, 'Napolitane,' 3 v. (Venice, 1587), canons of various kinds on two canti fermi of the first tonus (1st mode), 3-6 v. (Milan, 1611). In Lucino's Concerti, 1616 : Vias tuas, 2 v., Alta immensa, 4 v.

              E. V. D. S.

VALESI, JOHANN EVANGELIST (WALLIS-HAUSER, called VALESI) (b. Unterhattenhofen, Bavaria, Apr. 28, 1735; d. Munich, 1811), adopted son of the Rev. Count Valvasoni, pupil of Placidus Cammerloher at Munich, where he was originally sent for the study of theology. In 1754 he was appointed court singer to the Prince-Bishop of Freising. In 1755 he was acclaimed the greatest singer in Germany, and appeared with great success at Amsterdam and Brussels. In 1756 he became chamber singer to the Duke of Bavaria, who sent him for further studies to Padua, where he adopted the name of Valesi. In 1771 he appeared in opera at Florence and Siena. The famous Tibaldi travelled specially from Rome to Siena to hear him. He remained for five years in Italy, where he appeared with signal success at Milan, Parma, Genoa, Turin, Rome and Venice, where the famous Biancha Saccetti became his pupil. In 1776 he returned to Munich, and in 1777 visited Prague, Dresden and Berlin, where Frederick the Great offered him an engagement which he declined. From 1778 the Elector of Bavaria, fearing to lose him, would no longer

[1] Dr. A. D. Loman published nineteen songs with harmony (of which fourteen are Netherland tunes) from the 1626 edition of the 'Gedenck-clanck' in 1871. (See VEREENIGING.)

grant him leave of absence. In 1798 he was pensioned, and devoted himself henceforth entirely to teaching. He trained over 200 excellent singers, the most prominent being Valentin Adamberger. C. M. von Weber was also his pupil in 1798, and his son and four daughters all attained notable success as singers (Riemann : Schilling).

VALLA, GIORGIO (b. Piacenza c. 1450 (?); d. Venice, 1499), studied at Pavia, became professor humaniorum at Venice and practised as a doctor. He published a Latin translation of the introduction to harmony by Euclid under the name of Cleonidas (Cleonidae harmonicum introductorium, etc., Venice, 1497). In his collection of scientific essays (Venice, 1497-1501), De expetendis et fugiendis rebus, is also a treatise, De musica, lib. v., Sed primo de inventione et commoditate ejus. Boemus in his Carmen Salphicum of 1515 speaks of him as the composer of a 4-part hymn (Mendel; Q.-L.).

VALLARA, FRANCESCO MARIA, of Parma, Carmelite monk, still living at Mantua in 1733. He wrote two books on Gregorian chant, and one on the cantus fermus; also a collection ('Selva di varie composizioni,' etc., Parma, 1733) of church compositions in cantus fermus for a solo choir, and for 2 choirs in counterpoint (Q.-L.).

VALLERIA, ALWINA (b. Baltimore, U.S.A., Oct. 12, 1848; d. Nice, Feb. 17, 1925), a singer, whose real name was Schoening, entered the R.A.M., London, as Alwina Valleria Lohman in Sept. 1867.

She studied the piano with W. H. Holmes, and singing with Wallworth, and in Dec. 1867 gained the Westmorland Scholarship; received further instruction in singing from Arditi, and on June 2, 1871, made her first appearance in public at a concert of her master's in the Hanover Square Rooms, when she sang 'Gli angui d' inferno' from 'Zauberflöte' in the original key, after which she was promptly engaged for Italian opera at St. Petersburg, where she made her first appearance on the stage Oct. 23 of the same year, as Linda di Chamouni. Her next engagements were in Germany and at La Scala, Milan. She was afterwards engaged at Her Majesty's Opera, Drury Lane, for two seasons, and made her first appearance May 3, 1873, as Marta. In 1877-1878 she was engaged in Italian opera at Her Majesty's Theatre, making a great success as Micaela on the production of 'Carmen.' In 1879-82 she sang at Covent Garden, undertaking a large number of parts.

On Oct. 22, 1879, she made her début in New York as Margaret in 'Faust,' adding Aïda to her repertory in the same season. For the seasons 1882 and 1883 she sang in English opera under Carl Rosa in the 'Flying Dutchman' and 'Tannhäuser'; and on Apr. 9, 1883, was much praised for her spirited performance of Colomba, on the production of Mackenzie's opera in 1883 ; she also created the principal parts in Goring Thomas's ' Nadeshda ' in 1885, and in Mackenzie's ' Troubadour ' in 1886. After that date she virtually retired. She sang in oratorio for the first time on Dec. 26, 1882, at Manchester, in the ' Messiah,' and was very successful at the Handel and Leeds Festivals of 1883, at the Philharmonic and other concerts. Her voice, which extended from B♭ below the line to D in alt (in her earlier years to F'), was of considerable flexibility, fair power and volume and pleasant quality. She was, moreover, an admirable actress. On Aug. 23, 1879, she married R. H. P. Hutchinson, of Husband's Bosworth, near Rugby.   A. C.

VALLET (VALET, VALE), NICOLAS, a 17th-century French lutenist, who lived at Amsterdam, where he became also a publisher. He wrote an instruction book for the lute, *The Secret of the Muses*, which appeared in 1615 in a Dutch, a Latin and a French edition,[1] and contained a composition by Claude Lejeune ; ' Le second livre de la tablature de luth ' (1618 and 1619) ; ' Piété royale,' the 150 Psalms of David arranged for the lute (1620) ; 21 Psalms arranged for the voice and lute (1619); ' Apollinis süsse Leyer ' . . . for violin and bass (Amsterdam, Janssen, 1642) (*Q.-L.* ; *Mendel*).

VALLOTTI, P. FRANCESCO ANTONIO (*b.* Piedmont, June 11, 1697 ; *d.* Padua, Jan. 16, 1780), attained a high reputation as the best organist and one of the best church composers in Italy. To his skill on the organ he owed the appointment of maestro di cappella at the church of S. Antony, at Padua, which he held from 1730 to his death. He had been third organist for eight years before his appointment as maestro.[2] His compositions for the Church are very numerous. In 1770 he composed a Requiem for the funeral of Tartini ; but his *magnum opus* was a theoretical work, entitled *Della scienza teorica, e pratica, della moderna musica.* The original plan of this treatise embraced four volumes : Vol. I., treating of the scientific or mathematical basis of music ; Vol. II., of the ' practical elements ' of music, including the Scale, Temperament, the Cadences and the Modes, both ecclesiastical and modern ; Vol. III., of Counterpoint ; and Vol. IV., of the method of accompanying a Thorough-Bass. Vol. I. only was published, at Padua, in 1779 ; and its contents are valuable enough to make the loss of the remaining portions of the work a subject of deep regret. In this volume the mathematical proportions of the consonant and dissonant intervals are described with a clearness for which we seek in vain in most of the older treatises on the same

subject—not excepting that of Tartini himself. Many motets, etc., in MS. are noted in *Q.-L.*

An attempt to complete Vallotti's great work was made after his death by his disciple and successor, P. Luigi Antonio SABBATINI ; and his system of teaching was continued by his talented but somewhat eccentric pupil, the Abbé VOGLER.   W. S. R.

BIBL.—BURNEY, *Present State of Music in France and Italy* (p. 131); *General History*, iv. 576; SABBATINI, *Notizie sopra la vita e le opere del Rev. P. Fr. A. Vallotti* (1780); F. FANZAGO, *Tartini, Vallotti e Gozzi* (1792).

VALSE, see WALTZ.

VALVE (Fr. *piston* ; Ger. *Ventil*). The Latin word *valvae*, signifying a pair of folding leaves or doors, has, in the English singular form (valve), such an extended meaning as to include many mechanical devices for the diverting or otherwise controlling the passage of gases or fluids through pipes, which depart widely from the type of a hinged door shutting against a face. For the use of valves in bellows-blown instruments see ORGAN, HARMONIUM, etc. ; their application to other wind instruments is here considered.

Although the development of valve actions during the past century has revolutionised wind-instrument construction in certain directions, it is not easy to say when valves of some kind or other were first used to vary the length of a musical tube. As soon as an assemblage of tubes of various lengths (the Pan's pipe) gave place to a single tube varied in length by means of lateral holes covered by the fingers, the valve system was virtually introduced, and to this day there is no more perfectly acting valve than the natural pad of the finger-tip working from the natural hinge of the finger. The causes which operated in introducing valve-work, so far as instruments with side-holes are concerned, were these : (1) Key-modulation and chromatic notes were to a large extent impracticable so long as the difficulty remained of closing more than seven, or at the most eight, holes with the fingers, and at the same time supporting an instrument. (2) The limited stretch of the fingers rendered impossible the placing in their best positions of many of the holes on the larger instruments.

ANCIENT HISTORY.—Probably the earliest known example of mechanical means for controlling a number of ventages or finger-holes is a Greek or Roman tibia, one of four discovered in 1876 at Pompeii, and now in the Museum at Naples. This instrument is made of ivory, cased with silver or bronze : it is of cylindrical bore, and is pierced with eleven lateral holes. Fitting over the holes are eleven sliding sockets or shutters, any one or more of which can be closed. By means of these sliders the sequence of tones and semitones, and therefore the *mode*, could be varied. Passing to the time of Virdung (1511) we find an open-standing key or hinged valve worked by the little finger, used

---

[1] Mendel speaks of ' A French edition of earlier date.'
[2] *Q.-L.*

both on the flûte-à-bec and on the bombardt to extend the compass downwards. Praetorius (1616) also shows the larger flutes with one key only, but the great double-quint pommer (a bass double-reed instrument) is shown with four keys, all, however, for the extension of the compass downwards, and not to obviate the awkward placing of the customary six finger-holes. The $d\sharp$ key was added to the 'German' flute or flûte traversière about 1660, and during the 18th and 19th centuries the addition, both to reed instruments and to flutes, of valves worked by keys or levers, gradually extended. Whether the valves were covered with skin, or were carefully adjusted metal plugs with a conical seating, does not affect the principle, although it is to the latter only that the name 'valve' is usually given, both by instrumentalists and by instrument-makers, so far as wood instruments are concerned.

At the present day, when valve-instruments are named, all such lip-blown instruments with cupped mouth-pieces are generally understood as do not fall under the classification of natural horns, bugles, and trumpets, or of slide instruments (trombones). These, our distinctively modern brass instruments, date from early in the 19th century for their very inception, and for a considerable part of that century were used concurrently with key-bugles, serpents and ophicleides, the surviving representatives of the zinke or cornett class. In the larger zinken, as we find from Praetorius, the finger-holes were sometimes supplemented by a hole governed by an 'open-standing' key, and this key or valve, when closed, extended the compass downwards, just as a similar key did on the flûte-à-bec. From the cornetto torto or curved cornett the serpent was derived, at first having six finger-holes, which from their necessarily small size gave very poor tone and faulty intonation. By degrees keys were added both in addition to and in substitution for finger-holes, but it was not until the invention of the key-bugle by Joseph Halliday in 1810, and of the ophicleide, that the best result obtainable from key-work adapted to conical brass instruments of the bugle type was seen. Some years previous to this date similar keyed-valves had been applied both to the trumpet and the horn, but these instruments are eminently unsuitable for the system.

As every note on a wind instrument is derived as a harmonic from a given prime or fundamental note, the pitch of which is determined by the length of the tube, notes not in the harmonic series of the original prime can only be obtained by altering the length of the tube. Whether this alteration is by lengthening or shortening is not very material with flutes and reed instruments; but the characteristic tone of brass instruments is impaired unless every note speaks through the bell-mouth, and therefore the application of side-holes to *shorten*

the tube, whether covered by the fingers or by valves, has gradually become a thing of the past. The key-bugle, however, held an important position from 1820–35, and the ophicleide to a much later date; in short, until the initial difficulties encountered in the design of the various piston-valve actions to be presently described were thoroughly overcome. The alteration of length by means of added tube in the form of crooks as on the horn and trumpet, and by means of the telescoping slides of the trombone, was introduced for some centuries before any valve action to attain the same result, and the modern brass instrument valve can be most simply regarded as a means of instantaneously adding a crook or tubing of the length required to flatten the pitch of the instrument by one or more semitones.

THE MODERN USE.—The various forms of valves used in modern brass instruments differ essentially from the above-mentioned hinged or flap-valves used on wood instruments and such brass instruments as the ophicleide, inasmuch as while on these latter the cutting-off of the air-column at a side-hole prevents, in whole or in part, any tone proceeding from the bell-mouth, thereby disturbing uniformity of quality, the valves we now have to consider are so contrived as to leave the conditions at the bell-mouth unaffected. In this there is a distinct invention, very different from the gradual introduction of keywork as a supplement or alternative to the covering of side-holes with the fingers.

According to evidence adduced by J. G. KASTNER [1] (*q.v.*), Blümel, a Silesian, devised piston-valves for the horn about the year 1813, and sold his invention to Stölzel, a native of Breslau and a horn-player. Stölzel improved upon the idea and took out a patent in Germany. In these valves or their subsequent modifications, a cylindrical piston works vertically in a casing, and in the prevailing type of piston there are three ways or passages, one of which, when the piston is in its normal position, forms part of the main tubing of the instrument; the other two are so placed that when the piston is depressed they introduce into the circuit an extra length of tubing sufficient to lower the pitch one or more semitones. The early piston-valves were cumbrous, and the passages through them were either constricted in diameter, or so placed as to introduce sharp angles instead of gently flowing curves. The many attempts to overcome these defects resulted in various designs of valves, too numerous to mention; but in the 1851 International Exhibition in London Dr. J. P. Oates exhibited improved pistons designed on such sound principles that his ideas have been the basis of all the best work since. His pistons, which he described as 'equi-trilateral' valves (the name referring to the spacing of the passages), gained a prize medal. Patents were taken out by John Shaw in 1824 and in 1838, but his schemes aimed at substitutes for the piston-valve rather than improvements upon it.

The only alternative to the piston-valve is the rotary cylinder-valve, which has been and still is largely used on the continent and in America, although not in England. This valve, introduced about the year 1820, is simply a four-way stop-cock turning in a cylindrical case in the plane of the instrument, two of its four ways forming part of the main channel, the other two, on its rotating through a quadrant of the circle, admitting the air to the by-path. With this valve it is possible to produce a very close shake, but as the mechanism connecting the axle with the finger touch-piece is somewhat complicated and delicate it is liable to get out of order, and in this respect cannot be compared with the simplicity of the piston-valve, which has a rectilinear vertical traverse direct from the finger.

Whether the piston or the rotary cylinder valve is used, the practical result as regards the scale of the instrument is the same. The first valve lowers the pitch one tone, the second valve a semitone, and the third three semitones. When a fourth valve is added, it is adjusted to lower the pitch two tones and a semitone, or a perfect fourth. From each of these different fundamental pitches a new harmonic series can be produced, and also from the valves when used in combination; the ordinary three valves giving in addition to the changes noted above, a tone and a half with the first and second, two tones with the second and third, two and a half tones with the first and third, and three tones with the first, second and third valves depressed together.

The table here given shows the actual sounds corresponding to the 'open' and the valve notes of an instrument having the 8-foot C for its fundamental or pedal note, with the natural harmonics proper both to the normal length of the instrument and to the length or change in fundamental pitch due to the tubing added by the different valves or their combinations. The harmonic seventh to each prime is shown by a small figure seven, thus, 7b'♭, etc., but these notes are seldom used, as they are slightly flat for either just or tempered intonation. Column 6 is divided to show the similarity of result due to the use of the first and second valves combined, or the third valve used singly, the only difference being that the notes due to the third valve are all slightly flatter than those from the first and second combined.

This difference arises from an inherent difficulty in the valve system, for the tubing connected with each valve bearing a certain proportion to the normal length of the instrument is too short when this normal length is increased by the depression of a valve. In other words, valves in combination always give notes too sharp, and the effect is cumulative. The most obvious remedy is to use six separate valves in place of the usual three with their three combinations. This plan was introduced by Sax, but not with much success, and the growing use of the fourth valve, to complete the scale in

SCALE TABLE OF FINGERING FOR INSTRUMENTS WITH THREE VALVES

1 Chromatic scale with enharmonic equivalents.	2 Open notes.	3 Valve notes.	4 2nd valve, Semitone.	5 1st valve, One tone.	6 (a) 1st and 2nd valves, One and a half tone.	6 (b) 3rd valve.	7 2nd and 3rd valves, Two tones.	8 1st and 3rd valves, Two and a half tones.	9 1st, 2nd and 3rd valves, Three tones.
c''	c''	c''							
b'		b'	b'						
b'♭-a'♯		b'♭		b'♭					
a'		a'	7a'		a'	a'			
a'♭-g'♯		a'♭		7a'♭			a'♭		
g'	g'	g'			7g'	7g'		g'	
g'♭-f'♯		g'♭	f'♯				7g'♭		g'♭
f'		f'		f'				7f'	
e'	e'	e'			e'	e'			7f'♭
e'♭-d'♯		e'♭	d'♯				e'♭		
d'		d'		d'				d'	
d'♭-c'♯		d'♭			c'♯	c'♯			d'♭
c'	c'	c'					c'		
b		b	b					b	
b♭-a♯		b♭		b♭					b♭
a		a			a	a			
a♭-g♯		a♭					a♭		
g	g	g						g	
g♭-f♯		g♭	f♯						g♭
f		f		f					
e		e			e	e			
e♭-d♯		e♭					e♭		
d		d						d	
d♭-c♯		d♭							d♭
c	c	c							
B		B	B						
B♭-A♯		B♭		B♭					
A		A			A	A			
A♭-G♯		A♭					A♭		
G		G						G	
G♭-F♯		G♭							G♭
F									
E									
E♭-D♯									
D									
D♭-C♯									
C	C								

the pedal octave, with the increased difficulty of combined valves, led to many attempts to introduce means to compensate for the error. Some of these were theoretically sound, but practically cumbersome, and therefore were not largely adopted. The importance of improving the intonation of the lowest octave of the larger brass instruments especially, led the writer of this article to design for Boosey & Co. in 1874, with a modification patented in 1878, a system of 'Compensating Pistons' still increasingly used, which pistons were examined by the late Dr. W. H. Stone, whose description of them in the first edition of this Dictionary is as follows :

'In the ordinary arrangement the first valve lowers the pitch one tone ; the second half a tone ; and the third a tone and a half ; but as the length of the instrument should be, speaking roughly, in inverse proportion to the number of vibrations of the required notes, the desired result is not exactly obtained when two or three valves are used in combination. Thus, in an instrument in the key of C, the first valve lowers the pitch to B♭, the third valve lowers it to A♮. For the low G the first valve is used in combination with the third, but its tubing is tuned to give the interval from C to B♭, and as the instrument when the third valve is down is virtually in A♮, the tubing of the first valve is not sufficiently long to flatten the pitch a true tone from A to G. This defect is intensified when all three valves are used together to produce D♭ and G♭. A numerical illustration may make this more clear : let the first valve tubing be one-eighth the length of the instrument, and the third valve tubing one-fifth, the length of the instrument being unity ; one-fifth added thereto will lengthen it in the right proportion to lower its pitch a minor third— *i.e.* from C to A♮. To produce G, we should be able to lower the instrument one tone from A♮, but the first valve will increase the length only one-eighth of unity, and not one-eighth of 1+⅕. G will therefore be somewhat sharp.

'Thus far with reference to instruments with three valves, but the defect is aggravated in those with four. Any actual lengthening of the valve slides by mechanism connected with the valve is practically inadmissible, as the lightness and rapidity of action of the valve would be thereby interfered with, but in the compensating pistons a lengthening of the valve slides is brought about as follows. The tubing connected with the third valve is passed through the first and second in such a way that when the third is pressed down, the vibrating column of air passes through passages in the first and second, in addition to the two passages in the third, as in the common arrangement : and for the purpose of bringing additional tubing into action in connection with the first and second valves, as required for correct intonation (when they are either or both used in combination with the third), two air-passages are added to each of these valves, and in connection with each pair of passages a loop or circuit of tube of the required length, which is added to the effective length of the instrument only when the third valve is used in connection with the others. Such additional tubing compensates for the lowering of the pitch due to pressing down the third valve. No extra moving parts are introduced, and the established fingering is preserved.'

In the above description an instrument with three valves is assumed, but it will be readily understood that the system is applied to the greatest advantage on four-valved instruments. The illustrations show :

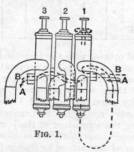

FIG. 1.

A set of saxhorn valves of the usual construction. The faint dotted line A . . . A and the strong dotted line B . . . B indicate respectively the air-passage for the 'open' notes, and the air-passage when the piston No. 1 is down.

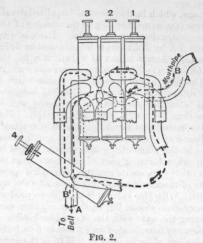

FIG. 2.

A set of four valves for the euphonium or tuba on the compensating system. The strong line B . . . B in this case indicates the air-passage when the piston No. 4 is down.

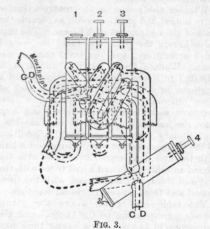

FIG. 3.

Indicates by the line D . . . D the air-passage when all pistons are down. The faint dotted line C . . . C indicates the air-passage for the 'open' notes in all cases.

In all the piston valves so far described the helical wire spring is under compression when the valve is pressed down, and this compression or closing of the spring introduces a tendency to a rotary movement which is checked by a pin working in a slot. The direct vertical action is thus preserved, but some friction necessarily results, and this detracts from the desired lightness and quickness of the valve action.

A patented design, No. 193729, to obviate this difficulty has been introduced by Boosey & Co. It is based upon an extension of the spring instead of the usual compression, and the connexion between the spring and the piston is so contrived as to relieve the latter of any friction due to the tendency to rotate inherent in the older system. A remarkably light, quick and noiseless action is thus obtained.

The only brass instrument which has gained nothing [1] from the introduction of the valve system is the TROMBONE. This instrument, from its peculiar proportions, lends itself admirably to the telescopic slide principle by which changes of pitch corresponding to those obtained by valves can be obtained by six different 'shifts.' It is impossible to apply the slide principle, however, to instruments which have little cylindrical tubing, and it is the invention of the valve which has made possible the variety in tone quality and the chromatic compass of modern brass instruments.

Under the article CLAGGET there is reference to a contrivance included in his patent of 1788 for combining two trumpets, in D and E♭ respectively, in such manner that they could be played with the same mouthpiece and the air-passage be diverted from one to the other by means of a valve. It has been suggested that credit should be given to Clagget as the inventor of the piston valve, and this in a limited measure is reasonable. The essence of the modern valve, however, is that its three windways allow of the use of one bell for a complete scale, which was impossible on Clagget's system.   D. J. B.

VALVERDE, JOAQUÍN (d. Madrid, Mar. 19, 1910), Spanish composer of light opera, whose 'Gran Via' (written in collaboration with CHUECA (q.v.), 1886), went the round of Europe. 'Cadiz,' the march from which was at one time almost the Spanish national anthem, has a delicious satire on English officers quartered there during the Peninsular War. In the combination of Chueca and Valverde, it was the latter who provided the knowledge of composition, the former the tunes.   J. B. T.

VAMP (verb), to extemporise an accompaniment to a song or instrumental solo. The name and the thing are confined to the least artistic class of musical performances, but real skill in 'vamping' requires no small knowledge of the usual harmonic transitions and great quickness in following the solo performer. The word is generally considered to be more or less slang of a modern date, but the following extract from a song in The Merry Musician or a Cure for the Spleen, vol. i., 1716, p. 68, shows that it has at least some degree of antiquity.

'Next Morphew the harper with his pig's face
Lies tickling a treble and vamping a base.'
        F. K.

VAMP-HORN, a form of speaking trumpet or megaphone used in certain churches in the 18th and early 19th centuries to increase the power of the voice either for leading the singing or giving out necessary notices. Specimens exist at Braybrook and Harrington, Northants;

[1] For attempts to apply the principle to the trombone, see TROMBONE.

Willoughton, Lincolnshire; Charing, Kent; and East Leake, Notts. They are made of tin and vary from 2 feet to 6 feet in length. (PLATE LXVIII. No. 5.)   F. W. G.

VAMPYR, DER, opera in 4 acts; words by C. G. Häser, music by Marschner. Produced Leipzig, Mar. 28, 1828; in London, Theatre Royal English Opera-House, in 3 acts, Aug. 25, 1829.   G.

VANBRUGHE, GEORGE, a popular song-composer in the early part of the 18th century. Besides many single songs, and those found in different collections, he issued two thin folio books of songs, the earlier being 'Mirth and Harmony; Consisting of Vocal and instrumental Musick; as songs, and ariets, for one and two voices,' London, Walsh, for the author, c. 1713. The latter is 'Modern Harmony or a desire to pleasing,' London, Walsh, c. 1720. No biographical details of him appear to be extant.   F. K.

VANHALL, JOHN BAPTIST, see WANHAL.

VANINI, FRANCESCA, see BOSCHI (2).

VANNEO, STEFFANO (b. Recanati, Ancona, 1493), Augustinian monk and choirmaster at the monastery of Ascoli; wrote a didactic treatise on music which ranks with the best of its time. Book 1 deals with Gregorian chant, solmisation and modes; Book 2 with the complete system of mensural music; Book 3 with counterpoint. The original, written in Italian and finished in 1531, was never published, but a Latin translation by Vincento Rosetti of Verona was published in 1533.   E. V. D. S.

VANNINI, FRA ELIA (b. Medicina, Province of Rome, 2nd half of 17th cent.), of a Jewish family, became a Carmelite monk, and was maestro di cappella, in 1692, at the church of Medicina, and from 1693–99 at the principal church of Ravenna. He composed: Litanies of the Holy Virgin in 4-6 parts, with violin ad lib.; Psalms and Vespers, 3-4 v.; 5 litanies a 6 and 8 v. with instruments, lib. 2, op. 4; Psalms (complete), 2-4 v. with symphonies, op. 5 (1699); Sonatas a 3, op. 1 (Bologna, 1691).   E. V. D. S.

VANNUCCI, DOMENICO FRANCESCO (b. Lucca, c. 1718; d. there, Aug. 7, 1775), an excellent violoncellist and composer; director of the seminary of the cathedral, teacher of L. Boccherini. He composed six oratorios, masses of 4 and 8 parts, responses, etc. (Q.-L.).

VARESI, FELICE (b. Calais), one of the leading baritones of his day in Italy, was taken at an early age to Milan, where he received a first-rate education. Varesi has a place of his own in operatic history, as at Venice, on Mar. 11, 1851, he was the first Rigoletto. Four years earlier at Florence he had created the title-rôle in Verdi's 'Macbeth.' It would seem that after his great success as Rigoletto he thought the part of the elder Germont in 'Traviata' unworthy of him. At any rate, on the rather disastrous first night of 'Traviata' at Venice, on Mar. 6, 1853, he gave a perfunctory performance, (see VERDI). Varesi came to London in 1864—too late for his fame, his fine voice had lost its freshness, but, according to Chorley, the touch of the artist was unmistakable.

His daughter, (2) ELENA, soprano, sang at Drury Lane in 1873 and again in 1875, having been first recommended to Mapleson by Madame Ristori. In 1875 she was Zerlina to the Don Giovanni of Jean de Reszke. She made no special success with the public in London—her opportunities were few—but discerning critics found in her a florid singer of consummate skill and the purest school.

S. H. P.

VARIANT (Ger. *Variante*) (1), the usual expression for varying versions or readings of a piece of music, such as frequently occur where an editor has to compile a text for publication from several manuscript sources.

(2) Similarly, students of folk-song to the several versions of songs preserved by aural tradition.

(3) Riemann thus described the sudden changes from major to minor, or *vice versa*, which occur frequently in modern music without involving modulation, and of which the ancient TIERCE DE PICARDIE is the prototype (cf. TRANSITION).

VARIATIONS. In the days when modern music was struggling in the earliest stages of its development, when most of the forms of art which are familiar in the present day were either unknown or in their crudest state of infancy, composers who aimed at making works of any size laboured under great disadvantages. They were as fully conscious as composers are now of the necessity of some system of structure or principle of art to unify the whole of each work, and to carry on the interest from moment to moment; but as they had not discovered any form which could extend for more than a few phrases or periods, their only means of making the music last any length of time was to repeat, and to disguise the repetition and give it fresh interest by artistic devices.

In choral music they took some old familiar piece of plain-song, or a good secular tune, put it into very long notes, and gave it to one of the voices to sing; and then made something ostensibly new upon this basis by winding round it ingenious and elaborate counterpoint for all the other voices. The movement lasted as long as the tune served, and for other movements—if the work happened to be a mass, or work necessarily divided into separate pieces —they either took a new tune and treated it in the same way, or repeated the former one, and sometimes sang it backwards for variety, with new turns of counterpoint each time.

Similarly, in instrumental music, as soon as their art was enough advanced to produce good, clear and complete dance-tunes and songs, they extended the musical performances by repeating the tunes, with such other touches of fresh interest as could be obtained by grace-notes and ornamental passages, and runs inserted in the bass or other parts. In this way the attention of composers came to be very much drawn to the art of varying a given theme, and presenting it in new lights; and they carried it to a remarkably advanced stage when scarcely any of the other modern forms of art had passed the period of incubation.

In choral music the art was limited to the practice of using a given tune as the central thread to hold the whole work together; and it almost died out when maturer principles of structure were discovered; but in instrumental music it has held its own ever since, and not only plays a part of great importance in the most modern sonatas and symphonies, but has given rise to a special form which has been a great favourite with all the greatest masters, and is known by the name of Variations.

THE ENGLISH VIRGINAL WRITERS.—The early masters had different ways of applying the device. One, which appears to have been a favourite, was to write only one variation at a time, and to extend the piece by joining a fresh theme to the end of each variation, so that a series of themes and single variations alternated throughout. In order to make the members of the series hang together, the variations to the different themes were often made in similar style; while the successive themes supplied some little contrast by bringing different successions of harmony into prominence. There are several pieces constructed in this fashion by Byrd, Bull and Orlando Gibbons, who were among the earliest composers of instrumental music in modern Europe; and they consist chiefly of sets of Pavans, or Galliards, or neat little tunes like Bull's 'Jewel.'[1] Many are interesting for ingenuity and originality of character, but the form in this shape never rose to any high pitch of artistic excellence. Another form, which will be noticed more fully later on, was to repeat incessantly a short clause of bass progression, with new figures and new turns of counterpoint over it each time; and another, more closely allied to the modern order of variations, was a piece constructed upon a theme like 'Sellenger's Round,' which did not come to a complete end, but stopped on the Dominant harmony and so returned upon itself; by which means a continuous flow of successive versions of the theme was obtained, ending with a coda.

These early masters also produced examples of a far more mature form of regular theme and variations, not unlike thoroughly modern works of the kind; in which they showed at once a very wide comprehension of the various prin-

---

[1] 'Fitzwilliam Virginal Book,' ii. 138. For the collections in which these English works of the 16th century are contained see VIRGINAL MUSIC.

ciples upon which variations can be constructed, and an excellent perception of the more difficult art of varying the styles of the respective members of the series so as to make them set off one another, as well as serve towards the balance and proportion of the whole set.

Two of the works which illustrate best the different sides of the question at this early date are Byrd's variations to the secular tune known as 'The Carman's Whistle' and Bull's set called 'Les Buffons.' These two represent respectively two of the most important principles upon which variations are made, since the first series is almost entirely melodic and the second structural; that is, each variation in the first series is connected with the theme mainly through the melody, whereas in the second the succession of the harmonies is the chief bond of connexion; both themes are well adapted to illustrate these principles, the tune of the first having plenty of definite character, and the harmonies of the second being planned on such broad and simple lines as are most likely to remain in the memory.

Byrd's series consists of eight variations, in all of which, except the last, the melody is brought very prominently forward; a different character being given to each variation by the figures introduced to accompany it. The way in which the various styles succeed one another is very happy. The first is smooth and full, and the second rugged and forcible; the third quiet and plaintive, and the fourth lively and rhythmic; and so on in similar alternation to the last, which is appropriately made massive and full, and is the only one which is based exclusively on the harmonies and ignores the tune. The two following examples give the opening bars of the fourth and sixth variations, and illustrate the style and way of applying the characteristic figures very happily. The upper part is the tune of the theme.

Ex. 1. Var. 4.

Ex. 2. Var. 6.

Byrd's variations are remarkable not only for their intrinsic qualities, but also as rare examples of melodic treatment in those early days, when composers were more inclined to notice the bass than the tune. Bull was by no means so great a genius as Byrd, but he had a vein of melody, a good deal of vivacity, and a considerable sense of effect. In 'Les Buffons' the former gift is scarcely brought into play, but the two latter are very serviceable. The theme is the simplest possible succession of chords, as follows:

Ex. 3.

Upon this fourteen variations are constructed, which are varied and contrasted with one another throughout, upon the same general principles of succession as in Byrd's series. Many of them are merely made of scale passages, or rather commonplace figures; but some are well devised, and the two following are interesting as examples of the freedom with which composers had learnt to treat structural variations even in such early days. Ex. 4 is the beginning of the second variation, and Ex. 5 is the thirteenth, which flows out of the one preceding it.

Ex. 4.

Ex. 5.

EARLY CONTINENTAL TYPES.—In the time which followed Byrd and Bull the best energies of composers were chiefly directed to the development of such instrumental forms as the suite and the canzona, and the earlier kinds of sonata ; and sets of variations were not so common.   There are a few examples among Frescobaldi's compositions ; as the 'Aria detta Balletto' in the second book of toccatas, canzonas, etc., which is curious on account of the way the variations are put into different times ; but his works of the kind are on the whole neither so interesting nor so satisfactory as Byrd's.   It is also common to meet with an occasional variation on one or more of the regular dance-movements in the suites ; and in that position they were commonly called 'doubles.'   There is a curious and unusual experiment in a suite of Kuhnau's in E minor, in which the courante in 6–4 time is a complete variation of the allemande in common time that precedes it.[1]   But the art of varying a theme of some sort was cultivated to a greater extent about this time under other guises.   In Germany composers were fond of harmonising their chorales in all sorts of ingenious ways, such as are found later in perfection in Bach's cantatas and passions ; they also used the chorales as a kind of canto fermo upon which they based elaborate movements for the organ, full of ingenious and effective figures and various devices of counterpoint ; and not a little of the great development of organ-playing, which culminated in J. S. Bach, was carried on by the cultivation of this form of art.

THE GROUND BASS.—Another form which was more obviously allied to the sets of variations, and indeed can in some cases hardly be distinguished from them, was the ground bass or *basso ostinato*, which was a very favourite form of art all over Europe during the greater part of the 17th century.   The principle of following the bass of the theme is indeed constantly made use of in variations, and in theory the only difference between the two forms is that in a ground bass the bass passage, which is repeated over and over again, is the whole bond of connexion which joins the series together ; while in variations the bass may change entirely so long as the theme is recognisable either by means of the melody or the succession of the harmonies.   But in practice, though there are many examples in which a good clear bass figure is made to persist with obstinate regularity in this form, it often gave place to the succession of the harmonies, or was itself so varied as to become scarcely recognisable. For instance, a ground in E minor by Blow, with twenty-eight divisions, begins with a section that is much more like a theme for variations ; and though the bass moves in good steps, it has no very decided figure.   A comparison of the first half of the so-called ground with

[1] In a sonata by Pergolesi in C minor the giga is a variation of the foregoing gavotte. Some suites of the same period have a virtual identity of theme throughout.

the corresponding part of the bass of the twentieth division will show that the view musicians then took of the repetitions was at least a liberal one :

Ex. 6.

In this case the outline of the bass as defined by the successive steps downwards is pretty well maintained, but in a few other divisions which are more elaborately constructed, not only is the bass altered, but even harmonies which do not strictly correspond with the originals are introduced.   Such treatment clearly destroys the individuality of the form of art, and makes the work to all intents a theme with variations, under limitations.   The real type of movement constructed on a ground bass has a decided character of its own, as the obstinate reiteration of a good figure is necessarily a striking bond of connexion throughout the piece ; and if the figures built upon it are well varied it can be made very amusing.   In Purcell's use of this form, which he was evidently fond of, the type is kept much purer, and the divisions on the ground are really what they pretend to be.   A quotation of the bass of a ground by him [2] will illustrate better than any description the difference between the real thing and a hybrid like Blow's :

Ex. 8.

But even so genuine a specimen as Purcell's is closely allied to a theme with variations ; and at a time when the form was so popular that it was not only a favourite with composers, but the constant resource of performers with any talent for extemporising to show off their skill in two directions at once, it seems very likely that the more elastic but less pure form adopted by Blow and others should have been easily allowed to pass in the crowd of experiments ; and thus composers were constantly developing the form of 'Theme and Variations' under another name.

CORELLI AND OTHERS.—A celebrated example which bears upon this question is the twelfth and last sonata of Corelli's Opera

[2] See Purcell Society's edition, vi p. 30, 'A New Ground'; also found in the song 'Here the Deities Approve' in 'Orpheus Britannicus'

Quínta, which is called ' La Follia.' This is sometimes described as a theme and twenty-two variations, and sometimes as divisions on a ground. The bass of the theme was well known in those days as ' Farinel's Ground (see Farinelli (2)), and was commonly used by musicians and composers, as for instance by Vivaldi. Hawkins speaks of it as ' the favourite air known in England as Farinelli's Ground,' showing a confusion in his mind even as to the difference between a ' ground ' and a tune. In Corelli's work the bass is not repeated at all regularly, so it is to all intents and purposes a series of free variations. These are most of them very simple, being different forms of arpeggios on the harmonies of the theme, but they are well devised so as to contrast and set off one another, and are effective in their way for the violin. The tempi vary from adagio and andante to allegro and vivace, and the time-signatures also as 3–4, 4–4 and. 3–8. Corelli evidently took an easy view of variations, for both in this set and in the chaconne in the twelfth sonata of op. 2 the harmonies are not at all strictly followed, and occasionally have next to nothing to do with the theme for several bars together ; and this appears to have been rather a characteristic of the Italian style of writing such things. The treatment of the form in this instance and in many others of nearly the same period (as those by Blow, and many by Locatelli and others a little later), together with the lax way in which Hawkins speaks of the subject, tend to the conclusion that this popular form of ground-bass movement was gradually becoming mixed up with the form of theme and variations, and trenching on its province. Even the length of the bass in the ' Follia ' and other examples is in favour of this view, because the effect of the ground bass is lost when it extends beyond very moderate limits. The best examples are after such a concise fashion as the bass quoted from Purcell, and such superb specimens as the ' Crucifixus ' in Bach's Mass, his passacaglia in C minor, and similar works by Buxtehude for the organ. If the ground bass has several clauses, as in Corelli's ' Follia ' or Blow's piece (Ex. 6), it loses its effect and has to be treated after the manner of a theme ; and the adoption of long periods led composers to that treatment, at the same time that the habit of looking at their subject in the direction of the bass rather than the upper part influenced their manner of dealing with variations.

THE GOLDBERG VARIATIONS.—This condition of things throws an interesting light upon J. S. Bach's thirty variations on an aria in G major [1] for a harpsichord with two rows of keys, which is the first very important work of its kind, and still remains the most remarkable in existence,

[1] Aria mit 30 Veränderungen,' known as the Goldberg Variations (see GOLDBERG, Johann Gottlieb).

though it is very seldom played in public in consequence of the difficulty of giving due effect on the single keyboard of the pianoforte to the rapid crossing passages which are written for two. The aria which serves for theme is not after the manner of a modern aria, but is a dance movement like those in the suites. It is in fact a sarabande of the expressive and elaborate kind familiar among Bach's works ; it has plenty of fine melody but no catching tune, and nothing to invite melodic variations of the modern kind. On the other hand, it is constructed of very broad and simple successions of harmony, with the bass moving a step of some sort in almost every bar ; and upon this motion of bass or harmonies the whole series of variations is really constructed. It is therefore actually almost as much of a ground-bass movement as Corelli's ' Follia ' or Blow's example. The actual bass figure is not repeated, but either the steps by which it moves or the regular changes of the harmony are always represented in some way under the elaborate texture of the figures. In fact, what Bach does is to take out the harmonic framework upon which the aria is built, and use it to build thirty other little movements upon. The way in which these are developed from the original will be best understood by a comparison of the opening bars of some of the variations with the corresponding portion of the bass of the theme.

The following is the bass of the first eight bars of the aria, with figures to represent the principal harmonies :

Ex. 9.

In a good many variations, such as the 1st 2nd, 4th, 12th and 22nd, these steps are very clearly maintained. The bass figure of the 2nd variation will serve to illustrate this :

Ex. 10.

It is very rare, however, that the same positions of the chords are rigidly adhered to throughout. All positions are held to be interchangeable. This would be less possible in dealing with a modern theme with weak or irregular motions of harmony ; but where the changes are so strict and clear, the successions are traceable even through a looser treatment of the original. An example which will illustrate Bach's method of interchanging positions of the same chords, and the ingenuity with which he builds one form upon another, is the opening of the tenth variation, which is a complete little four-part fughetta :

Ex 11.

In bar (b) the first position of the chord of the dominant is implied instead of its first inversion ; in bar (c) there is a similar interchange, and in bars (d) and (g) the principal emphasis of the bar falls upon a first inversion instead of a first position of the same chord.

In other variations he goes much further still. In the ninth the strict succession of chords is frequently altered, but in such a way that the character and general contour of the harmonic succession is still to be felt in the background. For instance, in the passage corresponding to bars (e) and (f) the harmonies of E minor and G are forced in, in the place of those of G and A. Then the harmony of C and A, which really represents bar (f), is driven into the bar corresponding with (g) ; and in order to make the final chord of the cadence answer in position with the original, all that appears of the chord corresponding to bar (g) is the last quaver. The following example will show the nature of the change, beginning at the half-bar corresponding with (d) where the first half close falls, up to the first close in the principal key in bar (h) :

Ex. 12.

This appears to be rather an extreme instance, but in reality the change is caused by nothing more than the happy idea of turning the passing note in bar (d) in an opposite direction and so leading to the intrusion of the chord of E ; thus causing the chords of G and C, which follow in their proper order, to come one step too late, and forcing the penultimate chord of the cadence into very close quarters. But the form of the cadence is preserved all the same, and so the change turns out to be more in superficial appearance than reality ; while the regularity of the succession is still sufficiently obvious to identify the theme.

The manner in which all the variations are written is contrapuntal, and in many cases they are cast in some one or other of the old contrapuntal forms. Every third variation throughout, except the last, is a canon of some sort, with a free bass which generally follows the outlines of the bass of the theme. These take all the intervals in regular order—a canon at the unison in the 3rd variation, a canon at the second in the 6th, and so on up to a canon at the ninth in the 27th variation, the canons at the fourth and fifth being complicated by making them in contrary motion. Variation 10 is a complete fughetta, and variation 16 an overture after the French model, managed by making the part which represents the first half of the theme into the maestoso movement, and the latter part into the fugal one. The last variation is a ' Quodlibet ' ; that is, a movement in which several bits of familiar tunes are worked in together. The tunes are ' Volkslieder ' of a very bright and happy type. It begins with one to the words ' Ich bin so lang nicht bei dir g'west,' on the top of which another, ' Kraut und Rüben haben mich vertrieben,' is introduced ; and the fragments of the two, and probably bits of others which are not identified, are mixed up together in amusing but artistic confusion throughout, always following the harmonic succession of the original aria. After the Quodlibet the theme is directed to be played again, so as to make the cycle complete—a plan followed by Beethoven more than once, most notably in the last movement of his sonata in E, op. 109. Every variation in the series has a perfectly distinct character of its own, and is knit together closely and compactly by the figures used ; which vary from the most pointed vivacity to the noblest dignity and calm ; and are so distributed as to keep the action always going, and the interest alive at every step ; the result of this many sided technical workmanship being a perfectly mature art-form.

In this respect, as in many others, Bach seems to sum up in his own lifetime the labours of several generations, and to arrive at a point of artistic development which the next generation fell far behind ; for a height equal to that of his work was not again reached till Beethoven's time. But the aspect of Bach's work is peculiar to himself and his time. The technical side is brought into extreme prominence. This is shown most obviously in the canons and fugues, but it is also shown in the texture of the other variations. Some few are extremely expressive and beautiful, but it was not with the paramount object of making them all so that Bach attacked his problem, for his variations are rather developments of ideas embodied in vigorous and regular rhythmic figures than romantic or dramatic types. Both the ideas and the way of treating them belong to the old contrapuntal school, and that style of variation-writing which is most richly and comprehensively shown in this series of variations comes to an end with Bach.

He produced several other sets in the same manner, notably the famous chaconne in the suite in D for violin solo ; but it is not necessary to analyse that work, since the same principles are observed throughout, even to the repetition of the theme at the end to clench it all together. As in the previous case, the basis of the variation is the harmonic framework of the theme ; and the melody hardly ever makes its reappearance till its resumption at the end. The bass steps are just as freely dealt with as in the previous case, from which it may be gathered that Bach considered the harmonic structure the chief thing in a chaconne (which has the reputation of being a movement on a ground-bass) as much as in a regular theme and variations. He also produced an example of a different kind, in a little set of eight variations on a very beautiful and melodious theme in A minor. In this the harmonic framework is not nearly so noticeable, and the variations are not made to depend upon it so much as in the other cases. Some few of them are constructed on the same principles as the great set of thirty, but more often the melody of the theme plays an unmistakable part. This may be seen from a comparison of the melody of the 3rd, 4th and 5th bars of the theme, with the same portion of the third variation.

Ex. 13.

The influence of the tune is similarly apparent in several other variations, putting a new complexion upon variation-making, in the direction cultivated by the next generation ; but the result is neither so vigorous nor so intrinsically valuable as in other works more after Bach's usual manner, though historically interesting as an experiment in a line which Bach generally thought fit to let alone.

HANDEL AND RAMEAU.—Handel's way of treating variations was very different from Bach's, and more like the methods of the Italian school, as illustrated by Corelli. In most cases, indeed, he regarded the matter from the same point of view as Bach, since he looked upon the harmonic framework as the principal thing to follow ; but he reduced the interest of his representation of that frame-work in new figures to a minimum. Where Bach used ingenious and rhythmical figures, and worked them with fascinating clearness and consistency, Handel was content to use mere empty arpeggios in different forms. In many of his sets of variations, and other works of the same kind, he makes the effect depend chiefly upon the way in which the quickness of the notes varies, getting faster and faster up to the brilliant but empty conclusion. The set which has most musical interest is the ' Harmonious Blacksmith ' [1] in the suite in E ; and in this the usual characteristic is shown, since the variations begin with semiquavers, go on to triplet semiquavers, and end with scale passages of demisemiquavers. The extraordinary popularity of the work is probably owing chiefly to the beauty of the theme, partly also to the happy way in which the style of the variations hits the mean between the elaborate artistic interest of such works as Bach's and the emptiness of simple arpeggios, and partly to the fact that their very simplicity shows to advantage the principles upon which a succession of variations can be knit together into an effective piece, by giving all the members of the series some relative bearing upon each other. In this set the connexion and function of each is so thoroughly obvious that the most ordinary musical intelligence can grasp it, and it is to such grounds of effect that Handel trusted in making all his sets, whether in such an example as the passacaglia in the G minor suite or the chaconne with sixty variations. Only in very few cases does he even appear to attempt to make the separate numbers of the series interesting or musically characteristic, and yet the series as a whole is almost always effective. He is more inclined to allow the tune of his theme to serve as a basis of effect than Bach was. In the variations in the suite in D it is very prominent, and in the earlier variations of the ' Harmonious Blacksmith ' is clearly suggested ; and in this way he illustrates the earlier stage of the tendency which came to predominate in the next generation. The following are types of the figures used by Handel in more than one set :

---

[1] The name is a publisher's invention not found earlier than 1820. The separate publication of the air and variations under this title has been a powerful agent in securing popularity.   c.

Another composer showed this tendency to follow the tune even more markedly. This was Rameau, who was born two years before Handel and Bach, but was brought more strongly under the rising influences of the early sonata period, through his connexion with the French operatic school, and the French instrumental school, of which Couperin was the happiest representative. These French composers were almost the first of any ability in Europe to give their attention unreservedly to tunes, and to make tune, and character of a tuneful kind, the object of their ambition. Rameau produced a number of charming tuneful pieces of a harmonic cast, and naturally treated variations also from the point of view of tune, studying to bring the tune forward, and to make it, rather than the harmonic successions, the basis of his variations. When operatic influences came into play and influenced the instrumental music of German composers, and when the traditions of the Protestant school gave place to those of the southern and Catholic Germans, the same result followed.

PREVALENCE OF THE MELODIC STYLE.—Other circumstances also affected the form unfavourably. The cause of the falling off in vigour, depth of feeling and technical resource from the standard of Handel and Bach is obvious enough in other departments; since men were thrown back, as they had been after Palestrina's time, through having to cope with new forms of art. In the case of variations—by this time an old and established form—the cause of such falling off is not easy to see; but in reality variations were just as amenable to unfavourable influences as the rest of instrumental music, since composers began to try to treat them in the same style as their sonata movements. They dropped the contrapuntal methods, with the opportunities afforded by them, and as they had not yet developed the art of expressing effective musical ideas in the modern style apart from the regular sonata form, their works of the kind seem, by the side of Bach's, to be sadly lacking in interest. Moreover, the object of writing them was changing. Bach wrote up to the level of his own ideas of art, without thinking what would please the ordinary public; but the composers of the middle of the 18th century wrote their clavier music chiefly for the use or pleasure of average amateurs, on whom first-rate art would be thrown away; and aimed at nothing more than respectable workmanship and easy agreeable tunefulness. The public were losing their interest in the rich counterpoint and massive nobility of style of the older school, and were setting their affections more and more on tune and simply intelligible form; and composers were easily led in the same direction. The consequences were happy enough in the end, but in the earlier stages of the new style varia-

tion-making appears to have suffered; and it only regained its position in rare cases, when composers of exceptional genius returned, in spite of the tendency of their time, to the method of building a fair proportion of their variations on the old principles, and found in the harmonic framework equal opportunities to those afforded by the tunes.

HAYDN'S CONTRIBUTION.—How strongly Haydn and Mozart were drawn in the prevailing direction is shown by the number of cases in which they took simple and popular tunes as themes, and by the preponderance of the melodic element in their variations. This is even more noticeable in Mozart than in Haydn, who took on the whole a more serious and original view of the form. True, he did not write nearly so many sets as his younger contemporary, and several that he did write are of the very slightest and most elementary kind—witness that which forms the last movement of the clavier sonata in E♭, that on a tune in 'tempo di minuetto' in a sonata in A, and that in a sonata for clavier and violin in C. In these cases he is obviously not exerting himself at all, but merely treating the matter lightly and easily. But when he set about his work seriously, it has far more variety, interest and many-sided ingenuity than Mozart's. This is the case with several of the sets in the string quartets, and with the remarkable one for clavier alone in F minor, and the beautiful slow movement in the sonata for clavier and violin in F. The things most noticeable in these are the remarkable freedom with which he treats his theme, and the original means adopted to combine the sets into complete and coherent wholes. Probably no one except Beethoven, Schumann and Brahms took a freer view of the limits of fair variation; the less essential chords and root harmonies of the theme are frequently changed, even without the melody being preserved to make up for the deviation, and in certain cases whole passages appear to be entirely altered, and to have little if any connexion with the theme beyond observance of the length of its prominent periods, and the fact that the final cadences come in the right forms and places. This occurs most naturally in a minor variation of a major theme, or vice versa, where a passage in the relative major is made to correspond with a passage in the dominant key, and the succession of chords is necessarily altered to a different course to make the passage flow back to the principal key at the same place, both in variation and theme. There is an extremely interesting example of such changes in the slow movement of the quartet in E♭, No. 22 Trautwein. The theme is in B♭, and the first variation in B♭ minor. The second half of the theme begins in F, and has a whole period of eight bars, closing in that key, before going back to B♭. The correspond-ng part of the first variation begins with the same notes transferred from first violin to violoncello, and has the same kind of motion, and similar free contrapuntal imitation ; but it proceeds by a chain of closely interlaced modulations through Eb minor and Ab, and closes in Db. And not only that, but the portion which corresponds with the resumption of the principal idea begins in the original key in Db, and only gets home to the principal key for the last phrase of four bars, in which the subject again appears. So that for eleven bars the variation is only connected with the theme by the fact that the successive progressions are analogous in major and minor modes, and by a slight similarity in the character of the music. This was a very important position to take up in variation-writing, and by such action Haydn fully established a much broader and freer principle of representing the theme than had been done before. The following examples are respectively the first eight bars of the second half of the theme, and the corresponding portion of the 1st variation :

Ex. 17.
Theme.
(1) (2) (3)
(4) (5) (6) (7) (8) etc.

Ex. 18.
Var. 1.
(1) (2) (3)
etc.
(4) (5) (6) (7) (8)

The other noticeable feature of Haydn's treatment of the variation-form is illustrated very happily by the ' Andante con variazioni ' in F minor for clavier solo, and by the movement in the F major sonata for clavier and

violin ; both showing how strongly he regarded the form as one to be unified in some way or other beyond the mere connexion based on identity of structure or tune which is common to all the members of the series. The first of these is really a set of variations on two themes ; since the principal theme in the minor is followed by a slighter one contrasting with it, in the major. The variations on these two themes alternate throughout, and end with a repetition of the principal theme in its original form, passing into an elaborate coda full of allusions to its principal figures. Thus there is a double alternation of modes and of styles throughout binding the members together ; and the free development of the features of the theme in the coda gives all the weight and interest necessary to clench the work at the end. The slow movement for clavier and violin is somewhat different in system, but aims at the same object. After the theme comes an episode, springing out of a figure in the cadence of the theme and modulating to the dominant ; then comes the first variation in full, followed by another episode modulating to Bb, with plenty of development of characteristic figures of the theme, coming back (after about the same length as the first episode) to a pause on the dominant chord of the principal key, and followed by another variation with demisemiquaver ornamental passages for the pianoforte. This variation deviates a little at the end, and pauses on the dominant chord again ; and then the beautiful and serene theme is given out once more in its original form. This is therefore an ingenious kind of rondo in the form of variations. The short contrasting episodes are quite in rondo-form, the only difference being that the two middle repetitions of the theme are made unusually interesting by appearing in a fresh guise. One more point worth noting about Haydn's works of this kind is that some of his themes are so rich and complex. In a few of the sets in the quartets the theme is not so much a tune as a network of figures combined in a regular harmonic scheme—see Ex. 17 ; and the same holds true of the ' Andante con variazioni ' mentioned above, which is long, and full of the most various and remarkable figures. It may be said finally that there is no branch of composition in which Haydn was richer and more truly polyphonic than in his best sets of variations.

MOZART'S STYLE.—Mozart, on the other hand, represents the extreme of the melodic form of variations. If in many of Haydn's slighter examples this tendency was perceptible in Mozart it comes to a head. The variations which he makes purely out of ornamental versions of the tune of the theme are at least four times as many as his harmonic and more seriously conceived ones. As has been said before, Mozart wrote far more sets than Haydn and many of them were probably *pièces d'occasion*—trifles upon which there was neither time nor need to spend much thought.   It is scarcely too much to say, moreover, that variation-writing was not Mozart's best province.   Two of his greatest gifts, the power of moulding his form with the most refined and perfect accuracy, and spontaneous melody, have here no full opportunity.   The themes which necessarily decide the form are in many cases not his own, and, except in rare instances, it does not seem to have entered into his head to try to make new and beautiful melodies on the foundation of their harmonic framework.   He seems rather to have aimed at making variations which would be easily recognisable by moderately gifted amateurs ; and it must be allowed that it takes a good deal of musical intelligence to see the connexion between a theme and a variation which is well enough conceived to bear frequent hearing.   It is also certain that the finest variations have been produced by scarcely any but composers of a very deep and intellectual organisation, like Beethoven, Bach and Brahms.   Mozart was gifted with the most perfect and refined musical organisation ever known ; but he was not naturally a man of deep feeling or intellectuality, and the result is that his variation-building is neither impressive nor genuinely interesting.   Its chief merits are delicate manipulation, illustrating the last phase of harpsichord-playing as applied to the Viennese type of pianoforte with shallow keys, and he obtains the good balance in each set as a whole without any of Haydn's interesting devices.   A certain similarity in the general plan of several of the independent sets suggests that he had a regular scheme for laying out the succession of variations.   The earlier ones generally have the tune of the theme very prominent ; then come one or two based rather more upon the harmonic framework, so as to prevent the recurrence becoming wearisome ; about two-thirds of the way through, if the theme be in the major, there will be a minor variation, and *vice versa* ; then, in order to give weight to the conclusion and throw it into relief, the last variation but one has a codetta of some sort or an unbarred cadenza, or else there is an unbarred cadenza dividing the last variation from the final coda, which usually takes up clearly the features of the theme. These unbarred cadenzas are a characteristic feature of Mozart's sets of variations, and indicate that he regarded them as show pieces for concerts and such occasions, since they are nothing but pure finger-flourishes to show off the dexterity and neatness of the performer. There are two—one of them a very long one— in the set on Paisiello's 'Salve tu Domine,' another long one in that on Sarti's 'Come un agnello,' a long one in that on ' Lison dormait,' and others of more moderate dimensions in the

sets on Gluck's ' Unser dummer Pöbel meint,' Duport's minuet, ' Je suis Lindor,' and others. In his treatment of the harmonic framework, Mozart is generally more strict than Haydn, but he is by no means tied by any sense of obligation in that respect, and even makes excellent point out of harmonic digression.   A most effective example, which contains a principle in a nutshell, is his treatment of the most characteristic phrase of ' Unser dummer Pöbel ' in the fourth variation.   The phrase is as follows :

Ex. 19.

To this he gives a most amusing turn by, as it were, missing the mark by a semitone :

Ex. 20.

then he goes on to the end of the half of the variation which contains the passage, and begins it again as if for repeat ; and then again overshoots the mark by a semitone :

Ex. 21.

There is probably no simpler example of an harmonic inconsistency serving a definite purpose in variations.   In a less obvious way there are some in which very happy effect is obtained by going an unexpected way round between one essential point of harmony and another, and in such refinements Mozart is most successful.

When he introduces sets of variations into sonatas and such works as his clarinet quintet, he seems to have taken more pains with them ; there are proportionately more free and harmonic variations among them ; and the element of show illustrated by the unbarred cadenza is not so prominent.   There are good examples of variety of treatment and success in balancing the various members of the series in the variations in the fine sonata in F for violin and pianoforte.   True, the basis of the variations is for the most part melodic, but the principle is treated with more solid effect than usual.   The same remark applies to the last movement of the pianoforte sonata in D, written in 1777.   This contains some extremely happy examples of the exclusive use of the harmonic principle, as in the 9th variation, in which the vigour and individuality of the figure give the variation all the appearance of an independent piece.   Similarly in the 11th, adagio cantabile, and in the last, in which the time is changed from 4-4 to 3-4, the melody is so devised as to appear really new, and not merely the theme in an ornamental dress.

An excellent use to which Mozart frequently puts variations is that of presenting the subjects of sonata-movements in new lights, or adding to their interest by new turns and ornaments when they reappear a second or third time in the course of the movement. One example is the recurrence of the theme in the 'Rondo en Polonaise' which forms the middle movement in the sonata in D just referred to. Another is the slow movement of the well-known sonata in C minor, connected with the fantasia in the same key.

The cases in which Mozart ventured to give a variation a thoroughly independent character are rare. He seems to have thought it better to keep always in sight of his theme, and though he invented some charming and effective devices which have been used by later composers, as a rule the variations wait upon the theme too subserviently, and the figures are often too simple and familiar to be interesting. The following ('Je suis Lindor') is a fair sample of his way of ornamenting a tune:

Ex. 22.
Theme.

Variation.

BEETHOVEN'S CONSUMMATION.—Beethoven's work forms an era in the history of variation-making. It was a branch of art eminently congenial to him; for not only did his instinct for close thematic development make him quick to see the various ways of treating details, but his mind was always inclined to present the innermost core of his idea in different forms. This is evinced plainly enough in the way in which he perfects his subjects. His sketchbooks show how ideas often came to him in the rough; and how, sometimes by slow degrees, he brought them to that refined and effective form which alone satisfied him. The substratum of the idea is the same from first to last, but it has to undergo many alterations of detail before he finds the best way to say it. Even in this his practice differed extremely from Mozart's, but in the treatment of the actual form of theme and variations it differed still more. In principle Beethoven did not leave the line taken up by the composers of the

sonata period, but he brought the old and new principles more to an equality than before, and was also very much more daring in presenting his model in entirely new lights. The proportion of purely ornamental variations in his works is small; and examples in which the variations follow the theme very closely are more conspicuous in the early part of his life than later; but even among such comparatively early examples as the first movement of the sonata in A♭ (op. 26), or the still earlier ones in the sonata in G (op. 14, No. 2), and the set on Righini's air, there is a fertility of resource and imagination, and in the last case a daring independence of style, which far outstrip anything previously done in the same line.

In some sets the old structural principle is once more predominant, as in the well-known 32 in C minor (1806), a set which is as much of a chaconne as any by Corelli, Bach or Handel. The theme is in chaconne time, and the strong steps of the bass have the old ground-bass character. It is true he uses the melody of the theme in one or two instances—it would be almost impossible to avoid it at a time when melody counted for so much; but in the large majority the variation turns upon the structural system of the harmonies. Among other points this set is remarkable as a model of coherence; almost every variation makes a perfect complement to the one that precedes it, and sets it off in the same way. In several cases the variations are grouped together, externally as well as in spirit, by treating the same figures in different ways; as happens with the 1st, 2nd and 3rd, with the 7th and 8th, and with the 26th and 27th and others. The 12th marks a new departure in the series, being the first in the major, and the four that follow it are closely connected by being variations upon that variation; while at the same time they form the single block in the major mode in the whole series. Every variation hangs together as closely as those in Bach's great set of thirty by the definite character of the figures used, while the whole resembles that set in the vigour of the style.

In most of the other remarkable sets the principles of treatment are more mixed. For instance, in that on the ballet air from the 'Men of Prometheus,' some have a technical interest like Bach's, and some have an advanced ornamental character after the fashion of Mozart's. Among ingenious devices which may fairly be taken as types, the sixth variation is worth noting. The tune is given intact at most available points in its original pitch and original form, but the harmonies are in a different key. A marked feature in the series is that it has an introduction consisting merely of the bass of the theme, and three variations on that are given before the real theme makes its appearance; as happens also in the last movement of the Eroica symphony, which has the same subject, and some of the same variations, but is not a set of variations in the ordinary sense of the word, since it has various episodes, fugal and otherwise, as in the movement from Haydn's violin and pianoforte sonata described above.

Others of Beethoven's sets have original external traits ; such as the set in F (op. 34), in which all the numbers are in different keys except the theme and the last two variations, the others going in successive steps of thirds downwards. The variations themselves are for the most part based on the melody, but a most ingenious variety of character is kept up throughout, partly by changing the time in each successively.

BEETHOVEN'S LAST PERIOD.—The sets so far alluded to belong to the early or middle period of Beethoven's life, but the finest examples of his work of this kind belong to the last period, such as those in the quartet in E♭, and the variations 'In modo lidico' in the quartet in A (op. 132), those in the trio in B♭, in the sonatas in E (op. 109), and C minor (op. 111), the two in the ninth symphony, and the thirty-three on the waltz by Diabelli. These last five are the finest and most interesting in existence, and illustrate all manner of ways of using the form. In most cases the treatment of the theme is very free, and is sometimes complicated by the structure of the movement. In the slow movement of the ninth symphony for instance the theme and variations are interspersed with episodes formed on a different subject and by passages of development based on the principal theme itself. In the choral part the variations are simply based upon the idea, each division corresponding to a variation being really a movement made out of a varied version of the theme adapted in style to the sentiment of the words, and developed without regard to the structure of the periods or plan of the tune.

The sets in the two sonatas are more strict, and the harmonic and structural variations are in about equal proportions. Their coherence is quite as strong as that of the thirty-two in C minor, or even stronger ; while there is infinitely more musical interest in them. In fact, there is a romantic element which colours each set and gives it a special unity. The individual character given to each variation is as strong as possible, and such as to give it an interest of its own beyond its connexion with the theme ; while it is so managed that whenever the freedom of style has a tendency to obliterate the sense of the theme, a variation soon follows in which the theme is brought forward clearly enough to re-establish the sense of its presence as the idea from which the whole series springs.

The set in op. 109 is an excellent model of the most artistic way of doing this, without the device being so obvious as it is in the works of the earlier masters. The first variation has such a marked melody of its own that it necessarily leads the mind away from the theme. But the balance is re-established by the next variation, which is a double one, the repeats of the theme being given with different forms of variations, severally like and unlike the original. The next variation is also double, but in a different sense, the repeats being given in full with different treatment of the same figures. Moreover, the balance is still kept up, since the first half is chiefly structural, and the second resumes the melody of the theme more clearly. The next two are more obscure, and therefore serve all the better to enhance the effect of the very clear reappearance of the theme in the final variation.

This plan of making double variations was a favourite one with Beethoven, and he uses it again in the fourth variation in op. 111, and in the Diabelli set. In op. 111 it is worth noticing that there is an emotional phase also. The first two variations gradually work up to a vehement climax, culminating in the third. After this outburst there comes a wonderful stillness in the fourth (9-16), like the reaction from a crisis of passion, and this stillness is maintained throughout, notwithstanding the two very different manners of the double variation. Then there is a codetta and a passage wandering through mazes of curious short transitions, constantly hinting at figures of the theme ; out of which the theme itself emerges at last, sailing with wind and tide in perfect fruition of its freedom ; the last variation of all seems to float away into the air as the tune sings through the haze of shakes and rapid light passages that spin round it, and the whole ends in quiet repose. In such a sense Beethoven gave to his variations a dramatic or emotional texture, which may be felt, by those who understand it, to be true of the innermost workings of their emotions, but can hardly be explained in words.

DIABELLI VARIATIONS ANALYSED. — Technically the most remarkable set of all is that of thirty-three on the Diabelli waltz. In this appear many traits recalling those in Bach's set of thirty. For instance, there is a fughetta, cast in the structural mould of the theme ; there are imitative variations, of thoroughly modern type ; and there are also examples of the imitations being treated by inversion in the second half, as was the manner of Bach. But in style there is little to recall the methods of the older master, and it is useless to try and lay down hard and fast technical rules to explain the detailed connexion of theme and variation. In all these last sets, and in the Diabelli set especially, Beethoven is making transformations rather than variations. He takes the theme in all its phases—harmonic, melodic, or rhythmic—and having the idea well in his mind, reproduces it with unlimited variety in different aspects. At one moment a variation may follow the melody of the theme, at another the harmonic structure, at another it will be enough that some special trait like the persistence of an inner portion of the harmony in thirds or otherwise is reproduced, as in the second phrase of variation No. 8. At other times he will scarcely do more than indicate clearly the places where the cadences and signs of the periods fall, as in variation 13, with the long pauses ; while at other times he works by nothing more than analogy, as in the relations of the end of the first half and beginning of the second half of variation 5, and the beginnings of the second halves of Nos. 9, 13 and 22. In other cases there are even more complicated reasons for the connexion. An example occurs as early as the first variation. The strong type of figure, moving by diatonic steps, adopted at the beginning, is worked out in longer reaches in the second half, until it forces the harmony away from the lines of the theme into short transitional digressions. These occur in two successive periods, which are brought round again and rendered externally as well as ideally intelligible by the way in which the periods are made to match. In a few other cases nothing but the strong points of the periods is indicated, and the hearer is left in doubt till he hears the strong cadence of the period, and then he feels himself at home again directly, but only to be immediately bewildered by a fresh stroke of genius in a direction where he does not expect it. The happiest example of this is variation 13, already alluded to, which is principally rhythmic, just indicating by a sort of suggestion here and there a humorous version of the theme, and making all the progressions seem absurdly wrong at first sight, though they come perfectly right in the end.

Another most wonderful variation is the twentieth, in which again there is a mere suggestion of the theme woven into mazes of transitions, passing away from the harmony of the theme in the less essential points, but always restoring the balance at the close, melodic and structural principles being mixed up almost inextricably. In almost all the variations except the fugue (No. 32) the periods are kept quite clear, and match the original faithfully ; and this is the strongest point in helping the hearer or reader to follow the connexion. The free fugue, which comes last but one, is exactly in the very best place to break any sense of monotony in the recurrence of these exact periods, while the last variation sets the balance even again in a very distinct and weighty way, in favour of the plan and melody of the theme.

In connexion with the point illustrated by the fugue in this set, it is noticeable that Beethoven from the first seems to have aimed at relieving in some striking and decisive way the monotony which is liable to result from the constant recurrence of short sections, and the persistence of one key. His codas are frequently very long and free, and often contain extra variations mixed up with telling passages of modulation. The early set of variations on a theme by Righini (1790) affords one remarkable illustration of this, and the twelve on the Russian air from ' Das Waldmädchen ' (1797), another. In the last movement of op. 111 the same end is gained by the string of transitions in the body of the movement before the last two variations ; a similar passage occurs in the slow movement of the ninth symphony ; and in a few instances he gained the same end by putting some of the variations in a different key, as in those of the E♭ quartet, which also contain a modulating episode near the end.

The history of variations seems to be summed up in the set we have just been considering. In the earlier stages of the art the plan of the bass and the harmonies indicated by it was generally the paramount consideration with composers, and great technical ingenuity was expended. In characteristic sets of the earlier sonata-period the melody became paramount, and technical ingenuity was scarcely attempted. In Beethoven's latest productions structural and melodic elements are brought to a balance, and made to minister in all the ways that artistic experience and musical feeling could suggest to the development of the ideas which lie in the kernel of the theme, and to the presentation of them in new lights.

LATER COMPOSERS.—Several composers in the generation after Beethoven produced isolated examples, which are really musical and interesting. Schubert is particularly happy in the variations on the ' Tod und Mädchen ' theme in the D minor quartet, in which there is great beauty of sound, charm of idea, and contrast of style, without anything strikingly original or ingenious in principle. Weber produced numbers of very effective and characteristic sets for pianoforte. Mendelssohn left one or two artistic works of the kind, of which the ' Variations sérieuses ' is the best. In this set there are happy instrumental effects, and the whole makes an effective pianoforte piece ; but Mendelssohn's view of this branch of art was only at the level of the simple standard of Mozart, and not even so free and spontaneous as Haydn's ; and in his application of melodic and structural principles he is extremely strict. Far more interesting is Schumann's treatment of the form in such examples as the Andante and Variations for two pianos, and the well-known ' Études symphoniques.' His view of the art tended to independence as much as Mendelssohn's did to rigidity, and at times he was even superfluously free in his rendering of the structural aspect of the theme. His devices are less noticeable for ingenuity than for the boldness with which he gives a thoroughly warm, free, and romantic version of the theme, or works up some of its characteristic figures into a movement of nearly equal proportions with it.

BRAHMS.—By far the finest variations since Beethoven are the numerous sets by Brahms, who was akin to Beethoven more especially in those characteristics of intellect and strong emphatic character, which seem to make variations one of the most natural modes of expressing ideas. In the Variations and Fugue on a theme of Handel (op. 24), the superb set for orchestra on a theme of Haydn (op. 56a), those for four hands on a theme of Schumann (op. 23), the two Paganini sets, and the fine set on an original theme in D (op. 21, No. 1), he not only showed complete mastery and perception of all aspects of the form, but a very unusual power of presenting his theme in different lights, and giving a most powerful individuality both of rhythm and figure to the several members of each series. His principles are in the main those of Beethoven, while he applies such devices as condensation of groups of chords, anticipations, inversions, analogues, sophistication by means of chromatic passing notes, etc., with an elaborate but fluent ingenuity which sometimes makes the tracing of the theme in a variation quite a difficult intellectual exercise. But analysis almost always proves the treatment to be logical, and the general impression is sufficiently true to the theme in broad outline for the principle of the form to be intelligible. He uses double variations with the happiest effect, as in those on the theme by Haydn, where the characteristic repetition of halves is sometimes made specially interesting by building one variation upon another, and making the repetition a more elaborate version of the first form of each half of the variations. Where the variations are strongly divided from one another, and form a string of separate little pieces, the contrasts and balances are admirably devised. In some cases again the sets are specially noticeable for their continuity, and for the way in which one variation seems to glide into another; while they are sometimes connected by different treatment of similar figures, so that the whole presents a happy impression of unity and completeness. Brahms is also, like Beethoven, most successful in his codas. Two very large ones are the fugue in the Handel set, and the fine, massive coda on a ground-bass derived from the first phrase of the theme, in the Haydn variations. Another on a large scale, but in different style, is that which concludes the Hungarian set (op. 21, No. 2).

In the following examples—which show the first four bars of the theme, and the corresponding portion of the third variation in the first Paganini set—the nature of several very characteristic devices, such as anticipation, insertion of new chords between essential points of the harmonic succession, doubling the variation by giving the repetition of each half in full, with new touches of effect, etc., is illustrated.

A peculiar adaptation of the variation-principle to the details of other forms of art remains to be noticed. In this also Beethoven led the way. A very fine example is the conclusion of the Marcia funebre of the Eroica symphony, where the subject is made to express a terrible depth of grief by the constant breaks of the melody, which seem to represent sobs. A similar device—in that case amounting to a complete variation—is the repetition of the short 'Arioso dolente' in Ab minor in the middle of the final fugue in the sonata in Ab (op. 110). Here again the object is obviously to intensify the sadness of the movement by constant breaks and irregularities of rhythm. Another passage of the same kind is the end of the overture to 'Coriolan.'

INCIDENTAL DEVELOPMENTS.—With a similar view Berlioz has given varied forms of his 'idée fixe' in the 'Épisode de la vie d'un artiste,' adapting it each time to the changed conditions implied by the movement in which it appears. Its original form is as follows :

Ex. 25.

In the ball scene it takes a form appropriate to the dance motion :

Ex. 26.

Another form occurs in the ' Scène aux champs,' and in the final ' Nuit de Sabbat ' it is purposely brutalised into the following :

Ex. 27.

Wagner, carrying out the same method on a grander scale, has made great use of it in adapting his ' leitmotiven ' to the changed circumstances of the individuals or ideas to which they belong. One of the most remarkable instances is the change from one of Siegfried's tunes as given by his own horn in his early days, representing his light-hearted boyish stage of life—

Ex. 28.

to the tune which represents him as the full-grown hero bidding adieu to Brünnhilde, which is given with the whole force of the orchestra.

Ex. 29.

Liszt has frequently made characteristic variations of his prominent figures for the same purposes, as in the ' Faust ' symphony, and ' Les Préludes.'

Among the devices known as ' æsthetic,' variations again play a most prominent part ; movements of symphonies and sonatas, etc., being often linked together by different forms of the same idea. Interesting examples of this are to be met with in Schumann's Symphonies in D minor and C, and again in Brahms's Symphony in D (see SYMPHONY).

In such a manner the principle of variation has pervaded all musical art from its earliest days to its latest, and appears to be one of its most characteristic and interesting features. In its early stages it was chiefly a mechanical device, but as the true position of ideas in music has come more and more to be felt and understood, the more obvious has it become that they can be represented in different phases. Thus the interest of the development of instrumental movements in modern symphonies and sonatas is frequently enhanced by the way in which the subjects are varied when they are reintroduced according to the usual principles of structure ; in operas and similar works ever since Mozart's time characteristic features are made all the more appropriate by adapting them to different situations ; and it is even possible that after all its long history the variation still affords one of the most favourable opportunities for the exercise of their genius by composers of the future.   C. H. H. P.

MODERN VARIATIONS

The prophecy of Sir Hubert Parry's last sentence has been fulfilled ; he himself played no small part in its fulfilment. But the above article was written when the romantic movement in music had reached its height, when the symphonic poem was held to be typical of the modern trend of the art, and adherence to the older and stricter forms was generally regarded as reactionary. It will be noticed that while Parry's estimate of Brahms as a writer of variations is accurate his record of Brahms's achievement is necessarily incomplete. Neither the clarinet quintet nor the fourth symphony were then written and both end with variations. The finale to the symphony in E minor is indeed the apotheosis of the chaconne type which traces its descent from Corelli's ' La folia ' through Bach's violin sonata in D minor. In that finale Brahms brought back into modern music a form which Beethoven had left unexplored and produced a work which may be placed beside Beethoven's Diabelli variations and Bach's Goldberg variations, and in right of which a place may be claimed for Brahms of equal honour with these earlier masters.

Nothing else in the epoch comes within range of this finale for originality of design and masterliness of handling, although several composers made good use of the established form. Dvořák's ' Symphonic Variations ' for orchestra, and the popular set in Tchaikovsky's third suite are noteworthy, but far more important in the latter's output is the ' Tema con variazioni,' followed by ' Variazione finale e coda ' of the trio for pianoforte and strings in A minor (op. 50). This fine work may be held to be the modern counterpart of the Mozart type, just as Brahms's several works are of the Beethoven and Bach types, for Tchaikovsky relies mainly on the capacities of the tune for rhythmic variation as against the German reliance on the harmonic structure. In every one of them the contour of the principal phrase makes its appearance and is instantly recognisable, *e.g.*

Ex. 30. Theme.

Variation II.

Variation III.

Variation VI. *Tempo di Valse.*
Strgs.

Piano. etc.

Variation VIII. *Fuga.*

Variation X. *Tempo di mazurka.*

a method which incorporates the transformation principle of Berlioz and Liszt (see above) with Mozart's method of melodic variation.

It is claimed for César Franck that he was a master of

'la *grande variation*, n'ayant rien de commun disons-le bien vite, avec le " thème varié," qui fit la joie des auditeurs d'Haydn et le tourment des pianistes romantiques, avait été entrevue par J. S. Bach, esprit universel, et quelques très rares compositeurs,' [1]

but it is not easy for those outside the immediate circle of discipleship to see in what way Franck added to the resources of variation form. His 'Variations symphoniques' is a wholly delightful work which employs a good deal of the rhythmic transformation illustrated above from the Tchaikovsky variations and in its rhapsodic treatment of the theme, a composite one, is akin to Schumann. His variation here and elsewhere is generally in the nature of a free development. The use of the term 'Symphonic,' which both Franck and Dvořák adopted, prompts the question, what is the difference between symphonic and other variations ? The answer cannot be very precise. It may be suggested, however, that composers tend to use the qualifying adjective to describe their desire for a greater measure of continuity between the several numbers than

[1] Vincent d'Indy, *César Franck*, p. 61.

the variation form with its clear-cut divisions generally implies. Tchaikovsky's variations in the trio aim primarily at direct contrasts of mood, while Franck's 'Variations symphoniques' grow out of one another. Parry's fine set of 'Symphonic Variations' for orchestra (1897) shows the intention with exceptional clearness, for in them the numbers fall naturally into groups corresponding with the contrasted movements of a symphony, and distinguished by the directions, 'Maestoso energico,' 'Allegretto grazioso,' 'Allegro scherzando vivace' and 'Largo appassionato' leading into a finale which begins 'Moderato' soon to become 'Vivace.' The method is to a certain extent that of Brahms, though the whole flavour of the work, as well as this element in its design, is a very personal contribution to the style.

A further phase of the variation form is that in which the technical method is allied with ideas which bring this strictest of designs within the range of PROGRAMME MUSIC (*q.v.*). Another English example, Elgar's 'Enigma' variations for orchestra (1899), may be pointed to as representative of the new phase. Each one of its fourteen numbers bears initials or other device indicating that it is a character study of a personal friend, and it is said that in addition to the theme which unites their contrasted characteristics there is another theme never heard but with which all are mentally consonant (see ELGAR). Technically the style relates to that of Tchaikovsky for each of the exquisite little miniatures takes its principle of cohesion direct from the simple germs of the tune

Ex. 31.

subjected to a number of rhythmic transformations and combined with counter-subjects. Compare the following, Var. V., with Tchaikovsky's 'Tempo di valse,' quoted from above.

Ex. 32. Vln.

Vol. C.B.

Incidentally it is noticeable that Elgar modifies and weakens the tune in bar 2 to make the counterpoint fit.

This is a consideration by which his masterful contemporary, Richard Strauss, was untroubled in the work which effected the union between the variation form and the symphonic poem, ' Don Quixote (Introduzione, Tema con variazioni e finale) fantastische, Variationen über ein Thema ritterlichen Characters für grosses Orchester ' (op. 35). It actually appeared in the year before Elgar's ' Enigma.' Here the ' programme ' idea takes complete control of the form. It is no mere question of contrasted moods ; the aim is definitely pictorial,[1] but the pictures are arranged in such a way as to accord with the traditions of developing a highly complex theme in a series of variations. Many later examples of the use of the form in one or other of its several aspects might be cited. No composer has applied himself to the form with greater seriousness than Max REGER (q.v.), and his several large sets bring a 20th-century view of harmony and counterpoint to bear on models evolved by Bach and Brahms. Others have recurred to it more sporadically, and it has been adapted to such different psychological situations as are represented by Vaughan Williams's ' Fantasia on a theme by Tallis' and Dohnanyi's ' Variations on a Nursery Song,' the one brooding in an atmosphere of mystical religion, the others sparkling with vivacious humour. But such things hardly mark a further development in the form. The 19th century made the form plastic in the hands of the individual composer, and after ' Don Quixote ' all things are possible.   c.

VARLAMOV, ALEXANDER IGOROVICH (b. Moscow, Nov. 15/27, 1801 ; d. St. Petersburg, Oct. 1848), song-writer, was the son of a nobleman of Moldavian extraction. He entered the court choir as a chorister at ten years of age, and his uncommon abilities soon attracted the attention of Bortniansky. His voice having broken and failing to regain its sweetness and power, he left the Imperial choir in 1819, and was appointed director of the choir of the chapel of the Russian embassy at The Hague, being also attached to the court of the Princess (Anna Pavlovna) of Orange. He returned to Russia in 1823, and settled in Moscow as a teacher. Besides singing, he taught also the violin and the guitar. From 1829–31 Varlamov was again employed in the Imperial court choir as teacher of choral singing. But he soon drifted back to his native town where he now settled once more as a teacher. His first nine songs were published about 1833, and soon became popular. Varlamov died suddenly of heart disease.

[1] It is to be observed, however, that in the score itself only the names of Don Quixote and Sancho Panza attached to themes indicate the pictorial intention. But the variations describing the episodes of the windmills, the flocks of sheep, the penitents, Dulcinea, the ride through the air and the death of the knight would all be sufficiently intelligible to readers of Cervantes without the explanation which has been given by commentators.

The entire collection of his songs, numbering 223, was published by Stellovsky in twelve books. Numerous other editions exist. In style and technical method they are closely allied to the songs of Alabiev. In the majority of them the use of Russian sentiment and colour is very superficial. The most famous is the ' Red Sarafan,' which is often mistaken for a genuine folk-song, and is known all over the world. This air and another one by the same composer (' I saddle the horse ') have been used by Wieniawski in his popular fantasia for violin ' Souvenir de Moscou.'   R. N.

VARNEY, (1) PIERRE JOSEPH ALPHONSE (b. Paris, Dec. 1, 1811 ; d. there, Feb. 7, 1879), was educated at the Conservatoire as a violinist, and was a pupil of Reicha for composition. He was successively conductor at the Théâtre historique and the Théâtre lyrique, at Ghent, The Hague, Rouen, the Bouffes Parisiens, and at Bordeaux (1865–78). Several short operas and operettas of slight construction by him were brought out at the various places where he worked. He is best known as having furnished the music for the celebrated Chant des Girondins, ' Mourir pour la Patrie,' the words of which were by Dumas, and which played so important a part in the revolution of 1848.

His son, (2) LOUIS (b. Paris, c. 1844 ; d. Cauterets, Aug. 20, 1908), wrote upwards of thirty-five operettas, most of them produced with success in Paris from 1876 onwards. The three-act ' Les Forains ' (1894) was given at Vienna in 1895, as ' Olympia,' and in the same year at Berlin as ' Die Gaukler.' ' Le Pompier de service ' (1897) and ' Les Demoiselles de Saint Cyr ' (1898) were very successful (Baker).   M.

VAROTTI (VAROTUS), MICHELE (b. Novara, 16th cent.), canon at Novara Cathedral ; composed masses, Magnificats, Lamentations, etc., between 1563 and 1595 (Fétis ; Q.-L.).

VARSOVIANA, a dance very similar in character to the Polka, Mazurka and Redowa. It is probably of French origin, and seems to have been introduced by a dancing-master named Désiré in 1853. Somewhat later it was much danced at the Tuileries balls, and is said to have been a favourite with the Empress Eugénie. The music is characterised by strong accents on the first notes of the second and fourth bars, corresponding with marked pauses in the dance. The tempo is rather slow. The following is the tune to which the Varsoviana was generally danced :

W. B. S.

VASCELLO FANTASMA, IL, an Italian version of Wagner's FLIEGENDE HOLLÄNDER (*q.v.*).

VASCONCELLOS, JOAQUIM DE, Portuguese historian. His most important work is the biographical dictionary of Portuguese musicians, *Os musicos portuguezes* (1870), in which he corrected many mistakes made by Fétis and others on Portuguese music. He also wrote a life of the 18th-century singer Luiza TODI (*q.v.*) (1873) ; Notes on the Catalogue of the Library of King John IV. (lost in the Lisbon earthquake), and later a facsimile, and commentary (1874-76) and index (1905) of this catalogue, which is of great importance to students of the history of Portuguese and Spanish music.

J. B. T.

VASQUEZ, JUAN (*b.* Badajoz, 16th cent.), Spanish composer, studied at Seville, and is said to have been maestro de capilla at Burgos, though he never describes himself as such in any of his works. His villancicos (3-5 v.) are compositions in which ' the chief singing part ' is often a folk-song, while the other voices supply a contrapuntal background. The melody is repeated over and over again in an unaltered form, as in some of the motets of MORALES, while the other parts are constantly varied. He published

Villancicos i Canciones de Iuan Vasquez, a 3 y a 4. Osuna, 1551. Partbooks. (Madrid, Bibl. Medinaceli.)
Recopilación de sonetos y villancicos a 4 y a 5 de Iuan Vasquez. Seville, 1560   Partbooks.   (Madrid : Bibl. Medinaceli.)

Transcriptions and other arrangements for the *vihuela* (Spanish lute) are found in the tablature-books of Daza, Enriquez, Fuenllana, Milan and Pisador. He also published :

Agenda Defunctorum. Seville, 1556. (Barcelona, Bibl. de la Diputació.)

J. B. T.

VASSILENKO, SERGIUS NIKIPHOROVICH (*b.* Moscow, 1872), Russian composer. After taking up law at the university, he entered the Conservatoire in 1896, where he studied under S. Taneiev and Ippolytov-Ivanov. In his last year (1901) he was awarded a gold medal for his cantata ' The Legend of the City of Kitezh,' which he remodelled as an opera, afterwards produced at the Private Opera, Moscow, of which he was the conductor. He organised and conducted a series of Historical Concerts in connexion with the Imperial Russian Music Society. He was appointed professor at the Moscow Conservatoire.

Vassilenko's early works were very interesting, and suggested that, breaking away from the Tchaikovsky tradition, he might create an original style of his own. His ' Legend of Kitezh ' and the ' Epic Poem ' for orchestra show a profound knowledge of the old Russian church music and are penetrated by a mediæval and mystical atmosphere. His symphony in E minor, op. 10, shows a departure from the national style, and in the symphonic poem based on Oscar Wilde's ' The Garden of Death,' he enters upon a period of complete reaction from the religious and archaic tendencies of his youth. His suite ' Au Soleil,' which discloses the influence of the French impressionists, was produced by Sir Henry J. Wood, at a Promenade Concert, Sept. 11, 1917. Vassilenko's works comprise :

2 symphonies, E min., op. 10, and F maj., op. 22 ; epic poem for orchestra, op. 4 ; 2 symphonic poems, ' The Garden of Death,' op. 12, and ' Hyrcus Nocturnus ' (The Witches' Flight), op. 15 ; suite for orchestra, ' Au Soleil,' op. 17 ; violin concerto, op. 14 ; songs and incidental music.

R. N.

VATERLÄNDISCHE KÜNSTLER-VEREIN (Society of Artists of the Fatherland), a name which has become famous through Beethoven's op. 120. ' The Fatherland ' here means Austria.

Schindler (*Life of Beethoven*, ii. 34) says that in the winter of 1822–23, the publishing firm of DIABELLI (*q.v.*) in Vienna formed a plan for issuing a collective set of variations for the pianoforte. No fewer than fifty-one composers, among whom were the first Viennese masters of the time,[1] consented to contribute to the collection, which was published in two large oblong books (Nos. 1380-81) under the title of

' Vaterländische Künstlerverein, Veränderungen über ein vorgelegtes Thema, componirt von den vorzüglichsten Tonsetzern und Virtuosen Wiens und der k. k. österreichischen Staaten.' [2]

It is an indication of the position held by Beethoven among the musicians of Vienna, that the whole of the first book is taken up with his variations, thirty-three in number, while the other fifty composers are represented by a single variation each. Beethoven's composition has the separate title :

' 33 Veränderungen über einen Walzer für das Pianoforte componirt und der Frau Antonia von Brentano, gebornen Edlen von Birkenstock, hochachtungsvoll zugeeignet von Ludwig van Beethoven. 120 Werk. Wien bey Cappi und Diabelli.'

(For a full discussion of it, see VARIATIONS, subsection DIABELLI VARIATIONS ANALYSED.) The work was published in June 1823. On the 16th of the month an elaborate advertisement [3] appeared in the *Österreichisch-kaiserliche priviligirte Wiener Zeitung.*

The original manuscript of op. 120, formerly in the possession of C. A. Spina, subsequently in that of Dr. Steger of Vienna, was offered for sale at 42,000 marks (£2100) by Karl W. Hiersemann of Leipzig and in the *Zeitschrift* of the Int. Mus. Ges. of Sept. 1908. Interesting information concerning the sketches for the composition is given in Nottebohm's *Zweite Beethoveniana*, Leipzig, 1887. Beethoven was fond of presenting copies of the printed work to his friends, and the writer possesses two such copies with autograph dedications.

The second book of the variations appeared in the latter half of 1823 or early in 1824.

[1] It is curious that the names of Seyfried and Weigl are not in the list.
[2] Society of Artists of the Fatherland. Variations on a given theme, written by the most prominent composers and performers of Vienna and the Imperial States of Austria.
[3] It was quoted in former editions of this Dictionary. It is merely a eulogy of Beethoven's handling of the variation form.

Anton Diabelli, the composer and publisher, had meanwhile dissolved partnership with Cappi, and the name of the firm was now ' A. Diabelli & Co.' As in the first book (Beethoven's portion) so here the theme by Diabelli precedes the variations. It consists of thirty-two bars, and, although of slight importance in itself, is well fitted for variation-writing. The waltz is followed by fifty variations :

(1) Ignatz Assmayer ; (2) Carl Maria von Bocklet ; (3) Leopold Eustache Czapek ; (4) Carl Czerny ; (5) Joseph Czerny ; (6) Moritz Graf Dietrichstein [1] ; (7) Joseph Drechsler ; (8) A. Emanuel Förster (' his last composition ') ; (9) Jakob Freystaedtler ; (10) Johann Gänsbacher ; (11) Abbé Gelinek ; (12) Anton Halm ; (13) Joachim Hoffmann ; (14) Johann Horzalka ; (15) Joseph Hugelmann ; (16) J. N. Hummel ; (17) Anselm Hüttenbrenner ; (18) Frederic Kalkbrenner (' written during his stay in Vienna ') ; (19) Friedrich August Kanne ; (20) Joseph Kerzkowsky ; (21) Conradin Kreutzer ; (22) Eduard Baron von Lannoy ; (23) M. J. Leidesdorf ; (24) Franz Liszt (' a boy of eleven years old, born in Hungary ') ; (25) Joseph Mayseder ; (26) Ignatz Moscheles ; (27) Ignatz F. Edler von Mosel ; (28) W. A. Mozart *fils* ; (29) Joseph Panny ; (30) Hieronymus Payer ; (31) J. P. Pixis ; (32) Wenzel Plachy ; (33) Gottfried Rieger ; (34) P. J. Riotte ; (35) Franz Rozer ; (36) Johann Schenk ; (37) Frank Schoberlechner ; (38) Franz Schubert ; (39) Simon Sechter (' Imitatio quasi Canon a tre voci ') ; (40) S. R. D. ; (41) Abbé Stadler ; (42) Joseph de Szalay ; (43) Wenzel Tomaschek ; (44) Michael Umlauf ; (45) Fr. Dionysius Weber ; (46) Franz Weber ; (47) Ch. A. de Winkhler ; (48) Franz Weiss ; (49) Johann Wittassek ; (50) J. H. Worzischek.

A long coda by Carl Czerny is appended to the variations. The MS. of Schubert's variation, No. 38, which is in the Imperial Library of Vienna, bears the date Mar. 1821. According to this the later date given by Schindler for the inception of the plan must be incorrect.

M. F.

VAUCORBEIL, AUGUSTE EMMANUEL (real name, VEAUCORBEILLE) (*b.* Rouen, Dec. 15, 1821 ; *d.* Nov. 2, 1884), composer, was the son of an actor long a favourite at the Gymnase under the name of Ferville.

Vaucorbeil entered the Paris Conservatoire in 1835, where he was patronised by Queen Marie Amélie, who made him an allowance. Here he studied seven years, Dourlen being his master for harmony, while Cherubini gave him some advice on composition. He took the second solfeggio prize in 1838. His first publication was twenty - two songs, of which ' Simple Chanson ' had some success at the time. His chamber music—two string quartets, some sonatas for PF. and violin, and one for viola, and two suites for PF—was well spoken of by J. d'Ortigue in the *Journal des Débats*. He wrote a three-act opéra-comique, ' La Bataille d'Amour ' (Apr. 13, 1863), and a *scena* with chorus, ' La Mort de Diane,' sung by Mme. Krauss at a Conservatoire concert (1870). Of an unpublished opera, ' Mahomet,' we know only some fragments played in 1877, but, as far as we can judge, the qualities required for success on the stage were not possessed by Vaucorbeil. In 1871 he became professor of vocal ensemble at the Conservatoire, and in 1872 accepted the post of Government commissary of the subsidised theatres. In 1878 he

obtained the title of Inspector des Beaux-Arts, and soon after was made director of the Opéra for seven years, entering on his functions by agreement with Halanzier, July 16, 1879.

G. C. ; rev. M. L. P.

VAUDEVILLE, a French word, which has had successively four meanings : (1) a popular song, generally satirical ; (2) couplets inserted in a play ; (3) the play itself ; and lastly (4) a theatre for plays of this kind, with songs. Most etymologists derive the word from Vaux de Vire, the name given to songs sung in the valleys (*vaux*) near Vire by a certain fuller and song-writer named Olivier Basselin, who was probably born at Vire at the end of the 14th or beginning of the 15th century. His songs were collected and published in 1610 by an *avocat* named Jean le Houx.[2] They contain such lines as these :

> ' Faisant l'amour, je ne saurais rien dire
> Ni rien chanter, sinon un *vau de vire*.'

Others [3] maintain that vaudeville comes from *voix de ville*, quoting as their authority the ' Recueil des plus belles et excellentes chansons en forme de voix de villes ' (Paris, 1575) by Jean Chardavoine, a musician of Anjou, but we, with Ménage, prefer the former derivation. It is at any rate certain that the word ' vaudeville ' was employed by writers in the 16th century to denote a song sung about the town, with a catching tune. Many lampoons, such as the *Mazarinades*, are vaudevilles. The word was used in this sense for some time, as is evident from a passage from Rousseau's *Confessions* ;

' A complete collection of the vaudevilles of the court and of Paris for over fifty years, contains a host of anecdotes which might be sought in vain elsewhere, and supplies materials for a history of France, such as no other nation could produce.'

It was about 1700 that the mere street-song passed into ' topical ' verses in a dramatic piece. The plays at the fairs of St. Germain and St. Laurent contained vaudevilles, generally adapted to well - known tunes so as to ensure their immediate popularity. Occasionally fresh music was written for them, and the vaudevilles composed by Joseph Mouret (a Provençal, called by his contemporaries ' le musicien des Graces '), Gillier, Quinault the elder and Blavet had great success in their day.

The next step was to conclude the play with a *vaudeville finale*, in which each character sang a verse in turn. Of this Beaumarchais's *Mariage de Figaro* (1784) gives a well-known example.

The rage for vaudevilles gave rise to pieces entirely in verse and parodies of operas, and largely contributed to the creation of the opéra-comique. To distinguish between these different

---

[1] The Graf Dietrichstein, mentioned under No. 6, was the leading aristocratic musician of the time. Schubert's ' Erlkönig ' is dedicated to him. The initials S. R. D. under No. 40 probably indicate the name of some other aristocratic amateur.

[2] The *Vaux de Vire of Jean Le Houx of Vire* were published in English by J. P. Muirhead (London, 1875).

[3] See Fétis, *Biographie*, under ' Leroy,' p. 280b.

classes of pieces the name *comédies à ariettes* was given to what are now called opéras-comiques, and the others became successively ' pièces en vaudevilles,' ' comédies mêlées de vaudevilles,' then 'comédies vaudevilles ' and finally 'vaudevilles.'

It is thus evident that the word would afford material for a book embracing some most curious chapters in the history of French dramatic literature ; for the vaudeville includes all styles—the comedy of intrigue, scenes of domestic life, village pieces, *tableaux* of passing events, parodies and so forth. It was therefore natural that from having found a home wherever it could, it should at last have a special house erected for it. The Théâtre du Vaudeville was built in 1792, on the site of a dancing-saloon called 'Vauxhall d'hiver ' or the ' Petit Panthéon,' between the Rue de Chartres and the Rue St. Thomas du Louvre, on the site of the Hôtel Rambouillet and on ground now occupied by the Galerie Septentrionale, and by a part of the new court of the Louvre. This theatre was burnt down in 1838, when the company removed to the Théâtre des Nouveautés, in the Place de la Bourse. This new Théâtre du Vaudeville having disappeared in its turn was replaced by the house in the Boulevard des Capucines, at the corner of the Rue de la Chaussée d'Antin. We cannot enumerate here the authors who have contributed to its success ; suffice it to say that *vaudeville*, born so to speak simultaneously with the French Revolution, crystallised into one of the most characteristic forms of the old French ' esprit ' ; that later, as has been justly remarked, it launched boldly into all the speculations of modern thought, from the historic plays of Ancelot and Rozier, and the Aristophanesque satires of 1848, down to the works— as remarkable for variety as for intense realism —of Émile Augier, Dumas fils, Théodore Barrière, Octave Feuillet, Georges Sand and Victorien Sardou.

This last period, so interesting from a literary and philosophical point of view, is, musically, wellnigh barren, while the early days of vaudeville were enlivened by the flowing and charming inspirations of Chardin (or Chardiny) and Wecht, Doche (father and son), Henri Blanchard and others less known. Most of the vaudevilles composed by these musicians are to be found in ' La Clé du caveau ' (1st ed., 1807 ; 4th and most complete, 1872). The airs are in notation without accompaniment. In the library of the Paris Conservatoire is a MS. collection of vaudevilles in eighteen volumes, with an index, made by Henri Blanchard. These have an accompaniment for four strings.

The comédie vaudeville or vaudeville proper has now been abandoned for the comédie de genre, but it is not improbable that it may be revived. At any rate the couplet is not likely

to die in a land where, as Beaumarchais said, everything ends with a song. Since his day manners in France have, it is true, greatly changed, but the taste for light, amusing, satirical verses with a catching refrain remains, and is likely to remain. Unfortunately the vaudeville, in the old sense of the word, has taken refuge in the café concerts, where the music is generally indifferent and the words poor, if not objectionable. Occasionally in the revues at the small Paris theatres a smart and witty vaudeville may still be heard.   G. C.

BIBL.—LUDWIG KRAUS, *Das deutsche Liederspiel in den Jahren 1800–30* (Halle Dissertation, 1921).

VAUGHAN, THOMAS (*b.* Norwich, 1782 ; *d.* Birmingham, Jan. 9, 1843), tenor singer, was a chorister of Norwich Cathedral under Dr. BECKWITH (*q.v.*). In June 1799 he was elected a lay-clerk of St. George's Chapel, Windsor. On May 28, 1803, he was admitted a gentleman of the Chapel Royal, and about the same time obtained the appointments of vicar-choral of St. Paul's and lay-vicar of Westminster Abbey. In Mar. 1806 he resigned his place at Windsor and in the same year married Miss Tennant, who had appeared as a soprano singer about 1797, and from 1800 had sung at the Concert of Ancient Music and the provincial festivals, for some years occupying a good position. In 1813 Vaughan was chosen to succeed Samuel HARRISON (*q.v.*) as principal tenor at the Concert of Ancient Music and the provincial festivals, which position he occupied for more than a quarter of a century. His voice was a genuine tenor, the deficiency of natural power in which was concealed by purity of tone, great distinctness of pronunciation and faultlessness of intonation. Vaughan sang the tenor part in Beethoven's Ninth Symphony on its production by the Philharmonic Society, London, Mar. 21, 1825. He was buried Jan. 17, 1843, in the west cloister of Westminster Abbey.

W. H. H.

VAUGHAN WILLIAMS, RALPH (*b.* Down Ampney, Gloucestershire, Oct. 12, 1872), composer, son of the Rev. Arthur Vaughan Williams, was educated at Charterhouse (1887–1890) and Trinity College, Cambridge (1892–1895).

The two years between school and university (1890–92) were spent in musical study at the R.C.M. Vaughan Williams took the degree of B.Mus. at Cambridge while still an undergraduate (1894), and returned to the R.C.M. for further study, 1895–96. Composition was always his main object ; he studied with Charles Wood at Cambridge and with Parry and Stanford at the R.C.M. He also learnt the organ from Alan Gray at Cambridge and Parratt at the R.C.M., and the piano, merely as a necessary acquisition, from other teachers at the R.C.M. The piano has indeed had as little influence on his output as it is possible for that all-pervading instrument to have on a composer of to-day. The organ has had a little more; he held an organistship (South Lambeth Church) for three years after leaving the R.C.M., but they were not years in which he was shut up to the organ loft, for during part of that time he was in Berlin studying at the Akademie der Künste and taking composition lessons from Max Bruch. The organistship may have shown Vaughan Williams how great was the need for a fine tune to Bishop Walsham How's hymn 'For all the Saints.' Certainly it contributed some valuable experiences when at a later date (1905–06) he undertook the musical editorship of 'The English Hymnal.' His 'Sine Nomine'[1] written for that work is one of the noblest melodies of English hymnody. Amongst his published compositions are 'Three preludes for organ, founded on Welsh Tunes,' and certain other organ works of his have been played from MS. Their style, however, does not suggest that they are the outcome of a close practical acquaintance with the instrument.

The fact that he was not faced with the immediate necessity for earning a living may have retarded his development or have made it possible. He was not forced to equip himself quickly with a serviceable technique either as composer or performer. At the R.C.M. he belonged to a generation which included Coleridge Taylor, William Hurlstone and Gustav Holst, and his compositions there certainly made less mark than those of these contemporaries. He visited Bayreuth in 1896 and there heard Wagner practically for the first time. After he left the R.C.M. he was comparatively free to extend his period of studentship according to inclination and for a time he undertook little in the way of executive work beyond the organistship already mentioned and some lecturing on music for the University Extension. He was profoundly dissatisfied with his own efforts as a composer, and most of his work of that time has been withdrawn or withheld from publication. He found that the music he had been taught alike in England and in Germany did not enable him to say what he wanted to say. He took his D.Mus. degree at Cambridge in 1901; the fact may be named as marking the end of his scholastic career.

At about that time he began to discover the language of the English folk-song and to make it his own. He was not an original member of the FOLK-SONG SOCIETY (q.v.) founded in 1899, but he joined it in 1904. His own songs written at about that time, of which 'Linden Lee' is typical, show clearly the modal and rhythmic influences of the folk-song. But more than that, from the folk-song has sprung that style which Vaughan Williams has evolved for himself, a style in which vocal melodies are

[1] English Hymnal, No. 641.

woven in a polyphony which at times seems recklessly oblivious of harmonic consequences.

In No. 7 of the Folk-song Society's Journal there are, amongst many others, a number of tunes noted by Vaughan Williams at King's Lynn, Norfolk, in Jan. 1905. The result of these researches was something more practical than the recovery of half-forgotten melodies and their bestowal in an antiquarian pigeon-hole. On his folk-song excursions Vaughan Williams lived in the country and among the people. The orchestral 'Impression,' 'In the Fen Country,' and the three 'Norfolk Rhapsodies' for orchestra were the result. The latter take their thematic material from some of the finest and most diversified of the folk-tunes he gathered, but whereas in many essays of a similar kind by his contemporaries the tunes have the character of quotations amongst more or less extraneous matter, in Vaughan Williams's rhapsodies the idiom of the tunes chosen permeates the whole melodic outline, and decides the harmonic structure. 'In the Fen Country' claims no folk-song origin; it is the first of many works, of which the 'Pastoral' symphony (1922) is the greatest example, in which Vaughan Williams's creative power seems to have been set free by his converse with the folk-singer. He did not adopt the folk-song manner as a conscious nationalistic pose; he merely found at King's Lynn his own musical language, for which he had searched the schools of London and Berlin in vain.

A natural corollary to this was Vaughan Williams's interest and active participation in the spread of the COMPETITION FESTIVALS (q.v.) throughout the country. The Leith Hill (Dorking) Festival has been from its foundation under his personal care.[2] Started as a village institution it has grown into a four days' festival in which competition and practice lead to excellent performances by combined choirs and instrumentalists, but Vaughan Williams's horror of the sophistication by which excessive organisation destroys artistic impulse has kept it simple. In all his activities he has refused to be bound by material restrictions. The fact that a work of his own is published will not prevent his altering a passage, and if he writes a programme note[3] to a new work his chief desire seems to be to avoid giving his hearers a cut and dried interpretation of his musical thought.

The successful production at the Leeds Festival (1907) of Vaughan Williams's first important work for choir and orchestra, 'Toward the Unknown Region,' inevitably brought him some of the responsibilities and trammels of publicity. He was marked down as a 'coming composer,' and 'A Sea Symphony,' at the

[2] There is no record of the Leith Hill festival in the Year Book (1925) of the British Federation of Musical Competition Festivals.
[3] See his notes to 'Flos campi.' New Queen's Hall Orchestra Symphony Concert, Oct. 10, 1925.

next festival (1910) declared his arrival. The latter work, however, was not undertaken as successor to the former. The large-hearted aspiration and the rugged speech of Walt Whitman had captured his imagination at an earlier date. He made up his mind that Whitman was the poet for him, just as, when he first heard 'Bushes and Briars,' he had 'said to himself that that was the music for him.'[1] The setting of poems from *Leaves of Grass* had been in his mind at least from 1903, and the composition of 'A Sea Symphony' occupied some six years from that date. 'Toward the Unknown Region' may be regarded as an essay in the direction of the larger work and a comparison of it with the finale of the symphony called 'The Explorers,' shows at once the similarity of mood and aim. Two influences apart from those already named are discernible as concomitants in the individual style of these choral works; they are Purcell and Parry. Vaughan Williams had been editing the 'Welcome Odes' of the former for the PURCELL SOCIETY (*q.v.*) during the years of the Sea Symphony's gestation, and something of Purcell's declamatory directness is felt in the symphony, notably in the first baritone solo. Parry's manner of marshalling the choral masses in exuberant contrapuntal climaxes was in the blood of the Yorkshire festivals. Its presence here needs no accounting for.

Very different from the massive style of these choral works is the intimate cycle of six songs for tenor voice, string quartet, and PF., 'On Wenlock Edge' (from Housman's poems *A Shropshire Lad*) first sung by Gervase Elwes in London on Nov. 15, 1909. Its production followed a time spent by Vaughan Williams in Paris for the purpose of study with Maurice Ravel; consequently every one was prepared to find that his work had become 'Frenchified,' and many declared that they found what they expected, and attributed what was new in 'On Wenlock Edge' to Ravel. Never was a critical shaft more ill-directed. Abroad and in Paris itself this was the work which first called attention to Vaughan Williams as a new voice and a very English one. Its English qualities were only unrecognisable at first by Londoners, because they had forgotten their native musical language. Vaughan Williams's personal faith on the vexed question of nationality in art has been succinctly stated in an essay which he wrote for a students' magazine in 1912. There he took to task the British composer's acquisitiveness and condemned 'the desire to "do it too" whenever the newest thing comes over from abroad.'[2] His recourse to Ravel as a teacher had nothing to do with acquiring

Ravel's personal style for future reproduction. His self-criticism had told him while he was in the act of fashioning 'A Sea Symphony' that his own technique was still clumsy and inchoate. He went to the man whose suppleness of mind could help him to clear away what was stodgy and incommunicative in his own. He came back with his powers of expression clarified.

The works produced at a series of Three Choirs Festivals, that is to say the Fantasia on a theme by Tallis[3] for strings (Gloucester 1910), the Five Mystical Songs (Herbert) for baritone solo,[4] choir and orchestra (Worcester 1911) and the Fantasia on Christmas Carols also for baritone solo,[5] choir and orchestra (Hereford 1912) are all fraught with that quality of inward reflection which marks Vaughan Williams's art as something distinct from the strident appeal to the senses so characteristic of most modern music, but his reflections are not detached from common life; it is indeed the common life which generates them. Even when he joins hands with George Herbert in the Mystical Songs his music assumes no pose of cloistral devotion; it remains homely like Herbert's verse.

The music to *The Wasps* of Aristophanes, from which an orchestral suite has been made and the overture from which has been much played, was a contribution to that free and easy presentation of Greek drama which is characteristic of the English Universities (see GREEK PLAYS, MUSIC TO). Incidentally it served to bring Vaughan Williams into touch with the requirements of the theatre. Two much larger works were to complete this period of his career as composer, his first purely orchestral symphony and his first opera. 'A London Symphony' received its first performance on Mar. 27, 1914, when it was conducted by Geoffrey Toye at one of a series of concerts given by F. B. Ellis (a keen amateur musician), for the purpose of bringing forward music, particularly native works, which the regular concert-giving institutions tended to neglect. Vaughan Williams was by this time in no way dependent for a hearing on such a special occasion as this, but he was heart and soul with the younger men, who indeed regarded him as a leader; he allowed his symphony to be produced in these conditions and under a comparatively untried conductor, preferring the enthusiasm of friends to the more public *réclame* which might have been secured elsewhere. The symphony was well played and well received, but no immediate repetition was called for, and it was not heard again until 1918 when Adrian Boult gave it with the London Symphony Orchestra. Its real life began with its publication by the Carnegie Trust, and by that time the

[1] *Music and Letters*, vol. i. p. 84. Article on Vaughan Williams by A. H. Fox Strangways, in which many of the earlier works are analysed.
[2] *R.C.M. Magazine*, vol. 9, No. 1. 'Who wants the British Composer?' by R. Vaughan Williams.

[3] Third mode melody. *English Hymnal*, No. 92.
[4] Sung by Campbell McInnes at the first performance.
[5] *Ibid.*

composer had made very extensive alterations[1] in the score, cutting out the second trio of the scherzo and considerably condensing the finale.

The question has been raised as to how far 'A London Symphony' is to be regarded as 'programme' music, since the composer has claimed a purely subjective intention while including a number of objective details, such as the Westminster chimes, the cry of the lavender seller, the jingle of bells on a hansom cab, and the suggestion of a mouth organ or concertina. Without discussing the question here we may quote again from the article already alluded to a passage which seems to bear directly on the case.

'Have not we all about us forms of musical expression which we can take and purify and raise to the level of great art ? For instance, the lilt of the chorus at a music-hall joining in a popular song, the children dancing to a barrel organ, the rousing fervour of a Salvation Army hymn, St. Paul's and a great choir singing in one of its festivals, the Welshmen striking up one of their own hymns whenever they win a goal at an international football match, the cries of the street pedlars, the factory girls singing their sentimental songs. Have all these nothing to say to us ?'[2]

In 'A London Symphony' Vaughan Williams has shown how much such things have to say to him, while the work viewed from the formal side draws its strength from the balanced structure of the classical type (see SYMPHONY, p. 241).

The quotation may also serve to show why Vaughan Williams had the ambition to write an opera in which an English boxing-match was the central feature of the action. He found a sympathetic librettist in Harold Child, and 'Hugh the Drover,' a work brimming with the life of the English countryside, expressed in frank untiring melody,[3] was the result. Composer and librettist worked together, and the published score describes it as 'a romantic ballad opera in two acts by Harold Child and R. Vaughan Williams.' Though mainly written and composed between 1911–14 it had to wait for completion, publication and presentation until after the war.

In 1914 Vaughan Williams, at the age of 42 entered the army as an orderly in the Territorial R.A.M.C. In this corps he served in Macedonia 1916–17, was recommended for a commission in the Artillery, and after a course in Heavy Gunnery in England served in France through the campaign of 1918 as Lieutenant R.G.A. Besides the break in his personal career which these facts indicate, the change in musical conditions at home wrought by these years made his position on his return a very different one. He had been a leader of the young men and several of the best of his group

had been killed. The older generation of musicians, too, was passing away. Allen had succeeded Parry as Director of the Royal College of Music and was quick to secure Vaughan Williams as teacher of composition amongst the staff which had to be re-formed. He soon became a member of the Board of Professors there, and also succeeded Allen in 1920 as conductor of the London Bach choir. These activities he still (1927) pursues, and since the death of Cecil Sharp he has directed the music of the English Folk-dance Society.

In 1920 the first annual congress of the newly formed BRITISH MUSIC SOCIETY (q.v.) chose 'A London Symphony' as the chief native work for presentation, and a fine performance of it was given at Queen's Hall (May 4) under Albert Coates. In the gradual revival of the several provincial festivals Vaughan Williams's vocal works took a place of increasing importance, the 'Sea Symphony' especially. Continental musicians increased their knowledge of his music through its performances at the congresses of the INTERNATIONAL SOCIETY FOR CONTEMPORARY MUSIC (q.v.), and, moreover, several English conductors, Wood,[4] Boult, Coates and others, gave it in their programmes in various continental cities. The first new work of first-rate importance to appear was the 'Pastoral Symphony,' given under Adrian Boult by the Royal Philharmonic Society (Queen's Hall, Jan. 26, 1922). In the following year Vaughan Williams accepted the invitation of Mr. Stoechel to visit America and produce this symphony at the Norfolk Conn. Festival.

The opera 'Hugh the Drover' was taken up by the R.C.M., which undertook the cost of publication and its production in the theatre equipped by the Council in memory of Parry. It was given there in a series of 'dress rehearsals' in July 1924, and while the preparation of these was in progress the British National Opera Company decided on its public presentation, and brought it out (His Majesty's Theatre, July 14, 1924) aided by facilities offered by the R.C.M. Since then the B.N.O.C. has performed it in most of the larger cities of Great Britain in which the company tours.

Previously (1922) the R.C.M. had produced on its own stage another operatic essay, 'The Shepherds of the Delectable Mountains,' a scene from the *Pilgrim's Progress*, which may be grouped with the 'Pastoral Symphony,' and the splendid Mass in G minor *a cappella* (first performed by R. R. Terry at Westminster Cathedral in 1923)[5] as representative of Vaughan Williams's mind in composition after the break which the war had caused. 'The Shepherds' is

---

[1] The original version was analysed by G. S. Kaye Butterworth in a programme note to the first performance. The published score is dedicated to his memory.

[2] *R.C.M. Magazine*, vol. 9, No. 1.

[3] There are allusions to nine traditional tunes in 'Hugh the Drover.' Most of them are no more than allusions, and all are quite subsidiary to the purely original music.

[4] Sir Henry Wood gave 'A London Symphony' in his programmes of the 'Bowl' concerts in California, 1924–25.

[5] At Westminster it was sung liturgically. The Mass has been frequently heard in concert performances. It has been given at Leipzig in the Thomas-Kirche by STRAUBE (q.v.).

no 'opera' in the generally received sense of the term ; it is a dialogue *en tableau*. Were it not for its stage setting it might have been called an oratorio with at least as much appropriateness as attaches to the use of that term in connexion with 'Sancta Civitas,' Vaughan Williams's latest (1925) work for solo voices, choir and orchestra. The two are indeed alike in their subject-matter, since it is the far-off vision of the Holy City as the Pilgrim approaches which gives the chief occasion for music to 'The Shepherds of the Delectable Mountains.' The choice of subjects for these works ('Sancta Civitas' is the Apocalyptic vision) and the general tone and manner of the treatment shows the deepening of that mystical side of Vaughan Williams's nature manifested earlier in the Herbert songs and in the Tallis Fantasia. But all these works, and not least the 'Pastoral Symphony' which had no literary subject and is purely orchestral,[1] show a style matured, unified and in a sense simplified. It may be that certain harmonic devices, the parallel fifths and 'false relations,' are inclined sometimes to stiffen into mannerisms. But such incidents apart, it is the very personal quality of all this music which gives it its peculiar eloquence. The suggestions from without, the influences of folk-song and of modal polyphony, have become assimilated, and each work as it appears shows something more of the man. Moreover, to place side by side such contrasted works as 'The Shepherds' and the ballet 'Old King Cole' is to realise at once to what diverse purposes of seriousness and of fun the Vaughan Williams idiom is amenable.[2] This is not the place for analysis [3] nor, happily, has the time come for a summary of Vaughan Williams's output. Of the latest phase of his art, however, including the strangely attractive suite 'Flos campi' for viola, voices and orchestra, and the 'Concerto Accademico,' a thoroughly unacademic work for violin and orchestra, it may be said that it is the fulfilment of the earlier ; it holds the attention in a distracted age as the work of one who has admitted no distraction from his course, and who steers 'for the deep waters only.'

Works by Vaughan Williams, including particulars of first productions :

CHORAL

'Toward the Unknown Region' (Whitman). (Leeds Fest., 1907.)
'Willow Wood' (Rossetti). Baritone solo, women's voices, orch. (Comp. 1903, Mus. League Fest., Liverpool, 1909.)
'A Sea Symphony' (Whitman). Sop. and baritone soli, ch. and orch. (Leeds Fest., 1910.)
Five Mystical Songs (Herbert). Baritone solo, ch. and orch. (Worcester Fest., 1911.)
Fantasia on Christmas Carols. Baritone solo, ch. and orch. (Hereford Fest., 1912.)

---

[1] There is a sort of chant or cantilation for soprano or tenor voice in the finale which may be played alternatively on the clarinet.
[2] These two works were given together in the operatic performances organised by Napier MILES (*q.v.*) in the Theatre Royal, Bristol, Oct. 1926.
[3] An analytical study of the 'Pastoral Symphony' by Herbert HOWELLS will be found in *Music and Letters*, vol. iii. No. 2.

Motets. 'O Praise the Lord.' Double choir. (London Church Choirs Ass., St. Paul's Cathedral, 1913.)
'O clap your hands.' Ch., brass and organ.
'Lord, Thou hast been our refuge.' Ch., semi-ch., orch. (or organ).
Mass in G minor. (Westminster Cathedral, 1923.)
'Sancta Civitas' (The Holy City), an oratorio. Words from the Authorized Version, with additions from Taverner's Bible and other sources. Ten. and baritone soli, ch., semi-ch. and orch. (Oxford, May 7, 1926, and in London by the Bach Choir, June 9, 1926).
Partsongs, choral arrangements of English folk-songs, carols, etc.

ORCHESTRAL

Serenade. Small orch. (Bournemouth, 1901.)
Bucolic Suite. (Bournemouth, 1902.)
Two Orchestral Impressions : (1) 'Harnham Down' ; (2) 'Boldrewood.' (Queen's Hall, 1907.)
Three Norfolk Rhapsodies : No. 1 (Queen's Hall Promenade, 1906); Nos. 2 and 3 (Cardiff Fest. 1907.)
Symphonic Impression, 'In the Fen Country.'
Fantasia on a Theme by Tallis. Strings. (Queen's Hall, Beecham, 1909 ; Gloucester Fest., 1910.)
'A London Symphony.' (G. Toye, Queen's Hall, 1914 ; rev. version, B.M.S., A. Coates conducting, Queen's Hall, May 4, 1920.)
'The Lark ascending.' Romance. Vln. and orch. (Comp. 1914, first perf., B.M.S., vln. Marie Hall, A. Boult conducting, Queen's Hall, June 14, 1921.)
'A Pastoral Symphony.' (R. Philh., A. Boult, Queen's Hall, Jan. 26, 1922.)
Suite, 'Flos campi.' Viola solo, small orch., including voices. (Queen's Hall, Tertis viola, Wood conducting, Oct. 10, 1925.)
Concerto Accademico. Vln. and orch. (Aeolian Hall, vln. Jelly D'Aranyi, Anthony Bernard conducting, Nov. 6, 1925.)

STAGE WORKS

Choruses and Incidental Music to *Paris Anniversary* (Ben Jonson) (Stratford-on-Avon, 1905.)
Incidental Music, *The Wasps* (Aristophanes). (Cambridge. 1909.)
'The Shepherds of the Delectable Mountains,' a scene from *The Pilgrim's Progress*, set as an opera in one act. (R.C.M., 1922.)
Ballet. 'Old King Cole.' (Cambridge, 1923.)
'Hugh the Drover,' ballad opera in 2 acts, libretto by Harold Child (Comp. 1911–14, produced privately R.C.M. 1924, in public by B.N.O.C., M. Sargent conducting, His Majesty's Theatre, London, July 14, 1924.)

CHAMBER MUSIC

Quintet, PF. and strings in C minor.
Quartet for strings in G minor.
Fantasy Quintet for strings.

'On Wenlock Edge' (Housman, *A Shropshire Lad*). A cycle of songs for tenor voice, string quartet, and PF. (London, 1909.)
'Four Hymns' for tenor voice and stringed orch. or PF. with viola obb. (Worcester Fest., 1920.)
Many songs, including 'The House of Life' (6 sonnets of Rossetti) ; 'Songs of Travel' (Stevenson), two vols. ; three Rondels, 'Merciless Beautee.'

C.

VAUTOR, THOMAS, one of the latest of the English madrigal composers, published in 1619 :

'The *First Set* : Beeing Songs of diuers Ayres and Natures, of Fiue and Sixe parts : Apt for *Vyols* and *Voyces* . . . London : Printed by *Thomas Snodham*, for *Matthew Lownes* and *Iohn Browne*.'

In the Dedication to George Villiers, Marquess (afterwards Duke) of Buckingham, the composer tells his patron that he was

'an indiuiduall appendant of your . . . noble Mothers house and name,'

and says of his songs that

'some were composed in your tender yeares, and in your most worthy Fathers house, (from whom, and your most honourable Mother, for many yeares, I receiued part of my meanes and liuelyhoode).'

From this it seems that Vautor must have been a domestic musician in the house of Sir George Villiers (the father of Buckingham) and his wife. She was Mary, daughter of Anthony Beaumont of Glenfield, Leicestershire, and before her marriage had been a waiting-woman in the household of her cousin, Lady Beaumont (of Cole Orton) ; another member of which branch of the Beaumont family was Sir Thomas Beaumont of Stoughton (*d.* 1614) ; his death is celebrated by Vautor in

'An Elegie, on the death of his right worshipfull Master, Sir Thomas *Beaumont*, Knight of Stoughton in Leicestershire.'

Sir George Villiers died in 1606, and after his

death Lady Villiers lived with her sons at Goadby, a village in the north-eastern corner of the county: this connexion with both Stoughton and Goadby entitles Vautor to be regarded as a Leicestershire musician. The only other biographical details that are known about him are that on May 11, 1616, he was dispensed for not hearing the lectures of the 'praelector musicae' at Oxford, 'being in practice in the country' and that on the same day he supplicated for the degree of Bachelor of Music, being described as of Lincoln College. His request was granted by grace, on the condition that he should compose 'hymnum choralem sex partium'; he was admitted Mus.B. on July 4, 1616.

So far, no music by Vautor has been discovered except the work published in 1619, which is one of the rarest music-books of the early 17th century. It is reprinted in ENGLISH MADRIGAL SCHOOL, vol. xxxiv. The compositions contained in it show a curious striving after originality, displayed not only in the selection of the words set, but also in a fondness for various musical devices peculiar to the composer. The last number in the collection, the great six-part madrigal 'Shepherds and Nymphs of Diana' is a direct imitation in its words of the 'Oriana' madrigals published eighteen years earlier, while its music echoes, not unsuccessfully, the style of Wilbye. But probably the real Vautor may be better detected in the five-part 'Sweet Suffolk Owle' and the Latin 'Mira cano,' with its curious effects of full chords repeated ten times in succession. Though he was evidently far below the greater English musicians of his day, Vautor is an interesting figure, and deserves to be better known.   w. b. s.

VAUTROLLIER, THOMAS (d. before Mar. 1587), an early printer, who printed several music-books in England during Elizabeth's reign. He was a Huguenot, came from either Paris or Rouen, and settled in London about 1564, although his first book is dated 1570. His printing-office was at Blackfriars, and his wife appears to have greatly assisted him in his business; for, leaving her in charge of his affairs, he went to Edinburgh, and traded there as a bookseller. After his return he again went to Scotland and established a press at Edinburgh in 1584. In 1586 he came back to London and died shortly before March 1587.

According to Johnson's *Typographia*, 1824, Vautrollier printed, in octavo, *A Brief Introduction to Musicke*. Another book bearing his imprint is 'Cantiones quae argumento Sacrae Vocantur, quinque et sex partium,' by Tallis and Byrd. This beautifully printed music-book is in oblong 8vo, and dated 1575. It contains at the end of the book the full text of the patent of music-printing granted to Tallis and Byrd. Besides the copy in the British Museum,

there is one in the York Minster library. With the date 1587 there were two editions of the 'Psalmes of David in metre,' printed by Vautrollier, or his wife.   F. K.

VAUXHALL GARDENS. In 1615 one Jane Vaux, widow of John Vaux, was tenant, as a copyholder of the manor of Kennington, of a tenement situate near to the Thames. About 1660 this house, with the grounds attached to it, was opened as a place of public entertainment. The earliest mention of it as such is in Evelyn's Diary, under date July 2, 1661: 'I went to see the New Spring Garden at Lambeth, a pretty contrived plantation.' Pepys at later dates frequently mentions it, and from him we learn that there was an older place of the same name and description in the neighbourhood. On May 29, 1662, he says,

'With my wife and the two maids and the boy took boat and to Fox-hall. . . . To the old Spring Garden. . . . Thence to the new one, where I never was before, which much exceeds the other.'

The musical entertainment appears to have been of the most primitive description. Pepys (May 28, 1667) says,

'By water to Fox-hall and there walked in Spring Garden. . . . But to hear the nightingale and other birds, and here fiddles, and there a harp, and here a Jew's trump,[1] and here laughing and there fine people walking, is mighty diverting.'

Addison, in *The Spectator*, mentions the place as much resorted to. In 1730 Jonathan Tyers obtained a lease of it and opened it June 7, 1732, with an entertainment termed a 'Ridotto al fresco,' then a novelty in England, which was attended by about 400 persons. This became very attractive, and was frequently repeated in that and following seasons; and the success attending it induced Tyers to open the Gardens in 1736 every evening during the summer. He erected a large covered orchestra, closed at the back and sides, with the front open to the Gardens, and engaged a good band. Along the sides of the quadrangle in which the orchestra stood were placed covered boxes, open at the front, in which the company could sit and sup or take refreshments. These boxes were adorned with paintings by Hayman from designs by Hogarth. There was also a rotunda in which the concert was given in bad weather.

In 1737 an organ was erected in the orchestra in the Gardens, and James WORGAN (q.v.) appointed organist. An organ concerto formed, for a long series of years, a prominent feature in the concerts. On the opening of the Gardens on May 1, 1738, Roubiliac's statue of Handel (expressly commissioned by Tyers), was first exhibited.[2] In 1745 Tyers increased the

[1] See JEW'S HARP.
[2] This statue remained in the Gardens, in various situations, sometimes in the open air and sometimes under cover, until 1818, when it was removed to the house of the Rev. Jonathan Tyers Barrett, D.D. (to whom the property in the Gardens had devolved, and who then contemplated a sale of it), in Duke Street, Westminster, where it remained until his death. It was purchased at auction in 1833 by Brown, a statuary, who in 1854 sold it to the Sacred Harmonic Society. It now (1925) decorates the staircase of the business premises of Novello (160 Wardour Street).

orchestra and introduced instrumental solos; Arne was engaged as composer, and Mrs. Arne, Reinhold and Lowe as singers. Richard Collet led the band, Hebden played the bassoon, Valentine Snow the trumpet and Thomas Vincent the oboe. In 1749 Tyers adroitly managed, by offering the loan of all his lanterns, lamps, etc., and the assistance of thirty of his servants at the display of fireworks in the Green Park on the rejoicings for the peace of Aix-la-Chapelle, to obtain permission to have the music composed by Handel for that occasion publicly rehearsed in Vauxhall, before its performance in the Green Park. The rehearsal took place on Friday, Apr. 21, by a band of 100 performers, before an audience of 12,000 persons admitted by 2s. 6d. tickets. The throng of carriages was so great that the traffic over London Bridge (then the only metropolitan road between Middlesex and Surrey) was stopped for nearly three hours. After Lowe withdrew, Vernon was the principal tenor singer. On the death of Jonathan Tyers in 1767 he was succeeded in the management by his two sons, one of whom, Thomas, who had written the words of many songs for the Gardens, soon afterwards sold his interest in the place to his brother's family.

In 1774 HOOK (*q.v.*) was engaged as organist and composer, and held these appointments until 1820. In his time the singers were Mrs. Martyr, Mrs. Wrighten, Mrs. Weichsell, Miss Poole (Mrs. Dickons), Miss Leary, Mrs. Mountain, Mrs. Bland (probably the most universally favourite female singer who ever appeared in the Gardens), Miss Tunstall, Miss Povey, Vernon, Incledon, Dignum, Charles Taylor, Collyer, Mahon, etc. etc. Parke, the oboist, was for many years the principal solo instrumentalist. On May 29, 1786, the Gardens were opened for the season, for the first time under the name 'Vauxhall Gardens' (the old name of 'Spring Garden' having been continued up to that time), with a jubilee performance in commemoration of their first nightly opening by Tyers fifty years before. In 1798 fireworks were occasionally introduced, and afterwards became one of the permanent attractions of the place. The favour shown by the Prince of Wales (afterwards George IV.), made the Gardens the resort of the fashionable world, and the galas given during the Regency, on the occasions and the anniversaries of the several victories over Napoleon, attracted immense numbers of persons. During that period the prosperity of the establishment culminated. In 1815 the celebrated performer on the tight rope, Madame Saqui, appeared, and excited universal astonishment by her ascent on the rope to the summit of the firework tower (60 feet high), during the pyrotechnic display. She continued one of the principal attractions of the Gardens for many years.

In 1818, the Gardens having become the property of the Rev. Dr. Jon. Tyres Barrett, who deemed the receipt of an income from them inconsistent with his sacred calling, they were submitted to auction (on Apr. 11), but bought in. In 1822, however, they passed into the hands of Bish, Gye and Hughes. Great changes then took place in the character of the entertainments ; and a theatre was erected, in which at first ballets, and afterwards vaudevilles, were performed. The concert, however, was retained as a leading feature, and in 1823 the singers were Miss Tunstall, Miss Noel, Miss Melville, Goulden, Collyer, Clark and Master Longhurst. In 1826 Miss Stephens, Mme. Vestris, Braham, Sinclair, De Begnis, etc., were engaged. In 1827 horsemanship was introduced and a mimic representation of the Battle of Waterloo (which proved attractive for several seasons), given on the firework ground. Miss Graddon, T. Phillips, Horn and Mr. and Mrs. Fitzwilliam were the singers, and Blewitt, T. Cooke and Horn the composers. In 1828 Blewitt, T. Cooke and R. Hughes were the composers, and Misses Helme, Knight and Coveney, Benson, Williams and Tinney the singers. In 1829 Rossini's 'Il Barbiere di Siviglia' was performed in the theatre by Miss Fanny Ayton, Mesdames Castelli and De Angioli, and Signori Torri, Giubilei, De Angioli and Pellegrini ; the orchestral concert being supported by Misses Helme and P. Horton (afterwards Mrs. German Reed), George Robinson, W. H. Williams and George Smith ; Blewitt and T. Cooke continuing as composers.

In 1830 Bishop was placed at the head of the musical department, and continued so for three years. He produced during that period the vaudevilles of 'Under the Oak,' and 'Adelaide, or the Royal William,' 1830 ; 'The Magic Fan,' 'The Sedan Chair,' and 'The Battle of Champagne,' 1832, and many single songs, amongst which was the still popular ballad, 'My pretty Jane,' written for the sweet-toned alto voice of George Robinson. His singers included Miss Hughes and Mrs. Waylett. Balloon ascents formed a main feature of the attractions a few years later. As far back as 1802 Garnerin had made an ascent from the Gardens, but that was an isolated case. In 1835 Charles Green ascended and remained in the air all night. On Nov. 7, 1836, Green, Monck Mason and Holland ascended in the large balloon, afterwards known as the 'Nassau,' and descended next morning near Coblentz, having travelled nearly 500 miles in eighteen hours. In July 1837 Green ascended, with Cocking attached in a parachute beneath the balloon, when the latter was killed in his descent by the failure of his machinery. The Gardens now rapidly declined. In 1840 an attempt was made to sell them, but they were bought in at £20,000.

In 1843 they were under the management of Wardell; masquerades, frequented by the most disreputable classes of the community, were given; matters grew worse and worse, until in 1855 they came into the hands of Edward Tyrrell Smith, and reached their lowest depth of degradation. The musical arrangements were beneath contempt; a platform for promiscuous dancing was laid down; and everything lowered in quality. They were not afterwards regularly opened, but speculators were forthcoming who ventured to give entertainments for a few nights in each year, 'for positively the last nights,' until 1859, when the theatre, orchestra, and all the fittings were sold by auction. On July 25 in that year the trees were felled and the site handed over to builders. Vauxhall Gardens had a longer existence than any public gardens in England, and assisted in maintaining a taste for music as a source of rational enjoyment, although they did little or nothing towards promoting its advancement.   W. H. H.

Arne and Worgan seem to have begun the practice of publishing books of songs sung at Vauxhall about 1750; they were followed by Walsh and Johnson. James Hook issued one or two books annually from 1769 till early in the 19th century; they were published successively by Welcker, Thomson, Preston, Bland & Weller and Dale. On Bland & Weller's issues are pretty vignettes of the gardens. Other views are in Bickham's 'Musical Entertainer,' and several are reproduced in Wroth's *London Pleasure Gardens*, 1896.   F. K.

VECCHI, GIUSEPPE, was a Papal singer, and maestro di cappella in 1683.

VECCHI, LORENZO (*b.* Bologna, 1566), received his scientific and musical education as *alumnus* of St. Petronio, where he was 'mansionarius' and maestro di cappella in 1605, when he published his first book of masses, 8 v. Two pieces by him are contained in Lucino's 'Le gemme'; and a Requiem, 5 v., as well as a Sanctus, Agnus and Postcommunio, all in MS., are in the library of Augsburg Cathedral.   E. V. D. S.

VECCHI (VECCHII), ORAZIO [1] (*b.* ? Modena *c.* 1551; *d.* there, Feb. 19, 1605), became the pupil of a monk named Salvatore Essenga, who was himself not unknown as a composer, and who published a volume of 'Madrigali,' containing a piece (doubtless his first essay) by Vecchi, in 1566.

The latter entered holy orders and was made first, in 1586, canon, and then, five years later, archdeacon, of Correggio. Soon afterwards, however, he seems to have deserted his office in order to live at his native town; and

[1] Orazio's separate compositions are indexed in Eitner's *Bibliographie des xvi. und xvii. Jahrhunderts*, pp. 890-895; they consist of sixty-two Italian and forty-four Latin numbers; besides forty-two (in German collections) with German words, many of which are presumably identical with compositions differently entitled in Italian or Latin.

by Apr. 1595 he was punished for his non-residence by being deprived of his canonry. Possibly the real reason of his absence or of his deprivation, or both, was the singular excitability and quarrelsomeness of his disposition, of which several stories are told. Be this as it may, in Oct. 1596 he was made maestro di cappella of Modena Cathedral; and two years later received the same post in the court, in which capacity he had not only to act as music-master to the ducal family, but also to furnish all sorts of music for solemn and festival occasions, grand mascarades, etc. Through this connexion his reputation extended widely. He was summoned at one time to the court of the Emperor Rudolf II.; at another he was requested to compose some particular music for the King of Poland. In 1604 he was supplanted in his office by the intrigue of a pupil, Geminiano Capi-Lupi; and within a year he died, it is said, of mortification at his ill-treatment.

Among Orazio's writings the work which calls for special notice, and which gives him an important place in the history of music, is his 'Amfiparnasso, commedia harmonica,' which was produced at Modena in 1594 and published at Venice three years later. The 'Amfiparnasso' has been claimed as the first example of a real opera, but on insufficient grounds. It is an attempt to translate into music the 'commedia dell' arte,' the characteristic figures of which (Pantalone, Arlecchino, Brighella, the Dottor Graziano, etc.) were to be seen at every village fair in North Italy, during the 16th and 17th centuries. The work is a series of madrigals, grouped in three acts and preceded by a prologue, in which it is clearly and unmistakably stated that the work is intended to appeal to the ear only, and not to the eye. The lines

'Ma voi sappiat' intanto
Che questo di cui parlo
Spettacolo si mira con la mente
Dov' entra per l' orecchie, e non per gl' occhi,'

are proof positive that it was never intended to be acted, even in dumb show, as has generally been suggested. The characters of the comedy would be as well known to an Italian audience as Punch and Judy are to English children, and the various dialects employed would differentiate the characters at once, especially as Vecchi has represented their characteristic rhythms and cadences in his music with great skill. The 'Amfiparnasso,' although deservedly ranked as a masterpiece, is by no means the first attempt in this style. Orlando Lassus had already treated the same subject on a smaller scale, and Striggio's 'Cicalamento delle Donne al Bucato' appeared as early as 1567. For a complete analysis of the 'Amfiparnasso' see the *Monthly Musical Record* for Mar. and Apr. 1906. Specimens of Vecchi's madrigals are in the second volume of Torchi's

'L'arte musicale in Italia,' and the third of 'Arion.'   R. L. P.; addns. E. J. D.

'Amfiparnasso' has been reprinted by Eitner in 'Die Oper,' and by Torchi, 'L'arte musicale,' vol. iv. The madrigal publications of Vecchi's lifetime include

Four books of Canzonettes. (4 v.) 1580, etc.
A book of Madrigals. (6 and 7 v.) 1583.
A book of Madrigals. (5 v.) 1589.
'Selva di varia recreatione.' 1590.
Two books of Canzonettes. (3 v.) 1597.
'Convito musicale.' (3-8 v.). 1597.
'Le veglie di Siena.' (4-6 v.) 1604.
Lamentations.
Motets, Masses.   (See List in Q.-L.)

BIBL.—JOHANNES HOL, *Horatio Vecchi als weltlicher Komponist*; Part I., *Vecchi's Leben.* (Basle Dissertation, 1917.)

VECCHI, ORFEO (*b.* Milan *c.* 1540; *d.* there, before 1604), an important and prolific church composer, and maestro di cappella of the church of Santa Maria della Scala (from which the famous Scala theatre received its name). Apart from some 5-part madrigals which appeared in 1604 in 'Scielta di madrigali,' and are the only secular music known to be by him, his published works are a Mass, Vesper Psalms, Magnificat, motet, etc., and fauxbourdons, 8 v. (1590); 3 books of 5-part masses (1588, 1598, 1602); 1 book of Psalms, 2 Magnificats, 4 antiphons, and fauxbourdons, 5 v. (1596); motets, 5 v., book 2 (1598); motets and other excellent pieces, 5 v., book 1 (1599; other edition, 1603); motets, 6 v., book 3 (1598); the complete Psalms, 5 v. (1598), another edition with 2 Magnificats, fauxbourdons and antiphons, with basso continuo (1614); 7 penitential Psalms 6 v. (1601); motets, 4 v. (1603); cantiones sacrae, 6 v. (Antwerp, 1603); cantiones sacrae, 5 v. (Antwerp, 1608). Many of these have appeared in various editions, some of his works appear in collective volumes, and a considerable number are preserved in MS. in the library of Milan Cathedral and other libraries (*Mendel*; *Q.-L.*; *Riemann*).

VECSEY, FRANZ VON (*b.* Budapest, Mar. 23, 1893), violin virtuoso. He was a pupil of his father and afterwards of Hubay and Joachim. He made a tour as a 'wonder-child' at the age of 10 (Berlin, Oct. 17, 1903), soon afterwards appeared in London, and is now one of the most esteemed violinists in Germany. Eberhardt in one of his excellent books on violin technique speaks of him as one of the greatest living masters of his instrument.   W. W. C.

VEICHTNER, FRANZ ADAM (*b.* probably Prussia, 1745; *d.* St. Petersburg ?). He studied the violin under Franz Benda, and composition under Riepel. About 1763–64 he was engaged by the Russian Count Kaiserling at Königsberg, Prussia, and there he composed some violin concertos mentioned by Reichardt (*Autobiography*). In 1771 he was Konzertmeister at the court of the Duke of Courland at Mitau. When the orchestra was dissolved he went to Italy, where he met with signal success, especially in some concerts at Milan. From Italy he went as Kapellmeister

to St. Petersburg, where he is said to have remained to the time of his death. His cantata 'Cephalus and Procris' (words by Ramler) was performed in 1780 in Berlin. He also wrote an oratorio, a 'Hymn to God'; about 60 symphonies in 10 parts, whereof 4 are published (Leipzig, 1777); also two Russian symphonies in 8 parts, a violin concerto (Leipzig, 1771); 3 quartets, op. 3 (St. Petersburg, 1802, and Berlin, Hummel); 24 fantasias, op. 7, for violin and bass, books 1 and 2 (Leipzig, Breitkopf & Härtel); 24 sonatas for violin and bass, 4 books, op. 8. Two 'Divertissements' for orchestras, soli for violin and bass, etc., remained in MS.   E. V. D. S.

VEILED PROPHET OF KHORASSAN, THE, opera in 3 acts; words by W. Barclay Squire, after Moore (see also LALLA ROOKH); music by Stanford. Produced Court Theatre, Hanover, as 'Der verschleierte Prophet' (German version by Ernst Frank, Feb. 6, 1881); in an Italian version by G. Mazzucato as 'Il profeta velato,' Covent Garden, July 26, 1893.
    G.

VEILED VOICE (*Voce velata*). A voice is said to be veiled when it is not clear, but sounding as if it passed through some interposed medium. The definition found in some dictionaries, namely, 'a husky voice,' is incorrect. Huskiness is produced by an obstruction somewhere along the line of the vocal cords, a small quantity of thick mucus which obstinately adheres to them, or an abrasion of the delicate membrane which lines them, from cold or over-exertion. But the veil is due to a special condition, temporary or permanent, of the entire surface of the vocal chords, which affects the tone itself without producing a separate accompanying sound. There are two distinct kinds of veil—that which is natural, proceeding from the special aforesaid condition of the vocal cords in a healthy state, and that which proceeds from a defective position of the vocal organs (bad production), overwork or disease. Almost every fine dramatic voice has a very slight veil upon it, scarcely recognisable as such, but imparting to it a certain richness and pathos often wanting in voices of crystalline clearness. It is in sound like atmosphere in a picture. The veil is therefore not a defect in every degree. Some great singers have had it to a considerable extent. Amongst these, Pasta, one of the first who united classic acting to fine singing, could never overcome a veil that was sufficient at times to be very much in the way, but was counterbalanced by her other great qualities; and Dorus-Gras, the French soprano, was a remarkable instance of the possession of large powers with a veil upon the voice, that would in most cases have been a serious impediment to vocal display. She, however, made the most brilliant singing pierce the impediment, like the sun shining through the mist. The slight veil on the voice of Jenny Lind gave it volume and consistency, and the same may be said of Salvini the actor, who had, perhaps, the finest speaking voice that ever was heard.   H. C. D.

VELLUTI, GIOVANNI-BATTISTA (b. Monterone, Ancona, 1781; d. Italy, Feb. 1861), was the last of the great male soprani of Italy. At the age of 14 he was taken up by the Abbate Calpi, who received him into his house and instructed him in music. After the traditional six years of solfeggi, he made his début, in the autumn of 1800, at Forlì; and for the next two or three years continued to sing at the little theatres of the Romagna. In 1805, appearing at Rome, he earned a great success in Nicolini's ' Selvaggia '; and two years later, in the same city, he sang the ' Trajano ' of the same composer, by which he established his position as the first singer of the day. With no less éclat he appeared in 1807 at the San Carlo in Naples, and at La Scala in Milan, during the Carnival of 1809, in ' Coriolano,' by Nicolini, and ' Ifigenia in Aulide,' by Federici. After singing at Turin, and again at Milan, he appeared in 1812 at Vienna, where he was crowned, medallised and celebrated in verse. On his return to Italy, he continued to reap golden honours at Milan and other places until 1825, when he came to London. Here he was the first sopranist whom that generation of opera-goers had ever heard, the last (Roselli) having ceased to sing in 1800, at the King's Theatre; and a strong prejudice was rather naturally felt against the new singer.

' His first reception at concerts was far from favourable, the scurrilous abuse [1] lavished upon him before he was heard, cruel and illiberal; and such was the popular prejudice and general cry that unusual precautions [2] were deemed necessary to secure a somewhat partial audience, and prevent his being driven from the stage on his very first entry upon it. The very first note he uttered gave a shock of surprise, almost of disgust, to inexperienced ears, but his performance was listened to with attention and great applause throughout, with but few audible expressions of disapprobation, speedily suppressed. The opera he had chosen (performed July 23, 1825) was " Il crociato in Egitto," by a German composer named Mayerbeer (sic), till then totally unknown in this country.' [3]

It must be remembered that Velluti at this time was no longer young, and doubtless had lost much of the vigour and freshness of his splendid voice, which had formerly been one of large compass. When he first sang in England, the middle notes had begun to fail, and many of them were harsh and grating to the ear, though the upper register was still exquisitely sweet, and he had retained the power of holding, swelling, and diminishing his tone with delightful effect. The lower notes were full and mellow, and he showed great ingenuity in passing from one register to the other, and

avoiding the defective portions of his scale. His manner was florid, but not extravagant; his embellishments, tasteful and neatly executed, and not commonplace. His usual style was suave, but rather wanting in variety; he never rose to bravura. In appearance he had been remarkably handsome, and was still good-looking. Velluti received £600 for his services during that (part) season, but was re-engaged for the next at a salary of £2300, as director of the music as well as singer. He then appeared in Morlacchi's ' Tebaldo ed Isolina,' which he considered his best opera. He was much less admired, however, in this than in the former work; and his favour sensibly declined. For his benefit he sang in Rossini's ' Aureliano in Palmira,' but in connexion with this got into a dispute about extra pay to the chorus, and the case was decided against him in the Sheriff's Court.

In 1829 Velluti came to London once more and sang on a few occasions. On one of these he was heard by Mendelssohn,[4] with an effect only of intense loathing. His voice, indeed, had completely lost its beauty, and he was not engaged. He returned to Italy, and died in the early part of Feb. 1861. It is strange that no fine portrait should exist of so great a singer and so handsome a man : there is an oval by Jügel, after Mouron, representing him as Trajano, and a woodcut, in which he appears as Tebaldo.[5]   J. M.

VELOCE, CON VELOCITÀ, VELOCISSIMO— ' Swiftly; with the utmost rapidity.' A term exploited by the ' Romanticists,' generally used of an ad libitum passage in a quick movement, as, for instance, a scale-passage, or similar figure, in a cadenza. It indicates an increased rate of speed—not, like accelerando, a gradual quickening of the time, but an immediate access of celerity, lasting evenly until the end of the passage or figure to which it is applied. The original time is then resumed without the words a tempo being required. In the large majority of cases the term is only applied to loud passages, as frequently in the works of Chopin, and in the finale of Schumann's Sonata in $F\sharp$ minor, op. 11; but in one instance at least, the slow movement of his second concerto, the former composer applies it to a soft passage, coupling velocissimo with delicatissimo. In Chopin's ' Là ci darem ' Variations it is applied to an entire variation. Under such conditions it must be regarded as equivalent to Presto con fuoco. It is worthy of notice that in Czerny's ' Études de la vélocité ' the direction occurs only once, and then in the superlative, applying, moreover, to an entire study. It is also found in Clementi's ' Gradus.'   M.

[1] The wits of the day called him ' non vir, sed veluti.'
[2] This statement is contradicted by Ebers (Seven Years).
[3] Lord Mount-Edgcumbe.

[4] Letter of May 19, 1829, to Devrient. See also MENDELSSOHN, Vol. III. p. 385.
[5] Another portrait, as well as a ' Cavatina a voce sola con pianoforte ' of his composition, is preserved in the Autograph Grasnick in the State Library, Berlin (Q.-L.).

VELUT, GILET (EGIDIUS), an early 15th-century church composer (probably Nether-lander), of whom some MS. compositions are preserved at Bologna, Vienna, and 5 songs in the Bodleian Library. One of the latter, ' Je voel servir,' has been republished in score by Stainer (Q.-L.).

VENEGAS DE HENESTROSA, LUYS (16th cent.), Spanish lutenist (*vihuelista*), author of a book in tablature entitled :

Libro de cifra nueva para tecla, harpa y vihuela. Alcalá de Henares, 1557. (Bibl. Nac., Madrid.)

The *cifra nueva* (new tablature) for ' key-board, harp or lute ' was on the same principle as that used by CABEZÓN, and not real lute-tablature. The lines drawn across the page do not represent the strings of the instrument, but the parts for the different voices. A composi-tion in 3-part counterpoint is written on 3 lines ; 4-part on 4 lines, etc. The figures represent, not the frets of the lute, but the notes of the scale. The key is indicated at the beginning of each piece. When this is F, the figure ' 1 ' re-presents F, ' 2 ' G, ' 3 ' A, etc. The particular octave to which the figures referred was distin-guished by dots and other signs : thus 1· was an octave higher than 1, 1' an octave higher than 1·. Accidentals fol owed the notes they affected instead of preceding them. Venegas gives transcriptions for keyboard, harp or vihuela of several old Spanish ballads, *diferencias* (variations), together with church music by Morales, Josquin des Prés, Soto and Vila. (*v.* PISADOR, for the importance of lute tran-scriptions for chromatic alteration.)

J. B. T.

VENETIAN SWELL. The first Swell Organ produced its effect by placing the front of the box containing the pipes under the control of the player, who by means of a pedal could raise or lower the panel at will, so releasing or muffling the sound. This plan was first adopted in the organ at St. Magnus, London Bridge, built in 1712. (See ORGAN : SWELL ORGAN.) The first Harpsichord Swell made its crescendo by the raising of the lid. These clumsy contrivances were superseded by the Venetian Swell, an in-vention patented by Shudi in 1769 (see SWELL ; HARPSICHORD), and so called from its re-semblance to the laths of a Venetian blind. This ingenious device was first applied to the harpsichord, but was soon adopted by organ-builders. The louvres were generally in hori-zontal rows and so hung as to close by their own weight ; but in very large Swell Organs the size and number of these shutters made them too heavy for control by tne foot, and they are now placed vertically and closed by a spring. The old form of Swell could only be left either quite open or completely closed : a balanced Swell has been introduced which allows the shutters to be left at any angle. In almost all cases the control is given to the foot of the player—generally the right foot.[1] This arrangement has had disastrous effects upon the pedalling of many players. Several ingenious attempts have been made to enable the organist to open and close the box by other means. In the large organ built by Willis for the 1862 Exhibition, a crescendo could be made by blowing into a small pipe. This, however, was liable to inconvenient sudden sforzandos. R. H. M. Bosanquet used a movable back attached to the seat by a hinge. A strap fastened to this was passed over one shoulder and under the other arm of the player. When the player leant forward he pulled on the back of the seat, and this opened the Swell. The action of the back Swell and Swell Pedal were distinct, so that acting on the former might not depress the latter.

W. Pᴬ.

VENICE. The frequent and laudatory references made by foreigners to the Conserva-tori of Venice abundantly prove the reputa-tion which they enjoyed during the 17th and 18th centuries. The President de Brosses, in his *Lettres historiques* (vol. i.), speaks of the pleasure he received from Venetian music generally :

' The music *par excellence* is the music of the Hospitals ; . . . the girls sing like angels ; they play the violin, the flute, the organ, the hautboy, the violoncello, the bassoon, in short no instrument is large enough to frighten them.'

Casotti (*Lettere*, July 29, 1713) assures us that at Vespers in the Incurabili they do not chant, they enchant (non cantano ma incan-tano). Rousseau (*Confessions*, vii.) bears similar testimony to the charm of the singing in the Venetian Conservatori ; and readers of Dr. Burney's letters will not have forgotten his reference to the Incurabili, ' where Bura-nello and his nightingales . . . poured balm into my wounded ears.' Finally, at the close of the 18th century, Mancini wrote :

' I am of opinion that in all Italy there are no schools of music worthy the name, save the Con-servatori of Venice and Naples and the school conducted by Bartolommeo Nucci of Pescia.'

The Venetians were always a music-loving race, and the city long possessed schools of music in the choir of St. Mark's, in the theatres, and above all in the four great Scuole or Con-servatori, which were attached to the pious foundations of the Pietà, the Mendicanti, the Ospedaletto and the Incurabili. So famous did these schools become that the greatest masters of Italy, and even of Europe, applied for the post of director. The names of Lotti, Galuppi, Scarlatti, Hasse, Porpora, Jommelli, Cimarosa, to take a few only, must always shed a lustre upon the Conservatori over which they presided ; and there is a tradition that Mozart promised an oratorio for the Incurabili choir.

[1] Frequently now (1925) swell pedals are placed above the centre of the pedal-board where they may be reached by either foot.

The four hospitals were not, in their origin, designed as schools of music. They were built and endowed by the munificence of private citizens to receive the poor and infirm ; their position as Conservatori was only gradually developed. The Pietà at San Giovanni in Bragola was founded in the year 1348 by Fra Pierazzo d' Assisi as a branch of the Foundling Hospital at San Francesco della Vigna. After the death of Pierazzo both hospitals were united at San Giovanni and placed under the ducal supervision. The institution was supplied with wood and corn free of charge, and enjoyed a rental of nearly three hundred thousand ducats. The children of the hospitals were taught singing, and the school of music gradually developed until it came to enjoy the highest reputation in Venice. At the time of de Brosses's visit the Pietà possessed the finest orchestra in the city. The Hospital of the Pietà was the only one of the Conservatori which survived the downfall of the republic and escaped the financial collapse which overtook so many pious foundations of Venice.

The Hospital of the Mendicanti was first founded in the 13th century, for the reception of lepers. As leprosy gradually disappeared from Venice, the institution and its funds were devoted to the assistance of mendicants and impotent persons. In the 17th century Bartolommeo Bontempelli and Domenico Biava, two wealthy citizens, built and endowed the Hospital at SS. Giovanni e Paolo. The school of music at the Mendicanti sprang up in the same way as the school at the Pietà had grown, and towards the close of the 18th century it had acquired a high repute. In the year 1775, on May 28, the Emperor Joseph II. was entertained at the Mendicanti, and a new oratorio was performed in his honour. The contemporary account of the visit describes how

'the Emperor and his brother, the Grand Duke of Tuscany, attempted to enter the choir. They were not recognised at first by the lady guardians of that door, forbidden to all men without distinction of person, and admittance was refused. The Emperor, however, was presently recognised and admitted. He amused himself by turning over the leaves of the music, and by taking part in a full chorus with his own well-modulated voice.'

In the year 1777, owing to financial difficulties, the hospital of the Mendicanti was closed, though the choir continued to take part in concerts and oratorios. The buildings of the Mendicanti now form part of the Civic Hospital of Venice.

The Ospedaletto was founded in 1527, at SS. Giovanni e Paolo, as a poorhouse and orphanage. S. Girolamo Miàni was among its early benefactors, and so too, by report, was Ignatius Loyola. The Conservatoire of the Ospedaletto seems to have been the least renowned of the four Venetian Schools, though Dr. Burney expresses himself much satisfied with the singing which he heard there, ranking it after the Incurabili.

The Incurabili, on the Zattere, a hospital for incurables, was founded in 1522 by two noble ladies, Maria Malipiero and Maria Grimani, under the inspiration of San Gaetano Thiene. The first building was of wood ; but the new church was begun in 1566 and finished in 1600. The education of the girls who were admitted to the hospital was supervised by a committee of twelve noble ladies. Dr. Burney gives the palm to the orchestra and choir of the Incurabili. This Conservatoire was raised to its high position by the labours of the two famous masters, Lotti and Galuppi. Galuppi, called Il Buranello, was the last maestro of the Incurabili choir, and wrote for it the last oratorio performed before the closing of the institution in 1776, the ' Moyses de Sinai revertens.' Six years later the concert-room of the Incurabili was opened once more for a performance of Galuppi's ' Tobias,' in honour of Pope Pius IV.

The pupils were divided into two classes, the novices and the *provette* or pupil teachers, whose duty it was to instruct the novices in the rudiments of music under the guidance of the maestro. The number of scholars in each Conservatorio varied from sixty to eighty. Every Saturday and Sunday evening the choirs performed full musical Vespers or a motet, usually written by their own maestro. The churches were crowded, and the town divided into factions which discussed, criticised and supported this or that favourite singer. On great festivals an oratorio was usually given. The choir sang behind a screen and was invisible. Admission to the choir was forbidden to all men except the maestro ; but, Rousseau, by the help of le Blond, French Consul, succeeded in evading this rule and was enabled to visit the choir of the Mendicanti and to make the acquaintance of the young singers whose voices had so delighted him. Special tribunes, called Coretti, were reserved for ambassadors and high State officials. Inside the church applause was forbidden.

At present (1927) the chief school of music in Venice is the LICEO BENEDETTO MARCELLO, which, founded in 1877, acquired a high reputation under the guidance of its director and professor of composition, Wolf-Ferrari—the composer of ' Le donne curiose ' and ' I giojelli della Madonna '—who held the position from 1902–12.

LA FENICE, the most important of the Venetian theatres, was built in 1790 by Antonio Selva and burnt before completion. It was reconstructed on Selva's plans by Tommaso Meduna in 1792. Most notable first performances given at La Fenice are Rossini's ' Tancredi ' (1813) and ' Semiramide ' (1823) ;

Verdi's 'Ernani' (1844), 'Rigoletto' (1851) and 'Traviata' (1853).

BIBLIOGRAPHY

P. CANAL: *Della musica in Venezia.* Printed in *Venezia e le sue lagune,* vol. i. part 2, p. 471.
FRANCESCO CAFFI: Letter to E. Cicogna. Printed in Cicogna, *Iscrizioni veneziane,* vol. v. p. 326.
E. CICOGNA: *Iscrizioni veneziane,* vol. v. p. 297, where a full list of all the oratorios performed at the Incurabili will be found.
DR. BURNEY: *The Present State of Music in France and Italy; History of Music.*
DE BROSSES: *Lettres historiques,* vol. i.
ROUSSEAU: *Confessions,* lib. vii.
FÉTIS: *Biographie universelle des musiciens.*
BOURNET: *Venise, notes prises dans la bibliothèque d'un vieux Vénitien,* p. 275.
MOLMENTI: *La storia di Venezia nella vita privata,* cap. x.
TASSINI: *Curiosità veneziane,* s.v. Pietà, Mendicanti, Ospedaletto, Incurabili.
H. KRETZSCHMAR: *Weitere Beiträge zur Geschichte der venetianischen Oper, J.M.P.,* 1910; and *Schlussbeitrag, J M.P.,* 1911.

H. F. B.; rev., with addns., F. B.

VENI CREATOR SPIRITUS, the popular hymn written by Rutanus Maurus and used at Whitsuntide, Ordinations, etc. The English version, by Bishop Cosyn, in the Book of Common Prayer—'Come, Holy Ghost, our souls inspire'—is in Long Measure, answering, so far, to the eight syllables of the original hymn, and susceptible of adaptation to the plain-song melody.

VENI SANCTE SPIRITUS, a Prose or Sequence sung on Whitsunday, and during the Octave of Pentecost (see SEQUENCE (2)).

VENITE, the name familiarly given to the 95th Psalm—in the Vulgate 'Venite exultemus Domino'—which in the Anglican Service is sung immediately before the Psalms of the day at Matins. (See SERVICE.)

VENOSA, CARLO GESUALDO, see GESUALDO.

VENTADOUR THEATRE, see PARIS, Vol. IV. p. 46.

VENTIL is the German term for the valve in brass instruments. 'Ventilhorn' and 'Ventil-trompet' are therefore equivalent to Valve-horn and Valve-trumpet. (See VALVE.)   G.

VENTO, IVO DE, a contemporary of Orlando Lassus at the Bavarian court. His nationality and birthplace have not been ascertained, though he may more reasonably be considered a Netherlander by birth than a Spaniard. He is first heard of in 1568 as Kapellmeister to the Chapel of Duke William of Bavaria at Landshut. In 1569 he was appointed organist to the Ducal Chapel at Munich where Lassus was Kapellmeister. His name appears in the Chapel accounts preserved in the Munich archives till 1575, when his death is indicated as having taken place after Michaelmas.[1] Vento's works, all published by Adam Berg of Munich, consist of Latin motets and German sacred and secular songs, with titles and dates as follows:

1. Latinae Cantiones quas vulgo Motteta vocant 4 voc, suavissima melodia etiam instrumentis . . . 1569.
2. Latinae Cantiones . . . 5 voc. 1570.
3. Liber Motetorum, 4 vocum. 1571.
4. Mutetae aliquot sacrae, 4 voc. 1574.
5. Quinque Motetae, duo Madrigalia, Gallicae cantiones duae et quatuor Germanicae. 5-8 voc . . . 1576.
6. Neue Teutsche Liedlein mit 5 Stim. 1569.

7. Neue Teutsche Lieder mit 4, 5, 6 Stim. 1570.
8. Neue Teutsche Lieder mit 4 St. sampt 2 Dialogen mit 7 u. 8 Stim. 1570.
9. Schöne auserlesene neue Teutsche Lieder mit 4 Stim. 1572.
10. Neue Teutsche Lieder mit 3 Stim. 1572.
11. Teutsche Lieder mit 5 Stim. sampt einem Dialogo mit 8. 1573.

Vento's German songs would appear to have been received with much favour, as repeated editions of each book appeared from time to time up to 1591. Eitner considers them to have more of German character and sentiment in them than the similar works of Scandelli or Regnart. Commer, in his collection 'Geistliche und weltliche Lieder aus dem xvi.-xvii. Jahrhundert' has republished five, two with sacred texts *a* 5, and three secular *a* 4. Schöberlein's *Schatz* contains a setting *a* 4 of 'Also hat Gott die Welt geliebt.' Of the Latin works there is only a short Motet *a* 4, 'Factum est silentium,' republished in Lück's 'Sammlung.' Various masses by Vento have remained in MS.

J. R. M.

BIBL.—SANDBERGER, *Beiträge zur Geschichte der Bayerischen Hofkapelle* (Documents vol. iii.); KURT HUBER, *Ivo de Vento,* pp. iii. 118 (Munich Dissertation, Lindenberg, 1918). See review in *Z.M.W.* Apr. 1919, pp. 425, 426.

VENTO, MATTHIAS (*b.* Naples, *c.* 1735-1736; *d.* London, Nov. 22, 1776[2]), an Italian musician who came to England at the suggestion of Giardini about 1763. He composed a number of operas, as 'Demofoönte,' 1764, 'La conquista de Messico,' 1767, 'Artaxerxes,' *c.* 1771, etc. His collections of 'Lessons' for the harpsichord and similar pieces were very numerous; he also composed vocal duets and solo songs. Most of his work was published by Bremner, and afterwards by Welcker. Burney speaks not very highly of his music, but implies that Vento's numerous scholars were sufficient to enable him to publish his pieces successfully.   F. K.

VENTURI, POMPILIO, a 16th-century composer of Siena, who wrote 3 books of villanelle; book 2 published in 1571, book 3 in 1583 (Venice, Scotto).

VENTURI, STEFANO, a composer of the 16th-century Venetian school. He published several books of madrigals *a* 4 and 5 from 1592-98. Two of his madrigals *a* 5 adapted to English texts appeared, one in Yonge's 'Musica transalpina' 1597, the other in Morley's collection of 1598. Morley also refers to him approvingly in his *Plain and Easy Introduction,* classing him as a madrigalist along with Vecchi, Giovanelli and Croce. No independent publication of sacred works by Venturi is known, but in Caspar Hassler's Collection, 'Symphoniae sacrae,' 1600, there appeared three motets by him, one *a* 7, two *a* 8, which have since been republished in modern times by F. Commer.

J. R. M.

VENTURINI, FRANCISCUS (*d.* Hanover, Apr. 18, 1745), a distinguished violinist-composer, pupil of J. B. FARINELLI at Hanover, where Venturini was married in 1697. He is described in the church register as ' Gallus.' In 1698 he was a member of the Electoral Chapel, and succeeded Farinelli as ' director of the Instrumentalists' in 1713, afterwards becoming court Kapellmeister. Mattheson relates that he made his acquaintance at the Hanoverian court on June 5, 1706. These data, communicated from state documents by Dr. Fischer, are curiously contrasted with the documents of the Würtemburg court chapel, published by Sittard, according to which Francesco Venturini appears as violinist in the lists of the court musicians at Stuttgart, and is pensioned as such on Feb. 1, 1745. No explanation of this mystery has been found so far. A ' C. Venturini ' was engaged as bass singer at the court at Hanover in 1667. Franciscus wrote 12 concerti da camera for 4-9 instruments, op. 1, dedicated to the Duke of Brunswick and Luneburg. He left in MS. a concerto for 6 instruments, a sonata I., overtures for 8 instruments, overtures for 5 instruments, and 4 violin concertos (*Q.-L.*).

E. v. d. s.

VÊPRES SICILIENNES, LES, opera in 5 acts ; libretto by Scribe and Duveyrier ; music by Verdi. Produced June 13, 1855, Opéra, Paris ; in Italian as ' Giovanna de Guzman,' Scala, Milan, Feb. 4, 1856 ; Drury Lane, July 27, 1859 ; New York, Academy of Music, Nov. 7, 1859.

G.

VERACINI, (1) ANTONIO, a violinist and composer who lived during the second half of the 17th century at Florence, one of the most eminent and influential composers of that time. His sonatas are of particular importance and prove a complete command of the technical resources of the violin, while their form shows a transition from the older to the newer form. The movements are more articulate, and there is a freer flow of melody in the slow movements than in the works of his predecessors, and even of his contemporaries. He was in the service of the Grand Duchess Victoria of Tuscany. His sonatas for 2 violins and violone (v'cl.) or archlute, with bass for the organ, op. 1 (Florence, 1692), are dedicated to the Grand Duchess, and bear the arms of the Grand Duke (Ferdinand II.) and his wife ' Vittoria ' on the covers. The dedication is dated ' Firenze, 8th Dec. 1692.' The second violin and organ parts are in the British Museum. Other existing compositions of his are : ' Sonate da chiesa ' for violin and violoncello or basso continuo, op. 2 (Amsterdam ; Roger—copy of original edition) ; ten ' Sonate da camera ' for violin and violone, or archlute, with basso for the harpsichord, op. 3 (Modena, 1696). Gustav Jensen edited one of the trio-sonatas, op. 1 (Augener). According to Fétis he published three sets of sonatas. His nephew and pupil,

(2) FRANCESCO MARIA (*b.* Florence, *c.* 1685 ; *d.* ? Pisa, 1750 [1]), a celebrated violinist and composer, was known as ' Il Fiorentino.' He appears to have settled early at Venice, where TARTINI (*q.v.*) was so much impressed by his style as to leave Venice without appearing in public, and retire to Ancona for further study after the model of Veracini. He visited England for the first time in 1714, acting as leader of the Italian Opera band, and appearing as soloist between the acts. He was then ' regarded as the greatest violinist in Europe.' [2] His début at the King's Theatre took place on Saturday, Jan. 23, 1714, when he was advertised as ' The Famous Signor Veracini lately arrived from Italy.' He continued to play ' symphonies ' between the acts of the operas at the King's Theatre until Dec. 24, 1714. He played for the BARONESS (*q.v.*) at her benefit concert of Mar. 17, and gave his own benefit concert at Hickford's Rooms on Apr. 22, when he performed

' an Extraordinary concert of Music both vocal and instrumental of his own compositions, viz. several solos for violin never performed before.'

In 1720 he accepted an appointment as soloplayer to the Elector of Saxony at Dresden. There he threw himself out of a high window, and in consequence was lamed for life. According to one version he did this in a fit of insanity ; but another report goes to the effect that PISENDEL (*q.v.*), the leading German musician at Dresden, in order to prepare a humiliation to Veracini, who by his conceit and arrogance had incurred the hostility of the Germans, asked him to play a concerto at sight before the court, and afterwards made a violinist of the orchestra repeat the piece. As the latter had carefully prepared his music, the audience, to Veracini's mortification, gave the preference to his performance and applauded him greatly. Be this as it may, Veracini left Dresden for Prague (1723) and Italy. In 1735 we find him again in London, where he achieved a signal success as a composer. His opera ' Adriano ' was first performed at the King's Theatre ' by his Majesty's command ' on Nov. 25, 1735, and given 17 times during the season. The artists who took part were Farinelli, Senesino, Bertolli, Montagnana and Cuzzoni. Many of the songs from this opera were printed separately by Walsh. As a violinist Geminiani, then a rising star, appears to have impaired his success. Dr. Burney heard Veracini lead the band in Hickford's Rooms in 1745. He seems to have been greatly impressed with the veteran violinist's bold style. He is reported to have died in reduced circumstances.

Veracini's compositions show him to have been a musician of remarkable originality and solid attainments.

---

[1] '*Q.-L.*, quoting Fürstenau (*Beiträge zur Geschichte der Kgl. Sächs. Kapelle*), says that Veracini died in London in 1750.
[2] Burney, *Hist.* vol. .v. p. 640.

He published two sets of twelve sonatas each (Dresden and Amsterdam, 1721 ; London and Florence, 1744). For London he composed the operas ' Adriano,' 1735 ; ' Roselinda,' 1744 ; ' L' errore di Salomone,' 1744. A number of concertos, sonatas, and symphonies for two violins, viola, violoncello and basso have remained in manuscript, and some of them are in the public libraries of Florence and Bologna. A set of Veracini's sonatas for violin and flute was published in Venice in 1716. He also wrote two cantatas, ' Nice e Tirsi ' and ' Parla al ritratto dell' Amante,' a canon for two sopranos, ' Ut relevet miserum,' and an air for soprano and quartet, 'M' assalgono affanno fierezza.' The ' Sonate accademiche a violino solo ' (London and Florence, 1744), op. 2, are dedicated to Augustus III., Elector of Saxony, Veracini's patron, and were licensed for publication in England by George II. on Mar. 13, 1744. An engraved portrait of Veracini playing the violin faces the title-page of these sonatas. Some of his sonatas have been edited by Ferd. David (Breitkopf & Härtel) and von Wasielewski (Senff, Simrock), and have been played by Joachim and others.

BIBL.—M. CAFFI, Storia di San Marco ; MATTHESON, Grundlage einer Ehrenpforte ; BURNEY, History of Music ; FÜRSTENAU, Beiträge zur Geschichte der Kgl. Sächs. Kapelle ; Daily Courant, from Mar. 21 to Dec. 24, 1714 ; WASIELEWSKI, Die Violine ; DU-BOURG, The Violin ; VIDAL, Les Instruments à archet ; HART, The Violin ; LAHEE, Famous Violinists ; FÉTIS, Biog. des mus., Choron and Fayolle, etc.

P. D. ; addns. E. H.-A. and E. v. d. S.

VERBONNET, JEAN, 15th-16th century Netherlandish composer. Of his compositions are known only : ' Hy sit die wertste,' 4 v. from Susato's ' Muziek Boexken ' (1551) ; a fine four-part setting of ' Dulces exuviae,' etc., from Virgil's Aeneid ; a Salve Regina, 4 v., 2 masses and 4 songs in the Codex Basevi (16th century) one of which is superscribed ' Io Ghisling alias Verbonnet ' ; which has led to his being identified with GHISELIN (q.v.) ; but Ambros points out that the word ' alias ' was sometimes used for ' or ' where uncertainty existed about the authorships, and that the style of these two masters was totally different. A three-part Mass signed 'Verbenet' in the Cod. 1594 of the Leipzig University Library may probably have to be attributed to Verbonnet. (Ambros, iii. 251 ; Riemann.)

VERDELOT,[1] PHILIPPE, a Flemish composer of the early part of the 16th century, appears to have settled in Italy when young, since his first work—a motet—was printed in the ' Fior de' motetti e canzoni ' published, as is believed, at Rome in 1526, and since he is found to have resided at Florence, as maestro di musica in San Giovanni, some time between 1530 and 1540. It is certain, however, that he was previously attached to the singing staff of the

church of S. Mark at Venice, and we have the authority of Guicciardini [2] for the statement that he was already dead by the year 1567. His earliest composition is in a collection of Juntas in 1526,[3] and his latest publication, ' Electiones diversorum motetorum,' is dated 1549.

Verdelot is commemorated by Cosmo Bartoli and by Vincenzo Galilei, who printed two lute-pieces by him in ' Fronimo.' His works had reached France and were printed in French collections as early as the year 1530. Verdelot's [4] remarkable skill in the science of music is well shown in the fifth part which he added to Jannequin's ' Bataille.'

Antonio Gardano, the publisher, when introducing in 1541 the reprint of a collection of six-part madrigals by Verdelot, describes them on the title-page as the most divine and most beautiful music ever heard (' la più divina e più bella musica che se udisse giammai '). On the general question of precedence in the composition of the madrigal, see MADRIGAL. Besides the fact insisted on by Eitner [5] that only a very few of Willaert's secular compositions are properly madrigals, the most of them being rather in the lighter style of villanellas, his first composition of the kind appeared only in 1538, while as early as 1536 Willaert himself had arranged in lute tablature for solo voice and lute accompaniment twenty-two madrigals by Verdelot (' Intavolatura degli Madrigali di Verdelotto da cantare et sonare nel lauto . . . per Messer Adriano,' Venice, 1536). Apart from the early mention of the name in the 14th century, the earliest known volume of musical pieces described as madrigals bears the date 1533, and Verdelot is the chief contributor. It is entitled ' Madrigali novi de diversi excellentissimi Musici.' [6] Costanzo Festa also appears as a contributor to this volume, and his name otherwise as a composer appears earlier in print than that of Verdelot. (It should be mentioned that this first book of madrigals is not perfectly preserved, two part-books only existing in the Staatsbibliothek at Munich.) From 1537 onwards various collections of Verdelot's madrigals for four, five and six voices were made by enterprising publishers, such as Scotto and Gardano, but generally mixed up with the works of other composers. Eitner says that no independent collection of Verdelot's madrigals is known to exist (but see Q.-L.). Out of the miscellaneous collections he reckons up about 100 as composed by Verdelot, although with regard to many of them some uncertainty prevails from the carelessness of the publishers in affixing names, and perhaps also their wish to pass off inferior compositions as

1 Two notices cited by Van der Straeten, La Musique aux Pays-Bas, vol. vi. p, 322, suggest that the name of ' Verdelot ' is an appellative ; if so we are ignorant of the composer's real name. One of the cases referred to is connected with the town of Bruges.

2 Quoted by Van der Straeten. vol. i. p. 44.
3 Ambros, Gesch. vol. iii. p. 287.
4 Ambros, Geschichte der Musik, vol. ii. p. 513.
5 M.f.M., vol. xix. p. 85.
6 See Eitner Bibliographie der Sammelwerke, p. 27.

the work of the more celebrated masters. Jannequin's 'Bataille,' with Verdelot's added fifth part, first appeared in Tylman Susato's tenth book of 'Chansons,' published at Antwerp in 1545, and has been reprinted in modern times by Commer. Besides madrigals, Verdelot appears as composer of motets in the various collections made by publishers from 1532 onwards. Forty are enumerated in Eitner's *Bibliographie*, several of them imperfectly preserved. Of the complete works which Ambros examined, he praises the masterly construction and the finely developed sense for beauty and pleasing harmony. Only one Mass by Verdelot is known, one entitled 'Philomena,' in a volume of five masses published by Scotto, Venice, in 1544. Fétis and Ambros say that several exist in manuscript in the archives of the Sistine Chapel at Rome; but Codex 38, to which Fétis refers, is shown by Haberl's *Katalog der Musikwerke im päpstlichen Archiv*, pp. 18, 171 and 172, to contain only three motets by Verdelot.[1] Three of Verdelot's madrigals are contained in Ott's Liederbuch, 1544, reprinted by Eitner, and one of these also reappeared in 'Arion,' vol. iii.　　　　　　　　　R. L. P. and J. R. M.

VERDI, GIUSEPPE (*b.* Le Roncole, Italy, Oct. 10, 1813; *d.* S. Agata, near Busseto, Jan. 27, 1901), one of the greatest and most popular operatic composers of the 19th century.

Unlike many musicians who have passed their infancy and childhood amongst artistic surroundings, Verdi's musical genius had to fight for its development against many difficulties. His father, Carlo Verdi, kept a small shop at Le Roncole, a little hamlet in the province of Parma. Once a week Carlo Verdi walked up to Busseto, making his chief purchases from a certain Barezzi, who was destined to serve as a bridge to Giuseppe Verdi over many a chasm.

Giuseppe, though good and obedient, was rather of a melancholy character; one thing only, we are told, could rouse him from his habitual indifference, and that was the occasional passing through the village of a grinding organ; to the child who in after years was to afford an inexhaustible repertory to those instruments for half a century all over the world, this was an irresistible attraction. This slight hint of his musical aptitude must have been accompanied by others which the traditions of Le Roncole have not transmitted, since we know that even in early childhood the boy was possessed of a spinet.

Another evidence of Giuseppe's musical aptitude is given by the following fact, which occurred when he was only 7 years old. He was then assisting the priest at the Mass in the little church of Le Roncole. At the very moment of the elevation of the Host, the

harmonies that flowed from the organ struck the child as so sweet that he stood motionless in ecstasy. 'Water,' said the priest to the acolyte; and the latter evidently not heeding him, the demand was repeated. Still no reply. 'Water,' a third time said the priest, kicking the child so brutally that he fell headlong down the steps of the altar, knocked his head against the floor, and was brought unconscious into the sacristy. After this event Giuseppe's father engaged Baistrocchi, the local organist, to give him music lessons. At the end of a year Baistrocchi made a declaration to the effect that the pupil had learned all that the teacher could impart, and thereupon resigned his position as Verdi's teacher.

Two years after, having completed this first stage in his musical education, Verdi—then but ten years old—was appointed as organist in the room of old Baistrocchi. The dream of his parents was thus for the time realised: yet before long the mind of the elder Verdi began to be haunted with the thought that some knowledge of the three R's could but bring good to his son in after life: and after debating his scheme with his wife, he resolved upon sending Giuseppe to a school in Busseto. This would have been beyond the small means of the good Verdi, but for the fact that at Busseto lived a countryman and friend—a cobbler named Pugnatta. This Pugnatta took upon himself to give Giuseppe board and lodging, and send him to the principal school of the town, all at the very moderate price of threepence a day. And to Pugnatta's Giuseppe went: and while attending the school most assiduously, kept his situation as organist of Le Roncole, walking there every Sunday morning, and back to Busseto after the evening service.

One night, while the poor lad was walking towards Le Roncole, worn out by fatigue and want of sleep or food, he did not notice that he was in the wrong track, and of a sudden, missing his ground, he fell into a deep canal. It was dark, it was bitter cold, and his limbs were absolutely paralysed; and but for an old woman who was passing by the spot and heard his cries for help, the exhausted and chilled boy would have been carried off by the current.

The following story of another and earlier very narrow escape from death we give on the entire responsibility of Pougin. In 1814 Russian and Austrian troops had been passing through Italy, leaving death and destruction everywhere. A detachment having stopped for a few hours at Le Roncole, all the women took refuge in the church; but not even that holy place was respected by these savages. The doors were unhinged, and the poor helpless women and children ruthlessly wounded and killed. Verdi's mother, with the little Giuseppe in her arms, was among those who took refuge in the church; but when the door was burst open she did not

1 See also Van der Straeten, *Musique aux Pays-Bas*, vol. vi. p. 473.

lose her spirits, but ascending the narrow stair-case of the belfry, hid herself and her baby among some timber that was there, and did not leave her hiding-place until the drunken troops were far beyond the village.

EDUCATION. — Giuseppe Verdi, after two years' schooling at Busseto, had learned to write, read and cypher: whereupon the above-mentioned Barezzi began to take much interest in the talented Roncolese, gave him employ-ment in his business, and opened a way to the development of his musical faculty.

Music was uppermost in the minds of the Bussetesi. Barezzi himself was first flute in the cathedral orchestra. His house was the residence of the Philharmonic Society, of which he was the president and patron, and it was there that all rehearsals were held, and all Philharmonic concerts given, under the con-ductorship of Ferdinando Provesi, organist of the cathedral.

This was the fittest residence for a lad of Verdi's turn of mind, and he immediately felt it. Without neglecting his chief occupation, he regularly attended the rehearsals, and under-took the task of copying out the parts from the score; and all this in such earnest that old Provesi began to notice Giuseppe with approval, and give him the foundation of a sound musical knowledge. Provesi was the first man in Busseto to understand Verdi's real vocation, and to advise him to devote himself to music. Don Pietro Seletti, the boy's Latin teacher, bore a grudge to Provesi. The fact that Provesi encouraged Verdi to study music was therefore enough for Don Pietro to dissuade him as strongly from it.

But a short time after this admonition there was to be a Mass at a chapel in Busseto where Don Pietro Seletti was the officiating priest. The organist was unable to attend, and Don Pietro was induced to let Verdi play the organ. The Mass over, Don Pietro sent for him. 'Whose music did you play?' said he; 'it was a most beautiful thing.' 'Why,' timidly answered the boy, 'I had no music, and I was playing extempore, just as I felt.' 'Ah! indeed,' rejoined Don Pietro; 'well, I am a fool, and you cannot do better than study music.'

Under the intelligent guidance of Provesi, Verdi studied until he was 16. During this period he often came to the help of his old master both as organist and as conductor of the Philharmonic Society. The archives of the society still contain works written by Verdi at that time, and composed, copied, taught, rehearsed, and conducted by himself.

It became evident that Busseto was too narrow a field for the aspirations of the young composer, and efforts were made to afford him the means of going to Milan, the most im-portant Italian town, musically speaking. The financial question came again to the front, and, thanks to the good-will of the Bussetesi, it had a happy solution. The Monte di Pietà, an institution granting four premiums of 300 francs a year, each given for four years to promising young men wanting means for undertaking the study of science or art, was induced by Barezzi to award one of the four premiums to Verdi, with the important modification of allowing him 600 francs a year for two years, instead of 300 for four years. Barezzi himself advanced the money necessary for music lessons, board, and lodging in Milan; and Seletti gave him an introduction to his nephew, a professor there, who most heartily welcomed him.

We come now to an incident of Verdi's artistic life to which a very undue importance has been often attached; we mean his being refused a scholarship at the Conservatorio di Musica of Milan, on the ground of his showing no special aptitude for music.

To a vacant scholarship—for pianoforte, singing, or composition—there is always a number of candidates, occasionally amounting to as many as a hundred. A committee of professors under the presidency of the Principal is appointed to examine all the competitors, and choose the best. The committee can only select one amongst those that have the fewest disqualifications, but nobody can accuse them of ignorance or ill-will if the chosen candidate, after five years' tuition, turns out to be a mere conductor of operettas, while one of the ninety-nine dismissed, after ten years' hard study elsewhere, writes a masterpiece of operatic or sacred music. Let us then bear no grudge to Basily, the then principal of the Conservatorio of Milan, for not having the foresight to recog-nise in the young organist of Le Roncole the man who was destined to write 'Rigoletto.'

But though failing to be admitted to the Conservatorio, Verdi stuck to the career which he had undertaken, and, on the advice of Ales-sandro Rolla, then conductor of La Scala, he asked Signor Lavigna to give him lessons in composition and orchestration. Lavigna was a distinguished musician and a composer of no ordinary merit, his operas having been per-formed several times with success. He con-sented to give the lessons, and to him actually belongs the honour of being the teacher of Verdi.

This was in 1831, when Verdi was 18. The two years 1831–33 passed in an uninter-rupted succession of exercises in harmony, counterpoint and fugue, and a daily study of Mozart's 'Don Giovanni.' In 1833 Ferdi-nando Provesi died. The trustees of the Monte di Pietà of Busseto, and the other contributors towards Verdi's musical training, had acted with the intention that, after Provesi's death, Verdi should be his successor both as maestro di cappella and organist of the Cathedral, and

LXXXV

VERDI

From a painting by Giovanni Boldini (1886), in the Home of Rest for Aged Musicians, Milan

also conductor of the Philharmonic Society. Verdi felt very sorry for the death of Provesi; with him he had lost the man who first taught him the elements of his art, and showed him the way to excellence; and though Verdi felt a call to something nobler in life, yet he kept his word to his countrymen and went to Busseto to fill the place left vacant by his deceased professor. The appointment rested with the authorities of the Cathedral, men who had little liking for Verdi, whom they called 'the fashionable maestrino,' and preferred Verdi's competitor, one Giovanni Ferrari.

Verdi next fell in love with Margherita, Barezzi's eldest daughter, whose father, unlike most fathers, did not oppose Margherita's union to a talented though very poor young man. In 1836 they were married.

AUTOBIOGRAPHY.—In 1838 Verdi, with his wife and two children, left Busseto and settled in Milan, in the hope of performing his opera 'Oberto Conte di S. Bonifacio.' We are fortunately able to give the relation of this most important period of an artist's career, in words that may be said to be Verdi's own.

The first part of the narrative refers to the time when he was in Milan, studying with Lavigna. On his return there his kind old master was gone—died while his pupil was at Busseto. And here is Verdi's narrative:

'About the year 1833 or 1834 there was in Milan a Philharmonic Society composed of first-rate vocalists, under the direction of one Masini. The Society was then in the bustle and hurry of arranging a performance of Haydn's "Creation," at the Teatro Filodrammatico. Signor Lavigna, my teacher of composition, asked me whether I should like to attend the rehearsals, in order to improve my mind, to which I willingly answered in the affirmative. Nobody would notice the young man sitting in the darkest corner of the hall. Three maestri shared the conducting between them; but one day it happened that neither of the three was present at the time appointed for rehearsal. The ladies and gentlemen were growing fidgety, when Masini, who did not feel himself equal to accompanying from the full orchestral score, desired me to be the accompanist for the evening: and as perhaps he believed in my skill as little as he did in his own, he added, "It will be quite enough to play the bass only." I was fresh from my studies, and certainly not puzzled by a full orchestral score; I therefore answered, "All right," and took my place at the piano.

'The rehearsal began, and in the course of it I gradually warmed up, so that at last, instead of confining myself to the mere piano part, I played the accompaniment with my left hand, while conducting most emphatically with my right. It was a tremendous success, all the more because quite unexpected. The re-hearsal over, everybody congratulated me upon it. In short, whether the three maestri were too busy to attend the rehearsals, or whether there was some other reason, I was appointed to conduct the performance, which was so welcomed by the audience that it had to be repeated in the large and beautiful hall of the Casino dei Nobili, in presence of the Arch-duke and Archduchess Ranieri.

'A short time afterwards, I was engaged by Count Renato Borromeo to write the music for a cantata for chorus and orchestra, on the occasion of the marriage of some member of the Count's family—if I remember right. I must say, however, that I never got so much as a penny out of all that, because the whole work was a gratuitous one.

'Masini next urged me to write an opera, and handed me a libretto, which, after having been touched up by Solera, became "Oberto, Conte di San Bonifacio."

'I closed immediately with the proposition, and went to Busseto, where I was obliged to remain nearly three years, and during that time I wrote out the whole opera. The three years over, I took my way back to Milan, carrying with me the score, and the solo parts copied out by myself.

'But here difficulties began. Masini being no longer conductor, my chance of seeing my opera produced there was at an end. However, whether Masini had confidence in my talents, or wished to show me some kindness, he assured me he would not leave a stone unturned until my opera was brought out at La Scala.

'The result was that the opera was put down for the spring of 1839, to be performed at La Scala for the benefit of the Pio Istituto; and among the interpreters were the four excellent artists Mme. Strepponi, Moriani, Giorgio Ronconi and Marini.

'After a few rehearsals Moriani fell seriously ill, everything was brought to a standstill, and all hope of a performance gone! I broke down utterly, and was thinking of going back to Busseto, when one fine morning one of the theatre attendants knocked at my door and said sulkily, "Are you the maestro from Parma who was to give an opera for the Pio Istituto? Come with me to the theatre; the impresario wants to speak to you."

'The impresario was Bartolemeo Merelli.

'On my entering his room, he abruptly told me that having heard my "Oberto" spoken of very favourably he was willing to produce it during the next season, provided I would make some slight alterations in the compass of the solo parts, as the artists engaged were not the same who were to perform it before. His only condition was that he should share with me the sale of the copyright. This was not asking much for the work of a beginner. And in fact, even after its favourable reception, Ricordi would give no more than 2000 Austrian livres (£67) for it.

' Though " Oberto " was not extraordinarily successful, yet it was well received by the public, and was performed several times ; and Merelli even found it convenient to extend the season and give some additional performances of it. The principal interpreters were Mme. Marini, Salvi and Marini. I had been obliged to make some cuts, and had written an entirely new number, the quartet, on a situation suggested by Merelli himself ; which proved to be one of the most successful pieces in the whole work.

' Merelli next made me an offer which, considering the time at which it was made, may be called a splendid one. He proposed to engage me to write three operas, one every eight months, to be performed either at Milan or Vienna, where he was the impresario of both the principal theatrical houses : he to give me 4000 livres (£134) for each opera, and the profits of the copyright to be divided between us. I agreed to everything, and shortly afterwards Merelli went to Vienna leaving instructions to Rossi to write a libretto for me, which he did, and it was the " Proscritto." I had not yet brought myself to begin to set it to music, when Merelli, coming hurriedly to Milan during the spring of 1840, told me that he was in want of a comic opera for the next autumn, that he would send me a libretto, and that I was to write it before the " Proscritto." I could not well say no, and so Merelli gave me several librettos of Romani to choose from, all of which had already been set to music, though owing to failure or other reasons, they could safely be set again. I read them and did not like any : but there was no time to lose, so I picked out one that seemed to me not so bad as the others, " Il finto Stanislao," a title which I changed into " Un giorno di regno."

' At that period of my life I was living in an unpretentious little house near the Porta Ticinese, and my small family was with me—that is, my young wife and my two sons. As soon as I set to work I had a severe attack of angina, that confined me to my bed for several days, and just when I began to get better I remembered that quarter-day was only three days off, and that I had to pay fifty crowns. Though in my financial position this was not a small sum, my illness had prevented me from taking the necessary steps ; and the means of communication with Busseto—the mail left only twice a week—did not allow me time enough to write to my excellent father-in-law Barezzi, and get the money from him. It vexed me so much to let the quarter-day pass by without paying the rent, that my wife, seeing my anxieties, took the few valuable trinkets she had, went out, and a little while after came back

with the necessary amount. I was deeply touched by this tender affection, and promised myself to buy everything back again, which I could have done in a very short time, thanks to my agreement with Merelli.

' But now terrible misfortunes crowded upon me. At the beginning of April my child falls ill, the doctors cannot understand what is the matter, and the dear little creature goes off quickly in his mother's arms. Moreover, a few days after the other child is taken ill too, and he too dies, and in June my young wife is taken from me by a most violent inflammation of the brain, so that on the 19th June I saw the third coffin carried out of my house. In a very little over two months, three persons so very dear to me had disappeared for ever. I was alone, alone ! My family had been destroyed ; and in the very midst of these trials I had to fulfil my engagement and write a comic opera ! " Un giorno di regno " proved a dead failure ; the music was, of course, to blame, but the interpretation had a considerable share in the fiasco. In a sudden moment of despondency, embittered by the failure of my opera, I despaired of finding any comfort in my art, and resolved to give up composition. To that effect I wrote to Dr. Pasetti (whom I had not once met since the failure of the opera) asking him to persuade Merelli to tear up the agreement.

' Merelli thereupon sent for me and scolded me like a naughty child. He would not even hear of my being so much disappointed by the cold reception of my work : but I stuck to my determination, and in the end he gave me back the agreement saying, " Now listen to me ; I can't compel you to write if you don't want to do it ; but my confidence in your talent is greater than ever ; nobody knows but some day you may return on your decision and write again : at all events if you let me know two months in advance, take my word for it your opera shall be performed."

' I thanked him very heartily indeed ; but his kindness did not shake my resolution, and away I went. I took up a new residence in Milan near the Corsia de' Servi. I was utterly disheartened, and the thought of writing never once flashed through my mind. One evening, just at the corner of the Galleria De Cristoforis, I stumbled upon Merelli, who was hurrying towards the theatre. It was snowing beautifully, and he, without stopping, thrust his arm under mine and made me keep pace with him. On the way he never left off talking, telling me that he did not know where to turn for a new opera ; Nicola was engaged by him, but had not begun to work because he was dissatisfied with the libretto.

' " Only think," says Merelli, " here is Solera's libretto ! such a beautiful subject ! Take it, just take it, and read it over."

' " What on earth shall I do with it ? . . . I am in no humour to read librettos."

' " . . . It won't kill you ; read it, and then bring it back to me again." And he gives me the manuscript. It was written on large sheets in big letters, as was the custom in those days. I rolled it up, and went away.

' While walking home I felt rather queer ; there was something that I could not well explain about me. I was burdened with a sense of sadness. I got into my room, and throwing the manuscript angrily on the writing-table, I stood for a moment motionless before it. The book as I threw it down, opened, my eyes fell on the page, and I read the line

"Va, pensiero, sull' ali dorate."

I read on, and was touched by the stanzas inasmuch as they were almost a paraphrase of the Bible, the reading of which was the comfort of my solitary life.

' I read one page, then another ; then, decided as I was to keep my promise not to write any more, I did violence to my feelings, shut up the book, went to bed, and put out the candle. I tried to sleep, but " Nabucco " was running a mad career through my brain, and sleep would not come. I got up, and read the libretto again—not once, but two or three times, so that in the morning I could have said it off by heart. Yet my resolution was not shaken, and in the afternoon I went to the theatre to return the manuscript to Merelli.

' " Isn't it beautiful ? " says he.

' " More than beautiful, wonderful."

' " Well, set it to music."

' I looked rather blank, but not knowing what to do went home with " Nabucco " in my pocket. One day a line, the next day another line, a note, a bar, a melody . . . at last I found that by imperceptible degrees the opera was done !

' It was then the autumn of 1841, and calling to mind Merelli's promise, I went straight to him to announce that " Nabucco " was ready for performance, and that he might bring it out in the coming Carnival.

' Merelli emphatically declared that he would stick to his word ; but at the same time he called my attention to the fact that it was impossible to bring out the opera during the Carnival, because the repertory was all settled, and no less than three new operas by known composers already on the list ; to give, together with them, a fourth, by a man who was almost a débutant, was a dangerous business for everybody, especially for me ; it would therefore be safer to put off my opera till Easter. This, however, I peremptorily refused:—either during the Carnival or never ; for I knew very well that during the spring it was utterly impossible to have two such good artists as Strepponi and Ronconi, on whom, knowing they were engaged for the Carnival season, I had mainly built my hopes of success.

' The issue was, that after a long succession of vacillations, one fine morning I saw the posters on the walls and " Nabucco " not there.

' I was young and easily roused, and I wrote a nasty letter to Merelli, wherein I freely expressed my feelings. No sooner was the letter gone than I felt something like remorse, and besides, a certain fear lest my rashness had spoiled the whole business.

' Merelli sent for me, and on my entering his office he says in an angry tone : " Is this the way you write to your friends ? . . . Yet you are right ; I'll give ' Nabucco ' ; but you must remember that because of the outlay on the other operas, I absolutely cannot afford new scenes or new costumes for you, and we must be content to make a shift with what we have in stock."

' I was determined to see the opera performed, and therefore agreed to what he said, and new posters were printed, on which " Nabucco " appeared with the rest.

' At the end of February 1842 we had the first rehearsal, and twelve days later, on March 9, the first performance. The principal interpreters were Mmes. Strepponi and Bollinzaghi, and Signori Ronconi, Miraglia, and Derivis.

' With this opera my career as a composer may rightly be said to have begun ; and though it is true that I had to fight against a great many difficulties, it is no less true that " Nabucco " was born under a very good star.' So far the maestro's own narrative.

OPERATIC CAREER.—Eleven months later (Feb. 11, 1843), Verdi achieved a still more indisputable success with ' I Lombardi alla prima Crociata,' interpreted by Mme. Frezzolini-Poggi, and Guasco, Severi and Derivis. Solera had taken the plot from the poem of Tommaso Grossi, the author of ' Marco Visconti.' This opera gave Verdi his first experience in the difficulty of finding libretti unobjectionable to the Italian governments. Though five years had still to elapse before the breaking out of the Milan revolt, yet something was brewing throughout Italy, and no occasion was missed by the patriots in giving vent to their feelings. As soon as the Archbishop of Milan got wind of the subject of the new opera he sent a letter to the chief of the police, Torresani, saying that he knew the libretto to be a profane and irreverent one, and that if Torresani did not veto the performance, he himself would write straight to the Austrian Emperor.

Merelli, Solera and Verdi were forthwith summoned to appear before Torresani and hear from him what alterations should be made in the opera. Verdi, in his usual blunt manner, took no notice of the peremptory summons,

' I am satisfied with the opera as it is,' said he, ' and will not change a word or a note of it. *It shall be given as it is, or not given at all!'* Thereupon Merelli and Solera went to see Torresani—who, to his honour be it said, besides being the most inflexible agent of the government, was an enthusiastic admirer of art and artists—and so impressed him with the responsibility he would assume by preventing the performance of a masterpiece of all masterpieces, like ' I Lombardi,' that at the end Torresani got up and said, ' I am not the man to prevent genius from getting on in this world. Go on ; I take the whole thing upon myself ; only put *Salve Maria* instead of *Ave Maria*, just to show the Archbishop that we are inclined to please him ; and as for the rest, it is all right.' The opera had an enthusiastic reception, and the chorus,

'O Signore, dal tetto natio,'

had to be repeated three times. The Milanese, the pioneers of the Italian revolution, always on the look out, knew very well that the Austrian Governor could not miss the meaning of the applause to that suggestively worded chorus.

Of Verdi's first three operas ' I Lombardi ' has stood its ground the best. In Italy it is still very often played. On Nov. 26, 1847, it was performed with considerable alterations in the music, and a libretto adapted by Vaez and Royer, but with little success, under the title of ' Jérusalem,' at the French Opéra. The experiment of retranslating the work into Italian was not a happy one, and ' Gerusalemme ' in Italy was little better welcomed than ' Jérusalem ' had been in Paris.

Verdi's works were soon eagerly sought after by all the impresarios, and the composer gave the preference to Venice, and wrote ' Ernani ' (Mar. 9, 1844) for the Fenice theatre there. The success was enormous, and during the following nine months it was produced on fifteen different stages. The libretto, borrowed from Victor Hugo's *Hernani*, was the work of F. Piave of Venice, of whom we shall have occasion to speak again. The police interfered before the performance, and absolutely would not allow a *conspiracy* on the stage. This time many expressions in the poem, and many notes in the music, had to be changed ; and besides the annoyances of the police, Verdi had some trouble with a Count Mocenigo, whose aristocratical susceptibility treated the blowing of the horn by Sylva in the last act as a disgrace to the theatre. In the end, after much grumbling, the horn was allowed admittance. The chorus ' Si ridesti il Leon di Castiglia ' gave the Venetians an opportunity for a political manifestation in the same spirit as that at the production of ' I Lombardi ' at Milan.

' I due Foscari ' (Nov. 3, 1844) followed close on ' Ernani.' It was brought out in Rome at the Argentina, but notwithstanding several beauties, the opera is not reckoned amongst the maestro's best. Three months after ' I due Foscari,' ' Giovanna d' Arco ' was given at the Scala in Milan (Feb. 15, 1845). The overture alone survives. ' Alzira ' (Aug. 12, 1845), performed at the San Carlo at Naples, neither added to nor detracted from its author's popularity ; while ' Attila ' (Mar. 17, 1846), produced at the Fenice, was the most successful after ' Ernani.' In this opera a cue to political demonstration was given by the aria,

'Cara Patria già madre e Regina,'

and by the no less popular line,

'Avrai tu l' Universo, resti l' Italia a me.'

The habitués of Covent Garden have little idea what ' enthusiastic applause ' means in Italy, and in Venice especially, and in what acts of sheer frenzy the audiences of 1846 would indulge to give the Austrian Government an unmistakable sign of their feelings. The overcrowded house was in a perfect roar—the noise often entirely covering the sound of both orchestra and chorus, and lasting till the police could restore order, or till there was no breath left in the audience.

' Attila ' was followed by ' Macbeth ' (Mar. 14, 1847), at the Pergola of Florence. The book was again the work of Piave, though to please the poet and composer, Andrea Maffei, the renowned translator of Byron, Moore, Schiller and Goethe, did not disdain to write some portions of it. This opera, owing chiefly to the lack of a tenor part, received scant justice in Italy, and still less abroad.

Verdi's fame was now firmly established, and Lumley, the manager of Her Majesty's Theatre, London, proposed to him to write a new opera, an offer which the composer gladly accepted. ' King Lear ' was first named as a fit subject for an English audience, but as love—the steampower of all operatic engines—had no share in the plot, it was feared that the work would want the first requisite for success. It was therefore settled to take the plot from Schiller's ' Robbers.' Maffei himself was engaged to write the poem, and no less famous artists than Jenny Lind, Lablache and Gardoni to interpret it. On this occasion the Muse did not smile on her devotee, and the first performance in London (July 22, 1847) proved no more than what in theatrical jargon is called a *succès d'estime* ; a judgment afterwards endorsed by many audiences. ' I masnadieri ' was not only Verdi's first work for the English stage, but was the last opera conducted by Costa at Her Majesty's previous to his joining the rival house at Covent Garden. This coincidence all but shunted Verdi's intellectual activity into a new track. Lumley, deserted by the fashionable conductor, made a liberal offer to Verdi, if he would act for three years as conductor. Verdi had a strong inclination to accept the offer, but there was a drawback in the fact that he had agreed with Lucca, the publisher, of Milan, to write two operas for him. Negotiations were set on foot with the view of breaking off the agreement, but Lucca would not hear of it, and Verdi had therefore to leave London, take a house at Passy, and write the ' Corsaro ' and the ' Battaglia di Legnano.'

' Il corsaro ' (Oct. 25, 1848, Trieste) was a failure. ' La Battaglia di Legnano ' (Jan. 27, 1849, Rome), though welcomed on the first night, was virtually another failure. During the summer of 1849, when the cholera was making ravages in France, Verdi, at his father's request, left Paris and went home, and he then bought the villa of S. Agata, his favourite residence, of which we shall give a description farther on.

It was in the solitude of the country near Busseto that ' Luisa Miller ' was composed for the San Carlo of Naples, where it was produced with great and deserved success on Dec. 8, 1849. The poem, one of the best ever accepted by an Italian composer, was the work of Cammarano, who took the plot from Schiller's *Kabale und Liebe* and adapted it most effectively to the operatic stage.

In connexion with ' Luisa Miller ' we shall relate an authentic incident illustrating the way in which the superstitious blood of the south can be stirred. The word ' jettatore ' is familiar to anybody acquainted with Naples. It means somebody still more to be dreaded than an evil angel, a man who comes to you with the best intentions, and who yet, by the ' evil eye,' or a charm attached to his person, unwittingly brings all kinds of accidents and misfortunes upon you. There was, at this time, one Capecelatro, an amateur composer, and a frantic admirer of all musicians, and, welcome or not welcome, an unavoidable friend to them. He was looked upon as a ' jettatore,' and it was an accepted fact in all Neapolitan circles that the cold reception of ' Alzira ' at San Carlo four years before was entirely due to his shaking hands with Verdi, and predicting a great triumph. To prevent the repetition of such a calamity, it was evident that Capecelatro must not be allowed to see, speak or write to Verdi on any pretence whatever before the first performance of ' Luisa Miller ' was over. Therefore a body of volunteers was levied amongst the composer's many friends, whose duty was to keep Capecelatro at a distance. Upon setting his foot on Neapolitan ground, Verdi found himself surrounded by this legion of friends ; they never left him alone for a minute ; they stood at the door of his hotel ; they accompanied him to the theatre and in the street ; and had

more than once to contend fiercely against the persistent and unreasonable Capecelatro. All went smoothly with the rehearsals, and the first performance was wonderfully good. During the interval before the last act—which, by the bye, is one of Verdi's most impressive and powerful creations—a great excitement pervaded the house, and every one was anxious to see the previous success crowned by a still warmer reception of the final terzetto. Verdi was standing on the stage in the centre of his guards, receiving congratulations from all, when suddenly a man rushed frantically forward, and crying out ' At last ! ' threw his arms fondly round Verdi's neck. At the same moment a side-scene fell heavily on the stage, and had it not been for Verdi's presence of mind, throwing himself back with his admirer hanging on him, both would have been crushed. We need not say that the admirer was Capecelatro, and that the last act of ' Luisa Miller ' had, compared to the others, a very cold reception.

' Stiffelio ' (Nov. 16, 1850, Trieste) was a failure ; and even after being rewritten and reproduced under the title of ' Aroldo ' (Aug. 16, 1857, Rimini) it did not become popular, though the score contains some remarkable passages, amongst others a great *pezzo concertato* and a duet for soprano and bass, which would be almost sufficient themselves, nowadays, to ensure the success of an Italian opera.

We are now going to deal with the period of the artist's career in which he wrote the masterpieces that have given him his world-wide fame —' Rigoletto,' ' Trovatore,' and ' La traviata.' Wanting a new libretto for La Fenice, Verdi requested Piave to adapt the ' Le Roi s'amuse ' of Victor Hugo, and one was soon prepared, with the suggestive French title changed into ' La maledizione.' Widely open to criticism as is Victor Hugo's drama, the situations and plot are yet admirably fit for opera-goers who do not trouble themselves about the why and the wherefore, but are satisfied with what is presented to them, provided it rouses their interest. Verdi saw the advantages offered by the libretto, and forthwith sent it to Venice for approval. But after the political events of 1848–49 the police kept a keener eye than before on all performances, and an opera in which a king is made to appear under such a light as François I. in ' Le Roi s'amuse ' was met by a flat refusal. The direction of La Fenice and the poet were driven almost mad by the answer ; the season was drawing near, and they would probably have to do without the *grand' opera d' obbligo*. Other subjects were proposed to the composer, who, with his Olympian calm, always refused on principle, saying, ' Either " La maledizione " or none.' Days went on without any solution to the problem, when it was brought to an unexpected end in a quarter where help seemed least likely. The chief of the Austrian police, Martello—who, like Torresani, had as great a love for the interests of art as he had hatred to patriotic ideas—came one morning into Piave's room with a bundle of papers under his arm, and patting him on the shoulder, said, 'Here is your business ; I have found it, and we shall have the opera.' And then he began to show how all the necessary alterations could be made without any change in the dramatic situations. The king was changed into a duke of Mantua, the title into 'Rigoletto,' and all the curses were made to wreak their fury on the head of the insignificant duke of a petty town. Verdi accepted the alterations, and after receiving the complete libretto, went to Busseto and set furiously to work. And his inspiration served him so well that in forty days he was back at Venice with 'Rigoletto' ready, and its production took place on Mar. 11, 1851. This was as great and genuine a success as was ever achieved by any operatic composer ; since no change, either of time or artistic taste, has been able to dim the beauty of this masterpiece.

Nearly two years passed before the appearance of 'Il trovatore,' which was performed at Rome at the Teatro Apollo on Jan. 19, 1853 ; and in little more than a month later 'La Traviata' was brought out at the Fenice at Venice (Mar. 6, 1853). The reception of the two works was very different : 'Il trovatore' from the very first hearing was appreciated in full ; 'La traviata' was a dead failure. 'Caro Emanuele,' wrote Verdi to his friend and pupil Muzio, 'Traviata last night made a fiasco. Is the fault mine or the actors' ? Time will show.' Time showed that the responsibility was to be laid entirely to the singers, though they were amongst the best of the day. The tenor, Graziani, took cold and sang his part throughout in a hoarse and almost inaudible voice. Varesi, the baritone, having what he would call a secondary rôle, took no trouble to bring out the dramatic importance of his short but capital part, so that the effect of the celebrated duet between Violetta and Germont in the second act was entirely missed. Mme. Donatelli, who impersonated the delicate, sickly heroine, was one of the stoutest ladies on or off the stage, and when at the beginning of the third act the doctor declares that consumption has wasted away the young lady, and that she cannot live more than a few hours, the audience was thrown in a state of perfectly uproarious glee, a state very different from that necessary to appreciate the tragic action of the last act. Yet the failure at Venice did not prevent the opera from being received enthusiastically elsewhere. In connexion with the 'Traviata' we may add that at its first performance in French, at Paris, Oct. 27, 1864, the heroine was Christine Nilsson, who then made her first appearance before the public.

Next to the 'Traviata' Verdi wrote 'Les Vêpres Siciliennes,' which appeared in Paris on June 13, 1855. It is strange that writing for the French stage an Italian composer should have chosen for his subject a massacre of the French by the Sicilians. Scribe and Duveyrier may be complimented upon their poetry, but not upon their common sense in offering such a drama to an Italian composer, who, writing for the first time for the Opéra, could hardly refuse a libretto imposed on him by the then omnipotent Scribe. However, the music was appreciated to its value by the French public, who, overlooking the inopportune argument, welcomed heartily the work of the Italian maestro. In Italy — where the opera was reproduced with a different libretto, and under the title of 'Giovanna di Guzman,' the Austrian police not allowing a poem glorifying the revolt of Sicily against oppressors—it did not actually fail, but its many beauties have never been fully appreciated.

'Simone Boccanegra'—by Piave, expressly composed by Verdi for La Fenice and produced Mar. 12, 1857—was a total failure, though the prologue and last act may be ranked amongst his most powerful inspirations. The failure was owing to the dull and confused libretto, and to a very bad interpretation. Both book and music were afterwards altered — the former by Arrigo Boito—and the opera was revived with success in Milan on Mar. 24, 1881.

'Un ballo in maschera,' though written for the San Carlo of Naples, was produced at the Teatro Apollo of Rome. Its original title was 'Gustavo III.'; but during the rehearsals occurred the attempt of Orsini against Napoleon III. (Jan. 13, 1858), and the performance of an opera with so suggestive a title was interdicted. Verdi received a peremptory order from the police to adapt his music to different words, and upon his refusal the manager of San Carlo brought an action against him for 200,000 francs damages. When this was known, together with the fact that he had refused to ask permission to produce his work as it was, there was very nearly a revolution in Naples. Crowds assembled under his window, and accompanied him through the streets, shouting 'Viva Verdi,' i.e. 'Viva Vittorio Emmanuele Re D' Italia.'

In this crisis Jasovacci, the enterprising impresario of Rome, called on Verdi, and taking the responsibility of arranging everything with the Roman police, entered into a contract to produce the work at Rome. Richard, Governor of Boston, was substituted for Gustavus III. ; the opera was re-christened 'Un ballo in maschera,' was brought out (Feb. 17, 1859), and Verdi achieved one of his greatest successes.

His next three were written for St. Petersburg, Paris and Cairo.

' La forza del destino '—the plot borrowed by Piave from ' Don Alvar,' a Spanish drama by the Duke of Rivas—was performed with moderate success on Nov. 10, 1862, at St. Petersburg. Seven years later Verdi had the libretto modified by Ghislanzoni, and after various alterations in the music, the opera was again brought before the public.

' Don Carlos,' the words by Méry and Du Locle, was enthusiastically received at the Opéra in Paris, Mar. 11, 1867. Verdi afterwards (1883) introduced some changes in the score, materially shortening the opera.

G. M. ; rev. and abridged by F. B.

THE REQUIEM AND 'AÏDA.'—Shortly after Rossini's death (1868) Verdi suggested that his memory should be honoured with the composition of a Requiem in which all the most eminent Italian composers of the time should contribute one number. The scheme seemed at first acceptable. But it was not an easy matter to gather together thirteen composers of some standing, and of the names which appear in the original list, apart from Verdi, only two or three are still remembered to-day.[1] There was also a significant omission. Boito, whose ' Mefistofele ' had been unsuccessfully performed at La Scala the very year in which Rossini died, was then looked upon as a revolutionary and ignored, while far less gifted men were asked to contribute. When all the numbers were assembled, the faults of the scheme, the inevitable want of homogeneity, the clash of different styles, were but too evident. The idea was then dropped. But when Alessandro Manzoni died in Milan in 1873, Verdi, who had always admired the poet most deeply and sincerely, thought again of the ' Libera me ' he had written for Rossini and decided to complete the Requiem. Between the writing of the last number for the proposed Rossini Requiem and the completion of the Manzoni Requiem, Verdi, however, added another opera to his repertory. The Egyptian Government desiring to inaugurate the new opera-house in Cairo with special pomp asked him to write an opera for the occasion on a story suggested by the French Egyptologist, Mariette Bey. Verdi accepted, and the score of ' Aïda ' was ready by the autumn of 1870. The outbreak of war between France and Prussia, however, delayed the performance,

since the stage decorations had been prepared in Paris. 'Aïda' was first produced in December 1871 under the conductorship of Bottesini at Cairo,[2] and in Feb. 1872 at La Scala conducted by Verdi.

'Aïda' was immediately accepted as the most finished and most typical work of its composer. There was no definite break with the Italian tradition which demands that the claims of the singer and of lyrical expression should stand foremost. But the melody of 'Aïda,' if it flows not less easily, has greater distinction than the melody of 'Traviata' or 'Don Carlos,' and there are no such lapses into the frankly popular vein which are noticeable now and again in ' Rigoletto.'

Before proceeding to the two last and greatest operas of Verdi it is necessary to revert to the Requiem, which when first heard produced not a little stir and provoked a good deal of hostile criticism in Germany and elsewhere. Two facts gave some semblance of reason to the objections raised against it. In the first place it was known that Verdi, whatever his views on religion, was not by any means an ardent Catholic and had identified himself with the Liberals. In the second place it was urged that his art was not fitted for religious service for the very qualities which made it admirable for the theatre. The answer to such criticism is simple enough. Antagonism to Church party, or to what was then the policy of the Church, does not constitute irreligion. No one has stigmatised policy in more unambiguous terms than Dante, yet he remains the greatest Christian of his time. The second objection falls before the evidence of the common source of church and theatre music. The only question we have a right to ask is whether the composer was sincere in his expression. The years that have gone have answered it conclusively. The manner may be that of a Latin, impetuous, impulsive, picturesque, but the sincerity of the Requiem is above question. Nor could it be otherwise, for Verdi was sincere in all things. Adverse criticism gained strength at the time owing to the onslaught of Bülow who, in the *Allgemeine Zeitung*, 1874, defined the Requiem as a monstrosity. Brahms, however, who had not heard it, on reading Bülow's notice, bought the score, read it through, and declared it to be the work of genius. It must be added that some years later Bülow wrote a repentant letter to Verdi (1892) declaring himself to have been before blinded by fanaticism and partisanship, and frankly owning that even an inadequate performance of the Requiem had since moved him profoundly. He was answered by Verdi with equal frankness and generosity. Both letters deserve to be closely studied for their

---

[1] The list of contributors was as follows :

1. Requiem aeternam (G minor), Buzzola.
2. Dies irae (C minor), Bazzini.
3. Tuba mirum (E♭ minor), Pedrotti.
4. Quid sum miser (A♭ major), Cagnoni.
5. Recordare (F major), Ricci.
6. Ingemisco (A minor), Nini.
7. Confutatis (D major), Boucheron.
8. Lacrymosa (G major, C minor), Coccia.
9. Domine Jesu (C major), Gaspari.
10. Sanctus (D♭ major), Platania.
11. Agnus Dei (F major), Petrella.
12. Lux aeterna (A♭ major), Mabellini.
13. Libera me (C minor), Verdi.

[2] CAST : Aïda, Pozzoni-Anastasi ; Amneris, Grossi ; Radames Mongini ; Ramfis, Medini ; Amonasro, Costa ; the King, Steller.

bearing on criticism as well as for the characteristic nobility of mind they reveal.

RELATIONS WITH BOITO.—The years which passed between 'Aïda' and the next opera, 'Otello,' were years of quiet and perhaps unconscious preparation in which Verdi found at last his ideal librettist, Boito. The relations between the two had been somewhat strained at first, as could be expected in view of the fact that Boito was the leader of the young and revolutionary, while Verdi ever believed that the pace of evolution should not be forced, and that progress is not achieved by rushing blindly forward, but by a deeper understanding of the fundamental laws which have governed music in all ages. Boito in his young days had also turned the popular tenor song in 'Rigoletto,' 'La donna è mobile,' into a polka—which was not likely to endear him to Verdi. But in 1862 the two were brought together in the composition of the 'Inno delle Nazioni' which Verdi wrote for the London Exhibition on words of Boito. In the following year, however, Boito in a toast expressed views which Verdi interpreted as an attack on himself. Boito probably meant nothing of the kind, but he was sanguine, fiery and apt to express his ideas very forcibly. Verdi, on the other hand, kept his temper, but having come to the conclusion that Boito looked upon his art with little respect, if not with contempt, could not be easily induced to believe the opposite. Ever since La Scala performance of 'Aïda' Boito had professed himself ready to write a libretto for Verdi. He would consider himself 'honoured and highly fortunate' to write for Verdi, although he would not write a line for anybody else. For long nothing came of it. When the subject of 'Otello' was suggested to Verdi by his publisher Ricordi and the conductor Faccio (1879), the composer did not seem very enthusiastic. Boito submitted a first sketch, which Verdi liked, but although he advised the poet to continue the work he would not accept it definitely. When the text was finished it was shown to Verdi, who then promised to set it to music. But the relations between poet and composer were destined to have yet another set-back. A banquet was given to Boito after the first performance of 'Mefistofele' at the S. Carlo Theatre in Naples, and the composer, pressed to say something on the subject of 'Jago'—this was the first title of 'Otello'—was reported as having expressed regret at not being able to write the music for it himself. Verdi saw in this a reflection on his own ability to write an adequate setting, and immediately offered to return the libretto to Boito. The latter wrote at length pointing out that the pretended slur was not in anything he had actually said, but only in the fantastic interpretation of his words by an irresponsible reporter. Verdi, still protesting

that he was too old, that he could not promise to set to work again, that he had served the public too long, accepted nevertheless the explanation. 'Otello' was finished on Nov. 1, 1886, and performed at La Scala in Feb. 1887, conducted by Franco Faccio, with Pantaleoni, Petrovich, Tamagno and Maurel as principal performers. The success was immediate. The opera was acknowledged as marking the highest point ever reached by Italian opera, and 'Otello' triumphed soon after in all the great European theatres.

VERDI'S ULTIMATE STYLE.—Technically it marks a distinct advance on 'Aïda.' Still greater is the advance it marks as regards Verdi's outlook on music and opera. It is known that he had once cherished the idea of setting to music 'King Lear,' and that he had finally put it aside because it had not a love interest in its tragic story, and love, he thought then, was essential to opera. In 'Otello' he proved that opera is possible without a love interest, for the theme of 'Otello' is not love but jealousy. Specially is this the case in Boito's version of the tragedy, which in its inevitable compression ignores the first doubts of the Moor and his desperate longing to trust Desdemona rather than Jago. Another point which may be made here, although it applies equally to 'Falstaff,' concerns Verdi's style. It has been said sometimes that his operas fall into three periods and that the later works show traces of Wagnerian influence. Nothing could be further from the truth. The texture of Wagner's music is essentially contrapuntal, while the texture of Verdi is ever melodic and harmonic. The orchestration of Wagner is based on the contrapuntal style of many threads of equal value being skilfully drawn together; the orchestration of Verdi is founded on the assumption that the singer, and melody with him, are the chief considerations to which the orchestra is subservient. The difference between the earlier and the later operas of Verdi is not one of method but of manner. The accompaniment which before was often colourless and even threadbare becomes ornate, characteristic, picturesque. Once it was the humble slave of the melody; later it becomes its helper, sharing its moods, adding to its power without, however, presuming to take its place. One has only to compare the accompaniment to 'Morire si Pura e Bella' in 'Aïda' with the love duet in 'Otello' to see the difference between the two conceptions. Verdi was in favour of certain reforms advocated by Wagner, but he held that it would be unwise for Italians to follow a foreign example. And his evolution followed Italian precedent, for the problem which, as the internal evidence of his operas shows, concerned him most was essentially the same which had attracted Monteverdi—the importance of the recitative and the tyranny of pure lyricism. Verdi never felt anything like a revolt against the old system of arias, cabalettas and recitatives. He held, in fact, that if there is to be such a thing as a stereotyped plan for opera, one system may be as good as another. But he laboured unceasingly to bring the recitative into line with lyricism and give it a real and living interest. From this point of view his work shows a continuous progress culminating in ' Otello ' and ' Falstaff.' The question of a dramatic recitative to take the place of lyrical expression was much to the fore when ' Otello ' was first produced, and critics were found who demurred to the lyricism of ' Ora e per sempre ' on the ground that it impeded the dramatic progress of the action. The objection is baseless for the reason that a lyrical expression at this point of the drama has its *raison d'être* not in the whim or desire of the composer, but in the psychology of the character, and is hence fully justified.

Verdi was delighted with the reception of ' Otello,' and he derived particular satisfaction from its success in London. He was afraid that Shakespeare's countrymen might find something to say about the way Boito had handled the text. Critics, however, took a broad view, and neither the omission of the first act of the tragedy nor the interpolation of the ' Credo ' of Jago provoked unfavourable comment. And the good fortune of ' Otello ' made him look upon ' Falstaff ' more favourably from the first. Boito suggested it as far back as 1889, and although Verdi appeared to fear lest his age might prevent him from carrying out his part, he was evidently anxious to set to work, and in the following year some progress was made, Verdi protesting that he was writing merely to while away the time. He was exceedingly satisfied with Boito's libretto, and for the first time in his long career he wrote the music without asking the poet to alter a syllable. He had long wished to write a comic opera, and he had possibly given some consideration to the subject of ' The Merry Wives of Windsor ' more than once. A rumour was spread that he was composing an opera on ' Falstaff ' in 1868 ; it may have been less completely erroneous than was then thought. It is interesting to note in a letter written in 1891 that Verdi thought a great theatre like La Scala damaging to the effect of ' Falstaff.' It may well be that the comparative coldness with which the opera was then received by the public at large was due to the inadequacy of a large stage for a work abounding in fine, subtle points. In London a performance given by students of the R.C.M. in a comparatively small theatre has evoked more genuine enthusiasm than the elaborate performances at Covent Garden.

' Falstaff ' was performed at La Scala on Feb. 9, 1893, conducted by Edoardo Mascheroni, and sung by Mmes. Zilli, Stehle, Pasqua, Guerrini and MM. Garbin, Maurel, Paroli, Pini-Corsi, Pelagalli - Rossetti and Arimondi. It revealed a new aspect of Verdi's genius of which there is not a glimmer in his other operas. Fra Melitone, the comic character in ' La forza del destino,' is caricature. The essence of ' Falstaff ' is humour not caricature. The one needs characterisation while the other implies exaggeration and distortion of character. Every scene abounds in happy strokes. From the first merry bustle which opens the opera to the last glittering fugue proclaiming that ' all in the world is a jest,' it is a succession of wonderful touches where music adds not only charm and eloquence to the word but often completes the thought of the poet. We need only quote Ford's monologue as an example of this subtle yet indissoluble bond between word and notes. Throughout the monologue runs the figure associated with Falstaff's words : ' I'll bamboozle him, neatly, neatly.' Ford grows quite lyrical in praise of his own jealousy and his own foresight, and the orchestra immediately follows this up with the phrase which before accompanied the words : ' And yet they say that jealous husbands are fools ! ' The fear of dishonour, the belief in his own wisdom, the desire of revenge, all are in the music as thoughts recurring and haunting the unfortunate Ford. There are also very different elements, such as the mellow sadness of the scene which precedes the final punishment of Falstaff in Windsor Park, and the exquisite grace of the love duets between Fenton and Anne Ford which give to the comedy its rich humanity. Above all stands the admirable characterisation. The Falstaff of Boito and Verdi may not be a faithful reproduction of the Falstaff of Shakespeare —but like him he is a diverting and forgivable rogue. Such he was conceived and painted by the composer, who at once grasped the drift of his collaborator and emphasised those traits which make him absurdly plausible and a cause of fun in others.

The first performance of ' Falstaff ' was a great personal triumph, and Verdi was recalled times without number. He was also offered a marquisate which he refused without thanks. But he knew the theatre and audiences too well not to realise that somehow ' Falstaff ' had not stirred the people as ' Otello ' and ' Aïda ' had done. It was played and well received all over Italy and in the principal musical centres abroad, but it failed to arouse the enthusiasm of Verdi's other operas. It seemed too fine and aristocratic to appeal to the average audience. Verdi began to feel that his work was done, and the thought lay heavier on him than his years. He prepared with Boito the French translation of ' Falstaff,' but ' it is useless,' he wrote, 'as we shall certainly not go to Paris,' and in a letter to Mme. Zilli, who had sung the part of Alice, he recalled the happy days spent in preparing for the first performance of 'Falstaff,' and how when parting he knew that 'as artists we shall meet no more,' concluding with the phrase 'everything is ended,' underlined. In Nov. 1897 his second wife, who had always been a dear companion, died after a short illness, and left him sadder than he had ever been. The loneliness of old age was all around him, and although he was not physically ill the extraordinary vitality which had kept him young in mind and body so long was slowly ebbing away, and he complained of failing strength and the uselessness of living while unable to read, to see, to feel. He died at S. Agata on Jan. 27, 1901, after a long and painful agony. Boito, who was near him, wrote of his end :

'The Master is dead, and has taken with him a large share of vital warmth and light. We were all sunned by his olympic old age. He died magnificently like a dumb, formidable wrestler. The silence of death fell on him a week before he breathed his last. With bent head he seemed to take the measure of the dreaded adversary and withstand his attack. His resistance was heroic. . . . He fought up to the last moment magnificently against death. . . . I have never felt before such hatred and contempt for this mysterious power, blind, senseless. . . .'

MISCELLANY.—Verdi wrote a great many compositions between the ages of 13 and 18, that is, before coming to Milan. Amongst them are Marches for brass band, short symphonies, six concertos and variations for pianoforte ; many serenate, cantate, arie, and a great many duetti, terzetti and church compositions, including a Stabat Mater. During the three years he remained at Milan he wrote amongst other things two symphonies which were performed there, and a cantata. Upon his return to Busseto, he wrote a 'Messa' and a 'Vespro,' three settings of Tantum Ergo and other sacred compositions, as well as choruses to Alessandro Manzoni's tragedies and 'Il cinque Maggio.' Everything is lost with the exception of a few 'symphonies,' probably 'overtures,' and the music to Manzoni's poems.

To this must be added the 'Inno delle nazioni' (Her Majesty's Theatre, 1862) ; a group of sacred works, consisting of an Ave Maria a 4, upon the 'scala enigmatica' (treated

like a canto fermo, each voice having the scale in turn) ; a Stabat Mater a 4 with orchestra ; 'Laudi alla Vergine Maria' for four-part female chorus ; a Te Deum for two four-part choirs and orchestra, 1898, first sung at the Paris Opéra on Apr. 7, 1898 ; and a string quartet (Naples, 1873) which does not deserve the complete neglect into which it has fallen.

The most important recent contribution to literature about Verdi is the volume *I copialettere di Giuseppe Verdi*, edited by Gaetano Cesari and Alessandro Luzio, consisting of the copy of letters written by Verdi between the years 1844–1900. It was Verdi's habit to write and keep a copy of every letter he sent out. These copies, filling five thick volumes, now collected and published, give us an extraordinary insight into the mind and character of a man whose simplicity, honesty and far-sightedness deserve in themselves to be called great. From these we see how clear a conception he had of his craft, of the theatre, and how a work for the theatre should be prepared. We can follow the correspondence with the poets who wrote his libretti ; his suggestions for changes of scenes and dialogue ; his description of the action, of the entrances and exits, of the characters—follow him in fact step by step in his long career and in his relations with other men, with humble impresarios, and with his famous collaborators—a publication more important and infinitely more truthful than many an autobiography.

Verdi's dicta have been often discussed and less often understood. 'There will be progress in going back to the old' does not mean that we are to adopt the manner of the old composers, but that in the old composers is the surest foundation of musical art. He did not believe in the 'realism' that became fashionable with 'Cavalleria rusticana,' hence his 'it is better to invent reality than to copy it,' and he pointed to Shakespeare, who 'created' his characters instead of seeking them ready to his hand, as the supreme arbiter. If his opinions on foreign schools have seemed at times unfair or exaggerated, it should be remembered that they were generally meant as a protest against fashions which Verdi felt could not but lead his own countrymen astray.

He was a just and charitable man. The great bulk of his fortune was left in trust for the Casa di Riposo for old musicians which he himself had founded in Milan.　　　F. B.

OPERAS

Oberto Conte di S. Bonifacio, Nov. 17, 1839. **Milan.**
Un giorno di regno, Sept. 5, 1840. **Milan.**
Nabucodonosor, Mar. 9, 1842. **Milan.**
I Lombardi, Feb. 11, 1843. **Milan.**
Ernani, Mar. 9, 1844. Venice
I due Foscari, Nov. 3, 1844. Rome.
Giovanna d' Arco, Feb. 15, 1845. **Milan.**
Alzira, Aug. 12, 1845. Naples.
Attila, Mar. 17, 1846. Venice.
Macbeth, Mar. 14, 1847. Florence.
I masnadieri, July 22, 1847. London.
Jérusalem, Nov. 26, 1847. Paris.
Il corsaro, Oct. 25, 1848. Trieste.
La battaglia di Legnano, Jan. 27 1849. **Rome.**
Luisa Miller, Dec. 8, 1849. Naples.
Stiffelio, Nov. 16, 1850. Trieste.
Rigoletto, Mar. 11, 1851. Venice.
Il trovatore, Jan. 19, 1853. Rome.
La traviata, Mar. 6, 1853. Venice.
Les Vêpres Siciliennes, June 13, 1855. **Paris.**
Simone Boccanegra, Mar. 12, 1857. Venice.
Aroldo, Aug. 16, 1857. Rimini.
Un ballo in maschera, Feb. 17, 1859. **Rome.**

La forza del destino, Nov. 10, 1862. St. Petersburg
Macbeth (revised), Apr. 21, 1865. Paris.
Don Carlos, Mar. 11, 1867. Paris.
Aida, Dec. 24, 1871. Cairo.
Simone Boccanegra (revised), Apr. 1881. Milan.
Otello, Feb. 5, 1887. Milan.
Falstaff, Feb. 9, 1893. Milan.

DRAWING-ROOM MUSIC

Sei romanze.—Non t' accostare all' urna. More Elisa, lo stanco
    poeta. In solitaria stanza. Nell' orror di notte oscura.
    Perduta ho la pace. Deh pietosa.
L' esule, a song for bass.
La seduzione, a song for bass.
Notturno a tre voci. S.T.B. Guarda che bianca luna, with flute
    obbligato.
Album di sei romanze. Il tramonto. La zingara. Ad una stella.
    Lo spazza camino. Il mistero. Brindisi.
Il poveretto. Romanza.
Tu dici che non m' ami. Stornello.

CHAMBER MUSIC

String Quartet. (1873.)

VOCAL MUSIC

' Suona la tromba.' (1848.)
Inno delle nazioni (for the London Exhibition). (1862.)

SACRED MUSIC

Requiem. (1874.)
Pater Noster for 5-part chorus. } (1880.)
Ave Maria (soprano and string acc.) }
Ave Maria (scala enigmatica, four parts).
Stabat Mater (chorus and orchestra). } (1st perf. Paris, 1898.)
Te Deum (double chorus and orchestra) }
Laudi alla Vergine (on Dante's Paradiso). }

BIBLIOGRAPHY

C. Bellaigue : Verdi-biografia critica. (Milan.)
A. Bonaventura : G. Verdi. (Livorno.)
Brazaguolo e Betrazzi : La vita di G. Verdi. (Milan.)
Monaldi : Conversazioni Verdiane. (Milan.)
Roncaglia : G. Verdi. (Naples.)
H. Joffredini : Le opere di G. Verdi (Milan.)
I. Pizzi : Verdi centenario. (Latter Torius.)
G. Cesari e A. Luzis : I copialettere di G. Verdi. (Commissione
    Executiva, Milan, 1913.)
Adolf Weissmann : Verdi. (Klassiker der Musik, Stuttgart,
    Berlin, 1922.)
See also : Stanford, Studies (London) ; Pizzetti, Saggi critici,
    (Milan) ; C. Ricci, A. Boito (Milan).

VERDINA, Pietro (d. Vienna, July 1643),
singer in 1619 in the Imperial Chapel, Vienna;
from 1634–35 vice-Kapellmeister. In 1641 the
emperor presented him with a gold medal. A
mass of his in MS. is in the library of Kremsmünster, and Giac. Vincenti's ' Lilia sacra,'
etc. (1618), contains two motets and 2 canzons,
3 v. (Q.-L.).

VERDONCK (Verdonk, Verdoncq
and other forms of spelling), Cornelius
(b. Turnhout, Belgium, 1563; d. Antwerp,
July 4, 1625). From 1579 or 1580 Verdonck
belonged to the service of Corneille Pruenen,
treasurer (afterwards sheriff) of the city of
Antwerp, who died in 1598. He then passed
to the service of Pruenen's nephews, Arnold
de Cordes (1598–1601) and Jean de Cordes
(1601–25). This makes Verdonck's sojourn in
Spain [1] as moço de capilla (singer), then oratorio
singer at the court of Madrid, very doubtful.
There exists, however, another musician of the
same name, contemporary, and possibly related,
living in Spain as singer in the Royal Chapel
' moyo de oratorio de Sa. Magestad.' It may
also be he who was a prebend of the church at
Eindhoven.

As a musician he must have been highly
appreciated by his contemporaries, as the

[1] Q.-L., Van der Straeten.

following epitaph, inscribed to his memory in
the Carmelite Church [2] at Antwerp, shows :

D. O. M. S.
SISTE GRADUM VIATOR
UT PERLEGAS QUAM OB REM HIC LAPIS LITTERATUS SIET
MUSICORUM DELICIAE
CORNELIUS VERDONCKIUS
TURNHOLTANUS HOC CIPPO EHEU ! CLAUSUS
PERPETUUM SILET
QUI DUM VIXIT
VOCE ET ARTE MUSICA
MORTEM SURDA NI ESSET FLEXISSET
QUAM DUM FRUSTRA DEMULCET
COELI CHORIS VOCEM AETERNAM SACRATURUS
ABIT
IV NON. JUL. ANNO MDCXXV AETAT. LXII
AT TU·LECTOR BENE PRECARE ET VALE
CLIENTI SUO MOESTUS PONEBAT
DE CORDES.

His compositions consist chiefly of madrigals
for four, six and up to nine voices, many of
which appear in the miscellaneous collections
published at Antwerp by Hubert Waelrant and
Peter Phalèse between 1585 and 1610. A book
of ' Poésies françoises ' a 5, with one a 10,
was published in 1599, and a set of 6-part
madrigals in 1603. One of his madrigals was
received into Young's English collection
entitled ' Musica transalpina,' published in
London, 1588. A few sacred compositions
also appear among the published works of
Verdonck. A Magnificat a 5 appeared at
Antwerp in 1584. An Ave Maria of his for
four voices is printed in Proske's ' Musica
divina,' Annus ii. Liber ii. 1874.   J. R. M.

Bibl.—Van der Straeten, La Musique aux Pays-Bas, iii. ;
Goovaerts, Histoire et bibliographie de la typographie musicale
dans les Pays-Bas ; Paul Bergmans, La Biographie des compositions
Corneille Verdonck, 1563–1625, with full list of compositions
(Brussels, 1919).

**VEREENIGING VOOR NEDER-
LANDSCHE MUZIEKGESCHIEDENIS** (Association for the History of Dutch Music) is the
literary branch of the national Society for the
Advancement of Music (see Maatschappij tot
Bevordering der Toonkunst). It was separated in 1868–69 for the purpose of collecting and
publishing materials for the musical history of
the Dutch Netherlands, especially during the
period extending from Obrecht (1450) to Sweelinck (1621). Its publications are as follows :

1. Sweelinck, Regina Coeli (ed. H. A. Viotta, 1869).
2. Old Dutch Songs, from the lute-book of Adrianus Valerius (ed. A. D. Loman, 1871).
3. Organ compositions, by Sweelinck and Scheidt (ed. R. Eitner, 1871).
4. Twelve Geuzeliedjes, songs of the Gueux during the Spanish oppression (ed. A. D. Loman, 1872).
5. Three madrigals by Schuijt, and two chansons by Sweelinck (ed. R. Eitner, 1873)
6. Eight Psalms by Sweelinck with Life by F. H. L. Tiedeman (1876).
7. Chanson by Sweelinck (ed. R. Eitner, 1877).
8. Selections from Johannes Wanning, 'LII Sententiae' (ed. R. Eitner, 1878).
9. Mass ' Fortuna desperata,' by Jacob Obrecht (ed. R. Eitner, 1880).
10. Old Dutch Dances arranged for piano (four hands) by J. C. M. van Riemsdijk (1882).
11. Const. Huygens, ' Pathodia sacra et profana ' (ed. W. J. A. Jonckbloet and J. P. N. Laud, 1883).
12. Six Psalms by Sweelinck, in four parts (ed. R. Eitner, 1884).
13. J. A. Reincken, ' Hortus musicus ' (ed. J. C. M. van Riemsdijk, 1886).
14. J. A. Reincken, Partita diverse sopra l'aria: 'Schweiget mir vor Weibernehmen ' (1887).
15. J. P. Sweelinck, Cantio sacra, ' Hodie Christus natus est,' five parts.
(Without No.) J. P. Sweelinck, 'O Sacrum Convivium,' five-part motet.

[2] Now disappeared. Copy was supplied by M. Goovaerts, keeper
of the public archives.

16. 24 Songs of the 15th and 16th centuries, for one voice with accompt. (ed. J. C. M. van Riemsdijk).

17. J. P. Sweelinck, Ps. cl., for eight voices.

18. Obrecht, Passio Domini (St. Matthew), for four voices.

19. A. van Noordt, 'Tabulaturbuch,' Psalms and Fantasias (1659) (ed. Max Seiffert).

20. Old Dutch 'Boerenliedjes' and 'Contradansen,' for violin with PF. accompt. (ed. Julius Röntgen), first set.

21. Marches used in Holland during the War of the Spanish Succession, 1702–1713, collected by J. W. Enschedé, arranged for PF. duet by A. Averkamp.

22. 50 Psalms by Cornelis Boskoop (1568), (ed. Max Seiffert).

23. Old Dutch 'Boerenliedjes' and 'Contradansen' (ed. Julius Röntgen), second set (cf. No. 20).

24. Six-part madrigals by Jan Tollius (1597) (ed. Max Seiffert).

25. Netherlandish Dances of the 16th century (arranged for PF. duet by J. Röntgen), first set.

26. A Dutch Music-book (1572) (ed. Fl. van H. Duyse).

27. Netherlandish Dances of the 16th century (arranged for PF. duet by J. Röntgen), second book.

28. Scherzi musicali per la viola da gamba, by Johan

29. First Music-book of Tielman (Tylman) Susato after the edition of 1551 (ed. Fl. van Duyse).

30. 25 Three-voiced old Dutch Songs, 15th century (ed. Julius Wolf).

31. Two sonatas for violin with piano accompt. by Pietro Locatelli da Bergamo (ed. Julius Röntgen).

32. Compositioni musicali per il cembalo. Divisi in due parti di Corrado Federigo Hurlebusch (ed. Max Seiffert).

33. Old Dutch 'Boerenliedjes' and 'Contradansen' (ed. Julius Röntgen), third and fourth sets, cf. No. 20.

34. Orchestral compositions by Dutch masters of the early 17th century. 'Paduanen' and 'Galliarden' by Melchior Borchgreving, Benedictus Grep and Nicolaus Gistow (ed. H. F. Wirth).

35. 'Missa super Benedicta,' by Adrian Willaert, for 5-voiced mixed choir (ed. Ant. Averkamp).

36. Old Dutch 'Boerenliedjes' and 'Contradansen' (ed. J. Röntgen. Fifth set, cf. No. 20.

37. Old Dutch clavier music from the Music-book of Anna Maria van Eyl (1671) (ed. Julius Röntgen).

38. 'Missa ad modulum benedicta' (6 v.) : Philippo de Monte (ed. A. Smijers).

Schenk (ed. Dr. Hugo Leichentritt).

The Vereeniging has also published complete collections of the works of Sweelinck (ed. Max Seiffert) and Obrecht (ed. Joh. Wolff). The collected works of Josquin des Prés (ed. A. Smijers are (1927) in progress. Other publications are a volume entitled *Musique et musiciens au XVIIᵉ siècle. Correspondance et œuvres musicales de Constantin Huygens, publiées par W. J. A. Jonckbloet et J. P. N. Land* (1882). Besides these works, transactions (*Bouwsteenen*) were published from 1869–1881. Their place was taken by a regular journal (*Tijdschrift*), publication of which was begun in 1882 and is still continued.   R. L. P.

VERHEYEN, PIERRE (*b.* Ghent, 1750; *d.* there, Jan. 11, 1819), son of a singer at St. Bavon, Ghent. Leonard Boutmy gave him his first music lessons. He went to Maestricht to prepare for the University, but his love for music prevailed, and soon after he became tenor singer at Bruges Cathedral, where he produced also some masses and psalms of his own. The paucity of his pay turned his attention towards the theatre, and after some successful tours in Flanders, Northern France and Holland he obtained an engagement at the theatre at Brussels through Witzthumb, who also became his first master in the art of composition, which he continued to study under F. Krafft at Ghent, where, in 1786, he became solo tenor at the cathedral and composer to the Bishop, Prince Lobkowitz. After holding a post of Kapellmeister at Maestricht for some time, he returned in 1790 to Ghent to fill a similar post at Ste Pharailde. On the invasion of the French he lost this position, became organist at the 'Temple de la Raison,'

and began to compose operas, which were given at various theatres, chamber music and a number of songs (*romances*). When order had once more been restored to the country, Verheyen resumed his position at Ghent, and composed chiefly for the Church, including 15 masses with full orchestra, 12 masses with organ, a Requiem for Haydn, a Te Deum, numerous psalms, etc. He also composed a cantata, 'La Bataille de Waterloo,' 1816, and in this year a medal was struck in his honour ; but in spite of all this he lived and died in very straitened circumstances.

    E. v. d. s.

VERHULST, JOHANNES JOSEPHUS HERMAN (*b.* The Hague, Mar. 19, 1816 ; *d.* there, Jan. 17, 1891), was one of the earliest students at the Royal School of Music there, where he learned violin and theory. He afterwards played in the orchestra of the French Opéra under Charles Hanssen, and wrote many pieces, amongst others an Overture in B minor which was published by the Maatschappij tot Bevordering der Toonkunst. An allowance from the king enabled him to go first to Cologne, where he studied with Joseph Klein, and then to Leipzig, where he arrived Jan. 12, 1838, and was well received by Mendelssohn, and soon after made director of the important ' Euterpe ' Concerts. There and in Germany he remained till 1842, when he returned to The Hague and was at once decorated by the King with the order of the Lion and made Director of the Music at court. Subsequently he resided at Rotterdam, where he became director of the Maatschappij tot bevordering der Toonkunst, at The Hague and at Amsterdam, where for many years he conducted the Felix Meritis Society, the concerts of the 'Maatschappij' and the Cecilia Concerts, as well as the Diligentia Society at The Hague (from 1860). As a conductor he was very famous in his own country. He retired in 1866. His compositions comprise symphonies, overtures, quartets, much church music (amongst other pieces a Requiem for men's voices), songs and part-songs to Dutch words. Verhulst's music is little known out of his own country. In England the writer only remembers to have heard one piece, an intermezzo for orchestra called ' Gruss aus der Ferne,' performed occasionally at the Crystal Palace. Verhulst's friendship with Schumann was one of the greatest events of his life. How close and affectionate it was may be judged from the many letters given in Jansen's *Davidsbündler,* and especially the following note written at the end of one of Schumann's visits to Holland :

Dear Verhulst,—Good-bye. It delighted me to find you in your old spirits. Unfortunately you cannot say the same of me. Perhaps my good genius may yet bring me back to my former condition. It delighted me too to find that you have got so dear a wife : in that matter we are both equally fortunate. Give her a nice message from me and take a hearty greeting and embrace for yourself from your old

ROBERT SCH.

Scheveningen, Sept. 8, 1852.

Schumann's ' Overture, Scherzo, and Finale ' (op. 52) is dedicated to Verhulst, who possessed the autograph, with the following inscription [1] :

J. J. Verhulst
übergiebt die Partitur des alten Opus
mit alten Sympathien.
Rotterdam d. 18 Dec. 1853.   R. Schumann.

G.

VERKAUFTE BRAUT, DIE (see PRODANÁ NEVĚSTA).

VERMONT, PIERRE, Netherlandish composer, singer in the Papal Chapel from 1529–30, singer in the Royal Chapel, Paris, 1532, and in 1547 appears in an account of the obsequies of Francis I. as ' chapelain des hautes messes ' (chanter). In Attaingnant's collections of motets and of chansons, 1533–35, there are 8 numbers signed *Vermont primus* and 3 signed *Vermont* only ; whether they both refer to *Pierre* Vermont, since he appears in the lists of singers, has yet to be established. Henry Expert has re-edited a chanson by Vermont *primus* from the Collection of Chansons of 1520 (*Fétis* ; *Q.-L.*).

VERNE, the name adopted in 1893 by the two younger sisters of Marie WURM (*q.v.*).

(1) MATHILDE, a pupil of Mme. Schumann, has had a successful career in London as pianist and teacher. She is well known as a chamber-music player and for many years has organised and appeared at the ' Tuesday, 12 o'clock ' concerts, a series of well-diversified programmes given during the winter months in London.

In 1909 Miss Mathilde Verne started her school of pianoforte-playing at Kensington, which she has maintained successfully ever since.

(2) ADELA, was a pupil of her sister Mathilde and first appeared in London in 1898. She pursued a brilliant career as a concert pianist and toured successfully all over the world. Later she has taken part in the training offered by her sister's school.   C.

VERNIZZI, OTTAVIO (*b.* Bologna, *c.* 1580), organist of S. Petronio from about 1603–48. He was one of the earliest dramatic composers, and wrote 5 ' Azioni dramatiche,' the first interludes performed at Bologna between 1617 and 1625, the last one being ' Intermezzi della coronazione di Apollo per Dafne convertita in lauro.' His other works are : motets, 5-10 v., with an organ part for the double chorus motets, lib. 1, 1603 ; Armonia ecclesiasticorum, motets, 2-4 v., with organ, op. 2, 1604 ; Angelici concentus, motets, 2-4 v., op. 3, 1606 (other editions, 1611 and 1631) ; Coelestium applausus, motets with basso continuo for organ, op. 4, 1612 ; concerti spirituali, 2-4 v., op. 6, 1648. Adr. Banchieri, who was his

friend, included a Concerto ossia Mottetto in his ' Nuovi pensieri,' 1613 (*Fétis* ; *Q.-L.*).

VERNON, JOSEPH (*b.* Coventry, *c.* 1738 ; *d.* South Lambeth, Mar. 19, 1782), singer, is believed to have been a chorister at St. Paul's Cathedral, London, under William Savage, master of the children ; he originally appeared at Drury Lane as a soprano singer in 1751. On Feb. 23 he sang in 'Alfred' (music by Arne and others), and on Nov. 19 performed the part of Thyrsis in Dr. Boyce's ' Shepherd's Lottery.' In 1754 he became a tenor singer. In the early part of 1755 he married, at the Savoy Chapel, Miss Poitier, a singer at Drury Lane. There was some irregularity in the performance of the ceremony which infringed the law for the prevention of clandestine marriages, and Wilkinson, the chaplain of the Savoy, and Grierson, his curate, the actual celebrant, were tried, convicted, and transported. Vernon had been compelled to appear as a witness against Grierson upon his trial, and the public, unjustly suspecting him of having instigated the prosecution, refused to allow him to appear upon the stage. His enforced retirement lasted until the end of 1756, when he was permitted to return, and became an established favourite.

He had an indifferent voice, but sang with such excellent taste and judgment as to render his organic defect almost imperceptible. He was, moreover, an admirable actor, and was constantly allotted parts in which no singing was required. This rare union of the qualities of singer and actor peculiarly fitted him for such parts as the Clown in ' Twelfth Night,' and Autolycus in ' The Winter's Tale,' in both of which he excelled. He was the original Cymon in Michael Arne's opera of that name, and in 1762 created the part of Apollo in ' Midas.' Linley composed for him the well-known song in ' The School for Scandal.' He sang in Michael Arne's ' Fairy Tale ' in 1764, and in the same year succeeded Lowe as the tenor singer at Vauxhall. He remained a favourite singer there until the winter of 1781. He composed, and in 1772 published in a volume,

' The New Songs in the Pantomime of The Witches ; the celebrated Epilogue in the Comedy of Twelfth Night ; a Song in The Two Gentlemen of Verona ; and two favourite Ballads sung by Mr. Vernon at Vauxhall.'

His wife, as ' Mrs. Vernon,' was singing at Drury Lane in ' Thomas and Sally,' in 1760, and a few years later, in other Drury Lane operas, including ' Midas,' 1764, as ' Miss Poitier.'

W. H. H. ; rev. F. K.

VÉRON, LOUIS DÉSIRÉ (*b.* Paris, Apr. 5, 1798 ; *d.* there, Sept. 27, 1867), the son of a stationer, studied medicine on leaving school, and took his doctor's degree in 1823. He had been intimate with the chemist Regnauld, and on his death bought the patent of his ' Pâte Regnauld,' and made a fortune. In 1828 he gave up doctoring, and took to writing for the press. In 1829 he founded the *Revue de Paris*, and became a personage of importance. In spite of this, however, he gave up journalism, and became (Mar. 2, 1831) director of the Opéra for five years, with a subsidy of 810,000 francs for the first year, 760,000 francs for the second, and 710,000 francs (respectively £32,500, £30,500 and £28,500) for the last three. Thus at his ease in money matters, with an excellent body of artists, and an able coadjutor in Edmond Duponchel (*b.* 1795; *d.* 1868), who looked after the *mise en scène*, his usual luck did not fail him, for the first work he produced was 'Robert le Diable' (Nov. 21, 1831). The success of Meyerbeer's first masterpiece is well known, but it is not so well known that the manager of the Opéra exacted from the composer a large sum in consideration of the expenses of mounting the opera. With much energy and tact Véron at once set to work to vary and renew the repertory, beginning in 1832 with the ballet ' La Sylphide ' and ending with the production, Feb. 23, 1835, of 'La Juive,' with Falcon, Nourrit and Levasseur —his greatest success after ' Robert.' Véron relinquished his licence to Duponchel, and took to politics. Failing to secure his election as a Deputy in 1838 he returned to journalism, and became in turn manager, editor and sole proprietor (1844) of the *Constitutionnel*. Véron was twice elected a member of the Corps Législatif. While attending the Chamber he found time to write his own life under the title of *Mémoires d'un bourgeois de Paris* (Paris, 1854, 6 vols. 8vo), which obtained a *succès de curiosité*, and encouraged his author to further works : *Cinq cent mille francs de rente* (1855, 2 vols. 8vo), a novel of manners ; a sequel to the *Mémoires* (1856) ; a political treatise, *Quatre ans de règne. Où allons-nous ?* (1857) ; and, finally, one coming more within the scope of this Dictionary, *Les Théâtres de Paris* (from 1806–60) (1860, 8vo). These books are all forgotten, but ' Mimi Véron ' (his nickname at the Opéra balls), the man of business and purveyor of pleasures under Louis Philippe, was a characteristic personage in his day, and a typical ' Bourgeois de Paris,' both in his industry and his vanity. G. C.

VEROVIO, MICHEL ANGELO (called MICHEL-ANGELO DEL VIOLINO), a Roman violinist of the beginning of the 17th century. According to Arteaga (*La rivulazione del teatro musicale*, etc., vol. i. p. 345), he enlarged the resources of violin-playing by the introducton of shakes, 'nordents, vibrato and other graces. Pietro della Valle and G. B. Doni likewise give accounts of his playing. E. V. D. S.

VEROVIO, SIMONE, a music printer and publisher at Rome, 1586–1604. He was apparently the first who used engraved copper-plates, with Martin van Buyten, a Hollander, as his engraver. A list of his publications appears in *Q.-L.*

VERSCHIEBUNG (Ger., literally *shoving aside*) ; see UNA CORDA and MUTE.

VERSCHWORENEN, DIE (*i.e.* The Conspirators)—a one-act play, with dialogue, adapted by Castelli from the French, and composed by Schubert. The MS. in the British Museum has the date Apr. 1823 at the end. The title was changed by the licensers to the less suggestive one of ' Der häusliche Krieg ' (*i.e.* The Domestic Struggle), but the piece was not adopted by the management, and remained unperformed till Mar. 1, 1861, when Herbeck produced it at a Musikverein concert. It was brought out on the stage at Frankfort, Aug. 29, 1861 ; in Paris, as ' La Croisade des dames,' Feb. 3, 1868 ; at a Crystal Palace Concert (' The Conspirators '), Mar. 2, 1872. G.

VERSE, a term used in church music to signify a passage sung by one or more solo voices. This use came from the Latin into the English services, where the compounds ' Verse-service ' and ' Verse-anthem ' were applied to compositions which included portions for one or more solo voices with instrumental accompaniment. (See ANTHEM and SERVICE.)

VERSICLE (Lat. *versiculum*), see RESPONSE.

VERSO, ANTONIO IL, a 16th-17th century composer of Piazza, Sicily, lived chiefly at Palermo, and was a pupil of Pietro Vinci. He composed 15 books of madrigals for 3 to 6 v., published between 1594 and 1619 ; 1 book of motets, 3-6 v. (1606) ; 4 books of sacred songs, 2-4 v., book 4 with a dialogue, 6 v., and bass for the organ (1611) ; 1 book villanelle, 3 v. (1612) (*Fétis* ; *Q.-L.*).

VERSTOVSKY, ALEXIS NICHOLAEVICH (*b.* Govt. of Tambov, Feb. 18/Mar. 1, 1799 ; *d.* Moscow, Nov. 5/17, 1862), probably the most gifted of Glinka's predecessors, was born at his father's manorial mansion in the Government of Tambov.

He was educated at the Institute of Civil Engineers in St. Petersburg, but managed to work fairly steadily at music while carrying on his studies there. His masters for the pianoforte were Field and Steibelt ; the violin he learnt from Böhm, singing from Tarquini, and theory from Brandt and Tseiner. Yet with all these advantages Verstovsky remained, like his contemporary Alabiev, merely an accomplished amateur as regards the technique of the art. At nineteen he composed his first vaudeville, and his pleasing, tuneful music soon became the fashion and was much imitated by other less talented composers. In 1824 he was appointed Inspector of the Imperial Opera, Moscow, and in 1842 he married a Russian actress, very famous in her day, Nadejda Repin, who left the stage soon after her marriage. Between 1825 and 1832 Verstovsky wrote the music for a number of typical vaudevilles. In 1828 he tried his hand for the first time at opera and produced

'Pan Tvardovsky' with considerable success. He followed this up by five more operas: 'Vadim' (1832), 'Askold's Tomb' (1835), 'Home-sickness' (1835), 'The Boundary Hills' (1841), and 'Gromoboi' (1845). Of all these works 'Askold's Tomb' was the most deservedly popular.

At this time Russian society so ardently desired the regeneration of national music that it was easily persuaded to believe that a truly representative composer had arisen in the person of Verstovsky. In the first twenty-five years of its existence 'Askold's Tomb' was given four hundred times in Moscow, and reached its two hundredth performance in St. Petersburg. It has never completely passed out of the repertory of national opera, and was revived with some success by the Private Opera Company of Moscow in 1897. It is not grand opera, the music being interspersed with spoken dialogue, and the style throughout, with its mixture of half-gipsy, half-street melodies, is exceedingly patchy. In the episodes which deal with the supernatural it is easy to trace the influence of Weber. The orchestration is very elementary. Yet, with all its weaknesses, 'Askold's Tomb' contains melody which must have seemed fresh, and even original, at the time it was written, and touches of humour which show its composer to have been the true forerunner of Dargomijsky and Moussorgsky. To hail him as the founder of national opera was somewhat premature. Russian music, like Russian literature at that period, was still destined to move a few years longer in grooves of routine and imitation, before Glinka appeared with his higher ideals to lift national opera above the superficial conception of it which we find in Verstovsky and his predecessors. Besides six operas and twenty-two vaudevilles, Verstovsky wrote several dramatic scenas, melodramas, and cantatas. Of his twenty-nine songs the most famous is his setting of Poushkin's Byronic poem 'The Black Shawl.'   R. N.

VESI, SIMON, of Forlì, chaplain in 1646 at Padua Cathedral, and from 1648 maestro di cappella to Giorgio Cornaro, Bishop of Padua, Count di Piove, di Sacco, etc. Composed masses, motets, psalms and other church music; also 'Le mascherate di . . .,' 2-4 v., with 2 violins ad lib., op. 5 (1660).

           E. V. D. S.

VESPA, GIROLAMO, of Naples, a 16th-century Franciscan monk. From 1589 he calls himself maestro di cappella of the arch-diocese of Fermo, and in 1591 of the Cathedral of Osimo. He composed 4 books of 5-part madrigals (1570–91); vesper psalms (1589); cantiones sacrae; motets, 5-8 v. (1594); some motets, etc., in collective volumes (Q.-L.).

VESPERALE—the Vesperal. This Latin Service-book, strictly speaking, need not contain more than the single service of Vespers or Evensong; but in practice it as a rule contains besides this (and the music belonging to it) the service of Compline, and may even include parts of the Lesser Hours as well of Prime, Terce, Sext, and None, and even of Lauds and Mattins for special occasions.   W. H. F.

VESPERS (Lat. Officium Vesperarum, Vesperae, Oratio vespertina, Ad Vesperas); the last but one and most important of the 'Horae Diurnae' or 'Day hours,' in the Antiphonarium.

The music sung at Vespers, though in itself far less considerable than the music of Mattins, has through force of circumstances become more elaborated than the music used at any other of the Hours. The plain-song is found in the Vesperal (see VESPERALE), but this service is the chief opportunity for introducing into the Hour Services other music than the plain-song. The Psalmody, for example, is often treated in Faux Bourdon. Many such settings by the great composers are still extant.

The great polyphonic composers wrote Magnificats which were necessarily very elaborate; for during the Canticle the High Altar is censed, and sometimes other altars also—a ceremony which often occupies a considerable time. (See MAGNIFICAT.)

The hymns for the various seasons have also been frequently set, in very elaborate form, by the polyphonic composers; Palestrina's 'Hymni totius anni' is a complete collection, of unapproachable beauty. Some fine isolated specimens will also be found among the works of Tallis, Byrd and other composers of the English school; and Proske has published many interesting examples, collected from various sources. The four 'Antiphons of Our Lady' —Alma Redemptoris, Ave Regina, Regina Coeli and Salve Regina—have been treated by many good writers, including Palestrina, Anerio and O. Lassus, in the form of highly developed motets.   W. S. R.; rev. W. H. F.

VESPRI SICILIANI, see VÊPRES SICILIENNES, LES.

VESQUE VON PÜTTLINGEN, JOHANN (J. HOVEN) (b. Opole, July 23, 1803; d. Vienna, Oct. 29, 1883), composer of operas, was born of a noble family of Belgian origin at Opole, the residence of Prince Alexander Lubomirski. His parents went to live in Vienna in 1804, and at 12 years old he was sent to the Löwenbürgische Convict there for about a year. He began his musical studies in 1816, learning successively from Leidesdorf, Moscheles and Worzischek. In 1822 he went to the University of Vienna in order to study for the civil service, which he entered in 1827. As early as 1830 he completed an opera, on the libretto of Rossini's 'Donna del Lago,' which was performed by amateurs in a private house. In 1833 he studied counterpoint, etc., with Sechter, and in Oct. 1838 a two-act opera, 'Turandot,' was given with success at the

Kärnthnerthor Theatre. In this and his other musical compositions he adopted the pseudonym of ' J. Hoven.' Two years later a third opera, ' Jeanne d'Arc,' in three acts, was given in Vienna. The work was considered worthy of being performed at Dresden in 1845, with Johanna Wagner in the principal part. His other operas are ' Der Liebeszauber,' four acts, 1845 ; ' Ein Abenteuer Carl des II., ' one act, 1850 ; ' Burg Thayer,' three acts, apparently not performed ; ' Der lustige Rath,' two acts, 1852, produced at Weimar by Liszt ; ' Lips Tellian,' one act, 1854. In 1872 he retired from the civil service, and in 1879 received the title of ' Geheimrath.' He enjoyed the friendship of nearly all the musicians of his time ; he corresponded with Mendelssohn, Schumann, Berlioz, Liszt, and many other distinguished men. His compositions of various kinds reach the opus number 58, besides two masses, and other works unpublished. He also published a book, *Das musikalische Autorrecht*. The above information is obtained from a sketch of his life published by Holder of Vienna, 1887, bearing no author's name.　　M.

VESTALE, LA, lyric tragedy in 3 acts ; words by Jouy ; music by Spontini. Produced Opéra, Paris, Dec. 15, 1807.　　G.

VESTRIS (VESTRI), a family of Italian musicians and dancers, originally of Florence. Of the eight children of Marie Hippolyte Vestris and Violante Béatrix de Dominique Bruscagli, his wife, the four best known settled in Paris in 1747 with their mother and eldest brother, Jean-Baptiste, called the ' cuisinier ' of the family.

(1) GAËTAN APOLLINE BALTHASAR (*b*. Florence, Apr. 18, 1729 ; *d*. Paris, Sept. 23, 1808), dancer and Italian choreograph, appeared at the Paris Opéra in 1747; was first dancer of the King's ballets in 1749, and in 1751 succeeded his master, Dupré, the ' *diou* de la danse,' who had begun the reform which raised the dance to a higher level. Vestris travelled much, however. He was in Berlin and in Italy (1754) ; at Stuttgart, where he directed the ballet with Noverre in 1760 ; at Vienna (Jan. and Sept. 1767 : Leopold Mozart speaks of him at this time) and at Warsaw.

Master and ' compositeur des ballets ' (1770–1775), first dancer (1776–81), Vestris retired May 12, 1782. From 1776 he had received a salary of 4500 livres as first dancer at the court. He appeared again in 1795, 1799 and 1800, for the débuts of his grandsons.

He married (June 16, 1792) Mlle Heinel (*b*. Bayreuth, Oct. 4, 1753 ; *d*. Paris, Mar. 17, 1808), a dancer at the Opéra from 1766–82, by whom he had one son (*b*. May 9, 1791).

Vestris contributed, like Noverre, to the reform of the ballet. He suppressed the masks of the dancers, and brought more sincerity into the costume. Called by his brother ' le *diou* de

la danse,' like Dupré of old he was ' grand, très bel homme et parfait dans la danse noble.' [1]

(2) MARIE JEAN AUGUSTIN (called Auguste ; also Vestr' Allard (*b*. Mar. 27, 1760 ; *d*. Montmartre, Paris, Dec. 5, 1842), natural son of Vestris (1) and of Marie Allard (a dancer at the Opéra from 1761–81). He made his début at the Opéra at the age of 12. As ' danseur seul ' (1776) and ' premier sujet ' (1780), Augustin was considered the first dancer of his time.[2] He created the style called ' demi-caractère comique.'

In 1780 Augustin spent some time in England with his father. His benefit alone brought him in 12,000 guineas. Of a capricious, difficult nature he was imprisoned on July 16, 1784, for refusing to play before the court and the King of Sweden at the Opéra.

At the Revolution he went over to England and became ballet - master at the King's Theatre at the same time that Haydn was composer there. After his retirement from the Opéra (Sept. 27, 1816) he fell into great misery and was even imprisoned for debt (July 22, 1819). He was the husband of the dancer Anne Catherine Augier (called Aimée) (1777–1809). She had made her début at the Opéra in 1793, and was separated from him. Augustin married again in 1823. His second wife, Jeanne Marie Tuillière, died before him, May 4, 1842. He reappeared for one night at the Opéra in ' Paul et Virginie ' (1826) as Domingo. Under Louis Philippe he tried in vain to get himself nominated ballet-master at the court (1833) ; but he was professor from 1821 till *c*. 1826 to the École ' de Perfectionnement ' and to the École ' de grâce ' at the Opéra. Among his pupils may be mentioned La Taglioni and the dancer Parrot, whose portrait, by Adèle Romance, was exhibited at the Exposition des Femmes Peintres du XVIIIᵉ siècle, Paris, May 1926.

(3) AUGUSTE ARMAND (*b*. Paris, 1788 ; *d*. 1825), son of the preceding, made his début at the Opéra, Mar. 1, 1800, beside his father and grandfather. Protected by Mme. Bonaparte, he resigned this post (Oct. 20, 1803) in order to travel first to Italy, then to England, where he married the singer Lucia Elizabeth Bartolozzi (see VESTRIS, Mme.). He then became ballet-master at the King's Theatre. He returned to Paris with his wife, leaving her about 1820.

(4) MARIE FRANÇOISE THÉRÈSE (*b*. Florence, Feb. 1, 1726 or 1731 ; *d*. Paris, Jan. 18, 1808), a dancer. After travelling in Italy and visiting Vienna and Dresden, she was the first of the family to arrive in Paris in 1746. She was admitted to the ' ballets du roi ' in 1749, and made her début at the Opéra in a *pas de deux* with her brother Gaëtan (1) (Apr. 1, 1751). She remained there until 1766.

----

[1] Mme. Lebrun, *Mémoires*, i. 132.
[2] See Noverre, *Lettre sur les ballets*, also Mme. Lebrun, *Mémoires*, i. 132.

(5) MARIE CATHERINE VIOLANTE (or VIOLAN-TINA) (b. Florence, c. 1732; d. Paris, Apr. 23, 1791), singer and dancer. She arrived in Paris in 1748; sang first at the court, then at the Concert Spirituel (Aug. 15, 1752), accompanied on the flute by her brother Angiolo (5). In December of the same year she was in London, where she married the celebrated violinist Felice de GIARDINI (q.v.). She appeared later in the Concert Spirituel up to 1757 as an Italian singer, under the name of Vestris-Giardini. Her name is also found as Jardiny.

(6) ANGIOLO MARIA GASPARO (b. Florence, Nov. 19, 1730; d. Paris, June 10, 1809) brother of Gaëtan Vestris (1), flautist, dancer and actor, was admitted to the ballets (1753–1757) after having appeared at the Concert Spirituel as flautist (see VESTRIS 4 and 5). He danced at Stuttgart (1758), was engaged there (1761) and married there in 1766 Françoise Rose Gourgaud (b. Marseilles, Apr. 7, 1743; d. Paris, Oct. 5, 1804) the future celebrated actress of the Théâtre-Français, step-sister of Dugazon. Angiolo left the Opéra for the Comédie-Italienne (1769–80), at which he was but a mediocre actor.

(7) CHARLES (b. Paris, 1797), a dancer, pupil and son (or nephew) of Augustin (2), made his début at the age of 12 at the Opéra in ' La Caravane ' (Oct. 3, 1809) and remained there until 1813. He then went abroad.

BIBL.—CAMPARDON, L'Académie Royale de Musique au XVIIIe siècle. C. PITON, Paris sous Louis XV, 5 vols., 1905–14. G. CAPON, Les Vestris, le ' diou ' de la danse et sa famille (1730–1808), 1908.

J. G. P.

VESTRIS, MME. LUCIA ELIZABETH (ELIZA LUCY[1]) (b. London, Jan. 3 or Mar. 2, 1797; d. Fulham, Aug. 8, 1856), daughter of Gaetano Stefano Bartolozzi, and granddaughter of Francesco Bartolozzi, the celebrated engraver. On Jan. 28, 1813, she married Auguste Armand Vestris (3 above), dancer and ballet-master at the King's Theatre and grandson of Gaëtan Vestris. It was on the occasion of his bene-fit at that theatre (July 20, 1815) that his wife, having received instruction in singing from Corri, made her first appearance in public as Proserpine in Winter's ' Il ratto di Proserpina.' Her success that season was great, in spite of her then limited ideas of acting and want of vocal cultivation. She reappeared in 1816 in Win-ter's ' Proserpina ' and ' Zaira,' Martini's ' Cosa rara,' and Mozart's 'Così fan tutte' and 'Nozze' (Susanna), but with less success, her faults be-coming more manifest with familiarity. In the winter she appeared at the Italian Opera, Paris, and at various theatres there, including the Français, where she played Camille in ' Les Horaces,' with Talma as Horace. About this time Vestris deserted her. On Feb. 19, 1820, she made her début at Drury Lane as Lilla in ' The Siege of Belgrade '; made an immediate success in that and in Adela (' The Haunted

Tower '), ' Artaxerxes,' ' Macheath ' and ' Gio-vanni in London,' and remained for many years a favourite at the patent theatres, not only in opera, but in musical farces and comedies.

In certain of these she introduced well-known songs—' Cherry ripe,' ' I've been roaming,' ' Meet me by moonlight alone,' and others, which gained their popularity at the outset through her very popular ballad singing. During her engagements with Elliston, Charles Kemble, etc., with their permission she re-appeared at the King's Theatre, and played in Rossini's operas on their production in England, viz. as Pippo (in 'La Gazza'), Mar. 10, 1821; Malcolm Graeme (in ' Donna del lago '), Feb. 18, 1823; Zamira (in ' Ricardo e Zoraide '), June 5, 1823; Edoardo (in ' Matilde di Shabran '), July 3, 1823; Emma (in ' Zelmira '), at Mme. Colbran-Rossini's début, Jan. 24, 1824; and Arsace, with Pasta as Semiramide, July 15, 1824. She played there also in 1825, and on Apr. 12, 1826, she played Fatima on the pro-duction of ' Oberon.' In 1827 she appeared in English at Covent Garden, as George Brown in ' The White Maid ' (' La Dame blanche '), Jan. 2, a part played in Paris by the tenor Ponchard, and Blonde in ' The Seraglio,' a mutilated ver-sion of Mozart's ' Entführung,' Nov. 24. With her subsequent career as manager of the Olym-pic, Covent Garden and Lyceum, we cannot deal, save to mention that during her tenancy of Covent Garden, in conjunction with Charles Mathews the younger (whom she married July 18, 1838), opera was occasionally performed, viz. ' Artaxerxes,' ' Comus,' etc., English ver-sions of ' Norma,' ' Elena di Feltre ' (Merca-dante), and ' Figaro,' with Miss Kemble, Miss Rainforth, etc., and with Benedict as conductor. In ' Figaro ' she played Cherubino, but resigned ' Voi che sapete ' to Miss Kemble. She had appeared in Dublin in 1824, 1831, 1836, 1841, 1843 and 1845; and took a farewell benefit there in 1847. She is buried at Kensal Green.

' As a girl she was extremely bewitching, if not faultlessly beautiful—endowed with one of the most musical, easy, rich contralto voices ever bestowed on a singer, and retaining its charm to the last—full of taste and fancy for all that was luxurious, but either not willing, or not able to learn, beyond a certain depth.' [2]

At the Italian Opera, says Chorley,[3]

' If she had possessed musical patience and energy, she might have queened it, because she possessed (half Italian by birth) one of the most luscious of low voices, great personal beauty, an almost faultless figure, which she adorned with consummate art, and no common stage address. But a less arduous career pleased her better; so she could not—or perhaps would not—remain on the Italian stage.

A. C.

VIADANA (LODOVICO GROSSI) (b. Viadana, c. 1564; d. Gualtieri on the Po, May 2, 1645), took his name from the place of his birth. He was (according to Parazzi's mono-graph, 1876) a pupil of Costanzo Porta, in 1594 was maestro in the cathedral of Mantua, an office he retained for fifteen years, visiting Venice and Rome during that period. In 1596 he entered the Franciscan order, and in 1609 was appointed maestro at Concordia, whence in 1612 he went to the cathedral at Fano. From 1615 he lived at Piacenza, and died in the Franciscan convent at Gualtieri. He composed and published a number of volumes of canzonets (1590, 1594), madrigals (1591 and 1593), psalms (1595, 1604, 1612), canticles and masses (1596, etc.) ; but the work upon which his historical significance rests is a collection of

' Cento concerti ecclesiastici a 1, a 2, a 3, e a 4 voci, con il basso continuo per sonar nell' organo. Nova inventione commoda per ogni sorte di cantori e per gli organisti,'

published at Venice, 1602, in partbooks. In consequence of this publication Viadana has been commonly regarded as the inventor of the (unfigured) *basso continuo* to accompany the voice on an instrument—a judgment expressed, but, as Ambros [1] thinks, unfairly, in the remark of a contemporary, Praetorius. As a matter of fact, *basso continuo* had been employed in the accompaniment of recitative two years earlier by Caccini and Peri and others before them. Viadana mentions in his preface, however, that his concerti had been performed in Rome 5 or 6 years before, that they were admired and imitated and that imitations were printed. Therefore Peri, Caccini and Cavalieri [2] may have got the idea from him. The question is discussed at length under THOROUGH-BASS). Whatever way the claim of priority be decided, the method enabled Viadana to employ a freer and lighter style than his contemporaries of the Roman school. Building up his compositions (in his ' Cento concerti ') from the bass instead of from a cantus firmus, he succeeded in creating real self-contained melodies ; and if he cannot be justly regarded as the inventor of the notion of *basso continuo*, he at least was led by it to a not far-off view of the modern principle of melodic, as opposed to contrapuntal, composition. (See Q.-L. for list of works.) Parazzi mentions a portrait of Viadana which was in the Franciscan convent of the town of Viadana about the middle of the 18th century, also another portrait in the possession of G. Grossi, the last of the family, who died 1814, aged 93. This was afterwards presented to the church, Archiprelate Plebena del Castello di Viadana, where it was hung in the sacristy.

R. L. P. ; addns. F. W. A.

BIBL.—MAX SCHNEIDER, *Die Anfänge des Basso continuo und seiner Bezifferung*, 1918.

VIAGGIO A REIMS, IL, OSSIA L' ALBERGO DEL GIGLIO D' ORA, opera in one act ; words by Balocchi ; music by Rossini. Produced

[1] *Geschichte der Musik*, vol. iv. p. 248, etc.
[2] Guidotti in his edition of Cavalieri's ' Rappresentazione ' (1600), uses the term ' basso continuato.'

Théâtre-Italien, Paris, June 19, 1825. The music was afterwards adapted to the new libretto of ' LE COMTE ORY ' (*q.v.*).   G.

VIANESI, AUGUSTE CHARLES LÉONARD FRANÇOIS (*b.* Leghorn, Nov. 2, 1837 ; *d.* New York City, Nov. 11, 1908), who was naturalised a Frenchman in 1885, had been for many years the conductor of various Italian opera companies before finally becoming first conductor at the Opéra in Paris. He was the son of a musician, and was taught music by the advice of Pacini and Döhler, and became a chorusmaster in Italy. In 1857 he came to Paris furnished with a letter of introduction to Rossini from Pasta, and in Paris he completed his musical education. In 1859 he was called to London to conduct the orchestra at Drury Lane. He then went to New York, and was afterwards engaged at the Imperial Theatre at Moscow. He made a short stay in St. Petersburg, and then for twelve years conducted the Italian opera at Covent Garden. On July 1, 1887, Vianesi was chosen by the directors of the Opéra to replace ALTÈS as conductor. In 1892 and 1893 he conducted opera in New York and Philadelphia.   A. J.

VIARDOT-GARCIA, (1) MICHELLE FERDINANDE PAULINE (*b.* Paris, July 18, 1821; *d.* there, May 17/18, 1910), a great lyric actress and singer, younger sister of Maria Malibran, and daughter of the famous Spanish tenor and teacher, Manuel del Popolo GARCIA (*q.v.*), and of his wife, Joaquina Sitchez, an accomplished actress. She received her names from her sponsors, Ferdinand Paër, the composer, and the Princess Pauline Galitzin.

The child showed extraordinary intelligence, with a marvellous aptitude for learning and retaining everything. She learned languages as if in play. Her facility for painting, especially portrait-painting, was equally great. Her earliest pianoforte lessons were given her by Marcos Vega, at New York, when she was not 4 years old. At 8, after her return from Mexico, she played the accompaniments for her father at his singing-lessons, ' and I think,' she wrote afterwards, ' I profited by the lessons even more than the pupils did.' She thus acquired a knowledge of Garcia's method, although she never was his pupil in the usual sense, and assures us that her mother was her ' only singing-master.' Her father worked her hard, however, as he did every one. In his drawing-room operettas, composed for his pupils, there were parts for her, ' containing,' she said, ' things more difficult than any I have sung since. I still preserve them as precious treasures.' The piano she studied for many years with Meysenberg, and afterwards with Liszt ; counterpoint and composition with Reicha.

After the death of her father and sister she lived with her mother at Brussels, where, in 1837, she made her first appearance as a singer,

LXXXVI

PAULINE VIARDOT-GARCIA

From a lithograph by N. Ploszczynski

SONTAG AS 'DONNA ANNA'

From an engraving by F. Girard, after P. Delaroche

under the auspices of her brother-in-law, Charles de Bériot. She afterwards sang for him on a concert tour, and in 1838 at the Théâtre de la Renaissance in Paris, at a concert, where her powers of execution were brilliantly displayed in a 'Cadence du Diable' framed on the 'Trillo del Diavolo' of Tartini. On May 9, 1839, she appeared at Her Majesty's Theatre as Desdemona in 'Otello,' and with genuine success, which increased at each performance. A certain resemblance to her sister MALIBRAN (q.v.) in voice and style won the favour of her audience, while critics were not wanting who discerned in her, even at that early age, an originality and an intellectual force all her own. In the autumn of the same year she was engaged for the Théâtre-Italien by the impresario Louis Viardot (b. Dijon, Côte d'Or, 1800 ; d. May 5, 1883), a distinguished writer and critic, founder of the *Revue Indépendante*, director of the Théâtre-Italien from 1838. She appeared there on Oct. 8, 1839. There, chiefly in the operas of Rossini, she shared in the triumphs of Grisi, Persiani, Rubini, Tamburini and Lablache. Her face lacked regularity of feature ; her voice, a mezzo-soprano, but so extended by art as to compass more than three octaves, from tenor C to F in alt, was neither equal nor always beautiful in tone. It had probably been overworked in youth : although expressive it was thin and sometimes even harsh, but she could turn her very deficiencies to account. Her picturesque weirdness and statuesque grace, her inventive power and consummate mastery over all the resources of her art, nay, her voice and face, irregular, but full of contrast and expression—all these appealed to the imagination, and formed an ensemble irresistible in its piquancy and originality.

In 1841 she married Viardot, who resigned the Opera management, and accompanied her to Italy, Spain, Germany, Russia and England. At Berlin, after her performance of Rahel, in 'La Juive,' one of her greatest parts, she was serenaded by the whole orchestra. Here, too, she astounded both connoisseurs and public by volunteering at a moment's notice to sing the part of Isabelle in 'Robert le Diable' for Fräulein Tuczek, in addition to her own part of Alice—a bold attempt, vindicated by its brilliant success.

She returned to Paris in 1849 for the production of Meyerbeer's 'Prophète.' She had been specially chosen by the composer for Fidès, and to her help and suggestions he was more indebted than is generally known. She was indeed, as Moscheles wrote, 'the life and soul of the opera, which owed to her at least half of its great success.' She played Fidès more than 200 times in all the chief opera-houses in Europe.

From 1848–58 she appeared every year in London. In Paris, 1851, she created the title-part in Gounod's 'Sapho.' In 1859 Carvalho,

director of the Théâtre-Lyrique, revived the 'Orphée' of Gluck, which had not been heard for thirty years. The part of Orphée, restored (by Berlioz) from a high tenor to the contralto for which it was written, was taken by Mme. Viardot, who achieved in it a triumph perhaps unique.[1] This revival was followed in 1861 by that of Gluck's 'Alceste' at the Opéra. The music of this—as Berlioz calls it—'wellnigh inaccessible part,' was less suited than that of Orphée to Mme. Viardot's voice, but it was perhaps the greatest of all her achievements, and a worthy crown to a repertory which had included Desdemona, Cenerentola, Rosina, Norma, Arsace, Camilla ('Orazi'), Amina, Romeo, Lucia, Maria di Rohan, Ninette, Leonora ('Favorita'), Azucena, Donna Anna, Zerlina, Rahel, Iphigénie, Alice, Isabelle, Valentine, Fidès and Orphée.

In 1863 Mme. Viardot fixed her abode at Baden, and sang no more at the Opera, though she appeared at concerts, and was heard in London as late as 1870. She composed a great deal, and several operettas, the books of which were written for her by Turgeniev, were represented in her little private theatre by her pupils and her children. One of these, 'Le Dernier Sorcier,' translated into German by Richard Pohl as 'Der letzte Zauberer,' was performed in public at Weimar, Carlsruhe and Riga. In 1871 she was obliged, as the wife of a Frenchman, to leave Germany, and after that lived in Paris. She devoted much time to teaching, and taught singing at the Paris Conservatoire, 1871–75. Among her pupils may be named Désirée Artôt, Orgeni, Marianne Brandt and Antoinette Sterling. Mme. Viardot published several collections of original songs, and vocal transcriptions of some of Chopin's mazurkas, made famous by her own singing of them and by that of Jenny Lind. Her daughter,

(2) LOUISE PAULINE MARIE HÉRITTE-VIARDOT (b. Paris, Dec. 14, 1841 ; d. Heidelberg, Jan. 1918), was a teacher of singing successively in the Conservatoire of St. Petersburg, Dr. Hoch's conservatorium at Frankfort and at Berlin. She married, 1862, the 'General-Consul,' Héritte. Her comic opera 'Lindoro' was given at Weimar in 1879, a cantata, 'Das Bacchusfest,' at Stockholm in 1880, and many songs, etc., have been published. Another daughter, Marianne, married the composer and pianist, Alphonse DUVERNOY. Her son,

(3) PAUL VIARDOT (b. Courtavenel, July 20, 1857), a pupil of Léonard, appeared with success in London and elsewhere as a violinist. He conducted at the Opéra in Paris occasionally.

Mme. Viardot was the centre of a distinguished circle of friends, by whom she was as much beloved for her virtues as admired for

---

[1] The reader is referred to Chorley's *Thirty Years' Recollections of the Opera* and to Berlioz's *A travers chants*, for detailed descriptions of her wonderful performance, which was repeated over 140 times.

her genius. Not one of her least distinctions was that Schumann dedicated to her his beautiful Liederkreis, op. 24. She was the first interpreter of the solo part in Brahms's 'Rhapsodie,' op. 53.   F. A. M. ; rev. M. L. P.

BIBL.—H. DE CURZON, *Croquis d'artistes* (Paris, 1898); LOUIS HÉRITTE DE LA TOUR, *Une Famille de grands musiciens; mémoires de Louise Héritte-Viardot* (Paris, 1923); IVAN TURGENIEV, *Lettres à Madame Viardot* (Paris).

VIBRATO (Ital. from *vibrare*, ' to vibrate ') is used to mean the pulsation of a note by slight and rapidly recurring variations of pitch.

I. INSTRUMENTAL.—(*a*) It belongs essentially to the art of the string-player who produces a throbbing effect on sustained notes by the rapid oscillating motion from the wrist of the finger stopping the note. As an emotional effect produced by physical means it has obvious dangers, but no string-player's technique is complete without its acquirement.   C.

Vibrato has undoubtedly been known to stringed-instrument players for over three centuries. Its origin is a matter for speculation, although Leopold Mozart (*Violinschule*, 1756), gracefully disposed of the question in the phrase ' Nature herself suggested it to man.' We can trace the use of the ' vibrato ' as far back as 1636, when Mersenne (*Harmonie universelle*) eulogises ' Les Sieurs Bocan Lazarin ' and others, who played with a *tremblement qui ravissent l'esprit*. The viol-players of Mersenne's time also employed the vibrato with circumspection. Christopher Simpson (*The Division Violinist*, 1659) advocates its use in ' any movement of the voice imitated by the viol.' A glimpse of the progress of the ' vibrato ' is afforded us by Geminiani (*The Art of Violin Playing*, 1751), who attempts a minute description of the ' vibrato ' under the heading : ' Of the Shake,' in which he embodies the modern elements of the art. Baillot (*L'Art du violon*) calls it *l'ondulation de la main gauche*. In fact the term ' vibrato ' is a modern description of a well-established practice.   O. R.

(*b*) The *vibrato* is obtainable to a limited extent on wind instruments, notably flute and cornet, by an irregularity in the supply of wind which causes the pitch to waver. The mechanism known as TREMULANT (*q.v.*) on the organ has a similar effect, as also stops such as the VOIX CÉLESTES (*q.v.*), where two ranks of pipes slightly out of tune with one another are heard simultaneously.

II. VOCAL.—(*a*) This vibrato, more commonly called TREMOLO (*q.v.*), seems to be a natural property of some voices and has been cultivated (often with deplorable results) by others. Obviously the first necessity of the singer with a natural tendency to waver in pitch is to secure control. The vibrato tends to appear in moments of emotional intensity, and such appearances in a voice generally under control have their force. The artificial simulation of emotion is as offensive as the incapacity to sustain a note at its true pitch.   C.

(*b*) The singer's vibrato, corresponding to the string-player's tremolo, is an alternate partial extinction and re-enforcement of the note. This was a legitimate figure used rhythmically of the *fioriture* of the Farinelli and Caffarelli period. It was introduced with wonderful effect by Jenny Lind in ' La figlia del reggimento.' In the midst of a flood of vocalisation these groups of notes occurred,

executed with the same brilliance and precision as they would be on the pianoforte.

        H. C. D., rev.

VICARS-CHORAL, ' the assistants or deputies of the canons or prebendaries of [English] collegiate churches, in the discharge of their duties, especially, though not exclusively, those performed in the choir or chancel, as distinguished from those belonging to the altar and pulpit.' (Hook.)

The vicars-choral answer to the κανονικοὶ ψαλ-ταί of the early Church. Originally each member of the capitular body had a vicar-choral or minor canon attached to his dignity, whose appointment only lasted during his own life ; but in process of time the numbers of these inferior ecclesiastical corporations became diminished. The difference between minor canons and vicars-choral appears to be that whereas for the former, only clergy are eligible, 'the latter post can be held by either laymen or clerics. The former term is generally found in cathedrals of the new foundation, where the lay-members are termed ' lay-clerks,' the name ' vicars-choral ' being chiefly confined to cathedrals of the old foundation. St. Patrick's (Dublin) and Hereford have both minor canons and vicars-choral; in the former the two bodies form distinct corporations, in the latter they are united. In all cathedrals of the old foundation in England, in St. David's, and in twelve Irish cathedrals, the vicars-choral form a distinct corporation, the members of which vary in number from twelve to three : these corporations are distinct from the chapter as regards property, but in subjection to it as to the performance of the services. Formerly the members of these ecclesiastical colleges lived in common in collegiate buildings, some of which (as at Hereford, Wells and York) still exist. The 42nd Canon orders that the vicars-choral shall ' be urged to the study of the Holy Scriptures, and every one of them to have the New Testament, not only in English, but also in Latin.' The name is entirely confined to the Anglican Church. (Jebb on *Choral Service*; Hook's *Church Dictionary*, etc.)   W. B. S.

VICENTINO, Nicola (*b.* Vicenza, 1511 or 1512).[1] If we are to believe the title he gives himself in his first publication, as ' unico discepolo ' to Adrian Willaert,[2] he had his musical education at Venice ; but as the ' unico ' is plainly false, we may perhaps question the ' discepolo.' He became ordained, entered the service of Ipolito of Este, cardinal of Ferrara, and accompanied him to Rome, where he lived, it seems, for many years. In 1546 he published a volume of five-part madrigals, with explanatory directions, written with the design of restoring the Greek modes. He then invented a peculiar instrument, the ' archicembalo,' with several keyboards, in order to illustrate his system, and employed a private choir to practise it. He published also a theoretical work entitled *L' antica musica ridotta alla moderna prattica* (Rome, 1555). His efforts were, however, rewarded with scant success, and he experienced much opposition. One contest into which he was led in defence of his theory, and in which he was defeated—that, namely, with Lusitano—is famous. (See DANKERTS.) The cardinal, his patron, is said to have looked on Vicentino's discomfiture as a personal affront ; he took him back to Ferrara, and appointed him maestro di cappella in his court. This post he appears to have held until his death. If we may judge by a medal struck in his honour, which describes him as ' perfectae musicae divisionisque inventor,' he must have enjoyed a certain amount of fame ; but there is a story that the medal was his own device. His real eminence was that of a performer on the clavichord, and it is difficult to quarrel with the criticism of J. B. Doni and Apostolo Zeno, who ridiculed him for pretending to be anything more than a performer. At best his theories belong only to a passing phase in the history of music.[3]   R. L. P.

VICTIMAE PASCHALI, see SEQUENCE (*b*), section (1).

VICTORIA, Tomás Luis de (*b.* Avila, *c.* 1535 or 1540 ; *d.* Madrid, Aug. 27, 1611), Spanish church composer, who has hitherto been more generally known in musical history by his name in its Italianised form, Vittoria, Tommaso Ludovico da. In Spanish documents his name sometimes appears as Vitoria, but never Vittoria. In his Latin publications it is always given as Thomas Ludovicus de (or à) Victoria.

As a composer Victoria has usually been reckoned as belonging to the Roman school of Palestrina, and allowed to be next to Palestrina, the greatest musician of the school. But

Spanish by birth, he always remained Spanish in feeling, though like Escobedo, Morales, Soto, and other Spanish musicians, he made Rome for a considerable time the chief sphere of his musical activity, and as a younger contemporary of Palestrina was naturally influenced by him to some extent. It is a striking coincidence, and may be regarded as a symbol of the close connexion of the Spanish music of the 16th century with Spanish religion that Avila, the birthplace of St. Teresa, the most striking embodiment of the Spanish religious spirit, was also the birthplace of Victoria, the noblest representative of Spanish music. The mystic-ascetical spirit peculiar to Spain is common to both. It is the expression of this spirit in Victoria's music that vindicates his claim to an independent position of his own alongside of Palestrina and redeems him from the charge of being merely a subordinate member of the school like Anerio and Soriano. Avila, in Old Castile, is inferred to have been his birthplace from the designation Abulensis being always appended to his name in the Latin titles of his works. Various documents unearthed by Perez Pastor and quoted by Pedrell appear to show that Sanchidrian, a small village near Avila, was the home of his family, but as Sanchidrian itself is also described as ' tierra de la ciudad de Avila,' this may be sufficient to warrant the acceptance of Avila as the place of his birth, as no doubt it would also be the place of his early education. The precise date of his birth has not been ascertained, but the known facts of his life have induced most authorities to place it about 1540. F. Pedrell, the modern editor of his works, is inclined to place it earlier, sometime between 1530 and 1535. About his earlier life in Spain we have no authentic record. It may be conjectured with some degree of probability that his teacher in musical composition was Bartolomeo Escobedo, who after serving in the Sistine Chapel choir from 1536 had retired to Spain in 1554, and been provided with a church benefice in Segovia, within easy reach of Avila. The more celebrated Spanish master Christobal Morales cannot have been his teacher, as, leaving Rome in 1545, Morales had died in 1553 after a somewhat unsettled life between Toledo, Seville and Malaga. H. Collet, the French biographer of Victoria, indulges in the interesting speculation whether, and how far, while still in Spain, Victoria may have been acquainted with and influenced by St. Teresa and the reforming religious movement associated with her name. It was in 1554 that what Teresa describes as her ' conversion,' the beginning of her mystical experiences, took place, and 1562 is the date of her first foundation at Avila of a religious house of reformed Carmelites. It appears too that in her book of the ' Foundations,' she mentions Augustin de Victoria, who is known to be a brother of the

---

[1] The place has been incorrectly given as Rome, and the date as 1513 ; but the latter is fixed to a year or two earlier by the notice in his ' Antica musica,' 1555, that he was then in his 44th year.

[2] Caffi has singularly inverted the relation, making Vicentino Willaert's *master : Storia della musica sacra nella già cappella ducale di san Marco in Venezia,* i. 83, 135 ; Venice, 1854.

[3] A manuscript notice furnished in 1826 by Abbate Todeschini of Vicenza to the Gesellschaft der Musikfreunde in Vienna, and now preserved in the library of that society, adds nothing to our knowledge of Vicentino's biography.

composer, as one who had greatly befriended her and her religious houses. It is probable that some time before 1565 Victoria was ordained to the priesthood, but our first authentic piece of information with regard to him consists of a privilege from King Philip II., dated Dec. 14, 1565, granting to Maestro Tomé de Victoria an allowance from the royal exchequer, apparently to enable him to proceed to Rome for the further study of music.

In 1566 Victoria appears engaged as a chaplain-singer at the Collegium Germanicum in Rome. This institution had been founded in 1552 by Ignatius Loyola for the training of German priests to combat Lutheranism, and specially for service in Bavaria and the Rhineland. It continued to flourish under the fostering care of the two Spanish successors of Ignatius, Diego Lainez and Francisco Borgia, and afterwards owed much to the patronage of Dukes Albert and William of Bavaria, also to Otto Truchsess, Bishop of Augsburg and Roman cardinal, who had for a time the Flemish musician Jacques de Kerle of Ypres in his service. With such patrons it was natural that music should occupy a prominent place in the studies of the institution. In 1571 Victoria became choirmaster, and in 1572 dedicated to Otto Truchsess as his chief patron a book of motets, 14 numbers a 4, 9 a 5, 9 a 6 and 1 a 8, 33 in all. This book already contains the majority of Victoria's works in the free motet form, to which only small additions were made in later publications. It opens with the well-known ' O quam gloriosum ' and includes the very beautiful and expressive ' O vos omnes,' which has been mistakenly ascribed to Morales, though it reappears as Victoria's own work in his later publication of 1583 and in the Dillingen editions of his motets in 1589. Mention may also be made of the very pathetic piece for Holy Week, ' Vere languores nostros,' but the whole contents of this work are of first-rate quality and show Victoria as already the fully fledged master in his own particular style of religious composition. There is no trace of his having had personally to work himself free from any trammels of Netherland scholasticism ; he appears to have entered at once into the heritage of a style of greater simplicity and expressiveness, which may have been partly indicated previously in works of Arcadelt and Morales, but was only first completely illustrated by Palestrina in his motets of 1563 and 1569. The date of publication of Victoria's work is sufficient to dispose of the suggestion that in the adoption of this style he was influenced by such other members of the Roman school as Nanino or Marenzio. On the other hand, the general resemblance of his motet style to that of Palestrina is so striking that many of his works might easily be mistaken for compositions of Palestrina. There is only this difference, that in

Victoria there is often a greater immediate warmth or tenderness of devotional feeling, an ascetically restrained ardour of mystical rapture with perhaps less of outward artistic grace, and less cultivation of contrapuntal art for its own sake. Victoria is often more interested in the appropriate use of expressive homophonic harmony than in the mere flow of melodic polyphony. It may also be claimed that if Victoria's general style is based on that first fully developed by Palestrina, Palestrina in his turn was partly influenced by Victoria in his later adoption of what he himself described as a more ardently passionate style (' usus sum genere aliquanto alacriore ') for his motets from the canticles published in 1584. It is interesting in this respect to compare Victoria's 'Vadam et circuibo ' and ' Vidi speciosam,' both a 6, from the book of 1572, with some of Palestrina's motets from the canticles on similar texts.

The Collegium Germanicum was for some time amalgamated with the Collegium Romanum, the other institution of Ignatius, but in 1573 Pope Gregory XIII. reorganised and re-endowed the former as a separate institution, and we are told in some detail how on the occasion of the transfer of the *alumni Germanici* to the new abode provided for them there was a solemn ceremony of parting between them and their *Italiani convittori*, when with the help of some members of the Sistine Chapel a psalm by Victoria a 8 for two choirs, ' Super flumina Babylonis,' was sung. Another change of domicile took place in 1575, when Gregory presented to the college the Palazzo San Apollinare with the church attached to it.

In 1576 Victoria dedicated to Duke Ernest of Bavaria, Count Palatine of the Rhine and Administrator of the Bishoprics of Freising and Hildesheim, afterwards Archbishop of Cologne, a miscellaneous collection of masses, Magnificats and motets, which, however, reappear in later separate publications and may then be more conveniently noticed. The Bavarian dukes showed their interest in the German college by appointing those who had been its pupils to important ecclesiastical positions in Bavaria and the Rhineland, which had the further result of spreading Victoria's reputation as a Church composer throughout Germany.

For what reason Victoria in 1578 retired from the Collegium Germanicum was not previously known, but a document of 1611 recently brought to light and quoted by R. Mitjana [1] appears to show that in that year Victoria received the appointment of chaplain to the widowed Empress Maria, daughter of Charles V. and sister of Philip II. of Spain. Where at first he exercised his duties in this capacity is not stated. It was not till 1581 that the Empress returned to Spain, and, after paying a visit to her brother Philip, then in Lisbon, definitely

[1] *Estudios sobre algunos musicos españoles del siglo xvi.* (1918.)

settled in Madrid in 1582, to take up her abode along with her daughter the Infanta Margaret in the convent of Franciscan nuns founded by her sister Doña Juana of Portugal, which was afterwards known as the house of the Descalzas Reales. The Infanta became a professed nun in this house Mar. 25, 1584. Until her definite settlement in Madrid, Victoria may not have been in constant attendance on the Empress, and as it is not till 1583 that in one of his dedications he speaks of himself as about to return to Spain ('natale solum revisurus'), he may have had leisure in Rome from 1581–83 to superintend the publication of several of his works. It would also appear from the same document that besides being chaplain to the Empress, from 1586 he acted as choirmaster to the chapel of the Descalzas Reales.

Meantime, in 1581, two comprehensive works of Victoria appeared in print at Rome. One, bearing the title 'Cantica B. Virginis per annum,' contains two sets of Magnificats on the eight tones, one set with the odd verses, the other with the even verses composed; also eight settings *a* 5 and 8 of the four Marian antiphons, 'Alma Redemptoris,' 'Ave Regina,' 'Regina Coeli' and 'Salve Regina.' The Magnificats are *a* 4, but with some verses *a* 3, probably for solo voices, and the last verse usually *a* 5 or 6, with an occasional canon. This work was dedicated to Michael Bonello, otherwise known as Cardinal Alessandrino, a nephew of Pope Pius V., who had been one of the early pupils of the Collegium Germanicum. In the dedication the composer declares his whole ambition to be to employ music solely as an instrument to raise the mind pleasantly to the contemplation of divine truth. Unlike his Roman contemporaries, Nanino, Anerio and Marenzio, who occupied themselves with the composition of madrigals, and following more in the wake of his Spanish predecessors, Morales and Guerrero, Victoria seems to have disdained to occupy himself with secular music even as an occasional relaxation. His other publication of 1581 is 'Hymni totius anni secundum sanctae Romanae ecclesiae consuetudinem,' which contains 32 settings *a* 4 of the Latin hymns usually sung at the vespers of festivals and saints' days, the even verses only being composed, while the others are understood to be sung to the unison plain-song. The last hymn, 'Pange lingua,' is described as being '*more Hispano*,' the *cantus firmus* being an old Spanish melody to the hymn of a very popular character, different from the usual plain-song. To the Hymns are appended four of the vesper psalms *a* 8 set for double choir. In the dedication to Pope Gregory XIII. Victoria describes himself as driven by a sort of natural instinct ('naturali quodam feror instinctu') to the exclusive cultivation of sacred music, and modestly refers to the

approbation which his labours in that field have met with. As bearing on the artistic relations of Victoria and Palestrina, it may be noted in passing that these comprehensive publications of Magnificats and Hymns appeared several years before the similar publications of Palestrina, 1589 and 1591. The hymns of Victoria may also be thought to have a character of greater austerity and less elaboration than those of Palestrina.

In 1583 appeared two further publications of Victoria. One consists of motets and psalms, 53 numbers *a* 4 to 12, most of which had already appeared in 1572 and 1576. Of the few new works in this collection may be specially mentioned two simple but very beautiful motets for equal voices—one for Trinity Sunday, 'Duo Seraphim,' the other a motet for Communion, 'Domine non sum dignus'—also 'Trahe me post to' *a* 6, set with some appropriateness to the text as a double canon for four of the voices. The last number is the psalm 'Laetatus sum' *a* 12, for three choirs. This may have been the psalm for three choirs reported as having been sung on the occasion of the entrance of the Collegium Germanicum into possession of the Church San Apollinare in 1575, though wrongly described as 'Confitemini Domino.' The dedication of this collection of motets and psalms is peculiar. It is addressed

'to the Blessed Virgin Mother of God and to all the Saints reigning in heavenly felicity with Christ, to celebrate their praises on occasion of their festivals, and to animate with greater sweetness the devotion of the faithful.'

Victoria subscribes himself here for the first time as 'reverendus Dominus, Presbyter Abulensis.' From this H. Collet drew the somewhat hasty conclusion that the year 1583 marked a special mystical crisis in Victoria's life which induced him to seek the priesthood. But this suggestion now falls to the ground with the discovery that Victoria had been appointed some years previously as chaplain to the Empress Maria, and further evidence supplied by Pedrell justifies the assertion that he had already been ordained a priest in the diocese of Avila before leaving Spain in 1565. The other publication of 1583 is a book of masses dedicated to Philip II. From the title, 'Missarum libri duo,' etc., taken in conjunction with the language used in the dedication, it might be inferred that he had originally intended to publish two books together, of which, however, only Liber I. then actually appeared. Although, too, in the dedication he makes no mention of his appointment as private chaplain to the Empress, his language would imply that the discharge of his duties as chaplain would henceforth give him no reason for any further occupation with the composition and publication of music. Reviewing his career and once more repeating that he had been led by a secret natural instinct and impulse ('ipsa me natura

tacito quodam instinctu impulsuque ducebat ')
to devote himself exclusively to the composition
of Church music, in which, as it appeared, he
had given satisfaction to those best qualified to
judge, he declares himself now weary and
desirous of repose so as to give his mind more
to the divine contemplation befitting a priest ;
but, being about to return to Spain, in order not
to return empty he desires to present to the
King in person this book of masses as the final
fruits of his talent (' postremum hunc ingenii
partum '). With the composition of masses he
had thought it most fitting to terminate his
labours (' in hoc meos labores placuit terminare ').

He thus thought of himself as then bidding
farewell to music, but, happily, it was not to be
as he anticipated. In fulfilling his duties as
chaplain to the Empress, he also became choirmaster to the house of the Descalzas Reales.
This first book of masses contains nine, of
which, however, five had already appeared in
the miscellaneous collection of 1576, so that
only four are really new. There are five a 4,
' Quam pulchri,' ' O quam gloriosum,' ' Simile
est regnum,' ' Ave Maris Stella ' and ' Pro
defunctis '; two a 5, ' De Beata Virgine ' and
' Surge Propera '; two a 6, ' Dum complerentur '
and ' Gaudeamus.' It is noticeable that none
of Victoria's masses take their themes from
secular songs. His themes are taken from his
own or other motets or from plain-song. All
these masses are distinguished by a careful
and concise declamation of the text, without
relapsing too much into mere homophonic
utterance, beautiful themes with fine harmony
resulting from their various combinations. In
the final Agnus Victoria usually makes a
discreet use of canon without any parade of
unnecessary ingenuity. They are mostly
canons in unison or at the octave. The best
known of these masses is perhaps the ' O quam
gloriosum,' based on his own early motet of
1572, very concise throughout, with a wonderfully simple and beautiful ' Et incarnatus.'
P. Wagner [1] points out how freely Victoria deals
with his own motet themes by only using those
which are more appropriate to the text of the
mass, and specially by not always beginning
each part of the mass with exactly the same
themes, as was the general fashion of the time.
The ' Ave Maris Stella ' is remarkable for
the fine melody of its themes borrowed from
the liturgical hymn. In the first Hosanna
Victoria takes the liberty of making the tenor
sing the hymn with its own text, while in the
second Agnus a 5 a second tenor voice sings
the hymn tune throughout to the proper words
of the mass. ' Simile est regnum,' which has
also very fine melodies, concludes with a second
Agnus a 8, in which four additional voices sing
together a responsive four - part canon in
unison. The mass ' Gaudeamus ' is remarkable

[1] Geschichte der Messe, Bd. i. pp. 425-8.

for the use made of the short liturgical theme
' Gaudeamus ' as a cantus firmus. In the
first Kyrie the alto voice announces the theme
by first singing it to its text ' Gaudeamus.'
Elsewhere the theme is sung to the proper
words of the mass, except in the concluding
Agnus a 7, in which two voices sing in canon at
the octave nothing else but both theme and
text ' Gaudeamus,' while the other voices sing
the usual words of the mass. This work would
thus seem to have been intended for All Saints'
Day, or for some of the other saints' days,
when the mass begins with the introit ' Gaudeamus.' A prominent theme at the beginning
of some parts of this mass is the ' io son ferito '
theme of Palestrina's popular madrigal, which
may have been intended as an act of homage
to the Roman master, unless its adoption be
purely accidental.

In 1585 appeared at Rome one of Victoria's
most important publications, that which bears
the title ' Officium hebdomadae sanctae.'
This contains in order the chief music for Palm
Sunday and the last three days of Holy Week.
For Palm Sunday there is the motet ' Pueri
hebraeorum,' a 4, for the preliminary service
of Benediction of Palms ; the ' Passio secundum Matthaeum,' in which only the ' Turba '
verses are composed, very simply a 4, but with
considerable dramatic appropriateness, followed
by the very expressive Communion motet, ' O
Domine Jesu Christe,' a 6. For the three last
days of Holy Week there are the nine Lamentation Lessons of the First Nocturns of Matins
for each day, set a 4 to 8, and the 18 Responsoria
of the Second and Third Nocturns, a 4 and 3, all
of these in Victoria's most refined style of devotional pathos and tenderness of sentiment.
For the mass of Holy Thursday there is a
' Tantum ergo,' a 5, based on the popular
Spanish ' Pange lingua ' tune. For Good
Friday, besides the ' Passio secundum Ioan-
nem,' a 4, there is the very lovely motet
' Vere languores,' a 4, taken over from the book
of 1572, to be sung at the Adoration of the
Cross, and a very simple setting of the Impro-
peria similar to that of Palestrina. The last
piece in the book is the hymn ' Vexilla regis '
(more Hispano), a 4 to 6, which has another old
Spanish melody quite different from the familiar
Roman. The whole work would thus seem to
have been intended for Spanish use, either in
Spain itself or in the Spanish churches in Rome.
The Lamentations, however, were copied into
the Sistine Chapel choir-books, two of them
appearing in an earlier form than that in which
they were afterwards published. They may
thus have been in use there before those of
Palestrina, which were only published in 1588.
The ' Officium hebdomadae sanctae ' bears no
dedication beyond what may be implied by the
beautiful engraving of the Crucifixion on the
title-page, accompanied on another page by the

last verse of the hymn ' Vexilla regis.' The work itself testifies to the thoroughly devotional liturgical spirit which inspired all the musical labours of the composer.

Another publication of 1585 bears the title ' Motetta festorum totius anni cum communi Sanctorum.' This was dedicated to Charles Emanuel, Duke of Savoy, a distinguished prince of the time, who was just then returning from Spain after having concluded a temporary alliance with Philip II. as against France. In the dedication the composer, with a curious allusion to the significance of his own name ('Victoriae nomine'), expresses the hope that his book might meet the Duke as a good omen on his return. He mentions that he had only been induced to offer his book for the Duke's acceptance by the persuasions of one with whom he was bound in ties of close friendship, Juvenal Ancina, a native of Fossano in the Duke's Piedmontese territories. Ancina was then a well-known priest at the Roman oratory of St. Philip Neri, and afterwards editor of a book of ' Laude spirituali ' for the use of the oratory, and at a later time Bishop of Saluzzo. The dedication is followed by what is described as a ' Protrepticon epigramma,' written by Ancina, consisting of 22 couplets of elegiac verse addressed to the Duke, extolling in extremely laudatory terms the merits of Victoria and his works. He describes Victoria as

'Servus Christi ardens, Abulae gloria magna suae . . . quem pia Roma colit, praecentorum urbis decus immortale recentum,' etc.

After this tribute to the composer's renown, it is perhaps matter for surprise that the contents of the book are not wholly new, but mainly consist of a reprint of the motets of a festival character from his earlier publications, with only 10 new pieces, all excellent of their kind. The more important may be the seven specially composed for the Commune Sanctorum, the high quality of which is vouched for by their inclusion in Proske's ' Musica divina.' The book also includes two pieces by other masters, one a 4 by his countryman Guerrero, choirmaster of Seville Cathedral, and one a 8 by Soriano, a Roman pupil of Palestrina, which would seem to show that Victoria took some interest in the works of his contemporaries.

From 1585–92 Victoria published nothing new, but in 1589 two important editions of his motets and psalms, reprints of his own book of 1583, appeared at Dillingen and Milan, testifying to the spread of his reputation both in Germany and northern Italy. The publisher of the Dillingen edition, in dedicating it to the Dean of Augsburg Cathedral, describes Victoria as acknowledged to be one of the greatest masters of the time in sacred music. In 1592 Victoria himself emerges once more to the light of day by the publication at Rome of his

second book of masses, dedicated to the Prince Cardinal Albert, sixth son of the Empress Maria. This prince was for some time Archbishop of Toledo and Primate of Spain, until by dispensation he was allowed to resign his ecclesiastical functions in order to marry and become lay Viceroy of Portugal for the King of Spain. In the dedication the composer mentions for the first time his appointment as chaplain to the Empress. He also states that it was in response to a request from the Cardinal himself that he presents to him this new work. At the same time he makes a mysterious allusion to other works of his which had been published under the patronage of the Cardinal, and were in the hands of all,[1] but what these works were we have no knowledge. Along with a setting of the ' Asperges ' and ' Vidi aquam ' for the preliminary ceremonies of the mass, the book contains seven masses: three a 4, ' Quarti toni,' ' O magnum mysterium' and ' Pro defunctis'; two a 5, ' Trahe me post te ' and ' Ascendens Christus'; one a 6, ' Vidi speciosam '; and one a 8, ' Salve Regina.' The mass ' Quarti toni ' is remarkable for its very expressive use of the so-called Hypophrygian Mode. It may be noted generally in Victoria's works that without overstepping the then recognised limits of the diatonic system, he makes freer use of chromatic modulations for the sake of expressive harmony than Palestrina, who relies so much on beautiful flow of melody, usually does. On this mass Proske remarks :

' Every note betrays the master who in devout contemplation served the sanctuary and among all the Roman contemporaries of Palestrina stood next to him in spiritual nobility. Work and prayer, genius and humility are here blended in perfect harmony.'

Of the other masses in this book, the ' Vide speciosam,' based on his own fine motet, may be thought to be the finest, but the ' Salve Regina ' a 8 is also a work of exceptional beauty, based on a very free handling of the beautiful phrases of his motet of 1576, which have so much the expression of spiritual aspiration. In ' O magnum mysterium ' the composer adopts in the Gloria and Credo the parlando homophonic style of text declamation, and makes much less use than we might have expected of the themes of the beautiful Christmas motet after which the mass is named. The mass ' Pro defunctis ' is the same as that in 1583 with a new responsorium added, ' Peccantem me quotidie.' The liturgical melody is in the soprano part of the mass throughout, and the responsoria are set with alternate unison plain-song.

With royal and other patronage Victoria had been enabled to bring out his works in magnificent folio editions. A document of 1598 quoted by Pedrell gives us full details of the contract entered into between Victoria and a

[1] ' Sicut caetera opera quae, tuo edita patrocinio, jamdudum in omnium manibus versantur.'

printing house at Madrid for the publication of his book of 1600 dedicated to King Philip III. This book consists of a miscellaneous collection of masses, Magnificats, motets, psalms and hymns, a considerable quantity of new work being mixed up with a republication of earlier. The works contained in the book were evidently meant for performance in the chapel of the Descalzas Reales ; as in the dedication the composer expresses the pious hope that they ' may tend to the increase of true devotion in clarissimo hoc templo augustissimae amitae tuae Joanne.' As most of them are composed on a large scale, viz., for 8 and 12 voices, royal patronage must have enabled the nuns to maintain a considerable choir. Among the new works are two masses *a* 8 for two choirs, ' Alma Redemptoris ' and ' Ave Regina,' one *a* 9 for two choirs of five and four voices respectively, entitled ' Pro Victoria,' one *a* 12 for three choirs, ' Laetatus sum.' Of these the most peculiar is the mass ' Pro Victoria ' with its strange intermixture of different styles, some parts written in the most sedate *a cappella* style, others in a fanfare fashion after the manner of Jannequin's battle-pieces with rapid parlando homophonic declamation. No contrast could be greater than that between the first two sections of the Kyrie and the third, or between the quiet opening of the Agnus and the excited parlando declamation of the ' Dona nobis pacem.' The work would seem to be less one of thanksgiving for a victory, for which, indeed, there was little occasion towards the disastrous end of the reign of Philip II. than an impassioned supplication for victory, not only from the peculiar setting of the ' Dona nobis ' but from the stress also laid upon the words ' suscipe deprecationem nostram ' in the Gloria, perhaps too from the parlando setting of the ' in nomine Domini ' of the Benedictus. But this mass has also a very beautiful ' Et incarnatus ' in the composer's usual better style.

Another special feature of the whole book is the provision of an organ accompaniment, which, however, is only a duplication of the voice parts of one or other of the two or three choirs. With regard to the mass ' Laetatus sum ' *a* 12 it may be mentioned that it has little connexion thematically with the psalm *a* 12 beginning with these words with which in this very book it is associated. Victoria is less strict in these matters than Palestrina. He does not lay such stress as Palestrina usually does on the exact thematic connexion of the different movements of the mass with one another or with the motets after which they are named. Yet in this respect he only follows the example first set by Palestrina himself in his Missa Papae Marcelli, in which the different sections of the mass have little direct thematic connexion with one another. There

are two new Magnificats in this book, one *a* 8 one *a* 12, with all the verses composed more or less antiphonally, also a simple Nunc Dimittis *a* 4. In the case of the psalms written for two or more choirs, the organ accompaniment would in case of necessity take the place of one of the choirs. It was this growing practice towards the end of the 16th century of composing the Vesper Psalms and Magnificat for antiphonal choirs that gradually led to the giving of a more independent position to organ accompaniment and to the invention of the system of figured bass. (See THOROUGH-BASS.)

Of the other new pieces of 1600 we need only mention a beautiful new setting of the hymn ' Ave Maris Stella ' which has the peculiarity of the proper melody being given complete in every verse to the soprano part, differing in this respect from the older custom of putting it more in the tenor. In Victoria's earlier setting of 1581 only one of the verses has the melody in the soprano. In this matter, as in that of organ accompaniment, Victoria with all his strict ecclesiasticism otherwise was yet evidently more open to modernising influences than Palestrina.

In March 1603 took place the death of the Empress Maria, and as a tribute to her memory Victoria composed and in 1605 published at Madrid what Proske and others have described as ' the crown of all his works,' ' the greatest triumph of his genius,' ' Officium defunctorum sex vocibus in obitu et obsequiis Sacrae Imperatricis.' It was appropriately dedicated to the Princess Margaret, daughter of the Empress, who ever since 1584 had been a professed nun of the Descalzas Reales. The title gives us sufficient reason for believing that the mass was sung at the funeral of the Empress, although the contemporary record of the funeral ceremonies quoted by Pedrell makes no mention of Victoria or his music. The work consists of those parts of the Requiem mass then usually composed, the Introit with the Kyrie, the Gradual, Offertorium, Sanctus, Benedictus, Agnus and Communio, each part preceded by the unison plain-song intonation, but also with the plain-song melody continued more or less freely in the second soprano. The hymn ' Dies Irae,' which figures so prominently in later requiems, is not composed by Victoria, and if then sung at all, would be sung in its plain-song setting. But besides the mass Victoria has composed a touchingly expressive motet *a* 6. ' Versa est in luctum,' also the responsorium ' Libera me ' with alternate plain-song, and an extremely pathetic setting in simple homophonic harmony *a* 4, of the Second Lesson of the Vigil Office ' Taedet animam meam.' He had previously published in 1583 and 1592 a very good Requiem Mass *a* 4, and indeed incorporates into his later work the small trio movement of the ' Libera '

'Tremens factus sum,' but the work of 1605 being for 6 voices is composed on a larger scale, and gives occasion for more powerful and expressive harmonies. The whole work is justly reckoned as a masterpiece of the highest order. There is no display of art for art's sake, but its artistic merit just consists in its subordination of art to the sincere expression of religious devotion. After the death of the Empress, Victoria continued to occupy the modest position of chaplain to the Princess Margaret and the house of the Descalzas, but seems to have retired from the position of choirmaster, while retaining that of organist. By her will the Empress bequeathed to him a pension chargeable on the revenues of certain bishoprics, and in this way as well as by gifts from distinguished patrons he was enabled to live comfortably. Although in the dedication of the work of 1605 he had described it as his 'swan-song,' he had at the same time expressed his desire and hope that if his life were prolonged, he might yet be able to offer for Princess Margaret's acceptance other greater works. But so far as we have any knowledge, this hope was not fulfilled. During the remainder of his life, he issued no new publication, and we have no mention of new compositions. Previously there was much uncertainty as to the date of his death, but recent investigation has now ascertained it to have taken place August 27, 1611.

With the almost too sudden change of musical style and outlook which began to prevail from the beginning of the 17th century, Victoria shared in the general oblivion which soon overtook the works of the older masters of vocal polyphony. A certain degree of interest was first reawakened by musical historians towards the end of the 18th century, which afterwards under the influence of the romantic movement at the beginning of the 19th century took the more practical form of a renewed publication of some of their works and the revival of them in public performance. Victoria began to be more generally known by one very delightful short motet a 4, 'Jesu dulcis memoria,' universally attributed to him, though it does not appear in any of his own published works, and its original source is nowhere specified. A fuller knowledge and appreciation of him first became possible by the labours of Canon Proske of Ratisbon, who in his 'Musica divina' (1853–61) published a large and excellent selection of his works, masses, motets, responsoria, etc. At the instance of the late F. X. Haberl the publication of a complete edition of Victoria's works was undertaken by Breitkopf and Härtel in 1896 under the editorship of F. Pedrell of Barcelona, the contents of which are as follows :

Vol. I.—Motets, a 4-8, 44 nos., without reckoning second parts separately.
Vol. II.—Ten masses, a 4-5.

Vol. III.—Eighteen Magnificats, a 4-12, with a Nunc Dimittis, a 4.
Vol. IV.—Five masses, a 6-8.
Vol. V.—Hymns, 34 nos. a 4, and the 'Officium Hebdomadae Sanctae.'
Vol. VI.—Three masses, a 8-12, and the two masses.' Pro Defunctis, with the smaller pieces attached to them.
Vol. VII.—Ten psalms and sequences, a 8-12, and ten settings of the Marian Antiphons, a 5 and 8, with three smaller works.
Vol. VIII.—Has a lengthy bio-bibliographical study of the composer, provided with the necessary documents, and a musical supplement of five other works, gleaned from various quarters, a 'Missa Dominicalis,' a 4, composed with alternate plain-song, two of the Lamentation Lessons in their earlier version from the Sistine Chapel archives, the motet, 'Jesu dulcis memoria,' and two others, 'Ave Maria,' 'Benedicam Dominum,' taken over from Proske's 'Musica divina' without any indication of source.

Victoria's separate works thus reckoned up just come short of 180, a small number as compared with those of Palestrina, over 700, or those of O. de Lassus, over 1200, but all or nearly all of the highest value.

RECENT BIBLIOGRAPHY

R. Mitjana: La Musique en Espagne (extracted from Lavignac, Encyclopédie de la musique). (1914.)
H. Collet : Victoria. (Paris, 1914.)
F. Pedrell : T. L. de Victoria Abulense. (Madrid, 1918.)
R. Mitjana : Estudios sobre algunos músicos Españoles del siglo xv. (Madrid, 1918.)   J. R. M.

VICTORINUS, Georgius (b. Huldschön, Bavaria, c. middle of 16th cent. ; d. Munich, 1624). About 1591 he was living in the Jesuit monastery of St. Michael as Musicus praefectus. On July 7, 1597, the day of the consecration of the church of St. Michael, a sacred play was given by students in the place in front of the church, for which Victorinus had composed the music. Nine hundred singers performed the choruses. Costumes and decorations were specially produced for the occasion, and the fall of the angels into the burning hell created quite a sensation. The play was afterwards repeated several times, but nothing but the scenario has been preserved. A few only of Victorinus's compositions are still in existence. A Magnificat, 6 v., of 1591, and 3 litanies, 4-10 v., in MS., are in the Munich library, and some 20 songs of his are contained in his valuable collection of church music by various authors, viz. : 'Thesaurus litaniarum' (1596), 'Siren coelestis' (1616 ; English edition by Wm. Braythwait, London, 1638) and 'Philomela coelestis' (1624).   E. v. d. s.

VIDAL, a name borne by several French musicians and writers on music. The earliest (1) B. Vidal, whose initial only is known (d. Paris, Feb. 1800), was a talented guitarplayer and teacher during the last quarter of the 18th century, and published sonatas, short pieces, and a method for his instrument, Nouvelle Méthode de guitare dédiée aux amateurs (Paris).

(2) Jean Jacques (b. Sorrèze, Mar. 7, 1789 ; d. June 14, 1867), a clever violinist formed in Kreutzer's school, won the first prize for violin at the Conservatoire in 1808, and the second Grand Prix de Rome for composition in 1809. He was for twenty years in Baillot's quartet-party, belonged to the Opéra orchestra and that of the Société des Concerts ; conducted

the orchestra of the Théâtre Italien from 1829–1831, played first violin in Louis Philippe's band, and was a valued teacher.

(3) Louis Antoine (b. Rouen, July 10, 1820; d. Paris, Jan. 7, 1891) was an erudite musical historian, author of copious and valuable works on the violin. He was an excellent amateur musician (he studied the violoncello with Franchomme), an accomplished linguist, and he was a friend of J. B. Vuillaume. In 1876 the first volume of his great work Les Instruments à archet, dealing with the history of the violin, was published by J. Claye, Rue Saint-Benoit, Paris. The second volume appeared in 1877, and dealt exhaustively with the subject of makers, while the third volume, dated 1878, discoursed of musical typography and gave not only biographies of musical composers, but also a magnificent bibliography of chamber music. These three sumptuous volumes were illustrated by Frédéric Hillemacher, and the edition was limited to 500 copies. In 1878 part of the above work was published under the title Les Vielles Corporations de Paris (Quantin). It forms a complete and exhaustive history of the Corporation of St. Julien des Ménétriers and the French Minstrels. In response to a demand for a separate edition of that part of Les Instruments à archet which dealt with the history and manufacture of the violin, Quantin published, in 1889, La Lutherie et les luthiers, of which as before only 500 copies were printed. Vidal was member of the Société de l'Histoire de Paris et de l'Île-de-France. He was compiling a history of the pianoforte when he died.   E. H.-A.; rev. M. P.

(4) Francois (b. Aix, July 14, 1832), Provençal poet, the author of Lou Tambourin (Avignon, 1864), an interesting work on the Tambourine of Provence, and the Galoubet, or pipe. It is in the Provençal dialect, with a French translation.   G. C.

(5) Paul Antonin (b. Toulouse, Haute-Garonne, June 16, 1863), passed brilliantly through the Paris Conservatoire, and took successively the first harmony prize in 1879, the first counterpoint and fugue prize in 1880, and the first Grand Prix de Rome in 1883, with the cantata 'Le Gladiateur.' He was assistant chorus-director at the Opéra, 1889–92; director of the singing and conductor there, 1892–1906. He taught at the Conservatoire, solfège (1894), accompaniment (1896), and composition, from 1910 onwards. His activity as a composer has extended in many directions. At the Opéra he gave 'La maladetta' (ballet, Feb. 24, 1893), 'La Burgonde' (Dec. 23, 1898); at the Opéra-Comique, 'Guernica' (1895). He has composed incidental music for various plays, such as 'Le Baiser' (Banville), 'La Reine Fiammette' (Mendès), etc., performed at the Théâtre des Marionnettes, Cercle funambulesque, etc.;

pantomimes, 'Pierrot assassin,' 'Colombine pardonnée (1888), etc.; 2 'Mystères,' 'Noël ou le Mystère de la Nativité (1890), 'Les Mystères d'Eleusis' (1894); an operetta, 'Eros' (1892). He founded the Concerts de l'Opéra with G. Marty, 1895–97, for which he arranged a series of old dances. A successful 'Suite de danses' (music by Chopin) was orchestrated by him, in co-operation with A. Messager (Opéra, June 23, 1913). As a composer of sacred music, he has composed motets, a cantata, 'Ecce Sacerdos magnus' (choir, organ, string orchestra). He has published many arrangements of old music. His pedagogic works as yet published are: 52 Leçons d'harmonie de Luigi Cherubini, in 3 volumes (Paris, Enoch). A Manuel pratique d'harmonie and Notes et observations sur la composition et l'exécution is in preparation.

His brother (6) Joseph Bernard (b. Toulouse, Nov. 15, 1859; d. Paris, Dec. 18, 1924) was a military bandmaster and won the first trombone prize at the Paris Conservatoire, 1882. He composed operetta, 'Le Mariage d'Yvette' (1896), 'Le Chevalier de Fontenoy,' etc. A collection of songs, 'Marches et chansons des soldats de France' (with J. Jouvin and Captain Gillet), appeared in 1919 (Paris, Plon).   M. L. P.

VIEIRA, Ernesto, Portuguese musical biographer, whose Diccionario biographico de musicos portuguezes (1900) supplements the dictionary of Vasconcellos, and to a certain extent replaces it.   J. B. T.

VIELLE, see Hurdy Gurdy.

VIENNA. The perennial importance of Vienna in musical history is evidenced by the number of great composers who lived and worked there. Schubert, Lanner and Johann Strauss were born there; Beethoven and Brahms made it their second home. Gluck, Mozart, Haydn, Bruckner, Hugo Wolf and Mahler lived in Vienna and all are buried there. Richard Strauss has settled there, and it continues to be an important centre of musical life, despite the political straits through which Austria and its capital have passed.

The following is a summary of its main musical institutions:

Staatsoper (State opera, formerly Hofoper), built by van der Nüll and Siccardsburg, opened May 25, 1869, holds 2260 persons. Its directors have been: Herbeck (1870–75); Jauner (1875–80); Jahn, Hans Richter (1880–1896); Gustav Mahler (1896–1907); Felix Weingartner (1907–11); Hans Gregor (1911–1918); Franz Schalk (1918 up to the present time, 1926); during 1920–24 Dr. Richard Strauss together with Franz Schalk. Since its foundation the ensemble consisted of the most famous singers, and the orchestral and choral staffs have been trained and selected with the utmost care and especially developed through Hans Richter and Gustav Mahler. Hans

Richter, including in the repertory the works of Gluck, Mozart and Wagner, disposed of an ensemble of world-famed artists : Winkelmann, Reichmann, Scaria, van Dyck, Schrödter, Lucca, Materna, Renard, Schläger. The genius of Gustav Mahler fully developed the forces which made the Vienna Opera capable of unsurpassed performances. Alfred Roller, Franz Schalk and Bruno Walter worked with him. Through systematic and untiring effort the ideal of performance was realised, and not only did Mahler inaugurate cyclical performances of the unshortened works by Mozart and Wagner, but he encouraged as well the production of his contemporaries (Strauss, Pfitzner, Rezniček, Zemlinsky, Bittner). Felix Weingartner, following Mahler, brought the performance of ' Elektra ' by Richard Strauss. During 1911–18 (Direktor Gregor) were first given Debussy's ' Pelléas et Mélisande,' Strauss's ' Salomé,' ' Rosenkavalier,' ' Ariadne.' In 1919 the Opera celebrated in a great and successful musical festival its fifty years' foundation. During the period Strauss-Schalk the repertory became enriched through ' Die Frau ohne Schatten ' (first performance), ' Josephs - Legende,' ' Schlagobers,' all by Strauss ; ' Palestrina,' by Pfitzner ; Puccini's three-act operas ; ' Die Gezeichneten ' and ' Der Schatzgräber,' by Schreker ; ' Die tote Stadt,' by Korngold ; ' Die Kohlhaymerin ' and ' Das Rosengärtlein,' by Bittner ; ' Der Zwerg,' by Zemlinsky ; ' Fredegundis,' by Schmidt ; Moussorgsky's ' Boris Godounov ' ; ' Pulcinella,' by Stravinsky ; ' André Chénier,' by Giordano ; ' Höllisch Gold,' by Bittner ; ' Don Gil,' by Braunfels. Besides Schalk, the present conductors are Reichenberger, Heger, Alwin. The famous Viennese tradition for the works especially of Mozart, Beethoven and Wagner has been kept fully alive. Notwithstanding the continual economic struggle, the Viennese Opera conducted by Franz Schalk has lately confirmed its reputation outside its own city by performances given with the utmost success at Salzburg, Geneva, Paris and Cologne.

Here must also be mentioned the VOLKSOPER, a private theatre opened in 1904 and capable of holding 1840 persons ; temporary directors : Rainer Simons, Weingartner, Dr. Stiedry, Blech.

ORCHESTRAL CONCERTS. — The famous orchestra of the ' Wiener Philharmoniker ' consists of members of the Staatsoper orchestra only. It gives eight symphony concerts each season, besides one extra concert for the benefit of its pension fund. The Philharmonic Concerts were founded by Otto Nicolai. The first concert was given by the Philharmonische Akademie, Mar. 18, 1842, in the Redoutensaal. The orchestra became an independent organisation in 1860, and since then its programmes have been remarkable for catholicity and

progress. Wagner's name appeared for the first time in 1861 with the Faust overture, Brahms two years later with the second Serenade (op. 16). In 1863 Wagner appeared as conductor of the prelude and ' Liebestod ' from Tristan. List of its most famous conductors : Otto Nicolai (1842 – 47), Georg Hellmesberger (1847–48), Otto Dessoff (1860–1875), Hans Richter (1875–82), Gustav Mahler (1898–1901), Joseph Hellmesberger (1901–03), Franz Schalk (1903, 1905–08), Muck (1904–06), Mottl (1904–07), Strauss (1906–08), Weingartner since 1908 ; Schalk, Furtwängler and Walter appearing as guest conductors. The orchestra is self-governing, choosing its own conductor and committee of twelve members. It has pension and sick funds, and has done much in the cause of Austrian charities.

GESELLSCHAFT DER MUSIKFREUNDE.—This institution was suggested in 1812 and founded 1813 mainly through Dr. Joseph von Sonnleitner after two great performances of Handel's ' Alexander's Feast.' The first patron was the Cardinal Archduke Rudolph, Beethoven's pupil and patron (1814–31). The ' Musikfeste ' (oratorios only with 1000 performers) were repeated in the Riding-school every year until 1847. In 1830 the Society, having meanwhile founded a conservatorium, a musical library and museum, moved into a house of its own, but having far outgrown it, removed in 1870 to the present large building (by Hansen) ' An-der-Wien,' where, besides its own concerts, many other large concerts are now held. The ' Singverein,' a choral society of 300-350 members, was founded by the Gesellschaft in 1858, the ' Orchesterverein ' established in 1860. Both perform the so-called ' Gesellschaftsconcerte,' amounting to eight oratorio concerts given each season without interruption from 1860 onward. Down to 1848 the concerts were conducted by the best musicians among the members in turn, but in 1851 Hellmesberger was appointed as professional conductor. His successors were Herbeck (1859–70, 1875–77), Anton Rubinstein (1871–72), Johannes Brahms (1872–75), E. Kremser (1878–80), W. Gericke (1880–84) (first performance of Liszt, Dante Symphony, and Berlioz's Requiem), Hans Richter (1885–90) (Bach, Mass in B minor and ' Christmas oratorio,' Weber Centenary Festival, 1886), W. Gericke (1890–95) (Mozart Festival, 1891, Bruckner, Mass F minor), R. von Perger (1895–1900), F. Löwe (1900–04), Franz Schalk (1904–21) (first complete performance of Bach's ' St. Matthew Passion,' Bach Festival, 1912 ; Beethoven Festival, 1920). Present conductors are W. Furtwängler and L. Reichwein.

The WIENER KONZERTVEREIN, founded 1900, gives its concerts in the new ' Wiener Konzerthaus ' (opened 1913), founded by the Wiener Konzerthausgesellschaft. Ferdinand LÖWE, the famous interpreter of Bruckner, was the artistic guide up to 1924 (*d.* 1925). Present conductors, Dirk Fock, Rudolf Nilius. The Wiener Konzerthaus contains three concert-halls for 2100, 900 and 420 people.

The WIENER TONKÜNSTLER ORCHESTER, founded in 1907 by Oskar NEDBAL, gives its concerts in the building of the 'Gesellschaft der Musikfreunde,' whose three concert halls contain 2000, 600 and 200 people. Present conductors are Clemens Krauss (Frankfort) and Hans Knappertsbusch (Munich). Sunday concerts, Anton Konrath.

The WIENER SYMPHONIE ORCHESTER, uniting the two orchestras above mentioned since 1919, gives the majority of all orchestral concerts in Vienna.

CHORAL SOCIETIES.—The most prominent are the SINGVEREIN DER GESELLSCHAFT DER MUSIKFREUNDE and the WIENER SINGAKA-DEMIE, both founded 1858, devoted to the study and performance of old and new classical choral music (Handel, Bach, Haydn, Beethoven, Schumann, Bruckner, Brahms, Wolf). (See above.) Conductors of the Singakademie were, amongst others, Brahms (1864), Stegmayer, Dessoff, Weinwurm, Heuberger, Mandyczewski, Ochs and Walter. The present conductor is Paul von Klenau.

The PHILHARMONISCHE CHOR, founded by Franz Schreker, gives its care to modern choral music exclusively (Schönberg, Mahler).

The ORATORIEN-VEREINIGUNG has Rudolf Nilius for its leader. Two old and famous male choirs complete this list : the WIENER MÄNNERGESANGSVEREIN (conductor, Luze), founded in 1843, and the SCHUBERTBUND, founded in 1863 (conductor, Keldorfer).

There exist innumerable other vocal societies for the performance of church music (Palestrina, Haydn, Schubert, Bruckner, Liszt) and musi-cal societies of working people, all testifying to the deeply rooted musical sense of the Viennese population.

CHAMBER MUSIC.—The principal chamber-music organisation inheriting the great tradi-tion of the Joachim quartet is the ROSÉ QUARTET (*q.v.*) (Rosé, Fischer, Ruszitska, Walter). Others are the Fitzner Quartet, Buxbaum Quartet, Sedlak-Winkler Quartet and many more. Special care is given to the literature for wind instruments by the 'Bläser-vereinigung der Wiener Philharmoniker,' with Professor Wunderer as chief.

EDUCATION : UNIVERSITY. — The Musik-historische Seminar, devoted to purely scientific and theoretical work, was founded by the eminent scientist Professor Guido ADLER (*q.v.*), president of the society for the publication of musical monuments in Austria and chief of the university's seminary for musical history. This institution contains a large library and has produced a great number of well-known

scientists and artists in and outside of Austria who continue the work of their leader. (Rietsch, Kurth, Fischer, Wellesz, Orel, Haas, Weigl, Kornauth, Grosz, Pisk, Gál).

HOCHSCHULE and AKADEMIE FÜR MUSIK UND DARSTELLENDE KUNST.—This establish-ment has its origin in the Conservatorium founded by the Gesellschaft der Musikfreunde in 1817 (with Antonio Salieri as first leader) as a school for singing, and quickly developing into importance, it enlarged itself in 1819 through a violin class, which was followed in 1821 by a school for all instruments, Joseph Böhm teach-ing from the beginning. Ernst, Joachim, Grün, Hellmesberger were his pupils (see VIOLIN-PLAYING). In 1870 it was again enlarged by an opera school, and in 1874 by a dramatic school. Guided for a long time by a com-mittee, its first real director was Gottfried Preyer (1843–47). Reorganised through Hell-mesberger (1851–93, followed by Fuchs, 1893–1899), it became world famous, having as teachers S. Sechter, J. Herbeck, A. Bruckner, O. Dessoff, H. Grädener, A. Door, T. Epstein, R. Fuchs, E. Mandyczewski, G. Bachrich, R. Heuberger. Innumerable artists have gone forth from this venerable school, amongst the most important of which we name Ernst, Staudigl, Goldmark, Richter, Mottl, Wolf, Mahler, Brodsky, Löwe, Nikisch, Josef Schalk, Franz Schalk, Rosé, Fritz Kreisler and many more.

Since 1908 the Conservatorium has become the property of the State, changing its name into 'Akademie für Musik und darstellende Kunst.' Reorganised in 1924, it is now a university with Professor Joseph Marx as rector and Professor Franz Schmidt as director of the academy. The instruction includes every instrumental and theoretical branch. Since 1910 a department for church music has been added to the State academy at Kloster-neuburg, with Professor Max Springer as leader. There are besides more than 100 private music schools in Vienna, amongst which are the Neue Wiener Konservatorium, founded by Professor Richard Robert and Fr. Ondriček.

LIBRARIES AND COLLECTIONS.—The collec-tions of the Gesellschaft der Musikfreunde con-sist of an archive, a library and a museum, its possessions having gradually increased to its present enormous extent. Its library, founded in 1819, the society acquiring the valuable collection of E. L. Gerber, quickly developed its importance through gifts and legacies. The society came into possession of the Spaun-Witteczek collection of Schubert, of Köchel's Mozart collection and of the library of Johannes Brahms. The society inherited the precious collection of autographs in posses-sion of its first protector, the Archduke Rudolph, and the original of all the Schubert symphonies, bequeathed by Nicolaus Dumba. The archive now contains nearly 40,000 pieces of music, printed or manuscript, divided into seventeen classes and 10,000 printed vols. The valuable museum includes fragments of J. S. Bach, Haydn's Ten Commandments, Mass in B♭, a great cantata and six string quartets (1771), Mozart's PF. concerto in D minor, a quintet, his last cantata (Nov. 1791), Beethoven's first violin concerto (a fragment), many songs, the sonata op. 81 (first part), a quantity of sketches, the Eroica of Beethoven, choruses by Gluck and Handel, Schubert's opera 'Alfonso und Estrella,' Singspiele, chamber music, symphonies and many songs. The museum possesses besides a large collection of letters, pictures and engravings of celebrated musicians and a collection of ancient musical instruments, medals, busts, etc., from all countries. C. F. Pohl was its archivist and librarian from 1866 until his death in 1887, when he was followed by Dr. Eusebius Mandyczewski, who holds this important office at the present day.

The music collection of the Nationalbibliothek (formerly Hofbibliothek) was founded 1829, and includes numerous autographs of earlier date, ancient and new musical prints and an extensive library. Lately the collection of manuscripts has become considerably enriched, especially through the bequest of Anton Bruckner's original scores (see LIBRARIES). In close connexion with the Nationalbibliothek are the archives of the Staatsoper, the Hofkapelle, the Theater an der Wien, the old Kärntnertortheater. At the head of the music collection is Dr. Robert Haas. The renowned Estensian collection of musical instruments has been placed in the new imperial Burg. The music department of the Wiener Stadtbibliothek (library of the city of Vienna, custos Dr. Alfred Orel) is chiefly occupied with the collection of such documents and facts as concern the musical life in Vienna during the 19th century, possessing many valuable manuscripts connected with it.

POPULAR EDUCATION.—The Wiener Volksbildungsverein (founded 1887), the Societies 'Volksheim' and Urania, popular lectures at the University and at the Academy, together with workmen's symphony concerts, spread the musical education among the broad masses of the people, a work to which great care and much time is devoted. K. R.

VIERDANCK, JOHANN, a 16th-century composer. He was a choir-boy in the court chapel at Dresden, and in 1628 was sent to Vienna to study under Sansoni. From about 1640 he was organist at St. Mary's Church, Stralsund. He wrote: 'Erster Theil neuer Pavanen Gagliarden,' 'Balletten und Correnten,' for 2 violins and violon (violoncello) with basso continuo (Rostock, 1637 and 1641);

'Ander Theil' (second part of former), containing some capriccios, canzons and sonatas for from 2 to 5 instruments, with and without basso continuo (1641); 'Erster Thiel geistlicher Concerten,' 2-4 v. (1642), several more editions; 'Geistliche Concerten,' 3-9 v., with basso continuo (1643); 'Ander Theil geistlicher concerten,' 3-9 v. (1643). Schilling compares him with Leo Hassler, whom he resembles closely in style and manner, and Mattheson speaks of him in terms of the highest praise. E. v. d. s.

VIERLING, GEORG (b. Frankenthal, Bavarian Palatinate, Sept. 15, 1820; d. Wiesbaden, May 1, 1901), son of Jakob Vierling (1796–1867), schoolmaster and organist, studied the organ under J. H. C. Rinck of Darmstadt and under A. B. Marx at Berlin, and in 1847 became organist of the Oberkirche at Frankfort-on-the-Oder, and conducted the Singakademie there. After passing a short time at Mainz he took up his permanent residence in Berlin, and founded the Bach-Verein, which did much to advance the study of the great master. He was made royal music-director in 1859, and in 1882 professor and a member of the Berlin Academy.

His works, all in the classical style, include :

Symphony, op. 33 ; Overtures to 'The Tempest,' 'Maria Stuart,' 'Im Frühling,' 'Hermannschlacht,' and 'Die Hexe'; a PF. trio, op. 51 ; 'Hero and Leander,' 'The Rape of the Sabines,' 'Alarichs Tod,' and 'Konstantin' for chorus and orchestra; in addition to numerous soli and partsongs, pianoforte pieces, etc. A pilgrims' song of the 7th century, 'O Roma Nobilis,' for 6-part chorus a cappella, is op. 63. G.

VIERLING, JOHANN GOTTFRIED (b. Metzels, Meiningen, Jan. 25, 1750; d. Schmalkalden, Nov. 22, 1813), studied at Schmalkalden under the organist Fischer, whom he succeeded afterwards in office. He employed a prolonged leave of absence to study under C. P. E. Bach at Hamburg, and Kirnberger at Berlin, whence he returned to his modest position which he retained to the time of his death. He was accounted one of the greatest organists of his time and a composer of sterling merit. He wrote a four-part Hymn-book with a short introduction to thorough-bass (1789); an attempt at an instruction book for improvising (präludieren) for the unpractised (1794); an Instruction in Thorough-bass (1805); several books of organ pieces, many of which have appeared in modern editions; 127th Psalm for 3-part chorus and orchestra; about 40 cantatas for chorus, solo voices and orchestra, a Magnificat, etc. (MS.); a singspiel, 'Empfindung und Empfindelei'; Harvest Festival music (MS.); songs in K. W. Justi's 'Gedichte' (1810); 2 pianoforte trios, op. 1 (1781); one quartet for pianoforte, 2 violins and bass, op. 4; 6 sonatas for pianoforte, dedicated to Kirnberger (Leipzig, Breitkopf, 1781); Riemann mentions a pianoforte quintet, but apparently in mistake for the quartet. E. v. d. s.

BIBL.—KARL PAULKE, Johann Gottfried Vierling, 1750–1813, A.M., Oct. 1922, pp. 143-55. With a catalogue of his compositions.

VIERNE, (1) Louis (b. Poitiers, 1870), organist, studied at the Paris Conservatoire under Franck and Widor. After acting as assistant to the latter at St. Sulpice he was appointed to Notre Dame, Paris. His compositions include a Mass for chorus and orchestra, a symphony, a string quartet, sonatas for violin and piano and violoncello and piano, and many smaller instrumental and vocal pieces. For the organ he has written 5 symphonies and about 30 short pieces. The best of his organ works are brilliantly effective and of considerable harmonic originality.

(2) René, brother of the above (b. Lille, Mar. 11, 1878 ; d. Verdun), organist. He fell in the European war. He was organist at Notre Dame des Champs, Paris, and wrote for the organ some sets of short pieces which, though mainly simple, and in some cases designed for manuals only, show freshness and originality.

H. G.

VIEUX, Maurice Edgard (b. Savy-Berlette, Apr. 14, 1884), viola-player. After brilliant studies at the Paris Conservatoire he took the first viola prize in 1902. On the death of his master, Laforge (1918), he took on his class, of which he is now the regular professor. Maurice Vieux has for long been viola soloist in the Société des Concerts du Conservatoire, and has taken part in the most important chamber-music performances. His qualities of style and of technique are of the first order, but he is chiefly distinguished for the beauty and fullness of his tone.   M. P.

VIEUXTEMPS, (1) Henri (b. Verviers, Belgium, Feb. 20, 1820 [1] ; d. Mustapha-lez-Alger, Algiers, June 6, 1881), celebrated violinist and composer for his instrument.

His father, a retired officer, was an instrument-maker and piano-tuner. Through the kindness of one Genin he had instruction from Lecloux, a competent local musician, and by the time he was 6 played Rode's 5th concerto in public with orchestra. In the winter of 1827 he and his father made a tour with Lecloux, in the course of which the boy was heard by De Bériot, who at once adopted him as his pupil, devoted himself to his thorough musical education, and in 1828 took him to Paris and produced him in public. On De Bériot's departure to Italy in 1831, the boy returned to Brussels, where he remained for some time, studying and practising hard, but without any guidance but his own. In 1833 his father took him on a lengthened tour through Germany—the first of an enormous series—in the course of which he met Guhr, Spohr, Molique and other musicians, and heard much music, amongst the rest ' Fidelio.' The journey extended as far as Munich and Vienna, where he excited surprise,

[1] The materials for this sketch are supplied by Vieuxtemps's autobiography published in the Guide Musical, and translated in the Musical World, June 25, 1881, and following nos., by Philharmonic Programmes, the A.M.Z. and other sources.

not only for his fullness of tone, purity of intonation, and elegance of style, but also for the ready way in which he played off a MS. piece of Mayseder's at sight (A.M.Z., 1834, p. 160). He remained in Vienna during the winter, and while there took lessons in counterpoint from Sechter. There, too, he made the acquaintance of Mayseder, Czerny and others. He also played Beethoven's violin concerto (at that time a novelty) at the Concert Spirituel. The party then returned northwards by Prague, Dresden, Leipzig (where Schumann welcomed him in a genial article in his Neue Zeitschrift), Berlin and Hamburg.

In the spring of 1834 he was in London at the same time with De Bériot, and played for the first time at the Philharmonic on June 2.[2] Here, too, he met Paganini. The winter of 1835 was spent in Paris, where he made a long stay, studying composition under Reicha. After this he began to write, and his compositions were brought forward in Holland in 1836. In 1837 he and his father made a second visit to Vienna, and in 1838 they took a journey to Russia, by Warsaw, travelling for part of the way with Henselt. The success was so great as to induce another visit in the following year, when he made the journey by Riga, this time with Servais. On the road he made the acquaintance of Richard Wagner. But a little later, at Narva, he was taken with a serious illness which delayed his arrival for some months, and lost him the winter season of 1838. The summer was spent in the country, mostly in composition—concerto in E, Fantaisie-Caprice, etc.—both which he produced in the following winter amid the most prodigious enthusiasm ; which was repeated in his native country when he returned, especially at the Rubens Fêtes in Antwerp (Aug. 1840), where he was decorated with the Order of Leopold, and in Paris, where he played the concerto at the Concert du Conservatoire, Jan. 12, 1841. He then made a second visit to London, and performed at the Philharmonic concert of Apr. 19, and at two others of the same series—a rare proof of the strong impression he made.

The next few years were taken up in another enormous continental tour, and in a voyage to America in 1844. A large number of compositions (opp. 6 to 19) were published after regaining Brussels ; but the strain of the incessant occupation of the tour necessitated a long Kur at Stuttgart. During this he composed his A major concerto (op. 25) and played it at Brussels in Jan. 1845. In the following autumn he married Miss Josephine Eder, an eminent pianist of Vienna. Shortly after this he accepted an invitation to settle in St. Petersburg as solo violinist to the Emperor, and professor in the Conservatoire, and in Sept. 1846 quitted Western Europe for Russia. In 1852,

[2] Moscheles, Life, i. 304 ; and Philh. Programmes.

however, he threw up this strange contract and returned to his old arena and his incessant wanderings. 1853 saw the composition of his concertó in D minor (op. 31). 1855 was spent in Belgium, and at a property which he had acquired near Frankfort. In 1857 he again visited the United States in company with Thalberg, and in the winter of 1858 was once more in Paris occupied in finishing his 5th concerto in A minor (op. 37). The next ten years were occupied in constant touring all over central Europe, and, somewhat later, Italy. Serious affliction now overtook his hitherto prosperous course. First his father, and then—June 29, 1868—his beloved wife, died. To divert his mind from the shock of these losses he engaged in another enormous tour over Europe, and that again was followed, in Aug. 1870, by a third expedition to the United States, from which he returned in the spring of 1871 to find Paris in ruins. This was the last of his huge tours. From 1871–73, on the invitation of Gevaert, who had succeeded Fétis at the Brussels Conservatoire, he acted as teacher to the violin class there, and as director of the popular concerts ; but this sphere of activity was suddenly ended by a paralytic attack which disabled the whole of his left side, and in consequence made playing impossible. His passion for travelling, however, remained to the last, and it was at Mustapha-lez-Alger, in Algiers, that he died, leaving a 6th concerto, in G, dedicated to Mme. Norman-Néruda, by whom it was first played. In 1872 Vieuxtemps was elected member of the Académie Royale of Belgium, on which occasion he read a memoir of Étienne Jean Soubre.

Vieuxtemps was one of the greatest violinists of modern times, and with De Bériot heads the French school. He had all the great qualities of technique so characteristic of that school. His intonation was perfect, his command of the bow unsurpassed. An astonishing staccato —in up and down bow—was a speciality of his ; and in addition he had a tone of such breadth and power as is not generally found with French violinists. He was fond of strong dramatic accents and contrasts, and, generally speaking, his style was better adapted to his own compositions and those of other French composers than to the works of the great classical masters. At the same time it should be said that he gained some of his greatest successes in the concertos of Beethoven and Mendelssohn, and was by no means unsuccessful as a quartet-player.

As a composer for the violin he had a wider success than almost any one since Spohr ; and the fact that not a few of his works, though written more than half a century ago, are still stock-pieces of the repertories of many violinists, shows such vitality as to lift him out of the rank of composers of merely ephemeral

productions of the virtuoso genre. It must be granted that their value is very unequal. While De Bériot, with his somewhat flimsy workmanship but undeniable charm of sentimental melody, has often been compared to Bellini and Donizetti, Vieuxtemps might not improperly be called the Meyerbeer among composers for the violin. He appears to share the good and the bad qualities of that great opera-writer. On the one hand, no lack of invention, beauty of melody, extremely clever calculation of effect ; and on the other, a somewhat bombastic and theatrical pathos, and occasional lapses into triviality.

The best-known of his works are the concertos, No. 1, in E (op. 10) ; No. 2, in F♯ minor (op. 19) ; No. 3, in A (op. 25) ; No. 4, in D minor (op. 31) ; No. 5, in A minor (op. 37) ; No. 6, in G (op. 47) ; the Fantaisie Caprice and Ballade et Polonaise. He also published a sonata for piano and violin, three cadenzas for Beethoven's violin concerto, and a large number of concert pieces. A statue was erected to his memory at Verviers in 1898.   P. D.

BIBL.—TH. RADOUX, H. Vieuxtemps, sa vie et ses œuvres (1891); PAUL BERGNANS, Henri Vieuxtemps (Turnhout, 1920). (Les Grands Belges.)

The brothers of Henri Vieuxtemps were :

(2) JEAN JOSEPH LUCIEN (b. July 5, 1828 ; d. Brussels, Jan. 1901), pianist, teacher and composer for the piano.

(3) JULES JOSEPH ERNEST (b. Brussels, Mar. 1832 ; d. Belfast, Mar. 20, 1896), violoncellist, who for many years was solo violoncellist at the Italian Opera in London and later in the Hallé orchestra at Manchester. (Riemann.)

VIGANO, SALVATORE (b. Naples, Mar. 29, 1769 ; d. Milan, Aug. 10, 1821), a famous dancer, and composer both of the action and the music of ballets, who will have a longer reputation than is otherwise his due, owing to his connexion with Beethoven. He began his career at Rome in female parts, women being then forbidden the stage there. We next find him at Madrid—where he married Maria Medina, a famous dancer—Bordeaux, London and Venice. At Venice in 1791 he brought out an opera, ' Raoul, sire de Créqui,' both words and music his own. Thence he came to Vienna, where he and his wife made their début, May 13, 1793. He then travelled in Germany, and returned to Vienna in 1799. Here he attracted the notice of the Empress, and the result was his ballet of The Men of Prometheus, ' Gli uomini di Prometeo,' or ' Die Geschöpfe des Prometheus ' (music by Beethoven), the subject of which is said to have been suggested by Haydn's ' Creation ' (Schöpfung), then in its first fame. The piece is called an heroic allegorical ballet, in two acts. It was produced at the Court Theatre, Mar. 28, 1801, and the two ' creations ' were danced by Vigano and Mlle. Cassentini, his wife being then passée. It had a remarkable run, being performed sixteen times in 1801, and thirteen times in 1802. Vigano was evidently a man of great ability, and made a real reputation for his abandonment of the old artificial Italian style of ballet in favour of a 'closer imitation of nature.' Ten ballets of his are mentioned in the *A.M.Z.*, and no doubt these are not all that he composed. How solid was his success may be judged from a passage in one if the letters of Henri Beyle (Stendhal) : 'Vigano has been immensely prosperous ; 4000 francs are the usual income of a ballet composer, but he has had 44,000 for the year 1819 alone.'

Vigano seems to have given his name to a kind of minuet in 4–4 time ; at least, if we may so interpret the title of a set of twelve Variations on a Minuet 'a la Vigano,' which Beethoven published in Feb. 1796.

The minuet was certainly danced, for the names of the dancers are given,[1] and is as certainly in Common time :

Allegretto.

It is worth noting that Beethoven has put the concluding variation and coda into triple time :

Allegro.

There is a life of Vigano—*Commentarii della vita*, etc., by Carlo Ritorni, 8vo, Milan, 1838 ; and much information on him and on the ballet of Prometheus (from which the above is chiefly compiled) is given by Thayer in his *Beethoven*, vol. ii. pp. 124-6 and 380-84 (1st ed.). See also *Krehbiel*, i. 283 *et seq.*   G.

VIGNATI, GIUSEPPE, an early 18th-century opera composer of Bologna. Only text-books of his operas between 1702 and 1726 are in existence. Some cantatas and church music works are preserved in MS. (*Q.-L.*).

VIGNERS, E., see LATVIAN MUSIC.

VIGUERIE, BERNARD (*b.* Carcassone, Languedoc, *c.* 1761 ; *d.* Paris, Mar. 1819), pupil of Charpentier at Paris, where he settled as teacher and music publisher. He wrote a considerable number of pianoforte sonatas,

with and without accompaniment of the violin ; 'Ouverture et chasse ' for pianoforte, violin and bass (*ad lib.*), op. 11. He contributed also to the notorious ' battle-piece ' literature by ' La Bataille de Maringo,' which was published in London as ' The Battle of Marengo, a sonata . . . with additions by the Marquis of Salvo ' ; 2 caprices for PF., op. 3. In Le Céne's 6 concerti he is also represented. His Tutor for the pianoforte appeared in a large number of editions, and attained great popularity. Most of his works were published by himself.   E. v. d. s.

VIHAN (WIHAN), HANUŠ, see BOHEMIAN STRING QUARTET.

VIHUELA, a guitar-shaped instrument, the Spanish equivalent of the lute. It had a flat back and a comparatively short neck though the head with the pegs was bent backwards at an angle of about 135°. From the 13th to the 16th centuries there were three kinds of vihuela : (1) *vihuela de péndola* (see PLATE XXVIII. No. 2), played with a plectrum, like the modern mandoline, and .the Calabrian *chitarra battente* ; (2) *vihuela de arco* (see PLATE XLVI. No. 1), played with a bow, *i.e.* a viol ; and (3) *vihuela de mano*, played with the hand. It was the last which became the universal instrument in 16th-century Spain and for which music of all sorts was arranged. The lute proper, as it was known in other parts of Europe, was only played in Spain by strangers and was called *vihuela de Flandes* (Flemish lute).

At the time of Luis MILAN (*q.v.*), author of the earliest Spanish book of lute-tablature (1535), the vihuela had six strings (5 double and one single), usually tuned at intervals of a 4th with a major 3rd between the third and fourth strings :

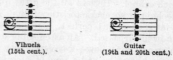

Vihuela   Guitar
(15th cent.).   (19th and 20th cent.).

Music of the Spanish *vihuelistas* may therefore be played on the modern guitar by (*a*) transposing the instrument up a minor 3rd (which is frequently done by modern players and easily accomplished by means of a *capotasto*, Span. *cejuela*, fastened round the neck at the level of the third string) ; and (*b*) by lowering the third string a semitone. The late Dr. Oscar Chilesotti used to play old Italian lute-music on the guitar to friends who visited him at Bassano ; and old Spanish music for the vihuela is sometimes included in modern Spanish programmes for the guitar.

The vihuela was generally the instrument of elegant and polite society. The popular instrument, even as early as the time of Luis Milan, was the GUITAR (*q.v.*). At first it had only four strings tuned like the inner ones of the vihuela. It was called 'Spanish' when it regularly began to be made with five strings; and from that time forward, the vihuela began to disappear. Ten books of tablature for the vihuela were published in Spain between 1535 and 1578; but FUENLLANA (*q.v.*) writing in 1554 already includes pieces for the guitar, and by the end of the 16th century the vihuela was practically obsolete. Now that the guitar has six strings (the sixth was added about 1800) it is as difficult to play, and as effective when well played, as the vihuela is ever likely to have been.

The following books of tablature for the vihuela were published in Spain :

A. IN ITALIAN LUTE-TABLATURE

MILAN, LUIS. Libro de musica de vihuela de mano intitulado El Maestro. Valencia, 1535–6. (B.M.; Bibl. Nat., Paris; Bibl. Nac. and Bibl. Real, Madrid; Bibl. Diputació, Barcelona.)

NARVAEZ, LUIS DE. Los seys libros del Delphin de Musica. Valladolid, 1538. (B.M.; Bibl. Nac., Madrid; Bibl. Prov., Toledo.)

MUDARRA, ALONSO DE. Tres libros en cifras para vihuela. Seville, 1546. (Bibl. Nac., Madrid; Bibl. Escurial.)

ENRIQUEZ DE VALDERRABANO, ENRIQUE. Libro de musica de vihuela, intitulado Silva de Sirenas. Valladolid, 1547. (B.M.; Bibl. Nac., Madrid; Bibl. Univ. Barcelona; Staatsbibl., Vienna.)

PISADOR, DIEGO. Libro de musica de vihuela. Salamanca, 1552. (B.M.; Bibl. Nat., Paris; Bibl. Nac., Madrid; Bibl. Escurial.)

FUENLLANA, MIGUEL DE. Libro de musica de vihuela intitulado Orphenica Lyra. Seville, 1554. (B.M.; Bibl. Nac. and Conserv., Paris; Bibl. Nac., Madrid; Bibl. Escurial; Bibl. Diputació, Barcelona; Staatsbibl., Vienna; Bibl. Wiesbaden; Bibl. Univ., Innsbruck.)

DAZA, ESTEBAN. Libra de musica en cifras para vihuela intitulado El Parnaso. Cordoba, 1576. (Bibl. Nac., Madrid.)

B. IN ORGAN-TABLATURE

VENEGAS DE HENESTROSA, LUYS. Libro de cifra nueva para tecla, harpa, y vihuela. Alcala, 1557. (Bibl. Nac., Madrid.)

SANTA MARIA, THOMAS DE. Libro llamado Arte de tañer fantasia, assi para tecla como para vihuela. Valladolid, 1565. (B.M.; Glasgow; Berlin; Bibl. Escurial; Bibl. Medinaceli, Madrid; Bibl. Univ., Barcelona.

CABEZON, ANTONIO. Obras de musica para tecla, arpa, y vihuela. Madrid, 1578. (B.M.; Bibl. Berlin; Bibl. Royale, Brussels; Bibl. Nac., Madrid; Bibl. Univ., Barcelona.)

See MORPHY, *Les Luthistes espagnols* (Leipzig, 1902); Villalba, *10 Canciones españolas de los siglos XV y XVI* (Madrid); *Luis Milan and the Vihuelistas* (Oxford, 1925). A complete edition of the Spanish vihuelistas is in course of publication by E. M. Torner (Junta para Ampliación de Estudios, Madrid).

J. B. T.

VILA, PEDRO ALBERTO (*b.* ? Barcelona, 1517; *d.* there, Nov. 16, 1582), Spanish madrigalist, organist and canon of the Cathedral at Barcelona, who published a set entitled

Odarum quas vulgo madrigales appellamus . . . lib. I. Barcelona, 1561. (Barcelona, Bibl. de la Diputació; alto only.)

The words of this curious collection are in Spanish, Catalan, Italian or French. A few pieces in MS. are preserved in the same library ; and in the library of the Orfeó Català, Barcelona; while organ-works are printed in the tablature of VENEGAS (*q.v.*).   J. B. T.

VILAR, JOSEPH TEODOR (*b.* Barcelona, Aug. 10, 1836 ; *d.* there, Oct. 21, 1905), studied with Ramon Vilanova (1801–70), the cathedral organist, himself a composer of church music of some distinction. In 1859 he went to Paris to continue his education with Henri Herz for piano and Bazin and Halévy for composition. On his return to his native city in 1863 he wrote an abridgment of musical history, played at concerts, and wrote a considerable number of zarzuelas. ' La Romeria de Racasens ' (1867),

' L'Ultim Rey de Magnolia ' (1868), ' El Pescadors de San Pol ' (1869), ' Una Prometensa,' ' La Rambla de las Flores,' and ' Pot mes qui piuta ' (1870), ' La Lluna en un cove,' ' L' Esca del pecat,' and ' La Torre del amor ' (1871). He was second conductor at one of the subordinate theatres, and afterwards rose to be chorus-master and finally conductor at the Teatro Principal. Later on he devoted himself exclusively to teaching and composition.   M.

VILBAC, ALPHONSE CHARLES RENAUD DE, (*b.* Montpellier, June 3, 1829 ; *d.* Brussels, Mar. 19, 1884), entered the Paris Conservatoire in 1842, and in 1844 took the first organ-prize, and the Prix de Rome at the same time as Victor Massé. The favourite pupil of Halévy, and remarkably industrious, he first became known as a composer of pianoforte pieces, more brilliant than original, but, like all young prize-winners on their return from Italy, he aspired to the stage. It was not, however, till Sept. 4, 1857, that he produced his first work, ' Au clair de la lune,' a pretty operetta in one act (Bouffes Parisiens), followed closely by his last, ' Don Almanzor ' (Théâtre Lyrique, Apr. 16, 1858). He found his true vocation as organist of Saint-Eugène (1855–71), where he rivalled Lefébure-Wély in improvisation, and equalled him in execution. Unfortunately he became a mere music-publisher's hack, and amateur pianists are familiar with his mosaïques, fantaisies, etc., for two and four hands, with such titles as ' Beautés de l'Opéra,' etc. This journeyman's work did not even pay, and he died in poverty. So brilliant and agreeable a talker deserved a better fate. He became nearly blind, but to the last retained his charming manner and his ability as a musician. The library of the Conservatoire contains the MSS. of his cantata ' Le Renégat de Tangier ' and a ' Messe solennelle ' (Aug. 1847). He also left printed scores of several orchestral works, 'Pompadour gavotte,' ' Chanson cypriote,' ' Marche serbe,' etc.   G. C.

VILLAGE ROMEO AND JULIET, A, opera in a prologue and 3 acts, text (after Gottfried Keller) and music by Frederick Delius. Produced Berlin Komische Oper, 1907 ; Covent Garden, in English, Feb. 22, 1910.

VILLALBA, P. LUIS (*b.* Valladolid, 1873 ; *d.* Madrid, Jan. 9, 1921), Spanish composer and musical historian. He came of a family of musicians, but entered the Augustinian order at the age of 14 and was a monk in the Escurial until shortly before his death. He renounced his order and went to live in Madrid, though he still remained a priest. His historical work was printed mainly in *La Ciudad de Dios*— ' The City of God,' a review published at the Escurial, and notable for its studies of Spanish musical history. It includes a course of lectures on chamber music in Spain (*La Música*

de cámara en España) and a study of the organ
in Spain in the 15th and 16th centuries. He
edited a set of songs from the *vihuelistas*
(Spanish lutenists) of the 16th century (*v.*
VIHUELA) and an 'Antología de organistas
clásicos españolas,' besides numerous transcriptions of old music which have never been
collected.   J. B. T.

VILLANCICO, a Spanish musical term
which has had different meanings at different
times. (1) A form of Spanish verse, similar
to (or identical with) the Spanish Arabic
muwashshah and *zajal*, *i.e.* having the refrain
at the beginning and (in the latter) repeated
after every verse, together with a complicated
rhyme-pattern ; (2) The music to which these
types of verse was sung : first monodic (cf.
ALFONSO X.) then a madrigalesque composition
for 3-5 v., the melody often being treated as a
solo and accompanied by the other voices, as in
Byrd's 'Psalms, Sonnets and Songs,' 1588.
(cf. VASQUEZ). (3) A composition resembling
a cantata, with soli and chorus, accompanied
by strings and organ, and sometimes with wind
instruments as well. The words are always in
Spanish (never in Latin) ; the favourite subject
is the visit of the Shepherds to the Manger,
singing in rustic dialects from different parts of
Spain. The *villancico*, however, is not exclusively Christmas music.   J. B. T.

VILLANELLA (Ital., a country girl), an unaccompanied partsong, of light rustic character, sharing, in about equal proportions, the
characteristics of the Canzonetta and the Bal-
letta. The looseness of the style is forcibly
described by Morley, who, in Part III. of his
Introduction to Practicall Musicke, speaks of it
thus :

> 'The last degree of grauity (if they have any at all)
> is given to the *villanelle*, or country songs, which are
> made only for the ditties sake : for, so they be aptly
> set to expresse the nature of the ditty, the composer
> (though he were never so excellent) will not stick to
> take many perfect cords of one kind together, for,
> in this kind they think it no fault (as being a kind of
> keeping *decorum*) to make a clownish musick to a
> clownish matter : and though many times the ditty
> be fine enough, yet because it carrieth that name
> *Villanella*, they take those disallowances as being
> good enough for a plow and cart.'

This severe criticism is, however, applicable
only to villanelle of the very lowest order. The
productions of Kapsberger—whose attempts in
this direction were very numerous—and of
other composers wanting the delicate touch
necessary for the successful manipulation of a
style so light and airy, are certainly not free
from reproach. But the villanelle of Pomponio
Nenna, Stefano Felis, and other masters of the
Neapolitan School,[1] differ but little from the
charming canzonetti, the canzone alla Napolitana, and the balletti, for which they are so
justly celebrated, and may be fairly classed

[1] The Stadtbibliothek at Munich contains a large number of
these works, by Giovanni de Antiquis, and fourteen other Neapolitan composers ; printed at Venice in 1574, in two very rare vols.
obl. 8vo.

among the most delightful productions of the
lighter kind that the earlier half of the 17th
century has bequeathed to us. Among the
lighter madrigals of Luca Marenzio—such as
'Vezzos' augelli'—there are many which exhibit almost all the more prominent characteristics of the villanella in their most refined
form : and the greater number of the canzone
of Giovanni Feretti, and the balletti of Gastoldi
—to which Morley is generally believed to have
been indebted for the first suggestion of his own
still more charming ballets—differ from true
villanelle only in name. The same may be
said of Morley's own compositions in the same
style. (See MADRIGAL.)   W. S. R.

VILLANI, GABRIELE, a 16th-century composer of Piacenza, who wrote 2 books of
'Toscanelle,' 4 v. (Venice, 1587, 1591).

VILLANI, GASPARO (*b.* Piacenza, late 16th
cent.), organist at Piacenza Cathedral in 1610 ;
wrote: 'Missa, Psalmi ad Vesperas et Motecta,'
16 v., lib. 2 (1610) ; 3 books of psalms, op. 3
(12 v.), lib. 5 (8 v.), op. 7 (5 v.) ; litanies, 8 v.,
lib. 1 (1610) ; 'Ad Deum opt. max. ad Dei-
paramque Virginem . . .' lib. 4, 20 v. (1611),
containing a Mass, Hymnus, Te Deum ; 5
eight-part masses, lib. 6 (1612) (*Q.-L.*).

VILLAROSA, IL MARCHESE DI, the author
of a Dictionary of Neapolitan musicians, entitled *Memorie dei compositori di musica del
Regno di Napoli, raccolte dal Marchese di Villarosa*. Napoli, 1840. He was also the author
of a work on Pergolesi (2nd ed., Naples, 1843),
and to him is due the first certain knowledge of
the place and date of the birth of that great
composer.   G.

VILLI, LE, opera in 2 acts, text by Fontana ;
music by Puccini. Produced, in its original
form in one act, Teatro dal Verme, Milan, May
31, 1884 ; in 2 acts, Reggio Theatre, Turin,
Dec. 26, 1884 ; New York, Metropolitan Opera
House, Dec. 17, 1908. Adam's ballet 'Giselle'
and Loder's 'Night Dancers' have the same
subject.

VILLOTA (VILLOTTA), a Venetian folk-
song of which the melody, according to Karl
Somborn's monograph on the form, was used
for many different sets of words.

VILLOTEAU, GUILLAUME ANDRÉ (*b.* Bel-
lême, Dept. de l'Orne, Sept. 6, 1759 ; *d.* Tours,
Apr. 27, 1839), a French writer on music. After
the death of his father he was put, at 4 years
of age, into the maîtrise of the Cathedral of Le
Mans, and afterwards into the town school,
under the Fathers of the Oratory. He declined,
however, to enter a seminary, enlisted as a
dragoon, but was totally unfitted for a military
life, and ultimately went up for three years to
the Sorbonne, and obtained a place in the choir
of Notre Dame. The outbreak of the Revolution brought this employment to an end, and
in 1792 he entered the chorus of the Opéra, and
remained there till offered a place as musician

among the savants who accompanied Napoleon on his expedition to Egypt.

This musical mission opened to him a congenial sphere for his very considerable abilities. Having studied on the spot ancient music, both Egyptian and Oriental, he returned to Paris, and continued his researches in the public libraries. As a member of the Institut de l'Égypte, he was anxious, before taking part in the great work which that body was commissioned by Government to draw up, to publish a *Mémoire sur la possibilité et l'utilité d'une théorie exacte des principes naturels de la musique* (Paris, 1809, 88 pp. 8vo), which he had read before the Société libre des Sciences et des Arts. This was followed by *Recherches sur l'analogie de la musique avec les arts qui ont pour objet l'imitation du langage (ibid.*, 1807, 2 vols. 8vo), in which he developed some of his favourite ideas. This huge book, in four parts, with all its tediousness, purposeless digressions and false philosophy, is crammed full of learning, and contains ideas which at that date were new and original.[1]

Villoteau's fame rests not on this book, but on his share in *La Description de l'Égypte*, the magnificent work in twenty vols. folio (eleven being plates), which took seventeen years to publish (1809–26), and which reflected so much credit on Conté and Jomard, the distinguished secretaries of the commission. The musical portions are : (1) On the present condition of music in Egypt ; researches and observations historical and descriptive made in the country (240 pp., October 1812) ; (2) A description, historical, technical and literary, of musical instruments in use among the Orientals (170 pp., 1813, with three plates engraved by Dechamel) ; (3) A dissertation on the different kinds of musical instruments to be seen on the ancient monuments of Egypt, and on the names given them in their own language by the first inhabitants of the country (26 pp.) ; (4) The music of ancient Egypt (70 pp., 1816).

As a student, and unversed in matters of business, Villoteau made no profit either out of his position or his labours. Three-parts ruined by a notary, whom he had commissioned to buy him a property in Touraine, he had to leave Paris for Tours, where he owned a small house. Here he lived on his own slender resources, and on certain small sums allowed him by government for a French translation of Meibom's *Antiquae musicae auctores VII* (1652), which, however, was never published. The MS., now in the library of the Conservatoire, is in three columns, the original Greek, and translations into Latin and French, all in Villoteau's hand.

[1] According to Fétis, its success was so small that the publisher exported or destroyed all the unsold copies, a fact which would account for its present scarcity, but as the copyright was Villoteau's own property, and it had been entered at Galland's, it is difficult to believe a story so much to the discredit of a respectable bookseller like Renouard.

During his last years Villoteau wrote a *Traité de phonéthésie*, now lost, which was not approved by the Institut de France, and consequently not published.   G. C.

VINÀ, see INDIAN MUSIC, subsection INSTRUMENTS. (*PLATE XXXVII.*)

VINACESI, CAVALIERE BENEDETTO (*b.* Brescia, *c.* 1670; *d.* Venice, 1719), maestro di cappella to Prince Francesco Gonzaga di Castiglione. He was appointed to the second organ of St. Mark's, Venice, on Sept. 7, 1704, at 200 ducats per annum which, in 1714, was raised to 300 ducats, and from 1706 he was also choirmaster at the Conservatorio dell' Ospedaletto (female orphanage). He composed a great deal of church music, including motets for 2 and 3 voices (1714), a motet for solo voice with 3 viols (MS. in Berlin Library), 2 oratorios, several operas, including 'ScipioneAfricano,' composed in conjunction with Franc. Cavalli (Venice, 1678), and a book of church sonatas, 'Sfere armoniche,' for 2 violins, violoncello and basso continuo for organ (1696) (*Fétis*; Schilling; *Q.-L.*).

VINCENT, a family of English musicians who were all recognised composers and performers during the early part of the 18th century, and consisted of (1) RICHARD, (2) THOMAS, (3) JAMES, and (4) THOMAS, junior. All these signed, in the order given, the trust deed of the ROYAL SOCIETY OF MUSICIANS in Aug. 1739. As the contemporary publications frequently merely gave the name of the composer of a piece of music as ' Mr. Vincent,' it is exceedingly difficult to separate these members of the family.

(1) RICHARD was probably the uncle and (2) THOMAS the father of Thomas, junior, the oboist, whose father was, according to Burney,[2] a bassoon-player in the Guards. (3) JAMES (*d.* Oct. 6, 1749[3]), the brother of Thomas (4), was, according to the same authority, ' Joint organist of the Temple with Stanley, and a brilliant performer.' He died young. Several songs ' composed by Mr. Vincent ' are to be found in Watt's ' Musical Miscellany,' vol. iv. 1730, but it is not clear whether they are by James, whose full name appears on single songs. There was also a Richard Vincent, junior. A notice of the death of a Richard Vincent occurs in the *Gentleman's Magazine* under date Aug. 10, 1783 :

' In Tottenham Court Road, aged eighty-two, Mr. Richard Vincent, the oldest musician belonging to Covent Garden playhouse, and to Vauxhall Gardens, who enjoyed till the last years of his life a remarkable flow of spirits.'

(4) THOMAS (*b. circa* 1720 ; *d.* ? May 10, 1783), oboist and composer, became the pupil of SAMMARTINI, who taught him his method of playing, by which the oboe, hitherto of coarse

[2] *General History of Music*, iv. 487.
[3] See *London Magazine*, Oct. 1749.   W. H. G. F.

tone, became valuable as a solo instrument. His first publication was

'Six Solos for a Hautboy, German Flute, Violin, or Harpsichord, with a Thorough Bass, Composed by Thomas Vincent, junior, opera prima, London. Printed by Wm. Smith at the Golden Bass in Middle Row, Holborn, and sold by the author at his house in Golden Square.'

His opera secunda, with a copyright dated Oct. 27, 1748, was

'A Sett of Familiar Lessons for the Harpsichord,' op. 2, published by John Cox, London, and 'Six Solos for a Hautboy, German Flute, Violin, or Harpsichord.'

Thomas had entered the King's band as a hautboy-player in 1735. He was there also in 1758; the Thomas Vincent who was in this band in 1778 was possibly his son.

Alfred Moffat[1] published an arrangement of a sonata, in A minor, for the violin, by Thomas Vincent, in his 'Old English Violin Music' (Novello).   F. K.

VINCENTI, GIACOMO, an important 16th-17th-century music publisher and printer of Venice, in partnership with Ricciardo Amadino from 1583-86, when they separated, each continuing under his own name. G. Vincenti can be traced until Dec. 24, 1618, when he was succeeded by Alessandro Vincenti. Giacomo published a considerable number of collective volumes of sacred and secular vocal music mostly compiled and edited by himself (Eitner; E. Vogel, *Bibliothek*, etc.; *Q.-L.*).

VINCI, LEONARDO (*b.* Strongoli, Calabria, 1690; *d.* Naples, May 28, 1730), was a pupil of Gaetano Greco at the Conservatorio dei Poveri di Gesù Cristo in Naples. His first known work was a comic opera in Neapolitan dialect, 'Lo cecato fauzo' (Il falso cieco), produced at the Teatro de' Fiorentini in 1719. The *Gazzetta di Napoli* of Apr. 25 informs us that the opera met with a great success, and that the composer was maestro di cappella to the Prince of Sansevero. The latter, it will be remembered, was also a patron of Alessandro Scarlatti. This opera was followed by others of the same sort, 'Le zite 'n galera' (1722) being the earliest of which the music has survived. Florimo mentions a serious opera, 'La Stratonice,' as having been produced in 1720, but no trace of it is to be found. The earliest extant example of his serious style is 'Silla dittatore,' produced on tne birthday of Charles VI. at the Teatro S. Bartolomeo in 1723, in which the principal parts were sung by Nicolo Grimaldi and Maria Benti-Bulgarelli, generally known as La Romanina. His connexion with the Teatro Fiorentini terminated after 1722, and the new Teatro della Pace (afterwards the scene of so many of Logroscino's triumphs) was inaugurated on May 15, 1724, with his comic opera 'La mogliera fedele.' He seems, however, to have devoted himself for the rest of his life mainly to *opera seria*, and the few comic operas which appeared later at the Teatro Nuovo (the special theatre of Leo's

comic muse) were in most cases revivals of earlier works. On the death of A. Scarlatti in 1725 he became pro-vice-maestro of the royal chapel, the post becoming vacant by the promotion of Mancini and Sarro; this appointment he held until his death. Florimo states that he was maestro, but this was not possible, as Mancini, who succeeded Scarlatti, did not die until 1738 or 1739. In 1728 (according to Florimo) Vinci entered the Congregation of the Rosary in the monastery of S. Caterina a Formiello, but apparently this did not prevent his continuing to write for the stage. The date of his death has been erroneously given by Fétis and others as 1734 or 1732, and it has been supposed that he was poisoned by a relative of a Roman lady with whom he had a liaison. But F. Piovano[2] demonstrated clearly that he must have been dead before June 1731, and definite information is given by the curious inscription on a caricature of him by Ghezzi in the Vatican Library, reproduced in the *R.M.I.* for 1904, fasc. 2. From this we learn that he died at Naples on Sunday, May 28, 1730. Ghezzi, whose comments on his sitters are as brutal as his portraits, says nothing whatever about either poison or a love-affair:

'He died of colic pains so suddenly that he could not even make his confession, and if the sister of Cardinal Ruffo had not given some assistance he could not even have been buried, not even three paoli being found on him, since he was a man who would have gambled his eyes away.'

Burney rightly praises Vinci for his strong sense of dramatic expression. Of the immediate followers of Scarlatti he is certainly the most vigorous, and his short career as a composer is long enough to give a very clear view of the gradual development of the aria-form from the type of Scarlatti as shown in 'Silla dittatore' (1723) to that generally associated with the name of Pergolesi, but found in Vinci ('Astianatte' 1725 and 'Artaserse' 1730) before the other had been heard of as a composer. There can be little doubt that this extension of the aria form owed its first inception to Farinelli. The great singer was equally celebrated for his agility and for his sustaining power; and in almost all the airs composed for him by Vinci, as well as in the few that he sang in Scarlatti's later operas, we may note that the desire to display these two qualities has gradually led to a sharper differentiation of two contrasting subjects, treated in the conventional binary form. The form $A_1 B_2 A_2 B_1 \|$ contrasting section $\|$ Da Capo may be traced in Scarlatti's earlier chamber cantatas; but it is not until the time of Vinci that the subjects A and B are made to contrast almost as strongly as they would in a sonata of Mozart. The well-known air 'Vo solcando un mar crudele' is a good example. This extension of the aria-form by Farinelli and Vinci is

---

[1] To whose researches are due many of the facts here recorded.

[2] *Sammelbände* of the Int. Mus. Ges. viii. 70.

important on account of its powerful influence on the forms of the concerto and the symphony.[1] In addition to the works of Vinci, mentioned in *Q.-L.*, there are several of his operas at Münster (Santini's Library) and at Montecassino.

E. J. D.

VINCI, Leonardo da (*b.* Vinci, 1452; *d.* chateau Clos-Lucé, Amboise, near Paris, May 2, 1519), the great painter and universal genius, was also an excellent singer, lutenist and viola da gamba player. He made several improvements in the construction of the viols, especially with regard to the finger-board, and constructed a new species of lute which, however, did not prove successful.

E. v. d. s.

VINCI, Pietro (*b.* Nicosia, *c.* 1540; *d.* there [2] or Palermo,[3] *c.* 1584), maestro di cappella at San Maria Maggiore, Bergamo, 1571, and from the end of 1581 in a similar position at Nicosia. He was a prolific church composer, a long list of whose works, masses, motets and madrigals appears in *Fétis* and in *Q.-L.* Some compositions of his pupils, Ambrosio Marien and Antonio il Verso, are included among his own madrigals and motets (*Fétis*; Schilling; *Q.-L.*).

VINER, William [4] (*d.* Nov.[5] 1716), a violinist and composer for that instrument in considerable favour in Ireland during the early part of the 18th century, and master of the State Music there, 1703-16, when he died.[4] About 1730-35, Walsh published a set of solos for violin and bass by him. He was the arranger of a piece in 'Aria di camera' (*c.* 1727), and is mentioned in very high terms in a poem by Pilkington, *The Progress of Musick in Ireland*, Dublin, 1730. The following is an extract from a lengthy panegyric on Viner in the poem mentioned :

'The Muses now from Albion's Isle retreat,
And here, with kind indulgence, fix their seat;
Then Viner rose, with all their warmth inspired,
A Bard caress'd by all, by all admir'd.

While round in crowds the fair creation stand
The polish'd Viol trembling in his hand,
While swift as thought, from note to note he springs,
Flies o'er the unerring Tones, and sweeps the sounding strings,' etc.

F. K.

VINER, William Letton (Litton) (*b.* Bath, May 14, 1790; *d.* Westfield, Mass., U.S.A., July 24, 1867), a composer, chiefly of hymn tunes and sacred music. He was a pupil of Charles Wesley, and in 1820 became organist of St. Michael's, Bath, after having, even in early life, made considerable progress both as a composer and as performer on the organ. He left Bath for Cornwall, and on Dec. 2, 1835, was appointed organist at St. Mary's Chapelry, Penzance. In 1859 he emigrated to America. He wrote an overture for 'Rob Roy' while at Bath, but though constantly performed at the theatre

there, it does not appear to have been published. Other secular pieces are of his composition, but he is best known by his collections of hymn and psalm tunes. These are, 'One Hundred Psalm and Hymn Tunes in score,' 1838; 'A Useful Selection from the most approved Psalms,' 1846, and 'The Chanter's Companion,' 1857, etc.

F. K.

VINES, Ricardo (*b.* Lérida, Feb. 5, 1875), Spanish pianist, studied in Paris, one of the first to understand the music of Debussy and Ravel and to make it convincing through his brilliant technique.

J. B. T.

VINGT-QUATRE VIOLONS. No reader of French 'mémoires' of the 17th century can be ignorant of the part played by ballets at the courts of Henri IV., Louis XIII. and Louis XIV. The ballet combined the pleasures of music, dancing and the play, gave great opportunities for magnificent display, and was for nearly a century the favourite diversion of princes and *grands seigneurs*, thus preparing the way for opera. The passion for *ballets de cour* and dancing led to the formation of a special band for violinists, who, under Louis XIII., bore the name of the 'band of 24 violins of the King's chamber.' Its members, no longer mere *ménestriers* (see Roi des Violons), became *musiciens en charge*, with a prospect of being eventually admitted to the Chapelle du Roi. Their functions were to play for the dancing at all the court-balls, as well as to perform airs, minuets and rigadoons, in the King's antechamber, during his *lever* and public dinner on New Year's Day, May 1, the King's fête-day, and on his return from the war, or from Fontainebleau.

No complete list of 'the 24 violins' who enlivened the court of the melancholy Louis XIII. has yet been made, but some of their airs may be seen in the MS. collection of Philidor aîné (*q.v.*)—one of the precious possessions of the Conservatoire library. The composers' names are Michel Henri, Constantin, Dumanoir, Robert Verdié, Mazuel, Le Page, Verpré, de la Pierre, de la Vallez and Lazarin, all, we conjecture, among the 24. The violinists occasionally acted in the ballets, as in the 'Ballet des doubles femmes' (1625), when they walked in backwards, dressed as old women with masks at the back of their heads, so as to look as if they were playing behind their backs. This had a great success, and was revived by Taglioni (the father) in the masked ball in Auber's 'Gustave III.' in 1833.

In Louis XIV.'s reign the band of 24 violins was called the 'grande bande,' and on Dumanoir's appointment as Roi des Violons, the King made him conductor, with the title of '25me violon de la Chambre.' The post, however, was suppressed at the same time with that of the Roi des ménestriers (May 22, 1697). The 'grande bande,' again called 'the 24 violins,'

[1] A complete discussion of this question will be found in D F. Tovey's pamphlet *The Classical Concerto.*
[2] *Q.-L.*   [3] *Fétis.*
Information from W. H. G. F.
His will was proved Nov. 30, 1716   W. H G. F

VOL. V   2 L

continued to exist till 1761, when Louis XV. dissolved it by decree (Aug. 22). During the rage for French fashions in music which obtained in Charles II.'s reign, the '24 violins' were imitated here in the 'King's music,' and became the 'four-and-twenty fiddlers all of a row' of the nursery rhyme. Meantime a dangerous rival had sprung up in its own home. In 1655 Lully obtained the direction of a party of sixteen violins, called the 'petite bande.' As violinist, leader and composer he soon eclipsed his rival, and his brilliant career is well known. The modest position of conductor of a few musicians, whose duty was simply, like that of the 'grande bande,' to play at the King's *levers*, dinners, and balls, satisfied him at first, but only because it brought him in contact with the nobility, and furthered his chance of becoming 'Surintendant de la Musique' to Louis XIV. This point once gained, nothing further was heard of the 'petite bande,' and by the beginning of the next reign it had wholly disappeared.

The 24 violins remained, but as time went on they became old-fashioned and distasteful to the courtiers. Accordingly, as fast as their places fell vacant they were filled by musicians from the Chapelle du Roi, and thus the band became independent of the community of St. Julian. After 1761 the only persons privileged to play symphonies in the King's apartments were the musicians of his 'chamber' and 'chapel.'   G. C.

VINNING, LOUISA (*b.* Kingsbridge, Devon, Nov. 10, 1836[1]; *d.* London, 1904), sang at the Plymouth Theatre when only two and a half years old, and appeared in public from 1840–1842, under the title of the 'Infant Sappho,' as a singer and harpist at the Adelaide Gallery, Polytechnic, and elsewhere. She afterwards received instruction in singing from Frank Mori, and on Dec. 12, 1856, was brought prominently into notice by taking the soprano part in the second and third parts of the 'Messiah' at the Sacred Harmonic Society's Concert, at a moment's notice, and 'with credit to herself,' in place of the singer engaged, who became suddenly indisposed during the performance. Miss Vinning afterwards sang at the Crystal Palace, the Worcester Festival, 1857, the Monday Popular Concerts (1861), and elsewhere until her marriage with J. S. C. Heywood, in or about 1865. At her concert, on July 5, 1860, Mme. Montigny-Rémaury first appeared in England.   A. C.

VIOL (Fr. *viole*; Ital. *viola*), the generic English name of the bowed instruments which succeeded the mediæval fiddle and preceded, at any rate as far as their literature was concerned if not in actual invention, the VIOLIN FAMILY (*q.v.*). The viol was invented in the 15th century, and passed out of general use in the 18th. It differs from the violin in having

deeper ribs, and a flat back, which is sloped off at the top, and was strengthened internally by cross-bars and a broad centre-piece, on which the sound-post rests. The shoulders curve upwards, joining the neck at a tangent, instead of at right angles, as in the violin. The neck is broad and thin, the finger-board was fitted originally with movable frets; the number of strings is varied, six being the normal number; the peg-box is usually surmounted by a carved head. The SOUND-HOLES (*q.v.*) are of the C pattern. The viol was made in three principal sizes—Bass (*viola da gamba*), tenor (*viola da braccio*) and treble or descant. These are the types belonging to the CHEST OF VIOLS (*q.v.*) and employed in the old English school of concerted chamber music. To these must be added the double bass (violone), as well as sundry subsidiary types enumerated below (see *PLATES LXXXVII.* and *LXXXVIII.*).

(1) BASS VIOL (Ital. *viola da gamba*), the most important of the series, since it was the one most used for solo work and produced many notable virtuosi, was the popular instrument of accompaniment[2] after the lute, and the foundation of the ensemble. The bass viol is about the size of the violoncello but with longer neck,[3] the strings measuring about 30 inches from nut to bridge. As its Italian name implies, it is held violoncello-wise in performance. Its six catgut strings were tuned like the lute:

This was the classical tuning, but the lowest string was sometimes tuned down to C, and some continental instruments had a seventh string tuned to G above the highest here shown. Christopher SIMPSON (*q.v.*) gives in his *Division Viol* (2nd edition, 1667) a complete description of the technique of performance as well as information about the English school of composers, for whom he claims pre-eminence. Of special importance is his description of the method of bowing,[4] the bow being held underhand, a method which long survived in playing the double bass. The bass viol retained its popularity in England longer than elsewhere. By the time that Simpson wrote it was already being supplanted in Italy. But in England it survived Simpson by more than a century. C. F. ABEL (*q.v.*) was the last of the great virtuosi here. The scores of J. S. Bach contain noteworthy uses of it for special effects,[5]

2 See title-page to Dowland's *First Booke of Songs*, 'so made that all the parts together, or each of them severally, may be sung to the lute, opherian, or viol de gambo.'
3 See Dolmetsch, *The Interpretation of the Music of the XVIIth and XVIIIth Centuries*, p. 449.
4 Quoted *ibid.* p. 447.
5 See three sonatas for clavier and gamba, B-G., vol. ix.; the introduction to the cantata 'Gottes Zeit' for 2 gambas and flutes; the 6th Brandenburg concerto for 2 viole da braccia, 2 viole da gamba, v'cl., violone; the air 'Komm süsses Kreuz' in the 'St. Matthew Passion' with an obbligato for a seven-string instrument of which the lowest string is A below the bass stave.

LXXXVII

Galpin Collection

1. ARABIAN REBAB. 2. TRUMPET MARINE (French, 17th cent.). 3. REBEC (14th-16th cent.). 4. CRWTH (Owain Tudur [Tudor], 19th cent.). 5. SORDINO or KIT (French, 17th cent.). 6. QUINTON VIOL (Fleury, Paris, 1764). 7. VIOL (Henry Jaye, Southwark, 1632). 8. LYRA VIOL (W. Addison, 1665). 9. BASS VIOL (C. Pierray, 1764). 10. VIOLA D' AMORE (G. Grancino, 1696). 11. HURDY-GURDY or VIELLE (French, 19th cent.).

but Bach wrote considerably after the classical era of the viols was over. For an account of tablature applied to the bass viol see LYRA VIOL.

(2) TENOR VIOL (Ital. *viola da braccio*), as its Italian name implies, is held by the arm, and is an instrument generally similar to the bass viol, but of small size proportioned to its higher pitch. Its tuning is

Its position was that of the middle member of the ensemble in the old English chamber music, and it never had any independent existence to speak of as a solo instrument in this country. In the 18th century its lowest string was discarded, and with five strings its compass was approximated to that of the modern viola, which gradually superseded it. (See also VIOLA DA SPALLA under VIOLIN FAMILY.)

(3) TREBLE or DESCANT VIOL, tuned an octave above the six-stringed bass viol, and therefore when properly built just half its size, formed the upper parts, one or more, of the ensemble. In England it had no vogue as a solo instrument ; in France the *dessus de viole* became fashionable, and a smaller size (*pardessus de viole*) tuned a fourth higher than the *dessus* was much used.[1]

(4) DOUBLE-BASS VIOL (*violone*), a six-stringed instrument tuned like the bass viol, but sounding an octave lower, was common in Italy and Germany.[2] It has been customary to speak of the modern double-bass (see under VIOLIN FAMILY) of the orchestra as the last of the viols. It retained characteristics of the double-bass viol in its shape, its tuning by fourths and the method of bowing. Its body being strengthened, its strings thickened and their number reduced to three (then augmented again to four), it became a sort of hybrid between the old violone and the violin family.

Subsidiary types of later usage are as follows :

(5) VIOLA BASTARDA, a bass viol mounted with sympathetic strings like the viola d' amore. It afterwards developed into the BARYTON (*q.v.*).

According to Michael Praetorius (*Syntagma musicum*, 1614–20) the viola bastarda had six strings and was made in five different pitches.

We give a normal tuning. He also states that it was to this instrument that the English first applied sympathetic strings. Engel (*The Violin Family*, 1883) says that the viola bastarda was somewhat like the

viola da gamba in shape, but slightly longer and narrower. He states that the six strings were tuned as above.

(6) VIOLA D' AMORE[3] (Fr. *viole d'amour*), a tenor viol with sympathetic strings. It usually has seven stopped strings. The sympathetic strings, of fine steel or brass, pass through small holes drilled in the lower part of the bridge, and under the finger-board : their number varies from seven to fourteen. They are tuned to a diatonic or chromatic scale. We give an ordinary tuning of the gut strings, though tunings were very variable[4] and it was a common practice to tune to the key of the piece. The sympathetic strings, tuned to the scale (in this case of D), diatonic or chromatic,

are sometimes screwed up by pegs similar to those of the gut strings : but the better plan is to attach them to wrest-pins driven into the sides of the peg-box.

As Praetorius (*Syntagma musicum*) describes several sizes of the viola bastarda, one of the smaller members of the family may, perhaps, be claimed as the true ancestor of the viola d' amore. According to the English authority —John Playford—who describes the instrument in his *Musicks Recreation on the Viol, Lyra-way*, 1661, Daniel Faurant, the inventor of the ' Poliphant ' and the ' Stump,' created the viola d' amore. Yet, to go further back, the ' Bourdons ' of centuries anterior to Praetorius and Playford may equally claim a place in the ancestry of this instrument.

On the authority of Evelyn, the viola d' amore had five strings, and made its début in England in the latter half of the 17th century. He records in his Diary under Nov. 20, 1679, that he dined at Mr. Slingsby's, Master of the Mint, who provided some excellent music for his guests ; among those artists who took part Evelyn enumerates

' Nicholas, on the Violin, but, above all for sweetness and novelty, the Viola d' Amore of five wire strings played on with a bow being but an ordinary violin played on lyra-way by a German.'

It is worthy of note that neither Mattheson nor Evelyn mentions the sympathetic strings. Burney[5] also speaks of the instrument as a novelty in 1716, when he says, Signor Attilio Ariosti played ' a symphony ' between the acts of the opera ' Amadis,' on July 12, the last night of the season. He played again some years later, and composed six sonatas for viola d' amore, which were published by subscription

---

1 Dolmetsch, *Inter.retation*, p. 451.
2 Praetorius, *Syntagma musicum*, distinguishes between viola di gamba ' and ' vio.ono ' or ' contrabasso di gamba.'

3 Eugène de Bricqueville, *La Viole d'amour* (Paris, 1908), suggests that the original name was ' viola da Mori ' (viol of the Moors), which might point to the derivation of the instrument itself from the several Oriental instruments employing sympathetic strings.
4 Mattheson, *Das neu-eröffnete Orchester* (Hamburg, 1713), directs the instrument to be tuned to the chord of C, major or minor.
5 *Gen. Hist. of Mus.* iv. 257.

in London, in 1728, under the title 'Cantatas, and a Collection of Lessons for the Viola d' Amore.' By the end of the 18th century this viol, according to Laborde,[1] was obsolete. He says it had four metal strings placed below the regular gut strings.

But the instrument has never become wholly obsolete. Hector Berlioz praised its tone quality and Meyerbeer included it in an air in 'Les Huguenots.' Later composers have recurred to it for special effects in orchestral works, notably Richard Strauss (' Sinfonia domestica ') and Loeffler (' The Death of Tintageles '). In the 19th century it had, too, its famous exponents (see Van WAEFELGHEM and ZOELLER).   E. J. P., E. H.-A. ; rev. C.

VIOLA, see VIOLIN FAMILY (2).

VIOLA, ALESSANDRO DELLA, see MERLO.

VIOLA, ALFONSO DELLA (b. Ferrara, early 16th cent. ; d. there (?) after 1567). He was maestro di cappella in the service of Hercules II., Duke of Este, at Ferrara, and appears to have been the first who accompanied dramatic action throughout with music. He may be regarded, therefore, as one of the pioneers of the opera, although it was not until Cavalieri, Peri and Monteverdi that the stilo rappresentativo, the arte nova, provided composers with the means of individual characterisation. In Alfonso's dramas the dialogue was sung by choruses in madrigal form. The first of his tragedies, ' Orbecche,' was performed in 1541 at his own house, in the presence of the Duke Hercules II. and Cardinal Ravenne Salviati (Allacci, Dramaturgia, p. 577). The second work for which he composed the music was Il sacrificio (the book published Ferrara, Fr. Rossi, 1555), performed on Feb. 11 and Mar. 4, 1554, at the palace of the Duke Francis d'Este. His third work was ' Arethusa,' a pastoral by Lollio, performed at the palace of Schivanoja in 1563 for the benefit of the students, in the presence of Alfonso II., Duke of Ferrara, and his brother, Cardinal Louis. The text-book only was published at Ferrara in 1566. A second pastoral, ' Lo sfortunato,' by Agost. Argenti Edelmann of Ferrara, set to music by Alfonso, was performed in 1557. Apart from the libretti nothing has survived of these dramas. Two books of madrigals (1539, 1540) and some motets and songs in collective volumes are still in existence (Fétis ; Q.-L.).

VIOLA, FRANCESCO DALLA or DELLA (b. Ferrara, 1st half of 16th cent.), probably related to Alfonso. He was a pupil of Willaert, a collection of whose motets and madrigals he edited and published at Ferrara in 1558 under the title ' Musica nova.' Zarlino [2] tells us that Francesco was maestro di cappella to Alfonso d'Este, Duke of Ferrara, who was his great admirer, and whom he accompanied to

Venice in Apr. 1562. This may also account for Cyprian de Rore's retirement from the court of Ferrara after the death of Hercules II. Francesco dalla Viola composed : madrigals a 4 v., lib. i. (1567) ; madrigals 4 and 5 v. (1575, 2nd ed. 1599). Three masses and some motets in MS. are in the Estense Library at Modena ; also a number of songs in collective volumes (Fétis ; Valdrighi ; Q.-L.).

VIOLA BASTARDA, see BARYTON (1); VIOL (5).

VIOLA DA BRACCIO, see VIOL (2): TENOR VIOL.

VIOLA DA GAMBA (1), see VIOL (1): BASS VIOL.

VIOLA DA GAMBA (2), see ORGAN : VOCABULARY OF STOPS.

VIOLA D' AMORE, see VIOL (6).

VIOLA DI BORDONE (VIOLA BASTARDA), see BARYTON (1); VIOL (5).

VIOLA DI FAGOTTO (BASSOON VIOL), a name sometimes given to the Viola Bastarda. See VIOL (5).   E. J. P.

VIOLA POMPOSA, see VIOLIN FAMILY (9).

VIOL D'ORCHESTRE, a string - toned organ-stop of 8 ft. pitch, and very small scale. This stop is one of the bearded Gamba tribe. (See ORGAN : VOCABULARY OF STOPS.)

VIOLET, a name sometimes given to the viola d' amore (see VIOL (6)). L. Mozart calls the viola d' amore with chromatic sympathetic apparatus the ' English Violet ': a singular denomination, for, as in the case of the Cor anglais, the instrument appears never to have been made, and seldom used in this country.   E. J. P.

VIOLETTA, the French version of Verdi's ' La traviata,' by M. E. Duprez ; produced at the Théâtre-Lyrique, Oct. 27, 1864.   G.

VIOLETTA MARINA, a viola with sympathetic strings.   (See VIOL.)

VIOLETTA PICCOLA. Michael Praetorius mentions this instrument amongst the viols he enumerates in his Syntagma musicum, 1614–20. He calls it ' Cant Viol de Gamba (Violetta Piccola),' and mentions four kinds, some with six, some with five, four and three strings. It answered in tone ' partly to the tenor and partly to the violin.' A violetta piccola was shown at the special Exhibition of Musical Instruments, held at South Kensington Museum in 1872.   E. H.-A.

VIOLIN DIAPASON, an organ stop of 8 ft. pitch, in scale between the open diapason and the dulciana. The pipes are open, and have a slot near the top. (See ORGAN : VOCABULARY OF STOPS.)   W. Pᴬ.

VIOLIN FAMILY. The violin and viol descended from a common ancestry, which is to be found in the various earlier forms of the late 15th and early 16th centuries. Both are the outcome of a gradual evolution and emerged in their perfect forms within some 15 years from

1 Essai sur la musique, 1780.
2 Dimostrazioni armoniche, p. 1.

each other about the middle of the 16th century.[1] The viols on the title page of Ganassi dal Fontego's '*Fontegara*,' 1535, are practically perfect in shape (more so than those shown on the title-page of his Regola Rubertina of 1543), and Dr. Kinsky (Heyer Cat. II. p. 369) gives the date of the first example of a perfect viola da gamba, by Duiffoprugcar as *c*. 1550, while the first description of violins, with four strings tuned in fifths, occurs in Philibert Jambe-de-Fer's 'Epitome musical,' etc., published at Lyons, 1556. Count Valdrighi (*Nomocheliurgografia*) mentions the use of '*violini*' in Italian monasteries during the early 16th century, and *joueurs de violons* occur in documents of the Dukes of Lorraine as early as 1490. In both cases, however, the name is applied to viols. The frontispiece [2] of a rare chap-book, *La violina con la sua risposta*,' Brescia, *c*. 1550, belonging to Mr. E. Heron-Allen, proves the use of the word in that sense, as it shows Apollo playing on a lyra. This is significant in another way as the Lira da braccio (see LIRA) was the immediate progenitor of the violin. An interesting fact is that Ventura Linarolo, Venice, the maker of a beautiful *lirone da braccio*, dated 1577, in the Wm. Heyer Museum (formerly Cologne, now Leipzig), made also a perfect violin in 1587, now in the collection of ancient musical instruments in Vienna. This is one of the oldest existing examples of a genuine violin with *f* holes crossed in the centre, which is not the case with the *ff*'s of the *lirone* although they are far more elegant in shape. Dr. Kinsky mentions also a violin, apparently of Bohemian origin, dated 1575, now in the Bach house at Eisenach. It is evident that the violin had already reached its final form by then, but whether the *violons* mentioned in the accounts of the wedding of Henry II. of France with Catherine of Medici at Rouen in 1550, of the eight 'vyolons,' etc., of Francis I. (1515–47), and of the *joueurs de violons* at the court of Lorraine in 1555, refer to violins proper cannot

be decided with certainty, although, considering Jambe-de-Fer's book, it appears possible.

It is not known who first constructed a perfect violin, but as it required only slight alterations to change the lyra into the violin and the idea was, so to speak, in the air, it probably occurred to several makers at various places at almost the same time. Several authorities assume with good reason that the first instruments of the violin type were of a pattern corresponding in size to the lyra da braccio, or a large viola, and that it was possibly Gasparo Bertolotti, called from his birthplace da Salò (1540–1609), who evolved therefrom the model of the modern violin. His workmanship in this was characterised by rugged strength, the centre bouts shortened and rather shallow, the sound-holes cut wide, the scroll inelegant, but the wood, especially of the tables, of the finest quality and even grain, and his instruments are covered with a choice brownish varnish. His first violins were highly arched, but repeated experiments convinced him of the advantages of a lower arching until eventually he adopted a comparatively flat model. Gasparo, apart from viols, made, however, more violas and violones which are still greatly valued.

Giovanni Paolo Maggini (1580–*c*. 1640), the pupil of Gasparo,[3] worked at first upon his master's lines but soon made great advances upon the latter's work, especially in the shape of the sound-holes, the scroll and the cutting of the wood for tables and backs. His model, at first fairly high, became flatter in his later work. His varnish, of excellent quality, is of a golden brown or yellow colour, and many of his instruments have two rows of purfling. He was also famed for his violones as well as for his violins. Other Brescian masters who worked on his lines, beside his son Pietro Santo Maggini, were Matteo Bente, Domenico and Antonio Pasta, Giovita Rodiani and Pellegrino Zanetto.

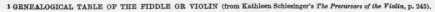

[1] GENEALOGICAL TABLE OF THE FIDDLE OR VIOLIN (from Kathleen Schlesinger's *The Precursors of the Violin*, p. 245).

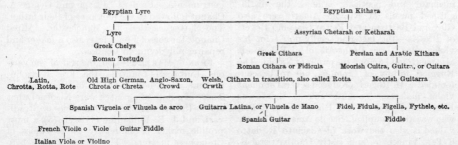

The above Table, compiled by Miss Schlesinger, shows that the lyre, with a vaulted sound-chest, was the ancestor of all boat-shaped instruments, while the kithara, with the tripartite shallow sound-chest, composed of back, ribs and table, led, through various evolutionary stages, to the viol and the violin.

[2] Reproduced in E. van der Straeten's *The Romance of the Fiddle*.
[3] According to a document of 1602, see Rev. R. H. Haweis, *Old Violins*, p. 31.

THE CREMONA MAKERS.[1]—Cremona's undying fame as the classical town of violin-makers, began with the Amati dynasty. The first of this famous family was Andrea Amati (c. 1520–c. 1580) whose work was closely related to that of the early Brescians. The achievements of Andrea and his sons Antonio and Girolamo are fully described under their own names. This extraordinary family reached the height of its artistic achievements in Nicolo (1596–1684), the son of Girolamo, who not only inherited his father's genius, but started out to construct a new model of his own, and after many attempts succeeded in producing those wonderful violins known as the 'Grand Amatis,' in which he was surpassed only by his pupil Antonio STRADIVARI (q.v.), that greatest of all violin-makers. His greatest and most original pupils were Carlo Bergonzi and Domenico Montagnana, who afterwards settled at Venice ; other pupils of distinction were (1) Alessandro Gagliano, who went to Naples, where his son Niccolo worked after him but on original lines, and was followed by his son Ferdinando ; (2) Lorenzo Guadagnini, and his son Giovanni Battista, who settled at Piacenza ; (3) his sons Francesco and Omobono. Francesco Gobetti, Venice (1690–1715) is also considered to have been a pupil of Stradivari. Among the pupils of Niccolo Amati was also his son Girolamo, the last violin-maker of that famous family ; Paolo Grancino of Milan, more important than the former but surpassed by his son Giovanni ; Andrea Guarneri, like Andreas Amati, the first of a great family of violin-makers, and an excellent master who was, however, surpassed by his sons Giuseppe Giovan Battista and Pietro Giovanni, both makers of distinct individuality. Pietro Guarneri, son of Giuseppe filius Andreæ, was also an excellent maker, but the greatest of the family was Giuseppe Antonio, better known as Giuseppe del Gesù, who shares the palm with Stradivari, whose instruments he surpasses in power and brilliance of tone in his latter period. Stradivari's violins, however, are sweeter, more intimate and poetical. Among the distinguished pupils of Niccolo Amati were also Giovanni Battista and Pietro Giacomo Rogeri of Brescia—the latter specially noted for his violoncellos,—and Paolo Albani of Palermo is also mentioned among the pupils of Nicolo. The Ruggieri family of Cremona, not to be confounded with Rogeri, produced several eminent violin-makers ; foremost among them was Francesco Ruggieri (also Ruger) detto il Per, who was also a pupil of Niccolo Amati. Greatly valued is also the work of Giacinto R. detto il Per, Vincenzo—and lastly Gambattista R. detto il Per. The Testore family of Milan, consisting of Carlo Giuseppe (c. 1690–1720), Carlo

1 See the articles under the names of principal makers for details of their individual styles.

Antonio (1730–64), his son Giovanni and his brother Paolo Antonio were excellent makers, and so were several members of the Tononi family of Bologna.

ENGLISH MAKERS. — Jacob Rayman, who probably came from the Tyrol and settled in London about 1620, may be looked on as the father of violin-making in England. Thomas Urquhart, Edward Pemberton and Christopher Wise belong to the mid - 17th century. Edward Pamphilon worked in London from c. 1680. Daniel Parker made good instruments (c. 1700–30), still obtainable at a moderate price. Barak Norman (1688–1740) was essentially viol-maker, but made also violins and especially violoncellos of excellent workmanship. Nathaniel Cross (1700–50), worked for many years together with Barak Norman. Daniel Parker, John Barrett, early Stradivari copyists, John Hare and Peter Wamsley were excellent makers of the early 18th century.

Benjamin Banks of Salisbury (1727–95), was the greatest English violin - maker ; his sons Benjamin, James and Henry were of average merit. Edmund Aireton, Edward Betts, Richard Duke, Thomas Dodd (instruments bearing his name were made by John Lott and Bernard Fendt, but covered with very fine varnish by him), John Dickeson, William Forster and his son William, John, and his son Henry John Furber, Samuel Gilkes, Charles Harris, Thomas Smith, Richard Tobin, were excellent makers of the late 18th and early 19th centuries.

The longest line of violin-makers is that of the Hill family, of whom Joseph Hill, a pupil of Wamsley, William (c. 1741), and Lockey (1800–40), were makers of note. William Ebsworth Hill, son of Lockey, and his sons, now living, are chiefly noted as repairers and dealers. John Thomas Hart (1805–74), a pupil of Gilkes, and his descendants were and are chiefly repairers and dealers. The Kennedy family · Alexander (1700–86), John (1730–1816), Thomas (1784–c. 1870), and George Crash of Manchester were prolific makers of good second - class instruments. Frederic, Joseph and George A. Chanot followed in the footsteps of their father. The latter settled in Manchester. Alfred Chanot, the son of Frederic, is also a maker and repairer now living in London.

FRENCH MAKERS.—Like the rest of the various European countries the French violin-makers were but copyists of the Italians. Those of outstanding merit were Nicolas Lupot (1758–1824), unrivalled in his copies of Stradivari, and J. B. Vuillaume (1798–1875), a most prolific maker of eminently clever copies of Cremonese masters. The nearest approach to the work of these two masters was that of Pièrre Silvestre (1801–59), a pupil of Lupot and, like his master, a copyist of Stradivari. His brother Hippolyte, for some time his

partner, and their nephew Hippolyte Chrétien
Silvestre, succeeded him in business. Other
distinguished French makers were : Seb. Phil.
Bernardel, Jacques Bocquay, C. Boullangier,
François Chanot, who made a violin of guitar
shape, his brother Georges, a clever copyist of
Stradivari and Guarneri, and Georges, the
son of the latter, who settled in London (see
supra) where he was succeeded by his sons,
Charles Henry, Charles Jacquot, Koliker,
Charles Maucotel, who settled in London, and
his brother, Charles Ad. Maucotel, François
Médard, Claude Aug. Miremont, Didier Nicolas,
Claude Pierray, F. S. Pique, a copyist of
Stradivari of high merit. Finally we must
mention Jacques Pièrre Thibout, a maker of
merit, who encouraged Tarisio to bring his rare
Italian instruments to Paris.

GERMAN MAKERS.—The ravages of the Thirty
Years War, which had devastated the whole
country, had completely extinguished the rare
lute and viol-makers' art which during the 15th
and 16th centuries stood highest in Europe.
Only the Tyrolean Mountains had enjoyed
comparative immunity from the horrors of
that time. There, in the quiet village of Absam,
was Jacob Stainer, the most famous German
violin-maker, born, 1621, and in the same year
Mathias Albani, an excellent maker, first saw
the light of day at Bozen ; he was, however,
far surpassed by his son Mathias (*c.*1650–1680),
who worked on the lines of Amati and produced
a number of very fine instruments.

18th-century German makers of merit were :
Paul Alletsee (Aletzie) Munich ; his oldest
known violins are dated 1698. About 1720 he
appears to have worked temporarily at Venice,
as the beautiful viole d'amour, which belonged
to L. van WAEFELGHEM (*q.v.*) had a label
which read ' Paolo Aletzie, Venetia, 1720 ' ;
workmanship and varnish were of the finest
quality. He was especially famed for his
basses. His son-in-law, Joh. Andr. Kämbl,
succeeded him as court instrument-maker in
Munich in 1738. Anton Bachmann (1716–1800),
court instrument-maker, Berlin, and his son
Carl Ludwig B. worked on Italian models ;
the latter was chiefly noted for his violas.
Martin Diel of Mainz was the first of a long
line of violin-makers, extending over a period of
more than 150 years. Martin and his son
Nicolaus made some good violas and violoncellos. Friedrich Diehl (as the name was
spelled by later members of the family) received
a bronze medal at the Paris exhibition in 1867.
Nicolaus Döpfer, the master and father-in-law
of Martin Diel, made some good large violas.
Joh. Andr. Dörffel was founder of the Graslitzer
violin - making industry. Johann Udalric
Eberle was a good copyist of Italian masters,
noted for his fine violes d'amour. Thomas
Edlinger of Augsburg worked at Prague and
was the master of Eberle.

Christoph Friedrich Hunger, Leipzig (1718–
1787), excellent maker, specially noted for his
violas. Joh. Jauch, Mathias Klotz Mittenwald
(1653–1743), founder of Mittenwald violin industry, studied in Italy, achieved good workmanship on the Stainer model. He was surpassed by his son Sebastian (1696–1743), and
the latter's son Joseph (*c.* 1743, *d.* after 1808),
noted for fine workmanship, and a flatter
model. Georg, brother of Sebastian, was also
a good maker but careless in the selection of
wood. Other members of the family are more
or less indifferent. Leonard Maussiel, Stainer
pattern, work resembling Tecchler's ; Sympert
Niggell, flat model.

Johann Gottlob Pfretzschner (1753–1823),
member of a violin-maker's family of several
generations, was the first Markneukirchen
maker to abandon the Stainer model in favour
of that of Stradivari.

Daniel Achatius Stadlmann of Vienna and
Widhalm of Nuremberg were both excellent
imitators of Stainer.

19th-century makers : Ludw. C. A. Bausch,
Leipzig, chiefly repairer and famous bow-maker;
W. H. Hammig, Leipzig ; Karl A. Hörlein,
Würzburg ; Gabriel Lemböck, Vienna ; Neuner,
Berlin ; Jac. Aug. Otto, head of a numerous
family of violin-makers, author of a book on
the construction of the violin—other notable
members of this family were Ludwig O. of
Cologne, afterwards Petersburgh, his son Her-
mann, and Louis O., Düsseldorf ; Béla
Szepessy, known as Béla, who settled in
London.

NETHERLANDISH MAKERS.—Mattys Hof-
mans, worked at Antwerp *c.* 1685–1725 ; Hendrick (also referred to as Peter) Jakobsz, latter
17th to early 18th century, copied Niccolo
Amati with great skill and is said to be the first
who used whalebone for his purfling ; Pieter
Rombouts, Amsterdam (1674–*c.* 1740), produced fine workmanship and varnish ; he also
used whalebone for purfling. Jan Koeuppers
worked at the Hague between 1755–1780, and
the Frenchman, Lefebre, at Amsterdam between 1720–1735.

In the above article we have only been able
to mention the most important makers of those
countries in which violin - making attained a
high degree of excellence. For that reason we
cannot include the names of wholesale manu-
facturers who work at the great industrial
centres of violin-makers, Markneukirchen, Mittenwald, Klingenthal, in Germany, Graslitz in
Austria and Mirecourt in France. Further
particulars about the most important of those
named may be found under their several
names in this Dictionary, while these as well
as all the rest may be found in the works
of Hart v. Lütgendorff, and Dr. Kinsky's
Catalogue of the Wm. Heyer Museum, vol. ii.
(See below : Bibliography.)

DESCRIPTION OF INSTRUMENTS

The name ' violin ' was in the first instance applied to a type and not a species, and this type, like that of the viol, the lute, the recorder, and of most other instruments, repeated itself in at least four different species, corresponding with the four parts of the human voice. As in the case of all stringed instruments, so in the violin family the construction of an instrument of a fairly low compass preceded that of the highest and lowest instruments of its type, and the word violin was first applied to an alto instrument. (See VIOLA below.) We have therefore (1) the treble violin, afterwards called violin by preference ; (2) the alto violin, called viola by the Italians, alto by the French, tenor by the English, as it represented that part when the real tenor violin disappeared, and Bratsche, from viola da braccio, or Viola by the Germans ; (3) the tenor violin, which became obsolete early in the 18th century ; (4) the bass violin, to which the Italian word violoncello, meaning a small bass, is now generally applied, while (5) the large bass retained in Italy the name of the contrabass viol= violone ; in England it is generally referred to as double-bass, but the more correct word contrabass is now frequently used, as the equivalent basse contre is in France.

CONSTITUENT PARTS OF THE VIOLIN.—It will be clear from the above that the description of the model holds good for all members of the family as they only differ in size but not in shape.

The wood used in the construction of the violin is : sycamore (maple) for the back, neck, ribs and bridge ; pine for the table, bass bar, blocks, linings and soundpost ; ebony for the finger-board, tail-piece, nut and pegs. The latter were formerly often of boxwood while in latter years they are often made of rosewood, which is least subject to slipping. The nut was in former times frequently made of ivory, which resists the wear from the strings better than ebony. For the back and the ribs the 17th- and 18th-century makers often used pear-wood (cf. *PLATE LXXVIII.*).

The strings are made from sheepgut which after undergoing an elaborate process of preparation is cut into thin strands, which then are twisted together by a ropemaker's wheel, three to four strands being used for a violin E string, four for an A string, six to nine for a D string, and proportionately more for the strings of the larger instruments. The finest strings were formerly made in Italy, but for some years past it has been found that England[1] produces the best gut, and the Germans the best makers, and the best Italian strings of

[1] An English enterprise which deserves mention here is the method of testing strings invented by James Kelway Toms, of Wellington, Somerset, which has given these strings, issued under the name of the inventor's late father, John R. Toms, a world-wide reputation. c.

to-day are those made of English gut by German makers.

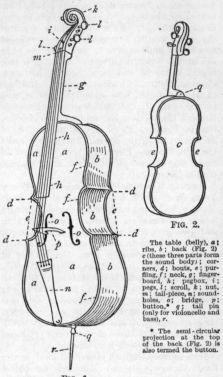

FIG. 2.

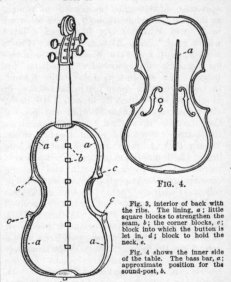

FIG. 1.

The table (belly), *a*; ribs, *b* ; back (Fig. 2) *c* (these three parts form the sound body) ; corners, *d*; bouts, *e* ; purfling, *f* ; neck, *g*; finger-board, *h* ; pegbox, *i*; pegs, *l*; scroll, *k* ; nut, *m*; tail-piece, *n*; sound-holes, *o*; bridge, *p*; button,* *q* ; tail pin (only for violoncello and bass), *r*.

* The semi-circular projection at the top of the back (Fig. 2) is also termed the button.

FIG. 4.

FIG. 3.

Fig. 3, interior of back and the ribs. The lining, *a* ; little square blocks to strengthen the seam, *b*; the corner blocks, *c*; block into which the button is let in, *d*; block to hold the neck, *e*.

Fig. 4 shows the inner side of the table. The bass bar, *a*; approximate position for the sound-post, *b*.

FUNCTIONS OF VARIOUS PARTS.—The vibrations of the strings caused by the friction of the bow are communicated to the bridge, transmitted by the latter to the table, and by this to the surrounding air, outside as well as inside the instrument. The inner air, as well as the sound-post and ribs cause the back to vibrate, the sound-post and ribs receiving their vibrations from the table as well as the inner air. Both the nut and the bridge must be high enough to allow the strings to vibrate freely without rattling against the finger-board, yet not so high as to cause undue exertion of the fingers in stopping the notes. As the vibrations of the fourth string are greater than those of the others, the finger-board is cut away a little under this string to allow of the necessary space. The feet of the bridge, which are most essential in the transmission of the vibrations to the table, must be shaped to the arching of the latter so as to insure perfect contact ; this must also be the case with the sound-post with respect to both the table and the back, as the object of that cylindrical rod is not only the transmission of the vibrations, as stated above, but also the support of the right foot of the bridge. The left foot of the latter is supported by the bass bar, which transmits its vibrations over the whole length of the instrument, and restores the balance between the vibrations of the table and the stronger vibrations of the lower strings. With the raising of the pitch, the use of thicker strings and of a higher bridge, which came into vogue in the early 19th century, the pressure upon the table was considerably increased, so that the bass bar, in order adequately to perform its functions under the altered circumstances, had to be made both longer and deeper, and the bass bars in old instruments had to be replaced by those of larger dimensions. The tone power depends chiefly upon the vibrations of the table and the back, the ribs being of little account in this respect, but their height is an important fact r in determining the volume of air enclosed in the sound-body. The sound- or f-holes have the double function of bringing the enclosed air of the body into communication with the outer air, and of making the narrow waist of the table between the centre bouts sufficiently flexible.

The corner blocks were introduced to strengthen the finely tapering projections at the extremities of the centre bouts, as well as to hold the table and the back firmly glued to the ribs, and the latter is also the purpose of the linings, consisting of fine strips of wood glued to the inner edges of the ribs which thus provide a greater surface for that purpose and strengthen the whole structure of the body.

The varnish has very little, if any, influence upon the tone of the violin, but it provides a protective covering for the wood, and considerably enhances the beauty of the instrument.

MEMBERS OF THE FAMILY

(1) The VIOLIN has three gut strings, and a fourth, or bass string, covered with plated copper or silver wire. They are tuned 𝄞.

(For special tunings see SCORDATURA.) Steel wire or silk strings are often used for the first or E string of late, on account of their durability, but such strings cannot compare with gut strings in quality of tone. The total length of the violin has been determined by the average length of the human arm, in a slightly bent position so as to ensure free action of all its muscles as well as those of the hand and fingers. The average measurements of a full size violin are : total length, $23\frac{1}{2}$ in. ; length of body, 14 in.; width of upper bouts, $6\frac{9}{16}$ in.; do. of lower bouts, $8\frac{3}{16}$ in. ; height of ribs at top, $1\frac{3}{16}$ in.; at bottom, $1\frac{1}{4}$ in. There are also three-quarter and half-size violins for the use of children.

(2) The VIOLA, also called tenor in English ; French= Alto, German= Bratsche, from viola da braccio. The tuning is 𝄢 ; the measurements of a Stradivari viola of 1723 are : length of body, $16\frac{3}{16}$ in. ; widths : upper bouts, $7\frac{5}{8}$ in.; centre bouts, $5\frac{5}{32}$ in.; lower bouts, $9\frac{1}{2}$ in.; height of ribs, at top, $1\frac{17}{32}$ in.; at bottom, $1\frac{9}{16}$ in.; total length, c. 26 in. The violas in general use have a body length of 16 in. or even a little less. The instrument is only $\frac{1}{7}$ larger than the violin, although this is much too little for the thickness and weight of its strings and the fact that it is tuned a fifth lower than the violin, which gives a ratio of 3 : 2. The result is a slightly veiled and reedy tone, rather nasal in the smaller instruments, but of sympathetic and penetrating quality. The small violas, which for various reasons are more convenient for the player, have not the real tenor quality, and this occasioned Berlioz's remonstrance in his book on orchestration against their use. The music for the viola is mostly written in the alto, or C clef on the third line, but the notes in the higher compass of the instrument are written in the G, or treble clef. The viola is the oldest member of the violin family. It was at first called violino (the diminutive of viola), until the smaller treble instrument came into use, when the name was transferred to the latter, but both words were used indiscriminately for many years.

Giovanni Gabrieli in his 'Sacrae symphoniae,' 1597, has a ' violino ' part written in the alto clef and demanding the compass of the viola, and L. Zacconi in his *Musica prattica*, 1596, uses the word in the same sense. Even Carlo FARINA (q.v.) between 1620 and 1630 calls himself *violinista* on his title-pages, and *violista* in a dedication. There were originally three instruments for the middle parts which Mersenne (*Harmonie universelle*, 1636) calls Cinquième, Haute-contre, and Taille, and he reproduces a fantasia by Henri Le Jeune, showing the use and compass of all the members of the violin family in which they appear with clefs and compass, used in the piece, as follows:

He explains in another place that the tuning of the Dessus, the Cinquième and the Haute-Contre is the same, viz.: *g, d', a', e"*; that of the Taille, *c, g, d', a',* and that of the Basse-contre B♭, F, *c, g,* and adds:

'The Cinquième is the smallest of the three which are in unison. The 24 violins of the King called it Haute-contre, the Haute-Contre Taille and the Taille Cinquième.'

This shows how much confusion there was still in the designation of the violins in the early 17th century. Soon, however, the Haute-contre became the alto, and the Taille the tenor violin, of which we shall speak presently.

The viola was only used in the orchestra, where it merely doubled either the bass or the second violin, until Bach and Handel gave it greater prominence, but it was not until it became an integral part of the string quartet under Haydn and Mozart that it developed a distinct individuality, and chiefly through C. Stamitz (1746–1801) rose even to the dignity of a solo instrument, as which it shines at the present time in the hands of that brilliant master Lionel TERTIS.

(3) The VIOLONCELLO (Ital. *violoncello*; Fr. *violoncelle*; Ger. *Violoncell*). The word is the diminutive of violone, and the frequently used word ' cello ' is a senseless mutilation of violoncello. The tuning is ⟨notation⟩; the average dimensions are: total length, 48½ in.; length of body, *c.* 30 in.; widths: upper bouts, 13½ in., lower bouts, 17⅛ in.; height of ribs, at the top, 4⅘; at the bottom, 5 in. For the use of pupils, half-size and three-quarter size instruments are made, and slightly smaller full-size instruments are often used by women. The violoncello came into existence together with the other members of the family, and two beautiful instruments by Andrea Amati, made between 1560–70, are still in existence. In its early times the instrument was often referred to as ' violoncino,' ' violunzel,' ' bass-violin,' or simply as ' bass.' Until the end of the 17th century it merely filled the bass part in the

orchestra, and its tuning sometimes underwent slight modifications. Purcell was the first English composer who preferred the violoncello to the viola da gamba, but the latter was not superseded by the former in this country until the arrival of Cervetto, Caporale and other Italian violoncellists. The first solos written for the instrument are probably the sonatas and ricercare by Domenico Gabrieli, dated 1689 (MS. in Estense Library, Modena). Bach and Handel made important use of the violoncello as a solo instrument, and since then it has become as such second only to the violin (see VIOLONCELLO - PLAYING). The music for the instrument, on account of its large compass, requires the use of the bass, the tenor and the treble clefs. The latter, if following the bass clef, is written according to classical usage an octave higher than it sounds. In the 18th century the soprano and mezzo-soprano C clefs were also used occasionally.

Old Italian violoncellos of a large pattern, even such by famous masters, are sometimes found to have had a small circular hole in the centre of the back, which has since been filled up. They were in former times used in church processions, suspended from the neck of the player by a little metal hook attached to a strap.

(4) The DOUBLE-BASS or Contrabass (Ital. *contrabasso*; Fr. *contrebasse*; Ger. *Kontrabass*). This is the Proteus of the violin family which has been constructed from its first appearance, and still exists, in a greater variety of sizes, patterns and tunings than any other of its members. A real contrabass is depicted in Jost Amman's ' Turnirbuch ' of 1566. The double-bass has retained several features of the contrabass viol, the violone, and even the name was frequently used in several countries, including England and Germany, as late as the 19th century. It retained the sloping shoulders, the flat back and corners of the viol, although it adopted the *f* holes and scroll of the violin. From the 17th century downward we meet with many various combinations of the viol and the violin model. Some show the latter in every detail, others with the only difference of sloping shoulders, or with these and a flat back, etc. While the average total length of a full-size double-bass is about 6 feet, there are innumerable deviations from this measurement apart from smaller sizes ranging downward to about 4½ feet in length, with other measurements in proportion. The number of strings varied between three and six, with a very large variety of tunings. In the modern orchestra we meet chiefly with four-stringed basses tuned

⟨notation⟩ sounding an octave lower; in a few cases a fifth string giving the lower C is added. Apart from these, three-stringed basses, which were in great favour during the 19th century, are frequently to be met with tuned 𝄞 -or- . What these lose in compass, they gain in brightness of tone on account of the smaller pressure upon the table. The double-bass is the only transposing instrument of the violin family; it is always written an octave higher than it sounds, and represents in the orchestra the 16-foot register of the organ. Down to the end of the 18th century the neck of the double-bass was always fretted in the manner of the older contrabass viol, but with the increasing technique of the players, and more florid figuration in orchestral bass parts, frets have been abandoned. In most cases the double-basses strengthen the bass of the violoncellos by doubling their part in the lower octave ; but when the latter have very rapid passages, the contrabass part must be reduced [1] to fundamental notes, as the heavy strings are slow at changing their rate of vibration. Where the latter is not implied, as in tremolo or repeated notes, their rapid succession is very effective. The first known use in the orchestra was by Baltazarini (q.v.), whose band of 20 violins included one contrabass ; and a contrabass was also included in Louis XIV.'s 24 violins. M. Pignolet de Monteclair introduced it into the orchestra of the Paris Opera c. 1706. The first virtuoso on the instrument was Joseph Kämpfer in the latter part of the 18th century, but to Domenico Dragonetti (1763-1846) belongs the credit of having developed the higher technique. The next great virtuoso, Giovanni Bottesini (1821-1889), introduced the use of a bow made after the pattern, and held in the manner of, the violoncello bow. Sergei Kussevitzky (q.v.) is the greatest living virtuoso of the double-bass.

Subsidiary Members of the Family and Obsolete Instruments

Of the numerous variations of which specimens may be found in the various museums of Europe and America only those can be mentioned which were of particular interest.

(1) Savart's trapezoid-violin, constructed by Felix Savart of Paris in 1819. This instrument, which was constructed on scientific principles, had a sound-body in trapezoid form and straight longitudinal sound-holes, and was pronounced by a jury, including Cherubini, Catel, Lesueur and a number of celebrated scientists, to be equal to the best Cremonese violins. Guitar-shaped violins were constructed by the French naval engineer,

(2) Francis Chanot, after years of experiments, from 1817. The French Academy gave a very favourable opinion on the instrument, for which Chanot was granted a patent. It

had many admirers, and several noted instrument-makers of the period imitated his theory.

(3) The Violon d'amour was a small viole d'amour (see under Viol, Viola d' amore) of violin shape. It had five strings, tuned , and six sympathetic strings, and was used in the 18th century.

(4) The Quinton, or quinte, used in France during the 18th century, was a violin strung and tuned like the above, but without sympathetic strings. (See *PLATE LXXXVII.* No. 6.)

(5) The Hardanger violin is an ordinary violin mounted with four gut strings and four sympathetic strings of steel. The finger-board, tail-piece and edges of the table are often inlaid with designs in mother-of-pearl and different coloured wood. They are used by Norwegian fiddlers. The Museum of the Brussels Conservatoire, has a fine specimen by Anders Heldahl of Bergen dated 1851, and also a collection of Norwegian Folk-dances which gives two alternate tunings for the instrument.

Gut strings.   Steel strings.

(6) Silent violins which were, and are still, made for practising, have only the upper part of the violin without the ribs and back ; others have in place of the sound-body only an open frame, following the outlines of the table. There were also violins made in fayence, china, tortoiseshell and various metals, but they are of no practical value.

(7) The Viola alta is a large tenor, constructed by K. A. Hörlein of Würzburg (1872–1875), according to instructions given him by Hermann Ritter, who played it in the Bayreuth Festival Orchestra. The instrument has a powerful tone of fine quality, but on account of its size it requires a player with a fairly long arm, and is somewhat tiring to hold for a great length of time. The dimensions are : total length, 26 in. ; body c. 18⅞ in. In 1898 Ritter added a fifth string to his viola corresponding to the violin e'' string, so that his instrument combined the compass of both those instruments. Michael Balling was an eminent performer on the viola alta.

F. Chanot and Dr. Alfred Stelzner have both made violas in their respective special models.

(8) The Tenor violin was the real tenor instrument of the violin family, for which D. Hizler, in his *Newe Musica*, Tübingen, 1628, gives the tuning as . In the Wm. Heyer Museum (formerly at Cologne, now at Leipzig) there are three specimens : one by

---

Joseph Meyer zu Graffenhausen (?), A[n]no 1668—total length, $27\frac{1}{2}$ in.; body, $16\frac{21}{32}$ in.; width of upper bouts, $8\frac{1}{16}$ in.; lower bouts, $9\frac{1}{2}$ in.; height of ribs, 2 in.; one by a Bavarian maker of the first half of the 18th century—total length, $27\frac{14}{16}$ in.; body, $17\frac{14}{16}$ in. The third is a six-stringed instrument by Gio. Picinetti fio, anno 1682, for which Dr. G. Kinsky, in his catalogue, gives the tuning as

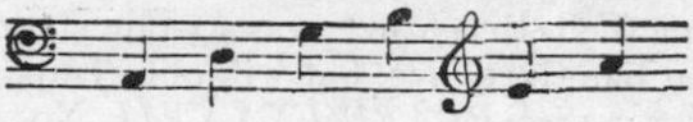

The dimensions do not differ much from those of the two former.

The tenor violin was used by Handel and J. S. Bach, but became obsolete by the middle of the 18th century. A long *viola* passage, written in the bass clef, in Joh. Christian Bach's Overture (symphony), op. 18 No. 3, seems to indicate that he must have still used a tenor violin with the tuning given by Hizler.

(9) The VIOLA POMPOSA, which Bach invented to facilitate the playing of quick and high violoncello passages, exceeding the skill of his violoncellists, was a five-stringed instrument with a total length of *c.* $30\frac{1}{2}$ in. and body length of *c.* $17\frac{14}{16}$ in.; height of ribs, *c.* $3\frac{1}{2}$ in.; tuned 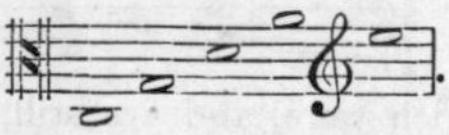. Georg PISENDEL (*q.v.*) was the only remarkable executant on this instrument, which had but a short existence. (See *PLATE LXXXVIII.* No. 6.)

(10) The VIOLA DA SPALLA was a viola of only slightly smaller proportions than the viola pomposa, but it had only four strings, tuned like the ordinary viola. It derived its name from the fact that it was held across the chest suspended from a strap over the right shoulder (Ital. *Spalla*). It was used largely by wandering musicians during the 17th and early 18th centuries.

(11) The VIOLOTTA was constructed by Dr. Alfred Stelzner of Dresden to fill the gap which occurs in the modern string quartet between the viola (alto) and the violoncello (bass). It is a real tenor violin, built on the model invented and applied by him to all the members of the violin family, employing, for acoustic reasons, the ellipse and parabola instead of circular segments for the outlines of the body.[1] The tone of the violotta is full and of beautiful quality; it is tuned 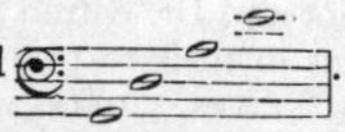. Measurements: total length, $28\frac{2}{16}$ in.; body, *c.* 16 in.; width of upper bouts, $9\frac{1}{4}$ in.; lower bouts, $11\frac{1}{16}$ in.; height of ribs, at top, $1\frac{3}{4}$ in.; middle, *c.* $2\frac{3}{8}$ in.; bottom, *c.* $2\frac{1}{8}$ in. Felix Dräseke, Arnold Krug, Jul. Major and others have written for it in chamber music, and Max Schillings has made effective use of it in his opera 'Der Pfeifertag.'

More or less successful experiments in the construction of tenor violins have been made also by J. B. Vuillaume, Paris (1855), B. Dubois, Paris (1833), Hopf, Josephstadt (Bohemia, *c.* 1800), Valentino de Zorzi, Florence (1908). All these are played under the chin, and tuned like the violotta. Hermann Ritter has also constructed a tenor violin with the same tuning but held between the knees.

(12) The VIOLONCELLO PICCOLO was used by Bach and others in the late 17th and 18th centuries as offering greater facilities to the player, when the technique of violoncello-playing was still in its infancy. It was in reality merely a half-size violoncello with a total length of about 3 feet, and corresponding other measurements. These instruments often showed features of the viols in the flame-shape sound-holes, sometimes combined with a rosette in the upper part of the table and the absence of projecting edges of the table and back. They are now used only by juvenile students.

(13) The ARPEGGIONE or GUITAR VIOLONCELLO constructed by Joh. Georg Stanfer of Vienna about 1824 is a six-stringed instrument tuned 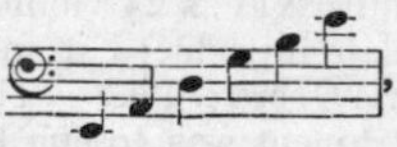, which suggests the model invented by F. Chanot both in outline and the shape of the sound-holes. The neck was provided with 24 metal frets. Its total length is *c.* $3\frac{1}{2}$ feet; length of body, $25\frac{1}{2}$ in.; upper width, $12\frac{3}{4}$ in.; lower width, $14\frac{14}{16}$ in.; height of ribs, $4\frac{1}{2}$ in. (See *PLATE LXXXVIII.* No. 3.) Franz Schubert wrote a beautiful sonata in A minor for it which was played by Vinc. Schuster, who also published a tutor for the arpeggione, which deservedly fell into disuse after an existence of about ten years.

(14) The CELLONE is a bass violoncello belonging to the family of the Stelzner instruments (see VIOLOTTA above), and exhibits the same model as these. It was intended chiefly as a contrabass for chamber music and used as such by the same composers, who also employed the violotta. The tuning is 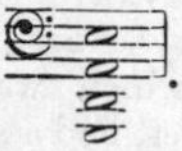. Total length, 3 feet $10\frac{1}{4}$ in.; length of body, *c.* $30\frac{3}{4}$ in.; width of upper bouts, $15\frac{10}{16}$ in.; lower bouts, *c.* 18 in.; height of ribs, $6\frac{1}{8}$ in.

(15) The OCTOBASS, constructed by J. B. Vuillaume in Paris in 1849, was a double-bass 4 metres high; with three strings tuned 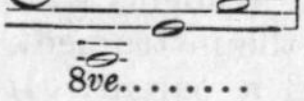
8ve........
; the notes were stopped by means of a system of levers and 8 pedals. In 1851 Vuillaume made a similar instrument on an

[1] For detailed description see Kathleen Schlesinger, *The Instruments of the Modern Orchestra*, pp. 194-201.

1. VIOLA DA GAMBA (Gaspar Tieffenbrucker, *c.* 1550).   2. BARYTON (D. Stadlmann, 1715).
3. ARPEGGIONE (J. Staufer, 1824).   4. LIRA DA GAMBA (*c.* 1650).
5. LIRA DA BRACCIO (J. Kerlino, 1452).   6. VIOLA POMPOSA (J. C. Hoffmann, 1732).

1, 5. Donaldson Collection, Royal College of Music.   2, 3, 4, 6. Heyer Museum, formerly Cologne, now Leipzig.

improved system, an Italian 17th-century three-stringed double-bass known as the giant, now in the Victoria and Albert Museum ; it measures 103 inches in length. Similar giant basses have been made from time to time in all European countries, and John Geyer, a German-American, made one in 1889 4½ metres in length.

BIBLIOGRAPHY

The following is a list of important works selected from an immense literature of the subject. The most essential are marked with an asterisk.

ABELE, H. : *Die Violine, ihre Geschichte und ihr Bau* (Neuberg, 1864, 1874) ; translation by Geoffrey Alwyn. (London, 1905, Strad Library.)
ARMSTRONG, R. B. : *Musical Instruments* (fine plates). (Edinburgh, 1904.)
BECKMANN, G. : *Das Violinspiel in Deutschland vor 1700*. (Leipzig, 1918.)
BOLTSHAUSER, H. : *Geschichte der Geigenbaukunst in der Schweiz* (Leipzig, 1923.)
DAVIDSON, P. : *The Violin*. (Glasgow, 1871–81.)
DRÖGEMEIER, A. : *Die Geige*. (Bremen, 1891, 1892, 1903.)
DUBOURG, G. : *The Violin*. (London, 1836, 1878.)
*ÉCORCHEVILLE, J. : *Quelques documents sur la musique de la Grande Écurie du Roy*, Int. Mus. Ges., *Sammelbände*, ii. (4), pp. 602-42
*EICHBORN, DR. HERMANN : *Zur Geschichte der Instrumentalmusik*. (Leipzig, 1885.)
ENGEL, CARL : *Researches into the Early History of the Violin Family*. (London, 1883.)
*FÉTIS, F. J. : *Antoine Stradivari* (Paris, 1856) ; translation, J. Bishop (London, 1864.)
FLEMING, J. M. : *Old Violins*. (London, 1883–90.)
FOLEGATTI, E. : *Storio del violino*. (Bologna, 1873–74.)
GALLAY, J. : *Les Luthiers italiens* (Paris, 1869) ; *Les Instruments des écoles italiens* (Paris, 1872.)
GONTERSHAUSEN, WELKER VON : *Neues öffnetes Magazin musikalischer Tonverkzeuge*. (Frankfort.)
*GRILLET, L. : *Les Ancêtres du violon*. 2 vols. (Paris, 1901.)
*HART, G. : *The Violin*. (London, 1875, 1880, 1885, 1887.)
HAWEIS, REV. H. R. : *Old Violins and New*. (Edinburgh, 1905.)
*HERON-ALLEN, EDW. : *Opuscula fidiculorum. The Ancestry of the Violin* (London, 1882–90) ; *De fidiculis opuscula* (London, 1890–93.)
*HILL, A. F. : *Antonio Stradivari*. (London, 1902.)
LAWRENCIE, L. DE LA : *L'École française du violon*. 2 vols. (Paris, 1922, 1923.)
*LUTGENDORFF, FREIHERR W. L. VON : *Die Geigen- und Lautenmacher vom Mittelalter bis zur Gegenwart*, 2 vols. (Frankfort, 1922) ; *Die Geigen- und Lautenmacher von Mittenwald* (Frankfo , 1904
*MERSENNE, MARIN : *Harmonie universelle*, vols. v.–vii. (Paris, 1636.)
MORDRET, L. *La Lutherie artistique* (Paris, 1889) ; *Les Violons de Crémone* (Rouen, 1894).
MORRIS, W. M. : *British Violin Makers*. (London, 1894.)
MOSER, ANDREAS : *Das Violino Piccolo*, *Zeitschr. f. Musikwissenschaft*, Apr. 1919, pp. 377-80.
NEF, C. : *Zur Geschichte der deutschen Instrumentalmusik*, Int. Mus. Ges. Beiheft 5. (Leipzig, 1902.)
NIEDERHEITMANN, F. : *Crémona*, 6th ed. (Leipzig, 1922) ; translation (London, 1894).
PETONG, DR. R. *The Arts and Crafts Book of the Worshipful Guild of Violinmakers of Markneukirchen from the year 1677 to the year 1772*, translated and edited by Edw. and Marianne Heron-Allen. (London, 1894.)
PETHERICK, H : *Joseph Guarnerius* (London, 1906) ; *Antonio Stradivarius* (London, 1900).
*POUGIN, A. : *Les Violinistes et la musique de violon du XVIe au XVIIIe siècle*. (Paris, 1924.)
*PRAETORIUS, M. : *De organographia* (*Syntagma musicum*, part II.) (Wolfenbüttel, 1618–19) ; *Syntagma musicum*, 4 tom. (Wittenberg, 1615–19) ; *Theatrum instrumentorum* (Wolfenbüttel, 1620).
RETBERG, R. VON : *Zur Geschichte der Musikinstrumente*. (Nürnberg, 1860.)
*RUKLMANN, JULIUS : *Zur Geschichte der Bogeninstrumente* (with Atlas). (Braunschweig, 1882.)
SANDYS, WM., and FORSTER. S. A. : *History of the Violin*. (London, 1864.)
*SCHLESINGER, KATHLEEN : *The Precursors of the Modern Violin Family* (London, 1896) ; *Modern Orchestral Instruments* (London, 1898).
STAINER, C. : *A Dictionary of Violin Makers*. (London, Novello's Music Primers.)
.TOLBECQUE, A. : *Notice historique sur les instruments à cordes et à archet*. (Paris, 1898.)
*VALDRIGHI, COUNT L. F. : *Nomocheliurgografia* (Modena, 1884–94) ; *Capelle, concerti e musiche di casa d' Este* (Modena, 1884).
*VIDAL, A. : *Les Instruments à archet*. (Paris, 1876–78.)
*WASIELEWSKI, W. VON : *Die Violine*, 6th ed. (Leipzig, 1920) ; *Die Violine im 17. Jahrhundert* (Leipzig, 1904).
WHITE, A. W. : *The Violin*. (Boston, Mass., 1892.)

Technical—
COURVOISIER, C. : *Technics of Violin Playing* (London, 1906) ; German ed., *Die Violin-Technik* (Cologne, 1878).
THISTLETON, F. : *The Art of Violin Playing*. (London, 1924 (?)).

Viola—
*STRAETEN, E. VAN DER : *The Viola* (*History and Literature*). (London, *The Strad*, 1912–May 1916.)
ADEMA, E. : *Hermann Ritter und seine Viola Alta*. (Würzburg, 1881.)
*RITTER, H. : *Die Geschichte der Viola*. (Leipzig, 1877.)

Violoncello—
Anon. (WM. ENGEL) : *Violoncellisten der Gegenwart*. (Hamburg, 1903.)
FORINO, L. : *Il violoncello*. (Milan, 1905.)
LIÉGEOIS, C. ET E. NOGUÉ : *Le Violoncelle*. (Paris.)
*STRAETEN, E. VAN DER : *Violoncello Technics*. 4th ed. (1924) ; *The History of the Violoncello* (London, 1916).
VALDING, M., and M. MERSEBURGER : *Das Violoncello*. (Leipzig, 1920.)
*WASIELEWSKI, W. VON : *Das Violoncell* (Leipzig) ; translation by J. S. E. Stigand (London, 1894.)

Double-bass—
WHITE, A. CHS. : *The Double-Bass* (London) ; Novello's Music Primers, Nos. 32 and 32a.
APPIAN-BENNEWITZ, P. O. : *Die Geige*, etc. (Weimar, 1892.)

Violin Making—
*BACHMANN, O. : *Theoretisch-praktisches Handbuch des Geigenbaues*. (Quedlinburg, 1835.)
BAGATELLA, A. : *Regole per costruzione di violini* (Padua, 1786, 1883) ; extracts with diagrams in Abele, *The Violin*.
BEVAN, G. P., and RIMBAULT, E. : *Musical Instruments. British Manufacturing Industries*. (London, 1876.)
COVENTRY, W. B. : *Notes on the Construction of the Violin*. (London, 1903.)
FOUCHER, G. : *Treatise on the History and Construction of the Violin*. (London, 1897.)
HEPWORTH, W. : *Information for Players, Owners, Dealers and Makers of Bow Instruments*. (London, 1899.)
*HERON-ALLEN, EDW. : *Violin Making as it was and is* (London, 1884–1900) ; *The Violin Makers of Markneukirchen* (London, 1894).
MANGIN, J. C., and A. W. MAIGNE : *Manuel du luthier* (Paris, 1834, 1869, 1894.)
MAYSON, M. H. : *Violin Making*. (London, 1902.)
MIGGE, O. : *Das Geheimniss der berühmten italienischen Geigenbauer*. (Frankfort, 1894.)
*OTTO, J. A. : *Über den Bau und die Erhaltung der Geige* (Halle, 1817) ; *Über den Bau der Bogeninstrumente* (Jena, 1828, 1873, 1886) ; translations (London, 1833, 1848, 1860, 1875).
*SIBIRE, A. : *La Chélomanie*. (Bruxelles, 1885.)
SIMOUTRE, N. E. : *Historique et la construction du violon*. (Bâle, 1883.)
TOLBECQUE, A. : *Quelques considérations sur la lutherie*. (Paris, 1890.)
*VIDAL, A. : *La Lutherie et les luthiers*. (Paris, 1889.)
WETTENGEL, G. A. : *Lehrbuch der Anfertigung, etc., von italienischen und deutschen Geigen*. (Ilmenan, 1828 ; Weimar, 1869.)
YOUSSOUPOFF, N. : *Lutomonographie*. (Frankfort, 1856.)
Zeitschrift für Instrumentenbau, ed. Paul de Wit. (Leipzig, 1880.)

E. v. d. s.

VIOLINO PICCOLO, a violin of small size, usually tuned a fourth higher than the ordinary violin, its open strings being an octave above those of the viola.

Among the thirty-six musical instruments employed by Claudio Monteverdi in the orchestra of his opera ' Orfeo,' published in 1609, and reissued in 1615, the score includes *Piccoli Violini alla Francese*. This title, written by an Italian, has caused a slight confusion as to the nationality of the violin proper, and at the same time given credence to a conjecture that the violin was a French invention. Naturally the correctness of the surmise rests upon the kind of instrument Monteverdi intended to designate by the appellation *Piccolo Violino*. The directions given in the published score of ' Orfeo ' indicate that the composer introduced several instruments into the orchestra solely for the purpose of imparting greater dramatic power and contrast than had hitherto been attained. Bearing this in mind—also the facts that Monteverdi was himself an Italian, that he lived in his native country where violins were being made by Gasparo da Salò more than forty years previous to the composition of ' Orfeo,' and that no French violin-maker or violinist is on record at this date—it is more than probable that the *Piccoli Violini alla Francese* indicated were none other than the POCHETTE (*q.v.*) (see also KIT), which 17th-century French dandies and dancing-masters were accustomed to carry in their pockets to madrigal parties and lessons. Famous makers of the French pochettes in the first half of the 17th century were Pierre Le Duc and Du Mesnil of Paris.

Leopold Mozart says the Quart-geige is smaller than the ordinary violin, and is used by children.

'Some years ago,' he continues, 'Concertos were written for these little violins, called by the Italians Violino Piccolo : and as they have a much higher compass than the ordinary violin, they were frequently used in open-air serenades (*Nachtstücke*) with a flute, harp and other similar instruments. Now, however [1756], the small violin can be dispensed with. Everythin : is played on the common violin in the higher positions.' (*Violinschule*, p. 2.)

The 'Three-quarter Fiddle' is still used by children, but is always abandoned as early as possible. In its more normal or violin shape J. S. Bach occasionally employed the violino piccolo in his church cantatas and also in the first Brandenburg Concerto (F major), sometimes treating it as a solo instrument.

F. W. G. ; incorporating material from E. J. P. and E. H.-A.

VIOLIN-PLAYING. For technique see the articles FINGERING and BOWING. The following is an historical summary.   C.

In order to gain an idea of the way the violin was played in its first period, we naturally look to the scores of contemporaneous composers. But here we meet with a difficulty. Down to the end of the 16th century we do not find the instruments specified by which the different parts are to be played. On the titles of the earlier works of A. and G. Gabrieli (1557–1613) we read : ' Sacrae Cantiones, tum viva voce tum omnis generis Instrumentis cantatu commodissimae ' (most convenient for the voice, as for all kinds of instruments), or ' Sacrae Symphoniae tam vocibus quam instrumentis ' (for voices as well as instruments) ; or ' Psalmi tum omnis generis instrumentorum tum ad vocis modulationem accommodati ' (Psalms for all kinds of instruments and the voice) ; or ' Buone da cantare e suonare,' or other similar directions.[1]

The earliest instance of a part being specially marked for ' Violino,' we find in ' Concerti di Andrea e Giovanni Gabrieli—per voci e stromenti musicali. Venetia, 1587.' In Gabrieli's scores the cornetti (See CORNETT) alternate with the violins in taking the lead. His instrumental compositions may roughly be divided into two classes, the one evidently based on his vocal style, the other decidedly instrumental in character. In a ' Sonata ' belonging to the first class, we find an instrumental double choir, a cornetto and three trombones forming the first choir, a violin and three trombones the second, the two being employed antiphonally ; the setting is contrapuntal

[1] These expressions are exactly equivalent to the words so often found on the title-pages of English madrigals of the 17th century—' Apt for viols and voices.'

throughout, and the effect not unlike that of a motet for double choir. The violin part does not materially differ from that for the cornetto. To the second class belong the sonatas and canzoni for two or three violins with bass. Here the setting is much more complicated, mostly in fugato-form (not regular fugues), reminding us to a certain extent of organ-style, and certainly not vocal in character, but purely instrumental. The scores of Gabrieli contain the first beginnings of the modern art of instrumentation, and mark an epoch in the history of music. Not content with writing, in addition to the voices, obbligato instrumental parts, he takes into consideration the quality (timbre) of the various instruments. That this should have been brought about at the very period in which the violin came into general use, can certainly not be considered a mere accident, although it may be impossible to show which of the two was cause and which effect. Once the violin was generally accepted as the leading instrument of the orchestra, its technique appears soon to have made considerable progress. While Gabrieli never exceeds the third position, we find but a few years later, in a score of Claudio Monteverdi (1610), passages going up to the fifth position : after an obbligato passage for two cornetti, enter the violins (1st and 2nd) :

The manner in which, in this example, the violins are used ' divisi ' is worthy of notice. In another work of Monteverdi, ' Combattimento di Tancredi e Clorinda, di Claudio Monteverde. Venezia, 1624,'[2] we find modern violin effects introduced in a still more remark-

[2] See MONTEVERDI, Vol. III. p. 505.

able way. Here we have recitatives accompanied by *tremoli* for violins and bass, *pizzicati* marked thus, ' Qui si lascia l' arco, e si strappano le corde con duoi diti ' ; and afterwards, ' Qui si ripiglia l' arco.' That violinists were even at that time expected to produce gradations of tone with the bow is proved by the direction given respecting the final pause of the same work : ' Questa ultima nota va in arcata morendo.'

The earliest known solo composition for the violin is contained in a work of Biagio MARINI, published in 1620. It is a ' Romanesca per Violino Solo e Basso se piaci ' (*ad lib.*) and some dances. The Romanesca [1] is musically poor and clumsy, and, except that in it we meet with the shake for the first time, uninteresting. The demands it makes on the executant are very small. The same may be said of another very early composition for violin solo, ' La sfera armoniosa da Paolo Quagliati ' (Rome, 1623).

Of far greater importance, and showing a great advance in execution, are the compositions of Carlo FARINA, who has justly been termed the founder of the race of violin virtuosi. He published in 1627, at Dresden, a collection of violin pieces, dances, French airs, ' Quodlibets,' etc., among which a ' capriccio stravagante ' is of the utmost interest, both musically and technically. Musically it represents one of the first attempts at tone-picturing (*Klangmalerei*), and, however crude and even childish, the composer evidently was well aware of the powers of expression and character pertaining to his instrument. He employs a considerable variety of bowing, double-stopping and chords. The third position, however, is not exceeded, and the fourth string not yet used. Tarquinio MERULA (about 1640) shows a technical advance in frequent change of position, and especially in introducing octave passages. Paolo UCELLINI, in his canzoni (1649), goes up to the sixth position, and has a great variety of bowing.

Hitherto (the middle of the 17th century) the violin plays but an unimportant part as a solo instrument, and it is only with the development of the sonata-form (in the old sense of the term) that it assumes a position of importance in the history of music. (See SONATA.) Towards the year 1630 we find the first compositions containing rudimentally the form of the classical violin sonata. Among the earliest specimens may be counted the sonatas of Giov. Battista Fontana (published about 1630), a sinfonia by Mont' Albano (1629), canzoni by Tarquinio Merula (1639), canzoni and a sonata by Massimiliano Neri (1644 and 1651). From about 1650, the name Canzone falls out of use, and Sonata is the universally accepted term for

violin compositions. Massimiliano NERI appears to have been the first to have made the distinction between ' sonata da chiesa ' (church sonata) and ' sonata da camera ' (chamber sonata). The first great master of the Violin Sonata is Giovanni Battista VITALI (1644–92). He cultivated chiefly the Chamber Sonata, and his publications bear the title of ' balletti, balli, correnti, etc., da camera,' but in some of his works the transition from the suite-form to the later sonata da camera, so closely allied to the church sonata, is already clearly marked. In musical interest Vitali's compositions are greatly superior to those of his predecessors and contemporaries. His dances are concise in form, vigorous in character, and occasionally he shows remarkable powers as a composer. (See VITALI.) His demands on execution are in some instances not inconsiderable, but on the whole he does not represent in this respect any material progress. The Ciaccona, with variations for violin solo by his son T. Antonio VITALI, is justly famous.

The first beginnings of violin-playing in an artistic sense in Germany were doubtless owing to Italian influence. As early as 1626 Carlo Farina was attached to the court of Dresden. About the middle of the century a certain Johann Wilhelm FURCHEIM is mentioned in the list of members of the Dresden orchestra, under the title of ' Deutscher Konzertmeister,' implying the presence of an Italian leader by his side. Gerber, in his Dictionary, mentions two publications of his for the violin : (1) ' Violin-Exercitium aus verschiedenen Sonaten, nebst ihren Arien, Balladen, Allemanden, Couranten, Sarabanden und Giguen, von 5 Partieen bestehend, Dresden, 1687 '; and (2) ' Musikalische Tafelbedienung (dinner-service), Dresden, 1674.'

Thomas BALTZAR was, according to Burney,[2] ' the first great violinist we had ever heard in England.' He appears to have greatly astonished his audiences, especially by his then unknown efficiency in the shift, in which, however, he did not exceed the third position. Of far greater importance than Baltzar are two German violinists, Johann Jacob WALTHER (b. 1650), and Franz Heinrich BIBER (d. 1698). WALTHER appears to have been a sort of German Farina, with a technique much farther developed ; he ascends to the sixth position and writes difficult double-stops, arpeggios and chords. His compositions are, however, clumsy and poor in the extreme, and if we consider that he was a contemporary of Corelli, we cannot fail to notice the much lower level of German art as compared with that of Italy. Biber was no doubt an artist of great talent and achievement. (See SONATA, Vol. IV. p. 810). His technique was in some respects in advance of that of the best Italian violinists

---

[1] Reprinted in the Appendix of Wasielewski's *Die Violine im XVII. Jahrhundert.*

[2] *Gen. Hist. of Music,* iii. 579.

of the period, and from the character of his compositions we are justified in assuming that his style of playing combined with the pathos and nobility of the Italian style that warmth of feeling which has ever been one of the main characteristics of the great musical art of Germany.

In tracing the further progress of violin-playing we must return to Italy. After Vitali it is TORELLI (1657–1716) who chiefly deserves our attention. In his concerti da camera and concerti grossi we find the form of the sonata da chiesa preserved, but the solo violins (one or two) are accompanied not only by a bass, as in the sonata, but by a stringed band (two orchestral or ripieno violins, viola and bass), to which a lute or organ part is sometimes added, an arrangement which on the whole was followed by Vivaldi, Corelli and Handel. If no remarkable progress in the technique of the instrument was effected by the introduction of the concerto, it is all the more striking to notice how henceforth the best composers for the Church contribute to the literature of the violin. We have, in fact, arrived at a period in which the most talented musicians, almost as a matter of course, were violinists. The most eminent representative of this type of composer violinist is Arcangelo CORELLI (1653–1713). His works, though in the main laid out in the forms of his predecessors, and, as far as technique goes, keeping within modest limits, yet mark an era both in musical composition and in violin-playing. He was one of those men who seem to sum up in themselves the achievements of their best predecessors. Corelli's place in the history of instrumental music is fully discussed elsewhere. (See CORELLI; SONATA, Vol. IV. p. 811.) The technical difficulties contained in his works are not great, and in this respect Corelli's merit does not lie in the direction of innovation, but rather of limitation and reform. We have seen how the violin at the beginning of its career simply adopted the style of the vocal music of the period, how later on it took in the orchestra the place of the cornetto, and how, though very gradually, a special violin style began to be formed. Now followed a period of experiments—all more or less tending towards the same end—a style which should correspond to the nature, ideal and mechanical, of the instrument. In both respects, as we have seen, remarkable progress was made; although exaggeration was not always avoided. The virtuoso *par excellence* made his appearance even at this early period. Corelli, by talent and character, had gained a position of authority with his contemporaries, which has but few parallels in the history of music. This authority he used to give an example of artistic purity and simplicity, to found a norm and model of violin-playing which forms the basis of all succeeding legiti-

mate development of this important branch of music.

Before mentioning the most important of Corelli's pupils we have to consider the influence exercised on violin-playing by the Venetian VIVALDI (*d.* 1743). Though by no means an artist of the exalted type of Corelli, his extraordinary fertility·as a composer for the violin, his ingenuity in making new combinations and devising new effects, and especially his undoubted influence on the further development of the concerto-form, give him an important position in the history of violin-playing. While in the concerti grossi of Torelli and Corelli the solo violins are treated very much in the same manner as the orchestral violins — the solo passages being usually accompanied by the bass alone—Vivaldi not only gives to the solo violins entirely distinct passages of a much more brilliant character, but he also adds to his orchestra oboes and horns, which not merely double other parts, but have independent phrases and passages to perform—thereby giving the earliest instance of orchestration as applied to the concerto.

As an executant the Florentine Francesco Maria VERACINI exercised a greater influence than Vivaldi. Veracini, a man of passionate temperament, threw into his performances and compositions an amount of personal feeling and life, which in his own day brought on him the charge of eccentricity, but which to us appears as one of the earliest manifestations of a style which has made the violin, next to the human voice, the most powerful exponent of musical feeling. His violin sonatas are remarkable for boldness of harmonic and melodic treatment, and of masterly construction. The demands he makes on execution, especially in the matter of double stops and variety of bowing, are considerable. His influence on Tartini — after Corelli the greatest representative of the Italian school—we know to have been paramount. TARTINI (1692–1770) by a rare combination of artistic qualities of the highest order, wielded for more than half a century an undisputed authority in all matters of violin-playing, not only in Italy, but in Germany and France also. He was equally eminent as a performer, teacher and composer for the violin. Standing, as it were, on the threshold of the modern world of music, he combines with the best characteristics of the old school some of the fundamental elements of modern music. Himself endowed with a powerful individuality, he was one of the first to assert the right of individualism in music. At the same time we must not look in his works for any material change of the traditional forms. His concertos are laid out on the plan of those of Corelli and Vivaldi, while his sonatas, whether he calls them 'da chiesa' or 'da camera,' are invariably in the accepted form of the 'sonata da chiesa.' The sonata da camera in the proper sense, with its dance forms, he almost entirely abandons The difference between Tartini's style and Corelli's is not so much one of form as of substance. Many of Tartini's works bear a highly poetical and even dramatic character, qualities which, on the whole, are alien to the beautiful but colder and more formal style of Corelli. His melodies often have a peculiar charm of dreaminess and melancholy, but a vigorous and manly tone is equally at his command. His subjects, though not inferior to Corelli's in conciseness and clear logical structure, have on the whole more breadth and development. His quick passages are freer from the somewhat exercise-like, dry character of the older school ; they appear to be organically connected with the musical context, and to grow out of it. As an executant Tartini marks a great advance in the use of the bow.

While no material change has been made in the construction of the violin since the beginning of the 16th century, the bow has undergone a series of modifications, and only toward the end of the 18th century attained its present form, which combines in such a remarkable degree elasticity with firmness. (See Bow; TOURTE.) Whether Tartini himself did anything to perfect the bow, we are not aware, but the fact that old writers on musical matters frequently speak of 'Tartini's bow,' seems to point that way. At any rate, we know that in his time the bow gained considerably in elasticity, and in some letters and other writings of Tartini's we have direct evidence that he made a more systematic study of bowing than any one before him. If we consider the character of Tartini's compositions, we cannot but see what great and new claims on expression, and consequently on bowing, are made in them. That these claims were fulfilled by Tartini in an extraordinary degree is the unanimous opinion of his contemporaries : in the production of a fine tone in all its gradations, as well as in perfect management of a great variety of bowing, he had no rival.

He appears to have adhered to the holding of the violin on the right side of the string-holder, a method which was a barrier to further development of the technique of the left hand. With him the exclusive classical Italian school of violin-playing reached its culminating point, and the pupils of Corelli and Tartini form the connecting links between that school and the schools of France and Germany. In this respect the Piedmontese SOMIS (1676–1763) must be considered the most important of Corelli's pupils. We do not know much of him as a player or composer, but as the teacher of GIARDINI (1716–96), and of PUGNANI (1727–1803), the teacher of VIOTTI (1753–1824), his influence reaches down to SPOHR, and thence to our own day. The most brilliant representa-

tives of Italian violin-playing after Tartini were GEMINIANI and NARDINI. The former was a pupil of Corelli, the latter of Tartini. Their style is decidedly more modern and more brilliant than are those of their great masters. Nardini's influence in Germany—where he passed many years—contributed much towards the progress of violin-playing in that country. Geminiani (1680–1761), who for a long time resided in London, was the first to publish a violin-school of any importance. Compared with that of Leopold MOZART which appeared a few years later, and is on the whole a work of much higher merit, Geminiani's ' school ' shows an advance in some important points of technique. Here for the first time the holding of the violin on the left side of the string-holder is recommended—an innovation of the greatest importance, by which alone the high development of modern technique was made possible. He goes up to the seventh position. As affording the only direct evidence of Corelli's method and principles (which in all main respects have remained ever since the basis of all legitimate and correct treatment of the instrument), Geminiani's book is still of the greatest interest. In LOCATELLI (1693–1764), another pupil of Tartini, a curious instance is afforded of how, in spite of the strongest school-influence, a powerful individuality will now and then, for better or worse, strike out a path for itself. While some of Locatelli's compositions afford clear evidence of his sound musicianship and genuine musical feeling, he shows himself in others, especially in a set of Caprices, to have been, to say the least, an experimentalist of the boldest type. In overstepping to an astonishing degree the natural resources and limits of the instrument, these caprices afford one of the earliest instances of charlatanism in violin-playing.

The beginnings of violin-playing in France date from a very early period. Yet to judge from the extreme simplicity of the violin parts in the scores of Lully, who in 1652 was appointed Director of the Royal Chapel (see VINGT-QUATRE VIOLONS), the general level of skill in performance was not great. As late as 1753 a certain Paris musician, Corrette, writes that when Corelli's violin sonatas came to Paris, no violinist was to be found who could play them. The violin compositions of Frenchmen of the same period, among which the suites of REBEL (1687), a pupil of Lully, were counted the best, are in every respect inferior to the average of Italian and even of German productions of the same period. François FRANCŒUR, in his sonatas (1715), shows decided progress in both respects. (As a curiosity it may be noticed that Francœur, in order to produce certain chords, adopted the strange expedient of placing the thumb on the strings.) As was the case in Germany, it was

owing to the influence of the Italian school
that violin-playing in France was raised to real
excellence. The first French violinist of note
who made his studies in Italy under Corelli was
Baptiste ANET (about 1700). Of much greater
importance, however, was Jean Marie LECLAIR
(1697–1764), a pupil of Somis, who again was a
direct pupil of Corelli. As composer for the
violin Leclair has hardly a rival among Frenchmen down to Rode. If most of his works are
characterised by vivacity, piquancy and grace,
he also shows in some instances a remarkable
depth of feeling. His technique shows itself,
within certain limits—he does not go beyond
the third position—to be quite as developed
as that of his Italian contemporaries. By the
frequent employment of double-stops a remarkable richness of sound is produced, and
the bow is used in a manner requiring that
agility and lightness of management for which
at a later period the French school gained a
special reputation.

Among other French violinists, directly or
indirectly formed by the Italian school, may
be mentioned PAGIN (b. 1721), TOUCHEMOULIN
(1727–1801), LAHOUSSAYE (1735–1818), BAR-
THÉLEMON (d. 1808), and BERTHAUME (1752–
1828). Meanwhile an independent French
school began to be formed, of which Pierre
GAVINIÉS (1728–1800) was the most eminent
representative. Of his numerous compositions,
‘ Les Vingt-quatre Matinées ’—a set of studies
of unusual difficulty—have alone survived.
Without partaking of the eccentricity of Locatelli's Caprices, these studies show a tendency
towards exaggeration in technique. Beauty
of sound is frequently sacrificed—difficulty
is heaped on difficulty for its own sake, and
not with the intention of producing new effects.
At the same time, so competent a judge as
Fétis ascribes to Gaviniés a style of playing
both imposing and graceful.

Not directly connected with any school, but
in the main self-taught, was Alexandre Jean
BOUCHER (1770–1861). He was no doubt a
player of extraordinary talent and exceptional
technical proficiency, but devoid of all artistic
earnestness, and was one of the race of char-
latan violinists which has had representatives
from the days of Farina down to our own time.
If they have done harm by their example, and
by the success they have gained from the
masses, it must not be overlooked that, in not
a few respects, they have advanced the technique of the violin. The advent of VIOTTI
(1753–1824) marks a new era in French violin-
playing. His enormous success, both as player
and composer, gave him an influence over his
contemporaries which has no parallel, except
in the cases of Corelli and Tartini before him,
and in that of Spohr at a later period.

In Germany the art of Corelli and Tartini
was spread by numerous pupils of their school,

who entered the service of German princes.
In Berlin we find J. G. GRAUN (1698–1771), a
direct pupil of Tartini, and F. BENDA (1709–
1786), both excellent players and eminent
musicians. In the south, the school of Mannheim numbered among its representatives
Johann Carl STAMITZ (1719–61), and his two
sons Carl and Anton (the latter settled in
Paris, and was the teacher of R. Kreutzer) ;
Chr. CANNABICH (1731–98), well known as
the intimate friend of Mozart ; Wilhelm
CRAMER (1745–99), member of a very distinguished musical family, and for many years
the leading violinist in London ; Ignaz FRÄNZL
(b. 1736) and his son Ferdinand (1770–1833).
The Mannheim masters, however, did not contribute anything lasting to the solo literature
of the violin. On the whole, the sonata, as
cultivated by Tartini, remained the favourite
form of violin composition. At the same time
the concerto (in the modern sense) came more
and more into prominence. The fact that
W. A. Mozart, who from early childhood practised almost every form of composition then in
use, wrote so many concertos for violin and
orchestra, is a clear indication of the growing
popularity of the new form. Mozart in his
younger years was hardly less great as a
violinist than at the keyboard, and his violin
concertos are the most valuable compositions
in that form anterior to Beethoven and Spohr.
Mozart, however, in his later years gave up
violin-playing altogether, and although, like
Haydn, he has shown in his chamber music
how thoroughly in sympathy he was with the
nature of the violin, he did not contribute to
the literature of the instrument any works
wherein he availed himself of the technical
proficiency attained by the best violinists of
his time. In this respect it is significant that
Spohr, whose unbounded admiration for Mozart
is well known, seems never to have played his
violin concertos in public. Viotti and Rode
were Spohr's models for his earlier concertos.

Towards the end of the 17th century Paris
became the undisputed centre of violin-playing,
and the Paris school—represented by Viotti
as depository of the traditions of the classical
Italian school, by KREUTZER (1766–1831), who,
though born at Versailles, was of German
parentage, and a pupil of Anton Stamitz, and
by RODE (1774–1830) and BAILLOT (1771–
1842), both Frenchmen—assumed a truly international character. The single circumstance
that four violinists of such eminence lived and
worked together at the same place, and nearly
the same time, would be sufficient to account
for their essential influence on the taste and
style of this period. Differing much in artistic
temperament, they all took the same serious
view of their art, and shared that musical
earnestness which is averse to mere technical
display for its own sake, and looks on execution

as the means of interpreting musical ideas and emotions. As teachers at the newly founded Conservatoire, Rode, Kreutzer and Baillot formally laid down the principles of violin-playing as they prevail to this day. It is to Germany that we have to look for their true successors, apparently because their style, founded on a broad and truly musical basis, irrespective of national peculiarities, found its most congenial soil in the country of the great composers, who in their works are truly international, as all art of the very first rank must be ; while the strongly pronounced national character of French violinists was bound sooner or later to assert itself, and to return to a characteristically French style of playing. Baillot, in his *L'Art du violon*, points out as the chief distinction between the old and the modern style of violin-playing, the absence of the dramatic element in the former, and its predominance in the latter. In so far as this means that the modern style better enables the player to bring out those powerful contrasts, and to do justice to the enlarged horizon of ideas and emotions in modern musical compositions, it merely states that executive art has followed the progress, and shared in the characteristic qualities of the creative art of the period. A comparison of Mozart's string quartets with those of Beethoven illustrates to a certain extent this difference. The style of playing which was admirably adapted for the interpretation of the works not only of Corelli and Tartini, but also of Handel, and even Mozart, could not cope with Haydn, and still less with Beethoven. The great merit of the masters of the Paris school was that they recognised this call for a freer and bolder treatment of the instrument, and approached their task in a truly musical and artistic spirit.

The manner and style of the Paris school were brought to Germany by Viotti and Rode, who both travelled a great deal, and by their performances effected a considerable modification in the somewhat antiquated style then prevailing in that country. The Mannheim school, as already mentioned, was the most important centre of violin-playing in Germany during the second half of the 18th century. It produced a number of excellent players, such as the Stamitz family, Chr. Cannabich, Ferd. Fränzl. They had adhered more closely than the French players to Tartini's method and manner, and not only Spohr, but before him Mozart, speaks of their style as old-fashioned, when compared with that of their French contemporaries. The fact that the last and final improvements in the bow, as made by TOURTE of Paris, were probably unknown to them would account for this. Another remarkable player belonging to this school was J. F. ECK (*b.* 1766), whose brother and pupil Franz ECK (1774–1809) was the teacher of Spohr. Both

the Ecks appear to some extent to have been under the influence of the French school. Spohr in his Autobiography speaks of Franz Eck as a French violinist. Spohr therefore can hardly be reckoned as of the Mannheim school, and we know that later on he was greatly impressed by Rode, and for a considerable time studied to imitate him. His earlier concertos are evidently worked after the model of Rode. Thus—granting the enormous difference of artistic temperament—Spohr must be considered as the direct heir of the art of Viotti and Rode. At the same time, his individuality was so peculiar that he very soon formed a style of his own as a player no less than as a composer. As a composer he probably influenced the style of modern violin-playing even more than as a player. His concertos were, with the single exception of Beethoven's concerto, by far the most valuable contributions to the literature of the violin, as a solo instrument, hitherto made. Compared even with the best of Viotti's, Rode's or Kreutzer's concertos they are not merely improvements, but in them the violin concerto itself is lifted into a higher sphere, and from being more or less a show-piece, rises to the dignity of a work of art, to be judged as much on its own merits as a musical composition as by its effectiveness as a solo-piece. Without detracting from the merits of the works of the older masters, it is not too much to say that there is hardly enough musical stuff in them to have resisted the stream of superficial virtuoso music which more than ever before flooded the concert-rooms during the first half of the 19th century. We believe that it was mainly owing to the sterling musical worth of Spohr's violin compositions that the great qualities of the classical Italian and the Paris schools have been preserved to the present day, and have prevented the degeneration of violin-playing. Spohr had great powers of execution, but he used them in a manner not wholly free from one-sidedness, and it cannot be said that he made any addition to the technique of the instrument. He set a great example of purity of style and legitimate treatment of the instrument.

Next to Spohr no one had a greater influence on the style of modern violin-playing than PAGANINI (1784–1840). The sensation he created wherever he appeared was unprecedented. By his marvellous execution, and his thoroughly original and eccentric personality and style, he for a time held Europe spellbound. His influence on the younger violinists of the period could not fail to be considerable—more so in France than in Germany, where the more serious spirit prevailing among musicians and the presence of such a master as Spohr, were powerful enough to keep the influence within bounds. The growing importance and popularity of chamber music for the violin, especially of the string quartet, since Haydn, Mozart and Beethoven were another barrier against the predominance of an exclusive virtuoso style of violin-playing in Germany. French violinists, especially Baillot, were certainly anxious enough to attack these highest tasks of the violinist, but there can be no doubt that in their hands the works of the German classics assumed an aspect which was too frequently more in accordance with the French character of the performers than with the intentions of the composers. In this respect the minute directions which Baillot gives for the performance of a great number of passages extracted from the works of most eminent composers is extremely curious and instructive. It was but natural that Paganini should have a number of imitators, who copied with more or less success his harmonics and double-harmonics, his long and quick staccatos, *pizzicati* with the left hand—in fact, all those technical feats which, though not invented by him, he brought to perfection. The style of the man, which had its source in his genius and originality, was inimitable. He could not, and did not start a school. SIVORI (*b.* 1817) claimed to be his only actual pupil. But, pupils or no pupils, Paganini caused nothing short of a revolution in the technique of the French school. The striking change which the general style of violin-playing underwent in France during the third decade of the 19th century has, however, other and deeper causes, and finds its explanation in the complete revolution in musical taste which took place at that period. The classical Paris school was in reality the school of Italy, which for the time being had made Paris, as it were, its headquarters. Founded by Viotti, the Italian, at a time when German instrumental music, in the persons of Haydn and Mozart, was occupying the attention of the whole musical world, this school hardly reflected the salient points of the French national character, although it harmonised well with the classical tendencies of the sister arts in that country. In Baillot's *L'Art du violon* we cannot fail to recognise already a leaning towards a style which was more in harmony with the genius of the French nation — a style, brilliant, showy, full of shrewdly calculated effects, elegant and graceful, aiming chiefly at a highly polished execution, and distinguished by what they themselves untranslatably call *élan*. At the same time, the French school gained, in what might be termed its classical period, a basis and a systematic method for the technical training of violinists, the advantages of which are still so apparent in the highly finished technique of a large number of French violin-players of the present day.

Two most eminent representatives of the French school, DE BÉRIOT (1802–70) and H. VIEUXTEMPS (1820–81), were of Belgian nationality. The Belgian school of violin-playing is, however, in reality but a branch, though a most important one, of the Paris school. De Bériot's style as a composer for the violin seems to have been formed under the influence of the modern Italian opera composers, especially of Rossini, Donizetti and Bellini ; and his concertos and ' Airs variés,' which attained an immense popularity all over the world, share the strong and weak points of contemporary Italian music. They have plenty of melody, though of a somewhat sentimental kind, and their general style, without affording much difficulty to the player, is most brilliant and effective. If De Bériot's ideas are on the whole superficial and often not free from triviality, they are also unpretentious and unaffected. The same can hardly be said of Vieuxtemps. He certainly was a great violinist, and as a musician decidedly superior to De Bériot. His compositions contain ideas of great beauty and are often cleverly worked out, but at the same time there is in them too frequently an element of theatrical bombast and pretension which is analogous to Meyerbeer's grand-opera style, just as De Bériot's is to the spontaneous melody of Italian opera. De Bériot's treatment of the instrument, though often commonplace, does not go against its nature, while Vieuxtemps not unfrequently seems to do violence to it, and in some of his *tours de force* oversteps the boundaries of the beautiful. Both these great artists travelled much, and gained by the great excellence of their performances universal success in almost every European country. Vieuxtemps was also the first violinist, of the highest rank, who visited America. De Bériot, as leader at the Brussels Conservatoire, formed a great number of excellent violinists, the best known of whom are the Spaniard MONASTERIO (*b.* 1836). SAURET (*b.* 1852), SCHRADIECK (*b.* 1846) and HEERMAN (*b.* 1844). Jean BECKER (*b.* 1833) and LAUTERBACH (*b.* 1832) also studied for some time under him.

Among Bailiot's pupils F. A. HABENECK (1781–1849) attained a great reputation as conductor and as teacher. He counts among his pupils SAINTON (*b.* 1813), PRUME (1816–49), ALARD (1815–88) and LÉONARD (*b.* 1819). The two last, with MASSART (*b.* 1811), a pupil of Kreutzer, headed the Franco-Belgian school as teachers at the Paris Conservatoire. Alard's most eminent pupil was SARASATE (1844–1908). MARSICK and DENGREMONT (*b.* 1866) studied under Léonard ; WIENIAWSKI, LOTTO and TERESINA TUA were pupils of Massart.

In Germany we find the schools of Cassel, Leipzig and Vienna taking the lead. Spohr at Cassel had a great number of pupils, but his manner and style were too exclusively individual to form a school. His most eminent pupil was Ferdinand DAVID (1810–73), who as founder of the Leipzig school exercised great influence on violin-playing in Germany. It can hardly be said that he perpetuated in his pupils Spohr's method and style. Entirely differing from his great master in musical temperament, enjoying from his early youth close intercourse with Mendelssohn, and strongly imbued with the spirit of Beethoven's music, he represented a more modern phase in German violin-playing and an eclecticism which has avoided one-sidedness not less in matters of technique than in musical taste and judgment generally. He was the first who played Bach's violin solos, and all the last quartets of Beethoven (not even excepting the fugue) in public. Schubert's quartets and quintet were on the programmes of his chamber concerts at the time when they had not yet been heard in public, except perhaps at Vienna. As a teacher his chief aim was to give to his pupils a thorough command of the technique of the violin, and to arouse and develop their musical intelligence. There as elsewhere the classical works of violin literature naturally formed the main stock of teaching material. At the same time David laid great stress on the study of the French masters, maintaining that, irrespective of musical value, their works, being as a rule written with the aim of bringing out the capabilities of the violin, contain a large amount of useful material for technical training, which in the end must benefit and improve the execution of music of any style. The correctness of this theory was strikingly proved by JOACHIM, who, as Boehm's pupil at Vienna, was made thoroughly familiar with the technique of the French school, while he studied most of his classical repertory at Leipzig under David's guidance, and in what we may term Mendelssohn's musical atmosphere. Joachim's unlimited command over technical difficulties in music of any style, which enabled him to do equal justice to Paganini and Bach, was undoubtedly largely owing to the fact that his early training was free from one-sidedness, and that he gained through the study of brilliant music the highest finish as well as the completest mastery. David trained a large number of good violinists : Japha (Cologne), Röntgen (Leipzig), Jacobsohn (Bremen), Schradieck (who succeeded him at Leipzig), F. Hegar (Zürich) and many more. By far the most eminent of his pupils was WILHELMJ (1845–1908), a virtuoso of the very first rank, who combined a fine broad tone with a technique of the left hand unrivalled by any contemporary violinist.

A most powerful influence on the style of the German violinists was exercised by the Vienna school, more especially by the pupils of BOEHM (1798–1876). Although it is difficult to trace any direct connexion between the Viennese violin-players of the 18th century and the

school of Italy, Italian violinists came very early to Vienna, and the local players adopted their method and style. We know that Tartini was for three years in the service of Count Kinsky, a Bohemian noble, and also that Trani, Ferrari and other Italian virtuosi came to Vienna. It is remarkable that the leading Viennese composers of the 18th century, down to Haydn, were almost without exception violinists. Some of them, like Anton Wranitzky and Dittersdorf, were virtuosi of high rank, but most of them were in the first place composers and leaders, and in the second place only violinists. Naturally they excelled less as solo-players than in the performance of chamber music, which at that period hardly enjoyed anywhere so much popularity as at Vienna. It was the time of preparation for the great classical period which opened with Haydn, and the circumstance that the violin was even then cultivated in Vienna far more in connexion with good and serious music than merely as a solo instrument, has undoubtedly contributed much towards giving to the later representatives of that school their thoroughly musical character, and towards making Vienna the earliest home of quartet-playing. As a quartet-player SCHUPPANZIGH (1776–1830), a pupil of Wranitzky, attained great reputation, and may be regarded as standing first on the roll of great quartet-players. For many years in close intercourse with Haydn and Beethoven, enjoying the advice and guidance of these great masters in the production of their quartets, he established the style of quartet-playing which has been handed down by the most eminent Vienna violinists to our days. His greatest pupil was MAYSEDER (1789–1863), a brilliant solo-player, of a style more elegant than powerful. Among his pupils the best known are MISKA HAUSER (1822–87) and DE AHNA (1835–92). (See JOACHIM QUARTET.)

ERNST (1814–65), G. HELLMESBERGER, sen., DONT, sen. (1815–88), JOACHIM, LUDWIG STRAUS, RAPPOLDI and GRÜN all studied under Boehm. Boehm himself can hardly be reckoned as belonging to the old Vienna school, since he made his studies under Rode, and no doubt was also influenced by Spohr, who resided at Vienna in 1813, 1814 and 1815. The Vienna school, therefore, though certainly not uninfluenced by the musical traditions of Vienna, appears in reference to technique and specific violin-style to be based on the principles of the classical French school. Counting among its representatives players of a great diversity of talent and artistic temperament, who afterwards formed more or less a style of their own, the Vienna school, or, strictly speaking, Boehm's school, can hardly be said to have been directly continued at Vienna. Boehm, although a thoroughly competent violinist, was not a player of great genius, but he was possessed of an eminently sound and correct taste and judgment in musical and technical matters, and had a rare talent for teaching. Ernst, next to Joachim the most famous of his pupils, came largely under the influence of Paganini, whose style he for some time closely imitated. Undoubtedly a violinist of the first rank, and by no means exclusively a bravura-player, he did not to any extent affect the prevailing style of violin-playing, nor did he train pupils. An enormous influence on modern violin-playing, and on the general musical life of Germany and England, was exercised by Joachim.[1] He combined in a unique degree the highest executive powers with the most excellent musicianship ; and while through his brilliant example he may truly be said to have given to modern German violin-playing a peculiar character, it has not been without effect even on the style of the French school. Unsurpassed as a master of the instrument, he used his powers of execution exclusively in the service of art. First musician, then violinist, seemed the motto of his life and the gist of his teaching. His performances undoubtedly derived their charm and supreme merit from the strength of his talent and of his artistic character, and were stamped with a striking originality of conception ; at the same time fidelity to the text, and careful endeavour to enter into the spirit and feeling of the composer, were the principles of executive art which Joachim through his long career invariably practised. With Ernst, and still more with Joachim, an element derived from the national Hungarian, and from Hungarian gipsy music, came into prominence. It is fiddle music *par excellence*, and if introduced into serious music with such judgment and discretion as in Joachim's Hungarian concerto and transcriptions of Brahms's Hungarian Dances, it opens a field for telling and beautiful violin effects. It evinces the same desire to make the resources of popular national music available for artistic purposes, which showed itself in Chopin's idealisations of the Polish element, and later in Sarasate's adaptations of Spanish melodies and dances.[2]

In addition to Boehm's pupils, the Vienna school produced a number of eminent violinists, such as Joseph HELLMESBERGER,[3] a pupil of his father, who was for a great many years the leading violinist at Vienna, enjoying a special reputation for quartet-playing ; Leopold AUER (*b.* 1845), pupil of Dont, jun., and others. Leopold JANSA (1797-1875) deserves to be specially mentioned as the teacher of Wilma Norman NERUDA (*b.* 1840). Madame Neruda (Lady Hallé), possessing a highly finished technique, was not merely a brilliant soloist but

a thorough musician, versed in the whole range of musical literature, an admirable quartet-player and the first woman to attain front rank as a violinist.

The school of Prague—started by F. W. PIXIS (1786–1842), a pupil of Fränzl at Mannheim, and of Viotti—has produced several violinists of note : J. W. KALLIWODA (1800–66), M. MILDNER (1812–65), who succeeded Pixis as professor of the violin at the Prague Conservatoire, and FERDINAND LAUB (1832–75) a violinist of the very first rank. For the later development of this school see ŠEVČÍK.

P. D., with addns.

The attempt to continue further the history of violin-playing by reference to its famous exponents leads inevitably to a digression in which testimonials to the personal powers of great artists obscure the view of the art. Rather than perpetuate the digression of former editions of this Dictionary and intensify it by a fruitless effort to keep pace with time, a summary of facts, including some recorded by previous contributors, must be made here.

In the first place it must be pointed out that all the circumstances of artistic life have so changed that the differentiation of 'schools' which served for classification from the birth of the violin until the middle of the 19th century no longer has the same historical significance. The schools of the past were sharply distinguished by the fact that their members were trained for the performance of particular kinds of music in local conditions and before certain kinds of audience. Members of a school, therefore, grew up sharing views in common, and they devised technical methods to suit their requirements. Even the enumerations given above show the lines of demarcation crossed and recrossed as history approaches modern times. The nationality of the individual and of his school are increasingly at variance, and the distinctions of national schools become more nominal than real. They may be traced in the Berlin school of Joachim and the Brussels school of Eugene YSÄYE, which towards the end of the 19th century were regarded as rivals ; these represented contrasted ideals to a certain extent based on national conceptions of music and its interpretation. But when we come to AUER[4] and ŠEVČÍK,[5] who number among their pupils a large proportion of the violinists who made great personal reputations in the first quarter of the 20th century, it is quite evident that we are dealing with methods which may be regarded as personal or as cosmopolitan but in no sense as national. In fact national schools have given way to the training of international artists on personal methods.

Violin technique has made no perceptible

---

[1] Among many pupils of repute trained by Joachim were J. Ludwig, Johann Kruse, Willy Hess, R. Gompertz, Marie Soldat, Halir, Adela d'Aranyi.
[2] Compare also the Bohemian Dances of Ševčík. It is a curious fact that composers have tended to stress national characteristics the more while performance has become increasingly cosmopolitan.
[3] Hellmesberger was the teacher of KREISLER (*q.v.*).

[4] Representative pupils of Auer are Mischa ELMAN, Ephraim ZIMBALIST, Kathleen PARLOW, Jascha HEIFETZ, Toscha SEIDEL.
[5] Representative pupils of Ševčík are KUBELIK, KOCIAN Marie HALL, Daisy KENNEDY.

advance (that was scarcely possible) after Paganini. What has advanced is its diffusion among the enlarged ranks of the artists who lay no claim to virtuosity. The gap between the solo-player and the orchestral player no longer exists. Every musical college in Europe and America turns out annually pupils trained in the highest branches of solo work but who have to be content to fill places at the last desks of good orchestras. The supply of excellent players exceeds the demand for their services. The virtuosi and able executants are separated by their personal qualities as interpreters rather than by any sharply drawn line of technical accomplishment. So widely spread is the latter that it is no longer asked what a new-comer can do but how he does it. Though certain details of his style in bowing and phrasing may be traceable to the traditions of the school in which he was trained, the question is answered far more by the evidences of his or her own artistic disposition.

The literature of ' methods ' and instructional works generally is enormous. The following are named as illustrative of points touched on above :

Spohr, *Violin School* (Eng. ed. by Henry Holmes).
Baillot, Kreutzer and Rode, *Méthode du violon.* (Officially issued by the Paris Conservatoire.)
Baillot, *L'Art du violon.* (1834.)
De Bériot, *École transcendentale de violon. Grande Méthode.* (Paris, 1858.)
Joachim and Moser, *Methodik des Violinspiels.* 2 parts. (Berlin, 1920.)
Ševčík, *Schule von Violintechnik.* 4 parts. (Prague, 1883.)
Schule von Bogentechnik (including 4000 exercises), in 6 books. (Prague, 1903.)
Auer, *Violin Playing as I Teach It.* (New York, 1921.)
Rivarde, *The Violin and its Technique.* (London, 1921.)   C.

VIOLONCELLO, see Violin Family (3).

VIOLONCELLO PICCOLO, see Violin Family (12).

VIOLONCELLO-PLAYING. Though the manufacture of the bass violin or violoncello followed closely on the invention of the tenor and treble violins, nearly a century elapsed before the violoncello took its proper rank in the family of stringed instruments. This is due to the fact that the six-stringed viola da gamba (see Viol), the established chamber and orchestral bass of the 17th century, was a very popular instrument, and more easily handled than the violoncello, though inferior to it in power and quality of tone. The larger and more thickly strung violoncello was at first employed to strengthen the bass part in vocal music, particularly in the music of the Church.

It was in Italy that the instrument first took a higher position. The stepping-stone appears to have been the basso continuo which formed the usual accompaniment to solos for the violin. The ringing tones of the violin demanded a more powerful accompaniment than the viola da gamba could give ; and with many violin solos of the latter part of the century we find bass parts of some difficulty, which were played on the violoncello by accompanists who made this department of music a

special study. Corelli is said to have had a violoncello accompaniment to his solo performances, though his basso continuo is obviously written in the first instance for the viola da gamba : but it is not until after the death of Corelli that we hear of the first solo violoncello-player. This was one Franciscello (1713–1740), of whom little is known except that he played solos in the principal European capitals. The name of Vandini has also come down to us as the violoncello accompanist of the solos of Tartini, and it may be assumed that it was from its association with the violin as a bass that the violoncello itself became a model instrument, and that the methods of violin-playing came to be applied to it.

Among the earliest compositions for the violoncello may be mentioned the sonatas of Antoniotto of Milan, an Amsterdam edition of which is dated 1736, and of Salvatore Lanzetti, violoncellist to the King of Sardinia (1730–50). According to Vidal [1] we trace in these masters the first decided recognition of the capacities of the instrument. The left hand stops an octave and a half (upper E) on the first string, necessitating the use of the thumb, which is the special characteristic of the higher positions of the violoncello (see Fingering). Canavasso and Ferrari, two other Italian players, appeared in Paris between 1750 and 1760. There already lived in Paris a player whose name stands by tradition at the head of the French school. This was the famous Berteau (*d.* 1756). He is always recognised as the first of the French school of violoncello-players. Cupis, Tillière, the two Jansons, and the elder Duport were among his pupils. Among the classical composers, Handel and Bach first employed the instrument in its wider range ; it is only necessary to mention the famous six suites of the latter, while well-known instances of its use by the former are the obbligato parts to ' O Liberty ' (' Judas '), ' What passion cannot music raise ' (' St. Cecilia's Day '), and ' But O ! sad virgin ' (' L'Allegro '). Pepusch's ' Alexis ' was for long a favourite.

With the creation of the stringed quartet the violoncello gained the greater prominence, which is exemplified in the chamber music of Haydn and Boccherini. The latter master was himself a soloist of considerable ability ; he played at the Concert Spirituel in Paris in 1768. Gluck is said to have been a violoncellist, but no predilection for the instrument appears in his works.

The true method of violoncello-playing was first worked out by the younger Duport (*q.v.*), and laid down in his famous *Essai sur le doigter du violoncelle, et la conduite de l'archet.* Before Duport much confusion had existed in fingering and bowing the instrument ; many players, it

[1] *Les Instruments à Archet.* vol. i. p. 327.

appears, endeavoured to get over the difficulties of the scales by fingering the violoncello like the violin, *i.e.* stopping whole tones with successive fingers, thus throwing the hand into a false position, and losing that *aplomb* which is indispensable alike to certainty of fingering and solidity of tone. Duport, recurring to the practice of the old viola da gamba players, laid down the principle that the true fingering was by semitones, only the first and second fingers being as a rule allowed to stretch a whole tone where necessary ; and he overcame the inherent difficulties of the scales by dividing the positions into four so-called ' Fractions,' and by adopting a methodical system of shifting, the violin fingering being only retained in the higher ' thumb ' positions, where the fingering is similar to the first position of the violin, the thumb acting as a movable nut. The *Essai* of Duport formed an epoch in violoncello-playing. The compliment of Voltaire to Duport, who visited him when at Geneva on a musical tour, aptly illustrates the change which was taking place in the treatment of the instrument. 'Monsieur,' he is reported to have said, ' vous me faites croire aux miracles : vous savez faire d'un bœuf un rossignol ! '

In Germany Bernhard Romberg and Stiastný, contemporaries of Duport, worked upon his method, while Levasseur, Lamare, Norblin, Platel, Baudiot and others represented the school in France. The Italians were slower in the cultivation of the violoncello, and Burney in his *Tour* remarks that the Italian players retained the underhand grasp of the bow while elsewhere the overhand grasp, founded on that of the violin, was generally adopted. Since the time of Duport, the tendency of players and composers has been to make the violoncello more and more a bass violin, *i.e.* to assimilate its treatment more and more closely to that of the treble instrument. Merk, Franchomme, Kummer, and Dotzauer ranked among the best bravura players of their times, but the greatest master of the mid-nineteenth century was undoubtedly A. F. Servais (*d.* 1866), under whose large and vigorous hand, says a critic, the violoncello vibrated with the facility of a kit : the staccato in single notes, in thirds, in octaves, all over the finger-board, even to the most acute tones, came out with irreproachable purity ; there was never a hesitation or a doubtful note. He was an innovator in every sense of the word ; never, before him, had the violoncello yielded such effects. His compositions will remain as one of the most marvellous monuments of the instrumental art of his time.[1] It is needless to catalogue here the names of the numerous fine players of the latter part of the century whose personal attainments are chronicled under their own names. That of Alfredo Piatti (*q.v.*) must

[1] Vidal, *Instruments à archet*, vol. i. p. 371.

be mentioned, since by his playing and his teaching he did a peculiar work for the propagation of the art in this country.

The violoncello affords less scope than the violin for displaying skill in bowing, the bow being shorter than that of the violin, though the instrument itself is very much larger ; while the bowing is to some extent reversed, because in the violin the bow points in the downward direction of the scales, *i.e.* towards the lowest string, while in the violoncello, which is held in a reversed position, the bow points in the upward direction, towards the highest string. The rule of the old viola da gamba players, however—to bow strictly the reverse way to the violin, *i.e.* to begin the bar with an up-bow—is not applicable to the violoncello.

One small mechanical invention, the ' tail pin ' now universally used to support the instrument, has had a far-reaching effect in the spread of violoncello-playing, particularly by making the instrument available for women. It is scarcely too much to say that without the aid of this simple appliance we should have been deprived of the many fine performances by women violoncellists which to-day are everywhere admired. May Mukle (*q.v.*) was a pioneer of a movement in this country. Others who must be named are Beatrice Harrison, and, perhaps most conspicuously, Guilhermina Suggia, who has inherited the traditions of her teacher, Casals. The adjustable ' tail pin ' itself seems to have been first used by Servais as an aid, when age and physique made difficult the old method of holding the violoncello between the knees. Hausmann and some of his pupils refused its use, but the manifest freedom and ease of position which it secured for the player quickly assured its general adoption.

E. J. P. ; rev. I. J.

With the advent of Pablo Casals (*q.v.*) a new era may be said to have begun, and the violoncello took quite a different position among solo instruments. His art was such that the six suites for violoncello by Bach were revived and made to live—those who have had the privilege of hearing them played by him have realised at once not only what beauty there is in these works, and how wonderfully they are written for the instrument, but also what beauty there is in the instrument itself. The importance of Casals's art cannot perhaps yet be adequately gauged. In addition to the suites of Bach he revived the Haydn concerto, the Schumann concerto, the Dvořák concerto—(to mention only three important works) and a violoncellist aspiring to reach the front rank must now have all these works in his repertory—yet it is only as recently as the beginning of the 20th century that such things as fantasias on opera tunes were the chief resource in the repertory of the solo violoncellist. Again, what must be attributed to Casals's influence is evident in the interest contemporary composers are taking in this instrument, as many new works are being written—chiefly duet sonatas with piano, showing a greatly advanced knowledge of the possibilities of the violoncello in every register.

It is of interest to trace the evolution of modern violoncello-playing as shown by the influence of Casals. There are many good methods for beginners to study, such as those by Kummer, Lee, Piatti, etc., but in the more advanced stages it is undoubtedly from Duport and his school of technique that Casals has evolved the wonderful beauty of his art. Duport's *Essai* and his manner of fingering the violoncello are the germs from which the present-day players derive their inspiration, and it is through the Latin school rather than through the Teutonic that the violoncello has travelled to its present state.

Besides the *Essai* by Duport, there exists a very exhaustive technical treatise by Massau and more recently an exposition by Diran Alexanian of the principles which Casals not only revived, but to a great extent created.

The concertos of Romberg still serve their purpose, but apart from their usefulness as a means of study in giving extra technical control, the technique he invented was actually a *cul de sac*, and no musical progress has been made along those lines ; other violoncellist composers, such as Davidoff, Goltermann and Klengel, have also written concertos and pieces which are important as a means of gaining more control in technique and tone, but of no musical value whatever. Popper was a violoncellist who wrote many light pieces which have served a useful purpose in helping players to acquire facility. The studies of Dotzauer are of the first importance, and he may be called the Czerny of the violoncello ; excellent studies are also those by Franchomme, Kummer, Grutzmacher, de Swert and Piatti.

Piatti set in motion a valuable movement (which has resulted in a good deal of research into the work of the old virtuosi composers) by editing many of the works of Boccherini, Porpora, Valentini, Marcello ; and this has been continued more recently by others, bringing within the reach of violoncellists many ancient solo sonatas, prominent among which are those by Sammartini, Eccles, Vivaldi, Marais and many more. This research has enriched the repertory of the violoncellist, and has provided at least the beginning of a musical library which has taken the place of the wretched operatic fantasias and other worthless arrangements so much the vogue in the latter part of the nineteenth century.

The first sonatas for piano and violoncello of any musical importance were those by Beethoven, who wrote five. Schumann, Chopin and Mendelssohn wrote sonatas or pieces of fair interest ; but the two sonatas of Brahms are next in musical importance to those of Beethoven. Effective sonatas have also been written by Rubinstein, Grieg, Saint-Saëns and Strauss, but their value musically is not great.

Recently many important contributions of the kind have come from such composers as Dohnányi, Hurlstone, Tovey, Emmanuel Moor, Ropartz, Huré, Debussy, Delius, Frank Bridge, John Ireland, Arnold Bax, and the concerto literature has been enriched by Delius and Elgar. A few works have also appeared for violoncello alone, such as the sonata in D major of Donald F. Tovey, three unaccompanied suites by Max Reger, and a sonata by Kodály.

A number of works have been written for more than one violoncello ; Popper wrote a suite for two and a ' Requiem ' for three violoncellos and piano ; Emmanuel Moor has written a concerto for two violoncellos and orchestra, a suite for two and a quartet for four violoncellos, while Thomas F. Dunhill has written a suite for six violoncellos.   I. J.

VIOLONE (1) See DOUBLE BASS. (2) An organ stop of 16-ft. pitch, with open pipes of smaller scale than those of the Open Diapason. Generally in the Pedal organ.   w. pᴬ.

VIOLOTTA, see VIOLIN FAMILY (11).

VIOTTI, JEAN BAPTISTE (GIOVANNI BATTISTA) (*b*. Fontanetto, near Crescentino, Canton of Piedmont, May 23, 1753 ; *d*. London, Mar. 3, 1824), founder of the modern school of violin-playing. The baptismal certificate states that he was the ' legitimate son of Antonio Viotti and his wife Maria Magdalena, Milano,' and that he was baptized by Johannes Domenico Roseno, on June 25, 1753. Alphonso Barberis, a lawyer, was the godfather, and Antonia Maria, his wife, godmother. Viotti's father, says Fétis, was a blacksmith, who played the horn and taught his son the elements of music. In Viotti's autograph MS. summary of his life, entitled *Précis de la vie de J. B. Viotti, depuis son entrée dans le monde jusqu'au 6 mars, 1789* (a kind of *apologia pro vita sua*, written at Schönfeldz for the information of the British Consul at Teneriffe after his banishment from England in 1798, and now in the possession of the present writer), he refers to Lombardy as the ' home of his birth.' This bears out the statement of Viotti's biographers, Miel, Fétis and others, that he showed his aptitude for music at an early age, and at the age of 8 years took pleasure in playing on a small violin that had been purchased for him at a fair held at Crescentino.

When he was 11 years old, a roving lute-player named Giovannini, who was a good all-round musician, established himself at Fontanetto, and from him the boy received instruction. Unfortunately, this Giovannini was called away at the end of a year's residence in Fontanetto, to take up a professorship at the Ivrée Academy of Music. In the MS. autobiography (to which we shall have frequent recourse for the purposes of this article) Viotti makes no mention of any of his masters, but he confirms the statement that in 1766 he went to Turin for his studies and lodged at the house of the Prince of Cisterna. This happy aid to the development of Viotti's talent was really brought about by Francisco Rora, Bishop of Strambo, who afterwards became Bishop of Turin. The story goes that a flautist named Jean Pavia introduced the talented child to this patron, who took such a fancy to him that he gave him an introduction to the Marquis de Vogliera in Turin, who was seeking a *compagnon d'étude* for his son Alphonso del Pozzo, Prince of Cisterna, then 18 years of age. It seems that Viotti's youth went so much against him with the Prince when they met, that it was at first decided that the lad should return from whence he came. Fortunately Colognetti, a distinguished musician of the Chapel Royal, chanced to hear Viotti play a sonata of Besozzi at sight in a manner worthy of a professor. He complimented the lad, who replied simply that it was a small thing to do. This remark induced the Prince to set a difficult sonata by Ferrari before the intrepid young violinist, who executed it with such skill that Colognetti was charmed, and persuaded the Prince to reconsider his unfavourable decision. He lodged Viotti in his palace, sent him to study with Pugnani, who was then in his prime, and, according to Viotti's own statement, paid for 'an education that cost twenty thousand francs before it was completed.' No one knows who taught Viotti composition, but at the age of 14, whether with or without theoretical knowledge, he wrote his first concerto for the violin ; the one in A minor, now published as No. 3. As soon as Viotti was sufficiently advanced to be heard in public Pugnani showed his affection for his pupil by taking him on tour with him. In his Autobiography Viotti himself makes no mention of his master being with him on this early tour. According to his own account the first place he visited was Geneva, in 1780. 'The encouragement I received,' says he,

'made me resolve to pursue my route. Already a little celebrity had preceded me at Berne ; I did not retard my arrival there. I was received with all the kindness that I could desire, and the love of voyaging grew more and more upon me.'

It is of the period of this Geneva visit that most biographers recount the doubtful anecdote of Voltaire and Viotti. It seems that Voltaire, on hearing Viotti and Pugnani play together, was so struck with the contrast the elegant young man made standing by his grotesque-looking master (Pugnani had a huge nose, and was of an ungainly habit), that he purposely mistook the pupil for the teacher and addressed all his eulogies to the former, calling him 'célèbre Pugnani.' From Switzerland Viotti states that he went to Dresden, where he was presented to the Elector, and thence to Berlin. Frederick the Great honoured Viotti with a hearing, and himself frequently played in concerted music with the violinist. In the same year (1780) Viotti left Germany and arrived at Warsaw, loaded with letters of introduction, and from thence to St. Petersburg, where the Prince Potemkin presented him to the Empress Catherine. About 1781 Viotti states that he left Russia, and after again visiting some of the northern cities, where he had been successful, he finally arrived in Paris, where he intended to pass a few months to allow himself to be heard in that great city. 'I delayed my departure from month to month, and year to year, and remained ten years.' He was first heard in Paris at a small private concert, and those who were present placed his playing above anything they had previously heard. It was on Mar. 15, 1782, that Viotti made his public début in the French capital at the Concert Spirituel. 'A true execution, a precise finish and an admirable quality of tone in the Adagio, have placed this artist amongst the greatest masters,' says the writer of the *Mémoires secrets pour servir à l'Histoire de la République*, under the date Mar. 13, 1782. On Mar. 24 the same authority announces that 'Viotti in a concerto on Sunday sustained the high reputation he had previously acquired in France.' According to an anecdote quoted in Ginguené's *Notice sur Piccini* (Paris, 1800, p. 144), Viotti was at one time leader of Prince Guémenée's band, and later 1st violin in the band of the Prince de Soubise. On Apr. 29, 1783, Viotti had a benefit concert at which he was assisted by Mlle. Buret and Mons. Legros. Madame Mara was announced to sing, but it is said that being jealous of the success Viotti had previously gained at her own benefit, she refused to appear at the last moment. In the following year (1783) Viotti's reputation as the greatest violinist of his day in France was firmly established. The *Mercure de France* became entirely convinced of the value of the artist, and records with unstinting praise how Viotti was received 'with triumphs of delight.' Yet the highest fee he received was 100 francs per concert, a sum that appears still more ridiculously small when contrasted with the 15,000 francs that Paganini was paid for each appearance but twenty years or so later. Curiously enough, Viotti, in the midst of adulation and success, suddenly ceased to appear at the Concert Spirituel. The precise reasons that decided Viotti to take this step have never been really discovered. Eymar (author of *Anecdotes sur Viotti*), who was his contemporary, and witnessed his triumphs, says that Viotti disdained public applause on account of its indiscriminate character. He refused the solicitations of people who moved in the highest society, and who wished to hear him, because he found so few among them who could see anything deeper than an artist's superficial qualities. Miel [1] says that Viotti's retirement was caused by the appearance of an inferior violinist who was applauded while Viotti was neglected. But this seems a doubtful solution of the mystery, as Pougin, after diligent research, has failed to find any account of this supposed rival. It was in 1784 that Marie Antoinette requested Viotti to play to her, 'and when I had determined,' says Viotti,

'to play no longer in public, and consecrate myself entirely to the service of this Sovereign, she in recompense obtained for me, during the time that Mons. de Calonne was Minister, a pension of 150 pounds sterling, though I had given up playing for some time.'

This consecration of his service to the Queen may perhaps explain Viotti's true motive in relinquishing his public appearances; in any case, it is certain that Viotti was very proud of his own talents, and much sickened by the artistic and social superficiality by which he was surrounded. But, for those who understood and loved true art, he was ever ready to play. When he was living with his great friend Cherubini, in 1785, at No. 8 Rue de la Michodière, all the musicians and violinists in Paris went to the musical auditions which were held at his house entirely on their behalf. In 1787 Viotti's 'Symphonies concertantes' for two violins were performed at the Concert Spirituel by his friends, Guerillot and Imbault, amidst great enthusiasm, and on Dec. 24 of the same year, his concerto for piano was played at these concerts by Mlle. Davion.

Although Viotti gave up his concert appearances, his name was ever before the public as an active factor in the world of music. In 1788 he was induced to join the Gascon, Léonard—Queen Marie Antoinette's skilful hairdresser, whose real name was Autier—in the management of the Théâtre de Monsieur, patronised by Monsieur le Comte de Provence, the King's brother. It was then ten years since Italian opera had been heard in Paris. Viotti with his high art ideals immediately conceived the plan of organising a superlative company of artists. Many celebrated names figured on the opera programmes, and the venture might have proved a success if it had not been for the Revolution. He writes:

'Having placed almost all I possessed in an enterprise for an Italian Theatre, what terrible fears assailed me at the approach of the terrible flood; what cares I had, and what arrangements I had to enter into before I could pull myself out of the difficulty.'

Yet in spite of the ominous atmosphere around

[1] Bio. Michaud.

him Viotti refused to emigrate as others were doing, because he considered that

'A man should die at his post; for good sense always taught me that if honest men quitted their posts, the wicked gained an immense triumph.'

He donned the uniform of the National Guard, and followed the fortunes of the Théâtre de Monsieur, until 1791, when it was removed to the Rue Feydeau.

At last, on the eve of the arrest of the King and Queen, Viotti left Paris, and arrived in London on July 21 or 22, 1792. A year later, in July 1793, he revisited his native country on the death of his mother, so as to put in order his own affairs and those of his brothers, who were still children, and then turned his face towards Switzerland, Germany and Flanders, arriving in London once more at the end of December, firmly resolved never to leave it again. The decision against playing in public, to which Viotti had previously adhered so strictly, was broken in London. He was heard at nearly all Salomon's concerts in 1794 and in 1795, and began to take part in the direction of the King's Theatre, where Italian opera was being played; in addition, he came under the most beneficial influence that ever affected his life, the sincere friendship of Mr. and Mrs. Chinnery. On the retirement of Cramer, Viotti succeeded him as leader at the King's Theatre, and life for a few years flowed peacefully and evenly with the great violinist until 1798, when the King's officers informed him one evening, as he sat with his cherished friends, that he must at once leave England. He had fallen under suspicion of being in league with some of the Revolutionary leaders in Paris. He was accused of encouraging hostile schemes against the Directory, and was even publicly charged with using 'heinous and sanguinary expressions against the King.' No accusation could have been more ill-founded or unjust. The general trend of Viotti's life and habits gave the most unequivocal contradiction to his accusers. In reality the suspicions of his enemies rested on some letters Viotti had written to France 'in innocence, and freedom from any thought of harm.' He was compelled to leave England and remain in obscurity at a small place near Hamburg, named Schönfeldz, for nearly three years. During this period of enforced loneliness he spent much time in composition, wrote many letters to Mrs. Chinnery and her children, many of which are in the possession of the writer, and composed small pianoforte pieces for her daughter Caroline Chinnery. One of the great pleasures he had while in exile was in teaching the young violinist François Guillaume Pixis, who came and resided near him, entreating him to complete his education.

At length, in 1801, Viotti was allowed to

return to England, where he found himself once again surrounded by friends. There is a certain amount of obscurity enveloping Viotti's doings at this period. He seems to have found difficulty in taking up his former position as an artist, and consequently, on the recommendation of Mrs. Chinnery, established himself as a wine merchant, a business in which he lost heavily. In 1802 Viotti revisited Paris, and allowed his fellow-artists there to hear the latest duos and trios he had written at Schönfeldz. Baillot, who heard him, speaks of him in terms of generous admiration, saying expressively that he had ' un archet de coton, dirigé par le bras de Hercule.' Before the end of the same year Viotti was back in London among his friends, and it was in the following year (1803) that Mme. Lebrun mentions in her *Mémoires* the delight she had experienced during a visit to Gilwell, in hearing the beautiful Mrs. Chinnery and Viotti play. It was at this time that she painted the celebrated portrait of Viotti now in the possession of the Greene family, who are descended from Mrs. Chinnery. From 1803, and many years following, Viotti's ever-increasing financial difficulties, in which his wine business had involved him, seem to have drawn him farther and farther away from his public career. In 1813 he, however, began to identify himself with musical enterprise once again. He was then living at 10 Charles Street, Mortimer Square,[1] and with all his fine instinct for the greatest aim in art, he took an active interest in the formation of the Philharmonic Society, which gave its first concert on Mar. 8, 1813. Viotti took a modest part in the orchestra (Salomon was leader), but that did not prevent him from conducting occasionally, and giving a quartet of his own composition at one of the concerts of the first year.

Still, his love of travel caused him to take frequent journeys to Paris. In 1814 he paid a visit there which was so hasty that the members of the Conservatoire never knew he was in the city until just upon the eve of his departure, yet, in spite of the short space of time left, Viotti's passionate admirer, Baillot, assembled a number of artists to hear his idol. Viotti appeared among the great musicians of the day ' like a father among his children.' At the end of a scene of great enthusiasm the climax was reached when Viotti embraced his close friend Cherubini before the assemblage. Four years later, at the moment when he was doubtless completely ruined by his unfortunate commercial enterprise, he grew anxious to remedy his fortunes in Paris, the scene of his former triumphs. Again he was the recipient of a touching artistic reception organised by Baillot, who states that Viotti's playing reduced many

of those present to tears. Aided by his old patron the Comte de Provence, who had mounted the throne of France as Louis XVIII., Viotti was at length appointed Director of the opera, but misfortune still dogged his efforts. A year after his nomination, the opera-house became the scene of the assassination of the King's nephew, the Duc de Berry, on Feb. 13, 1820, and in consequence closed its doors to a public that ever after shunned the ill-starred building. Consequently, Italian opera was forced to find a new home at the Théâtre Favart, and, as these premises proved unsatisfactory, changed its quarters again to the Théâtre Louvois. All these changes were a most serious misfortune to the manager, whose financial position, according to a letter written by Viotti to the Baron de Ferté, was far from satisfactory. In this letter, dated Jan. 27, 1821, poor Viotti pleads for some furniture to be sent him as—after an absence of twenty-nine years—he finds himself without household effects, and without the means of obtaining any. Viotti's connexion with the opera was a period of disenchantment and mortification. All Viotti's great gifts were powerless against the blows of adverse fate. At last, in the spring of 1822, Viotti, worn out with the failure of his theatrical enterprises, returned to London. His health began to fail seriously. Year by year he grew feebler, until at last he fell into a decline and died on Mar. 3, 1824, at Mrs. Caroline Chinnery's house, No. 5 Berkeley Street, Portman Square, at 7 o'clock in the morning.[2] A great deal of painstaking research has failed to elucidate the mystery of his burial-place, but it is believed to have been St. Pancras cemetery. In Viotti's will (now in the possession of the present writer) dated Paris, Mar. 13, 1822, the story of his losses is pathetically unfolded. In it he states that he dies without fortune. He dedicates his last wishes to his friends Gustave Gasslar, living at 17 Boulevard Poissonnière ; and Guillaume Chinnery, living at Havre, and in default of him to George Fobert Chinnery. He cries out that his soul is torn to pieces in the agony of feeling that he dies in debt to Madame Chinnery *née* Tresilian, to the amount of twenty-four thousand francs, which she lent him to assist him in his wine business.

' If I die before I can pay off this debt, I pray that everything I have in the world may be sold off, realised, and sent to Madame Chinnery, or her heirs, praying only that they shall pay to my brother, André Viotti, the sum of 800 francs, that I owe him.'

He desired that his friends should reserve nothing for his burial ; ' a little earth will suffice for such a miserable creature as myself.' He mentions two manuscript concertos among his belongings, and two violins; a 'Clotz' belonging to Mrs. Chinnery, and a Stradivarius,[3] which

---

[1] *Vide* seven letters from H.R.H. Adolphus Frederick, Duke of Cambridge, to Viotti, in the possession of the present writer.

[2] *Vide Viotti*, by Van der Straeten, in *Die Musik*, June 1902.

[3] An interesting account of Viotti's most celebrated instrument, a superb Stradivarius (but whether the one referred to in his will we do not know), now in the possession of W. E. Hill & Sons, is to be found in their monumental work upon Stradivari.

he considered should realise a large sum. Two gold snuff-boxes, and a gold watch—all of which are bequeathed to Mrs. Chinnery—complete his list of valuable possessions.

Physically and mentally, nature was bountiful to Viotti. His head was grand and powerful, his face—though lacking in perfect regularity of feature—was expressive, amiable and radiant; his figure was well-proportioned and graceful, his manners were distinguished, his conversation animated and polished, and he had a wonderful knack of telling a story so that the incident lived again in the telling. In spite of the decadent atmosphere in which he lived at the court of France, Viotti never lost his fresh kindliness, or frank fearlessness of disposition.

As a violinist, Viotti was undoubtedly not only the greatest classical player of his day, but the founder and originator of the modern school of classical violin-playing. Pugnani instilled into his pupil the traditions of the grand Italian school founded by Corelli, but, outside of his teaching, the classic style was inbred in Viotti. He played with a simple dignity that commanded instant attention. There was something so grand, so inspiring, in his playing, says Miel, that even the cleverest artists shrank in his presence, and became mediocre. The same nobility reveals itself in Viotti's compositions, which, if they lack striking originality, are filled with the dignity of fine ideals; in them he shows how thoroughly Tartini's maxim, *Per ben suonare, bisogna ben cantare*, appealed to him. Finally, Viotti was one of the first to compose violin concertos that drew fully upon the resources of the accompanying orchestra. The following were among his pupils: Rode, Pixis, Alday, Vacher, Cartier, Labarre, Libon, Mori, Pinto and Roberrechts.

COMPOSITIONS.—Twenty-nine concertos for violin and orchestra. Two sets of six Sonatas for violin and piano; two *Symphonies Concertantes* for two principal violins, two violins, alto, bass, horn and hautbois *ad lib.*; three *Divertissemens*, for violin alone, dedicated to his friend L. Duport; three popular airs for violin and piano, *Les Trois Fermiers, Au bord d'une fontaine,* and *Marlbrough*; Four books, each containing six duos for two violins; Ten books, each containing three duos for two violins. Six Serenades for two violins. One book containing six trios for two violins and bass. Ten books of three trios for two violins and bass. Seven books of string quartets. A set of six string quartets founded on popular airs. Ten concertos for the pianoforte. Three books containing three sonatas each for the pianoforte. Three Divertissemens for the violoncello with pianoforte accompaniment. Three duos for two violoncellos (transcription of violin duets, op. 6). Two books of duos for two violoncellos. Songs: *La Polacca de Viotti. Air de la Casa Rara,* with accompaniment for pianoforte or harp. (This was sung in Martini's Opera of that name at the Théâtre Feydeau, 1791.) *Air de la Parisienne en Espagne* (this, according to M. Pougin, was another air of Viotti's that was inserted in a dramatic composition of that name).

BIBLIOGRAPHY.—MSS. Documents relating to Viotti in the author's possession: *Précis de la Vie de J. B. Viotti, depuis son entrée dans le monde jusqu'au 6 mars, 1798.* Donné à Hambourg à Mons. Coleman Macgregor, Consul Britannique à Ténériffe. Viotti's will, dated Paris, Dec. 13, 1822. Letters from Viotti to Miss Caroline Chinnery, Walter Chinnery, Monsieur le Baron de Ferté, and Mons. L. Jadin. The description by himself of the origin of the 'Ranz des Vaches' written out by him for Mrs. Chinnery. Seven letters from H.R.H. Adolphus Frederick, Duke of Cambridge, to Viotti.

PUBLISHED AUTHORITIES.—EYMAR, *Anecdotes sur Viotti*; FAYOLLE, *Notice sur Tartini, etc.*: BERTOLOTTI, *Gaetano Pugnani*; DELDEVEZ, *La Société des concerts du Conservatoire*; *Mémoire à consulter et consultation pour le Sieur Martin . . . contre le Sieur Léonard, Chaillot des Arènes et Viotti. Observations désintéressées sur l'administration du Théâtre Royal Italien adressés à M. Viotti*; BAILLOT, *Notice sur J. B. Viotti*; MIEL, *Notice historique sur J. B. Viotti* (taken from the *Biographie Universelle*, Michaud); VIOTTI, *Mémoire au Roi, concernant l'exposition du privilège de l'Opéra*; CONSOLO, *Accademia del R. Instituto Musicale di Firenze*; ESCUDIER, *Vie et Aventures des Cantatrices Célèbres* (pp. 63-7, Viotti à Londres);

MONTROND, *Les Musiciens les plus célèbres*; HOGARTH, *Musical History*; PARKE, *Musical Memoirs*; ESCUDIER, *Un Musicien en vacances*: POUGIN, *Viotti et l'école moderne*; *The English Cyclopædia* (edited by Charles Knight); GINGUENÉ, *Notice sur Piccini*; *The Harmonicon*, vol. ii. p. 33 . . . 1824. *Musical Standard, Viotti and the Italian School of Violin-playing*, vol. xxxiii. New Series, 1889. *The Quarterly Musical Magazine and Review*, London, 1819, No. 5, p. 52; *Memoir of Viotti: Leipziger Tageblatt und Anzeiger,* No. 106, Apr. 16, 1890. *Ein Geigen Solo.*

PORTRAITS OF VIOTTI.—A portrait of Viotti painted by Trossarelli in London and engraved by Meyer is considered by Miel to be the best likeness. This was also lithographed by Peyre and published in 1843 by Mme. Veuve Lanner. A portrait by Mme. Lebrun. A portrait of Viotti engraved by Lambert from the original of P. Guérin which formerly belonged to M. Cartier faces the title-page of Fayolle's *Notices sur Tartini*, and a bust portrait lithographed by Maurin appeared in the *Galerie des Musiciens célèbres*, published by Fétis. An excellent portrait faces the six duos concertants pour deux violins, composed by Viotti, and dedicated to Mr. and Madame Chinnery, written and published during his exile. The sculptor Flatters executed a bust of Viotti in 1813. The writer possesses a series of seven small portraits of Viotti, sent to him by Mr. Julian Marshall, drawn from life by a member of his orchestra in Paris.　　　　　　　　　　　　　　　E. H.-A.

VIRCHI, PAOLO (*b.* Brescia; *d.* ? Mantua, *c.* 1610), organist at Brescia, 1570; at the courts of Modena and Ferrara from about 1584–1591, and finally at Mantua, where he was appointed to the church of S. Barbara. He was also a famous chitarrone player, for which instrument he wrote a book of ricercari, madrigali, etc., in tablature (1584), and composed 2 books of madrigals 5 v. (1584, 1588), and 1 book of madrigals 6 v. (1591).

VIRDUNG, SEBASTIAN, author of the oldest work describing the precursors of modern musical instruments. It is entitled

'Musica getutscht und auszgezogen durch Sebastianum Virdung Priesters von Amberg und alles gesang ausz den noten in die tabulaturen diser benanten dryer Instrumenten der Orgeln: der Lauten: und den Flöten transferieren zu lernen. Kurtzlich gemacht zu eren dem hochwirdigen hoch gebornen fürsten unnd herren: herr Wilhalmen Bischove zum Strazzburg seynem gnedigen herren.'

We read in the dedication that the Bishop in 1510 had required of Virdung that he should send to him the 'Gedicht der deutschen Musica.' Virdung replied that on account of the great cost he had decided to postpone printing the great work, but to pacify the Bishop and his own friend Andreas Sylvanus, he sends this present extract, in which the latter appears as the interlocutor. The place of publication is Basle; the date 1511. The work, which is written in dialogue, begins with a description of the keyboard instruments; then follow the others in use at the time. He describes the keyboard, the organ and clavichord, concluding with the tablature of those instruments and of the lute and flute.

The woodcuts, taken in their order, will best briefly indicate the nature of the book. The clavicordium is the clavichord 'gebunden,' or fretted, as is obvious from the twisted keys, and he explains this peculiarity in the text. It shows its monochord origin by the strings being all of the same length. The sound-board is very narrow. The virginal is an instrument of the same oblong form, but has a triangular scale of stringing, by an error of the engraver turned the wrong way (an error repeated by Agricola, Luscinius and Rimbault). The sound-board, psaltery-wise, covers the interior. The compass of keyboard of both these instruments is three octaves and a note from the bass clef-note f to g''', the lowest $f\sharp$ being omitted; but

Virdung goes on to say that the compass had already, in 1511, been extended by repeating the lowest octave, that is, descending to F below the bass clef. The clavicimbalum is like the virginal, but with different compass (the organ short octave), apparently from B♮ in the bass clef to *d′′′* ; but the B, we believe, sounded G. (See SHORT OCTAVE ; SPINET ; VIRGINAL.) This is the ' clavicimbanum ' of Sagudino, on which he tells us little Mary Tudor played : the Italian *spinetta* ; French *espinette*. The claviciterium is figured as an upright virginal, with the same keyboard ; but the keyboards of all these instruments and the organs also are inverted in the printing. Virdung says it has jacks (' federkile ') like a virginal, but catgut strings. It was, he says, newly invented ; he had only seen one. This is the only early reference we have anywhere met with to the clavicytherium. Rimbault's early dates for it in his *History of Music* and the chronological order of keyboard instruments, are alike without foundation and misleading ; and further to confuse matters, he has been deceived by a blunder in Luscinius, the Latin translator (1536) of Virdung, by which the horizontal clavicimbalum appears as the claviciterium, and *vice versa*. Count Correr's interesting upright virginal, or spinetta, to be ascribed to the last years of the 15th century, shown in the Loan Collection of the International Inventions Exhibition, 1885, and now in the Victoria and Albert Museum, has Virdung's compass, but adds the bass E and F♯, which we assume to represent C and D short octave. Virdung appears to know nothing about the harpsichord or later clavicembalo, yet there is a fine and authentic specimen of this two-unisons instrument, dated 1521, of Roman make, in South Kensington Museum. Virdung's lyra is the hurdy gurdy. His lute has 11 strings, 5 pairs and chanterelle, 6 notes ; his quintern, or treble lute, 10 strings, or 5 notes. The Gross Geigen is a bass viol with the bridge omitted by the draughtsman. The Harffen is the regular mediæval David's harp, such as John Egan was still making in Dublin as a revival or fancy instrument from 1803 to 1839. The Psalterium is a triangular small harp strung across. The Hackbrett shows the common dulcimer. The ' Clein ' Geigen is a small viol ; the Trumscheit, or Tromba Marina a kind of bowed monochord. The last-named instruments being without frets Virdung regards as useless. The wind instruments follow : — Schalmey, Bombardt (oboes), Schwegel, Zwerchpfeiff (German flute), Flöten (set of flauti dolci or recorders), Ruszpfeiff, Krumhorn, Hemsen horn, Zincken (ancient cornets), Platerspil, Krumhörner (set of Cromornes, the origin of the ' Cremona ' in the modern organ), Sackpfeiff (bag - pipes), Busaun (trombone), Felttrumet (cavalry trumpet), Clareta (clarion), Thurner horn (a kind of French horn). The

organs are Orgel (with 3 divisions of pipes), Positive (a chamber organ), Regale (a reed organ) and Portative (pipe regal), with, as we have said, short-octave compass like the clavicimbalum, the keyboards being reversed in the printing. The organ and portative end at *g′* instead of *d′′′*. Lastly are Ampos, Zymeln und Glocken (anvil and various bells, Virdung appearing to believe in the anvil myth). He has trusted to his own or another's imagination in reproducing St. Jerome's instruments, only the drums and perhaps psalteries being feasible. His keyboards come next, and are evidently trustworthy. His diagram of the diatonic keyboard, with two B♭s only, agreeing with Guido's hand, is the only evidence we are acquainted with for this disposition of the clavichord with twenty natural and two raised keys, which Virdung says lasted long. The latter part of the book is occupied with the Tablatures. His lute rules meet with objections from Arnold Schlick the younger, *Tabulatur etlicher Lobgesänge* (Mentz, 1512). Mendel's *Lexicon* says that copies of Virdung's book are only to be found in the Berlin and Vienna Libraries. However, the late Alfred Littleton owned an original copy, and another is in the library of J. C. Matthew. A facsimile reproduction of 200 copies was brought out in 1882 at Berlin, edited by Robert Eitner, being the eleventh volume published for the Gesellschaft für Musikforschung, who had previously published Arnold Schlick's ' Spiegel der Orgelmacher,' also of 1511, and referred to by Virdung.

Mendel further says there are at Munich four 4-part German songs by Virdung in the rare collection of Peter Schoeffer (Mentz, 1513). They are numbered 48, 49, 52 and 54.

A. J. H.

VIRGIL PRACTICE CLAVIER, THE, an American invention, produced in a rudimentary form in 1872, under the name of ' Techniphone.' It was patented by Almon Kincaid Virgil in 1892, as the ' Practice Clavier,' and was brought to England in 1895, when the inventor gave a practical demonstration, on May 25, in the small Queen's Hall. A ' Virgil Clavier School ' was subsequently established in London at 12 Princes Street, Hanover Square. The instrument is in the form of a small piano, having nearly the full compass of the keyboard. The keys are dumb (the pressure being regulated as in the DIGITORIUM (*q.v.*)), but the special property of the contrivance is that any inequality of touch in legato playing can be easily corrected. The key can be made to produce a little ' click ' as it descends, and another ' click ' as it ascends (both sets of clicks can be used, or caused to cease, at discretion), so that a perfect legato touch can be produced by almost mechanical means, for when the click of the rising key coincides exactly with that of the falling key it is manifest that on an ordinary piano the passage from one note to the other would be perfectly smooth.   M.

VIRGINAL or VIRGINALS (Fr. *clavecin rectangulaire*). Virdung (*Musica getutscht und auszgezogen*; Basel, 1511) is the oldest authority we can cite who describes this keyboard instrument. His woodcut of it shows a rectangular or oblong spinet, which agrees in form with what we are told of the spinetta of 1503, said by Banchieri (*Conclusione nel suono dell' organo*; Bologna, 1608) to have been the invention of the Venetian Spinetti. Banchieri derives the name 'spinetta' from this maker; in later Italian the oblong SPINET (*q.v.*), which is the same as Virdung's virginal, is called 'spinetta tavola.' Virdung's virginal is, in fact, of the same shape as his clavichord, and has the same arrangement of keyboard (from the bass clef note F), but the sound-board of the clavichord is narrow; the jack-action of the virginal is derived from the psaltery plectrum, while the tangent of the clavichord comes from the monochord bridge. Virdung confesses he knows nothing of the invention of either, by whom or where. The 'proverb' quoted by Rimbault,[1] as formerly inscribed on a wall of the Manor House of Leckingfield, Yorkshire, is of the time of Henry VIII. (*c.* 1518), and contains a reference to the virginal of the period. This proverb reads :

'A slac strynge in a Virginall soundithe not aright,
  It doth abide no wrestinge it is so loose and light ;
  The sound-borde crasede, forsith the instrumente,
  Throw misgovernance, to make notes which was not
    his intente.'

According to Praetorius, who wrote early in the 17th century, virginal was then the name of the quadrangular spinet in England and in the Netherlands. In John Minshen's *Ductor in Linguas,* 1617, against 'Virginalls' we read,

'instrumentum Musicum propriè Virginum . . . so called because virgins and maidens play on them. Latin, Clavicymbalum, Cymbaleum Virginaeum.'

Other lexicographers follow. Most to the purpose is Blount, *Glossographia,* 1656 :

'Virginal (virginalis), maidenly, virginlike, hence the name of that musical instrument called Virginals, because maids and virgins do most commonly play on them.'

But another reason may be given for the name ; that keyed stringed instruments were used to accompany the hymn 'Angelus ad Virginem,' as similar instruments without keys, the psaltery, for instance, had been before them. (See Chaucer's *Miller's Tale.*) From Henry VII.'s time to nearly the close of the 17th century, 'Virginal' in England included all quilled keyboard instruments, the harpsichord and trapeze-shaped spinet, as well as the rectangular virginal of Virdung and Praetorius.

For instance, in the *Privy Purse Expenses of Henry the Eighth* [2] there is an entry :

'1530 (April) Item the vj daye paied to William Lewes for ii payer of Virginalls in one coffer with iiii stoppes, brought to Grenwiche iii *li* . . . and for a little payer of Virginalls brought to the More, etc.'

This two pair of virginals in one case with four stops looks very like a double harpsichord. Again, in the inventory [3] of the same king's musical instruments, compiled by Philip Van WILDER (*q.v.*), 'a payre of new long virginalls made harp fashion of Cipres,[4] with keys of Ivory, etc.' Still later, in 1638, from 'Original unpublished papers illustrative of the life of Sir Peter Rubens' (London, 1859), we find a correspondence between Sir F. Windebanck, private secretary to Charles I., and the painter Gerbier, relating to a Ruckers 'virginal' the latter had undertaken to procure :

'C'est une double queue ainsi nommée [*i.e.* 'virginal'] ayant quatre registres et le clavier placé au bout.'

There can be no doubt about either of these ; although called virginals, they were at the same time also harpsichords. Huyghens [5] shows how invariably the clavicimbal or espinette was 'virginal' in England. Henry VIII. played well, according to contemporary authority, on the virginal, and he had a virginal player attached to the court, one John Heywood, who died at Mechlin about 1565.[6] The same Heywood was one of Edward VI.'s *three* virginals players. Mary, Elizabeth, and James I. retained as many. Queen Mary is said to have equalled, if not surpassed, Queen Elizabeth in music, playing the regals and lute, as well as the virginals. One Cowts used to repair her virginals.[7] The first engraved music for this tribe of instruments, including harpsichords, was 'PARTHENIA, the first musicke that ever was printed for the Virginals'; London, 1611. After the restoration of the Stuarts, we find, in different publications for the harpsichord and virginal, the instruments clearly separated.

John Playford, in *Musick's Handmaid,* distinguishes them, and in 1672, *Introduction to the skill of Musick,* names Mr. Stephen Keen as a maker of 'Harpsycons and Virginals.' John Loosemore, Adam Leversidge, and Thomas White appear to have been at that time foremost English makers ; they adopted the Italian coffer-shaped instrument, combining with it Flemish fashions in painting.

---

[1] Rimbault's *History of the Pianoforte.* The house is destroyed, but the inscriptions are preserved in a MS. at the British Museum.

[2] Sir N. H. Nicholas, editor ; London, 1827.
[3] MS. in the British Museum.
[4] A fine virginal in Cipres *temp.* Henry VIII. is in the possession of Miss Margaret Glynn.   E. J. H[8].
[5] *Correspondance,* Jonkbloet et Land ; Leyden, 1882.
[6] W. H. J. Weale owns a medal struck for Michael Mercator of Venloo in 1539. An engraving of this medal is to be seen in the index to *Musical Instruments, Historic, Rare and Unique,* by A. J. Hipkins. The virginal referred to—now in the Victoria and Albert Museum—is shown in the same book. Mercator (*b.* 1491 ; *d.* 1544) was maker of virginals to Floris d'Egmont, Cardinal Wolsey, and Henry VIII.
[7] *Privy Purse Expenses of the Princess Mary,* ed. Sir F. Madden : London, 1831.

Pepys, describing (Sept. 2, 1666) the flight of the citizens at the time of the Great Fire, says :

'I observed that hardly one lighter or boat in three that had the goods of a house in, but there was a paire of virginals in it.'

The plural, or rather dual, in organs, regals, virginals, with the following 'pair,' signifies a graduation or sequence, as nowadays 'a pair of stairs.' In spite of the interesting statement of Pepys the destruction of virginals by this terrible catastrophe must have been very great, for very few musical instruments are found in this country anterior in date to the Great Fire. In Queen Anne's reign we hear no more of the virginal; the 'spinnet' is the favourite domestic instrument.

'Queen Elizabeth's Virginal,' which bears her royal arms and was the property of the Gresley family,[1] is really a pentagonal spinet, evidently of Italian make.

Notwithstanding the statement of Prætorius, we have not found the name virginal common in the Netherlands. The 'Clavecin Rectangulaire ' is ' Vierkante Clavisimbal.' The RUCKERS (q.v.), as well as other Antwerp makers, made these oblong instruments and so called them.[2]

A. J. H.

A LIST OF ENGLISH VIRGINALS OF THE 17TH CENTURY KNOWN AS STILL EXISTING (1926)

The instruments are all of rectangular coffer-shape and, except in one instance (No. 3), with domed or slightly convex lids, painted within. The case is of oak, decorated with embossed pasteboard gilt, and is one with the instrument : the sound-board generally has as sound-holes one or more ornamental 'roses ' and is painted in tempera with designs of flowers, fruits, birds, etc., after the style of the Flemish harpsichords. The fronts of the natural keys are usually gilded. In several examples the original stand of oak, on which the instrument rests, is preserved, and the brass strapwork of the hinges in the later specimens is very fine.

No.	Date.	Maker's Name.	Length and Width of Case.	Compass.	Details.	Present Owner.
1	1641	GABRIELL TOWNSEND .	5' 9¼" × 1' 9¼"	C–e''' (53 keys)	No stand : boxwood naturals, ebony sharps. Lid painting : Orpheus and the animals : bears the Plantagenet Royal Arms with E.R., having probably been made for Elizabeth, Queen of Bohemia and daughter of James I. Illustrated in the Dictionary of English Furniture (Country Life), 1927.	Conservatoire de Musique, Brussels.
2	1651	THOMAS WHITE . .	5' 6" × 1' 8"	B,–d''' (52 keys)	No stand : boxwood naturals, ebony sharps. The monograms of the clef signs are marked on the F, C and G keys : also G gamut. Short octave from G,. Lid painting : landscape with river and castle. Illustrated in Old English Instruments of Music (Galpin), 1911. (See note (a).)	The York Philosophical Society.
3	1653	THOMAS WHITE . .	5' 6" × 1' 8½"	C–e''' (49 keys)	Stand not original : boxwood naturals, brown wood sharps inlaid with ivory. Flat lid with painting : Orpheus and the animals. Over the keyboard ' Mary Byard ' a former owner's name. Exhibited at South Kensington, 1872, by the late Mr. S. H. Gell of Nottingham.	The Duke of Devonshire at Hardwick Hall.
4	1655	JOHN LOOSEMORE .	5' 8½" × 1' 8½"	C–d''' (51 keys)	Original stand : boxwood naturals, ebony sharps. Lid painting : Adam and Eve with a hunting scene and sea fight. Illustrated on PLATE LXXXIX. (See note (b).	Victoria and Albert Museum, South Kensington.
5	1656	JAMES WHITE .	5' 5¼" × 1' 8¼"	B,–c''' (50 keys)	Stand not original : boxwood naturals, light wood sharps inlaid with ivory. Short octave from G,. The embossed pasteboard has the Plantagenet Royal Arms frequently repeated in its designs. Lid painting : hunting scene. Exhibited at the Inventions Exhibition, South Kensington, 1885.	Mr. R. Temple Bourne, Clifton.
6	1664	THOMAS WHITE . .	5' 6" × 1' 9¼"	B,–f''' (55 keys)	Original stand with four turned legs : boxwood naturals, ebony sharps inlaid with ivory. Short octave from G,. Lid painting : Orpheus and the animals (see No. 3). Once the property of G. Kendrick Pyne and illustrated in the Boddington Collection Catalogue, 1888.	The Hon. F. G. Wynn, Llanwnda, North Wales.
7	1666	ADAM LEVERSIDGE .	5' 2" × 1' 8"	B,–d''' (52 keys)	Original stand with turned legs and stretchers : boxwood naturals, ebony sharps. Short octave from G,. Lid painting : The Mall, St. James's Park. Said to have belonged to Nell Gwyn. Illustrated in the Catalogue of the Musicians Company's Exhibition, Fishmonger's Hall (Novello), 1909. Former owners : Dr. Rimbault, Messrs. Chappell, W. A. F. Hill. (See note (c).)	Miss B. Skinner, Springfield, Mass., U.S.A.

(a) Rimbault (The Pianoforte, p. 397) gives the following details of this maker from the obituary of Richard Smyth (Camden Society, 1848) 1660. Janua. 5. Tho. White, virginal maker in Old Jury, buried. 1665. Septem. 2. Mary White, ye relict of Thom. White, virginall maker, my late tenant in Old Jury, buried ex peste.
From the inscription on No. 6 of the above list it is evident that the widow continued the business in her husband's name after his death, James White may have been a son or brother, but the virginal No. 5 came from Teesdale. It is possible that he succeeded Townsend (No. 1) and used his embossed pasteboard, omitting E.R.
(b) John Loosemore (1613–81) was also an eminent organ-builder : in 1665 he erected the famous organ at Exeter Cathedral. See Hopkins and Rimbault (The Organ, p. 61). A large Regal, probably by him, is figured on PLATE LXV.
(c) Adam Leversidge was a London maker as shown by the choice of his lid paintings.

---

[1] Now in Victoria and Albert Museum, South Kensington. The badge or arms of the Queen Mother (Anne Boleyn), a dove holding a sceptre, is found on the right-hand side.   E. J. H⁶.   [2] See De Liggeren der Antwerpsche Sint Lucasgilde, by Rombouts and Van Lerius. Antwerp and the Hague, 1872.

ENGLISH VIRGINAL BY JOHN LOOSEMORE, 1655
Victoria and Albert Museum, South Kensington

No.	Date.	Maker's Name.	Length and Width of Case.	Compass.	Details.	Present Owner.
8	1668	STEPHEN KEENE .	5′ 11¼″×1′ 9½″	$F_{,}$–d'' (57 keys)	No stand: dark redwood naturals, ivory sharps with ebony slip. Lowest $F_{,}$ key omitted. Lid painting: park scene with house and lake, probably St. James's Park. (See note (*d*).)	Mr. H. C. Moffatt, Goodrich Court, Ross.
9	1670	ADAM LEVERSIDGE .	5′ 7½″×1′ 9½″	$B_{,}$–f''' (55 keys)	Stand as in No. 7: boxwood naturals, ebony sharps. Short octave from $G_{,}$. Lid painting: The Mall. Illustrated in the Dictionary of English Furniture (*Country Life*), 1927.	Mr. Arthur F. Hill, London.
10	1671	PHILIP JONES . .	5′ 9″×1′ 10″	$B_{,}$–f''' (55 keys)	No stand: dark redwood naturals, ivory sharps. Short octave from $G_{,}$. Lid painting: park scene with house and lake (St. James's Park ?). Exhibited at the Inventions Exhibition, 1885, by Lord de Tabley. Illustrated in a painting by J. Fulleylove, 'A 17th Century Virginal.'	Mr. Leicester Warren, Tabley Hall, Knutsford.
11	1675	CHARLES REWALLIN .	5′ 4½″×1′ 9″	$B_{,}$–d''' (52 keys)	Original stand: boxwood naturals, black walnut sharps. Short octave from $G_{,}$. Lid painting: landscape with tower and bridge. Formerly belonged to Arthur Hull, Chard: illustrated in the *Connoisseur* 1916. (See note (*e*).)	Somerset County Museum, Taunton.
12	——	[CHARLES HAWARD ?] .	5′ 9½″×1′ 7½″	$B_{,}$–f''' (55 keys)	No stand, and name and date board missing: ebony naturals, ivory sharps: the keys alphabetically lettered in accordance with Haward's custom (see SPINET). Lid painting: a garden scene with musicians. Motto upon the jack rail, 'Musica dei donum.' (See note (*f*).)	Municipal Museum, Warrington.

(*d*) The name of Stephen Keene—possibly father and son—was prominently connected with the making of virginals and spinets from 1668–1719. Playford (*Introduction to the Skill of Music*, 1671) informs us 'Mr. Stephen Keen, maker of harpsycons and virginals, dwelleth now in Threadneedle Street at the sign of the Virginal, who maketh them exactly good, both for sound and substance.' The compass of this virginal is unusual, but the keyboard appears to be original.

(*e*) Charles Rewallin was married in Exeter Cathedral, 1657, and died in that city in 1697. See Art. G. H. St. George Gray in *The Connoisseur*, Oct. 1916.

(*f*) Charles Haward (Hayward) lived in Aldgate Street, London, and was patronised by Samuel Pepys, who bought of him a small spinet in 1668.

In addition to the names of 17th-century makers above mentioned the writer has been informed by Mr. Arthur Hill—to whom, as to his many other correspondents, he is much indebted—that in 1906 Mr. Hill inspected a coffer-shaped virginal in poor condition bearing the name Roberthus Hatley. At that time it apparently belonged to a Mr. Parkyn, a dealer in Cromer Street, Gray's Inn Road, London. About the year 1915 a similar instrument—also in poor condition—was seen at Bushey, being the property of a lady. In both cases the writer has failed to discover their present existence or ownership. In Scotland John Davidson and Alexander ADAM appear as virginal makers in 1652 and 1659: possibly their instruments were similar to those then made in England, but the name was often loosely applied to harpsichord and spinets.

F. W. G.

VIRGINAL MUSIC, COLLECTIONS OF. (1) FITZWILLIAM VIRGINAL BOOK.—The most remarkable, and in many respects the most valuable collection of English 17th-century instrumental music is that contained in the volume known in the 19th century by the misleading name of 'Queen Elizabeth's Virginal Book,' and now called the 'Fitzwilliam Virginal Book.' This book, which is preserved in the Fitzwilliam Museum at Cambridge, is a small folio volume containing 220 folios of paper ruled by hand for music in 6-line staves, 209 of which are filled with music written in a small but distinct handwriting. The volume measures $33\frac{9}{10}$ centimetres in height by 22 centimetres in breadth, and the binding (a fine specimen of English 17th-century workmanship) is of crimson morocco, enriched with beautiful gold tooling, the sides being sprinkled with fleurs-de-lis. The water-mark on the paper is a crozier-case, measuring 4½ inches in height and 2½ inches in its widest part. It is possible that this mark indicates that the paper was manufactured at Basle, as the arms of that town are similar to it. The manuscript has in places been cut by the binder, but the binding is probably not of later date than the bulk of the book. Nothing is known of the history of the volume before the early part of the 18th century, when it was first noticed as being in the possession of Dr. Pepusch, but there is sufficient evidence to prove that it can never have belonged, as was generally supposed, to Queen Elizabeth, a statement for which Hawkins seems to be responsible. The whole of the manuscript is in one handwriting; in many cases the compositions it contains bear the dates at which they were composed, and these dates (as will be seen from the list printed below) are in no sort of chronological order. The latest dated composition contained in the collection is an 'Ut, re, mi, fa, sol, la, a 4 voci,' by the Amsterdam organist Jehan Peterson Sweelinck (1562–1621), which occurs on page 216 [ii. p. 26],[1] and bears the date 1612, nine years after the death of Queen Elizabeth, to whom the book is said to have belonged. But there is another piece in the volume which was held to prove that the collection must have been written even later

[1] The references in square brackets are to the printed edition of the 'Fitzwilliam Virginal Book,' edited by J. A. Fuller Maitland and W. Barclay Squire.

than this. At page 255 [ii. p. 128] is a short
composition by Dr. John Bull, entitled ' D.
Bull's Juell ' (*i.e.* ' Dr. Bull's Jewel '). Another
setting of the same tune occurs on folio 49*b*
of a manuscript collection of Bull's instrumental music in B.M. Add. MSS. 23,623, which
is particularly valuable as containing the dates
at which most of the compositions were
written, and this copy bears the inscription
' Het Juweel van Doctor Jan Bull quod fecit
anno 1621. December.'

Chappell, at the beginning of his work on
the *Popular Music of the Olden Time*[1] (p. xv)
surmises that this collection may have been
made for, or by, an English resident in the
Netherlands, and that Dr. Pepusch obtained it
in that country. This conjecture he founds
upon the fact that the only name which occurs
in an abbreviated form throughout the book is
that of Tregian, and that a sonnet signed ' Fr.
Tregian ' is prefixed to Verstegan's *Restitution
of Decayed Intelligence*, which was published at
Antwerp in 1605. The abbreviated name
occurs as follows : at p. 111 [i. p. 226] is a composition of William Byrd's headed ' Treg.
Ground ' ; at p. 152 [i. p. 321] is a ' Pavana
Dolorosa. Treg.,' set by Peter Philips and dated
1593 ; at p. 196 [i. p. 415] is a short piece
entitled ' Heaven and Earth,' to which no composer's name is given besides the syllable ' Fre '
(possibly a contraction of ' F. Tregian ') ; and
at p. 297 [ii. p. 237] in the margin, the initials
' F. Tr.' are written against the first line of a
jig by William Byrd ; on p. 315 [ii. p. 278]
' Mrs. Katherin Tregian's Pauen ' is written in
the margin against a Pavana Chromatica by
William Tisdall. These few clues certainly
point to some connexion of the volume with
the Tregian family, and it so happens that the
history of at least two individuals of the name
of F. Tregian is known with a considerable
degree of certainty.[2]

It is now known that the connexion of the
Tregian family with the Netherlands was even
closer than Chappell suspected, but it was impossible that the Virginal book could have
been written by the elder Francis Tregian, who

(according to Oliver) was the author of the
sonnet prefixed to Verstegan's work. Whoever
the actual scribe was, the series of dated pieces
by Peter Philips (pp. 134-165 [i. 280-346]),
who was an English Catholic ecclesiastic settled
in the Netherlands, and possibly a connexion
of Morgan Philips, one of the first Professors
of the Douay College, the note (p. 284 [ii. 204])
to the Pavana of Byrd's (who was all his life a
Catholic),[3] the heading of the jig (p. 306 [ii.
257]), ' Doctor Bull's myselfe ' (Bull went to
Holland in 1613), all point to the conclusion
that the collection was formed by some one
who was intimate with the Roman Catholic
refugees of the period, while the probable connexion of the book with the Tregian family
lends to it a value beyond that of its musical
contents.

The earliest account of this collection of
virginal music occurs in the Life of Dr. John
Bull in Ward's *Lives of the Gresham Professors*
(1740), in which is printed a list of Bull's compositions contained in it. Ward states that his
information was derived from Dr. Pepusch,
who communicated the contents of the volume
to him, describing it as ' a large *folio* neatly
written, bound in red Turkey leather, and
guilt.' In this no mention is made of the book
having belonged to Queen Elizabeth. In 1762
it was bought for 10 guineas at the sale of
Dr. Pepusch's collection by R. Bremner, who
gave it to Lord Fitzwilliam, in whose possession
it was in 1783. It is next noticed in Hawkins's
History (1776), where it is first stated to have
been in Queen Elizabeth's possession. Hawkins
also tells the story (repeated by Burney) of
Pepusch's wife, Margherita de l'Épine, having
attempted to play the music it contained, but
although an excellent harpsichord player, never
having been able to master the first piece, Bull's
variations on ' Walsingham.' Burney (1789)
adds the well-known account of Elizabeth's
playing to Sir James Melvil, with the remark
that if she could execute any of the pieces in the
Virginal Book, she must have been a very great
player, as some are so difficult that it would be
hard to find a master in Europe who would play
them without a month's practice. Burney's
remarks have been repeated by several writers,
amongst others by Steevens, in his notes to
A Winter's Tale (1803), but with the exception
of Chappell's conjecture nothing further has
been discovered with regard to the origin or history of the book. A MS. index of its contents
was in the possession of Bartleman, and from
this a copy was made in 1816 by Henry Smith,

[1] The edition of this work referred to in this article is that published by Chappell & Co. in two volumes, without a date. The full
title-page runs as follows: ' The Ballad Literature and Popular
Music of the Olden Time : a History of the Ancient Songs, Ballads,
and the Dance Tunes of England, with numerous Anecdotes and
entire Ballads. Also a Short Account of the Minstrels. By W.
Chappell, F.S.A. The whole of the Airs harmonised by G. A. Macfarren.'

[2] The Tregians were a rich and powerful Roman Catholic family
whose seat was at Golden or Volveden near Trewithan in Cornwall.
The elder Francis Tregian suffered despoliation and imprisonment.
After his release he visited Douay, taking Douay on his way (1606)
and died at Lisbon, Sept. 25, 1608. The younger Francis (eldest
son) was educated at Eu and entered Douay, Sept. 29, 1586. The
story of the sufferings of the family was recorded at some length
in former editions of this Dictionary. Further information as to
the Tregian family may be found in the following works : Oliver's
Catholic Religion in Cornwall ; Polwhele's *History of Cornwall*, vols.
iv. and v. ; *Catholic Miscellany* for June 1823 ; Morris, *Troubles
of our Catholic Forefathers* (1872–77) ; Knox, *Records of the English
Catholics* (1878–82) ; Gilbert, *Historical Survey of Cornwall* (1817) ;
The Oeconomy of the Fleete (Camden Soc., 1879) : also in Add MSS.
21,203, and in the *State Papers*, particularly Domestic Series,
James I., 1619, vol. xli.. and 1620, vol. cxvi. Historical MSS.
Commission, House of Lords, Sup. Cal., Report IV. (1874), p. 120.
Ditto, Marquis of Salisbury's papers, Report VI. Appendix (1877),
p. 272a. Report VII. (1879), p. 185b.

[3] This much may be said with certainty. The question of
Byrd's religion presents difficulties only to those who do not realise
that it was possible for Englishmen, whose personal preferences
were for the old order and the Latin ritual, to serve the Church of
England loyally throughout the reigns of Elizabeth and James I.
The trivial fines incurred by Byrd and his family probably show
where their preferences lay (see vol. i. p. 511). The fact of his
holding the lease of Stonden, sequestrated on account of its owner's
complicity in a Popish plot, sufficiently attests his political loyalty,
and his continued service in the Chapel Royal shows him to have
been in communion with the national Church.   G.

and inserted at the end of the original volume. In Warren's edition of Boyce's 'Cathedral Music' (1849), a list of its contents was printed in the notes to the Life of Byrd, but this is in many respects inaccurate. In framing the following list some attempt has been made to give a few references to similar collections in which other copies of the compositions indexed may be found. The compositions mostly consist of airs and variations, the different sections of which are numbered consecutively. Thus the first piece in the book consists of twenty-nine variations on the air 'Walsingham,' but as in the MS. the air itself is numbered '1,' the number of sections is stated in the index to be thirty. The references to Chappell's work are to the edition already mentioned. The spelling of the MS. is generally retained, but in a few instances abbreviations have been omitted.

VOL. I. OF PRINTED EDITION

Page of MS.	Number.	Page of printed ed.	Description.	Composer.
1	1	1	Walsingham	Dr. Jhon Bull.[1]
10	2	19	Fantasia	John Munday.
12	3	23	Fantasia	" [2]
14	4	27	Pauana	Ferdinand Richardson.[3]
15	5	29	Variatio	"
16	6	32	Galliarda	" [4]
17	7	34	Variation	"
19	8	37	Fantasia	William Byrd.
21	9	42	'Goe from my Window'	Thomas Morley.[5]
23	10	47	'Jhon, come kiss me now'	W. Byrd.[6]
27	11	54	Galliarda to my L. Lumley's Pauen, Pag. 76	Doctor Bull.[7]
28	12	57	Nancie	T. Morley.[8]
30	13	62	Pauana	Doctor Bull.[9]
32	14	65	Alman	"
32	15	66	Robin	Jhon Munday.
33	16	68	Pauana	M. S.
34	17	70	Galiarda	Dr. Bull.[10]
35	18	72	Barafostus Dreame	[11]
37	19	74	Muscadin	[12]
37	20	75	Alman	"
38	21	77	Galliarda	[13]
39	22	80	Praeludium	"
40	23	81	Praeludium. El. Kidermister	"
41	24	83	Praeludium	[William Byrd].[14]
41	25	85	Praeludium	"
42	26	87	The Irish Ho-hoane	[15]
43	27	87	Pauana	Ferdinando Richardson.
44	28	90	Variatio	"
46	29	93	Galiada	"
47	30	95	Variatio	"

Page of MS.	Number.	Page of printed ed.	Description.	Composer.
49	31	99	The Quadran Pauen	Dr. Bull.[16]
54	32	107	Variation of the Quadran Pauen	"
59	33	117	Galiard to ye Quadran Pauan	"
63	34	124	Pauana. Do.	"
66	35	129	Galiard to the Pauen	"
67	36	131	St. Thomas Wake	" [17]
69	37	135	In Nomine	"
70	38	138	....	[18]
72	39	141	Pauana	Rob. Jhonson. Sett by Giles Farnabie.
74	40	144	The Woods so Wilde [19]	"
76	41	149	Pauana of My L. Lumley	Doctor Bull.[20]
78	42	153	'Goe from my Window'	Jhon Munday.[21]
80	43	158	Praeludium	Doctor Bull.[22]
81	44	160	Gloria Tibi Trinitas	" [23]
82	45	163	Saluator Mundi	" [24]
86	46	170	Galliarda	"
87	47	173	Variatio	"
89	48	177	Galiarda to the Pauen. Pag. 63. Dor.	"
91	49	180	Praeludium	Thomas Oldfield.[25]
91	50	181	In Nomine	William Blithman.[26]
92	51	183	Vt, re, mi, fa, sol, la	Doctor Bull.[27]
94	52	188	Fantasia	William Byrd.
98	53	196	The K(ing's) Hunt	Giles Farnabie.[28]
100	54	199	Spagnioletta	"
101	55	202	For 2 Virg.	" [29]
102	56	203	Passamezzo Pauana	W. Byrd.[30]
104	57	209	Galiardus Passamezzo	"
106	58	214	The Carman's Whistle	" [31]
108	59	218	The Hunt's Up	" [32]
111	60	226	Treg. Ground	" [33]
114	61	234	Monsieur's Alman	" [34]
116	62	238	Variatio	"
119	63	245	Alman	"
120	64	248	Sellinger's Round	" [35]
123	65	254	Fortune	" [36]
125	66	258	O Mistris myne	" [37]
127	67	263	The Woods so Wild	" 1590.[38]
129	68	267	Walsingham	" [39]
132	69	274	The Bells	"
134	70	280	(1) Tirsi di Luca Marenzio. 1a parte. Intau olata di Pietro Philippi	Peeter Philips.

1 Chappell, p. 121. Ward (*Lives of the Gresham Professors*) says, 'This tune was first composed by William Byrde with twenty-two variations; and afterwards thirty others were added to it by Dr. Bull.' Another copy is in Benjamin Cosyn's Virginal Book, p. 139. See also Forster's Virginal Book, p. 74.

2 Contains 80 bars of music descriptive of a storm. The different sections are headed, Faire Wether, Lightning, Thunder, Calme Wether, Lightning, Thunder, Faire Wether, Lightning, Thunder, Faire Wether, Lightning, Thunder, A Cleare Day. (See PROGRAMME MUSIC.)

3 A copy of this is in Add. MS. 30,485, fol. 75b.

4 Add. MS. 30,485, fol. 76b.

5 Chappell, p. 140, 142. A setting by Wm. Byrd is in B. Cosyn's Virginal Book, p. 139. See also No. 42. Another setting (by Francis Pilkington, Mus.B.) is in lute tablature in Add. MSS. 31,392, fol. 26.

6 Chappell, pp. 122, 147, 218, 660, 771.

7 Mentioned in Ward's List. A copy is in B. Cosyn's Virginal Book, p. 120.

8 Chappell, p. 149.   9 In Ward's List.

10 In Ward's List.

11 See No. 131.

12 Chappell, pp. 240, 775. *Vide infra*, p. 241.

13 *Vide infra*, p. 410.

14 This prelude is assigned to Byrd in 'Parthenia.'

15 *i.e.* 'Ochone.' Chappell, p. 793.

16 Chappell, p. 104. A different setting by Dr. Bull is in Cosyn's Virginal Book, p. 94. See also Add. MSS. 29,485, p. 34; 30,485, fol. 175; 31,392, fol. 20; and Forster's Virginal Book, pp. 96 and 202; also *infra* No. 133. This and the next seven pieces are in Ward's List.

17 Also in 'Parthenia.'

18 In Ward's List this is called 'Fantasia upon a Plain Song.'

19 Only one bar of the fifth section has been written in, the rest of the page is left blank. Chappell, p. 66. A copy of this is in Add. MSS. 31,403, which gives the name of Orlando Gibbons as the composer. See also Forster's Virginal Book, p. 118; Lady Nevell's Virginal Book, fol. 109; and Add. MSS. 30,485, fol. 67; also *infra*, No. 67.

20 Vide the Galliard to this Pauen, pag. 27 ' (note in the MS.) In Cosyn's Virginal Book, p. 15, this Pavan and its Galliard have Cosyn's initials to them. It is mentioned in Ward's List.

21 ' Vide p. 21.' This is the same composition as that on p. 21, attributed to Morley, but the copy on p. 21 wants the final section. Another setting (by Byrd) is in Forster's Book, p. 324, and in Cosyn's Book, p. 157.

22 Ward calls this ' Praeludium to Gloria Tibi Trinitas.'

23 This and the following three pieces are in Ward's List.

24 There are two similarly named compositions by Bull in Add. MSS. 23,623, fol. 19, and 31,403 respectively, but all three are different.

25 This composer is totally unknown.

26 Written on the same plain-song as In Nomines by Blytheman in Add. MSS. 31,403 and 30,485.

27 In Ward's List.

28 Chappell, p. 60. See also Cosyn's Book, p. 75.

29 A curious little piece of eight bars for two Virginals.

30 This Pavan and the following Galliard also occur in Lady Nevell's Book, fol. 92, and Will Forster's Book, p. 217. See also p. 142, No. 76.

31 This celebrated piece has been often printed. Copies of it are in Lady Nevell's Book, fol. 149, and in Add. MSS. 31,403 and 30,485, and Forster's Book, p. 130. Chappell, pp. 137-140, 428.

32 Chappell, pp. 53 60-62, 196; a copy is in Lady Nevell's Book, fol. 46. Another setting by Byrd is No. 276 (ii. 430), where it is called ' Pescodd Time.'

33 A copy of this is in Lady Nevell's Book, fol. 153b, where it is called ' Hughe Astons grownde.'

34 A different setting of this is in Forster's Book, p. 244. A different setting is in Lady Nevell's Book, fol. 173b, of which a copy is also in Forster's Virginal Book, p. 366.

35 Chappell, p. 69, where the melody is printed in Byrd's arrangement. A copy is in Lady Nevell's Book, fol. 166b.

36 Chappell, p. 162.

37 *Ibid.* p. 209.

38 A different setting from that contained in p. 74, *v. supra*. Copies in Lady Nevell's Book, fol. 109 and Add. MSS. 30,485 and 31,403. See also Will Forster's Virginal Book, p. 118.

39 See No. 1. Other copies of this setting are in Lady Nevell's Book, fol. 31, and Will Forster's Book, p. 74.

Page of MS.	Number.	Page of printed ed.	Description.	Composer
135	71	283	(2) Freno, 2ª parte .	Peeter Philips.
137	72	286	(3) Cosi Moriro, 3ª parte	"
138	73	288	(4) Fece da voi a 6 .	"
139	74	291	(5) Pauana Pagget .	"
141	75	296	(6) Galiarda .	"
142	76	299	(7) Passamezzo Pauana .	" 1592.
146	77	306	(8) Galiarda Passamezzo	" 40
148	78	312	(9) Chi fara fede al cielo di Alessandro Striggio	Peter Philips.
150	79	317	(10) Bon Jour mon Cueur di Orlando	" 1602.
152	80	321	(11) Pauana Dolorosa. Treg.	" 1593.
154	81	327	(12) Galiarda Dolorosa .	"
155	82	329	(13) Amarilli di Julio Romano 41	" 1603.
156	83	332	(14) Margotte Laborez .	" 1605.
158	84	335	(15) Fantasia . .	"
161	85	343	(16) Pauana . .	" 1580.42
162	86	346	(17) Le Rossignuol . .	" 1595.
164	87	351	(18) Galliarda . .	"
165	88	354	(19) Galliarda . .	" 1582.
167	89	357	(1) Fantasia . .	Nicholas Strogers.
168	90	359	Alman . .	Martin Peereson.
169	91	361	Pauana Bray .	W. Byrd.
170	92	365	Galiarda . .	"
171	93	367	Pauana. Ph. Tr.	"
173	94	371	Galiarda . .	"
174	95	373	Toccata . .	Giovanni Pichi.43
181	96	378	Praeludium Toccata 1	Jehan Pieterson Swellinck.
183	97	384	Pauana 1 . .	Thomas Warrock.
185	98	388	Galiarda 2 . .	"
186	99	391	Praeludium . .	Galeazzo.
186	100	394	Praeludium to ye Fancie. Pag. 94 44	Wm. Byrd.
187	101	395	Vt, re, mi, fa, sol, la .	W. Byrd.45
190	102	401	Vt, mi, re . .	"
192	103	406	Fantasia . .	"
194	104	411	All in a Garden green .	" 46
196	105	415	Heauen and Earth .	Fre.
197	106	418	Preludium . .	Dr. Bull.
198	107	421	Veni . .	"
199	108	423	Fantasia . .	Dr. Bull.47
201	109	427	Foelix Namque. 1um .	ThomasTallis,15648

VOL. II. OF PRINTED EDITION

Page of MS.	Number.	Page of printed ed.	Description.	Composer
205	110	1	Foelix Namque. 2m .	ThomasTallis,156449
209	111	12	Exercise . .	Anon.
210	112	12	Daphne. 5 . .	Giles Farnabie. 50
212	113	17	Pawles Wharfe. 6 .	Giles Farnaby.
213	114	19	Quodling's Delight. 7 .	" 51
214	115	22	Praeludium . .	Dr. Bull.52
215	116	23	Praeludium Dor. .	" 53
215	117	25	Praludium . .	"
216	118	26	Vt, re, mi, fa, sol, la, a 4 voci. 2	Jehan Peterson Swelling, 1612.
219	119	34	In Nomine . .	Dr. Bull.
221	120	40	Praeludium . .	"
222	121	42	Pauana Lachrymae .	John Dowland, sett foorth by Wm. Byrd.54
223	122	47	Galiarda . .	James Harding, sett foorth by Wm. Byrd.55

Page of MS.	Number.	Page of printed ed.	Description.	Composer.
225	123	51	Pauana. 1 . .	Thomas Tomkins.
227	124	57	Fantasia . .	Thomas Morley.
229	125	64	Christe Redemptor .	Dr. Bull.56
231	126	67	The Mayden's Song .	Wm. Byrd.57
233	127	72	Putt vp thy dagger Jemy. 8	Giles Farnaby
235	128	77	Bony Sweet Robin. 9 .	" 58
237	129	82	Fantasia. 10 . .	"
239	130	87	A Grounde. 2 . .	Thomas Tomkins.
241	131	94	Barafostus Dreame. 3 .	" 59
244	132	100	The Hunting Galliard. 4	"
245	133	103	Quadran Pauen . .	Wm. Byrd.60
248	134	111	Galiard to the Quadran Pauen	" 61
250	135	116	The King's Hunt .	Dr. Bull.62
252	136	121	Pauana . .	"
254	137	125	Galiarda . .	"
255	138	128	D. Bull's Juell .	" 63
256	139	131	The Spanish Pauen .	" 64
257	140	135	In Nomine. 1 .	Persons.65
259	141	138	Woondy-Cock. 11 .	Giles Farnaby.66
262	142	146	The Duke of Brunswick's Alman	Dr. Bull.67
262	143	148	Rosasolis. 12 .	Giles Farnaby.68
264	144	151	Psalme. 3. . .	Jehan Pieterson Swelling.
266	145	158	Alman . .	Robert Johnson.
267	146	159	Alman. 2 . .	"
267	147	160	Alman. 2 . .	R. Johnson. Sett by Giles Farnaby.
267	148	161	The New Sa-hoo.69 13	Giles Farnaby.
268	149	162	Nobodyes Gigge. 1 .	Richard Farnaby, sonne to Giles Farnaby.
269	150	166	Malt's come downe .	William Byrd.70
270	151	169	Praeludium . .	"
271	152	171	Alman . .	Thomas Morley
272	153	173	Pauana . .	"
274	154	177	Galiarda . .	"
275	155	180	La Volta . .	William Byrd.71
276	156	182	Alman . .	Wm. Byrd.
276	157	184	Wolsey's Wilde .	" 72
277	158	186	Callino Casturame .	W. Byrd.73
278	159	188	La Volta. T. Morley	"
278	160	190	Rowland . .	" 74
279	161	192	Why aske you 75 .	"
280	162	193	The Ghost . .	Byrd.
281	163	196	Alman . .	"
281	164	198	Galliard . .	"
282	165	200	Pauana . .	"
283	166	202	Galiarda . .	"
284	167	204	Pauana . .	" 76
285	168	207	Galiarda . .	W. Byrd.
286	169	209	Pauana . .	Thomas Morley.
288	170	213	Galliarda . .	"
289	171*	217	The Queenes Alman .	Wm. Byrd.
291	172	220	A Medley . .	"
293	173	226	Pauana . .	"
294	174	228	Galliarda . .	"

* The numbers from * to * are wrongly noted in the printed edition. There is there no number 171, and two numbers 182.

40 See vol. iii. p. 664.   41 i.e. Caccini.

42 In the margin is the following note (part of which has been cut by the binder) : ' The first one Philips made.'

43 Part of p. 176, and pp. 177, 178, 179, and 180 are blank. The numeration of the pieces leaves off here.

44 i.e. No. 52.

45 This piece consists of seventeen quite short sections. At the foot of p. 189 is written ' Perge.'

46 Chappell, p. 110. Occurs in Lady Nevill's Book, fol. 142b.

47 In Ward's List.

48 In Add. MSS. 30,485, a collection of Virginal Music headed ' Extracts from Lady Nevil's Music Book,' but containing much besides, is a ' Felix Namque ' by Tallis, against which (in a later hand) is written ' 1562. In the Virginal Book,' but this is a different composition from either this or the following.

49 A copy of this, entitled ' Felix Numquam,' is in Forster's Virginal Book (p. 24) with no composer's name to it. Another ' Felix Namque ' is in Benjamin Cosyn's Book (p. 150); this is different from any of the above, bringing up the number of Tallis's settings to four. (See ante, p. 13a.)

50 No. 4 of Giles Farnaby's ' Canzonets to Foure Voyces ' (1598) is ' Daphne on the Rainebow.'   51 Chappell, pp. 456, 782, 794.

52 In Ward's List.   53 Ibid.

54 Add. MSS. 31,392 (fol. 35) has ' Dowland's Lachrymae ' in lute tablature. The tune is to be found in nearly every Elizabethan collection, and is frequently alluded to by writers. It occurs at fol. 71a of Add. MS. 30,485, and a setting by Cosyn is in his Virginal Book, p 8. See Chappell, p. 92, and infra. Morley's setting is No. 153, and Farnaby's is No. 290.

55 Occurs as ' Hardings Galiard,' without Byrd's name in Forster's Book, p. 380. Two fancies by James Harding are in Add. MSS. 30,485, ff. 47 and 50.

56 In Ward's List.

57 Occurs at fol. 113a of Lady Nevill's Book. A copy is in Add. MS. 31,403.

58 Chappell, p. 233. In Add. MSS. 23,623 is (fol. 13b) ' Bonn well Robin van Doct. Jan Bull,' dated Jan. 18, 1627. A setting by Munday is No. 15.

59 Vide supra, No. 35 ; this is a different setting.

60 Vide supra, No. 31. A copy is in Forster's Book, p. 288.

61 A copy is in Forster's Book, p. 302.

62 This and the following four pieces are in Ward's List.

63 This occurs in Add. MSS. 23,623 (fol. 49b), where it is entitled ' Het Juweel van Doctor Jan Bull quod fecit anno 1621. December.' Ward, who prepared a list of the contents of this MS., inserts the date ' 12,' before the name of the month. A slightly different version occurs at p. 124 of Cosyn's Virginal Book.

64 Chappell, pp. 240, 776.

65 ' Parsons.' In Nomine by Byrd in Forster's Book, 46.

66 Chappell, p. 793.

67 In Ward's List.

68 At fol. 17b of Add. MSS. 23,623 is a different setting of this air entitled ' Rose a solis van Joan (sic) Bull Doct.' The sections of this piece are termed ' variations.'

69 The theme of this occurs in Hilton's ' Catch that catch can,' as a catch ' Slaves to the World,' ascribed to Edmund Nelham.

70 Chappell, p. 74.

71 Occurs under the name ' Leualto ' at p. 20 of Forster's Virginal Book.

72 Chappell, p. 86. See Forster's Book (p. 70).

73 Chappell, p. 793. This tune, the Irish origin of which is denoted by its name (' Colleen oge asthore '), is referred to in Shakespeare's Henry V. Another copy is at fol. 96b of Add. MSS. 30,485.

74 Chappell, pp. 114 and 770. Occurs under the name ' Lord Willobies welcome home,' at fol. 46b of Lady Nevill's Virginal Book and at p. 22 of Forster's Book. Against the bass line is written in the margin ' 300 to S. T. by Tom.'

75 Vide infra, No. 286.

76 In the margin is written ' the first t(hat) euer hee m(ade).' The letters in brackets have been cut by the binder.

Page of MS.	Number.	Page of printed ed.	Description.	Composer.
294	175	230	Miserere, 3 Parts	Wm. Byrd.
295	176	232	Miserere, 4 Parts	"
296	177	234	Pakington's Pownde 77	
297	178	236	The Irishe Dumpe 78	
297	179	236	Watkins Ale 79	
297	180	237	A Gigg	W. Byrd.80
298	181*	238	Pipers Pauen	Martin Peerson.
299	182	242	Pipers Galliard	Dr. Bull.81
300	183	244	Variatio eiusdem	"
302	184	248	Praeludium. D.	"
303	185	249	Galliarda	"
304	186	251	Galiarda	"
305	187	253	Allemanda	Marchant.
306	188	256	Can shee	"
306	189	257	A Gigge. Dr. Bulls my-selfe	Dr. Bull.83
306	190	258	A Gigge	"
307	191	258	Sr Jhon Grayes Galiard	W. B.83
307	192	259	Praeludium	Dr. Bull.84
307	193	260	A Toy 85	"
308	194	260	Giles Farnaby's Dreame.	Giles Farnaby.
308	195	261	His Rest. Gallard	Giles Farnabie.
308	196	262	His Humour	Giles Farnaby.
309	197	263	Fayne would I wedd	Richard Farnabye
309	198	264	A Maske	Giles Farnabye.
310	199	265	A Maske	"
310	200	266	An Almain	
310	201	266	Corranto	
310	202	266	Alman	
311	203	267	Corranto	
311	204	267	Corranto 86	
311	205	268	Corranto	
311	206	268	Daunce 87	
312	207	269	Worster Braules	Thomas Tomkins.
312	208	270	Fantasia	Giles Farnabye.88
313	209	273	A Maske	"
314	210	274	Praeludium	Dr. Bull.89
314	211	274	....	"
314	212	275	Martin sayd to his man 90	"
315	213	276	Almand	William Tisdall.
315	214	278	Pauana Chromatica	91
317	215	281	Vt, re, mi, fa, sol, la	Dr. Bull.92
321	216	292	Gipseis Round	Wm. Byrd.93
324	217	297	Fantasia. 4	Jhon Pieterson Sweeling, Organista a Amstelreda94
327	218	305	Corranto	William Byrd sett.94
328	219	306	Pauana. Clement Cottō. 3	Wm. Tisdall.
328	220	307	Pauana. 4	"
329	221	308	Corranto	
329	222	309	Alman	Hooper.
329	223	309	Corranto	
329	224	310	Corranto	
330	225	310	Corranto	
330	226	311	Corranto	
330	227	312	Alman	
331	228	312	Corranto	Hooper.
331	229	313	Fantasia. 20	Giles Farnaby.
333	230	317	Loth to depart. 21	Giles Farnaby.95
334	231	320	Fantasia. 22	"
335	232	323	" 23	"
335	233	330	" 24	"
340	234	333	" 25	"
341	235	336	Walter Earle's Pauen. 26	"
343	236	340	Fantasia. 27	"
344	237	343	" 28	"
346	238	347	" 29	"
347	239	350	L. Zouches Maske. 30	"
349	240	353	A Grounde. 31	"
351	241	359	Corranto	W. Byrd.
352	242	360	Vp T(ails) All. 32	Giles Farnaby.96
355	243	366	Thomson's Medley	Edward Jhonson.
356	244	369	Nowel's Galliard	"
357	245	371	Tower Hill	Giles Farnaby.
358	246	372	Praeludium. 33	"
358	247	373	The King's Morisco	"
359	248	374	A Duo	Richard Farnaby.
359	249	375	Alman	"
359	250	375	A Galliard Ground. 1	William Inglot.
362	251	381	The Leaues bee greene. 2	"

Page of MS.	Number.	Page of printed ed.	Description.	Composer.
364	252	384	Pauana	W. Byrd.
365	253	387	Galiarda	"
366	254	389	Pauana	"
367	255	392	Galiarda	"
368	256	394	Pauana	"
370	257	398	Pauana Fant(asia)	"
370	258	400	Galiarda	"
371	259	402	The Earle of Oxford's Marche	" 97
373	260	405	Gallarda	Jehan Oystermayre.
374	261	406	Fantasia	W. Byrd.98
377	262	412	The Duchesse of Brunswick's Toye	Dr. Bull.99
377	263	413	A Toye	
378	264	414	Corranto	
378	265	414	Corranto Lady Riche	
378	266	415	Corranto	
379	267	416	A Gigge	Giles Farnaby.
379	268	418	A Toye	
380	269	419	Galiarda	
381	270	421	A Toye	
381	271	422	The Primerose	Martin Peerson.
382	272	423	The Fall of the Leafe	Martin Peereson.
383	273	424	Farnaby's Conceit	Giles Farnabye.
383	274	424	Allemanda	"
384	275	427	Pauana. Canon. 2 parts in one	Wm. Byrd.
385	276	430	Pescodd Time	" 100
388	277	436	Pauana Delight	Edward Johnson. Sett by Will.Byrd.
390	278	440	Galiarda	Ed. Johnson. Sett by William Byrd.
391	279	442	Miserere, 3 parts	Dr. Bull.101
393	280	446	Tell mee, Daphne	Giles Farnaby.102
394	281	447	Mal Sims	103
395	282	449	Munday's Gioy	Munday.
396	283	450	Rosseter's Galiard	Sett by Giles Farnaby.104
397	284	453	The Flatt Pauan	Giles Farnaby.
398	285	456	Pauana	" 105
401	286	462	Why aske you	" 106
403	287	465	Farmers Pauen	Giles Farnaby.
405	288	470	Dalling Alman	"
405	289	471	The Old Spagnoletta	Giles Farnaby.
406	290	472	Lachrimae Pauan	J. D.107 Sett by Giles Farnaby.
408	291	477	Meridian Alman	Sett by Giles Farnaby.108
409	292	479	Pauana	Orlando Gibbons.
410	293	481	Muscadin	Giles Farnaby.109
411	294	483	Lady Montegle's Pauen	Wm. Byrd.
412	295	486	Galiarda. 5	Wm. Tisdall.
413	296	489	Fantasia	Giles Farnaby.
416	297	494	Hanskin	Richard Farnaby.110

The complete contents of the MS. were published by B. & H. in monthly instalments, between 1894 and 1899. They occupy two folio volumes, and were edited by J. A. Fuller Maitland and W. Barclay Squire. A description of the MS., with analysis of its contents, by Dr. E. W. Naylor, was published by Dent & Co.

The music ends on p. 418. At the end of the volume is an index of the contents signed ' Henry Smith Richmond, scripsit, from a MS. Index in the possession of Mr. Bartleman. 24 March, 1816.' In this, pieces, of which copies occur in Lady Nevell's book, are marked with an asterisk.

77 Chappell, pp. 123 and 771. Another copy is at p. 46 of Cosyn's Virginal Book, where it is signed with his initials.
78 Chappell, p. 793.
79 Ibid. p. 136. Occurs at p. 460 of Forster's Book.
80 Against the first line in the margin is written ' F. Tr.'
81 This and the four following pieces are in Ward's List.
82 In Ward's List.
83 Undoubtedly William Byrd.   84 In Ward's List.
85 Virtually identical with No 199.   86 See No. 193.
87 The melody is that given as ' Dulcina ' in Giles Earle's Songbook, 1626 : see Wooldridge's ' Old English Popular Music,' i. 160.
88 In the margin are some words which Chappell reads ' R. Rysd silas.'
89 In Ward's List.   90 Chappell, p. 76.
91 In the margin is written ' Mrs. Katherin Tregian's Pauen.'
92 Ward calls this ' Fantasia with 23 Variations upon Ut, re, mi, fa, sol, la.'
93 Chappell, pp. 171, 772.
94 The melody is the well-known ' Belle qui tient ma vie.'
95 Chappell, pp. 173, 708, 772.   96 Ibid. pp. 196, 773.

97 Burney says this is the same as ' The Marche before the Batell ' at fol. 135 of Lady Nevell's Book.
98 In the margin is written ' Vide P. Philippi sopr. la medesima fuga, pag. 158.' The subject is the same as that of Philips' Fantasia (No. 84). Against the third line is written ' . . . (illegible) la fuga e fuggira.'
99 In Ward's List. A copy is in Cosyn's Book, p. 199.
100 Chappell, p. 196. Same air as No. 59. See Lady Nevell's Book, fol. 46.
101 Chappell, p. 196.   102 Chappell, p. 158.
103 Ibid. pp. 177, 789.
104 Rosseter published a volume of ' Consort Lessons ' in 1609.
105 In the margin is written ' Vedi Mor. 287.' This refers to a curious piece of plagiarism, section 3 of Morley's Pavan, on p. 287 [i. 212] being nearly identical with section 3 of Farnaby's on p. 400.
106 At p. 59 of Cosyn's Book is a setting of this air signed ' B. C.', and at fol. 955 of Add. MS. 30,485 is another by Bull. Vide supra No. 161.
107 i.e. John Dowland.   108 Vide supra, No. 121.
109 The air of this is the same as that of No. 19.
110 Chappell, p. 23

(2) MY LADYE-NEVELLS BOOKE.—This valuable collection of Byrd's virginal music belongs to the Marquess of Abergavenny. It was published by permission of Lord Henry Nevill and edited by Miss Hilda Andrews (Curwen, 1926). It formerly belonged to Dr. Burney, and was sold at his sale for £11 : 0 : 6 to T. Jones, at whose sale it was lot 342 (Feb. 13, 1826). It is an oblong folio volume, beautifully bound in morocco enriched with gold, green and red, and lined with blue watered silk. On the title-page is an illuminated coat of arms and the monogram ' H. N.' The music is written on a 6-line stave in square-headed notes, and was copied by John Baldwin of Windsor, a fine volume of whose transcribing is preserved in the Royal Library, British Museum. Hawkins[1] states that the book was given by Byrd to his scholar, Lady Nevill, but there is no evidence in support of this assertion. The MS. was examined by Chappell when writing *Popular Music of the Olden Time*, in which volumes it is frequently referred to. The following is a list of its contents :

No.	Name.	Folio.	Composer.
1	My Ladye Nevel's grownde	1	Mr. W. Birde.
2	Qui passe : for my Ladye Nevel	8	,,
3	The Marche before the battel.[2]	13b	
4	The Souldiers Sommons : the Marche of Footemen	19	
	The Marche of Horsmen .	20	
	Now foloweth the Trumpetts : the Trumpetts	21	
	The Irishe Marche . .	22b	
	The Bagpipe . . .	24	
	And the Drone . . .	24	
	The Flute and the Droome	25	
	The Marche to the Fighte .	28	
	The Retreat. Now foloweth a Galliarde for the Victorie		
5	The Galliarde . . .	32	Mr. W. Birde.
6	The Barelye Breake . .	34	Mr. W. Birde Gentleman of Her Maiestie's Chappel.
7	A Galliards Gygge . .	43	Mr. W. Birde organiste of Her Maiestie's Chappell.
8	The Huntes Upp . .	46	Mr. W. Birde. Laus sit Deo.[3]
9	Ut re mi fa sol la . .	46b	Finis Mr. W. Birde.
10	The First Pauian . .	58b	
11	The Galliard foloweth .	61b	,,
12	The II Pauian . . .	63	,,
13	The Galliarde . . .	65	,,
14	The III Pauian . .	67	,,
15	The Galiarde to the same .	69b	,,
16	The IIII Pauian . .	71b	,,
17	The Galliard heer followeth	73b	Mr. W. Birde. Homo memorabilis.
18	The V Pauian . . .	75b	Mr. W. Birde. Laudes Deo.
19	The Galliarde . . .	78b	
20	Pauana the VI. Kinbrugh. Goodd	80b	Mr. W. Birde.
21	The Galliarde folows . .	84	Laus sit Deo. Mr. W. Birde.
22	The Seventh Pauian . .	86	Mr. W. Birde Gentleman of the Chappell.
23	The Eighte Pauian . .	89	Mr. W. Birde of the Chappell[4]
24	The passinge mesures Pauian of Mr. W. Birdes	92	Mr. W. Birde.
25	The Galliarde foloweth. The Galliarde	99b	Mr. W. Birde of the Chappell.

[1] *History of Music*, vol. iii. p. 288, and vol. iv p. 386.
[2] A copy of numbers 3, 4 and 5 is in Ch. Ch. This curious piece was known as ' Mr. Byrd's Battle.' At fol. 29b occur the words : ' Tantara tantara, the battels be ioyned.' Hawkins, vol. iv. 386. In the published edition (1926) three numbers from the Eliz. Rogers Virginal Book are added. These are ' The buriing of the dead,' ' The Morris ' and ' Ye souldiers dance.'
[3] Fitzwilliam Virginal Book, No. 59.
[4] Forster's Virginal Book, p. 217. Fitzwilliam Virginal Book, No. 56.

No.	Name.	Folio.	Composer.
26	A Voluntarie for my Ladye Nevell	105b	Finis Mr. W. Birde.[5]
27	Will you walke the woods so wylde	109	Finis Mr. W. Birde. Anno 1590.
28	The Maidens songe . .	113	Mr. W. Birde.[6]
29	A Lesson of Voluntarie .	119b	Finis. Mr. W. Birde.
30	The Seconde Grownde	126	Mr. W Bird.
31	Haue with you to Walsinghame	135	Finis Maister W, Birde.[7]
32	All in a garden grine .	142b	Mr W. Bird.[8]
33	Lord Willobies welcome home	146b	Finis Maister Willm. Birde.[9]
34	The Carman's Whistle .	149	Finis Maister Willm. Birde.[10]
35	Hugh Astons Grownde .	153b	Mr. W. Birde.[11]
36	A fancie	161	
37	Sellinger's Rownde . .	166b	Finis Mr. W. Birde.[12]
38	Munser's Almaine . .	173b	Finis Mr. W Birde[13]
39	The Tennthe Pauian : Mr. W. Peter	180b	Finis. The Galliarde followeth.
40	The Galliard . . .	184b	Finis Mr. W. Birde.
41	A Fancie . . .	186b	
42	A Voluntarie . . .	191	Finis Mr. W. Birde. Gentleman of the Queen's Chappell.

At the end of the volume is ' The Table for this booke,' after which is the following colophon :

' Ffinished and ended the leventh of September in the yeare of our Lorde God 1591 and in the 33 yeare of the raigne of our sofferaine ladie Elizabeth by the grace of God queene of Englande, etc. By me Jo. Baldwine of Windsore. Laudes Deo.'

(3) WILL. FORSTER'S VIRGINAL BOOK.—This volume, which belongs to His Majesty the King, is preserved in the Royal Library, British Museum, and consists of 238 octavo folios ruled in 6-line staves. The water-marks are a shield surmounted by a coronet, bearing a fleur-de-lis on the escutcheon, and a pot with the initials ' E. O. R.' The book probably belonged to Sir John Hawkins, and has been bound in modern times in half red morocco and paper boards. At the beginning is a ' Table of the Lessons,' written in the same hand as the rest of the book, and signed ' 31 Januarie 1624. Will. Forster.' The following is a list of the contents of the volume :

No.	Name	Page.	Composer.
1	A Grounde of Mr. Bird's .	2	Byrd.
2	I. The French Coranto .	14	,,
3	The Second French Coranto .	16	,,
4	The 3rd French Coranto .	18	,,
5	A Levolto[14] . . .	20	,,
6	Lo. Wiliobies wellcome home .	22	,,
7	Felix Nunquam[15] . .	24	
8	A Horne pipe . . .	50	Byrd.
9	Kapasse	63	,,
10	Wilson's Wilde[16] . .	70	
11	An Almaine . . .	72	Byrd.
12	As I went to Walsingham[17] .	74	Byrd.

[5] Fitzwilliam Virginal Book, No. 67.
[6] A copy of this is in Add. MSS. 31,403.
[7] Fitzwilliam Virginal Book, No. 68. Forster's Virginal Book, p. 74. Add. MSS. 30,485.
[8] On fol. 145b is written : ' Here is a falte, a pointe left out wch ye shall finde prickte, after the end of the nexte songe, upon the 148 leafe.' Fitzwilliam Virginal Book, p. 194.
[9] Forster's Virginal Book, p. 22.
[10] Fitzwilliam Virginal Book, No. 58. Forster's Virginal Book, p. 130. Add. MSS. 31,403 and 30,485.
[11] Fitzwilliam Virginal Book, No. 60.
[12] Fitzwilliam Virginal Book, p. 120.
[13] Forster's Virginal Book, p. 366. A different setting in Fitzwilliam Virginal Book, p. 114.
[14] *i.e.* a Lavolta.
[15] This composition is attributed in Fitzwilliam Book to Tallis, and dated 1564 (see p. 345a, notes 15, 16).
[16] The first note only has been written in. In the Table of Lessons, this composition *is* attributed to Byrd.
[17] In the ' Table ' called ' Walsingham ' only.

No.	Name.	Page.	Composer.
13	Galliardo	88	Thomas Morley
14	Quadro Pavine . . .	96	,,
15	Almayne	110	,,
16	Pavin	114	Byrd.
17	The Wood soe wylde [1]	118	
18	Pavin	127	Byrd.
19	. . . .	130	,, [2]
20	Parludam	136	
21	A Galliard	137	
22	The New Medley . .	143	
23	3 voc. Praise the Lord. Psalme 103	150	John Ward.
24	The Lord executeth righteousness. a 3 voc.	152	,,
25	For looke howe highe. a 3 voc.	154	,,
26	The Dales of Man. a 3 voc.	156	,,
27	The Lord. a 3 voc.	158	,, 3
28	Have Mercie. a 3 voc.	160	,, 4
29	Behould	162	,, 5
30	Turne Thye Face . .	164	,,
31	Deliver mee	166	,, 6
32	The Marchant's Dreame .	170	7 ,,
33	Rogero	176	
34	. . . .	182	
35	. . . .	186	8
36	. . . .	188	Byrd.
37		196	Englitt.
38	The Quadrant Pavin . .	202	Bull.
39	Passa Measures Pavin .	217	Byrd.
40	Passa Measures Galliard .	230	,,
41	Mr. Bird's Galliard . .	240	,,
42	Mounser's Alman . .	244	,,
43	Fortune	252	,,
44	A Grounde	258	,,
45	A Ground	263	,,
46	Parsons Innominey (sic) .	272	,, 9
47	Johnson's delighte . .	276	,,
48	The Galliard to the Pavin aforesaid	284	,,
49	Quadrant Pavin . . .	288	,,
50	The Galliard . . .	302	,, 10
51	Pavin	311	,,
52	The Galliard . . .	319	,,
53	A Galliard	322	,,
54	Goe from my Windoe .	324	,, 11
55	Lachramie	331	,,
56	A Pavan	340	
57	Doctor Bull's Gall(iard) .	347	Bull.
58	. . . .	352	
59		360	
60	Mounser's Alman . .	366	Byrd.
61	Harding's Gall(iard) . .	368	
62	A Parludam . . .	386	Byrd.
63	A Grounde	390	,,
64	A Pavin	404	
65	Galliard	412	
66	An Alman	416	
67	A pavin	420	
68	The Galliard . . .	426	
69	Robbin Hood . . .	430	
70	If my Complaints, or Pyper's Galliard	442	
71	The King's Hunt . . .	447	Bull.
72	. . . .	456	
73	Praeludiam	458	
74	Watkins Ale . . .	460	
75	. . . .	462	
76	. . . .	464	
77	The same a noate lower .	466	
78	. . . .	468	

(4) Benjamin Cosyn's Virginal Book.—
This fine folio volume, like the last-mentioned
collection, is the property of His Majesty, and
is preserved at Roy. Lib. B.M. The binding
is of English workmanship, and contemporary
with the MS. It consists of calf with gold
tooling. The letters ' B. C.' are stamped both
on the front and the back, and part of the
tooling has been stamped above the letters
' M. O.' — probably the initials of an earlier
owner. The book has been shut by brass
clasps, but these are now broken off. At the
beginning is an index, divided into ' A Table
of these Lessons followinge made and sett forth

[1] A mistake is made in the pagination here. Pages 118 and 119 are the same.
[2] In the Table this is called ' Ground.' It is the well-known Carman's Whistle.'
3 ' The 5th and last of the 103 Psalme.'
4 ' The 1 of the 51 Psalme.'
5 ' 2 of ye 51 Psalme.'
6 ' The last of the 51 Psalme.'
7 ' Marchant's Dreame ' (Table).
8 ' Byrd ' (Table).
9 A Pavan.
10 ' The Galliard to it ' (Table).
11 ' Lachramy ' (Table).

by Ben Cos,' ' A Table of these Lessons followinge made by Mr. Docter Bull,' ' A Table of
these Lessons following made by Mr. Or.
Gibbons,' ' These lessons following are made by
Tallis and Byrd,' after which comes a list of
six services contained in the same volume, at the
end of which is written 'These are y[e] six services
for the Kings Royall Chappell.' The same page
also contains ' A Catch of 9 parts in one,' ' Let
us goe pray for John Cook's soul,' and 'A Table
of all these Lessons generally contained in this
Booke are in Nomber : 96. By me Beniamin
Cosyn Right owner of this Booke.' Hawkins [12]
says that Cosyn was ' a famous composer of
lessons for the harpsichord, and probably an
excellent performer on that instrument,' that
he flourished about the year 1600, and that
' there are many of his lessons extant that seem
in no respect inferior to those of Bull.' The
last statement looks as if Hawkins had been
acquainted with the Virginal Book. Researches [13]
have shown that Benjamin Cosyn was organist
of Dulwich College from 1622–24, and the first
organist of the Charterhouse in 1626–43.

The following is a complete list of the contents
of the volume: as the old pagination is in places
irregular, the pages have been numbered freshly.
The titles of the index are sometimes different
from those in the body of the book ; when these
variations occur, they have been noted in the
last column.

No.	Name	Page.	Composer.	Title in Index.
1	A Prelude . . .	1	Benj. Cosyn	
2	A Pavin . . .	2	,,	In E. La, Mi.
3	The Galliard to itt .	5	,,	In A, Re.
4	Lacrime Pavin . .	8	,,	
5	The Galliard to itt .	12	,,	
6	A Pavin . . .	15	,,	The Lo. Lumlye's Pavin
7	The Galliard to itt .	19	,,	
8	A Grounde . . .	22	,,	In A, Re.
9	A Grounde . . .	29	,,	In Gam, Ut.
10	Sermone Blando .	38	,,	
11	A Galliard . . .	42	,,	In Ff, fa, ut
12		43	,,	In D, sol, re.
13	Pakinton's Pownde.	46	,,	
14	A Galliard . . .	49	,,	A cross-handed Galliard.
15	Dum Aurora . .	54	,,	
16	Whie aske you .	59	,,	' Why aske yu.'
17	The Queene's Commande	62	Orl. Gibbons	In the Index attributed to Cosyn.
18	Filliday Floutes me.	64	Benj. Cosyn	18. ' Fillida.'
19	My Self . . .	65	,,	
20	Miserere . . .	68	,,	
21	What you Will .	71	,,	
22	A Galliard . . .	73	,,	' My Lo. Rich. his Galliard.'
23	The Kings Hunt .	75	,,	
24	Thomas Lupoes Galliard	78	,,	
25	My Lo. Burrows Galliard	80	,,	
26	Ut, re, mi, fa, sol, la	82	Orl. Gibbons	In the Index attributed to Cosyn.
27	A Galliard . . .	88	Benj. Cosyn	' Sir Robert Southwell's Gall.'
28	Mr. Stroude's Galliard	90	,,	
29	The Galliard to Doct. Bulle's Fantastick Pavin	92	,,	
30	Preludiem . . .	93	Doctor Bull	' A Prelude in Gamut.'
31	The Quadren Pavin.	94	,,	
32	The Galliard to itt .	101	,,	
33	Pavana . . .	106	'Finis. Doct. Bulles Ffantasticall Pavine'	' The Phantasticall Pavin.'

[12] History vol. iii. p. 421.
[13] Some MS. voluntaries by him were in Dr. W. H. Cummings's collection. See Mus. T., 1903, pp. 780, 781.

No.	Name.	Page.	Composer.	Title in Index.
34	A Pavin in A, re	110	Doctor Bull	
35	The Galliard to itt	113	,,	
36	Pavana	114	,,	'A Pavin in D. sol. re.'
37	Galliard	114a	,,	'The Galliard to itt.'
38	Brunswick's Toy	114b	,,	'The Duke of Brunswick.'
39	Pavana	115	,,	'The Trumpet Pavin.'
40	Galliardo	116	,,	'The Galliard to it.'
41	Pavana	118	,,	'The Lo. Lumlies Pavin.'
42	The Galliard	120	,,	'The Galliard to it'
43	Wake Galliard	122	,,	'Wake's Galliard.'
44	Docter Bulle's Jewel	124	,,	
45	Duretto	125	,,	
46	A Galliard	126	Doctor Bull	'The Lo. Hunsden's Galliard.'
47	A Prelude	127	,,	In ff, fa, ut.
48	A Galliard	128	,,	The Galliard to Pavan No. 70.'
49	Fantasia	130	,,	'A Fancy.'
50	Pavana	135	,,	'The Mallincholy Pavin.'
51	The Galliard to itt	137	,,	
52	As I went to Wallsingham	139	,,	
53	Felix Namque	150	Thos. Tallis	
54	Goe from my windoe	157	Will Byrd	
55	1. Galliarda	160	Orl.Gibbons, 'Bachellor of Musik.'	
56	2.	162	Orl. Gibbons	'The Hunt's up.'
57	3. A Maske	167	,,	
58	4. Galliard	168	,,	
59	5. ,,	170	,,	'The La. Hatten's Galliard.'
60	6. A Fancy	171	,,	
61	7 A Toy	171	,,	
62	8. Galliard		,,	
63	9. Almaine			Attributed to Orlando Gibbons in the Index.
64	10. Almaine			'The Ffrench Allmaine.'
65	11. Allmaine		Orl. Gibbons	'Another Allmaine '
66	12. Fantasia		,,	'A Fancy.'
67	Galliard		Benj. Cosyn	'Sir Richard Latener's Galliard.'
68	The Goldfinch			
69	Pavana		Doctor Bull	'A Pavin in Gamut flatt.'
70	Pavana		Mr.Yves sett forth by B. Cosyn	'Mr.Yves his Allmaine.'
71	Allmaine			'The Coranto to itt.'
72	Galliard		Orl. Gibbons	
73	Fantasia		,,	'A Fancy.'
74	Preludem		,,	'A Prelude.'
75	Fantasia		,,	'A Fancy.'
76	In Nomine		,,	
77	Fantasia		,,	'A Fancy.'
78	An Allmaine		,,	
79	Allmaine		,,	
80	A Fancy for a Double Orgaine		,,	
81	Fantasia		,,	'A Fancy in Gamut flatt.'
82	,,		,,	'A Fancy in C, fa, ut.'
83	,,		,,	'Another Fancy in C, fa, ut.'
84	,,		,,	'A Fancy in A, re.'
85	Galliard		Doctor Bull	'The Galliard to no. 87.'
86	,,		,,	'The La. Lucie's Galliard.'
87	Pavana		,,	'Queene Elizabeth's Pavin.'
88	In Nomine		,,	
89	Dr. Bulles Greefe		,,	
90	Galliard		,,	'The Vauting Galliard.'
91	Mr. Bevan's Morning and Evening Service		Bevin	
92	O my sonne Absolon		,,	
93	Morning and Evening Service in D		Tallis	
94	Morning and Evening Service in D		Strogers	
95	Morning and Evening Service in D		Byrd	
96	Venite in F		Benj.Cosyn [1]	
97	Morning and Evening Service in F		Orl. Gibbons	
98	Morning Service in F		Tho. Weelks	

[1] Cosyn's name does not occur in the Index ; No. 96 consists of a T.D., B., K., C., M. and N.D., and the whole service is attributed to Gibbons.

W. B. S.

VIRTUOSO (from Lat. *virtus*), one who has attained the highest mastery over the technical side of his art, whether of singing, playing an instrument or in modern times of conducting an orchestra. In England especially the term has acquired a depreciatory meaning as suggesting the display of such a mastery for its own sake.

VISCONTI, GASPARO (*b.* Cremona), a 17th-18th century violinist who lived in London in the early 18th century, and wrote a book of violin sonatas with violoncello or harpsichord op. 1, dedicated to the Duke of Devonshire (Amsterdam, 1703). Three violin concertos with string orchestra and some solos and sonatas in MS. are in the libraries of Dresden and Schwerin (*Q.-L.*; E. v. d. Straeten, *18th century Violin Sonatas*: *The Strad*).

VISÉE, (1) ROBERT DE, French lutenist, player on the guitar and theorbo to the Dauphin (1680), chamber musician to the King (1686 ?), held this post until 1721; his son, François, succeeding him. In 1709 he was appointed 'chantre ordinaire de la musique du roi.' He published a 'livre de guitarre,' dedicated to the King (1682); another book with the same title (1686); some ' Pièces de théorbe et de luth, mises en partition' (1716); these are really trios. These three works are in ordinary notation. Some ' airs' by him were published between 1731 and 1732 in the 'Concerts parodiques divisés en 6 suites.'

(2) FRANÇOIS, his son, succeeded him as singer to Jean-Louis Marais on Oct. 25, 1733.

BIBL.—*Fétis*, viii.; *Eitner*, ix.; CHILESOTTI, *Sammelb. der I.M.G.* Oct. 1907, with musique; MICHEL BRENET, *R.M.I.*, 1898-99.

J. G. P.

VISETTI, ALBERT ANTHONY (*b.* Salona, Dalmatia, May 13, 1846), teacher of singing. His mother was English; he studied composition under Alberto Mazzucato at the Conservatorio of Milan, where he gained two scholarships. His exercise for his degree was a cantata to words by his friend Arrigo Boïto. His first engagement was as conductor at Nice. He then went to Paris, where A. Dumas prepared specially for him a libretto for an opera from his ' Trois Mousquetaires.' The score was hardly completed when it was burnt in the siege of the Commune. Visetti then came to London, where he has since resided, and has devoted himself chiefly to teaching singing. He joined the first Board of Professors at the R.C.M., and also taught at the G.S.M., the Watford School and various other institutions. He was also, in 1878-90, director and conductor of the Bath Philharmonic Society, to which he devoted an immensity of time, money and ability. Visetti has published Italian translations of Hullah's *History of Modern Music*, of Hueffer's *Musical Studies*, Parry's ' Blest pair of Sirens' and of other works. The King of Italy in 1880 conferred on him the order of the Corona d' Italia.

G., addns.

VITALI, ANGELO. This name is known in connexion with the following work, of which only the libretto seems to have survived :

' Tomiri, drama per musica, da rappresentarsi nel Teatro di S. Casciano, l' anno M.DC.LXXX., di

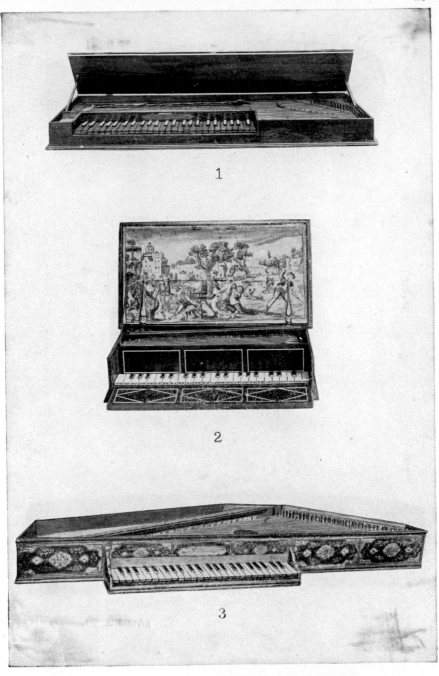

1. ENGLISH CLAVICHORD (P. Hicks, *c.* 1715).

2. OCTAVE VIRGINAL (H. Ruckers ? *c.* 1610).

3. ITALIAN VIRGINAL or SPINET (B. Floriani, 1571).

1. Victoria and Albert Museum, South Kensington.   2, 3. Heyer Museum, formerly Cologne, now Leipzig.

Antonio Medolago. Consecrato all' illustriss. et eccell. Sig. Gio: Francesco Morosini, dignissimo e meritissimo Cavalier, e Procurator di S. Marco. In Venetia, M.DC.LXXX. Per Francesco Nicolini.'

In the prefatory letter occurs the statement

' La musica è del S.D. Angelo Vitale, nelle noti del cui bizzaro contrapunto conoscerai, che non hà degradato da gli altri suoi spiritosi talenti,' etc.

A copy of this work is in the British Museum ; a later edition was published in Venice by Francesco Batti. Music is not mentioned in the play itself, probably only the songs were set to music.

From a passage in a letter in Angelo Berardi's *Il perche musicale*, 1693, p. 15, addressed to Signor Angelo Vitale, Orvieto, it appears that he was maestro di cappella there :

' Havendo V.S. biasimato quel suo Anversario con taccia d' ignorante nel segnare le sue proportioni con un numero solo, hà dimostrato l' ottima intelligenza, che deve havere il perito Maestro di cappella ne' fondamenti armonici.'

                                                 C. S.

VITALI, Filippo (*b.* Florence, end of 16th century), a priest and an esteemed composer. His first volume of madrigals appeared in 1616, and with the exception of short visits to Venice and Rome he remained at Florence, working at composition. He had already published eight volumes of vocal music when he was called to Rome, being nominated a tenor singer in the Papal Choir on June 10, 1631.[1] During his residence in Rome, where he was attached to the household of Cardinal Francesco Barberini as musician and composer, he wrote two sacred works, his Hymni in 1636, and the Salmi a 5 voci in 1641. He was recalled to Florence in Feb. 1642, to succeed Marco da Gagliano as maestro di cappella to the Duke, and at the Cathedral of S. Lorenzo.[2] On Apr. 1, 1653, he was presented to a canonry of the Cathedral, and entitled S. Ambrogio.[3]

Among Vitali's works, the ' favola in musica,' ' L' Aretusa,' attracts attention, for its performance at the palace of Monsignor Ottavio Corsini in the presence of nine Cardinals and the principal ladies of Rome, was practically the first appearance in Rome of a definite attempt at lyrical drama.[4] The publication was dedicated to Cardinal Borghese :

' L' Aretusa, favola in musica di Filippo Vitali, rappresentata in Roma in casa di Monsignor Corsini. Dedicata all' illmo. et rmo. Sig. Card. Borghese. In Roma. Luca Ant. soldi. 1620.'

In the preface [5] Vitali states that the libretto was written, the music composed, the parts distributed and learnt, and the first performance given, all in forty-four days, for on Dec. 26, 1619, he began the work, and on Feb. 8, 1620, it was performed. The instruments he used were two cembali, two theorbos, two violins, one lute and one viola da gamba, and he declares

---

1 Adami, *Osservazioni*, 1711, p. 201.
2 Vogel, *Vierteljahrsschrift*, v. 1889, p. 509.
3 Cianfogni, *Memorie*, 1804, p. 236.
4 A. Ademollo, *I teatri di Roma*, 1888, p. 4.
5 See Vogel, *Bibl. weltlichen Vokalmusik Italiens*, 1892.

that in his music he was a humble follower of Peri and Caccini of Florence.

Hugo Goldschmidt [6] points out that in the employment of two violins instead of viols, for the Discant or treble parts in ' Aretusa,' Vitali was distinctly in advance of his time ; in other respects the music is poor and shows signs of the haste with which it had been written.

A less important work opening with thirty-two bars of a sinfonia in five-part writing is the following :

' Intermedi di Filippo Vitali. Fatti per la commedia degl' Accademici inconstanti recitata nel palazzo del Casino, dell' illmo. e revmo. S. Cardinale de Medici l' anno 1622. In Firenze. Pietro Cecconcelli, 1623.'

Other publications were :

Il primo libro de madrigali a cinque voci. **Venezia**. Bartolomeo Magni. 1616.
Musiche a due, tre e sei voci. Firenze. Zanobi Pignoni. 1617. Some of these compositions contain Ritornelli for instruments alone ; and one introduces, with a sinfonia for five instruments, an unaccompanied madrigal for six voices.
Musiche a una e due voci. Libro secondo. Roma. G. B. Robletti. 1618.
F. H. Gevaert, Les Gloires d'Italie, No. 23, reprints a Canzonetta for solo voice with basso continuo from this work.
Musiche a una, due e tre voci per cantare nel cimbalo ò in altri stromenti simili con l' alfabeto per la chitarra in quelle più a proposito per tale stromento. Libro terzo. Roma. L. A. soldi. 1620.
Arie a 1, 2, 3 voci. Da cantarsi nel chitarrone chitarra spagnuola & altri stromenti. Libro quarto. Venetia, 1622. Gardano. In the dedication, dated from Venice, Vitali says he composed the work during his brief stay in Venice.
Varie musiche. Libro quinto. Stampo del Gardano. In Venetia, 1625. Bartolomeo Magni.
Italian and Latin compositions for 1 to 4 voices.
Il terzo libro de madrigali a cinque voci. Opera quarta decima. Venetia, 1629. Bartolomeo Magni.
Concerto di Filippo Vitali, madrigali et altri generi di canta a 1, 2, 3, 4, 5 & 6 voci. Libro primo. In Venetia, 1629. Bartolomeo Magni. Copies of this work in the Bologna and in the Breslau libraries have the dedication to Gio. Romena by F. V. dated from Florence, Apr. 1, 1629. The Canto and Quinto partbooks in the British Museum are dedicated to Gio. Giorgio Costanti by F. V. and dated from Venice, July 1, 1629.
Arie a una, due e tre voci, di Filippo Vitali musico della cappella di sua Santità. In Orvieto. Ad istantia di G. B. Robletti. 1632.
Arie a tre voci, etc. In Roma. Paolo Masotti. 1635.
Arie a tre voci, etc. In Roma. Vincenzo Bianchi. 1639.
Libro quinto di arie a tre voci. Firenze. Landi. 1647.
Sacrae cantiones a sex vocibus. Cum basso ad organum, Liber 1, Venetia, 1625.
Hymnos Urbani VIII. Pont. Max. jussu editos ; in musicos modos ad templorum usum digestos ; a Philippo Vitali Florentino Pontificii Sacelli musico ; ejusdemq. S. D. N. addictos, dicatos. Romae, ex typographia R.C. Apostolicae. An. 1636.
Psalmi ad vesperas quinque vocibus cum basso ad organum si placet. Authore Philippo Vitalio, Capellae Pontificiae Musico. Romae apud Vincentium Blancum. 1641.   C. S.

VITALI (1), Giovanni Battista (*b.* Cremona, *c.* 1644 or earlier; *d.* Modena, Oct. 12, 1692 [7]), a musician and composer, who produced an extraordinary amount of dance music, balletti and sonatas. He was a pupil of Maurizio Cazzati for counterpoint (as Gaspari gathers from Vitali's earliest work, published in 1666). Cazzati was maestro di cappella at the church of S. Petronio in Bologna from 1658–71, and Vitali himself was sonatore or ' musico di violone da brazzo ' at the same church from 1666, probably until he became ' maestro di cappella del santissimo Rosario di Bologna,' a title he is given on the title pages of his works in 1673 and 1674. Marino Silvani in the eulogistic preface he wrote to Vitali's ' Balletti, correnti, gighe,' etc., 1671, alludes to his violin-playing, ' eccellente nell' arte del suono,' and adds that it is not only those who hear him who admire ' le sue prodigiose virtu,' but also those who

---

6 *Sammelbände* of the Int. Mus. Ges., 1900–01, p. 35.
7 Eitner states that this date given in a manuscript in the Biblioteca Estense, Modena, had a note appended to the effect that he died at an advanced age.

examine his compositions, worthy of the highest praise. From 1667 Vitali was a member of the Bologna Accademia de' Filaschisi and Accademia de' Filarmonici.

On Dec. 1, 1674, he was appointed vice-maestro di cappella to the Duke Francesco II. of Modena, and ten years later was able to call himself maestro di cappella to the Duke, a post he was only to occupy for a short time. Among Vitali's published works, the sonatas naturally arouse most interest, both those contained in opus 2, dated 1667, and the more elaborate compositions in opus 5, first printed in 1669. They show in fact the first hesitating footsteps on the long road that eventually led to the present perfection of form. (See SONATA.) Constant and rapid changes from quick to slow movement mark the various sections. For instance ' La Campori,' sonata for two violins, passes in quick succession from allegro to grave, grave to vivace, and a sonata, ' La Guidoni,' is marked allegro, grave, allegro, grave, allegro.

Moreover, there is another point of interest to be considered : it is quite possible that these sonatas were the compositions on which Purcell modelled his sonatas ' in imitation of the Italian Masters ' which were published in 1683, for Nicola Matteis, the violin-player, may have introduced his compatriot's music into England. (See PURCELL.)

An extensive collection of Vitali's compositions, printed and in manuscript, is in the Biblioteca Estense, Modena ; the Bologna Library also possesses a large number of the following works :

Correnti e balletti da camera a due violini col suo basso continuo per spinetta ò violone da G. B. Vitali, sonatore di violone da brazzo in S. Petronio di Bologna & Accademico filaschese. Opera prima. In Bologna, per Marino Silvani. 1666.
Two editions were published in Venice in 1670 and in 1677, and another in Bologna by Giacomo Monti in 1680.
Wasielewski (' Instrumentalsätze,' 1874, No. 25) reprinted a balletto from this work.
Sonate a due violini col suo basso per l' organo, di G. B. V. musico di violone da Brazzo . . . & accademico filaschese. Opera seconda. In Bologna, per Giacomo Monti. 1667. Gratefully dedicated by Vitali to Vincenzo Maria Carrati, from whom he had received so many benefits, and who had admitted him to the Accademia of which he was the founder. (The Accademia dei Filarmonici was inaugurated at Carrati's house in Bologna, 1666.) Later editions were published at Venice in 1668, 1671 and 1682.
Wasielewski included a sonata from this work in the ' Instrumentalsätze,' 1874, No. 26. Another was published by Hugo Riemann in ' Alte Kammermusik,' 1898, vol. iv.
Balletti, correnti alla francese, gagliarde e brando per ballare. Balletti, correnti da camera a quatro stromenti di G. B. V., musico di violone da Brazzo, etc. Opera terza. In Bologna, per Giacomo Monti.
An edition of 1674 entitled Vitali ' maestro di capella del Santissimo Rosario di Bologna & Accademico filaschese.' Another edition published 1680.
Balletti, correnti, gighe, allemande e sarabande a violino e violone, ò spinetta con il secondo violino a beneplacito. Del G. B. V., musico di violone da brazzo, etc. Opera quarta. In Bologna, per Giacomo Monti. 1668. Other editions published in 1671, 1673, 1677 and 1678.
Livre cinquième du recueil des dances, ballets, allemandes, brandes, courantes, etc. des diverses autheurs de ce temps, à deux parties. Et aucunes à deux violons avecq. la basse continue pour les espinettes ou basse violon, du Gio. Battista Vitali. Anvers, chez les héritiers de P. Phalèse. 1668.
Sonate a due, tre, quattro e cinque stromenti di G. B. V., musico di violone da brazzo, etc. Opera quinta. Bologna, per Giacomo Monti. 1669. Other editions in 1677 and 1683. Wasielewski (' Instrumentalsätze,' 1874, Nos 27 and 28) reprinted the Sonata ' La Graziani ' and the Capriccio ' Il Molza ' from this work.
Salmi concertati a due, tre, quattro e cinque voci, con stromenti consecrati all' A. S. Francesco II. Duca di Modena, etc. Da G. B. V., vice maestro di capella di S.A.S. & accademico filaschese. Opera sesta. Bologna. Giacomo Monti. 1677. Ten partbooks as well as a MS. score by G. Busi are in the Bologna Library.
Varie partite del passo a mezzo, ciaccona capricci e passagalli a 3 : due violini, e violone, ò spinetta. Opera settima. Modena, 1682. Gasparo Ferri.

Balletti, correnti e capricci per camera a due violini e violone del Sig. G. B. V., vice maestro di capella, etc. & accademico filaschese e filarmonico. Opera ottava. In Venetia, 1683. Stampa del Gardano.
Some authors mention as opus 9 : ' Sonate a due violini e basso per l' organo,' published at Amsterdam.
Fétis also records opus 10 : Inni sacri per tutto l' anno, a voce sola con cinque stromenti. Modena, 1681.
Varie sonate alla francese & all' itagliana a sei stromenti da G. B. V., maestro di capella dell' A.S. di Sig. duca di Modena & accademico filaschese. Opera undecima. In Modena, per Gio. Gasparo Ferri. 1684.
Balli in stile francese à cinque stromenti consecrati alla sacra real maestà di Maria Beatrice d' Este Stuarda, regina della Gran Bretagna. Da G. B. V. maestro di cappella, etc. Opera duodecima. In Modena, per Antonio Vitaliani. 1685.
Artificii musicali ne quali si contengono canoni in diverse maniere, contrapunti dopii, inventioni curiose, capritii e sonate di G. B.V Opera decimaterza. In Modena, per gli eredi Cassiani stampator episcopali. 1689.
Sonate da camera a tre, due violini e violone di G. B. V. Opera decimaquarta. In Modena, 1692, per Christoforo Canobi, stampatore di musica ducale. The dedication, dated Dec. 1692, is written by Tommaso Antonio Vitali, son of Gio. Battista, who states that owing to the death of his father he had undertaken the publication of this work.
Twelve MS. ' Sonate a due violini del vitali ' are in the Bodleian Library : MS. Mus. Sch. d. 257. Torchi (' L' arte musicale in Italia,' 1908, vol. 7), reprinted nine short movements for two violins and viola.
Two oratorios, ' Agar ' and ' Gefte,' composed in 1671 and 1672 (C. Ricci, I teatri di Bologna, p. 342).
In his catalogue of the operas in the Brussels Conservatoire Library, Wotquenne gives the following :
Olocausto d' encomi offerto da sign. Accademici Unanimi al loro gran protettore San Nicolo il Magno nell' Accademia di Belle Lettere e Musica, fatti la sera delli 17 Marzo, 1672. In Bologna, per Gio. Recaldini, 1672. The sinfonia preceding an oratorio, ' Il trionfo della fede,' was composed by G. B. Vitali.
L' ambitione debellata overo la caduta di Monmouth, oratorio per musica, di G. A. Canal, Venitiano, posto in musica dal sig. Gio. Battista Vitali, V. maestro di cappella di S.A.S. In Modena per gli eredi Soliani stampatore ducale. 1686.
A MS. score of the music is in Bibl. Estense, Modena. Fétis also states that ' Il Giona,' oratorio for seven voices, chorus and instruments, the music by G. B. V., was performed in Modena in 1689. MS score in Modena.

C. S.

(2) TOMMASO ANTONIO (b. Bologna, c. mid. 17th cent.), a son of Gio. Battista, was a fine violin-player, and when his father moved to Modena in 1674, Tommaso became a member of the court cappella, and eventually its director under the Dukes Francesco II. and Rinaldo I. He calls himself their ' servitore attuale ' in his works published 1693–1701. He was a member of the Accademia de' filarmonici of Bologna from 1706. He is said to have had many distinguished violin pupils, but the name of only one is known, that of Girolamo Nicolò Laurenti.

Copies of his three known published volumes of sonatas are in the library of the Liceo musicale, Bologna. (Gaspari's Catalogue, vol. iv.) :

Sonate a tre, doi violini e violoncello col basso per l' organo consecrate all' Altezza Serenissima di Francesco II, Duca di Modona, Reggio, etc., da Tomaso Antonio Vitali, bolognese servitore attuale della medema altezza. In Modona, 1693, per Antonio Ricci, stampatore di musica ducale.
The dedication shows that this was his first work.
Sonati a doi violini, col basso per l' organo, consecrate all' Altezza serenissima del Sig. Prencipe de Parma Odoardo Farnese, da T. A. V. etc., as above. Opera seconda. In Modona, 1693. Per Christoforo Canobi, stampatore di musica ducale.
Concerto di sonate a violino, violoncello e cembalo consecrate all' eminentissimo e rever. Sig. Cardinale Ottoboni da T. A. V. etc., as above. Opera quarta. In Modona, 1701. Nella stampa di Fortuniano Rosati, stampatore ducale di musica.

Tommaso also edited a volume of his father's sonatas in 1692.

A sonata by Tommaso for two violins and basso was included in the Corona di dodici fiori armonici tessuta da altertanti ingegni sonori a tre strumenti. Bologna, 1706.

His best-known work at the present time is the characteristic ' Ciaccona ' for violin solo, with figured bass, edited by Ferdinand David (' Die hohe Schule,' 1867, No. 13), which has been much played at concerts by eminent violinists. One of the rare autographs included in the International Musical Exhibition at Bologna in 1888 (Succi's Catalogue, p. 174) was a letter from Tommaso to Count Pirro Albergati, of Bologna, dated Mar. 17, 1711.   c. s.

VITOLS, J., see LATVIAN MUSIC.

VITRY, PHILIPPE DE (b. Champagne, c. 1285–1295 ; d. Paris, 1361), author of the earliest treatises expounding the Ars nova, was born of a noble family in Champagne. He was secretary to two kings of France, Charles IV. and Philip VI., and to the latter's son John, Duke of Normandy, afterwards King John II. He took part in various diplomatic missions, and in 1350 negotiated a meeting between the French king and the Pope at Avignon. It is supposed that he remained at the Papal Court and received holy orders there, as he was shortly afterwards nominated Bishop of Meaux.

Philippe de Vitry was celebrated in his own day not only as a theorist but also as a poet and composer. Petrarch, in a letter addressed to him in 1350, preserved at the Bibliothèque Nationale in Paris, calls him 'poeta nunc unicus Galliarum.' Very little of his verse has survived to our own day, and his musical compositions are lost. It is believed that a MS. formerly at Strassburg, which was destroyed in a fire during the Prussian bombardment of the city in 1870, contained music by him.

Four musical treatises attributed to Philippe de Vitry (Philippus de Vitriaco) are extant : Ars nova, Ars perfecta, Liber musicalium and Ars contrapunctus. They are contained in de Coussemaker's Scriptorum de musica medii aevi novam seriem, etc., vol. iii. According to J. Wolf, Geschichte der Mensural-Notation, vol. i. part ii., the Ars perfecta is probably not by him, but Wolf admits the genuineness of the Ars nova and Liber musicalium. Although the 'New Art' in music was, as Wolf says, less an invention than a development of the older art (ars antiqua), the innovations introduced by Philippe de Vitry are of considerable importance in the history of music. They concern rhythm and the method of representing it in notation, and may be summarised as follows :

1. Recognition of the independence of the minima as a note form.

2. Extension of the principle of the Ars antiqua by which a longa might be 'imperfected' by a brevis, i.e. one longa followed by one brevis loses one-third of its value—normally $\sqcap = \sqcap \sqcap \sqcap$, but $\sqcap \sqcap = \sqcap \sqcap \sqcap$—to the smaller note values, so that a semibrevis might now imperfect a brevis, and a minima a semibrevis.

3. Introduction from Italian usage of the rhythms known as quaternaria ($\sqcap = \circ \circ$ = ♩ ♩ ♩ ♩) and senaria perfecta ($\sqcap = \circ \circ \circ$ = ♩ ♩ ♩ ♩ ♩ ♩).

4. Introduction, in addition to the ideas of modus perfectus (longa = three breves) and imperfectus (longa = two breves), and tempus perfectum (brevis = three semibreves) and imperfectum (brevis = two semibreves), of the idea of prolatio maior (semibrevis = three minimae) and minor (semibrevis = two minimae).

The Ars antiqua recognised only perfect, i.e. triple, rhythm, and demanded that all music should be written in one of the six RHYTHMIC MODES (q.v.). When the art-music invented in France was first introduced into Italy, the influence of native Italian folk-music upon it was so strong that duple as well as triple rhythms were allowed. The idea of binary rhythm, originated in Italy, was probably introduced into France at the time of the transference of the Papal See from Rome to Avignon (1309). The importance of Philippe de Vitry's work lies in the fact that he recognised and adopted the principle of binary rhythm and was the earliest theorist to expound and develop that principle in his treatises, thus helping his contemporaries to free themselves from the restrictions of the earlier methods of composition, and especially from the rhythmic modes.

His method of notation is very fully treated of in Wolf, op. cit. vol. i. part ii. His contribution to the history of harmony is less important. A good summary of the principles of composition advocated by him and his contemporaries is given in J. Combarieu's Histoire de la musique, vol. i. chapter xxiv. p. 390. As stated above, his own compositions have been lost, but his theories are well illustrated in the works of his contemporary, Guillaume de MACHAUT (q.v.).   B. S.

VITTORIA, TOMASO DE, see VICTORIA.

VITZTHUMB (WITZTHUMB) IGNACE (b. Baden, near Vienna, July 20, 1723; d. Brussels, Mar. 23, 1816), studied at the school of the Scottish Oratorians at Vienna, and served during the Seven Years' War as kettledrummer in a regiment of Prince Charles of Lorraine, to whose chapel in Brussels he went. In 1771 he became joint manager with Louis Compain of the Théâtre de la Monnaie, which, under him, experienced a period of splendour and prosperity ; but he failed in 1777. After a short period of conductorship at the Ghent theatre, c. 1780, where his daughter, Mme. Mees, appeared as singer, he was appointed Kapellmeister at the Théâtre de la Monnaie, Brussels, in 1786. The French Revolution deprived him of his position as well as of his pension from the Austrian court. After some years of activity as Kapellmeister and stage manager at the Amsterdam theatre, he returned to Brussels where he died in straitened circumstances. Among his pupils he counted the Flemish composer Verheyen. He composed a number of masses, motets and other church music, symphonies, and opéras - comiques, some of which were very successful. E. van der Straeten gives his portrait in *La Musique aux Pays-Bas*. (See also E. G. Grégoir, *Les Artistes musiciens*, etc., and *Q.-L.*)

VIVACE (Vivo, Vivacissimo), 'Lively, in the liveliest manner possible.' A direction used either alone, and indicating a rate of speed between *Allegro* and *Presto*, or as qualifying some other direction, as *Allegro* or *Allegretto*. *Allegro vivace* will be taken quicker than Allegro (*q.v.*) by itself, but not so quick as *Allegro assai*.

VIVALDI, Antonio (*b.* Venice, latter half of 17th cent.), surnamed 'Il prete rosso,' was the son of Giovanni Battista Vivaldi, a violinist in St. Mark's at Venice. There is no evidence in support of the statement that he went to Germany. He entered the service of the landgrave of Hesse-Darmstadt,[1] who was then resident in Italy. On his return to his native city in 1713 Vivaldi was appointed maestro de' concerti at the Ospedale della Pietà, a post which he held until his death in 1743. The institution, which was a foundling-hospital for girls, possessed a choir and a good orchestra composed entirely of females. (See Venice.) Vivaldi's own instrument was the violin, for which he wrote very largely ; he is stated also to have contributed something to the development of its technical manipulation. The publications on which his fame rests are all works in which the violin takes the principal part. Fétis [2] enumerates the following :

Op.	Op.
1. 12 trios for 2 violins and violoncello. Paris, 1737.	8. ' Le quattro staggioni, ovvero il cimento dell' armonia
2. 12 sonatas for violin solo with bass.	e dell' invenzione, in 12 concerti a quattro e
3. ' Estro armonico, ossia 12 concerti a 4 violini, 2 viole, violoncello e basso continuo per l' organo.'	cinque.'
	9. ' La cetra, ossia 6 concerti ' for the same.
	10. 6 concerti for flute, violin, viola, violoncello and
4. ' 12 concerti a violino solo, 2 violini ripieni, viola e basso per l' organo.'	organ.
	11, 12. Each consisting of 6 concertos for the same instru-
5. Sonatas for the same.	ments, with the addition
6, 7. Each consisting of 6 concerti for the same instruments.	of the violoncello.

Besides these works,[3] twenty-eight operas by Vivaldi are named (he was in Rome in 1735 for the performance of one of 'them), and a few cantatas and even motets will be found scattered in various manuscript collections.

As a writer for the violin Vivaldi held apart from the classical Roman school lately founded by Corelli. He sought and won the popularity of a virtuoso ; and a good part of his writings is vitiated by an excessive striving after display, and effects which are striking simply in

so far as they are novel. His 'stravaganze' for the violin solo, which were much played in England during the 18th century, are, according to Dr. Burney,[4] nothing better than show-pieces. The 'Cimento' (op. 8) illustrates another fault of the composer : ' The first four concertos,' says Sir John Hawkins,[5]

' are a pretended paraphrase in musical notes of so many sonnets on the four seasons, wherein the author endeavours, by the force of harmony and particular modifications of air and measure, to excite ideas correspondent with the sentiments of the several poems.'

Vivaldi in fact mistook the facility of an expert performer (and as such he had few rivals among contemporaries) for the creative faculty, which he possessed but in a limited degree. His real distinction lies in his mastery of form, and in his application of this mastery to the development of the concerto. It is thus that we find his violin concertos constantly studied in Germany, for instance by Benda and Quantz [6]; and the best proof of their sterling merits is given by the attraction which they exercised upon Sebastian Bach, who arranged sixteen [7] of them for the clavier and four for the organ, and developed one into a colossal concerto for four claviers and a quartet of strings.[8] (See Arrangement.)

A portrait of Vivaldi is in Hawkins's *History*.

R. L. P., rev.

Bibl.—W. Altmann, *Thematischer Katalog der gedruckten Werke Antonio Vivaldis nebst Angabe der Neuausgaben und Bearbeitungen. A.M.Z.* Apr. 1922, pp. 262-79.

VIVANDIÈRE, LA, opéra-comique in 3 acts ; text by Henri Cain ; music by Benjamin Godard. Produced, Opéra - Comique, Paris, Apr. 1, 1895 ; in England by the Carl Rosa Company, Court Theatre, Liverpool, Mar. 10, 1896 ; Garrick Theatre, London, Jan. 20, 1897.

VIVES, Amadeo (*b.* Catalonia), Spanish composer of light opera ; teacher of composition at the Conservatoire, Madrid. Besides his comic operas (which are good), he has attempted more serious work in ' Maruxa,' and in a set of songs (' Canciones epigramáticas ') to words from some of the greatest Spanish poets. His lyric comedy ' Doña Francisquita ' was inspired by Lope de Vega's play, *La discreta enamorada*. A book of essays, *Sofía* (Madrid, 1923), shows that his capacity for clear thinking is not confined to his music.

J. B. T.

VIVIANI, Giovanni Bonaventura, of Florence. In 1688 and 1690 he calls himself

---

[1] *Riemann* describes him as Kapellmeister to the Duke Philipp von Hessen, and concludes therefore that he was at Mantua from 1707-13.

[2] *Fétis*, vol. viii. p. 369a.

[3] A concerto and a sinfonia in 3-5 parts for viola d' amore and lute also exist in manuscript. A transcript is in the British Museum Add. MS. 31,305, f. 10.

[4] *History*, ii. 561 ; 1789.

[5] *History*, etc., ii. 837 ; ed. 1875.

[6] Burney, *Present State of Music in Germany*, ii. 134, 166 ; 2nd ed. 1775.

[7] Modern criticism has assigned many of the originals to other composers : Prince Ernst of Saxe-Weimar, Telemann, Marcello. See A. Schering, *Zur Bachforschung, Sammelb. Int. Mus. Ges.* iv. and v. No. 4 is an arrangement of the same work as the clavier concerto, No. 13.

[8] This has commonly been mistaken for an original work of Bach : see Forkel, *Life of Bach*, p. 99, English translation, 1820. Fétis says that he possessed the manuscripts of two other arrangements by Bach, namely, of two concerti in the ' Estro armonico,' for clavier, 2 violins, alto and bass. These do not appear in the catalogue of the Fétis Library.

maestro di cappella of Pistoja Cathedral and *Nobile del sacro Romano Impero*. He had previously been in the emperor's service at Toscana. Fétis, who differs from the above, says that he lived for some time at Innsbruck about 1680. He wrote an oratorio (1690), psalms, motets, solfeggi and several operas, including 'Scipione Africano,' in collaboration with Cavalli (1678) (*Fétis*; *Q.-L.*).

VIVIER, EUGÈNE LÉON (*b.* Ajaccio, 1821 ; *d.* Nice, Mar. 4, 1900), a remarkable horn-player. His father was a tax-collector, and intended him for a similar career, but his passion for music made him throw aside all restraints and go to Paris. He knew enough of the horn to gain admittance to the orchestra of the Italiens, and then of the Opéra, and after some instruction from Gallay appeared at concerts as a solo-player. His extraordinary humour and imagination soon showed themselves, and endeared him to society, in the best circles of which he mixed largely. He was also master of a curious discovery or trick upon the horn, the secret of which he never divulged, by which he could produce three and even four notes at once, so as to play pieces for three horns, with full, sonorous triads, and chords of the 6 and 6-4 from the one instrument. Vivier soon made his entrance at court, and his horn in E, with which he used to play before Louis Philippe at the Château d'Eu, is still preserved at the Conservatoire. From this time forward his fame steadily increased at home and abroad. Among other artistic *tournées* he came several times to England after 1844, and was a great favourite in London for his drollery as much as his music. Philippe Gille wrote the preface for Vivier's pamphlet, *Un peu de ce qui se dit tous les jours* (Motteroz), printed in green and black, and now extremely scarce. It was a collection of the ready-made phrases which it is so difficult to avoid, and which are the bane of ordinary conversation.   G. C.

VIVO, see VIVACE.

VOCAL ASSOCIATION, THE, established in 1856 at a meeting at Store Street Music Hall, attended by about 300 amateurs, with the view of founding in England an association answering to the German 'Gesangverein.' Benedict was elected conductor ; Chas. E. Horsley subsequently shared the duties. In 1857 the Society gave a series of concerts at the Crystal Palace, including Mendelssohn's 'First Walpurgis Night,' and it subsequently gave performances at St. James's Hall, at one of which the conductor's opera, 'The Lily of Killarney,' was sung. The concerts included vocal and instrumental solos, and occasionally there was an orchestra, the choir usually numbering 200 voices. The Association has ceased to exist for many years.   C. M.

VOCAL CONCERTS, THE (1792–1822). These concerts, the first of which was given on Feb. 11, 1792, originated in the secession of HARRISON from the ANCIENT CONCERTS (*q.v.*) in 1789. Harrison was joined by Miss Cantelo, whom he subsequently married, and in 1791 by Bartleman, and at the close of that year they circulated proposals for the new concerts, which were begun at Willis's Rooms under the management of Harrison and Knyvett senior. The accompaniments at first were furnished by the pianoforte, at which the elder Knyvett presided as conductor, and a quartet of two violins, viola and violoncello, led by François Cramer. Mr. and Mrs. Harrison and Bartleman were the principal singers, and were assisted in the glees, which formed the principal feature of the concerts, by the Knyvetts and others. Callcott, Crotch, Spofforth, Dr. Clarke and Stevenson contributed new works to the programmes, and Italian music was added. In 1793 Mme. Dussek and Miss Poole (afterwards Mrs. Dickons) joined the vocalists, and the brothers Leander, then the most celebrated horn-players in Europe, were added to the little band. The concerts, ten of which were given each season, were abandoned at the end of 1794, the subscriptions (of three guineas) having fallen off, and Harrison and his wife and Bartleman returned to the Ancient Concerts, the cause of their failure being the competition of Salomon's concerts (with Haydn's music and Mme. Mara among the singers), the Professional Concerts (with Pleyel and Billington) and the Ancient Concerts. In 1801 the Vocal Concerts were revived with the additional attractions of a complete orchestra and chorus. The band was led by Cramer ; Greatorex was organist and general conductor ; and among the principal singers, besides the two directors, Harrison and Bartleman, were Mrs. Harrison, Mrs. Bianchi, Miss Parke, Miss Tennant and W. Knyvett. The programmes provided a wider variety of excellent music than was ever before given in a single series of concerts. As an episode in their history it may be mentioned that an opposition series, under the name of 'Messrs. Knyvett and Vaughan's Vocal Subscription Concerts,' was begun in 1811 with six or seven hundred subscribers, including the Dukes of Kent, Sussex and Cambridge ; the programmes of 1812 included the first acts of 'Don Juan' and 'Figaro,' the finale to the second act of 'Don Juan' and other pieces from Mozart's operas ; but in 1812 the death of Harrison led to a union of the two schemes, which was accomplished in 1813.   C. M.

VOCALION ; an 'organ' or instrument of the free-reed kind, exhibited by James Baillie Hamilton in the International Inventions Exhibition, London, 1885. The first patent was taken out Nov. 13, 1872, by John Farmer (of Harrow) for a combination of reed with string or wire—either as a continuation of the reed or as a coil fastened to the back thereof—

and was succeeded by many more, taken out in the names of Hamilton and others. The first attempts gave a beautiful and very peculiar quality of sound, but by degrees the combination of reed and string from which this proceeded had to be given up, for practical and commercial reasons, and the instrument as exhibited was virtually a harmonium with broad reeds, giving great rigidity of action and therefore purity of tone, and large channels, and acted on by high pressure of wind—not suction. A main peculiarity of the vocalion is that the reeds are placed above the pallets and below the slides, and that though the sliding ' plug ' of three reeds is only of the width of the groove, the cavities are more than twice as wide. (See AMERICAN ORGAN.) This is expressed in one of Hamilton's patents (U.S.A., Mar. 25, 1884) as

' the combination of pallets, soundboard and reeds with cavity-boards, one above the other, the lower one containing the nostrils and the upper one the mouths, and an intermediate controlling slide.'

The vocalion exhibited was 6 ft. square, and stood on a somewhat larger pedestal containing the bellows, wind-chest, etc. It had three manuals, denominated choir, great and swell; two stops in the pedals and three in each manual, as well as three extra ones of lighter quality called ' complementary.' In the successive steps of the invention since 1874, it is understood that Baillie Hamilton was much assisted by the practical knowledge and skill of Hermann Smith. (See *Mus. Assoc. Proc.*, 1882–83, p. 59.)   G.

VOCALISE (Fr.), VOCALIZZO (Ital.), see SOLFEGGIO.

VOCAL SOCIETY, THE, established 1832

' to present the vocal music of the English school, both ancient and modern, including that of the church, the chamber and the theatre, with the addition of foreign compositions of excellence.'

Its first programme at the King's Concert Rooms, Hanover Square, on Monday, Jan. 7, 1833, included the sestetto and chorus from Webbe's ' Ode to St. Cecilia '; Bennet's madrigal, ' All creatures now '; Attwood's glee, ' In this fair vale '; Cooke's glee, ' Deh dove '; Bishop's serenade, 'Sleep, gentle lady'; Webbe's catch, ' Would you know ' ; solos from Haydn, Hummel, Mozart and Purcell, and an instrumental quintet of Beethoven. T. Cooke was leader ; at the organ and pianoforte were Turle, Goss and Horncastle ; and the vocalists included Miss Clara Novello, Mrs. Bishop, Miss George, and Bennett, Parry, Phillips, Hobbs and Braham. The original intention of presenting mainly English music was departed from in the first year of the Society's existence, for we find in its programmes the names of Palestrina, Pergolesi, Bononcini, Beethoven, Mozart and other foreign composers, and from a notice of the last concert given in 1833 we learn that, ' with the exception of three glees and a madrigal, the performance consisted entirely of

the works of foreign artists.' (See HANOVER SQUARE ROOMS.)   C. M.

VOCE DI PETTO, CHEST - VOICE (Ger. *Bruststimme*) ; VOCE DI TESTA, HEAD - VOICE (Ger. *Kopfstimme*) ; see SINGING, subsection REGISTER.

VOGEL, CHARLES LOUIS ADOLPHE (*b.* Lille, May 17, 1808 ; *d.* Paris, Sept. 1892), though of German origin, is accounted a Franco-Belgian composer. He studied at the Paris Conservatoire. His opera, ' Le Podestat,' was produced at the Opéra-Comique in Paris in 1833, and a grand oratorio, ' Le Jugement dernier,' represented with costumes and scenery, had a good deal of success. ' La Siège de Leyde ' came out at the Hague in 1847 ; ' La Moissonneuse ' at the Théâtre Lyrique in 1853 ; ' Rompons,' a piece in one act, at the Bouffes-Parisiens in 1857 ; ' Le Nid de cicognes ' at Baden-Baden in 1858 ; ' Gredin de Pigoche ' at the Folies-Marigny, Paris, 1866 ; and ' La Filleule du Roi ' first in Brussels and afterwards in Paris in 1875. He wrote numerous songs, of which one of his earliest, ' Les Trois Couleurs,'[1] celebrating the return of the tricolour after the revolution of 1830, had a peculiar fame. He also wrote several symphonies, quartets and quintets for strings which gained the Prix Trémont at the Académie, and other things.   M., addns.

VOGEL, JOHANN CHRISTIAN (*b.* Nuremberg, *c.* 1756; *d.* Paris, June 28, 1788), studied at Ratisbon under Riepel, who made him familiar with the works of Graun and Hasse. In 1776 he entered the service of the Duke of Montmorency at Paris, and afterwards the Count of Valentinois. He became an enthusiastic admirer of Gluck, whom he took for his model, and imitated with such skill that Gluck even admitted his dramatic talent, and accepted the dedication of his opera, ' Le Toison d'Or,' which was not performed, however, until 1786, when it went through a number of performances, and was afterwards revived as ' Medea in Colchis.' Before its first appearance he had already started on another opera, ' Démophon,' but his irregular habits retarded the progress of the work, which was not finished until shortly before his death, and was first performed in 1789. Fétis speaks of the overture as one of the finest works of its kind. He composed also symphonies, concertos for various instruments, quartets, trios, duos, etc. (*Mendel* ; *Fétis* ; *Q.-L.*).

VOGL, (1) HEINRICH (*b.* Au, near Munich, Jan. 15, 1845 ; *d.* Munich, Apr. 21, 1900), began life as a schoolmaster, and received instruction in singing from Franz Lachner, and in acting from Jenk, stage manager of the Royal Theatre, Munich, where he made his début on Nov. 5, 1865, as Max, in ' Der Freischütz.' His success was immediate, and he remained at Munich

---

[1] Words by Adolphe Blanc, sung by Chollet at the Théâtre de Nouveautés (Place de la Bourse, Paris).

throughout his career, making the usual tours in Germany and Austria in company with his wife, whom he married in 1868. He excelled pre-eminently in the operas of Wagner, and played Loge and Siegmund on the production respectively of 'Rheingold' (Sept. 22, 1869) and 'Walküre' (June 26, 1870) at Munich. He sang at the Beethoven Centenary Festival at Bonn in 1871. He was the first Tristan (after the four performances by Schnorr von Carolsfeld), and for some years the only representative of the part. On the production of the trilogy at Bayreuth in 1876 he again played the part of Loge, and made a great hit by his fine declamation and admirable acting. On May 5, 1882, he made his first appearance in England at Her Majesty's in the same part, and subsequently in Siegfried, and on May 18 was heard with pleasure in Handel's 'Total Eclipse' and songs by Franz, etc., at a symphony concert at St. James's Hall. He composed many songs, and an opera, 'Der Fremdling,' was produced at Munich, May 7, 1899, with himself and Ternina in the chief parts. A biographical sketch, by Baron Hermann von Pfordten, appeared in the same year.

His wife, (2) THERESE, whose maiden name was THOMA (b. Tutzing, Lake Starnberg, Bavaria, Nov. 12, 1845 ; d. Munich, Sept. 29, 1921), learnt singing from Hauser at the Munich Conservatorium, and in 1865 first appeared in opera at Carlsruhe. In Dec. 1866 she made her début at Munich as Casilda (Auber's 'Part du Diable'), became very popular as a dramatic soprano, and remained there until her retirement in 1892. She was for some years the only Isolde, and was the original Sieglinde at Munich. On May 6, 1882, she made her first appearance in England at Her Majesty's, as Brünnhilde, and played the part throughout the trilogy with great success. In the second 'cycle' of performances she played with equal success her old part of Sieglinde, having resigned Brünnhilde to Mme. Reicher-Kindermann (since deceased), who had been the Fricka in the first cycle.   A. C.

VOGL, JOHANN MICHAEL (b. Steyer, Upper Austria, Aug. 10, 1768 ; d. Vienna, Nov. 19, 1840), distinguished opera-singer, and, with Baron von Schönstein, one of the principal interpreters of Schubert's songs. He had his general education in the monastery of Kremsmünster, and took part there in little Singspiele by Süssmayer, giving considerable promise both as singer and actor. He next went to the University of Vienna, and was about to take a permanent post in the magistracy of the city when Süssmayer engaged him for the court opera. He played with the German opera company formed by Süssmayer in the summer of 1794, and made his début as a regular member of the court opera in the following May. From that period till his retirement in 1822 (his last appearance was in Grétry's 'Barbe - bleue,'

1821) he was a great favourite, and held an important position as a singer and an actor in both German and Italian opera. Gifted with a baritone voice of sympathetic quality, his method was excellent, and his phrasing marked by breadth, intelligence and great dramatic expression. Such parts as Oreste ('Iphigénie en Tauride'), Jakob ('Schweizerfamilie'), Count Almaviva ('Le Nozze di Figaro'), Micheli ('Deux Journées'), Kreon ('Médée'), Telasco ('Ferdinand Cortez') and Jacob (Méhul's 'Joseph'), show the range of his powers.

He became acquainted with Schubert somewhere about 1816, through the latter's friend Schober. Vogl recognised Schubert's genius, urged him to produce, and did his best to make him known by singing his songs both in public and private. The 'Erl-König' was first introduced by him to the general public at a musical entertainment at the Kärnthnerthor Theatre (Mar. 7, 1821), though it had been sung before at a soirée of the Gesellschaft der Musikfreunde (Jan. 25) by von Gymnich, an excellent amateur. Vogl in his diary calls Schubert's compositions 'truly divine inspirations, utterances of a musical clairvoyance,' and Schubert, writing to his brother Ferdinand, says, 'when Vogl sings and I accompany him we seem for the moment to be one, which strikes the good people here as something quite unheard of.' In the summer of 1825 the two friends met at Steyer, and made a walking tour through Upper Austria and Styria, singing Schubert's songs like a couple of wandering minstrels at all their resting-places, whether monasteries or private houses. Schubert publicly testified his esteem by dedicating to Vogl three Lieder (op. 6), published in 1821.

Vogl's early conventual education left its traces in his fondness for serious study, to which all his spare time was devoted, his favourite authors being Goethe and the Greek classics. In 1823 he went to Italy, and on his return in the following spring astonished his friends by announcing his marriage with the daughter of the former director of the Belvedere, whom he had long treated as a sort of pupil. One of his last appearances in public was at a soirée of the Gesellschaft der Musikfreunde in 1833, when he sang the 'Wanderer.' He died in 1840, Nov. 19, on the same day on which his friend Schubert had departed twelve years before, and was buried in the churchyard of Matzleinsdorf, where rest Gluck and his wife (1787), Salieri (1825), and the eminent singers Forti (1859), Staudigl (1861), and Ander (1864).   C. F. P.

VOGLER, GEORG JOSEPH, the Abbé (b. Würzburg, June 15, 1749 ; d. Darmstadt, May 6, 1814), is one of the most curious figures in the annals of music. He evinced from an early age a religious cast of mind and an aptitude for music, and his attachment to the organ dated from his tenth year. Both his father and his step-father, one Wenceslaus Stautinger, were violin-makers. While learning the organ his stepfather let him have pedals attached to his harpsichord, and Vogler practised with such determination all night that no one would live on the floor below.

At the same time his independent turn of mind exhibited itself. He elaborated a new system of fingering, and contrived to learn the violin and other instruments without a teacher; and even while a pupil at the Jesuits' College he played much in the churches, and made a name for himself in the contrapuntal preludes which were regarded as the test of an organist's skill.[1] How long this sort of life lasted is not very clear, but Vogler himself declares that he was at Würzburg as late as 1769.

STUDIES.—His departure must have taken place very shortly after this. He proceeded in the first place to Bamberg to study law. In 1771 he went from Bamberg to Mannheim, then one of the chief musical centres of Germany, and obtained permission to compose a ballet for the Court Theatre, which produced such an impression that the Elector, Karl Theodor, was led to provide him with funds to go to Bologna and study counterpoint under Padre Martini. Starting about the beginning of 1773 Vogler travelled by way of Venice. He there met Hasse, and also a pupil of VALLOTTI (q.v.), from whom he first heard of the system of harmony that he subsequently advocated with such vehemence.[2] The original object of his journey was not achieved, for, though kindly received by Martini, they speedily conceived a repugnance for each other. Vogler could not tolerate a slow and graduated course of counterpoint ; and Martini complained that his pupil had neither perseverance nor aptitude. Vogler soon abandoned the trial, and repaired to Padua with a view of studying for Orders, and learning composition from Vallotti, who had been for nearly fifty years musical director of San Antonio. But the old organist's method of teaching was wholly distasteful to his disciple, and in five months Vogler went on to Rome, where he was ordained priest at the end of 1773.[3] In the Papal city he was made Apostolic Protonotary and Chamberlain to the Pope, knight of the Order of the Golden Spur, and member of the Academy of the Arcadians. He also found time to gain some instruction from the Bohemian musician Mysliweczek, and armed with these ecclesiastical credentials and musical experience he returned in 1775 to Mannheim.[4] The Elector at once appointed him court chaplain, and he proceeded forthwith to compose a ' Miserere '

with orchestral accompaniments, and was made second Kapellmeister, a result partly owing to the influence of some ladies of the court, if Mozart may be trusted.[5]

It was at Mannheim that he first put himself forward as a teacher, and established the first of his three schools. He maintained that most previous teachers had pursued erroneous methods, and promised to make his pupils composers by a quicker system. All this naturally provoked much opposition, but his school must have had some merits, for amongst those who were actually students or came directly under its influence were Winter, Ritter, Kraus, Danzi and Knecht—an ardent disciple. At Mannheim Vogler made enemies as well as friends, and it is probable that when Mozart visited Mannheim in the winter of 1777 he fell into that section of the musical world there. On no other supposition can we fully explain the tone in which he speaks of Vogler in his letters, which will not allow the Abbé a single redeeming feature. Vogler at any rate was studiously attentive to Mozart, and after having several times in vain invited Mozart to call on him, put his pride in his pocket, and went to call on the newcomer.[6] During Mozart's visit the Elector-Palatine became Elector of Bavaria, and in the same year (1778) removed the court to Munich. Vogler's devotion to his school kept him at Mannheim, and he did not, in all probability, go to Munich till 1780. His five years at Mannheim are marked by other achievements than the Tonschule. At the end of 1777 we find him opening a new organ built after his design at Frankfort. The next year, in all likelihood, he was summoned to Darmstadt by the heir-apparent—the Prince who provided him with a home in his last years—to compose the music for a melodrama called ' Lampedo ' (or ' Lampredo ').[7] Another work was the overture and entr'actes to ' Hamlet,' brought out at Mannheim in 1779. These were succeeded by an operetta, ' Der Kaufmann von Smirna,' written about 1780 for the theatre at Mainz.

TRAVELS.—The next twenty years of Vogler's life present great difficulties to his biographer. Although nominally settled at Stockholm from 1786 or 1787-99, he was really constantly travelling, and the records of his journeys are so fragmentary and contradictory, that it is impossible to construct a complete narrative. Thus, though he undoubtedly extended his travels to Spain, Portugal, Greece and Africa, nay, even to Armenia and Greenland,[8] the authorities are by no means agreed as to when he went. One writer[9] gives it in 1783–86, another[10] in 1792, while the dates at which he appears in other distant spots make it difficult

1 See also the Graduale (De Profundis) of the Missa Pastorica.
2 The account in the text follows the statements usually made with reference to Vogler's proceedings at Bologna and Padua. But in the Musikalische Correspondenz of Spires for 1790, No. 15, Professor Christmann asserts that the Elector Palatine himself directly recommended Vogler to Vallotti.
3 A.M.Z. vol. vi. p. 250.
4 According to a statement in his Choral System (p. 6), it was in this year that he learnt the basis for his system from Vallotti.

5 Letter, Nov. 13, 1777.   6 Mozart's Letter of Jan. 17, 1778.
7 For a detailed account see the A.M.Z. vol. i. Nos. 23 and 24.
8 A.M.Z. vol. iii. p. 268 ; vol. ix. p. 386.
9 Fétis.   10 A.M.Z. vol. xxiii. p. 257

to understand how such an extensive tour could have been managed at all.

About 1780 Vogler followed the Electoral court to Munich. He there employed himself in perfecting the education of the celebrated singer Madame Lange, in teaching composition to B. A. Weber, and in composing an opera in five acts entitled 'Albert III. von Baiern,' which was represented at the Court Theatre in 1781. It did not prove successful, and disgust at the want of appreciation that he found in Germany seems to have induced him to appeal to foreign musicians. With this view he submitted an exposition of his system to the Académie Royale des Sciences, probably in 1781, and to the Royal Society in 1783.[1] In 1782 he was in Paris[2] and the next year perhaps crossed the Channel to England.[3] Returning from England, if indeed he really visited it at this time, he again attempted to obtain success as an opera composer. But his comic opera 'La Kermesse,' produced at the Théâtre de la Comédie Italienne on Nov. 15, 1783, proved a dead failure, and could not even be finished. Another effort in Germany was crowned with success. 'Castor and Pollux,' produced at Munich in 1784, was not only received with applause but continued a favourite for years.[4] The close of 1784 and beginning of 1785 appear to have been occupied with the journey to Africa, Greece and the East. At all events the next definite trace of him is on Nov. 22, 1785, at a great organ recital in Amsterdam, for which no fewer than 7000 tickets were sold.[5] In the next year he entered the service of the King of Sweden as Kapellmeister, resigning his posts at Munich, where he had become chief Kapellmeister on the death of Holzbauer in 1783.[6] At Stockholm he established his second Tonschule, but neither that nor his official duties put much check on his roving propensities. He signalised his arrival with a French opera, 'Eglé,' produced in 1787, but the next year he is at St. Petersburg,[7] and in Nov. 1789 at Amsterdam.

ENGLAND.—He arrived in London at the beginning of 1790, and was very successful. His performances were applauded and he was entrusted with the reconstruction of the organ in the Pantheon. According to Gerber[8] he intro-

duced organ pedals into this country, and their introduction by the organ-builder, England, certainly belongs to the year of his visit. (See ORGAN, Vol. III. p. 753.) His last performance at the Pantheon took place on May 31, and the proceeds of his visit amounted to £1000 or £1200. One of his most admired performances was 'The pastoral festival interrupted by a storm,' which seems to be the piece by Knecht which was the precursor of Beethoven's Pastoral Symphony. (See KNECHT.) He went to the Handel Festival in Westminster Abbey,[9] but was not much impressed. The Festival ended on June 3, and he next appeared at Warsaw. In the early part of September he was giving concerts at Coblenz, Mainz and Frankfort. From thence he journeyed on, through Worms, Carlsruhe, Durlach and Pforzheim, to Esslingen, where the enthusiastic inhabitants presented him with the 'wine of honour' usually reserved for sovereigns.[10] Rackwitz remained at Frankfort, making a free-reed stop for the Carmelite church,[11] but Vogler probably rejoined him in time for the coronation of Leopold II. on Oct. 9. The Abbé now began to be held in honour in his own country. At Frankfort his 'Hallelujah' fugue fairly astonished both friends and enemies.[12] It was at this time he projected a return to London with the view of establishing a manufactory of free reeds.[13] This intention was not carried out : he returned to Stockholm, and was followed by B. A. Weber, who gave up his position as conductor at Hanover to obtain further instruction from his old master. The early part of 1791 was employed in the composition of 'Athalie' and 'Gustav Adolf,' and in September he was giving organ recitals in Hamburg. The assassination of Gustavus Adolphus III., whom he liked and respected,[14] on Mar. 16, 1792, only a few days after the production of his opera, started him off with Weber on another long tour through Sweden, Norway, Denmark and the Netherlands.[15] In the next year[16] he undertook a course of lectures on harmony, and in 1794 betook himself to Paris to hear the choruses accompanied by wind instruments with which the new-born republic solemnised its fêtes, and to add the result of his observations to his 'Polymelos or characteristic music of divers nations.' At St. Sulpice he gave an organ performance for the poor, the receipts of which were 15,000 livres. On his return he gave a second course of lectures in 1795,[17] and in 1796[18] erected his

1 *Choral System*, pp. 1-5. The records of the Royal Society afford no trace of communication from Vogler or anything else bearing on the question. The *Journal des Sçavans* for 1782 has an anonymous article comparing the Tonometers of Pythagoras, the Greeks, and the Abbé Vogler, which states that his instrument had been presented to the Académie Royale des Sciences together with the inventor's new musical system, which he proposed to publish shortly.
2 So at least we may infer from the date of his *Essai de diriger le goût*, etc., published in Paris.
3 *Choral System*, p. 5.
4 Fétis assumes that 'Castor and Pollux' was produced at Mannheim in 1791, but contradicts himself elsewhere (see his account of Mlle. Kreiner). For the date here given see *A.M.Z.* vol. viii. p. 318.
5 *A.M.Z.* vol. i. p. 575.
6 Fétis speaks as if Vogler resigned his Bavarian appointments in 1782. This is at variance with the title page of Knecht's *Portrait Musical* (for which see PROGRAMME-MUSIC), published in 1784 (see KNECHT). Moreover Winter, who succeeded Vogler as Kapellmeister, obtained the post in 1788. (*A.M.Z.* vol. xxviii. p. 358.)
7 *A.M.Z.* vol. xxv. p. 152.
8 *Lexicon der Tonkünstler*. The Lutheran Chapel had an organ with pedals in 1772. W. H G. F.

9 On Vogler's performances in London see *The Gazetteer and New Daily Advertiser*, for May 8, 22 and 29, 1790.
10 Christmann and Schubart, in *Musik. Correspondenz* for 1790, Nos. 15, 16.
11 Compare with the authorities just quoted, *A.M.Z.* vol. xxv. p. 153.
12 Christmann and Schubart, *l.c.*, give several instances.
13 Christmann. 14 Christmann.
15 To this date some assign his travels in the East.
16 Fétis says 1792.
17 This is explicitly stated by himself. See *Intelligenz-Blatt* attached to *A.M.Z.* of June 25, 1800.
18 *A.M.Z.* vol. xxv. p. 153.

orchestrion at Stockholm. About this time his ten years' engagement as royal music-director came to an end, and he proposed to leave Sweden. But his school was considered so successful [1] that the Regent prevailed on him to prolong his stay till the spring of 1799.[2] In that year he received from the Swedish court an annual pension of 500 dollars, departed for Denmark, and made an unusually protracted stay in the Danish capital, during which he brought out an important work for the church, and another for the stage.

The former was his *Choral-System*, in which he reviewed Fux, Kirnberger and Rameau, and professed to demonstrate that all the Protestant Choral-melodies were written in the Greek modes. Of this work the Danish government ordered 100 copies for distribution gratis to organists. The latter was the music to ' Hermann von Unna.' This, though originally written to a Swedish libretto by Spöldebrand, had not been performed in Sweden. It now proved a great success. Though the ticket office did not open till 4 in the afternoon, people began to assemble round it at 6 A.M.

VIENNA AND GERMANY.—After these achievements Vogler proceeded, in the summer of 1800, to Berlin. There he gave ' Hermann ' several times in German by way of attracting the general public, appealed to the *savants* by his ' Data zur Akustik,' and to the religious world by his proposals to reduce the cost of organ-building. He was entrusted with the reconstruction of the organ in St. Mary's,[3] and gave a performance on it on Nov. 28, 1800. The King of Prussia commissioned him to build an organ at Neu-Ruppin. But this did not keep him in Prussia. He set off to Leipzig, gave three organ recitals in the spring of 1801, and then went on about June to Prague. At Prague he was received with great honour, and made governor of a musical school. It was perhaps in consequence of the failure of his orchestrion that he left Prague for Vienna, arriving about the end of 1802.[4] He was reported to be invited to Vienna to write an opera, and rumours of the forthcoming work were constant throughout 1803. ' Samori,' however, did not actually appear till May 17, 1804, at the Theatre an-der-Wien, after more than fifty rehearsals. It enjoyed a moderate success, but on the course of operatic history at Vienna it exercised no influence at all. Two

other of Vogler's works were given there, ' Castor and Pollux ' (with additions and alterations), in a concert-room on Dec. 22 and 23, 1803, and ' Athalie ' at the Redoutensaal in Nov. 1804. Neither made much impression. While at Vienna, Vogler celebrated the thirtieth anniversary of his ordination. An interesting circumstance connected with his stay there is his meeting with Beethoven, and their extemporising in turn on the piano. (See BEETHOVEN, Vol. I. p. 282.) Another is that here Gänsbacher, and, through him, C. M. von Weber,[5] became his pupils. Weber made the PF. arrangement of ' Samori.' Vogler had now been more than two years in Vienna, and his wandering instincts revived. He spent the summer of 1805 at Salzburg, *en route* for Munich.[6] There he gave organ recitals, and at Christmas had his Pastoral Mass performed in the Court Chapel. When Napoleon, on his return from Austerlitz, paused at Munich to celebrate the marriage of Eugène Beauharnais with the Princess Augusta of Bavaria, the Abbé was the musical hero of the hour, and ' Castor and Pollux ' was performed on the wedding day, Jan. 14, 1806.[7] He made some little stay in Munich, occupying himself as usual in simplifying organs and publishing theoretical works. In Sept. 1807 he turns up at Frankfort, and shortly afterwards [8] received an invitation from the Grand Duke of Darmstadt, Louis I., for whom he had written ' Lampedo ' nearly thirty years before, to settle in that town. The Duke gave him a salary of 3000 florins, a house, with dinner and supper every day from his own kitchen, four wax candles a day and firewood *ad libitum*, the titles of Kapellmeister, and Privy Councillor for Ecclesiastical Affairs, and the Order of Merit of the first class. In return for these honours and emoluments he was not expected to perform any duties, or to take part in the opera unless at the performance of one of his own works. The Duke thought himself well repaid by the mere presence of such a celebrity.

Here he opened his last and most successful Tonschule ; and in the remaining six and a half years of his life became very fond of the dull old town. It contained, in fact, everything necessary to make it a haven of rest. The accusations of charlatanism that he had so often combated down to 1802,[9] at any rate did not penetrate to Darmstadt. In 1810 he visited Frankfort, Mainz, Hanau and Offenbach, with Weber, and made another visit to Frankfort for the production of his pupil's opera ' Silvana ' on Sept. 17. Two years later he journeyed through Munich to Vienna,

[1] B. A. Weber is the only musician of note who studied under Vogler at Stockholm. The School in 1796 consisted of seventeen pupils, while the orchestra of the Academy consisted of twenty-eight Swedes. Four of these Swedes, whose total ages did not exceed thirty-six years, executed one of Vogler's quartets in public, while mere children of the singing school performed several entire operas ! Perhaps Vogler did more real service to Swedish music by giving excellent performances of Gluck's music. (*A.M.Z.* vol. xxiii. p. 257.)
[2] He was at Stockholm, Apr. 28, 1799 (*A.M.Z.* vol. i. p. 592). In July he was travelling between Copenhagen and Hamburg (see his attack on Müller in *A.M.Z.* vol. i., *Intell.-Blatt.* xviii. p. 95), and was at Copenhagen on Nov. 1, 1799 (*A.M.Z.* vol. ii., *Intell.-Blatt.* vi.).
[3] The specification of this organ may be found in the *Intelligenz-Blatt* attached to the *A.M.Z.* for Feb. 4, 1801.
[4] This date is taken from *A.M.Z.* vol. v. p. 374. The *Biographie* Gänsbacher states that Vogler came to Vienna about the end of 1803.

[5] *Life of C. M. v. Weber*, by his son. Gänsbacher (*Biographie*) says that he first made acquaintance with Weber at Vogler's house.
[6] Fétis's statement that Vogler left Vienna in consequence of the war is refuted by dates.
[7] One of the pieces in ' Polymelos ' is written in commemoration of this marriage.
[8] Vogler is found in Darmstadt in 1806. (*A.M.Z.* vol. xxv. p. 153.)
[9] See the Preface to the *Handbuch zur Harmonielehre*.

where it was noticed that he 'preserved his long acknowledged mastery' of the organ. He employed himself in composing for stage, concert-room and church, and his best work, the Requiem, was the occupation of his last days. On May 4, 1814, his friend Gottfried Weber visited him on passing through Darmstadt and remained till mid-day on the 5th. The following day (May 6), at half-past four in the morning, the old musician died of apoplexy. He was buried on the evening of the 7th, quietly, amid tokens of respect and grief from those who knew him, from his old scholar, the Grand Duchess, downwards. Wherever one of his numerous pupils was to be found, the intelligence came like a heavy blow, for it announced the loss of a musician zealous for his art and of a man devoted to his friends.[1]

PERSONALIA.—Vogler was short in stature, and latterly became corpulent. His arms were of great length, his hands enormous, and his general aspect has been described as that of a large fat ape. His singular character was strongly tinged with vanity, and not without a touch of arrogance. He delighted to array himself in his purple stockings and gold buckles, with his black silk ecclesiastical mantle and the grand cross of the Order of Merit given him by the Grand Duke of Hesse.[2] He would take his prayer-book with him into society, and often kept his visitors waiting while he finished his devotions. Beneath his quaint exterior lay remarkable mental gifts, a great insight into character, and a powerful memory. Nor were his egotism and affectation without counterbalancing excellences. He was always anxious to avoid a quarrel, ready to acknowledge the merits of brother artists,[3] and to defend them, even if they had opposed him, provided their music was good. The civility which he showed to Mozart is in marked contrast to Mozart's behaviour towards him. Moreover, his vanity did not blind him to his own defects. He was well aware that harmony, not melody, was the department in which he excelled. 'Had I your flow of melody,' he said to Sterkel, 'and you my science, we should be both great men.'

An enthusiastic contemporary[4] calls him 'an epoch-making man.' The expression is too strong, but as a musical iconoclast Vogler certainly did excellent service. His incessant attacks on the pedantic methods of musical instruction and systems of harmony in vogue, and on the old methods of organ-building, were often extravagant and untrue. His attacks

on rooted prejudices stimulated not only his pupils Weber and Meyerbeer, but acted indirectly on a wide circle.

COMPOSITIONS.—As a composer it was his aim to retain the simple and severe beauty of the old church music and yet enrich it with the wealth of harmony at the command of modern music. He was thus most happy in his treatment of a canto fermo. He brought to this task a facility in vocal counterpoint gained in the ecclesiastical schools of Italy, and an intimate acquaintance with the resources and effects of an orchestra acquired as Kapellmeister at Mannheim. His Symphony in C and his Requiem are his best works, and contain original and striking music. The former was played at the Gewandhaus under Mendelssohn in 1838 and 1839, and by the Euterpe in the season 1844–45. The overture to 'Samori,' whose insignificant themes and fine development make it a type of its composer, was performed later still, in 1847, and the characteristic Pastoral Mass was both popular and impressive. A striking success was achieved by the Psalm 'Ecce quam bonum' at Choron's first Sacred Concert at Paris in 1827, and though the programme included works by Scarlatti, Marcello, Handel, Haydn and Mozart, we are told that the honours rested with Vogler.[5]

INNOVATIONS IN THE ORGAN.—But it was as an organist and theorist that Vogler made most stir. He would travel about playing in the most *ad captandum* style such things as 'Cheu-Tew, a Chinese song,' a 'Hottentot melody in three notes,' 'The Fall of the walls of Jericho,' 'Thunder-storms,' and the like,[6] as if with the design of concealing his complete command of the highest ranges of organ-playing. His extempore playing never failed to create an impression, and in the elevated fugal style he easily distanced all rivals. 'One was amazed at his performance in the severe style,' says Rink; and his study of the construction of the organ gave him an unerring instinct in the selection of stops. The ill-natured criticism of Mozart in his letter to his father of Jan. 17, 1778, is by no means generally endorsed by other contemporary writers. They declare that in transposing and accompanying, Vogler had remarkable readiness and skill, and that as a reader at sight he 'was perhaps unsurpassed and unique.'[7]

In organ-building,[8] his first practical efforts were made in 1784. Five years later he completed an instrument which he called the Orchestrion, and gave performances on it at

1 See the touching letters of Gottfried and C. M. v. Weber on receiving the news of Vogler's death. In the former, by the way, Vogler's age seems wrongly given. In 1845 the Historical Society of Würzburg placed a tablet in the house in which Vogler was born, with the inscription 'Geburtshaus des Tonkünstlers Georg Joseph Vogler, geboren den 15. Juni 1749, gestorben den 6. Mai 1814.'
2 The analysis prefixed to 'Die Scala' has a sort of facsimile of Vogler's signature attached to it. The autograph is as eccentric as the man, being encircled with the most comical flourishes.
3 See Christmann's report of a conversation with Vogler.
4 Schubart, Ästhetik.

5 *A.M.Z.* vol. xxix. p. 558.
6 Christmann mentions a performance intended to represent 'The Last Judgment *according to Rubens*.' Pictorial music has perhaps never been pushed beyond this.
7 Once at least, Vogler met Beethoven, viz. at Sonnleithner's house in the winter of 1803–04. (See BEETHOVEN.) Gänsbacher, who then heard both extemporise for the first time, admired Beethoven, but was perfectly enchanted with the adagio and fugue thrown off by Vogler. So excited was he that he could not go to bed after it, and knocked up his friends at unseasonable hours to quiet his excitement by describing what he had heard (*Biographie*).
8 *Data zur Akustik.*

various dates at Amsterdam, London, Stockholm and Prague. It is described as being 9 feet square, 6 feet high on each side, and 9 in the centre. This box contained about 900 pipes, and had shutters for *crescendos* and *diminuendos*. The reed-stops were free reeds, and variety of power in their case was gained by three canvas screens in the wind-trunk. As to the effect produced, opinions were much divided. At Amsterdam it was asserted to be the *non plus ultra* of organ - building, at Prague it was declared a failure. Vogler was also prepared to 'simplify' old organs. He claimed to work such a metamorphosis in an instrument in three weeks that its effect would be largely enhanced, though many of the old pipes were removed. The cost of an organ on his system was alleged to be a third of that of one built in the old way. Such pretensions were sure to provoke keen opposition. At Berlin he was charged with stealing the pipes removed in 'simplifying' the organ in St. Mary's Church. The falsity of the charge was demonstrated, but it shows the feeling against him.

His proposals were fourfold : viz. (1) to avoid the use of expensive large pipes ; (2) to introduce free reeds ; (3) to arrange the pipes in a different order on the wind-chest, and (4) to remove mutation stops.

(1) The means by which the cost of organs was diminished without depriving them of their resources lay in Tartini's theory that just as a note gives certain harmonics, so the harmonics of a note if combined give the fundamental note. The first harmonics of a pipe of 32 feet would be represented by pipes of 16 feet and of $10\frac{2}{3}$ feet. It was therefore possible by employing a pipe of 16 feet and a pipe of $10\frac{2}{3}$ feet together to obtain a 32-foot sound without having to use a 32-foot pipe. Time appears, on the whole, to have decided in favour of Tartini and Vogler on this point. It is true that some organ-builders and organists still hold that the 'third sound' is but a poor apology for the real pipe-produced sound, and that every organ of any pretensions still contains large pipes. On the other hand, a quint on the pedal organ undoubtedly enjoys great favour as an adjunct to or substitute for the 32-foot stop.

(2) The free reed was derived from a Chinese organ, and was applied about 1780 to organ reed-stops by a Copenhagen organ-builder named Kirsnick, who had settled at St. Petersburg. Vogler was so impressed with Kirsnick's experiment that he induced Rackwitz, Kirsnick's assistant, to follow him to Stockholm, and make several stops on this principle. When Vogler returned to Germany in 1799 he carried the invention with him wherever he went, and it was through his advocacy that people first realised its capabilities. To this initiative must be attributed not only the free-reed stops in organs, but also the HARMONIUM (*q.v.*) and its varieties.

(3) Vogler arranged the pipes of an organ in semitonal order—the large pipes at the left end of the sound-board, and the small pipes at the right end. Most organ-builders adhere to the old system; but Vogler's arrangement has found adherents.

(4) On the fourth point Vogler has achieved an undoubted success. The mixtures still found in organs are not the overwhelming ones that he assailed. Outside the particular questions raised by Vogler, his influence on organ-building was considerable, and much of the improvement therein in the last hundred years may be ascribed to his attacks.

THEORETIC TEACHING.—As a theorist Vogler developed the tenets of Vallotti. His system of harmony was founded on acoustics, and its fundamental principle was that not only the triad (common chord), but also the discords of the seventh, ninth and eleventh could be introduced on any degree of the scale without involving modulation. He went even beyond this, and allowed chromatically altered forms of these chords and inversions of them. But his system never took much root. According to Knecht, its most ardent advocate, it was full of practical advantages, placed in a clear light the formation of the scales, simplified figuring and thorough-bass, and got rid of all sorts of meaningless and confusing terms, 'dominants that do not dominate, Vorschlags, Nachschlags, etc.' Two other writers have founded their systems on that of Vogler, F. J. C. Schneider and Jelensperger ; but it has passed into oblivion.

It is as a teacher that Vogler has most claims on posterity, for no musician has ever had so many remarkable pupils. As a teacher of singing he was in great request, and the celebrated Madame Lange (Aloysia Weber) owed almost everything that was admirable in her singing to his instruction.[1] It was, however, to the teaching of composition that he directed his greatest efforts ; and from his Schools at Mannheim, Stockholm and Darmstadt came forth Winter,[2] Ritter, Kraus, Danzi, Kornacher, B. A. Weber, Baron von Poisel, Gänsbacher, C. M. von Weber and Meyerbeer. Sterkel also received lessons from Vogler, and Knecht the organist and Gottfried Weber were very directly influenced by him. His pupils conceived the deepest regard for him. 'Mere association with him,' says Gänsbacher, 'was a kind of school.' Vogler was not only a most judicious and sagacious teacher,[3] he was also the kindest and most generous of friends, and he reaped the reward of his kindness by finding that his old pupils

[1] Schubart, *Ästhetik*, p. 135.
[2] Winter afterwards objected to be called a pupil of Vogler, apparently without good reason. Compositions of his appear in the *Mannheimer Tonschule*.
[3] As for instance when he made C. M. v. Weber go back to the study of the great old masters in 1803

after passing into the world were ever ready to return to his side.[1] Few scenes of artistic life are more charming than the picture of the details of Vogler's last Tonschule at Darmstadt. After the Abbé had said Mass, at which one of his scholars played the organ, all met for a lesson in counterpoint. Then subjects for composition were given out, and finally each pupil brought up his piece to receive the criticism of his master and fellow-pupils.[2] Every day a work of some great composer was analysed. Sometimes the Abbé would propound a theme for improvisation. Not unfrequently he would play himself, as he never played except when alone with his 'three dear boys,' in the empty church. From the mind of one of these 'boys' the impression of these performances was never effaced, for Weber always described them as a thing not to be forgotten. Anon we get glimpses of Weber at work on 'Abu Hassan' or on 'Papa's' biography, while the 'old gentleman' looks on, and advises or composes, consuming 'enormous quantities of snuff.' By way of varying the regular routine the master would take his scholars with him to organ recitals in neighbouring towns. The pupils, in their turn, would diversify the common round by writing an ode to celebrate 'Papa's' birthday.[3] A happier household can hardly be imagined. When the master died, his pupils felt as if they had lost a father. 'Reiner . . . announced to me yesterday,' wrote Weber to Gänsbacher (May 13, 1814), 'that on the 6th our beloved master Vogler was suddenly snatched from us by death. . . . He will ever live in our hearts.'

A list of Vogler's works in various departments is appended.

OPERATIC WORKS

(Arranged as far as possible in chronological order, with the places where they were first performed.)

Ino, cantata by Ramler. Darmstadt, 1779.
Lampedo (or Lampredo), a melodrama. Darmstadt, about 1779.
Hamlet, overture and entr'actes for the play of. At Mannheim, 1779.
Der Kaufmann von Smirna, operetta. At Mannheim, 1771.
Albert III. von Baiern, opera in 5 acts. At Munich, 1780.
La Kermesse, opera. At the Comédie Italienne in Paris, Nov. 15, 1783.
Le Patriotisme, opera. Versailles, 'on occasion of Siege of Gibraltar,' 1783.
Castor and Pollux, opera in 3 acts. At the Italian Opera in Munich, during the Carnival of 1784.[4]
Eglé, French opera. At Stockholm, 1787.
Le Patriotisme, opera. Written for the Paris Académie in 1788, but rejected, or, at all events, not performed.
Athalie, choruses in Racine's play of. At Stockholm, 1791.
Gustav Adolf, Swedish opera. At Stockholm, Mar. 1792.
Hermann von Unna, overture, choruses, dances and one song. At Copenhagen, in the early part of 1800.
Die Hussiten vor Naumburg im Jahr 1432. 'Schluss-Chor' to Kotzebue's drama. At Leipzig, Sept. 1802.
Samori, opera in 2 acts, words by F. X. Huber. At the Theatre an-der-Wien, Vienna, May 17, 1804.
Der Admiral, comic opera. Darmstadt, 1810.

---

[1] E.g. Kraus in 1779, B. A. Weber in 1790, C. M. von Weber in 1809, Gänsbacher in 1810.
[2] Gänsbacher tells us that Moses Mendelssohn's Translation of the Psalms was a favourite text-book for the daily exercise at Darmstadt. 'At first,' he adds, 'we took the exercises in the afternoon, but the Abbé, who almost daily dined with the Grand Duke, used to go to sleep, pencil in hand. We therefore agreed to take our exercises to him henceforward in the morning.'
[3] In 1810. Weber wrote the words, Gänsbacher two solos, Meyerbeer a terzet and chorus.
[4] This was one of Vogler's most successful works. The chorus of Furies was sufficiently popular in 1821 to lead an unscrupulous manager at Munich to introduce it into the *finale* of the second act of 'Don Giovanni'!

Epimenides.—Erwin und Elmire.—Der gewonnene Prozess.—Les Rendezvous de Chasse.—Die Kreuzfahrer; overture.—Der Eremit auf Formentarra, ditto.—Prolog, Comödie—Scena de Fulvia—Jägerballet.—Schmied-ballet.

Also probably a number of similar works, of which particulars are not now attainable. Certainly an overture for a play called 'Die Kreuzfahrer,' and either an opera called 'Agnes Bernauerin' or incidental music to a play of that name. A letter of Weber, Jan. 1811, says 'Papa is composing a little opera . . . it will be ready in a few days.'

CHURCH MUSIC

1. MASSES

No. 1, Missa solennis in D min., for 4 Voices, Orchestra and Organ.
No. 2, Missa pastoricia in E, for 4 Voices, Orchestra and Organ.
Missa de Quadragesima in F, for 4 Voices and Organ *ad lib.*
Missa pro Defunctis (Requiem) in E♭, for 4 Voices and Orchestra.[5]
Missa Agnus Dei.
German Mass, for 4 Voices and Organ (about 1778).
German Mass, for 4 Voices and Orchestra.

2. PSALMS AND MOTETS

Psalms.—Psalmus Miserere decantandus a quatuor vocibus cum Organo et basis, S. D. Pio VI. Pontifici compositus (about 1777).
Miserere in E♭, for 4 Voices, Orchestra and Organ.
Miserere, 'Ps. 4.'—In exitu. 'Ps. 5.'
Memento Domine, orch.—Psalm, 'Jehova's Majestät.'
Davids Buss-Psalm, nach Moses Mendelssohns Übersetzung im Choral-Styl. For 4 real parts, one, the Tenor, *ad lib.* (about 1807).
Ecce quam bonum (133rd Psalm), for 4 Men's Voices with PF. *ad lib.*
Motets.—Suscepit Israel (composed for Concert Spirituel at Paris apparently before 1780).
Rorate Coeli, for 4 Voices with PF. (ed. by G. Weber, with German words; with English and Latin words in Vocal Anthology).
Ave Regina, for 4 Voices with Org. or PF. (Latin and German words.)
Cantate Domino, for 4 Voices with Org. or PF. (Ditto.)
Laudate, for Soprano solo, chorus, Organ obbligato and Orchestra.
Postquam impleti (Sereniss. Puerperae sacrum), 4 Voices and Orch.

3. HYMNS, ETC.

Te Deum in D, for 4 Voices and Orchestra.
Kyrie, with Orch. (Oct. 1776).
Magnificat, with Orch. (1777).
Stabat Mater, with Orch. acc.
Ecce panis angelorum (about 1777).
Ave Maris Stella, and Crudelis Herodes, for 2 Choirs with Org. or PF.[6]
Veni Sancte Spiritus, Graduale in B♭, for 4 Voices, Orchestra and Organ.
Beatam me dicent, Orch.
Alma Redemptoris, Orch.
Jesu Redemptor, Orch.
Regina coeli and Laudate Dominum, Orch.
Ave Regina, Org.
Salve Regina, for 4 Voices with Org. or PF. *ad lib.*
Salve Regina, Ave Regina, and Alma Redemptoris, for 4 Voices with Org. or PF. *ad lib.*
Cantus processionalis pro festo corporis Christi.
Vesperae de Paschale (14 Apr. 1805).
Vesperae chorales modulis musicis ornatae, with Orch. acc. (These Vespers *may* be identical with the work next mentioned.)
Vesperae chorales, 4 Vocum cum Organo.
4 Latin Hymns, for 4 Voices with PF. *ad lib.*
6 Hymns, for 4 Voices with Org. or PF. *ad lib.* (Latin and German words—ed. by Gottfr. Weber.)
12 Church Hymns, for 3, 4, or 8 Voices unacc. (First Series).
6   ,,   ,,   ,,   (Second Series).
6   ,,   ,,   ,,   (Third Series).
6   ,,   ,,   ,,   (Fourth Series).
6   ,,   ,,   ,,   (Fifth Series).
3 Hymns, for 4 Voices with PF. *ad lib.*: Defectio tenuit (F min.); Deus caritas est (A); O Salutaris (C).
Heilig (1809).—Chorale (1813).—O God vi lofve dig, Orch.—Hessische Vater unser, Orch.
Die Auferstehung Jesu.

4. MISCELLANEOUS

Paradigma modorum ecclesiasticorum (about 1777).
Fugues a 4, on themes of Pergolesi's Stabat Mater (about 1777).
S. Kilian's Lied (for 2 Choirs).[7]

INSTRUMENTAL MUSIC

Op. 1. 6 Trios, PF., Violin and Bass.—Duos for Flute and Violin.
Op. 2. 6 easy Sonatas, PF.
Op. 3. 6 easy Sonatas PF. and Violin.
Op. 4. 6 Sonatas, in the form of Duets, Trios and Quartets, PF. Violin, Viola and Bass.

---

[5] The composition of this Requiem for himself occupied most of Vogler's later years. It was esteemed his finest work, and is a very striking composition. Besides the ordinary constituents of a Requiem, it contains Agnus (2 settings), a 'Libera me, Domine,' in 4 movements and an 'Absolutio ad Tumbam.'
[6] In the library at Darmstadt is a 'Crudelis Herodes,' with orch., dated Jan. 1776, and also a 'Hymnus Ave Maris stella, a 4 vocibus senza istromenti,' possibly identical with the works in the text.
[7] A.M.Z. 1820, Beylage V. June 21.

Op. 5. 6 Concertos, PF. (in two books, each containing 3 pieces).
Op. 6. 6 Trios, PF., Violin and Bass.
Op. 7. 6 Trios, PF., Violin and Bass.
Op. 8. 12 easy Divertissements of national character, PF. (two books, six in each).—Concerto, PF. (played before the Queen of France).
Op. 9. 112 easy Preludes for Organ or PF. (about 1804).
Concerto, PF., printed with a Concerto by Kornacher about 1784.—Nocturne, PF. and Strings.—Quatuor Concertante, PF., Violin, Viola and Bass.—6 Sonatas for 2 PF. (1794).—Sonata, PF. (4 hands).—Sonata (Der eheliche Zwiet), PF. with Strings (C).—Pièces. PF.—Air de Marlborough, var. PF. March with var. PF. 15 Var. (Lied aus dem Lügner) PF.—16 Var. PF. (F).—Pastorella, PF. (about 1807).—Canzonetta Veneziana varié (about 1807).—Var. (March and Swedish air) PF. (about 1812).²—Polonaise favorite, PF. (D) (about 1812).—5 Var. on March from 'Samori,' PF., Viol. and Violoncello (F).—6 Var. Duo (Was brauchen wir) in 'Samori,' PF., Violin and Violoncello (D). 6 Var. on Duo in 'Samori,' PF., Viol. and Violoncello (G).—6 Var. on Trio (Sanfte Hoffnung) in 'Samori,' PF., Violin and Violoncello (A).—7 Var. on Theme from the Overture to 'Samori,' PF., Violin and Violoncello (C).
Polymelos, or characteristic music of different nations, PF. and Strings (1792?).—Polymelos, a characteristic organ-concert, arranged for PF. with Violin and Violoncello ad lib. (1806?).³
Var. PF., with Orch. acc.—Var. on 'Ah que dirai-je Maman,' PF. with Orch. acc.—Symphony in G (1779).—Do. in D min.—Do. in C.—Baierische Nationalsymphonie.—L'Invocazione, for Guitar.⁵
(See D.D.T. 2nd Series xv. and xvi., Mannheim Chamber Music, ed. Riemann.)

THEORETICAL WORKS

Tonwissenschaft und Tonsetzkunst. Mannheim, 1776.
Stimmbildungskunst. Mannheim, 1776.
Churpfälzische Tonschule. Mannheim, 1778.⁶
Mannheimer Tonschule. Offenbach.⁷
Betrachtungen der Mannheimer Tonschule. Spire,⁸ (1778–80).
Essai de diriger le goût des amateurs de musique. Paris, 1782.
Introduction to the Theory of Harmony (Swedish). Stockholm, 1795.
Method of Clavier and Thorough Bass (Swedish). Stockholm, 1797.
Organ School (Swedish). Stockholm, 1797.
Choral System. Copenhagen, 1800.
Data zur Akustik. Offenbach, 1800.
Handbuch zur Harmonie Lehre, und General-Bass. Prague, 1802.⁹
Äusserung über Hrn. Knechts Harmonik. Prague, 1802.
Erklärung der Buchstaben die in Grundriss der . . . neu zu erbauenden S Peters Orgel in München vorkommen. Munich, 1806.
Vergleichungsplan der vorigen mit der nun umgeschaffenen Orgel in Hofbethause zu München. Munich, 1807.
Über die harmonische Akustik. Munich, Offenbach, 1807.
Gründliche Anleitung zum Clavierstimmen. Stuttgart, Vienna, 1807.
Deutsche Kirchenmusik die vor 30 Jahren zu 4 Singstimmen und der Orgel komponiert, und mit einer modernen Instrumental-begleitung bereichert. Munich, 1807.¹⁰
System für den Fugenbau. Offenbach, 1811.¹⁰
Über Chorale und Kirchengesänge. Ein Beitrag zur Geschichte der Tonkunst im 19ⁿ Jahrhundert. Munich, 1814.
To this class of works the following may also be fitly assigned : Verbesserung der Forkelschen Veränderungen (of 'God save the King'?), 1793.
32 Preludes for Organ in every key, with an analysis. Munich, 1806.
12 Chorals of J. S. Bach (arranged by Vogler and analysed by C. M. v. Weber). Leipzig, about 1810.

Amongst Vogler's contributions to current musical literature may be noticed, besides those

---

¹ Gänsbacher says that 'Vogler's Quintet ' was played at the soirée in Sonnleithner's house at which Vogler and Beethoven met. (See Vol. I. p. 282.) This Nocturne is perhaps meant.
² The march is described as 'd. l'ordre d. Seraphins,' but this appears to be only a short way of putting 'marche des Chevaliers de l'ordre des Seraphins.' The Seraphin is the oldest Swedish Order.
³ It is quite possible that the staple, at any rate, of the two works styled Polymelos is the same. The latter originated from and is practically the substance of an organ recital given by Vogler at Munich on Mar. 29 and 31, 1806. Its contents consist of sixteen numbers, viz. No. 1, Volkslied ; No. 2, Swedish Air ; No. 3, Bavarian Vater Unser ; No. 4, Venetian Barcarolle ; No. 5, Volkslied ; No. 6, Swiss Ranz des Vaches ; No. 7, An African Air ; No. 8 ; No. 9, Bavarian Volkslied ; No. 10, Scotch Air ; No. 11, Jan. 14—A Bridal Song ; No. 12, A Cossack Air ; No. 13, The Return of the Wounded Bavarian Knight ; No. 14, Moorish Air ; No. 15, Greenland Air ; No. 16, Chinese Air. Each of these appears to have had variations appended, and the variations on Nos. 2 and 15 were published separately. The 'Greenland Air ' is said to have been noted down by Vogler in that country, while the seven Bavarian Volkslieder were the Abbé's own composition ; No. 11 is a piece commemorative of the marriage of Eugène Beauharnais with the Princess of Bavaria on Jan. 14, 1805, and No. 13 was published separately as an ' Ode.'
⁴ The last movement in this Symphony is called ' The Scala.' The Symphony was not published till after Vogler's death. At Knyvett's concert in Willis's Rooms on Feb. 25, 1811, the Second Part opened with a ' New Symphonie for 2 clarinets, 2 oboes, 2 flutes, 2 horns and trumpet (obbligati) '—' never performed in this country '—by Vogler, but what this was it seems impossible to ascertain.
⁵ This may be the work of some musician of like name. Christmann also speaks of a Sonata for Harp, with accompaniment for Flutes and Violoncello. Rink, in his Autobiography, mentions Variations for Clavier on a Swedish March in E major.
⁶ This embodies the last-named work.
⁷ This embodies the three preceding works.
⁸ A magazine recording the progress of the school, 1776–79.
⁹ A translation from the Swedish.
¹⁰ Fétis declares that this work was not published till after the author's death. The preface, however, is dated ' Darmstadt, 1811. It seems to have been written for the instruction of Meyerbeer.

---

which were reprinted separately, and have been already mentioned :

Several short notices in the Wetzlarische Conzertanzeiger (1779–1780).
Von der Musik in Frankreich, in Kramer's Magazin der Musik.
Antwort auf verschiedene sein Sistem betreffende Fragen in Musik. Korrespondenz No. 2, 1790.
Bemerkungen über die der Musik vortheilhafteste Bauart eines Musikchor, in Journal von und für Deutschland, No. 2, 1792.

The following treatise not improbably belongs to this class :

Ästhetisch-kritische Zergliederung des wesentlich vierstimmigen Singe-satzes des vom Knecht in Musik gesetzen ersten Psalms.

Lichtenthal also ascribes to Vogler the article Über den Choralgesang der Böhmischen Kirche zu Johann Hussens Zeiten, in the A.M.Z. for Apr. 6, 1803.

MISCELLANEOUS WORKS

Die Scala oder personificirte Stimmbildungs- und Singkunst, for Soprano Solo, Chorus and Orchestra.¹¹
Der Rheinübergang der Allirten am Neujahrstag, 1814. Cantata with accompaniment for full Orchestra.
Teutonia oder Kriegslied, 1814, with Orch. acc.
Tricordium und Trias Harmonica oder Lob der Harmonie.¹²
Frohe Empfindungen bei der Zurückkunft eines Vielgeliebten. Chorus, with Orch. acc.
Wielands Grab, gedichtet von Ch. Westphalen. Chorus for 4 voices.
Empfindungen des Hessen an 14 Juni. Chorus for 4 Voices.
Der Altarberg. For 4 Voices, with PF. acc.
Sangstücke für d. 19 Augusti. Drottingholm, 1786.
Sangstücke.
L' Invocazione del Sole alla mezza notte in Laponia.¹³
Friedenslied (about 1807)—Der schöne Morgen ; Die volle Mondsnacht. Two songs with PF. accompaniment.
Hessischer Kriegertraum. Song with PF. accompaniment.¹⁴
' Declamatorium '—' Tuiskon ist erwacht.' ¹⁵

BIBL., consulted by the writer : The monograph on Vogler by Th. Nisard (the Abbé Normand), and the Life of C. M. v. Weber by his son ; the vast mass of information relating to Vogler and his views contained in the A.M.Z. ; the articles in Nos. 15 and 16 of the Musikalische Correspondenz for 1790 by Christmann and Schubart; the MS. Biographie Gänsbacher in the possession of Dr. Gänsbacher of Vienna; letters of Vogler belonging to the same. In one of Weber's letters to Gänsbacher he states that he was working hard at Vogler's biography, but the result of his work seems to have completely disappeared. All these are superseded by Prof. Schafhäutl's monograph, Abt Georg Joseph Vogler (Augsburg, 1888).   J. H. M.

VOGLER, JOHN and GERARD, possibly brothers of the Abbé Vogler, came to London, and about 1770 were established as music-sellers and music-publishers in Glasshouse Street, near Burlington Gardens. Gerard was composer of a once popular song, ' Tell me, babbling Echo.' Robert Wornum succeeded to their business probably about 1775.   F. K.

VOGRICH, MAX WILHELM KARL (b. Szeben, Austria, Jan. 24, 1852 ; d. New York, June 10, 1916), Austrian pianist and composer. Having

---

¹¹ The analysis prefixed to this work, after stating that it was finished at Darmstadt on Aug. 25, 1810, declares that the author had in 1777 offered a prize of 100 louis d'or for the discovery of a device by which 4 voices should each sing a scale up and down in only 16 chords, and that no one had been able to find out the secret. The solution given by ' Die Scala ' is certainly ingenious.
¹² A Cantata for Voices and Full Orchestra to words by Professor Meissner. Rousseau's air of three notes is used as the foundation of the whole composition, which extends to eleven numbers Vogler made use of this air as the theme of a piece of considerable dimensions at a concert in Stockholm, Apr. 28, 1799, and published it in five real parts in the A.M.Z. for June 12 in the same year.
¹³ A terzetto published in the A.M.Z. for June 12, 1799.
¹⁴ The publisher's advertisement gives ' Treue ' for ' Traum.'
¹⁵ This piece, an orchestral accompaniment to a declaimed poem, was probably one of Vogler's last works, as it was brought out at Mannheim early in 1814. The poem was by Madame Bürger.

made his début as pianist at the age of 7, he later studied at the Leipzig Conservatory, and toured as a pianist. The latter part of his life was chiefly devoted to composition; he lived successively in New York, Weimar, London and again in New York.   w. s. s.

VOGT, AUGUSTUS STEPHEN (b. Washington, Ontario, Aug 14, 1861; d. Toronto, Sept. 17, 1926), studied music at the New England Conservatory, Boston, and at the Leipzig Conservatorium under Reinecke and Jadassohn. Returning to Canada he held an organistship in Toronto and particularly interested himself in the practice of a cappella choral music. In 1894 he founded the Mendelssohn Choir in Toronto, beginning with 180 singers, all carefully chosen for vocal ability and musicianship, and conducted it from its foundation until 1917, when he resigned and was succeeded by H. A. FRICKER (q.v.).

From the first, Vogt set the highest standard before his singers, and the high reputation of the Mendelssohn Choir was the result of his brilliant abilities as a choral trainer. Under him the Choir not only performed a wide repertory at home, but made many highly successful appearances in the principal cities of the United States.   c.

VOGT, GUSTAVE (b. Strassburg, Mar. 18, 1781; d. Paris, May 30, 1879), French oboe-player, studied at the Paris Conservatoire under Sallantin, and took the first oboe-prize in 1799. While in Rey's class he began to play in public, and was appointed oboe-solo at the Opéra Italien in 1801, and co-professor at the Conservatoire in 1802. In 1805 he entered the band of the Imperial Guard, was present at Austerlitz, and during the occupation of Vienna made the acquaintance of Haydn and Beethoven. After the peace of Tilsit he returned to Paris, and never left it again for any distance. After some time at the Théâtre Feydeau, he succeeded his friend and master Sallantin as first oboe at the Opéra (1814), and professor at the Conservatoire, where he taught with marked success from Apr. 1, 1816, to Nov. 1, 1853. His fame spread, and in 1825 the Philharmonic Society invited him to London, and he played in their concerts. His tone was thought to be thin, harsh and forced, but his execution was astonishing,[1] and he was engaged again in 1828. He was an original member of the Société des Concerts du Conservatoire, and played there regularly till his resignation in 1844, often producing with success compositions of his own. As first oboe in the Chapelle du Roi from 1815–30 he received the Legion of Honour in 1829. He formed many talented pupils, including Brod,[2] Vinit, Verroust, Barré, Lavigne, Delabarre,

Cras, Colin, Berthélemy and Bruyant. Vogt left a considerable number of pieces for the oboe. The library of the Conservatoire has the MS. of his *Method for the Oboe*, and the Museum contains his oboe, cor anglais and baryton.   G. C.

VOICES. (1) For classification according to compass see table given under singing, Vol. IV. p. 763.

(2) For notes on the several types of voice see SOPRANO; MEZZO-SOPRANO; CONTRALTO, ALTO (countertenor); TENOR; BARITONE; BASS-BARITONE; BASS. Also FALSETTO; CASTRATO.

(3) For ancient classification of voices in composition see POLYPHONY; MOTET; PART-BOOKS.

VOICING, a term used in organ-building to express the method of obtaining a particular quality of tone in an organ pipe, and of regulating a series of pipes so that their tone shall be uniform throughout.

The quality of the tone of flue-pipes is mainly dependent on (1) their general shape, (2) their scale; but, after the pipe-maker has turned out a set of pipes of true proportion, the voicer can produce a great variety of qualities by regulating (1) the quantity of wind admitted to the pipe, (2) the thickness of the 'sheet of wind,' (3) the angle at which it impinges on the upper lip, (4) by imparting a special surface to the edge of the lip itself or by cutting it higher and in other ways.

The voicing of reed-pipes is dependent chiefly on (1) the quantity of air admitted, (2) the shape, curve and thickness of the tongue, (3) its position, (4) the relation between the length of tube and the pitch of the note produced.

Voicing thus requires both a delicate ear and skilful hand; it is, in fact, the most artistic part of an organ-builder's work. But few are equally good voicers both of reed- and flue-pipes, and better voicing is obtained from a specialist than from a general hand. In testing the voicing of an organ-stop, an opinion should first be formed as to the merit of the particular quality selected by the voicer; next, the pipes should be consecutively sounded in order to ascertain whether the quality of tone is uniform. This applies both to flue- and reed-pipes.   J. S.

VOIGT, (1) HENRIETTE, *née* KUNZE (b. 1809; d. Oct. 15, 1839), a distinguished German amateur musician, and prominent figure in the musical life of Leipzig.

She was the pupil of L. Berger, and became a remarkable performer, and the warm friend of her teacher.[3] Schumann was introduced to her by Ludwig Schunke, who almost lived in the Voigts' house, and their intimacy became very close. A characteristic story illustrating this is told in the article on SCHUMANN (q.v.),

1 *Harmonicón*, 1825.
2 Henri Brod, a great French oboe-player (b. 1799; d. 1889). Maître, Brod est mort,' said a pupil to Cherubini. ' Ah,' replied the stern old Italian, ' petit son, petit son.'
3 See his letter of 1836, given by Schumann, *N.Z.M.* xi. 159.

and we may here quote Schumann's own expression—'Ich dichte, wenn ich an Sie denke,' which may be rendered, 'The thought of you inspires me.' He alludes [1] to her occasionally in his 'Davidsbündler' articles under the name of 'Eleonore'; and her entry in her album was very characteristic, consisting only of a huge crescendo mark ⸻ reaching across the whole page, with his name below it. This, on inquiry, he explained to predict the continual increase of their friendship. Mendelssohn's contribution to her album was the first sketch of the Gondellied in F♯ minor (op. 30, No. 6); and though there is no mention of her either in his collected Letters or in the *Familie Mendelssohn* there is ample testimony to his esteem for her talents and her person in his *Eight Letters* to her, published in 1871.[2] Hauptmann [3] and C. Löwe have also left the most appreciative references to her ability and taste: indeed she was, with Madame Frege, at the head of the amateurs of Leipzig in that brilliant time.

Her husband, (2) CARL (*d.* June 15, 1881), to whom she was married in Nov. 1830, was a Leipzig merchant, and as great an enthusiast for music as herself. He died in his seventy-sixth year, leaving £300 to the Gewandhaus Concerts for a performance of Beethoven's Ninth Symphony every year, or at the least every two years. A few words about that Symphony, attributed to him, will be found in Schumann's *Ges. Schriften*, 1st ed. i. 27.

(3) WOLDEMAR (*b.* Leipzig, Sept. 2, 1850), son of Carl by his second wife, became professor of physics at Göttingen, formed a Bach choir at Göttingen and wrote on the music of Bach. (*Riemann.*)

VOIGTLÄNDER, GABRIEL (*b. circa* 1580; *d.* ? Sorö, Jan. 1643, court field-trumpeter and chamber musician to Prince Christian of Denmark. He arranged and edited a collection of odes and songs to melodies and airs of the best Italian, French, English and German composers. An important collection of 93 melodies with bass appeared in five editions between 1642 and 1664. A 4-part St. Matthew Passion and songs remained in MS.

E. v. d. s.

VOIX CÉLESTES,[4] VOX CŒLESTIS, VOX ANGELICA, UNDA MARIS; an organ stop with two ranks of pipes, one tuned about three beats a second sharper than the other. The pipes are sometimes of the Dulciana type; sometimes (generally in the case of French organ-builders) two small Gambas, and occasionally the ranks are dissimilar, one a Keraulophon, and one a Dulciana. The custom is to tune one rank with the organ and one sharper,

but this has the effect of making the organ sound disagreeably flat after using the stop, and the plan advocated by Sedley Taylor of tuning one rank slightly above and one below the general pitch of the organ is no doubt preferable, though it precludes the use of either alone, or in combination with the other stops. The Voix Célestes has its proper place in the swell organ, and in large buildings its wavy floating effect is not unpleasing. Like other 'fancy' stops it should be used with great reserve. The name Vox Angelica is ambiguous, some builders making it a synonym for Voix Célestes, and others for the rank of pipes which is tuned to the rest of the organ. It often refers to a stop of two ranks, of which the 'beating' rank is tuned flat, the 'beating' rank of the Voix Célestes being tuned sharp. w. pᴬ.; addns. т. е.

VOLBACH, FRITZ (*b.* Wippelfürst, Rhineland, Dec. 17, 1861), studied at the Cologne Conservatorium and elsewhere, and in 1886 joined the Royal Institute of Church-music at Berlin. Here he remained until 1892, when he accepted the responsible post of music-director at Mainz, where he conducted several choral societies, removing to Tübingen to take up professional work in 1907. During the war (1914–18) he conducted symphony concerts at rest camps, and in 1919 became professor in the University of Münster. He has done much editorial work and published many educational books, notably on orchestration. (See *Riemann.*)

Volbach's style in composition is distinguished for melody, a warm expression, pleasant fancy, and clear individuality. He brings to bear upon his work a full knowledge of vocal and orchestral effects, and a power of embodying his thoughts in scoring which is both effective and artistic.

In England he became known by the symphonic poem, op. 21, played in London at a Promenade Concert in 1901: 'Easter,' for organ and orchestra, was given at the Sheffield Festival of 1902, and in a revised form at a Promenade Concert in 1904, in which season 'Alt Heidelberg' was also played. The frequent hearing of 'Easter' since established it as a popular work. A set of three 'Stimmungsbilder' for choir and orchestra was heard under the composer's direction at the R.C.M. in Dec. 1904. His chief works are as follows:

Symphonic poems: 'Easter,' organ and orchestra; 'Es ware zwei Königskinder'; 'Alt Heidelberg, du feine.'
Symphony in B minor.
Quintet for wind and PF. in E flat.
    ,,   for strings and PF. in D minor.
Comedy opera, 'Die Kunst zu lieben.' (Düsseldorf, 1910.)
Choral ballad, 'Der Troubadour,' male ch. and orch.
    ,,   'Am Siegfrieds Brunnen,' male ch. and orch.
    ,,   'König Laurins Rosengarten,' baritone, male ch. and orch.
'Hymne au Maria' (Dante), ch., solo instruments and organ.
'Raffael,' ch., orch. and organ.
Ballad cycle, 'Vom Pagen und der Königstöchter.'

D. H., addns.

BIBL.—GREGOR SCHWAKE, *Fritz Volbachs Werke*. (Münster, i. W., 1921.)

---

[1] A sketch of her by Schumann appeared in the *Neue Zeitschrift*, Nov. 15, 1839, reprinted in *Ges. Schriften*.
[2] *Acht Briefe und ein Facsimile*, etc. Leipzig, Grunow, 1871. Translated by M. E. von G. in *Macmillan's Magazine*, No. 140.
[3] *Letters to Hauser*, No. 43.
[4] The final *s* is sometimes omitted, but the original French name is undoubtedly in the plural.

VOLKERT, Franz (b. Friedland, near Bunzlau, Feb. 2, 1767; d. Vienna, Mar. 22, 1845), organist and Kapellmeister at the Theater an-der-Wien, wrote graduals, 4 v., organ pieces and about 150 singspiele, musical farces, melodramas, pantomimes, etc., which were very popular in their time; also pianoforte trios, variations, songs, etc. (*Riemann*).

VOLKMANN, (1) Friedrich Robert (b. Lommatzsch, Saxony, Apr. 6, 1815; d. Pest, Oct. 30, 1883). His father, cantor and schoolmaster of the town, taught the boy music, with such effect that by the time he was twelve he took the services in church. He then had instruction from Friebel, the 'Town musician,' in violin and violoncello, and later from A. F. Anacker, music-director of the Seminary at Freiberg. In 1836 he went to Leipzig to study systematically, and made the acquaintance of C. F. Becker, and also of Schumann, who exercised great influence on him; in 1837 he published his first work, 'Phantasiebilder,' in Leipzig. His next step was to visit Prague as teacher in the family of Countess Stainlein-Saalenstein, where he remained from 1839–41. He afterwards went to Pest, where he set up as a teacher and composer, holding various offices from 1841–54. From 1854–58 he resided at Vienna, producing many compositions. He was appointed professor of composition in the Landes-musik-akademie of Buda-Pest in 1878. In spite of its great popularity on the Continent for many years, Volkmann's music has not obtained a permanent place in the estimation of musicians. Fluent, graceful, clever, and not without originality, it yet misses the qualities that make music immortal. A complete list of works follows :

LIST OF VOLKMANN'S COMPOSITIONS

Op.
1. Six Phantasiebilder, pf.
2. Five Songs.
3. First Trio in F for pf. and strings.
4. Dithyrambe and Toccata for pf.
5. Second Trio in B flat minor, for pf. and strings.
6. ' Souvenir de Maróth,' for pf.
7. Romance for violoncello and pf
8. Nocturne for pf.
9. First String Quartet. A minor.
10. Chant du troubadour for vln. and pf.
11. Musikalisches Bilderbuch, pf. 4 hands.
12. Sonata, pf.
13. Three Songs.
14. Second String Quartet, G minor.
15. Allegretto capriccioso, vln. and pf.
16. Three Songs.
17. Buch der Lieder, for pf.
18. Deutsche Tanzweisen, pf.
19. Cavatina and Barcarole for pf.
20. Hungarian Songs for pf.
21. ' Vioegrád ' for pf.
22. Four Marches, pf.
23. Wanderskizzen, pf.
24. Seven Hungarian Sketches, pf. 4 hands.
25. Phantasie and Intermezzo, pf.
26. Variations on a theme of Handel, pf.
27. Lieder der Grossmutter, pf.
28. First Mass for male voices. D major.
29. Second Mass for male voices. A flat.
30. Six Songs for male choir.
31. Rhapsodie for vln. and pf.
32. Three Songs.
33. Violoncello Concerto.
34. Third String Quartet, G.
35. Fourth String Quartet, E minor.
36. Three Improvisationen, pf.
37. Fifth String Quartet, F. minor.
38. Three Geistliche Chöre, with pf. acct.
39. ' Die Tageszeiten,' for pf. 4 hands.
40. Three Marches, for pf. 4 hands.
41. ' Au Tombeau du Comte Széchenyi,' pf.

Op.
42. Concertstück, pf.
43. Sixth String Quartet, E flat.
44. First Symphony, D minor.
45. ' An die Nacht,' alto solo and orch.
46. Liederkreis, for alto.
47. Offertorium, sopr. solo, choir and orch.
48. Three Songs for male choir.
49. ' Sappho,' for sopr. and orch.
50. Fest ouvertüre.
51. Ballade and Scherzetto, pf.
52. Three Lieder for soprano or tenor.
53. Second Symphony, B flat.
54. ' Die Bekehrte,' for sopr.
55. Rondino and Marsch-Caprice, for pf. 4 hands.
56. Two Songs for mezzo-sop., v'cl. and pf.
57. Sonatina for pf. 4 hands.
58. Two Songs for male choir.
59. Weihnachtslied, for choir and soli.
60. First Sonatina, vln. and pf., A minor.
61. Second Sonatina, vln. and pf.
62. First Serenade for string orchestra, C.
63. Second Serenade for string orchestra, F.
64. Altdeutscher Hymnus for male voices, double choir.
65. Kirchenarie for high bass and orchestra.
66. Three Songs, sopr.
67. Six Duets for sopr. and tenor.
68. Overture to Richard III.
69. Third Serenade for string orchestra and v'cl. solo, D minor
70. Two Geistliche Lieder for choir.
71. Three Hochzeitslieder for choir.
72. Three Songs for tenor.
73. Entr'actes for Richard III.
74. Capriccio, v'cl. and pf.
75. Two Songs for choir.
76. Schlummerlied for harp, clarinet, and horn.

Without Opus Numbers
Two Songs.
Variations on the Rheinweinlied for pf.
Capriccietto for pf.
Concert-overture, C.
Four Songs for male choir.
Weihnacht for three-part children's choir.   G.

BIBL.—Hans Volkmann, *Robert Volkmann* (1903); a smaller work (1922); Letters edited by the same.

(2) Hans (b. Apr. 29, 1875), grand-nephew of the above, and his biographer, studied art and musical history at Munich and Berlin. His researches with regard to Astorga (*q.v.*) have cleared away the legends which surrounded the career of that composer.   c.

VOLKSLIED, see Song, subsection Germany.

VOLKSTÜMLICHES LIED, see Song, subsection Germany.

VOLLWEILER, (1) Johann Georg, (b. 1770; d. Frankfort, Nov. 17, 1847), an esteemed professor of music in Frankfort. He was the author of two instruction-books, one in PF.-playing, and one in singing for schools; both published by Schott. Vollweiler was the teacher of two renowned musicians, Aloys Schmitt and Ferdinand Hiller.

His son, (2) Carl (b. 1813; d. Heidelberg, Jan. 27, 1848), had a varied musical career in Germany, Austria and Russia. A MS. symphony, two trios, and many pianoforte pieces are mentioned in *Riemann*.   G.

VOLTA, Prima, Seconda—First, or second time; more commonly seen in the abbreviated forms, '1ma,' '2da,' or with the numerals alone—an indication that the portion of an instrumental movement which is to be repeated is to undergo certain modifications at the close of its repetition, instead of being repeated exactly. The words ' Prima volta,' or the figure 1, are placed over the first version, and ' Seconda volta,' or simply 2, over the second. At first the player goes straight on to the repeat, but the second time he passes from the beginning of the line where ' Prima volta ' stands, to the double bar, so that the portion after the double bar is played instead of that before it.　　　　M.

VOLTE, a kind of ancient dance, in three-time, so called from the figure containing many turns (*volti*). Thoinot Arbeau, in his ' Orché-sographie,' gives the following air of a Volte :

The pieces called ' La Volta,' ' Lavolta,' and sometimes ' Levalto ' in collections of Virginal Music, derive their name from this word.　G.

VOLTI (VOLTI SUBITO)—' Turn over,' ' Turn over quickly.' This direction, or the initials V.S., is used in manuscript and old printed music, at the bottom of a page where, without it, it might be supposed, for one cause or another, that the piece had come to an end. In the appendix to vol. i. of C. H. Bitter's Life of J. S. Bach, part of a song, ' Bist du bei mir,' from the music-book of Anna Magdalena, Bach's second wife, is given in facsimile of the composer's writing. A double bar closes the page, but evidently the song does not end there ; the composer, to prevent any mistake, has added the words ' Volti cito,' the meaning of which is precisely the same as the more usual version of the direction.　　　　M.

VOLUMIER,[1] JEAN BAPTISTE (b. 1677 ; d. Dresden, Oct. 7, 1728), a musician of Belgian extraction, chiefly remembered for his acci-dental connexion with John Sebastian Bach, said to have been born in Spain, and brought up at the French court.[2] He entered the Electoral Chapel of Prussia, Nov. 22, 1692, and soon became *Maître de Concert* and Director of the dance music at the Berlin court, and was renowned for his Ballets. On June 28, 1709, he was appointed Konzertmeister to the court of Dresden. Here he kept up his former reputation for dance music and divertissements, but was also celebrated as a violin-player, especially of French compositions, and a per-former on an instrument of the Hackbrett kind, of his own invention. He was on friendly terms with Bach and an enthusiastic admirer of his genius, and it was during his residence at Dresden, and also at his instigation, that the famous match was arranged between Bach and Marchand the French player, which resulted in the flight of the latter.

BIBL.—FÜRSTENAU, *Zur Geschichte Musik . . . am Hofe Dresdens*; MATTHESON, *Ehrenpforte* ; FORKEL, *J. S. Bach*.　　　　G.

VOLUNTARY, an organ solo played in connexion with a church service. To-day it is so regular a feature that the term has little meaning ; but originally, no doubt, the

[1] The name is said to have been originally Woulmyer.
[2] Mendel.

voluntary was so called because it was merely a casual adjunct to a service, limited to special occasions or dictated by convenience. The use of the word as a musical term seems to have been confined to this country, and its signi-ficance in the matter of form was extremely vague. At the hands of its chief exponents, *e.g.* Benjamin Cooke, Thomas Adams, William Russell, the Wesleys, etc., the voluntary took on a variety of shapes, comprising the prelude and fugue, the hymn tune varied, a group of movements suggestive of the suite or sonata, etc. It is worth noting that when the music publishers, Coventry and Hollier, asked Mendels-sohn to write some organ music, their request was for ' three Voluntaries.' The change of title was due to the composer, who wrote (Aug. 29, 1844) :

' I have been busy about the organ pieces which you wanted me to write for you, and they are nearly finished. I should like you to call them, "Three Sonatas for the Organ" instead of "Voluntaries." Tell me if you like this title as well ; if not, I think the name of "Voluntaries" will suit the pieces also, the more so as I do not know what it means precisely.'

Though the term apparently did not come into general use until the 18th century, many of the pieces by Byrd, Gibbons and other early keyboard writers were obviously designed for use as voluntaries. As English organs at that time had no pedal board, composers often wrote indiscriminately for organ and virginal ; and there is little difference in style between pieces called ' Voluntary,' ' Fancy,' ' In Nomine,' Fantasia and Prelude. Two of the earliest accessible examples of English organ music of the voluntary type are a ' Glorificamus ' (in which a plain-song theme occurs in the alto) by John REDFORD (c. 1486–1540) and a Voluntary by Richard ALWOOD (q.v.), both issued in John E. West's series of ' Old English Organ Music.'

The voluntary is now used only at the beginning and end of a service. For a long period, however, it was a prominent feature during the service, being called the ' Middle Voluntary.' An entry in a ' Vestry Book,' Boston (Lincs.), under date Apr. 29, 1717, is of interest as showing that the voluntary has long had a recognised place in the musical arrangements of a parish church :

' Ye organist who shall be chosen to serve in ye Parish Church of Boston shall play :—Upon Sundays, Holy Daies, and as often as there shall happen to be a Sermon or Homily, One short Voluntary before ye service begins, and another immediately after ye First Lesson . . . and a Voluntary immediately ye service is finished. Also on Communion Daies, a Voluntary between ye Sermon and ye beginning of ye Communion Service, a Short Voluntary at ye finishing of ye Communion.'

Austere in its early days, the voluntary fell from grace during the 18th century, when, despite some admirable examples that are still well worth playing, the general style was superficial. As evidence of its triviality during this period may be cited the well-known essay in the *Spectator* of Mar. 28, 1712, on ' Merry Epilogues after Tragedies, and Jigging Voluntaries.' Similar complaints may be found in periodicals as late as the middle of the 19th century, at which time the custom arose of using transcriptions from all kinds of sources, often inappropriate. There is now a better and rapidly improving standard, owing to the general recognition of the principle that a voluntary should justify itself on the grounds of (*a*) musical quality, and (*b*) fitness for use in connexion with divine service. The ideal is reached when the principle of fitness is developed from the general to the particular, and voluntaries are chosen to suit the liturgical season—and even a given Sunday or holy day. This may be done without great difficulty, as there is now a large repertory of admirable English, German and French organ music based on liturgical themes from plain-song and chorales to modern hymn tunes and carols. Thanks to this wide field of choice, a service may now open and close with organ music not less appropriate than the hymns and anthems. Thus used, the voluntary amply justifies itself, both as a decorative accessory and an aid to devotion.

For examples of the 17th and 18th century ' Voluntary ' at its best, see the large collection of John E. West alluded to above (Novello).

H. G.

VOMÁČKA, BOLESLAV (*b.* Mlada Boleslav, 1887), Czechoslovak composer and writer. He is a doctor of law and practised as a solicitor until he entered the civil service in 1919 (the Ministry of Social Welfare). He studied music at the Prague Conservatoire under Vít. NOVÁK (*q.v.*), and acted as musical critic to the journals *Čas* and *Lidové Noviny.* At present he edits the *Listy Hudebni Matice,* the monthly journal of the musical section of Umělecka Besedá (the Society of Arts). He composes at infrequent intervals, and his works accord with the views which he advocates strongly as regards modern music — that it must now avoid the excessive subjectivity and personal lyricism too freely exploited by the earlier generation, and adapt itself to a more detached and universal expression. He began as a disciple of Schönberg, but soon formed an individual style ; a little harsh, as might be expected from his reluctance to show the least sign of sentimentality, but full of vitality, courage, and robust independence. His workmanship is too firmly based on a sound traditional culture to degenerate into merely freakish experimentalism. His fine pianoforte sonata, introduced to Paris by Mlle. Blanche Selva, has made its way on the Continent. His chief compositions are :

Symphonic Poem ' Mlada ' (Youth) ; Pianoforte Sonata ; Violin and Pianoforte Sonata ; Cycle for Pianoforte, ' Hledani ' (The

Quest) ; Song Cycle, ' 1914 ' ; short Choral Works ; all published by Hudebni Matice, Prague.

R. N.

VOPELIUS, GOTTFRIED (*b.* Herwigsdorf, near Zittau, Jan. 28, 1645 ; *d.* Leipzig, Feb. 3, 1715), became cantor at St. Nicholas, Leipzig, in 1675. He wrote some original tunes to hymns previously set to other music, but is chiefly known as a harmoniser of older melodies in four voice-parts. He adopts the more modern form of regular rhythm (generally 3–2), and freely uses the subdominant and major dominant even in minor keys, and the accidental ♯ and ♮. He published in 1682 the ' Neu Leipziger Gesangbuch,' which contains besides other tunes 100 hymns from Schein's Cantional oder Gesangbuch ' of 1627. R. M.

VORHALT, see APPOGGIATURA.

VORSCHLAG, see APPOGGIATURA ; ORNAMENTS, GERMAN.

VORSPIEL (Ger.), see PRELUDE.

VORTRAG (Ger., lit. a drawing-out), a term used purely in reference to the performance or interpretation of a musical work. The best English equivalent is perhaps ' interpretation ' or ' reading.' Vortrag embraces not only all that belongs to differences of rates of speed and force, but all that lies beyond the mere execution of the written notes in the proper rhythm. ' Vortragsbezeichnungen ' are the directions for the various shades of force and kinds of expression. M.

VOSS, CHARLES (*b.* Schmarsow, near Demmin, Sept. 20, 1815 ; *d.* Aug. 29, 1882), received his musical education at Berlin, and settled in Paris in 1846, where he had a successful career as pianist and teacher, turning out a great number of pianoforte pieces to suit the taste of the day. He also wrote a concerto in F minor which was highly praised by Mendelssohn. (*Riemann* and *Baker.*) M.

VOSS (VOSSIUS), (1) GERHARD JOHANN (*b.* in or near Heidelberg, *c.* 1577 ; *d.* Amsterdam, Mar. 19, 1649), was professor of rhetoric at Leyden in 1618. He was presented by Laud to a canonry at Canterbury in 1629, and became professor of history at Amsterdam in 1633. His works bearing on music are : *De artis poeticae natura ac constitutione,* 1647, and *De quatuor artibus popularibus grammatica, gymnastica, musica et graphica liber,* 1650.

His seventh child, (2) ISAAC (*b.* Leyden, 1618 ; *d.* Windsor, Feb. 21, 1688–89), was in 1649–52 at the court of Christina of Sweden, was given the degree of D.C.L. at Oxford in 1670, and was presented by Charles II. to a vacant prebend in the royal chapel of Windsor on May 12, 1673. In the same year appeared, anonymously, his important contribution to musical literature, *De poematum cantu et viribus rythmi,* a treatise on the alliance of poetry with music. There are some curious criticisms on the work by Roger North in the B.M. Add. MSS. 32,531, fol. 53. For the details of his career, and the list of his works, see *D.N.B.*　　M.

VOWEL SOUNDS. In speaking and singing there is an essential difference between consonants and vowels. A vowel is a continuous sound which can be sustained for as long as may be desired, and will retain throughout the characteristics by which it is distinguished from another vowel. A consonant is in general merely a method of beginning or ending a vowel and cannot be maintained. Consider, for instance, such a word as *book*. The letter *b* represents a particular kind of explosion at the beginning of the vowel sound, and the letter *k* represents another kind of explosion at the end of the vowel. Both these are momentary, whilst the vowel sound can be prolonged indefinitely, and is recognised as *oo* whether the beginning and end are heard or not. Each vowel sound has a characteristic similar to what is called tone or quality in the case of musical notes. We distinguish between *a* and *o*, for instance, in the same way as we distinguish between the note of a violin and that of a flute.

There are certain consonants, such as *s*, *f*, *v*, *m*, etc., sometimes called semi-vowels, which can be maintained, though not in singing, as most of them are merely hisses. What is said below does not apply to these.

It has been shown by Helmholtz that the tone of a musical instrument is dependent on the relative strengths of such harmonic overtones as may be present along with the fundamental (see ACOUSTICS), and it must be some similar feature that gives its special character to any one vowel. The cavity of the mouth serves as a resonator, which intensifies one or more of the constituents of the complex note produced by the vocal cords. The pitch of the note strengthened can be varied by altering the position of the tongue or by varying the extent to which the lips and teeth are separated. Further, by raising the centre of the tongue the cavity of the mouth can be converted into two connected chambers, whereby two distinct notes can be strengthened.

Helmholtz maintained that each vowel is characterised by the presence of overtones strengthened by the mouth resonance. He believed that some vowels have only one such resonance tone, whilst others have two, and that these tones have a definite fixed pitch for any one vowel whatever may be the pitch of the larynx note on which the vowel is sung. His theory is known as the Fixed Pitch Theory.

Other physicists maintain that the overtones which give the vowel its character rise and fall with the larynx note, always remaining at the same intervals above it. This is known as the Variable Pitch Theory and makes the difference between two vowels result from the same cause as gives rise to the differences of quality of the same note played on different instruments.

The exact cause of vowel differences cannot be said to be settled. The majority of physicists, however, regard Helmholtz's Fixed Pitch Theory as being correct as a first approximation, but the matter is probably not quite so simple as Helmholtz imagined it to be.

J. W. C.

VOX HUMANA (VOIX HUMAINE), an organ stop of 8-feet tone and of the reed family, but with very short capped pipes, which therefore reinforce only the overtones of the fundamental. The pipe for the CC note, which would in the case of an ordinary reed-stop be nearly 8 feet in length, is here often only 13 inches. The pipes vary little in length, and there are perceptible breaks in the timbre.

As its name implies, the stop is supposed to resemble the human voice. Burney,[1] speaking of the specimen in the Haarlem organ, says:

'It does not at all resemble a human voice, though a very good stop of the kind : but the world is very apt to be imposed upon by names ; the instant a common hearer is told that an organist is playing upon a stop which resembles the human voice, he supposes it to be very fine, and never inquires into the propriety of the name or the exactness of the imitation. However, I must confess, that of all the stops I have yet heard which have been honoured by the appellation of Vox humana, no one, in the treble part, has ever yet reminded me of anything human so much as of the cracked voice of an old woman of ninety, or, in the lower parts, of Punch singing through a comb.'

This description is by no means out of date. In acoustically favourable buildings, and when only just audible, the stop has sometimes a weird effect which is not unimpressive, but distinctness is quite fatal. The Vox humana should be placed in a box of its own inside the swell box. It is nearly always used with the tremulant. Opinions differ as to its capacity for combining pleasantly with other registers, and this depends upon the kind of stop. There are instances where it gives a piquant quality to other light stops. Its voicing is very delicate and it is liable to get soon out of tune, but a great improvement in this respect can be made by careful scaling, and by giving attention to the consonance of the tube. (See ORGAN: VOCABULARY OF STOPS.)　　W. Pᴬ.

VOZ, LAURENT DE (*b.* Antwerp, 1533 ; *d.* Cambrai, Jan. 1580), brother of the painter Martin de Vos. After having been engaged for some years as a musician at Antwerp Cathedral, Laurent de Voz was appointed master of the children and director of music at Cambrai Cathedral by Archbishop Louis de Berlaymont. His attachment to the latter caused him, during the troublous times which followed, to compose a motet, in which the text was compiled from the Psalms in such a manner as to describe the banishment of Berlaymont, the usurpation of Inchy, his iniquities, the murder of citizens, the vain hope of release

[1] *Present State, Germany,* vol. ii. p. 303.

through the Duc d'Alençon and the probable short duration of the reign of the wicked. The motet, written for a large choir, was performed after vespers in the presence of the usurper, who had him seized and hanged without trial. Lacroix du Maine (*Bibliothèque Française*) mentions de Voz as composer of published motets and chansons, but only one motet, *a* 5 v., published by Phalèse in ' Concentum sacrorum,' etc. (1591), has been discovered so far (*Fétis*; *Mendel*).

VOZIKA, a 17th-18th century chamber musician at the Court of Würtemberg, whence he was dismissed ' on account of his cynical character,' [1] and was appointed to the chapel of the Archbishop of Trèves at Coblenz. He is described as the first soloist on the contrabass, for which he composed some soli. He was still living in 1750.   E. v. d. s.

VRCHLICKY, JAROSLAV (*b.* 1853 ; *d.* 1912), the initiating spirit in modern Czech poetry whose writings have inspired a great number of musical works, and who, in turn, has been inspired by music. He was a remarkable linguist and a felicitous translator. The following are a few of the more important compositions which owe to Vrchlicky their literary idea— Dvořák : the opera ' Armida,' based on the poet's translation of Tasso's *Jerusalem Delivered* ; the oratorio ' St. Ludmila.' Fibich : the melodramas ' Hakon,' ' Queen Emma,' the trilogy ' Hippodameia ' ; comedy overture, ' A Night at Karlstein ' ; incidental music to the poet's ' Pietro Aretino.' J. B. Foerster : the opera ' Jessica ' (founded on Vrchlicky's translation of Shakespeare's *The Merchant of Venice*); melodramas, ' The Three Riders,' ' The Legend of St. Julia.' Karel Bendl : opera, ' Švanda Dudák ' (The Merry Piper). Vít. Novák : opera, ' A Night in Karlstein ; symphonic overture, ' Lady Godiva.' Janáček : ' Amarus,' solo, orchestra and mixed chorus. Many lyrics and brief choral works.   R. N.

VREDEMAN, JACOB, teacher of music at Leuwarden from about 1600–40. He wrote a book of madrigals, canzons and villanelle *a* 4 v. (1603), and a musical instruction book, ' Isagoge musicae ' (1618) (*Riemann*).

VREEDEMAN, SEBASTIAN, of Malines, was appointed, May 12, 1589, composer at Brussels for the carillons of the corporation. He wrote two books of dance tunes for the cither, published by Phalèse in 1568 and 1569 (*Q.-L.*).

VREULS, VICTOR (*b.* Verviers, Belgium, Feb. 4, 1876), viola-player, composer and conductor, studied music at the École de Musique in his native town ; then at the Conservatoire at Liège ; then in Paris with Vincent d'Indy. For seven years he was professor of the viola and of harmony at the Schola Cantorum in Paris. From 1906 he was director at the Luxembourg

Conservatoire. His production is already considerable, his chief works being :

An overture ; a prelude ; 3 symphonic poems ; a symphony with violin solo (Eugene Ysaÿe prize, 1904) ; pieces for various instruments with orchestral accompaniment ; an adagio, and 2 pieces for str. orch. For voice : a cantata, a ' Tryptyque,' 2 songs with orch. ; a number of songs with PF. ; a quartet with PF. ; a str. quartet ; 2 trios ; 2 sonatas for vln. and PF. ; one for v'cl. For the theatre he has produced a lyric drama in 3 acts, ' Olivier le Simple ' (La Monnaie, Mar. 9, 1922), ' Un Songe de nuit d'été,' a fairy comedy in 3 acts (La Monnaie, Dec. 17, 1925).

BIBL.—VICTOR VREULS, *Revue musicale Belge*, i.. Dec. 8, 1925. *S.I.M.*, May 1911.

M. P.

VROYE, THÉODORE JOSEPH DE (*b.* Villers-la-Ville, Belgium, Aug. 19, 1804 ; *d.* Liège, July 19, 1873), Belgian writer on music, was ordained priest in 1828, and devoted all his spare time to the study of plain-song and the liturgical singing of the church. In 1835 he was appointed canon and precentor of the Cathedral of Liège, and conducted the services with a care and taste which produced remarkable results. He published a ' Vespéral ' (1829), a ' Graduel ' (1831), and a ' Processionale ' (1849) which passed through many editions in Belgium ; also, a ' Traité du Plain-Chant ' (1839), a ' Manuale Cantorum ' (1849) and a ' Rituale Romanum ' (1862). His last work, ' De la musique religieuse ' (1866), written in conjunction with the Chevalier Van Elewyck, was a collection of documents and observations relating to the Congresses of Paris (1860) and Mechlin (1863–64) on service music.

VUELTA, see SONG, subsection SPAIN (2).

VUILLAUME, (1) JEAN BAPTISTE (*b.* Mirecourt, Vosges, Oct. 7, 1798 ; *d.* Paris, Feb. 19,[2] 1875), violin-maker, learnt his craft from his father, Claude Vuillaume (*b.* 1772 ; *d.* Mirecourt, 1834), a descendant of Claude Vuillaume of Mirecourt (1625), who had married a daughter of the old violin-maker, François Médard, of Nancy, and was the founder of the business.

At the age of 19, Jean Baptiste went to Paris, where he worked with François Chanot, and in 1821 joined Lété, the organ-builder. Lété had been a member of the firm Chanot-Lété—Simon aîné et Payonne, and besides his organ-building dabbled in fiddle-making with Vuillaume, at 20 Rue Pavée St. Sauveur, where his business was known as Lété et Vuillaume. In 1828 Vuillaume ended this association, establishing himself at 46 Rue Croix des Petits Champs, and in the same year he married Adèle Guesnet, of Clermont. The frequent intercourse which Vuillaume had with such men as Pique and Savart, during his partnership with Lété, familiarised him with the methods and styles of the old Italian luthiers to an extent that eventually made him one of the most expert connoisseurs of his time. As soon as he left Lété, Vuillaume attempted to put his knowledge and technical skill to practical use. But there being then a

---

[1] Schubart.

[2] The date, Mar. 19, given by Vidal, Pougin and others, is incorrect.

demand for old Italian instruments, his own original work was at a discount. Instead, however, of fighting against the prevailing demands, Vuillaume turned them to good account by placing on the market a Stradivarius-model violin of extraordinary merit, bearing the master's label within, in facsimile. For this instrument he charged 300 frs. This speculation proved a complete success. Orders poured in, and there is little doubt that in the desire to meet his clients' demands he adopted the practice of baking the wood from which he made some of his fiddles, improving their immediate appearance, but proving fatal to them as time went on. So brilliant was the success of Vuillaume's venture that he was soon able to put a 500 frs. violoncello on the market, which found equal favour, and this was the foundation of his fortunes. The fidelity of his copies increased, so that even experts found it difficult to distinguish between the copy and the original when they were placed side by side. Vuillaume was an inventor as well as a dealer and maker. A ponderous and eccentric steel bow, of which apparently but a solitary specimen survives, is in the Victoria and Albert Museum. In 1885 he introduced a new model for the tenor, constructed on the scientific principles of Dr. Felix Savart, so built that the mass of air contained within gave the note F 341·33 vibrations to the second. But the instruments hardly recommended themselves to players on account of their bulk. His mute, patented under the name of the *sourdine pédale* (Paris Exhibition, 1867), was an ingenious combination of mute and tail-piece, allowing the player to mute the instrument by a push with the chin, without ceasing from playing. A copy of his huge double-bass, known as the octobasse, the large proportions of which necessitated a complicated but ingenious invention of machinery for tuning, is in the Musée of the Paris Conservatoire. He also invented a machine for regulating the manufacture of gut-strings in such a manner that false strings should be entirely done away with. In 1827 Vuillaume was awarded a silver medal at the Paris Exhibition; he obtained another in 1834 and in 1839, and in 1844 two gold medals. At the London Exhibition of 1851 he obtained the ' Council medal,' for his perfected octobasse and a magnificent quartet of stringed instruments, receiving in the same year the cross of the Legion of Honour. Finally in 1855 at the Exposition Universelle in Paris, Vuillaume carried off the 'grand médaille d'honneur,' and from that moment he was pronounced *hors concours*. During the latter part of his career Vuillaume established himself in the Rue Demours No. 3, aux Thermes. Here many violins were made by his workmen which passed through his hands for supervision only. These bear the label ' St. Cécile des

Thermes,' with the date and number. Vuillaume is said to have issued from his workshops no less than 3000 instruments before his death, which took place at Rue Demours. One of his daughters married Delphin Alard. Vuillaume's brothers, Nicolas, Nicolas François, and Claude François, all became luthiers.

The first of these three—(2) NICOLAS (*b.* Mirecourt, 1800; *d.* 1871)—worked with Jean Baptiste for ten years, but returned to M recourt in 1824, establishing a successful business there in cheap violins. (3) NICOLAS FRANÇOIS (*b.* May 13, 1812; *d.* Brussels, Jan. 14, 1876) likewise served an apprenticeship in his brother's workshop, and eventually settled in Brussels at No. 30 Rue de l'Évêque. He was appointed luthier to the Conservatoire, and several medals were awarded him. He was made Chevalier of the Order of Leopold. (4) CLAUDE FRANÇOIS VUILLAUME (*b.* Mirecourt, 1807; *d.* 1862) was a pupil of his father. He made fiddles for some years, but finally gave himself up entirely to organ-making. His son, (5) SEBASTIAN (*b.* Paris, 1835; *d.* Nov. 17, 1875), was an excellent violin-maker, who had a workshop for many years at No. 27 Boulevard Bonne Nouvelle in Paris. He also gained several medals, and was the possessor of the unique machine for bending bows invented by his uncle Jean Baptiste Vuillaume. (See TARISIO.)

BIBL.—SIMOUTRE, *Un Progrès en lutherie*; LA FAGE. *Quinze visites musicales à l'Exposition Universelle*; GALLAY, *Les Instruments a archet*; FOLEGATTI, *Storia del violino* (2nd part); VON LUTGENDORFF, *Die Geigen- und Lautenmacher*; FÉTIS, *Notice sur Nicolo Paganini*; HAWEIS, *Old Violins*; POUGIN, *Supplement to Fétis's Biog. des Mus.*; ANON. (Hill & Sons), *The Salabue Strad*; ANON. (Volckmann), *Was Gaspar Duiffoprougcar really the first Violin maker?*; VIDAL, *Les Instruments à archet*.
E. H.-A.

VULPIUS, MELCHIOR (*b.* Wasungen, Henneberg territory, *c.* 1560; *d.* Weimar, Aug. 7, 1615), became cantor at Weimar from 1602–15, and held this position till his death (he was buried on Aug. 7, 1615). He composed some Chorals, notably ' Jesu Leiden, Pein und Tod,' ' Christus der ist mein Leben,' and ' Weltlich Ehr und zeitlich Gut,' (see CHORALE); but accomplished much more in harmonising tunes for many voices, in which he showed himself a sound contrapuntist. His chief works are ' Cantiones Sacrae cum 6, 7 et 8 vocibus,' Jena, 1602; ' Cantiones Sacrae 5, 6 et 8 vocum,' 2 pts., Jena, 1603–04; ' Kirchengesänge und geistliche Lieder D. Lutheri und Anderer mit 4 und 5 Stimmen,' Leipzig, 1604, of which the second enlarged edition bears the title ' Ein schön geistlich Gesangbuch,' Jena, 1609, and has the melody in the discant, whereas most of his settings have it in the tenor; ' Canticum B.V. Mariae 4, 5, 6 et pluribus vocibus,' Jena, 1605; wedding hymns to Latin words, 1608, 1609 and 1614; ' Opusculum novum,' 1610; two books of ' Deutsche Sonntägliche Evangelische Sprüche,' for the whole year (1612 and 1614), and a Passion oratorio (St. Matthew) (1613), in which the narrator has a tenor voice.

His *Musicae compendium* (1610) went through many editions. (For details of printed and MS. music see *Q.-L.*) It is interesting to note that Goethe's wife was '*née* Vulpius of Weimar.'　　　　R. M. ; addns. E. V. D. S.

VYCPÁLEK, LADISLAV (*b.* Vršovice, near Prague, 1882), one of the most original of contemporary Czech composers ; doctor of philosophy, and secretary of the University Library, Prague. Vycpálek studied music at the Prague Conservatoire, where his master for composition was Vít. NOVAK (*q.v.*). A mystic and earnest thinker, his development has been deep and slow, and his output comparatively small. A fleeting attraction to impressionism soon gave way to independent and settled convictions, the outcome of his profound sympathy with suffering humanity and his sane democratic outlook. The quality of his art is somewhat ascetic ; and although it is based on the folk spirit it makes no compromise with superficial popular taste. The essence of Vycpálek's style is polyphony ; a rigorous and logical adherence to contrapuntal writing which, when the parts move at his volition without regard to accepted principles, sometimes involves him in a certain harmonic harshness. His methods reflect himself. Colour is a secondary consideration ; orchestral opulence and glitter are voluntarily abnegated. In his music—which has a serious ethical relation to life—the chief values are spiritual. Vycpálek, in fact, may be called a spiritual descendant of the Unity of Bohemian Brethren. Therefore it is not surprising that the operatic traditions of the Czechs have taken no root in him, and that his best work—by no means lacking in dramatic significance—is a devout cantata : ' Of the Last Things of Man' ('O posledních věcech Clověká '). It was written in 1920, and is the outcome of that inevitable reaction after the victory when, in his own words :

'The seeds of war were still putting forth strong growths—the greed of humanity for money, the inconsiderate impatience for the fulfilment of individual interests, all the brutal materialism born of war, still threatened to choke everything higher and less aggressive. The cantata, which originated like a secret thing, came forth as an ardent and poignant protest against materialism.'[1]

The text is based upon several Moravian folk-songs. The cantata is a continuous work, which falls, however, into three sections : the Triumph of Materialism, the Triumph of Death, the Triumph of Faith. The music is chiefly built upon two main subjects : the theme of Death and the Soul's theme. It is written for mixed chorus, alternating with solos for soprano and baritone. Besides this cantata, Vycpálek has composed several Songcycles :

'Tícha Usmírení' (Quiet Reconcilement); 'Tuchy Vidiny' (Visions), op. 5; 'V Boží Dlani' (In God's Hand), words by the Russian poet, V. Brussov, op. 14 ; five Moravian Ballads, op. 12 ; ten Moravian Folk-songs (descriptive of the soldier's fate), op. 13 ; Pianoforte Pieces, op. 9 ; choruses for mixed and male voice choir ; 'Tulácí' (Tramps); ' Sírotek' (The Orphan); ' Naše Jaro' (Oui Springtide), op. 15, No. 1 ; 'Boj nynější' (The Conflict of To-day) op. 15, No. 2 ; mostly published by Hudební Matice, Prague.

　　　　　　　　　　　　　　　　　R. N.

[1] For a full account of this cantata see R. Newmarch, *Som. Czechoslovak Choral Works* (11), *Mus. T.*, Mar. 1, 1923

W

WACHTEL, (1) THEODOR (b. Hamburg, Mar. 10, 1823/24; d. Nov. 14, 1893), opera singer. He was the son of a stable-keeper, and began life by driving his father's cabs. He learnt to sing from Mme. Grandjean, and obtained operatic engagements at Schwerin, Dresden, Hanover (1854), Berlin, Darmstadt, Vienna, etc. On June 7, 1862, he made his début in England at the Royal Italian Opera as Edgardo in 'Lucia,' and failed completely. He sang there again in the seasons of 1864 and 1865 with better results; and indeed obtained a certain popularity, more on account of his fine and powerful voice than from any artistic use he made of it. His principal attraction was the way he produced a C in alt direct from the chest instead of by the customary falsetto; he brought out the note with stentorian vigour and great success, especially when he played Manrico or Arnold. Of his other parts may be named Stradella on the production of Flotow's opera of that name at the Royal Italian Opera, June 4, 1864, and Vasco da Gama on the production of 'L'Africaine' in England, July 22, 1865. He reappeared in 1870, and again in 1877, at Her Majesty's. In 1869 he sang in Paris with very indifferent results, but was successful in America both in German and Italian opera.

His son, (2) THEODOR (b. 1841; d. Jan. 1871), began life as a clockmaker, and at one period of his life was a tenor singer of the same calibre as his father. He died of consumption.   A. C.

WADDINGTON, SIDNEY PEINE (b. Lincoln, July 23, 1869), studied at the R.C.M. (where he won a scholarship) from 1883–88. In 1889 the College sent him for a time to Germany, and he stayed two months in Frankfort and six in Vienna. In 1890 he was elected to the Mendelssohn Scholarship, which he held until 1893. He was choirmaster of St. Mary of the Angels, Bayswater, from 1894–1905. He conducted an amateur operatic society about 1896, and some years before that date had been chosen to complete the score of Goring Thomas's 'Golden Web.' He holds the appointment of teacher of harmony and counterpoint at the R.C.M., where latterly he has been also master of the opera class. From about 1896 he was maestro al pianoforte to the Royal Opera, Covent Garden. He is a member of the Associated Board of the R.A.M. and R.C.M., and one of the most experienced of the Board's examiners. His clever setting of 'John Gilpin' for chorus and orchestra was heard at a R.C.M. concert in Nov. 1894. He has written violin and violoncello sonatas, a string trio and quartet, a quintet for PF. and wind, a fantasia for piano solo, a beautiful suite for PF. duet, a concerto for PF. and orchestra, an overture and an 'Ode to Music' for soprano solo, choir and orchestra.   M., with addns.

WADE, JOSEPH AUGUSTINE (b. Dublin, end of 18th or beginning of 19th cent.[1]; d. London, July 15, 1845). Having published songs in 1813–14 and collaborated with Dr. Smith in an opera (Dec. 4, 1820), he migrated to London (1821), where his talents soon brought him into notice. From intercourse with orchestral performers he acquired sufficient confidence to undertake to conduct the opera during Monck Mason's regime, a position he did not long retain. He had been engaged by the firm of Chappell, at a salary of £300 a year, to make himself generally useful; but he made no use of his gifts as poet, musician and scholar, and the house reaped little advantage from him. He once returned to his native city—in Dec. 1840—travelling with Lavenu's touring party. It included Liszt, Richardson the flautist, the Misses Steele and Bassano, John Parry and J. P. Knight; two or three of Wade's concerted pieces were included in the concerts, at which, however, he did not appear, even as accompanist. He returned to London, where he died, at 350 Strand,[2] in destitution.

There is little doubt that Wade was a man of remarkable gifts and acquirements. His personal appearance was much in his favour; he was witty and quick in perception, and had acquired some knowledge of the Latin classics, as well as of one or two modern languages, and also had a smattering of anatomy. His memory was retentive in the extreme, and he possessed a gift for creating melody. The following is a list of his chief works, with their approximate dates:

'A Series of Select Airs,' etc., c. 1818; 'The Prophecy,' an oratorio (Drury Lane, 1824); 'The Two Houses of Granada' (ib. 1826); 'The Pupil of Da Vinci' (operetta by Mark Lemon), 1831; 'Polish Melodies' (words and music), 1831; 'Convent Belles' (with Hawes), 1833; 'A woodland life' (polacca interpolated in 'Der Freischütz' and sung by Braham); 'Meet me by moonlight alone' (sung by Vestris and published 1826); the duet 'I've wandered in dreams.'

This last obtained a popularity equalling the preceding ballad, which enjoyed an extraordinary vogue for many years. He wrote a Handbook to the Pianoforte which was dedicated to Liszt, whose portrait figured in the frontispiece. A new issue, edited by John Barnett, appeared in 1850. As early as 1831 he projected a History of Music, but it was never printed. He contributed to Bentley's Miscellany, the Illustrated London News and other periodicals. He was associated with Dr. Crotch and G. A. Macfarren in the pianoforte arrangement of the earlier issues of Chappell's 'National English Airs,' 1838. He appears to have occasionally signed his first name as

1 About 1796 is the usual date given, but the register of death at Somerset House goes to support the theory that 1801 is the year of birth. See Mus. T., 1898, p. 597.
2 Musical World, 1845, p. 501.

John, but there is no reason to doubt that it was really Joseph.

R. P. S.; addns., F. K.; W. H. G. F.; D.N.B., etc.

WAEFELGHEM, Louis van (b. Bruges, Jan. 13, 1840 ; d. Paris, June 19, 1908), Belgian violinist, viola and viole d'amour player (see Viol (6)). He was educated at the Athénée of Bruges and entered the Conservatoire of Brussels at the age of 17, studying the violin under Meerts and composition under Fétis. In 1860 he appeared successfully at Weimar, after which he settled in Dresden, attracted thither by his friend C. J. Lipinski. He was offered the professorship of the violin at Lemberg, in the Conservatoire, but refused the post to become solo-violinist at the Opera in Buda-pest. He left this post on the death of his father, but in 1863 he went to Paris, where he abandoned the violin for the viola. He played the viola in the Opéra orchestra in 1868, and at the Pasdeloup concerts, and finally settled down as examiner for the viola in the Conser-vatoire. After the Franco-German war Van Waefelghem came to London, where he played in the Opera orchestra, and in chamber con-certs of the Musical Union with Joachim, Auer, Vieuxtemps, Sivori and Sarasate. In 1875 he was a member of a quartet society with Mar-sick, Rémé and Delsart. He also played the viola in Ovide Musin's quartet, with Metzger and Van der Gucht. He was in London every season for many years until 1895, when he resigned his position in Lamoureux's orchestra and devoted himself exclusively to the revival and study of the viole d'amour.

He speedily became probably the greatest artist of the 19th century upon this instrument, and being highly endowed with the enthusiasm of research, restored to the world a complete library of music for the instrument which had sunk into oblivion. He played upon a superb instrument dated 1720, made by Paul Aletzie, a Munich maker who settled in Venice. A minute description of this instrument is to be found in L. Grillet's Les Ancêtres du violon. Grillet was to the vielle (or hurdy-gurdy) what Van Waefelghem was to the viole d'amour, and played it to perfection. (His father was vielle-player to Louis XVI., and a pupil of Naudot, the great vielle-player of the time of Louis XV.) Van Waefelghem, Grillet, Diémer (harpsichord) and Delsart (viola da gamba) founded the Société des Instruments Anciens, and toured the whole of Europe with great success. On May 2, 1895, they made their début at the Salle Pleyel in Paris ; in the summer of 1897 they gave concerts at the Salle Erard in London. A number of Van Waefelghem's viole d'amour solos have been published in Paris, and a Romance and a Melody of his (' Soir d'au-tomne ') for viole d'amour or viola are pub-lished by Durand. Schott published a ' pas-

torale ' and ' rêverie ' of his for violin and pianoforte. He was a Knight of the Legion of Honour, and of the Order of Leopold. The writer is indebted to Van Waefelghem's life-long friend, E. van der Straeten, for the information contained in this article, as also to his personal reminiscences of its subject. (See also E. G. Grégoire, Les Artistes musiciens belges.)

E. H.-A.

WAELRANT, Hubert (b. Tongerloo,[1] Kempenland, North Brabant, c. 1518 ; d. Ant-werp, Nov. 19, 1595 [2]), one of the most dis-tinguished of the second generation of the great Flemish masters. An old tradition relates that he went in his youth to Venice, and there studied under the guidance of his great fellow-countryman Adrian Willaert ; but this lacks confirmation, and may very possibly be as apocryphal as the similar story usually told with reference to Sweelinck's sojourn at Venice, and the lessons he had from Zarlino later on in the century. Be this as it may, Waelrant is found in the year 1544 estab-lished in Antwerp, as a singer in the choir of the chapel of the Virgin at Notre-Dame. Three years later he had a school of music there, where he introduced a new method of solmisation, that known as bocedisation or the voces Belgicae.[3] (See Solmisation.) He is said now to have entered partnership with J. de Laet as a publisher of music ; but this was more prob-ably not until 1554.[4] The association lasted until 1558, when he retired. Waelrant was twice married—first in 1551, and again before 1568 ; by his first wife he had six children.

Among contemporaries Waelrant was held in very high repute, not only as a teacher of music but more especially as a composer, chiefly of madrigals and motets. Guicciardini, in his Descrittione di tutti i Paesi bassi,[5] includes him in a list of the greatest living musicians of his time. His first musical works were : ' Chansons,' published by Phalesius at Louvain, 1553–54, and ' Il primo libro de madrigali e canzoni francezi (sic) a cinque voci ; Anversa, Huberto Waelrant e J. Latio, 1558.' It is remarkable, however, that of the numerous volumes of music which he published—Psalms, ' Cantiones sacrae,' ' Jardin musiqual,' etc.— only two (of the ' Jardin ') include composi-tions by himself. He seems in fact to have preferred to publish either by Tylman Susato or Phalesius. Seven of the collections of the latter contain works by Waelrant. One of these was also edited by him under the follow-ing title, ' Symphonia angelica di diversi

[1] The discovery of Waelrant's birthplace is due to the researches of A. Goovaerts, Histoire et bibliographie de la typographie musicale dans les Pays-bas, pp. 38-40, Antwerp, 1880. A confusion with a namesake had led to the opinion previously universally accepted, that the musician was a native of Antwerp (see Fétis, s.v. ; Mendel and Reissmann; Musikalisches Conversations-Lexikon, xi. 233, 2nd ed. 1880 ; and also E. van der Straeten, La Musique aux Pays-bas, iii. 201-4, 1875.
[2] Sweertius, l.c.
[3] See F. Sweertius, Athenae Belgicae, p. 350, Antwerp, 1628, folio ; E. van der Straeten, i. 62, 1867 ; Mendel and Reissmann, xi. 234.
[4] Goovaerts, p. 42.   [5] Page 42, ed. Antwerp, 1588 folio.

eccellentissimi Musici, a quattro, cinque e sei voci ; Nuovamente raccolta per Uberto Waelrant, 1585.'[1]   R. L. P.

WAERT, DE, see WERT, DE.

WAGENAAR, JOHAN (b. Utrecht, Nov. 1, 1862), composer. He was a pupil of Richard Hol, and as Hol's successor remained a long time in Utrecht as a conductor, organist and teacher. In 1918 he was invited to The Hague as director of the Royal Conservatoire. Wagenaar's cantatas and humorous-burlesque operas show originality, while his virtuoso orchestral works are under the influence of Berlioz, Strauss and Mahler—the best known of these is the overture to ' Cyrano de Bergerac.' Wagenaar is an Hon. Doctor of Utrecht University, in acknowledgment of which honour he dedicated a sinfonietta to the faculty of philosophy.
                                        R. MᶜG.

WAGENSEIL, GEORG CHRISTOPH (b. Vienna, Jan. 15, 1715 ; d. Mar. 1, 1777[2]). He studied the clavier and organ with Wöger, and the science of composition with Fux and Palotta, the former of whom recommended him for a court scholarship in 1736, and as court composer in 1739, a post which he retained till his death. He was also organist to the Dowager Empress Elizabeth Christine from 1741 to her death in 1750, and music-master to the Empress Maria Theresa and the Imperial princesses, with a life salary of 1500 florins. Among his pupils were Steffan, then court Kapellmeister, and Leopold Hoffmann, afterwards Kapellmeister of the cathedral. When Mozart, a little boy of 6, was playing before the court in 1762, he inquired, ' Is not Herr Wagenseil here ? he knows all about it '; and when the latter came forward, he said, ' I am playing a concerto of yours ; you must turn over for me.' In old age Wagenseil suffered from sciatica, which confined him to his room, and nearly lost the use of his left hand from gout. Nevertheless when Burney visited him he managed to play several of his compositions ' in a masterly manner, and with great fire.'[3] In his day he was a favourite composer for the clavier with both amateurs and artists. He modelled his church music after Hasse and Scarlatti, his dramatic music after Leo and his instrumental after Rameau. Of the latter many pieces were engraved in Paris, London, Amsterdam and Vienna. There are several MS. works of his in the court library and in the archives of the Gesellschaft der Musikfreunde in Vienna, both vocal (cantatas, Italian arias, etc.) and instrumental (trios, quartets, divertimenti, symphonies, etc.). Two oratorios, ' La Redenzione,' 1755, and ' Gioas, rè di Giuda,' are in the court library at Vienna ; a Requiem and two

---

[1] For the complete bibliography see Q.-L.
[2] He was thus in his 63rd year at the time of his death, and not 92 as Gerber states (vol. i.), and after him Fétis. Neither was he 58, as Burney supposed when he visited him in 1772. (Present State . . . Germany, i. 326.)
[3] Present State . . . Germany, vol. i. p. 325, etc.

masses are at Berlin, and many MSS. of psalms, motets, etc., are mentioned in Q.L., where fifteen operas are enumerated. Examples of his instrumental works are published in D.D.T., 2nd series, xv. Of permanent value are ' Suavis artificiose elaboratus,' etc., in six parts (Bamberg, 1740) ; ' Tre divertimenti per cembalo ' (Vienna, 1761) ; ' Divertissement musical,' six sonatas for harpsichord, op. 1 (Nuremberg, Haffner) ; and four numbers, each containing ' VI divertimenti da cembalo,' dedicated to his pupils the Archduchesses Mariana, Marie Cristina, Elizabeth and Amalia (all 1760), finely engraved on copper by Giorgio Nicolai for Agostino Bernardi the Viennese publisher. (See list in Q.-L.) The claim that Wagenseil wrote the theme of the ' Harmonious Black-smith ' is disposed of by the dates.
                                   C. F. P., with addns.

BIBL.—R. SONDHEIMER, Die formale Entwicklung der vorklassischen Sinfonie. A.M.Z., Jan. 1922, pp. 91, 92.

WAGENSEIL, JOHANN CHRISTOPH (b. Nuremberg, Nov. 26, 1633 ; d. Altdorf, Oct. 9, 1708), historian and librarian, is noteworthy for his Buch von der Meistersinger holdseligen Kunst (1697). The work, containing the melodies of Frauenlob, Müglin, Murner and Regenbogen, is important as one of the chief sources of information on the methods of the Meistersinger (see SONG : GERMANY).

BIBL.—H. THOMPSON, Wagner and Wagenseil (London, 1927).

WAGNER, GEORG GOTTFRIED (b. Mühlberg, Saxony, Apr. 5, 1698 ; d. Plauen i. V., Mar. 23, 1756), pupil of Kuhnau at the school of St. Thomas, Leipzig, from 1712–19, studying theology there until 1726. In the latter year he became cantor at Plauen i. V. at the recommendation of J. S. Bach, in whose orchestra he had been principal violin. His motet ' Lob und Ehre ' was published by Breitkopf & Härtel in 1819 as J. S. Bach's work. He also composed cantatas, oratorios, overtures, concertos, trios, solos, etc., which were held in high esteem, but remained in MS. (Riemann ; Q.-L.).

WAGNER, GOTTHARD (b. Erding, 1679 ; d. Tegernsee, 1739), Benedictine monk at the monastery of Tegernsee from 1700, wrote several collections of sacred songs with instrumental accompaniment, viz. : ' Cygnus Marianus ' (1710), 86 German airs ; ' Musikalischer Hofgarten ' (1717), 100 airs, 2 v. and basso continuo ; ' Der Marianische Springbrunnen ' (1720), 31 airs ; ' Das Marianische Immelein ' (1730), 52 airs, 4 v., with instruments ; also a cantata, 4 v., with instruments, of which the MS. is in the Brussels Conservatoire Library (Lipowsky ; Q.-L.).

WAGNER, JACOB KARL (b. Darmstadt, Feb. 22, 1772 ; d. Nov. 24, 1822), son of a Darmstadt court musician. He was apprenticed in the court chapel at Darmstadt in 1788, joined the orchestra as oboist, became music-master and accompanist for the vocal music at the court in 1800, and court Kapellmeister in 1811. In 1820 he was pensioned. He composed operas, Singspiele, melodramas, music to Goethe's 'Götz von Berlichingen,' overture to *As You Like It*, and a large number of vocal and instrumental works, including symphonies, concertos, concertantes, overtures, pianoforte pieces, etc. (*Q.-L.* ; *Riemann*).

WAGNER, PETER JOSEF (*b.* Trèves, Aug. 19, 1865), writer on musical subjects, more particularly ancient ecclesiastical music, was educated at the University of Strassburg and pursued his studies further at Berlin under Bellermann and Spitta. He became professor in the University of Freiburg (Switzerland) in 1897, and founded there (1901) a Gregorian academy for research and practical study. His publications include important works on Gregorian and mediæval music, together with *Geschichte der Messe* (part i., 1914).

WAGNER, (1) WILHELM RICHARD (*b.* Leipzig, May 22, 1813 ; *d.* Venice, Feb. 13, 1883).

The materials of the following article have been thus arranged : I. Biographical, personal. II. Literary. III. Musical. IV. Chronological and Bibliographical Lists.

I. Wagner's ancestors were natives of Saxony,[1] fairly well educated and fairly well-to-do. The grandfather, Gottlob Friedrich Wagner (*d.* 1795), was *Accisassistent*, and later on *Kurfürstlich Sächsischer Generalacciseinnehmer* (Receiver-General of Excise), in plain words *Thorschreiber* (clerk at the town gates of Leipzig) ; he married in 1769 Johanna Sophia Eichel, daughter of Gottlob Friedrich Eichel, *Schulhalter* (keeper of a school). Of their children, two sons and a daughter, the eldest son, Carl Friedrich Wilhelm Wagner (*b.* Leipzig, 1770), was the father of the poet-composer. He is described as *Actuarius bei den Stadtgerichten* (clerk to the city police courts) ; a ready linguist, whose command of French stood him in good stead during the occupation of Leipzig, when Davoust made him chief of police ; fond of poetry and of theatricals, in which he occasionally took an active part—as, for instance, in the private performance of Goethe's ' Die Mitschuldigen,' given by Leipzig dilettanti in Thomé's house, near the famous Auerbach's Keller, facing the Marktplatz. He married in 1798 Johanna Rosina Pätz[2] (*b.* Weissenfels ; *d.* Feb. 1848), by whom, between 1799 and 1813, he had nine children :

1. Carl Albert Wagner, 1799–1874, studied medicine at the University of Leipzig ; actor and singer

at Würzburg and Dresden ; finally stage manager at Berlin ; father of Johanna Jachmann-Wagner, the well-known singer.
2. Carl Gustav Wagner, 1801, died early.
3. Johanna Rosalie Wagner, distinguished actress (Frau Dr. Gotthard Oswald Marbach), 1803–37.
4. Carl Julius Wagner, 1804, became a goldsmith ; died at Dresden, 1862.
5. Luise Constanze Wagner (Frau Friedrich Brockhaus), 1805–71.
6. Clara Wilhelmine Wagner (Frau Wolfram), a singer, 1807–75.
7. Maria Theresia Wagner, 1809, died 1814.
8. Wilhelmine Ottilie Wagner (Frau Professor Hermann Brockhaus[3]), 1811–83.
9. WILHELM RICHARD WAGNER, May 22, 1813.

The last of these dates[4] is inscribed on a white marble slab between the first and second stories of a quaint old house *Der rothe und weisse Löwe*[5] in the Brühl at Leipzig, No. 88, where the poet-composer was born. After the battle of Leipzig, Oct. 16, 18 and 19, 1813, an epidemic fever, attributed to the carnage, fell upon the town, and just six months after Richard's birth, on Nov. 22, the ' Herr Actuarius ' died of it. His widow was left in sad straits. The eldest son was but 14 ; she had no private means, and her pension was small. In 1814 she became the wife of Ludwig Geyer (*b.* Eisleben, Jan. 21, 1780), actor, playwright and amateur portrait-painter. He had formerly been a member of ' Seconda's troupe,' which used to give theatrical performances alternately at Dresden and Leipzig. At the time of the marriage he was a member of the Königl.-Sächs-Hoftheater, and accordingly the family removed to Dresden.[6] Richard Wagner frequently spoke of him with affectionate reverence, treasured his portrait by the side of that of his mother, and was delighted at the surprise performance of one of Geyer's little plays, ' Der Bethlehemitische Kindermord,' which was privately got up at Bayreuth in celebration of his sixtieth birthday, 1873. ' My schoolbooks at the Dresden Kreuzschule,' Wagner said to the writer, ' were marked Richard Geyer, and I was entered under that name.'[7]

---

[3] Hermann Brockhaus, the well-known Orientalist and translator of Somadeva, etc.

[4] At Wagner's birth Beethoven was 42 years old, Spohr 29, Weber 27, Marschner 17, Spontini 38, Rossini 21, Auber 29, Meyerbeer 22, Bellini 11, Berlioz 10, Mendelssohn and Chopin 4, Schumann 3, Liszt 2.

[5] In 1885 the house in the Brühl was condemned as unsafe and pulled down ; a tablet has been placed in the building which has been erected on or near the same spot.

[6] There was also a child of the second marriage, Caecilie Geyer (*b.* 1815), who appears as Frau Avenarius in Wagner's correspondence.

[7] It was no uncommon occurrence for a boy to be thus entered under the name of his stepfather, and the circumstance gives no support to the theory that Wagner was in reality the son of the clever actor. Mrs. Burrell's book gives ocular demonstration, by a very remarkable similarity between the composer and a portrait of a Wagner uncle, that the boy was actually the son of the ' Actuarius.' The whole question of Wagner's paternity has been dealt with by Ernest Newman in *Wagner as Man and Artist* (London, 1914), and still more fully in the second edition (1926). It is also dealt with in Wallace's *Richard Wagner* (London, 1925), Appx. B. The question depends entirely upon surmise, and direct evidence is at this time obviously impossible. The assertion, said to have originated with Nietzsche (or, according to some, Mottl), that Wagner in his autobiography described himself as the son of Geyer, has been proved false, for a comparison made by Fuller Maitland between a copy of the privately printed edition of 1870 and the edition published in 1911, showed that the passage in question had not been altered. The point would have no real importance but for the suggestion that the Geyer parentage brought a strain of Jewish blood into the composer, but Bournot, in his book on Geyer, has traced his family back to 1700, and shown that throughout that time the Geyers were all of the Evangelical faith, married Germans, and had ' Christian ' as a favourite family name,

---

[1] See *Richard Wagner und seine erste ' Elisabeth ' Johanna Jachmann-Wagner. Ein neuer Beitrag zur Wagnerforschung*, edited by Dr. Julius Kapp and Hans Jachmann, Berlin, 1927, which contains a genealogical table of the Wagner family from Samuel Wagner, 1643–1705.

[2] All Wagner's biographers have followed one another in giving this name as Bertz : Mrs. Burrell has shown that the above is the correct version. (See her *Life of Wagner*, p. 19.) Wagner himself, in the autobiography, gives it as Bertz.

'Geyer [1] wanted to make a painter of me, but I was very unhandy at drawing ; I had learnt to play " Ueb' immer Treu und Redlichkeit" and the " Jungfern-kranz " (" Freischütz "), which was then quite new. The day before his death (30th Sept. 1821) I had to play these to him in an adjoining room, and I heard him faintly saying to my mother, " Do you think he might have a gift for music ? " '

In Dec. 1822 (aet. 9) Richard had begun to attend the Kreuzschule, a ' classical school.' He did well there, and became the favourite of Herr Silig, the professor of Greek, to whose de-light (aet. 13) he translated the first twelve books of the *Odyssey* out of school hours.[2] His progress in Latin seems to have been compara-tively slow, still his gifts attracted attention. ' I was considered good *in litteris*.' At German verses he was unusually quick. The boys were asked to write commemorative verses on the death of a schoolfellow, and after the removal of much bombast Richard's were printed (aet. 11). ' I was now bent upon becoming a poet ; I sketched tragedies in Greek form in imitation of Apel's "Polyeidos," "Die Aetolier," etc. I attempted a metrical translation of Romeo's monologue, by way of learning English, etc.' German versions of Shakespeare were then, as now, much read. The boy's fancy was excited, and he secretly began a grand tragedy (aet. 14). It was made up of Hamlet and Lear ; forty-two men died in the course of it, and some of them had to return as ghosts so as to keep the fifth act going.[3] Weber's music also took hold of him. He knew the airs from ' Der Freischütz ' by heart, and played the overture ' with atroci-ous fingering.'

' When Weber passed our house on his way to the theatre, I used to watch him with something akin to religious awe.' [4]

It appears that Weber now and then stepped in to have a chat with the delicate-featured and intelligent Frau Geyer. ' Her sweet ways and lively disposition had a specia charm for artists.' But the pleasant life at Dresden was not to last long. Geyer's salary had been a small one, and soon after his decease pecuniary troubles arose. Three of the grown-up children took to the theatre, and when the elder sister Rosalie got a good engagement as ' erste Lieb-haberin ' at Leipzig, the mother followed with the younger members of the family. Richard attended the Kreuzschule till the autumn of 1827, and entered the Nicolaischule at Leipzig early in the following year (aet. 15). The change proved unfortunate. He had sat in ' Secunda ' at Dresden, and was now put back to ' Tertia ' ; his feelings were hurt, and he came to dislike the school and the masters.

' I grew negligent, and scamped the work ; nothing interested me except my big tragedy.'

1 *Autobiographische Skizze*, 1842.
2 The autobiography mentions 12 books, the school archives give the number as 3. After over forty years Wagner's memory may have played him false, and it seems unnecessary to convict him of dishonesty on the strength of this slip. But see Wallace (*supra*), at p. 13 and Appx. A, in which he deals at great length with Wagner's knowledge of the Classics.
3 It was called ' Leubold, ein Trauerspiel ' (Mrs. Burrell, p. 83).
4 For Wagner's early years see A. Schilling's *Aus. R. W.'s Jugend-zeit* (Bibliography, below).

At the Gewandhaus Concerts he first heard Beethoven's symphonies, and the impression upon him ' was overwhelming.' Music such as that to ' Egmont ' appeared to be the very thing needful for the tragedy. He found a copy of Logier's ' Thorough-bass ' at a circulating library, and studied it assiduously ; but some-how the ' System ' could not be turned to account. At length a master was engaged, Gottlieb Müller, subsequently organist at Alten-burg ; Richard composed a quartet, a sonata and an aria, under his guidance : but it does not appear how far Müller was really respon-sible for these pieces. The lessons did not last long. Müller thought his pupil wilful and eccen-tric, and in return was accounted a stupid pedant. The ferment in Richard's mind now took a literary direction. The writings of E. T. A. Hoffmann engrossed his attention, and it is curious to note that so early as in his 16th year he became acquainted with some of the subjects which he treated later on. Thus, Hoffmann's ' Serapions Brüder,' in vol. ii., con-tains a story about the legendary contest of ' Meistersinger ' (Hoffmann's misnomer for 'Minnesinger ') at Wartburg (2nd act of ' Tann-häuser ') ; and sundry germs of Wagner's ' Meistersinger ' are to be found in Hoffmann's ' Meister Martin der Küfer von Nürnberg.'— Ludwig Tieck's narrative poem ' Tannhäuser ' was read at the same time.—A performance of Beethoven's Pastoral Symphony led to an at-tempt at a music pastoral, the dramatic aspect of which was suggested by Goethe's ' Laune des Verliebten.' In 1830 Richard attended the ' Thomasschule ' with results little more satis-factory than at the ' Nicolai.' Practically his philological studies went no further ; ' I chose to write overtures for grand orchestra, and to bluster about politics with young literati like Heinrich Laube.' An overture (in B♭, 6-8) was performed under H. Dorn at the theatre in a Christmas Day concert [5] (1830, aet. 17).

' This was the culminating point of my absurdities. The public was fairly puzzled by the persistence of the drum-player, who had to give a tap *fortissimo* every four bars from beginning to end ; people grew impatient, and finally thought the thing a joke.' [6]

When he matriculated at the University of Leipzig (Feb. 23, 1831),[7] Wagner had the good luck to find a proper master, Theodor Weinlig, cantor at the Thomasschule, an admirable musician and a kindly intelligent man, who at once gained his pupil's confidence and led him in the right direction. Wagner felt deeply in-debted to Weinlig, and held his memory in great esteem. In 1877 he spoke at length about the lessons :

' Weinlig had no special method, but he was clear-headed and practical. Indeed you cannot *teach* com-position, you may show how music gradually came to be what it is, and thus guide a young man's judgment,

5 See Mrs. Burrell, p. 99.   6 *Autobiographische Skizze*.
7 This is shown to be the true date, notwithstanding the state-ment in Wagner's *Mein Leben*, as Mrs. Burrell gives facsimiles from the University books, p. 109, etc.

but this is historical criticism, and cannot directly result in practice. All you can do is, to point to some working example, some particular piece, set a task in that direction, and correct the pupil's work. This is what Weinlig did with me. He chose a piece, generally something of Mozart's, drew attention to its construction, relative length and balance of sections, principal modulations, number and quality of themes, and general character of the movement. Then he set the task :—you shall write about so many bars, divide into so many sections with modulations to correspond so and so, the themes shall be so many, and of such and such a character. Similarly he would set contrapuntal exercises, canons, fugues—he analysed an example minutely and then gave simple directions how I was to go to work. But the true lesson consisted in his patient and careful inspection of what had been written. With infinite kindness he would put his finger on some defective bit and explain the why and wherefore of the alterations he thought desirable. I readily saw what he was aiming at, and soon managed to please him. He dismissed me, saying, you have learnt to stand on your own legs. My experience of young musicians these forty years has led me to think that music should be taught all round on such a simple plan. With singing, playing, composing, take it at whatever stage you like, there is nothing so good as a proper example, and careful correction of the pupil's attempts to follow that example. I made this the basis of my plan for the reorganisation of the Music-school at Munich, etc.' [1]

The course with Weinlig lasted barely six months. A sonata in four movements B♭, op. 1, and a polonaise for four hands in D, op. 2, were printed at Breitkopf & Härtel's—straightforward music, solid school-work, without a trace of Wagner. A fantasia in F♯ minor, where Weinlig's controlling hand is less visible, remains in MS.

Whilst this musical work was going on, philology and æsthetics, for which his name was set down at the University, were neglected. He plunged into the gulf of German students' dissipations (curious details are given in *Mein Leben*), but soon felt disgusted, and worked all the more steadily at music. In the course of 1830 he made a pianoforte transcription of Beethoven's ninth symphony, which was offered to Messrs. Schott in a letter dated Oct. 6. In 1831, feeling sure of his competence to do such work, he addressed a letter in very modest terms to the Bureau de Musique (Peters) offering his services as ' corrector for the press and arranger.' [2] Dorn [3] gives a pleasant account of his enthusiasm for Beethoven in those early days.

' I doubt whether there ever was a young musician who knew Beethoven's works more thoroughly than Wagner in his 18th year. The master's overtures and larger instrumental compositions he had copied for himself in score. He went to sleep with the quartets, he sang the songs and whistled the concertos (for his pianoforte-playing was never of the best) ; in short, he was possessed with a *furor teutonicus*, which, added to a good education and a rare mental activity, promised to bring forth rich fruit.'

A ' Concert-ouvertüre mit Fuge ' in C (MS.) was written in 1831 ; and another MS. overture in D minor (Sept. 26, amended Nov. 4) was performed Dec. 25, 1831.

In 1832 (aet. 19) he wrote a symphony in

four movements (C major).[4] ' Beethoven,' he says of it, ' and particular sections of Mozart's C major symphony were my models, and in spite of sundry aberrations, I strove for clearness and power.' In the summer of this year he took the scores of the symphony and the overture in C to the ' Music-town,' Vienna—probably with a view to some small post. He found Herold's ' Zampa ' and Strauss's potpourris upon it rampant there, and beat a hasty retreat. On the way home he stopped at Prague, and made the acquaintance of Dionys WEBER (*q.v.*), director of the Conservatorium, whose pupils rehearsed the symphony. The score was then submitted to the directors of the Gewandhaus Concerts at Leipzig. The managing director, Hofrath Rochlitz, editor of the *Allgemeine Musikalische Zeitung*, an authority in musical matters, invited the composer to call.

' When I presented myself to him, the stately old gentleman raised his spectacles, saying, "You are a young man indeed ! I expected an older and experienced composer." He proposed a trial performance at the meetings of a junior institution, the " Euterpe," and a fortnight afterwards (Jan. 10, 1833) my Symphony figured in the programme of a Gewandhaus Concert.'

The sequel of the story of the work is as follows. In 1834–35 Wagner, being on a visit to Leipzig, presented the score to Mendelssohn, who was then conducting the Gewandhaus Concerts ; or rather, he forced it upon him in the hope of getting a critical opinion, and perhaps another performance. Mendelssohn, though repeatedly meeting Wagner later on, never mentioned the score and Wagner did not care to ask him about it. After Mendelssohn's decease the MS. appears to have been lost, and inquiries proved fruitless. In 1872 an old trunk was discovered at Dresden which had been left by Wagner during the disturbances of 1849. It contained musical odds and ends, together with a set of orchestral parts almost complete, which proved to be those of the missing symphony in the handwriting of a Prague copyist of 1832. A new score was compiled from these parts, and after nearly half a century a private performance of the work was given by the orchestra of the Liceo Marcello at Venice on Christmas Eve, 1882, Wagner conducting. Apart from its biographical interest the symphony has few claims to attention. In 1883, ' for the benefit of the curious,' Wagner quoted a fragment of the andante, and then dismissed the whole as ' an old-fashioned *ouvrage de jeunesse*.' [5]

Whilst at Prague (summer of 1832) he wrote his first libretto for an opera, ' Die Hochzeit.'

' It was of tragic import. An infuriated lover climbs to the window of the bedroom of his beloved, who is his friend's bride. She is awaiting the arrival of the bridegroom. The bride wrestles with the

[1] These and other words of Wagner's not otherwise authenticated, were uttered in conversation with the writer in the spring and summer of 1877, and are here first made public.
[2] Herr Tappert, in his admirable brochure *Richard Wagner, sein Leben und seine Werke*, gives the entire letter (Aug. 6, 1831).
[3] In a contribution to Schumann's *Neue Zeitschrift*, 1838, No. 7.

[4] As to the ' Polonia ' overture, written about this time, see the *Mus. T.*, 905, p. 117. It was performed with the ' Columbus ' and ' Rule, Britannia ' overtures at the Queen's Hall, Jan. 2, 1905.
[5] Details in *Ges. Schriften*, vol. x., *Bericht über die Wiederaufführung eines Jugendwerkes*, pp. 399-405 (*Prose Works*, vi. 313).

madman, and precipitates him into the courtyard below. At the funeral rites the bride, with a wild cry, falls dead over the corpse.'

On his return to Leipzig he began writing the music. There was a grand septet, which pleased Weinlig ; but Wagner's sister Rosalie disapproved of the story, and the verses were destroyed. An autograph presentation copy to the Würzburger Musikverein, consisting of the introduction, chorus and septet (not sextet), 36 pages, is extant.

With the year 1833 (aet. 20) begins Wagner's career as a professional musician. The elder brother Albert, who had a high tenor voice, was engaged at the theatre of Würzburg as actor, singer and stage manager. Richard paid him a visit [1] lasting from February until January 1834, and was glad to take the place of chorus-master with a pittance of 10 florins per month. Albert's experience of theatrical matters proved useful ; the Musikverein performed several of Richard's compositions ; his duties at the theatre were light, and he had ample leisure to write the words and music to an opera in three acts, ' Die Feen.' The plot of this opera is constructed on the lines of Gozzi's ' La donna serpente, Fiaba teatrale in tre atti,' with a characteristic change in the *dénouement*. In Gozzi's play, as in the Scottish ballad *The Laidly Worm*, a fairy is ready to forgo her immortality for a mortal lover, but she can do so only under certain conditions. The lover shall not disown her, no matter how unworthy she may happen to appear. The fairy is turned into a snake, which the lover courageously kisses. Wagner alters this ; the fairy is not changed into a snake but into a stone, and she is disenchanted by the power of music.

' Beethoven, Weber and Marschner were my models. The *ensemble* pieces contained a good deal that seemed satisfactory, and the finale of the second act especially promised to be effective.'

Excerpts were tried at Würzburg in 1834. On his return to Leipzig Wagner offered the opera to Ringelhardt, the director of the theatre, who accepted but never performed it. The autograph score was in the possession of the King of Bavaria. ' Die Feen ' was produced at Munich in 1888.

In the spring of 1834 Wilhelmine Schröder-Devrient appeared at Leipzig. Her performances, both as actress and as singer, gave a powerful impulse to Wagner's talents. He had seen her as Fidelio in 1832.[2] Her rare gifts appear to have suggested to him that intimate union of music with the drama which he afterwards achieved. During six important years (1842-48 and 1849), when she was engaged as principal singer and he as Kapellmeister at Dresden, he was in almost daily communication with her. As late as 1872 he stated that her example had constantly been before him :

' Whenever I conceived a character I saw *her*.' In 1834 she sang the part of Romeo in Bellini's ' Montecchi e Capuletti.' The young enthusiast for Beethoven perceived the weakness of Bellini's music clearly enough, yet the impression Mme. Devrient made upon him was powerful and artistic. The Leipzig theatre next brought out Auber's ' La Muette de Portici ' (Masaniello). To his astonishment Wagner found that the striking scenes and rapid action of this opera proved effective and entertaining from beginning to end, even without the aid of a great artist like Mme. Devrient. This set him thinking. He was ambitious, and longed for an immediate and palpable success ;—could he not take hints from Bellini and Auber, and endeavour to combine the merits of their work ? Heroic music in Beethoven's manner was the true ideal ; but it seemed doubtful whether anything approaching it could be attained in connexion with the stage. The cases before him showed that effective music can certainly be produced on different lines and on a lower level ; the desiderata, as far as he then saw them, were : to contrive a play with rapid and animated action ; to compose music that would not be difficult to sing and would be likely to catch the ear of the public. His sole attempt in such a direction—' Das Liebesverbot,' an opera in two acts after Shakespeare's ' Measure for Measure ' (the part of Isabella intended for Mme. Devrient)—has not had a fair chance before the footlights. He sketched the libretto during the summer holidays, and worked at the score in 1835 and 1836. Details of the plot and the rather licentious tendency of the whole are described in his *Ges. Schriften*, vol. i. (*Prose Works*, vii. 5). The music is curiously unlike his former models, and it is easy to trace the influence of ' La Muette,' and even of ' Il pirata ' and ' Norma.' [3]

In the autumn of 1834 Wagner undertook the duties of Musikdirektor at the Magdeburg theatre. The troupe of actors and singers, mostly young people, was not a bad one ; they liked him, and the curious life behind and before the scenes afforded interest and amusement. At concerts under his direction the overture to ' Die Feen ' and a new overture to Apel's play, ' Columbus ' (1835), were performed [4] ; he wrote music for the celebration of New Year's Day, 1835, songs to a fantastic farce, ' Der Berggeist,' etc., and came to be liked by the public as well as the artists. In the summer of 1835 he went on a tour to find new singers, and was promised ' a benefit performance ' as a set-off against expenses. During this tour he again met Mme. Schröder-Devrient when she appeared at Nuremberg as Fidelio, and as Emmeline in Weigl's ' Schweizerfamilie.' The theatre at Magdeburg was supported by a small subven-

---

[1] In Mrs. Burrell's collection was the MS of a septet written at Würzburg. A tablet was affixed in 1890 to the house where he lived.   [2] See *Mein Leben*, p. 49.

[3] See Int. Mus. Ges. Quarterly, Jan. 1912, p. 348.
[4] On this overture see *Mus. T.*, 1905, p. 117. It was played at the Queen's Hall, Jan. 2, 1905.

tion from the court of Saxony and managed by a committee. But in spite of such assistance and supervision the worthy director, Bethmann, was ever on the brink of bankruptcy. He had a habit of disappearing when pay-day came round, and the troupe was in a bad plight during the spring season of 1836. ' We meant to close,' writes Wagner,

' towards the end of April with my opera, and I worked hard to get score and parts finished in good time. But as early as March the leading members threatened to leave ; for my sake they agreed to remain till the end of the month and to study my work. This, however, was not an easy task. No *Singspiel*, but music after the manner of La Muette ! Herr Bethmann represented that he would be put to sundry expenses for stage properties, etc., and claimed the first night for *his* benefit. I was to profit by the second.'

There were twelve days left, and the preparations went on incessantly ; rehearsals at the theatre, rehearsals at every private lodging ; all Magdeburg excited ; yet no man knew his part, and the ensembles were hopeless. At the general rehearsal Wagner's conducting, gesticulating and prompting kept things together somehow. Not so at the performance (Mar. 29, 1836)—a crowded house, and utter chaos. The repetition for the composer's benefit was duly announced, but collapsed ere the curtain could rise—few people in the auditorium, and a free fight behind the scenes [1] !

Wagner had many debts and no means to pay. He repaired to Leipzig, hoping that the long connexion of members of his family with the theatre there would smooth the way for ' Das Liebesverbot.' He was advised to offer the part of Marianne to the daughter of the director ; but Ringelhardt, after perusing the libretto, stated that his paternal conscience would not permit him to sanction the appearance of his daughter ' in a piece of such frivolous tendency.' Wagner next applied to the Königstädter Theater at Berlin—equally in vain. Penniless, he left Berlin for the Prussian town of Königsberg, where colleagues from Magdeburg—Frau Pollert the prima donna, and his special friend Wilhelmina or ' Minna ' Planer the actress (erste Liebhaberin) —had found engagements. With a view to the conductorship he arranged concerts at the Schauspielhaus, at one of which an overture of his, presumably ' Columbus,' was performed. At length the appointment as conductor was promised, and he forthwith married Fräulein Planer [2] (Nov. 24, 1836), the third daughter of the ' Mechanicus ' Gothilf Planer of Dresden. ' I wasted a year at Königsberg amid petty cares, worrying myself and others An overture, " Rule, Britannia," [3] is the only thing I wrote.'

[1] For a droll account of the performance, see ' *Bericht über eine erste Opernaufführung*,' *Ges. Schriften*, vol. i. (*P.W.* vii. 5) ; *Mein Leben*, p. 138.
[2] She was born at Oederan, near Chemnitz, Sept. 5, 1809, and was therefore nearly four years older than her husband. She died Jan. 25, 1866, and was buried in the Anna Friedhof in Dresden. (Kietz's *Reminiscences*, p. 135.)
[3] See *Mus. T.*, 1905, p. 117, and programme of the Queen's Hall concert of Jan. 2. 1905.

How to get out of this groove of mediocrity ? He longed for Paris. In those days success in the operatic world began in France. Had not Meyerbeer recently cleared 300,000 francs by ' Les Huguenots ' ? Wagner sent sketches for an opera in four acts—' Die hohe Braut,' after a novel of Heinrich König's—to Scribe the librettist, hoping thus to approach the Parisian Opéra.[4] Of course Scribe took no notice. About Michaelmas the director at Königsberg followed Herr Bethmann's example and declared himself bankrupt.

Wagner eagerly grasped at a chance which presented itself from the Russian side of the Baltic. A theatre was about to be started under Karl v. Holtei at Riga. On the recommendation of Dorn, who had gone thither some years before, Wagner was chosen First Musikdirektor, and his wife and her sister, Therese Planer, were engaged for the ' Schauspiel.' As compared with Magdeburg or Königsberg, Riga was a wealthy place, and the salaries were liberal. Wagner found all that was needful to attain good performances, and set to work energetically. During the winter season he conducted orchestral concerts [5] ; his overtures ' Columbus' and ' Rule, Britannia ' were played; he wrote various arias for the vocalists ; and the text to a comic opera in two acts, ' Die glückliche Bärenfamilie.' [6] Dec. 11 is the date of a ' Benefizvorstellung von Bellinis Norma, für Herrn Musikdirector Wagner.' During the summer of 1838 he rehearsed Méhul's ' Joseph ' ' with great love and enthusiasm for the work ' —and completed the book of ' Rienzi.'

' When in the autumn I began the music to "Rienzi," my sole care was to do justice to the subject. I had so laid it out that a first performance would be impossible at a second-rate theatre. I had Paris in view. The thought of conscious triviality, even for a single bar, was intolerable. The character of Rienzi, ardent, aspiring, amid barbarous surroundings, interested me. I approached it by way of the grand opera ; still my first care was to depict it in accordance with my feelings.' [7]

In the spring of 1839, at the termination of his contract, the first two acts were finished. He returned to Königsberg (July 1839), repaired to the port of Pillau, and took berths, on board a sailing vessel [8] bound for London, for himself, his little wife, and a huge Newfoundland dog, *en route* for Paris.

' I shall never forget the voyage : it lasted three weeks and a half, and was rich in disasters. Three times we suffered from the effects of heavy storms. The passage through the Narrows made a wondrous impression on my fancy. The legend of the "Flying Dutchman" [he had read it in Heine's *Salon*] was

[4] In 1842 these sketches were carried out in light verse to oblige Kapellmeister Reissiger, Wagner's colleague at Dresden. In 1848 the opera, entitled (' Bianca und Giuseppe,' or) ' Die Franzosen in Nizza,' in four acts, and with sundry alterations enforced by the Austrian censorship, music by Kapellmeister J. F. Kittl, was performed at Prague with considerable and lasting success.
[5] As to Wagner's orchestration of a Rossini duet for a concert in Mar. 1838 see Int. Mus. Ges. Monthly Journal, June 1912, p. 309, art. by Einstein.
[6] L. Nohl found the MS. at Riga in 1872, together with sketches for bits of the music—' à la Adam.' These are quoted in *Neue Zeitschrift* (1884, p. 244).
[7] See *Eine Mittheilung an meine Freunde*.
[8] The *Thetis*, an English vessel.

confirmed by the sailors, and the circumstances gave it a distinct and characteristic colour in my mind. We stopped eight days in London to recover from the trying effects of the voyage.   I was interested above all things in the aspect of the town and the Houses of Parliament ; of the theatres I saw nothing.' [1]

At Boulogne he made the acquaintance of Meyerbeer, and remained four weeks to cultivate it.   How far the music to ' Rienzi ' pleased Meyerbeer does not appear, and the saying attributed to him that ' Rienzi ' is the best opera-book extant is not sufficiently authenticated.   Meyerbeer provided Wagner with letters of introduction to the directors of the Opéra and the Théâtre de la Renaissance, to Schlesinger the music publisher and proprietor of the *Revue et Gazette musicale*, and to M. Gouin his agent, ' *l'alter ego* du grand maître.' Assertions in German journals that Wagner was then or at a later period under pecuniary obligations to Meyerbeer are groundless, and have been publicly contradicted.   The true relations of the two men will be described farther on.

PARIS.—Wagner arrived in Paris in Sept. 1839 and remained till Apr. 7, 1842 (aet. 26-29). His hopes and plans were not realised ; yet, for the growth of his power as an artist this was an important and eventful time.

' Except for the sake of my poor wife, whose patience was sorely tried, I have no reason to regret the adventure.   At two distinct periods we felt the pinch of poverty severely—actually suffered from cold and hunger.   I did a good deal of work, mere drudgery for the most part, but I also studied and wrote assiduously, and the performances of Beethoven at the Conservatoire were invaluable to me.'

They found lodgings in an out-of-the-way quarter, Rue de la Tonnellerie, ' au fond d'un appartement garni d'assez triste apparence,' in an old house which claims to have been the birthplace of Molière.   Patronised and introduced by Meyerbeer, Wagner was received with marked politeness.

' Léon Pillet [director of the Opéra, at that time called ACADÉMIE ROYALE DE MUSIQUE, *q.v.*] lui tend les bras, Schlesinger lui fait mille offres de service, Habeneck [conductor at the Opéra and the Conservatoire] le traite d'égal à égal.'

But he soon found that fine speeches meant anything rather than help or goodwill.   In fact Meyerbeer's intervention seems to have told against, rather than for him.   ' Do you know what makes me suspicious of this young man ?' said Heine : ' it is that Meyerbeer recommends him.' [2]   When told of Wagner's antecedents and his sanguine hopes of success, Heine devoutly

[1] They lodged for a night at the Hoop and Horseshoe, 10 Queen Street, Tower Hill, still existing ; then stayed at the King's Arms boarding-house, Old Compton Street, Soho, from which place the dog disappeared, and turned up again after a couple of days, to his master's frantic joy.   Wagner's accurate memory for localities was puzzled when he wandered about Soho with the writer in 1877 and failed to find the old house.   Mr. J. Cyriax, who has zealously traced every step of Wagner in London 1839, 1855 and 1877, states that the premises have been pulled down.   (See F. G Edwards, *Musical Haunts in London*, p. 50 ; *Mein Leben*, p. 199.)
[2] On the authority of Theodor Hagen, late editor of the New York *Musikzeitung*.   No other well-authenticated utterance of Heine regarding Wagner has come to light.   The so-called letter to Laube which appeared in *Das Orchester* (Dresden), and was reprinted by Herr Kastner in *Parsifal*, is not a letter at all, but a concoction made up of Laube's words.

folded his hands in admiration of a German's faith.   There was no chance whatever for '. Rienzi ' at the Opéra.

' Quand il lui détaille les merveilles de son *Rienzi*, le directeur de l'académie enveloppe sa phrase laudative d'épithètes plus réservées : quand il insiste et demande une audition à jour fixe, son interlocuteur recule visiblement, et redouble d'aménités oratoires pour éviter un engagement formel.'

A writer for the *Variétés* undertook a translation of the libretto of ' Das Liebesverbot ' for the Théâtre de la Renaissance.   Three numbers were tried and found acceptable.

' Wagner quitte à la hâte la rue de la Tonnellerie, trop éloignée de ce monde d'artistes avec lequel il va se trouver journellement en contact.   Il achète des meubles et s'établit triomphalement rue du Helder.'

On the very day of his removal M. Joli the director failed, and the doors of the theatre were closed.   Wagner attempted to gain a footing at one of the Boulevard theatres.   There was a talk of his setting a vaudeville of Dumanoir's, ' La Descente de la Courtille,' and a beginning was made.

' Malheureusement, les choristes du théâtre ne s'étaient pas aguerris encore à cette époque avec la musique de *La Belle Hélène*, et après quelques répétitions dérisoires, on déclara celle du jeune Allemand parfaitement inexécutable.   On en conserva seulement une chanson : " Allons à la Courtille ! " qui eut son heure de célébrité.' [3]

Wagner offered himself as a ' choriste ' at a still smaller Boulevard theatre.

' I came off worse than Berlioz when he was in a similar predicament.   The conductor who tested my capabilities discovered that I could not sing at all, and pronounced me a hopeless case all round.'

He tried song-writing with a view to the Salons.   A French version of Heine's ' Die beiden Grenadiere ' was made for him, and he set it, in 1839, introducing the ' Marseillaise ' at the close—a rather difficult and not altogether satisfactory composition, refused by professional singers with sufficient reason.   It appears strange, however, that neither singers nor publishers would have anything to do with three other simple and lovely songs to French words : the delicious little Berceuse ' Dors, mon enfant,' Ronsard's ' Mignonne ' and Victor Hugo's ' Attente.'   These were, literally, too good for the market.   For ' Mignonne ' Wagner in the end got a few francs when the song was printed in the music pages of a French periodical. Subsequently (1841-42) it appeared, together with ' Attente ' and ' Dors, mon enfant,' in the ' Beilagen ' to Lewald's *Europa*.   Apr. 1, 1841, is the date of a touching letter to the editor of *Europa*, to whom Wagner submits the three songs, requesting speedy payment of the ' maximum ' fee paid for such contributions, since prices are known to vary from 5 to 9 florins (about 10s. to 18s.), ' Ein Schelm, wer sich besser giebt, als er ist : mich hat man hier so zugerichtet ! '

On Feb. 4, 1840, the score of a superb orches-

[3] Gasperini, *R. Wagner*, p. 27.   The chanson has not been traced.

tral piece, published 15 years later as 'Eine Faust Ouvertüre,' was finished. This is the first work that has the true stamp of Wagner. It was conceived after a rehearsal of Beethoven's ninth symphony at the Conservatoire in the winter of 1839 (aet. 26), and is in some sense a piece of autobiography written in music. As originally planned it was to form the first movement of a Faust symphony. After a trial performance at Dresden, July 22, 1844, it was laid aside till 1855, when a revised version was published bearing a motto from Goethe's 'Faust '—

'Und so ist mir das Dasein eine Last,
  Der Tod erwünscht, das Leben mir verhasst!'

It is a masterpiece of construction and instrumentation. The influence of Beethoven is apparent in the concise power of the themes and the plain direct manner in which they are set forth, yet the work is Wagner's own from beginning to end.

Performances in Paris were not so good as he had anticipated :

'The Académie savours of mediocrity ; the *mise en scène* and decorations are better than the singing. At the Opéra-Comique the representations have a completeness and a physiognomy of their own such as we know nothing of in Germany, but the music written for that theatre is perhaps the worst that has yet been produced in these days of decadence. The miserable quadrille rhythms which now (1842) rattle across the stage have banished the grace of Méhul, Isouard, Boieldieu and *young* Auber. For a musician there is but one thing worth attention —the orchestral concerts at the Conservatoire ; but these stand alone, and nothing springs from them.'

His remarks about the stars at the Opéra— Duprez, Dorus-Gras, Rubini ' with his sempiternal shake ' — are rarely without a sting. The facile success of virtuosi annoyed him. Liszt, with whom he was to be so closely connected in after days, and who was then at the height of his fame as a virtuoso, appeared quite antipathetic. Wagner called once only at Liszt's lodgings, and left them in a state of irritation. ' Take Liszt to a better world and he will treat the assembly of angels to a Fantaisie sur le Diable.' Paris at the time harboured many Germans—artists, savants, literati—in needy circumstances for the most part, but warm-hearted and impulsive. In such circles Wagner found congenial associates.[1] ' I met with many proofs of true friendship in Paris '—and the words may be taken to explain how it was that he and his ' bildhübsche kleine Frau ' [2] did not actually starve during that first winter. The dog was stolen before they left the Rue de la Tonnellerie.[3]

Having no immediate prospects, he set to work to complete the music to ' Rienzi,' and for its ultimate performance cast his eye on Dresden, where his name might be supposed to have some little weight. On Nov. 19 the score was completed, and on Dec. 4 he despatched it to Herr v. Lüttichau, the Intendant. In the meantime, to keep the wolf from the door, he did all manner of odd work for Schlesinger, reading proofs, arranging rubbish for various instruments—the cornet-à-piston among the number—making *partitions de piano* of operas, etc. In 1841 he began to write for the *Gazette musicale* a clever novelette, *Une visite à Beethoven,* ' fut très remarqué par Berlioz, qui en parla avec éloge dans le *Journal des débats.*' Such things improved his position in the estimation of musicians, and preserved his self-respect. But the pay was small and partly absorbed by the expenses of translation ; for Wagner, like most Germans, knew enough French for everyday purposes, but could not write the language effectively. His contributions to the *Gazette* were—to give their German titles : ' Der Virtuos und der Künstler,' ' Der Künstler und die Öffentlichkeit,' ' Ein glücklicher Abend,' ' Der Freischütz,' ' Eine Pilgerfahrt zu Beethoven,' ' Das Ende eines deutschen Musikers in Paris.' The original German of the two latter has been preserved in the *Dresdener Abendzeitung* of Theodor Hell (Hofrath Winkler) for 1841 ; the other articles have been translated back into German by Frau Cosima Wagner. Further articles written in Paris which the author thought worth reprinting are : Rossini's ' Stabat Mater,' dated Dec. 15, 1841, and signed H. Valentino (Schumann's *Neue Zeitschrift für Musik*), ' Le Freischütz,' ' Bericht nach Deutschland ' (*Ges. Schrift.* vol. i. *P.W.* vii.),[4] ' Über die Ouvertüre ' (ditto, do.). A series of gossiping articles in Lewald's *Europa* signed V. Freudenfeuer, and styled ' Pariser Amusements ' and ' Pariser Fatalitäten für Deutsche,' also the correspondence written for the *Dresdener Abendzeitung*—' Nachrichten aus dem Gebiete der Künste und Wissenschaften,' have been cancelled [5]—with the one exception of an article on Halévy's ' Reine de Chypre,' Dec. 31, 1841 (*Ges. Schrift.* vol. i. *P.W.* vii. 205).

On Feb. 4, 1841, Wagner's overture ' Columbus ' was performed at the annual concert to which the publisher Schlesinger used to invite the subscribers to the *Gazette musicale.*[6] This, by the way, was the only performance of one of Wagner's works at Paris during his first residence there. Score and parts disappeared at that time, and were discovered in Paris about 1880.

When Meyerbeer returned in the summer of 1840, Wagner was in great distress. Meyerbeer again introduced him to the director of the Opéra, Pillet. This time it was a personal intro-

---

[1] Hallé, who was one of these associates, has recorded his recollections of Wagner : see *Life and Letters of Sir Charles Hallé*, 1896, p. 59.
[2] So described by Friedrich Pecht, the painter.
[3] See *Richard Wagner an Theodor Apel*, p. 72, for a letter describing Wagner's sufferings in Paris.

[4] According to Kastner, this was a contribution to the *Augsburger Abendzeitung*—on Wolzogen's authority it should be *Dresdener Abendzeitung*, 1841.
[5] They are translated in *P.W.* viii.
[6] Pillet's account of the fiasco is in W. A. Ellis's *Life of Wagner* i. 311.

duction, and the reception accordingly was still
more polite and encouraging. On Meyerbeer's
advice Wagner submitted detailed sketches
for the libretto to an opera, ' Der fliegende
Holländer,' with the proposal that a French
text-book should be prepared for him to set to
music. Wagner had come to an understanding
about the treatment of the story with Heine,
who had a claim to be consulted, inasmuch as it
was Heine who had recently related it and had
suggested a new and touching *dénouement* which
Wagner wished to adopt. In Heine's *Memoiren
des Herrn von Schnabelewopski* the imaginary
hero witnesses the beginning and end of a play
about the ' Ahasuerus of the ocean ' at some
theatre at Amsterdam, and reports that in the
course of that performance the salvation of the
doomed captain was brought about by the
devotion of a woman ' faithful unto death.' [1]
Matters at the Opéra apparently progressed
just as Wagner desired. His sketches were
accepted, and the names of various *arrangeurs*
were mentioned. Meyerbeer again left Paris,
and soon after his departure Pillet astonished
Wagner by telling him that he had taken a
liking to ' Le Vaisseau-fantôme,' and was therefore anxious to dispose of it in favour of a composer to whom he had long ago promised a good
libretto. Wagner refused to listen to any such
proposition, and demanded his manuscript back.
But this again did not suit Pillet, and so the
matter remained in abeyance, Wagner consoling
himself with the hope that Meyerbeer would
ultimately set it straight. In the spring of
1841 Wagner, pressed by creditors, sub-let his
rooms in the Rue du Helder, and took lodgings
in the suburbs, at Meudon. Accidentally he
heard that the plans for the ' Holländer ' had
been handed to Paul Foucher for versification,
and that if he did not choose to give his consent
to what was going on, he might be left in the
cold altogether. Protests proved useless, and
in the end Pillet paid £20 by way of compen-
sation !

Wagner lost no time in completing his own
poem and setting it to music. In seven weeks
the score of the entire opera, except the overture, was finished. But £20, even at Meudon,
cannot last for ever. Before Wagner could find
leisure to write the overture he had to do two
months more of journeyman work (*partitions
de piano* of Halévy's ' Guitarrero,' ' La Reine
de Chypre,' etc.).

' I did it all cheerfully enough, corresponded with
the artists at Dresden, and looked forward to my
deliverance. I offered the book of the " Holländer "
to the managers at Munich and Leipzig; they refused
it as unfit for Germany. I had fondly hoped it would
touch chords that respond quickest with Germans ! '

At Berlin a word from Meyerbeer sufficed to

get it ' accepted,' but without prospect of
immediate performance.

After the composition of the ' Holländer ' he
cast about for other subjects. During a course
of historical reading he met with the story of
the conquest of Apulia and Sicily by Manfred,
son of the Emperor Frederick II. The picturesque semi-Oriental circumstances of the story
attracted him, and he sketched a libretto, ' Die
Sarazener,' in which a prophetess, Manfred's
half-sister by an Arabian mother, kindles the
enthusiasm of the Saracens and leads to victory
and to Manfred's coronation. Mme. Devrient,
to whom some years later he submitted the
fully developed plan, objected to the *dénouement*, and it was dropped altogether.

By a lucky chance the popular version
(Volksbuch) of the story of ' Tannhäuser ' now
came into his hands and took possession of his
fancy. It has already been said that he was
familiar with the subject ; in early youth he
had read Tieck's rhymed ' Erzählung ' of Tannhäuser, and Hoffmann's novel ' Der Sängerkrieg ' ; he was also aware that Weber had
planned an opera on the legend of Tannhäuser.

' When I re-read Tieck's altogether modern poem,
I saw clearly why its mystical coquetry and frivolous
catholicism had formerly repelled me. The Volksbuch
and the plain Tannhäuserlied [2] present the figure of
Tannhäuser in far clearer and simpler outlines.'

He was especially struck by the connexion of
Tannhäuser with the contest of Minnesänger at
Wartburg, which the Volksbuch establishes in
a loose sort of way. Thereupon he endeavoured
to trace the story of the ' Sängerkrieg ' to its
source. A German philologist of his acquaintance happened to possess a copy of the mediæval German poem. It interested him greatly,
and he was tempted to pursue the subject
further. One of the MS. copies of the ' Wartburgkrieg ' [3] introduces the poem of ' Loherangrin.' [4] Wagner was led to the study of Wolfram von Eschenbach's 'Parzival' and 'Titurel';
' and thus an entirely new world of poetical
matter suddenly opened before me.' [5]

DRESDEN (1842–49, aet. 29-36).—Before the
ensemble rehearsals for ' Rienzi ' began in July,
Wagner made an excursion to the Bohemian
hills, and at Teplitz completed the sketches for
the book of ' Tannhäuser.' ' Rienzi ' had found
friends in the person of Herr Fischer the chorus-
master, and of Josef Tichatschek the tenor, who
felt sure that his ' trumpet tones ' would tell in
the title - rôle. Mme. Schröder - Devrient, in
spite of her ' contours tant soit peu maternels,' [6]
would make the most of Adriano. There was
ample opportunity for novel scenic effects,
dumb show and the display of choral masses.

[1] It was, however, not a Dutch play at Amsterdam, but, as
Hueffer has shown, an English play of Fitzball's at the Adelphi in
London which Heine witnessed in 1827, and which furnished him
with the outlines of the story. Still the ingenious *dénouement* is
Heine's own. But see an article, *From Fitzball to Wagner*, by
W. A. Ellis, in *The Meister*. Feb. 1892, p. 4.

[2] For the original ' Tannhäuserlied ' see Uhland's *Alte hoch- und
nieder-deutsche Volkslieder*, bk. v. p. 297.
[3] See Simrock's edition of *Der Wartburgkrieg* (1858) and his
version into modern German of Wolfram von Eschenbach's *Parzival
und Titurel* (xvi. ' Loherangrin,' 3rd ed. 1857).
[4] Printed by Görres in 1813, and in 1858 again edited by Rückert.
[5] As to the sources of these dramas, see *The Legends of the Wagner
Drama ; Studies in Mythology and Romance*, by Jessie L. Weston,
1896.   [6] Berlioz, *Mémoires*, p. 274.

The chorus-master and the stage manager were ready to make special efforts; Reissiger, the conductor, was well disposed, and had a good orchestra; in short, the night of Oct. 20, 1842, proved a memorable one. The performance began at 6, and came to an end just before midnight, amid immense applause. 'We ought all to have gone to bed,' relates a witness, 'but we did nothing of the kind.' Early next morning Wagner appeared in the band-room to make excisions. In the afternoon he reappeared to see whether they had been properly indicated in the parts; the copyist excused himself on the plea that the singers objected! 'Ich lasse mir nichts streichen,' said Tichatschek, 'es war zu himmlisch!' During the next ten days two repetitions were given to crowded houses at increased prices. When Reissiger, after the fifth [1] performance, offered Wagner the baton, the enthusiasm redoubled. Wagner was the hero of the day. By and by 'Rienzi' came to occupy two evenings: acts 1 and 2—and 3, 4, 5. The attraction at Dresden has continued more or less ever since. But it was five years before the work was performed at Berlin, Oct. 26, 1847; it was produced at Hamburg, 1844; at Königsberg, 1845; at Munich and Cassel, 1870; at Vienna, 1871. [2]

Nov. 26, 1842, a soirée [3] was given at the Gewandhaus, Leipzig, by Sophie Schröder the tragedian (Mme. Devrient's mother), at which Tichatschek sang Rienzi's prayer and Mme. Devrient the air of Adriano. Wagner's literary friend Laube ('Der sich gar nichts daraus machte wie etwas klang') mistook a duet from Marschner's 'Templer und Jüdin' for another extract from 'Rienzi,' and reported that the three pieces 'were rather dry and poor in thought.' Laube was about to assume the editorship of the Zeitung für die elegante Welt, and asked Wagner for materials towards a biographical article. This was the origin of the Autobiographische Skizze, repeatedly quoted above and reprinted in vol. i. of Wagner's collected writings. It was printed verbatim in the 5th and 6th numbers of that journal, Feb. 1 and 8, 1843, and was accompanied by a portrait 'after Kietz.'

The managers of the Dresden theatre were now eager to bring out 'Der fliegendeHolländer.' The opera was hastily prepared, and Wagner conducted the first performance on Jan. 2, 1843 (Senta, Mme. Schröder-Devrient).

'I had aimed at presenting the action in its simplest traits, and at avoiding needless details and everything that might flavour of intrigue; the incidents of the story were to tell their own tale.'

The public had expected a second 'Rienzi,' and were disappointed. It was by no means a

failure, nor was it a succès d'estime: some were deeply touched, others simply astonished. Schumann's paper reported that Mme. Devrient's Senta 'was the most original representation she has perhaps ever given.' Wagner's own words tend to show that she made too much of her part; the rest, especially the representative of the Holländer, Wächter, too little, and that in spite of applause and recalls the performance was unsatisfactory. The work was repeated in due course, and never quite disappeared from the repertory. [4] The poem was submitted to Spohr, who pronounced it 'a little masterpiece,' and asked for the music, which he conducted at Cassel, June 5, 1843. Wagner wrote a warm letter of thanks, and a pleasant correspondence ensued. Altogether Spohr appears to have been the only eminent musician of an earlier generation who cordially held out his hand to young Wagner. Spohr's Selbstbiographie (ii. 272, Eng. trans. ii. 245) contains extracts from a letter to his friend Lüder, written whilst the rehearsals were going on:

'"Der fliegende Holländer" interests me in the highest degree. The opera is imaginative, of noble invention, well written for the voices, immensely difficult, rather overdone as regards instrumentation, but full of novel effects; at the theatre it is sure to prove clear and intelligible. . . . I have come to the conclusion that among composers for the stage pro tem. Wagner is the most gifted.'

The 'Holländer' was originally meant to be performed in one act [5] as a 'dramatic Ballade.' A reference to the score will show that the division into three acts is made by means of crude cuts, and new starts equally crude.

When 'Rienzi' was produced, the death of Kapellmeister Morlacchi (1841) and of Musikdirector Rastrelli (1842) had left two vacancies at Dresden. The names of Schindelmeisser, Gläser and Wagner were put forward as candidates. Wagner appears at first to have tried for the lesser post of Musikdirektor, with a salary of 1200 thalers (£180). But von Lüttichau the Intendant supported him, and in the end he was appointed Hofkapellmeister with a salary of 1500 thalers (£225). [6] On Jan. 10, 1843, he gave the customary 'trial performance' by rehearsing and conducting Weber's 'Euryanthe'; and, whilst the rival candidate, Schindelmeisser, was busy with Spontini's 'La Vestale,' he repaired to Berlin to press forward 'Rienzi' and the 'Holländer.' But it appeared that the managers of the Royal Prussian Opera did not care to risk a performance of either work just then, their acceptance of Wagner's libretti having been a mere act of politeness towards Meyerbeer. Before the end of Jan.

---

[1] The performance conducted by Wagner was the sixth. See Ellis's Life, i. 351, and the Familien Briefe, p. 86.
[2] For the further history of 'Rienzi' see an article by O. Eichberg in the Bayreuth Taschenbuch for 1892, p. 5.
[3] Mendelssohn (who conducted his overture to 'Ruy Blas') wrote about it to his mother, Nov. 28.

[4] On May 22, 1843, it was given at Riga; in 1844 at Berlin. As to its further history, see Eichberg's article in Bayreuther Taschenkalender, 1893, p. 139.
[5] The first reading was restored in Dec. 1898 at the Lyceum Theatre, at a students' performance of the R.C.M.; and the same admirable arrangement was carried out at Bayreuth in 1901, 1902 and 1914.
[6] At court theatres in Germany the title Hofkapellmeister usually implied an appointment for life, with a retiring pension in proportion to salary and duration of service.

Wagner's appointment at Dresden was ratified by the authorities. The ceremony of installation took place on Feb. 2—the day after Berlioz's arrival—and it was the first of Wagner's official acts to assist Berlioz at the rehearsals for his concerts.[1]

Wagner had scruples as to whether he would prove the right man for the place. With every appearance of reason his wife and friends urged that no one in his circumstances could afford to slight a permanent appointment with a fixed salary. No doubt he would have been the right man if the Königliche sächsische Hofoperntheater had in reality been what it professed to be—an institution subsidised for the sake of art. But the words ' Operatic Theatre, Royal and subsidised ' or otherwise, and ' Art for Art's sake,' convey widely divergent notions. Wagner had experience enough to know as much. He held his peace, however, and accepted—' froh und freudig ward ich königlicher Kapellmeister.' The duties were heavy; performances every evening all the year round—at least three plays, and generally three, sometimes four, operas per week—besides the music at the Hofkirche and occasional concerts at court. The Musikdirector led at the plays, and looked after the church music on week - days; the two Kapellmeister conducted at church on Sundays and festivals, and each was responsible for certain operas. During his seven years' service Wagner rehearsed and conducted ' Euryanthe,' ' Freischütz,' 'Don Juan,' 'Zauberflöte,' ' Clemenza di Tito,' ' Fidelio,' Spontini's ' La Vestale,' Spohr's ' Jessonda,' Marschner's ' Hans Heiling ' and 'Adolf von Nassau,' Winter's ' Unterbrochenes Opferfest,' Mendelssohn's ' Sommernachtstraum ' and ' Antigone,' Gluck's ' Armida,' etc. He made a special arrangement of ' Iphigenia in Aulis,' performed Feb. 22, 1847, in which he revised the text, retouched the instrumentation, condensed certain bits, added sundry connectinglinks and changed the close. The arrangement has been published and generally adopted. At the Pensionskonzerte given by the Hofkapelle his reading of Beethoven's symphonies—' Eroica,' C minor, A major and F major, and particularly of the Choral Symphony—attracted much attention. ' It was worth while to make the journey from Leipzig merely to hear the recitative of the contrabasses,' said Niels Gade concerning the last.[2]

Wagner had not much to do with the music at the Hofkirche, but he detested the routine work there. The Catholic court chose to have none but Catholics in the choir, women's voices were excluded, and the soprano and alto parts were taken by boys. All told, the choir con-

sisted of 24 or 26—14 men and 10 or 12 boys. The accompaniments were played by a full orchestra—on festive occasions as many as 50 performers, including trumpets and trombones !

' The echoes and reverberations in the building were deafening. I wanted to relieve the hard-worked members of the orchestra, add female voices, and introduce true Catholic church music *a cappella*. As a specimen I prepared Palestrina's Stabat Mater, and suggested other pieces, but my efforts failed.[3]
' There was an odd relic of bygone days there, a *musico*, a great fat *soprano*. I used to delight in his extreme conceit and silliness. On holidays and festivals he refused to sing unless some aria was especially set apart for him. It was quite wonderful to hear the ancient colossus trill that florid stuff of Hasse's : a huge pudding, with a voice like a cracked cornet-à-piston. But he had a virtue for which we may well envy him ; he could sing as much in one breath as any normal singer I ever met with in two.' [4]

Wagner became leader of the Liedertafel (a choir of male voices established 1839) and was chosen conductor of the Männergesangfest, which took place in July 1843, and for which he wrote ' Das Liebesmahl der Apostel —eine biblische Scene.' This work requires three separate choirs of male voices, which begin *a cappella* and are ultimately supported by the full orchestra. It is dedicated to Frau Charlotte Weinlig, ' der Wittwe seines unvergesslichen Lehrers.' [5]

In 1844 the remains of C. M. von Weber were exhumed and brought from London to Dresden. Wagner had taken an active part in the movement, and the musical arrangements for the solemn reception of the body and the interment, Dec. 14, were carried out under his direction.

Meantime ' Tannhäuser ' was completed (Apr. 13, 1844 ; first revision, Dec. 23 ; further revision of close, Sept. 4, 1846). He had worked at it arduously and finished it with the greatest care ; so much so that he ventured to have the full score lithographed from his manuscript. In July 1845 he forwarded a copy to Carl Gaillard at Berlin, with a long and interesting letter [6] :

' Pianoforte arrangement, etc., has already been prepared, so that on the day after the first performance I shall be quite free. I mean to be lazy for a year or so, to make use of my library and produce nothing. . . . If a dramatic work is to be significant and original it must result from a step in advance in the life and culture of the artist ; but such a step cannot be made every few months ! '

He desired to rest and read ; but he returned from Teplitz after the summer holidays with sketches for ' Die Meistersinger ' and ' Lohengrin.' The first performance of ' Tannhäuser ' took place at Dresden, Oct. 19, 1845. It was not an unqualified success—even the executants confessed themselves bewildered. Tichatschek

---

[1] See Berlioz's letter to D'Ortigue, Feb. 28, 1843 (*Correspondance and Mémoires*), Lettre à Ernst. Translated in K. F. Boult's *Life of Hector Berlioz*, 1903, p. 182.
[2] Some interesting particulars of the rehearsal, etc., of this performance are given in Kietz's *Reminiscences*, p. 45 f.

[3] In conversation with the writer. The German translation of the Stabat Mater given in Wagner's edition is by the late C. Riedel.
[4] Inquiries at Dresden show that this *Soprano*, Mose Tarquinio, was a member of the Köngl. Sächs. musica., Kapelle till Apr. 30, 1845 ; also that Angelo Ciccarelli, another *musico*, acted as instructor to the choir-boys, under Wagner. This is due to the kindness of Herr Moritz Fürstenau, custos of the Royal Library of Music at Dresden.
[5] See *Mus. T.*, 1899, p. 165.
[6] Quoted by Tappert in *Musicalisches Wochenblatt*, 1877, p. 411

sang the part of Tannhäuser, Mme. Devrient that of Venus, Johanna Wagner (Richard Wagner's niece) that of Elisabeth, Mitterwurzer that of Wolfram. The scene in the Venusberg fell flat. ' You are a man of genius,' said Mme. Devrient, ' but you write such eccentric stuff, it is hardly possible to sing it.' The second act, with the march, fared best ; the third act, with the ' pointless and empty recitation of Tannhäuser ' (*i.e.* the story of the pilgrimage to Rome, which now holds people spellbound), was pronounced a bore. Critics discovered that Wagner had no melody, no form ; ' this sort of music acts on the nerves.' ' A distressing, harassing subject '—' art ought to be cheerful and consoling '—' why should not Tannhäuser marry Elisabeth ? ' The Intendant explained to Wagner that his predecessor, ' the late Kapellmeister ' Weber, had managed matters better, ' since he understood how to let his operas end satisfactorily ! ' The public was fairly puzzled. ' A feeling of complete isolation overcame me,' writes Wagner. ' It was not my vanity—I had knowingly deceived myself, and now I felt numbed. I saw a single possibility before me : *induce the public to understand and participate in my aims as an artist.*' And this is the root of his subsequent literary and theoretical efforts.

Liszt conducted the overture to ' Tannhäuser ' at Weimar, Nov. 12, 1848, and produced the entire work Feb. 16, 1849. Other leading theatres followed at intervals—Wiesbaden, 1852 ; Munich, 1855 ; Berlin, 1856 ; Vienna (Thalia Theater and Theater in der Josefstadt, 1857), Hofoperntheater, Nov. 19, 1859 ; Paris, Mar. 13, 1861.[1]

Spohr brought out ' Tannhäuser ' in 1853.[2] 'The opera,' he wrote, ' contains much that is new and beautiful, also several ugly attacks on one's ears. . . .[3] A good deal that I disliked at first I have got accustomed to on repeated hearing—only the absence of definite rhythms (das Rhythmuslose) and the frequent lack of rounded periods (Mangel an abgerundeten Perioden) continue to disturb me,' etc. Mendelssohn witnessed a performance, and said to Wagner ' that a canonical answer in the adagio of the second finale had given him pleasure.' Moritz Hauptmann (Weinlig's successor at the Thomasschule) pronounced the overture ' quite atrocious (ganz grässlich), incredibly awkward, long and tedious.'[4] Schumann (who settled in Dresden in the autumn of 1844) wrote to Heinrich Dorn, Jan. 7, 1846 :

' I wish you could see " Tannhäuser " ; it contains deeper, more original and altogether an hundredfold better things than his previous operas—at the same time a good deal that is musically trivial. On the whole, Wagner may become of great importance and significance to the stage, and I am sure he is possessed

of the needful courage. Technical matters, instrumentation, I find altogether remarkable, beyond comparison better than formerly. Already he has finished a new text-book, " Lohengrin." ' [5]

About 1845–46 pecuniary troubles again began to press upon Wagner. The success of ' Rienzi ' had naturally led him to hope that his operas would soon find their way to the leading theatres. To facilitate this he had entered into an agreement with a firm of music publishers (C. F. Meser, Dresden) to print the pianoforte scores of ' Rienzi ' and the ' Holländer.' The pianoforte arrangement and the full score of ' Tannhäuser ' were now added to these. The conditions of the contract have not been made public ; the results, however, proved disastrous. Issued at high prices, and by publishers whose business relations were not very extensive, the editions did not sell well, and Wagner became liable for a considerable sum. His professional duties, too, began to grow irksome. He had gradually drifted into the position of an agitator and a party leader. The more gifted among his musical colleagues admired and liked him, but to the majority his excitable temperament was antipathetic and his restless activity was found inconvenient. No one disputed his personal ascendancy, yet he was made to feel the effects of jealousy and ill-will. The press did its best to confuse matters, and to spread damaging gossip. The accredited critic at Dresden, Reissiger's friend J. Schladebach, was the champion of existing usages, which he chose to call classical traditions. A person of some education and an experienced writer, Schladebach cannot be accused of having treated Wagner unfairly, as journalism goes. At first he was inclined to be rather patronising ; in course of time he took care to minimise whatever might tell in Wagner's favour and to accentuate everything that looked like a departure from the beaten tracks. Unfortunately he was the principal Dresden correspondent of the musical and literary journals of Leipzig, Berlin, etc. Thus the effect of his reports was more detrimental to Wagner's prospects than perhaps he intended it to be. Managers of theatres and German musicians generally took their cue from the journals, and in the end Wagner came to be regarded as an eccentric and unruly personage difficult to deal with. The libretti and scores he submitted were hardly glanced at ; in sundry cases indeed the parcels were returned unopened !

Except the performance of Gluck's ' Iphigenia in Aulis,'[6] arranged by Wagner, and of

[1] The *Bayreuther Taschenkalender*, 1891, contains a monograph on ' Tannhäuser ' and a chronological table of events relating to the history of the work.
[2] *Selbstbiographie*, ii. 356. [3] Letter to Hauptmann, *ibid.*
[4] Letter to Spohr, Apr. 21, 1846.

[5] It is curious to compare with these just and generous words the following extracts from a letter of Schumann written some years later (1853) and quoted by Herr Kastner (*Richard Wagner Katalog*): ' Wagner is, if I am to put it concisely, not a good musician (kein guter Musiker) ; he is wanting in the proper sense for form and for beauty of sound. . . . Apart from the performance the music is poor (gering), quite amateurish, empty and repelling (gehaltlos und widerwärtig),' etc.
[6] For details concerning Wagner's reading of the overture, and for a description of his ' arrangement ' of the entire opera, see *Ges. Schriften*, v. 143 (*P.W.* iii. 153), and Glasenapp, p. 226.

Beethoven's Choral Symphony, which was repeated at the Pensionskonzert, there was nothing remarkable in the musical doings of 1847. Wagner led a more retired life than heretofore, and worked steadily at 'Lohengrin.' On Aug. 28 the introduction was written, and the instrumentation of the entire work completed during the winter and early spring. He knew that he had made a considerable step in advance since 'Tannhäuser,' but he was also conscious of having moved still further away from the standards of contemporary taste. It is enough to state that, whilst he was writing 'Lohengrin,' the repertory at Dresden consisted in a large measure of Donizetti. A letter written early in 1847 exhibits an almost apologetic tone :

'I am inclined rather to doubt my powers than to overrate them, and I must look upon my present undertakings as experiments towards determining whether or not *the opera is possible*.'

The management at Dresden did not care for such experiments, and indefinitely put off the production of 'Lohengrin'; so that the finale to the first act, which was performed on the 300th anniversary of the Kapelle, Sept. 22, 1848, was all he heard of the work.

At Berlin 'Tannhäuser' had been refused as 'too epic,' whatever that may mean. After six years' delay preparations were begun there for 'Rienzi,' and the King of Prussia's birthday, Oct. 5, 1847, was fixed for the first performance. When Wagner arrived to superintend rehearsals he was received in a singularly lukewarm manner ; personal attacks and injurious insinuations appeared in the local journals, and it soon became evident that 'Rienzi' was foredoomed. The management discovered that political catchwords—'liberty,' 'fraternity' and the like—could be culled from the libretto ; another opera was chosen for the royal fête, and 'Rienzi' postponed till Oct. 26, when the court did not attend and 'General-Musikdirector Meyerbeer thought fit to leave town.' A large miscellaneous audience applauded vigorously, but the success proved ephemeral and Wagner's hopes of bettering his pecuniary position were disappointed.

In 1848 the universal distress and political discontent told upon musical matters at Dresden as it did elsewhere. The repertory showed signs of rapid deterioration. Flotow's 'Martha' attracted the public. With the exception of three subscription concerts given by the orchestra, at the first of which, in January, Wagner conducted Bach's 8-part motet 'Singet dem Herrn ein neues Lied,' nothing of interest was performed. Towards the end of March, when the instrumentation of 'Lohengrin' was finished, his restless mind had already begun to brood upon new subjects. Sketches for 'Jesus von Nazareth'[1]—a tentative effort in the direction

of 'Parsifal'—were laid aside, as he failed to find a satisfactory mode of treating the subject. For the last time the conflicting claims of history and of legend presented themselves— Frederick Barbarossa on the one side and Siegfried on the other. The former subject would have been particularly opportune at a time when the name of the great emperor was in everybody's mouth ; but Wagner's historical studies regarding Barbarossa had no other result than a curious essay treating of that vague borderland which separates historical fact from mythical tradition, entitled *Die Wibelungen, Weltgeschichte aus der Sage*. It was written in 1848 and printed in 1850.[2] To students for whom the growth of a great man's mind is almost as interesting as the ultimate result, this essay presents many points of interest ; to others it cannot be attractive, except as evidence of Wagner's peculiar earnestness of purpose and his delight in hard work.

He decided to dramatise the myths of the Nibelungen, and made his first grip at the subject in a prose version (1848), 'Der Nibelungen-Mythus als Entwurf zu einem Drama.'[3] This was immediately followed by 'Siegfrieds Tod,'[4] in three acts and a prologue (autumn, 1848), written in alliterative verse, and subsequently incorporated with many additions and emendations in 'Götterdämmerung.' Sundry germs of the music, too, were conceived at this early period.

Wagner entertained hopes that the general desire for political reform might lead to a better state of things in musical and theatrical matters. Accordingly he wrote out an elaborate plan for the organisation of a 'national theatre.' His objects were : thorough reform of the theatre at Dresden ; amalgamation of the existing art institutions of Saxony, with headquarters at Dresden ; increase of efficiency and reduction of expenditure. Supported throughout by detailed statements of facts and figures, his proposals appear eminently practical, and might have been carried out entire or in part with obvious advantage. The new liberal Minister of the Interior, Herr Oberländer, sympathised with Wagner, but had little hope of surmounting the initial difficulty, viz. to detach the finances of the theatre from those of the court and get an annual grant of public money in place of the subsidies from the King's privy purse. Derisory pencil notes on the margin of the manuscript showed that it had been read by certain people at court, but no action was taken by the Ministry, and the political catastrophe of May 1849 ere long put an end to all projects of reform, social or artistic.[5]

---

[1] Published in 1887 and translated in *P.W.* viii. 283.

[2] *Ges. Schriften*, ii. (*P.W.* vii. 257).
[3] *Ibid.* ii. (*P.W.* vii. 299).   [4] *Ibid.* (*P.W.* viii. 1).
[5] Extracts, *Sittliche Stellung des Musik zum Staat, Zahl der Theatervorstellungen, Die katholische Kirchenmusik*, were communicated by Theod. Uhlig to the *Neue Zeitschrift für Musik*, vol. xxxiv., and the entire document is given in *Ges. Schriften* vol. ii. (*P.W.* vii. 319).

Wagner was less concerned with politics proper than is generally supposed.[1] The speech—one of two—which he delivered in the Vaterlandsverein, a political club, June 14, 1848, and which was then reported in full in the *Dresden Anzeiger*, has been unearthed and reprinted by Herr Tappert (*R. W.* pp. 33-42).[2] Its tone is moderate enough, and it had no further consequences than a reprimand from the police authorities, who thought it undesirable that a ' königlicher Kapellmeister ' should speak in such a place. In May 1849, when the court of Saxony fled and Prussian troops were despatched to coerce the rioters at Dresden, Wagner was much excited ; but the tale of his having carried a red flag and fought on the barricades is not corroborated by the ' acts of accusation ' preserved in the Saxon police records. Alarming rumours, however, reached him that a warrant for his arrest was being prepared, and he thought it prudent to get out of the way and await the turn of events. He went quietly to Weimar, where Liszt was busy with ' Tannhäuser.' On the 19th May, in course of a rehearsal, news came from Dresden that orders for Wagner's arrest as a ' politically dangerous individual ' had been issued. There was no time to lose ; Liszt procured a passport and escorted Wagner as far as Eisenach on the way to Paris.[3]

EXILE (1849-61, aet. 36-48).—' It is impossible to describe my delight, after I had got over the immediate painful impressions, when I felt free at last—free from the world of torturing and ever-unsatisfied wishes, free from the annoying surroundings that had called forth such wishes.'

The hopes which Liszt indulged, that Wagner might now be able to gain a footing in Paris, proved futile. Wagner's desire to publish a series of articles in a French periodical ' on the prospects of art under the Revolution ' met with no response. Paris, said the editor of the *Journal des débats*, would laugh at any attempt to discuss the notions of a German musician about the relation of art to politics. Music altogether was at a low ebb in France, and no one cared to risk the production of a tragic opera.

In June 1849 Wagner went to Zürich, where several of his Dresden friends had found refuge, and where his wife joined him. In Oct. 1849 he became a citizen of Zürich. The first years of his residence there are marked by a long spell of literary work : *Die Kunst und die Revolution*, 1849 ; *Das Kunstwerk der Zukunft, Kunst und Klima, Das Judenthum in der*

Musik, 1850 ; *Über die Goethe Stiftung, Ein Theater in Zürich, Erinnerungen an Spontini*, 1851 ; *Über die Aufführung des Tannhäuser, Bemerkungen zur Aufführung der Oper Der fliegende Holländer, Oper und Drama*, 1852. ' My mental state,' writes Wagner, looking back upon these books and essays,

' resembled a struggle. I tried to express, theoretically, that which under the incongruity of my artistic aims as contrasted with the tendencies of public art, especially of the opera, I could not properly put forward by means of direct artistic production.' [4]

An account of the main contents of these writings belongs to Part II. of this article, and it will suffice here to touch upon a few minor points which are of biographical interest.

Too many side-issues have been raised with regard to *Das Judenthum in der Musik*, an article which first appeared in the *Neue Zeitschrift* under the pseudonym K. Freigedank. It is a far less intemperate and injudicious production than might be supposed from the *succès de scandale* it met with when Wagner signed and republished it with additions nineteen years later. In spite of his belief to the contrary, it did not at first attract much attention ; the *Zeitschrift*, then edited by Franz Brendel, had only a few hundred subscribers, and no other German journal, as far as the writer is aware, reproduced it. The only immediate effect was a vindictive feeling in musical circles against Brendel. Eleven masters at the Leipzig Conservatorium, where Brendel was engaged as lecturer on the History of Music, signed a letter [5] requesting him either to give up his post or to divulge the name of the writer. Brendel refused to accept either alternative. Wagner's authorship, however, was suspected, and the attitude of many professional journalists towards him grew bitterly hostile. When he issued the augmented edition in 1869 dozens of articles and pamphlets appeared in reply ; yet none of these attempted to deal with the artistic questions he had raised. The actual contents of the article were ignored ; but Wagner was persistently reproached with having attempted a disgraceful defamation of rival composers ' because of their Hebrew origin ' ! It remains significant that amongst his staunchest and most intelligent friends there were many of Jewish descent, who may have wished he had left the subject alone, but who nevertheless saw no reason to disagree with him in the main. The noise in the newspapers had an odd result : other writings of his, hitherto a drug on the market, suddenly began to sell, and continued to do so.

With regard to the fierce attack upon Meyerbeer in *Oper und Drama*, it should not be overlooked that Wagner's strictures concern Meyerbeer the musician, not Meyerbeer the man. The following extracts from a private letter of 1847

---

1 See Ellis's *Wagner Sketches, 1849 : a Vindication*, London, 1892; the same writer's *Life*, iv. 236, for a detailed account of Wagner's association with the Dresden riots ; also the Wagner-Liszt Correspondence, Letter 20 (Eng. trans. i. 31).
2 Translated in *P.W.* iv. 136, together with a letter written four days later to Von Lüttichau, the director of the court theatre. See also Praeger's *Wagner as I knew him*, p. 156.
3 Some particulars of Wagner's flight are given in Kietz's *Reminiscences*, p. 172.

4 *The Music of the Future*, p. 32.
5 Written by Julius Rietz and printed in *Moscheles Leben*, ii. 217 (trans. ii. 21 f).

comprise everything Wagner thought fit to state publicly later on :

'I am on a pleasant footing with Meyerbeer, and have every reason to value him as a kind and amiable man. But if I attempt to express all that is repellent in the incoherency and empty striving after outward effect in the operatic music of the day, I arrive at the conception " Meyerbeer."
'Whoever mistakes his way in the direction of triviality has to do penance towards his better self, but whoever consciously seeks triviality is lost.'

Did Wagner really act as an ungrateful and ill-conditioned person towards Meyerbeer ? The two men never were friends in the true sense of the word. The time they actually spent together can hardly amount to a hundred hours. In 1839–42 at Boulogne and Paris, Meyerbeer, the senior by twenty-two years, was the patron and Wagner the client ; and for the next decade this state of things apparently continued. Meyerbeer had spoken well of Wagner, and in return it was expected that Wagner should make himself useful as a partisan. But this Wagner would not and could not do ; the broadest hints produced no effect upon him. When Wagner sought Meyerbeer's acquaintance the latter was surrounded by a host of literary adherents, willing champions in the press, with whom his agent and his publisher could manœuvre as they pleased. But the support of real musicians was wanting. Masters like Spohr and Marschner, Mendelssohn and Schumann, pronounced Meyerbeer's music an ingeniously contrived sham, and would have nothing to do with it ; they attributed a good deal of the success of ' Robert,' etc., to Meyerbeer's business talents and to the exertions of his literary ' bureau.' [1] Thus to secure the services of a promising young musician was a matter of some moment, and Wagner was regarded as the right sort of man to enlist. What did Meyerbeer do by way of patronage ? He wrote a letter introducing Wagner to Pillet, fully aware that there was not a ghost of a chance for an unknown German at the Opéra. To foist Wagner, with his ' Liebesverbot,' upon Antenor Joly and the Théâtre de la Renaissance, was, in the eyes of Parisians, little better than a practical joke ; twice or thrice in the year that rotten concern had failed and risen again : ' mon théâtre est mort, vive mon théâtre,' was Joly's motto. Meyerbeer introduced Wagner to his publisher, Schlesinger. And this is all that came to pass at Paris—unless the fact be taken into account that Scribe imitated an important scene from ' Rienzi ' in ' Le Prophète ' [2] without acknowledgment. At Dresden a letter from Meyerbeer to Herr v. Lüttichau, dated Mar. 18, 1841,[3] turned the scales in favour of ' Rienzi,' and both ' Rienzi ' and the ' Holländer ' were accepted (but not performed) on his recommendation at Berlin. After the surprising success of ' Rienzi,' open hostility was shown by certain sections of the press. As time went on, Wagner traced some queer attacks to their source, and came upon members of Meyerbeer's ' bureau ' ! No one who is aware of the large and complicated interests at stake with regard to the success or failure of a grand opera will be surprised at the existence of press scandals, and it is of course impossible to say at present whether or not Meyerbeer was personally concerned. Wagner certainly thought he was, but chose to remain silent. It was not until 1850–1852 that Meyerbeer's people came to know in their turn whom they were dealing with. By this time, when ' Le Prophète ' was pitted in Germany against ' Lohengrin,' the words ' friendship ' or ' personal obligation ' cannot have conveyed the usual meaning to Wagner's mind ; yet there is little that savours of revenge or recrimination in *Oper und Drama* and *Das Judenthum*. Serious questions of art are treated, and Meyerbeer's works are quoted as glaring examples of operatic good and evil.

Besides the vast mass of theoretical and critical writing, Wagner got through much other work during the first two years at Zürich. He completed the prose version of a drama in three acts, ' Wieland der Schmidt ' (meant to be carried out in French verse with a view to performance in Paris), conducted orchestral concerts, superintended the performances at the Stadttheater (where his young disciples, Carl Ritter and H. von Bülow, acted as conductors), lectured on the musical drama (reading the poem of ' Siegfrieds Tod ' by way of illustration), and kept up a lively correspondence with German friends.

The first performance of ' Lohengrin ' took place under Liszt at Weimar, Aug. 28, 1850. The date chosen was that of Goethe's birth and of the inauguration of the statue to Herder ; Liszt had invited musical and literary friends from all parts of Europe, and the work, performed (for once) without cuts, made a powerful impression. From that memorable night dates the success of the Wagner movement in Germany.[4] The reception of ' Lohengrin ' by the musical profession, the press and the general public resembled that of ' Tannhäuser,' described above. It is not worth while to give details here. The following words of Wagner are strictly applicable, not only to ' Lohengrin ' but to the first performances of every subsequent work of his :

'Musicians had no objection to my dabbling in poetry, poets admitted my musical attainments ; I have frequently been able to rouse the public ; professional critics have always disparaged me.'

' Lohengrin ' was given at Wiesbaden, 1853 ; at Leipzig, Schwerin, Frankfort, Darmstadt, Breslau, Stettin, 1854 ; at Cologne, Hamburg,

---

[1] Concerning the ' bureau ' see H. Laube's *Erinnerungen*.
[2] See *Oper und Drama*, I , in *Ges. Schriften*, iii. 373, etc. (*P.W.* H. 98).
[3] Printed in Tappert, p. 20 ; translated in Ellis's *Life*, i. 315.

[4] On Liszt's relations to Wagner see LISZT, Vol. III. p. 209.

Riga, Prague, 1855; Munich, Vienna, 1858; Berlin, Dresden, 1859. The full score and the piano score (by Th. Uhlig) were sold for a few hundred thalers to Breitkopf & Härtel, and published in 1852.

Wagner fitly closed the literary work of this period with the publication of a letter to the editor of the *Neue Zeitschrift*,—*Über musikalische Kritik*, and of *Eine Mittheilung an meine Freunde* (1852).[1] Written simultaneously with *Oper und Drama*, the latter production forms the preface to three operatic poems—'Holländer,' 'Tannhäuser' and 'Lohengrin'; it is a fascinating piece of psychological autobiography, indispensable for a right knowledge of his character.

His magnum opus, 'Der Ring des Nibelungen,' now occupied him entirely.

'When I tried to dramatise the most important moment of the mythos of the Nibelungen in "Siegfrieds Tod," I found it necessary to indicate a vast number of antecedent facts so as to put the main incidents in the proper light. But I could only *narrate* these subordinate matters—whereas I felt it imperative that they should be embodied in the action. Thus I came to write "Siegfried." But here again the same difficulty troubled me. Finally I wrote "Die Walküre" and "Das Rheingold," and thus contrived to incorporate all that was needful to make the action tell its own tale.'[2]

The poem was privately printed early in 1853. 'During a sleepless night at an inn at Spezia the music to "Das Rheingold" occurred to me; straightway I turned homeward and set to work.'[3] He advanced with astonishing rapidity. In May 1854 the score of 'Das Rheingold' was finished. In June he began 'Die Walküre,' and completed the composition, all but the instrumentation, during the winter 1854-55. The full score was finished in 1856. The first sketches of the music to 'Siegfried' belong to the autumn of 1854. In the spring of 1857 the full score of Act I. of 'Siegfried,' and of the larger part of Act II., was finished.

Up to this point there have been but few interruptions to the work, viz. rehearsals and performances of 'Tannhäuser' at Zürich, Feb. 1855; an attack of erysipelas,[4] May 1856; a prolonged visit from Liszt[5] (at St. Gallen, Nov. 3, 1856, Wagner conducted the 'Eroica' and Liszt his 'Poèmes symphoniques,' 'Orphée' and 'Les Préludes'); and the eight concerts of the Philharmonic Society in London, Mar.-June 1855.

In Jan. 1855 Mr. Anderson, one of the directors of the London Philharmonic Society, arrived at Zürich to invite Wagner to conduct the coming season's concerts. The Society, it appeared, was at its wits' end for a conductor of reputation—Spohr could not come, Berlioz was re-engaged by the New Philharmonic, and it had occurred to the directors that Wagner might possibly be the man they were in want of. Davison, of *The Times* and the *Musical World*, and Chorley, of the *Athenæum*, thought otherwise. Wagner arrived in London towards the end of Feb. The dates of the concerts he conducted are: Mar. 12 and 26, Apr. 16 and 30, May 14 and 28, June 11 and 25, 1855.[6]

'A magnificent orchestra as far as the principal members go. Superb tone—the leaders had the finest instruments I ever heard—a strong *esprit de corps*—but no distinct style. The fact is the Philharmonic people—orchestra and audience—consumed more music than they could possibly digest. As a rule an hour's music takes several hours' rehearsal—how can any conductor with a few morning hours at his disposal be supposed to do justice to monster programmes such as the Directors put before me? two symphonies, two overtures, a concerto and two or three vocal pieces at each concert! The Directors continuously referred me to what they chose to call the Mendelssohn traditions. But I suspect Mendelssohn had simply acquiesced in the traditional ways of the Society. One morning when we began to rehearse the "Leonora" overture I was surprised; everything appeared dull, slovenly, inaccurate, as though the players were weary and had not slept for a week. Was this to be tolerated from the famous Philharmonic Orchestra? I stopped and addressed them in French, saying I knew what they could do and I expected them to do it. Some understood and translated—they were taken aback, but they knew I was right and took it good-humouredly. We began again and the rehearsal passed off well. I have every reason to believe that the majority of the artists really got to like me before I left London.'

Among the pieces he conducted were Beethoven's 3rd, 4th, 5th, 6th, 7th, 8th and 9th symphonies; overture 'Leonora,' No. 3, the 2nd PF. concerto in B♭ and violin concerto; Mozart's symphonies in E♭ and C, and overture 'Zauberflöte'; Weber's overtures 'Oberon,' 'Freischütz,' 'Euryanthe,' 'Ruler of the Spirits' and 'Preciosa'; Mendelssohn's Italian and Scotch symphonies, the overtures 'Isles of Fingal' and 'A Midsummer Night's Dream' and the violin concerto; Spohr's symphony in C minor; Potter's in G minor[7]; the overture to 'Tannhäuser' (twice) and a selection from 'Lohengrin' (Introduction, Bridal Procession, Wedding Music and Epithalamium).[8] He occupied rooms at 31 Milton Street, Dorset Square, and at 22 Portland Terrace, Regent's Park, at which latter address a large portion of the instrumentation of 'Die Walküre' was completed. Karl KLINDWORTH (*q.v.*),

[1] *P.W.* i. 267.
[2] The same thing is said more explicitly in *Eine Mittheilung an meine Freunde.*
[3] Letter to Arrigo Boito, Nov. 7, 1871.
[4] As to Wagner's health and the ill-effects of eye-strain see Ellis's *Life*, vi. 41 f., also p. 423, note. At pp. 53-4 is an account of a visit to Messrs. Critchett in 1877, when Wagner was found to be suffering from astigmatism.
[5] In a private letter to Dr. Gille of Jena referring to a subsequent visit (Lucerne, 1857), Liszt writes: 'I am with Wagner all day long—his Nibelungen music is a glorious new world which I have long wanted to know. Some day the coolest persons will grow enthusiastic about it.' And again (1875, letter to Herr Gobbi of Pest): '"The Ring of the Nibelungen" rises above and dominates our entire art-epoch, as Mont Blanc dominates the surrounding mountains.'

[6] Vol. v. of Ellis's *Life* is practically given up entirely to a detailed account of the London visit. In *Richard Wagner to Minna Wagner* (the letters written to his wife from London are Nos. 76 to 102) are many interesting details. Hueffer's *Half a Century of Music in England*, 1889, chap. ii., may be consulted. See also *Mus. T.*, 1877, p. 162; *Studies in Music*, p. 168; and *Richard Wagner*, by W. Wallace, 1925, p. 164. From the last-named it appears that Wagner's fee was £200, the highest paid by the Society till then.
[7] Chas. Lucas conducted his own symphony at the fourth concert.
[8] He conducted also Macfarren's 'Chevy Chase' overture, to which he refers in complimentary terms in the autobiography.

who had settled in London the previous year and with whom Wagner became intimate, now began his pianoforte scores of the ' Nibelungen.'[1]

Whilst at work upon ' Die Walküre ' (1854) the stories of ' Tristan und Isolde ' and ' Parsifal ' had already taken possession of Wagner's mind, and the plan for ' Tristan ' was sketched. In the summer of 1857 he resolved to put aside ' Die Nibelungen ' and to proceed with ' Tristan.' Various causes contributed to this resolution.[2] He was tired ' of heaping one silent score upon the other,' tired of the monotony of the task too—if he lived to finish it, how should his colossal work ever be performed ? He longed to hear something of his own ; he had, moreover, pecuniary needs, which made it desirable that he should again write something that stood a chance of performance. Finally, a curious incident concluded the matter. A *soi-disant* agent of the Emperor of Brazil called : would Wagner compose an opera for an Italian troupe at Rio Janeiro ? would he state his own terms and promise to conduct the work himself ? Much astonished, Wagner hesitated to give a decisive answer ; but he forthwith began the poem to ' Tristan ' ![3]

Wagner looked upon ' Tristan ' as an accessory to the ' Nibelungen,' inasmuch as it presents certain aspects of the mythical matter for which in the main work there was no room. He was proud of the poem, proud of the music :

' I readily submit this work to the severest test based on my theoretical principles. Not that I constructed it after a system—for I entirely forgot all theory—but because I here moved with entire freedom, independent of theoretical misgivings, so that even whilst I was writing I became conscious how far I had gone beyond my system.[4] There can be no greater pleasure than an artist's perfect abandonment whilst composing—I have admitted no repetition of words in the music of "Tristan"—the entire extent of the music is as it were prescribed in the tissue of the verse—that is to say, the melody (*i.e.* the vocal melody) is already contained in the poem, of which again the symphonic music forms the substratum.'[5]

The poem was finished early in 1857 ; in the winter of the same year the full score of the first act was forwarded to Breitkopf & Härtel to be engraved. The second act was written at Venice, where Wagner, with the permission of the Austrian authorities, had taken up his residence, and is dated Venice, Mar. 2, 1859 ; the third, Lucerne, Aug. 1859.

In connexion with ' Tristan,' attention must be called to the strong and lasting impression made upon Wagner's mind by the philosophical writings of Schopenhauer. ' Tristan ' represents the emotional kernel of Schopenhauer's view of life as reflected in the mind of a poet

and a musician. Even in ' Die Meistersinger ' (Hans Sachs's monologue, Act III.) there are traces of Schopenhauer, and the spirit of his Buddhistic quietism pervades ' Parsifal.' The publication of Schopenhauer's *Parerga und Paralipomena* in 1851 took the intellectual public of Germany by surprise, and roused a spirit of indignation against the official representatives of ' Philosophy ' at the universities and their journals, who had secreted Schopenhauer's *Die Welt als Wille und Vorstellung* (1818 and 1844). The little colony of refugees at Zürich was among the first to hail Schopenhauer's genius as a moralist. Wagner accepted his metaphysical doctrine, and in 1854 forwarded to Schopenhauer at Frankfort a copy of ' Der Ring des Nibelungen ' as a token of ' thanks and veneration.' Wagner adhered to Schopenhauer's teaching to the end, and has even further developed some of its most characteristic and perhaps questionable phases.[6] It will be seen in the sequel that Wagner had more trouble in connexion with the performance of ' Tristan ' than with any other of his works. At first the difficulty was to get permission to return to Germany ; even the solicitations of the Grand Dukes of Weimar and of Baden in his favour had no effect upon the court of Dresden. Projects for producing ' Tristan ' at Strassburg and Carlsruhe came to nothing.

PARIS.—In Sept. 1859 (aet. 46) Wagner again went to Paris, with a faint hope of producing his new work there with the help of German artists, or perhaps getting ' Tannhäuser ' or ' Lohengrin ' performed in French. M. Carvalho, director of the Théâtre Lyrique, seemed inclined to risk ' Tannhäuser ' :

' Il avait témoigné à Wagner le désir de connaître sa partition.[7] Un soir, en arrivant chez lui Rue Matignon j'entends un vacarme inusité. Wagner était au piano ; il se débattait avec le formidable finale du second acte ; il chantait, il criait, il se démenait, il jouait des mains, des poignets, du coude. M. Carvalho restait impassible, attendant avec une patience digne de l'antique que le sabbat fût fini La partition achevée, M. Carvalho balbutia quelques paroles de politesse, tourna les talons et disparut.'

Determined to bring some of his music forward, Wagner made arrangements for three orchestral and choral concerts at the Théâtre Impérial Italien,[8] Jan. 25, Feb. 1 and 8, 1860. The programme, consisting of the overture to ' Der Holländer,' four pieces from ' Tannhäuser,' the prelude to ' Tristan ' and three numbers from ' Lohengrin,' was thrice repeated :

' De nombreuses répétitions furent faites à la salle Herz, à la salle Beethoven, où H. de Bülow conduisait les chœurs.
' Un parti très-ardent, très-actif, s'était formé autour de Wagner ; les ennemis ne s'endormaient pas davantage, et il était évident que la bataille serait acharnée.'

The performances conducted by Wagner

---

[1] See *Mus. T.*, 1898, p. 513.
[2] As to the chief cause, the personal influence of Frau Wesendonck, see *Richard Wagner to Mathilde Wesendonck*, London, 1905 ; also Ellis's *Life*, vi. 315. etc.
[3] The offer from Rio appears to have been genuine ; the Emperor of Brazil subsequently became a patron of the theatre at Bayreuth and witnessed a performance of the ' Ring ' there.
[4] *The Music of the Future*, pp. 36, 37 (*P.W.* iii. 326).
[5] *Ibid.* (*P.W.* iii. 331).

[6] See *Beethoven*, particularly the supplement to the English translation (by E. Dannreuther, 1880 ; also *Religion und Kunst*), 1880–81 (*P.W.* vi. 211).   [7] Gasperini, p. 53.
[8] This was the old Salle Ventadour, at which, as the Théâtre de la Renaissance, ' Das Liebesverbot ' was to have been given twenty years previously. It is now a Bureau d'escompte. (See VENTADOUR.)

made a great sensation—'Wagner avait réussi à passionner Paris, à déchaîner la presse'—but the expenses had been inordinate and there was a deficit of something like £400, which he had to meet with part of the honorarium paid by Messrs. Schott for the copyright of 'Der Ring des Nibelungen.' Two similar programmes were conducted by him at the Brussels Opera House in Mar. 1860—also, it would seem, with unsatisfactory results.

Unexpected events, however, sprang from the exertions at Paris. 'Sur les instances pressantes de Mme. de Metternich, l'empereur avait ordonné la mise à l'étude de "Tannhäuser" à l'Opéra.'[1] A substantial success seemed at last within Wagner's reach. Preparations on a vast scale were begun. Edmond Roche and Ch. Nuitter translated the text; the management met every wish of Wagner; sumptuous scenery and stage properties were prepared; Wagner was invited to choose his own singers, and to have as many rehearsals as he might think fit. He chose Niemann for Tannhäuser, Mlle. Saxe for Elisabeth, Mlle. Tedesco for Venus, Mlle. Reboux for the shepherd, Cazaux for the Landgraf and Morelli for Wolfram. The number of rehearsals, according to the official record, was 164: 73 at the pianoforte, 46 choral, 27 with the vocalists on the stage but without orchestra, 4 for scenic changes and 14 full, with orchestra.[2] The total costs appear to have amounted to something like £8000. Wagner entirely rewrote the opening scene in the Venusberg, and made a number of minor changes. On the advice of M. Villot (curateur des musées impériaux) he also published Quatre poèmes d'opéras traduits en prose française, précédés d'une lettre sur la musique, giving a résumé of his aims and opinions.[3] After numerous interruptions, misunderstandings and quarrels, including a complete rupture with the conductor Dietsch—the quondam chorus-master and composer of 'Le Vaisseau-fantôme,' who proved incompetent, and whom Wagner could not get rid of—the performances began Mar. 13, 1861. 'Une cabale très-active, très-puissante, très-déterminée, s'était organisée de bonne heure. Un certain nombre d'abonnés de l'opéra qui savaient que la pièce n'avait pas de ballet,' etc. The scandal need not be repeated here. After the third performance Wagner withdrew his work.

'The less said the better as to the complicated causes of the disaster. But it was a blow to me: everybody concerned had been paid per month; my share was to consist in the usual honorarium after each performance, and this was now cut short.[4] So I left Paris

1 See Princess Pauline Metternich's *The Days that are no more. Some Reminiscences* (London, 1921). Ch. iv. gives her own account of the event.
2 'Les 164 répétitions et les 3 représentations du "Tannhäuser" à Paris,' par Ch. Nuitter. (See *Bayreuther Festblätter* for 1884.)
3 See Dannreuther's English translation: *The Music of the Future.*
4 The customary remuneration for each performance of a new opera at Paris was 500 francs, so that 1500 francs would have been Wagner's share for the three evenings; but it had been arranged that for the first twenty performances half of the remuneration was to be paid to the translators of the libretto: thus 750 francs was the sum Wagner received for something like a year's work.

with a load of debt, not knowing where to turn. Apart from such things, however, my recollections of this distracting year are by no means unpleasant.'

On Wednesday evenings the little house[5] he inhabited with his wife in the Rue Newton, near the Arc-de-Triomphe, welcomed many remarkable Parisians,—'c'est ainsi,' reports Gasperini, 'que j'ai vue M. Villot [to whom Wagner dedicated his *Music of the Future*], Émile Ollivier, Mme. Ollivier [Liszt's daughter], Jules Ferry, Léon Leroy; et Berlioz, et Champfleury, et Lorbac, et Baudelaire,' etc.[6]

Princess Metternich's enthusiasm had a further result: whilst at work upon the additions to 'Tannhäuser,' permission arrived for Wagner 'to re-enter German states other than Saxony.' It was not till Mar. 1862 (*i.e.* after thirteen years) that the ban was completely raised and he got leave, in truly paternal phrase, 'to return to the kingdom of Saxony without fear of punishment.'

RETURN TO GERMANY, 1861 (aet. 48).—The disaster in Paris produced a strong reaction. Wagner was received with enthusiasm wherever he appeared. Yet the three years to come until 1864, when he was suddenly called to Munich, must be counted among the most distressing of his entire career. His hopes and prospects lay in a successful performance of 'Tristan,' and all his efforts to bring about such a performance failed. At Vienna, after fifty-seven rehearsals, 'Tristan' was definitely shelved, owing to the incompetence, physical or otherwise, of the tenor Ander; at Carlsruhe, Prague and Weimar the negotiations did not even lead to rehearsals. He found it impossible to make both ends meet, and had to seek a precarious subsistence by giving concerts. A few words will explain this strange state of things at a time when his works were so unmistakably popular. The customary honorarium on the first performance of an opera in Germany varied from 10 to 50 or 60 louis-d'or (£8 to £48), according to the rank and size of the theatre. On every subsequent repetition the author's share consisted either of some little sum agreed upon or of a small percentage on the receipts—generally five per cent, occasionally seven—never more than ten per cent. As most German towns possess a theatre, a successful opera on its first round may produce a considerable amount; but afterwards the yield is small. It is impossible to run the same piece night after night at a court or town theatre; the prices of admission are always low, and the system of subscription per season or per annum tends to reduce the number of performances allowed to any single work.

5 Now demolished.
6 Ch. Baudelaire's article in the *Revue européenne*, augmented and reprinted as a pamphlet, Apr. 1861, *Richard Wagner et Tannhäuser*, is a masterpiece. One very interesting episode of this sojourn in Paris is told at length in E. Michotte's *Souvenirs personnels, La Visite de Richard Wagner à Rossini* (Paris, 1906). In the *Zeitsch.* of the Int. Mus. Ges., 1907 (ix. 71), are two letters written by Wagner in Paris a few days after the fiasco.

'My operas were to be heard right and left ; but I could not live on the proceeds. At Dresden "Tannhäuser" and the "Holländer" had grown into favour ; yet I was told that I had no claim with regard to them, since they were produced during my Kapellmeistership, and a Hofkapellmeister in Saxony is bound to furnish an opera once a year ! When the Dresden people wanted "Tristan" I refused to let them have it unless they agreed to pay for "Tannhäuser." Accordingly they thought they could dispense with "Tristan." Afterwards, when the public insisted upon "Die Meistersinger," I got the better of them.'

On May 15, 1861, Wagner heard 'Lohengrin' for the first time at Vienna. Liszt and a large circle of musicians welcomed him at the Tonkünstler Versammlung at Weimar in August.[1] His long-cherished plan of writing a comic opera was now taken up. He elaborated the sketch for 'Die Meistersinger von Nürnberg,' which dates from 1845, and was intended to be a comic pendant to the contest of Minnesinger in 'Tannhäuser.' The poem was finished during a temporary stay at Paris in the winter of 1861–62. Messrs. Schott of Mayence secured the copyright, and the poem was printed in 1862 for private circulation.[2] Wagner settled opposite Mainz at Biebrich-am-Rhein to proceed with the music.[3] On Nov. 1 of the same year (1862) he appeared at a concert given by Wendelin Weissheimer in the Gewandhaus at Leipzig, to conduct the overture to 'Die Meistersinger.' The writer, who was present, distinctly remembers the half-empty room, the almost complete absence of professional musicians, the wonderful performance, and the enthusiastic demand for a repetition, in which the members of the orchestra took part as much as the audience.

'That curious concert at Leipzig was the first of a long series of such absurd undertakings to which my straitened means led me. At other towns the public at least appeared en masse, and I could record an artistic success ; but it was not till I went to Russia that the pecuniary results were worth mentioning.'

Dates of such concerts, at which he conducted Beethoven symphonies, fragments of the 'Nibelungen' and 'Die Meistersinger,' etc., are Dec. 26, 1862, and first weeks in Jan. 1863, Vienna ; Feb. 8, Prague ; Feb. 19, Mar. 6,[4] 8, St. Petersburg ; March, Moscow ; July 23, 28, Pest ; Nov. 14, 19, Carlsruhe, and a few days later Löwenberg ; Dec. 7, Breslau. Towards the end of Dec. 1863, at a concert of Carl Tausig's, he astonished the Viennese public with the true traditional reading of the overture to 'Der Freischütz.'[5]

In his fiftieth year (whilst living at Penzing, near Vienna, at work upon 'Die Meistersinger')

Wagner published the poem to 'Der Ring des Nibelungen,' 'as a literary product.'

'I can hardly expect to find leisure to complete the music, and I have dismissed all hope that I may live to see it performed.'

His private affairs went from bad to worse. In the spring of 1864 his power of resistance was almost broken ; he determined to give up his public career, and accepted an invitation to a country home in Switzerland.

MUNICH and LUCERNE, 1864–72 (aet. 51–59). —The poem of 'Der Ring des Nibelungen,' with its preface, must have got into the hands of the young King Ludwig II. of Bavaria. The King was acquainted with Beethoven's symphonies, and in his sixteenth year had heard 'Lohengrin.' One of the first acts of his reign was to despatch a private secretary to find Wagner, with the message, 'Come here and finish your work.' Wagner had already left Vienna in despair—had passed through Munich on his way to Zürich—and for some reason had turned about to Stuttgart. The secretary tracked and there found him.[6] In May the Augsburger allgemeine Zeitung brought the news that King Ludwig had allowed to the composer Richard Wagner a 'Sustentationsgehalt von 1200 Gulden aus der Kabinetscasse' (a stipend of about £100, from the privy purse). Here was relief at last. Wagner's hopes revived ; his enthusiasm returned and redoubled.

'My creditors were quieted, I could go on with my work,—and this noble young man's trust made me happy. There have been many troubles since—not of my making nor of his—but in spite of them I am free to this day—and by his grace. (1877.)'

Cabals without end were speedily formed against Wagner—some indeed of a singularly disgraceful character ; and he found it impossible to reside at Munich, although the King's favour and protection remained unaltered.[7] There can be no doubt that the 'Nibelungen Ring' would not have been completed, and that the idea of Bayreuth would not have come to any practical result (the exertions of the Wagner Societies notwithstanding), if it had not been for the steady support of the royal good wishes and the royal purse. It must suffice here to indicate the dates and events which are biographically interesting.

Wagner was naturalised as a Bavarian subject in 1864. He settled in Munich, and composed the 'Huldigungsmarsch,' for a military band[8] ; at the King's request he wrote an essay, Über Staat und Religion,[9] and the report concerning a 'German music school to be established at Munich' (Mar. 31, 1865). In the autumn of 1864 he was formally commissioned to com-

1 See Weissheimer, Erlebnisse mit Richard Wagner, etc. (Stuttgart and Leipzig, 1898), p. 72.
2 The final version differs considerably from this. Messrs. Schott have published a facsimile of Wagner's autograph of the poem. See Zademek, Die Meistersinger von Nürnberg: R. Wagners Dichtung und ihre Quellen, Berlin, 1921, and H. Thompson, Wagner and Wagenseil (London, 1927).
3 See Weissheimer, Erlebnisse mit Richard Wagner, etc., p. 94 f., and as to the Leipzig concert, p. 194.
4 A facsimile programme of this concert, with particulars of the Russian visit, is given in Mus. T., 1901, p. 594.
5 See Über das Dirigiren (P.W. iv. 289), and Glasenapp, ii. p. 113.

6 The circumstances of this meeting are detailed in Weissheimer's Erlebnisse, p. 265 f. Another version may be found in Angelo Neumann's Erinnerungen, p. 6.
7 See Glasenapp, ii. ch. 3, for true details regarding the extraordinary means employed to oust Wagner.
8 Not published in that form.
9 P.W. iv. 3.

plete the 'Nibelungen'; and, further to ease his pecuniary affairs, the stipend was increased,[1] and a little house in the outskirts of Munich, 'bevor den Propyläen,' was placed at his disposal.[2] Dec. 4, 1864, the 'Holländer' was given for the first time at Munich; Dec. 11, Jan. 1, and Feb. 1, 1865, Wagner conducted concerts there. In Jan. 1865 his friend Semper the architect was consulted by the King about a theatre to be erected for the 'Nibelungen.'[3] With a view to the performance of 'Tristan,' von Bülow was called to Munich, and under his direction, Wagner supervising, the work was performed, exactly as Wagner wrote it, on June 10, 1865, and repeated June 13 and 19 and July 1—Tristan, Ludwig Schnorr v. Carolsfeld[4]; Isolde, Frau Schnorr. In July 1865 the old Conservatorium was closed by the King's orders, and a commission began to deliberate as to the means of carrying out Wagner's proposals for a new 'music school.' But nothing tangible came of this; owing, it would seem, to ill-will on the part of Franz Lachner and other Munich musicians, and also, as was alleged, to the insufficiency of the available funds.[5] In Dec. 1865 Wagner left Munich and settled, after a short stay at Vevey and Geneva, at Triebschen, near Lucerne, where he remained with little change until he removed to Bayreuth in Apr. 1872. At Triebschen the 'Meistersinger' was completed (full score finished Oct. 20, 1867), twenty-two years after the first sketches! (see *ante*). Hans Richter[6] arrived there in Oct. 1866 to copy the score, and the sheets were at once sent off to Mainz to be engraved.

The 'Meistersinger' was performed at Munich under von Bülow (H. Richter chorusmaster), Wagner personally supervising everything, on June 21, 1868—

'Eva, Frl. Mallinger; Magdalena, Frau Dietz; Hans Sachs, Betz; Walther, Nachbauer; David, Schlosser; Beckmesser, Hölzel,'

a perfect performance; the best that has hitherto[7] been given of any work of the master's, 'Parsifal' at Bayreuth not excepted.

Before Wagner had quite done with the 'Meistersinger' he published a series of articles in the *Süddeutsche Presse* (one of the chief editors of which was his former Dresden colleague Musikdirektor Aug. Roeckel) entitled *Deutsche Kunst und deutsche Politik* (*P.W.* iv. 35).

During the quiet residence at Triebschen, the unfinished portion of 'The Ring' progressed steadily. Early in 1869 the instrumentation of the third act of 'Siegfried' was completed, and the composition of the 'Vorspiel' and first act of 'Götterdämmerung' finished, June 1870.

Aug. 25, 1870, is the date of Wagner's marriage to Cosima von Bülow, *née* Liszt (b. Dec. 25, 1837), his first wife, Minna Wagner, having died Jan. 25, 1866; after close upon twenty-five years of married life she had retired to Dresden in 1861.[8]

In 1869 he published *Über das Dirigiren*[9] in the *Neue Zeitschrift für Musik. Beethoven*[10] appeared in Sept. 1870, during the Franco-Prussian War. The King's plan to build a special theatre for the 'Nibelungen Ring' at Munich being abandoned,[11] Wagner fixed upon Bayreuth.

BAYREUTH (1872–83).—The municipality of this little Franconian town did its best to further Wagner's objects; he left Triebschen and settled there in April, and on his sixtieth birthday, May 22, 1872, he was able to celebrate the foundation of his theatre with a magnificent performance of Beethoven's Choral Symphony and his own 'Kaisermarsch.'[12] A large portion of the funds for the theatre was got together by private subscription. The sum originally estimated, 300,000 thalers (£45,000), was to be raised in accordance with Carl Tausig's plan upon 1000 'Patronatscheine,' *i.e.* 1000 certificates of patronage, each entitling the holder to a seat at the three complete performances contemplated. A considerable number of these were taken up before Tausig's death; then Emil Heckel of Mannheim suggested 'Wagner Societies,' and started one himself.[13] It appeared at once that all over Germany there were numbers of people who were ready to contribute their share of work and money, but to whom individually the 300 thalers asked for by Tausig would have been impossible. Societies sprang up on all sides—not only in German towns, but in the most unexpected quarters—St. Petersburg, Warsaw, New York, Amsterdam, Brussels, Paris, Stockholm, Cairo, Milan, London,[14] etc.

In connexion with the efforts of the societies, Wagner conducted concerts at Mannheim, Vienna, Hamburg, Schwerin, Berlin, Cologne,

---

1 The exact amount has not been made public.
2 It was returned to the K. Kabinetscassa in 1866.
3 The model of the proposed theatre is now in the National Museum, Munich (see Semper, M., *Das Münchener Festspielhaus. Gottfried Semper und Richard Wagner*, Hamburg, 1906). The Prinz-Regenten Theater, the first to be erected after the Bayreuth plan, was opened in 1901, and is not far from the site originally chosen by King Ludwig II.
4 Schnorr died suddenly at Dresden on July 21, 1865, and 'Tristan' was again 'impossible' until Herr and Frau Vogl sang it in June 1869.
5 The present Conservatorium, opened under von Bülow in 1867, is practically the old institution, and does not carry out Wagner's ideas.
6 In the *Mus. T.*, 1899, p. 443, are some of Richter's recollections of his stay at Triebschen.
7 This refers to 1889, when Dannreuther's article was first published in this Dictionary.

8 Dannreuther's extreme reticence may be supplemented by a statement of the facts as related by Ernest Newman, *Wagner as Man and Artist*, p. 118: 'On the 10th April, 1865, a daughter, Isolde, was born to Cosima. Bülow believed the child to be his own (see *Hans von Bülow; Briefe*, iv. 24), and Wagner became its godfather. In reality the child was Wagner's own. (A second child, Eva, was born to them 18th February, 1867, at Triebschen; Siegfried was born 6th June, 1869.)' c.
9 *P.W.* iv. 289. 10 *Ibid.* v. 57.
11 'Rheingold' and 'Walküre' were performed at the Munich Hoftheater in 1869 and 1870 respectively.
12 In 1874 Wagner took up his abode in 'Wahnfried,' the house he built in the Hofgarten at Bayreuth.
13 See Wagner's *Letters to Heckel, with a Brief History of the Bayreuth Festival* (London, 1899).
14 The London Wagner Society's Orchestral Concerts (conducted by E. Dannreuther) took place Feb. 19, 27, May 9, Nov. 14, Dec. 12, 1873: and Jan. 23, Feb. 13, Mar. 13, May 13, 1874.

etc. In Nov. 1874 the instrumentation of 'Götterdämmerung' was completed; and preliminary rehearsals with the vocalists had already produced satisfactory results. The ensemble rehearsals, with full orchestra, in the summer of 1875 under Hans Richter (Wagner always present) left no doubt as to the possibility of a performance in exact accordance with the master's intentions. The scenery and stage machinery promised well, and the effects of sonority in the auditorium proved excellent.[1]

It had at first been a matter of some doubt whether the invisible orchestra would answer for the more subtle effects of orchestration; but it turned out eventually that all details were perfectly audible; and, moreover, that certain shortcomings of customary orchestra arrangements had been removed. Flutes, oboes, clarinets and bassoons were heard more distinctly, and the explosive blare which ordinarily seems inseparable from a sudden *forte* of trumpets and trombones, was less apparent. It may be well here to record the disposition of the 'Nibelungen' orchestra: conductor (quite invisible from the auditorium) facing the orchestra and the stage; to left of him, 1st violins; to right, 2nd violins; violas near violins; violoncellos and basses flanking to left and right; in the middle of the orchestra, somewhat nearer the stage, the wood-wind; behind these again, partially under the stage, the brass and percussion instruments. Total, exclusive of conductor, 114.[2]

A notion of the auditorium may be gained by fancying a wedge, the thin end of which is supposed to touch the front of the stage, the thick end the back of the auditorium; the seats arranged in a slight curve, each row farther from the stage raised a little above the one in front of it, and the several seats so placed that every person seated can look at the stage between the heads of two persons before him; all seats directly facing the stage; no side boxes or side galleries, no prompter's box. Total number of seats, 1500; a little over 1200 for the patrons, the rest, about 300, for distribution gratis to young musicians, etc.

In Nov. and Dec. 1875 Wagner superintended rehearsals of 'Tannhäuser' and 'Lohengrin' at Vienna, which were performed, without cuts, on Nov. 22 and Dec. 15. 'Tristan,' also under his supervision, was given at Berlin on Mar. 20, 1876.

At last, twenty-eight years after its first conception—on Aug. 13, 14, 16, 17, again from 20 to 23 and from 27 to 30, 1876—'Der Ring des Nibelungen' was performed entire at Bayreuth.

'Wotan, Betz; Loge, Vogl; Alberich, Hill; Mime, Schlosser; Fricka, Frau Grün; Donner and Gunther, Gura; Erda and Waltraute, Frau Jaïde; Siegmund, Niemann; Sieglinde, Frl. Schefzky; Brünnhilde, Frau Materna; Siegfried, Unger; Hagen, Siehr; Gutrune, Frl. Weckerlin; Rheintöchter, Frl. Lili and Marie Lehmann and Frl. Lammert; Norns, Fr. Johanna Jachmann-Wagner, Frl. Schefzky, Fr. Grün. Leader of strings, Wilhelmj; Conductor, Hans. Richter.'

From a musical point of view the performances were correct throughout—in many instances of surpassing excellence; sundry shortcomings on the stage were owing more to want of money than to anything else. In spite of the sacrifices readily made by each and all of the artists concerned, there was a heavy deficit, £7500, the responsibility for which passed upon Wagner. He had hoped to be able to repeat the performances in the following summer; this proved impossible, and his efforts to discharge the debts of the theatre failed for the most part. The largest of these efforts, the so-called Wagner Festival at the Albert Hall in London, 1877, came near to involving him in further difficulties.

LONDON, May 1877.—Herr Wilhelmj believed that a series of concerts on a large scale under Wagner's personal supervision would pay; but the sequel proved all too clearly that his acquaintance with the ins and outs of musical matters in London was superficial.[3] Messrs. Hodge and Essex of Argyll Street acted as entrepreneurs. The Albert Hall was chosen, and six prodigious programmes were advertised for the 7th, 9th, 12th, 14th, 16th and 19th May. Copious extracts, of his own making, from all his works were to represent and illustrate Wagner as poet and composer: selections from 'Rienzi,' the 'Holländer,' 'Tannhäuser,' 'Lohengrin,' 'Meistersinger,' 'Tristan,' in the first part of the programmes; and from 'Der Ring des Nibelungen' in the second part. An orchestra of 170 (wood-wind double) and several of the singers who had taken leading parts at Bayreuth (Frau Materna, Frau Grün, Herren Hill, Schlosser, Unger), besides sundry subordinates, were engaged; Wagner himself was to conduct the first half of each programme, and Hans Richter the second. The expenditure for advertisements and salaries to vocalists was lavish; the attendance, though always large, nothing like what had been anticipated; the result of the six concerts, a difficulty in making both ends meet. Thereupon the promoters were persuaded to try again: that is, to give two further concerts (May 28 and 29) with a minimum of expenditure all round, reduced prices, and programmes made up of the most telling pieces. This saved the venture, and enabled Wagner to forward a little over £700 to Bayreuth. After his departure, and without his knowledge, an attempt was made to get up

---

[1] As to the Bayreuth rehearsals in 1875–76 see Fricke's *Bayreuth vor 30 Jahren* (Dresden, 1906), Kietz's *Richard Wagner in der Jahren 1842–9 und 1873–5* (Dresden, 1905), and Julius Hey's *Richard Wagner als Vortragsmeister* (Leipzig, 1911).

[2] Interesting plans may be seen in Adolphe Jullien's *Wagner*.

[3] The writer, whose name has been mentioned in Glasenapp's Biography and elsewhere in connexion with this 'London episode,' desires to state that he had *nothing whatever* to do with the planning of the 'festival,' nor with the business arrangements. All he did was to attend to the completion of the orchestra with regard to the 'extra' wind instruments, and at Wagner's request to conduct the preliminary rehearsals.

a testimonial. A considerable sum was speedily subscribed, but before it reached him ' another way out of the difficulty had been found '—viz. that the honorarium and *tantièmes* to come from performances of the ' Ring ' at Munich should be set aside to cover the debt of the Bayreuth theatre—and the promoters of the testimonial had the satisfaction of returning the contributions with a warm letter of thanks from Wagner ' to his English friends.' [1] During this third residence in London (Apr. 30 to June 4) Wagner resided at 12 Orme Square, Bayswater.[2]

. 'Erinnerungen,' he wrote from Ems on June 29, ' so weit sie sich nicht auf die Ausübung meiner kleinen Kunstfertigkeiten beziehen, herrlich.' The expression ' kleine Kunstfertigkeiten ' (little artistic attainments) was a hint at his conducting at the Albert Hall, which had been a good deal commented upon. Was Wagner really a great conductor ? . There can be no doubt that he was ; particularly with regard to the works of Weber and Beethoven. His perfect sympathy with these led him to find the true tempi as it were by intuition.[3] He was thoroughly at home in the orchestra, though he had never learnt to play upon any orchestral instrument. He had an exquisite sense for beauty of tone, nuances of tempo, precision and proportion of rhythm. His beat was distinct, and his extraordinary power of communicating his enthusiasm to the executants never failed. The writer was present at one of the *great* occasions when he appeared as conductor —the rehearsals and performance of the Ninth Symphony at Bayreuth, May 22, 1872—and felt that for spirit, and perfection of phrasing, it was the finest musical performance within the whole range of his experience.[4] But at the Albert Hall Wagner did not do himself justice. His strength was already on the wane. The rehearsals fatigued him, and he was frequently faint in the evening. His memory played him tricks, and his beat was nervous. Still there were moments when his great gifts appeared as of old. Those who witnessed his conducting of the ' Kaisermarsch ' at the first rehearsal he attended (May 5) will never forget the superb effect.

Wagner brought the manuscript of the poem of ' Parsifal ' with him to London and read it for the first time entire to a circle of friends at Orme Square (May 17). It was published in Dec. 1877.

A plan for a sort of school for the performance of classical orchestral music, together with classical operas, and ultimately of his own works at Bayreuth, came to nothing. Greatly against his wish he was obliged to permit ' Der Ring des Nibelungen ' to take its chance at the German theatres.[5] The first number of *Bayreuther Blätter*, a monthly periodical edited by von Wolzogen and published by and for the Wagner Verein, appeared in Jan. 1878. Wagner, whilst at work upon ' Parsifal,' found time to contribute a delightful series of essays : *Was ist Deutsch ? Modern ; Publikum und Popularität ; Das Publikum in Zeit und Raum*, 1878 ; *Wollen wir hoffen ? Über das Dichten und Komponiren ; Über das Opern-Dichten und Komponiren im besonderen ; Über die Anwendung der Musik auf das Drama*, 1879.[6]—A more elaborate work, a sort of comment upon the ethical and religious doctrine of ' Parsifal,' *Religion und Kunst*, with its sequel, *Was nützt diese Erkenntniss ? Erkenne dich selbst*, and *Heldenthum und Christenthum* (1880–81), he did not live to finish—a fragment only of the concluding part was written in 1883. It is given under the heading *Über das Weibliche im Menschlichen*, in a posthumous publication, *Entwürfe, Gedanken, Fragmente, aus nachgelassene Papieren zusammengestellt* [7] (Leipzig, Sept. 1885), pp. 125-9.

Wagner began the music to ' Parsifal ' in his sixty-fifth year. The sketch of the first act was completed early in the spring of 1878, and the greater part of the second act by the middle of June (completed on Oct. 11) ; the third act was begun after Christmas, and completed Apr. 1879. Towards the end of the year his old enemy erysipelas reappeared in a severe form, and he sought relief in Southern Italy. The instrumentation to ' Parsifal ' was continued (the Vorspiel had already been performed privately by the Meiningen orchestra under Wagner, at Bayreuth, Christmas 1878), and was finished during the next winter's sojourn in the south, at Palermo, Jan. 13, 1882.

In July and Aug. 1882—six years after ' Der Ring des Nibelungen '—sixteen performances of ' Parsifal,' everything under Wagner's supervision, were given; the artists alternating :

' Parsifal, Winkelmann, Gudehus, Jäger; Kundry, Frau Materna, Frl. Brandt, Frl. Malten ; Gurnemanz, Scaria, Siehr ; Amfortas, Reichmann, Fuchs; Klingsor, Hill, Degele, Plank. Conductors, H. Levi and Franz Fischer.'

(For the dates of the repetition of the work at Bayreuth, see BAYREUTH, Vol. I. p. 250 ; see also PARSIFAL, Vol. IV. p. 65.)

During the residence at Venice (Palazzo Vendramini on the Grand Canal) in the autumn and winter of 1882–83, the state of Wagner's health was not satisfactory, though no unusual symptoms appeared. He wrote for the *Bayreuther Blätter*, and was strong enough to

1 (Aug. 22, 1877.) 'Strange things happen in the realms of music,' wrote a surprised subscriber.
2 The residence of E. Dannreuther, the writer of the article. In the *Mus. T.*, 1898, p. 651, Dannreuther gives some of his recollections of the visit. See also *Briefe an Hans Richter* (1924), p. 151 *et seq.*
3 See the striking testimony of the veteran violoncellist Dotzauer and of Weber's widow as to ' Der Freischütz,' in *Über das Dirigiren*.
4 For interesting particulars concerning it see H. Porges' *Über die Aufführung der neunten Symphonie unter R. Wagner in Bayreuth.*

5 A full account of the introduction of the ' Ring ' in Leipzig, Berlin, London and other cities may be read in Angelo Neumann's *Erinnerungen* (Leipzig, 1907).
6 *P.W.* vi.   7 *Ibid.* vi. 335.

rehearse and conduct a private performance of his symphony in C (mentioned above, p. 581) at the Liceo Marcello on Christmas Eve. Late in the afternoon of Feb. 13, 1883, the great heart suddenly ceased to beat.[1] On Feb. 18 the body was laid in the little ivy-covered vault he had built long ago at Bayreuth in a retired spot of the garden at the rear of his house ' Wahnfried.'

Apart from a host of letters, and the *Lebenserinnerungen*, an autobiography covering fully two-thirds of his life,[2] there are no MS. literary remains of importance. Reports of his having read or recited scenes from the poem to a Buddhistic drama ' Die Sieger,' or ' Die Büsser,' intended to follow ' Parsifal,' rest upon vague hearsay. The fact is simply that in 1856–57 he came across a story in Burnouf's *Introduction à l'histoire du Buddhisme* which interested him, and that he took note of the leading incidents with a view to dramatic treatment ; but the plan was never matured, and what little of it had taken shape in his mind was incorporated in ' Parsifal.' For a short sketch of ' Die Sieger,' dated ' Zürich, 16 Mai, 1856,' see *Entwürfe, Gedanken, Fragmente* (Leipzig, 1885), pp. 97, 98.[3] Cancelled articles and unpublished musical works of early date will be found enumerated in the Chronological Lists, pp. 607-10.

Wagner disliked sitting for his portrait, so that of the numerous likenesses current few are at first hand. Two excellent paintings exist : one, by Lenbach (with the old German cap), is now at Bayreuth (see *PLATE XCI.*); the other, by Herkomer (1877), is (or was) at the German Athenæum, London (replica at Bayreuth). A bust (aet. 28) by Kietz, of Dresden (a pupil of Delaroche whom Wagner met in Paris in 1840–41), is also of interest (at Bayreuth); the portrait sketch for it was reproduced in the *Zeitung für die elegante Welt*, 1842, where it accompanied the *Autobiographische Skizze* (see *ante*, p. 587).[4] The best photographs are (1) a large half-length published in the revised edition of the Clavierauszug of ' Tannhäuser ' (Berlin, Fürstner); (2) full-length profile (rare), aet. 52, seated at a table reading, a dog at his feet (Munich, Hanfstängl); (3) carte and cabinet sizes, aet. 64 (Elliot & Fry, London, 1877); and the last of all, aet. 69 (A. V. Gross, Bayreuth, 1882).[5]

Like Beethoven, Wagner was slightly under middle height, well built, quick in movement, speech and gesture. His carriage was usually erect, his aspect commanding, and he made the impression of being somewhat taller than he actually was. After the political disturbances

of 1849, when he was ' wanted ' by the Saxon police, the following ' Signalement ' was issued.

' Wagner is 37 to 38 years old, of middle height, has brown hair, wears glasses ; open forehead ; eyebrows brown ; eyes grey-blue ; nose and mouth well proportioned ; chin round. Particulars : in moving and speaking he is hasty. Clothing : surtout of dark-green buckskin, trousers of black cloth, velvet waistcoat, silk neckerchief, the usual felt hat and boots.'

Like Beethoven, too, he at once made the impression of an original and powerful individuality. The fascination of his talk and his ways increased on acquaintance. When roused to speak of something that interested him he *looked* what he meant, and his rich voice gave a musical effect to his words. His presence in any circle apparently dwarfed the surroundings. His instinctive irrepressible energy, self-assertion and incessant productivity went hand in hand with simple kindness, sympathy and extreme sensitiveness. Children liked to be near him. He had no pronounced manners, in the sense of anything that can be taught or acquired by imitation. Always unconventional, his demeanour showed great refinement. His habits in private life are best described as those of a gentleman. He liked domestic comforts, had an artist's fondness for rich colour, harmonious decoration, out-of-the-way furniture, well-bound books and music, etc.[6] The good things of this world distinctly attracted him, but nothing could be farther from the truth than the reports about his ways and tastes current in German newspapers. The noble and kindly man as his friends knew him, and the aggressive critic and reformer addressing the public, were as two distinct individuals. Towards the public and the world of actors, singers, musicians, his habitual attitude was one of defiance. He appeared on the point of losing his temper, showed impatience and irritation, and seemed to delight in tearing men and things to pieces. His violence often stood in the way of his being heard ; indeed he has not yet been heard properly, either on questions of art so near and dear to him, or on questions farther off regarding things political, social or religious. It has been said with much truth that wherever Wagner was brought to a stand a social problem lies buried ; hitherto, however, it is only his vehement protestations that have attracted attention, whilst most of the problems, social or religious, remain unsolved. Regarding the state of music and the theatre in Germany, those who have access to the facts can account for a large part of his excitement and irritation. One has but to remember that from his eighteenth year onwards his life was mixed up with that most equivocal institution the German *Operntheater*. As a professional conductor, and

---

[1] The immediate cause of death seems to have been an attack of angina pectoris. For a minute account of the last days see Wallace's *Richard Wagner* (1925), at p. 253 *et seq.*
[2] See Bibliography, *infra.*
[3] *P.W.* viii. 385.
[4] As to Renoir's sketch see *Mus. T.*, 1921, p. 570.
[5] Thirty-four reproductions of photographs are in *Richard Wagners photographische Bildnisse mit Vorwort von A. Vanselow* (Munich, 1908).

[6] Amusing examples of his love for fine clothing and bright colours are to be found in *Briefe Richard Wagners an eine Putzmacherin* (Vienna, 1906). Autographs of the letters on this subject have been acquired by the Library of Congress, Washington, U.S.A.

WAGNER

From the painting by F. von Lenbach, in the possession of the Wagner family

subsequently as the recipient of *tantièmes* (percentage on the receipts)—for a long time his sole source of income—he could not afford to break the connexion. Here the idealist, the passionate poet, there the opera and the operetta. How could the most disastrous misunderstandings fail to arise ? The composer of ' Tristan ' confronted by the Intendant of some Hoftheater, fresh from a performance of Flotow's ' Martha ' ! A comic picture, but unfortunately a typical one, implying untold suffering on Wagner's part. Moreover he, the most irritable of men, impatient and fretting in his false position, was for years the object of personal attacks in the press, the ' best abused ' man in Europe, the object of wilful misrepresentation and calumny—' it was like having to walk against the wind with sand and grit and foul odours blowing in one's face.' [1]

All his life long Wagner was a great reader. 'Whatever is worth reading is worth re-reading,' he said. Thus, though never a systematic student or even a good linguist (which as regards Greek he greatly regretted),[2] he nevertheless became thoroughly familiar with all he cared for, and his range was a very wide one He retained whatever touched him sympathetically, and could depend upon his memory. The classics he habitually read in translations. With Shakespeare (in German, of course) he was as familiar as with Beethoven. To hear him read an act or a scene was a delight never to be forgotten. The effect, to use his own words about Shakespeare, was that of ' an improvisation of the highest poetical value.' When in particularly good spirits he would take up a comic scene and render it with the exuberant merriment of a child. A list of the principal books in the expensive and very choice library at Bayreuth would give a fair idea of his literary tastes, for he kept nothing by him that was not in some way connected with his intellectual existence. The handiest shelves held Sanskrit, Greek and Roman classics ; Italian writers, from Dante to Leopardi; Spanish, English, French dramatists; philosophers from Plato to Kant and Schopenhauer. A remarkably complete collection of French and German mediæval poems and stories, Norse sagas, etc., together with the labours of German and French philologists in those departments, occupied a conspicuous position ; history and fiction old and new were well represented ; translations of Scott, Carlyle, etc.

In a Dictionary of Music it would be out of place to speak of Wagner's power as a poet or as a writer on matters foreign to music. All that can be done is to point out the leading features of his practice and theory as a musical dramatist. We may begin with his theoretical pro-

ductions, premising merely that in his case, as in that of other men who have had new things to say and found new ways of saying them, Practice goes before Theory ; artistic instincts lead the way, and criticism acts in support and defence.

II. Broadly stated, Wagner's aim is *Reform of the Opera from the standpoint of Beethoven's music*.[3]

Can the modern spirit produce a theatre that shall stand in relation to modern culture as the theatre of Athens stood to the culture of Greece? This is the central question, the multifaced problem he set himself to solve. Whether he touches upon minor points connected with it ; speaks of the mode of performance of a play or an opera ; proposes measures of reform in the organisation of existing theatres ; discusses the growth of operatic music up to Mozart and Weber, or of instrumental music up to Beethoven ; treats of the efforts of Schiller and Goethe to discover an ideal form for their dramatic poems : whether he sweeps round the problem in wide circles, comparing modern, social and religious institutions with ancient, and seeking free breathing-space for his artistic ideals, he arrives at results tending in the same direction—his final answer is in the affirmative. Starting from the vantage of symphonic music, he asserts that we *may* hope to rise to the level of Greek tragedy : our theatre *can* be made to embody our ideal of life. From the opera at its best a drama can be evolved that shall express the vast issues and complex relations of modern life and thought, as the Greek stage expressed the life and thought of Greece.

The theatre is the centre of popular culture. For good or for evil it exerts the chief influence —from it the arts, as far as they affect the people, take their cue. Practically its power is unlimited. But who wields this power ? for what ends and for whom is it wielded ? Wagner's experience in Germany and in Paris furnished an answer. He had found corruption in every direction. In front of the scenes, the stolid German Philistine, or the bored Parisian roué clamouring for novelty, athirst for excitement ; behind the scenes, confusion and anarchy, sham enthusiasm, labour without aim or faith—the pretence, art ; the true end, money. Looking from the German stage to the German public, from the public to the nation, the case appeared hopeless, unless some violent change should upset the social fabric. A hasty and, as it proved, mistaken diagnosis of the political situation . in Germany in 1849 led Wagner to become a revolutionary for art's sake. Leaving the politics of the day to take care of themselves, he endeavoured to set forth his artistic ideals In *Die Kunst und die Revolution* he points to the theatre of Aeschylus

---

[1] Consult Herr Tappert's *Ein Wagner Lexikon; Wörterbuch der Unhöflichkeit*, etc. (Leipzig, 1877), for an astonishing record of the length to which such things can go in Germany.
[2] See ' *Brief an Fr. Nietzsche* ' *Ges. Schriften*, vol ix. (*P.W.* v. 292)

See also OPERA, Vol. III. p. 704.

and Sophocles, searches for the causes of its decline, and finds them identical with the causes that led to the decline of the ancient state itself. An attempt is then made to discover the principles of a new social organisation that might bring about a condition of things in which proper relations between art and public life might be expected to revive.

This pamphlet was followed by an elaborate treatise, *Das Kunstwerk der Zukunft* (The Artwork of the Future), which occupied him for several months. The first edition (1850) begins with a dedicatory letter to Ludwig Feuerbach (since cancelled), in which the author returns enthusiastic thanks for the instruction afforded by that philosopher's works.[1] Unfortunately Wagner was tempted to adopt Feuerbach's terminology, and to use it in a sense of his own. The result is bewildering, and the book, though rich in matter, warm in style and well worth reading, is in every respect difficult. The main argument, as far as art is concerned, might be sketched as follows : Poetry, mimetics and music were united in the drama of the Greeks ; the drama disappeared with the downfall of the Athenian State ; the union of the arts was dissolved, each had an existence of its own, and at times sank to the level of a mere pastime. Attempts made during the Renaissance, and since, to reunite the arts, were more or less abortive, though the technique and the width of range of most of the arts increased. In our day each 'separate branch of art' has reached its limits of growth, and cannot overstep them without incurring the risk of becoming incomprehensible, fantastic, absurd. At this point each art demands to be joined to a sister art—poetry to music, mimetics to both ; each will be ready to forgo egotistical pretensions for the sake of an 'artistic whole,' and the *musical* drama may become for future generations what the drama of Greece was to the Greeks.

Wagner's next work, *Oper und Drama* (his principal critical and theoretical production), contains little of the revolutionary and pseudo-philosophical ferment. It was originally issued in three parts : containing (1) a quasi-historical criticism of the opera ; (2) a survey of the spoken drama ; (3) an attempt to unite the results obtained, and to construct the theory of the musical drama. To us who have witnessed the 'Nibelungen' and 'Tristan,' the entire book is easy reading ; even the third and concluding part is readily intelligible and of very great interest. A generation ago, however, the case was different ; especially with regard to the third and, in the author's eyes, the most important part, which consists in the main of abstract statements about the new departure in art, the relation of verse to music, the func-

tion of the orchestra, etc. Wagner could not illustrate and support his assertions by concrete examples ; he thus laid himself open to misunderstanding, and was misunderstood indeed ! Part the Second abounds in acute observations on the elements of the dramatist's art, with copious references to Shakespeare, Schiller and Goethe. It seems to have attracted the attention of students of literature here and there, but on the whole it fell flat. The First Part, however, caused a disturbance in the musical world such as had not occurred since the paper war between the Gluckists and Piccinnists. It is sufficiently evident now that it was not the propositions seriously put forward, nor the brilliant literary powers displayed, that attracted attention. People were, or pretended to be, scandalised by the references to living composers, the biting satire, the fierce attack on Meyerbeer, etc. But Wagner's name was henceforth in everybody's mouth.

The course of musical history has already in so large a measure confirmed and endorsed Wagner's opinions regarding the opera that a short résumé will answer the present purpose. The *thesis* of *Oper und Drama* is as follows : —In the opera the means of expression (*music*) has been taken for the sole aim and end, while the true aim (*the drama*) has been neglected for the sake of particular musical forms. The dramatic cantata of Italy is the root of the opera. The scenic arrangements and the action formed the pretext for the singing of arias, *i.e.* people's songs artistically arranged. The composer's task consisted in writing arias of the accepted type to suit his subject or to suit this or that vocalist. When the ballet was added to the conglomerate of airs, it was the composer's business to reproduce the popular dance forms. The airs were strung together by means of recitatives, mostly conventional. The ballet tunes were simply placed side by side. Gluck's reform in the main consisted in his energetic efforts to place his music in more direct *rapport* with the action. He modified the melody in accordance with the inflections and accents of the language employed. He put a stop to the exhibition of mere vocal dexterity, and forced his singers to become the spokesmen of his dramatic intentions. But as regards the *form* of his musical pieces (and this is the cardinal point) he left the opera as he found it. The entire work remains a congeries of recitatives, arias, choruses, dance tunes, just as before. Gluck's librettists furnished words for airs, etc., in which the action was not lost sight of ; but it was considered to be of secondary importance. Gluck's great successors, Méhul, Cherubini, Spontini, cultivated the dramatic musical ensemble, and thus got rid of the incessant monologue which the arias of the elder opera had necessitated. This was an important step forward, and in essential

1 Wagner came across a copy of Feuerbach's *Das Wesen der Religion* in the writer's library : 'Solch confuses Zeug liesst sich leicht in jüngeren Jahren—ist an- und aufregend—ich habe lang daran gezehrt ; jetzt [1877] wär' mir's aber unverdaulich.'

matters the development of the opera is therewith at an end. For, although Mozart produced richer and more beautiful music than Gluck, there can be no doubt that the factors of Mozart's opera are essentially those of Gluck's. Subsequently, in the hands of Weber and Spohr, Rossini, Bellini, Auber, Meyerbeer, etc., the history of the opera is the history of the transformation of 'operatic melody.'

Subject and form in the spoken drama are investigated in the Second Part. With regard to subject Wagner traces two distinct factors ; first the mediæval romance and its offspring the modern novel ; secondly the Greek drama, or rather the formal essence thereof as given by Aristotle in his Poetics. He points to the plays of Shakespeare as being for the most part dramatised stories, and to those of Racine as constructed on the lines of Aristotle. In the course of the argument the works of Schiller and Goethe are examined, and the conclusion is arrived at that historical subjects present special difficulties to the dramatist. 'The modern stage appeals to our sensuous perceptions rather than to the imagination.' Thus Schiller was over-burdened with the mass of historical facts in his 'Wallenstein' ; whereas 'Shakespeare, appealing to the spectator's imagination, would have represented the entire Thirty Years War in the time o: cupied by Schiller's trilogy.' An interesting parallel is drawn between the rhetorical art of Racine and Gluck's opera. Racine puts forward the motives for action, and the effects of it, without the action proper. 'Gluck's instincts prompted him to translate Racine's tirade into the aria.' In view of the difficulties experienced by Goethe and Schiller in their efforts to fuse historical matter and poetic form, Wagner asserts that mythical subjects are best for an ideal drama, and that music is the ideal language in which such subjects are best presented. In the Third Part he shows that it is only the wonderfully rich development of music in our time, totally unknown to earlier centuries, which could have brought about the possibility of a musical drama such as he has in view. The conclusions arrived at in Oper und Drama are again discussed in his lecture 'On the Destiny of the Opera,' where particular stress is laid on the fact that music is the informing element of the new drama. Further statements regarding the main heads of the argument of the concluding part of Oper und Drama, and of the lecture 'Über die Bestimmung der Oper,' will be found incorporated later on in this article, where details as to Wagner's method and practice as playwright and musician are given.

Nineteen years after his Oper und Drama Wagner published Beethoven (1870). This work contains his contributions towards the metaphysics of music, if indeed such can be said

to exist. It is based on Schopenhauer's view of music,[1] which that philosopher candidly admitted to be incapable of proof, though it satisfied him. Wagner accepts it and supplements it with quotations from Schopenhauer's Essay on Visions and Matters connected therewith,[2] which contains equally problematic matter. Apart, however, from metaphysics, the work is an 'exposition of the author's thoughts on the significance of Beethoven's music.' It should be read attentively.

One of the finest of his minor publications, and to a professional musician perhaps the most instructive, is Über das Dirigiren, a treatise on style ; giving his views as to the true way of rendering classical music, with minute directions how to do it and how not to do it, together with many examples in music type from the instrumental works of Beethoven, Weber, Mozart, etc.[3]

Zum Vortrag der 9ten Symphonie (P.W. v. 231) is of great interest to students of instrumentation.

The general reader will be interested in Wagner's smaller essays and articles : Zukunftsmusik, Über die Bestimmung der Oper, Über das Dichten und Komponiren, Über das Opern-Dichten und Komponiren im besonderen—and especially in his graphic Erinnerungen, recollections of contemporaries, Spohr, Spontini, Rossini, Auber. Three of the latter are excerpts from his Lebenserinnerungen—apparently improvisations, showing the master-hand in every touch, valuable for their width of range and exquisite fidelity. Intending readers had better begin with these and Über das Dirigiren.

III. Regarding Wagner's weight and value as a musician, it is enough to state that his technical powers, in every direction in which a dramatic composer can have occasion to show them, were stupendous. He does not make use of Bach's forms nor of Beethoven's ; but this has little if anything to do with the matter. Surely Bach would salute the composer of 'Die Meistersinger' as a contrapuntist, and the poet-composer of the 'Eroica' and the 'Pastoral' would greet the author of 'Siegfried' and of 'Siegfrieds Tod.' Wagner is best compared with Beethoven. Take Schumann's saying, 'You must produce bold, original and beautiful melodies' as a starting-point, and supplement it with 'You must also produce bold and beautiful harmonies, modulations, contrapuntal combinations, effects of instrumentation.' Let excerpts be made under these heads from Beethoven's mature works, and a similar number of examples be culled from 'Die Meistersinger,' 'Tristan' and the 'Nibelungen'

[1] Die Welt als Wille und Vorstellung (1818), vol. i. 52 (ibid. vol. ii. chap. 39).
[2] Parerga und Paralipomena, Berlin, 1851. (See the Appendix to the English translation of Beethoven by E. Dannreuther, 1873.)
[3] See the English translation, On Conducting (London, 1885); also P.W. iv. 289.

—could it be doubtful that the aspect of such lists would be that of a series of equivalents? and as for originality, who can study the score of 'Tristan' and find it other than original from the first bar to the last?

Wagner's musical predilections may perhaps be best shown by a reference to the works that were his constant companions, and by a record of a few of his private sayings. Everyday friends, household words with him, were Beethoven's quartets, sonatas and symphonies; Bach's 'Wohltemperirtes Clavier'; Mozart's 'Zauberflöte,' 'Entführung,' 'Figaro' and 'Don Juan'; Weber's 'Freischütz' and 'Euryanthe'; and Mozart's symphonies in E♭, G minor and C. He was always ready to point out the beauties of these works, and inexhaustible in supporting his assertions with quotations from them [1]:

'Give me Beethoven's quartets and sonatas for intimate communion, his overtures and symphonies for public performance. I look for homogeneity of materials, and equipoise of means and ends. Mozart's music and Mozart's orchestra are a perfect match; an equally perfect balance exists between Palestrina's choir and Palestrina's counterpoint; and I find a similar correspondence between Chopin's piano and some of his Études and Preludes. I do not care for the "Ladies'-Chopin," there is too much of the Parisian salon in that; but he has given us many things which are above the salon.

'Schumann's peculiar treatment of the pianoforte grates on my ear: there is too much blur; you cannot produce his pieces unless it be *mit obligatem Pedal*. What a relief to hear a sonata of Beethoven's. In early days I thought more would come of Schumann. His *Zeitschrift* was brilliant, and his pianoforte works showed great originality. There was much ferment, but also much power, and many bits are quite unique and perfect. I think highly, too, of many of his songs, though they are not as great as Schubert's. He took pains with his declamation—no small merit a generation ago. Later on I saw a good deal of him at Dresden; but then already his head was tired, his powers on the wane. He consulted me about the text to "Genoveva," which he was arranging from Tieck's and Hebbel's plays, yet he would not take my advice—he seemed to fear some trick.'

Mendelssohn's overture 'The Hebrides' was a prime favourite of Wagner's, and he often asked for it at the piano.[2]

'Mendelssohn was a landscape-painter of the first order, and the "Hebriden" overture is his masterpiece. Wonderful imagination and delicate feeling are here presented with consummate art. Note the extraordinary beauty of the passage where the oboes rise above the other instruments with a plaintive wail like sea-winds over the seas. "Meeresstille und glückliche Fahrt" also is beautiful; and I am very fond of the first movement of the Scotch symphony. No one can blame a composer for using national melodies when he treats them so artistically as Mendelssohn has done in the scherzo of this symphony. His second themes, his slow movements generally, where the human element comes in, are weaker. As regards the overture to "A Midsummer Night's Dream," it must be taken into account that he wrote it at seventeen; and how finished the form is already! etc.

'Schubert has produced model songs, but that is no reason for us to accept his pianoforte sonatas or his ensemble pieces as really solid work, no more than we need accept Weber's songs, his pianoforte quartet or the trio with a flute because of his wonderful operas. Schumann's enthusiasm for Schubert's trios and the like was a mystery to Mendelssohn. I remember Mendelssohn speaking to me of the note of Viennese bonhomie (*bürgerliche Behäbigkeit*) which runs through those things of Schubert's. Curiously enough Liszt still likes to play Schubert. I cannot account for it; that Divertissement à la Hongroise verges on triviality, no matter how it is played.

'I am not a learned musician; I never had occasion to pursue antiquarian researches; and periods of transition did not interest me much. I went straight from Palestrina to Bach, from Bach to Gluck and Mozart—or, if you choose, along the same path backwards. It suited me personally to rest content with the acquaintance of the principal men, the heroes and their main works. For aught I know this may have had its drawbacks; any way, my mind has never been stuffed with "music in general." Being no learned person I have not been able to write to order. Unless the subject absorbs me completely I cannot produce twenty bars worth listening to.'

The latter part of this was said after a performance of the 'Centennial, Philadelphia, March,' at the Albert Hall (1877), and that March was the case in point.

'In instrumental music I am a *réactionnaire*, a conservative. I dislike everything that requires a verbal explanation beyond the actual sounds. For instance, the middle of Berlioz's touching *scène d'amour* in his "Romeo and Juliet" is meant by him to reproduce in musical phrases the lines about the lark and the nightingale in Shakespeare's balcony scene, but it does nothing of the sort—it is not intelligible as music. Berlioz added to, altered and spoilt his work. This so-called *Symphonie dramatique* of Berlioz's as it now stands is neither fish nor flesh—strictly speaking it is no symphony at all. There is no unity of matter, no unity of style. The choral recitatives, the songs and other vocal pieces have little to do with the instrumental movements. The operatic finale, Père Laurent especially, is a failure. Yet there are beautiful things right and left. The *convoi funèbre* is very touching and a masterly piece. So, by the way, is the offertoire of the Requiem. The opening theme of the *scène d'amour* is heavenly; the garden scene and fête at the Capulets enormously clever: indeed Berlioz was diabolically clever (*verflucht pfiffig*). I made a minute study of his instrumentation as early as 1840, at Paris, and have often taken up his scores since. I profited greatly, both as regards what to do and what to leave undone.'

'Whenever a composer of instrumental music loses touch of tonality he is lost.' To illustrate this (*Bayreuther Blätter*, 1879 [3]), Wagner quotes a dozen bars from 'Lohengrin,' Scene 2, bars 9 to 12, and then eight bars, 'mit züchtigem Gebahren' to 'Er soll mein Streiter sein,' as an example of very far-fetched modulation, which in conjunction with the dramatic situation is readily intelligible, whereas in a work of pure instrumental music it might appear as a blemish.

'When occasion offered I could venture to depict strange, and even terrible things in music, because the action rendered such things comprehensible; but music apart from the drama cannot risk this, for fear of becoming grotesque. I am afraid my scores will be of little use to composers of instrumental music; they cannot bear condensation, still less dilution; they are likely to prove misleading, and had better be left alone. I would say to young people who wish to write for the stage, "Do not, as long as you are young, attempt dramas—write 'Singspiele.'"'

[1] See *Die Musik und ihre Classiker in Aussprüchen Richard Wagners* (Leipzig, n.d.), 1878.
[2] Herr v. Wolzogen (*Erinnerungen an Richard Wagner*) gives a capital résumé of his sayings on such occasions (An appreciative notice of 'St. Paul,' written by Wagner on its performance at Dresden in 1843, is given in *P.W.* viii. 279; also in *Mus. T.*, 1899, p. 171.)
[3] *Ges. Schriften*, vol. x. p. 248 (*P.W.* vi. 189).

It has already been said that Wagner looks at the drama from the standpoint of Beethoven's music. Bearing this in mind it is easy to see where and how he would apply his lever to lift and upset the opera, and what his ideal of a musical drama would be. In early days the choice of subject troubled him much. Eventually he decided that mythical and legendary matter was better for music than historical; because the emotional elements of a mythical story are always of a simple nature and can be readily detached from any side issue; and because it is only the heart of a story, its emotional essence, that is suggestive to a musician. The mythical subject chosen (say the story of Volsungs and Niblungs, or Tristan and Isolde), the first and hardest thing to do is to condense the story, disentangle its threads and weave them up anew. None but those who are familiar with the sources of Wagner's dramas can have any idea of the amount of work and wisdom that goes to the fusing and welding of the materials. When this formidable preliminary task is finished, the *dramatis personae* stand forth clearly, and the playwright's task begins. In planning acts and scenes, Wagner never for a moment loses sight of the stage; the actual performance is always present to his mind. No walking gentlemen shall explain matters in general, nothing shall be done in the background and subsequently accounted for across the footlights. Whatever happens during the progress of the play shall be intelligible then and there. The dialogue in each scene shall exhibit the inner motives of the characters. Scene by scene the progress of the story shall be shown to be the result of these motives; and a decisive event, a turning-point in the story, shall mark the close of each act. The play being sketched, the leading motives of the dialogue fixed, Wagner turns to the verse. Here the full extent of the divergence of his drama from the paths of the opera becomes apparent. He takes no account of musical forms as the opera has them—recitative, aria, duet, ensemble, etc. If only the verse is emotional and strongly rhythmical, music can be trusted to absorb and glorify it. With Wagner as with Aeschylus, the verse is conceived and executed in the orgiastic spirit of musical sound. There is no need of, indeed there is no room for, subtleties of diction, intricate correspondence of rhyme and metre; music can supply all that and much more. Whilst working on the 'Ring' he found that alliterative verse as it exists in the poems of the elder Edda, in Beowulf, etc., was best suited to his subject, and that such verse could be written in German without offering violence to the language. In ' Tristan ' and ' Parsifal ' he makes use of a combination of alliteration, assonance and rhyme. Firm and concise, abounding in strong accents, the lines seem to demand music; indeed musical emphasis and prolongation of sound render them more readily intelligible and more impressive.

The poem finished, Wagner began the music, or rather began to *write* the music, for it is obvious that whereas in his case playwright and musician are one, the musical conception will go hand in hand with the poetic, will perhaps even precede it. Together with the first conception of the characters and situations at a very early stage in the growth of the work, certain musical phrases suggest themselves. These phrases, themes, ' Leitmotive,' [1] are the musician's equivalents for the dominant emotions or characteristics of the *dramatis personae*. Together with other musical germs of kindred origin they are the *subjects*—in a technical sense the themes— which the dramatic symphonist manipulates, using the full resources of Beethoven's orchestra, and adding thereto whatever the dramatic action may suggest. The pictures and actions on the stage are as visions induced by the symphonic music. The orchestra prepares for and floats the action, enforces details, recalls bygones, is, as it were, the artistic conscience of the whole performance.

Wagner's treatment of the voice, his vocal melody, has undergone many a change. First he tried to find melodies effective from a vocalist's point of view; then, in the ' Holländer,' and more consciously in ' Tannhäuser,' the melodic ebb and flow is regulated by the action; in ' Lohengrin ' the emotions expressed, as much as any peculiarity of melody, attract attention, whilst characteristic harmony and instrumentation enforce the melodic outlines. In the later works the vocal melody often springs direct from the words; it is frequently independent of the orchestra; in some cases indeed it is but an intensified version of the actual sounds of the German language.

From the blatant and at times almost vulgar style of ' Rienzi ' there is a steady and truly astonishing increase in power and concentration, subtlety and delicacy. The ' Nibelungen,' ' Tristan ' and subsequent works abound in harmonic, melodic and rhythmical combinations of great beauty and striking originality. The innovations in harmony and melody peculiar to Wagner are mainly due to the free use of chromatics. Besides bold chromatic and enharmonic progressions, he constantly employs chromatic anticipatory, changing and passing notes, which have a melodic significance only. For purposes of analysis such chromatic notes should be eliminated—the harmonic framework

---

[1] See the article LEIT-MOTIF, Vol. III. p 134. The term is v. Wolzogen's, not Wagner's, and should be used cautiously. At Bayreuth, in the summer of 1877, after warmly praising v. Wolzogen's *Thematische Leitfäden* for the interesting information they afford, and for the patience displayed in the attempts at thematic analysis, Wagner added : ' To a musician this naming and tracing of themes is not particularly significant. If dilettanti are thus induced to study a pianoforte arrangement a little more attentively, I can have no objection, but that does not concern us musicians (*für uns Musiker ist das aber nichts*). It may be worth while to look at the complex combinations of themes in some of my scores, to see how music can be applied to the drama ;—this, however, is a matter for private study.'

will then stand forth clearly and prove perfectly consistent (see HARMONY). The greater part of Wagner's chromatic or enharmonic progressions will be found to be based upon correct diatonic progressions in minor or major. Exceptionally, the chromatic progression of parts upwards or downwards, or in contrary motion ('Tristan,' PF. arrt. p. 25, lines 1, 2, etc.), forms a sufficient link between apparently contradictory chords. The exigencies and suggestions of the dramatic action fully account for sudden and far-fetched modulations, enharmonic changes, rhythmical elisions (as when a beat or a chord is dropped, the phrase being intelligible though not logically complete, 'Tristan,' p. 150, bars 3 to 4 *et seq.*), interrupted cadences, expansion or condensation of time ('Tristan,' PF. arrt. pp. 210-12 and 226-8), sequences of chromatically altered chords and other peculiarities ('Siegfried,' PF. arrt. p. 65 *et seq.*). In pure instrumental music such eccentric and apparently extravagant things would not have sufficient *raison d'être*; but in their right place they require no apology, nor do they present special difficulties from the point of view of musical grammar. Indeed Wagner as he advanced grew more and more careful with regard to diction, and it is not too much to say that among the hundreds of unusual and complex combinations in 'Tristan,' 'Siegfried,' 'Götterdämmerung' and 'Parsifal' it would be difficult to point to a single crude one.

Wagner is a supreme master of instrumentation, of orchestral colour. His orchestra differs from Beethoven's in the quality of tone emitted; over and above effects of richness obtained by the more elaborate treatment of the inner part of the string quartet, the frequent subdivision of violins, violas, violoncellos, the use of chromatics in horn and trumpet parts, etc., there is a peculiar charm in the very sound of Wagner's wood-wind and brass. It is fuller than Beethoven's, yet singularly pure. And the reason for this is not far to seek. Wagner rarely employed instruments unknown to Beethoven, but he completed each group or family of wind instruments with a view to getting full chords from each group. Thus the two clarinets of Beethoven's orchestra are supplemented by a third clarinet and a bass clarinet if need be; the two oboes by a third oboe or a corno-inglese (alto oboe); the two bassoons by a third bassoon and a contra-fagotto; the two trumpets by a third trumpet and a bass trumpet, etc. The results got by the use of these additional instruments are of greater significance than at first appears, since each set of instruments can thus produce complete chords and can be employed in full harmony without mixture of *timbre* unless the composer so chooses.

To account for the exceptional array of extra instruments in the scores of the 'Nibelungen' it is enough to say that they are used as special means for special ends. Thus at the opening of the 'Rheingold' the question is what sound will best prepare for and accord with dim twilight and waves of moving water? The soft notes of horns might be a musician's answer; but to produce the full smooth wave-like motion upon the notes of a single chord, the usual two or four horns are not sufficient. Wagner takes eight, and a unique and beautiful effect is secured. Again, in the next scene, the waves change to clouds; from misty mountain heights the gods behold Walhall in the glow of the morning sun. Here subdued solemn sound is required. How to get it? Use brass instruments *piano*. But the trumpets, trombones and tuba of Wagner's usual orchestra cannot produce enough of it; he therefore supplements them by other instruments of their family; a bass trumpet, two tenor and two bass tubas, a contrabass trombone and contrabass tuba; then the full band of thirteen brass instruments is ready for one of the simplest and noblest effects of sonority in existence. At the close of 'Rheingold' Donner with his thunder-hammer clears the air of mist and storm-clouds; a rainbow spans the valley of the Rhine, and over the glistening bridge the gods pass to Walhall. What additional sounds shall accompany the glimmer and glitter of this scene? The silvery notes of harps might do it: but the sounds of a single harp would appear trivial, or would hardly be audible against the full chant of the orchestra. Wagner takes six harps, writes a separate part for each, and the desired effect is attained.

In the 'Ring,' in 'Tristan,' the 'Meistersinger' and 'Parsifal' the notation of all that pertains to execution, tempi, gradations of sonority, etc., has been carried out in the most complete manner possible. The composer's care and patience are truly extraordinary. Nothing is left to chance. If the conductor and the executants strictly follow the indications given in the scores, a correct performance cannot fail to ensue. The tempo and the character of each movement, and every modification of tempo or character, are indicated in unmistakable German (for instance, in 'Rheingold,' p. 1, 'Ruhig heitere Bewegung,' which in the conventional Italian terms would have been 'Allegretto piacevole,' or something equally misleading); doubtful changes of time; cases where the notation would seem to suggest a change of tempo—whereas only a change of metre occurs, while the musical pulsation, the actual beat, remains the same—are indicated by equivalents in notes and elucidatory words. Thus in 'Tristan,' p. 69, where 2-2 changes to 6-8, the latter is marked ♩.=♩; that is to say, the dotted crotchets shall now be taken at the rate of the preceding minims.[1] The number of

[1] Many a disastrous *quid pro quo* might be avoided if this simple method of noting the relation of one tempo to another were universally adopted.

strings necessary to balance the wind instruments employed is given—in the ' Nibelungen ' it is 16 first violins, 16 seconds, 12 violas, 12 violoncellos and 8 contrabasses. When the violins or other strings are divided, the number of desks that shall take each part is shown. To secure specially delicate effects the number of single instruments required out of the total is indicated, etc. etc.

' If I had a chance,' said Wagner in 1877, ' to get up the " Meistersinger " with an intelligent company of young people, I would first ask them to read and act the play ; then only would I proceed with the music in the usual way. I am certain we should thus arrive at a satisfactory performance in a very short time.' The desiderata are simple enough. Keep the work apart from the ordinary repertory, clear the stage for at least a week, and during that time let every one concerned give his attention to the task in hand and to nothing else ; give the work entire, and aim at reproducing the score exactly as it stands.[1]

IV. CHRONOLOGICAL LISTS

FOR THE STAGE

Die Hochzeit : fragment of an opera; introduction, chorus and septet.[2] Unpublished ; autograph copy of the score, 36 pages, dated Mar. 1, 1833, was presented by Wagner to the Musik-verein of Würzburg.

Die Feen : romantische Oper, in 3 acts ; 1833. Never performed ; the overture only was played at Magdeburg, 1834. Unpublished ; original score in possession of the King of Bavaria. Produced in Munich, June 29, 1888 ; published by Breitkopf.

Das Liebesverbot : sketched in the summer of 1834, music composed 1835 and 1836. Performed once only, at Magdeburg, Mar. 29, 1836. Original score in the possession of the King of Bavaria. A song from the opera, ' Carnevalslied,' was printed in Lewald's *Europa*, 1837, p. 240, and pirated at Brunswick and Hanover. Published by Breitkopf.

Rienzi, der letzte der Tribunen, grosse tragische Oper, in 5 acts. Music begun at Riga, July 26, 1838. Acts 1 and 2 finished 1839 at Riga and Mitau ; Acts 3, 4 and 5 at Paris, Nov. 19, 1840. First performed at Dresden, Oct. 20, 1842.

Der fliegende Holländer : romantische Oper, in 3 acts. Original sketch, 1 act, May 1841 : poem, May 1841 : completed, Meudon, Paris, Sept. 13, 1841. First performed at Dresden, Jan. 2, 1843. Published in lith., Dresden, 1844, and by Meser, Dresden, in 1861.

Tannhäuser, und der Sängerkrieg auf Wartburg : romantische Oper, in 3 acts. First sketches in summer of 1842 ; poem finished May 22, 1843 ; score completed Apr. 13, 1845. First performed at Dresden, Oct. 19, 1845. Pub. 1845 in lith. ; the Venusberg scene written in Paris, Jan. 1861.

Lohengrin, romantische Oper, in 3 acts. Poem written at Dresden, 1845 ; music begun Sept. 9, 1846. Introduction written Aug. 28, 1847 ; instrumentation of the entire work completed during the ensuing winter and spring. First performed Aug. 28, 1850, at Weimar, under Liszt. Score published by Breitkopf, 1866.

Das Rheingold. Part I. of ' Der Ring des Nibelungen.' Poem of ' Der Ring ' begun at Dresden, 1848, executed in reverse order (' Siegfrieds Tod,' ' Siegfried,' ' Walküre,' ' Rheingold ') ; finished at Zürich, 1851–52. Music to ' Das Rheingold ' begun in the autumn of 1853 at Spezia ; score finished in May 1854. First performed at Munich, Sept. 22, 1869. PF. score published 1861 ; full do. 1873.

Die Walküre. Part II. of ' Der Ring des Nibelungen,' in 3 acts. Score begun in June 1854 ; finished at Zürich, 1856. First performed June 25, 1870, at Munich. PF. score published 1865 ; full do. 1873.

Tristan und Isolde : in 3 acts. Poem written at Zürich, 1857 ; music begun 1857. Score of Act 1 finished in the autumn of 1857 at Zürich ; Act 2, Mar. 1859 at Venice ; Act 3, Aug. 1859 at Lucerne. First performed June 10, 1865, at Munich, under von Bülow. PF. and full score published 1860.

Siegfried. Part III. of ' Der Ring des Nibelungen,' in 3 acts. Music begun at Zürich, before ' Tristan.' Act 1 finished Apr. 1857 ; part of Act 2, up to the ' Waldweben,' written in 1857 ; laid aside in June ; Act 2 completed at Munich, June 21, 1865 ; sketch of Act 3 finished in 1869, score completed Feb. 5, 1871. First performed Aug. 16, 1876, at Bayreuth, under Richter. PF. score published 1871 ; full do. 1876.

Die Meistersinger von Nürnberg : in 3 acts. Sketch 1845 ; poem begun winter 1861–62 at Paris, printed as MS. 1862 : music begun 1862 ; score finished Oct. 24, 1867. First performed

June 21, 1868, at Munich, under von Bülow. PF. score published 1867 ; full do. 1868.

Götterdämmerung. Part IV. of ' Der Ring des Nibelungen.' (The first sketches to ' Siegfrieds Tod ' dated June 1848.) Music begun 1870 at Lucerne. Sketch of Introduction and Act 1 completed Jan. 20, 1871. Sketch of full score finished at Bayreuth, June 22, 1872. Instrumentation completed Nov. 21, 1874. First performed Aug. 17, 1876, at Bayreuth, under Richter. PF. score published 1875 ; full do. 1876.

Parsifal : Ein Bühnenweihfestspiel, in 3 acts (the first sketches of Charfreitagszauber belong to the year 1857, Zürich). Poem written at Bayreuth, 1876–77 ; sketch of music begun at Bayreuth, 1877 ; completed Apr. 25, 1879. Instrumentation finished Jan. 13, 1882, at Palermo. First performed July 26, 1882, at Bayreuth, under Levi. PF. score published 1882 ; full do. 1884.

ORCHESTRAL AND CHORAL WORKS [3]

Overture B♭ (6–8). (' Paukenschlagouvertüre.') Unpublished. Performed 1830 at Leipzig. Score apparently lost.

Overture D minor (4–4). Unpublished. Performed Feb. 23, 1832, at the Gewandhaus, at Leipzig. Score at Bayreuth.

Overture to Raupach's drama : ' König Enzio.' Finished Feb. 3, 1832 ; performed in the Royal Theatre, Leipzig, Mar. 16, 1832. Score published by Breitkopf, 1907.

Overture in C (' Konzert - Ouverture — ziemlich fugirt '). Unpublished ; performed for the first time at a Euterpe concert at Leipzig, then at the Gewandhaus, Apr. 30, 1832, and May 22, 1873, at Bayreuth.

Overture ' Polonia.' C major (4–4). Not published until 1904, when it was brought forward with two other overtures. (See *Mus. T.*, 1905, p. 117.) Written 1832 at Leipzig (qu. 1836 at Riga ?). Score at Bayreuth.

Symphony in C. Unpublished. Written 1832 at Leipzig, and performed at Prague, summer 1832 ; Dec. 1832 at the Euterpe ; and Jan. 10, 1833, at the Gewandhaus, Leipzig ; Dec. 24, 1882, at Venice.

New Year's Cantata. Introduction and two choral pieces. Unpublished. Performed at Magdeburg on New Year's Eve, 1834–35, and at Bayreuth, May 22, 1873.

Overture ' Columbus.' Unpublished. Written early in 1835 and performed at Leipzig, Apr. 2, 1835 ; at Magdeburg, May 2, 1835 ; Leipzig, May 25, 1835 ; Riga, 1838 ; and Paris, Feb. 4, 1841. After the last performance score and parts disappeared and were eventually discovered in Paris. Now published by Metzler & Co. (See *Mus. T.*, 1894, p. 50.)

Incidental music—songs—to a ' Zauberposse,' by Gleich, ' Der Berggeist, oder Die drei Wünsche.' Magdeburg, 1836. (See Ellis's *Life*, i. 195, where he suggests 1835 as the more likely date.) (Unpublished ; MS. probably lost.)

Overture ' Rule, Britannia.' Written at Königsberg and finished Mar. 15, 1837. Performed there in Mar. 1837. Sent to the London Philharmonic Society in 1840 : subsequently lost until the parts were discovered among the papers of C. B. Gamble of Leicester. It was published in 1904. See *The Times* of May 16, 1904 ; *Mus. T.* for 1904, p. 372. The Hon. Mrs. Burrell possessed another set of parts, and a third, with the score, is at Bayreuth.

' Eine Faust Ouverture.' Written in Paris, 1839–40 ; first performed July 22, 1844, at Dresden ; rewritten 1855 in Zürich, and performed there Jan. 23. Published by Breitkopf, 1855.

Huldigungsmarsch. Written 1864 at Starnberg. Published 1869 (? 1871). The original score, for a military band, remains in MS. The published version for the usual full orchestra was begun by Wagner and finished by Raff in 1871.

Siegfried Idyll. Written 1870 at Triebschen. First performed there Dec. 25, 1870. Published 1877.

Kaisermarsch. 1871 at Triebschen. First performed at Berlin, Apr. 14, 1871.

Grosser Festmarsch (Centennial Exhibition, Philadelphia). Sketched at Bayreuth : finished at Berlin, Mar. 17, 1876. First performed at Philadelphia, May 10, 1876.

Das Liebesmahl der Apostel. Eine biblische Scene für Männerchor und grosses Orchester. First performance, Dresden, July 6, 1843, at a festival of the male voice choirs of Saxony. (See *P.W.* viii. 277 for sketch of libretto.)

Gelegenheits Cantate. For unveiling of bronze statue representing King Friedrich August at Dresden, June 7, 1843. Unpublished.

Gruss an den König, 1844. Published (*a*) for four male voices ; (*b*) as a song with PF. Performed at Dresden, Aug. 12, 1844, or the King of Saxony's return from England.

An Webers Grabe. (*a*) Trauermarsch for wind instruments or motives from ' Euryanthe ' ; (*b*) double quartet for voices, 1844. Score of (*b*) published 1872. Performed Dec. 15, 1844.

PIANOFORTE PIECES

Sonata, B♭. Written 1831. Published 1832.

Polonaise, D. Four hands. Written 1831. Published 1832.

Fantasie, F♯ minor. Unpublished. Written 1831.

Album-Sonate, for Frau Mathilde Wesendonck, in E♭. Written 1853. **Albumblatt**, ' Ankunft bei den schwarzen Schwänen ' for Countess Pourtalès, in A♭. Published 1877.

Ein Albumblatt, for Fürstin Metternich, in C. Written 1861. Published 1871.

Albumblatt, for Frau Betty Schott, in E♭. Written Jan. 1, 1875. Published 1876.

SONGS

' Carnevalslied,' from ' Das Liebesverbot,' 1835–36. Reprinted at Brunswick, 1885.

' Dors, mon enfant ' ; ' Mignonne ' ; ' Attente.' Paris, 1839–40. Appeared as ' Musikbeilagen ' to Lewald's *Europa*, 1841 and 1842. Republished with a German translation, 1871.

' Les deux Grenadiers.' (Heine's *Die beiden Grenadiere*.) Paris, 1839. Dedicated to Heine. Music fits the French version.

Der Tannenbaum 1838. See Ellis's *Life*, i. 253. Published 1871.

Kraft-Liedchen (1871), a little humorous vote of thanks to Herr Kraft of Leipzig. Printed in Müller v. der Werra's Reichscommersbuch.

---

[1] It is perhaps worth while to point out that public taste has decreed the restoration of every note in special performances of the ' Ring,' etc. A new method of bringing the ' Ring ' within ordinary theatre hours was tried by the British National Opera Company in 1925, by giving it in six sections instead of four.

[2] Not sextet.

[3] For details concerning the orchestral works see Müller-Reuter *Lexikon der deutschen Konzertliteratur*, 1909. p. 435 *et seq.*

Fünf Gedichte. 1. Der Engel; 2. Stehe still; 3. Im Treibhaus (Studie zu Tristan und Isolde); 4. Schmerzen; 5. Träume (Studie zu Tristan und Isolde). 1862. English by Francis Hueffer.

ARRANGEMENTS, Etc.

Gluck. Iphigénie en Aulide. 1846. ' Nach der Bearbeitung von Richard Wagner.' PF. arrt. by H. von Bülow. (Published 1859.)
Score of close to overture published 1859.
Mozart. Don Juan—revised dialogue and recitatives—performed at Zürich, 1850. Unpublished.
Palestrina. Stabat Mater, mit Vortragsbezeichnungen eingerichtet. 1848. Score published 1877.
Allegro zur Arie des Aubrey, in dem Vampyr von Marschner (in F min.). Score, 142 bars of additional text and music, instead of the 58 bars of the original, dated Würzburg, Sept. 23, 1833. in the possession of Herr W. Tappert, Berlin.
Beethoven. Ninth Symphony, Clavierauszug. 1830. Unpublished.
Donizetti. La Favorite. PF. score, Paris.
    ,,   Elisir d' amore, PF. score.
Halévy. La Reine de Chypre. PF. score, Paris, 1841.
  ,,   Le guittarero. PF. score, Paris, 1841.

ARTICLES, LIBRETTI, Etc., NOT CONTAINED IN THE GERMAN COLLECTED WRITINGS, OR CANCELLED

Die deutsche Oper. 1834. Laube's Zeitung für die elegante Welt. (P.W. viii. 55.) [1]
Pasticcio von Canto Spianato, Nov. 1834 (Bay. Bl., 1884, pp. 337-42.) (P.W. viii. 59.)
Die glückliche Bärenfamilie ; a libretto for a comic opera, after a story in the Arabian Nights. 1839 (MS.).
Pariser Amusements. (P.W. viii. 70.)
Berlioz. May 5, 1841. (Bay. Bl., 1884, pp. 65-8.) (P.W. viii. 131.)
Bellini. (Bay. Bl., Dec. 1885.) (P.W. viii. 67.)
Pariser Fatalitäten für Deutsche, signed V. Freudenfeuer. Appeared 1841 in Lewald's Europa. (P.W. viii. 87.)
' Bianca e Giuseppe,' oder ' Die Franzosen in Nizza.' Libretto for an opera after H. S. König's novel, Die hohe Braut. Sketch made in 1836, sent to Scribe in 1838. Put into verse for Kapellmeister Reissiger at Dresden ; subsequently set to music by J. F. Kittl and performed at Prague, 1848.
' Die Sarazenen ' ; plan for libretto of a 5-act tragic opera. First sketch of poem, 1841 ; detailed plan, 1843, given in the Nachgelassene Schriften. (P.W. viii. 251.)
' Friedrich Rothbart ' ; sketch for a 5-act drama. MS. 1848.
' Rede gehalten im Vaterlands-Verein zu Dresden,' June 14, 1848. (Tappert, pp. 33-42 ; P.W. iv. 136.)
' Jesus von Nazareth,' a poetic draft. Written between Nov. 1843 and the early part of 1849. First published in 1887. See P.W. viii. 283.
Theaterreform. Dresdener Anzeiger, Jan. 16, 1849. (Tappert, pp. 44-7. P.W. viii. 222.)
' Gräfin Egmont.' Ballet von Rota. An article in the Österreichische Zeitung, signed P. C. (Peter Cornelius), but partly written by Wagner.
Grabschrift für Carl Tausig. 1873.
Richard Wagner. Entwürfe. Gedanken. Fragmente. Aus den nachgelassenen Papieren zusammengestellt. 1885.

COLLECTED LITERARY WORKS
(Ten volumes. Leipzig, 1871-85 ; 2nd ed., Leipzig, 1887-88.)

Vol. I.

Vorwort zur Gesammtherausgabe. (P.W. i. xv.)
Einleitung. (P.W. vii. 1.)
Autobiographische Skizze (bis 1841). (P.W. i. 1 : see also Mrs. Burrell, p. 45.)
' Das Liebesverbot.' Bericht über eine erste Opernaufführung (extracted from autobiography). (P.W. vii. 5.)
Rienzi, der letze der Tribunen.
Ein deutscher Musiker in Paris. Novellen und Aufsätze (1840 und 1841). 1. Eine Pilgerfahrt zu Beethoven. 2. Ein Ende in Paris. 3. Ein glücklicher Abend. 4. Über deutsches Musikwesen. 5. Der Virtuos und der Künstler. 6. Der Künstler und die Öffentlichkeit. 7. Rossini's ' Stabat Mater.' (P.W. vii. 1a.)
Über die Ouvertüre. (P.W. vii. 151.)
Der Freischütz, in Paris (1841). 1. ' Der Freischütz.' An das Pariser Publikum. 2. ' Le Freischütz.' Bericht nach Deutschland. (P.W. vii. 167.)
Bericht über eine neue Pariser Oper (' La Reine de Chypre ' von Halévy). (P.W. vii. 205. See another article in P.W. viii. 175.)
Der fliegende Holländer.

Vol. II.

Einleitung. (P.W. vii. 223.)
Tannhäuser und der Sängerkrieg auf Wartburg.
Bericht über die Heimbringung der sterblichen Überreste Karl Maria von Webers aus London nach Dresden. Rede an Webers letzter Ruhestätte. Gesang nach der Bestattung. (Extracted from the autobiography.) (P.W. vii. 227.)
Bericht über die Aufführung der neunten Symphonie von Beethoven, im Jahre 1846, nebst Programm dazu. (From autobiography.) (P.W. vii. 239.)
Lohengrin.
Die Wibelungen. Weltgeschichte aus der Saga. (Written 1848. published 1850.) (P.W. vii. 257.)
Der Nibelungen-Mythus. Als Entwurf zu einem Drama. (P.W. vii. 299.)
Siegfrieds Tod. (P.W. vii. 1.)
Trinkspruch am Gedenktage des 300jährigen Bestehens der königlichen musikalischen Kapelle in Dresden. (P.W. vii. 313.)
Entwurf zur Organisation eines deutschen Nationaltheaters für das Königreich Sachsen (1849). (P.W. vii. 319.)

Vol. III.

Einleitung zum dritten und vierten Bande. (P.W. i. 23.)
Die Kunst und die Revolution. (P.W. i. 30.)

----

[1] This and similar references are to the English translation, Richard Wagner's Prose Works, by W. Aston Ellis, as to which see below.

Das Kunstwerk der Zukunft. (P.W. i. 69.)
' Wieland der Schmiedt,' als Drama entworfen. (P.W. i. 215.)
Kunst und Klima. (P.W. i. 249.)
Oper und Drama, erster Theil : Die Oper und das Wesen de. Musik. (P.W. ii. 21.)

Vol. IV.

Oper und Drama, zweiter und dritter Theil : Das Schauspiel und das Wesen der dramatischen Dichtkunst.—Dichtkunst und Tonkunst im Drama der Zukunft. (P.W. ii. 117.)
Eine Mittheilung an meine Freunde. (P.W. i. 267.)

Vol. V.

Einleitung zum fünften und sechsten Bande. (P.W. iii. 1.)
Über die ' Goethestiftung.' Brief an Franz Liszt. (P.W. iii. 5.)
Ein Theater in Zürich. (P.W. iii. 23.)
Über musikalische Kritik. Brief an den Herausgeber der ' Neuen Zeitschrift für Musik.' (P.W. iii. 59.)
Das Judenthum in der Musik. (P.W. iii. 76.)
Erinnerungen an Spontini. (P.W. iii. 123.)
Nachruf an L. Spohr und Chordirektor W. Fischer. (P.W. iii. 145.)
Gluck's Ouvertüre zu ' Iphigenia in Aulis.' (P.W. iii. 153.)
Über die Aufführung des ' Tannhäuser.' (P.W. iii. 167.)
Bemerkungen zur Aufführung der Oper ' Der fliegende Holländer.' (P.W. iii. 207.)
Programmatische Erläuterungen. 1. Beethoven's ' Heroische Symphonie.' 2. Ouvertüre zu ' Koriolan.' 3. Ouvertüre zum ' Fliegenden Holländer.' 4. Ouvertüre zu ' Tannhäuser.' 5. Vorspiel zu ' Lohengrin.' (P.W. iii. 219.)
Über Franz Liszt's symphonische Dichtungen. (P.W. iii. 235.)
Das Rheingold. Vorabend zu dem Bühnenfestspiel : Der Ring des Nibelungen.

Vol. VI.

Der Ring des Nibelungen, Bühnenfestspiel. Erster Tag: Die Walküre. Zweiter Tag : Siegfried. Dritter Tag : Götterdämmerung.
Epilogischer Bericht über die Umstände und Schicksale die Ausführung des Bühnenfestspieles ' Der Ring des Nibelungen ' bis zur Veröffentlichung der Dichtung desselben begleiteten (P.W. iii. 255.)
Tristan und Isolde. (P.W. iii. 285.)
Ein Brief an Hector Berlioz. (P.W. iii. 285.)
' Zukunftsmusik.' An einen französischen Freund (Fr. Villot) als Vorwort zu einer Prosa-Übersetzung meiner Opern Dichtungen. (P.W. iii. 293.)
Bericht über die Aufführung des ' Tannhäuser ' in Paris (Brieflich). (P.W. iii. 347.)
Die Meistersinger von Nürnberg.
Das Wiener Hof-Operntheater. (P.W. iii. 361.)

Vol. VIII.

Dem königlichen Freunde, Gedicht. (P.W. iv. 1.)
Über Staat und Religion. (P.W. iv. 3.)
Deutsche Kunst und deutsche Politik. (P.W. iv. 35.)
Bericht an Seine Majestät den König Ludwig II. von Bayern über eine in München zu errichtende deutsche Musikschule. (P.W. iv. 171.)
Meine Erinnerungen an Ludwig Schnorr von Carolsfeld. (P.W. iv. 225.)
Zur Widmung der zweiten Auflage von ' Oper und Drama.' (P.W. ii. 3.)
Censuren : 1. W. H. Riehl. (P.W. iv. 253.) 2. Ferdinand Hiller. (P.W. iv. 261.) 3. Eine Erinnerung an Rossini. (P.W. iv. 269.) 4. Eduard Devrient. (P.W. iv. 275.) 5. Aufklärungen über ' Das Judenthum in der Musik.' (P.W. iii. 77.)
Über das Dirigiren. (1869.) (P.W. iv. 289.)
Drei Gedichte : 1. Rheingold. 2. Bei der Vollendung des ' Siegfried.' 3. Zum 25. August 1870. (P.W. iv. 368.)

Vol. IX.

An das deutsche Heer vor Paris (Januar 1871). (P.W. v. 1.)
Eine Kapitulation. Lustspiel in antiker Manier. (P.W. v. 3.)
Erinnerungen an Auber. (P.W. v. 35.)
Beethoven. Published Dec. 2, 1870. (P.W. v. 57.)
Über die Bestimmung der Oper. (The account of Wilhelmine Schroeder-Devrient is from the autobiography.) (P.W. v. 127.)
Über Schauspieler und Sänger. (P.W. v. 157.)
Zum Vortrag der neunten Symphonie Beethovens. (P.W. v. 229.)
Sendschreiben und kleinere Aufsätze : 1. Brief über das Schauspielerwesen an einen Schauspieler. 2. Ein Einblick in das heutige deutsche Opernwesen. 3. Brief an einen italienischen Freund über die Aufführung des ' Lohengrin ' in Bologna. 4. Schreiben an den Bürgermeister von Bologna. 5. An Friedrich Nietzsche, ord. Prof. der klass. Philologie in Basel. 6. Über die Benennung ' Musikdrama.' 7. Einleitung zu einer Vorlesung der ' Götterdämmerung ' vor einem ausgewählten Zuhörerkreise in Berlin. (P.W. v. 255.)
' Bayreuth ' : 1. Schlussbericht über die Umstände und Schicksale, welche die Ausführung des Bühnenfestspieles ' Der Ring des Nibelungen ' bis zur Gründung von Wagner-Vereinen begleiteten. 2. Das Bühnenfestspielhaus zu Bayreuth nebst einem Bericht über die Grundsteinlegung desselben. (P.W v. 307.)

Vol. X.

Über eine Opernaufführung in Leipzig. Brief an den Herausgeber des ' Musikalischen Wochenblattes.' (P.W. vi. 1.)
Bayreuth. Bayreuther Blätter : 1. An die geehrten Vorstände der Richard Wagner-Vereine. 2. Entwurf, veröffentlicht mit den Statuten des Patronatvereines. 3. Zur Einführung (Bayreuther Blätter, Erstes Stück). 4. Ein Wort zur Einführung der Arbeit Hans von Wolzogens, ' Über Verrottung und Errettung der deutschen Sprache.' 5. Erklärung an die Mitglieder des Patronatvereines. 6. Zur Einführung in das Jahr 1880. 7. Zur Mittheilung an die geehrten Patrone der Bühnenfestspiele in Bayreuth. 8. Zur Einführung der Arbeit des Grafen Gobineau ' Ein Urtheil über die jetzige Weltlage.' (P.W. vi. 13.)
Was ist deutsch ? (1865-78). (P.W. vi. 149.)
Modern. (P.W. vi. 49.)
Publikum und Popularität. (P.W. vi. 51.)
Ein Rückblick auf die Bühnenfestspiele des Jahres 1876. (P.W vi. 95.)

Wollen wir hoffen ? (1879). (*P.W.* vi. iii.)
Über das Dichten und Komponiren. (*P.W.* vi. 131.)
Über das Opern Dichten und Komponiren im besonderen. (*P.W.* vi. 149.)
Über die Anwendung der Musik auf das Drama. (*P.W.* vi. 173.)
Offenes Schreiben an Herrn Ernst von Weber, Verfasser der Schrift : ' Die Folterkammern der Wissenschaft.' (*P.W.* vi. 193.)
Religion und Kunst (1880) : ' Was nützt diese Erkenntniss ? ' Ein Nachtrag zu ' Religion und Kunst.' Ausführungen zu ' Religion und Kunst ' (1881). 1. ' Erkenne dich selbst.' 2. Heldenthum und Christenthum. (*P.W.* vi. 211.)
Brief an H. v. Wolzogen. (*P.W.* vi. 285.)
Offenes Schreiben an Herrn Friedrich Schön in Worms. (*P.W.* vi. 293.)
Das Bühnenfestspiel in Bayreuth, 1882. (*P.W.* vi. 301.)
Bericht über die Wiederaufführung eines Jugendwerkes. An den Herausgeber des ' Musikalischen Wochenblattes.' (*P.W.* vi. 313.)
Brief an H. v. Stein. (*P.W.* vi. 323.)
Parsifal.
(Lebenserinnerungen. This is the privately printed autobiography from which the extracts in vols. i., ii. and ix. mentioned above are taken.)[1]

An English translation by W. Ashton Ellis of the *Gesammelte Schriften*, excluding, with some minor exceptions, the poems, but including some additional essays, was published in 1892–99. The eight volumes appear under the general title *Richard Wagner's Prose Works* and have the following subtitles :
Vol. I. (1892). The Art-work of the Future, etc.
Vol. II. (1893). Opera and Drama.
Vol. III. (1894). The Theatre.
Vol. IV. (1895). Art and Politics.
Vol. V. (1896). Actors and Singers.
Vol. VI. (1897). Religion and Art.
Vol. VII. (1898). In Paris and Dresden.
Voi. VIII. (1899). Posthumous, etc.

SELECTED BOOKS, Etc.

GLASENAPP, C. F., und H. v. STEIN. *Wagner Lexicon.* Stuttgart, 1883. (An admirable compendium of Wagner's writings.)
GLASENAPP, C. F. *Richard Wagners Leben und Wirken.* 2 vols. 2nd ed. Leipzig, 1882. Based on an intimate acquaintance with Wagner's writings and a diligent study of periodicals, etc. Somewhat verbose and only partially trustworthy. 3rd and 4th editions, 1894 to 1911. 6 vols. As to the English version by W. A. Ellis, see below.
KASTNER, E. *Wagner Katalog.* 1878.
Briefe Richard Wagners an seine Zeitgenossen (1830–83) chronologische geordnet 1885. (A valuable list, but very far from complete.) A later edit on appeared in 1897 comprising 1470 letters.
ÖSTERLEIN, NIC. *Katalog einer R. Wagner Bibliothek.* 4 vols. Leipzig, 1882–95.
NIETZSCHE, FR. *Richard Wagner in Bayreuth (Unzeitgemässe Betrachtungen,* 4tes Stück). Chemnitz, 1876. *Die Geburt der Tragödie aus dem Geiste der Musik.* 1872. 2nd edition. Chemnitz, 1878.
Der Fall Wagner. 1888.
Nietzsche contra Wagner. 1889. (All are in the complete translation of Nietzsche's works.)
LISZT. *Lohengrin à Tannhäuser.* Leipzig, 1851.
Der fliegende Holländer (1854). *Das Rheingold* (1855). Vol. iii. of Liszt's *Gesammelte Schriften.* Leipzig, 1881.
BÜLOW, HANS VON. *Über R. Wagners Faust-Ouvertüre.* Leipzig, 1860.
MAYRBERGER, KARL. *Die Harmonik Richard Wagners.* Chemnitz, 1882.
SCHURÉ, ED. *Le Dramé musical.* 2 vols. Paris, 1875.
POHL, RICH. *Richard Wagner, ein Lebensbild.* Leipzig, 1883.
Richard Wagner. Studien und Kritiken. Leipzig, 1883.
TAPPERT, W. *Richard Wagner. Sein Leben und seine Werke.* Elberfeld, 1883
Ein Wagnerlexicon — Wörterbuch der Unhöflichkeit, enthaltend grobe, höhnende, gehässige und verläumderische Ausdrücke, welche gegen den Meister Richard Wagner von der Feinden und Spöttern gebraucht worden sind. Leipzig, 1877.
WOLZOGEN, H. v. *Erinnerungen an Richard Wagner.* Vienna, 1883.
Richard Wagners Lebensbericht. (Original of ' The Work and Mission of my Life,' *North American Review,* for Aug. and Sept. 1879. Sanctioned by Wagner, but apparently not written by him.) Leipzig, 1884.
Die Sprache in Richard Wagners Dichtungen. Leipzig, 1878. Full of valuable information.
Poetische Lautsymbolik. Leipzig, 1876.
Der Nibelungen Mythos in Sage und Literatur. Berlin, 1876.
Thematische Leitfäden : Nibelungen, Tristan, Parsifal.
PORGES, H. *Die Aufführung von Beethovens ixte. Symphonie unter Richard Wagner in Bayreuth.* Leipzig, 1872.
Die Buhnenproben zu den Festspielen im Jahre 1876. i. and ii. Chemnitz, 1883.
GASPERINI, A. DE. *Richard Wagner.* Paris, 1866.
BAUDELAIRE CH. *R. Wagner et Tannhäuser à Paris.* 1861.
WAGNER. *Quatre Poèmes d'opéra traduits en prose française, précédés d'une lettre sur la musique par Richard Wagner.* Paris, 1861.
MÜLLER, FRANZ. *Tannhäuser und Wartburgkrieg.* 1853.
Richard Wagner und das Musikdrama. 1861.
Der Ring des Nibelungen. 1862.
Tristan und Isolde. 1865.
Lohengrin und Die Meistersinger von Nürnberg. Munich, 1869.
HUEFFER, F. *Richard Wagner and the Music of the Future.* London, 1874. (Translated into German as *Die Poesie in der Musik.* Leipzig, 1874.)
Richard Wagner. London, 1881.
Parsifal : An Attempt at Analysis. London, 1884.

---

[1] It is founded on, or identical with, the brochure *Mein Leben,* of which only three copies were supposed to exist. Mrs. Burrell proves that there were many more (one in her possession), and that it is in many details untrustworthy. *Mein Leben* was published in 1911, see *infra*.

Richard Wagner's Letter on Liszt's Symphonic Poems. Translated by F. Hueffer. London, 1881.
WAGNER, R. *The Music of the Future.* Translated by E. Dannreuther. London, 1873.
Beethoven. Translated by E. Dannreuther. London, 1880.
On Conducting. Translated by E. Dannreuther. London, 1885.

Since the above article was written the mass of Wagner literature has increased enormously. From it a few of the more important works may be selected, with a preference for those in the English language.

(a) BIOGRAPHIES

WAGNER, R. *Mein Leben.* 2 vols. Munich, 1911.
My Life. 2 vols. London, 1911.
This is the autobiography up to the year 1864, dictated by Wagner to his wife, and privately printed in 1870. The English translation is not satisfactory, and a carefully revised edition is much to be desired. See Irvine's *Two Essays on Wagner.* London, 1912.
JULLIEN, ADOLPHE. *Richard Wagner, sa vie et ses œuvres.* Paris, 1886. (Profusely illustrated ; original lithographs by Fantin Latour.)
FINCK, H. T. *Wagner and his Works. The Story of his Life with Critical Comments.* 2 vols. New York, 1893.
CHAMBERLAIN, H. S. *Richard Wagner.* Munich, 1896. English translation, London and Philadelphia, 1900. (From the standpoint of a thorough-going disciple ; in close touch with the Bayreuth traditions ; not judicial, but accurate. Profusely illustrated : fine reproductions of Lenbach's portraits.)
ELLIS, W. ASHTON. *Life of Richard Wagner.* London, 1902–08. (This most exhaustive biography began as ' an authorised English version of C. F. Glasenapp's *Das Leben Richard Wagner*,' but as the original plan was widened in scope Glasenapp's name was, from the 4th volume onwards, omitted from the title-page. With the 6th volume, the last tc be published, the biography is brought down to the year 1859, from which some idea of the scale on which it was planned may be obtained. Though enthusiastic in tone, and very diffuse, it is generally accurate in all matters of fact.)
BURRELL, the HON. MRS. *Richard Wagner's Life and Works, 1813–34.* In 1898 a sumptuous book, the first portion of a projected life of the master, was issued (100 copies only), as a memorial of the author, who had devoted many years and much money to obtaining authoritative materials. A second instalment is promised, and a reprint of the first at an ordinary price is to be desired. The volume is engraved throughout, and every statement made is fully substantiated by facsimiles of the documents referred to. Many mistakes, copied from one book to another, have been finally corrected.
HIGHT, GEORGE AINSLIE. *Richard Wagner : a Critical Biography.* London, 1925. 2 vols. (The fullest completed biography as yet published in English.)
RUNCIMAN, J. F. *Richard Wagner, Composer of Operas.* London, 1913. (A highly individualised view of Wagner's art.)
NEWMAN, ERNEST. *Wagner as Man and Artist.* London, 1914. A second (revised) edition was published in New York in 1924 ; in London, 1926. (A brilliant appreciation of Wagner's art ; a less enthusiastic appreciation of his personal character.)
WALLACE, WILLIAM. *Richard Wagner as he lived.* London, 1925. (A valuable contribution, though not exhaustive ; following on Newman's lines, but containing the results of much careful research and correcting a good many errors in earlier writers.)
KAPP, JULIUS. *Richard Wagner und die Frauen. Eine erotische Biographie.* Berlin, 1912.
ENGEL, ERICH W. *Richard Wagners Leben und Werke im Bilde.* 2 vols. Vienna and Leipzig, 1913. 2nd ed. 1922. (A collection of over 500 illustrations : portraits, places, opera bills, autographs, scenes, costumes, etc.)

(b) CORRESPONDENCE
(English translations are given when such exist.)

Correspondence of Wagner and Liszt. Translated by Franck Hueffer. 2 vols. London, 1888.
Richard Wagner's Letters to his Dresden Friends, Theodor Uhlig, Wilhelm Fischer and Ferdinand Heine. Translated by J. S. Shedlock. London, 1890.
Richard Wagner's Letters to August Roeckel. Translated by Eleanor C. Sellar. Bristol, n.d.
Richard Wagner : Letters to Wesendonck et al. Translated by W. Ashton Ellis. London, 1899.
Letters of Richard Wagner to Emil Heckel, with a brief history of the Bayreuth Festivals. Translated by W. Ashton Ellis. London, 1899.
Richard Wagner to Mathilde Wesendonck. Translated by W. Ashton Ellis. London, 1905.
Familienbriefe von Richard Wagner, 1832–74. Berlin, 1907. C. F. Glasenapp. Transl. by W. Ashton Ellis. London, 1911.
Bayreuther Briefe von Richard Wagner, 1871–83. Berlin and Leipzig, 1907. C. F. Glasenapp. Transl. by C. V. Kerr London, n.d. (1913).
Richard Wagner an Minna Wagner. 2 vols. Berlin and Leipzig, 1908. N. von Wolzogen. English translation by W. A. Ellis. London, 1909.
Richard Wagner an seine Künstler. Erich Kloss. Berlin, 1908.
Richard Wagner an Eliza Wille. Berlin : new ed., 1908. W. Golther.
Richard Wagner an Freunde und Zeitgenossen. Berlin ; 2nd ed., 1909. Erich Kloss.
Richard Wagner an Theodor Apel. Leipzig, 1910.
The Nietzsche-Wagner Correspondence. London, 1922. Elizabeth Foerster-Nietzsche. Translated by C. V. Kerr.
Richard Wagner an Hans Richter (1868–83). Berlin and Vienna, 1925. Ludwig Karpath.
Richard Wagner an Julie Ritter.
Richard Wagner und Albert Niemann. (Berlin, 1924. W. Altmann.)
Richard Wagner und seine erste ' Elisabeth ' Johanna Jachmann-Wagner. Ein neuer Beitrag zur Wagnerforschung : edited by

Dr. Julius Kapp and Hans Jachmann (Dom-Verlag, Berlin,
1927). In 2 parts : (1) Richard Wagner's relations with his
brother Albert's family, by Dr. Kapp ; (2) Johanna Jachmann-
Wagner, a biography by H. Jachmann. Contains many letters
of Wagner hitherto unpublished, several illustrations, and a
genealogical table of the Wagner family from Samuel Wagner,
1643–1705.

———

A chronological summary of Wagner's letters may be found in
W. Altmann's *Richard Wagners Briefe nach Zeitfolge und Inhalt.*
See also Kastner's *Briefe Richard Wagners* (*supra*). A complete
edition of all Wagner's letters is promised by Breitkopf & Härtel.

(c) PERSONAL RECOLLECTIONS

FRICKE, R. *Bayreuth vor dreissig Jahren. Erinnerungen an
Wahnfried und aus dem Festspielhause.* (Includes 10 letters
from Wagner.) Dresden, 1906.
GAUTHIER, JUDITH. *Wagner at Home.* Translated by E. D.
Massie. (London, 1910.)
HEY, HANS. *Richard Wagner als Vortragsmeister.* (Leipzig, 1911.)
KIETZ, G. A. *Richard Wagner in den Jahren 1842–49 und 1873–
1875.* Dresden, 1905.
METTERNICH, PRINCESS PAULINE. *The Days that are no more. Some
Reminiscences.* London, 1921. Ch. iv. contains an account
of the Paris production of ' Tannhäuser ' in 1861.
MICHOTTE, E. *Souvenirs personnels. La Visite de R. Wagner
à Rossini (Paris, 1860).* Paris, 1906.
NEUMANN, A. *Erinnerungen an Richard Wagner.* Leipzig, 1907.
(Deals more particularly with the introduction of the ' Ring'
in various cities soon after the first Bayreuth performances
of 1876, including the introduction of that work to London
in 1882. Many of Wagner's letters are given.) Published in
an English translation in 1909.
PERL, HENRY. *Richard Wagner in Venedig. Mosaikbilder aus
seinen letzten Lebenstagen* Augsburg, 1883.
PRAEGER, F. *Wagner as I knew him.* London, 1892. (The
accuracy of this book has been seriously called in question,
and the German version was on this account withdrawn by
the publishers. See H. S. Chamberlain, ' Echte Briefe an
Ferdinand Praeger.' Bayreuth, 1894.)
SCHILLING, A. *Aus Richard Wagners Jugendzeit.* Berlin, n.d.
1898. (Derived chiefly from the recollections of Wagner's
step-sister, Caecilie Avenarius.)
STEINER, A. *Richard Wagner in Zürich.* (New Year's publications
of the Allgemeine Musik Gesellschaft in Zürich, 1901, 1902,
1903 : Zürich, Orell Füssli.)
WEISSHEIMER, W. *Erlebnisse mit Richard Wagner, Franz Liszt
und vielen anderen Zeitgenossen, nebst deren Briefen.* Stuttgart
and Leipzig, 1898.
WILLE, ELIZA. *Richard Wagner und Eliza Wille. Fünfzehn
Briefe des Meisters nebst Erinnerungen und Erläuterungen.*
WOLZOGEN, H. VON. *Recollections of Richard Wagner.* Translated
by A. and C. Simpson. Bayreuth, 1894.

(d) MISCELLANEOUS

BOURNOT, OTTO. *Ludwig Heinrich Christian Geyer, der Stiefvater
Richard Wagners.* Leipzig, 1913. (Already referred to as
demonstrating the German antecedents of the Geyer family.)
GRAND-CARTERET, J. *Richard Wagner en caricatures. 130 Re-
productions de caricatures, etc.* Paris, n.d.
KREHBIEL, H. E. *Studies in the Wagnerian Drama.* London, 1891.
KREOWSKI, E., and FUCHS, E. *Richard Wagner in der Karikatur.*
Berlin, 1907. (230 reproductions.)
NEWMAN, E. *A Study of Wagner.* London, 1899. (Appreciative
but critical.)
The Music of the Masters. Wagner. London. n.d. 1904.
(A concise critical survey.)
SHAW, G. B. *The Perfect Wagnerite : a Commentary on the Nib-
lung's Ring.* London, 1898 ; 2nd edition, 1903. (A very
individual interpretation.)
VANSELOW, A. *Richard Wagners photographische Bildnisse.*
Munich, 1908. (A collection of 34 photographic portraits of
Wagner.)
WEINGARTNER, F. *Bayreuth (1876–96).* 2nd ed. Leipzig, 1904.
DANNREUTHER, E. *Oxford History of Music,* vol. vi. ch. xiv., on
Wagner's earlier operas.
BULTHAUPT, H. *Dramaturgie der Oper.* 1902 : vol. ii.
The Meister, the Quarterly Journal of the London Branch of
the Wagner Society, first appeared in 1888 and ended with the
8th volume in 1895. It contains, in addition to sundry Wagneriana,
some translations which afterwards appeared in the ' Prose Works.'
Of commentaries on the music dramas there is no end, but these
do not come within the scope of the present article.
For exact details of composition, first performances, publication
and orchestration of the purely orchestral works (including the
overtures to the operas) see Müller-Reuter, *Lexicon der deutschen
Konzert-literatur,* vol. i., 1909, pp. 440 *et seq.*
Mention should be made of some carefully produced facsimiles
of Wagner's autograph scores, issued by the Drei Masken Verlag,
Munich. ' Tristan,' ' Meistersinger' and the ' Siegfried Idyll'
have thus appeared.
For a fuller bibliography see G. A. HIGHT's *Richard Wagner,
a Critical Biography.*

SOME FRENCH PUBLICATIONS

Among the more important publications which have appeared
in France may be mentioned the following :
SILÈGE, HENRI. *Bibliographie Wagnérienne française.* 1902.
Includes all French works from 1851–1902.
PROD'HOMME J. G., HOLL, CAILLÉ et VAN VASSENHOVE. *Œuvres
en prose.* 1908–25. 13 vols. (Transl. of the *Gesammelte
Schriften.*)
VALENTIN, N., and SCHENK, A. *Ma Vie.* 1911. 3 vols. (Transla-
tion of ' Mein Leben.')
PROD'HOMME, J. G. *Richard Wagner et la France* (1920).
CURZON, H. DE. *L'Œuvre de Richard Wagner à Paris et ses inter-
prètes (1850–1914).* Paris, n.d. (1920).
DAURIAC, L. *Le Musicien-poète Richard Wagner. Étude de
psychologie suivie d'une bibliographie raisonnée* (1908).
MARNOLD, J. *Le Cas Wagner* (1917).

E. D. ; with addns. and corrs. by H. T.

(2) JOHANNA (*b.* Hanover, Oct. 13, 1826 ;
d. Würzburg, Oct. 16, 1894), niece of Richard
Wagner and daughter of Albert Wagner, a
dramatic tenor. He married Elise Gollmann,
who had a voice of the abnormal compass of
three octaves and two notes, and who in her
very short career is said to have sung the parts
of Tancredi and of the Queen of Night with
equal fullness of tone.

Johanna appeared at the age of 6 as Salome in
the ' Donauweibchen.' In 1843 her uncle heard
her sing the part of Myrrha in Winter's ' Unterbrochenes Opferfest,' and in May 1844 obtained
a temporary engagement for her at the Royal
Opera at Dresden.[1] Though but 18 she had
such success as Irma in ' Maurer und Schlosser,'
and Agathe in ' Der Freischütz,' that she was not
only engaged for three years, but the manage
ment paid the fine necessary to release her from
her contract at the Ducal Theatre at Bernburg.
She spent the summer with her uncle near
Dresden, studying his ' Tannhäuser ' scene by
scene, as he composed it, and had the honour
of creating the part of Elisabeth when only 17.
Her uncle had intended the first performance
to take place on her nineteenth birthday, but
the illness of a singer postponed it until Oct. 21,
1845. However, when his friends assembled
at his house for supper that night, Johanna
found, hidden under her napkin, a little gold
bracelet engraved with her name and the date,
a proof of his satisfaction with her performance,
which was always her greatest treasure.

Such hopes were founded upon the talents
of the young singer that the King of Saxony
sent her to Paris to study under Garcia. She
left Dresden, Feb. 1, 1847, accompanied by
her father, who until then had been her instructor. Returning in six months she appeared as Norma, singing in Italian, her uncle
conducting. She now added to her repertory
Fidelio, Valentine, Adriano, Susanna, Reiza,
Favorita, Donna Anna, Recha, Euryanthe,
Ernani, Sextus, Weisse Dame, etc. Her
uncle's part in the revolutionary troubles of
1849, and consequent exile, making it unpleasant for her to remain in Dresden, she
accepted an engagement at Hamburg ; there
she sang the part of Fidès in the first German
production of the ' Prophète,' and gave it
fifty times in succession. In 1850 she was permanently engaged at the Royal Opera House in
Berlin, with an exceptional contract giving her
six months' leave each year.

In 1852 she came to England, but owing
to a lawsuit concerning her contract she was
precluded from singing at either of the
opera houses. In 1856 she appeared at Her
Majesty's Theatre as Tancredi, Lucrezia Borgia
and Romeo.[2]

———

[1] See *Familien Briefe,* p. 135, where in a letter of July 28, 1844,
Wagner mentions Johanna's fine singing of the part of Irene in
' Rienzi.' [2] See Chorley's *Recollections,* ii. 175, 242.

In 1859 she married Landrath Jachmann, and two years later had the misfortune to lose her voice suddenly and completely. She then bravely entered upon a second artistic career, as an actress, her very exceptional gifts enabling her to do so with brilliant success. This lasted for eleven years, at the same theatre at Berlin. Meantime her voice had returned to a great extent, and on May 22, 1872, at her uncle's request, she went to Bayreuth, to take part in the performance of Beethoven's Ninth Symphony, which he gave to celebrate the laying of the first stone to his theatre there. She sang the solo alto part, as she had done on Palm Sunday twenty-six years before, at his performance of the same symphony at Dresden. In 1876, at the opening of the Festspielhaus at Bayreuth, she took the minor parts of Schwertleite and first Norn.

In 1882 Baron von Perfall, Intendant of the Royal Opera at Munich, offered her the professorship of dramatic singing, in the Royal School of Music there. This appointment she accepted (to quote her own words) ' in the hope of training young artists in the spirit and traditions of my uncle, to be worthy interpreters of his works.' In 1884 she retired from this post, and went to live in Berlin. M. B.

(3) HELFERICH SIEGFRIED RICHARD (b. Triebschen, June 6, 1869), son of Richard Wagner and Cosima, was at first intended for an architect, and actually designed the monument to his grandfather, Liszt, at Bayreuth ; he preferred to follow in his father's footsteps, although at a considerable distance, and after studying with Humperdinck and Kniese, acted as subconductor at Bayreuth in 1894 and subsequent years, directing some of the performances from 1896 onwards. The control of the theatre and its festivals naturally passed into his hands when Mme. Wagner relinquished her personal responsibility. (See BAYREUTH.) A symphonic poem, ' Sehnsucht,' was brought out in 1895, and played with fair success wherever his father's music was most ardently admired. His first opera, ' Der Bärenhäuter,' was played at Munich in 1899, a second, ' Herzog Wildfang,' at the same place in 1901, and ' Der Kobold ' at Hamburg in 1904. Since then he has maintained a fairly steady output of composition, chiefly for the stage, but including a few concerted instrumental works. His later operas include :

'Bruder Lustig.' (Hamburg, 1905.)
'Sternengebot.' (Hamburg, 1908.)
Barradietrich.' (Carlsruhe 1910.)
'Der Heiden König.' (1915.)
An allem ist Hütchen Schuld.' (1916.)
'Schwarzschwarrenreich.' (Carlsruhe, 1918.)
'Der Schmied von Marienberg.' (1920.)

BIBL.—CARL FRIEDRICH GLASENAPP, Siegfried Wagner und seine Kunst, etc., 3 series (Leipzig, 1911, 1913, 1919) ; PAUL PRETYSCH,. Die Kunst Siegfried Wagners. Ein Führer durch seine Werke (Leipzig, 1919) ; S. WAGNER, Erinnerungen (Stuttgart, 1923).

WAILLY, LOUIS AUGUSTE PAUL DE (b. Amiens, Somme. May 16, 1854), French com-

poser, studied law and was self-taught in music. He was recommended by Romain Bussine (one of the founders of the Société Nationale de Musique), at the age of 27, to César Franck, who became his only master in composition. He remained faithful all his life to the principles of the latter's school.

P. de Wailly's principal works were first performed at the Société Nationale de Musique ; his début there was ' Hylas, idylle antique,' in 2 tableaux (1882), words by J. Lorrain. He has composed chamber music (sonatas, quintet, octet, etc.), 3 symphonies, church music, a few songs and a dramatic oratorio, ' L'Apôtre,' 4 acts (Paris, Eschig), performed at the Théâtre des Champs Élysées, Paris, Dec. 1924.
M. L. P.

WAINWRIGHT, HARRIET, afterwards Mrs. Colonel Stewart, composer, flourished between 1780–1840. She was probably one of the Cheshire Wainwrights (see below). She composed ' Comâla,' a dramatic poem from Ossian (1803), choruses, a glee, songs, duets, trios, etc. She also wrote Critical Remarks on the Art of Singing (Brown and Stratton). E. v. d. s.

WAINWRIGHT, (1) JOHN (d. Jan. 1768), a native of Stockport, Cheshire, settled in Manchester about the middle of the 18th century, and on May 12, 1767, was appointed organist and singing-man of the Collegiate Church, now the cathedral. He composed anthems, chants and psalm-tunes, a collection of which he published in 1766.

His three sons were : (2) ROBERT, Mus.D. (b. Stockport, 1748 ; d. July 15, 1782), accumulated the degrees of Mus.B. and Mus.D. at Oxford, Apr. 29, 1774. On Mar. 1, 1775, he was appointed organist of St. Peter's, Liverpool. He succeeded his father as organist of the Collegiate Church, Manchester, in 1768. He composed services and anthems, and an oratorio, ' The Fall of Egypt,' performed at Liverpool in 1780 and 1801.

(3) RICHARD (b. Manchester, 1758 ; d. Aug. 20, 1825), was organist of St. Ann's, Manchester. In Sept. 1782 he was chosen to succeed his brother, Robert, as organist of St. Peter's, Liverpool, which he afterwards quitted for the organistship of St. James's, Toxteth Park, Liverpool, but in 1813 resumed his place at St. Peter's. He published a collection of hymn-tunes of his composition. His glee, ' Life's a bumper,' was very popular. His execution was remarkable — more remarkable perhaps than his taste.

(4) WILLIAM (b. Stockport ; d. July 2, 1797), was a singing-man at the Collegiate Church, Manchester, and also a performer on the double bass, besides carrying on the business of musicselling in Manchester, in partnership with Sudlow. W. H. H.

WAISSEL (WAISSELIUS), MATTHEUS (b. Bartenstein), a 16th-century lutenist, at one time pastor at Lackheim (?). In 1573 he calls himself Moderator of the School of Schippenbell (now Schippenbeil, district of Königsberg). He wrote :

'Tabulatura continens . . . cantiones 4, 5 et 6 vocum, testudini aptatas, ut sunt Praeambula, Phantasiae, Cantiones, germanicae, italicae, gallicae et latinae, Passamesiae, Gagliardiae et Choreae ' (Frankfort a/O, 1573) ;
'Tabulatura oder Lautenbuch allerley künstlicher Präambula, auserlesener teutscher und polnischer Täntze,' etc. (1592—according to Riemann a second edition of above) ;
'Lautenbuch, darinnen von der Tabulatur und Application der Lauten gründlicher und voller Unterricht : sampt auserlesenen deutschen und polnischen Tentzen ' ; . . . etc. (1592) ;
'Tabulatura Guter gemeiner Deudtscher Tentze ' for one and two lutes, durch Quarten, zusammen zu schlagen (1592).

E. v. d. s.

WAIT (WAYTE, WAIGHT), an obsolete musical instrument of the hautboy type used by the WAITS (q.v.) or watchmen and identical with the earlier SHAWM. According to Henry Davey's Hist. Eng. Mus., the statutes of Edward I. (before 1296) provided for the City of London that each gate shall be ' shut by the servant dwelling there and each servant shall have a wayte, at his own expense.' In a Nominale of the 15th century the low Latin word Calamaula, a reed-pipe—whence the word Shawm—is translated ' wayte pipe,' and in a 17th-century MS. (Harl. 2029) there is a sketch of a reed-pipe to which is appended the threefold title ' a Howboye or a Wayte or a Shawm.'

. On the Minstrels' Pillar in St. Mary's Church, Beverley, is represented the figure of a minstrel with his 'wait.'

F. W. G.

WAITS, THE. (1) In early times Waits were the night guards stationed at city gates. They were provided with a reed instrument, of the hautboy kind, for the purpose of signalling, or sounding at regular intervals to proclaim ' All's Well.'

Gradually, we may assume that musical effects were produced by the original instruments and by others added to them. In the 15th and 16th centuries the Waits had developed into paid bands of musicians supported by the towns and cities for the purpose of playing at civic functions, etc. They were accustomed to welcome distinguished visitors into the towns, and many of the entries in MS. books of household expenses are donations to the Waits of different towns. This practice had not died out in the 18th century, for in Humphrey Clinker, Matthew Bramble is welcomed to Bath by the Town Waits calling at his lodgings and playing. At Christmas it was the custom for the Town Waits to visit the houses of notables, playing and singing suitable music, and the term ' Christmas Waits ' survives as applied to these players and their imitators. In the 16th and 17th centuries it is quite evident that members of the Town

Waits were skilled musicians. William Kemp, in his account of his nine days' Morris from London to Norwich in 1599, speaks of being welcomed by the City Waits. He further says :

' Such Waytes (under Benedicitie be it spoken) few citties in the Realme haue the like, none better ; who besides their excellency in wind instruments, their rare cunning on the Vyoll and Violin, theyre voices be admirable, euerie one of them able to serue in any Cathedrall Church in Christendome for Quiresters.' [1]

Several distinguished musicians have arisen from the ranks of the Waits. The father of Orlando Gibbons was one of the Waits at Cambridge ; the father of John Banister was one of St. Giles in the Fields ; and John Ravenscroft, a composer of some clever triple time hornpipes and one of the band belonging to Goodmans Fields Theatre, was a Wait of the Tower Hamlets.

In certain places silver badges bearing the town's arms were issued to the official Waits. Leeds maintained four Waits in the 17th century, and one of the silver badges is still in existence.

(2) The name was also applied to pieces of music supposed to have been played or sung by the Waits of particular towns or cities, as especially associated with these places. Thus we get ' London Waits,' ' Chester Waits,' ' Colchester Waits,' ' Worksop Waits,' ' Oxford Waits,' ' Bristol Waits,' ' York Waits ' and so on. Many of these are preserved in 17th- and 18th-century country dance-books, the earliest specimen in print known to the writer being one named ' The Waits ' in the 3rd edition of the Dancing Master, 1665, among the tunes at the end.

In the reissue of this part of the book under the title Apollo's Banquet the air is named ' London Waits.'

The Waits.

From 'The Dancing Master,' 1665.

A more famous air for four voices, also named ' The Waits,' is by Jeremy Savile, and is published in Playford's Musical Companion, 1672–73.

It is a fine melody, and is sung to the syllables ' Fa, la, la.' The meetings of the Madrigal Society maintain the custom of concluding their music with the singing of this piece four times.

F. K.

WAKE, WILLIAM, organist about 1640–50 of Exeter Cathedral, when Matthew LOCKE (q.v.)

[1] Nine Daies Wonder, 1600.

was a choirboy there. Wake was sworn in as a gentleman of the Chapel Royal, Aug. 7, 1663. It was he who encouraged Locke to write his 'Little Consort' in three parts for viols or violins (published by Playford in 1656), as the latter tells us in the preface, where he speaks of Wake as 'an intimate friend and great Master in Musick.'   E. V. D. S.

WAKEFIELD, AUGUSTA MARY (b. Sedgwick, near Kendal, Westmorland, Aug. 19, 1853; d. Grange-over-Sands, Sept. 16, 1910), studied singing under Randegger, Henschel, Blumenthal, and with Alari at Rome, where she also had piano lessons from Sgambati; she made a remarkable success as an amateur contralto singer and composer of songs, and after appearing at many charity concerts in London and elsewhere, was engaged at the Gloucester Festival of 1880, and sang at various important concerts. Her voice was of rich quality, and her artistic temperament carried conviction to all her hearers.

In 1885 she established the first of the competitive festivals with which her name is inseparably connected. The occasion was a modest competition at her home at Sedgwick, but in the following year the event was transferred to Kendal where it has flourished ever since. This Westmorland festival became the model for a far-reaching movement (see COMPETITION FESTIVALS). It grew so rapidly that in later years Mary Wakefield's energies became well-nigh exclusively devoted to it. Meantime in 1890 she had definitely adopted the profession of lecturer on music, illustrating her own lectures with great success. She edited an anthology called *Ruskin on Music*, and contributed to various periodicals.   M., addns.

BIBL.—ROSA NEWMARCH, *Mary Wakefield—a Memoir*. (Kendal, 1912.)

WALD, DER, opera in one act; words and music by Ethel M. Smyth. Produced, Dresden, Sept. 1901; Covent Garden, July 18, 1902; Metropolitan Opera-House, New York, Mar. 1903.

WALDERSEE, PAUL, GRAF VON (b. Potsdam, Sept. 3, 1831; d. Königsberg, June 14, 1906), a distinguished editor of the musical classics. In 1848-71 he was an officer in the Prussian army, but after the latter date devoted himself wholly to music, taking an active part in the preparation of Breitkopf & Härtel's great editions of Mozart and Beethoven. He also edited the enlarged reprint of Köchel's Mozart-catalogue. An important publication for which he was mainly responsible was the *Sammlung musikalischer Vorträge*, which appeared from 1879-84, and included monographs by various distinguished writers on the great masters, partly biographical and partly analytical. He contributed to the most important musical periodicals of Germany. M.

WALD FLUTE, an open treble wood organ stop of 8-feet and 4-feet pitch, rather similar to the Clarabella, but having the splay of the mouth inverted, *i.e.* inside the pipe.   T. E.

WALDHORN, the German name for the large circular hunting-horn or *cor de chasse* (see HORN).   D. J. B.

WALDSTEIN, COUNT FERDINAND ERNST GABRIEL (b. Mar. 24, 1762; d. Aug. 29, 1823), one of Beethoven's earliest friends, immortalised by the dedication of the PF. Sonata in C, op. 53, now usually known as the 'Waldstein Sonata.' Ferdinand was the youngest of the four sons of Emmanuel Philipp, Graf Waldstein und Wartemberg von Dux. He was born just eight years before Beethoven, and his father died in 1775, leaving the property to the eldest son Joseph Carl Emmanuel. Ferdinand when of age (24 according to the German law) entered the 'German order' (Deutscher Orden) as a career; in 1812, however, he obtained a dispensation from his vows and married, but, like all his brothers, died without male issue, and thus with this generation the house of Waldstein von Dux became extinct. Count Ferdinand spent the year of his novitiate (1787-88 [1]) at the court of the Elector at Bonn, and it was then that he became acquainted with BEETHOVEN (q.v.). Vol. I. p. 261. In 1791 or 1792 Beethoven composed twelve variations for four hands on the PF. on an air of the Count's, and in 1804 or 1805 he wrote the Sonata which has made the name of Waldstein so familiar. In this splendid work (published May 1805) the well-known 'Andante Favori' in F was originally the slow movement; but Beethoven took it out, as too long, and substituted the present Adagio for it. The Adagio is in a different coloured ink from the rest of the autograph.   G.

WALDTEUFEL, EMIL (b. Strassburg, Dec. 9, 1837; d. Paris, Feb. 12, 1912), a pupil of the Paris Conservatoire under Marmontel and Laurent, was afterwards employed in a piano factory, and was appointed pianist to the Empress Eugénie. His first waltzes, 'Joies et peines' and 'Manola,' were published at his own expense, and were such a success that he devoted himself exclusively to the production of similar things, which eventually reached many hundreds.   M.

WALEY, SIMON WALEY (b. London, Aug. 23, 1827; d. Dec. 30, 1875), composer and pianist. He was a pupil successively of Moscheles, Bennett and G. A. Osborne for the piano, and of W. Horsley and Molique for theory and composition. He began composing very early, and wrote several elaborate PF. pieces before he was 12. His first published work, 'L'Arpeggio,' a PF. study, appeared in 1848. It was speedily followed by a number

[1] Thayer, i. 178 (2nd ed. i. 213-18); *Krehbiel*, i. 102.

of songs and pianoforte pieces, including a
concerto with orchestral accompaniment, and
two pianoforte trios, op. 15 in B♭ and op. 20 in
G minor (published by Schott & Co.). Simon
Waley was an accomplished pianist, and frequently performed at the concerts of the
Amateur Musical Society, conducted by Henry
Leslie. His compositions abound in the plaintive melody characteristic of Mendelssohn;
they exhibit great finish, and a richness of
detail and harmony not unworthy of the best
disciples of the Leipzig school. He was a
prominent member of the London Stock
Exchange, and for many years took an active
part on the committee. He is buried in the
Jewish Cemetery at Ball's Pond. He belonged
to the Jewish faith, and was a leading member
of that community during the critical period
of its emancipation from civil disabilities. One
of his finest works is a choral setting of the
117th and 118th Psalms for the Synagogue
service.

His published works, besides those already
mentioned, contain a large number of pieces
for piano, solo and duet; two duets for violin
and piano; songs and duets, etc. etc. The
choruses for the Synagogue mentioned above
are published in vol. i. of the *Musical Services
of the West London Synagogue*. Besides the
printed works some orchestral pieces remain in
MS.   G.

WALKELEY, ANTONY (*b*. Wells, 1672;
d. Jan. 16, 1717–18), was a chorister and afterwards a vicar-choral of Wells Cathedral. In
1698 he was appointed organist of Salisbury
Cathedral as successor to Daniel Roseingrave.
His Morning Service in E♭ is preserved in the
Tudway Collection (Harl. MS. 7342), and
anthems by him are in MS. at Ely Cathedral
and in the R.C.M.   W. H. H.

WALKER, EBERHARDT FRIEDRICH, an
organ-builder at Cannstadt, Stuttgart, in the
middle of the 18th century, with his son, of the
same names, was one of the best builders in
Germany. In 1820 he removed to Ludwigsburg. His European reputation is due to the
fine organ which he built in 1833 for the church
of St. Paul at Frankfort-on-the-Main. In 1856
he completed a large organ for Ulm Cathedral
of 100 stops on four manuals and two pedals,
and a new movement for drawing out all the
stops in succession to produce a *crescendo*. This
can be reversed for a *diminuendo*. In 1863
he carried his fame to the New World by
erecting a large organ in the Music Hall,
Boston, U.S.   V. DE P.

WALKER, ERNEST, D.Mus. (*b*. Bombay,
July 15, 1870), pianist, composer and writer on
music, was educated at Balliol College, Oxford,
where he graduated B.A. in *Lit. Hum.* in 1891.
He took his D.Mus. in 1898 and has been
closely associated with his College and University throughout his career, since from 1900–

1925 he was director of the music at Balliol and
presided over the Sunday concerts of chamber
music, which have been a potent factor in the
musical life of Oxford. In 1926 he was elected
to an honorary fellowship of Balliol. As an
examiner, a member of the Board of Studies
for music and a teacher in the University his
academic work has been important.

Walker educated himself in music by close
and practical study of the classics, and the
German masters (particularly Beethoven and
Brahms) and German literature formed the
ground plan of his studies. But with a mind
too active to be confined to one school, however
great, he has extended his outlook to other
methods and other times, and is a scholar
alike of the new and the old. For a few years
(1899–1902) he edited a quarterly periodical,
the *Musical Gazette*; in 1905 he wrote *Beethoven*
(*Music of the Masters*, John Lane), a monograph which touches with a sure hand on the
principal compositions of its subject. But his
most important literary work is *A History
of Music in England* (1907, second revised
edition, 1923), which is a standard work of
reference and deals trenchantly with every
phase of musical composition from 'Sumer
is i-cumen in' to modern times. He was an
important contributor to the second edition of
this Dictionary as also to the present one.

The greater number of Walker's compositions are in MS. He has been content to
write thoughtfully and finely without care for
publicity, and his chamber music compositions,
heard only occasionally in London, Oxford and
elsewhere, deserve a wider recognition. In
such songs as 'Bluebells from the clearings'
and 'Corinna going a-maying' he exhibits a
vein of intimate feeling for the implications
of English poetry and an instinct for apt
musical expression which place him high
among the song-writers of his generation. His
vocal quartets (with PF. accomp.) from 'England's Helicon' are equally fascinating and
have been widely sung. The following is a
list of his principal compositions:

Stabat Mater for soli, chorus, and orch.
Hymn to Dionysus (Euripides), for chorus and orch. (Novello.)
Ode to a Nightingale (Keats), for baritone solo, chorus and orch.
   (Novello.)
Concert-Overture in F minor for orch.
Quintet in A for piano and strings.
Quintet in B flat minor for horn and strings.
Quartets in C minor and D for piano and strings.
Fantasia in D for string quartet.
Trio in C minor for piano and strings.
Sonatas in A minor and E flat for violin and PF. (Williams.)
Variations for viola and piano. (Schott.)
Variations for piano and viola.
Sonata in F minor for v'cl. and piano.
Songs from 'England's Helicon' for four solo voices and piano.
Music to Euripides' *Rhesus*, for soli, chor. and orch.
'Neptune's Empire' (Campion), for chor. and orch.
Variations on a Theme of Joachim, for vln. and PF.
Album of Songs (Acott, Oxford), and many smaller instrumental
   and vocal works of all kinds.
(See *B.M.S. Ann.* 1920.)

                                          C.

WALKER, GEORGE. The founder of an
extensive music-publishing business, established towards the end of the 18th century, at
106 Great Portland Street, and at 9 Brook

Street. The latter address only occurs on a few early imprints. He was at 106 Great Portland Street about 1790, and remained there until 1824, having, in 1822, additional premises at 64 Burlington Street. In 1824 he removed to 17 Soho Square, and as ' George Walker & Son ' the firm remained here until the 'thirties and 'forties.

It is probable that he was the originator of the absurd practice of marking sheet-music at double what it was sold for ; this is gathered from the statement in the London Directory that he is ' publisher of music at " half-price." ' He was author of several novels, *Cinthela, The Three Spaniards, Don Raphael,* etc., and a book of *Poems on Various Occasions.* William Walker of 116 Portland Street, probably a relative, published sheet-music about 1794.

F. K.

WALKER & SONS, JOSEPH W., organ-builders in Francis Street, Tottenham Court Road, London. This business was originated by George England in 1740, who was succeeded by his son and his son-in-law, H. Nicholls, to whom J. W. Walker was apprenticed. Walker took over the business after Nicholls' death in 1820, established it in Museum Street in 1828, removed it to 166 High Holborn in 1830, and in 1838 to Francis Street, W.C. He died in 1870, and the factory was carried on by his son, James John (*b.* Aug. 21, 1846 ; *d.* Sept. 19, 1922). The latter, a practical scientist, who had worked .is way through every stage of the business, was responsible for a very large number of famous organs and for the high position which the firm still occupies. See *Mus. T.,* Nov. 1922, p. 807.

v. de P., addns.

WALKÜRE, DIE, see RING DES NIBE-LUNGEN.

WALLACE (GRACE), LADY (*b.* Apr. 1815 ; *d.* 1878), daughter of John Stein of Edinburgh, married in 1836 Sir James Maxwell Wallace, who died 1867.

She translated the following musical works :

Two vols. of Mendelssohn's Letters : *From Italy and Switzerland* (1862) ; *From 1833 to 1847* (1863) ; *Letters of Mozart,* 2 vols. (1865) ; *Reminiscences of Mendelssohn,* by Elise Polko (1865) ; *Letters of Beethoven,* 2 vols. (1866) ; *Letters of distinguished Musicians,* from a collection by Ludwig Nohl (1867) ; Nohl's *Life of Mozart* (1877). All published by Longman & Co., London.

G.

WALLACE, WILLIAM (*b.* Greenock, July 3, 1860), is the son of the late James Wallace, M.D., an eminent Scottish surgeon. He was educated at Fettes College, where he gained a Trustees' Exhibition to Edinburgh University. This he resigned and entered Glasgow University, where he graduated M.B. and M.Ch. in 1886, and went to Vienna to study ophthalmic surgery. He graduated with honours in Glasgow in 1888, and was on the staff of eye hospitals both in Glasgow and London. He abandoned this profession for music, however, only resuming it temporarily during the war

(1914–18) when he served with the British Red Cross and in the R.A.M.C. (Captain) as inspector of ophthalmic centres.[1]

In 1889 he entered the R.A.M. as a student, but did not long remain there. Nevertheless his connexion with the institution was maintained ; he was successively elected A.R.A.M. and F.R.A.M. and is now (1927) on the professorial staff. He has also been closely associated with the ROYAL PHILHARMONIC SOCIETY (*q.v.*), to whose affairs he has devoted much time and energy both as Honorary Secretary and later as Trustee. Wallace's public career as a composer was begun when his scena for baritone solo and orchestra, ' Lord of Darkness,' was given at a R.A.M. students' concert, and an orchestral suite, ' The Lady from the Sea ' (Ibsen), was given by the Stock Exchange Orchestra in 1892. In this year, too, his first symphonic poem, ' The Passing of Beatrice,' said to be the first British work with that generic title, was heard at the Crystal Palace. A series of orchestral works appeared on several occasions (see list below) and in 1899 the production of certain works at New Brighton (see BANTOCK) including the ' Freebooter Songs ' made him famous. Of his several symphonic poems ' Villon ' (1909) is generally considered to be the most representative, and has been the most widely played both in England and America. A man of many parts, Wallace has devoted his scholastic attainments and literary powers to several aspects of music in *The Threshold of Music* (1908), *The Musical Faculty* (1914), *A Study of Wagner* (1925). The following is a list of his principal compositions :

INSTRUMENTAL

Symphony. ' The Creation.' (New Brighton, 1899.)
Symphonic Poems—
  1. ' The Passing of Beatrice.' Dante, *Paradiso,* canto **xxxi.** (Crystal Palace, 1892.)
  2. ' Anvil or Hammer,' Goethe, *Kophtisches Lied.* (Crystal Palace, 1896.)
  3. ' Sister Helen.' Rossetti. (Crystal Palace, 1899.)
  4. ' To the New Country.' (London Philharmonic, 1901.)
  5. ' Wallace, A.D. 1305–1905.' (Queen's Hall Promenades, 1905.)
  6. ' Villon.' (New Symphony Orch., London, 1909.)
Suite. ' The Lady from the Sea.' Ibsen. (London, 1892.)
Symphonic Prelude to the *Eumenides* of Aeschylus. (Crystal Palace, 1893.)
Overture. ' In Praise of Scottish Poesie.' (1894.)
2 Suites in olden style. Small orch.
' A Scots Fantasy,' for orch.
Trio in A. PF. and strings. (1892.)

VOCAL

Scena. ' Lord of Darkness.' Baritone and orch. (London, 1890.)
' Spanish Songs.' Vocal quartet. (1893.)
' My soul is an enchanted boat.' Voice, vln. and PF. (1896.)
Scena. ' The Rhapsody of Mary Magdalene ' (words from the composer's mystery play, *The Divine Surrender*). (London, 1896.)
Song Cycles—
  1. ' Freebooter Songs,' originally with orch. (New Brighton, 1899.)
  2. ' Jacobite Songs.' (1900.)
  3. ' Lords of the Sea.' (Bournemouth, 1902.)
' The Massacre of the Macpherson.' Burlesque ballad, male ch. and orch. (Leeds Musical Union.)
Scena. ' The Outlaw.' Male voices and orch.
' Brassolis.' Lyric tragedy in one act.
Choral Symphony. ' Koheleth.'
Many songs and short choral pieces. (See *R.M.S. Ann.* 1920.)

C., incorporating material from M.

[1] Wallace's ophthalmological researches are recorded in contributions to several scientific journals and in 100 water-colour sketches by him presented to the Army Medical War Museum.

WALLACE, WILLIAM VINCENT (b. Waterford, Ireland, Mar. 11, 1812 [1]; d. Château de Bagen, Oct. 12, 1865), was composer of ' Maritana ' and other remarkably popular operas. His father, a bandmaster [2] and skilful bassoonplayer, migrated to Dublin, and was engaged in the band of the Adelphi Theatre there, where his second son Wellington played second flute.

Vincent had displayed considerable talent as organist before quitting Waterford, and his skill and steadiness as a violinist were so appreciated in the Dublin theatre, that we find him leading the band dressed in a boy's jacket whenever the regular *chef* was belated. In June 1829 Wallace sustained the violin part in Herz and Lafont's duo on Russian airs at a public concert in Dublin, and continued to appear at concerts there, and at the festival held in 1831, when Paganini was engaged. In 1831 Wallace married Isabella Kelly,[3] of Frescati, Blackrock, near Dublin, who survived him, dying in Dublin, July 25, 1900.[4] He turned his knowledge of the violin to account by playing a concerto of his own composition at a concert in Dublin in May 1834 ; but Dublin offered little field for an aspiring artist, and so, wearying of such mechanical labours as adding symphonies and accompaniments to songs for the Dublin publishers, he quitted Ireland in 1835, with his wife and her sister, and transferred his household to an abode in the bush far to the west of Sydney, New South Wales. During one of his visits to Sydney, some friends accidentally hearing him play, were amazed to discover in a simple emigrant a violinist of the first rank, and Wallace was induced to give a concert, which had enormous success. He met with various romantic adventures in different parts of the world.[5]

In 1845 we find him in London, in a costume somewhat unusual for the private box of a theatre. ' It consisted,' says Heyward St. Leger, ' of a white hat with a very broad brim, a complete suit of planter's nankeen, and a thick stick in his hand.' Wallace recognised St. Leger immediately. They at once renewed their intimacy, which dated from the days when Wallace had led the Dublin orchestra. Inquiring of his friend whether he thought him capable of composing an opera, ' Certainly,' replied the other, ' twenty.' ' Then what about a libretto ? ' ' Come over now to Fitzball with me, and I will introduce you.' Accordingly they called on the poet at his house in Portland Road. Fitzball at once gave him the book of ' Maritana ' (Drury Lane, Nov. 15, 1845), which proved a great success, and still keeps the stage. In 1847 he

[1] The register of birth is quoted by w. H. G. F., *Mus. T.*, July 1912, p. 448.
[2] Army records show that Wallace sen. joined the 29th Regiment in 1822, was promoted sergeant 1823, and purchased his discharge 1826 (*Mus. T.*, July 1912, p. 448).
[3] Their separation (1835), and Wallace's subsequent connexion with Hélène Stoepel (pianist), by whom he had two sons, has occasioned several mis-statements by his biographers.
[4] A concert for her benefit was organised by W. H. Gregory, at the Queen's Hall, in 1896. Her son was nominated to the Charterhouse about the same time.
[5] See Pougin's Biography.

produced ' Matilda of Hungary,' of which the libretto was, even for Bunn, outrageously bad. In 1849 we find him at the head of a concert party in South America. On his return he went to Germany, where he remained fourteen years. To this period belongs most of his pianoforte music, partaking of the dreamy style of Chopin, the ornate *cantabile* of Thalberg, and his own charming manner. Part of the opera, ' Lurline ' too was now written, in the romantic district it describes. An unpublished opera, ' The Maid of Zurich,' dates also from this period. The Irish composer now received a high compliment —a commission from the Opéra of Paris. He began to write, but his eyesight failing he abandoned his pen, and once more went abroad, visiting both North and South America, and giving concerts with great success. He was nearly blown up in a steamboat in 1850, and lost all his savings by the failure of a pianoforte factory in New York. His concerts there, however, proved very lucrative. He returned to London in 1853, his pianoforte music being in high repute and eagerly sought for by the publishers. In 1860 he brought forward his ' Lurline ' (Covent Garden, Feb. 23) ; it met with even greater success than ' Maritana,' equally overflowing with melody, and being in addition a really fine piece of art-work. In 1861 appeared ' The Amber Witch ' (Her Majesty's, Feb. 28) ; in 1862 ' Love's Triumph ' (Covent Garden, Nov. 3) ; in 1863 ' The Desert Flower ' (Covent Garden, Oct. 12). This was his last completed work, but of an unfinished opera, called ' Estrella,' some fragments remain. A detailed list of his pianoforte and other compositions will be found in *Brit. Mus. Biog.* His health had been breaking for some time, and he was ordered to the Pyrenees, where he died at the Château de Bagen. He was buried in Kensal Green Cemetery on Oct. 23.

R. P. S. ; addns. and corr. W. H. Gregory; w. H. G. F. ; *D.N.B.*, etc.

BIBL.—A. POUGIN, *William Vincent Wallace* (1866) ; W. H. GRATTAN FLOOD, *Memoir of W. V. Wallace* (1912) ; *W. V. Wallace —a Centenary Notice* (*Mus. T.*, July 1912) ; Correspondence arising from the last named (*Mus. T.*, Sept. 1912, p. 595) ; CECIL FORSYTH, *Music and Nationalism*, containing criticism of Wallace's operas.

WALLASCHEK, RICHARD (b. Brünn, Nov. 16, 1860 ; d. Vienna, Apr. 24. 1917), studied law and philosophy at Vienna, Heidelberg and Tübingen, took the degree of Dr. in both faculties, taught in the university of Freiburg in 1886, in which year appeared his *Ästhetik der Tonkunst*. In 1890–95 he lived in London, studying the music in the British Museum. He went to Vienna in 1896, and was for some time teacher of the æsthetics of music in the conservatorium of the Gesellschaft der Musikfreunde. His most important works on music were published in London : *On the Origin of Music* (1891), *Natural Selection and Music* (1892), *On the Difference of Time and Rhythm in Music* (1893), and *Primitive Music* (1893). Many articles of value appeared in the *Vierteljahrs-*

schrift, the *Contemporary Review*, etc. In 1903 his treatise on *Primitive Music* appeared in an enlarged German edition as *Anfänge der Tonkunst*. His subsequent German works include *Geschichte der Wiener Hofoper* (1907–08), and several volumes on æsthetics and psychology as applied to music. (See *Riemann*.)   M.

BIBL.—R. LACH, *Zur Erinnerung au R. Wallaschek*. 1917.

WALLERSTEIN, ANTON (*b*. Dresden, Sept. 28, 1813; *d*. Geneva, Mar. 30, 1892), began life early as a violinist, and in 1827 was much noticed during a visit to Berlin. In 1829 he entered the court band at Dresden, and in 1832 that at Hanover, but various wanderings to Hamburg, Copenhagen and other places led to the resignation of his post in 1841.

He began to write in 1830, and from that time till 1877 poured forth a constant flood of dance music, chiefly published by Schott & Co., of Mainz. His 275th opus is entitled ' Souvenir du pensionnat. Cinq petites pièces faciles en forme de danse pour piano. Leipzig, Kahnt.' With this piece his name disappears from the publishing list. His dances had a prodigious vogue during their day in Germany, France and England, in all classes of society. Among the best known are ' La Coquette,' ' Redova Parisienne,' ' Studentengalopp,' ' Erste und lezte Liebe,' etc. His songs also were popular, especially ' Das Trauerhaus ' and ' Sehnsucht in die Ferne.'   G.

WALLIS, DR. JOHN (*b*. Ashford, Kent, Nov. 23, 1616 ; *d*. Oxford, Oct. 28, 1703), professor of mathematics at Oxford University in 1649. He edited : *Tractatus elenchticus adversus Marci Meibomii dialogum de proportionibus* (1657) ; *Claudii Ptolemaei harmonicarum libri III* (Greek 1662), with an appendix ; *De veterum harmonia ad hodiernam comparata* ; *Porphyrii in harmonica Ptolemaei commentarius*; *Manuelis Bryennii harmonica* (also reproduced in his collected works, 3 vols. 1699). A number of acoustical investigations in philosophical transactions (1672–98) ; *De loquela, seu sonorum formatione, tractatus, Lugduni*, 1740.

WALLISER, CHRISTOPH THOMAS (*b*. Strassburg, Apr. 17, 1568 ; *d*. there, Apr. 27, 1648), was a pupil of Melchior Vulpius and Tobias Kindler ; he was a teacher in the Academy and director of music in two churches in Strassburg from 1599. It was no doubt his academic post which suggested the composition of choruses from the *Clouds* of Aristophanes, and to various other plays on the classical model, such as *Andromeda, Elias* and *Charicles*. His ' Teutscher Psalmen ' (*a* 5) were published in 1602 ; his ' Hexastichon ' (*a* 6) in 1610 ; his ' Musicae figuralis praecepta brevia,' for 2 - 6 voices, appeared in 1611 ; and his ' Sacrae modulationes' for Christmas in 1613. His chief work is :

' Ecclesiodae, das ist Kirchengesang, nemblich die gebreuchlichsten Psalmen Davids so nicht allein viva voce, sondern auch zu musikalischen Instrumenten christlich zu gebrauchen, mit 4, 5, 6 Stimmen componirt,' Strassburg, 1614.

It consists of fifty German psalms set in the old contrapuntal style on the melodies to which they were sung in the protestant services in Strassburg. Two of them are republished in Schöberlein and Riegel's ' Schatz des liturgischen Chorgesangs,' and one (' Ein' feste Burg,' Luther's version of the 46th Psalm) in Kade's Notenbeilagen to Ambros's *Geschichte der Musik*. In 1625 Walliser published

' Ecclesiodae Novae, darinn • die Catechismusgesang, andere Schrifft und geistliche Lieder samt dem Te Deum, und der Litania . . . mit 4, 5, 6, 7 Stimmen gesetzt.'

Similar publications appeared in 1617, 1627 and 1641, and many works in MS. are extant. (See *Q.-L.*)   M.

WALMISLEY, (1) THOMAS FORBES (*b*. Westminster, May 22, 1783 ; *d*. July 23, 1866), son of William Walmisley, Clerk of the Papers to the House of Lords, was a chorister in the Abbey and was sent to Westminster School. At 14 he began his musical education, and studied the organ, piano and counterpoint under ATTWOOD (*q.v.*). Walmisley achieved success as a musical teacher and glee-writer. The *Spectator* for Aug. 28, 1830, thus characterises a volume of glees published by Walmisley at that time :

' These compositions, though displaying the attainments of a skilful musician, are not the dull effusions of a pedant. Though formed upon the best models, they are no servile copies, but the effusions of good taste matured and nurtured by study.'

In 1810–14 he was assistant organist to the Female Orphan Asylum, and in the latter year he became organist at St. Martin-in-the-Fields, an appointment he held until Mar. 1854, when he retired on a pension. His name appears on the list of musicians assembled at Weber's funeral in 1826. He lived to edit his more famous son's ' Cathedral Music.' He is buried in Brompton Cemetery.

The following printed works appear in the Catalogue of the British Museum, with dates of publication :

Six glees, 1814. Round, Underneath this stone (Ben Jonson), 1815. Song, Taste life's glad moments, 1815. Trio, The fairy of the dale, 1815. Song, Sweet hope, 1817. Glee, From flower to flower, 1819. Canzonet, The soldiers, 1819. Glee, Say, Myra, 1822. Song, The wild hyacinth, 1825. A collection of glees, trios, rounds and canons, 1826. Song, I turn from pleasure's witching tone, 1827. Song, Home, dearest home, 1828. By those eyes of dark beauty, 1829. Glee, Bright while smiles the sparkling wine, 1830. Six glees, 1830. Six glees, 1830. Round, O'er the glad waters, 1835. Glee, I wish to tune, 1835. Glee, Thou cheerful bee, 1835. Song, To Zuleika, 1835. Three canons, 1840. Duet, Tell me, gentle hour of night, 1840. Sacred songs, poetry by E. B. Impey, 1841. Glee, To-morrow, 1845. Glee, The traveller's return (Southey), 1856.

His eldest son, (2) THOMAS ATTWOOD (*b*. London, Jan. 21, 1814 ; *d*. Hastings, Jan. 17, 1856), showed at an unusually early age such a rare aptitude for music that his father secured for him the advantage of studying composition under his godfather, Thomas Attwood. The lad rapidly attained proficiency as a pianist. In 1830 he became organist of Croydon Church, and attracted the notice of Thomas Miller, who encouraged his literary tastes and persuaded him to combine mathematical with musical studies. At this time an attempt was made by Monck Mason to secure him for English opera, but Walmisley decided to try his fortune at Cambridge. In 1833 he was elected organist of Trinity and St. John's Colleges, and composed an exercise, 'Let God arise,' with full orchestra, for the degree of Mus.B. He then entered Corpus Christi College, where he distinguished himself in the mathematical examinations. He subsequently migrated to Jesus College, and though unsuccessful as a competitor for the University Prize Poem, fully justified the wisdom of Miller's advice that his love of literature should not be entirely sacrificed to professional duties. The then system concentrated the duties of several persons in one, and the young organist submitted to a slavery which it is now difficult to realise. He took without any remuneration Pratt's duties as organist in King's College Chapel and St. Mary's, and his Sunday work deserves to be recorded : St. John's at 7.15 A.M.; Trinity, 8 ; King's, 9.30 ; St. Mary's, 10.30 and 2 ; King's, 3.15 ; St. John's, 5 ; Trinity, 6.15. In 1834 he wrote the anthem ' O give thanks,' for the Commemoration at Trinity, and his Service in B flat. In 1835 he composed the Ode, written by the Bishop of Lincoln, for the Installation of Lord Camden as Chancellor—a serious interruption to his mathematical studies.

His election to the professorial chair of Music, vacated by the death of Dr. Clarke-Whitfeld, took place in 1836 ; in 1838 he took his B.A. degree, and in 1841 his M.A. On two other occasions it fell to his lot to compose music for Odes written for the Installation of Chancellors of the University. In 1842, the words, in honour of the Duke of Northumberland, were written by the Rev. T. Whytehead ; in 1847, for the Installation of the Prince Consort, they were by Wordsworth, then Laureate. Poetry and music written for such occasions are seldom long-lived, but a quartet from the Ode of 1842, ' Fair is the warrior's mural crown,' would certainly be an effective concert-piece at any time. In 1848 he took the degree of Mus.D., and continued working at Cambridge until within a short period of his death, which took place at Hastings, Jan. 17, 1856. He was buried at Fairlight, and a brass tablet to his memory was erected in Trinity College Chapel in 1888.

His intimacy with Mendelssohn was a source of great pride to him, though a rebuff administered by Mendelssohn weighed unduly on his mind, and deterred him from orchestral writing. Walmisley asked Mendelssohn to look at a symphony written for the Philharmonic Society. Before he would consent, Mendelssohn asked how many he had written already. On hearing that it was a first attempt : ' No. 1 ! ' exclaimed Mendelssohn, ' let us see what No. 12[1] will be first ! '

[1] Mendelssohn's Symphony in C minor, with which he made his début at the Philharmonic in 1829, though known as ' No. 1,' is really his 13th, and is so inscribed on the autograph.

Walmisley was one of the first English organists of his day, and in a period of church music made memorable by the compositions of Wesley and Goss, his best anthems and services are little, if at all, inferior to the compositions of these eminent men. As instances of fine writing we may cite the Service in B♭, the Dublin Prize Anthem, his anthem ' If the Lord himself ' and the madrigal ' Sweete Floweres,' a work which Henry Leslie's choir did much to popularise. His position at Cambridge no doubt acted prejudicially. A larger professional area, a closer neighbourhood with possible rivals, would have ensured a deeper cultivation of powers which bore fruit but promised a still richer harvest. In general cultivation and knowledge of musical history he was far in advance of most English musicians. He was one of the first to inaugurate the useful system of musical lectures illustrated by practical examples. In a series of lectures on the ' Rise and Progress of the Pianoforte,' he spoke incidentally of Bach's Mass in B minor as ' the greatest composition in the world,' and prophesied that the publication of the cantatas (then in MS.) would show that his assertion of Bach's supremacy was no paradox.

The volume of anthems and services published by his father after the son's death are a first-class certificate of sound musicianship. Amongst his unpublished manuscripts are some charming duets for pianoforte and oboe, written for Alfred Pollock, a Cambridge undergraduate, whose remarkable oboe - playing Walmisley much admired.

His published works in the Catalogue of the British Museum are as follows :

Song, When nightly my wild harp I bring, 1835 (?). Ode at the installation of the Duke of Northumberland as Chancellor, 1842. Chants and Responses in use at King's, Trinity and St. John's Colleges, Cambridge, 1845. Three anthems arranged from Hummel's Masses, 1849. Ode at the installation of Prince Albert as Chancellor, 1849. Attwood's Cathedral Music : 4 services, 8 anthems, etc., arranged by T. A. Walmisley, 1852. Two trios for trebles—1. The approach of May ; 2. The Mermaid, 1852. Choral hymn, 4 v. and organ, 1853. Madrigal, Sweete floweres. Four songs—1. Gay festive garments ; 2. Sing to me then ; 3. Farewell, sweet flowers ; 4. The sweet spring day, 1854. Cambria, 1857. Cathedral Music, edited by T. F. Walmisley, 1857. Song, There is a voice, 1858.

A. D. C. ; addns. from *D.N.B.*, etc.

WALMSLEY, P., see WAMSLEY.

WALOND, (1) WILLIAM, Mus.B. (*b.* 1725 ; *d.* 1770 [2]), was admitted to the privileges of the University of Oxford, June 25, 1757, being described as ' organorum pulsator ' (whence we may suppose him to have been organist or assistant organist of one of the churches or colleges at Oxford), and on July 5 following took his degree as of Christ Church. In 1758 he published his setting of Pope's ' Ode on St. Cecilia's Day,' believed to be the first setting of that poem in its original form. (See GREENE, Maurice ; CECILIA, St.) Three sets of voluntaries for organ or harpsichord were also published. (2) WILLIAM (*d.* Chichester, Feb. 9, 1836), possibly a son of William (1),

[2] Dates given by W. H. G F.

became deputy organist in 1775 and organist in 1794 of Chichester Cathedral, which post he resigned in 1801. After his resignation he resided in Chichester in extreme poverty and seclusion (subsisting upon an annuity raised by the sale of some houses, and being rarely seen abroad) until his death. Some fragments of church compositions by him remain in MS. in the choir - books of Chichester Cathedral. (3) RICHARD (b. 1754), son of William (1), matriculated from Christ Church, Oxford, July 14, 1770. He was a clerk of Magdalen College, Oxford, from Mar. 24, 1775, until 1776. On Mar. 14, 1776, he took the degree of B.A. as of New College, and was subsequently a vicar-choral of Hereford Cathedral. (4) GEORGE, another son of William (1), was a chorister of Magdalen College, Oxford, from Apr. 13, 1768, until 1778.

w. h. h.

WALPURGISNACHT, DIE ERSTE; Goethe's ballad set for chorus and orchestra by Mendelssohn, op. 60; produced Berlin, Jan. 1833; re-scored, with English words by Bartholomew, Philharmonic Society, July 8, 1844.

WALSH, (1) JOHN (d. Mar. 13, 1736), a famous London music-publisher during the first half of the 18th century. He was established at the 'Harp and Hoboy,' in Catherine Street, Strand, and was there publishing engraved music. Walsh was, in all probability, of Irish extraction, and appears to have had court favour, for he was the first, so far as the writer can ascertain, to be named 'Musical instrument - maker and music - seller to the King' (William III.).[1] The royal appointment extended to himself and his son through all succeeding reigns, including the first few years of George III. On one early imprint the name is spelled 'Welch,' but as this only occurs on one item it may be safely assumed that it is merely a misprint. On the early imprints, down to 1705, the sign stands as 'The Golden Harp and Hoboy.' John Playford was dead, and his son merely dragging on the remains of the once large business, so Walsh had no serious rival in the trade, which he pushed forward with unprecedented vigour.

He reprinted from Dutch sources popular continental music (Corelli, for example) at low prices, using, no doubt, pewter instead of the more costly copper. Hawkins states that he began stamping pewter plates in 1710, instead of engraving them, as Thomas CROSS (q.v.) was then doing. The date is not confirmed, but it is quite a probable one. Walsh's shop was quite distant from St. Paul's Churchyard and Temple Bar, where the usual music-trade congregated, and no doubt this isolation enabled him to build up a business that may

[1] C. H. de Lafontaine's *The King's Musick* finds the earliest reference to Walsh in an entry to the effect that he was appointed musical-instrument maker to the King in place of John Shaw, surrendered on June 24, 1692. F. K.

be aptly compared with the largest of our modern music-publishing firms. Hawkins in his *History* has no good word for Walsh. He intimates that he was mean and illiterate, and with him he includes John Hare, who was more or less associated with Walsh. Whether Hawkins's prejudices enter into this condemnation or not it is difficult to tell.

Walsh's earliest productions are frequently adorned with elaborately engraved titles and frontispieces : many very artistic, others in the Dutch style then so popular. Some of these title-pages were used over again for different publications, the altered titles printed from smaller inserted plates. Most of Walsh's early imprints also bear the name of John Hare, and, later, John and Joseph HARE (q.v.). Afterwards these were erased from the plates. John Hare lived in Freeman's Yard, Cornhill, and had a shop in St. Paul's Churchyard, 'The Golden Viall.' He was succeeded by his son Joseph in Freeman's Yard. Walsh was thus able to get both the City as well as the West End trade. Whether the Hares were partners with Walsh is uncertain.

About 1710 Walsh associated himself with P. Randall, who, a few years before, was established at 'The Violin and Lute without Temple Bar.' There are indications that Randall married the elder Walsh's sister, leaving a son, William Randall, who ultimately succeeded to the Walsh business. P. Randall gave up his shop near Temple Bar and remained with Walsh.

In 1710 Walsh was in full trade, publishing single songs and the Italian operas, instrumental works and the whole range of current music. Handel, coming over to England, naturally turned to him as the principal publisher, and 'Rinaldo' appeared in 1711, by which it is said that Walsh made one thousand pounds. Walsh senior was intimately connected with Handel from this time to the date of the former's death. They appear to have continually squabbled, as is proved by Handel publishing by subscription, through Cluer and through Meares, being evidently dissatisfied with Walsh's treatment.

Walsh was buried in the vaults of St. Mary Le Strand. *The Gentleman's Magazine* announces that he left £30,000. F. K.

(2) JOHN (d. Jan. 15, 1766), his son, succeeded to the business left by his father, and also to the royal appointments as music-seller and instrument-maker. Although Johnson and other great rivals had sprung up there was no falling off of the business. The younger Walsh continued it on the same lines as his father. The engraving and the paper were of the best, and even after a century and a half's usage it is pleasant to turn over the clearly printed sheets on excellent paper that bear his imprints. Walsh junior continued the Handel

publications. The *Public Advertiser* stated that on his death his fortune amounted to £40,000. The business was taken over by William Randall, who was, presumably, the son of P. Randall and cousin to the last Walsh. Randall went into partnership with one Abell, in 1767–68, but this lasted only for about a year. He republished from the old plates all the Walsh publications that were of marketable value, and made but few additions to the stock. On his death, before 1781, his widow, Elizabeth Randall, succeeded, and before 1784 Wright and Wilkinson were at the address, reprinting from the old plates, mainly Handel's works. Hermond Wright remained here until about 1800, when the old premises, after being a music-publishing house for over a century, knew music no more. The later imprints show the number to have been 13, which appears to have been on the right-hand side going up from the Strand. All traces of the site of Walsh's shop and of Catherine Street itself are lost. Walsh and his son had apprentices as engravers, and many of these, including William Smith and Caulfield, set up for themselves. Robert Birchall was assistant to Randall, and Samuel Chappell assistant to Birchall.   F. K.

WALSINGHAM, THOMAS DE (*b.* Norfolk, early 15th cent.), entered the Benedictine monastery of St. Alban about 1440 and became precentor of the Abbey Church. He is apparently identical [1] with the author of the treatise : *Regule Magistri Thome Walsingham* in the Waltham Holy Cross, now Lansdowne MS. 763, from about 1460, in which he says that the *newly introduced* crotchet would be of no use if musicians would remember that no subdivision of notes should be made beyond the minim (*Hawkins* ; *Q.-L.*).

WALTER, ALBERT (*b.* Coblenz), an 18th century clarinettist-composer, occupied various positions at Paris from 1795, becoming bandmaster of the chasseurs of the Imperial Guards in 1805. He composed symphonies, concertante for 2 clarinets, quartets, trios for 2 violins and bass, duets, variations, etc. (*Fétis* ; *Q.-L.*).

WALTER, BRUNO (*b.* Berlin, Sept. 15, 1876), a distinguished conductor, both of opera and the symphonic orchestra, received his musical education at the Stern Conservatorium. After a wide experience gained through appointments at several German opera-houses, including the Royal Opera at Berlin, Walter became director at the Vienna Hofoper (1901–12). In 1911 he also conducted the Singakademie there (see VIENNA). He followed Mottl as general music director at Munich (1913–22), and there his power as an organiser of operatic enterprise over and above his purely musical abilities were displayed in many festival performances.

Walter first appeared in England at a concert

of the Royal Philharmonic Society on Mar. 3, 1909, when he gained so instant a success that the Society secured him for further concerts in the autumn. In this first programme was the overture to Ethel Smyth's ' The Wreckers,' and Walter conducted when that opera was given at Covent Garden in the spring of 1910. In that season, one given by Beecham, he also conducted ' Tristan.' He was not again heard in opera in this country, however, until 1924, when he took charge of the German opera season at Covent Garden (the first since 1914) with such brilliant musical results that the newly formed London Opera Syndicate wisely secured his services for their first season in 1925 and again in 1926. In these last years he has appeared frequently in concert work with the London Symphony Orchestra.   c.

WALTER, GUSTAV (*b.* Bilin, Bohemia, Feb. 11, 1834; *d.* Vienna, Jan. 30, 1910), learned singing at the Prague Conservatorium from Franz Vogl, and made his first appearance in opera as Edgar at a private representation of ' Lucia.' He played at Brünn for a short time, and in July 1856 appeared at Vienna in Kreutzer's ' Nachtlager.' He remained there throughout his career, and attained great popularity as a lyric tenor both on the stage and in the concert-room. He came to London in 1872, and made his first appearance on May 13, at the Philharmonic, where he was favourably received in songs of Mozart, Riedel and Rubinstein. He also sang at the Crystal Palace, etc. He retired in 1887, but continued to sing in concert, and took part in a performance of Bach's ' St. Matthew Passion ' by the Gesellschaft der Musikfreunde under Richter in 1890. His daughter MINNA, a pupil of Madame Marchesi, had a successful career in various cities (Vienna, Frankfort, etc.).   A. C.

WALTER, (1) IGNAZ (*b.* Radowitz, Bohemia, 1759 ; *d.* Ratisbon, Apr. 1832), a famous tenor singer and composer ; pupil of Starzer, Vienna. He sang at Prague (1783), Mainz (1789), and in Grossmann's Company at Hanover (1793). After the death of Grossmann he took over the company which appeared at Frankfort-on-M. and at Ratisbon. Walter wrote about a dozen Singspiele for his troupe, the first ' Faust' opera based on Goethe's drama, a memorial music for Schiller, a coronation cantata for the Emperor Leopold (1791), masses, chamber music, etc. His wife (2) JULIANE, *née* ROBERTS, of Brunswick, was also a noted singer, who held her own even by the side of the famous Mme. Schick at Mainz. While Walter was managing the theatre at Bremen his wife became blind, and both went to Ratisbon, where Walter was engaged with his troupe in 1804, and lived there in retirement from 1822 (Schilling ; *Q.-L.*).

WALTER, JOHN, organist of Eton College at the end of the 17th century, composed an anthem in MS. at Ely, and a psalm, ' O give thanks,' in the Fitzwilliam Museum, Cambridge. He was the first music-master of John Weldon.   w. h. h.

WALTHER, Johann (b. Cola, Thuringia,[1] 1496 ; d. before Apr. 24, 1570), Luther's friend, and one of the earliest of the composers in the Lutheran Church. In 1524 he was bass singer in the choir at Torgau, and in the following year Kapellmeister, or ' Sängermeister,' to the Elector of Saxony. In 1548 he was sent to Dresden to organise and lead a choir of singers for Moritz of Saxony, and remained till 1554, when he returned with a pension to Torgau, and there lived till his death.

In 1524 he was called to Wittenberg by Luther to assist him in framing the German Mass. The result of this was his ' Geystlich Gesangk Buchleyn ' for four voices (1524), the earliest Protestant hymn-book. His other works are ' Cantio septem vocum,' etc. (1544) ; ' Ein gar schöner geistlicher und christlicher Bergkreyen ' (1552) ; ' Magnificat octo tonorum ' (1557); ' Ein newes christliches Lied ' (1561) ; ' Das christlich Kinderlied Dr. Martin Luthers, Erhalt uns Herr bei Deinem Wort . . . mit etlichen lateinischen und deutschen Sängen gemehret ' (1566). Other pieces are included in the collections of Rhaw and Forster, ' Montan-Neubers Psalmenwerk,' 1538, and ' Motettensammlung,' 1540. Poems appeared in 1538 and 1564. (See Q.-L.)   g.

Some instrumental compositions discovered (1912) in the library of the Thomasschule at Leipzig will be published in D.D.T. (Riemann).

Bibl. Robert Haas, Zu Walthers Choralpassion nach Matthäus. A.M.Z. Jan. 1922, pp. 24-47 ; Adolf Aber, Die Pflege der Musik unter den Wettinern, 1922. Aber produces evidence to show that Walther was the real founder of the musical liturgy of the Lutheran church.

WALTHER, (1) Johann Gottfried (b. Erfurt, Sept. 18, 1684 ; d. Weimar, Mar. 23, 1748), a very skilful contrapuntist [2] and famous musical lexicographer. He was a pupil of Jacob Adlung and J. Bernhard Bach in 1702 ; became in 1702 organist of the Thomaskirche at Erfurt, and July 29, 1707, town organist of Weimar (in succession to Heintze) and teacher of the son and daughter of the Grand Duke ; and in 1720 ' Hofmusicus.' Walther was a relative of J. S. Bach, and during Bach's residence in Weimar (1708–14) they became very intimate, and Bach was godfather to his eldest son. The meagre notice of Bach in Walther's Lexicon seems to show that the intimacy did not last. Mattheson's judgment of Walther, in his Ehrenpforte, is a very high one ; he regards him as ' a second Pachelbel, if not in art the first.' In the arrangement and variation of chorales on the organ he certainly stands next to Bach himself. An anecdote preserved by one of Bach's sons shows that he was once able to puzzle even that great player.[3]

[1] According to his tombstone.
[2] See the instances given by Spitta, Bach (Engl. transl.), ii. 384.
[3] Ibid. ii. 388.

He printed the following pieces : clavier concerto without accompaniment (1741) ; prelude and fugue (1741) ; four chorales with variations ; and a mass of compositions remains in MS. in the Berlin library and elsewhere. (See Q.-L.)

But Walther's most lasting work is his Dictionary—Musicalisches Lexicon oder musicalische Bibliothec (Leipzig, 1732), the first to combine biography and musical subjects, a work of great accuracy and merit and the ground-work to many a subsequent one. (See Dictionaries of Music.) This work was the production of his leisure hours only. He published a first sketch, of 68 pages, in 1728, under the title of Alte und neue musikalische Bibliothek oder musikalisches Lexikon. Walther had prepared elaborate corrections and additions for a second edition of his great work, and after his death they were used by Gerber (q.v.) in the preparation of his Lexicon. They ultimately came into the possession of the Gesellschaft der Musikfreunde at Vienna. g.

(2) Johann Christoph (b. Weimar, July 8, 1715 ; d. there, Aug. 25, 1771), son of the above, music director and organist of the cathedral at Ulm (1751–70), published three sonatas for clavier, 1766. (Riemann.)

WALTHER, Johann Jakob (b. Witterda, near Erfurt, Thuringia, 1650), violinist and composer, styles himself on the title of one of his works ' Italian Secretary to the Elector of Mainz.' We find him first as a member of the band of the Elector of Saxony at Dresden, and later on attached to the court of the Elector of Mainz. The place and date of his death are unknown.[1] Two sets of violin compositions of his have been preserved :

1. Scherzi da Violino solo, con il Basso Continuo per l' Organo ò Cimbalo, accompagnabile anche con una Viola ò Leuto, di Giovanni Giacomo Valther, Primo Violinista di Camera di sua Altezza Elettorale di Sassonia MDCLXXVI.
2. Hortulus Chelicus, uni Violino, duabus, tribus et quatuor subinde chordis simul sonantibus harmonice modulanti. Studiosa varietate consitus a Johanne Jacobo Walthero, Eminentis. Celsitud. Elector. Maguntin. Secretario Italico. Maguntiae, sumptibus Lud. Bourgeat. Academi. Bibliopol. 1688.

The musical interest of these compositions is but small. They consist chiefly of short preludes, pieces in dance-forms (gavottes, sarabandes, etc.) and sets of variations. In some respects they remind us of the works of Farina, who was his predecessor at Dresden. Like Farina he appears fond of realistic tone-pictures —he imitates the cuckoo, the nightingale, the crowing of the cock and other sounds of nature. In a set of variations we meet with imitations of the guitar by pizzicatos, of pipes by passages going up to the sixth position on the first string ; of the trumpet by fanfares on the fourth string ; farther on he introduces echo-effects, the lyre, the harp, and winds up with a ' Coro ' in full chords. Besides these childish efforts, it is true, we find some more serious pieces, which, as far as invention, harmonic and metrical treatment go, are decidedly an advance on

Farina's style. Walther's importance for the history of the development of violin-playing consists exclusively in the advanced claims his writings make on execution. He ascends to the sixth position, frequently employs difficult double-stoppings and uses a variety of bowing. (See VIOLIN-PLAYING.)   P. D.

WALTHEW, RICHARD HENRY (b. London, Nov. 4, 1872), was for some time a pupil of the G.S.M., and in 1890 gained an open scholarship at the R.C.M., where he studied for the following four years under Parry. A setting of Browning's ' Pied Piper,' for soli, chorus and orchestra, was performed by the Highbury Philharmonic Society in 1893 with great success ; it was afterwards repeated at the Crystal Palace and elsewhere. In 1894 he introduced a pianoforte concerto of his own at a concert given by the Strolling Players at Queen's Hall ; various orchestral works were performed by the Stock Exchange Orchestral Society. He was musical director of the Passmore Edwards Settlement for five years (1900–04). In 1907 he was appointed music professor at Queen's College, later became conductor of the University College Musical Society, and in 1905 conductor of the Operatic Class at the G.S.M., where he raised the level of performances to a remarkable degree of efficiency. In 1909 he became conductor of the South Place Orchestra, Finsbury ; and the SOUTH PLACE CONCERTS (q.v.), at which his chamber music, the most important class of his compositions, has been constantly played, owe much to his interest and guidance, and to his well-written programme notes. His cantatas, especially the ' Pied Piper,' have been popular with choral societies of the smaller kind. Most of his major compositions are in MS. The following is a list of the chief among them :

ORCHESTRA

Variations in B flat.
Overture, ' Friend Fritz.'
Overture and Entr'actes to ' Aladdin.'
Three ' Night Scenes.'
Concerto in E flat.   PF. and orch.
Caprice Impromptu.   Vln. and orch.

CHAMBER MUSIC

Trio in C min.   PF., vln. and clar. (or vla.).
Trio in G.   PF., vln., v'cl.
Quintet in F min.   PF. and strings.
Quartet in G min.   PF. and strings.
String Quartets in E, B flat and E flat.
Six Lyrical Pieces for string quartet.
Sonata in A flat.   Vln. and PF.
Prelude, Sarabande and Fugue for string trio.
Quintet.   PF., vln., vla., v'cl., double bass.   (Stainer & Bell.)
Prelude and Fugue.   2 clar. and bassoon (v'cl.).
Five Diversions for string trio.
Quintet.   Clar. and strings.
Sonata.   V'cl. and PF.
Serenade Sonata.   Vln. and PF.

VOCAL

Operettas : ' The Enchanted Island ' ; ' The Gardeners.'
Cantatas : ' Ode to a Nightingale ' (Keats) ; ' The Pied Piper '
   (Browning) ; ' The Fair Maids of February ' ; ' John o' Dreams.'
Many songs, duets, vocal quartets and partsongs.   (See B.M.S.
   Ann., 1920.)   M., with addns.

WALTON, WILLIAM TURNER (b. Oldham, Lancashire, Mar. 29, 1902), entered Christ Church Cathedral Choir School at Oxford, and subsequently became an undergraduate of Christ Church. He studied for a time with Sir Hugh Allen, but from the age of 16 he has been self-taught, save that he received helpful advice at various times from Ansermet and from Busoni.

As a composer he first became known in 1923 through two works of very different character. The first was a string quartet, which the jury of the INTERNATIONAL SOCIETY FOR CONTEMPORARY MUSIC selected from many works submitted for the annual Festival at Salzburg in August. The other work, entitled ' Façade,' was a setting of a number of poems by Edith Sitwell. The mode of presentation was that the platform was divided from the auditorium by a curtain painted to represent a mask, the mouth of which was the orifice of a megaphone. Through this the concealed reciter (in the first instance Miss Sitwell herself) spoke the verses in a strict rhythm, the patterns of which had a close affinity with those of music. For instance, one entitled ' Hornpipe ' is spoken in the rhythm of the familiar nautical type of hornpipe. To these poems Walton wrote an accompaniment to be played behind the curtain by trumpet, flute, clarinet, saxophone, violoncello and percussion. After several performances in private, ' Façade ' was presented in this form at the Aeolian Hall, June 12, 1923. Since then it has been completely revised, and again performed in 1926. The composer has also arranged an orchestral suite for concert use, in which form it is in the repertory of the Diaghilev Ballet as an Interlude. In 1924 the Carnegie Trust recommended the publication of an earlier work, the quartet for strings and pianoforte written when the composer was sixteen years old, and giving little indication of the course his development would take. In 1925 Walton composed an overture, ' Portsmouth Point,' which again found favour with the jury of the International Society for Contemporary Music, and was performed at the Zürich Festival of 1926, where it met with warm appreciation. In the autumn of the same year a new composition for chamber orchestra, entitled ' Siesta,' was included in the programme of the Guy Warrack concerts at the Aeolian Hall. Of these various works it is ' Façade ' which has attracted the most attention, because of its novelty. The spirit it breathes is wholly different from that of the string quartet, a work of deep seriousness, concluding with a very elaborate fugue. The thoroughness with which the ideas are worked out gives it an excessive length, but the skill displayed, and also a certain affinity with modes of thought current on the Continent obviously swayed the International Jury to a decision which caused some surprise in musical circles at home, Walton's name then being unknown. ' Portsmouth Point ' was given as an interlude during the Diaghilev season at His Majesty's Theatre in the summer of 1926.

                                        E. E.

WALTZ (Fr. *valse*; Ger. *Walzer*; Ital. *valzero*). The origin of the Waltz is wrapped in even more obscurity than is usually the case with the best-known dances. The immense popularity which it achieved in the 19th century —a popularity which had the effect of almost banishing every other dance—has given rise to a dispute as to the historical genesis of the waltz, into which national antipathies have to a certain extent entered. It would have been thought that French writers could not ignore the evidence of a German origin given by the name *waltz*, derived from *waltzen*, to turn; but in the face of the etymology of the word an ingenious theory has been invented by which it is sought to prove that the dance and the name were originally borrowed by Germany from France, and then reintroduced, as a foreign invention, from the former to the latter country.

This theory apparently was first propounded by Castil Blaze, and was adopted by Fétis, Littré and Larousse. The French account of the origin of the waltz is that the dance is a descendant of the VOLTA (*q.v.*)—known to the Elizabethans as Lavolta—a dance described by Thoinot Arbeau in his *Orchésographie*, and said to have been a native of Provence, whence it was introduced into Paris under Louis VII. It remained in fashion up to the 16th century, at which period it was (according to Larousse) introduced into Germany, the name *Volta* being changed into *Waltzer*. The obvious Italian origin of the word 'volta' has been overlooked by the French writers. The German authorities, on the other hand, trace the waltz back to the *Drehtanz*, or turning dance, a modification of the old form of dances which (like the English country dances) were danced by couples standing face to face, or holding one another by one hand only.

Great confusion exists in the German accounts of these early dances. The Volta, the Langaus and the Allemande are all mentioned as being the ancestors of the waltz, but none of these seems to be satisfactorily connected with the modern dance. That the volta and the spring-tanz were identical seems pretty certain: in both the indecency of the performance seems to have been a characteristic feature, as a comparison of the descriptions in Thoinot Arbeau's *Orchésographie* and Johann von Münster's

Traktat vom ungottseligen Tanz (1594) clearly shows; but this feature is different from that which was held up to reprobation in the waltz in later days by Lord Byron and other English writers on its introduction into England. The German dances, like the French, in the 15th and 16th centuries, were either of a solemn and slow character, or consisted in unseemly leapings and jumpings; as Chapman in his *Alphonsus Emperour of Germany* makes one of his characters say:

'We *Germans* have no changes in our dances,
An Almain and an upspring that is all.'

In course of time the latter became so objectionable that it was not only preached and written against, but was made the subject of local edicts, notably in the towns of Nuremberg, Amberg and Meissen. The Almain or Allemande was introduced into France after the conquest of Alsace by Louis XIV., but the dance had nothing in common with the modern waltz, and the spring-tanz, which, as has been mentioned, was identical with the volta, no longer occurs in the 17th and 18th centuries. This break in the imaginary genealogy of the waltz has not been made clear by the writers who have treated the subject.

It is generally admitted that the modern dance first made its appearance about the year 1780, and the only attempt at connecting the old and the new dances is the suggestion that because the song 'Ach du lieber Augustin'(which was one of the first tunes to which waltzes were danced) was addressed to a wandering musician who lived in 1670, therefore the modern dance was contemporary with the tune. The attempts at tracing the waltz from such a widely spread dance as the volta or spring-tanz have led to further confusion with regard to the humble Ländler or Schleifer, which is its real ancestor. That it springs from a class of country dances, and not from the ancient stock of the volta, must be obvious upon many grounds. The dance itself is first heard of in Bohemia, Austria and Bavaria in the latter part of the 18th century; in Bohemia it seems first to have become fashionable, since on Mar. 18, 1785, it was forbidden by an Imperial edict as 'sowohl der Gesundheit schädlich, als auch der Sünden halber sehr gefährlich,' in spite of which it found its way into Vienna, and was danced in the finale to Act ii. of Vicente Martin y Solar's 'Una cosa rara' by four of the principal characters (Lubino, Tita, Chita and Lilla). On its first appearance in Vienna the music of the waltz was played quite slowly; the tempo in Martin's opera is marked Andante con moto, but in Vienna the character of the dance was changed, and a Geschwindwalzer was introduced which finally led to a Galoppwalzer in 2–4 time. But in spite of the changes that the dance underwent, what it was originally like can still be seen at any Austrian or Bavarian village festival at the present day, where it will be found, perhaps called a Ländler or Schleifer, or some other local name, but still danced to the old slow rhythms which were imitated by Mozart, Beethoven and (to a less degree) Schubert in their waltzes written for the Viennese in the early days of the dance's fashionable career. Crabb Robinson's account of the manner in which he saw it danced at Frankfort in 1800 agrees with the descriptions of the dance when it found its way to England.

'The man places the palms of his hands gently against the sides of his partner, not far from the armpits. His partner does the same, and instantly with as much velocity as possible they turn round, and at the same time gradually glide round the room.' [1]

In England the name and the tune of the dance made their first appearance about the year 1791. In that year an advertisement appeared, on another piece of music, of ' Four favourite Waltzes for 1791' and 'Four favourite Schleifers for 1792.' About 1795–1800 a number of waltzes were published (a collection is in the Brit. Mus., g. 231). The collection of Preston's Country Dances published in 1797 contains ' The new German Waltz' and 'The Princess of Wales's Waltz,' both of which are real waltz tunes, though how different the dances were may be gathered from the directions for dancing the former :

'Set and hands across and back again, lead down the middle up again to the top, turn your partner with the right hand quite round, then with the left, hands 4 round at bottom right and left.'

The same collection also contains a dance called ' Miss Simpson's Waltz,' the tune of which is written in common time. It was not until 1812 that the dance in its modern form made its appearance in England, when it was greeted with a storm of abuse as ' a fiend of German birth,' ' destitute of grace, delicacy and propriety,' a ' disgusting practice,' and called forth a savage attack from Lord Byron.[2] In spite of this reception it seems to have won a speedy victory. In France the waltz made its appearance during the war with Germany (1792–1801), which ended with the Peace of Lunéville, after which it was said that the Germans had ceded even their national dance to the French. It was first danced at the Opéra in Gardel's ballet 'La Dansomanie' (1800), for which Méhul wrote the music. Beyond the changes introduced in Vienna by Schubert, Strauss, etc., and adopted all over Europe, the form of the dance has not undergone any material alteration in France, though it was probably there that the misnamed 'Valse à deux temps' (i.e. a faster form of the dance, containing six steps to every two of the waltz ' à trois temps') was first introduced towards the middle of the century.

The music of the waltz originally consisted of

two sections, each consisting of 8 bars in 3-4 or 3-8 time. Good examples of these primitive forms will be found in Beethoven's and Mozart's Deutsche Tänze. The next development of the music was the stringing together of several of the 16-bar waltzes and the addition of trios and a coda. This was first effected by Hummel in a waltz in 9 numbers, which he wrote in 1808 for the opening of the Apollo Saal in Vienna, but this isolated example cannot have had much influence upon the development of the waltz, since it is not until the time of Schubert that it possesses any intrinsic musical value. The dances of this composer form really the basis of the later waltz music. Though in the main they adhere to the old 16-bar form, yet the beginnings of development are apparent in them, not only in their immense musical superiority to any of their predecessors, but also in the numerous extensions and improvements of the original form which are to be found in them, and which have since become the commonplaces of every writer of dance music. For instance, in op. 9b, Waltz No. 15, instead of having an 8-bar phrase repeated in each section, has two sections of 16 bars each. The next number (16) has two introductory bars of bass solo before the 16-bar melody begins—a device which is nowadays too familiar to be noticed, though when Schubert wrote, it was probably bsolutely novel. A careful analysis of these beautiful compositions would probably reveal many such points of departure ; indeed, in comparing them with the works of his contemporaries, such as LANNER and the elder STRAUSS (q.v.), it is extraordinary to find how Schubert anticipated their effects.

But if Schubert had so great an influence on the Viennese school of dance composers, it is to Weber that the waltz owes what, musically speaking, is its most important development. The composition of the ' Aufforderung zum Tanz ' marks the adoption of the waltz-form into the sphere of absolute music, and prepared the way for the stream of pianoforte and vocal waltzes, not intended as accompaniments to dancing, the best examples of which are the waltzes of Chopin and Rubinstein, though this form of composition has been adopted by most writers of ' brilliant ' music. The waltzes of Brahms, Kiel and other German composers of the same generation belong more to the Schubert type. Brahms indeed may be said to have introduced a new class in his ' Liebeslieder ' for pianoforte duet and vocal quartet ; but the original type of these is the same as Schubert's dances.

In the early part of the 19th century the composition of waltzes for dancing was almost entirely in the hands of the Viennese composers. Johann Strauss the elder introduced the habit of giving names to waltzes, and it was at Vienna,

---

[1] Diary, i. 76.
[2] 'The Waltz : an apostrophic hymn,' published 1818.

under the Strauss family, Lanner, Labitzky and Gung'l, that the waltz became fixed in the form in which we now know it, *i.e.* an introduction generally in a slow tempo, foreshadowing the principal motive of the composition, and followed by five or six separate waltzes ending with a coda recapitulating the best numbers. Vienna has, moreover, always preserved the tradition of playing what a modern writer aptly describes as ' those irresistible waltzes that first catch the ear, and then curl round the heart, till on a sudden they invade and will have the legs.' France has produced a few good waltzes, but more for operatic or vocal purposes than for dancing, while England is very far below either country in compositions of this kind.　　　w. b. s.

WALTZ, Gustavus, a German, who seems to have acted as Handel's cook, and after some time to have come out as a singer. He appeared [1] as Polyphemus in Handel's ' Acis and Galatea,' when it was performed as an ' English Pastoral Opera,' under Arne, at the ' new English theatre in the Haymarket,' May 17, 1732, showing that his voice was a large bass. Seven years later (1739) he and Reinhold sang ' The Lord is a man of war ' at the performance of ' Israel in Egypt,' their names being pencilled by Handel over the duet. He also sang Abinoam in ' Deborah,' Abner in ' Athaliah,' and Saul, on the production of those oratorios. His portrait was painted by Hauck and engraved by Müller. He is seated with a violoncello, a pipe and a pot of beer on the table beside him. It belonged to the late Mr. J. W. Taphouse, of Oxford, and was exhibited in the Loan Collection of the Inventions Exhibition, 1885.

Handel, on one occasion, speaking to Mrs. Cibber, said of Gluck : ' He knows no more of contrapunta than my cock Waltz.' This very impolite speech is often misquoted,[2] and given as if Handel had said ' no more *music* ' ; but its force as uttered is very much altered when we recollect that Gluck was no contrapuntist, and that Waltz must have been a considerable musician to take such parts as he did at Handel's own choice.　　　G.

WAMSLEY (Walmsley; Warmsley), Peter, one of the best English luthiers of the 18th century. (See Violin Family.) He worked in London from about 1720–60, becoming renowned for his excellent violoncellos and altos, which he made upon the Stainer model. His workshop was in Piccadilly in 1727, at ' Ye Golden Harp,' a sign that was subsequently changed to ' The Harp and Hautboy.' He used a yellowish-brown varnish, and often drew lines round his instruments, after the manner of Jacobs of Amsterdam, instead of inlaying purfling. Wamsley sought

to age his instruments artificially by making the plates too thin, and the wood he employed has consequently not always lasted well.　　　e. h.-a.

In 1741 his business in Piccadilly was carried on by Mrs. Walmsley,[3] which points to Peter being dead. His name as ' P. Warmsley at Ye Harp in Piccadilly ' is on the imprint of ' The Songs in Hurlothrumbo ' (1729). In 1741 De Fesch's ' Eight Concertos ' are advertised as sold by him. He appears to have been in business relations with John Barrett, who worked at the Harp and Crown, also in Piccadilly, as a violin-maker and music-seller at a contemporary date ; also with William Smith the music-engraver, as the three names are frequently conjoined on imprints of works issued about 1720–30.

It is stated that Walmsley was succeeded at the ' Harp and Hautboy ' by Thomas Smith, a pupil, some of whose labels bear the date 1756.　　　F. K.

Bibl.—Hart, *The Violin*; Meredith Morris, *British Violin-Makers*; Heron-Allen, *Violin-Making*; Von Lutgendorff, *Die Geigen und Lautenmacher*.

WANHAL (in English publications Vanhall), John Baptist (b. Nechanicz, Bohemia, May 12, 1739 ; d. Vienna, Aug. 26, 1813), a contemporary of Haydn, was of Dutch extraction. His instructors were two local worthies, Kozák and Erban, and his first instruments the organ and violin. His early years were passed in little Bohemian towns near the place of his birth. At one of these he met a good musician, who advised him to stick to the violin, and also to write for it ; both which he did with great assiduity. In 1760 he was taken to Vienna by the Countess Schaffgotsch, and here his real progress began ; he studied under Dittersdorf, read all the works he could get at, played incessantly, composed with great enthusiasm and what was then thought extravagance, and was soon taken up by many of the nobility. One of these, the Freiherr Riesch, sent him to Italy for a long journey, of which he took full advantage. On his return to Vienna he fell into a state of mental depression, which for some time affected him greatly. It was thus that Burney found him in 1772.[4] Life in Vienna then was very much what it was fifty years later, and Wanhal's existence was passed, like Beethoven's or Schubert's, in incessant work, varied by visits to Hungary or Croatia, where the Count Erdödy, the immediate predecessor of Beethoven's friend, received him. Though somewhat younger than Haydn, his music arrived in England first. Burney mentions this fact [5] and speaks of his symphonies as ' spirited, natural and unaffected,' and of the quartets and other music for violins of this excellent composer as ' deserving a place among the first productions in which unity of melody, pleasing harmony and a free and manly style are constantly preserved.'

1 He had previously sung in Lampe's ' Amelia,' Mar. 13, 1732.　　w. h. g. f.

2 As, for instance, by Berlioz in his *Autobiography*, chap. xx.

3 Old newspaper advt.
4 *Present State*, etc. p. 358.　　5 *Hist.* iv. 599,

Burney's expressions about Haydn in the next paragraph show, however, how far higher he placed him than Wanhal or any other composer of that time. It would seem, from the fact that some of his compositions were published at Cambridge, that he may have visited England. Further information concerning such a visit is not forthcoming.

The list of his works is enormous. Dlabacz, the author of the Dictionary of Bohemian Musicians, gives no less than 100 symphonies, 100 string quartets, 25 masses and 2 Requiems, 30 Salve Reginas and 36 offertories, 1 Stabat Mater, 1 oratorio, 2 operas, and many other works. (See list in *Q.-L.*) Many of the symphonies and sonatas were produced a dozen at a time, a practice to which Beethoven gave the death-blow. They must not therefore be judged of from too serious a point of view.

G.

WANLESS, (1) JOHN (late 16th and early 17th cent.), English organist and composer of church music, possibly the father of Thomas (2). He was organist of Lincoln Cathedral in 1616, and was still there in some capacity in 1625, when the Gate House Chambers in Vicar's Court were assigned to him at a rent of 10s. per annum (West's *Cath. Org.*). An anthem by him, 'Plead thou my cause,' is in Tenb. O.B./453, and he was possibly also the composer of the funeral anthem, 'I am the Resurrection.' J. M^K.

(2) THOMAS, Mus.B. (*d.* 1721[1]), English organist and composer of church music, possibly the son of John (1). If, as seems likely, he is the same as the 'Thomas Wanlesse' who was summoned to appear before the 'Corporation for regulating the Art and Science of Music' in 1663, he must have died an old man, and was probably born some time about, or most probably before, 1640. Under the date Feb. 3, 1663, there is the following reference to him in the minutes of the Corporation (Harl. MS. 1911/2):

'Ordered by the Marshall, Wardens and Assistants of the Art and Science of Musique that Joseph Gallaway, John Howard, Thomas Wanlesse and Thomas (?) be and are hearby fined for their non appearance upon sumons three pounds each person.
'(Signed) HENRY COOKE, Dep[uty] Marshall.'

He was appointed organist of York Minster, Apr. 18, 1691, and is described in the Chapter books there as 'in musicis experium.' He held this post until 1715, when he was succeeded by Charles Murgatroyd (West's *Cath. Org.*). He graduated in 1698, and a 3-part verse anthem with instrumental accompaniment, 'Awake up, my glory,' in the Tudway collection (Harl. MS. 7341/129) is described as 'compos'd by Tho. Wanless, Organist of York, for his Batchelour of Musick's Degree, in Cambridge.' The score of another anthem, 'I am the Resur-

[1] C. F. Abdy Williams, *Degrees in Music.*

rection,' from a Funeral Service, is also in the British Museum (Add. MSS. 17,820/107*b*) and is referred to simply as by 'Wanless.' This probably is by Thomas, although it may be the work of his father. In 1703 he published at York a collection of the words of anthems sung in the Minster, and the year previously had published at London a psalter as below :

' The Metre Psalm-tunes in 4 parts. Compos'd for the use of the Parish Church of St. Michael's of Belfrey's in York.' . . . J. Heptinstall, for Thomas Baxter : London, 1702.

He was also the composer of the 4-part 'York Litany,' no two versions of which agree. Jebb printed three in his 'Choral Responses and Litanies' (1846), and there is another in R.C.M. 813/104. J. M^K.

WANNENMACHER, JOHANNES (*d.* Interlaken, *c.* 1551), whose surname is also Latinised into Vannius, was of Swiss descent. In 1510 he was living in Berne, when he was elected cantor by the Canons of the Collegiate foundation of St. Vincent. His duties were to conduct the choir, to maintain and instruct the choir boys, and to provide new compositions for the church. He was then in Orders and was required to say Mass there three or four times a week. A trivial dispute induced him to leave Berne, and in 1514 he was canon and cantor of St. Nicolas at Freiburg in Breisgau. Here he joined a circle of Humanist scholars, and made the acquaintance of Glarean, who highly esteemed him as a musician. In 1519, for some reason unknown, he secretly left Freiburg to offer his services to Cardinal Schinner, Bishop of Sion (Sitten), but was persuaded to return to Freiburg. Afterwards, coming under the influence of the reformer Zwingli, with whom he entered into correspondence, he imbibed the reforming opinions, and in 1530 publicly renounced Catholicism, which led to his being imprisoned and subjected to the torture of the rack ; he was ultimately banished from the place. He took refuge in Berne, which had embraced protestantism, but no longer finding there any prospect of a musical appointment, was fain to accept in 1531 the position of town clerk at Interlaken, which was offered him, where he remained till his death.

Wannenmacher was a composer of some consequence, though he has left few works behind him. Glarean in his *Dodecachordon* has inserted as a good example of polyphonic composition in the Hypomixolydian mode a considerable motet *a* 4 in two parts by Wannenmacher, 'Attendite, populus meus,' which he says was publicly performed in 1516 at Freiburg, and greatly pleased the cultured people of the place ; meaning, no doubt, the Humanist scholars then living there and their sympathisers. He seems also to hint at the motet having had a political significance, the words selected from various Psalms being intended as a dissuasive to the Swiss from entering into any alliance with Francis I. of France. A still more important work by Wannenmacher is his setting of Wolfgang Dachstein's metrical version of the 137th Psalm, 'An Wasserflüssen Babylon,' in five divisions *a* 3-6, which appeared in Ott's 'Liederbuch' of 1544. This piece alone enables us to form a very favourable judgment of Wannenmacher's merits as a polyphonic composer. After his death there was published a small collection of German songs, sacred and secular, *a* 2, under the title 'Bicinia sive duo Germanica ad aequales. . . . Berne, 1553.' J. R. M.

WANNINGUS, JOHANN (*b.* Kampen, Overyssel, 16th cent. ; *d. c.* 1604), Kapellmeister at S⁺. Mary's church, Danzig, 1580–90 ; pensioned in 1602. He composed Sacrae cantiones 5-8 v. (1580) ; two books 'Sententiae insigniores,' etc., motets on texts from the gospels, 5, 6 and 7 v. (1584 and 1590) ; Sacrae cantiones, 5 and 6 v. in MS. ; a 5-part mass, 7-part Jubilate, and motets in organ-tablature ; five Sententiae in score, edited by Eitner in *Annals of the Netherlandish Society for Musical History* (1878) (*Q.-L.*).

WANSKI, JEAN NÉPOMUCÈNE (*b.* Grand Duchy of Poe, beginning of 19th cent.; *d.* ? Aix, Provence), a Polish violinist and composer, son of Jean Wanski (*b.* 1762 ; *d.* after 1800), also a composer and violinist, who gained a great popularity in his own country at the end of the 18th century as a writer of national songs, polonaises, mazurkas and military marches.

The younger Wanski was educated at Kalisz and Warsaw, and leaving Poland for Paris, became a pupil of Baillot. His studies completed, and being gifted with a considerable talent, he toured in Spain, France, Italy and Sicily. Extending his travels as far as Malta, he returned to France, visiting Florence and Rome on his way. At the latter place he was made a member of the Academy of St. Cecilia. He again toured in France, before visiting Switzerland. The profits accruing from Wanski's voyages were apparently small, and when a severe illness seized him at Saint Gall he was found alone and in a dying condition by a compatriot, Count Alexander Sobanski. Hearing that a fellow-countryman of his was lying in poverty and sickness, the Count sought out the unfortunate artist to render him assistance. In 1839 Wanski settled at Aix, in Provence, where he married a French woman, and gave himself up to teaching and composition. He wrote two 'Méthodes' for the violin ; one for the alto ; also *Gymnastique des doigts et de l'archet*, and numerous brilliant studies and pieces for the violin. (Pougin, Supplement to Fétis's *Biog. des Mus.*) E. H.-A.

WARD, JOHN, published in 1613

'The *First Set* of English Madrigals To 3. 4. 5. and 6. parts apt both for Viols and Voyces. With a Mourning Song in memory of *Prince Henry*. Newly

Composed by *Iohn Ward. . . . Printed by* Thomas Snodham, 1613.'

The work—in six partbooks—is dedicated 'To the Honorable Gentleman, and my very good Maister, Sir *Henry Fanshawe*, Knight,' and in the dedication the composer tells his patron that

'These . . . are the primitiae of my Muse, planted in your pleasure, and cherisht by the gentle calme of your Fauour.'

Sir Henry Fanshawe (1569 ?–1616), Remembrancer of the Exchequer, of Ware Park, Herts, and Warwick Lane, London, was a personal friend of Prince Henry and a prominent member of the protestant party at the beginning of the 17th century. His daughter-in-law, Anne, Lady Fanshawe, says in her *Memoirs* (1830, p. 42) that he

'was a great lover of music, and kept many gentlemen that were perfectly well qualified both in that and the Italian tongue, in which he spent some time.'

John Ward was evidently one of these gentlemen of the Fanshawe household. He witnessed Sir Henry's will (dated Nov. 13, 1613), by which the testator left to his heir all his musical instruments 'except the greate Wind Instrument in my howse in Warwyck Lane' ; and from Lady Fanshawe's will (dated Feb. 20, 1629) it seems that he was a trustee for her jointure, for she states that by deed dated May 20, James I. (1607), she had assigned a lease of the Dengey Hall estate to her son-in-law, her nephew, and her 'ancient servant John Ward gent,' in trust for the uses of her will. On July 8, 1619, Ward was granted the arrears of a rent of £8 : 6 : 8 payable to the King out of the Manor of Bengeo, Herts. (Cal. Dom. James I. CIX. Sign. Man. x. No. 19) ; according to Sir Henry Fanshawe's will this manor had been conveyed to trustees as part of his wife's jointure. Ward was a witness of Lady Fanshawe's will, among the bequests of which are sums of £10 apiece to John Ward and two others, 'three of my feoffees,' and of mourning to John Ward 'and the rest of my own servants.' Apart from his musical compositions this is all that is known of Ward's biography ; he must have died before 1641, for in that year John Barnard printed an Evening Service and two Anthems by him in his collection of Church Music, which only contained music by deceased composers. W. B. S.

The value and importance of Ward's work as a madrigal writer was not realised before the publication of his set of madrigals in ENG. MADR. SCH. vol. xix. It is in his writing for five and six voices more especially that he exhibits a definitely individual style, and several of these madrigals are to be placed in the very first rank. 'Die not, fond man' has long been a popular favourite, and deservedly so, but it is by no means the finest of the set. 'If the deep sighs' is a superb and very moving piece of music; like many of Ward's madrigals it is of great length; especially beautiful is the passage, ' Nor not a river weeps not at my tale.' Another magnificent madrigal is ' I have entreated and I have complained '; the words are by Walter Davison, and the final passage is very beautiful. ' Out from the vale ' and ' Upon a bank with roses set ' are also first-rate madrigals. A characteristic feature of Ward's work is his use of suspensions; and he also uses passing notes sometimes in a very individual manner; an example of this is to be found at the words ' And die I shall ' in ' Flora, fair nymph.' Remarkable examples of Ward's use of suspensions occur in the closing passage of ' Upon a bank '; at the words, ' her cruelty hath lost' in ' Out from the vale '; and at ' with miseries opprest ' in ' If the deep sighs.' Very fine massive effects are built up in this manner, and not infrequently six different notes of the scale are simultaneously employed. But suspended discords of all kinds, simple, double and triple are found throughout Ward's madrigals. He showed great taste in selecting words, and seems to have had a special preference for the poems of Sidney and Drayton, and poems by both Walter and Francis Davison are among his madrigals.

Ward wrote a good number of Fantazias for viols, notably those in B.M. Add. MSS. 29,372-7, as well as pieces for the virginals, and a fine collection of Fancies for 4, 5 and 6 viols is at Ch. Ch.[1] Many of the string pieces are attractive, but none have been printed. Compositions by him are to be found in Foster's Virginal Book, B.M. Roy. Lib. (see VIRGINAL MUSIC). Little of Ward's church music is known to-day, yet a fair amount of it has survived. He contributed ' O let me tread ' (a 4), and ' O Lord, consider' (a 5) to Leighton's ' Teares or Lamentacions,' and Barnard printed his ' First Evening Service,' and ' I will praise the Lord ' and ' Let God arise ' in 1641. Appended is a list of his church music in MS.

SERVICES

T.D., K., C. B.M. Add. MSS. 29,289 fo. 107.
1st Verse Service. R.C.M. 1049 fo. 168.
2nd Evening Service. Tenb. 791 fo. 292.

ANTHEMS

Bow down.
Down caitiff wretch.
How long wilt thou forget.
How long shall I seek counsel.
I heard the voice of a great multitude.
O let me tread.
O, Lord, consider my great moans.
Praise the Lord, O my soul, O Lord.
Praise the Lord, O my soul, and all.
This is a joyful day.
Unto Thee, O Lord.
Exsurge Domine.

E. H. F.

WARING, WILLIAM, translator of ROUSSEAU's *Dictionnaire de Musique—A Complete Dictionary of Music, consisting of a copious explanation of all the words necessary to a true knowledge and understanding of Music.*

[1] See Arkwright, *Cat. of Music in Library of Ch. Ch., Oxford,* Part I. (MS. Music), pp. 119, 120, pub. by Oxford Univ. Press.

London, 1770. 8vo. In the 2nd edition (1779) Waring's name as translator was added to the title.   G.

WARLOCK, PETER, see HESELTINE.

WARNER, H. WALDO (b. Northampton, Jan. 4, 1874), viola-player and composer. The family moved to London in 1880, but although the boy was passionately fond of music, his training was not seriously taken in hand until he entered the G.S.M. in 1888. He then studied the violin with Alfred Gibson, and composition with R. Orlando Morgan. He won many distinctions, including the associateship and gold medal, and was afterwards appointed a professor, but had to relinquish this post in 1920 owing to the touring engagements of the LONDON STRING QUARTET, in which he has played the viola since its foundation in 1907. For some years he also played as principal viola in the New Symphony and Royal Philharmonic orchestras. His first public appearances, however, were as a violinist. As a student he wrote an opera, ' The Royal Vagrants,' which was performed at the G.S.M. Since then he has become best known as a writer of chamber music. His name occurs more than once as prize-winner in the list of compositions in phantasy - form due to the initiative of W. W. COBBETT (q.v.), and as the recipient of a commission to write a specified work. His chamber works include three pianoforte trios, of which one obtained a Cobbett, and another the Coolidge prize of $1000 in 1921; a string quartet in C minor which was awarded the first prize in the ' War Time ' competition of 1916; three phantasies for string quartet, in F, D, and G minor, the third being based on folk-songs in accordance with the terms of the Cobbett competition in which it was a successful entry; a suite, ' The Pixy-Ring,' for string quartet; a rhapsody for viola solo and string quartet; a violin sonata, a viola sonata, numerous short pieces for each instrument and also for violoncello. He has also written several suites for orchestra, one of which, ' Three Elfin Dances ' (Elves, Nymphs and Gnomes), has been performed at the Promenade Concerts and elsewhere; and upwards of a hundred songs and partsongs.   B. E.

WARNOTS, (1) HENRY (b. Brussels, July 11, 1832; d. Mar. 3, 1893), was taught music first by his father, and in 1849 became a pupil at the Brussels Conservatoire, in harmony, pianoforte-playing and singing. In 1856 he appeared in opera at Liège as a light tenor, and was engaged for a short period at the Opéra-Comique, Paris, as the titular hero of Boieldieu's ' Jean de Paris.' He next sang at Strassburg, and on Jan. 24, 1865, an operetta of his composition, ' Une Heure du mariage,' was performed there. He also composed a patriotic cantata sung at Ghent in 1867, and in that year he was engaged at the National Theatre,

Brussels; in October he sang in Flemish the hero's part in De Miry's 'Franz Ackermann.' In December of the same year he obtained a professorship at the Conservatoire, and retired from the stage. In 1869 he was appointed director of the orchestra of the Brussels City Musical Society, and in 1870 he founded a school of music at St. Josse-ten-Noode-Schaernbeeck, a suburb of Brussels. His daughter and pupil,

(2) ELLY (ELISABETH) (b. Liège, 1862) made her début, Sept. 9, 1878, as Anna ('Dame Blanche') at the Théâtre de la Monnaie, Brussels. She sang there for two seasons, and in 1881 she was engaged at the Pergola, Florence; on May 17 of the same year she made her first appearance in England at the Royal Italian Opera as Marguerite de Valois in the 'Huguenots.' During the season she also played the part of the same Queen in Hérold's 'Pré aux Clercs,' and was favourably received. After that she was frequently heard at the Promenade Concerts, at the Crystal Palace, and elsewhere. For some years she was a regular visitor to London.   A. C.

WARREN, JOSEPH (b. London, Mar. 20, 1804; d. Bexley, Kent, Mar. 8, 1881), in early life began the study of the violin, which he gave up for the pianoforte and organ. In 1834 he became organist of St. Mary's (R.C.) Chapel, Chelsea, and composed some masses for its service. He was author of *Hints to Young Composers*, *Hints to Young Organists*, *Guide to Singers*, and other similar works, and editor of Hilton's 'Ayres, or Fa las' for three voices (for the Musical Antiquarian Society), an English version of Beethoven's 'Christus am Ölberge,' Boyce's 'Cathedral Music,' for which he wrote new biographies of the composers, including, in most cases, exhaustive lists of their compositions, and many other works. He also compiled a *Biographical Dictionary of Deceased Musicians*, issued in two parts by R. Cocks & Co. in 1845.

W. H. H.; addns. F. K.

WARREN, THOMAS (d. circa 1794), the editor of a famous collection of Catches and Glees, published annually in oblong folio volumes between 1763 and 1794, in which latter year he probably died. He was Secretary to the Noblemen's and Gentlemen's CATCH CLUB (q.v.) from its foundation in 1761 to 1794, being succeeded by S. Webbe. Warren's collection of 'Catches, Canons and Glees' was begun in 1763, and the volumes were engraved and printed for the editor, by different publishers. It is a valuable work, containing 652 pieces; many of the volumes are of extreme rarity. A selection from its contents, under the title 'Vocal Harmony,' was published by Welcker, who also published Warren's 'Monthly Collection'   F. K.

WARROCK, THOS., see WARWICK.

WARTEL, (1) PIERRE FRANÇOIS (b. Versailles, Apr. 3, 1806; d. Paris, Aug. 12, 1882). From 1823–28 he was a pupil in Choron's School of Music, and afterwards at the Conservatoire under Banderali and Nourrit, where he obtained a first prize for singing. From 1831–46 he played small tenor parts at the Opéra. He afterwards sang with success in Germany, but on his return to Paris devoted himself entirely to teaching. He was considered one of the best teachers of the day, and among his pupils must be named Christine Nilsson, Trebelli, Mlle. Hisson (Opéra), etc. Wartel has another claim to distinction, as having introduced into France and popularised Schubert's songs. Indeed it was he who drew the attention of the Viennese to them in 1842, at a time when Schubert was completely eclipsed by Proch, Hackel, etc., and an occasional performance of the 'Wanderer' was the only sign of his existence.[1] His wife,

(2) ALDA-THÉRÈSE-ANNETTE, née Adrien (b. July 2, 1814; d. Paris, Nov. 6, 1865), was the daughter of a violinist at the Opéra, and leader of the Conservatoire band. She received instruction in music at the Conservatoire, was appointed accompanist there, and in 1831 obtained a professorship, which she resigned in 1838. She was the first female instrumentalist ever engaged at the Société des Concerts. In 1859 she visited England with her husband, and gave a concert at the house of Mr. Grote, where she played Mendelssohn's Pianoforte Trio in D minor with Joachim and Piatti. She composed Studies and other works, including her Lessons on the Pianoforte Sonatas of Beethoven. Their son,

(3) LOUIS ÉMILE (b. Paris, Mar. 31, 1834), was engaged at the Théâtre Lyrique from 1858–65, and afterwards established a vocal school of his own.   A. C.

WARWICK (WARWICKE, WARROCK), THOMAS. There were probably two musicians of this name, father and son, living in the 16th and 17th centuries. They were descendants of an old Cumberland family whose seat was at Warwick Hall, some four miles from Carlisle. The elder Thomas married Elizabeth, daughter of John Somerville, of Aston Somerville, and by her was the father of Sir Philip Warwick (b. 1609) who was Secretary to the Treasury to Charles II. He succeeded John Bull as organist of Hereford Cathedral in 1586, and held this post until 1589. His name appears among the benefactors to the library of the vicars-choral at Hereford (West's Cath. Org.). The younger Thomas (b. beginning of 17th cent.; d. 1660) succeeded Orlando Gibbons as organist of the Chapel Royal. Gibbons died in 1625, but there is no indication of Warwick's appointment until 1630, when, on Mar. 29, he had to forfeit a month's salary

[1] Hanslick, *Concertwesen*, p. 346.

' because he presumed to play verses on the organ at service tyme, being formerly inhibited by the Deane from doinge the same, by reason of his insufficiency for that solemn service.'

In 1641, he appears as musician ' for the Virginall,' and on Nov. 17, 1660, a warrant was issued ' to admit Christopher Gibbons musician upon the virginalls in place of Thomas Warwick deceased, with the yearly wages of £86 to be paid quarterly ' (H. C. de Lafontaine, *The King's Musick*). He contributed a ' Pavano ' and ' Galiardo ' to the Fitzwilliam Virginal Book, and Thomas Tomkin's madrigal, ' When I observe,' included in his ' Songs of 3, 4, 5 and 6 parts,' 1622, is dedicated to ' Mr. Thomas Warwicke.' He is said by Hawkins to have composed a song in 40 parts performed before Charles I. about 1635, and Anthony Wood refers to him as organist of Westminster Abbey, but this is unsupported by the Abbey records.

ANTHEMS

I lift mine eyes, *a* 5. Ch. Ch. 56-60. Bass part wanting ; Harl· 6343/14. Words only.
I lift my hart up to the hills, *a* 5. B.M. Add. MSS. 29,366-8. Cantus, bassus and altus parts only.
O God of my salvation, *a* 5. P.H. ; Durh. ; Ch. Ch. 56-60. Bass part wanting ; B.M. Add. MSS. 30,478-9. Tenor cantoris part only ; Harl. 6343/139. Words only.   J. M^K.

WASIELEWSKY, JOSEPH W. VON (*b.* Gross Leesen, near Dantzig, June 17, 1822 ; *d.* Dec. 13, 1896), author, violin-player and conductor. On Apr. 3, 1843, he entered the Conservatorium at Leipzig under Mendelssohn's personal teaching. Other branches he learned under David and Hauptmann, and remained in the Conservatorium till Easter, 1845. He acted as musical critic for the *Signale*, *Leipziger Zeitung*, *Dresdener Journale*, etc. He played in the orchestras of the theatre, the Gewandhaus and the Euterpe concerts, till 1850, when he left for Düsseldorf at the invitation of Schumann, and remained there for two years. In May 1852, he removed to Bonn, and became conductor of the Concordia, the Gesangverein and the Beethoven-Verein. After three years he exchanged this for Dresden. In 1869 he was recalled to Bonn as ' town music-director.' He withdrew from this appointment in 1884 and retired to Sondershausen. In 1858 he published his biography of Schumann (2nd and 3rd eds., 1869 and 1880) ; in 1869 his excellent book on *Die Violine und ihre Meister* (B. & H.), 2nd ed. considerably augmented 1883, 3rd, 1893. In 1874 appeared *Die Violine im xvii. Jahrhundert und die Anfänge der Instrumental-composition* (Bonn), with an interesting collection of ' Instrumentalsätze ' by way of supplement to it ; *Geschichte der Instrumentalmusik im xvi. Jahrhundert* (1878) : *Musikalische Fürsten vom Mittelalter bis zu Beginn des xix. Jahrhundert* (1879) : *Schumanniana* (1883) ; *Beethoven* (1888) ; *Das Violoncell und seine Geschichte* (1889) ; *Karl Reinecke* (1892) ; *Aus siebzig Jahren* (1897). He contributed much to musical periodicals, and as a composer wrote some partsongs and a nocturne for violin and piano.

He had a decoration from the Duke of Meiningen (1871) ; and was a royal music-director (1873) and a member of the ' Accademia filarmonica ' at Bologna.   G.

WASSERMANN, HEINRICH JOSEPH (*b.* Schwarzbach, near Fulda, Hesse, Apr. 3, 1791 ; *d.* Riehen near Basle, Aug. 1838), violinist-composer. He was the son of a village musician, and studied under cantor Henkel at Fulda, and Spohr at Gotha. He was violinist at the court of Hechingen, Kapellmeister at Zürich, chamber musician at Donaueschingen, Kapellmeister at Geneva, and finally at Basle. He composed three quartets, one with flute ; violin duets ; dances for orchestra ; fantasias and variations for violin and string quartet, also with pianoforte (*Fétis* ; *Mendel*).

WASTE VALVE, a safety valve to organ bellows.   T. E.

WATER CARRIER, THE, the English version of Cherubini's LES DEUX JOURNÉES.

WATER MUSIC, THE, a series of instrumental movements composed by HANDEL (*q.v.*). The Water Music consists of twenty-one movements ; the original autograph has disappeared ; but two movements undated, and differing considerably from the printed copies, will be found in B.M. Add. MSS. 30,310. The earliest printed edition is that of Walsh, published in 1740.   W. S. R.

WATKIN-MILLS, ROBERT (*b.* Painswick, Gloucestershire, Mar. 5, 1856), was taught singing by Edwin Holland in London, by Federico Blasco in Milan, and on his return to London by Blume. On May 17, 1884, he made his début at a Crystal Palace concert, and on the 21st he made a single appearance on the stage at Birmingham with the Carl Rosa Company as Baldassare in an English version of ' La Favorita,' and was offered a permanent engagement, which he declined in favour of a concert career. On Jan. 1, 1885, he created a favourable impression at the Albert Hall in the ' Messiah.' On Feb. 14 he first appeared at the Popular Concerts. In the autumn of the same year he sang at the Birmingham Festival in the production of Stanford's ' Three Holy Children,' etc. Thenceforward he became a favourite bass-baritone singer at all the principal concerts and festivals, and after 1894 made several tours in Canada, the United States and Australasia, etc., with the greatest success. He ultimately settled at Toronto, Canada, as a teacher, and with his wife, organist of the Knox Presbyterian Church, established the Watkin-Mills Music Club.   A. C.

WATLEN, JOHN, a composer and music-publisher who proclaimed on many of his title-pages 'Late of the Royal Navy.' He was living in Edinburgh in 1788, and about and before this time was composing sonatas for the harpsichord and programme music. Some of this, of various dates of composition, include ' The Siege of

Toulon,' ' Battle of Trafalgar,' etc. In Edinburgh he was at one time an assistant to Corri & Co., music-publishers, and was a tuner and music-teacher until he opened a music-shop at 17 Princes Street. From this address he published many arrangements and selections of Scottish Songs, including his ' Circus Tunes.' He removed to 13 North Bridge, and this imprint appears on a great number of Scots Songs, either arranged or entirely composed by himself. In 1798 he failed in business and retired to Abbeyhill, a sanctuary from arrest near Holyrood. Here he taught music and issued sundry sheet songs. About 1800 he removed to London, where, in partnership with a person named Cobb, he was again publishing. Cobb and Watlen were at 19 Tavistock Street, Covent Garden, in 1805: in 1807 Watlen had set up business on his own account at 5 Leicester Place, Leicester Square. Watlen was the first secretary of the Edinburgh Musical Fund. F. K.

WATSON, THOMAS (d. circa 1592), put forth in 1590

' The first sett of Italian Madrigalls Englished, not to the sense of the originall dittie, but after the affection of the Noate. By Thomas Watson. There are also heere inserted two excellent Madrigals of Master William Byrd's composed after the Italian vaine at the request of the sayd Thomas Watson.'

It is dedicated in a Latin metrical epistle to Robert Devereux, Earl of Essex, and there is also a similar epistle addressed to Luca Marenzio, the celebrated Italian madrigal composer, from whose works twenty-three of the twenty-eight madrigals included in the publication were taken. Watson is conjectured to have been identical with Thomas Watson, a native of London, who after studying poetry for some time at Oxford, returned to London to study law. A collection of sonnets by him entitled *Hecatompathia*, or *Passionate Centurie of Love*, was licensed in 1581, and some poems by him were inserted in *England's Helicon*, 1614. W. H. H.

WATTS, JOHN, a famous bookseller and printer with whom Benjamin Franklin served as a journeyman, when he was in London. Watts was established in Wild's Court, Lincoln's Inn Fields, before 1726, and in conjunction with Jacob Tonson published plays and miscellaneous works. The introduction of the ballad opera at Lincoln's Inn Fields Theatre brought Watts into brisk trade in the publication of the operas performed there. He published the first and later editions of the ' Beggar's Opera,' 1727–28 (music engraved), and after this practically the whole of the series of ballad operas as they were performed. These editions have the airs for the songs in the operas printed from engraved wood blocks, and are especially valuable for giving the old names of the tunes. They range in date from 1727–39. Another important work in six volumes is ' The Musical Miscellany,' 1729–31. After Watt's death this was reissued with different titles to the volumes (' The Harp,'

' The Spinnet,' ' The Violin,' etc.) by a person named Wren, c. 1750. Some of the operas were also reissued (1765, etc.) by J. and R. Tonson. F. K.

WAYLETT, HARRIETT (b. Bath, Feb. 7, 1800 ; d. Kensington, Apr. 26, 1851), an actress and soprano singer, principally of ballads of the Vauxhall type. She was the daughter of an upholsterer named Cooke. She became the pupil of one of the Loder family, and made her début on the Bath stage, Mar. 16, 1816, performing in provincial theatres for the next three or four years. At this time she made considerable reputation by her playing and singing in the character of Margery, in the opera ' Love in a Village,' in which she afterwards appeared at Drury Lane. She made her first appearance on a London stage at the Adelphi in October 1820. She had previously (1819) married an actor named Waylett, who proved a very unsuitable husband, and she experienced many misfortunes through her marriage, which ended in separation. In 1826 she married George Alexander Lee, the composer. She appeared at the Dublin Theatre Royal almost every season from 1826–36. In Oct. 1835 she got £800 for a three weeks' engagement. F. K. ; addn. W. H. G. F.

WAYLETT, HENRY, a London music-publisher, established before 1740, at ' The Black Lyon ' in Exeter Change. He was an extensive publisher of half-sheet songs, collections of songs, tutors, etc. He had the honour of issuing the first edition of ' Rule, Britannia ' which formed part of the following publication

' The music in the Judgment of Paris . . . to which (by particular desire of several encouragers of this work) are added the celebrated Ode in Honour of Great Britain, call'd Rule Britannia, and Sawney and Jenny, a favourite dialogue in the Scotch stile, the whole compos'd by Thomas Augustine Arne, opera sesta,'

folio, the patent dated Jan. 29, 1740–41. Waylett also published sets of country dances (one is for 1751), ' The Muses Choice ' by Joseph Bryan, two books 1756–58, solos by Thomas Davis, etc. etc. He appears to have been succeeded by Francis Waylett, who at another address (' his music shop opposite Suffolk Street, Pall Mall ') reissued publications by the elder Waylett. In 1769 (and probably long before) Richard Bride was established at The Black Lyon in Exeter Change, publishing on his own account, and republishing the early Waylett publications. F. K.

WEALE (WHEALE), WILLIAM (d. Bedford, 1727), was organist of St. Paul's, Bedford, from about 1715, and took the degree of Mus.B. at Cambridge in 1719. He deserves mention as the composer of the hymn-tune ' Bedford,' which seems to have equal authenticity in both its versions, in triple and duple time. (*Brit. Mus. Biog.*) M.

WEAVER, JOHN (b. Shrewsbury, July 21, 1673 ; d. there, Sept. 24, 1760), a dancing master. In 1706 he published in quarto a translation of Feuillet's *Chorégraphie*, under the title of *Orchesography, or the Art of Dancing by Characters and Demonstrative Figures*. This was the first attempt of the sort in England. A second edition without date appeared some ten years later. In the same year, 1706, he published *A Small Treatise of Time and Cadence in Dancing, reduc'd to an Easy and Exact Method*, consisting of eight quarto pages of text and four of choregraphic examples. He also published a number of dances in the new character with their tunes, but the only one that bears his name is

'The Union, a New Dance compos'd by Mr. Isaac, perform'd at Court on Her Majestie's Birth day, Febr. ye 6th, 1707, and writt down in Characters by John Weaver.'

This is a dance in fifteen couplets engraved on copper plates. Weaver's next literary effort was *An Essay towards an History of Dancing*, 8vo, 1712. This is largely concerned with the Pantomime of the ancient Romans. In speaking of Country Dances he describes them as 'the peculiar growth of this [English] nation ; tho' now transplanted into almost all the Courts of Europe.' Before publication he had written a letter to the *Spectator* dated Mar. 19, 1711–12, describing the book, and he managed to get it noticed again on Aug. 25, as 'now ready to be published.'[1] The *History of Dancing* was followed by *Anatomical and Mechanical Lectures upon Dancing*, 8vo, 1721, and this again by

'The History of the Mimes and Pantomimes. To which will be added a List of the Modern Entertainments that have been exhibited on the English Stage, either in imitation of the ancient *Pantomimes*, or after the manner of the Modern *Italians* ; when and where first Perform'd, and by whom Compos'd,' 8vo, 1728.

This List of Entertainments is of interest, for in it Weaver claims to have been the first to introduce drama in dumb show on the English stage. He says :

'The first Entertainment that appeared on the *English* stage, where the Representation and Story was carried on by Dancing, Action and Motion only, was performed in Grotesque Characters, after the manner of the Modern Italians, such as Harlequin, Scaramouch, etc., and was called The Tavern Bilkers. Composed by Mr. Weaver, and first performed in Drury Lane Theatre, 1702. The next was many years after, and was an attempt in Imitation of the ancient *Pantomimes*, and the first of that kind that had appeared since the time of the Roman Emperors, and was called The Loves of Mars and Venus. Composed by Mr. Weaver. First perform'd on the theatre in Drury Lane, 1716.'

'The Tavern Bilkers' was played at Drury Lane with Farquhar's 'The Constant Couple' on Oct. 23, 1702. It was revived in conjunction with the same play on Mar. 8, 1715–16, when it is described as 'a mimick night scene, after the Italian manner, as it was performed 14 years ago,' and again at Goodman's Fields on Jan. 13, 1732–33, with Woodward as First Drawer.[2] Harlequin and Scaramouch had long been known on the English stage as speaking

[1] See *Spectator*, Nos. 334 and 466.
[2] See Genest, *History of the English Stage*, ii. 254, 576, and iii. 399.

characters : the novelty consisted in the representation of an entire drama in dumb show.

'The Loves of Mars and Venus' was produced with symphonies by Symonds, and the 'musical airs of the dancing parts' were composed by Firbank. It was so well received that in the following season Weaver produced 'Orpheus and Eurydice, a Dramatick Entertainment in Dancing after the manner of the ancient Pantomimes,' and in 1719 a similar pantomime entitled 'Cupid and Bacchus.' He did not, however, entirely abandon the modern Italian style, for on Apr. 2, 1717, he produced at Drury Lane 'Perseus and Andromeda, a Burlesque Entertainment in Dancing, in Grotesque Characters,' with Mrs. Bignall as Andromeda. This was played with Beaumont and Fletcher's 'The Humorous Lieutenant.' If one may judge of the piece by a description printed about 1780 it consisted of two distinct plays, each in five interludes, the one serious, representing the classical story of Perseus and Andromeda, the other comic and modern, introducing Harlequin, Columbine, Clown and other characters. Each interlude of the serious was followed by an interlude of the comic play, and in the latter a song of Weaver's beginning 'In London town there lived, well known, a Doctor old and wary,' was sung to the tune of 'Thomas, I cannot.' 'Harlequin turned Judge' was another grotesque pantomime of Weaver's produced in 1717.

In 1719 Weaver seems to have severed his connexion with Drury Lane and to have been succeeded by another dancing master named John Thurmond, but we hear of one other pantomime of his, 'The Judgment of Paris,' produced at Drury Lane on Feb. 6, 1732–33. Pantomimic entertainments in dumb show were just then the favourite diversions of the town : see the *Gentleman's Magazine* for 1732, p. 761.   J. F. R. S.

WEBB, REV. RICHARD, M.A. (*d.* near Windsor, Apr. 13, 1829), a clergyman and musician; author of a valuable collection of 15th- and 16th-century madrigals, 3-6 v. (London, 1808), and another collection of 3, 4 and 5-part madrigals in 1814. He also composed a set of four glees for 3 voices (Brown and Stratton).
                                            E. v. d. s.

WEBB, WILLIAM, a 17th-century English composer. His songs are in John Playford's 'Select Musical Ayres and Dialogues,' 1652 ; 'Select Ayres,' etc., editions of 1653 and 1659; Hilton's 'Catch that Catch Can' of 1658, and J. Playford's edition of 1667 ; Playford's 'The Musical Companion,' 1673 (3-part songs), and a three-part song in *A-B. Philo-Mus. Synopsis of Vocal Musick*, 1680.   E. v. d. s.

WEBBE, (1) SAMUEL (*b.* 1740 ;[3] *d.* London,

[3] He is generally said to have been born in Minorca, but the obituary notice in the *Gentleman's Magazine* of 1816 (quoted in *Mus. T.*, 1897, p. 678) implies that his father died after accepting a government position in Minorca, before his wife and son could join him there.

May 25, 1816), was, at 11 years of age, apprenticed to a cabinet-maker, but upon the expiration of his time quitted that calling, and copied music for a livelihood, being employed by Welcker in Soho, through whose instrumentality he had lessons from Barbandt, organist of the Bavarian ambassador's chapel. He also studied the Latin, French and Italian languages, which were afterwards supplemented by German, Greek and Hebrew. He first appeared as a composer about 1763, devoting himself chiefly to the production of unaccompanied vocal music. In 1766 the CATCH CLUB (*q.v.*) awarded him a prize medal for his canon ' O that I had wings,' and in subsequent years twenty-six other medals for the following compositions :

'The man and the woman,' catch, 1767 ; 'From everlasting,' canon, and 'A generous friendship,' glee, 1768 ; 'Alzate o porte,' canon, 1770 ; 'Iddio i quel che mi cingo,' canon, 1771 ; 'Discord, dire sister,' glee, 1772 ; 'To the old, long life,' catch, and 'Who can express,' canon, 1774 ; 'Now I'm prepared,' glee, 1775 ; 'You gave me your heart,' and ''Tis beauty calls,' glees, 1776 ; 'Glory be to the Father,' canon, and 'Rise, my joy,' glee, 1777 ; 'Great Bacchus,' and 'Hail, music,' glees, 1778 ; 'Neighbours, come,' catch, and 'O all ye works,' canon, 1781 ; 'My Lady Rantum,' catch, 1782 ; 'To Thee all angels,' canon, 1783 ; 'When youthful Harriet,' catch, and 'The fragrant painting,' glee, 1784 ; 'O Lord, show Thy mercy,' canon, and 'Swiftly from the mountain's brow,' glee 1789 ; 'Juliet is pretty,' catch, and 'Non fidi al mar,' glee, 1790 ; and 'Tell me,' catch, 1794.

More than half of these compositions are catches and canons, and but three of the glees can be ranked among Webbe's best. His finest works,—his glees ' When winds breathe soft,' ' The mighty conqueror,' ' Come live with me,' ' Thy voice, O Harmony,' ' To me the wanton girls,' and ' Hence, all ye vain delights,' and his catches, ' Dear father, the girl you desire me in marriage,' and ' Would you know my Celia's charms,'—are not to be found in the list of his prize compositions.

On the death of Thomas Warren Horne in 1784 he became secretary to the Catch Club, and held the office until his death. On the establishment of the GLEE CLUB (*q.v.*) in 1787 he became its librarian and wrote and composed for it his glee ' Glorious Apollo,' which during the whole existence of the club enjoyed the distinction of being the first glee performed at every meeting. He was also organist of the chapel of the Sardinian embassy. In the *Laity's Directory* for 1793 (quoted in *The Tablet*, 1817), is an advertisement which supports this statement, and the publication of music used in this chapel, as well as of music used in the Portuguese chapel, seems to imply that he was organist of both. He published in 1792 'A Collection of Motetts or Antiphons,' and 'A Collection of Masses for small choirs,' principally composed by himself. He published at various periods, beginning 1764, nine books of glees, etc., which were subsequently republished with additions in 3 vols. folio. Twenty-five glees, thirty-six catches, and nine canons by him are included in Warren's collections. He also composed several excellent songs, of which ' The Mansion of Peace ' enjoyed a long-continued popularity. Various other publications are mentioned in *Q.-L.* He died at his chambers in Gray's Inn, and was buried in Old St. Pancras churchyard. William Linley wrote an ode upon his death, for the best setting of which a prize was offered. Seven competitors entered the lists, viz. William Beale, Lord Burghersh, James (?) Elliott, C. S. Evans, William Hawes, William Knyvett and William Linley ; the prize being won by Evans. Webbe stands in the foremost rank of glee-writers, and his works will maintain that position as long as a taste for that style of composition shall endure. As a man he was much beloved and respected for his social virtues.

(2) SAMUEL (*b.* London, *c.* 1770 ; *d.* Liverpool, Nov. 25, 1843), his eldest son, studied principally under his father and became a good pianist and organist. Like his father he early devoted himself to the practice of vocal composition, and in 1794 obtained from the Catch Club prizes for a catch, ' Ah Friendship,' and a canon, ' Resonate Jovem,' and in 1795 for a canon, ' Come follow me.' About 1798 he settled in Liverpool, and became organist of the Unitarian Chapel, Paradise Street. About 1817 he returned to London and joined LOGIER (*q.v.*) in teaching on the latter's system, and became organist of the Spanish ambassador's chapel. Some years afterwards he again settled in Liverpool, where he became successively organist of St. Nicholas' Church and of St. Patrick's Roman Catholic Chapel, Toxteth Park. He composed many glees possessing great merit (among which ' Come away, Death ' is conspicuous), songs, motets, etc. He edited the collection of glees, etc., entitled ' Convito Armonico.' (See *Q.-L.*)

W. H. H.

WEBBER, AMHERST (*b.* Cannes, Oct. 25, 1867), was educated at Marlborough College, and New College, Oxford, where he took an ordinary and a musical degree. He then went to Dresden to study composition with J. L. Nicodé, and in the winter of 1889–90 was at the Paris Conservatoire under Guiraud. He was engaged as *maestro al piano* for several years at Covent Garden and the Metropolitan Opera-House, New York, and did valuable work in ' coaching ' various eminent singers in the Wagner repertory. He composed a symphony, performed by the Philharmonic Orchestra in Warsaw in 1904, and at Boston by the Symphony Orchestra under Gericke in 1905. His one-act comic opera, ' Fiorella,' to a libretto by Sardou, was produced at the Waldorf Theatre, London, June 7, 1905. Various songs in English and French have become popular with the refined singers to whom they appeal. ' Aubade ' and ' La Première ' are two of the most successful as well as the best.   M.

WEBER. The several members of that family of musicians, of whom Carl Maria, the composer of ' Der Freischütz ' and founder of German Romantic Opera was the most outstanding figure, are described below [1] in order according to the following table.

(7) CONSTANZE (*b.* Zell, 1763 ; *d.* Salzburg, Mar. 6, 1842), became Mozart's wife. See MOZART (4).

(8) SOPHIE(*b.*1764;*d.*Salzburg,1843),married Haibl, tenor and composer, attached to Schikaneder's theatre. During widowhood she lived

(1) Johann Baptist (*cr.* Freiherr)

(2) Joseph Franz Xaver

(3) Fridolin (*d.* 1754)

(4) Fridolin (*b.* 1733)

(9) Franz Anton von (*b.* 1734 ; *d.* 1812)

(5) Josepha (6) Aloysia (7) Constanze (8) Sophie (10) Fritz (11) Edmund (12) Carl Maria (*b.* 1786 ; *d.* 1826)

The earliest known member of the family, (1) JOHANN BAPTIST, a man of property in Lower Austria during the latter half of the 16th century, was made Freiherr by the Emperor Ferdinand II. in 1622. The family was, and remained, Roman Catholic. We know nothing of Johann Baptist's musical tastes or faculties, but his younger brother (2) JOSEPH FRANZ XAVER, apparently living in Upper Swabia, is said to have been a great amateur of music and the drama. The title of the elder brother was not transmitted till 1738, and of the younger one's descendants, one, (3) FRIDOLIN, was in the service of Freiherr von Schönau-Zella, near Freiburg im Breisgau, in the 18th century, and died in 1754. He was passionately devoted to music—sang, and played the violin and organ. Of his two sons, the elder (4) FRIDOLIN (*b.* Zell, 1733) (and also a singer and violin player) succeeded his father as manager of the Schönau-Zella estates, and apparently dropped the *von*, which his brother's family retained. He with his brother was a member of the Electoral chapel at Mannheim. In 1756 he married Marie Cæcilie Stamm of Mannheim, by whom he had four daughters (see below), all excellent singers. The eldest,

(5) JOSEPHA (*d.* 1820) was a bravura singer with a high and flexible voice, but a poor musician. Mozart wrote for her the part of the Queen of Night in the ' Zauberflöte ' and a bravura air (Köchel, No. 580). She married in 1789 Hofer, violinist at Schikaneder's theatre, and after his death Meyer, a bass-singer, who sang Pizarro in ' Fidelio.' The second,

(6) ALOYSIA (*b.* 1750 ; *d.* Salzburg, 1839), was Mozart's first love. Her voice was exceptionally high and extremely pleasant in tone, though perhaps rather weak for the stage. In 1780 she was engaged for the opera in Vienna, and married an actor at the court theatre, named Lange, who died in 1827. Mme. Lange made several professional tours before her final retirement in 1808. Mozart wrote for her the part of Constanze in the ' Entführung,' six airs (Köchel, Nos. 294, 316, 383, 418, 419, 538), and a rondo (No. 416). The third,

with Constanze at Salzburg. She was present at Mozart's death, and in 1825 wrote, at Nissen's request, a touching account of the last sad moments.

(9) FRANZ ANTON VON WEBER (*b.* 1734 ; *d.* Mannheim, Apr. 16, 1812), became the father of Carl Maria, who was thus connected by marriage with Mozart. Franz Anton must have been a violinist of more than common ability, as we find him included, by those qualified to speak, amongst the most distinguished viola-players of the time.[2] He was also a virtuoso on the double-bass. He took military service with the Elector Palatine, Karl Theodor, at Mannheim, on the understanding that he was to assist in the celebrated court band. He fought against Frederick the Great at Rosbach (1756) and was slightly wounded, after which he left the army, and entered the service of the Elector Clement Augustus at Cologne. In 1758 he became Steward to the Prince-Bishop, and Court-Councillor at Steuerwald, near Hildesheim. His devotion to music, which was such that he would even play the violin while walking in the fields with his family, caused him to neglect the duties of his office, and he was deprived of it. From 1768–73 he lived at Hildesheim as an ordinary citizen, and there decided, despite his age and numerous family, on becoming a practical musician. He appears to have started on a tour as a viola-player,[3] and then settled in Lübeck, where he published ' Lieder mit Melodien fürs Clavier ' (1774), compositions apparently not without talent, as they were noticed nine years after.[4] In 1778 he was musical director of the theatre at Lübeck, and from 1779–83 Kapellmeister to the Prince-Bishop of Eutin. In 1784 he went to Vienna, made acquaintance with Joseph Haydn, and entrusted to him his two eldest sons, (10) FRITZ and (11) EDMUND,[5] both of

[1] Some details previously given by C. F. P., under separate headings, are incorporated here.

[2] Forkel's *Musikalischer Almanach* for 1783, p. 93.
[3] Gerber's *Lexicon*, ii. 771.
[4] Forkel, p. 68, and elsewhere. M. M. von Weber, in his biography of his father (*Lebensbild*), i. 13, conjectures that Franz Anton had played under an assumed name up to 1778, as no trace of him is found before. Apparently he did not know of the passage in Forkel's *Almanach*. Gerber also mentions as compositions of Franz Anton a cantata, ' Das Lob Gottes in der Natur,' and pieces for the viola, both in MS.
[5] Haydn was specially attached to Edmund, and wrote in his album—

whom showed talent for music (see HAYDN, Vol. II. p. 572). In 1785 he married again in Vienna, returned to Eutin, and undertook the post of director of the town-band.

(12) CARL MARIA FRIEDRICH ERNST, VON (b. Eutin, Dec. 18, 1786 ; d. London, June 5, 1826), was the first child of Franz Anton's second marriage. The father had always longed to have a child that should turn out a prodigy, such as Mozart had been. All his children, daughters as well as sons, showed talent for music and the stage, and his two eldest sons became really good musicians. But Franz Anton could not disguise from himself that so far none of his children surpassed mediocrity, and he was all the more anxious to discern in Carl Maria talent of a high order. Inconstant by nature, his character was an odd mixture of vanity and a pretentious vein of comedy with the most brilliant and versatile gifts, forming a most unsatisfactory whole. Such a disposition was little adapted to the training of a gifted child.

Carl Maria was early set to learn music, principally under his father, who after all was but an amateur. The talent so ardently longed for, however, would not appear in the delicate, nervous child. There is a tradition that after taking great pains with him in vain, his elder brother Fritz exclaimed on one occasion, ' Carl, you may become anything else you like, but a musician you never will be.' The father now tried him with the plastic arts, and put him to drawing, painting in oil, pastel and engraving. Weber, in his autobiography, says that he followed this with some success,[1] but the specimens preserved in the family show nothing beyond a certain manual dexterity, with no sign of real talent.

His father had left Eutin in 1787, and was leading a restless life as director of a dramatic troupe mainly consisting of his own grown-up children. During the next few years he is to be found in Vienna, Cassel, Meiningen, Nuremberg, Erlangen and Augsburg. Bad as the influence of this roving life must have been on the whole, it had its advantages for Carl Maria in the special line to which he was to devote himself, for he may be said to have grown up behind the scenes. From his childhood he was at home in the stage-world as none of the great opera-composers have been—not even Mozart. That instinct for the stage, so obvious in all his dramatic conceptions, no doubt sprang from these early impressions. In 1794, the father being at Weimar with his family, Carl Maria's mother Genoveva, then 26, was engaged

as a singer at the theatre under Goethe's direction, and appeared, on June 16, as Constanze in Mozart's ' Entführung.' The engagement was, however, cancelled in September, and Franz Anton left Weimar, to his subsequent regret.[2] He went, it appears, to Erlangen, and in 1796 to Hildburghausen. There the boy of 9 found his first scientific and competent teacher in HEUSCHKEL (q.v.), an eminent oboist, a solid pianist and organist, and a composer who thoroughly understood his art. An organ-piece by him on the chorale ' Vom Himmel hoch,' [3] shows little fancy, but a complete mastery of the technique of composition. Carl Maria did not at first like the hard, dry studies to which his teacher inexorably bound him, but he soon found that he was making progress, and the father at last beheld with astonishment the dawn of that genuine musical talent which he had himself tried in vain to evoke. Weber never forgot what he owed to Heuschkel. In his autobiographical sketch, written in 1818, he says that from him he had received the best possible, indeed the only true, foundation for a style of pianoforte playing, at once powerful, expressive, and full of character, especially the equal cultivation of the two hands. Heuschkel on his part followed with justifiable pride the subsequent triumphs of his pupil, and one of his published compositions is a piece for wind instruments on themes from Rossini's ' Semiramide ' and Weber's ' Euryanthe ' (Schott).

STUDY UNDER MICHAEL HAYDN.—Unfortunately this instruction lasted but a short time, as Franz Anton moved on in the autumn with his company to Salzburg. Here there was a training-school for chorister-boys, similar to St. Stephen's Cantorei in Vienna, in which the brothers Joseph and Michael Haydn were educated. Michael Haydn had been in the service of the Archbishop of Salzburg since 1762, first as Konzertmeister, and afterwards cathedral organist also. One of his duties was to teach singing to the choristers, among whom the young Weber soon found a place, speedily exciting the attention of Haydn. He asked him to his house and set him to play a concerto of Kozeluch's, which he had studied with Heuschkel, and other pieces, including a recitative from Graun's ' Tod Jesu.' The upshot was that after repeated requests from the father he consented to give the boy gratuitous instruction in composition.

As a teacher, the mere fact of his sixty years put Michael Haydn at too great a distance from his eleven-year-old pupil for anything like the same results as had been obtained with Heuschkel. Still, he seems to have been satisfied with six fughettas, composed apparently under his own eye, and the proud father had them printed

---

' Fear God, love thy neighbour, and thy
Master Joseph Haydn who loves thee heartily.'
Estoras (sic), May 22, 1788.

C. F. Pohl's *Joseph Haydn*, ii. 204.   The general opinion of Edmund von Weber is somewhat opposed to Spohr's judgment on making his acquaintance in Berne in 1816.   He says ' he is said to be a good theoretical musician ; as a violinist and conductor he is weak.' Spohr's *Selbstbiographie*, i. 253.
[1] Weber's *Litterarische Arbeiten*, p. 175.   (Leipzig, Kiel, 1866.)

[2] Pasqué's *Goethes Theaterleitung in Weimar*, ii. 20, 223.   Leipzig, Weber.   1863.
[3] Spitta possessed a copy.

in score. The dedication, showing evident traces of the father's hand, runs :

' To Herr Edmund von Weber, my beloved brother in Hessen-Cassel. To you as connoisseur, as musician, as teacher and more than all as brother, these first-fruits of his musical labours are dedicated, in the eleventh year of his age, by your tenderly loving brother, Karl Maria von Weber, Salzburg, Sept. 1, 1798.' [1]

Carl Maria's mother had died on Mar. 13, of consumption, and her death perhaps occasioned a trip to Vienna in April, on which Carl Maria accompanied his father. Here they heard the 'Creation' (Apr. 29 or 30), and probably entered into personal relations with Haydn. Immediately after his return, in the beginning of July at the latest, the father began to talk of leaving Salzburg, for ' one cannot exist under this hierarchy,' and in the autumn they all moved to Munich. As the lessons in composition from Michael Haydn only began in January 1798, they cannot have lasted more than six months. Franz Anton had gradually tired of his stage-managing. ' I have bid good-bye to the good old theatre,' he writes,[2] ' and have returned, though without pay, to my old military life.' This consisted in his adoption of the title of Major, to which he had no sort of right. In Munich Carl Maria had two new teachers, the singer Wallishauser (Italianised into Valesi) and Johann Nepomuck Kalcher, afterwards court-organist. With the latter he made more progress in composition than with Michael Haydn, and always retained a grateful recollection of him. He soon began to play at concerts with success. Under Kalcher's eye he wrote his first opera, ' Die Macht der Liebe und des Weins,' a Mass, PF. sonatas, and variations, violin trios, and songs ; but the MSS. have all disappeared[3]; apparently he burnt them himself. One work of his time has survived, a set of variations for PF. (op. 2), dedicated to Kalcher, and specially interesting as lithographed by himself. He had been led to this kind of work by his acquaintance with Aloys Senefelder, the inventor of lithography, in whose shop he frequently occupied himself, even imagining that he had discovered some improvements in the method of mechanical reproduction. Indeed, his interest in lithography became so keen, that for a time he neglected composition. The father, always restless and whimsical, thought of carrying out the new discovery on a large scale, and it was decided to move to Freiberg in Saxony, where the necessary materials were more easily procurable.

[1] M. M. von Weber, i. 41, and elsewhere, thinks his father made him out intentionally a year younger than he was, but of this piece of dishonesty he may be acquitted. The careless mistake of speaking of a person as of the age of the current year instead of that of the year last completed is very frequent in Germany. The expression ' in the eleventh year of his age ' may well have meant the same as eleven years old.
[2] Jan. 19, 1799, to Hofkammerrath Kirms at Weimar.
[3] M. von Weber, i. 49, etc., says that they were accidentally destroyed in Kalcher's house. See, however, Biedenfeld's *Komische Opera*, p. 134 (Leipzig, Weigel, 1848), and R. Muziol in the *Neue Berliner Musikzeitung* for 1879, No. 1, etc.

The plan was carried into effect in 1800, Carl Maria giving concerts on the way with success at Leipzig and other towns in Central Germany. Arrived in Freiberg he speedily lost his interest in lithography, partly owing to an opening which occurred for producing a dramatic work. The large and well-selected company of Ritter von Steinsberg, whom the Webers had met before, had been playing there since the summer. Steinsberg had written an opera-book, ' Das Waldmädchen,' which he handed over to Carl Maria, then just 13, and the first performance took place on Nov. 24. Public expectation had been roused to a high pitch by Franz Anton's manœuvres, and seems to have been barely satisfied by the result. Two Freiberg musicians entered into a newspaper correspondence with the composer, whose pen was obviously guided by his father, for the intemperate, impertinent tone of the letters is wholly unlike anything in Carl Maria's character. The opera succeeded better at Chemnitz (Dec. 5, 1800), and was evidently appreciated in Vienna (Leopoldstadt Theatre, 1805), where it was given eight times during the month of December. It was also performed at Prague, and even in St. Petersburg, but negotiations with Weimar fell through. Carl Maria was quite aware afterwards of the small value of this youthful work. In his autobiographical sketches, he calls it ' a very immature production, not perhaps without occasional marks of invention, the second act of which I wrote in ten days,' adding, ' this was one of the many unfortunate consequences of the marvellous tales of the great masters, which made so great an impression on my juvenile mind, and which I tried to imitate.'

Freiberg in its turn was abandoned, possibly towards the end of 1800, certainly by the beginning of 1801. The last we hear of him there is that he wrote on Dec. 9 to Artaria of Vienna offering him his lithographic invention, the advantages of which were, in his own words,

' 1. I can engrave music on stone in a manner quite equal to the finest English copper-plate engraving, as the enclosed specimens will show. 2. One workman can complete from two to three plates a day in winter, and from three to four in summer when the days are longer. 3. A plate can be used again, by which I mean entirely erased, over thirty times. 4. Two men can take as many thousand impressions a week as in common printing. 5. One hundred thalers will cover the whole outlay for machinery.'

He also offered the Viennese publishers several compositions for strings and for piano. Artaria took no notice of the letter.[4] After this the father and son seem to have made some stay in Chemnitz, as we have letters from the former there dated Apr. 24, and May 17, 1801. By November they were again in Salzburg, where Carl Maria composed the opera ' Peter Schmoll und seine Nachbarn,' produced in Augsburg

[4] Nohl's *Musiker-Briefe*, 2nd ed., 1777.

(probably in 1803) without any special success. In a letter of Nov. 25, 1801, Carl Maria calls himself a pupil of Michael Haydn, ' and of several other great masters in Munich, Dresden, Prague and Vienna,' but who these masters were has not been ascertained. As far as Vienna, Prague and Dresden are concerned, it can refer only to short temporary relations with musicians, as up to this time no stay had been made in any of these places. The passage, however, is fresh evidence of the continual restlessness in which Weber's youth was passed.

In the summer of 1802 he went with his father to North Germany, and in October paid a fortnight's visit to his birthplace. Here he saw much of Johann Heinrich Voss, a fact worthy of note, because of the admirable settings he afterwards composed to some of Voss's poems. On the return journey he composed at Hamburg, also in October, his two first Lieder—' Die Kerze,' by Matthisson, and ' Umsonst,' of which the latter only has been printed. At Coburg, where the court was very musical, he tried to procure a hearing for his two operas, but whether successfully or not cannot be ascertained. More important than the actual musical results of this tour were the theoretical studies on which he embarked during its progress. He collected books on theory, and soon his letters are full of Emanuel Bach's *Versuch über die wahre Art das Clavier zu spielen*, of Agricola (apparently his revision of Tosi's *Opinioni*), of Kirnberger, and others. Thus he began to cultivate independence of thought on matters of art. His newly acquired knowledge of theory was indeed rudely shaken in Augsberg, where he arrived November 1802, and made some stay. Here he formed a close friendship with a certain Dr. Munding, who in all their conversations on art had a disturbing habit of demanding the reason for every rule propounded, which Weber was not at that time competent to give. This, however, stimulated him to clear up his own views on the fundamental laws of art.

VOGLER AT VIENNA.—The most striking fact about him at this time was the extraordinary activity of his mind in every direction. He took great interest in musical criticism, and in December 1802 was busy with preparations for a musical dictionary. A Salzburg friend, Ignaz Susan, wrote to encourage him in a plan for a musical periodical, and was soon afterwards employed in procuring him materials for a history of music in Vienna, whither he betook himself early in 1803. The most important acquaintance he made on this visit was that of the Abbé VOGLER (*q.v.*), who was then composing his opera ' Samori.' This gifted, many-sided man, exercised a more stimulating effect than any other artist on Weber, who attached himself to him with all the enthusiasm of youth. ' By Vogler's advice,' he says,

' I gave up—and a great privation it was—working at great subjects, and for nearly two years devoted myself to diligent study of the various works of the great masters, whose method of construction, treatment of ideas, and use of means, we dissected together, while I separately made studies after them to clear up the different points in my own mind.'

Vogler himself put great confidence in his pupil. After Weber's arrival one evening in October 1803, Vogler suddenly ran into the inner room, closed the doors, shut the shutters, and set to work at something with great secrecy. At length he brought out a bundle of music, and after Weber had promised absolute silence, played him the overture and some other pieces from his new opera. Finally he commissioned him to prepare the PF. score. ' I am now sitting down to it, studying, and enjoying myself like the devil,' Weber writes to Susan.[1]

The relations with Joseph Haydn were also renewed.

' He is always cheerful and lively, likes to talk of his experiences, and particularly enjoys having rising young artists about him. He is the very model of a great man.'

These words of Weber perhaps explain the fact that neither in his letters, which often go into great detail on the state of music in Vienna, nor in his biographical sketch, does he mention Beethoven. That he was personally acquainted with him there is no manner of doubt.[2] But Beethoven was difficult of access, and his rough ways may have repelled the delicate, refined and graceful youth. That Vogler used underhand means to keep them asunder is probably an unfounded assumption, but a certain irritation against Beethoven clung to Weber for many a year, till it gave way in manhood to an unreserved admiration and hearty veneration. Among other musicians of note in Vienna Weber mentions Hummel, just made Kapellmeister to Prince Esterhazy, whom he calls the ' most elegant pianoforte-player in Vienna.' This opinion he modified on hearing him again in Prague in 1816. His precision and his pearly runs he still admired, but thought ' Hummel had not studied the intrinsic nature of the instrument.' Of Weber's own works during this time in Vienna but few exist, and of these few most are connected with Vogler, e.g. the PF. score of ' Samori'; PF. variations on themes from ' Samori,' and ' Castor and Pollux,' another opera of Vogler's.[3] That he was studying hard is certain, but this was not incompatible with a youthful enjoyment both of life and natural beauty. He became acquainted with a young officer, Johann Baptist Gänsbacher, a musical amateur, also a pupil of Vogler, and the acquaintance soon ripened into an intimate and life-long friendship. Weber's son and biographer also has something to say of a ' tender connection with a lady of position ' in Vienna. Possibly a song, ' Jüngst sass ich am Grab der

1 Nohl's *Mosaik*, p. 68, etc.   Leipzig ; Senff, 1882.
2 *Ibid.* p. 78, note.   3 See Jähns, Nos. 39, 40, 43.

Trauten allein,' composed immediately after his departure from Vienna, had something to do with this affair. Vogler had recommended him for the post of Kapellmeister of the theatre at Breslau, and by May 8, 1804, before he was quite 17½, the arrangements were concluded. He went first to Salzburg to fetch his old father, and there, in the rooms of his friend Susan, composed the song just mentioned. On June 5 he was in Augsburg, and travelled on the 14th by Carlsbad to Breslau.[1]

APPOINTMENT AT BRESLAU. — If his biographer is correct in stating that Weber did not enter upon his post at Breslau before November 1804, he must either have been living there for more than three months without occupation, or have been touring about as an artist from June to October. But there is no indication of his having taken either of these courses. The Breslau theatre was kept up by a company chiefly consisting of better-class citizens. The head manager in 1804 was J. G. Rhode, Professor at the Kriegsschule. Previous to Weber's appointment, Carl Ebell had acted as director of music, but he, originally a lawyer, had returned to an official career. The orchestra and chorus were sufficient for ordinary demands. Weber, on this his first entrance on practical life, showed great talent for direction and organisation, though from over-zeal and inexperience he made many mistakes. He had from the first to contend with the prejudices of the managing committee, and with strong opposition in the chief musical circles of the town. The leader of this opposition was Joseph Schnabel, formerly first violinist, and deputy-conductor of the theatre, and appointed Cathedral-organist in 1805. Schnabel left the theatre on Weber's arrival, probably from vexation at not being Kapellmeister himself, and, as a man of 37, declining to serve under a lad of 18. The two continued on awkward terms, and some rudenesses of which Weber was guilty towards Schnabel, a respectable and much-respected man, did not raise him in the estimation of the better part of the public. Among the managing company he had roused opponents, by insisting on several expensive alterations. Rhode, indeed, was well disposed towards him, and wrote a libretto, ' Rübezahl,' on which Weber set to work at Breslau.

In spite of Rhode, however, a regular breach ensued in the spring of 1806, and Weber's resignation was accepted. With the best intentions he had done little to raise the state of music in Breslau ; but the years spent there were of great importance to his own development. Not only was his great gift for conducting first made apparent to himself and others, but it was chiefly at Breslau that the original and gifted pianist and composer, whom his con-

temporaries admired, and posterity venerates, was formed. Although somewhat isolated socially, his gifts and his amiable disposition attracted round him a small circle of musical people. Carl Ebell was one of the number, but his closest friends were F. W. Berner and J. W. Klingohr, both little older than himself, and both admired pianists, Berner being also chief organist of the church of St. Elizabeth, a talented composer, and in a certain sense a pupil of Vogler. The three young men formed a close bond, and endeavoured to make their intimacy mutually profitable. Klingohr's strong points were sweetness, correctness and grace ; Berner's, power and depth of thought ; Weber excelled in brilliancy, fascination and unexpectedness. In genius he far surpassed the others, but Berner had had the solid training which he lacked. All three exercised themselves diligently in extempore playing, then justly considered the highest qualification for a good pianoforte-player and organist. In this branch also Weber proved the most gifted ; in spite of risky harmonies, and even awkward counterpoint, detected by critical hearers, he carried all before him by the charm of his melodies, and the originality of his whole musical nature. He had also acquired considerable skill on the guitar, on which he would accompany his own mellow voice in songs, mostly of a humorous character, with inimitable effect. This talent was often of great use to him in society, and he composed many Lieder with guitar accompaniment. His fine voice, however, he nearly lost in Breslau. • One day, in the early part of 1806, he had invited Berner to spend the evening with him, and play over the newly completed overture to ' Rübezahl,' but on Berner's arrival he found his friend insensible on the floor. Wanting a glass of wine he had taken by mistake some nitric acid, used by his father for experiments in etching. He was with difficulty restored to consciousness, when it was found that the vocal organs were impaired, and the inside of the mouth and air-passages seriously injured. He recovered after a long illness, but his singing-voice remained weak, and even his speaking-voice never regained its full power. Beyond a few numbers of ' Rübezahl,' Weber composed little in Breslau. An ' Overtura Chinesa,' lost in its original form, was remodelled in 1809 as the overture to ' Turandot.'

After his withdrawal from the theatre he remained at Breslau without any regular employment, living on the hard-earned proceeds of music-lessons. Having his father to provide for, and encumbered with debts accumulated while he was endeavouring to live a somewhat fast life on a salary of 600 thalers a year, he found himself hard-pressed, and determined to try a concert-tour. One of his pupils, Fräulein von Belonde, was lady-in-waiting to the wife of

---

[1] M. von Weber is incorrect here, i. 87. Also the Variations, op. 6, were completed earlier than stated by Jähns (No. 43, p. 57). They were undoubtedly finished by May 1804.

Duke Eugene of Würtemberg, then living at Schloss Carlsruhe in Silesia, where he kept up a great deal of music. The lady's influence procured for Weber the title of Musik-Intendant, which would, it was hoped, be a help to him on his tour, but that prospect having been destroyed by the war, the Duke invited Weber to Schloss Carlsruhe. Here he found not only a refuge for himself, his father, and an aunt, but a most desirable atmosphere for the cultivation of his art. He took up his abode there about midsummer, and though the Duke was summoned to the army in September, the war was expected to be so soon over that at first no change was made in the peaceful life at the Castle.

In these few months Weber wrote a considerable number of instrumental pieces, chiefly for the excellent artists who composed the small chapel of the Duke. To Jan. 1807 belong two orchestral symphonies (his only ones, both in C major [1]), and these had been preceded by some variations for viola and orchestra (Dec. 19), and a small concerto for horn and orchestra (Nov. 6, 1806). Possibly, too, the well-known variations on Bianchi's ' Vien quà, Dorina bella ' belong to the last few weeks at Carlsruhe.[2]

SECRETARYSHIP AT STUTTGART.—This happy time came to an end in Feb. 1807, after Napoleon's decisive victory over the Prussians, when the state of universal insecurity made it necessary to dismiss the band. But the Duke, with true nobility of mind, showed himself anxious to provide for his musicians, and through his intervention Weber was installed as private secretary at Stuttgart to Duke Ludwig, brother to Duke Eugene, and to the king (Frederic) of Würtemberg. As things were, he could not hesitate to accept a post which promised him, even at the cost of a temporary exile from his art, a certain income, doubly necessary now that he had his father to provide for. As he was not required at Stuttgart till Sept. 1, he made use of the interval after his departure from Carlsruhe on Feb. 23, for a concert-tour. The war made concerts a matter of great difficulty, but after several vain attempts, he succeeded at Anspach, Nuremberg, Bayreuth and Erlangen. He then turned in the direction of Stuttgart, where he arrived July 17, and entered on his new post August 1.

Duke Ludwig was a frivolous man of pleasure who habitually spent more than his income, and did not scruple to resort to underhand and desperate expedients to extricate himself from his embarrassments. The corruption of morals at the dissipated court of Stuttgart was terrible,

and Weber's position was a dangerous one from many points of view. His duties were to manage the Duke's private correspondence, keep his accounts, furnish him, sometimes by most unpleasant means, with money to satisfy or put off his numerous creditors—all things for which Weber was too ignorant and inexperienced, and which formed a ruinous exhibition of dissolute life for so young a man. His natural tendency to dissipation and gaiety was fostered by this immoral life, all the more because his title of Freiherr at once gained him admittance to the circles of the corrupt young nobility. Thus involved he lost sight of his own proper life-object—music,—or like a mere dilettante, treated his art as an amusement. He had besides, great social gifts, and was always a welcome guest. He ran great risk of giving up all serious effort, and yet it was indispensable to him, on account of his irregular and defective training. It is not to be wondered at that a sterling artist like Spohr, who knew him in Stuttgart, should have formed a low, or wholly unfavourable, impression of his artistic powers.

Stuttgart abounded in opportunities for improving his general cultivation, and procuring fresh nutriment for his active and receptive mind. He made acquaintance with the principal authors, artists and scientific men of the place. Hauy and Reinbeck, Dannecker and Hötsch, J. C. Schwab, Spittler and Lehr, all enjoyed intercourse with so agreeable a youth. Lehr, the court-librarian, opened to him the treasures of the royal collection of books, among which Weber's preference was for philosophical works. He read Wolf, Kant and Schelling, with attention and profit, and formed on them his own modes of thinking and expressing himself.

His great gift for music naturally became known, and Duke Ludwig made him music-master to his children. The Kapellmeister of the opera (from 1807) was Franz Danzi, a melodious composer, an excellent violoncellist, and sociable, though of regular life. Though twenty-three years older than Weber, ne speedily formed an intimacy with him, and tried to exercise a calming and restraining influence over him, while both by precept and example he was of great service to him in his art. His friendship with Danzi brought Weber into connexion with the company of the Stuttgart court-theatre, a circumstance which, while it stimulated him to fresh dramatic production, involved him in the loose life of a bohemian set. A violent reciprocal attachment for the singer Margarethe Lang [3] led him into all sorts of follies, causing him to neglect cultivated and intellectual society, and ruining him financially. Another personage of importance in his artistic career was Franz Carl

---

[1] See Jähns, Nos. 50 and 51.

[2] Weber states in his autobiographical sketch that he composed at Schloss Carlsruhe two Symphonies, several Concertos, and ' Harmoniestücke ' (pieces for wind without strings). If we include the viola variations, much in the form of a concerto, we get two concertos, but the Harmoniestücke are missing. A ' Tusch ' (flourish of trumpets) of four bars, for twenty trumpets, printed by Jähns No. 47 A, p. 61, probably counted as one of them. The autograph of this is in the collection of Dr. W. H. Cummings.

[3] Not the daughter, as M. M. v. Weber states (i. 159), but the sister of Theobald Lang the violinist, and in consequence aunt to Josephine Lang-Köstlin, Mendelssohn's friend, and composer of many Lieder

Hiemer, the dramatic author. Both he and
Weber belonged to a society of lively young
men, who called themselves 'Fausts Höllen-
fahrt.' Each member assumed a special
name; the president, a Dr. Kellin, was 'Dr.
Faust,' Hiemer 'Reimwol,' Weber 'Krautsalat'
and Danzi, who had been persuaded to join,
'Rapunzel.' Among Weber's papers was
found a comic musical epistle, 'from Krautsalat to Rapunzel,'[1] which gives a striking
picture of his irrepressible spirits in such
society. Hiemer had had some previous success as a librettist, and undertook to write a
romantic-comic opera for him. 'Das Waldmädchen' was the subject chosen, and Hiemer
seems to have adhered pretty closely to Steinsberg's book, which Weber had set in Freiberg.
The new work, 'Silvana' by name, seems to
have made slow progress amid the distractions
of Weber's life. It was begun, as far as can be
ascertained, on July 18, 1808, and finished Feb.
23, 1810.[2]

Through Danzi's intervention the opera was
accepted for the court theatre, and was about
to be put into rehearsal, when an incident, to
be related shortly, ruined all. Whilst busy
with his opera, Weber composed what under
the circumstances must be considered a large
number of other works—a strong proof of the
increasing force of his productive power. The
most important was 'Der erste Ton,' a poem
by Rochlitz, for declamation, with orchestra
and concluding chorus. He remodelled the
overture to 'Peter Schmoll,' and published
it as a separate work; also the 'Overtura
Chinesa,' which was made to serve as the introduction to 'Turandot,' a play by Gozzi and
Schiller, for which he also wrote six short
incidental pieces.[3] Of PF. music, by far the
most important piece is the Polonaise in E♭,
op. 21, completed June 4, 1808, at Ludwigsburg, and dedicated to Margarethe Lang. With
her, too, are connected the 'Variations on an
original theme,' op. 9; the clever 'Momento
capriccioso,' op. 12, and the charming 'Six
pièces pour le pianoforte à quatre mains' (Nov.
27, 1809). His solitary PF. quartet (in B♭)[4]
was also of this period, as well as the 'Variations for PF. and violin on a Norwegian theme,'
an 'Andante and Rondo Ungarese' for viola
and orchestra, not published in this form, a
Potpourri for violoncello and orchestra, and
thirteen Lieder with accompaniment, several
of which are of perfect beauty.

King Frederic lived on bad terms with his
brother, Duke Ludwig, whose frivolity and extravagance were specially irritating, as the King
had several times had to extricate him from
his embarrassments for the sake of the family

honour. His displeasure also descended on the
Duke's secretary, who generally had the unpleasant task of informing the King of his
brother's difficulties. On these occasions the
King would load the unfortunate Weber with
most unkingly abuse. This roused Weber to
revenge himself by various little spiteful tricks.
On leaving the Cabinet in a great rage after one
of these violent scenes, he met an old woman
in the corridor who asked him for the laundress's room. 'There,' said Weber, pointing to
the door of the King's apartments, 'the royal
laundress lives in there,' and went off. The
woman went in, and, being angrily received
by the King, stammered out that a young
gentleman who had just left the room had
directed her there. Enraged at this affront,
the King ordered him into arrest, but he was
begged off by the Duke, and nothing more
was done at the time. That the King did not
forget his impertinence he learnt afterwards to
his cost.

As Duke Ludwig's financial position became
worse, he was driven to still more questionable
expedients. The King having made a decree by
which the only persons exempt from military
service were the members of the royal household, these appointments were much sought
after, and many parents were willing to pay a
considerable sum for the reversion of one. It
was observed that about this time there was a
sudden accession to the Duke's household of
young noblemen who bore official titles without
any corresponding duties. Just then Weber had
been endeavouring to obtain a loan from one of
his acquaintances, in order to discharge a debt
of his father's, who had been living with him
since 1809. On the gentleman's refusal a former
servant of his offered Weber to procure it for a
consideration, and then assured his late employer that the Secretary, if obliged in the
matter of the loan, would secure his son an
appointment in the Duke's household. On this
understanding the loan was effected; but when
no appointment ensued, and the son was drawn
for a soldier, the father in his indignation made
the affair known. The King had long been dissatisfied with the state of his brother's household, and believing Weber to be the real culprit,
determined to make an example of him. The
preparations for 'Silvana' were in progress,
and Weber was at the theatre, when, on the
evening of Feb. 9, 1810, he was arrested and
thrown into prison. An inquiry ensued, and
Weber's innocence, of which indeed all Stuttgart had been convinced, was completely estab
lished; but the King, on Feb. 26, sentenced him
and his father to perpetual banishment from
Würtemberg. This hard stroke of fate might be
looked upon as a punishment for so many
frivolous years, and for sins committed against
the guiding genius of his art; and it was in
this light that Weber took it. Henceforth his

[1] Printed entire by M. M. von Weber, i. 146.
[2] Jähns, pp. 101 and 103.
[3] Three of the pieces are marches. All are founded more or less
on a Chinese melody taken from Rousseau's *Dict. of Music* (vol. ii.
Plate N). The overture was first performed at Strassburg, Dec. 31,
1814.   [4] Jähns. No. 76.

youthful follies were laid aside, and he settled down conscientiously and perseveringly to the life of an artist in earnest pursuit after his ideal. ' From this time forward,' he said, eight years afterwards, ' I can count pretty tolerably on having settled matters with myself ; and all that time has since done or can do for me, is to rub off corners, and add clearness and comprehensibility to the principles then firmly established.'

MANNHEIM FRIENDSHIPS. — Danzi, a real friend in need, gave him introductions to Mannheim, where Peter Ritter was Kapellmeister, and Gottfried WEBER (*q.v.*, p. 673), afterwards so well known as a musical theoretician. Received in a kindly spirit by all, in Gottfried Weber he found a friend for life. Under his auspices concerts were at once arranged for Mar. 9 and Apr. 2, and at these the ' Erster Ton ' was produced for the first time, the words being declaimed by the actor Esslair. His first symphony, too, was a great success, as well as his pianoforte-playing. On a trip to Heidelberg he made the acquaintance of Alexander von Dusch, a brother-in-law of Gottfried Weber, and a violoncello-player of great taste, who, after finishing his studies at Easter 1810, came to settle in Mannheim. The three friends spent a few happy weeks in lively intellectual intercourse, and in April Weber moved to Darmstadt, where Vogler had been living since 1807. Here he met his friends Gänsbacher and Meyerbeer from Berlin. Weber did not return to the old relations of master and pupil with Vogler, but sought to profit by intercourse with him. His respect for him was undiminished, though he could no longer agree with all that he practised and taught, and was quite aware of the weaknesses of his character.

' May I succeed in placing before the world a clear idea of his rare psychological development, to his honour, and the instruction of young artists ! '

Weber had the intention of writing a life of Vogler as far back as 1810, and the words just quoted show that he still retained the idea in 1818, though it was never carried out. (See VOGLER, p. 562 ff.)

On June 21, 1810, Weber undertook a small literary work at Vogler's instigation. Vogler had remodelled some of the Chorals in Breitkopf's second edition (1784–86) of J. S. Bach's Chorals, published under Emanuel Bach's supervision, honestly thinking that Bach was open to great improvement on the score of beauty and correctness. He now begged his former pupil to write a commentary on his revisions, and publish them for the benefit of students. That Weber embarked on the work [1] with any amount of eagerness there is no evidence to show ; probably not, his mind being entirely practical and by no means

pedagogic. As a matter of fact the analyses were done very perfunctorily, nor were they all his own, for Choral VII. was done by Gottfried Weber, and part of Choral IX. and all Choral X. by Vogler himself.[2] Weber felt his unfitness for the task, and so expressed himself in the introduction. If any part of it interested him it was the comparison of Vogler's supposed systematic and philosophical methods with Bach's mode of proceeding by instinct. He had been long seeking for something on which to ground a system ; a fact for which there is a very simple explanation in the uncertainty of his musical instincts, particularly as regards the sequence of harmonies, an uncertainty arising from his desultory early training, and never wholly overcome. That he considered Vogler's alterations improvements is not surprising ; for his acquaintance with Bach, like his knowledge of history in general, was small ; and he knew as little as Vogler did of the original intention of the Chorals in question.

Weber's attraction towards literary work, of which traces may be seen as far back as 1802, was very marked about this time. He came forward frequently as an author between 1809 and 1818, after that at longer intervals, and not at all after 1821. In Stuttgart he began a musical novel, *Tonkünstlers Leben*, which had been accepted by Cotta of Tübingen, and was to have been ready by Easter 1811 ; but the time went by, and it was never finished. A fragment published in the *Morgenblatt* for Dec. 1809 contains some severe remarks on Beethoven's third and fourth symphonies. Mozart was Weber's ideal musician, and at that time he was quite impervious to Beethoven's music. Nägeli of Zürich having pointed out a subtle resemblance between Weber and Beethoven (which really is observable, in the Momento Capriccioso for instance, and still more in his later works), Weber wrote to him from Mannheim :

' Flattering as this might appear to many, it is not agreeable to me. In the first place, I detest everything in the shape of imitation : and in the second, my ideas are so opposite to Beethoven's that I cannot imagine it possible we should ever meet. His fervid, almost incredible, inventive powers, are accompanied by so much confusion in the arrangement of his ideas, that his early works alone interest me ; the later ones are to me a bewildering chaos, an obscure straining after novelty, lit up it is true by divine flashes of genius, which only serve to show how great he might be if he would but curb his riotous imagination. I, of course, cannot lay claim to the genius of Beethoven ; all I hope is . . . that each separate stroke of mine tells.' [3]

This passage shows that Weber by no means over-appreciated himself, but was anxious to guard his own independence and uttered his opinions in a straightforward manner.

CRITICISM.—He began now to appear more frequently as a critic. All criticism on himself he paid great attention to, and was fully

---

[1] Published in the same year by Peters of Leipzig.   ' Zwölf Chorāle von Sebastian Bach, umgearbeitet von Vogler, zergliedert von Carl Maria von Weber,' etc.

[2] Jähns, p. 454.
[3] Nohl's *Musikerbriefe*, 2nd ed. p. 178.

convinced of the value of good musical censure, so he set to work with his friends to elevate the art in general. Towards the close of 1810, he, Gottfried Weber, Alexander von Dusch and Meyerbeer founded the so-called 'Harmonischer Verein,' with the general object of furthering the cause of art, and the particular one of extending thorough and impartial criticism. The regularly constituted members were required to be both composers and literary men, but writers were admitted, if possessed of sufficient musical knowledge. The motto of the Society was 'the elevation of musical criticism by musicians themselves,' a sound principle, then promulgated for the first time in musical Germany. In this branch Weber was the direct precursor of Schumann. He and Gottfried Weber also considered the foundation of a musical journal, and though the plan was never carried out, it was long before Weber gave it up. He was still occupied with it even during the Dresden period of his life. Other members of the Society were Gänsbacher, Berger the singer, Danzi and Berner. The existence of the Society was a secret, and each member adopted a *nom de plume*. Weber signed himself Melos; Gottfried Weber, Giusto; Gänsbacher, Triole, etc. Here, again, we are reminded of Schumann and the 'Davidsbündler.' The two Webers were active in their exertions, and their efforts were undeniably successful.

Vogler was proud of his disciples, especially of Weber and Meyerbeer. 'Oh,' he is said to have exclaimed, 'how sorry I should have been if I had had to leave the world before I formed those two. There is within me a something which I have never been able to call forth, but those two will do it.' Weber, however, found existence at Darmstadt hard after the pleasant never-to-be-forgotten days at Mannheim. He got away as often as he could, gave concerts at Aschaffenburg, Mannheim, Carlsruhe and Frankfort, and found time also to compose. Ideas flowed in upon him, many to be used only in much later works. For instance, the ideas of the first chorus of fairies, and of the ballet music in the third act of 'Oberon,' and the chief subject of the 'Invitation à la valse' were in his mind at this period. While on the look-out for a subject for an opera he and Dusch hit upon 'Der Freischütz,' a story by Apel, then just published, and Dusch set to work to turn it into a libretto. For the present, however, it did not get beyond the beginning; not till seven years later did Weber begin the work which made his reputation. He succeeded in bringing out 'Silvana' at Frankfort on Sept. 16, 1810,[1] when, in spite of unpropitious circumstances, it produced a very favourable impression. The part of Silvana was taken by Caroline Brandt, Weber's future wife; and Margarethe

Lang was the first soprano. Having completed by Oct. 17 six easy sonatas for piano and violin, for which André had given him a commission, Weber soon after set out for Offenbach, but had the mortification of having them refused, on the ground that they were too good for André's purpose.[2] At André's he saw for the first time an autograph of Mozart's, and his behaviour on the occasion touchingly expressed his unbounded veneration for Mozart's genius. He laid it carefully on the table, and on bended knees pressed his forehead and lips to it, gazed at it with tears in his eyes, and then handed it back with the words, 'Happy the paper on which his hand has rested!'

For a short time there seemed a prospect of Weber's securing a permanent appointment in his beloved Mannheim. At a concert there on Nov. 19, he produced his remodelled overture to 'Peter Schmoll,' and played for the first time his PF. Concerto in C, completed on Oct. 4. Among the audience was Princess Stephanie of Baden, whose father, the Crown Prince Ludwig of Bavaria, Weber had met a few months before at Baden-Baden. The Prince had been delighted with him, and had walked about with him all night, while he sang serenades to his guitar. The Princess also was anxious to hear him in this capacity, and after the concert he sang her a number of his best songs to the guitar, making so great an impression that she promised to procure him the post of Kapellmeister in Mannheim, or make him an allowance of 1000 gulden from her privy purse. All this, however, ended in nothing, for a few weeks later he received a message from the Princess to say that she found her promise had been made too hastily.

The cause of Weber's so soon giving up the 'Freischütz,' which Dusch was to prepare for him, was that he had been busy for some time with a new opera, or rather comic Singspiel, in one act, called 'Abu Hassan,' the libretto of which Franz Hiemer sent him, Mar. 29, 1810, from Stuttgart. He composed one number, the Creditors' chorus, at Mannheim, Aug. 11, left it untouched till Nov. 1, and completed it at Darmstadt, Jan. 12, 1811. By Vogler's advice the work was dedicated to the Grand Duke Ludwig, who, although an enthusiastic devotee and connoisseur of music (he used to conduct the rehearsals at the opera himself), had hitherto declined to have much to do with Weber, possibly because the latter had not shown sufficient deference to his authority on matters of art. Now he seemed much more kindly disposed, sent a handsome fee for the score, and gave permission for a concert at the Schloss (Feb. 6, 1811), himself taking 120 tickets. For it Weber composed an Italian duet for two altos (Mesdames Mangold and Schönberger) and small orchestra, with clarinet

1 According to the register of the theatre.   Jähns, p. 103.

2 Published later by Simrock of Bonn.

obbligato played by Heinrich Bärmann of Munich. The duet pleased greatly, and was encored, but all this success did not end in a permanent appointment, as Weber had at one time hoped would be the case. Meyerbeer had left on Feb. 12 for a tour; outside the court the inhabitants had little feeling for music; Weber did not care to be left wholly to Vogler; and on Feb. 14 he finally left a place where he had never felt thoroughly at home, and started on a grand concert tour.

At this period he often felt sorely the restless, uncertain conditions of his life, the inconstant nature of all human relations, and the loneliness to which he seemed doomed by the sudden snatching away of friends as soon as he became attached to them. During his last visit but one to Mannheim, he composed a song called 'Weber's Abschied'[1] (Dec. 8, 1810) to words by Dusch.

At Darmstadt, on the night of Jan. 12, 1811, he wrote down more connectedly some of the thoughts which surged through his mind. His childhood came up before him, and his life, so full of disappointments, and so near failure. 'My path in life,' says he,

'was cast from my birth in different lines from that of any other human being; *I* have no happy childish days to look back upon, no free open boyhood; though still a youth I am an old man in experience, learning everything through my own feelings and by myself, *nothing* by means of others.'[2]

To Gänsbacher he writes a few months later:

'You live in the midst of your own people, I stand *alone*; think then how much a word from you refreshes and revives me.'

His elastic temperament, however, soon recovered itself, as the smallest piece of good fortune was enough to feed his hopes, and the consciousness that he had at last laid firm hold of art—his own proper aim in life—was a constant encouragement. Nothing could distract him from this, nor from the continuous endeavour to work out his moral education. The touching tone of piety and trust which runs through his later life is now first noticeable. He closes the year 1810 with the following avowal:

'God has sent me many vexations and disappointments, but He has also thrown me with many good kind people, who have made life worth living. I can say honestly and in all quietness, that within the last ten months I have become a *better* man.'

CONCERT TOURS.—Weber travelled through Frankfort to Giessen, where he gave a well-attended concert on Feb. 18, and Hanau, where he saw a 'bad play' on the 23rd; went next day to Aschaffenburg, where he stayed two days, and made acquaintance with Sterkel, an adherent of Volger's; and by Mar. 3 was at Würzburg. Thence he went to Bamberg, where he met E. T. A. Hoffmann, and Bader the tenor, both of whom reappear in the Freischütz

period; and by Nuremberg and Augsburg to Munich, arriving Mar. 14. Here he stayed nearly five months, finding powerful stimulus in the society of Bärmann, the greatest clarinet-player of his time, for whom he wrote within the next few months no fewer than three concertos. The first, in C minor and E♭,[3] was played at his first concert (Apr. 5) as well as his PF. concerto, one of his symphonies, and the 'Erster Ton.' Bärmann played the second,[4] in F minor, at a concert given by Kaufmann the pianoforte-maker of Dresden (June 13), and again at Weber's second (Aug. 7). These compositions procured him warm adherents, not only among the general public, but also in the Munich orchestra, celebrated for its haughty reserve. One of the band having spoken slightingly of the F minor concerto at rehearsal as an 'amateur work,' the rest fell upon him, and would have turned him bodily out of the orchestra if Weber had not interposed. There was also a successful performance of 'Abu Hassan' under Winter on June 4, and during the preparations Weber learned that it was to be given before the court at Ludwigsburg in the beginning of May, but not under his name. 'Is not that miserable?' he writes to Gottfried Weber, 'and how stupid! all the papers will announce it as mine. *Item*, God's will be done.'

On Aug. 9 he started for a tour in Switzerland, during which he gave himself up to the enjoyment of nature rather than of music. By the beginning of November he was again in Munich and gave a brilliantly successful concert on the 11th. For it he had composed a new concert rondo, which he afterwards used for the finale to the clarinet concerto in E♭,[5] and remodelled the overture to 'Rübezahl,' a piece of work which he declared to be the clearest and most powerful of anything he had yet done. Besides these he composed some vocal pieces, chiefly for his patroness Queen Caroline, and a complete bassoon concerto (op. 75) for Brandt, the court player. On Dec. 1 he started again, this time in company with Bärmann, for Central and North Germany.

In Prague he met Gänsbacher, then living there, formed some ties which became of importance when he settled there later, composed variations for PF. and clarinet on a theme from 'Silvana' (op. 33), and gave with Bärmann a largely attended concert on Dec. 21. Passing through Dresden they arrived, Dec. 27, at Leipzig, where Weber met Rochlitz and other musical authors, and fostered his own inclination for literary work. Indeed, so strong was this that he seriously thought of staying in Leipzig and devoting himself exclusively to literature. His ideas, however, soon took a different turn. The Crown Prince Ludwig of

---

[1] Published later by Schlesinger of Berlin as 'Des Künstlers Abschied.'
[2] Nohl's *Musikerbriefe*, p. 195.

[3] Known as the Concertino, op. 26. Jähns, No. 109.
[4] Concerto No. 1, op. 73. Jähns, No. 114.
[5] Concerto No. 2, op. 74. Jähns, No. 118.

Bavaria, on whom he had evidently made a deep impression, had written about him to Duke Emil Leopold August of Saxe Gotha, and the result was an invitation for himself and Bärmann to Gotha, where they arrived Jan. 17, 1812. The Duke was devoted to the arts, a poet and composer, but whimsical and given to extremes —in fact a Jean-Paul kind of man, and a great admirer of Jean-Paul's works. Intercourse with him was exciting but very wearing, as Weber discovered, although just now it was only for a short time that he enjoyed the privilege of almost uninterrupted access to him. The Duke took great pleasure in his society, but, having at the time many claims on his time, invited Weber to return in the autumn and make a longer stay. In Gotha Weber met Spohr, who since 1805 had been Konzertmeister—the court had then no opera—and had married in 1806 Dorette Scheidler, a harpist, and daughter of Madame Scheidler, the court singer. Spohr had not retained a very favourable impression of Weber's music at Stuttgart, but received him in true brotherly fashion. On Jan. 20 they passed some pleasant hours together at Spohr's house, and on the 24th played before the court Weber's variations on a Norwegian theme (op. 22), on which Weber remarks in his diary, 'Spohr played gloriously.' From Gotha the two musicians went to Weimar, were kindly received at court, and gave a concert. If Weber had been hoping for inspiration from Weimar's great poets, his only chance was with Wieland, for Goethe behaved coldly, or rather took no notice at all of him. His diary contains an entry:

' Jan. 29. Early to the Princess [Maria Paulowna]. Goethe there and spoke. I did not like him.'

Spohr indeed had met with scarcely better treatment some little time before, but this may have arisen from Goethe's lack of interest in music. Against Weber he was personally prejudiced, possibly because of former circumstances about his father and his family, and the feeling was fostered by Zelter. Indeed, Weber never succeeded in approaching Goethe. By the beginning of February Weber and Bärmann were in Dresden, but left it with no very favourable impression ; indeed, they are reported to have said, ' Dresden shall not catch us again '— very contrary to the fact, as far as Weber was concerned.

On Feb. 20 they arrived in Berlin, where Weber had hopes of producing ' Silvana.' It had been tried through some months before by Righini, but ' went so confusedly that all pronounced it perfect rubbish.' [1] He had thus to meet a prejudice against his work, and, still worse, a personal one of the Kapellmeister against himself. Bernhard Anselm Weber especially, an able and cultivated man, and

himself a pupil of Vogler, was by no means kindly disposed to his young comrade ; but difficulties were gradually overcome, two arias were added, and the performance took place on July 10. Weber conducted in person, and succeeded in inspiring both band and singers, and the public gave the work a warm reception, in spite of its startling novelty. Weber had been much depressed by some sharp criticism of Herr von Drieberg's and had rigidly tested his work, so he was much encouraged by its success. He writes in his diary :

' While duly acknowledging my faults, I will not in future lose confidence in myself, but bravely, prudently, and watchfully march onwards on my art-career.'

Even before this he had made many friends in Berlin, and the two concerts given by himself and Bärmann, though not well attended, had roused great interest. He was introduced to the ' Singakademie' and the ' Liedertafel,' and wrote for the latter a composition which even gained the approval of Zelter.[2] Meyerbeer's parents from the first treated him as a son, and he stayed in their house the whole time he was in Berlin. His most valuable acquaintance was Lichtenstein, Professor of Zoology, who was the first to recognise his genius in Berlin. As one of the foremost members of the Singakademie he had no difficulty in introducing Weber to cultivated and musical families, where he soon became a favourite for his pleasant manners, his admirable pianoforte-playing and extemporising, his inspiriting way of leading concerted music, and, above all, his songs and his guitar. For these private circles he composed five charming partsongs. He used often to play to his new friends, with an almost inexhaustible variety of *nuances*, his sonata in C, composed in Berlin. He himself taught (on Aug. 26) the soldiers at the barracks near the Oranienburg gate, to sing his ' Kriegs-Eid,' a chorus for men's voices with wind instruments in unison, which he dedicated to the Brandenburg Brigade. While he was in Berlin his old father died at Mannheim (Apr. 16, 1812), an event which brought back in full force his homelessness and loneliness, and made him touchingly grateful for any proof of friendship. Bärmann had left him on Mar. 28 for Munich, and on Aug. 31 he himself also left Berlin, stayed some few days in Leipzig, where he found a publisher for some of his compositions and had a talk with Rochlitz, and then, passing through Weimar, arrived on Sept. 6 at Gotha.

The Duke's treatment was politeness itself, but instead of having, as he hoped, a quiet time for composition, Weber found the constant attendance on the Duke's inspired moments exciting and exhausting. In the midst of this he received an invitation from the Princess

---

[1] Weber to Gänsbacher.

[2] ' Das Turnierbankett,' Jähns, No. 132.

Maria Paulowna to come to Weimar and teach her some of his works, including the sonata in C, which he had dedicated to her. On this subject he writes to Lichtenstein (Nov. 1):

'The Princess often says that she does not believe she will ever play the sonata properly as long as she lives. If she were not a Princess, I should be at liberty to tell her that I *fully agree* with her.'

He had to give her a lesson each morning for a week, and the rest of his time he spent with the company at the theatre, among whom P. A. Wolf specially attracted him, and with Wieland, who was a sympathetic listener to his playing. One of the effects which Weber carried to a pitch of excellence never heard before was a long crescendo, beginning with an almost inaudible pianissimo, and passing through every gradation of loudness up to a thundering fortissimo. The effect of this was irresistible, and Wieland, having asked for it, found himself gradually drawn off his chair as by some demoniacal agency.

In Gotha he had much stimulating intercourse with Spohr, and also with Albert Methfessel, then passing through. His diary contains some interesting remarks on Spohr's compositions. Thus the evening of Sept. 16 was passed in going with Spohr through the latter's 'Last Judgment' (produced at Erfurt, Aug. 15). Weber did not much like the work, and calls it 'laboured, tedious, full of unnecessary modulations, and modelled entirely upon Mozart.' On Sept. 27, however, he writes:

'Spohr played his new Quartet in G minor very finely; it is well composed; much flow and unity. Afterwards a fine Sonata with his wife.'

At Spohr's he also met Hermstadt, the clarinet-player from Sondershausen, who played a concerto of Spohr's in masterly style, but seems to have been inferior to Bärmann in purity of tone and expression. As a rule, the quick-witted, far-seeing Weber was more just towards Spohr's compositions than the more ponderous and short-sighted Spohr was to his. But personal dislikes never lasted with Spohr. He could distinguish between a man and his work, and was always a loyal friend to Weber.

The Duke's younger brother, Prince Friedrich, an admirer of Italian music, had brought a singing-master back with him from Italy, and often had Weber to go through Italian operas with him. He had a good tenor voice, and for him Weber composed an Italian *scena ed aria*, with chorus, from an opera 'Ines de Castro,' performed at a court concert on Dec. 17. Other works written at Gotha were the celebrated PF. Variations on a theme from Méhul's ' Joseph,' the first two movements of the PF. concerto in E, and a hymn, ' In seiner Ordnung schafft der Herr,' to Rochlitz's words. Spohr having recently started on a concert tour, Weber left Gotha, on Dec. 19, for Leipzig, where he produced this hymn at a Gewandhaus concert

(Jan. 1, 1813); and played the E♭ concerto, 'with a success,' he writes himself, ' such as was perhaps scarcely ever known in Leipzig before. It is pronounced to be the first of concertos for effect and novelty. Truly these people, once so cold, have quite adopted me.' Thus the new year opened to him under happy auspices.

This year, 1813, was the greatest turning-point in Weber's short career. Hitherto his life had been that of a wandering minstrel or troubadour. Roving restlessly from place to place, winning all hearts by his sweet, insinuating, lively melodies, his eccentricities making him an imposing figure to the young of both sexes, and an annoyance to the old, exciting the attention of everybody, and then suddenly disappearing, his person uniting in the most seductive manner aristocratic bearing and tone with indolent dissipation, his moods alternating between uproarious spirits and deep depression—in all ways he resembled a figure from some romantic poem, wholly unlike anything seen before in the history of German art. In talking of Weber, people have in their minds, as a rule, only the last period of his life, beginning with ' Der Freischütz ' and ending with ' Oberon,' but from that point of view the work becomes too prominent, and the man of too little importance. As a man his versatile gifts made more effect in the first half of his artistic career than in the second. The love of the antique, whether in history, the life of the people, or national melody, was then newly awakened in Germany, and gave its stamp to the period. Weber became the embodiment of the ancient troubadour who, in Eichendorff's words, went through the country singing his melodies from house to house.

APPOINTMENT AT PRAGUE.—In 1813 this roving life came to an end, and was succeeded by a settled existence, with ties of place and circumstance, and definite duties. The wandering impulse was indeed too ingrained in his nature not to have a secret influence on his after life, but henceforth it was sufficiently under control to admit of that collectedness of spirit without which the creation of great and enduring works of art is impossible. On Jan. 12, 1813, Weber arrived at Prague, intending to go on by Vienna to Venice, Milan and the rest of Italy, and then back through Switzerland and France. This tour he calculated to take fully two years, and from it he hoped for great results. At Prague, however, there was a vacancy for a Kapellmeister of the theatre, owing to Wenzel Müller's resignation. Liebich, the director, knew Weber's value, and offered him the post, with a salary of 2000 gulden (about £200), a vacation of two or three months, an annual benefit guaranteed at 1000 gulden, and absolute independence of the opera. This gave him not only a fixed income, but the prospect of paying off the debts contracted at Breslau and Stuttgart, a decisive consideration to a man of his honourable nature. The grand tour, planned with so much expectation, was given up, and Liebich's offer accepted.

Under Müller's direction the opera had deteriorated to such a degree that Liebich determined to disband the company and entirely reorganise it. For this task he selected Weber, who started for Vienna on Mar. 27, furnished with full powers to engage good musicians and German singers.[1] In Vienna he met Meyerbeer, heard Hummel and Moscheles, whose playing he thought ' fine, but too smooth,' and gave a concert of his own on Apr. 25, but was principally occupied with the main object of his journey. The whole company, with the exception of three members, was new, and included Caroline Brandt, Weber's future wife. He entirely reorganised the whole system, and developed a marvellous capacity for that kind of work. It now became evident that it was not in vain that he had passed his childhood behind the scenes, and been a Kapellmeister at 18. His wide experience and energy helped him to conquer the singers and musicians, who were at first amazed by his strictness and the inflexibility of his rules. Among them were a number of Czechs, and in order to be able to grumble at him with impunity, they talked to each other at rehearsal in Czech. This Weber soon perceived, and set to work to learn the language, which in a few months he had mastered sufficiently for his purpose. Not only did he manage, arrange, and direct the music even to the smallest details, but he also superintended the administration, the scene-painting and the stage-management, and proved to demonstration that all these were really within his province. So completely were all theatrical details at his finger-ends, that on the prompter's sudden illness, Weber supplied his place. By this means he ensured an accuracy and a unity in all the dramatic representations which had never been seen before, and which the public did not fail to recognise. He was perhaps quite as great a conductor as a composer, and was the first of the great German musicians whose talent was conspicuous in this direction. In this matter also he was a virtuoso. The first opera he put on the stage at Prague was Spontini's ' Cortez ' (Sept. 10, 1813), then produced for the first time there. Between that date and Dec. 19 followed seven, and between that and Mar. 27, ten, newly studied operas and Singspiele. Of each he made a *scenario*, including the smallest details.

His aim was to reinstate the Prague opera in the position it occupied between 1780 and 1790 (see MOZART, Vol. III. p. 551). He was quite the man to do it, if only the times had been the same ; but unfortunately this was not the case.

[1] The Italian Opera of Prague ceased to exist in 1806.

During the war, society ceased to cultivate music, and lost its power of discrimination, and the only way of keeping up its traditional reputation for taste was to maintain a dignified reserve on all artistic productions. Weber, accustomed to more sympathy, soon discovered this, and it put him out of tune. Besides, he had not managed to form comfortable relations for himself. Gänsbacher had left, and Weber, to whom a friend was an absolute necessity, felt deserted. With the Prague musicians, KOŽELUH, Dionys (see WEBER, Friedrich Dionysus), TOMASCHEK (*q.v.*) and others, he did not hit it off. The real cause of his discomfort was that he could not at once fall into the regular ways of professional life. Passages in his letters make this clear.

' My incessant occupation, and my life of utter solitude, have made me morose, gloomy, and misanthropical. If Heaven does not soon thrust me violently back among my fellow-men, I shall become the most abominable Philistine on the face of the earth.' (Jan. 29, 1814.)
' The few composers and scholars who live here groan for the most part under a yoke which has reduced them to slavery and taken away the spirit which distinguishes the true free-born artist.' (May 5.)

The outward advantages of his position he fully acknowledged.

' I reason myself by main force into a sort of contentment, but the naturally cheerful state of mind which steels all one's nerves, and sends one's spirits bubbling up of themselves, *that* one cannot give oneself.' (Apr. 22.)

After bringing out seven more operas between Apr. 19 and June 26 (1814), Weber, who had been out of health for some time, went on July 8 to take the baths at Liebwerda. But the impulse to join the great world was too strong to allow him to stay there, and, pushing on, he arrived in Berlin on Aug. 3, a couple of days before the King of Prussia's return from the Allied Armies' victorious expedition to Paris after the battle of Leipzig. Unlike Prague, where a few official ceremonies formed all the notice taken of the victory over Napoleon, Berlin was in a tumult of joy, and Weber had before him the spectacle of a great people hailing their reconquered freedom with transport. He was carried away like the rest, and thoroughly enjoyed it. To increase his happiness he met with an enthusiastic reception from his friends, whose circle now included Tieck and Brentano, with whom he had formed an intimacy in Prague in 1813. Brentano began to arrange a libretto on the Tannhäuser legend for him, but other things intervened, and the work was laid aside. He gave a concert on Aug. 24, and received permission to invite the King, the Crown Prince, and other princes and princesses. Several great personages were interested in him, and there was some talk of making him Kapellmeister of the Court Opera, in place of Himmel, who had just died. ' Silvana ' was given again on Sept. 5, and Weber left Berlin, happy in many a proof of heartfelt sympathy, and loaded with impressions destined to bear fruit later on.

At that period patriotic songs were naturally enough the order of the day, and in this direction Weber could hardly fail to be led. An invitation from the Duke took him to Gotha on Sept. 11, and the next day to Gräfentonna, the Duke's hunting seat. Here, finding a little repose for the first time for many months, he composed on the 13th two Lieder from Körner's ' Leyer und Schwert,' followed by eight others during the journey home and in the first few months after his return. Six of these are for four men's voices, and four for a single voice and PF., and in them he has recorded the impressions made on his mind by the surging national movement. It was his first opportunity of showing how great a power he had of absorbing the feelings of the masses and giving them artistic expression. The effect of these songs on the whole people of Germany, and especially on the youth, was extraordinary. Wherever they were sung they roused the most fervid enthusiasm. All the other patriotic compositions, in which the time abounded, paled before the brilliancy, swing and pathos of these Songs of War and Fatherland. Weber's own cantata even yields to them in effect. The choruses from the ' Leyer und Schwert ' are still among the most favourite of such works for men's voices, and are indeed so bound up with the development of the male choral societies in Germany that only with them can they cease to be heard.

Before his trip to Berlin Weber had entered into closer relations with Caroline Brandt, but there were difficulties in the way of marriage. Caroline, a talented soubrette, and a good deal spoiled by the public, was somewhat whimsical, and had imperfect views both as to the dignity of art in itself, and Weber's importance as an artist. Neither did she like his requiring her to leave the stage before they married. This uncertainty about an object he so ardently desired added to his discontent with Prague, and made him anxiously look out for some opening which should lead to his removal. In the meantime he made use of his summer holiday in 1815 for an expedition to Munich, and it was there that the news of the battle of Waterloo reached him. The outburst of joy and enthusiasm which followed incited him to a great composition in honour of the event. Gottfried Wohlbrück the actor provided him with the words, and in August, before leaving Munich, he wrote the first two numbers of ' Kampf und Sieg.' The last two days of his stay were embittered by a letter from Caroline, conveying her conviction that they had better part. This seems to justify what Weber had written to Gänsbacher:

' I see now that her views of high art are not above the usual pitiful standard—namely, that art is but a means of procuring soup, meat and shirts.'

Her ' conviction,' however, did not last long. When Weber returned to Prague her real affection for him overcame all scruples, and he was able to look forward with confidence to a time when she should be all his own.

' Lina is behaving extremely well, and honestly trying to become better. If God will only bestow on me some post without cares, and with a salary on which a man can live ; and if she is as brave in a year and a day as she is at this moment, she is to leave the stage, and become my faithful *Hausfrau*. You shake your head ! A year is a long time, and a person who can hold out so long is really brave.' [1]

The cantata was quickly completed, and performed for the first time at Weber's benefit concert (Dec. 22). The immediate effect was very great, though, for reasons hereafter to be explained, not so lasting as that of the Körner songs. Beethoven had composed his orchestral picture in honour of the battle of Vittoria, and this had been performed shortly before in Prague. At the close of ' Kampf und Sieg,' General Nostiz went up to Weber and said, ' With you I hear nations speaking; with Beethoven, only big boys playing with rattles.' This criticism, though too severe [2] on Beethoven, has in it elements of justice, for in this *pièce d'occasion* Weber has in truth outdone his great contemporary.

With the completion of his cantata Weber decided to give up his post at Prague. The main object of his labours, the reorganisation of the opera on a solid basis, was accomplished. To produce first-rate results, and make it one of the chief institutions for promoting German dramatic art, was out of the question under the circumstances in which he was placed, and with the means at his disposal. But he thought that it could be maintained at its then state of efficiency without his aid ; and as Prague had nothing to offer for himself and the furtherance of his own artistic life, he resigned his post on Sept. 30, 1816. Projects of a grand tour or a summons to some other great art-institution again floated through his mind. He had been again in Berlin during the summer, and had produced his cantata on the anniversary of Waterloo with such success that it was repeated on the 23rd June. Count Brühl, Iffland's successor as Intendant of the court theatres, was devoted to both Weber and his music, and tried, though vainly, to procure him the appointment of Kapellmeister *vice* Himmel. The post was occupied provisionally by Bernhard Romberg, and not even a title from the Prussian court could be had for Weber. On his return journey to Prague he made the acquaintance at Carlsbad of Count Vitzthum, Marshal to the Saxon court, and he opened to him a prospect of an invitation to Dresden. After a formal farewell to Prague he accompanied his *fiancée* to Berlin on a star engage-

1 Letter to Gänsbacher, Aug. 4, 1816.
2 But compare Grove's strictures on ' Wellington's Victory' under BEETHOVEN, Vol. I. p. 290.

ment, and remained there for the rest of the year busily engaged in composition. The PF. sonatas in A♭ and D minor, the grand duo for PF. and clarinet, and several charming songs with PF. accompaniment, belong to this time. On Dec. 21, just before starting on a *tournée* to Hamburg and Copenhagen, he received the news that the King of Saxony had appointed him Kapellmeister of the German opera at Dresden.

GERMAN OPERA AT DRESDEN. — Weber's work at Dresden, which was to last for nine years and terminate only with his premature death, is of the highest importance. Not only did he there bestow on his countrymen those works which, with Mozart's, form the main basis of German national opera, but he founded an institution for the performance of German opera at one of the most musically distinguished courts of Germany, which did not possess one before. In all the other courts where music was cultivated German opera had for long stood on an equal footing with Italian. Vienna, Berlin, Munich, Mannheim and other places had had a national opera by the end of the 18th century, and in most cases the rise of the German opera had put an end to the separate existence of its rival. In Dresden alone matters were different. From the beginning of the 18th century, when Italian opera had reached a perfection scarcely to be surpassed even in Italy, it had reigned there supreme, and by 1765 had even ceased to belong exclusively to the court.

Towards the end of the century, German Singspiele were occasionally performed in Dresden, but only by second-rate actors, at a small theatre in the so-called Linkesche Bad, the court Kapellmeister being expressly prohibited from taking part in the performance. After King Friedrich August's return from the war in 1815 his Intendant Count Heinrich Vitzthum induced him to found a German opera, though only as an addition to the Italian, and it was this institution which Weber was called on to organise. Such a work naturally could not be carried out without violent opposition from the Italians, who had hitherto had it all their own way in Dresden, with the court and nobility almost exclusively on their side. The post of Kapellmeister had been filled since 1811 by a born Italian named Francesco MORLACCHI (*q.v.*). Weber had hardly entered on his new office before he discovered that powerful foes were actively though secretly engaged against him. In accepting the post he had made it a *sine qua non* that he and his institution should be ranked on terms of perfect equality with Morlacchi and his, and had expressly stipulated for the title of Kapellmeister, which was held by the other. These conditions were agreed to, and yet when the appointment was gazetted he found himself styled 'Musikdirector,' a title which, according to general usage, made him

subordinate to Morlacchi. Weber at once stated with decision that he must decline the post. He, however, allowed himself to be persuaded, for the sake of the object, to fill the office provisionally, until either a substitute had been engaged in his place, or he himself had been formally pronounced Kapellmeister. By Feb. 10, 1817, he had the satisfaction of learning that the King had given way. His salary (1500 thalers, = about £220) had been from the first on an equality with Morlacchi's, and on Sept. 13 the appointment was confirmed for life. In Dresden he had a first-rate orchestra and a tolerable body of singers at his disposal, and found ample opportunity for turning his knowledge and experience to account.

German opera having generally had spoken dialogue, often forming a large proportion of the work, a custom had arisen of filling the parts with actors who could sing. The style was not a very perfect one, the profession of an actor being so wearing for the voice, and hence small parts alone were fit for these singing actors. Of such materials Weber's company at first exclusively consisted. He was indeed allowed, with special permission, to make use of the members of the Italian opera, but this availed him little, because the Italians could rarely speak German and were unfamiliar with German music. As for the chorus, it was at first non-existent. A few supers with voices, and two or three subordinate solo-singers, constituted the basses and tenors, while the sopranos and altos were supplied by schoolboys, as was once the custom at all German theatres. With such materials it needed all Weber's gifts of organisation and direction to produce results which might bear comparison with the far better appointed Italian theatre, and keep alive, or rather kindle, an interest in German opera among cultivated people.

The way in which he set about his task made it clear that musical life in Dresden now possessed a man of power, who would keep steadfastly in view the success of his undertaking, without concerning himself as to whether he were breaking with old traditions, abolishing old and convenient usages, or even giving personal offence. He knew that, in order to prosper, German opera must command the sympathy of the German people. The court, he was also aware, took but a languid interest in it, while the aristocracy considered foreign music more *distingué*, and had as a body no community of feeling with the people. For this reason his first step, a very startling one to Dresden society, was to publish in the *Abendzeitung*, a literary paper with a large circulation, an article addressed to the 'Amateurs of Dresden,' laying down the conditions necessary to his undertaking. Modestly bespeaking the indulgence of the public for the first attempts of a new institution, and frankly owning that real excellence would only be attained after many failures, the whole article shows how clearly he perceived the goal at which he was aiming, and how energetically he directed his course towards it from the very first. 'The Italians and the French,' he says,

'have fashioned for themselves a distinct form of opera, with a framework which allows them to move with ease and freedom.   Not so the Germans.   Eager in the pursuit of knowledge, and constantly yearning after progress, they endeavour to appropriate anything which they see to be good in others.   But they take it all so much more seriously.   With the rest of the world the gratification of the senses is the main object ;   the German wants a work of art complete in itself,   with each part rounded off and compacted into a perfect whole.   For him, therefore, a fine *ensemble* is the prime necessity.'

It had been so much the habit hitherto in Dresden for society to look to the court, and mould its tastes in fashion in accordance with those set from above, that it was almost an impossibility for a court official to talk about his work as if he were in any sense personally responsible for it, or wished to be considered the head of his own institution. People were aware that Weber had been leading a free and restless life as an independent artist : and that his songs of war and liberty had endeared him to the heart of young Germany.   Hence he was set down as a revolutionary spirit aiming at dangerous political innovations ; though as a fact he was no politician, and never went beyond the general interest natural to a cultivated man in forms of government, social conditions and the universal rights of man. Another of his actions which excited remark was the giving a very gay dinner and ball to his staff, himself tho life and soul of the party. How could he expect to keep up the respect of his subordinates, if he began by treating them in this way ? His singers and actors were indeed very much surprised by his strictness and punctuality in all business matters. At first this aroused much dissatisfaction, but when it was found that he could make an opera go in all its parts, that at rehearsal his ears and eyes were everywhere at once, that he was as familiar with the details of acting, dressing and scenery as he was with the music, and master of all the ins and outs of the opera as a whole, then a higher ideal gradually dawned upon the company, and an immense respect for their new director.

The first opera he produced was Méhul's 'Joseph' (Jan. 13, 1817). As had been his successful habit in Prague, he published two days beforehand in the *Abendzeitung* an article giving some information about the new opera. The performance was excellent ; indeed, all that could be desired, as far as the *ensemble* went, though the solo-singers were but indifferent. The engagement of competent leading artists was his next care. Here he acted upon the principle that German opera was not to be confined to native works only, but should also produce Italian and French operas. To this end a numerous, well-trained and thoroughly cultivated body of artists was requisite, and he felt it necessary to engage at least three leading sopranos, one first-rate tenor and one first-rate bass. His Intendant sent him in Mar. 1817 on a mission to Prague, with the view of engaging Frl. Grünbaum, then singing at the theatre there.   On the 28th he conducted his ' Silvana,' and was enthusiastically received, the people of Prague taking every means of showing how much they felt his loss.   Immediately after his return he went to Leipzig, and played his concerto in E♭ at a Gewandhaus concert, his scena from ' Atalia ' and his 'Kampf und Sieg ' being also in the programme.   Grünbaum sang in Dresden, but was not engaged ; various other stars were unsuccessful, and the year 1817 came to a close without any real acquisition having been made.   However, Weber had secured a regular chorus and chorusmaster, the post being filled first by Metzner, and then towards the close of 1819 by Johannes Micksch.   The latter had studied in Italy, and was considered a first-rate teacher of singing ; his principal object, however, was not so much expression as the production of a full and even tone, which occasioned some differences of opinion between him and Weber.   On the whole, however, he proved an excellent teacher, and was duly appreciated.

A third reform undertaken by Weber in the early part of 1818 was the re-arrangement of the orchestra.   The band had been hitherto placed in the same manner as at the Italian opera, but this disposition he wished to alter for one more suited to the component parts of a modern orchestra, and to the greater importance assigned to the instrumental part of an opera.   The change was at first strongly opposed, and he was obliged for the time to desist by the King's express command.   Bit by bit, however, he made the changes he wanted, and his new arrangement having proved itself perfect, was permanently maintained.

Weber's work in Dresden very nearly came to an end in a few months' time, for on June 27, 1817, a post as Kapellmeister in Berlin fell vacant, and Count Brühl the Intendant at once entered into negotiations with him on the subject.   It was an appointment he was strongly inclined to accept. Berlin had many attractions for him, and so far society in Dresden had done little to make his residence there agreeable.   The burning of the Berlin theatre on July 31, however, put a stop to the negotiations, and though several times renewed, nothing came of them.   One result at any rate was that his appointment at Dresden was made for life, and that he was also admitted to a share in the direction of the musical services at the Catholic Chapel Royal. He conducted for the first time Sept. 24, 1817, the music being a

Salve Regina by Schuster and a litany by Naumann, for whose church music Weber had a great admiration. It is an evidence of his devout turn of mind that before this his first official participation in divine service he confessed and received Communion. Now that he was often called on to compose for court festivities, the duties of his post became varied and extensive, and absorbed much time. His colleague Morlacchi had frequent leave of absence, and passed long periods of time in Italy (*e.g.* from Sept. 1817 to June 1818), and then all his work fell upon Weber. A man loving freedom from restraint as he did would have found it very hard to carry on his work with the cheerfulness and elasticity of spirit so remarkable in him, if he had not had a constant spring of happiness and refreshment in married life. His union with Caroline Brandt took place at Prague, Nov. 4, 1817. On their wedding tour the young couple gave concerts at Darmstadt and Giessen, appeared in Gotha before the Duke, and then went home to Dresden, which they reached Dec. 20.

To the early years of his work in Dresden belong most of Weber's *compositions d'occasion.* His sincere devotion to the royal family made him hail opportunities of showing his loyalty, so that several of these works were undertaken of his own motion, and did not always meet with proper acknowledgment. The fullest year in this respect was that of 1818, the 50th anniversary of the King's accession. Besides two or three smaller works, Weber composed a grand Mass in E♭ for the King's name-day, and for the accession-day (Sept. 20) a grand Jubel-Cantata, which the King did not allow to be performed, so he added the well-known Jubel-Ouvertüre.[1] The Mass in G may also be counted as belonging to this year, since it was finished on Jan. 4, 1819, for the golden wedding of the King and Queen. These official duties were not despatched perfunctorily, or as mere obligations. Into each he put his full strength, though well aware, as he wrote to Gänsbacher (Aug. 24, 1818), 'that they were but creatures of a day in the world of art, and from their ephemeral nature always disheartening.' Shortly after the performance of the Mass in G he was asked to write a festival opera for the marriage of Prince Friedrich August. He took up the idea with great earnestness, chose for his subject the tale of Alcindor in the *Arabian Nights,* and had already begun to think out the music, when he found (June 28) that his commission had been withdrawn, and Morlacchi requested to prepare an Italian piece for the ceremony (Oct. 9).

COMPOSITION OF 'DER FREISCHÜTZ.'—Had 'Alcindor' been written, Weber and Spontini might have been directly rivals, for Spontini's opera of that name, composed a few years later

at Berlin, is drawn from the same source. Perhaps also the work on which Weber's world-wide fame rests, and which was to give him a triumph over Spontini, might have taken another form, or never have been written at all. He had already been at work on it for two years. Soon after his removal to Dresden he became intimate with Friedrich Kind, who, after throwing up his employment as an advocate in Leipzig, had been living in Dresden solely by literature. Weber having proposed to him to write a libretto, Kind heartily assented, and the two agreed on Apel's novel of 'Der Freischütz,' which came out in 1810 and had excited Weber's attention. Kind wrote the play in seven days ; on Feb. 21, 1817, he and Weber sketched the plan together, and by Mar. 1 the complete libretto was in Weber's hands. The composition did not proceed with equal celerity ; on the contrary, Weber took longer over this than over any other of his operas. Bit by bit, and with many interruptions, it advanced to completion. The sketch of the first number—the duet between Agathe and Aennchen, with which the second act begins—was written July 2 and 3, 1817. Nothing more was done that year, except the sketch of the terzet and chorus in the first act ('O, diese Sonne ') and Agathe's grand air in the second (Aug. 6 to 25).[2] In 1818 he only worked at the opera on three days (Apr. 17, 21 and 22). On Mar. 13, 1819, he wrote the sketch of Caspar's air in D minor, which ends the first act. Then follows another six months' pause, after which he set to work continuously on Sept. 17, and the last number, the overture, was completed on May 13, 1820.

The court compositions of 1818 may have hindered his progress in that year, but in the summer of 1819, without any pressure from without, solely following the bent of his own genius, he wrote several of his finest PF. compositions for two and four hands, including the Rondo in E♭, op. 62, the 'Aufforderung zum Tanze,' op. 65, and the Polacca brillante in E, op. 72. The PF. Trio also and many charming Lieder belong to this summer, which Weber passed, like those of 1822, 1823 and 1824, in a little country place, Hosterwitz, near Pillnitz.[2] By the time 'Der Freischütz' was at last finished, his delight in dramatic production had reached such a pitch that he at once began and completed another dramatic work, and started at any rate on a third. Count Brühl, Intendant of the Berlin theatres, had asked him for some new music to Wolff's play of 'Preciosa,' Eberwein's not being satisfactory. Weber did as he was requested, and wrote the music—' a heavy piece of work and an important one, more than half an opera,' as he says himself—between May 25 and July 15, 1820. In the meantime he was working at a comic opera, 'Die drei

Pintos,' the libretto by Theodor Hell, a Dresden poet, whose real name was Karl Winkler. This work was still progressing in the following year.

Count Brühl, who had a great esteem for Weber, informed him in the summer of 1819 that it was his intention to produce ' Der Frei-schütz ' at the opening of the new theatre, then in course of erection by Schinkel. The building was to have been finished in the spring of 1820, but was not ready till a year later. Weber had intended to take the opportunity of his visit to Berlin for making a professional tour, but it did not seem advisable to postpone this for so long. For the last two years he had been out of health, and disquieting symptoms of the malady which brought his life to a premature close had begun to show themselves. Relaxation and refresh-ment were urgently necessary. He also wished, after this interval of ten years, to appear again in public as a pianist. He started with his wife July 25, 1820, went first to Leipzig, to his inti-mate friend Rochlitz, then on to Halle. His settings of Körner's ' Leyer und Schwert ' had made Weber the darling composer of the German student, as he discovered at Halle. The greatest enthusiasm prevailed at the con-cert he gave there, July 31. Among the students with whom he formed relations was J. C. G. Loewe, afterwards the greatest of German ballad-composers, who took the whole arrange-ments for the concert off his hands.[1] Still more enthusiastic was his reception by the students of Göttingen, where he arrived Aug. 11, and gave a concert Aug. 17. After it he was serenaded by the students, who sang his Lied ' Lützow's wilde Jagd,' and, on his coming down to talk with them, crowded round him cheering. Thence they went by Hanover to Bremen, Oldenburg and Hamburg, where he left his wife, going on to Lübeck, Eutin (his birthplace, which he had not visited since 1802) and Kiel, from whence he crossed over to Copenhagen. This was the most brilliant point of his journey. He was presented to the King and Queen, played at court on Oct. 4, and at a public concert Oct. 8, overwhelmed with applause on both occasions. After another concert at Hamburg on his way back, he reached Dresden, Nov. 4.

As a great pianist Weber was often asked to give lessons, and did so. Pupils in the higher sense of the word, that is to say, artists stamped with his own sign-manual as composers or pianists, he had none. For this his artistic

disposition was too peculiar, his character too restless and unmethodical. We find a pupil named Freytag from Berlin studying the piano and composition with him in Prague in 1816, and are told that he made his début at a concert of Weber's (Mar. 29), to his master's satisfac-tion, but we never hear of him again from that day forwards.[2] MARSCHNER (q.v.) communi-cated with him in 1818, sending him his opera ' Heinrich IV. und D'Aubigné ' from Pressburg, and coming himself, Aug. 18, 1819. Weber was much interested in the opera, and secured its performance at Dresden, where it was given for the first time, July 19, 1820.[3] Marschner settled in Dresden in the beginning of Aug. 1821, and in 1824 was appointed Musik-director of the opera, a post he retained till Weber's death. The two maintained an inter-course which at times was animated, though Weber never found Marschner a congenial companion. Marschner was undoubtedly strongly influenced by Weber's music ; it is evident in all his compositions during his stay in Dresden, and also in his opera ' Der Vampyr.' And yet he cannot be called a pupil of Weber. When he settled in Dresden he was 26, and a formed musician, so that after passing through the Weber period he recovered his independence in the ' Templer und Jüdin ' and ' Hans Heiling.' Weber's most devoted and only real pupil was Jules Benedict of Stuttgart. He came to Weber in Feb. 1821, and his account of their first interview is so charming that we venture to transcribe it.

' I shall never forget the impression of my first meeting with him. Ascending the by no means easy staircase which led to his modest home, on the third storey of a house in the old market-place, I found him sitting at his desk, and occupied with the pianoforte arrangement of his " Freischütz." The dire disease which but too soon was to carry him off had made its mark on his noble features ; the pro-jecting cheek-bones, the general emaciation, told their own tale ; but in his clear blue eyes, too often concealed by spectacles, in his mighty forehead fringed by a few straggling locks, in the sweet expression of his mouth, in the very tone of his weak but melodious voice, there was a magic power which attracted irresistibly all who approached him. He received me with the utmost kindness, and, though overwhelmed with double duties during Morlacchi's absence, found time to give me daily lessons for a considerable period.' [4]

Benedict goes on to relate how Weber played him ' Freischütz ' and ' Preciosa,' works then unknown to the world, and what a fascinating effect both he and his compositions made on him ; but what impressed him even more was his

' rendering of Beethoven's sonatas, with a fire and precision and a thorough entering into the spirit of the composer, which would have given the mighty Ludwig the best proof of Weber's reverence and admiration for his genius.'

PRODUCTION OF ' DER FREISCHÜTZ.'— Benedict was fortunate enough to share the

---

[1] Some papers entitled *Scenes from Dr. Karl Loewe's Life* have been published by Dr. Max. Runze (from MS. notes by Loewe's daughter) in the *Musikwelt* (Berlin, 1881). No. 11 (Apr. 9, 1881) contains a charming picture of Weber's concert at Halle, and the part Loewe took in it. Unfortunately it is historically inaccurate. Dr. Runze makes Weber play in July 1820 his Concertstück in F minor, which was not written till 1821, and played in public for the first time, June 25, in Berlin. Nor is this all ; Dr. Runze declares that in this his own composition Weber could not keep time with the orchestra, and says that in the fire of playing he accelerated the tempo, the band hurried after him, but by and by fell behind, and Loewe had to stop Weber and start them again. Dr. Runze's description would apply to the playing of a bad amateur, not to that of a finished Kapellmeister like Weber. All this, too, about the execution of a piece not then in existence !

[2] Weber's *Literarische Arbeiten*, p. 109 (*Lebensbild*, vol. iii.).
[3] Weber also wrote an article in its behalf : see p. 224 of the *Lebensbild*, and elsewhere.
[4] *The Great Musicians*, edited by Francis Hueffer ; *Weber*, by Sir Julius Benedict, p. 61 (London, 1881).

brightest and most triumphant bit of Weber's short life with him.   After 'Preciosa' had been played for the first time with Weber's music (Mar. 14, 1821) at the Berlin opera-house, and very well received, the day drew near for the opening of the new theatre, in which 'Der Freischütz' was to be the first opera performed.[1] Weber had been invited to rehearse and conduct the opera himself, and for this purpose arrived in Berlin, May 4.   Benedict followed two or three weeks later.

SPONTINI (q.v.) was at that time the ruling spirit in operatic matters at Berlin.   The King was a great admirer of his music, and he had many adherents among the court and in society. In the rest of the world, however, opinions were mingled.   During the war a strong feeling of nationality had developed in Germany, and there was a prejudice against foreigners, especially against foreigners hailing from Paris. Hence that a Franco-Italian should be installed, on terms of unusual liberality, in the chief musical post in the capital gave great umbrage. There is no question that Spontini, apart from his blunders, was made a scapegoat, and that the dislike of the people of Berlin was as much due to political and social as to musical reasons.

All at once Weber stepped on the scene with his new opera.   We can quite understand how ardently the patriots of Berlin must have longed for a brilliant success, if only as a counterpoise to Spontini.   Obviously, too, it was impossible to prevent a certain anxiety lest Weber was not man enough to sustain with honour this conflict with the foreigner.   He was known as a gifted composer of songs and instrumental music, but his earlier operas had not been un-disputed successes, and for the last ten years he had done nothing at all in that line.   On all these grounds the first performance of 'Der Freischütz' was looked forward to with a wide-spread feeling of suspense and excitement.

Weber thus could not but feel that much was at stake, both for himself and for the cause of German art.   As if to point the contrast still more forcibly between himself and Spontini, between native and foreign art, Spontini's 'Olympie,' entirely remodelled by the composer after its production in Paris, had been given for the first time in Berlin (May 14) only a month before 'Der Freischütz,' with a success which, though not enduring, was enormous at the time. Weber's friends were full of dismay, fearing that 'Freischütz' would not have a chance ; Weber alone, as if with a true presentiment of the event, was always in good spirits.   The rehearsals began on May 21, and the perform-ance was fixed for June 18, a day hailed by Weber as of good omen, from its being that of the battle of Waterloo.   So entirely was he free

from anxiety, that he employed his scanty leisure in composing one of his finest instru-mental works, the Concertstück in F minor, finishing it on the morning of the day on which 'Der Freischütz' was produced.   Benedict relates how he was sitting with Weber's wife when the composer came in, and played them the piece just finished, making remarks as he went, and what an indelible impression it made on him.   ' He was certainly one of the greatest pianists who ever lived,' he adds.[2]

Weber's presentiment did not fail him.   The 18th of June was as great a day of triumph as ever fell to the lot of a musician.   The applause of a house filled to the very last seat was such as had never been heard before, in Germany at any rate.   That this magnificent homage was no outcome of party spirit was shown by the en-during nature of the success, and by the fact that it was the same wherever ' Der Freischütz ' was heard.   No sooner had it been produced in Berlin than it was seized upon by nearly all the principal theatres in Germany.   In Vienna it was given on Oct. 3, and, though to a certain extent mutilated and curtailed, was received with almost greater enthusiasm than in Berlin. The feeling reached its height when Weber, on a visit to Vienna, conducted the performance in person, Mar. 7, 1822.   There is an entry in his diary :

' Conducted the "Freischütz" for Schröder's benefit.   Greater enthusiasm there cannot be, and I tremble to think of the future, for it is scarcely possible to rise higher than this.[3]   To God alone the praise ! '

Weber thought it desirable to appear in public at a concert before leaving Berlin.   The second representation of ' Der Freischütz ' took place on the 20th, and the third on the 22nd, of June.   On the 25th he gave his concert in the hall of the new theatre, and played his Concert-stück, completed that day week, for the first time in public.   Others of his compositions heard on the same occasion were the Italian scena from ' Atalia,' and the Variations for PF. and violin on a Norwegian theme.   His colleague in the latter piece was the eccentric violinist, Alexandre Boucher, who, having asked permis-sion to introduce a cadenza of his own in the finale of the variations, improvised on themes from ' Der Freischütz,' but wandered off so far that he could not get back again, seeing which, he put down his violin, and throwing his arms round Weber exclaimed enthusiastically, ' Ah, grand maître ! que je t'aime, que je t'admire ! ' The audience joined in with loud cheers for Weber.

Weber returned to Dresden, July 1, 1821.   In comparison with other places in Germany, Dresden was in no special hurry to produce ' Der Freischütz,' though it had not been able altogether to shut its ears to the reports of its

---

[1] It was not the first actual performance.   That distinction fell to Goethe's 'Iphigenia' (May 26), succeeded for the next few days by one or two other plays.

[2] Benedict's *Weber*, p. 65.
[3] He had undertaken to write a new opera ' Euryanthe ' for Vienna.

colossal success. The composer, in spite of all the pains he took to show his loyalty, was no favourite with the King and court. He was the singer *par excellence* of Körner's lyrics, and anything which called up reminiscences of the war that inspired those songs could not but be painful to the King of Saxony. He tried to be just towards Weber, and acknowledged his services in many ways, but his sentiments were well known and had their influence on the courtiers. From the time of the first appearance of ' Der Freischütz ' till Weber's death, there is not a sign that at court the smallest pride was felt in the fact of Dresden possessing so great a composer. He was all but allowed to accept the post of court Kapellmeister at Cassel, with the liberal salary of 2500 thalers (£375)—1000 thalers more than he received at Dresden. The Minister at last offered him an increase of 300 thalers, calculating that with his attachment to Dresden that would be sufficient inducement to him to remain ; and he was not deceived. The additional salary, however, was deprived of all value as a distinction by its being also bestowed on Morlacchi. This took place in August and September of the year in which ' Der Freischütz ' saw the light, but even some years later Weber's official superiors would not see that the Kapellmeister of the Dresden German opera was a man of world-wide fame. Perhaps they really did not see it. When Weber was in Berlin, Dec. 1825, for the production of ' Euryanthe,' his Intendant, von Lüttichau, happened to be present when Weber was leaving the theatre after rehearsal, and seeing a large crowd waiting at the door, and all hats raised with the greatest respect, he turned to him and said with astonishment, ' Weber, are you then really a celebrated man ? '

' Der Freischütz ' was performed in Dresden for the first time, Jan. 26, 1822, and met with a more enthusiastic reception than had ever been known there before. At the close of the performance the storm of applause defied all restraint. A few isolated cases were found of people who did not like it, but their comments were unheard in the general approval. Kind, the librettist, could not bear the music, because it threw his own merits into the shade, and its ever-increasing success irritated the petty vanity of this *bel esprit* to such an extent as to end in a complete breach of his friendship with Weber. Spohr, who had moved to Dresden [1] with his family, Oct. 31, 1821, heard it there for the first time, and was not favourably impressed. His failure to understand Weber's music has been mentioned already, and this is fresh evidence of it ; but, as before, it made no difference in their relations. On the contrary, Weber showed his esteem for Spohr by warmly

[1] Thus all the three representatives of German romantic opera, Weber, Spohr and Marschner, were living in the same place.

recommending him to Generaldirector Feige, of Cassel, for the post of Kapellmeister, which he had himself declined, but which, as is well known, Spohr accepted, and filled with credit up to a short period before his death.

Ludwig Tieck, too, then resident in Dresden, never could reconcile himself thoroughly to ' Der Freischütz,' though he heartily appreciated ' Euryanthe.' The two men, much as they differed in their views on dramatic art, formed a lasting friendship, expressed with frankness on both sides. Weber was seldom absent from Tieck's dramatic readings of great works, and was a most attentive listener. Speaking generally, he was on excellent terms with the poets of the day. With Goethe indeed he never got on, though they met several times ; but with Jean Paul, and also with Achim von Arnim, he was intimate. Arnim, like Tieck, belonged to the romantic school, and it was natural that there should be sympathy between them ; but Weber was also very friendly with Wilhelm Müller, author of the ' Müllerlieder ' and the ' Winterreise.' Müller visited him in Dresden and dedicated a volume of poems to him in the autumn of 1824, but not one of these did Weber set. His day for writing Lieder was over. Of Tieck's poems he only composed one (' Sind es Schmerzen, sind es Freuden,' from ' Die schöne Magelone ').

COMPOSITION OF ' EURYANTHE.'—During the latter half of 1821 Weber was at work upon the comic opera ' Die drei Pintos,' begun in 1820, but never to be finished by him. He was drawn off towards work of a different kind. The criticisms on ' Der Freischütz ' were almost always on points of form, and mainly resolved themselves into this, that the opera did not contain enough of those larger, artistically constructed, forms which betray the hand of the master. Hence, was it certain that Weber was really master of his art, or did he not owe his great success mainly to his heaven-sent genius ? Weber was very sensitive to public criticism, even when so ignorant, one-sided and absurd as this, and he determined to write a grand opera, and show the world what he was capable of. When, therefore, an invitation to write a new opera arrived (Nov. 11, 1821) from Barbaja, of the Kärnthnerthor theatre in Vienna, he seized the opportunity with avidity. The libretto was to be written by Frau Helmina von Chezy, who had been in Dresden since 1817, well received in literary circles, and not without poetical talent. She offered him several subjects, and he selected ' Euryanthe.' After several attempts, in which Weber gave her active assistance, she succeeded in putting her materials into something like the shape he desired. His idea of an opera was that the music should not be so entirely dominant as in Italian opera, but that the work should be a drama, in which the words should have a real interest of their own, and in which action, scenery and decorations should all contribute to the vividness and force of the general impression : in short, that the impression made by an opera should be based on a carefully balanced combination of poetry, music and the descriptive arts. These principles he had endeavoured to carry out in ' Der Freischütz '; in ' Euryanthe ' he hoped to realise them fully. The words of the first act were ready by Dec. 15, 1821, and Weber set to work with all his might.

Thinking it well to study the circumstances under which his new work was to appear, he started, Feb. 10, 1822, for Vienna, stopping on the way to conduct ' Der Freischütz ' (Feb. 14) at Prague, with unmeasured success. He attended a performance of the same opera in Vienna on the 18th, but found it far from edifying. How he conducted it himself on Mar. 9, and what a reception it had, has been already mentioned. This one work gave him a popularity in Vienna that became almost burdensome. He was urged to settle there altogether, and undertake the direction of the German opera. There also he received an invitation to write a grand opera for Paris. In the midst of all this excitement he fell ill with a violent sore throat. That his disease was making progress was evident. Still he appeared in public on two occasions besides the ' Freischütz ' performance, once at a concert given by Böhm the violinist, on Mar. 10—when he conducted his ' Jubel-Ouvertüre,' and the men's choruses from the ' Leyer und Schwert,' with enormous success—and once at a concert of his own (Mar. 19), when he played his Concertstück, which, oddly enough, was not equally appreciated. By Mar. 26 he was again at home.

All the summer he remained at Hosterwitz, and there was composed by far the greatest part of ' Euryanthe,' for he had the same house the following summer. His most important piece of official work at this time was the production of ' Fidelio.' That opera, though composed in 1805, and reduced to its final shape in 1814, had never been given in Dresden, for the simple reason that till Weber came there was no German opera. Though it was impossible for him to ignore that the music is not throughout essentially dramatic, he felt it to be a sublime creation, for which his admiration was intense, and he strained every nerve to secure a performance worthy of the work. An animated correspondence ensued between him and Beethoven. Weber's first letter was dated Jan. 28, 1823 ; Beethoven replied Feb. 16, and Weber rejoined on the 18th. After that there were letters from Beethoven of Apr. 9, June 5 and 9, and Aug. 11, the last enclosing a sonata and variations of his own composition. Weber was a great admirer and a remarkable exponent of Beethoven's PF. music, especially of his

sonatas, a fact which Beethoven seems to have known. The correspondence has been lost, except a fragment of a rough copy of Weber's,[1] conclusively proving his high opinion of ' Fidelio.' The score sent by Beethoven, Apr. 10, is still at the Dresden court theatre. The first performance took place Apr. 29, with Wilhelmine Schröder as Leonore.

In Sept. 1823 Weber started for Vienna to conduct the first performance of ' Euryanthe.' Benedict accompanied him. Barbaja had assembled a company of first-rate Italian singers and was giving admirable performances of Italian operas, especially Rossini's. Rossini had been in Vienna, and had rehearsed his operas himself. The public was almost intoxicated with the music, and it was performed so admirably that even Weber, who had previously been almost unjustly severe on Rossini's operas, was obliged, to his vexation, to confess that he liked what he heard there. It was unfortunate that the singers cast for ' Euryanthe,' though as a whole efficient, were stars of the second order. Still, ' Der Freischütz ' had prepossessed the public, and the first performance of the new work was enthusiastically applauded. But the enthusiasm did not last. The plot was not sufficiently intelligible, people found the music long and noisy, and after the second and third representations, which Weber conducted with great success, the audiences gradually became cold and thin. After his departure Conradin Kreutzer compressed the libretto to such an extent as to make the opera a mere unintelligible conglomeration of isolated scenes, and after dragging through twenty performances, it vanished from the boards.

After the enormous success of the ' Freischütz,' ' Euryanthe ' was virtually a fiasco. Neither had Weber much consolation from his fellow-artists. In many instances envy prevented their seeing the grand and beautiful ideas poured forth by Weber in such rich abundance ; and there were artists above the influence of any such motive, who yet did not appreciate the work. Foremost among these was Schubert ; even if his own attempts at opera had not shown the same thing before, his seeing no merit in ' Euryanthe ' would prove to demonstration that a man may be a great composer of songs and yet know nothing of dramatic [2] music. The only really satisfactory part of the visit was his intercourse with Beethoven, who welcomed him heartily.[3] At one time Beethoven had not valued Weber's compositions at a high rate, but his opinion of the composer of ' Der Freischütz ' had risen enormously. He did not go to ' Euryanthe ' :

1 Given by Max von Weber in the *Biographie*, ii. 466. The dates given are not entirely in accordance with those in the biography but I have followed Jähns's careful epitome of Weber's diary, now in the State Library of Berlin.
2 See SCHUBERT, Vol. IV. p. 602.
3 See BEETHOVEN, Vol. I. p. 296.

there would have been no object in his doing so, now that his troubles with his hearing had settled down into total deafness.

Weber left Vienna Nov. 5, conducted the 50th representation of ' Der Freischütz ' in Prague on the 7th, and arrived in Dresden on the 10th. By his desire Benedict remained in Vienna, to keep him informed of the progress of ' Euryanthe '; but what he heard was so far from pleasant that he did not venture to report it. Weber had put his full strength into the work, intending it as a demonstration of his power and capacity. With the keenest anxiety he followed its progress, marking the impression it produced, not only in Vienna, but in every theatre which performed it. When he found that in most places it received only a succès d'estime, and that opinions as to its value were divided, even amongst unbiassed connoisseurs, he fell into deep depression. Benedict, on his return from Vienna, thought him looking ten years older, and all the symptoms of his malady had increased. To illness it was undoubtedly to be attributed that all his old energy, nay, even his love of music, for the time abandoned him. His compositions seemed to recede into the far distance, and in the summer of 1824 he writes in a bitter mood to his wife from Marienbad, where he was taking the waters, ' I have not an idea, and do not believe I ever composed anything. Those operas were not mine after all.' When asked how he did, he would reply, ' I cough, and am lazy.' During fifteen months he composed absolutely nothing, except one little French romance.

Many disappointments, however, as ' Euryanthe ' brought him, there were places where it was at once valued as it deserved. In Dresden the first performance took place Mar. 31, 1824, with a success that equalled Weber's highest expectations. As an instance, Tieck pronounced it to contain passages which Gluck and Mozart might have envied. And as in stage matters the first impression is apt to be the lasting one, even down to a later generation, the people of Dresden continued to understand and love ' Euryanthe.' In Leipzig it was much the same, the opera occupying a place in the repertory from May 1824. Rochlitz heard it May 24, 1825, and next day wrote Weber almost the best and most discerning criticism of the time.[1] In Berlin there was considerable delay in producing the opera, for which Spontini received more than his share of the blame. The first performance took place on Dec. 23, 1825, and in Berlin too, where Weber's most devoted adherents were to be found, the effect it produced was great and lasting. The composer conducted in person, though, suffering as he was from mortal illness, it took all his indomitable energy to make the

mind rise superior to the body. It was his last appearance in Berlin.

THE INVITATION TO LONDON.—Weber knew that his days were numbered. His great desire was to leave enough to place his family above fear of poverty. It was his love for them which roused him from the languor and depression into which he had fallen after the completion of ' Euryanthe.' The immediate impulse was a letter from Charles Kemble, then lessee of Covent Garden Theatre, inviting him to write an opera in English. London had also participated in the ' Freischütz ' mania, no fewer than three theatres playing it at the same time. Kemble added a request that he would come to London to produce the new opera in person, and conduct ' Der Freischütz ' and ' Preciosa.' Weber did not hesitate long, and the two soon agreed on ' Oberon ' as the subject of the opera, the libretto to be drawn up by Planché. The terms took longer to arrange. Kemble's offer of £500 Weber considered too low, and Kemble thought Weber's demands much too high. At last, however, he agreed to give £1000.[2] Before the affair was concluded Weber consulted his physician, Dr. Hedenus, as to the possibility of the journey in his then state of health. The reply was that if he would give up conducting and composing, and take a year's complete rest in Italy, his life might be prolonged for another five or six years. If, on the other hand, he accepted the English commission, his life would be measured by months, perhaps by weeks. Weber replied by his favourite motto, ' As God will,' and settled to go.

Although he had undertaken to compose this opera from a desire to make money, he would not have been the high-minded artist he was if he had not set to work at it with all his might. So much was he in earnest that, at the age of 37, and with one foot in the grave, he began to learn English systematically, and was soon able to carry on his own correspondence in English, and when in London astonished everybody by the ease with which he spoke.

The first and second acts reached him Jan. 18, 1825, and the third on Feb. 1. He set to work Jan. 23, the first number he composed being Huon's grand air in the first act. He laid the work aside during the summer, but resumed it Sept. 19. The last number, the overture, was completed in London, Apr. 29, 1826.

By medical advice he took the waters at Ems in the summer of 1825, starting from Dresden on July 3. His route lay through Naumburg to Weimar, where he made a last unsuccessful attempt to enter into close relations with Goethe, and was warmly welcomed by Hummel and his family. Thence he went by Gotha to Frankfort, greeting his old friend Gottfried Weber for the last time, and then by

---

[1] Jähns (p. 369) gives the most important part of his letter.

[2] So says Benedict, p. 106, and elsewhere. Max von Weber's account varies slightly.

Wiesbaden to Ems. This journey must have convinced him of his extraordinary popularity. People of all ranks vied with each other in showing him kindness, respect and admiration. At Ems he was admitted into the circle of that accomplished man the Crown Prince of Prussia (afterwards Frederick William IV.), and his wife, an unusual distinction. But the musician tottering to his grave was no longer able to enjoy the sunshine which shone so brightly on his last days.

The time for Weber's departure for England drew on. On Feb. 5 he conducted ' Der Freischütz ' in Dresden for the last time, and took leave of his band, all except Fürstenau, the well-known flute-player, who was to travel with him. He chose the route through Paris, and made the acquaintance of the principal musicians there, specially enjoying the attentions of Cherubini, for whom he had always had a high respect. A performance of Boieldieu's ' La Dame blanche ' enchanted him. ' What grace ! what wit ! ' he writes to Theodor Hell, at Dresden, ' no such comic opera has been written since " Figaro." '

PRODUCTION OF ' OBERON.'—On Mar. 5[1] he arrived in London, and was most hospitably received by Sir George Smart, then organist of the Chapel Royal. On the 6th he went to Covent Garden Theatre to view the scene of his future labours ; he was recognised, and the cheers of the spectators must have assured him of his popularity in London. On Mar. 8 he conducted a selection from ' Der Freischütz ' at one of the ' oratorio concerts,' and here his reception was even more enthusiastic, nearly every piece from the opera being encored. On the 9th the rehearsals for ' Oberon ' began, and Weber perceived at once that he had at his disposal all the materials for a first-rate performance. To please Braham, who took the part of Huon, he composed two additional pieces, a grand scena and aria (' Yes, even love '), which Braham substituted for the grand air in the first act, and the prayer in the second act (' Ruler of this awful hour '). The former is never sung in Germany, being far inferior in beauty to the original air, but the prayer is retained, and is indeed one of the gems of the work. The first performance took place Apr. 12. The music went beautifully, and the composer had an even more enthusiastic reception than that bestowed on Rossini two or three years before. The aristocracy alone, with few exceptions, held aloof. Weber was not the man to show himself obsequious, and on the other hand his look and manner were too unpretending to be imposing. By May 29 ' Oberon '[2] had reached its twenty-eighth performance, the first twelve having been conducted by himself according

to his contract. The following appeared in *The Harmonicon* in an article by Scudo on ' Oberon ' :

' It is impossible to quote an instance of a great man in literature or in the arts whose merit was entirely overlooked by his contemporaries. As for the death of Weber it may be explained by fatigue, by grief without doubt, but, above all, by an organic disease from which he had suffered for years.'

Nevertheless the enthusiasm exhibited by the public at the first performance of ' Oberon ' was not maintained at the following representations. The masterpiece of the German composer experienced much the same fate as ' Guillaume Tell ' in Paris. In a letter to his wife, written on the very first night of performance, Weber says,

' My dear Lina, Thanks to God and to His all-powerful will I obtained this evening the greatest success of my life. The emotion produced by such a triumph is more than I can describe. To God alone belongs the glory. When I entered the orchestra, the house, crammed to the roof, burst into a frenzy of applause. Hats and handkerchiefs were waved in the air. The overture had to be executed twice, as had also several pieces in the opera itself. At the end of the representation I was called on to the stage by the enthusiastic acclamations of the public ; an honour which no composer had ever before obtained in England. All went excellently, and every one around me was happy.'

Though his strength was constantly declining, he was always ready to lend his name or his services when he could be of assistance to others. Thus he took part in concerts given Apr. 27, May 1, 10 and 18 by Miss Hawes, Fürstenau, Kemble and Braham, even at one of Miss Paton's on May 30, six days before his death. A concert of his own on May 26 was a failure. The day was badly chosen, and Weber in his state of utter exhaustion had omitted two or three social formalities. Among other music given at this concert was his Jubel-Cantata (1818), put to different words, and a song (' From Chindara's warbling fount ') just composed for Miss Stephens, who sang it to his accompaniment. It was his last composition, and the last time his fingers touched the keyboard.[3]

The preparations for his journey home were made in haste, for Weber was filled with an inexpressible longing to see his family once more. But his own words to a friend before leaving Germany, that he ' was going to London to die,' were fulfilled. Far from home and kindred he sank under his sufferings during the night of June 4, 1826. The following certificate of Weber's death was among the papers of Sir Julius Benedict :

' On examining the body of Carl M. von Weber we found an ulcer on the left side of the larynx. The lungs almost universally diseased, filled with tubercles, of which many were in a state of suppuration, with two vomicae, one of them about the size of a common egg, the other smaller, which was a quite sufficient cause of death. (Signed) F. Tencken, M.D. ; Chas. F. Forbes, M.D. ; P. M. Kind, M.D. ; Wm. Robinson, Surgeon. 91 Great Portland Street, June 5, 1826, 5 o'clock.'

---

1 Benedict (p. 115) says Mar. 6, but he is wrong.
2 Concerning Mrs. Keeley's appearance in the part of the Mermaid, see *Mus. T.*, 1899, p. 140.

3 See *Mus. T.*, 1901, p. 162.

His body was laid in the grave at Moorfields Chapel, to the strains of Mozart's Requiem, on June 21. The funeral ceremonies were conducted as if for a person of the highest rank, and there was an enormous crowd. In 1844 the coffin was removed to Germany, and interred in the family vault at Dresden. (See WAGNER, p. 588.) The application for this transference was made by the widow to the Home Secretary, Oct. 5, 1844. A tablet was affixed to the house in Great Portland Street.

WEBER'S OPERAS.—To form a right estimate of Weber's music it is necessary to look upon him as a dramatic composer. Not that his other compositions are of no importance— quite the contrary ; but in one and all may be discerned more or less plainly that dramatic genius which was the essence of his nature, and which determined their form, and gave them that stamp whereby they differ so strikingly from the productions of other artists. Composers gifted with the true dramatic instinct have always been rare in Germany, and it was this that Weber possessed in a high degree, higher perhaps even than Mozart. Being his most prominent characteristic, we will deal with his operas first.

1. The earliest, ' Die Macht der Liebe und des Weins,' was destroyed, apparently by himself. Of the second, 'Das Waldmädchen,' composed in Freiberg, there are extant three autograph fragments, containing in all 214 bars, the originals of some and copies of others being now in the State Library at Berlin.[1] These fragments seem to bear out Weber's own verdict that the opera was an immature production, not perhaps wholly devoid of invention. Although played several times, no complete score can now be found.

2. The libretto of ' Peter Schmoll und seine Nachbarn ' was adapted by a certain Joseph Türke from a novel of the same name by Carl Gottlob Cramer (2 vols., Rudolstadt, 1798–1799). The book was one of the romances of knights and robbers with which the market was flooded after the success of ' Götz von Berlichingen ' and ' Die Räuber.'[2] Cramer's ' Peter Schmoll ' has no artistic merit, but it is less crude and sensational than some others of its class. The scene is laid not in the Middle Ages, but in the period of the French Revolution. Türke arranged the plot in two acts, and treated it after the fashion of the German Singspiel, with spoken dialogue. All this part, however, has been lost, the words of the songs alone being preserved in the score. The verses are rarely Türke's own, but were taken from the novel, which was interlarded, in the then fashion, with songs. Such verses as he did write are more than commonplace,

especially when intended to be comic ; refined comedy being a rarity in German drama long after Peter Schmoll's day. The music shows great talent, perhaps artificially matured, but naturally so great and so healthy that not even the hot-house treatment to which it had been subjected could injure it permanently. Weber was impelled to produce operas before he had fully developed the feeling for logical harmonic progressions, nay, before he had mastered musical orthography itself, to say nothing of the skill necessary to construct musico-dramatic forms on a large scale. 'Peter Schmoll' affords a good opportunity for comparing the unequal, unpropitious developments of Weber's powers with those of Mozart. In Mozart the mastery of external means advanced step by step with the development of mental power. From the first he always had the two. Weber, at the time he composed ' Peter Schmoll,' had much to say that was original, but was without the technical training necessary to enable him to say it. To one capable of piercing through the defective form to the thought beneath, the unmistakable features of his individuality will often be discernible. Real dramatic characterisation is not to be expected from a boy of 14 ; so far his music is rather stagey than dramatic, but still he had, even then, unquestionably a brilliant talent for the stage. This is mainly apparent in the treatment of general situations, such as the second scene of the first act, where Schmoll, Minette and Hans Bast play at blindman's-buff in the dark. The melodies are throughout catching, often graceful and charming, always related to the German Lied, and never reflecting the Italian style. He puts almost all he has to say into the voice parts ; the accompaniments being unimportant, at least as regards polyphony. There is much originality in the harmony, and the colouring is individual and full of meaning. Now it is precisely with harmony and colouring that Weber produces his most magical effects in his later operas. In his autobiography he relates how an article he read in a musical periodical about this time suggested to him the idea of writing in a novel manner, by making use of old and obsolete instruments. The instrumentation in ' Peter Schmoll ' is indeed quite peculiar, No. 14, a terzet ('Empfanget hier des Vaters Segen '), being accompanied by two flauti dolci (see FIPPLE FLUTE), two bassethorns, two bassoons and string-quartet. His motive was not a mere childish love of doing something different from other people, but he had an idea that these strange varieties of tone helped to characterise the situation. In the passage named the peculiar combination of wind instruments does produce a peculiarly solemn effect. Again, in certain comic, and also in some mysterious passages, he uses two piccolos with excellent effect, giving almost a forecast of the spirit of ' Der Freischütz.' Minette sings

1 The Weber collection, amassed with so much diligence by Prof. Jähns, was purchased some years ago for the Berlin State Library.
2 The best-known work of the kind was ' Rinaldo Rinaldini ' by Goethe's brother-in-law Vulpius.

in the first act a mournful song of a love-lorn maiden, and as the voice ceases the last bar is re-echoed softly by a single flute, solo, a perfect stroke of genius to express desolation, loneliness and silent sorrow, and recalling the celebrated passage in the third act of ' Euryanthe,' where the desolation of the hapless Euryanthe is also depicted by a single flute. Weber adapted the music of this romance to the song ' Wird Philomele trauern ' (No. 5), in ' Abu Hassan,' and used some other parts of the opera in his later works, for instance the last song in the third finale of ' Oberon.' The overture to ' Peter Schmoll ' was printed, after Weber's thorough revision of it, in 1807, and also a revised form of the duet ' Dich an dies Herz zu drücken,' in 1809.[1]

3. The subject of 'Rübezahl,' a two-act opera begun by Weber in Breslau, but never finished, was taken from a legend of the Riesengebirge, dramatised by J. G. Rhode. The versification is polished and harmonious, but the action drags sadly. Rübezahl, the spirit of the mountain, having fallen in love with a mortal Princess, lures her into his castle, and keeps her prisoner there, but woos her in vain. Having managed to secure his magic sceptre, she gets rid of him by bidding him count the turnips in the garden, which at her request he turns into human beings for her companions. As soon as he is gone she summons a griffin, who carries her down again to her own home, and thus outwits Rübezahl. For variety's sake the poet has introduced the father, lover and an old servant of the Princess, who penetrate in disguise to the castle, and are hired by Rübezahl as servants ; but they do not influence the plot, and have to be got rid of at the close.

These weaknesses, however, are redeemed by some supernatural situations, excellent for musical treatment. Of this libretto Weber says that he had composed ' the greater part,'[2] though the overture and three vocal numbers alone have been preserved.[3] Even of these the second vocal number is unfinished, while the overture exists complete only in a revised form of later date.[4] Those familiar with ' Der Freischütz ' and ' Oberon ' know Weber's genius for dealing with the spirit-world ; but the Rübezahl fragments show extraordinarily few traces of the new language he invented for the purpose. The music, indeed—always excepting the revised form of the overture—is less Weberish than a great deal in 'Peter Schmoll,' nor is there any marked advance in the technique of composition. In a quintet for four soprani and bass,[5] the princess bewails her loneliness, and sighs for her girl-companions, when Rübezahl bids her plant three turnips, and call them Clärchen, Kunigunde and Elsbeth ; he then touches them with his wand, and her three friends rise out of the ground and rush to her amid a lively scene of mutual recognition, Rübezahl standing by and making his reflections. The manner in which he has treated this scene indicates very clearly the state of Weber's development at the time. The phantoms evoked from the turnips sing like mortals, in strains differing in no degree from those of the princess. Twenty years later such a scene would inevitably have produced a series of the most individual tone-pictures, contrasting sharply with everything of mortal interest. As it is, the future dramatist and composer is but in the chrysalis stage, and the quintet is merely a very lively and effective stage scene, with some clever passages in it (the middle subject, ' schön sind der sterblichen Gefühle,' particularly fine), but with no traces of Weber's individuality.

4. With the next opera, ' Silvana,' we take leave of boyish compositions, and reach a higher stage of development. ' Silvana ' and ' Abu Hassan ' form the middle group of Weber's dramatic works, while ' Freischütz,' ' Preciosa,' ' Euryanthe' and ' Oberon' constitute the third and last. We have stated already that in ' Silvana' he used some material from ' Das Waldmädchen,' the libretto of which has been lost, except the few verses preserved in the score.

This opera, with its mediæval romanticism, is the precursor of ' Euryanthe,' and therefore of great interest in Weber's development. Independent of this, however, its merit as a work of art is considerable. The story of Silvana deals with emotions which are natural, true and intelligibly expressed, and the situations are not less fitted for musical treatment because they belong to a bygone period—seen through a legendary haze, but still an heroic period of great and lasting interest. Another point in favour of Hiemer's poem is that the plot develops itself naturally and intelligibly, the interest is well kept up, and there is the necessary variety of sensation. That Weber transferred to it musical ideas from ' Das Waldmädchen ' can be verified in two instances only, one being the overture, the autograph of which is docketed ' renovata il 23 Marzo, 1809,' a term which must necessarily apply to the ' Waldmädchen ' overture. The ' renovation ' cannot have been of a very startling nature, judging by the music, which is neither interesting nor original. The second case is the air assigned to Krips the Squire, ' Liegt so ein Unthier ausgestreckt ' (No. 2), the opening of which is identical with a ritornel in one of the ' Waldmädchen ' fragments. It may therefore be assumed that the adaptation of old material was of a very limited description. The fact of there having been any adaptation at all may

---

[1] PF. score by Jähns (Berlin, Schlesinger).
[2] His autograph list shows that the first act contained 15 scenes, the second 12.
[3] A chorus of spirits, a recitative and arietta and a quintet. (See Jähns's list Nos. 44, 45, 46 and 122, Anhang 2, No. 27.)
[4] ' The Ruler of the Spirits,' the original existing MS. consisting of only the last eleven bars of the violin part.
[5] With PF. accompaniment by Jähns (Schlesinger).

partly explain the extreme inequality between the separate numbers in ' Silvana,' but we must also take into account the inevitable distractions and interruptions among which it was composed at Stuttgart. The opera undoubtedly does not give the impression of having been conceived all at once, and this damages the general effect.

The progress in dramatic characterisation made by Weber since ' Rübezahl ' and ' Peter Schmoll ' is obvious. The knights of the period are more or less typical personages, and do not require much individualising. A composer's chief difficulty would lie in maintaining the particular tone adapted to each character consistently throughout the drama, and in this Weber has succeeded thoroughly. Count Adelhart especially, and Krips the Squire, are drawn with a master hand. The power of indicating a character or situation by two or three broad strokes, afterwards so remarkable in Weber, is clearly seen in ' Silvana.' For instance, the very first bar of the duet between Mechthilde and Adelhart, ' Wag' es, mir zu widerstreben ' (Act ii. No. 9), seems to put the violent, masterful knight bodily before us. Another crucial point is the winding up of a dénouement, by massing the subjects together in a general movement which shall keep the interest of the spectator at a stretch ; and of this we have an excellent specimen in the finale of Act ii. Speaking of the music simply as music, though by no means perfect in form, the ideas are abundant and original. The melodies partake of the Volkslied character, there is a riotous fancy combined with the drollest comedy, and a grace peculiarly Weberish, while the instrumentation is dainty, full of colour and melodious. Good examples of the first quality are the Huntsmen's Chorus (Act i. No. 3), and the Drinking Chorus in the finale of the same act ; and of comedy the whole part of the cowardly bully Krips. His Arietta in E♭, No. 14, is capital, and also interesting as a specimen of the distinction between Weber's *vis comica* and Mozart's as shown in the ' Entführung ' and ' Zauberflöte.' The dances allotted to Silvana (Nos. 1, 8, 12) are most graceful and charming.

Another remarkable point in the opera is the musical illustration of pantomime, even in the vocal numbers, a device for connecting the music and the action together, which is well known to have been carried to such an extent by Wagner that he is generally considered the inventor of it. Weber, however, has in ' Silvana ' turned it to account most effectively. A striking example is the scene where Rudolf meets Silvana in the forest. He addresses her in gentle tones, to which she replies only by signs, accompanied by orchestral strains of the most expressive nature, with a great deal of violoncello solo. The whole scene is full of

genius, and continually suggests a comparison with Wagner, especially where Rudolf sings, ' Wenn du mich liebtest, o welch' ein Glück ! O lass mich deine Augen fragen !' while Silvana, to a melting strain from the violoncello, ' looks at him sweetly and tenderly,' a passage which recalls the first meeting of Siegmunde and Sieglinde in the ' Walküre.' Other passages, in which the music follows the action step by step, are to be found in Weber's great operas, especially in ' Euryanthe.' Strange to say, they seem to have attracted little attention, even in the latter case. The composer prepared two PF. editions of ' Silvana,'[1] the former of which (1812) is incomplete, and both now very rare.

5. ' Abu Hassan,' the second in the middle group of Weber's operas, was adapted by Hiemer from an Arabian fairy-tale, with occasional reminiscences of Weisse's ' Dorfbarbier.' The story of this one-act Singspiel is closely connected with certain experiences of both Weber and Hiemer in Stuttgart. It must have been easy to Weber to find appropriate melodies for a creditor dunning a light-minded impecunious debtor ; and curiously enough, the first number of the opera he set was the Creditors' Chorus, ' Geld, Geld, Geld, ich will nicht länger warten ' (Aug. 11, 1810). The little piece consisted originally of the overture and eight vocal numbers, the duet ' Thränen sollst du nicht vergiessen ' being added in 1812, and the air ' Hier liegt, welch martervolles Loos ' in 1823.

The fun in German comic opera has always been somewhat boisterous : for more refined comedy we must generally go to the French, but ' Abu Hassan ' is almost the only German work which produces a hearty laugh, and at the same time charms by its grace and refinement, and by the distinction of its musical expression. Perhaps the best bit is the scene between Abu Hassan and his creditors, but the duet between Omar and Fatima (No. 6), the final terzetto (No. 7) and Fatima's additional air (No. 8) are all of great merit. The last air, it should be borne in mind, was composed twelve years after the rest, and bears the stamp of the matured composer. Various little instances of want of finish appear in the music, but defects of this kind may well be overlooked for the sake of the invention, so spontaneous and *spirituel*, and the downright hearty fun of the whole, mingled as it is with rare and touching tenderness.[2]

6. Between the completion of ' Abu Hassan ' and the beginning of ' Der Freischütz ' intervene no less than six years—a long period in so short a life—during which Weber composed no opera. Not that the dramatic impulse had abandoned him. ' I am anxiously looking

---

[1] Schlesinger, Berlin.
[2] A complete PF. score is published by Simrock.

out for another good libretto,' he writes after the production of ' Abu Hassan ' at Munich, ' for I cannot get on at all without an opera in hand.' We know he had several projects, and that he had a ' Tannhäuser ' in his mind in 1814 ; but his restless life, and the unsatisfactory nature of his position at Prague, prevented his bringing anything to maturity. Nevertheless his dramatic powers did not lie absolutely fallow. Six grand Italian arias with orchestra, some with chorus also, composed during this period, though intended for the concert-room, may be classed with his dramatic works, because they presuppose a scene or situation in which some distinct person gives expression to his or her feelings. The same is true of three Italian duets, which mark an important stage in his development, as it was through them that he gained dexterity in handling the larger forms of vocal music. As we have seen, he was somewhat clumsy at this in ' Silvana.' Several of the six concert arias are of high merit, particularly the one composed for Prince Frederic of Gotha, ' Signor, se padre sei,' the *scena ed aria* for ' Atalia,' ' Misera me,' and the *scena ed aria* for Méhul's ' Hélène,' ' Ah, se Edmundo fosse l' uccisor.' The three duets with PF. accompaniment are also worthy of notice, as showing Weber's perfect familiarity with the Italian style, while retaining intact his German individuality, a combination which gives them a special interest. One— ' Si il mio ben, cor mio tu sei '—was originally composed for two altos, with clarinet obbligato, and an accompaniment of string quartet and two horns. It was performed at Weber's concert in Darmstadt in 1811, when he writes to Gottfried Weber, ' a duet so confoundedly Italian in style that it might be Farinelli's ; however, it pleased them infernally.' This is, however, unjust to himself, for though here and there the Italian cast of melody is obvious, the main body is thoroughly Weberish. The allegro with its contrasting subjects, one sustained and flowing, and the other light, graceful and piquant, recalls the duet between Agathe and Aennchen in ' Freischütz.'

Besides his Italian compositions, among which we may include three canzonets for single voice and PF., Weber exercised his dramatic vein twice between 1811 and 1817, in the composition of Lieder, and in his cantata ' Kampf und Sieg ' (1815). These important works are of course only indirectly dramatic.

7. With ' Der Freischütz ' Weber laid the foundation of German romantic opera. To explain this statement we must first define precisely what we mean by the term ' romantic.' Originally borrowed from the Spanish and French mediæval chronicles of chivalry, the word primarily denoted anything marvellous, surprising, knight - errant - like or fantastic. Operas were often founded on stories of this kind

in the 18th century, the first being a libretto called ' Lisouart und Dariolette,' adapted by Schiebler from Favart, and set by J. A. Hiller (Hamburg, 1766). The French taste for fairy-tales and eastern stories penetrated to Germany, and such subjects were used in opera. Thus the story of Zemire and Azor was set in 1775, and that of Oberon's Magic Horn in 1790. The ' Zauberflöte,' too, as is well known, was founded on an eastern fairy-tale, and that *chef-d'œuvre* made fairy-operas a recognised fashion. All these, from the nature of their subjects, might be called romantic operas, and indeed were so at the time. Weber himself speaks of Mozart, Cherubini and even Beethoven as romantic composers, but this was not in the sense in which the word has been used since his time in Germany. The fairy and magic operas, of which Vienna was the headquarters, were popular because their sensational plots and elaborate scenery delighted a people as simple as a set of grown-up children. They were, in fact, pretty fantastic trifles, and Mozart, though he introduces serious tones in them, did not alter their essential character. The romantic opera, in the later restricted sense of the word, differs from these earlier fairy-operas in that whatever is introduced of the marvellous, whether narrative, legend or fairy-tale, is treated seriously, and not as a mere matter of amusement. The ultimate cause of this change of ideas was the entire transformation of the intellectual life of Germany during the end of the 18th and beginning of the 19th centuries. After its long state of dependence on foreign countries the mind of Germany awoke to consciousness, began to know something of its own history, its legends and myths, its natural language and customs, and to prize them as precious heirlooms. It again grasped the peculiar — almost pantheistic — relations with nature, which distinguished the Teutonic from the classic and Latin peoples. This change of ideas was greatly accelerated by the gradual transference of the predominating influence in music from the lively light-hearted South Germans, to the more serious and thoughtful inhabitants of North Germany. Lastly, individual composers, Weber among them, came under the influence of the poets of the romantic school. As these latter, breaking away from the classicalism of Goethe and Schiller, sought their ideals of beauty in national art, history and myth, primarily German, and afterwards Indian, Italian, Spanish, French or English, so the composers of the romantic school also found an attraction in the same class of subjects partly because of their very unfamiliarity. Thus, consciously or unconsciously, they applied to music the dictum of Novalis with regard to romantic poetry—that it was the art of surprising in a pleasing manner.

Subjects for romantic opera require a certain

expansiveness of the imagination ; a capacity of soaring beyond the commonplace events of daily life. Presupposing also, as they do, a healthy and not over-refined taste, they accommodate themselves with ease to the manners and speech of the people. This is how it happens that other elements of the German popular plays—the comic and amusing—which have no inherent connexion with the serious conception of a romantic subject, find a place in romantic opera. Again, in contradistinction to the antique-classical drama, which revealed to the spectators an ideal world without restrictions of time or space, romantic subjects laid the utmost stress on peculiarities of race or epoch, social relations or distinctions. Thus it followed that there were in romantic opera four principal elements—the imaginative, the national, the comic and the realistic. The fusion of these elements by means of the imagination into one whole is what constitutes German romanticism.

In ' Silvana,' Weber had already trenched upon the domain of romantic opera, in the sense in which we have just expounded it, but had not yet found adequate musical expression for German romanticism. Next came Spohr's ' Faust ' in 1813, and ' Zemire und Azor ' in 1818. In both these the subjects are conceived with earnestness, and a dreamy twilight tone runs through the whole, so that they undoubtedly possess some of the distinguishing marks of the romantic opera ; but Spohr's music is much too rounded off in form, and too polished, and he had a positive aversion to anything popular. Nor had he sufficient versatility and flexibility, boldness or *vis comica*. Strictly speaking, therefore, he is only half a roman ticist. ' Freischütz ' was a revelation ; from the date of its production there was no question as to what a romantic opera really was.

Kind did not draw on his own invention for the libretto. The history of the subject is still incomplete, but we know that the story can be traced back as far as the 17th century. It was published in the beginning of the 18th, in a book called *Unterredungen vom Reiche der Geister*, of which a second edition appeared in Leipzig in 1731. The statement there made, that the occurrence took place in a town of Bohemia in 1710, carries no weight. From this book Johann August Apel took the story, and published it as a narrative called ' Der Freischütz, a legend of the people ' [1] (1810), handling it so cleverly that it again became popular. In 1819 Gerle took it up and wrote ' Der braune Jäger.' [2] In 1821 it was turned into a tragedy by Count von Reisch, and performed Aug. 17, 1821, at Würzburg, two months after the first performance of the opera in Berlin. Kind mainly followed Apel : his poem, with explanatory notes, ran through

two editions in 1822 and a third in 1823 (Göschen). Twenty years later he prepared the last edition for his ' Freischütz-book,' and added to it a mass of cognate matter by no means uninteresting.

Apel's story had a later revival, and finding how much Kind borrowed from it, people have been apt to disparage both him and his libretto. Ambros's [3] remarks on this point, for instance, are most unjust. Neither originality of ideas nor literary skill are so important to a librettist as the faculty of arranging his materials in a really dramatic form. This Kind had in a high degree, and it ought to be sufficient. His own alterations and additions, too, are most successful, having the threefold advantage of conducing to the musical development, suiting Weber's special gifts, and hitting the ideal of German national opera. The parts of Caspar, Aennchen and the Hermit are entirely his own, while that of Agathe is greatly strengthened, and Samiel is brought forward to meet the requirements of the music. The motives and action of the plot also diverge considerably from Apel's romance. Caspar, being jealous of Max, tries to engage him in a compact with Satan, but the Evil One is frustrated by the pure-minded and devout Agathe, and in her stead Caspar becomes the victim. Thus Kind contrived a happy termination instead of Apel's tragic one. The plot, as it now stands—its main interest centred in a couple of true-hearted lovers, living in an honest forester's cottage, on a background of German forest, with all its delights and all its weird associations, lit up now by sunbeams glinting on a frolicsome peasantry, now by lurid flashes revealing the forms of the powers of darkness—appeals with irresistible attraction to every German heart. The most important point in the opera, however, and the secret of its success, is the strongly marked religious element which at once raised it to an altogether higher level than any earlier opera, and gave it a kind of sacred character. During the war a spirit of religious enthusiasm had taken hold of the people of Germany, and become so far a ruling passion that any one who succeeded in giving expression to it in music was sure of striking home to the national heart. Looked at from this point of view, the part of the hermit, Kind's own invention, acquires considerable significance. The opening of the opera was originally intended to be quite different from what it is now. The curtain drew up on a forest scene with a hermit's cell, having close by a turf altar with a cross or image at the back, covered with white roses. The hermit praying before the altar sees in a vision the Prince of Darkness lying in wait to entrap Agathe, ' the spotless lamb,' and her Max. At this point Agathe enters, bearing bread, milk and fruit for

---

[1] Published in vol. i. of the *Gespensterbuch*, edited by Apel and Laun (Leipzig, Göschen, 1810).
[2] To be found in No. 68 of the *Freimüthigen für Deutschland*, edited by Müchler and Symanski (Berlin, 1819).

[3] See his *Bunte Blätter*, i. (Leipzig, Leuckart, 1872) ; also the New Series, 33 (*ibid.*, 1874), and Wustmann in the *Grenzboten*, i., 1874, p. 414.

the hermit. After warning her that danger is near, he gives her his blessing and two or three of the roses, which have the power of working miracles. A duet between the two concludes the scene. Weber did not compose either the duet or the hermit's monologue ; but, by his *fiancée's* advice, began the opera with the village fête. By this means he certainly secured a more effective introduction, though the appearance of the hermit in the last act now seems somewhat abrupt and out of place.

The religious sentiment of Weber's day was entirely of a romantic kind, made up partly of a sort of mediæval fanatical Catholicism, partly of an almost pantheistical nature - worship. What a gift he had for giving expression to this sentiment Weber perhaps scarcely knew before he wrote the 'Freischütz.' It was an advantage to him to be a member, and a conscientious one, of the Roman Catholic Church, and to have also a naturally serious and devout disposition. Hence the character of Agathe has a virgin sweetness, an unearthly purity, such as was never put on the stage before. As an interpreter of nature Weber's position in the dramatic world is like that of Beethoven in the symphony ; nay, the infinite variety of nature-pictures contained in ' Der Freischütz,' ' Preciosa,' ' Euryanthe ' and ' Oberon ' is quite new of its kind, and each equally surpasses even the manifestations of genius of the Pastoral Symphony. Nobody had ever depicted with the same truth as he a sultry moonlight night, the stillness broken only by the nightingale's trill and the solemn murmur of the trees, as in Agathe's grand scena ; or a gruesome nightscene in the gloomy forest ravine, such as that in the finale of the second act. With this descriptive faculty went hand in hand consummate skill in orchestration. There is something original and intoxicating in the sound he brings out of the orchestra, a complete simplicity, combined with perfect novelty. He was able, as it were, to transport himself into the soul of the instruments, and make them talk to us like human beings, each in its own language, each speaking when it alone has power to lay bare the very heart of the action. Orchestral colouring handled in this masterly manner naturally served principally to characterise situations, but it was also used for the personages. Nothing distinguishes Weber as a born dramatist more than the way he appropriated to a character from its first entrance upon the stage a certain mode of musical expression, which he maintained as a kind of keynote through all the varying emotions of the opera. A good example is the opening of the duet between Agathe and Aennchen. With the very first phrase each strikes a note which completely exemplifies their different characters, and to which they remain true to the end. The very first musical phrase sung by each gives a

tone perfectly in keeping with their different characters, and held firm to the end of the opera. With all this distinctness of characterisation, however, Weber's creations keep to general lines ; he draws types rather than individuals. His figures have not the sharpness of outline that distinguishes Mozart's ; they resemble rather the characters in Schiller's dramas, while Mozart's may be compared to Shakespeare's.

Weber had a wonderful talent for inventing popular melodies, as he has shown in many parts of ' Der Freischütz.' The Lied-form is introduced four times in the first act, and twice in the last, besides appearing as an element of a larger whole in Agathe's aria (' Leise, leise, fromme Weise ') and the finale of the third act (' Die Zukunft soll mein Herz bewähren '). These are precisely the numbers which have attained the greatest popularity. We need only mention the Bridesmaids' and Huntsmen's choruses, the waltz in the first act, and the Peasants' march. This latter is taken direct from the people's music, and is an air which Weber must have heard when conducting the opera in Prague. At least, between 1816 and 1824, the musical population of Bohemia were addicted to a march, the first part of which is identical with that in ' Freischütz.' [1]

Perfect as are these smaller musical forms, it must in justice be conceded that Weber did not always succeed with his larger ones, which often have a sort of piecemeal effect. The construction of a piece of music in grand, full proportions was to him a labour, and rarely a successful one. He does not so much develop from within as superimpose from without, and not unfrequently the musical flow stagnates. The finale of the third act may be cited as an instance of his way of falling short in this respect. For the most part, however, this is only true of his music when considered simply as music without regard to dramatic fitness, and such defects are therefore much less noticeable in performance, so accurately does he hit the appropriate musical development for each moment of the action. He has also a wonderful power of keeping up one prevailing idea throughout the piece, so that amid all the variety of successive emotions there is unity. A striking example of his ingenuity is the duet between Agathe and Aennchen in the beginning of the second act, where two wholly different and equally characteristic melodies are given in the most charming manner. For this, however, he had a model in the duet (*à la polonaise*) between Verbel and Florestan in ' Lodöiska,' by Cherubini, a composer to whom he looked up with great admiration.

8. The play of ' Preciosa ' was adapted from a novel (1613) of Cervantes by an actor named

[1] This discovery is due to Ambros ; see his *Cultur-historische Bilder aus dem Musikleben der Gegenwart*, p. 47 (Leipzig, Matthes, 1860), and *Bunte Blätter*, p. 22.

Pius Alexander Wolff, of Weimar, engaged in Berlin in 1816. Before Weber undertook, at Count Brühl's desire, to write music for it, he had several times used his pen in a similar way. Mention may be made of his music for Schiller's 'Turandot,' consisting of an overture and six smaller instrumental pieces (1809); for Müllner's 'König Yngurd,' 11 Nos. (1817); and for Gehe's 'Heinrich IV.,' 9 Nos. (1818), besides many smaller works of the same kind, all bearing witness to his extraordinary talent for illustrating a dramatic situation in the clearest and most distinct manner by music. A predilection for Spanish subjects is observable in Weber about this period, and may be attributed to the influence of Tieck. Columbus, Pizarro, Don Juan of Austria and the Cid, all passed before him, as subjects for operas, and in 1820–21 he completed a sketch of the first act, and a duet out of the second, of 'Die drei Pintos,' a Spanish comic opera. This, however, he laid aside for 'Euryanthe' and 'Oberon,' and died without completing a work full of promise.[1] It was, therefore, in all probability, its Spanish local colouring which attracted him to 'Preciosa.' One of the signs of his natural gift for dramatic composition was his love for strong contrasts, not only between different parts of the same work, but between the different works he took in hand. The phrase 'local colouring' in music may be defined as that which conjures up before our mind the associations connected with certain scenes, races and epochs. Weber's unusual gift for this kind of illustration was most probably connected with the peculiar manner in which his musical faculties were set in motion. This is a point on which we are thoroughly informed by means of his own expressions preserved by his son and biographer. As a rule, it took place through external impressions, presented to his imagination as tone-pictures. As he sat in his travelling carriage, the scenery through which he passed would present itself to his inner ear as a piece of music, melodies welling up with every hill or valley, every fluttering bush, every waving field of corn. With him any external impression at once clothed itself in musical form, and this peculiarity of mental constitution undoubtedly contributed to give his music its individual character.

The music to 'Preciosa' does, no doubt, reflect the then prevailing idea of Spain, its scenery, its people and its art. In fact, he hit the keynote of Spanish nationality in a marvellous manner. The prevailing impression is heightened by the introduction of gipsy-rhythms and Spanish national airs. Instances

of the former are the march, appearing first in the overture, and then as No. 1, No. 9a and No. 10a; of the latter the three dances forming No. 9. This method of characterisation he had made use of several times before, as in 'Turandot,' which has a Chinese melody running all through, in the 'Freischütz' peasants' march, and in 'Oberon' an Arabian and a Turkish melody. We may add that the 'Preciosa' music has lately been augmented by a little dance, intended as an alternative to the first of the three contained in No. 9. True, this charming little piece does not exist in Weber's own hand, but its origin is betrayed by the resemblance to it of the first chorus in the third act of Marschner's 'Templer und Jüdin.' When writing his first great opera Marschner was strongly under the influence of Weber's music which he had been hearing in Dresden, and reminiscences from it not unfrequently cropped up in his own works. Moreover, he knew the little valse to be Weber's.[2]

9. The original source of the libretto of 'Euryanthe' was the *Roman de la violette*, by Gilbert de Montreuil (13th century), reprinted textually by Francisque Michel (Paris, 1834). The subject was used several times by early writers. Boccaccio borrowed from it the main incident of one of the stories of the *Decameron* (Second day, Ninth tale), and thence it found its way into Shakespeare's *Cymbeline*. Count Tressan remodelled it in 1780 for the second volume of the *Bibliothèque universelle des Romains*, and in 1804 it was published at Leipzig, under the title *Die Geschichte der tugendsamen Euryanthe von Savoyen*, in the collection of mediæval romantic poems edited by Schlegel. The translator was Helmina von Chezy, who compiled the libretto for Weber. After completing the latter she republished her translation, with many alterations.[3]

The libretto has been much abused, and when we consider that it was remodelled nine times, and at last brought into shape only by Weber's own vigorous exertions, it is evident that the authoress was not competent to create a dramatic masterpiece. It does not follow that with the help of Weber's ability and experience she was not able to concoct something tolerable for the purpose. The utter inadequacy of her poem having been reiterated *ad nauseam,* the time seems to have arrived for setting forth the opposite view, and maintaining that it is on the whole a good, and in some respects an excellent, libretto. It is curious to see the naïf way in which for the last hundred years German critics have been in the habit of considering the libretto and the music of an opera as two

---

[1] The autograph sketches were in the possession of Weber's grandson, Capt. Freiherr von Weber, at Leipzig. Reissiger added an accompaniment to a duet 'So wie Blumen, so wie Blüthen,' which was published in this form in the Weber-Album edited by the Sarrische Schiller-Verein. For an exhaustive account of these interesting fragments see Jähns, Nos. 417 to 427. The opera, completed by the composer's grandson and August Mahler, was produced at Leipzig, Jan. 20, 1888.

[2] The first two editions of the score of 'Preciosa' were full of mistakes. A third, prepared with great care by Ernst Rudorff (Berlin, Schlesinger, 1872), contains this previously unknown dance in an appendix.

[3] *Euryanthe von Savoyen*, from a MS. in the National Library at Paris called *Histoire de Gerard de Nevers et de la belle et vertueuse Euryant de Savoye, sa mie* (Berlin, 1823). Michel's edition of the *Roman de la violette* is in verse.

distinct things, the one of which may be condemned and the other extolled, as if a composer had no sort of responsibility with regard to the words he sets. 'Do you suppose that any proper composer will allow a libretto to be put into his hand like an apple?' are Weber's own words. It is, moreover, obvious that a libretto which satisfied a man of such high culture, and a composer of so eminently dramatic organisation, could not have been utterly bad. Nevertheless, the verdict against 'Euryanthe' was all but unanimous. The first who ventured to speak a decided word in its favour is Gustav Engel. He says:

'"Euryanthe" is an opera full of human interest. Truth and a fine sense of honour, jealousy, and envy, mortified love and ambition, above all the most intense womanly devotion—such are its leading motives. There is indeed one cardinal error, which is that when Euryanthe is accused of infidelity in the second Act, she remains silent, instead of explaining the nature of her comparatively small offence. This may, however, arise from the confusion into which so pure and maidenly a nature is thrown by the suddenness of the fate which overwhelms her. In the main, however, the story is a good one, though it starts with some rather strong assumptions.'

The 'cardinal error,' however, is no error at all, but a trait in perfect keeping with Euryanthe's character. It is more difficult to understand why she does not find the opportunity to enlighten Adolar, when he has dragged her off into the wilderness in the third act. Other plausible objections are the too great intricacy of the story, and its being partly founded on events which do not come within the range of the plot, viz. the story of Emma and Udo. Weber was aware of this defect, and intended to remedy it by making the curtain rise at the slow movement of the overture, and disclose the following tableau:

'The interior of Emma's tomb; a kneeling statue is beside her coffin, which is surmounted by a 12th-century baldacchino. Euryanthe prays by the coffin, while the spirit of Emma hovers overhead. Eglantine looks on.'

The opera contains four principal characters, Adolar and Lysiart, Euryanthe and Eglantine. Eglantine has most vitality, the others being types rather than individuals; but this would be no defect in Weber's eyes, being, as we have seen, in accordance with his own mode of treating his personages. The poem abounds in opportunities for the descriptive writing in which he so much delighted and excelled. The characters are not the main attraction, they seem mere condensations of the poetry of the situation, and are carried along by the scene, rather than work it out for themselves. 'Euryanthe,' like all Weber's operas, is an epic procession, an enchanted panorama, representing the life of one special period, that of mediæval chivalry. Looked at from this point of view it can be thoroughly enjoyed.[1]

'Euryanthe' is Weber's sole grand opera, both because it is without spoken dialogue, and because it is much the fullest and longest. He meant to put his best into it, and he did. 'It is his heart's blood,' says Robert Schumann.[2] There is no question that 'Euryanthe' is richer, more varied, deeper, grander, than all the rest of Weber's dramatic works. All that gives distinction to 'Der Freischütz' is found here again; Lieder at once dignified and easily comprehensible, melodies genuine in feeling and full of fire, orchestral colouring as new as it is charming, instrumentation both bold and *spirituel*, an intuitive grasp of the situation and complete mastery in treating it, such as genius alone is capable of. In many passages, and particularly in the scena and cavatina in the third act, where Euryanthe is abandoned in the wilderness, the colours are used with masterly skill. The long wailing notes of the solo bassoon, and the solitary flute wandering aimlessly about, incline one to re-echo Schumann's words, 'What a sound comes from the instruments! they speak to us from the very depths of all being.' The accompaniment to 'Hier dicht am Quell,' consisting only of the string-quartet and one bassoon, but producing the most extraordinary effect of sound, is a striking example of what genius can do with small means. Quite different again is the colouring for Euryanthe's narrative in the first act; four muted solo-violins, whose long sustained notes are supported by quivering violins and violas, also muted, with stifled moans from low flutes, suggest a spectral form, only half visible in the moonlight, hovering overhead and muttering words which die away indistinctly on the breeze.

Each of the four principal characters has its own language, to which it adheres strictly throughout the opera, and which is accentuated by the orchestral colouring employed liberally, though not exclusively, for the purpose. As we have previously remarked, one prevailing tone runs through the whole opera, sharply distinguishing it from any other of Weber's.

One point in which the music of 'Euryanthe' is far superior to that of 'Der Freischütz' is in the use of the larger dramatic forms. Here we have recitative, full of expression, passion and movement, such as had come from no German pen since Gluck's; arias, duets, *ensemble* pieces, and splendidly constructed finales. The Lied- or cavatina-form is used freely for the parts of Adolar and Euryanthe; but Lysiart and Eglantine never express themselves except in the grand dramatic forms; and the higher the passion rises the more exclusively do these two characters occupy the stage. In this

---

[1] This Goethe did not do; he says (*Gespräche mit Eckermann*, i. 148): 'Karl Maria von Weber should never have composed "Euryanthe"; he ought to have seen at once that it was a bad subject, with which nothing could be done.' After what I have said it is unnecessary to point out the injustice of this remark. Goethe had not musical insight enough to understand what it was in the libretto that attracted Weber, against whom, moreover, he had a prejudice. Still, even he allowed 'Der Freischütz' to be a good subject (Eckermann, ii. 16).

[2] *Gesammelte Schriften* iv. 290.

respect the second act is the climax : Lysiart's *scena ed aria*, his duet with Eglantine ; Adolar's air, in such wonderful contrast, and the duet with Euryanthe ; lastly the finale, in which a perfect tempest of passions seems let loose. The third act also has dramatic forms of the first order, especially Euryanthe's air, ' Zu ihm, und weilet nicht,' with the chorus ending *diminuendo* (a very striking point) and the duet and chorus with the clashing swords— ' Trotze nicht, Vermessener.' Weber's large dramatic pieces are freer as regards form than Mozart's, because he follows the poet more closely, almost indeed word by word. Though it cannot be said that there are no little roughnesses, or bits of dull or unformed work, any such are completely submerged in the overwhelming flood of beauties.

10. Although Weber wrote his last opera at the request of Kemble, he chose the subject himself, and was aware how completely it suited his own individuality. Since the publication of Wieland's poem in 1780, two German operas had been composed on Oberon. The first, Wranitzky's (1790), was one of those childish fairy - pieces, whose lively music, harlequin-tricks, scene-painting and machinery were long the delight of the simple-minded people of Vienna. The other, composed for Copenhagen (1790, with the second title of ' Holger Danske ') by Kunzen, Schulz's talented successor, and J. F. Reichardt's friend, was a far more serious work, and can be spoken of in connexion with Weber's, though the latter put it so completely into the background as virtually to obliterate it.

Weber's librettist, Planché, likewise worked on Wieland's ' Oberon,' or rather on Sotheby's translation. Though satisfied with the poem in detail, Weber could not reconcile himself to English opera as such.

' The cut of an English opera is certainly very different from a German one ; the English is more a drama with songs,'

he writes (in English) to Planché on Jan. 6, 1825 ; and again on Feb. 19 :

' I must repeat that the cut of the whole is very foreign to all my ideas and maxims. The intermixing of so many principal actors who do not sing, the omission of the music in the most important moments—all deprive our Oberon of the title of an opera, and will make him unfit for all other theatres in Europe.'

These words contain a very just criticism on the libretto. The continual change of scene, which keeps the spectator in a state of restlessness, is certainly a mistake. Weber intended to remodel the opera for Germany, when he would have put it into a form more in accordance with his own ideas, giving the music a larger share in the course of the plot, but simplifying the plot so that it should run more smoothly and consecutively. Whether he would also have endeavoured to strengthen the dramatic interest is doubtful. As it stands it is an epic poem dramatised, rather than a drama. But no subject dealing with fairyland can admit of dramatic treatment beyond a limited extent, for the characters, instead of moving independently and of their own free will, act under the guidance of supernatural powers, who visibly interfere with their destiny on all occasions. Weber required not so much characters full of dramatic action, as suggestive situations and picturesque scenes, and these Planché's libretto supplied to the full. That he had the German form in his mind all the time he was setting the English, is evident from the fact that he had each number, as fast as he composed it, translated by Theodor Hell, of Dresden, instructing him to make the words correspond as closely as possible with the melody. Hell's workmanship was not of the best, and Weber was too much occupied to correct all his blunders. One glaring instance occurs in Reiza's grand scena (' Ocean, thou mighty monster ') ; a beam from the setting sun parts the storm-clouds, and she exclaims, ' And now the sun bursts forth,' which Hell translates, ' Und nun die Sonn' geht auf ' (rises). Thus the astonished spectator, having been told that it is morning, shortly beholds the sun set in the same quarter from which it has just risen. Nevertheless the passage is always so sung in Germany, and the absurdity, if noticed at all, is laid at the door of the English librettist. Weber got his translator to make a reduction in the number of the personages introduced. In the quartet, ' Over the dark blue waters,' Planché gave the bass to a sea-captain, and in the duet, ' On the banks of sweet Garonne,' associated a Greek fellow-slave with Fatima, in both cases because the original Sherasmin was a poor singer. These makeshifts find no place in the German version, or in the English revival at Her Majesty's in 1860. Then again, the song ' Yes, even love to fame must yield,' composed in London for Braham in place of ' From boyhood trained in battle-field,' is omitted in the German, while another addition, the prayer in the second act, ' Ruler of this awful hour,' is retained. The first was a concession on the part of the composer, who did not care for this ' battle-picture ' ; but he saw that the prayer was not only a passage of great beauty, but materially strengthened the part of Huon.[1]

The music to ' Oberon,' though the work of a man dying by inches, bears no traces of mental exhaustion. Indeed it is delightfully fresh and original throughout, and entirely different from all the rest of Weber's compositions. The keynote of the whole is its picture of the mysteries

1 Hell's translation was published almost simultaneously with the original libretto, the preface to which is dated ' Brompton Crescent, Apr. 10, 1826.' The German title runs ' Oberon, King of the Elves, a romantic fairy-opera in three acts. Translated for the German stage by Theodor Hell from the English original by J. R. Planché, set to music by Capellmeister Freyherr Karl Maria von Weber ' (Arnold, Dresden and Leipzig, 1826). With a long preface by the translator.

of Elf-land, and the life of the spirits of air, earth and water. True, this note is touched in 'Der Freischütz' and 'Euryanthe,' but in 'Oberon' it is struck with full force, and vibrates with an almost intoxicating sweetness. What Weber did in this direction was absolutely new, and a valuable addition to his art, and many composers have followed in the same track. His melody, the chords of his harmony, the figures employed, the effects of colour so totally unexpected—all combine to waft us with mysterious power into an unknown land. Anybody acquainted with the adagio of the overture will see what we mean. Of a charm almost unparalleled is the introduction to the first act, with the elves flitting hither and thither, softly singing as they keep watch over Oberon's slumbers. The second act is specially rich in delicious pictures of nature, now in her tender and dreamy, now in her savage and sublime, moods. Puck's invocation of the spirits, the roar of the tempest, the magnificent picture in Reiza's grand scena of the gradual calming of the waves beneath the rays of the setting sun ; lastly, the finale, with the mermaids' bewitching song, and the elves dancing in the moonlight on the strand—these are musical treasures which have not yet been exhausted. Mendelssohn, Gade, Bennett, drew the inspiration for their romantic scenes of a similar kind from 'Oberon,' but none of them attained the depth or the individuality of their prototype. Even Schumann trod in his footsteps in isolated passages of 'Paradise and the Peri,' the ballad 'Vom Pagen und der Königstochter' and 'Manfred.' Of German opera composers I say nothing ; their imitation of him is patent.

SONGS AND VOCAL WORKS.—Next after Weber's operas come into consideration his Lieder, the Lied-form playing, as was natural with a German, so important a part in his operas. He left seventy-eight German Lieder for single voice with PF. or guitar accompaniment, besides two or three Italian canzonets, a French romance, and a song from *Lalla Rookh*, 'From Chindara's warbling fount I come,' his last composition, with the accompaniment merely sketched in.[1] We do not include his ten Scots airs arranged with accompaniment for PF., flute, violin and violoncello. Among the partsongs should be singled out sixteen Lieder for men's voices, and three Volkslieder for two voices with accompaniment.

It was at the suggestion of Vogler that Weber first made a study of the songs of the people, and this study, added to his own intuitive perception of what was intrinsically good and individual in popular music, enabled him to hit off the characteristic tone of the Volkslied as nobody had done before. 'Mein Schatz ist

auf die Wanderschaft hin,' 'Herzchen, mein Schätzchen, bist tausendmal mein,' 'Wenn ich ein Vöglein wär,' 'Ich hab' mir eins erwählet,' 'O Berlin, ich muss dich lassen,' ''Sis nichts mit den alten Weibern,' are songs in which every variety of feeling is expressed with a freshness and originality rarely met with. His musical treatment, too, of songs in dialect, especially those of a humorous or rollicking character, was excellent ; instances are 'Trariro, der Sommer, der ist do,' 'Mein Schatzerl is hübsch' and 'Ich und mein junges Weib.' The form of these songs is most simple, and generally strophical ; the accompaniment frequently for the guitar.

Besides these Lieder, Weber composed other songs of a more ambitious character, with PF. accompaniment, each stanza having a different melody. Weber's vocal compositions contain the two main elements of which German opera is constituted—the Lied and the dramatic song. These, too, appear in turn in the ten splendid songs from Körner's 'Leyer und Schwert,' four of which are for single voice and PF. and six for male chorus unaccompanied. Of the single songs, 'Vater ich rufe dich' and 'Die Wunde brennt' are magnificent tone-pictures in Weber's own style. Even in the strophical choruses there are touches of great power. The beginning of 'Du Schwert an meiner Linken' rings like a sword-thrust. 'Lützow's wilde Jagd' contains a complete dramatic scene within a single stanza of twenty-one bars. The horsemen plunge forward out of the forest gloom, rush by in tearing haste, shout one wild hurrah, and are gone.

It has often been felt as a difficulty that Weber should pass straight from such operas as 'Silvana' and 'Abu Hassan' to a masterpiece like 'Der Freischütz.' One explanation of this sudden and startling progress may probably be found in the songs which were his main occupation from 1811-17. Another important landmark is the cantata 'Kampf und Sieg' (1815). This is not a cantata in the modern sense—*i.e.* an essentially lyric vocal piece—but one rather in the sense of the 17th and 18th centuries, when the word signified solo songs representing a specific character in a specific situation. The only difference was that Weber employed the full resources of solo-singers, chorus and orchestra. The central idea is the battle of Waterloo, with various episodes grouped round it, and a chorus, 'Herr Gott dich loben wir,' as finale. The description of the battle forms what we should now call a grand dramatic scene, an opera finale, only without action.

Between 1810 and 1815 Weber wrote six concert airs with Italian words, and these also have their share in explaining the extraordinary maturity of 'Der Freischütz.' Several are of high artistic merit, notably the fourth ('Signor

[1] Schlesinger of Berlin published a complete edition in two vols. of Weber's songs. Two or three unimportant ones for single voice are omitted, but the two-part songs, Italian duets, numerous choruses for men's voices (arranged), partsongs for various voices with accompaniments, bring up the number to 100.

se padre sei '), composed in 1812 for Prince Frederic of Gotha.[1] It is written for tenor and double chorus, and is in fact a dramatic scena. None of these Italian airs, however, come up to a German scena written in 1818 for insertion in Cherubini's 'Lodoïska.' It was intended for Frau Milder-Hauptmann, then in Berlin, and was to be the first number in the second act. It is a work of the first rank, and of itself proves that the creator of 'Der Freischütz' had now attained his full stature. How it comes to be now wholly forgotten it is difficult to understand.

Among Weber's remaining vocal compositions we have still some cantatas and the two masses to consider. 'Der erste Ton' (1818), words by Rochlitz, must be mentioned among the cantatas, although the term scarcely applies to it. The greater part of the poem is declaimed to an orchestral accompaniment, but a four-part chorus is introduced near the end. The form is peculiar and new. It cannot be called a melodrama, because the poem is narrative and not dramatic. The nearest approach to it is in some of the descriptive recitatives in Haydn's oratorios. The descriptive part of the music shows already, though indistinctly, that plasticity which he was presently to make use of in such an incomparable way. The closing chorus does not satisfy the requirements of art, and Weber himself spoke of it as 'rough' part-writing. Another hymn of Rochlitz's, 'In seiner Ordnung schafft der Herr,' is a fine work of art. It was composed in 1812, and dedicated to the Musik-Gesellschaft of Zurich, which had elected him an honorary member. At first the composer has evidently had a difficulty in warming to his work, on account of the half-dogmatic, half-descriptive nature of the words; and the hearer, though occasionally interested, is not carried away by the earlier movements. The introduction of the chorale 'Drum lerne still dich fassen' (to the tune of 'O Haupt voll Blut und Wunden ') is scarcely to be justified on æsthetic grounds. But then comes the chorus 'Gelobt sei Gott,' and all that has hitherto failed to please is forgotten, and the hearer is swept away in the rushing torrent of music. The fugue of this chorus, 'Im Wettersturm, im Wogendrang,' is a character-piece of the first rank.[2]

Of the six occasional cantatas composed for the court of Saxony, the Jubel-Cantata, written for the 50th anniversary of Friedrich August's accession (1818), is the most important, both in size and matter. The four choral movements, Nos. 1, 4, 7 and 9, are ripe examples of Weber's talent for delineating a specific situation, and make one regret that the work as a whole, from the circumstances of its origin, is unavailable for general use. It is essentially a Saxon, nay,

almost a Dresden composition, and no sympathy is now felt for Friedrich August. Wendt's attempt to turn it into a harvest cantata proved fairly successful in one or two cases, especially Nos. 4 and 7 ; but the music is, as a rule, too closely wedded to the words to be divorced from them, unless at great sacrifice.[3]

CHURCH MUSIC.—As to Weber's masses, those acquainted with the state of Catholic church music at the beginning of the 19th century will not expect to find them written in a pure church style. Fine music they contain in abundance. As previously mentioned, they were produced within a short time of each other, in 1818 and 1819. After Weber's fashion they contrast sharply with each other, while each has one prevailing tone running consistently through to the end. The year 1818 being the 50th of the King's reign, he gave to the E♭ Mass a tone of solemnity and splendour noticeable specially in the Sanctus. That in G, being for a family festival, is quite idyllic in character. 'I mean to keep before myself,' he wrote to Rochlitz, 'the idea of a happy family party kneeling in prayer, and rejoicing before the Lord as His children.' It is worth while to examine the Mass, and see how this idea is worked out. The Kyrie, Sanctus (with an exquisite Benedictus) and Agnus Dei are delightful music. Occasional suggestions of well-known passages in his operas jar on a modern ear, but a composer is scarcely to be blamed for retaining his identity even in a mass. His love of contrast, and habit of never remaining long occupied with one musical idea, give these pieces a somewhat restless and piecemeal effect, and for this reason those who were accustomed to Haydn's and Mozart's masses felt these too 'secular.'[4]

ORCHESTRAL AND CHAMBER MUSIC.—When a youth of 20 Weber wrote two symphonies, clever and to a certain extent interesting, but parti-coloured and without form. The indications they gave of his future position as an orchestral composer were very inadequate, and in later years they by no means satisfied himself. Of wholly different import are his ten overtures :

'Peter Schmoll' (remodelled 1807 as 'Grande Ouverture à plusieurs instruments '), 'Rübezahl' (remodelled 1811 as 'Ouvertüre zum Beherrscher der Geister,' 'Ruler of the Spirits '), 'Overtura Chinesa' (remodelled 1809 for 'Turandot '), 'Silvana,' 'Abu Hassan,' 'Jubel-Ouvertüre,' 'Freischütz,' 'Preciosa,' 'Euryanthe' and 'Oberon.'

Of these, 'Peter Schmoll' and 'Silvana' are unimportant and immature. In 'Turandot' the local colouring furnished by a Chinese air is pushed into an extreme which becomes ugly. The remaining seven are very fine, and excepting perhaps 'Rübezahl' and 'Abu Hassan,' all have been most popular. They hold a middle

---

[1] Op. 53, Schlesinger, Berlin, vocal score.
[2] Score, parts, and PF. score, published by Schlesinger of Berlin.
[3] The score, with the two sets of words, and preceded by the Jubel-Ouvertüre, is published by Schlesinger (Berlin). A full analysis with ample quotations is given in the *Monthly Musical Record*, 1873.
[4] The score of the E♭ Mass was published by Richault (Paris), that of the one in G by Haslinger (Vienna, *édition de luxe*).

position between simple introductions and abstract orchestral works, sounding equally well in the concert-room and the theatre. This they share with the overtures of Mozart and Cherubini. There are, however, important differences of style between these overtures and those of Mozart and Cherubini. This is not so much because Weber constructed them out of the materials of the opera, though some have with great injustice gone so far as to maintain that they are mere elegant potpourris. Each is a complete conception, and—some unimportant passages apart—carved out of one block. That what looks like mosaic may have been constructed organically is proved by Cherubini's 'Anacreon' overture, in which—a little-known fact—there is not a single bar not contained in the opera. Weber's natural way of working was not to develop continuously, but to proceed from one strong contrast to another. His musical ideas are seldom adapted for thematic treatment, being always full of meaning, but with few capacities of development. The instant one idea is given out decisively it calls up another absolutely opposed to it. Illustrations of this may be found in the opening of the 'Rübezahl' overture, as well as in the Eb movement of the allegro in that to 'Der Freischütz.' This method of progression by continual contrasts is undoubtedly the sign-manual of Weber's dramatic genius; and to it his works owe as much of their stimulating effect and fascination as they do to the variety, tenderness and brilliance of the instrumentation.

This explains why Weber produced so little chamber music. The quiet thoughtfulness, the refinements of instrumental polyphony, the patient development of a subject, which are the essence of this branch of art, were not congenial to one who liked to be up and away. He did not write a single string quartet; and his PF. quartet, string quintet with clarinet, and trio for PF., violoncello and flute, are, for him, unimportant compositions, and not always in the true chamber-music style. Jähns appositely observes that the trio is pastoral in character, and the last three movements almost dramatic. By this he means not so much that the composer had in his mind specific figures or scenes, but that the subjects are almost like spoken phrases, and the contrasts singularly life-like. Many movements of Beethoven's chamber music were inspired by some definite poetical idea (as the adagios of the quartets in F major (No. 1) and E minor), but these are all genuine chamber music. The third movement of the trio, headed 'Schäfers Klage' (Shepherd's Lament), is a series of clever variations on a simple melody of eight bars. The writer believes—though Jähns does not agree—that this is the air of a real Lied, and suspects it to be a setting of Goethe's 'Da droben auf jenem Berge,' but whether

Weber's or not we have at present no means of determining. Amongst his chamber music must not be forgotten six sonatas for PF. and violin, published in 1811. Though of modest dimensions, and occasionally somewhat immature, they contain a host of charming thoughts.

PIANOFORTE MUSIC.—Weber was one of the greatest and most original pianists of his day. After his thorough grounding when a boy he never became the pupil of any of the principal virtuosi, and all the finishing part of his education was his own work. He formed himself neither on Clementi nor Hummel; indeed his feeling with regard to the latter was one of decided opposition. After hearing him in Vienna in 1813, he wrote in his diary: 'Hummel improvised—dry but correct.' After a concert of Hummel's in 1816, Weber wrote that

'Hummel seemed to set the most store on plenty of runs executed with great clearness. Drawing out and developing the higher resources of the instrument, he perhaps undervalues too much.' [1]

In private letters he spoke still more openly, saying plainly that 'Hummel had not made a study of the nature of the pianoforte.' This he himself had done most thoroughly, and in consequence obtained a number of effects at once new and thoroughly in accordance with the nature of the instrument. This was the principal cause of the unexpectedness which was so striking in his playing, besides its brilliancy, fire and expression. Wide stretches, easy to his long flexible fingers, bold jumps from one part of the keyboard to another, rapid passages of thirds for one hand (the Eb concerto), or of thirds, sixths and octaves for both, runs with accompanying chords for the same hand (first movement of the sonata in C)—such are some of his technical resources, all of real value because used to express really new ideas. His pianoforte style also shows, within reasonable limits, a leaning to the orchestral. For instance, in the finale of the sonata in D minor he must certainly have had the violoncello and clarinet in mind, when he wrote the *cantabile*, and the still more beautiful counter-subject. Again, in the first movement of the sonata in C his mental ear has evidently been filled with the sound of the orchestra from bar 4.

The four sonatas (in C, Ab, D minor and E minor) are pronounced by Marx to excel in some respects even the sonatas of Beethoven. This is going too far. In perfection of form Weber is always far behind Beethoven, and though his ideas may be equally original, they are far less solid and not so varied. His sonatas therefore cannot be considered models of the type, which Beethoven's are in the highest degree. They are rather fantasias in sonata-form, and their very irregularities give them a kind of air of improvisation, which is their chief charm. Each has its distinctive character,

[1] *Lebensbild,* iii. 117.

consistently maintained throughout. When we say that no one of Beethoven's sonatas resembles another, we mean something quite different from this. The divergence between his various creations goes far deeper ; with Weber certain favourite phrases are frequently repeated, and his sphere of ideas is far less extensive. His sonatas contrast more in form and colour than in essence ; in each he gives us his whole self, but from a different point of view.

Next to the sonatas in importance are his ten sets of variations.[1] Weber did not attempt —as Bach did in the ' Goldberg ' variations, or Beethoven in the ' Eroica ' ones and those on Diabelli's waltz (see VARIATIONS)—to enlarge the bounds of variation, but clung to the simple old-fashioned form. This makes it all the more wonderful that he could cram so much that was new within such narrow limits. In the invention of new figures and striking harmonies he is inexhaustible, and—a main point—each has its own distinctive and sharply defined stamp. His dramatic genius never left him. His variations on ' Vien quà Dorina bella,' op. 7 ; on 'A peine au sortir de l'enfance,' op. 28 ; and on ' Schöne Minka,' op. 40, are among the finest specimens of the kind.

His talent shone most conspicuously whenever he had a poetical idea to interpret musically, and nowhere do we see this more clearly than in his two Polonaises, in E♭ and E, and above all in his ' Invitation à la valse,' known all over the world. The ' Rondo brillant,' op. 62, and the ' Momento capriccioso,' op. 12, though not unattractive, scarcely come up to the other three pieces. Of pianoforte music for four hands his only examples are opp. 3, 10 and 60, containing six, six and eight pieces respectively. Op. 60 is a collection of little pieces which for invention and fascination of sound do not yield to Schubert's best work of the kind.

CONCERTOS.—Finally, Weber takes high rank as a composer of concertos. As a pianist it was of course an object with him to find scope for his own instrument with an orchestra. Of his three concertos, the one in F minor, op. 79 (Concertstück), is to this day a stock-piece with virtuosi, and has left its mark on later composers. Mendelssohn would probably not have written his G minor concerto but for this predecessor. Not the least of its many attractions is its form (Larghetto, Allegro, March, Finale), diverging so materially from that of all previous concertos. Then, too, though complete in itself as a piece of music, it is prompted by a poetical idea, for a whole dramatic scene was in the composer's mind when he wrote it. What this was we are told by Benedict, who on the morning of the first performance of ' Der Freischütz ' sat listening with Weber's wife while he played them the Concertstück, then just finished.

' The Châtelaine sits all alone on her balcony gazing far away into the distance. Her knight has gone to the Holy Land. Years have passed by, battles have been fought. Is he still alive ? will she ever see him again ? Her excited imagination calls up a vision of her husband lying wounded and forsaken on the battlefield. Can she not fly to him and die by his side ? She falls back unconscious. But hark ! what notes are those in the distance ? Over there in the forest something flashes in the sunlight—nearer and nearer. Knights and squires with the cross of the Crusaders, banners waving, acclamations of the people ; and there—it is he ! She sinks into his arms. Love is triumphant. Happiness without end. The very woods and waves sing the song of love ; a thousand voices proclaim his victory.' [2]

The part which the different movements take in this programme is obvious enough. The music is quite independent of the idea which prompted it, but a knowledge of the programme adds greatly to the pleasure of listening ; and the fact of his having composed in this manner is an interesting point in the study of Weber's idiosyncrasy.

The other two concertos, in C and E♭, have been unduly neglected for the ' Concertstück.' The former, composed in 1810, is indeed not so brilliant, but its delightfully original finale would alone make it a valuable work. The other owes its origin apparently to Beethoven's concerto in E♭. This came out in Feb. 1811, and we learn from Weber's diary that he bought a copy in Leipzig on Jan. 14, 1812. His own concerto in E♭ was finished in December of the same year at Gotha. The choice of the key, the remote key of B major for the adagio, and still closer resemblances between parts of the movements of the two, show how deep an impression Beethoven's work had made on the younger artist. Still it was only suggestion, and did not affect Weber's identity. The differences between the two will be found quite as decided as the resemblances.

When once Mozart had introduced the clarinet into the higher range of music it rapidly became a favourite solo-instrument. Germany had at the beginning of the century two pre-eminent clarinet-players—Hermstedt of Sondershausen and Bärmann of Munich. Spohr composed for the former, Weber for the latter.[3] Hermstedt was an excellent player as far as technique went, but a man of limited intellect, while Bärmann, with an equally brilliant technique, was a thorough artist in temperament and a man of refined taste. Spohr's clarinet compositions are good work, but, perhaps because he was in the habit of composing for Hermstedt, he never seems to have got at the heart of the instrument. This Weber did, and to such an extent that he is still the classical composer for the clarinet. It is a remarkable instance of his power of penetrating into the nature of instruments that

---

[1] I include the variations for PF. and violin, op. 22, and for PF. and clarinet, op. 33.

[2] Benedict's Weber.

[3] Of Weber's six works for clarinet solo, five are dedicated to his friend Bärmann ; the sixth, op. 48, bears no dedication. It seems probable from Jähns (p. 434, No. 57) that this was composed for Hermstedt at his own request, but that Weber would not dedicate it to him out of consideration for Bärmann.

though not able to play the clarinet himself, he should have so far developed its resources that since his day no substantial advance has been made by composers in handling the instrument. His three clarinet concertos (opp. 26, 73 and 74, the first a concertino) were all written in 1811, when he was living in Munich in constant intercourse with Bärmann. We have also two works for PF. and clarinet, Variations on a theme from 'Silvana,' and a fine 'Duo concertante' in three movements, op. 48. Seldom as these are heard, those he wrote for other wind instruments are never played at all. And yet the concertos for horn, bassoon and flute testify very remarkably to his wonderful gift for penetrating into the nature of an instrument.

LITERARY WORKS.—Weber's turn for literary composition, developed most strongly between the years 1809 and 1818, has been already mentioned.[1] As a rule his pen was naturally employed on musical matters, only one of his newspaper articles being on a general subject—*Über Baden-Baden*, Aug. 1, 1810. His talent for authorship was undoubtedly considerable. His narrative is clear and intelligible, his style correct, elegant and lively, with a certain freedom not at all unbecoming. Now and then, too, he wrote successful verses.

In this respect, as in so many others, Weber was the first of a new generation of artists. It pleased him to reveal the ideas with which his mind was crowded in words as well as in music. This is evident from his active correspondence. Weber's letters are more amusing and contain more information than those of any other German musician. As an author he was the precursor of Schumann and Wagner, over whose music, too, his own exercised so great an influence. But unlike them he did not concentrate his literary powers; his nature was too restless, and his life too unsettled. It is a pity that his musical novel, *Tonkünstlers Leben*, remained unfinished, for as he himself was the 'musician' whose 'life' he described, we should have gained an artistically drawn autobiography of inestimable value. What remains of the novel is interesting and tantalising, on account of its many acute and profound observations on art. Not that Weber could philosophise and systematise like Wagner; he touches lightly on subjects, sometimes indeed superficially, but in every word you see the man of intellectual cultivation capable of forming his own judgment. His literary affinity is closer to Schumann than to Wagner. The imagination, the humour, the kindness and cordiality towards his juniors, the absence of jealousy towards equals, are as characteristic of Weber as of Schumann. He helped materi-

ally to launch Meyerbeer and Marschner, exerted himself heartily to extend the knowledge of Spohr's music (a service Spohr did not return in kind), and though as a youth he passed a hasty judgment on Beethoven, he amply repaired the oversight in maturer years. When 'Fidelio' was being performed in Dresden, he wrote to Beethoven (Jan. 28, 1823):

'Each representation will be a festival to me, giving me the opportunity of offering to your noble spirit a homage springing from my inmost heart, which is filled with mingled admiration and affection for you.'

And Weber was no man to pay empty compliments. Like as he was to Schumann in many respects, they were very different in others. Besides the sense of humour characteristic of both, Weber had a strong satirical vein, a caustic wit and a love of fun, which he shared with Mozart. He was also more mercurial and brilliant than Schumann, who by his side seems almost slow. He took wider views of life, was more a man of the world, often with a kind of chivalrous gallantry; but far more fickle than his younger comrade in art. He wrote on all sorts of subjects—critical, polemical, historical, theoretical; most often perhaps to introduce new works and prepare the public mind for their reception. The mechanical construction of instruments was always an interesting subject to him, and he wrote newspaper articles on Capeller's improved flutes, on Kaufmann's [2] trumpets, chiming-clocks and harmonichord, and on Buschmann's 'Terpodion.' He even went so far as to compose a Concertstück (adagio and allegretto in F) for Kaufmann's harmonichord, a piece which shows very clearly his wonderful feeling for beauty of sound.

SUMMARY OF WEBER'S COMPOSITIONS [3]

I. OPERAS

1. Das Waldmädchen; 3 fragments only remaining. Unprinted. 1800.
2. Peter Schmoll und seine Nachbarn. Unprinted. 1801.
3. Rübezahl; only 3 numbers in existence, the last a Quintet published by Schlesinger. 1804, 1805.
4. Silvana; PF. score. Schlesinger. 1810.
5. Abu Hassan; PF. score. Simrock, Bonn. 1811.
6. Der Freischütz. 1820.
7. Die drei Pintos. Sketch only, unfinished. 1821. (See above p. 472b, note 2.)
8. Euryanthe. 1823.
9. Oberon. 1826.

II. OTHER DRAMATIC WORKS

1. Music to Schiller's 'Turandot'; overture and 6 short instrumental pieces. 1809.
2. Music to Müllner's 'König Yngurd'; 10 instrumental pieces and 1 vocal piece. 1817.
3. Music to Gehe's 'Heinrich IV., König von Frankreich'; 8 instrumental pieces. 1818.
4. Music to Rublack's play 'Lieb' um Liebe'; 4 vocal pieces, 1 march and 1 melodrama. 1818.
5. Music to Houwald's tragedy 'Der Leuchtthurm'; 2 melodramas and 2 interludes for harp, all short. 1820.
6. Music to Wolff's 'Preciosa'; overture, 4 choruses, 1 song, 3 melodramas and dances. 1820.
7. Music to a Festspiel by Ludwig Robert; instrumental movement and 5 choruses. 1822.
8. Rondo alla Polacca for tenor voice; for Haydn's opera 'Freibrief.'
9. 4 Lieder for single voice and guitar, Über die Berge mit Unge-, stüm; Rase, Sturmwind, blase; Lass mich schlummern Herzlein, schweige; Umringt vom mutterfüllten Heere: from Kotzebue's *Der arme Minnesinger*. 1811.

---

[1] Weber's posthumous writings came out originally in three vols. (Arnold, Dresden and Leipzig), and were republished as vol. iii. of Max von Weber's *Lebensbild*.

[2] Father and son, of Dresden.
[3] Based on Jähns's *C. M. von Weber in seinen Werken*. Berlin, 1871.

10. 2 Lieder, Mein Weib ist capores. and Frau Liesere guhe ; from Anton Fischer's *Travestirte Aeneas*. 1815.
11. 2 Lieder, Wer stets hinte' Ofen kroch, and Wie wir voll Glut uns hier zusammenfinden ; from Gubitz's *Lieb und Versöhnen*. 1815.
12. Ballad for single voice and harp, Was stürmt die Haide herauf ? from Reinbach's tragedy *Gordon und Montrose*. 1815.
13. Ariette to Huber's *Sternenmädchen im Maidlinger Walde*. 1816.
14. Romance for single voice and guitar, Ein König einst gefangen sass ; from Castelli's *Diana von Poitiers*. 1816.
15. Lied, Hold ist der Cyanenkranz ; from Kind's *Weinberg an der Elbe*. 1817.
16. Chorus with wind instruments, Heil dir Sappho ; from Grillparzer's tragedy *Sappho*. 1818.
17. Lied for single voice and guitar, Ein Mädchen ging die Wies' entlang ; from Kind's *Der Abend am Waldbrunnen*. 1818.
18. Chorus with wind instruments, Agnus Dei ; from Graf von Blankensee's tragedy *Carlo*. 1820.
19. Lied for 3 women's voices and guitar, Sagt woher stammt Liebesluste (Tell me where is fancy bred) ; from Shakespeare's *Merchant of Venice*.
20. Music and recitative, Doch welche Töne steigen jetzt hernieder ; for Spontini's ' Olympia.' 1825.
21. Recitative and Rondo for soprano and orchestra, Il momento s' avvicina. 1810.
22. Scena ed aria for soprano and orchestra, Misera me ; from ' Atalia.' 1811.
23. Scena ed aria for tenor, men's chorus and orchestra, Qual altro attendi. 1811.
24. Scena ed aria for tenor, 2 choruses and orchestra, Signor se padre sei ; for ' Ines de Castro.' 1812.
25. Scena ed aria for soprano and orchestra, Ah, se Edmondo fosse l' uccisor ; for Méhul's ' Hélène.' 1815.
26. Scena ed aria for soprano and orchestra, Non paventar, mia vita ; for ' Ines de Castro.' 1815.
27. Scena ed aria for soprano and orchestra, Was sag'ich ? Schaudern macht mich der Gedanke l for Cherubini's ' Lodoïska.' 1818.
28. Three duets for 2 soprani and PF., Se il mio ben ; Mille volte mio tesoro ; Va, ti consola. 1818.

III. CANTATAS

1. Der erste Ton ; by Rochlitz ; orchestral music for declamation and final chorus. 1808.
2. Hymn, In seiner Ordnung schafft der Herr ; by Rochlitz : soli, chorus and orchestra. 1812.
3. Kampf und Sieg ; by Wohlbrück ; in commemoration of June 18, 1815 : soli, chorus and orchestra. 1815.
4. L' Accoglianza ; for the wedding of the Hereditary Grand Duke Leopold of Tuscany and Princess Maria Anna Carolina of Saxony, words by Celani : 6solo-voices, chorus and orchestra. Oct. 29, 1817.
5. Natur und Liebe ; by Kind ; for the name-day of King Friedrich August of Saxony : 2 sopranos, 2 tenors, 2 basses and PF. 1818.
6. Jubel-Cantata, Erhebt den Lobgesang ; by Kind ; for the 50th anniversary of King Friedrich August's accession : soli, chorus and orchestra. 1818.
7. Du, bekränzend unsre Laren ; by Kind ; for Duchess Amalia von Zweibrücken's birthday : solo and chorus, with PF. and flute. 1821.
8. Wo nehm' ich Blumen her ; by Heil ; for Princess Therese of Saxony's birthday : 3 solo-voices and PF. 1823.

IV. MASSES

1. In E♭ ; 4 solo-voices, chorus and orchestra ; for the King of Saxony's name-day. 1818.
1a. Offertoire to the same ; soprano solo, chorus and orchestra. 1818.
2. In G : 4 solo-voices, chorus and orchestra ; for the golden wedding of the King and Queen of Saxony. 1818–19.
2a. Offertoire to the same ; soprano solo, chorus and orchestra. 1818.

V. LIEDER, BALLADS AND ROMANCES FOR ONE OR TWO VOICES, WITH PIANO OR GUITAR
(Alphabetically arranged).

1. Ach wär' ich doch zu dieser Stund. 1816.
2. Ach wenn ich nur ein Liebchen hätte. 1809.
3. Ah, dove siete, oh luci belle. Canzonet (guitar). 1811.
4. Alles in mir glühet zu lieben. 1814.
5. Auf die stürmche See hinaus (guitar). 1810.
6. Ch' io mai vi possa. Canzonet (guitar). 1811.
7. Das war ein recht abscheuliches Gesicht. 1820.
8. Der Gaishirt steht am Felsenrand. 1822.
9. Der Holdseligen sonder Wank. 1813.
10. Der Tag hat seinen Schmuck. Volkslied. 1819.
  Die Temperamente beim Verlust der Geliebten. 1816.
11. *a*. Der Leichtmüthige (Lust entfloh, und hin ist hin).
12. *b*. Der Schwermüthige (düge Zeiten).
13. *c*. Der Liebemüthige (Verrathen !).
14. *d*. Der Gleichmüthige (Nun bin ich befreit, wie behäglich !).
15. Die Wunde brennt, die bleichen Lippen beben. Sonnet from Leyer und Schwert. 1814.
16. Düst're Harmonieen hör' ich klingen. *Ibid.* 1816.
17. Du liebes, holdes, himmelsüsses Wesen. Sonnet. 1812.
18. Ein Echo kenn' ich. 1808.
19. Ein' fromme Magd von gutem Stand. Volkslied. 1818.
20. Ein König einst gefangen sass (guitar). 1816. See II. 14.
21. Ein Mädchen ging die Wies' entlang (guitar). 1818. See II. 17.
22. Ein neues Lied, ein neues Lied ; MS. 1810.
23. Ein steter Kampf ist unser Leben. 1808.
24. Ein Veilchen blüht im Thale. 1817.
25. Ei, wenn ich doch ein Maler wär'. 1820.
26. Elle était simple et gentillette. 1824.
27. Endlich hatte Damon sie gefunden (guitar). 1810.
28. Entfliehet schnell von mir ; MS. 1803.
29. Es sitzt die Zeit im weissen Kleid (guitar). 1810.
30. Es stürmt auf der Flur, es brauset im Hain. 1813.
31. Frage mich immer, fragest umsonst. 1813.
32. Frei und froh mit muntern Sinnen. 1812.

33. From Chindara's warbling fount I come ; MS. 1826.
34. Herzchen, mein Schätzchen, bist tausendmal mein. **Volkslied.** 1819.
35. Herz, lass dich nicht zerspalten. Leyer und Schwert. **1814.**
36. Herz, mein Herz ermanne dich. 1820.
37. Horch ! leise horch, Geliebte, horch ! (guitar). **1809.**
38. Ich denke dein, wenn durch den Hain. 1806.
39. Ich empfinde fast ein Grauen. 1818.
40. Ich hab' mir eins erwählet. Volkslied. **1817.**
41. Ich sah ein Röschen am Wege stehen. 1809.
42. Ich sah sie hingesunken ; MS. 1804.
43. Ich tummle mich auf der Haide. 1819.
44. In der Berge Riesenschatten (guitar). 1812.
45. Judäa, hochgelobtes Land. 1819.
46. I und mein junges Weib können schön tanza. **Volkslied** (guitar). 1812.
47. Jüngst sass ich am Grabe der Trauten allein. 1804.
48. Keine Lust ohn' treues Lieben. Triolet. 1819.
49. Lass mich schlummern, Herzlein schweige (guitar). 1811. See II. 9.
50. Mädel, schau' mir ins Gesicht (guitar). 1807.
51. Maienblümlein so schön. 1811.
52. Meine Lieder, meine Sänge. 1809.
53. Mein Schatz, der ist auf der Wanderschaft hin. Volkslied. **1818**
54. Mein Schatzerl ist hübsch. Volkslied. 1818.
55. Ninfe, se liete. Canzonet (guitar). 1811.
56. O Berlin, ich muss dich lassen. Volkslied, 2-part. 1817.
57. Rase, Sturmwind, blase (guitar). 1811. MS. See II. 9.
58. Rosen im Haare, den Becher zur Hand. 1818.
59. Sagt mir an, was schmunzelt ihr. 1813.
60. Sanftes Licht, weiche nicht (guitar). 1813.
61. Schlaf, Herzenssöhnchen, mein Liebling bist du (guitar). 1810.
62. Sicché t' inganni, o Clori. Canzonet. 1810.
63. Sind es Schmerzen, sind es Freuden. 1813.
64. Sind wir geschieden, und ich muss leben ohne dich. Volkslied. 1819.
65. 'Sis nichts mit den alten Weibern. Volkslied. 1817.
66. So geht es im Schnützelputz-Häusel. Volkslied, 2-part. 1817.
67. Süsse Ahnung dehnt den Busen. 1809.
68. Trariro, der Sommer der ist do. Volkslied, 2-part. 1817.
69. Traurig, einsam weikst du hin. 1809.
70. Über die Berge mit Ungestüm (guitar). 1811. See II. 9.
71. Um Rettung bietet ein güldnes Geschmeide. 1812.
72. Umringt vom mutherfüllten Heere. Lied with chorus (guitar). 1811. See II. 9.
73. Umsonst entsagt ich der lockenden Liebe. 1802.
74. Ungern fliebt das süsse Leben ; MS. 1802.
75. Vater ich rufe dich. Leyer und Schwert. 1814.
76. Vöglein, einsam in dem Bauer. 1816.
77. Vöglein hüpfet in dem Haine. 1816.
78. Was bricht hervor, wie Blüthen weiss. 1819.
79. Was stürmet die Haide herauf (harp). 1815. See II. 12.
80. Was zieht zu deinem Zauberkreise. 1809.
81. Weile, Kind, ich will nicht rauben. 1816.
82. Weil es Gott also gefügt ; MS. 1809.
83. Weine, weine, weine nur nicht. Volkslied. 1818.
84. Wenn, Brüder, wie wir täglich sehn. Lied with chorus. 1809.
85. Wenn die Maien grün sich kleiden. 1818.
86. Wenn ich die Blümlein schau. 1817.
87. Wenn ich ein Vöglein wär'. Volkslied. 1818.
88. Wenn Kindlein süssen Schlummers Ruh. 1821.
89. Wo ist des Sängers Vaterland ? Leyer und Schwert. 1814.
90. Wollt ihr sie kennen, soll ich sie nennen. 1808.

VI. PARTSONGS FOR MEN'S VOICES

1. Bald heisst es wieder : Gute Nacht. 4-part. 1819
2. Das Volk steht auf, der Sturm bricht los. Leyer und Schwert ; 4-part. 1814.
3. Du Schwert an meiner Linken. Leyer und Schwert ; -part. 1814.
4. Ei, ei, wie scheint der Mond so hell. Volkslied ; 3-part. 1818.
5. Ein Kind ist uns geboren. 4-part. 1819.
6. Flüstert lieblich, Sommerlüfte. 4-part. with PF. 1817.
7. Freunde, dass Glut liebend uns trage. 4-part. 1814.
8. Frisch auf, frisch auf, mit raschem Flug. Leyer und Schwert. 1814
9. Füllet die Humpen, muthige Knappen (Turnierbankett). 1812.
10. Hinaus, hinaus, zum blut'gen Strauss. 4-part. 1825.
11. Hörnerschall ! Überfall ! 4-part. 1825.
12. Hör' uns, Allmächtiger ! Leyer und Schwert ; 4-part. 1814.
13. Husaren sind gar wackre Truppen. 4-part. 1821.
14. Ja freue dich, so wie du bist. 4-part. 1819.
15. Schlacht, du brichst an. Leyer und Schwert ; 4-part. 1814.
16. Schöne Ahnung ist erglommen. 4-part. 1818.
17. Sohn der Ruhe, sinke nieder. 4-part. 1822.
18. Was glänzt dort vorm Walde im Sonnenschein. (Lützow.) Leyer und Schwert ; 4-part. 1814.
19. Wir stehn vor Gott, der Meineids Frevel rächt. Unison with wind instruments. 1812.

VII. LIEDER AND PARTSONGS FOR VARIOUS VOICES WITH AND WITHOUT ACCOMPANIMENT

1. Canons zu zwey sind nicht drey. Canon *a* 3 (printed by Jähns, No. 90). 1810.
2. Die Sonate soll ich spielen. Canon *a* 3 (Jähns, No. 89). 1810.
3. Ein Gärtchen und ein Häuschen drin. Soprano, tenor and bass, without accompaniment ; MS. 1803.
4. Geiger und Pfeiffer. Swabian Dance-song : soprano, 2 tenors and bass. 1812.
5. Heisse, stille Liebe schwebet. Soprano, 2 tenors and bass. 1812.
6. Hörst du der Klage dumpfen Schall. Mixed chorus and wind instruments ; MS. 1811.
7. Leck' mich im Angesicht. Canon *a* 3 (Jähns, No. 95). 1810.
8. Leis' wandeln wir, wie Geisterhauch. Dirge : soprano, 2 tenors and bass, with wind instruments. 1803.
9. Lenz erwacht und Nachtigallen. 2 soprani, 2 tenors and 2 basses, with PF. ; MS. 1814.
10. Mädchen, ach meide Männerschmeichelein. Canon *a* 3 (Jähns, No. 35). 1802.
11. Scheiden und meiden ist einerlei. Canon *a* 4 (Jähns, No. 167). 1814.

12. Weil Maria Töne hext. Canon *a* 3 ; MS. 1816.
13. Zu dem Reich der Töne schweben. Canon *a* 4 (Jähns, No. 164). 1814.
14. Zur Fremde ward geboren. Soprano, 2 tenors and bass. 1812.

VIII. SCOTCH SONGS, ACCOMPANIMENTS TO, FOR FLUTE, VIOLIN, VIOLONCELLO AND PF., 1825

1. The soothing shades of gloaming.
2. Glowing with love, on fire for fame.
3. O poortith cauld and restless love.
4. True-hearted was he.
5. Yes thou mayst walk.
6. A soldier am I.
7. John Anderson my jo.
8. O my Luve's like the red red rose.
9. Robin is my joy.
10. Where hae ye been a' day.

IX. SYMPHONIES, OVERTURES, ORCHESTRAL DANCES AND MARCHES

1. First Symphony, C major: Allegro con fuoco ; Andante; Scherzo, presto ; Finale, presto. 1806–7.
2. Second Symphony, C major : Allegro ; Adagio ma non troppo ; Menuetto, allegro ; Finale, scherzo presto. 1807.
3. Grande Ouverture à plusieurs instruments, B♭—E♭. 1807. See I. 2.
4. Overture, Beherrscher der Geister ; D minor. 1811. See I. 3.
5. Jubel-Ouverture ; E. 1818.
6. Waltz for wind instruments ; E♭. MS. The trio is Weber's Lied ' Maienblümlein so schön.' 1812.
7. Deutscher for full orchestra ; D. Subject same as the second of the Lieder II. 10. 1815.
8. Tedesco for full orchestra ; D. Unprinted ; used for the ' Preciosa ' music. 1816.
9. Marcia vivace, for 10 trumpets ; D. Unprinted ; used for ' Euryanthe.' 1822.
10. March, for wind instruments ; C. Subject partly the same as XI. 22 (5). 1826.

X. CONCERTOS AND CONCERTED PIECES WITH ORCHESTRA

1. First PF. concerto ; C. Allegro ; Adagio ; Finale, presto, 1810.
2. Second PF. concerto ; E♭. Allegro maestoso ; Adagio ; Rondo, presto. 1812.
3. Concertstück for PF. ; F minor. Larghetto affettuoso ; Allegro passionato ; Marcia e Rondo giojoso. 1821.
4. Concertino for clarinet ; C minor—E♭. Adagio ma non troppo ; Thema (Andante) with variations, and Finale, allegro. 1811.
5. First concerto for clarinet ; F minor. Allegro moderato ; Adagio ma non troppo ; Rondo, allegretto. 1811.
6. Second concerto for clarinet ; E♭. Allegro ; Romanze ; Alla Polacca. 1811.
7. Quintet for clarinet and string-quartet ; B♭. Allegro ; Fantasia Adagio ; Menuetto ; Rondo, allegro giojoso. Classed here as being of the nature of a concerto. 1815.
8. Concerto for bassoon ; F major. Allegro ma non troppo ; Adagio ; Rondo, allegro. 1811.
9. Adagio e Rondo Ungarese, for bassoon ; C minor Revision of No. 13. 1813.
10. Concertino for horn ; E minor. Adagio ; Andante con moto with variations ; Polacca. 1815.
11. Romanza Siciliana for flute ; G minor. 1805.
12. Six variations for viola on the Volkslied ' A Schüsserl und a Reind'rl ' ; C. 1806.
13. Andante and Rondo Ungarese for viola C minor. See No. 9. 1809.
14. Potpourri for violoncello ; D. Maestoso ; Andante with variations ; Adagio ; Finale, allegro. 1808.
15. Andante and variations for violoncello ; D minor, F major. 1810.
16. Adagio and Rondo for the harmon chord ; F major. 1811.

XI. PIANOFORTE MUSIC
A. For two hands

1. First Sonata ; C. Allegro ; Adagio ; Menuetto, allegro ; Rondo, presto. 1812.
2. Second Sonata ; A♭. Allegro moderato con spirito ed assai legato ; Andante ; Menuetto capriccio ; Rondo, moderato e molto grazioso. 1816.
3. Third Sonata ; D minor. Allegro feroce ; Andante con moto ; Rondo, presto. 1816.
4. Fourth Sonata ; E minor. Moderato ; Menuetto ; Andante quasi Allegretto ; Finale, La Tarantella. 1822.
5. Six variations on an original theme ; C. 1800.
6. Eight variations on a theme from Vogler's ' Castor and Pollux ' ; F. 1804.
7. Six variations on a theme from Vogler's ' Samori ' ; B♭. 1804.
8. Seven variations on Bianchi's ' Vien quà Dorina bella ' ; C. 1807.
9. Seven variations on an original theme ; F. 1808.
10. Seven variations on a theme from Méhul's ' Joseph ' ; C. 1812.
11. Nine variations on a Russian air, ' Schöne Minka ' ; C minor. 1815.
12. Seven variations on a Gipsy air ; C. 1817.
13. Momento capriccioso ; B♭. 1808.
14. Grande Polonaise ; E♭. 1808.
15. Polacca brillante ; E major. 1819.
16. Rondo brillante ; E♭. 1819.
17. Aufforderung zum Tanze, Rondo brillant ; D♭. 1819.
18. Six Fughetti, op. 1. 1798.
19. Twelve Allemandes (Valses, Nos. 11 and 12, for 4 hands). 1801.
20. Six Écossaises. 1802.
21. Eighteen Valses (Valses favorites de l'Impératrice de France). 1812.

B. For four hands

22. Six easy little pieces : (1) Sonatina, C ; (2) Romanze, F: (3) Menuetto, B♭ ; (4) Andante con variazioni, G ; (5) Marcia, maestoso, C ; (6) Rondo, E♭.

23. Six pieces : (1) Moderato, E♭ ; (2) Andantino con moto, C minor ; (3) Andante con variazioni, G ; (4) Masurik, C ; (5) Adagio, A ; (6) Rondo, E♭. 1809.
24. Eight pieces : (1) Moderato, D ; (2) Allegro, C ; (3) Adagio, F ; (4) Allegro, A minor ; (5) Alla Siciliana, D minor ; (6) Tema variato (Ich hab' mir eins erwählet, see V. 40), E ; (7) Marcia, G minor ; (8) Rondo, B♭. 1818–19.

XII. PIANOFORTE MUSIC WITH ACCOMPANIMENT

1. Nine variations on a Norwegian air ; D minor. PF. and violin. 1808.
2. Six Sonatas for PF. and violin : (1) F, Allegro, Romanze, Rondo amabile ; (2) G. Moderato, Adagio, Rondo allegro ; (3) D minor, Allegretto moderato, Rondo presto ; (4) E♭, Moderato, Rondo vivace ; (5) A. Andante con moto with variations, Finale Siciliano ; (6) C, Allegro con fuoco, Largo, Polacca. 1810.
3. Seven variations for PF. and clarinet ; B♭. 1811.
4. Grand Duo concertant for PF. and clarinet ; E♭. Allegro con fuoco. Andante con moto, Rondo allegro. 1816.
5. Divertimento assai facile for PF. and guitar ; (1) Andante, C ; (2) Valse, A minor ; (3) Andante con variazioni, G ; (4) Polacca, A major. 1816.

P. S.

BIBLIOGRAPHY

F. W. JÄHNS : *C. M. von Weber in seinen Werken* (Thematic catalogue of works). Berlin, 1871.
T. HELL : *Hinterlassene Schriften von C. M. von Weber.* 1828.
J. BENEDICT : *Weber* (Great Musicians). London, 1881.
G. KAISER : *Sämtliche Schriften von C. M. von Weber.* 1908.
C. RUDORFF : *Briefe Webers an H. Lichtenstein.* 1900.
G. KAISER : *Briefe v. Webers an den Grafen K. von Brühl.* 1911.
MAX VON WEBER : *C. M. von Weber, ein Lebensbild,* 3 vols. (1864–66). New edition by R. Pechel, 1912 ; trans. English by Palgrove.
L. KIRSCHBERG : *Die Kriegsmusik der deutschen Klassiker und Romantiker* (1919). Contains references to previously unknown works of Weber.
LUCIEN BOUEGUÈS and AL. DÉNÉREAZ : *La Musique et la vie intérieure.* Paris, 1921.
A. COEUROY : *Weber* (with a general bibliography). Paris, 1925.

WEBER, BERNHARD ANSELM (*b.* Mannheim, Apr. 18, 1766 ; *d.* Berlin, Mar. 23, 1821). He was a pupil of Abbé Vogler and Holzbauer, studied theology and law at Heidelberg about 1781. After touring for some time as a virtuoso on Röllig's *Xänorphika*,[1] he became, in 1787, musical director of Grossmann's theatrical company which played alternately at Hanover, Cassels and Pyrmont, and it was during that time that he produced his first works for the stage. In 1790 he joined Abbé Vogler in a tour through Holland, Scandinavia and Germany, continuing at the same time, under the latter, his studies in counterpoint. After a prolonged sojourn in Stockholm they returned to Hamburg, where Weber appeared with great success as pianoforte virtuoso. Thence he went to Berlin as Kapellmeister, conjointly with Wessely of the National theatre. In 1793 he was sent to Vienna to engage singers for the Berlin theatre, and it was then that he wrote the essay on the Vienna theatre and the singers of that town, for the *Berliner Musikzeitung* (1793, p. 131). In Vienna he became acquainted with Salieri, whose experiences with regard to the theatre were of great value to him. He also heard during that time some of Gluck's operas, and on his return to Berlin he used all his influence to have them performed there. This became only possible when he succeeded in inducing the famous Mme. Schick (STRINASACCHI *q.v.*) to exchange the Italian for the German Opera. She sang the title rôle in ' Iphigenia in Tauris,' the first of Gluck's operas given in Berlin under Weber's direction and conductorship, Feb. 24, 1795. In 1796 he refused an engagement for Rheinsberg, and henceforth his

[1] One of the many abortive attempts to construct a clavier instrument in which the tone is produced by friction, as in the hurdy-gurdy cf. SOSTINENTE PIANOFORTE.

salary in Berlin was raised to 1000 thaler. In 1800 he went on a concert tour to Breslau with the violinist Ernst Schick (*q.v.*) and his wife, and in 1803 he visited Paris with the famous dramatist Kotzebue. On the fusion of the Italian and the National Operas he became royal Kapellmeister, and in 1816 he was decorated with the iron cross on a white ribbon (non-combatant). In 1818 he was attacked by a serious malady which compelled him to withdraw gradually from his official duties. He was a prolific composer of operas, Singspiele, songs, etc. (List in Ledebur, *Tonkünstler Lexikon Berlins*, p. 627-28), but he lacked the qualities necessary to ensure their permanence. Some of his songs have retained their popularity, and the melodies to ' Mit dem Pfeil dem Bogen,' and ' Rasch tritt der Tod den Menschen an,' from his music to Schiller's *Tell*, first performed in Berlin, 1804, have even become folksongs. (Ledebur, *Berliner Tonkünstler Lexikon Q.-L.*)   E. V. D. S.

WEBER, Bernhard Christian, organist at Tennstedt, Thuringia, at the beginning of the 18th century, deserves mention as the composer of ' Das wohltemperirte Klavier,' a set of fugues with preludes in all keys major and minor, the MS. dated 1689 in the library of the Brussels Conservatoire. See *Monatshefte für Musikgeschichte*, 1898, No. 10, and 1899, No. 8 (*Riemann*).

WEBER, Franz (*b.* Cologne, Aug. 26, 1805 ; *d.* there, Sept. 18, 1876), pupil of Bernhard Klein, organist of Cologne Cathedral, and conductor of the Cologne Male Choir, which he raised to a high degree of efficiency and brought over to London for a very successful series of concerts. In 1875 he received the title of professor. He composed the 57th Psalm, 4 v., and choruses for male voices.   E. V. D. S.

WEBER, Friedrich Dionysus (*b.* Velichov, Bohemia, Oct. 9, 1766 ; *d.* Prague, Dec. 25, 1842), a pupil of Vogler (*q.v.*), composer and music teacher in Prague, was one of the founders and the first director of the Prague Conservatoire. When Wagner, as a young musician, visited Prague in 1832 with his symphony in C, Weber assembled the orchestra of the Conservatoire to give it a first hearing. His works include light operas, music for wind instruments, military band, etc., and several theoretic books. (See Weber, Carl Maria 12, p. 646.)

WEBER, Georg (*b.* Mühlhausen, Thuringia,[1] early 16th cent.), studied at Leipzig *c.* 1554, became cantor of Weissenfels in 1572. He was the greatest Weissenfels cantor before the Thirty Years' War, and composed German sacred songs and psalms (1588 ; 2nd ed., 1596) ; German Psalms of David, 4-6 v. (1568 and 1569).

Bibl. — A. Werner, *Städtische und fürstliche Musikpflege in Weissenfels* (1911) (*Mendel*; *Q.-L.*).

[1] Riemann says *b.* Weissenfels.

WEBER, Georg (*b.* Dahlen, near Meissen, 17th cent.), studied at Königsberg, Prussia, becoming vicar and succentor of Magdeburg cathedral. He was an excellent poet and composer, and wrote a number of books of sacred songs, 1-5 v. The first two books, with accompaniments for several instruments, published in 1640 and 1645 at Stockholm, where also the dedications are signed, show that he was living there at the time. Four books appeared in 1648 at Danzig, 3 at Königsberg, 1649 ; 3 melodies from these have been republished. Two other books appeared at Leipzig, 1652 and 1653 (*Q.-L.*).

WEBER, Gottfried (*b.* Freinsheim, near Mannheim, Mar. 1, 1779 ; *d.* Sept. 21, 1839), Doctor of Laws and Philosophy, composer, theorist and practical musician, studied and travelled until, in 1802, he settled in Mannheim as a lawyer and holder of a Government appointment.

It was here that his namesake, Carl Maria von Weber, sought a refuge after his banishment from Würtemberg (1810), that in the house of Gottfried's father an asylum was found for old Franz Anton until his death in 1812, and that a lasting friendship was formed between Gottfried Weber, then aged 31, and Carl Maria, eight years his junior. A year previously the lawyer, proficient on the piano, flute and violoncello, and well versed in the scientific branches of musical knowledge, had founded, out of two existing societies, the ' Museum,' a band and chorus of amateurs who, under his able direction and with some professional help, did excellent work. Gottfried's influence gained for the young composer a hearing in Mannheim, and the artists and amateurs, carried away by the spirit and fire of their conductor, did much towards establishing Carl Maria's fame in their city. For a lengthy account of the relations, both lively and severe, between these distinguished men, their influence on each other's work, their pleasant wanderings in company with other choice spirits, singing their newest songs to the guitar as serenades ; their establishment of a so-called secret society (with high aims) of composer-literati, in which Gottfried adopted the pseudonym of Giusto ; and of their merry meetings at the ' Drei Könige ' or at Gottfried's house—the reader may be referred to Max v. Weber's life of his father (Carl Maria). Some of Gottfried's best songs had been inspired by this intercourse, and were no doubt exquisitely interpreted by his (second) wife, *née* v. Dusch. Besides these songs, strophic in form and sometimes provided with guitar accompaniment, Weber's compositions include three masses, other sacred music, sonatas and concerted pieces for various instruments. He held various legal posts at Mainz from 1814, and at Darmstadt from 1818, and in 1832 was given

the title of ' Grossherzoglicher Generalstaats-
prokurator.'

In the intervals of founding the Mannheim
Conservatoire, superintending the court church
musical services, and doing occasional duty as
conductor at Mainz, he laid the basis of his
reputation by a profound study of the theory
of music, the result of which appeared in the
Versuch einer geordneten Theorie (1817–21), of
which translations subsequently appeared in
French, Danish and English (Warner, Boston,
1846, and J. Bishop, London, 1851) ; *Allgemeine Musiklehre* (1822) ; *Die Generalbasslehre
zum Selbstunterricht* (1833) ; *Ergebnisse der
bisherigen Forschungen über die Echtheit des
Mozartschens Requiems* (1826),[1] and other
volumes, and articles published in *Caecilia*, the
musical periodical published by Schott in
Mainz, and edited by Gottfried Weber from its
beginning in 1824 until his death (1839) (see
PERIODICALS). Weber's examination of musical theories led to his work on time-measure-
ments and the ' tempo - interpreter ' (*Über
chronometrische Tempobezeichnung*, 1817) (see
METRONOME), and his study of acoustics to
certain improvements or inventions in wind-
instrument making. A full list of his writings
and compositions is given in *Riemann* and *Q.-L.*
                                        L. M. M.

WEBER, JOHANNES (*b.* Brumath, Alsace,
Sept. 6, 1818 ; *d.* Paris, Mar. 19 or 20, 1902),
writer on music. He was secretary to Meyerbeer in Paris, and was musical critic of *Le
Temps* from 1861–95. He wrote *Grammaire
musicale*, and other theoretical books, *La
Situation musicale en France* (1884); *Meyerbeer,
notes et souvenirs d'un de ses secrétaires* (Paris,
1898) ; *Les Illusions musicales et la vérité sur
l'expression* (1899, 2nd ed.).   M. L. P.

WEBER, LUDWIG (*b.* Nüremberg, Oct. 13,
1891), composer, largely self - taught, has
brought out a symphony in B minor, ' Hymnen
an die Nacht,' a large work for choir and
orchestra, two string quartets, PF. music,
organ music, songs and a 1-act opera, 'Midas'
(*Riemann*).

WEBERN, ANTON VON (*b.* Vienna, Dec. 3,
1883), composer, became a research student
under Guido Adler and took his degree of Ph.D.
at Vienna University in 1906, the same year as
Carl Horwitz and two years before Egon
Wellesz. All three were pupils of Schönberg,
whose influence is shown in their works at
different periods, but Webern was the first, and
has remained the most loyal, adherent. Berg
and Webern were working with him at a critical
phase, when, according to Erwin Stein, ' they
actually experienced the absolute necessity
that gave birth to a new music, and could
therefore not help making Schönberg's style
their own.' Webern was for a time a theatrical

conductor. Apart from his first published work,
a Passacaglia for orchestra, op. 1, his compositions are mostly of small, not to say minute
dimensions, within which he seeks to concentrate the utmost intensity of expression,
though in subdued tones which have led the
writer quoted above to describe him as the
' composer of the pianissimo espressivo.' The
best-known example of this is the 'Five Movements ' for string quartet, op. 5, brief spells of
hypersensitive colour, which demand the most
patient and thorough rehearsal and pass in a
few moments. A characteristic example of his
latest development is the ' Geistliche Lieder '
for soprano with flute, clarinet, trumpet, harp
and double bass. His works are as follows :

Orchestral —' Passacaglia,' op 1. Six Pieces, op. 6. Five Pieces,
        op. 10.
Choral. —' Entflieht auf leichten Kähnen,' *a cappella*, op. 2.
String Quartets.—Five Movements, op. 5. Six Bagatelles, op. 9.
Other Chamber Music.—Four pieces for vln. and PF., op. 7. Three
        little pieces for vcl. and PF., op. 11.
Songs.—Opp. 3 and 4 with PF., opp. 8 and 13 with orch. and PF.,
        opp. 14, 15 and 16 ('Geistliche Lieder ') with various solo instr.
                                              E. E.

WEBER'S LAST WALTZ, see REISSIGER.
WECHSELNOTE, see NOTA CAMBITA.
WECKER, GEORG KASPAR (*b.* Nuremberg,
Apr. 2, 1632 ; *d.* there, Apr. 20, 1695). His
father, who had some ability as an instrumental
musician, gave him his first instruction in
clavier-playing. He received his further instruction in organ-playing and composition
generally from Erasmus Kindermann, then
organist to the Egidienkirche of Nuremberg.
At the age of 19 Wecker obtained his first appointment as organist to one of the Nuremberg
churches, and afterwards passing from one
church to another, at last in 1686 obtained the
highest post in Nuremberg, that of organist to
the Sebaldkirche, where he remained till his
death. He was in great request as a teacher,
and numbered among his pupils Johann Krieger
and Pachelbel. It was only at the urgent
request of his friend and pupil, W. M. Endter,
who was also his publisher, that in the last year
of his life he prepared for publication a work
with the following title :

XVIII Geistliche Concerten, mit 2 bis 4 Vocal-Stimmen und 5
instrumentis ad libitum, zu musiciren, auf die Heiligen Festtäge
des gantzen Jahres gerichtet samt etlichen anderen, so bei vorfälligen
Kirchensolennitäten zu gebrauchen. . . Nürnberg, 1695.

The publisher introduces the work with a
preface in which he gives directions as to
various ways of performance. These ' Spiritual
Concertos ' are in reality church cantatas, and
like similar works by Buxtehude and others,
show the form in its intermediate stage between
Heinrich Schütz and Sebastian Bach. They
begin with a short instrumental prelude entitled ' Sonatina,' and have similar interludes
entitled ' Ritornelli,' and short solo arias
between the choruses. Two of these cantatas
are given in *D.D.T.*, 2nd series, vi. i., which contain works of various Nuremberg masters of
the latter part of the 17th century. Another
from a MS. source on the hymn ' Allein Gott

---

[1] Weber's connexion with the controversy on Mozart's Requiem
is fully dealt with in Dr. W. Pole's *Story of Mozart's Requiem* (1879).

in der Höh' sei Ehr',' with a fuller complement of instruments, though with little use of the familiar tune, and evidently designed for a great festival occasion, is also given in the modern publication. Several 'Geistliche Lieder' by Wecker for one voice with basso continuo appeared in the Nuremberg hymn-books of the time. Only one short organ fugue of his composition has come down to us in MS. It is printed in Ritter's *Geschichte des Orgelspiels*, Ex. 79.   J. R. M.

WECKERLIN, JEAN BAPTISTE THÉODORE (b. Guebwiller, Alsace, Nov. 9, 1821; d. Trottberg, near Guebwiller, May 20, 1910), son of a manufacturer. So strong were his musical instincts, that though educated for trade, he ran away to Paris in 1843, and in 1844 entered the Conservatoire, where he learned harmony under Elwart, singing under Ponchard, and composition under Halévy. Not succeeding in the Conservatoire examinations, he left the school, and took to teaching and composition. Eager to produce, and very industrious, he let slip no opportunity of making himself known, and attempted all branches of composition, though soon finding that success at the theatre was out of the question, in spite of the fact that his one-act piece, 'L'Organiste dans l'embarras,' was performed at the Théâtre Lyrique one hundred times in 1853. Musical bibliography was his main resource, and he brought to light many curious old compositions, such as the 'Ballet comique de la Royne,' which was given with others of the same class, at the concerts of the Société de Sainte Cécile, of which he was chorus-master from 1850–1855.[1] He also made a fine collection of scarce books of poetry, with airs in notation, and song-writers, which he turned to account in his collections of national airs. In 1863 he was selected to form the library of the newly-founded Société des Compositeurs de Musique, of which he became archivist, and in 1869 was placed by Auber in the Library of the Conservatoire, of which he became head-librarian Sept. 9, 1876 — a post which he filled with success until 1905. His first composition of importance was performed at the Salle du Conservatoire, Paris, Dec. 5, 1847 ('Roland,' heroic scenes for solo, chorus and orchestra— not published).

His vocal and operatic works include 6 operas; 2 ode-symphonies; 2 antique dramas; a large number of choruses for female voices and for male do.; 6 'Quatuors de salon'; various extensive collections of pieces, and over 300 airs for voice and PF.; a Mass and sundry motets. His instrumental works comprise a symphony and suite, both for full orchestra; arrangements, etc.

His bibliographical works are as follows :
'Chansons populaires des provinces de la

[1] Beghers (1801–81) was conductor.

France' (1860), with Champfleury; 'Les Échos du temps passé,' 3 vols.; 'Les Échos d'Angleterre,' 1877; 'Album de la grand-maman,' twenty old melodies; 'Chansons et rondes pour les enfants' (1885); 'Chansons de France pour les petits Français' (1885): revised editions of 'Ballet comique de la Reine'; Cambert's operas 'Pomone' and 'Les Peines et les plaisirs de l'amour'; 'Le Bourgeois gentil-homme,' divertissements by Molière and Lully. Various articles in the 'Bulletin de la Société des Compositeurs'; 'Chansons populaires de l'Alsace,' 2 vols. (1883); and 'La Bibliothèque du Conservatoire de Musique,' 1 vol. 8vo (1885), a *catalogue raisonné* of the books in the Réserve. Books on French folk-song appeared in 1886, 1887, 1904, etc., and three series of *Musiciana* were published in 1877, 1890, and 1899.   G. C., with addns.

WECKMANN, MATTHIAS (b. ? Oppers-hausen,[2] Thuringia, 1621; d. Hamburg, 1674). At an early age he was received into the Electoral Chapel at Dresden as soprano singer, and enjoyed the instruction of Heinrich Schütz. On the recommendation of Schütz he was sent in 1637, at the expense of the Elector Johann Georg I., to receive further instruction in organ-playing and composition from Jacob Praetorius in Hamburg. After his return to Dresden in 1640 he was appointed organist to the Electoral Chapel, and had the further duty of training the choir boys. A visit of the Crown Prince of Denmark to Dresden was the occasion of Weckmann's being permitted to go for a time to serve as Kapellmeister to the Crown Prince at Nykjöbing in Denmark. He returned to his Dresden duties in 1647, but in 1654 the occasional friction between Germans and Italians in the Electoral Chapel induced him to apply for the vacant organistship of St. James's, Hamburg, which in 1655 the Elector permitted him to accept. With the exception of an occasional visit to Dresden, Weckmann remained at Hamburg for the rest of his life, living an exceptionally busy musical life till his death in 1674.

In conjunction with the other organists and musicians of the town, such as Scheidemann, Praetorius, Selle, Schop and Bernhard, and with the hearty support of all the citizens of highest social standing, he founded the Collegium Musicum, a musical society which gave frequent performances of the best and newest native and foreign music, vocal and instrumental, the beginning of the system of public concerts in Hamburg. As an organist and clavier-player generally, Weckmann enjoyed great reputation in his day. Mattheson gives an account of a trial of skill which took place at Dresden between Weckmann and Froberger, who parted from each other with

[2] Some doubt is thrown on the alleged place of birth, because his father, who was a Lutheran pastor, was not appointed to Oppers-hausen till 1628, and his name is not found in the baptismal register.

expressions of mutual respect, Froberger declaring his competitor to be a real virtuoso. None of Weckmann's works were printed in his lifetime, and only eight of his larger works for voices and instruments have been preserved. Five of them are due to the diligence with which Gustaf Düben, the Swedish Kapellmeister at Stockholm, collected the works of North German musicians for the use of his chapel, and these are now in the Royal library at Upsala. Düben made Weckmann's personal acquaintance at Hamburg in 1664, and was afterwards in correspondence with him. The other three works Weckmann took with him to Dresden in 1667 as a gift to the Elector Johann Georg II., and they are now in the library at Dresden. These eight works are all in the sacred concerto style of Heinrich Schütz, and have now been published in modern form in *D.D.T.* vi. Besides these, only a few choral-treatments for organ have been preserved, of which one now appears in Straube's ' Choral-Vorspiele alter Meister' (Peters).   J. R. M.

WEDDING OF CAMACHO, THE, see HOCHZEIT DES CAMACHO, DIE.

WEELKES, THOMAS (*d.* London, Nov. 30, 1623), is not heard of before 1597, when his book of 'Madrigals to 3. 4. 5. & 6. Voyces' was published. In the dedication of this book to George Phillpot (of Thruxton near Andover) Weelkes describes the contents as 'the first fruicts of my barren ground.' In 1598 he was in the service of Edward Darcye, Groom of the Privy Chamber, to whom he dedicated his 'Balletts and Madrigals, to fiue voyces.' As he speaks here of his 'yeeres yet unripened,' we may perhaps place his birth between 1570 and 1580. Two books appeared in 1600 ; the first, a set of 5-part madrigals, is dedicated to Henry, Lord Winsor, Baron of Bradenham. In this dedication he says, ' I confess my conscience is untouch with any other arts,' though other musicians try to be more than musicians ; ' this small faculty of mine is alone in me, and without the assistance of other more confident sciences.' The other volume of this year is a set of 6-part madrigals dedicated to George Brooke. Weelkes now describes himself as 'of the Colledge at Winchester, organist.' His name occurs only once in the College books in reference to the mending of the window of his room in College ; it also appears from the books that the organist's stipend in the years 1600–02 was 13s. 4d., with his daily commons and his lodging.

To 'The Triumphes of Oriana,' 1601, Weelkes contributed a 6-part madrigal, ' As Vesta was from Latmos,' one of the finest madrigals in the collection. He seems to have been on terms of intimacy with Morley, the editor of the collection, for on his death he composed a setting of a verse beginning ' Death hath deprived me of my dearest friend,' published

as ' A Remembrance of his friend, Thomas Morley' in the 'Ayeres or Phantasticke Spirites' of 1608. On July 13, 1602, Weelkes took his degree of Bachelor of Music at Oxford from New College. The entry in the University Register which records the granting of the grace (Feb. 12, 1601–02) mentions his sixteen years' study and practice of music. Soon afterwards he was appointed organist to Chichester Cathedral. The Chapter Records of Chichester have perished, but it is evident from the Subdeanery Registers that he was at Chichester with his family in 1603, for the baptism of Thomas Weelkes is entered there on June 9 ; another child ' Alles ' was baptized Sept. 17, 1606. In 1608 appeared his ' Ayeres or Phantasticke Spirites for three voices,' in which he describes himself as 'Gentleman of his Majesty's Chapel, Bachelor of Music, and Organist of the Cathedral Church of Chichester.' The name of Weelkes, however, is not to be found in the *Old Cheque Book of the Chapel Royal* (edited by Rimbault, 1872). He contributed two pieces to Leighton's ' Teares or Lamentacions,' 1614, —' Most mighty and all,' *a* 4, and ' O happy he,' *a* 5. Though these were his last publications it is probable that to this period of his life belong the numerous anthems which still for the most part remain in MS. ; one anthem at any rate bears the date Mar. 9, 1617 (' Deliver us, O Lord,' R.C.M.). The burial of ' Eliza: Welkes, the wyfe of Mr. Tho: Welkes, organist of the Cathedriall Church,' is entered in the Subdeanery Registers, Sept. 7, 1622.

G. E. P. A.

Weelkes died, while on a visit to London, at the house of his friend Henry Drinkwater, in the parish of St. Bride's, Fleet Street. His will is dated Nov. 30, 1623, and the registers of St. Bride's show that he was buried there on Dec. 1 ; these facts point to his having died on Nov. 30. His will was proved on Dec. 5 in the Dean's Peculiar Court at Chichester (vol. iii. fo. 174) and is printed in full in Arkwright's OLD ENGLISH EDITION, Part xiii., Preface. He made Drinkwater his executor, and left legacies to his children Thomas, Katherine and Alice.

On the occasion of his tercentenary commemorations in 1923 memorial tablets were placed on the walls of St. Bride's Church, the Cloisters of Winchester College, and the North Transept of Chichester Cathedral.

Weelkes's Madrigals (1597) were reprinted by the Mus. Ant. Society in 1843. The Ballets and Madrigals (1598) and the ' Ayeres or Phantasticke Spirites (1608) were reprinted in Arkwright's OLD ENGLISH EDITION. These three, together with the two sets of madrigals (1600), were reprinted in Fellowes's ENG. MAD. SCH. (vols. ix.-xiii.).[1] ' Ay me, my wonted joys.' from the 1597 set, was printed in Sessa

---

[1] See *Mus. Ass. Proc.*, 1916, paper by E. H. Fellowes ; and *Eng. Madr. Composers.*

d'Aranda's ' Il primo libro de madrigali a quattro voci, con uno di Thomas Weelkes Inglese, Elmstat 1605.' A second edition of the ballets (1598) appeared in 1608.

As a madrigal-writer Weelkes holds very high rank; indeed, some regard him as the greatest of all madrigalists, although others would prefer the claims of the great stylist WILBYE (*q.v.*). Weelkes showed his genius especially in his daring use of what in his time were novel harmonies, as well as in the fertility of his imagination, which gave colour to the expression of ideas and even to single words and phrases. This aspect of his work is to be seen at its best in his wonderful madrigal, ' O Care, thou wilt despatch me,' or in the very expressive three-part work, ' Cease, sorrows, now.' But it is a mistake to affect to see the true Weelkes only in his more highly coloured chromatic work; he was as well able as any of his contemporaries to build up broad and massive effects with the conventional limitations of simple harmony. Examples of such writing are ' Like two proud armies ' or ' Mars in a fury.' In contrast to these is the exquisite delicacy of ' On the plains fairy trains.' As a writer of ballets he was at least the equal of Morley, and no higher praise is possible, while his ' Ayeres or Phantasticke Spirites ' show him in yet another light, that of a witty satirist.

A few additional madrigals survive in MS. Among these the ballet ' Grace, my lovely one,' was recently printed under the editorship of W. Barclay Squire.

Weelkes wrote a large amount of church music. As many as ten of his Services have survived in fragments, but unfortunately not one of them is complete; indeed, only the simple four-voice Service, which is quite devoid of individuality, can be satisfactorily reconstructed, and the alto part of that is missing. This is the more to be regretted because the material that does exist clearly shows that Weelkes was remarkably original in developing the form of the SERVICE (*q.v.*), and in employing various devices for giving variety and interest to this class of composition. Verse passages with independent organ accompaniment are introduced, and various antiphonal effects are devised such as are found in the work of few other composers of his time.

Thomas Tomkins alone followed him in extending the conventional scope of the Cathedral service. This is all the more remarkable when it is recalled that for nearly two centuries after the death of Weelkes English church musicians, with scarcely any exception, followed the old conventional form of the ' short ' service of Tudor days as defined by Cranmer.

The ' full ' sections of the Service ' for two trebles ' can easily be put together from the available material, and this Service would be a very valuable addition to the Cathedral repertory if only it could be completed. One of the two treble parts and the organ part are available, but it is difficult if not impossible to surmise the composer's intention as to these sections, and the verse parts may not all have been limited to two trebles. The meaning of the term ' in medio chori ' in No. 5 of these Services has been lost; the direction occurs in contrast to sections marked ' Verse ' or ' Full.' Possibly it may mean the trebles alone singing in chorus, but this is a mere conjecture.

SERVICES

1. ' 1st Service for Verses to the organs in gam ut.' T.D., K., C.: Tenb. 791 fo. 407v (organ); M., N.D.: Tenb. 791 fo. 411 (organ).
2. ' 2nd Service with verses to the organs in D sol re.' T.D., B., K., C.: Tenb. 791 fo. 412v (organ); M., N.D.; Tenb. 791 fo. 134v.
3. M., N.D. ' with verses to the organ in F fa ut ': Tenb. 791 fo. 416 (organ).
4. Service of 5 parts ' for two trebles.' T.D.: Tenb. 791 fo. 403v (organ); M., N.D.: Tenb. 791; Durh. A fo. 54 (organ); Durh. Cl fo. 185; PH. 34 fo. 51 (Medius); PH. 39 fo. 41v; fo. 57v (Altus); Durh. C13 fo. 104 rev (Tenor); Durh. C18 fo. 75; PH. 33 fo. 45v; 38 fo. 53 (Bass).
5. M., N.D. ' in medio chori ': Tenb. 791 fo. 400v (organ).
6. T.D., M. ' with verses for a meane.' T.D.: Wimb. Alto fo. 25, Tenor fo. 36, Bass fo. 11. Mag.: Wimb. Tenor fo. 90 Bass fo. 32v and fo. 39v.
7. M., N.D. ' in verse for 2 contratenors.' Wimb Alto fo. 63, Tenor fo. 83, Bass fo. 28.
8. V., T.D., J., M., N.D. ' of 4 parts.' V.: B.M. Add. MSS. 29,289. T.D., J.: Durh. A6 fo. 324 (organ); B.M. Add. MSS. 29,289 (Alto); Durh. C13 fo. 145 (Tenor); M., N.D.: PH. 45 fo. 114 (Medius); Durh. C13; PH. 43 fo. R5 (Tenor); PH. 36 fo. R5 (Bass); Ch. Ch. 437 (organ). Score of V., T.D., and J.: B.M. Roy. Lib. Cosyn. MS.
9. T.D., J., M., N.D., ' Mr. Weelkes' 5 parts ': T.D., J.: Tenb. 791 fo. 336 (organ); M., N.D.: Tenb. 791 fo. 132.
10. M., N.D. ' of 7 parts ': Durh. Cl fo. 308; PH. 34 fo. 53 (Medius); PH. 39 fo. 60 (1st Alto); PH. 39 fo. 43 (2nd Alto); Durh. C15 fo. 80; PH. 38 fo. 54v (1st Bass); PH. 33 fo. 46 (2nd Bass).

Weelkes has left a large number of anthems, but as an anthem writer his work seems to show some inequality. The greater number of his anthems have not as yet been scored, and it is not possible, for this reason, to judge accurately of their value as a whole. Yet nothing could be more splendid than his noble ' Hosanna to the Son of David '; and almost equally fine is the Christmas anthem ' Gloria in excelsis . . . Sing, my soul.' In contrast to these is the tender little Collect, ' Let thy merciful ears.' The following anthems by Weelkes have been printed : ' O Lord, grant the king,' by Barnard in 1641 ; ' All people clap your hands ' and ' When David heard ' (both edited by Rimbault), by the Mus. Ant. Society ; ' Hosanna,' ' Gloria in excelsis . . . Sing, my soul ' and, ' Let Thy merciful ears ' (ed. by Fellowes) and ' Alleluia, Salvation ' (ed. by S. T. Warner), in the Tudor Church Music Series.

The instrumental works of Weelkes include :

A set of pieces for 5 viols (R.C.M.). 2 Pavans and one other piece for 5 viols (B.M. Add. MSS. 17,786-91 and 17,792-6). 2 In Nomines *a* 5 (Bodl. MS. Mus. Sch. c64-69. These last with another In Nomine *a* 4 (Bodl. MS. Mus. Sch. d212-6. Lacrimæ *a* 5 (B.M. Add. MSS. 30,480-4)

ANTHEMS

All laud and praise. R.C.M.; Tenb. 791 fo. 74 and fo. 419v.
All people clap your hands. Rimbault, Mus. Ant. Soc., 1843.
Alleluia, I heard a voice. B.M. Add. MSS. 29,372-7; Ch. Ch. 56-60.
An earthly tree. Tenb. 791 fo. 421v.
Behold how good and joyful. Rimbault, Mus. Ant. Soc., 1843.
Behold, O God our defender. Durh. C7.
Behold, O Israel. Rimbault, Mus. Ant. Soc., 1843.
Blessed be the man. Tenb. 791 fo. 415.
Blessed is he. Tenb. 791 fo. 409.
Christ rising. Tenb. 791 fo. 418.
Deal bountifully. Tenb. 791 fo. 354.
Deliver us, O Lord. R.C.M.
Give ar, O Lord. Tenb. 791 fo. 54; B.M. Add. MSS. 29,372-7.
Give one King thy judgements. B.M. Add. MSS. 30,478-9; R.C.M.; Durh.; Tenb. 791 fo. 63.

Gloria in excelsis. Sing, O my soul. B.M. Add. MSS. 17,786-91;
 Ch. Ch. 56-60 ; Tenb. 807-11.
Hosanna to the Son. B.M. Add. MSS. 17,786-91 ; Tenb. 807-11,
 295 ; Ch. Ch. 56-60.
I lift my heart. R.C.M. 1051.
I love the Lord. Tenb. 791 fo. 424.
If King Manasses. R.C.M. ; Tenb. 791 fo. 64v.
If ye be risen again. Tenb. 791 fo. 430.
In Thee, O Lord. Tenb. 791 fo. 427 ; Durh.
Laborari. Tenb. 807-11.
Let Thy merciful ears. PH. 36, 43 and 45.
Let us lift up our eyes. Clifford, 1664 (words only).
Lord, to Thee I make my moan. Ch. Ch. 56-60 ; R.C.M.
Most mighty and all-knowing. B.M. Add. MSS. 31,418.
O happy be. B.M. Add. MSS. 29,372-7.
O how amiable. Durh. ; PH.
O Jonathan. B.M. Add. MSS. 29,372-7 ; Ch. Ch. 56-60 ; Tenb.
 1162-7.
O Lord, arise. B.M. Add. MSS. 17,786-91, 17,792-6 ; R.C.M.
O Lord God Almighty. Ch. Ch. 1220-4, 1001.
O Lord, grant the king. Barnard ; B.M. Add. MSS. 30,478-9 ;
 R.C.M. ; Ely ; Ch. Ch. 1001.
O Lord, how joyful is the King. B.M. Add. MSS. 30,478-9 ; Durh.
O Lord, preserve Thee. Rimbault, Mus. Ant. Soc., 1843.
O Lord, rebuke me not. Rimbault, Mus. Ant. Soc., 1843.
O Lord, turn not away. Tenb. 791 fo. 420.
O mortal man. R.C.M.
Plead Thou my cause. R.C.M.
Rejoice in the Lord (mentioned by Bumpus, organ part only).
Sing unto the Lord. Clifford, 1663 and 1664 (words only).
 successive course. B.M. Add. MSS. 30,478-9.
Thy mercies great. Clifford, 1664 (words only).
What, by so true. R.C.M. ; Tenb. 791 fo. 423.
When David heard. B.M. Add. MSS. 29,372-7 ; Tenb. 807-11,
 1162-7 ; Ch. Ch. 56-60.
With all our hearts (mentioned by Bumpus), bass only.

E. H. F.

WEERBECKE (VEERBECKE DI FIANDRA ;
WARBECK), GASPAR (GASPARD, JASPER)
(b. Audenaerde, Flanders, c. 1440), educated
at the maîtrise at Audenaerde. G. Crespel,
in his lament on Okeghem's death, enumerates
Weerbecke among the latter's pupils. On his
compositions he generally signed himself
merely Gaspard. We meet him first under
the name of Gaspare de Alemania as rectore
de la ducale at St. Gothard, where he appears
also as custodian of the watch in 1469. In
1472 and 1474 he is mentioned as maestro di
cappella at Milan Cathedral, and in the former
year (in letters) also as a singer at the ducal
court of Milan. The letters describe him as a
cleric of Tournay. He must, therefore, have
taken holy orders before he went to Italy. In
1475 the duke sent him to Picardy and Flanders
to engage singers for his court, and in 1480 he
was prebendary of St. Donat, Bruges, probably
an honorary sinecure. From Oct. 1481 to
Apr. 1489 he was singer in the Papal Chapel.
At the marriage of Galeas Sforza to Isabella of
Arragon in 1488, allegorical-mythological plays
and interludes were performed at the court of
Milan, looked upon by Arteaga as the origin of
musical drama. To these Weerbecke contributed at least part of the music, and probably
took part in them also as organiser and singer.
In 1490 he revisited Audenaerde, where he
was received on Nov. 14 with great rejoicings
by the citizens and council, who presented him
with four stoups of wine. On Aug. 18, 1498,
he was again furnished with letters patent
from the duke to engage singers from abroad
for the court. Van der Straeten (Musiciens
aux Pays-Bas, p. 36) states that on Mar. 12,
1536, he conducted a choir of 24 singers at the
investiture of Pierre Aaron at Bergamo. The
date appears rather late for Weerbecke.
Petrucci published between 1505 and 1509 a

number of Weerbecke's masses, motets and
lamentations. A Stabat Mater is contained
in a magnificently decorated MS. volume of
1490. Some masses of his in MS. are in the
Papal Chapel library (Motta ; van der Straeten ;
Q.-L.).   E. v. d. s.

WEGELER, FRANZ GERHARD (b. Bonn,
Aug. 22, 1765 ; d. Coblenz, May 7, 1848), professor of medicine at Bonn University at the
age of 19. After the dissolution of the University in 1794, he became rector, and afterwards
general practitioner at Coblenz. Wegeler and
Beethoven were friends from their youth. The
former married Eleonore von Breuning, and
published, together with Ferdinand Ries,
Biographical Notes on Ludwig van Beethoven
(1838, etc., several editions in various languages)
(see BEETHOVEN, Vol. I., p. 310).

WEHLI (WEHLE), KARL (b. Mar. 17, 1825 ;
d. Paris, June 3, 1883), a brilliant pianist, was
the son of a merchant in Prague, learned the
PF. under Moscheles and Kullak, composed
very much, and exhibited his talent in Europe,
America, Australia, India, etc. Paris was for
long his headquarters. The list of his works
given by Pougin comprises a Sonata (op. 38),
Impromptus (10, 73), Ballades (11, 79), Nocturnes, Waltzes and Allegro hongroise (81),
etc. etc.   G.

WEICHENBERGER, JOHANN GEORG, of
Vienna, a 17th-century lutenist, mentioned by
Baron. Of two 17th-century MS. lute-books
in French tablature in the Benedictine monastery of Raigern, one, containing a 'Lauthen
Concert,' bears his name and place of residence,
the other contains some pieces by him, and
another MS. book of the same period, also in
French lute-tablature, at Kremsmünster, contains pieces by Du Faut, Lauffensteiner and
W . . . (Weichenberger ?). Breitkopf's MS.
Catalogue contains a Partita a liuto solo by
him (Q.-L.).

WEICHMANN (WICHMANN), JOHANN
(b. Wolgast, Pomerania, Jan. 9, 1620 ;
d. Königsberg, Prussia, July 24, 1652), visited
the school at Hameln, studied music and
science at Danzig, and, after returning for a
time to Königsberg, became cantor and organist
at Wehlau, where he was in 1643. In 1647 he
was appointed cantor and director of the choir
at the Altstadt (old town) of Königsberg. He
composed several books of motets, sacred and
secular songs, two books of ballets, courants,
allemands and sarabands in 2 parts (1649).

E. v. d. s.

WEICHSELL, MRS., a popular vocalist,
mother of Mrs. Billington, and wife of Carl
Weichsell, a German, who was principal oboist
of the King's Theatre in the Haymarket, and
appeared in public as a clarinet-player in 1763.[1]
Mrs. Weichsell became a popular ballad-singer
at Vauxhall as early as 1766, three years

[1] Pohl, ii. 373.

earlier than generally supposed. She continued singing at Vauxhall until 1784. Besides her daughter Elizabeth, who became Mrs. BILLINGTON, she had a son, Charles, who was a talented violinist and led the band at the King's Theatre, occasionally conducting at Covent Garden when his sister was singing there.   F. K.

WEIDEMAN, CHARLES (or CHARLES FREDERICK), a popular composer and flute-player during the middle of the 18th century. Burney says he came over to England about 1726, and that he was long the principal solo-player on the German flute. Further, that he was a good musician, but his productions never ' rose above that mediocrity to which his instrument seems confined.' Scattered through many 18th-century works such as : ' The Delightful Pocket Companion for the German Flute ' (John Simpson, *circa* 1740–45) are numbers of airs of the Minuet and Gavotte type of his composition. Walsh published some concertos in 7 or 8 parts for flutes and violins by him, and Bremner issued duets, trios, and quartets for flutes. There are also some vocal compositions by him.

It was Weideman who, with Festing, first conceived the idea of a musical benevolent society, which ultimately took form as the ROYAL SOCIETY OF MUSICIANS (*q.v.*). Weideman's name is on the deed of trust dated 1739. He was conductor of the King's Band of Musick in 1778 at a salary of £100 yearly. Burney and others spelt his name incorrectly. His own signature and all contemporary publications of his works spell it as in the heading of this article.   F. K.

WEIDEMANN, KARL FRIEDRICH (*d.* London, 1782), a celebrated flautist and prolific composer, came to London in 1726. He wrote 6 concertos in 7 parts, op. 2, 6 concertos in 8 parts, several books of flute sonatas, duets, solos, also some songs for Vauxhall Gardens, etc. He was for many years the greatest soloist on his instrument who appeared at the concerts at Hickford's Room and the Swan and Castle concerts in the City. Burney describes him as a good musician but a mediocre composer.
                                              E. V. D. S.

WEIGL, JOHANN BAPTIST (*b.* Hahnenbach, Bavaria, Mar. 26, 1783), church composer and organist. He studied at Amberg, and Preising, near Ratisbon ; became organist at Amberg, and in 1805 pastor and teacher at St. Ulrich, Ratisbon. Soon after, he returned to Amberg as professor at the college (gymnasium). His masses, cantatas, Te Deum, offertories and other sacred music, as well as his canons, songs, etc., are spoken of in terms of praise (Schilling ; Mendel).

WEIGL, (1) JOSEPH (*b.* Bavaria, Mar. 19, 1740 ; *d.* Jan. 25, 1820), entered Prince Esterhazy's band at Eisenstadt as first violon-

cellist in 1761, left in 1769 for the orchestra of the Imperial Opera at Vienna, and was admitted member of the Imperial Chapel, 1792. He was a great friend of Joseph Haydn, who stood godfather to his eldest son.

(2) JOSEPH (*b.* Eisenstadt, Mar. 28, 1766 ; *d.* Feb. 3, 1846). Joseph's first teacher was Sebastian Witzig, choirmaster of Korneuburg, and later he studied with Albrechtsberger and Salieri. At 16 he wrote his first small opera, ' Die betrogene Arglist,' which was produced at Gluck's recommendation, and secured him the favour of the Emperor Joseph, of which he had henceforth repeated proofs, including a present of 100 ducats (about £50) for his first Italian opera ' Il pazzo per forza ' (1788). A letter of congratulation written him by Haydn on the production of his ' Principessa d' Amalfi ' is well known. Weigl was also fortunate enough to gain admittance to the performances of classical music under Mozart's direction, at Baron van Swieten's house. Salieri took a special interest in him, and employed him up to 1790 as assistant-conductor of the National Court Theatre. In 1792 he became composer to the Opera with a salary of 1000 florins, then Kapellmeister, finally conductor. This post he resigned in 1823, and in 1827 was appointed vice-court Kapellmeister. Before that date he had composed a series of operas, German and Italian, and ballets, many of which became exceedingly popular. Amongst these, special mention must be made of the ' Schweizerfamilie ' (1809), which long kept the boards, and by its pleasing melodies won all hearts. Reichardt [1] gives a pointed description of Weigl :

' He is a really charming, affectionate, good-hearted Viennese, and his eye and whole expression are thoroughly in keeping with his tender, graceful, pleasing melodies.'

Other favourite operas were ' Das Waisenhaus,' ' Nachtigall und Rabe ' (1818), ' Der Bergsturz,' ' L' Amor marinaro' (1797), and ' L' Uniforme.' Beethoven has preserved the air ' Pria ch' io impegno ' in the ' Amor marinaro ' from oblivion, by taking it as the theme for the finale of his clarinet trio, op. 11. (See BEETHOVEN, Vol. I. p. 277.) ' L' Uniforme ' (libretto by Carpani) was composed at the request of Maria Theresa, produced at Schönbrunn (in 1798), and repeated in concert-form (1805) with the Empress in the principal part (Pauline). Treitschke translated it into German, and ' Die Uniforme ' was given at both court theatres, and in many foreign towns. Weigl was a special favourite of the Empress (to whom Beethoven dedicated his Septet), and had to preside at the piano at all chamber-concerts, besides composing cantatas and small ballets for many court festivities. He had an advantageous offer for Stuttgart, but the

Empress, to retain him, made his appointment for life. Soon after her death (1807) he accepted the post of Kapellmeister at Dresden, but the negotiations were broken off, and Morlacchi was appointed in his stead.[1] Weigl was twice invited to Milan to compose for La Scala—in 1807, when he produced two operas, 'Cleopatra' and 'Il rivale di sè stesso,' and 1815, when he produced 'L' imboscata,' and a cantata, 'Il ritorno d'Astrea,' all with great success. Of his earlier cantatas, 'Minerva e Flora' was given at Prince Auersperg's in honour of a visit from the King and Queen of Sicily (1791), and 'Venere ed Adone' at Esterhaz in 1792, when the Archduke (afterwards Emperor) Joseph was staying with Prince Esterhazy at his country seat on the Neusiedlersee. Haydn was at the time in London, so Weigl was called upon to supply his place. This cantata figured several times in the programmes of the Tonkünstler-Societät concerts. Of his two oratorios, 'La Passione di Gesù Cristo' (libretto by Carpani), first produced at Court (1804), was performed at Prince Lobkowitz's, at the Burg Theatre (1811), at an extra concert of the Gesellschaft der Musikfreunde (1821), and in Prague and Milan. After 1827 he wrote only for the church, composing his last Mass in his seventy-first year. Weigl received many distinctions, amongst others the large gold Ehrenmedaille (1839) and the freedom of the city of Vienna. He was an honorary member of the Conservatoire of Milan, the St. Cecilia Academy of Rome, the Gesellschaft der Musikfreunde, and other musical societies of Austria. His works include 13 Italian and 18 German operas, 17 ballets, 2 oratorios, 12 Italian and 7 German cantatas, 9 masses, 6 graduales, 6 offertoires ; scenas in various languages ; airs for insertion in operas ; songs, airs and duets with PF. accompaniment ; and various instrumental pieces. (See list in Q.-L.) His younger brother,

(3) THADDÄUS (b. 1776), wrote a number of operas and ballets for the Leopoldstadt Theatre and the two court theatres, and was at one time Kapellmeister and director of the musical archives of the court theatre. His name lives, however, not as a musician, but as a music publisher. He set up in business in 1801, and devoted himself chiefly to supporting the Kunst- und Industrie-Comptoir in its endeavour to establish a home trade in music, for which Haydn gave him a flattering testimonial (dated Eisenstadt, 1801). After the production of his last ballet, 'Bacchus und Ariadne' (Dec. 1803), he withdrew from the theatre, and occupied himself entirely with his business till 1826, when he resigned it to his second son Peter. Later it passed into Diabelli's hands. Thaddäus Weigl published Schubert's opp. 57, 58, 88, 95 and 130.　　　　　　　　C. F. P.

[1] A letter from Griesinger, dated Dresden, Feb. 11, 1810.

WEILAND, JOHANN JULIUS (d. Brunswick, Apr. 2, 1663), appointed court musician at Brunswick, Mar. 5, 1655, was vice-Kapellmeister in 1655, but in 1661 he calls himself simply musician. He wrote psalms and songs in 4 to 10 parts, with and without instruments ; also 'Uns ist ein Kind geboren,' in 13 parts, divided into 3 choirs (Wolfenbüttel, 1/1/1663) (Q.-L.).

WEIMAR. The 'German Athens' under the patronage of its art-loving Grand Dukes of Saxe-Weimar-Eisenach, had a long musical history, the record of its court orchestra going back to the 16th century. J. S. Bach was a violinist there in 1703 and director of music in 1708. Johann Gottfried Walther was organist at the great church of Weimar from 1707–48. Hummel was Hofkapellmeister from 1819–37.

Perhaps because the greater attention was paid to poetry and the drama in the period of Weimar's greatness (the end of the 18th and beginning of the 19th centuries) its most brilliant era of music came later. This was in the years between 1847 and 1861, when Liszt settled there as chief Kapellmeister and gathered round him the group which included Hans von Bülow, Cornelius, Raff and (for a time) Joachim. Liszt had produced Berlioz's 'Benvenuto Cellini,' which apparently gave an impetus to the new German movement of which Cornelius became the leading spirit under Liszt, and the Neue Zeitschrift für Musik (see BRENDEL) its organ of expression. Liszt produced Cornelius's 'Barbier von Bagdad' on December 15, 1858. Liszt was succeeded by Eduard Lassen, during whose term of office Saint-Saëns's 'Samson et Delila' was first produced. In more recent times the most noteworthy production has been Humperdinck's 'Hansel und Gretel,' first given on Dec. 23, 1893, at Weimar.

The present opera house, formerly Hoftheater, now Deutsches Nationaltheater, was built in 1907 from plans by M. Littmann, and was opened in the following year. The present general music director is Dr. Praetorius, with E. Latzko and Ferdinand Hertz as Kapellmeister. The theatre receives a subvention from the Thuringian state. The principal orchestra, the Weimarer Staatskapelle (Prof. R. Reitz), serves the double purpose of opera and symphony orchestra. It numbers fifty-three performers. There are two other orchestras in Weimar—the Professional Orchestra (Peters) and the Orchesterverein (B. Branco). The Gesellschaft für Musikfreunde (President Dr. Gumprecht) organises regular concerts during the season. Weimar has frequently been the scene of musical festivals, one of the more important of late years being the Tonkünstlerfest of 1921, when Schönberg's 'Four pieces for Orchestra' was produced. The Deutsche Festspiele, the purpose of which is to promote the performance of German operas, took place at Weimar in July 1926. The principal choirs are the Volkschor (Pretorius) and the Kirchenchor St. Jakob (C. Thiem).

The Staatliche Musikschule zu Weimar (with its renowned orchestral school) is under the control of the Thuringian Ministry of Education. It was founded in 1872 and is intended to form an educational background to the Nationaltheater. The present director is Professor Bruno Hinze-Reinhold, who has a staff of about thirty teachers. The associations of Liszt with Weimar are preserved in the Liszt Museum (Prof. R. Wetz) and those of Max Reger in the Reger Archiv (F. Martin).

H. G. D.

WEIMAR, GEORG PETER (b. Stotternheim, Saxe Weimar, Dec. 16, 1734; d. Erfurt, Dec. 19, 1800), pupil of Adlung, Fasch and Höck (violin). He was chamber-musician and court cantor at Zerbst in 1758; cantor at Kaufmannskirche, Erfurt, 1763, and, in addition, music director at the *Gymnasium* in 1774, and from 1776 also at the Catholic *Gymnasium*. He wrote an operetta with pianoforte; cantatas; motets; vocal exercises for schools; a book of Chorals for the Protestant church was edited by Joh. Chr. Kittel in 1803; a number of church compositions, including a Passion, remained in MS. (*Mendel*; *Q.-L.*).

WEINER, LEO (b. Budapest, Apr. 16, 1885), has made a name for himself by the enterprising nature of his chamber music. His string quartet in F sharp minor (op. 13) won the Coolidge Prize in 1921, and has been much played abroad by the Budapest String Quartet.

Weiner studied (1901–06) at the Landesakademie in Budapest, and afterwards joined its teaching staff. Among his published works are a serenade for orchestra (op. 3), a string quartet (op. 4), 'Fasching,' humoreske for orchestra (op. 5), string trio (op. 6), piano pieces, etc. (*Riemann.*)

WEINGARTNER (PAUL), FELIX (Edler von Münzberg) (b. Zara, Dalmatia, June 2, 1863), eminent conductor, composer and writer of important literary works on musical subjects, studied composition at Graz under W. A. Remy, and entered the university of Leipzig in 1881 as a student of philosophy.

He passed over very soon to the Conservatorium, went to Liszt at Weimar in 1883, and there his first opera, 'Sakuntala,' was brought out in 1884, in which year he undertook the post of Kapellmeister at Königsberg; in 1885–87 he was in the same capacity at Danzig, in 1887–89 at Hamburg, and in 1889–91 at Mannheim. In the latter year he was appointed court Kapellmeister of the Opera at Berlin, as well as director of symphony concerts of the royal band. Here he remained until 1898, when the opposition of old-fashioned musicians to his operatic conduct-

ing induced him to give up the theatrical appointment, though he kept that of the orchestral concerts. He went to live at Munich in that year and became conductor of the Kaim concerts there. In 1907 he was appointed to succeed Mahler as conductor of the Hofoper at Vienna, and was thus compelled to give up the Berlin concerts. He entered on his duties in Jan. 1908, but retired from the Opera in 1910, retaining the conductorship of the symphony concerts of the Opera orchestra. In 1919–20 he was director of the Vienna Volksoper. Other appointments which he occupied in these years were those of Kapellmeister of the Hamburg Stadt-theatre (1912–14) and general Musikdirector of the Grand Ducal concerts at Darmstadt (1914).

Meantime his international reputation as a conductor was built up by innumerable visits to other countries of Europe and to America. He first visited London in May 1898, when his quiet mastery of the orchestra and his sane readings of the classics made a profound impression. Since then he has been a frequent visitor, and his performances with the ROYAL PHILHARMONIC SOCIETY, the LONDON SYMPHONY ORCHESTRA and the SCOTTISH ORCHESTRA have confirmed the impression, especially as regards the symphonies of Beethoven. In 1905 he conducted four concerts of the New York Philharmonic Society, made a tour with the Symphony Society (see NEW YORK) in 1906, and in 1912–13 conducted opera at Boston.

Weingartner's literary works, beginning with the famous pamphlet *Über das Dirigiren* (1895) (see CONDUCTING), are largely concerned with matters of performance and artistic interpretation. His power of applying an intellectual analysis to the processes of artistic intuition has given him his commanding position among the musical interpreters of his generation. Despite the preoccupations of his busy executive life, which has included much musical editing, notably of the collected edition of Berlioz, he has continued to compose and has produced works on a large scale both for the stage and the concert room, such as the dramatic trilogy from Æschylus on the one hand, and five symphonies for orchestra on the other. He has been described as an eclectic [1] among composers, which means that a mind steeped in the work of all the great masters commands too many tools for its own individual work. Weingartner's compositions have every virtue comprised in the word 'musicianship,' and sometimes rise to the distinction which lies beyond technical accomplishment. His early songs, such as 'Motten' (op. 25), 'Plauderwäsche' (op. 27) and the three 'Handwerkerlieder' (op. 28) first showed his qualities to English hearers.

The following is a summary of Weingartner's principal works.

[1] *Riemann.*

Sakuntala. (Weimar, 1884.)
Malawika. (Munich, 1886.)
Genesius. (Berlin, 1892.)
Trilogy after the *Oresteia* of Aeschylus. (Athens, 1925.)
' Agamemnon.'
' Das Totenopfer.'
' Die Erinnyen.' (Leipzig, 1902.)
' Kain und Abel.' (Darmstadt, 1914.)
' Die Dame Kobold.' (Darmstadt, 1916.)
Incidental music to the *Antigone* of Sophocles.
    „   „   Voss's *Frühlingsmärchenspiel*. (Weimar, 1908.)
    „   „   *Faust* (Pts. I. and II.). (Weimar, 1908.)

Symphonies : No. 1 in G (op. 23) ; No. 2 in E flat (op. 29) ; No. 3
    in E (op. 49) ; No. 4 in F ; No. 5 in C minor (op. 71).
Symphonic Poems : ' König Lear ' (op. 20) ; ' Das Gefilde der
    Seligen,' (op. 21).
Violin concerto in G (op. 53).
' Lüstige Ouvertüre.'
' Aus schwerer Zeit ' (overture). Vienna, 1914.
Serenade for stringed orchestra.
Arrangement for orch. of Weber's ' Invitation à la valse.'

String quartets : op. 24 in D minor ; op. 26 in F minor; op. 34 in F.
String quintet, op. 40 in C.
Quintet. Clar., PF. and strings. Op. 50 in G minor.
Sextet. PF. and strings. Op. 33 in E minor.
Two sonatas. Vln. and PF. Op. 42 in D and F sharp minor.
Pianoforte pieces, opp. 1-5.

' Traumnacht,' ' Sturmhymnus.' 8-part choir.
Three male choruses.
Songs with orchestra, opp. 12, 35, 36, 39.
Songs with PF. (in sets), opp. 13, 15, 16, 17, 18, 19, 22, 25, 27, 28,
    31, 32, 37, 41, 45, 46, 47, 48, 51. (For further details see *Baker*.)

Die Lehre von der Wiedergeburt und das musikalische Drama. 1895.
Über das Dirigiren. 1895, fourth ed. 1913.
Bayreuth, 1876–96. 1896, rev. ed. 1904.
Die Symphonie nach Peethoven. 1897, rev. ed. 1909. (Trans.
    French, C. Chevillard ; English, M. B. Dutton, 1904.)
Ratschläge für Aufführungen der Sinfonien Beethovens. 1906. (Trans.
    English, J. Crosland, 1907). 2nd ed. 1916.
Musikalische Walpurgisnacht (satirical comedy). 1907.
Golgotha (drama in 2 parts). 1908.
Akkorde (collected essays). 1912.
Erlebnisse eines K. Kapellmeisters in Berlin. 1913.
Ratschläge für Aufführungen klavisches Symphonien (devoted to
    Schubert and Schumann; published as part II. of *Ratschläge*
    above). 1919.
Do.   Part III. (devoted to Mozart). 1923.
Eine Künstlerfahrt nach Südamerika, Tagebuch Juni-Nov. 1 20.
    1921.
Lebenserinnerungen. 1923.

C., incorporating material from M.

WEINLIG, (1) CHRISTIAN EHREGOTT
(*b.* Dresden, Sept. 30, 1743 ; *d.* there, Mar. 14,
1813), organist, was a pupil of Homilius at the
Kreuzschule at Dresden, and after holding posts
at Leipzig, Thorn and the Frauenkirche at
Dresden, succeeded his old master as cantor of
the Kreuzschule. He composed Passion music,
oratorios, cantatas, etc., but only some clavier
pieces and flute sonatas were published during
his life. His nephew, (2) CHRISTIAN THEODOR
(*b.* Dresden, July 25, 1780 ; *d.* Leipzig, Mar. 7,
1842), was instructed first by his uncle and then
by Padre Mattei at Bologna. In 1814–17 he
was cantor of the Kreuzschule at Dresden, and
in 1823 he succeeded SCHICHT as cantor of the
Thomas-School at Leipzig, and remained there
till his death. He published a German Magnificat for soli, chorus and orchestra, some
singing exercises, and a treatise of some value,
Anleitung zur Fuge für den Selbstunterricht (2nd
ed. 1852). But it is as a teacher of theory and
as the master of Wagner for six months in 1830
that his name will be remembered. Wagner
has left his recollections of Weinlig's teaching
on record in words which deserve to be pondered
by all teachers of theory. (See WAGNER.)

G. ; addns. *Riemann*.

WEISS (*recte* SCHNEEWEISS), AMALIE
(*b.* Marburg, Styria, May 10, 1839 ; *d.* Berlin,
Feb. 3, 1899), made her stage-début at Troppau
in 1853, in 1854 was engaged at Hermannstadt,
and in the same year appeared at the Kärnthnerthor Theatre, Vienna, where she assumed
the name by which she was known until her
marriage with JOACHIM (*q.v.*). She was engaged
at the Opera at Hanover, 1862, and her betrothal
to Joachim, early in the following year, was
artistically celebrated by a remarkable performance of Gluck's ' Orpheus,' in which she sang
the title-part, Joachim conducting. Her farewell of the stage took place on May 30, 1863, in
the part of Fidelio, and on June 10 tne twc
great artists were married. After her marriage
she had a career of the utmost brilliance and
usefulness as a concert-singer and teacher, obtaining world-wide fame as a singer of Schumann's songs, and later on of those of Brahms.
The tragic misunderstandings which resulted in
a separation of the husband and wife in 1882
may have been the cause of her not visiting
England after her successful appearances here
in 1870 and 1878. She went to America for a
short time about 1890 and taught there, but
never quitted Germany as a residence. She
accepted the post of professor of singing in the
Klindworth - Scharwenka Conservatorium in
Berlin. Perhaps the most memorable of her
performances in England was that of the air
from Bach's Matthew-Passion, ' Erbarme dich,'
with Joachim's violin obbligato ; but her singing of Schubert's ' Tod und das Mädchen ' and
of Beethoven's ' Faithfu' Johnie ' was scarcely
less perfect in its interpretative and emotional
power. Her voice was a contralto of singular
richness; her technique left nothing to be desired.   M.

WEISS, FRANZ (*b.* Silesia, Jan. 18, 1788 ;
d. Vienna, Jan. 25, 1830), a distinguished viola-
player, and long a member of the celebrated
string-quartet maintained by Prince RASOU-
MOWSKY (*q.v.*) at his palace in Vienna. By these
distinguished players most of Beethoven's
quartets were studied for the first time, SCHUP-
PANZIGH (*q.v.*) taking the first violin, the Prince
himself the second, and Linke the violoncello.
Weiss was also a composer of merit, and published, among other works, ' Variations brillantes ' for violin and orchestra, op. 13 (Vienna,
Artaria), quartet (Vienna, Haslinger and Offenbach, André), duets for flutes and for violins,
and PF. sonatas. A symphony of his for flute,
bassoon and trumpet *concertante* with orchestra,
was played with great success by the brothers
Alois, Joseph and Anton Khayll.   C. F. P.

WEISS, KAREL (*b.* Prague, Feb. 13, 1862),
composer and conductor. He studied at the
Prague Conservatoire, where he took up the
violin and horn. Thence he passed on to the
Organ School (1878–81), where he worked
under Skuherský and Fibich. After finishing

his courses, he occupied a variety of posts : organist of St. Stephen's and of the chief synagogue, teacher at the music school at Kroměříž, member of the orchestra of the National Theatre, Prague, and, from 1886–87, conductor at the National Theatre, Brno (Brünn). He also toured as accompanist with Fr. Ondřiček. Weiss began to compose early in life. His choral scene 'Triumfator' led the way to his first essay in opera, 'Viola' (from Shakespeare), 1892. It is comedy opera verging on operetta, having some affinity with Nicolai's 'Merry Wives of Windsor,' and met with great success for a time. It was revised later under the title 'The Twins.' His second opera, 'The Polish Jew' (Erckmann-Chatrian), produced in 1901, became very popular at home and abroad. The musical material is strongly touched with nationalism. Smetana and Dvořák have contributed to its inspiration. It is, however, temperamental music ; strong in rhythm, impulsive and effective. It has the qualities which please at first hearing. Weiss followed it up some years later by 'The Attack on the Mill' (1912), the libretto based on Zola's tale *L'Attaque du moulin.* An opera on a national subject, 'The Black Smith of Lešetin,' appeared in 1920. Weiss has neglected opera for a lighter style. His operettas 'Die Dorfmusikanten' (1904), 'Revisor' (after Gogol, 1907) are oftener heard in Germany. Apart from the stage, his compositions include : a symphonic poem, 'Helios and Selene' ; a violin sonata ; a string quartet ; for pianoforte, Cotillon, Serenade, op. 13 ; four pieces, op. 15 ; ten pieces, op. 18 ; Dance Sketches, op. 21—all sparkling and rather superficial salon music; collections of folk-songs, 'Blat'ácké,' opp. 31, 32 and 33 ; 'Prástky,' a folk-song for chorus and orchestra.   R. N.

WEISS, Sylvius Leopold (*b.* Breslau, Oct. 12, 1686 ; *d.* Dresden, Oct. 15, 1750), was by many, including Gerber and the sister of Frederic the Great, declared to be the greatest lutenist of all times. He accompanied the Polish Prince Alex. Sobiesky to Rome *c.* 1708, and remained with him until his death at the end of 1714. In 1715 he was for a short time at the court of Hesse-Cassel, whence he was invited to Düsseldorf by the Elector Johann Wilhelm. At the end of 1716 or beginning of 1717 he visited the court of Dresden, where he was induced to overstay his leave, and received from the Elector on Apr. 3, 1718, a letter of apology to Johann Wilhelm, such as the latter had given to Handel on a similar occasion. Soon afterwards we find him at the Saxon Court, where he served under Antonio Lotti, Hasse, Porpora and even Gluck. In Sept. 1718 a special band of 12, including, besides Weiss, Hebenstreit, Pisendel and Zelenka, was sent for the Crown Prince's music to Vienna, and Weiss was always in great demand for all the special festivals of the various courts. In 1719 he was at Dresden again when Handel visited the court. Early in 1722 an enraged French violinist, to whom Weiss had shown much kindness, bit his right thumb, nearly severing the top joint, and it was not until the end of the year that he could play again on a visit to Munich. In 1723 he played with Quantz and H. Graun in Fux's opera for the Emperor's coronation as King of Bohemia at Prague. He was famous for his art of improvising, and Reichard relates that at Dresden on one occasion he even competed therein with J. S. Bach. His compositions for the lute were much sought after, but as they were mostly copied in MS., few have survived. They are mentioned in *Q.-L.* erroneously under two headings (Sylvius, W., and Sylvius, Leopold W.). His brother Siegmund was likewise an excellent lutenist, as well as viola da gambist, violinist and composer. A portrait engraving exists, made from a painting by Denner (Hans Volkmann, *Die Musik*, vol. 23, p. 273).   E. v. d. s.

WEISS, (1) Willoughby Hunter (*b.* Liverpool, Apr. 2, 1820 ; *d.* Oct. 24, 1867), son of Willoughby Gaspard Weiss, professor of the flute and music-publisher. He learnt singing from Sir George Smart and Balfe, and on May 5, 1842, made his first appearance in public at a concert of his own at Liverpool. He next sang in London at the concerts of Balfe, Thalberg, etc., and then joined the farewell tour of Miss Adelaide Kemble, and made a successful début on the stage at Dublin, July 2, as Oroveso in 'Norma.' On Dec. 26 he made his first London appearance in opera at the Princess's as the Count in an English version of 'Sonnambula.' He established a reputation both as an operatic and concert singer. In the former capacity he sang in the various English operatic enterprises of Bunn, Maddox, Jullien, Pyne and Harrison, and the English Opera Company, Limited, and in various operas of Auber, Balfe, Benedict, Hatton, Macfarren, etc. But he was best in oratorio, in which his rich voice and musicianly feeling showed to advantage. He made his first appearance in oratorio in 1844 at the Gloucester Festival, and was continually engaged at the London oratorio concerts and provincial festivals until close upon his death. Weiss also composed songs and ballads, of which 'The Village Blacksmith' became very popular. He also arranged a PF. edition of Weber's Mass in G. His wife,

(2) Georgina Ansell (*née* Barrett) (*b.* Gloucester, 1826 ; *d.* Brighton, Nov. 6, 1880), the daughter of a musician in Gloucester, was a pupil at the R.A.M. (1842–45), and first attracted notice at the Gloucester Festival of 1844. On Sept. 15, 1845, she married Weiss. On Dec. 20, 1847, she made her first appearance on the stage at Drury Lane as Queen Elizabeth in Balfe's 'Maid of Honour,' and later sang

with her husband at the Prince's and Covent Garden. In 1856 she sang at the Philharmonic, in the production of Schumann's 'Paradise and the Peri.' According to Chorley, who was not prejudiced in her favour, 'she had the honours of the evening' (*Athenœum*). She married again, Feb. 13, 1872, C. Davis of New Malden, Surrey.   A. C.

WEISSENBURG (Weysenbergh), Hainz, see Albicastro, Henrico.

WEISSENSEE, Friedrich (*b.* Schwerstedt, Thuringia, *c.* 1560; *d.* Altenweddingen, 1622), rector of the Latin college at Gebesee *c.* 1590, and at Magdeburg town school, 1596. About 1601–02 he became pastor at Altenweddingen. He is one of the greatest German masters of his time, and a disciple of the great Venetians. He wrote a large number of motets, a list of which appears in *Q.-L.* (See also *Riemann*.)

WEISSHAN (Winsheim), Abraham, a 16th-17th-century lutenist, at first at the court of Duke Frederic on the Grimmenstein, near Gotha. In a letter of Apr. 9, 1568, the Elector August of Saxony asks for his transference to his court at Dresden, where he still was in Aug. 1611. He wrote 'Silvae musicalis libri VII.,' preludes, fantasias, ballets, etc. (Cologne, 1603) (*Q.-L.*).

WEISSMANN, Julius (*b.* Freiburg, Breisgau, Dec 26, 1879), was a pupil of Seyffart, Rheinberger and Bussmeyer in Munich; of Herzogenberg in Berlin; and finally of Thuille in Munich. Inspired by the romance of poetry and possessed of a pronounced inclination to musical absoluteness, his music is characterised by a graciously subtle rhythm. His works include :

A symphony in B min., op. 19; three pieces for orch., op. 57; a concerto for v'cl. in D min., op. 36; a concerto for PF.; variations and fugue on an old 'Ave Maria,' for PF. and orch., op. 37; a sonata for v'cl. and pf.; a string quartet in F maj., op. 24; PF. trios, opp. 27 and 77; v'cl. sonatas in F major, op. 28, and in F sharp min., op. 47; a solo vln. sonata in D min., op. 30; variations for oboe and PF., op. 39; songs, opp. 1, 2, 3, 4, 5, 6, 13, 15, 16, 22, 23, 29, 40, 43, 67; choral works with orch., op. 10; 'Hymne an den Mond,' op. 11; 'On a grave,' op. 12; sacred cantata, op. 34; male choir, op. 31; female choir, op. 65; pieces for PF., opp. 17, 21, 25, 27, 32, 35, 48; variations for 2 PF's. in A maj., op. 64.   K. D. H.

WEIST-HILL, (1) Thomas Henry (*b.* London, Jan. 23, 1828; *d.* Dec. 25, 1891), was taught violin-playing by Sainton at the R.A.M., and in 1845 was elected King's Scholar. He first appeared at an Academy Concert in 1847, in Spohr's 9th Concerto, and subsequently went to America, where he introduced Mendelssohn's Violin Concerto. He afterwards undertook a professional tour in Europe, and in 1849 became a member of Costa's band at the Royal Italian Opera and elsewhere. In 1871 he followed his old conductor to Drury Lane, where he filled the post of director of the Ballet Music, and then to Her Majesty's till 1879.[1] In 1874–76 he was conductor at the Alexandra Palace, and displayed great energy in that department, giving performances of Handel's

[1] In 1878 he conducted at Her Majesty's the winter season of English opera.

'Esther' and 'Susanna,' Gade's 'Spring Fantasia,' Berlioz's 'Danse des sylphes,' compositions of Saint-Saëns, etc. Weist-Hill introduced to the British public important works of Bizet and Massenet   British composers were invited by the Alexandra Palace Company to compete for the composition of the two best symphonies, and the prizes were awarded to F. W. Davenport and C. V. Stanford by Joachim and G. A. Macfarren, as judges. In 1878–79 Weist-Hill was conductor of Mme. Viard-Louis's orchestral concerts, and gained much reputation for himself and his orchestra during the short life of the undertaking. In 1880 he was appointed Principal of the G.S.M. Under his energetic direction the number of pupils rose to upwards of 2500. Two sons of his, (2) Ferdinand, a violinist, pupil of the Brussels Conservatoire, and (3) Thomas, a violoncellist, scholar of the R.C.M., have won success in London.   A. C.

WEITZMANN, Karl Friedrich (*b.* Berlin, Aug. 10, 1808; *d.* there, Nov. 7, 1880), a learned and excellent writer on musical subjects, was a pupil of Henning Klein, Spohr and Hauptmann. He rose by various posts and labours, till in 1848 he established himself as a teacher and writer in Berlin, where he resided till his death. Three operas, 'Räuberliebe,' 'Walpurgisnacht,' and 'Lorbeer und Bettelstab,' were performed at Reval; he published a volume of 1800 preludes and modulations. His literary works include : *Der übermässige Dreiklang* (1853); *Der verminderte Septimenaccord* and *Geschichte des Septimenaccords* (1854); *Geschichte des griechischen Musik* (1855); *Geschichte der Harmonie* (1849); *Harmoniesystem* (1860); *Die neue Harmonielehre*; *Geschichte des Klavierspiels*, etc. (1863); *Der letzte der Virtuosen* (1868). A pupil, E. M. Bowman, published in 1877 in New York a work entitled *C. F. Weitzmann's Manual of Musical Theory* (*Riemann*). He contributed the fourth variation, in canon, to Liszt's 'Todtentanz.'   G.

WEKERLIN, Jean-Baptiste Theodore, see Weckerlin.

WELCH, John Bacon (*b.* Pattishall Vicarage, Northampton, Dec. 26, 1839; *d.* July 1, 1887), a teacher of singing, began his musical education in London, and in 1861 went to Milan, and studied for three years under Nava. Ultimately he settled in London, where he had a large number of private pupils, and was professor of singing at the G.S.M. Among his most successful pupils may be mentioned Miss Anna Williams, Miss A. Marriott, Miss Santley (Hon. Mrs. R. Lyttelton), H. Blower, Bridson, Brereton, H. Piercy.   G.

WELCKER, a family of London music-publishers in the latter half of the 18th century.

Peter (1) was the first, and his shop was in Gerrard Street, St. Anne's, Soho; afterwards

numbered 17. He was established before 1764, and published much of the instrumental music of the day. He died in (or about) 1775, leaving his widow, Mary, to continue the business.

His son, (2) JOHN, about this time leaving his mother's business, probably under the management of James Blundell, who had married one of his sisters, set up as music-seller and publisher at 9 (afterwards 10) Haymarket, four doors below the Opera House. Besides the class of music which came from the Gerrard Street house, John Welcker issued the opera dances and ballets performed at the Haymarket Theatre. He also reissued (with an added volume) 'Clio and Euterpe.' In 1780–81 he removed to 18 Coventry Street, where he still was in 1785–86. The Haymarket shop was taken over by James Blundell, his brother-in-law. As the imprints of the Welcker publications frequently merely give the surname it is sometimes difficult to place their period of issue.   F. K.

WELCKER VON GONTERSHAUSEN, HEINRICH (b. Gontershausen, Grand Duchy of Hesse-Darmstadt. 1811 ; d. there, June 15, 1873), court pianoforte-maker to the Grand Duke of Hesse, and a writer on the construction and history of musical instruments, particularly the pianoforte. His published works include :

1. Der Flügel oder die Beschaffenheit des Pianos in allen Formen. Eine umfassende Darstellung der Forte-Piano-Baukunst vom Entstehen bis zu den neuesten Verbesserungen mit specieller Hinweisung auf die rationelle Praxis für Bearbeitung und Zusammensetzung der Mechanismen, nebst gründlicher Anweisung zur Intonirung, Stimmung, und Saitenbemessung. Mit 75 Zeichnungen. Frankfurt am Main, 1853 (neue vermehrte Ausgabe, 1856).
2. Die musikalischen Tonwerkzeuge in technischen Zeichnungen aller Saiten-, Blas-, Schlag-, und Frictions-Instrumente, mit spezieller Beschreibung ihres Baues, Tonumfangs, und fasslicher Angabe ihrer Behandlung und Erhaltung. Mit 160 Abbildungen. Frankfurt am Main, 1855.
3. Der Ratgeber für Ankauf, Behandlung und Erhaltung der Pianoforte (1857).
4. Die Clavierbau in seiner Theorie, Technik und Geschichte, unter Hinweisung seiner Beziehungen zu den Gesetzen der Akustik. Mit 91 Abbildungen. Frankfurt am Main (vierte mit einem Nachtrag vermehrte Ausgabe, 1870).
5. Über den Bau der Saiteninstrumente und deren Akustik, nebst Übersicht der Entstehung und Verbesserung der Orgel. Ein Anhang zum Clavierbau in seiner Theorie, Technik und Geschichte. Frankfurt am Main, 1876.

These very meritorious works bear witness to Welcker's great industry. They are not, however, to be always accepted as authorities, and a comparison of the fourth with the first shows that the earlier works, for which he had presumably his note-books at hand, are more trustworthy than the later ones.   A. J. H.

WELDON, GEORGINA (b. Clapham, May 24, 1837 ; d. Brighton, Jan. 11, 1914). Her maiden name was Thomas, which was afterwards changed to Treherne. On Apr. 21, 1860, she married Captain Weldon, of the 18th Hussars. For many years she was known in society as the possessor of a lovely voice, and she afterwards adopted music as a profession on charitable grounds, and made her first appearance in public in 1870. She undertook a tour in Wales with her pupil, Miss Gwendoline Jones, and became a member of Leslie's choir, in which she sang the solo in Mendelssohn's 'Hear my prayer,' on Mar. 9, 1871. She afterwards sang at the Popular Concerts, the Crystal Palace, the Philharmonic, and elsewhere. In 1872 she took the solo soprano part in Gounod's 'Gallia' at Notre Dame, the Opéra-Comique and the Conservatoire, Paris. Her romantic friendship with Gounod is well known. She assisted in training his choir in London, and established an orphanage at her residence, in order to give musical instruction to poor children, with objects and on principles which she fully described in a letter to the Ménestrel, and with a zeal and energy rarely equalled. She also published songs by Gounod and other composers in aid of her orphanage, among which was Clay's popular setting of 'The Sands o' Dee.' She also composed songs translated from the French by herself, viz. 'Choses du soir,' 'Le Chant du passereau,' 'Le Petit Garçon et le nid du rougegorge'; also 'The Brook' (poetry by Tennyson), etc. In 1879 she sang at Rivière's Promenade Concerts, with a female choir trained and directed by herself. This transaction gave rise to a protracted lawsuit, which was matter of considerable notoriety. Her last professional engagement was at a popular music hall in 1884.   A. C.

WELDON, JOHN (b. Chichester, Jan. 19, 1676 ; d. London, May 7, 1736), was educated at Eton College, and whilst there studied music under John Walton, the college organist. He afterwards became a pupil of Henry Purcell. In 1694 he was appointed organist of New College, Oxford. In 1700 he gained the first of the four prizes offered for the best compositions of Congreve's masque, 'The Judgment of Paris,' the others being awarded to John ECCLES, Daniel PURCELL and Godfrey FINGER (q.v.). Weldon's music was not printed, with the exception of Juno's song, 'Let ambition fire thy mind,' the air of which was adapted by Arne to the opening duet of 'Love in a Village.' On June 6, 1701, Weldon was sworn in a gentleman extraordinary of the Chapel Royal. In 1702 he resigned his appointment at New College. Upon the death of Dr. Blow in 1708, Weldon was appointed his successor as organist of the Chapel Royal, and on Aug. 8, 1715, upon the establishment of a second composer's place there, he was sworn into it. He was also organist of St. Bride's, Fleet Street, and in 1726 was appointed to the same office at St. Martin's-in-the-Fields. He was buried in the churchyard of St. Paul, Covent Garden. Weldon's principal compositions are for the Church ; he published, under the title of 'Divine Harmony,' six solo anthems composed for Richard Elford; other anthems are printed in the collections of Boyce, Arnold and Page, and many are still in manuscript in the books of the Chapel Royal and some of the cathedrals. The two anthems printed by Boyce—'In Thee, O Lord,' and 'Hear my cry·

ing '—are admirable compositions, combining pure melody, fine harmony, and just expression. Weldon published three books of his songs, and many other songs are contained in the collections of the period. A song by him, 'From grave lessons,' is printed in Hawkins's *History*. He wrote music for four operas, besides the masque already mentioned : 'She would and she would not,' 1703 ; 'The Fair Unfortunate,' and 'Orpheus and Eurydice,' 1710 ; and 'The Agreeable Disappointment,' 1715. There is a portrait of Weldon among the Music School portraits in the Bodleian Library, Oxford.

W. H. H.

WELLESZ, EGON (*b.* Vienna, Oct. 21, 1885), composer and research student, studied musical science and history with Guido Adler at Vienna University, harmony with Carl Frühling, counterpoint with Arnold Schönberg and composition with Bruno Walter, and graduated as Ph.D. at Vienna in 1908, with a thesis 'Gius. Bonno,' which was published in the 1910 volume of the International Musical Society. In 1910 he edited, for the *D.T.Ö.*, J. J. Fux's opera 'Costanza e fortezza.' In 1913 he became lecturer on musical history at Vienna University. He is the author of many historical essays on the baroque period, and has made a special study of old Byzantine music, on which he published an important volume in 1922. (See BYZANTINE MUSIC : BIBLIOGRAPHY.) He has played a prominent part in the musical life of Vienna, using his pen and his influence in furthering the knowledge of contemporary music generally, and he was one of the group of Viennese musicians to whose initiative was due the meeting at Salzburg in 1922, from which developed the INTERNATIONAL SOCIETY FOR CONTEMPORARY MUSIC (*q.v.*). As a composer he is usually included among those acknowledging the leadership of Schönberg, but his adoption of their creed is much looser than is the case with other Schönberg pupils. His early works reveal other influences, notably that of Mahler and occasionally of Reger. He developed an enthusiasm for Debussy and the French school, traces of which are still discernible, though less abundantly than at that time. Since then a modified form of expressionism has definitely claimed him. Parallel with this development in his methods, the predilection for sharply defined rhythmic phrases which appeared in the early works has led to the composition of several ballets and of a 'Dance-Suite' for violin solo and chamber orchestra. His most important works are :

STAGE

Operas.—' Die Prinzessin Girnara,' op. 27.   'Alkestis,' op. 35.
Ballets.—' Das Wunder der Diana,' op. 18.   Persian Ballet, op. 30.
 'Achilles auf Skyros,' op. 33.   'Die Nächtlichen' (Tanz-symphonie), op. 37.

ORCHESTRA

' Gebete der Mädchen zur Maria,' sop., chor. and orch., op. 5.
' Vorfrühling,' symphonic poem, op. 12.
Suite, vln., solo and chamber orch. op. 38.

CHAMBER MUSIC

Four String Quartets.
' Geistiges Lied,' v., PF. vln. and vla., op 23
Sonata for v'cl. solo, op. 31.
   „   vln. solo, op. 36.
Two clar. pieces, op. 34.

Numerous PF. pieces, notably opp. 4 (' Der Abend '), 9, 11 (' Eklogen '), 17 (' Epigrams '), 21 (' Idylls '), and 26.
Many songs, among which ' Wie ein Bild,' op. 3, cycle, ' Kirsch-blütenlieder,' op 8, and ' Aurora,' a song without words for coloratura voice.

E. E.

WELL-TEMPERED CLAVIER, see WOHL-TEMPERIRTE KLAVIER.

WELSH, THOMAS (*b.* Wells, Somerset, *c.* 1780; *d.* Jan. 24, 1848), became, when 6 years old, a chorister in the cathedral there. He made such rapid progress that in the course of a few years Wells became the resort of lovers of music attracted by the beauty of his voice and excellence of his singing. His fame drew the attention of Sheridan and Linley, and he appeared in 1792 at the Bath concerts, in the concerts given at the King's Theatre during the rebuilding of Drury Lane, and also on the stage in Attwood's 'Prisoner.' He subsequently performed at Drury Lane in Attwood's 'Adopted Child,' Storace's 'Lodoiska,' and other pieces. John Kemble thought highly of his abilities as an actor, and taught him to perform the part of Prince Arthur in Shakespeare's 'King John.' After the breaking of his boyish voice Welsh pursued his studies under C. F. Horn, John Cramer and Baumgarten. In 1802, his voice having become a deep and powerful bass, he was admitted a gentleman of the Chapel Royal. A few years later he essayed dramatic composition, and produced ' Twenty Years Ago,' a melodramatic entertainment, 1810 ; 'The Green-eyed Monster,' musical farce, and ' Kamtchatka,' musical drama, 1811. But his greatest reputation was gained as a singing master and instructor of pupils for the stage. Foremost among those whom he taught were John Sinclair, C. E. Horn, Miss Stephens and Miss Wilson. He joined Hawes in carrying on the Royal Harmonic Institution. (See ARGYLL ROOMS.) He published some glees and pianoforte pieces and a 'Vocal Instructor.' He married Miss WILSON (*q.v.*) (*d.* 1867), who had been his pupil, and had issue an only child, who became the wife of Alfredo Piatti, the eminent violoncellist.

W. H. H.

WELSH MUSIC. There is sufficient evidence to prove that at a very early period a musical culture existed in Wales ; a culture far in advance of what might have been expected in a country of rugged character, whose political conditions were continually plunging it into war. It has been asserted that this especial cultivation of scientific music was mainly due to the fact that the harp, an instrument of more capability than most primitive ones, was in popular use. Also it may be added that Wales possessed in its bards a race of men whose profession was the production of poetry and music for the purpose of inciting their country-men, by song and chant, to deeds of valour.

While much has been written regarding the bards, their poetry and music, in the earliest period of Welsh history, it must be confessed that we have really little evidence of the kind of music in use in these early bardic times. Notwithstanding this, several Welsh writers have freely dealt with the musical history of Wales from a very remote date, so remote, in fact, as to reach backward to Druidical times. Lengthy lists of bards dating from A.D. 60 are given in Edward Jones's *Musical and Poetical Relicks of the Welsh Bards* (1794) and elsewhere, with translations of their songs, and prose narratives, musical laws, rules for the govern-ment of their order, and many other intimate matters, with little reservation. Later writers copy these, and accept statements which more cautious antiquaries might wish to see better verified.

It is impossible here to enter into this bewildering mass of quotation and assertion, and to sift the likely from the unlikely. There is no doubt much worthy of all credence, but its absolute value can only be estimated by Welsh scholars having access to the manuscript and other real evidence that may still remain. Several points, however, stand out from the mass, such as the association of Irish with Welsh harpers, and the great interest shown by early Welsh rulers in the progress of the musical art in the country.

Prince Gruffydd ab Cynan, who lived in the 11th and 12th centuries, is credited with having put the professional music of Wales into some order, and with having made laws for the guidance and government of the bards and harpers, and others of the minstrel class. He is said to have enacted that certain 'measures' should be played to particular kinds of lyrics, and to have given names to these.

Another proof of the existence of an early Welsh school of music is found in a much-quoted passage from Giraldus Cambrensis who, at the end of the 12th century, wrote of Welsh music thus :

'The Britons do not sing in unison like the in-habitants of other countries, but in many different parts. So that when a company of singers, among the common people, meet to sing, as is usual in this country, as many different parts are heard as there are performers, who all at length unite in consonance with organic sweetness.'

(Other translations give ' unite in consonance under the softness of B flat.') [1]

Other proofs of Welsh musical activity are forthcoming in these early days, but space will not permit an entry into the difficult question, particularly where no example can be found that will give the modern musician authentic and tangible evidence of the class of music

[1] Wooldridge, *Oxf. Hist. Mus.* i. 162, quotes this passage from *Cambriae Descriptio*, cap. xiii. in Latin and English, and comments on its interpretation.

cultivated. The reader who wishes to examine such details as are available is referred to the *Historical Dissertation* prefixed to John Parry's 'Antient British Music' (1742),to Edward Jones's *Relicks* (1794), and *Bardic Museum* (1802), Bunt-ing's 'Ancient Music of Ireland' (1809 and 1840), and to other works contemporary with these. The more modern essays on the subject are mainly based upon the statements made in one or the other of these books, and much appears to be accepted without further independent research.

Of Welsh musical instruments we have better knowledge. The harp was pre-eminent, although it must not be forgotten that this instrument was equally in evidence among the Anglo-Saxons and among the Scots and Irish. The other musical instruments of Wales were much the same as those in use at contemporary periods in England, Ireland and Scotland. There was, however, one exception, the CRWTH (*q.v.*), a stringed instrument played with a bow,although it had become practically obsolete at the end of the 18th century. Jones, in 1794, mentioned that he had possessed one, which was accident-ally destroyed by fire ; and the Rev. William Bingley, in his *North Wales* (1804), tells us that he found an old man who played one, and de-scribes its tone as harsh and disagreeable. It had six strings, two of which were off the finger-board, but its flat bridge scarcely allowed any string to be touched singly by the bow, and the whole appears to have been chiefly played as an accompaniment for the harp, or for the voice.

The rest of the Welsh instruments, so far as we know, were the pibgorn or hornpipe (see PIBGORN ; STOCKHORN), the bagpipe, the bugle horn, and the tabret, a small drum. The harps were of different sizes, some being three or four feet long, though the usual size was large, six or seven feet high, and all had a varying number of strings.

In Queen Elizabeth's reign some of the single harps had twenty-nine strings. There were also double harps with two sets of strings, as well as the triple harp (see HARP) having three sets of strings ; this seems to have been in use among the more skilful performers only. Ac-cording to early laws certain kinds of harps were confined to learners, and one of these kinds was made of hardened leather. Jones gives a translation of a poem, said to belong to the 14th century, which condemns the leathern harps, and suggests that they bent while being played upon ; they were, the poem indicates, made of horse skin. A more credible reference is to be found in the remembrance of a person who told Jones that he used as a boy to play on a harp which was covered with ox skin. It is quite evident that the leathern harp, with the other instruments named (excepting the correct forms of harp) could not make very satisfactory music.

In furtherance of musical culture Welsh

musicians have, from early times, held musical meetings at which harpers and other performers from different parts of the country attended. Here they played in competitions, and settled the affairs of the profession. The modern revival of these meetings is the EISTEDDFOD (*q.v.*), which is so prominent a feature of musical life in Wales at the present day.

While in bardic times the office of the harper was to inspire the onslaught and to sing the deeds of valour done, as times grew more tranquil the professional harper wandered abroad and either took service with some wealthy family as domestic harper, or went from one country seat to another or to various fairs, markets or gatherings, picking up his living by such donations as might come in his way. It is important to remember this when considering the airs which now constitute Welsh national music.

Many of the harpers were blind, as in Scotland and Ireland, and indeed the affliction seemed to fix the calling of the man. Among others, two blind harpers may be mentioned as connected with the issue of important collections of Welsh airs, viz., John PARRY (*q.v.*) of Ruabon (*d.* 1782), and Richard Roberts of Carnarvon (*d.* 1855, aged 86).

Regarding the profession of a harper at a comparatively early date a curious commission may be quoted which was given by Queen Elizabeth to certain Welsh gentlemen in 1567. By it, it appears that

'vagrant and idle persons naming themselves Minstrels, Rythmers, and Bards are lately grown into such intolerable multitude within the principality of North Wales, that not only gentlemen and others by their shameless disorders are often disquieted in their habitations, but also the expert minstrels and musicians in tonge and cunynge thereby much discouraged to travaile in the exercise and practice of their knowledge ' ; etc.

It was therefore enacted that the silver harp, which had been bestowed by Sir William Mostyn and his ancestors upon the best minstrel at the assemblies held at ' Cayroes in the county of Flynt,' should be given annually at the said town of Cayroes on the Monday after Trinity, beginning in 1568, upon the advice of 'expert men in the faculty of Welsh music,' and that all who were considered unfit should be compelled to ' return to honest labour,' upon pain of being taken as sturdy and idle vagabonds.[1]

It may be now asked what authentic remnants of ancient Welsh music exist. In the 18th century there were several libraries of old Welsh manuscripts which, in at least two instances, suffered greatly by fires ; it does not, however, appear that among those destroyed were any manuscript musical collections which (as among English manuscripts) gave indication of the vocal or instrumental music of Wales at an early date, with the exception of two MSS. to

be presently dealt with. The most famous of these manuscripts is a volume, formerly in the possession of Lewis Morris and afterwards in that of the Welsh School, whence it passed to the British Museum in 1844. By an inscription it is judged to have been written about the middle of the 17th century. An early entry in the MS. states that ' this book was wrote by Robert ap Huw of Bodwigan in Anglesey in Charles ye First's time, some part of it copied out of William Penllyn's book.' William Penllyn was a harper who was one of the chief bards of North Wales in the ninth year of Elizabeth.[2] It purports to contain

' the music of the ancient Britons as settled by a congress of masters of music by order of Gruffydd ab Cynan about the year 1100, with some of the most ancient pieces of the Britons, supposed to have been handed down to us from the British Bards.'

However this may be, there are twenty-four lessons, or ' measures,' followed by twelve variations on a ground-bass. The whole is in a tablature used for organ music in the 16th and 17th centuries, though, in ignorance of this fact, John Parry in the ' Welsh Harper,' vol. i., refers to it as ' the most ancient specimen of Welsh musical notation extant,' and that ' the characters used are those of the ancient bardic alphabet.' He also mentions an article by Sir Samuel Meyrick, *On the Musical Notation of the Ancient Britons*, in a Welsh antiquarian journal, evidently founded upon the same MS. and tablature. There is a description of the manuscript in Dr. Burney's *History of Music* (vol. ii., 1782, pp. 110-14) with facsimiles and translations. It is, however, transcribed in full, in the third volume of *Myvyrian Archaiology of Wales* (1807), and again reprinted with a full translation in the 1870 edition. The most recent consideration of the MS. is in Miss M. H. Glyn's *Evolution of Musical Form*, 1909, where an independent translation of ' The Prelude to the Salt ' is given. She happily describes the whole of the music in the MS. as

' ceaseless reiteration of equal beat figures of a few notes, [which] suggest five-finger exercises rather than variation. Monotony pervades the whole range of the music, a fact which goes far to prove its authenticity.'

Burney, however, says of it : ' This counterpoint, artless as it may seem, is too modern for such remote antiquity as is given to it.' In the present article the age of the MS. need not be discussed, and the series of chords which make up the bulk of the music does not in any way resemble the popular Welsh airs. It has been suggested that the pieces contained in the MS. are for performance on the crwth, but this opinion is scarcely tenable ; it appears quite evident that it is harp music. Regarding this manuscript, Brinley Richards, in the 1884 edition of ' Songs of Wales,' says that he

[1] See the whole quoted in Evans's *Specimens of the Poetry of the Ancient Welsh Bards*, 1760.

[2] See note by Burney, *History of Music*, vol. ii. p. 110.

feels obliged to modify his former statements concerning the so-called 11th-century MSS., and he now believes that they are of more recent date, as the accounts of the congress of Prince Gruffydd ab Cynan, at which they are said to have been written, are unsupported by any authentic evidence.'

In the *Myvyrian Archaiology of Wales* also appear a transcript and a translation of another early musical MS., that of Rhys Jones, but the character of the music resembles that of the manuscript previously described.

Besides these MSS. there does not appear to be preserved any collections of Welsh music (save one or more general treatises on the art of music written in Welsh) before the early part of the 18th century. We are thus, unfortunately, in the dark as to the character of Welsh music before the harpers were influenced by the art of other countries. It is much to be regretted that we cannot trace, step by step, as we can in the music of England, by the aid of MSS. or printed books, the evolution of Welsh melody. Nevertheless, from a cause not now easy to discover, Welsh historians have claimed for Welsh melodies an antiquity far greater than that of any music current in the British Isles. So far as the present writer has been able to ascertain, this claim first made its appearance shortly before the middle of the 18th century. If Lewis Morris, the Welsh antiquary then living in London, did not first broach this theory he certainly did much to foster it. How much or how little truth there may be in the statement, for instance, that certain now popular Welsh airs have come down traditionally from Druidical times and are coeval with the Roman occupation of Britain, will always remain a matter of personal opinion. While not in any way disputing the fact that cultured music was commonly performed in Wales, it must be remembered that many of the old harpers were blind, and that therefore, to such, musical notation would be useless, also that it would require a very ample system and great skill to put down upon paper the florid music of which the harp, in the hands of a clever harper, is capable. There can be but little doubt that the music of Wales would be played entirely by ear, and subject to extemporaneous adornment or alteration by each player.

It is not very clear when Welsh music, considered as national music, began to have attention paid to it. Towards the end of the 17th century stress began to be laid upon the fact that certain tunes were of Scotch origin, and that others were in the 'Scotch taste,' but the present writer cannot find (save in one minor instance) that any attempt was made before 1742 to offer to the public a collection of melodies professedly of Welsh birth, although some Welsh tunes, indicated as such, occur at earlier date in certain London country dance books.

Blind John Parry of Ruabon, assisted by one Evan Williams, issued his ' Antient British Music ' in London in 1742. Lewis Morris, who, it is stated, first put the harp into the hands of Parry, had some share in this work, for he contributed an anonymous *Historical Dissertation*, and probably concocted the title which speaks of the melodies as ' supposed by the learned to be the remains of the music of the Antient Druids.' The airs (twenty-four in number) are unnamed, and were probably the general tunes then played by the harpers of North Wales.

Parry in London got some degree of fame, fostered by the belief that the tunes he played were of the highest antiquity. He was appointed harper to the king, and fired the poet Gray to write ' The Bard.' Gray, writing to a friend, says : ' Mr. Parry has been here and scratched out such ravishing blind harmony, such tunes of a thousand years old, with names enough to choke you.' No other musician after Parry's first volume ventured on a Welsh collection, but in 1781 (the year before he died) Parry issued a further collection, this time introducing a large number of variations for the harp. Edward Jones followed in 1784, 1794 and 1802, still claiming the melodies as ' Bardic tunes from very remote antiquity ' and ' Ancient war tunes of the Bards,' also that they were ' never before published.'

This insistence on the great age of the Welsh airs continued throughout all later collections. Richard Roberts in ' Cambrian Harmony ' (1829), speaks of his tunes as ' never before published, arranged as they were originally performed by the Ancient Britons.' The book, however, opens with ' The King's Joy,' which proves to be the well-known cavalier song ' When the King shall enjoy his own again,' and this is reprinted without remark in Parry's ' Welsh Harper ' (1848).

In ' Cambrian Minstrelsie ' (1893) (see BIBLIOGRAPHY below), great age for known Welsh melodies is asserted. For example, the note appended to ' Nos Galen ' is,

' This melody is of very great antiquity, dating, as some maintain, from the days of the Druids. It must, therefore, be at least between 2000 and 3000 years old.'

Many other quotations might be given from this and other works of a similar character.

With no wish to belittle either the beauty or the antiquity of the many charming Welsh melodies which the older collectors have placed before us, one is tempted to inquire more closely into the history of them, and here it becomes evident that there are many difficulties in reconciling these statements with facts. It is also quite clear that the earlier editors of Welsh collectors did not approach their subject with open minds, or with the method now expected in dealing with antiquarian subjects.

Structure of melody was not considered ; prior published collections of airs were not examined ; and the sources of their own airs not given. Edward Jones was the most laborious of these editors, and while his books are full of interesting material, this is badly arranged and difficult to sift. He gives many quotations from MSS. having reference to the musical affairs of Wales, yet neither here nor elsewhere have we any tangible evidence of the early existence of the present-known Welsh melodies, either in notation or as definitely named by title.

The earliest Welsh tunes that exist (apart from the Rhys Jones and the Penllyn MSS. referred to above, and these can scarcely be claimed as melodies) are found in Playford's ' Dancing Master,' from 1665 to 1718, a half dozen or so, and some few others in the London dance books. These, with the five in ' Aria di Camera ' (c. 1727), are the only ones before John Parry's Collection of 1742. We are thus more severely handicapped in our study of Welsh national music than in that of English, which possesses the advantage of being traceable, step by step, from the 13th century onward by actual noted examples.

The tunes Jones and the two Parrys give have evidently been taken down from the playing of harpers in North Wales, where the harp seems to have been in greatest favour. They appear to have considered that this instrument was the sole one worthy of attention (this may be due to the fact that they were themselves skilled performers on it), and that Welsh vocal music was of but little interest. They filled their books with pages of variations, and one frequently wonders what is claimed as genuinely old and what is admittedly modern. Also, sometimes a suspicion arises, as no sources are named, whether every tune inserted is purely traditional or whether the editors have been tempted silently to include compositions of their own.

In the early years of the 19th century it seems to have been recognised that, apart from the published Welsh tunes, a number of traditional Welsh melodies yet existed among the people, and at local eisteddfodau prizes were offered for MS. collections of these. Though no attempt at publication was made, one or two of these MS. collections fortunately still exist ; John Parry, the later, having used one for material for his ' Welsh Harper.' Miss Maria Jane WILLIAMS (q.v.) collected folk-tunes in South Wales, and in 1838 submitted her collection at an eisteddfod. She, however, did more, and a selection of forty-three of them was published in 1844. Her collection is now extremely rare, and only a small number of copies can have been issued. She noted a number of modal tunes, and had the true instinct of a modern folk-song collector, being distinctly in advance of her time in the appreciation of pure folk melody. Her collecting was done in Glamorganshire. It was not until 1896 that a further book of traditional Welsh folk melodies was published. Nicholas Bennett in that year issued ' Alawon fy Ngwled, or Lays of my Land.' This has over 400 melodies, without words, from traditional sources, though, as might be expected, there are in it a number of English folk-tunes, and some published English and other airs not folk tunes ; it is, however, an honest attempt at a much-needed work. Carl Engel, in his Literature of National Music (1879), drew attention to the desirability of searching Wales for traditional melodies, and he prints an air, ' Dixon's Hornpipe,' noted by himself at Llangollen, claiming it to be ' as fine as any of the finest Welsh tunes in popular favour.'

A ' Welsh Folk-song Society ' was subsequently formed with the object of collecting and publishing this class of music. In the collection of ' Welsh Melodies,' edited by Lloyd Williams and Arthur Somervell (Boosey & Co.), are some examples of genuine old tunes of fine quality.

Consideration may now be given to the sources of many of the fine tunes which make up the national music of Wales. Among these there are a great number of fine bold melodies of which any nation might be proud. The first printed sacred music of Welsh origin, or usage, occurs in Thomas Ravenscroft's ' Whole Booke of Psalmes,' etc., 1621 and 1633. Among the tunes marked as Welsh is ' Wrexham.' (See PSALTER.)

As before mentioned, Welsh secular airs began to be first printed in London books of country dances, and the earliest that may be referred to Wales that the present writer has discovered, is the tune ' Abergenie ' in the 1665 and later editions of Playford's ' Dancing Master.' ' Abergenie ' is probably Abergavenny in Monmouth, which is a sufficiently Welsh county in manner and customs to be musically included. Singularly enough, this air bears a strong resemblance to ' Cold and Raw.' ' The Bishop of Bangor's jig,' ' Lord of Carnarvon's jigg,' ' St. David's Day,' and ' Welch Whim ' are all in different editions of the ' Dancing Master,' and may, from their titles, be presumed to be of Welsh origin, although not reprinted in any Welsh collection. The fine melody ' Morva Ryddlan ' (The Marsh of Rhuddlan) is in ' Aria di Camera ' (c. 1727), which also includes the characteristic ' Meillionen ' ; this latter occurs also in several country dance books about 1735–40.

As ' Aria di Camera ' is a book of extreme rarity,[1] the earliest version of the first-named famous Welsh melody may be given from it ; it will be seen to have some difference from later copies.

[1] A copy was in the library of the writer.

Morva Ryddlan.

From 'Aria di Camera,' *cir.* 1727.

Very slow.

Another early version of it named 'An old Welsh Tune,' again having a difference, is printed in Francis Peacock's 'Fifty Scotch Airs' (1762).

The striking tune named 'Of noble race was Shenkin' first occurs in connexion with

Of Noble Race was Shenkin.

From 'Dancing Master,' 1703.

D'Urfey's comedy 'The Richmond Heiress,' acted 1693, where the song, in broken English, sung by Bowman, is put into the mouth of a comic Welshman, Rice ap Shenkin. The song is printed in Playford's 'Thesaurus Musicus,' book i. 1693, in different editions of 'Pills to Purge Melancholy' and 'The Dancing Master,' as well as on half-sheets of the period. In 'Pills' there is also another song to the same air. Henry Purcell and John Eccles wrote the music for 'The Richmond Heiress,' but whether a genuine Welsh air was employed for Shenkin's song is by no means certain. The tune, after being immensely popular in England, was first included in a Welsh collection in 1794 (Jones's), and named 'The Camp.' It is rather strange that John Parry (Bardd Alaw), in including it in his 'Two Thousand Melodies' (1841), No. 1980, names it, without further comment, 'Danish Air.' Parry had inserted it in his first Welsh collection, 1809, and there states that he is unable to trace its origin.

Blind Parry's first collection of twenty-four 'Arias,' unnamed, includes 'Lady Owen's Delight,' which is again repeated without name in his later collection of 'Twelve Airs for one and two Guitars' (c. 1760–65). In his 1781

edition it first bears the name 'Difyswch Arglwyddes Owen's.'

Lady Owen's Delight.

From Parry's 'Twelve Airs for one and two Guitars,' *cir.* 1760-65.

'The Mock Nightingale' is also in the 1742 edition, repeated in the 1781, and 'Glân Meddwdod Mwyn' ('Good humoured and fairly tipsy'), after being in the 'Twelve Airs' (1760–1765), occurs in the 1781 edition.

Others in this last-named work of Parry's printed for the first time are 'Nos Galen,' 'Sir Harry Ddû,' 'Mentra Gwen,' 'Merch Megan,' and other familiar airs, comprising forty-two in all.

In Jones's first edition of *Musical and Poetical Relicks of the Welsh Bards* (1784) is included 'Captain Morgan's March,' 'The Dimpled Cheek,' 'The Bend of the Little Horseshoe,' 'Winifreda,' 'Ar hyd y nos,' 'Dafyddy Garreg Wen,' 'Pen Rhaw,' etc. In the 1794 edition the whole plates are reprinted, with additions, and for the first time. 'Men of Harlech,' with

Gorhoffedd Gwyr Harlech.

(The March of the Men of Harlech.)

Jones's 'Welsh Bards,' 1794.

other now popular airs, sees the light for the first time. Among these is the following 'Eryri Wen ' (' White Snowdon ') from Jones's ' Welsh Bards ' (1794).

In Jones's *Bardic Museum* (1802) the pretty air 'Ash Grove' is first printed. In later works by different editors many fresh Welsh tunes find place ; those of Parry (Barrd Alaw) and Miss Williams especially contributing largely.

It is not necessary to reprint here the well-

Eryri Wen.
(White Snowdon.)
From Jones's 'Welsh Bards,' 1794.

known Welsh melodies which are to be found in the usual Welsh collections, but a couple of airs from Parry's 'Welsh Harper' will serve to give examples of two types of Welsh tunes.

Cywnvan y Wraig Weddw.
(The Widow's Lamentations.)
From 'The Welsh Harper,' vol. ii. 1848.

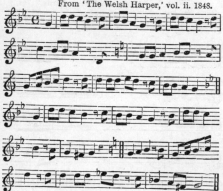

Divyrwch Gwyr Corwen.
(The Pastime of the Men of Corwen.)
From 'The Welsh Harper,' vol. ii. 1848.

DOUBTFUL MELODIES.—It now becomes necessary to consider the great number of tunes which have been classed as Welsh upon insufficient grounds. As a preliminary it must be recollected that Wales has at all times produced a large number of skilful performers on

the harp, who were accustomed to pick up a livelihood by travelling about the country in the exercise of their profession. It was from this class of men that the earlier collectors noted the melodies they published. It is impossible to assume that these wandering minstrels played nothing but Welsh tunes; they would, without doubt, please their audience or themselves with such airs as took their fancy. Those remaining among the mental stock in trade of harpers would become traditional and subject to such changes as affect traditional melody.

In a lengthy list of 'songs and melodies commonly used by the poets and harpers, in Wales, collected by Richard Morris, 1779' (B.M. Add. MSS. 14,939), are many titles of English melodies evidently, as the compiler of the list states, commonly used in Wales. Blind Parry, Jones and others, without inquiring into this matter, noted down numbers of English and Irish airs, apparently without the knowledge that they were merely traditional Welsh forms of such airs. The inclusion in these early Welsh works, especially with the words on their title-pages 'Never before published,' has caused them to be ranked among genuine Welsh music. A few of these cases may be here named, though the list could be largely extended did space permit.

'Pen Rhaw,' first published as Welsh in 1784, has considerable affinity to 'John, come kiss me now,' a tune common in England and Scotland in the 16th and 17th centuries. 'Torried y dydd' ('The dawning of the day'), 1781, is a well-known air, 'Windsor Tarras' (or Terrace), printed with the song in 'Pills,' vol. i., in Walsh's Dances for 1714, and elsewhere. 'Brenhines Dido' ('Queen Dido'), 1781, is a very imperfect remembrance of the ballad air 'Queen Dido,' or 'Troy Town,' as it is sometimes named; this was printed as early as 1660. 'Margaret that lost her garter' (1781) has great likeness to 'Franklin has fled away' of 1669. 'Good humoured and fairly tipsy,' which occurs in John Parry's 'Twelve Airs for one and two Guitars,' circa 1760, and again in his 1781 edition, is a slight deviation from a once favourite song, 'The women all tell me I'm false to my lass,' sung originally at Vauxhall in 1750 and printed with the song and air in the June supplement of the Universal Magazine for 1751. 'Hunting the Hare' (1794) has no Welsh claim; it is 'The Green Gown,' printed as early as 1652 in 'Musick's Recreation on the Viol,' and later, in a great number of other places.

'The Rising Sun' was published by Jones in 1794, with the note 'The subject of this air Mr. Handel has borrowed and introduced into the duet "Happy We" in his oratorio of "Acis and Galatea."' The duet is said to have been added by Handel to his pastoral in 1739; 'The Rising Sun' was printed in country dance-books about 1735, but it was not considered as Welsh before Jones published it in 1794. In any case the phrase is unimportant and probably had long been common property.

In a similar way an illogical proposition is made to the effect that the tune, ' Cease your funning,' in the ' Beggar's Opera ' (1727–28), is stolen from the air ' Llwyn Onn,' or ' Ash Grove,' which first appeared in the ' Bardic Museum ' (1802), without any account of its source, except that it was named after ' Mr. Jones's mansion near Wrexham.' The original of ' Cease your funning ' has been traced from the contemporary air ' Constant Billy ' or ' Lofty Mountains ' ; but while the resemblance to the Welsh tune is of the slightest, it is inconceivable that it can be founded on one of which no trace appears until over seventy years have passed. The error has been persistently repeated, down to the date of Brinley Richards. ' Drive the world before me ' (1794) is an Irish jig which is printed in Oswald's ' Caledonian Pocket Companion ' and elsewhere about the middle of the 18th century as ' Kick the world before you.' ' The First of August ' (1802) is a tune which figures in the ' Dancing Master ' as ' Frisky Jenny,' and under other titles has long been a favourite in England. The title ' The First of August ' was given to it by reason of its being sung to a song, so named, in commemoration of the Hanoverian succession, and not, as Jones suggests, in connexion with Lammas Day, or the payment of Welsh tithes. The air is probably Swedish.[1]

' Flaunting Two ' (1794) is the 17th-century country dance ' The Hemp Dresser,' and ' The Monks' March,' conjectured to be so named as one sung by the monks of Bangor who were massacred in 613, is really one named after General Monk, which occurs in the ' Dancing Master ' of 1665 as ' The L[ord] Monks March.' The Melody of ' Cynwyd ' (1794) is ' Dargason,' a tune of great antiquity, printed in the ' Dancing Master ' (1651, etc.). ' The Delight of the Men of Dovey ' (1781) is the Irish air ' Dear Catholic Brother,' and the list might be considerably prolonged. These tunes have, without evidence or comment, been included among Welsh national music at the dates above given. Succeeding editors have accepted the position, and where they have found them among earlier English music, have illogically suggested that they have been stolen from the Welsh. In one recent collection the editor has included ' The Princess Royal ' (' the Arethusa') without offering an explanation. Another illogical claim is for ' The Bells of Aberdovey ' (1844), which has long been included in Welsh collections as native of the soil, but is really the composition of Charles Dibdin, who, writing a song for it in broken Welsh, used it in his opera

' Liberty Hall ' (1785). Miss Williams, hearing it traditionally, published a version of it in her collection of 1844, and from that time onward it has been accepted as genuine Welsh. There is certainly no evidence to show that Dibdin used an existing tune (it was quite opposed to his practice), and no copy can be found except Dibdin's of a date before 1844.

A good example of the way in which great age is ascribed to tunes whose internal structure proclaims them of late date is seen in the air ' Captain Morgan's March,' included in every Welsh collection, and deservedly a great favourite. It was originally published by Jones in his 1784 edition, again repeated in that of 1794, while its terminal notes were altered to its present form in Parry's ' Welsh Melodies ' of 1809. The Welsh account of its origin, as given by Jane Williams, *History of Wales*, 1869, in mentioning the rising of Rhys ap Morgan, in Glamorganshire, in 1294, is that it ' was probably composed, or selected by this Prince to animate the march of his followers.' This early Morgan's connexion with the air is more or less suggested by all writers on the subject from Jones onward, and the passage from Williams's *History* is quoted by the editor of ' Cambrian Minstrelsie ' as late as 1893. It is somewhat strange that these historians skip all the Captain Morgans for five hundred years to fix upon this particular one renowned in Welsh history. The present writer makes the suggestion that the tune offers no structural evidence of an earlier date than the middle of the 18th century, and that it is most likely the composition of a regimental band-master, who has named it after some Captain Morgan associated with the regiment. Collectors of musical works do not need to be told that from about 1745–90 there was quite a run on military music, and that great numbers of marches of a similar character, named after military personages, were included in the flute and violin collections of the period.

Even if documentary evidence of a more trustworthy kind should be found in support of the theory that these tunes were of great antiquity, their internal evidence remains as a strong proof of their being, for the most part, of comparatively recent origin. In the two books of ' Welsh Melodies,' edited by Dr. J. Lloyd Williams [2] and Dr. Somervell (1907 and 1909), there are some fine tunes which are evidently old ; the lullaby, ' Suo-Gan ' and ' The Shepherd of Hafod ' (' Bugail yr Hafod ') are clearly older than any of the usually recognised Welsh airs ; and ' The Bard's Dream' (' Brenddwyd y Bardd ') is so purely Dorian in character that it must date from a time when the modes were in practical use.

---

[1] See article by the present writer in the *Mus. T.*, Sept. 1895, p. 593, and in the *Proceedings of the Musical Association*, 34th session, p. 89.

[2] See also a paper on ' Welsh National Melodies and Folk-Songs,' read by Dr. J. Lloyd Williams before the Honourable Society of Cymmrodorion on Jan. 22, 1908.

Of modern Welsh music the recognised national airs are ' Land of my Fathers,' ' God bless the Prince of Wales,' and ' Jenny Jones.' ' Land of my Fathers ' is the composition of James James, the Welsh words being written by Evan James of Pontypridd. They, with the tune, were printed in John Owen's ' Gems of Welsh Melody ' (1860), 1st series. ' God bless the Prince of Wales ' was composed (or compiled) by Brinley Richards in 1862. ' Jenny Jones ' was originally an instrumental piece for the harp, composed by John Parry (Bardd Alaw) in 1803, when it was named ' Cader Idris.' Charles Matthews the elder wrote the song ' Jenny Jones ' to the air and sang it in a musical play, ' He would be an Actor,' since when its popularity has been great.

PENNILLION SINGING. — There is one particular feature of Welsh music peculiar to the Principality ; this is ' Pennillion Singing ' —' pennil ' a stanza (' pennillion ' plural). This has been practised all over Wales from early times, and is still in vogue. There are two forms of it, one being more common in North Wales than in the South ; pennillion singing is generally a subject in musical competitions. The common method is this. A harper plays a well-known Welsh air—there are several tunes usually employed for the purpose, ' Pen Rhaw,' being one—in strict time, over and over again. Each of the company in turn adapts to the tune extempore words in rhyme, which are answered with a burden of ' fal lal la ' by the rest between the lines. This impromptu poetry must fit the melody in time and tune, and the subject is almost always expected to be humorous or familiar.

The North Wales manner, which is claimed to be the more correct one, is of greater difficulty. The singer must not only sing to the melody, but he must neither begin with it, nor on the first beat of a bar. Idris Vychan, who wrote a treatise on the art in 1866, laid down certain rules which are authoritative. Among them are the following : He (the singer) may begin at any portion of a bar he chooses, but must end with the melody. The instrumentalist must play the air continuously and markedly, and in correct time, whether with or without variations. The harper plays the air over each time a fresh one is introduced to give the singer time to adapt his stanza. No competitor is to use a stanza previously employed. Many of the Welsh collections give specimens of Pennillion singing.

A BIBLIOGRAPHY OF WELSH NATIONAL MUSIC
MANUSCRIPT

The Rhys Jones Manuscript, of unknown date. This is transcribed in the *Myvyrian Archaiology of Wales*, vol. iii., 1807, and again with a translation in the 1870 edition. The music is in tablature and similar in character to that contained in the MS. next mentioned.

The Penllyn or The Robert ab Huw MS. in the British Museum, described more fully in the body of the present article ; also transcribed and translated in the *Myvyrian Archaiology of Wales*, 1807 and 1870.

The Havod MSS., Nos. 3 and 24. These are treatises on the theory of music in Welsh, translated from works not yet identified. They were written some time in the early 17th or late 16th centuries. MS. No. 24 bears dates 1605, 1606 and 1608. Both are in the Cardiff Public Library.

The Jenkins MS. This is a collection of 187 airs, noted down by the Rev. John Jenkins, of Ceri in Montgomeryshire, during thirty years. In 1820 he presented it to John Parry (Bardd Alaw), who used many of the airs in his ' Welsh Harper.'

The Davies MS. A collection of Welsh airs, offered 'a competition at the National Eisteddfod at Llangollen in 1855, where it took the second prize ; the collector's name is not known. The sheets were unclaimed, and remained in the hands of the committee. Mr. Hartley, a commercial traveller of Bangor, bought them from some person for a shilling, had them bound, and afterwards presented them to Mr. Cadwaladr Davies in 1888. The MS. is now in the possession of Mrs. Mary DAVIES (*q.v.*), his widow. Several other MSS. of a like character and of late period are in the possession of Welsh gentlemen and ladies.

ENGRAVED AND PRINTED COLLECTIONS

c. 1727. **Aria di Camera**, being a choice Collection of Scotch, Irish and Welsh airs for the violin and German flute, by the following masters : Mr. Alex. Urquahart of Edinburgh, Mr. Dermot O'Connar of Limerick, Mr. Hugh Edwards of Carmarthen. London, printed for Dan Wright next the Sun Tavern in Holborn, and Dan Wright, junior, at the Golden Bass in St. Paul's Church Yard. 8vo. (In the library of Frank Kidson.)
Among the contents are the following Welsh airs, ' Welch Richard,' ' Welch Morgan,' ' Meillionen and Feriony'dd,' ' Morva Ryddlan,' and ' North Welch Morris.'

1742. **Antient British Music** or a Collection of tunes never before published, which are retained by the Cambro-Britons (more particularly in North Wales), and supposed by the learned to be the Remains of the music of the Antient Druids, so much famed in Roman History. Part I. containing twenty-four airs set for the harp, harpsichord, violin, and all within the compass of the German flute and figured for a thoroughbass. To which is prefixed an Historical Account, etc. Printed for and sold by the compilers, John Parry . . . and Evan Williams. . . . MDCCXLII. Sm. folio, pp. 64.
Contains 16 pp. music, having 24 airs, not named except as ' Aria I.,' etc. The dissertation was by Lewis Morris, and a copy in the British Museum has the Welsh names of the airs added in MS. evidently written in by Morris. Another copy, in the Euing Library, Glasgow, has also the names of the airs supplied in contemporary MS. The work includes ' Morva Ryddlan,' ' Lady Owen's Delight,' ' Meillion' and others not so well known.

c. 1760-65. A Collection of Welsh, English and Scotch Airs with new variations, also four new Lessons for the Harp or Harpsichord. Composed by John Parry, to which are added twelve airs for the Guittar. London, printed for and sold by John Johnson opposite Bow Church in Cheapside. Folio.
The Welsh Music included in this work is limited to ' Sweet Richard,' ' Rhyddian Marsh,' ' Of noble race was Shenkin,' ' Meillionen, or Sir Watkin's Delight,' and the twelve airs for the guitar which are untitled. John Parry (Bardd Alaw) and those who have copied him refer to the above two works as ' Parts I. and II.,' and the 1781 work by Parry of Rhuabon, as ' Part III.' There is no justification for this either on title-page or elsewhere ; they are quite independent works.

c. 1760-65. **Twelve Airs for one and two Guittars** composed by John Parry, harper to his Majesty. London, printed for H. Thorowgood under the North Piazza of the Royal Exchange, obl. 4to, in library of Frank Kidson.
This is a book of 5 pp., and contains the twelve airs mentioned in the title-page. There are only four out of the twelve arranged for two guitars, and the airs (unnamed) include those two which are known as ' Lady Owen's Delight,' and ' Good humoured and fairly tipsy ' (not harmonised). It is therefore a question whether Parry, by his title-page, did not profess himself the composer of them.

1781. **British Harmony** ; being a collection of Antient Welsh Airs, the traditional remains of those originally sung by the Bards of Wales ; carefully compiled and now first published with some additional variations by John Parry. . . . Printed for and sold by John Parry, Rhuabon, Denbighshire, and by P. Hodgson. . . . London, 1781. Folio. This is the last work issued by Parry ; he died in 1782. It contains 42 airs with Welsh titles, and is arranged with basses, and in some instances, with variations. It was afterwards reprinted from the old plates by Preston (see Cambrian Harmony).

1784. **The Musical and Poetical Relicks of the Welsh Bards**, preserved by tradition and authentic MSS. from very remote antiquity, never before published. To the bardic tunes are added variations for the harp, harpsichord, violin or flute . . . by Edward Jones. London, 1784. Folio.

1794. Ditto (second edition) with a larger number of tunes.

1800-08. Ditto, reprints of the 1794 edition. Also a Dublin pirated edition.

c. 1800. A Collection of Original Welsh Music for the harp, pianoforte, flute or violin . . . dedicated to the Prince of Wales. Published by S. Holden, 26 Parliament Street, Dublin. Folio. (In the Dundee Public Library.)

1802. **The Bardic Museum of primitive British Literature** . . . forming the second volume of the musical, poetical and historical Relicks of the Welsh Bards and Druids, with great pains now rescued from oblivion and never before published . . . by Edward Jones. London, 1802. Folio.
These two works have formed the basis of most subsequent collections. The first volume of ' The Welsh Harper,' 1839, was chiefly a reprint from these original plates.

c. 1804-05. **Cambro-British Melodies**, or the National Songs and Airs of Wales, enriched with curious historical illustrations of the airs. Harmonised with new basses . . . by Edward Jones. London. Folio.
A continuation of Jones's first two books.

c. 1800. Six Welch Airs with English words . . . by Mrs. Opie, harmonised for 2, 3 and 4 voices . . . by Ed. Smith Biggs. London, Birchall. Fol. (2 sets).

1804. North Wales, including its Scenery, Antiquities, Customs, and some sketches of its Natural History, by the Rev. W. Bingley. London. 2 vols. 8vo.
Contains, in the 2nd volume, 16 Welsh airs mainly from Jones.

1807. *Myvyrian Archæology of Wales*, vol. iii. 1807.
This contains transcripts of the Rhys Jones, and Penllyn MSS. The 1870 edition reprints the transcripts and gives translations and an article on the MSS. by John Thomas.

c. 1806–07. Specimens of various styles of music referred to in a course of lectures at Oxford and London . . . by W. Crotch, vol. i. Folio.
Contains 42 tunes, some noted by Malchair, others principally from Jones and Parry of Rhuabon.

c. 1809. A Selection of Welsh melodies with appropriate English words . . . with symphonies and accompaniments . . . by John Parry. London, Bland & Weller. Folio.
This was reprinted 1817–20 by Goulding and D'Almaine. This John Parry is 'Bardd Alaw' (1776–1851). In addition to those enumerated in this bibliography he issued many minor arrangements of Welsh melodies.

1809–1811–1814. A Select Collection of Original Welsh Airs adapted for the voice, united to characteristic English Poetry, never before published . . . accompaniments . . . chiefly by . Joseph Haydn. Vol. i. [ii. and iii.] London, Preston, and by G. Thomson, the editor and proprietor, Edinburgh. Folio.
George Thomson's collection in 3 vols., bearing the above dates respectively; practically all the airs are from printed sources.

c. 1810. Cambrian Harmony, being a Collection of ancient Welsh airs, the traditional remains of those originally sung by the Bards of Wales. . . . by John Parry [of Rhuabon]. London, Preston. 2 books. Folio.
A reprint of Parry's 'British Harmony,' 1781.

1810. Sixty of the most admired Welsh airs collected principally during his excursion into Wales, by the Rev. W. Bingley . . . the basses and variations arranged . . . by William Russell, junior, organist of the Foundling Hospital. London. Folio, 1810.

c. 1813–14. Twelve Favourite Welch Airs and melodies, arranged with variations as solos for the German Flute by Louis Jansen. London, G. Walker. Folio.

1817–20. A Selection of British Melodies, with symphonies and accompaniments by Clifton, and appropriate words by John F. M. Dovaston [1817]. Dublin, W. Power. Folio.
Second book, published by Clementi. London, dated (on cover only), 1820.

1822. A Selection of Welsh Melodies, with symphonies and accompaniments, by John Parry, and characteristic words by Mrs. Hemans. London, J. Power. Folio.

1829. A Third Volume of Welsh Melodies. The poetry by Mrs. Cornwall, Baron, Wilson ; the symphonies and accompaniments by John Parry. London, Goulding and D'Almaine.
The first of this series was published 1809, see above, and reprinted.

c. 1825. A Collection of Welsh Airs arranged on a plan never before attempted . . . also notes and observations on the mode of playing and singing the Welsh music . . . by John Parry. London, Goulding and D'Almaine. Folio.

1828. Cambrian Wreath, a selection of English poems on Welsh subjects . . . including Welsh melodies, illustrated by T. J. Llewelyn Prichard. 12mo. Aberystwith, 1828.
The book contains no music ; it is a collection of songs and poems in English, many being adapted to the Welsh melodies. The verses are by different authors.

1829. Cambrian Harmony, being a collection of Welch airs never before published, arranged as they were originally performed by the Ancient Britons . . . by Richard Roberts, Dublin, for the author, and to be had at his residence, Carnarvon. Folio.

1839. British Melodies, the composition of Master Hughes from the fourth to the ninth year of his age, with variations for the pianoforte, etc. and a collection of Cambrian Melodies. Folio.

1839 and 1848. The Welsh Harper, being an extensive collection of Welsh music, including most of the contents of the three volumes published by the late Edward Jones. . . . Also several airs from the publications of the late Mr. Parry of Ruabon . . . with many others never before published . . . by John Parry (Bardd Alaw). London, D'Almaine & Co. Folio, 2 vols.
The first volume, issued 1839, is a reprint from many of Jones's plates ; the 2nd, issued 1848, is a miscellaneous collection from various sources.

1844. Ancient National Airs of Gwent and Morganwg, being a collection of original Welsh melodies hitherto unpublished, which obtained the prize at the Eisteddfod held . . . Oct. 1838. To which are added the words usually sung thereto. Collected and arranged . . . by M. Jane Williams, Llandovery. London, 1844. Folio.
A valuable collection, independent of the earlier works ; it contains forty-three airs which Miss Maria Jane Williams obtained from direct oral tradition.

1845. The Cambrian Minstrel, being a collection of the melodies of Cambria with original words in English and Welsh, together with several original airs by John Thomas. Merthyr Tydvil, for the author, 1845. 4to.
The preface gives a list of some forty songs noted by himself from four people.

c. 1850–55. A Choice Collection of Welsh Airs by Edward Jones, harper to his late Majesty King George IV. when Prince of Wales. Carnarvon. Obl. 4to.
Two editions ; one contains twenty-five tunes, a later, forty-four taken from the original edition.

1860–64. Gems of Welsh Melody. A selection of Popular Welsh Songs with English and Welsh words. Specimens of Pennillion singing after the manner of North Wales and Welsh National Airs, ancient and modern, arranged by

John Owen (Owain Alaw). London, large 4to. First series 1860, second series 1861, third series 1862, fourth series 1864.
A later edition, 1873.

1862–74. Welsh Melodies with Welsh and English Poetry . . . harmonised by John Thomas. Folio, 4 vols. First and second vols. 1862, third 1870, fourth 1874.

1873. The Songs of Wales, edited by Brinley Richards. London, Boosey & Co. 8vo. [Fourth edition, 1879 ; a later, 1884.]

1893. Cambrian Minstrelsie, edited by Dr. Joseph Parry. Edinburgh, 6 vols., large 4to.

1896. Alawon fy Ngwlad ; Lays of My Land, collected by N. Bennett of Glanyrafon. Folio.
A collection of traditional melodies.

1906. The Minstrelsy of Wales, a collection of Welsh Songs, adapted to their traditional airs arranged . . . by Alfred Moffat. London, 8vo. Augener.

1907, 1909. Welsh Melodies, edited by J. Lloyd Williams and Arthur Somervell (two books, Boosey & Co.), contains many of the best Welsh tunes, and several that have not previously been included in collections.

1908. Welsh National Melodies and Folk-Song : a paper read before the Society of Cymmrodorion, Jan. 22, 1908, by J. Lloyd Williams, D.Sc., Director of Music, University College of North Wales.

1909. The publications of the Welsh Folk-Song Society.
To the above list might be added many collections of Welsh airs compiled from the books above named ; also many other publications by John Parry [Bardd Alaw], among which is his early work 'The British Fifer,' two parts, *circa* 1800. Also his musical plays, 'A Trip to Wales,' 1826, and 'The Welsh Girl,' 1833. In these some Welsh airs were used, as also in Attwood's opera, 'St. David's Day,' 1801.

F. K.

WELSH TRIPLE HARP, see HARP.

WENDLING, JOHANN BAPTIST (*b.* Alsace, *c.* 1720 ; *d.* Munich, Nov. 27, 1797), an excellent flautist, was first in the court chapel at Zweibrücken, and from 1754 in that at Mannheim. On the dissolution of the latter he followed the Elector to Munich. In 1771 he toured in Western Europe and also visited London. In Paris he appeared at the Concert Spirituel with his wife in 1751, 1752, 1780, and alone in 1778. He composed concertos, a trio, duets and sonatas for his instrument (list in *Q.-L.*). His wife, DOROTHEA SPOURNI (*b.* Stuttgart, 1737 ; *d.* Munich, Aug. 20, 1811), was a great operatic soprano and a successful teacher. Her sister, AUGUSTE ELISABETH (*d.* Mannheim, 1794), wife of the violinist Karl Wendling, was likewise an excellent singer, engaged at the Mannheim Opera. She died at the early age of 34 from consumption. Her husband remained at Mannheim when the electoral chapel was transferred to Munich in 1778, but Johann Franz, a brother of Joh. Baptist, violinist in the chapel since 1747, remained in it on its removal (*Riemann* ; *Q.-L.*).

WENNERBERG, GUNNAR (*b.* Lidköping, Oct. 2, 1817 ; *d.* Leckö, Aug. 22, 1901), a Swedish poet and composer, educated at the Upsala university. For many years he was a member of the Swedish legislature. As a musician he was entirely self-taught, and he published his first composition 'Frihetssänger' ('Songs of Freedom'), in 1847. This was followed by several works of which the best known is 'Gluntarne' (duets for male voices, descriptive of student life in Upsala). He subsequently wrote an oratorio entitled 'The Birth of Christ' and a Stabat Mater ; and set the Psalms of David in a simple and melodious form for soli and chorus with accompaniment. These Psalms are universally popular in Sweden, and they are sung both in North Germany and Scotland. In 1867 he became a

member of the Swedish Academy. His collected writings appeared in four volumes, 1881–
1885.   A. H. W.

BIBL.—S. ALMQUIST, *Om Gunnar Wennerberg. Hans tid och hans gärning.* Stockholm, 1917.

WERCKMEISTER, ANDREAS (*b.* Benneck-
enstein, Nov. 30, 1645; *d.* Halberstadt, Oct. 26,
1706), a clever organist and sound musician,
devoted his energies to elucidating the difficult
problem of the correct tuning of organs and
claviers.

His *Musicae mathematicae Hodegus curiosus*
in 1686 deals mathematically with everything
used in the construction of music, with intervals,
beats and temperament. This was followed by
another mathematical work *Musikalische Temperatur*, in 1691. The comprehensive survey
of Werckmeister's theories given in Mattheson's
Das forschende Orchestre, 1721, shows the
influence they exercised on his contemporaries.
As a composer Werckmeister is practically
unknown, for although in the catalogues
of new books published at Leipzig by
Gross and at Frankfort by Latomi in 1686, a
volume of his compositions is announced:
'Andrea Werckmeister's musikalische Privat-
kunst, bestehend in Sonatinen, Allemanden,
Cour, etc. Quedlinburg, Th. Ph. Calvisius,' no
copy of it seems to be now in existence.

He was the son of Joachim Werckmeister.
In 1658 he went to school at Benningen, his
uncle Christian, the organist there, teaching
him music. On Aug. 15, 1660, he joined the
school at Nordhausen under the Rector Hilde-
brand, and at the end of two years entered the
Gymnasium at Quedlinburg, where his uncle
Victor Werckmeister occupied the position of
cantor. On Dec. 24, 1664, he was appointed
organist at Hasselfelde, Brunswick, where he
remained for ten years. He refused posts
offered to him at Ellrich in 1670, and at Elbin-
gerode in 1674, but accepted one as Hoforganist
at Quedlinburg in 1675.

He was twice married, first on July 16, 1667,
to a wife who died in 1680, and again on Feb.
14, 1682; he had a family of two sons and four
daughters. It was not until 1696 that he
received his most important appointment, as
organist at St. Martin's Church at Halberstadt,
and as Inspector of all organs constructed in
the principality of Halberstadt.

A detailed account of his life is to be found in
the funeral oration given by Johann Melchior
Goetzen, which was published in 1707 under the
title *Der weitberühmte Musicus und Organista*,
etc.

Hawkins says of Werckmeister in his *History
of Music* :

'Mr. Handel, who was well acquainted with him,
was used to speak of him in terms of great respect,
and he was doubtless a learned and very skilful
musician.'

Werckmeister published in 1699–1700 at
Quedlinburg, a German translation of Agostino
Steffani's *Quanta certezza habbia da suoi principii
la musica, et in qual pregio fosse perciò presso
gli antichi* (Amsterdam, 1695). Under the
title of *D. A. Steffani . . . Sendschreiben*, it
was reissued with additions by J. L. Albrecht at
Mühlhausen in 1760.

The list of his published works opens with
the well-known *Orgelprobe*, on the construction,
testing, and tuning of organs, of which there
were several editions.

(1) Orgelprobe oder kurtze Beschreibung wie und welcher
Gestalt man die Orgel-Wercke von den Orgelmachern annehmen,
probiren, untersuchen, und der Kirchen liefern könne und solle,
benebenst einem kurtzen jedoch gründlichen Unterricht wie durch
Anweiss und Hülffe des Monochordi, ein Clavier wohl zu temperiren
und zu stimmen sei, etc. Frankfort and Leipzig. 1681, 12mo.
  Second edition : Andreae Werckmeisters Benic. Cherusci, p.t.
Musici und Organ. zu S. Martini in Halberstadt, erweiterte und
verbesserte Orgel-Probe, oder : Eigentliche Beschreibung, etc. Jetze
von dem Autore selbst übersehen, etc. Quedlinburg. In Verlegung
Th. Ph. Calvisii, 1698. 4to, 32 chapters, pp. 82.
  Third edition : Quedlinburg und Aschersleben. In Verlegung
G. E. Struntz, 1716. 4to, Gedruckt bey J. Th. Heinsio, Waldenburg.
32 chapters, pp. 82.
  Fourth edition : Leipzig, J. M. Teubner, 1754. 8vo, 32 chapters,
pp. 110.
  Another edition : Augsburg, J. J. Lotter, 1783. 32 chapters,
pp. 112.
  A Dutch translation was also published : Orgel-Proef of nauw-
keurige Beschrjving, etc. uit het Hoogduitsche vertaald door Jacob
Wilhelm Lustig. T'Amsteldam, A. Olofsen, 1755. 12mo, pp. 151.
Another edition, 1775.
  (2) Musicae mathematicae Hodegus curiosus, oder richtiger
musikalischer Weg-Weiser, das ist, wie 'man nicht alleine die
natürlichen Eigenschafften der musikalischen Proportionen, durch
das Monochordum, und Ausrechnung erlangen, sondern auch
vermittels derselben, natürliche und richtige Rationes über eine
musikalische Composition vorbringen könne, etc. Von A. W.
itziger Zeit Hoff-Organisten zu Quedlinburg. Franckfurt und
Leipzig. In Verlegung Th Ph. Calvisii. Merseburg, gedruckt
bey Christian Gottschicken, 1686. 4to, pp. 160. Another edition,
1698.
  (3) Der edlen Music-Kunst Würde, Gebrauch und Missbrauch, so
wohl aus der Heiligen Schrifft, als auch aus etlichen alten und
neubewährten reinen Kirchen-Lehrern, und dann aus den Music-
Gründen selbst eröffnet und vorgestellet von A. W. Stiffts-Hof-
Organisten in Quedlinburg. Franckfurt und Leipzig. Th. Ph.
Calvisii 1691. 4to, 12 chapters, pp. 41.
  Musikalische Temperatur, oder deutlicher und warer mathe-
matischer Unterricht, wie man durch Anweisung des Monochordi
ein Clavier, sonderlich die Orgel-Wercke, Positive, Regale, Spinetten,
und dergleichen wol temperirt stimmen könne, etc. Franckfurt
und Leipzig. Th. Ph. Calvisii, 1691. 4to, 34 chapters, pp. 91.
  (4) Hypomnemata musica oder musikalisches Memorial, welches
bestehet in kurtzer Erinnerung dessen, so bishero unter guten
Freunden discurs-weise, insonderheit von der Composition und
Temperatur möchte vorgangen seyn, etc. Von A. W. Benicosteinensi
Cherusc.; Jezziger Zeit bey der Haupt-Pfarr Kirche St. Martini in
Halberstat, bestallten Musico, und Organisten. Quedlinburg, Th.
Ph. Calvisius, 1697. 4to, 12 chapters, pp. 44.
  Die nothwendigsten Anmerckungen, und Regeln wie der Bassus
continuus, oder General-Bass wol könne tractiret werden, und ein
jeder, so nur ein wenig Wissenschaft von der Music und Clavier hat,
denselben von sich selbst erlernen könne, etc. Aschersleben,
1698, 4to.
  Another edition : Aschersleben, G. E. Struntz, Buchhändler.
Waldenburg druckts Joh. Th. Heinsius, 1715, pp. 75. The *Catalogus
universalis*, published at Leipzig, 1714–1715, calls this the second
edition.
  An undated edition : 'aniezzo mercklich vermehret . . . durch
Andreas Werckmeistern, M.u.O.z. S.M.i.H. Aschersleben, Verlegts
G. E. Struntz.'
  (5) A. W. Benic. Cherusci, p.t. Musici und Organ. zu S. Martini in
Halberstadt Cribrum musicum oder musikalisches Sieb, darinnen
einige Mängel eines halb gelehrten Componisten vorgestellet, und
das Böse von dem Guten gleichsam ausgesiebet und abgesondert
worden, etc. Durch Johann Georg Carl, bestalten Stadt-Musicum
in Halberstadt. Quedlinburg und Leipzig. Th. Ph. Calvisius, 1700.
Jena, gedruckt bey Paul Ehrichen. 4to, 16 chapters, pp. 60.
  Harmonologia musica oder kurtze Anleitung zur musikalischen
Composition, wie man vermittels der Regeln und Anmerckungen
bey den General-Bass einen Contrapunctum simplicem mit sonder-
bahrem Vortheil durch drey Sätze oder Griffe componiren, und
extempore spielen, etc. : wie man einen gedoppelten Contrapunkt
und mancherley Canones oder Fugas Ligatas, durch sonderbahre
Griffe und Vortheile setzten und einrichten möge, aus denen
mathematischen und musikalischen Gründen aufgesetzet, etc.
Durch A. W., Benicosteinensem Cheruscum, p.t. Organisten in
der Haupt-Pfarr Kirche zu S. Martini in Halberstadt. Franck-
furth und Leipzig, Th. Ph. Calvisius, 1702. Jena, gedruckt bey
Paul Ehrichen. 4to, pp. 142.
  Dietrich Buxtehude, the celebrated organist at Lübeck, a friend
of Werckmeister greatly esteemed this work. (*Vierteljahrsschrift*,
v. 573.)
  (6) Organum Gruningense redivivum, oder kurtze Beschreibung
des in der Grüningischen Schloss-Kirchen berühmten Orgel-Wercks,
wie dasselbe anfangs erbauet und beschaffen gewesen : und wie es
anitzo noch allergnädigsten Befehl Sr. Kön. Preussis. Magistät, ist
renovirt und mercklich verbessert worden . . . von A. W. Quedlinburg und Aschersleben. G. E. Struntz, 4to. The dedication is
dated : 'Halberstadt, den 16 Augusti, 1705.'
  (7) Musikalische Paradoxal-Discourse, oder ungemeine Vor-
stellungen, wie die Musica einen hohen und göttlichen Uhrsprung

tabe, und wie hingegen dieselbe so sehr gemissbraucht wird, etc.: von A. W. musico und organ. zu S. Martini in Halberstadt, Quedlinburg. Th. Ph. Calvisius, 1707. 4to, pp. 120. Published after Werckmeister's death.   C. S.

WERNER, GREGOR JOSEPH (d. Eisenstadt, Mar. 3, 1766),[1] was Haydn's immediate predecessor as Kapellmeister to Prince Esterhazy, his appointment dating from May 10, 1728. In 1761 Haydn became vice-Kapellmeister, but Werner retained his place to the time of his death. He was a prolific and talented composer, who wrote 18 oratorios, over 40 masses, 3 Requiems and a large quantity of other church music, symphonies and sonatas for 2 violins and bass, a string quartet, 2 pastorellas for 2 violins, harpsichord and organ, etc. Haydn arranged six of his fugues for string quartet, adding an introduction to each, and published them through Artaria (Mendel; Riemann; Q.-L.).

WERNER, JOHANN GOTTLOB (b. Hayn, near Leipzig, 1777; d. Chemnitz, July 19, 1822), was organist at Frohburg, near Leipzig, 1798; deputy of Cantor Tag at Hohenstein, near Chemnitz, 1804, and from about 1819 cathedral organist and music-director at Merseburg. On account of the gout he retired with a pension, and lived the last years of his life with a married daughter at Chemnitz. He wrote a number of successful Tutors for the organ and the pianoforte, harmony and accompaniment, and several books of organ pieces (Riemann; Q.-L.).

WERRECORE (VERECOREN), HERMANN MATTHIAS (1523–55). One of the puzzling cases in which it is difficult to decide if there is more than one composer in question, and if so, how many. The above is a different person from Mattheus Le MAISTRE (q.v.), first heard of in 1554; but his identity with the 'Matthias Hermannus,' the 'Hermannus' and 'Matthias,' whose compositions appear in various collections between 1538 and 1569, although probable, remains undecided.

In the British Museum are the four partbooks of Wolffgang Schmeltzel's collection of songs:

'Guter seltzamer, vñ künstreicher teutscher Gesang, sonderlich ettliche künstliche Quodlibet, Schlacht, vñ der gleichen, mit vier oder fünff Stimmen, biss her, im Truck nicht gesehen. Nürnberg J. Petreius, 1544.'

This contains the earliest known copy of Werrecore's descriptive composition, celebrating Francesco Sforza's victory in the struggle as to the fate of Milan. The music is simply written for four voices, soprano, alto, tenor and bass, without instrumental accompaniment, and is in three movements.

The appearance of Werrecore's composition in this work seems to require some explanation, for Schmeltzel was cantor or schulmeister in the Schottenkloster at Vienna; how did he hear of this piece of music, which could hardly have travelled so far afield?

[1] At the age of 56 according to his tombstone, but 71 according to the parish register.

Dr. Elsa Bienenfeld answers this question in her able paper [2] on Schmeltzel's Liederbuch; the connecting link is formed by Conrad Weichselbaum, a keen fighter, who had been through the campaign which culminated in the battles of Bicocca and Pavia. He was afterwards, 1528–42, Abbot of the Schottenkloster in Vienna, and would come into touch with Schmeltzel, who was certainly working there before 1540. In all probability Werrecore composed the music soon after his return from the war; it is here called 'Die Schlacht vor Pavia.' In each of the partbooks this is followed by the words, 'Matthias Herman Verecoiensis, qui et ipse in acie quaeque miserrima vidit, me obiter composuit' (Matthias Herman of Vereco, who was himself in the ranks and witnessed the utmost of the disaster, composed this on his way). The term Verecoiensis led Eitner to assume that Verecore or Werrecore was the composer's native place, and that either Matthias or Hermann was his surname,[3] but it will be seen that in every other instance the word Verecore is used as a surname, and though this of course does not prevent its being derived from the name of a birthplace, it is a curious thing that in spite of many plausible suggestions no town with a similar name has yet been discovered.

In 1549 the same composition was published under the title:

' La Bataglia Taliana composta da M. Mathias Fiamengo maestro di capella del domo di Milano, con alcune Villotte piacevole novamente con ogni diligentia stampate e corrette. A quatro voci. In Venetia apresso Antonio Gardane, 1549.'

The four partbooks are in the Wolfenbüttel herzogl. Bibl. Gardane in writing the dedication says:

' Hora ho deliberato meco stesso d' indirizzare a lei una battaglia Italiana, composta dall' eccellente M. Mathias e ho voluto aggiungere alcune altre compositioni,' etc.[4]

A second edition ('ristampate & corrette. Aggiontovi anchora una Villotta alla Padoana con quatro parte. A quatro voci') was published by Gardane in 1552; there is a complete copy in the Munich Library. An anonymous composition [5] in three movements for four voices, found in a manuscript Cantional of the year 1558, and inscribed 'Conflictus ad Ticinium,' was probably Werrecore's Bataglia Italiana; it began with the same words 'Signori e cavalieri,' etc. Muoni, in his list of Maestri di cappella del duomo di Milano (1883), states that, Jan. 5, 1523, 'Armanno Verecore detto Maestro Matthias fiammingo' was elected with a monthly salary of 12 lire, that he reorganised the cappella, which started on its new footing on Dec. 9, 1534. The next maestro is not mentioned before 1558, in that year,

[2] See Sammelbände of the Int. Mus. Ges. vi. 1904-05.
[3] As evidence that the family name existed, Van der Straeten (Pays-Bas, vii. 143) refers to a Pieter Werrekoren, printer at Sint-Martensdijk, Zeland, in 1478.
[4] Parisini, Cat. Bibl. Liceo Musicale, Bologna, iii. 243.
[5] See Becker's Hausmusik in Deutschland, 1840, p. 14.

therefore, Werrecore was no longer in possession of the post.

His only other complete work was published in 1555 :

'Cantuum quinque vocum (quos motetta vocant) Hermann Matthiae Werrecoren musici excellentissimi liber primus. Nunc primum in lucem editus. Mediolani apud Franciscum et Simonem Moschenios.'

The five partbooks are in the Hamburg Stadtbibliothek. Haberl (*M.f.M.*, 1871–72) described them and their contents in his excellent article on 'Matthias Hermann Werrecorensis' and gave Werrecore's dedication in full, also the score of the two movements of the motet 'Popule meus' (see the *Musikbeilage*). He states that the work is a most beautiful specimen of 16th-century music-printing. Two of the motets, 'O altitudo divitiarum' and 'Veni sancte spiritus,' are in manuscripts dated respectively 1573 and 1571, in the Proske Library. It will be noticed that this work was published at Milan. This alone would make one hesitate as to the identity of Le Maistre and Mathias Fiammengo, which was assumed by Fétis (*Biog. univ.*) and by Otto Kade (*Mattheus Le Maistre*, 1862) and leads to the theory that Mathias left Milan in 1554 to fill the post of Kapellmeister at Dresden. For nearly all Le Maistre's works were published at Dresden; and Kade, after giving a facsimile of a receipt for the 'Gesangbücher meines gnädigsten Herrn Hertzogen Augusts,' signed Matheus Le Maistre and written after his appointment as Kapellmeister at Dresden on Oct. 7, 1554, adds that Le Maistre never varied from this signature ; in no case had he found in his writing or in his printed works anything signed by his Christian name only. From this it seems justifiable to conclude that the single compositions by 'Matthias' already alluded to were by Werrecore and not by Le Maistre. Kade in his work published the first part, in score, of 'La Bataglia,' assuming that Matthias, the composer, was Le Maistre ; although, in his admirable account of the music, he repeatedly accentuates the difference in quality between this and everything else afterwards composed by Le Maistre, and also notices that the three Villotte included are totally different from his later style.

There is an interesting little allusion to Werrecore in Petrus Schoeffer's edition of *Cantiones quinque vocum selectissimae*, Argentorati, 1539. In the dedication Schoeffer mentions the valuable thesaurus of songs sent to him from Italy by Hermann Matthias Verrecoren, the learned master of music in the Cathedral of Milan :

'Jam vero tandem praeter spem quidem, ut non sine felici quodam auspicio thesaurus cantionum summi pretij ex Italia ad me perlatus est, quem D. Hermannus Mathias Verrecoren negocij musici primariae Ecclesiae Mediolani magister, vir, praeter alias virtutes, in ea arte maximopere doctus, nuper ad me misit,' etc.[1]

_____
[1] See Parisini's *Cataloso*, ii. 359.

The following works are those containing compositions under Werrecore's name :

1. 'Selectissimae necnon familiarissimae Cantiones. Augsburg, Kriesstein. 1540.'
   No. 1, Sex vocum : 'Congregati sunt.' Ad aequales voces. By 'Hermann Matthias Verrecoren.'
   No. 47, Quinque vocum, 'Ne vous chaille.' Ad aequales voces. 'Her. Math. Wer.'
2. Mutetarum divinitatis liber primus quae quinque absolutae vocibus ex multis praestantissimorum musicorum academiis collectae sunt. Mediolani, 1543' (and again in 1569). The motets 'Adsit nobis,' 'Beati omnes,' and 'In nomine Jesu,' by 'Her. Math. Vuer.' A manuscript copy of 'Beati omnes,' inscribed, 'Hermannus Cū,' and dated 1538, is in the Proske Library.
3. Secunda pars magni operis musici ... Noribergae, 1559.' Four motets by 'Herm. Math. Werrecoren.' These were taken from his work published in 1555.
4 Thesauri musici tomus quartus. Noribergae, 1564. Seven metets (from the 1555 work) and the 'In nomine Jesu' already published in 1543, by 'Matthias Hermannus Werrecoren,' and 'Hermanni Mat. Werre.'

Compositions by 'Matthias' will be found in the second and fourth book of motets published by Attaingnant in Paris, 1534 ; in the third book of motets, 'Motetti del fiore' (Lugduni, Modernus, 1538 and 1542) ; and in the third book, 'Selectissimarum sacrarum cantionum' (Lovanii, Phalesius, 1569). Also in 'Il primo libro dei madrigali di Maistre Jhan,' 1541, and in 'Il primo libro di madrigali d'Archadelt,' 1559, but it is doubtful if this Matthias is to be identified with Werrecore A Motet for five voices, 'Surrexit pastor bonus,' by 'Hermannus,' is in the 'Secundus tomus novi operis musici, 6, 5 et 4 vocum' (Noribergae, J. Otto, 1538), and this might possibly be Werrecore's work. Manuscript copies of it are in the Breslau Library, dated 1573.

It is generally thought that the two settings of 'Mein hertz und gmüt' for five voices, by Mathias Hermanus in G. Forster's work, 'Der fünffte Theil schöner, frölicher, frischer, alter und newer teutscher Liedlein,' Nürnberg, 1556 were composed by Werrecore.   C. S.

WERT, GIACHES DE (JACHES WERT), or as he more usually signs himself in his works, Giaches Vuert (*b.* ? Antwerp *c.* 1536 ; *d.* Mantua, May 23, 1596), madrigal composer, was sent to Italy at a very early age as a chorister in the house of Maria di Cardona, Marchese della Padulla, and when 9 years old became a member of the Novellara choir formed by Alfonso Gonzaga of Reggio.

Thirteen years later he published the first of his long series of volumes of madrigals, and must have taken up his residence in Mantua very shortly afterwards. His musical work in Mantua was principally in connexion with the church of Santa Barbara ; he is known to have composed music for the celebration of a church festival in Oct. 1564, and in 1565 he succeeded Giovanni Contino as maestro di cappella there ; to this was added the position of composer and maestro di cappella to the Duke Guglielmo Gonzaga, à post he retained until his death.

Canal's work, *Della musica in Mantova*, 1881 (see also Haberl's paper in the *Kirchenmusikalisches Jahrbuch*, 1886), throws a good deal of light on the details of Wert's life in Mantua, and on the various small journeys that he made

From July 3 to Sept. 19, 1565, he obtained leave of absence in order to visit ' la casa sua ' at Novellara, where his wife was still living. In the spring of 1566 he accompanied the Duke of Mantua to Augsburg, where the Italian and German princes had been convoked by the Emperor Maximilian II. to decide on defensive measures against Soliman and the Turks. Wert's musical gifts received general recognition, and the Emperor wished him to remain in his service, but Wert declined the offer and returned to Mantua in the autumn. On Feb. 3, 1567, another journey was made in the company of the Duke and other personages to Venice. Wert also passed some time at the court of Ferrara ; he makes reference to this in dedicating the eighth volume of his madrigals (1586) to Alfonso II. of Ferrara.

Wert's residence at Mantua does not appear to have been altogether peaceful, although on July 1, 1580, his long and faithful services were recognised by the presentation of the freedom of the city to him and his heirs for ever, and by the gift of a large sum of money. A letter of his, written from Novellara, on Aug. 27, 1567, contains bitter complaints of the intrigues and annoyance to which he was subjected by Italian musicians owing to his being a foreigner; and another, addressed to the Duke, dated Mar. 27, 1570, makes a more specific complaint as to the relations of one Agostino Bonvicino with Wert's wife ; Bonvicino eventually was dismissed from the ducal cappella. Another letter, quoted by Haberl, was written by Alfonso of Novellara, on Jan. 3, 1568, and asked for the loan of Wert for a few days to prepare singers and players for the performance of the Intermedii in a Commedia he had just written.

Duke Guglielmo Gonzaga, a great lover of music, was a personal friend of Palestrina, whom he met in Rome in 1572, and with whom he had been previously in correspondence. This probably brought Palestrina into touch with Wert, with whose music he was at any rate familiar, for in writing to the Duke in Feb. 1568, he referred to Wert as ' un virtuoso veramente raro.'

Theoretical writers contemporary with Wert and those writing early in the following century, find nothing but praise for his musicianship and especially for his skill in counterpoint. Under the name of Jacques de Vert he appears in Thomas Morley's *Plaine and Easie Introduction*, 1597, among the ' Practitioners, the moste parte of whose works we have diligently perused, for finding the true use of the Moods.' Artusi mentions Wert in his treatise *Delle imperfettioni della moderna musica*, 1600, p. 42 ; and Zacconi (*Prattica di musica*, 1622, p. 130) writes :

' Io ho cognosciuto quatro musici singolarissimi ne contrapunti, Costanza Porta, Jaches Vuert, . . . Jaches Vuert venne anch' egli in detta professione altro tanto singolare ; perche essendo egli maestro di cappella di Guglielmo, serenissimo duca di Mantova,

facendo detto duca profession di musico, e componendo molte cose, lo tenea suegghiato si, nelle cose de sudetti contrapunti, che bene spesso come dire il proverbio li facea sudar il fronte,' etc.

Again G. B. Doni (*Annotazioni*, 1640, p. 141) refers to Wert's madrigal for three voices ' Qual dall' usato,' ' il quale è mirabilmente soave.' Another interesting reference to Wert is to be found in the preface to the fine volume of sacred music by Francisco Sale, of which a copy is in the British Museum, the ' Tomus I. Missarum solenniorum,' published by Adam Berg at Munich in 1589. The passage is as follows :

' Aut aliquo intervallo, ad quintam puta, vel altiore vel demissiore, qua in re doctissimum nostra aetate musicum D. Jacobum Werthium, Belgam, utrumque imitari libuit, qui jam olim in comitiis Augustanis, coram divi Maximiliani Caesaris, et aliorum principum musicis, cum summa omnium admiratione ejus artis specimen ex tempore dedit.'

Nearly every collection of either sacred or secular music from 1564 up to the middle of the 17th century contained compositions by Wert. Although the earliest known edition of Wert's madrigals for four voices, of which there is a copy in the Munich Library, is dated 1561, one of the most popular madrigals in it had already been included in the ' Secondo libro delle muse a quattro voci,' Roma, 1558, ' Chi salira.' [1] In the same way, although Wert did not publish his first book of motets for five voices till 1566, the ' Motetta de Cipriani de Rore et aliorum auctorum quatuor vocibus,' Venice, 1563, contained ' Diligite justiciam ' by Jaches de Vuerth. The fine motets ' Egressus Jesus ' for seven voices, and ' Transeunte Domino ' for five voices, were published in Joannellus's ' Novi thesauri musici,' 1568 ; these have been reprinted by Commer (' Collectio operum mus.,' vols. ii. and iv.), but with the composer's name given as Jaches Vaet. In Stafford Smith's ' Musica antiqua,' i. p. 92, will be found ' Virgo Maria hodie,' scored from Wert's first book of motets for six voices, 1581, and in S. W. Dehn's ' Sammlung älterer Musik.' vi. Lieferung, 1836, the six-part motet ' Quiescat vox tua a ploratu.'

LIST OF WORKS

1558. Il primo libro de madrigali a cinque voci.   Venetia, Scotto. Dedicated to Alfonso Gonzaga.   Other editions were published by Gardane at Venice in 1564, 1571, and 1583.
1561. Il primo libro de madrigali a quattro voci di Giaches de Wert.   Venetia, Scotto.   Dedicated to the Marchese di Pescara.   Other editions were published by Gardane in 1562, 1564, 1570 and 1583.
1561. Il secondo libro de madrigali a cinque voci.   Venetia, Scotto. Dedicated to Ottavio Farnese, Duca di Parma e Piacenza. Reissued by Gardane in 1564, 1571, 1575 and 1596. Scotto also published both this and the first book with the title ' of ' Madrigali del fiore,' in 1561.
1563. Il terzo libro.   Published by Gardane, and again in 1572 and 1592.   The dedication to Consalvo Fernandes di Cordova, Duca di Sessa, states : ' havendomi V. E. degnata del governo di sua cappella e del nome di suo creato,' etc.
1567. Il quarto libro.   Gardane, and in 1568 and 1583.   Dedicated to Guglielmo Gonzaga, Duca di Mantova.
1571. Il quinto libro de madrigali a cinque, sei et sette voci. Gardane, and in 1580. Dedicated to the ' Signori academici di Verona detti Filharmonici . . . protettrici et amichi della musica.'
1577. Il sesto libro.   Scotto, and in 1584 and 1592.   Dedicated to the ' Principe di Mantova et Monferrato, mio signore.'
1581. Il settimo libro.   Gardano.   Dedicated to Margherita Farnesa Gonzaga, Principessa di Mantova, with the date ' Di Mantova il di 10 di Aprile, 1581.   Giaches Vuert.'
1586. L' ottavo libro.   Gardano, and in 1596.   The dedication to

[1] Republished by W. Barclay Squire as No. 19 of 'Ausgewählte madrigale.'   No. 40 of the same series is ' Un jour je m'en allai ' from Wert's ' Primo libro delle canzonette ' (1589).

the Duca di Ferrara states that many of these madrigals were composed in Ferrara, and mentions ' Tanti altri eccellenti & musici & cantori, che sono nella sua numerosissima e perfettissima cappella ' and the 'Si rare qualità della tre nobilissime giovanidame della sereniss. Signora Duchessa di Ferrara.'

1588. Il nono libro. Gardano. Dedicated to Vincenzo Gonzaga, Duca di Mantova a Monferrato.

1591. Il decimo libro. Gardano. Dedicated to Donna Ines d'Argotti Carretta, Marchese di Grana, dated from Venice, Sept. 10, 1591, signed Giaches Vuert.

1595. L' undecimo libro. Gardano, and in 1600. The dedication to Francesco Gonzaga, Principe di Mantova, has the following passage referring to Wert's age : ' Vecchio però tanto che non isperi di poter consacrare a suo tempo qualche nuovo lavoro anche ad un figlio di Francesco, non ha consecrato all' avo, al padre, e alla madre ; sicche ad ogni modo non doveva essere più là dal sessant' anni, perchè al principino non ne aven che nove.'

1566. Jaches Wert musici suavissimi ac chori illustriss. et excellentiss. Ducis Mantuae magistri musices, vel ut dicunt motectorum quinque vocum liber primus. Venetiis, 1566, apud Claudium Coregiatum et Faustum Bethanium Socios. The dedication to Guglielmo, Duca di Mantova, is signed Giaches de Vuert. A later edition was published at ' Noribergae apud Theodoricum Gerlatzenum,' 1569. This work with the two books following was included in the collected edition of 1583.

1581. Modulationum cum sex vocibus liber primus. Venetiis apud haeredem Hieronymi Scoti, 1581. Dedicated to the Prince Cardinal Alessandro Farnese.

1581. Di Jaches de Wert il secondo libro de motetti a cinque voci. In Vineggia appresso l' herede di Gir. Scotto. 1581.

1583. Jaches Wert musici suavissimi modulationum sacrarum quinque et sex vocum libri tres, in unum volumen redacti. Noribergae excudebant Catharina Gerlachin & haeredes Johannis Montani, 1583. In six separate part-books.

1589. Il primo libro delle canzonette, Villanelle a cinque voci. Venetia, Gardano. Dedicated to Leonora Medici Gonzaga, Duchessa di Mantova, and dated from ' Venetia il di 20 Genaro, 1589.' This work includes three French, two Spanish compositions and one Greek.

1653. Vana mundi beatitudo quam vocibus quatuor decantavit Giaches de Wert. Typis recudit Joannes Reusnerus acad. Regimontanae typogr. anno 1653. ' Sunt summo beati,' in four separate part-books in the Königsberg Library.

MANUSCRIPTS

Augsburg Library.—Seven motets.
British Museum.—Add. MS. 12,532, madrigals for five and six voices. Add. MSS. 31,407 and 31,412, ' Io non son pero ' for five voices. Add. MS. 31,992, f. 67b, in lute tablature ' Speremus meliora.'
Basle Library.—' Egressus Jesus,' in German organ tablature, written about 1593.
Breslau Stadtbibliothek.—Motets for five, six and seven voices, including ' Egressus Jesus ' and ' Transeunte Domino.'
Brieg Library.—MS. 49, dated 1579, ' Egressus Jesus '; MS. 28, ' Speremus meliora ' for five voices.
Dresden State Library.—' Angelus domini ' for five voices.
Frankfort Gymnasium-Bibliothek.—' Egressus Jesus.'
Grimma Library.—Four motets.
Liegnitz Ritteracademie-Bibliothek.—Motets for five and seven voices.
Milan Conservatoire Library.—A Mass for four voices, and another for six voices, inscribed with Wert's name.
Modena Bibl. palatina.—Some of Wert's compositions arranged for one or two voices with lute accompaniment.
Munich State Library.—Motets, some in organ tablature, and two madrigals.
New York Library.—' Ninfe ' madrigal for six voices, by Giaches de Vuert.
Nuremberg Lorenzkirche Bibliothek.—In MSS. dated 1582, three motets for five voices.
Proske Library.—Fifteen motets.
Vienna Royal Library.—MS. 16,704, ' Transeunte Domino,' and in MS. 16,705, ' O sacrum convivium,' motets for five voices.
Zwickau Library.—Five motets for five voices.
C. S.

WERTHER, lyric drama in 4 acts (after Goethe), text by Edouard Blau, Paul Milliet and Georges Hartmann ; music by Massenet. Produced Imperial Opera, Vienna, Feb. 16, 1892 ; Paris, Opéra-Comique, Jan. 16, 1893 ; New York, Apr. 19, 1894 ; Covent Garden, June 11, 1894 ; in English, His Majesty's Theatre (Beecham), May 27, 1910.

WESLEY, (1) CHARLES (b. Bristol, Dec. 11, 1757 ; d. May 23, 1834), son of the Rev. Charles Wesley and nephew of the celebrated Rev. John Wesley. His musical instinct displayed itself in early infancy, and at 2¾ years old he could play ' a tune on the harpsichord readily and in just time,' and ' always put a true bass to it.' He was taken to London, and Beard offered to get him admitted as a child of the Chapel Royal, but his father declined it, having then no intention of educating him as a musician. He

was also introduced to Stanley and Worgan, who expressed themselves very strongly as to his abilities. After receiving instruction from Kelway and Boyce, to the latter of whom he dedicated a set of string quartets and upon whose death he wrote a hymn, beginning ' Father of heroes,' he embraced music as his profession, and became an excellent performer on both organ and harpsichord. He held at various times the appointment of organist at South Street Chapel, Welbeck Chapel, Chelsea Hospital and St. Marylebone Church. Having attained to a certain degree of excellence as a performer he made no further progress. He composed a set of ' Six Concertos for the Organ or Harpsichord, op. 1,' a set of Eight Songs, a Concerto grosso, 1784, some anthems (one printed in Page's ' Harmonia Sacra '), music for ' Caractacus,' a drama, and other pieces.

His younger brother (2) SAMUEL (b. Bristol, Feb. 24, 1766 ; d. London, Oct. 11, 1837), although also a precocious performer, did not develop his faculties quite so early, for he was 3 years old before he played a tune, and did not attempt to put a bass to one until he had learned his notes. He proved to be, notwithstanding, the more gifted of the two brothers. (See *Mus. T.*, 1902, p. 524.) From his cradle he had the advantage of hearing his brother's performances upon the organ, to which, perhaps, his superiority might be partly ascribed. Before he was 5 years old he learned to read words by poring over Handel's oratorio, ' Samson,' and soon afterwards learned, without instruction, to write. When between 6 and 7 years of age he was taught to play by note by David Williams, a young organist of Bath. Before then (Sept. and Oct. 1774) he had composed some parts of an oratorio, ' Ruth ' (now in B.M. Add. MSS. 34,997), which he completed and penned down when about 8 years old, and which was highly commended by Dr. Boyce. About the same time he learned to play the violin, of which he became a master, but his chief delight was in the organ. He was now introduced into company as a prodigy, and excited general admiration.[1] The brothers gave concerts in their house in London from 1779.[2] In 1777 he published ' Eight Lessons for the Harpsichord,' and about the same time appeared an engraved portrait of him when 8 years old. Before he attained his majority he had become a good classical scholar, acquired some knowledge of modern languages, successfully cultivated a taste for literature, and obtained distinction as an extemporaneous performer upon the organ and pianoforte.

In 1784 he joined the Roman Catholic Church. In 1787 an accident befell him, the consequences of which more or less affected him during the remainder of his life, and from which

[1] See the Hon. Daines Barrington's *Miscellanies*, 1781, p. 291.
[2] See Add. MSS. 35,017, *Mus. T.*, 1902, p. 525 etc.

SAMUEL WESLEY

From a painting by J. Jackson, A.R.A., in the National Portrait Gallery

S. S. WESLEY

From a painting by W. R. Briggs, R.A., in the Royal College of Music

6

undoubtedly sprang those erratic and eccentric habits for which he became remarkable. Passing along Snow Hill one evening, he fell into a deep excavation prepared for the foundation of a new building, and severely injured his skull. He refused to undergo the operation of trepanning, and suffered for seven years from despondency and nervous irritability, which occasioned him to lay aside all his pursuits, even his favourite music. On his recovery he resumed his usual avocations, and became acquainted with the works of John Sebastian Bach, the study of which he pursued with enthusiasm, and to propagate a knowledge of which among English musicians he laboured assiduously. (See BACH GESELLSCHAFT). During 1808 and 1809 he addressed a remarkable series of letters to Benjamin JACOB (q.v.) upon the subject of the works of his favourite author, which was edited by his daughter, and published in 1875.[1] In 1810 he put forward, in conjunction with C. F. Horn, an arrangement of Bach's organ trios, and in 1813 an edition of the ' Wohltemperirtes Clavier,' and promoted the publication of an English translation of Forkel's Life of Bach (1820). (See FORKEL.)

In 1811 he was engaged as conductor and solo organist at Birmingham Festival, and lectured at the Royal Institution and elsewhere. In 1816 he suffered a relapse of his malady, and was compelled to abandon the exercise of his profession until 1823, when he resumed his pursuits until 1830, becoming in 1824 organist of Camden Chapel, Camden Town ; but a further attack again disabled him, and he was afterwards unable to do more than make occasional appearances. One of his latest public performances was at the concert of the Sacred Harmonic Society on Aug. 7, 1834, when at the organ he accompanied the anthem, ' All go unto one place,' which he had composed upon the death of his brother Charles. His actual last appearance was at Christ Church, Newgate Street, on Sept. 12, 1837. He had gone there to hear Mendelssohn play upon the organ, and was himself prevailed upon to perform. He died within a month afterwards, and was buried Oct. 17, in the vault in the graveyard of Old St. Marylebone Church, in which the remains of his father, mother, sister and brother had been previously deposited.

Wesley was indisputably the greatest English organist of his day, and both in his extemporaneous playing and in his performance of the fugues of Bach and Handel he was unrivalled. His compositions were numerous and varied, and some are of the highest excellence. His instrumental music shows that he was to a certain extent a pioneer of the symphonic style in England, but it has sunk into oblivion. He is remembered by a few of his choral works, notably the motets, of which one, the noble

[1] See Mus. T., 1902, pp. 798 ff.

eight part ' In exitu Israel,' still receives fairly frequent performance in English cathedrals and elsewhere even in the 20th century. S. Wesley's religious tenets have been matter of doubt. At a late period of his life he disclaimed having ever been a convert to Rome, observing that ' although the Gregorian music had seduced him to their chapels, the tenets of the Romanists never obtained any influence over his mind.' But the letter from Pope Pius VI. in acknowledgment of a Mass (now in B.M. Add. MSS. 35,000) is direct evidence that he had joined that Church. He left several children ; his eldest son, Rev. Charles Wesley, D.D. (b.1795 ; d. Sept. 14, 1859), was sub-dean of the Chapel Royal, and editor of a collection of words of anthems. An obituary notice appeared in the Gentleman's Magazine of Nov. 1837 ; see also D.N.B. and Mus. T., 1902, pp. 524 ff. and 798. A list of the MSS. in the B.M. relating to him and containing his works is given in D.N.B. The following list of his compositions was compiled with the assistance of his daughter, Miss Wesley.

Those marked with * are published.

Oratorios. Ruth (composed at 8 years old). Death of Abel. Parts 2 and 3 complete.

Masses. Missa solemnis (Gregorian) for voices only ; Missa, Kyrie eleison ; Missa de S. Trinitate ; Missa pro Angelis.

Motets. *In exitu Israel a 8; *Exultate Deo, a 5; *Dixit Dominus ; *Omnia Vanitas ; Tu es Sacerdos ; Te decet hymnus ; Hosanna in excelsis ; Domine salvum fac (org. obblig.), all a 4 ; Confitebor for soli, chorus, and orchestra ; *IV., In Nativitate Domini ; V. ; VI. ; VII. ; VIII. ; IX. ; X., In Epiphania ; XI. ; XII., In Festo Corporis Christi ; XIV., In Epiphania ; XVI. Ad Benedictum, for Corpus Christi ; XVII., XVIII., In Festo Corp. Christi ; Dixit Dominus ; Salve Regina ; Ad Magnificat ; Qualem ministrum ; Agnus Dei, in D (1812) ; Agnus Dei (1812) ; Hymnus in Festo Ascensionis. Versus 3 de Ps. cxxxvi. Ave Maria Stella (1786) ; Salve Regina ; Magna opera ; Omnes gentes. Deus Majestatis for double choir with accompaniment of strings and organ, dated Sept. 26, 1799 ; autograph in the collection of Dr. W. H. Cummings.

Services. *Morning and Evening Church Service in F a 4 ; also Te Deum, Sanctus, Kyrie, Nunc Dimittis and Burial Service a 4 ; Jubilate Deo ; Sanctus in F.

Anthems. *All go unto one place, Funeral Anthem for Charles Wesley ; *I am well pleased ; Behold how good (org. obblig.) ; *Thou, O God, art praised ; Who can tell ? (July 4, 1823) ; Hear, O Thou Shepherd ; Be pleased, O Lord ; I will take heed.

Choruses. My delight (Apr. 11, 1816) ; Thus through successive ages ; On the death of W. Kingsbury (1782) ; Why should we shrink? (Orch. May 1813).

Parochial Psalm-tunes, with interludes, *Bk. I. only ; Chorals or Psalm-tunes, 600 or more.

Ode on S. Cecilia's Day, for soli, chorus and orch. Words by Rev. S. Wesley.

Glees. For 4 voices :—Circle the bowl ; *O sing unto my roundelaic (Madr.) : No more to earth ; Now the trumpet's (1815) ; While every short-lived (1822) ; *Father of Light ; Here shall the morn ; Join with thee. For 3 voices : Thou happy wretch ; These are by fond mama (1778) ; Harsh and untuneful (1783) ; *Goosy, goosy, gander (1781) ; Adieu, ye soft ; When Orpheus went down ; When first thy soft lips (1783) ; What bliss to life (1807) ; When Friendship ; On the Salt Wave, (1793) ; Roses their sharp spines (1822) ; Say can power (1791) ; The rights of man ; Blushete mio caro ; How grand in age ; *from Anacreon ; Nella cara ; Life's a jest, dated Jan. 17, 1807. Autograph in the collection of Dr. W. H. Cummings.

Duets. Beneath a sleeping infant lies ; Belle Gabrielle (1792) ; Since powerful love (1783) ; Sweet constellations (1782).

Songs. *True Blue ; Within a cowslip's ; England, the spell ; Gentle warbling (1799) ; What shaft of Fate's relentless power ; In gentle slumbers ; Farewell, if ever fondest prayer ; Think of me ; Behold where Dryden ; Louisa, view ; *Come all my brave boys ; Election squib ; *The House that Jack built ; *Love and Folly ; *The Autophagos ; Adieu, ye jovial youths (1783) ; The world, my dear Mira (1784) ; Yes, Daphne ! (1781) ; When we see a lover languish (1783) ; Too late for redress (1783) ; Pale mirror of resplendent night ; Love's but the frailty ; Oh, how to bid ; Parting to death (1783) ; The white-robed hours (1783) ; Armin's lamentation (1784) ; Flutt'ring spread (1783) ; Might I in Thy sight appear (1807).

Symphonies. In D (1784) ; in Eb (1784) ; in Bb (1802) ; in A ; in D, unfinished.

Overtures. In D (1778) ; in C (1780) ; in D ; ' to the 2nd Act,' unfinished.

Organ Concertos. In Eb (1776) ; in D (1781) ; in G (1782) ; in Bb (1785). On Rule Britannia ; in G ; in Bb ; in Eb ; in G ; in C; in D (hornpipe).

Grand Duet, *No. 1 ; Do. No. 2 ; *Do. in 3 movements, insc. to F. Marshall.

Voluntaries. In D, in C, in C minor, in C, in E♭, in G minor, in F, in C (all in * op. 6) ; *Do. in G, in D, in D, in A, in F ; *3 Voluntaries ded. to W. Harding ; a 2nd set of do. ; *6 Voluntaries for young Organists ; *One do. insc. to Thos. Attwood ; *Do. in G minor insc. to W. Linley ; *Do. in G, insc. to H. J. Gauntlett ; *One do. insc. to W. Drummer, Esq. ; *A 2nd in D, insc. to the same ; *Easy Voluntaries ; *6 do. ; *A short and familiar Voluntary in A ; *12 short pieces with full Voluntary added ; *12 short pieces with Grand Fugue ; *A Book of Interludes ; *Fugue in D ; *Preludes and Fugues or Exercises ; *6 Introductory movements, and Fugue in D ; *Characteristic airs for the Seraphine ; Concerto in D for Organ and Violin (1800). Many of these have been reprinted, some adapted for pedal organ.

Pianoforte. *Eight lessons (1777) ; *Duet March in D, No. 25 ; 3 Sonatas, op. 3 ; 4 Sonatas and 2 Duets, op. 5 ; Sonata with fugue on subject of Salomon's ; 2 Sonatas for PF. or Harpsichord with acc. for Violin, op. 2 ; *Sonatina, ded. to Miss Meeking ; *Do. on air in Tekeli, in G ; Rondo in D, Off she goes ; *Do. in D, Lady Mary Douglas ; Do., Fly not yet ; Orphan Mary ; Patty Kavannah ; The young May moon ; *Do. in G minor, Kitty alone and I ; *Do. in A, I attempt from Love's sickness ; Do., Will Putty ; *Bellissima Signora ; *Pastorellis Polacca ; *Do. in B♭, the Lass of Richmond Hill ; Do. in D, Old Towler ; *Do. from an Organ Concerto ; *Do. on Polish Air, in D minor ; *Do. in G ; *Bay of Biscay (B♭) ; *Christmas Carol (E min.) ; *Moll Pately (in F) ; *Widow Waddle (in A) ; *La Mélange ; *Scots wha hae ; *The Deserter's Meditations ; *A favourite Air from ' Der Freischütz ' ; *Jacky Horner, with Flute ; Adagio, March, and Waltz ; *Duet in ' La cosa rara ' ; Divertimento, ded. to Miss Walker ; *Siege of Badajoz, with March in D ; Rondo in A (1773) ; Waltz, the Skyrocket ; *Do. the Coburg ; Introd. and Air, insc. to Mrs. Stirling ; Sweet Enslaver, with Vars. ; *Hornpipe and variations with Introd. ; *Variations on a fav. Italian air, in F ; *Grand Fugue with March from Ode on S. Cecilia's Day : Grand Coronation March ; *Do. in D ; New March as performed on Parade ; Preludes throughout the 8ve both major and minor ; *Fugue, insc. to J. B. Logier.

String Quintet, in A ; Do. Fugue in B♭ (1800). *Quartet* (1780) ; Do. (1799). *Trio,* Aria for Strings ; for Oboe, Violin and Violoncello ; *for PF. and 2 Flutes ; for 3 PF.'s. *Duet,* Violin and Violoncello. *Sonata* a Violino Solo, in A. *Solo* per Violino e Basso. *March,* Corni, Oboi, Bassoni, Serpent (1777).

W. H. H., addns.

(3) SAMUEL SEBASTIAN, Mus.D. (*b.* Aug. 14, 1810 ; *d.* Gloucester, Apr. 19, 1876), natural son of the above, whose genius he inherited. In his 10th year he was elected chorister of the Chapel Royal, St. James's ; in 1826 organist at St. James's, Hampstead Road ; in 1829 organist of St. Giles's, Camberwell, of St. John's, Waterloo Road, and in 1830 of Hampton-on-Thames, holding three of these appointments simultaneously. During these early years he had some experience as a theatrical conductor [1] and purveyor of incidental music.

In 1832 he became organist of Hereford Cathedral, conducting the festival there in 1834 (see THREE CHOIRS FESTIVALS), and a year later marrying the sister of Dean Merewether, when he migrated to Exeter, and remained at that cathedral for six years, during which period his reputation as the first English church composer and organist of his country became established. In 1839 he accumulated the degrees of Mus.B. and Mus.D. at Oxford. In 1842 he was induced by a good offer from Dr. Hook to accept the organistship of Leeds Parish Church. He had played at the opening of the organ in Oct. 1841 ; according to the Parish Church records he was engaged in 1839, but the *Leeds Intelligencer* of Oct. 16, 1841, speaks of the post as then vacant. During his tenure of the post he delivered lectures at the Liverpool Collegiate Institution. He wrote his famous service in E, and sold it in 1845 to Martin Cawood, an ironmaster, to whose wife he dedicated a set of satirical 'Jeux d'Esprit : Quadrilles à la Herz ' in 1846. In 1844 he was a candidate for the professorship of music in the University of Edinburgh, then vacant by the resignation of Sir Henry Bishop.

[1] See *Mus. T.,* 1900, pp. 298-99.

Among Wesley's testimonials on that occasion was the following from Spohr :

' His works show, without exception, that he is master of both style and form of the different species of composition, and keeps himself closely to the boundaries which the several kinds demand, not only in sacred art, but also in glees, and in music for the pianoforte. His sacred music is chiefly distinguished by a noble, often even an antique style, and by rich harmonies as well as by surprisingly beautiful modulations.'

On leaving Leeds in 1849 he entered into a contract with R. S. Burton, to sell the ' goodwill ' of his Leeds practice for 500 guineas.[2]

In 1849 he was appointed to Winchester Cathedral, where the school offered facilities for the education of his sons. On Aug. 10, 1850, he was appointed professor of the organ at the R.A.M. After fifteen years in Cathedral and School Chapel, Wesley, being consulted by the Dean and Chapter of Gloucester as to the claims of candidates for that organistship then (1865) vacant, intimated that he would himself accept it, an offer which was naturally taken advantage of. This post brought him more prominently forward in the musical world, as conductor *ex officio,* once in three years, of the Three Choirs Festivals, and the change seemed for a time to reanimate energies and powers which had not received adequate public recognition. In Jan. 1873 he received a Civil List pension of £100 per annum.

But the best years had been spent of a life which, to a less sensitive nature, might have been happier and more eventful ; and long-deferred hopes for restorations of founders' intentions, and for thorough reforms in Cathedral matters generally—reforms which, both with pen and voice, he warmly and constantly advocated—combined with other disappointments and cares, shortened his days, and after some ten years' tenure of his Gloucester post, he died there, his last words being : ' Let me see the sky '—words appropriate for one whose motto as a composer seemed always ' Excelsior.' According to his own wish he was buried at Exeter in the old cemetery by the side of an only daughter, who died in 1840. A tablet to his memory was placed on the north wall of the nave of the Cathedral, on which these words are inscribed :

' This monument has been placed here by friends as an expression of high esteem for his personal worth, and admiration of his great musical genius.'

There is also a window to his memory in Gloucester Cathedral. But a more lasting monument, of his own creation, exists in his works.[3]

As composer for the Church of England, Wesley may fairly be placed in the highest rank.

[2] See *Leeds Mercury* and *Leeds Intelligencer,* July 17, 1852, and *The Times,* July 16, for the report of the action which followed.
[3] The centenary of Wesley's birth was celebrated in Westminster Abbey by a commemorative service (June 29, 1910) at which eight of his finest anthems were sung under the direction of Sir J. F Bridge.

in his elaborate Service in E major, published, with an interesting and caustic preface, in 1845 whilst he was at Leeds, advantage is taken of modern resources of harmony and modulation, without departure from the lines of that true church school to which the composer had been so long habituated. (See ANTHEM and SERVICE.) And this judicious combination of ancient and modern is characteristic of his church music, in which he gives practical illustration of the reform which he was always urging. (See the pamphlet, etc., on church music named at the end of the list of his compositions.) His fame will chiefly rest on his volume of twelve anthems, published in 1853. Two of these, composed at Hereford, ' Blessed be the God and Father ' [1] and ' The Wilderness,' [2] are now universally recognised as standard works of excellence. Later in life Wesley soared even higher—for instance, in his noble ' O Lord, Thou art my God,' for eight voices, in his ' Ascribe unto the Lord,' composed in the Winchester period, and also in the exquisite little anthem, ' Thou wilt keep him in perfect peace,' wherein knowledge and the dignity of the true church style are so conspicuous, and which is one of the brightest gems in a collection of choral jewels. It should not be forgotten, too, that popular hymnody was much enriched by his fine tunes which combined the dignity of the Church style with a vocal ease which made them attractive to the masses. That known as ' Aurelia ' is the most famous.

As an organist, Wesley was for a considerable period acknowledged the first in this country. His touch was eminently *legato*, his style always noble and elevated. (See EXTEMPORISATION.) At Winchester he was heard to great advantage on Willis's fine organ. His extempore playing after the Psalms, before the Anthem, or after the Service, is a thing to be remembered, and various players after hearing him changed their style for the better, some of them catching a ray of the *afflatus divinus* which, as organist, may be fairly ascribed to him. His views, formed from early habit, on two important points in the construction of organs were curiously divergent from opinions widely held, for he was an advocate both of unequal temperament and of a ' G ' or ' F ' compass. But in supporting such exceptional views, he could give practical reasons for the belief that was in him.

Those well acquainted with Wesley could not fail, notwithstanding a manner at times reserved, retiring, or even eccentric, to appreciate his kindness and sympathy. To those he liked and trusted he could be an agreeable and interesting companion and friend, and these will not forget their pleasant intercourse with him,

[1] See *Mus. T.*, 1900, p. 522.
[2] See *Mus. T.*, 1899, p. 164, and 1900, pp. 300, 301.

even on occasions when music formed little or no part of conversation.[3] That he felt deeply and aimed high is proved in the devotional and masterly works with which, at a period when our ecclesiastical music was at a low ebb, he enriched the choral repertory of the Church of England.

The following is a list of Dr. Wesley's published compositions.

ANTHEMS, ETC.	Introduction and Fugue, in C♯ minor.
Ascribe unto the Lord.	Andante in G.
All go unto one place. (Funeral.) S.A.T.B.	,, in A (posthumous).
Blessed be the Lord God of Israel. (Christmas.) 4 voices.	,, in E minor (do.).
Blessed be the God and Father. SS.A.T.B.	National anthem, with variations. An Air, varied, composed for Holsworthy church bells (do.).
Cast me not away from thy presence. SS.A.TT.B.	' Studio ' for Organ.
Give the King Thy judgments. S.AA.TT.B.	Grave and Andante for *The Organist's Quarterly Journal* and some other contributions to collections.
Glory be to God on high. Full. 4 voices.	
God be merciful unto us. (Marriage.) 4 voices.	The Psalter, pointed for Chanting.
I am Thine, O save me. Full. 5 voices.	The European Psalmist. 1872.
I will arise ; and O remember not. Let us lift up our heart. 8 voices. Man that is born of a woman. S.A.T.B.	Ode to Labour, for the opening of an Industrial Exhibition, words by W. H. Bellamy. Agricultural Hall, Islington, Oct. 17, 1864.
O give thanks unto the Lord. S.A.T.B.	The praise of Music, for Gounod's Choir at Albert Hall, 1873.
O God, Whose nature and property. Full. 4 voices.	Numerous Chants and Hymn tunes.
O how amiable.	
O Lord, my God (Solomon's Prayer). S.A.T.B.	
O Lord, Thou art my God. 8 voices.	GLEES
Praise the Lord, O my soul. S.A.T.B.	I wish to tune my quiv'ring lyre. A.TT.BB.
The Face of the Lord. 8 voices.	When fierce conflicting passions.
The Lord is my shepherd.	Shall I tell you whom I love ?
The Wilderness. S.A.T.B.	
Thou wilt keep him in perfect peace. S.A.TT.B.	SONGS
Three Collects for the first three Sundays in Advent. Two for Treble, and one for Bass.	Shall I tell you whom I love ? (with Violoncello ad lib.).
Wash me throughly. S.A.TT.B.	When from the great Creator's hand (from the Ode).
The Hundredth Psalm, arranged with various harmony for choirs. Foundation-stone of Netley Hospital, 1856.	Strong in heart and strong in hand (Ditto). Silently, silently (from the Ode). There be none of beauty's daughters.
By the rivers of Babylon (Soprano solo).	Wert thou like me.
Ditto. (Alto solo.)	The Butterfly. Orphan hours, the year is dead. Hoher Muth und süsse Minne (with Violoncello ad lib.).
SERVICES, ETC.	
(In E.) T.D., J., K., S. and C., M. and N.D.	FOR PF.
(In F.) Chant Service. T.D. and J., M. and N.D.	Air and variations in E. March in C minor, and Rondo in C.
(In F.) Chant Service. Letter B. T.D., J., M. and N.D.	
(In G.) Chant Service. T.D., J., M. and N.D.	Also a pamphlet entitled *A Few Words on Cathedral Music and the Musical System of the Church*, with a plan of *Reform*. (Rivingtons, 1849.)
(In C.) Glory be to God on high. (Early work.)	*Reply to the Inquiries of the Cathedral Commissioners relating to improvement in the Music of Divine worship in Cathedral*. 1854.
FOR ORGAN	
Six Pieces for a Chamber Organ (Set 1 and 2).	

A few MS. sketches are preserved at Leeds Church and elsewhere.

BIBL.—E. DANNREUTHER, *The Romantic Period (Oxf. Hist. Mus.* vol. vi.) ; E. WALKER, *History of Music in England* (These alike include finely critical estimates of both the Wesleys.)

H. S. O. ; addns. from *D.N.B., Mus. T.*, etc.

WESSEL, CHRISTIAN RUDOLPH (*b.* Bremen, 1797 ; *d.* Eastbourne, Mar. 15, 1885), came to England in 1825, and established, with an amateur named Stodart, at No. 1 Soho Square, the firm of music-publishers Wessel & Stodart, for the popularisation of foreign music in this country. In 1838 Stodart retired and Wessel continued the business until 1839, when he took in Stapleton as a partner, and removed to 67

[3] *Mus. T.*, 1900, pp. 297, 369 and 452 ; anecdotes, etc., in the same, 1899, pp. 453, 485 ; *D.N.B.*, etc. Information from Herbert Thompson and others.

Frith Street, Soho. About this time the firm entered into a contract with Chopin for the exclusive right to publish his works in England, paying him £12 for each fresh composition. In 1845 Stapleton left the firm, and Wessel again carried on business by himself, from 1846 at 229 Regent Street, and from 1856 at 19 Hanover Square, until 1860, when he retired in favour of Edwin ASHDOWN and Henry John PARRY, both of them long in his employ. In 1882 Parry retired, and from that time it was in the hands of Ashdown alone. The business ultimately became the company known as ' Edwin Ashdown, Limited.'

Wessel was a great benefactor to the spread of music in England. Among composers whose works were introduced by him are Schubert, Schumann, Mendelssohn, Abt, Kücken, Gade, Schulhof, Heller, etc. Of the works of Heller, as of those of Chopin, Wessel and his successors held the exclusive copyright in England, though by a decision of the Court of Chancery in 1853, several important works were lost to them. (See BOOSEY & Co.) Since that period they have turned their attention to the publication of the works of resident composers. In 1867 they established a monthly musical magazine, *Hanover Square*. A. C.

WESSELY, BERNHARD (*b*. Berlin, Sept. 1, 1768 ; *d*. Potsdam, July 11, 1826). The house of his parents (a Jewish family) was a meeting-place for the great poets and philosophers of the time, and Lessing, Moses Mendelssohn, Ramler, etc., were frequent visitors. Wessely studied under J. A. P. Schulz, and in 1787 he went to Hamburg to conduct his coronation cantata. In 1788 he became music-director at the Royal National Theatre, Berlin. In 1796 Prince Henry engaged him as his Kapellmeister at Rheinsberg, and on the latter's death he abandoned his musical career, for family reasons, and became a government official at Potsdam, where he founded, with the secretary (Justiz Sekretär) Mödinger, the society for classical music, which in 1816, when he had been transferred to Magdeburg, prevailed upon the king to recall him. His compositions were very popular. Meyerbeer points him out as the real author of the famous lullaby, ' Schlafe mein Prinzchen,' attributed to Mozart. He composed 4 operas, incidental music to 3 plays, ballets, cantatas, songs, chamber music, etc. (Ledebur, *Mus. Lexikon* ; *Q.-L.*).

WESSELY, HANS (*b*. Vienna, Dec. 23, 1862; *d*. Innsbruck, Sept. 1926), violinist, began to learn the violin when 9 years of age. He received his musical training at the Vienna Conservatorium, and completed his studies there with the leading professor of that institution, J. M. Grün. His first important appearance in public was made at the age of 21 years, when he gave two orchestral

concerts in his native city, and was subsequently engaged to play Spohr's 7th Concerto at the Philharmonic Society (of Vienna) under Richter. He subsequently visited various countries in Europe and eventually found his way to London, making his début at the Crystal Palace concerts under Manns on Apr. 7, 1888. In 1889 he became a professor at the R.A.M., and attained the position of leading violin professor in that institution. His repertory as a soloist included all the great violin concertos, but it was as a quartet leader that he was best known. The Quartet bearing his name gave a series of concerts annually in London until 1914. He had a good technique, much force, and a serious conception of the masterpieces of chamber music which he was mainly engaged in interpreting. He played on a Stradivari violin of the best period. W. W. C.

WEST, BENJAMIN (*b*. Northampton), an 18th-century organist-composer, who wrote ' Sacra concerto,' or the voice of melody, containing an introduction to the grounds of music; also 41 psalm tunes and 10 anthems (London, 1760 ; second ed., with 12 anthems, 1769). E. V. D. S.

WEST, JOHN EBENEZER (*b*. Hackney, London, Dec. 7, 1863), organist and composer, is specially noteworthy for his valuable publication, *Cathedral Organists*, much quoted in this Dictionary.

He studied at the R.A.M. under his uncle, Prout and others, held successively several organistships in London, resigning that of St. Augustine's, Queen's Gate, in 1902 in order to devote himself to composition and editorial work. He joined the staff of Novello & Co. in 1884 and became musical editor and adviser to that firm in 1897. His compositions include Cantatas (two short works were produced at the Gloucester festivals of 1904 and 1907), over 70 church anthems published and several services. *Cathedral Organists*, which gives the most comprehensive, and at the same time concise record of the holders of that office in all English Cathedrals and Collegiate Churches, first appeared in 1899, and was reissued in a new and enlarged edition in 1921 (Novello). Its information is remarkably accurate and clearly set forth. C.

WEST (WESTE), WILLIAM (*d*. 1643), a gentleman of the Chapel Royal from 1612 until his death (H. C. de Lafontaine, *The King's Musick*). He is presumably the West whose ' Sharp ' Service (including T.D., K., C., M. and N.D.) and two anthems, ' Have mercy ' and ' Save me, O God,' are included in Barnard's MS. collection (R.C.M. 1045-51). This supposition is supported by the fact that these works are included in this collection and not in Barnard's ' Selected Church Music,' published in 1641. The latter included only works by composers then dead, and the MS. collection contains the nucleus of a second assembly by living composers, which Barnard intended to publish as a supplement to it.   J. M^K.

WESTBROOK, WILLIAM JOSEPH, Mus.D. (*b.* London, Jan. 1, 1831 ; *d.* Sydenham, Mar. 24, 1894). His instructor was R. Temple, a blind organist. In 1848 he became organist of St. Bartholomew's, Bethnal Green, which he exchanged in 1851 for St. Bartholomew's, Sydenham, where he remained until his death. He took his degree of B.Mus. at Cambridge in Feb. 1876, and his D.Mus. in May 1878, his exercise, ' Jesus, an oratoriette,' for solo voices, eight-part chorus, and orchestra, having been performed in the chapel of Queens' College, Cambridge. He was sub-organist at the Crystal Palace for some three years, and conductor for thirteen years of the South Norwood Musical Society. Westbrook published many organ-pieces, original or arranged ; songs, partsongs, madrigals, canons ; English text to many songs of Mozart, Schubert, Fesca, etc.; in part or entirely the English text of De Bériot's, Dancla's and Alard's Violin Schools ; Organ Tutors ; a large portion of the first 12 volumes of the ' Musical Standard.'   G.

WESTENHOLZ, (1) KARL AUGUST FRIEDRICH (*b.* Lauenburg,[1] 1736; *d.* Schwerin-Mecklenburg, Jan. 24, 1789), pupil of J. A. Kunzen for theory, and Fr. Xav. Voczitka for violoncello. From *c.* 1756 he was tenor singer in the Schwerin court chapel, of which he became Kapellmeister in 1768, as Hertel's successor. In 1770 he married the singer Lucietta Affabili (*d.* 1776) and in 1777 Eleonora Sophia Maria Fritscher, an excellent singer, harpsichord and glass-harmonica player, and composer of sonatas, songs and harpsichord pieces. At the court concerts she often presided at the harpsichord, and E. W. Wolf dedicated to her 6 harpsichord sonatas. Karl Westenholz composed concertos, sonatas and pieces for harpsichord, cantatas, psalms, chorales, birthday serenades, songs, etc. His son, (2) **FRIEDRICH** (*d.* Berlin, Mar. 12, 1840), was virtuoso on the oboe and chamber musician at the Berlin court ; and composed concertantes for oboe and flute, and oboe and bassoon, with orchestra, duets for violin with various instruments, etc. (*Mendel* ; *Q.-L.*)

WESTHOFF, JOHANN PAUL VON (*b.* Dresden, 1656 ; *d.* Weimar, Apr. 1705), son of a lutenist in the Dresden court chapel, who had been a captain in Gustav Adolph's army. He started his career as teacher of languages to the Saxon princes *c.* 1671, and ended it as professor of languages at Wittenberg University (after 1691), and, finally (1704), chamber secretary and chamber musician at Weimar. About 1674 he became chamber musician at Dresden, visited Sweden in 1679, and was induced to join the army in the Turkish cam-

[1] Mendel says Lüneburg.

paign in Hungary ; but returned to Dresden in 1680. He toured as a violinist all over Europe, coming to England *c.* 1684–85, and returning to Dresden in the latter year. He was a remarkable virtuoso, and composed 6 violin sonatas with basso continuo (Dresden, 1694). G. Beckmann re-edited a sonata in D minor and a solo Suite in A major (1921), and the latter was also re-edited by K. Gerhartz (1921) (Schilling ; *Riemann*).

WESTLAKE, FREDERICK (*b.* Romsey, Hants, Feb. 25, 1840 ; *d.* London, Feb. 12, 1898), pianist and composer. In 1855–59 he was a student at the R.A.M., of which institution in 1860 he was made sub-professor, then associate, and in 1863 professor. He played in public with success until the demands made on his time for teaching became too great. He re-appeared, Oct. 22, 1873, at W. H. Holmes's concert, and played, with his pupil Miss Agnes Channel, Chopin's Rondo for two Pianofortes, probably for the first time in England. He was a member of the Philharmonic Society and the Society of Musicians. His compositions include:

Mass in E♭ ; O Salutaris ; Kyrie and Gloria (with orchestra) ; hymns included in ' Hymns Ancient and Modern ' ; Duo Concertante for PF. and v'cl. ; Allegro con forza, nine ' Episodes,' and a Fugue in octaves for PF. ; Songs and Part Songs, ' Lyra Studentium.'

He also completed Sterndale Bennett's edition of Bach's 48 Preludes and Fugues.   A. C.

WESTMORLAND, JOHN FANE (*b.* Feb. 3, 1784 ; *d.* Oct. 16, 1859), ELEVENTH EARL (of the creation of 1624)—better known in the musical world by the courtesy title of LORD BURGHERSH, which he bore before his succession to the earldom. He entered the army and served in the various campaigns from 1805–15, and was subsequently envoy at Florence, and ambassador successively at Berlin and Vienna. His love for music manifested itself in early youth, and he became a good violinist. Whilst a student at Cambridge he obtained instruction from Dr. Hague, the University professor; he also studied under Zeidler at Berlin and Mayseder at Vienna. He essayed composition, and produced 6 Italian operas : 'Bajazet,' 'Il torneo,' 'Fedra,' 'L' eroe di Lancastro,' ' Il ratto di Proserpina,' and ' Lo scompiglio teatrale ' ; an English opera, ' Catherine ' ; a resetting of Cobb's ' Siege of Belgrade ' ; a Mass, a Service, a Magnificat, and two anthems, besides hymns, madrigals, songs, duets, etc. In 1817 he was one of the unsuccessful competitors for the prize offered for the best setting of William Linley's Ode on the death of Samuel Webbe.

His real claim to mention here, however, is not his musicianship, but the energy, perseverance and success with which he advocated, and ultimately succeeded in procuring, the establishment of an Academy of Music in London, and the zeal with which, as its President, he strove at all times to advance its interests. (See ROYAL ACADEMY OF MUSIC.) In 1832 he was appointed a director of the Concert of Antient Music. He succeeded to the earldom on the death of his father, Dec. 15, 1844.   w. h. h.

WESTPHAL, RUDOLF, GEORG HERMANN (b. Oberkirchen, Lippe-Schaumberg, July 3, 1826 ; d. Stadthagen, July 11, 1892), writer on music whose theories especially as regards the nature of GREEK MUSIC (q.v.) have occasioned considerable controversy.

Westphal studied classical philology at Marburg and from 1858–62 held a professorship at Breslau. In 1875 he held a similar post at Moscow in the Katkov Lycée (see MELGOUNOV), and returning to Germany in 1880, lived successively at Leipzig, Bäckeburg and Stadthagen. His special field of research was the metrical and rhythmical principles of ancient Greek music. He maintained for some time but ultimately abandoned the theory that polyphony was known to the Greeks.

His principal works relating to music are :

Metrik der griechischen Dramatiker und Lyriker, with Rossbach. 3 vols. 1854–65.
Theorie der musischen Künste der Hellenen, 3rd ed. of the above.
Die Fragmente und Lehrsaatze der griechischen Rhythmiker. 1861.
Geschichte der alten und mittelalterlichen Musik. 1864.
System der antiken Rhythmik. 1865.
Scriptores metrici Graeci. 1866.
Theorie der neuhochdeutschen Metrik. 1870.
Die Elemente des musikalischen Rhythmus mit Rücksicht auf unsre Opernmusik. 1872.
Allgemeine Theorie der musikalischen Rhythmik seit J. S. Bach. 1880.
Aristoxenos von Tarent.
Metrik und Rhythmik des klassischen Hellenentums. 2 vols. 1883–93.
Die Musik des griechischen Altertums. 1883.
Die Aristoxenische Rhythmuslehre. 1891. (See *Riemann*.)   C.

WESTROP, (1) HENRY (b. Lavenham, Suffolk, July 22, 1812 ; d. London, Sept. 23, 1879), is said to have made his first appearance at concerts in Norwich at 10 years old, and at 13 appeared at the Sudbury Theatre as pianist, violinist and singer. He afterwards became organist at St. Stephen's, Norwich ; in 1831 at Little Stanmore ; 1832, at Fitzroy Chapel, and Apr. 3, 1834, at St. Edmund, Lombard Street, which he held till his death. He was conductor of the Choral Harmonists' Society, and sub-conductor to Costa at the Sacred Harmonic ; he led the second violins at the Royal Italian opera and the Philharmonic Society.[1] He was a member of the Society of British Musicians and of the Philharmonic Society. Westrop's abilities as a composer were greater than his reception by musicians and the public would imply. His compositions include a symphony performed by the Society of British Musicians, but accidentally destroyed afterwards ; a considerable quantity of concerted chamber music ; an opera, 'The Maid of Bremen,' libretto by Fitzball, written for the Pyne and Harrison company (but not performed owing to the collapse of the undertaking) ; another opera, 'The Mariners,' was unfinished at his death. His daughter,

(2) KATE (Mrs. Allender), a pianist, succeeded to his post of organist, and was an associate of the Philharmonic Society. His younger

[1] See C. E. Stephens in the *Musical World*, Oct. 11, 1879.

brothers, (3) EAST JOHN (1804–56) and (4) THOMAS (1816–81) were also musicians.
                                     A. C., addns.

WEYSE, CHRISTOPH ERNST FRIEDRICH (b. Altona, Mar. 5, 1774 ; d. Oct. 7, 1842), was sent in 1789 to Copenhagen to complete his musical instruction under J. A. P. Schulz. From 1792 to his death, he was settled at Copenhagen as organist and music-teacher. He is chiefly known as the composer of Danish operas and operettas, in which there is a considerable infusion of the spirit of national romanticism. Along with Friedrich Kuhlau Weyse indeed is credited as one of the first to introduce the element of romanticism into Danish artistic music. He occupied himself in collecting and harmonising old Danish folk-songs, a work which was continued and so far completed by his pupil A. P. Berggreen. Weyse also wrote several books of studies, sonatas, and Allegri di Bravura for the pianoforte. Moscheles considered some of his Books of Studies as giving Weyse a claim to rank among the best pianoforte writers of the time ; and Schumann has also a very appreciative review of them in his *Gesammelte Schriften* of 1854, reprinted from the *Neue Zeitschrift* of 1836 and 1838. Some of these Books of Studies, and one of the sonatas have more recently been reprinted, edited by August Winding.   J. R. M.

WHEALE, see WEALE.

WHEATSTONE, a family of music-publishers, and instrument-makers, said to have been established in business in 1750. Of this family was (1) SIR CHARLES WHEATSTONE (b. Gloucester, Feb. 1802 ; d. Paris, Oct. 19, 1875), famous for his inventions in telegraphy. He was the son of a music-seller at Gloucester, came to London, evidently to relatives in the music trade, and professionally was a music instrument-maker, but soon turned his attention to scientific subjects, which included light optics, sound vibrations, and electricity. He invented the concertina, and the patent (June, 1829) was held by the Wheatstone firm for many years. He was knighted in 1868. His portrait is in the National Portrait Gallery.

The London music firms of Wheatstone were Charles Wheatstone and William Wheatstone, who, having separate businesses at first, appear to have amalgamated.

(2) CHARLES WHEATSTONE was a music-engraver, and was publishing sheet music about 1790 at 9 Whitehall. Other early addresses were 31 Newgate Street ; 20 Panton Street, Haymarket ; 83 St. James Street ; 14 Castle Street, Leicester Square ; and 3 Bedford Court, Covent Garden. All these addresses were held at different times before 1806. After this date he was at 436 Strand, and from here most of his publications were issued down to about 1830. The firm was now a partnership,

and was established at 20 Conduit Street. Besides a mass of sheet music, Wheatstone & Co. published many interesting collections of Glees, etc., one being 'The Harmonist' in 9 vols. (c. 1805–10). They have also been makers and dealers, extensively, in musical instruments.

(3) WILLIAM WHEATSTONE was a professor and manufacturer of German flutes, in the improvement of which he held patents. He was at 128 Pall Mall in 1821, and shortly after removed to Chester Street, St. James's, and about 1826 to 118 Jermyn Street. He published some books of airs for the flute, and possibly became a partner with the Charles Wheatstone above. F. K.

WHICHELLO (WICHELLO), ABIELL (d. circa 1745), a popular composer of songs in the early part of the 18th century. He was at one time deputy-organist to Philip Hart, and afterwards organist at St. Edmund the King. Hawkins refers to him as being a teacher of the harpsichord, and a performer at the concerts organised by Thomas BRITTON (q.v.). He published a set of 'Lessons for the Harpsichord, or Spinett,' 1710, a cantata named 'Apollo and Daphne,' circa 1730. Another named 'Vertumnus and Pomona,' and a large number of songs, many of which appear in such works as Watts's 'Musical Miscellany,' 1729–1731, Bickham's 'Musical Entertainer,' 1737, etc., also on single engraved half-sheets of about the same period. His song 'Contentment' ('No glory I covet') appears to have survived long after the rest of his compositions were forgotten. Hawkins states that he died about 1745. F. K.

WHISTLE, the simplest form of flageolet, or flûte-à-bec. It may be made of wood, cane, or metal; modern whistles are sometimes of celluloid. The principle is that of a tube plugged, or otherwise arranged, at the mouth so that a narrow slit only remains. A short distance below is a notch having a portion of the tube cut slantingly away, or if of metal deflected inwards, upon which the breath impinges and so produces a shrill sound dependent on the length and width of the tube for its pitch and power.

The short whistle, of the dog-whistle type, is not open at the end, and only produces one note. The old parish clerk's pitch-pipe (made of wood) was merely a whistle plugged at the end by a movable stopper, which, pushed upwards to certain fixed places, gave the required notes as a pitch for singing. The ordinary musical whistle (the 'tin' or 'penny' whistle) has six vents which are stopped by the fingers of both hands, and the fingering follows the same rule as for the fife, or flute without keys. The bird whistle (directions for playing which were published by Walsh early in the 18th century) is very short, and as a consequence

shrill. The whistles of savage nations are generally of cane, and sometimes blown with the nose instead of the mouth. F. K.

WHISTLING, KARL FRIEDRICH, a Leipzig publisher, initiated the useful Handbuch, with which his name and that of HOFMEISTER (q.v.) are associated. In 1817 Whistling brought out the first volume, under the title

'Handbuch der musikalischen Literatur, oder allgemeines systematisch geordnetes Verzeichniss gedruckter Musikalien, auch musikalischer Schriften und Abbildungen mit Anzeige des Verlegers und Preises, 8vo.'

This work was published anonymously by A. Meysel, and contains a tolerably complete list of the music published in Germany, with some additions from neighbouring countries, between the years 1780 and 1817. In 1819 the publication was bought by the elder Hofmeister, but in 1825 it was resold to Whistling. The 1817 volume was followed by ten yearly supplements, carrying the work down to 1827. In 1828 the second volume (or rather a new edition of that of 1817) appeared. This work, to which Whistling's name appears, is an 8vo volume of 1158 pages; it is divided into three parts, and was followed by a supplement, containing a list of the works published while the book was in the press.

In 1829 Whistling sold his whole business to the Hofmeisters, who brought out two more supplements, carrying it down to 1833 and 1838. In 1844 a third edition appeared under the following title:

'C. F. Whistlings Handbuch der musikalischen Literatur, oder allgemeines systematisch-geordnetes Verzeichniss der in Deutschland und in den angrenzenden Ländern gedruckten Musikalien auch musikalischen Schriften und Abbildungen, mit Anzeige der Verleger und Preise. Dritte, bis zum Anfang des Jahres 1844 ergänzte Auflage. Bearbeitet und herausgegeben von A. Hofmeister.'

This edition (a 4to volume) was published by Friedrich Hofmeister. It consists of three parts with separate pagination (Part I. pp. 144; Part II. pp. 336; Part III. pp. 340); the third part is dated 1845, and is preceded by a list of the changes which had taken place in the various firms of music-publishers during the period covered by the volume. In 1852 another volume (382 pp.) of the 4to edition carried the collection on from Jan. 1844 until the end of 1851. In 1860 a second volume (470 pp.) carried it down to the end of 1859, in 1868 a third (561 pp.) down to the end of 1867, in 1876 a fourth (575 pp.) down to the end of 1873, and in 1881 a fifth (684 pp.) down to the end of 1879, since when this series has been discontinued. W. B. S.

WHITAKER, JOHN (b. 1776; d. London, Dec. 4, 1847), was organist of St. Clement, East Cheap, and composer of the music of many popular dramatic pieces, amongst which were

'The Outside Passenger,' 1811; 'Orange Boven,' 1813; 'A Chip of the Old Block,' and 'My Spouse and I,' 1815; 'The Broken Sword,' 1816; 'A Friend in Need,' 1817; 'Three Miles from Paris,' 1818; 'A Figure of Fun,' 1821; 'The Apprentice's Opera,' 'The Rake's Progress,' 'Sixes and Sevens.'

He joined Reeve in composing music for 'Who's to have her?' and contributed some songs to 'Guy Mannering' (1816), amongst them the once popular 'Oh, slumber, my darling,' 'Dog Tray,' and 'O say not woman's heart is bought.' He also composed the music for several pantomimes, in one of which (produced at Sadler's Wells on Easter Monday, Apr. 12, 1819) occurred the famous Clown's song, 'Hot Codlins,' written for Grimaldi. His comic songs ('Darby Kelly,' 'Paddy Carey' and others adapted from Irish airs) were highly popular. He composed some anthems, music for English versions of the Odes of Anacreon and Æsop's Fables, The Seraph Collection of Sacred Music, 2 vols. (1818), and 12 Pedal Exercises for the Organ. He was a music publisher, being a partner in the firm of BUTTON & WHITAKER (q.v.). W. H. H.

WHITBROKE (WHYTBROKE), WILLIAM (1st half of 16th cent.), English ecclesiastic and composer of church music. He was at Cardinal College (now Christ Church), Oxford, in 1525, and was ordained priest in 1529. In 1530 he was commissioned by Higden, Dean of Cardinal College, to report on the musicianship of a certain John Benbow, who was a candidate for the post of master of the choristers there, in succession to TAVERNER (q.v.). On the suppression of Cardinal College, Whitbroke became sub-Dean of St. Pauls (June 29, 1531), a post usually held by a musical cleric (see PYGOTT and SAMPSON). He was also appointed to the vicarage of All Saints, Stanton, Suffolk, and possibly retired there in 1535 when he resigned from St. Paul's.[1] Ch. Ch. 979-83 contains a piece in 4 parts called 'Hugh Ashtons Maske,' in which Whitbroke's name is at the end of the contra-tenor part (see ASTON). He contributed to Day's 'Certaine Notes' (1560), a setting 'Let your light so shyne' (described as 'A thankesgeuyng for the poore'), for the first of the three Communion Services contained therein. In the 1565 edition (issued under a new title—see John DAY) his name is also appended to the Magnificat of the second Evening Service. It is probable that he also wrote the Nunc Dimittis which follows, as 'Knyght' (see KNIGHT) is given as the composer of both canticles of an alternative Evening Service. There is no evidence to show that Whitbroke was alive at the time of Day's publication, but he was a contemporary of Shepherd, Redford and Ludford, and composed chiefly for the Latin liturgy. The Magnificat in the list below was published as No. 898 of Novello's 'Parish Choir Book.'

Mass 'Apon ye square' (i.e. in 4 pts.). B.M. Add. MSS. 17,802-5.
M. B.M. Add. MSS. 30,480-3.
Sancte Deus, a 5. PH.
'Audivi media nocte.' B.M. Add. MSS. 17, 802-5. This setting is by Taverner, but the 'pars ad placitum' is by Whitbroke. J. MK.

WHITE, ALICE MARY MEADOWS, see SMITH, Alice Mary.

WHITE, HAROLD ROBERT (b. Dublin, Jan.

[1] See W. H. Grattan Flood, Early Tudor Composers, p. 91.

12, 1872), was a chorister in Christ Church Cathedral from 1881-87. As a boy he had a beautiful voice, and when it broke he was for a time a bass singer, being also successively organist of St. Andrew's and of St. Mary's, and musical critic. Owing to ill-health he went to Denver, Colorado (U.S.A.), in 1897, but returned within two years, and won prizes at the Feis Ceoil (1898), also a prize given by the Worshipful Company of Musicians (Fantasie Trio). He founded the Clef Club (1905), still flourishing, and composed much vocal and instrumental music. His chief work has been an Irish opera, 'Shaun the Post' (based on Boucicault's drama, Arrah na pogue), successfully produced by the Carl Rosa Company in August 1924 at the Theatre Royal, Dublin, and since included in the Company's repertory. W. H. G. F.

WHITE, JOHN (b. York, 1779; d. Leeds, Aug. 22, 1831), organist and composer, studied for the medical profession, but his performance on the violin, when a boy, showed that he had considerable musical ability, and medicine was therefore abandoned for music. As 'Master White' he played at concerts in York, Leeds and other Yorkshire towns. In 1794 he came under the patronage of the Earl of Harewood, who employed him as leader and director of his private concerts, and teacher to the family. Visiting London with the family, he took lessons on the pianoforte from Dussek, singing and the organ from John Ashley, violin from Raimondi, and the harp from Philip Meyer.

At some of the London concerts he played the violoncello in the absence of Lindley and Dahmen. He became organist of Harewood Church in 1804, and settled at Leeds in 1807 as organist of St. Paul's Church. He was leader of the Doncaster Meeting of 1812, and one of the assistant conductors of the great York Festivals of 1823, 1825 and 1828.

From 1793 to nearly the period of his death he was the main organiser and leader of concerts in the West Riding.

In 1821 he held, in addition to his Leeds appointment, the post of organist of Wakefield Parish Church. He was the writer of a few unimportant musical compositions, some of which were published by Muff of Leeds, and was probably the White who was in a partnership with the Knaptons of York as music-sellers there during the early twenties. His son was also in the musical profession, and in later years assisted his father. The wife of John White played the harp and published some compositions. F. K.

WHITE, LUKE (d. London, Feb. 25, 1824), a famous Dublin publisher and bookseller in the last quarter of the 18th century. In 1779 he issued, from 18 Crampton Court, the second English edition of Rousseau's Dictionary of Music, translated by William Waring. This work has numerous musical illustrations, in addition to two large engraved plates. Six years later he published Dr. Burney's *Account of the Musical Performances in Westminster Abbey and the Pantheon*. However, his best-known musical work is the fine quarto edition of J. C. Walker's *Irish Bards*, issued from 86 Dame Street in 1786. In 1790 he gave up publishing and became a lottery-broker, at 42 Dawson Street. In 1791 he removed to 19 Dawson Street, and between his success as publisher and as a lottery-broker he was reputed a millionaire in 1810. He subsequently purchased a seat for Leitrim and, in 1823, got his son, Thomas, elected M.P. for Dublin City. He became the founder of the Annaly peerage.

W. H. G. F.

WHITE, MATTHEW, was gentleman of the Chapel Royal in 1603 (see Rimbault, *Old Cheque-book of the Chapel Royal*, 1872). In 1613, when he was admitted Gospeller in the place of Robert Stone, he is described as ' Minister, and a Basse (from Welles [1]). He resigned his place in 1614. He is presumably the ' Matthew Wight of London,' who on July 18, 1619, received a share in a grant of the surveyorship of lands, etc., belonging to rectories, vicarages and rural prebends in England and Wales. On July 18, 1629, he accumulated the degrees of Bachelor and Doctor of Music at Oxford. Tudway calls him organist of Christ Church, Oxford, in 1611, and ascribes to him anthems really composed by Robert WHITE (*q.v.*). He has been assumed to be the ' Mr. White ' whose catches are printed in Hilton's ' Catch that catch can,' and in Playford's ' Musical Companion,' 1667, but there is nothing to show that they are his. It is very questionable whether any of the anthems to which his name is attached is rightly assigned to him, unless perhaps the fragmentary full anthem ' Zache stood forth,' which bears his name in Barnard's MS. collection (R.C.M. Husk, 1642), is his and not Robert White's.

G. E. P. A.

WHITE, MAUDE VALÉRIE (*b*. Dieppe, June 23, 1855), of English parentage, a successful song-writer.

After acquiring the rudiments of harmony and composition from W. S. Rockstro and Oliver May, she entered the R.A.M. in Oct. 1876, and studied composition under Sir G. A. Macfarren. In Feb. 1879 she was elected to the Mendelssohn Scholarship, which she held for two years, studying the while under Macfarren and F. Davenport. In Apr. 1881 ill-health compelled her to give up the scholarship and reside for a time in South America. Previously, however, to her departure, a portion of a Mass of hers was performed at a R.A.M. students' orchestral concert. In the winter of 1883 she completed her musical studies in Vienna.

Among the most popular of her early lyrics are ' Absent yet present,' ' The devout lover,' ' Ye Cupids ' and ' When passion's trance.' Her best songs are to words by Herrick and Shelley. For instance, for ' To Blossoms,' ' To Daffodils,' ' To Electra,' ' To Music, to becalm his fever ' she has written pure, quaint and measured music in thorough accord with Herrick's delicate and somewhat archaic turns of thought and language. But a song of greater scope and merit than any of these is to Shelley's words, ' My soul is an enchanted boat,' from ' Prometheus Unbound.' Here she completely caught the spirit of Shelley's beautiful song, and proved herself to be an adequate interpreter of a most exquisite lyric. And worthy of all praise is her thorough appreciation of the importance of the words of songs, an appreciation attested alike by the excellence of the poetry she sets to music, and by her own careful attention to the metre and accents of the verse.

Of Miss White's German and French songs we may mention Heine's ' Wenn ich in deine Augen seh',' and ' Im wunderschönen Monat Mai,' Victor Hugo's ' Chantez, chantez, jeune inspirée,' and ' Heureux qui peut aimer,' also a fine setting of Schiller's ' Ich habe gelebt und geliebet,' for soprano and orchestra.

Among her later compositions may be mentioned a vocal quintet, ' Du bist wie eine Blume,' a setting of Browning's ' King Charles,' some songs on Sicilian themes, and a few piano pieces. An opera, ' Jocelyn,' was projected, but seems not to have been finished.

A. H. W.

WHITE, ROBERT (*b. circa* 1530 ; *d*. London, Nov. 1574), was, next to Tye and Tallis, the most important English composer of the mid-16th century. The date of his birth cannot be placed earlier than 1530. His father, also called Robert White, has been identified, with great probability, with an organ-builder ' Magister White,' whose name is known through payments having been made to him between 1531 and 1545 for work done to the organ at Magdalen College, Oxford.[2] A certain amount of support is given to this identification by some entries in the Churchwarden's Books of the Parish of St. Andrew's, Holborn,[3] whence it appears that in the first year of Mary (1553–54) ' the parish gave young Whyte £5 for ye great orgaynes which his father gave to ye church.' In 1572 ' young Whyte ' pulled down these organs without the leave of the parish, and sold them for £10 : 10s. to Westminster Abbey ' wher they now stand and cannot be bought for any money so highly are they esteemed for their goodness.' Among the Westminster Abbey Muniments is a bond dated Dec. 29, 1572, which is connected with the sale of the St. Andrew's organs to ' Robert Whyte gentleman of Westminster,' and one John Thomas, yeoman.

<hr>

[1] On Jan. 30, 1611, he was admitted a perpetual Vicar-Choral of Wells.

W. H. G. F.

[2] *D.N.B.*   [3] *Mus. T.*, Mar. 1905.

As Robert White the composer was then master of the choristers at Westminster Abbey, and his father had been living with him for some time before 1574, the last-named Robert White may perhaps be identified with either the father or the son. The whole transaction is difficult to understand, but it seems highly probable that 'young Whyte' of the St. Andrew's documents was the composer.

The first certain fact recorded about Robert White is that he took his degree of Mus.B. at Cambridge, Dec. 13, 1560. The Grace speaks of his ten years' study in music, and he was required under penalty of a 40s. fine, to compose a Communion Service, to be performed at St. Mary's Church on Commencement Day ; 'omnia peregit' is added in the Grace-Book. Soon afterwards he was appointed master of the choristers at Ely Cathedral, in succession (as it seems) to Dr. Tye, who retired in the early part of 1561. The series of Treasurers' Rolls at Ely is incomplete, but that for Michaelmas, 1563 (in which is recorded the payment of White's yearly stipend of £10), proves that he had entered on his duties not later than Michaelmas, 1562. He remained at Ely till the beginning of 1566 : for John Farrant had succeeded to his place of Magister Choristarum by Michaelmas, 1566 ; and that White was still at Ely on Dec. 23, 1565, is proved by the entry of the baptism of Margery, daughter of Robert White, in the registers of Trinity Church, Ely. His wife, Ellen Tye, was probably the daughter of Dr. TYE (q.v.).

There is evidence tending to show that White, on leaving Ely, went to Chester. In a copy of Morley's *Plaine and Easie Introduction*, 1597, which once belonged to Thomas Tomkins and is now in the library of Dr. A. H. Mann, King's College, Cambridge, against the name of White, in the list of English Practitioners, is written in Tomkins's hand 'First of West Chester & Westminster.' It had been known from the researches of Dr. J. C. Bridge, that a musician named White was Magister Choristarum at Chester at this date, but hitherto no evidence has been found (such as that supplied by the Tomkins *Morley*) to connect him with Robert White. It appears from the Chester Cathedral Treasurers' Accounts that 'Mr. White' (without any official title) was paid £4 : 3 : 4 in Mar. 1567, the Magister Choristarum then being Richard Saywell, with a salary of £1 : 13 : 4. In June 1567 White appears as Magister Choristarum, and contributes 13s. 4d. to Saywell's salary. In 1567 and 1568 'Mr. White' took part in the Chester Whitsun plays, and on each occasion received 4s. for his services, which was higher pay than any of the other musicians received. The evidence of the account books in fact is held to show that 'Whyte' was thought a person of importance. His name is not found at Chester later than 1568, but the exact date of his disappearance from Chester is unknown, as the series of Treasurers' Account Books is incomplete.[1]

It would seem that Robert White was appointed master of the choristers at Westminster Abbey in 1570. The Abbey Muniments throw no light on the subject, but the entries in the registers of St. Margaret's, Westminster, record the baptism of 'Margaret Whyte daughter of Robert,' June 7, 1570.[2] 'Elizabeth daughter of Robert' was baptized Feb. 24, 1571 ; and 'Prudence daughter of Robert,' Aug. 23, 1573. All these children were buried in the end of 1574, when the plague was raging in Westminster, and nearly all the family was carried off. Robert White himself was buried at St. Margaret's, Nov. 11, 1574, and his widow died between the following Nov. 21 and Dec. 8. Only two daughters, Margery and Anne, survived their parents.

The will of Robert White, 'Bacheler of Musicke and Master of the Queristers of the Cathedrall Churche of St. Peter in the Cittie of Westminster,' is dated Nov. 7, 1574. He desires to be buried at St. Margaret's, Westminster, 'near unto my childrin' ; he leaves £3 to his father Robert White, 'and all such his household stufe and goodes wᶜʰ he did bringe vnto me at or before his cominge to me ' : he makes bequests •to his daughters Margery, Anne and Prudence, leaving to the first ' a mazer wᶜʰ was her late graundmother's.' To his wife Ellen he leaves property called ' Swallowfelde and Wilsnowes ' at Nuthurst, Sussex, and he makes her executrix ; and gives ' to every of my skollers to eche of them iiijd.' Prudence White was buried Nov. 7, the day on which her father's will was made. The will of Ellen White, the widow, is dated Nov. 21, 1574. She wishes to be buried at St. Margaret's, ' nere unto my late husband and children.' Among a number of small bequests is one to her father-in-law, Robert White ; to Richard Granwell, one of the Gentlemen of the Queen's Chapel, to whom she owed 20s.; to her aunt, Anne Dingley ; her sisters, Susan Fulke and Mary Rowley, and her brother-in-law Thomas Hawkes, citizen and pewterer of London ; and her mother Katherine Tye, who is to have charge of the daughters Margery and Anne ; or if she die, then Henry Barnarde, and after him John Croste, neighbours to the testatrix, are to have charge of them. A list of debts owing to Ellen White and her late husband includes the sum of £6, owed by ' Gabriell Cawood, Citizen and Stacyoner of London ' : Edwarde Parston Esquier ' owed xxxˢ· viijᵈ , and she hathe in Pawne a Jewell of golde ' : Robert Kene and John White are also named.

1 Information kindly contributed by Dr. J. C. Bridge : cf. also his paper on ' The Chester Miracle Plays,' *Chester Archæological Society's Journal*, 1903.
2 It does not follow that these daughters of Robert Whyte, a common name, were all children of the composer.

It has been suggested [1] with great probability that the large sum owing to White from Gabriel Cawood the printer was in payment for some of his musical compositions. An Edward Paston is known as the owner of 16th-century MSS., such as the Lute-Book in the R.C.M. (Husk, 1964). It is possible that White added to his income by copying music, and that Paston was among his employers.

White's contemporaries held him in the highest esteem. In the MS. Partbooks, dated 1581, now in Ch. Ch. (984-8), the copyist has written at the end of White's Lamentations:

'Non ita moesta sonant plangentis verba prophetae
Quam sonat authoris musica moesta mei.'

('Sad as the mourning Prophet's words fall on the ear
More sad to me the music's tones appear.')

Again, at the end of the Precamur, is written:

'Maxima musarum nostrarum gloria White
Tu peris, aeternum sed tua musa manet.'

('Thou diest, White, chief splendour of our art,
But what thy art hath wrought shall nevermore depart.')

The Roy. Lib. B.M. contains a MS. written in 1591 by John Baldwine, 'singing man of Windsor,' who says, in recounting the principal composers of his age:

'I will begine with White, Shepper, Tye, and Tallis, Parsons, Gyles, Mundie, th'oulde one of the queenes pallis.'

Morley, 1597, quotes him among 'those famous English men, who have beene nothing inferiour in Art' to various foreign writers; and gives him, with Orlandus Lassus, as an authority, for beginning a composition 'upon the sixt.' His name, however, seems to have been forgotten by the end of the 17th century, when his works are nearly always assigned to Matthew White. It was not until he was discovered by Burney that his merit was fully recognised; but ever since Burney's time he has taken his proper place in English histories of music, though even now but little of his music has been printed. His printed compositions are 'Lord, who shall dwell' (Burney, *Hist.* iii. 67); 'The Lord bless us' (Barnard, 1641; and *Old English Edition*, No. xxi.); 'O how glorious art Thou' (*Old English Edition*, No. xxi.). The 8-part 'O praise God in His holiness' is printed in Burns's 'Anthems and Services,' 2nd series, c. 1847. The second half of the 4-part version of this anthem, beginning 'Praise Him in the cymbals,' is given in vol. ii. of the *Oxf. Hist. Mus.*

It is not easy to prepare an accurate list of White's MS. works, partly because early copyists have been free in supplying new words to his music, and partly because great confusion exists between Robert White and two 17th-century musicians named Matthew WHITE and William WHITE.

The following list of compositions is based on

that compiled by Dr. J. H. Mee for the first edition of this Dictionary.

I. LATIN MOTETS AND SERVICES

Ad Te levavi, a 6. Ch. Ch., wanting tenor.
Appropinquet deprecatio, a 5. Ch. Ch.
Cantate Domino, a 3. R.C.M. (Husk, 1737), a piece without words (? part of Ps. 96). It is identical with the opening of Exaudiat te.
Christe Qui Lux. B.M. Add. MSS. 18,936-9. A piece without words. Two lute arrangements, Add. MSS. 29,246.
Deus misereatur, a 6. Ch. Ch., wanting tenor; MS. Bodl. Mus. Sch., E, 423, tenor only; Roy. Lib. B.M.
Domine non est exaltatum, a 6. MS. Bodl. Mus. Sch., E, 1-5; Ch. Ch., wanting tenor; MS. Bodl. Mus. Sch., E, 423, tenor only. Extracts, 'Domine non est' and 'Sicut ablactatus.' Ch. Ch. 45.
Domine quis habitabit. Three settings, Ch. Ch., wanting tenor. One of them is in MS. Bodl. Mus. Sch., E, 423, bassus only.
Exaudiat te, a 5. Ch. Ch.; Bodl. MS. Mus. Sch., E, 1-5; B.M. Add. MSS. 18,936-9. See 'Cantate' above.
Justus es, a 5. MS. Bodl. Mus. Sch., E, 1-5.
Letentur coeli. Roy. Lib. B.M., fragment ? of 'Cantate.'
Lamentations, a 5. Heth, peccatum peccavit, etc. Ch. Ch. (twice); MS. Bodl. Mus. Sch., E, 1-5; B.M. Add. MSS. 17,792-6; MS. Bodl. Mus. Sch., E, 423, contra-tenor only. Fragments, 'De excelso misit,' Add. MSS. 18,936-6; wanting tenor. Ch. Ch.
Libera me, a 4. B.M. Add. MSS. 17,802-5.
M. MS. Bodl. Mus. Sch., E, 423, tenor only, dated 1570 and ascribed to William Whyte. Tenbury MSS. Fragments, 'Quia fecit'; 'Et sanctum nomen'; 'Sicut locutus est'; and 'Sicut erat,' Ch. Ch. 45.
Manus Tuae, a 5. Ch. Ch. (twice); MS. Bodl. Mus. Sch., E, 1-5; B.M. Add. MSS. 18,936-9. Lute arrangement, B.M. Add. MSS. 29,246; MS. Bodl. Mus. Sch., E, 423, contra-tenor only. Extracts in R.C.M., Husk, 1737 (twice); Roy. Lib. B.M.; and Ch. Ch. 45 (Veniant mihi).
Miserere mei, a 5, with second part Cor mundum. MS. Bodl. Mus. Sch., E, 1-5; Ch. Ch.
Peccatum peccavit, a 5 (not the same as the Lamentations above). Lute MSS., B.M. Add. MSS. 29,246; and R.C.M., Husk, 1737 (twice), and without name; B.M. Add. MSS. 34,049 (cantus only).
Porcio mea, a 5. Ch. Ch. (twice).
Precamur sancte Domine, a 5. Ch. Ch. Four settings in Ch. Ch. MSS. 984-8 (Nos. 3, 4, 5 and 38): three settings in Ch. Ch. MSS. 979-83, wanting tenor. (The 2nd and 3rd settings in 984-8 are Nos. 78 and 76 in 979-83.) MS. Bodl. Mus. Sch., E, 423, contra-tenor only. An arrangement for lute, R.C.M. (Husk, 1964).
Regina coeli for men, a 5. Ch. Ch., imperfect.
Tota pulchra, a 5. Ch. Ch., wanting tenor.

II. ENGLISH ANTHEMS, Etc.

Behold now, praise the Lord. B.M. Add. MSS. 30,478-9; PH., ascribed to Matthew White.
If you love Me. B.M. Add. MSS. 29,289, alto only.
Lord, who shall dwell, a 5. Ch. Ch. Printed by Burney.
O, how glorious art Thou, a 5. Printed in Old English Edition. MS. Bodl. Mus. Sch., F, 11-15; B.M. Add. MSS. 30,478-9; PH., ascribed to Matthew White; Ch. Ch. (two organ scores).
O Lord, deliver me from mine enemies. Ch. Ch., wanting bass.
O Lord our governor. R.C.M. (Husk, 1642), by 'R. W.,' perhaps an adaptation from a Latin motet.
O praise God in His holiness, a 4. The 2nd half is printed in the *Oxford Hist. of Mus.*, vol. ii. B.M. Add. MSS. 30, 480-4; Ch. Ch. organ score, differing somewhat from the last, and from the 8-part version.
O praise God in His holiness, a 8. An enlarged version of the last: printed by Burns E.C.L., Hawkins's score, tenor-book, and organ score; PH., ascribed to Matthew White; B.M. Add. MSS 30,478-9; B.M. Harl. 7339 (Tudway), ascribed to Matthew White.
The Lord bless us, a 5. Printed by Barnard, and in Old English Edition. Ch. Ch.; B.M. Harl. 7339 (Tudway), ascribed to Matthew White; E.C.L., Hawkins's score and organ-book (Matthew White); Fitzw.; R.C.M. (Husk, 1642); B.M. Add. MSS. 30,478-9 and 22,597.

To these, possibly, should be added (see above, under Matthew WHITE):

Zache stood forth. R.C.M. (Husk, 1642); Barnard's MSS., ascribed to Matthew White.

Doubtful anthems and adaptations are:

I will wash my hands. Ch. Ch. 1205. An adaptation (by Aldrich ?) of 'O how glorious.'
Let Thy merciful ears. Ch. Ch., 1220-4. Cantus wanting and also in Fitzw., without composer's name. Words in B.M. Harl. 4142. It is merely an adaptation of 'O how glorious.'
O God, the heathen are come, referred to as in 'York Catalogue,' in the article WHITE in the first edition of this Dictionary. Nothing is known of this at York.
O Lord, rebuke me not. B.M. Harl. 7338 (Tudway), 'set to English words by the Rev. Dr. Aldrich,' also in Add. MSS. 17,842, as 'Husbands' from R. White. This is 'The Lord bless us,' with new words.
O sing unto the Lord, in Husk's Catalogue (R.C.M., 1642, Barnard MSS.), is apparently entered by mistake. There seems to be no such Anthem in the MS.
Praise the Lord, O my soul, R.C.M. (Husk, 1642), is an adaptation of 'Speret Israel,' from 'Domine non est.'

III. IN NOMINES, Etc.

In Nomine, a 5. Ch. Ch.; MS. Bodl. Mus. Sch., D, 212-16; B.M. Add. MSS. 29,401-5; Lute Add. MS. 29,246.
Three In Nomines, a 4. MS. Bodl. Mus. Sch., D, 212-16. The first of these is in Lute MS. B.M. Add. MSS. 29,246. In Nomine for lute (different), Add. MSS. 29,246. 6 Fantasias for lute, B.M. Add. MSS. 29,246.
Ut re mi fa sol la, for organ. Ch. Ch. 371.
Mr. Whyte his songe, a 5. B.M. Add. MSS. 31,390. 'Bitts of 3 part songs in Partition with ditties 11 without ditties 16.' Burney, vol. iii. p. 71. It is not known where this MS. is.

G. E. P. A.

WHITE, WILLIAM (first half of 17th cent.), was the composer of fantasias, pavans, etc., for viols, of which many exist in MS. in the Bodleian Music School Collection (with the date 1641) ; in Christ Church and elsewhere. To him may be assigned the fantasias, etc., in B.M. Add. MSS. 17,792-6. A verse anthem, *a* 6, in two parts, ' Almighty Lord ' and ' Bend down,' is in Myriell's collection, 1616 (B.M. Add. MSS. 29,372-7). Thomas Tomkins dedicated to him a five-part song in his set published in 1622. The name of William White with the date 1570 is attached to a Latin Magnificat in MS. Bodl. Mus. Sch., E, 423. This may be the work of an early William White, but the name is generally supposed to be a mistake for Robert White.

William White is named among the ' singing men ' of Westminster, to whom mourning was granted for the funeral of Queen Elizabeth.[1]

G. E. P. A.

WHITEHILL, CLARENCE (*b.* Marengi, Iowa, Nov. 5, 1871), distinguished dramatic bass. A pupil of H. D. Phelps in Chicago, he was in business in that city, and incidentally a church soloist, until 1896, when he went to Paris to study for the operatic stage under Giraudet and Sbriglia. His début was made at Brussels in 1899, as Friar Lawrence in Gounod's ' Romeo and Juliet,' and immediately afterwards he was the first American male singer to appear at the Paris Opéra-Comique. In 1900 he was the leading baritone with the Savage English Opera Company during its season in New York. After further study with Stockhausen at Frankfort, he went to Bayreuth for study of the Wagnerian repertory with Frau Wagner—rôles in which he has won especial eminence.

In 1903–08 he sang principal parts at Cologne ; in 1909–11 he was a member of the Metropolitan Opera Company in New York, and in 1911–15 of the Chicago Opera Company. Since 1916 he has again been with the Metropolitan forces. He has also sung Wagnerian rôles at Covent Garden during five seasons, and at Bayreuth and at Munich during three and two seasons respectively.   w. s. s.

WHITEHOUSE, WILLIAM EDWARD (*b.* London, May 20, 1859), violoncellist. After some early study of the violin, he took to the violoncello at the age of 13, studying for four years under Walter Pettitt. He entered the R.A.M. in 1877, receiving tuition from Piatti and Pezze, won the Bonamy Dobree prize in 1878, and joined the teaching staff in 1882. With a purity of style modelled on that of Piatti, his greatest successes were made in chamber music. He travelled in the provinces with Joachim, and was violoncellist to the Ludwig Quartet, the Bath Quartet Society (the oldest in England), and the ' London Trio '

1 See C. H. Lafontaine, *The King's Musick*, p. 44.

(Amina Goodwin, Simonetti, Whitehouse) with whom he toured in France and Italy. He resigned from the last of these organisations in 1925, being succeeded by Lebell. He holds the appointments of professor at the R.A.M., R.C.M. and Trinity College, and Examiner for the Associated Board, and has formed many distinguished pupils. The violoncello upon which he plays is a fine specimen of Francesco Ruggeri.   w. w. c.

WHITFELD, CLARKE-, see CLARKE, John.

WHITHORN (or MAY-HORN), a rustic oboe, the body constructed of green willow-bark twisted into a conical shape and fastened with hawthorn spines ; the double reed is also made of soft willow rind pressed together. This primitive instrument used to be employed in Oxfordshire in connexion with a local Whit-Monday Hunt in the forest.   F. W. G.

WHITING, ARTHUR (*b.* Cambridge, Mass., June 20, 1861), American pianist and composer. He studied at the New England Conservatory with Sherwood and Chadwick and later at the Munich Conservatorium with Rheinberger, Bussmayer and Abel. In 1885–95 he lived in Boston, devoting himself chiefly to composition. Since 1895 he has lived in New York, and since 1907 he has been largely occupied with the giving of concerts of chamber music designed to be definitely educational. His ' Expositions ' are a regular feature at Harvard, Yale and Princeton Universities. He has also become an authoritative exponent of music for harpsichord and clavichord.

With various American orchestras Whiting has played his pianoforte concerto, in D minor, and his Fantasy, B-flat minor. His other compositions include an overture, a suite for strings and horns, chamber music, vocal music and pianoforte pieces. He has also published valuable arrangements of classical harpsichord music for the piano.   w. s. s.

WHITING, GEORGE ELBRIDGE (*b.* Holliston, near Boston, U.S.A., Sept. 14, 1842 ; *d.* Cambridge, Mass., Oct. 14, 1923), an eminent American musician At the age of 15 he succeeded Dudley Buck as organist of the North Congregational Church at Hartford, Conn. There he founded the Beethoven Musical Society for church practice. In 1862 he began his Boston career, playing at Dr. Kirk's church, and afterwards at Tremont Temple, and giving concerts on the Music Hall organ, and on many other large organs, and meanwhile studying with G. W. Morgan, organist in New York. In 1863 he visited England to study with W. T. Best, and while there often deputised for Best in church. Returning to America he became organist of St. Joseph's Church, Albany, where Emma Lajeunesse (see ALBANI) was a member of his choir. After three years he returned to Boston, where he was organist and director of music at King's Chapel for five years, and at the Music Hall for one year. In 1874 he visited Berlin, and studied harmony with Haupt, and orchestration with Radecke. Returning to Boston again, he became principal organ-instructor in the New England Conservatory. He was also organist at the Cathedral of the Holy Cross, and conductor of the Foster Club, Boston. While Whiting was its director the club sang a number of his compositions, among others a setting of the prologue to Longfellow's ' Golden Legend,' and the first sketch of a cantata, ' The Tale of the Viking.' His compositions further included cantatas, church music and some symphonic works for orchestra. In 1879 he accepted a call from Theodore Thomas to take charge of the organ department in the College of Music at Cincinnati, of which Thomas was then director. In 1882 Whiting returned to Boston and the New England Conservatory.   w. h. d., abridged.

WHITTAKER, WILLIAM GILLIES, Mus.D. (b. Newcastle-on-Tyne, July 23, 1876), has particularly devoted himself to choral conducting in Northumberland and obtained conspicuously fine musical results from the choirs under his control. These have included classes at Armstrong College, the Newcastle and Gateshead Choral Union and the Newcastle Bach Choir. The last-named, a small body of picked singers, was founded and trained by him for the purpose of giving Bach's cantatas in conditions approximating to those for which they were intended. Whittaker brought his Bach Choir to London for a three days' festival in 1922. He gave the first complete performance of Byrd's ' Great Service ' at Newcastle and repeated it at St. Margaret's, Westminster, in 1924. He has published many choral arrangements of folk-songs (for list see B.M.S. Ann. 1920), as well as original choral pieces. A quintet for strings and PF. ' Among the Northumbrian Hills,' and ' A Lykewake Dirge ' (choir and orch.) are published by the Carnegie Trust. Whittaker is editor of the series of Bach's cantatas with English texts by C. Sanford TERRY (q.v.) in process of publication by the Oxford University Press.   c.

WHOLE-TONE SCALES. From the chromatic scale of twelve semitones can be extracted two scales, each consisting of six whole tones. The notation of them is quite arbitrary, and will normally depend on the context in which they are used.

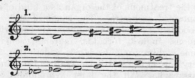

Although they are symmetrical with respect to each other, these scales have

no note in common and have therefore no mutual harmonic relations. There is also no interval of a perfect fifth within them, and they have thus no unambiguous associations with the classical major-minor systems. They have, however, been used for melodic and harmonic expression within their prescribed limits, and still more frequently in contrast with traditional idioms. Some of the possible harmonic inferences of certain whole-tone chords are given in the article on HARMONY.

                              G. D.

WHYTE, ROBERT, see WHITE, Robert.

WHYTE, WILLIAM, an Edinburgh music-publisher, ' at the sign of the Organ,' 1 South St. Andrew Street (this number was changed to 17 and then to 12), where he remained until 1826. In this year he removed to 13 George Street, having entered into partnership. He published great quantities of half-sheet and whole-sheet Scots songs, but he is best known as having engaged Haydn to arrange two collections of Scots songs, in rivalry of George Thomson's similar publication ; Thomson was much hurt at Haydn undertaking the work. The arrangements for Whyte were done in 1802–1803, and were sixty-five in number; they were issued in two folio volumes in 1806 and 1807, and for this Haydn received 500 florins.

                              F. K.

WHYTHORNE, THOMAS (b. 1528[1]; d. after 1590), composer. He seems to have been an amateur musician and a man of sufficient means to sustain the cost of printing his compositions. In 1571 he published :

' Songes, for three, fower, and fiue voyces composed and made by Thomas Whythorne, Gent. the which songes be of sundry sortes, that is to say, some long, some short, some hard, some easie to be songe, and some betwene both : also some solemne, and some pleasant or mery : so that according to the skill of the singers (not being Musitians) and disposition and delite of the hearers, they may here finde songes for their contentation and liking. Now newly published An. 1571. At London, Printed by John Daye, dwelling over Aldersgate.'

The preface, printed only in the tenor partbook,[2] shows that Whythorne had travelled 'in sundry forrein land ' [sic] paying special attention to various kinds of music,

' But cheefly the Italian, emong the which is one
   That called is Napolitane (a prety mery one).'

This volume has historical importance, for it is the only published set of secular vocal compositions in England between that of Wynkyn de Worde in 1530 and Byrd's ' Psalmes, Sonets and Songs ' in 1588. Nor does the music deserve the severe censure that has been heaped upon it. Burney described both the words and music of this set as being ' truly barbarous,' and other writers have followed Burney's lead rather blindly. Whythorne can scarcely be called a great composer, but it must not be forgotten that secular vocal music in England in 1571 cannot fairly be compared with that of 25 years later. Nevertheless the 1571 book contains some really

1 This date is calculated from the statement on his portrait.
2 Four partbooks (triplex, medius, tenor, bassus) are at Ch. Ch. The Bodleian contains only tenor partbook, of which the title-page is missing.

excellent songs, designed on the plan of the Ayre of a generation later rather than that of the madrigal; the melody is in the top voice part, the lower voices being of subordinate interest. 'As thy shadow itself apply'th' has a splendid flowing melody, and this song alone is sufficient to confute those who have so greatly undervalued Whythorne's work. Philip Heseltine has edited and published this song together with eleven others selected from this same set, and he claims that several of them are worthy to rank with the best of the Ayres of the lutenists who flourished some thirty years later.[1] Heseltine also points out that Whythorne's 'Buy new broom' is the earliest printed example of an English solo-song with instrumental accompaniment; the accompanying instruments in this instance were viols. There are 76 compositions in this set. Most of them are moral songs, but the Venite and some other psalms are also included.

Whythorne's second publication is of less interest. It was entitled:

'Duos, or Songs for two voices, composed and made by Thomas Whythorne Gent. Of the which, some be playne and easie to be sung, or played on Musicall Instruments, & be made for yong beginners of both those sorts. And the rest of these Duos be made and set foorth for those that be more perfect in singing or playing as aforesaid, all the which be deuided into three parts. That is to say:
'The first, which doth begin at the first song, are made for a man and a childe to sing, or otherwise for voices or Instruments of Musicke, that be of the like compasse or distance in sound.
'The second, which doth begin at the XXIII. song, are made for two children to sing. Also they be aptly made for two treble Cornets to play or sound: or otherwise for voices or Musicall Instruments, that be of the lyke compasse or distance in sound.
'And the third part which doth begin at the XXXVIII. song (being all Canons of two parts in one) be of diuers compasses or distances, and therefore are to be used with voices or Instruments of Musicke accordingly.
'Now newly published in An. Do. 1590. Imprinted at London by Thomas Este, the assigné of William Byrd. 1590.'

This set was dedicated to the Earl of Huntingdon, and the composer's portrait at the age of 40 was printed at the end of each of the partbooks. The first twelve pieces are psalms, but the remaining 40 numbers have only the opening words printed with the music.

E. H. F.

WIDERSPÄNSTIGEN ZÄHMUNG, DER —The Taming of the Shrew, opera in 4 acts; text adapted by J. V. Widmann from Shakespeare; music by Goetz; produced Mannheim Oct. 11, 1874; in English (Rev. J. Troutbeck), Carl Rosa Co., Her Majesty's Theatre, Jan. 20, 1880; New York, Metropolitan Opera House, 1916. G.

WIDMANN, ERASMUS (b. Hall, Würtemberg, 1572; d. Rothenburg a./d. Tauber, Oct. 1634), cantor-preceptor at Graz c. 1590, Kapellmeister to Count Hohenlohe at Weickersheim in 1604; from c. 1614 preceptor and cantor at the school of Rothenburg a./d. Tauber. In 1629 he styles himself 'P. L. Caes.' (Imperial poet-laureate.) He was a prolific composer of psalms, motets, hymns and other church music, also secular songs and instrumental music (canzons, intradas, ballets and courants), also

[1] Thomas Whythorne. An unknown Elizabethan composer, by Peter Warlock. Oxford University Press.

a theoretical treatise, Praecepta musicae latino-Germanica (Nuremberg, 1615). (Schilling; Riemann, Q.-L.). E. v. d. s.

WIDOR, CHARLES MARIE JEAN ALBERT (b. Lyons, Feb. 22, 1845), organist and composer. He studied first under his father (organist of St. François, Lyons) afterwards going to Brussels, where he was a pupil of Lemmens for organ and Fétis for composition. In 1870 he became organist of St. Sulpice, Paris. He succeeded Franck as organ professor at the Paris Conservatoire, and later followed Dubois as professor of composition. He soon distinguished himself, not only as a player, but also as a writer (he was critic for the Estafette) and a prolific composer in many fields. He is Permanent Secretary to the Académie des Beaux-Arts. His works comprise many pianoforte pieces, songs, symphonies in F and A for orchestra, ten symphonies for organ and one for organ and orchestra, concertos for pianoforte, violin and violoncello, a pianoforte quintet and trio, sonata for pianoforte and violin, a suite for flute, six duets for pianoforte and organ, a Mass for two choirs and two organs, Ps. cxii. for chorus, orchestra and organ, a ballet in 2 acts, 'La Korrigane' (produced at the Opéra, Dec. 1, 1880), an opera in 3 acts and 4 tableaux, 'Maître Ambros' (Opéra-Comique, May 1886), a 4-act opera, 'Les Pêcheurs de Saint Jean' (Opéra-Comique, Dec. 1905), a lyric drama 'Nerto' (Opéra, Oct. 27, 1924), incidental music to 'Conte d'Avril' and 'Les Jacobites,' a symphonic poem, 'Une Nuit de Valpurgis' (performed in London at a Philharmonic concert on Apr. 19, 1888, under the composer's direction), etc.

He is best known in this country as an organ composer, certain movements from his symphonies for that instrument having achieved great popularity. These works are among the most important in the organ repertory, both in scope and in the influence they have had on organ technique, idiom and registration. They date from two periods of the composer's life, Nos. 1-4 being op. 13, Nos. 5-8, op. 42, 'Symphonie gothique,' op. 70, 'Symphonie romane,' op. 73, and 'Sinfonia sacra' (for organ and orchestra), op. 81. The title 'symphony,' however, is sometimes inappropriate, especially in the case of some of the earlier set, which, consisting as they do of six or seven movements, some rather slight and short, would be better termed suites. Justification is perhaps found in the treatment of the organ as a kind of self-contained orchestra. The range of style and mood is very wide, the movements comprising canons, fugues, toccatas, marches, scherzos, some highly-wrought adagios and (in No. 9) a very fine set of variations—really a free kind of passacaglia. All the later symphonies, and certain sections in the first four, make severe demands on the resources of both player and

instrument—so much so that only lately have many of the best movements begun to receive due recognition. Some recent performances (1924) by prominent recitalists in England and America, of the whole set of symphonies in their entirety, bear witness to the growing appreciation of this important side of Widor's output.
                                                                        H. G.

WIECK, (1) FRIEDRICH (b. Pretsch, near Torgan, Saxony, Aug. 18, 1785; d. Dresden, Oct. 6, 1873), a remarkable pianoforte-teacher, and father of Clara SCHUMANN (q.v.), began life as a student of theology at Wittenberg, preacher and private tutor, and was for some time engaged in a piano factory and library at Leipzig.

His first wife was Marianne Tromlitz, and was the mother of Clara Josephine (2), his famous daughter, and of two sons, Alwyn (3) and Gustav. This union, however, was severed and the lady married Bargiel, father of Woldemar BARGIEL (q.v.). Wieck married again, July 31, 1828, Clementine Fechner, by whom he had three children, Cäcilie, Clemens (died young) and Marie (4). About 1844 he removed from Leipzig to Dresden, where he resided till his death, spending the summer at Löschwitz, and leading a very musical life, his house a rendezvous for artists. Mendelssohn endeavoured to secure him as professor of the piano in the Leipzig Conservatorium, but without success, and Moscheles was appointed instead.

Wieck began to teach the piano on Logier's system, but soon abandoned it for a method of his own, if that can be called a method which seems to have consisted of the application of the greatest care, sense and intelligence possible to the teaching of technique and expression. He embodied his views on the piano and singing in a pamphlet entitled Clavier und Gesang (1853, 2nd ed., Leipzig, 1875), translated into English by H. Krüger, of Aberdeen, with three portraits. Among Wieck's pupils may be mentioned Hans von Bülow, who, in a letter quoted in the translation just mentioned, speaks of him with respect and gratitude. But his daughter Clara was his best pupil, and his greatest glory.

An institution called the ' Wieck-Stiftung ' was founded in Dresden on Aug. 18, 1871, his eighty-sixth birthday, partly by funds of his own. He continued to see his friends almost up to the end of his life, and an amusing account of a visit to him in 1872 is given by Miss Amy Fay (Music Study in Germany, London, 1886, p. 147). He published some studies and dances for the piano, exercises in singing, and a few pamphlets, Verfall der Gesangkunst (Decay of the Art of Singing), etc. He edited a number of classical pianoforte works which are published anonymously, but distinguished by the letters D.A.S. (Der alte Schulmeister).

(2) CLARA JOSEPHINE (b. Leipzig, Sept. 13, 1819; d. Frankfort-on-Main, May 20, 1896), famous pianist, married Robert Schumann.

Sept. 12, 1840. Her career is traced under SCHUMANN.

BIBL.—B. LITZMANN, Clara Schumann, 3 vols., 1902–08; F. MAY, The Girlhood of Clara Schumann, 1912.

(3) ALWYN (b. Leipzig, Aug. 27, 1821; d. there, Oct. 21, 1885), studied the violin under David, was in the orchestra of the Italian Opera at St. Petersburg (1849–59), lived later in Dresden, and published (1875) Materialien zu Fr. Wieck's Pianofortemethodik. (See Riemann.)

(4) MARIE (b. Leipzig, Jan. 17, 1832; d. Dresden, Nov. 2, 1916), was educated by her father. She visited England in 1859 and 1864. She was much esteemed for many years in Dresden as a teacher both of the pianoforte and singing. She edited several of her father's works.
                                                          G., addns.

WIENIAWSKI (1), HENRI (b. Lublin, Poland, July 10, 1835; d. Moscow, Apr. 2, 1880), famous violinist, was the son of a medical man. His great musical talent showed itself so very early that his mother, a sister of the pianist Ed. Wolff, took him at the age of 8 to Paris, where he entered the Conservatoire, and was soon allowed to join Massart's class. As early as 1846, when only 11, he gained the first prize for violin-playing. He then made a tour through Poland and Russia, but returned to Paris to continue his studies, more especially in composition. In 1850 he began to travel with his brother Joseph (2), and appeared with great success in most of the principal towns of the Netherlands, France, England and Germany. In 1860 he was nominated solo-violinist to the Emperor of Russia, and for the next twelve years resided principally at St. Petersburg. In 1872 he started with Anton Rubinstein for a lengthened tour through the United States, and after Rubinstein's return to Europe, extended his travels as far as California. Returning to Europe (1874), he accepted the post of first professor of the violin at the Conservatoire of Brussels, as Vieuxtemps's successor; but after a few years quitted it again, and though his health was failing, resumed his old wandering life of travel. An incident connected with this last tour deserves record. During a concert which he gave at Berlin, he was suddenly seized by a spasm and compelled to stop in the middle of a concerto. Joachim, who happened to be among the audience, without much hesitation stepped on to the platform, took up Wieniawski's fiddle, and finished the programme amid the enthusiastic applause of an audience delighted by so spontaneous an act of good fellowship.

Struggling against his mortal disease, Wieniawski made for Russia, but broke down at Odessa, and was conveyed to Moscow, where he died.

Wieniawski was one of the most eminent violin-players ; a great virtuoso, distinguished from the mass of clever players by a striking and peculiar individuality. Technical difficulties did not exist for him—he mastered them in early childhood. Left hand and right arm were trained to perfection, and while the boldness of his execution astonished and excited his audience, the beauty and fascinating quality of his tone went straight to their hearts, and enlisted their sympathy from the first note. The impetuosity of his Slavonic temperament was probably the most prominent and most characteristic quality of his style, in which respect he much resembled his friend Rubinstein; but warm and tender feeling, as well as gracefulness and piquancy, were equally at his command. At the same time he was so thoroughly musical as to be an excellent quartet-player, though perhaps more in sympathy with the modern than with the older masters. Impetuous, warm-hearted, witty, an excellent story-teller —such was the man, and such were the qualities which shone through his performances. His fiery temperament led him sometimes to a certain exaggeration, especially in quick movements, or to such errors as the introduction of an enlarged cadenza in Mendelssohn's concerto; but who would not readily forgive such peccadilloes to so rare and genuine a talent?

His compositions—two concertos, a number of fantasias, pièces de salon, and some studies— are not of much importance, though much played. Among the most famous are:

Polonaise (op. 4); 'Souvenir de Moscou' (op. 6); Le Carnaval russe (op. 11); 'Légende' (op. 17); Fantasie on Gounod's 'Faust' (op. 20).

P. D.

(2) JOSEPH (b. Lublin, May 23, 1837; d. Brussels, Nov. 11, 1912), brother of the above, was an eminent pianist, trained at the Paris Conservatoire and with Liszt at Weimar. He toured much with his brother, held a professorship at the Moscow Conservatoire and later at the Brussels Conservatoire. He was the composer of some chamber music and pianoforte music.

BIBL.—L. DELCROIX, Joseph Wieniawski. 1908.

WIEPRECHT, WILHELM FRIEDRICH (b. Aschersleben, Aug. 8, 1802; d. Berlin, Aug. 4, 1872), was the inventor of several improvements in wind-instrument construction and reorganised the system of instrumentation of the Prussian military bands. He was made director of the music of the Prussian Guards. For an account of his innovations see WIND BAND.

WIETROWETZ, GABRIELE (b. Laibach, Jan. 13, 1866), violinist. In her 6th year she began to study the violin with her father, a military bandsman, who placed her, five years later, in the hands of Casper, director of a musical college in Styria. Here she distinguished herself, and after four years of study was assigned a stipend, which enabled her to go to Berlin, enter the Hochschule and take lessons of Joachim (in 1882). At the end of the first year she gained the Mendelssohn prize

(1500 marks), and achieved a similar success two years later. She spent three years in studying at the Hochschule, during which time she was engaged to play Bruch's 2nd concerto at the Berlin Philharmonic, and later gave a concert in which Joachim took part, playing with her Bach's double concerto and conducting the orchestra in concertos by Brahms and Spohr.

She made many concert tours in her own country (scoring a brilliant success at the St. Cecilia Festival in Münster in Brahms's Concerto), and in Switzerland, Norway, Sweden, etc. In 1892 she made her début in England at the Crystal Palace concerts, and led for the first time the Quartet of the Popular Concerts, revisiting London thirteen times in the course of the ensuing seven years. On the secession of Miss Emily Shinner (Mrs. Liddell) from the Quartet which bore her name, Fräulein Wietrowetz became the first violin. She became violin professor at the Hochscule at Berlin (1901–12), and upheld her position as a worthy representative of the Joachim school.

W. W. C.

WIGMORE HALL. This concert hall was built by the firm of BECHSTEIN (q.v.) as a part of their premises in Wigmore Street, and was originally known as Bechstein Hall. It was opened to the public on June 1, 1901, with a concert at which Ysaÿe, Busoni and Ben Davies took part, and has always been in great request for recitals and concerts of chamber music. The seating capacity is 600. For a short time during the war period, 1914–18, the hall was closed; it reopened in Jan. 1917 under the name it now bears. The hall is managed by W. J. K. Pearson, who has kindly supplied the above information.   N. C. G.

WIGTHORPE, WILLIAM (late 16th and early 17th cent.), English composer. A student of New College, Oxford, he graduated Mus.B. in 1605, after having studied music for 10 years.[1] B.M. Add. MSS. 17,786-91 contains the following madrigals by Wigthorpe (although 'To plead my faith' is attributed to D. Batchelor in Robert Dowland's 'Musicall Banquet,' 1610):

'Dowland's sorrow,' beginning 'Sorrow . . . come,' a 5; 'Come hither,' a dialogue a 6; 'Smithes are good fellowes,' a 5; 'Were I made Jurer,' a 5; 'To plead my faith,' a 5; 'I am not I of such beleefe,' a dialogue.

Two anthems by him, 'I musing stand' and 'O give thanks,' are included in the Batten Organ Book (see BATTEN), and the words of some others are given in Clifford's collection (1663).   J. M^K.

WIHAN, HANUŠ, see BOHEMIAN STRING QUARTET.

WIHTOL, JOSEPH (b. Wolmar, Latvia, July 26, 1863), is the national exponent of Lettish music, a pupil of Johannsen and Rimsky-Korsakov at the Conservatory in St. Peters-

---

[1] C. F. Abdy Williams, Degrees in Music.

Ďurg, where, in 1886, he was appointed professor of theory. The breakdown of the Russian Empire brought with it the formation of the little Baltic States, and since 1918 Wihtol has been the heart and soul of the Lettish musical movement in Riga, where he is the director of the National Opera and the Lettish Conservatory of Music. His works exhale the typically Lettish characteristic of a melancholy that is wholly apart in sentiment and quite different in mood from that of Russian music.

WORKS.—' Das Fest der Ligo ' (a symphonic poem on a Lettish theme), op. 4 ; Lettish overture, ' Spriditis,' op. 37 ; phantasy on Lettish folk-songs for v'cl. and orch., op. 42 ; dramatic overture, op. 21 ; a symphony in MS. ; string quartet, op. 27 ; five sonatas, opp. 30, 32, 33, 41 ; many choral works and Lettish folk-songs.

K. D. H.

WILBYE, JOHN (b. Diss, 1574 ; d. Colchester, Sept. 1638), madrigal composer. He was baptized at Diss, co. Norfolk, on Mar. 7, 1573/4. He was the third son of Matthew Wilbye, a tanner, who was in a prosperous position as a landowner at Diss, and there can be no doubt that this was the composer's birthplace. While still a youth he attracted the notice of the Cornwallis family, seated at Brome Hall in the same neighbourhood. Elizabeth, daughter of Sir Thomas Cornwallis, married Sir Thomas Kytson, son of the Sir Thomas who built Hengrave Hall, near Bury St. Edmunds, and not far distant from Brome over the Suffolk border. Wilbye became resident musician at Hengrave about the year 1595, and had the advantage of living in surroundings where music was greatly encouraged. The younger Kytson did much to improve the magnificence of Hengrave, and also owned a town house in Austin Friars, where Wilbye accompanied the family on their visits.

In spite of changes in ownership, Hengrave Hall has undergone surprisingly little alteration during the three centuries that have elapsed since Wilbye lived there ; the Kytson family portraits still hang on the walls, and many priceless documents have remained in the house. Among these are the very interesting inventories taken in 1602 and 1621 ; from these we learn exactly which room was occupied by Wilbye, and details as to the furniture of his apartment are recorded. There are also lists of the musical instruments, and books which would have been in his keeping. Among the papers belonging to this date are original letters of many notable people, including Sir Philip Sidney ; and of special interest to musicians is a holograph letter of Wilbye dated from Hengrave, Sept. 1628, and addressed to his friend Mistress Camocke at the house of Lady Rivers at Colchester (Hengrave Letter Book II., No. 131). This letter is reproduced in facsimile in ENG. MADR. SCH., vol. vi.

Wilbye continued to live at Hengrave until the death of Lady Kytson, who in her widow-hood kept up the establishment in great state. Her death took place in 1628. Wilbye then retired and spent the last ten years of his life at the house of Lady Rivers, the younger daughter of Sir Thomas Kytson, at Colchester. The house is described by Morant in his history of Colchester as ' the Great brick house ' opposite Holy Trinity Church. The house is still (1927) standing, and it was there that Wilbye died in Sept. 1638. He was buried at Holy Trinity, but there is nothing to show the position of his grave. Wilbye was a man of some substance at the time of his death. Many years previously the Kytsons had granted him a lease of the best sheep-farm on their estate in reward for long and faithful services ; and he owned land at Diss, Bury St. Edmunds, and elsewhere. He died unmarried. His will (P.C.C. 145 Lee) was dated Sept. 10, 1638, and proved Nov. 13 in the same year ; it is printed in full in the preface of ENG. MADR. SCH., vol. vi. Two Latin motets ' Homo natus,' a 6, and ' Ne reminiscaris,' a 5, a treble solo with instrumental accompaniment, were edited by Arkwright, and printed in No. xxi. of his OLD ENGLISH EDITION.

Except for two contributions to Leighton's ' Teares or Lamentacions ' (1614), Wilbye has left no English Church music, and only a fragment of a single instrumental piece by him is known. It is as a madrigal composer that he has won enduring fame, and in the opinion of many well-qualified judges he is considered the greatest of all madrigal writers, whether English or continental. For style and finish he is perhaps most nearly approached by Luca Marenzio, and certainly he stands as the greatest stylist of the English madrigalists.

It was in 1598 that Wilbye's first volume was published. It was entitled ' The First Set of English Madrigals to 3. 4. 5. and 6. voices.' The dedication was to Sir Charles Cavendish, who was a cousin of Michael CAVENDISH (q.v.), the lutenist and madrigalist. Sir Charles married Elizabeth, the elder daughter of Sir Thomas Kytson of Hengrave. The dedication is dated from Kytson's house in ' th' Augustine Fryers the xii of Aprill 1598.' The set contains 30 madrigals, of which 6 are for 3 voices, 6 for 4, 10 for 5, and 8 for 6 voices. Among the best are ' What needeth all this travail ' and ' Adieu, sweet Amaryllis,' ' Flora gave me fairest flowers ' and the six-part version of ' Lady, when I behold.' Eleven years later he published ' The Second Set of Madrigales to 3. 4. 5. and 6. parts apt both for Voyals and Voyces,' 1609. This set was dedicated to Lady Arabella Stuart, whose mother, Lady Lennox, was Elizabeth Cavendish, sister of Sir Charles the patron of Wilbye's first set. This second set contains 34 madrigals, 8 each for 3, 4, and 6 voices, and 10 for 5. Wilbye's style in this second volume is decidedly more mature and individual than in his earlier work ; a large proportion of the madrigals in this set belong to the very highest class. ' Draw on, sweet night,' ' Stay, Corydon ' and ' Softly, O softly drop,' which follow each other in the six-part section, are superb examples of madrigal writing. Almost equally fine are ' Happy, O happy he,' *a* 4, and ' Oft have I vowed,' *a* 5 ; the deservedly popular ' Sweet honey - sucking bees ' is also in the very first rank with its splendidly contrasted sections, its varied grouping of the voices and its strong and compelling sense of rhythm. There is scarcely one weak number in the set.

Wilbye's contribution to ' The Triumphes of Oriana ' was ' The Lady Oriana.' This six-part madrigal is characteristic of him in his brighter mood.

Of MS. music by Wilbye, there is an imperfect ' Oh, who shall ease me,' *a* 6, wanting the 2nd cantus and altus parts, in the Bodleian Library (MS. Mus. f, 20-24). The altus part of three Phantasias, *a* 4, is in B.M. Add. MSS. 29,427. A volume of Lessons for the Lute was sold in the library of the Rev. William Gostling of Canterbury in 1777, but it is not known whether it still exists.

Both Wilbye's sets of Madrigals were reprinted for the MUSICAL ANTIQUARIAN SOCIETY (*q.v.*) ; more recently they were printed as vols. vi. and vii. of ENG. MADR. SCH. The preface to vol. vi. gives many details concerning the life and family of Wilbye, including wills and other documents. For further information, see paper on Wilbye by Fellowes, *Mus. Ass. Proc.*, 1914, and Fellowes's *English Madrigal Composers*.

E. H. F.

WILD, FRANZ (*b.* Hollabrunn, Lower Austria, Dec. 31, 1791 ; *d.* Ober Döbling, near Vienna, 1860), tenor singer, as a boy entered the choir of the monastery at Klosterneuburg, near Vienna, and thence was promoted to the court chapel. His voice changed with extreme rapidity in his 16th year, the process only lasting two months, after which he became a chorus-singer, first at the Josefstadt, and then at the Leopoldstadt theatres. A happy accident brought him into notice. General excitement about the war prevailing at the time, some battle-songs by Collin (of Beethoven's ' Coriolan '), set to music by Weigl, were being sung at the theatre, when one night the solo-singer fell ill, and Wild, though unprepared, took his place, and sang so finely that he was received with acclamation. He was at once offered an engagement for the Kärnthnerthor theatre, to sing in the chorus and take subordinate parts. His powerful sonorous voice told with so much effect one night in the quartet in ' Uthal,' that Hummel recommended him to Prince Esterhazy (whose band at Eisenstadt Hummel was conducting), and he entered on an engagement for

six years from Oct. 11, 1810. Soon after, however, Count Ferdinand Palffy endeavoured to secure him for the theatre ' an der Wien,' but Prince Esterhazy declined to let him go. Wild pressed for his release, which was at last granted in Sept. 1811. In the meantime he had taken the law into his own hands, and was singing Ramiro in Isouard's ' Cendrillon ' at the above theatre, first ' als Gast ' (July 9), and then (Aug. 28) with a permanent engagement. His success was great, and when the theatre was united under one management with the Kärnthnerthor (1814) he removed thither, and as Jean de Paris (1815) excited universal admiration by the liquid tones of his voice. For two years he was acting there with those excellent singers FORTI and VOGL (*q.v.*), his last appearance being June 4, 1816, after which he started on a tour through Frankfort, Mainz, Leipzig, Berlin, Dresden, Hamburg and Prague. On Nov. 9, 1816, he appeared for the first time as Sargines at Darmstadt, having been made Kammersänger to the Grand Duke of Hesse. Here he remained till 1825. From Darmstadt he went to Paris, principally for the sake of further study with Rossini and Bordogni, and after this accepted an invitation to Cassel as Kammersänger. In July 1829 he went to Vienna, his engagement being made permanent on Nov. 1, 1830, and there he remained till 1845, except for occasional tours. One of these brought him to London in 1840, where he appeared with Staudigl and Sabine Heinefetter at the Princess's in ' Das Nachtlager,' ' Jessonda,' ' Iphigénie en Tauride,' and ' De Freischütz.' His last appearance on the stage was at the Kärnthnerthor theatre, Mar. 24, 1845, his part being Abayaldos in ' Dom Sebastian.' After this he became régisseur. Latterly his voice had acquired so much the tone of a baritone that he sang such parts as Don Juan, Zampa and Sever with irresistible power and energy. High notes he never forced, but preserved the full power and freshness of his middle register, which told most effectively in declamation and recitative. As a concert-singer he was always well received, but perhaps his best singing of all was in church. Those privileged to hear him sing the Lamentations during Holy Week will never forget how the full round tones of his superb voice floated forth in perfect devotional feeling.

One of the happiest events of Wild's life was his meeting with Beethoven in 1815, at a festival-concert on the birthday of the Empress of Russia. The last number of the programme was the quartet in ' Fidelio,' ' Mir ist so wunderbar.' Through some curious chance Beethoven himself appeared, and extemporised for the last time in public, before an audience of monarchs and statesmen. Wild had arranged to substitute ' Adelaide ' for an air of Stadler's : Beethoven was delighted, and at once offered to accompany it. ' His pleasure at my performance,' continues Wild, ' was so great that he proposed to instrument the song for orchestra. This never came off, but he wrote for me the cantata [1] " An die Hoffnung " (to Tiedge's words), which I sang to his accompaniment at a very select matinée.' On Apr. 20 of the next year, Wild gave a little musical party at which he sang the same songs ; Beethoven again accompanied him, and this was his farewell as an accompanist, as the other had been his farewell as a player. [2]   c. f. p.

WILDER, Jérôme Albert Victor van (b. Welteren, Belgium, Aug. 21, 1835 ; d. Paris, Sept. 8, 1892), lyric poet and musical critic. While studying for his doctor's degree in law and philosophy at the University of Ghent, he also frequented the Conservatoire. Having written for a time for the Journal de Gand he determined, like his countrymen Vaez and Gevaert, to push his way in Paris. He began by translating songs, and ended with adapting Wagner's works for the French stage. He wrote French words to Handel's ' Messiah ' and adapted for the French stage Mozart's ' Oca di Cairo'; Schubert's 'Häusliche Kreig'; Paisiello's ' Barbiere di Siviglia ' ; Weber's ' Silvana ' ; and Wagner's ' Meistersinger,' ' Tristan und Isolde,' ' Ring der Nibelungen' ('Rheingold,' 'Walküre,' ' Siegfried ' and ' Götterdämmerung '), and ' Parsifal.'

He wrote criticisms and feuilletons in L'Évènement, L'Opinion nationale, Le Parlement, and Le Gil Blas ; was a contributor to the Ménestrel from June 1871–84, and republished Mozart : l'homme et l'artiste (Paris, 1880, 8vo, and 1881, 12mo), and Beethoven : sa vie et son œuvre (Paris, 1883, 12mo). To him also we owe the publication of Mozart's ballet ' Les petits Riens.'   g. c., addns.

WILDER, Philip van (or Philip de Wildroe), a composer of the early 16th century, whose MSS. in England, often assigned to ' Mr. Phillips,' have been much confused with those of Peter Phillips (q.v.).

Van Wilder was appointed lutenist to King Henry VIII. in 1538, and in the inventory of goods (Harl. 1419) taken after the King's death he is described as keeper of the musical instruments at Westminster. In 1550 he appears as gentleman of the Privy Chamber to Edward VI., commissioned to collect children for the Chapel Royal. His identity with the earlier ' Mr. Phillips ' is established by a MS. of Baldwin's at Christ Church, Oxford, in which is a motet, ' Aspice Domine,' by ' Mr. Philips of the King's privi chamber.' The same motet occurs, ascribed to 'Phillips,' with the date 1568, in Sadler's MS. (Bodl. Mus. e. 1-5) and also in B.M. Add. MSS. 31,390. ' A booke of In nomines, and other

solfainge songes of v. vi. vii. and viii. parts for voyces and instruments,' which contains fifteen other pieces by the same composer. It is therefore safe to conclude that these, and the similar lute arrangements in the R.C.M. (Sac. Har. Cat. No. 1964), are all by Philip van Wilder. Music by him was printed in Antwerp and Paris collections of 1544, 1545, 1572 and 1597,[3] but the style of all these is earlier than that of Peter Philips, and there can be but small doubt that nothing by the latter composer dates from much earlier than the Pavana of 1580 in the ' Fitzwilliam Virginal Book,' described by the writer of the MS. as ' the first one Philips made.' It may be mentioned that besides Philip van Wilder a Peter van Wilder was appointed minstrel to Henry VIII. in 1519 ; his name is found among the royal musicians until the reign of Mary. A Robert Philip was also a pupil of Cornysshe in 1514 ; he was a singing-man at St. George's Chapel, Windsor, before 1550, and also a gentleman of Edward VI.'s Chapel Royal, but he is not known to have composed any music.   w. b. s.

WILDERER, Johann Hugo, organist in 1696 of the Elector Palatine, afterwards his Kapellmeister at Düsseldorf, Mannheim and Heidelberg until 1723. He composed a number of operas, also Modulationi sacre a 2, 3 e 4 voci e violini (Q.-L.).

WILHELM, Carl (b. Schmalkalden, Sept. 5, 1815 ; d. there, Aug. 16, 1873), was the composer of ' Die Wacht am Rhein ' to the verse of Max Schneckenburger. He directed the Liedertafel at Crefeld from 1840–65, composed his famous song in 1854, and received an annual pension of £150 for it in 1871.   g.

WILHELMJ, August Daniel Ferdinand Victor (b. Usingen, duchy of Nassau, Sept. 21, 1845 ; d. London, Jan. 22, 1908), famous violinist and teacher (see Violin-playing).

His father, who was a doctor of laws and for some time Attorney-General of Prussia, owned considerable property in vineyards at Hattenheim. Wilhelmj's mother, née Charlotte Petry, was an excellent pianist, a pupil of André, Offenbach and Chopin. Wilhelmj's earliest instruction in violin-playing was given him in 1849, by Konrad Fischer, who was then the Duke of Nassau's Kapellmeister, at Wiesbaden. He developed into an able violinist at an early age, indeed his talent was so precocious that when Henriette Sontag heard him in 1852 she embraced the seven-year-old child warmly, exclaiming : ' You will be the German Paganini.' Her prediction was destined to bear fruit speedily, for on Jan. 8, 1854, Wilhemj made his first public appearance at a charity concert given at Lumbourg-on-the-Lahn, when he created a great impression ; later his playing at the

---

[1] Op. 94, composed in 1816, not to be confounded with an earlier setting of the same poem, op. 32, composed 1805.
[2] Thayer, Beethoven ii. 327, 382 (first ed.); Krehbiel, ii. 305, 338.

[3] See Eitner's Sammelwerke. Van der Straeten conjectures that there may have been two Philip Van Wilders, one in the Netherlands and one in England.

Court Theatre, Wiesbaden, is said to have 'astounded his audience.' Prince Emil von Wittgenstein sent Wilhelmj to Liszt, who was so enchanted with the child's playing of Spohr's 8th concerto and Ernst's 'Airs hongroises,' that he sent him to David at Leipzig with the words : 'Let me present to you the future Paganini ! Look well to him !' This was in 1861. In the following year he played Ernst's 'Concerto pathétique' at a Conservatorium Concert, and on Nov. 24 of the same year he played Joachim's Hungarian concerto at a Gewandhaus concert with conspicuous and admitted success. He remained at the Conservatorium for three years, having Hauptmann and Richter to teach him harmony and composition. Then (in 1864) he went to Frankfort for further study with Raff.

The following year (1865) saw Wilhelmj begin the wandering life of a virtuoso. He first went to Switzerland ; then in 1866 to Holland, and in the summer—through Jenny Lind's influence—came to London, making his début, on Sept. 17, at one of Alfred Mellon's Promenade Concerts at Covent Garden, and receiving a rapturous ovation. He was equally successful in his first appearance at a Monday Popular Concert on Nov. 26 following, and likewise in his début at the Crystal Palace on Dec. 1. In 1867 Wilhelmj was in France and Italy. In Paris—through Joachim's introduction—he was first heard at Pasdeloup's concert, given at the Cirque Napoléon on Jan. 20. Then, in the autumn, he went to Florence, where he made his début on Dec. 15, 1867, at the Società del Quartetto. At the fourth concert of the Society, on Dec. 29, Wilhelmj was elected Protettore della Società. The 27th of Jan. 1868 saw the violinist's first appearance in St. Petersburg, whither, with Hector Berlioz, he had been invited by the Grand Duchess Helena Paulovna. The year 1869 was spent in revisiting France, Switzerland and Belgium ; the following year in touring through England, Scotland and Ireland, with Santley. From the British Isles Wilhelmj went—in 1871—for a tour that extended through Holland, Denmark, Norway and Sweden. During these travels he was elected a member of the Royal Academy of Stockholm : made a knight of the order of Gustavus Vasa, and decorated with the grand medal of Arts and Sciences—also at Stockholm. His first appearance before a Berlin audience was on Oct. 22, 1872, at a Singakademie concert, and on Mar. 22, 1873, he made his first appearance in Vienna.

In 1875 Wilhelmj was in England again. He played at the Philharmonic Society's concert in memory of Sterndale Bennett, and occupied himself during the year in propagating the cult of Wagner in England. In 1876 Wilhelmj led the orchestra at Bayreuth, coming to England again in 1877. In the same year he induced Wagner to journey to London and conduct the famous festival at the Albert Hall. Wilhelmj led the violins, and organised two extra concerts on a less lavish scale on May 28 and 29. After this, Wilhelmj suffered a serious illness. In 1878 he started on a tour round the world, which lasted until 1882, when he passed through London on his way to Germany, home to his villa at Mosbach-Biberich on the Rhine, after which he practically retired from public life for some time.

During his stay at Biberich, Wilhelmj founded a violin school in conjunction with R. Niemann, in the neighbouring Wiesbaden. In 1885 he was travelling again, and it was in this year that—at the invitation of the Sultan of Turkey—he had the unique experience of playing before the ladies of the Seraglio. Probably Wilhelmj was the only violinist to whom such a compliment had, until then, been paid. The Sultan decorated him with the order of the Medjidie of the second class, and also presented him with some fine diamonds. Blasewitz, near Dresden, became Wilhelmj's home from 1886–93, in which year he installed himself in London. In 1894 he was appointed principal violin professor at the G.S.M. He also taught privately, and although he never appeared at London concerts during the latter years of his life, Wilhelmj's massive, dignified figure, with its flowing grey hair, crowned with a wide-brimmed soft felt hat, was familiar to concert-goers as a member of the audience. He died after a short illness at his residence, 54 Priory Road, West Hampstead. He was twice married ; (1) to the Baroness Liphardt—a niece of Ferdinand David—on May 29, 1866 ; (2) to Miss Mariella Mausch-Jerret, a distinguished Dresden pianist, in 1895. His son ADOLF (b. Mar. 31, 1872) was appointed violin professor to the Belfast Conservatoire in 1895.

The qualities that combined to make Wilhelmj one of the greatest violinists of his day may be summed up in the force of his personality, the great certainty of his technique, his rich tone, cultured rendering and splendid poise. He stood for dignity and breadth. He believed that people wanted intellectual renderings, and he aimed at an exact balance of intellect and imagination, conveying a suggestion of reserve force that was essentially majestic.

In his later years he took an active interest in the technique of violin-making, and was a fervent patron and champion of more than one continental maker of the present day. He was convinced that the 'secret of the Cremona makers' lay in varnishing their violins whilst the backs and bellies were fixed only to the top and bottom blocks of the instruments, the final gluing taking place after the varnish was dry. His house in Avenue Road was (in 1894) a museum of modern-made violins, and he was for ever encouraging amateur violin-makers to devote themselves to the art.

He composed several pieces for the violin, and was very successful in arranging Wagner's 'Preislied' and other notable themes for the violin. He also wrote a 'Modern Violin School' with James Brown, which was published by Novello & Co., in six parts.

LIBL.—*Violin Times*, Feb. 1894; *Mus. T.*, June 1901; *To-day*, vol. i. No. 5, Sept. 1883; *Times*. Jan. 25, 1908; LAHEE, *Famous Violinists*; *Cenni storici intorno alla Società del Quartetto in Firenze*.

E. H.-A.

WILHELM VON HIRSAU (*b.* Bavaria; *d.* monastery of St. Aurelius, Hirsau, June 4, 1091), writer of legends to Othlos of Würzburg, *c.* 1032. He was first a monk of St. Emmeran's, Ratisbon, but from 1068–91 abbot of the Benedictine monastery at Hirsau in the Würtemberg part of the Black Forest, which was destroyed by the French. He was a man of great learning, who, apart from many philosophical and astronomical works, wrote the treatise published in Gerbert's *Scriptores* II. under the title *Musica S. Wilhelmi*, etc., in which he deals with the antique and mediæval tonal systems, and points out the errors of his predecessors, including Boëtius, whom even as much as to doubt was considered sacrilege during the whole of the Middle Ages. A second work, *De musica et tonis*, was contained in a 12th-century codex belonging to a Nuremberg antiquarian, von Murr, which has unfortunately been lost, and only a full description by von Murr, published at Nuremberg in 1801 under the title *Notitia duorum codicum*, dedicated to Haydn, is still in existence. From this it is apparent that the Guidonian hand existed long before GUIDO D'AREZZO (*q.v.*) (*Mendel*; Ambros).

WILHELMUS VAN NASSOUWE is the national anthem of Holland. The origin both of the words and the melody has given rise to much discussion.[1] It is still a point of controversy whether Marnix van St. Aldegonde wrote the words of the song, or whether, as Professor Enschedé surmises,[2] the words were originally written in French about 1568, and that Marnix translated them into Dutch in 1572. The melody has at length been conclusively proved to be of French origin, for the oldest version of the song, which appeared in the first edition of the *Geusenliedenboecxken* of 1581, bears the heading 'Naar de wijze van Chartres.' This is the tune of a song of derision, on the siege of Chartres, undertaken by Condé and his Huguenots in 1568, and entitled 'O la folle entreprise du Prince de Condé.'[3]

[1] In vol. v. of the *Tijdschrift der Vereeniging* the subject is discussed at full length by Loman, van Riemsdijk, Land, Enschedé, and van Duyse. Fifteen versions of the song are placed one under the other to show wherein they differ, and their various sources are stated. [2] *Tijdschrift*, etc., vol. vii. (1904).
[3] In an undated 'Recueil de Chansons spirituelles . . . avec autres Chansons des Victoires qu'il a pleu à Dieu de donner à notre très-christien roy, Charles IX . . . par Christofle de Bordeaux, Paris' (*c.* 1570) we find at No. 48, 'autre chanson de la ville du Chartres assiégée par le prince de Condé, sur un chant nouveau' beginning with the words ' O folle entreprise.' And in the collection of 1619 entitled 'La pieuse alouette avec son tire-lire' there is

And soldiers who were employed by Condé and afterwards by William of Orange evidently brought the melody from the North of France to the Netherlands, where it was adopted as a national song. The Wilhelmslied has undergone many changes, but the following version given by F. van Duyse in his *Oude Nederlandsche Lied*, ii. p. 1620, claims to be the best and oldest.[4]

WILHELMUS VAN NASSOUWE (1581)
Naar de wijse van Chartres.

Wil - hel - mus van   Nas - sou - we ben
den   Va - der - lant   ghe - trou - we blijf

ick van   Duy-tschen   bloet   een
ick tot   in - den   doot:

Prin-ce van   O-raen-gien ben ick vrij on-ver - veert, den

Co-ninck van Eis-paen-gien hab ick al-tijt ghe-eert.

The 'Nederlansche Volksliederenboek' gives a version of greater rhythmic complication.[5]

A. H. W.

WILHEM, GUILLAUME LOUIS BOCQUILLON (*b.* Paris, Dec. 18, 1781; *d.* Apr. 26, 1842), a musician known chiefly by his efforts to promote the popular teaching of singing. In early youth he was in the army, but an irresistible passion for music made him take to it as the pursuit of his life. After passing through the Paris Conservatoire he became one of the professors in the Lycée Napoléon, and afterwards had a post in the Collége Henri IV. His original compositions were few —chiefly settings of Béranger's lyrics. It was about the year 1815 that he began to interest himself in the class-teaching of music in schools, and through Béranger's influence was put in charge of the musical part of the work of a society for promoting general education, and

[a] hymn in honour of the Virgin fitted to the same 'folle entreprise' melody. Finally, in 'La Clef des chansonniers, ou recueil des vaudevilles depuis cent ans et plus' (Ballard, Paris, 1717), a song occurs called 'Mon Dieu, la belle entrée,' the air of which is the old reading of the Chartres song. All this proves that the song survived for many years also in France.
[4] Duyse thinks that in the beginning the Wilhelmus melody was a signal or trumpet-blast. With this Enschedé does not concur, although he admits it was essentially an army-song; and he quotes as the purest (though not the most beautiful) version the following German soldier song of 1607:

[5] Much of the above information was supplied by Professor J. W. Enschedé.

afterwards, as his plans broadened out, he was made director-general of music in the municipal schools of Paris. He threw himself into this cause with an enthusiasm which soon produced striking results. Besides the school teaching, he had classes which gave instruction to thousands of pupils, mainly working people ; and out of this presently grew the establishment of the ORPHÉON (q.v.), the vast organisation which has since covered France with singing-societies.

The speciality of Wilhem's system turned on the point of school organisation. The plan of ' Mutual Instruction,' as it was called, was then much in vogue in France as a way of economising teaching power, and the point of the Wilhem System was the application of this idea to the teaching of singing. His principal class-book, the *Manuel musical à l'usage des Colléges, des Institutions, des Écoles, et des Cours de Chant*, is an explanation of the ordinary written language of music, clefs, staves, signatures, time-symbols, etc., interspersed with a number of solfeggio exercises for class practice ; the explanations are of the kind usually found in musical instruction books. His special way of arranging the classes is explained in his *Guide de la méthode* (4th edition, dated 1839).   R. B. L.

WILIS, LES, see GISELLE, OU LES WILIS ; NIGHT DANCERS, THE ; VILLI, LE.

WILKINSON (WYLKYNSON), ROBERT (15th and early 16th cent.), English composer of church music. All that remains to us of his work is in an early 16th-century MS. in the Eton College Library. The index to this MS. shows that it originally contained 97 compositions, and of the 43 which remain, 4 are by Wilkinson. These are 2 ' settings of Salve Regina,' for 9 and 5 v., a 13-part ' Jesus autem transiens,' and an imperfect ' O virgo prudentissima.' The 13-part composition is in canon and is a setting of the Apostles' Creed prefixed by the words, ' Jesus autem transiens.' A part is assigned to each apostle, and their names are placed at the beginning of that part of the Creed which each is traditionally said to have written. A note in Latin gives the key to the Canon. A copy of this is in John BALDWIN'S (q.v.) Commonplace Book. The 9-part ' Salve Regina ' is similarly prefixed by a set of initials, each representing one of the 9 angelic hierarchies. As before, a voice is assigned to each. W. Barclay Squire (*Archæologia*, vol. lxi., from which most of these details are taken) refers to a man of this name who was a demy of Magdalen in 1502 and who took his bachelor's degree, Feb. 12, 1508 ; but there is a note in the Eton MS. (' Robert Wylkynson cu aleppiciet Dè ') which seems to indicate that he was dead before the MS. was written, probably some time during the first few years of the century.   J. MK.

WILKINSON, SARAH [1] (b. circa 1768 ; d. Hammersmith, July 3, 1841), singer and actress, who in 1787 married the violinist, Joseph MOUNTAIN (q.v.). Her parents were circus performers engaged at Sadler's Wells. As a young girl she was handed over to Charles Dibdin who trained her as a singer, and employed her in a little burletta named ' Mount Parnassus ' acted at his Royal Circus, where she made some success. Shortly afterwards, in 1782, she appeared at the Haymarket Theatre, and in 1784 went to Hull where she sought an engagement from Tate Wilkinson, who at first refused her. She obtained a public hearing at the benefit of one of his actors, and he then gave her a part in ' The Maid of the Mill.' She rapidly rose as a vocalist, and in 1786 was engaged at Covent Garden Theatre. Though her reception by the public while at Covent Garden was enthusiastic, yet for some reason the managers kept her considerably in the background, and she left the theatre to go to Dublin. In 1790 she again returned to the Haymarket Theatre, and Vauxhall. At this latter place she was a great acquisition, and her name figures as singer there from 1793–99. She again returned to Covent Garden, but left it in 1798, ultimately singing at the Haymarket and Drury Lane. In 1802, having had a monologue entertainment written for her, she went on tour.   F. K.

WILKINSON, THOMAS (late 16th and early 17th cent.), English composer, chiefly of church music. As most of what remains of his work is in MS. (Durh. ; and B.M. Add. MSS. 30,478-9, which contains the tenor cantoris volume of a set of partbooks made at Durham in 1664) it is possible that he was a singing man there. There is no record of him either as organist or choirmaster. B.M. Add. MSS. 29,366-8, which also contains a good deal of his music, is an early 17th-century MS. in the hand of Alfonso Ferrabosco the elder. Only the cantus, bassus and quintus partbooks of this set remain. The MS. also contains a madrigal, ' O Lovely, loveless sweet,' by him. Another 3-part one, ' Say, Galatea, since our comminge hither,' is in B.M. Add. MSS. 18,936-9 and 34,800. The cantus, altus and tenor parts of three 5-part Pavans by him are in B.M. Add. MSS. 30,826-8.

SERVICES, ETC.

Morning Service (T.D. ; B.). Durh. C. 12, 13. Incomp.
Evening Service (M. ; N.D.). Durh. A. 2, 6. Organ score.
Kyrie. (2) PH. 36/05. Incomp.

ANTHEMS

Behold, O Lord. PH. ; Durh. ; B.M. Add. MSS. 30,478-9.
Deliver me, O God. Durh. ; B.M. Add. MSS. 30,478-9 and 29,366-3.
*Hear my prayer, O God. PH. ; B.M. Add. MSS. 29,372-7 ; Ch. Ch. 56-60. Bass part wanting.
Heare my prayer, O Lord. B.M. Add. MSS. 30,478-9.
Helpe, Lord. PH. ; Durh. ; B.M. Add. MSS. 30,478-9 and 29,366-8.
I am the resurrection (verse anthem with 6-part chorus). Harl. 7340/36b. Score ; B.M. Add. MSS. 293,66-8.
In Thee, O Lord. Tenb. O. B/373.

* Contributed to Thomas Myriell's Collection, ' Tristitiae remedium,' 1616.

[1] The Christian name is given variously in contemporary biographical notices as Sarah, Sophia and Rosoman.

Lord, how are they increased. Durh.; B.M. Add. MSS. 30,478-9 and 29,366-8.
Lord, I am not highminded. PH. Incomp.
O Jerusalem. York.
O.Lord, consider. Durh.; B.M. Add. MSS. 30,478-9 and 29,366-8.
O Lord God of my salvation. PH.; Harl. 7340/44*b*. Score.
O Lord my God. Durh.; B.M. Add. MSS. 30,478-9 and 29,366-8.
Praise the Lord. Durh.; B.M. Add. MSS. 30,478-9 and 29,366-8.
*Preserve me, O Lord. Durh.; B.M. Add. MSS. 30,478-9, 29,372-7, and 29,366-8; Ch. Ch. 56-60. Bass part wanting.
*Put me not to rebuke. Durh.; B.M. Add. MSS. 30,478-9, 29,366-8, 37,402-6, and 29,372-7; Ch. Ch. 56-60. Bass part wanting.
Unto Thee, O Lord. Durh.; B.M. Add. MSS. 30,478-9.
Why art thou so full. York.

* Contributed to Thomas Myriell's Collection, 'Tristitiae remedium,' 1616.   J. M^K.

WILLAERT, ADRIAN (*b.* Flanders, *c.* 1480; *d.* Venice, Dec. 7, 1562), the founder of the Venetian school of musicians. His birthplace has been generally given as Bruges, a statement which, according to Fétis, rests on the authority of Willaert's own pupil Zarlino; but this reference appears to be an error: while on the other hand we have the express assertion of a contemporary, Jacques de Meyere (1531), that he was born at Roulers, or Rosselaere, near Courtrai.[1] Willaert was bred for the law and sent to Paris for the purpose of study; but his energies were soon turned into their natural channel, and he became the pupil[2] either of Jean Mouton or of Josquin des Prés—which, it is not certain—in the theory of music. Three compositions in MS. at Bologna are dated 1518. He returned to Flanders for a while, then went to Venice, Rome and Ferrara. It was during this visit to Rome, when Leo X. was Pope, that Willaert heard a motet of his own (' Verbum dulce et suave ') performed as the work of Josquin. As soon, it is added, as the choir learned its real authorship, they refused to sing it again. Willaert's name evidently had not yet become that power which it was soon to be, under the naturalised form of ' Adriano,' among Italian musicians. From Ferrara he went northward, and became cantor to King Lewis of Bohemia and Hungary; and as on Dec. 12, 1527, he was appointed maestro di cappella of St. Mark's at Venice by the doge Andrea Gritti, it is presumed[3] that he returned to Italy at the King's death in the previous year. In 1542 and 1556 he visited his native country. His career at Venice, where he lived until his death, is associated principally with the foundation of the singing-school which was soon to produce a whole dynasty of musicians of the highest eminence in their day. Among the first of these may be named Willaert's own pupils, Zarlino and Cyprian de Rore; the latter was Willaert's successor at St. Mark's.

Willaert's compositions are very numerous.[4] Those published at Venice include five masses,

1536; three collections of motets, 1539-45 and 1561; two of madrigals, 1546 and 1563; a volume of ' Musica nova,' 1559, containing both motets and madrigals; several books of psalms (1550, 1555) and of hymns (1542), Canzone Villanesche, 1545; Fantasie e Ricercari, 1559. Besides these a variety of his works may be found in different musical collections published during his lifetime at Antwerp, Louvain, Nuremberg, Strassburg and other places. (See *Q.-L.* for lists.) Willaert holds a remarkable position among those Flemish masters whose supremacy in the musical world made the century from 1450 to 1550 distinctively ' the century of the Netherlands.'[5] He did not merely take up the tradition of Josquin des Prés; he extended it in many directions. From the two organs and the two choirs of St. Mark's he was led to invent double choruses; and this form of composition he developed to a perfection which left little even for Palestrina to improve upon. His motets for 4, 5 and 6 voices are of the pure Belgian style, and written with singular clearness in the different parts. In one instance he advanced to the conception of an entire narrative, that of the history of Susannah, set for five voices.[6] It would be absurd to describe such a work as an oratorio, yet the idea of it is not dissimilar. Indeed, in departing to some extent from the severity of his predecessors and creating for himself a richer style of his own, Willaert ventured to be more distinctively declamatory than any one before him. The complexion, therefore, of his writing, though it might appear ' dry ' to Fétis, is markedly more modern than that of his masters. He is also of first-rate importance in the realm of the MADRIGAL (*q.v.*), and his compositions in this field are probably the best remembered of all he wrote. To contemporaries, however, if we may believe Zarlino, his church music appealed most strongly; his psalms, and in particular a Magnificat for three choirs, being peculiarly admired. A fine portrait of the musician is given by E. van der Straeten, *La Musique aux Pays-bas,* i. 258.

                   R. L. P.

WILLAN, HEALEY (*b.* Balham, 1880), organist and composer. After holding posts at St. John Baptist, Kensington, and other churches he went to Toronto, as head of the theory classes at the Conservatoire, and organist and choirmaster of St. Paul's. In 1914 he was appointed lecturer and examiner to the University of Toronto, and in 1919 became music director to the Hart House Players Club, in connexion with which he wrote incidental music for performances of classical plays. Since 1920 he has been Vice-Principal of Toronto Conservatoire. He has written much admirable church and organ music, among the latter being

---

1 See the opposite views in Fétis, viii. 470 (2nd ed., 1867), and E. van der Straeten, *La Musique aux Pays-bas*, i. 249-57. Sweertius, *Athenae Belgicae*, p. 104 (Antwerp, 1628, folio), also describes Willaert as of Bruges. Very possibly the discrepancy is to be explained by supposing Bruges to have been the seat of Willaert's family, and Roulers that of his actual birth.
2 See A. W. Ambros, *Geschichte der Musik*, iii. 502.
3 Fétis, viii. 471.
4 See the lists in Fétis *l.c.*, and, for those published in the Netherlands, Goovaerts's *Historie et bibliographie de la typographie musicale dans les Pays-bas*, under the different years.

5 Ambros, i. 3. See this writer's excellent criticism of Willaert vol. iii. 503-9.   6 Compare Fétis, viii. 471.

two fine preludes and fugues in C minor and B minor, an effective epilogue, and a broadly conceived introduction, passacaglia and fugue.   H. G.

WILLEMS, the surname of a family of Ghent violin-makers, consisting of Jooris, Hendrick—presumably his brother—and the latter's son, or nephew, Heyndrick. (1) JOORIS (worked 1634–42) was a cornett-player as well as a luthier, in which latter capacity he turned out very careful work. His model resembles that of the Amati School, but with stouter and more projecting edges. The varnish is brittle and pale in colour. A bass viol by Jooris is preserved in the Snoeck Collection, Berlin. His son (2) NICHOLAS was a viol-player in the Ghent Cathedral. (3) HENDRICK (1651–98) was the best maker of the trio. He followed the Stainer model, adhering to the high arch, sharp-edge and stiff sound-holes of the Brescian School. The work of this maker is excessively neat, and the wood of the table always well chosen, but the varnish is ordinary and roughly laid on. For the backs of his fiddles he employed maple wood, beech, lime and almond. Some of Hendrick Willems's work is preserved in the cathedral at Ghent, and in the Snoeck Collection in Berlin there is a Pochette of his dated 1679. He also made lutes. (4) HEYNDRICK (1717–1743), nephew or son of Hendrick (3), made fiddles and violoncellos on the Amati model. A certain J. B. Willems, who came to the fore as a maker of brass instruments in 1760, seems to have been a fiddle-maker also. The relationship is undefined.

BIBL.—VON LUTGENDORFF, *Die Geigen und Lautenmacher.*
E. H.-A.

WILLEMS, MISS, see ADDISON, John.

WILLIAM OF NEWARK (*d.* London (?), 1509), English composer, ' Master of the Song ' (master of the children, Chapel Royal), William Cornysh being his successor. He is represented in the Fayrfax (Thoresby) MS. in the British Museum by 7 songs. A madrigal, ' Thus musing,' was republished by Novello in 1894 (Davey; Brown and Stratton).

WILLIAMS, AARON (*b.* London (?), 1731; *d.* there, 1776), music teacher and engraver, and clerk to the Scottish church in London Wall. He wrote ' A New Christmas Anthem for 1, 2, 3 and 4 voices,' and edited several collections of psalms, anthems and other church music. (See list in Brown and Stratton.)

WILLIAMS, ANNA (*b.* London, Aug. 6, 1845; *d.* there, Sept. 3, 1924), a distinguished concert-singer, was the daughter of William Smith Williams, reader to Smith, Elder & Co., to whose insight the publication of *Jane Eyre* was due. She was taught singing by H. C. Deacon and J. B. Welch, and on June 27, 1872, took the first soprano prize at the National Prize Meeting Festival at the Crystal Palace. She afterwards studied for fifteen months at

Naples with Domenico Scafati, and on Jan. 17, 1874, reappeared at the Crystal Palace. She obtained a very high position as an oratorio- and concert-singer at the principal festivals and Musical Societies of the United Kingdom. Special mention must be made of her singing at three successive Birmingham Festivals in three new oratorios : in 1885 in Stanford's ' Three Holy Children ' ; in 1888 in Parry's ' Judith ' ; and in 1891, at very short notice, in Stanford's ' Eden.' On the last occasion she received from the committee a handsome present in acknowledgment of her readiness in taking extra work on account of the illness of Mme. Albani (*Brit. Mus. Biog.*). She sang occasionally in opera in the provinces, but it is as a refined and accomplished concert-singer that she was best known. Her powerful soprano voice was of $2\frac{1}{2}$ octaves in compass, and she used it like a true musician. On Oct. 13, 1897, while still in the plenitude of her powers, she made a farewell appearance, and devoted herself to teaching at the R.C.M. and elsewhere until 1904, when she resigned her appointment. She married Rodney John Fenessy in 1910.   A. C.

WILLIAMS, CHARLES FRANCIS ABDY (*b.* Dawlish, S. Devon, July 16, 1855; *d.* Milford, Lymington, Feb. 27, 1923), was educated at Sherborne School, and subsequently under the Rev. F. A. Radcliffe, Rector of Milston, near Amesbury, whose influence contributed, in no small degree, to foster his love of music. In 1875 he entered Trinity Hall, Cambridge, where he took the degrees of B.A. in 1878, M.A. in 1882 and Mus.B. in 1891. He also took the Oxford Mus.B. degree in 1889. While at Cambridge he took an active part in the management of the Cambridge University Musical Society, and played the violin and viola at its concerts. On taking his degree he went for health to New Zealand, where he was organist for some years at a church in Auckland, playing in the orchestra of the Auckland Choral Society, and founding a Glee Club. Returning to England in 1879 he resumed his studies for the Church ; but family opposition to the musical profession being overcome, he became organist and music-master at Dover College in 1881. In the following year he entered the Leipzig Conservatorium, and in 1885–91 was organist of St. Mary's, Boltons, S.W., where he did much to improve the standard of the music. He next devoted himself to the study of ancient Greek music, and especially plain-song, making tours for purposes of research in Italy, Belgium and France.

Articles and lectures by him on this subject led to his appointment, in 1895, as composer and director of the music of the Greek Theatre at Bradfield College, of which institution he afterwards became the organist. For the Greek plays he made use of ancient modes and rhythmical forms, besides reproducing, from ancient models, auloi and lyres, on which he taught the boys to play. In 1901, in consequence of ill-health, he retired, wrote many valuable books and did much to promote the revival of plain-song. He trained the body of priests of Capri in the Solesmes system in 1904, and directed the music of their Easter Mass; this led to the establishment of that system in the island, a work for which in 1907 he was received in private audience and thanked by the Pope.

His published compositions are few in number; they include a Magnificat and Nunc Dimittis in F, a Morning, Evening and Communion Service for alto, tenor and bass, the Choruses of the 'Antigone' of Sophocles in the Greek modes, as performed at Bradfield. Unpublished works are, a quartet in D minor, a violoncello sonata in F, and four canons for clarinet, violin and pianoforte, all performed at the Musical Artists' Society in 1887–88; the choruses of 'Alcestis' and 'Agamemnon' composed for Bradfield. His literary works are as follows: *A Historical Account of Musical Degrees at Oxford and Cambridge*, 1893; *The Music of the Greek Drama*, essay prefixed to the 'Antigone' choruses; Lives of *Bach* and *Handel*, in the Master Musicians series; *Notation, the Organ,* and *Organ Music*, in the Music Story series; *The Rhythm of Modern Music* (1909); Aristoxenas's *Theory of Musical Rhythm* (1913); contributions to the second edition of this Dictionary, to the *Classical Review* and to various musical periodicals, on Greek music, plain-song, etc., and kindred subjects.   M.

WILLIAMS, CHARLES LEE (b. Winchester, May 1, 1853), organist and composer of church music, was fifth son of the late Rev. David Williams, fellow of New College, Oxford, and rector of Alton Barnes, Wilts.

He was a chorister of New College in 1862–65, and a pupil and assistant organist to Dr. Arnold at Winchester Cathedral in 1865–70. In 1872 he went to Ireland as tutor and organist of St. Columba's College, where he stayed till 1875. He took the Mus.B. degree at Oxford in 1876. In 1876–82 he was organist and choirmaster of Llandaff Cathedral, and in the latter year entered upon his chief official position, that of organist of Gloucester Cathedral—a position he occupied with much distinction until 1898, conducting, in that time, five Gloucester Festivals, and taking part in the other THREE CHOIRS FESTIVALS (q.v.). He composed a considerable amount of church music, and the sacred cantatas 'Bethany,' 'Gethsemane,' 'A Dedication,' 'A Harvest Song,' and 'A Festival Hymn,' all of which have been produced at Gloucester or Worcester Festivals. Owing to ill-health he retired from active work in 1898, but retained his interest in the Three Choirs Festivals as a steward, a member of committee, and ultimately as Chairman of the Executive at Gloucester.

He also edited (with H. G. Chance, M.A.) the continuation of the *History of the Three Choirs*, bringing the record up to the year 1922.
                     M., addns.

WILLIAMS, GEORGE EBENEZER (b. 1783; d. Apr. 17, 1819), was a chorister of St. Paul's Cathedral under Richard Bellamy. On quitting the choir (about 1799) he became deputy organist for Dr. Arnold at Westminster Abbey. In 1805 he was appointed organist of the Philanthropic Society's chapel, and in 1814 succeeded Robert Cooke as organist of Westminster Abbey. He composed, when a boy, some chants and settings of the Sanctus, printed in 'Sixty Chants . . . composed by the Choristers of St. Paul's Cathedral,' 1795, and was author of 'An Introduction to the Pianoforte,' 1810, and 'Exercises for the Pianoforte,' 1815. He was buried, Apr. 24, 1819, in the south cloister of Westminster Abbey.   W. H. H.

WILLIAMS, JOHN GERARD (b. London, Dec. 10, 1888), composer, originally followed the profession of an architect, but devoted his spare time to music, joining choral societies and playing in orchestras as opportunities arose. When he first took to composition in 1911 he had had no other training than this, and that which he acquired from constantly reading music, but two years later he received some guidance from R. H. Walthew. In all essentials, however, he is a self-taught musician. Most of his music is in the smaller forms and of an intimate character, with something of the art of the miniaturist. Much of his best work is in his numerous songs, which have great lyrical charm. He has also written two string quartets, of which the second is published, and has orchestrated a set of his own piano pieces, ' Pot Pourri.' His other piano works comprise 'Miniatures' (also orchestrated), Preludes, 'Side-shows,' etc. A comic operetta, 'The Story of the Willow Pattern Plate,' is for children. Since then he has written a ballad-opera, 'Kate, the Cabin Boy' (Kingsway Theatre, London, 1924), based on traditional tunes, and he has arranged and orchestrated a ballet from a Beethoven sonata for Mme. Lopokova. In 1922 he gave a first recital of his own works at the Æolian Hall, London.   E. E.

WILLIAMS, MARIA JANE (b. Glamorganshire, Oct. 9, 1793; d. Nov. 10, 1873), a soprano singer of merit, who resided mostly in Glamorganshire. Her chief title to remembrance is her collection of traditional Welsh airs, which was offered in competition at an Eisteddfod held in Abergavenny in 1838. She published forty-three of the melodies, with Welsh words, in 1844, Llandovery (and D'Almaine's, London), but only a few copies seem to have been printed. The title runs:

'Ancient National Airs of Gwent, and Morganwg : being a collection of original Welsh Melodies, hitherto unpublished . . by M. Jane Williams,' 1844, folio.

See WELSH MUSIC.   F. K.

WILLIAMS, RALPH VAUGHAN, see VAUGHAN WILLIAMS.

WILLIAMS, THOMAS. In 1780 he published 'Harmonia coelestis,' a collection of anthems by Purcell, Blow, Croft, etc. (London); in 1789 he published 'Psalmodia Evangelica,' a collection of psalm and hymn tunes in 3 parts, preceded by a complete introduction and historical essay on Church Music, instructions in miniature for learning psalmody, etc.

E. v. d. s.

WILLIAMSON, T. G., a composer and music-publisher, at the end of the 18th century. About 1790 he had a music and 'fancy warehouse' at 20 Strand, from which he issued a number of sheet songs, and collections of music. He arranged two sets of 'Hindoostanee Airs,' 1797 and 1798, composed some vocal music, 'Six favourite sonatinas,' a set of marches and other music.

F. K.

WILLIAM TELL, see GUILLAUME TELL.

WILLING, CHRISTOPHER EDWIN (b. Feb. 28, 1830; d. Dec. 1, 1904), son of Christopher Willing, alto singer and assistant gentleman of the Chapel Royal (b. 1804; d. May 12, 1840), was admitted a chorister of Westminster Abbey under James Turle in 1839, and continued such until 1845, during which time he also sang in the chorus at the Concert of Ancient Music, the Sacred Harmonic Society, etc. Upon leaving the choir he was appointed organist of Blackheath Park Church, and assistant organist of Westminster Abbey. In 1847 he was engaged as organist at Her Majesty's Theatre, and held the post until the close of Lumley's management in 1858. In 1848 he was appointed organist to the Foundling Hospital, and shortly afterwards also director of the music. In 1857 he was invited to take the place of organist of St. Paul's, Covent Garden, which he held in conjunction with his appointment at the Foundling, but resigned it in 1860 to accept the post of organist and director of the music at All Saints', Margaret Street, which he held until 1868. In 1872 he was appointed organist, and afterwards also chorus-master, to the Sacred Harmonic Society. In the same year he was re-engaged as organist in the company of Her Majesty's Theatre (then performing at Drury Lane), and in 1868 was made in addition *maestro al piano*. In 1879 he resigned his appointment at the Foundling Hospital. For many years he was conductor of the St. Albans Choral Union, which held a triennial festival in St. Albans Abbey—now Cathedral.

W. H. H.

WILLIS, HENRY (b. Apr. 27, 1821; d. London, Feb. 11, 1901), a leading English organ-builder, was articled in 1835 to John GRAY. He was for some years organist of Christ Church, Hoxton, subsequently of Hampstead Parish Church, and Islington Chapel-of-Ease, which latter post he filled down to within a few years of his death.

In 1847, in which year he played the double-bass at the Gloucester Festival, he took the first step in his career by rebuilding the organ at Gloucester Cathedral, with the then unusual compass of twenty-nine notes in the pedals. In the Great Exhibition of 1851 he exhibited a large organ which was much noticed, and which led to his being selected to build that for St. George's Hall, Liverpool, which under the hands of Best became so widely known. The organ which he exhibited in the Exhibition of 1862 also procured him much fame, and became the nucleus of that at the Alexandra Palace, destroyed by fire on June 9, 1873, shortly after its completion. His next feat was the organ for the Royal Albert Hall (opened 1871), which in size, and for the efficiency of its pneumatic, mechanical and acoustic qualities, shared its high reputation with the second Alexandra Palace organ, which was constructed for the restoration of that building, and was opened in May 1875.

Willis supplied or renewed organs to nearly half the cathedrals of England and Scotland, viz. St. Paul's (1872), Canterbury (1886), Carlisle (1856), Durham (1877), Hereford (1879), Oxford (1884), Salisbury (1877), Wells (1857), Winchester (1853), Truro, St. David's (1881), Edinburgh (1879), Glasgow (1879), as well as many colleges, churches, halls, etc. He built the organ in Windsor Castle, with a double console, so that the instrument can be played from St. George's Hall or from the Private Chapel. The award of the Council Medal in 1851 specifies his application of an improved exhausting valve to the pneumatic lever, the application of pneumatic levers in a compound form, and the invention of a movement for facilitating the drawing of stops singly or in combination. In 1862 the Prize Medal was awarded to him for further improvements. In 1885 the Gold Medal was given him for 'excellence of tone, ingenuity of design and perfection of execution.' He took out seven patents between 1851 and 1868.

Willis was always a scientific organ-builder, and his organs are distinguished for their excellent engineering, clever contrivances and first-rate workmanship, as much as for their brilliance, force of tone and orchestral character. (See ORGAN, subsection 1851, EXHIBITION ORGANS, *et seq*.) (See *Mus. T.*, 1898, p. 297 ff. and 1901, p. 164.)

G.

The present (1926) head of the firm of Henry Willis and Sons is HENRY WILLIS (b. 1889), third of the name and grandson of the founder. His *chef d'œuvre* is the Liverpool Cathedral organ (168 speaking stops), and under him the firm maintains its high reputation. The firm publishes accounts of its achievements in a house periodical called *The Rotunda*.

C.

WILLIS, ISAAC, a Dublin music-publisher who, about 1815 or 1816, took over the premises, 7 Westmorland Street, formerly held by Goulding & Knevett, to whom he acted as agent. His business became extensive, and he removed to London about 1825, the firm being then 'Willis & Co.,' and their shop in a room, or rooms of the Egyptian Hall, Piccadilly. In 1827 they removed to 55 St. James Street, and at a later date to 75 Lower Grosvenor Street, and finally, before 1850, to 119 New Bond Street. The Dublin business was retained until 1835–36, when it passed to Robinson, Bussell, & Robinson. The music they issued was principally of the 'drawing-room' type, and dance music. Their principal collections are Fitzsimon's 'Irish Minstrelsy,' bk. 2, 1816 ; T. H. Bayly's 'Miniature Lyrics,' 3 books, 1823–25 ; 'Tyrolese Melodies,' 1827. Isaac Willis may have had some interest in 'Willis's Rooms,' in St. James Street, though in 1850 the proprietors were Frederick and Charles Willis.　　F. K.

WILLMAN, Thomas Lindsay (b. London, c. 1783 ; d. Nov. 28, 1840), a famous clarinettist, was the son of a German who, in the latter half of the 18th century, came to England and became master of a military band. Father and son were in Ireland, 1804–18. After being a member of a military band and of various orchestras the latter became principal clarinettist in the Opera and other chief orchestras of London, and also master of the Coldstream Guards' kand. His tone and execution were remarkably beautiful, and his concerto-playing admirable. His age was recorded in the register of deaths as 56, but, by comparison with his own statement made more than eight years before, when he joined the Royal Society of Musicians, it should have been 57.　　W. H. H.

WILLMERS, Heinrich Rudolf (b. Berlin, Oct. 31, 1821 ; d. Vienna, Aug. 24, 1878), pianist, a pupil of Hummel and Fr. Schneider, was widely known both as a brilliant player and composer for the PF., and was teacher at Stern's school in Berlin from 1864–66. He then resided in Vienna, where he died insane.　　G.

WILLY, John Thomas (b. London, July 24, 1812 ; d. there, Aug. 8, 1885), violin-player. He was for some time a pupil of Spagnoletti, and became a member of the King's Theatre band. He played under Costa as a first violin, and later as principal second, during the whole of his career. He led the 'Elijah' at Birmingham in 1846, and was leader at various other festivals ; at Jullien's and the London Wednesday Concerts, the new Philharmonic, the National Choral, the Society of British Musicians (of which he became a member in 1837), etc. etc. In 1849–50, and again in 1860, he gave classical chamber concerts at St. Martin's Hall, very much on the plan of the subsequent 'Popular Concerts.' Among the artists who appeared were Mesdames Goddard,

Louisa Pyne and Dolby ; Sims Reeves, Sterndale Bennett, Ernst, Piatti, Pauer, etc. He retired from active work in 1880, owing to failing health.　　A. C.

WILM, Nicolaj von (b. Riga, Mar. 4, 1834 ; d. Wiesbaden, Feb. 20, 1911), studied at the Leipzig Conservatorium in 1851–56, became in 1857 second conductor at the Stadttheater of Riga, and in 1860 teacher of pianoforte and theory in the Nikolai Institute at St. Petersburg. In 1875 he settled in Dresden, and in 1878 at Wiesbaden. His works are numerous, and some are important ; a string sextet, op. 27 ; a quartet, op. 4 ; two violin sonatas, opp. 83 and 92 ; a violoncello sonata, op. 111 ; two suites for violin and piano, opp. 88, 95, are among the best of his compositions, which include very many pianoforte pieces of a popular kind, and partsongs and motets for chorus, as well as single songs. (Riemann.)　　M.

WILMS, Johann Wilhelm (b. Witzhelden, near Solingen, Mar. 30, 1772 ; d. Amsterdam, July 19, 1847), studied with his father and brother, settled in Amsterdam as piano virtuoso and teacher in Aug. 1791, and continued his studies of composition under Hodermann. In 1808 he became a member of the institute of arts and science, and in 1824 organist of the Baptist church. As a composer his claim to posterity rests chiefly on the National Anthem, 'Wien Neerlands bloed,' but he also composed a symphony, a flute concerto, quartets, trios, sonatas, variations, etc. (Mendel ; Q.-L.).

WILSON, John (b. Apr. 5, 1595 [1] ; d. Westminster, Feb. 22, 1673/4). Anthony Wood calls him a native of Faversham, but the Faversham registers do not go back to so early a date, and nothing is to be learnt there about his family ; it would seem, however, that he was 'kinsman' to Walter Porter, the musician.[2] Wood's statement that he was 'naturally inclin'd in his youth to vocal and instrumental Musick' is corroborated by the fact that, before he was 20, he was employed to write music for

[1] 'The Maske of Flowers. Presented By the Gentlemen of Graies-Inne, at the Court of White-hall, in the Banquetting House, vpon Twelfe night, 1613 (i.e. 1614). Being the last of the Solemnities and Magnificences which were performed at the marriage of the right honourable the Earle of Somerset, and the Lady Francis daughter of the Earle of Suffolke, Lord Chamberlaine. London Printed by N. O. for Robert Wilson, and are to be sold at the Shop at Graies-Inne new gate. 1614.'

The music to some of the songs is given with the description of the Masque ; it has no composer's name, and it is often attributed to Coprario, but that it is by Wilson is proved by his having printed it as his, in a three-part arrangement, in his 'Cheerfull Ayres,' 1660. Possibly this is not the only stage-music written by Wilson in his youth ; for he printed several songs from plays among his later publications, including settings of Shakespeare's 'Take, O take those lips away,' and 'Lawn as white as driven snow.' Rimbault[3] indeed main-

[1] According to his tombstone.　[2] Wood, Fasti, anno 1608.　[3] Rimbault, Who was Jacke Wilson ? 1846.

tained (what is very likely to be the fact) that Wilson was the stage singer who took the part of Balthazar, the character who sings ' Sigh no more, ladies,' in some performance of *Much Ado about Nothing.* In the first folio edition of Shakespeare's Plays, 1623, the stage direction has ' Enter the Prince, Leonato, Claudio and Jacke Wilson.' This Jacke Wilson was most likely the same ' Mr. Willson yᵉ singer,' who was among the friends of Alleyn the actor,[1] and dined with him on his wedding anniversary, Oct. 22, 1620 [2]; and the same John Willson who was recommended to the Lord Mayor and Court of Aldermen by Henry Montague, Viscount Mandeville, as one of the ' Servants of the City for Music and voice,' Oct. 21, 1622.[3] The ' John Wilson Musitian' of the parish of St. Bartholomew the Less,' whose wife Jone was buried at St. Giles's, Cripplegate, July 17, 1624, and whose son was buried there the following Sept. 3, ' from the house of George Sommerset, musitian,' was probably the same, though J. Payne Collier [4] took him to be identical with an infant born 1585, son of one Nicholas Wilson, minstrel, of St. Giles's, Cripplegate. Except that the combination of names is a very common one, there seems to be no reason for doubting the identity of these Wilsons with the subject of this notice.

In 1635 John Wilson was made one of the King's Musicians. The Warrant for his Liveries is dated May 30, 1635, and a patent of £20 per annum ' to continue during life' bears the same date. His name recurs among the Musicians up to 1641, when he is fourteenth on the list of Musicians ' For Lutes, Violls and Voices,'[5] and on the list of His Majesty's Servants of the Chamber in Ordinary, 1641, printed in *The Musician,* May 12, 1897.

Wilson seems to have been a favourite with Charles I., and

' giving his Majesty constant attendance, had oftentimes just opportunities to exercise his hand on the Lute (being the best at it in all England) before him to his great delight and wonder; who, while he played, did usually lean or lay his hand on his shoulder.'

Other evidence of the King's appreciation of his singing is found in the verses prefixed to the ' Cheerfull Ayres.' During the Civil War Wilson went with the court to Oxford, where on Nov. 29, 1644, he signed receipts on behalf of the musicians. On the following Mar. 10 he was made Doctor of Music by the University, being ' now the most noted Musitian of England.' After the surrender of the garrison at Oxford in 1646, ' he spent some years in the family of

[1] It is possible that he may have been intimate with Ben Jonson, who on a presentation copy of his collected *Workes,* 1616 (sold by Messrs. Sotheby, Dec. 18, 1908), wrote the inscription, ' To his most worthy and learned friend, Mr. John Wilson, Ben Jonson's Guift and testimony of his love.'
[2] Diary in Young's *Hist. of Dulwich Coll.,* 1889.
[3] *Remembrancia,* p. 303.
[4] *Principal Actors in the Plays of Shakespeare,* 1846.
[5] Rev. H. C. de Lafontaine, *The King's Musick,* pp. 91, 101, etc. In the first edition of this Dictionary his name is said to be found in a list dated Apr. 17, 1641, of ' Musicians for the Waytes ' (*sic*), but it may be conjectured that the same appointment is meant.

Sir Will. Walter of Sarsden in the Parish of Churchill in Oxfordshire, who with his Lady, were great lovers of Musick.' While living there he contributed 'An Elegie to the memory of his Friend and Fellow, Mr. William Lawes,' to H. Lawes's ' Choice Psalmes,' 1648. It is probable that he devoted his time to composition during this period of retirement, for most of his published music appeared between 1648 and 1660. ' At length,' says Wood,

' upon the desire of Mr. Tho. Barlow of Qu. Coll. (then Lecturer at Churchill) made to his quondam Pupil Dr. Joh. Owen, Vicechancellour of this University, he was constituted Musick Professor thereof, an. 1656; which with other helps from some Royalists in these parts (he having then a Lodging in Ball. Coll.) found a comfortable subsistance.'

Wood mentions him among those who attended the weekly music meetings at Oxford in 1656 (' he sometimes play'd on the lute, but mostly presided the consort'); and describes the ' humoursome way ' in which he showed his admiration of Baltzar's violin-playing in 1658. Wilson held the professorship until 1661. In 1657 he published:

' Psalterium Carolinum. The Devotions of his Sacred Majestie in his Solitudes and Sufferings, Rendered in Verse. Set to Musick for 3 Voices and an Organ, or Theorbo, By John Wilson, Dr. and Musick Professor of Oxford. London, Printed for John Martin and James Allestrey, and are to be sold at the Bell in St. Paul's Church-yard, 1657.'

He speaks of this work as ' the last of his labours,' and Lawes in a commendatory poem urges him to call back his ' resolution of not composing more.' It may be, therefore, that his next publication was merely a collection of his early songs revised and rearranged. This was

' Cheerfull Ayres or Ballads First composed for one single Voice and since set for three Voices by John Wilson Dr in Musick Professor of the same in the University of Oxford. Oxford. Printed by W. Hall, for Ric Davis. Anno Dom. ᴍᴅᴄʟx.'

This is described as ' The first Essay (for ought we understand) of printing Musick that ever was in Oxford.'

At the Restoration Wilson returned to his place of Musician in Ordinary [6]; and on Oct. 22, 1662, was sworn as gentleman of the Chapel Royal in succession to Henry Lawes. Wood implies that he had been gentleman of the Chapel Royal at the beginning of his career, but there is no record of any such earlier appointment. Wood also says he was made ' one of the Choire at Westminster.' It was at Westminster Abbey that (on Jan. 31, 1670/71) he married Anne Penniall, widow of Matthew Penniall, who had been a gentleman of the Chapel Royal. In the marriage licence Wilson is described as ' of St. Margaret, Westminster, widower, about 66.' [7] He died at his house at the Horseferry, Westminster, and was buried on Feb. 27, 1673 /74, in the Little Cloister, Westminster Abbey. By his will, dated Apr. 30, 1671, and proved Mar. 18, 1673/74, he left all his property to his widow, with the exception of a bequest of 40s. to his daughter Rebecca Bowreman, ' to by her a Ring.'

[6] See *The King's Musick* for many references to him.
[7] Foster's *London Marriage Licenses,* 1887.

Besides the publications already mentioned, songs and snatches by Wilson appeared in his lifetime in Playford's 'Select Musicall Ayres and Dialogues,' 1652 and 1653, 'Select Ayres and Dialogues,' 1659, and 'The Treasury of Musick,' 1669; in Hilton's 'Catch that catch can,' 2nd edition, corrected and enlarged by J. Playford, 1658; and in Playford's 'Catch that catch can: or the Musical Companion,' 1667. The words of an anthem, 'Hearken, O God,' are in both editions of Clifford's *Services and Anthems*, 1663 and 1664. Much MS. music by Wilson exists in the British Museum and elsewhere; in particular there is a large volume in the Bodleian Library (MS. Mus. b, 1), to which it was presented by the composer before the Restoration, on condition 'that no person should peruse it, till after his death.'

Wilson, according to Wood, 'was a great Humourist and a pretender to Buffoonry'; and Sir N. L'Estrange's MS. *Merry Passages and Jeasts* (B.M. Harl. 6395) gives an anecdote of how 'Willson,' who may be supposed to be John Wilson, provoked a drunken quarrel, in the company of the brothers Lawes. But Henry Lawes, who evidently was intimate with him, presents him in a pleasanter light:

'From long acquaintance and experience, I
Could tell the world thy known integritv
Unto thy friend; thy true and honest heart,
Ev'n mind, good nature, all but thy great art,
Which I but dully understand.'

Wilson's great reputation among his contemporaries was doubtless due chiefly to his skill as lutenist and singer, though Wood calls him 'the greatest and most curious Judge of Musick that ever was,' and Lawes praises him as a pioneer, in words which seem more appropriate to Lawes himself than to Wilson:

'For this I know, and must say't to thy praise,
That thou hast gone in Musick, unknown wayes,
Hast cut a path where there was none before,
Like Magellan traced an unknown shore.
Thou taught'st our Language, first, to speak in Tune,
Gav'st the right accents and proportion.'

His songs are pleasant and melodious, and one or two of them (such as 'In the merry month of May') are still met with in anthologies, but it is probably as an early composer of music to Shakespeare's words that he is now best known. His portrait is in the Bodl. Mus. Sch.

G. E. P. A.

WILSON, JOHN (*b.* Edinburgh, Dec. 25, 1800[1]; *d.* Quebec, July 8, 1849), singer, famous for his Scottish 'table entertainments.' He was apprenticed to a printer, and afterwards became corrector of the press to Ballantyne & Co., in which capacity many of the Waverley novels passed through his hands. In 1816 he applied himself to the study of music. After officiating as precentor in a church, he became in 1824 a pupil of Finlay Dun, and soon after-

wards appeared at the Edinburgh concerts. In 1827 he began teaching singing. He studied under Crivelli, and in Mar. 1830 appeared at the Edinburgh theatre as Henry Bertram in 'Guy Mannering.' His success was so decided that he was straightway engaged for Covent Garden, where he came out Oct. 16, 1830, as Don Carlos in 'The Duenna.' He continued at that theatre until 1835, when he removed to Drury Lane, where he sang in Balfe's 'Siege of Rochelle' and other operas.

In 1838, in company with Miss Shirreff and Mr. and Mrs. E. Seguin, he visited America, where he was warmly welcomed. On his return to England he began giving those Scottish table entertainments with which his name subsequently became identified, and to which from May 1841 he exclusively devoted himself. He gave them throughout England and Scotland with the greatest success. Their titles were:

'A Nicht wi' Burns,' 'Anither Nicht wi' Burns,' 'Adventures of Prince Charlie,' 'Wandering Willie's Wallet,' 'Mary Queen of Scots,' 'Jacobite Relics,' 'The Jameses of Scotland,' 'The Wallace and the Bruce,' and 'A Haver wi' Jamie Hogg.'

Early in 1849 he revisited America. At Quebec he was attacked by cholera and died there. Wilson's voice was a pure, sweet-toned tenor, and he sang with great taste. W. H. H.

WILSON, MARY ANN (*b.* 1802; *d.* Goudhurst, Kent, Dec. 13, 1867), was taught singing by Thomas WELSH. Her first appearance in public at Drury Lane Theatre, Jan. 18, 1821, as Mandane in 'Artaxerxes,' caused an immediate furore, as much for her youth and looks as for her fresh voice and brilliant singing. She remained there until July 5, 'about 65 nights,' according to Geneste, 'wonderfully attractive.'[2] Her other parts were Rosetta ('Love in a Village'), Clara ('Duenna'), and Lady Gayland ('False Alarms'), etc. After an equally successful provincial tour she went the next year to Italy. The premature strain of her early exertions, however, soon ruined her health, and then destroyed her voice. But her short career was very lucrative, and in the year of her début she made the unprecedented sum of £10,000.[3] On June 9, 1827, she married Welsh, and by him had an only daughter, who married PIATTI (*q.v.*). A. C.

WILSON, (1) MATILDA ELLEN (known as Hilda Wilson) (*b.* Monmouth, Apr. 7, 1860; *d.* Dec. 1, 1918), the daughter of James Wilson, a musician and bandmaster of the local Volunteer Corps. She studied music at an early age, and her parents having removed to Gloucester, she sang in the choir of St. Mildred's there. In 1874–75 she appeared as a soloist with the Gloucester Choral Society. Later she studied singing under Shakespeare at the R.A.M., and the pianoforte under Morton.

---

[1] The date of birth has been established by James Love, who has found an entry in the Canongate Records of Edinburgh, to the effect that the singer was the son of John Wilson, a coach-driver, and was born Dec. 25, 1800, and baptized Jan. 4, 1801.

[2] According to the same authority, a 'novel mode of puffing was instituted by Elliston, by printing press notices on playbills in red ink'—called by the wags of the day—' Elliston's blushes.'

[3] Her own statement to Ella, quoted by Pougin in his Supplement to Fétis.

From 1880–82 she was the Westmorland Scholar there, and in 1882 was the holder of the Parepa-Rosa Prize. In 1880 she sang at the Gloucester Festival with such success that she was engaged the two following years for Worcester and Hereford. Later she sang as principal contralto at the Norwich and Birmingham Festivals in addition to those above named, with engagements at the Sacred Harmonic, Royal Choral Society, Crystal Palace, Philharmonic, and at various concerts throughout the United Kingdom. She became a great favourite, on account of her fine voice, the perfection of her style and phrasing, and of her musicianly feeling. On July 16, 1904, she married Ashley Richard Hart of Clifton.

Her sister (2) AGNES (b. Gloucester, Oct. 8, 1864 ; d. Apr. 27, 1907) studied singing under Visetti. She sang in the Lincoln, Hovingham and Hereford Festivals, and later became a teacher at the Blackheath and West London Conservatoires of Music. Her brother, (3) HENRY LANE WILSON (b. 1871 ; d. Jan. 8, 1915), won success as a baritone singer, composer and arranger of songs. He was originally an organist and pianist.   A. C.

WILSON, T[HOMAS] (17th cent.), English organist and composer of church music. A singing man of this name at Ripon Minster was appointed to play on the organ there from 1670–77 in place of the regular organist, Wanless, who had become deaf (West, *Cath. Org.*). *Q.-L.* refers to him as organist of Peterhouse, where much of his music, detailed below, is preserved :

V. and T.D. ; M. and N.D. (2 settings) ; Latin K., C. and S. ANTHEMS. ' Behold how good and joyful ' ; ' Behold now, praise the Lord ' ; ' Blessed is the man that feareth ' ; ' Christ rising ' ; ' Lord, Thou art become gracious ' ; ' Prevent us, O Lord ' ; ' Thy mercy, O Lord,' incomp. ; ' Turn thy face,' incomp. ; Settings of the Collects for the Feasts of the Circumcision, and St. John the Evangelist.

Single parts of the following are also at PH. : Latin Litany ; Collects for 2nd and 4th Sundays in Lent. Another anthem, ' By the waters of Babylon,' is at Durh.   J. M^K.

WILT, MARIE (*née* LIEBENTHALER) (b. Vienna, Jan. 30, 1833 ; d. Pest, Sept. 25, 1891), singer, was the daughter of poor parents, whom she lost in early life. She was adopted by a respectable couple named Tremier and was married to a civil engineer or architect, Franz Wilt. She first sang in concerts and made a notable success as Jemina in Schubert's ' Lazarus,' performed by the Vienna Singverein, under Herbeck. Advised by Mme. Artôt to adopt the operative stage, she received vocal instruction from Gänsbacher and Wolf, and in Dec. 1865 made her débuts at Graz, and at Berlin, in the following year, as Donna Anna.

On May 1, 1866, she made her début, under the name Vilda, at Covent Garden as Norma, with considerable success, and later as Lucrezia. She sang again in 1867 with less effect. Between these years she sang in Venice and Vienna, with

such success at the later as Leonora in ' Trovatore,' early in 1867, that she was permanently engaged there in the autumn. She became a great favourite both in dramatic and coloratura parts, though physically unfitted for the latter, on account of her corpulent person, to use the words of Dr. Hanslick.[1] On May 25, 1869, she sang, as Donna Elvira, at the opening of the new Opera-House. In 1874 she was the first Aïda there, and in 1875 the original Sulamith in Goldmark's ' Königin von Saba.' She was a great favourite in concerts, and in 1873 sang with great success at the Rhenish Festival at Aix-la-Chapelle and the Schumann Festival at Bonn. According to Hanslick, she was unrivalled in ' Alexander's Feast,' the Ode to St. Cecilia's Day, and Brahms's ' Requiem.' On the stage,

' she was a well-played musical instrument ; she delighted the ear ; a deeper impression she rarely made upon me. Not a vestige of dramatic talent or education.' [2]

In 1874 and 1875 she was again at Covent Garden as Donna Anna, Semiramide, Valentine, Alice, etc., with somewhat better success than before. But in spite of her wonderful voice of great volume and compass she did not make the success that was expected. Probably she would have succeeded better here, as a concert-singer, for she had, according to Deacon,[3] ' perfect production and style.' In 1878 she did not renew her engagement at Vienna for family reasons, but became engaged at Leipzig, where she added Brünnhilde to her repertory, later at Brünn and Pest, singing occasionally as a ' guest ' on the stage of her native city, and taking up her residence there on her retirement. She committed suicide there by throwing herself out of a fourth-floor window.   A. C.

WINCKWORTH, ARTHUR (b. Bath, 1866), started his musical career as a choir boy in Bath Abbey. He afterwards studied there as basso with Emilio Pieraccini and later went to Italy to study repertory with Bevignani. In 1894 he joined the Royal Carl Rosa Opera Co. as principal basso, and has appeared in about 60 operas with that company. He was also artistic director from 1916–21, and from that date on has been principal of the Carl Rosa School of Opera.

WIND-BAND. The history of the development of wind-instrument music is so closely interwoven with the political and social state of Europe in the Middle Ages, that it is almost impossible to sketch the one without touching upon the other. Before the 12th century music of a popular kind was almost entirely in the hands of the wandering or ' roving ' musicians, who, associated with actors, acrobats,

[1] *Aus meinem Leben*, vol. ii. cap. 1.
[2] ' Kleine Spur von schauspielerischem Talent, schauspielerischer Bildung ' (Hanslick).
[3] H. C. Deacon, article on Singing in the first edition of this Dictionary.

loose women, etc., led an unsettled life. That their free and lawless existence offered great temptations to those of an unstable character may be inferred from the fact that their numbers increased so much that severe imperial and provincial edicts were enacted for their repression. 'Roving men' were considered 'shadows,' and as such out of the pale of law; they could not inherit landed property, recover debts, nor partake of any Christian sacrament.

Yet by the agency of these wandering vagabonds many of the ancient tunes or songs that we have were preserved. If a new melody grew up like a wild-flower, these fifers, fiddlers or minstrels took it up and made it known far and wide. Although a social outcast, it was no breach of etiquette to allow the musician in the houses of high or low degree, and learn from him the last ballad or the newest dance-tune. On all great occasions, fêtes or church festivals, large numbers of them flocked together for the exercise of their merry calling. But their associating together as a 'band' was a matter of mere momentary convenience, and their performances only consisted of playing the melodies of songs, vocal dance tunes, and marches. Bag-pipes being favourite instruments in these bands, we can form an idea of the quality of the 'music.' Trumpets and kettle-drums were strictly forbidden to ordinary minstrels, being reserved for the exclusive use of princes and men of high rank.

These instruments predominated in the bands which officially performed on state occasions, or at royal banquets. It is said that King Henry VIII.'s band consisted of fourteen trumpets, ten trombones and four drums, in conjunction with two viols, three rebecs, one bagpipe and four tambourines. Queen Elizabeth's band consisted (1587), besides a small number of other instruments, of ten trumpets and six trombones.[1] The Elector of Saxony had in 1680 twenty court-trumpeters and three kettle-drums, with apprentices trained for the performances of each instrument. Other courts had their trumpeter-corps, and their respective numbers were considered an indication of the importance, wealth or power of the court. In the German Empire they formed the guild of 'Royal Trumpeters and Army Kettle-drummers,' which enjoyed many privileges and were under the special protection and jurisdiction of the Grand Marshal of the Empire, the Elector of Saxony. No one could be admitted to this corporation without having previously served an apprenticeship of several years.

As early as the 13th century those 'pipers' who were settled in towns, and who felt the ignominious position of being classed with the wandering vagabonds, combined and formed 'Innungen,' or corporations for their mutual protection, in Germany, France and England. The first of these, the 'Brotherhood of St. Nicolas,' was instituted at Vienna, 1288, and elected as 'protector' Count Peter von Ebersdorff, a high imperial official. He organised a 'Court of Musicians,' obtained an imperial charter for its perpetuation, elaborated a set of laws for the guidance of the members, and presided over it for twenty-two years.[2] In Paris a 'King of Minstrels' was appointed and statutes enacted for the incorporation of the 'Brotherhood of St. Julian,' 1321.[3] (See ROI DES VIOLONS.)

In England the appointment of 'Patron' of minstrels owed its origin to a curious circumstance. Randal, Earl of Chester, being suddenly besieged, 1212, in Rhydland Castle by the Welsh at the time of Chester fair, Robert de Lacy, constable of Chester, assembled the pipers and minstrels, who had flocked to the fair in great numbers, and marching at their head towards the castle so terrified the Welsh that they instantly fled. In honour of the event the earls of Chester received the title of 'patrons of the minstrels.'[4] This dignified title had, however, no influence whatever upon the progress of music, but merely perpetuated some useless public ceremonies once a year, down to the end of the 18th century.

The first guild at Vienna was imitated during the next two centuries by most of the large imperial towns, who established regular bands of 'townpipers,' or 'townmusicians,' under the leadership of the 'Stadtpfeifer,' who had to provide all 'musics' at civic or private festivities. Wandering musicians were strictly prohibited from playing within the boundaries of the corporation. In some towns the number of musicians was regulated according to the importance of the occasion, or the rank of the family requiring a band. The 'full band' could only officiate on civic state occasions, or in connexion with religious festivals. An alderman could only employ a reduced number; and if at a citizen's wedding more than from four to six pipers were employed, both the Stadtpfeifer and the offending citizen were mulcted in a fine. Kettle-drummers and trumpeters dared not perform except at a nobleman's requisition; the lowest rank of the social scale who could indulge in this luxury being a doctor-at-law. Although the town bands had as yet but poor instrumentation, consisting mostly of fifes, flutes, schalmey, bombard (a sort of tenor or bass oboe), zinken (or cornetti), bagpipes, viols and drums—yet they are the first germs from which modern bands originated.

[1] Lavoix, *Histoire de l'instrumentation depuis le XVI siècle jusqu'à nos jours.*

[2] Forkel, *Geschichte der Musik*, vol. i. 2ter Abschnitt, sec. 73 etc. (Leipzig, 1801).
[3] Schletterer, *Geschichte der Spielmannszunft in Frankreich*, p. 115 (Berlin, 1884).
[4] Dr. Burney, *General History of Music*, vol. ii. p. 358 (London, 1782).

In the year 1426 the Emperor Sigismund granted as ' an act of special grace ' to the town of Augsburg the privilege of maintaining a corps of ' town trumpeters and kettle-drummers,' a grant extended during the next century to most other free towns ; yet it does not seem that the results, in a musical sense, were of such importance as we might expect.

In the pieces written for a band, which date from about three centuries ago, we find a strange habit of keeping different classes of instruments separate. Flutes, reed instruments, trumpets and hunting-horns, were mostly treated as forming distinct bands. Louis XIV. entrusted Lully with the organisation of certain regimental bands, which were to form a part of the regular army Before that time the great officers commanding in the field engaged music, if they wanted it, at their own expense. These bands consisted at first of oboes (in four parts —treble, alto, tenor and bass, or bassoon) and regimental drums. The following march is one of the many written by Lully, the notation being that given by Kastner.[1]

Premier Air de la Marche Française pour les Hautbois fait par M. de Lully.

A more ambitious composition is the next piece, evidently written for town bands. The cornetto is the CORNETT (*q.v.*) or zinke.

Till the 17th century the music played by the bands of trumpeters was learned by ear, and transmitted without notation, as something of a secret nature. When princes took command of their armies in the field they were accompanied by their trumpeters, both for signalling (see MILITARY SOUNDS AND SIGNALS) and for enlivening the dreariness of the march or camp. As they served on horseback, the custom arose of looking upon trumpet-music as being specially appropriate to the cavalry service, and

1 Georges Kastner, *Manuel général de musique militaire*, etc. (Paris, 1848).

Johann Pezelius, *Fünfstimmige blasende Musik*, etc. (Frankfort, 1685).

eventually it became regularly attached to it. The music of these bands, consisting only of trumpets and kettle-drums, was naturally very simple.

example of the employment of a choir of five trombones, which weave around the simple four-part Choral a richly figured and most effective accompaniment. The diversity of

The denomination 'Trompano' in the above score is singular. The usual names for the four different parts of trumpet-music were—Clarino primo, Clarino secondo, Principale, and Toccato. In the example above, the fourth part is either for Trumpet (in which case the bars written 𝄐 are to be played in 'double tongue') or for kettle-drums, but probably for both combined.

The fact that all trumpet and horn music suffered from the absence of such important intervals as the third and seventh of the dominant chord, gave it a monotonous character. To obviate this the device was adopted of adding to the principal body of trumpets, in the key of the tonic, a few tuned in other keys. The adoption and extension of the custom of mixing in both trumpet- and horn-bands a variety of differently-tuned instruments made almost every harmonic progression possible, providing the band was numerous enough.

Although trombones were in frequent requisition they seem not to have been so often combined with either trumpet- or horn-bands as might have been expected. In a collection of Lutheran hymns by Johannes Krüger ('Psalmodia sacra,' publ. 1685) we meet with a fine

duties imposed upon town-bands—having not only to provide the music for all sorts of civic fêtes, but also on high church-festivals to take part in the musical portion of the sacred rites—necessarily led to an enlargement of the limits of ancient instrumentation. Trombones came into general use, and being combined with flutes, oboes, pommers, zinken (cornetti), and sometimes a couple of trumpets and kettle-drums, some very decent band-music emerged by slow degrees from the barbarous noise of former times. Instrumental music now began to be noted down, and we are enabled to trace its progress as we come nearer the 18th century. Bands separated more distinctly into three classes, each striving to perfect its own special mission—the full orchestra addressing itself to the cultivated musical intellect, whilst the military and brass bands appealed to the masses at large.

A new era begins with the invention and rapid improvement of the clarinet, which for wind-bands is as important as the violin is for the orchestra. Its brilliant tone, capable of every shade, from the softest to the loudest, and its large compass, extended by the introduction of the smaller clarinets as well as by tenor and bass clarinets, at once placed it in the rank of the leading instrument: thus the oboe was pushed into the second place. Two more instruments were so perfected in their construction as to become important additions to wind-bands, namely the bassoon and the French horn.

From 1763 military music assumed a definite form, and although still very rudimentary, we can trace in the instrumentation, as fixed by order of King Frederick II. of Prussia (Frederick the Great), the foundation upon which further development, in the shape of additions of other instruments, soon manifested itself. This first organisation comprised two oboes, two clarinets, two horns, and two bassoons, to which after a short time were added a flute, one or two trumpets and a contrafagotto. The French bands of the Republic (1795) consisted of one flute, six clarinets, three bassoons, two horns, one trumpet and one serpent, besides a number of side-drums. In the time of Napoleon military bands made rapid strides, both with regard to the augmentation of their numbers and to their executive capacity, and were admitted to be the best then in existence. It seems that between the years 1805 and 1808 the addition of bass-drum, cymbals and triangle was made ; and also into the Prussian bands that most useless of toys, the crescent, found its way.

England having in no way contributed to improve or even influence the progress of wind instrumental music, we have of necessity to pursue its course on the continent, from whence any important advance was simply adopted. It is difficult to trace the introduction of military bands into the English service. In 1783 the Coldstream Guards had a band of eight musicians—two oboes, two clarinets, two horns and two bassoons. The Duke of York, wishing to improve the musical service, imported from Germany what probably was the first 'full band' of twenty-four men, who, besides the above-named instruments, brought flute, trumpets, trombones and serpent. To these were added three negroes with tambourines and crescent.[1]

On the introduction of VALVES (q.v.) valve-trumpets were introduced here and there, but without creating a favourable impression. Thus it went on until two men came to the front—one as a reformer of military music, the other as the inventor of scientifically constructed brass instruments—WIEPRECHT and SAX (q.v.). The former had an anomalous position, for being a civilian his propositions for reforming a purely military establishment were received but coolly by the military authorities. However, persevering in his endeavours, he at last succeeded so far as to be allowed (at the expense of the commanding officer) to introduce his instrumentation in a German cavalry brass-band. It consisted of two high trumpets in B♭ (cornettini), two key-bugles in B♭, two alto-trumpets in E♭ (cornetti), eight trumpets in E♭, two tenor-horns in B♭, one bass-horn in B♭, and three trombones in B♭, the former all having two or three valves, the latter being slide-trombones. The great advantage of this innovation was so apparent that Wieprecht was requested to introduce it into the bands of the Prussian Life Guards, and he went so far as to give the members of these bands personal lessons, to be assured of a proper perception of his ideas. In 1838 he was appointed director of all the Guards' bands, and in this influential position he successfully dealt with the formation and style of playing of the military bands throughout Germany. The first grand effort of combining many bands for a monster performance, at which he officiated, was at a fête given at Berlin on May 12, 1838, to the Emperor Nicholas of Russia, who was on a visit to the King of Prussia, when Wieprecht conducted a performance of sixteen infantry and sixteen cavalry bands, consisting of 1000 wind-instruments, besides 200 side-drummers. He directed this great mass of musicians, all dressed in brilliant uniforms, in plain civilian garb, and it is said that the Emperor was so struck with the incongruity of the thing that Wieprecht hurriedly put into uniform to conduct a second performance before the crowned heads four days after.[2]

Without following in detail the many results of his well-directed efforts, we will only give the instrumentation of the first military (reed) band, as reformed by him.

2 Flutes.	2 Soprano Cornetti in E♭.
2 Oboes.	2 Altocornets in B♭.
1 A♭ (high) Clarinet.	2 Tenor Horns in B♭.
2 E♭ Clarinets.	1 Baritone Tuba (Euphonium).
8 B♭ Clarinets.	
2 Bassoons.	4 Bass Tubas (Bombardons).
2 Contrabassoons.	
2 Tenor Trombones.	4 Trumpets.
2 Bass Trombones.	4 French Horns.

2 Side Drums, Bass Drum, Cymbals and Crescent. (47 men in all.)

For the cavalry he organised the bands thus (trumpet-bands) :

Cavalry.	*Artillery.*
1 Cornettino in B♭.	3 Cornetti in B♭.
2 Cornettos in E♭.	3 Cornetti in E♭.
4 Cornets in B♭.	6 Cornets in B♭.
2 Tenor Horns.	6 Tenor Horns.
8 Trumpets.	3 Euphoniums.
1 Euphonium.	12 Trumpets.
3 Bombardons.	6 Tubas (Bombardons).
(21 men in all.)	(39 men in all.)

And for the light infantry (Jäger) the instrumentation was called 'horn-music,' consisting of—

1 Cornettino in B♭.	4 French Horns.
2 Cornetti in E♭.	3 Trumpets.
4 Cornets in B♭.	2 Euphoniums.
2 Tenor Horns.	3 Bombardons.

The regulation instrumentation of the Aus-

[1] Parke, *Musical Memoirs*, vol. ii. p. 239 (London, 1830) ; C. F. Pohl, *Haydn in London*, p. 163 (Wien, 1867).

[2] For a description of a similar performance see Berlioz, *Voyage musical*, Letter IX. Berlioz wrongly calls him Wibrecht.

trian bands at the same period differed from the above in so far that it regarded less the artistic completeness than the production of greater power or loudness. We find, therefore, no flute, oboes or bassoons. It consisted of—

Austrian Infantry Band, 1860.	The same, 1884.
1 Piccolo.	1 Piccolo in E♭.
1 high A♭ Clarinet.	1 Flute.
2 E♭ Clarinets.	1 high A♭ Clarinet.
4 E♭ Clarinets.	2 E♭ Clarinets.
2 Cornetti (B♭).	8 B♭ Clarinets (in 4 parts).
2 Cornetti (E♭).	4 Horns (E♭).
2 Cornets (B♭).	2 First Flügel Horns.
2 Tenor Horns.	2 Second ditto.
2 Euphoniums.	2 ditto. B♭ Bass (or Tenor Horns).
4 Bombardons.	2 Euphoniums.
4 Trumpets.	10 Trumpets E♭ (in 4 or 5 parts).
2 French Horns.	2 Bass Trumpets (B♭).
2 Tenor Trombones.	3 Bombardons in F.
2 Bass Trombones.	3 Tubas in E♭, C, or Contra B♭.
1 Side and 1 Bass Drum and one pair of Cymbals. (35 men in all.)	2 Side Drums and 1 Bass Drum and Cymbals. (47 men in all.[1])

This regulation number has, however, on nearly all occasions been overstepped, and there are frequently bands of from seventy to ninety performers.

Spontini recommended to the special commission for the reorganisation of the French military bands, at Paris, 1845, the following as the best instrumentation for bands of infantry regiments :

1 Piccolo.	4 Saxhorns in B♭ (Cornets)
2 Concert Flutes.	4 Ditto (Althorns).
2 E♭ Clarinets.	4 Bass Saxhorns in B♭ (Euphoniums).
8 or 10 First B♭ Clarinets.	
8 or 10 Second ditto.	4 Contrabass Saxhorns (Bombardons).
2 Alto Clarinets.	
2 Bass ditto.	2 Horns without valves.
4 First Oboes.	2 Ditto with 3 valves.
4 Second ditto.	3 Trombones (slide—alt., tenor and bass).
2 Bassethorns (Alt. Clarinet in F).	
2 First Bassoons.	3 Ditto, with valves (ditto).
2 Second ditto.	1 Serpent (Ophicleide).
2 high Saxhorns in E♭ (Cornettos)	1 or 2 Contrafagotts.

But it was not adopted.

Like Wieprecht in Germany, Sax in France created a revolution in the instrumentation of the military bands ; but, whereas the former was prompted by purely artistic motives, the latter acted from scientific knowledge and for mercantile purposes. (See SAX.) He adapted the valve to all classes of brass instruments, and gave them the generic name of Saxhorns, Saxtromba, Saxtuba, etc., ignoring the fact that valve-trumpets, valve-horns and various other forms of valve-brass instruments were known, although not in general use, long before he adopted them for his ' inventions.'. The bombardons (by him called Saxtubas) were designed by Wieprecht, and introduced into the Prussian army before ' Saxtubas ' were heard of.[2] However, by a unity of design and

a great number of ingenious improvements in the details of manufacture, he deservedly gained a great name as an instrument-maker. This, combined with influence at the court of Napoleon III., and the enthusiastic support of Berlioz, enabled him to bring about a complete reorganisation of the French military bands, he obtaining almost the monopoly of supplying the instruments. He designed a peculiar clarinet of metal, very wide in diameter and conical in shape, formidable-looking on account of a great number of keys, and called the SAXO-PHONE (q.v.).

The following lists of French infantry bands show that the instrumentation, as fixed by the government of the time, has since been considerably departed from :

In 1860.	In 1884.
2 Flutes.	2 Piccolos in E♭.
2 Piccolos.	1 Flute in D (concert).
4 Clarinets.	2 Oboes.
2 Oboes.	1 E♭ Clarinet.
2 Saxophones soprano.	4 B♭ Clarinets.
2 Do. alto.	1 Saxophone soprano.
2 Do. tenor.	1 Do. alto.
2 Do. baritone.	1 Do. tenor.
2 Cornets à pistons.	1 Do. baritone.
2 Trumpets (cylinder).	2 Bassoons.
3 Trombones.	1 Petit Bugle in E♭.
2 Saxhorns, B♭ alto.	2 Pistons in B♭.
3 Saxtromba, E♭.	2 Bugles in B♭.
2 Saxhorns, baritone B♭.	2 Horns in E♭.
3 Do. bass in B♭ (4 cylinders).	2 Trumpets in E♭.
1 Saxhorn, contrabass in E♭.	3 Altos in E♭.
	2 Barytones in B♭.
1 Saxhorn, contrabass in B♭.	3 Trombones.
	Bass in B♭ (Euphonium).
Side and Bass Drums and Cymbals.[3]	Contrabass in E♭.
	Do. in B♭.
	Drums and Cymbals.[4]

The bands of two more armies may be mentioned ; the first on account of a rather peculiar instrumentation, and the second as a curious illustration of the influence of European ideas upon a very distant people.

Spain.	Japan.
1 Piccolo in E♭ (D♭).	2 Flutes.
1 Flute in E♭.	1 Oboe.
1 E♭ Clarinet.	2 E♭ Clarinets.
10 B♭ Clarinets.	8 B♭ Clarinets.
2 Saxophones sopr. in B♭.	4 Saxophones in B♭.
2 Do. alto in E♭.	4 Do. in E♭.
2 Do. tenor in B♭.	2 Do. in B♭ (bass).
2 Do. bass in C.	2 Baritones in B♭.
2 Flügelhorns in B♭.	3 Cornets in B♭.
4 Cornets in B♭.	2 Trumpets in E♭.
3 Trumpets in E♭.	3 Trombones.
2 French Horns.	4 Euphoniums.
4 Tenor Trombones in C.	2 Bombardons in E♭.
1 Bass Trombone in F.	2 Contrabasses in B♭.
2 Euphoniums in B♭.	And 2 Drums, with Cymbals.[5]
2 Bombardons in E♭.	
2 Tubas in C.	
1 Tuba (Contra F).	
1 High (shallow) Side Drum.	
1 Do. (long old pattern)	
1 Bass Drum.	
1 Cymbal.	
1 Lyra Glockenspiel).	
(to which are added, for various instruments, 10 pupils under training.)	

[1] A. Kalkbrenner, *Wilhelm Wieprecht, sein Leben und Wirken,* tc. (Berlin, 1882).
[2] *Wieprechts Schriften.* Published letter (Berlin, 1867).
[3] Albert Perrin, *Military Bands,* etc. (London, 1863).
[4] A. Kalkbrenner, *Die Organisation der Militairmusikchöre, etc.* (Hanover, 1884).   [5] *Ibid.*

In 1878 Gilmore brought the band of the 22nd Regiment of New York to Europe, giving concerts at Liverpool, Dublin, the Crystal Palace, Paris, etc. Although the band had a great reputation, its performances surpassed the expectation of even the most fastidious critics.

Their instrumentation was as follows :

2 piccolos, 2 flutes, 2 oboes, 1 A♭ piccolo clarinet, 3 E♭ clarinets, 8 first, 4 second, and 4 third B♭ clarinets, 1 alto and 1 bass clarinet, 1 soprano, 1 alto, 1 tenor and 1 bass saxophone, 2 bassoons, 1 contra-fagotto, 1 E♭ cornetto, 2 first and 2 second B♭ cornets, 2 trumpets, 2 flügelhorns, 4 French horns, 2 E♭ alto horns, 2 B♭ tenor horns, 2 euphoniums, 3 trombones, 5 bombardons, 3 drums and cymbals—66 in all.

Military (Reed) bands are now constructed on the same system in all countries.

The following is the instrumentation of an English Military Band as at present (1927) in use at the ROYAL MILITARY SCHOOL OF MUSIC (q.v.) (Kneller Hall), Twickenham.

Piccolo.	1st B♭ Cornet.
Flutes.	2nd B♭ do.
1st E♭ Clarinet.	1st B♭ Trumpet.
2nd E♭ do.	2nd B♭ do.
1st Oboe.	1st Tenor Trombone.
2nd do.	2nd do. do.
Solo B♭ Clarinets.	Bass Trombone.
1st B♭ do.	Euphonium.
2nd B♭ do.	E♭ and B♭ Basses (play
3rd B♭ do.	from the same part).
E♭ Alto Saxophone.	Tympani, Side drum,
B♭ Tenor do.	Bass drum and the
1st Bassoon.	usual percussion and
2nd do.	effects.
1st Horn (F or E♭).	
2nd do. do.	
3rd do. do.	
4th do. do.	

With this may be compared the following scheme as given for an Italian Military Band, as well as the specimens of recently (1925) published scores for such bands in France, Spain and Germany.

Instrumentation of the Italian Military Band.

Ottavino in Re bemolle.
Due Flauti in Do.
Due Clarinetti Piccolo in La bemolle e Mi bemolle.
Tre Clarinetti Soprani in Si bemolle.
Due Clarinetti Contralti in Mi bemolle.
  Do. do.   Bassi (Claroni) in Si bemolle.
Quattro Saxofoni.
  Soprano in Si bemolle.
  Contralto in Mi bemolle.
  Tenore in Si bemolle.
  Baritono in Mi bemolle.
Contrabasso.
Quattro Corni in Mi bemolle.
Due Cornette in Si bemolle.
  Do. Trombe in Si bemolle.
  Do. do. in Mi bemolle.
  Do. Tromboni Tenori in Si bemolle.
Trombone Basso in Fa e Contrabasso in Si bemolle.
Flicorno Sopranino (Pistonino) in Mi bemolle.
Due Flicorni Soprani in Si bemolle.
  Do. do. Contralti (Genis) in Mi bemolle.
  Do. do. Tenori in Si bemolle.
Flicorno Baritono (Bombardino) in Si bemolle.
  Do. Basso (Eufonio) in Si bemolle.
Flicorni Bassi-Gravi in Fa e Mi bemolle.
  Do. Contrabassi in Si bemolle.
Timpani.
Tamburo.
Gran Cassa ; Piatti.

Instrumentation of Continental Military Bands.

French (' L'Apprenti Sorcier ').

Petite Flute.	1er 2e 3e et 4e Trombones
Grandes Flutes.	Petit Bugle.
1er et 2e Hautbois.	1er et 2e Bugle.
Petites Clarinettes.	1er et 2e Cors MI♭.
Clarinettes Soli.	1er 2e et 3e Altos.
1ers Clarinettes.	1er et 2e Barytons.
2e et 3e Clarinettes.	1re et 2e Basse SI♭.
Clarinette Alto (ad lib.).	C. Basse MI♭.
Do. Basse (ad lib.).	C. Basse SI♭.
Saxophone Alto.	Sarrusophone C. B. MI♭
1er et 2e Saxophone Tenors.	(ad lib.).
Saxophone Baryton.	Clavi-Timbres.
Do. Basse.	Timbales.
Bassons (ad lib.).	Triangle.
1er et 2e Trompettes en SI♭.	Grosse Caisse.
1er et 2e Cornets a Pistons.	Cymbales.

Spanish (' El dos de Mayo ' March).

Flatin.	Trombas en MI♭ (Trum
Flauta.	pets).
Oboe.	Trombones.
Requinto (E♭ Clarinet).	Fliscornos (Baritones).
Clarinettes 1os.	Trompas en MI♭ (Horns).
Do. 2os.	Bombardinos (Euph. and
Saxophones Alto MI♭.	Tuba).
Do. Tenores SI♭.	Bajos (Basses).
Do. Baritonos MI♭	Ruido (Drums).
Fagotes.	Cornetas (Bugles).
Cornetines (Cornets).	Tambores.

German (' Achtung : Die Garde kommt March ').

Flauto piccolo.	Corno in F, I, II, III and
Do. grand.	IV.
Oboe I and II.	Alt Cornett in Es, I and II.
Clarinetto in Es, I and II.	Tenorhorn in B, I and II.
Clarinette in B, I, II and	Baryton.
III.	Trombone Tenore, I and II.
Fagott I and II.	Do. Basso, I and II.
Cornett in B, I and II.	Tuba I and II.
Tromba in ,F, I, II, III	Tambour petit.
and IV.	Do. grand.
	Glockenspiel.

The assimilation of instrumentation in all countries has facilitated the publication of a large literature for wind-bands. Though the bulk of the best work still consists of arrangements from the orchestral repertory a few modern composers have produced original works for the wind-band, and English composers have been particularly encouraged in this direction in recent years by the more serious artistic attitude adopted by the ROYAL MILITARY SCHOOL OF MUSIC (q.v.).

J. A. K ; rev. C. with information
from H. E. A.

WIND - CHEST ; the box-like construction in an organ which receives the wind from the bellows, and supplies it to the pipes above when the pallets in the wind-chest are opened and the sliders drawn. (See ORGAN, sub-section 3, THE MODERN ORGAN.)   T. E.

WINDET, JOHN, a music and typographical printer, living in the reigns of Elizabeth and James I. His first address was at the White Bear in Adling Street. In 1594 he was at the ' Crosse Keyes ' at Paul's Wharf. He printed several editions of Sternhold's Psalms, and many musical works. He held an assignment of printing rights from William Barley. His works include Greaves's ' Songs of Sundrie Kindes,' 1604 ; Hume's ' Ayres French, Pollish, and others,' 1605 ; 'An Howres Recreation in

Musicke,' by Rd. Alison, 1606 ; John Bartlet's ' Booke of Ayres ' ; Michael East's ' Second Set of Madrigales,' 1606 ; Robert Jones's 'First Set of Madrigals,' 1607, and some others of a similar kind.   F. K.

WIND GAUGE, see TELL-TALE.

WIND-HOLE, the hole in the boot or foot of an organ pipe for admission of the wind.   T. E.

WIND INSTRUMENTS. This designation is by common consent held to include all instruments supplied with air from the lungs of the player, and to exclude instruments, such as the organ, harmonium and concertina, which receive their wind-supply from bellows fed with natural air. Certain instruments of the bagpipe family which are blown by bellows must, however, be regarded as exceptions to the rule.

Disregarding forms used among peoples whose music is to us either in a barbaric stage or but little removed therefrom (see PIPES, EVOLUTION AND DISTRIBUTION OF MUSICAL), all modern wind instruments of artistic value may be classified in two different ways, under either of which they fall into three distinct groups. In every wind instrument it is the column of air itself which is virtually the instrument, and not the tube of wood or metal which fixes its proportions and dimensions, and the acoustical properties of such columns, therefore, afford the means of determining one of these systems of classification. As is explained in the article ACOUSTICS, a cylindrical tube open at both ends, when excited to musical speech, can give a fundamental note whose wave length is twice that of the tube, and also upper notes following the lowest, or prime, in the harmonic series. If the tube be halved in length and closed at one end, the fundamental note remains the same, and also every alternate upper note, but the notes represented by the even numbers of the harmonic series are now absent. A conical tube complete to its apex is of the same pitch, and has the same series of natural tones as the cylindrical tube open at both ends. We have, therefore, the following results :

Harmonic series . 1 2 3 4 5 6 7 8 9 10, etc.
Open cylindrical tube and cone of same length } c c' g' c'' e'' g'' bb''c'''d'''e'''
Cylindrical tube closed at one end of half length of open tube } c g' e'' bb'' d'''

and the three divisions under which all wind instruments are grouped in this scheme may be held to be represented by the flute, the clarinet, and the horn. The stopped tube may be represented, however, by the pandean pipe instead of by the clarinet, and the cone may be represented by the bassoon instead of by the horn, and other variations might be instanced,

so that in practice it is found more convenient to classify instruments according to the manner in which the player's lips are applied for the production of the tone than by the three fundamental forms of resonating tubes, and we thus obtain the three great divisions of flute, reed and brass.

Of these primary divisions, the flute and reed in modern bands, both orchestral and military, are frequently grouped together as the ' wood wind,' leaving the ' brass wind ' as a division by itself. The material, however, has but little significance, as the ' wood wind ' may include flutes of silver, clarinets of ebonite or vulcanite and saxophones of brass, and the ' brass wind ' includes, or until late years included, serpents, ophicleides, and other forms of brass horns blown with cup mouth-pieces, made sometimes of wood, and sometimes of metal.

The Table of Classification on p. 738 shows the grouping and relationship of the majority of our modern wind instruments and of a few of the early types with which their connexion is easily traced. For the special characteristics of individual instruments or of families, the reader is referred to articles under each name, but characteristics which are common to many families in the different divisions are more conveniently treated here.

The one fundamental fact common to all wind instruments is that the scale is based upon the harmonic series of sounds, in which the interval between any two consecutive notes is measured by the same number of vibrations. The means of altering the normal length of an instrument so as to obtain a change of wave-length with corresponding change of pitch of harmonics, lies at the root of development from elementary types.

The various means of altering lengths, thereby completing the scale, and the different methods of tone-production, are here set forth under the three different divisions adopted in the Table.

1. FLUTES.—The source of tone in every instrument in this division is a thin stream, blade, or reed of air issuing either directly from the lips, or from a chink or slit as in the common penny whistle. The passing of this stream across the end of a tube as in the pandean pipe, or across a side mouth-hole as in the modern flute, sets up in the tube alternate rarefactions and condensations, or stationary waves, the fundamental pitch of which depends almost entirely upon the length of the tube, but somewhat upon the size of mouth-hole and other details, and also upon the force of blowing. With an open tube, an increase of force in blowing first slightly raises the prime or fundamental note ; the pitch then leaps to the octave or second note in the harmonic series, and subsequently to the twelfth or third harmonic. Higher notes can be obtained,

TABLE OF CLASSIFICATION OF WIND INSTRUMENTS

Division.	Class.		Family.	Subdivisions of Families and Special Examples.
FLUTE or Air-Reed.	Vertical or beaked (Flûte-à-bec).		Recorders or Flûtes-douces. Flageolets. Galoubets.	Soprano to Bass. Picco Pipe. Single, double, and triple. Tabor Pipe.
	Transverse (Flûte traversière).		Blown across open end {	Egyptian Này (open pipe). Pandean Pipe (closed pipe).
			Blown across side mouth-hole (modern flutes).	Flutes, Fifes, and Piccolos (both cone and cylinder).
REED. In all these Instruments, except the Bagpipes and Cromornes, the reeds are under the direct control of the lips.	Single Reed.	With Cylindrical Tube.	Arghool. Chalumeau. Clarinet.	{ Soprano to Bass. { Basset Horn.
		With Conical Tube.	Saxophone.	Soprano to Bass.
	Double Reed.	With Cylindrical Tube.	Aulos or Greek Flute.	Racket or Cervelat. Sourdine.
			With enclosed reed.	Cromorne or Krummhorn.
		With Conical Tube.	Pommers, including Shawm or Schalmey.	Wait or Waight. Musette. Oboe. Cor Anglais. Dulcian. Bassoon.
	Single and Double Reeds enclosed and in combination.	Bagpipe (Cylindrical and Conical tubes in combination).	Air-reservoir supplied from the lungs.	Cornemuse. Highland Bagpipe. Bignou. Zampogna.
			Air-reservoir supplied from bellows.	Musette. Northumbrian Bagpipe. Irish Bagpipe.
BRASS. Lips acting as reeds against cap-shaped mouth-pieces.	Tubes of fixed length.		Short, i.e. Lower harmonics chiefly used.	Oliphant. Bugle. Post-Horn.
			Long, i.e. Upper harmonics freely used.	Trumpet. French Horn.
	Length varied by side-holes closed by fingers or keys.		Cornetts or Zinken (chiefly of wood).	Cornetto diretto, Cornetto curvo, and Cornetto torto. Serpent.
			Metal Horns.	Key Bugle. Ophicleide. Bass Horn or Bassoon Russe.
	Length varied by slide.			Trumpet. Trombone.
	Length varied by valves.			Cornet. Trumpet. French Horn.
			Saxhorns { Bugle type { Wide bore type {	Flügel Horn. Tenor and Baritone Althorns. Euphonium. Tuba or Bombardon.

but are of no practical importance in flute-playing.

The completion of the scale in these instruments is obtained by the introduction of side holes, closed either by the fingers or by padded keys. By this means the speaking length of the tube is gradually shortened as the scale ascends.

2. REED.—In this division the lips act by controlling the vibration of a single or double blade of cane (see REED), and although there is necessarily a slight opening between the single reed and its mouth-piece, and between the two blades of a double reed, this opening is either almost or, altogether periodically closed during vibration, so that the associated instrument behaves as a tube stopped at one end. In conical tubes, whether with single or double reed, the series of tones is as on the flute, but when the reeds are associated with cylindrical tubes the even numbered notes of the harmonic series are absent. In all instruments in this division, side holes are used in the same way as in the flutes.

3. BRASS.—In the majority of instruments in this division the upper harmonics play a much more important part than on those included in divisions 1 and 2, the lips having the power of covering the range of three octaves or more without altering the mouthpiece. On a very short horn such as a natural ox-horn, or the mediæval oliphants, only the fundamental note of the harmonic series with its octave, and sometimes its twelfth, can be sounded, but the ease of producing relatively higher notes increases with increase of length until in the ordinary field bugle the sixth harmonic becomes easy, and the eighth possible. Increasing the length of the instrument yet more, as by the addition of a small cylindrical tube, so as to lower the fundamental pitch by an octave, we obtain an approximation to the trumpet, on which the twelfth harmonic is easy, being in this case of the same actual pitch as the sixth harmonic on our original bugle. On the French horn the length is further increased, and harmonics up to the sixteenth are available.

Instruments of fixed length such as the horn and trumpet can therefore give in their upper octave certain successive notes of the diatonic scale which it is impossible to produce on short natural horns, but such short horns on which only the lower harmonics are possible may be regarded as typical of the old cornetts or zinken. In these the scale was completed by side finger-holes in the same manner as on the flute and reed instruments, and the system was further extended by key-work on the serpent, key-bugle and ophicleide.

It is evident that a new fundamental note can be obtained by lengthening a given tube, as well as by shortening it. This lengthening, carried out by means of telescopic slides, is the principle adopted in the trombone, and it is an excellent one both musically and mechanically. It is, however, necessarily limited to instruments having a large proportion of cylindrical tubing, and therefore of a certain tone-quality. Instruments having a continuous taper are necessarily excluded from the slide action, and in these in early days the filling up of the scale was made possible by the introduction of side-holes as above described.

The disappearance of all lip-blown instruments with side-holes, the cornetts, serpents, ophicleides, etc., is undoubtedly the result of the introduction of the valve action in its various forms. A sketch of the development of the principle will be found under the article VALVE (q.v.) and of the chief instruments in which the valve is used under their respective names. It will be sufficient here to describe the action generally, and to note the grouping into which valve instruments naturally fall.

The idea on which the valve is based has more analogy to the slide than to any other contrivance, for the depression of a valve or valves opens air-ways into additional tubing, which virtually lengthens the instrument, so that the effect is similar to that produced by the extension of the trombone slide. The depression of a valve or valves flattens the pitch by one or more semitones, so that from each alteration of length a new harmonic series is obtained, and the chromatic scale in valve instruments is therefore built up of elements derived from many different harmonic scales. In an ordinary three-valve instrument there are, in addition to the harmonic scale proper to its natural length, six others due to the valves acting either singly or in combination, and the addition of a fourth valve gives six other harmonic scales subject to certain limitations noticed under the article VALVE.

The chief valve instruments may be grouped thus :

(a) Cornet : a hybrid instrument combining the qualities of a high-pitched trumpet and of the flügel-horn or bugle.

(b) Saxhorns of the bugle type, ranging in pitch from soprano to baritone.

(c) Saxhorns of wide bore, and consequently broad tone, and of bass and contrabass compass. These are known as euphoniums, tubas and bombardons, and take the place of the serpents, ophicleides and other bass horns formerly used.

(d) Horns, trumpets and trombones. The original proportions of these instruments are little changed by the introduction of the valve, but the quality of the trombone loses some distinctiveness, through a lessening of the force of the upper partials.

In group (c) owing chiefly to the large calibre, the pedal octave between the first and second notes of the harmonic series is available, whereas in all the other groups the pedal octave is practically unused. The instruments in group (c) have therefore a compass downwards of about one octave more than the other instruments.

In one respect wind instruments occupy a position midway between keyboard instruments and the bowed-string class. On a keyboard instrument the performer has little or no power of regulating either intonation or quality; the violinist, on the other hand, has absolute control over intonation and great control of quality. Mouth-blown instruments are susceptible of some slight control over intonation by the player; he can correct a note that is slightly sharp or flat, and he can also modify tone-quality.

The comparatively recent development of our wind instruments, as contrasted with the permanence of model of the violin since the days of Stradivarius, is to be explained in large measure by the difficulty early makers had in overcoming the limitations imposed by the natural number and stretch of the fingers. Of the ten fingers, two at least are required for the support of an instrument, leaving only eight for the control of the ventages required for a chromatic scale extending in instruments of the clarinet type through the compass of a twelfth. As a consequence we find that the older instruments were designed on a diatonic, rather than on a chromatic basis, and it is only with the introduction of modern mechanism that good chromatic scales have become possible. (For a general sketch of the different schemes of treatment of side-holes, see FINGERING.) D. J. B.

WINDSOR, or ETON TUNE. This famous psalm tune is first found complete (unless the assertion be true that its original form is in Nyland's ' Piae cantiones,' 1582) in Daman's music to the Psalms, 1591, harmonised in four parts, and set to Ps. cxvi. It is not in Daman's earlier work of 1579.[1] As no complete set of parts is known to exist, the melody only can be quoted :

This affords an example of Daman's method of prolonging a tune by repetition, of which Hawkins speaks.

In 1592 the tune appears in East's ' Whole Booke of Psalmes,' containing the Church Tunes and ' other short tunes usually sung in London, and most places of the Realme.' It is marked as being one of the latter, and must therefore have been in use for some little time previously.

[1] For an account of this extremely scarce work see Hawkins, *Hist. of Music*, chap. cxvii. ; also vol. i. p. 654.

In East's Psalter it is harmonised by George Kirby, the melody in the tenor. Daman and Kirby merely harmonised the melody, but whoever was its composer, it is only an adaptation of the tune set by TYE (*q.v.*) to the third chapter of

' The Actes of the Apostles, translated into Englyshe Metre . . . with notes to eche Chapter, to synge and also to play upon the Lute,' 1553.

Here we find the first, third and fourth strains of Windsor, and a fragment of the second. For the sake of comparison Dr. Tye's tune is subjoined, reduced into score in modern clefs.

In East's Psalter the tune has no distinctive name, but in 1615 it was inserted in the Scottish Psalter published by Andro Hart, as ' Dundie.' In Ravenscroft's Psalter, 1621, it is marked as an English Tune, and is doubly named ' Windsor

or Eaton.' The tune was popular in Scotland,[1] and this, coupled with the Scottish form of its earliest name, led to the belief that it was indigenous to that country.

In Hart's Psalter of 1615 the melody alone is given with slight variations, including the omission of the accidental leading note. This may have been done to assimilate its character to that of other tunes in the collection; but however this may be, the accidental was restored to the penultimate note of the last strain in Raban's Psalter, Aberdeen, 1633, and throughout the hymn in the harmonised Scottish Psalter of 1635. G. A. C.

WIND-TRUNK, a large wooden or metal tube for conveying the wind of an organ from the bellows to the wind-chest. T. E.

WINDWAY, the narrow slit or opening between the block or languid, and the cap or lower lip of a flue pipe of the organ. T. E.

WINGHAM, THOMAS (b. London, Jan. 5, 1846; d. London, Mar. 24, 1893), became organist of St. Michael's Mission Church, Southwark, at the age of 10, and in 1863 entered the London Academy of Music. Four years afterwards he went to the R.A.M. and became pupil of Sterndale Bennett for composition, and of Harold Thomas for piano. In 1871 he was appointed a professor of the piano in the school, and was subsequently elected a fellow. As early as 1864 he was appointed organist of All Saints, Paddington, and in 1882 was given the post of musical director at the Brompton Oratory, an office which he filled with much distinction until his death.

·His church compositions are marked by suavity rather than austerity, and it is rather as a pioneer of better things in the music of the Roman Church than as a composer that his name will be remembered. He raised the services at the Oratory to a very high standard. His Mass in D was composed for Antwerp Cathedral in 1876, and another Mass was written in the following year for the Oratory. A Te Deum, for voices, orchestra and organ, was brought out at the Oratory in 1884, and in the same year his fine motet, ' Amavit sapientiam ' was written for the tercentenary of St. Charles Borromeo at the church of St. Mary of the Angels, Bayswater.

He left four symphonies (in D minor, R.A.M. 1869; in B flat, Crystal Palace, 1872; in E minor, with choral finale, 1873; and in D, 1883). His six concert-overtures are as follows: No. 1, in C, Jubilee of the R.A.M., 1872; No. 2, in E (Eros), Crystal Palace, 1875; No. 3, in D, choral, Alexandra Palace, 1877; No. 4, in F (' Fair laughs the morn '), Crystal Palace, 1878; No. 5, in A, Brighton Festival,

[1] Burns, in his ' Cottar's Saturday Night,' refers to this tune:
Perhaps Dundee's wild warbling measures rise,
Or plaint' e Martyrs, worthy of the name.
Care must be taken not to confound it with the ' Dundee ' of Ravenscroft, which is the ' French' tune ' o₁ the Scottish Psalter.

1879; No. 6 (' Mors janua vitae '), Leeds Festival, 1880. An elegy on the death of Sterndale Bennett was performed at the Crystal Palace in 1875, and a serenade in E flat at the Philharmonic, 1885. A concert-capriccio for PF. and orch., two string quartets, a septet for piano and strings and wind, were completed, and an opera, ' Nala and Damayanti,' was left incomplete. (Brit. Mus. Biog. etc.) M.

WINKEL, DIETRICH NIKOLAUS (b. circa 1780; d. Amsterdam, Sept. 28, 1826), a mechanic who constructed several instruments for musical reproduction and was the inventor of the METRONOME (q.v.). (See also MAELZEL.)

WINKELMANN (1) HERMANN (b. Brunswick, Mar. 8, 1849; d. Vienna, Jan. 18, 1912), tenor singer. With the intention of becoming a pianoforte-maker he went to Paris for his training, but abandoned business for a vocal career. After lessons in singing from Koch at Hanover, he made his début in 1865 at Sondershausen. He sang successively at Altenburg, Darmstadt and Hamburg, where on Nov. 1, 1879, he made a great success as the hero on the production of Rubinstein's ' Nero.' On May 18, 1882, he made his début at Drury Lane, under Richter, as Lohengrin (in German), and attracted immediate attention on account of his fine tenor voice, manly presence and admirable acting. He sang also as Tannhäuser, and was the original Walther von Stolzing and Tristan in England; he was admired in all three parts. On June 20 he sang at a Richter Concert, St. James's Hall, with Frau Sucher in her husband's ' Waldfräulein,' and on June 26 in the Choral Symphony. On July 26 he was the original Parsifal at Bayreuth. In 1883 he was engaged at Vienna, the result of successful ' Gastspiele ' there before, in operas of Wagner, Meyerbeer, etc., and on Oct. 4 he and Materna were the first Tristan and Isolde in that city. He became a great favourite there. In operas new to Vienna he sang the tenor parts in Marschner's ' Vampyr,' Massenet's ' Cid,' Verdi's ' Otello,' Merlin, on production of Goldmark's opera of that name, Admetus in the revival of ' Alceste,' Rinaldo in the revival of ' Armida,' etc. On June 1, 1906, he retired on a pension. A. C.

(2) HANS, his son, is also an esteemed ' Heldentenor,' who appeared first at the Vienna Opera and later at Prague and elsewhere (Riemann).

WINN, WILLIAM (b. Bramham, Yorks, May 8, 1828; d. Willesden, June 4, 1868), bass singer, was taught singing by Sir G. Smart and Schira and made his first appearance in London in ' St. Paul,' Oct. 24, 1855, at St. Martin's Hall. He became popular in oratorio and glee music. In 1864 he was elected a gentleman of Her Majesty's Chapels Royal, and in 1867 vicar choral of St. Paul's. He was a member of the Noblemen and Gentlemen's Catch Club, and

Honorary Secretary of the Round, Catch and Canon Club. His song 'Nothing more,' and the prize glee, 'Go, Rose,' are well-known favourites. His elder daughter and pupil, FLORENCE (*b.* Nov. 1857), was a favourite contralto concert singer who made her début in 1881.　　　　　　　　　　　　　　　A. C.

WINNEBERGER, PAUL ANTON (*b.* Mergentheim a./d. Tauber, 1758 ; *d.* Hamburg, Feb. 8, 1821), violoncellist, organist and composer. He studied under Magister Heilig, Abbé Vogler and Holzbauer. At the age of 9 he was court altist at Mergentheim, at 14 organist at the Dominican church. He studied theology at Würzburg and Heidelberg Universities, and *c.* 1778 was teacher at the Music Seminary, organist at the Jesuit church and solo violoncello at the theatre, Mannheim. In 1780 he became solo violoncello and music director to Prince Wallerstein, and from 1783 teacher and violoncellist at the French Theatre, Hamburg. He composed an opera, violoncello concertos, quartets, trios, sonatas, etc. (*Mendel*; E. v. d. Straeten, *History of the Violoncello* ; Q.-L.).

WINSLATE, RICHARD, organist at Winchester Cathedral, *c.* 1550. Of his compositions, only a piece for organ or virginal, 'Lucem Tuam,' has been found, contained in the Redford MS., B.M. Add. MSS. 29,996.

　　　　　　　　　　　　　　　　E. v. d. s.

WINTER, PETER VON (*b.* Mannheim, 1755[1] ; *d.* Munich, Oct. 17, 1825), an opera composer, much esteemed in his day.

At 11 years old he was a violinist in the Elector Karl Theodor's celebrated band. He had some instruction in composition from the Abbé Vogler, but really formed himself as a composer later in life. In 1776 he became musik-director of the court theatre, and in this post made acquaintance with Mozart, to whom he took a great dislike, and whom he damaged later in Vienna by spreading false reports about his private life.[2] When the court removed from Mannheim to Munich Winter followed ; in 1794 he was made vice Kapellmeister, and in 1798 court Kapellmeister. This post he retained to his death, and was treated with the greatest consideration, receiving on more than one occasion leave of absence for two or three years. On one occasion he presumed too far on this leniency, and was thereby in disgrace for a time. He visited Vienna twice, first in 1781, when he produced three ballets, and again during the years between 1793 and 1797, when he had nine operas performed at the Burgtheater and Schikaneder's theatre, including 'Das unterbrochene Opferfest' (Burgtheater, June 14, 1796), and a cantata 'Timoteo o gli effetti della musica' (1796), by the Tonkünstler Societät. The intercourse he main-

tained with Salieri was important as inducing him to pay more attention to the vocal part of his compositions. This is perceptible in all the works written in Vienna. He also visited Italy (Naples and Venice, 1791 and 1793), Prague (1796), Paris (1802 and 1806), London (1803–05), and Italy again (Milan and Genoa, 1817–19). Besides a number of operas, of which the greatest and most lasting favourites were 'Maria von Montalban' (Munich, 1798) and the 'Das unterbrochene Opferfest,' popular on account of its catching melodies, Winter composed a quantity of church music, cantatas, lieder, partsongs and instrumental works (symphonies, overtures and concerted pieces for various instruments), most of which were printed, but have long since disappeared. His Singing Method (Schott, Mayence, with German, French and Italian words) is, however, still of value.

We append a list of his operas, classified according to the places where they were first produced :

MUNICH.—' Armida ' (1778), ' Cora ed Alonzo ' and ' Leonardo e Blandine ' (1779), ' Helena und Paris ' (German, 1780), ' Der Bettelstudent ' (German operetta, 1781), ' Bellerophon ' (German, 1782), ' Scherz, List, und Rache ' (operetta, 1784), ' Circe ' (1788), ' Jery und Bätely ' (German, 1790), ' Psyche ' and ' Der Sturm ' (Shakespeare's ' Tempest,' 1793), ' Marie von Montalban ' (German, 1798), ' Der Frauenbund ' (German, 1805), ' Colmal ' (1809), ' Die Blinden ' (German, 1810).

NAPLES.—' Antigone ' (1791).

VENICE.—' Catone in Utica ' (1791), ' I Fratelli rivali ' and ' Il Sacrificio di Creta ' (1792).

VIENNA.—' Armida und Rinaldo ' (German melodrama with chorus and dances, 1793), ' I due vedovi ' and ' Das unterbrochene Opferfest ' (German, 1796), ' Babylons Pyramiden ' (German, with Mederitsch, nicknamed Gallus, 1797), and ' Das Labyrinth ' (sequel to the ' Zauberflöte,' German, 1798).[3]

PRAGUE.—' Ogus, il trionfo del bel sesso ' (1796).

PARIS.—' Tamerlan ' (1802), ' Castor e Pollux ' (1806).

LONDON.—' Calypso ' (1803), ' Proserpina ' (1804), ' Zaire ' (1805).

MILAN.—' I due Valdomiri ' and ' Maometto ' (1817), ' Etelinda ' (1818), ' Sanger und Schneider,' written in Geneva but first produced in Munich (1820), his last work for the stage.

Besides the above, the following exist in various libraries (see *Q.-L.*) :

' La Belisa, ossia la fedeltà riconosciuta ' : ' Elise, Gräfin von Hilburg ' (1797) ; ' Heinrich IV.' (ballet) ; ' Ines de Castro ' (ballet) ; ' La Mort d'Hector ' (ballet) ; ' La Morte d'Orfeo ed Euridice ' (ballet with songs) ; ' Salomons Urteil ' ; ' Wittwer und Wittwe.'

Of his church works there are in the Royal Chapel at Munich 26 masses, 2 Requiems, 3 Stabat Maters, and a quantity of graduales, offertoires, vespers, etc. For the Protestant court chapel he wrote 7 cantatas, 2 oratorios, 'Der sterbende Jesus' and 'La Betulia liberata,' a German Stabat Mater, and smaller anthems. (See *Q.L.* for detailed list.)

Winter's strong points were just declamation, agreeable melody, brilliant choral writing and rich instrumentation, which he never suffered to overpower the voices. His weakness was in counterpoint, which he had never found an opportunity of mastering thoroughly. As a whole his church music is preferable to his operas ; which, though vocal and melodious, have neither originality, greatness, dramatic force, fire nor genius. His airs are specially weak, never seeming fully developed. Winter could amuse and entertain, but to seize the imagination, to touch, to agitate, was beyond

---

[1] The early dates have been fairly well established in Q.-L., which is here followed.

[2] Jahn's *Mozart*, 2nd ed. i. 363, 695.

[3] These two were written for Schikaneder's theatre.

him. This is why even his best and most popular works disappeared from the stage soon after his death. C. F. P.

WINTERFELD, KARL GEORG AUGUST VIVIGENS VON (b. Berlin, Jan. 28, 1784; d. there, Feb. 19, 1852), was educated for the law, which he studied at Halle. After holding a succession of official posts at Berlin and Breslau, he retired on a pension in 1847 and devoted himself to musical literature. He had made a large collection of materials in Italy, which he left at his death to the Berlin Library. His most important books are as follows :

Johannes Pierluigi von Palestrina (1832).
Johannes Gabrieli und sein Zeitalter (1834).
Der evangelische Kirchengesang und sein Verhältniss zur Kunst des Tonsatzes (1843–47).
Über K. Christian Friedrich Faschs geistliche Gesangswerke (1839).
Dr. Martin Luthers deutsche geistliche Lieder (1840).
Über Herstellung des Gemeinde- und Chorgesangs in der evangelischen Kirche (1848).
Zur Geschichte heiliger Tonkunst (1850–52).

(*Riemann.*) M.

WIPPERN, LOUISE (HARRIERS-WIPPERN) (b. Hildesheim or Bückeburg,[1] 1835 or 1837 ; d. Görbersdorf, Silesia, Oct. 5, 1878), made her first appearance at Berlin on June 16, 1857, and played Agathe in ' Der Freischütz,' and Alice in ' Robert le Diable,' with such success as to obtain a permanent engagement in Berlin in September of the same year. She kept the post until her retirement, and was a great favourite both in dramatic and in the lighter parts, viz. Iphigenia, Jessonda, Pamina, Susanna, Fidelio, Inez (' L'Africaine '), the Princess of Navarre (' John of Paris '), Mrs. Ankerstrom (' Gustavus III.'), Gretchen (' Faust '), Elizabeth (' Tannhäuser '), Valentine, etc. In Dec. 1859 she married at Bückeburg an architect named Harriers. She sang for three seasons in London at Her Majesty's, appearing first, June 11, 1864, as Alice. Her parts in London were but few, viz. Pamina (July 6, 1865), Amelia (' Un Ballo '), Leonora (' Trovatore '), Zerlina (' Don Giovanni ') ; but several of her best parts were in the hands of Mlle. Tietjens, then in the zenith of her fame and powers, and Mme. Harriers-Wippern was placed at great disadvantage. In May 1868, while at Königsberg, she was seized with diphtheria, which compelled her to visit Italy. She reappeared at Berlin, Jan. 5, 1870, and sang there for a year or more, but her voice and strength were so much impaired that she was compelled to retire from regular work. She died from another throat disease at the Hydropathic Establishment at Görbersdorf, Silesia. A. C.

WIRTH, EMANUEL (b. Luditz, near Karlsbad, Oct. 18, 1842 ; d. Berlin, Jan. 5, 1923), violinist, played viola in the JOACHIM QUARTET (q.v.).

After study under Mildner and Kittl at the Prague Conservatoire, he received his first engagement as leader of the orchestra at Baden Baden. In 1864 he was appointed leader of the German Opera and ' Society ' concerts at Rotterdam, and also undertook the duties of professor at the Conservatoire. In 1877 he accepted an invitation from Joachim to settle in Berlin as teacher at the Hochschule, and as viola in the Joachim Quartet. His popularity with Berlin audiences was shown on the occasion of his Jubilee in 1902. The ' Trio evenings,' which he founded in conjunction with Barth and Hausmann, were long a feature of Berlin musical life. In these he took the violin part, but it is as viola player in the Joachim Quartet that he will be best remembered. W. W. C.

WISE, MICHAEL (b. Wiltshire,[2] c. 1648 ; d. Salisbury, Aug. 24, 1687), was admitted a child of the Chapel Royal under Captain Cooke in 1660. In 1663 he became a lay-clerk of St. George's Chapel, Windsor. In 1668 he was appointed organist and master of the choristers of Salisbury Cathedral. On Jan. 6, 1675/76, he was admitted a gentleman of the Chapel Royal in the place of Raphael Courteville, deceased, being described in the cheque-book as ' a counter-tenor from Salisbury.' During the royal progresses of Charles II. Wise is said to have had the right to play the organ in any church visited by the King. At the time of the coronation of James II. (Apr. 23, 1685) he was suspended from his office, and Edward Morton officiated in his stead. The cause of such suspension is unknown. There is in the Bagford collection in the British Museum library a coarse political song, published in London in 1680, entitled ' The Wiltshire Ballad,'[3] from which it appears that Wise was supposed to have been engaged with other Wiltshire men in getting up a petition for calling a Parliament. It is possible that this siding with those opposed to the court policy may have been made the pretext for his suspension. On Jan. 27, 1686/87, Wise was appointed almoner and master of the choristers of St. Paul's Cathedral. But he did not hold those offices long. On Aug. 24, 1687, being at Salisbury, he had a dispute with his wife, in the heat of which he rushed out into the street, and the hour being late, was challenged by a watchman, with whom he began a quarrel, and received a blow on the head from the man's bill which killed him. He was buried near the west door of the Cathedral.

Six of his anthems, ' Prepare ye the way,' ' Awake, put on,' ' The ways of Sion,' ' Thy beauty, O Israel,' ' Awake up, my glory,' and ' Blessed is he,' are printed in Boyce's ' Cathedral Music,' and an Evening Service in E♭ in Rimbault's ' Cathedral Music.' Other anthems and services exist in MS. in the Tudway collection, the R.C.M., and the choir-books of many of the cathedrals. ' I charge you, O daughters,' is in Dering's ' Cantica sacra,'

---

[1] *Neue Berliner Musikzeitung.*

[2] Probably at Salisbury.
[3] Reprinted by the Ballad Society in *The Bagford Ballads.*

1674 ; ' I will sing ' is in Langdon's ' Divine
Harmony,' 1774.   See also *D.N.B.* and *Q.-L.*
Some catches by him are included in ' The
Musical Companion,' 1667, and his duet ' Old
Chiron thus preached to his pupil Achilles,' has
often been reprinted.   w. h. h.

WITKOWSKI, Georges Martin (*b.* Mosta-
ganem, Algeria, Jan. 6, 1867), began life as
an officer before becoming a composer. The
Grand Théâtre at Nantes produced his ' Le
Maître à chanter' (1 act) in 1891, but he felt
the need for serious musical study, and worked
with V. d'Indy at composition from 1894–97.
Having left the army he settled at Lyons where
he founded the Schola of Lyons (choral society)
and the Société des Grands Concerts, which he
conducts. He assumed also the direction of the
Conservatoire at Lyons. His first important
composition was a quintet (1897) unpublished
2 symphonies (1900, 1910), a quartet (1902),
a sonata (PF. and vln., 1907) followed. His
' Poème de la maison ' was first performed at
Lyons, Jan. 26, 1919. It is a vast composition
in 5 parts for solo voices, chorus and orchestra,
in the nature of a dramatic symphony or
oratorio, largely designed and very characteristic. Another work, ' Mon Lac, prélude,
variations et finale (PF. and orch ; 1st perf.
Lyons, Nov. 20, 1921, by the pianist B. Selva),
displays also the mark of a strong individuality.
His most recent compositions are ' Quatre
poèmes' (vln. and orch. op. 25 ; 1925).

Bibl.—*Revue musicale*, 1926, No. 5, M. Boucher, *G. M.
Witkowski* (with bibl. and list of works).
                                              M. L. P.

WITT, Christian Friedrich (*b.* Altenburg,
1660 ; *d.* there, Apr. 13, 1716), court Kapellmeister at Altenburg, and one of the best
composers of his time. A passacaglia of his
was published as the work of J. S. Bach. He
composed a number of cantatas which appear
to be lost. He also wrote : ' Psalmodia sacra '
(1715, and a later undated edition), 3 French
overtures, a 7-part sonata, 4 suites, organ and
harpsichord pieces (*Riemann* ; *Q.-L.*).

WITT, Friedrich (*b.* Haltenbergstetten,
Würtemberg, 1771 ; *d.* Würzburg, 1837), was
violinist at the court of Oettingen - Wallerstein,
c. 1790, toured to bring out his compositions,
and obtained in 1802, through the performance
of one of his oratorios, the post of Kapellmeister
at Würzburg. He wrote 2 operas, 2 oratorios,
masses, cantatas, symphonies, concertos for
various instruments, chamber music, pieces for
military band, etc. (*Mendel* ; *Q.-L.*).

WOELFL,[1] Joseph (*b.* Salzburg, *c.* 1772 ;
d. Great Marylebone Street, London, May 21,
1812). His instruction in composition and
pianoforte-playing was due to Leopold Mozart [2]

[1] The uncertainties that envelop Woelfl extend even to the
spelling of his name, which appears variously as Wölfl, Woefel,
Woelfle, Wölfel, Wolfell, Woelf, Woelft, Wulff and Woelfl, the last
of which, on the whole, seems most probably correct. The Parisians
despaired of either pronouncing or spelling his name, and called
him Wolf, as they spell Kreutzer *Kretsche*, and to this day persist in
writing *Listz*.
[2] In the Prospectus of ' The Harmonic Budget ' Woelfl is stated
to be ' a scholar of the great Mozart,' which seems most improbable.

and Michael Haydn. He was a chorister in
Salzburg Cathedral in 1783–86. No mention
of him occurs, however, in the correspondence
of Leopold Mozart and his son. In 1790 he
went to Vienna and was taken thence to
Warsaw by Count Oginsky. Here, in 1792 or
1793, he began his public career and subsequently in Vienna, where he was received with
favour, both as composer and performer. His
first opera, ' Der Höllenberg,' was composed
to a libretto by Schikaneder, and brought out
at this theatre in 1795. This was followed by
' Das schöne Milchmädchen ' for the National
Theatre in 1797, and ' Der Kopf ohne Mann '
at Schikaneder's in 1798. The value of these
pieces does not appear to have been great, but
they were successful at Vienna, and the last
two were performed at Leipzig, and ' Der Kopf
ohne Mann ' at Prague also.[3] To this period
the curious combination-piece, ' Liebe macht
kurzen Prozess,' may possibly belong. On the
whole, Woelfl was not of much account as a
composer for the stage. As a pianoforte virtuoso
he stepped into the first rank, and was even
able to contest the palm of supremacy with
Beethoven (*q.v.* Vol. I. p. 277). At Vienna
the young composer married, in 1798, Therese
Klemm, an actress at the National Theatre ;
and in the summer of the same year set out
on an extended tour, whether with or without
Madame Woelfl seems uncertain. He travelled
through Brunn to Prague, Leipzig, Dresden,
Berlin and Hamburg. He had intentions of
going on to London,[4] but seems to have left
Hamburg at the beginning of December with
Righini, probably for Berlin.[5]

The next clear mention of Woelfl is at a
concert in Leipzig, Oct. 21, 1800.[6] He arrived
in Paris in Sept. 1801, and soon began to
attract great attention. On the 5th Brumaire
(Oct. 26) the *Journal de Paris* described him as
' l'un des hommes les plus étonnans de l'Europe
sur le piano.' He speedily assumed a leading
position, and in the next spring was reported
to be writing an opera for the Théâtre-

[3] *A.M.Z.* vol. i. p. 448 and *Intell. Blatt*, xi. vol. iv. p. 253 ; vol. v.
p. 249.
[4] *A.M.Z.* p. 31.
[5] *Ibid.* p. 410. The statement here made differs from that of all
other biographers. Schilling seems to suggest that Woelfl returned
to Vienna, but all other writers assert that he went from Hamburg
to London, and from London to Paris, reaching the French capital
in 1801. The facts given in the text show that this account cannot
be correct, and it seems improbable that Woelfl went to London at
all at this time, though J. W. Davison, in the Preface to his
edition of the ' Non Plus Ultra ' sonata, declares, without giving
any authority, that the Military Concerto (op. 43) was composed in
London in 1800. On the other hand, the following circumstances
seem, taken together, to make strongly against the London visit :
(1) Woelfl left Hamburg in Dec. 1799 *with Righini* (*A.M.Z.* vol.
ii. p. 410). Now Righini almost certainly was going to Berlin to
produce ' Tigrane ' in the early part of 1800 (*A.M.Z.* vol. ii. p. 620).
(2) Woelfl's letter to Lodi (*A.M.Z.* vol. ii. *Intell. Blatt.* No. x.) is
dated ' Auf der Reise, den 15. Decemb. 1799,' which suggests that he
had left Hamburg and was on a journey in Germany. This is
exactly the date at which he would be travelling to Berlin with
Righini.
(3) A Berlin letter of Apr. 1800 (*A.M.Z.* vol. ii. p. 622) declares
that Woelfl had been there three separate times since the preceding
June ; it is hardly likely that he went three times from Hamburg
to Berlin and back again *between June and December* 1799.
(4) No trace of him in England at this time is forthcoming.
(5) The programme of the concert in London on May 27, 1805,
at which he appeared, pointedly asserts that it was ' his first performance in England ' (*Morning Chronicle*, May 27, 1805).
[6] Dörffel's *Geschichte*.

Feydeau.[1] This epoch may be regarded as the culminating point in his career. Henceforward he falls, in some strange way, under a cloud.

Whether this was the result of a *faux pas* cannot be exactly determined. Fétis's circumstantial story that Woelfl struck up a friendship at Paris with the bass-singer Ellmenreich, who was given to card-sharping, travelled to Brussels with him, got into trouble with the police and came to London in 1805, where Woelfl died in poverty, seems to be incorrect in almost every detail. That Woelfl was brought into relations with Ellmenreich by the project of the latter for establishing a German Opera in Paris is likely enough,[2] but Woelfl appears to have been in Paris throughout 1804,[3] whereas Ellmenreich left Paris at the end of 1803, and was at Vienna at the beginning of 1805.[4] Moreover, Woelfl had no reason to complain of his reception in England in 1805 ; he certainly did not die in obscurity, and it is not likely that he died in poverty.[5]

To return to certainties ; the three years and a half (Sept. 1801–April 1805) during which Paris was the centre of Woelfl's life were, on the whole, years of success. In the early part of 1804 his opera, ' L'Amour romanesque,' was produced at the Théâtre-Feydeau with success. In the next year he made his most considerable venture with an heroic opera in three acts, called 'Fernando, ou Les Maures,' which was brought out anonymously at the Théâtre-Feydeau. It was produced in very unfavourable circumstances, and was more of a failure than it deserved to be.[6] Perhaps this mischance led Woelfl to conceive a disgust for Paris. He certainly left the French capital within a month or two without any other apparent reason, and repaired to London,[7] where he arrived about the beginning of May 1805. The first trace of him is in an advertisement on May 18 of a benefit concert by Mr. and Mrs. Ashe, which states that he had just arrived in England, and would perform a concerto at this concert on May 27— ' his first performance in England.' Besides the

concerto (MS.), a grand symphony (MS.) by Woelfl was performed at the concert, and pianoforte concertos by him were played at other concerts on June 1 and June 5, on the former occasion by himself. He was received with the greatest applause,[8] and everything shows that he retained his popularity throughout his seven years' residence in London. In 1806 his concerto known as ' The Calm ' created a positive *furore*, being played at four concerts in about two months, and new compositions by him were almost annually put forward as attractions at the most important concerts.[9] In 1810 the prospectus of ' The Harmonic Budget' presents him as the fashionable composer of the day, and a portrait is one of the allurements to subscribers. As a composer for the stage Woelfl did not make any greater mark in London than in Vienna or Paris. Still, two ballets by him were produced at the King's Theatre, ' La Surprise de Diane,' on Dec. 21, 1805, and ' Alzire ' (founded on Voltaire's ' Alzire '), on Jan. 27, 1807. Both, especially the former, pleased. His abilities were fully appreciated by the artists and by the public, nor is any trace of a falling off in popular esteem discoverable. On May 16, 1812, a new concerto of his was played at Salomon's concert by Cudmore.[10] A week later *The Morning Chronicle* of May 23 contained the announcement,

' Died, on Thursday morning ' [*i.e.* May 21] ' after a short illness, at his lodgings in Great Mary-le-bone Street, Mr. Woelfl, the celebrated pianoforte player.' [11]

It is impossible, therefore, to understand the uncertainty as to the circumstances of Woelfl's death. An anxious discussion was maintained in the *A.M.Z.* in 1815 and 1816 [12] as to whether he was dead or not. It asserted that Woelfl had played at the Philharmonic Concerts, which did not begin till 1813, and the matter was only considered as settled by the marriage of Woelfl's widow to an oboist at Frankfort.[13]

Woelfl possessed remarkable qualifications for making a success in society. His portrait, about a year before his death, represents a handsome man, rather tall, somewhat stout, and of commanding presence.[14]

As a musician, Woelfl exhibits all the excellences that flow from a sound training. Like other composers of that time he wrote much trivial music, but his sympathies were steadily

---

[1] *A.M.Z.* vol. iv. p. 604.
[2] Cp. *A.M.Z.* vol. iv. pp. 111 and 320.
[3] *A.M.Z.* vol. vi. p. 478 ; vol. vii. p. 142.
[4] *Ibid.* vol. vi. pp. 281, 469, 502.
[5] It may be added that it is not easy to see when Woelfl and Ellmenreich could have been at Brussels together. At the beginning of 1802 both were in Paris. In the spring and summer Ellmenreich went to London (*A.M.Z.* vol. iv. pp. 323 and 781), but Woelfl stayed in Paris (*A.M.Z.* vol. iv. p. 604). However, in the autumn of 1802 Woelfl was at Amsterdam (*A.M.Z.* vol. v. p. 115), and was thought to be going to London, and it may have been about this time that the two got into trouble at Brussels. They are next heard of in Sept. 1803 (*A.M.Z.* vol. v. p. 865), and are then both in Paris. But Woelfl's position there seems just as good after this date as before it.
[6] See on the whole affair, *A.M.Z.* vol. vii. p. 422.
[7] One of the strangest of the romantic tales current about Woelfl must be mentioned here. Schilling asserts that he was named music-master to the Empress Josephine in 1804, and followed her after her divorce (*i.e.* of course, at the beginning of 1810) to Switzerland. Growing weary of the lonely mountain life, he went down the Rhine by boat, and so to England. This story seems to be a pure fiction. Woelfl may have been music-master to the Empress, but he went to London in 1805, and is to be found in London every year from that date to the time of his death. In 1810 he was engaged on a monthly publication, ' The Harmonic Budget,' which must have precluded long absence from London. Finally, the Empress Josephine did not go to Switzerland in 1810, or at any time after her divorce.

[8] *A.M.Z.* vol. vii. p. 756.
[9] Besides MS. works which may have been novelties, and sonatas, etc., we find the following ' first performances ' : Symphony (June 15, 1808, Ferrari's Concert) ; PF. Concerto (Apr. 19, 1809, Ferrari's Concert) : Symphony (Mar. 28, 1811, New Musical Fund Concert) ; PF. Concerto (May 16, 1812, five days before his death, Salomon's Concert).
[10] *Times*, May 16, 1812.
[11] A similar notice, giving the same date (May 21), appears in the *Gentleman's Magazine*.
[12] *A.M.Z.* vol. xvii. p. 311 ; vol. xviii. pp. 291 and 762.
[13] Mme. Woelfl appears to have been established as a singer at Frankfort since 1804 (*A.M.Z.* vol. vi. p. 402). Examination of the Philharmonic programmes reveals no trace of Woelfl as a performer.
[14] There was a portrait by Tielker. This, or another, engraved by Scheffner, was issued with the *A.M.Z.* for Feb. 19, 1806. The portrait in ' The Harmonic Budget ' was drawn by Pyne and engraved by Mayer. The original water-colour sketch by Pyne is in the Hope collection of portraits at Oxford. Much of what is stated in the text is due to reminiscences of Potter's conversations, kindly communicated by his son, Dr. Potter, and by A. J. Hipkins.

on behalf of a more elevated style. Pupils who wished him to teach them how to play the showy variations that conclude his celebrated 'Non Plus Ultra' sonata always met with a rebuff, and were not allowed to go on to the variations till they had mastered the opening allegro. The ease with which he threw off trifles to catch the popular ear did not blind him to their trivial character or impair his respect for his art. Consequently, much of his work [1]—sonatas, quartets, concertos and symphonies—is thoroughly solid, showing great instrumental effect and, especially, contrapuntal artifice.[2] The only pupil of Woelfl who attained much eminence was Cipriani POTTER (q.v.).　　　J. H. M.

WOHLTEMPERIRTE CLAVIER, DAS— 'The well-tempered Clavier'—better known in England as 'The 48 Preludes and Fugues'[3] of Johann Sebastian Bach, is in two parts, each containing twenty-four preludes and twenty-four fugues. The first part was completed at Cöthen in 1722 when Bach was in his thirty-eighth year, and to this alone he gave the above name. Subsequently (1744) he finished twenty-four more preludes and fugues 'through all the major and minor keys'; and so like in design to the former series are these, that they have come to be regarded as the second part, the entire collection being now universally known under the one title.

His own full title, very like that of an earlier work on similar lines by Bernhard Christian WEBER (q.v.), is as follows :

Das wohl temperirte Clavier oder *Praeludia* und *Fugen* durch alle *Tone* und *Semitonia* so wohl *tertiam majorem* oder *Ut Re Mi* anlangend, als auch *tertiam minorem* oder *Re Mi Fa* betreffend. Zum Nutzen und Gebrauch der Lehrbegierigen *Musical*ischen Jugend als auch derer in diesem *Studio* schon *habil* seyenden besondern Zeit Vertreib aufgesetzet und verfertiget von *Johann Sebastian Bach* p. t. Hochfürstl. Anhalt. Cöthenischen *Capell*-Meistern und *Directore* derer Cammer-*Musiquen. Anno* 1722.'[4]

It was Bach's intention by this work to test the system of equal temperament in tuning. To this end he furnishes a prelude and fugue in each key, the keys following one another not according to their relationship, but simply in the order of chromatic ascent.

A credible tradition says that most of the first part was written rapidly; in a place where Bach had no regular musical occupation, and where he was deprived of any musical instrument—probably when accompanying his prince. This tradition is supported by Gerber, whose father, Heinrich Gerber, was a pupil of Bach in Leipzig soon after 1722. Forkel, however, who probably possessed some general information on

[1] Previous editions of this Dictionary contained an elaborate and carefully annotated list of Woelfl's compositions.
[2] See *e.g.* the Minuet of the G minor Symphony.
[3] For a concise analysis of each number see *The '48,' Bach's Wohltemperirtes Clavier* ('Musical Pilgrim'), 2 vols., by J. A. Fuller Maitland (Oxford Univ. Press, 1926.)
[4] 'The Well-tempered Clavier, or preludes and fugues in all the tones and semitones, both with the major third or Ut, Re, Mi and with the minor third or Re, Mi, Fa. For the use and practice of young musicians who desire to learn, as well as for those who are already skilled in this study, by way of amusement: made and composed by Johann Sebastian Bach, Kapellmeister to the Grand Duke of Anhalt-Cöthen and director of his chamber-music, 1722.' The title is almost identical with that of the work by Bernhard Christian WEBER (q.v.).

the subject from Bach's sons, says that earlier compositions were used in compiling the first part. Many of the preludes had certainly already appeared as independent compositions. In re-writing these Bach often considerably lengthened them, the one in C♯ to the extent of nearly forty bars. Eleven of them were given in a short form in the Clavierbüchlein (1720), written for his son Friedemann. When used for the later work, they were, however, more fully developed, especially those in C major, C minor, D minor and E minor. The A minor fugue, too, is without doubt an earlier composition. Spitta considers it belongs to 1707 or 1708. It is an open copy of one in the same key by Buxtehude, and judging from the pedal at its conclusion, it was not at first intended for the clavichord. Perhaps it is therefore somewhat out of keeping with the rest of the work—written so manifestly for this instrument. Witness for instance the beginning of the 16th bar of the E♭ minor fugue, where the upper part stops short on C♭, evidently because D♭ was not available on most clavichords. Again, in the 30th bar of the A major fugue it is apparent that the imitation in the right hand is accommodated to a limited keyboard. In the second part of the work D♭ (C♯) above the line occurs but twice in the 25th bar of the fugue in C sharp, and in the 68th bar of the prelude in A flat. In compiling this, Bach again availed himself of earlier compositions, though not to such an extent as in the first part. The prelude in C is given, however, as a piece of 17 bars' length in a Clavierbuch of J. P. Kellner with the date '3 Juli 1726.' The fugue in C♯ major exists also in C major, and the prelude in D minor exists in another version. (See B.-G. xxxvi. 224-6.) The fugue in G had twice before been associated with other preludes. (See B.-G. xxxvi. 114 ff. and 220.) The A♭ fugue first stood in F; it was shorter by more than one-half, and it had another prelude. (See B. G. xxxvi. 113.) Other instances of a similar kind may be adduced.

Three or four original MSS. are existing of the first part of the work; not one (complete) exists of the second. Still, notwithstanding the many revisions Bach made of the first part, there is perhaps, as Carl von Bruyck says (*Technische und ästhetische Analysen*, p. 68), on the whole a richer and broader display of contrapuntal art in the fugues of the second part. (See also Sir Hubert Parry's *Johann Sebastian Bach*, chap xiii.)

The three oldest printed editions appeared in 1800-01. One was issued by Nägeli of Zürich, another by Simrock of Bonn and Paris, and the third by Kühnel (now Peters) of Leipzig. The first was dedicated to the Paris Conservatoire de Musique, the matter being supplied by Schwencke. In it the second part is placed first : many of the older readings are given, and it has the long versions of the preludes which most editions since have copied. The third was revised by Forkel, and it is to that he refers in his well-known treatise. The first English edition was that edited by S. Wesley and C. Horn, and published 1810–13.[1] The B.-G. xiv. (1865), by Franz Kroll, with an appendix of various readings, was issued without reference to the British Museum autograph of Part II. (see below) Its readings were incorporated in a subsequent volume of the B.-G. edition, xlv. (i.) which also contains the readings of the Zürich autograph.

Editors have not been slow to make alterations in the text of Bach. One of the most glaring of these is the bar introduced by Schwencke in the middle of the first prelude. Yet this bar has been retained by Czerny, by Wesley and Horn, and by many others. It is even used by Gounod in his 'Meditation.' As an editorial curiosity it is worth preserving:

father, the Marshal Lowendahl. ' He received an excellent education, having Lolli—whom he closely resembled in character and disposition —to teach him the violin. Owing to reverses of fortune, Woldemar became the head of a wandering troop of artists, who eventually settled at Clermont Ferrand, where Woldemar died. Without being a member of the staff, Woldemar wrote several articles on music for the *Courrier des Spectacles*, a theatrical journal of the Revolutionary period. It was in this publication that his *Commandements du violon*, a facetious imitation of the Decalogue, was printed. He also composed a number of pieces and concertos for the violin, and a *Grande Méthode de violon* (Paris, *Cochet*)—which is to-day difficult to meet with—*Le Nouvel Art de l'archet* (ibid.), and *L'Étude élémentaire de l'archet moderne*. Woldemar, like Lolli, attempted an extension of the compass of the violin by adding a lower fifth string (C in the

Bar 22.   SCHWENCKE.   Bar 23.

Of the First Part three autographs are known; one formerly belonging to Nägeli, and now in the Town Library of Zürich, another in the possession of Professor Wagener of Marburg and a third in the State Library of Berlin.[2] Of the Second Part no complete autograph is known to exist. The authenticity of the autographs of certain numbers in the Berlin State (Royal) Library is examined by A. Dörffel in the preface to B.-G. xlv. For many years there remained in comparative obscurity original autographs, now in the British Museum, of nearly all [3] the preludes and fugues of the Second Part. They were bought at Clementi's sale by Emett. During one of Mendelssohn's visits to England (June 1842) Emett showed them to him, and he at once recognised them as being in Bach's handwriting.[4] Later on, in or about 1855, Sterndale Bennett saw them, and he too pronounced them to be in the handwriting of Bach. After that they so far lapsed out of sight that they are not mentioned even by Spitta.   F. W.; addns. M.; rev. C.

WOLDEMAR, MICHAEL (*b.* Orleans, Sept. 17, 1750; *d.* Clermont Ferrand, Jan. 1816), violinist and composer, who came of a well-to-do mercantile family. It is said that his real name was Michael, and that he assumed that of Woldemar, at the request of his god-

bass), and for this instrument, which he called a 'violin-alto,' he wrote a concerto with orchestra. Urhan Chrétien (*b.* Feb. 16, 1790) often played on this instrument of Woldemar's invention at the Paris Conservatoire concerts.

BIBL.—HUET, *Écoles de violon*; POUGIN, *Supplément* to *Fétis*; *Biog. des Mus.*; MASON CLARKE, *Dic. Fiddlers*; FAYOLLE, etc.
E. H.-A.

WOLF, THE. (1) A term applied to the harsh howling sound of certain chords on keyed instruments, particularly the organ, when tuned by any form of unequal temperament.

The form of unequal temperament most widely adopted was the mean-tone system. The rule of this system is that its fifths are all a quarter of a comma flat. The major thirds are perfect, and are divided into two equal whole tones, each of which is a mean between the major and minor tones of the diatonic scale; hence the name Mean-tone System.

The total error of the whole circle of twelve fifths, at a quarter of a comma each, amounts to three commas. Since the circle of twelve perfect fifths fails to meet by about one comma, the circle of mean-tone fifths fails to meet by about two commas, or roughly, nearly half a semitone. In the mean-tone system on the ordinary key-board there is always one-fifth out of tune to this extent, usually the fifth G♯-E♭. There are also four false thirds, which are sharp to about the same extent, usually B-E♭, F♯-B♭, C♯-F and G♯-C. All chords into which any of these intervals enter are intolerable. (See TEMPERAMENT; TUNING).   R. H. M. B.

---

[1] Dr. Cummings has shown (*Mus. T.* Mar. 1885, p. 131) that the edition projected by Kollmann in 1799 was never published.
[2] See Spitta's *Bach* (Novello), ii. 665; B.-G. xiv. preface.
[3] Nos 4, 5 and 12 are wanting. An analysis of the readings differing from those of Kroll (B.-G. xiv.) was made by the writer (F. W.) and published in the first edition of this Dictionary.
[4] See Rockstro's *Life of Mendelssohn*, pp. 83, 84.

(2) In bowed instruments the Wolf occurs, owing to defective vibration of one or more notes of the scale. When it occurs, it is often found more or less in every octave and on every string. Different instruments have it in different places : it is most common at or near the fourth above the lowest note on the instrument, in the violin at C, in the violoncello at F. The more sonorous and brilliant the general tone, the more obtrusive it becomes ; if the tone be forced, a disagreeable jar is produced. Hence it is idle to attempt to play the wolf down : the player must humour the troublesome note. It is commonly believed that there is a wolf somewhere in all fiddles, and it is certain that it exists in some of the finest. Probably, however, it is always due to some defect in the construction or adjustment. The cause of the wolf is obscure, and probably not uniform : it may result from some excess or defect in the thicknesses, from unequal elasticity in the wood, from bad proportion or imperfect adjustment of the fittings, or from some defect in the proportions of the air chamber. It has also been suggested with a still greater show of probability that the wolf occurs on the note to which the body of the instrument acts as a resonating box, and that the particles of wood, set in vibration by this note, are unable to maintain the stretched string quite evenly. It may be palliated by reducing some of the thicknesses so as to diminish the general vibration, and by careful adjustment of the bar, bridge and soundpost ; but in the opinion of violin-makers where it is once established it cannot be radically cured.   E. J. P.

WOLF, ERNST WILHELM (b. Grossgehringen, near Gotha, 1735 ; d. Weimar, Dec. 7, 1792), Konzertmeister at Weimar, 1761, court Kapellmeister in 1768. He was a prolific composer in all branches of music, also author of a theoretical work, *Musikalischer Unterricht*, and *Auch eine Reise*, a musical journey. (List of works in Q.-L.)

WOLF, FERDINAND (b. Vienna, Dec. 8, 1796 ; d. there, Feb. 18, 1866), court librarian, wrote an important work for the study of mediæval monody, *Über die Lais, Sequenzen und Leiche*; also an essay on the music of the Arabs (*Mendel* ; *Riemann*).

WOLF, GEORG FRIEDRICH (b. Hainrode, Schwarzburg, c. 1762 ; d. Werningerode, 1814), Kapellmeister at Stolberg in 1785, and in 1802 at Werningerode. He composed pianoforte sonatas, motets, songs, etc., and wrote instruction books for pianoforte and singing, which appeared in several editions; also a musical dictionary (*Mendel* ; *Q.-L.*).

WOLF, HUGO (b. Windischgraz, south Styria, Mar. 13, 1860 ; d. Vienna, Feb. 22, 1903), the eminent song-writer, was the fourth son of a father of musical tastes, who was in a family leather business, and who intended tha the boy should eventually come into it too.

At an early age, however, Hugo showed that his real interests were in music and literature, and his conduct at the various schools through which he passed, disappointed his parents as much as his teachers. In 1875 the usual struggle over the question of his future career was fought, and ended in his father reluctantly consenting to let him enter the Vienna Conservatorium. One event in this year left a profound impression upon him. This was the visit of Wagner, who came to Vienna to conduct 'Tannhäuser' and 'Lohengrin.' He managed to see the great man for a moment, and although he got nothing for his pains but a more or less kindly snub, he became from this moment, and remained all his life, an ardent disciple. For the Conservatorium he had no more enthusiasm than he had for the schools, and he was expelled at the end of two years, which he had spent mainly in breaking the rules laid down for discipline and counterpoint. He was now thrown almost entirely on his own resources, for his father was able to do little for him, having had his business ruined by a fire. He eked out a living in his lodgings at Vienna by giving piano and violin lessons, but he could barely make enough to afford himself a meal a day, and the drudgery was so intolerable to him that he nearly emigrated to America. At this critical moment he was offered the post of second Kapellmeister at Salzburg, mainly through the influence of the composer Adalbert von Goldschmidt, who, with Mottl and the two Schalks, was kind to him in these Vienna days, lending him music and helping him to obtain pupils. But though he took the post he was back again in Vienna in two months' time, composing songs and sketching out his symphonic poem 'Penthesilea.' Some of his early work, consisting of miscellaneous piano and orchestral music, as well as of songs, was found amongst his papers after his death, some of it he seems to have destroyed.

The twelve 'Lieder aus der Jugendzeit' were written in 1877-78, and the collection of six 'Lieder für eine Frauenstimme' also dates from this period. But in these early years most of his time was given to reading rather than composing music. Bach, Beethoven, Mozart, Gluck and the other classics he devoured eagerly ; he worked hard at the songs of Schubert and Schumann, and for Berlioz and the French school he showed all his life such a predilection that he used to say in later years he must have had a few drops of Latin blood in his veins. He was able to make capital out of his strong musical tastes, for in 1886 he accepted the post of musical critic to the Vienna *Salonblatt*, and wrote for it for four years. He wrote, as well as felt, strongly, and while championing the cause of the older composers and breaking lances on behalf of Wagner and Bruckner, he poured scorn upon Boïto, Ponchielli, and the contemporary Italian operatic writers, he jeered mercilessly at the Philistines and the purveyors of conventional goods, and earned the undying hatred of Bülow as well as of the anti-Wagnerians by the outspoken terms in which he proclaimed his dislike of Brahms. But Wolf would never have attained the peculiar position he now holds amongst the great song-writers if he had given his attention solely to music. As a boy he was devoted to books, and his catholic taste, controlled by sound instinct, soon made him acquainted with the great writers of France and England, no less than with those of Germany. His favourite German poets were Goethe, Eichendorff, Kleist and Mörike, the popular Swabian pastor, who inspired Wolf to his first outburst of song-writing.

This was in 1888, the turning-point in his career. He had lost his father in the previous year (who died just too soon to see the publication of his son's first two volumes of songs), he had given up writing for the *Salonblatt* and had established himself in a friend's house at Perchtoldsdorf, a little village near Vienna. Suddenly the flood-gates were opened, and between Feb. and May of 1888 he wrote forty-three of his Mörike songs, and five months later finished the set in a single week, after composing a group of songs to words by Eichendorff. No sooner was the Mörike set completed than he turned to Goethe, and between October 1888 and February 1889 set fifty of his poems. After a break in the summer, during which he paid his third visit to Bayreuth (his first was in 1882 when he and Mottl went together), he composed forty-four songs on end from the 'Spanisches Liederbuch' of Heyse and Geibel, a volume of translations which had already inspired Schumann, Brahms, Cornelius and others. These were completed at the end of Apr. 1890. In June he set the six 'Alte Weisen' from poems of Gottfried Keller, who had just celebrated his seventieth birthday, and in the autumn he set to work on Heyse's 'Italienisches Liederbuch.' Of these, twenty-two were written without a break, and then—after this almost uninterrupted period of activity, in which something like 200 songs were written—came a silence which remained unbroken for more than three years. For that was how he composed. He would sit down to a volume of poems and work at white heat, flinging off songs day after day, hardly stopping to eat or sleep until the fit of inspiration had passed, when he would relapse into a fit of despondency and lethargy that lasted until the next furious outburst.

Meantime his work was gradually gaining recognition. Humperdinck had introduced him, in 1890, to the firm of Schott, who now arranged to publish his songs. Wolf recitals were given in Berlin, Stuttgart, Mannheim and other centres where there was less prejudice against the composer than in Vienna ; and in the autumn of 1890 he was commissioned to write incidental music for Ibsen's play *Das Fest auf Solhaug*. This was an effort to him to write, for he soon lost interest in the play, and was hampered by the restrictions imposed on him by the theatre. What he wanted to write was not incidental music to a play he did not care for, but an opera set to a text of his own choosing. He had been searching for one ever since 1882. He had thought at one time of setting *A Midsummer Night's Dream* and *The Tempest*, but gave up the idea. Mérimée's *Colomba* he rejected, and instinct told him that his friends Grohe and Liliencron might have offered him better alternatives for a hero than Buddha and Buffalo Bill. Eventually he found what he was looking for in *Der Dreispitz*, a translation of a novel by the Spanish author Pedro de Alarcon, in an adaptation by Frau Mayreder, which he had read and rejected five years earlier. He set feverishly to work on it on Mar. 3, 1895, and on July 9 he announced that he had finished it. The scoring occupied him till December, and the opera was given at Mannheim, with the title 'Der Corregidor,' on June 6, 1896. It appears to have been well received, but owing to operatic conditions it could not be repeated that season, and it was performed only once in his lifetime. The fit of inspiration which carried him through this opera with such incredible speed enabled him to complete the 'Italienisches Liederbuch'; and in the spring of 1897 he set to work on a German translation of some of Michelangelo's sonnets, and on the libretto of a new opera, 'Manuel Venegas,' also drawn from a novel by Alarcon. Three of the sonnets were written and half the first act of the opera was completed when his brain suddenly gave way. The furious mental energy which had manifested itself throughout his life in spasmodic outbursts now broke through its bonds, and in Sept. 1897 it was found necessary to confine him. He came out of the establishment the next year, and it was hoped that he would recover, but his sanity lasted only for a brief interval, and in the autumn of 1898 he entered the asylum at Vienna a raving lunatic. Paralysis soon overtook him, but he lingered on until Feb. 22, 1903, when he died at the age of 43. He was buried in the cemetery not far from the graves of Beethoven and Schubert.

It is as a song-writer that Wolf lives. His instrumental works consist only of the early symphonic poem 'Penthesilea'; a string quartet which, though still earlier, shows more signs of originality and power ; and a charming 'Italienische Serenade' for string-orchestra which was a later version of an early string quartet. The choral works include six sacred songs for unaccompanied voices to words by Eichendorff, written in 1881, and four compositions for chorus and orchestra : ' Christnacht,' ' Elfenlied ' (with words taken from *A Midsummer Night's Dream*), ' Der Feuerreiter,' and ' Dem Vaterland,' of which the last two had been conceived originally as songs for a solo voice. The two operas and the incidental music to Ibsen's play complete the list of his works apart from the songs, and the operas themselves are less in the nature of operas than of collections of songs. The characterisation is wonderfully strong, and the writing is as rich and free and complex as it is in the most striking of his songs. ' Der Corregidor ' is, in fact, a storehouse of beautiful things, but Wolf had little sense of the stage and not much capacity for adapting his methods to its requirements. His nature was entirely lyrical, and what stirred him to utterance was poetry, and poetry not spread over a situation but crystallised in a poem.

A song to him was poetry absorbed and recreated in terms of something which was neither melody by itself nor mere declamation but a fusion of the two. That is why each of his songs has a character of its own; each looks different on paper except in cases where a figure from one song is repeated in another with definite purpose, or where two songs, being cast in the same mould, are treated by similar methods. In the majority of cases, however, each of the poems and each group of poems has a distinctive character of its own, so that if one is familiar with Wolf's idiom it would hardly be possible to transfer a song from one group to another without making it look out of place. The music does not merely fit the words carefully ; though Wolf does make it do that more carefully than any other composer has done or tried to do ; his method is more fundamental than that. He makes one feel that he has composed the poetry as well as the music—that the poetry and music are the simultaneous product of one brain. That is, when he is at his best ; for sometimes the strain under which he worked makes itself felt in the writing, more especially in the songs of his middle period (some of the settings of Goethe, for instance) where the continuously chromatic harmony, the persistent repetition of a figure through an endless series of keys and the indications of hypersensitive anxiety that the subtlest *nuances* should not be left unexpressed, combine to leave an impression of restlessness ; the composer, one feels, has aimed at elaborating single, detached details too much, instead of trying to make all the details coalesce and illustrate the whole. But in the earlier songs set to Mörike's words or in the ' Italienisches Liederbuch,' where he tried to clarify his ideas and express himself simply in the manner of Mozart, his extraordinary capacity for hitting the right balance between the words and the music has produced a number of songs of widely different character which may be ranked with the very highest of their kind. The ' Spanisches Liederbuch ' is on the whole the most varied collection, and the Goethe songs show him in his most complex and subtle aspect, but whether he is simple or whether he is complex, he writes with the fullest understanding of the requirements of both singer and pianist. His habit of building up an accompaniment from a single rhythmical phrase and of repeating a single figure under various aspects does not involve the sacrifice of the singer ; both singer and pianist are consulted, for both have parts which are free and independent of each other, but are at the same time mutually involved because both have been conceived together as a single entity in the composer's brain, instead of having been thought of separately and been subsequently put together. The key to Wolf's attitude towards those for whom he wrote is to be found on the title-pages of his volumes, which contain not ' songs ' but ' songs for voice and piano.'

L. W. H.

BIBLIOGRAPHY

E. DECSEY : *Hugo Wolf.* 4 vols. 1903–06, in one vol. 1919. A complete biography.
ERNEST NEWMAN : *Hugo Wolf.* London, 1907. The standard book for English readers contains a full list of published works. Several volumes of Wolf's letters, his collected essays and many studies of his works have been published in Germany.

WOLF, JOHANNES (*b.* Berlin, Apr. 17, 1869), distinguished as a research student, editor and writer on music, was a pupil of Spitta in Berlin. He graduated at Leipzig (1893) with the thesis *Ein anonymer Musiktraktat des* 11. *bis* 12. *Jahrhundert.* Mediæval music and its notation has been his special study, and his research in this direction has led to the *Geschichte der Mensuralnotation von* 1250–1460, etc. (3 parts, 1905), and *Handbuch der Notationskunde* (Bd. i., 1913, Bd. 2, 1919). Wolf became a teacher in the University of Berlin in 1902 and professor in 1908. From 1899–1904 he edited with Oskar Fleischer the *Sammelbände* of the Int. Mus. Ges., and was responsible for several volumes of the *D.D.T.* and *D.T.Ö.* (see DENKMÄLER). In 1910 he published ' Deutsche Lieder des 15. Jahrhunderts,' and in 1915 became librarian and curator of the musical collection of the Prussian Staatsbibliothek. He has produced the collected edition of the works of Obrecht for the VEREENIGING (*q.v.*) and done other important work of the kind. (See *Riemann.*)

c.

WOLFF, ALBERT LOUIS (*b.* Paris, Jan. 19, 1884), conductor. He was a pupil at the Paris Conservatoire and left it in 1906 with a first prize for pianoforte accompaniment. He became conductor of the Opéra - Comique (making his first appearance on Apr. 26, 1911, in Laparra's ' La Jota '), and of the Concerts Pasdeloup in 1925. Wolff is a chevalier of the Légion d'honneur.

J. G. P.

WOLFF, Auguste Désiré Bernard (*b.* Paris, May 3, 1821 ; *d.* there, Feb. 3,[1] 1887), pianist and pianoforte-maker, was head of the firm of Pleyel-Wolff et Cie. At 14 he entered the Conservatoire, studied the piano with Zimmerman, and took a first prize in 1839. He was also a pupil of Leborne for counterpoint and Halévy for composition, and under these auspices composed several pianoforte pieces, published by Richault. At 21 he entered the staff of the Conservatoire as 'répétiteur '— teacher of pupils in dramatic singing—and kept it for five years, when he gave up teaching to become the pupil and partner of the well-known pianoforte-maker, Camille Pleyel, who, being old and infirm, was looking out for a dependable assistant. Wolff entered the business in 1850, became a member of the firm in 1852, and naturally succeeded to the headship of it on the death of Pleyel in 1855. From that time his exertions were unremitting ; with the scientific assistance of his friend Lissajous the acoustician, he devoted all his attention to increasing the volume of tone without losing sweetness. His repeated experiments on the tension of strings, on the best possible spot for the hammer to strike the string so as to get the fullest tone and the best ' partials,' on the damper, etc., proved very fruitful, and led him to patent several ingenious contrivances. (See Pleyel & Co.)　　　　　　　　　　a. j.

Bibl.—Constant Pierre, *Les Facteurs d'instruments de musique, les luthiers et la facture instrumentale.* (Paris, 1893).

WOLFF, Martin, an early 16th-century German composer, wrote motets and songs of great merit, published between 1513 and 1539 (*Q.-L.*).

WOLF-FERRARI, Ermanno (*b.* Venice, Jan. 12, 1876), of a German father and Italian mother, has made his reputation primarily as a composer of Italian opera.

He showed at an early age great love and aptitude for music, but his father, who was a distinguished painter, wished the son to follow in his own footsteps, and to that end sent him to an art school in Rome. This decision was hastened by the impression produced on Ermanno by the Bayreuth performances of the operas of Wagner, which stirred him so deeply as to cause a severe illness. Thus the boy had no responsible tuition in music before he had reached his fifteenth year. Then, however, the signs of talent and his devotion became so evident that it was decided to place him under the guidance of Rheinberger in Munich. There he soon made his mark, and returning to Venice in 1899 he had no difficulty in persuading the Philharmonic Society to perform his oratorio ' La Sulamite ' for soli, chorus and orchestra at the Teatro Rossini. The oratorio was favourably received, and its success paved the way for the production the following year at

the Teatro Fenice of an opera on the subject of Cinderella (' Cenerentola ') on a book by Maria Pezzè Pascolato. Partly owing to the inadequate rendering the opera was unsuccessful. Wolf-Ferrari felt keenly the failure of his hopes and went back to Germany, where a revised version of ' Cenerentola ' was given in Bremen under the title of ' Aschenbrödel ' on Jan. 31, 1902, and favourably received. In less than twelve months another opera, ' Le donne curiose,' on a libretto by L. Susana was given at the court theatre, Munich, and a third opera ' I quattro Rusteghi ' (libretto by Giuseppe Pizzolato on Goldoni's famous comedy) was produced in Munich in 1906. A cantata on Dante's *Vita Nuova* also belongs to this period, being performed in Munich for the first time in 1903.

After these successful operas, Wolf-Ferrari set to work on the one-act comedy by which he is best known in England. ' Il segreto di Susanna ' (words by E. Golisciani and Max Kalbeck) was first performed in Munich in Dec. 1909, and the favourable verdict of that audience was soon confirmed by other European opera houses. Although the plot is simple to the point of barrenness, the charm of the music, the odd mixture of modern effects and a Mozartian framework has been found singularly effective and ' Susanna's Secret ' is, so far, the most fortunate of all his operas. His next effort ' I giojelli della Madonna ' on a libretto by E. Golisciani and C. Zangarini has also met with a fair measure of success. It was first given in Berlin on Dec. 23, 1911, and has since been frequently performed in England—at Covent Garden during the Italian season, and by the Carl Rosa Company in the provinces. But it may be doubted whether the composer is at his best in dealing with a subject which carries the ' realistic ' tendencies of ' Cavalleria ' to excessive length. The story is lurid in the extreme, and without a redeeming feature. The music is passionate and picturesque, but no beauty of melody can turn the sordid, revolting plot into a tolerable story. The orchestral intermezzo which precedes the third act has met with greater popular success than any other prelude of the kind since Cavalleria. Another opera, ' Amor medico,' was successfully performed at Dresden, Dec. 4, 1913. Wolf-Ferrari has also written chamber music : two sonatas for pianoforte and violin (opp. 1 and 10), a quintet for pianos and strings (op. 6), a trio for piano, violin and violoncello (op. 7), four ' Rispetti ' for soprano voice and piano (op. 11), a ' chamber ' symphony for strings, piano, wood wind instruments and horn, and a number of violoncello and organ pieces.

In all these works Wolf-Ferrari shows that he possesses a talent of a very unusual kind. While his technique on the one hand is essentially that of to-day, his melodies are often

1 Fétis, *Supplement*, gives Feb. 4.

reminiscent in design of the art of the past. He gives the impression of a composer whose sense of beauty is so deeply rooted in the past that he is most individual when he can use the idiom of a bygone era. He evidently has a profound belief in the power of lyrical expression, and allows his lyrical vein to flow easily and unchecked. In his orchestral scores graceful touches are frequent, and in the comedies both harmony and orchestral colour often emphasise very effectively points of wit or humour.

In 1902 Wolf-Ferrari was appointed director of the Liceo Benedetto Marcello of his native city, a post which he held until 1912.   F. B.

WOLKENSTEIN, DAVID (b. Breslau, Nov. 19, 1534; d. Strassburg, Sept. 11, 1592), mathematician at Strassburg, wrote ' Primum Musicum volumen scholarum Argentoratensium,' 4th edition in 1585 ; psalms for churches and schools, in 4 parts, 1583 (Psalmen für Kirchen und Schulen, etc.) ; Harmonia Psalmorum Davidis, 4 v. (1583). Henry Faber's Compendium musicae, Strassburg, 1596, gave Wolkenstein's psalm tunes as an addition (Mendel).

WOLKENSTEIN, OSWALD VON (b. Tyrol, c. 1377 ; d. Aug. 2, 1445), one of the last of the Minnesinger, descended from a knightly family long settled in the Tyrol, lived a very stirring and adventurous life, in the course of which he had travelled over the greater part of Europe, and had even visited some parts of Asia and Africa. In one of his poems he boasts of being able to converse in ten different languages. From 1415 he was for several years in the service of King (afterwards Emperor) Sigismund, sometimes one of his immediate train, at other times sent on various embassies to Spain and Portugal. On his return home, in his constant desire to extend his own domains at the expense of his neighbours, he was from 1421-27 involved in various strifes and lawsuits, in the course of which he was twice subjected to arrest and imprisonment. A worse fate might have befallen him at the hands of Duke Frederick of Austria, but for the intercession of powerful friends. The circumstances of the various disputes in which he was engaged even up to the day of his death afford a curious picture of the wild and lawless life of the German Knights of the times. Long before his death he had in 1408 erected for himself a monument, which still exists, in the Cathedral Church of Brixen, probably in connexion with some endowment for a pious purpose which he had there founded.

It is surprising that in so troubled and adventurous a life from beginning to end he should have been able to devote himself to the cultivation of poetry and music. Many of his poems are spring- and love-songs, and some are devoted to the glorification of Margaret Queen of Aragon. There is in all of them the strong personal note, and it is mainly from his own poems that the details of his wandering and adventurous life are known. He invented the melodies to his poems, and these are no longer in the mere recitative style of his predecessors, but are real songs, many of them very fresh and pleasing, with a popular lilt about them. Oswald was not only an inventor of melodies, but was also skilled in all the intricacies of the mensural notation of his time, and set some of his songs in two and three-part counterpoint. There are occasionally slight canonic imitations, and a few pieces are expressly described as fugues, but the harmonies are very stiff and uncouth to modern ears, and the conduct of the parts generally, though it may be that one or other of the parts was only meant to be played on some instrument, and not sung, in which case the harmonies may not have been so disagreeable. There are two instances of apparently four-part writing, but they are meant to be sung or played in three parts, with one taken alternately with another. The most successful setting from a harmonic point of view is the three-part setting of the Latin words Ave Mater, O Maria, etc. The whole of Von Wolkenstein's compositions, both literary and musical, have now been edited with critical apparatus and various facsimiles in the D.T.Ö. ix.   J. R. M.

WOLLE, JOHN FREDERICK (b. Bethlehem, Pennsylvania, Apr. 4, 1863), is eminent for his enthusiasm in the propagation of Bach's choral music and his formation and direction of the important series of Bach festivals in Bethlehem.

Wolle studied music with Rheinberger at Munich (1884-85), and then becoming organist of the Moravian Church in his native place began his lifelong campaign for the advancement of Bach's music in America. The ' St. John Passion ' was given complete for the first time in 1888 ; the ' St. Matthew ' followed in 1892, the B minor Mass in 1900. During the period 1905-11 Wolle was in California as professor of the university, and there also he organised performances of the major works of Bach. On his return to Bethlehem the festivals were renewed. Their programmes have been expanded to include a large number of the church cantatas, the Brandenburg concertos played by the PHILADELPHIA ORCHESTRA (q.v.) and other important works.

BIBL.—WALTERS, Bethlehem Bach Choir (1918); Amer. Supp. articles on Bethlehem Bach Choir and Wolle.   C.

WOLLENHAUPT, HEINRICH [1] ADOLF (b. Schkeuditz, Sept. 27, 1827 ; d. New York, Sept. 18, 1865), studied at the Leipzig Conservatorium, and had a brilliant career as a pianist and a composer of drawing-room pieces of the lightest character. In 1845 he went to New York (Riemann).   M.

WOLLICK, NICOLAUS (b. Ancerville, near Bar-le-Duc), a 15th-16th-century writer on

[1] Baker gives Hermann.

Musica figurata, Gregorian chant, counterpoint, etc., in his works : *Opus aureum* (5 editions, Cologne, between 1501 and 1509) ; *Enchiridion musices* (appeared in Metz and Paris in 1508, and 2nd edition 1512). As a boy he was very poor, but was taken up and educated by Adam of Boppard, Regens of the College of Corneillian, near Air, Northern France. He became a master of philosophy, music and poetry, and lectured apparently at the universities of Paris, Metz and Cologne (*Q.-L.*).

WOLSTENHOLME, WILLIAM (*b.* Blackburn, Feb. 24, 1865), organist and composer. As an instance of musical precocity may be mentioned the fact that when 6 years old he used to improvise a melody on the piano, adding an accompaniment on a small harmonium at its side, playing the latter a half tone higher than the piano, owing to the instruments differing in pitch. He was trained at the College for the Blind, Worcester, and obtained the degree of Mus.B. at Oxford, being the only blind musician to take the Oxford degree since John Stanley. Elgar was much interested in him, and as visiting teacher at the College not only gave him violin lessons, but also helped him in preparing for his degree, acting as his amanuensis. On leaving the College, Wolstenholme returned to Blackburn, where for fifteen years he held the post of organist and choirmaster at St. Paul's. In 1902 he became organist at the King's Weigh House Church, going thence two years later to All Saints', Norfolk Square. At present (1926) he is organist at All Saints', St. John's Wood. In 1908 he made a successful tour of the United States. A brilliant pianist and organist, he is also among the most gifted of improvisers. His compositions include about twenty works for various chamber music combinations, seven for orchestra, one for military band, many vocal works, some church music, thirty pieces for pianoforte, and nearly a hundred for the organ. Naturally it is by the last named that he is best known. Worthy of special mention are the sonata in F, the sonata in D (in the style of Handel), the finale in B flat, the fantasia in E, and the prelude and fugue. But the general level through all this large output is high. There is a wealth of melodic invention, fresh and natural harmony, and, above all, a finished workmanship which is not too common in modern organ music. Wolstenholme no doubt owes much of his neatness in the technique of composition to his early training as a pianist and chamber musician. Perhaps to the piano may also be ascribed a less happy feature—his over-frequent use of octaves in the right hand. That, however, is but a trifling blemish on a large mass of organ music which has the unusual merit of appealing to the crowd by its tunefulness, and to the musician by its quality and skill.   H. G.

WOLTZ, JOHANN. On May 1, 1617, he calls himself church administrator and organist for over forty years at Heilbronn on the Neckar. He wrote a book of organ tablature, containing motets, canzons and fugues by German and Italian masters (Basle, 1617 ; *Mendel*; *Q.-L.*).

WOLZOGEN, HANS PAUL, FREIHERR VON (*b.* Potsdam, Nov. 13, 1848), the son of K. A. A. von Wolzogen (1823–83, the Intendant of the court theatre at Schwerin, author of several pamphlets, etc., on Mozart), studied comparative philology at Berlin in 1868–71. He eagerly embraced Wagner's doctrines and wrote many books, large and small, about the time of the opening of the theatre at Bayreuth in 1876. The most valuable of these is no doubt his *Thematischer Leitfäden*, published in English as *Guide through Der Ring des Nibelungen*, translated into very curious English by his brother, Ernst von Wolzogen. In 1877 he was called to Bayreuth to edit *Bayreuther Blätter*, the organ by which the campaign was carried on between the festivals. Among the author's many contributions to Wagnerian literature, his book on *Tristan* which appeared in 1880 may be mentioned, as well as a treatise, *Was ist Stil ? Was will Wagner ?* He wrote the libretto for Hans Sommer's 'Schloss der Herzen' (*Riemann*).

                                      M.

WOOD, CHARLES (*b.* Armagh, June 15, 1866 ; *d.* Cambridge, July 12, 1926), composer, professor of music in the University of Cambridge and professor of composition, etc., at the R.C.M., was the son of Charles Wood, lay vicar of Armagh Cathedral.

He began his education in harmony and counterpoint in 1880–81 under Dr. T. O. Marks, the organist of Armagh Cathedral. From 1883–1887 he was at the R.C.M., where he won the Morley Scholarship for composition. He studied there under Stanford for composition, Bridge for counterpoint, and Franklin Taylor for pianoforte. In 1888 he was appointed teacher of harmony at the R.C.M., where later he became a member of the Board of Professors and of the Associated Board of the R.A.M. and R.C.M. As teacher and examiner he exercised an important influence through these posts.

In 1888 he took up his residence in Cambridge, conducting the Cambridge University Musical Society from that year until 1894. He entered Cambridge through Selwyn College, but migrated to Caius College on his appointment as organist-scholar of Gonville and Caius College. 1889–94. In the latter year he was made a Fellow. He was bandmaster of the University Volunteers, 1889–97. In 1897 he was made university lecturer in harmony and counterpoint, and was elected to the professorship on the death of Stanford in 1924. He examined for the universities of Cambridge, Oxford and London. He took the degrees of B.A. and Mus.B. at Cambridge in 1890, of M.A.

and Mus.D. in 1894, and was given an honorary LL.D. degree at Leeds in 1904.

Wood's talent as a composer, his fastidious taste and his fine scholarship, were shown in a number of short works for voices and orchestra which belong to his early years. These include 'Ode to the West Wind,' for solo, chorus and orchestra, 1890 ; a setting of Swinburne's ' Ode on Music ' for the opening of the new building of the R.C.M., 1894 ; Milton's ' Ode on Time,' for chorus and orchestra, 1898. His ' Dirge for two Veterans ' had a great success at the Leeds Festival of 1901 and was revived at that of 1925 ; his ' Song of the Tempest ' for solo, chorus and orchestra, was performed at the Hovingham Festival of 1902, and his ' Ballad of Dundee ' at the Leeds Festival of 1904. A set of Symphonic Variations on ' Patrick Sarsfield ' was given at one of the Beecham Concerts in London in 1907.

He wrote music to the *Ion* of Euripedes for Cambridge (1890) and to *Iphigenia in Tauris* (1894) (see GREEK PLAYS, MUSIC TO), and essayed dramatic composition of a very different kind in a scene from *The Pickwick Papers* taken as the basis of a one-act comic opera and performed by the students of the R.C.M. in 1922. His works of concerted chamber music include three string quartets (A minor, E flat and F) heard occasionally in London, and in 1925 he reappeared as a 'festival' composer, conducting at Gloucester an unaccompanied motet ' Glory and Honour ' (8 voices). Among his smaller compositions may be mentioned a book of Irish Folk-songs published in 1897 ; some fine church music, many partsongs and solo songs, among the last being the very remarkable ' Ethiopia saluting the Colours ' to words by Walt Whitman.   M. ; addns. C.

WOOD, Sir HENRY JOSEPH (*b.* London, Mar. 3, 1870), eminent orchestral conductor, came of musical parents, was taught at first by his mother, and at 10 years of age acted as deputy organist of St. Mary, Aldermanbury. At 13 he was deputy organist at St. Sepulchre's, Holborn. At 17 he had his first appointment as organist of St. John's, Fulham. Before this he had given organ recitals at the Fisheries and Inventions Exhibitions, in 1883 and 1885 respectively. He studied for six terms at the R.A.M., working with Prout and Garcia, and apparently aiming at the career of a composer. He wrote several theatrical and other pieces, which were consigned to oblivion as soon as the main object of his life was found to be conducting.

A four months' tour with the Arthur Rousbey Opera Company in 1889 gave him his first experience of responsible conducting, and in 1890 he was engaged by Sullivan and D'Oyly Carte to superintend the rehearsals of ' Ivanhoe.' He became assistant conductor at the Savoy Theatre for a short time, and conducted opera at the

Crystal Palace on at least two occasions. In 1891 he conducted ' Carmen ' during Marie Roze's farewell tour with the Carl Rosa Company. In 1892 he conducted for an operatic enterprise of Mme. Georgina Burns and Leslie Crotty, and prepared an English version of Rossini's ' Cenerentola.' His next move was to the Olympic Theatre in London, where he conducted Lago's interesting but unfortunate season of Italian Opera. The engagement was most important for him, for it not only brought him under the notice of London musicians, but the first work performed, Tchaikovsky's 'Eugen Onegin,' was his first introduction to that Russian music with which he was afterwards to be so closely identified. After the collapse of the undertaking Wood taught singing, and formed operatic classes, etc., until in 1894 he came into contact with Mottl, and was appointed musical adviser for the Wagner Concerts organised by Schulz Curtius at the newly built QUEEN'S HALL (*q.v.*).

In 1895 he was engaged by Robert Newman to conduct a series of Promenade Concerts in the new hall, and from that moment began an association maintained unbroken till the death of Newman in 1926, which has had the most important effect on the musical life of London (see PROMENADE CONCERTS and NEW QUEEN'S HALL ORCHESTRA) and incidentally made Wood the most prominent personality in London music. In 1896 he conducted the run of Stanford's ' Shamus O'Brien ' at the Opéra-Comique Theatre, but his career was now shaped in the direction of symphonic work, and not only that at Queen's Hall (including with the Promenades, the Symphony Concerts and Sunday Concerts from 1897 onwards), but many other opportunities which he found or made in provincial cities, absorbed his energies. In 1897 a Command performance of the Queen's Hall Orchestra was given before Queen Victoria ; in the same year Wood was appointed director of the Nottingham Sacred Harmonic Society and he founded the Nottingham City Orchestra in 1899. He was made conductor of the Wolverhampton Festival Choral Society in 1900, of the Sheffield Festival (1902–11), and of the Norwich Festival in 1908. This last he was able to revive after the lapse of ten years in 1924. In 1926 he conducted the Handel Festival at the Crystal Palace, and himself scored the whole of the music for a three days' programme for an immense orchestra proportioned to the choir and the building.

He conducted symphony concerts at Birmingham in 1907, the festival there in 1912 and the Festival Choral Society from 1919 – 23. Other important provincial appointments have included the Westmorland Festivals (see WAKEFIELD, Mary), Cardiff Orchestral Concerts (1911–13), the Manchester ' Gentleman's Concerts ' and Brand Lane Concerts, the Liverpool Philharmonic, and Societies at Sheffield, Leicester and Hull.

In 1898 Wood married Olga, daughter of Princess Sofie Ouroussov (*née* Narishkin) (*d.* Dec. 20, 1909), a soprano singer whose charm of voice and style added distinction to many of her husband's earlier festival performances. She had been his pupil and became to a certain extent his teacher, for he owed much to her accomplishment and fine taste. She was no doubt partly responsible for the direction of Wood's attention to the great wealth of Russian orchestral music which was still practically unknown in England in the 'nineties. Another who contributed very definitely to the enlargement of Wood's musical horizon was Rosa NEWMARCH (*q.v.*) whose knowledge of the Russian and other Slavonic schools of composition has been constantly used to enrich the repertory of the Queen's Hall orchestra. These influences, together with the fact that after the production of Tchaikovsky's 'Pathetic' symphony the London public was ripe for the vivid colours and rich imagery of the Russians, contributed to found Wood's reputation as a conductor primarily on music of this kind. He was never, however, a specialist in the exclusive sense, and it may be hazarded that the conditions of his work as an English conductor have given him the widest repertory of any concert conductor in the world. As a musician his taste has constantly matured, so that while at 25 he attracted attention by sensational performances of Tchaikovsky, at 55 he is noted for finely tempered readings of the classics.

In 1911 Wood was knighted ; in the same year (two years after his first wife's death) he married Muriel, daughter of Major Greatorex, by whom he has two daughters. The years immediately before the war were remarkable for the great number of important new works which were produced under his direction at Queen's Hall. Richard Strauss, Debussy, Reger, Scriabin, Schönberg were among the more famous continental composers who visited England either to conduct their works with his orchestra or to hear them under his direction. Elgar's second symphony was first given at the London Festival of 1911, and the works of native composers too numerous to record were produced by him both in London and the provinces. After the war, when the armistice made possible the re-establishment of international relations amongst artists, Wood was able to carry English music abroad. He conducted with Nikisch and Pierné at the international festival given at Zürich in 1921. He was invited to conduct English music at Wiesbaden in 1925, and in the same year visited California for the same purpose. Elgar, Delius, Ethel Smyth, Holst, Vaughan Williams, nave been the principal composers represented in these programmes. In 1926 he received

the degree of Doctor of Music, *honoris causa*, from Oxford.

Wood has made a good many orchestral arrangements of works ranging from a suite of pieces by Purcell to Moussorgsky's ' Pictures at an Exhibition ' and Debussy's ' La Cathédrale engloutie.' A fantasia on British sea songs by him was for many years popular at the Promenade Concerts. Since 1923 he has found time to undertake the training in orchestral playing and conducting at the R.A.M. He has always been a man of hobbies, amongst which painting in oils and carpentry are conspicuous. Alike in his hobbies and his life-work of music the quality of thoroughness underlies all his activity. He has never been known to conduct a score without knowing it, or to conduct without a score in order to show how well he knows it. He takes infinite pains at rehearsal, is a firm disciplinarian and has cultivated so direct and indicative a style of conducting that his requirements can never be in doubt for an instant. Consequently, while his great work has been the training of an orchestra to play constantly under his direction, he is extraordinarily ready in getting results from strange players.

BIBL.—ROSA NEWMARCH, *Henry J. Wood: Living Masters of Music*, 1904) ; *A Quarter of a Century of Promenade Concerts* (1919). (Contains lists of first productions at Queen's Hall Promenade Concerts, 1895–1919.)

C. ; incorporating material from M.

WOOD, JOHN MUIR (*b.* Edinburgh, July 31, 1805 ; *d.* Annandale, Cove, June 25, 1892), head of a Scottish firm of music-publishers originally located in Edinburgh, but afterwards established in Glasgow, was the son of Andrew Wood, a music-publisher who named him after his partner, John Muir. John Muir Wood was closely associated with the musical life of Scotland, and took a keen interest in Scottish musical antiquities. He edited a new edition of Graham's ' Songs of Scotland,' 1884, in one volume (the original was issued by Wood & Co. of Edinburgh in 3 vols. 1848, etc.), and was the writer of the article ' Scottish Music ' and some others in the first edition of this Dictionary.

WOOD & Co., the above-mentioned firm of music-publishers, was started by James Muir at 16 George Street, Edinburgh, in May 1796. Difficulties having arisen, the business was taken over shortly after by his brother, John Muir, an ironmonger, who, advertising for a partner, associated himself with Andrew Wood and others. Muir, Wood & Co. were at 16 George Street in 1799, and were ' Musical instrument makers to His Majesty.' In 1804 they had removed to 7 Leith Street ; in 1811 the number was changed to 13, and here they remained until 1818. They were very active publishers, and published quantities of sheet music and collections of airs mostly Scottish.

The survivors of the firm were Wood & Co. of 12 Waterloo Place, Edinburgh, and J. Muir

Wood & Co. of 42 Buchanan Street, Glasgow, who were intimately connected, and were issuing, in the 'forties and 'fifties, many important Scottish musical works, among which were Graham's 'Songs of Scotland,' Surennes' 'Dance Music of Scotland,' and some others, which in their subject may now claim to be classic.　　　　　　　　　　　　　　　F. K.

WOOD, MRS., see PATON, Mary Anne.

WOODCOCK, ROBERT, is described by Hawkins as a celebrated flute-player. Little is known regarding him save that he composed twelve concertos in eight parts for flutes and strings. These concertos seem to have had considerable popularity, as they are advertised in Randalls' list for 1776 ; they were published with the imprint of Walsh and Joseph Hare about 1728–30. Alfred Moffat arranged one of the slow movements (in D minor) of the concertos as a violin solo in Bk. ii. of ' Pieces by English Masters of the 17th and 18th Centuries' (Augener). The dates of his birth and death have not been ascertained.

Hawkins also refers to Thomas Woodcock, an excellent performer on the violin, who kept a coffee-house at Hereford, and who died about 1750.　　　　　　　　　　　　　　　F. K.

WOODHOUSE, CHARLES (b. London, 1879), an artist of singular versatility. He has gained experience by playing violin, viola, piano, orchestral and chamber music, composing and arranging, with occasional conducting, and is one of the Examiners of the Associated Board. Best known as an orchestral player of the first rank, he is leader of the New Queen's Hall Orchestra, and a pianist in a small orchestra directed by Frederick Cassano. He belongs to several well-known quartets.
　　　　　　　　　　　　　　　w. w. c.

WOODS ('WODDS,' 'WOODES '), MICHAEL (?) (16th cent.), English organist and composer of church music. There are records of payments to a Michael Woods as ' organista ' of Chichester Cathedral from 1567 – 69 (West, Cath. Org.). B.M. Add. MSS. 29,426–7 is a collection of 16th-century motets, chiefly by English composers such as Taverner, Tallis, Fayrfax and Shepherd, arranged in Italian tablature, and contains the following by Woods :

' Effunde quaeso ' ; ' Exurge Domine ' ; ' Perfeci illud ' ; ' Verbi tui.'　All for 3 v.

The first of these is also in Tenb. 354-8, and a score of the second is in B.M. Add. MSS. 34,726/17 b. Copies of Nos. 2, 3 and 4 are in R.C.M. 2035, and also in the Commonplace Book of John BALDWIN (q.v.). The R.C.M. MS. also contains another motet by Woods : ' Igitur Jhesu,' a 3, and the Baldwin book still another, ' Esto Pater,' a 3.　　　　J. Mᴷ.

WOODSON, (1) LEONARD (b. Winchester ; d. 1641), English organist and composer of church music, described in the Batten Organ Book (see BATTEN), as ' organist of Eaton

College, and one of ye quire of Winzor who was born at Winchester.' That he was a singing man at St. George's Chapel, Windsor, under Nathaniel Giles, who was organist and master of the children there from 1585–1633, is confirmed by the following entry in the Chapter Acts for Apr. 5, 1605 :

' It is decreed, at the request of Nathanaell Giles, esquier, Master of the Choristers of this free Chapel, that Leonard Woodeson, one of the singing men of the same, shall have the teaching, keeping, dieting, ordering and lodging of the said choristers for so long time as it shall be thought meet by the Dean and Chapter. And whensoever the said Dean and Chapter shall mislike therewith then upon one quarters warning from them to be given to the said Nathanaell he shall take them again to his own ordering and government as before.'

It is probable that Woodson continued as deputy choirmaster until 1615, when he became organist of Eton College. He held this post until 1641 (West, Cath. Org.) and presumably died in this year, as a Te Deum by him is printed in Barnard's ' Selected Church Music,' declaredly a collection of music by composers dead at the time of publication (1641). An In Nomine by Woodson is at Oxford (Bodl. Mus. Sch.), a 3-part ' Ut re mi fa ' is in the Commonplace Book of John BALDWIN (q.v.), and a treble solo, ' The mary gould of golden hew,' is in Ch. Ch. 439.

(2) LEONARD, possibly a son of the above, was sworn a gentleman of the Chapel Royal, Aug. 15, 1681. He was appointed ' to the vocall musick ' July 17, 1689, and still held this position in 1699 under Dr. John Blow as ' composer ' (H. C. de Lafontaine, The King's Musick).　　　　　　　　　　　　　　J. Mᴷ.

WOODSON, THOMAS (late 16th and early 17th cent.), English composer, possibly the father of Leonard WOODSON (1). He was a gentleman of the Chapel Royal in 1581,[1] and continued as such, at any rate until 1603, when he was one of the gentlemen who had an ' allowance of mourning liverie given out to them on the funeral of Queen Elizabeth ' (H. C. de Lafontaine, The King's Musick). B.M. Add. MSS. 29,996/184 b contains a composition for organ by him described as ' Forty wayes of 2 parts in one on the " Miserere." ' Only 20 ' wayes ' are given, but another copy is in Ch. Ch. 371.　　　　J. Mᴷ.

WOODWARD, RICHARD (b. Dublin, 1744 ; d. there, Nov. 22, 1777). His father (also Richard Woodward) was a vicar choral of Christ Church and St. Patrick's Cathedrals. He (the younger Woodward) was a chorister of Christ Church Cathedral, of which he was afterwards appointed organist in 1765. In 1768 he took the degree of Bachelor in Music at Trinity College, Dublin, and proceeded to the Doctor's degree in 1771. He was appointed a vicar choral of St. Patrick's Cathedral in 1772.

[1] G. E. P. Arkwright, Catalogue of Mus., Ch. Ch.

In 1771 he published (with Welcker of Gerrard Street, St. Anne's, Soho) a folio volume of his church music, with a dedication to Archbishop Smyth. It is entitled :

'Cathedral music, consisting of one compleat Service, Seven Anthems, several Chants, and Veni Creator Spiritus, in score ; for one, two, three, four, five and six voices, composed by Richard Woodward, Mus.D., Organist of Christ Church Cathedral, Dublin. Opera Terza.'

At the present time his anthems are not often heard, although some of his chants (notably a double chant in D) are well known. He also published a collection of his songs, catches and canons. Woodward is buried at Christ Church Cathedral. On his monument in the Cathedral is engraved his Canon (4 in 2), ' Let the words of my mouth,' which had been awarded the gold medal of the Glee and Catch Club in 1764.

L. M'C. L. D.

WOODYATT, EMILY (b. 1814), daughter of a confectioner at Hereford, was taught singing by Sir G. Smart, and first attracted public attention in Jan. 1834, at a concert of the Vocal Association, and later at Hereford Festival the same year. She became a favourite singer of the second rank at the various festivals, oratorio and other concerts. In 1839 she became a member of the Female Society of Musicians, on its foundation, and in 1840 was elected an Associate of the Philharmonic Society at the instance of Sir G. Smart, Cramer, and Edward LODER (q.v.). On Oct. 27, 1841, she married William Loder the violoncellist (he died in 1851), and retired soon after her marriage.

A. C.

WOOLDRIDGE, HARRY· ELLIS (b. 1845 ; d. London, Feb. 13, 1917) was Slade Professor of Fine Arts at Oxford, a man of practical ability in several arts, especially painting, and a profound scholar of the mediæval period of polyphonic music. He revised and edited Chappell's ' Popular Music of the Olden Time ' with the title ' Old English Popular Music ' (1893), and collaborated with G. E. P. Arkwright in his researches. But Wooldridge's chief contribution to historical knowledge was his work on the polyphonic period which forms the first two volumes of the Oxford History of Music, and traces the developments of such music from Organum to the end of the sixteenth century.

C.

WORCESTER FESTIVAL, see THREE CHOIRS FESTIVAL.

WORCESTER MUSIC FESTIVALS (U.S.A.). The music festivals given by the Worcester County Musical Association annually in the city of Worcester, Massachusetts, are the offspring of institutions called musical conventions, which did much to raise the character of church music and its performance in the United States, especially in New England, in the earlier decades of the 19th century.

At these conventions there were gatherings of singing teachers and choristers sometimes to the number of several hundred, who, under the guidance of teachers of experience and better training than was the rule, went out from Boston and other large cities, studied singing from notes and some of the simpler principles of vocalisation, and made the acquaintance of selections from the oratorios, especially those of Handel and Haydn. After two or more days had been spent in study and discussion all the members of the Convention were wont to join in a concert, at which the new music that had been learned would be performed, with scanty and improvised instrumental accompaniments as a rule, but frequently with good effect, so far as the singing was concerned. Worcester had long been a centre of choral culture when the first of these conventions was held there in 1858. Indeed, inspired by the example of the Handel and Haydn Society of BOSTON (q.v.), singing societies were in existence, one of which, the Mozart Society, organised in 1850, had been founded for the express purpose of performing oratorios. But works of this kind were then associated in the public mind, as they still too widely are, with the notion of large numbers in the choir, and little was done in the way of oratorio until a union of choirs was effected in the conventions. At the first Musical Convention held in Worcester in 1858, hymns, glees, a cantata composed by the conductor (B. F. Baker, of Boston) and choruses from the ' Messiah ' and the ' Creation ' were sung, at the one public concert which was given. In 1860 there were two concerts, and by 1866 the meetings had taken on so much of the festival character that four concerts were not thought too many, and the new conductor, Carl ZERRAHN, ventured upon an entire oratorio, viz., Handel's ' Judas Maccabaeus.' For four years the organisation which arranged the conventions was a loose one, but in 1863 the Worcester County Musical Convention was formally established with representatives from twenty cities, towns and villages.

In 1871 the name was changed to the Worcester County Musical Association, and it was formally declared that thereafter the conventions should be called festivals—an ambition to imitate the English festivals having found an expression at the meeting of 1863, when it had also been resolved to perform oratorios in their entirety. It was long before this pious resolution could be carried out, for even after the choir, then made up of singers from Worcester and vicinity (the choir is now almost wholly local), was able to master one of the works of Handel or Haydn, the instrumental company was lacking. At first the pianoforte alone was used, then, when in 1864 a fine organ was presented by popular subscription to the Mechanics' Association in whose hall the meetings were held, that was also employed. When Zerrahn first brought forward 'Judas Maccabaeus' the orchestra consisted of six players—the Mendelssohn Quintet of Boston and a double-bass. The next year there was an orchestra of ten men, in 1868 of eighteen. Later the band consisted of between fifty and sixty members of the Boston Symphony Orchestra.

Zerrahn was conductor of the Worcester festivals from 1866–97 inclusive. After 1868 he had the help of different men to conduct the smaller works and the accompaniments to the miscellaneous solos. He was succeeded after his resignation in 1897 by George W. CHADWICK, who officiated 1898–1901. Wallace GOODRICH held the post in 1902–07, and was succeeded by Arthur MEES, who in turn was followed by Nelson P. COFFIN in 1919. Victor HERBERT was associate conductor from 1889–1891, and Franz KNEISEL from 1892–1908. Since 1866 a wide repertory of large choral works has been given, including most of the classics and many modern works, with those of native composers such as Horatio Parker, Chadwick, Converse and Hadley.

H. E. K., addns.

WORGAN, (1) JAMES (d. 1753), was organist of St. Botolph,[1] Aldgate, and St. Dunstan in the East. In 1737 he became organist of Vauxhall Gardens, which office he resigned about 1751.

(2) JOHN, Mus.D., his younger brother (b. 1724 ; d. London, Aug. 24, 1790), studied music under him and Thomas Roseingrave. He became organist of St. Andrew Undershaft with St. Mary Axe, about 1749, and of St. John's Chapel, Bedford Row (1760). He graduated as Mus.B. at Cambridge in 1748. In 1751 he succeeded his brother as organist at Vauxhall Gardens, and in 1753 also as organist of St. Botolph's, Aldgate. In 1753 he was appointed composer to Vauxhall Gardens, and continued so until 1761. In 1770 he was re-appointed to the office and held it until 1774, when he resigned both it and the organistship of the gardens. In 1775 he proceeded Mus.D. He died in his house in Gower Street, and was buried in St. Andrew Undershaft. He excelled as an organist, and whenever he played, crowds of professors and amateurs resorted to hear him. In a satirical song upon Joah Bates, written by Martin Madan and set by Samuel Wesley, he was placed upon an equality, as a player, with Handel :

'Let Handel or Worgan go thresh at the organ.'

His compositions include an Ode on the Rebellion in 1745, an anthem for a thanksgiving for victories, 1759 ; oratorios : 'The Chief of Maon,' 'Gioas' (incomplete) ; 'Hannah' (to words by Christopher Smart), produced at the Haymarket Theatre, 1764, and 'Manasseh,'

produced at the Lock Hospital Chapel, 1766 ; many books of songs composed for Vauxhall ; psalm tunes, glees, organ music, and harpsichord lessons. He left a treatise on composition, unfinished. A full biography, with a minute and laudatory analysis of his works, will be found in the Quarterly Musical Review, vol. v. p. 113.

W. H. H.

Other members of the Worgan family, also musical, were :

(3) JOHN, son of Dr. Worgan (2), who composed marches for the pianoforte, and some songs, about the junction of the 18th and 19th centuries. He married, Sept. 1, 1753, Sarah Macklean, whom he divorced,[2] June 1768.

(4) THOMAS DANVERS, another son (b. London, 1774 ; d. 1832), was author of a musical game with cards, 1807 ; 'The Musical Reformer,' 1829 ; besides other works of a technical character. He also composed songs, 'Vocal Sonatinas,' 'The Hero's Welcome,' a motet.

(5) RICHARD, another son, published a set of sonnets in 1810.

(6) GEORGE (b. 1802 ; d. Wellington, N.Z., Apr. 2, 1888), a grandson of Dr. John Worgan, went to New Zealand. He composed psalm and hymn tunes, songs, etc., and issued in 1841, 'Gems of Sacred Melody.' (See an obituary notice in Mus. T., 1888, p. 490.)

F. K.

WORMSER, ANDRÉ ALPHONSE TOUSSAINT (b. Paris, Nov. 1, 1851, d. Nov. 4, 1926), was a scholar of the Paris Conservatoire under Bazin and Marmontel, obtained the Prix de Rome in 1875 with his 'Clytemnestre,' and won success with many operas and other works ('Adèle de Ponthieu' was given at Aix-la-Chapelle in 1887, 'Rivoli' in Paris in 1896) : but none has achieved the success of the pantomime or wordless play, 'L'Enfant prodigue,' produced in Paris in 1890 (at the Cercle Funambulesque, June 14, and at the Bouffes Parisiens, June 21). It was produced at the Prince of Wales's Theatre, London, Mar. 31, 1891 (see RONALD, Sir Landon), and at Dresden in 1903. 'Amour,' a poem for voice and orchestra, was performed at the Lamoureux concerts in 1921. An extract from it, 'Solitude,' was published in 1922.

M., with addns.

WORNUM. The name is intimately connected with the invention and development of the upright piano, since it is Robert Wornum's action, patented in 1826, though not completed until the 'tie' was added in 1828, that produced cottage or pianino action. (See PIANOFORTE, Vol. IV. p. 160.)

(1) ROBERT (b. 1742 ; d. 1815), the father of the inventor, was of a Berkshire family, originally Wornham. He succeeded to the business established by J. and G. VOGLER, in Glasshouse Street, and published many small

1 Elected Dec. 22, 1738 ; was succeeded May 11, 1753, by Mrs. Mary Worgan, probably his widow (St. Dunstan's Vestry Books).
W. B. S.

2 F. Plowden, Criminal Court Biog i., 1830.   W. B. S.

books of dances, and airs for flute or violin. He moved to 42 Wigmore Street in 1777, and according to the *Musical Directory* of 1794, was a maker of violins and violoncellos.

His son (2) ROBERT (*b.* 1780 ; *d.* 1852) was the inventor of diagonally and upright-strung low upright pianos in 1811 and 1813, which he named, respectively, the 'Unique' and the 'Harmonic.' He brought out his 'piccolo' piano in 1827, and finally perfected his crank action in 1829. He was intended for the Church, but the mechanical bias prevailed, and he went into partnership with George Wilkinson in a pianoforte business in Oxford Street in 1810. A fire in 1812 caused a dissolution of this partnership. He ultimately established a warehouse and concert room in Store Street. The subsequent head of the firm of Robert Wornum & Sons, A. N. Wornum, succeeded to his grandfather's inventive talent.

A. J. H. ; addns. F. K.

WORZISCHEK, JOHANN HUGO (*b.* Wamberg, Bohemia, May 11, 1791 ; *d.* Vienna, Nov. 19, 1825), was first taught by his father, a schoolmaster. At the age of 8 he had attained to such remarkable facility in playing the organ, piano and violin that he was sent to Prague, where he had lessons from Tomaschek.

To attend lectures on philosophy and law and find the means of living, he had himself to give lessons before he had completed his musical studies. Worzischek went afterwards to Vienna (1813), and became intimate with Hummel, Meyerbeer and Moscheles ; and he was recommended by Hummel as a teacher to all his friends, when the great pianist left Vienna. He made a name as a pianist and conductor of the Gesellschaft der Musikfreunde. In 1822 he was appointed organist to the imperial chapel—but he died early.

Among his published works (which received unusual favour, and are still much liked by Viennese musicians) are a symphony, a duet for piano and violoncello, and a divertissement for two pianos ; he left many sacred works in manuscript. E. J. Hˢ.

WOTQUENNE, ALFRED (*b.* Lobbes, Hennegau, Jan. 25, 1867), was a pupil of the Brussels Conservatoire, under Brassin for piano, Mailly for organ, Dupont and Gevaert for theory ; he became in 1894 librarian of the institution, and under his care (till 1918) the library has become a model of organisation. It has constantly acquired works of importance, both original and MS. copies of rarities in other libraries ; and in no institution of the kind is a warmer welcome or more generous assistance given to research students. He has also published the following bibliographical works, which are indispensable to all students of musical history :

Catalogue de la Bibliothèque du Conservatoire de Bruxelles. 3 vols. 1888-1908.
Étude bibliographique sur les œuvres de Baldassare Galuppi. 1900.
Catalogue des livrets d'opéras et d'oratorios italiens du XVII. siècle. 1902.
Catalogue thématique de l'œuvre de Gluck. 1905.
Catalogue thématique de l'œuvre de C. P. E. Bach. 1906.
Table alphabétique des morceaux mesurés contenus dans les œuvres dramatiques de Zeno, Metastasio et Goldoni. 1906.
Étude bibliographique sur Luigi Rossi. 1909.

E. J. D.

WOTTON, (1) WILLIAM BALE (*b.* Torquay, Sept. 6, 1832 ; *d.* Deal, May 3, 1912), bassoon-player. His father was corporal-major in the 1st Life Guards, and he was thus brought up among the best regimental music. His fondness for the art showed itself very early ; he learnt the flute and cornet, and at the age of 13 entered the band of the regiment. The bassoon he learned with John Hardy, an excellent player, under whom he laid the foundation of that artistic style and charm of tone which distinguished him. He studied orchestral playing at the R.A.M. under Charles Lucas. His first appearance as a soloist was at the Town Hall, Windsor, where he and the late William Crozier (a most admirable player, who died Dec. 20, 1870, after having been for many years first oboe at the Crystal Palace) played a duet for oboe and bassoon under the direction of Dr. George Elvey. On the death of Baumann he would have accepted engagements with Jullien for the Promenade Concerts, and with Alfred Mellon for the Orchestral Union, if Waddell, his bandmaster, had not peremptorily forbidden it. He was then transferred from the bassoon to the saxophone, of which he was the earliest player in England. About 1870, by special permission of the colonel of his regiment, he joined the orchestra of the Crystal Palace, in which he played first bassoon for nearly thirty years. He was also a member of the orchestras of the Philharmonic, Albert Hall, and many others, and was professor of the bassoon at the R.C.M. until his retirement in 1904.

(2) T. E. WOTTON (*b.* 1852), succeeded to the various posts held by his brother (1), with whom he was associated in the Crystal Palace band from 1879. W. B. Wotton's son, (3) L. V. WOTTON, was also a bassoon-player. G.

WOTTON, WILLIAM, 'Orkyn maker,' in 1486 built a 'pair of organs' for Magdalen College, Oxford, for £28, and in 1487 agreed to make a similar instrument for Merton College, which was to be completed in 1489. V. DE P.

WRANITZKY, (1) PAUL (*b.* Neureisch, Moravia, Dec. 30, 1756 ; *d.* Vienna, Sept. 26, 1808), conductor of the orchestra at the two court theatres at Vienna, and a popular composer of operas and instrumental music. He was educated at the monastery close by, and at Iglau and Olmütz, where he perfected himself, especially in violin-playing. In 1776 he went to Vienna to study theology at the Imperial Seminary, and at once obtained a post as conductor. He next studied composition with Kraus, a Swedish composer then living in

Vienna, and produced a number of new works which attracted notice. Towards the end of 1780 he became conductor of the court theatres, and remained so till his death. He was also for many years Kapellmeister to Prince Lobkowitz. His operas were great favourites, and became known nearly throughout Germany. The one which was oftenest and longest performed was ' Oberon ' (May 23, 1791), a serio-comic fairy opera, libretto adapted by Giesecke from Wieland, which at one time ran the ' Zauberflöte ' hard. Special mention should also be made of ' Die gute Mutter,' comic opera (1795) ; ' Der Schreiner,' Singspiel (1799) ; ' Mitgefühl,' Liederspiel (1804) ; all produced at the court theatre, as were also many ballets, including ' Die Weinlese,' ' Das Urtheil des Paris,' ' Der Sabinerraub,' all between 1794 and 1800. Gerber gives a detailed catalogue of Wranitzky's operas, ballets and instrumental music. Among his many works, mostly published by André in Paris and Vienna, may be specified : 12 symphonies ; string-quintets, quartets and trios ; 3 trios for 2 flutes and violoncello, op. 83 ; concertos for violoncello, op. 27, flute, op. 24 ; and sonatas for pianoforte, violin and violoncello. He also left much music in MS. His connexion with the Tonkünstler-Societät must not be passed over. He entered it in 1793, and having become secretary undertook, at Haydn's instigation, to reorganise its affairs, then in a very bad state. In 1797 he completely effaced the difficulties which existed in 1779, when Haydn had thought of entering. Haydn had a great respect for him, both as a man and an artist, and expressly desired that he might lead the strings at the first performances of the ' Creation ' and the ' Seasons.'

His younger brother, (2) ANTON (b. Neureisch, 1761 ; d. Vienna, 1819), studied law at Brünn, where he began to compose. He went next to Vienna, where he was esteemed as a teacher. Prince von Lobkowitz made him his Kapellmeister in 1808. (See Dlabacz and Q.-L. for list of works of both brothers.)

C. F. P.

WRECKERS, THE (Les Naufrageurs ; Strandrecht) ; opera in 3 acts ; libretto by H. B. Leforestier (H. B. Brewster) ; music by Ethel Smyth. Produced Leipzig, Nov. 11, 1906 ; in English, His Majesty's Theatre, June 22, 1909.

WREST PLANK and WREST PINS. The wrest-plank or pin-block of a pianoforte is the carrier of the wrest- or tuning-pins. It is constructed of a number of layers of wood glued together so that the grain of any layer is at right angles to that of contiguous layers.

The plank so formed is rigidly fixed to the wooden framework of the piano, and the metal frame which carries the strings is placed over the plank.

The tuning-pins are in reality gripped by the wooden plank, the object of the cross-graining in which is to ensure sufficient friction to prevent the tuning-pins slackening off and so going out of tune.

Sometimes a space is provided in the metal frame to clear the tuning-pins. This is known as the ' Open Plank.' In general, the piano frame is continuous, and has holes drilled in it for the tuning-pins to pass through, these holes being generally bushed with wood, the object being to take some of the thrust set up by the string tension on the pins.

This method of gripping the tuning-pins in a wooden plank, although of considerable antiquity, is generally considered to be the most satisfactory of all methods.

Mechanical or worm-geared pins as used on such instruments as guitars or mandolines have been tried, but are unsatisfactory owing to the large forces to which they are subjected ; moreover, on account of the inevitable backlash between the worm and the worm-wheel, the process of tuning with such contrivances is exceedingly difficult to carry out. See under PIANOFORTE, the section on the modern frame.

L. A. B.

WRIGHT, DANIEL, father and son with the same Christian name, London music-publishers during the early part of the 18th century. Hawkins sums up the character of the elder Wright as a man ' who never printed anything that he did not steal ' (Hist. Music, Novello ed., p. 884). However this may be, the two Wrights published many now very interesting musical works.

Daniel Wright, the elder, was established by, or before, 1709 at the corner of Brook Street, next the Sun Tavern in Holborn, his sign being ' The Golden Bass Violin.' He died or gave up business about 1734. His son, Daniel Wright, junior, had a business on the north side of St. Paul's Churchyard, under the sign ' The Golden Bass,' and may have succeeded J. Clarke and John Hare, earlier publishers, who, in partnership, had a shop here also on the north side with the sign the ' Golden Viol.' Wright, junior, in due course changed his sign to that of the ' Violin and Flute.' He probably gave up trade about 1740, and there seems some likelihood that John JOHNSON of Cheapside founded his extensive business upon that of the younger Wright, though not on the same premises. For some years before the elder Wright's death, or retirement, both names appear on some of the imprints ; the elder at least claimed to be a musical instrument maker. Wright, senior, published Lully's ' Lessons for the Harpsichord or Spinnet,' ob. folio, c. 1710 ; the ' Songs in Hurlothrumbo,' c. 1729, folio ; John Humphries' ' Six Solos for a Violin,' 1726 ; some half-sheet songs, and many curious books of dances and airs for the flute or violin. His son followed much on the same lines. The elder Wright was also notorious for publishing musical works under the same title as, and in similar style to, those issued by Walsh. For instance, he published a ' British Musical Miscellany ' (1733), a ' Merry Musician,' and a ' Monthly Mask of Vocal Musick ' (1718), the latter with a rudely engraved pictorial title-page copied from Walsh. Hawkins speaks of the elder Wright impudently publishing a set of lessons for the harpsichord by Greene, without permission of the composer.

Besides the two Daniel Wrights, senior and junior, there was a musicseller named Thomas Wright—' At the Golden Harp and Violin, on London Bridge,' who published half-sheet engraved songs about 1730-35. Another early musicseller with the same surname was E. Wright, who, according to an elaborately engraved trade card, c. 1740, ' At her music shop under St. Dunstan's Church, Fleet Street, makes and sells all sorts of musical instruments.'   F. K.

WRIGHT, THOMAS (b. Stockton - on - Tees, Sept. 18, 1763; d. Wycliffe Rectory, near Barnard Castle, Nov. 24, 1829), organist and composer, was the son of Robert Wright (a pupil of Avison of Newcastle), who was organist in Stockton Church from 1766–97, the date of his death. Robert was the son of Thomas Wright, the elder, the first organist of Stockton, about 1758–60.

Thomas Wright, the younger, was instructed by his father, and at 11 years of age went to John Garth, at Sedgefield (nine miles from Stockton) as organ pupil ; he succeeded Garth at the organ, 1784–85. Previous to his appointment as full organist, he had been apprenticed to Thomas Ebdon at Durham Cathedral. Wright soon became famous for his extempore voluntaries, and in high repute as a teacher for the pianoforte, violin and organ. He succeeded his father at Stockton in 1797, and resigned the appointment and left Stockton in 1817. After a period of residence and an organ appointment at Kirkleatham, near Redcar, he returned to Stockton and resumed teaching. It was while on a professional engagement that a sudden seizure caused his death, at Wycliffe Rectory, near Barnard Castle. He had married in 1794 Elizabeth Foxton, a lady of some literary attainment who survived him.

Besides the hymn tune ' Stockton,' he composed ' A Concerto for the harpsichord or pianoforte . . . dedicated to the Hon. Miss Dundas,' 1795 ; ' An Anthem for thanksgiving for Peace ' (of Amiens, 1802) ; ' Overtures and Songs in a musical piece called Rusticity,' 1800 (written by his wife) ; ' A Musical Primer ' and ' Supplement,' etc. The 'Concerto' is remarkable for being (so far as the present writer can ascertain) the first music to contain metronome marks, indicating speed value. In the preface

attached, Wright explains his system, and claims that for simplicity and effectiveness it is superior to the chronomètres of Loulié, and of Sauveur (see METRONOME), and to the metronometres of later invention.

A simple pocket metronome consisting of a weighted string swinging across a wooden arc marked from zero in tens, was of his invention or adaptation. One bearing his name and the date 1795 is still in existence. Each movement of the concerto is marked with a speed mark ; and he explains that '28 $=\rho$' indicates that the vibration of a weighted string measured over twenty-eight keys of the harpsichord, goes to a minim. Wright also invented an organ attachment to a square pianoforte, which plays a set of organ pipes at will, without impairing its use as a pianoforte. This invention does not appear ever to have been made public ; his own instrument is in the possession of Miss Edith Wright,[1] of Wakefield, his granddaughter. He built for himself in 1789 a chamber organ, constructed two orreries for illustrating and calculating eclipses, and sent to the Society of Arts a model of a machine for raising coal, for which they had offered a premium.   F. K.

WRIGHT & CO., musicsellers and publishers who, after Elizabeth Randall, succeeded to the business of Walsh about 1782–84, at 13 Catherine Street. The senior partner was Hermond or Herman Wright, and the firm is notable for the reissue of Handel's works from the Walsh plates. About 1800 they removed to 386 Strand, and in 1802 the business was broken up, Preston buying the Handel plates ; some of these descended to J. A. Novello, who republished certain of the oratorios from the original or early plates.   F. K.

WRIGHTEN, MRS. (b. Feb. 1751 ; d. America, Aug. 11, 1796), a favourite vocalist at Vauxhall, from about 1776–88/89. She was much appreciated for her singing of ballads, and was the first to sing in public the popular ' Within a mile of Edinburgh town ' ; this was in the season of 1780. She was also famous in the hunting songs of the period, whose extended range, and heavy instrumental accompaniments, demanded great voice power.

     F. K.

She made her debut in ' The Recruiting Officer,' 1770. Her first husband was a prompter at one of the London theatres. She went to America, where in 1792 she joined John Henry's New York Company and married A. M. Pownall.   W. H. G. F.

WÜERST, RICHARD FERDINAND (b. Berlin, Feb. 22, 1824 ; d. Oct. 9, 1881), composer and critic, was a pupil of Rungenhagen at the Berlin Academy, of Hubert, Ries and David in violin, and of Mendelssohn in composition. After touring for a couple of years, he settled

[1] Much of the above information was kindly supplied by Miss Edith Wright.

at his native place and became in 1856 music director, in 1874 professor, and 1877 member, of the Academy of Arts. He was for many years teacher of composition in Kullak's Conservatorium. He contributed to the *Berliner Fremdenblatt*, and in 1874–75 edited the *Neue Berliner Musikzeitung*. His works comprise seven symphonies, overtures, quartets, etc. G.

WÜLLNER, (1) FRANZ (*b.* Münster, Jan. 28, 1832; *d.* Braunsels, on the Lahn, Sept. 7, 1902), pianist, conductor and composer, was the son of a distinguished philologist, director of the Gymnasium at Düsseldorf. Franz attended the Gymnasium of Münster till 1848, and passed the final examination; studying the piano and composition with Carl Arnold up to 1846, and afterwards with Schindler. In 1848 Wüllner followed Schindler to Frankfort, and continued his studies with him and F. Kessler till 1852. The winter of 1852–53 he passed in Brussels, frequently playing in public, and enjoying the society of Fétis, Kufferath, and other musicians. As a pianist he confined himself almost entirely to Beethoven's concertos and sonatas, especially the later ones. He then made a concert-tour through Bonn, Cologne, Bremen, Münster, etc., and spent some little time in Hanover and Leipzig. In Mar. 1854 he arrived in Munich, and on Jan. 1, 1856, became pianoforte professor at the Conservatorium there. In 1858 he became music-director of the town of Aix-la-Chapelle, being elected unanimously out of fifty-four candidates. Here he conducted the subscription concerts, and the vocal and orchestral unions. He turned his attention mainly to the orchestra and chorus, and introduced for the first time many of the great works to the concert-hall of Aix. In 1861 he received the title of Musikdirector to the King of Prussia, and in 1864 was joint-conductor with Rietz of the 41st Lower Rhine Festival.

In the autumn of 1864 Wüllner returned to Munich as court Kapellmeister to the King. His duty was to conduct the services at the court church, and while there he reorganised the choir, and added to the repertory many fine church works, especially of the early Italian school. He also organised concerts for the choir, the programmes of which included old Italian, old German and modern music, sacred and secular. In the autumn of 1867 he took the organisation and direction of the vocal classes in the king's new school of music, and on Bülow's resignation the whole production department came into his hands, with the title of 'Inspector of the School of Music,' and in 1875 of 'Professor Royal.' During this time he wrote his admirable 'Chorübungen der Münchener Musikschule,' an English edition of which, by A. Spengel, has been published.

When Wüllner succeeded Bülow at the court theatre in 1869, he found himself plunged into personal difficulties of all kinds connected with the production of Wagner's 'Rheingold'; but his tact and ability surmounted all, and the result was an unqualified success. The 'Rheingold' was followed by the 'Walküre,' one of the most brilliant achievements of the Munich stage, and in 1870 Wüllner was appointed court Kapellmeister in chief. He also succeeded Bülow as conductor of the concerts of the Academy of Music, and carried them on alone till Levi was associated with him in 1872. In 1877 he left Munich,[1] in order to succeed Rietz at Dresden as Kapellmeister of the court theatre, and artist director of the Conservatorium; but after five years he was deprived of his post at the opera, without any reason given; in 1882 he conducted the Lower Rhine Festival at Aix-la-Chapelle, and in 1883–84 the Philharmonic Orchestra in Berlin. On Oct. 1, 1884, he was appointed to succeed Hiller as head of the Cologne Conservatorium and conductor of the Gürzenich concerts there. He was succeeded by Steinbach.

Wüllner's works include — 'Heinrich der Finkler,' cantata for voice and orchestra—first prize at the competition of the Aix-la-Chapelle Liedertafel in 1864; PF. pieces for 2 and 4 hands, and chamber-music; several books of Lieder for single voice; important choral compositions, with and without orchestra, such as masses, motets, Lieder for mixed chorus, a Stabat Mater, a Miserere for double choir, op. 26; Psalm cxxv. for chorus and orchestra, op. 40, etc.; a new arrangement of Weber's 'Oberon,' the additional recitatives being compiled from materials in the opera (the libretto by F. Grandaur of Munich). In this form 'Oberon' has been put on the stage at several of the great German theatres. His editions of six of Haydn's symphonies Rieter-Biedermann) must not be overlooked.

His son, (2) LUDWIG (*b.* Münster, Aug. 19, 1858), studied philology, etc., at Munich, Berlin, and Strassburg, took the Doctor's degree, and became a teacher in the Münster Academy, 1884–87. After two years' study at the Cologne Conservatorium he went on the stage at Meiningen in 1889. In 1895 he adopted the career of a reciter, and in 1896 that of a singer; notwithstanding his many vocal shortcomings, his performances called forth great admiration for their dramatic intensity. M. F.

WULFSTAN, monk and precentor of St. Swithin's, Winchester, *c.* 1000. William of Malmesbury ascribes to him a treatise, *De tonorum harmonia*, which has not been rediscovered so far. E. V. D. S.

WURM, MARIE (*b.* Southampton, May 18, 1860), the daughter of a musician of that town, who died in 1892. Marie Wurm studied the piano and composition at the Stuttgart Conservatorium, with Franklin Taylor, Mme. Schumann, Joachim Raff and others. She appeared in Schumann's concerto at the Crystal

---

[1] The University conferred on him the honorary degree of Doctor.

Palace in 1882, and at the Popular Concerts in 1884, in which year she gained the Mendelssohn Scholarship. She gave successful pianoforte recitals in London and in Germany, which country has been her residence for a good many years past. On one of her later visits to England she gave a concert entirely consisting of music extemporised on themes given by the audience. She has composed a piano concerto and an orchestral overture ; a string quartet, a violoncello sonata, many pianoforte pieces, etc.

For her two younger sisters see VERNE. M.

WYDOW, ROBERT, Mus.B. (WEDOW, WIDOWS, WYDEWE, etc., and latinised into VIDUUS) (d. Oct. 4, 1505). According to Leland he was born at Thaxted, in Essex. He was educated by his stepfather, the master and proprietor of a school at Thaxted, who ultimately sent him to Oxford to complete his studies. While there he distinguished himself in literature and the arts, especially in poetry and music, finally taking the degree of Bachelor of Music. His is the first recorded degree of the kind at Oxford ; he was incorporated at Cambridge in the same degree in 1502. After his stepfather's death Robert Wydow succeeded him as master of the school, and is said to have turned out several illustrious pupils. Among his patrons, Wydow numbered Edward IV., who appointed him to one of the two chantries in the low chapel under le Croft in Christ Church, Canterbury, on Jan. 12, 1474.[1] As Edward had some connexion with Thaxted, being lord of a third of the manor, it is not unreasonable to suppose that it was owing to that monarch's good offices that he obtained the presentation to the vicarage of Thaxted on Dec. 22, 1481. This living, which was then worth about £28, Wydow resigned on Oct. 1, 1489. It was probably at this period that he travelled in France and Italy for the purposes of study, and added to those stores of learning which gained him the appellation of ' Grammaticus ' ; and it was perhaps on his return from the Continent that he was made ' Penitentiarius ' in St. Paul's Cathedral, if, as is generally believed, he really held that post. On Nov. 19, 1493, he was collated rector of Chalfont St. Giles, in Buckinghamshire, a place afterwards associated with the more illustrious names of John Milton and William Penn. After enjoying that living for rather more than three years, he was installed by proxy Canon and Confrater of Comba II., in Wells Cathedral, on Mar. 27, 1497 ; and a few months later (Sept. 10) was appointed Succentor in the place of Henry ABYNGDON. On Sept. 21, 1499, he obtained the vicarage of Chew Magna, in Somerset, which he held till his death. In 1499-1500 he was made one of the residentiary canons, and on May 25 in the latter year was installed Sub-Dean and Prebendary of Hol-

combe Burnell, in Devonshire. About the same time Robert Wydow was made deputy for the transaction of affairs between the Pope and the Cathedral and Chapter of Wells ; he was also granted the advowson of Wookey, in Somerset, the rectory and vicarage of which were together worth about £15. He also held about this time the offices of ' Scrutator Domorum ' and Librarian in the Chapter House. On Sept. 21, 1502, Wydow was made Seneschal, and shortly after Auditor, of the Chapter House. On Oct. 1, 1503, he was presented to the perpetual vicarage of Buckland Newton, in Dorset, which is the last event recorded in his life. He was a man of some wealth, if we may judge from his benefactions to the Carthusian Priory of Henton, near Bath, which were so considerable that a Requiem was ordered to be sung for his soul in every house of the Order throughout the kingdom. Edward Lee, Archbishop of York, who in his younger days had met Wydow, called him ' facile princeps ' among the poets of his day. Holinshed speaks of him as an ' excellent poet,' and classes him among the celebrities of Henry VII.'s reign. Wydow's chief poetical work was a rhythmical life of Edward the Black Prince, to which Leland refers in these words :

' Contulit Hectoreis arguta voce triumphis
Eduerdum Viduus doctissimus ille Nigellum
Et facti pretium tulit immortale poeta.'

This work is said to have been written by Wydow at the instigation of his royal patron. He also wrote a book of epigrams. No musical composition by this author is extant. A. H.-H.

WYLDE, HENRY (b. Bushey, Herts, May 22, 1822 ; d. London, Mar. 13, 1890), conductor and composer. Though intended for Holy Orders he had so strong a bent for music that he became organist of Whitchurch, was placed at 16 under Moscheles, and in 1843 became a student, under Cipriani Potter, at the R.A.M., of which he afterwards was appointed one of the professors of harmony. He was organist of St. Anne's, Aldersgate Street, and St. Agnes, Gresham Street, 1844-47, and in 1851 he accumulated the degrees of Mus.B. and Mus.D. at Cambridge. He acted as Juror in the Musical Instrument Section in the International Exhibitions of 1851 and 1862, and in 1863 was elected professor of music at Gresham College, London. In 1852 the NEW PHILHARMONIC SOCIETY (q.v.) was founded by Sir Charles Fox, and others, on the advice of Dr. Wylde. In 1858 he assumed the sole responsibility of the undertaking, and conducted its annual series of concerts till 1879. In 1861 Dr. Wylde founded the LONDON ACADEMY OF MUSIC (at first at St. James's Hall) and built St. George's Hall, Langham Place, for its purposes, which was opened in the summer of 1867. Dr. Wylde's musical compositions include a cantata on Milton's ' Paradise Lost ' for soli, chorus and orchestra, performed by the New Philharmonic Society, May 11, 1853, and May 1, 1854 ; and a cantata, ' Prayer and Praise,' for the same ; selection performed, June 9, 1852 ; pianoforte concerto in F minor, performed Apr. 14, 1852 ; pianoforte sonatas ; a ' Rhapsodie for piano ' (op. 2) ; ' Fantasia sur un air favori ' (op. 6) ; English songs from Goethe and Schiller ; English songs, ' The Sea Nymphs,' vocal duet, etc. Dr. Wylde was also the author of *The Science of Music* (1865) ; *Music in its Art Mysteries* (1867) ; *Modern Counterpoint* (1873) ; *Occult Principles of Music* (1881) ; *Music as an Educator* (1882) ; *Evolution of the Beautiful in Sound* (1887). He died in London and was buried in Kensal Green Cemetery. (*Brit. Mus. Biog.*, etc.)   A. C.

WYNGAERDE (VINEA), ANTONIUS, of Utrecht (*d.* Antwerp, 1499), a composer living at Antwerp, mentioned by Glarean, who reproduces his Ego dormio, 4 v., which appears also in Tschudi's MS., No. 463 in the library of St. Gall (*Q.-L.*).

WYNKYN DE WORDE (London, 15th-16th cent.), the first English music-printer. See PRINTING OF MUSIC.

WYNNE, JOHN, a musician and a music-seller, living at Cambridge at the middle of the 18th century. His address was in Regent's Walk, and his name is found on London imprints as selling particular musical works. His compositions comprise ' Ten English songs set to musick,' published by John Johnson, and dated 1754, before which, *circa* 1740–45, had been an earlier set of ' Twelve English Songs ' issued by John Simpson.   F. K.

WYNNE, (1) SARAH EDITH (called Eos Cymru —' the Welsh Nightingale ') (*b.* Holywell, Flintshire, Mar. 11, 1842 ; *d.* London, Jan. 24, 1897), was taught singing by Mrs. Scarisbrick of Liverpool, and by Pinsuti, at the R.A.M., where she was Westmorland Scholar, 1863–64.

She was subsequently taught by Romani and Vannuccini at Florence. She first sang in the provinces, and made her début in London (St. James's Hall) at John Thomas's Welsh concert, July 4, 1862. She sang with great success in the following year at Henry Leslie's Welsh concert, Feb. 4 ; at the Crystal Palace, Apr. 25 ; at Thomas's concert in his cantata ' Llewellyn,' June 29 ; and as the heroine on the production of Macfarren's ' Jessy Lea,' at the Gallery of Illustration, Nov. 2. She played Lady Mortimer at Drury Lane on the revival of *King Henry IV.* in 1864. She played a few times in English opera at the Crystal Palace in 1869–71 as Arline, Maritana, Lady Edith (in Randegger's ' Rival Beauties ') ; but she was chiefly noted for her singing of songs and ballads and especially in her own Welsh songs ; she was remarkable alike for her passionate expression and the simplicity of her pathos. She sang in the United States with the Pateys, Cummings and Santley, in 1871–72, and at the Boston Festival of 1874. After her marriage with Aviet Agabeg, at the Savoy Chapel, Nov. 16, 1875, she sang less frequently in public, and devoted herself to teaching. Her last appearances were at John Thomas's concert in 1894, and at Aberystwith in 1896.

Her sister (2) KATE (called Llinos Cwynedd— ' the Welsh Linnet ') was a favourite contralto singer. She retired in 1877, on her marriage with Harry Matthison of Birmingham. Their daughter is the well-known actress Edith Wynne-Matthison (Mrs. Charles Rann Kennedy).   A. C.

WYSSENBACH, RUDOLF, of Zürich, a 16th-century type-cutter (*Formschneider*), music printer and publisher, the compiler of a lute-book in tablature, 1550. Another edition, printed and published by Gessner, appeared at Zürich in 1563. Wyssenbach is mentioned only in the preface of this edition (*Q.-L.*).

X

XYLOPHONE (Fr. *xylophon, claquebois*; Ger. *Strohfiedel* or *Holzharmonika*; Ital. *zilafone, gigelira* or *sticcato*), *i.e.* Strawfiddle (also known as Ligneum Psalterium) is described by Mendel in his Lexicon as a very ancient and widespread instrument, found principally among the Russians, Poles and Tartars, consisting of a range of flat pieces of deal or glass,[1] of no settled number, tuned to the scale, arranged on belts of straw, and struck with two small hammers (cf. STICCADO PASTROLE). *(PLATE XXIV. No. 8.)*

Its sound was sweet and bell-like, but weak. Mendelssohn wrote, à propos of GUSIKOW'S performance upon it:

' With a few sticks, lying on straw and struck with other sticks, he does what is possible only on the most perfect instrument. How from such materials even the small tone produced—more like a Papageno-

---

[1] Burney (*Present State (Ger.*), vol. ii. p. 71) found it at Dresden, and, under the name of *Strofl*, describes it as made with glass, and played on with sticks, ' like the *sticcado.*'

fife than anything else—can be obtained, is a mystery to me.' [2]

Gusikow's Strohfiedel, however, seems to have been an improved kind. It was strong enough to bear the accompaniment of two violins and a violoncello. The Strohfiedel was introduced into the orchestra in Lumbye's ' Traumbildern.'

In its modern form, usually with a compass from to , the tone-quality has changed, being weird and sombre, suggesting the rattle of dry bones (see Saint-Saëns's 'Danse Macabre'), rather than the cheerfulness of bells and chimes. The bars are made of rosewood supported by resonators and are struck with beaters of willow or boxwood. The part is written on one stave in the treble clef and usually at the actual pitch required.

G. ; addns. D. J. B. and N. C. G.

[2] *Mendelssohn Family*, 1836, Feb. 12.

YANIEWICZ, FELIX, see JANIEWICZ.

YANKEE DOODLE. With an obsolete text, 'Yankee Doodle' can hardly be called a national song, but it is still one of the current national airs of the United States. Its vitality has not been impaired by criticism of its musical merits, and will not be as long as there is room in patriotic folk-music for humorous, indeed, burlesque utterances.

As 'Yankee Doodle' the air seems first to have been printed in the first volume of James Aird's 'Selection of Scotch, English, Irish and Foreign Airs,' Glasgow (1782), as Frank Kidson pointed out in his 'Old English Country Dances' (1890). Aird gives this form[1] :

Slightly different it appeared as 'Yankee Doodle' in Arnold's opera 'Two to One' (1784), and was sung there by John Edwin in the character of Dicky Ditto to the words 'Adzooks, old Crusty, why so rusty ? ' Again slightly different is the version in Charles Dibdin's 'Musical Tour' (1788), to the words 'I sing Ulysses and those chiefs,' and entitled 'The return of Ulysses to Ithaca.' This burlesque song Dibdin is said to have first introduced in his 'Reasonable Animals' (1780).

The question of the earliest American appearance in print of 'Yankee Doodle' is still open. In Moore's 'Songs and Ballads of the American Revolution' (1855), it is claimed that 'The Recess' appeared with this air as a music-sheet in 1779, but no such musical broadside has been found ; and the history of music-printing in America renders it doubtful if the air found its way into print here before forming an ingredient to Benjamin Carr's medley, 'Federal Overture,' composed 1794 and published 1795. The earliest printed American version extant is that published by G. Willig, Philadelphia (1798), together with the President's March (' Hail, Columbia ') in the following form, to the words ' Columbians all the present hour '.

After this, 'Yankee Doodle' became frequent in print, but, curiously enough, for decades nearly all versions differed slightly, and they differ also more or less from two early American MS. versions, the one dated 1790 (in private

[1] A full discussion of all possible sources of this song and summary of the bibliography relating thereto appeared in the second edition of this Dictionary. The reader is referred to *Report on* 'The Star-spangled Banner,' 'Hail, Columbia,' 'America,' 'Yankee Doodle,' by O. G. Sonneck (Library of Congress Publication, Washington, 1909).

hands, the other, possibly written as early as 1775, at the Boston Public Library. The form now used officially is the one given in Sousa's ' National . . . Airs ' (1890), and the smaller notes in the above example illustrate the differences from the Willig version. O. G. S.

YATES, WILLIAM, an 18th-century English composer, appeared in London at a concert given by himself in 1764. In Lent 1765, his masque, ' The Choice of Apollo,' was performed. He wrote a number of songs for Vauxhall and Marylebone Gardens, a collection of moral songs or hymns, 6 easy sonatas for the harpsichord, op. 3, etc. (Q.-L.).

YEOMEN OF THE GUARD, THE: or, THE MERRYMAN AND HIS MAID, opera in 2 acts ; words by W. S. Gilbert ; music by Sullivan. Produced Savoy Theatre, Oct. 3, 1888. M.

YON, PIETRO (b. Settimo-Vittone, Italy, Aug. 6, 1886), Italian organist and composer. He studied at the Conservatoires of Milan and Turin ; in 1904 he entered the Academy of St. Cecilia, where he studied organ with Renzi, piano with Sgambati and composition with de Sanctis. For two years he served as substitute organist at the Vatican and the Royal Church in Rome. Since 1907 he has been organist and choirmaster of the Church of St. Francis Xavier in New York, and he has won a wide reputation as concert-organist. In 1921 he was made honorary organist of the Basilica of St. Peter, Vatican, Rome. His compositions include a 'Concerto Gregoriane' for organ and orchestra ; masses ; choral music ; many organ pieces, pianoforte pieces and songs. W. S. S.

YONGE (YOUNG, YONG), NICHOLAS, (b. Lewes, Sussex ; d. Cornhill, London, Oct. 1619), the compiler of MUSICA TRANSALPINA, is probably identical with a Nicholas Young who was a singing-man at St. Paul's Cathedral in the time of Elizabeth. Burney, misled by a passage in the Dedication to the first book of 'Musica Transalpina,' a collection of 57 madrigals, translated and published in 1588, says that he was an Italian merchant, whereas all that Yonge says is :

' Since I first began to keepe house in this citie, a great number of Gentlemen and Merchants of good accompt (as well of this realme as of forreine nations) have taken in good part such entertainment of pleasure, as my poore abilitie was able to affoord them, both by the exercise of Musicke daily used in my house, and by furnishing them with Bookes of that kind yeerely sent me out of Italy and other places.'

Yonge's mother's maiden name was Bray. During the greater part of his life he lived in the parish of St. Michael, Cornhill: he had nine children, most of whom survived him and settled in the same parish, where his descendants remained until the 18th century, when some of them are found in that of St. James, Clerkenwell. His wife's name was Jane, and he was probably married about 1584. The title-page of the first Book of MUSICA TRANSALPINA (*q.v.*) has been already given under that heading, that of the second Book of 24 songs (1597) runs as follows :

'Musica Transalpina. The Second Booke of Madrigalles, to 5 and 6 Voices : translated out of sundrie Italian Authors. and newly published by Nicholas Yonge. At London Printed by Thomas Este. 1597.'

Lists of the contents of both volumes are printed (with many mistakes) in Rimbault's *Bibliotheca Madrigaliana* (1847). Both books (copies of which are in the B.M., R.C.M. and Huth Collections) seem to have been very successful. 'A. B.' printed the words of three of the madrigals in *England's Helicon* (1600), and Dr. Heather, in his portrait in the Bodl. Mus. Sch., is represented holding a volume lettered 'Musica Transalpina.' G. W. Budd began a complete reissue of the collection, but issued only six of the 81 pieces (1843). (*D.N.B.*) The text of the first book was issued in Arber's *English Garner*, vol. iii. Yonge's will (which was proved by his wife on Nov. 12) is dated Oct. 19, 1619, and he was buried at St. Michael's, Cornhill, on the 23rd of the same month.[1]

W. B. S.

YORKE TROTTER, THOMAS HENRY, (*b.* Nov. 6, 1854) M.A., D.Mus. Oxon, is principal of the London Academy of Music (Incorporated). He has devised a successful system for the practical education of children in the elements of music (see EXTEMPORISATION). Teachers of this system are trained at Dr. Yorke Trotter's Academy. His principles are embodied in the following publications :

Constructive Harmony; *Rhythmic Gradus*; *Ear Training and Sight Reading*; *The Making of Musicians* (1922); *Music and Mind* (1924).

C.

YORK MUSICAL FESTIVAL (1791–1835). The first festival was in 1791, and they were continued annually till 1803. After that no other festival took place until 1823,[2] when the performance was revived for the benefit of the York County Hospital, and the Infirmaries at Leeds, Sheffield and Hull. The scheme consisted of four sacred concerts, including the 'Messiah' in its entirety, held in the Cathedral on the mornings of Sept. 23 to 25, three secular evening

concerts, and two balls given in the Assembly Rooms. The vocalists were Mme. Catalani (who usurped ' Comfort ye,' ' Every valley,' and introduced ' Non più andrai '), Mrs. Salmon, Misses Stephens, D. Travis and Goodall, sopranos ; Knyvett and Buggins, altos ; Bellamy, Sherwood and Placci, bass. The band and chorus contained 180 instrumentalists and 285 vocalists ; in the former were Cramer and Mori, leaders ; Griesbach, Ella, Lindley, Dragonetti, Puzzi, Harper, etc., Greatorex was conductor, Matthew CAMIDGE (who had officiated in 1791) and his son John, Knapton and White, organists. The festival was rendered noteworthy from the receipts being larger than those at any previous meeting, viz. £16,174 : 16 : 8. The sum of £7200 was divided among the charities. A long and voluminous account is given of the above in a 4to volume by John Crosse, F.S.A.. York, 1825, to which we are indebted for the above information.[3]

A second festival was held in Sept. 1825. on a similar plan and for the same charities. The band and chorus were increased to 600, and among the vocalists who appeared for the first time were Madame Caradori-Allan, Madame Malibran (then Miss Garcia), Braham, Phillips and De Begnis. The receipts were still larger, viz. £20,876 : 10s. ; but owing to the cost of a concert-hall for the evening concerts, the profits were not in proportion, £1900 only being divided among the charities.

A third festival was held in Sept. 1828. Catalani reappeared, and Miss Paton, Madame Stockhausen and Edward Taylor sang for the first time. Beethoven's symphony in F was a novelty to the audience, and not so successful as the C minor in 1823. It was described in the *Harmonicon* as ' eccentric and very difficult,' and was coldly received. The receipts diminished to £16,769 : 11 : 6, and £1400 only was obtained for the charities. Another festival was given in 1835.

A. C.

YOST (JOST), MICHEL (*b.* Paris, *c.* 1754 : *d.* ? there, July 5, 1786), a famous clarinettist, studied under Beer. He appeared regularly as soloist at the Concert Spirituel. He composed a number of concertos, trios, duos and solos. which he simply signed Michel ; nearly all remained in MS. (*Q.-L.*).

YOULL, HENRY (*fl.* 1608), composer. Nothing is known of the personal history of this musician except what can be gathered from the dedication of his set of Canzonets to the four sons of Edward Bacon, who seems to have been his patron. On the title-page he is called a ' Practicioner in the Art of Musicke.' This volume of ' Canzonets to three voyces ' was published in 1608. It is reprinted in ENG. MADR. SCH., vol. xxviii. Copies are extremely scarce ; one is in the British Museum, one in

---

[1] The information contained in this article is chiefly derived from the Registers o' St. Michael's, Cornhill, and the Visitation of London, both published by the Harleian Society.

[2] See *Description of the Great Musical Festival held in York during Sept. 1823, by the editor of the 'York Courant,'* York, 1823.

[3] A satire on his somewhat bombastic style was published in London the same year, by an anonymous writer ' Outis.'

the Cambridge University Library, and the bass partbook is in the Bodleian Library. It contains some very attractive pieces, notably 'Pipe, shepherds, pipe,' a setting of Ben Jonson's 'Slow, slow, fresh fount,' and Sidney's 'Only joy, now here you are.' There are six ballets at the end of the book which are as good as anything of the kind for three voices.

E. H. F.

YOUNG, a family of musicians. (1) AN-THONY was organist of St. Clement Danes in 1707, and at another period of St. Catherine Cree, near the Tower. According to de Lafon-taine's *The King's Musick*, two boys, named Anthony Young and John Reading, left the Chapel Royal, on the breaking of their voices, at Michaelmas 1700 ; one of these is evidently the above Anthony Young. It is even possible that he may have been the son of William YOUNG who was a violinist in the King's private band.

Anthony Young composed songs, one being an excellent setting of 'Send home my long-strayed eyes,' which, along with Leveridge's tune, was published as half-sheet music about 1720.

He has been foolishly credited with being the composer of 'God save the King.' [1] He was probably the father of (2) CHARLES, organist of All Hallows, Barking, and (according to Dr. Burney) was father of the Misses Young, three singers in great repute about 1735-40. Hawkins, probably incorrectly, names Charles Young as their father.

They were (3) CECILIA (b. 1711 ; d. Oct. 6, 1789), the eldest, who married Dr. Arne in 1736. The second daughter, (4) ISABELLA, became the wife of J. F. Lampe, and (5) ESTHER married —— Jones, probably John Jones, organist of the Temple Church in 1749. (6) MARY (b. circa 1745 ; d. Sept. 20, 1799) may have been of the family. She married, in 1766, F. H. Barthéle-mon, and was a soprano vocalist, who appeared in opera at Drury Lane and Covent Garden.

F. K.

YOUNG, (1) JOHN, a music-publisher and a 'musical instrument seller' at the sign of the 'Dolphin and Crown,' at the west end of St. Paul's Church Yard. The earliest notice the present writer has found regarding him is an advertisement in the *London Gazette* of 1698, of

'The Compleat Tutor to the Violin, . . . by John Bannister, published by J. Young, at the Dolphin and Crown'

He also published 'A Choice Collection of Ayres,' by Blow, Piggot, Clarke, Barrett and Croft, 1700 (B.M.). 'The Flute Master Com-pleat ; Improved, or the Gentleman's Diver-sion,' 1706 (Bodl.). Later works are mostly issued with the names of Walsh & Hare, as well as Young on the imprint, as Jer. Clarke's 'Choice Lessons for the Harpsichord or

1 See R. Clark's *Account of the National Anthem*, 1822, and Dr. Cummings's work on the same subject, 1902.

Spinett,' 1711, Simpson's 'Compendium,' 'The Third Volume of the Dancing Master,' c. 1728, etc. etc. ; also many half-sheet songs. It is probable that he gave up business or died shortly after 1730. He had a son, (2) TALBOT, who helped, with Greene and others, to estab-lish a musical society, at first held at his father's house and afterwards at the Queen Head Tavern, and then at the Castle Tavern, both in Paternoster Row. He was a clever performer on the violin, and a witty catch was made upon father and son : it is printed in Henry Playford's 'Second Book of the Pleasant Musical Companion,' 1701, as follows :

'A CATCH UPON MR. YOUNG AND HIS SON.'—*Dr. Cæsar.*

'You scrapers that want a good fiddle well strung,
You should go to the man that is old while he's Young.
But if this same fiddle you fain wou'd play bold,
You must go to his son, who'll be Young when he's old.
There's old Young and young Young, both men of renown.
Old sells, and young plays the best fiddle in town.
Young and old live together and may they live long,
Young to play an old fiddle, Old to sell a new song'

In de Lafontaine's *The King's Musick*, is a record of a John Young being appointed musician in ordinary to the King, for the viola da gamba, on May 23, 1673, in place of one, Paul Bridges. It is quite probable that John Young, the musicseller, may be this same person.

F. K.

YOUNG, NICHOLAS, see YONGE.

YOUNG, THOMAS (b. Canterbury, 1809 ; d. Walworth, Aug. 12, 1872), received his musical education there, and from 1831-36 was first principal alto singer at the cathedral. In 1836 he became deputy and afterwards lay vicar at Westminster Abbey, and Mar. 3, 1848, first alto at the Temple. This last post he held until his death, with the exception of a year's interval, when he married the widow of a Canterbury alderman and went into business without success. Young was an excellent solo singer, and was successor in public favour to Knyvett and Machin, being the last male alto soloist of eminence. As such he was frequently heard at the Ancient and Sacred Harmonic Concerts. With the latter Society he sang for a period of ten years ; he first appeared Nov. 14, 1837, in the Dettingen Te Deum and Mozart's 'Twelfth Mass,' etc. He took the parts of Hamor and Joad on the respective revivals of 'Jephthah' and 'Athaliah.' He also sang in the revival of Purcell's Jubilate and in various anthems and services.   A. C.

YOUNG, WILLIAM (d. 1672), a skilled per-former on the viol and violin ; flourishing in the middle of the 17th century. He is said to have been in the service as domestic musician of the Count of Innsbruck. While there he composed and published a set of twenty-one sonatas for three violins, viola and bass. The title of the work is 'Sonate (21) a 3, 4, 5 voci con allemande, corrante, etc., a 3. Inspruck,

1653,' folio, dedicated to the Archduke Ferdinand Karl. A copy of this rare work is stated to be in the library of the University of Upsala, and is cited by Walther. Other detached pieces by William Young occur in Playford's 'Musical Banquet,' 1651, 'Musick's Recreation on the Lyra Viol,' 1652, and elsewhere in the Playford publications. Also there are some pieces in manuscript in the Music School collection at the Bodleian. On Playford's 'Treasury of Musick,' 1669, is advertised ' Mr. Will Young, his Fantazies for viols, of three parts.' This may be either a reprint of, or the original Innsbruck sonatas.

It is probable that Young returned to England about 1660, for in that year a William Young entered the King's private band as a flute-player.[1] In 1661 he was, in addition, appointed to the violin. In this early stage of his royal appointments he appears to have roused some ill feeling, for Nicholas Lanier, the master of His Majesty's Musick, was ordered to allow him and other musicians to use the practice chamber from which he had been excluded.

He was among the best players of the band, and on some occasions was selected to attend His Majesty, with certain violinists. In 1664 he was allowed, with others of the band, to attend at the theatre when Mr. Killigrew desired it. On his death Nicholas Staggins obtained his place.

He may have been the father of John YOUNG, the music-publisher, and of Anthony YOUNG.   F. K.

YOUNG PEOPLE'S SYMPHONY CONCERTS, see NEW YORK.

YRADIER, SEBASTIAN (d. Vittoria, Nov. 1865), a successful composer of Spanish songs, some of which it is known were in the hands of Bizet when he composed ' Carmen.' A collection of twenty-five of his most popular songs ('25 Chants avec paroles françaises ') was issued in Paris shortly after his death (Baker).   M.

YRIARTE, DON TOMAS DE (b. Teneriffe, Sept. 18, 1750; d. Santa Maria, near Cadiz, Sept. 17, 1791), was secretary of the archives in Madrid. He wrote poems under the anagram Tirso Imareta, and composed symphonies, quartets, songs and a ' monodrama,' ' Guzman el bueno.' His chief work is La Musica, a Spanish poem on music published in 1779. It is in irregular metre, and is divided into five cantos. The first two deal with elements such as the notes, scales and ornaments, and with musical expression in its various branches. In the third, which treats of church music, the writer distinguishes three principal species—(1) the Gregorian, having no measure of time in its five varieties ; (2) the Mixed or Florid, measured by common or triple time, admitting of various cadences and ornaments ; and (3)

the Organic, to some extent a combination of the two former, in which both voices and instruments were employed. Here the writer takes occasion to praise the Spanish composers Patiño, Roldan, Garcia, Viana, Guerrero, Victoria, Ruiz, Morales, Duron, Literes, San Juan and Nebra. The canto closes with a description of the examinations for admission to the Royal Chapel, from which it appears that candidates were required to show proficiency on the organ, violin, flute and hautboy, and to play sonatas at sight. The fourth canto treats of theatrical music : the shade of Jommelli appears, and after assigning to Spain the palm for pure vocal music, to Germany and Bohemia for instrumental, to France for science, and to Italy for the opera, gives a lengthened description of the orchestra, of recitative, ' greater than declamation, less than song,' which he limits to the compass of an octave, and of the aria with its various graces, the rondeau, cavatina, duos, trios, quartets, etc. Among dramatic authors the palm is assigned to Gluck, whose rivalry with Sacchini and Piccinni was distracting the musical world. The fifth and last canto, which treats of chamber music, contains a long eulogy of Haydn, who is said to have enjoyed special appreciation in Madrid, where prizes were given for the best interpretations of his compositions. The poem concludes with a wish for the establishment of an academy of music. It was translated into French, German and Italian ; and an English version by John Belfour, who acknowledges the assistance of Dr. Burney, Dr. Callcott, and S. Wesley, was published in 1807.   E. J. P.

YSAŸE, (1) EUGÈNE (b. Liège, July 16, 1858), famous violinist and conductor.

Ysaÿe's early lessons were given him by his father, Nicolas Ysaÿe, at the age of five. He then joined the Conservatoire of his native town and studied under Rodolphe Massart (violin) and Michel Dupuis (harmony), gaining a second prize with Ovide Musin in 1867. Two years earlier he had already made his first public appearance at a small concert given at Montègnée, near Liège, but it cannot be said that his performances as a youth attracted much attention. Then came two pieces of good fortune— the one in 1873 when he had the opportunity of studying under Wieniawski, the other in 1876 when Vieuxtemps, after hearing him play one of his concertos at Antwerp, and being much impressed by the talent displayed, used his influence to obtain a special subsidy from the Government which enabled him to study for another three years. During that period he received many private lessons from Vieuxtemps himself, who held Ysaÿe at all times in the highest esteem. This was evidenced in many ways, especially in his later days, when, being in Algiers and seeking to recuperate after serious illness, he expressed the desire (impossible

---
[1] De Lafontaine, The King's Musick.

of realisation) that Ysaÿe should be sent for to play some of his compositions to him, and was frequently heard to say that he was ' haunted by the *chanterelle* of Ysaÿe.' [1]

In 1879 Ysaÿe played at the concerts given by Pauline Lucca at Cologne and Aix-la-Chapelle, and made the acquaintance of Ferdinand Hiller, who introduced him to Joachim, before whom he played Vieuxtemps's fourth concerto to Hiller's accompaniment. Joachim listened in silence, but said, just before leaving, 'I never heard the violin played like that before.' The remark was ambiguous, but whether tinged with praise or blame, it serves to illustrate what was the salient feature of the art of Ysaÿe— viz. his originality in technique and in the conception and treatment of music.

Hiller took great interest in the young artist, and after obtaining for him an engagement in Oct. 1879, to play Mendelssohn's concerto at a festival of the Gürzenich concerts at Cologne, advised him to go to Frankfort, where he enjoyed some fruitful intercourse with Joachim Raff, and played, with Madame Schumann, Beethoven's C minor sonata.   In 1880 he was appointed leader of Bilse's orchestra in Berlin, an engagement which lasted a year, in the course of which he gained his first experiences as a conductor, after which (in 1881) he toured in Norway with Ole Bull's son as manager, and (in 1883) played at a concert of the Paris Conservatoire under Colonne.   In 1886 he accepted the post of violin professor at the Brussels Conservatoire, holding the appointment till 1898.   It was at this period that he founded the ' Ysaÿe Orchestral Concerts ' at Brussels, of which he was not only the conductor but also entrepreneur and manager, achieving success, both artistic and financial, in spite of the absence of either guarantee fund or subscription list.

His subsequent tours were very numerous, some in early days, of an adventurous nature. He met with enemies as well as friends—that was inevitable with his original style of playing— and the musical world only gradually awakened to an appreciation of his merits.   He first succeeded in impressing the Berlin critics, in Mar. 1899, by a striking performance of Bach's concerto in E at a Philharmonic concert conducted by Nikisch.   His free reading of Bach was recognised as containing elements of beauty which attracted even audiences accustomed to the more austere rendering of German artists.   The same may be said of his moving interpretation of Beethoven's great concerto in D, which has won him admirers in every musical centre in Europe.

He first visited America in 1894 and toured there subsequently with great success, declining an invitation, however, to succeed Seidl as conductor of the New York Philharmonic in

¹ Radoux's *Life of Vieuxtemps*.

1898.   In England his first appearance was in 1889 (in Beethoven's concerto) at a Philharmonic concert.   In the autumn of that year he appeared at the Popular Concerts for the first time, and in 1896 gave three concerts of his own (one orchestral), and another in 1899, etc.   In Feb. 1900 he led quartets at the Popular Concerts (with Inwards, Gibson and Ludwig), and the same year played trios in Queen's Hall (with Busoni and Becker).   In 1901 he brought from Brussels his own quartet (Marchot, Van Hout, and J. Jacob) and introduced several modern chamber works to London audiences.   Though the virtuoso element in his playing tended to undue prominence of the first violin part in quartets, his readings of the greater works of the chamber music repertory never failed to reveal a musical personality of remarkable interest.   Subsequently he gave many series of recitals and sonata concerts at Queen's Hall with Pugno and others.

In Paris, where he had an enthusiastic following, he found an audience for modern sonatas, mostly written by composers of the French and Belgian school.   César Franck's only sonata, which was composed for and dedicated to him, he may be said to have popularised, and he also won acceptance for the sonata written by his compatriot, Guillaume Lekeu.   His repertory was therefore very wide in range, though including less of the compositions of the neo-Russian school than that of most modern violinists.   A late addition to his achievements was his performance of the concerto of Brahms in Oct. 1909, of which he gave a strongly individual interpretation.   An appreciation of his style would be incomplete without mention of his considerable use of tempo rubato ; and it should be also mentioned that, though in the main fiery and impulsive, his playing at its best was kept well under control, as evidenced by his treatment of the vibrato, of which he made constant use, yet would play occasionally passages entirely without it, producing what he himself has called a ' white tone.'

Until 1914, when the war made Ysaÿe an exile, Brussels remained his headquarters, where he was the centre of a devoted circle of admirers and carried on his work, teaching and conducting (see VIOLIN-PLAYING).   He subsequently went to America and accepted (1918) the conductorship of the Cincinnati Orchestra.

He has played successively upon a J. B. Guadagnini violin, a Stradivari of large dimensions and late date, and an exceptionally fine J. Guarneri del Gesù, which has been for some years past his solo instrument, the Stradivari being kept in reserve for contingencies.   The latter, unfortunately, he no longer possesses, as it was stolen from the artists' room of a concert hall in St. Petersburg in 1908.   He is the owner, it may be added, of a fine collection of French violins.

He has composed many concertos for violin, which remain in MS., and has published some smaller pieces for violin solo, including 3 mazurkas, op. 11, and a ' Poème élégiaque.'

Ysaÿe has received many orders and decorations, including that of the Légion d'honneur.

w. w. c.

His brother, (2) THÉOPHILE (b. Verviers, 1865; d. Nice, Mar. 24, 1918), studied at the Conservatoire of Liège, at Berlin under Kullak, and in Paris with César Franck. He attained considerable skill as a pianist, and made a successful first appearance in London at a concert of his brother's in the spring of 1896. At later dates he appeared here in sonata programmes with his brother. His compositions include a ' Suite Wallonne,' a concerto for piano, a symphonic poem, a fantasia, etc., and a symphony (No. 1) in F minor, first performed at Brussels in Nov. 1904, was played in London at one of the concerts organised in June 1905 for the Ostend Kursaal band. M.

YSORE (ISORE), G., an early 16th-century composer, probably French. He wrote chansons, of which 5 were published in a collection by Attaingnant, 1529, and later editions; one in Gardano's collection, 1559; and one in Arcadelt's ' Madrigali,' 3 v., 1542 (Q.-L.).

YSSANDON, JEAN (b. Lesart, Ariège, 16th cent.), lived at Avignon in the palace of Cardinal d'Armagnac. He wrote Traité de la musique pratique, divisé en deux parties, etc., 1582; Le Roy et Rob. Ballard (Q.-L.).

YUSUPOV, NICOLAI BORISOVICH (PRINCE), (also YOUSSOUPOFF, JUSUPOF, JOUSSOUPOW, etc.) (b. St. Petersburg, 1827; d. Baden-Baden, Aug. 3, 1891), a Russian musical dilettante. He studied the violin with Vieuxtemps, and maintained an orchestra in his palace. He was the author of the monograph on the violin entitled Luthomonographie historique et raisonnée (first edition, Frankfort-on-Main, 1856 (printed at Munich) ; fifth edition, Paris, Bonhoure, n.d.), a well-meaning, but faulty essay, dedicated to de Bériot, illustrated with full-sized drawings of instruments, which are, perhaps, the most valuable part of the work. He also projected a work entitled Histoire de la musique et de son avenir en Russie, of which the first part, Musique sacrée suivi d'un choix de morceaux de chant d'Église (Paris, 1862), alone appeared. He composed a violin concerto, and a programme symphony with a violin solo entitled ' Gonzalvo de Cordova.' In 1863 he published a systematic catalogue of the books contained in the Imperial Library, St. Petersburg. His Analyse comparée des compositions des violinistes contemporains, announced for publication in 1856, never appeared. De Bériot wrote a set of six violin duets on motifs taken from Prince Yusupov's Ballet d'Espagne. The title-page of the later editions of his Luthomonographie announces him as Maître compositeur de la Société Philharmonique de Bologne, et Membre honoraire de l'Académie Philharmonique de St. Cécile à Rome. (Riemann; Fétis, Biog. des Mus.)

E. H.-A.

Z

ZACCONI, LUDOVICO (b. Pesaro, June 11, 1555; d. Mar. 23, 1627), one of the most learned musical theorists of the early Italian school. He spent the greater part of his life at Venice, where he was admitted to the priesthood, received the tonsure as a monk of the Order of S. Augustine, and officiated as maestro di cappella in the great church belonging to the Order. In 1592 he was in the service of Wilhelm, Duke of Bavaria, as 'musico,' and in 1593 he was invited to Vienna by the Archduke Charles, who made him his Kapellmeister some years later. In 1619 he returned to Venice, and devoted himself to the completion of his great theoretical work, the first portion of which was published before his departure to Vienna.

The work on which Zacconi's fame is based is entitled *Prattica di musica utile et necessaria si al compositore . . . si anco al cantore*, and is dedicated to Guglielmo Conte Palatino del Reno, Duca dell' alta e bassa Baviera, etc. The first part was published at Venice in 1592, and reprinted in 1596. The second part, also printed at Venice, first appeared in 1619. The contents of the work are divided into four books, wherein the treatment of consonant and dissonant progressions, the complications of mode, time and prolation, the laws of *cantus fictus*, with many like mysteries, are explained with a degree of lucidity for which we seek in vain in the works of other theoretical writers of the polyphonic period—the *Dodecachordon* of Glareanus and the *Musicae activae Micrologus* of Ornithoparcus alone excepted. It may, indeed, be confidently asserted that we are indebted to these two works, in conjunction with the *Prattica di musica*, for the most valuable information we possess on these subjects—information, in the absence of which Josquin's ' Missa didadi ' and portions even of Palestrina's ' Missa l'homme armé,' to say nothing of the enigmatical canons of the earlier Flemish schools, would be quite undecipherable.

Lib. I. of the *Prattica di musica* is subdivided into 80 chapters, 23 of which are occupied with dissertations on the origin and history of music, interspersed with definitions, and other introductory matter, of no great practical utility. Cap. xxiv. treats of the ' Harmonic Hand '; Cap. xxv. of the figures used in notation; Cap. xxvi. of the stave of five lines; and Cap. xxvii. of the clefs, of which several forms are given. Caps. xxviii.-xxxiii. treat of measure, time and various forms of rhythmic division (*misura, tatto, e battuta*). Caps. xxxiv.-xxxv. describe the time table, beginning with the *Maxima*, and ending with the *Semicroma*. Caps. xxxvi.-xxxvii. describe the time-signatures (*Segni del Tatto*). Caps.

xxxviii.-xl. treat of solmisation. Caps. xli.-xlii. describe the office of points generally, and especially that of the point of augmentation. Caps. xliii.-xlvi. furnish some very valuable information concerning the ligatures in common use towards the close of the 16th century. Cap. xlvii. treats of rests; xlviii.-xlix. of the B molle and B quadro; l.-li. of the diesis; and lii. of syncope. Caps. liii.-lv. are devoted to the consideration of certain difficulties connected with the matters previously discussed. Caps. lvi.-lvii. treat of canon, and the different ways of singing it. Caps. lviii.-lxvi. contain the rules to be observed by singers, illustrated by many examples and exercises, and throw great light upon the laws of *cantus fictus*, the management of complicated rhythmic combinations and other mysteries. Caps. lxvii.-lxxi. treat of the duties of the maestro di cappella and singers. Caps. lxxii.-lxxiii. describe the villanella and canzonetta, while Caps. lxxiv.-lxxx. state the mutual qualifications of singers and composers.

Lib. II. is divided into 58 chapters, of which the first 5 treat of the different species of mood, time and prolation. Caps. vi.-vii. describe the points of division, alteration and perfection. Cap. viii. corrects some prevalent errors in the matter of perfect time. Caps. ix.-xxxvii. treat of the mutual adaptation of mood, time and prolation, and the different kinds of proportion. In illustration of this subject, Cap. xxxviii. gives, as examples, the Kyrie, Christe, second Kyrie, the beginning of the Gloria, the Osanna and the Agnus Dei, of Palestrina's ' Missa l'homme armé,' with full directions as to the mode of their performance. Aided by Zacconi's explanations, Dr. Burney was able to score them.[1] Caps. xxxix.-lviii. bring the second book to an end, with the continuation of the same subject.

Lib. III. consists of 77 chapters, treating of the different kinds of proportion.

Lib. IV. is divided into 56 chapters, of which the first 37 treat of the twelve modes. Of these Zacconi, in common with all the great theoretical writers of the polyphonic school, admits the use of 6 Authentic and 6 Plagal forms, and no more; and, not content with expunging the names of the Locrian and Hypolocrian modes from his list, he expunges even their numbers, describing the Ionian mode as Tuono XI., and the Hypoionian as Tuono XII.[2] Caps. xxxviii.-xlvi. treat of instrumental music, as practised during the latter half of the 16th century, and are especially valuable as describing the compass and manner of using the various orchestral instruments as played by

[1] See Dr. Burney's ' Extracts,' B.M. Add. MSS. 11,581.
[2] See Vol. III. p. 482.

Peri, Monteverdi and their immediate successors, in their early essays in opera and oratorio. Caps. xlvii.-lv. treat of the tuning of musical instruments ; and the concluding chapter, lvi., furnishes us with a table, exhibiting on a great stave of eleven lines, the compass of the instruments most commonly used at the time the book was written. We subjoin the compass of each instrument, on an ordinary stave, and translated into modern notation :

Cornetti Bianchi e Negri.   Violini.[1]   Pifari.

Dolziane.   Corno torto.

Cornamuti torti. Fagotto chorista. Trombone.

Flauti.

Canto.   Tenore.   Basso.

Viole.[3]

Canto.[4]   Tenore.   Basso.

Doppiani.

Canto.   Tenore.   Basso.

The foregoing synopsis gives but a slight indication of the value of the *Prattica di musica*, which supplies information on every important subject connected with the music of the 16th century, information in many cases obtainable from no other source. The work is now extremely scarce and costly ; complete copies will, however, be found in the British Museum and the R.C.M. (For continental copies see *Q.-L.*)

W. S. R.

BIBL.—F. BATIELLI, *Un musicista pesarese nel seccolo XVI* (1905); idem, *Notizie su la vita e le opere di L. Zacconi* (1912); H. KRETZSCH-MAR, *L. Zacconi's Leben auf Grund seiner Autobiographie* (1910).

ZACHARIA (ZACCARIA), CESARE DE, of Cremona, lived *c.* 1590 at Munich. In 1594 he signs from ' Schera ' (Scheer) on the Danube, when he was probably at the court of Prince Henry of Fürstenberg. He composed canzonette, 4 v. (1590) ; patrocinium musices,

hymns, psalms, etc., 1594 ; hymns, 5 v., 1594 ; and fauxbourdons, litanies, etc., in collective volumes (*Q.-L.*).

ZACHAU [5] (ZACHOW), FRIEDRICH WILHELM (*b.* Leipzig, Nov. 19, 1663 ; *d.* Halle, Aug. 14, 1712), Handel's master. His father was *Stadtmusikus* in Leipzig. Under his direction Zachau learned to play on all the instruments then in general use, including violin, hautboy, harpsichord and organ, devoting his chief attention to the last two, on which he attained great proficiency. When about 10 years old the family removed to Eilenburg, between Halle and Leipzig, where he continued his studies. In 1684 he was elected organist of Liebfrauenkirche in Halle.

Here it was, if Mainwaring's account is to be trusted, that Handel was first taken to Zachau for instruction in music ' while he was yet under 7 years of age ' ; that is to say, some time before the end of 1692 (Chrysander places the event a little later). The circumstances which led to Handel's being placed under Zachau have already been narrated in detail and are too well known to need repetition (see HANDEL). There can be no doubt that Zachau took great interest in his pupil, who, Mainwaring tells us, ' pleased him so much that he never thought he could do enough for him.' That the child was placed under an excellent and thoroughly conscientious teacher is indeed conclusively proved, both by Mainwaring and Coxe.[6] The former says :

' Zachau had a large collection of Italian as well as German music. He showed his pupil the different styles of different nations ; the excellences and defects of each particular author ; and, that he might equally advance in the practical part he frequently gave him subjects to work, and made him copy, and play, and compose in his stead. And Zachau was glad of an assistant who, by his uncommon talents, was capable of supplying his place whenever he was inclined to be absent. It may seem strange to talk of an assistant at seven years of age. But it will appear much stranger that by the time he was nine he began to compose the Church Service for voices and instruments, and from that time actually did compose a service every week for three years successively.'

And in confirmation of this account, Coxe describes a volume, formerly in the possession of Lady Rivers, dated 1698, signed G. F. H., and filled with transcripts, in Handel's handwriting, of airs, fugues, choruses and other works, by Zachau, Frohberger, Krieger, Kerl, Heinrich Albert, Ebner, Adam Strungk and other composers of the 17th century. (See *Leichtentritt*, p. 28.)

Handel always spoke of his old master with the deepest respect ; visited him at Halle for the last time in 1710 ; and after his death sent ' frequent remittances ' to his widow. These tokens of esteem did not, however, preserve the

1 It will be seen that the violin is here treated in the First position only.
2 This note is omitted in the B.M. copy.
3 The tuning of the tenor and bass viols differs materially from the usual form.
4 The viola clef is wanting in the original.

5 Mainwaring has Zackaw ; Schoelcher, Sackau.
6 *Anecdotes of George Frederic Handel and John Christopher Smith*, by the Rev. W. Coxe. (London, 1799.)

memory of Zachau from a cruel aspersion, which originated in this wise. A certain Johann Christoph LEPORIN (*q.v.*), organist of the Dom-kirche zur Moritzburg at Halle, was dismissed from his office in 1702 on account of his dissolute life and neglect of duty. Handel, then 17 years of age, was chosen to supply his place. After Handel's death his biographers attributed Leporin's misdeeds to Zachau, accusing him of irregularities of which he was wholly innocent. Chrysander traces the libel to its source and proves it to be unfounded.

The Berlin Library possesses a large collection of Zachau's compositions, consisting principally of MS. church cantatas and pieces for the organ. Some fragments were printed by Chrysander and v. Winterfeld. They are not works of genius, but their style is thoroughly musician-like, and is marked both by good taste and earnestness of purpose. A complete edition of the works of Zachau was brought out in vols. xxi. and xxii. of the *D.D.T.*, edited by Max Seiffert. An interesting Mass, on the theme 'Christ lag in Todesbanden,' is assigned to 'Nikolaus Zachau' in the copy in the Berlin Library. It is accepted as F. W. Zachau's by Seiffert, but its authorship is doubted in *Q.-L.*

W. S. R.; rev. S. G.

ZACHEREWITSCH, MICHAEL (*b.* Ostroff, Russia, Aug. 26, 1879), violinist.

At the age of 15 he made an extraordinarily successful début at Odessa with Tchaikovsky, who conducted his own concerto. As a con-sequence the composer got up a subscription to send Zacherewitsch to Prague, where he studied for nine years under Ševčík. He had also the advantage of a few lessons from Ysaÿe. In 1893 he played at Amsterdam under Mengelberg, and in 1903 gave his first recital in London, after which he toured the English provinces. He returned in 1909 and frequently later, and played with success, displaying considerable breadth of style.   W. W. C.

ZAÏDE, operetta in 2 acts; text by Schacht-ner, probably from the French; music by Mozart, 1779 or 1780. It does not appear to have been produced till given at Frankfort in 1866.   G.

ZAIRE, opera in 3 acts; words by Romani; music by Bellini. Produced Parma, May 16, 1829.   G.

ZAJAL, see SONG, subsection SPAIN; VILLANCICO.

ŽAK, see SHACK.

ZAMBRA, an ancient dance of the Spanish Moors, danced with clasped hands to music of scabebas (Moorish flutes) and dulzainas (a name given to so many different instruments that its application here is doubtful), but probably a kind of oboe is meant.   H. V. H.

ZAMPA, OU LA FIANCÉE DE MARBRE (The Marble Bride), opéra-comique in 3 acts; libretto by Melesville, music by Hérold. Pro-duced Opéra-Comique, Paris, May 3, 1831; in

Italian, King's Theatre (with a new finale to the third act, by Hummel),[1] Apr. 19, 1833; in French, St. James's, Jan. 16, 1850; in English, Covent Garden, Apr. 19, 1833.   G.

ZAMPOGNA (CALABRIAN BAGPIPE), see BAGPIPE.

ZAMR, an Arab pipe with a conical tube, spreading bell and double reed. In most Mohammedan countries it is found under somewhat similar names : it is the prototype of the shawm and oboe. (*PLATE LXXV.* No. 10. See PIPES, EVOLUTION OF; subsection DOUBLE REED.)   F. W. G.

ZANDONAI, RICCARDO (*b.* Sacco, Trentino, May 28, 1883), Italian composer, studied at first with Gianferrari at Roveredo. In 1899 he went to Pesaro to complete his musical educa-tion at the Liceo, which had then Mascagni as its director. Zandonai was given the diploma of composition in 1902. Boïto, who met him in Milan, was struck by his early compositions and introduced him to the publisher Ricordi, who commissioned an opera. Zandonai wrote then his first work for the theatre, 'Il grillo sul farolare' (The Cricket on the Hearth), which was produced successfully at Turin in 1908 and later at Genoa and Nice. More clamorous was the success of his second opera, 'Conchita,' first produced at the Dal Verme Theatre in Milan in 1911. 'Melenis,' a tragic opera (1912), and 'La via della Finestra' a comic opera (1919), have not had equal good fortune ; but 'Fran-cesca da Rimini' (on the tragedy of D'Annunzio), first given in 1914, holds a foremost place in the modern Italian repertory, and 'Giulietta e Romeo' (Rome, Feb. 14, 1921) has been received with conspicuous favour by Italian audiences. 'I cavalieri di Ekebu' (La Scala, Milan, Mar. 7, 1925) had also a favourable reception.

A prolific composer, Zandonai has written also a Requiem Mass for voices (Rome, 1916) ; an album of melodies; a 'Serenade' for violoncello and small orchestra (1912) ; 'Our Father,' for chorus, organ and orchestra (1912); 'Ave Maria,' for voices and small orchestra; and other works. A 'concerto romantico' for violin and orchestra was performed at Rome (1921) ; a string quartet belongs to his early com-positions. In 1919 Zandonai was made an Associate of the Royal Academy of St. Cecilia of Rome.

The best operas of Zandonai show that characteristic flair for the theatre and for a dramatic situation which is so important a qualification for the operatic composer. He possesses, however, a rare skill in writing for the orchestra, and, like most modern Italians, he devotes the utmost care to the relations between word and music, with the result that the effect of the musical phrase is enhanced by the combination. These are qualities the

nature of which in the theatre cannot be over-
estimated.   F. B.

ZANDT, MARIE VAN (b. New York, Oct. 8,
1861 ; d. Cannes, 1920), operatic soprano. Her
mother, Mme. Vanzini, a well-known member
of the Carl Rosa Company in its early days,
was her first vocal teacher, and she also studied
with Lamperti.   Her début took place at
Turin in Jan. 1879, when her Zerlina in ' Don
Giovanni ' made a highly favourable impression. She was immediately engaged for Covent
Garden, and made her appearance there in May
of the same year as Amina in ' La Sonnambula,'
being then barely eighteen. Her voice, however,
was already well developed and of a pretty
quality, if of no great power ; while her execution was singularly neat and sure and her
acting enhanced in charm by her youth and
grace.   These were the gifts that made for the
success which she won as Mignon at the Opéra-
Comique in Mar. 1880, and for the popularity
that she enjoyed in Paris during the next five
years.   So enthusiastic were the French critics
over her Mignon, her Rosina, her Dinorah and
her Cherubino, that Delibes decided to entrust
her with the creation of the heroine in his
' Lakmé,' which she sang for the first time on
Apr. 14, 1883.   That part she made her own,
and her rendering of it has not been surpassed.
Her voice did not stand the strain of constant
work, and her long stay at the Opéra-Comique
was brought to a close in Mar. 1885.   She
nevertheless continued for several years to tour
in concerts and appear as ' guest ' at various
opera-houses, until her marriage with Prof.
Tcherinov in Moscow.   H. K.

BIBL.—H. DE CURZON, Croquis d'artistes (Paris, 1898).

ZANETTA, OU IL NE FAUT PAS JOUER AVEC
LE FEU, opéra-comique in 3 acts ; libretto by
Scribe and St. Georges ; music by Auber. Pro-
duced Opéra-Comique, Paris, May 18, 1840 ;
St. James's Theatre, Feb. 12, 1849.   G.

ZANETTI (ZANNETTI), FRANCESCO (b. Vol-
terra, 1740 ; d. London, 1790 [1]), singer and
composer.   In 1770 he was maestro di cappella
at Perugia Cathedral, but lost his post on
account of his connexion with the stage. He
married a singer, and both toured together as
operatic singers.   According to Fétis he was
in London in 1790.   As, however, his 6 string
quintets, op. 2, 5 books of sonatas for 2 violins
and bass, 6 sonatas for harpsichord, 6 solos for
flute and 4 solos for violin were all published
in London between 1770–75, it appears that
he paid an earlier visit there soon after leaving
Perugia.   In 1783 he was at Alexandrie de la
Paille for the performance of his opera, ' Le
Cognate in contesa.'   Besides several operas
he wrote also church music and songs (Q.-L.).
                                        E. V. D. S.

ZANETTO, opera in one act, founded on
Coppée's ' Le Passant,' by G. Targioni-Tozzetti

[1] Mendel.

and G. Menasci ; music by Mascagni. Produced
Liceo Musicale, Pesaro, Mar. 2, 1896 ; given
privately 7 Chesterfield Gardens, London, June
23, 1896.

ZANGIUS, NICOLAUS (d. Berlin (?), 1618 or
1619), Kapellmeister at Brunswick, 1597 ;
deputy organist at S. Mary's, Danzig, 1602,
1603, 1605 ; ' Aulicus ' (flautist) at the Imperial
court at Prague, 1609 ; from 1612 Kapellmeister
at the court of Berlin. He was a prolific composer of motets, and of sacred and secular
songs, some books of which appeared in several
editions.   A number of his motets, 5-20 v., a
7-part Mass and sacred songs remained in MS.
(Q.-L.).

ZANOTTI (JOANNOTI), CAMILLO, of Cesena,
from Aug. 1, 1586, till after 1591 he was vice-
Kapellmeister to the German Emperor Rudolph
II.   He composed masses, a 5 v., 1588 ; sacrae
symphoniae, 8 v. ;   motets for double chorus,
Nuremberg, 1562 ; 3 books of madrigals, 5 v.,
1587–89 ; 1 book madrigals, 6 v., 1589 ; madrigalia tam italica quam latina . . ., 5, 6 and 12 v.,
1590 (Mendel ; Q.-L.).

ZAPPA, FRANCESCO, of Milan, late 18th-
century eminent violoncellist, for some time in
the service of the Duke of York, composer of
symphonies, quartets, trios, sonata and duo for
violoncello, vocal romances, etc. (E. van der
Straeten, History of the Violoncello ; Q.-L.).

ZAPPASORGO, GIOVANNI, of Treviso, wrote
2 books of ' Neapolitane,' 3 v., which appeared
in several editions between 1571 and 1588
(Q.-L.).

ZARLINO, GIOSEFFE (b. Chioggia, Mar. 22,
1517 ; d. Venice, Feb. 14, 1590), one of the
most learned musical theorists of the 16th
century.   Chioggia being the Clodia of the
Romans, he was generally known as Zarlinus
Clodiensis.

By the wish of his father, Giovanni Zarlino,
he spent his youth in studying for the Church ;
was admitted to the Minor Orders in 1539,
and ordained Deacon in 1541.   In that year
he came to reside in Venice, where his proficiency as a theologian, aided by his intimate
acquaintance with the Greek and Hebrew
languages, and his attainments in philosophy,
mathematics, astronomy and chemistry, soon
gained him an honourable position.   But his
love for music, for which, as he himself tells
us in the dedication prefixed to his Istitutioni
armoniche, ' he had felt a natural inclination
from his tenderest years,' tempted him to forsake all other studies for his favourite pursuit ;
and he was at once accepted as a pupil by
Adriano Willaert, under whom he studied, in
company with Cipriano di Rore and other
promising neophytes.

On the removal of Cipriano di Rore to Parma,
Zarlino was elected, in 1565, first maestro di
cappella at S. Mark's.   The duties connected
with this appointment were not confined to the

Offices sung in the Cathedral. After the Battle of Lepanto, Oct. 7, 1571, Zarlino was commissioned to celebrate the victory with music worthy of the occasion. When Henri III. visited Venice, on his return to France from Poland in 1574, he was greeted, on board the Bucentaur, by a composition, the Latin verses for which were furnished by Rocco Benedetti and Cornelio Frangipani, and the music by Zarlino, who also composed the music sung in the Cathedral, and a dramatic piece, called 'Orfeo,'[1] which was performed with great splendour in the Sala del Gran Consiglio. Again, in 1577, when the Church of S. Maria della Salute was founded in memory of the plague, Zarlino was commissioned to compose a Mass for the solemn occasion. None of these works have been preserved, and we can only judge of their merits by the immense reputation the composer enjoyed.

But Zarlino did not neglect the duties of his ecclesiastical status. On the contrary, in 1582 he was elected a Canon of Chioggia; and, on the death of Marco de' Medici, Bishop of Chioggia, in 1583, he was chosen to fill the vacant See. This proceeding was, however, so strongly opposed by the Doge, Niccolo da Ponte, and the Senate, that Zarlino consented to retain his appointment at S. Mark's in preference to the proffered mitre; and he continued to perform the duties of maestro di cappella until his death. He was buried in the church of San Lorenzo. No inscription now marks the spot, but his bust has been placed in a corridor of the Doge's Palace; and during his lifetime a medal was struck in his honour, bearing his effigy, and, on the reverse, an organ, with the legend, *Laudate eum in chordis.*

Few compositions by Zarlino have been preserved to us, besides the examples given in his theoretical works; they include a MS. Mass for 4 voices, in the library of the Liceo filarmonico at Bologna, and a printed volume of 'Modulationes sex vocum' (Venice, 1566). Torchi (' Arte musicale in Italia ') has printed two motets (5 v.). His chief fame, however, rests upon three treatises, entitled : *Istitutioni armoniche* (Venice, 1558, reprinted 1562, and again, 1573, etc.); *Dimostrationi armoniche* (Venice, 1571, reprinted 1578); and *Sopplimenti musicali* (Venice, 1588). The best edition is the complete one, entitled *Tutte l' opere del R. M. Gioseffo Zarlino da Chioggia* (Venice, 1589).

The *Istitutioni* comprise 448 pp. fol.; and are divided into four sections.

Lib. I. contains 69 Chapters, chiefly devoted to a dissertation on the excellence of music; a mystical elucidation of the transcendental properties of the number six; and a description of the different forms of arithmetical, geometrical and harmonical proportion.

In Lib. II., comprising 51 chapters, Zarlino demonstrates the superiority of the system

[1] Caffi calls it an ' opera.'

known as the ' Syntonous, or Intense Diatonic,' of Ptolomy, above all other systems whatsoever. In this system the tetrachord is divided into a greater tone, a lesser tone, and a greater hemitone—the diatonic semitone of modern music—as represented by the fractions $\frac{8}{9}$, $\frac{9}{10}$, $\frac{15}{16}$. The system was not a new one, and Zarlino, naturally enough, made no attempt to claim the honour of its invention. The constitution of the lesser tone had been demonstrated, by Didymus, as early as the 60th year of the Christian era. The misfortune was, that Didymus placed the lesser below the greater; an error which was corrected about the year 130, by Claudius Ptolomy, who gave his name to the system. The merit of Zarlino lay in his clear recognition of the correctness of this division of the tetrachord, which, in Lib. II. Cap. xxxix. p. 147 of the complete edition, he illustrates as in Fig. 1.[2]

By following the curves in Fig. 1 we may

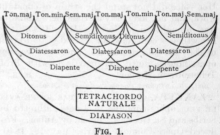

FIG. 1.

ascertain the exact proportions, in just intonation, of the diatonic semitone, the greater and lesser tone, the major and minor third, the perfect fourth, and the perfect fifth, in different parts of the octave. Like Pietro Aron (*Toscanello della musica*, Venice, 1523), Ludovico Fogliano (*Musica teoretica*, Venice, 1529), and other theoretical writers of the 16th century, Zarlino was fond of illustrating his theses by diagrams of this kind : and it was, no doubt, the practical utility of the custom that tempted Des Cartes to illustrate this self-same system by the ' Canonical Circle ' (Fig. 2), which later theorists extended, so as to include the proportions, in commas,[3] of every possible diatonic interval within the limits of the octave (Fig. 3).

It needs but a very slight examination of the accompanying diagrams to prove that the

[2] Want of space compels us to omit one or two unimportant details of the Diagram, as given in the edition of 1589.
[3] A comma is the ninth part of a Greater Tone.

'Syntonous Diatonic' of Ptolomy coincided, to the minutest particular, with the system advocated by Kepler (*Harmonices mundi*, Lib. III.,

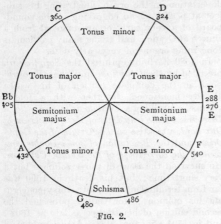

FIG. 2.

Cap. 7). Mersenne (*Harm. univers.* Lib. II.), Des Cartes (*Compendium musicae*), and all the most learned theoretical writers of later date, who, notwithstanding our acceptance of equal

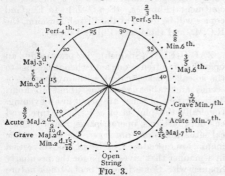

FIG. 3.

temperament as a practical necessity, entertain but one opinion as to the true division of the scale in just intonation—the opinion defended by Zarlino.

Lib. III. of the *Istitutioni* treats of the laws of counterpoint, which, it must be confessed, are not always set forth here with the clearness for which Zacconi is so justly remarkable. In the examples with which this part of the work is illustrated an interesting use is made of the well-known *canto fermo* which forms so conspicuous a feature in ' Non nobis Domine,' and so many other works of the 16th and 17th centuries.

FIG. 4.

Lib IV. treats of the modes, more especially in the later forms introduced by the Early

Christians, and systematised by S. Ambrose and S. Gregory. In common with Glareanus, and all the great theorists of the polyphonic school, Zarlino insists upon the recognition of 12 modes, and 12 only ; rejecting the Locrian and Hypolocrian forms as inadmissible, by reason of the false fifth inseparable from the one, and the tritonus which forms an integral part of the other. But, though thus entirely at one with the author of the *Dodecachordon* on the main facts, he arranges the modes in a different order of succession [1] (see MODES, ECCLESIASTICAL). Instead of beginning his series with the Dorian mode, he begins with the Ionian, arranging his series thus :

Authentic Modes.	Plagal Modes.
I. Ionian. Final, C.	II. Hypoionian. Final, C
III. Dorian. Final, D.	IV. Hypodorian. Final, D.
V. Phrygian. Final, E.	VI. Hypophrygian. Final, E.
VII. Lydian. Final, F.	VIII. Hypolydian. Final, F.
IX. Mixolydian. Final, G.	X. Hypomixolydian. Final, G.
XI. Æolian. Final, A.	XII. Hypoæolian. Final, A.

This arrangement—which no other great theorist of the century has followed—would almost seem to have been dictated by a prophetic anticipation of the change which was to lead to the abandonment of the modes, in favour of a newer tonality : for the series here begins with a form which corresponds exactly with our modern major mode, and ends with the prototype of the descending minor scale of modern music.

In the course of the work Zarlino introduces some very valuable memoranda, and occasionally records as facts some very curious superstitions. In one place he tells us that the human pulse is the measure of the beats in music—a statement fortunately corroborated by other early writers, and furnishing us with a comparative estimate of the duration of the two beats which are included in the normal semibreve. In another he asserts that Josquin treated the fourth as a consonance. In a third he records his observation that untaught singers always sing the third and sixth major —which is in all probability true. Occasionally, too, he diverges into the region of romance, and assures us that deer are so delighted with music that hunters use it as a means of capturing them.

The *Dimostrationi armoniche*, occupying 312 folio pages, is disposed in the form of five dialogues, carried on by Adriano Willaert, Claudio Merulo and Francesco Viola, maestro di cappella of Alfonso d'Este, Duke of Ferrara. Zarlino tells us that in the year 1562 the friends met at the house of Willaert, who was then laid up with the gout ; and that their

1 See Lib. IV. cap. x. p. 399, in edition of 1589.

conversation is faithfully reported in the five Ragionamenti of the *Dimostrationi*. The first of these treats chiefly of the proportions of intervals ; the second and third, of the ratios of the consonances, and lesser intervals ; the fourth, of the division of the monochord ; and the fifth, of the Authentic and Plagal modes.

Not long after the publication of these works Vincenzo GALILEI (*q.v.*)—who had formerly been Zarlino's pupil—printed at Florence a tract entitled *Discorso intorno alle opere di messer Gioseffe Zarlino di Chioggia*, in which he violently attacked his former master's principles ; and in 1581 he followed up the subject in his famous *Dialogo della musica antica et della moderna*, in the second edition of which (Fiorenza, 1602), the title-page bore the words, ' in sua difesa contra Joseffo Zarlino.' Galilei attacked, in very uncourteous terms, the division of the scale advocated by Zarlino ; and proposed to substitute for it the Ditonic Diatonic Tetrachord, consisting of two greater tones and a Limma[1] ; as set forth by Pythagoras—a division which all modern theorists agree in rejecting. While accusing Zarlino of innovation, he inconsistently complained that the Syntonous Diatonic was advocated by Lodovico Fogliano half a century before his time. This is perfectly true[2] : and in all probability it was this division of the scale that the Aristoxenians unconsciously sang by ear. But Galilei was not satisfied with an empirical scale ; and his admiration for the Greeks blinded him to the fact that his theory, reduced to practice, would have been intolerable. His favourite instrument, the lute, required some reasonable power of temperament : and Zarlino, who was in every respect in advance of his age, actually proposed that for the lute the octave should be divided into 12 equal semitones—that is to say, he advocated in the 16th century the practice that we have only seen universally adopted within the 19th. That he extended the system to the organ is sufficiently proved by the fact that his organ at S. Mark's remained in the condition in which it was left by Monteverdi.[3] It is evident, therefore, that he advocated equal temperament for keyed instruments, and just intonation for unaccompanied vocal music and instruments of the violin tribe.

In defence of his principles, and in answer to Galilei's caustic diatribes, Zarlino published in 1588 his *Sopplimenti musicali*, containing 330 pages of valuable and interesting matter, much of which is devoted to the reinforcement of the principles laid down in the *Istitutioni* and the *Dimostrationi*. The system of equal temperament, as applied to the lute, is set forth in detail in Lib. IV. Cap. xxvii. *et seq.* In Lib.

VI. the author recapitulates much of what he has previously said concerning the modes ; and in Lib. VIII. he concludes the volume with a dissertation on the organ, illustrating his subject at p. 291 by an engraving of the soundboard of a very early organ removed from a church at Grado ; and giving many particulars concerning organs of very early date.

In 1589 Zarlino reprinted the *Sopplimenti*, preceded by the *Istitutioni* and the *Dimostrationi*, in the complete edition of his works already mentioned, together with a fourth volume, containing a *Trattato della pazienzia*, a *Discourse on the true Date of the Crucifixion of Our Lord*, a treatise on *The Origin of the Capuchins*, and the *Resolution of some Doubts concerning the correctness of the Julian Calendar*. He survived the issue of the 4 volumes but a very short time ; but his death in 1590 was far from terminating the controversy concerning his opinions ; for Galilei published the second edition of his *Dialogo* as late as 1602 ; and in 1704 Giovanni Maria Artusi published an equally bitter attack at Bologna, entitled *Impresa del R. P. Gio. Zarlino di Chioggia*, etc. The works of Zarlino are now scarce and costly, though copies[4] exist in a number of continental libraries. (See *Q.-L.*) In England copies will be found at the British Museum, the R.C.M., and the Leeds Public Library.

W. S. R.

ZARZUELA (Spanish), is practically an opéra bouffe, often in one act (when it belongs to the so-called *genero chico*), with any number of scenes and tableaux, lasting about an hour. Three or four of these are given in an evening. Generally the plot is of a comic nature, and customs, fashions, operas, plays, novels, political situations and, not least, the tauromachic mania, are reproduced, satirised and travestied in a manner that gives scope for the peculiarly Spanish wit. Sometimes plots of a tragic nature are written, sometimes melodramatic, sometimes fantastic ; but it would be quite an exception if one were produced without its element of humour. Scarcely any successful play, opera or novel is not somehow or other burlesqued in the form of a zarzuela.

The best performances of zarzuelas take place in Madrid, in the theatre which is now invariably called the Teatro de la Zarzuela. It was built at the instigation of the composers Barbieri and Gaztambide, the singer Salas and the poet Olona, and was opened on Oct. 10, 1857, in the presence of Doña Isabel ; her consort, Don Francisco, and their court. On that occasion the performance consisted of a symphony on

---

[1] The Limma or remaining portion of a perfect fourth, after two greater tones have been subtracted from it, is less than a diatonic semitone by one comma.

[2] See Fogliano's *Musica teorica* (Venice, 1529), Sect. II De utilitate toni majoris et minoris.

[3] Bontempi, *Hist. Mus.* Parte 1ma, Coroll. IV

[4] The only existing translations of Zarlino's *Istitutioni armoniche* are two French ones, both MSS. in the National Library, Paris : fr. 1361 attributed to Claude Hardy, fr. 19101 by Jehan Le Fort (Michel Brenet, *Deux traductions françaises inédites de Zarlino. L'Année musicale*, 1911). On the erroneous attribution to Sweelinck of the Dutch translation, consult · Max Seiffert, *Sweelinck und seine direkten Schüler* (Vierteljahrsschrift für Musikwissenschaft, vii. 1891). Of the German translation by Johann Caspar Trost there seems to be no trace   M. L. P.

themes from zarzuelas for orchestra and military band composed by Barbieri ; a cantata by Arrieta to words by Olona and Hurtado ; a zarzuela in one act, ' El Sonámbulo,' by Hurtado and Arrieta, and an allegory in one act, ' La Zarzuela,' text by Hurtado and Olona, with music by Gaztambide, Barbieri, Arrieta and Rossini. Another theatre where good performances are given is the Apolo, built on the site of a convent, and for that reason formerly avoided from religious feeling by many Madrileños.

Zarzuelas are sometimes in two or more acts ; and such works as ' La Fille de Mme Angot,' ' H.M.S. Pinafore,' etc., have been produced and announced as zarzuelas, but the piece in one act is by far the most frequent and popular. The music is almost always of vivid Spanish colouring, sparkling and bright ; ' Flamenco,' Aragonese, Basque or whatever the occasion demands, but always restless, somewhat lacking in the elegance that characterises the music of the more successful operettas of other countries, a little blatant in orchestration and apt to be vague in form when the national dance and folk-song forms are avoided. There is, in fact, a discontent and want of repose apparent in this phase of art in Spain, as in almost everything in the country.

The libretti are sometimes written in verse, but more frequently not, and the author often depends on the actors' own invention and ingenuity for presenting the public with a good character, and the custom of ' gagging ' and improvising ' encore ' verses to a song is so freely indulged in that the actors themselves, as well as the audience, are constantly in roars of laughter during the early stages of the run of a new piece. The acting is less conventional and more unstudied and natural than in other forms of dramatic performance. The intimacy between actors and audience is so close and informal that a course of repartee between one of the former and members of the latter is at times started and kept up for quite a long time.

The best-known authors and composers in Spain have contributed to the zarzuela, and among the most successful composers may be mentioned Arrieta, Gaztambide, Barbieri, Oudrid, Margués, Caballero, Chapi, Chueca, Torregosa, Barrera and the Valverdes, father and son. Perhaps the most successful zarzuela has been that called ' Gigantes y Cabezudos,' written in verse by the illustrious and venerated Miguel Echegaray, with music by Caballero. It deals with a subject dear to every Spanish heart, that of the fiestas of the Virgin of Saragossa, Santa Maria del Pilar. It has had many a long run on many a stage, and is constantly revived, and sometimes for a special occasion or a gala performance it is given a place in the programme at the Royal Opera-House in Madrid. Of its kind it is a gem, and, as the name of its author would suggest, has none of the extravagance, the vulgarity or the morbidity of many popular zarzuelas. Another favourite, ' La gran via,' has overrun the theatres of Italy, and been given in various other European countries, besides being produced in London a few years ago in a distorted and elongated form.　　　　H. V. H., abridged.

ZARZYCKI, ALEXANDER (b. Lemberg, Feb. 21, 1834 ; d. Warsaw, Oct. 13, 1895), for some years director of the conservatorium of Warsaw. He is favourably known by his violin pieces, notably a mazurka that has won great success, and he also wrote a piano concerto and many pieces of a more or less slight kind (Riemann).　　　　　　　　　　　　M.

ZAUBERFLÖTE, DIE (Il flauto magico, La Flûte enchantée, The Magic Flute), opera by Mozart in 2 acts ; the text by Schikaneder.[1] Produced Theater-auf-der-Wieden, Vienna, Sept. 30, 1791 ; Paris, as ' Les Mystères d'Isis,' Aug. 20, 1801 (see LACHNITH) ; in Italian, King's Theatre, June 6, 1811 ; in English, New York, Park Theatre, Apr. 17, 1833 ; in German, Covent Garden, May 27, 1833 ; in English, Drury Lane, Mar. 10, 1838.　　G.

ZAVERTAL, the original Bohemian name (Zavrtal) of a musical family, several members of which became prominent both in Germany and England. (1) JOSEPH RUDOLF (b. Polep, Leitmeritz, Bohemia, Nov. 5, 1819), horn-player, was educated at the Prague Conservatorium. He entered the Austrian army as bandmaster in 1840. In 1846 he established the Pension Society for bandmasters of the Austrian army. After several promotions, in 1864 he became director of military music to Maximilian, Emperor of Mexico. Shortly after this he left Austria for England, and in 1868 was made bandmaster of the 4th King's Own Regiment, and in 1871 was placed at the head of the band (wind and string) of the Royal Engineers. (2) WENCESLAS HUGO (b. Polep, Aug. 31, 1821), clarinettist and composer, brother of the foregoing. Among various important posts in Austria and Italy, he held those of director of the Conservatorio of Treviso and principal of the School of Music at Modena. In 1866 he quitted the service, and in 1874 came to Great Britain, where he resided at Helensburgh, near Glasgow, much esteemed as a teacher of music, and where his compositions were much relished. In 1847 he married Carlotta Maironi Nobile da Poule (d. 1873), an eminent musician. His son (3) LADISLAUS (b. Milan, Sept. 29, 1849) was taught music by his parents, and first appeared at Milan in 1864. Four years later he produced an opera at Treviso. Next year he was made conductor and composer to the theatre at Milan. In 1871 he removed to Glasgow, where

---

[1] As to Giesecke's claim to authorship, see Dent, *Mozart's Operas*, p. 355 *et seq.*

he remained teaching and conducting for ten years. In 1881 he succeeded James Smythe as master of the band (wind and string) of the Royal Artillery at Woolwich. He initiated the Sunday Concerts in the Albert Hall and conducted them for 10 years, and by introducing many new works to English audiences, and maintaining a high standard of artistic excellence, raised the Artillery Band to the high position it now holds. He filled the post with distinction and much artistic success until Dec. 1906. At the last concert of the Artillery Band conducted by him, his second symphony was performed. An opera of his, ' Una notte a Firenze,' was successfully produced at Prague in 1886, and another, ' Myrrha,' at the same city, Nov. 7, 1886. An operetta, ' Love's Magic,' was performed at Woolwich in Feb. 1890. He was made a Commendatore of the Order of the Crown of Italy, and received the Ernestine Order for Art and Science from the late Duke of Coburg. (See *Memoirs of the Royal Artillery Band.*)　　　　　　　　　　　G.

ZECKWER, RICHARD (b. Stendal, Apr. 30, 1850; d. Philadelphia, 1922), educated at Leipzig, migrated to America and settled in Philadelphia as pianist and teacher. He joined the staff (1876) of the newly opened Musical Academy and later became its director, resigning this post in 1917. His son,

(2) CAMILLE (b. Philadelphia, June 26, 1875 ; d. there, Aug. 7, 1924), pianist and composer, studied with Dvořák in New York (1893–95) and with P. Scharwenka in Berlin. He settled as a teacher in his native city and became director of the Musical Academy in conjunction with F. E. Hahn. He was the composer of several symphonic works played by the Philadelphia Orchestra ; his symphonic poem ' Jade Butterflies ' won a Chicago prize and was played by the Chicago Orchestra ; he also wrote chamber music and an opera, ' Jane and Janetta ' (*Amer. Supp.*).　　　　　　　　　9.

ZEISLER, FANNIE BLOOMFIELD (b. Bielitz, Austria, July 16, 1863), an American pianist who was taken to the United States in 1868 by her parents, who settled in Chicago. She studied there under Bernhard Ziehn and Carl Wolfsohn ; and in 1878 went to Leschetizky in Vienna, with whom she studied for five years. She returned to the United States in 1883, and at once made a name as a public pianist. In 1893 she undertook a concert tour in Germany and repeated it the next year. She appeared in London in 1898, and in that year also in the Lower Rhine Music Festival in Cologne, and has made European tours in subsequent years. She married Siegmund Zeisler, a lawyer of Chicago, in 1885. She is a cousin of Moriz Rosenthal, the pianist.

Mme. Bloomfield-Zeisler's style is one of individuality, fiery intensity, and incisiveness ; that of a nervously high-strung artist. R. A

ZELENKA, JOHANN DISMAS (b. Launowicz, Bohemia, 1681 [1]; d. Dresden, Dec. 22-3, 1745), composer.

He was educated at the Jesuit College in Prague, was in the service of Freiherr Joseph Ludwig von Hartig as musician there in 1690, entered the band of the Dresden Hofkapelle as double-bass player in 1710, and obtained leave of absence in 1716 in order to study composition with J. J. Fux at Vienna. In the same year he was taken in the suite of the Prince Elector to Italy, and became a pupil of Lotti, but returned to Vienna in 1717, and to Dresden in 1719. In 1723, for the coronation of Karl VI. at Prague, he wrote music to a Latin comedy, ' Melodrama de Sancto Wenceslao.' He succeeded Heinichen (whose coadjutor he had been since 1719) as director of church music in 1729, and received the title of court composer in 1733. He was a voluminous composer, leaving no fewer than 21 masses, 108 psalms, motets, etc. Three Italian oratorios, ' I penitenti al sepolcro,' ' Il serpente di bronzo,' ' Giesu al Calvario,' three cantatas, ' Immisit Dominus,' ' Deus dux,' and ' Attendite et videte,' besides a serenata and the ' melodrama ' above mentioned, with other compositions in his autograph, were kept in a special cupboard in the Catholic Church at Dresden, and the State Library there has the largest collection of his manuscript compositions. Hardly any of them appear to have been published (*Q.-L.*).　　M.

ZELENKA, LADISLAV (b. Mar. 11, 1881), a Czech violoncellist, professor at the Prague Conservatoire, and, since 1913, a member of the CZECH (BOHEMIAN) STRING QUARTET (*q.v.*).
　　　　　　　　　　　　　　　　R. N.

ZELMIRA, opera in 2 acts ; words by Tottola, music by Rossini. Produced Naples, Feb. 16, 1822.　　　　　　　　　　　　G.

ZELTER, CARL FRIEDRICH (b. Berlin, Dec. 11, 1758 ; d. May 15, 1832), director of the Berlin Singakademie, and founder of the Liedertafeln now so general throughout Germany.

He was the son of a mason. He has recorded the first indelible impression that he received on hearing Graun's opera ' Phaeton,' to which his parents treated him in the Carnival of 1770.

' The grand powerful masses of tone riveted my attention far more than the melody and construction of the airs. . . . I thought the orchestra a riddle as wonderful as it was beautiful. I was seated amongst the musicians . . . I swam in a sea of delight.'

Of the opera itself he says little, except that the sweet unknown Italian words added to the magic of the whole, so that he afterwards agreed with the Great Frederick as to the profanity of allowing Art to speak in the vulgar tongue, and sympathised heartily with the royal dislike of the German opera. When nearly 14, his father sent him to the Gymnasium, but here, though the lessons got on tolerably well, his relations with his fellow-students were so stormy that

[1] According to Dlabacz ; *Riemann* gives Oct. 16, 1679.

the place became too hot to hold him ; he was next handed over to the organist of the Gymnasium, who had a school of his own. This was only a temporary expedient, for Zelter returned to the Gymnasium, where some of the masters were well disposed towards him, notwithstanding his taste for practical jokes. At the age of 17, after another course of the organist's teaching, he left school, and now his real education began. Though apprenticed to his father's trade, he was but a half-hearted mason. He made friends with any one who happened to have musical proclivities, and amongst others with the town musician, George, an original even in those days. In his household Zelter was always a welcome guest ; George appreciated his musical skill and enthusiasm, and gave him free access to all his musical instruments. Meantime Zelter was ripening into a capable musician.

In 1777 his apprenticeship was declared over, and a great longing seized him to join his friend Hackert, the artist, in a journey to Italy, a longing which often returned upon him through his life, though he never fulfilled it. Hackert went without him, and he remained at home to do a good deal of love-making. His love affairs, described minutely in his autobiography, are of little interest, except perhaps his flirtation with an artistic Jewess, at whose father's house Moses Mendelssohn and other scholars used to meet. The lady and her lover quarrelled over the theory of suicide, and parted company because they differed about Goethe's treatment of Werther, who, in Zelter's opinion, ought to have shot Albrecht instead of himself. The episode is worth recording, as it marks the first connexion of the names of Goethe and Mendelssohn with that of Zelter. In spite of such distractions, Zelter passed his examination easily and successfully, and was made a master mason in consequence. When he was 18, his first cantata was performed in St. George's Church, and Marpurg the theorist thought so highly of it that Zelter applied to Kirnberger and Fasch for further instruction in musical science. In gratitude for his old master's teaching, he ultimately became the biographer of Karl Friedrich Christian Fasch,[1] the original founder of the Berlin Singakademie. From 1792–1800, Zelter acted as accompanist to that institution, and at the death of Fasch he succeeded to the directorship. In 1806 he was appointed assessor to the Akademie, and in 1807 he established a ' Ripienschule ' for orchestral practice. A few years previously, Zelter's music to some of Goethe's songs had so attracted the poet, that a correspondence began which shows that Goethe was capable of a real affection for at least one of his blindest worshippers.[2]

There are frequent allusions in these letters to the progress of the Singakademie, over which in his later years Zelter reigned as a musical dictator from whose decision there was no appeal. The Akademie consisted originally of only 30 members, who met weekly at different private houses, and during Fasch's life they practised little except his compositions. It was reserved for Zelter to enlarge the area of selection, and under him some of the greatest works of the time were added to the repertory. The Liedertafel, which was definitely founded in 1809, at first consisted of 25 men, singers, poets and composers. The society met once a month for supper and music, the songs were the compositions of the guests themselves, and the gatherings are amusingly described in Zelter's letters to Goethe. In the same year he received the professorial title, and was made a member of the Akademie. In 1819 he founded the Königliche Institut für Kirchenmusik, and conducted it until his death.

As the teacher and friend of Felix Mendelssohn, Zelter is entitled to lasting gratitude, for though his judgment of contemporary art was at times mistaken, his faith in his pupil never waned. For his share in the revival of the choral music of J. S. Bach see BACH GESELLSCHAFT. The joint enthusiasm of Mendelssohn and Devrient for Bach's music had been kindled by the study of the score of the ' Passion,' which Zelter had bought years before. Zelter rashly ventured on simplifying some of the recitatives and choral parts, after the method of Graun. The purity of the work was saved by Felix Mendelssohn's grandmother, who prevailed on the fortunate possessor of the score to present the treasure to her grandson. Not only was the work well bestowed and rescued from sacrilege, but its publication and performance inaugurated a fresh era in the art of music. The expediency of printing the work was discussed at a dinner party given by Schlesinger, the publisher. Marx was appealed to for an opinion. ' All I can say is, that it is the greatest thing I know in church music,' was his reply, whereupon old Schlesinger struck the table with his fist, and called out, ' I will publish it, should it cost me three thousand thalers. I will do it for the honour of the house.'

The zeal of Mendelssohn and Devrient, in league to prevail on Zelter to allow a public performance, eventually triumphed over every obstacle. Their old teacher was at first incredulous ; it may well have been that he was conscious of the original sin of tampering with the score, and felt that the ' lynx eyes ' of Felix had silently convicted him. The concession was wrung from him with difficulty, but once given he put the forces of the Akademie at his pupil's disposal. The first and ever-memorable performance of the ' Passion' music was given Mar. 11, 1829, under Mendelssohn's baton, his

---

[1] *Karl Friedrich Christian Fasch*, von Karl Friedrich Zelter, 4to Berlin, 1801, with a portrait (drawn by Schadow).
[2] *Briefwechsel zwischen Goethe und Zelter*, 6 vols. Berlin, 1833–34. Translated by A. D. Coleridge, 1887.

friend Edward Devrient singing the part of Christ.

Zelter composed songs and quartets for the Liedertafel of Berlin, and set many of Goethe's songs to music. These songs were interpreted in their day by Mara and other great singers. Amongst his numerous works, now forgotten, was a cantata on the death of Frederick the Great, which seems, by the account of it in a journal of 1786, to have been thought worthy of the occasion. He also wrote an oratorio called 'The Ascension,' a Requiem, a Te Deum and several other works which were never published. A list of these is to be found in *A Sketch of the Life of Carl Friedrich Zelter, arranged from Autobiographical MSS.*, by Rintel (Janke, Berlin, 1861). (See also *Q.-L.*)

A. D. C., rev. with addns.

ZÉMIRE ET AZOR, a fairy comedy in 4 acts ; words by Marmontel ; music by Grétry. Produced Fontainebleau, Nov. 9, 1771, and Les Italiens, Paris, Dec. 16 ; revived, the libretto reduced by Scribe to 2 acts, and the score reinforced by Adam, Feb. 21, 1832 ; again revived, in 4 acts, June 29, 1846.

The story is that of ' Beauty and the Beast,' and has been set to music under the above title by Baumgarten (1775), Neefe (Beethoven's teacher) (1778), Tozzi (1792), Seyfried (1818) and Spohr (Apr. 4, 1819). The last, under the name of ' Azor and Zemira, or the Magic Rose,' was produced at Covent Garden Theatre, Apr. 5, 1831. G.

ZEMLINSKY, ALEXANDER VON (*b.* Vienna, Oct. 4, 1872), studied at the Vienna Conservatorium and became conductor first at the Volksoper (1906), then at the Hofoper (1908). After holding a similar position at Mannheim, Zemlinsky settled at Prague as conductor at the German Opera House, where he has done distinguished work. The German Opera under him has maintained a high level, and he still (1927) directs it (see PRAGUE). Zemlinsky has composed several stage works which have been given at VIENNA (*q.v.*) and elsewhere with success. ' Sarema ' (Luitpold prize) was produced at Munich in 1897 ; ' Es war einmal ' (1900) and ' Kleider machen Leute ' (Volksoper 1910) were produced in Vienna, and ' Der Zwerg ' (1921) at Frankfort. C.

ZENATELLO, GIOVANNI (*b.* Verona, Feb. 22, 1878 or 1879),[1] operatic tenor. He was trained as a baritone and made his début as such at the Teatro Mercadante, Naples. Two months later he exchanged the part of Silvio in ' Pagliacci ' for that of Canio, and astonished the Neapolitan critics by proving himself a genuine robust tenor, in which capacity he appeared in various opera-houses in Southern Italy for three years. Then only did he begin serious vocal study at Milan, and fit himself for the worthy employment of a magnificent organ.

[1] *Baker.*

After a highly successful reappearance at Mantua as Andrea Chénier, he went to South America and entered upon the most brilliant part of his career, being engaged on his return for La Scala, Milan, where he sang regularly from 1903–07. In the latter year he sang for Hammerstein at the Manhattan Opera House, New York, following up there the successes which he had won at Covent Garden in 1905–06. He made a good impression here, both by his acting and singing, on his début in ' Un ballo in maschera ' (100th performance at Covent Garden, Oct. 6, 1905) ; but achieved a more marked triumph three years later when he sang Otello with Melba and Scotti as Desdemona and Jago. He was also very fine that season as Radamès with Destinn as Aïda, and these two Verdi rôles were considered his best in a repertory of some fifty characters. He was for many years a member of the Boston Opera Company, and whilst in America married (1913) the well-known Spanish prima donna, Maria Gay. He supports a conservatory in Verona for the free tuition of talented students.

BIBL.—*International Who's Who in Music*; NORTHCOTT, *Covent Garden and the Royal Opera.*　H. K.

ZERETEIEV, see LAWROWSKA.

ZERLINE, OU LA CORBEILLE D'ORANGES (The Basket of Oranges), opera in 3 acts ; libretto by Scribe ; music by Auber. Produced Académie Nationale, May 16, 1851 ; in Italian, Her Majesty's Theatre, July 22, 1851. G.

ZERR, ANNA (*b.* Baden-Baden, July 26, 1822 ; *d.* Winterbach, near Oberkirch, Baden, June 14, 1881), singer.

She was taught by Bordogni, and first appeared in opera at Carlsruhe, in 1839, where she remained until 1846, and was subsequently engaged at Vienna. In 1851 she obtained leave of absence, and made her first appearance in England on May 19, at Catherine Hayes' Concert, at the Hanover Square Rooms, and sang with great success there and at other concerts, including one given for the benefit of the Hungarian Refugees. On this account, on her return to Vienna, she was deprived of her diploma of court chamber singer, and was not permitted to sing again at the opera during the remainder of her engagement. On July 10 she made her début with great effect at the Royal Italian Opera as Astrifiammante on the production of ' Zauberflöte.' She reappeared in 1852 in the same part, and in that of Lucia ; on July 15 as Rosa on the revival of Spohr's ' Faust ' ; on Aug. 17 as Catherine on the production of ' Pietro il Grande ' (Jullien). She afterwards sang at the Birmingham Festival, at Jullien's concerts, went to America, and retired from public life in 1857. A. C.

ZERRAHN, CARL (*b.* Malchow, Mecklenburg-Schwerin, July 28, 1826 ; *d.* Milton, Mass., U.S.A., Dec. 29, 1909). As conductor of important choral societies in New England he executed a powerful influence on the spread of music in the country of his adoption (see WORCESTER MUSIC FESTIVALS, U.S.A.)

He came to the United States in 1848 as a member of the Germania Orchestra, playing the flute. He was elected conductor of the Handel and Haydn Society in 1854, and conducted the concerts of this choral society for 42 years. He conducted the concerts of the Worcester, Mass. Musical Festivals for 30 years (1866–97) and the Harvard Symphony Concerts during the entire period of their existence. He was also the conductor of many Musical Festivals in the States. He retired in 1898.   H. E. K.

ZEUGHEER, JAKOB (known also as J. Z. HERRMANN) (b. Zürich, 1805 ; d. Liverpool, June 15, 1865), violinist.

He learned the violin first from Wassermann in his native town, and in 1818 was placed at Munich under Ferdinand Fränzel, for the violin, and Gratz for composition and musical science. A visit to Vienna in 1823 confirmed his enthusiasm for chamber-music and Beethoven, who remained through life the object of his highest veneration. The example of SCHUP-PANZIGH (q.v.), and of the four brothers Moralt, suggested to Zeugheer the idea of attempting the same with his friends in Munich, as 'das Quartett Gebrüder Herrmann.' Zeugheer was leader ; Joseph Wex of Immenstadt, second violin ; Carl Baader, viola ; and Joseph Lidel (grandson of Andreas Lidl, the eminent performer on the BARYTON), violoncello. They started Aug. 24, 1824, for the south, and gave performances at the towns of south Germany and Switzerland, and along the Rhine to Holland and Belgium. In the spring of 1826 they played in Paris, before Cherubini and Baillot, and gave a public performance assisted by Mlle. Sontag and M. Boucher. They first performed in Paris Spohr's double quartet in D minor, the second quartet being played by Boucher and his three sons. From Boulogne they crossed the Channel ; in England they seem to have been successful, at Dover, Ramsgate, and especially at Brighton, where they resided for five months. They gave concerts throughout the South and West of England, and in Ireland from Cork to Dublin, where they arrived in Nov. 1827. Early in 1828 they proceeded by Belfast to Glasgow, Edinburgh and London. In London they had only a few engagements in private houses ; Wex retired ill, and the quartet was broken up till a new violinist was found in Anton Popp of Würzburg. The concerts began again with a series of six at Liverpool in the summer of 1829, and were continued through the northern counties. But in the spring of 1830 the 'brothers' had had enough of a roving life. Zeugheer and Baader settled at Liverpool, Lidel and Popp at Dublin. Zeugheer resided in Liverpool till his death, Baader till his retirement in 1869.

In 1831 Zeugheer took the conductorship of the Gentlemen's Concerts at Manchester, which he retained till 1838. The Liverpool Philharmonic Society, originally a private society, began in Jan. 1840 to give public concerts with an orchestra, and in 1843 appointed Zeugheer director. He conducted their concerts from that date to Mar. 28, 1865, shortly before his death. But the great work of his life at Liverpool was tuition.

Zeugheer's playing was very pure in tone and refined in expression, though the work of his career was not favourable to original composition. He wrote 2 symphonies, 2 overtures, a cantata, 2 sets of entr'actes, a violin concerto, op. 28, a potpourri for violin and orchestra, op. 6, an instrumental quartet, an andante and rondo for piano and violin, op. 21, and a polacca for 4 voices, few of them published. In Liverpool he wrote an opera, 'Angela of Venice,' to Chorley's words, but it was neither produced nor published, owing to the badness of the libretto. He published 2 sets of waltzes, a vocal duet, 'Come, lovely May,' and other songs and glees.   R. M.

ZIANI, (1) MARC ANTONIO (b. Venice, c. 1653 ; d. Vienna, Jan. 22, 1715), maestro di cappella at S. Barbara, and at the theatre of Mantua whence he was dismissed Sept. 28, 1686. He became vice-Kapellmeister at the Viennese court, Apr. 1, 1700, and first Kapellmeister Jan. 1, 1712. He composed oratorios, masses, motets and other church music as well as 45 operas, serenades and cantatas (Riemann ; Q.-L.).

(2) PIETRO ANDREA (b. Venice, early 17th cent.), uncle of the preceding. He was organist at S. Salvator, Venice, 1640 ; from May 1657 till 1659 or 1660 he was maestro di cappella of San Maria Maggiore, Bergamo ; from Dec. 20, 1666 to Jan. 20, 1667, he conducted some of his church works at the wedding of the hereditary Prince of Saxony at Dresden. In 1669 he succeeded Cavalli as second organist of S. Mark's, Venice, and when he was not appointed first organist, on the death of the former in 1676, he went to Naples. From that time reliable data are not obtainable ; those given by various biographers are not substantiated. He composed 23 operas, 3 oratorios, masses, psalms, instrumental sonatas of 3 to 6 parts, overtures, organ pieces (Riemann ; Q.-L.).

ZICH, OTAKAR (b. Kralové Městec, 1879), a Czech composer who began life as a secondary schoolmaster, proceeded to the University of Brno (Brünn), took the degree of Ph.D., and was appointed professor of æsthetics at that institution. He has collected and published the folk-songs of the Chods (inhabitants of E. Bohemia) and other districts. His realistic opera 'Vina' (The Sin), a setting of Jaroslav Hilbert's remarkable episode from modern life, was produced at the National Theatre, Prague,

1922, and awakened considerable controversy. He has also composed two works for chorus and orchestra, ' Osudna svatba ' (The ill-fated Marriage) and ' Polka jedé ' (Polka Rides) ; an earlier opera, ' Maliřský nápad ' (The Painter's Downfall) ; and vocal settings of poems by Jan Neruda.   R. N.

ZIEGLER, JOSEPH, an 18th-century vioiinist-composer ; in Vienna, c. 1750. He was the master of Dittersdorf. Of his compositions are still in existence 5 motets, 4 masses, 2 litanies, 1 Salve Regina, 1 violin concerto with string accompaniment, and a violin sonata with basso continuo (Q.-L.).

ZIEHN, BERNHARD (b. Erfurt, Germany, Jan. 20, 1845 ; d. Chicago, U.S.A., Sept. 8, 1912), German-American musical theorist. In 1868–70 he taught higher mathematics, German, and music-theory at the German Lutheran School in Chicago.

After 1871 Ziehn occupied himself with the theory of music, the technique of composition and of piano-playing, and with writing concerning it. Busoni said of him : ' He is a theoretician who points to the possibilities of undiscovered lands—a prophet through logic. As a master of harmony he stands alone.' Besides his master-work, *Harmonie und Modulationslehre* (1888), his books include : *System der Übungen für Klavierspieler* (1881) ; *Lehrgang für den ersten Klavierunterricht* (1881) ; *Five-and Six-Part Harmonies, How to use Them* (1911) ; and *Canonical Studies, a New Technic of Composition* (1912).   W. S. S.

ZILCHER, HERMANN (b. Frankfort-on-Main, Aug. 18, 1881), son of the composer Paul Zilcher who gave him his first musical training. He went later to the Hoch Conservatorium (Kwast, Scholz, Knorr). In 1901 he gained the ' Mozart Prize for Composition.' He toured Europe and America with Vecsey and Petschnikof, etc. In 1905 he was appointed teacher at the Hoch Conservatorium and in 1908 was called to the Academy in Munich as professor for PF. and composition. He has been Director of the Conservatorium of Music in Würzburg since 1920. In his compositions he is at his best in the numerous song cycles which reveal a profound study of Brahms allied to a strong influence of the Neo-Romantic and Impressionistic School.

Song cycles (opp. 10, 12, 13, 14, 25, 28, 29, 30, 31, 35a, 35b, 36, 37, 40, 41) ; a German Folk-song Play (for solo, quartet, PF.); ' Aus dem Hohelied Salomonis ' (for alto, baritone, str. quartet and PF.) ; PF. pieces (opp. 5, 6, 8, 26, 34) ; vln. sonata ; PF. quintet ; symphonietta ; suite (for orch.) ; symphony in A maj. ; symphony in F min. ; double concerto for two vlns. ; vln. concerto. ; suite (for two vlns. and orch.) ; v'cl. concerto ; ' Klage ' (for vlns. and orch.) ; PF. concerto ; ' Night and Morning ' (for two PFs., orch. and kettle-drums) ; 'Reinhart,' chor. work ; ' The Love Mass, (chor. work) : ' Filzebutze ' (Dream Play), (Mannheim, 1903) ; Incidental music to 'As You Like It,' ' A Winter's Tale,' and ' Dr. Eisenbart ' (Mannheim, 1922).   K. D. H.

ZIMBALIST, EFREM (b. Rostoff on the Don, Russia, May 7, 1889), violinist.

After receiving some lessons from his father, an orchestral leader, he entered in 1901 the St. Petersburg Conservatorium, where he studied continuously for 6 years under Leopold Auer, and gained a gold medal and a scholarship of 1200 roubles. After 1907, when he left the Conservatorium, he toured in Germany, England (his first appearance in London was in Dec. 1907), and Belgium with considerable success, playing most of the great concertos with a purity of style and freedom from extravagance remarkable in one so young. He went to America in 1911, playing on Oct. 27 Glazounov's concerto in A minor with the Boston Symphony Orchestra. He ultimately settled there and married (1914) Alma Gluck, a soprano singer. He plays on a Stradivari violin of the best period.   W. W. C., addns.

ZIMBALON, see DULCIMER.

ZIMMERMAN, PIERRE JOSEPH GUILLAUME (b. Paris, Mar. 17, 1785 ; d. there, Oct. 29, 1853), distinguished pianist and teacher.

The son of a pianoforte-maker, he entered the Conservatoire in 1798, studied the piano with Boieldieu, and harmony with Rey and Catel. In 1800 he carried off first prize for piano, Kalkbrenner taking the second. His musical education was completed by a course of advanced composition under Cherubini. In 1811 he was appointed ' répétiteur,' or undermaster of the pianoforte at the Conservatoire, became joint-professor in 1817, and professor in chief in 1820. This post he held till 1848, when he retired with the title of honorary inspector of pianoforte classes. During this long period he fulfilled his duties with indefatigable zeal and entire devotion, so much so, indeed, that for the sake of his constantly increasing pupils he entirely gave up appearing in public, and found little time for composition. He did, however, produce at the Opéra-Comique in 1830 ' L'Enlèvement,' in 3 acts, libretto by Saint-Victor, Scribe and d'Épagny, wholly forgotten, and composed ' Nausicaa,' a grand opera, which was never performed. He also wrote a number of pianoforte pieces of various kinds, but his most important work is the *Encyclopédie du pianiste*, which comprises a complete method of pianoforte-playing, and a treatise on harmony and counterpoint. In 1811 Zimmerman won the post of professor of fugue and counterpoint thrown open to competition on the death of Eler, but satisfied with the honour of victory decided to retain his favourite piano class. A daughter of his became Mme. Charles Gounod.   A. J.

ZIMMERMANN, AGNES MARIE JACOBINA (b. Cologne, July 5, 1847 ; d. London, Nov. 14, 1925), pianist and composer, came to England very early, and at 9 became a student at the R.A.M., under Cipriani Potter and Steggall. Later she learnt from Pauer and Sir George Macfarren.

Her works were often heard at the R.A.M. Students' concerts. In 1860 and 1862 she obtained the King's Scholarship, and on Dec. 5,

1863, made her first public appearance at the Crystal Palace in two movements of Beethoven's E♭ concerto. In 1864 she followed this up by playing at the Gewandhaus, Leipzig, and elsewhere in Germany. Though occasionally travelling abroad (as in 1879–80 and 1882–83), and always with success, she made England her home, where her name became for many years a household word for purity of interpretation and excellent musicianship. In playing she always devoted herself to the classical school, once or twice in a very interesting manner. Thus it was she who performed (for the first and only time in England) Beethoven's transcription of his violin concerto for the pianoforte at the Crystal Palace, Dec. 7, 1872. Her compositions are also chiefly in the classical form and style, and include 3 sonatas for piano and violin (opp. 16, 21 and 23), a sonata for piano, violin and violoncello (op. 19), a sonata for piano solo (op. 22), a mazurka (op. 11), and Presto alla Tarantella (op. 15); also several songs, duets and 4-part songs, and various arrangements of instrumental works, etc.

She edited the sonatas of Mozart and Beethoven and the complete pianoforte works of Schumann for Novello.   G.

ZINCK, (1) BENEDIKT FRIEDRICH (b. Husum, Holstein, May 23, 1743; d. Ludwigslust, Mecklenburg, June 23, 1801). At first organist at Schleswig; in Aug. 1783 he signs himself Court Musician at Ludwigslust. He composed a considerable number of symphonies, mostly for full orchestra, the 103d Psalm for voices and orchestra, harpsichord sonatas, duets for various instruments, etc. He was also the inventor of the ' Coelestina,' a clavier or organ-harmonika (Mendel; Q.-L.).

(2) HARNAK OTTO CONRAD (b. Husum, July 2, 1746; d. Copenhagen, Feb. 15, 1832), a brother of the former. He was a singer at Hamburg, 1768; flautist and chamber-musician at Ludwigslust, Mecklenburg - Schwerin; went to Copenhagen in 1787 as singing-master at the Royal Theatre; was organist at St. Saviour's church 1789–1801; and music master at the Blaagard Seminary 1791–1811. He published the authorised Danish Hymn-book; composed oratorios, cantatas, songs, clavier - sonatas, trio sonatas, divertiments for violin and harpsichord, etc.; and wrote Die nordische Harfe, an essay on Scandinavian music (Mendel; Q. L.).

ZINGARA, LA, an Italian version of Balfe's BOHEMIAN GIRL (q.v.).   G.

ZINGARELLI, NICCOLÒ ANTONIO (b. Naples, Apr. 4, 1752; d. Torre del Greco, May 5, 1837), eldest son of Riccardo Tota Zingarelli, a tenor singer and teacher of singing.

In 1759 his father died, leaving his mother with four children and very poor. The eldest boy was chief clerk in the Musical College of S. Maria di Loreto, and Niccolò was at once admitted there as a resident pupil. Here he

and Cimarosa learnt composition under Fedele Fenaroli. By the rules of his College he was bound to study an instrument, and he selected the violin, on which he soon became very proficient. Among his teachers was Speranza, a learned contrapuntist and the best pupil of Durante. Before leaving his College, Zingarelli produced his first opera, or rather intermezzo —' I quattro pazzi '—which was performed by the pupils in the Conservatorio in 1768.

Soon after his departure from the Conservatorio in 1769 we find him teaching the violin in the Gargano family at Torre Annunziata, near Naples. Later on he gave lessons to the Duchess of Castelpagano, under whose patronage he produced his first work at the San Carlo in 1779, the cantata ' Pigmalione,' which met with some success. On Aug. 13, 1781, his first opera, ' Montesuma,' was represented at the same house. It shows a style of the greatest simplicity and purity; and when afterwards performed in Vienna, Haydn praised it greatly, and foretold a career of success to its composer. Strongly recommended to the Archduchess Beatrice of Austria, he went to Milan, and was well received at the vice-regal court. Milan was to be henceforth the scene of Zingarelli's many triumphs, and for La Scala he wrote most of his serious and all his comic operas. He began there with ' Alsinda ' in 1785, which greatly pleased the Milanese public, though composed in seven days and in ill-health, if we are to believe Carpani, who wrote most of Zingarelli's libretti, and asserts that he was an ocular witness, not only of the above feat, but also of the composition of the whole of ' Giulietta e Romeo ' in forty hours less than ten days. This really astounding facility was the result of Speranza's method of obliging his pupils to write the same composition many times over, with change of time and signature, but without any change in its fundamental poetical ideas. ' Alsinda ' was soon followed by ' Armida,' ' Annibale,' ' Ifigenia in Aulide,' and ' Ricimero,' all given at La Scala during the two following years with enormous success.

Whilst thus satisfying the theatrical public, Zingarelli did not neglect his more congenial work of writing sacred music, and in 1787 he composed an oratorio of ' The Passion,' given at the church of S. Celso in Milan. From 1786 to 1788 he wrote 9 cantatas, ' Alceste,' ' Hero,' ' Sappho,' ' Nice d' Elpino,' ' L'amor filiale,' ' Alcide al bivio,' ' Telemaco,' ' Oreste ' and ' Il trionfo di David '; all in Milan, except the last, which was given at San Carlo, Naples.

In 1789 Zingarelli was called to Paris to compose an opera for the Académie Royale de Musique. He arrived in the thick of the fight between the Piccinnists and Gluckists. Marmontel wrote for him the book of ' L'Antigone,' which was represented on Apr. 30, 1790. This opera was performed in Paris only 3 times consecutively. Zingarelli, as both a conservative and a religious man, soon fled from revolutionary Paris, and returned to Milan through Switzerland at the beginning of 1791. There he produced at La Scala ' La morte di Cesare,' and in the following year 'L' oracolo sannita' and 'Firro.'

In 1792 there was an open competition in Milan for the place of maestro di cappella of the Duomo, the subject being a canon for 8 voices, and Zingarelli was appointed. Among his many pupils of this time we may mention F. Pollini, to whom he dedicated his ' Partimenti ' and his ' Solfeggi,' which soon became recognised text-books.

With ' La secchia rapita ' in 1793, Zingarelli began a series of comic operas, which made his name popular, not only in Italy but throughout Germany, where they were widely performed. ' Il mercato di Monfregoso ' soon followed, and is reputed his best opera buffa. In 1794 he composed ' Artaserse ' for Milan, the ' Orazi e Curiazi ' for the Teatro Reale of Turin, and ' Apelle e Campaspe ' for the theatre La Fenice of Venice, in which opera Crescentini made his début. The ' Conte di Saldagna ' was unsuccessfully produced in 1795 at the same theatre in Venice ; but this failure was grandly retrieved the following year by the performance of his greatest work, ' Giulietta e Romeo,' at La Scala. Its beauty and popularity are shown by the fact that it was played all over the continent for the greater part of a century.

Zingarelli was appointed in 1794 maestro di cappella at Loreto, which place he held for 10 years. Here he wrote many operas, of which we may mention ' Clitennestra,' written expressly for Catalani, and ' Inez de Castro,' for Silva. His principal work, however, during these ten years was sacred music, to which he was inclined by his nature and by the duties of his office. In the archives of the Santa Casa of Loreto is accumulated an immense quantity of manuscript music, known by the name of ' Annuale di Loreto.' To this great collection Zingarelli contributed the astounding number of 541 works, inclusive of 28 masses, which are still sung in that church. As it is forbidden to copy the music of the ' Annuale,' the outside world must remain ignorant of its merits. Zingarelli's masses, to those who heard them, have a spontaneity of expression, an easy facility of style, a simplicity, and, above all, a most entrancing melody.

In 1804 Zingarelli succeeded Guglielmi as maestro di cappella of the Sistine Chapel in Rome. Here he set to music passages from the great Italian poets. Tancredi's Lamento, from the twelfth Canto of Tasso's *Gerusalemme Liberata*, was performed in Naples in 1805, in the Palace of the Prince di Pantelleria, where Zingarelli met Mme. de Staël, whom he had previously known in Paris as Mlle. Necker. The same year he gave in Rome ' La distru-

zione di Gerusalemme ' at the Valle theatre, where it kept the boards for 5 consecutive years. He produced, 7 years after, in Florence, ' La Riedificazione di Gerusalemme,' one of his very few failures. His opera ' Baldovino ' was given in 1810 at the Argentina theatre, and the following year ' Berenice ' at the Valle theatre, both in Rome. ' Berenice ' was Zingarelli's last opera, and had a run of over a hundred consecutive representations ; a thing unheard of in the thinly populated towns of Italy. But it was not his last work, as he continued writing to the last day of his life. ' Berenice ' was composed after leaving Rome for Città Vecchia on his forced journey to Paris ; and one of its finest numbers, the finale of the first act, ' Già sparir vedo la sponda,' was written on board ship.

We have now arrived at a memorable epoch of Zingarelli's life, when his already well-known name became illustrious among those of Italian patriots. When Napoleon, in the zenith of his imperial power, gave his son the title of ' King of Rome,' he ordered rejoicings throughout all his dominions. A Te Deum was therefore arranged to be sung at St. Peter's in Rome ; but when the authorities, both French and Italian, were assembled for the performance, it was found to their consternation that the maestro di cappella refused to have anything to do with it, and that nothing could induce him to acknowledge the rule of the Corsican usurper. He was arrested and, by Napoleon's orders, taken to Paris, where he was immediately set free and granted a pension. This he owed to the fact that Napoleon was fond, above all other, of Zingarelli's music, which he had heard at Loreto in 1796, in Vienna in 1805 and in Paris in 1809. On the last occasion, when Crescentini sang the part of Romeo, Napoleon, much affected, sent him from his own breast the star of the order of the Iron Crown. He also ordered Zingarelli to compose for his imperial chapel a Mass that should not last more than 20 minutes, had it rehearsed in his presence, and was so pleased with it as to give the composer 6000 francs. During his stay in Paris, Zingarelli was replaced at Rome by Fioravanti. In Feb. 1813 he was appointed director of the Real Collegio di Musica in Naples. In 1816 he succeeded Paisiello as maestro di cappella of the Neapolitan cathedral ; and held both these places until his death.

For the Birmingham Festival of 1829 Zingarelli wrote a cantata on the 12th chapter of Isaiah. As he could not take it to England himself he entrusted his pupil, COSTA (*q.v.*), with the mission, and this was the occasion of Costa's introduction to the English public. Zingarelli's next composition was a Hymn to commemorate the inauguration of the Philharmonic Society of Naples in Jan. 1835. His oratorio, ' The Flight into Egypt,' was written and performed only a few weeks before his death in 1837.

Of his very numerous masses, without reckoning the 28 in the 'Annuale di Loreto,' the best are : that of Novara; that of Dresden (commissioned by the King of Saxony, and performed in 1835 under the direction of Morlacchi, one of his pupils); a Requiem for the Neapolitan minister Medici ; and another Requiem, composed for his own funeral.

Although in his 'Mercato di Monfregoso' and in his 'Secchia rapita' Zingarelli gives many proofs of a comic musical vein, he shone more in serious operas, and most of all in his numberless sacred compositions. The adaptation of profane music to religious services, so common in Italian churches, he strenuously combated.

The following is a list of Zingarelli's operas and oratorios. (See also *Q.-L.*)

OPERAS

Date.	Name.	First Performed.
1771	I quattro pazzi	Conservatorio, Naples.
1781	Montesuma	S. Carlo, Naples.
1785	Alsinda	Scala, Milan.
1786	Armida	Do.
1787	Annibale	Do.
„	Ifigenia in Aulide	Do.
„	Ricimero	Do.
1790	Antigone	Opera, Paris.
1791	Morte di Cesare	Scala, Milan.
1792	L' oracolo Sannita	Do.
„	Pirro	Do.
1793	La secchia rapita	Do.
„	Il mercato di Monfregoso	Do.
1794	Artaserse	Do.
„	Apelle e Campaspe	Fenice, Venice.
„	Orazi e Curiazi	Reale, Turin.
1795	Conte di Saldagna	Fenice, Venice.
1796	Giulietta e Romeo	Scala, Milan.
„	La Danaide	Do.
„	Meleagro	Do.
„	Mitridate	Fenice, Venice.
1798	Carolina e Menzikoff	Do.
1799	Edipo a Colona	Do.
„	Il ritratto	Scala, Milan.
1800	Il ratto delle Sabine	Do.
1801	Clitennestra	Do.
1803	Il bevitore fortunato	Do.
„	Le nozze di Dorina	Do.
„	Inez di Castro	Do.
1810	Baldovino	Torre Argentina, Rome.
1811	Berenice	Valle, Rome.

ORATORIOS AND CANTATAS

Date.	Name.	First Performed.
1779	Pigmalione	S. Carlo, Naples.
1786	Alceste	Milan.
„	Hero	Do.
„	Sappho	Do.
1787	The Passion	S. Celso, Milan.
„	Nice d' Elpino	Do.
„	L' amor filiale	Do.
„	Alcide al bivio	Do.
„	Telemaco	Do.
1788	Oreste	Do.
„	Il trionfo di David	S. Carlo, Naples.
1804	Francesca da Rimini	Rome.
1805	Tancredi al sepolcro di Clorinda	Naples.
„	La distruzione di Gerusalemme	Valle, Rome
1809	Conte Ugolino	Paris.
1812	La riedificazione di Gerusalemme	Florence.
1829	Isaiah	Birmingham.
1833	Saul	S. Michael, Rome.
1835	Hymn of Inauguration	Philharmonic Soc., Naples.
1837	The Flight into Egypt	Naples.

Also 541 MS. works in the 'Annuale di Loreto,' a detailed and complete list of which, obtained from and certified by the maestro di cappella at Loreto, is in the R.C.M.   L. R.

ZINKE, CORNETTO, CORNET À BOUQUIN, see CORNETT.

ZIPOLI, DOMENICO (*b.* Nola, Naples, *c.* 1675) studied at the conservatorio dei Turchini, Naples; went to Rome in 1696, where he became organist at the Jesuit church. He composed 'Sonate d' intavolatura per organo e cimbalo,' 2 parts, the 2nd part dance suites ; six suites of Italian lessons for the harpsichord, etc. (Walsh, 1725 ?) a third collection of toccatas, voluntaries and fugues for the organ or harpsichord (Walsh, 1715 ?). His organ-pieces were held in great esteem (*Mendel*; *Q.-L.*).

ZIRYÁB, 'ALI IBN NÁFI (*b.* Baghdád, *c.* 800; *d.* Córdoba), a celebrated Persian singer and composer, who was a pupil of IṢHÁQ and eventually removed to Spain (821), became the idol of 'Abd-ar-Raḥmán II. (822–852) of Córdoba. His fertility of composition was attributed to the jinn, who visited him in his sleep and whispered melodies in his ear. On waking he called his two slave musicians and taught them the song; then he wrote the words and went back to bed. As a teacher of singing Ziryáb divided his instruction into three courses : rhythm, melody and ornamentation. The pupil had first to pass certain tests, one of which was to sing a prolonged *ah* on all degrees of the scale. Then he began by learning the words and metre ; he spoke the words while he beat time with a tambourine, marking the strong and the weak accents and the pace of the different movements. Then he was taught the melody in its simplest form with no ornaments, and only when he could sing it perfectly was he allowed to study the shakes, vocalises, scale-passages and appoggiaturas with which the master embellished the song, and the nuances he introduced to give it expression and charm. Ziryáb's method gives some indication of what the music of his time was like—how it appeared to his pupils and how it was appraised by his admirers. His life is related by al-Maqqarí, ABU'L FARAJ and other writers.   J. B. T.

ZÍTEK, OTA (*b.* Prague, 1892), Czech writer on music and composer. He pursued his studies at the Universities and Conservatoires of Prague and Vienna, and afterwards specialised in questions concerning the staging of drama and opera, on which subject he contributed many articles to Czech periodicals, and wrote a book, *Modern Opera*. His works are mostly published by Hudební Matice, Prague. Operas: 'Vznešené srdce' (The Heart a-flame), 1918 ; 'Pád Petra Královce' (The Downfall of Peter Kralence), 1921 ; song cycles.   R. N.

ZITHER, a modern member of the great family of stringed instruments plucked with a plectrum, which are undoubtedly among the most ancient of musical instruments. It is unnecessary in this place to trace the development of the modern zither from the CITHER of two centuries ago, or from the Greek κιθάρα, but it is remarkable that the method of exciting the vibrations of the strings is practically identical in all the instruments similarly named at various dates, though the bare finger is used, as in the GUITAR, and in the modern zither a kind of open thumb-ring with a pointed end is worn. This plectrum is the main distinction between the real zither, or 'Schlagzither' as it is sometimes called, and the 'Streichzither' which can be played with a bow, and is a more or less hybrid invention of recent times.

The zither may be called the national instrument of Bavaria, Styria and Tyrol, for it is played by all classes, and no inn is without one. It consists of a flat box which lies on the table, strung with 5 metal strings passing over frets, and from 27 to 40 strings of various kinds played as open strings plucked with the fingers, to form the accompaniment to the melody which is played with the plectrum, on the strings nearest the performer. There are many slight varieties in the make of the instrument, and every professor has his own preferences; the form most commonly seen is that shown on *PLATE I. No. 5.* The 'Concert-Zither' is rather longer, more powerful in tone, and has from 36 to 42 strings; a yet longer variety of the instrument is the 'Elegy-Zither,' which is tuned a third or fourth lower than the others. The tuning of the melody-strings is as follows, the two highest being nearest to the player:

The two A's are of steel, the D of brass, the G of steel covered with silver wire, and the C of brass covered with copper wire. This is the standard or 'Munich' arrangement of the strings, but the 'Viennese' tuning is as follows:

and was adopted, in order to facilitate certain effects at first peculiar to Styrian Ländler. These strings are stopped (by the fingers of the left hand) on 29 frets, arranged in semitones. The accompaniment strings are arranged in what at first sight seems to be an arbitrary and most complicated order. The 12 or 13 strings nearest the player (the highest 8 of gut, the rest of silk covered with silver wire) are called the 'harmony-strings,' and in the 'Munich' tuning are thus arranged:

The 'bass strings' which lie again beyond the 'harmony-strings' are tuned, roughly speaking, in octaves with them, adding some notes tuned semitonically in the extreme bass.

The accompaniment strings are played with the three middle fingers of the right hand, and are plucked towards the player, whose thumb is occupied with the melody-strings. The arrangement shown, which is by fifths and fourths (transpositions of an octave being arranged for convenience, and so as to keep the whole within ordinary limits, allows the whole chord in any usual major triad, to be played, for the fourth finger (the little finger is not used) plucks the bass-note of a triad, the middle finger the third, and the forefinger the fifth and octave together, in whatever position the chords may lie. The minor triads are more difficult to manage, and other harmonies have to be specially studied.[1] The present type of zither with its 30 strings has apparently [2] only been in use for about 80 years, and before then 18 strings were the average. A mountain-zither of the 17th century is in the National Museum at Munich, and has 4 strings on the keyboard, and 13 for accompaniment. PETZMAYER (*q.v.*), the 'Paganini of the zither,' used only 18 strings in all.

The musical effect of the zither is greatly enhanced by the picturesque and romantic circumstances in which it is usually heard. The metal 'melody-strings' have a naturally plaintive tone, and their 'singing' quality contrasts very agreeably with the more harp-like tones of the accompaniment, while the resonance of the whole is considerably increased by the characteristic sympathetic vibrations of the open strings. It has been introduced into orchestras for special purposes in imitations of national music; and is a pleasant accompaniment to the voice, either in soli, or in choruses of moderate size.

It would be impossible to enumerate the varieties of the zither which have been brought before the public from time to time. From the 'Arion' zither, with a slightly different shape, and a powerful tone, to the toy known as the 'auto-harp,' the principle of the instrument is the same. A more important variation is that of the 'Streichzither,' played with a bow. This necessitates a different shaping of the body, with a 'waist' like that of the violin family. It was made in three several sizes, but does not appear to have won much permanent favour.

M.

ZOCCA, GAETANO (*b.* Ferrara, 1784; *d.* there, Sept. 14, 1834), a distinguished violinist, was first a pupil of Jean Ballo, and afterwards went to Rolla, at Milan.

In 1816 Zocca was nominated conductor of

[1] The way in which these ordinary chords are arranged will be found in convenient tabular form in Dr. Charles Maclean's admirable article on the zither in the *Zeitschr.* of the Int. Mus. Ges. x. p. 345.   [2] *Ibid.*

the theatre and cathedral orchestras in Milan, and successively became conductor of the Philharmonic Society of Ferrara, and member of the Philharmonic Academy of Bologna. He advanced the art of violin-playing considerably in Italy, doing much to reform the art of bowing in that country.   E. H.-A.

ZOELLER, CARLI (b. Berlin, Mar. 28, 1840 ; d. London, July 13, 1889), bandmaster, composer and performer on the viole d'amore.

His musical studies were pursued entirely at the Berlin Conservatorium, where Hubert Ries, W. Gärich and Grell were his masters for violin, harmony and counterpoint respectively. He travelled for some time in Germany, with an Italian opera-troupe, settling eventually in London, in 1873. In 1879 Zoeller became bandmaster of the 7th (Queen's Own) Hussars ; in 1884 he was elected a member of the Accademia di Sta. Cecilia, of Rome ; and in 1885 a similar honour was conferred on him by the Istituto Musicale di Firenze. Zoeller wrote a comic operetta, ' The Missing Heir ' ; a lyrical drama, ' Mary Stuart of Fotheringay' ; a scena for soprano and orchestra, ' The Rhine King's Daughter ' ; four overtures and other orchestral pieces, also a concerto for violin and orchestra, a string quartet and quintet, several songs, church music, etc. He did much towards reviving the cult of the viola d'amore, which he himself played, and for which he wrote a scholarly Method, preceded by an erudite and concise history of the instrument and its origin entitled *The Viole d'Amour, Its Origin and History, and Art of Playing it.* In Mar. 1889 he wrote an admirable lecture on the viole d'amore, which was read at a meeting of the original Cremona Society, illustrated by many instruments and accessories and works relating to the instrument, of which a catalogue was published by the Society. He was at this time bandmaster of the 2nd Life Guards, and editor of the *United Services Military Band Journal.* (See VIOL.) He died as the result of an accident which befell him at the Military Tournament at Islington in the month of July of the same year.   E. H.-A.

ZOILO, ANNIBALE (b. Rome, mid. 16th cent.) maestro di cappella at S. Giovanni di Lateran (according to Fétis from 1561–70). In 1563 he calls himself maestro di cappella at S. Luigi. On July 5, 1570, he entered the Papal Chapel as singer, in which he remained until 1581–82. From that time onward he devoted himself entirely to composition, but only a few masses, his second book of madrigals and a number of songs and madrigals in collective volumes are still in existence (*Q.-L.*).

ZOILO, CESARE, an early 17th-century Roman composer who wrote madrigals a 5 v., Venice 1620 (several editions) ; motets in collective volumes (*Q.-L.*).

ZOLOTARIEV, VASSILY ANDREIEVICH

(b. Taganrog (Govt. of the Don Cossacks), Feb. 23 - Mar. 7, 1873), composer. He entered the school of the court chapel, St. Petersburg, as chorister, studied the violin, but had to give it up because of an injury to his hand. He worked at composition under Liadov and Balakirev ; also under Rimsky-Korsakov, at the St. Petersburg Conservatoire, from 1898–1900. In 1900 he won the Rubinstein Memorial Prize with his cantata ' Paradise and the Peri.' He was a professor at the Moscow Conservatoire, but now (1925) lives in the Caucasus. His chief works are :

Symphony, op. 8 ; Overture, 'A Rustic Festival' (Fête villageoise), Promenade Concerts, Oct. 2, 1917 (condr., Sir Henry J. Wood) : String quintet, D min., op. 19 ; String quartets, D maj., op. 5 : A maj., op. 6 ; D maj., op. 25 ; B flat min., op. 33 ; PF. quartet, D maj., op. 13 ; PF. trio, E min., op. 28 ; PF. sonata, G maj., op. 10 ; PF. pieces and songs.   R. N.

ZOPF, *i.e.* ' pigtail,' a German term for an old-fashioned obsolete style in music.

The word is generally used of a particularly conventional style, which was very common through the 18th century, especially in it-latter part.[1] The tendency, which may be perceived in composers like Durante, Vinci, Jommelli, Graun, and many others, to substitute a mechanical kind of expression for the utterances of genuine emotion, found a very common outlet in the trick of writing for two soprano voices usually following one another about in thirds, over a bass a long way below them. This was not done as a result of poverty of ideas, for it occurs side by side with music that is earnest and workmanlike. It seems to have been demanded by the fashionable people of the day, and to have been just such a guarantee of respectability as a wig or a pigtail at the same date. Much the same lack of originality gave rise to Wagner's term of ' Kapellmeistermusik.'   M.

ZOPFF, HERMANN (b. Glogau, Silesia, June 1, 1826 ; d. Leipzig, July 12, 1883), was composer and critic and editor of the *Neue Zeitschrift für Musik* after Brendel.

Though he had received a complete university education, his father wished him to be a farmer ; but his own predilections inclined him to music. At length the successful performance of an overture composed by him removed his father's opposition, and from the age of 24 he devoted himself exclusively to music. He placed himself under the tuition of A. B. Marx and Kullak, and was soon engaged to fill an important post on the teaching staff of their new Conservatorium at Berlin. He had also other appointments in the musical circles of that city ; but his ambition drew him in 1864 towards Leipzig, and he gladly accepted an offer from Brendel to edit the *Neue Zeitschrift für Musik,* which necessitated his removal thither. There he toiled until within a short time of his death, as editor, critic, conductor, composer, and professor of singing and

_____
[1] See the *Oxf. Hist. Mus.* vol. iv. pp. 62, 63, etc.

composition. The character and tone which had been imparted to the *Neue Zeitschrift* by Brendel were continued by Zopff, for both editors were strenuous advocates of the new German school. But Zopff was no narrow partisan ; he was ready to do full justice to every musician of high aims.

Zopff's compositions cover a wide range of form, from the simplest pianoforte pieces or songs to the largest polyphonic or dramatic works, and all bear the mark of a thorough, scientific musician. But for a certain want of spontaneity and grace, they would probably have been much better known and oftener performed. Among his numerous choral works with orchestral or pianoforte accompaniment, we may mention his ' Brauthymne,' ' Frühlingshymne,' and ' Triumph der Liebe.' Of his larger works, approaching the oratorio form, we may cite ' Anbetung Gottes,' ' Evangelium der That,' and ' Alexandera.' It is clear from his operas, ' Carloman,' ' Muhammed,' ' Judas Makkabeus ' and ' Constantin,' that his strength was especially concentrated on dramatic forms ; but as regards popularity his symphonic poem ' Tell,' the ' Idyllen für kleines Orchester,' and the ' Traum am Rhein ' have been most fortunate. Zopff was a careful and prolific writer of critical, theoretical and didactic essays ; his *Theorie der Oper* is a good illustration of the industry with which he collected and utilised valuable information.

A. H. W.

ZOPPA, ALLA, *i.e.* halting or limping, a term applied to a rhythm in which the second quaver in a bar of 2–4 time is accentuated, as in certain Hungarian pieces, or the modern American ' rag-time.' (See MAGYAR.)   G.

ZORTZIKO (ZORZIKO), see SONG, subsection SPAIN (5).

ZUFFOLO, a more or less generic name for a whistle, pipe or flageolet ; in the scores of Keiser's ' Croesus' (1710), and ' Jodelet ' (1726), the instrument is used, and seems to have been some kind of shrill oboe. In Grassineau's dictionary (1740) it is given as the name of a small flute or flageolet, used for teaching birds to whistle.   M.

ZULEHNER, CARL (*c.* 1770–*c.* 1830), is notorious for the share he took in compiling and foisting on the public several masses which he ascribed to MOZART (*q.v.*) (subsection SPURIOUS AND DOUBTFUL WORKS.)   M.

ZUMPE, HERMANN (*b.* Taubenheim, Saxony, Apr. 9, 1850 ; *d.* Munich, Sept. 4, 1903), was educated at the teachers' Seminary at Bautzen, was a schoolmaster at Weigsdorf in 1870–71, from thence going to Leipzig, and playing the triangle in the Stadttheater there ; he was one of those who helped Wagner in the preparation of the ' Ring ' at Bayreuth in the years 1873–1876, and after this he conducted in the theatres of Salzburg, Würzburg, Magdeburg,

Frankfort and Hamburg (in 1884–86). In 1891 he went to Stuttgart as Court Kapellmeister, taking over the conductorship of the Society for Classical Church Music, in lieu of Faisst who was ill. In 1895 he became conductor of the Kaim Concerts in Munich, and was made court Kapellmeister at Schwerin in 1897. He visited London to conduct the Wagner performances at Covent Garden in 1898. In 1900 he received the most important appointment of his career, that of court Kapellmeister at Munich. Here he was especially active in directing the famous Wagner performances at the Prinz Regenten Theater up to 1903, when he died suddenly. Among his compositions the most important are : a fairy opera ' Anhana ' (Berlin, 1880), ' Die verwünschene Prinzessin,' operettas ' Farinelli ' (Hamburg, 1886), ' Karin ' (Hamburg, 1888), and ' Polnische Wirtschaft ' (Berlin, 1891). At his death the score of another opera, ' Sawitri,' was found incomplete, and was scored by Gustav von Rosseler, and produced at Schwerin. (*Riemann.*)   M.

ZUMPE, JOHANNES, a German in the employ of the London harpsichord maker, Shudi, who about the year 1760 began the manufacture of square pianos. If he was not actually the inventor of the type, it was he who popularised it as a domestic instrument. (See PIANOFORTE, subsection THE SQUARE PIANO.)

ZUMSTEEG, JOHANN RUDOLF (*b.* Sachsenflur, Mosbach district of Baden, Jan. 10, 1760 ; *d.* Stuttgart, Jan. 27, 1802).

His father being a valet to Duke Carl of Würtemberg, he was admitted into the Carlschule, at ' The Solitude,' near Stuttgart, where he received a good general education, and formed a close friendship with Schiller, also a pupil there. He was originally intended for a sculptor, but the love of music proved too strong, and he studied first the violoncello, and then composition with Poli, whom he succeeded in 1792 as Kapellmeister, and director of the Opera. His chief claim to a place in the history of music is that he was the pioneer of the ballad, a form afterwards carried to perfection by Reichardt, Zelter and, pre-eminently, Löwe. Zumsteeg's best, and in his day widest-known, ballads were—' Leonore,' ' Des Pfarrers Tochter von Taubenhayn,' ' Kolma,' ' Die Büssende,' ' Ritter Toggenburg,' ' Elwina ' and ' Die Entführung.' Of his operas the following were frequently performed : ' Die Geisterinsel,' ' Das Pfauenfest ' and ' Ebondokani, the Calif of Bagdad.' ' Der Betrug aus Liebe,' ' Die Frühlingsfeier ' (an ode by Klopstock for recitative with orchestra) and ' Zalsor ' were other pieces of his, and many ballads and odes were published separately from the seven books of his ' Balladen und Lieder ' published by Breitkopf & Härtel. Other works deserving mention are—Choruses for Schiller's *Räuber*, 18 church cantatas, a concerto and duet for violoncello.[1]   C. F. P., addns.

ZUR MÜHLEN, RAIMUND VON (*b.* Livonia, Nov. 10, 1854), singer.

He was born on the property of his father and received his education in Germany. In his 21st year he began to learn singing at the Hochschule, Berlin, and continued the study under Stockhausen at Frankfort, and Bussine in Paris. He made a speciality of the German Lied, particularly the songs of Schubert and Schumann, the latter of which he studied with Madame Schumann. His voice had a peculiar and sympathetic quality; but what gave Zur Mühlen's singing its chief charm was the remarkable clearness of his pronunciation, and the way in which he contrived to identify the feeling of the words with the music. He sang in London first in 1882, and was a frequent visitor later.   G.

ZVONAŘ, JOSEF LEOPOLD (*b.* Kublov, near Prague, 1824; *d.* Prague, 1865), Czech musical pedagogue and composer, director of the Organ School, Prague, and one of the founders of the famous choral society Hlahol (1861) and the Umělěcká Beseda (Society of Arts). He composed songs, masses, two

Requiems and several humorous choruses, but is more highly valued as a theorist. His chief books were educational. A valuable publication is *Monuments of Early Czech Music* (1860–1864), which drew attention to the old contrapuntal school of Bohemian composers. R. N.

ZWEERS, BERNARD (*b.* Amsterdam, May 18, 1854; *d.* Dec. 9, 1924), composer. He was at first self-taught, but finished his studies, 1881, with Jadassohn in Leipzig. He then returned to Amsterdam, where he worked first as a choral conductor, and later chiefly as a teacher of theory and composition. Zweers, who was much influenced by Wagner's music, has written, amongst other works, three symphonies, music to Vondel's 'Gysbrecht van Amstel,' and many choral works. His third symphony, for a large orchestra, 'To my Fatherland' (1890), gave him a distinctive place amongst Dutch composers.   R. Mᵍ.

ZWISCHENSPIEL—something played between. The German term for INTERLUDE (*q.v.*). That the term had sometimes a wider meaning than Interlude is evident from a notice in the *Wiener Zeitung* for Apr. 1, 1795, referring to Beethoven's concerto in B♭:

'In the interval (*zum Zwischenspiel*), on the first evening, the famous Herr Beethoven won the unanimous applause of the public by an entirely new Pianoforte Concerto of his own.'

G.

[1] Haydn had a high esteem for Zumsteeg. Griesinger wrote to Härtel: 'Haydn is much distressed at Zumsteeg's death; he had plenty of imagination, and a fine sense of form.'

THE END